The Norton Anthology of English Literature

FOURTH EDITION

VOLUME 2

The Norton Anthology of English Literature

FOURTH EDITION

M. H. Abrams, *General Editor*

E. Talbot Donaldson

Hallett Smith

Robert M. Adams

Samuel Holt Monk

Lawrence Lipking

George H. Ford

David Daiches

VOLUME 2

W·W·NORTON & COMPANY · NEW YORK · LONDON

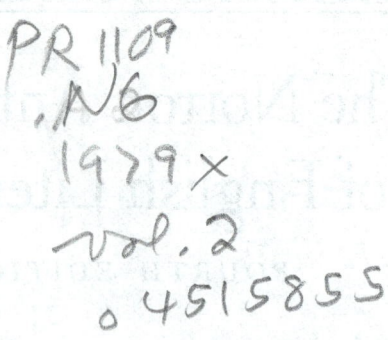

END PAPER MAP BY A. KARL/H. GEORGE

BOOK DESIGN BY JOHN WOODLOCK

Library of Congress Cataloging in Publication Data
Abrams, Meyer Howard, ed.
　The Norton anthology of English literature.
　Bibliography: p.
　Includes index.
　1. English literature.　I. Title.
PR1109.A2 1979　　　820'.8　　　78-27117

ISBN 0 393 95043 3 cloth edition
ISBN 0 393 95051 4 paper edition

1 2 3 4 5 6 7 8 9 0

Contents

[handwritten annotation:] Might add *The Song of Los* and "*Auguries of Innocence.*"

Contents · *xiii*

The Victorian Age (1832-1901) 927

The Twentieth Century

Contents · xxix

Preface
to the Fourth Edition

The intention of *The Norton Anthology of English Literature* from the beginning has been to maintain continuity, yet to allow for change. Its continuing aim is to provide, for the indispensable courses which introduce students to the greatness and variety of English literature, the major works in verse and prose from *Beowulf* to the present day, ordered chronologically, and presented in accurate and readable texts. A vital literary culture, however, is always on the move. The interests of readers change; new texts are discovered; old texts are better edited; new scholarly information and critical viewpoints become available; teachers and students want fresh materials that invite experimentation in the way literature is to be presented and studied. The policy, accordingly, has been to issue periodic revisions which, without violating the principle that only major writings be represented, are designed to keep the anthology in the mainstream of contemporary literary, cultural, and intellectual knowledge and concerns.

The strength of this collection is that its contents and editorial matter are grounded, not on theoretical views of what might be taught in an introduction to English literature, but on long experience in actually teaching such a course. The first edition in 1962 was the product of a decade of experimentation by several of its editors, and some of them (including the general editor) have proceeded to test each new edition by using it in the classroom. And ever since 1962 we have received a steady flow of voluntary suggestions from hundreds of users, students as well as teachers, who view the anthology with a loyal but critical eye. For this edition, we have also solicited detailed judgments about the utility of materials in the last version, together with recommendations for new materials, from almost one hundred critics—some of them experts in individual periods, but most of them instructors who use the book in a course. With each new edition, *The Norton Anthology* thus becomes more and more the product of a sustained collaboration between editors, teachers, and students.

The criteria for the choice, editing, and printing of texts remain what they were for the original edition: (1) that the selection make possible a study in depth of the major English writers in prose and verse, in the context of the chief literary modes and traditions of each age; (2) that the works selected be so far as feasible complete, and copious enough to allow instructors to select from the total those that they prefer to teach; (3) that the student be provided the most accurate texts available, edited so as to make them immediately accessible, and printed in a format that is easy to the hand and inviting to the eye; (4) that introductions and glosses be adequate to make an understanding of the texts independent of a reference library, so that the anthology may be read anywhere—in the student's room, in a coffee lounge, or under a tree; and (5) that the book, in size and weight, be comfortably portable, for if students won't carry the anthology to class, lectures are lamed and discussions rendered profitless.

Some earlier selections, which our canvass of teachers showed to have been assigned infrequently or not at all, have been dropped from this edition. Only three of these omissions are prominent ones. (1) In the third edition, we undertook to represent Victorian fiction by long excerpts from the novels of Dickens and from George Eliot's *Mill on the Floss*. This was, we believe, a worthwhile experiment; but in the almost unanimous judgment of teachers, the experiment failed, and the selections languished unassigned. (2) The "Topics," designed to exhibit the social and intellectual ambiance of each period, had begun to outlive their usefulness, and have in this edition been deleted. There are two exceptions. Since it is impossible to understand the greater part of Victorian literature outside the context of its dominant social, scientific, and religous concerns, the "Topics" of "Evolution" and "Industrialism" have been retained under the more accurate heading "Victorian Issues" and have been supplemented by a third issue, "The Woman Question." Also, the attested and varied usefulness of "Romantic Poems in Process" has been enhanced, by extending it to include authors from the 17th century to the present, and by including a section of pertinent "Poems in Process" in each of the two volumes. (3) In the preceding editions, the examples of 16th- and 17th-century prose were selected mainly to illustrate prominent subjects of discussion and debate, such as "The Dispute over Natural Law." In the present edition, we simply represent, chronologically, the best writers of each period, chosen also to represent the diversity of the prose styles current at that time.

The various deletions have provided the space for a number of additions to the anthology, and for completing items hitherto represented by excerpts. Almost all of the additions are in response to many requests; a few of them, as veteran users of the anthology will recognize, are selections which had been dropped from the first or second editions but are reintroduced by widespread demand. An overview here of the more important changes may help the teacher to appraise the teaching opportunities that this new edition provides.

Medieval selections now include the complete *Pearl* (in a new translation by Marie Borroff); a retranslaticn of *Piers Plowman*, with two passages on the Deadly Sins replacing "The Harrowing of Hell"; and new translations of three Old English poems. Among the added materials in the 16th century is the text of *Hero and Leander* as, according to the scholar, Louis L. Martz, it was originally written in a complete form, by Christopher Marlowe, with Chapman's unwarranted division into "Sestiads" deleted. The *Mutabilitie Cantos* of Spenser's *Faerie Queene* are now printed in their entirety, thereby providing a possible alternative to assigning the complete Book I, which is retained in this edition. The sections of More's *Utopia* are presented in Robert M. Adams's cogent new translation. There are new prose selections from Thomas Nashe's *Pierce Penniless* and from Hoby's influential translation of Castiglione's *The Courtier*. There are also addi-

tions to the lyrics by various poets and, in response to insistent demands, a
number of changes in our representation of Shakespeare's sonnets. In a
major innovation, Ben Jonson's *Volpone* has been added to the four Elizabethan and Jacobean plays in the previous edition, thereby creating a mini-
anthology of the golden age of English dramatic literature. Other new items
in the 17th century are Donne's complete *Anatomy of the World*; a
number of songs from the plays of Beaumont and Fletcher; poems by
Donne, Jonson, various Cavalier lyrists, Traherne, and Cowley; five poems
by Herbert (attesting to the great current interest in that craftsman in
verse); as well as a number of poems by Andrew Marvell (several on a
single, related subject). The writings in prose now include Bacon's essay
on *Masques and Triumphs*, and, to demonstrate the development of a
prose adapted to practical and scientific exposition, selections from Sprat's
History of the Royal Society and Isaac Newton's letter to the Society
announcing his "New Theory about Light and Colors." The selections from
Paradise Lost (already including four complete Books) have also been augmented so as to clarify the evolving relations between Adam and Eve, by
Book V, lines 377–505 (before the Fall) and the concluding section of
Book X (after the Fall).

In accord with many recommendations, Congreve's *The Way of The
World* has been replaced by his more simply and coherently plotted *Love
for Love*. Two poems by Lady Wortley Montagu, hitherto known mainly
through footnotes to the writings of Alexander Pope, show her to have
been a trenchant exponent of what women are, as against what male poets
suppose them to be. There is an added poem by Jonathan Swift (*Stella's
Birthday, 1721*), and Pope's *Essay on Criticism* is now printed in its entirety.
Additional essays are included from the *Tatler* and the *Spectator*, while Dr.
Johnson's writings have been supplemented by his *Brief to Free a Slave* and
by materials from his great achievement, *A Dictionary of the English Language*—important sections of the Preface, as well as some of the more
notable definitions. The selections from Thomson's *Seasons* and Cowper's
Task have been improved. We have also added the "Peter Grimes" story
from Crabbe's *The Borough*, as well as new odes by Thomson, Gray, and
Collins.

To the Romantic section have been added two writers: Mary Wollstonecraft (the central sections from her pioneering treatise, *A Vindication of
the Rights of Woman*, together with selections from her *Letters Written
in Sweden*) and Mary Shelley (her remarkable Introduction to *Frankenstein* and a Gothic tale of the supernatural, *Transformation*). Two additional long works are Byron's complete *Manfred* and Shelley's urbane dialogue with Byron in his poem *Julian and Maddalo*. In response to numerous
suggestions, we have added Burns's poem of homely realism, *To a Louse*,
as well as several early Romantic poems written in the deliberately simple
style—two more of Blake's *Songs of Innocence* and another of Wordsworth's
lyrical ballads, *Simon Lee*, in the version of 1798. We have also included
three short items by Blake on natural religion and deism, added a third
letter, and replaced the excerpts from *Jerusalem* by a complete and more
readily intelligible instance of Blake's prophetic mode, *America: A Prophecy*.
Wordsworth's *Prelude* is still represented (though in newly edited texts)
by its first and last versions of 1799 (complete) and 1850; but the latter has
been supplemented by some 300 lines, so as to reveal the complex internal

design of that poem. Two new poems by Wordsworth exemplify moments of vision: *The Two April Mornings* and *Nutting*. The selections from Coleridge include an added section of *Biographia Literaria* on "rustic" language, and two excerpts from *The Statesman's Manual* on "Symbol and Allegory" and the "Satanic Hero." Shelley's *Prometheus Unbound* has been supplemented by a passage on Prometheus's temptation by the Furies (Act I); Byron's *Childe Harold* has been expanded; and in his *Don Juan*, while Canto XVI (infrequently assigned) has been deleted, other Cantos have been supplemented: Canto II, for example, now includes Byron's description of cannibalism at sea. In the writings by Lamb, Hazlitt, and De Quincey, furthermore, some essays have been replaced by others which, on the testimony of instructors, will be of greater use and interest to students.

The most conspicuous addition in the Victorian period is a complete play, Oscar Wilde's *The Importance of Being Earnest*, but there are numerous other innovations. Among the prose writings, we now have selections from Carlyle's *French Revolution*, an added passage from Ruskin's *Modern Painters*, and Pater's *The Child in the House*, which serves as a revealing introduction to that writer's characteristic concerns and literary artistry. *St. Agnes' Eve* has been added to Tennyson's poems; in response to persistent demand, there are also five new passages from *Maud*, and six additional sections from *In Memoriam* (6, 8, 12, 29, 105, 113) which clarify the structure, and bring the total selections to more than two-thirds of the entire poem. Other poets whose works are more fully represented are Elizabeth Barrett Browning, George Meredith (six additional sonnets from *Modern Love*), Dante and Christina Rossetti, and William Morris. W. S. Gilbert has been added to the group now entitled "Light Verse." In a major reorganization, the section on "The Nineties" has been transferred from "The Twentieth Century" to the end of the Victorian section (where it belongs); it is strengthened not only by adding to the poems of Wilde and Dowson, but also by representing more fully the "hearty" writers of that decade—Rudyard Kipling and a new writer, William Ernest Henley.

The writers in "The Twentieth Century," like those in "The Victorian Age," have been reordered so as to make them more readily locatable. Conrad's long (and, to most students, too familiar) *Heart of Darkness* has been replaced by two short stories and a passage of critical comment on fiction; similarly, D.H. Lawrence's *The Fox* has been replaced by a new story, *The Princess*, a selection from the travel book *Mornings in Mexico*, and several often-demanded poems. As befits a major writer, the representation of Virginia Woolf has been signally increased: to *The Mark on the Wall* we add the title sketch from the one volume of short fiction she herself published, *Monday or Tuesday*, as well as *An Unwritten Novel* and several pieces of social and literary criticism, including an excerpt from *A Room of One's Own*. For the earlier selections from Yeats's autobiographic writings, we have substituted others which are more central to his life and work, and have replaced Joyce's short story, *Clay*, by his more lucid *Counterparts*. In line with a strong current interest, there is a substantial new section of "Poetry of World War I" which, in addition to poets in the previous edition (Brooke, Edward Thomas, Owen, Jones), now includes Siegfried Sassoon, Ivor Gurney, and Isaac Rosenberg. Other writers of verse and prose added in the present edition are Edith Sitwell, Katherine Mansfield, F. R. Leavis (a complete essay), Stevie Smith, and George Orwell. Shaw's *Major*

Barbara has been replaced by the more teachable (and in its vigorous feminism, a very topical) play, *Mrs. Warren's Profession*. Samuel Beckett is now represented by a most characteristic short story, *The End*; and we have added to our long array of dramas Harold Pinter's very "modern" play, *The Dumb Waiter*. The selections from Robert Graves and Hugh MacDiarmid have been altered. Finally, the passage of time and an emerging critical consensus have provided greater assurance in the choice of writers and writings for "Poetry after Mid-Century." The reconstituted section now includes two new poets, Molly Holden and Elaine Feinstein, as well as more recent selections by Donald Davie, Philip Larkin, Thom Gunn, Ted Hughes, Jon Silkin, Geoffrey Hill, and Seamus Heaney.

It should be noted that the number and variety of the works included in the anthology make possible not only a chronological approach to major writers, but also generic or topical ways of organizing a course, or parts of a course. English poetry, in all its species and magnitudes, is of course represented fully, and now supplemented by the diversely useful sections on "Poems in Process." The broad spectrum of plays, augmented by four new titles, constitutes an overview of English drama in its various modes, starting with *The Second Shepherds' Play* and *Everyman*, ranging through Marlowe, Shakespeare (a history play and a tragedy), Jonson, Webster, two masques (Jonson's *Pleasure Reconciled to Virtue* and Dryden's *Secular Masque*), a Restoration comedy of manners, two Romantic closet dramas (*Manfred*, complete, and *Prometheus Unbound*), Wilde's great farce, and Shaw's satiric social drama, and ending with a contemporary play by Harold Pinter. It is also possible to study the evolution of shorter forms of prose fiction, from *Pilgrim's Progress* through the narrative papers in the *Tatler* and *Spectator*, Defoe's *Mrs. Veal*, Swift's *Gulliver's Travels*, Johnson's *Rasselas*, and a great variety of short stories, including a Gothic tale by Mary Shelley and the diverse stories by Conrad, Forster, Woolf, Joyce, Mansfield, Beckett, and Lessing.

The third edition of the anthology undertook to redress the neglect of women in traditional literary study; the present edition has enlarged the representation of these authors, as well as of writings that deal with women in western culture. Literature centrally concerned with the social and sexual roles of women may be studied in a range from "the marriage group" in the *Canterbury Tales*, through many intervening works (e.g., *Paradise Lost*, *The Rape of the Lock, Rasselas*), to a number of poems and stories in our own age. Social and literary criticism specifically addressed to the situation of women is represented by selections from two classic works, Mary Wollstonecraft's *A Vindication of the Rights of Woman* and J. S. Mill's *The Subjection of Women*; by documents by George Eliot, Florence Nightingale, and other Victorians in the new section "The Woman Question," and by selections from Virginia Woolf. And the earlier list of women poets and writers of fiction has been enlarged by the inclusion of Lady Mary Wortley Montagu, Mary Shelley, Molly Holden, and Elaine Feinstein.

Many other topics can be profitably studied from materials in the present anthology, including such matters of current interest as: (1) the imaginative response of writers to the changing aspects of war, from *Beowulf* and *The Battle of Maldon*, to the many poems in "Poetry of World War I"; (2) the visionary mode in literature, as exemplified by Spenser's *Mutabilitie Cantos*, several 17th-century visionary poets, Christopher Smart, William

Blake, a number of Romantic and Victorian representations, in verse and prose, of visions and dreams, and the poems and autobiographic writings of Yeats; (3) the persistent but ever-altering form of spiritual autobiography, crisis, and the quest for identity, as represented in Bunyan's *Grace Abounding*, Wordsworth's *Prelude*, De Quincey's *Confessions*, Carlyle's *Sartor Resartus*, Mill's *Autobiography*, Pater's *The Child in the House*, Tennyson's *In Memoriam*, Joyce's *Portrait of the Artist*, and Eliot's *Little Gidding*.

The organization of the contents in each period of English literature has been simplified by putting in chronological order the authors, whether they wrote in verse or prose, as well as the titles written by each author; there are a few exceptions to this principle, most of them instances when it has seemed helpful to group short, related items under such headings as "Sixteenth-Century Lyrics," Victorian "Light Verse," or "Poetry of World War I."

In accord with our policy to adopt improved texts as they become available, we now print Jonathan Wordsworth's revised versions of *The Prelude* of 1799 and 1850 (from *Wordsworth's Prelude, 1799, 1805, 1850: A Norton Critical Edition*, edited by Wordsworth, M. H. Abrams, and Stephen Gill, 1979); Jack Stillinger's new edition of Keats's *Poems* (Harvard University Press, 1978); the poems of Gerard Manley Hopkins as edited by W. H. Gardner and N. H. MacKenzie (Oxford University Press, 4th edition, 1970); and the stories from Joyce's *Dubliners* in the definitive edition by Robert Scholes (1968). To make texts as accessible as possible to student readers, we have normalized spelling and capitalization (and, very sparingly, punctuation) according to modern American usage. There are two kinds of exceptions to this procedure. (1) We have left unaltered texts in which modernization would change semantic, phonological, or metric qualities, or would affect distinctive features of the original publications. Thus the verse of Spenser, Burns, Hopkins, MacDiarmid, and David Jones, as well as the prose of Dorothy Wordsworth's *Journals* and of the writings of Carlyle, Joyce, and Shaw have been reproduced exactly. Only minor changes required for ready intelligibility (mainly in punctuation) have been made in the poems etched by William Blake. The works of Chaucer and other writers in Middle English that are not too difficult for the novice have also been left in the original language; each word, however, is consistently spelled in that variant of its scribal forms which is closest to modern English. (2) We have also left unaltered certain texts for which we use specially edited versions (identified in a headnote or footnote): Wollstonecraft's *Vindication* and *Letters from Sweden*, the two versions of Wordsworth's *Prelude*, all the verse and prose of Shelley and Keats, and the selections from Mary Shelley.

Each editor has reconsidered and rewritten (in some instances, radically) his introductory essays and headnotes and has revised his footnotes, both to take advantage of recent scholarship and in a continuing effort to make them as informative and clear as possible. In selected instances editorial headnotes or footnotes briefly indicate interpretations of a difficult work or passage. The reason for this procedure is a practical one. The anthology includes some of the most complex and difficult writings in the language, and the normal procedure is to assign some texts which there is not time to discuss adequately—or sometimes, to discuss at all—in the classroom. We therefore undertake to give an essential modicum of guidance to the student, but to present it in such a way as to open out possibilities for independent judgment and to provide, not definitive readings, but points of departure for dialogue in the classroom.

We continue other editorial procedures which have proved their usefulness in earlier editions. The historical and biographical introductions, although succinct, are informative enough to eliminate the need for supplementary books on the lives of authors and on the literary, social, and cultural history of England. In most introductions we identify at the beginning a few dates which are important for orienting the student. After each work we cite (when known) the date of composition on the left and the date of first publication on the right; in some instances the latter is followed by the date of a revised reprinting. Texts which include a large proportion of unfamiliar words are glossed in the margin, so that readers may assimilate the translation without interrupting the flow of their reading. In the limited instances when part of a work has been omitted, that fact is indicated by the word *From* before the title, and the place of the omission in the text is indicated by three asterisks.

The selected bibliographical guides at the end of each volume are designed to encourage students to read further on their own, and also to serve as points of departure in assigned essays. In this edition all the bibliographies have been brought up to date, and the authors and subgroups within each period have been put in alphabetic order. In both volumes a brief glossary of terms is provided under the title "Poetic Forms and Literary Terminology."

We have also added, in Volume I, illustrations of two subjects in which graphic representations are of special value: a schematic drawing of the universe according to Ptolemy, and exterior and interior views of a London playhouse of Shakespeare's time (drawn especially for us by C. Walter Hodges, author of *The Globe Restored*).

To the hundreds of teachers throughout the United States and Canada who have helped us to design and improve these volumes, the editors express their deep gratitude; we cannot name every one of them here, but all will recognize the changes that they have suggested. A separate list of "Acknowledgments" names advisors who provided detailed critiques of the anthology as a whole or of particular periods, or were especially helpful in the preparation of texts and editorial matter. We wish to mention here the assistance of Jennifer Sutherland, Valerie Eads, John W. N. Francis, and of Diane O'Connor, Marjorie Flock, Nelda Freeman, Marian Johnson, Tam Putnam, Josepha Gutelius, Roy Tedoff, Hugh O'Neill, and James Mairs of Norton's production department; we also owe thanks to Norman McAfee, to Julie Aidelberg of Cornell University; to Susan Metzger of the Harvard University Press; to Barbara Zimmerman; and to Barbara and Paul Bodin. Our greatest debt is to George P. Brockway and John Benedict of W. W. Norton and Company, Inc., who have helped mitigate the chronic dilemmas in the continuing process of representing, justly, accurately, and in accord with changing interests and advancing knowledge, the immense scope of English literature within a single book.

M. H. ABRAMS

Acknowledgments

Among our many critics, advisors, and friends, the following were of especial help in providing critiques of particular periods or of the anthology as a whole, or assisted in preparing texts and editorial matter: Barry B. Adams (Cornell University); Paul Alpers (University of California, Berkeley); Judith H. Anderson (Indiana University); Colin B. Atkinson; Paula Backscheider (University of Rochester); Sheridan Baker (University of Michigan); Jerome Beaty (Emory University); Miriam J. Benkovitz (Skidmore College); Marie Borroff (Yale University); A. T. J. Cairns (University of Calgary); Jenni Calder (Edinburgh University); Angus Calder(The Open University); Tom J. Collins (University of Arizona); Rebecca Crump (Louisiana State University); Stuart Curran (University of Washington); Beth Darlington (Vassar College); Roman R. Dubinski (University of Waterloo); Dwight Eddins (University of Alabama); Scott Elledge (Cornell University); Hubert M. English, Jr. (University of Michigan); John P. Farrell (University of Texas at Austin); Barbara Charlesworth Gelpi (Stanford University); Marilyn Gaull (Temple University); Stephen Gill (Lincoln College, Oxford); Homer B. Goldberg (State University of New York at Stony Brook); Nancy M. Goslee (University of Tennessee); Donald J. Gray (Indiana University); David V. Harrington (Gustavus Adolphus College); Carolyn G. Heilbrun (Columbia University); Richard Helgerson (University of California, Santa Barbara); Robert D. Hume (Cornell University); J. Paul Hunter (Emory University); Joel Hurstfield (University of London); Robert Kiely (Harvard University); Ruth P. M. Lehmann (University of Texas at Austin); William T. Liston (Ball State University); James R. McAdams (Pennsylvania State University); N. H. MacKenzie (Queen's University); Hugh Maclean (State University of New York at Albany); Leslie H. Martin (University of Notre Dame); Dorothy Mermin (Cornell University); Helene Moglen (State University of New York College at Purchase); David Novarr (Cornell University); Robert O'Clair (Manhattanville College); William Park (Sarah Lawrence College); Reeve Parker (Cornell University); Carol H. Poston (University of Illinois at Chicago Circle); Jon A. Quitslund (George Washington University; Donald H. Reiman (The Carl H. Pforzheimer Library); M. L. Rosenthal (New York University); H. Grant Sampson (Queen's University); Ronald A. Sharp (Kenyon College); David Shore (University of Ottawa); Sally K. Slocum (University of Akron); Jon Stallworthy (Cornell University); Jack Stillinger (University of Illinois at Urbana-Champaign); E. E. Stokes, Jr. (Texas A&M University); Roger G. Swearingen (University of North Carolina at Chapel Hill); Nina L. Thiess (Santa Monica College); Charles H. Vivian (Bentley College); Jonathan Wordsworth (Exeter College, Oxford).

The Romantic Period

(1798-1832)

1789–1815: Revolutionary and Napoleonic period in France. 1789: The Revolution begins with the assembly of the States-General in May and the storming of the Bastille on July 14.—1793: King Louis XVI executed; England joins the alliance against France.—1793–94: The Reign of Terror under Robespierre.—1804: Napoleon crowned emperor. 1815: Napoleon defeated at Waterloo.

1798: *Lyrical Ballads* published anonymously by William Wordsworth and Samuel Taylor Coleridge.

1811–20: The Regency—George, Prince of Wales, acts as regent for George III, who was declared incurably insane.

1820: Accession of George IV.

1832: The Reform Bill carried in Parliament.

THE POLITICAL BACKGROUND: REVOLUTION AND REACTION

Following the common usage of historians of English literature, we will denote by the "Romantic period" the span between the year 1798, in which Wordsworth and Coleridge published their *Lyrical Ballads*, and 1832, when Sir Walter Scott died, when other major writers of the earlier century were either dead or no longer productive, and when the passage of the first Reform Bill inaugurated the Victorian era of cautious readjustment of political power to the economic and social realities of a new industrial age. This was a turbulent period in political and economic history, during which England was experiencing the ordeal of the change from a primarily agricultural society, where wealth and power had been largely concentrated in the landholding aristocracy, to a modern industrial nation, in which the balance of economic power was shifted to large-scale employers, who found themselves ranged against an immensely enlarging and increasingly restive working class. And this change occurred in a context first of the American and then of the much more radical French Revolution, of wars, of economic cycles of inflation and depression, and of the constant threat to the social structure from imported revolutionary ideologies to which the ruling

1

classes responded by heresy-hunts and the repression of traditional liberties.

The early period of the French Revolution, marked by the Declaration of the Rights of Man and the storming of the Bastille to release the imprisoned political offenders, evoked enthusiastic support from English liberals and radicals alike. Two influential books indicate the radical social thinking stimulated by the Revolution. Tom Paine's *Rights of Man* (1791–92) justified the French Revolution against Edmund Burke's attack in his *Reflections on the Revolution in France* (1790), and advocated for England a democratic republic which was to be achieved, if lesser pressures failed, by popular revolution. More important for its influence on Wordsworth, Shelley, and other poets was William Godwin's *Inquiry Concerning Political Justice* (1793), which foretold an inevitable but peaceful evolution of society to a final stage in which all property would be equally distributed and all government would wither away. Later, however, English sympathizers dropped off as the Revolution followed its increasingly grim and violent course: the accession to power by the Jacobin extremists; the "September Massacres" of the imprisoned and helpless nobility in 1792, followed by the execution of the royal family; the invasion by the French Republic of the Rhineland and Netherlands, and its offer of armed assistance to all countries desiring to overthrow their governments, which brought England into the war against France; the guillotining of thousands in the Reign of Terror under Robespierre; and after the execution in their turn of the men who had directed the Terror, the emergence of Napoleon first as dictator and then as emperor of France. As Wordsworth wrote in *The Prelude* (XI.206–9),

> become oppressors in their turn,
> Frenchmen had changed a war of self-defence
> For one of conquest, losing sight of all
> Which they had struggled for * * *

For Wordsworth and all the English of liberal inclinations, these events posed a dilemma which has become familiar since the 1920's, in our parallel era of wars, revolutions, and the struggle by competing social ideologies —liberals had no side they could wholeheartedly espouse. Napoleon, the child and champion of the French Revolution, had become an arch-aggressor, a despot, and the founder of a new dynasty; yet almost all those who opposed him did so for the wrong reasons, so that his final defeat at Waterloo in 1815 proved to be the triumph, not of progress and reform, but of reactionary despotisms throughout continental Europe.

In England this period was one of harsh repressive measures. Public meetings were prohibited, habeas corpus suspended for the first time in over a hundred years, and advocates of even moderate measures of political change were charged with high treason in time of war. The Napoleonic wars put an end to reform, and to almost all genuine political life in England, for more than three decades.

Yet this was the very time when profound economic and social changes were creating a desperate need for corresponding changes in political arrangements and politics, and new classes—manufacturing, rather than agricultural—were beginning to demand a power in goverment proportionate to their wealth. The "Industrial Revolution"—the shift in methods of manufacturing which resulted from the invention of power-driven machinery to replace hand labor—had begun in the mid-18th century with improvements in machines for processing textiles, and was given immense impetus when James Watt perfected the steam engine in 1765. In the succeeding decades steam replaced wind and water as the primary source of power in one after another type of manufacturing; and at once, after centuries of almost imperceptibly slow change, there began that constantly accelerating alteration in economic and social conditions which shows no signs of slowing down in the foreseeable future. A new laboring population massed in the sprawling mill towns which burgeoned in central and northern England. In rural communities the destruction of home industry was accompanied by a rapid growth of the process—lamented by Oliver Goldsmith in *The Deserted Village* as early as 1770—of enclosing the old open-field and communally worked farms into privately owned agricultural holdings. This process was necessary for the more efficient methods of agriculture and animal breeding required to supply a growing population (although some of the land thus acquired was turned into vast private parks); in any case, it created a new landless class which either migrated to the industrial towns or remained as farm laborers, subsisting on starvation wages eked out by an inadequate dole. The landscape of England began to take on its modern appearance: the hitherto open rural areas subdivided into a checkerboard of fields enclosed by hedges and stone walls, and the factories of the industrial and trading cities casting a pall of smoke over vast areas of jerry-built houses and slum tenements. Meanwhile, the population was becoming increasingly polarized into what Disraeli later called the "Two Nations"—the two classes of capital and labor, the large owner or trader and the possessionless wageworker, the rich and the poor.

No attempt was made to regulate this movement from the old economic world to the new, not only because of inertia and the power of vested interests, but because even the liberal reformers were dominated by the social philosophy of laissez faire. This theory of "let alone" holds that the general welfare can be ensured only by the free operation of economic laws; the government must maintain a policy of strict noninterference and leave each man to pursue his own private interests. For the great majority of the laboring class the results of this policy were inadequate wages, long hours of work under harsh discipline in sordid conditions, and the large-scale employment of women and children for tasks which destroyed both the body and the spirit. Reports by investigating committees on the coal mines, with male and female children of ten or even five years of age harnessed to heavy coal-sledges which they dragged by crawling on their hands and knees, read like scenes from Dante's *Inferno*. In 1815 the conclusion of the French war, when the enlargement of the working force by demobilized troops coincided with the fall in the wartime demand for goods, brought on the first modern industrial depression. Since the workers had no vote and were prevented from unionizing by law, their sole recourse was to petitions, protest meetings, agitation, and hunger riots, which only frightened the ruling class into more repressive measures. In addition the introduction of new machines caused technological unemployment, and this provoked sporadic attempts by dispossessed workers to destroy the machines. After one such outbreak the House of Lords—despite Lord Byron's eloquent protest—passed a bill (1812) making death the penalty for destroying the frames used for weaving in the stocking industry. In 1819 meetings of workers were organized to demand Parliamentary reform. In August of that year, a huge but orderly assembly at St. Peter's Fields, Manchester, was wantonly charged by troops, who killed nine and severely injured hundreds more; this was the notorious "Peterloo Massacre," so named as a parody on the Battle of Waterloo. The event incited Shelley to write his great poems for the working class, *England in 1819, Song: "Men of England,"* and *To Sidmouth and Castlereagh.*

Suffering was largely confined to the poor, however, for all the while the landed classes, the industrialists, and many of the merchants prospered. In London the Regency period (1811–20) was for the leisure class a time of lavish display and moral laxity. In the provinces, the gentry in their great country houses carried on their familial and social concerns—reflected in the novels of Jane Austen—almost untouched by great national and international events.

As in earlier English history, women constituted a deprived class which cut across social classes, for they were widely regarded as inferior to men in intellect and in all but domestic talents, were provided limited schooling and no facilities for higher education, had only lowly vocations open to them, and possessed (especially after marriage) very few legal rights. In the revolutionary period, women finally acquired a strong and eloquent champion. Mary Wollstonecraft, who in 1790 wrote an early defense of the French Revolution, *A Vindication of the Rights of Men,* followed this two years later with *A Vindication of the Rights of Woman,* a founding classic of the feminist movement. Wollstonecraft asserted that women possess equal intellectual capacity and talents with men, and demanded for them greater equality of social, educational, and vocational privileges. The cause of women's rights, however, was not taken up by effective proponents until the Victorian era, and even partial achievement of its aims was delayed until well along in the 20th century.

But the pressures for reform in the privileges of men could not be eliminated in the early 19th century, especially since political disabilities were not limited to the working class. Gradually the working-class reformers acquired the support of the middle classes and the liberal Whigs. Finally, at a time of acute economic distress, and after unprecedented agitation and disorders that threatened to break out into revolution, the first Reform Bill was carried in 1832, amid widespread rejoicing. It eliminated the rotten boroughs (depopulated areas whose seat in Commons was at the disposal of a nobleman), redistributed parliamentary representation to include the new industrial cities, and extended the vote. Although about half the middle class, almost all the working class, and all women remained still without a franchise, the principle of peaceful adjustment of conflicting interests by Parliamentary majority had been firmly established; and reform was to go on until, by stages, England acquired universal adult suffrage.

All attempts at a single definition of Romanticism fall far short of matching the variegated facts of a time which exceeds almost all ages of English literature in the range and diversity of its achievements. No writer in Wordsworth's lifetime thought of himself as a "Romantic"; the word was not applied until half a century later, by English historians. Contemporary critics and reviewers treated them as independent individuals, or else grouped them (often invidiously, but with some basis in fact) into a number of separate schools: "the Lake School" of Wordsworth, Coleridge, and Robert Southey; "the Cockney School" of Leigh Hunt, Hazlitt, and associated writers, including John Keats; and "the Satanic School" of Byron, Shelley, and their followers.

Many of the major writers, however, did feel that there was something distinctive about their time—not a shared doctrine or literary quality, but a pervasive intellectual climate, which some of them called "the spirit of the age." They had the sense that (as Keats said in one of his sonnets) "Great spirits now on earth are sojourning," and that there was evidence all about of that release of energy, experimental boldness, and creative power which marks a literary renaissance. In his *Defence of Poetry* Shelley claimed that the literature of the age "has arisen as it were from a new birth," and that "an electric life burns" within the words of its best writers, which is "less their spirit than the spirit of the age." Shelley explained this literary spirit as the accompaniment of political and social revolution; and other writers agreed. Francis Jeffrey, foremost conservative reviewer of the day, connected "the revolution in our literature" with "the agitations of the French Revolution, and the discussions as well as the hopes and terrors to which it gave occasion." William Hazlitt, who published a book of essays called *The Spirit of the Age*, described how, in his early youth, the French Revolution seemed "the dawn of a new era, a new impulse had been given to men's minds." The new poetry of the school of Wordsworth, he maintained, "had its origin in the French Revolution. * * * It was a time of promise, a renewal of the world—and of letters."

The imagination of Romantic writers was, indeed, preoccupied with the fact and idea of revolution. In the early period of the French Revolution all the leading English writers except Edmund Burke were in sympathy with it, and Robert Burns, William Blake, Wordsworth, Coleridge, Southey, and Mary Wollstonecraft were among its fervent adherents. Later, even after the first boundless expectations had been disappointed by the events in France, the younger writers, including Hazlitt, Hunt, Shelley, and Byron, felt that its example, when purged of its errors, still comprised man's best hope. The Revolution generated a pervasive feeling that this was a great age of new beginnings when, by discarding inherited procedures and outworn customs, everything was possible; and not only in political and social arrangements, but in intellectual and literary enterprises as well. In his *Prelude* Wordsworth wrote the classic description of the intoxicating spirit of the early 1790's, with "France standing on the top of golden hours, / And human nature seeming born again," so that "the whole Earth, / The beauty wore of promise." Something of this sense of suddenly expanding horizons and of limitless possibilities survived the shock of first disappointment at events in France and carried over to the year 1797, when Wordsworth and Coleridge, in excited daily communion, set out to revolutionize the theory and practice of poetry. The product of these discussions was the *Lyrical Ballads* of 1798.

POETIC THEORY AND POETIC PRACTICE

Wordsworth undertook to justify the new poetry by a critical manifesto or statement of poetic principles, in the form of an extended Preface to the second edition of *Lyrical Ballads* in 1800, which he enlarged still further in the third edition of 1802. In it he set himself in opposition to the literary *ancien régime*, those writers of the preceding century who, to his view, had imposed on poetry artificial conventions which distorted its free and natural development. Many of Wordsworth's later critical writings were attempts to clarify, buttress, or qualify points made in his first declaration. Coleridge declared that the Preface was "half a child of my own brain"; and although he soon developed doubts about certain of Wordsworth's unguarded statements, and undertook to correct them in *Biographia Literaria* (1817), he did not question the necessity of Wordsworth's attempt to overturn the reigning tradition. In the course of the 18th century there had been increasing opposition to the neoclassic tradition of Dryden, Pope, and Dr. Johnson, and especially in the 1740's and later, there had emerged many of the critical concepts, as well as a number of the poetic subjects and forms, which were later exploited by Wordsworth and his contemporaries. Wordsworth's Preface nevertheless deserves its reputation as a turning point in English literature, for Wordsworth gathered up isolated ideas, organized them into a coherent theory based on explicit critical principles, and made them the rationale for his own massive achievements as a poet. We can conveniently use the concepts in this extremely influential essay as points of departure for a survey of distinctive elements in the theory and poetry of the Romantic period.

1. *The Concept of Poetry and of the Poet.*

In neoclassic theory, poetry had been regarded as primarily an imitation of human life—in a favorite figure, "a mirror held up to nature"—in a form designed to instruct and give artistic pleasure to the reader. Wordsworth, in a reiterated statement, described all good poetry as "the spontaneous overflow of powerful feelings." In a reversal of earlier aesthetic theory, he thus located the source of poetry not in the outer world, but in the individual poet, and identified as its essential material not men and their actions, but the fluid feelings of the author himself, or else natural and human objects as they are modified by the author's feelings. Other Romantic theories, however various, concurred in this crucial point by referring to the mind and feelings of the individual writer, instead of to the outer world, for the origin and defining attributes of a poem. Many writers identified poetry (in metaphors parallel to Wordsworth's "overflow") as the "expression" or "utterance" or "exhibition" of emotion. Blake and Shelley described a poem as the poet's imaginative vision, which they opposed to the ordinary world of public experience. Coleridge introduced into English criticism an organic theory of the imaginative process and the poetic product, based on the model of a growing plant. That is, he conceived a great work of literature as a self-originating and self-organizing process which begins with a seedlike idea in the poet's imagination, grows by assimilating the most diverse materials of sense-experience, and evolves into an organic form in which the parts are integrally related to each other and to the whole.

In accordance with the view that poetry expresses the poet's own mind, imagination, and emotion, Romantic poems take as their subject matter, not the actions of other men, but the experiences, thoughts, and feelings of the poets who wrote them. The lyric poem written in the first person, which had earlier been regarded as a minor poetic kind, became a major Romantic form and was usually described as the most essentially poetic of all the genres. And in the Romantic lyric the "I" is often not a mere *dramatis persona*, a typical lyric speaker such as the Petrarchan lover or Cavalier gallant of Elizabethan and 17th-century love poems, but is recognizably the poet in his private person. In the poems of Coleridge and Keats, for example, the experiences and states of mind expressed by the lyric speaker often accord closely with the personal confessions in the poets' letters and journals. Even in his ostensibly fictional writings, narrative and dramatic, Byron usually invites his readers to identify the hero with the author, whether the hero is presented romantically (as in *Childe Harold*, *Manfred*, or the Oriental tales) or in an ironic perspective (as in *Don Juan*). An extreme instance of this tendency is Wordsworth's *Prelude*, which is a poem of epic length and epic seriousness about the growth of the poet's own mind.

The Prelude exemplifies two other important tendencies in the period. Like Blake, Coleridge in his early poems, and later on Shelley, Wordsworth presents himself as what he calls "a chosen son," or "Bard." That is, he assumes the persona and voice of a poet-prophet, modeled on Milton and the prophets in the Bible, and puts himself forward as a spokesman for traditional Western civilization at a time of profound crisis—a time, as Wordsworth said in Book II of *The Prelude*, "of dereliction and dismay" and the "melancholy waste of hopes o'erthrown." As bards, Wordsworth and his visionary fellow poets set out to revise the Biblical promise of divine redemption by reconstituting the grounds of hope and pronouncing the coming of a time in which a renewed humanity will inhabit a renovated earth on which men and women will feel thoroughly at home. *The Prelude* also represents a central form of English, as of European Romanticism —a long work about the formation of the self, often centering on a crisis, and presented in the radical metaphor of the poet's interior journey in quest of his true identity and destined spiritual home. Major examples of this form are Blake's *Milton*, the crucial episode of Asia's underground journey in Shelley's *Prometheus Unbound*, and Keats' *Endymion* and the *Fall of Hyperion*. In contemporary prose, we find equivalent developments: the subjectivity of the personal essays of Lamb, Hazlitt, and Leigh Hunt, and the currency of spiritual autobiography, whether fictionalized (Thomas Carlyle's *Sartor Resartus*) or presented as fact (Coleridge's *Biographia Literaria*, Thomas De Quincey's *Confessions of an English Opium Eater* and *Autobiographic Sketches*).

2. *Poetic Spontaneity and Freedom.*

Wordsworth defined good poetry not merely as the overflow but as "the *spontaneous* overflow" of feelings. In traditional aesthetic theory, poetry had been regarded as supremely an art; an art which in modern times could be practiced successfully only by a craftsman who had assimilated classical precedents, was aware of the "rules" governing the kind of poem he was writing, and (except for the felicities which, as Pope said, are "beyond the reach of art") deliberately employed tested means to achieve foreknown effects upon his audience. But to Wordsworth, although the writing of a poem may be preceded by reflection and followed by second thoughts, the immediate act of composition must be spontaneous—that is, arising from impulse, and free from all rules and the artful manipulation of means to foreseen ends—if the product is to be a genuine poem. Other important Romantic critics also voiced declarations of artistic independence. Keats listed as an "axiom" that "if poetry comes not as naturally as the leaves to a tree it had better not come at all." Blake insisted that he wrote from "Inspiration and Vision," and that his long "prophetic" poem, *Milton*, was given to him by an agency not himself, and "produced without Labor or Study." Shelley also maintained that it is "an error to assert that the finest passages of poetry are produced by labor and study," and suggested instead that they are the products of an unconscious creativity: "A great statue or picture grows under the power of the artist as a child in the mother's womb." "The definition of genius," Hazlitt remarked, "is that it acts unconsciously." The surviving work-sheets of the Romantic poets, however, as well as the testimony of observers, show that they worked and reworked their texts no less arduously—if perhaps more immediately under the impetus of first conception—than the craftsmen of earlier ages. Coleridge, who believed that truth lies in a union of opposites, came closer to the facts of Romantic practice when he claimed that the act of composing poetry involves the psychological contraries "of passion and of will, of *spontaneous* impulse and of *voluntary* purpose."

The emphasis in this period on the free activity of the imagination is related to an insistence on the essential role of instinct, intuition, and the feelings of "the heart" to supplement the judgments of the purely logical faculty, "the head," whether in the province of artistic beauty, philosophical and religious truth, or moral goodness. "Deep thinking," Coleridge wrote, "is attainable only by a man of deep feeling, and all truth is a species of revelation"; hence, "a metaphysical solution that does not tell you something in the heart is grievously to be suspected as apocryphal."

3. *Romantic "Nature Poetry."*

In his Preface Wordsworth wrote that "I have at all times endeavored to look steadily at my subject"; and in a supplementary Essay he complained that, from Dryden through Pope, there is scarcely an image from external nature "from which it can be inferred that the eye of the poet had been steadily fixed on his object." A glance at the table of contents of any collection of Romantic poems will indicate the degree to which the natural scene has become a primary poetic subject, while Wordsworth, Shelley, and even more Coleridge and Keats, described natural phenomena with an accuracy of observation which had no earlier match in its ability to capture the sensuous nuance.

Because of the prominence of landscape in this period, "Romantic poetry" has to the popular mind become almost synonymous with "nature poetry." Neither Romantic theory nor practice, however, justifies the opinion that the aim of this poetry was description for its own sake. Wordsworth in fact insisted that the ability to observe and describe objects accurately, although a necessary, is not at all a sufficient condition for poetry, "as its exercise supposes all the higher qualities of the mind to be passive, and in a state of subjection to external objects." And while most of the great Romantic lyrics—Wordsworth's *Tintern Abbey* and *Ode: Intimations of Immortality*, Coleridge's *Frost at Midnight* and *Dejection*, Shelley's *Ode to the West Wind*, Keats's *Nightingale*—begin with an aspect or change of aspect in the natural scene, this serves only as stimulus to the most characteristic human activity, that of thinking. Romantic "nature poems" are in fact meditative poems, in which the presented scene usually serves to raise an emotional problem or personal crisis whose development and resolution constitute the organizing principle of the poem. As Wordsworth said in his Prospectus to *The Recluse*, not nature, but "the Mind of Man" is "my haunt, and the main region of my song."

In addition, Romantic poems habitually imbue the landscape with human life, passion, and expressiveness. In part such descriptions represent the poetic equivalent of the metaphysical concept of nature, which had developed in deliberate revolt against the world views of the scientific philosophers of the 17th and 18th centuries, who had posited as the ultimate reality a mechanical world consisting of physical particles in motion. What is needed in philosophy, Coleridge wrote, is "the substitution of life and intelligence * * * for the philosophy of mechanism, which, in everything that is most worthy of the human intellect, strikes *Death*. * * *" But for many Romantic poets it was clearly also a matter of immediate experience to respond to the outer universe as a living entity which shares the feelings of the observer. James Thomson and other descriptive poets had described the created universe as giving direct access to God, and even as itself possessing the attributes of divinity; in *Tintern Abbey* and other poems Wordsworth exhibits toward the landscape attitudes and sentiments which men had earlier felt not only for God, but also for a father, a mother, or a beloved woman. Elsewhere, as in the great passage on crossing Simplon Pass (*The Prelude* VI.624 ff.), Wordsworth also revives the ancient theological concept that God's creation constitutes a symbol system, a physical revelation parallel to Revelation in the Scriptures—

> Characters of the great Apocalypse,
> The types and symbols of Eternity,
> Of first, and last, and midst, and without end.

This view of natural objects as corresponding to the spiritual world served also as the understructure for a tendency, especially by Blake and Shelley, to write a symbolist poetry in which a rose, a sunflower, a mountain, a cave, or a cloud are presented as objects instinct with a significance beyond themselves. "I always seek in what I see," Shelley said, "the likeness of something beyond the present and tangible object." And by Blake mere nature, as perceived by the physical eye and un-humanized by the imagination, was spurned "as the dirt upon my feet, no part of me."

4. The Glorification of the Commonplace.

In two lectures on Wordsworth, Hazlitt declared that the school of poetry founded by Wordsworth was the literary equivalent of the French Revolution, translating political changes into poetical experiments. "Kings and queens were dethroned from their rank and station in legitimate tragedy or epic poetry, as they were decapitated elsewhere. * * * The paradox [these poets] set out with was that all things are by nature equally fit subjects for poetry; or that if there is any preference to be given, those that are the meanest and most unpromising are the best."

Hazlitt had in mind Wordsworth's statement that the aim of *Lyrical Ballads* was "to choose incidents and situations from common life," and to use a "selection of language really spoken by men," for which the source and model is "humble and rustic life." As Hazlitt shrewdly saw, this was more a social than a distinctively literary definition of the proper materials and language for poetry. Versifiers of the later decades of the 18th century had experimented in the simple treatment of simple subjects, and Robert Burns —like Wordsworth, a sympathizer with the French Revolution—had achieved great poetic success in the serious representation of humble life in a language really spoken by rustics. But Wordsworth buttressed his poetic practice by a theory which inverted the traditional hierarchy of poetic genres, subjects, and style by elevating humble and rustic life and the plain style, earlier appropriate to the lowly pastoral, into the principal subject and medium for poetry in general. And in his own practice, as Hazlitt also noted, Wordsworth went even further, and turned for the subjects of his serious poems not only to humble people but to the ignominious, the outcast, the delinquent—to "convicts, female vagrants, gypsies * * * idiot boys and mad mothers," as well as to "peasants, peddlers, and village barbers." Hence the outrage of Lord Byron, who alone among his great contemporaries insisted that Dryden and Pope had laid out the proper road for poetry, and who—in spite of his liberalism in politics—maintained allegiance both to aristocratic proprieties and traditional poetic decorum:

> "Peddlers," and "Boats," and "Wagons"! Oh! ye shades
> Of Pope and Dryden, are we come to this?

But in his democratization of poetry, Hazlitt insisted, Wordsworth was "the most original poet now living." And certainly Wordsworth in *Lyrical Ballads* was in this respect, more radical than any of his contemporaries. He effected an immense enlargement of our imaginative sympathies and brought into the province of serious literature a range of materials and interests which are still being explored by writers of the present day.

It should be noted, however, that Wordsworth's aim in *Lyrical Ballads* was not a mere reproductive realism, but as he announced in his Preface, to

throw over "situations from common life * * * a certain coloring of imagination, whereby ordinary things should be presented to the mind in an
unusual aspect." As this passage indicates, Wordsworth's concern in his
poetry was not only with "common life" but with "ordinary *things*"; no
one can read his poems without noticing the extraordinary reverence which
he attaches to words which in earlier writers had been derogatory—words
like "common," "ordinary," "everyday," "humble," whether applied to
people or to objects in the visible scene. His aim throughout is to shake us,
out of the lethargy of custom so as to refresh our sense of wonder—indeed,
of divinity—in the everyday, the trivial, and the familiar. In one of the
events Wordsworth called "a spot of time," when he entered London for
the first time, he describes how the "vulgar men about me, trivial forms
* * * mean shapes" suddenly assumed a "weight and power" that lasted
only a moment, "yet with Time it dwells, / And grateful memory, as a
thing divine" (*The Prelude* VIII.545-59).

Dr. Johnson had said that "wonder is a pause of reason," and that "all
wonder is the effect of novelty upon ignorance." But for many Romantic
critics, to arouse in the sophisticated mind that sense of wonder felt by the
ignorant and the innocent was a primary power of imagination and a major
function of poetry. Commenting on the special imaginative quality of
Wordworth's early poetry (*Biographia*, Chapter VI), Coleridge commented: "To combine the child's sense of wonder and novelty with the
appearances, which every day for perhaps forty years had rendered familiar
* * * this is the character and privilege of genius," and its prime service is
to awaken in the reader "freshness of sensation" in the representation of
"familiar objects." Poetry, said Shelley in his *Defence of Poetry*, "reproduces the common universe" but "purges from our inward sight the film of
familiarity which obscures from us the wonder of our being," and "creates
anew the universe, after it has been blunted by reiteration." And in Carlyle's *Sartor Resartus* (1833-34), the chief—indeed the only—effect of the
conversion of the protagonist from despairing unbelief is that he is able to
sustain a sense of the "Natural Supernaturalism" in ordinary experience and
so overcome the "custom" which "blinds us to the miraculousness of daily-
recurring miracles." The great power of the imagination is that it makes the
old world new again.

5. *The Supernatural and "Strangeness in Beauty."*

In most of his poems Coleridge, like Wordsworth, dealt with the everyday things of this world, and in *Frost at Midnight* he showed how well he
too could achieve the effect of wonder in the familiar. But according to the
agreed division of labor in *Lyrical Ballads*, Coleridge's function, he tells us,
was to achieve wonder by a frank violation of natural laws and the ordinary
course of events, in poems of which "the incidents and agents were to be,
in part at least, supernatural." And in *The Ancient Mariner*, *Christabel*,
and *Kubla Khan*, Coleridge opened up the realm of mystery and magic, in
which ancient folklore, superstition, and demonology are used to impress
upon the reader the sense of occult powers and unknown modes of being.
Such poems are usually set in the distant past or in faraway places, or both;

the milieu of *Kubla Khan*, for example, exploits the exoticism both of the Middle Ages and of the Orient. Next to Coleridge, the greatest master of this Romantic mode—in which supernatural events have a profound psychological import—was John Keats. In *La Belle Dame sans Merci* and *The Eve of St. Agnes* he adapted the old forms of ballad and romance to modern sophisticated use and, like Coleridge, established a medieval setting for events that violate the natural order. Hence the term "the medieval revival," frequently attached to the Romantic period, which comprehends also the ballad imitations and some of the verse tales and historical novels of Sir Walter Scott.

Another side of the tendency which Walter Pater later called "the addition of strangeness to beauty" was the Romantic interest in unusual modes of experience, of a kind which earlier writers had largely ignored as either too trivial or too aberrant for serious literary concern. Blake, Wordsworth, and Coleridge in their poetry explored visionary states of consciousness which are common among children but violate the standard categories of adult judgment. Coleridge was interested in mesmerism (what we now call hypnotism), and like Blake and Shelley, studied the literature of the occult and the esoteric. Coleridge also shared with De Quincey a concern with dreams and nightmares; both authors exploited in their writings the heightened consciousness and distorted perceptions they experienced under their addiction to opium. Byron exploited the fascination of the forbidden and the appeal of the terrifying Satanic hero. And Keats was extraordinarily sensitive to the ambivalences of human experience—to the mingling, at their highest intensity, of pleasure and pain, to the destructiveness of love, and to the erotic quality of the longing for death. These phenomena had already been crudely explored by 18th-century writers of terror tales and Gothic fiction, and later in the 19th century all of them, sometimes exaggerated to blatant perversity, became the special literary province of Charles Baudelaire, Algernon Charles Swinburne, and writers of the European "Decadence."

INDIVIDUALISM, NONCONFORMITY, AND APOCALYPTIC EXPECTATION

Through the greater part of the 18th century, man had for the most part been viewed as a limited being in a strictly ordered and essentially unchanging world. A variety of philosophical and religious systems in this century coincided in a distrust of radical innovation, a respect for the precedents established through the ages by the common sense of mankind, and the recommendation to set accessible goals and avoid extremes, whether in politics, intellect, morality, or art. Many of the great literary works of the period joined in attacking "pride," or man's aspirations beyond the limits natural to his species. "The bliss of man," Pope wrote in *An Essay on Man*, "(could pride that blessing find) / Is not to act or think beyond mankind."

> This kind, this due degree
> Of blindness, weakness, Heaven bestows on thee.
> Submit.

The Romantic period, the age of burgeoning free enterprise and revolutionary hope, was also an age of radical individualism, in which both the

philosophers and poets put an immensely higher estimate on man's potentialities and on his proper aims. In German post-Kantian philosophy, which
generated many of the characteristic ideas of European Romanticism, the
mind of man—what was called the "Subject" or "Ego"—took over various
functions which had hitherto been the sole prerogative of Divinity. Most
prominent was the rejection of a central 18th-century concept of the mind
as a mirrorlike recipient of a universe already created and its replacement by
the new concept of the mind as itself the creator of the universe it perceives. The English founders of the new poetry also described the mind as
creating its own experience. In Blake, the mind creates its proper milieu
only if it rejects the material world; in Coleridge and Wordsworth, the
mind creates in collaboration with something given to it from without.
Mind, wrote Coleridge in 1801, is "not passive" but "made in God's
Image, and that too in the sublimest sense—the Image of the *Creator*."
And Wordsworth declared in *The Prelude* (II.257–60) that the individual
mind

> Doth like an agent of the one great Mind
> Create, creator and receiver both,
> Working but in alliance with the works
> Which it beholds. * * *

Many Romantic writers also agreed that man's mind has access beyond
sense to the infinite, through a special faculty they called either Reason or
Imagination. In *The Prelude* (VI.601 ff.) Wordsworth describes a flash of
imagination "that has revealed / The invisible world," and affirms:

> Our destiny, our being's heart and home,
> Is with infinitude, and only there;
> With hope it is, hope that can never die,
> Effort, and expectation, and desire,
> And something evermore about to be.

The aspect of man which, to the moralists of the preceding age, had been
his essential sin, or his tragic error, now becomes his glory and his triumph:
he refuses to submit to his limitations and, though finite, persists in setting
infinite, hence inaccessible goals. Wordsworth characteristically goes on to
declare that "under such banners militant, the soul / Seeks for no trophies,
struggles for no spoils"; for him, the militant striving ends in physical quietism and moral fortitude. But for other writers, especially in Germany,
man's proper destiny is ceaseless activity—a *"Streben nach dem Unend-
lichen,"* a striving for the infinite. This view is epitomized by Goethe's
Faust, who in his quest for the unattainable violates ordinary moral limits,
yet wins salvation by his very insatiability, which never stoops to contentment with any possibilities offered by this finite world. Man's infinite longing—in Shelley's phrase, "the desire of the moth for a star"—was a recurrent theme also in the English literature of the day. "Less than everything," Blake announced, "cannot satisfy man." Shelley's *Alastor* and Keats's
Endymion both represent the quest for an indefinable and inaccessible goal,
and Byron's *Manfred* has for its hero a man whose "powers and will" reach
beyond the limits of that human clay "which clogs the ethereal essence," so
that "his aspirations / Have been beyond the dwellers of the earth."

In the contemporary theory of art, we find critics rejecting the neoclassic ideal of a limited intention, perfectly accomplished, in favor of "the glory of the imperfect," in which the artist's very failure attests the largeness of his aim. And in their own work, Romantic writers deliberately put themselves in competition with their greatest predecessors, and experimented boldly in poetic language, versification, and design. Especially in their longer poems, they struck out in new directions, and in the space of a few decades produced an astonishing variety of forms constructed on novel principles of organization and style. Blake's symbolic lyrics and visionary "prophetic" poems; Coleridge's haunting ballad-narrative of sin and retribution, *The Ancient Mariner*; Wordsworth's epiclike spiritual autobiography, *The Prelude*; Shelley's cosmic symbolic drama, *Prometheus Unbound*; Keats's great sequence of *Odes* on the irreconcilable conflict in basic human desires; Byron's ironic survey of all European civilization, *Don Juan*—one can say of each of them, as Shelley said of *Don Juan*, that it was "something wholly new and relative to the age."

The great neoclassic writers had typically dealt with men as members of an organized, and usually an urban, society; of this society the author regarded himself as an integral part, its highest standards were those he spoke for, and to it as his audience he addressed himself. Some Romantic writers, on the other hand, deliberately isolated themselves from society in order to give scope to their individual vision. Wordsworth's projected masterwork he entitled *The Recluse*, and he described himself as "musing in solitude" on its subject, "the individual Mind that keeps her own / Inviolate retirement." And in almost all Wordsworth's poems, long or short, the words "single," "solitary," "by oneself," "alone" constitute a leitmotif; his imagination is released by the sudden apparition of a single figure or object, stark against an undifferentiated background. Coleridge also, and still more strikingly, Byron and Shelley, represented a solitary protagonist who is separated from society because he has rejected it, or because it has rejected him; these poets introduced what became a persistent theme in many Victorian and modern writers—the theme of exile, of the disinherited mind which cannot find a spiritual home in its native land and society or anywhere in the modern world. The solitary Romantic nonconformist was sometimes also a great sinner. Writers of that time were fascinated by the outlaws of myth, legend, or history—Cain, Satan, Faust, the Wandering Jew or the great, flawed figure of Napoleon—about whom they wrote and on whom they modeled a number of their villains or their heroes. In Coleridge's *Ancient Mariner* (as in Wordsworth's *Guilt and Sorrow* and *Peter Bell*) the guilty outcast—"alone, alone, all, all alone"—is made to realize and expiate his sin against the community of living things, so that he may reassume his place in the social order. But in Byron the violator of conventional laws and limits remains proudly unrepentant. His hero Manfred, a compound of guilt and superhuman greatness, cannot be defeated by death, successfully defying the demons who, in the tradition of Marlowe's *Dr. Faustus*, have come to drag his soul to hell: I "was my own destroyer, and will be / My own hereafter * * * / Back, ye baffled fiends!" A more reputable Romantic hero, who turns up frequently in Byron and other writers and is made the protagonist of Shelley's greatest poem, is the Prometheus of Greek mythology. He shares with Satan the status of superlative nonconformity, since he sets himself in opposition to deity itself; unlike Satan, however, he is the champion rather than the enemy of the human race.

Nowhere is the Romantic combination of boundless aspiration and the reliance on the power of the individual mind better exhibited than in the literary treatment of the ultimate hope of mankind. The French Revolution had aroused in many sympathizers the millennial expectations which are profoundly rooted in Hebrew and Christian tradition. "Few persons but those who have lived in it," Robert Southey reminisced in 1824, "can conceive or comprehend what the memory of the French Revolution was, nor what a visionary world seemed to open upon those who were just entering it. Old things seemed passing away, and nothing was dreamt of but the regeneration of the human race." Southey's language—like that of Wordsworth, Coleridge, Hazlitt, and other writers when they described their early Revolutionary fervor—is Biblical; and it reflects the extent to which, in England, the Revolution was championed especially by members of radical Protestant sects, who envisioned it on the model of Biblical prophecy.

The Bible ends with the book of Apocalypse (literally, "Revelation"), prophesying a return of man to his lost Edenic felicity, first in the millennium ("a thousand years") of an earthly kingdom, then in the eternity of "a new heaven and a new earth"; this consummation of history is symbolized as a marriage between the New Jerusalem and Christ the Lamb. At the outbreak of the French Revolution, Joseph Priestley and other Unitarian leaders hailed that event as the stage preceding the millennium prophesied in Revelation. Coleridge and Wordsworth, in their early poems, also interpreted the Revolution as the violent preliminary to the new earth and heaven of apocalyptic prophecy. And Blake's *The French Revolution* (1791) and *America, a Prophecy* (1793) represented both these revolutions as apocalyptic portents of the last days of the fallen world.

When the later events in France dashed their faith in political revolution as a means to the millennium, a number of Romantic writers salvaged their apocalyptic hope by giving it a new interpretation. They transferred the agency of apocalypse from mass action to the individual mind—from a political to a spiritual revolution—and proposed that "the new earth and new heaven" of Revelation is available here, now, to each man, if only he can make his visionary imagination triumph over his senses and his sense-bound understanding. Hence the extraordinary Romantic emphasis on a new way of *seeing* (which is the restoration of a lost earlier way of seeing) as man's chief aim in life. Blake's "Prophetic Books," for example, all deal with some aspects of the Fall and Redemption, and represent apocalypse as the recovery of the imaginative vision of things as they really are, seen "through and not with the eye." "The Nature of my Work is Visionary or Imaginative; it is an Endeavor to Restore what the Ancients called the Golden Age." This concept of the imaginative recreation of the old earth is still expressed by Romantic poets in the original Biblical metaphor of a marriage—although now it is not a marriage of the New Jerusalem with the Lamb, but a reintegration of man's inner faculties into spiritual unity, or else a marriage between man's mind and the external world. Coleridge put this latter version succinctly, in *Dejection: An Ode*; it is the inner condition of "Joy," at life's highest moments, "Which, wedding nature to us, / gives in dower / A new earth and new heaven." Wordsworth announced as the "high argument" for *The Recluse* (the same theme serves as underpattern for *The Prelude*) that "Paradise, and groves Elysian" are not "a history only of departed things"—

> For the discerning intellect of Man
> When wedded to this goodly universe
> In love and holy passion, shall find these
> A simple produce of the common day.

In Shelley's *Prometheus Unbound*, Prometheus represents archetypal man, whose total change of heart frees his imaginative capacity to envision, and to achieve, a regenerate world; the fourth act symbolizes this event in the mode of a marriage celebration in which the whole cosmos participates. Carlyle's *Sartor Resartus*, to mention one other example, is the history of an individual's savage spiritual crisis and conversion, which turns out to be the achievement of an individual apocalypse: "And I awoke to a new Heaven and a new Earth." But, as Carlyle goes on to indicate, this new earth is the old earth, seen by his protagonist as though miraculously recreated, because he has learned to substitute the "Imaginative" faculty for what Carlyle represents as the chief faculty of the 18th-century Enlightenment, the "Logical, Mensurative faculty," or "Understanding." Writing in 1830–31, at the close of the period historians have labeled "Romantic," Carlyle thus summed up the tendency of a generation of writers to retain the ancient faith in apocalypse, but to interpret it not as a change in the world, but as a change in man's imaginative vision, or world view.

THE FAMILIAR ESSAY

At the close of the 18th century the reviews and magazines were written largely by hacks who acceded to the political bias and financial interests of the publisher and advertisers. The essays they included were weak imitations of the type established nearly a century earlier by the single-essay periodicals, the *Tatler* and the *Spectator*. In 1802, however, the *Edinburgh Review* inaugurated the modern type of periodical publication. It allowed considerable latitude to its writers, set its literary standards high, and was able to meet these standards by paying for contributions at rates good enough to command the best talents of the day.

The great and immediate success of this new enterprise stimulated the founding of rival reviews and magazines. (A "review," usually issued four times yearly, consisted primarily of essays on important books and discussions of contemporary issues; a "magazine" was a monthly publication which printed more miscellaneous materials, including a high proportion of original essays, poems, and stories.) In 1820 appeared the *London Magazine*, liberal in politics and contemporary in literary interests; in its short but notable career until 1829, it printed the work of a group of brilliant writers, including the three men who soon established themselves as the greatest essayists of the age—Lamb, Hazlitt, and De Quincey.These magazines, and others like them, elevated the essay in literary dignity and quality and revolutionized its form and substance. They competed strenuously for talent, paying well enough so that an author (at least if he were as prolific as Hazlitt) could earn a living as a free-lance essayist. Since allotment of space was flexible, each topic could find its appropriate length, instead of being held to the Procrustean brevity of the earlier essays modeled on Addison and Steele; in consequence, the new essays tended to be from two to four times as long as the 18th-century form. And writers were treated as serious craftsmen who were competent, within broad limits, to write as they pleased.

Under these new conditions the familiar essay—a commentary on a nontechnical subject written in a relaxed and intimate manner—flourished, and in a fashion that to some degree paralleled the course of Romantic poetry. Each of the major essayists was in fact closely associated with important poets and supported at least some of the new poetic developments in critical commentaries whose perceptiveness and discrimination render them permanently valuable. Like the poets, these essayists were personal and subjective; their essays are often candidly autobiographical, reminiscent, self-analytic; and when the writers treated other matters than themselves, they did so impressionistically, so that the material is seen reflected in the temperament of the essayist. The subject matter of the essays, like that of the poetry, exhibits an extension of range and sympathy far beyond the earlier limits of the leisure class and its fashionable concerns, to comprehend clerks, chimney sweeps, poor relations, handball players, prizefighters, and murderers. Most strikingly, the essayists resemble the poets in rebelling against 18th-century conventions to revive prose forms long disused and to develop new prose styles and structural principles. The result was a notable variety of achievement, ranging from Hazlitt's hard-hitting plain style and seemingly casual order of topics, through Lamb's delicately contrived rhetoric and meticulously controlled organization, to De Quincey's elaborate experiments in applying to prose the rhythms, harmonies, and thematic structure of music.

DRAMA

Although favorable to the essay, literary conditions in the early 19th century were unfavorable in the extreme to writing for the stage. By a licensing act which was not repealed until 1843, only the Drury Lane and Covent Garden theaters had the right to produce "legitimate"—that is to say, spoken—drama; the other theaters were restricted by law to entertainments in which there could be no dialogue except to music, and so put on mainly dancing, pantomime, and various types of musical plays. The two monopoly theaters were vast and ill-lighted, and their audiences were noisy and unruly; as a result, actors played in a grandiose and orotund style. To succeed under such conditions, plays had also to be blatant and magniloquent, so that the drama of that period (fettered also by rigid moral and political censorship) tended to the extremes of either farce or melodrama. None of the plays written by the professional playwrights of the time have survived, except in the limbo of scholarly monographs on the history of the theater.

Nonetheless, attracted irresistibly by the example of their idolized Shakespeare, all the major Romantic poets, and many minor ones, tried their hand at poetic plays. Some of these were deliberate closet dramas—Byron's *Manfred* and Shelley's *Prometheus Unbound*, for example, can hardly be visualized, much less produced—but others were expressly written for the stage. The poets, however, lacked experience with the hard necessities of the practical theater, and they were unable to throw off the artifice of an archaic style dominated by Elizabethan and Jacobean models.

Above all, the genius of an age which excelled in subjective or visionary literary forms was ill adapted to the theater, which is a peculiarly social genre and must represent a variety of men other than the author himself. Even Byron, the only important poet of his generation to produce major work in a literary kind—satire—which requires a highly developed social sensibility, did not succeed as a practical dramatist. His stage plays, while readable, mainly exhibit various aspects of the Byronic hero; they lack theatrical vigor and variety, and their thin-skinned author wisely refused to let them be put on before the merciless and demonstrative audiences of his day. Coleridge achieved a minor hit with his tragedy *Remorse*, which ran for twenty nights at the Drury Lane in 1813. The most successful Romantic dramatist was, surprisingly, Shelley. In *The Cenci* (1820) Shelley, with extraordinary tact and genuine theatrical acumen, converts a true story of the Italian Renaissance—of a monstrous father who violates his daughter and is in turn murdered by her—into a powerful version of his own central fable of the instinctive desire of evil to destroy, by degrading, the defiant individual, and of the moral triumph of the unconquerable single spirit, even in death. The play was not acted, however, until long after Shelley had died.

THE NOVEL

Two new types of fiction were prominent in the late 18th century. One was the "Gothic novel," which had been inaugurated in 1764 by Horace Walpole's *Castle of Otranto, A Gothic Story*, and continued by Clara Reeve in *The Champion of Virtue, A Gothic Story* (1777). The term derives from the frequent setting of these tales in a gloomy castle of the Middle Ages, but it has been extended to a larger group of novels, set somewhere in the past, which exploit the possibilities of mystery and terror in sullen, craggy landscapes; decaying mansions with dank dungeons, secret passages, and stealthy ghosts; chilling supernatural phenomena; and often, persecution of a beautiful maiden by an obsessed and haggard villain. The best of these novels opened up to later fiction the dark, irrational side of human nature—the savage egoism, the perverse impulses, and the nightmarish terrors that lie beneath the controlled and ordered surface of the conscious mind. In her *Mysteries of Udolpho* (1794), and better still in *The Italian* (1797), Ann Radcliffe developed the figure of the mysterious and solitary *homme fatal*, torturing others because himself tortured by unspeakable guilt, who, though a villain, usurps the place of the hero in the reader's interest. Matthew Gregory Lewis in *The Monk* (1797), which he wrote at the age of 20, has a similar protagonist, and brings to the fore the elements of diabolism, sensuality, and sadistic perversion which were pungent but submerged components in Mrs. Radcliffe's Gothic formula. Gothicism is apparent also in Romantic poetry: in Coleridge's medieval terror poem *Christabel*, in Byron's recurrent hero-villain, and in Shelley's inclinations (fostered by his early love for Gothic tales and his own youthful trials in that form) toward the fantastic, the macabre, and the exploration of the realm of the unconscious mind and of aberrations such as incest.

The second fictional mode popular at the turn of the century was the novel of purpose, often written to propagate the new social and political theories current in the period of the French Revolution. The best examples combine didactic intention with elements of Gothic terror. William Godwin, the political philosopher, wrote *Caleb Williams* (1794) to illustrate the thesis that the lower classes are helplessly subject to the power and privilege of the ruling class, but he did so in the form of a chilling story about the relentless pursuit and persecution by a wealthy squire of his young secretary who has come upon evidence that the squire has committed murder. Mary Shelley—Shelley's wife and the daughter of Mary Wollstonecraft, author of *A Vindication of the Rights of Woman*—wrote a thematic novel of terror which is not only a literary classic, but has become a popular myth. Her *Frankenstein* (1817) transforms a story about a fabricated monster into a powerful representation of the moral distortion imposed on an individual who, because he diverges from the norm, is rejected by society.

The Romantic period produced two major novelists, Jane Austen and Sir Walter Scott. Jane Austen (1775–1817) is one of the greatest of English novelists, yet she is the only important author who, untouched by the political, intellectual, and artistic revolutions of her age, stayed serenely within the culture and the literary traditions of the neoclassic past. Charlotte Brontë, speaking for the Romantic sensibility, complained that Jane Austen's novels lack warmth, enthusiasm, energy; "she ruffles her reader by nothing vehement, disturbs him by nothing profound. The passions are perfectly unknown to her. * * * " But Austen deliberately elected to work within the circumference of her own experience—the life of provincial English gentlefolk—and to maintain the decorum of the aloof and ironic novel of manners, based on such 18th-century antecedents as the comedy of manners of William Congreve and Richard Brinsley Sheridan and the novels of earlier women authors, Fanny Burney and Maria Edgeworth. Within these elected limits both of subject and form, Austen achieved a fully particularized setting within which to examine the values men and women live by in their everyday social lives.

Sense and Sensibility and *Northanger Abbey* poke fun at two latter 18th-century deviations from the humanistic norm, the cult of sensibility and the taste for Gothic terrors. Austen's other novels, published between 1813 and 1818—*Mansfield Park, Persuasion,* and best of all, *Pride and Prejudice* and *Emma*—all deal with the subject of getting married. This was in fact the central preoccupation and problem for the young leisure-class lady of that age, who had no career open to her outside of domesticity; Austen, however, chose the subject because it provided her with the best available opportunities for testing her heroines' practical sense and moral integrity, their degree of knowledge of the world and of themselves, and their capacity to demonstrate grace under pressure.

Sir Walter Scott (1771–1832) was contemporary with Jane Austen, and admired her greatly, but his work in fiction was at the opposite extreme from hers. In 1814, with the anonymous *Waverly*, he turned from narrative verse (in which Byron had displaced him in popularity) to narrative prose, and managed to write almost thirty long works of fiction in the eighteen years before he died. They are in the mode which he himself defined as romance, "the interest of which turns upon marvelous and uncommon incidents," in contrast to the novel such as Jane Austen wrote, in which "the events are accommodated to the ordinary train of human events, and the modern state of society." Scott's great originality lay in opening up to fiction the realm of history; he sometimes alters the order of events for novelistic purposes, yet he maintains fidelity to the spirit of the past and a meticulous accuracy in antiquarian detail. His great series of Scottish novels, including *Guy Mannering, The Antiquary, Old Mortality, Rob Roy* and (best of all) *The Heart of Midlothian*, are rooted in historical events from the 17th century up to his own time; *Ivanhoe* is set in 13th-century England and *Kenilworth* in the age of Elizabeth; and *Quentin Durward*, the best of his Continental romances, has for background the French Court of the 15th century.

Like his friend Byron, Scott wrote with dash and grandiosity in a kind of sustained improvisation; his plotting is often loose, his romantic lovers pallid, and his kings and chieftains large-scale puppets. But in his great scenes of action there is a scope and sweep that was not to be exceeded in fiction until the appearance of Leo Tolstoy's *War and Peace* in the 1860's. And although, unlike his liberal Romantic contemporaries, Scott's political sympathies were aristocratic and feudal, his most vivid and convincing characters are members of the middle and lower classes. His tradesmen, servants, peasantry, social outcasts, and demented old women, speaking a rich Scottish vernacular (Scott's language, like Robert Burns's in verse, tended to become stilted and conventional when he wrote in standard English), compose a populous world in which each person is an individual, rooted in the circumstances of his time and place and class and occupation. Scott had an immense international vogue, equaling that of Byron and Goethe, and became the acknowledged master of some of the greatest 19th-century novelists, including Balzac and Tolstoy. Jane Austen, on the other hand, during her lifetime was admired only by a limited group of English readers. Her novels have, however, demonstrated greater staying power. Scott's combination of casualness in design and prodigality in detail puts off many readers who have formed their sensibilities on the well-made novel of the present century. But even after the achievements of such craftsmen in the form as Henry James, Jane Austen remains the sovereign of the intricate, spare, and graceful art of the novel of manners.

WILLIAM BLAKE

(1757–1827)

1783:   *Poetical Sketches*, his first book of poems.
1794:   *Songs of Innocence and of Experience*.
1804–20: The two last and greatest "prophetic" poems,
          Milton and *Jerusalem*.

What Blake called his "Spiritual Life" was as varied, free, and dramatic as his "Corporeal Life" was simple, limited, and unadventurous. His father was a London haberdasher. His only formal education was in art: at the age of 10 he entered a drawing school and later studied for a time at the school of the Royal Academy of Arts. At 14 he apprenticed for seven years to a well-known engraver, James Basire, read widely in his free time, and began to try his hand at poetry. At 24 he married Catherine Boucher, daughter of a market gardener. She was then illiterate, but Blake taught her to read and to help him in his engraving and printing. In the early and somewhat sentimentalized biographies, Catherine is represented as an ideal wife for an unorthodox and impecunious genius. Blake, however, must have been a trying domestic partner, and his vehement attacks on the torment caused by a possessive, jealous female will, which reached their height in 1793, and remained prominent in his writings for another decade, probably reflect a troubled period at home. The couple were childless.

The Blakes for a time enjoyed a moderate prosperity while Blake gave drawing lessons, illustrated books, and engraved designs made by other artists. When the demand for his work slackened, Blake in 1800 moved to a cottage at Felpham, on the Sussex seacoast, under the patronage of the wealthy poetaster, biographer, and amateur of the arts, William Hayley, who with the best of narrow intentions tried to transform Blake into a conventional artist and breadwinner. But the caged eagle soon rebelled. Hayley, Blake wrote, "is the Enemy of my Spiritual Life while he pretends to be the Friend of my Corporeal."

At Felpham in 1803 occurred an event that left a permanent mark on Blake's mind and art. He had an altercation with one John Schofield, a private in the Royal Dragoons. Blake ordered the soldier out of his garden and, when the soldier replied with threats and curses against Blake and his wife, pushed him the fifty yards to the inn where he was quartered. Schofield brought charges that Blake had uttered seditious statements about King and country. Since England was at war with France, sedition was a hanging offense. Blake was acquitted; an event, according to a newspaper account, "which so gratified the auditory that the court was * * * thrown into an uproar by their noisy exultations." Nevertheless Schofield, his fellow-soldier Cock, and other participants in the trial haunted Blake's imagination and were enlarged to demonic characters who play a sinister role in *Jerusalem*. The event exacerbated Blake's sense that ominous forces were at work in the contemporary world and led him to complicate the symbolic obliquities by which he veiled the unorthodoxy of his religious and moral opinions, as well as the radicalism of the many allusions to contemporary affairs that he worked into his poems.

After three years at Felpham Blake moved back to London, determined to follow his "Divine Vision" though it meant a life of isolation, misunderstanding, and poverty. When his one great bid for public recognition, a one-man show put on in 1809, proved a total failure, Blake passed into almost complete obscurity. Only when he was in his 60's did he finally attract a small but devoted group of young painters who served as an audience for his work and his talk. Blake's old age was serene, self-confident, and joyous, largely free from the bursts of irascibility with which he had earlier responded to the shallowness and blindness of the English public. He died in his seventieth year.

Blake's first book of poems, *Poetical Sketches*, which he had printed when he was 26 years old, showed his dissatisfaction with the reigning poetic tradition and his restless quest for new forms and techniques. For lyric models he turned back to the Elizabethan and early 17th-century poets, to the Ossianic poems, and to Collins, Thomas Chatterton, and other 18th-century writers outside the tradition of Pope; he also experimented with partial rhymes and novel rhythms and employed bold figures of speech that at times approximate symbols. In *Songs of Innocence* (1789) Blake inaugurated the method of publication he used for his later original works, a procedure he had partly invented. He covered a copper plate with acid-proof wax, engraved away the wax from a design that incorporated both text and pictorial illustration, then applied acid so that the design was left in relief. With this plate he printed a page, which he later colored with water colors by hand and bound with the other pages to make up a volume. The procedure of making the plates was laborious and time-consuming, and Blake struck off very few copies of his works; for example, of *Songs of Innocence and Experience* 27 copies (both complete and incomplete) are known to exist; of *The Book of Thel*, 15; of *The Marriage of Heaven and Hell*, 9; and of *Jerusalem*, 5. It must be remembered that to read Blake's poem in a printed text is to see only an abstraction from an integral and mutually illuminating combination of words and design. In 1794 Blake supplemented the earlier songs of innocence and published a work he called *Songs of Innocence and Experience*. The two groups of poems represent the world as it is envisioned by what he calls "two contrary states of the human soul." In the best of the songs of experience, such as *The Tyger* and *London*, Blake achieved his mature lyric technique of compressed metaphor and symbol which explode into a multiplicity of reference.

Gradually Blake's thinking about human history and his experience of life and suffering articulated themselves in the "Giant Forms" and their actions, which constitute a complete mythology. As Los said, speaking for all imaginative artists, "I must Create a System or be enslaved by another Man's." This coherent but constantly altering and enlarging system composed the subject matter, first of Blake's "minor prophecies," completed by

1795, and then of the major prophetic books on which he continued working until about 1820: *The Four Zoas, Milton,* and *Jerusalem.*

In his 60's Blake gave up poetry to devote himself to pictorial art. In the course of his life he produced hundreds of paintings and engravings, many of them illustrations for the work of other poets, including a representation of Chaucer's Canterbury pilgrims, a superb set of designs for the Book of Job, and a series of illustrations of Dante, on which he was still hard at work when he died. At the time of his death Blake was little known as an artist and almost entirely unknown as a poet. In the mid-19th century he acquired a group of admirers among the Pre-Raphaelites, who regarded him as a precursor. Since the mid 1920's, Blake has finally come into his own, both in poetry and painting, as one of the most dedicated, intellectually challenging, and astonishingly original of artists.

The explication of Blake's cryptic and complex prophetic books has been the preoccupation of many scholars. Blake wrote them in the persona, or "voice," of "the Bard / Who Present, Past, & Future sees"—that is, as a British poet who follows Spenser, and especially Milton, in a lineage going back to the prophets of the Bible. "The Nature of my Work," he said, "is Visionary or Imaginative." What Blake meant by the key terms "vision" and "imagination," however is often misrepresented by taking literally what he, speaking the traditional language of his great predecessors, intended in a figurative sense. "That which can be made Explicit to the Idiot," Blake declared, "is not worth my care." Blake was a born ironist who enjoyed mystifying his well-meaning but literal-minded friends and who took a defiant pleasure in shocking the dull and complacent "angels" of his day by being deliberately outrageous in representing his work and opinions.

Blake declared that "all he knew was in the Bible," and that "The Old & New Testaments are the Great Code of Art." This is an exaggeration of the truth that all his prophetic writings deal, in various formulations, with some aspects of the over-all Biblical plot of the creation and fall of man, the history of the generations of man in the fallen world, redemption, and the promise of a recovery of Eden and of a New Jerusalem. These events, however, Blake interprets in what he calls "the spiritual sense." For such a procedure he had considerable precedent, not in the Neoplatonic and occult thinkers with which some modern commentators align him, but in the "spiritual" interpreters of the Bible among the radical Protestant sects in 17th- and 18th-century England. In *The French Revolution, America: A Prophecy, Europe: A Prophecy,* and the trenchant prophetic satire, *A Marriage of Heaven and Hell*—all of which Blake wrote in the early 1790's while he was an ardent supporter of the French Revolution—he, like Wordsworth, Coleridge, Southey, and a number of radical English theologians, represented the contemporary Revolution as the purifying violence that, according to Biblical prophecy, was the portent of the imminent redemption of humanity and the world. In Blake's later poems, Orc, the fiery spirit of revolution, gives way as a central personage to Los, the type of the visionary imagination in the fallen world. Even in his early writings, however, Blake had represented historical revolution as correlative with a radical change effected within the mind and imagination of man, so that the replacement of Orc by Los does not indicate Blake's recantation of former beliefs, but a shift of emphasis from an apocalypse by revolution to an apocalypse by imagination.

BLAKE'S MATURE MYTH

Blake's first attempt to articulate his full myth of mankind's present, past, and future was *The Four Zoas*, begun in 1796 or 1797. A passage from the opening statement of its theme exemplifies the long verse line (what Blake called "the march of long resounding strong heroic verse") in which he wrote his Prophetic Books and will serve also to outline the myth, or visualizable imaginative form, in which Blake's thought embodied itself:

> Four Mighty Ones are in every man: a Perfect Unity
> Cannot Exist, but from the Universal Brotherhood of Eden,
> The Universal Man. To Whom be Glory Evermore, Amen.* * *
> Los was the fourth immortal starry one, & in the Earth
> Of a bright Universe Empery attended day & night
> Days & nights of revolving joy, Urthona was his name
> In Eden: in the Auricular Nerves of Human life
> Which is the Earth of Eden, he his Emanations propagated.* * *
>   Daughter of Beulah, Sing
> His fall into Division & his Resurrection to Unity.

Blake's mythical premise, or starting point, is not a transcendent God but "The Universal Man" who is himself God and who incorporates the cosmos as well. (Blake elsewhere describes this founding image as "the Human Form Divine" and names him "Albion.") The fall, in this myth, is not the fall of man away from God but a falling apart of primal man, a "fall into Division." In this event the original sin is what Blake calls "Selfhood," the attempt of an isolated part to be self-sufficient. The break-up of the all-inclusive Universal Man in Eden into exiled parts, it is evident, identifies the fall of man with the creation—both of man and of nature, as we ordinarily know them, as well as of a sky god who is alien from humanity. Universal Man divides first into the "Four Mighty Ones" who are the Zoas, or chief powers and component aspects of man, and these in turn divide sexually into male Spectres and female Emanations. (Thus in the quoted passage the Zoa known in the unfallen state of Eden as Urthona, the imaginative power, separates into the form of Los in the fallen world.) In addition to Eden there are three successively lower "states" of being in the fallen world, which Blake calls Beulah (a pastoral condition of easy and relaxed innocence, without clash of "contraries"), Generation (the realm of common human experience, suffering, and conflicting contraries), and Ulro (Blake's hell, the lowest state, or limit, of bleak rationality, tyranny, static negation, and isolated Selfhood). The fallen world moves through the cycles of its history, successively approaching and falling away from redemption, until, by the agency of the Redeemer (who is equated with the human imagination and is most potently operative in the prophetic poet), it will culminate in an apocalypse. In terms of his controlling image of the Universal Man, Blake describes this apocalypse as a return to the original, undivided condition, "his Resurrection to Unity."

Blake, although he did not know it, shared with a number of contemporary German philosophers the point of view—it has in our own time become the prevailing point of view—that man's fall (or the malaise of modern culture) is essentially a mode of psychic disintegration and of resultant alienation from oneself, one's world, and one's fellow-men, and that man's hope of recovery lies in a process of reintegration. As an imaginative poet, however, Blake does not present this view in abstract conceptual terms, but embodies it in picturable agents acting out an epic plot. What is confusing to many readers is that Blake uses different ways of representing the same vision of man in the world. For example, Blake alternates with his image of the division of Primal Man, the representation of the fall as a catastrophic alteration, in individual human beings, from imaginative vision to physical eyesight. The result of this alteration was that the cosmos, which in the original mode of unified imaginative perception, had been beheld as human and one, came to be seen as a multitude of isolated individuals in a de-humanized and alien nature. Conversely, the apocalypse toward which Blake—the imaginative artist who as an individual represents the mythical type-figure Los—is always working, is to enable all men to break through to a restored unity of vision. By such a vision all beings, together with the world they inhabit, will again be perceived as sharing the one life and the one humanity of that "Universal Brotherhood," the Human Form Divine, who is imaged as creating such a universe by the very act of so envisioning it.

Blake decries, as the mythical being "Vala," what we ordinarily mean by "nature," the material universe perceived by the senses. It is, however, a mistake to equate his views with ascetic other-worldliness. Blake does not look forward to a consummation that will wipe out the natural world and replace it by a transcendental substitute. Blake maintained, on the contrary, that we achieve redemption by liberating and intensifying the bodily senses —as he said, by "an improvement of sensual enjoyment"—and by attaining and sustaining that mode of vision that does not cancel the fallen world, but transfigures it, by revealing the lineaments of its eternal imaginative form. That is what Blake means when, in *A Vision of the Last Judgment* (included below), he says that "The Nature of my Work is Visionary or Imaginative," and that in the moment of apocalyptic redemption "Error or Creation will be Burnt Up & then & not till then Truth or Eternity will appear. It is Burnt up the Moment Men cease to behold it." Accordingly, in the apocalypse that concludes *Jerusalem*, the reunion of Albion the Universal Man with Jerusalem, his emanation, is accompanied by a freeing of man's senses and results in the recovery of a lost mode of vision that sees a nature which, because it is humanized, is a place where individual men, united as One Man, can feel at home.

The text for all of Blake's writings is that of *The Poetry and Prose of William Blake*, edited by David V. Erdman and Harold Bloom (New York, 1965). Blake's erratic spelling and punctuation have been altered when the original form might mislead the reader.

From POETICAL SKETCHES[1]

Song

How sweet I roam'd from field to field,
　And tasted all the summer's pride,
'Till I the prince of love[2] beheld,
　Who in the sunny beams did glide!

He shew'd me lilies for my hair,　　　　　　5
　And blushing roses for my brow;
He led me through his gardens fair,
　Where all his golden pleasures grow.

With sweet May dews my wings were wet,
　And Phoebus fir'd my vocal rage;[3]　　10
He caught me in his silken net,
　And shut me in his golden cage.

He loves to sit and hear me sing,
　Then, laughing, sports and plays with me;
Then stretches out my golden wing,　　　15
　And mocks my loss of liberty.

　　　　　　　　　　　　　　　1783

To the Evening Star

Thou fair-hair'd angel of the evening,
Now, while the sun rests on the mountains, light
Thy bright torch of love;[4] thy radiant crown
Put on, and smile upon our evening bed!
Smile on our loves; and, while thou drawest the　　5
Blue curtains of the sky, scatter thy silver dew
On every flower that shuts its sweet eyes
In timely sleep. Let thy west wind sleep on

1. *Poetical Sketches*, Blake's only volume of poems to be set in type, went to press in 1783, but was never put on sale. A preface written by an anonymous friend apologized for the poems on the ground that they had been composed between the ages of 12 and 20. Although, like the work of other youthful poets, they echo earlier writers (especially Spenser, Shakespeare, and Milton), many of them show remarkable originality. Some are radical experiments in meter and rhyme; *To the Evening Star* is a sonnet without rhyme, and shows great boldness in its use of metaphor (lines 8–10); while in this same sonnet (lines 11–14) and in the *Song* ("How sweet I roam'd") and *Mad Song*, the images begin to assume the added reach of meaning that characterizes Blake's mature symbolism.
2. In Greek myth, Eros or Cupid.
3. Fervor.
4. The evening star is Venus, goddess of love.

The lake; speak silence with thy glimmering eyes,
And wash the dusk with silver. Soon, full soon,   10
Dost thou withdraw; then the wolf rages wide,
And the lion glares thro' the dun forest:
The fleeces of our flocks are cover'd with
Thy sacred dew: protect them with thine influence.[5]

1783

Song[6]

Memory, hither come,
   And tune your merry notes;
And, while upon the wind,
   Your music floats,
I'll pore upon the stream,   5
Where sighing lovers dream,
And fish for fancies as they pass
Within the watery glass.

I'll drink of the clear stream,
   And hear the linnet's song;   10
And there I'll lie and dream
   The day along:
And, when night comes, I'll go
   To places fit for woe;
Walking along the darken'd valley,   15
   With silent Melancholy.

1783

Mad Song[7]

The wild winds weep,
   And the night is a-cold;
Come hither, Sleep,
   And my griefs infold:
But lo! the morning peeps   5
   Over the eastern steeps,
And the rustling birds of dawn
   The earth do scorn.

5. In astrology, the technical term for the occult power of stars over men.
6. Cf. *Under the Greenwood Tree* in *As You Like It* II.v.
7. Cf. the songs of the Fool in Shakespeare's great scene of madness and incipient madness in *King Lear*, Act. III. In a marginal comment on Spurzheim's *Observations on Insanity* (1817), Blake wrote: "Cowper came to me & said, 'O that I were insane always; I will never rest. * * * You retain health & yet are as mad as any of us all—over us all—mad as a refuge from unbelief—from Bacon Newton & Locke.'" (Cowper, like the other 18th-century poets Christopher Smart and William Collins, went genuinely insane.)

Lo! to the vault
　　Of pavéd heaven,   10
With sorrow fraught
　　My notes are driven:
They strike the ear of night,
　　Make weep the eyes of day;
They make mad the roaring winds,   15
　　And the tempests play.

Like a fiend in a cloud
　　With howling woe,
After night I do croud,
　　And with night will go;   20
I turn my back to the east,
From whence comforts have increas'd;
For light doth seize my brain
With frantic pain.

　　　　　　　　　　　　　　　　　　1783

To the Muses

Whether on Ida's[8] shady brow,
　　Or in the chambers of the East,
The chambers of the sun, that now
　　From antient melody have ceas'd;

Whether in Heav'n ye wander fair,   5
　　Or the green corners of the earth,
Or the blue regions of the air,
　　Where the melodious winds have birth;

Whether on chrystal rocks ye rove,
　　Beneath the bosom of the sea   10
Wand'ring in many a coral grove,
　　Fair Nine,[9] forsaking Poetry!

How have you left the antient love
　　That bards of old enjoy'd in you![10]
The languid strings do scarcely move!   15
　　The sound is forc'd, the notes are few!

　　　　　　　　　　　　　　　　　　1783

---

8. Ida is a mountain in southern Phrygia, celebrated in classical mythology.
9. The nine Muses.
10. The poem is Blake's lament, in the diction of latter 18-century poetry, over the failure of the inspiration manifested by the "bards," the older British poet-prophets.

There Is No Natural Religion[1]

The Author & Printer W. Blake

[a]

The Argument. Man has no notion of moral fitness but from Education. Naturally he is only a natural organ subject to Sense.

I. Man cannot naturally Percieve but through his natural or bodily organs.

II. Man by his reasoning power can only compare & judge of what he has already perciev'd.

III. From a perception of only 3 senses or 3 elements none could deduce a fourth or fifth.

IV. None could have other than natural or organic thoughts if he had none but organic perceptions.

V. Man's desires are limited by his perceptions; none can desire what he has not perciev'd.

VI. The desires & perceptions of man, untaught by any thing but organs of sense, must be limited to objects of sense.

Conclusion. If it were not for the Poetic or Prophetic character the Philosophic & Experimental would soon be at the ratio[2] of all things, & stand still unable to do other than repeat the same dull round over again.

There Is No Natural Religion

[b]

I. Man's perceptions are not bounded by organs of perception; he percieves more than sense (tho' ever so acute) can discover.

II. Reason, or the ratio of all we have already known, is not the same that it shall be when we know more.

[III lacking]

IV. The bounded is loathed by its possessor. The same dull

---

1. These three sets of axioms were etched by Blake in 1788. They are his critique of 18th-century Deism, or "natural religion," which bases the tenets of religion not on revelation, but on evidences derived from the constitution of the natural, or "organic" world. In the first set, Blake presents his version, and critique, of English empiricism, which derives all mental content (including the evidences by which man's reason proves the existence of God) from sense-perceptions of natural objects. In the second set, he presents his contrary tenets, which are grounded not on the finite senses, but on the infinity of man's desire and his God-like capacity for vision. In the third set, Blake ironically accepts the Deistic view that all positive religions are variants of one true religion, but attributes the common elements of truth not to reasoning from sense-experience, but to the possession by all men of "Poetic Genius"—that is, a capacity for imaginative vision.

2. In Latin, *ratio* signifies both "calculation" and "reasoning." Blake applies the term derogatorily to the 18th-century concept of reason as a calculating faculty whose operations are limited to sense-perceptions.

round even of a universe would soon become a mill with complicated wheels.

V. If the many become the same as the few when possess'd, More! More! is the cry of a mistaken soul. Less than All cannot satisfy Man.

VI. If any could desire what he is incapable of possessing, despair must be his eternal lot.

VII. The desire of Man being Infinite, the possession is Infinite & himself Infinite.

Application.   He who sees the Infinite in all things sees God. He who sees the Ratio only sees himself only.

Therefore God becomes as we are, that we may be as he is.

All Religions Are One

The Voice of one crying in the Wilderness[3]

The Argument.   As the true method of knowledge is experiment the true faculty of knowing must be the faculty which experiences. This faculty I treat of.

PRINCIPLE 1st. That the Poetic Genius is the true Man, and that the body or outward form of Man is derived from the Poetic Genius. Likewise that the forms of all things are derived from their Genius, which by the Ancients was call'd an Angel & Spirit & Demon.

PRINCIPLE 2d. As all men are alike in outward form, So (and with the same infinite variety) all are alike in the Poetic Genius.

PRINCIPLE 3d. No man can think write or speak from his heart, but he must intend truth. Thus all sects of Philosophy are from the Poetic Genius, adapted to the weaknesses of every individual.

PRINCIPLE 4. As none by travelling over known lands can find out the unknown, So from already acquired knowledge Man could not acquire more. Therefore an universal Poetic Genius exists.

PRINCIPLE 5. The Religions of all Nations are derived from each Nation's different reception of the Poetic Genius, which is every where call'd the Spirit of Prophecy.

PRINCIPLE 6. The Jewish & Christian Testaments are An original derivation from the Poetic Genius. This is necessary from the confined nature of bodily sensation.

PRINCIPLE 7th. As all men are alike (tho' infinitely various), So all Religions & as all similars have one source.

The true Man is the source, he being the Poetic Genius.

1788

---

3. Applied in the Gospels (e.g., Matthew iii.3) to John the Baptist, regarded as fulfilling the prophecy in Isaiah xxxix.3. Blake applies the phrase to himself, as a later prophetic voice in an alien time.

From SONGS OF INNOCENCE AND OF EXPERIENCE [1]
SHEWING THE TWO CONTRARY STATES OF THE HUMAN SOUL

From Songs of Innocence
1789
The Author & Printer   W Blake

Introduction

Piping down the valleys wild
Piping songs of pleasant glee
On a cloud I saw a child,
And he laughing said to me,

"Pipe a song about a Lamb";   5
So I piped with merry chear;
"Piper pipe that song again"—
So I piped, he wept to hear.

"Drop thy pipe thy happy pipe
Sing thy songs of happy chear";   10
So I sung the same again
While he wept with joy to hear.

"Piper sit thee down and write
In a book that all may read"—
So he vanish'd from my sight.   15
And I pluck'd a hollow reed,

---

1. *Songs of Innocence* was etched in 1789, and in 1794 was combined with additional poems under the title *Songs of Innocence and Experience*; this collection was republished at various later times with varying arrangements of the poems. In his songs of innocence Blake assumes the stance that he is writing "happy songs / Every child may joy to hear," but they do not all depict an innocent and happy world; many of them incorporate injustice, evil, and suffering. These aspects of the fallen world, however, are represented as they appear to a "state" of the human soul that Blake calls "innocence," and which he expresses in a simple pastoral language, in the tradition of Isaac Watts's widely read *Divine Songs for Children* (1715). The vision of the same world, as it appears to the "contrary" state of the soul that Blake calls "experience," is an ugly and terrifying one of poverty, disease, prostitution, war, and social, institutional, and sexual repression, epitomized in the ghastly representation of modern London. Though each stands as an independent poem, a number of the songs of innocence have a matched counterpart, or "contrary," in the songs of experience. Thus *Infant Joy* is paired with *Infant Sorrow*, and the meek *Lamb* reveals its other aspect of divinity in the flaming, wrathful *Tyger*.

In Blake's later writings the "contrary states" become a dialectic of contraries, according to which naïve innocence must necessarily pass through and assimilate the opposing state of experience if it is to move on, by an act of imagination, to the third state, comprehending but transcending both the others, which he called "organized innocence."

And I made a rural pen,
And I stain'd the water clear,
And I wrote my happy songs
Every child may joy to hear.

20
1789

The Lamb

Little Lamb, who made thee?
  Dost thou know who made thee?
Gave thee life & bid thee feed,
By the stream & o'er the mead;
Gave thee clothing of delight,
Softest clothing wooly bright;
Gave thee such a tender voice,
Making all the vales rejoice!
  Little Lamb who made thee?
  Dost thou know who made thee?

Little Lamb I'll tell thee,
Little Lamb I'll tell thee!
He is calléd by thy name,
For he calls himself a Lamb:
He is meek & he is mild,
He became a little child:
I a child & thou a lamb,
We are calléd by his name.
  Little Lamb God bless thee.
  Little Lamb God bless thee.

5

10

15

20
1789

The Little Black Boy

My mother bore me in the southern wild,
And I am black, but O! my soul is white;
White as an angel is the English child:
But I am black as if bereav'd of light.

My mother taught me underneath a tree,
And sitting down before the heat of day,
She took me on her lap and kisséd me,
And pointing to the east, began to say:

"Look on the rising sun: there God does live,
And gives his light, and gives his heat away;
And flowers and trees and beasts and men receive
Comfort in morning, joy in the noon day.

"And we are put on earth a little space,
That we may learn to bear the beams of love,

5

10

And these black bodies and this sun-burnt face   15
Is but a cloud, and like a shady grove.

"For when our souls have learn'd the heat to bear,
The cloud will vanish; we shall hear his voice,
Saying: 'Come out from the grove, my love & care,
And round my golden tent like lambs rejoice.' "   20

Thus did my mother say, and kisséd me;
And thus I say to little English boy:
When I from black and he from white cloud free,
And round the tent of God like lambs we joy,

I'll shade him from the heat till he can bear   25
To lean in joy upon our father's knee;
And then I'll stand and stroke his silver hair,
And be like him, and he will then love me.

1789

The Chimney Sweeper

When my mother died I was very young,
And my father sold me while yet my tongue
Could scarcely cry " 'weep! 'weep! 'weep! 'weep!" [2]
So your chimneys I sweep & in soot I sleep.

There's little Tom Dacre, who cried when his head   5
That curl'd like a lambs back, was shav'd, so I said,
"Hush, Tom! never mind it, for when your head's bare,
You know that the soot cannot spoil your white hair."

And so he was quiet, & that very night,
As Tom was a-sleeping he had such a sight!   10
That thousands of sweepers, Dick, Joe, Ned, & Jack,
Were all of them lock'd up in coffins of black;

And by came an Angel who had a bright key,
And he open'd the coffins & set them all free;
Then down a green plain, leaping, laughing they run,   15
And wash in a river and shine in the Sun;

Then naked & white, all their bags left behind,
They rise upon clouds, and sport in the wind.
And the Angel told Tom, if he'd be a good boy,
He'd have God for his father & never want joy.   20

And so Tom awoke; and we rose in the dark
And got with our bags & our brushes to work.
Tho' the morning was cold, Tom was happy & warm;
So if all do their duty, they need not fear harm.

1789

2. The child's lisping attempt at the chimney sweeper's street cry, "Sweep! Sweep!"

Laughing Song

When the green woods laugh with the voice of joy
And the dimpling stream runs laughing by,
When the air does laugh with our merry wit
And the green hill laughs with the noise of it;

When the meadows laugh with lively green   5
And the grasshopper laughs in the merry scene,
When Mary and Susan and Emily
With their sweet round mouths sing Ha, Ha, He;

When the painted birds laugh in the shade
Where our table with cherries and nuts is spread,   10
Come live & be merry and join with me
To sing the sweet chorus of Ha, Ha, He.

1789

The Divine Image

To Mercy, Pity, Peace, and Love,
All pray in their distress:
And to these virtues of delight
Return their thankfulness.

For Mercy, Pity, Peace, and Love,   5
Is God, our father dear:
And Mercy, Pity, Peace, and Love,
Is Man, his child and care.

For Mercy has a human heart,
Pity, a human face: 10
And Love, the human form divine,
And Peace, the human dress.

Then every man of every clime,
That prays in his distress,
Prays to the human form divine,   15
Love, Mercy, Pity, Peace.

And all must love the human form,
In heathen, Turk, or Jew.
Where Mercy, Love, & Pity dwell,
There God is dwelling too.   20

1789

Holy Thursday[3]

'Twas on a Holy Thursday, their innocent faces clean,
The children walking two & two, in red & blue & green,
Grey headed beadles[4] walkd before with wands as white as snow,
Till into the high dome of Paul's they like Thames' waters flow.

O what a multitude they seemd, these flowers of London town!   5
Seated in companies they sit with radiance all their own.
The hum of multitudes was there, but multitudes of lambs,
Thousands of little boys & girls raising their innocent hands.

Now like a mighty wind they raise to heaven the voice of song,
Or like harmonious thunderings the seats of heaven among.   10
Beneath them sit the aged men, wise guardians of the poor;
Then cherish pity, lest you drive an angel from your door.[5]

ca. 1784   1789

Nurse's Song

When the voices of children are heard on the green
And laughing is heard on the hill,
My heart is at rest within my breast
And everything else is still.

"Then come home my children, the sun is gone down   5
And the dews of night arise;
Come, come, leave off play, and let us away
Till the morning appears in the skies."

"No, no, let us play, for it is yet day
And we cannot go to sleep;   10
Besides, in the sky, the little birds fly
And the hills are all coverd with sheep."

"Well, well, go & play till the light fades away
And then go home to bed."
The little ones leapéd & shouted & laugh'd   15
And all the hills ecchoéd.

ca. 1784   1789

---

3. In the English church, the Thursday celebrating the ascension of Jesus (forty days after Easter). It was the custom on this day to march the children from the charity schools of London to a service at St. Paul's Cathedral.

4. Lower church officers, one of whose duties is to keep order.
5. Hebrews xiii.2:"Be not forgetful to entertain strangers: for thereby some have entertained angels unawares."

Infant Joy

"I have no name,
I am but two days old."
What shall I call thee?
"I happy am,
Joy is my name." 5
Sweet joy befall thee!

Pretty joy!
Sweet joy but two days old,
Sweet joy I call thee;
Thou dost smile, 10
I sing the while—
Sweet joy befall thee.

1789

From Songs of Experience

1794

The Author & Printer   W Blake

Introduction

Hear the voice of the Bard!
Who Present, Past, & Future sees;
Whose ears have heard
The Holy Word
That walk'd among the ancient trees;[6] 5

Calling the lapséd Soul
And weeping in the evening dew,
That might controll
The starry pole,
And fallen, fallen light renew![7] 10

"O Earth, O Earth, return!
Arise from out the dewy grass;

6. Genesis iii.8: "And [Adam and Eve] heard the voice of the Lord God walking in the garden in the cool of the day." The Bard, or poet-prophet, whose imagination is not bound by time, has heard the voice of the Lord in Eden. The call (the syntax leaves it ambiguous whether it is "the Bard" or "the Holy Word" whose voice does the calling) is to the fallen ("lapsèd") soul and to the fallen earth; the behest is to turn full to the light and stop the endless natural cycle of alternating light and darkness.

7. The likely syntax is that "Soul" is the subject of "might controll"; the sense would be that the fallen Soul could, if it would, renew the fallen light.

Night is worn,
And the morn
Rises from the slumberous mass.   15

"Turn away no more;
Why wilt thou turn away?
The starry floor
The watry shore[8]
Is giv'n thee till the break of day."   20

1794

Earth's Answer[9]

Earth rais'd up her head,
From the darkness dread & drear.
Her light fled:
Stony dread!
And her locks cover'd with grey despair.   5

"Prison'd on watry shore
Starry Jealousy does keep my den,
Cold and hoar
Weeping o'er
I hear the Father of the ancient men.[10]   10

"Selfish father of men,
Cruel, jealous, selfish fear!
Can delight
Chain'd in night
The virgins of youth and morning bear?   15

"Does spring hide its joy
When buds and blossoms grow?
Does the sower
Sow by night,
Or the plowman in darkness plow?   20

"Break this heavy chain
That does freeze my bones around;
Selfish! vain!
Eternal bane!
That free Love with bondage bound."   25

1794

8. In Blake's recurrent symbolism, the starry sky ("floor") signifies rigid rational order, and the sea signifies chaos.
9. The Earth's answer explains why she, the natural world, cannot by her unaided endeavors renew the fallen light.

10. This is the character that Blake named "Urizen" in his prophetic works. He imposes the perceptual and moral tyranny that binds the mind to time and space and imposes on sexual desire (as on all modes of human energy) the bondage of selfishness, fear, secrecy, shame, and jealousy.

The Clod & the Pebble

"Love seeketh not Itself to please,
Nor for itself hath any care;
But for another gives its ease,
And builds a Heaven in Hell's despair."

So sang a little Clod of Clay,   5
Trodden with the cattle's feet;
But a Pebble of the brook,
Warbled out these metres meet:

"Love seeketh only Self to please,
To bind another to its delight;   10
Joys in another's loss of ease,
And builds a Hell in Heaven's despite."

                                        1794

Holy Thursday

Is this a holy thing to see,
In a rich and fruitful land,
Babes reducd to misery,
Fed with cold and usurous hand?

Is that trembling cry a song?   5
Can it be a song of joy?
And so many children poor?
It is a land of poverty!

And their sun does never shine,
And their fields are bleak & bare,   10
And their ways are fill'd with thorns;
It is eternal winter there.

For where-e'er the sun does shine,
And where-e'er the rain does fall,
Babe can never hunger there,   15
Nor poverty the mind appall.

                                        1794

The Chimney Sweeper

A little black thing among the snow
Crying "'weep, 'weep," in notes of woe!
"Where are thy father & mother? say?"
"They are both gone up to the church to pray.

"Because I was happy upon the heath,   5
And smil'd among the winter's snow;
They clothéd me in the clothes of death,
And taught me to sing the notes of woe.

"And because I am happy, & dance & sing,
They think they have done me no injury,   10
And are gone to praise God & his Priest & King,
Who make up a heaven of our misery."

1790–92   1794

Nurse's Song

When the voices of children, are heard on the green
And whisprings are in the dale,
The days of my youth rise fresh in my mind,
My face turns green and pale.

Then come home my children, the sun is gone down   5
And the dews of night arise;
Your spring & your day are wasted in play,
And your winter and night in disguise.

1794

The Sick Rose

O Rose, thou art sick.
The invisible worm
That flies in the night
In the howling storm

Has found out thy bed   5
Of crimson joy,
And his dark secret love
Does thy life destroy.

1794

The Tyger

Tyger! Tyger! burning bright
In the forests of the night,
What immortal hand or eye
Could frame thy fearful symmetry?

In what distant deeps or skies   5
Burnt the fire of thine eyes?
On what wings dare he aspire?
What the hand, dare seize the fire?

And what shoulder, & what art,
Could twist the sinews of thy heart?   10
And when thy heart began to beat,
What dread hand? & what dread feet?

What the hammer? what the chain?
In what furnace was thy brain?
What the anvil? what dread grasp   15
Dare its deadly terrors clasp?

When the stars threw down their spears,
And water'd heaven with their tears,
Did he smile his work to see?
Did he who made the Lamb make thee?   20

Tyger! Tyger! burning bright
In the forests of the night,
What immortal hand or eye
Dare frame thy fearful symmetry?

1790–92   1794

Ah Sun-Flower

Ah Sun-flower! weary of time,
Who countest the steps of the Sun,
Seeking after that sweet golden clime
Where the traveller's journey is done;

Where the Youth pined away with desire,   5
And the pale Virgin shrouded in snow,
Arise from their graves and aspire,
Where my Sun-flower wishes to go.

                                                             1794

The Garden of Love

I went to the Garden of Love,
And saw what I never had seen:
A Chapel was built in the midst,
Where I used to play on the green.

And the gates of this Chapel were shut,   5
And "Thou shalt not" writ over the door;
So I turn'd to the Garden of Love,
That so many sweet flowers bore,

And I saw it was filled with graves,
And tomb-stones where flowers should be: 10
And Priests in black gowns were walking their rounds,
And binding with briars my joys & desires.

                                                             1794

London

I wander thro' each charter'd [1] street,
Near where the charter'd Thames does flow,

---

1. "Given liberty," but also, ironically, "pre-empted as private property, and
rented out."

And mark in every face I meet
Marks of weakness, marks of woe.

In every cry of every Man,   5
In every Infant's cry of fear,
In every voice, in every ban,[2]
The mind-forg'd manacles I hear.

How the Chimney-sweeper's cry
Every blackning Church appalls;   10
And the hapless Soldier's sigh
Runs in blood down Palace walls.

But most thro' midnight streets I hear
How the youthful Harlot's curse
Blasts the new-born Infant's tear,[3]   15
And blights with plagues the Marriage hearse.[4]

1794

The Human Abstract[5]

Pity would be no more,
If we did not make somebody Poor;
And Mercy no more could be,
If all were as happy as we;

And mutual fear brings peace,   5
Till the selfish loves increase;
Then Cruelty knits a snare,
And spreads his baits with care.

He sits down with holy fears,
And waters the ground with tears;   10
Then Humility takes its root
Underneath his foot.

Soon spreads the dismal shade
Of Mystery over his head;
And the Catterpiller and Fly   15
Feed on the Mystery.

2. The various meanings of "ban" are relevant (political and legal prohibition, curse, public condemnation) as well as "banns" (marriage proclamation).
3. Implying prenatal blindness, resulting from a parent's venereal disease (the "plagues" of line 16) by earlier infection from the harlot.
4. In the older sense of "hearse": converts the marriage bed into a bier. Or possibly, since the current sense of the word had also come into use in Blake's day, "converts the marriage coach into a funeral hearse."
5. The matched contrary to *The Divine Image* in *Songs of Innocence*. The virtues of the earlier poem, "Mercy, Pity, Peace, and Love," are now seen as exploitation, cruelty, conflict, and hypocritical humility—the seed in the human brain of the Tree of Mystery, which darkens both the moral and natural world.

And it bears the fruit of Deceit,
Ruddy and sweet to eat;
And the Raven his nest has made
In its thickest shade.   20

The Gods of the earth and sea,
Sought thro' Nature to find this Tree,
But their search was all in vain:
There grows one in the Human Brain.

1790–92   1794

Infant Sorrow

My mother groand! my father wept.
Into the dangerous world I leapt:
Helpless, naked, piping loud;
Like a fiend hid in a cloud.

Struggling in my father's hands,   5
Striving against my swadling bands,
Bound and weary I thought best
To sulk upon my mother's breast.

                                                                          1794

A Poison Tree

I was angry with my friend:
I told my wrath, my wrath did end.
I was angry with my foe:
I told it not, my wrath did grow.

And I waterd it in fears,   5
Night & morning with my tears;
And I sunnéd it with smiles,
And with soft deceitful wiles.

And it grew both day and night,
Till it bore an apple bright.   10
And my foe beheld it shine,
And he knew that it was mine,

And into my garden stole,
When the night had veild the pole;
In the morning glad I see   15
My foe outstretchd beneath the tree.

                                                                          1794

To Tirzah[6]

Whate'er is Born of Mortal Birth
Must be consuméd with the Earth
To rise from Generation free;
Then what have I to do with thee?[7]

The Sexes sprung from Shame & Pride,   5
Blow'd[8] in the morn: in evening died;
But Mercy changd Death into Sleep;
The Sexes rose to work & weep.

Thou, Mother of my Mortal part,
With cruelty didst mould my Heart,   10
And with false self-deceiving tears
Didst bind my Nostrils, Eyes, & Ears.

Didst close my Tongue in senseless clay
And me to Mortal Life betray.
The Death of Jesus set me free,   15
Then what have I to do with thee?

                                        ca. 1805

A Divine Image[9]

Cruelty has a Human Heart
And Jealousy a Human Face,
Terror, the Human Form Divine,
And Secrecy, the Human Dress.

The Human Dress is forgéd Iron,   5
The Human Form, a fiery Forge,
The Human Face, a Furnace seal'd,
The Human Heart, its hungry Gorge.[10]

1790–91

6. Tirzah was the capital of the northern kingdom of Israel and is conceived by Blake in opposition to Jerusalem, capital of the southern kingdom of Judah, whose tribes had been redeemed from captivity. In this poem, which was added to late versions of *Songs of Experience*, Tirzah represents the natural mother of the mortal body, with its limited senses and enslaved desires. Blake anticipates his emancipation from this bondage to the cycle of generation by the redemptive triumph of the imaginative over the natural body.
7. Echoing the words of Christ to his mother at the marriage in Cana, John ii.4: "Woman, what have I to do with thee? mine hour is not yet come."
8. Blossomed.
9. After etching this poem Blake omitted it from *Songs of Experience*, probably because *The Human Abstract* served as a more comprehensive and subtle contrary to *The Divine Image*, in *Songs of Innocence*.
10. Maw, stomach.

The Book of Thel [1]

The Author & Printer Willm Blake, 1789

PLATE i [2]

THEL'S MOTTO

Does the Eagle know what is in the pit?
Or wilt thou go ask the Mole?
Can Wisdom be put in a silver rod?
Or Love in a golden bowl? [3]

PLATE 1

I

The daughters of Mne [4] Seraphim led round their sunny flocks,
All but the youngest; she in paleness sought the secret air,

1. Although Blake dated the engraved poem 1789, its composition probably extended to 1791, so that he was working on it at the time he was writing the *Songs of Innocence* and some of the *Songs of Experience. The Book of Thel* treats the same two "states" and implies the need to pass from primitive innocence through experience in order to achieve a higher, organized innocence; now, however, Blake employs the narrative instead of the lyrical mode and embodies aspects of the developing myth which was fully enacted in his later prophetic books. And like the major prophecies, this poem is written in the fourteener, a long line of seven stresses.

Thel—her name probably derives from a Greek word for "wish" or "will" and suggests the timid failure of a desire to fulfill itself—is a virgin dwelling in the Vales of Har, which is equivalent to the sheltered condition of pastoral peace and innocence in Blake's *Songs of Innocence* and will develop into the "Beulah" of his prophetic books. In the fragile beauty of this realm of unrealized potentiality, Thel lives a two-dimensional mirror image of existence (line 9). The Lily of the Valley and the Cloud try to comfort her by describing their content with their roles in the cycle of innocent existence. Thel, however, since she is a human potentiality, finds such comfort inapplicable to her condition of unfulfillment and uselessness, as a virgin without a male contrary and as a shepherdess whose sheep run no risks and need no care. The Clod of Clay then speaks for her child, the voiceless Worm, an emblem of phallic generation and a devourer of the mortal body in the fallen world; but the maternal Clay sees the role of the Worm, as well as her own, only from the perspective of

essential ignorance: "But how this is, sweet maid, I know not, and I cannot know." In her capacity, however, as the substance from which is formed the mortal body of man, the Clay invites Thel to try the experiment of dying into embodied life. With an abrupt and brutal shift in language and tone, Part IV expresses the shock of the revelation to Thel of the world of Generation and Experience—a revelation from which she flees in terror back to her sheltered, if inadequate, paradise.

The reader does not need to be an adept in Blakean mythology to recognize the symbolic reach of this poem in ordinary human experience—the elemental failure of nerve to meet the challenge of life as it is, the timid incapacity to risk the conflict, physicality, pain, and loss without which there is no possibility either of growth or of any kind of creativity.

2. The plate numbers identify the page, each with its own pictorial design, as originally printed by Blake. They are reproduced here because they are frequently used for reference to Blake's writings.

3. Ecclesiastes xii. 5–6 describes a time when "fears shall be in the way * * * and desire shall fail: because man goeth to his long home, and the mourners go about the streets: Or ever the silver cord be loosed, or the golden bowl be broken." Blake presumably changed the silver cord to a rod in order to make it, with the golden bowl, a sexual symbol.

4. In his earlier poem *Tiriel*, Blake adopted the name "Mnetha" for the goddess of the vales of Har. Thel, the abbreviated form of this name indicates, is one of the daughters of the angelic Mnetha. In the Bible, Seraphim are the highest order of angels.

To fade away like morning beauty from her mortal day;
Down by the river of Adona [5] her soft voice is heard,
And thus her gentle lamentation falls like morning dew: 5

"O life of this our spring! why fades the lotus of the water?
Why fade these children of the spring? born but to smile & fall.
Ah! Thel is like a watry bow, and like a parting cloud,
Like a reflection in a glass, like shadows in the water,
Like dreams of infants, like a smile upon an infant's face,   10
Like the dove's voice, like transient day, like music in the air.
Ah! gentle may I lay me down, and gentle rest my head,
And gentle sleep the sleep of death and gentle hear the voice
Of him that walketh in the garden in the evening time."[6]

The Lilly of the valley, breathing in the humble grass,   15
Answer'd the lovely maid and said: "I am a watry weed,
And I am very small, and love to dwell in lowly vales;
So weak, the gilded butterfly scarce perches on my head;
Yet I am visited from heaven, and he that smiles on all
Walks in the valley and each morn over me spreads his hand,   20
Saying: 'Rejoice, thou humble grass, thou new-born lilly flower,
Thou gentle maid of silent valleys and of modest brooks;
For thou shalt be clothed in light, and fed with morning manna,
Till summer's heat melts thee beside the fountains and the springs
To flourish in eternal vales.' Then why should Thel complain?   25

PLATE 2

Why should the mistress of the vales of Har utter a sigh?"

She ceasd & smild in tears, then sat down in her silver shrine.

Thel answerd: "O thou little virgin of the peaceful valley,
Giving to those that cannot crave, the voiceless, the o'ertired;
Thy breath doth nourish the innocent lamb, he smells thy milky
        garments,   5
He crops thy flowers, while thou sittest smiling in his face,
Wiping his mild and meekin [7] mouth from all contagious taints.
Thy wine doth purify the golden honey; thy perfume,
Which thou dost scatter on every little blade of grass that springs,
Revives the milkéd cow, & tames the fire-breathing steed.   10
But Thel is like a faint cloud kindled at the rising sun:
I vanish from my pearly throne, and who shall find my place?"

"Queen of the vales," the Lilly answered, "ask the tender cloud,
And it shall tell thee why it glitters in the morning sky,

---

5. Possibly suggesting an equation of the Vales of Har to Spenser's Garden of Adonis in *The Faerie Queene* III.vi, as well as to the paradisal garden in Genesis (in line 14).

6. Genesis iii.8: "And they heard the voice of the Lord God walking in the garden in the cool of the day."

7. Humble.

And why it scatters its bright beauty thro' the humid air.   15
Descend, O little cloud, & hover before the eyes of Thel."

The Cloud descended, and the Lilly bowd her modest head,
And went to mind her numerous charge among the verdant grass.

PLATE 3

II

"O little Cloud," the virgin said, "I charge thee tell to me,
Why thou complainest not when in one hour thou fade away:
Then we shall seek thee but not find; ah, Thel is like to Thee.
I pass away, yet I complain, and no one hears my voice."

The Cloud then shew'd his golden head & his bright form emerg'd, 5
Hovering and glittering on the air before the face of Thel.

"O virgin, know'st thou not our steeds drink of the golden springs
Where Luvah[8] doth renew his horses? Look'st thou on my youth,
And fearest thou, because I vanish and am seen no more,
Nothing remains? O maid, I tell thee, when I pass away,   10
It is to tenfold life, to love, to peace, and raptures holy:
Unseen descending, weigh my light wings upon balmy flowers,
And court the fair eyed dew, to take me to her shining tent;
The weeping virgin trembling kneels before the risen sun,
Till we arise link'd in a golden band, and never part,   15
But walk united, bearing food to all our tender flowers."

"Dost thou O little Cloud? I fear that I am not like thee;
For I walk through the vales of Har and smell the sweetest flowers,
But I feed not the little flowers; I hear the warbling birds,
But I feed not the warbling birds; they fly and seek their food; 20
But Thel delights in these no more, because I fade away,
And all shall say, 'Without a use this shining woman liv'd,
Or did she only live to be at death the food of worms?' "

The Cloud reclind upon his airy throne and answer'd thus:

"Then if thou art the food of worms, O virgin of the skies,   25
How great thy use, how great thy blessing! Every thing that lives
Lives not alone, nor for itself; fear not, and I will call
The weak worm from its lowly bed, and thou shalt hear its voice.
Come forth, worm of the silent valley, to thy pensive queen."

The helpless worm arose, and sat upon the Lilly's leaf,   30
And the bright Cloud saild on, to find his partner in the vale.

8. The earliest mention in Blake's work of one of his "Giant Forms," the Zoas. Luvah, the mythical embodiment of the passional and sexual aspect of man, repairs to the Vales of Har simply in order to rest and water his horses. The cloud in this passage describes the cycle of water, from cloud to rain and (by the vaporizing action of the sun on the dew and other forms of water) back to the cloud.

PLATE 4

III

Then Thel astonish'd view'd the Worm upon its dewy bed.

"Art thou a Worm? Image of weakness, art thou but a Worm?
I see thee like an infant wrapped in the Lilly's leaf;
Ah, weep not, little voice, thou can'st not speak, but thou can'st weep.
Is this a Worm? I see thee lay helpless & naked, weeping,   5
And none to answer, none to cherish thee with mother's smiles."

The Clod of Clay heard the Worm's voice, & raisd her pitying head;
She bow'd over the weeping infant, and her life exhal'd
In milky fondness; then on Thel she fix'd her humble eyes.

"O beauty of the vales of Har! we live not for ourselves;   10
Thou seest me the meanest thing, and so I am indeed.
My bosom of itself is cold, and of itself is dark;

PLATE 5

But he that loves the lowly, pours his oil upon my head,
And kisses me, and binds his nuptial bands around my breast,
And says: 'Thou mother of my children, I have lovéd thee,
And I have given thee a crown that none can take away.'
But how this is, sweet maid, I know not, and I cannot know;   5
I ponder, and I cannot ponder; yet I live and love."

The daughter of beauty wip'd her pitying tears with her white veil,
And said: "Alas! I knew not this, and therefore did I weep.
That God would love a Worm, I knew, and punish the evil foot
That, wilful, bruis'd its helpless form; but that he cherish'd it   10
With milk and oil I never knew; and therefore did I weep,
And I complaind in the mild air, because I fade away,
And lay me down in thy cold bed, and leave my shining lot."

"Queen of the vales," the matron Clay answerd, "I heard thy sighs,
And all thy moans flew o'er my roof, but I have call'd them down.   15
Wilt thou, O Queen, enter my house? 'Tis given thee to enter
And to return; fear nothing, enter with thy virgin feet."

PLATE 6

IV

The eternal gates' terrific porter lifted the northern bar: [9]
Thel enter'd in & saw the secrets of the land unknown.
She saw the couches of the dead, & where the fibrous roots

9. Homer, in *Odyssey* XIII, described the Cave of the Naiades, of which the northern gate is for men and the southern gate for gods. The Neoplatonist Porphyro had allegorized it as an account of the descent of the soul into matter. Blake has Thel use the northern gate to pass from the state before birth into incarnate life.

Of every heart on earth infixes deep its restless twists:
A land of sorrows & of tears where never smile was seen.   5

She wanderd in the land of clouds thro' valleys dark, listning
Dolours & lamentations; waiting oft beside a dewy grave,
She stood in silence, listning to the voices of the ground,
Till to her own grave plot she came, & there she sat down,
And heard this voice of sorrow breathéd from the hollow pit: 10

"Why cannot the Ear be closed to its own destruction?
Or the glistning Eye to the poison of a smile?
Why are Eyelids stord with arrows ready drawn,
Where a thousand fighting men in ambush lie?
Or an Eye of gifts & graces, show'ring fruits & coinéd gold?   15
Why a Tongue impress'd with honey from every wind?
Why an Ear, a whirlpool fierce to draw creations in?
Why a Nostril wide inhaling terror, trembling, & affright?
Why a tender curb upon the youthful burning boy?
Why a little curtain of flesh on the bed of our desire?" [1]   20

The Virgin started from her seat, & with a shriek
Fled back unhinderd till she came into the vales of Har.

THE END

1789–91

1. From Thel's grave issues, apparently, the voice of Thel herself, expressing how experience would seem to her timid and shrinking temperament, should she elect to live out her life in the human world. The catalogue of experience runs through the various senses to end with touch, the primary sexual sense.

The Marriage of Heaven and Hell   This, the most immediately accessible of Blake's longer works, is a vigorous, deliberately outrageous, and at times comic, onslaught against the timidly conventional and self-righteous members of society, as well as against many of the stock opinions of orthodox Christian piety and morality. The seeming simplicity of Blake's satiric attitude, however, is deceptive.

Initially, Blake accepts the terminology of middle-class Christian morality ("what the religious call Good & Evil") but reverses its values. In this conventional use Evil, which is manifested by the class of beings called Devils and which consigns a man to the orthodox Hell, is everything associated with the body and its desires and consists essentially of energy, abundance, act, freedom. And conventional Good, which is manifested by Angels and guarantees its adherents a place in the orthodox Heaven, is associated with the Soul (regarded as entirely separate from the body) and consists of the contrary qualities of reason, restraint, passivity, and prohibition. Blandly adopting this current nomenclature, Blake elects to assume the diabolic persona—what he calls "the voice of the Devil"—and to utter "Proverbs of Hell." This ironic stance produces a vein of satire which is in the great 18th-century tradition of sustained ironic reversal, represented by works such as Jonathan Swift's *Modest Proposal*.

But the transvaluation of standard criteria is only a first stage in Blake's complex irony, designed to startle the reader into recognizing the inadequacy of standard moral categories and stock responses. As he also says in the opening summary of his total argument, "Without Contraries is no progression," and "Reason and Energy" are both "necessary to Human existence." It turns out that Blake subordinates his satiric reversal of conventional values under a more inclusive point of view, according to which the real Good, as distinguished from the merely ironic Good, is not simply freedom from restraint, but a "marriage" of the contrary extremes of desire and restraint, energy and reason, the promptings of Hell and the limitations of Heaven—or as Blake calls these contraries, in the comprehensive terms he introduces in Plate 16, "the Prolific" and "the Devouring." These two classes, he adds, "should be enemies," and "whoever tries to reconcile them seeks to destroy existence." When Blake speaks not as moral satirist but as serious moralist, the good life is that abundant and strenuous life he describes as the sustained conflict, without victory or suppression, of simultaneous opposites.

Blake was stimulated to write this unique work in response to the books of the visionary Swedish theologian, Emanuel Swedenborg, whom he had at first admired but then had come to recognize as a conventional Angel in the disguise of a radical Devil. In Plate 3, the writings of Swedenborg are described as the winding clothes Blake discards as he is resurrected from the tomb of his past self, as a poet-prophet who heralds the apocalyptic promise of his age. For Blake wrote *The Marriage of Heaven and Hell* in the early 1790's, during the bright early years of the French Revolution, when he shared the expectations of a number of radical Englishmen, including the young poets Wordsworth, Coleridge, and Southey, that the Revolution was the universal violence which had been predicted by the Biblical prophets as a stage immediately preceding the millennium. The double role of *The Marriage* as both satire and revolutionary prophecy is made explicit in *A Song of Liberty*, which Blake engraved in 1792 and added as a coda.

The Marriage of Heaven and Hell

PLATE 2

The Argument

Rintrah [1] roars & shakes his fires in the burdend air;
Hungry clouds swag[2] on the deep.

Once meek, and in a perilous path,
The just man kept his course along
The vale of death.   5

1. Rintrah plays the role of the angry Old Testament prophet Elijah as well as of John the Baptist, the voice "crying in the wilderness" (Matthew iii), preparing the way for Christ the Messiah. It has been plausibly suggested that stanzas 2–5 summarize the course of biblical history to the present time. "Once" (line 3) refers to Old Testament history after the fall of man; "Then" (line 9) is the time of the birth of Christ; "Till" (line 14) identifies the era when Christianity was perverted into an institutional religion; and "Now" (line 17) is the time of the wrathful portent of the French Revolution. In this final era, the hypocritical serpent represents the priest of the "angels" in the poem, while "the just man" is embodied in Blake himself, a raging poet and prophet in the guise of a Devil.
2. Sag or sway (or both).

Roses are planted where thorns grow,
And on the barren heath
Sing the honey bees.

Then the perilous path was planted,
And a river, and a spring,
On every cliff and tomb;   10
And on the bleached bones
Red clay[3] brought forth;

Till the villain left the paths of ease,
To walk in perilous paths, and drive   15
The just man into barren climes.

Now the sneaking serpent walks
In mild humility,
And the just man rages in the wilds
Where lions roam.   20

Rintrah roars & shakes his fires in the burdend air;
Hungry clouds swag on the deep.

PLATE 3

As a new heaven is begun, and it is now thirty-three years since
its advent, the Eternal Hell revives.[4] And lo! Swedenborg is the
Angel sitting at the tomb; his writings are the linen clothes folded
up. Now is the dominion of Edom, & the return of Adam into
Paradise; see Isaiah xxxiv & XXXV Chap.[5]

Without Contraries is no progression. Attraction and Repulsion,
Reason and Energy, Love and Hate, are necessary to Human existence.

3. In Hebrew, the literal meaning of "Adam," or created man. There is a probable reference to the birth of the Redeemer, the new Adam.

4. The Swedish scientist and religious philosopher, Emanuel Swedenborg (1688–1772) had predicted, on the basis of his visions, that the Last Judgment and the coming of the Kingdom of Heaven would occur in 1757. This was precisely the year of Blake's birth. Now, in 1790, Blake is thirty-three, the age at which Christ had been resurrected from the tomb; appropriately, Blake rises from the tomb of his past life in his new role as imaginative artist who will redeem his age. But, Blake ironically comments, the works he will engrave in his resurrection will constitute the Eternal Hell, the contrary inevitably brought into simultaneous being by Swedenborg's limited New Heaven.

5. Isaiah xxxiv prophesies "the day of the Lord's vengeance," a time of violent destruction and bloodshed; Isaiah xxxv

prophesies the redemption to follow, in which "the desert shall * * * blossom as the rose," "in the wilderness shall waters break out, and streams in the desert," and "no lion shall be there," but "an highway shall be there * * * and it shall be called the way of holiness." (Cf. "The Argument," lines 3–11, 20.) Blake combines with these chapters Isaiah lxiii, in which "Edom" is the place from which comes the man whose garments are red with the blood he has spilled; for as he says, "the day of vengeance is in mine heart, and the year of my redeemed is come." Blake interprets this last phrase as predicting the time when Adam would regain his lost Paradise.

With reference to affairs in 1790, Edom represents France, and the red man coming from Edom (to England) is the spirit of the French Revolution, which Blake represents as a portent of apocalyptic redemption and of the recovery of Paradise.

From these contraries spring what the religious call Good & Evil. Good is the passive that obeys Reason. Evil is the active springing from Energy.

Good is Heaven. Evil is Hell. — *Traditional Definitions.*

PLATE 4

The voice of the (Devil)

All Bibles or sacred codes have been the causes of the following Errors:

1. That Man has two real existing principles; Viz: a Body & a Soul.

2. That Energy, calld Evil, is alone from the Body, & that Reason, calld Good, is alone from the Soul.

3. That God will torment Man in Eternity for following his Energies. But the following Contraries to these are True:

1. Man has no Body distinct from his Soul; for that calld Body is a portion of Soul discernd by the five Senses, the chief inlets of Soul in this age.

2. Energy is the only life, and is from the Body; and Reason is the bound or outward circumference of Energy.

3. Energy is Eternal Delight

———

PLATE 5

Those who restrain desire, do so because theirs is weak enough to be restrained; and the restrainer or reason usurps its place & governs the unwilling.

And being restraind, it by degrees becomes passive, till it is only the shadow of desire.

The history of this is written in *Paradise Lost*,[6] & the Governor or Reason is call'd Messiah.

And the original Archangel, or possessor of the command of the heavenly host, is calld the Devil or Satan, and his children are call'd Sin & Death.[7]

But in the Book of Job, Milton's Messiah is call'd Satan.[8]

For this history has been adopted by both parties.

It indeed appear'd to Reason as if Desire was cast out; but the Devil's account is, that the Messi[PL 6]ah fell, & formed a heaven of what he stole from the Abyss.

This is shewn in the Gospel, where he prays to the Father to send the comforter or Desire that Reason may have Ideas to build

6. What follows, to the end of this section, is Blake's "diabolical" reading of Milton's *Paradise Lost*.
7. Satan's giving birth to Sin and then incestuously begetting Death upon her is described in *Paradise Lost* II.745 ff.;

the war in heaven, referred to three lines below, in which the Messiah defeated Satan and drove him out of heaven, is described in VI.824 ff.
8. Satan plays the role of the moral accuser and physical tormentor of Job.

on; [9] the Jehovah of the Bible being no other than he who dwells in flaming fire. Know that after Christ's death, he became Jehovah.

But in Milton, the Father is Destiny, the Son, a Ratio of the five senses,[1] & the Holy-ghost, Vacuum!

Note. The reason Milton wrote in fetters when he wrote of Angels & God, and at liberty when of Devils & Hell, is because he was a true Poet and of the Devil's party without knowing it.

A Memorable Fancy [2]

As I was walking among the fires of hell, delighted with the enjoyments of Genius, which to Angels look like torment and insanity, I collected some of their Proverbs; thinking that as the sayings used in a nation mark its character, so the Proverbs of Hell shew the nature of Infernal wisdom better than any description of buildings or garments.

When I came home, on the abyss of the five senses, where a flat sided steep frowns over the present world, I saw a mighty Devil folded in black clouds, hovering on the sides of the rock; with cor-[PL. 7]roding fires he wrote the following sentence [3] now perceived by the minds of men, & read by them on earth:

Point of view of Perception.

> How do you know but ev'ry Bird that cuts the airy way,
> Is an immense world of delight, clos'd by your senses five?

Proverbs of Hell [4]

In seed time learn, in harvest teach, in winter enjoy.
Drive your cart and your plow over the bones of the dead.
The road of excess leads to the palace of wisdom.
Prudence is a rich ugly old maid courted by Incapacity.
He who desires but acts not, breeds pestilence.
The cut worm forgives the plow.
Dip him in the river who loves water.
A fool sees not the same tree that a wise man sees.
He whose face gives no light, shall never become a star.
Eternity is in love with the productions of time.
The busy bee has no time for sorrow.
The hours of folly are measur'd by the clock; but of wisdom, no

9. Possibly John xiv.16–17, where Christ says he "will pray the Father, and he shall give you another Comforter * * * even the Spirit of truth."
1. The Latin *ratio* means both "reason" and "sum." Blake applies the term to the 18th-century view, following the empirical philosophy of John Locke, that the content of the mind is limited to the sum of the experience acquired by the five senses.

2. A parody of what Swedenborg called "memorable relations" of his literal-minded visions of the eternal world.
3. The "mighty Devil" is Blake, as he sees himself reflected in the shiny plate on which he is etching this very passage with "corroding fires"—i.e., acid. See also the third from last sentence in Plate 14.
4. A "diabolic" version of the Book of Proverbs in the Old Testament.

clock can measure.

All wholsom food is caught without a net or a trap.

Bring out number, weight, & measure in a year of dearth.

No bird soars too high, if he soars with his own wings.

A dead body revenges not injuries.

The most sublime act is to set another before you.

If the fool would persist in his folly he would become wise.

Folly is the cloke of knavery.

Shame is Pride's cloke.

PLATE 8

Prisons are built with stones of Law, Brothels with bricks of Religion.

The pride of the peacock is the glory of God.

The lust of the goat is the bounty of God.

The wrath of the lion is the wisdom of God.

The nakedness of woman is the work of God.

Excess of sorrow laughs. Excess of joy weeps.

The roaring of lions, the howling of wolves, the raging of the stormy
    sea, and the destructive sword, are portions of eternity too great
    for the eye of man.

The fox condemns the trap, not himself.

Joys impregnate. Sorrows bring forth.

Let man wear the fell of the lion, woman the fleece of the sheep.

The bird a nest, the spider a web, man friendship.

The selfish, smiling fool & the sullen, frowning fool shall be both
    thought wise, that they may be a rod.

What is now proved was once only imagin'd.

The rat, the mouse, the fox, the rabbit watch the roots; the lion, the
    tyger, the horse, the elephant, watch the fruits.

The cistern contains: the fountain overflows.

One thought fills immensity.

Always be ready to speak your mind, and a base man will avoid you.

Every thing possible to be believ'd is an image of truth.

The eagle never lost so much time as when he submitted to learn of
    the crow.

PLATE 9

The fox provides for himself, but God provides for the lion.

Think in the morning, Act in the noon, Eat in the evening, Sleep in
    the night.

He who has sufferd you to impose on him knows you.

As the plow follows words, so God rewards prayers.

The tygers of wrath are wiser than the horses of instruction.

Expect poison from the standing water.

You never know what is enough unless you know what is more than
    enough.

Listen to the fools reproach! it is a kingly title!

The eyes of fire, the nostrils of air, the mouth of water, the beard of
    earth.

The weak in courage is strong in cunning.

The apple tree never asks the beech how he shall grow, nor the lion the horse, how he shall take his prey.

The thankful reciever bears a plentiful harvest.

If others had not been foolish, we should be so.

The soul of sweet delight can never be defil'd. [5]

When thou seest an Eagle, thou seest a portion of Genius; lift up thy head!

As the catterpiller chooses the fairest leaves to lay her eggs on, so the priest lays his curse on the fairest joys.

To create a little flower is the labour of ages.

Damn braces: Bless relaxes.

The best wine is the oldest, the best water the newest.

Prayers plow not! Praises reap not!

Joys laugh not! Sorrows weep not!

PLATE 10

The head Sublime, the heart Pathos, the genitals Beauty, the hands & feet Proportion.

As the air to a bird or the sea to a fish, so is contempt to the contemptible.

The crow wish'd every thing was black, the owl that every thing was white.

Exuberance is Beauty.

If the lion was advised by the fox, he would be cunning.

Improvement makes strait roads, but the crooked roads without Improvement are roads of Genius.

Sooner murder an infant in its cradle than nurse unacted desires.

Where man is not, nature is barren.

Truth can never be told so as to be understood, and not be believ'd.

Enough! or Too much.

PLATE 11

The ancient Poets animated all sensible objects with Gods or Geniuses, calling them by the names and adorning them with the properties of woods, rivers, mountains, lakes, cities, nations, and whatever their enlarged & numerous senses could percieve.

And particularly they studied the genius of each city & country, placing it under its mental deity.

Till a system was formed, which some took advantage of & enslav'd the vulgar by attempting to realize or abstract the mental deities from their objects; thus began Priesthood,

Choosing forms of worship from poetic tales.

And at length they pronounced that the Gods had ordered such things.

Thus men forgot that All deities reside in the human breast.

5. Repeated in *America* 8.14, below.

PLATE 12

A Memorable Fancy[6]

The Prophets Isaiah and Ezekiel dined with me, and I asked them how they dared so roundly to assert that God spake to them; and whether they did not think at the time that they would be misunderstood, & so be the cause of imposition.

Isaiah answer'd: "I saw no God, nor heard any, in a finite organical perception; but my senses discover'd the infinite in every thing, and as I was then perswaded, & remain confirm'd, that the voice of honest indignation is the voice of God, I cared not for consequences, but wrote."

Then I asked: "Does a firm perswasion that a thing is so, make it so?"

He replied: "All poets believe that it does, & in ages of imagination this firm perswasion removed mountains; but many are not capable of a firm perswasion of any thing."

Then Ezekiel said: "The philosophy of the East taught the first principles of human perception. Some nations held one principle for the origin & some another; we of Israel taught that the Poetic Genius (as you now call it) was the first principle and all the others merely derivative, which was the cause of our despising the Priests & Philosophers of other countries, and prophecying that all Gods [PL 13] would at last be proved to originate in ours & to be the tributaries of the Poetic Genius; it was this that our great poet, King David, desired so fervently & invokes so patheticly, saying by this he conquers enemies & governs kingdoms; and we so loved our God, that we cursed in his name all the deities of surrounding nations, and asserted that they had rebelled; from these opinions the vulgar came to think that all nations would at last be subject to the Jews."

"This," said he, "like all firm perswasions, is come to pass, for all nations believe the Jews' code and worship the Jews' god, and what greater subjection can be?"

I heard this with some wonder, & must confess my own conviction. After dinner I ask'd Isaiah to favour the world with his lost works; he said none of equal value was lost. Ezekiel said the same of his.

I also asked Isaiah what made him go naked and barefoot three years? He answerd, "the same that made our friend Diogenes, the Grecian."[7]

I then asked Ezekiel why he eat dung, & lay so long on his right & left side?[8] He answered, "the desire of raising other men into a

---

6. Blake parodies Swedenborg's accounts, in his *Memorable Relations*, of his conversations with the inhabitants during his spiritual trips to heaven.
7. In Isaiah xx.2–3, the prophet, at the command of the Lord, walked "naked and bare-foot" for three years. Diogenes was the 4th-century Greek Cynic, whose extreme repudiation of civilized customs gave rise to anecdotes that he had renounced clothing.
8. The Lord gave these instructions to **the prophet Ezekiel, iv.4–6.**

perception of the infinite; this the North American tribes practise, & is he honest who resists his genius or conscience only for the sake of present ease or gratification?"

PLATE 14

The ancient tradition that the world will be consumed in fire at the end of six thousand years is true, as I have heard from Hell.

For the cherub with his flaming sword is hereby commanded to leave his guard at [the] tree of life;[9] and when he does, the whole creation will be consumed, and appear infinite and holy, whereas it now appears finite & corrupt.

This will come to pass by an improvement of sensual enjoyment.

But first the notion that man has a body distinct from his soul is to be expunged; this I shall do, by printing in the infernal method, by corrosives, which in Hell are salutary and medicinal, melting apparent surfaces away, and displaying the infinite which was hid.[10]

If the doors of perception were cleansed every thing would appear to man as it is, infinite.

For man has closed himself up, till he sees all things thro' narrow chinks of his cavern.

PLATE 15

A Memorable Fancy

I was in a Printing house in Hell & saw the method in which knowledge is transmitted from generation to generation.

In the first chamber was a Dragon-Man, clearing away the rubbish from a cave's mouth; within, a number of Dragons were hollowing the cave.

In the second chamber was a Viper folding round the rock & the cave, and others adorning it with gold, silver, and precious stones.

In the third chamber was an Eagle with wings and feathers of air; he caused the inside of the cave to be infinite; around were numbers of Eagle-like men, who built palaces in the immense cliffs.

In the fourth chamber were Lions of flaming fire, raging around & melting the metals into living fluids.

In the fifth chamber were Unnam'd forms, which cast the metals into the expanse.

There they were receiv'd by Men who occupied the sixth chamber, and took the forms of books & were arranged in libraries.[11]

---

9. In Genesis iii.24, when the Lord drove Adam and Eve from the Garden of Eden, he had placed Cherubims and a flaming sword at the eastern end "to keep the way of the tree of life."
10. See "A Memorable Fancy," Plates

6–7 above, footnote 3.
11. In this Memorable Fancy Blake allegorizes his procedure in designing, etching, printing, and binding works of imaginative genius.

PLATE 16

The Giants who formed this world into its sensual existence, and now seem to live in it in chains, are in truth the causes of its life & the sources of all activity; but the chains are the cunning of weak and tame minds which have power to resist energy; according to the proverb, the weak in courage is strong in cunning.

Thus one portion of being is the Prolific, the other, the Devouring: to the Devourer it seems as if the producer was in his chains; but it is not so, he only takes portions of existence and fancies that the whole.

But the Prolific would cease to be Prolific unless the Devourer as a sea received the excess of his delights.[1]

Some will say, "Is not God alone the Prolific?" I answer, "God only Acts & Is, in existing beings or Men."

These two classes of men are always upon earth, & they should be enemies; whoever tries [PL 17] to reconcile them seeks to destroy existence.

Religion is an endeavour to reconcile the two.

Note. Jesus Christ did not wish to unite but to separate them, as in the Parable of sheep and goats! & he says, "I came not to send Peace but a Sword."[2]

Messiah or Satan or Tempter was formerly thought to be one of the Antediluvians[3] who are our Energies.

A Memorable Fancy

An Angel came to me and said: "O pitiable foolish young man! O horrible! O dreadful state! consider the hot burning dungeon thou art preparing for thyself to all eternity, to which thou art going in such career."

I said: "Perhaps you will be willing to shew me my eternal lot, & we will contemplate together upon it and see whether your lot or mine is most desirable."

So he took me thro' a stable & thro' a church & down into the church vault at the end of which was a mill; thro' the mill we went, and came to a cave; down the winding cavern we groped our tedious way till a void boundless as a nether sky appeard beneath us, & we held by the roots of trees and hung over this immensity, but I said: "If you please, we will commit ourselves to this void, and see whether Providence is here also, if you will not I will." But he answerd: "Do not presume, O young man, but as we here remain, behold thy lot which will soon appear when the darkness passes

---

1. The "Giants" in this section are man's creative energies, called "the Prolific," which are necessarily limited by their contrary, "the Devourer."

2. The parable of the sheep and the goats is in Matthew xxv.32–33; the saying of Christ, in Matthew x.34.
3. Men who lived before Noah's flood.

away." 4

So I remain with him sitting in the twisted [PL 18] root of an oak; he was suspended in a fungus which hung with the head downward into the deep.

By degrees we beheld the infinite Abyss, fiery as the smoke of a burning city; beneath us at an immense distance was the sun, black but shining; round it were fiery tracks on which revolv'd vast spiders, crawling after their prey, which flew, or rather swum in the infinite deep, in the most terrific shapes of animals sprung from corruption; & the air was full of them, & seemd composed of them; these are Devils, and are called Powers of the air. I now asked my companion which was my eternal lot? he said, "Between the black & white spiders."

But now, from between the black & white spiders a cloud and fire burst and rolled thro the deep, blackning all beneath, so that the nether deep grew black as a sea & rolled with a terrible noise; beneath us was nothing now to be seen but a black tempest, till looking east between the clouds & the waves, we saw a cataract of blood mixed with fire, and not many stones throw from us appeard and sunk again the scaly fold of a monstrous serpent. At last to the east, distant about three degrees, appeard a fiery crest above the waves. Slowly it reared like a ridge of golden rocks till we discovered two globes of crimson fire, from which the sea fled away in clouds of smoke; and now we saw it was the head of Leviathan; his forehead was divided into streaks of green & purple like those on a tyger's forehead: soon we saw his mouth & red gills hang just above the raging foam, tinging the black deep with beams of blood, advancing toward [PL 19] us with all the fury of a spiritual existence.

My friend the Angel climb'd up from his station into the mill; I remain'd alone, & then this appearance was no more, but I found myself sitting on a pleasant bank beside a river by moon light, hearing a harper who sung to the harp, & his theme was: "The man who never alters his opinion is like standing water, & breeds reptiles of the mind."

But I arose, and sought for the mill, & there I found my Angel, who surprised asked me how I escaped?

I answered: "All that we saw was owing to your metaphysics: for when you ran away, I found myself on a bank by moonlight hearing a harper. But now we have seen my eternal lot, shall I shew you yours? He laughd at my proposal; but I by force suddenly caught

4. The "stable" is that where Jesus was born, which, allegorically, leads to the "church" founded in his name and to the "vault" where this institution effectually buried him. The "mill" in Blake is a symbol of mechanical and analytic philosophy; through this the pilgrims pass into the twisting cave of rationalistic theology and descend to an underworld which is an empty abyss. The point of this Blakean equivalent of a carnival fun house is that only after you have thoroughly confused yourself by this tortuous approach, and only if you then (as in the next two paragraphs) stare at this topsy-turvy emptiness long enough, will the void gradually assume the semblance of the comic horrors of the fantasied hell of angelic orthodoxy.

him in my arms, & flew westerly thro' the night, till we were elevated above the earth's shadow; then I flung myself with him directly into the body of the sun; here I clothed myself in white, & taking in my hand Swedenborg's volumes, sunk from the glorious clime, and passed all the planets till we came to Saturn; here I staid to rest & then leap'd into the void between Saturn & the fixed stars.[5]

"Here," said I, "is your lot, in this space, if space it may be calld." Soon we saw the stable and the church, & I took him to the altar and open'd the Bible, and lo! it was a deep pit, into which I descended, driving the Angel before me; soon we saw seven houses of brick;[6] one we enterd; in it were a [PL 20] number of monkeys, baboons, & all of that species, chaind by the middle, grinning and snatching at one another, but withheld by the shortness of their chains: however, I saw that they sometimes grew numerous, and then the weak were caught by the strong, and with a grinning aspect, first coupled with & then devour'd, by plucking off first one limb and then another till the body was left a helpless trunk. This, after grinning & kissing it with seeming fondness, they devour'd too; and here & there I saw one savourily picking the flesh off of his own tail; as the stench terribly annoyd us both, we went into the mill, & I in my hand brought the skeleton of a body, which in the mill was Aristotle's Analytics.[7]

So the Angel said: "Thy phantasy has imposed upon me, & thou oughtest to be ashamed."

I answerd: "We impose on one another, & it is but lost time to converse with you whose works are only Analytics."

Opposition is true Friendship.

PLATE 21

I have always found that Angels have the vanity to speak of themselves as the only wise; this they do with a confident insolence sprouting from systematic reasoning.

Thus Swedenborg boasts that what he writes is new; tho' it is only the Contents or Index of already publish'd books.

A man carried a monkey about for a shew, & because he was a little wiser than the monkey, grew vain, and conciev'd himself as much wiser than seven men. It is so with Swedenborg; he shews the folly of churches & exposes hypocrites, till he imagines that all are religious, & himself the single [PL 22] one on earth that ever broke a net.

Now hear a plain fact: Swedenborg has not written one new truth. Now hear another: he has written all the old falsehoods.

5. In the Ptolemaic world picture, Saturn was in the outermost planetary sphere; beyond it was the sphere of the fixed stars.
6 The "seven churches which are in Asia," to which John addresses the Book of Revelation i.4. Blake now forces upon the angel his own diabolic view of angelic Biblical exegesis, theological speculation and disputation, and Hell—a view, Harold Bloom has remarked, which "makes monkeys out of the theologians."
7. Aristotle's treatises on logic.

And now hear the reason: He conversed with Angels who are all religious, & conversed not with Devils, who all hate religion, for he was incapable thro' his conceited notions.

Thus Swedenborg's writings are a recapitulation of all superficial opinions, and an analysis of the more sublime, but no further.

Have now another plain fact: Any man of mechanical talents may from the writings of Paracelsus or Jacob Behmen[8] produce ten thousand volumes of equal value with Swedenborg's, and from those of Dante or Shakespear, an infinite number.

But when he has done this, let him not say that he knows better than his master, for he only holds a candle in sunshine.

A Memorable Fancy

Once I saw a Devil in a flame of fire, who arose before an Angel that sat on a cloud, and the Devil utterd these words:

"The worship of God is, Honouring his gifts in other men, each according to his genius, and loving the [PL 23] greatest men best; those who envy or calumniate great men hate God, for there is no other God."

The Angel hearing this became almost blue; but mastering himself, he grew yellow, & at last white, pink, & smiling, and then replied:

"Thou Idolater, is not God One? & is not he visible in Jesus Christ? and has not Jesus Christ given his sanction to the law of ten commandments, and are not all other men fools, sinners, & nothings?"

The Devil answer'd; "Bray a fool in a mortar with wheat, yet shall not his folly be beaten out of him;[9] if Jesus Christ is the greatest man, you ought to love him in the greatest degree; now hear how he has given his sanction to the law of ten commandments: did he not mock at the sabbath, and so mock the sabbath's God? murder those who were murderd because of him? turn away the law from the woman taken in adultery? steal the labor of others to support him? bear false witness when he omitted making a defence before Pilate? covet when he pray'd for his disciples, and when he bid them shake off the dust of their feet against such as refused to lodge them?[1] I tell you, no virtue can exist without breaking these

8. Paracelsus (1493–1541), a Swiss physician and a pioneer in empirical medicine, was also a prominent theorist of the occult. Behmen is Jakob Boehme (1575–1624), a German shoemaker who developed a theosophical system which has had great and persisting influence both on theological and metaphysical speculation.
9. "Though thou shouldst bray a fool in a mortar among wheat with a pestle, yet will not his foolishness depart from him" (Proverbs xxvii.22). "Bray": pound into small pieces.
1. See Mark ii.27 ("the sabbath was made for man * * * "); John viii.2 ff. (on the woman taken in adultery); Matthew xxv.13–14 (Christ's silence before Pilate); Matthew x.4 ("whosoever shall not receive you * * * when ye depart * * * shake off the dust of your feet").

ten commandments. Jesus was all virtue, and acted from im[PL24] pulse, not from rules."

When he had so spoken, I beheld the Angel, who stretched out his arms, embracing the flame of fire, & he was consumed and arose as Elijah.[2]

Note. This Angel, who is now become a Devil, is my particular friend; we often read the Bible together in its infernal or diabolical sense, which the world shall have if they behave well.

I have also The Bible of Hell,[3] which the world shall have whether they will or no.

One Law for the Lion & Ox is Oppression.

1790–93   1790–93

PLATE 25

A Song of Liberty[4]

1. The Eternal Female groan'd! it was heard over all the Earth.
2. Albion's[5] coast is sick, silent; the American meadows faint!
3. Shadows of Prophecy shiver along by the lakes and the rivers and mutter across the ocean: France, rend down thy dungeon![6]
4. Golden Spain, burst the barriers of old Rome!
5. Cast thy keys, O Rome,[7] into the deep down falling, even to eternity down falling,
6. And weep.[8]
7. In her trembling hands she took the new born terror, howling.
8. On those infinite mountains of light now barr'd out by the Atlantic sea,[9] the new born fire stood before the starry king!
9. Flag'd with grey brow'd snows and thunderous visages, the jealous wings wav'd over the deep.
10. The speary hand burned aloft, unbuckled was the shield, forth went the hand of jealousy among the flaming hair, and [PL 26] hurl'd the new born wonder thro' the starry night.

2. In II Kings ii.11, the prophet Elijah "went up by a whirlwind into heaven," borne by "a chariot of fire."
3. I.e., the poems and designs that Blake is working on.
4. Blake etched this poem in 1792 and sometimes bound it as an appendix to *The Marriage of Heaven and Hell.* It recounts the birth, manifested in the contemporary events in France, of the flaming Spirit of Revolution (whom Blake later called Orc), and describes his conflict with the tyrannical sky god (whom Blake later called Urizen). The poem ends with the portent of the Spirit of Revolution shattering the ten commandments, or prohibitions against

political, religious, and moral liberty, and bringing in a free and joyous new world. These matters are developed in his prophetic poem, *America.*
5. England's.
6. The political prison, the Bastille, was destroyed by the French revolutionaries in 1789.
7. The keys of Rome, a symbol of Papal power.
8. John xi.35: "Jesus wept."
9. The legendary continent of Atlantis, sunk beneath the sea; Blake uses it to represent the condition before the fall. Blake often uses the stars, in their fixed courses, as symbol of the law-governed Newtonian universe.

11. The fire, the fire, is falling!

12. Look up! look up! O citizen of London, enlarge thy countenance! O Jew, leave counting gold! return to thy oil and wine. O African! black African! (Go, wingéd thought, widen his forehead.)

13. The fiery limbs, the flaming hair, shot like the sinking sun into the western sea.

14. Wak'd from his eternal sleep, the hoary element[1] roaring fled away:

15. Down rushd, beating his wings in vain, the jealous king; his grey brow'd councellors, thunderous warriors, curl'd veterans, among helms, and shields, and chariots, horses, elephants; banners, castles, slings and rocks,

16. Falling, rushing, ruining! buried in the ruins, on Urthona's[2] dens;

17. All night beneath the ruins; then, their sullen flames, faded, emerge round the gloomy king,

18. With thunder and fire, leading his starry hosts thro' the waste wilderness [PL 27] he promulgates his ten commands, glancing his beamy eyelids over the deep in dark dismay,

19. Where the son of fire in his eastern cloud, while the morning plumes her golden breast,

20. Spurning the clouds written with curses, stamps the stony law[3] to dust, loosing the eternal horses from the dens of night, crying:

Empire is no more! and now the lion & wolf shall cease.[4]

CHORUS

Let the Priests of the Raven of dawn, no longer in deadly black, with hoarse note curse the sons of joy. Nor his accepted brethren, whom, tyrant, he calls free, lay the bound or build the roof. Nor pale religious letchery call that virginity, that wishes but acts not!

For every thing that lives is Holy.

1792   1792

1. The sea, which to Blake represents a devouring chaos, such as swallowed Atlantis.
2. In the later Prophetic Books, Urthona is the unfallen form of Los, who in the fallen world represents the poetic imagination, the agent working for the regeneration of humanity.
3. I.e., the ten commandments (verse 18), which the "finger of God" had

written on "tables [tablets] of stone" (Exodus xxxi.18).
4. Cf. Isaiah's prophecy, lxv.17–25, of "new heavens and a new earth," when "the wolf and the lamb shall feed together, and the lion shall eat straw like the bullock." Repeated in *America* 6.15.
5. Repeated in *America* 8.3.

America: A Prophecy   *America* is one of Blake's early prophetic poems, and the first which he himself entitled "a prophecy." Like the related poems *The French Revolution* and *Europe* (a sequel to *America*), also written in the early 1790's, it deals with the revolutionary movements of the time, but treats temporal history imaginatively, as embodying the permanent form of all revolutions. Like the later prophetic books, *America* is written in what Blake called the "long resounding line" of seven stresses which he adapted from the early English measure known as "fourteeners."

Blake etched *America* in the years 1791–93, which encompassed the early period of the French Revolution when Blake, like Wordsworth, Coleridge, and other enthusiastic poets and intellectuals, interpreted the Revolution as initiating the millenium that had been prophesied in the apocalyptic books of the Bible. By the time Blake completed the poem, however, England had declared war on France (January, 1793), and the government had on May 21 passed harshly oppressive laws against "divers wicked and seditious writings."

The poem, after a "Preludium" (or prelude) on the coming-of-age of the spirit of revolution, covers the period from the Boston Massacre of 1770 through the American Revolution and the contagion of the revolutionary impulse among radical groups in England; it ends with a reference to the outbreak of the French Revolution and a prediction of the spread of revolution through Europe and all the world. In *Blake, Prophet against Empire* (1954), David Erdman details the many veiled references to historical events of the time. But Blake treats these facts freely, as instances of eternal archetypes whose manifestations are not tied to a particular time or place, and whose significance applies not only to history, but also to mental powers and events in the life of each man and woman. By many echoes and allusions to the Bible, Blake assimilates current history to Biblical history and millennial prophecy; he also attributes the initiative in the revolutionary combat to early versions of his own "Giant Forms" (symbolizing universal aspects of the human mind), and especially to the antagonists Orc and Urizen. These and other figures of the Blakean myth which are mentioned in *America* play altered and greatly expanded roles in his later prophetic books, *The Four Zoas*, *Milton*, and *Jerusalem*. The universal or "prophetic" aspects of the events of his age are also developed by Blake in another medium, the brilliantly colored illustrations with which he illuminated his text in the etched plates. A full-color facsimile of *America* as Blake printed it is available in the series published by the Blake Trust.

Blake did not invent his narrative strategy, but adapted to his own original purposes a traditional mode of "polysemantic" narration—the sustaining of multiple references by a single narrative line—which had fallen into disuse after the 17th century. The procedure had been elaborated over centuries of Biblical exegesis, and had been employed by many preachers and by writers such as Bunyan, whose *Pilgrim's Progress* simultaneously recounts the life of each person and of Everyman. The mode of narrative on several levels had also been exploited by earlier poets such as Dante in *The Divine Comedy*, William Langland in *Piers Plowman*, and Edmund Spenser in *The Faerie Queene*. In our own century James Joyce, in *Finnegans Wake* (1939), developed a new form of this ancient narrative method by employing mythical figures, complex allusions, and an equivocal vocabulary in which two or more words were conflated into a single invented expression.

America

A PROPHECY

Printed by William Blake in the year 1793

PLATE 1

Preludium

The shadowy daughter of Urthona stood before red Orc,[1]
When fourteen suns[2] had faintly journey'd o'er his dark abode;
His food she brought in iron baskets, his drink in cups of iron;
Crown'd with a helmet & dark hair the nameless female[3] stood;
A quiver with its burning stores, a bow like that of night,   5
When pestilence is shot from heaven; no other arms she need;
Invulnerable tho' naked, save where clouds roll round her loins
Their awful folds in the dark air. Silent she stood as night;
For never from her iron tongue could voice or sound arise,
But dumb till that dread day when Orc assay'd[4] his fierce
    embrace.   10

"Dark virgin," said the hairy youth, "thy father stern abhorr'd
Rivets my tenfold chains while still on high my spirit soars;
Sometimes an eagle screaming in the sky, sometimes a lion
Stalking upon the mountains, & sometimes a whale I lash
The raging fathomless abyss; anon a serpent folding   15
Around the pillars of Urthona,[5] and round thy dark limbs,
On the Canadian wilds I fold; feeble my spirit folds.
For chaind beneath I rend these caverns; when thou bringest
    food
I howl my joy! and my red eyes seek to behold thy face—
In vain! these clouds roll to & fro, & hide thee from my sight."   20

PLATE 2

Silent as despairing love, and strong as jealousy,
The hairy shoulders rend the links, free are the wrists of fire;
Round the terrific loins he siez'd the panting struggling womb;

1. Orc is the spirit of all human energy (including sexual energy) which, when repressed, breaks out into revolutionary violence. Here he is represented as alienated from Urthona, who has cruelly imprisoned him. In the later prophetic books Urthona, one of the four Zoas, is the unfallen form of Los, the poetic imagination.
2. Orc, at the age of 14, has achieved sexual maturity. Erdman, in *Blake, Prophet Against Empire* (p. 239), proposes that the 14 years are the period between the appearance of Rousseau's *Social Contract* in 1762 (symbolizing the birth of the revolutionary spirit) and the American Declaration of Inde-

pendence in 1776.
3. Nature, who in her separation from mankind is represented as a mute virgin, the "shadowy daughter of Urthona" (line 1). As in various folktales, the jailer's daughter pities and gives food and drink to her father's prisoner. Since Urthona, in Blake's mythology, is a blacksmith, he has presumably fashioned the iron vessels (line 3) in which his daughter carries the food and drink.
4. Attempted, dared.
5. Eagle, lion, whale, and serpent are metamorphic guises in which Orc appears (see 2.12–14); all are emblems on various revolutionary flags.

It joy'd; she put aside her clouds & smiled her first-born smile,
As when a black cloud shews its light'nings to the silent deep.   5

Soon as she saw the terrible boy, then burst the virgin cry:

"I know thee, I have found thee, & I will not let thee go;
Thou art the image of God who dwells in darkness of Africa,
And thou art fall'n to give me life in regions of dark death.
On my American plains I feel the struggling afflictions   10
Endur'd by roots that writhe their arms into the nether deep;
I see a serpent in Canada, who courts me to his love;
In Mexico an Eagle, and a Lion in Peru;
I see a Whale in the South-sea, drinking my soul away.
O what limb-rending pains I feel![6] Thy fire & my frost   15
Mingle in howling pains, in furrows by thy lightnings rent;
This is eternal death; and this the torment long foretold."

The stern Bard ceas'd, asham'd of his own song; enrag'd he
     swung
His harp aloft sounding, then dash'd its shining frame against
A ruin'd pillar in glittring fragments; silent he turn'd away,   20
And wander'd down the vales of Kent in sick & drear
     lamentings.[7]

PLATE 3

A Prophecy

The Guardian Prince of Albion[8] burns in his nightly tent;
Sullen fires across the Atlantic glow to America's shore,
Piercing the souls of warlike men, who rise in silent night.
Washington, Franklin, Paine & Warren, Gates, Hancock &
     Green[9]
Meet on the coast glowing with blood from Albion's fiery
     Prince.[1]   5

6. When Nature is forcibly embraced by Orc (1.10, 2.3 ff.), her virginal innocence and silence flare into revolutionary fervor and outcry in America (2.10). The geographical references in 2.12–14 are to others of her natural domains where oppression is causing rebellious stirrings, signified by various animal metamorphoses of Orc.

7. These last four lines appear in only four or five of the more than 20 printed copies of *America*. "The stern Bard" (line 18) is Blake himself. Erdman (p. 264) conjectures that they were added by Blake after completion of the poem in 1793, in a moment of shame and despair because of the suppression of radical opinion in England. Blake wrote in his notebook at the time: "I say I shan't live five years, And if I live one it will be a Wonder."

8. England. "The Guardian Prince" is the tutelary spirit of England, represented as encamped in a tent, preparing for oppressive war.

9. Thomas Paine was the author of *The Rights of Man* (1792); Joseph Warren was a soldier killed at Bunker Hill; Horatio Gates commanded the army which defeated Burgoyne at Saratoga; John Hancock, of Boston, was a signer of the Declaration of Independence and a member of the Continental Congress; Nathaniel Greene was an effective general in the Revolutionary Army.

1. The allusion is probably to the Boston Massacre of 1770.

Washington spoke: "Friends of America, look over the Atlantic
    sea;
A bended bow is lifted in heaven, & a heavy iron chain
Descends link by link from Albion's cliffs across the sea to bind
Brothers & sons of America, till our faces pale and yellow,
Hands deprest, voices weak, eyes downcast, hands work-bruis'd,   10
Feet bleeding on the sultry sands, and the furrows of the whip
Descend to generations that in future times forget."
The strong voice ceas'd; for a terrible blast swept over the heav-
    ing sea.
The eastern cloud rent; on his cliffs stood Albion's wrathful
    Prince,
A dragon form clashing his scales; at midnight he arose,   15
And flam'd red meteors round the land of Albion beneath.
His voice, his locks, his awful shoulders, and his glowing eyes,

PLATE 4

Appear to the Americans upon the cloudy night.

Solemn heave the Atlantic waves between the gloomy nations,
Swelling, belching from its deeps red clouds & raging Fires.

Albion is sick! America faints! enrag'd the Zenith grew.
As human blood shooting its veins all round the orbéd heaven   5
Red rose the clouds from the Atlantic in vast wheels of blood,
And in the red clouds rose a Wonder o'er the Atlantic sea,[2]
Intense! naked! a Human fire, fierce glowing as the wedge
Of iron heated in the furnace; his terrible limbs were fire
With myriads of cloudy terrors, banners dark, & towers   10
Surrounded; heat but not light went thro' the murky atmos-
    phere.

The King of England looking westward trembles at the vision.

PLATE 5

Albion's Angel[3] stood beside the Stone of night, and saw
The terror like a comet, or more like the planet red
That once inclos'd the terrible wandering comets in its sphere.
Then, Mars, thou wast our center, & the planets three flew round
Thy crimson disk; so[4] e'er the Sun was rent from thy red sphere.   5
The Spectre[5] glowd, his horrid length staining the temple long
With beams of blood; & thus a voice came forth, and shook the
    temple:

PLATE 6

"The morning comes, the night decays, the watchmen leave
    their stations;

---

2. I.e., Orc rises from the sea.
3. The tutelary "Prince" of 3.1. He is
standing beside a pulpitlike "stone," in
a darkness into which red Orc flares.

4. I.e., "and so it was * * *" Lines
2–5 are a speculative account of the
origin of the solar system.
5. I.e., Orc.

The grave is burst, the spices shed, the linen wrapped up;[6]
The bones of death, the cov'ring clay, the sinews shrunk & dry'd
Reviving shake, inspiring move, breathing, awakening,
Spring like redeemed captives when their bonds & bars are
    burst.[7]   5
Let the slave grinding at the mill run out into the field;
Let him look up into the heavens & laugh in the bright air;
Let the inchained soul shut up in darkness and in sighing,
Whose face has never seen a smile in thirty weary years,
Rise and look out; his chains are loose, his dungeon doors are
    open.   10
And let his wife and children return from the opressor's scourge;
They look behind at every step & believe it is a dream,
Singing: "The Sun has left his blackness, & has found a fresher
    morning,
And the fair Moon rejoices in the clear & cloudless night;
For Empire is no more, and now the Lion & Wolf shall cease."[8] 15

PLATE 7
In thunders ends the voice. Then Albion's Angel wrathful burnt
Beside the Stone of Night; and like the Eternal Lion's howl
In famine & war, reply'd: "Art thou not Orc, who serpent-form'd
Stands at the gate of Enitharmon to devour her children?[9]
Blasphemous Demon, Antichrist, hater of Dignities,   5
Lover of wild rebellion, and transgresser of God's Law,
Why dost thou come to Angels' eyes in this terrific form?"

PLATE 8
The terror answer'd: "I am Orc, wreath'd round the accursed
    tree.[1]
The times are ended, shadows pass, the morning gins to break;
The fiery joy, that Urizen perverted to ten commands
What night he led the starry hosts thro' the wide wilderness,[2]
That stony law I stamp to dust, and scatter religion abroad   5
To the four winds as a torn book, & none shall gather the leaves;

6. The reference to the watchmen, spices, and linen assimilate the outbreak of revolution to the accounts of the resurrection of Christ from his sepulcher in the concluding chapters of the Gospels; see, e.g., Luke xxiii.52–xxiv.12.
7. Lines 3–5 are an allusion to Ezekiel's vision, xxxvii.1–10, of the resurrection of the skeletons in the valley of bones: "And when I beheld, lo, the sinews and the flesh came upon them, and the skin covered them above. * * * So I prophesied as he commanded me, and the breath came into them, and they lived. * * *"
8. A repetition of verse 20, *A Song of Liberty*, above; it echoes Isaiah's millenial prophecy (lxv.17–25) of "new heavens and a new earth" when "the wolf and the lamb shall feed together,

and the lion shall eat straw like the bullock."
9. Albion's Angel identifies Enitharmon with the "woman clothed with the sun" in Revelation xii.1–4, and charges Orc with being the "great red dragon" (i.e., Satan) who waited "to devour her child as soon as it was born."
1. Orc replies (8.1ff.) that he is in fact the serpent wreathed around the tree of the forbidden fruit in Eden, and that he is tempting mankind to break the commandments of a tyrant god.
2. The fallen Zoa Urizen, representing the constricting reason which imposes limits, prohibitions, and measure upon joyous human energy, is here identified with the Moses of Exodus, who brought the stone tablets of the ten commandments down from Sinai.

But they shall rot on desart sands & consume in bottomless deeps
To make the desarts blossom & the deeps shrink to their foun-
tains,
And to renew the fiery joy, and burst the stony roof;
That pale religious letchery, seeking Virginity,   10
May find it in a harlot, and in coarse-clad honesty
The undefil'd, tho' ravish'd in her cradle night and morn;
For every thing that lives is holy,[3] life delights in life;
Because the soul of sweet delight can never be defil'd.[4]
Fires inwrap the earthly globe, yet man is not consumd;   15
Amidst the lustful fires he walks; his feet become like brass,
His knees and thighs like silver, & his breast and head like gold."[5]

PLATE 9

"Sound, sound, my loud war-trumpets & alarm my Thirteen
Angels![6]
Loud howls the eternal Wolf! the eternal Lion lashes his tail!
America is darkned, and my punishing Demons, terrified,
Crouch howling before their caverns deep like skins dry'd in the
wind.
They cannot smite the wheat, nor quench the fatness of the
earth;   5
They cannot smite with sorrows, nor subdue the plow and spade;
They cannot wall the city, nor moat round the castle of princes;
They cannot bring the stubbed oak to overgrow the hills;
For terrible men stand on the shores, & in their robes I see
Children take shelter from the lightnings, there stands Washing-
ton   10
And Paine and Warren, with their foreheads reard toward the
east.
But clouds obscure my aged sight. A vision from afar!
Sound, sound, my loud war-trumpets & alarm my thirteen
Angels.
Ah vision from afar! Ah rebel form that rent the ancient
Heavens, Eternal Viper self-renew'd,[7] rolling in clouds!   15
I see thee in thick clouds and darkness on America's shore,
Writhing in pangs of abhorréd birth; red flames the crest rebel-
lious
And eyes of death; the harlot womb, oft opened in vain,
Heaves in enormous circles; now the times are return'd upon
thee,

3. Repeated in the Chorus of *A Song
of Liberty*.
4. Repeated in the "Proverbs of Hell,"
The Marriage of Heaven and Hell,
Plate 9.
5. These last three lines echo Daniel
iii.23–27 (the account of the three men
who walked unscathed inside Nebuchadnezzar's fiery furnace) and ii.32–
33 (Daniel's description of the king's
dream of a great image whose "head

was of fine gold, his breast and his
arms of silver, his belly and his thighs
of brass").
6. The speaker of lines 1–27 is Albion's
Angel, calling on his representatives
("Thirteen Angels") in the 13 American colonies to suppress the revolutionary stirrings.
7. In his serpent form, Orc renews
himself by shedding his skin.

Devourer of thy parent, now thy unutterable torment renews. 20
Sound, sound, my loud war-trumpets & alarm my thirteen Angels!
Ah terrible birth! a young one bursting! where is the weeping
    mouth?
And where the mother's milk? Instead those ever-hissing jaws
And parched lips drop with fresh gore. Now roll thou in the
    clouds;
Thy mother lays her length outstretch'd upon the shore
    beneath.[8] 25
Sound, sound, my loud war-trumpets & alarm my thirteen Angels!
Loud howls the eternal Wolf; the eternal Lion lashes his tail."

PLATE 10

Thus wept the Angel voice, & as he wept the terrible blasts
Of trumpets blew a loud alarm across the Atlantic deep.
No trumpets answer, no reply of clarions or of fifes.
Silent the Colonies remain and refuse the loud alarm.

On those vast shady hills between America & Albion's shore, 5
Now barr'd out by the Atlantic sea, call'd Atlantean hills,[9]
Because from their bright summits you may pass to the Golden
    world,
An ancient palace, archetype of mighty Emperies,
Rears its immortal pinnacles, built in the forest of God
By Ariston, the king of beauty for his stolen bride.[1] 10

Here on their magic seats the thirteen Angels sat perturb'd,
For clouds from the Atlantic hover o'er the solemn roof.

PLATE 11

Fiery the Angels rose, & as they rose deep thunder roll'd
Around their shores, indignant burning with the fires of Orc;
And Boston's Angel cried aloud as they flew thro' the dark night.

He cried: "Why trembles honesty, and like a murderer,
Why seeks he refuge from the frowns of his immortal station? 5
Must the generous tremble & leave his joy to the idle, to the
    pestilence,
That mock him? Who commanded this? what God? what
    Angel?
To keep the gen'rous from experience till the ungenerous
Are unrestraind performers of the energies of nature;
Till pity is become a trade, and generosity a science 10
That men get rich by, & the sandy desert is giv'n to the strong.

8. Albion's Angel sees Orc as varying in form between a serpent and a youth.
9. The fabled island of Atlantis in the western ocean was the beautiful seat of a great and prosperous empire until, because of the impiety of its inhabitants, it sank beneath the sea (Plato, *Timaeus*). Blake locates Atlantis between England and America, which it had once connected as parts of a single continent, and describes it as accessible still as a meeting place for the Angels of the 13 colonies (lines 11–12).
1. Ariston, King of Sparta, stole the wife of his best friend, according to the Greek historian, Herodotus.

What God is he, writes laws of peace, & clothes him in a tempest?
What pitying Angel lusts for tears, and fans himself with sighs?
What crawling villain preaches abstinence & wraps himself
In fat of lambs? No more I follow, no more obedience pay!"   15

PLATE 12

So cried he, rending off his robe & throwing down his scepter
In sight of Albion's Guardian; and all the thirteen Angels
Rent off their robes to the hungry wind, & threw their golden
    scepters
Down on the land of America. Indignant they descended
Headlong from out their heav'nly heights, descending swift as
    fires   5
Over the land. Naked & flaming are their lineaments seen
In the deep gloom; by Washington & Paine & Warren they
    stood,
And the flame folded roaring fierce within the pitchy night
Before the Demon red,[2] who burnt towards America,
In black smoke, thunders, and loud winds, rejoicing in its terror, 10
Breaking in smoky wreaths from the wild deep, & gath'ring thick
In flames as of a furnace on the land from North to South.

PLATE 13

What time the thirteen Governors that England sent convene
In Bernard's[3] house; the flames coverd the land; they rouze, they
    cry,
Shaking their mental chains they rush in fury to the sea
To quench their anguish; at the feet of Washington down fall'n
They grovel on the sand and writhing lie, while all   5
The British soldiers thro' the thirteen states sent up a howl
Of anguish, threw their swords & muskets to the earth, & ran
From their encampments and dark castles seeking where to hide
From the grim flames and from the visions of Orc; in sight
Of Albion's Angel who, enrag'd, his secret clouds open'd   10
From north to south, and burnt outstretched on wings of wrath,
    cov'ring
The eastern sky, spreading his awful wings across the heavens;
Beneath him roll'd his num'rous hosts, all Albion's Angels
    camp'd
Darkend the Atlantic mountains, & their trumpets shook the
    valleys,
Arm'd with diseases of the earth to cast upon the Abyss,   15
Their numbers forty millions, must'ring in the eastern sky.

PLATE 14

In the flames stood & view'd the armies drawn out in the sky
Washington, Franklin, Paine & Warren, Allen, Gates & Lee,
And heard the voice of Albion's Angel give the thunderous command.

2. I.e., Orc.

3. Sir Francis Bernard, Governor of Massachusetts Bay Colony (1760–71).

His plagues, obedient to his voice, flew forth out of their clouds,
Falling upon America as a storm to cut them off, 5
As a blight cuts the tender corn when it begins to appear.
Dark is the heaven above, & cold & hard the earth beneath;
And as a plague wind fill'd with insects cuts off man & beast,
And as a sea o'erwhelms a land in the day of an earthquake,

Fury, rage, madness, in a wind swept through America, 10
And the red flames of Orc that folded roaring fierce around
The angry shores, and the fierce rushing of th'inhabitants together.
The citizens of New-York close their books & lock their chests;
The mariners of Boston drop their anchors and unlade;[4]
The scribe of Pennsylvania casts his pen upon the earth; 15
The builder of Virginia throws his hammer down in fear.[5]

Then had America been lost,[6] o'erwhelm'd by the Atlantic,
And Earth had lost another portion of the infinite;
But all rush together in the night, in wrath and raging fire;
The red fires rag'd, the plagues recoil'd, then rolld they back with fury 20

PLATE 15
On Albion's Angels; then the Pestilence began in streaks of red
Across the limbs of Albion's Guardian, the spotted plague smote Bristol's[7]
And the Leprosy London's Spirit, sickening all their bands.
The millions sent up a howl of anguish and threw off their hammerd mail,
And cast their swords & spears to earth, & stood a naked multitude. 5
Albion's Guardian writhed in torment on the eastern sky,
Pale, quivring toward the brain his glimmering eyes, teeth chattering,
Howling & shuddering, his legs quivering, convuls'd each muscle & sinew;
Sick'ning lay London's Guardian and the ancient miter'd York,
Their heads on snowy hills, their ensigns sick'ning in the sky. 10
The plagues creep on the burning winds, driven by flames of Orc,
And by the fierce Americans rushing together in the night,
Driven o'er the Guardians of Ireland and Scotland and Wales.
They, spotted with plagues, forsook the frontiers, & their banners seard

4. Unload (their cargo).
5. The attack echoes Milton's description of the onslaught by the Messiah against the rebel angels in heaven. Christ used as his weapon "ten thousand thunders, which he sent / Before him, such as in their souls infixed / plagues" (*Paradise Lost*, VI.834ff.); Blake implies that the Messiah, acting under the command of Jehovah, represented a tyrant deity, and that Satan and his rebel Angels were the types of Orc and the rebel colonies. The use of plagues as a weapon also recalls the plagues with which Jehovah punished the Egyptian pharoah, when he refused to liberate the Israelites (Exodus vii–xi).
6. I.e., would have been lost.
7. Bristol was a major seaport in the trade with America.

With fires of hell, deform their ancient heavens with shame &   15
    woe.
Hid in his caves the Bard of Albion[8] felt the enormous plagues,
And a cowl of flesh grew o'er his head, & scales on his back &
    ribs;
And rough with black scales all his Angels fright their ancient
    heavens.
The doors of marriage are open, and the Priests in rustling scales
Rush into reptile coverts, hiding from the fires of Orc   20
That play around the golden roofs in wreaths of fierce desire,
Leaving the females naked and glowing with the lusts of youth.

For the female spirits of the dead, pining in bonds of religion,
Run from their fetters reddening, & in long drawn arches sitting
They feel the nerves of youth renew, and desires of ancient times 25
Over their pale limbs as a vine when the tender grape appears.[9]

PLATE 16
Over the hills, the vales, the cities, rage the red flames fierce;
The Heavens melted from north to south; and Urizen, who sat
Above all heavens in thunders wrap'd, emerg'd his leprous head
From out his holy shrine, his tears in deluge piteous
Falling into the deep sublime. Flag'd with grey-brow'd snows   5
And thunderous visages, his jealous wings wav'd over the deep;
Weeping in dismal howling woe he dark descended, howling
Around the smitten bands, clothed in tears & trembling, shud-
    d'ring cold.
His stored snows he poured forth, and his icy magazines
He open'd on the deep, and on the Atlantic sea, white, shiv'ring. 10
Leprous his limbs, all over white, and hoary was his visage,
Weeping in dismal howlings before the stern Americans,
Hiding the Demon red with clouds & cold mists from the earth;[1]
Till Angels & weak men twelve years should govern o'er the
    strong:
And then their end should come, when France reciev'd the
    Demon's light.[2]   15

Stiff shudderings shook the heav'nly thrones! France, Spain, &
    Italy
In terror view'd the bands of Albion, and the ancient Guardians
Fainting upon the elements, smitten with their own plagues.

8. Probably the official English poet laureate, who at the time was the minor poet, Henry James Pye.
9. The triumph of Orc is one of release from all authoritarian limits on human energy: political, social, religious, and sexual. The last line echoes the *Song of Songs* ii.13: "* * * and the vines with the tender grape give a good smell. Arise, my love, my fair one, and come away."
1. Roused to action by the failure of

the lesser tyrants of whom he is the archetype, Urizen succeeds in temporarily freezing into stasis the revolutionary movement.
2. The "twelve years" are probably the period between the American triumph at Yorktown in 1781 and the execution by the French revolutionists of King Louis XVI in 1793; in this period, the "weak men" continue to govern in France.

They slow advance to shut the five gates[3] of their law-built
  heaven,
Filled with blasting fancies and with mildews of despair,   20
With fierce disease and lust, unable to stem the fires of Orc;
But the five gates were consum'd, & their bolts and hinges
  melted,
And the fierce flames burnt round the heavens, & round the
  abodes of men.[4]

FINIS

1791–93

Poems from BLAKE'S NOTEBOOK[1]

Never Pain to Tell Thy Love

Never pain to tell thy love
Love that never told can be,
For the gentle wind does move
Silently, invisibly.

I told my love, I told my love,   5
I told her all my heart,
Trembling, cold, in ghastly fears—
Ah, she doth depart.

Soon as she was gone from me
A traveller came by   10
Silently, invisibly—
O, was no deny.

I Askéd a Thief

I askéd a thief to steal me a peach,
He turned up his eyes;
I ask'd a lithe lady to lie her down,
Holy & meek she cries.

3. I.e., the five human senses, which set
finite limits to man's infinite imaginative vision. Cf. *Marriage of Heaven
and Hell*, Plate 14: "If the doors of
perception were cleansed every thing
would appear to man as it is, infinite.
/ For man has closed himself up, till
he sees all things thro' narrow chinks
of his cavern."
4. The poem ends in the historical
moment of 1793, with the fires of revolution burning but the outcome of the
war against oppression, both in the

individual human mind and in human
history, as yet unresolved.
1. A commonplace book in which Blake
drew sketches and jotted down verses
and memoranda between the late 1780's
and 1810. It is known as the "Rossetti
Manuscript" because it later came into
the possession of the poet and painter
Dante Gabriel Rossetti. These poems
were first published in imperfect form in
1863, then transcribed from the manuscript by Geoffrey Keynes in 1935.

As soon as I went   5
An angel came.
He wink'd at the thief
And smild at the dame—

And without one word said
Had a peach from the tree   10
And still as a maid
Enjoy'd the lady.

1796

Mock on, Mock on, Voltaire, Rousseau

Mock on, Mock on, Voltaire, Rousseau;[2]
Mock on, Mock on, 'tis all in vain.
You throw the sand against the wind,
And the wind blows it back again.

And every sand becomes a Gem   5
Reflected in the beams divine;
Blown back, they blind the mocking Eye,
But still in Israel's paths they shine.

The Atoms of Democritus
And Newton's Particles of light[3]   10
Are sands upon the Red sea shore,
Where Israel's tents do shine so bright.

Morning

To find the Western path
Right thro the Gates of Wrath
I urge my way;
Sweet Mercy leads me on,
With soft repentant moan
I see the break of day.   5

The war of swords & spears
Melted by dewy tears
Exhales on high;
The Sun is freed from fears   10
And with soft grateful tears
Ascends the sky.

2. Blake regards both Voltaire and Rousseau as representing rationalism and Deism.
3. Democritus (460–362 B.C.) proposed that atoms were ultimate components of the universe; Newton in his *Opticks* hypothesized that light consisted of minute material particles.

The Mental Traveller[1]

I traveld thro' a Land of Men
A Land of Men & Women too
And heard & saw such dreadful things
As cold Earth wanderers never knew

For there the Babe is born in joy   5
That was begotten in dire woe
Just as we Reap in joy the fruit
Which we in bitter tears did sow

And if the Babe is born a Boy
He's given to a Woman Old   10
Who nails him down upon a rock
Catches his shrieks in cups of gold

She binds iron thorns around his head
She pierces both his hands & feet
She cuts his heart out at his side   15
To make it feel both cold & heat

---

1. A useful clue to this cryptic narrative is Blake's assertion in *A Vision of the Last Judgment*: "Man passes on but States remain for ever. He passes thro them like a traveller who may ... suppose that the places he has passed thro exist no more. ... Every thing is Eternal." In the poem, the Mental Traveller is a visitor from another country—the "eternal" realm of imagination—to our fallen, temporal world. His travelogue describes the temporal sequence of States that he discovers, but which "cold Earth wanderers never knew" (line 4) because their knowledge of their lot is that of delusory sense-experience, not of imaginative vision. These States are the persisting forms through which all earthly existence passes; in Blake's prophetic poems they are named Beulah, Generation, and Ulro (see the headnote to Blake, above). The Traveller describes man's passage through the States as a revolving cycle in time; in the prophetic poems, this circling constitutes what scholars call the Orc cycle, in which the spontaneous, all-demanding, rebellious infant Orc matures inevitably into the rigid, materialistic, and isolated old man, Urizen, who then reverts to infancy and so begins the cycle anew. This temporal world is "A Land of Men & Women too" (line 2). That is, the sexes have fallen into separation and Selfhood, and the female character in the poem represents both human women and the alien-ated human environment, which Blake elsewhere calls the delusory "Nature, Mother of all." The female principle is represented in the predominant guise in which she appears to the male perspective, at each stage of his development. The female cycle is thus complementary and opposite to that of the male, moving from an old, cruel, oppressive mother-figure (or wicked stepmother), through the form of mistress and prolific wife, to that of female infant, and on to oppressive crone again. The only way to break out of blind bondage to time is by a triumph of imagination that will provide the vision of the Mental Traveller—and of Blake the Bard.

The cycle in time is the form of each individual life, as well as of each historical culture. Blake's description of the cycle also involves pagan myth (especially the myth of Prometheus, lines 11 ff.), fairy-tales, and the Gospel story of Christ, as read in its literal and historical instead of in what Blake calls its "spiritual sense" (e.g., lines 13 ff., 93 ff.). But the full significance of this travelogue, like that of Blake's other myths, is open-ended rather than explicit. As Blake said in his letter to Dr. Trusler (below), "What is not too explicit is the fittest for instruction, because it rouzes the faculties to act."

This poem was not engraved by Blake, but it survived in what is known as the Pickering manuscript.

Her fingers number every Nerve
Just as a Miser counts his gold
She lives upon his shrieks & cries
And she grows young as he grows old   20

Till he becomes a bleeding youth
And she becomes a Virgin bright
Then he rends up his Manacles
And binds her down for his delight

He plants himself in all her Nerves   25
Just as a Husbandman his mould
And she becomes his dwelling place
And Garden fruitful seventy fold

An aged Shadow soon he fades
Wandring round an Earthly Cot²   30
Full filled all with gems & gold
Which he by industry had got

And these are the gems of the Human Soul
The rubies & pearls of a lovesick eye
The countless gold of the akeing heart   35
The martyrs groan & the lovers sigh

They are his meat they are his drink
He feeds the Beggar & the Poor
And the wayfaring Traveller
For ever open is his door   40

His grief is their eternal joy
They make the roofs & walls to ring
Till from the fire on the hearth
A little Female Babe does spring

And she is all of solid fire   45
And gems & gold that none his hand
Dares stretch to touch her Baby form
Or wrap her in his swaddling-band

But She comes to the Man she loves
If young or old or rich or poor   50
They soon drive out the aged Host
A Beggar at anothers door

He wanders weeping far away
Untill some other take him in
Oft blind & age-bent sore distrest   55
Untill he can a Maiden win

---

2. Cottage.

And to allay his freezing Age
The Poor Man takes her in his arms
The Cottage fades before his sight
The Garden & its lovely Charms   60

The Guests are scattered thro' the land
For the Eye altering alters all
The Senses roll themselves in fear
And the flat Earth becomes a Ball[3]

The Stars Sun Moon all shrink away   65
A desart vast without a bound
And nothing left to eat or drink
And a dark desart all around

The honey of her Infant lips
The bread & wine of her sweet smile   70
The wild game of her roving Eye
Does him to Infancy beguile

For as he eats & drinks[4] he grows
Younger & younger every day
And on the desart wild they both   75
Wander in terror & dismay

Like the wild Stag she flees away
Her fear plants many a thicket wild
While he pursues her night & day
By various arts of Love beguild   80

By various arts of Love & Hate
Till the wide desart planted oer
With Labyrinths of wayward Love
Where roams the Lion Wolf & Boar

Till he becomes a wayward Babe   85
And she a weeping Woman Old
Then many a Lover wanders here
The Sun & Stars are nearer rolld

The trees bring forth sweet Extacy
To all who in the desert roam   90
Till many a City there is Built
And many a pleasant Shepherds home

But when they find the frowning Babe
Terror strikes thro the region wide

3. Blake claimed that the post-Coperni-
can and Newtonian conception of the
earth "as of a Globe rolling thro Void-
ness . . . is a delusion of Ulro" (*Milton*,
Plate 29).

4. Man eats and drinks "the bread and
wine" of line 70—the delusive communion of the female as seductive harlot.

They cry the Babe the Babe is Born   95
And flee away on Every side

For who dare touch the frowning form
His arm is withered to its root
Lions Boars Wolves all howling flee
And every Tree does shed its fruit   100

And none can touch that frowning form
Except it be a Woman Old
She nails him down upon the Rock
And all is done as I have told

ca. 1803   1863

And Did Those Feet[1]

And did those feet in ancient time
Walk upon England's mountains green?
And was the holy Lamb of God
On England's pleasant pastures seen?

And did the Countenance Divine   5
Shine forth upon our clouded hills?
And was Jerusalem builded here,
Among these dark Satanic Mills?[2]

Bring me my Bow of burning gold:
Bring me my Arrows of desire:
Bring me my Spear: O clouds unfold!   10
Bring me my Chariot of fire!

I will not cease from Mental Fight,
Nor shall my Sword sleep in my hand,
Till we have built Jerusalem
In England's green & pleasant Land.   15

ca. 1804–10   ca. 1804–10

1. These quatrains occur in the Preface to Blake's prophetic poem *Milton*. There is an ancient belief, still current in parts of England, that Jesus came to England with Joseph of Arimathea. Blake adapts the legend to his own conception of a spiritual Israel, in which the significance of Biblical events are as relevant to England as to Palestine. By a particularly Blakean irony, this poem of mental war in the service of apocalyptic desire is widely used as a hymn by those of us whom Blake called "angels."

2. There may be an allusion here to industrial England; but the mill is primarily Blake's symbol for a mechanistic and utilitarian world view, according to which, as he said elsewhere, "the same dull round, even of a universe" becomes "a mill with complicated wheels."

A Vision of The Last Judgment[1]

For the Year 1810
Additions to Blake's Catalogue of Pictures &c

The Last Judgment [will be] when all those are Cast away who trouble Religion with Questions concerning Good & Evil or Eating of the Tree of those Knowledges or Reasonings which hinder the Vision of God turning all into a Consuming fire. When Imaginative Art & Science & all Intellectual Gifts, all the Gifts of the Holy Ghost, are lookd upon as of no use & only Contention remains to Man then the Last Judgment begins & its Vision is seen by the Imaginative Eye of Every one according to the situation he holds.

[PAGE 68] The Last Judgment is not Fable or Allegory but Vision. Fable or Allegory are a totally distinct & inferior kind of Poetry. Vision or Imagination is a Representation of what Eternally Exists, Really & Unchangeably. Fable or Allegory is Formd by the daughters of Memory. Imagination is Surrounded by the daughters of Inspiration who in the aggregate are calld Jerusalem. [P 69] Fable is Allegory but what Critics call The Fable is Vision itself. [P 68] The Hebrew Bible & the Gospel of Jesus are not Allegory but Eternal Vision or Imagination of All that Exists. Note here that Fable or Allegory is Seldom without some Vision. Pilgrim's Progress is full of it, the Greek Poets the same; but Allegory & Vision ought to be known as Two Distinct Things & so calld for the Sake of Eternal Life. Plato has made Socrates say that Poets & Prophets do not know or Understand what they write or Utter; this is a most Pernicious Falshood. If they do not, pray is an inferior Kind to be calld Knowing? Plato confutes himself.[2]

The Last Judgment is one of these Stupendous Visions. I have represented it as I saw it. To different People it appears differently as [P 69] every thing else does for tho on Earth things seem Permanent they are less permanent than a Shadow as we all know too well.

1. In this essay Blake describes and comments on his painting of the Last Judgment, now lost, which is said to have measured seven by five feet and to have included a thousand figures. The text has been transcribed and rearranged, as the sequence of the pages indicate, from the scattered fragments in Blake's Notebook. The opening and closing parts are reprinted here as Blake's fullest, although cryptic, statements of what he means by vision. These sections deal with the relations of imaginative vision to allegory, Greek fable, and the Biblical story; to un-curbed human passion and intellectual power; to conventional and coercive virtue; to what is seen by the "corporeal" eye; to the arts; and to the Last Judgment and the apocalyptic redemption of man and the created world —an apocalypse which is to be achieved by the triumph over the bodily eye of human imagination, as manifested in the creative artist.

2. In Plato's diologue *Ion*, in which Socrates traps Ion into admitting that, since poets compose by inspiration, they do so without knowing what they are doing.

The Nature of Visionary Fancy or Imagination is very little Known & the Eternal nature & permanence of its ever Existent Images is considered as less permanent than the things of Vegetative & Generative Nature; yet the Oak dies as well as the Lettuce, but Its Eternal ·Image & Individuality never dies, but renews by its seed. Just so the Imaginative Image returns by the seed of Contemplative Thought. The Writings of the Prophets illustrate these conceptions of the Visionary Fancy by their various sublime & Divine Images as seen in the Worlds of Vision. * * *

Let it here be Noted that the Greek Fables originated in Spiritual Mystery [P 72] and Real Visions Which are lost & clouded in Fable & Allegory while the Hebrew Bible & the Greek Gospel are Genuine, Preservd by the Saviour's Mercy. The Nature of my Work is Visionary or Imaginative. It is an Endeavour to Restore what the Ancients calld the Golden Age.

[PAGE 69] This world of Imagination is the World of Eternity; it is the Divine bosom into which we shall all go after the death of the Vegetated body. This World of Imagination is Infinite & Eternal whereas the world of Generation or Vegetation is Finite & for a small moment Temporal. There Exist in that Eternal World the Permanent Realities of Every Thing which we see reflected in this Vegetable Glass of Nature.

All Things are comprehended in their Eternal Forms in the Divine [P 70] body of the Saviour, the True Vine of Eternity, The Human Imagination, who appeard to Me as Coming to Judgment among his Saints & throwing off the Temporal that the Eternal might be Establishd. Around him were seen the Images of Existences according to a certain order suited to my Imaginative Eye. * * *

[PAGE 87] Men are admitted into Heaven not because they have curbed & governd their Passions or have No Passions but because they have Cultivated their Understandings. The Treasures of Heaven are not Negations of Passion but Realities of Intellect from which All the Passions Emanate Uncurbed in their Eternal Glory. The Fool shall not enter into Heaven let him be ever so Holy. Holiness is not The Price of Enterance into Heaven. Those who are cast out Are All Those who, having no Passions of their own because No Intellect, Have spent their lives in Curbing & Governing other People's by the Various arts of Poverty & Cruelty of all kinds. Wo Wo Wo to you Hypocrites. Even Murder the Courts of Justice, more merciful than the Church, are compelld to allow is not done in Passion but in Cool Blooded Design & Intention.

The Modern Church Crucifies Christ with the Head Downwards.

[PAGE 92] Many Persons such as Paine & Voltaire with some of the Ancient Greeks say we will not converse concerning Good & Evil we will live in Paradise & Liberty. You may do so in Spirit but not in the Mortal Body as you pretend, till after the Last Judgment; for in Paradise they have no Corporeal & Mortal Body; that originated with the Fall & was calld Death & cannot be removed but by a Last Judgment; while we are in the world of Mortality we Must Suffer. The Whole Creation Groans to be deliverd; there will always be as many Hypocrites born as Honest Men & they will always have superior Power in Mortal Things. You cannot have Liberty in this World without what you call Moral Virtue & you cannot have Moral Virtue without the Slavery of that half of the Human Race who hate what you call Moral Virtue.

The Nature of Hatred & Envy & of All the Mischiefs in the World are here depicted. No one Envies or Hates one of his Own Party; even the devils love one another in their Way; they torment one another for other reasons than Hate or Envy; these are only employd against the Just. Neither can Seth Envy Noah, or Elijah Envy Abraham, but they may both of them Envy the Success [P 93] of Satan or of Og or Molech. The Horse never Envies the Peacock nor the Sheep the Goat but they Envy a Rival in Life & Existence whose ways & means exceed their own, let him be of what Class of Animals he will; a Dog will envy a Cat who is pamperd at the expense of his comfort, as I have often seen. The Bible never tells us that Devils torment one another thro Envy; it is thro this that they torment the Just; but for what do they torment one another? I answer, For the Coercive Laws of Hell, Moral Hypocrisy. They torment a Hypocrite when he is discovered; they Punish a Failure in the tormentor who has suffered the Subject of his torture to Escape. In Hell all is Self Righteousness; there is no such thing there as Forgiveness of Sin; he who does Forgive Sin is Crucified as an Abettor of Criminals, & he who performs Works of Mercy in Any shape whatever is punishd & if possible destroyd, not thro Envy or Hatred or Malice but thro Self Righteousness that thinks it does God service, which God is Satan. They do not Envy one another; they contemn & despise one another.

Forgiveness of Sin is only at the Judgment Seat of Jesus the Saviour, where the Accuser is cast out, not because he Sins but because he torments the Just & makes them do what he condemns as Sin & what he knows is opposite to their own Identity.

It is not because Angels are Holier than Men or Devils that makes them Angels but because they do not Expect Holiness from one another but from God only.

The Player is a liar when he Says Angels are happier than [P 94] Men because they are better. Angels are happier than Men & Devils because they are not always Prying after Good & Evil in one Another & eating the Tree of Knowledge for Satan's Gratification.

Thinking as I do that the Creator of this World is a very Cruel Being, & being a Worshipper of Christ, I cannot help saying: "the

Son O how unlike the Father!" First God Almighty comes with a Thump on the Head. Then Jesus Christ comes with a balm to heal it.

The Last Judgment is an Overwhelming of Bad Art & Science. Mental Things are alone Real; what is Calld Corporeal Nobody Knows of its dwelling Place; it is in Fallacy & its Existence an Imposture. Where is the Existence Out of Mind or Thought? Where is it but in the Mind of a Fool? Some People flatter themselves that there will be No Last Judgment & [P 95] that Bad Art will be adopted & mixed with Good Art, That Error or Experiment will make a Part of Truth, & they Boast that it is its Foundation. These People flatter themselves; I will not Flatter them. Error is Created. Truth is Eternal. Error or Creation will be Burned Up, & then & not till then Truth or Eternity will appear. It is Burnt up the Moment Men cease to behold it. I assert for My self that I do not behold the Outward Creation & that to me it is hindrance & not Action; it is as the Dirt upon my feet, No part of Me. "What," it will be Questiond, "When the Sun rises do you not see a round Disk of fire somewhat like a Guinea?" O no no, I see an Innumerable company of the Heavenly host crying "Holy Holy Holy is the Lord God Almighty." I question not my Corporeal or Vegetative Eye any more than I would Question a Window concerning a Sight. I look thro it & not with it.

1810   1810

[Three Letters on Sight and Vision[1]]

To Dr. John Trusler (August 23, 1799)

Revd Sir

I really am sorry that you are falln out with the Spiritual World Especially if I should have to answer for it. I feel very sorry that your Ideas & Mine on Moral Painting differ so much as to have made you angry with my method of Study. If I am wrong I am wrong in good company. I had hoped your plan comprehended All Species of this Art & Especially that you would not regret that Species which gives Existence to Every other, namely Visions of Eternity. You say that I want somebody to Elucidate my Ideas. But you ought to know that What is Grand is necessarily obscure to Weak

1. Blake wrote each of these pronouncements about the difference between "corporeal" sight and imaginative vision at a time when a friend, a patron, or the need for money was putting pressure on him to turn from his visionary art to more fashionable modes of representation. The first letter is a passionate response to John Trusler (1735–1820), clergyman, bookseller, and author, who had objected to Blake's illustrations for one of Trusler's books.

men. That which can be made Explicit to the Idiot is not worth my care. The wisest of the Ancients considerd what is not too Explicit as the fittest for Instruction because it rouzes the faculties to act. I name Moses Solomon Esop Homer Plato.

But as you have favord me with your remarks on my Design permit me in return to defend it against a mistaken one, which is, That I have supposed Malevolence without a Cause.[2]—Is not Merit in one a Cause of Envy in another & Serenity & Happiness & Beauty a Cause of Malevolence? But Want of Money & the Distress of A Thief can never be alledged as the Cause of his Thievery, for many honest people endure greater hard ships with Fortitude. We must therefore seek the Cause elsewhere than in want of Money for that is the Misers passion, not the Thiefs.

I have therefore proved your Reasonings Ill proportiond, which you can never prove my figures to be. They are those of Michael Angelo Rafael & the Antique & of the best living Models. I percieve that your Eye is perverted by Caricature Prints, which ought not to abound so much as they do. Fun I love but too much Fun is of all things the most loathsom. Mirth is better than Fun & Happiness is better than Mirth—I feel that a Man may be happy in This World. And I know that This World Is a World of Imagination & Vision. I see Every thing I paint In This World, but Every body does not see alike. To the Eyes of a Miser a Guinea is more beautiful than the Sun & a bag worn with the use of Money has more beautiful proportions than a Vine filled with Grapes. The tree which moves some to tears of joy is in the Eyes of others only a Green thing that stands in the way. Some See Nature all Ridicule & Deformity & by these I shall not regulate my proportions, & Some Scarce see Nature at all. But to the Eyes of the Man of Imagination Nature is Imagination itself. As a man is So he Sees. As the Eye is formed such are its Powers. You certainly Mistake when you say that the Visions of Fancy are not to be found in This World. To Me This World is all One continued Vision of Fancy or Imagination & I feel Flatterd when I am told So. What is it sets Homer Virgil & Milton in so high a rank of Art? Why is the Bible more Entertaining & Instructive than any other book? Is it not because they are addressed to the Imagination which is Spiritual Sensation & but mediately to the Understanding or Reason? Such is True Painting and such was alone valued by the Greeks & the best modern Artists. Consider what Lord Bacon says, "Sense sends over to Imagination before Reason have judged & Reason sends over to Imagination before the

2. Blake had made for Trusler a water-color drawing (which has survived), illustrating Malevolence. As Blake described this design in an earlier letter: "A Father, taking leave of his Wife & Child, Is watch'd by two Fiends incarnate, with intention that when his back is turned they will murder the mother & her infant."

Decree can be acted." See Advancem^t of Learning, Part 2, P. 47 of first Edition.

But I am happy to find a Great Majority of Fellow Mortals who can Elucidate My Visions & Particularly they have been Elucidated by Children, who have taken a greater delight in contemplating my Pictures than I even hoped. Neither Youth nor Childhood is Folly or Incapacity. Some Children are Fools & so are some Old Men. But There is a vast Majority on the side of Imagination or Spiritual Sensation.

To Engrave after another Painter is infinitely more laborious than to Engrave ones own Inventions. And of the Size you require my price has been Thirty Guineas & I cannot afford to do it for less. I had Twelve for the Head I sent you as a Specimen, but after my own designs I could do at least Six times the quantity of labour in the same time, which will account for the difference of price, as also that Chalk Engraving is at least six times as laborious as Aqua tinta. I have no objection to Engraving after another Artist. Engraving is the profession I was apprenticed to, & should never have attempted to live by any thing else, If orders had not come in for my Designs & Paintings, which I have the pleasure to tell you are Increasing Every Day. Thus If I am a Painter it is not to be attributed to Seeking after. But I am contented whether I live by Painting or Engraving.

I am Revd Sir Your very obedient servant

William Blake

To Thomas Butts[1] *(November 22, 1802)*

[With Happiness Stretchd Across the Hills]

Dear Sir

After I had finishd my Letter I found that I had not said half what I intended to say, & in particular I wish to ask you what subject you choose to be painted on the remaining Canvas which I brought down with me (for there were three) and to tell you that several of the Drawings were in great forwardness; you will see by the Inclosed Account that the remaining Number of Drawings which you gave me orders for is Eighteen. I will finish these with all possible Expedition, if indeed I have not tired you or, as it is politely calld, Bored you too much already; or if you would rather

---

1. Thomas Butts (d. 1845) was a staunch supporter who, though only a chief clerk in the Public Record Office, bought more of Blake's works than did any other contemporary. To this friend Blake expresses his anguish at the demands of William Hayley (1745–1820), a well-to-do writer and patron of the arts who, after having settled the Blakes at Felpham in Sussex, was trying to impose on the artist, for what he thought were Blake's best interests, his own conventional standards and tastes.

cry out Enough, Off Off! tell me in a Letter of forgiveness if you
were offended, & of accustomd friendship if you were not. But I will
bore you more with some Verses which My Wife desires me to
Copy out & send you with her kind love & Respect they were Composed above a twelve-month ago while Walking from Felpham to
Lavant to meet my Sister:[2]

With happiness stretchd across the hills
In a cloud that dewy sweetness distills
With a blue sky spread over with wings
And a mild sun that mounts & sings
With trees & fields full of Fairy elves   5
And little devils who fight for themselves
Remembring the Verses that Hayley sung
When my heart knockd against the root of my tongue
With Angels planted in Hawthorn bowers
And God himself in the passing hours   10
With Silver Angels across my way
And Golden Demons that none can stay
With my Father hovering upon the wind
And my Brother Robert just behind
And my Brother John the evil one[3]   15
In a black cloud making his mone
Tho dead they appear upon my path
Notwithstanding my terrible wrath
They beg they intreat they drop their tears
Filld full of hopes filld full of fears   20
With a thousand Angels upon the Wind
Pouring disconsolate from behind
To drive them off & before my way
A frowning Thistle implores my stay
What to others a trifle appears   25
Fills me full of smiles or tears
For double the vision my Eyes do see
And a double vision is always with me

2. This poem expresses Blake's distress at the vexations of his mundane life, and the conflict he felt between the need to provide for the material wants of his family and the betrayal this seemed to involve of his own artistic genius, which manifests itself to him in outward form as the accusing figure of Los. The poem distinguishes four ways of viewing the natural world. Its last six lines indicate that these four modes, from single up to fourfold vision, are related to the four "States" of human consciousness—from Ulro (the world view of Newtonian science), through Generation, and Beulah, to the ulti-mate imaginative vision, Eden, in which the objects of the world of nature, freed from the illusory catego-ries of time and space, are revealed in their eternal and human forms. This highest "fourfold vision" is correlated also, in Blake's mythology, with the "expanded" and integral vision of the world as perceived by the "human four-fold"—that is, by the four Zoas when they have been reintegrated into the redeemed Albion.

3. Blake's father, James, had died in 1784. Three years later his brother, Rob-ert, died of consumption; Blake, who was devoted to him and attended him on his deathbed for two sleepless weeks, said that all his life thereafter Robert conversed with him "daily and hourly in the spirit." "Brother John" was the ne'er-do-well of the family; he had en-listed as a soldier and died soon after.

With my inward Eye 'tis an old Man grey
With my outward a Thistle across my way   30
"If thou goest back," the thistle said,
"Thou art to endless woe betrayd
For here does Theotormon lower
And here is Enitharmons bower
And Los the terrible[4] thus hath sworn   35
Because thou backward dost return
Poverty Envy old age & fear
Shall bring thy Wife upon a bier
And Butts shall give what Fuseli gave
A dark black Rock & a gloomy Cave."[5]   40

I struck the Thistle with my foot
And broke him up from his delving root
"Must the duties of life each other cross
Must every joy be dung & dross
Must my dear Butts feel cold neglect   45
Because I give Hayley his due respect
Must Flaxman[6] look upon me as wild
And all my friends be with doubts beguild
Must my Wife live in my Sisters bane
Or my sister survive on my Loves pain[7]   50
The curses of Los the terrible shade
And his dismal terrors make me afraid"

So I spoke & struck in my wrath
The old man weltering upon my path
Then Los appeard in all his power   55
In the Sun he appeard descending before
My face in fierce flames in my double sight
Twas outward a Sun: inward Los in his might[8]

"My hands are labourd day & night
And Ease comes never in my sight   60
My Wife has no indulgence given
Except what comes to her from heaven
We eat little we drink less
This Earth breeds not our happiness
Another Sun feeds our lifes streams   65

4. Theotormon was one of the four sons
of Los and his Emanation, Enitharmon.
These personages serve here as guardians
of Blake's fidelity to the promptings of
his poetic genius.
5. The rock and cave are among Blake's
recurrent symbols for the fallen, or "unimaginative," world. Henry Fuseli was a
fellow-artist, friend, and admirer of
Blake, but the two had recently quarreled; the threat is that Butts will do
likewise, and so destroy his imaginative
state.

6. John Flaxman was a well-known
sculptor of the time; like Fuseli, he admired Blake's work and helped him in
his profession, but the relations between
the two artists were sometimes strained.
7. Blake's sister, Catherine, lived with
Blake and his wife at Felpham, and the
two Catherines did not get along with
each other.
8. To the poet's "twofold" vision, the
material sun is recognized, in its spiritual form, as Los.

We are not warmed with thy beams
Thou measurest not the Time to me
Nor yet the Space that I do see
My Mind is not with thy light arrayd
Thy terrors shall not make me afraid"   70

When I had my Defiance given
The Sun stood trembling in heaven
The Moon that glowd remote below
Became leprous & white as snow
And every Soul of men on the Earth   75
Felt affliction & sorrow & sickness & dearth
Los flamd in my path & the Sun was hot
With the bows of my Mind & the Arrows of Thought
My bowstring fierce with Ardour breathes
My arrows glow in their golden sheaves[9]   80
My brothers & father march before
The heavens drop with human gore

Now I a fourfold vision see
And a fourfold vision is given to me
Tis fourfold in my supreme delight   85
And threefold in soft Beulahs night
And twofold Always. May God us keep
From Single vision & Newtons sleep

I also inclose you some Ballads by Mr Hayley with prints to them
by Your H^ble. Servt.[1] I should have sent them before now but
could not get any thing done for You to please myself, for I do
assure you that I have truly studied the two little pictures I now
send & do not repent of the time I have spent upon them.
    God bless you.

                                            Yours
                                              W B

P.S. I have taken the liberty to trouble you with a letter to my
Brother which you will be so kind as to send or give him & oblige
yours, W B

To George Cumberland[2] (*April 12, 1827*)

Dear Cumberland
    I have been very near the Gates of Death & have returned very
weak & an Old Man feeble & tottering, but not in Spirit & Life not
in The Real Man The Imagination which Liveth for Ever. In that I

9. Compare the bow and arrows of
"Mental Fight" in the poem, "And Did
Those Feet," above.
1. *Designs to a Series of Ballads written
by William Hayley*, with engravings by
Blake, was published in 1802.

2. Cumberland, a businessman, was an
old and loyal friend of Blake and a
buyer of his illuminated books. Blake
wrote this letter only four months
before his death on August 4, 1827.

am stronger & stronger as this Foolish Body decays. I thank you for the Pains you have taken with Poor Job.[3] I know too well that a great majority of Englishmen are fond of The Indefinite which they Measure by Newton's Doctrine of the Fluxions of an Atom,[4] a Thing that does not Exist. These are Politicians & think that Republican Art[5] is Inimical to their Atom. For a Line or Lineament is not formed by Chance; a Line is a Line in its Minutest Subdivision[s]; Strait or Crooked, It is Itself & Not Intermeasurable with or by any Thing Else. Such is Job, but since the French Revolution Englishmen are all Intermeasurable One by Another; certainly a happy state of Agreement, to which I for One do not Agree. God keep me from the Divinity of Yes & No too, The Yea Nay Creeping Jesus, from supposing Up & Down to be the same Thing as all Experimentalists must suppose.

You are desirous I know to dispose of some of my Works & to make [them] Please. I am obliged to you & to all who do so. But having none remaining of all that I had Printed, I cannot Print more Except at a great loss, for at the time I printed those things I had a whole House to range in; now I am shut up in a Corner, therefore am forced to ask a Price for them that I scarce expect to get from a Stranger. I am now Printing a Set of the Songs of Innocence & Experience for a Friend at Ten Guineas, which I cannot do under Six Months consistent with my other Work, so that I have little hope of doing any more of such things. The Last Work I produced is a Poem Entitled Jerusalem the Emanation of the Giant Albion, but find that to Print it will Cost my Time the amount of Twenty Guineas. One I have Finishd; it contains 100 Plates but it is not likely that I shall get a Customer for it.[6]

As you wish me to send you a list with the Prices of these things they are as follows

	£	s	d
America	6.	6.	0
Europe	6.	6.	0
Visions &c	5.	5.	0
Thel	3.	3.	0
Songs of Inn. & Exp.	10.	10.	0
Urizen	6.	6.	0

6. Cumberland was trying to interest his friends in buying a set of Blake's etchings, *Illustrations of the Book of Job*.

4 . Isaac Newton's "Method of Fluxions" (1704) announced his discovery of the infinitesimal calculus. To Blake, Newton was the arch-representative of materialist philosophy.

5. I.e., a free art, not subject to authoritarian control.

6. This single colored copy of Blake's *Jerusalem* survives in the Yale University Library.

The Little Card I will do as soon as Possible,[1] but when you Consider that I have been reduced to a Skeleton from which I am slowly recovering you will I hope have Patience with me.

Flaxman[2] is Gone & we must All soon follow, every one to his Own Eternal House, Leaving the Delusive Goddess Nature & her Laws to get into Freedom from all Law of the Members into The Mind in which every one is King & Priest in his own House. God Send it so on Earth as it is in Heaven.

I am Dear Sir Yours Affectionately

WILLIAM BLAKE

1. A small illustrated name-card which Blake executed for Cumberland; it was his last engraving.
2. John Flaxman (1755–1826), a famous sculptor and book-illlustrator of that time, was a friend and admirer of Blake. He had died the preceding December.

ROBERT BURNS
(1759–1796)

1786: *Poems, Chiefly in the Scottish Dialect* (Kilmarnock edition).
1787: Begins collecting, editing, and writing songs for *The Scots Musical Museum*.

A favorite myth of later 18th-century primitivists was that there existed natural poets who warbled their native woodnotes wild, independent of art or literary tradition. These artless poets were sought among peasants and proletarians, whose caste or rural habitation, it was thought, protected them from contamination by the artificialities of civilized life and culture. When Robert Burns published his first volume of *Poems*, in 1786, he was at once hailed by the literati of Edinburgh as an instance of the natural genius, a "Heaven-taught plowman" whose poems were the spontaneous overflow of his native feelings. Burns himself sometimes fostered this belief, and rather enjoyed playing the role of the poet by instinct. But in fact he was a well-read (although largely self-educated) man, whose quick intelligence and sensibility enabled him to make the most of limited opportunities. And although he broke clear of the contemporary conventions of decayed English neoclassicism, he did so not by instinct but as a deliberate craftsman who turned to two earlier traditions for his models —the Scottish oral tradition of folklore and folk song, and the highly developed Scottish literary tradition, which goes back to the late Middle Ages.

His father—William Burnes, as he spelled his name—was a God-fearing and hard-working farmer of Ayrshire, a county in southwestern Scotland, who could not make a go of it in a period of hard times and high rents, and died in 1784, broken in body and spirit. Robert, with his brother Gilbert, was forced to do the toil of a man while still a boy, and began to develop the heart trouble of which he was to die when only 37. Although his father had the Scotsman's esteem for education and saw to it that his sons attended school whenever they could, Burns's education in literature, theology, politics, and philosophy came mainly from his own reading. At the age of 15 he fell in love, and was immediately inspired by that event to write his first song. "Thus," Burns said, "with me began Love and Poesy." After he reached maturity, Burns cultivated assiduously both these propensities. He began a series of amorous affairs, producing in 1785 the first of a number of illegitimate children; he also extended greatly the range and quantity of his attempts at poetry. So rapid was his development as a poet that by the time he published the Kilmarnock edition, at the age of 27, he had written all but a few of his greatest long poems.

The Kilmarnock volume (so named from the town in which it was published) was one of the most extraordinary first volumes by any British poet, and it had a great and immediate success. Burns was at once acclaimed "Caledonia's Bard" and was lionized by the intellectuals and gentlefolk when he visited Edinburgh soon after his book came out. In this milieu the peasant-poet soon demonstrated that he could more than hold his own as a brilliant conversationalist and debater. But he was also wise enough to realize that once the novelty wore off, his eminence in this society would not endure. He had a fierce pride which was quick to resent any hint of contempt or condescension toward himself as a man of low degree. His sympathies were democratic, and he was an outspoken admirer of the American Revolution and of the republican experiment in France. In religion, too, he was a radical, professing "the Religion of Sentiment and Reason" in opposition to the strict Calvinism in which he had been raised, and he offended many pious Presbyterians by his devastating satires against the rigid tenets and the moral authoritarianism of the Scottish kirk. Furthermore, his sexual irregularities were notorious, less because they were out of the common order at that time than because of his bravado in flaunting them before the "unco guid"—as his biographer, DeLancey Ferguson, has said, "it was not so much that he was conspicuously sinful as that he sinned conspicuously." Most of Burns's friends in high station quickly fell away, and his later visits to Edinburgh did not repeat the social success of the first.

In 1788 Burns was given a commission as Excise officer, or tax inspector, and he settled down with Jean Armour, his former mistress—now his wife—at Ellisland, near Dumfries, combining his official duties with farming. This was the fourth farm on which Burns had worked; and when it, like the others, failed, he moved his family to the lively country town of Dumfries. Here he was fairly happy, despite recurrent illness and a chronic shortage of money. He performed his official duties efficiently and was respected by his fellow townspeople and esteemed by his superiors; he was a devoted family man and father; and he accumulated a circle of intimates to whom he could repair for conversation and conviviality. In 1787 James Johnson, an engraver, had enlisted Burns's aid in collecting

Scottish folk songs for an anthology called *The Scots Musical Museum*. Burns soon became the real editor for several volumes of this work, devoting all of his free time to collecting, editing, restoring, and imitating traditional songs, or writing verses of his own to traditional dance tunes. Almost all of his creative work, during the last twelve years of his life, went into the writing of songs for the *Musical Museum* and for George Thomson's *Select Collection of Original Scottish Airs*. This was for Burns a devoted labor of love and patriotism, done anonymously, for which he refused to accept any pay, although badly in need of money; and he continued the work when he was literally on his deathbed.

Burns's best work was written in Scots, a northern dialect of English spoken by Scottish peasants and (on other than formal occasions) by most 18th-century Scottish gentlemen as well. When Burns attempted to write in standard English the result—except in an occasional lyric such as the lucid and graceful *Afton Water*—was stilted and conventional, with all the stock phrasing, sententiousness, and sentimentality of the genteel poetic tradition of his day. He is often considered a "pre-Romantic" who, anticipating Wordsworth, revived the English lyric, exploited the literary forms and legends of folk culture, and wrote in the language really spoken by the common man. But this reputation is based primarily on his songs. By far the major portion of the poems Burns published under his own name are concerned with men and manners and fall, technically, in the favorite genres of 18th-century poets; they include brilliant satire in a variety of forms, a number of fine verse epistles to friends and fellow poets, and one masterpiece of mock-heroic (or at least, seriocomic) narrative, *Tam o' Shanter*. The claim could be supported that, next to Pope, Burns is the greatest 18th-century master of these literary types. Yet Burns's writings in satire, epistle, and mock-heroic are very remote from Pope's, in their heartiness and verve, no less than in their dialect and intricate stanza forms. The reason for the difference is that Burns turned for his models not to Horace and the English neoclassic tradition, but to the native tradition which had been established in the golden age of Scottish poetry by Robert Henryson, William Dunbar, Gavin Douglas, and other Scottish Chaucerians of the 15th and 16th centuries. He knew this literature through his 18th-century Scottish predecessors, especially Allan Ramsay and Robert Fergusson, who had collected some of the ancient poems and written new ones based on the ancient models. Burns improved on these predecessors, but he derived from them much that is characteristic in his literary forms, subjects, diction, and stanzas.

Burns's songs, however, are more widely known than his longer poems, and have in themselves been adequate to sustain his reputation as a major poet. He wrote over 300 of them, in unequaled abundance and variety. In them he surrenders himself wholeheartedly to the emotion of the moment, evoked by all the great lyric subjects: love, drink, work, friendship, patriotism, and bawdry. His poetic character is hearty, generous, rollicking, tender, with a sympathy that encompasses men of all types, from national heroes to tavern roarers; like all the great poets of humanity, Burns had that poetical character which Keats described: "It lives in gusto, be it foul or fair, high or low, rich or poor, mean or elevated. It has as much delight in conceiving an Iago as an Imogen." Burns is not only the national poet of Scotland but also a song writer for all English-speaking people. Everywhere in the world on New Year's Eve when, helped by drink and the reminder of their bondage to time, men indulge their instinct of a common humanity, they join hands and sing a song of Burns.

To a Mouse

ON TURNING HER UP IN HER NEST WITH
THE PLOW, NOVEMBER, 1785[1]

Wee, sleekit,° cow'rin', tim'rous beastie,   *sleek*
O, what a panic's in thy breastie!
Thou need na start awa sae hasty,
   Wi' bickering brattle![2]
5 I wad be laith° to rin an' chase thee   *loath*
   Wi' murd'ring pattle!°   *plowstaff*

I'm truly sorry man's dominion
Has broken Nature's social union,
An' justifies that ill opinion
10   Which makes thee startle
At me, thy poor, earth-born companion,
   An' fellow mortal!

I doubt na, whiles,° but thou may thieve;   *sometimes*
What then? poor beastie, thou maun° live!   *must*
15 A daimen-icker in a thrave[3]
   'S a sma' request:
I'll get a blessin' wi' the lave,°   *remainder*
   And never miss 't!

Thy wee-bit housie, too, in ruin!
20 Its silly° wa's the win's are strewin'!   *feeble*
An' naething, now, to big° a new ane,   *build*
   O' foggage° green!   *moss*
An' bleak December's winds ensuin',
   Baith snell° an' keen!   *bitter*

25 Thou saw the fields laid bare and waste,
An' weary winter comin' fast,
An' cozie here, beneath the blast,
   Thou thought to dwell,
Till crash! the cruel coulter° passed   *cutter-blade*
30   Out-through thy cell.

That wee-bit heap o' leaves an' stibble°   *stubble*
Has cost thee mony a weary nibble!

---

1. Burns's brother said that this poem was composed on the occasion it describes.
2. With headlong scamper.
3. An occasional ear in 24 sheaves.

Now thou's turned out, for a' thy trouble,
        But° house or hald,⁴   *without*
35 To thole° the winter's sleety dribble,   *endure*
        An' cranreuch° cauld!   *hoarfrost*

But Mousie, thou art no thy lane,⁵
In proving foresight may be vain:
The best-laid schemes o' mice an' men
40   Gang aft a-gley,⁶
An' lea'e us nought but grief an' pain,
        For promised joy.

Still thou art blest compared wi' me!
The present only toucheth thee:
45 But och! I backward cast my e'e
        On prospects drear!
An' forward though I canna see,
        I guess an' fear!

1785   1786

To a Louse

ON SEEING ONE ON A LADY'S BONNET AT CHURCH

Ha! whare ye gaun, ye crowlan° ferlie!°   *crawling/wonder*
Your impudence protects you sairly:°   *sorely*
I canna say but ye strunt° rarely,   *strut*
    Owre gauze and lace;
5 Tho' faith, I fear ye dine but sparely,
    On sic a place.

Ye ugly, creepan, blastit wonner,°   *wonder*
Detested, shunn'd, by saunt an' sinner,
How daur ye set your fit° upon her,   *foot*
10   Sae fine a Lady!
Gae somewhere else and seek your dinner,
    On some poor body.

Swith,° in some beggar's haffet° squattle;° *swift/locks/sprawl*
There ye may creep, and sprawl, and sprattle,° *struggle*
15 Wi' ither kindred, jumping cattle,
    In shoals and nations;
Whare horn nor bane¹ ne'er daur unsettle,
    Your thick plantations.

Now haud you there, ye're out o' sight,
20 Below the fatt'rels,° snug and tight,   *ribbon-ends*

---

4. Hold, holding (i.e., land).
5. Not alone.
6. Go oft awry.

1. I.e., fine-tooth comb made of horn or bone ("bane").

Na faith ye yet![2] ye'll no be right,
    Till ye've got on it,
The vera tapmost, towrin height
    O' Miss's bonnet.

25 My sooth! right bauld ye set your nose out,
    As plump an' gray as onie grozet:°   *gooseberry*
    O for some rank, mercurial rozet,°   *rosin*
    Or fell,° red smeddum,°   *sharp/powder*
    I'd gie you sic a hearty dose o't,
30   Wad dress your droddum!°   *buttocks*

I wad na been surpriz'd to spy
You on an auld wife's flainen toy;[3]
Or aiblins° some bit duddie° boy,   *perhaps/ragged*
    On 's wylecoat;°   *undershirt*
35 But Miss's fine Lunardi,[4] fye!
    How daur ye do't?

O Jenny dinna toss your head,
An' set your beauties a' abroad!°   *abroad*
Ye little ken what cursed speed
40   The blastie's° makin!   *creature's*
Thae° winks and finger-ends, I dread,   *those*
    Are notice takin!

O wad some Pow'r the giftie gie us
To see oursels as others see us!
45 It wad frae monie a blunder free us
    An' foolish notion:
What airs in dress an' gait wad lea'e us,
    And ev'n Devotion![5]

1785   1786

Green Grow the Rashes[6]

Chorus
Green grow the rashes, O;
    Green grow the rashes, O;
The sweetest hours that e'er I spend,
Are spent amang the lasses, O!

5 There's nought but care on ev'ry han',
    In ev'ry hour that passes, O:

2. Confound you!
3. Flannel cap.
4. A balloon-shaped bonnet, named after Vincenzo Lunardi, who made a number of balloon flights in the mid-

1780's.
5. I.e., even pretended piety.
6. **Burns's revision of a song long current in a number of versions, most of them bawdy. "Rashes": rushes.**

What signifies the life o' man,
   An' 'twere na for the lasses, O.
            (Chorus)

The warly° race may riches chase,   **worldly**
10   An' riches still may fly them, O;
An' though at last they catch them fast,
   Their hearts can ne'er enjoy them, O.
            (Chorus)

But gie me a canny° hour at e'en,   **quiet**
   My arms about my dearie, O;
15 An' warly cares, an' warly men,
   May a' gae tapsalteerie,° O!   **topsy-turvy**
            (Chorus)

For you sae douce,° ye sneer at this,   **sober**
   Ye're nought but senseless asses, O:
The wisest man[7] the warl' saw,
20   He dearly loved the lasses, O.
            (Chorus)

Auld nature swears, the lovely dears
   Her noblest work she classes, O:
Her prentice han' she tried on man,
   An' then she made the lasses, O.
            (Chorus)

1784   1787

Holy Willie's Prayer[1]

O thou, wha in the Heavens dost dwell,
Wha, as it pleases best thysel',
Sends ane to heaven and ten to hell,
         A' for thy glory,
5 And no for ony guid or ill
         They've done afore thee!

I bless and praise thy matchless might,
Whan thousands thou hast left in night,
That I am here afore thy sight,
10   For gifts an' grace
A burnin' an' a shinin' light,
         To a' this place.

7. King Solomon.
1. This satire, in the form of a dramatic monologue, was inspired by one William Fisher, a self-righteous elder in the parish of Mauchline, and is directed against a basic Calvinist tenet of the old Scottish kirk. Holy Willie assumes that he is one of the small minority, God's "elect"; in other words, that he has been predestined for grace, no matter what he does in this vale of tears.

What was I, or my generation,
That I should get sic exaltation?
15 I, wha deserve most just damnation,
      For broken laws,
Sax° thousand years 'fore my creation,   *six*
      Through Adam's cause.

When frae my mither's womb I fell,
20 Thou might hae plungéd me in hell,
To gnash my gums, to weep and wail,
      In burnin' lakes,
Where damnéd devils roar and yell,
      Chained to their stakes;

25 Yet I am here a chosen sample,
To show thy grace is great and ample;
I'm here a pillar in thy temple,
      Strong as a rock,
A guide, a buckler, an example
30   To a' thy flock.

O Lord, thou kens what zeal I bear,
When drinkers drink, and swearers swear,
And singin' there and dancin' here,
      Wi' great an' sma':
35 For I am keepit by thy fear
      Free frae them a'.

But yet, O Lord! confess I must
At times I'm fashed° wi' fleshly lust;   *troubled*
An' sometimes too, in warldly trust,
40   Vile self gets in;
But thou remembers we are dust,
      Defiled in sin.

O Lord! yestreen, thou kens, wi' Meg—
Thy pardon I sincerely beg;
45 O! may't ne'er be a livin' plague
      To my dishonor,
An' I'll ne'er lift a lawless leg
      Again upon her.

Besides I farther maun° allow,   *must*
50 Wi' Lizzie's lass, three times I trow—
But, Lord, that Friday I was fou,°   *drunk*
      When I cam near her,
Or else thou kens thy servant true
      Wad never steer°her.   *molest*

55 May be thou lets this fleshly thorn
Beset thy servant e'en and morn
Lest he owre high and proud should turn,
      That he's sae gifted;
If sae, thy hand maun e'en be borne,
60   Until thou lift it.

Lord, bless thy chosen in this place,
For here thou hast a chosen race;
But God confound their stubborn face,
   And blast their name,
65 Wha bring thy elders to disgrace
   An' public shame.

Lord, mind Gawn Hamilton's[2] deserts,
He drinks, an' swears, an' plays at cartes,°   *cards*
Yet has sae mony takin' arts
70   Wi' grit° an' sma',   *great*
Frae God's ain priest the people's hearts
   He steals awa'.

An' when we chastened him therefor,
Thou kens how he bred sic a splore°   *disturbance*
75 As set the warld in a roar
   O' laughin' at us;
Curse thou his basket and his store,
   Kail° and potatoes.   *broth*

Lord, hear my earnest cry an' pray'r,
80 Against that presbyt'ry o' Ayr;
Thy strong right hand, Lord, make it bare
   Upo' their heads;
Lord, weigh it down, and dinna spare,
   For their misdeeds.

85 O Lord my God, that glib-tongued Aiken,
My very heart and soul are quakin',
To think how we stood sweatin', shakin',
   An' pissed wi' dread,
While he, wi' hingin'° lips and snakin',°   *hanging / sneering*
90   Held up his head.

Lord, in the day of vengeance try him;
Lord, visit them wha did employ him,
And pass not in thy mercy by them,
   No hear their pray'r:
95 But, for thy people's sake, destroy them,
   And dinna spare.

But, Lord, remember me and mine
Wi' mercies temp'ral and divine,
That I for gear° and grace may shine   *goods, wealth*
100   Excelled by nane,
And a' the glory shall be thine,
   Amen, Amen!

1785   1789, 1799

---

2. Burns's friend Gavin Hamilton, whom "Holy Willie" had brought up on moral charges before the Kirk Session of the Presbytery of Ayr; Hamilton was successfully defended by his counsel, Robert Aiken (referred to in line 85).

Tam o' Shanter[1]

Of Brownyis and of Bogillis full is this Buke.
—Gavin Douglas

When chapman billies[2] leave the street,
And drouthy° neebors neebors meet,   *thirsty*
As market days are wearing late,
An' folk begin to tak the gate;°   *road*
5 While we sit bousing at the nappy,°   *strong ale*
An' getting fou° and unco° happy,   *drunk / very*
We think na on the lang Scots miles,
The mosses, waters, slaps,° and stiles, *gaps (in walls)*
That lie between us and our hame,
10 Where sits our sulky sullen dame,
Gathering her brows like gathering storm,
Nursing her wrath to keep it warm.
  This truth fand° honest Tam o' Shanter, *found*
As he frae Ayr ae night did canter
15 (Auld Ayr, wham ne'er a town surpasses
For honest men and bonnie lasses).
  O Tam! hadst thou but been sae wise
As ta'en thy ain wife Kate's advice!
She tauld thee weel thou was a skellum,[3]
20 A bletherin', blusterin', drunken blellum;° *babbler*
That frae November till October,
Ae market day thou was na sober;
That ilka melder[4] wi' the miller
Thou sat as lang as thou had siller;° *silver, money*
25 That every naig° was ca'd° a shoe on, *nag / driven*
The smith and thee gat roarin' fou on;
That at the Lord's house, even on Sunday,
Thou drank wi' Kirkton Jean till Monday.
She prophesied that, late or soon,
30 Thou would be found deep drowned in Doon;

---

1. This poem was written to order for a book on Scottish antiquities, and was based on a witch story told about Alloway Kirk, an old ruin near Burns's house in Ayr. As a mock-heroic rendering of folk material. *Tam o' Shanter* is comparable to the Nun's Priest's Tale of Chaucer, in excellence as well as genre. Burns recognized that the poem was his most sustained and finished artistic performance; it discovers "a spice of roguish waggery," but also shows "a force of genius and a finishing polish that I despair of ever excelling." The verve and seriocomic sympathy with which Burns manages this misadventure of a confirmed tippler won Wordsworth, a water-drinker, to passionate advocacy against the moralists who objected to Burns's ribaldry: "Who but some impenetrable dunce or narrow-minded puritan in works of art ever read without delight the picture which he has drawn of the convivial exaltation of the rustic adventurer, Tam o' Shanter? * * * I pity him who cannot perceive that, in all this, though there was no moral purpose, there is a moral effect" (letter to a friend of Burns, 1816).
2. Peddler fellows.
3. Good-for-nothing; "bletherin' ": chattering.
4. A "melder" is the amount of corn processed at a single grinding. "Ilka": every.

Or catched wi' warlocks° in the mirk°   wizards / night
By Alloway's auld haunted kirk.
    Ah, gentle dames! it gars° me greet°   makes / weep
To think how mony counsels sweet,
35 How mony lengthened sage advices,
The husband frae the wife despises!
    But to our tale: Ae market night,
Tam had got planted unco right,
Fast by an ingle,° bleezing° finely,   fireplace / blazing
40 Wi' reaming swats,⁵ that drank divinely;
And at his elbow, Souter° Johnny,   Cobbler
His ancient, trusty, drouthy crony;
Tam lo'ed him like a very brither;
They had been fou for weeks thegither.
45 The night drave on wi' sangs and clatter,
And ay the ale was growing better:
The landlady and Tam grew gracious,
Wi' favors secret, sweet, and precious;
The souter tauld his queerest stories;
50 The landlord's laugh was ready chorus:
The storm without might rair° and rustle,   roar
Tam did na mind the storm a whistle.
    Care, mad to see a man sae happy,
E'en drowned himsel amang the nappy.
55 As bees flee hame wi' lades o' treasure,
The minutes winged their way wi' pleasure;
Kings may be blest, but Tam was glorious,
O'er a' the ills o' life victorious!
    But pleasures are like poppies spread—
60 You seize the flow'r, its bloom is shed;
Or like the snow falls in the river—
A moment white, then melts forever;
Or like the borealis race,
That flit ere you can point their place;
65 Or like the rainbow's lovely form
Evanishing amid the storm.
Nae man can tether time nor tide;
The hour approaches Tam maun° ride;   must
That hour, o' night's black arch the keystane,
70 That dreary hour, he mounts his beast in;
And sic a night he taks the road in,
As ne'er poor sinner was abroad in.
    The wind blew as 'twad blawn its last;
The rattling show'rs rose on the blast;
75 The speedy gleams the darkness swallowed;
Loud, deep, and lang, the thunder bellowed:
That night, a child might understand,
The Deil had business on his hand.
    Weel mounted on his gray mare, Meg,

5. Foaming new ale.

80 A better never lifted leg,
   Tam skelpit° on through dub° and mire,   *slapped / puddle*
   Despising wind, and rain, and fire;
   Whiles holding fast his gude blue bonnet;
   Whiles crooning o'er some auld Scots sonnet;
85 Whiles glowring° round wi' prudent cares,   *staring*
   Lest bogles° catch him unawares.   *hobgoblins*
   Kirk-Alloway was drawing nigh,
   Whare ghaists° and houlets° nightly cry.   *ghosts / owls*
     By this time he was cross the ford,
90 Where in the snaw the chapman smoored;[6]
   And past the birks° and meikle stane,[7]   *birches*
   Where drunken Charlie brak's neck bane;
   And through the whins,[8] and by the cairn,[8a]
   Where hunters fand the murdered bairn;
95 And near the thorn, aboon the well,
   Where Mungo's mither hanged hersel.
   Before him Doon pours all his floods;
   The doubling storm roars through the woods;
   The lightnings flash from pole to pole;
100 Near and more near the thunders roll:
   When, glimmering through the groaning trees,
   Kirk-Alloway seemed in a bleeze;
   Through ilka bore° the beams were glancing;   *hole*
   And loud resounded mirth and dancing.
105   Inspiring bold John Barleycorn!
   What dangers thou canst make us scorn!
   Wi' tippenny,[9] we fear nae evil;
   Wi' usquebae,° we'll face the devil!   *whisky*
   The swats sae reamed in Tammie's noddle,
110 Fair play, he cared na deils a boddle![1]
   But Maggie stood right sair astonished,
   Till, by the heel and hand admonished,
   She ventured forward on the light;
   And, vow! Tam saw an unco° sight!   *strange*
115 Warlocks and witches in a dance!
   Nae cotillon brent° new frae France,   *brand*
   But hornpipes, jigs, strathspeys,[2] and reels,
   Put life and mettle in their heels.
   A winnock-bunker° in the east,   *window seat*
120 There sat auld Nick, in shape o'beast—
   A touzie tyke,[3] black, grim, and large!
   To gie them music was his charge:
   He screwed the pipes and gart° them skirl.°   *made / screech*
   Till roof and rafters a' did dirl.°   *rattle*
125 Coffins stood round like open presses,

6. The peddler smothered.
7. Big stone.
8. Furze (an evergreen shrub).
8a. Stones heaped up as a memorial.
9. Twopenny (of drink).

1. I.e., he didn't care a farthing about
devils (a "boddle" is a very small copper coin).
2. Slow Highland dance.
3. Shaggy dog.

That shawed the dead in their last dresses;
And by some devilish cantraip° sleight   *charm, trick*
Each in its cauld hand held a light,
By which heroic Tam was able
130 To note upon the haly° table   *holy*
A murderer's banes in gibbet airns;°   *irons*
Twa span-lang,[4] wee, unchristened bairns;
A thief new-cutted frae the rape°—   *rope*
Wi' his last gasp his gab° did gape;   *mouth*
135 Five tomahawks, wi' blude red rusted;
Five scimitars, wi' murder crusted;
A garter, which a babe had strangled;
A knife, a father's throat had mangled,
Whom his ain son o' life bereft—
140 The gray hairs yet stack to the heft;
Wi' mair of horrible and awfu',
Which even to name wad be unlawfu'.
    As Tammie glowred, amazed, and curious,
The mirth and fun grew fast and furious:
145 The piper loud and louder blew;
The dancers quick and quicker flew;
They reeled, they set, they crossed, they cleekit,°   *joined hands*
Till ilka carlin° swat and reekit,   *old woman*
And coost her duddies to the wark,[5]
150 And linkit° at it in her sark!°   *tripped lightly / shirt*
    Now Tam, O Tam! had thae been queans,°   *girls*
A' plump and strapping in their teens;
Their sarks, instead o' creeshie flannen,[6]
Been snaw-white seventeen hunder[7] linen!
155 Thir° breeks o' mine, my only pair,   *these*
That ance were plush, o' gude blue hair,
I wad hae gi'en them off my hurdies,°   *buttocks*
For ae blink o' the bonnie burdies!°   *maidens*
    But withered beldams, auld and droll,
160 Rigwoodie° hags wad spean° a foal,   *bony / wean*
Louping° and flinging on a crummock,°   *leaping / staff*
I wonder didna turn thy stomach.
    But Tam kent what was what fu' brawlie°   *finely*
There was ae winsome wench and walie°   *strapping*
165 That night enlisted in the core,°   *corps*
Lang after kent on Carrick shore!
(For mony a beast to dead she shot,
And perished mony a bonnie boat,
And shook baith meikle corn and bear,°   *barley*
170 And kept the countryside in fear.)
Her cutty° sark, o' Paisley harn,°   *short / yarn*
That while a lassie she had worn,
In longitude though sorely scanty,

4. Span-long (i.e., the distance from outstretched thumb to little finger).
5. Cast off her clothes for the work.
6. Greasy flannel.
7. Very fine linen, woven on a loom with 1700 strips.

It was her best, and she was vauntie.°   **proud**
175 Ah! little kent thy reverend grannie
 That sark she coft° for her wee Nannie   **bought**
 Wi' twa pund Scots ('twas a' her riches)
 Wad ever graced a dance of witches!
  But here my muse her wing maun cour;° **lower**
180 Sic flights are far beyond her pow'r—
 To sing how Nannie lap and flang
 (A souple jade she was, and strang);
 And how Tam stood, like ane bewitched,
 And thought his very een enriched;
185 Even Satan glowred, and fidged fu' fain,[8]
 And hotched° and blew wi' might and main: **jerked**
 Till first ae caper, syne° anither,   **then**
 Tam tint° his reason a' thegither,   **lost**
 And roars out, "Weel done, Cutty-sark!"
190 And in an instant all was dark!
 And scarcely had he Maggie rallied,
 When out the hellish legion sallied.
  As bees bizz out wi' angry fyke°   **fuss**
 When plundering herds° assail their byke,° **herdsmen / hive**
195 As open° pussie's mortal foes   **begin to bark**
 When pop! she starts before their nose,
 As eager runs the market crowd,
 When "Catch the thief!" resounds aloud.
 So Maggie runs; the witches follow,
200 Wi' mony an eldritch° skriech and hollow. **unearthly**
  Ah, Tam! ah, Tam! thou'll get thy fairin'!° **deserts**
 In hell they'll roast thee like a herrin'!
 In vain thy Kate awaits thy comin'!
 Kate soon will be a woefu' woman!
205 Now do thy speedy utmost, Meg,
 And win the keystane o' the brig:°   **bridge**
 There at them thou thy tail may toss,
 A running stream they darena cross.
 But ere the keystane she could make,
210 The fient a tail she had to shake![9]
 For Nannie, far before the rest,
 Hard upon noble Maggie pressed,
 And flew at Tam wi' furious ettle;°   **intent**
 But little wist she Maggie's mettle!
215 Ae spring brought off her master hale,° **whole**
 But left behind her ain gray tail:
 The carlin claught° her by the rump,   **clutched**
 And left poor Maggie scarce a stump.
  Now, wha this tale o' truth shall read,
220 Each man and mother's son, take heed;
 Whene'er to drink you are inclined,
 Or cutty-sarks rin in your mind,

8. Fidgeted with pleasure.   9. I.e., she had no tail left at all.

Think! ye may buy the joys o'er dear;
Remember Tam o' Shanter's mare.

1790   1791

Afton Water[1]

Flow gently, sweet Afton, among thy green braes,
Flow gently, I'll sing thee a song in thy praise;
My Mary's asleep by thy murmuring stream,
Flow gently, sweet Afton, disturb not her dream.

Thou stock-dove whose echo resounds through the glen,   5
Ye wild whistling blackbirds in yon thorny den,
Thou green-crested lapwing, thy screaming forbear,
I charge you disturb not my slumbering fair.

How lofty, sweet Afton, thy neighboring hills,
Far marked with the courses of clear winding rills;   10
There daily I wander as noon rises high,
My flocks and my Mary's sweet cot[2] in my eye.

How pleasant thy banks and green valleys below,
Where wild in the woodlands the primroses blow;
There oft as mild evening weeps over the lea,   15
The sweet-scented birk[3] shades my Mary and me.

Thy crystal stream, Afton, how lovely it glides,
And winds by the cot where my Mary resides;
How wanton thy waters her snowy feet lave,
As gathering sweet flowerets she stems thy clear wave.   20

Flow gently, sweet Afton, among thy green braes,
Flow gently, sweet river, the theme of my lays;
My Mary's asleep by thy murmuring stream,
Flow gently, sweet Afton, disturb not her dream.

1789   1792

Ae Fond Kiss[4]

Ae fond kiss, and then we sever!
Ae fareweel, and then forever!
Deep in heart-wrung tears I'll pledge thee,
Warring sighs and groans I'll wage thee.
Who shall say that fortune grieves him   5

1. The Afton is a small river in Ayrshire. "Braes": slopes, hillsides.
2. Cottage.
3. Birch.
4. Written to Mrs. M'Lehose, with whom Burns had been engaged in a sentimental correspondence, on the occasion of her departure to rejoin her husband in the West Indies.

While the star of hope she leaves him?
Me, nae cheerfu' twinkle lights me,
Dark despair around benights me.

I'll ne'er blame my partial fancy,
Naething could resist my Nancy;   10
But to see her was to love her,
Love but her, and love forever.
Had we never loved sae kindly,
Had we never loved sae blindly,
Never met—or never parted,   15
We had ne'er been broken-hearted.

Fare thee weel, thou first and fairest!
Fare thee weel, thou best and dearest!
Thine be ilka joy and treasure,
Peace, enjoyment, love, and pleasure!   20
Ae fond kiss, and then we sever;
Ae fareweel, alas, forever!
Deep in heart-wrung tears I'll pledge thee,
Warring sighs and groans I'll wage thee.

1791   1792

Ye Flowery Banks[1]

Ye flowery banks o' bonnie Doon,
   How can ye blume sae fair?
How can ye chant, ye little birds,
   And I sae fu' o' care?

5 Thou'll break my heart, thou bonnie bird,
   That sings upon the bough;
Thou minds me o' the happy days,
   When my fause° luve was true.   *false*

Thou'll break my heart, thou bonnie bird,
10 That sings beside thy mate;
For sae I sat, and sae I sang,
   And wist na o' my fate.

Aft hae I roved by bonnie Doon,
   To see the woodbine twine,
15 And ilka° bird sang o' its luve,   *every*
   And sae did I o' mine.

Wi' lightsome heart I pu'd° a rose   *pulled*
   Frae aff its thorny tree;
But my fause luver staw° my rose,   *stole*
20 And left the thorn wi'me.

1. Burns wrote several versions of this song; the present one is the simplest and the best.

Wi' lightsome heart I pu'd a rose
   Upon a morn in June;
And sae I flourished on the morn,
   And sae was pu'd ere noon.

                       1792, 1808

Scots, Wha Hae[2]

Scots, wha hae wi' Wallace[3] bled,
Scots, wham Bruce has aften led,
Welcome to your gory bed,
   Or to victorie.

Now's the day, and now's the hour;   5
See the front o' battle lour;
See approach proud Edward's power—
   Chains and slaverie!

Wha will be a traitor-knave?
Wha can fill a coward's grave?
Wha sae base as be a slave?   10
   Let him turn and flee!

Wha for Scotland's King and law
Freedom's sword will strongly draw,
Freeman stand, or freeman fa',   15
   Let him follow me!

By oppression's woes and pains!
By your sons in servile chains!
We will drain our dearest veins,
   But they shall be free!   20

Lay the proud usurpers low!
Tyrants fall in every foe!
Liberty's in every blow!
   Let us do, or die!

1793   1794, 1815

For A' That and A' That[1]

Is there, for honest poverty,
   That hangs his head, and a' that?

2. In this best-known of Burns's patriotic songs, Robert Bruce is addressing his army before the great victory at Bannockburn (1314), at which the English were driven from Scotland.
3. Sir William Wallace (ca. 1272–

1305), the great Scottish warrior in the wars against the English.
1. Burns's vigorous affirmation of the radical ideas of liberty, equality, and fraternity may have been based on Tom Paine's *Rights of Man*.

The coward slave, we pass him by,
  We dare be poor for a' that!
5   For a' that, and a' that,
      Our toils obscure, and a' that;
    The rank is but the guinea's stamp,
      The man's the gowd° for a' that.   *gold*

What though on hamely fare we dine,
10   Wear hodden-gray,[2] and a' that;
Gie fools their silks, and knaves their wine,
    A man's a man for a' that:
    For a' that, and a' that,
      Their tinsel show, and a' that;
15   The honest man, though e'er sae poor,
      Is king o' men for a' that.

Ye see yon birkie,° ca'd a lord,   *brisk young fellow*
  Wha struts, and stares, and a' that;
Though hundreds worship at his word,
20   He's but a coof° for a' that: *dolt*
    For a' that, and a' that,
      His riband, star, and a' that,
    The man of independent mind,
      He looks and laughs at a' that.

25 A prince can mak a belted knight,
  A marquis, duke, and a' that;
But an honest man's aboon° his might,   *above*
  Guid faith he mauna fa' that![3]
    For a' that, and a' that,
30   Their dignities, and a' that,
    The pith o' sense, and pride o' worth,
      Are higher rank than a' that.

Then let us pray that come it may,
  As come it will for a' that,
35 That sense and worth, o'er a' the earth,
  May bear the gree,[4] and a' that.
    For a' that, and a' that,
      It's coming yet, for a' that,
    That man to man the warld o'er
40   Shall brothers be for a' that.

1794   1795, 1799

A Red, Red Rose[1]

O My Luve's like a red, red rose,
  That's newly sprung in June;

---

2. A coarse cloth of undyed wool.
3. Must not claim that.
4. Win the prize.

1. Like many of Burns's songs, this one incorporates elements from several current folk songs.

O My Luve's like the melodie
    That's sweetly played in tune.

As fair art thou, my bonnie lass,   5
    So deep in luve am I;
And I will luve thee still, my dear,
    Till a' the seas gang dry.

Till a' the seas gang dry, my dear,
    And the rocks melt wi' the sun: 10
O I will love thee still, my dear,
    While the sands o' life shall run.

And fare thee weel, my only luve,
    And fare thee weel awhile!
And I will come again, my luve,   15
    Though it were ten thousand mile.

1796

Auld Lang Syne[1]

Should auld acquaintance be forgot,
    And never brought to min'?
Should auld acquaintance be forgot,
    And days o' lang syne?

Chorus

5   For auld lang syne, my dear,
    For auld lang syne,
    We'll tak a cup o' kindness yet,
    For auld lang syne.

We twa hae run about the braes,°   *slopes*
10   And pu'd the gowans° fine,   *daisies*
But we've wandered mony a weary foot,
    Sin' auld lang syne.

    (*Chorus*)

We twa hae paidled i' the burn,°   *stream*
    From morning sun till dine;°   *dinner, noon*
15 But seas between us braid° hae roared,   *broad*
    Sin' auld lang syne.

    (*Chorus*)

And there's a hand, my trusty fiere,°   *friend*
    And gie's a hand o' thine;
And we'll tak a right gude-willie waught,[2]
20   For auld lang syne.

    (*Chorus*)

And surely ye'll be° your pint-stowp,°   *pay for / pint-cup*
    And surely I'll be mine;

1. Long ago.   2. A very hearty swig.

And we'll tak a cup o' kindness yet,
For auld lang syne.
(*Chorus*)

1788   1796

MARY WOLLSTONECRAFT
(1759–1797)

1792: A *Vindication of the Rights of Woman.*

Wollstonecraft's father inherited a substantial fortune and set himself up as
a gentleman farmer. He was, however, both extravagant and incompetent,
and as one farm after another failed, he became ever more moody and violent and sought solace in heavy bouts of drinking and in tyrannizing over
his submissive wife. Mary was the second of five children and the oldest
daughter. She later told her husband, William Godwin, that she used to
throw herself in front of her mother to protect her from her father's blows,
and that she sometimes slept outside the door of her parents' bedroom in
order to intervene if her father should break out in a drunken rage. The
solace of Mary's early life was her fervent attachment to Fanny Blood, an
accomplished girl two years her senior; their friendship, which began when
Mary was 16, endured and deepened until Fanny's death.

At the age of 19, Mary Wollstonecraft left home to take a position as
companion to Mrs. Dawson, a well-to-do widow living in Bath, where she
for the first time had the opportunity to observe—and scorn—the social life
of the upper classes at the most fashionable of English resort cities. Having
left her job in 1780 in order to nurse her dying mother through a long and
harrowing illness, Wollstonecraft next went to live with the Bloods, where
her work helped to sustain the struggling family. Her sister Eliza meanwhile had married, and in 1784, after the birth of a daughter, suffered a
nervous breakdown. Convinced that her sister's collapse was the result of
her husband's cruelty and abuse, Wollstonecraft persuaded her to abandon
husband and child and flee to London; since a divorce at that time was not
commonly available, and a fugitive wife could be forced to return to her
husband, the two women hid in secret quarters while awaiting the grant of
a legal separation. The infant, who was automatically given into the father's
custody, died before she was a year old.

The penniless women, together with Fanny Blood and Wollstonecraft's
other sister, Everina, established a girls' school at Newington Green, near
London. The project flourished at first, and at Newington Wollstonecraft
was befriended by the Reverend Richard Price, a leading radical author and
reformer whose kindly guidance helped to shape her social and political
opinions. Fanny Blood, although already ill with tuberculosis, went to
Lisbon to marry her longtime suitor, Hugh Skeys, and quickly became preg-

nant. Wollstonecraft rushed to Lisbon to attend her friend's childbirth, only to have Fanny die in her arms; the infant died soon afterward. The loss threw Wollstonecraft (already subject to bouts of depression) into black despair, which was heightened when she found that the school at Newington was in bad financial straits and had to be closed. Tormented by creditors, Mary rallied her energies to write her first book, *Thoughts on the Education of Daughters* (1786), a conventional and pious series of essays, and took up a position as governess for several daughters in the Anglo-Irish family of Viscount Kingsborough, a man of great wealth whose seat was at County Cork, Ireland.

The Kingsboroughs were well-intentioned and did their best to introduce Wollstonecraft into the busy trivialities of their social life. But her ambiguous position as governess, halfway between a servant and member of the family, was galling to her. An antagonism developed between Wollstonecraft and the beautiful Lady Kingsborough, in part because the children feared their mother and adored their governess. Wollstonecraft was dismissed, and returned to London, where Joseph Johnson in 1788 published her first novel, *Mary, a Fiction*, a partly autobiographical but conventionally sentimental novel written while she was in Ireland, as well as a book for children, *Original Stories from Real Life*. The latter was a considerable success, was translated into German, and quickly achieved a second English edition illustrated with engravings by the young William Blake. Wollstonecraft was befriended and subsidized by Johnson, the major publisher in England of radical and reformist books, and she took a prominent place among the notable writers whom he regularly entertained at his rooms in St. Paul's Churchyard. She published translations from French and German (she had taught herself both languages) and began reviewing books for Johnson's newly founded journal, the *Analytical Review*. Though still in straitened circumstances, she helped support her two sisters and her improvident and importunate father, and was also generous with funds—and with advice—to one of her brothers and to the indigent family of Fanny Blood.

In 1790 Edmund Burke's *Reflections on the Revolution in France*—an eloquent and powerful attack on the French Revolution and its English sympathizers—quickly evoked Wollstonecraft's response, *A Vindication of the Rights of Men*. This was a formidable piece of journalistic propaganda; its most potent passages are those which represent the disabilities and sufferings of the English lower classes and malign the motives and sentiments of Burke, who had heightened Wollstonecraft's ire by his attacks on her old friend, Richard Price. This work, the first book-length reply to Burke, scored an immediate success, although it was soon submerged in the flood of other replies, especially Tom Paine's classic *The Rights of Man* (1791–92). In 1792 Wollstonecraft focused her defense of the underprivileged on her own sex and wrote, in six weeks of intense effort, *A Vindication of the Rights of Woman*.

Earlier writers both in France and England had proposed that, given an equivalence in education, women would equal men in achievement; Wollstonecraft was particularly indebted to Catharine Macaulay's *Letters on Education* (1790), of which she had written an enthusiastic review. But Wollstonecraft's *Vindication* was unprecedented in its firsthand observations of the disabilities and indignities suffered by women, and in the articulateness and passion with which it exposed and decried such injustice. Wollstonecraft's views were conspicuously radical at a time when women had no political rights, were limited to a few lowly vocations as servants, nurses, governesses, and petty shopkeepers, and were legally nonpersons who lost their property to their husbands at marriage and were incapable of instituting an action in the courts of law. An impressive feature of her book, for all its vehemence, is the clear-sightedness and balance of her analysis of the social conditions of the time, as they affect men as well as women. She perceives that women constitute an oppressed class that cuts across the standard hierarchy of social classes; she shows that women, because they are denied political and domestic privileges, have been forced to seek their ends by means of coquetry and cunning; and she recognizes that men, no less than women, inherit their roles, and that the wielding of irresponsible power corrupts the oppressor no less than it distorts the oppressed. Hence her surprising but apt comparisons between women on the one hand, and men of the nobility and military on the other, as classes whose values and behavior have been distorted because their social roles prevent them from becoming fully human. In writing this pioneering work Wollstonecraft had found the cause that she was to pursue the rest of her life.

In December of 1792 Wollstonecraft went to Paris to observe the French Revolution at first hand. The years 1793–94 that she lived in France were those in which the early years of revolutionary moderation were succeeded by extremism and violence. In Paris she joined a group of English, American, and European expatriates sympathetic to the Revolution, and fell deeply in love with Gilbert Imlay, a tall, lean, and personable American who had been briefly an officer in the American revolutionary army and was the author of a widely read book on the Kentucky backwoods, where he had been an explorer. He played the role in Paris of an American frontiersman and child of nature amid the ancient corruptions of Europe, but was in fact an adventurer who had left America to avoid prosecution for debt and for freewheeling speculations in Kentucky land; he was also unscrupulous in his relations with women. The two became lovers, and Wollstonecraft bore a daughter, Fanny Imlay, in May, 1794. Imlay, who was often absent on mysterious business deals, left mother and daughter for a visit to London that he kept protracting. After the publication of her book, *An Historical and Moral View of the Origin and Progress of the French Revolution* (1795), Wollstonecraft followed Imlay to London where, persuaded that he no longer loved her, she tried to commit suicide; the attempt, however, was discovered and prevented by Imlay. In order to give Wollstonecraft a function and change of scene—as well as to clear the way for his love affair with a strolling actress—he persuaded her to take a trip as his business envoy to the Scandinavian countries. This was then a region relatively unknown in England, with poor and sometimes impassable roads and, outside the cities, very primitive accommodations. But she intrepidly set out, taking with her the year-old Fanny and accompanied only by the infant's French nurse, Marguerite.

Back in London after a four-month tour, Wollstonecraft discovered that Imlay was living with his new mistress. Confronting her lover, she was finally convinced he was lost to her, rowed to Putney bridge, and hurled herself into the Thames; she was rescued by a passerby just as she lost consciousness. Imlay evaded the difficulty of his situation by taking his actress off to Paris. But Wollstonecraft, resilient as always, had gotten him to return her letters, including those she had written him during her Scandinavian journey, and used these in composing her *Letters Written during a Short Residence in Sweden, Norway, and Denmark*, published by Joseph Johnson in 1796. The book is a notable achievement in the ancient genre of travel literature, whose antecedents go back to Greek and Roman times. Her observations on life in the northern countries, and especially on the lot of women, are sharp and shrewd; she is sensitive to the nuance and detail of the austere northern landscape; and she projects into her descriptions her own valiant and vibrant character.

In the same year Wollstonecraft renewed an earlier acquaintance with the social philosopher William Godwin. His *Inquiry concerning Political Justice* (1793), the most drastic proposals for restructuring the political and social order yet published in England, together with his novel of terror *Caleb Williams* (1794), which embodies his social views, had made him the most famed radical writer of his time. Godwin, then 40, was solemn, pedantic, and gauche in his social demeanor. But the austerely rationalistic philosopher had an unexpected capacity for deep feeling, and what began as a flirtation soon ripened into affection and (as their letters show) passionate physical love. She wrote Godwin, with what was for the time remarkable outspokenness on the part of a woman: "Now by these presents [i.e., this document] let me assure you that you are not only in my heart, but my veins, this morning. I turn from you half abashed—yet you haunt me, and some look, word or touch thrills through my whole frame. * * * When the heart and reason accord there is no flying from voluptuous sensations, do what a woman can." Wollstonecraft was soon again with child, and Godwin (who had in his *Inquiry* attacked the institution of marriage as a base form of property rights in human beings) braved the ridicule of his radical friends and conservative enemies by marrying her.

They set up a household together, but Godwin kept separate quarters in which to do his writing, and they further salvaged their principles by agreeing to live a separate social life in the company of both sexes. Wollstonecraft, secure in her husband's affection, and once more busy writing, was happy for a brief six months. On August 30 she gave birth to Mary Wollstonecraft Godwin. The delivery was not difficult, but the placenta was not discharged, and medical efforts to remove it resulted in massive blood poisoning. After ten days of agony, she lapsed into a coma and died. Her last whispered words were about her husband: "He is the kindest, best man in the world." Godwin wrote to a friend, announcing her death: "I firmly believe that there does not exist her equal in the world. I know from experience we were formed to make each other happy."

To distract himself in his grief Godwin wrote, and published in 1798, his *Memoirs of the Author of "A Vindication of the Rights of Woman"* in which he told, with the total candor on which he prided himself, of her affairs with Imlay and himself, her attempts at suicide, and her free thinking in matters of religion and sexual relationships; in four companion vol-

umes of her *Posthumous Works* he included her outspoken love letters to
Imlay. The unintended result was to saddle Wollstonecraft with a scandalous reputation so enduring that, through the Victorian era, advocates of
women's rights circumspectly avoided references to her *Vindication*; even
John Stuart Mill, in his *Subjection of Women* (1869), neglected to mention the work. It is only in the present century, and especially in recent decades, that Wollstonecraft's *Vindication* has achieved the recognition it
deserves.

From A Vindication of the Rights of Woman[1]

Introduction

After considering the historic page, and viewing the living world
with anxious solicitude, the most melancholy emotions of sorrowful
indignation have depressed my spirits, and I have sighed when
obliged to confess, that either nature has made a great difference
between man and man, or that the civilization which has hitherto
taken place in the world has been very partial. I have turned over
various books written on the subject of education, and patiently
observed the conduct of parents and the management of schools;
but what has been the result?—a profound conviction that the
neglected education of my fellow-creatures is the grand source of the
misery I deplore; and that women, in particular, are rendered weak
and wretched by a variety of concurring causes, originating from
one hasty conclusion. The conduct and manners of women, in fact,
evidently prove that their minds are not in a healthy state; for, like
the flowers which are planted in too rich a soil, strength and usefulness are sacrificed to beauty; and the flaunting leaves, after having
pleased a fastidious eye, fade, disregarded on the stalk, long before
the season when they ought to have arrived at maturity.—One
cause of this barren blooming I attribute to a false system of education, gathered from the books written on this subject by men who,
considering females rather as women than human creatures, have
been more anxious to make them alluring mistresses than affectionate wives and rational mothers; and the understanding of the sex
has been so bubbled by this specious homage, that the civilized
women of the present century, with a few exceptions, are only anxious to inspire love, when they ought to cherish a nobler ambition,
and by their abilities and virtues exact respect.

In a treatise, therefore, on female rights and manners, the works
which have been particularly written for their improvement must

1. The text is from the second revised
edition of 1792, as edited by Carol H.
Poston for the Norton Critical Edition
of *A Vindication* (1975). The editor
gratefully acknowledges Professor Poston's permission to make use of the
information in her annotations.

not be overlooked; especially when it is asserted, in direct terms, that the minds of women are enfeebled by false refinement; that the books of instruction, written by men of genius, have had the same tendency as more frivolous productions; and that, in the true style of Mahometanism, they are treated as a kind of subordinate beings, and not as a part of the human species,[2] when improveable reason is allowed to be the dignified distinction which raises men above the brute creation, and puts a natural sceptre in a feeble hand.

Yet, because I am a woman, I would not lead my readers to suppose that I mean violently to agitate the contested question respecting the equality or inferiority of the sex; but as the subject lies in my way, and I cannot pass it over without subjecting the main tendency of my reasoning to misconstruction, I shall stop a moment to deliver, in a few words, my opinion.—In the government of the physical world it is observable that the female in point of strength is, in general, inferior to the male. This is the law of nature; and it does not appear to be suspended or abrogated in favour of woman. A degree of physical superiority cannot, therefore, be denied—and it is a noble prerogative! But not content with this natural pre-eminence, men endeavour to sink us still lower, merely to render us alluring objects for a moment; and women, intoxicated by the adoration which men, under the influence of their senses, pay them, do not seek to obtain a durable interest in their hearts, or to become the friends of the fellow creatures who find amusement in their society.

I am aware of an obvious inference: —from every quarter have I heard exclamations against masculine women; but where are they to be found? If by this appellation men mean to inveigh against their ardour in hunting, shooting, and gaming, I shall most cordially join in the cry; but if it be against the imitation of manly virtues, or, more properly speaking, the attainment of those talents and virtues, the exercise of which ennobles the human character, and which raise females in the scale of animal being, when they are comprehensively termed mankind;—all those who view them with a philosophic eye must, I should think, wish with me, that they may every day grow more and more masculine.

This discussion naturally divides the subject. I shall first consider women in the grand light of human creatures, who, in common with men, are placed on this earth to unfold their faculties; and afterwards I shall more particularly point out their peculiar designation.

I wish also to steer clear of an error which many respectable writ-

---

2. It was a common but mistaken opinion among Europeans that the Koran, the sacred text of the Mohammedans, teaches that women have no souls.

ers have fallen into; for the instruction which has hitherto been addressed to women, has rather been applicable to *ladies*, if the little indirect advice, that is scattered through Sandford and Merton,[3] be excepted; but, addressing my sex in a firmer tone, I pay particular attention to those in the middle class, because they appear to be in the most natural state.[4] Perhaps the seeds of false-refinement, immorality, and vanity, have ever been shed by the great. Weak, artificial beings, raised above the common wants and affections of their race, in a premature unnatural manner, undermine the very foundation of virtue, and spread corruption through the whole mass of society! As a class of mankind they have the strongest claim to pity; the education of the rich tends to render them vain and helpless, and the unfolding mind is not strengthened by the practice of those duties which dignify the human character. —They only live to amuse themselves, and by the same law which in nature invariably produces certain effects, they soon only afford barren amusement.

But as I purpose taking a separate view of the different ranks of society, and of the moral character of women, in each, this hint is, for the present, sufficient, and I have only alluded to the subject, because it appears to me to be the very essence of an introduction to give a cursory account of the contents of the work it introduces.

My own sex, I hope, will excuse me, if I treat them like rational creatures, instead of flattering their *fascinating* graces, and viewing them as if they were in a state of perpetual childhood, unable to stand alone. I earnestly wish to point out in what true dignity and human happiness consists—I wish to persuade women to endeavour to acquire strength, both of mind and body, and to convince them that the soft phrases, susceptibility of heart, delicacy of sentiment, and refinement of taste, are almost synonymous with epithets of weakness, and that those beings who are only the objects of pity and that kind of love, which has been termed its sister, will soon become objects of contempt.

Dismissing then those pretty feminine phrases, which the men condescendingly use to soften our slavish dependence, and despising that weak elegancy of mind, exquisite sensibility, and sweet docility of manners, supposed to be the sexual characteristics of the weaker vessel, I wish to shew that elegance is inferior to virtue, that the first object of laudable ambition is to obtain a character as a human being, regardless of the distinction of sex; and that secondary views

3. *The History of Sandford and Merton*, by Thomas Day, was a very popular story for children, published in three volumes (1786–89). In it a tutor, the Rev. Mr. Barlow, frequently cites the superiority in moral principles of Harry Sandford, the son of a poor farmer, over Tommy Merton, the spoiled son of a rich family.
4. The middle class is viewed as more "natural" than the upper classes because uncorrupted by the artificialities of leisure-class life.

should be brought to this simple touchstone.

This is a rough sketch of my plan; and should I express my conviction with the energetic emotions that I feel whenever I think of the subject, the dictates of experience and reflection will be felt by some of my readers. Animated by this important object, I shall disdain to cull[5] my phrases or polish my style;—I aim at being useful, and sincerity will render me unaffected; for, wishing rather to persuade by the force of my arguments, than dazzle by the elegance of my language, I shall not waste my time in rounding periods,[6] or in fabricating the turgid bombast of artificial feelings, which, coming from the head, never reach the heart.—I shall be employed about things, not words!—and, anxious to render my sex more respectable members of society, I shall try to avoid that flowery diction which has slided from essays into novels, and from novels into familiar letters and conversation.

These pretty superlatives, dropping glibly from the tongue, vitiate the taste, and create a kind of sickly delicacy that turns away from simple unadorned truth; and a deluge of false sentiments and overstretched feelings, stifling the natural emotions of the heart, render the domestic pleasures insipid, that ought to sweeten the exercise of those severe duties, which educate a rational and immortal being for a nobler field of action.

The education of women has, of late, been more attended to than formerly; yet they are still reckoned a frivolous sex, and ridiculed or pitied by the writers who endeavour by satire or instruction to improve them. It is acknowledged that they spend many of the first years of their lives in acquiring a smattering of accomplishments; meanwhile strength of body and mind are sacrificed to libertine notions of beauty, to the desire of establishing themselves,—the only way women can rise in the world,—by marriage. And this desire making mere animals of them, when they marry they act as such children may be expected to act:—they dress; they paint, and nickname God's creatures.[7]—Surely these weak beings are only fit for a seraglio!—Can they be expected to govern a family with judgment, or take care of the poor babes whom they bring into the world?

If then it can be fairly deduced from the present conduct of the sex, from the prevalent fondness for pleasure which takes place of ambition and those nobler passions that open and enlarge the soul; that the instruction which women have hitherto received has only tended, with the constitution of civil society, to render them insig-

5. Be selective in.
6. I.e., in rounding out elaborate sentences. A "period" is a formal sentence composed of balanced clauses.
7. Hamlet, charging Ophelia with the faults characteristic of women, says:

"You jig, you amble, and you lisp; you nickname God's creatures and make your wantonness your ignorance" (*Hamlet* III.i.150 ff.). "Seraglio": harem, the women's quarters in a Moslem household.

nificant objects of desire—mere propagators of fools!—if it can be proved that in aiming to accomplish them, without cultivating their understandings, they are taken out of their sphere of duties, and made ridiculous and useless when the short-lived bloom of beauty is over,[8] I presume that *rational* men will excuse me for endeavouring to persuade them to become more masculine and respectable.

Indeed the word masculine is only a bugbear: there is little reason to fear that women will acquire too much courage or fortitude; for their apparent inferiority with respect to bodily strength, must render them, in some degree, dependent on men in the various relations of life; but why should it be increased by prejudices that give a sex to virtue, and confound simple truths with sensual reveries?

Women are, in fact, so much degraded by mistaken notions of female excellence, that I do not mean to add a paradox when I assert, that this artificial weakness produces a propensity to tyrannize, and gives birth to cunning, the natural opponent of strength, which leads them to play off those contemptible infantine airs that undermine esteem even whilst they excite desire. Let men become more chaste and modest, and if women do not grow wiser in the same ratio, it will be clear that they have weaker understandings. It seems scarcely necessary to say, that I now speak of the sex in general. Many individuals have more sense than their male relatives; and, as nothing preponderates where there is a constant struggle for an equilibrium, without it has[9] naturally more gravity, some women govern their husbands without degrading themselves, because intellect will always govern.

From *Chap. II. The Prevailing Opinion of a Sexual Character Discussed*

To account for, and excuse the tyranny of man, many ingenious arguments have been brought forward to prove, that the two sexes, in the acquirement of virtue, ought to aim at attaining a very different character: or, to speak explicitly, women are not allowed to have sufficient strength of mind to acquire what really deserves the name of virtue. Yet it should seem, allowing them to have souls, that there is but one way appointed by Providence to lead *mankind* to either virtue or happiness.

If then women are not a swarm of ephemeron[1] triflers, why should

---

8. "A lively writer, I cannot recollect his name, asks what business women turned of forty have to do in the world?" [Wollstonecraft's note]. Poston, in her edition of the *Vindication*, suggests that Wollstonecraft is recalling a passage in Fanny Burney's novel *Evelina* (1778), where the licen-

tious Lord Merton exclaims: "I don't know what the devil a woman lives for after thirty; she is only in other folks' way."
9. I.e., "unless it has * * *"
1. A flying insect that lives only one day.

they be kept in ignorance under the specious name of innocence? Men complain, and with reason, of the follies and caprices of our sex, when they do not keenly satirize our headstrong passions and groveling vices. —Behold, I should answer, the natural effect of ignorance! The mind will ever be unstable that has only prejudices to rest on, and the current will run with destructive fury when there are no barriers to break its force. Women are told from their infancy, and taught by the example of their mothers, that a little knowledge of human weakness, justly termed cunning, softness of temper, *outward* obedience, and a scrupulous attention to a puerile kind of propriety, will obtain for them the protection of man; and should they be beautiful, every thing else is needless, for, at least, twenty years of their lives.

Thus Milton describes our first frail mother; though when he tells us that women are formed for softness and sweet attractive grace,[2] I cannot comprehend his meaning, unless, in the true Mahometan strain, he meant to deprive us of souls, and insinuate that we were beings only designed by sweet attractive grace, and docile blind obedience, to gratify the senses of man when he can no longer soar on the wing of contemplation.

How grossly do they insult us who thus advise us only to render ourselves gentle, domestic brutes! For instance, the winning softness so warmly, and frequently, recommended, that governs by obeying. What childish expressions, and how insignificant is the being—can it be an immortal one? who will condescend to govern by such sinister methods! 'Certainly,' says Lord Bacon, 'man is of kin to the beasts by his body; and if he be not of kin to God by his spirit, he is a base and ignoble creature!'[3] Men, indeed, appear to me to act in a very unphilosophical manner when they try to secure the good conduct of women by attempting to keep them always in a state of childhood. Rousseau[4] was more consistent when he wished to stop the progress of reason in both sexes, for if men eat of the tree of knowledge, women will come in for a taste; but, from the imperfect cultivation which their understandings now receive, they only attain a knowledge of evil.

Children, I grant, should be innocent; but when the epithet is applied to men, or women, it is but a civil term for weakness. For if it be allowed that women were destined by Providence to acquire human virtues, and by the exercise of their understandings, that sta-

2. Milton asserts the authority of man over woman, on the grounds that "for contemplation he and valor formed, / For softness she and sweet attractive grace, / He for God only, she for God in him" (*Paradise Lost* IV.295 ff.).
3. Francis Bacon, essay *Of Atheism* (1597).
4. Jean-Jacques Rousseau (1712–78),

who proposed limiting the role of rationality, as against reliance on intuition and instinct. Rousseau's opinions about women and their appropriate education, as alluded to in this chapter, are expressed in his treatise *Emile* (1762), especially Book V, "Sophy, or Woman."

bility of character which is the firmest ground to rest our future hopes upon, they must be permitted to turn to the fountain of light, and not forced to shape their course by the twinkling of a mere satellite. Milton, I grant, was of a very different opinion; for he only bends to the indefeasible right of beauty, though it would be difficult to render two passages which I now mean to contrast, consistent. But into similar inconsistencies are great men often led by their senses.

> 'To whom thus Eve with *perfect beauty* adorn'd.
> 'My Author and Disposer, what thou bidst
> '*Unargued* I obey; So God ordains;
> 'God is *thy law, thou mine*: to know no more
> 'Is Woman's *happiest* knowledge and her *praise.*'[5]

These are exactly the arguments that I have used to children; but I have added, your reason is now gaining strength, and, till it arrives at some degree of maturity, you must look up to me for advice— then you ought to *think*, and only rely on God.

Yet in the following lines Milton seems to coincide with me; when he makes Adam thus expostulate with his Maker.

> 'Hast thou not made me here thy substitute,
> 'And these inferior far beneath me set?
> 'Among *unequals* what society
> 'Can sort, what harmony or true delight?
> 'Which must be mutual, in proportion due
> 'Giv'n and receiv'd; but in *disparity*
> 'The one intense, the other still remiss
> 'Cannot well suit with either, but soon prove
> 'Tedious alike: of *fellowship* I speak
> 'Such as I seek, fit to participate
> 'All rational delight[6] —

In treating, therefore, of the manners of women, let us, disregarding sensual arguments, trace what we should endeavour to make them in order to co-operate, if the expression be not too bold, with the supreme Being.

By individual education, I mean, for the sense of the word is not precisely defined, such an attention to a child as will slowly sharpen the senses, form the temper,[7] regulate the passions as they begin to ferment, and set the understanding to work before the body arrives at maturity; so that the man may only have to proceed, not to begin, the important task of learning to think and reason.

To prevent any misconstruction, I must add, that I do not

5. *Paradise Lost* IV.634–38 (Wollstonecraft's italics).
6. *Paradise Lost* VIII.381–92 (Wollstonecraft's italics).
7. Temperament, character.

believe that a private education can work the wonders which some sanguine writers have attributed to it. Men and women must be educated, in a great degree, by the opinions and manners of the society they live in. In every age there has been a stream of popular opinion that has carried all before it, and given a family character, as it were, to the century. It may then fairly be inferred, that, till society be differently constituted, much cannot be expected from education. It is, however, sufficient for my present purpose to assert, that, whatever effect circumstances have on the abilities, every being may become virtuous by the exercise of its own reason; for if but one being was created with vicious inclinations, that is positively bad, what can save us from atheism? or if we worship a God, is not that God a devil?

Consequently, the most perfect education, in my opinion, is such an exercise of the understanding as is best calculated to strengthen the body and form the heart. Or, in other words, to enable the individual to attain such habits of virtue as will render it independent. In fact, it is a farce to call any being virtuous whose virtues do not result from the exercise of its own reason. This was Rousseau's opinion respecting men: I extend it to women, and confidently assert that they have been drawn out of their sphere by false refinement, and not by an endeavour to acquire masculine qualities. Still the regal homage which they receive is so intoxicating, that till the manners of the times are changed, and formed on more reasonable principles, it may be impossible to convince them that the illegitimate power, which they obtain, by degrading themselves, is a curse, and that they must return to nature and equality, if they wish to secure the placid satisfaction that unsophisticated affections impart. But for this epoch we must wait—wait, perhaps, till kings and nobles, enlightened by reason, and, preferring the real dignity of man to childish state,[8] throw off their gaudy hereditary trappings: and if then women do not resign the arbitrary power of beauty—they will prove that they have *less* mind than man.

I may be accused of arrogance; still I must declare what I firmly believe, that all the writers who have written on the subject of female education and manners from Rousseau to Dr. Gregory,[9] have contributed to render women more artificial, weak characters, than they would otherwise have been; and, consequently, more useless members of society. I might have expressed this conviction in a lower key; but I am afraid it would have been the whine of affectation, and not the faithful expression of my feelings, of the clear result, which experience and reflection have led me to draw. When I come to that division of the subject, I shall advert to the passages

8. Pomp, costly display.
9. Dr. John Gregory, Scottish author of a widely read book on the education of women, *A Father's Legacy to His Daughters* (1774).

that I more particularly disapprove of, in the works of the authors I have just alluded to; but it is first necessary to observe, that my objection extends to the whole purport of those books, which tend, in my opinion, to degrade one half of the human species, and render women pleasing at the expense of every solid virtue.

Though, to reason on Rousseau's ground, if man did attain a degree of perfection of mind when his body arrived at maturity, it might be proper, in order to make a man and his wife *one*, that she should rely entirely on his understanding; and the graceful ivy, clasping the oak that supported it, would form a whole in which strength and beauty would be equally conspicuous. But, alas! husbands, as well as their helpmates, are often only overgrown children; nay, thanks to early debauchery, scarcely men in their outward form —and if the blind lead the blind, one need not come from heaven to tell us the consequence.

Many are the causes that, in the present corrupt state of society, contribute to enslave women by cramping their understandings and sharpening their senses. One, perhaps, that silently does more mischief than all the rest, is their disregard of order.

To do every thing in an orderly manner, is a most important precept, which women, who, generally speaking, receive only a disorderly kind of education, seldom attend to with that degree of exactness that men, who from their infancy are broken into method, observe. This negligent kind of guess-work, for what other epithet can be used to point out the random exertions of a sort of instinctive common sense, never brought to the test of reason? prevents their generalizing matters of fact—so they do to-day, what they did yesterday, merely because they did it yesterday.

This contempt of the understanding in early life has more baneful consequences than is commonly supposed; for the little knowledge which women of strong minds attain, is, from various circumstances, of a more desultory kind than the knowledge of men, and it is acquired more by sheer observations on real life, than from comparing what has been individually observed with the results of experience generalized by speculation. Led by their dependent situation and domestic employments more into society, what they learn is rather by snatches; and as learning is with them, in general, only a secondary thing, they do not pursue any one branch with that persevering ardour necessary to give vigour to the faculties, and clearness to the judgment. In the present state of society, a little learning is required to support the character of a gentleman; and boys are obliged to submit to a few years of discipline. But in the education of women, the cultivation of the understanding is always subordinate to the acquirement of some corporeal accomplishment; even while enervated by confinement and false notions of modesty, the body is prevented from attaining that grace and beauty which relaxed half-formed limbs never exhibit. Besides, in youth their faculties are not brought forward by emulation; and having no serious scientific study, if they have natural sagacity it is turned too soon on life and manners. They dwell on effects, and modifications, without tracing them back to causes; and complicated rules to adjust behaviour are a weak substitute for simple principles.

As a proof that education gives this appearance of weakness to females, we may instance the example of military men, who are, like them, sent into the world before their minds have been stored with knowledge or fortified by principles. The consequences are similar; soldiers acquire a little superficial knowledge, snatched from the muddy current of conversation, and, from continually mixing with society, they gain, what is termed a knowledge of the world; and this acquaintance with manners and customs has frequently been confounded with a knowledge of the human heart. But can the crude fruit of casual observation, never brought to the test of judgment, formed by comparing speculation and experience, deserve such a distinction? Soldiers, as well as women, practice the minor virtues with punctilious politeness. Where is then the sexual difference, when the education has been the same? All the difference that I can discern, arises from the superior advantage of liberty, which enables the former to see more of life.

* * *

Probably the prevailing opinion, that woman was created for man, may have taken its rise from Moses's poetical story;[1] yet, as very few, it is presumed, who have bestowed any serious thought on the subject, ever supposed that Eve was, literally speaking, one of Adam's ribs, the deduction must be allowed to fall to the ground; or, only be so far admitted as it proves that man, from the remotest antiquity, found it convenient to exert his strength to subjugate his companion, and his invention to shew that she ought to have her neck bent under the yoke, because the whole creation was only created for his convenience or pleasure.

Let it not be concluded that I wish to invert the order of things; I have already granted, that, from the constitution of their bodies, men seem to be designed by Providence to attain a greater degree of virtue.[2] I speak collectively of the whole sex; but I see not the shadow of a reason to conclude that their virtues should differ in respect to their nature. In fact, how can they, if virtue has only one eternal standard? I must therefore, if I reason consequentially, as

1. The story of the creation of Eve from the rib of Adam (Genesis ii.21–22). Traditionally, the first five books of the Old Testament were attributed to the authorship of Moses.

2. In the third paragraph of her "Introduction" (above), Wollstonecraft had said that men are, in general, physically stronger than women.

strenuously maintain that they have the same simple direction, as that there is a God.

It follows then that cunning should not be opposed to wisdom, little cares to great exertions, or insipid softness, varnished over with the name of gentleness, to that fortitude which grand views alone can inspire.

I shall be told that woman would then lose many of her peculiar graces, and the opinion of a well known poet might be quoted to refute my unqualified assertion. For Pope has said, in the name of the whole male sex,

> 'Yet ne'er so sure our passion to create,
> 'As when she touch'd the brink of all we hate.'[3]

In what light this sally places men and women, I shall leave to the judicious to determine; meanwhile I shall content myself with observing, that I cannot discover why, unless they are mortal, females should always be degraded by being made subservient to love or lust.

To speak disrespectfully of love is, I know, high treason against sentiment and fine feelings; but I wish to speak the simple language of truth, and rather to address the head than the heart. To endeavour to reason love out of the world, would be to out Quixote Cervantes,[4] and equally offend against common sense; but an endeavour to restrain this tumultuous passion, and to prove that it should not be allowed to dethrone superior powers, or to usurp the sceptre which the understanding should ever coolly wield, appears less wild.

Youth is the season for love in both sexes; but in those days of thoughtless enjoyment provision should be made for the more important years of life, when reflection takes place of sensation. But Rousseau, and most of the male writers who have followed his steps, have warmly inculcated that the whole tendency of female education ought to be directed to one point:—to render them pleasing.

Let me reason with the supporters of this opinion who have any knowledge of human nature, do they imagine that marriage can eradicate the habitude of life? The woman who has only been taught to please will soon find that her charms are oblique sunbeams, and that they cannot have much effect on her husband's heart when they are seen every day, when the summer is passed and gone. Will she then have sufficient native energy to look into herself for comfort, and cultivate her dormant faculties? or, is it not more rational to expect that she will try to please other men; and, in the emotions raised by the expectation of new conquests, endeav-

3. Alexander Pope, *Moral Essays* II, *Of the Characters of Women*, lines 51–52.

4. I.e., to outdo the hero of Cervantes' *Don Quixote* (1605) in trying to accomplish the impossible.

our to forget the mortification her love or pride has received? When the husband ceases to be a lover—and the time will inevitably come, her desire of pleasing will then grow languid, or become a spring of bitterness; and love, perhaps, the most evanescent of all passions, gives place to jealousy or vanity.

I now speak of women who are restrained by principle or prejudice; such women, though they would shrink from an intrigue with real abhorrence, yet, nevertheless, wish to be convinced by the homage of gallantry that they are cruelly neglected by their husbands; or, days and weeks are spent in dreaming of the happiness enjoyed by congenial souls till their health is undermined and their spirits broken by discontent. How then can the great art of pleasing be such a necessary study? it is only useful to a mistress; the chaste wife, and serious mother, should only consider her power to please as the polish of her virtues, and the affection of her husband as one of the comforts that render her task less difficult and her life happier.—But, whether she be loved or neglected, her first wish should be to make herself respectable,[5] and not to rely for all her happiness on a being subject to like infirmities with herself.

The worthy Dr. Gregory fell into a similar error. I respect his heart; but entirely disapprove of his celebrated Legacy to his Daughters.

He advises them to cultivate a fondness for dress, because a fondness for dress, he asserts, is natural to them. I am unable to comprehend what either he or Rousseau mean, when they frequently use this indefinite term.[6] If they told us that in a pre-existent state the soul was fond of dress, and brought this inclination with it into a new body, I should listen to them with a half smile, as I often do when I hear a rant about innate elegance.—But if he only meant to say that the exercise of the faculties will produce this fondness—I deny it.—It is not natural; but arises, like false ambition in men, from a love of power.

Dr. Gregory goes much further; he actually recommends dissimulation, and advises an innocent girl to give the lie to her feelings, and not dance with spirit, when gaiety of heart would make her feel eloquent without making her gestures immodest. In the name of truth and common sense, why should not one woman acknowledge that she can take more exercise than another? or, in other words, that she has a sound constitution; and why, to damp innocent vivacity, is she darkly to be told that men will draw conclusions which she little thinks of?[7]—Let the libertine draw what inference he pleases; but, I hope, that no sensible mother will restrain the natural frank-

5. I.e., morally worthy of respect.
6. I.e., the term "natural."
7. In *A Father's Legacy to His Daughters*, Dr. John Gregory had advised a girl, when she dances, not "to forget the delicacy of [her] sex," lest she be "thought to discover a spirit she little dreams of."

ness of youth by instilling such indecent cautions. Out of the abundance of the heart the mouth speaketh;[8] and a wiser than Solomon hath said, that the heart should be made clean,[9] and not trivial ceremonies observed, which it is not very difficult to fulfill with scrupulous exactness when vice reigns in the heart.

Women ought to endeavour to purify their heart; but can they do so when their uncultivated understandings make them entirely dependent on their senses for employment and amusement, when no noble pursuit sets them above the little vanities of the day, or enables them to curb the wild emotions that agitate a reed over which every passing breeze has power? To gain the affections of a virtuous man is affectation necessary? Nature has given woman a weaker frame than man; but, to ensure her husband's affections, must a wife, who by the exercise of her mind and body whilst she was discharging the duties of a daughter, wife, and mother, has allowed her constitution to retain its natural strength, and her nerves a healthy tone, is she, I say, to condescend to use art and feign a sickly delicacy in order to secure her husband's affection? Weakness may excite tenderness, and gratify the arrogant pride of man; but the lordly caresses of a protector will not gratify a noble mind that pants for, and deserves to be respected. Fondness is a poor substitute for friendship!

In a seraglio, I grant, that all these arts are necessary; the epicure must have his palate tickled, or he will sink into apathy; but have women so little ambition as to be satisfied with such a condition? Can they supinely dream life away in the lap of pleasure, or the languor of weariness, rather than assert their claim to pursue reasonable pleasures and render themselves conspicuous by practising the virtues which dignify mankind? Surely she has not an immortal soul who can loiter life away merely employed to adorn her person, that she may amuse the languid hours, and soften the cares of a fellow-creature who is willing to be enlivened by her smiles and tricks, when the serious business of life is over.

Besides, the woman who strengthens her body and exercises her mind will, by managing her family and practising various virtues, become the friend, and not the humble dependent of her husband; and if she, by possessing such substantial qualities, merit his regard, she will not find it necessary to conceal her affection, nor to pretend to an unnatural coldness of constitution to excite her husband's passions. In fact, if we revert to history, we shall find that the women who have distinguished themselves have neither been the most beautiful nor the most gentle of their sex.

8. Matthew xii.34.
9. Psalms xxiv (attributed to David, the "wiser than Solomon"), 3–4: "Who shall ascend into the hill of the Lord? or who shall stand in his holy place? He that hath clean hands, and a pure heart * * * "

Nature, or, to speak with strict propriety, God, has made all things right; but man has sought him out many inventions to mar the work. I now allude to that part of Dr. Gregory's treatise, where he advises a wife never to let her husband know the extent of her sensibility or affection. Voluptuous precaution, and as ineffectual as absurd.—Love, from its very nature, must be transitory. To seek for a secret that would render it constant, would be as wild a search as for the philosopher's stone, or the grand panacea:[1] and the discovery would be equally useless, or rather pernicious to mankind. The most holy band of society is friendship. It has been well said, by a shrewd satirist, "that rare as true love is, true friendship is still rarer."[2]

This is an obvious truth, and the cause not lying deep, will not elude a slight glance of inquiry.

Love, the common passion, in which chance and sensation take place of choice and reason, is, in some degree, felt by the mass of mankind; for it is not necessary to speak, at present, of the emotions that rise above or sink below love. This passion, naturally increased by suspense and difficulties, draws the mind out of its accustomed state, and exalts the affections; but the security of marriage, allowing the fever of love to subside, a healthy temperature is thought insipid, only by those who have not sufficient intellect to substitute the calm tenderness of friendship, the confidence of respect, instead of blind admiration, and the sensual emotions of fondness.

This is, must be, the course of nature.—Friendship or indifference inevitably succeeds love.—And this constitution seems perfectly to harmonize with the system of government which prevails in the moral world. Passions are spurs to action, and open the mind; but they sink into mere appetites, become a personal and momentary gratification, when the object is gained, and the satisfied mind rests in enjoyment. The man who had some virtue whilst he was struggling for a crown, often becomes a voluptuous tyrant when it graces his brow; and, when the lover is not lost in the husband, the dotard, a prey to childish caprices, and fond jealousies, neglects the serious duties of life, and the caresses which should excite confidence in his children are lavished on the overgrown child, his wife.

In order to fulfil the duties of life, and to be able to pursue with vigour the various employments which form the moral character, a master and mistress of a family ought not to continue to love each other with passion. I mean to say, that they ought not to indulge those emotions which disturb the order of society, and engross the

1. A medicine reputed to cure all diseases. "The philosopher's stone," in alchemy, had the power of transmuting base metals into gold.

2. Maxim 473 of La Rochefoucauld (1613–80), the great French writer of epigrams.

thoughts that should be otherwise employed. The mind that has never been engrossed by one object wants vigour—if it can long be so, it is weak.

A mistaken education, a narrow, uncultivated mind, and many sexual prejudices, tend to make women more constant than men; but, for the present, I shall not touch on this branch of the subject. I will go still further, and advance, without dreaming of a paradox, that an unhappy marriage is often very advantageous to a family, and that the neglected wife is, in general, the best mother.[3] And this would almost always be the consequence if the female mind were more enlarged: for, it seems to be the common dispensation of Providence, that what we gain in present enjoyment should be deducted from the treasure of life, experience; and that when we are gathering the flowers of the day and revelling in pleasure, the solid fruit of toil and wisdom should not be caught at the same time. The way lies before us, we must turn to the right or left; and he who will pass life away in bounding from one pleasure to another, must not complain if he acquire neither wisdom nor respectability of character.

Supposing, for a moment, that the soul is not immortal, and that man was only created for the present scene,—I think we should have reason to complain that love, infantine fondness, ever grew insipid and palled upon the sense. Let us eat, drink, and love, for to-morrow we die, would be, in fact, the language of reason, the morality of life; and who but a fool would part with a reality for a fleeting shadow? But, if awed by observing the improbable[4] powers of the mind, we disdain to confine our wishes or thoughts to such a comparatively mean field of action; that only appears grand and important, as it is connected with a boundless prospect and sublime hopes, what necessity is there for falsehood in conduct, and why must the sacred majesty of truth be violated to detain a deceitful good that saps the very foundation of virtue? Why must the female mind be tainted by coquetish arts to gratify the sensualist, and prevent love from subsiding into friendship, or compassionate tenderness, when there are not qualities on which friendship can be built? Let the honest heart shew itself, and *reason* teach passion to submit to necessity; or, let the dignified pursuit of virtue and knowledge raise the mind above those emotions which rather imbitter than sweeten the cup of life, when they are not restrained within due bounds.

I do not mean to allude to the romantic passion, which is the

3. Wollstonecraft's point is that a woman who is not preoccupied with her husband (and his attentions to her) has more time and attention for her children.

4. Poston points out that this may be a misprint in the second edition for "improvable," which occurs in the first edition.

concomitant of genius.—Who can clip its wing? But that grand passion not proportioned to the puny enjoyments of life, is only true to the sentiment, and feeds on itself. The passions which have been celebrated for their durability have always been unfortunate. They have acquired strength by absence and constitutional melancholy. —The fancy has hovered round a form of beauty dimly seen—but familiarity might have turned admiration into disgust; or, at least, into indifference, and allowed the imagination leisure to start fresh game. With perfect propriety, according to this view of things, does Rousseau make the mistress of his soul, Eloisa, love St. Preux, when life was fading before her;[5] but this is no proof of the immortality of the passion.

Of the same complexion is Dr. Gregory's advice respecting delicacy of sentiment,[6] which he advises a woman not to acquire, if she have determined to marry. This determination, however, perfectly consistent with his former advice, he calls *indelicate*, and earnestly persuades his daughters to conceal it, though it may govern their conduct;—as if it were indelicate to have the common appetites of human nature.

Noble morality! and consistent with the cautious prudence of a little soul that cannot extend its views beyond the present minute division of existence. If all the faculties of woman's mind are only to be cultivated as they respect her dependence on man; if, when a husband be obtained, she have arrived at her goal, and meanly proud rests satisfied with such a paltry crown, let her grovel contentedly, scarcely raised by her employments above the animal kingdom; but, if, struggling for the prize of her high calling, she look beyond the present scene, let her cultivate her understanding without stopping to consider what character the husband may have whom she is destined to marry. Let her only determine, without being too anxious about present happiness, to acquire the qualities that ennoble a rational being, and a rough inelegant husband may shock her taste without destroying her peace of mind. She will not model her soul to suit the frailties of her companion, but to bear with them: his character may be a trial, but not an impediment to virtue.

If Dr. Gregory confined his remark to romantic expectations of constant love and congenial feelings, he should have recollected that experience will banish what advice can never make us cease to wish for, when the imagination is kept alive at the expence of reason.

5. In Rousseau's *Julie, ou la Nouvelle Héloise* (1761), Julie, after a life of fidelity to her husband, reveals on her deathbed that she has never lost her passion for St. Preux, her lover when she was young. Wollstonecraft accepts the common opinion that Julie represents Madame d'Houdetot, with whom Rousseau was in love when he wrote the novel.

6. I.e., too elevated and refined an expectation of what to expect in a man.

I own it frequently happens that women who have fostered a romantic unnatural delicacy of feeling, waste their[7] lives in *imagining* how happy they should have been with a husband who could love them with a fervid increasing affection every day, and all day. But they might as well pine married as single—and would not be a jot more unhappy with a bad husband than longing for a good one. That a proper education; or, to speak with more precision, a well stored mind, would enable a woman to support a single life with dignity, I grant; but that she should avoid cultivating her taste, lest her husband should occasionally shock it, is quitting a substance for a shadow. To say the truth, I do not know of what use is an improved taste, if the individual be not rendered more independent of the casualties of life; if new sources of enjoyment, only dependent on the solitary operations of the mind, are not opened. People of taste, married or single, without distinction, will ever be disgusted by various things that touch not less observing minds. On this conclusion the argument must not be allowed to hinge; but in the whole sum of enjoyment is taste to be denominated a blessing?

The question is, whether it procures most pain or pleasure? The answer will decide the propriety of Dr. Gregory's advice, and shew how absurd and tyrannic it is thus to lay down a system of slavery; or to attempt to educate moral beings by any other rules than those deduced from pure reason, which apply to the whole species.

Gentleness of manners, forbearance and long-suffering, are such amiable Godlike qualities, that in sublime poetic strains the Deity has been invested with them; and, perhaps, no representation of his goodness so strongly fastens on the human affections as those that represent him abundant in mercy and willing to pardon. Gentleness, considered in this point of view, bears on its front all the characteristics of grandeur, combined with the winning graces of condescension; but what a different aspect it assumes when it is the submissive demeanour of dependence, the support of weakness that loves, because it wants protection; and is forbearing, because it must silently endure injuries; smiling under the lash at which it dare not snarl. Abject as this picture appears, it is the portrait of an accomplished woman, according to the received opinion of female excellence, separated by specious reasoners from human excellence. Or, they[8] kindly restore the rib, and make one moral being of a man and woman; not forgetting to give her all the 'submissive charms.'[9]

---

7. "For example, the herd of Novelists" [Wollstonecraft's note]. The author's reference is to women who have formed their expectations on love as it is misrepresented in the sentimental novels of her time.
8. "*Vide* [see] Rousseau and Swedenborg" [Wollstonecraft's note]. Rousseau's view was that a wife constituted an integral moral being only in concert with her husband. Emmanuel Swedenborg (1688–1772), the Swedish theosophist, held that in the married state in heaven, male and female are embodied in a single angelic form.
9. Milton says of Adam and Eve in *Paradise Lost* IV.497–99 that "he in delight / Both of her beauty and submissive charms / Smiled with superior love * * * "

How women are to exist in that state where there is to be neither marrying nor giving in marriage,[1] we are not told. For though moralists have agreed that the tenor of life seems to prove that *man* is prepared by various circumstances for a future state, they constantly concur in advising *woman* only to provide for the present. Gentleness, docility, and a spaniel-like affection are, on this ground, consistently recommended as the cardinal virtues of the sex; and, disregarding the arbitrary economy of nature, one writer has declared that it is masculine for a woman to be melancholy. She was created to be the toy of man, his rattle, and it must jingle in his ears whenever, dismissing reason, he chooses to be amused.

To recommend gentleness, indeed, on a broad basis is strictly philosophical. A frail being should labour to be gentle. But when forbearance confounds right and wrong, it ceases to be a virtue; and, however convenient it may be found in a companion—that companion will ever be considered as an inferior, and only inspire a vapid tenderness, which easily degenerates into contempt. Still, if advice could really make a being gentle, whose natural disposition admitted not of such a fine polish, something towards the advancement of order would be attained; but if, as might quickly be demonstrated, only affectation be produced by this indiscriminate counsel, which throws a stumbling-block in the way of gradual improvement, and true melioration of temper, the sex is not much benefited by sacrificing solid virtues to the attainment of superficial graces, though for a few years they may procure the individuals regal sway.

As a philosopher, I read with indignation the plausible epithets which men use to soften their insults; and, as a moralist, I ask what is meant by such heterogeneous associations, as fair defects, amiable weaknesses, &c.?[2] If there be but one criterion of morals, but one archetype for man, women appear to be suspended by destiny, according to the vulgar tale of Mahomet's coffin;[3] they have neither the unerring instinct of brutes, nor are allowed to fix the eye of reason on a perfect model. They were made to be loved, and must not aim at respect, lest they should be hunted out of society as masculine.

But to view the subject in another point of view. Do passive indolent women make the best wives? Confining our discussion to the present moment of existence, let us see how such weak creatures perform their part. Do the women who, by the attainment of a few superficial accomplishments, have strengthened the prevailing prejudice, merely contribute to the happiness of their husbands? Do they

---

1. "For in the resurrection they neither marry, nor are given in marriage, but are as the angels in heaven" (Matthew xxii.30).
2. In *Paradise Lost* X.891–92, the fallen Adam refers to Eve as "this fair defect / Of Nature"; and in *Moral Essays* II.44 Pope describes women as "Fine by defect, and delicately weak."
3. A legend has it that Mohammed's coffin hovers suspended in his tomb.

display their charms merely to amuse them? And have women, who have early imbibed notions of passive obedience, sufficient character to manage a family or educate children? So far from it, that, after surveying the history of woman, I cannot help, agreeing with the severest satirist, considering the sex as the weakest as well as the most oppressed half of the species. What does history disclose but marks of inferiority, and how few women have emancipated themselves from the galling yoke of sovereign man?—So few, that the exceptions remind me of an ingenious conjecture respecting Newton: that he was probably a being of a superior order, accidentally caged in a human body.[4] Following the same train of thinking, I have been led to imagine that the few extraordinary women who have rushed in eccentrical directions out of the orbit prescribed to their sex, were *male* spirits, confined by mistake in female frames. But if it be not philosophical to think of sex when the soul is mentioned, the inferiority must depend on the organs; or the heavenly fire, which is to ferment the clay, is not given in equal portions.

But avoiding, as I have hitherto done, any direct comparison of the two sexes collectively, or frankly acknowledging the inferiority of woman, according to the present appearance of things, I shall only insist that men have increased that inferiority till women are almost sunk below the standard of rational creatures. Let their faculties have room to unfold, and their virtues to gain strength, and then determine where the whole sex must stand in the intellectual scale. Yet let it be remembered, that for a small number of distinguished women I do not ask a place.

* * *

From *Chap. IV. Observations on the State of Degradation to Which Woman Is Reduced by Various Causes*

* * *

In the middle rank of life, to continue the comparison,[5] men, in their youth, are prepared for professions, and marriage is not considered as the grand feature in their lives; whilst women, on the contrary, have no other scheme to sharpen their faculties. It is not business, extensive plans, or any of the excursive flights of ambition, that engross their attention; no, their thoughts are not employed in rearing such noble structures. To rise in the world, and have the liberty of running from pleasure to pleasure, they must marry advantageously, and to this object their time is sacrificed, and their persons often legally prostituted. A man when he enters any profession has

---

4. A possible reminiscence of Pope's *Essay on Man* II.31–34: "Superior beings [i.e., angels] * * * / Admired such wisdom in an earthly shape, / And showed a Newton as we show an ape."

5. I.e., her comparison between the social conditions of men and of women, which conduce to the degradation of women.

his eye steadily fixed on some future advantage (and the mind gains great strength by having all its efforts directed to one point), and, full of his business, pleasure is considered as mere relaxation; whilst women seek for pleasure as the main purpose of existence. In fact, from the education, which they receive from society, the love of pleasure may be said to govern them all; but does this prove that there is a sex in souls? It would be just as rational to declare that the courtiers in France, when a destructive system of despotism had formed their character, were not men, because liberty, virtue, and humanity, were sacrificed to pleasure and vanity.—Fatal passions, which have ever domineered over the *whole* race!

The same love of pleasure, fostered by the whole tendency of their education, gives a trifling turn to the conduct of women in most circumstances: for instance, they are ever anxious about secondary things; and on the watch for adventures, instead of being occupied by duties.

A man, when he undertakes a journey, has, in general, the end in view; a woman thinks more of the incidental occurrences, the strange things that may possibly occur on the road; the impression that she may make on her fellow-travellers; and, above all, she is anxiously intent on the care of the finery that she carries with her, which is more than ever a part of herself, when going to figure on a new scene; when, to use an apt French turn of expression, she is going to produce a sensation.—Can dignity of mind exist with such trivial cares?

In short, women, in general, as well as the rich of both sexes, have acquired all the follies and vices of civilization, and missed the useful fruit. It is not necessary for me always to premise, that I speak of the condition of the whole sex, leaving exceptions out of the question. Their senses are inflamed, and their understandings neglected, consequently they become the prey of their senses, delicately termed sensibility, and are blown about by every momentary gust of feeling. Civilized women are, therefore, so weakened by false refinement, that, respecting morals, their condition is much below what it would be were they left in a state nearer to nature. Ever restless and anxious, their over exercised sensibility not only renders them uncomfortable themselves, but troublesome, to use a soft phrase, to others. All their thoughts turn on things calculated to excite emotion; and feeling, when they should reason, their conduct is unstable, and their opinions are wavering—not the wavering produced by deliberation or progressive views, but by contradictory emotions. By fits and starts they are warm in many pursuits; yet this warmth, never concentrated into perseverance, soon exhausts itself; exhaled by its own heat, or meeting with some other fleeting passion, to which reason has never given any specific gravity, neutrality ensues. Miserable, indeed, must be that being whose cultivation of mind has only tended to inflame its passions! A distinction should be made between inflaming and strengthening them. The passions thus pampered, whilst the judgment is left unformed, what can be expected to ensue?—Undoubtedly, a mixture of madness and folly!

This observation should not be confined to the *fair* sex; however, at present, I only mean to apply it to them.

Novels, music, poetry, and gallantry, all tend to make women the creatures of sensation, and their character is thus formed in the mould of folly during the time they are acquiring accomplishments, the only improvement they are excited, by their station in society, to acquire. This overstretched sensibility naturally relaxes the other powers of the mind, and prevents intellect from attaining that sovereignty which it ought to attain to render a rational creature useful to others, and content with its own station: for the exercise of the understanding, as life advances, is the only method pointed out by nature to calm the passions.

Satiety has a very different effect, and I have often been forcibly struck by an emphatical description of damnation:—when the spirit is represented as continually hovering with abortive eagerness round the defiled body, unable to enjoy any thing without the organs of sense. Yet, to their senses, are women made slaves, because it is by their sensibility that they obtain present power.

And will moralists pretend to assert, that this is the condition in which one half of the human race should be encouraged to remain with listless inactivity and stupid acquiescence? Kind instructors! what were we created for? To remain, it may be said, innocent; they mean in a state of childhood.—We might as well never have been born, unless it were necessary that we should be created to enable man to acquire the noble privilege of reason, the power of discerning good from evil, whilst we lie down in the dust from whence we were taken, never to rise again.—

It would be an endless task to trace the variety of meannesses, cares, and sorrows, into which women are plunged by the prevailing opinion, that they were created rather to feel than reason, and that all the power they obtain, must be obtained by their charms and weakness:

'Fine by defect, and amiably weak!'[6]

And, made by this amiable weakness entirely dependent, excepting what they gain by illicit sway, on man, not only for protection, but advice, is it surprising that, neglecting the duties that reason alone points out, and shrinking from trials calculated to strengthen their

6. Pope's actual words were: "Fine by defect, and delicately weak" (*Moral Essays* II.44).

minds, they only exert themselves to give their defects a graceful covering, which may serve to heighten their charms in the eye of the voluptuary, though it sink them below the scale of moral excellence?

Fragile in every sense of the word, they are obliged to look up to man for every comfort. In the most trifling dangers they cling to their support, with parasitical tenacity, piteously demanding succour; and their *natural* protector extends his arm, or lifts up his voice, to guard the lovely trembler—from what? Perhaps the frown of an old cow, or the jump of a mouse; a rat, would be a serious danger. In the name of reason, and even common sense, what can save such beings from contempt; even though they be soft and fair?

These fears, when not affected, may produce some pretty attitudes; but they shew a degree of imbecility which degrades a rational creature in a way women are not aware of—for love and esteem are very distinct things.

I am fully persuaded that we should hear of none of these infantine airs, if girls were allowed to take sufficient exercise, and not confined in close rooms till their muscles are relaxed, and their powers of digestion destroyed. To carry the remark still further, if fear in girls, instead of being cherished, perhaps, created, were treated in the same manner as cowardice in boys, we should quickly see women with more dignified aspects. It is true, they could not then with equal propriety be termed the sweet flowers that smile in the walk of man; but they would be more respectable members of society, and discharge the important duties of life by the light of their own reason. 'Educate women like men,' says Rousseau, 'and the more they resemble our sex the less power will they have over us.'[7] This is the very point I aim at. I do not wish them to have power over men; but over themselves.

In the same strain have I heard men argue against instructing the poor; for many are the forms that aristocracy assumes. 'Teach them to read and write,' say they, 'and you take them out of the station assigned them by nature.' An eloquent Frenchman has answered them, I will borrow his sentiments. But they know not, when they make man a brute, that they may expect every instant to see him transformed into a ferocious beast.[8] Without knowledge there can be no morality!

Ignorance is a frail base for virtue! Yet, that it is the condition for which woman was organized, has been insisted upon by the writ-

---

7. In *Émile,* his influential treatise on education. Rousseau means this as a warning to women that if they are brought up to be like men, they will lose their sexual power over men.

8. Poston suggests that Wollstonecraft has in mind the comment by Mirabeau, the Revolutionary statesman, to the Abbé Siéyès, who had been rudely treated in the French Constituent Assembly in 1790: "My dear abbé, you have loosed the bull: do you expect he is not to make use of his horns?"

ers who have most vehemently argued in favour of the superiority of man; a superiority not in degree, but essence; though, to soften the argument, they have laboured to prove, with chivalrous generosity, that the sexes ought not to be compared; man was made to reason, woman to feel: and that together, flesh and spirit, they make the most perfect whole, by blending happily reason and sensibility into one character.

And what is sensibility? 'Quickness of sensation; quickness of perception; delicacy.' Thus is it defined by Dr. Johnson;[9] and the definition gives me no other idea than of the most exquisitely polished instinct. I discern not a trace of the image of God in either sensation or matter. Refined seventy times seven,[1] they are still material; intellect dwells not there; nor will fire ever make lead gold!

I come round to my old argument; if woman be allowed to have an immortal soul, she must have, as the employment of life, an understanding to improve. And when, to render the present state more complete, though every thing proves it to be but a fraction of a mighty sum, she is incited by present gratification to forget her grand destination, nature is counteracted, or she was born only to procreate and rot. Or, granting brutes, of every description, a soul, though not a reasonable one, the exercise of instinct and sensibility may be the step, which they are to take, in this life, towards the attainment of reason in the next; so that through all eternity they will lag behind man, who, why we cannot tell, had the power given him of attaining reason in his first mode of existence.

* * *

Another argument that has had great weight with me, must, I think, have some force with every considerate benevolent heart. Girls who have been thus weakly educated, are often cruelly left by their parents without any provision; and, of course, are dependent on, not only the reason, but the bounty of their brothers. These brothers are, to view the fairest side of the question, good sort of men, and give as a favour, what children of the same parents had an equal right to. In this equivocal humiliating situation, a docile female may remain some time, with a tolerable degree of comfort. But, when the brother marries, a probable circumstance, from being considered as the mistress of the family, she is viewed with averted looks as an intruder, an unnecessary burden on the benevolence of the master of the house, and his new partner.

Who can recount the misery, which many unfortunate beings, whose minds and bodies are equally weak, suffer in such situations

---

9. In his *Dictionary of the English Language* (1747).
1. Jesus replies, when asked whether a brother's repeated sin should be for-given "till seven times": "I say not unto thee, Until seven times; but, Until seventy times seven" (Matthew xviii.22).

—unable to work, and ashamed to beg? The wife, a cold-hearted, narrow-minded, woman, and this is not an unfair supposition; for the present mode of education does not tend to enlarge the heart any more than the understanding, is jealous of the little kindness which her husband shews to his relations; and her sensibility not rising to humanity, she is displeased at seeing the property of *her* children lavished on an helpless sister.

These are matters of fact, which have come under my eye again and again. The consequence is obvious, the wife has recourse to cunning to undermine the habitual affection, which she is afraid openly to oppose; and neither tears nor caresses are spared till the spy is worked out of her home, and thrown on the world, unprepared for its difficulties; or sent, as a great effort of generosity, or from some regard to propriety, with a small stipend, and an uncultivated mind, into joyless solitude.

These two women may be much upon a par, with respect to reason and humanity; and changing situations, might have acted just the same selfish part; but had they been differently educated, the case would also have been very different. The wife would not have had that sensibility, of which self is the centre, and reason might have taught her not to expect, and not even to be flattered by, the affection of her husband, if it led him to violate prior duties. She would wish not to love him merely because he loved her, but on account of his virtues; and the sister might have been able to struggle for herself instead of eating the bitter bread of dependence.

I am, indeed, persuaded that the heart, as well as the understanding, is opened by cultivation; and by, which may not appear so clear, strengthening the organs; I am not now talking of momentary flashes of sensibility, but of affections. And, perhaps, in the education of both sexes, the most difficult task is so to adjust instruction as not to narrow the understanding, whilst the heart is warmed by the generous juices of spring, just raised by the electric fermentation of the season; nor to dry up the feelings by employing the mind in investigations remote from life.

With respect to women, when they receive a careful education, they are either made fine ladies, brimful of sensibility, and teeming with capricious fancies; or mere notable women.[2] The latter are often friendly, honest creatures, and have a shrewd kind of good sense joined with worldly prudence, that often render them more useful members of society than the fine sentimental lady, though they possess neither greatness of mind nor taste. The intellectual world is shut against them; take them out of their family or neighbourhood, and they stand still; the mind finding no employment, for literature affords a fund of amusement which they have never

2. I.e., energetic in running a household.

sought to relish, but frequently to despise. The sentiments and taste of more cultivated minds appear ridiculous, even in those whom chance and family connections have led them to love; but in mere acquaintance they think it all affectation.

A man of sense can only love such a woman on account of her sex, and respect her, because she is a trusty servant. He lets her, to preserve his own peace, scold the servants, and go to church in clothes made of the very best materials. A man of her own size of understanding would, probably, not agree so well with her; for he might wish to encroach on her prerogative, and manage some domestic concerns himself. Yet women, whose minds are not enlarged by cultivation, or the natural selfishness of sensibility expanded by reflection, are very unfit to manage a family; for, by an undue stretch of power, they are always tyrannizing to support a superiority that only rests on the arbitrary distinction of fortune. The evil is sometimes more serious, and domestics are deprived of innocent indulgences, and made to work beyond their strength, in order to enable the notable woman to keep a better table, and out-shine her neighbours in finery and parade. If she attend to her children, it is, in general, to dress them in a costly manner—and, whether this attention arise from vanity or fondness, it is equally pernicious.

Besides, how many women of this description pass their days; or, at least, their evenings, discontentedly. Their husbands acknowledge that they are good managers, and chaste wives; but leave home to seek for more agreeable, may I be allowed to use a significant French word, *piquant*[3] society; and the patient drudge, who fulfils her task, like a blind horse in a mill, is defrauded of her just reward; for the wages due to her are the caresses of her husband; and women who have so few resources in themselves, do not very patiently bear this privation of a natural right.

A fine lady, on the contrary, has been taught to look down with contempt on the vulgar employments of life; though she has only been incited to acquire accomplishments that rise a degree above sense; for even corporeal accomplishments cannot be acquired with any degree of precision unless the understanding has been strengthened by exercise. Without a foundation of principles taste is superficial, grace must arise from something deeper than imitation. The imagination, however, is heated, and the feelings rendered fastidious, if not sophisticated; or, a counterpoise of judgment is not acquired, when the heart still remains artless, though it becomes too tender.

These women are often amiable; and their hearts are really more sensible to general benevolence, more alive to the sentiments that civilize life, than the square-elbowed family drudge; but, wanting a

3. Stimulating.

due proportion of reflection and self-government, they only inspire love; and are the mistresses of their husbands, whilst they have any hold on their affections; and the platonic friends of his male acquaintance. These are the fair defects in nature; the women who appear to be created not to enjoy the fellowship of man, but to save him from sinking into absolute brutality, by rubbing off the rough angles of his character; and by playful dalliance to give some dignity to the appetite that draws him to them.—Gracious Creator of the whole human race! hast thou created such a being as woman, who can trace thy wisdom in thy works, and feel that thou alone art by thy nature exalted above her,—for no better purpose?—Can she believe that she was only made to submit to man, her equal, a being, who, like her, was sent into the world to acquire virtue?—Can she consent to be occupied merely to please him; merely to adorn the earth, when her soul is capable of rising to thee?—And can she rest supinely dependent on man for reason, when she ought to mount with him the arduous steeps of knowledge?—

Yet, if love be the supreme good, let women be only educated to inspire it, and let every charm be polished to intoxicate the senses; but, if they be moral beings, let them have a chance to become intelligent; and let love to man be only a part of that glowing flame of universal love, which, after encircling humanity, mounts in grateful incense to God.

* * *

1792

From Letters Written during a Short Residence in Sweden, Norway, and Denmark[1]

From *Letter III.* [*Social Conditions in Sweden*]

The population of Sweden has been estimated from two millions and a half to three millions; a small number for such an immense tract of country: of which only so much is cultivated, and that in the simplest manner, as is absolutely necessary to supply the necessaries of life; and near the seashore, from whence herrings are easily procured, there scarcely appears a vestige of cultivation. The scattered huts that stand shivering on the naked rocks, braving the pitiless elements, are formed of logs of wood, rudely hewn; and so little pains are taken with the craggy foundation, that nothing like a pathway points out the door.

Gathered into himself by the cold, lowering his visage to avoid

---

1. Reprinted from the edition by Carol H. Poston (University of Nebraska Press, 1976).

the cutting blast, is it surprising that the churlish pleasure of drinking drams[2] takes place of social enjoyments amongst the poor, especially if we take into the account, that they mostly live on high-seasoned provisions and rye bread? Hard enough, you may imagine, as it is only baked once a year. The servants also, in most families, eat this kind of bread, and have a different kind of food from their masters, which, in spite of all the arguments I have heard to vindicate the custom, appears to me a remnant of barbarism.

In fact, the situation of the servants in every respect, particularly that of the women, shews how far the Swedes are from having a just conception of rational equality. They are not *termed* slaves; yet a man may strike a man with impunity because he pays him wages; though these wages are so low, that necessity must teach them to pilfer, whilst servility renders them false and boorish. Still the men stand up for the dignity of man, by oppressing the women. The most menial, and even laborious offices, are therefore left to these poor drudges. Much of this I have seen. In the winter, I am told, they take the linen down to the river, to wash it in the cold water; and though their hands, cut by the ice, are cracked and bleeding, the men, their fellow servants, will not disgrace their manhood by carrying a tub to lighten their burden.

You will not be surprised to hear that they do not wear shoes or stockings, when I inform you that their wages are seldom more than twenty or thirty shillings per annum. It is the custom, I know, to give them a new year's gift, and a present at some other period; but can it all amount to a just indemnity for their labour? The treatment of servants in most countries, I grant, is very unjust; and in England, that boasted land of freedom, it is often extremely tyrannical. I have frequently, with indignation, heard gentlemen declare that they would never allow a servant to answer them; and ladies of the most exquisite sensibility, who were continually exclaiming against the cruelty of the vulgar to the brute creation, have in my presence forgot that their attendants had human feelings, as well as forms. I do not know a more agreeable sight than to see servants part of a family. By taking an interest, generally speaking, in their concerns, you inspire them with one for yours. We must love our servants, or we shall never be sufficiently attentive to their happiness; and how can those masters be attentive to their happiness, who living above their fortunes, are more anxious to outshine their neighbours than to allow their household the innocent enjoyments they earn.

It is, in fact, much more difficult for servants who are tantalized by seeing and preparing the dainties of which they are not to partake, to remain honest, than the poor, whose thoughts are not led from their homely fare; so that, though the servants here are com-

2. Small glasses of liquor.

monly thieves, you seldom hear of house-breaking, or robbery on the highway. The country is, perhaps, too thinly inhabited to produce many of that description of thieves termed footpads, or highwaymen. They are usually the spawn of great cities; the effect of the spurious desires generated by wealth, rather than the desperate struggles of poverty to escape from misery.

* * *

From *Letter VIII.* [*The Sea*]

Tonsberg was formerly the residence of one of the little sovereigns of Norway; and on an adjacent mountain the vestiges of a fort remain, which was battered down by the Swedes; the entrance of the bay lying close to it.

Here I have frequently strayed, sovereign of the waste, I seldom met any human creature; and sometimes, reclining on the mossy down, under the shelter of a rock, the prattling of the sea amongst the pebbles has lulled me to sleep—no fear of any rude satyr's[3] approaching to interrupt my repose. Balmy were the slumbers, and soft the gales, that refreshed me, when I awoke to follow, with an eye vaguely curious, the white sails, as they turned the cliffs, or seemed to take shelter under the pines which covered the little islands that so gracefully rose to render the terrific[4] ocean beautiful. The fishermen were calmly casting their nets; whilst the seagulls hovered over the unruffled deep. Every thing seemed to harmonize into tranquillity—even the mournful call of the bittern was in cadence with the tinkling bells on the necks of the cows, that, pacing slowly one after the other, along an inviting path in the vale below, were repairing to the cottages to be milked. With what ineffable pleasure have I not gazed—and gazed again, losing my breath through my eyes—my very soul diffused itself in the scene—and, seeming to become all senses, glided in the scarcely-agitated waves, melted in the freshening breeze, or, taking its flight with fairy wing, to the misty mountains which bounded the prospect, fancy tript[5] over new lawns, more beautiful even than the lovely slopes on the winding shore before me. —I pause, again breathless, to trace, with renewed delight, sentiments which entranced me, when, turning my humid[6] eyes from the expanse below to the vault above, my sight pierced the fleecy clouds that softened the azure brightness; and, imperceptibly recalling the reveries of childhood, I bowed before the awful throne of my Creator, whilst I rested on its footstool.

You have sometimes wondered, my dear friend, at the extreme affection of my nature—But such is the temperature of my soul—It

3. In Greek myth, a lecherous woodland creature with the horns and legs of a goat.

4. Terrifying.
5. I.e., [my] fantasy moved nimbly.
6. Moist.

is not the vivacity of youth, the hey-day of existence. For years have I endeavoured to calm an impetuous tide—labouring to make my feelings take an orderly course.—It was striving against the stream. —I must love and admire with warmth, or I sink into sadness. Tokens of love which I have received have rapt me in elysium[7]— purifying the heart they enchanted.—My bosom still glows. —Do not saucily ask, repeating Sterne's question, "Maria, is it still so warm?"[8] Sufficiently, O my God! has it been chilled by sorrow and unkindness—still nature will prevail—and if I blush at recollecting past enjoyment, it is the rosy hue of pleasure heightened by modesty; for the blush of modesty and shame are as distinct as the emotions by which they are produced.

I need scarcely inform you, after telling you of my walks, that my constitution has been renovated here; and that I have recovered my activity, even whilst attaining a little *embonpoint*.[9] My imprudence last winter, and some untoward accidents just at the time I was weaning my child, had reduced me to a state of weakness which I never before experienced.[1] A slow fever preyed on me every night, during my residence in Sweden, and after I arrived at Tonsberg. By chance I found a fine rivulet filtered through the rocks, and confined in a bason for the cattle. It tasted to me like a chalybeat,[2] at any rate it was pure; and the good effect of the various waters which invalids are sent to drink, depends, I believe, more on the air, exercise and change of scene, than on their medicinal qualities. I therefore determined to turn my morning walks towards it, and seek for health from the nymph of the fountain; partaking of the beverage offered to the tenants of the shade.

Chance likewise led me to discover a new pleasure, equally beneficial to my health. I wished to avail myself of my vicinity to the sea, and bathe; but it was not possible near the town; there was no convenience. The young woman whom I mentioned to you, proposed rowing me across the water, amongst the rocks; but as she was pregnant, I insisted on taking one of the oars, and learning to row. It was not difficult; and I do not know a pleasanter exercise. I soon became expert, and my train of thinking kept time, as it were, with the oars, or I suffered the boat to be carried along by the current, indulging a pleasing forgetfulness, or fallacious hopes. —How

7. In Greek myth, the happy abode of the blessed after death.
8. In Laurence Sterne's *Sentimental Journey through France and Italy* (1768), the traveler Yorick drenches his handkerchief with his tears at hearing Maria tell her sad story. She offers to wash it, and when he inquires where she will then dry it, she replies, in her bosom. Yorick asks, "And is your heart still so warm, Maria?"

9. Plumpness.
1. Wollstonecraft's letters to Imlay from Paris, in early 1795, describe how she undertook to wean her illegitimate infant while suffering from a heavy cold, and at a time when she had begun to fear that Imlay's long absence indicated he no longer loved her.
2. Spring water impregnated with iron, sometimes used as a medicine.

fallacious! yet, without hope, what is to sustain life, but the fear of annihilation—the only thing of which I have ever felt a dread—I cannot bear to think of being no more—of losing myself—though existence is often but a painful consciousness of misery; nay, it appears to me impossible that I should cease to exist, or that this active, restless spirit, equally alive to joy and sorrow, should only be organized dust—ready to fly abroad the moment the spring snaps, or the spark goes out, which kept it together. Surely something resides in this heart that is not perishable—and life is more than a dream.

Sometimes, to take up my oar, once more, when the sea was calm, I was amused by disturbing the innumerable young star fish[3] which floated just below the surface: I had never observed them before; for they have not a hard shell, like those which I have seen on the sea-shore. They look like thickened water, with a white edge; and four purple circles, of different forms, were in the middle, over an incredible number of fibres, or white lines. Touching them, the cloudy substance would turn or close, first on one side, then on the other, very gracefully; but when I took one of them up in the ladle with which I heaved the water out of the boat, it appeared only a colourless jelly.

I did not see any of the seals, numbers of which followed our boat when we landed in Sweden; for though I like to sport in the water, I should have had no desire to join in their gambols.

* * *

Letter XV. [*The Cascade Near Fredericstadt*]

I left Christiania yesterday. The weather was not very fine; and having been a little delayed on the road, I found that it was too late to go round, a couple of miles, to see the cascade near Fredericstadt, which I had determined to visit. Besides, as Fredericstadt is a fortress, it was necessary to arrive there before they shut the gate.

The road along the river is very romantic, though the views are not grand; and the riches of Norway, its timber, floats silently down the stream, often impeded in its course by islands and little cataracts, the offspring, as it were, of the great one I had frequently heard described.

I found an excellent inn at Fredericstadt, and was gratified by the kind attention of the hostess, who, perceiving that my clothes were wet, took great pains to procure me, as a stranger, every comfort for the night.

It had rained very hard; and we passed[4] the ferry in the dark, without getting out of our carriage, which I think wrong, as the

3. What Wollstonecraft calls starfish were apparently jellyfish.   4. Crossed over on.

horses are sometimes unruly. Fatigue and melancholy, however, had made me regardless whether I went down or across the stream; and I did not know that I was wet before the hostess remarked it. My imagination has never yet severed me from my griefs—and my mind has seldom been so free as to allow my body to be delicate.[5]

How I am altered by disappointment! —When going to Lisbon,[6] the elasticity of my mind was sufficient to ward off weariness, and my imagination still could dip her brush in the rainbow of fancy, and sketch futurity in glowing colours. Now—but let me talk of something else—will you go with me to the cascade?

The cross road to it was rugged and dreary; and though a considerable extent of land was cultivated on all sides, yet the rocks were entirely bare, which surprised me, as they were more on a level with the surface than any I had yet seen. On inquiry, however, I learnt that some years since a forest had been burnt. This appearance of desolation was beyond measure gloomy, inspiring emotions that sterility had never produced. Fires of this kind are occasioned by the wind suddenly rising when the farmers are burning roots of trees, stalks of beans, &c. with which they manure the ground. The devastation must, indeed, be terrible, when this, literally speaking, wild fire, runs along the forest, flying from top to top, and crackling amongst the branches. The soil, as well as the trees, is swept away by the destructive torrent; and the country, despoiled of beauty and riches, is left to mourn for ages.

Admiring, as I do, these noble forests, which seem to bid defiance to time, I looked with pain on the ridge of rocks that stretched far beyond my eye, formerly crowned with the most beautiful verdure.

I have often mentioned the grandeur, but I feel myself unequal to the task of conveying an idea of the beauty and elegance of the scene when the spiral tops of the pines are loaded with ripening seed, and the sun gives a glow to their light green tinge, which is changing into purple, one tree more or less advanced, contrasting with another. The profusion with which nature has decked them, with pendant honours,[7] prevents all surprise at seeing, in every crevice, some sapling struggling for existence. Vast masses of stone are thus encircled; and roots, torn up by the storms, become a shelter for a young generation. The pine and fir woods, left entirely to nature, display an endless variety; and the paths in the wood are not entangled with fallen leaves, which are only interesting whilst they are fluttering between life and death. The grey cobweb-like appearance of the aged pines is a much finer image of decay; the fibres whitening as they lose their moisture, imprisoned life seems to be

---

5. "When the mind's free, / The body's delicate" [Wollstonecraft's note] (*King Lear* III.iv.11–12).
6. Wollstonecraft had gone to Lisbon

in 1785 to attend her friend, Fanny Blood Skeys, during childbirth.
7. Ornaments (the reference is to the pine cones).

stealing away. I cannot tell why—but death, under every form, appears to me like something getting free—to expand in I know not what element; nay I feel that this conscious being must be as unfettered, have the wings of thought, before it can be happy.

Reaching the cascade, or rather cataract, the roaring of which had a long time announced its vicinity, my soul was hurried by the falls into a new train of reflections. The impetuous dashing of the rebounding torrent from the dark cavities which mocked the exploring eye, produced an equal activity in my mind: my thoughts darted from earth to heaven, and I asked myself why I was chained to life and its misery? Still the tumultuous emotions this sublime object excited, were pleasurable; and, viewing it, my soul rose, with renewed dignity, above its cares—grasping at immortality—it seemed as impossible to stop the current of my thoughts, as of the always varying, still the same, torrent before me—I stretched out my hand to eternity, bounding over the dark speck of life to come.

We turned with regret from the cascade. On a little hill, which commands the best view of it, several obelisks are erected to commemorate the visits of different kings. The appearance of the river above and below the falls is very picturesque, the ruggedness of the scenery disappearing as the torrent subsides into a peaceful stream. But I did not like to see a number of saw-mills crowded together close to the cataracts; they destroyed the harmony of the prospect.

The sight of a bridge erected across a deep valley, at a little distance, inspired very dissimilar sensations. It was most ingeniously supported by mast-like trunks, just stript of their branches; and logs, placed one across the other, produced an appearance equally light and firm, seeming almost to be built in the air when we were below it; the height taking from the magnitude of the supporting trees give them a slender, graceful look.

There are two noble estates in this neighbourhood, the proprietors of which seem to have caught more than their portion of the enterprising spirit that is gone abroad. Many agricultural experiments have been made; and the country appears better enclosed and cultivated; yet the cottages had not the comfortable aspect of those I had observed near Moss, and to the westward. Man is always debased by servitude, of any description; and here the peasantry are not entirely free.

Adieu!

I almost forgot to tell you, that I did not leave Norway without making some inquiries after the monsters said to have been seen in the northern sea; but though I conversed with several captains, I could not meet with one who had ever heard any traditional description of them, much less had any ocular demonstration of their existence. Till the fact be better ascertained, I should think the account of them ought to be torn out of our Geographical Grammars.[8]

1796

8. In the old sense: books that present, in methodical form, the principles of a body of knowledge.

WILLIAM WORDSWORTH
(1770–1850)

1791–92: In France during the early period of the Revolution.
1797: With his sister Dorothy at Alfoxden House, Somersetshire, near Coleridge at Nether Stowey.
1798: First edition of *Lyrical Ballads*.
1799: William and Dorothy settle at Grasmere, in the Lake District.
1800: Second edition of *Lyrical Ballads* in two volumes, with the famous Preface.
1807: *Poems in Two Volumes*; end of the great decade.

Wordsworth was born in Cockermouth in West Cumberland, just on the northern fringe of the English Lake District; when his mother died, the 8-year-old boy was sent to school at Hawkshead, near Esthwaite Lake, in the heart of that thinly settled region which he and Coleridge were to transform into the poetic center of England. William and his three brothers boarded in the cottage of Ann Tyson, who gave the boys simple comfort, ample affection, and freedom to roam the countryside at will. A vigorous, willful, and sometimes moody boy, William spent his free days and sometimes "half the night" in the sports and rambles described in the first two books of *The Prelude*, "drinking in" (to use one of his favorite metaphors) the natural sights and sounds, and getting to know the cottagers, shepherds, and solitary wanderers who moved through his imagination and dreams into his later poetry. He also found time to read voraciously in the books owned by his young headmaster, William Taylor, who encouraged him in his inclination to poetry.

John Wordsworth, the poet's father, died suddenly when William was 13, leaving to his five children mainly the substantial sum owed him by Lord Lonsdale, whom he had served as attorney and as steward of the huge Lonsdale estate. That harsh and litigious nobleman managed to keep from paying the debt until he died in 1802. Wordsworth was nevertheless able to go up to St. John's College, Cambridge, in 1787, where he found very little in the limited curriculum of that time to appeal to him. He took his A.B. degree in 1791 without distinction.

During the summer vacation of his third year at Cambridge (1790), Wordsworth and his closest college friend, the Welshman Robert Jones, journeyed on foot through France and the Alps (described in *The Prelude* VI) at the time when Frenchmen were joyously celebrating the first anniversary of the fall of the Bastille. Upon completing his course at Cambridge, Wordsworth spent four months in London, set off on another walking tour with Robert Jones through Wales (the time of the memorable ascent of Mount Snowdon in *The Prelude* XIV), and then went back alone to France in order to master the language and qualify as a traveling tutor.

In that year (between November, 1791, and December, 1792) Wordsworth became a fervent "democrat" and proselyte of the French Revolution —which seemed to him, as to many other generous spirits, to promise a "glorious renovation"—and he had a passionate love affair with Annette Vallon, the impetuous and warm-hearted daughter of a French surgeon at Blois. It seems clear that Wordsworth and Annette planned to marry, despite their difference in religion and political inclinations (Annette belonged to an old Catholic family whose sympathies were Royalist). But almost immediately after a daughter, Caroline, was born, lack of funds forced Wordsworth back to England. The outbreak of war between England and France made it impossible for him to rejoin Annette until they had drifted so far apart in sympathies that a permanent union no longer seemed practicable. Wordsworth's agonies of guilt, his divided loyalties between England and France, his gradual disillusion with the course of the Revolution in France—as he describes them in *The Prelude* X and XI —brought him to the verge of an emotional breakdown, when "sick, wearied out with contrarieties," he "yielded up moral questions in despair." His suffering, his near-collapse, and the successful effort, after his sharp break with his own past, to re-establish "a saving intercourse with my true self" are the experiences which underlie many of Wordsworth's greatest poems.

At this critical point a young friend, Raisley Calvert, died and left Wordsworth a sum of money just sufficient to enable him to live by his poetry. He settled in a rent-free cottage at Racedown, Dorsetshire, with his beloved sister Dorothy, who now began her long career as confidante, inspirer, and secretary. At that same time Wordsworth met Samuel Taylor Coleridge; two years later he moved to Alfoxden House, Somersetshire, to be near Coleridge, who lived four miles away at Nether Stowey. Here, his recovery complete, he entered at the age of 27 upon the delayed springtime of his poetic career.

Even while he had been an undergraduate at Cambridge, Coleridge had detected signs of genius in Wordsworth's rather conventional poem about his tour in the Alps, *Descriptive Sketches*, published in 1793. Now he hailed Wordsworth unreservedly as "the best poet of the age." The two men met almost daily, talked for hours about poetry, and composed prolifically. So close was their association that they lost almost all sense of individual proprietorship in a composition. We find the same phrases occurring in poems of Wordsworth and Coleridge, as well as in the remarkable journals that Dorothy kept at the time; the two poets collaborated in some writings and freely traded thoughts and passages for others; and Coleridge even undertook to complete a few poems that Wordsworth had left unfinished.

The result of their joint efforts was a small volume, published anonymously in 1798, *Lyrical Ballads, With a Few Other Poems*. It opened with Coleridge's *Ancient Mariner*, included three other poems by Coleridge, a number of Wordsworth's verse anecdotes and psychological studies of humble people, some lyrics in which Wordsworth celebrated impulses from a vernal wood, and closed with Wordsworth's great descriptive and meditative poem in blank verse (not a "lyrical ballad," but one of the "other poems" of the title), *Tintern Abbey*. No other book of poems in English so plainly announces a new literary departure. William Hazlitt said that when he heard Coleridge read some of these newly written poems aloud, "the sense of a new style and a new spirit in poetry came over me," with something of the effect "that arises from the turning up of the fresh soil, or of the first welcome breath of spring." The professional reviewers were less enthusiastic. Nevertheless *Lyrical Ballads* sold out in two years, and Wordsworth published over his own name a new edition, dated 1800, to which he added a second volume of poems, many of them written in homesickness during a long, cold, and friendless winter he and Dorothy had spent in Goslar, Germany, 1798–99. In his famous Preface to this edition, planned, like so many of the poems, in close consultation with Coleridge, Wordsworth enunciated the principles of the new criticism which served as rationale for the new poetry. Notable among the other works written in this prolific period is the austere and powerful tragic poem *The Ruined Cottage*.

Late in 1799 Wordsworth and Dorothy moved back permanently to their native lakes, settling at Grasmere in the little house later named Dove Cottage; Coleridge, following them, rented Greta Hall at Keswick, thirteen miles away. In 1802 Wordsworth finally came into his father's inheritance and, after an amicable settlement with Annette Vallon, married Mary Hutchinson, a Lake Country girl whom he had known since childhood. The course of his existence after that time was broken by various disasters: the drowning in 1805 of his favorite brother John, a sea captain whose ship was wrecked in a storm; the death of two of his five children in 1812; a gradual estrangement from Coleridge, culminating in an open quarrel (1810) from which they were not completely reconciled for almost two decades; and, from the 1830's on, the physical and mental decline of his sister Dorothy. The life of his middle age, however, was one of steadily increasing prosperity and reputation, as well as of political and religious conservatism. In 1813 an appointment as Stamp Distributor (that is, revenue collector) for Westmoreland was concrete evidence of his recognition as a national poet. Gradually Wordsworth's residences, as he moved into more and more commodious quarters, became standard places of resort for tourists; he was awarded honorary degrees and, in 1843, appointed poet laureate. He died in 1850 at the age of 80; only then did his executors publish his masterpiece, *The Prelude*, the autobiographical poem which he had written in two parts in 1799 and then expanded to its full length in 1805, but which he continued to revise almost to the last decade of his long life.

Most of Wordsworth's greatest poetry had been written by 1807, when he published *Poems in Two Volumes*; and after *The Excursion* (1814) and the first collected edition of his poems (1815), although he continued to write voluminously, there is a conspicuous decline in his powers as a poet. The causes of what is often called "Wordsworth's anti-climax" have been much debated; the principal cause seems to be inherent in the very nature of his most characteristic writing. Wordsworth is above all the poet of the remembrance of things past, or as he himself put it, of "emotion recollected in tranquility." Some object or event in the present triggers a sudden renewal of feelings he had experienced in youth; the result is a poem exhibiting the sharp discrepancy between what Wordsworth called "two consciousnesses": himself as he is now and as he once was. But one's early emotional experience is not an inexhaustible resource for poetry. As Basil Willey has said, Wordsworth as a poet "was living upon capital"; and he knew it. As he says in *The Prelude* XII, while describing the recurrence of "spots of time" from his memories of childhood:

> The days gone by
> Return upon me almost from the dawn
> Of life: the hiding places of man's power
> Open; I would approach them, but they close.
> I see by glimpses now; when age comes on,
> May scarcely see at all. * * *

The past which Wordsworth recollected was one of emotional turmoil which is ordered, in the calmer present, into a hard-won equilibrium. The result was a poetry of excitation in calm; genius, as Wordsworth said, is "born to thrive by interchange / Of peace and excitation" (*Prelude* XIII.1–10). As time went on, however, the precarious equilibrium of his great creative period became a habit, and Wordsworth finally gained what, in the *Ode to Duty* (composed in 1804), he longed for, "a repose which ever is the same"—but at the expense of the agony and excitation which, under the calm surface, empowers his best and most characteristic poems.

Occasionally in his middle and later life a jolting experience would revive the intensity of Wordsworth's remembered emotion, and also his earlier poetic strength. The moving sonnet *Surprised by Joy*, for example, was written in his forties at the abrupt realization that time was beginning to diminish his grief at the death some years earlier of his little daughter Catherine. And when Wordsworth was 65 years old, the sudden report of the death of James Hogg called up the memory of other and greater poets whom Wordsworth had loved and outlived; the result was an "Extempore Effusion," written in a return to the simple quatrains of the early *Lyrical Ballads* and with a recovery of the great elegiac voice which had uttered the dirges to Lucy, 35 years before.

From Lyrical Ballads of 1798

Simon Lee[1]

The Old Huntsman

WITH AN INCIDENT IN WHICH HE WAS CONCERNED

In the sweet shire of Cardigan,[2]
Not far from pleasant Ivor Hall,
An old man dwells, a little man,
I've heard he once was tall.
Of years he has upon his back,   5
No doubt, a burden weighty;
He says he is threescore and ten,
But others say he's eighty.

A long blue livery-coat[3] has he,
That's fair behind, and fair before;   10
Yet, meet him where you will, you see
At once that he is poor.
Full five and twenty years he lived
A running huntsman merry;
And, though he has but one eye left,   15
His cheek is like a cherry.

No man like him the horn could sound,
And no man was so full of glee;
To say the least, four counties round
Had heard of Simon Lee;   20
His master's dead, and no one now
Dwells in the hall of Ivor;
Men, dogs, and horses, all are dead;
He is the sole survivor.

His hunting feats have him bereft   25
Of his right eye, as you may see:
And then, what limbs those feats have left
To poor old Simon Lee!
He has no son, he has no child,

1. "This old man had been huntsman to the Squires of Alfoxden, which, at the time we occupied it, belonged to a minor. * * * I have, after an interval of 45 years, the image of the old man as fresh before my eyes as if I had seen him yesterday. The expression when the hounds were out, "I dearly love their voices," was word for word from his own lips" [Wordsworth's comment, 1843]. Wordsworth and Dorothy had lived at Alfoxden House, Somerset-shire, in 1797–98; at the time it had been inherited by a "minor" (someone not of legal age).

Wordsworth revised and reordered this poem many times between 1798 and 1845. It is reprinted here in the original version of the first edition of *Lyrical Ballads*.
2. Wordsworth relocated the incident from Somersetshire to Cardiganshire in Wales.
3. A servant's uniform.

His wife, an aged woman,   30
Lives with him, near the waterfall,
Upon the village common.

And he is lean and he is sick,
His little body's half awry;
His ankles they are swoln and thick,   35
His legs are thin and dry.
When he was young he little knew
Of husbandry or tillage;
And now he's forced to work, though weak,
—The weakest in the village.   40

He all the country could outrun,
Could leave both man and horse behind;
And often, ere the race was done,
He reeled and was stone-blind.[4]
And still there's something in the world   45
At which his heart rejoices;
For when the chiming hounds are out,
He dearly loves their voices!

Old Ruth works out of doors with him,
And does what Simon cannot do;   50
For she, not over stout of limb,
Is stouter of the two.
And though you with your utmost skill
From labor could not wean them,
Alas! 'tis very little, all   55
Which they can do between them.

Beside their moss-grown hut of clay,
Not twenty paces from the door,
A scrap of land they have, but they
Are poorest of the poor.   60
This scrap of land he from the heath
Enclosed when he was stronger;
But what avails the land to them,
Which they can till no longer?

Few months of life has he in store,   65
As he to you will tell,
For still, the more he works, the more
His poor old ankles swell.
My gentle reader, I perceive
How patiently you've waited,   70
And I'm afraid that you expect
Some tale will be related.

4. I.e., totally blind.

O reader! had you in your mind
Such stores as silent thought can bring,
O gentle reader! you would find   75
A tale in every thing.
What more I have to say is short,
I hope you'll kindly take it;
It is no tale; but should you think,
Perhaps a tale you'll make it.   80

One summer day I chanced to see
This old man doing all he could
About the root of an old tree,
A stump of rotten wood.
The mattock tottered in his hand;   85
So vain was his endeavor
That at the root of the old tree
He might have worked forever.

"You're overtasked, good Simon Lee.
Give me your tool," to him I said;   90
And at the word right gladly he
Received my proffered aid.
I struck, and with a single blow
The tangled root I severed,
At which the poor old man so long   95
And vainly had endeavored.

The tears into his eyes were brought,
And thanks and praises seemed to run
So fast out of his heart, I thought
They never would have done.   100
—I've heard of hearts unkind, kind deeds
With coldness still returning.
Alas! the gratitude of men
Has oft'ner left me mourning.

1798   1798

We Are Seven[1]

—A simple Child,
That lightly draws its breath,
And feels its life in every limb,
What should it know of death?

I met a little cottage Girl:
She was eight years old, she said;   5
Her hair was thick with many a curl
That clustered round her head.

1. "Written at Alfoxden in the spring
of 1798. * * * The little girl who
is the heroine I met within the area of
Goodrich Castle in the year 1793"
(Wordsworth). Wordsworth also tells
us that he composed the last line of the
last stanza first, and that Coleridge
contributed the initial stanza.

She had a rustic, woodland air,
And she was wildly clad:
Her eyes were fair, and very fair;
—Her beauty made me glad.   10

"Sisters and brothers, little Maid,
How many may you be?"
"How many? Seven in all," she said,
And wondering looked at me.   15

"And where are they? I pray you tell."
She answered, "Seven are we;
And two of us at Conway dwell,
And two are gone to sea.   20

"Two of us in the churchyard lie,
My sister and my brother;
And, in the churchyard cottage, I
Dwell near them with my mother."

"You say that two at Conway dwell,   25
And two are gone to sea,
Yet ye are seven! I pray you tell,
Sweet Maid, how this may be."

Then did the little Maid reply,
"Seven boys and girls are we;   30
Two of us in the churchyard lie,
Beneath the churchyard tree."

"You run about, my little Maid,
Your limbs they are alive;
If two are in the churchyard laid,   35
Then ye are only five."

"Their graves are green, they may be seen,"
The little Maid replied,
"Twelve steps or more from my mother's door,
And they are side by side.   40

"My stockings there I often knit,
My kerchief there I hem;
And there upon the ground I sit,
And sing a song to them.

"And often after sunset, sir,   45
When it is light and fair,
I take my little porringer,[2]
And eat my supper there.

"The first that died was sister Jane;
In bed she moaning lay,   50
Till God released her of her pain;
And then she went away.

_____
2. Bowl for porridge.

"So in the churchyard she was laid;
And, when the grass was dry,
Together round her grave we played,   55
My brother John and I.

"And when the ground was white with snow,
And I could run and slide,
My brother John was forced to go,
And he lies by her side."   60

"How many are you, then," said I,
"If they two are in heaven?"
Quick was the little Maid's reply,
"O master! we are seven."

"But they are dead; those two are dead!   65
Their spirits are in heaven!"
'Twas throwing words away; for still
The little Maid would have her will,
And said, "Nay, we are seven!"

1798   1798

Lines Written in Early Spring

I heard a thousand blended notes,
While in a grove I sate reclined,
In that sweet mood when pleasant thoughts
Bring sad thoughts to the mind.

To her fair works did Nature link   5
The human soul that through me ran;
And much it grieved my heart to think
What man has made of man.

Through primrose tufts, in that green bower,
The periwinkle[3] trailed its wreaths;   10
And 'tis my faith that every flower
Enjoys the air it breathes.

The birds around me hopped and played,
Their thoughts I cannot measure—
But the least motion which they made,   15
It seemed a thrill of pleasure.

The budding twigs spread out their fan,
To catch the breezy air;
And I must think, do all I can,
That there was pleasure there.   20

3. A trailing evergreen plant with small blue flowers (U.S. myrtle).

If this belief from heaven be sent,
If such be Nature's holy plan,[4]
Have I not reason to lament
What man has made of man?

1798   1798

Expostulation and Reply[1]

"Why, William, on that old gray stone,   *Wordsworth is
Thus for the length of half a day,   *personally involved as a*
Why, William, sit you thus alone,   *character in this poem.*
And dream your time away?

Importance   "Where are your books?—that light bequeathed   5
of books and   To beings else forlorn and blind!
of book learning   Up! up! and drink the spirit breathed
From dead men to their kind.

"You look round on your Mother Earth,
As if she for no purpose bore you;   10
As if you were her first-born birth,
And none had lived before you!"

One morning thus, by Esthwaite lake,
When life was sweet, I knew not why,
To me my good friend Matthew[2] spake,   15
And thus I made reply:

"The eye—it cannot choose but see;   *Importance of*
We cannot bid the ear be still;   *Nature as a Teacher*
Our bodies feel, where'er they be,   *to man.*
Against or with our will.   20

"Nor less I deem that there are Powers
Which of themselves our minds impress;
That we can feed this mind of ours
In a wise passiveness.

"Think you, 'mid all this mighty sum   25
Of things forever speaking,
That nothing of itself will come,
But we must still be seeking?

4. The version of these lines printed in
the *Lyrical Ballads* of 1798 mentioned
neither heaven nor holiness: "If I these
thoughts may not prevent, / If such
be of my creed the plan."
1. This and the following companion-
poem have often been attacked—and defended—as Wordsworth's solemn deliverance on the comparative merits of nature
and of books. But they are a dialogue
between two friends who are intimate
enough to rally one another by the usual

device of overstating parts of a whole
truth. Wordsworth said that the pieces
originated in a conversation "with a
friend who was somewhat unreasonably
attached to modern books of moral philosophy," and also that the lore of "a
wise passiveness" made the poem a favorite among Quakers.
2. A schoolmaster who plays a role in
others of Wordsworth's early poems;
see, e.g., *The Two April Mornings*.

"—Then ask not wherefore, here, alone,
Conversing[3] as I may,   30
I sit upon this old gray stone,
And dream my time away."

1798   1798

The Tables Turned

AN EVENING SCENE ON THE SAME SUBJECT

Up! up! my friend, and quit your books,
Or surely you'll grow double;
Up! up! my friend, and clear your looks;
Why all this toil and trouble?

The sun, above the mountain's head,   5
A freshening luster mellow
Through all the long green fields has spread,
His first sweet evening yellow.

Books! 'tis a dull and endless strife:
Come, hear the woodland linnet,[1]   10
How sweet his music! on my life,
There's more of wisdom in it.

And hark! how blithe the throstle[2] sings!
He, too, is no mean preacher;
Come forth into the light of things,   15
Let Nature be your teacher.

She has a world of ready wealth,
Our minds and hearts to bless—
Spontaneous wisdom breathed by health,
Truth breathed by cheerfulness.   20

One impulse from a vernal wood
May teach you more of man,
Of moral evil and of good,
Than all the sages can.

Sweet is the lore which Nature brings;   25
Our meddling intellect
Misshapes the beauteous forms of things—
We murder to dissect.

Enough of Science and of Art;
Close up those barren leaves;   30
Come forth, and bring with you a heart
That watches and receives.

1798   1798

[handwritten marginal note: The doctrine of the Romantics]

---

3. In the old sense of "communing"   1. A small finch, common in Europe.
(with the "things forever speaking").   2. The song thrush.

Lines[1]

COMPOSED A FEW MILES ABOVE TINTERN ABBEY
ON REVISITING THE BANKS OF THE WYE
DURING A TOUR. JULY 13, 1798

Five years have passed; five summers, with the length
Of five long winters! and again I hear
These waters, rolling from their mountain-springs
With a soft inland murmur. Once again
Do I behold these steep and lofty cliffs,   5
That on a wild secluded scene impress
Thoughts of more deep seclusion; and connect
The landscape with the quiet of the sky.
The day is come when I again repose
Here, under this dark sycamore, and view   10
These plots of cottage ground, these orchard tufts,
Which at this season, with their unripe fruits,
Are clad in one green hue, and lose themselves
'Mid groves and copses. Once again I see
These hedgerows, hardly hedgerows, little lines   15
Of sportive wood run wild; these pastoral farms,
Green to the very door; and wreaths of smoke
Sent up, in silence, from among the trees!
With some uncertain notice, as might seem
Of vagrant dwellers in the houseless woods,   20
Or of some Hermit's cave, where by his fire
The Hermit sits alone.

　　　　　　　These beauteous forms,
Through a long absence, have not been to me
As is a landscape to a blind man's eye;
But oft, in lonely rooms, and 'mid the din   25
Of towns and cities, I have owed to them,
In hours of weariness, sensations sweet,
Felt in the blood, and felt along the heart;
And passing even into my purer mind,
With tranquil restoration—feelings too   30
Of unremembered pleasure; such, perhaps,
As have no slight or trivial influence
On that best portion of a good man's life,

Handwritten marginal notes: Untouched, unspoiled Nature. · Aloofness from society seems good to the Romantics. · Solitary figure in Nature. · How the persona has used his memories of these natural scenes while he was pent-up in the city.

1. "No poem of mine was composed under circumstances more pleasant for me to remember than this. I began it upon leaving Tintern, after crossing the Wye, and concluded it just as I was entering Bristol in the evening, after a ramble of 4 or 5 days, with my sister. Not a line of it was altered, and not any part of it written down till I reached Bristol" (Wordsworth). The poem was printed as the last item in *Lyrical Ballads.*
Wordsworth had first visited the Wye valley and the ruins of Tintern Abbey, in Monmouthshire, while on a solitary walking tour in August of 1793, when he was 23 years old. The puzzling difference between the present landscape and the remembered "picture of the mind" (line 61) gives rise to an intricately organized meditation, in which the poet reviews his past, evaluates the present, and (through his sister as intermediary) anticipates the future, until he ends by rounding back quietly upon the scene which had been his point of departure.

His little, nameless, unremembered, acts
Of kindness and of love. Nor less, I trust,   35
To them I may have owed another gift,
Of aspect more sublime; that blessed mood,
In which the burthen of the mystery,
In which the heavy and the weary weight
Of all this unintelligible world,   40
Is lightened—that serene and blessed mood,
In which the affections gently lead us on—
Until, the breath of this corporeal frame
And even the motion of our human blood
Almost suspended, we are laid asleep   45
In body, and become a living soul;
While with an eye made quiet by the power
Of harmony, and the deep power of joy,
We see into the life of things.

                    If this
Be but a vain belief, yet, oh! how oft—   50
In darkness and amid the many shapes
Of joyless daylight; when the fretful stir
Unprofitable, and the fever of the world,
Have hung upon the beatings of my heart—
How oft, in spirit, have I turned to thee,   55
O sylvan Wye! thou wanderer through the woods,
How often has my spirit turned to thee!

   And now, with gleams of half-extinguished thought
With many recognitions dim and faint,
And somewhat of a sad perplexity,   60
The picture of the mind revives again;
While here I stand, not only with the sense
Of present pleasure, but with pleasing thoughts
That in this moment there is life and food
For future years. And so I dare to hope,   65
Though changed, no doubt, from what I was when first
I came among these hills; when like a roe
I bounded o'er the mountains, by the sides
Of the deep rivers, and the lonely streams,
Wherever nature led—more like a man   70
Flying from something that he dreads than one
Who sought the thing he loved. For nature then
(The coarser pleasures of my boyish days,
And their glad animal movements all gone by)
To me was all in all.—I cannot paint   75
What then I was. The sounding cataract
Haunted me like a passion; the tall rock,
The mountain, and the deep and gloomy wood,
Their colors and their forms, were then to me
An appetite; a feeling and a love,   80
That had no need of a remoter charm,

By thought supplied, nor any interest
Unborrowed from the eye.—That time is past,
And all its aching joys are now no more,
And all its dizzy raptures.[2] Not for this   85
Faint[3] I, nor mourn nor murmur; other gifts
Have followed; for such loss, I would believe,
Abundant recompense. For I have learned
To look on nature, not as in the hour
Of thoughtless youth; but hearing oftentimes   90
The still, sad music of humanity,
Nor harsh nor grating, though of ample power
To chasten and subdue. And I have felt
A presence that disturbs me with the joy
Of elevated thoughts; a sense sublime   95
Of something far more deeply interfused,
Whose dwelling is the light of setting suns,
And the round ocean and the living air,
And the blue sky, and in the mind of man:
A motion and a spirit, that impels   100
All thinking things, all objects of all thought,
And rolls through all things. Therefore am I still
A lover of the meadows and the woods,
And mountains; and of all that we behold
From this green earth; of all the mighty world   105
Of eye, and ear—both what they half create,[4]
And what perceive; well pleased to recognize
In nature and the language of the sense
The anchor of my purest thoughts, the nurse,
The guide, the guardian of my heart, and soul   110
Of all my moral being.

                    Nor perchance,
If I were not thus taught, should I the more
Suffer my genial spirits[5] to decay:

Handwritten marginal notes:
- *Now he is different.* (line 84–85)
- *His current attitude toward Nature.* (line 89–91)
- *The presence of a kind of god or divinity in Nature, a godhood.* (line 94–96)

2. Lines 66 ff. contain Wordsworth's famous description of the three stages of his growing up, defined in terms of his evolving relations to the natural scene: the young boy's purely physical responsiveness (lines 73–74); the post-adolescent's aching, dizzy, and equivocal passions—a love which is more like dread (lines 67–72, 75–85: this was his state of mind on the occasion of his first visit); his present state (lines 85 ff.), in which for the first time he adds thought to sense. All his knowledge of human suffering, so painfully acquired in the interim, chastens him while it enriches the visible scene like a chord of music, and he has gained also awareness of an immanent "presence" which links his mind and all the elements of the external world.

3. Lose heart.

4. The fact that apparent changes in the sensible world have turned out to be projected by the changing mind of the observer gives evidence that the faculties "half create" the world; the part that is "perceived" (line 107) is what has remained unchanged between the two visits. This view that the "creative sensibility" contributes to its own perceptions is often reiterated in the early books of *The Prelude*.

5. "Genial" is here the adjectival form of the noun "genius" ("native powers"). The sense of lines 111–13 is: "Perhaps, even if I had not learned to look at nature in the way I have just described, I would not have suffered a decay in my creative powers."

For thou art with me here upon the banks
Of this fair river; thou my dearest Friend,[6]   115
My dear, dear Friend; and in thy voice I catch
The language of my former heart, and read
My former pleasures in the shooting lights
Of thy wild eyes. Oh! yet a little while
May I behold in thee what I was once,   120
My dear, dear Sister! and this prayer I make,
Knowing that Nature never did betray
The heart that loved her; 'tis her privilege,
Through all the years of this our life, to lead
From joy to joy: for she can so inform   125
The mind that is within us, so impress
With quietness and beauty, and so feed
With lofty thoughts, that neither evil tongues,
Rash judgments, nor the sneers of selfish men,
Nor greetings where no kindness is, nor all   130
The dreary intercourse of daily life,
Shall e'er prevail against us, or disturb
Our cheerful faith, that all which we behold
Is full of blessings. Therefore let the moon
Shine on thee in thy solitary walk;   135
And let the misty mountain winds be free
To blow against thee: and, in after years,
When these wild ecstasies shall be matured
Into a sober pleasure; when thy mind
Shall be a mansion for all lovely forms,   140
Thy memory be as a dwelling place
For all sweet sounds and harmonies; oh! then,
If solitude, or fear, or pain, or grief
Should be thy portion, with what healing thoughts
Of tender joy wilt thou remember me,   145
And these my exhortations! Nor, perchance—
If I should be where I no more can hear
Thy voice, nor catch from thy wild eyes these gleams
Of past existence[7]—wilt thou then forget
That on the banks of this delightful stream   150
We stood together; and that I, so long
A worshiper of Nature, hither came
Unwearied in that service; rather say
With warmer love—oh! with far deeper zeal
Of holier love. Nor wilt thou then forget,   155
That after many wanderings, many years
Of absence, these steep woods and lofty cliffs,
And this green pastoral landscape, were to me
More dear, both for themselves and for thy sake!

1798   1798

---

6. His sister Dorothy.
7. I.e., his own "past experience" five years before; see lines 116–19.

Preface to *Lyrical Ballads* (1802)

To the first edition of *Lyrical Ballads*, published jointly with Coleridge in 1798, Wordsworth prefixed an "Advertisement" which asserted that the majority of the poems were "to be considered as experiments" to determine "how far the language of conversation in the middle and lower classes of society is adapted to the purposes of poetic pleasure." In the second, two-volume edition of 1800 Wordsworth, relying on frequent conversations with Coleridge, expanded the Advertisement into a Preface which justified the new poetry not as experiments, but by reference to the principles of all good poetry. The Preface was enlarged for the third edition of *Lyrical Ballads*, published two years later; this version of 1802 is the one that is reprinted here.

The Preface deserves its reputation as a revolutionary manifesto in the theory of poetry. Like most radical statements, however, it claims to go back to the implicit principles which informed the great poetry of the past but have been perverted in recent practice. Most discussions of the Preface, following the lead of Coleridge in his *Biographia Literaria*, have focused on Wordsworth's assertions about the valid language of poetry, on which he bases his attack on the "poetic diction" of 18th-century poets. As Coleridge pointed out, Wordsworth's argument about this issue is far from clear. It is apparent, however, that Wordsworth undertook to overthrow the basic theory, as well as the reigning practice, of neoclassic poetry. That is, his Preface implicitly denies the assumption that the poetic genres constitute a hierarchy, from epic and tragedy at the top down through comedy, satire, pastoral, to the short lyric at the lower reaches of the poetic scale; he also rejects the traditional principle of "decorum," according to which the subject-matter (especially the social class of the protagonists) and the level of diction of a poem must conform to the status of the literary kind on the poetic scale.

When Wordsworth asserted in the Preface that he deliberately chose to represent "incidents and situations from common life," he translated his democratic sympathies into critical terms, justifying his use of peasants, children, outcasts, criminals, and idiot boys as serious subjects of poetic and even tragic concern. He also undertook to write in "a selection of language really used by men," on the grounds that there can be no "essential difference between the language of prose and metrical composition." In making this claim, Wordsworth subverted the neoclassic principle that the language of a poem must be elevated over standard speech by a special diction and by artful figures of speech, in order to match the language to the height and dignity of a particular genre. Wordsworth's own views about the valid language of poetry are based on the new and radical premise that "all good poetry is the spontaneous overflow of powerful feelings"—spontaneous, that is, at the moment of composition, even though the process is influenced by prior thought and acquired poetic skill. The equivalence which Wordsworth claims, therefore, between the valid language of poems and the prose language "really spoken by men" is not one of vocabulary nor of syntax, but an equivalence in emotional genesis—both, according to Wordsworth, are not contrived and artful constructions, but originate spontaneously, as the words and figures which, as Keats later put it, are "the true voice of feeling."

Wordsworth's assertions about the materials and diction of poetry have been immensely influential in expanding the range of serious literature to include the common man and ordinary things and events, as well as in justifying a poetry of sincerity rather than of artifice, expressed in the ordinary language of its time. But in the long view, other aspects of his Preface have been no less significant in establishing its importance, not only as a turning point in English criticism but also as a central document in modern culture. Wordsworth attributed to imaginative literature the primary role in keeping man emotionally alive and morally sensitive—that is, keeping him essentially human—in the face of the pressures of a technological and increasingly urban society, with its mass media and mass culture that threaten, as he presciently foresaw, to blunt the mind's "discriminatory powers" and to "reduce it to a state of almost savage torpor." However radical their literary application by Wordsworth, the values which permeate his Preface are the central humanistic values of the 18th-century Enlightenment—that is, the normative reference to that which is essential, simple, universal, and permanent in human nature. The great subjects of poetry, Wordsworth claims, are "the essential passions of the heart" and "the great and simple affections," as these qualities interact with "the beautiful and permanent forms of nature" and are expressed in a "naked and simple" language that is "adapted to interest mankind permanently." The great poet is not the practitioner of an artistic craft designed to satisfy the refined "taste" of a literary connoisseur. He is instead, Wordsworth says in a memorable phrase, "a man speaking to men," who is actuated by and affirms the primal human values—the joy of life, reverence for all manifestations of life, and the grandeur of the pleasure-principle which is the expression of the life-force and the natural sign of any activity that enhances life. The poet, he says, "rejoices more than other men in the spirit of life," and pays homage to "the naked dignity of man" and (in a phrase Wordsworth deliberately echoes from St. Paul) "to the grand elementary principle of pleasure, by which he knows and feels, and lives, and moves." In opposition to all the modern forces that tend to divide—or, as we now say, to "alienate" —man from his own essential nature, from outer nature, and from his fellow men, Wordsworth places the burden of sustaining human connections primarily on the poet: "He is the rock of defense of human nature; an upholder and preserver, carrying everywhere with him relationship and love."

From Preface to *Lyrical Ballads, with Pastoral and Other Poems* (1802)

The first volume of these poems has already been submitted to general perusal. It was published, as an experiment, which, I hoped, might be of some use to ascertain, how far, by fitting to metrical arrangement a selection of the real language of men in a state of vivid sensation, that sort of pleasure and that quantity of pleasure may be imparted, which a poet may rationally endeavor to impart.

I had formed no very inaccurate estimate of the probable effect of those poems: I flattered myself that they who should be pleased with them would read them with more than common pleasure: and, on the other hand, I was well aware, that by those who should dislike them they would be read with more than common dislike. The result has differed from my expectation in this only, that I have pleased a greater number, than I ventured to hope I should please.

For the sake of variety, and from a consciousness of my own weakness, I was induced to request the assistance of a friend, who furnished me with the poems of the *Ancient Mariner*, the *Foster-Mother's Tale*, the *Nightingale*, and the poem entitled *Love*. I should not, however, have requested this assistance, had I not believed that the poems of my friend would in a great measure have the same tendency as my own, and that, though there would be found a difference, there would be found no discordance in the colors of our style; as our opinions on the subject of poetry do almost entirely coincide.[1]

Several of my friends are anxious for the success of these poems from a belief, that, if the views with which they were composed were indeed realized, a class of poetry would be produced, well adapted to interest mankind permanently, and not unimportant in the multiplicity, and in the quality of its moral relations: and on this account they have advised me to prefix a systematic defense of the theory upon which the poems were written. But I was unwilling to undertake the task, because I knew that on this occasion the reader would look coldly upon my arguments, since I might be suspected of having been principally influenced by the selfish and foolish hope of *reasoning* him into an approbation of these particular poems: and I was still more unwilling to undertake the task, because, adequately to display my opinions, and fully to enforce my arguments, would require a space wholly disproportionate to the nature of a preface. For to treat the subject with the clearness and coherence, of which I believe it susceptible, it would be necessary to give a full account of the present state of the public taste in this country, and to determine how far this taste is healthy or depraved; which, again, could not be determined, without pointing out, in what manner language and the human mind act and re-act on each other, and without retracing the revolutions, not of literature alone, but likewise of society itself. I have therefore altogether declined to enter regularly upon this defense; yet I am sensible, that there would be some impropriety in abruptly obtruding upon the public,

---

1. "The friend" of course is Coleridge. When he read this preface and the new poems included in this 1802 edition of *Lyrical Ballads*, Coleridge wrote to Robert Southey that although Wordsworth's Preface of 1800 had been "half a child of my own brain," he now suspects that "there is a radical difference in our theoretical opinions respecting poetry—this I shall endeavor to go to the bottom of." The results of this endeavor are Coleridge's discussions of Wordsworth's Preface in *Biographia Literaria*, chapters XIV and XVII.

without a few words of introduction, poems so materially different from those, upon which general approbation is at present bestowed.

It is supposed, that by the act of writing in verse an author makes a formal engagement that he will gratify certain known habits of association; that he not only thus apprises the reader that certain classes of ideas and expressions will be found in his book, but that others will be carefully excluded. This exponent or symbol held forth by metrical language must in different eras of literature have excited very different expectations: for example, in the age of Catullus, Terence and Lucretius, and that of Statius or Claudian;[2] and in our own country, in the age of Shakespeare and Beaumont and Fletcher, and that of Donne and Cowley, or Dryden, or Pope. I will not take upon me to determine the exact import of the promise which by the act of writing in verse an author, in the present day, makes to his reader; but I am certain, it will appear to many persons that I have not fulfilled the terms of an engagement thus voluntarily contracted. They who have been accustomed to the gaudiness and inane phraseology of many modern writers, if they persist in reading this book to its conclusion, will, no doubt, frequently have to struggle with feelings of strangeness and awkwardness: they will look round for poetry, and will be induced to inquire by what species of courtesy these attempts can be permitted to assume that title. I hope therefore the reader will not censure me, if I attempt to state what I have proposed to myself to perform; and also, (as far as the limits of a preface will permit) to explain some of the chief reasons which have determined me in the choice of my purpose: that at least he may be spared any unpleasant feeling of disappointment, and that I myself may be protected from the most dishonorable accusation which can be brought against an author, namely, that of an indolence which prevents him from endeavoring to ascertain what is his duty, or, when his duty is ascertained, prevents him from performing it.

The principal object, then, which I proposed to myself in these poems was to choose incidents and situations from common life, and to relate or describe them, throughout, as far as was possible, in a selection of language really used by men; and, at the same time, to throw over them a certain coloring of imagination, whereby ordinary things should be presented to the mind in an unusual way; and, further, and above all, to make these incidents and situations interesting by tracing in them, truly though not ostentatiously, the primary laws of our nature: chiefly, as far as regards the manner in which we associate ideas in a state of excitement.[3] Low and rustic

2. Wordsworth's implied contrast is between the naturalness and simplicity of the first three Roman poets (who wrote in the last two centuries B.C.) and the elaborate artifice of the last two Roman poets (Statius wrote in the 1st and Claudian in the 4th century A.D.).
3. Cf. Coleridge's account of their plan in *Biographia Literaria*, the beginning of Chapter XIV.

Why W. writes of rural life.

life was generally chosen, because in that condition, the essential passions of the heart find a better soil in which they can attain their maturity, are less under restraint, and speak a plainer and more emphatic language; because in that condition of life our elementary feelings coexist in a state of greater simplicity, and, consequently, may be more accurately contemplated, and more forcibly communicated; because the manners of rural life germinate from those elementary feelings; and, from the necessary character of rural occupations, are more easily comprehended; and are more durable; and lastly, because in that condition the passions of men are incorporated with the beautiful and permanent forms of nature. The language, too, of these men is adopted (purified indeed from what appear to be its real defects, from all lasting and rational causes of dislike or disgust) because such men hourly communicate with the best objects from which the best part of language is originally derived; and because, from their rank in society and the sameness and narrow circle of their intercourse, being less under the influence of social vanity they convey their feelings and notions in simple and unelaborated expressions. Accordingly, such a language, arising out of repeated experience and regular feelings, is a more permanent, and a far more philosophical language, than that which is frequently substituted for it by poets, who think that they are conferring honor upon themselves and their art, in proportion as they separate themselves from the sympathies of men, and indulge in arbitrary and capricious habits of expression, in order to furnish food for fickle tastes, and fickle appetites, of their own creation.[4]

I cannot, however, be insensible of the present outcry against the triviality and meanness both of thought and language, which some of my contemporaries have occasionally introduced into their metrical compositions; and I acknowledge that this defect, where it exists, is more dishonorable to the writer's own character than false refinement or arbitrary innovation, though I should contend at the same time that it is far less pernicious in the sum of its consequences. From such verses the poems in these volumes will be found distinguished at least by one mark of difference, that each of them has a worthy *purpose*. Not that I mean to say, that I always began to write with a distinct purpose formally conceived; but I believe that my habits of meditation have so formed my feelings, as that my descriptions of such objects as strongly excite those feelings, will be found to carry along with them a *purpose*. If in this opinion I am mistaken, I can have little right to the name of a poet. For all good poetry is the spontaneous overflow of powerful

language of W's poetry

Poetry should have a purpose

Definition of poetry 1.

4. "It is worthwhile here to observe that the affecting parts of Chaucer are almost always expressed in language pure and universally intelligible even to this day" [Wordsworth's note].

feelings: but though this be true, poems to which any value can be attached, were never produced on any variety of subjects but by a man, who being possessed of more than usual organic sensibility, had also thought long and deeply. For our continued influxes of feeling are modified and directed by our thoughts, which are indeed the representatives of all our past feelings; and, as by contemplating the relation of these general representatives to each other we discover what is really important to men, so, by the repetition and continuance of this act, our feelings will be connected with important subjects, till at length, if we be originally possessed of much sensibility, such habits of mind will be produced, that, by obeying blindly and mechanically the impulses of those habits, we shall describe objects, and utter sentiments, of such a nature and in such connection with each other, that the understanding of the being to whom we address ourselves, if he be in a healthful state of association, must necessarily be in some degree enlightened, and his affections ameliorated.

I have said that each of these poems has a purpose. I have also informed my reader what this purpose will be found principally to be: namely, to illustrate the manner in which our feelings and ideas are associated in a state of excitement. But, speaking in language somewhat more appropriate, it is to follow the fluxes and refluxes of the mind when agitated by the great and simple affections of our nature. This object I have endeavored in these short essays to attain by various means; by tracing the maternal passion through many of its more subtile windings, as in the poems of the *Idiot Boy* and the *Mad Mother*; by accompanying the last struggles of a human being, at the approach of death, cleaving in solitude to life and society, as in the poem of the *Forsaken Indian*; by showing, as in the stanzas entitled *We Are Seven*, the perplexity and obscurity which in childhood attend our notion of death, or rather our utter inability to admit that notion; or by displaying the strength of fraternal, or to speak more philosophically, of moral attachment when early associated with the great and beautiful objects of nature, as in *The Brothers*; or, as in the Incident of *Simon Lee*, by placing my reader in the way of receiving from ordinary moral sensations another and more salutary impression than we are accustomed to receive from them. It has also been part of my general purpose to attempt to sketch characters under the influence of less impassioned feelings, as in the *Two April Mornings, The Fountain, The Old Man Traveling, The Two Thieves*, &c. characters of which the elements are simple, belonging rather to nature than to manners, such as exist now, and will probably always exist, and which from their constitution may be distinctly and profitably contemplated. I will not abuse the indulgence of my reader by dwelling longer upon this subject;

but it is proper that I should mention one other circumstance which distinguishes these poems from the popular poetry of the day; it is this, that the feeling therein developed gives importance to the action and situation, and not the action and situation to the feeling. My meaning will be rendered perfectly intelligible by referring my reader to the poems entitled *Poor Susan* and the *Childless Father*, particularly to the last stanza of the latter poem.

I will not suffer a sense of false modesty to prevent me from asserting, that I point my reader's attention to this mark of distinction, far less for the sake of these particular poems than from the general importance of the subject. The subject is indeed important! For the human mind is capable of being excited without the application of gross and violent stimulants; and he must have a very faint perception of its beauty and dignity who does not know this, and who does not further know, that one being is elevated above another, in proportion as he possesses this capability. It has therefore appeared to me, that to endeavor to produce or enlarge this capability is one of the best services in which, at any period, a writer can be engaged; but this service, excellent at all times, is especially so at the present day. For a multitude of causes, unknown to former times, are now acting with a combined force to blunt the discriminating powers of the mind, and unfitting it for all voluntary exertion to reduce it to a state of almost savage torpor. The most effective of these causes are the great national events which are daily taking place, and the increasing accumulation of men in cities, where the uniformity of their occupations produces a craving for extraordinary incident, which the rapid communication of intelligence hourly gratifies.[5] To this tendency of life and manners the literature and theatrical exhibitions of the country have conformed themselves. The invaluable works of our elder writers, I had almost said the works of Shakespeare and Milton, are driven into neglect by frantic novels, sickly and stupid German tragedies,[6] and deluges of idle and extravagant stories in verse.—When I think upon this degrading thirst after outrageous stimulation, I am almost ashamed to have spoken of the feeble effort with which I have endeavored to counteract it; and, reflecting upon the magnitude of the general evil, I should be oppressed with no dishonorable melancholy, had I not a deep impression of certain inherent and indestructible qualities of the human mind, and likewise of certain powers in the great and permanent objects that act upon it, which are equally inherent

5. This was the period of the wars against France, of industrial urbanization, and of the rapid proliferation in England of daily newspapers.
6. Wordsworth had in mind the "Gothic" terror novels by writers such as Ann Radcliffe and Mathew Gregory Lewis, and the sentimental melodrama, then immensely popular in England, of August von Kotzebue and his German contemporaries.

and indestructible; and did I not further add to this impression a belief, that the time is approaching when the evil will be systematically opposed, by men of greater powers, and with far more distinguished success.

Having dwelt thus long on the subjects and aim of these poems, I shall request the reader's permission to apprise him of a few circumstances relating to their *style,* in order, among other reasons, that I may not be censured for not having performed what I never attempted. The reader will find that personifications of abstract ideas rarely occur in these volumes; and, I hope, are utterly rejected as an ordinary device to elevate the style, and raise it above prose. I have proposed to myself to imitate, and, as far as is possible, to adopt the very language of men; and assuredly such personifications do not make any natural or regular part of that language. They are, indeed, a figure of speech occasionally prompted by passion, and I have made use of them as such; but I have endeavored utterly to reject them as a mechanical device of style, or as a family language which writers in meter seem to lay claim to be prescription. I have wished to keep my reader in the company of flesh and blood, persuaded that by so doing I shall interest him. I am, however, well aware that others who pursue a different track may interest him likewise; I do not interfere with their claim, I only wish to prefer a different claim of my own. There will also be found in these volumes little of what is usually called poetic diction[7]; I have taken as much pains to avoid it as others ordinarily take to produce it; this I have done for the reason already alleged, to bring my language near to the language of men, and further, because the pleasure which I have proposed to myself to impart is of a kind very different from that which is supposed by many persons to be the proper object of poetry. I do not know how, without being culpably particular, I can give my reader a more exact notion of the style in which I wished these poems to be written, than by informing him that I have at all times endeavored to look steadily at my subject, consequently, I hope that there is in these poems little falsehood of description, and that my ideas are expressed in language fitted to their respective importance. Something I must have gained by this practice, as it is friendly to one property of all good poetry, namely good sense; but it has necessarily cut me off from a large portion of phrases and figures of speech which from father to son have long been regarded as the common inheritance of poets. I have also thought it expedient to restrict myself still further, having abstained from the use of many expressions, in themselves proper and beautiful, but which

---

7. In the sense of words, phrases, and figures of speech, not commonly used in conversation or prose, which are re- garded as especially appropriate to poetry.

have been foolishly repeated by bad poets, till such feelings of disgust are connected with them as it is scarcely possible by any art of association to overpower.

If in a poem there should be found a series of lines, or even a single line, in which the language, though naturally arranged, and according to the strict laws of meter, does not differ from that of prose, there is a numerous class of critics, who, when they stumble upon these prosaisms, as they call them, imagine that they have made a notable discovery, and exult over the poet as over a man ignorant of his own profession. Now these men would establish a canon of criticism which the reader will conclude he must utterly reject, if he wishes to be pleased with these volumes. And it would be a most easy task to prove to him, that not only the language of a large portion of every good poem, even of the most elevated character, must necessarily, except with reference to the meter, in no respect differ from that of good prose, but likewise that some of the most interesting parts of the best poems will be found to be strictly the language of prose, when prose is well written. The truth of this assertion might be demonstrated by innumerable passages from almost all the poetical writings, even of Milton himself. I have not space for much quotation; but, to illustrate the subject in a general manner, I will here adduce a short composition of Gray, who was at the head of those who, by their reasonings, have attempted to widen the space of separation betwixt prose and metrical composition, and was more than any other man curiously elaborate in the structure of his own poetic diction.[8]

> In vain to me the smiling mornings shine,
> And reddening Phoebus lifts his golden fire:
> The birds in vain their amorous descant join,
> Or cheerful fields resume their green attire.
> These ears, alas! for other notes repine;
> *A different object do these eyes require;*
> *My lonely anguish melts no heart but mine;*
> *And in my breast the imperfect joys expire;*
> Yet morning smiles the busy race to cheer,
> And new-born pleasure brings to happier men;
> The fields to all their wonted tribute bear;
> To warm their little loves the birds complain.
> *I fruitless mourn to him that cannot hear,*
> *And weep the more because I weep in vain.*

It will easily be perceived that the only part of this sonnet which is of any value is the lines printed in italics: it is equally obvious, that,

<hr>

8. Thomas Gray had written, in a letter to Richard West, that "the language of the age is never the language of poetry." The poem that follows is Gray's *Sonnet on the Death of Richard West.*

except in the rhyme, and in the use of the single word "fruitless" for fruitlessly, which is so far a defect, the language of these lines does in no respect differ from that of prose.

By the foregoing quotation I have shown that the language of prose may yet be well adapted to poetry; and I have previously asserted that a large portion of the language of every good poem can in no respect differ from that of good prose. I will go further. I do not doubt that it may be safely affirmed, that there neither is, nor can be, any essential difference between the language of prose and metrical composition. We are fond of tracing the resemblance between poetry and painting, and, accordingly, we call them sisters: but where shall we find bonds of connection sufficiently strict to typify the affinity betwixt metrical and prose composition? They both speak by and to the same organs; the bodies in which both of them are clothed may be said to be of the same substance, their affections are kindred, and almost identical, not necessarily differing even in degree; poetry[9] sheds no tears "such as Angels weep,"[1] but natural and human tears; she can boast of no celestial Ichor[2] that distinguishes her vital juices from those of prose; the same human blood circulates through the veins of them both.

Taking up the subject, then, upon general grounds, I ask what is meant by the word "poet"? What is a poet? To whom does he address himself? And what language is to be expected from him? He is a man speaking to men: a man, it is true, endued with more lively sensibility, more enthusiasm and tenderness, who has a greater knowledge of human nature, and a more comprehensive soul, than are supposed to be common among mankind; a man pleased with his own passions and volitions, and who rejoices more than other men in the spirit of life that is in him; delighting to contemplate similar volitions and passions as manifested in the goings-on of the universe, and habitually impelled to create them where he does not find them. To these qualities he has added a disposition to be affected more than other men by absent things as if they were present; an ability of conjuring up in himself passions, which are indeed far from being the same as those produced by real events, yet (especially in those parts of the general sympathy which are pleasing and delightful) do more nearly resemble the passions pro-

---

9. "I here use the word 'Poetry' (though against my own judgment) as opposed to the word prose, and synonymous with metrical composition. But much confusion has been introduced into criticism by this contradistinction of poetry and prose, instead of the more philosophical one of poetry and matter of fact, or science. The only strict antithesis to prose is meter; nor is this, in truth, a *strict* antithesis; because lines and passages of meter so naturally occur in writing prose that it would be scarcely possible to avoid them, even were it desirable" [Wordsworth's note].
1. *Paradise Lost* I. 620.
2. In Greek mythology, the fluid in the veins of the gods.

duced by real events, than anything which, from the motions of
their own minds merely, other men are accustomed to feel in themselves; whence, and from practice, he has acquired a greater readiness and power in expressing what he thinks and feels, and especially those thoughts and feelings which, by his own choice, or from
the structure of his own mind, arise in him without immediate
external excitement.

But, whatever portion of this faculty we may suppose even the
greatest poet to possess, there cannot be a doubt but that the language which it will suggest to him, must, in liveliness and truth, fall
far short of that which is uttered by men in real life, under the
actual pressure of those passions, certain shadows of which the poet
thus produces, or feels to be produced, in himself. However exalted
a notion we would wish to cherish of the character of a poet, it is
obvious, that, while he describes and imitates passions, his situation
is altogether slavish and mechanical, compared with the freedom
and power of real and substantial action and suffering. So that it
will be the wish of the poet to bring his feelings near to those of
the persons whose feelings he describes, nay, for short spaces of
time perhaps, to let himself slip into an entire delusion, and even
confound and identify his own feelings with theirs; modifying only
the language which is thus suggested to him, by a consideration
that he describes for a particular purpose, that of giving pleasure.
Here, then, he will apply the principle on which I have so much
insisted, namely, that of selection; on this he will depend for removing what would otherwise be painful or disgusting in the passion; he
will feel that there is no necessity to trick out or to elevate nature:
and, the more industriously he applies this principle, the deeper will
be his faith that no words, which his fancy or imagination can suggest, will be to be compared with those which are the emanations
of reality and truth.

But it may be said by those who do not object to the general
spirit of these remarks, that, as it is impossible for the poet to produce upon all occasions language as exquisitely fitted for the passion
as that which the real passion itself suggests, it is proper that he
should consider himself as in the situation of a translator, who
deems himself justified when he substitutes excellences of another
kind for those which are unattainable by him; and endeavor occasionally to surpass his original, in order to make some amends for
the general inferiority to which he feels that he must submit. But
this would be to encourage idleness and unmanly despair. Further,
it is the language of men who speak of what they do not understand; who talk of poetry as a matter of amusement and idle pleasure; who will converse with us as gravely about a *taste* for poetry, as
they express it, as if it were a thing as indifferent as a taste for

rope-dancing, or Frontiniac[3] or sherry. Aristotle, I have been told, hath said, that poetry is the most philosophic of all writing:[4] it is so: its object is truth, not individual and local, but general, and operative; not standing upon external testimony, but carried alive into the heart by passion; truth which is its own testimony, which gives strength and divinity to the tribunal to which it appeals, and receives them from the same tribunal. Poetry is the image of man and nature. The obstacles which stand in the way of the fidelity of the biographer and historian, and of their consequent utility, are incalculably greater than those which are to be encountered by the poet who has an adequate notion of the dignity of his art. The poet writes under one restriction only, namely, that of the necessity of giving immediate pleasure to a human being possessed of that information which may be expected from him, not as a lawyer, a physician, a mariner, an astronomer or a natural philosopher, but as a man. Except this one restriction, there is no object standing between the poet and the image of things; between this, and the biographer and historian there are a thousand.

Nor let this necessity of producing immediate pleasure be considered as a degradation of the poet's art. It is far otherwise. It is an acknowledgment of the beauty of the universe, an acknowledgment the more sincere, because it is not formal, but indirect; it is a task light and easy to him who looks at the world in the spirit of love: further, it is a homage paid to the native and naked dignity of man, to the grand elementary principle of pleasure, by which he knows, and feels, and lives, and moves.[5] We have no sympathy but what is propagated by pleasure: I would not be misunderstood; but wherever we sympathize with pain it will be found that the sympathy is produced and carried on by subtle combinations with pleasure. We have no knowledge, that is, no general principles drawn from the contemplation of particular facts, but what has been built up by pleasure, and exists in us by pleasure alone. The man of science, the chemist and mathematician, whatever difficulties and disgusts they may have had to struggle with, know and feel this. However painful may be the objects with which the anatomist's knowledge is connected, he feels that his knowledge is pleasure; and where he has no pleasure he has no knowledge. What then does the poet? He considers man and the objects that surround him as acting and re-acting upon each other, so as to produce an infinite complexity of pain and pleasure; he considers man in his own nature and in his ordinary life as contemplating this with a certain quantity of immediate knowledge, with certain convictions, intuitions, and deductions

3. A sweet wine made from muscat grapes.
4. Aristotle in fact said that "poetry is more philosophic than history, since its statements are of the nature of universals, whereas those of history are singulars" (*Poetics* 1451b).
5. A bold echo of the words of St. Paul, that in God "we live, and move, and have our being" (Acts xvii.28).

which by habit become of the nature of intuitions; he considers him as looking upon this complex scene of ideas and sensations, and finding everywhere objects that immediately excite in him sympathies which, from the necessities of his nature, are accompanied by an overbalance of enjoyment.

To this knowledge which all men carry about with them, and to these sympathies in which without any other discipline than that of our daily life we are fitted to take delight, the poet principally directs his attention. He considers man and nature as essentially adapted to each other,[6] and the mind of man as naturally the mirror of the fairest and most interesting qualities of nature. And thus the poet, prompted by this feeling of pleasure which accompanies him through the whole course of his studies, converses with general nature with affections akin to those, which, through labor and length of time, the man of science has raised up in himself, by conversing with those particular parts of nature which are the objects of his studies. The knowledge both of the poet and the man of science is pleasure; but the knowledge of the one cleaves to us as a necessary part of our existence, our natural and unalienable inheritance; the other is a personal and individual acquisition, slow to come to us, and by no habitual and direct sympathy connecting us with our fellow-beings. The man of science seeks truth as a remote and unknown benefactor; he cherishes and loves it in his solitude: the poet, singing a song in which all human beings join with him, rejoices in the presence of truth as our visible friend and hourly companion. Poetry is the breath and finer spirit of all knowledge; it is the impassioned expression which is in the countenance of all science. Emphatically may it be said of the poet, as Shakespeare hath said of man, "that he looks before and after."[7] He is the rock of defense of human nature; an upholder and preserver, carrying everywhere with him relationship and love. In spite of difference of soil and climate, of language and manners, of laws and customs, in spite of things silently gone out of mind and things violently destroyed, the poet binds together by passion and knowledge the vast empire of human society, as it is spread over the whole earth, and over all time. The objects of the poet's thoughts are everywhere; though the eyes and senses of man are, it is true, his favorite guides, yet he will follow wheresoever he can find an atmosphere of sensation in which to move his wings. Poetry is the first and last of all knowledge—it is as immortal as the heart of man. If the labors of men and science should ever create any material revolution, direct or indirect, in our condition, and in the impressions which we habitually receive, the poet will sleep then no more than at present, but he will be ready

6. On the mutual adaptation of man's mind and nature, see Wordsworth's Prospectus to *The Recluse*, lines 63–71.
7. *Hamlet* IV.iv.37.

to follow the steps of the man of science, not only in those general indirect effects, but he will be at his side, carrying sensation into the midst of the objects of the science itself. The remotest discoveries of the chemist, the botanist, or mineralogist, will be as proper objects of the poet's art as any upon which it can be employed, if the time should ever come when these things shall be familiar to us, and the relations under which they are contemplated by the followers of these respective sciences shall be manifestly and palpably material to us as enjoying and suffering beings.[8] If the time should ever come when what is now called science, thus familiarized to men, shall be ready to put on, as it were, a form of flesh and blood, the poet will lend his divine spirit to aid the transfiguration, and will welcome the being thus produced, as a dear and genuine inmate of the household of man.—It is not, then, to be supposed that anyone, who holds that sublime notion of poetry which I have attempted to convey, will break in upon the sanctity and truth of his pictures by transitory and accidental ornaments, and endeavor to excite admiration of himself by arts, the necessity of which must manifestly depend upon the assumed meanness of his subject.

What I have thus far said applies to poetry in general; but especially to those parts of composition where the poet speaks through the mouths of his characters; and upon this point it appears to have such weight that I will conclude, there are few persons of good sense, who would not allow that the dramatic parts of composition are defective, in proportion as they deviate from the real language of nature, and are colored by a diction of the poet's own, either peculiar to him as an individual poet, or belonging simply to poets in general, to a body of men who, from the circumstance of their compositions being in meter, it is expected will employ a particular language.

It is not, then, in the dramatic parts of composition that we look for this distinction of language; but still it may be proper and necessary where the poet speaks to us in his own person and character. To this I answer by referring my reader to the description which I have before given of a poet. Among the qualities which I have enumerated as principally conducing to form a poet, is implied nothing differing in kind from other men, but only in degree. The sum of what I have there said is, that the poet is chiefly distinguished from other men by a greater promptness to think and feel without immediate external excitement, and a greater power in expressing such thoughts and feelings as are produced in him in that manner. But these passions and thoughts and feelings are the general passions and thoughts and feelings of men. And with what are they con-

8. Wordsworth is at least right in anticipating the poetry of the machine; he himself wrote an early instance, the sonnet *Steamboats, Viaducts, and Railways.*

nected? Undoubtedly with our moral sentiments and animal sensations, and with the causes which excite these; with the operations of the elements and the appearances of the visible universe; with storm and sunshine, with the revolutions of the seasons, with cold and heat, with loss of friends and kindred, with injuries and resentments, gratitude and hope, with fear and sorrow. These, and the like, are the sensations and objects which the poet describes, as they are the sensations of other men, and the objects which interest them. The poet thinks and feels in the spirit of the passions of men. How, then, can his language differ in any material degree from that of all other men who feel vividly and see clearly? It might be *proved* that it is impossible. But supposing that this were not the case, the poet might then be allowed to use a peculiar language when expressing his feelings for his own gratification, or that of men like himself. But poets do not write for poets alone, but for men. Unless therefore we are advocates for that admiration which depends upon ignorance, and that pleasure which arises from hearing what we do not understand, the poet must descend from this supposed height, and, in order to excite rational sympathy, he must express himself as other men express themselves. * * *

I have said that poetry is the spontaneous overflow of powerful feelings: it takes its origin from emotion recollected in tranquility: the emotion is contemplated till by a species of reaction the tranquility gradually disappears, and an emotion, kindred to that which was before the subject of contemplation, is gradually produced, and does itself actually exist in the mind. In this mood successful composition generally begins, and in a mood similar to this it is carried on; but the emotion, of whatever kind and in whatever degree, from various causes is qualified by various pleasures, so that in describing any passions whatsoever, which are voluntarily described, the mind will upon the whole be in a state of enjoyment. Now, if nature be thus cautious in preserving in a state of enjoyment a being thus employed, the poet ought to profit by the lesson thus held forth to him, and ought especially to take care, that whatever passions he communicates to his reader, those passions, if his reader's mind be sound and vigorous, should always be accompanied with an overbalance of pleasure. Now the music of harmonious metrical language, the sense of difficulty overcome, and the blind association of pleasure which has been previously received from works of rhyme or meter of the same or similar construction, an indistinct perception perpetually renewed of language closely resembling that of real life, and yet, in the circumstance of meter, differing from it so widely, all these imperceptibly make up a complex feeling of delight, which is of the most important use in tempering the painful feeling which will always be found intermingled with powerful descriptions of the deeper passions. This effect is always produced in pathetic and impassioned poetry; while, in lighter compositions, the ease and gracefulness with which the poet manages his numbers are themselves confessedly a principal source of the gratification of the reader. I might perhaps include all which it is *necessary* to say upon this subject by affirming, what few persons will deny, that, of two descriptions, either of passions, manners, or characters, each of them equally well executed, the one in prose and the other in verse, the verse will be read a hundred times where the prose is read once.

* * *

I know that nothing would have so effectually contributed to further the end which I have in view, as to have shown of what kind the pleasure is, and how the pleasure is produced, which is confessedly produced by metrical composition essentially different from that which I have here endeavored to recommend: for the reader will say that he has been pleased by such composition; and what can I do more for him? The power of any art is limited; and he will suspect, that, if I propose to furnish him with new friends, it is only upon condition of his abandoning his old friends. Besides, as I have said, the reader is himself conscious of the pleasure which he has received from such composition, composition to which he has peculiarly attached the endearing name of poetry; and all men feel an habitual gratitude, and something of an honorable bigotry for the objects which have long continued to please them; we not only wish to be pleased, but to be pleased in that particular way in which we have been accustomed to be pleased. There is a host of arguments in these feelings; and I should be the less able to combat them successfully, as I am willing to allow, that, in order entirely to enjoy the poetry which I am recommending, it would be necessary to give up much of what is ordinarily enjoyed. But, would my limits have permitted me to point out how this pleasure is produced, I might have removed many obstacles, and assisted my reader in perceiving that the powers of language are not so limited as he may suppose; and that it is possible that poetry may give other enjoyments, of a purer, more lasting, and more exquisite nature. This part of my subject I have not altogether neglected; but it has been less my present aim to prove, that the interest excited by some other kinds of poetry is less vivid, and less worthy of the nobler powers of the mind, than to offer reasons for presuming, that, if the object which I have proposed to myself were adequately attained, a species of poetry would be produced, which is genuine poetry; in its nature well adapted to interest mankind permanently, and likewise important in the multiplicity and quality of its moral relations.

From what has been said, and from a perusal of the poems, the reader will be able clearly to perceive the object which I have proposed to myself: he will determine how far I have attained this object; and, what is a much more important question, whether it be worth attaining: and upon the decision of these two questions will rest my claim to the approbation of the public.

1802

Strange Fits of Passion Have I Known[1]

Strange fits of passion have I known:
And I will dare to tell,
But in the Lover's ear alone,
What once to me befell.

When she I loved looked every day   5
Fresh as a rose in June,
I to her cottage bent my way,
Beneath an evening moon.

Upon the moon I fixed my eye,
All over the wide lea;   10
With quickening pace my horse drew nigh
Those paths so dear to me.

And now we reached the orchard plot;
And, as we climbed the hill,
The sinking moon to Lucy's cot   15
Came near, and nearer still.

In one of those sweet dreams I slept,
Kind Nature's gentlest boon!
And all the while my eyes I kept
On the descending moon.   20

My horse moved on; hoof after hoof
He raised, and never stopped:
When down behind the cottage roof,
At once, the bright moon dropped.

What fond and wayward thoughts will slide   25
Into a Lover's head!
"O mercy!" to myself I cried,
"If Lucy should be dead!"[2]

1799   1800

1. This and the four following pieces are often grouped by editors as the "Lucy poems," even though *A Slumber Did My Spirit Steal* does not identify the "she" who is the subject of that poem. All but the last were written in 1799, while Wordsworth and Dorothy were in Germany, and homesick. There has been diligent speculation about the identity of Lucy, but it remains speculation; the one certainty is that she is not the girl of Wordsworth's *Lucy Gray*, below. "Fits of passion": in an archaic sense, "sudden moods of intense grief."

2. An additional stanza in an earlier MS. version demonstrates how a poem may profit by omitting a passage which is, in itself, excellent poetry: "I told her this: her laughter light / Is ringing in my ears; / And when I think upon that night / My eyes are dim with tears."

She Dwelt Among the Untrodden Ways

She dwelt among the untrodden ways
    Beside the springs of Dove.[3]
A Maid whom there were none to praise
    And very few to love;

A violet by a mossy stone   5
    Half hidden from the eye!
—Fair as a star, when only one
    Is shining in the sky.

She lived unknown, and few could know
    When Lucy ceased to be;   10
But she is in her grave, and, oh,
    The difference to me!

1799   1800

Three Years She Grew

Three years she grew in sun and shower,
Then Nature said, "A lovelier flower
On earth was never sown;
This Child I to myself will take;
She shall be mine, and I will make   5
A Lady of my own.[4]

"Myself will to my darling be
Both law and impulse: and with me
The Girl, in rock and plain,
In earth and heaven, in glade and bower,   10
Shall feel an overseeing power
To kindle or restrain.

"She shall be sportive as the fawn
That wild with glee across the lawn
Or up the mountain springs;   15
And hers shall be the breathing balm,
And hers the silence and the calm
Of mute insensate things.

"The floating clouds their state shall lend
To her; for her the willow bend;   20
Nor shall she fail to see
Even in the motions of the Storm
Grace that shall mold the Maiden's form
By silent sympathy.

3. There are several rivers by this
name in England, including one in the
Lake Country.
4. I.e., Lucy was three years old when

Nature made this promise; line 37 makes
clear that Lucy had reached the maturity
foretold in the sixth stanza when she
died.

"The stars of midnight shall be dear   25
To her; and she shall lean her ear
In many a secret place
Where rivulets dance their wayward round,
And beauty born of murmuring sound
Shall pass into her face.   30

"And vital feelings of delight
Shall rear her form to stately height,
Her virgin bosom swell;
Such thoughts to Lucy I will give
While she and I together live   35
Here in this happy dell."

Thus Nature spake—the work was done—
How soon my Lucy's race was run!
She died, and left to me
This heath, this calm, and quiet scene;   40
The memory of what has been,
And never more will be.

1799   1800

A Slumber Did My Spirit Seal

A slumber did my spirit seal;
   I had no human fears:
She seemed a thing that could not feel
   The touch of earthly years.

No motion has she now, no force;   5
   She neither hears nor sees;
Rolled round in earth's diurnal[1] course,
   With rocks, and stones, and trees.

1799   1800

I Traveled Among Unknown Men

I traveled among unknown men,
   In lands beyond the sea;
Nor, England! did I know till then
   What love I bore to thee.

'Tis past, that melancholy dream!   5
   Nor will I quit thy shore
A second time; for still I seem
   To love thee more and more.

Among thy mountains did I feel
   The joy of my desire;   10
And she I cherished turned her wheel
   Beside an English fire.

1. Daily.

Thy mornings showed, thy nights concealed,
    The bowers where Lucy played;
And thine too is the last green field   15
    That Lucy's eyes surveyed.

ca. 1801   1807

Lucy Gray[1]

OR SOLITUDE

Oft I had heard of Lucy Gray:
And, when I crossed the wild,
I chanced to see at break of day
The solitary child.

No mate, no comrade Lucy knew;   5
    She dwelt on a wide moor,
—The sweetest thing that ever grew
    Beside a human door!

You yet may spy the fawn at play,
    The hare upon the green;
But the sweet face of Lucy Gray   10
    Will never more be seen.

"Tonight will be a stormy night—
    You to the town must go;
And take a lantern, Child, to light   15
    Your mother through the snow."

"That, Father! will I gladly do:
    'Tis scarcely afternoon—
The minster[2] clock has just struck two,
    And yonder is the moon!"   20

At this the Father raised his hook,
    And snapped a faggot band;[3]
He plied his work—and Lucy took
    The lantern in her hand.

Not blither is the mountain roe;   25
    With many a wanton stroke
Her feet disperse the powdery snow,
    That rises up like smoke.

The storm came on before its time;
    She wandered up and down;   30

1. Written in 1799 while Wordsworth was in Germany, and founded on a true account of a young girl who drowned when she lost her way in a snowstorm. "The body however was found in the canal. The way in which the incident was treated and the spiritualizing of the character might furnish hints for contrasting the imaginative influences which I have endeavored to throw over common life with Crabbe's matter-of-fact style of treating subjects of the same kind" (Wordsworth). Compare Wordsworth's statement (in the Preface to Lyrical Ballads) of his undertaking to throw over ordinary things "a certain coloring of imagination."
2. Church.
3. Cord binding a bundle of sticks to be used for fuel.

And many a hill did Lucy climb,
But never reached the town.

The wretched parents all that night
Went shouting far and wide;
But there was neither sound nor sight   35
To serve them for a guide.

At daybreak on a hill they stood
That overlooked the moor;
And thence they saw the bridge of wood,
A furlong⁴ from their door.   40

They wept—and, turning homeward, cried,
"In heaven we all shall meet";
—When in the snow the mother spied
The print of Lucy's feet.

Then downwards from the steep hill's edge   45
They tracked the footmarks small;
And through the broken hawthorn hedge,
And by the long stone wall;

And then an open field they crossed:
The marks were still the same;   50
They tracked them on, nor ever lost;
And to the bridge they came.

They followed from the snowy bank
Those footmarks, one by one,
Into the middle of the plank;   55
And further there were none!

—Yet some maintain that to this day
She is a living child;
That you may see sweet Lucy Gray
Upon the lonesome wild.   60

O'er rough and smooth she trips along,
And never looks behind;
And sings a solitary song
That whistles in the wind.

1799   1800

The Two April Mornings¹

We walked along, while bright and red
Uprose the morning sun;
And Matthew stopped, he looked, and said,
"The will of God be done!"

4. One eighth of a mile.

1. In this poem and another called *Matthew*, both written in 1799, the central figure is named after a onetime schoolmaster at Hawkshead School, which Wordsworth attended.

A village schoolmaster was he,   5
With hair of glittering gray;
As blithe a man as you could see
On a spring holiday.

And on that morning, through the grass,
And by the steaming rills,[2]   10
We traveled merrily, to pass
A day among the hills.

"Our work," said I, "was well begun,
Then, from thy breast what thought,
Beneath so beautiful a sun,   15
So sad a sigh has brought?"

A second time did Matthew stop;
And fixing still his eye
Upon the eastern mountaintop,
To me he made reply: 20

"Yon cloud with that long purple cleft
Brings fresh into my mind
A day like this which I have left
Full thirty years behind.

"And just above yon slope of corn   25
Such colors, and no other,
Were in the sky, that April morn,
Of this the very brother.

"With rod and line I sued the sport
Which that sweet season gave,   30
And, to the churchyard come, stopped short
Beside my daughter's grave.

"Nine summers had she scarcely seen,
The pride of all the vale;
And then she sang—she would have been   35
A very nightingale.

"Six feet in earth my Emma lay;
And yet I loved her more,
For so it seemed, than till that day
I e'er had loved before.   40

"And, turning from her grave, I met,
Beside the churchyard yew,
A blooming girl, whose hair was wet
With points of morning dew.

2. Small streams.

"A basket on her head she bare;   45
Her brow was smooth and white:
To see a child so very fair,
It was a pure delight!

"No fountain from its rocky cave
E'er tripped with foot so free;   50
She seemed as happy as a wave
That dances on the sea.

"There came from me a sigh of pain
Which I could ill confine;
I looked at her, and looked again: 55
And did not wish her mine!"

Matthew is in his grave, yet now,
Methinks, I see him stand,
As at that moment, with a bough
Of wilding[3] in his hand.   60

1799   1800

Nutting[1]

————It seems a day
(I speak of one from many singled out)
One of those heavenly days that cannot die;
When, in the eagerness of boyish hope,
I left our cottage threshold, sallying forth   5
With a huge wallet o'er my shoulders slung,
A nutting-crook in hand; and turned my steps
Tow'rd some far distant wood, a figure quaint,
Tricked out in proud disguise of cast-off weeds[2]
Which for that service had been husbanded,   10
By exhortation of my frugal Dame[3]—
Motley accouterment, of power to smile
At thorns, and brakes, and brambles—and, in truth,
More ragged than need was! O'er pathless rocks,
Through beds of matted fern, and tangled thickets, 15
Forcing my way, I came to one dear nook
Unvisited, where not a broken bough
Drooped with its withered leaves, ungracious sign
Of devastation; but the hazels rose
Tall and erect, with tempting clusters hung,   20
A virgin scene!—A little while I stood,
Breathing with such suppression of the heart

3. A wild apple tree.
1. Wordsworth said that this passage, written in Germany in 1798, was "intended as part of a poem on my own mind [i.e., *The Prelude*], but struck out as not being wanted there."

He published it in the second edition of *Lyrical Ballads*, 1800.
2. Clothes.
3. Ann Tyson, with whom Wordsworth lodged while at Hawkshead grammar school.

As joy delights in; and, with wise restraint
Voluptuous, fearless of a rival, eyed
The banquet—or beneath the trees I sate   25
Among the flowers, and with the flowers I played;
A temper known to those who, after long
And weary expectation, have been blessed
With sudden happiness beyond all hope.
Perhaps it was a bower beneath whose leaves   30
The violets of five seasons reappear
And fade, unseen by any human eye;
Where fairy water-breaks[4] do murmur on
Forever; and I saw the sparkling foam,
And—with my cheek on one of those green stones   35
That, fleeced with moss, under the shady trees,
Lay round me, scattered like a flock of sheep—
I heard the murmur and the murmuring sound,
In that sweet mood when pleasure loves to pay
Tribute to ease; and, of its joy secure,   40
The heart luxuriates with indifferent things,
Wasting its kindliness on stocks[5] and stones,
And on the vacant air. Then up I rose,
And dragged to earth both branch and bough, with crash
And merciless ravage: and the shady nook   45
Of hazels, and the green and mossy bower,
Deformed and sullied, patiently gave up
Their quiet being: and, unless I now
Confound my present feelings with the past,
Ere from the mutilated bower I turned   50
Exulting, rich beyond the wealth of kings,
I felt a sense of pain when I beheld
The silent trees, and saw the intruding sky.—
Then, dearest Maiden,[6] move along these shades
In gentleness of heart; with gentle hand   55
Touch—for there is a spirit in the woods.

1798   1800

4. I.e., where the flow of a stream is   mate things.")
broken by rocks.   6. In a manuscript passage, originally
5. Tree stumps. ("Stocks and stones")   intended to lead up to *Nutting*, the
is a conventional expression for "inani- maiden is called Lucy.

The Ruined Cottage   Wordsworth wrote *The Ruined Cottage* in
1797–98, but revised it several times before he finally published an expanded rendering of the story as Book I of *The Excursion*, in 1814. Not
until 1949 was *The Ruined Cottage*, as an independent poem, made available in the fifth volume of *The Poetical Works of William Wordsworth*,
edited by Ernest de Selincourt and Helen Darbishire, who printed a version
known as "MS. B." The version reprinted here is, however, from "MS. D,"

dating 1799 or 1800, as transcribed by Jonathan Wordsworth in *The Music of Humanity: A Critical Study of Wordsworth's "Ruined Cottage"* (1969).

This is a shorter and better poem than the one reprinted in *The Poetical Works.* The latter lacks the great concluding passage, lines 493–538, and includes in Part I more than 250 lines describing the youthful development of the peddler that are extraneous to the narrative proper and soften the hard naturalism of the story by introducing into it, at considerable length, the peddler's faith that nature teaches "deeply the lesson deep of love." The version in the first book of *The Excursion* is longer still, and attempts to mitigate the impact of Margaret's sufferings even more by attributing to her a Christian piety which is conventional rather than deeply realized. In the version reprinted here, however, we confront the blank facts of "a tale of silent suffering"—suffering which is undeserved, unrationalized, and irremissive. Like the narrating poet, we attend in "the impotence of grief" as the peddler describes how Margaret's fierce hope for the return of her husband slowly bends and then breaks her spirit, before destroying her life. Her deterioration under this relentless pressure is a moral one, measured by the bleak details of the correlative deterioration of her untended garden and cottage. The event is "a common tale," and it poses the implicit question, What are we to make of human life, in which such things happen?

The peddler's recovery of heart turns, unexpectedly, on his recognition that this human tragedy takes place within the unceasing and neutral operation—as the narrator says, "the calm oblivious tendencies"—of nature, which silently goes about the process of assimilating the human artifacts that have been wrought from it back into its own independent and continuing life. In a reversal as extreme as Wordsworth could make it, the peddler declares: "I turned away, / And walked along my road in happiness." By his artistry Wordsworth carries us along in imagination so that we too, whatever our own beliefs, feel what it is to be able to look upon and master the fact of human suffering, unsupported by any consoling creed of a beneficent power, whether in or out of nature.

Beyond any of Wordsworth's writings, even *Michael, The Ruined Cottage* demonstrates that distinctive quality which Walter Raleigh identified more than a half century ago as Wordsworth's "calm and almost terrible strength."

The Ruined Cottage

First Part

'Twas Summer and the sun was mounted high.
Along the south the uplands feebly glared
Through a pale steam, and all the northern downs,
In clearer air ascending, shewed far off
Their surfaces with shadows dappled o'er   5
Of deep embattled clouds. Far as the sight
Could reach those many shadows lay in spots
Determined and unmoved, with steady beams
Of clear and pleasant sunshine interposed—

Pleasant to him who on the soft cool grass   10
Extends his careless limbs beside the root
Of some huge oak whose aged branches make
A twilight of their own, a dewy shade
Where the wren warbles while the dreaming man,
Half conscious of that soothing melody,   15
With sidelong eye looks out upon the scene,
By those impending branches made more soft,
More soft and distant.

                                Other lot was mine.
Across a bare wide Common I had toiled
With languid feet which by the slipp'ry ground   20
Were baffled still, and when I stretched myself
On the brown earth my limbs from very heat
Could find no rest, nor my weak arm disperse
The insect host which gathered round my face
And joined their murmurs to the tedious noise   25
Of seeds of bursting gorse that crackled round.
I rose and turned towards a group of trees
Which midway in that level stood alone;
And thither come at length, beneath a shade
Of clustering elms that sprang from the same root   30
I found a ruined house, four naked walls
That stared upon each other. I looked round
And near the door I saw an aged Man,
Alone and stretched upon the cottage bench,
An iron-pointed staff lay at his side.   35
With instantaneous joy I recognized
That pride of nature and of lowly life,
The venerable Armytage, a friend
As dear to me as is the setting sun.

                                Two days before
We had been fellow travelers. I knew   40
That he was in this neighborhood, and now
Delighted found him here in the cool shade.
He lay, his pack of rustic merchandise
Pillowing his head. I guess he had no thought
Of his way-wandering life. His eyes were shut,   45
The shadows of the breezy elms above
Dappled his face. With thirsty heat oppressed
At length I hailed him, glad to see his hat
Bedewed with waterdrops, as if the brim
Had newly scooped a running stream. He rose   50
And pointing to a sunflower, bade me climb
The [   ] wall where that same gaudy flower
Looked out upon the road.

                                It was a plot
Of garden ground now wild, its matted weeds   55
Marked with the steps of those whom as they passed,
The gooseberry trees that shot in long lank slips,

Or currants hanging from their leafless stems
In scanty strings, had tempted to o'erleap
The broken wall. Within that cheerless spot, 60
Where two tall hedgerows of thick alder boughs
Joined in a damp cold nook, I found a well
Half covered up with willow flowers and grass.
I slaked my thirst and to the shady bench
Returned, and while I stood unbonneted 65
To catch the motion of the cooler air,
The old Man said, "I see around me here
Things which you cannot see. We die, my Friend,
Nor we alone, but that which each man loved
And prized in his peculiar nook of earth 70
Dies with him, or is changed, and very soon
Even of the good is no memorial left.
The Poets, in their elegies and songs
Lamenting the departed, call the groves,
They call upon the hills and streams to mourn, 75
And senseless rocks—nor idly, for they speak
In these their invocations with a voice
Obedient to the strong creative power
Of human passion. Sympathies there are
More tranquil, yet perhaps of kindred birth, 80
That steal upon the meditative mind
And grow with thought. Beside yon spring I stood,
And eyed its waters till we seemed to feel
One sadness, they and I. For them a bond
Of brotherhood is broken; time has been 85
When every day the touch of human hand
Disturbed their stillness, and they ministered
To human comfort. When I stooped to drink
A spider's web hung to the water's edge,
And on the wet and slimy footstone lay 90
The useless fragment of a wooden bowl.
It moved my very heart.

    The day has been
When I could never pass this road but she
Who lived within these walls, when I appeared,
A daughter's welcome gave me, and I loved her 95
As my own child. Oh Sir, the good die first,
And they whose hearts are dry as summer dust
Burn to the socket. Many a passenger
Has blessed poor Margaret for her gentle looks
When she upheld the cool refreshment drawn 100
From that forsaken spring, and no one came
But he was welcome, no one went away
But that it seemed she loved him. She is dead,
The worm is on her cheek, and this poor hut,
Stripped of its outward garb of household flowers, 105
Of rose and sweetbriar, offers to the wind
A cold bare wall whose earthy top is tricked

With weeds and the rank spear grass. She is dead,
And nettles rot and adders sun themselves
Where we have sate together while she nursed   110
Her infant at her breast. The unshod colt,
The wandring heifer and the Potter's ass,
Find shelter now within the chimney wall
Where I have seen her evening hearthstone blaze
And through the window spread upon the road   115
Its cheerful light. You will forgive me, sir,
But often on this cottage do I muse
As on a picture, till my wiser mind
Sinks, yielding to the foolishness of grief.

She had a husband, an industrious man,   120
Sober and steady. I have heard her say
That he was up and busy at his loom
In summer ere the mower's scythe had swept
The dewy grass, and in the early spring
Ere the last star had vanished. They who passed   125
At evening, from behind the garden fence
Might hear his busy spade, which he would ply
After his daily work till the daylight
Was gone, and every leaf and flower were lost
In the dark hedges. So they passed their days   130
In peace and comfort, and two pretty babes
Were their best hope next to the God in Heaven.

You may remember, now some ten years gone,
Two blighting seasons when the fields were left
With half a harvest. It pleased heaven to add   135
A worse affliction in the plague of war,
A happy land was stricken to the heart,
'Twas a sad time of sorrow and distress.
A wanderer among the cottages,
I with my pack of winter raiment saw   140
The hardships of that season. Many rich
Sunk down as in a dream among the poor,
And of the poor did many cease to be,
And their place knew them not. Meanwhile, abridged
Of daily comforts, gladly reconciled   145
To numerous self-denials, Margaret
Went struggling on through those calamitous years
With cheerful hope. But ere the second autumn
A fever seized her husband. In disease
He lingered long, and when his strength returned   150
He found the little he had stored to meet
The hour of accident, or crippling age,
Was all consumed. As I have said, 'twas now
A time of trouble: shoals of artisans
Were from their daily labor turned away   155
To hang for bread on parish charity,
They and their wives and children, happier far

Could they have lived as do the little birds
That peck along the hedges, or the kite
That makes her dwelling in the mountain rocks.   160

Ill fared it now with Robert, he who dwelt
In this poor cottage. At his door he stood
And whistled many a snatch of merry tunes
That had no mirth in them, or with his knife
Carved uncouth figures on the heads of sticks,   165
Then idly sought about through every nook
Of house or garden any casual task
Of use or ornament, and with a strange
Amusing but uneasy novelty
He blended where he might the various tasks   170
Of summer, autumn, winter, and of spring.
But this endured not, his good humor soon
Became a weight in which no pleasure was,
And poverty brought on a petted mood
And a sore temper. Day by day he drooped,   175
And he would leave his home, and to the town
Without an errand would he turn his steps,
Or wander here and there among the fields.
One while he would speak lightly of his babes
And with a cruel tongue, at other times   180
He played with them wild freaks of merriment,
And 'twas a piteous thing to see the looks
Of the poor innocent children. 'Every smile,'
Said Margaret to me here beneath these trees,
'Made my heart bleed.' "   185

                At this the old Man paused,
And looking up to those enormous elms
He said, " 'Tis now the hour of deepest noon.
At this still season of repose and peace,
This hour when all things which are not at rest
Are cheerful, while this multitude of flies   190
Fills all the air with happy melody,
Why should a tear be in an old man's eye?
Why should we thus with an untoward mind,
And in the weakness of humanity,
From natural wisdom turn our hearts away,   195
To natural comfort shut our eyes and ears,
And, feeding on disquiet, thus disturb
The calm of Nature with our restless thoughts?"
      END OF THE FIRST PART

Second Part

He spake with somewhat of a solemn tone,
But when he ended there was in his face   200
Such easy cheerfulness, a look so mild,
That for a little time it stole away
All recollection, and that simple tale

Passed from my mind like a forgotten sound.
A while on trivial things we held discourse,   205
To me soon tasteless. In my own despite
I thought of that poor woman as of one
Whom I had known and loved. He had rehearsed
Her homely tale with such familiar power,
With such an active countenance, an eye   210
So busy, that the things of which he spake
Seemed present, and, attention now relaxed,
There was a heartfelt chillness in my veins.
I rose, and turning from that breezy shade
Went out into the open air, and stood   215
To drink the comfort of the warmer sun.
Long time I had not stayed ere, looking round
Upon that tranquil ruin, I returned
And begged of the old man that for my sake
He would resume his story.   220

                                    He replied,
"It were a wantonness, and would demand
Severe reproof, if we were men whose hearts
Could hold vain dalliance with the misery
Even of the dead, contented thence to draw
A momentary pleasure, never marked   225
By reason, barren of all future good.
But we have known that there is often found
In mournful thoughts, and always might be found,
A power to virtue friendly; were't not so
I am a dreamer among men, indeed   230
An idle dreamer. 'Tis a common tale
By moving accidents uncharactered,
A tale of silent suffering, hardly clothed
In bodily form, and to the grosser sense
But ill adapted, scarcely palpable   235
To him who does not think. But at your bidding
I will proceed.

                        While thus it fared with them
To whom this cottage till that hapless year
Had been a blessed home, it was my chance
To travel in a country far remote;   240
And glad I was when, halting by yon gate
That leads from the green lane, again I saw
These lofty elm trees. Long I did not rest:
With many pleasant thoughts I cheered my way
O'er the flat common. At the door arrived,   245
I knocked, and when I entered, with the hope
Of usual greeting, Margaret looked at me
A little while, then turned her head away
Speechless, and sitting down upon a chair
Wept bitterly. I wist not what to do,   250
Or how to speak to her. Poor wretch, at last

She rose from off her seat, and then, oh Sir,
I cannot tell how she pronounced my name.
With fervent love, and with a face of grief
Unutterably helpless, and a look   255
That seemed to cling upon me, she enquired
If I had seen her husband. As she spake
A strange surprise and fear came to my heart,
Nor had I power to answer ere she told
That he had disappeared—just two months gone.   260
He left his house: two wretched days had passed,
And on the third by the first break of light,
Within her casement full in view she saw
A purse of gold.[1] 'I trembled at the sight,'
Said Margaret, 'for I knew it was his hand   265
That placed it there. And on that very day
By one, a stranger, from my husband sent,
The tidings came that he had joined a troop
Of soldiers going to a distant land.
He left me thus. Poor Man, he had not heart   270
To take farewell of me, and he feared
That I should follow with my babes, and sink
Beneath the misery of a soldier's life.'

This tale did Margaret tell with many tears,
And when she ended I had little power   275
To give her comfort, and was glad to take
Such words of hope from her own mouth as served
To cheer us both. But long we had not talked
Ere we built up a pile of better thoughts,
And with a brighter eye she looked around,   280
As if she had been shedding tears of joy.
We parted. It was then the early spring:
I left her busy with her garden tools,
And well remember, o'er that fence she looked,
And, while I paced along the footway path,   285
Called out and sent a blessing after me,
With tender cheerfulness, and with a voice
That seemed the very sound of happy thoughts.

    I roved o'er many a hill and many a dale
With this my weary load, in heat and cold,   290
Through many a wood and many an open ground,
In sunshine or in shade, in wet or fair,
Now blithe, now drooping, as it might befall;
My best companions now the driving winds
And now the 'trotting brooks' and whispering trees,   295
And now the music of my own sad steps,
With many a short-lived thought that passed between
And disappeared.

1. The "bounty" that her husband had been paid for enlisting in the militia. The shortage of volunteers and England's sharply rising military needs had in some counties forced the bounty up from about £1 in 1757 to more than £16 in 1796 (J. R. Western, *English Militia in the Eighteenth Century*, 1965, p. 276).

I came this way again
Towards the wane of summer, when the wheat
Was yellow, and the soft and bladed grass   300
Sprang up afresh and o'er the hay field spread
Its tender green. When I had reached the door
I found that she was absent. In the shade,
Where we now sit, I waited her return.
Her cottage in its outward look appeared   305
As cheerful as before, in any shew
Of neatness little changed, but that I thought
The honeysuckle crowded round the door,
And from the wall hung down in heavier tufts,
And knots of worthless stonecrop started out   310
Along the window's edge, and grew like weeds
Against the lower panes. I turned aside
And strolled into her garden. It was changed.
The unprofitable bindweed spread his bells
From side to side, and with unwieldy wreaths   315
Had dragged the rose from its sustaining wall
And bent it down to earth. The border tufts,
Daisy, and thrift, and lowly camomile,
And thyme, had straggled out into the paths
Which they were used to deck.   320

                              Ere this an hour
Was wasted. Back I turned my restless steps,
And as I walked before the door it chanced
A stranger passed, and guessing whom I sought,
He said that she was used to ramble far.
The sun was sinking in the west, and now   325
I sate with sad impatience. From within
Her solitary infant cried aloud.
The spot though fair seemed very desolate,
The longer I remained more desolate;
And looking round I saw the cornerstones,   330
Till then unmarked, on either side the door
With dull red stains discolored, and stuck o'er
With tufts and hairs of wool, as if the sheep
That feed upon the commons thither came
Familiarly, and found a couching place   335
Even at her threshold.

                        The house clock struck eight:
I turned and saw her distant a few steps.
Her face was pale and thin, her figure too
Was changed. As she unlocked the door she said,
'It grieves me you have waited here so long,   340
But in good truth I've wandered much of late,
And sometimes, to my shame I speak, have need
Of my best prayers to bring me back again.'

While on the board she spread our evening meal,
She told me she had lost her elder child, 345
That he for months had been a serving boy,
Apprenticed by the parish. 'I perceive
You look at me, and you have cause. Today
I have been traveling far, and many days
About the fields I wander, knowing this 350
Only, that what I seek I cannot find.
And so I waste my time: for I am changed,
And to myself,' she said, 'have done much wrong,
And to this helpless infant. I have slept
Weeping, and weeping I have waked. My tears 355
Have flowed as if my body were not such
As others are, and I could never die.
But I am now in mind and in my heart
More easy, and I hope,' she said, 'that heaven
Will give me patience to endure the things 360
Which I behold at home.'

                It would have grieved
Your very soul to see her. Sir, I feel
The story linger in my heart. I fear
'Tis long and tedious, but my spirit clings
To that poor woman. So familiarly 365
Do I perceive her manner and her look
And presence, and so deeply do I feel
Her goodness, that not seldom in my walks
A momentary trance comes over me,
And to myself I seem to muse on one 370
By sorrow laid asleep or borne away,
A human being destined to awake
To human life, or something very near
To human life, when he shall come again
For whom she suffered. Sir, it would have grieved 375
Your very soul to see her: evermore
Her eyelids drooped, her eyes were downward cast,
And when she at her table gave me food
She did not look at me. Her voice was low,
Her body was subdued. In every act 380
Pertaining to her house affairs appeared
The careless stillness which a thinking mind
Gives to an idle matter. Still she sighed,
But yet no motion of the breast was seen,
No heaving of the heart. While by the fire 385
We sate together, sighs came on my ear,
I knew not how, and hardly whence they came.
I took my staff, and when I kissed her babe
The tears stood in her eyes. I left her then
With the best hope and comfort I could give: 390
She thanked me for my will, but for my hope
It seemed she did not thank me.

                                    I returned
And took my rounds along this road again
Ere on its sunny bank the primrose flower
Had chronicled the earliest day of spring.   395
I found her sad and drooping. She had learned
No tidings of her husband; if he lived,
She knew not that he lived; if he were dead,
She knew not he was dead. She seemed the same
In person or appearance, but her house   400
Bespoke a sleepy hand of negligence.
The floor was neither dry nor neat, the hearth
Was comfortless,
The windows too were dim, and her few books,
Which one upon the other heretofore   405
Had been piled up against the corner panes
In seemly order, now with straggling leaves
Lay scattered here and there, open or shut,
As they had chanced to fall. Her infant babe
Had from its mother caught the trick of grief,   410
And sighed among its playthings. Once again
I turned towards the garden gate, and saw
More plainly still that poverty and grief
Were now come nearer to her. The earth was hard,
With weeds defaced and knots of withered grass;   415
No ridges there appeared of clear black mould,
No winter greenness. Of her herbs and flowers
It seemed the better part were gnawed away
Or trampled on the earth. A chain of straw,
Which had been twisted round the tender stem   420
Of a young apple tree, lay at its root;
The bark was nibbled round by truant sheep.
Margaret stood near, her infant in her arms,
And, seeing that my eye was on the tree,
She said, 'I fear it will be dead and gone   425
Ere Robert come again.'

                              Towards the house
Together we returned, and she inquired
If I had any hope. But for her Babe,
And for her little friendless Boy, she said,
She had no wish to live—that she must die   430
Of sorrow. Yet I saw the idle loom
Still in its place. His Sunday garments hung
Upon the selfsame nail, his very staff
Stood undisturbed behind the door. And when
I passed this way beaten by Autumn winds,   435
She told me that her little babe was dead,
And she was left alone. That very time,
I yet remember, through the miry lane
She walked with me a mile, when the bare trees

Trickled with foggy damps, and in such sort 440
That any heart had ached to hear her, begged
That wheresoe'r I went I still would ask
For him whom she had lost. We parted then,
Our final parting; for from that time forth
Did many seasons pass ere I returned 445
Into this tract again.

                Five tedious years
She lingered in unquiet widowhood,
A wife and widow. Needs must it have been
A sore heart-wasting. I have heard, my friend,
That in that broken arbor she would sit
The idle length of half a sabbath day; 450
There, where you see the toadstool's lazy head;
And when a dog passed by she still would quit
The shade and look abroad. On this old Bench
For hours she sate, and evermore her eye 455
Was busy in the distance, shaping things
Which made her heart beat quick. Seest thou that path?—
The green sward now has broken its gray line—
There to and fro she paced through many a day
Of the warm summer, from a belt of flax 460
That girt her waist, spinning the long-drawn thread
With backward steps. Yet ever as there passed
A man whose garments shewed the Soldier's red,
Or crippled Mendicant in Sailor's garb,
The little child who sate to turn the wheel 465
Ceased from his toil, and she, with faltering voice,
Expecting still to hear her husband's fate,
Made many a fond inquiry; and when they
Whose presence gave no comfort, were gone by,
Her heart was still more sad. And by yon gate, 470
Which bars the traveler's road, she often stood,
And when a stranger horseman came, the latch
Would lift, and in his face look wistfully,
Most happy if from aught discovered there
Of tender feeling she might dare repeat 475
The same sad question.

                Meanwhile her poor hut
Sunk to decay; for he was gone, whose hand
At the first nippings of October frost
Closed up each chink, and with fresh bands of straw
Chequered the green-grown thatch. And so she lived 480
Through the long winter, reckless and alone,
Till this reft house, by frost, and thaw, and rain,
Was sapped; and when she slept, the nightly damps
Did chill her breast, and in the stormy day
Her tattered clothes were ruffled by the wind 485
Even at the side of her own fire. Yet still

She loved this wretched spot, nor would for worlds
Have parted hence; and still that length of road,
And this rude bench, one torturing hope endeared,
Fast rooted at her heart. And here, my friend,   490
In sickness she remained; and here she died,
Last human tenant of these ruined walls."

The old Man ceased: he saw that I was moved.
From that low bench rising instinctively,
I turned aside in weakness, nor had power   495
To thank him for the tale which he had told.
I stood, and leaning o'er the garden gate
Reviewed that Woman's sufferings; and it seemed
To comfort me while with a brother's love
I blessed her in the impotence of grief.   500
At length towards the cottage I returned
Fondly, and traced with milder interest,
That secret spirit of humanity
Which, 'mid the calm oblivious tendencies
Of nature, 'mid her plants, her weeds and flowers,   505
And silent overgrowings, still survived.
The old man seeing this resumed, and said,
"My friend, enough to sorrow have you given,
The purposes of Wisdom ask no more:
Be wise and cheerful, and no longer read   510
The forms of things with an unworthy eye.
She sleeps in the calm earth, and peace is here.
I well remember that those very plumes,
Those weeds, and the high spear grass on that wall,
By mist and silent raindrops silvered o'er,   515
As once I passed, did to my mind convey
So still an image of tranquillity,
So calm and still, and looked so beautiful
Amid the uneasy thoughts which filled my mind,
That what we feel of sorrow and despair   520
From ruin and from change, and all the grief
The passing shews of being leave behind,
Appeared an idle dream that could not live
Where meditation was. I turned away,
And walked along my road in happiness."   525

     He ceased. By this the sun declining shot
A slant and mellow radiance, which began
To fall upon us where beneath the trees
We sate on that low bench. And now we felt,
Admonished thus, the sweet hour coming on: 530
A linnet warbled from those lofty elms,
A thrush sang loud, and other melodies
At distance heard, peopled the milder air.
The old man rose and hoisted up his load.
Together casting then a farewell look   535

Upon those silent walls, we left the shade;
And, ere the stars were visible, attained
A rustic inn, our evening resting place.

THE END

1797–ca. 1799   1968

Michael[1]

A PASTORAL POEM

If from the public way you turn your steps
Up the tumultuous brook of Greenhead Ghyll,[2]
You will suppose that with an upright path
Your feet must struggle; in such bold ascent
The pastoral mountains front you, face to face.   5
But, courage! for around that boisterous brook
The mountains have all opened out themselves,
And made a hidden valley of their own.
No habitation can be seen; but they
Who journey thither find themselves alone   10
With a few sheep, with rocks and stones, and kites[3]
That overhead are sailing in the sky.
It is in truth an utter solitude;
Nor should I have made mention of this dell
But for one object which you might pass by,   15
Might see and notice not. Beside the brook
Appears a straggling heap of unhewn stones!
And to that simple object appertains
A story—unenriched with strange events,
Yet not unfit, I deem, for the fireside,   20
Or for the summer shade. It was the first
Of those domestic tales that spake to me
Of Shepherds, dwellers in the valleys, men
Whom I already loved—not verily
For their own sakes, but for the fields and hills   25
Where was their occupation and abode.
And hence this Tale, while I was yet a Boy
Careless of books, yet having felt the power
Of Nature, by the gentle agency
Of natural objects, led me on to feel   30

1. This poem is founded on the actual misfortunes of a family at Grasmere. For the account of the sheepfold, see Dorothy Wordsworth's *Grasmere Journals*, Oct. 11, 1800. Wordsworth wrote to Thomas Poole, on April 9, 1801, that he had attempted to picture a man "agitated by two of the most powerful affections of the human heart; the parental affection, and the love of property, *landed* property, including the feelings of inheritance, home, and personal and family independence." The subtitle shows Wordsworth's shift of the term "pastoral" from aristocratic make-believe to the tragic suffering of people in what he called "humble and rustic life."
2. Greenhead Ghyll (a ghyll is a ravine forming the bed of a stream) is not far from Wordsworth's cottage at Grasmere. The other places named in the poem are also in that vicinity.
3. Hawks.

For passions that were not my own, and think
(At random and imperfectly indeed)
On man, the heart of man, and human life.
Therefore, although it be a history
Homely and rude, I will relate the same   35
For the delight of a few natural hearts;
And, with yet fonder feeling, for the sake
Of youthful Poets, who among these hills
Will be my second self when I am gone.

   Upon the forest side in Grasmere Vale   40
There dwelt a Shepherd, Michael was his name;
An old man, stout of heart, and strong of limb.
His bodily frame had been from youth to age
Of an unusual strength: his mind was keen,
Intense, and frugal, apt for all affairs,   45
And in his shepherd's calling he was prompt
And watchful more than ordinary men.
Hence had he learned the meaning of all winds,
Of blasts of every tone; and oftentimes,
When others heeded not, he heard the South   50
Make subterraneous music, like the noise
Of bagpipers on distant Highland hills.
The Shepherd, at such warning, of his flock
Bethought him, and he to himself would say,
"The winds are now devising work for me!"   55
And, truly, at all times, the storm, that drives
The traveler to a shelter, summoned him
Up to the mountains: he had been alone
Amid the heart of many thousand mists,
That came to him, and left him, on the heights.   60
So lived he till his eightieth year was past.
And grossly that man errs, who should suppose
That the green valleys, and the streams and rocks,
Were things indifferent to the Shepherd's thoughts.
Fields, where with cheerful spirits he had breathed   65
The common air; hills, which with vigorous step
He had so often climbed; which had impressed
So many incidents upon his mind
Of hardship, skill or courage, joy or fear;
Which, like a book, preserved the memory   70
Of the dumb animals, whom he had saved,
Had fed or sheltered, linking to such acts
The certainty of honorable gain;
Those fields, those hills—what could they less? had laid
Strong hold on his affections, were to him   75
A pleasurable feeling of blind love,
The pleasure which there is in life itself.

His days had not been passed in singleness.
His Helpmate was a comely matron, old—
Though younger than himself full twenty years.   80
She was a woman of a stirring life,
Whose heart was in her house; two wheels she had
Of antique form: this large, for spinning wool;
That small, for flax; and, if one wheel had rest,
It was because the other was at work.   85
The Pair had but one inmate in their house,
An only Child, who had been born to them
When Michael, telling o'er his years, began
To deem that he was old—in shepherd's phrase,
With one foot in the grave. This only Son,   90
With two brave sheep dogs tried in many a storm,
The one of an inestimable worth,
Made all their household. I may truly say,
That they were as a proverb in the vale
For endless industry. When day was gone,   95
And from their occupations out of doors
The Son and Father were come home, even then,
Their labor did not cease; unless when all
Turned to the cleanly supper board, and there,
Each with a mess of pottage and skimmed milk,   100
Sat round the basket piled with oaten cakes,
And their plain homemade cheese. Yet when the meal
Was ended, Luke (for so the Son was named)
And his old Father both betook themselves
To such convenient work as might employ   105
Their hands by the fireside; perhaps to card
Wool for the Housewife's spindle, or repair
Some injury done to sickle, flail, or scythe,
Or other implement of house or field.

   Down from the ceiling, by the chimney's edge,   110
That in our ancient uncouth country style
With huge and black projection overbrowed
Large space beneath, as duly as the light
Of day grew dim the Housewife hung a lamp;
An aged utensil, which had performed   115
Service beyond all others of its kind.
Early at evening did it burn—and late,
Surviving comrade of uncounted hours,
Which, going by from year to year, had found,
And left, the couple neither gay perhaps   120
Nor cheerful, yet with objects and with hopes,
Living a life of eager industry.
And now, when Luke had reached his eighteenth year,
There by the light of this old lamp they sate,
Father and Son, while far into the night   125

The Housewife plied her own peculiar work,
Making the cottage through the silent hours
Murmur as with the sound of summer flies.
This light was famous in its neighborhood,
And was a public symbol of the life   130
That thrifty Pair had lived. For, as it chanced,
Their cottage on a plot of rising ground
Stood single, with large prospect, north and south,
High into Easedale, up to Dunmail Raise,
And westward to the village near the lake;   135
And from this constant light, so regular,
And so far seen, the House itself, by all
Who dwelt within the limits of the vale,
Both old and young, was named The Evening Star.

Thus living on through such a length of years,   140
The Shepherd, if he loved himself, must needs
Have loved his Helpmate; but to Michael's heart
This son of his old age was yet more dear—
Less from instinctive tenderness, the same
Fond spirit that blindly works in the blood of all—   145
Than that a child, more than all other gifts
That earth can offer to declining man,
Brings hope with it, and forward-looking thoughts,
And stirrings of inquietude, when they
By tendency of nature needs must fail.   150
Exceeding was the love he bare to him,
His heart and his heart's joy! For oftentimes
Old Michael, while he was a babe in arms,
Had done him female service, not alone
For pastime and delight, as is the use   155
Of fathers, but with patient mind enforced
To acts of tenderness; and he had rocked
His cradle, as with a woman's gentle hand.

And in a later time, ere yet the Boy
Had put on boy's attire, did Michael love,   160
Albeit of a stern unbending mind,
To have the Young-one in his sight, when he
Wrought in the field, or on his shepherd's stool
Sate with a fettered sheep before him stretched
Under the large old oak, that near his door   165
Stood single, and, from matchless depth of shade,
Chosen for the Shearer's covert from the sun,
Thence in our rustic dialect was called
The Clipping Tree, a name which yet it bears.
There, while they two were sitting in the shade,   170
With others round them, earnest all and blithe,
Would Michael exercise his heart with looks
Of fond correction and reproof bestowed

Upon the Child, if he disturbed the sheep
By catching at their legs, or with his shouts
Scared them, while they lay still beneath the shears. 175

   And when by Heaven's good grace the boy grew up
A healthy Lad, and carried in his cheek
Two steady roses that were five years old;
Then Michael from a winter coppice[4] cut 180
With his own hand a sapling, which he hooped
With iron, making it throughout in all
Due requisites a perfect shepherd's staff,
And gave it to the Boy; wherewith equipped
He as a watchman oftentimes was placed 185
At gate or gap, to stem or turn the flock;
And, to his office prematurely called,
There stood the urchin, as you will divine,
Something between a hindrance and a help;
And for this cause not always, I believe, 190
Receiving from his Father hire of praise;
Though nought was left undone which staff, or voice,
Or looks, or threatening gestures, could perform.

   But soon as Luke, full ten years old, could stand
Against the mountain blasts, and to the heights, 195
Not fearing toil, nor length of weary ways,
He with his Father daily went, and they
Were as companions, why should I relate
That objects which the Shepherd loved before
Were dearer now? that from the Boy there came 200
Feelings and emanations—things which were
Light to the sun and music to the wind;
And that the old Man's heart seemed born again?

   Thus in his Father's sight the Boy grew up:
And now, when he had reached his eighteenth year, 205
He was his comfort and his daily hope.

   While in this sort the simple household lived
From day to day, to Michael's ear there came
Distressful tidings. Long before the time
Of which I speak, the Shepherd had been bound 210
In surety for his brother's son, a man
Of an industrious life, and ample means;
But unforeseen misfortunes suddenly
Had pressed upon him; and old Michael now
Was summoned to discharge the forfeiture, 215
A grievous penalty, but little less
Than half his substance. This unlooked-for claim,
At the first hearing, for a moment took

4. Grove of small trees.

More hope out of his life than he supposed
That any old man ever could have lost.   220
As soon as he had armed himself with strength
To look his trouble in the face, it seemed
The Shepherd's sole resource to sell at once
A portion of his patrimonial fields.
Such was his first resolve; he thought again,   225
And his heart failed him. "Isabel," said he,
Two evenings after he had heard the news,
"I have been toiling more than seventy years,
And in the open sunshine of God's love
Have we all lived; yet, if these fields of ours   230
Should pass into a stranger's hand, I think
That I could not lie quiet in my grave.
Our lot is a hard lot; the sun himself
Has scarcely been more diligent than I;
And I have lived to be a fool at last   235
To my own family. An evil man
That was, and made an evil choice, if he
Were false to us; and, if he were not false,
There are ten thousand to whom loss like this
Had been no sorrow. I forgive him—but   240
'Twere better to be dumb than to talk thus.

"When I began, my purpose was to speak
Of remedies and of a cheerful hope.
Our Luke shall leave us, Isabel; the land
Shall not go from us, and it shall be free;   245
He shall possess it, free as is the wind
That passes over it. We have, thou know'st,
Another kinsman—he will be our friend
In this distress. He is a prosperous man,
Thriving in trade—and Luke to him shall go,   250
And with his kinsman's help and his own thrift
He quickly will repair this loss, and then
He may return to us. If here he stay,
What can be done? Where everyone is poor,
What can be gained?"
               At this the old Man paused,   255
And Isabel sat silent, for her mind
Was busy, looking back into past times.
There's Richard Bateman,[5] thought she to herself,
He was a parish boy—at the church door
They made a gathering for him, shillings, pence,   260
And halfpennies, wherewith the neighbors bought
A basket, which they filled with peddler's wares;

5. "The story alluded to here is well known in the country. The chapel is called Ings Chapel and is on the road leading from Kendal to Ambleside" [Wordsworth's note].

And, with this basket on his arm, the lad
Went up to London, found a master there,
Who, out of many, chose the trusty boy   265
To go and overlook his merchandise
Beyond the seas; where he grew wondrous rich,
And left estates and monies to the poor,
And, at his birthplace, built a chapel floored
With marble, which he sent from foreign lands.   270
These thoughts, and many others of like sort,
Passed quickly through the mind of Isabel,
And her face brightened. The old Man was glad,
And thus resumed: "Well, Isabel! this scheme
These two days has been meat and drink to me.   275
Far more than we have lost is left us yet.
We have enough—I wish indeed that I
Were younger—but this hope is a good hope.
Make ready Luke's best garments, of the best
Buy for him more, and let us send him forth   280
Tomorrow, or the next day, or tonight:
If he *could* go, the Boy should go tonight."

      Here Michael ceased, and to the fields went forth
With a light heart. The Housewife for five days
Was restless morn and night, and all day long   285
Wrought on with her best fingers to prepare
Things needful for the journey of her son.
But Isabel was glad when Sunday came
To stop her in her work; for, when she lay
By Michael's side, she through the last two nights 290
Heard him, how he was troubled in his sleep;
And when they rose at morning she could see
That all his hopes were gone. That day at noon
She said to Luke, while they two by themselves
Were sitting at the door, "Thou must not go;   295
We have no other Child but thee to lose,
None to remember—do not go away,
For if thou leave thy Father he will die."
The Youth made answer with a jocund voice;
And Isabel, when she had told her fears,   300
Recovered heart. That evening her best fare
Did she bring forth, and all together sat
Like happy people round a Christmas fire.

      With daylight Isabel resumed her work;
And all the ensuing week the house appeared
As cheerful as a grove in spring; at length   305
The expected letter from their kinsman came,
With kind assurances that he would do
His utmost for the welfare of the Boy;

To which requests were added that forthwith   310
He might be sent to him. Ten times or more
The letter was read over; Isabel
Went forth to show it to the neighbors round;
Nor was there at that time on English land
A prouder heart than Luke's. When Isabel   315
Had to her house returned, the old Man said,
"He shall depart tomorrow." To this word
The Housewife answered, talking much of things
Which, if at such short notice he should go,
Would surely be forgotten. But at length   320
She gave consent, and Michael was at ease.

    Near the tumultuous brook of Greenhead Ghyll,
In that deep valley, Michael had designed
To build a Sheepfold;[6] and, before he heard
The tidings of his melancholy loss,   325
For this same purpose he had gathered up
A heap of stones, which by the streamlet's edge
Lay thrown together, ready for the work.
With Luke that evening thitherward he walked;
And soon as they had reached the place he stopped,   330
And thus the old Man spake to him: "My son,
Tomorrow thou wilt leave me: with full heart
I look upon thee, for thou art the same
That wert a promise to me ere thy birth,
And all thy life hast been my daily joy.   335
I will relate to thee some little part
Of our two histories; 'twill do thee good
When thou art from me, even if I should touch
On things thou canst not know of. After thou
First cam'st into the world—as oft befalls   340
To newborn infants—thou didst sleep away
Two days, and blessings from thy Father's tongue
Then fell upon thee. Day by day passed on,
And still I loved thee with increasing love.
Never to living ear came sweeter sounds   345
Than when I heard thee by our own fireside
First uttering, without words, a natural tune;
While thou, a feeding babe, didst in thy joy
Sing at thy Mother's breast. Month followed month,
And in the open fields my life was passed   350
And on the mountains; else I think that thou
Hadst been brought up upon thy Father's knees.
But we were playmates, Luke; among these hills,
As well thou knowest, in us the old and young
Have played together, nor with me didst thou   355
Lack any pleasure which a boy can know."

---

6. Pen for sheep. "A sheepfold in these   stone walls, with different divisions"
mountains is an unroofed building of   [Wordsworth's note].

Luke had a manly heart; but at these words
He sobbed aloud. The old Man grasped his hand,
And said, "Nay, do not take it so—I see
That these are things of which I need not speak.   360
Even to the utmost I have been to thee
A kind and a good Father: and herein
I but repay a gift which I myself
Received at others' hands; for, though now old
Beyond the common life of man, I still   365
Remember them who loved me in my youth.
Both of them sleep together; here they lived,
As all their Forefathers had done; and, when
At length their time was come, they were not loath
To give their bodies to the family mold.   370
I wished that thou shouldst live the life they lived,
But 'tis a long time to look back, my Son,
And see so little gain from threescore years.
These fields were burthened⁷ when they came to me;
Till I was forty years of age, not more   375
Than half of my inheritance was mine.
I toiled and toiled; God blessed me in my work,
And till these three weeks past the land was free.
It looks as if it never could endure
Another master. Heaven forgive me, Luke,   380
If I judge ill for thee, but it seems good
That thou shouldst go."
                          At this the old Man paused;
Then, pointing to the stones near which they stood,
Thus, after a short silence, he resumed:
"This was a work for us; and now, my Son,   385
It is a work for me. But, lay one stone—
Here, lay it for me, Luke, with thine own hands.
Nay, Boy, be of good hope—we both may live
To see a better day. At eighty-four
I still am strong and hale; do thou thy part;   390
I will do mine. I will begin again
With many tasks that were resigned to thee:
Up to the heights, and in among the storms,
Will I without thee go again, and do
All works which I was wont to do alone,   395
Before I knew thy face. Heaven bless thee, Boy!
Thy heart these two weeks has been beating fast
With many hopes; it should be so—yes—yes—
I knew that thou couldst never have a wish
To leave me, Luke; thou hast been bound to me   400
Only by links of love; when thou art gone,
What will be left to us!—But I forget
My purposes. Lay now the cornerstone,
As I requested; and hereafter, Luke,

7. I.e., mortgaged.

When thou art gone away, should evil men   405
Be thy companions, think of me, my Son,
And of this moment; hither turn thy thoughts,
And God will strengthen thee; amid all fear
And all temptation, Luke, I pray that thou
May'st bear in mind the life thy Fathers lived,   410
Who, being innocent, did for that cause
Bestir them in good deeds. Now, fare thee well—
When thou return'st, thou in this place wilt see
A work which is not here: a covenant
'Twill be between us; but, whatever fate   415
Befall thee, I shall love thee to the last,
And bear thy memory with me to the grave."

     The Shepherd ended here; and Luke stooped down,
And, as his Father had requested, laid
The first stone of the Sheepfold. At the sight   420
The old Man's grief broke from him; to his heart
He pressed his Son, he kisséd him and wept;
And to the house together they returned.
Hushed was that House in peace, or seeming peace
Ere the night fell; with morrow's dawn the Boy   425
Began his journey, and, when he had reached
The public way, he put on a bold face;
And all the neighbors, as he passed their doors,
Came forth with wishes and with farewell prayers,
That followed him till he was out of sight.   430

     A good report did from their kinsman come,
Of Luke and his well-doing; and the Boy
Wrote loving letters, full of wondrous news,
Which, as the Housewife phrased it, were throughout
"The prettiest letters that were ever seen."   435
Both parents read them with rejoicing hearts.
So, many months passed on; and once again
The Shepherd went about his daily work
With confident and cheerful thoughts; and now
Sometimes when he could find a leisure hour   440
He to that valley took his way, and there
Wrought at the Sheepfold. Meantime Luke began
To slacken in his duty; and, at length,
He in the dissolute city gave himself
To evil courses; ignominy and shame   445
Fell on him, so that he was driven at last
To seek a hiding place beyond the seas.

     There is a comfort in the strength of love;
'Twill make a thing endurable, which else
Would overset the brain, or break the heart;   450
I have conversed with more than one who well
Remember the old Man, and what he was

Years after he had heard this heavy news.
His bodily frame had been from youth to age
Of an unusual strength. Among the rocks   455
He went, and still looked up to sun and cloud,
And listened to the wind; and, as before,
Performed all kinds of labor for his sheep,
And for the land, his small inheritance.
And to that hollow dell from time to time   460
Did he repair, to build the Fold of which
His flock had need. 'Tis not forgotten yet
The pity which was then in every heart
For the old Man—and 'tis believed by all
That many and many a day he thither went,   465
And never lifted up a single stone.

There, by the Sheepfold, sometimes was he seen
Sitting alone, or with his faithful Dog,
Then old, beside him, lying at his feet.
The length of full seven years, from time to time,   470
He at the building of this Sheepfold wrought,
And left the work unfinished when he died.
Three years, or little more, did Isabel
Survive her Husband: at her death the estate
Was sold, and went into a stranger's hand.   475
The Cottage which was named The Evening Star
Is gone—the plowshare has been through the ground
On which it stood; great changes have been wrought
In all the neighborhood; yet the oak is left
That grew beside their door; and the remains   480
Of the unfinished Sheepfold may be seen
Beside the boisterous brook of Greenhead Ghyll.
Oct. 11–Dec. 9, 1800   1800

Written in March[1]

WHILE RESTING ON THE BRIDGE AT THE FOOT
OF BROTHER'S WATER

The cock is crowing,
The stream is flowing,
The small birds twitter,
The lake doth glitter,
The green field sleeps in the sun;   5
The oldest and youngest
Are at work with the strongest;
The cattle are grazing,
Their heads never raising;
There are forty feeding like one!   10

1. For the composition of this poem, see Dorothy Wordsworth's *Grasmere Journals*, Apr. 16, 1802.

> Like an army defeated
> The snow hath retreated,
> And now doth fare ill
> On the top of the bare hill;
> The plowboy is whooping—anon—anon: 15
> There's joy in the mountains;
> There's life in the fountains;
> Small clouds are sailing,
> Blue sky prevailing;
> The rain is over and gone!   20

1802   1807

Resolution and Independence[1]

1

There was a roaring in the wind all night;
The rain came heavily and fell in floods;
But now the sun is rising calm and bright;
The birds are singing in the distant woods;
Over his own sweet voice the stock dove broods;   5
The jay makes answer as the magpie chatters;
And all the air is filled with pleasant noise of waters.

2

All things that love the sun are out of doors;
The sky rejoices in the morning's birth;
The grass is bright with raindrops; on the moors   10
The hare is running races in her mirth;
And with her feet she from the plashy earth
Raises a mist; that, glittering in the sun,
Runs with her all the way, wherever she doth run.

3

I was a Traveler then upon the moor;   15
I saw the hare that raced about with joy;
I heard the woods and distant waters roar;
Or heard them not, as happy as a boy:
The pleasant season did my heart employ;
My old remembrances went from me wholly;   20
And all the ways of men, so vain and melancholy.

1. For the meeting with the old leech-gatherer, see Dorothy Wordsworth's *Grasmere Journals*, Oct. 3, 1800. Wordsworth himself tells us that "I was in the state of feeling described in the beginning of the poem, while crossing over Barton Fell from Mr. Clarkson's, at the foot of Ullswater, towards Askam. The image of the hare I then observed on the ridge of the Fell." Eighteen months later (see *Grasmere Journals*, May 4 and 7, 1802), these events, recollected in tranquility, were transformed into this poem of personal crisis, mastered by an imaginative process of spontaneous mythmaking. The metamorphosis of the still old man (stanzas 8 ff.) ends when he modulates into the archetypal figure of the eternal and haunted wanderer, of whom Coleridge's Ancient Mariner had been the most recent embodiment. Unlike Coleridge's, however, Wordsworth's is a natural supernaturalism, for the old leech-gatherer remains stubbornly matter-of-fact.

4

But, as it sometimes chanceth, from the might
Of joy in minds that can no further go,
As high as we have mounted in delight
In our dejection do we sink as low;
To me that morning did it happen so;   25
And fears and fancies thick upon me came;
Dim sadness—and blind thoughts, I knew not, nor could name.

5

I heard the skylark warbling in the sky;
And I bethought me of the playful hare:
Even such a happy Child of earth am I;   30
Even as these blissful creatures do I fare;
Far from the world I walk, and from all care;
But there may come another day to me—
Solitude, pain of heart, distress, and poverty.   35

6

My whole life I have lived in pleasant thought,
As if life's business were a summer mood;
As if all needful things would come unsought
To genial faith, still rich in genial good;
But how can he expect that others should   40
Build for him, sow for him, and at his call
Love him, who for himself will take no heed at all?

7

I thought of Chatterton,[2] the marvelous Boy,
The sleepless Soul that perished in his pride;
Of him who walked in glory and in joy
Following his plow, along the mountainside;[3]   45
By our own spirits are we deified:
We Poets in our youth begin in gladness,
But thereof come in the end despondency and madness.

8

Now, whether it were by peculiar grace,
A leading from above, a something given,   50
Yet it befell that, in this lonely place,
When I with these untoward thoughts had striven,
Beside a pool bare to the eye of heaven
I saw a Man before me unawares:
The oldest man he seemed that ever wore gray hairs.   55

9

As a huge stone is sometimes seen to lie
Couched on the bald top of an eminence;

2. Thomas Chatterton (1752–70), a
poet of great talent who, in his loneliness and dire poverty, poisoned himself at the age of 17 and so became the
prime Romantic symbol of neglected

young genius.
3. Robert Burns, also considered at
that time as a natural poet who died
young and poor, without adequate recognition.

Wonder to all who do the same espy,
By what means it could thither come, and whence;   60
So that it seems a thing endued with sense:
Like a sea beast crawled forth, that on a shelf
Of rock or sand reposeth, there to sun itself;

10

Such seemed this Man,[4] not all alive nor dead,
Nor all asleep—in his extreme old age;   65
His body was bent double, feet and head
Coming together in life's pilgrimage;
As if some dire constraint of pain, or rage
Of sickness felt by him in times long past,
A more than human weight upon his frame had cast.   70

11

Himself he propped, limbs, body, and pale face,
Upon a long gray staff of shaven wood;
And, still as I drew near with gentle pace,
Upon the margin of that moorish flood
Motionless as a cloud that old Man stood,   75
That heareth not the loud winds when they call,
And moveth all together, if it move at all.

12

At length, himself unsettling, he the pond
Stirred with his staff, and fixedly did look
Upon the muddy water, which he conned,   80
As if he had been reading in a book;
And now a stranger's privilege I took,
And, drawing to his side, to him did say,
"This morning gives us promise of a glorious day."

13

A gentle answer did the old Man make,   85
In courteous speech which forth he slowly drew;
And him with further words I thus bespake,
"What occupation do you there pursue?
This is a lonesome place for one like you."
Ere he replied, a flash of mild surprise   90
Broke from the sable orbs of his yet-vivid eyes.

14

His words came feebly, from a feeble chest,
But each in solemn order followed each,
With something of a lofty utterance dressed—
Choice word and measured phrase, above the reach   95

4. In Wordsworth's own analysis of this passage, he says that the stone is endowed with something of life, the sea beast is stripped of some of its life to assimilate it to the stone, and the old man divested of enough life and motion to make "the two objects unite and coalesce in just comparison". He used the passage to demonstrate his theory of how the "conferring, the abstracting, and the modifying powers of the Imagination * * * are all brought into conjunction" (Preface to the *Poems* of 1815). Compare Coleridge's analysis of the imagination in *Biographia Literaria*, Chapter XIII.

Of ordinary men; a stately speech;
Such as grave livers[5] do in Scotland use,
Religious men, who give to God and man their dues.

15

He told, that to these waters he had come
To gather leeches,[6] being old and poor: 100
Employment hazardous and wearisome!
And he had many hardships to endure:
From pond to pond he roamed, from moor to moor;
Housing, with God's good help, by choice or chance;
And in this way he gained an honest maintenance.   105

16

The old Man still stood talking by my side;
But now his voice to me was like a stream
Scarce heard; nor word from word could I divide;
And the whole body of the Man did seem
Like one whom I had met with in a dream;   110
Or like a man from some far region sent,
To give me human strength, by apt admonishment.

17

My former thoughts returned: the fear that kills;
And hope that is unwilling to be fed;
Cold, pain, and labor, and all fleshly ills;   115
And mighty Poets in their misery dead.
—Perplexed, and longing to be comforted,
My question eagerly did I renew,
"How is it that you live, and what is it you do?"

18

He with a smile did then his words repeat;
And said that, gathering leeches, far and wide   120
He traveled, stirring thus about his feet
The waters of the pools where they abide.
"Once I could meet with them on every side,
But they have dwindled long by slow decay;
Yet still I persevere, and find them where I may."   125

19

While he was talking thus, the lonely place,
The old Man's shape, and speech—all troubled me:
In my mind's eye I seemed to see him pace
About the weary moors continually,   130
Wandering about alone and silently.
While I these thoughts within myself pursued,
He, having made a pause, the same discourse renewed.

20

And soon with this he other matter blended,
Cheerfully uttered, with demeanor kind,   135

---

5. Those who live gravely.
6. Leeches were used to draw blood for curative purposes. A leech-gatherer, barelegged in shallow water, stirred the water to rouse them, and then picked them off his skin.

But stately in the main; and, when he ended,
I could have laughed myself to scorn to find
In that decrepit Man so firm a mind.
"God," said I, "be my help and stay[7] secure;   140
I'll think of the Leech Gatherer on the lonely moor!"
May 3–July 4, 1802   1807

Yew Trees[1]

There is a Yew Tree, pride of Lorton Vale,
Which to this day stands single, in the midst
Of its own darkness, as it stood of yore:
Not loath to furnish weapons for the bands
Of Umfraville or Percy ere they marched   5
To Scotland's heaths; or those that crossed the sea
And drew their sounding bows at Azincour,
Perhaps at earlier Crecy, or Poictiers.
Of vast circumference and gloom profound
This solitary Tree! a living thing   10
Produced too slowly ever to decay;
Of form and aspect too magnificent
To be destroyed. But worthier still of note
Are those fraternal Four of Borrowdale,
Joined in one solemn and capacious grove;   15
Huge trunks! and each particular trunk a growth
Of intertwisted fibers serpentine
Up-coiling, and inveterately convolved;
Nor uninformed with Phantasy, and looks
That threaten the profane—a pillared shade,   20
Upon whose grassless floor of red-brown hue,
By sheddings from the pining umbrage[2] tinged
Perennially—beneath whose sable roof
Of boughs, as if for festal purpose decked
With unrejoicing berries—ghostly Shapes   25
May meet at noontide; Fear and trembling Hope,
Silence and Foresight; Death the Skeleton
And Time the Shadow—there to celebrate,
As in a natural temple scattered o'er
With altars undisturbed of mossy stone,   30
United worship; or in mute repose
To lie, and listen to the mountain flood
Murmuring from Glaramara's[3] inmost caves.

ca. 1803   1815

---

7. Support (a noun).
1. An evergreen tree; its wood was used for the bows which won the English victories mentioned in the poem, in the late medieval wars against Scotland and France. In the *Biographia Literaria*, Chapter XXII, Coleridge cited lines 13 ff. as a prime example of the faculty of imagination, in which Wordsworth "stands nearest of all modern writers to Shakespeare and Milton; and yet in a kind perfectly unborrowed and his own."
2. Foliage that casts a shade.
3. Mountain rising from Borrowdale valley, in the Lake Country.

I Wandered Lonely as a Cloud[4]

I wandered lonely as a cloud
That floats on high o'er vales and hills,
When all at once I saw a crowd,
A host, of golden daffodils;
Beside the lake, beneath the trees,   5
Fluttering and dancing in the breeze.

Continuous as the stars that shine
And twinkle on the milky way,
They stretched in never-ending line
Along the margin of a bay: 10
Ten thousand saw I at a glance,
Tossing their heads in sprightly dance.

The waves beside them danced; but they
Outdid the sparkling waves in glee;
A poet could not but be gay,   15
In such a jocund company;
I gazed—and gazed—but little thought
What wealth the show to me had brought:

For oft, when on my couch I lie
In vacant or in pensive mood,   20
They flash upon that inward eye
Which is the bliss of solitude;
And then my heart with pleasure fills,
And dances with the daffodils.

1804   1807

My Heart Leaps Up

My heart leaps up when I behold
    A rainbow in the sky:
So was it when my life began;
So is it now I am a man;
So be it when I shall grow old,   5
    Or let me die!
The Child is father of the Man;
And I could wish my days to be
Bound each to each by natural piety.[1]

March 26, 1802   1807

4. The last stanza describes the kind of recollection in tranquillity from which this poem arose, two years after the original experience, which Dorothy Wordsworth described in her *Grasmere Journals* for Apr. 15, 1802.
1. As distinguished from piety based on the Scriptures, in which God makes the rainbow the token of his covenant with Noah and all his descendants. The religious sentiment that binds Wordsworth's mature self to that of his childhood is a continuing responsiveness to the miracle of ordinary things.

Ode: Intimations of Immortality "This was composed during my residence at Town End, Grasmere; two years at least passed between the writing of the four first stanzas and the remaining part. To the attentive and competent reader the whole sufficiently explains itself; but there may be no harm in adverting here to particular feelings or *experiences* of my own mind on which the structure of the poem partly rests. Nothing was more difficult for me in childhood than to admit the notion of death as a state applicable to my own being. I have said elsewhere

> —A simple child,
> That lightly draws its breath,
> And feels its life in every limb,
> What should it know of death!—

But it was not so much from [feelings] of animal vivacity that *my* difficulty came as from a sense of the indomitableness of the spirit within me. I used to brood over the stories of Enoch and Elijah, and almost to persuade myself that, whatever might become of others, I should be translated, in something of the same way, to heaven. With a feeling congenial to this, I was often unable to think of external things as having external existence, and I communed with all that I saw as something not apart from, but inherent in, my own immaterial nature. Many times while going to school have I grasped at a wall or tree to recall myself from this abyss of idealism to the reality. At that time I was afraid of such processes. In later periods of life I have deplored, as we have all reason to do, a subjugation of an opposite character, and have rejoiced over the remembrances, as is expressed in the lines—

> Obstinate questionings
> Of sense and outward things,
> Fallings from us, vanishings; etc.

To that dreamlike vividness and splendor which invest objects of sight in childhood, everyone, I believe, if he would look back, could bear testimony, and I need not dwell upon it here: but having in the Poem regarded it as presumptive evidence of a prior state of existence, I think it right to protest against a conclusion, which has given pain to some good and pious persons, that I meant to inculcate such a belief. It is far too shadowy a notion to be recommended to faith, as more than an element in our instincts of immortality. But let us bear in mind that, though the idea is not advanced in revelation, there is nothing there to contradict it, and the fall of Man presents an analogy in its favor. Accordingly, a pre-existent state has entered into the popular creeds of many nations; and, among all persons acquainted with classic literature, is known as an ingredient in Platonic philosophy. Archimedes said that he could move the world if he had a point whereon to rest his machine. Who has not felt the same aspirations as regards the world of his own mind? Having to wield some of its elements when I was impelled to write this Poem on the 'Immortality of the Soul,' I took hold of the notion of pre-existence as having sufficient foundation in humanity for authorizing me to make for my purpose the best use of it I could as a Poet" (Wordsworth).

As Wordsworth says, Plato held the doctrine that the soul is immortal and exists separately from the body both before birth and after death. But while the *Ode* proposes that the soul only gradually loses "the vision splendid" after birth, Plato maintained the contrary: that the knowledge of the eternal Ideas, which the soul had acquired by direct acquaintance, is totally lost at the instant of birth, and must be gradually "recollected" by philosophical discipline in the course of this life (*Phaedo* 73–77). Wordsworth's concept resembles more closely the view of some Neo-Platonists that the glory of the unborn soul is gradually quenched by its descent into the darkness of matter.

Wordsworth was troubled by objections to the Christian heterodoxy of this apparent claim for the pre-existence, as against the orthodox belief in the survival, of the soul. He insisted that he did not intend to assert this as doctrine, but only to use it as a poetic postulate, enabling him to deal "as a poet" with an experience to which everyone, as he says, "if he would look back, could bear testimony." This experience is a universal human one: that the loss of youth involves the loss of a freshness and radiance investing all experience. Coleridge's *Dejection: An Ode*, which he wrote after he had heard the first four stanzas of Wordsworth's poem, employs a similar figurative technique for a comparable, though more devastating, experience of loss. As with all poems so large and rich as this one, there are divergent interpretations of its purport, emphases, and organization. But most commentators agree that the poem offers two different perspectives on the fact that growing up is also a stage on the way to death, and almost all agree that it is one of the greatest instances of the very difficult form of the irregular Pindaric ode. The Catholic poet G. M. Hopkins remarked: "For my part I should think St. George and St. Thomas of Canterbury wore roses in heaven for England's sake on the day that *Ode*, not without their intercession, was penned."

The original version of this poem had as its title only "Ode," and then as epigraph "*Paulo maiora canamus*" ("Let us sing of somewhat higher things") from Virgil's *Eclogue IV*.

Ode

INTIMATIONS OF IMMORTALITY FROM RECOLLECTIONS OF EARLY CHILDHOOD

> The Child is father of the Man;
> And I could wish my days to be
> Bound each to each by natural piety.[1]

1

There was a time when meadow, grove, and stream,
 The earth, and every common sight,
   To me did seem
   Apparelled in celestial light,
The glory and the freshness of a dream.
It is not now as it hath been of yore—   5
   Turn wheresoe'er I may,
    By night or day,
The things which I have seen I now can see no more.

---

1. The concluding lines of Wordsworth's *My Heart Leaps Up*.

2

The Rainbow comes and goes,   10
  And lovely is the Rose,
  The Moon doth with delight
Look round her when the heavens are bare,
  Waters on a starry night
  Are beautiful and fair;   15
The sunshine is a glorious birth;
But yet I know, where'er I go,
That there hath passed away a glory from the earth.

3

Now while the birds thus sing a joyous song,
  And while the young lambs bound
    As to the tabor's sound,[2]   20
To me alone there came a thought of grief:
A timely utterance[3] gave that thought relief,
  And I again am strong:
The cataracts blow their trumpets from the steep;   25
No more shall grief of mine the season wrong;
I hear the Echoes through the mountains throng,
The Winds come to me from the fields of sleep,[4]
  And all the earth is gay;
    Land and sea   30
  Give themselves up to jollity,
    And with the heart of May
  Doth every Beast keep holiday—
    Thou Child of Joy,
Shout round me, let me hear thy shouts, thou happy   35
  Shepherd-boy!

4

Ye blessed Creatures, I have heard the call
  Ye to each other make; I see
The heavens laugh with you in your jubilee;
  My heart is at your festival,
    My head hath its coronal,[5]   40
The fullness of your bliss, I feel—I feel it all.
    Oh, evil day! if I were sullen
    While Earth herself is adorning,
      This sweet May morning,
    And the Children are culling   45
      On every side,
  In a thousand valleys far and wide,
  Fresh flowers; while the sun shines warm,

2. A tabor is a small drum often used to beat time for dancing.
3. Perhaps *My Heart Leaps Up*, perhaps *Resolution and Independence*, perhaps not a poem at all.
4. Of the many suggested interpretations, the simplest is "from the fields where they were sleeping." Wordsworth often associated a rising wind with the revival of spirit and poetic inspiration; see, e.g., the opening passage of *The Prelude*.
5. Circlet of wild flowers, with which the shepherd boys trimmed their hats in May.

And the Babe leaps up on his Mother's arm—
    I hear, I hear, with joy I hear!
    —But there's a Tree, of many, one,   50
A single Field which I have looked upon,
Both of them speak of something that is gone:
    The Pansy at my feet
    Doth the same tale repeat:
Whither is fled the visionary gleam?   55
Where is it now, the glory and the dream?

5

Our birth is but a sleep and a forgetting:
The Soul that rises with us, our life's Star,[6]
    Hath had elsewhere its setting,   60
    And cometh from afar:
    Not in entire forgetfulness,
    And not in utter nakedness,
But trailing clouds of glory do we come
    From God, who is our home: 65
Heaven lies about us in our infancy!
Shades of the prison-house begin to close
    Upon the growing Boy
    But he
Beholds the light, and whence it flows,
    He sees it in his joy;   70
The Youth, who daily farther from the east
    Must travel, still is Nature's Priest,
    And by the vision splendid
    Is on his way attended;
At length the Man perceives it die away,   75
And fade into the light of common day.

6

Earth fills her lap with pleasures of her own;
Yearnings she hath in her own natural kind,
And, even with something of a Mother's mind,   80
    And no unworthy aim,
    The homely[7] Nurse doth all she can
To make her foster child, her Inmate Man,
    Forget the glories he hath known,
And that imperial palace whence he came.   85

7

Behold the Child among his newborn blisses,
A six-years' Darling of a pygmy size!
See, where 'mid work of his own hand he lies,
Fretted[8] by sallies of his mother's kisses,
With light upon him from his father's eyes!   90
See, at his feet, some little plan or chart,
Some fragment from his dream of human life,

6. The sun, as metaphor for the soul.
7. In the old sense, "simple and friendly."
8. "Irritated," or possibly in the old sense, "checkered over."

Shaped by himself with newly-learned art;
A wedding or a festival,
A mourning or a funeral;   95
And this hath now his heart,
And unto this he frames his song;
Then will he fit his tongue
To dialogues of business, love, or strife;
But it will not be long   100
Ere this be thrown aside,
And with new joy and pride
The little Actor cons another part;
Filling from time to time his "humorous stage"[9]
With all the Persons, down to palsied Age,   105
That Life brings with her in her equipage;
As if his whole vocation
Were endless imitation.

8

Thou, whose exterior semblance doth belie
Thy Soul's immensity;   110
Thou best Philosopher, who yet dost keep
Thy heritage, thou Eye among the blind,
That, deaf and silent, read'st the eternal deep,
Haunted forever by the eternal mind—
Mighty Prophet! Seer blest!   115
On whom those truths do rest, ·
Which we are toiling all our lives to find,
In darkness lost, the darkness of the grave;
Thou, over whom thy Immortality
Broods like the Day, a Master o'er a Slave,   120
A Presence which is not to be put by;
Thou little Child, yet glorious in the might
Of heaven-born freedom on thy being's height,
Why with such earnest pains dost thou provoke
The years to bring the inevitable yoke,   125
Thus blindly with thy blessedness at strife?
Full soon thy Soul shall have her earthly freight,
And custom lie upon thee with a weight,
Heavy as frost, and deep almost as life!

9

O joy! that in our embers   130
Is something that doth live,
That nature yet remembers
What was so fugitive!
The thought of our past years in me doth breed
Perpetual benediction: not indeed   135
For that which is most worthy to be blest;
Delight and liberty, the simple creed

9. From a sonnet by Samuel Daniel, Elizabethan poet. In Daniel's age, "humerous" meant "capricious," and also referred to the various characters and temperaments ("humors") represented in drama.

Of Childhood, whether busy or at rest,
With new-fledged hope still fluttering in his breast—
      Not for these I raise   140
      The song of thanks and praise;
   But for those obstinate questionings
   Of sense and outward things,
   Fallings from us, vanishings;
   Blank misgivings of a Creature[1]   145
Moving about in worlds not realized,
High instincts before which our mortal **Nature**
Did tremble like a guilty Thing surprised;
      But for those first affections,
      Those shadowy recollections,
     Which, be they what they may,   150
Are yet the fountain light of all our day,
Are yet a master light of all our seeing;
   Uphold us, cherish, and have power to make
Our noisy years seem moments in the being   155
Of the eternal Silence: truths that wake,
      To perish never;
Which neither listlessness, nor mad endeavor,
      Nor Man nor Boy,
Nor all that is at enmity with joy,   160
Can utterly abolish or destroy!
      Hence in a season of calm weather
      Though inland far we be,
Our Souls have sight of that immortal sea
      Which brought us hither,   165
      Can in a moment travel thither,
And see the Children sport upon the shore,
And hear the mighty waters rolling evermore.

      10

Then sing, ye Birds, sing, sing a joyous song!
      And let the young Lambs bound
      As to the tabor's sound!   170
We in thought will join your throng,
      Ye that pipe and ye that play,
      Ye that through your hearts today
      Feel the gladness of the May!
What though the radiance which was once so bright   175
Be now forever taken from my sight,
      Though nothing can bring back the hour
Of splendor in the grass, of glory in the flower;
      We will grieve not, rather find   180
      Strength in what remains behind;
      In the primal sympathy
      Which having been must ever be;
      In the soothing thoughts that spring
      Out of human suffering;   185

1. Not seeming real; see Wordsworth's comment in the headnote to the *Ode*.

In the faith that looks through death,
In years that bring the philosophic mind.

11

And O, ye Fountains, Meadows, Hills, and Groves,
Forebode not any severing of our loves!
Yet in my heart of hearts I feel your might;   190
I only have relinquished one delight
To live beneath your more habitual sway.
I love the Brooks which down their channels fret,
Even more than when I tripped lightly as they;
The innocent brightness of a newborn Day   195
      Is lovely yet;
The clouds that gather round the setting sun
Do take a sober coloring from an eye
That hath kept watch o'er man's mortality;
Another race hath been, and other palms are won[2].   200
Thanks to the human heart by which we live,
Thanks to its tenderness, its joys, and fears,
To me the meanest flower that blows can give
Thoughts that do often lie too deep for tears.

1802–4   1807

Ode to Duty[1]

*Jam non consilio bonus, sed more eo perductus, ut non tantum recte facere possim,
sed nisi recte facere non possim.*

Stern Daughter of the Voice of God![2]
O Duty! if that name thou love

2. In Greece, foot races were often run for the prize of a branch or wreath of palm. Wordsworth's line echoes Paul, 1 Corinthians ix.24, who uses such races as a metaphor for life: "Know ye not that they which run in a race run all, but one receiveth the prize?"

1. "This Ode * * * is on the model of Gray's *Ode to Adversity* which is copied from Horace's *Ode to Fortune.* Many and many a time have I been twitted by my wife and sister for having forgotten this dedication of myself to the stern lawgiver" (Wordsworth).

This poem merits its reputation as a departure from Wordsworth's earlier poems and ideas. In it he abandons the descriptive-meditative pattern of his *Tintern Abbey* and *Ode: Intimations of Immortality* and reverts to the standard 18th-century form of an ode addressed to a personified abstraction. The moral idea of this poem also represents Wordsworth's reversion from his youthful reliance on natural impulse to a more orthodox ethical tradition. The poem makes no reference to that "Nature" which earlier had constituted for Wordsworth "both law and impulse," and, in *Tintern Abbey*, had been called "The guide, the guard-

ian of my heart, and soul / Of all my moral being." The Duty, "Stern Daughter of the Voice of God," to which Wordsworth now commends himself, is the same concept as Milton's "right reason," God's representative in man, which Christian humanists had developed by combining the stern morality of the pagan Stoics with the concept of the inner voice of the Christian "conscience." (In one MS. variant Wordsworth described Duty as "sent from God" to keep us to the road "which conscience hath pronounced the best.")

The epigraph is translated, "Now I am not good by taking thought, but have been brought by habit to such a point that it is not so much that I am able to act rightly, but that I am unable to act other than rightly." Added in 1837, it is an adaptation from *Moral Epistles* CXX.10 by Seneca (4 B.C.–A.D. 65), Stoic philosopher and writer of tragedies.

2. Cf. *Paradise Lost* IX.652–54: "God so commanded, and left that Command / Sole Daughter of his voice; the rest, we live / Law to ourselves, our Reason is our Law."

Who are a light to guide, a rod
To check the erring, and reprove;
Thou, who art victory and law
When empty terrors overawe;   5
From vain temptations dost set free;
And calm'st the weary strife of frail humanity!

There are who ask not if thine eye
Be on them; who, in love and truth,
Where no misgiving is, rely   10
Upon the genial sense[3] of youth:
Glad Hearts! without reproach or blot;
Who do thy work, and know it not:
Oh! if through confidence misplaced   15
They fail, thy saving arms, dread Power! around them cast.

Serene will be our days and bright,
And happy will our nature be,
When love is an unerring light,
And joy its own security.   20
And they a blissful course may hold
Even now, who, not unwisely bold,
Live in the spirit of this creed;
Yet seek thy firm support, according to their need.

I, loving freedom, and untried,   *Self-analysis.*   25
No sport of every random gust,
Yet being to myself a guide,
Too blindly have reposed my trust;   } *Resolves to*
And oft, when in my heart was heard   } *be more attentive*
Thy timely mandate, I deferred   } *to his duty* 30
The task, in smoother walks to stray;
But thee I now would serve more strictly, if I may.

Through no disturbance of my soul,
Or strong compunction[4] in me wrought,
I supplicate for thy control;   35
But in the quietness of thought:
Me this unchartered freedom tires;
I feel the weight of chance desires:
My hopes no more must change their name,   *He longs for a*
I long for a repose that ever is the same.   *consistency of purpose.*   40

Stern Lawgiver! yet thou dost wear
The Godhead's most benignant grace;
Nor know we anything so fair
As is the smile upon thy face:
Flowers laugh before thee on their beds   45
And fragrance in thy footing treads;

---

3. Innate vitality.
4. In the older sense, "sting of conscience," "remorse."

Almost an acceptance of Quietistic mysticism.

Thou dost preserve the stars from wrong;[5]
And the most ancient heavens, through thee, are fresh and strong.

To humbler functions, awful Power!
I call thee: I myself commend
Unto thy guidance from this hour;   50
Oh, let my weakness have an end!
Give unto me, made lowly wise,[6]
The spirit of self-sacrifice;
The confidence of reason give;   55
And in the light of truth thy Bondman let me live!
1804   1807

The Solitary Reaper[1]

Behold her, single in the field,
Yon solitary Highland Lass!
Reaping and singing by herself;
Stop here, or gently pass!
Alone she cuts and binds the grain,   5
And sings a melancholy strain;
O listen! for the Vale profound
Is overflowing with the sound.

No Nightingale did ever chaunt
More welcome notes to weary bands   10
Of travelers in some shady haunt,
Among Arabian sands;
A voice so thrilling ne'er was heard
In springtime from the Cuckoo bird,
Breaking the silence of the seas   15
Among the farthest Hebrides.

Will no one tell me what she sings?[2]—
Perhaps the plaintive numbers flow
For old, unhappy, far-off things,
And battles long ago;   20
Or is it some more humble lay,

5. Wordsworth's parallel between the moral law and the laws governing the motion of the stars is illuminated by Kant's famous statement: "Two things fill the mind with ever new and increasing admiration and awe * * * the starry heavens above and the moral law within."

6. Another echo from Milton, whose Christian-humanist ethic pervades this ode. The angel Raphael had advised Adam (*Paradise Lost* VIII.173–74), "Be lowly wise: / Think only what concerns thee and thy being."

1. One of the rare poems not based on Wordsworth's own experience. Wordsworth tells us that it was suggested by a passage in Thomas Wilkinson's *Tour of Scotland* (1824), which he had seen in MS.: "Passed by a female who was reaping alone, she sung in Erse [the Gaelic language of Scotland] as she bended over her sickle, the sweetest human voice I ever heard. Her strains were tenderly melancholy, and felt delicious long after they were heard no more."

2. I.e., the poet does not understand Erse, the language in which she sings.

Familiar matter of today?
Some natural sorrow, loss, or pain,
That has been, and may be again?

Whate'er the theme, the Maiden sang   25
As if her song could have no ending;
I saw her singing at her work,
And o'er the sickle bending—
I listened, motionless and still;
And, as I mounted up the hill,   30
The music in my heart I bore,
Long after it was heard no more.

November 5, 1805   1807

Elegiac Stanzas

SUGGESTED BY A PICTURE OF PEELE CASTLE, IN A STORM,
PAINTED BY SIR GEORGE BEAUMONT[1]

I was thy neighbor once, thou rugged Pile!
Four summer weeks I dwelt in sight of thee:
I saw thee every day; and all the while
Thy Form was sleeping on a glassy sea.

So pure the sky, so quiet was the air!   5
So like, so very like, was day to day!
Whene'er I looked, thy Image still was there;
It trembled, but it never passed away.

How perfect was the calm! it seemed no sleep;
No mood, which season takes away, or brings: 10
I could have fancied that the mighty Deep
Was even the gentlest of all gentle Things.

Ah! then, if mine had been the Painter's hand,
To express what then I saw; and add the gleam,
The light that never was, on sea or land,   15
The consecration, and the Poet's dream;

I would have planted thee, thou hoary Pile
Amid a world how different from this!
Beside a sea that could not cease to smile;
On tranquil land, beneath a sky of bliss.   20

1. Sir George Beaumont, a wealthy landscape painter, was Wordsworth's patron and close friend. Peele Castle is on a promontory opposite Rampside, Lancashire, where Wordsworth had spent a month in 1794, eleven years before he saw Beaumont's painting. A current tendency is to interpret this poem as an expression of Wordsworth's loss of faith in nature. It should be noted, however, that the focus of the poem is not on an altered view of nature, but on an altered knowledge of life and on the moral values necessary to manage the certainty of loss and suffering.

Thou shouldst have seemed a treasure house divine ·
Of peaceful years; a chronicle of heaven—
Of all the sunbeams that did ever shine
The very sweetest had to thee been given.

A Picture had it been of lasting ease,   25
Elysian[2] quiet, without toil or strife;
No motion but the moving tide, a breeze,
Or merely silent Nature's breathing life.

Such, in the fond illusion of my heart,
Such Picture would I at that time have made,   30
And seen the soul of truth in every part,
A steadfast peace that might not be betrayed.

So once it would have been—'tis so no more;
I have submitted to a new control:
A power is gone, which nothing can restore;   35
A deep distress hath humanized my Soul.[3]

Not for a moment could I now behold
A smiling sea, and be what I have been:
The feeling of my loss will ne'er be old;
This, which I know, I speak with mind serene.   40

Then, Beaumont, Friend! who would have been the Friend,
If he had lived, of him whom I deplore,[4]
This work of thine I blame not, but commend;
This sea in anger, and that dismal shore.

O 'tis a passionate Work!—yet wise and well,   45
Well chosen is the spirit that is here;
That Hulk which labors in the deadly swell,
This rueful sky, this pageantry of fear!

And this huge Castle, standing here sublime,
I love to see the look with which it braves,   50
Cased in the unfeeling armor of old time,
The lightning, the fierce wind, and trampling waves.

Farewell, farewell the heart that lives alone,
Housed in a dream, at distance from the Kind![5]
Such happiness, wherever it be known,   55
Is to be pitied; for 'tis surely blind.

But welcome fortitude, and patient cheer,
And frequent sights of what is to be borne!
Such sights, or worse, as are before me here.—
Not without hope we suffer and we mourn.   60
1805   1807

2. Elysium, in classical mythology, was the peaceful place where those favored by the gods dwelled after death.
3. Captain John Wordsworth, Wil-

liam's brother, had been drowned in a shipwreck on February 5, 1805. He is referred to in lines 41–42.
4. Mourn.
5. Mankind.

SONNETS

Composed upon Westminster Bridge, September 3, 1802[1]

Earth has not anything to show more fair:
Dull would he be of soul who could pass by
A sight so touching in its majesty;
This City now doth, like a garment, wear
The beauty of the morning; silent, bare,   5
Ships, towers, domes, theaters, and temples lie
Open unto the fields, and to the sky;
All bright and glittering in the smokeless air.
Never did sun more beautifully steep
In his first splendor, valley, rock, or hill;   10
Ne'er saw I, never felt, a calm so deep!
The river glideth at his own sweet will:
Dear God! the very houses seem asleep;
And all that mighty heart is lying still!

1802   1807

It Is a Beauteous Evening[2]

It is a beauteous evening, calm and free,
The holy time is quiet as a Nun
Breathless with adoration; the broad sun
Is sinking down in its tranquility;
The gentleness of heaven broods o'er the Sea: 5
Listen! the mighty Being is awake,
And doth with his eternal motion make
A sound like thunder—everlastingly.
Dear Child! dear Girl! that walkest with me here,
If thou appear untouched by solemn thought,   10
Thy nature is not therefore less divine:
Thou liest in Abraham's bosom[3] all the year,
And worship'st at the Temple's inner shrine,
God being with thee when we know it not.

1802   1807

1. The date of this experience was not Sept. 3, but July 31, 1802; its occasion was a trip to France. See Dorothy Wordsworth's *Grasmere Journals* for July, 1802. The conflict of feelings attending Wordsworth's brief return to France, where he had once been a revolutionist and the lover of Annette Vallon, evoked a number of personal and political sonnets, among them the two which follow.
2. The girl walking with Wordsworth is Caroline, his natural daughter by Annette Vallon. For the event described, see *Grasmere Journals* for July, 1802.
3. Where the souls destined for heaven rest after death. Luke xvi.22: "And it came to pass, that the beggar died, and was carried by the angels into Abraham's bosom."

London, 1802[4]

Milton! thou shouldst be living at this hour:
England hath need of thee: she is a fen
Of stagnant waters: altar, sword, and pen,
Fireside, the heroic wealth of hall and bower,
Have forefeited their ancient English dower   5
Of inward happiness. We are selfish men;
Oh! raise us up, return to us again;
And give us manners, virtue, freedom, power.
Thy soul was like a Star, and dwelt apart;
Thou hadst a voice whose sound was like the sea: 10
Pure as the naked heavens, majestic, free,
So didst thou travel on life's common way,
In cheerful godliness; and yet thy heart
The lowliest duties on herself did lay.

September, 1802   1807

The World Is Too Much with Us

The world is too much with us; late and soon,
Getting and spending, we lay waste our powers;
Little we see in Nature that is ours;
We have given our hearts away, a sordid boon![5]
This Sea that bares her bosom to the moon,   5
The winds that will be howling at all hours,
And are up-gathered now like sleeping flowers,
For this, for everything, we are out of tune;
It moves us not.—Great God! I'd rather be
A Pagan suckled in a creed outworn;   10
So might I, standing on this pleasant lea,
Have glimpses that would make me less forlorn;
Have sight of Proteus rising from the sea;
Or hear old Triton blow his wreathéd horn.[6]

1807

Surprised by Joy[7]

Surprised by joy—impatient as the Wind
I turned to share the transport—Oh! with whom

---

4. One of a series "written immediately after my return from France to London, when I could not but be struck, as here described, with the vanity and parade of our own country * * * as contrasted with the quiet, and I may say the desolation, that the revolution had produced in France" (Wordsworth).

5. Gift; it is the act of giving the heart away that is sordid.

6. Proteus: an old man of the sea who (in the *Odyssey*) can assume a variety of shapes. Triton: a sea deity, usually represented as blowing on a conch shell. The description of Proteus echoes *Paradise Lost* III.603–604, and that of Triton echoes Spenser's *Colin Clout's Come Home Again*, lines 244–45. Spenser and Milton are the two English poets to whom Wordsworth specifically allied himself.

7. "This was in fact suggested by my daughter Catherine, long after her death" (Wordsworth). Catherine Wordsworth died June 4, 1812, at the age of 4.

But thee, deep buried in the silent tomb,
That spot which no vicissitude can find?
Love, faithful love, recalled thee to my mind— 5
But how could I forget thee? Through what power,
Even for the least division of an hour,
Have I been so beguiled as to be blind
To my most grievous loss!—That thought's return
Was the worst pang that sorrow ever bore, 10
Save one, one only, when I stood forlorn,
Knowing my heart's best treasure was no more;
That neither present time, nor years unborn
Could to my sight that heavenly face restore.

1815

Mutability [1]

From low to high doth dissolution climb,
And sink from high to low, along a scale
Of awful notes, whose concord shall not fail;
A musical but melancholy chime,
Which they can hear who meddle not with crime, 5
Nor avarice, nor over-anxious care.
Truth fails not; but her outward forms that bear
The longest date do melt like frosty rime,
That in the morning whitened hill and plain
And is no more; drop like the tower sublime 10
Of yesterday, which royally did wear
His crown of weeds, but could not even sustain
Some casual shout that broke the silent air,
Or the unimaginable touch of Time.

1821   1822

Steamboats, Viaducts, and Railways [2]

Motions and Means, on land and sea at war
With old poetic feeling, not for this,
Shall ye, by Poets even, be judged amiss!
Nor shall your presence, howsoe'er it mar
The loveliness of Nature, prove a bar 5
To the Mind's gaining that prophetic sense
Of future change, that point of vision, whence
May be discovered what in soul ye are.

1. This great sonnet interrupts a rather pedestrian sequence, *Ecclesiastical Sonnets*, dealing with the history and ceremonies of the church in England.
2. In late middle age Wordsworth demonstrates, as he had predicted in the Preface to *Lyrical Ballads*, that the poet will assimilate to his subject matter the "material revolution" produced by science. Unlike most poets, furthermore, he boldly accepts as evidences of man's progress even the unlovely encroachments of technology upon his beloved natural scene.

In spite of all that beauty may disown
In your harsh features, Nature doth embrace   10
Her lawful offspring in Man's art; and Time,
Pleased with your triumphs o'er his brother Space,
Accepts from your bold hands the proffered crown
Of hope, and smiles on you with cheer sublime.

1833   1835

Extempore Effusion upon the Death of James Hogg[1]

When first, descending from the moorlands,
I saw the Stream of Yarrow[2] glide
Along a bare and open valley,
The Ettrick Shepherd[3] was my guide.

When last along its banks I wandered,   5
Through groves that had begun to shed
Their golden leaves upon the pathways,
My steps the Border-minstrel[4] led.

The mighty Minstrel breathes no longer,
'Mid moldering ruins low he lies;   10
And death upon the braes[5] of Yarrow,
Has closed the Shepherd-poet's eyes:

Nor has the rolling year twice measured,
From sign to sign, its steadfast course,
Since every mortal power of Coleridge   15
Was frozen at its marvelous source;

The rapt One, of the godlike forehead,
The heaven-eyed creature sleeps in earth:
And Lamb, the frolic and the gentle,
Has vanished from his lonely hearth.   20

Like clouds that rake the mountain summits,
Or waves that own no curbing hand,
How fast has brother followed brother,
From sunshine to the sunless land!

Yet I, whose lids from infant slumber   25
Were earlier raised, remain to hear

1. Wordsworth's niece relates how Wordsworth was deeply moved by finding unexpectedly in a newspaper the account of the death of the poet James Hogg. "Half an hour afterwards he came into the room where the ladies were sitting and asked Miss Hutchinson [his sister-in-law] to write down some lines which he had just composed." All the poets named here, several of Wordsworth's closest friends among them, had died between 1832 and 1835.
2. A river in the southeast of Scotland.
3. James Hogg, the "Ettrick Shepherd" (he was born in Ettrick Forest, and was for a time a shepherd), was discovered as a writer by Sir Walter Scott, and became well known as a poet, essayist, and editor.
4. Sir Walter Scott.
5. The sloping banks of a stream.

A timid voice, that asks in whispers,
"Who next will drop and disappear?"

Our haughty life is crowned with darkness,
Like London with its own black wreath,
On which with thee, O Crabbe![6] forth-looking,   30
I gazed from Hampstead's breezy heath.

As if but yesterday departed,
Thou too art gone before; but why,
O'er ripe fruit, seasonably gathered,
Should frail survivors heave a sigh?   35

Mourn rather for that holy Spirit,
Sweet as the spring, as ocean deep;
For her[7] who, ere her summer faded,
Has sunk into a breathless sleep.   40

No more of old romantic sorrows,
For slaughtered Youth or lovelorn Maid!
With sharper grief is Yarrow smitten,
And Ettrick mourns with her their Poet dead.

November 21, 1835   1835

Prospectus
to *The Recluse*[1]

On Man, on Nature, and on Human Life,
Musing in solitude, I oft perceive
Fair trains of imagery before me rise,

---

6. George Crabbe, the poet of rural and village life.

7. Felicia Hemans, a minor but prolific poetess, who died when only 42. She is best known in America for *The Landing of the Pilgrim Fathers* and "The Boy Stood on the Burning Deck."

1. Through most of his poetic life Wordsworth labored intermittently at a long philosophic poem called *The Recluse,* which he intended to be his masterwork. As Wordsworth described this project in the Preface to *The Excursion* (1814), it was to consist of an autobiographical introduction (the poem now called *The Prelude*) and three long parts; of these three he completed only Book I of Part I ("Home at Grasmere") and Part II, called *The Excursion.* In the Preface to *The Excursion,* Wordsworth printed this long extract (the concluding section of "Home at Grasmere") to serve "as a kind of *Prospectus* of the design and scope of the whole Poem"—i.e., of the entire *Recluse.*

The first version of this "Prospectus" may have been drafted as early as 1798 or 1800. In language thronged with echoes from *Paradise Lost,* Wordsworth announces an undertaking which he conceives to be no less inspired and sublime than Milton's. In it he will move higher than Milton's heaven and deeper than Milton's hell, past scenes evoking greater fear than Erebus and greater awe than Jehovah; but without ever leaving "the Mind of Man— / My haunt, and the main region of my song" (lines 40–41). And his "high argument" is that Paradise can be regained; not, however, as in Revelation xxi, and in Milton, by the marriage between the New Jerusalem and Christ the Lamb, but by a marriage between the "intellect of Man" and "this goodly universe," and the resulting new "creation * * * which they with blended might / Accomplish" (lines 47–71). In no other passage does Wordsworth reveal so clearly the extent to which he assimilates to his poetry the Biblical scheme of Milton's epic—assigning, however, the active role, from creation to redemption, to the human faculties, in their vital interaction with the external universe.

Accompanied by feelings of delight
Pure, or with no unpleasing sadness mixed;   5
And I am conscious of affecting thoughts
And dear remembrances, whose presence soothes
Or elevates the Mind, intent to weigh
The good and evil of our mortal state.
—To these emotions, whencesoe'er they come,   10
Whether from breath of outward circumstance,
Or from the Soul—an impulse to herself—
I would give utterance in numerous verse.[2]
Of Truth, of Grandeur, Beauty, Love, and Hope,
And melancholy Fear subdued by Faith;   15
Of blessed consolations in distress;
Of moral strength, and intellectual Power;
Of joy in widest commonalty spread;
Of the individual Mind that keeps her own
Inviolate retirement, subject there   20
To Conscience only, and the law supreme
Of that Intelligence which governs all,
I sing—"fit audience let me find though few!"[3]
    So prayed, more gaining than he asked, the Bard—
In holiest mood. Urania,[4] I shall need   25
Thy guidance, or a greater Muse, if such
Descend to earth or dwell in highest heaven!
For I must tread on shadowy ground, must sink
Deep—and, aloft ascending, breathe in worlds
To which the heaven of heavens[5] is but a veil.   30
All strength—all terror, single or in bands,
That ever was put forth in personal form—
Jehovah—with his thunder, and the choir
Of shouting Angels, and the empyreal thrones—
I pass them unalarmed. Not Chaos, not   35
The darkest pit of lowest Erebus,[6]
Nor aught of blinder vacancy, scooped out
By help of dreams—can breed such fear and awe
As fall upon us often when we look
Into our Minds, into the Mind of Man—   40
My haunt, and the main region of my song.
—Beauty—a living Presence of the earth,
Surpassing the most fair ideal Forms
Which craft of delicate Spirits hath composed
From earth's materials—waits upon my steps;   45
Pitches her tents before me as I move,

---

2. Harmonious verse; an echo of *Paradise Lost* V.150. The inspiring "breath of outward circumstance" parallels the "correspondent breeze" in the opening passage of *The Prelude*, just below.
3. *Paradise Lost* VII.31.
4. The Muse whom Milton had invoked in *Paradise Lost* vii.1–39.

5. In *Paradise Lost* the dwelling place, beyond the visible heaven, of God and his angels. For line 34, see *Paradise Lost* II.430: "O progeny of Heaven, empyreal thrones!"
6. In classical myth, a dark region of the underworld; often used as a name for hell by Christian writers.

An hourly neighbor. Paradise, and groves
Elysian,[7] Fortunate Fields—like those of old
Sought in the Atlantic Main—why should they be
A history only of departed things,   50
Or a mere fiction of what never was?
For the discerning intellect of Man,
When wedded to this goodly universe
In love and holy passion, shall find these
A simple produce of the common day.   55
—I, long before the blissful hour arrives,
Would chant, in lonely peace, the spousal[8] verse
Of this great consummation—and, by words
Which speak of nothing more than what we are,
Would I arouse the sensual from their sleep   60
Of Death, and win the vacant and the vain
To noble raptures; while my voice proclaims
How exquisitely the individual Mind
(And the progressive powers perhaps no less
Of the whole species) to the external World   65
Is fitted—and how exquisitely, too—
Theme this but little heard of among men—
The external World is fitted to the Mind;
And the creation (by no lower name
Can it be called) which they with blended might   70
Accomplish—this is our high argument.[9]
—Such grateful haunts foregoing, if I oft
Must turn elsewhere—to travel near the tribes
And fellowships of men, and see ill sights
Of madding passions mutually inflamed;   75
Must hear Humanity in fields and groves
Pipe solitary anguish; or must hang
Brooding above the fierce confederate storm
Of sorrow, barricadoed[1] evermore
Within the walls of cities—may these sounds   80
Have their authentic comment; that even these
Hearing, I be not downcast or forlorn!—
Descend, prophetic Spirit! that inspir'st
The human Soul of universal earth,
Dreaming on things to come;[2] and dost possess   85
A metropolitan[3] temple in the hearts
Of mighty Poets: upon me bestow

---

7. **Elysium, in Greek myth, was the** place where men favored by the gods live a happy life after death. It was sometimes identified with the "Islands of the Blessed," reputed to be located far out in the western sea—hence "sought in the Atlantic Main." See Horace, *Epodes* XVI.
8. Marital; hence a "spousal verse" is an epithalamion.
9. Theme, as in *Paradise Lost* I.24:

"the height of this great argument."
1. Barricaded, as in *Paradise Lost* VIII.241: "Fast we found, fast shut / The dismal gates, and barricadoed strong * * *"
2. Cf. "the prophetic soul / Of the wide world dreaming on things to come" (Shakespeare, *Sonnet* CVII).
3. Designating the principal seat of a religion.

A gift of genuine insight; that my Song
With starlike virtue in its place may shine,
Shedding benignant influence, and secure,   90
Itself, from all malevolent effect
Of those mutations that extend their sway
Throughout the nether sphere![4]—And if with this
I mix more lowly matter; with the thing
Contemplated, describe the Mind and Man   95
Contemplating; and who, and what he was—
The transitory Being that beheld
The Vision; when and where, and how he lived[5]—
Be not this labor useless. If such theme
May sort with highest objects, then—dread Power!   100
Whose gracious favor is the primal source
Of all illumination—may my Life
Express the image of a better time,
More wise desires, and simpler manners—nurse
My Heart in genuine freedom—all pure thoughts   105
Be with me—so shall thy unfailing love
Guide, and support, and cheer me to the end!

ca. 1798–1814   1814

4. In the Ptolemaic world picture, the spheres of the heavenly bodies were immutable, and only the earth (the "nether sphere," or region below the sphere of the moon) was subject to change. Compare *Paradise Lost* VII.375 and X.656–64.

5. Wordsworth thus justifies *The Prelude* and the autobiographical sections of *The Recluse*.

The Prelude

The Prelude is Wordsworth's crowning achievement, the greatest and most original long poem since Milton's *Paradise Lost*. Its existence, however, was unknown to the public until after Wordsworth's death in 1850. When, three months later, *The Prelude* was published from manuscript, its title was given to it by the poet's wife; Wordsworth himself had referred to it variously as "the poem to Coleridge," "the poem on the growth of my own mind," and "the poem on my own poetical education."

For some 75 years this posthumous publication of 1850 was the only known text of *The Prelude*. Then in 1926 Ernest de Selincourt, working from manuscripts, printed an earlier version of the poem that Wordsworth had completed in 1805. Since that time other scholars have established the existence of a still earlier and much shorter version of *The Prelude*, in two parts, which Wordsworth had composed in 1798–99. The following seems to have been the process of composition that produced the three extant versions of the poem:

1. The *Two-Part Prelude* of 1799. Wordsworth originally planned, early in 1798, to include an account of his own development as a poet in his projected but never-completed philosophical poem *The Recluse* (see the title footnote to the "Prospectus" for *The Recluse*, above). While living in Germany during the autumn and winter of 1798–99, he composed a number of passages about his early experiences with nature. What had

been intended to be part of *The Recluse*, however, quickly evolved into an independent autobiographical poem, and by late 1799, when Wordsworth settled with his sister, Dorothy, at Grasmere, he had written a poem in two parts, 978 lines in length, which takes his life from infancy, through his years at Hawkshead School, to the age of 17. This poem survives in two fair copies (MS. U and MS. V), and its two parts correspond, by and large, to the contents of Books I and II of the later versions of *The Prelude*. We print this earliest form of *The Prelude* in its entirety.

2. The 1805 *Prelude*. Late in 1801 Wordsworth began to expand the poem on his poetic life, and in 1804 he set to work intensively on the project. His initial plan was to write it in five books. Before he completed the five-book poem, however, he decided to enlarge it still further, to incorporate an account of his experiences in France and of his mental crisis after the failure of his hopes in the French Revolution, and to end the poem with his settlement at Grasmere and his taking up the great task of *The Recluse*. He completed this poem, in 13 books, in May of 1805. This is the version that Wordsworth read to Coleridge after his return from Malta (see *To William Wordsworth*, below).

3. The 1850 *Prelude*. For the next 35 years Wordsworth tinkered with the text, polishing the style and qualifying some of its radical statements about the divine sufficiency of the human mind in its communion with nature; he did not, however, in any essential way alter its subject matter or overall design. *The Prelude* that was published in July, 1850, is in 14 books and was printed from a fair copy; it incorporated Wordsworth's latest revisions, which had been made in 1839, as well as some alterations introduced by his literary executors. (Note that in the conventional short references "the 1805 *Prelude*" specifies the date of completion, and "the 1850 *Prelude*" specifies the date of publication.) Selections from each of the books of this final version of *The Prelude* are reprinted below; they were chosen to show the overall design of the poem, as well as to include its main operative concepts and its most distinctive passages of poetry.

The Two-Part Prelude (1799)

This work was composed 1798–99, soon after Wordsworth had discovered in *Tintern Abbey* (July, 1798) his distinctive voice and subject: the blank-verse poem of the remembrance of things past, in which the forming of an identity is presented as a continuing interaction between the solitary mind and the natural world. It is not certain whether Wordsworth considered this text to be a finished poem. At the opening the narrator plunges into the middle of things with a rhetorical question—"Was it for this * * *?"—twice repeated, in which "this" lacks an antecedent reference. Wordsworth very likely had in mind to add an introductory section that would correspond in function to the opening of the 1805 and 1850 *Preludes*; in these later poems the "this" refers back to his frustration in his attempts to write a great work that would fulfill his obligation as an elected poet-prophet. (See the 1850 *Prelude*, below, I.1–274.) The ending of Part II, on the other hand, in which the narrator sums up the circumstances which have given him his assured stance and function in a time of troubles, has both the content and cadence of a valediction intended to conclude the poem.

Whether or not, however, Wordsworth thought to end his work at this point, *The Prelude* of 1799 is thematically an entity, narrating the key episodes, from the poet's infancy to the threshold of his maturity, by which nature has provided him with the "gift" of contentment with his life, a "visionary" capacity, and a confidence in human nature which he bespeaks "in these times of fear" and "of dereliction and dismay" (II.478–92). This text, unlike the later versions (which, for altered structural purposes, relocate some of the episodes in later books), allows us to read the unbroken sequence of his "spots of time"; that is, revelatory moments of early experience which turn out, in retrospect, to mark crucial stages in the growth of the poet's mind. And in this version much of the poetry, especially in Part I (recounting his solitary communings with the external world up to the age of 10), has a terse power which was weakened by Wordsworth's later attempts to smooth out the syntax and heighten the style, and to elaborate the detail of passages which had originally been simple and direct. The footnotes below make it easy to compare Wordsworth's first and last versions of *The Prelude*, by identifying the passages of 1799 which correspond to the selections of 1850.

This text of *The Two-Part Prelude* was edited from the manuscripts by Jonathan Wordsworth and Stephen Gill, and is reprinted from *The Prelude: 1799, 1805, 1850: A Norton Critical Edition*, edited by Jonathan Wordsworth, M. H. Abrams, and Stephen Gill (1979). The manuscript text has not been modernized, with the exception that (since Wordsworth's capitalization of many common nouns was inconsistent) the initial capitals have been retained only for "God" and "Nature," and for terms that Wordsworth clearly intended to be personifications.

The Two-Part Prelude (1799)

[First Part]

Was it for this
That one, the fairest of all rivers,[1] loved
To blend his murmurs with my nurse's song,
And from his alder shades and rocky falls,
And from his fords and shallows, sent a voice   5
That flowed along my dreams? For this didst thou,
O Derwent, travelling over the green plains
Near my 'sweet birthplace',[2] didst thou, beauteous stream,
Make ceaseless music through the night and day,
Which with its steady cadence tempering   10
Our human waywardness, composed my thoughts
To more than infant softness, giving me
Among the fretful dwellings of mankind
A knowledge, a dim earnest, of the calm

1. The river Derwent, which flowed past the garden of his father's house at Cockermouth, Cumberland, on the northern border of the Lake District. Lines 1–198

correspond to the passage from the 1850 *Prelude* (below), I.269–475.
2. Echoing Coleridge's *Frost at Midnight* (below), line 28.

Which Nature breathes among the fields and groves?   15
Beloved Derwent, fairest of all streams,
Was it for this that I, a four years' child,
A naked boy, among thy silent pools
Made one long bathing of a summer's day,
Basked in the sun, or plunged into thy streams,   20
Alternate, all a summer's day, or coursed
Over the sandy fields, and dashed the flowers
Of yellow grunsel;[3] or, when crag and hill,
The woods, and distant Skiddaw's[4] lofty height,
Were bronzed with a deep radiance, stood alone   25
A naked savage in the thunder-shower?

    And afterwards ('twas in a later day,
Though early), when upon the mountain slope
The frost and breath of frosty wind had snapped
The last autumnal crocus, 'twas my joy   30
To wander half the night among the cliffs
And the smooth hollows where the woodcocks ran
Along the moonlight turf. In thought and wish
That time, my shoulder all with springes[5] hung,
I was a fell destroyer. Gentle powers,   35
Who give us happiness and call it peace,
When scudding on from snare to snare I plied
My anxious visitation, hurrying on,
Still hurrying, hurrying onward, how my heart
Panted; among the scattered yew-trees and the crags   40
That looked upon me, how my bosom beat
With expectation! Sometimes strong desire
Resistless overpowered me, and the bird
Which was the captive of another's toils[6]
Became my prey; and when the deed was done   45
I heard among the solitary hills
Low breathings coming after me, and sounds
Of undistinguishable motion, steps
Almost as silent as the turf they trod.

    Nor less in springtime, when on southern banks   50
The shining sun had from his knot of leaves
Decoyed the primrose flower, and when the vales
And woods were warm, was I a rover then
In the high places, on the lonesome peaks,
Among the mountains and the winds. Though mean   55
And though inglorious were my views,[7] the end
Was not ignoble. Oh, when I have hung
Above the raven's nest, by knots of grass

---

3. A plant, also known as ragwort.
4. A mountain nine miles east of Cocker-mouth.
5. Bird snares.

6. Either "snares" or "labors."
7. His intention was to steal ravens' eggs. "End": result.

Or half-inch fissures in the slipp'ry rock   60
But ill sustained, and almost, as it seemed,
Suspended by the blast which blew amain,
Shouldering the naked crag, oh, at that time,
While on the perilous ridge I hung alone,
With what strange utterance did the loud dry wind
Blow through my ears; the sky seemed not a sky   65
Of earth, and with what motion moved the clouds!

    The mind of man is fashioned and built up
Even as a strain of music. I believe
That there are spirits which, when they would form
A favored being, from his very dawn   70
Of infancy do open out the clouds
As at the touch of lightning, seeking him
With gentle visitation—quiet powers,
Retired, and seldom recognized, yet kind,
And to the very meanest not unknown—   75
With me, though rarely, in my boyish days
They communed. Others too there are, who use,
Yet haply aiming at the self-same end,
Severer interventions,[8] ministry
More palpable—and of their school was I.   80

    They guided me: one evening led by them
I went alone into a shepherd's boat,
A skiff, that to a willow-tree was tied
Within a rocky cave, its usual home.
The moon was up, the lake was shining clear   85
Among the hoary mountains; from the shore
I pushed, and struck the oars, and struck again
In cadence, and my little boat moved on
Just like a man who walks with stately step
Though bent on speed. It was an act of stealth   90
And troubled pleasure. Not without the voice
Of mountain echoes did my boat move on,
Leaving behind her still on either side
Small circles glittering idly in the moon,
Until they melted all into one track   95
Of sparkling light. A rocky steep uprose
Above the cavern of the willow-tree,
And now, as suited one who proudly rowed
With his best skill, I fixed a steady view
Upon the top of that same craggy ridge,   100
The bound of the horizon—for behind

8. Wordsworth here introduces the distinction between the two antithetic "powers" of nature—the "gentle visitation" (line 73), as opposed to "severer interventions"—which cooperate in forming the poet's mind and imagination; see, e.g., I.194–98, 430–35; II.371–76. The incident that follows is an example of a severer intervention.

Was nothing but the stars and the grey sky.
She was an elfin pinnace;[9] twenty times
I dipped my oars into the silent lake,
And as I rose upon the stroke my boat   105
Went heaving through the water like a swan—
When from behind that rocky steep, till then
The bound of the horizon, a huge cliff,
As if with voluntary power instinct,
Upreared its head. I struck, and struck again,   110
And, growing still in stature, the huge cliff
Rose up between me and the stars, and still,
With measured motion, like a living thing
Strode after me. With trembling hands I turned,
And through the silent water stole my way   115
Back to the cavern of the willow-tree.
There in her mooring-place I left my bark,
And through the meadows homeward went with grave
And serious thoughts; and after I had seen
That spectacle, for many days my brain   120
Worked with a dim and undetermined sense
Of unknown modes of being. In my thoughts
There was a darkness—call it solitude,
Or blank desertion—no familiar shapes
Of hourly objects, images of trees,   125
Of sea or sky, no colours of green fields,
But huge and mighty forms that do not live
Like living men moved slowly through my mind
By day, and were the trouble of my dreams.

　　Ah, not in vain ye beings of the hills,   130
And ye that walk the woods and open heaths
By moon or star-light, thus, from my first dawn
Of childhood, did ye love to intertwine
The passions that build up our human soul
Not with the mean and vulgar[1] works of man,   135
But with high objects, with eternal things,
With life and Nature, purifying thus
The elements of feeling and of thought,
And sanctifying by such discipline
Both pain and fear, until we recognise   140
A grandeur in the beatings of the heart.
Nor was this fellowship vouchsafed to me
With stinted kindness. In November days,
When vapours rolling down the valleys made
A lonely scene more lonesome, among woods   145
At noon, and 'mid the calm of summer nights
When by the margin of the trembling lake

---

9. I.e., a small boat.　　　　　　1. Commonplace.

Beneath the gloomy hills I homeward went
In solitude, such intercourse was mine.

And in the frosty season, when the sun   150
Was set, and visible for many a mile
The cottage windows through the twilight blazed,
I heeded not the summons. Clear and loud
The village clock tolled six; I wheeled about
Proud and exulting, like an untired horse   155
That cares not for its home. All shod with steel
We hissed along the polished ice in games
Confederate, imitative of the chace
And woodland pleasures, the resounding horn,
The pack loud bellowing, and the hunted hare.   160
So through the darkness and the cold we flew,
And not a voice was idle. With the din,
Meanwhile, the precipices rang aloud;
The leafless trees and every icy crag
Tinkled like iron; while the distant hills   165
Into the tumult sent an alien sound
Of melancholy, not unnoticed; while the stars,
Eastward, were sparkling clear, and in the west
The orange sky of evening died away.

Not seldom from the uproar I retired   170
Into a silent bay, or sportively
Glanced sideway,[2] leaving the tumultuous throng,
To cut across the shadow[3] of a star
That gleamed upon the ice. And oftentimes
When we had given our bodies to the wind,   175
And all the shadowy banks on either side
Came sweeping through the darkness, spinning still
The rapid line of motion, then at once
Have I, reclining back upon my heels
Stopped short—yet still the solitary cliffs   180
Wheeled by me, even as if the earth had rolled
With visible motion her diurnal[4] round.
Behind me did they stretch in solemn train,[5]
Feebler and feebler, and I stood and watched
Till all was tranquil as a summer sea.   185

Ye powers of earth, ye genii[6] of the springs,
And ye that have your voices in the clouds,
And ye that are familiars of the lakes
And of the standing pools, I may not think
A vulgar hope was yours when ye employed   190

2. Moved off at an angle.
3. Reflection.
4. Daily.
5. Sequence.
6. Guardian spirits of a particular place.
   "Familiars" (line 188): attendant spirits.

Such ministry—when ye through many a year
Thus, by the agency of boyish sports,
On caves and trees, upon the woods and hills,
Impressed upon all forms the characters[7]
Of danger or desire, and thus did make   195
The surface of the universal earth
With meanings of delight, of hope and fear,
Work[8] like a sea.

          Not uselessly employed,
I might pursue this theme through every change
Of exercise and sport to which the year   200
Did summon us in its delightful round.
We were a noisy crew; the sun in heaven
Beheld not vales more beautiful than ours,
Nor saw a race in happiness and joy
More worthy of the fields where they were sown.   205
I would record with no reluctant voice
Our home amusements by the warm peat fire
At evening, when with pencil and with slate,
In square divisions parcelled out, and all
With crosses and with cyphers scribbled o'er,   210
We schemed and puzzled, head opposed to head,
In strife too humble to be named in verse;[9]
Or round the naked table, snow-white deal,[1]
Cherry, or maple, sate in close array,
And to the combat—lu or whist[2]—led on   215
A thick-ribbed army, not as in the world
Discarded and ungratefully thrown by
Even for the very service they had wrought,
But husbanded through many a long campaign.
Oh, with what echoes on the board they fell—   220
Ironic diamonds, hearts of sable hue,[3]
Queens gleaming through their splendour's last decay,
Knaves wrapt in one assimilating gloom,
And kings indignant at the shame incurred
By royal visages. Meanwhile abroad   225
The heavy rain was falling, or the frost
Raged bitterly with keen and silent tooth,
And, interrupting the impassioned game,
Oft from the neighbouring lake the splitting ice,
While it sank down towards the water, sent   230
Among the meadows and the hills its long

---

7. Signs.
8. Seethe.
9. Ticktacktoe; Wordsworth parodies neoclassic decorum by dignifying with high-flown phrases things too lowly to be named in poetry.
1. Boards cut from fir or pine.

2. Loo and whist are card games. Wordsworth's description of these games, as played by boys with bedraggled cards, is a takeoff on Pope's mock-heroic description of the game of ombre in *The Rape of the Lock*, III.25 ff
3. I.e., the red hearts are black with dirt.

And frequent yellings, imitative some
Of wolves that howl along the Bothnic main.[4]

    Nor with less willing heart would I rehearse
The woods of autumn, and their hidden bowers   235
With milk-white clusters hung; the rod and line—
True symbol of the foolishness of hope—
Which with its strong enchantment led me on
By rocks and pools, where never summer star
Impressed its shadow, to forlorn cascades   240
Among the windings of the mountain-brooks;
The kite in sultry calms from some high hill
Sent up, ascending thence till it was lost
Among the fleecy clouds—in gusty days
Launched from the lower grounds, and suddenly   245
Dashed headlong and rejected by the storm.
All these, and more, with rival claims demand
Grateful acknowledgement. It were a song
Venial,[5] and such as—if I rightly judge—
I might protract unblamed, but I perceive   250
That much is overlooked, and we should ill
Attain our object if, from delicate fears
Of breaking in upon the unity
Of this my argument,[6] I should omit
To speak of such effects as cannot here   255
Be regularly classed, yet tend no less
To the same point, the growth of mental power
And love of Nature's works.

                  Ere I had seen
Eight summers—and 'twas in the very week
When I was first transplanted to thy vale,   260
Beloved Hawkshead;[7] when thy paths, thy shores
And brooks, were like a dream of novelty
To my half-infant mind—I chanced to cross
One of those open fields which, shaped like ears,
Make green peninsulas on Esthwaite's lake.   265
Twilight was coming on, yet through the gloom
I saw distinctly on the opposite shore,
Beneath a tree and close by the lake side,
A heap of garments, as if left by one
Who there was bathing. Half an hour I watched   270
And no one owned them; meanwhile the calm lake
Grew dark with all the shadows on its breast,
And now and then a leaping fish disturbed

4. The Gulf of Bothnia is a northern arm
of the Baltic Sea.
5. Trivial, readily forgivable.
6. Theme.

7. Where Wordsworth boarded and at-
tended school. In biographical fact,
Wordsworth was nine when he went to
Hawkshead.

The breathless stillness. The succeeding day
There came a company, and in their boat   275
Sounded with iron hooks and with long poles.
At length the dead man, 'mid that beauteous scene
Of trees and hills and water, bolt upright
Rose with his ghastly face.[8] I might advert
To numerous accidents in flood or field,[9]   280
Quarry or moor, or 'mid the winter snows,
Distresses and disasters, tragic facts
Of rural history, that impressed my mind
With images to which in following years
Far other feelings were attached—with forms   285
That yet exist with independent life,
And, like their archetypes,[1] know no decay.

    There are in our existence spots of time
Which with distinct preeminence retain
A fructifying virtue,[2] whence, depressed   290
By trivial occupations and the round
Of ordinary intercourse, our minds—
Especially the imaginative power—
Are nourished and invisibly repaired;
Such moments chiefly seem to have their date   295
In our first childhood. I remember well
('Tis of an early season that I speak,
The twilight of rememberable life),
While I was yet an urchin, one who scarce
Could hold a bridle, with ambitious hopes   300
I mounted, and we rode towards the hills.
We were a pair of horsemen: honest James[3]
Was with me, my encourager and guide.
We had not travelled long ere some mischance
Disjoined me from my comrade, and, through fear   305
Dismounting, down the rough and stony moor
I led my horse, and stumbling on, at length
Came to a bottom[4] where in former times
A man, the murderer of his wife, was hung
In irons. Mouldered was the gibbet-mast;   310
The bones were gone, the iron and the wood;
Only a long green ridge of turf remained
Whose shape was like a grave. I left the spot,
And reascending the bare slope I saw
A naked pool that lay beneath the hills,   315

8. Wordsworth later transferred the passage on the drowned man in Esthwaite (lines 258–79) to Book V of *The Prelude* of 1805 and 1850.
9. "Wherein I spake of most disastrous chances, / Of moving accidents by flood and field" (*Othello* I.iii.134–35).

1. The reference is back to "tragic facts" (line 282), as distinguished from the feelings later attached to those facts (line 285).
2. A power to make fruitful, productive.
3. An accompanying servant.
4. Valley.

The beacon on the summit, and more near
A girl who bore a pitcher on her head
And seemed with difficult steps to force her way
Against the blowing wind. It was in truth
An ordinary sight, but I should need   320
Colours and words that are unknown to man
To paint the visionary dreariness
Which, while I looked all round for my lost guide,
Did at that time invest the naked pool,
The beacon on the lonely eminence,   325
The woman and her garments vexed and tossed
By the strong wind.

               Nor less I recollect—
Long after, though my childhood had not ceased—
Another scene which left a kindred power
Implanted in my mind. One Christmas-time,   330
The day before the holidays began,[5]
Feverish, and tired, and restless, I went forth
Into the fields, impatient for the sight
Of those three horses which should bear us home,
My brothers and myself. There was a crag,   335
An eminence, which from the meeting-point
Of two highways ascending overlooked
At least a long half-mile of those two roads,
By each of which the expected steeds might come—
The choice uncertain. Thither I repaired   340
Up to the highest summit. 'Twas a day
Stormy, and rough, and wild, and on the grass
I sate half sheltered by a naked wall.
Upon my right hand was a single sheep,
A whistling hawthorn on my left, and there,   345
Those two companions at my side, I watched
With eyes intensely straining, as the mist
Gave intermitting prospects of the wood
And plain beneath. Ere I to school returned
That dreary time, ere I had been ten days   350
A dweller in my father's house, he died,
And I and my two brothers, orphans then,
Followed his body to the grave. The event,
With all the sorrow which it brought, appeared
A chastisement; and when I called to mind   355
That day so lately passed, when from the crag
I looked in such anxiety of hope,
With trite reflections of morality,
Yet with the deepest passion, I bowed low
To God who thus corrected my desires.   360

5. In December, 1783; Wordsworth, 13, was at Hawkshead school with two of his brothers.

And afterwards the wind and sleety rain,
And all the business of the elements,
The single sheep, and the one blasted tree,
And the bleak music of that old stone wall,
The noise of wood and water, and the mist   365
Which on the line of each of those two roads
Advanced in such indisputable shapes[6]—
All these were spectacles and sounds to which
I often would repair, and thence would drink
As at a fountain. And I do not doubt   370
That in this later time, when storm and rain
Beat on my roof at midnight, or by day
When I am in the woods, unknown to me
The workings of my spirit thence are brought.[7]

    Nor, sedulous[8] as I have been to trace   375
How Nature by collateral interest,
And by extrinsic passion, peopled first
My mind with forms or beautiful or grand
And made me love them, may I well forget
How other pleasures have been mine, and joys   380
Of subtler origin—how I have felt
Not seldom, even in that tempestuous time,
Those hallowed and pure motions of the sense
Which seem in their simplicity to own
An intellectual[9] charm, that calm delight   385
Which, if I err not, surely must belong
To those first-born affinities that fit
Our new existence to existing things,
And, in our dawn of being, constitute
The bond of union betwixt life and joy.   390

    Yes, I remember when the changeful earth
And twice five seasons on my mind had stamped
The faces of the moving year, even then,
A child, I held unconscious intercourse
With the eternal beauty, drinking in   395
A pure organic pleasure from the lines
Of curling mist, or from the level plain
Of waters coloured by the steady clouds.
The sands of Westmoreland, the creeks and bays
Of Cumbria's[1] rocky limits, they can tell   400

6. Pronounced *indisputáble shápes*; i.e., shapes one didn't dare question.
7. Wordsworth transferred these two "spots of time" (lines 288–374) to Book XII of the 1850 *Prelude* (below, XII.208–335). This drastic relocation was impelled by the new design of *The Prelude* as a crisis-autobiography: having related how his Imagination was "impaired," Words-

worth now describes how it was "restored" by the "renovating virtue" of such remembered moments of early experience.
8. Careful; "collateral": incidental. Lines 375–442 correspond to the 1850 *Prelude*, I.544–612 (below).
9. Spiritual.
1. Cumberland's.

How when the sea threw off his evening shade
And to the shepherd's hut beneath the crags
Did send sweet notice of the rising moon,
How I have stood, to images like these
A stranger, linking with the spectacle   405
No body of associated forms,
And bringing with me no peculiar sense
Of quietness or peace—yet I have stood
Even while my eye has moved o'er three long leagues[2]
Of shining water, gathering, as it seemed,   410
Through the wide surface of that field of light
New pleasure, like a bee among the flowers.

    Thus often in those fits of vulgar joy
Which through all seasons on a child's pursuits
Are prompt attendants, 'mid that giddy bliss   415
Which like a tempest works along the blood
And is forgotten, even then I felt
Gleams like the flashing of a shield. The earth
And common face of Nature spake to me
Rememberable things—sometimes, 'tis true,   420
By quaint associations, yet not vain
Nor profitless, if haply they impressed
Collateral objects and appearances,
Albeit lifeless then, and doomed to sleep
Until maturer seasons called them forth   425
To impregnate and to elevate the mind.
And if the vulgar joy by its own weight
Wearied itself out of the memory,
The scenes which were a witness of that joy
Remained, in their substantial lineaments   430
Depicted on the brain, and to the eye
Were visible, a daily sight. And thus
By the impressive agency of fear,
By pleasure and repeated happiness—
So frequently repeated—and by force   435
Of obscure feelings representative
Of joys that were forgotten, these same scenes,
So beauteous and majestic in themselves,
Though yet the day was distant, did at length
Become habitually dear, and all   440
Their hues and forms were by invisible links
Allied to the affections.[3]

                I began
My story early, feeling, as I fear,
The weakness of a human love for days

2. A league is approximately three miles.　|　3. Feelings.

Disowned by memory—ere the birth of spring   445
Planting my snowdrops among winter snows.[4]
Nor will it seem to thee, my friend,[5] so prompt
In sympathy, that I have lengthened out
With fond and feeble tongue a tedious tale.
Meanwhile my hope has been that I might fetch   450
Reproaches from my former years, whose power
May spur me on, in manhood now mature,
To honourable toil.[6] Yet should it be
That this is but an impotent desire—
That I by such inquiry am not taught   455
To understand myself, nor thou to know
With better knowledge how the heart was framed
Of him thou lovest—need I dread from thee
Harsh judgements if I am so loth to quit
Those recollected hours that have the charm   460
Of visionary things,[7] and lovely forms
And sweet sensations, that throw back our life
And make our infancy a visible scene
On which the sun is shining?

Second Part

Thus far, my friend, have we retraced the way
Through which I travelled when I first began
To love the woods and fields; the passion yet
Was in its birth, sustained, as might befal,
By nourishment that came unsought—for still   5
From week to week, from month to month, we lived
A round of tumult. Duly[2] were our games
Prolonged in summer till the daylight failed:
No chair remained before the doors, the bench
And threshold steps were empty, fast asleep   10
The labourer and the old man who had sate
A later lingerer, yet the revelry
Continued and the loud uproar. At last,
When all the ground was dark and the huge clouds
Were edged with twinkling stars, to bed we went   15
With weary joints and with a beating mind.
Ah, is there one who ever has been young
And needs a monitory voice to tame
The pride of virtue and of intellect?[2]
And is there one, the wisest and the best   20

4. I.e., he fears that he may have been
attributing later thoughts and feelings to
a time of life he can no longer remember.
5. Coleridge, to whom this, like the later
versions of the poem, is addressed.
6. An indication that the opening question, "Was it for this?" referred to delays in undertaking his major poetic enterprise.
7. Things seen in a vision.
1. Appropriately.
2. I.e., does anyone who was once young
need to be admonished not to overrate
the achievements of older age?

Of all mankind, who does not sometimes wish
For things which cannot be, who would not give,
If so he might, to duty and to truth
The eagerness of infantine desire?
A tranquillizing spirit presses now   25
On my corporeal frame, so wide appears
The vacancy between me and those days,
Which yet have such self-presence in my heart
That sometimes when I think of them I seem
Two consciousnesses—conscious of myself,   30
And of some other being.[3]

                    A grey stone
Of native rock, left midway in the square
Of our small market-village, was the home
And centre of these joys; and when, returned
After long absence thither I repaired,   35
I found that it was split and gone to build
A smart assembly-room[4] that perked and flared
With wash and rough-cast,[5] elbowing the ground
Which had been ours. But let the fiddle scream,
And be ye happy! Yet I know, my friends,   40
That more than one of you will think with me
Of those soft starry nights, and that old dame
From whom the stone was named,[6] who there had sate
And watched her table with its huckster's wares,
Assiduous, for the length of sixty years.   45

    We ran a boisterous race, the year span round
With giddy motion; but the time approached
That brought with it a regular desire
For calmer pleasures—when the beauteous scenes
Of Nature were collaterally attached   50
To every scheme of holiday delight,
And every boyish sport, less grateful else
And languidly pursued. When summer came
It was the pastime of our afternoons
To beat along the plain of Windermere[7]   55
With rival oars; and the selected bourn[8]
Was now an island musical with birds
That sang for ever, now a sister isle
Beneath the oak's umbrageous[9] covert, sown
With lilies-of-the-valley like a field,   60
And now a third small island where remained

---

3. The "two consciousnesses" are his present self and, co-present with it, the past self of his memory.
4. The Town Hall, built in 1790 on the Hawkshead Market Square.
5. "Wash": a wall paint with a water base; "rough-cast": a coarse mixture of mortar and gravel.
6. It was called "the Stone of Rowe."
7. The surface of Lake Windermere.
8. Terminus of a journey.
9. Shady.

An old stone table and one mouldered cave—
A hermit's history. In such a race,
So ended, disappointment could be none,
Uneasiness, or pain, or jealousy;   65
We rested in the shade, all pleased alike,
Conquered or conqueror. Thus our selfishness
Was mellowed down, and thus the pride of strength
And the vainglory of superior skill
Were interfused with objects which subdued   70
And tempered them, and gradually produced
A quiet independence of the heart.
And to my friend who knows me I may add,
Unapprehensive of reproof, that hence
Ensued a diffidence and modesty,   75
And I was taught to feel—perhaps too much—
The self-sufficing power of solitude.

    No delicate viands sapped our bodily strength:
More than we wished we knew the blessing then
Of vigorous hunger, for our daily meals   80
Were frugal, Sabine fare[1]—and then, exclude
A little weekly stipend, and we lived
Through three divisions of the quartered year
In pennyless poverty. But now, to school
Returned from the half-yearly holidays,   85
We came with purses more profusely filled,
Allowance which abundantly sufficed
To gratify the palate with repasts
More costly than the dame of whom I spake,
That ancient woman, and her board, supplied.   90
Hence inroads into distant vales, and long
Excursions far away among the hills,
Hence rustic dinners on the cool green ground—
Or in the woods, or by a river-side
Or fountain[2]—festive banquets, that provoked   95
The languid action of a natural scene
By pleasure of corporeal appetite.[3]

    Nor is my aim neglected if I tell
How twice in the long length of those half-years
We from our funds perhaps with bolder hand   100
Drew largely, anxious for one day at least
To feel the motion of the galloping steed;
And with the good old innkeeper, in truth
I needs must say, that sometimes we have used
Sly subterfuge, for the intended bound   105

1. Modest meals, like those served at
Horace's Sabine farm. "Exclude": leave
out of account.

2. Spring.
3. I.e., the pleasure of eating enhanced
the effect ("action") of the scenery.

Of the day's journey was too distant far
For any cautious man: a structure famed
Beyond its neighbourhood, the antique walls
Of a large abbey,[4] with its fractured arch,
Belfry, and images, and living trees—   110
A holy scene. Along the smooth green turf
Our horses grazed. In more than inland peace,
Left by the winds that overpass the vale,
In that sequestered ruin trees and towers—
Both silent and both motionless alike—   115
Hear all day long the murmuring sea that beats
Incessantly upon a craggy shore.

    Our steeds remounted, and the summons given,
With whip and spur we by the chantry[5] flew
In uncouth race, and left the cross-legged knight   120
And the stone abbot, and that single wren
Which one day sang so sweetly in the nave
Of the old church that, though from recent showers
The earth was comfortless, and, touched by faint
Internal breezes, from the roofless walls   125
The shuddering ivy dripped large drops, yet still
So sweetly 'mid the gloom the invisible bird
Sang to itself that there I could have made
My dwelling-place, and lived for ever there,
To hear such music. Through the walls we flew   130
And down the valley, and, a circuit made
In wantonness of heart, through rough and smooth
We scampered homeward. O, ye rocks and streams,
And that still spirit of the evening air,
Even in this joyous time I sometimes felt   135
Your presence, when, with slackened step, we breathed[6]
Along the sides of the steep hills, or when,
Lightened by gleams of moonlight from the sea,
We beat with thundering hoofs the level sand.

    There was a row of ancient trees, since fallen,   140
That on the margin of a jutting land
Stood near the lake of Coniston, and made,
With its long boughs above the water stretched,
A gloom through which a boat might sail along
As in a cloister. An old hall[7] was near,   145
Grotesque and beautiful, its gavel-end[8]
And huge round chimneys to the top o'ergrown

---

4. Furness Abbey, 21 miles south of Hawkshead.
5. A chapel endowed so that masses would be sung for the donor.
6. Stopped to let our horses catch their breath.
7. The Hall of Coniston, ancient seat of the Le Fleming family.
8. Gable.

With fields of ivy. Thither we repaired—
'Twas even a custom with us—to the shore,
And to that cool piazza. They who dwelt   150
In the neglected mansion-house supplied
Fresh butter, tea-kettle and earthernware,
And chafing-dish with smoking coals; and so
Beneath the trees we sate in our small boat,
And in the covert eat our delicate meal   155
Upon the calm smooth lake. It was a joy
Worthy the heart of one who is full grown
To rest beneath those horizontal boughs
And mark the radiance of the setting sun,
Himself unseen, reposing on the top   160
Of the high eastern hills. And there I said,
That beauteous sight before me, there I said
(Then first beginning in my thoughts to mark
That sense of dim similitude which links
Our moral feelings with external forms)   165
That in whatever region I should close
My mortal life I would remember you,
Fair scenes—that dying I would think on you,
My soul would send a longing look to you,
Even as that setting sun, while all the vale   170
Could nowhere catch one faint memorial gleam,
Yet with the last remains of his last light
Still lingered, and a farewell lustre threw
On the dear mountain-tops where first he rose.
'Twas then my fourteenth summer, and these words   175
Were uttered in a casual access
Of sentiment, a momentary trance
That far outran the habit of my mind.[9]

    Upon the eastern shore of Windermere
Above the crescent of a pleasant bay   180
There was an inn,[1] no homely-featured shed,
Brother of the surrounding cottages,
But 'twas a splendid place, the door beset
With chaises, grooms, and liveries, and within
Decanters, glasses and the blood-red wine.   185
In ancient times, or ere the hall was built
On the large island, had the dwelling been
More worthy of a poet's love, a hut
Proud of its one bright fire and sycamore shade;
But though the rhymes were gone which once inscribed   190
The threshold, and large golden characters
On the blue-frosted signboard had usurped
The place of the old lion, in contempt

9. Wordsworth transferred a shortened   *Prelude*, Book Eighth.
version of lines 140–178 to the 1850   1. The White Lion Inn at Bowness.

And mockery of the rustic painter's hand,
Yet to this hour the spot to me is dear   195
With all its foolish pomp. The garden lay
Upon a slope surmounted by the plain
Of a small bowling-green; beneath us stood
A grove, with gleams of water through the trees
And over the tree-tops—nor did we want   200
Refreshment, strawberries and mellow cream—
And there through half an afternoon we played
On the smooth platform, and the shouts we sent
Made all the mountains ring. But ere the fall
Of night, when in our pinnace we returned   205
Over the dusky lake, and to the beach
Of some small island steered our course, with one,
The minstrel of our troop, and left him there,
And rowed off gently, while he blew his flute
Alone upon the rock, oh, then the calm   210
And dead still water lay upon my mind
Even with a weight of pleasure, and the sky,
Never before so beautiful, sank down
Into my heart and held me like a dream.

    Thus day by day my sympathies increased,   215
And thus the common range of visible things
Grew dear to me: already I began
To love the sun, a boy I loved the sun
Not as I since have loved him—as a pledge
And surety of my earthly life, a light   220
Which while I view I feel I am alive—
But for this cause, that I had seen him lay
His beauty on the morning hills, had seen
The western mountain touch his setting orb
In many a thoughtless hour, when from excess   225
Of happiness my blood appeared to flow
With its own pleasure, and I breathed with joy.
And from like feelings, humble though intense,
To patriotic and domestic love
Analogous, the moon to me was dear;   230
For I would dream away my purposes
Standing to look upon her, while she hung
Midway between the hills as if she knew
No other region but belonged to thee,
Yea, appertained by a peculiar right   235
To thee and thy grey huts,[2] my native vale.

    Those incidental charms which first attached
My heart to rural objects, day by day

2. Gray stone cottages.

Grew weaker, and I hasten on to tell
How Nature, intervenient till this time   240
And secondary, now at length was sought
For her own sake. But who shall[3] parcel out
His intellect by geometric rules,
Split like a province into round and square?
Who knows the individual hour in which   245
His habits were first sown even as a seed?
Who that shall point as with a wand, and say
'This portion of the river of my mind
Came from yon fountain'? Thou, my friend, art one
More deeply read in thy own thoughts, no slave   250
Of that false secondary power[4] by which
In weakness we create distinctions, then
Believe our puny boundaries are things
Which we perceive, and not which we have made.
To thee, unblinded by these outward shews,   255
The unity of all has been revealed;
And thou wilt doubt with me, less aptly skilled
Than many are to class the cabinet[5]
Of their sensations, and in voluble phrase
Run through the history and birth of each   260
As of a single independent thing.
Hard task to analyse a soul, in which
Not only general habits and desires,
But each most obvious and particular thought—
Not in a mystical and idle sense,   265
But in the words of reason deeply weighed—
Hath no beginning.

              Blessed the infant babe—
For my best conjectures I would trace
The progress of our being—blest the babe
Nursed in his mother's arms, the babe who sleeps   270
Upon his mother's breast, who, when his soul
Claims manifest kindred with an earthly soul,[6]
Doth gather passion from his mother's eye.
Such feelings pass into his torpid life
Like an awakening breeze, and hence his mind,   275
Even in the first trial of its powers,
Is prompt and watchful, eager to combine
In one appearance all the elements
And parts of the same object, else detached
And loth to coalesce. Thus day by day   280
Subjected to the discipline of love,
His organs and recipient faculties

---

3. Is able to.
4. The analytic faculty, as opposed to the power to apprehend "the unity of all" (line 256).
5. To classify, as if in a display-case.
6. I.e., another human being.

Are quickened, are more vigorous; his mind spreads,
Tenacious of the forms[7] which it receives.
In one beloved presence—nay and more,   285
In that most apprehensive habitude[8]
And those sensations which have been derived
From this beloved presence—there exists
A virtue which irradiates and exalts
All objects through all intercourse of sense.   290
No outcast he, bewildered and depressed;
Along his infant veins are interfused
The gravitation and the filial bond
Of Nature that connect him with the world.
Emphatically such a being lives,   295
An inmate of this *active* universe.
From Nature largely he receives, nor so
Is satisfied, but largely gives again;
For feeling has to him imparted strength,
And—powerful in all sentiments of grief,   300
Of exultation, fear and joy—his mind,
Even as an agent of the one great mind,
Creates, creator and receiver both,
Working but in alliance with the works
Which it beholds. Such, verily, is the first   305
Poetic spirit of our human life—
By uniform control of after years
In most abated and suppressed, in some
Through every change of growth or of decay
Preeminent till death.[9]   310

From early days,
Beginning not long after that first time
In which, a babe, by intercourse of touch
I held mute dialogues with my mother's heart,[1]
I have endeavoured to display the means
Whereby this infant sensibility,   315
Great birthright of our being, was in me
Augmented and sustained. Yet is a path
More difficult before me, and I fear
That in its broken windings we shall need
The chamois'[2] sinews and the eagle's wing.   320
For now a trouble came into my mind
From obscure causes: I was left alone

---

7. Visual images.
8. I.e., in that customary mode of most sensitive perception.
9. Compare the 1850 version (II.232–65, below). The infant, secure in his mother's arms, experiences objects of sense which are irradiated by his assurance of maternal love, and so comes to feel at home in a world to which his mind has contributed, and which his own perceptions, therefore, in part create.
1. I.e., both the infant and the mother who clasps him feel the pulse of the other's heart.
2. A nimble, antelopelike animal inhabiting mountainous regions of Europe.

Seeking this visible world, nor knowing why.
The props of my affections were removed,[3]
And yet the building stood, as if sustained   325
By its own spirit. All that I beheld
Was dear to me, and from this cause it came
That now to Nature's finer influxes
My mind lay open—to that more exact
And intimate communion which our hearts   330
Maintain with the minuter properties
Of objects which already are beloved,
And of those only.

Many are the joys
Of youth, but oh, what happiness to live
When every hour brings palpable access   335
Of knowledge, when all knowledge is delight,
And sorrow is not there. The seasons came,
And every season brought a countless store
Of modes and temporary qualities
Which but for this most watchful power of love   340
Had been neglected, left a register
Of permanent relations else unknown.
Hence life, and change, and beauty, solitude
More active even than 'best society',[4]
Society made sweet as solitude   345
By silent inobtrusive sympathies,
And gentle agitations of the mind
From manifold distinctions, difference
Perceived in things where to the common eye
No difference is, and hence, from the same source,   350
Sublimer joy. For I would walk alone
In storm and tempest, or in starlight nights
Beneath the quiet heavens, and at that time
Would feel whate'er there is of power in sound
To breathe an elevated mood, by form   355
Or image unprofaned; and I would stand
Beneath some rock, listening to sounds that are
The ghostly[5] language of the ancient earth,
Or make their dim abode in distant winds.
Thence did I drink the visionary power.   360
I deem not profitless these fleeting moods
Of shadowy exaltation; not for this,
That they are kindred to our purer mind

3. Wordsworth's mother had died the month before his eighth birthday. The reference to "a trouble * * * / From obscure causes" (lines 321–22) makes it unclear whether he is referring to the loss of his mother (in whose arms he had come to feel secure in the world) or to an indefinite sense of being cut off from outer reality, such as he describes in lines 399–401, and later in the *Intimations Ode* (above, lines 143–47).
4. In *Paradise Lost* IX.249, Adam says to Eve that "solitude sometimes is best society."
5. Disembodied, or spiritual.

And intellectual life,[6] but that the soul—
Remembering how she felt, but what she felt   365
Remembering not—retains an obscure sense[7]
Of possible sublimity, to which
With growing faculties she doth aspire,
With faculties still growing, feeling still
That whatsoever point they gain they still   370
Have something to pursue.[8]

                          And not alone
In grandeur and in tumult, but no less
In tranquil scenes, that universal power
And fitness in the latent qualities
And essences of things, by which the mind   375
Is moved with feelings of delight, to me
Came strengthened with a superadded soul,
A virtue not its own. My morning walks
Were early: oft before the hours of school
I travelled round our little lake, five miles   380
Of pleasant wandering—happy time, more dear
For this, that one was by my side, a friend
Then passionately loved.[9] With heart how full
Will he peruse these lines, this page—perhaps
A blank to other men—for many years   385
Have since flowed in between us, and, our minds
Both silent to each other, at this time
We live as if those hours had never been.[1]
Nor seldom did I lift our cottage latch
Far earlier, and before the vernal thrush   390
Was audible,[2] among the hills I sate
Alone upon some jutting eminence
At the first hour of morning, when the vale
Lay quiet in an utter solitude.
How shall I trace the history, where seek   395
The origin of what I then have felt?
Oft in those moments such a holy calm
Did overspread my soul that I forgot
The agency of sight, and what I saw
Appeared like something in myself, a dream,   400
A prospect[3] in my mind.

                      'Twere long to tell
What spring and autumn, what the winter snows,

---

6. I.e., not because they are related to
the purer (the nonsensuous, or "intellectual") part of our mind.
7. Pronounced *obscŭre sénse*.
8. Compare the revelation that our destiny is with "something evermore about
to be" in Wordsworth's later passage
about crossing Simplon Pass (1850 *Prelude*, below, VI.604–8).

9. A note in the 1850 *Prelude* identifies
this friend as John Fleming.
1. I.e., in our separation we now live as
if we had never shared those morning
walks.
2. So early in the morning that the thrush
had not begun his spring song.
3. Scene.

And what the summer shade, what day and night,
The evening and the morning, what my dreams
And what my waking thoughts, supplied to nurse   405
That spirit of religious love in which
I walked with Nature. But let this at least
Be not forgotten, that I still retained
My first creative sensibility,[4]
That by the regular action of the world   410
My soul was unsubdued. A plastic[5] power
Abode with me, a forming hand, at times
Rebellious, acting in a devious mood,
A local spirit of its own, at war
With general tendency, but for the most   415
Subservient strictly to the external things
With which it communed. An auxiliar light
Came from my mind, which on the setting sun
Bestowed new splendour; the melodious birds,
The gentle breezes, fountains that ran on   420
Murmuring so sweetly in themselves, obeyed
A like dominion, and the midnight storm
Grew darker in the presence of my eye.
Hence my obeisance, my devotion hence,
And *hence* my transport.[6]   425

                    Nor should this, perchance,
Pass unrecorded, that I still[7] had loved
The exercise and produce of a toil
Than analytic industry to me
More pleasing, and whose character I deem
Is more poetic, as resembling more   430
Creative agency—I mean to speak
Of that interminable building reared
By observation of affinities
In objects where no brotherhood exists
To common minds. My seventeenth year was come,   435
And, whether from this habit rooted now
So deeply in my mind, or from excess
Of the great social principle of life
Coercing all things into sympathy,
To unorganic natures I transferred   440
My own enjoyments, or, the power of truth
Coming in revelation, I conversed
With things that really are, I at this time
Saw blessings spread around me like a sea.
Thus did my days pass on, and now at length   445
From Nature and her overflowing soul
I had received so much that all my thoughts
Were steeped in feeling. I was only then

4. As described in lines 301–6.   6. Exaltation.
5. Shaping, formative.   7. Always.

Contented when with bliss ineffable
I felt the sentiment of being spread   450
O'er all that moves, and all that seemeth still,
O'er all that, lost beyond the reach of thought
And human knowledge, to the human eye
Invisible, yet liveth to the heart
O'er all that leaps, and runs, and shouts, and sings,   455
Or beats the gladsome air, o'er all that glides
Beneath the wave, yea, in the wave itself
And mighty depth of waters. Wonder not
If such my transports were, for in all things
I saw one life, and felt that it was joy;   460
One song they sang and it was audible—
Most audible then when the fleshly ear,
O'ercome by grosser prelude of that strain,
Forgot its functions and slept undisturbed.[8]

If this be error, and another faith   465
Find easier access to the pious mind,[9]
Yet were I grossly destitute of all
Those human sentiments which make this earth
So dear if I should fail with grateful voice
To speak of you, ye mountains, and ye lakes   470
And sounding cataracts, ye mists and winds
That dwell among the hills where I was born.
If in my youth I have been pure in heart,
If, mingling with the world, I am content
With my own modest pleasures, and have lived   475
With God and Nature communing, removed
From little enmities and low desires,
The gift is yours; if in these times of fear,
This melancholy waste[1] of hopes o'erthrown,
If, 'mid indifference and apathy   480
And wicked exultation, when good men
On every side fall off we know not how
To selfishness, disguised in gentle names
Of peace and quiet and domestic love—
Yet mingled, not unwillingly, with sneers   485
On visionary minds—if, in this time
Of dereliction and dismay, I yet
Despair not of our nature, but retain
A more than Roman confidence, a faith
That fails not, in all sorrow my support,   490
The blessing of my life, the gift is yours
Ye mountains, thine O Nature. Thou hast fed
My lofty speculations, and in thee
For this uneasy heart of ours I find

---

8. For the later version of lines 401–
64, see the 1850 *Prelude*, below, II.352–
418.

9. Cf. lines 458–66 to *Tintern Abbey*
(above), lines 43–50.
1. Wasteland.

A never-failing principle of joy   495
And purest passion.

              Thou, my friend, wast reared
In the great city, 'mid far other scenes,[2]
But we by different roads at length have gained
The self-same bourne. And from this cause to thee
I speak unapprehensive of contempt,   500
The insinuated scoff of coward tongues,
And all that silent language which so oft
In conversation betwixt man and man
Blots from the human countenance all trace
Of beauty and of love. For thou hast sought   505
The truth in solitude, and thou art one
The most intense of Nature's worshippers,
In many things my brother, chiefly here
In this my deep devotion. Fare thee well:
Health and the quiet of a healthful mind   510
Attend thee, seeking oft the haunts of men—
But yet more often living with thyself,
And for thyself—so haply shall thy days
Be many, and a blessing to mankind.

End of the second Part

1798–99   1974, 1979

2. A reminiscence of Coleridge's *Frost*   I was reared / In the great city, pent
at Midnight (below), lines 51–52: "For   'mid cloisters dim."

The Prelude (1850) When Wordsworth enlarged the two-part *Prelude* of 1799 into 13 books (1805) and then into 14 books (1850), he not only made it a poem of epic length but also heightened the style and introduced various thematic parallels with earlier epics, especially *Paradise Lost*. (For a central example, see Wordsworth's version of Milton's enterprise to "justify the ways of God to men," in the 1850 *Prelude*, below, XIV.157–70, 384–89). The expanded poem, however, is a personal history which turns on a mental crisis and recovery, and for such a narrative design the chief prototype is not the classical or Christian epic, but the spiritual autobiography of crisis. St. Augustine's *Confessions* established this great Christian form late in the 4th century, and it has had an uninterrupted history in European literature ever since. Among the scores of prose versions of the spiritual autobiography are the Catholic Dante's *Vita Nuova* (*The New Life*) and the Puritan Bunyan's *Grace Abounding to the Chief of Sinners*. Its greatest poetic instance is Dante's *Divine Comedy*, an allegorical account of the narrator's spiritual journey from earth through hell, purgatory, and paradise, back to earth.

    As in *The Divine Comedy*, and in Augustine's *Confessions* itself, Wordsworth's recurrent metaphor is that of a journey, whose end—as T. S. Eliot put it in *Four Quartets*, his adaptation of the same form—is in its beginning, and in which it turns out that the end of the journey is "to arrive where we started / And know the place for the first time" (see the Quartet *Little Gidding*, below, lines 241–44). Wordsworth's *Prelude* opens with a literal journey whose chosen goal (I.72, 106–7) is "a known Vale, whither my feet should turn"—that is, the Vale of Grasmere. There are a number of later journeys, of which the most important are the crossing of the Alps in Book VI and, at the beginning of the final book, the ascent of Mount Snowdon which culminates in a definitive vision. In the course of the poem, however, such literal journeys become the metaphoric vehicle for an interior journey in a quest, both within the poet's memory and in his poetic enterprise itself, for his lost early self and his proper spiritual home. The poem ends by adverting to its own beginning, and leaves the poet settled in the Vale of Grasmere, ready finally to begin his great enterprise, *The Recluse* (XIV.302–11, 374–85).

In reading *The Prelude* as autobiography, we readily forget how traditional it is in both voice and form; and in our understandable preoccupation with its great poetic moments we are apt to overlook the artistry of its overall structure. Although the narrator is the actual Wordsworth, addressing himself to the English people of his own troubled age, he adopts a personal and a prophetic stance that goes back through Milton and Spenser to the poets and prophets of the Bible. And although the separate episodes are events from Wordsworth's own life, he does not describe these events as they had seemed to him at the time, but as they are interpreted in distant retrospect, re-ordered in sequence, and shaped into the inherited design of crisis and recovery, from which the author emerges as a different self in a transformed world.

Wordsworth, however, changes the traditional spiritual history in a radical way: he converts what had earlier been the supernatural Christian agencies of its providential plot into secular and humanistic terms. The true protagonist in Wordsworth's poem turns out, in fact, to be a power of his own mind which is capable of transforming the natural world with which it interacts; he calls this power "Imagination." "This faculty," he reveals in the last book (XIV.193 ff.), "hath been the feeding source of our long labor," and he goes on to say that the account of its appearance, development, loss, and restoration has constituted the submerged plot of the poem in its entirety. *The Prelude* has been called the greatest religious poem of the 19th century. Its religion, however, despite some pious phrases and passages that Wordsworth cautiously inserted into the 1850 text, is not an inherited creed, nor even a religion of Nature, but rather a faith in the redeeming power of "the mind of man" which, the closing lines declare, compared with the unchanging earth, is "In beauty exalted, as it is itself / Of quality and fabric more divine."

The text of the 1850 *Prelude* reprinted here was established by Jonathan Wordsworth, with the assistance of Stephen Gill, for *The Prelude: 1799, 1805, 1850: A Norton Critical Edition*, edited by Jonathan Wordsworth, M. H. Abrams and Stephen Gill (1979). The text is reproduced without modernization. By referring to the surviving printer's copy, the editors have eliminated a number of alterations of Wordsworth's text which were introduced by the literary executors who saw the first edition through the press in 1850. As the result of these corrections, the line count differs somewhat from that of earlier reprints of the 1850 *Prelude* in Books I, IV, V, XI, and XIV.

From The Prelude
or
Growth of a Poet's Mind

AN AUTOBIOGRAPHICAL POEM

(1850)

From *Book First. Introduction—Childhood and School-time*

O there is a blessing in this gentle breeze, [1]
A visitant that while he fans my cheek
Doth seem half-conscious of the joy he brings
From the green fields, and from yon azure sky.
Whate'er his mission, the soft breeze can come   5
To none more grateful than to me; escaped
From the vast city,[2] where I long had pined
A discontented sojourner: now free,
Free as a bird to settle where I will.
What dwelling shall receive me? in what vale   10
Shall be my harbour? underneath what grove
Shall I take up my home? and what clear stream
Shall with its murmur lull me into rest?
The earth is all before me.[3] With a heart
Joyous, nor scared at its own liberty,   15
I look about; and should the chosen guide
Be nothing better than a wandering cloud,
I cannot miss my way. I breathe again!
Trances of thought and mountings of the mind
Come fast upon me: it is shaken off,   20
That burthen of my own unnatural self,

1. Wordsworth says, lines 46–50, that the preceding lines were uttered in the circumstances they describe. Until recently it was the standard opinion that the occasion was September of 1795 when Wordsworth, released from financial worries by a legacy, was on his way to find a home in Racedown, Dorset. It is much more likely, however, that the lines refer primarily to his walk to what was to be his home at Grasmere, deliberately fused with details from an earlier trip to Racedown, in order to make the walk the symbol of a new stage in the journey of his life. In 1804 this passage was adopted as the preamble for *The Prelude*, where it replaces the epic device (as in *Paradise Lost*) of the opening prayer to the Muse for inspiration. To be "inspired" is, in its literal sense, to be blown into by a divinity: Wordsworth begins his poem with a literal wind, the "breath of heaven," which (lines 33–42) becomes the stimulus for a correspondent inner breeze, marking both a springlike revival of the spirit after a wintry season and a burst of poetic power which Wordsworth equates with the inspiration of the Biblical prophets when touched by the Holy Spirit (lines 50–54). The revivifying breeze, material and spiritual, recurs as a kind of leitmotif in *The Prelude*, and also serves as the radical metaphor of Coleridge's *Dejection: An Ode* and Shelley's *Ode to the West Wind*.
2. Primarily London; but like the journey, the city serves as a type, symbolizing a release from spiritual bondage.
3. One of many echoes from *Paradise Lost*, where the line describes Adam and Eve beginning their new life after the expulsion from Eden: "The world was all before them" (XII.646).

The heavy weight of many a weary day
Not mine, and such as were not made for me.
Long months of peace (if such bold word accord
With any promises of human life),   25
Long months of ease and undisturbed delight
Are mine in prospect; whither shall I turn
By road or pathway, or through trackless field,
Up hill or down, or shall some floating thing
Upon the river point me out my course?   30

Dear Liberty! Yet what would it avail
But for a gift that consecrates the joy?
For I, methought, while the sweet breath of heaven
Was blowing on my body, felt within
A corresondent breeze, that gently moved   35
With quickening virtue,⁴ but is now become
A tempest, a redundant⁵ energy,
Vexing its own creation.⁶ Thanks to both,
And their congenial powers, that, while they join
In breaking up a long-continued frost,   40
Bring with them vernal promises, the hope
Of active days urged on by flying hours,—
Days of sweet leisure, taxed with patient thought
Abstruse, not wanting punctual service high,
Matins and vespers, of harmonious verse!⁷   45

Thus far, O Friend!⁸ did I, not used to make
A present joy the matter of a song,⁹
Pour forth that day my soul in measured strains
That would not be forgotten, and are here
Recorded: to the open fields I told   50
A prophecy: poetic numbers came
Spontaneously to clothe in priestly robe
A renovated spirit singled out,
Such hope was mine, for holy services.
My own voice cheered me, and, far more, the mind's   55
Internal echo of the imperfect sound;
To both I listened, drawing from them both
A cheerful confidence in things to come.

Content and not unwilling now to give
A respite to this passion, I paced on   60
With brisk and eager steps; and came, at length,

4. Reviving power.
5. Abounding, exuberant.
6. Kindred.
7. I.e., work on his planned major poem,
The Recluse.
8. Samuel Taylor Coleridge, to whom the
entire poem is addressed as a kind of

immense verse letter. For Coleridge's
reply, see *To William Wordsworth.*
9. His poetry, Wordsworth said in the
Preface to *Lyrical Ballads*, usually originates as "emotion recollected in tranquility," not, as in the preamble above,
during the experience it describes.

To a green shady place, where down I sate
Beneath a tree, slackening my thoughts by choice,
And settling into gentler happiness.
'Twas autumn, and a clear and placid day,   65
With warmth, as much as needed, from a sun
Two hours declined towards the west; a day
With silver clouds, and sunshine on the grass,
And in the sheltered and the sheltering grove
A perfect stillness. Many were the thoughts   70
Encouraged and dismissed, till choice was made
Of a known Vale,[1] whither my feet should turn,
Nor rest till they had reached the very door
Of the one cottage which methought I saw.
No picture of mere memory ever looked   75
So fair; and while upon the fancied scene
I gazed with growing love, a higher power
Than Fancy gave assurance of some work
Of glory there forthwith to be begun,
Perhaps too there performed. Thus long I mused,   80
Nor e'er lost sight of what I mused upon,
Save when, amid the stately grove of oaks,
Now here, now there, an acorn, from its cup
Dislodged, through sere leaves rustled, or at once
To the bare earth dropped with a startling sound.   85
From that soft couch I rose not, till the sun
Had almost touched the horizon; casting then
A backward glance upon the curling cloud
Of city smoke, by distance ruralised;
Keen as a Truant or a Fugitive,   90
But as a Pilgrim resolute, I took,
Even with the chance equipment of that hour,
The road that pointed toward the chosen Vale.
It was a splendid evening, and my soul
Once more made trial of her strength, nor lacked   95
Æolian visitations;[2] but the harp
Was soon defrauded, and the banded host
Of harmony dispersed in straggling sounds,
And lastly utter silence! 'Be it so;
Why think of any thing but present good?'   100
So, like a home-bound labourer I pursued
My way beneath the mellowing sun, that shed
Mild influence;[3] nor left in me one wish
Again to bend the Sabbath of that time[4]
To a servile yoke. What need of many words?   105
A pleasant loitering journey, through three days

1. Grasmere.
2. I.e., influences to which his soul responded like an Eolian harp (as in lines 33–38).
3. *Paradise Lost* VII.374–75: "the Pleiades before him danced / Shedding sweet influence."
4. That time of rest.

Continued, brought me to my hermitage.
I spare to tell of what ensued, the life
In common things—the endless store of things,
Rare, or at least so seeming, every day   110
Found all about me in one neighbourhood—
The self-congratulation,5 and, from morn
To night, unbroken cheerfulness serene.
But speedily an earnest longing rose
To brace myself to some determined aim,   115
Reading or thinking; either to lay up
New stores, or rescue from decay the old
By timely interference: and therewith
Came hopes still higher, that with outward life
I might endue some airy phantasies   120
That had been floating loose about for years,
And to such beings temperately deal forth
The many feelings that oppressed my heart.
That hope hath been discouraged; welcome light
Dawns from the east, but dawns to disappear   125
And mock me with a sky that ripens not
Into a steady morning: if my mind,
Remembering the bold promise of the past,
Would gladly grapple with some noble theme,
Vain is her wish; where'er she turns she finds   130
Impediments from day to day renewed.6

                    * * * Then a wish,
My best and favourite aspiration, mounts
With yearning toward some philosophic song
Of Truth that cherishes our daily life;7   230
With meditations passionate from deep
Recesses in man's heart, immortal verse
Thoughtfully fitted to the Orphean lyre;8
But from this awful burthen I full soon
Take refuge and beguile myself with trust   235
That mellower years will bring a riper mind
And clearer insight. Thus my days are past
In contradiction; with no skill to part
Vague longing, haply bred by want of power,
From paramount impulse not to be withstood,   240
A timorous capacity from prudence,
From circumspection, infinite delay.9
Humility and modest awe themselves

5. Self-rejoicing.
6. In the omitted passage, the poet considered various possible subjects for poetic treatment.
7. I.e., *The Recluse*.
8. The lyre of Orpheus, who in Greek myth was able to enchant not only men but the natural world by his singing and playing.
9. The syntax is complex and inverted; in outline, the sense of lines 238–42 is: "With no ability ('skill') to distinguish longing from impulse, timid capacity from prudence, delay from carefulness ('circumspection')."

Betray me, serving often for a cloak
To a more subtle selfishness; that now   245
Locks every function up in blank reserve,[1]
Now dupes me, trusting to an anxious eye
That with intrusive restlessness beats off
Simplicity and self-presented truth.
Ah! better far than this, to stray about   250
Voluptuously[2] through fields and rural walks,
And ask no record of the hours, resigned
To vacant musing, unreproved neglect
Of all things, and deliberate holiday.
Far better never to have heard the name   255
Of zeal and just ambition, than to live
Baffled and plagued by a mind that every hour
Turns recreant to her task; takes heart again,
Then feels immediately some hollow thought
Hang like an interdict[3] upon her hopes.   260
This is my lot; for either still I find
Some imperfection in the chosen theme,
Or see of absolute accomplishment
Much wanting, so much wanting, in myself,
That I recoil and droop, and seek repose   265
In listlessness from vain perplexity,
Unprofitably travelling toward the grave,
Like a false steward who hath much received
And renders nothing back.[4]

                    Was it for this[5]
That one, the fairest of all rivers, loved   270
To blend his murmurs with my nurse's song,
And, from his alder shades and rocky falls,
And from his fords and shallows, sent a voice
That flowed along my dreams? For this, didst thou,
O Derwent! winding among grassy holms[6]   275
Where I was looking on, a babe in arms,
Make ceaseless music that composed my thoughts
To more than infant softness, giving me
Amid the fretful dwellings of mankind
A foretaste, a dim earnest, of the calm   280
That Nature breathes among the hills and groves.
When he had left the mountains and received
On his smooth breast the shadow of those towers
That yet survive, a shattered monument
Of feudal sway, the bright blue river passed   285
Along the margin of our terrace walk;[7]

1. Absolute inaction.
2. Luxuriously, sensuously.
3. Pronounced "interdite": prohibition.
4. The reference is to the parable of the false steward in Matthew XXV.14–30.
5. Lines 269–475 correspond to the *Two-*
Part Prelude, above, I.1–198.
6. Flat ground next to a river.
7. The Derwent River flows by Cockermouth Castle and then past the garden terrace behind Wordsworth's father's house in Cockermouth, Cumberland.

A tempting playmate whom we dearly loved.
Oh, many a time have I, a five years' child,
In a small mill-race severed from his stream,
Made one long bathing of a summer's day;   290
Basked in the sun, and plunged and basked again
Alternate, all a summer's day, or scoured [8]
The sandy fields, leaping through flowery groves
Of yellow ragwort; or when rock and hill,
The woods, and distant Skiddaw's[9] lofty height,   295
Were bronzed with deepest radiance, stood alone
Beneath the sky, as if I had been born
On Indian plains, and from my mother's hut
Had run abroad in wantonness, to sport
A naked savage, in the thunder shower.   300

　　Fair seed-time had my soul, and I grew up
Fostered alike by beauty and by fear:[1]
Much favoured in my birth-place, and no less
In that beloved Vale[2] to which erelong
We were transplanted—there were we let loose   305
For sports of wider range. Ere I had told
Ten birth-days, when among the mountain slopes
Frost, and the breath of frosty wind, had snapped
The last autumnal crocus, 'twas my joy
With store of springes[3] o'er my shoulder hung   310
To range the open heights where woodcocks ran
Along the smooth green turf. Through half the night,
Scudding away from snare to snare, I plied
That anxious visitation;—moon and stars
Were shining o'er my head. I was alone,   315
And seemed to be a trouble to the peace
That dwelt among them. Sometimes it befel
In these night wanderings, that a strong desire
O'erpowered my better reason, and the bird
Which was the captive of another's toil[4]   320
Became my prey; and when the deed was done
I heard among the solitary hills
Low breathings coming after me, and sounds
Of undistinguishable motion, steps
Almost as silent as the turf they trod.   325

8. Ran swiftly over.
9. A mountain nine miles east of Cockermouth.
1. Wordsworth introduces here a dialectic that plays a central role in the
evolution of *The Prelude*. He represents
his mind, confronting nature, as fostered
in its growth by two antithetic principles,
one associated with love and the other
with fear. These principles correspond to
the two main categories, "the beautiful"
(or "the fair") and "the sublime," into

which theorists of the landscape during
the preceding century had classified the
antithetic aspects of the natural scene.
See, e.g., I.351–56, 466–75, 545. In the
concluding Book, this antithesis is finally
resolved; see below, XIV.162–70 and
note.
2. The valley of Esthwaite, the location
of Hawkshead, where Wordsworth attended school.
3. Bird snares.
4. "Snare," or else "labor."

Nor less when spring had warmed the cultured[5] Vale,
Roved we as plunderers where the mother-bird
Had in high places built her lodge; though mean
Our object and inglorious, yet the end[6]
Was not ignoble. Oh! when I have hung   330
Above the raven's nest, by knots of grass
And half-inch fissures in the slippery rock
But ill-sustained, and almost (so it seemed)
Suspended by the blast that blew amain,
Shouldering the naked crag, oh, at that time   335
While on the perilous ridge I hung alone,
With what strange utterance did the loud dry wind
Blow through my ear! the sky seemed not a sky
Of earth—and with what motion moved the clouds!

Dust as we are, the immortal spirit grows   340
Like harmony in music; there is a dark
Inscrutable workmanship that reconciles
Discordant elements, makes them cling together
In one society. How strange that all
The terrors, pains, and early miseries,   345
Regrets, vexations, lassitudes interfused
Within my mind, should e'er have borne a part,
And that a needful part, in making up
The calm existence that is mine when I
Am worthy of myself! Praise to the end!   350
Thanks to the means which Nature deigned to employ;
Whether her fearless visitings, or those
That came with soft alarm, like hurtless light
Opening the peaceful clouds; or she may use
Severer interventions, ministry   355
More palpable, as best might suit her aim.[7]

One summer evening (led by her) I found
A little boat tied to a willow tree
Within a rocky cave, its usual home.
Straight I unloosed her chain, and stepping in   360
Pushed from the shore. It was an act of stealth
And troubled pleasure, nor without the voice
Of mountain-echoes did my boat move on;
Leaving behind her still, on either side,
Small circles glittering idly in the moon,   365
Until they melted all into one track
Of sparkling light. But now, like one who rows,
Proud of his skill, to reach a chosen point
With an unswerving line, I fixed my view

5. Cultivated.
6. Outcome.
7. A restatement of the double ministry
of nature described in line 302; what follows is a second example of discipline by
fear.

Upon the summit of a craggy ridge,   370
The horizon's utmost boundary; for above
Was nothing but the stars and the grey sky.
She was an elfin pinnace;[8] lustily
I dipped my oars into the silent lake,
And, as I rose upon the stroke, my boat   375
Went heaving through the water like a swan;
When, from behind that craggy steep till then
The horizon's bound, a huge peak, black and huge,
As if with voluntary power instinct
Upreared its head.[9] I struck and struck again,   380
And growing still in stature the grim shape
Towered up between me and the stars, and still,
For so it seemed, with purpose of its own
And measured motion like a living thing,
Strode after me. With trembling oars I turned,   385
And through the silent water stole my way
Back to the covert of the willow tree;
There in her mooring-place I left my bark,—
And through the meadows homeward went, in grave
And serious mood; but after I had seen   390
That spectacle, for many days, my brain
Worked with a dim and undetermined sense
Of unknown modes of being; o'er my thoughts
There hung a darkness, call it solitude
Or blank desertion. No familiar shapes   395
Remained, no pleasant images of trees,
Of sea or sky, no colours of green fields;
But huge and mighty forms, that do not live
Like living men, moved slowly through the mind
By day, and were a trouble to my dreams.   400

   Wisdom and Spirit of the universe!
Thou Soul that art the eternity of thought,
That givest to forms and images a breath
And everlasting motion, not in vain
By day or star-light thus from my first dawn   405
Of childhood didst thou intwine for me
The passions that build up our human soul;
Not with the mean and vulgar[1] works of man,
But with high objects, with enduring things—
With life and nature, purifying thus   410
The elements of feeling and of thought,
And sanctifying, by such discipline,

---

8. Small boat.
9. In order to direct his boat in a straight line, the rower has fixed his eye on a point in the ridge of the nearby shore, which blocks out the landscape behind. As he moves farther out, the black peak suddenly rears into his altering angle of vision and seems to stride closer with each stroke of the oars. "Instinct": endowed.
1. Commonplace.

Both pain and fear, until we recognise
A grandeur in the beatings of the heart.
Nor was this fellowship vouchsafed to me   415
With stinted kindness. In November days,
When vapours rolling down the valley made
A lonely scene more lonesome, among woods
At noon, and 'mid the calm of summer nights,
When, by the margin of the trembling lake,   420
Beneath the gloomy hills homeward I went
In solitude, such intercourse was mine;
Mine was it in the fields both day and night,
And by the waters, all the summer long.

   And in the frosty season, when the sun   425
Was set, and visible for many a mile
The cottage windows blazed through twilight gloom,
I heeded not their summons: happy time
It was indeed for all of us—for me
It was a time of rapture! Clear and loud   430
The village clock tolled six,—I wheeled about,
Proud and exulting like an untired horse
That cares not for his home. All shod with steel,
We hissed along the polished ice in games
Confederate, imitative of the chase   435
And woodland pleasures,—the resounding horn,
The pack loud chiming, and the hunted hare.
So through the darkness and the cold we flew,
And not a voice was idle; with the din
Smitten, the precipices rang aloud;   440
The leafless trees and every icy crag
Tinkled like iron; while far distant hills
Into the tumult sent an alien sound
Of melancholy not unnoticed, while the stars[5]
Eastward were sparkling clear, and in the west   445
The orange sky of evening died away.
Not seldom from the uproar I retired
Into a silent bay, or sportively
Glanced sideway,[2] leaving the tumultuous throng,
To cut across the reflex[3] of a star   450
That fled, and, flying still before me, gleamed
Upon the glassy plain; and oftentimes,
When we had given our bodies to the wind,
And all the shadowy banks on either side
Came sweeping through the darkness, spinning still   455
The rapid line of motion, then at once
Have I, reclining back upon my heels,
Stopped short; yet still the solitary cliffs
Wheeled by me—even as if the earth had rolled

---

2. Moved off obliquely.   3. Reflection.

With visible motion her diurnal[4] round! 460
Behind me did they stretch in solemn train,[5]
Feebler and feebler, and I stood and watched
Till all was tranquil as a dreamless sleep.

    Ye Presences of Nature in the sky
And on the earth! Ye Visions of the hills! 465
And Souls of lonely places![6] can I think
A vulgar hope was yours when ye employed
Such ministry, when ye through many a year
Haunting me thus among my boyish sports,
On caves and trees, upon the woods and hills, 470
Impressed upon all forms the characters[7]
Of danger or desire; and thus did make
The surface of the universal earth
With triumph and delight, with hope and fear,
Work[8] like a sea? 475

* * *

    Nor, sedulous[9] as I have been to trace
How Nature by extrinsic passion first 545
Peopled the mind with forms sublime or fair,[1]
And made me love them, may I here omit
How other pleasures have been mine, and joys
Of subtler origin; how I have felt,
Not seldom even in that tempestuous time, 550
Those hallowed and pure motions of the sense
Which seem, in their simplicity, to own
An intellectual[2] charm; that calm delight
Which, if I err not, surely must belong
To those first-born[3] affinities that fit 555
Our new existence to existing things,
And, in our dawn of being, constitute
The bond of union between life and joy.

    Yes, I remember when the changeful earth,
And twice five summers on my mind had stamped 560
The faces of the moving year, even then
I held unconscious intercourse with beauty
Old as creation, drinking in a pure
Organic pleasure from the silver wreaths

---

4. Daily.
5. Succession.
6. Wordsworth referred both to a single "Spirit" or "Soul" of the universe as a whole (e.g., lines 401–2, above) and to plural "Presences" and "Souls" inanimating the various parts of the universe. See the earlier version of this passage in *The Two-Part Prelude* (above), I.186 ff.
7. Signs.
8. Seethe.

9. Diligent.
1. The passion at first was "extrinsic" because felt not for nature itself, but for nature as associated with the outdoor activities he loved. He now goes on to distinguish other "subtler" pleasures, felt in the very process of sensing the natural objects themselves.
2. Spiritual, as opposed to sense perceptions.
3. Innate.

Of curling mist, or from the level plain   565
Of waters coloured by impending[4] clouds.

    The sands of Westmoreland, the creeks and bays
Of Cumbria's[5] rocky limits, they can tell
How, when the Sea threw off his evening shade,
And to the shepherd's hut on distant hills   570
Sent welcome notice of the rising moon,
How I have stood, to fancies such as these
A stranger, linking with the spectacle
No conscious memory of a kindred sight,
And bringing with me no peculiar sense   575
Of quietness or peace; yet have I stood,
Even while mine eye hath moved o'er many a league[6]
Of shining water, gathering as it seemed
Through every hair-breadth in that field of light
New pleasure like a bee among the flowers.   580

    Thus oft amid those fits of vulgar[7] joy
Which, through all seasons, on a child's pursuits
Are prompt attendants, 'mid that giddy bliss
Which, like a tempest, works along the blood
And is forgotten; even then I felt   585
Gleams like the flashing of a shield;—the earth
And common face of Nature spake to me
Rememberable things; sometimes, 'tis true,
By chance collisions and quaint accidents
(Like those ill-sorted unions, work supposed   590
Of evil-minded fairies), yet not vain
Nor profitless, if haply they impressed
Collateral[8] objects and appearances,
Albeit lifeless then, and doomed to sleep
Until maturer seasons called them forth   595
To impregnate and to elevate the mind.
—And if the vulgar joy by its own weight
Wearied itself out of the memory,
The scenes which were a witness of that joy
Remained in their substantial lineaments   600
Depicted on the brain, and to the eye
Were visible, a daily sight; and thus
By the impressive discipline of fear,
By pleasure and repeated happiness,
So frequently repeated, and by force   605
Of obscure feelings representative
Of things forgotten, these same scenes so bright,
So beautiful, so majestic in themselves,

---

4. Overhanging.
5. Cumberland's.
6. A league is approximately three miles.

7. Ordinary, commonplace.
8. Accompanying but subordinate.

Though yet the day was distant, did become
Habitually dear, and all their forms   610
And changeful colours by invisible links
Were fastened to the affections.[9]

                    I began
My story early—not misled, I trust,
By an infirmity of love for days
Disowned by memory[1]—fancying flowers where none,   615
Not even the sweetest, do or can survive,
For him at least whose dawning day they cheered.
Nor will it seem to thee, O Friend! so prompt
In sympathy, that I have lengthened out
With fond and feeble tongue a tedious tale.   620
Meanwhile, my hope has been, that I might fetch
Invigorating thoughts from former years;
Might fix the wavering balance of my mind,
And haply meet reproaches too, whose power
May spur me on, in manhood now mature,   625
To honourable toil. Yet should these hopes
Prove vain, and thus should neither I be taught
To understand myself, nor thou to know
With better knowledge how the heart was framed
Of him thou lovest; need I dread from thee   630
Harsh judgements, if the song be loth to quit
Those recollected hours that have the charm
Of visionary things, those lovely forms
And sweet sensations that throw back our life,
And almost make remotest infancy   635
A visible scene, on which the sun is shining?

    One end at least hath been attained; my mind
Hath been revived, and if this genial[2] mood
Desert me not, forthwith shall be brought down
Through later years the story of my life.   640
The road lies plain before me;—'tis a theme
Single and of determined bounds; and hence
I choose it rather at this time, than work
Of ampler or more varied argument,
Where I might be discomfited and lost: 645
And certain hopes are with me, that to thee
This labour will be welcome, honoured Friend!

---

9. Feelings.
1. I.e., he fears that he may have been
attributing later thoughts and feelings to
a time of life he can no longer remember.
2. Productive, creative.

From *Book Second. School-time (Continued)*

* * *

Ah! is there one who ever has been young,
Nor needs a warning voice to tame the pride   20
Of intellect and virtue's self-esteem? [1]
One is there, [2] though the wisest and the best
Of all mankind, who covets not at times
Union that cannot be;—who would not give,
If so he might, to duty and to truth   25
The eagerness of infantine desire?
A tranquillising spirit presses now
On my corporeal frame, so wide appears
The vacancy between me and those days
Which yet have such self-presence [3] in my mind,   30
That musing on them, often do I seem
Two consciousnesses, conscious of myself
And of some other Being. * * *

Blest the infant Babe
(For with my best conjecture I would trace
Our Being's earthly progress), [4] blest the Babe,
Nursed in his Mother's arms, who sinks to sleep   235
Rocked on his Mother's breast; who with his soul
Drinks in the feelings of his Mother's eye!
For him, in one dear Presence, there exists
A virtue which irradiates and exalts
Objects through widest intercourse of sense.   240
No outcast he, bewildered and depressed:
Along his infant veins are interfused
The gravitation and the filial bond
Of nature that connect him with the world.
Is there a flower, to which he points with hand   245
Too weak to gather it, already love
Drawn from love's purest earthly fount for him
Hath beautified that flower; already shades
Of pity cast from inward tenderness
Do fall around him upon aught that bears   250
Unsightly marks of violence or harm.
Emphatically such a Being lives,
Frail creature as he is, helpless as frail,
An inmate of this active universe.
For feeling has to him imparted power   255

1. I.e., does anyone who has once been young need to be warned not to overrate the achievements of age?
2. I.e., "is there anyone * * * ?"
3. Actuality, existence.
4. Like the modern psychologist, Wordsworth recognizes the importance of earliest infancy in the development of the individual mind, although he had then to invent the terms with which to analyze infant psychology. See the early version of this passage, *The Two-Part Prelude* (above), II.267 ff.

That through the growing faculties of sense
Doth like an agent of the one great Mind
Create, creator and receiver both,
Working but in alliance with the works
Which it beholds.[5]—Such, verily, is the first   260
Poetic spirit of our human life,
By uniform control of after years,
In most, abated or suppressed; in some,
Through every change of growth and of decay,
Pre-eminent till death.   265

                              * * *
                                    'Twere long to tell
What spring and autumn, what the winter snows,
And what the summer shade, what day and night,
Evening and morning, sleep and waking thought,   355
From sources inexhaustible, poured forth
To feed the spirit of religious love
In which I walked with Nature. But let this
Be not forgotten, that I still retained
My first creative sensibility;[6]   360
That by the regular action of the world
My soul was unsubdued. A plastic[7] power
Abode with me; a forming hand, at times
Rebellious, acting in a devious mood;
A local spirit of his own, at war   365
With general tendency, but, for the most,
Subservient strictly to external things
With which it communed. An auxiliar light
Came from my mind, which on the setting sun
Bestowed new splendour; the melodious birds,   370
The fluttering breezes, fountains that ran on
Murmuring so sweetly in themselves, obeyed
A like dominion, and the midnight storm
Grew darker in the presence of my eye:
Hence my obeisance, my devotion hence,   375
And hence my transport.[8]

                              Nor should this, perchance,
Pass unrecorded, that I still[9] had loved
The exercise and produce of a toil,
Than analytic industry to me
More pleasing, and whose character I deem   380

---

5. The infant, in the sense of security and love shed by his mother's presence on outer things, perceives what would otherwise be an alien world as a place to which he has a relationship like that of a son to a mother (lines 238–44). On such grounds Wordsworth asserts that the mind partially creates, by altering, the world it seems simply to perceive. In the succeeding passage (lines 360–74) Wordsworth repeats this concept in various metaphors signifying the give-and-take of outer world and inner mind and emotion.
6. I.e., the creative perception manifested by the babe in his mother's arms, above.
7. Shaping, formative.
8. Exaltation.
9. Always.

Is more poetic as resembling more
Creative agency. The song would speak
Of that interminable building reared
By observation of affinities
In objects where no brotherhood exists   385
To passive minds. My seventeenth year was come;
And, whether from this habit rooted now
So deeply in my mind, or from excess
In the great social principle of life
Coercing all things into sympathy,   390
To unorganic natures were transferred
My own enjoyments; or the power of truth
Coming in revelation, did converse
With things that really are;[1] I, at this time,
Saw blessings spread around me like a sea.   395
Thus while the days flew by, and years passed on,
From Nature overflowing on my soul,
I had received so much, that every thought
Was steeped in feeling; I was only then
Contented, when with bliss ineffable   400
I felt the sentiment of Being spread
O'er all that moves and all that seemeth still;
O'er all that, lost beyond the reach of thought
And human knowledge, to the human eye
Invisible, yet liveth to the heart;   405
O'er all that leaps and runs, and shouts and sings,
Or beats the gladsome air; o'er all that glides
Beneath the wave, yea, in the wave itself,
And mighty depth of waters. Wonder not
If high the transport, great the joy I felt,   410
Communing in this sort through earth and heaven
With every form of creature, as it looked
Towards the Uncreated with a countenance
Of adoration, with an eye of love.[2]
One song they sang, and it was audible,   415
Most audible, then, when the fleshly ear,
O'ercome by humblest prelude of that strain,
Forgot her functions, and slept undisturbed.[3]

If this be error, and another faith
Find easier access to the pious mind,   420
Yet were I grossly destitute of all
Those human sentiments that make this earth

1. Wordsworth is careful to indicate that there are alternative explanations for his sense that life pervades the inorganic as well as the organic world: it may be the result either of a way of perceiving habitual since infancy, or a projection of his own inner life, or it may be the perception of an objective truth.

2. Wordsworth did not add lines 412–14, giving a Christian frame to his experience of the "one life," until the last revision of *The Prelude*, 1839. For the early version of this passage, see *The Two-Part Prelude* (above), II.445 ff.
3. Cf. *Tintern Abbey*, lines 41–49.

So dear, if I should fail with grateful voice
To speak of you, ye mountains, and ye lakes
And sounding cataracts, ye mists and winds   425
That dwell among the hills where I was born.
If in my youth I have been pure in heart,
If, mingling with the world, I am content
With my own modest pleasures, and have lived
With God and Nature communing, removed   430
From little enmities and low desires,
The gift is yours; if in these times of fear,
This melancholy waste[4] of hopes o'erthrown,
If, 'mid indifference and apathy
And wicked exultation, when good men   435
On every side fall off we know not how,
To selfishness, disguised in gentle names
Of peace and quiet and domestic love,
Yet mingled not unwillingly with sneers
On visionary minds; if, in this time   440
Of dereliction and dismay,[5] I yet
Despair not of our nature, but retain
A more than Roman confidence, a faith
That fails not, in all sorrow my support,
The blessing of my life; the gift is yours,   445
Ye winds and sounding cataracts! 'tis yours,
Ye mountains! thine, O Nature! Thou hast fed
My lofty speculations; and in thee,
For this uneasy heart of ours, I find
A never-failing principle of joy   450
And purest passion.

* * *

From *Book Third. Residence at Cambridge*

* * *

The Evangelist St. John my patron was:[1]
Three Gothic courts are his, and in the first
Was my abiding-place, a nook obscure;
Right underneath, the College kitchens made
A humming sound, less tuneable than bees,   50
But hardly less industrious; with shrill notes
Of sharp command and scolding intermixed.
Near me hung Trinity's[2] loquacious clock,
Who never let the quarters, night or day,
Slip by him unproclaimed, and told the hours   55

4. Wasteland.
5. The era, some ten years after the outbreak of the French Revolution, was one of violent reaction, in which many earlier sympathizers were recanting their earlier radical beliefs.
1. Wordsworth was a student at St. John's College, Cambridge University, from 1787 to 1791.
2. Trinity College adjoins St. John's. Roubiliac's statue of Newton, holding the prism with which he had conducted the experiments described in his *Optics*, stands in the west end of Trinity chapel.

Twice over with a male and female voice.
Her pealing organ was my neighbour too;
And from my pillow, looking forth by light
Of moon or favouring stars, I could behold
The antechapel where the statue stood   60
Of Newton with his prism and silent face,
The marble index of a mind for ever
Voyaging through strange seas of Thought, alone.

Of College labours, of the Lecturer's room
All studded round, as thick as chairs could stand,   65
With loyal students faithful to their books
Half-and-half idlers, hardy recusants,
And honest dunces—of important days,
Examinations, when the man was weighed
As in a balance! of excessive hopes,   70
Tremblings withal and commendable fears,
Small jealousies, and triumphs good or bad,
Let others that know more speak as they know.
Such glory was but little sought by me,
And little won. Yet from the first crude days   75
Of settling time in this untried abode,
I was disturbed at times by prudent thoughts,
Wishing to hope without a hope, some fears
About my future worldly maintenance,
And, more than all, a strangeness in the mind,   80
A feeling that I was not for that hour,
Nor for that place. * * *

* * * Companionships,
Friendships, acquaintances, were welcome all.   250
We sauntered, played, or rioted;[3] we talked
Unprofitable talk at morning hours;
Drifted about along the streets and walks,
Read lazily in trivial books, went forth
To gallop through the country in blind zeal   255
Of senseless horsemanship, or on the breast
Of Cam[4] sailed boisterously, and let the stars
Come forth, perhaps without one quiet thought.

* * *
Thus in submissive idleness, my Friend!
The labouring time of autumn, winter, spring,
Eight months! rolled pleasingly away; the ninth
Came and returned me to my native hills.   635

---

3. This was a period of low ebb in the intellectual vigor and discipline of Cambridge, so that Wordsworth was able to indulge generously in the fringe activi-ties of university life.
4. The river Cam, which flows through Cambridge.

From *Book Fourth. Summer Vacation*[1]

* * *

As one who hangs down-bending from the side
Of a slow-moving boat, upon the breast
Of a still water, solacing himself
With such discoveries as his eye can make
Beneath him in the bottom of the deep,   260
Sees many beauteous sights—weeds, fishes, flowers,
Grots, pebbles, roots of trees, and fancies more,
Yet often is perplexed and cannot part
The shadow from the substance, rocks and sky,
Mountains and clouds, reflected in the depth   265
Of the clear flood, from things which there abide
In their true dwelling; now is crossed by gleam
Of his own image, by a sun-beam now,
And wavering motions sent he knows not whence,
Impediments that make his task more sweet;   270
Such pleasant office have we long pursued
Incumbent o'er the surface of past time
With like success, nor often have appeared
Shapes fairer or less doubtfully discerned
Than these to which the Tale, indulgent Friend!   275
Would now direct thy notice.[2] * * *

              Yes, that heartless chase
Of trivial pleasures was a poor exchange
For books and nature at that early age.
'Tis true, some casual knowledge might be gained   300
Of character or life; but at that time,
Of manners put to school[3] I took small note,
And all my deeper passions lay elsewhere.
Far better had it been to exalt the mind
By solitary study, to uphold   305
Intense desire through meditative peace;
And yet, for chastisement of these regrets,
The memory of one particular hour
Doth here rise up against me. 'Mid a throng
Of maids and youths, old men, and matrons staid   310
A medley of all tempers, I had passed
The night in dancing, gaiety, and mirth,
With din of instruments and shuffling feet,
And glancing forms, and tapers glittering,
And unaimed prattle flying up and down;   315

1. Wordsworth spent his first summer vacation from the university at Hawkshead.
2. In this extended simile, Wordsworth describes his attempts to distinguish facts from fancies, and his current from his former self, in his remembrance of things past.
3. I.e., human manners made a subject of study.

Spirits upon the stretch, and here and there
Slight shocks of young love-liking interspersed,
Whose transient pleasure mounted to the head,
And tingled through the veins. Ere we retired,
The cock had crowed, and now the eastern sky   320
Was kindling, not unseen, from humble copse
And open field, through which the pathway wound,
And homeward led my steps. Magnificent
The morning rose, in memorable pomp,
Glorious as e'er I had beheld—in front,   325
The sea lay laughing at a distance; near
The solid mountains shone, bright as the clouds,
Grain-tinctured,[4] drenched in empyrean light;
And in the meadows and the lower grounds
Was all the sweetness of a common dawn—   330
Dews, vapours, and the melody of birds,
And labourers going forth to till the fields.

   Ah! need I say, dear Friend! that to the brim
My heart was full; I made no vows, but vows
Were then made for me; bond unknown to me   335
Was given, that I should be, else sinning greatly,
A dedicated Spirit. On I walked
In thankful blessedness, which yet survives.

                    * * *
                  Once, when those summer months
Were flown, and autumn brought its annual show   370
Of oars with oars contending, sails with sails,
Upon Winander's[5] spacious breast, it chanced
That—after I had left a flower-decked room
(Whose in-door pastime, lighted up, survived
To a late hour), and spirits overwrought[6]   375
Were making night do penance for a day
Spent in a round of strenuous idleness—
My homeward course led up a long ascent,
Where the road's watery surface, to the top
Of that sharp rising, glittered to the moon   380
And bore the semblance of another stream
Stealing with silent lapse to join the brook
That murmured in the vale. All else was still;
No living thing appeared in earth or air,
And, save the flowing water's peaceful voice,   385
Sound there was none—but, lo! an uncouth shape,
Shown by a sudden turning of the road,
So near that, slipping back into the shade

---

4. Crimson. The "empyrean" was, in
ancient thought, the outer sphere of the
universe, composed of pure fire.
5. Lake Winander's.

6. Worked up to a high pitch. Wordsworth is describing a party; the "pastime" has been dancing.

Of a thick hawthorn, I could mark him well,
Myself unseen. He was of stature tall,   390
A span[7] above man's common measure tall,
Stiff, lank, and upright; a more meagre[8] man
Was never seen before by night or day.
Long were his arms, pallid his hands; his mouth
Looked ghastly[9] in the moonlight: from behind,   395
A mile-stone propped him; I could also ken
That he was clothed in military garb,
Though faded, yet entire. Companionless,
No dog attending, by no staff sustained,
He stood, and in his very dress appeared   400
A desolation, a simplicity,
To which the trappings of a gaudy world
Make a strange back-ground. From his lips, ere long,
Issued low muttered sounds, as if of pain
Or some uneasy thought; yet still his form   405
Kept the same awful steadiness—at his feet
His shadow lay, and moved not. From self-blame
Not wholly free, I watched him thus; at length
Subduing my heart's specious cowardice,[1]
I left the shady nook where I had stood   410
And hailed him. Slowly from his resting-place
He rose, and with a lean and wasted arm
In measured gesture lifted to his head
Returned my salutation; then resumed
His station as before; and when I asked   415
His history, the veteran, in reply,
Was neither slow nor eager; but, unmoved,
And with a quiet uncomplaining voice,
A stately air of mild indifference,
He told in few plain words a soldier's tale—   420
That in the Tropic Islands[2] he had served,
Whence he had landed scarcely three weeks past;
That on his landing he had been dismissed,
And now was travelling towards his native home.
This heard, I said, in pity, 'Come with me.'   425
He stooped, and straightway from the ground took up
An oaken staff by me yet unobserved—
A staff which must have dropt from his slack hand
And lay till now neglected in the grass.
Though weak his step and cautious, he appeared   430
To travel without pain, and I beheld,
With an astonishment but ill suppressed,
His ghostly figure moving at my side;

7. About 9 inches (the distance between extended thumb and little finger).
8. Lean, emaciated.
9. Ghostly.
1. I.e., he had been deceiving himself that the cause for his dallying had been other than cowardice.
2. The West Indies; many thousands of British soldiers there were rendered unfit for service by tropical fevers.

Nor could I, while we journeyed thus, forbear
To turn from present hardships to the past,   435
And speak of war, battle, and pestilence,
Sprinkling this talk with questions, better spared,
On what he might himself have seen or felt.
He all the while was in demeanour calm,
Concise in answer; solemn and sublime   440
He might have seemed, but that in all he said
There was a strange half-absence, as of one
Knowing too well the importance of his theme,
But feeling it no longer. Our discourse
Soon ended, and together on we passed   445
In silence through a wood gloomy and still.
Up-turning, then, along an open field,
We reached a cottage. At the door I knocked,
And earnestly to charitable care
Commended him as a poor friendless man,   450
Belated and by sickness overcome.
Assured that now the traveller would repose
In comfort, I entreated that henceforth
He would not linger in the public ways,
But ask for timely furtherance and help   455
Such as his state required. At this reproof,
With the same ghastly mildness in his look,
He said, 'My trust is in the God of Heaven,
And in the eye of him who passes me!'

    The cottage door was speedily unbarred,   460
And now the soldier touched his hat once more
With his lean hand, and in a faltering voice,
Whose tone bespake reviving interests
Till then unfelt, he thanked me; I returned
The farewell blessing of the patient man,   465
And so we parted. Back I cast a look,
And lingered near the door a little space,
Then sought with quiet heart my distant home.

* * *

From *Book Fifth. Books*

    * * * Oh! why hath not the Mind   45
Some element to stamp her image on
In nature somewhat nearer to her own?
Why, gifted with such powers to send abroad
Her spirit, must it lodge in shrines so frail?[1]

---

1. Wordsworth is describing his recurrent fear that some holocaust might wipe
out all books, the frail and perishable re-
positories of all man's wisdom and poetry.

One day, when from my lips a like complaint   50
Had fallen in presence of a studious friend,
He with a smile made answer, that in truth
'Twas going far to seek disquietude;
But on the front of his reproof confessed
That he himself had oftentimes given way   55
To kindred hauntings. Whereupon I told,
That once in the stillness of a summer's noon,
While I was seated in a rocky cave
By the sea-side, perusing, so it chanced,
The famous history of the errant knight   60
Recorded by Cervantes,[2] these same thoughts
Beset me, and to height unusual rose,
While listlessly I sate, and, having closed
The book, had turned my eyes toward the wide sea.
On poetry and geometric truth,   65
And their high privilege of lasting life,
From all internal injury exempt,
I mused, upon these chiefly: and at length,
My senses yielding to the sultry air,
Sleep seized me, and I passed into a dream.   70
I saw before me stretched a boundless plain
Of sandy wilderness, all black and void,
And as I looked around, distress and fear
Came creeping over me, when at my side,
Close at my side, an uncouth shape appeared   75
Upon a dromedary, mounted high.
He seemed an Arab of the Bedouin tribes:
A lance he bore, and underneath one arm
A stone, and in the opposite hand, a shell
Of a surpassing brightness. At the sight   80
Much I rejoiced, not doubting but a guide
Was present, one who with unerring skill
Would through the desert lead me; and while yet
I looked and looked, self-questioned what this freight
Which the new-comer carried through the waste   85
Could mean, the Arab told me that the stone
(To give it in the language of the dream)
Was 'Euclid's Elements';[3] and 'This', said he,
'Is something of more worth'; and at the word
Stretched forth the shell, so beautiful in shape,   90
In colour so resplendent, with command
That I should hold it to my ear. I did so,
And heard that instant in an unknown tongue,
Which yet I understood, articulate sounds,

A loud prophetic blast of harmony; 95
An Ode, in passion uttered, which foretold
Destruction to the children of the earth
By deluge, now at hand. No sooner ceased
The song, than the Arab with calm look declared
That all would come to pass of which the voice 100
Had given forewarning, and that he himself
Was going then to bury those two books:
The one that held acquaintance with the stars,
And wedded soul to soul in purest bond
Of reason, undisturbed by space or time; 105
The other that was a god, yea many gods,
Had voices more than all the winds, with power
To exhilarate the spirit, and to soothe,
Through every clime, the heart of human kind.
While this was uttering, strange as it may seem, 110
I wondered not, although I plainly saw
The one to be a stone, the other a shell;
Nor doubted once but that they both were books,
Having a perfect faith in all that passed.
Far stronger, now, grew the desire I felt 115
To cleave unto this man; but when I prayed
To share his enterprise, he hurried on
Reckless[4] of me: I followed, not unseen,
For oftentimes he cast a backward look,
Grasping his twofold treasure.—Lance in rest, 120
He rode, I keeping pace with him; and now
He, to my fancy, had become the knight
Whose tale Cervantes tells; yet not the knight,
But was an Arab of the desert too;
Of these was neither, and was both at once. 125
His countenance, meanwhile, grew more disturbed;
And, looking backwards when he looked, mine eyes
Saw, over half the wilderness diffused,
A bed of glittering light: I asked the cause:
'It is', said he, 'the waters of the deep 130
Gathering upon us'; quickening then the pace
Of the unwieldly creature he bestrode,
He left me: I called after him aloud;
He heeded not; but, with his twofold charge
Still in his grasp, before me, full in view, 135
Went hurrying o'er the illimitable waste,
With the fleet waters of a drowning world
In chase of him; whereat I waked in terror,
And saw the sea before me, and the book,
In which I had been reading, at my side. 140

* * *

4. Neglectful.

There was a Boy:[5] ye knew him well, ye cliffs 365
And islands of Winander!—many a time
At evening, when the earliest stars began
To move along the edges of the hills,
Rising or setting, would he stand alone
Beneath the trees or by the glimmering lake, 370
And there, with fingers interwoven, both hands
Pressed closely palm to palm, and to his mouth
Uplifted, he, as through an instrument,
Blew mimic hootings to the silent owls,
That they might answer him; and they would shout 375
Across the watery vale, and shout again,
Responsive to his call, with quivering peals,
And long halloos and screams, and echoes loud,
Redoubled and redoubled, concourse wild
Of jocund din; and, when a lengthened pause 380
Of silence came and baffled his best skill,
Then sometimes, in that silence while he hung
Listening, a gentle shock of mild surprise
Has carried far into his heart the voice
Of mountain torrents; or the visible scene 385
Would enter unawares into his mind,
With all its solemn imagery, its rocks,
Its woods, and that uncertain heaven, received
Into the bosom of the steady lake.[6]

This Boy was taken from his mates, and died
In childhood, ere he was full twelve years old. 390
Fair is the spot, most beautiful the vale
Where he was born; the grassy churchyard hangs
Upon a slope above the village school,
And through that churchyard when my way has led
On summer evenings, I believe that there 395
A long half hour together I have stood
Mute, looking at the grave in which he lies!

* * *

The tales that charm away the wakeful night
In Araby,[7] romances; legends penned
For solace by dim light of monkish lamps;
Fictions, for ladies of their love, devised
By youthful squires; adventures endless, spun 500
By the dismantled warrior[8] in old age,
Out of the bowels of those very schemes

---

5. In an early MS. version of this passage, Wordsworth uses the first-person pronoun; the experience he describes was thus apparently his own.
6. Coleridge wrote of the last line and a half ("that uncertain heaven * * * lake"): "Had I met these lines running wild in the deserts of Arabia, I should instantly have screamed out, 'Wordsworth.' "
7. I.e., the tales told in *The Arabian Nights.*
8. I.e., the warrior when he no longer wears a suit of armor.

In which his youth did first extravagate;[9]
These spread like day, and something in the shape
Of these will live till man shall be no more.   505
Dumb yearnings, hidden appetites, are ours,
And *they must* have their food. Our childhood sits,
Our simple childhood, sits upon a throne
That hath more power than all the elements.[1]
I guess not what this tells of Being past,   510
Nor what it augurs of the life to come;
But so it is, and, in that dubious hour,
That twilight when we first begin to see
This dawning earth, to recognise, expect,
And in the long probation that ensues,   515
The time of trial, ere we learn to live
In reconcilement with our stinted powers,
To endure this state of meagre vassalage;
Unwilling to forego, confess, submit,
Uneasy and unsettled, yoke-fellows   520
To custom, mettlesome, and not yet tamed
And humbled down; oh! then we feel, we feel,
We know where we have friends. Ye dreamers, then,
Forgers of daring tales! we bless you then,
Imposters, drivellers, dotards, as the ape   525
Philosophy will call you:[2] *then* we feel
With what, and how great might ye are in league,
Who make our wish, our power, our thought a deed,
An empire, a possession,—ye whom time
And seasons serve; all Faculties; to whom   530
Earth crouches, the elements are potters' clay,
Space like a heaven filled up with northern lights,
Here, nowhere, there, and everywhere at once.

* * *

Here must we pause: this only let me add,
From heart-experience, and in humblest sense   585
Of modesty, that he, who in his youth
A daily wanderer among woods and fields
With living Nature hath been intimate,
Not only in that raw unpractised time
Is stirred to extasy, as others are,   590
By glittering verse; but further, doth receive,
In measure only dealt out to himself,
Knowledge and increase of enduring joy
From the great Nature that exists in works
Of mighty Poets.[3] Visionary power   595
Attends the motions of the viewless winds,

9. Wander.
1. Natural forces.
2. I.e., the kind of philosophical rationalism which derogates imaginative fiction.

3. Having found a set of symbols in nature, Wordsworth now finds nature in
the symbol systems of "mighty poets."

Embodied in the mystery of words:
There, darkness makes abode, and all the host
Of shadowy things work endless changes there,
As in a mansion like their proper home.   600
Even forms and substances are circumfused
By that transparent veil with light divine,
And, through the turnings intricate of verse,
Present themselves as objects recognised,
In flashes, and with glory not their own.   605

* * *

From *Book Sixth. Cambridge and the Alps*

* * *

When the third summer freed us from restraint,[1]
A youthful friend, he too a mountaineer,
Not slow to share my wishes, took his staff,
And sallying forth, we journeyed side by side,   325
Bound to the distant Alps. A hardy slight
Did this unprecedented course imply
Of college studies and their set rewards;[2]
Nor had, in truth, the scheme been formed by me
Without uneasy forethought of the pain,   330
The censures, and ill-omening of those
To whom my worldly interests were dear.
But Nature then was sovereign in my mind,
And mighty forms, seizing a youthful fancy,
Had given a charter[3] to irregular hopes.   335
In any age of uneventful calm
Among the nations, surely would my heart
Have been possessed by similar desire;
But Europe at that time was thrilled with joy,
France standing on the top of golden hours,   340
And human nature seeming born again.

* * *

That very day,
From a bare ridge we also first beheld
Unveiled the summit of Mont Blanc, and grieved   525
To have a soulless image on the eye
That had usurped upon a living thought
That never more could be.[4] The wondrous Vale

1. After reviewing briefly his second and third years at Cambridge, Wordsworth here describes his trip through France and Switzerland with a college friend, Robert Jones, in the succeeding summer vacation, 1790. France was then in the "golden hours" of the early period of the Revolution; the fall of the Bastille had occurred on July 14 of the preceding year.
2. English universities allow much longer vacations than those in America, on the optimistic assumption that they will be used primarily for intensive study. Wordsworth is facing his final examinations in the next college year.
3. Privileged freedom.
4. The "image" is the actual sight of Mont Blanc, as against what the poet has imagined the famous Swiss mountain to be. Chamonix (see line 529) is a valley in eastern France, north of Mont Blanc.

Of Chamouny stretched far below, and soon
With its dumb cataracts and streams of ice,   530
A motionless array of mighty waves,
Five rivers broad and vast, made rich amends,
And reconciled us to realities;
There small birds warble from the leafy trees,
The eagle soars high in the element,   535
There doth the reaper bind the yellow sheaf,
The maiden spread the haycock in the sun,
While Winter like a well-tamed lion walks,
Descending from the mountain to make sport
Among the cottages by beds of flowers.   540

    Whate'er in this wide circuit we beheld,
Or heard, was fitted to our unripe state
Of intellect and heart. With such a book
Before our eyes, we could not choose but read
Lessons of genuine brotherhood, the plain   545
And universal reason of mankind,
The truths of young and old. Nor, side by side
Pacing, two social pilgrims, or alone
Each with his humour,[5] could we fail to abound
In dreams and fictions, pensively composed: 550
Dejection taken up for pleasure's sake,
And gilded sympathies, the willow wreath,[6]
And sober posies of funereal flowers,
Gathered among those solitudes sublime
From formal gardens of the lady Sorrow,   555
Did sweeten many a meditative hour.

    Yet still in me with those soft luxuries
Mixed something of stern mood, an under-thirst
Of vigour seldom utterly allayed.
And from that source how different a sadness   560
Would issue, let one incident make known.
When from the Vallais we had turned, and clomb
Along the Simplon's steep and rugged road,[7]
Following a band of muleteers, we reached
A halting-palce, where all together took   565
Their noon-tide meal. Hastily rose our guide,
Leaving *us* at the board; awhile we lingered,
Then paced the beaten downward way that led
Right to a rough stream's edge, and there broke off;
The only track now visible was one   570
That from the torrent's further brink held forth
Conspicuous invitation to ascend

5. Temperament, or state of mind.   small branches of flowers.
6. Symbolizing sorrow. "Gilded": laid   7. The Simplon Pass through the Alps;
on like gilt; i.e. superficial. "Posies":   "clomb": climbed.

A lofty mountain. After brief delay
Crossing the unbridged stream, that road we took,
And clomb with eagerness, till anxious fears   575
Intruded, for we failed to overtake
Our comrades gone before. By fortunate chance,
While every moment added doubt to doubt,
A peasant met us, from whose mouth we learned
That to the spot which had perplexed us first   580
We must descend, and there should find the road,
Which in the stony channel of the stream
Lay a few steps, and then along its banks;
And, that our future course, all plain to sight,
Was downwards, with the current of that stream.   585
Loth to believe what we so grieved to hear,
For still we had hopes that pointed to the clouds,
We questioned him again, and yet again;
But every word that from the peasant's lips
Came in reply, translated by our feelings,   590
Ended in this,—*that we had crossed the Alps.*[8]

   Imagination—here the Power so called
Through sad incompetence of human speech,
That awful Power rose from the mind's abyss
Like an unfathered vapour[9] that enwraps,   595
At once, some lonely traveller. I was lost;
Halted without an effort to break through;
But to my conscious soul I now can say—
'I recognise thy glory': in such strength
Of usurpation, when the light of sense   600
Goes out, but with a flash that has revealed
The invisible world, doth greatness make abode,
There harbours, whether we be young or old.
Our destiny, our being's heart and home,
Is with infinitude, and only there;   605
With hope it is, hope that can never die,
Effort, and expectation, and desire,
And something evermore about to be.[1]
Under such banners militant, the soul
Seeks for no trophies, struggles for no spoils   610
That may attest her prowess, blest in thoughts
That are their own perfection and reward,

8. As Dorothy Wordsworth baldly put it later on, "The ambition of youth was disappointed at these tidings." The visionary experience that follows (lines 592–616) occurred not in the Alps but at the time of writing the passage, as the 1805 text explicitly says: "Imagination! lifting up itself / Before the eye and progress of my Song."
9. Sudden vapor from no apparent source.

1. I.e., the imaginative vision reveals that his hitherto inexplicable disappointment—in that his hopes continued to point upward, although the trail led downward—signifies that man's glory and tragic dignity consist in sustaining an infinite striving against the limits of his finite possibilities.

Strong in herself and in beatitude [2]
That hides her, like the mighty flood of Nile
Poured from his fount of Abyssinian clouds   615
To fertilise the whole Egyptian plain.

    The melancholy slackening that ensued
Upon those tidings by the peasant given
Was soon dislodged. Downwards we hurried fast,
And, with the half-shaped road which we had missed,   620
Entered a narrow chasm. The brook and road
Were fellow-travellers in this gloomy strait,
And with them did we journey several hours
At a slow pace. The immeasurable height
Of woods decaying, never to be decayed,   625
The stationary blasts of waterfalls,
And in the narrow rent at every turn
Winds thwarting winds, bewildered and forlorn,
The torrents shooting from the clear blue sky,
The rocks that muttered close upon our ears,   630
Black drizzling crags that spake by the way-side
As if a voice were in them, the sick sight
And giddy prospect of the raving stream,
The unfettered clouds and region of the Heavens,
Tumult and peace, the darkness and the light—   635
Were all like workings of one mind, the features
Of the same face, blossoms upon one tree;
Characters of the great Apocalypse, [3]
The types and symbols of Eternity,
Of first, and last, and midst, and without end. [4]   640

* * *

From *Book Seventh. Residence in London* [1]

* * *

    As the black storm upon the mountain top
Sets off the sunbeam in the valley, so   620
That huge fermenting mass of human-kind
Serves as a solemn back-ground, or relief,
To single forms and objects, whence they draw,
For feeling and contemplative regard,
More than inherent liveliness and power.   625
How oft, amid those overflowing streets,

---

2. The ultimate blessedness or happiness.
3. The objects in this natural scene, exhibiting a coincidence of all opposites, are like the written words of the Apocalypse—i.e., of the Book of Revelation, the last book of the New Testament.
4. Cf. Revelation i.8: "I am Alpha and Omega, the beginning and the ending, saith the Lord"; the phrase is re-

peated in xxi.6, after the fulfillment of the last things. In *Paradise Lost* V.153–65 Milton says that the things created declare their Creator, and calls on all to extol "him first, him last, him midst, and without end."
1. Wordsworth spent three and a half months in London in 1791.

Have I gone forward with the crowd, and said
Unto myself, 'The face of every one
That passes by me is a mystery!'
Thus have I looked, nor ceased to look, oppressed   630
By thoughts of what and whither, when and how,
Until the shapes before my eyes became
A second-sight procession, such as glides
Over still mountains, or appears in dreams;
And once, far-travelled in such mood, beyond   635
The reach of common indication, lost
Amid the moving pageant, I was smitten
Abruptly, with the view (a sight not rare)
Of a blind Beggar, who, with upright face,
Stood, propped against a wall, upon his chest   640
Wearing a written paper, to explain
His story, whence he came, and who he was.
Caught by the spectacle my mind turned round
As with the might of waters; an apt type   645
This label seemed of the utmost we can know,
Both of ourselves and of the universe;
And, on the shape of that unmoving man,
His steadfast face and sightless eyes, I gazed,
As if admonished from another world.

       * * * From these sights   675
Take one,—that ancient festival, the Fair,
Holden where martyrs suffered in past time,
And named of St. Bartholomew;[2] there, see
A work completed to our hands, that lays,
If any spectacle on earth can do,   680
The whole creative powers of man asleep!—
For once, the Muse's help will we implore,
And she shall lodge us, wafted on her wings,
Above the press and danger of the crowd,
Upon some showman's platform. What a shock   685
For eyes and ears! what anarchy and din,
Barbarian and infernal,—a phantasma,[3]
Monstrous in colour, motion, shape, sight, sound!
Below, the open space, through every nook
Of the wide area, twinkles, is alive   690
With heads; the midway region, and above,
Is thronged with staring pictures and huge scrolls,

---

2. This huge fair was long held in Smithfield, the place where, on St. Bartholomew's Day, August 24, Protestants had been executed in Queen Mary's reign (1553–58). The scene, which for Wordsworth laid "the whole creative powers of man asleep" (line 681), is exactly the kind that most stimulates those writers (including Chaucer, Shakespeare, and Dickens) who take inspiration from the vigor and bustle of variegated humanity. But "before it could touch [Wordsworth] near," as Walter Raleigh said, "an experience had to be simple and isolated."
3. Fantasy of a disordered mind.

Dumb proclamations of the Prodigies;
With chattering monkeys dangling from their poles,
And children whirling in their roundabouts;[4]   695
With those that stretch the neck and strain the eyes,
And crack the voice in rivalship, the crowd
Inviting; with buffoons against buffoons
Grimacing, writhing, screaming,—him who grinds
The hurdy-gurdy,[5] at the fiddle weaves,   700
Rattles the salt-box, thumps the kettle-drum,
And him who at the trumpet puffs his cheeks,
The silver-collared Negro with his timbrel,[6]
Equestrians, tumblers, women, girls, and boys,
Blue-breeched, pink-vested, with high-towering plumes.   705
All moveables of wonder, from all parts,
Are here—Albinos, painted Indians, Dwarfs,
The Horse of knowledge,[7] and the learned Pig,
The Stone-eater, the man that swallows fire,
Giants, Ventriloquists, the Invisible Girl,   710
The Bust that speaks and moves its goggling eyes,
The Wax-work,[8] Clock-work, all the marvellous craft
Of modern Merlins,[9] Wild Beasts, Puppet-shows,
All out-o'-the-way, far-fetched, perverted things,
All freaks of nature, all Promethean[10] thoughts   715
Of man, his dullness, madness, and their feats
All jumbled up together, to compose
A Parliament of Monsters, Tents and Booths
Meanwhile, as if the whole were one vast mill,
Are vomiting, receiving, on all sides,   720
Men, Women, three-years Children, Babes in arms.

    Oh, blank confusion! true epitome
Of what the mighty City is herself
To thousands upon thousands of her sons,
Living amid the same perpetual whirl   725
Of trivial objects, melted and reduced
To one identity, by differences
That have no law, no meaning, and no end—
Oppression, under which even highest minds
Must labour, whence the strongest are not free.   730
But though the picture weary out the eye,
By nature an unmanageable sight,
It is not wholly so to him who looks

4. Merry-go-rounds.
5. A stringed instrument, sounded by a turning wheel covered by rosin. "Salt box": a wooden box, rattled and beaten with a stick.
6. Tambourine.
7. A horse trained to tap out answers to numerical questions, etc.
8. In 1802 Madame Tussaud had opened in London her exhibition of wax sculptures of the leaders and victims of the French Revolution.
9. Magicians. Merlin was the magician in the Arthurian romances.
10. Creative, or highly inventive. Prometheus, in Greek mythology, made man out of clay and taught him the arts.

In steadiness, who hath among least things
An under-sense of greatest; sees the parts   735
As parts, but with a feeling of the whole.

* * *

From *Book Eighth. Retrospect.—Love of Nature Leading to Love of Man*[1]

* * *

For me, when my affections first were led
From kindred, friends, and playmates, to partake
Love for the human creature's absolute self,
That noticeable kindliness of heart
Sprang out of fountains, there abounding most   125
Where sovereign Nature dictated the tasks
And occupations which her beauty adorned,
And Shepherds were the men that pleased me first;

    * * * A rambling school-boy, thus
I felt his presence in his own domain,
As of a lord and master, or a power,
Or genius,[2] under Nature, under God,
Presiding; and severest solitude   260
Had more commanding looks when he was there.
When up the lonely brooks on rainy days
Angling I went, or trod the trackless hills
By mists bewildered, suddenly mine eyes
Have glanced upon him distant a few steps,   265
In size a giant, stalking through thick fog,
His sheep like Greenland bears;[3] or, as he stepped
Beyond the boundary line of some hill-shadow,
His form hath flashed upon me, glorified
By the deep radiance of the setting sun:[4]   270
Or him have I descried in distant sky,
A solitary object and sublime,
Above all height! like an aerial cross
Stationed alone upon a spiry rock
Of the Chartreuse, for worship.[5] Thus was man   275

1. In this book Wordsworth reviews the first 21 years of his life in order to trace the transfer of his earlier feelings for nature to shepherds and other humble people who carry on their lonely duties almost as though they were animate parts of the landscape (cf. *Michael*, lines 1–39). Wordsworth's central concern is to describe the early development in his relatively inexperienced mind of an Image, or conceptual model, of the largeness, worth, and almost sacred dignity of generic Man (lines 256–81); an Image which proved invulnerable to the acid bath of his later experience of the vulgarity, meanness, and evil of which individual men are capable (lines 317–22).
2. Presiding spirit.
3. Polar bears.
4. A "glory" is a mountain phenomenon in which the enlarged figure of a person is seen projected by the sun upon the mist, with a radiance about its head. Cf. Coleridge's *Dejection*, line 54.
5. In his tour of the Alps Wordsworth had been deeply impressed by the Chartreuse, a Carthusian monastery in the French Alps, with its soaring cross visible against the sky. There is an overtone here of the Christlike divinity investing the "common" man (line 289).

Ennobled outwardly before my sight,
And thus my heart was early introduced
To an unconscious love and reverence
Of human nature; hence the human form
To me became an index of delight,   280
Of grace and honour, power and worthiness.
Meanwhile this creature—spiritual almost
As those of books, but more exalted far;
Far more of an imaginative form
Than the gay Corin[6] of the groves, who lives   285
For his own fancies, or to dance by the hour,
In coronal, with Phyllis in the midst—
Was, for the purposes of kind,[7] a man
With the most common; husband, father; learned,
Could teach, admonish; suffered with the rest   290
From vice and folly, wretchedness and fear;
Of this I little saw, cared less for it,
But something must have felt.

                  Call ye these appearances—
Which I beheld of shepherds in my youth,
This sanctity of Nature given to man—   295
A shadow, a delusion, ye who pore
On the dead letter, miss the spirit of things;
Whose truth is not a motion or a shape
Instinct with vital functions, but a block
Or waxen image which yourselves have made,   300
And ye adore! But blessed be the God
Of Nature and of Man that this was so;
That men before my inexperienced eyes
Did first present themselves thus purified,
Removed, and to a distance that was fit: 305
And so we all of us in some degree
Are led to knowledge, whencesoever led,
And howsoever; were it otherwise,
And we found evil fast as we find good
In our first years, or think that it is found,   310
How could the innocent heart bear up and live!
But doubly fortunate my lot; not here
Alone, that something of a better life
Perhaps was round me than it is the privilege
Of most to move in, but that first I looked   315
At Man through objects that were great or fair;
First communed with him by their help. And thus
Was founded a sure safeguard and defence
Against the weight of meanness, selfish cares,
Coarse manners, vulgar passions, that beat in   320

6. "Corin" and "Phyllis," dancing in
their "coronals," or wreaths of flowers,
were stock characters in earlier pastoral
literature.
7. I.e., in carrying out the tasks of
humankind.

On all sides from the ordinary world
In which we traffic. * * *

   Yet deem not, Friend! that human kind with me   340
Thus early took a place pre-eminent;
Nature herself was, at this unripe time,
But secondary to my own pursuits
And animal activities, and all
Their trivial pleasures;[8] and when these had drooped   345
And gradually expired, and Nature, prized
For her own sake, became my joy, even then—
And upwards through late youth, until not less
Than two-and-twenty summers had been told—
Was Man in my affections and regards   350
Subordinate to her, her visible forms
And viewless[9] agencies: a passion, she,
A rapture often, and immediate love
Ever at hand; *he*, only a delight
Occasional, an accidental grace,   355
His hour being not yet come. * * *

From *Book Ninth. Residence in France*[1]

Even as a river,—partly (it might seem)
Yielding to old remembrances, and swayed
In part by fear to shape a way direct,
That would engulph him soon in the ravenous sea—
Turns, and will measure back his course, far back,   5
Seeking the very regions which he crossed
In his first outset; so have we, my Friend!
Turned and returned with intricate delay.
Or as a traveller, who has gained the brow
Of some aerial Down,[2] while there he halts   10
For breathing-time, is tempted to review
The region left behind him; and, if aught
Deserving notice have escaped regard,
Or been regarded with too careless eye,
Strives, from that height, with one and yet one more   15
Last look, to make the best amends he may:
So have we lingered. Now we start afresh
With courage, and new hope risen on our toil.
Fair greetings to this shapeless eagerness,
Whene'er it comes! needful in work so long,   20

8. Cf. Wordsworth's account of the stages of his development in *Tintern Abbey*, lines 65–92 and note.
9. Invisible.
1. Wordsworth's second visit to France, while he was 21 and 22 years of age (1791–92), came during a crucial period of the French Revolution. This book deals with Wordsworth's stay at Paris, Orléans, and Blois, when he developed his passionate partisanship for the French people and the revolutionary cause.
2. Treeless high land.

Thrice needful to the argument which now
Awaits us! Oh, how much unlike the past![3]

* * *

France lured me forth; the realm that I had crossed
So lately, journeying toward the snow-clad Alps.   35
But now, relinquishing the scrip and staff,[4]
And all enjoyment which the summer sun
Sheds round the steps of those who meet the day
With motion constant as his own, I went
Prepared to sojourn in a pleasant town,   40
Washed by the current of the stately Loire.[5]

Through Paris lay my readiest course, and there
Sojourning a few days, I visited,
In haste, each spot of old or recent fame,
The latter chiefly; from the field of Mars   45
Down to the suburbs of St. Anthony,
And from Mont Martyr southward to the Dome
Of Genevieve.[6] In both her clamorous Halls,
The National Synod[7] and the Jacobins,
I saw the Revolutionary Power   50
Toss like a ship at anchor, rocked by storms;
The Arcades I traversed, in the Palace huge
Of Orleans;[8] coasted round and round the line
Of Tavern, Brothel, Gaming-house, and Shop,
Great rendezvous of worst and best, the walk   55
Of all who had a purpose, or had not;
I stared and listened, with a stranger's ears,
To Hawkers and Haranguers, hubbub wild!
And hissing Factionists with ardent eyes,
In knots and pairs, or single. Not a look   60
Hope takes, or Doubt or Fear are forced to wear,
But seemed there present; and I scanned them all,
Watched every gesture uncontrollable,
Of anger, and vexation, and despite,

3. This preface parallels in function Milton's preface to the equivalent ninth book of *Paradise Lost*, in which he announces that, having narrated the blameless life of Adam and Eve, he "now must change / Those notes to tragic," and tell of their fall. "Argument": theme.
4. The "scrip" (the bag or knapsack) and the "staff" are the traditional emblems of the foot pilgrim.
5. Orléans, on the Loire River, where Wordsworth stayed from December, 1791, until he moved to Blois early the next year.
6. The "field of Mars" (the Champ de Mars), where Louis XVI swore fidelity to the new constitution. "The suburbs of St. Anthony": Faubourg St. Antoine, near the Bastille, a working-class quarter and center of revolutionary violence. "Mont Martyr": Montmartre, a hill on which revolutionary meetings were held. The "dome of Geneviève" became the Panthéon, a burial place for notable Frenchmen.
7. The newly formed National Assembly. "Jacobins": the club of radical democratic revolutionists, named for the ancient convent of St. Jacques, their meeting place.
8. The arcades in the courtyard of the Palais d'Orléans, a fashionable shopping center and Parisian rendezvous.

All side by side, and struggling face to face,   65
With gaiety and dissolute idleness.

   Where silent zephyrs sported with the dust
Of the Bastile,[9] I sate in the open sun,
And from the rubbish gathered up a stone,
And pocketed the relic, in the guise   70
Of an enthusiast; yet, in honest truth,
I looked for something that I could not find,
Affecting more emotion than I felt;
For 'tis most certain, that these various sights,
However potent their first shock, with me   75
Appeared to recompense the traveller's pains
Less than the painted Magdalene of Le Brun, [1]
A beauty exquisitely wrought, with hair
Dishevelled, gleaming eyes, and rueful cheek
Pale and bedropped with everflowing tears.   80

      * * * For myself, I fear
Now in connection with so great a theme
To speak (as I must be compelled to do)
Of one so unimportant; night by night
Did I frequent the formal haunts of men,
Whom, in the city, privilege of birth   115
Sequestered from the rest; societies
Polished in arts, and in punctilio[2] versed;
Whence, and from deeper causes, all discourse
Of good and evil of the time was shunned
With scrupulous care; but these restrictions soon   120
Proved tedious, and I gradually withdrew
Into a noisier world, and thus ere long
Became a patriot;[3] and my heart was all
Given to the people, and my love was theirs.

      * * * Yet not the less,
Hatred of absolute rule, where will of one
Is law for all, and of that barren pride
In them who, by immunities unjust,
Between the sovereign and the people stand,   505
His helper and not theirs, laid stronger hold
Daily upon me, mixed with pity too
And love; for where hope is, there love will be
For the abject multitude. And when we[4] chanced

---

9. The political prison of the Bastille had
been demolished, after it had been
stormed and sacked on July 14, 1789.
1. A theatrical painting of the weeping
Mary Magdalene by Charles Le Brun
(1619–90), then regarded as a religious
masterpiece.
2. The niceties of social manners.

3. I.e., became committed to the people's side in the Revolution.
4. Wordsworth is accompanied by Michel Beaupuy, one of the few republican
sympathizers among the officer corps of
the regular army. By doctrine and force
of character he did much to shape
Wordsworth's radical views.

One day to meet a hunger-bitten girl,   510
Who crept along fitting her languid gait
Unto a heifer's motion, by a cord
Tied to her arm, and picking thus from the lane
Its sustenance, while the girl with pallid hands
Was busy knitting in a heartless mood   515
Of solitude, and at the sight my friend
In agitation said, ' 'Tis against *that*
That we are fighting', I with him believed
That a benignant spirit was abroad
Which might not be withstood, that poverty   520
Abject as this would in a little time
Be found no more, that we should see the earth
Unthwarted in her wish to recompense
The meek, the lowly, patient child of toil.
All institutes for ever blotted out   525
That legalised exclusion, empty pomp
Abolished, sensual state and cruel power,
Whether by edict of the one or few;
And finally, as sum and crown of all,
Should see the people having a strong hand   530
In framing their own laws; whence better days
To all mankind.⁵ * * *

From *Book Tenth. Residence in France—Continued*¹

* * *

Cheered with this hope,² to Paris I returned,
And ranged, with ardour heretofore unfelt,
The spacious city, and in progress passed   50
The prison³ where the unhappy Monarch lay,
Associate with his children and his wife
In bondage; and the palace, lately stormed
With roar of cannon by a furious host.
I crossed the square (an empty area then!)   55
Of the Carrousel, where so late had lain
The dead, upon the dying heaped, and gazed
On this and other spots, as doth a man
Upon a volume whose contents he knows

---

5. The following political aims constituted the radicalism of Wordsworth and
Beaupuy: elimination of the extreme of
poverty; the rewards of tillage to go to
the tiller of the land; all careers opened
to talents; abolition of absolute power,
whether by a monarch or an oligarchy;
and a greatly extended franchise.
1. At this period, October, 1792–August,
1794, Wordsworth's revolutionary enthusiasm was at its height.
2. The Parisian mob had stormed the
Tuileries; the king had been deposed and

imprisoned; and the Commune had organized the "September Massacres," in
which 3,000 Royalist suspects were murdered. Wordsworth's "hope" was that
the moderates were now taking over and
would eliminate further violence.
3. I.e., the "Temple" (it had once housed
the religious Order of Templars), where
Louis XVI was held prisoner. "The palace" is the Tuileries; in front of this is
the great square of "the Carrousel,"
where a number of the mob storming the
palace had been killed.

Are memorable, but from him locked up, 60
Being written in a tongue he cannot read,
So that he questions the mute leaves with pain,
And half upbraids their silence. But that night
I felt most deeply in what world I was,
What ground I trod on, and what air I breathed. 65
High was my room and lonely, near the roof
Of a large mansion or hotel,[4] a lodge
That would have pleased me in more quiet times;
Nor was it wholly without pleasure then.
With unextinguished taper I kept watch, 70
Reading at intervals; the fear gone by
Pressed on me almost like a fear to come.
I thought of those September massacres,
Divided from me by one little month.
Saw them and touched:[5] the rest was conjured up 75
From tragic fictions or true history,
Remembrances and dim admonishments.
The horse is taught his manage,[6] and no star
Of wildest course but treads back his own steps;
For the spent hurricane the air provides 80
As fierce a successor; the tide retreats
But to return out of its hiding-place
In the great deep; all things have second birth;
The earthquake is not satisfied at once;
And in this way I wrought upon myself, 85
Until I seemed to hear a voice that cried,
To the whole city, 'Sleep no more'.[7] The trance
Fled with the voice to which it had given birth;
But vainly comments of a calmer mind
Promised soft peace and sweet forgetfulness. 90
The place, all hushed and silent as it was,
Appeared unfit for the repose of night,
Defenceless as a wood where tigers roam.

* * *

In this frame of mind,
Dragged by a chain of harsh necessity,
So seemed it,—now I thankfully acknowledge,
Forced by the gracious providence of Heaven,—
To England I returned,[8] else (though assured 225
That I both was and must be of small weight,
No better than a landsman on the deck
Of a ship struggling with a hideous storm)
Doubtless, I should have then made common cause

---

4. A town house.
5. I.e., his imagination of the September Massacres was so vivid as to be palpable.
6. The French *manège*, the prescribed action and paces of a trained horse.
7. "Methought I heard a voice cry, 'Sleep no more! / Macbeth does murder sleep' " (*Macbeth* II.ii.34–36).
8. Forced by the "harsh necessity" of a lack of money, Wordsworth returned to England late in 1792.

With some who perished; haply, perished too,[9]   230
A poor mistaken and bewildered offering,—
Should to the breast of Nature have gone back,
With all my resolutions, all my hopes,
A Poet only to myself, to men
Useless, and even, beloved Friend! a soul   235
To thee unknown![1]

* * *

What, then, were my emotions, when in arms
Britain put forth her free-born strength in league,
Oh, pity and shame! with those confederate Powers![2]   265
Not in my single self alone I found,
But in the minds of all ingenuous youth,
Change and subversion from that hour. No shock
Given to my moral nature had I known
Down to that very moment; neither lapse   270
Nor turn of sentiment that might be named
A revolution, save at this one time;
All else was progress on the self-same path
On which, with a diversity of pace,
I had been travelling: this a stride at once   275
Into another region. As a light
And pliant harebell, swinging in the breeze
On some grey rock—its birth-place—so had I
Wantoned, fast rooted on the ancient tower
Of my beloved country, wishing not   280
A happier fortune than to wither there:
Now was I from that pleasant station torn
And tossed about in whirlwind. I rejoiced,
Yea, afterwards—truth most painful to record!—
Exulted, in the triumph of my soul,   285
When Englishmen by thousands were o'erthrown,
Left without glory on the field, or driven,
Brave hearts! to shameful flight.[3] It was a grief,—
Grief call it not, 'twas anything but that,—
A conflict of sensations without name,   290
Of which *he* only, who may love the sight
Of a village steeple, as I do, can judge,
When, in the congregation bending all
To their great Father, prayers were offered up,

9. Wordsworth had allied his sympathies with the party of the Girondins, almost all of whom were guillotined, or committed suicide.
1. Wordsworth did not meet Coleridge, the "beloved Friend," until 1795.
2. England joined the war against France in February, 1793. The great moral crisis which almost wrecked Wordsworth's life began with this sudden split between his profound attachments to the English land (the development of which he had described in the early books of *The Prelude*) and his later but heartfelt identification with the cause of the French Revolution. What had seemed a single and coherent development suddenly became split into conflicting parts.
3. The French defeated the English in the battle of Hondschoote, September 6, 1793.

Or praises for our country's victories;   295
And, 'mid the simple worshippers, perchance
I only, like an uninvited guest
Whom no one owned, sate silent, shall I add,
Fed on the day of vengeance yet to come.

* * *

   Domestic carnage now filled the whole year
With feast-days; old men from the chimney-nook,
The maiden from the bosom of her love,
The mother from the cradle of her babe,
The warrior from the field—all perished, all—   360
Friends, enemies, of all parties, ages, ranks,
Head after head, and never heads enough
For those that bade them fall.[4] They found their joy,
They made it proudly, eager as a child,
(If light desires of innocent little ones   365
May with such heinous appetites be compared),
Pleased in some open field to exercise
A toy that mimics with revolving wings
The motion of a wind-mill; though the air
Do of itself blow fresh, and make the vanes   370
Spin in his eyesight, *that* contents him not,
But, with the plaything at arm's length, he sets
His front against the blast, and runs amain,
That it may whirl the faster.

* * *

Most melancholy at that time, O Friend!
Were my day-thoughts,—my nights were miserable;
Through months, through years, long after the last beat
Of those atrocities, the hour of sleep   400
To me came rarely charged with natural gifts,
Such ghastly visions had I of despair
And tyranny, and implements of death;
And innocent victims sinking under fear,
And momentary hope, and worn-out prayer,   405
Each in his separate cell, or penned in crowds
For sacrifice, and struggling with forced mirth
And levity in dungeons, where the dust
Was laid with tears. Then suddenly the scene
Changed, and the unbroken dream entangled me   410
In long orations, which I strove to plead
Before unjust tribunals,—with a voice
Labouring, a brain confounded, and a sense,
Death-like, of treacherous desertion, felt
In the last place of refuge—my own soul.   415

* * *

4. A description of the height of the
Reign of Terror under Robespierre; in
1794, 1,376 people were guillotined in
Paris in 49 days. "Feast-days" (line
357): i.e., festivals celebrated by human
slaughter ("carnage").

From *Book Eleventh. France—Concluded*[1]

* * *

O pleasant exercise of hope and joy![2]   105
For mighty were the auxiliars which then stood
Upon our side, we who were strong in love!
Bliss was it in that dawn to be alive,
But to be young was very Heaven! O times,
In which the meagre, stale, forbidding ways   110
Of custom, law, and statute, took at once
The attraction of a country in romance!
When Reason seemed the most to assert her rights
When most intent on making of herself
A prime enchantress—to assist the work,   115
Which then was going forward in her name!
Not favoured spots alone, but the whole Earth,
The beauty wore of promise—that which sets
(As at some moments might not be unfelt
Among the bowers of Paradise itself)   120
The budding rose above the rose full blown.[3]
What temper at the prospect did not wake
To happiness unthought of? The inert
Were roused, and lively natures rapt away![4]
They who had fed their childhood upon dreams,   125
The play-fellows of fancy, who had made
All powers of swiftness, subtilty, and strength
Their ministers,—who in lordly wise had stirred
Among the grandest objects of the sense,
And dealt with whatsoever they found there   130
As if they had within some lurking right
To wield it;—they, too, who of gentle mood
Had watched all gentle motions, and to these
Had fitted their own thoughts, schemers more mild,
And in the region of their peaceful selves;—   135
Now was it that *both* found, the meek and lofty
Did both find helpers to their hearts' desire,
And stuff at hand, plastic[5] as they could wish,—
Were called upon to exercise their skill,
Not in Utopia,—subterranean fields,—   140
Or some secreted island, Heaven knows where!
But in the very world, which is the world

---

1. Book XI deals with the year from August, 1794, through September, 1795: Wordsworth's growing disillusionment with the French Revolution, his recourse to abstract theories of man and politics, his despair and nervous breakdown, and the beginning of his recovery when he moved from London to Racedown.
2. Wordsworth in this passage turns back to the summer of 1792, when his enthusiasm for the Revolution was at its height.
3. A statement of the Romantic theme of the glory of the imperfect, which sets a higher value on promise than on achievement. "Temper": temperament.
4. Enraptured; carried away by enthusiasm.
5. Malleable.

Of all of us,—the place where, in the end,
We find our happiness, or not at all!

Why should I not confess that Earth was then   145
To me, what an inheritance, new-fallen,
Seems, when the first time visited, to one
Who thither comes to find in it his home?
He walks about and looks upon the spot
With cordial transport, moulds it and remoulds,   150
And is half pleased with things that are amiss,
'Twill be such joy to see them disappear.

* * *

But now, become oppressors in their turn,
Frenchmen had changed a war of self-defence
For one of conquest, losing sight of all
Which they had struggled for:[6] and mounted up,
Openly in the eye of earth and heaven,   210
The scale of liberty.[7] I read her doom,
With anger vexed, with disappointment sore,
But not dismayed, nor taking to the shame
Of a false prophet. While resentment rose
Striving to hide, what nought could heal, the wounds 215
Of mortified presumption, I adhered
More firmly to old tenets, and, to prove[8]
Their temper, strained them more; and thus, in heat
Of contest, did opinions every day
Grow into consequence, till round my mind   220
They clung, as if they were its life, nay more,
The very being of the immortal soul.

This was the time, when, all things tending fast
To depravation, speculative schemes—
That promised to abstract the hopes of Man   225
Out of his feelings, to be fixed thenceforth
For ever in a purer element—
Found ready welcome.[9] Tempting region *that*
For Zeal to enter and refresh herself,
Where passions had the privilege to work,   230
And never hear the sound of their own name.
But, speaking more in charity, the dream

6. In late 1794 and early 1795 French troops had successes in Spain, Italy, Holland, and Germany—even though, in the constitution written in 1790, they had renounced all foreign conquest.
7. I.e., the desire for power now outweighed the love of liberty.
8. Test; the figure is that of testing a tempered steel sword.
9. I.e., schemes which undertook to separate ("abstract") people's hopes for future happiness from reliance on the emotional part of human nature, and instead to ground those hopes on their rational natures ("a purer element"). The allusion is primarily to William Godwin's *Inquiry Concerning Political Justice* (1793), which attempted to ground ethical and political principles, and the expectation of human progress, on rational principles.

Flattered the young, pleased with extremes, nor least
With that which makes our Reason's naked self
The object of its fervour. * * *   235

I summoned my best skill, and toiled, intent
To anatomise[1] the frame of social life,   280
Yea, the whole body of society
Searched to its heart. Share with me, Friend! the wish
That some dramatic tale, endued with shapes
Livelier, and flinging out less guarded words
Than suit the work we fashion, might set forth   285
What then I learned, or think I learned, of truth,
And the errors into which I fell, betrayed
By present objects, and by reasonings false
From their beginnings, inasmuch as drawn
Out of a heart that had been turned aside   290
From Nature's way by outward accidents,
And which was thus confounded more and more,
Misguided and misguiding. So I fared,
Dragging all precepts, judgments, maxims, creeds,
Like culprits to the bar; calling the mind,   295
Suspiciously, to establish in plain day
Her titles[2] and her honours; now believing,
Now disbelieving; endlessly perplexed
With impulse, motive, right and wrong, the ground
Of obligation, what the rule and whence   300
The sanction; till, demanding formal *proof*,
And seeking it in every thing, I lost
All feeling of conviction, and, in fine,[3]
Sick, wearied out with contrarieties,
Yielded up moral question in despair.   305

     This was the crisis of that strong disease,
This the soul's last and lowest ebb; I drooped,
Deeming our blessed reason of least use
Where wanted most: * * *

               * * * Then it was—
Thanks to the bounteous Giver of all good!—
That the beloved Sister[4] in whose sight   335
Those days were passed, now speaking in a voice
Of sudden admonition—like a brook
That does but *cross* a lonely road, and now
Seen, heard, and felt, and caught at every turn,
Companion never lost through many a league—   340

1. Analyze.
2. Legal entitlements.
3. In the end.
4. After a long separation, from 1791 to
1794, Dorothy Wordsworth came to live
with her brother at Racedown in 1795,
and continued a member of his household until her death.

Maintained for me a saving intercourse
With my true self;[5] for, though bedimmed and changed
Both as a clouded and a waning moon,
She whispered still that brightness would return,
She, in the midst of all, preserved me still   345
A Poet, made me seek beneath that name,
And that alone, my office upon earth;
And, lastly, as hereafter will be shown,
If willing audience fail not, Nature's self,
By all varieties of human love   350
Assisted, led me back through opening day
To those sweet counsels between head and heart
Whence grew that genuine knowledge, fraught with peace,
Which, through the later sinkings of this cause,
Hath still upheld me, and upholds me now   355
In the catastrophe (for so they dream,
And nothing less), when, finally to close
And rivet down the gains of France, a Pope
Is summoned in, to crown an Emperor[6]—

* * *

From *Book Twelfth. Imagination and Taste,*
How Impaired and Restored[1]

Long time have human ignorance and guilt
Detained us, on what spectacles of woe
Compelled to look, and inwardly oppressed
With sorrow, disappointment, vexing thoughts,
Confusion of the judgment, zeal decayed,   5
And, lastly, utter loss of hope itself
And things to hope for! Not with these began
Our song, and not with these our song must end.[2]—
Ye motions of delight, that haunt the sides
Of the green hills; ye breezes and soft airs,   10
Whose subtle intercourse with breathing flowers,
Feelingly watched, might teach Man's haughty race
How without injury to take, to give
Without offence; ye who, as if to show
The wondrous influence of power gently used,   15
Bend the complying heads of lordly pines,
And, with a touch, shift the stupendous clouds
Through the whole compass of the sky; ye brooks,

5. Dorothy and the renewed influence of nature (line 349) healed the inner fracture between his earlier and later self, which Wordsworth had described in Book X.268 ff.
6. The ultimate blow to liberal hopes for France occurred when on December 2, 1804, Napoleon summoned Pope Pius VII to officiate at the ceremony elevating him to Emperor. At the last moment,

Napoleon took the crown and donned it himself.
1. Book Twelfth reviews the "impairment" and gradual recovery of Wordsworth's creative sensibility in response to the natural world.
2. The reference is back to the joyous preamble with which *The Prelude* began. Wordsworth goes on (line 10) to invoke the breeze described in the opening line.

Muttering along the stones, a busy noise
By day, a quiet sound in silent night;   20
Ye waves, that out of the great deep steal forth
In a calm hour to kiss the pebbly shore,
Not mute, and then retire, fearing no storm;
And you, ye groves, whose ministry it is
To interpose the covert of your shades,   25
Even as a sleep, between the heart of man
And outward troubles, between man himself,
Not seldom, and his own uneasy heart:

* * *

In such strange passion, if I may once more   75
Review the past, I warred against myself—
A bigot to a new idolatry—
Like a cowled monk who hath forsworn the world,
Zealously laboured to cut off my heart
From all the sources of her former strength;   80
And as, by simple waving of a wand,
The wizard instantaneously dissolves
Palace or grove, even so could I unsoul
As readily by syllogistic words[3]
Those mysteries of being which have made,   85
And shall continue evermore to make,
Of the whole human race one brotherhood.

    What wonder, then, if, to a mind so far
Perverted, even the visible Universe
Fell under the dominion of a taste   90
Less spiritual, with microscopic view
Was scanned, as I had scanned the moral world?[4]

* * *

I speak in recollection of a time
When the bodily eye, in every stage of life
The most despotic of our senses, gained
Such strength in *me* as often held my mind   130
In absolute dominion. Gladly here,
Entering upon abstruser argument,
Could I endeavour to unfold the means
Which Nature studiously employs to thwart
This tyranny, summons all the senses each   135
To counteract the other, and themselves,
And makes them all, and the objects with which all
Are conversant, subservient in their turn
To the great ends of Liberty and Power.[5]

---

3. Logical reasoning.
4. I.e., the habit of logical analysis perverted his perception of the natural world.
5. I.e., the ways in which Nature uses an individual's other senses to counteract the tyranny of the eye—as well as the tyranny of any other single sense—so as to make all the senses (and the external objects they enable us to perceive) subordinate to the free, creative power of the human mind. In lines 203–6, below, Wordsworth attributes this power of free creativity to the imagination.

* * * I had known
Too forcibly, too early in my life,
Visitings of imaginative power
For this to last: I shook the habit off
Entirely and for ever, and again   205
In Nature's presence stood, as now I stand,
A sensitive being, a *creative* soul.

There are in our existence spots of time,[6]
That with distinct pre-eminence retain
A renovating virtue, whence, depressed   210
By false opinion and contentious thought,
Or aught of heavier or more deadly weight,
In trivial occupations, and the round
Of ordinary intercourse, our minds
Are nourished and invisibly repaired;   215
A virtue, by which pleasure is enhanced,
That penetrates, enables us to mount,
When high, more high, and lifts us up when fallen.
This efficacious spirit chiefly lurks
Among those passages of life that give   220
Profoundest knowledge to what point, and how,
The mind is lord and master—outward sense
The obedient servant of her will. Such moments
Are scattered everywhere, taking their date
From our first childhood. I remember well,   225
That once, while yet my inexperienced hand
Could scarcely hold a bridle, with proud hopes
I mounted, and we journeyed towards the hills:
An ancient servant of my father's house
Was with me, my encourager and guide: 230
We had not travelled long, ere some mischance
Disjoined me from my comrade; and, through fear
Dismounting, down the rough and stony moor
I led my horse, and, stumbling on, at length
Came to a bottom,[7] where in former times   235
A murderer had been hung in iron chains.
The gibbet-mast[8] had mouldered down, the bones
And iron case were gone; but on the turf,
Hard by, soon after that fell deed was wrought,

6. These are moments of experience of what is in itself ordinary (line 254), but becomes luminous with a profound significance that, since it is bestowed by the perceiver, evidences the freedom and creative power of the imaginative mind (lines 220–23, 275–77). The recollection of such scenes nourishes and repairs the mind in those periods of depression or distraction when the imagination flags (lines 210–15). Wordsworth also recognizes (lines 277–86) that the recollection of such spots of time from his own early experience is the source of his greatest poetry, and that this source is not inexhaustible.

For Wordsworth's terse early description of these two spots of time, see *The Two-Part Prelude*, I.288–374 and the note to line 374.
7. Valley.
8. The post of the T-shaped structure used for hangings.

Some unknown hand had carved the murderer's name. 240
The monumental letters were inscribed
In times long past; but still, from year to year,
By superstition of the neighbourhood,
The grass is cleared away, and to that hour
The characters were fresh and visible: 245
A casual glance had shown them, and I fled,
Faltering and faint, and ignorant of the road:
Then, reascending the bare common, saw
A naked pool that lay beneath the hills,
The beacon on its summit, and, more near, 250
A girl, who bore a pitcher on her head,
And seemed with difficult steps to force her way
Against the blowing wind. It was, in truth,
An ordinary sight; but I should need
Colours and words that are unknown to man, 255
To paint the visionary dreariness
Which, while I looked all round for my lost guide,
Invested moorland waste, and naked pool,
The beacon crowning the lone eminence,
The female and her garments vexed and tossed 260
By the strong wind. When, in the blessed hours
Of early love, the loved one [9] at my side,
I roamed, in daily presence of this scene,
Upon the naked pool and dreary crags,
And on the melancholy beacon fell 265
A spirit of pleasure and youth's golden gleam;
And think ye not with radiance more sublime
For these remembrances, and for the power
They had left behind? So feeling comes in aid
Of feeling, and diversity of strength 270
Attends us, if but once we have been strong.
Oh! mystery of man, from what a depth
Proceed thy honours. I am lost, but see
In simple childhood something of the base
On which thy greatness stands; but this I feel, 275
That from thy self it comes, that thou must give,
Else never canst receive. The days gone by
Return upon me almost from the dawn
Of life: the hiding-places of man's power
Open; I would approach them, but they close. 280
I see by glimpses now; when age comes on,
May scarcely see at all; and I would give,
While yet we may, as far as words can give,
Substance and life to what I feel, enshrining,
Such is my hope, the spirit of the Past 285
For future restoration.—Yet another
Of these memorials:—

9. Mary Hutchinson, who became Wordsworth's wife.

One Christmas-time,[1]
On the glad eve of its dear holidays,
Feverish and tired, and restless, I went forth
Into the fields, impatient for the sight   290
Of those led palfreys[2] that should bear us home;
My brothers and myself. There rose a crag,
That, from the meeting-point of two highways
Ascending, overlooked them both, far stretched;
Thither, uncertain on which road to fix   295
My expectation, thither I repaired,
Scout-like, and gained the summit; 'twas a day
Tempestuous, dark, and wild, and on the grass
I sate half-sheltered by a naked wall;
Upon my right hand couched a single sheep,   300
Upon my left a blasted hawthorn stood;
With those companions at my side, I sate
Straining my eyes intensely, as the mist
Gave intermitting prospect of the copse
And plain beneath. Ere we to school returned,—   305
That dreary time,—ere we had been ten days
Sojourners in my father's house, he died,[3]
And I and my three brothers, orphans then,
Followed his body to the grave. The event,
With all the sorrow that it brought, appeared   310
A chastisement; and when I called to mind
That day so lately past, when from the crag
I looked in such anxiety of hope;
With trite reflections of morality,
Yet in the deepest passion, I bowed low   315
To God, Who thus corrected my desires;
And, afterwards, the wind and sleety rain,
And all the business[4] of the elements,
The single sheep, and the one blasted tree,
And the bleak music of that old stone wall,   320
The noise of wood and water, and the mist
That on the line of each of those two roads
Advanced in such indisputable shapes;[5]
All these were kindred spectacles and sounds
To which I oft repaired, and thence would drink,   325
As at a fountain; and on winter nights,
Down to this very time, when storm and rain
Beat on my roof, or, haply, at noon-day,
While in a grove I walk, whose lofty trees,
Laden with summer's thickest foliage, rock   330

---

1. In 1813; Wordsworth was 13, and at Hawkshead School with two of his brothers.
2. Small saddle horses.
3. John Wordsworth died on December 30, 1783; William's mother had died five years earlier.
4. Busy-ness; motions.
5. Pronounced *indísputáble shápes*; i.e., shapes one did not dare question.

In a strong wind, some working of the spirit,
Some inward agitations thence are brought,
Whate'er their office, whether to beguile
Thoughts over busy in the course they took,
Or animate an hour of vacant ease.   335

From *Book Thirteenth. Imagination and Taste,*
How Impaired and Restored—Concluded

From Nature doth emotion come, and moods
Of calmness equally are Nature's gift:
This is her glory; these two attributes
Are sister horns that constitute her strength.[1]
Hence Genius, born to thrive by interchange   5
Of peace and excitation, finds in her
His best and purest friend; from her receives
That energy by which he seeks the truth,
From her that happy stillness of the mind
Which fits him to receive it when unsought.   10

* * *

        Here, calling up to mind what then I saw, [2]
A youthful traveller, and see daily now
In the familiar circuit of my home,
Here might I pause, and bend in reverence
To Nature, and the power of human minds,   225
To men as they are men within themselves.
How oft high service is performed within,
When all the external man is rude in show,—
Not like a temple rich with pomp and gold,
But a mere mountain chapel, that protects   230
Its simple worshippers from sun and shower.
Of these, said I, shall be my song; of these,
If future years mature me for the task,
Will I record the praises, making verse
Deal boldly with substantial things; in truth   235
And sanctity of passion, speak of these,
That justice may be done, obeisance paid
Where it is due: thus haply shall I teach,
Inspire, through unadulterated[3] ears
Pour rapture, tenderness, and hope,—my theme   240

1. In the Old Testament, the horn of an
animal signifies power. "Genius" (line
5): the individual capable of creativity.
2. Wordsworth has described, as part of
his imaginative recovery, his learning to
look again with sympathy upon "the
unassuming things that hold / A silent
station in this beauteous world," and his
finding again "in Man an object of delight." Now he shows how, in reaction
against his concern with great actions detached from moral purpose which constituted the French Revolution, he came to
embrace the poetic doctrines of the Preface to *Lyrical Ballads*. He will write of
simple, lowly men, whose patient endurance of suffering redounds to the glory
of human kind, and who speak a language which is the spontaneous overflow
of powerful feeling (lines 264–65).
3. Uncorrupted.

No other than the very heart of man,
As found among the best of those who live,
Not unexalted by religious faith,
Nor uninformed by books, good books, though few,
In Nature's presence: thence may I select   245
Sorrow, that is not sorrow, but delight;
And miserable love, that is not pain
To hear of, for the glory that redounds
Therefrom to human kind, and what we are.
Be mine to follow with no timid step   250
Where knowledge leads me: it shall be my pride
That I have dared to tread this holy ground,
Speaking no dream, but things oracular;
Matter not lightly to be heard by those
Who to the letter of the outward promise   255
Do read the invisible soul;[4] by men adroit
In speech, and for communion with the world
Accomplished; minds whose faculties are then
Most active when they are most eloquent,
And elevated most when most admired.   260
Men may be found of other mould than these,
Who are their own upholders, to themselves
Encouragement, and energy, and will,
Expressing liveliest thoughts in lively words
As native passion dictates.[5] * * *

Moreover, each man's Mind is to herself
Witness and judge; and I remember well
That in life's every-day appearances
I seemed about this time to gain clear sight
Of a new world—a world, too, that was fit   370
To be transmitted, and to other eyes
Made visible; as ruled by those fixed laws
Whence spiritual dignity originates,
Which do both give it being and maintain
A balance, an ennobling interchange   375
Of action from without and from within;
The excellence, pure function, and best power
Both of the object seen, and eye that sees.

From *Book Fourteenth. Conclusion*

In one of those excursions (may they ne'er
Fade from remembrance!) through the Northern tracts

4. I.e., this doctrine will not be lightly accepted by those who judge a man's inner worth by his exterior seeming.
5. In his Preface to *Lyrical Ballads* of 1800, Wordsworth said that he chose characters from low and rustic life because in them "the essential passions of the human heart * * * are less under restraint and speak a plainer and more emphatic language."

Of Cambria ranging with a youthful friend, [1]
I left Bethgelert's huts at couching-time,
And westward took my way, to see the sun   5
Rise from the top of Snowdon. To the door
Of a rude cottage at the mountain's base
We came, and roused the shepherd who attends
The adventurous stranger's steps, a trusty guide;
Then, cheered by short refreshment, sallied forth.   10

    It was a close, warm, breezeless summer night,
Wan, dull, and glaring,[2] with a dripping fog
Low-hung and thick that covered all the sky;
But, undiscouraged, we began to climb
The mountain-side. The mist soon girt us round,   15
And, after ordinary travellers' talk
With our conductor, pensively we sank
Each into commerce with his private thoughts:
Thus did we breast the ascent, and by myself
Was nothing either seen or heard that checked   20
Those musings or diverted, save that once
The shepherd's lurcher,[3] who, among the crags,
Had to his joy unearthed a hedgehog, teased
His coiled-up prey with barkings turbulent.
This small adventure, for even such it seemed   25
In that wild place and at the dead of night,
Being over and forgotten, on we wound
In silence as before. With forehead bent
Earthward, as if in opposition set
Against an enemy, I panted up   30
With eager pace, and no less eager thoughts.
Thus might we wear a midnight hour away,
Ascending at loose distance each from each,
And I as chanced, the foremost of the band;
When at my feet the ground appeared to brighten,   35
And with a step or two seemed brighter still;
Nor was time given to ask or learn the cause,
For instantly a light upon the turf
Fell like a flash, and lo! as I looked up,
The Moon hung naked in a firmament   40
Of azure without cloud, and at my feet
Rested a silent sea of hoary mist.

1. Wordsworth climbed Mt. Snowdon—
the highest peak in Wales ("Cambria"),
and some 10 miles from the sea—with
Robert Jones, the friend with whom he
had also tramped through the Alps (Book
Sixth). The climb started from the village of Bethgelert at "couching time,"
the time of night when the sheep lie
down to sleep. This event had taken
place in 1791 (or possibly 1793); Wordsworth presents it out of its chronological
order to introduce at this point a great
natural "type" or "emblem" (lines 66,
70) for the mind, and especially for the
activity of the imagination, whose "restoration" he has described in the two preceding Books.
2. In north-of-England dialect, "glairie,"
applied to the weather, means dull, rainy.
3. A crossbred dog, used to hunt hares.

A hundred hills their dusky backs upheaved
All over this still ocean;[4] and beyond,
Far, far beyond, the solid vapours stretched,   45
In headlands, tongues, and promontory shapes,
Into the main Atlantic, that appeared
To dwindle, and give up his majesty,
Usurped upon far as the sight could reach.
Not so the ethereal vault; encroachment none   50
Was there, nor loss;[5] only the inferior stars
Had disappeared, or shed a fainter light
In the clear presence of the full-orbed Moon,
Who, from her sovereign elevation, gazed
Upon the billowy ocean, as it lay   55
All meek and silent, save that through a rift—
Not distant from the shore whereon we stood,
A fixed, abysmal, gloomy, breathing-place—
Mounted the roar of waters, torrents, streams
Innumerable, roaring with one voice   60
Heard over earth and sea, and, in that hour,
For so it seems, felt by the starry heavens.

　　When into air had partially dissolved
That vision, given to spirits of the night
And three chance human wanderers, in calm thought   65
Reflected, it appeared to me the type
Of a majestic intellect, its acts
And its possessions, what it has and craves,
What in itself it is, and would become.
There I beheld the emblem of a mind   70
That feeds upon infinity, that broods
Over the dark abyss, intent to hear
Its voices issuing forth to silent light
In one continuous stream; a mind sustained
By recognitions of transcendent power,   75
In sense conducting to ideal form,
In soul of more than mortal privilege.[6]
One function, above all, of such a mind
Had Nature shadowed there, by putting forth,
'Mid circumstances awful and sublime,   80
That mutual domination which she loves
To exert upon the face of outward things,
So moulded, joined, abstracted, so endowed
With interchangeable supremacy,

---

4. In Milton's description of the creation
of the world, "the mountains huge appear / Emergent, and their broad backs
upheave / Into the clouds * * *" (*Paradise Lost*, VII.285–87).
5. The mist projected in various shapes
over the Atlantic Ocean, but did not

"encroach" upon the heavens overhead.
6. The sense of lines 74–77 seems to be
that the mind of a man who is gifted
beyond the ordinary lot of mortals recognizes its power to transcend the sense
by converting sensory objects into ideal
forms.

That men, least sensitive, see, hear, perceive, 85
And cannot choose but feel. The power, which all
Acknowledge when thus moved, which Nature thus
To bodily sense exhibits, is the express
Resemblance of that glorious faculty
That higher minds bear with them as their own.[7] 90
This is the very spirit in which they deal
With the whole compass of the universe:
They from their native selves can send abroad
Kindred mutations; for themselves create
A like existence; and, whene'er it dawns 95
Created for them, catch it, or are caught
By its inevitable mastery,
Like angels stopped upon the wing by sound
Of harmony from Heaven's remotest spheres.
Them the enduring and the transient both 100
Serve to exalt; they build up greatest things
From least suggestions; ever on the watch,
Willing to work and to be wrought upon,
They need not extraordinary calls
To rouse them; in a world of life they live, 105
By sensible impressions not enthralled,
But by their quickening impulse made more prompt
To hold fit converse with the spiritual world,
And with the generations of mankind
Spread over time, past, present, and to come, 110
Age after age, till Time shall be no more.
Such minds are truly from the Deity,
For they are Powers; and hence the highest bliss
That flesh can know is theirs—the consciousness
Of Whom they are, habitually infused 115
Through every image and through every thought
And all affections,[8] by communion raised
From earth to heaven, from human to divine;
Hence endless occupation for the Soul,
Whether discursive or intuitive;[9] 120
Hence cheerfulness for acts of daily life,
Emotions which best foresight need not fear,
Most worthy then of trust when most intense.
Hence, amid ills that vex and wrongs that crush
Our hearts—if here the words of Holy Writ 125
May with fit reverence be applied—that peace

---

7. The "glorious faculty" is the imagination, which in its exhibition of mastery over sense—through its power to alter and re-create what is given to it in perception (lines 93–106)—is analogous to that aspect of the outer scene, in which the ordinary landscape is transfigured by the moonlit mist. Compare the mind as "lord and master" of outward sense in XII.221–23.

8. Feelings, emotions.

9. An echo of *Paradise Lost* V.488. The "discursive" reason undertakes to reach truths through a logical sequence of premises, observations, and conclusions; the "intuitive" reason comprehends truths immediately.

Which passeth understanding,[1] that repose
In moral judgments which from this pure source
Must come, or will by man be sought in vain.

   Oh! who is he that hath his whole life long   130
Preserved, enlarged, this freedom in himself?
For this alone is genuine liberty:
Where is the favoured being who hath held
That course unchecked, unerring, and untired,
In one perpetual progress smooth and bright?—   135
A humbler destiny have we retraced,
And told of lapse and hesitating choice,
And backward wanderings along thorny ways:
Yet—compassed round by mountain solitudes,
Within whose solemn temple I received   140
My earliest visitations, careless then
Of what was given me; and which now I range,
A meditative, oft a suffering man—
Do I declare—in accents which, from truth
Deriving cheerful confidence, shall blend   145
Their modulation with these vocal streams—
That, whatsoever falls my better mind,
Revolving[2] with the accidents of life,
May have sustained, that, howsoe'er misled,
Never did I, in quest of right and wrong,   150
Tamper with conscience from a private aim;
Nor was in any public hope the dupe
Of selfish passions; nor did ever yield
Wilfully to mean cares or low pursuits,
But shrunk with apprehensive jealousy   155
From every combination which might aid
The tendency, too potent in itself,
Of use and custom to bow down the soul
Under a growing weight of vulgar sense,
And substitute a universe of death[3]   160
For that which moves with light and life informed,
Actual, divine, and true. To fear and love,
To love as prime and chief, for there fear ends,
Be this ascribed;[4] to early intercourse,

1. Philippians iv.7: "the peace of God, which passeth all understanding." This passage of Christian piety was added by Wordsworth in a late revision.
2. An allusion to the ancient concept of fortune's revolving wheel.
3. Milton's description of hell in *Paradise Lost*, II.622–23: "A universe of death, which God by curse / Created evil * * *"
4. Wordsworth's mind, he had said early in *The Prelude*, had been "fostered alike by beauty and by fear" (I.302 and footnote); that is, by the opposing but equally necessary principles of the beautiful and terrifying, or "sublime," aspects of nature. Now, in his conclusion, the principles of fear and pain are said to be mistakenly equated with "evil," and to be ultimately transcended by their "adverse principles" of love and joy. This passage is equivalent to the theodicy of *Paradise Lost*—Milton's justification of evil and pain ("the ways of God to men," I.26) by reference to the fall and redemption—but is translated by Wordsworth into a natural theodicy of the interaction of man's mind with the external world. Cf. the Prospectus to *The Recluse*, above, lines 8–9, and the title footnote.

In presence of sublime or beautiful forms,   165
With the adverse principles of pain and joy—
Evil as one is rashly named by men
Who know not what they speak. By love subsists
All lasting grandeur, by pervading love;
That gone, we are as dust, * * *   170

   This spiritual Love acts not nor can exist
Without Imagination,[5] which, in truth,
Is but another name for absolute power   190
And clearest insight, amplitude of mind,
And Reason in her most exalted mood.
This faculty hath been the feeding source
Of our long labour: we have traced the stream
From the blind cavern whence is faintly heard   195
Its natal murmur; followed it to light
And open day; accompanied its course
Among the ways of Nature, for a time
Lost sight of it bewildered and engulphed:
Then given it greeting as it rose once more   200
In strength, reflecting from its placid breast
The works of man and face of human life;
And lastly, from its progress have we drawn
Faith in life endless, the sustaining thought
Of human Being, Eternity, and God.[6]

   Imagination having been our theme,
So also hath that intellectual Love,
For they are each in each, and cannot stand
Dividually.[7]—Here must thou be, O Man!
Power to thyself; no Helper hast thou here;   210
Here keepest thou in singleness thy state:
No other can divide with thee this work:
No secondary hand can intervene
To fashion this ability; 'tis thine,
The prime and vital principle is thine   215
In the recesses of thy nature, far
From any reach of outward fellowship,
Else is not thine at all. * * *

   And now, O Friend![8] this history is brought
To its appointed close: the discipline
And consummation of a Poet's mind,
In everything that stood most prominent,   305
Have faithfully been pictured; we have reached
The time (our guiding object from the first)

5. Cf. Shelley's *Defence of Poetry*: "The great secret of morals is love; or a going out of our own nature. * * * The great instrument of moral good is the imagination."
6. In the 1805 version, this read: "The feeling of life endless, the great thought / By which we live, Infinity and God."
7. Separately.
8. Coleridge, to whom the "thy" in lines 431–32 also refers.

When we may, not presumptuously, I hope,
Suppose my powers so far confirmed, and such
My knowledge, as to make me capable   310
Of building up a Work that shall endure.

                          * * *
                                   Having now
Told what best merits mention, further pains
Our present purpose seems not to require,
And I have other tasks. Recall to mind
The mood in which this labour was begun,   375
O Friend! The termination of my course
Is nearer now, much nearer; yet even then,
In that distraction and intense desire,
I said unto the life which I had lived,
Where art thou? Hear I not a voice from thee   380
Which 'tis reproach to hear?[9] Anon I rose
As if on wings, and saw beneath me stretched
Vast prospect of the world which I had been
And was; and hence this Song, which like a lark
I have protracted, in the unwearied heavens   385
Singing, and often with more plaintive voice
To earth attempered and her deep-drawn sighs,
Yet centring all in love, and in the end
All gratulant, if rightly understood.[1]

                          * * *
Oh! yet a few short years of useful life,
And all will be complete, thy race be run,
Thy monument of glory will be raised;
Then, though (too weak to tread the ways of truth)   435
This age fall back to old idolatry,
Though men return to servitude as fast
As the tide ebbs, to ignominy and shame
By nations sink together,[2] we shall still
Find solace—knowing what we have learnt to know,   440
Rich in true happiness if allowed to be
Faithful alike in forwarding a day
Of firmer trust, joint labourers in the work
(Should Providence such grace to us vouchsafe)
Of their deliverance,[3] surely yet to come.   445

9. As he approaches the end, Wordsworth recalls the beginning of *The Prelude*. The reproachful voice is that which asked the question, "Was it for this?" in I.269 ff. This query called forth a vision of his remembered life, which he proceeded to explore in search both of the sources of his poetic powers and the impediments to their fulfillment. The "song" describing this quest, which he then began, is the poem he is now completing.

1. The poet finds that suffering and frustration are justified, when seen as part of the overall design of the life he has just reviewed. The passage echoes the conclusion of Pope's theodicy (the justification of evil) in *An Essay on Man*, I.291–92: "All discord, harmony not understood; / All partial evil, universal good." "Gratulant": expressive of joy.

2. I.e., though men—whole nations of them together—sink to ignominy and shame.

3. In the 1805 *Prelude*, the term was "redemption." Wordsworth reaffirms his belief in a millennial outcome of human history, though he now bases that belief not on political "revolution," but on a revolution in the mind of man.

Prophets of Nature, we to them will speak
A lasting inspiration, sanctified
By reason, blest by faith: what we have loved,
Others will love, and we will teach them how;
Instruct them how the mind of man becomes   450
A thousand times more beautiful than the earth
On which he dwells, above this frame of things
(Which, 'mid all revolutions in the hopes
And fears of men, doth still remain unchanged)
In beauty exalted, as it is itself   455
Of quality and fabric more divine.[4]

1798–1839   1850

4. Cf. Wordsworth's assertion that "the
Mind of Man" is "My haunt, and the
main region of my song" in the Prospectus to *The Recluse*, lines 40–41.

DOROTHY WORDSWORTH

(1771–1855)

Dorothy Wordsworth has an enduring place in English literature even
though she wrote not a single word for publication. Not until long after her
death did scholars gradually retrieve and print her letters, a few poems (one
written for children in her brother's household), and above all a series of
journals that she kept sporadically between 1798 and 1828 because, she
wrote, "I shall give William Pleasure by it." It has always been known,
from tributes to her by Wordsworth and Coleridge, that she exerted an
important influence on the lives and writings of both these men. It is now
apparent that she also possessed a power exceeding that of the two poets
for precise observation of people and the natural world, together with a
genius for terse, luminous, and delicately nuanced description in prose. Her
hastily scribbled journals are an incomparable record of what Coleridge, in
Frost at Midnight called "all the numberless goings on of life" in "sea, hill,
and wood" as well as in the "populous village," as noted by one who lived
her life among rural folk, and as reflected in her own ardent and compassionate spirit.

Dorothy was born on Christmas day, 1771, 21 months after William; she
was the only girl of five Wordsworth children. From her seventh year,
when her mother died, she lived with various relatives—some of them tolerant and affectionate, others rigid and tyrannical—and saw William and her
other brothers only occasionally, during the boys' summer vacations from
school. In 1795, when she was 24, the bequest to William by Raisely Calvert enabled her to carry out a long-held plan to join her brother in a cottage at Racedown, and the two spent the rest of their long lives together,
first in Dorsetshire, then in their beloved Lake Country.

Suddenly, after a severe illness in 1835, Dorothy suffered a physical and
mental collapse, which is now diagnosed as the result of a hardening of

arteries in the brain. She spent the rest of her existence in bed or in a wheelchair, huddled over a blazing fire even in the hottest weather. Hardest for her family to endure was the drastic change in her temperament: from a high-spirited and uncomplaining woman she became (save for brief intervals of lucidity) torpid, querulous, demanding. In this half-life she lingered for 20 years, attended devotedly by William until his death five years before her own in 1855.

Our selections are from the journal Dorothy kept in 1798 at Alfoxden, Somersetshire, where the Wordsworths had moved from Racedown in order to be near Coleridge at Nether Stowey, as well as from her journals while at Grasmere, (1800–1803), with Coleridge residing some 13 miles away at Greta Hall, Keswick. This is the period when both men emerged as major poets, and in their achievements Dorothy played an indispensable role. In Book XI of *The Prelude* Wordsworth says that, in the time of his spiritual crisis, Dorothy "maintained for me a saving intercourse / With my true self" and "preserved me still a Poet"; and, in a letter of 1797, Coleridge stressed the delicacy and tact in the responses of Wordsworth's "exquisite sister" to the world of sense: "Her manners are simple, ardent, impressive. . . . Her information various—her eye watchful in minutest observation of nature—and her taste a perfect electrometer—it bends, protrudes, and draws in, at subtlest beauties & most recondite faults.

The passages from the journals reprinted below include many verbal sketches of natural appearances which turn up also in Wordsworth's and Coleridge's poems. Of at least equal importance for Wordsworth was their chronicling of the busy wayfaring life of rural England in the early 19th century. These were exceedingly hard times for country people, when the remorseless displacement of small farms and of household crafts by large-scale farms and mass industries was accelerated by the economic distress caused by protracted Continental wars. (See Wordsworth's comment in *The Ruined Cottage*, above, lines 133 ff.) Peddlers, maimed war veterans, leech-gatherers, adult and infant beggars, ousted farm families, fugitives, women abandoned by husbands or lovers streamed endlessly along the rural roads and into Wordsworth's brooding poetic imagination—often by way of Dorothy's prose records.

The excerpts from the journals also show the intensity of Dorothy's love for her brother. Inevitably, in our era, the mutual devotion of the orphaned brother and sister has evoked psychoanalytic speculation. It is important to note, however, that Mary Hutchinson, a gentle and open-hearted girl, had been Dorothy's closest friend ever since childhood, and that Dorothy encouraged Wordsworth's courtship and marriage, even though she realized that it entailed her own displacement as the focus of her brother's life. All the evidence indicates that their life in a single household never strained the affectionate relationship between the two women; indeed, Dorothy, until she became an invalid, added to her former functions as Wordsworth's chief support, adviser, and amanuensis a loving ministration to her brother's children.

Since the manuscript of the Alfoxden journal has disappeared, the text below is from the transcript published by William Knight in 1897. The selections from the Grasmere journals reproduce Mary Moorman's exact reprint of the manuscripts in the Wordsworth Library at Dove Cottage (Oxford University Press, 1971).

From The Alfoxden Journal

Jan. 31, 1798. Set forward to Stowey[1] at half-past five. A violent storm in the wood; sheltered under the hollies. When we left home the moon immensely large, the sky scattered over with clouds. These soon closed in, contracting the dimensions of the moon without concealing her.[2] The sound of the pattering shower, and the gusts of wind, very grand. Left the wood when nothing remained of the storm but the driving wind, and a few scattering drops of rain. Presently all clear, Venus first showing herself between the struggling clouds; afterwards Jupiter appeared. The hawthorn hedges, black and pointed, glittering with millions of diamond drops; the hollies shining with broader patches of light. The road to the village of Holford glittered like another stream. On our return, the wind high—a violent storm of hail and rain at the Castle of Comfort.[3] All the Heavens seemed in one perpetual motion when the rain ceased; the moon appearing, now half veiled, and now retired behind heavy clouds, the stars still moving, the roads very dirty.

* * *

Feb. 3. A mild morning, the windows open at breakfast, the redbreasts singing in the garden. Walked with Coleridge over the hills. The sea at first obscured by vapour; that vapour afterwards slid in one mighty mass along the sea-shore; the islands and one point of land clear beyond it. The distant country (which was purple in the clear dull air), overhung by straggling clouds that sailed over it, appeared like the darker clouds, which are often seen at a great distance apparently motionless, while the nearer ones pass quickly over them, driven by the lower winds. I never saw such a union of earth, sky, and sea. The clouds beneath our feet spread themselves to the water, and the clouds of the sky almost joined them. Gathered sticks in the wood; a perfect stillness. The redbreasts sang upon the leafless boughs. Of a great number of sheep in the field, only one standing. Returned to dinner at five o'clock. The moonlight still and warm as a summer's night at nine o'clock.

Feb. 4. Walked a great part of the way to Stowey with Coleridge. The morning warm and sunny. The young lasses seen on the hill-tops, in the villages and roads, in their summer holiday clothes —pink petticoats and blue. Mothers with their children in arms, and the little ones that could just walk, tottering by·their side. Midges or small flies spinning in the sunshine; the songs of the lark and redbreast; daisies upon the turf; the hazels in blossom; honeysuckles budding. I saw one solitary strawberry flower under a hedge.

---

1. Coleridge's cottage at Nether Stowey, three miles from Alfoxden.
2. See Coleridge's *Christabel*, lines 16–19.

3. A tavern, halfway between Holford and Nether Stowey.

The furze gay with blossom. The moss rubbed from the pailings by the sheep, that leave locks of wool, and the red marks with which they are spotted, upon the wood.[4]

* * *

Feb. 8. Went up the Park, and over the tops of the hills, till we came to a new and very delicious pathway, which conducted us to the Coombe.[5] Sat a considerable time upon the heath. Its surface restless and glittering with the motion of the scattered piles of withered grass, and the waving of the spiders' threads.[6] On our return the mist still hanging over the sea, but the opposite coast clear, and the rocky cliffs distinguishable. In the deep Coombe, as we stood upon the sunless hill, we saw miles of grass, light and glittering, and the insects passing.

Feb. 9. William gathered sticks.

Feb. 10. Walked to Woodlands, and to the waterfall. The adder's-tongue and the ferns green in the low damp dell. These plants now in perpetual motion from the current of the air; in summer only moved by the drippings of the rocks.[7] A cloudy day.

* * *

Mar. 7. William and I drank tea at Coleridge's. A cloudy sky. Observed nothing particularly interesting—the distant prospect obscured. One only leaf upon the top of a tree—the sole remaining leaf—danced round and round like a rag blown by the wind.[8]

Mar. 8. Walked in the Park in the morning. I sate under the fir trees. Coleridge came after dinner, so we did not walk again. A foggy morning, but a clear sunny day.

Mar. 9. A clear sunny morning, went to meet Mr and Mrs Coleridge. The day very warm.

Mar. 10. Coleridge, Wm, and I walked in the evening to the top of the hill. We all passed the morning in sauntering about the park and gardens, the children playing about, the old man at the top of the hill gathering furze; interesting groups of human creatures, the young frisking and dancing in the sun, the elder quietly drinking in the life and soul of the sun and air.

Mar. 11. A cold day. The children went down towards the sea. William and I walked to the top of the hills above Holford. Met the blacksmith. Pleasant to see the labourer on Sunday jump with the friskiness of a cow upon a sunny day.

* * *

1798   1897

4. See Wordsworth's *The Ruined Cottage*, lines 330–336.
5. Hodder's Combe in the Quantock Hills, near Alfoxden; a "combe" (pronounced "koom") is a deep valley on the flank of a hill.
6. Cf. Coleridge's *The Ancient Mariner*,

line 184: "Like restless gossameres."
7. See the description of the dell in Coleridge's *This Lime-Tree Bower*, lines 13–20.
8. Cf. *Christabel*, lines 49 ff.: "The one red leaf, the last of its clan. . . ."

From The Grasmere Journals

1800

May. 14. Wm and John set off into Yorkshire[1] after dinner at
½ past 2 o'clock, cold pork in their pockets. I left them at the turning of the Low-wood bay under the trees. My heart was so full that
I could hardly speak to W. when I gave him a farewell kiss. I sate a
long time upon a stone at the margin of the lake, and after a flood
of tears my heart was easier. The lake looked to me I knew not why
dull and melancholy, and the weltering on the shores seemed a
heavy sound. I walked as long as I could amongst the stones of the
shore. The wood rich in flowers. A beautiful yellow, palish yellow
flower, that looked thick round and double, and smelt very sweet—I
supposed it was a ranunculus—Crowfoot, the grassy-leaved Rabbit-
toothed white flower, strawberries, geranium—scentless violet, anemones two kinds, orchises, primroses. The heckberry very beautiful,
the crab coming out as a low shrub. Met a blind man, driving a
very large beautiful Bull and a cow—he walked with two sticks.
Came home by Clappersgate. The valley very green, many sweet
views up to Rydale head when I could juggle away the fine houses,
but they disturbed me even more than when I have been happier.
One beautiful view of the Bridge, without Sir Michael's.[2] Sate
down very often, though it was cold. I resolved to write a journal of
the time till W. and J. return, and I set about keeping my resolve
because I will not quarrel with myself, and because I shall give Wm
Pleasure by it when he comes home again. At Rydale a woman of
the village, stout and well dressed, begged a halfpenny—she had
never she said done it before, but these hard times— —Arrived at
home with a bad head-ach, set some slips of privett. The evening
cold, had a fire—my face now flame-coloured. It is nine o'clock. I
shall soon go to bed. A young woman begged at the door—she had
come from Manchester on Sunday morn with two shillings and a
slip of paper which she supposed a Bank note—it was a cheat. She
had buried her husband and three children within a year and a half
—all in one grave—burying very dear—paupers all put in one place
—20 shillings paid for as much ground as will bury a man—a stone
to be put over it or the right will be lost—11/6 each time the
ground is opened. Oh! that I had a letter from William!

* * *

Oct. 3. Very rainy all the morning. Little Sally learning to mark.
Wm walked to Ambleside after dinner. I went with him part of the
way—he talked much about the object of his Essay for the 2nd

1. William and his younger brother,
John Wordsworth, on the way to visit
Mary Hutchinson, whom William was to
marry two years later.
2. Sir Michael le Fleming's estate, Rydal
Hall.

volume of LB.[3] I returned expecting the Simpsons—they did not come. I should have met Wm but my teeth ached and it was showery and late—he returned after 10. Amos Cottle's[4] death in the Morning Post. Wrote to S. Lowthian.[5]

N.B. When Wm and I returned from accompanying Jones we met an old man almost double,[6] he had on a coat thrown over his shoulders above his waistcoat and coat. Under this he carried a bundle and had an apron on and a night cap. His face was interesting. He had dark eyes and a long nose. John who afterwards met him at Wythburn took him for a Jew. He was of Scotch parents but had been born in the army. He had had a wife 'and a good woman and it pleased God to bless us with ten children'. All these were dead but one of whom he had not heard for many years, a sailor. His trade was to gather leeches, but now leeches are scarce and he had not strength for it. He lived by begging and was making his way to Carlisle where he should buy a few godly books to sell. He said leeches were very scarce partly owing to this dry season, but many years they have been scarce—he supposed it owing to their being much sought after, that they did not breed fast, and were of slow growth. Leeches were formerly 2/6 [per] 100; they are now 30/. He had been hurt in driving a cart, his leg broke his body driven over his skull fractured. He felt no pain till he recovered from his first insensibility. 'It was then late in the evening, when the light was just going away.'

* * *

Oct. 11. A fine October morning. Sat in the house working all the morning. Wm composing—Sally Ashburner learning to mark. After Dinner we walked up Greenhead Gill in search of a sheepfold.[7] We went by Mr Oliff's and through his woods. It was a delightful day and the views looked excessively chearful and beautiful chiefly that from Mr Oliff's field where our house is to be built. The colours of the mountains soft and rich, with orange fern—the Cattle pasturing upon the hill-tops Kites sailing as in the sky above our heads—Sheep bleating and in lines and chains and patterns scattered over the mountains. They come down and feed on the little green islands in the beds of the torrents and so may be swept away. The Sheepfold is falling away it is built nearly in the form of a heart unequally divided. Look down the brook and see the drops

3. The Preface to the second edition of *Lyrical Ballads*, 1800.
4. The brother of Joseph Cottle, Bristol publisher of the first edition of *Lyrical Ballads*.
5. Sally Lowthian, who had been a servant in the house of Wordsworths' father.
6. Wordsworth's *Resolution and Independence*, composed one and a half years later, incorporated various details of Dorothy's description of the leech-gatherer. See below, May 4 and 7, 1802, for Wordsworth working on the poem he originally called *The Leech Gatherer*.
7. The sheepfold, in Wordsworth's *Michael*; lines 1–17 of the poem describe the walk up Greenhead Ghyll.

rise upwards and sparkle in the air, at the little falls the higher sparkles the tallest. We walked along the turf of the mountain till we came to a Cattle track—made by the cattle which come upon the hills. We drank tea at Mr Simpson's returned at about nine—a fine mild night.

Oct. 12. Beautiful day. Sate in the house writing in the morning while Wm went into the Wood to compose. Wrote to John in the morning—copied poems for the LB,[8] in the evening wrote to Mrs Rawson. Mary Jameson and Sally Ashburner dined. We pulled apples after dinner, a large basket full. We walked before tea by Bainriggs to observe the many coloured foliage the oaks dark green with yellow leaves, the birches generally still green, some near the water yellowish. The Sycamore crimson and crimson-tufted, the mountain ash a deep orange, the common ash Lemon colour but many ashes still fresh in their summer green. Those that were discoloured chiefly near the water. William composing in the Evening. Went to bed at 12 o'clock.

* * *

1801

Nov. 24, 1801. A rainy morning. We all were well except that my head ached a little and I took my Breakfast in bed. I read a little of Chaucer, prepared the goose for dinner, and then we all walked out. I was obliged to return for my fur tippet and Spenser[9] it was so cold. We had intended going to Easedale but we shaped our course to Mr Gell's cottage. It was very windy and we heard the wind everywhere about us as we went along the Lane but the walls sheltered us. John Green's house looked pretty under Silver How. As we were going along we were stopped at once, at the distance perhaps of 50 yards from our favorite Birch tree. It was yielding to the gusty wind with all its tender twigs, the sun shone upon it and it glanced in the wind like a flying sunshiny shower. It was a tree in shape with stem and branches but it was like a Spirit of water. The sun went in and it resumed its purplish appearance the twigs still yielding to the wind but not so visibly to us. The other Birch trees that were near it looked bright and chearful, but it was a creature by its own self among them. We could not get into Mr Gell's grounds—the old tree fallen from its undue exaltation above the Gate. A shower came on when we were at Benson's. We went through the wood—it became fair—there was a rainbow which spanned the lake from the Island house to the foot of Bainriggs. The village looked populous and beautiful. Catkins are coming out

8. *Lyrical Ballads.*
9. A "Spencer" was a close-fitting jacket worn by women and children.

palm trees budding—the alder with its plumb coloured buds. We came home over the stepping stones. The Lake was foamy with white waves. I saw a solitary butter flower in the wood. *I* found it not easy to get over the stepping stones. Reached home at dinner time. Sent Peggy Ashburner some goose. She sent me some honey —with a thousand thanks. 'Alas! the gratitude of men has etc.'[1] I went in to set her right about this and sate a while with her. She talked about Thomas's having sold his land. 'Ay,' says she I said many a time 'He's not come fra London to buy our Land however.' Then she told me with what pains and industry they had made up their taxes interest etc. etc.—how they all got up at 5 o'clock in the morning to spin and Thomas carded, and that they had paid off a hundred pound of the interest. She said she used to take such pleasure in the cattle and sheep. 'O how pleased I used to be when they fetched them down, and when I had been a bit poorly I would gang out upon a hill and look over t' fields and see them and it used to do me so much good you cannot think.' Molly said to me when I came in 'poor Body.' She's very ill but one does not know how long she may last. Many a fair face may gang before her. We sate by the fire without work for some time then Mary read a poem of Daniell[2] upon Learning. After tea Wm read Spenser now and then a little aloud to us. We were making his waistcoat. We had a note from Mrs C., with bad news from poor C. very ill. William walked to John's Grove. I went to meet him—moonlight but it rained. I met him before I had got as far as John Baty's—he had been surprized and terrified by a sudden rushing of winds which seemed to bring earth sky and lake together, as if the whole were going to enclose him in—he was glad he was in a high Road.

In speaking of our walk on Sunday Evening the 22nd November I forgot to notice one most impressive sight. It was the moon and the moonlight seen through hurrying driving clouds immediately behind the Stone man upon the top of the hill on the Forest side. Every tooth and every edge of Rock was visible, and the Man stood like a Giant watching from the Roof of a lofty castle. The hill seemed perpendicular from the darkness below it. It was a sight that I could call to mind at any time it was so distinct.

* * *

1802

Mar. 4. Before we had quite finished Breakfast Calvert's man brought the horses for Wm.[3] We had a deal to do to shave—pens to make—poems to put in order for writing, to settle the dress pack

---

1. A quotation from Wordsworth's *Simon Lee*: "Alas! the gratitude of men / Hath oftener left me mourning."
2. Samuel Daniel's long poem *Musophi-* *lus: Containing a General Defense of Learning* (1599).
3. For a journey to Keswick, to visit Coleridge.

up etc. The man came before the pens were made and he was obliged to leave me with only two. Since he has left me (at ½ past 11) it is now 2 I have been putting the Drawers into order, laid by his clothes which we had thrown here and there and everywhere, filed two months' newspapers and got my dinner 2 boiled eggs and 2 apple tarts. I have set Molly on to clear the garden a little, and I myself have helped. I transplanted some snowdrops—The Bees are busy—Wm has a nice bright day. It was hard frost in the night. The Robins are singing sweetly. Now for my walk. I *will* be busy, I *will* look well and be well when he comes back to me. O the Darling! Here is one of his bitten apples! I can hardly find in my heart to throw it into the fire. I must wash myself, then off—I walked round the two Lakes crossed the stepping stones at Rydale Foot. Sate down where we always sit. I was full of thoughts about my darling. Blessings on him. I came home at the foot of our own hill under Loughrigg. They are making sad ravages in the woods. Benson's Wood is going and the wood above the River. The wind has blown down a [?small] fir tree on the Rock that terminates John's path—I suppose the wind of Wednesday night. I read German after my return till tea time. After tea I worked and read the LB, enchanted with the Idiot Boy. Wrote to Wm then went to Bed. It snowed when I went to Bed.

* * *

Mar. 22. A rainy day. William very poorly. Mr Luff came in after dinner and brought us 2 letters from Sara H. and one from poor Annette. I read Sara's letters while he was here. I finished my letters to M. and S. and wrote to my Br Richard. We talked a good deal about C. and other interesting things. We resolved to see Annette, and that Wm should go to Mary.[4] We wrote to Coleridge not to expect us till Thursday or Friday.

Mar. 23. A mild morning. William worked at the Cuckow poem.[5] I sewed beside him. After dinner he slept I read German, and at the closing in of day went to sit in the orchard. He came to me, and walked backwards and forwards. We talked about C. Wm repeated the poem to me. I left him there and in 20 minutes he came in, rather tired with attempting to write. He is now reading Ben Jonson I am going to read German it is about 10 o'clock, a quiet night. The fire flutters and the watch ticks I hear nothing else save the Breathing of my Beloved and he now and then pushes his book forward and turns over a leaf. Fletcher is not come home. No letter from C.

4. It had been arranged several months earlier that William was to marry Mary Hutchinson ("Sara H." in this entry is Mary's sister, with whom Coleridge had fallen in love). Now the Wordsworths resolve to go to France to settle affairs with Annette Vallon, mother of William's natural daughter, Caroline. William did not conceal the facts of his early love affair from his family, nor from Mary Hutchinson.
5. *To the Cuckoo.*

Apr. 15. It was a threatening misty morning—but mild. We set off after dinner from Eusemere. Mrs Clarkson went a short way with us but turned back. The wind was furious and we thought we must have returned. We first rested in the large Boat-house, then under a furze Bush opposite Mr Clarkson's. Saw the plough going in the field. The wind seized our breath the Lake was rough. There was a Boat by itself floating in the middle of the Bay below Water Millock. We rested again in the Water Millock Lane. The hawthorns are black and green, the birches here and there greenish but there is yet more of purple to be seen on the Twigs. We got over into a field to avoid some cows—people working, a few primroses by the roadside, wood-sorrel flower, the anemone, scentless violets. strawberries, and that starry yellow flower which Mrs C. calls pile wort. When we were in the woods beyond Gowbarrow park we saw a few daffodils[6] close to the water side. We fancied that the lake had floated the seeds ashore and that the little colony had so sprung up. But as we went along there were more and yet more and at last under the boughs of the trees, we saw that there was a long belt of them along the shore, about the breadth of a country turnpike road. I never saw daffodils so beautiful they grew among the mossy stones about and about them, some rested their heads upon these stones as on a pillow for weariness and the rest tossed and reeled and danced and seemed as if they verily laughed and the wind that blew upon them over the lake, they looked so gay ever glancing ever changing. This wind blew directly over the lake to them. There was here and there a little knot and a few stragglers a few yards higher up but they were so few as not to disturb the simplicity and unity and life of that one busy highway. We rested again and again. The Bays were stormy, and we heard the waves at different distances and in the middle of the water like the sea. Rain came on—we were wet when we reached Luffs but we called in. Luckily all was chearless and gloomy so we faced the storm—we *must* have been wet if we had waited—put on dry clothes at Dobson's. I was very kindly treated by a young woman, the Landlady looked sour but it is her way. She gave us a goodish supper. Excellent ham and potatoes. We paid 7/ when we came away. William was sitting by a bright fire when I came downstairs. He soon made his way to the Library piled up in a corner of the window. He brought out a volume of Enfield's Speaker,[7] another miscellany, and an odd volume of Congreve's plays. We had a glass of warm rum and water. We enjoyed ourselves and wished for Mary. It rained and blew when we went to bed. N.B. Deer in Gowbarrow park like skeletons.

6. Wordsworth did not compose his poem on the daffodils, *I Wandered Lonely as a Cloud,* until two years later; comparison with the poem will show how extensive was his use of Dorothy's prose description.

7. William Enfield's *The Speaker* (1774), a volume of selections suitable for elocution.

Apr. 16 (Good Friday). When I undrew my curtains in the morning, I was much affected by the beauty of the prospect and the change. The sun shone, the wind has passed away, the hills looked chearful, the river was very bright as it flowed into the lake. The Church rises up behind a little knot of Rocks, the steeple not so high as an ordinary 3 story house. Trees, in a row in the garden under the wall. After Wm had shaved we set forward. The valley is at first broken by little rocky woody knolls that make retiring places, fairy valleys in the vale, the river winds along under these hills travelling not in a bustle but not slowly to the lake. We saw a fisherman in the flat meadow on the other side of the water. He came towards us and threw his line over the two arched Bridge. It is a Bridge of a heavy construction, almost bending inwards in the middle, but it is grey and there is a look of ancientry in the architecture of it that pleased me. As we go on the vale opens out more into one vale with somewhat of a cradle Bed. Cottages with groups of trees on the side of the hills. We passed a pair of twin Children 2 years old—Sate on the next bridge which we crossed a single arch. We rested again upon the Turf and looked at the same Bridge. We observed arches in the water occasioned by the large stones sending it down in two streams. A Sheep came plunging through the river, stumbled up the Bank and passed close to us, it had been frightened by an insignificant little Dog on the other side, its fleece dropped a glittering shower under its belly. Primroses by the roadside, pile wort that shone like stars of gold in the Sun, violets, strawberries, retired and half buried among the grass. When we came to the foot of Brothers water I left William sitting on the Bridge and went along the path on the right side of the Lake through the wood. I was delighted with what I saw. The water under the boughs of the bare old trees, the simplicity of the mountains and the exquisite beauty of the path. There was one grey cottage. I repeated the Glowworm[8] as I walked along. I hung over the gate, and thought I could have stayed for ever. When I returned I found William writing a poem descriptive of the sights and sounds we saw and heard. There was the gentle flowing of the stream, the glittering lively lake, green fields without a living creature to be seen on them, behind us, a flat pasture with 42 cattle feeding to our left the road leading to the hamlet, no smoke there, the sun shone on the bare roofs. The people were at work ploughing, harrowing and sowing—lasses spreading dung, a dog's barking now and then, cocks crowing, birds twittering, the snow in patches at the top of the highest hills, yellow palms, purple and green twigs on the Birches, ashes with their glittering spikes quite bare. The hawthorn a bright green with black stems under the oak. The moss of the oak glossy.

8. Wordsworth's poem beginning "Among all lovely things my Love had been," composed four days earlier; "my Love" in this line is Dorothy.

We then went on, passed two sisters at work, *they first passed us*, one with two pitch forks in her hand. The other had a spade. We had some talk with them. They laughed aloud after we were gone perhaps half in wantonness, half boldness. William finished his poem before we got to the foot of Kirkstone.[9] * * *

          * * *

Apr. 29. A beautiful morning. The sun shone and all was pleasant. We sent off our parcel to Coleridge by the waggon. Mr Simpson heard the Cuckow today. Before we went out after I had written down the Tinker (which William finished this morning)[1] Luff called. He was very lame, limped into the kitchen—he came on a little Pony. We then went to John's Grove, sate a while at first. Afterwards William lay, and I lay in the trench under the fence—he with his eyes shut and listening to the waterfalls and the Birds. There was no one waterfall above another[2]—it was a sound of waters in the air—the voice of the air. William heard me breathing and rustling now and then but we both lay still, and unseen by one another. He thought that it would be as sweet thus to lie so in the grave, to hear the *peaceful* sounds of the earth and just to know that our dear friends were near. The Lake was still. There was a Boat out. Silver How reflected with delicate purple and yellowish hues as I have seen Spar. Lambs on the island and running races together by the half dozen in the round field near us. The copses green*ish*, hawthorn green.—Came home to dinner then went to Mr Simpson. We rested a long time under a wall. Sheep and lambs were in the field—cottages smoking. As I lay down on the grass, I observed the glittering silver line on the ridges of the Backs of the sheep, owing to their situation respecting the Sun—which made them look beautiful but with something of strangeness, like animals of another kind—as if belonging to a more splendid world. Met old Mr S. at the door—Mrs S. poorly. I got mullens and pansies. I was sick and ill and obliged to come home soon. We went to bed immediately—I slept up stairs. The air coldish where it was felt somewhat frosty.

          * * *

May 4. William had slept pretty well and though he went to bed nervous and jaded in the extreme he rose refreshed. I wrote the Leech Gatherer[3] for him which he had begun the night before and of which he wrote several stanzas in bed this Monday morning. It was very hot, we called at Mr Simpson's door as we passed but did not go in. We rested several times by the way, read and repeated the Leech Gatherer. We were almost melted before we were at the

9. See the joyous lyric *Written in March*, above.

1. Wordsworth never published his comic poem *The Tinker*; it was first printed in 1897.

2. I.e., no waterfull could be heard individually.

3. The poem that was published as *Resolution and Independence*; for its origin, see the entry for October 3, 1800.

top of the hill. We saw Coleridge on the Wytheburn side of the water. He crossed the Beck to us. Mr Simpson was fishing there. William and I ate a Luncheon, then went on towards the waterfall. It is a glorious wild solitude under that lofty purple crag. It stood upright by itself. Its own self and its shadow below, one mass—all else was sunshine. We went on further. A Bird at the top of the crags was flying round and round and looked in thinness and transparency, shape and motion like a moth. We climbed the hill but looked in vain for a shade except at the foot of the great waterfall, and there we did not like to stay on account of the loose stones above our heads. We came down and rested upon a moss covered Rock, rising out of the bed of the River. There we lay ate our dinner and stayed there till about 4 o'clock or later. Wm and C. repeated and read verses. I drank a little Brandy and water and was in Heaven. The Stags horn is very beautiful and fresh springing upon the fells. Mountain ashes, green. We drank tea at a farm house. The woman had not a pleasant countenance, but was civil enough. She had a pretty Boy a year old whom she suckled. We parted from Coleridge at Sara's Crag after having looked at the Letters which C. carved in the morning. I kissed them all. Wm deepened the T with C.'s penknife.[4] We sate afterwards on the wall, seeing the sun go down and the reflections in the still water. C. looked well and parted from us chearfully, hopping up upon the side stones. On the Rays we met a woman with 2 little girls one in her arms the other about 4 years old walking by her side, a pretty little thing, but half starved. She had on a pair of slippers that had belonged to some gentleman's child, down at the heels—it was not easy to keep them on but, poor thing! young as she was, she walked carefully with them. Alas too young for such cares and such travels. The Mother when we accosted her told us that her husband had left her and gone off with another woman and how she '*pursued*' them. Then her fury kindled and her eyes rolled about. She changed again to tears. She was a Cockermouth woman 30 years of age—a child at Cockermouth when I was. I was moved and gave her a shilling—I believe 6[d] more than I ought to have given. We had the crescent moon with the 'auld moon in her arms'.[5] We rested often always upon the Bridges. Reached home at about 10 o'clock. The Lloyds had been here in our absence. We went soon to bed. I repeated verses to William while he was in bed—he was soothed and I left him. 'This is the spot'[6] over and over again.

* * *

4. The rock, which has since been blasted away for a new road, contained the carved letters: W.W., M.H., D.W., S.T.C., J.W., S.H. (M.H. and S.H. are Mary and Sara Hutchinson; J.W. is John Wordsworth.)

5. From the *Ballad of Sir Patrick Spens*; Coleridge cited the stanza of which this phrase is part as epigraph to *Dejection: An Ode*.

6. Wordsworth never completed this poem.

May 6. A sweet morning. We have put the finishing stroke to our Bower and here we are sitting in the orchard. It is one o'clock. We are sitting upon a seat under the wall which I found my Brother building up when I came to him with his apple—he had intended that it should have been done before I came. It is a nice cool shady spot. The small Birds are singing, Lambs bleating, Cuckow calling. The Thrush sings by Fits. Thomas Ashburner's axe is going quietly (without passion) in the orchard. Hens are cackling, Flies humming, the women talking together at their doors: Plumb and pear trees are in Blossom—apple trees greenish the opposite woods green, the crows are cawing. We have heard Ravens. The ash trees are in blossom, Birds flying all about us. The stitchwort is coming out, there is one budding Lychnis, the primroses are passing their prime. Celandine violets and wood sorrel for ever more little geraniums and pansies on the wall. We walked in the evening to Tail End to enquire about hurdles for the orchard shed and about Mr Luff's flower. The flower dead—no hurdles. I went to look at the falling wood—Wm also when he had been at Benson's went with me. They have left a good many small oak trees but we dare not hope that they are all to remain. The Ladies are come to Mr Gell's cottage. We saw them as we went and their light when we returned. When we came in we found a Magazine and Review and a letter from Coleridge with verses to Hartley and Sara H. We read the Review,[7] etc. The moon was a perfect Boat a silver Boat when we were out in the evening. The Birch Tree is all over green in *small* leaf more light and elegant than when it is full out. It bent to the breezes as if for the love of its own delightful motions. Sloe-thorns and Hawthorns in the hedges.

May 7. William had slept uncommonly well so, feeling himself strong, he fell to work at the Leech gatherer. He wrote hard at it till dinner time, then he gave over tired to death—he had finished the poem.[8] * * *

* * *

[*July*.] On Thursday morning, 29th, we arrived in London.[9] Wm left me at the Inn—I went to bed. Etc. etc. After various troubles and disasters we left London on Saturday morning at ½ past 5 or 6, the 31st of July (I have forgot which). We mounted the Dover Coach at Charing Cross. It was a beautiful morning. The City, St Paul's, with the River and a multitude of little Boats, made a most beautiful sight as we crossed Westminster Bridge. The houses were not overhung by their cloud of smoke and they were spread out endlessly, yet the sun shone so brightly with such a pure

7. Probably the journal *Monthly Review*.
8. Later entries show, however, that Wordsworth kept working on the manuscript until July 4.
9. On the way to France to visit Annette Vallon and Caroline; see the entry for March 22, 1802.

light that there was even something like the purity of one of nature's own grand spectacles.[1] We rode on chearfully now with the Paris Diligence before us, now behind. We walked up the steep hills, beautiful prospects everywhere, till we even reached Dover. * * *

* * * We arrived at Calais at 4 o'clock on Sunday morning, the 31st of July.[2] We stayed in the vessel till ½-past 7, then Wm went for Letters, at about ½ past 8 or 9 we found out Annette and C. chez Madame Avril dans la Rue de la Tête d'or. We lodged opposite two Ladies in tolerably decent-sized rooms but badly furnished, and with large store of bad smells and dirt in the yard, and all about. The weather was very hot. We walked by the sea-shore almost every evening with Annette and Caroline or Wm and I alone. I had a bad cold and could not bathe at first but William did. It was a pretty sight to see as we walked upon the sands when the tide was low perhaps a hundred people bathing about ¼ of a mile distant from us, and we had delightful walks after the heat of the day was passed away—seeing far off in the west the Coast of England like a cloud crested with Dover Castle, which was but like the summit of the cloud. The Evening star and the glory of the sky. The Reflections in the water were more beautiful than the sky itself, purple waves brighter than precious stones for ever melting away upon the sands. * * *

* * *

[*Sept.* 24.] Mary first met us in the avenue. She looked so fat and well that we were made very happy by the sight of her. Then came Sara, and last of all Joanna.[3] Tom was forking corn standing upon the corn cart. We dressed ourselves immediately and got tea —the garden looked gay with asters and sweet peas. I looked at everything with tranquillity and happiness—was ill on Saturday and on Sunday and continued to be during most of the time of our stay. Jack and George came on Friday Evening 1st October. On Saturday 2nd we rode to Hackness, William Jack George and Sara single, I behind Tom. On Sunday 3rd Mary and Sara were busy packing. On Monday 4th October 1802, my Brother William was married to Mary Hutchinson. I slept a good deal of the night and rose fresh and well in the morning. At a little after 8 o'clock I saw them go down the avenue towards the Church. William had parted from me upstairs. I gave him the wedding ring—with how deep a blessing! I took it from my forefinger where I had worn it the whole of the

---

1. See Wordsworth's sonnet *Composed upon Westminster Bridge.*
2. The actual date was August 1. One of the walks by the sea that Dorothy goes on to describe was the occasion for the sonnet *It Is a Beauteous Evening.*
3. The Wordsworths have come to Gallow Hill, Yorkshire, for the marriage of William and Mary. The people mentioned are Mary's sisters and brothers (Sara, Joanna, Tom, Jack, and George Hutchinson). Out of consideration for Dorothy's overwrought feelings, only Joanna, Jack, and Tom attended the ceremony at Brampton Church.

night before—he slipped it again onto my finger and blessed me fervently. When they were absent my dear little Sara prepared the breakfast. I kept myself as quiet as I could, but when I saw the two men running up the walk, coming to tell us it was over, I could stand it no longer and threw myself on the bed where I lay in stillness, neither hearing or seeing anything, till Sara came upstairs to me and said 'They are coming'. This forced me from the bed where I lay and I moved I knew not how straight forward, faster than my strength could carry me till I met my beloved William and fell upon his bosom. He and John Hutchinson led me to the house and there I stayed to welcome my dear Mary. As soon as we had breakfasted we departed.[4] It rained when we set off. Poor Mary was much agitated when she parted from her Brothers and Sisters and her home. Nothing particular occurred till we reached Kirby. We had sunshine and showers, pleasant talk, love and chearfulness. * * * It rained very hard when we reached Windermere. We sate in the rain at Wilcock's to change horses, and arrived at Grasmere at about 6 o'clock on Wednesday Evening, the 6th of October 1802. Molly was overjoyed to see us, for my part I cannot describe what I felt, and our dear Mary's feelings would I dare say not be easy to speak of. We went by candle light into the garden and were astonished at the growth of the Brooms, Portugal Laurels, etc. etc. etc. The next day, Thursday, we unpacked the Boxes. On Friday 8th we baked Bread, and Mary and I walked, first upon the Hill side, and then in John's Grove, then in view of Rydale, the first walk that I had taken with my Sister.

* * *

Dec. 24 1802, Christmas Eve. William is now sitting by me at ½ past 10 o'clock. I have been beside him ever since tea running the heel of a stocking, repeating some of his sonnets to him, listening to his own repeating, reading some of Milton's and the Allegro and Penseroso. It is a quiet keen frost. Mary is in the parlour below attending to the baking of cakes and Jenny Fletcher's pies. Sara is in bed in the toothache, and so we are—beloved William is turning over the leaves of Charlotte Smith's sonnets, but he keeps his hand to his poor chest pushing aside his breastplate. Mary is well and I am well, and Molly is as blithe as last year at this time. Coleridge came this morning with Wedgwood.[5] We all turned out of Wm's bedroom one by one to meet him. He looked well. We had to tell him of the Birth of his little Girl, born yesterday morning at 6 o'clock.[6] W. went with them to Wytheburn in the Chaise, and M.

---

4. Dorothy accompanied William and Mary on the three-day journey back to their cottage at Grasmere.

5. Tom Wedgwood, whose father had founded the famous pottery works, was a friend and generous patron of Coleridge.

6. Coleridge's daughter, Sara (1802–52).

and I met Wm on the Rays. It was not an unpleasant morning to the feelings—far from it. The sun shone now and then, and there was no wind, but all things looked chearless and distinct, no meltings of sky into mountains—the mountains like stonework wrought up with huge hammers.—Last Sunday was as mild a day as I ever remember. We all set off together to walk. I went to Rydale and Wm returned with me. M. and S.[7] went round the Lakes. There were flowers of various kinds the topmost bell of a fox-glove, geraniums, daisies—a buttercup in the water (but this I saw two or three days before) small yellow flowers (I do not know their name) in the turf a large bunch of strawberry blossoms. Wm sate a while with me, then went to meet M. and S.—Last Saturday I dined at Mr Simpson's also a beautiful mild day. Monday was a frosty day, and it has been frost ever since. On Saturday I dined with Mrs Simpson. It is today Christmas-day Saturday 25th December 1802. I am 31 years of age.—It is a dull frosty day.

* * *

1800–1803

7. Mary and her sister Sara Hutchinson.

SAMUEL TAYLOR COLERIDGE
(1772–1834)

1797: At Nether Stowey, Somersetshire; the Wordsworths settle nearby, at Alfoxden.
1798: *Lyrical Ballads*, which included *The Ancient Mariner* and several other poems by Coleridge.
1800: Moves to Greta Hall, Keswick, thirteen miles from the Wordsworths at Grasmere.
1816: Final residence at Highgate, near London, under the care of Dr. James Gillman.
1817: *Biographia Literaria*.

In *The Prelude* Wordsworth, recording his gratitude to the mountains, lakes, and winds "that dwell among the hills where I was born," commiserates with Coleridge because "thou, my Friend! wert reared / In the great city, 'mid far other scenes." Coleridge had in fact been born in the small town of Ottery St. Mary, in rural Devonshire; but upon the death of his father he had been sent to school at Christ's Hospital, in London. He was a dreamy, enthusiastic, and extraordinarily precocious schoolboy; Charles Lamb, his schoolmate and lifelong friend, in his essay on Christ's Hospital has given us a vivid sketch of Coleridge's loneliness, his learning, and his eloquence. When in 1791 Coleridge went up to Jesus College, Cambridge, he was an accomplished scholar; but he found little intellectual stimulation at the university, fell into idleness, dissoluteness, and debt, and in despair fled to London and enlisted in the Light Dragoons under the alias of Silas Tomkyn Comberbacke—probably the most inept cavalryman in the long history of the British army. Although rescued by his brothers and sent back to Cambridge, he left in 1794 without a degree.

In June, 1794, Coleridge met Robert Southey, then a student at Oxford who, like himself, had poetic aspirations, was a radical in religion and politics, and sympathized with the republican experiment in France. Together the two young men planned to establish an ideal democratic community in America for which Coleridge coined the name "Pantisocracy," signifying an equal rule by all. A plausible American real-estate agent persuaded them that the ideal location would be on the banks of the Susquehanna, in Pennsylvania. Twelve men undertook to go; and since perpetuation of the scheme required offspring, hence wives, Coleridge dutifully became engaged to Sara Fricker, conveniently at hand as the sister of Southey's fiancée. The Pantisocracy scheme collapsed, but at Southey's insistence Coleridge went through with the marriage, "resolved," as he said, "but wretched." Later Coleridge's radicalism waned, and he became a conservative—a highly philosophical one—in politics, and a staunch Anglican in religion.

Despite its inauspicious beginning, Coleridge was at first happy in his marriage. When Wordsworth (whom Coleridge met in 1795, and almost immediately judged "the best poet of the age") brought his sister Dorothy to settle at Alfoxden, only three miles from the Coleridges at Nether Stowey, the period of intimate communication and poetic collaboration began which was the golden time of Coleridge's life. An annuity of £150, granted to Coleridge by Thomas and Josiah Wedgwood, sons of the founder of the famous pottery firm, came just in time to deflect him from assuming a post as a Unitarian minister. After their momentous joint publication of *Lyrical Ballads* in 1798, Coleridge and the Wordsworths spent a winter in Germany, where Coleridge attended the University of Göttingen and began the lifelong study of Kant and the post-Kantian German philosophers and critics which helped to alter profoundly his thinking about philosophy, religion, and aesthetics.

Back in England, Coleridge in 1800 followed the Wordsworths to the Lake District, settling at Greta Hall, Keswick. He had become gradually disaffected from his wife, and in 1799 he fell helplessly and hopelessly in love with Sara Hutchinson, whose sister, Mary, Wordsworth married three years later. All his life Coleridge had suffered from numerous painful physical ailments; Wordsworth has described how sometimes, in a sudden spasm of agony, Coleridge would "throw himself down and writhe like a worm upon the ground." According to the standard medical prescription of the time, Coleridge had long been taking laudanum (opium dissolved in alcohol). In 1800–1801 heavy dosages taken for attacks of rheumatism made opium a necessity to him, and Coleridge soon recognized that the drug was a worse evil than the diseases it did not cure. *Dejection: An Ode*, published in 1802, was Coleridge's despairing farewell to health, happiness, and poetic creativity. A two-year sojourn on the Mediterranean island of Malta, intended to restore his health, instead completed his decline. When he returned to England in the late summer of 1806 he was a broken man, an inveterate drug addict, estranged from his wife, suffering from agonies of remorse, and subject to terrifying nightmares of guilt and despair from which his own shrieks awakened him. A bitter quarrel with Wordsworth in 1810 marked the nadir of his life and expectations.

Under these conditions Coleridge's literary efforts, however sporadic and fragmentary, were little short of heroic. In 1808 he gave his first course of public lectures in London, and in the next eleven years followed these with other series on both literary and philosophical topics. He wrote for newspapers and singlehandedly undertook to write, publish, and distribute a periodical, *The Friend*, which lasted for some fourteen months after January, 1809. A tragedy, *Remorse*, had in 1813 a very successful run of twenty performances at the Drury Lane Theatre. In 1816 he took up residence at Highgate, a northern suburb of London, under the supervision of the excellent and endlessly patient physician James Gillman, who managed to control, although not to eliminate, Coleridge's consumption of opium. The next three years were Coleridge's most sustained period of literary activity: while continuing to lecture and to write for the newspapers on a variety of subjects, he published the *Biographia Literaria*, *Zapolya* (a drama), a book consisting of the essays in *The Friend* (revised and greatly enlarged), two collections of poems, and several important treatises on philosophical and religious subjects; in these he undertook to establish a metaphysical basis for the Trinitarian theology to which he had turned after his youthful period of Unitarianism.

The remaining years of his life, which he spent with Dr. and Mrs. Gillman, were quieter and happier than any he had known since the turn of the century. He came to a peaceful understanding with his wife and was reconciled to Wordsworth, with whom he toured the Rhineland in 1828. His rooms at Highgate became a center for friends, for the London literati, and for a steady stream of pilgrims from England and America. They came to hear one of the wonders of the age, the Sage of Highgate's conversation—or monologue—for even in his decline, Coleridge's talk never entirely lost the almost incantatory power which Hazlitt has immortalized in *My First Acquaintance with Poets*. When he died, Coleridge left his friends with the sense that an incomparable intellect had vanished from the world. "The most *wonderful* man that I have ever known," Wordsworth declared, his voice breaking; and Charles Lamb: "His great and dear spirit haunts me. * * * Never saw I his likeness, nor probably the world can see again."

Coleridge's friends, however, abetted by Coleridge's own merciless self-judgments, set current the opinion, still common, that Coleridge was great in promise but not in performance. Even in his buoyant youth, before opium had drained his strength and weakened his will, Coleridge described his own character as "indolence capable of energies"; and it is true that while his mind was incessantly active and fertile, he lacked application and staying power, and he manifested early in life a profound sense of guilt and a need for public expiation. After drug addiction sapped Coleridge's strength and will, even while it reinforced his emotional problems, Coleridge often adapted (or simply adopted) passages from other writers, with little or no acknowledgment, and sometimes in a context that seems designed at once to obfuscate his literary obligations and to reveal the subterfuge. Whatever the tangled motives for his procedure, Coleridge has repeatedly been charged with plagiarism, from his day to our own. After *The Ancient Mariner*, most of the poems he completed were written, like the first version of *Dejection: An Ode*, in a spasm of intense effort. Writings which required sustained planning and application were either left unfinished or, like the *Biographia Literaria*, made up of brilliant sections eked out with filler, sometimes lifted from other writers, in a desperate effort to meet a deadline. Many of his best speculations Coleridge merely confided to his notebooks and the ears of his friends, incorporated in letters, and poured out upon the margins of his own and other people's books.

Even so, it is only when measured against his own immense potentialities that Coleridge's achievements appear limited. In opposition to the prevailing British philosophy of empiricism and associationism, Coleridge for most of his mature life expounded his views of the mind as creative in perception, intuitive in its discovery of the first premises of metaphysics and religion, and capable of a poetic re-creation of the world of sense by the fusing and formative power of the "secondary imagination." Within the decade after Coleridge died, John Stuart Mill, the most acute student of contemporary thought, announced that Coleridge was one of "the two great seminal minds of England," the most important instigator and representative of the conservative intellectual movement of the day. Time has proved Mill's estimate of Coleridge to be just, for his influence is strongly evident in 19th-century English and American traditions of philosophical idealism, enlightened political conservatism, and liberal interpretations of Trinitarian theology. By present consensus, Coleridge is also one of the greatest and most influential of literary theorists; his ideas became central points of reference even in many of the New Critics of the middle of the present century who depreciated the Romantic poetry for which Coleridge, in his criticism, attempted to provide a rationale. And Coleridge's writings in verse, though small in bulk, are the work of a major and notably original poet.

Here, too, we tend to underestimate Coleridge's versatility—this time because of our preoccupation with his three poems of mystery and demonism, *The Ancient Mariner*, *Christabel*, and *Kubla Khan*. These are indeed great and unprecedented achievements, but Coleridge wrote them all within a few years, and then dropped the mode. No less impressive in their own way are the blank-verse poems of the lonely and meditative mind which, by an extension of his term for one of them, are called "Conversation Poems"; in the best of these, *Frost at Midnight*, Coleridge perfected that characteristic pattern of integrally related description and meditation which Wordsworth immediately adopted in *Tintern Abbey*. Coleridge himself adapted this pattern to the larger requirements of *Dejection*, a high achievement in a genre in which few poets have been successful, the irregular Pindaric ode. The verse epistle *To William Wordsworth* is at once the most insightful comment ever made about *The Prelude*, a superb tribute to a friend whom Coleridge thought the greatest poet since Milton, and a moving elegy on the death of his own poetic power. But even when he had mainly given up poetry, after 1805, Coleridge continued to write occasional short lyrics (represented below) which are remarkable equally for their quality, their diversity, and the extent to which they have been neglected by anthologists.

Sonnet to the River Otter[1]

Dear native Brook! wild Streamlet of the West!
   How many various-fated years have past,
     What happy and what mournful hours, since last
I skimmed the smooth thin stone along thy breast,
Numbering its light leaps! yet so deep impressed   5
Sink the sweet scenes of childhood, that mine eyes
   I never shut amid the sunny ray,
But straight with all their tints thy waters rise,
   Thy crossing plank, thy marge with willows grey,
And bedded sand that veined with various dyes   10
Gleamed through thy bright transparence! On my way,
   Visions of Childhood! oft have ye beguiled
Lone manhood's cares, yet waking fondest sighs:
   Ah! that once more I were a careless Child!

1793?   1796

The Eolian Harp[2]

Love of Nature leads to a kind of understanding of God. —

COMPOSED AT CLEVEDON, SOMERSETSHIRE

My pensive Sara! thy soft cheek reclined
Thus on mine arm, most soothing sweet it is
To sit beside our Cot, our Cot o'ergrown
With white-flowered Jasmin, and the broad-leaved Myrtle,
(Meet emblems they of Innocence and Love!)   5
And watch the clouds, that late were rich with light,

1. Coleridge's model was W. L. Bowles's *To the River Itchin*. For the great impact of Bowles's sonnets on Coleridge's poetic theory and practice, see his *Biographia Lietraria*, Chapter 1. Coleridge expanded this poetic mode of natural description interwoven with memory and meditation into his "conversation poems," such as *The Eolian Harp*, *This Lime-Tree Bower*, and *Frost at Midnight*.
2. Named for Aeolus, god of the winds, the harp has strings stretched over a rectangular sounding box. The strings are tuned in unison. When placed in an opened window, the harp (also called "Eolian lute," "Eolian lyre," "wind harp") responds to the altering wind by sequences of musical chords. This instrument, which seems to voice nature's own music, was a favorite household furnishing in the period, and was repeatedly alluded to in Romantic poetry; see Geoffrey Grigson, *The Harp of Aeolus and Other Essays* (1947). It served also as one of the recurrent Romantic images for the mind—either the

mind in poetic inspiration, as in the last stanza of Shelley's *Ode to the West Wind*, or else the mind in perception, responding to an intellectual breeze by trembling into consciousness, as in this poem, lines 44–48. Coleridge, however, no sooner puts forward this concept than he retracts it, for it comes too close to the heresy of pantheism, which identifies God with the nature that, in the orthodox view, is His creation.

Coleridge wrote this poem to Sara Fricker, whom he married on October 4, 1795, and took to a cottage at Clevedon, overlooking the Bristol Channel. He later several times expanded and altered his original version; the famous lines 26–33, for example, were not incorporated until 1817. The poem was Coleridge's first achievement in the important Romantic form of the sustained blank-verse lyric of description and meditation, in the mode of conversation addressed to a silent auditor, which he perfected in *Frost at Midnight*, and which Wordsworth adopted for *Tintern Abbey*.

Slow saddening round, and mark the star of eve
Serenely brilliant (such should Wisdom be)
Shine opposite! How exquisite the scents
Snatched from yon bean-field! and the world *so* hushed!   10
The stilly murmur of the distant Sea
Tells us of silence.

             And that simplest Lute,
Placed length-ways in the clasping casement, hark!
How by the desultory breeze caressed,
Like some coy maid half yielding to her lover,   15
It pours such sweet upbraiding, as must needs
Tempt to repeat the wrong! And now, its strings
Boldlier swept, the long sequacious[3] notes
Over delicious surges sink and rise,   20
Such a soft floating witchery of sound
As twilight Elfins make, when they at eve
Voyage on gentle gales from Fairy-Land,
Where Melodies round honey-dropping flowers,
Footless and wild, like birds of Paradise,[4]   25
Nor pause, nor perch, hovering on untamed wing!
O! the one Life within us and abroad,
Which meets all motion and becomes its soul,
A light in sound, a sound-like power in light,
Rhythm in all thought, and joyance everywhere—   30
Methinks, it should have been impossible
Not to love all things in a world so filled;
Where the breeze warbles, and the mute still air
Is Music slumbering on her instrument.

    And thus, my Love! as on the midway slope
Of yonder hill I stretch my limbs at noon,   35
Whilst through my half-closed eyelids I behold
The sunbeams dance, like diamonds, on the main,
And tranquil muse upon tranquillity:
Full many a thought uncalled and undetained,
And many idle flitting phantasies,   40
Traverse my indolent and passive brain,
As wild and various as the random gales
That swell and flutter on this subject Lute!

    And what if all of animated nature
Be but organic Harps diversely framed,   45
That tremble into thought, as o'er them sweeps
Plastic and vast, one intellectual breeze,
At once the Soul of each, and God of all?

    But thy more serious eye a mild reproof
Darts, O belovèd Woman! nor such thoughts   50
Dim and unhallowed dost thou not reject,

3. Successive
4. Brilliantly colored birds, found in New Guinea and adjacent islands. The native practice of removing the legs when preparing the skin led Europeans to believe that the birds were footless and spent their lives hovering in the air and feeding on nectar.

And biddest me walk humbly with my God.
Meek Daughter in the family of Christ!
Well hast thou said and holily dispraised
These shapings of the unregenerate mind; 55
Bubbles that glitter as they rise and break
On vain Philosophy's aye-babbling spring.
For never guiltless may I speak of him,
The Incomprehensible! save when with awe
I praise him, and with Faith that inly *feels*; 60
Who with his saving mercies healéd me,
A sinful and most miserable man,
Wildered and dark, and gave me to possess
Peace, and this Cot, and thee, heart-honored Maid!

1795–1817   1796, 1817

[handwritten margin note: Maunderings about Nature lead him to an acceptance of traditional christian values.]

This Lime-Tree Bower My Prison

[handwritten margin note: The power of Nature + the power of imagination]

ADDRESSED TO CHARLES LAMB, OF THE INDIA HOUSE, LONDON

In the June of 1797 some long-expected friends paid a visit to the author's cottage; and on the morning of their arrival, he met with an accident, which disabled him from walking during the whole time of their stay. One evening, when they had left him for a few hours, he composed the following lines in the garden-bower.[1]

Well, they are gone, and here must I remain,
This lime-tree bower my prison! I have lost
Beauties and feelings, such as would have been
Most sweet to my remembrance even when age
Had dimmed mine eyes to blindness! They, meanwhile, 5
Friends, whom I never more may meet again, *[handwritten note: A bit of Frame]*
On springy[2] heath, along the hill-top edge,
Wander in gladness, and wind down, perchance,
To that still roaring dell, of which I told;
The roaring dell, o'erwooded, narrow, deep, 10
And only speckled by the mid-day sun; *[handwritten note: His imagination can transport him.]*
Where its slim trunk the ash from rock to rock
Flings arching like a bridge;—that branchless ash,
Unsunned and damp, whose few poor yellow leaves
Ne'er tremble in the gale, yet tremble still, 15
Fanned by the waterfall! and there my friends
Behold the dark green file of long lank weeds,
That all at once (a most fantastic sight!)
Still nod and drip beneath the dripping edge
Of the blue clay-stone.[3]

1. The time was in fact July 1797; the visiting friends were William and Dorothy Wordsworth and Charles Lamb; the accident was the fault of Mrs. Coleridge —"dear Sara," Coleridge wrote, "accidentally emptied a skillet of boiling milk on my foot"; and the bower consisted of lime (i.e., linden) trees in the garden of Thomas Poole, next door to Coleridge's cottage at Nether Stowey. Coleridge related these facts in a letter to Robert Southey, July 17, 1797, in which he transcribed the first version of this fine "conversation poem."
2. "*Elastic*, I mean" [Coleridge's note].
3. Compare Dorothy Wordsworth's description of the "low damp dell" in her *Alfoxden Journal* for February 10, 1798.

                    Now, my friends emerge   20
Beneath the wide wide Heaven—and view again
The many-steepled tract magnificent
Of hilly fields and meadows, and the sea,
With some fair bark, perhaps, whose sails light up
The slip of smooth clear blue betwixt two Isles   25
Of purple shadow! Yes! they wander on
In gladness all; but thou, methinks, most glad,
My gentle-hearted Charles! for thou hast pined
And hungered after Nature, many a year,
In the great City pent,[4] winning thy way   30
With sad yet patient soul, through evil and pain
And strange calamity![5] Ah! slowly sink
Behind the western ridge, thou glorious Sun!
Shine in the slant beams of the sinking orb,
Ye purple heath-flowers! richlier burn, ye clouds!   35
Live in the yellow light, ye distant groves!
And kindle, thou blue Ocean! So my friend
Struck with deep joy may stand, as I have stood,
Silent with swimming sense; yea, gazing round
On the wide landscape, gaze till doth seem   40
Less gross than bodily; and of such hues
As veil the Almighty Spirit, when yet he makes
Spirits perceive his presence.

                    A delight
Comes sudden on my heart, and I am glad
As I myself were there! Nor in this bower,
This little lime-tree bower, have I not marked   45
Much that has soothed me. Pale beneath the blaze
Hung the transparent foliage; and I watched
Some broad and sunny leaf, and loved to see
The shadow of the leaf and stem above   50
Dappling its sunshine! And that walnut-tree
Was richly tinged, and a deep radiance lay
Full on the ancient ivy, which usurps
Those fronting elms, and now, with blackest mass
Makes their dark branches gleam a lighter hue   55
Through the late twilight: and though now the bat
Wheels silent by, and not a swallow twitters,
Yet still the solitary humblebee
Sings in the bean-flower! Henceforth I shall know
That Nature ne'er deserts the wise and pure;   60
No plot so narrow, be but Nature there,
No waste so vacant, but may well employ
Each faculty of sense, and keep the heart
Awake to Love and Beauty! and sometimes
'Tis well to be bereft of promised good,   65

4. Despite Cole...ge's claim, Lamb eminently preferred London over what he
called "dead Nature"; see his Let...
Wordsworth, January 30, 1801.

5. Some ten months earlier Charles
Lamb's sister, Mary, had stabbed her
...er to death in a fit of insanity.

That we may lift the soul, and contemplate
With lively joy the joys we cannot share.
My gentle-hearted Charles! when the last rook
Beat its straight path along the dusky air
Homewards, I blessed it! deeming its black wing   70
(Now a dim speck, now vanishing in light)
Had crossed the mighty Orb's dilated glory,
While thou stood'st gazing; or, when all was still,
Flew creeking o'er thy head, and had a charm
For thee, my gentle-hearted Charles, to whom   75
No sound is dissonant which tells of Life.

1797   1800

The Rime of the Ancient Mariner[1]

IN SEVEN PARTS

Facile credo, plures esse Naturas invisibiles quam visibiles in rerum universitate. Sed horum [sic] *omnium familiam quis nobis enarrabit? et gradus et cognationes et discrimina et singulorum munera? Quid agunt? quae loca habitant? Harum rerum notitiam semper ambivit ingenium humanum, nunquam attigit. Juvat, interea, non diffiteor, quandoque in animo, tanquam in tabulâ, majoris et melioris mundi imaginem contemplari: ne mens assuefacta hodiernae vitae minutiis se contrahat nimis, et tota subsidat in pusillas cogitationes. Sed veritati interea invigilandum est, modusque servandus, ut certa ab incertis, diem a nocte, distinguamus.*
T. BURNET, *Archaeol. Phil.* p. 68.[2]

Argument

How a Ship, having first sailed to the Equator, was driven by storms to the cold Country towards the South Pole; how the Ancient Mariner cruelly and in contempt of the laws of hospitality killed a Sea-bird and how he was followed by many and strange Judgments: and in what manner he came back to his own Country.

1. Coleridge describes the origin of this poem in the opening section of Chapter XIV of *Biographia Literaria.* In a comment made to the Rev. Alexander Dyce in 1835, and in a note on *We Are Seven* dictated in 1843, Wordsworth added some details. The poem, based on a dream of Coleridge's friend Cruikshank, was originally planned as a collaboration between the two friends, to pay the expense of a walking tour they took with Dorothy Wordsworth in November of 1797. Before he dropped out of the enterprise, Wordsworth suggested the shooting of the albatross and the navigation of the ship by the dead men; he also contributed lines 13–16 and 226–27.
The version of *The Ancient Mariner* printed in *Lyrical Ballads* (1798) contained many archaic words and spellings. In later editions Coleridge greatly improved the poem by pruning the archaisms, and by other revisions; he also added the Latin epigraph and the marginal glosses.

2. Latin epigraph: "I readily believe that there are more invisible than visible Natures in the universe. But who will explain for us the family of all these beings, and the ranks and relations and distinguishing features and functions of each? What do they do? What places do they inhabit? The human mind has always sought the knowledge of these things, but never attained it. Meanwhile I do not deny that it is helpful sometimes to contemplate in the mind, as on a tablet, the image of a greater and better world, lest the intellect, habituated to the petty things of daily life, narrow itself and sink wholly into trivial thoughts. But at the same time we must be watchful for the truth and keep a sense of proportion, so that we may distinguish the certain from the uncertain, day from night." Adapted by Coleridge from Thomas Burnet, *Archaeologiae philosophicae* (1692).

Part I

*An ancient Mar-
iner meeteth
three Gallants
bidden to a wed-
ding feast, and
detaineth one.*

It is an ancient Mariner
And he stoppeth one of three.
—"By thy long gray beard and glittering eye,
Now wherefore stopp'st thou me?

The Bridegroom's doors are opened wide,   5
And I am next of kin;
The guests are met, the feast is set:
May'st hear the merry din."

He holds him with his skinny hand,
"There was a ship," quoth he.   10
"Hold off! unhand me, graybeard loon!"
Eftsoons³ his hand dropped he.

*The Wedding
Guest is spell-
bound by the eye
of the old seafar-
ing man, and
constrained to
hear his tale.*

He holds him with his glittering eye—
The Wedding Guest stood still,
And listens like a three years' child: 15
The Mariner hath his will.⁴

The Wedding Guest sat on a stone:
He cannot choose but hear;
And thus spake on that ancient man,
The bright-eyed Mariner.   20

"The ship was cheered, the harbor cleared,
Merrily did we drop
Below the kirk,⁵ below the hill,
Below the lighthouse top.

*The Mariner
tells how the
ship sailed south-
ward with a good
wind and fair
weather, till it
reached the Line.*

The Sun came up upon the left,   25
Out of the sea came he!
And he shone bright, and on the right
Went down into the sea.

Higher and higher every day,
Till over the mast at noon⁶—"   30
The Wedding Guest here beat his breast,
For he heard the loud bassoon.

*The Wedding
Guest heareth
the bridal music;
but the Mariner
continueth his
tale.*

The bride hath paced into the hall,
Red as a rose is she;
Nodding their heads before her goes   35
The merry minstrelsy.

---

3. At once.
4. I.e., the Mariner has gained control
of the will of the Wedding Guest by
hypnosis—or, as it was called in Coleridge's time, by "mesmerism."
5. Church.
6. I.e., the ship had reached the equator
(the "Line").

The Wedding Guest he beat his breast,
Yet he cannot choose but hear;
And thus spake on that ancient man,
The bright-eyed Mariner.   40

The ship driven by a storm toward the South Pole.

"And now the STORM-BLAST came, and he
Was tyrannous and strong;
He struck with his o'ertaking wings,
And chased us south along.

With sloping masts and dipping prow,   45
As who pursued with yell and blow
Still treads the shadow of his foe,
And forward bends his head,
The ship drove fast, loud roared the blast,
And southward aye we fled.   50

And now there came both mist and snow,
And it grew wondrous cold:
And ice, mast-high, came floating by,
As green as emerald.

The land of ice, and of fearful sounds where no living thing was to be seen.

And through the drifts the snowy clifts   55
Did send a dismal sheen:
Nor shapes of men nor beasts we ken—
The ice was all between.

The ice was here, the ice was there,
The ice was all around: 60
It cracked and growled, and roared and howled,
Like noises in a swound![7]

Till a great sea bird, called the Albatross, came through the snow-fog, and was received with great joy and hospitality.

At length did cross an Albatross,
Thorough the fog it came;
As if it had been a Christian soul,   65
We hailed it in God's name.

It ate the food it ne'er had eat,
And round and round it flew.
The ice did split with a thunder-fit;
The helmsman steered us through!   70

And lo! the Albatross proveth a bird of good omen, and followeth the ship as it returned northward through fog and floating ice.

And a good south wind sprung up behind;
The Albatross did follow,
And every day, for food or play,
Came to the mariners' hollo!

In mist or cloud, on mast or shroud,[8]   75
It perched for vespers nine;
Whiles all the night, through fog-smoke white,
Glimmered the white Moon-shine."

---

7. Swoon.   8. Rope supporting the mast.

*The ancient Mar-
iner inhospitably
killeth the pious
bird of good
omen.*
"God save thee, ancient Mariner!
From the fiends, that plague thee thus!—
Why look'st thou so?"—With my crossbow
I shot the ALBATROSS.   80

Part II

The Sun now rose upon the right:[9]
Out of the sea came he,
Still hid in mist, and on the left   85
Went down into the sea.

And the good south wind still blew behind,
But no sweet bird did follow,
Nor any day for food or play
Came to the mariners' hollo!   90

*His shipmates
cry out against
the ancient Mar-
iner, for killing
the bird of good
luck.*
And I had done a hellish thing,
And it would work 'em woe:
For all averred, I had killed the bird
That made the breeze to blow.
Ah wretch! said they, the bird to slay,   95
That made the breeze to blow!

*But when the fog
cleared off, they
justify the same,
and thus make
themselves ac-
complices in the
crime.*
Nor dim nor red, like God's own head,
The glorious Sun uprist:
Then all averred, I had killed the bird
That brought the fog and mist.   100
'Twas right, said they, such birds to slay,
That bring the fog and mist.

*The fair breeze
continues; the
ship enters the
Pacific Ocean,
and sails north-
ward, even till it
reaches the Line.*
The fair breeze blew, the white foam flew,
The furrow followed free;
We were the first that ever burst   105
Into that silent sea.

*The ship hath
been suddenly
becalmed.*
Down dropped the breeze, the sails dropped down,
'Twas sad as sad could be;
And we did speak only to break
The silence of the sea!   110

All in a hot and copper sky,
The bloody Sun, at noon,
Right up above the mast did stand,
No bigger than the Moon.

Day after day, day after day,   115
We stuck, nor breath nor motion;
As idle as a painted ship
Upon a painted ocean.

9. I.e., having rounded Cape Horn, the ship heads north into the Pacific.

*And the Alba-
tross begins to
be avenged.*

Water, water, everywhere,
And all the boards did shrink;   120
Water, water, everywhere,
Nor any drop to drink.

The very deep did rot: O Christ!
That ever this should be!
Yea, slimy things did crawl with legs   125
Upon the slimy sea.

About, about, in reel and rout
The death-fires[1] danced at night;
The water, like a witch's oils,
Burnt green, and blue and white.   130

And some in dreams assuréd were
Of the Spirit that plagued us so;
Nine fathom deep he had followed us
From the land of mist and snow.

*A Spirit had
followed them;
one of the invis-
ible inhabitants
of this planet,*

*neither departed souls nor angels; concerning whom the learned Jew, Josephus, and
the Platonic Constantinopolitan, Michael Psellus, may be consulted. They are very
numerous, and there is no climate or element without one or more.*

And every tongue, through utter drought,   135
Was withered at the root;
We could not speak, no more than if
We had been choked with soot.

Ah! well-a-day! what evil looks
Had I from old and young!   140
Instead of the cross, the Albatross
About my neck was hung.

*The shipmates,
in their sore dis-
tress, would fain
throw the whole
guilt on the an-
cient Mariner: in*

sign whereof they hang the dead sea bird round his neck.

Part III

There passed a weary time. Each throat
Was parched, and glazed each eye.
A weary time! a weary time!
How glazed each weary eye,   145
When looking westward, I beheld
A something in the sky.

*The ancient Mar-
iner beholdeth a
sign in the ele-
ment afar off.*

At first it seemed a little speck,
And then it seemed a mist;
It moved and moved, and took at last   150
A certain shape, I wist.[2]

A speck, a mist, a shape, I wist!
And still it neared and neared:

1. The corposant, or St. Elmo's fire, an atmospheric electricity on a ship's mast or rigging, believed by the super- stitious sailor to portend disaster.
2. Knew.

As if it dodged a water sprite,   155
It plunged and tacked and veered.

At its nearer approach, it seemeth him to be a ship; and at a dear ransom he freeth his speech from the bonds of thirst.

With throats unslaked, with black lips baked,
We could nor laugh nor wail;
Through utter drought all dumb we stood!
I bit my arm, I sucked the blood,   160
And cried, A sail! a sail!

With throats unslaked, with black lips baked,
Agape they heard me call:

A flash of joy;

Gramercy![3] they for joy did grin,
And all at once their breath drew in,   165
As they were drinking all.

And horror follows. For can it be a ship that comes onward without wind or tide?

See! see! (I cried) she tacks no more!
Hither to work us weal;[4]
Without a breeze, without a tide,
She steadies with upright keel!   170

The western wave was all aflame.
The day was well nigh done!
Almost upon the western wave
Rested the broad bright Sun;
When that strange shape drove suddenly   175
Betwixt us and the Sun.

It seemeth him but the skeleton of a ship.

And straight the Sun was flecked with bars,
(Heaven's Mother send us grace!)
As if through a dungeon grate he peered
With broad and burning face.   180

And its ribs are seen as bars on the face of the setting Sun.

Alas! (thought I, and my heart beat loud)
How fast she nears and nears!
Are those *her* sails that glance in the Sun,
Like restless gossameres?[5]

The Specter-Woman and her Deathmate, and no other on board the skeleton ship.

Are those *her* ribs through which the Sun   185
Did peer, as through a grate?
And is that Woman all her crew?
Is that a DEATH? and are there two?
Is DEATH that woman's mate?

Like vessel, like crew!

Her lips were red, *her* looks were free,   190
Her locks were yellow as gold:
Her skin was as white as leprosy,
The Nightmare LIFE-IN-DEATH was she,
Who thicks man's blood with cold.

Death and Life-in-Death have diced for the ship's crew, and she (the latter) winneth the ancient Mariner.

The naked hulk alongside came,   195
And the twain were casting dice;
"The game is done! I've won! I've won!"
Quoth she, and whistles thrice.

---

3. From the French *grand-merci*, "great thanks."   4. Benefit.
5. Filmy cobwebs floating in the air.

No twilight within the courts of the Sun.	The Sun's rim dips; the stars rush out:
	At one stride comes the dark;
	With far-heard whisper, o'er the sea,
	Off shot the specter bark.

No twilight within the courts of the Sun.

The Sun's rim dips; the stars rush out:
At one stride comes the dark;   200
With far-heard whisper, o'er the sea,
Off shot the specter bark.

At the rising of the Moon,

We listened and looked sideways up!
Fear at my heart, as at a cup,
My lifeblood seemed to sip!   205
The stars were dim, and thick the night,
The steersman's face by his lamp gleamed white;
From the sails the dew did drip—
Till clomb above the eastern bar
The hornéd Moon, with one bright star   210
Within the nether tip.[5a]

One after another,

One after one, by the star-dogged Moon,
Too quick for groan or sigh,
Each turned his face with ghastly pang,
And cursed me with his eye.   215

His shipmates drop down dead.

Four times fifty living men,
(And I heard nor sigh nor groan)
With heavy thump, a lifeless lump,
They dropped down one by one.

But Life-in-Death begins her work on the ancient Mariner.

The souls did from their bodies fly—   220
They fled to bliss or woe!
And every soul, it passed me by,
Like the whizz of my crossbow!

Part IV

The Wedding Guest feareth that a Spirit is talking to him;

"I fear thee, ancient Mariner!
I fear thy skinny hand!   225
And thou art long, and lank, and brown,
As is the ribbed sea-sand.

I fear thee and thy glittering eye,
And thy skinny hand, so brown."—

But the ancient Mariner assureth him of his bodily life, and proceedeth to relate his horrible penance.

Fear not, fear not, thou Wedding Guest!   230
This body dropped not down.

Alone, alone, all, all alone,
Alone on a wide wide sea!
And never a saint took pity on
My soul in agony.   235

He despiseth the creatures of the calm,

The many men, so beautiful!
And they all dead did lie:
And a thousand thousand slimy things
Lived on; and so did I.

5a. An omen of impending evil.

And envieth that
they should live,
and so many lie
dead.

I looked upon the rotting sea,   240
And drew my eyes away;
I looked upon the rotting deck,
And there the dead men lay.

I looked to heaven, and tried to pray;
But or ever a prayer had gushed,   245
A wicked whisper came, and made
My heart as dry as dust.

I closed my lids, and kept them close,
And the balls like pulses beat;
For the sky and the sea, and the sea and the sky   250
Lay like a load on my weary eye,
And the dead were at my feet.

But the curse
liveth for him in
the eye of the
dead men.

The cold sweat melted from their limbs,
Nor rot nor reek did they:
The look with which they looked on me   255
Had never passed away.

An orphan's curse would drag to hell
A spirit from on high;
But oh! more horrible than that
Is the curse in a dead man's eye!   260
Seven days, seven nights, I saw that curse,
And yet I could not die.

The moving Moon went up the sky,
And nowhere did abide:

In his loneliness
and fixedness he
yearneth towards
the journeying
Moon, and the
stars that still
sojourn, yet still
move onward;
and everywhere
the blue sky be-
longs to them,
and is their ap-
pointed rest, and
their native
country and their own natural homes, which they enter unannounced, as lords that are
certainly expected and yet there is a silent joy at their arrival.

Softly she was going up,   265
And a star or two beside—

Her beams bemocked the sultry main,
Like April hoar-frost spread;
But where the ship's huge shadow lay,
The charmèd water burnt alway   270
A still and awful red.

By the light of
the Moon he be-
holdeth God's
creatures of the
great calm.

Beyond the shadow of the ship,
I watched the water snakes:
They moved in tracks of shining white,
And when they reared, the elfish light   275
Fell off in hoary flakes.

Within the shadow of the ship
I watched their rich attire:
Blue, glossy green, and velvet black,
They coiled and swam; and every track   280
Was a flash of golden fire.

O happy living things! no tongue
Their beauty might declare:

A spring of love gushed from my heart,
And I blessed them unaware: 285
Sure my kind saint took pity on me,
And I blessed them unaware.

He blesseth them in his heart.

The selfsame moment I could pray;
And from my neck so free
The Albatross fell off, and sank   290
Like lead into the sea.

The spell begins to break.

Part V

Oh sleep! it is a gentle thing,
Beloved from pole to pole!
To Mary Queen the praise be given!
She sent the gentle sleep from Heaven,   295
That slid into my soul.

The silly[6] buckets on the deck,
That had so long remained,
I dreamt that they were filled with dew;
And when I awoke, it rained.   300

By grace of the holy Mother, the ancient Mariner is refreshed with rain.

My lips were wet, my throat was cold,
My garments all were dank;
Sure I had drunken in my dreams,
And still my body drank.

I moved, and could not feel my limbs: 305
I was so light—almost
I thought that I had died in sleep,
And was a blessed ghost.

And soon I heard a roaring wind:
It did not come anear;   310
But with its sound it shook the sails,
That were so thin and sere.

He heareth sounds and seeth strange sights and commotions in the sky and the element.

The upper air burst into life!
And a hundred fire-flags sheen,[7]
To and fro they were hurried about!   315
And to and fro, and in and out,
The wan stars danced between.

And the coming wind did roar more loud,
And the sails did sigh like sedge;[8]
And the rain poured down from one black cloud;   320
The Moon was at its edge.

The thick black cloud was cleft, and still
The Moon was at its side:
Like waters shot from some high crag,
The lightning fell with never a jag,   325
A river steep and wide.

6. In the archaic sense: blessed, happy.
7. Shone. These are the Aurora Australis, or Southern Lights.
8. A rushlike plant growing in wet soil.

The bodies of the ship's crew are inspirited, and the ship moves on;

The loud wind never reached the ship,
Yet now the ship moved on!
Beneath the lightning and the Moon
The dead men gave a groan.   330

They groaned, they stirred, they all uprose,
Nor spake, nor moved their eyes;
It had been strange, even in a dream,
To have seen those dead men rise.

The helmsman steered, the ship moved on;   335
Yet never a breeze up-blew;
The mariners all 'gan work the ropes,
Where they were wont to do;
They raised their limbs like lifeless tools—
We were a ghastly crew.   340

The body of my brother's son
Stood by me, knee to knee:
The body and I pulled at one rope,
But he said nought to me.

"I fear thee, ancient Mariner!"   345

But not by the souls of the men, nor by demons of earth or middle air, but by a blessed troop of angelic spirits, sent down by the invocation of the guardian saint.

Be calm, thou Wedding Guest!
'Twas not those souls that fled in pain,
Which to their corses[9] came again,
But a troop of spirits blest:

For when it dawned—they dropped their arms,   350
And clustered round the mast;
Sweet sounds rose slowly through their mouths,
And from their bodies passed.

Around, around, flew each sweet sound,
Then darted to the Sun;   355
Slowly the sounds came back again,
Now mixed, now one by one.

Sometimes a-dropping from the sky
I heard the skylark sing;
Sometimes all little birds that are,   360
How they seemed to fill the sea and air
With their sweet jargoning![1]

And now 'twas like all instruments,
Now like a lonely flute;
And now it is an angel's song,   365
That makes the heavens be mute.

It ceased; yet still the sails made on
A pleasant noise till noon,
A noise like of a hidden brook

---

9. Corpses.   1. In Middle English, "warbling."

In the leafy month of June,
That to the sleeping woods all night   370
Singeth a quiet tune.

Till noon we quietly sailed on,
Yet never a breeze did breathe:
Slowly and smoothly went the ship,   375
Moved onward from beneath.

*The lonesome
Spirit from the
South Pole car-
ries on the ship
as far as the
Line, in obedi-
ence to the an-
gelic troop, but
still requireth
vengeance.*
Under the keel nine fathom deep,
From the land of mist and snow,
The spirit slid: and it was he
That made the ship to go.   380
The sails at noon left off their tune,
And the ship stood still also.

The Sun, right up above the mast,
Had fixed her to the ocean:
But in a minute she 'gan stir,   385
With a short uneasy motion—
Backwards and forwards half her length
With a short uneasy motion.

Then like a pawing horse let go,
She made a sudden bound: 390
It flung the blood into my head,
And I fell down in a swound.

*The Polar
Spirit's fellow
demons, the in-
visible inhabit-
ants of the ele-
ment, take part
in his wrong;
and two of them
relate, one to the
other, that pen-
ance long and
heavy for the
ancient Mariner
hath been ac-
corded to the
Polar Spirit, who
returneth south-
ward.*
How long in that same fit I lay,
I have not[2] to declare;
But ere my living life returned,   395
I heard and in my soul discerned
Two voices in the air.

"Is it he?" quoth one, "Is this the man?
By him who died on cross,
With his cruel bow he laid full low   400
The harmless Albatross.

The spirit who bideth by himself
In the land of mist and snow,
He loved the bird that loved the man
Who shot him with his bow."   405

The other was a softer voice,
As soft as honeydew:
Quoth he, "The man hath penance done,
And penance more will do."

Part VI

FIRST VOICE

"But tell me, tell me! speak again,
Thy soft response renewing—   410

2. I.e., have not the knowledge.

What makes that ship drive on so fast?
What is the ocean doing?"

SECOND VOICE

"Still as a slave before his lord,
The ocean hath no blast;   415
His great bright eye most silently
Up to the Moon is cast—

If he may know which way to go;
For she guides him smooth or grim.
See, brother, see! how graciously   420
She looketh down on him."

FIRST VOICE

*The Mariner
hath been cast
into a trance;
for the angelic
power causeth
the vessel to
drive northward
faster than hu-
man life could
endure.*

"But why drives on that ship so fast,
Without or wave or wind?"

SECOND VOICE

"The air is cut away before,
And closes from behind.   425

Fly, brother, fly! more high, more high!
Or we shall be belated:
For slow and slow that ship will go,
When the Mariner's trance is abated."

*The supernatural
motion is re-
tarded; the Mar-
iner awakes, and
his penance be-
gins anew.*

I woke, and we were sailing on   430
As in a gentle weather:
'Twas night, calm night, the moon was high;
The dead men stood together.

All stood together on the deck,
For a charnel-dungeon fitter: 435
All fixed on me their stony eyes,
That in the Moon did glitter.

The pang, the curse, with which they died,
Had never passed away:
I could not draw my eyes from theirs,   440
Nor turn them up to pray.

*The curse is
finally expiated.*

And now this spell was snapped: once more
I viewed the ocean green,
And looked far forth, yet little saw
Of what had else been seen—   445

Like one, that on a lonesome road
Doth walk in fear and dread,
And having once turned round walks on,
And turns no more his head;
Because he knows, a frightful fiend   450
Doth close behind him tread.

But soon there breathed a wind on me,
Nor sound nor motion made:
Its path was not upon the sea,
In ripple or in shade.   455

It raised my hair, it fanned my cheek
Like a meadow-gale of spring—
It mingled strangely with my fears,
Yet it felt like a welcoming.

Swiftly, swiftly flew the ship,   460
Yet she sailed softly too:
Sweetly, sweetly blew the breeze—
On me alone it blew.

And the ancient Mariner behold- eth his native country.

Oh! dream of joy! is this indeed
The lighthouse top I see?   465
Is this the hill? is this the kirk?
Is this mine own countree?

We drifted o'er the harbor bar,
And I with sobs did pray—
O let me be awake, my God!   470
Or let me sleep alway.

The harbor bay was clear as glass,
So smoothly it was strewn!
And on the bay the moonlight lay,
And the shadow of the Moon.   475

The rock shone bright, the kirk no less,
That stands above the rock:
The moonlight steeped in silentness
The steady weathercock.

And the bay was white with silent light,   480
Till rising from the same,

The angelic spirits leave the dead bodies,

Full many shapes, that shadows were,
In crimson colors came.

And appear in their own forms of light.

A little distance from the prow
Those crimson shadows were: 485
I turned my eyes upon the deck—
Oh, Christ! what saw I there!

Each corse lay flat, lifeless and flat,
And, by the holy rood![3]
A man all light, a seraph man,   490
On every corse there stood.

This seraph band, each waved his hand:
It was a heavenly sight!

3. Cross. "Seraph": a shining celestial being, highest in the ranks of the angels.

They stood as signals to the land,
Each one a lovely light; 495

This seraph band, each waved his hand,
No voice did they impart—
No voice; but oh! the silence sank
Like music on my heart.

But soon I heard the dash of oars, 500
I heard the Pilot's cheer;
My head was turned perforce away
And I saw a boat appear.

The Pilot and the Pilot's boy,
I heard them coming fast: 505
Dear Lord in Heaven! it was a joy
The dead men could not blast.

I saw a third—I heard his voice:
It is the Hermit good!
He singeth loud his godly hymns 510
That he makes in the wood.
He'll shrieve my soul, he'll wash away
The Albatross's blood.

Part VII

The Hermit of the Wood

This Hermit good lives in that wood
Which slopes down to the sea. 515
How loudly his sweet voice he rears!
He loves to talk with marineres
That come from a far countree.

He kneels at morn, and noon, and eve—
He hath a cushion plump: 520
It is the moss that wholly hides
The rotted old oak stump.

The skiff boat neared: I heard them talk,
"Why, this is strange, I trow!
Where are those lights so many and fair, 525
That signal made but now?"

Approacheth the ship with wonder.

"Strange, by my faith!" the Hermit said—
"And they answered not our cheer!
The planks looked warped! and see those sails,
How thin they are and sere! 530
I never saw aught like to them,
Unless perchance it were

Brown skeletons of leaves that lag
My forest-brook along;
When the ivy tod[4] is heavy with snow, 535

4. Clump of ivy.

And the owlet whoops to the wolf below,
That eats the she-wolf's young."

"Dear Lord! it hath a fiendish look,"
The Pilot made reply,
"I am a-feared"—"Push on, push on!"   540
Said the Hermit cheerily.

The boat came closer to the ship,
But I nor spake nor stirred;
The boat came close beneath the ship,
And straight a sound was heard.   545

The ship sud-
denly sinketh.

Under the water it rumbled on,
Still louder and more dread:
It reached the ship, it split the bay;
The ship went down like lead.

The ancient
Mariner is saved
in the Pilot's
boat.

Stunned by that loud and dreadful sound,   550
Which sky and ocean smote,
Like one that hath been seven days drowned
My body lay afloat;
But swift as dreams, myself I found
Within the Pilot's boat.   555

Upon the whirl, where sank the ship,
The boat spun round and round;
And all was still, save that the hill
Was telling of the sound.

I moved my lips—the Pilot shrieked   560
And fell down in a fit;
The holy Hermit raised his eyes,
And prayed where he did sit.

I took the oars: the Pilot's boy,
Who now doth crazy go,   565
Laughed loud and long, and all the while
His eyes went to and fro.
"Ha! ha!" quoth he, "full plain I see,
The Devil knows how to row."

And now, all in my own countree,   570
I stood on the firm land!
The Hermit stepped forth from the boat,
And scarcely he could stand.

The ancient
Mariner ear-
nestly entreateth
the Hermit to
shrieve him; and
the penance of
life falls on him.

"O shrieve me, shrieve me, holy man!"
The Hermit crossed his brow.[5]   575
"Say quick," quoth he, "I bid thee say—
What manner of man art thou?"

5. Made the sign of the cross on his forehead; "shrieve me": hear my confession and grant me absolution.

Forthwith this frame of mine was wrenched
With a woeful agony,
Which forced me to begin my tale;   580
And then it left me free.

And ever and
anon throughout
his future life an
agony constrain-
eth him to travel
from land to
land;

Since then, at an uncertain hour,
That agony returns:
And till my ghastly tale is told,
This heart within me burns.   585

I pass, like night, from land to land;
I have strange power of speech;
That moment that his face I see,
I know the man that must hear me:
To him my tale I teach.   590

What loud uproar bursts from that door!
The wedding guests are there:
But in the garden-bower the bride
And bridemaids singing are:
And hark the little vesper bell,   595
Which biddeth me to prayer!

O Wedding Guest! this soul hath been
Alone on a wide wide sea:
So lonely 'twas, that God himself
Scarce seeméd there to be.   600

O sweeter than the marriage feast,
'Tis sweeter far to me,
To walk together to the kirk
With a goodly company!—

To walk together to the kirk,   605
And all together pray,
While each to his great Father bends,
Old men, and babes, and loving friends
And youths and maidens gay!

And to teach, by
his own exam-
ple, love and rev-
erence to all
things that God
made and loveth.

Farewell, farewell! but this I tell   610
To thee, thou Wedding Guest!
He prayeth well, who loveth well
Both man and bird and beast.

He prayeth best, who loveth best
All things both great and small;   615
For the dear God who loveth us,
He made and loveth all.[6]

6. Coleridge said in 1830, answering the objection of the poet, Mrs. Barbauld. that the poem "lacked a moral": "I told her that in my own judgment the poem had too much; and that the only, or chief fault, if I might say so, was the obtrusion of the moral sentiment so openly on the reader as a principle or cause of action in a work of pure imagi-nation. It ought to have had no more moral than the *Arabian Nights'* tale of the merchant's sitting down to eat dates by the side of a well and throwing the shells aside, and lo! a genie starts up and says he *must* kill the aforesaid merchant *because* one of the date shells had, it seems, put out the eye of the genie's son."

The Mariner, whose eye is bright,
Whose beard with age is hoar,
Is gone: and now the Wedding Guest   620
Turned from the bridegroom's door.

He went like one that hath been stunned,
And is of sense forlorn:[7]
A sadder and a wiser man,
He rose the morrow morn.   625

1797–1816

1798, 1817

Kubla Khan

OR A VISION IN A DREAM. A FRAGMENT

The following fragment is here published at the request of a poet of great and deserved celebrity,[1] and, as far as the author's own opinions are concerned, rather as a psychological curiosity, than on the ground of any supposed *poetic* merits.

In the summer of the year 1797, the author, then in ill health, had retired to a lonely farmhouse between Porlock and Linton, on the Exmoor confines of Somerset and Devonshire. In consequence of a slight indisposition, an anodyne had been prescribed, from the effects of which he fell asleep in his chair at the moment that he was reading the following sentence, or words of the same substance, in *Purchas's Pilgrimage*: "Here the Khan Kubla commanded a palace to be built, and a stately garden thereunto. And thus ten miles of fertile ground were inclosed with a wall."[2] The author continued for about three hours in a profound sleep, at least of the external senses,[3] during which time he has the most vivid confidence that he could not have composed less than from two to three hundred lines; if that indeed can be called composition in which all the images rose up before him as *things*, with a parallel production of the correspondent expressions, without any sensation or consciousness of effort. On awaking he appeared to himself to have a distinct recollection of the whole, and taking his pen, ink, and paper, instantly and eagerly wrote down the lines that are here preserved.

7. Forsaken.
1. Lord Byron.
2. "In Xamdu did Cublai Can build a stately Palace, encompassing sixteene miles of plaine ground with a wall, wherein are fertile Meddowes, pleasant springs, delightfull Streames, and all sorts of beasts of chase and game, and in the middest thereof a sumptuous house of pleasure, which may be removed from place to place." From Samuel Purchas, *Purchas his Pilgrimage* (1613). The historical Kublai

Khan founded the Mongol dynasty in China in the 13th century.
3. In a note on a manuscript copy of *Kubla Khan*, Coleridge gave a more precise account of the nature of this "sleep": "This fragment with a good deal more, not recoverable, composed, in a sort of reverie brought on by two grains of opium, taken to check a dysentery, at a farmhouse between Porlock and Linton, a quarter of a mile from Culbone Church, in the fall of the year, 1797."

At this moment he was unfortunately called out by a person on business from Porlock, and detained by him above an hour, and on his return to his room, found, to his no small surprise and mortification, that though he still retained some vague and dim recollection of the general purport of the vision, yet, with the exception of some eight or ten scattered lines and images, all the rest had passed away like the images on the surface of a stream into which a stone has been cast, but, alas! without the after restoration of the latter!

> Then all the charm
> Is broken—all that phantom world so fair
> Vanishes, and a thousand circlets spread,
> And each misshape[s] the other. Stay awhile,
> Poor youth! who scarcely dar'st lift up thine eyes—
> The stream will soon renew its smoothness, soon
> The visions will return! And lo, he stays,
> And soon the fragments dim of lovely forms
> Come trembling back, unite, and now once more
> The pool becomes a mirror.
>
> [From Coleridge's *The Picture; or, the Lover's Resolution*,
> lines 91–100]

Yet from the still surviving recollections in his mind, the author has frequently purposed to finish for himself what had been originally, as it were, given to him. Σαμερον αδιον ασω: but the to-morrow is yet to come.[4]

In Xanadu did Kubla Khan
A stately pleasure dome decree:
Where Alph,[5] the sacred river, ran
Through caverns measureless to man
    Down to a sunless sea.
So twice five miles of fertile ground   5
With walls and towers were girdled round:
And there were gardens bright with sinuous rills,
Where blossomed many an incense-bearing tree;
And here were forests ancient as the hills,   10
Enfolding sunny spots of greenery.

But oh! that deep romantic chasm which slanted
Down the green hill athwart a cedarn cover!

4. A number of Coleridge's assertions in this preface have been debated by critics: whether the poem was written in 1797 or later; whether it was actually composed in a "dream" or opium reverie; even whether it is a fragment or in fact complete. All critics agree, however, that this visionary poem of daemonic inspiration is much more than a mere "psychological curiosity."

The Greek may be translated, "I shall sing a sweeter song today." In the edition of 1834, Σαμερον ('today') was changed to αὔριον ("tomorrow"). Coleridge had in mind Theocritus, *Idyls* I.145: ἐς ὕστερον ἄδιον ᾀσῶ ("I shall sing a sweeter song on a later day").

5. Derived probably from the Greek river Alpheus, which flows into the Ionian Sea. Its waters were fabled to rise again in Sicily as the fountain of Arethusa; see Milton's *Lycidas*, lines 85 and 132.

A savage place! as holy and enchanted
As e'er beneath a waning moon was haunted   15
By woman wailing for her demon lover!
And from this chasm, with ceaseless turmoil seething,
As if this earth in fast thick pants were breathing,
A mighty fountain momently was forced:
Amid whose swift half-intermitted burst   20
Huge fragments vaulted like rebounding hail,
Or chaffy grain beneath the thresher's flail:
And 'mid these dancing rocks at once and ever
It flung up momently the sacred river.
Five miles meandering with a mazy motion   25
Through wood and dale the sacred river ran,
Then reached the caverns measureless to man,
And sank in tumult to a lifeless ocean:
And 'mid this tumult Kubla heard from far
Ancestral voices prophesying war!   30
　　The shadow of the dome of pleasure
　　Floated midway on the waves;
　　Where was heard the mingled measure
　　From the fountain and the caves.
It was a miracle of rare device,   35
A sunny pleasure dome with caves of ice!

　　A damsel with a dulcimer
　　In a vision once I saw:
　　It was an Abyssinian maid,
　　And on her dulcimer she played,   40
　　Singing of Mount Abora.[6]
Could I revive within me
　　Her symphony and song,
To such a deep delight 'twould win me,
That with music loud and long,   45
I would build that dome in air,
That sunny dome! those caves of ice!
And all who heard should see them there,
And all should cry, Beware! Beware!
His flashing eyes, his floating hair!   50
Weave a circle round him thrice,[7]
And close your eyes with holy dread,
For he on honeydew hath fed,
And drunk the milk of Paradise.[8]

ca. 1797–98   1816

6. Apparently a reminiscence of *Paradise Lost* IV.280–82: "where Abassin Kings their issue guard, / Mount Amara, though this by some supposed / True Paradise under the Ethiop Line."
7. A magic ritual, to protect the inspired poet from intrusion.

8. Lines 50 ff. echo in part the description, in Plato's *Ion* 533–4, of inspired poets, who are "like Bacchic maidens who draw milk and honey from the rivers when they are under the influence of Dionysus but not when they are in their right mind."

Christabel[1]

Preface

The first part of the following poem was written in the year 1797, at Stowey, in the county of Somerset. The second part, after my return from Germany, in the year 1800, at Keswick, Cumberland. It is probable that if the poem had been finished at either of the former periods, or if even the first and second part had been published in the year 1800, the impression of its originality would have been much greater than I dare at present expect. But for this I have only my own indolence to blame. The dates are mentioned for the exclusive purpose of precluding charges of plagiarism or servile imitation from myself. For there is amongst us a set of critics, who seem to hold that every possible thought and image is traditional; who have no notion that there are such things as fountains in the world, small as well as great; and who would therefore charitably derive every rill they behold flowing from a perforation made in some other man's tank. I am confident, however, that as far as the present poem is concerned, the celebrated poets[2] whose writings I might be suspected of having imitated, either in particular passages, or in the tone and the spirit of the whole, would be among the first to vindicate me from the charge, and who, on any striking coincidence, would permit me to address them in this doggerel version of two monkish Latin hexameters.

> 'Tis mine and it is likewise yours;
> But an if this will not do;
> Let it be mine, good friend! for I
> Am the poorer of the two.

I have only to add that the meter of Christabel is not, properly speaking, irregular, though it may seem so from its being founded on a new principle: namely, that of counting in each line the accents, not the syllables.[3] Though the latter may vary from seven

1. Coleridge had planned to publish *Christabel* in the second edition of *Lyrical Ballads* (1800), but had not been able to complete the poem. When *Christabel* was finally published in 1816 in its present fragmentary state, Coleridge still had hopes of finishing it, for the Preface contained this sentence (deleted in the edition of 1834): "But as, in my very first conception of the tale, I had the whole present to my mind, with the wholeness, no less than the liveliness of a vision, I trust that I shall be able to embody in verse the three parts yet to come, in the course of the present year."
2. Sir Walter Scott and Lord Byron, who had read and admired *Christabel*

while it circulated in manuscript. Coleridge has in mind Scott's *Lay of the Last Minstrel* (1805) and Byron's *Siege of Corinth* (1816), which showed the influence of *Christabel*, especially in their meter.
3. Much of the older English versification, following the example of Anglo-Saxon poetry, had been based on stress, or "accent," and some of it shows as much freedom in varying the number of syllables as does *Christabel*. The poem, however, is a radical departure from the theory and practice of versification in the 18th century, which had been based on a recurrent number of syllables in each line.

to twelve, yet in each line the accents will be found to be only four. Nevertheless, this occasional variation in number of syllables is not introduced wantonly, or for the mere ends of convenience, but in correspondence with some transition in the nature of the imagery or passion.

Part I

'Tis the middle of night by the castle clock,
And the owls have awakened the crowing cock;
Tu—whit!——Tu—whoo!
And hark, again! the crowing cock,
How drowsily it crew.   5

Sir Leoline, the Baron rich,
Hath a toothless mastiff bitch;
From her kennel beneath the rock
She maketh answer to the clock,
Four for the quarters, and twelve for the hour;   10
Ever and aye, by shine and shower,
Sixteen short howls, not over loud;
Some say she sees my lady's shroud.

Is the night chilly and dark?
The night is chilly, but not dark.   15
The thin gray cloud is spread on high,
It covers but not hides the sky.
The moon is behind, and at the full;
And yet she looks both small and dull.
The night is chill, the cloud is gray: 20
'Tis a month before the month of May,
And the spring comes slowly up this way.

The lovely lady, Christabel,
Whom her father loves so well,
What makes her in the wood so late,   25
A furlong from the castle gate?
She had dreams all yesternight
Of her own betrothéd knight;
And she in the midnight wood will pray
For the weal[4] of her lover that's far away.   30

She stole along, she nothing spoke.
The sighs she heaved were soft and low,
And naught was green upon the oak
But moss and rarest mistletoe:[5]
She kneels beneath the huge oak tree,   35
And in silence prayeth she.

The lady sprang up suddenly,
The lovely lady, Christabel!

4. Well-being.
5. In Celtic Britain the mistletoe (a parasitic plant) had been held in veneration when it was found growing—as it rarely does—on an oak tree (its usual host is the apple tree).

It moaned as near, as near can be,
But what it is she cannot tell.—
On the other side it seems to be,
Of the huge, broad-breasted, old oak tree. 40

The night is chill; the forest bare;
Is it the wind that moaneth bleak?
There is not wind enough in the air 45
To move away the ringlet curl
From the lovely lady's cheek—
There is not wind enough to twirl
The one red leaf, the last of its clan,
That dances as often as dance it can, 50
Hanging so light, and hanging so high,
On the topmost twig that looks up at the sky.

Hush, beating heart of Christabel!
Jesu, Maria, shield her well!
She folded her arms beneath her cloak, 55
And stole to the other side of the oak.
    What sees she there?

There she sees a damsel bright,
Dressed in a silken robe of white,
That shadowy in the moonlight shone: 60
The neck that made that white robe wan,
Her stately neck, and arms were bare;
Her blue-veined feet unsandaled were,
And wildly glittered here and there
The gems entangled in her hair. 65
I guess, 'twas frightful there to see
A lady so richly clad as she—
Beautiful exceedingly!

"Mary mother, save me now!"
Said Christabel, "And who art thou?" 70

The lady strange made answer meet,
And her voice was faint and sweet—
"Have pity on my sore distress,
I scarce can speak for weariness:
Stretch forth thy hand, and have no fear!" 75
Said Christabel, "How camest thou here?"
And the lady, whose voice was faint and sweet,
Did thus pursue her answer meet—

"My sire is of a noble line,
And my name is Geraldine: 80
Five warriors seized me yestermorn,
Me, even me, a maid forlorn:
They choked my cries with force and fright,
And tied me on a palfrey white.

The palfrey was as fleet as wind,   85
And they rode furiously behind.
They spurred amain,[6] their steeds were white:
And once we crossed the shade of night.
As sure as Heaven shall rescue me,
I have no thought what men they be;   90
Nor do I know how long it is
(For I have lain entranced, I wis[7])
Since one, the tallest of the five,
Took me from the palfrey's back,
A weary woman, scarce alive.   95

"Some muttered words his comrades spoke:
He placed me underneath this oak;
He swore they would return with haste;
Whither they went I cannot tell—
I thought I heard, some minutes past,   100
Sounds as of a castle bell.
Stretch forth thy hand," thus ended she,
"And help a wretched maid to flee."

Then Christabel stretched forth her hand,
And comforted fair Geraldine: 105
"O well, bright dame! may you command
The service of Sir Leoline;
And gladly our stout chivalry
Will he send forth and friends withal
To guide and guard you safe and free   110
Home to your noble father's hall."

She rose: and forth with steps they passed
That strove to be, and were not, fast.
Her gracious stars the lady blessed,
And thus spake on sweet Christabel: 115
"All our household are at rest,
The hall as silent as the cell;
Sir Leoline is weak in health,
And may not well awakened be,
But we will move as if in stealth,   120
And I beseech your courtesy,
This night, to share your couch with me."

They crossed the moat, and Christabel
Took the key that fitted well;
A little door she opened straight,   125
All in the middle of the gate;
The gate that was ironed within and without,
Where an army in battle array had marched out.
The lady sank, belike through pain,

6. At top speed.
7. I believe; Coleridge's minsinterpre-
tation of the Middle English adverb
"ywis," meaning "certainly."

And Christabel with might and main
Lifted her up, a weary weight,
Over the threshold of the gate:[8]
Then the lady rose again,
And moved, as she were not in pain.

So free from danger, free from fear,
They crossed the court: right glad they were.
And Christabel devoutly cried
To the lady by her side,
"Praise we the Virgin all divine
Who hath rescued thee from thy distress!"
"Alas, alas!" said Geraldine,
"I cannot speak for weariness."
So free from danger, free from fear,
They crossed the court: right glad they were.

Outside her kennel, the mastiff old
Lay fast asleep, in moonshine cold.
The mastiff old did not awake,
Yet she an angry moan did make!
And what can ail the mastiff bitch?
Never till now she uttered yell
Beneath the eye of Christabel.
Perhaps it is the owlet's scritch:
For what can ail the mastiff bitch?

They passed the hall, that echoes still,
Pass as lightly as you will!
The brands were flat, the brands were dying,
Amid their own white ashes lying;
But when the lady passed, there came
A tongue of light, a fit of flame;
And Christabel saw the lady's eye,
And nothing else saw she thereby,
Save the boss of the shield of Sir Leoline tall,
Which hung in a murky old niche in the wall.
"O softly tread," said Christabel,
"My father seldom sleepeth well."

Sweet Christabel her feet doth bare,
And jealous of the listening air
They steal their way from stair to stair,
Now in glimmer, and now in gloom,
And now they pass the Baron's room,
As still as death, with stifled breath!
And now have reached her chamber door;
And now doth Geraldine press down
The rushes[9] of the chamber floor.

130

135

140

145

150

155

160

165

170

8. She cannot cross the threshold by her
own power because it has been blessed
against evil spirits; this is the first of
several indications that Geraldine is a
malign being.
9. Often used as a floor-covering in the
Middle Ages.

The moon shines dim in the open air,   175
And not a moonbeam enters here.
But they without its light can see
The chamber carved so curiously,
Carved with figures strange and sweet,
All made out of the carver's brain,   180
For a lady's chamber meet:
The lamp with twofold silver chain
Is fastened to an angel's feet.

The silver lamp burns dead and dim;
But Christabel the lamp will trim.   185
She trimmed the lamp, and made it bright,
And left it swinging to and fro,
While Geraldine, in wretched plight,
Sank down upon the floor below.

"O weary lady, Geraldine,   190
I pray you, drink this cordial wine!
It is a wine of virtuous powers;
My mother made it of wild flowers."

"And will your mother pity me,
Who am a maiden most forlorn?"   195
Christabel answered—"Woe is me!
She died the hour that I was born.
I have heard the gray-haired friar tell
How on her deathbed she did say,
That she should hear the castle bell   200
Strike twelve upon my wedding day.
O mother dear! that thou wert here!"
"I would," said Geraldine, "she were!"
But soon with altered voice, said she—
"Off, wandering mother! Peak and pine!   205
I have power to bid thee flee."
Alas! what ails poor Geraldine?
Why stares she with unsettled eye?
Can she the bodiless dead espy?
And why with hollow voice cries she,   210
"Off, woman, off! this hour is mine—
Though thou her guardian spirit be,
Off, woman, off! 'tis given to me."

Then Christabel knelt by the lady's side,
And raised to heaven her eyes so blue—   215
"Alas!" said she, "this ghastly ride—
Dear lady! it hath 'wildered you!"
The lady wiped her moist cold brow,
And faintly said, " 'tis over now!"

Again the wild-flower wine she drank: 220
Her fair large eyes 'gan glitter bright,

And from the floor whereon she sank,
The lofty lady stood upright:
She was most beautiful to see,
Like a lady of a far countree.   225

And thus the lofty lady spake—
"All they who live in the upper sky,
Do love you, holy Christabel!
And you love them, and for their sake
And for the good which me befell.   230
Even I in my degree will try,
Fair maiden, to requite you well.
But now unrobe yourself; for I
Must pray, ere yet in bed I lie."
Quoth Christabel, "So let it be!"   235
And as the lady bade, did she.
Her gentle limbs did she undress,
And lay down in her loveliness.

But through her brain of weal and woe
So many thoughts moved to and fro,   240
That vain it were her lids to close;
So halfway from the bed she rose,
And on her elbow did recline
To look at the lady Geraldine.

Beneath the lamp the lady bowed,   245
And slowly rolled her eyes around;
Then drawing in her breath aloud,
Like one that shuddered, she unbound
The cincture[1] from beneath her breast:
Her silken robe, and inner vest,   250
Dropped to her feet, and full in view,
Behold! her bosom and half her side——
A sight to dream of, not to tell!
O shield her! shield sweet Christabel!

Yet Geraldine nor speaks nor stirs;   255
Ah! what a stricken look was hers!
Deep from within she seems halfway
To lift some weight with sick assay,[2]
And eyes the maid and seeks delay;
Then suddenly, as one defied,   260
Collects herself in scorn and pride,
And lay down by the maiden's side!—
And in her arms the maid she took,
          Ah well-a-day!
And with low voice and doleful look   265
These words did say:
"In the touch of this bosom there worketh a spell,
Which is lord of thy utterance, Christabel!

1. Belt.   2. Attempt.

Thou knowest tonight, and wilt know tomorrow,
This mark of my shame, this seal of my sorrow;   270
    But vainly thou warrest,
      For this is alone in
    Thy power to declare,
      That in the dim forest
    Thou heard'st a low moaning,   275
And found'st a bright lady, surpassingly fair;
And didst bring her home with thee in love and in charity,
To shield her and shelter her from the damp air."

The Conclusion to Part I

It was a lovely sight to see
The lady Christabel, when she   280
Was praying at the old oak tree.
    Amid the jagged shadows
    Of mossy leafless boughs,
    Kneeling in the moonlight,
    To make her gentle vows;   285
Her slender palms together pressed,
Heaving sometimes on her breast;
Her face resigned to bliss or bale[1]—
Her face, oh call it fair not pale,
And both blue eyes more bright than **clear**,   290
Each about to have a tear.

With open eyes (ah woe is me!)
Asleep, and dreaming fearfully,
Fearfully dreaming, yet I wis,
Dreaming that alone, which is—   295
O sorrow and shame! Can this be she,
The lady, who knelt at the old oak tree?
And lo! the worker of these harms,
That holds the maiden in her arms,
Seems to slumber still and mild,   300
As a mother with her child.

A star hath set, a star hath risen,
O Geraldine! since arms of thine
Have been the lovely lady's prison.
O Geraldine! one hour was thine—   305
Thou'st had thy will! By tairn[2] and rill,
The night birds all that hour were still.
But now they are jubilant anew,
From cliff and tower, tu—whoo! tu—whoo!
Tu—whoo! tu—whoo! from wood and fell![3]   310

And see! the lady Christabel
Gathers herself from out her trance;
Her limbs relax, her countenance

---

1. Evil, sorrow.   3. Elevated moor, or hill.
2. Tarn, a mountain pool.

Grows sad and soft; the smooth thin lids
Close o'er her eyes; and tears she sheds—
Large tears that leave the lashes bright!   315
And oft the while she seems to smile
As infants at a sudden light!

Yea, she doth smile, and she doth weep,
Like a youthful hermitess,
Beauteous in a wilderness,   320
Who, praying always, prays in sleep.
And, if she move unquietly,
Perchance, 'tis but the blood so free
Comes back and tingles in her feet.
No doubt, she hath a vision sweet.   325
What if her guardian spirit 'twere,
What if she knew her mother near?
But this she knows, in joys and woes,
That saints will aid if men will call:
For the blue sky bends over all!   330

Part II

"Each matin bell," the Baron saith,
"Knells us back to a world of death."
These words Sir Leoline first said,
When he rose and found his lady dead:
These words Sir Leoline will say   335
Many a morn to his dying day!

And hence the custom and law began
That still at dawn the sacristan,
Who duly pulls the heavy bell,
Five and forty beads must tell[4]   340
Between each stroke—a warning knell,
Which not a soul can choose but hear
From Bratha Head to Wyndermere.[5]

Saith Bracy the bard, "So let it knell!
And let the drowsy sacristan   345
Still count as slowly as he can!
There is no lack of such, I ween,
As well fill up the space between.
In Langdale Pike[6] and Witch's Lair,
And Dungeon Ghyll[7] so foully rent,   350
With ropes of rock and bells of air
Three sinful sextons' ghosts are pent,
Who all give back, one after t'other,
The death note to their living brother;
And oft too, by the knell offended,   355

4. Pray while "telling" (keeping count on) the beads of a rosary. "Sacristan": sexton.
5. These and the following names are of localities in the English Lake Country.
6. Peak.
7. Ravine forming the bed of a stream.

Just as their one! two! three! is ended,
The devil mocks the doleful tale
With a merry peal from Borodale."

The air is still! through mist and cloud   360
That merry peal comes ringing loud;
And Geraldine shakes off her dread,
And rises lightly from the bed;
Puts on her silken vestments white,
And tricks her hair in lovely plight,[8]   365
And nothing doubting of her spell
Awakens the lady Christabel.
"Sleep you, sweet lady Christabel?
I trust that you have rested well."

And Christabel awoke and spied   370
The same who lay down by her side—
O rather say, the same whom she
Raised up beneath the old oak tree!
Nay, fairer yet! and yet more fair!
For she belike hath drunken deep   375
Of all the blessedness of sleep!
And while she spake, her looks, her air
Such gentle thankfulness declare,
That (so it seemed) her girded vests
Grew tight beneath her heaving breasts.   380
"Sure I have sinned!" said Christabel,
"Now heaven be praised if all be well!"
And in low faltering tones, yet sweet,
Did she the lofty lady greet
With such perplexity of mind   385
As dreams too lively leave behind.

So quickly she rose, and quickly arrayed
Her maiden limbs, and having prayed
That He, who on the cross did groan,
Might wash away her sins unknown,   390
She forthwith led fair Geraldine
To meet her sire, Sir Leoline.

The lovely maid and the lady tall
Are pacing both into the hall,
And pacing on through page and groom,   395
Enter the Baron's presence-room.

The Baron rose, and while he pressed
His gentle daughter to his breast,
With cheerful wonder in his eyes
The lady Geraldine espies,   400
And gave such welcome to the same,
As might beseem so bright a dame!

8. Plait.

But when he heard the lady's tale,
And when she told her father's name,
Why waxed Sir Leoline so pale,   405
Murmuring o'er the name again,
Lord Roland de Vaux of Tryermaine?

Alas! they had been friends in youth;
But whispering tongues can poison truth;
And constancy lives in realms above;   410
And life is thorny; and youth is vain;
And to be wroth with one we love
Doth work like madness in the brain.
And thus it chanced, as I divine,
With Roland and Sir Leoline.   415
Each spake words of high disdain
And insult to his heart's best brother:
They parted—ne'er to meet again!
But never either found another
To free the hollow heart from paining—   420
They stood aloof, the scars remaining,
Like cliffs which had been rent asunder;
A dreary sea now flows between—
But neither heat, nor frost, nor thunder,
Shall wholly do away, I ween,   425
The marks of that which once hath been.

Sir Leoline, a moment's space,
Stood gazing on the damsel's face:
And the youthful Lord of Tryermaine
Came back upon his heart again.   430

O then the Baron forgot his age,
His noble heart swelled high with rage;
He swore by the wounds in Jesu's side
He would proclaim it far and wide,
With trump and solemn heraldry,   435
That they, who thus had wronged the dame,
Were base as spotted infamy!
"And if they dare deny the same,
My herald shall appoint a week,
And let the recreant traitors seek   440
My tourney court—that there and then
I may dislodge their reptile souls
From the bodies and forms of men!"
He spake: his eye in lightning rolls!
For the lady was ruthlessly seized; and he kenned   445
In the beautiful lady the child of his friend!

And now the tears were on his face,
And fondly in his arms he took
Fair Geraldine, who met the embrace,
Prolonging it with joyous look.   450

Which when she viewed, a vision fell
Upon the soul of Christabel,
The vision of fear, the touch and pain!
She shrunk and shuddered, and saw again—
(Ah, woe is me! Was it for thee,   455
Thou gentle maid! such sights to see?)

Again she saw that bosom old,
Again she felt that bosom cold,
And drew in her breath with a hissing sound:
Whereat the Knight turned wildly round,   460
And nothing saw, but his own sweet maid
With eyes upraised, as one that prayed.
The touch, the sight, had passed away,
And in its stead that vision blest,
Which comforted her after-rest   465
While in the lady's arms she lay,
Had put a rapture in her breast,
And on her lips and o'er her eyes
Spread smiles like light!
                              With new surprise,
"What ails then my belovéd child?"   470
The Baron said—His daughter mild
Made answer, "All will yet be well!"
I ween, she had no power to tell
Aught else: so mighty was the spell.

Yet he, who saw this Geraldine,   475
Had deemed her sure a thing divine:
Such sorrow with such grace she blended,
As if she feared she had offended
Sweet Christabel, that gentle maid!
And with such lowly tones she prayed   480
She might be sent without delay
Home to her father's mansion.
                                "Nay!
Nay, by my soul!" said Leoline.
"Ho! Bracy the bard, the charge be thine!
Go thou, with music sweet and loud,   485
And take two steeds with trappings proud,
And take the youth whom thou lov'st best
To bear thy harp, and learn thy song,
And clothe you both in solemn vest,
And over the mountains haste along,   490
Lest wandering folk, that are abroad,
Detain you on the valley road.

"And when he has crossed the Irthing flood,
My merry bard! he hastes, he hastes
Up Knorren Moor, through Halegarth Wood,   495
And reaches soon that castle good
Which stands and threatens Scotland's wastes.

"Bard Bracy! bard Bracy! your horses are fleet,
Ye must ride up the hall, your music so sweet,
More loud than your horses' echoing feet!
And loud and loud to Lord Roland call,   500
Thy daughter is safe in Langdale hall!
Thy beautiful daughter is safe and free—
Sir Leoline greets thee thus through me!
He bids thee come without delay
With all thy numerous array   505
And take thy lovely daughter home:
And he will meet thee on the way
With all his numerous array
White with their panting palfreys' foam:
And, by mine honor! I will say,   510
That I repent me of the day
When I spake words of fierce disdain
To Roland de Vaux of Tryermaine!—
For since that evil hour hath flown,
Many a summer's sun hath shone;   515
Yet ne'er found I a friend again
Like Roland de Vaux of Tryermaine."

The lady fell, and clasped his knees,
Her face upraised, her eyes o'erflowing;
And Bracy replied, with faltering voice,   520
His gracious Hail on all bestowing!—
"Thy words, thou sire of Christabel,
Are sweeter than my harp can tell;
Yet might I gain a boon of thee,
This day my journey should not be,   525
So strange a dream hath come to me,
That I had vowed with music loud
To clear yon wood from thing unblest,
Warned by a vision in my rest!
For in my sleep I saw that dove,   530
That gentle bird, whom thou dost love,
And call'st by thy own daughter's name—
Sir Leoline! I saw the same
Fluttering, and uttering fearful moan,
Among the green herbs in the forest alone.   535
Which when I saw and when I heard,
I wondered what might ail the bird;
For nothing near it could I see,
Save the grass and green herbs underneath the old tree.   540

"And in my dream methought I went
To search out what might there be found;
And what the sweet bird's trouble meant,
That thus lay fluttering on the ground.
I went and peered, and could descry   545

No cause for her distressful cry;
But yet for her dear lady's sake
I stooped, methought, the dove to take,
When lo! I saw a bright green snake
Coiled around its wings and neck.   550
Green as the herbs on which it couched,
Close by the dove's its head it crouched;
And with the dove it heaves and stirs,
Swelling its neck as she swelled hers!
I woke; it was the midnight hour,   555
The clock was echoing in the tower;
But though my slumber was gone by,
This dream it would not pass away—
It seems to live upon my eye!
And thence I vowed this selfsame day   560
With music strong and saintly song
To wander through the forest bare,
Lest aught unholy loiter there."

Thus Bracy said: the Baron, the while,
Half-listening heard him with a smile;   565
Then turned to Lady Geraldine,
His eyes made up of wonder and love;
And said in courtly accents fine,
"Sweet maid, Lord Roland's beauteous dove,
With arms more strong than harp or song,   570
Thy sire and I will crush the snake!"
He kissed her forehead as he spake,
And Geraldine in maiden wise
Casting down her large bright eyes,
With blushing cheek and courtesy fine   575
She turned her from Sir Leoline;
Softly gathering up her train,
That o'er her right arm fell again;
And folded her arms across her chest,
And couched her head upon her breast,   580
And looked askance at Christabel——
Jesu, Maria, shield her well!

A snake's small eye blinks dull and shy;
And the lady's eyes they shrunk in her head,
Each shrunk up to a serpent's eye,   585
And with somewhat of malice, and more of dread,
At Christabel she looked askance!—
One moment—and the sight was fled!
But Christabel in dizzy trance
Stumbling on the unsteady ground   590
Shuddered aloud, with a hissing sound;
And Geraldine again turned round,
And like a thing, that sought relief,

Full of wonder and full of grief,
She rolled her large bright eyes divine   595
Wildly on Sir Leoline.

The maid, alas! her thoughts are gone,
She nothing sees—no sight but one!
The maid, devoid of guile and sin,
I know not how, in fearful wise,   600
So deeply had she drunken in
That look, those shrunken serpent eyes,
That all her features were resigned
To this sole image in her mind:
And passively did imitate   605
That look of dull and treacherous hate!
And thus she stood, in dizzy trance,
Still picturing that look askance
With forced unconscious sympathy
Full before her father's view—   610
As far as such a look could be
In eyes so innocent and blue!

And when the trance was o'er, the maid
Paused awhile, and inly prayed:
Then falling at the Baron's feet,   615
"By my mother's soul do I entreat
That thou this woman send away!"
She said: and more she could not say:
For what she knew she could not tell,
O'ermastered by the mighty spell.   620

Why is thy cheek so wan and wild,
Sir Leoline? Thy only child
Lies at thy feet, thy joy, thy pride,
So fair, so innocent, so mild;
The same, for whom thy lady died!   625
O by the pangs of her dear mother
Think thou no evil of thy child!
For her, and thee, and for no other,
She prayed the moment ere she died:
Prayed that the babe for whom she died,   630
Might prove her dear lord's joy and pride!
    That prayer her deadly pangs beguiled,
            Sir Leoline!
    And wouldst thou wrong thy only child,
            Her child and thine?   635

Within the Baron's heart and brain
If thoughts, like these, had any share,
They only swelled his rage and pain,
And did but work confusion there.
His heart was cleft with pain and rage,
His cheeks they quivered, his eyes were wild,   640

Dishonored thus in his old age;
Dishonored by his only child,
And all his hospitality
To the wronged daughter of his friend   645
By more than woman's jealousy
Brought thus to a disgraceful end—
He rolled his eye with stern regard
Upon the gentle minstrel bard,
And said in tones abrupt, austere—   650
"Why, Bracy! dost thou loiter here?
I bade thee hence!" The bard obeyed;
And turning from his own sweet maid,
The agéd knight, Sir Leoline,
Led forth the lady Geraldine!   655

The Conclusion to Part II

A little child, a limber elf,
Singing, dancing to itself,
A fairy thing with red round checks,
That always finds, and never seeks,
Makes such a vision to the sight   660
As fills a father's eyes with light;
And pleasures flow in so thick and fast
Upon his heart, that he at last
Must needs express his love's excess
With words of unmeant bitterness.   665
Perhaps 'tis pretty to force together
Thoughts so all unlike each other;
To mutter and mock a broken charm,
To dally with wrong that does no harm.
Perhaps 'tis tender too and pretty   670
At each wild word to feel within
A sweet recoil of love and pity.
And what, if in a world of sin
(O sorrow and shame should this be true!)
Such giddiness of heart and brain   675
Comes seldom save from rage and pain,
So talks as it's most used to do.

1797–1801   1816

Frost at Midnight[1]

The Frost performs its secret ministry,
Unhelped by any wind. The owlet's cry
Came loud—and hark, again! loud as before.
The inmates of my cottage, all at rest,
Have left me to that solitude, which suits   5

---

1. The scene is Coleridge's cottage at   his son Hartley.
Nether Stowey; the infant in line 7 is

Abstruser musings: save that at my side
My cradled infant slumbers peacefully.
'Tis calm indeed! so calm, that it disturbs
And vexes meditation with its strange
And extreme silentness. Sea, hill, and wood,   10
This populous village! Sea, and hill, and wood,
With all the numberless goings-on of life,
Inaudible as dreams! the thin blue flame
Lies on my low-burnt fire, and quivers not;
Only that film,[2] which fluttered on the grate,   15
Still flutters there, the sole unquiet thing.
Methinks its motion in this hush of nature
Gives it dim sympathies with me who live,
Making it a companionable form,
Whose puny flaps and freaks the idling Spirit   20
By its own moods interprets, everywhere
Echo or mirror seeking of itself,
And makes a toy of Thought.

                 But O! how oft,
How oft, at school, with most believing mind,
Presageful, have I gazed upon the bars,   25
To watch that fluttering *stranger!* and as oft
With unclosed lids, already had I dreamt
Of my sweet birthplace,[3] and the old church tower,
Whose bells, the poor man's only music, rang
From morn to evening, all the hot fair-day,   30
So sweetly, that they stirred and haunted me
With a wild pleasure, falling on mine ear
Most like articulate sounds of things to come!
So gazed I, till the soothing things, I dreamt,
Lulled me to sleep, and sleep prolonged my dreams!   35
And so I brooded all the following morn,
Awed by the stern preceptor's face,[4] mine eye
Fixed with mock study on my swimming book:
Save if the door half opened, and I snatched
A hasty glance, and still my heart leaped up,   40
For still I hoped to see the *stranger's* face,
Townsman, or aunt, or sister more beloved,
My playmate when we both were clothed alike![5]

    Dear Babe, that sleepest cradled by my side,
Whose gentle breathings, heard in this deep calm,   45
Fill up the interspersèd vacancies
And momentary pauses of the thought!
My babe so beautiful! it thrills my heart

---

2. "In all parts of the kingdom these films are called *strangers* and supposed to portend the arrival of some absent friend" [Coleridge's note]. The "film" is a piece of soot fluttering on the bar of the grate.
3. Coleridge was born at Ottery St. Mary, Devonshire, but went to school in London, beginning at the age of 9.
4. The "stern preceptor" at Coleridge's school, Christ's Hospital, was the Rev. James Boyer, whom Coleridge describes in *Biographia Literaria*, Chapter I.
5. I.e., when both Coleridge and his sister Ann still wore infant clothes.

With tender gladness, thus to look at thee,
And think that thou shalt learn far other lore, 50
And in far other scenes! For I was reared
In the great city, pent 'mid cloisters dim,
And saw nought lovely but the sky and stars.
But *thou*, my babe! shalt wander like a breeze
By lakes and sandy shores, beneath the crags 55
Of ancient mountain, and beneath the clouds,
Which image in their bulk both lakes and shores
And mountain crags: so shalt thou see and hear
The lovely shapes and sounds intelligible
Of that eternal language, which thy God 60
Utters, who from eternity doth teach
Himself in all, and all things in himself.
Great universal Teacher! he shall mold
Thy spirit, and by giving make it ask.

Therefore all seasons shall be sweet to thee, 65
Whether the summer clothe the general earth
With greenness, or the redbreast sit and sing
Betwixt the tufts of snow on the bare branch
Of mossy apple tree, while the nigh thatch
Smokes in the sun-thaw; whether the eave-drops fall 70
Heard only in the trances of the blast,
Or if the secret ministry of frost
Shall hang them up in silent icicles,
Quietly shining to the quiet Moon.

February, 1798

Somewhat self-pitying? 1798

Dejection: An Ode[1]

Late, late yestreen I saw the new Moon,
With the old Moon in her arms;
And I fear, I fear, my master dear!
We shall have a deadly storm.
Ballad of Sir Patrick Spence

1

Well! If the bard was weather-wise, who made
The grand old ballad of Sir Patrick Spence,
This night, so tranquil now, will not go hence

1. This poem originated in a verse letter of 340 lines, called *A Letter to ———*, which Coleridge wrote on the night of April 4, 1802, after hearing the opening stanzas of *Ode: Intimations of Immortality*, which Wordsworth had just composed. The *Letter* was addressed to Sara Hutchinson (whom Coleridge sometimes called "Asra"), the sister of Wordsworth's fiancée Mary. It picked up the theme of a loss in the quality of perceptual experience which Wordsworth had presented at the beginning of his *Ode*. In his original poem, Coleridge lamented at length his unhappy marriage and the hopelessness of his love for Sara Hutchinson. In the next six months Coleridge deleted more than half the original lines, revised and reordered the remaining passages, and so transformed a long verse confession into the compact and dignified *Dejection: An Ode*. He published the *Ode*, in substantially its present form, on October 4, 1802, Wordsworth's wedding day—and also the seventh anniversary of Coleridge's own disastrous marriage to Sara Fricker. Coleridge's implicit concern with the marital relation emerges in the marriage metaphors of lines 49 and 67–70.

Unroused by winds, that ply a busier trade
Than those which mold yon cloud in lazy flakes,
Or the dull sobbing draft, that moans and rakes   5
Upon the strings of this Aeolian lute,[2]
    Which better far were mute.
  For lo! the New-moon winter-bright!
  And overspread with phantom light,   10
  (With swimming phantom light o'erspread
  But rimmed and circled by a silver thread)
I see the old Moon in her lap, foretelling
  The coming-on of rain and squally blast.
And oh! that even now the gust were swelling,   15
  And the slant night shower driving loud and fast!
Those sounds which oft have raised me, whilst they awed,
    And sent my soul abroad,
Might now perhaps their wonted[3] impulse give,
Might startle this dull pain, and make it move and live!   20

2

A grief without a pang, void, dark, and drear,
  A stifled, drowsy, unimpassioned grief,
  Which finds no natural outlet, no relief,
    In word, or sigh, or tear—
O Lady![4] in this wan and heartless mood,   25
To other thoughts by yonder throstle wooed,
  All this long eve, so balmy and serene,
Have I been gazing on the western sky,
  And its peculiar tint of yellow green:
And still I gaze—and with how blank an eye!   30
And those thin clouds above, in flakes and bars,
That give away their motion to the stars;
Those stars, that glide behind them or between,
Now sparkling, now bedimmed, but always seen:
Yon crescent Moon, as fixed as if it grew   35
In its own cloudless, starless lake of blue;
I see them all so excellently fair,
I see, not feel, how beautiful they are!

[handwritten annotation: Extreme state of melancholy.]

3

  My genial[5] spirits fail;
  And what can these avail
To lift the smothering weight from off my breast?   40
  It were a vain endeavor,
  Though I should gaze forever
On that green light that lingers in the west:
I may not hope from outward forms to win
The passion and the life, whose fountains are within.   45

2. A stringed instrument played upon by the wind; see Coleridge's *The Eolian Harp*, note 1.
3. Customary.
4. In the original version "Sara"—i.e., Sara Hutchinson. After intervening versions, in which the poem was addressed first to "William" (Wordsworth) and then to "Edmund," Coleridge introduced the noncommittal "Lady" in 1817.
5. In its old use as the adjective form of "genius": "My innate powers fail."

4

O Lady! we receive but what we give,
　And in our life alone does Nature live:
Ours is her wedding garment, ours her shroud![6]   *— Importance of the individual's perception.*
　　And would we aught behold, of higher worth,   50
Than that inanimate cold world allowed
To the poor loveless ever-anxious crowd,
　　Ah! from the soul itself must issue forth
A light, a glory,[7] a fair luminous cloud
　　　Enveloping the Earth—   55
And from the soul itself must there be sent
　A sweet and potent voice, of its own birth,
Of all sweet sounds the life and element!

5

O pure of heart! thou need'st not ask of me
What this strong music in the soul may be!   60
What, and wherein it doth exist,
This light, this glory, this fair luminous mist,
This beautiful and beauty-making power.
　　Joy,[8] virtuous Lady! Joy that ne'er was given,
Save to the pure, and in their purest hour,   65
Life, and Life's effluence, cloud at once and shower,
Joy, Lady! is the spirit and the power,
Which wedding Nature to us gives in dower
　　A new Earth and new Heaven,[9]
Undreamt of by the sensual and the proud—   70
Joy is the sweet voice, Joy the luminous cloud—
　　　We in ourselves rejoice!
And thence flows all that charms or ear or sight,
　All melodies the echoes of that voice,
All colors a suffusion from that light.   75

6

There was a time when, though my path was rough,
　This joy within me dallied with distress,
And all misfortunes were but as the stuff   *Past*
　Whence Fancy made me dreams of happiness:
For hope grew round me, like the twining vine,   80
And fruits, and foliage, not my own, seemed mine.
But now afflictions bow me down to earth: *— Present.*

---

6. I.e., whether nature is experienced as "inanimate" (line 51) or in living interchange with the observer depends on the apathy or joyous vitality of the observer's own spirit.
7. Coleridge commonly used "glory" not in the sense of a halo, merely, but as a term for a mountain phenomenon in which a walker sees his own figure projected by the sun in the mist, enlarged, and with a circle of light around its head.
8. Coleridge often uses "Joy" for a sense of abounding vitality and of harmony between one's inner life and the life of nature. He sometimes calls the contrary "exsiccation," or spiritual dryness.
9. The sense becomes clearer if line 68 is punctuated in the way that Coleridge himself punctuated it when quoting the passage in one of his essays: "Which, wedding Nature to us, gives in dower." I.e., "Joy" is the condition which (overcoming the alienation between mind and its milieu) marries us to "Nature," and gives by way of wedding portion ("dower") the experience of a renovated world.

Nor care I that they rob me of my mirth;
  But oh! each visitation
Suspends what nature gave me at my birth,   85
  My shaping spirit of Imagination.
For not to think of what I needs must feel,
  But to be still and patient, all I can;
And happly by abstruse research to steal
  From my own nature all the natural man—   90
This was my sole resource, my only plan:
Till that which suits a part infects the whole,
And now is almost grown the habit of my soul.

7

Hence, viper thoughts, that coil around my mind,
  Reality's dark dream!   95
I turn from you, and listen to the wind,
  Which long has raved unnoticed. What a scream
Of agony by torture lengthened out
That lute sent forth! Thou Wind, that rav'st without,
  Bare crag, or mountain tairn,[1] or blasted tree, 100
Or pine grove whither woodman never clomb,
Or lonely house, long held the witches' home,
  Methinks were fitter instruments for thee,
Mad lutanist! who in this month of showers,
Of dark-brown gardens, and of peeping flowers,   105
Mak'st devils' yule,[2] with worse than wintry song,
The blossoms, buds, and timorous leaves among.
  Thou actor, perfect in all tragic sounds!
Thou mighty poet, e'en to frenzy bold!
  What tell'st thou now about?   110
  'Tis of the rushing of an host in rout,
  With groans, of trampled men, with smarting wounds—
At once they groan with pain, and shudder with the cold!
But hush! there is a pause of deepest silence!
  And all that noise, as of a rushing crowd,   115
With groans, and tremulous shudderings—all is over—
  It tells another tale, with sounds less deep and loud!
  A tale of less affright,
  And tempered with delight,
As Otway's[3] self had framed the tender lay—   120
  'Tis of a little child
  Upon a lonesome wild,
Not far from home, but she hath lost her way:
And now moans low in bitter grief and fear,
And now screams loud, and hopes to make her mother hear. 125

8

'Tis midnight, but small thoughts have I of sleep:
Full seldom may my friend such vigils keep!

---

1. Tarn, or mountain pool.
2. Christmas, in the perverted form in which it is celebrated by devils.
3. Thomas Otway (1652–85), a dram- atist noted for the pathos of his tragic passages. The poet originally named was "William," and the allusion was probably to Wordsworth's *Lucy Gray*.

Visit her, gentle Sleep! with wings of healing,
  And may this storm be but a mountain birth,[4]
May all the stars hang bright above her dwelling,   130
    Silent as though they watched the sleeping Earth!
      With light heart may she rise,
        Gay fancy, cheerful eyes,
    Joy lift her spirit, joy attune her voice;
To her may all things live, from pole to pole,   135
  Their life the eddying of her living soul!
    O simple spirit, guided from above,
  Dear Lady! friend devoutest of my choice,
  Thus mayest thou ever, evermore rejoice.

April 4, 1802   1802, 1817

The Pains of Sleep[1]

Ere on my bed my limbs I lay,
It hath not been my use to pray
With moving lips or bended knees;
But silently, by slow degrees,
My spirit I to Love compose,   5
In humble trust mine eye-lids close,
With reverential resignation,
No wish conceived, no thought exprest,
Only a sense of supplication;
A sense o'er all my soul imprest   10
That I am weak, yet not unblest,
Since in me, round me, every where
Eternal Strength and Wisdom are.

But yester-night I prayed aloud
In anguish and in agony,   15
Up-starting from the fiendish crowd
Of shapes and thoughts that tortured me:
A lurid light, a trampling throng,
Sense of intolerable wrong,
And whom I scorned, those only strong!   20

Thirst of revenge, the powerless will
Still baffled, and yet burning still!

4. Probably, "May this be a typical mountain storm, short though violent," although it is possible that Coleridge intended an allusion to Horace's phrase, "the mountain labored and brought forth a mouse."

1. Coleridge included a draft of this poem in a letter to Robert Southey, September 11, 1803, in which he wrote that "my spirits are dreadful, owing entirely to the Horrors of every night—I truly dread to sleep. It is no shadow with me, but substantial Misery foot-thick, that makes me sit by my bedside of a morning, & cry—. I have abandoned all opiates except Ether be one; & that only in *fits.* . . ." The last sentence indicates what Coleridge did not know—that his guilty nightmares were probably what we now call "withdrawal symptoms" from opium. The dreams he describes are very similar to those that De Quincey represents as "The Pains of Opium" in his *Confessions.*

Desire with loathing strangely mixed
On wild or hateful objects fixed.
Fantastic passions! maddening brawl!   25
And shame and terror over all!
Deeds to be hid which were not hid,
Which all confused I could not know
Whether I suffered, or I did:
For all seemed guilt, remorse or woe,   30
My own or others still the same
Life-stifling fear, soul-stifling shame.

So two nights passed: the night's dismay
Saddened and stunned the coming day.
Sleep, the wide blessing, seemed to me   35
Distemper's worst calamity.
The third night, when my own loud scream
Had waked me from the fiendish dream,
O'ercome with sufferings strange and wild,
I wept as I had been a child;   40
And having thus by tears subdued
My anguish to a milder mood,
Such punishments, I said, were due
To natures deepliest stained with sin,—
For aye entempesting anew   45
The unfathomable hell within,
The horror of their deeds to view,
To know and loathe, yet wish and do!
Such griefs with such men well agree,
But wherefore, wherefore fall on me?   50
To be beloved is all I need,
And whom I love, I love indeed.
1803   1816

Phantom[3]

All look and likeness caught from earth
All accident of kin and birth,
Had passed away. There was no trace
Of aught on that illumined face,
Upraised beneath the rifted stone   5
But of one spirit all her own—
She, she herself, and only she,
Shone through her body visibly.
1805   1834

---

3. A notebook Coleridge kept at Malta
in 1804 makes it clear that the poem
describes the appearance of Sara Hutchinson in a dream.

To William Wordsworth

COMPOSED ON THE NIGHT AFTER HIS RECITATION OF A POEM
ON THE GROWTH OF AN INDIVIDUAL MIND[1]

Friend of the wise! and teacher of the good!
Into my heart have I received that lay
More than historic, that prophetic lay
Wherein (high theme by thee first sung aright)
Of the foundations and the building up   5
Of a Human Spirit thou hast dared to tell
What may be told, to the understanding mind
Revealable; and what within the mind
By vital breathings secret as the soul
Of vernal growth, oft quickens in the heart   10
Thoughts all too deep for words![2]—

                              Theme hard as high!
Of smiles spontaneous, and mysterious fears
(The first-born they of Reason and twin birth),
Of tides obedient to external force,
And currents self-determined, as might seem,   15
Or by some inner Power; of moments awful,
Now in thy inner life, and now abroad,
When power streamed from thee, and thy soul received
The light reflected, as a light bestowed—
Of fancies fair, and milder hours of youth,   20
Hyblean[3] murmurs of poetic thought
Industrious in its joy, in vales and glens
Native or outland, lakes and famous hills!
Or on the lonely highroad, when the stars
Were rising; or by secret mountain streams,   25
The guides and the companions of thy way!

Of more than Fancy, of the Social Sense
Distending wide, and man beloved as man,
Where France in all her towns lay vibrating
Like some becalmèd bark beneath the burst   30
Of Heaven's immediate thunder, when no cloud
Is visible, or shadow on the main.
For thou wert there, thine own brows garlanded,
Amid the tremor of a realm aglow,
Amid a mighty nation jubilant,   35

---

1. This was the poem (later called *The Prelude*) addressed to Coleridge, which Wordsworth had completed in 1805. After Coleridge returned from Malta, very low in health and spirits, Wordsworth read the poem aloud to him on the evenings of almost two weeks. Coleridge wrote most of his poem immediately the reading was completed, on January 7, 1807.

2. Wordsworth had described the effect on his mind of the animating breeze ("vital breathings") in *The Prelude*, I.1-44 "Thoughts * * * words" echoes the last line of his *Intimations* ode. Coleridge goes on to summarize the major themes and events of *The Prelude*.

3. Sweet; Hybla, in ancient Sicily, was famous for its honey.

When from the general heart of human kind
Hope sprang forth like a full-born deity!
——Of that dear Hope afflicted and struck down,
So summoned homeward, thenceforth calm and sure
From the dread watchtower of man's absolute self,   40
With light unwaning on her eyes, to look
Far on—herself a glory to behold,
The Angel of the vision! Then (last strain)
Of Duty, chosen Laws controlling choice,
Action and joy!—An Orphic song[4] indeed,   45
A song divine of high and passionate thoughts
To their own music chaunted!

                          O great bard!
Ere that last strain dying awed the air,
With steadfast eye I viewed thee in the choir
Of ever-enduring men. The truly great   50
Have all one age, and from one visible space
Shed influence! They, both in power and act,
Are permanent, and Time is not with them,
Save as it worketh for them, they in it.
Nor less a sacred roll, than those of old,   55
And to be placed, as they, with gradual fame
Among the archives of mankind, thy work
Makes audible a linkéd lay of Truth,
Of Truth profound a sweet continuous lay,
Not learnt, but native, her own natural notes!   60
Ah! as I listened with a heart forlorn,
The pulses of my being beat anew:
And even as Life returns upon the drowned,[5]
Life's joy rekindling roused a throng of pains—
Keen pangs of Love, awakening as a babe   65
Turbulent, with an outcry in the heart;
And fears self-willed, that shunned the eye of Hope;
And Hope that scarce would know itself from Fear;
Sense of past Youth, and Manhood come in vain,
And Genius given, and Knowledge won in vain;   70
And all which I had culled in wood-walks wild,
And all which patient toil had reared, and all,
Commune with thee had opened out—but flowers
Strewed on my corse, and borne upon my bier
In the same coffin, for the selfsame grave!   75

    That way no more! and ill beseems it me,
Who came a welcomer in herald's guise,
Singing of Glory, and Futurity,

---

4. As enchanting and oracular as the song of the legendary Orpheus. There may also be an allusion to the Orphic mysteries, involving spiritual death and rebirth; see lines 61–66. "The Angel of the Vision" probably alludes to "the great vision of the guarded mount" in Milton's *Lycidas*, line 161.

5. A death-in-life is also described in, e.g., *Dejection* and *Epitaph*.

To wander back on such unhealthful road,
Plucking the poisons of self-harm! And ill   80
Such intertwine bescems triumphal wreaths
Strewed before thy advancing!

              Nor do thou,
Sage bard! impair the memory of that hour
Of thy communion with my nobler mind[6]
By pity or grief, already felt too long!   85
Nor let my words import more blame than needs.
The tumult rose and ceased: for Peace is nigh
Where Wisdom's voice has found a listening heart.
Amid the howl of more than wintry storms,
The Halcyon[7] hears the voice of vernal hours   90
Already on the wing.

           Eve following eve,[8]
Dear tranquil time, when the sweet sense of Home
Is sweetest! moments for their own sake hailed
And more desired, more precious, for thy song,
In silence listening, like a devout child,   95
My soul lay passive, by thy various strain
Driven as in surges now beneath the stars,
With momentary stars of my own birth,
Fair constellated foam, still darting off
Into the darkness; now a tranquil sea,   100
Outspread and bright, yet swelling to the moon.

And when—O friend! my comforter and guide!
Strong in thyself, and powerful to give strength!—
Thy long sustainéd song finally closed,
And thy deep voice had ceased—yet thou thyself   105
Wert still before my eyes, and round us both
That happy vision of belovéd faces—
Scarce conscious, and yet conscious of its close
I sate, my being blended in one thought
(Thought was it? or aspiration? or resolve?)   110
Absorbed, yet hanging still upon the sound—
And when I rose, I found myself in prayer.

1807   1817

Recollections of Love

1

How warm this woodland wild recess!
Love surely hath been breathing here;
And this sweet bed of heath, my dear!

6. I.e., during the early association between the two poets (1797-98).
7. A fabled bird, able to calm the sea, where it nested in winter.
8. The evenings during which Wordsworth read his poem aloud.

Swells up, then sinks with faint caress,
　　As if to have you yet more near.　　　　　　　　　5

2

Eight springs have flown since last I lay
　　On seaward Quantock's heathy hills,[9]
　　Where quiet sounds from hidden rills
Float here and there, like things astray,
　　And high o'erhead the skylark shrills.　　　　　10

3

No voice as yet had made the air
　　Be music with your name; yet why
　　That asking look? that yearning sigh?
That sense of promise every where?
　　Belovéd! flew your spirit by?　　　　　　　　　15

4

As when a mother doth explore
　　The rose mark on her long-lost child,
　　I met, I loved you, maiden mild!
As whom I long had loved before—
　　So deeply had I been beguiled.　　　　　　　　20

5

You stood before me like a thought,
　　A dream remembered in a dream.
　　But when those meek eyes first did seem
To tell me, Love within you wrought—
　　O Greta,[1] dear domestic stream!　　　　　　　25

6

Has not, since then, Love's prompture deep,
　　Has not Love's whisper evermore
　　Been ceaseless, as thy gentle roar?
Sole voice, when other voices sleep,
　　Dear under-song in clamor's hour.　　　　　　　30

ca. 1807　　　　　　　　　　　　　　　　　　　1817

On Donne's Poetry[2]

With Donne, whose muse on dromedary[3] trots,
Wreathe iron pokers into truelove knots;
Rhyme's sturdy cripple, fancy's maze and clue,
Wit's forge and fire-blast, meaning's press and screw.

ca. 1818　　　　　　　　　　　　　　　　　　　1836

---

9. Near Nether Stowey, Somerset, where
Coleridge had lived 1796–98.
1. The river Greta, which flowed past
Coleridge's home in Keswick, in the
Lake Country.
2. Donne as a poet had been in eclipse
for most of the 18th century. This terse
and penetrating comment shows the Romantic poet's great, though ironically
qualified, respect for the master of the
metaphysical style.
3. The one-humped Arabian camel,
trained for riding.

Work Without Hope

LINES COMPOSED 21ST FEBRUARY 1825

All Nature seems at work. Slugs leave their lair—
The bees are stirring—birds are on the wing—
And Winter slumbering in the open air
Wears on his smiling face a dream of Spring!
And I the while, the sole unbusy thing,   5
Nor honey make, nor pair, nor build, nor sing.

Yet well I ken the banks where amaranths[4] blow,
Have traced the fount whence streams of nectar flow.
Bloom, O ye amaranths! bloom for whom ye may,
For me ye bloom not! Glide, rich streams, away!   10
With lips unbrightened, wreathless brow, I stroll:
And would you learn the spells that drowse my soul?
Work without Hope draws nectar in a sieve,
And Hope without an object cannot live.

1825   1828

Constancy to an Ideal Object

Since all that beat about in Nature's range
Or veer or vanish, why should'st thou remain
The only constant in a world of change,
O yearning Thought! that liv'st but in the brain?
Call to the Hours, that in the distance play,   5
The faery people of the future day——
Fond[1] Thought! not one of all that shining swarm
Will breathe on thee with life-enkindling breath,
Till when, like strangers shelt'ring from a storm,
Hope and Despair meet in the porch of Death!   10
Yet still thou haunt'st me; and though well I see,
She[2] is not thou, and only thou art she,
Still, still as though some dear embodied Good,
Some living Love before my eyes there stood
With answering look a ready ear to lend,   15
I mourn to thee and say—"Ah! loveliest friend!
That this the meed[3] of all my toils might be,
To have a home, an English home, and thee!"
Vain repetition! Home and thou are one.
The peaceful'st cot the moon shall shine upon,   20
Lulled by the thrush and wakened by the lark,
Without thee were but a becalméd bark,
Whose Helmsman on an ocean waste and wide
Sits mute and pale his moldering helm beside.

---

4. Mythical flowers that bloom perpetually.
1. Foolish.

2. Sara Hutchinson.
3. Reward.

And art thou nothing? Such thou art, as when   25
The woodman winding westward up the glen
At wintry dawn, where o'er the sheep-track's maze
The viewless snow-mist weaves a glist'ning haze,
Sees full before him, gliding without tread,
An image with a glory round its head,[4]   30
The enamored rustic worships its fair hues,
Nor knows he makes the shadow he pursues!

                                          1828

Epitaph[5]

Stop, Christian passer-by!—Stop, child of God,
And read with gentle breast. Beneath this sod
A poet lies, or that which once seemed he.
O lift one thought in prayer for S. T. C.;
That he who many a year with toil of breath   5
Found death in life, may here find life in death!
Mercy for praise—to be forgiven for[6] fame
He asked, and hoped, through Christ. Do thou the same!

1833   1834

From Biographia Literaria[1]
From *Chapter I*

The discipline of his taste at school—Bowles's sonnets—Comparison between the poets before and since Mr. Pope.

    * * * At school I enjoyed the inestimable advantage of a very

---

4. A projected image of oneself in the mist. See Coleridge's *Dejection: An Ode,* line 54.
5. Written by Coleridge the year before he died. One version that he sent in a letter had as title: "Epitaph on a Poet little known, yet better known by the Initials of his name than by the Name Itself."
6. " 'For' in the sense of 'instead of' " [Coleridge's note].
1. In March, 1815, Coleridge was preparing a collected edition of his poems, and planned to include "a general preface * * * on the principles of philosophic and genial criticism." Characteristically, the materials developed as Coleridge worked on them, until, on July 29, he declared that the preface had been extended into a complete work, "an Autobiographia Literaria"; it was to consist of two main parts, "my literary life and opinions, as far as poetry and *poetical* criticism [are] concerned," and a critique of Wordsworth's theory of poetic diction. This work was ready by 17 September 1815, but the *Biographia Literaria*, in two volumes, was not published until July, 1817. The delay was caused by a series of miscalculations by his printer, which forced Coleridge to add miscellaneous materials needed to eke out the length of his original manuscript.

The critique of Wordsworth's theory of diction, which Coleridge had been planning ever since 1802, when he had detected "a radical difference in our theoretical opinions respecting poetry," is long, detailed, and subtly reasoned. In the selection from Chapter XVII, below, Coleridge agrees with Wordsworth's general aim of reforming the artifices of modern poetic diction, but he sharply denies Wordsworth's claim that there is no essential difference between the language of poetry and the language really spoken by men. The other selections printed here are devoted mainly to the central principle of Coleridge's own critical theory, the distinction between the mechanical

sensible, though at the same time a very severe master. He[2] early molded my taste to the preference of Demosthenes to Cicero, of Homer and Theocritus to Virgil, and again of Virgil to Ovid. He habituated me to compare Lucretius (in such extracts as I then read), Terence, and, above all, the chaster poems of Catullus not only with the Roman poets of the so-called silver and brazen ages but with even those of the Augustan era; and, on grounds of plain sense and universal logic, to see and assert the superiority of the former in the truth and nativeness both of their thoughts and diction. At the same time that we were studying the Greek tragic poets, he made us read Shakespeare and Milton as lessons; and they were the lessons, too, which required most time and trouble to *bring up*, so as to escape his censure. I learnt from him that poetry, even that of the loftiest and, seemingly, that of the wildest odes, had a logic of its own as severe as that of science; and more difficult, because more subtle, more complex, and dependent on more, and more fugitive, causes. In the truly great poets, he would say, there is a reason assignable, not only for every word, but for the position of every word; and I well remember that, availing himself of the synonyms to the Homer of Didymus,[3] he made us attempt to show, with regard to each, *why* it would not have answered the same purpose, and *wherein* consisted the peculiar fitness of the word in the original text.

In our own English compositions (at least for the last three years of our school education) he showed no mercy to phrase, metaphor, or image unsupported by a sound sense, or where the same sense might have been conveyed with equal force and dignity in plainer words. Lute, harp, and lyre, muse, muses, and inspirations, Pegasus, Parnassus, and Hippocrene were all an abomination to him. In fancy I can almost hear him now, exclaiming, "Harp? Harp? Lyre? Pen and ink, boy, you mean! Muse, boy, muse? Your nurse's daughter, you mean! Pierian spring? Oh, aye! the cloister pump, I suppose!" Nay, certain introductions, similes, and examples were placed by name on a list of interdiction. Among the similes there was, I remember, that of the manchineel fruit,[4] as

---

"fancy" and the organic "imagination." Thus the biographical section of the *Biographia* (Chapters I and IV), dealing with the development of his poetic taste and theory, describes his gradual realization, climaxed by his first exposure to Wordsworth's poetry, "that fancy and imagination were two distinct and widely different faculties." The conclusion to Chapter XIII tersely summarizes this distinction, and the definition of poetry, at the end of Chapter XIV, develops at somewhat greater length the nature of the process and products of the "synthetic and

magical power * * * of imagination." These cryptic paragraphs have proved to be the most widely discussed and influential passages ever written by an English critic.

2. "The Rev. James Boyer, many years Head Master of the Grammar School, Christ's Hospital" [Coleridge's note]. See also Charles Lamb's essay, *Christ's Hospital Five-and-Thirty Years Ago*.

3. Didymus of Alexandria (ca. 65 B.C.–A.D. 10) was the author of a commentary on the text of Homer.

4. Poisonous, though attractive in appearance.

suiting equally well with too many subjects, in which, however, it yielded the palm at once to the example of Alexander and Clytus,[5] which was equally good and apt whatever might be the theme. Was it ambition? Alexander and Clytus! Flattery? Alexander and Clytus! Anger? Drunkenness? Pride? Friendship? Ingratitude? Late repentance? Still, still Alexander and Clytus! At length the praises of agriculture having been exemplified in the sagacious observation that, had Alexander been holding the plow, he would not have run his friend Clytus through with a spear, this tried and serviceable old friend was banished by public edict *in secula seculorum*.[6] I have sometimes ventured to think that a list of this kind or an *index expurgatorius* of certain well-known and ever returning phrases, both introductory and transitional, including the large assortment of modest egotisms and flattering illeisms,[7] etc., etc., might be hung up in our law courts and both Houses of Parliament with great advantage to the public as an important saving of national time, an incalculable relief to his Majesty's ministers; but, above all, as insuring the thanks of country attorneys and their clients, who have private bills to carry through the House.

Be this as it may, there was one custom of our master's which I cannot pass over in silence, because I think it imitable and worthy of imitation. He would often permit our theme exercises, under some pretext of want of time, to accumulate till each lad had four or five to be looked over. Then placing the whole number *abreast* on his desk, he would ask the writer why this or that sentence might not have found as appropriate a place under this or that other thesis; and if no satisfying answer could be returned and two faults of the same kind were found in one exercise, the irrevocable verdict followed, the exercise was torn up, and another on the same subject to be produced, in addition to the tasks of the day. The reader will, I trust, excuse this tribute of recollection to a man whose severities, even now, not seldom furnish the dreams by which the blind fancy would fain interpret to the mind the painful sensations of distempered sleep; but neither lessen nor dim the deep sense of my moral and intellectual obligations. He sent us to the university excellent Latin and Greek scholars and tolerable Hebraists. Yet our classical knowledge was the least of the good gifts which we derived from his zealous and conscientious tutorage. He is now gone to his final reward, full of years and full of honors, even of those honors which were dearest to his heart as gratefully bestowed by that school, and still binding him to the interests of that school in which he had been himself educated and to which

---

5. Plutarch's *Life* of Alexander the Great relates that the king killed his friend Clytus in a drunken quarrel.
6. Forever ("for centuries of centuries").
7. Excessive use of the pronoun "he" (in Latin, *ille*).

during his whole life he was a dedicated thing. * * *

I had just entered on my seventeenth year when the sonnets of Mr. Bowles,[8] twenty in number, and just then published in a quarto pamphlet, were first made known and presented to me by a schoolfellow who had quitted us for the university and who, during the whole time that he was in our first form (or in our school language, a Grecian[9]), had been my patron and protector. I refer to Dr. Middleton, the truly learned and every way excellent Bishop of Calcutta. * * *

It was a double pleasure to me, and still remains a tender recollection, that I should have received from a friend so revered the first knowledge of a poet by whose works, year after year, I was so enthusiastically delighted and inspired. My earliest acquaintances will not have forgotten the undisciplined eagerness and impetuous zeal with which I laboured to make proselytes, not only of my companions, but of all with whom I conversed, of whatever rank and in whatever place. As my school finances did not permit me to purchase copies I made, within less than a year and a half, more than forty transcriptions, as the best presents I could offer to those who had in any way won my regard. And with almost equal delight did I receive the three or four following publications of the same author.

Though I have seen and known enough of mankind to be well aware that I shall perhaps stand alone in my creed, and that it will be well if I subject myself to no worse charge than that of singularity, I am not therefore deterred from avowing that I regard and ever have regarded the obligations of intellect among the most sacred of the claims of gratitude. A valuable thought, or a particular train of thoughts, gives me additional pleasure when I can safely refer and attribute it to the conversation or correspondence of another. My obligations to Mr. Bowles were indeed important and for radical good. At a very premature age, even before my fifteenth year, I had bewildered myself in metaphysics and in theological controversy. Nothing else pleased me. History and particular facts lost all interest in my mind. Poetry (though for a schoolboy of that age I was above par in English versification and had already produced two or three compositions which, I may venture to say without reference to my age, were somewhat above mediocrity, and which had gained me more credit than the sound good sense of my old master was at all pleased with), poetry itself, yea novels and romances, became insipid to me. In my friendless wanderings on our leave-days (for I was an orphan, and had scarce

8. William Lisle Bowles (1762–1850) published in 1789 two editions of a collection of sonnets setting forth the meditations evoked from a traveler by the changing scene.
9. Gifted students in the final class at Christ's Hospital who were being prepared for a university.

any connections in London), highly was I delighted if any passenger, especially if he were dressed in black,[10] would enter into conversation with me. For I soon found the means of directing it to my favorite subjects

> Of providence, foreknowledge, will, and fate,
> Fixed fate, free will, foreknowledge absolute,
> And found no end, in wandering mazes lost.[1]

This preposterous pursuit was, beyond doubt, injurious both to my natural powers and to the progress of my education. It would perhaps have been destructive had it been continued; but from this I was auspiciously withdrawn, partly indeed by an accidental introduction to an amiable family,[2] chiefly however by the genial influence of a style of poetry so tender and yet so manly, so natural and real, and yet so dignified and harmonious, as the sonnets, etc., of Mr. Bowles! Well were it for me, perhaps, had I never relapsed into the same mental disease; if I had continued to pluck the flower and reap the harvest from the cultivated surface, instead of delving in the unwholesome quicksilver mines of metaphysic depths. But if in after time I have sought a refuge from bodily pain and mismanaged sensibility in abstruse researches, which exercised the strength and subtlety of the understanding without awakening the feelings of the heart; still there was a long and blessed interval, during which my natural faculties were allowed to expand and my original tendencies to develop themselves; my fancy, and the love of nature, and the sense of beauty in forms and sounds.

The second advantage which I owe to my early perusal and admiration of these poems (to which let me add, though known to me at a somewhat later period, the *Lewesdon Hill* of Mr. Crow)[3] bears more immediately on my present subject. Among those with whom I conversed there were, of course, very many who had formed their taste and their notions of poetry from the writings of Mr. Pope and his followers: or to speak more generally, in that school of French poetry condensed and invigorated by English understanding which had predominated from the last century. I was not blind to the merits of this school, yet as from inexperience of the world and consequent want of sympathy with the general subjects of these poems they gave me little pleasure, I doubtless undervalued the *kind*, and with the presumption of youth withheld from its masters the legitimate name of poets. I saw that the excellence of this kind

10. I.e., if he were a clergyman.
1. *Paradise Lost* II.559–61.
2. The family of Mary Evans, with whom Coleridge fell deeply in love in 1788.
3. William Crow(e) (1745–1829) published in 1788 *Lewesdon Hill*, a long poem in blank verse which, like Bowles's sonnets, combined descriptions of the natural scene with associated moral and personal reflections.

consisted in just and acute observations on men and manners in an artificial state of society as its matter and substance, and in the logic of wit conveyed in smooth and strong epigrammatic couplets as its *form*. Even when the subject was addressed to the fancy or the intellect, as in the *Rape of the Lock* or the *Essay on Man*; nay, when it was a consecutive narration, as in that astonishing product of matchless talent and ingenuity, Pope's translation of the *Iliad*; still a *point* was looked for at the end of each second line, and the whole was as it were a sorites or, if I may exchange a logical for a grammatical metaphor, a *conjunction disjunctive*,[4] of epigrams. Meantime the matter and diction seemed to me characterized not so much by poetic thoughts as by thoughts *translated* into the language of poetry. On this last point I had occasion to render my own thoughts gradually more and more plain to myself by frequent amicable disputes concerning Darwin's *Botanic Garden*,[5] which for some years was greatly extolled, not only by the *reading* public in general, but even by those whose genius and natural robustness of understanding enabled them afterwards to act foremost in dissipating these "painted mists" that occasionally rise from the marshes at the foot of Parnassus. During my first Cambridge vacation I assisted a friend in a contribution for a literary society in Devonshire, and in this I remember to have compared Darwin's work to the Russian palace of ice, glittering, cold, and transitory. In the same essay too I assigned sundry reasons, chiefly drawn from a comparison of passages in the Latin poets with the original Greek from which they were borrowed, for the preference of Collins's odes to those of Gray, and of the simile in Shakespeare:

> How like a younker or a prodigal
> The scarfed bark puts from her native bay,
> Hugged and embraced by the strumpet wind!
> How like the prodigal doth she return,
> With over-weathered ribs and ragged sails,
> Lean, rent and beggared by the strumpet wind![6]

to the imitation in the *Bard*:

> Fair laughs the morn, and soft the zephyr blows
> While proudly riding o'er the azure realm
> In gallant trim the gilded vessel goes;
> Youth on the prow, and Pleasure at the helm;
> Regardless of the sweeping whirlwind's sway,
> That, hushed in grim repose, expects its evening prey.[7]

---

4. "Sorites": a sequence of interconnected syllogisms; "*conjunction disjunctive*": a word which connects the parts of a sentence but expresses an alternative or opposition: "or," "but," "lest." etc.

5. Published in 1789–91 by Erasmus Darwin (1731–1802); a long poem in closed couplets, presenting the science of botany in elaborate allegories.
6. *Merchant of Venice* II.vi.14–19.
7. Thomas Gray, *The Bard* (1757).

(In which, by the bye, the words "realm" and "sway" are rhymes dearly purchased.) I preferred the original, on the ground that in the imitation it depended wholly in the compositor's putting, or not putting, a small capital both in this and in many other passages of the same poet whether the words should be personifications or mere abstracts. I mention this because, in referring various lines in Gray to their original in Shakespeare and Milton, and in the clear perception how completely all the propriety was lost in the transfer, I was at that early period led to a conjecture which, many years afterwards, was recalled to me from the same thought having been started in conversation, but far more ably, and developed more fully, by Mr. Wordsworth; namely, that this style of poetry which I have characterized above as translations of prose thoughts into poetic language had been kept up by, if it did not wholly arise from, the custom of writing Latin verses and the great importance attached to these exercises in our public schools. Whatever might have been the case in the fifteenth century, when the use of the Latin tongue was so general among learned men that Erasmus is said to have forgotten his native language; yet in the present day it is not to be supposed that a youth can think in Latin, or that he can have any other reliance on the force or fitness of his phrases but the authority of the author from whence he had adopted them. Consequently he must first prepare his thoughts and then pick out from Virgil, Horace, Ovid, or perhaps more compendiously, from his *Gradus*,[8] halves and quarters of lines in which to embody them.

I never object to a certain degree of disputatiousness in a young man from the age of seventeen to that of four or five and twenty, provided I find him always arguing on one side of the question. The controversies occasioned by my unfeigned zeal for the honor of a favorite contemporary, then known to me only by his works, were of great advantage in the formation and establishment of my taste and critical opinions. In my defense of the lines running into each other instead of closing at each couplet, and of natural language, neither bookish nor vulgar, neither redolent of the lamp nor of the kennel, such as *I will remember thee*; instead of the same thought tricked up in the rag-fair finery of

>———Thy image on her wing
>Before my Fancy's eye shall Memory bring,

I had continually to adduce the meter and diction of the Greek poets from Homer to Theocritus inclusive; and still more of our elder English poets from Chaucer to Milton. Nor was this all. But

---

8. *Gradus ad Parnassum* ("Stairway to Parnassus"), a dictionary of Latin words, synonyms, and descriptive epithets, illustrated from the Latin poets. It was long used as a school text in Latin composition.

as it was my constant reply to authorities brought against me from later poets of great name that no authority could avail in opposition to Truth, Nature, Logic, and the Laws of Universal Grammar; actuated too by my former passion for metaphysical investigations, I labored at a solid foundation on which permanently to ground my opinions in the component faculties of the human mind itself and their comparative dignity and importance. According to the faculty or source from which the pleasure given by any poem or passage was derived I estimated the merit of such poem or passage. As the result of all my reading and meditation, I abstracted two critical aphorisms, deeming them to comprise the conditions and criteria of poetic style: first, that not the poem which we have *read*, but that to which we *return* with the greatest pleasure, possesses the genuine power and claims the name of *essential* poetry. Second, that whatever lines can be translated into other words of the same language without diminution of their significance, either in sense of association or in any worthy feeling, are so far vicious in their diction. Be it however observed that I excluded from the list of worthy feelings the pleasure derived from mere novelty in the reader, and the desire of exciting wonderment at his powers in the author. Oftentimes since then, in perusing French tragedies, I have fancied two marks of admiration at the end of each line, as hieroglyphics of the author's own admiration at his own cleverness. Our genuine admiration of a great poet is a continuous undercurrent of feeling; it is everywhere present, but seldom anywhere as a separate excitement. I was wont boldly to affirm that it would be scarcely more difficult to push a stone out from the pyramids with the bare hand than to alter a word, or the position of a word, in Milton or Shakespeare (in their most important works at least), without making the auther say something else, or something worse, than he does say. One great distinction I appeared to myself to see plainly, between even the characteristic faults of our elder poets and the false beauties of the moderns. In the former, from Donne to Cowley, we find the most fantastic out-of-the-way thoughts, but in the most pure and genuine mother English; in the latter, the most obvious thoughts, in language the most fantastic and arbitrary. Our faulty elder poets sacrificed the passion and passionate flow of poetry to the subtleties of intellect and to the starts of wit; the moderns to the glare and glitter of a perpetual yet broken and heterogeneous imagery, or rather to an amphibious something, made up half of image and half of abstract[9] meaning. The one sacrificed the heart to the head, the other both heart and head to point and drapery. * * *

9. "I remember a ludicrous instance in the poem of a young tradesman: 'No more will I endure Love's pleasing pain, / Or round my *heart's leg* tie his galling chain' " [Coleridge's note].

From *Chapter IV*

*Mr. Wordsworth's earlier poems—On fancy and imagination—
The investigation of the distinction important to the fine arts.*

* * * During the last year of my residence at Cambridge I became acquainted with Mr. Wordsworth's first publication, entitled *Descriptive Sketches;*[1] and seldom, if ever, was the emergence of an original poetic genius above the literary horizon more evidently announced. In the form, style, and manner of the whole poem, and in the structure of the particular lines and periods, there is a harshness and acerbity connected and combined with words and images all aglow which might recall those products of the vegetable world, where gorgeous blossoms rise out of the hard and thorny rind and shell within which the rich fruit was elaborating. The language was not only peculiar and strong, but at times knotty and contorted, as by its own impatient strength; while the novelty and struggling crowd of images acting in conjunction with the difficulties of the style demanded always a greater closeness of attention than poetry (at all events than descriptive poetry) has a right to claim. It not seldom therefore justified the complaint of obscurity. In the following extract I have sometimes fancied that I saw an emblem of the poem itself and of the author's genius as it was then displayed:

> 'Tis storm; and hid in mist from hour to hour,
> All day the floods a deepening murmur pour,
> The sky is veiled, and every cheerful sight;
> Dark is the region as with coming night;
> And yet what frequent bursts of overpowering light!
> Triumphant on the bosom of the storm,
> Glances the fire-clad eagle's wheeling form;
> Eastward, in long perspective glittering, shine
> The wood-crowned cliffs that o'er the lake recline;
> Wide o'er the Alps a hundred streams unfold,
> At once to pillars turned that flame with gold;
> Behind his sail the peasant strives to shun
> The West, that burns like one dilated sun,
> Where in a mighty crucible expire
> The mountains, glowing hot, like coals of fire.[2]

The poetic Psyche, in its process to full development, undergoes as many changes as its Greek namesake, the butterfly.[3] And it is remarkable how soon genius clears and purifies itself from the

---

1. Published 1793, the year before Coleridge left Cambridge; a long descriptive-meditative poem in closed couplets, describing Wordsworth's walking tour in the Alps in 1790. See also *The Prelude* VI.

2. *Descriptive Sketches* (1815 version), lines 332 ff.
3. "In Greek, Psyche is the common name for the soul and the butterfly" [Coleridge's note].

faults and errors of its earliest products; faults which, in its earliest compositions, are the more obtrusive and confluent because, as heterogeneous elements which had only a temporary use, they constitute the very *ferment* by which themselves are carried off. Or we may compare them to some diseases, which must work on the humors and be thrown out on the surface in order to secure the patient from their future recurrence. I was in my twenty-fourth year when I had the happiness of knowing Mr. Wordsworth personally;[4] and, while memory lasts, I shall hardly forget the sudden effect produced on my mind by his recitation of a manuscript poem which still remains unpublished, but of which the stanza and tone of style were the same as those of *The Female Vagrant* as originally printed in the first volume of the *Lyrical Ballads*.[5] There was here no mark of strained thought or forced diction, no crowd or turbulence of imagery, and, as the poet hath himself well described in his lines on revisiting the Wye, manly reflection and human associations had given both variety and an additional interest to natural objects which in the passion and appetite of the first love they had seemed to him neither to need or permit.[6] The occasional obscurities which had risen from an imperfect control over the resources of his native language had almost wholly disappeared, together with that worse defect of arbitrary and illogical phrases, at once hackneyed and fantastic, which hold so distinguished a place in the *technique* of ordinary poetry and will, more or less, alloy the earlier poems of the truest genius, unless the attention has been specifically directed to their worthlessness and incongruity. I did not perceive anything particular in the mere style of the poem alluded to during its recitation, except indeed such difference as was not separable from the thought and manner; and the Spenserian stanza which always, more or less, recalls to the reader's mind Spenser's own style, would doubtless have authorized in my then opinion a more frequent descent to the phrases of ordinary life than could, without an ill effect, have been hazarded in the heroic couplet. It was not however the freedom from false taste, whether as to common defects or to those more properly his own, which made so unusual an impression on my feelings immediately, and subsequently on my judgment. It was the union of deep feeling with profound thought; the fine balance of truth in observing with the imaginative faculty in modifying the objects observed; and above all the original gift of spreading the tone, the *atmosphere*, and with it the depth and height of the ideal world, around forms,

4. The meeting occurred in September, 1795.
5. *Salisbury Plain* (1793–4), which was left in manuscript until Wordsworth published a revised version in 1842 under the title *Guilt and Sorrow*. An excerpt from *Salisbury Plain* was printed as *The Female Vagrant*, in *Lyrical Ballads* (1798).
6. Wordsworth's *Tintern Abbey*, lines 76 ff.

incidents, and situations of which, for the common view, custom had bedimmed all the luster, had dried up the sparkle and the dewdrops. "To find no contradiction in the union of old and new, to contemplate the Ancient of Days and all his works with feelings as fresh as if all had then sprang forth at the first creative fiat, characterizes the mind that feels the riddle of the world and may help to unravel it. To carry on the feelings of childhood into the powers of manhood; to combine the child's sense of wonder and novelty with the appearances which every day for perhaps forty years had rendered familiar:

> With sun and moon and stars throughout the year
> And man and woman;[7]

this is the character and privilege of genius, and one of the marks which distinguish genius from talents. And therefore it is the prime merit of genius, and its most unequivocal mode of manifestation, so to represent familiar objects as to awaken in the minds of others a kindred feeling concerning them, and that freshness of sensation which is the constant accompaniment of mental no less than of bodily convalescence. Who has not a thousand times seen snow fall on water? Who has not watched it with a new feeling from the time that he has read Burns' comparison of sensual pleasure:

> To snow that falls upon a river
> A moment white—then gone forever![8]

In poems, equally as in philosophic disquisitions, genius produces the strongest impressions of novelty while it rescues the most admitted truths from the impotence caused by the very circumstance of their universal admission. Truths of all others the most awful and mysterious, yet being at the same time of universal interest, are too often considered as *so* true, that they lose all the life and efficiency of truth and lie bedridden in the dormitory of the soul side by side with the most despised and exploded errors." *The Friend*, p. 76, No. 5.[9]

This excellence, which in all Mr. Wordsworth's writings is more or less predominant and which constitutes the character of his mind, I no sooner felt than I sought to understand. Repeated meditations led me first to suspect (and a more intimate analysis of the human faculties, their appropriate marks, functions, and effects, matured my conjecture into full conviction) that fancy and imagination were two distinct and widely different faculties, instead of being, according to the general belief, either two names with one meaning, or at furthest the lower and higher degree of one and the same power. It is not, I own, easy to conceive a more apposite

7. Altered from Milton's sonnet *To Mr. Cyriack Skinner upon his Blindness.*
8. Altered from Burns, *Tam o' Shanter,* lines 61–62.
9. *The Friend* was a periodical published by Coleridge (1809–10).

translation of the Greek *phantasia* than the Latin *imaginatio*; but it is equally true that in all societies there exists an instinct of growth, a certain collective unconscious good sense working progressively to desynonymize those words originally of the same meaning which the conflux of dialects had supplied to the more homogeneous languages, as the Greek and German, and which the same cause, joined with accidents of translation from original works of different countries, occasion in mixed languages like our own. The first and most important point to be proved is that two conceptions perfectly distinct are confused under one and the same word, and (this done) to appropriate that word exclusively to one meaning, and the synonym (should there be one) to the other. But if (as will be often the case in the arts and sciences) no synonym exists, we must either invent or borrow a word. In the present instance the appropriation had already begun and been legitimated in the derivative adjective: Milton had a highly *imaginative*, Cowley a very *fanciful*, mind. If therefore I should succeed in establishing the actual existence of two faculties generally different, the nomenclature would be at once determined. To the faculty by which I had characterized Milton we should confine the term *imagination*; while the other would be contra-distinguished as *fancy*. Now were it once fully ascertained that this division is no less grounded in nature than that of delirium from mania, or Otway's

> Lutes, lobsters, seas of milk, and ships of amber,[1]

from Shakespeare's

> What! have his daughters brought him to this pass?[2]

or from the preceding apostrophe to the elements, the theory of the fine arts and of poetry in particular could not, I thought, but derive some additional and important light. It would in its immediate effects furnish a torch of guidance to the philosophical critic, and ultimately to the poet himself. In energetic minds truth soon changes by domestication into power; and from directing in the discrimination and appraisal of the product becomes influencive in the production. To admire on principle is the only way to imitate without loss of originality. * * *

From *Chapter XIII*

On the imagination, or esemplastic[3] power.

* * * The IMAGINATION, then, I consider either as primary, or secondary. The primary IMAGINATION I hold to be the living power and prime agent of all human perception, and as a repetition in

---

1. Thomas Otway, in *Venice Preserved* (1682), wrote "laurels" in place of "lobsters" (V.ii.151).
2. *King Lear* III.iv.63.
3. Coleridge coined this word and used it to mean "molding into unity."

the finite mind of the eternal act of creation in the infinite I AM. The secondary I consider as an echo of the former, coexisting with the conscious will, yet still as identical with the primary in the *kind* of its agency, and differing only in *degree*, and in the *mode* of its operation. It dissolves, diffuses, dissipates, in order to re-create; or where this process is rendered impossible, yet still, at all events, it struggles to idealize and to unify. It is essentially *vital*, even as all objects (*as* objects) are essentially fixed and dead.

FANCY, on the contrary, has no other counters to play with but fixities and definites. The fancy is indeed no other than a mode of memory emancipated from the order of time and space; and blended with, and modified by that empirical phenomenon of the will which we express by the word CHOICE. But equally with the ordinary memory it must receive all its materials ready made from the law of association.[4] * * *

Chapter XIV

Occasion of the Lyrical Ballads, and the objects originally proposed—Preface to the second edition—The ensuing controversy, its causes and acrimony—Philosophic definitions of a poem and poetry with scholia.[5]

During the first year that Mr. Wordsworth and I were neighbors[6] our conversations turned frequently on the two cardinal points of poetry, the power of exciting the sympathy of the reader by a faithful adherence to the truth of nature, and the power of giving the interest of novelty by the modifying colors of imagination.[7] The sudden charm which accidents of light and shade, which moonlight or sunset diffused over a known and familiar landscape, appeared to represent the practicability of combining both. These are the poetry of nature. The thought suggested itself (to which of us I do not recollect) that a series of poems might be composed of two sorts. In the one, the incidents and agents were to be, in part at least, supernatural; and the excellence aimed at was to consist in the interesting of the affections by the dramatic truth of such emotions as would naturally accompany such situations, supposing them real. And real in *this* sense they have been to every

---

4. Coleridge conceives God's creation to be a continuous process, which has an analogy in the creative perception ("primary imagination") of all human minds. The creative process is repeated, or "echoed," on still a third level, by the "secondary imagination" of the poet, which dissolves the products of primary perception in order to shape them into a new and unified creation—the imaginative passage or poem. The "fancy," on the other hand, can only manipulate

"fixities and definites" which, linked by association, come to it ready-made from perception. Its products, therefore, are not re-creations (echoes of God's original creative process), but mosaic-like reassemblies of existing bits and pieces.
5. Additional remarks, after a philosophic demonstration.
6. At **Nether Stowey and Alfoxden**, Somerset, in 1797.
7. Cf. Wordsworth's account in his Preface to *Lyrical Ballads*.

human being who, from whatever source of delusion, has at any time believed himself under supernatural agency. For the second class, subjects were to be chosen from ordinary life; the characters and incidents were to be such as will be found in every village and its vicinity where there is a meditative and feeling mind to seek after them, or to notice them when they present themselves.

In this idea originated the plan of the *Lyrical Ballads*; in which it was agreed that my endeavors should be directed to persons and characters supernatural, or at least romantic; yet so as to transfer from our inward nature a human interest and a semblance of truth sufficient to procure for these shadows of imagination that willing suspension of disbelief for the moment, which constitutes poetic faith. Mr. Wordsworth, on the other hand, was to propose to himself as his object to give the charm of novelty to things of every day, and to excite a feeling analogous to the supernatural, by awakening the mind's attention from the lethargy of custom and directing it to the loveliness and the wonders of the world before us; an inexhaustible treasure, but for which, in consequence of the film of familiarity and selfish solicitude, we have eyes yet see not, ears that hear not, and hearts that neither feel nor understand.[8]

With this view I wrote the *Ancient Mariner*, and was preparing, among other poems, the *Dark Ladie*, and the *Christabel*, in which I should have more nearly realized my ideal than I had done in my first attempt. But Mr. Wordsworth's industry had proved so much more successful and the number of his poems so much greater, that my compositions, instead of forming a balance, appeared rather an interpolation of heterogeneous matter.[9] Mr. Wordsworth added two or three poems written in his own character, in the impassioned, lofty, and sustained diction which is characteristic of his genius. In this form the *Lyrical Ballads* were published; and were presented by him, as an *experiment*,[1] whether subjects which from their nature rejected the usual ornaments and extra-colloquial style of poems in general might not be so managed in the language of ordinary life as to produce the pleasurable interest which it is the peculiar business of poetry to impart. To the second edition[2] he added a preface of considerable length; in which, notwithstanding some passages of apparently a contrary import, he was understood to contend for the extension of this style to poetry of all kinds, and to reject as vicious and indefensible all phrases and forms of style that were not included in what he (unfortunately, I think, adopting an equivocal expression) called the language of *real* life. From this

8. Cf. Isaiah vi.9–10.
9. The first edition of *Lyrical Ballads*, published anonymously in 1798, contained nineteen poems by Wordsworth, four by Coleridge.

1. "Experiments" was also the word used by Wordsworth in his "Advertisement" to the first edition.
2. Of 1800.

preface, prefixed to poems in which it was impossible to deny the presence of original genius, however mistaken its direction might be deemed, arose the whole long continued controversy.[3] For from the conjunction of perceived power with supposed heresy I explain the inveteracy and in some instances, I grieve to say, the acrimonious passions with which the controversy has been conducted by the assailants.

Had Mr. Wordsworth's poems been the silly, the childish things which they were for a long time described as being; had they been really distinguished from the compositions of other poets merely by meanness of language and inanity of thought; had they indeed contained nothing more than what is found in the parodies and pretended imitations of them; they must have sunk at once, a dead weight, into the slough of oblivion, and have dragged the preface along with them. But year after year increased the number of Mr. Wordsworth's admirers. They were found too not in the lower classes of the reading public, but chiefly among young men of strong sensibility and meditative minds; and their admiration (inflamed perhaps in some degree by opposition) was distinguished by its intensity, I might almost say, by its *religious* fervor. These facts, and the intellectual energy of the author, which was more or less consciously felt where it was outwardly and even boisterously denied, meeting with sentiments of aversion to his opinions and of alarm at their consequences, produced an eddy of criticism which would of itself have borne up the poems by the violence with which it whirled them round and round. With many parts of this preface, in the sense attributed to them and which the words undoubtedly seem to authorize, I never concurred; but, on the contrary objected to them as erroneous in principle, and as contradictory (in appearance at least) both to other parts of the same preface and to the author's own practice in the greater number of the poems themselves. Mr. Wordsworth in his recent collection[4] has, I find, degraded this prefatory disquisition to the end of his second volume, to be read or not at the reader's choice. But he has not, as far as I can discover, announced any change in his poetic creed. At all events, considering it as the source of a controversy in which I have been honored more than I deserve by the frequent conjunction of my name with his, I think it expedient to declare once for all in what points I coincide with his opinions, and in what points I altogether differ. But in order to render myself intelligible I must previously, in as few words as possible, explain my ideas, first, of a POEM; and secondly, of POETRY itself, in *kind* and in *essence*.

3. The controversy over Wordsworth's theory and poetical practice in the literary journals of the day.

4. Wordsworth's *Poems*, two volumes, 1815.

The office of philosophical *disquisition* consists in just *distinction*; while it is the privilege of the philosopher to preserve himself constantly aware that distinction is not division. In order to obtain adequate notions of any truth, we must intellectually separate its distinguishable parts; and this is the technical *process* of philosophy. But having so done, we must then restore them in our conceptions to the unity in which they actually coexist; and this is the *result* of philosophy. A poem contains the same elements as a prose composition; the difference therefore must consist in a different combination of them, in consequence of a different object proposed. According to the difference of the object will be the difference of the combination. It is possible that the object may be merely to facilitate the recollection of any given facts or observations by artificial arrangement; and the composition will be a poem, merely because it is distinguished from prose by meter, or by rhyme, or by both conjointly. In this, the lowest sense, a man might attribute the name of a poem to the well-known enumeration of the days in the several months:

> Thirty days hath September
> April, June, and November, etc.

and others of the same class and purpose. And as a particular pleasure is found in anticipating the recurrence of sounds and quantities, all compositions that have this charm superadded, whatever be their contents, *may* be entitled poems.

So much for the superficial *form*. A difference of object and contents supplies an additional ground of distinction. The immediate purpose may be the communication of truths; either of truth absolute and demonstrable, as in works of science; or of facts experienced and recorded, as in history. Pleasure, and that of the highest and most permanent kind, may *result* from the *attainment* of the end; but it is not itself the immediate end. In other works the communication of pleasure may be the immediate purpose; and though truth, either moral or intellectual, ought to be the *ultimate* end, yet this will distinguish the character of the author, not the class to which the work belongs. Blessed indeed is that state of society in which the immediate purpose would be baffled by the perversion of the proper ultimate end; in which no charm of diction or imagery could exempt the Bathyllus even of an Anacreon, or the Alexis of Virgil,[5] from disgust and aversion!

But the communication of pleasure may be the immediate object of a work not metrically composed; and that object may have been in a high degree attained, as in novels and romances. Would

5. The reference is to poems of homosexual love. "Bathyllus" was a beautiful boy praised by Anacreon, a Greek lyric poet (ca. 560–475 B.C.); "Alexis" was a young man loved by the shepherd Corydon in Virgil's *Eclogues* II.

then the mere superaddition of meter, with or without rhyme, entitle *these* to the name of poems? The answer is that nothing can permanently please which does not contain in itself the reason why it is so, and not otherwise. If meter be superadded, all other parts must be made consonant with it. They must be such as to justify the perpetual and distinct attention to each part which an exact correspondent recurrence of accent and sound are calculated to excite. The final definition then, so deduced, may be thus worded. A poem is that species of composition which is opposed to works of science by proposing for its *immediate* object pleasure, not truth; and from all other species (having *this* object in common with it) it is discriminated by proposing to itself such delight from the *whole* as is compatible with a distinct gratification from each component *part.*

the concept of the organic whole

Controversy is not seldom excited in consequence of the disputants attaching each a different meaning to the same word; and in few instances has this been more striking than in disputes concerning the present subject. If a man chooses to call every composition a poem which is rhyme, or measure, or both, I must leave his opinion uncontroverted. The distinction is at least competent to characterize the writer's intention. If it were subjoined that the whole is likewise entertaining or affecting as a tale or as a series of interesting reflections, I of course admit this as another fit ingredient of a poem and an additional merit. But if the definition sought for be that of a *legitimate* poem, I answer it must be one the parts of which mutually support and explain each other; all in their proportion harmonizing with, and supporting the purpose and known influences of metrical arrangement. The philosophic critics of all ages coincide with the ultimate judgment of all countries in equally denying the praises of a just poem on the one hand to a series of striking lines or distichs,[6] each of which absorbing the whole attention of the reader to itself disjoins it from its context and makes it a separate whole, instead of a harmonizing part; and on the other hand, to an unsustained composition, from which the reader collects rapidly the general result unattracted by the component parts. The reader should be carried forward, not merely or chiefly by the mechanical impulse of curiosity, or by a restless desire to arrive at the final solution; but by the pleasurable activity of mind excited by the attractions of the journey itself. Like the motion of a serpent, which the Egyptians made the emblem of intellectual power; or like the path of sound through the air; at every step he pauses and half recedes, and from the retrogressive movement collects the force which again carries him onward. "*Praecipi-*

6. Pairs of lines.

tandus est liber spiritus," says Petronius Arbiter most happily.[7] The epithet *liber* here balances the preceding verb; and it is not easy to conceive more meaning condensed in fewer words.

But if this should be admitted as a satisfactory character of a poem, we have still to seek for a definition of poetry. The writings of Plato, and Bishop Taylor, and the *Theoria Sacra* of Burnet,[8] furnish undeniable proofs that poetry of the highest kind may exist without meter, and even without the contradistinguishing objects of a poem. The first chapter of Isaiah (indeed a very large proportion of the whole book) is poetry in the most emphatic sense; yet it would be not less irrational than strange to assert that pleasure, and not truth, was the immediate object of the prophet. In short, whatever *specific* import we attach to the word poetry, there will be found involved in it, as a necessary consequence, that a poem of any length neither can be, nor ought to be, all poetry.[9] Yet if a harmonious whole is to be produced, the remaining parts must be preserved *in keeping* with the poetry; and this can be no otherwise effected than by such a studied selection and artificial arrangement as will partake of *one*, though not a *peculiar*, property of poetry. And this again can be no other than the property of exciting a more continuous and equal attention than the language of prose aims at, whether colloquial or written.

My own conclusions on the nature of poetry, in the strictest use of the word, have been in part anticipated in the preceding disquisition on the fancy and imagination. What is poetry? is so nearly the same question with, what is a poet? that the answer to the one is involved in the solution of the other. For it is a distinction resulting from the poetic genius itself, which sustains and modifies the images, thoughts, and emotions of the poet's own mind. The poet, described in *ideal* perfection, brings the whole soul of man into activity, with the subordination of its faculties to each other, according to their relative worth and dignity. He diffuses a tone and spirit of unity that blends and (as it were) *fuses*, each into each, by that synthetic and magical power to which we have exclusively appropriated the name of imagination. This power, first put in action by the will and understanding and retained under their irremissive, though gentle and unnoticed, control (*laxis ef-*

The poetic nature.

7. "The free spirit [of the poet] must be hurled onward." From the *Satyricon*, by the lively Roman satirist, Petronius Arbiter (1st century A.D.).
8. Bishop Jeremy Taylor (1613–67), author of *Holy Living* and *Holy Dying;* Thomas Burnet, author of *The Sacred Theory of the Earth* (1681–89). Coleridge greatly admired the elaborate and sonorous prose of both these writers; he took from a work by Burnet the Latin motto for *The Ancient Mariner*.
9. Coleridge does not use the word "poetry" in the usual way, as a term for the class of all metrical compositions, but to designate those passages, whether in verse or prose, produced by the mind of genius in its supreme moments of imaginative activity.

fertur habenis[1]) reveals itself in the balance or reconciliation of opposite or discordant qualities:[2] of sameness, with difference; of the general, with the concrete; the idea, with the image; the individual, with the representative; the sense of novelty and freshness, with old and familiar objects; a more than usual state of emotion, with more than usual order; judgment ever awake and steady self-possession, with enthusiasm and feeling profound or vehement; and while it blends and harmonizes the natural and the artificial, still subordinates art to nature; the manner to the matter; and our admiration of the poet to our sympathy with the poetry. "Doubtless," as Sir John Davies observes of the soul (and his words may with slight alteration be applied, and even more appropriately, to the poetic IMAGINATION):

> Doubtless this could not be, but that she turns
> Bodies to spirit by sublimation strange,
> As fire converts to fire the things it burns,
> As we our food into our nature change.
>
> From their gross matter she abstracts their forms,
> And draws a kind of quintessence from things;
> Which to her proper nature she transforms
> To bear them light on her celestial wings.
>
> Thus does she, when from individual states
> She doth abstract the universal kinds;
> Which then reclothed in divers names and fates
> Steal access through our senses to our minds.[3]

Finally, GOOD SENSE is the BODY of poetic genius, FANCY its DRAPERY, MOTION its LIFE, and IMAGINATION the SOUL that is everywhere, and in each; and forms all into one graceful and intelligent whole.

From *Chapter XVII*

Examination of the tenets peculiar to Mr. Wordsworth—Rustic life (above all, low and rustic life) especially unfavorable to the formation of a human diction—The best parts of language the products of philosophers, not clowns or shepherds—Poetry essentially ideal and generic—The language of Milton as much the language of real life, yea, incomparably more so than that of the cottager.

1. I.e., driven with loosened reins.
2. Here Coleridge introduces into English criticism the concept that the highest poetry incorporates and reconciles opposite or discordant elements; under the names of "irony" and "paradox," this concept became a primary criterion of the American New Critics.

Although admittedly derived from Coleridge, the concept, by a further irony, has usually been employed to derogate Romantic poetry.
3. Adapted from John Davies' *Nosce Teipsum* ("Know Thyself"), a philosophical poem (1599).

As far then as Mr. Wordsworth in his preface contended, and most ably contended, for a reformation in our poetic diction, as' far as he has evinced the truth of passion, and the *dramatic* propriety of those figures and metaphors in the original poets which, stripped of their justifying reasons and converted into mere artifices of connection or ornament, constitute the characteristic falsity in the poetic style of the moderns; and as far as he has, with equal acuteness and clearness, pointed out the process by which this change was effected and the resemblances between that state into which the reader's mind is thrown by the pleasurable confusion of thought from an unaccustomed train of words and images and that state which is induced by the natural language of impassioned feeling, he undertook a useful task and deserves all praise, both for the attempt and for the execution. The provocations to this remonstrance in behalf of truth and nature were still of perpetual recurrence before and after the publication of this preface. * * *

My own differences from certain supposed parts of Mr. Wordsworth's theory ground themselves on the assumption that his words had been rightly interpreted, as purporting that the proper diction for poetry in general consists altogether in a language taken, with due exceptions, from the mouths of men in real life, a language which actually constitutes the natural conversation of men under the influence of natural feelings.[4] My objection is, first, that in *any* sense this rule is applicable only to *certain* classes of poetry; secondly, that even to these classes it is not applicable, except in such a sense as hath never by anyone (as far as I know or have read) been denied or doubted; and, lastly, that as far as, and in that degree in which it is *practicable*, yet as a *rule* it is useless, if not injurious, and therefore either need not or ought not to be practiced. * * *

As little can I agree with the assertion that from the objects with which the rustic hourly communicates the best part of language is formed. For first, if to communicate with an object implies such an acquaintance with it, as renders it capable of being discriminately reflected on; the distinct knowledge of an uneducated rustic would furnish a very scanty vocabulary. The few things, and modes of action, requisite for his bodily conveniences, would alone be individualized; while all the rest of nature would be expressed by a small number of confused general terms. Secondly, I deny that the words and combinations of words derived from the objects, with which the rustic is familiar, whether with distinct or confused knowledge, can be justly said to form the *best* part of language. It is more than

4. Wordsworth, Preface to *Lyrical Ballads* (1800): "A selection of the real language of men in a state of vivid sensation. * * * Low and rustic life was generally chosen. * * * The language too of these men is adopted. * * *"

probable that many classes of the brute creation possess discriminating sounds, by which they can convey to each other notices of such objects as concern their food, shelter, or safety. Yet we hesitate to call the aggregate of such sounds a language, otherwise than metaphorically. The best part of human language, properly so called, is derived from reflection on the acts of the mind itself. It is formed by a voluntary appropriation of fixed symbols to internal acts, to processes and results of imagination, the greater part of which have no place in the consciousness of uneducated man; though in civilized society, by imitation and passive remembrance of what they hear from their religious instructors and other superiors, the most uneducated share in the harvest which they neither sowed or reaped. * * *

Here let me be permitted to remind the reader that the positions which I controvert are contained in the sentences—"a selection of the REAL language of men"; "the language of these men (i.e., men in low and rustic life) I propose to myself to imitate, and as far as possible to adopt the very language of men." "Between the language of prose and that of metrical composition there neither is, nor can be any essential difference." It is against these exclusively that my opposition is directed.

I object, in the very first instance, to an equivocation in the use of the word "real." Every man's language varies according to the extent of his knowledge, the activity of his faculties and the depth or quickness of his feelings. Every man's language has, first, its *individualities*; secondly, the common properties of the *class* to which he belongs; and thirdly, words and phrases of *universal* use. The language of Hooker, Bacon, Bishop Taylor, and Burke differs from the common language of the learned class only by the superior number and novelty of the thoughts and relations which they had to convey. The language of Algernon Sidney[5] differs not at all from that which every well-educated gentleman would wish to write, and (with due allowances for the undeliberateness and less connected train of thinking natural and proper to conversation) such as he would wish to talk. Neither one or the other differ half as much from the general language of cultivated society as the language of Mr. Wordsworth's homeliest composition differs from that of a common peasant. For "real" therefore we must substitute *ordinary*, or *lingua communis*.[6] And this, we have proved, is no more to be found in the phraseology of low and rustic life than in that of any other class. Omit the peculiarities of each, and the result of course must be common to all. And assuredly the omissions and changes to be made in the language of rustics before it

5. Algernon Sidney (1622-83), republican soldier and statesmen, author of *Discourses Concerning Government*.
6. "The common language."

could be transferred to any species of poem, except the drama or other professed imitation, are at least as numerous and weighty as would be required in adapting to the same purpose the ordinary language of tradesmen and manufacturers. Not to mention that the language so highly extolled by Mr. Wordsworth varies in every county, nay, in every village, according to the accidental character of the clergyman, the existence or nonexistence of schools; or even, perhaps, as the exciseman, publican, or barber happen to be, or not to be, zealous politicians and readers of the weekly newspaper *pro bono publico*.[7] Anterior to cultivation the *lingua communis* of every country, as Dante has well observed, exists everywhere in parts and nowhere as a whole.[8]

Neither is the case rendered at all more tenable by the addition of the words "in a state of excitement."[9] For the nature of a man's words, when he is strongly affected by joy, grief, or anger, must necessarily depend on the number and quality of the general truths, conceptions, and images, and of the words expressing them, with which his mind had been previously stored. For the property of passion is not to *create*, but to set in increased activity. At least, whatever new connections of thoughts or images, or (which is equally, if not more than equally, the appropriate effect of strong excitement) whatever generalizations of truth or experience the heat of passion may produce, yet the terms of their conveyance must have pre-existed in his former conversations, and are only collected and crowded together by the unusual stimulation. It is indeed very possible to adopt in a poem the unmeaning repetitions, habitual phrases, and other blank counters which an unfurnished or confused understanding interposes at short intervals in order to keep hold of his subject which is still slipping from him, and to give him time for recollection; or in mere aid of vacancy, as in the scanty companies of a country stage the same player pops backwards and forwards, in order to prevent the appearance of empty spaces, in the procession of *Macbeth* or *Henry VIIIth*. But what assistance to the poet or ornament to the poem these can supply, I am at a loss to conjecture. Nothing assuredly can differ either in origin or in mode more widely from the apparent tautologies of intense and turbulent feeling in which the passion is greater and of longer endurance than to be exhausted or satisfied by a single representation of the image or incident exciting it. Such repetitions I admit to be a beauty of the highest kind; as illustrated by Mr. Wordsworth himself from the song of Deborah. "At her feet he

7. "For the public welfare."
8. In *De vulgari eloquentia* ("On the Speech of the People") Dante discusses —and affirms—the fitness for poetry of the unlocalized Italian vernacular.
9. Wordsworth: "the manner in which we associate ideas in a state of excitement."

bowed, he fell, he lay down: at her feet he bowed, he fell: where he bowed, there he fell down dead."[10]

1815   1817

From Lectures on Shakespeare[1]
[Fancy and Imagination in Shakespeare's Poetry]

In the preceding lecture we have examined with what armor clothed and with what titles authorized Shakespeare came forward as a poet to demand the throne of fame as the dramatic poet of England; we have now to observe and retrace the excellencies which compelled even his contemporaries to seat him on that throne, although there were giants in those days contending for the same honor. Hereafter we shall endeavor to make out the title of the English drama, as created by and existing in Shakespeare, and its right to the supremacy of dramatic excellence in general. I have endeavored to prove that he had shown himself a *poet*, previously to his appearance [as] a dramatic poet—and that had no *Lear*, no *Othello*, no *Henry the Fourth*, no *Twelfth Night* appeared, we must have admitted that Shakespeare possessed the chief if not all the requisites of a poet—namely, deep feeling and exquisite sense of beauty, both as exhibited to the eye in combinations of form, and to the ear in sweet and appropriate melody (with the exception of Spenser he is [the sweetest of English poets]); that these feelings were under the command of *his own will*—that in his very first productions he projected his mind out of his own particular being, and felt and made others feel, on subjects [in] no way connected with himself, except by force of contemplation, and that sublime faculty, by which a great mind becomes that which it meditates on. To this we are to add the affectionate love of nature and natural objects, without which no man could have observed so steadily, or painted so truly and passionately the very minutest beauties of the external world. Next, we have shown that he possessed fancy, considered as the faculty of bringing together images dissimilar in the main by some one point or more of likeness distinguished.[2]

---

10. Judges v.27. Cited by Wordsworth in a note to *The Thorn* as an example of the natural tautology of "impassioned feelings."

1. Although Coleridge's series of public lectures on Shakespeare and other poets contained much of his best criticism, he published none of this material, leaving only fragmentary remains of his lectures in notebooks, scraps of manuscript, and notes written in the margins of books. The following selections, which develop some of the basic ideas presented in *Biographia Literaria*, are taken from T. M. Raysor's edition, based on Coleridge's manuscripts and on contemporary reports, of *Coleridge's Shakespearean Criticism* (1930).

2. Coleridge here applies the distinction between fancy and imagination presented in *Biographia Literaria*, Chapter XIII. This passage from the narrative poem *Venus and Adonis* (lines 361–64) is an instance of fancy because the elements brought together remain an assemblage of recognizable and independent "fixities and definites," despite the isolated points of likeness which form the grounds of the comparison.

> Full gently now she takes him by the hand,
> A lily prisoned in a jail of snow,
> Or ivory in an alabaster band—
> So white a friend engirts so white a foe.

Still mounting, we find undoubted proof in his mind of imagination, or the power by which one image or feeling is made to modify many others and by a sort of *fusion to force many into one*—that which after showed itself in such might and energy in *Lear*, where the deep anguish of a father spreads the feeling of ingratitude and cruelty over the very elements of heaven. Various are the workings of this greatest faculty of the human mind—both passionate and tranquil. In its tranquil and purely pleasurable operation, it acts chiefly by producing out of many things, as they would have appeared in the description of an ordinary mind, described slowly and in unimpassioned succession, a oneness, even as nature, the greatest of poets, acts upon us when we open our eyes upon an extended prospect. Thus the flight of Adonis from the enamored goddess in the dusk of evening—

> Look how a bright star shooteth from the sky—
> So glides he in the night from Venus' eye.[3]

How many images and feelings are here brought together without effort and without discord—the beauty of Adonis—the rapidity of his flight—the yearning yet hopelessness of the enamored gazer—and a shadowy ideal character thrown over the whole.[4]—Or it acts by impressing the stamp of humanity, of human feeling, over inanimate objects * * *

> Lo, here the gentle lark, weary of rest,
> From his moist cabinet mounts up on high
> And wakes the morning, from whose silver breast
> The sun ariseth in his majesty;
>   Who doth the world so gloriously behold
>   That cedar tops and hills seem burnished gold.

And lastly, which belongs only to a great poet, the power of so carrying on the eye of the reader as to make him almost lose the consciousness of words—to make him *see* everything—and this without exciting any painful or laborious attention, without any *anatomy* of description (a fault not uncommon in descriptive poetry) but with the sweetness and easy movement of nature.

Lastly, he previously to his dramas, gave proof of a most pro-

3. *Venus and Adonis*, lines 815–16.
4. An instance of imagination, Coleridge claims, because the component parts—the shooting star and the flight of Adonis, together with the feelings with which both are perceived—dissolve into a new and seamless unity, different in character from the sum of its parts. In the following instance (lines 853–58), the imagination is said to fuse the neutral and inanimate objects with the human nature and feelings of the observer.

found, energetic, and philosophical mind, without which he might
have been a very delightful poet, but not the great dramatic poet
* * * But chance and his powerful instinct combined to lead
him to his proper province—in the conquest of which we are to
consider both the difficulties that opposed him, and the advantages.

ca. 1808

[Mechanic vs. Organic Form]⁵

The subject of the present lecture is no less than a question submitted to your understandings, emancipated from national prejudice: Are the plays of Shakespeare works of rude uncultivated
genius, in which the splendor of the parts compensates, if aught
can compensate, for the barbarous shapelessness and irregularity
of the whole? To which not only the French critics, but even his
own English admirers, say [yes]. Or is the form equally admirable
with the matter, the judgment of the great poet not less deserving
of our wonder than his genius? Or to repeat the question in other
words, is Shakespeare a great dramatic poet on account only of
these beauties and excellencies which he possesses in common with
the ancients, but with diminished claims to our love and honor to
the full extent of his difference from them? Or are these very differences additional proofs of poetic wisdom, at once results and
symbols of living power as contrasted with lifeless mechanism, of
free and rival originality as contradistinguished from servile imitation, or more accurately, [from] a blind copying of effects instead
of a true imitation of the essential principles? Imagine not I am
about to oppose genius to rules. No! the comparative value of these
rules is the very cause to be tried. The spirit of poetry, like all other
living powers, must of necessity circumscribe itself by rules, were
it only to unite power with beauty. It must embody in order to
reveal itself; but a living body is of necessity an organized one—
and what is organization but the connection of parts to a whole,
so that each part is at once end and means! This is no discovery
of criticism; it is a necessity of the human mind—and all nations

---

5. Coleridge is opposing the earlier
view that, because he violates the critical "rules" based on classical drama,
Shakespeare is a highly irregular dramatist whose occasional successes are the
result of innate and untutored genius,
operating without artistry or judgment.
Coleridge's refutation is based on his
distinction between the "mechanical
form" conceived by neoclassical criticism, and "organic form." Mechanical
form results from imposing a pattern
of pre-existing rules on the literary
material. Shakespeare's organic form,
on the other hand, evolves like a plant
by an inner principle, according not to
rules but to the laws of its own growth.
until it achieves an organic unity—a
living interdependence of parts and
whole in which, as Coleridge says,
"each part is at once end and means."
The concept of "organic form," in one
or another interpretation, has become
a cardinal principle in much modern
criticism.

have felt and obeyed it, in the invention of meter and measured sounds as the vehicle and involucrum[6] of poetry, itself a fellow growth from the same life, even as the bark is to the tree.

No work of true genius dare want its appropriate form; neither indeed is there any danger of this. As it must not, so neither can it, be lawless! For it is even this that constitutes its genius—the power of acting creatively under laws of its own origination. How then comes it that not only single Zoili,[7] but whole nations have combined in unhesitating condemnation of our great dramatist, as a sort of African nature, fertile in beautiful monsters, as a wild heath where islands of fertility look greener from the surrounding waste, where the loveliest plants now shine out among unsightly weeds and now are choked by their parasitic growth, so intertwined that we cannot disentangle the weed without snapping the flower. In this statement I have had no reference to the vulgar abuse of Voltaire,[8] save as far as his charges are coincident with the decisions of his commentators and (so they tell you) his almost idolatrous admirers. The true ground of the mistake, as has been well remarked by a continental critic,[9] lies in the confounding mechanical regularity with organic form. The form is mechanic when on any given material we impress a predetermined form, not necessarily arising out of the properties of the material, as when to a mass of wet clay we give whatever shape we wish it to retain when hardened. The organic form, on the other hand, is innate; it shapes as it develops itself from within, and the fulness of its development is one and the same with the perfection of its outward form. Such is the life, such the form. Nature, the prime genial artist, inexhaustible in diverse powers, is equally inexhaustible in forms. Each exterior is the physiognomy of the being within, its true image reflected and thrown out from the concave mirror. And even such is the appropriate excellence of her chosen poet, of our own Shakespeare, himself a nature humanized, a genial[10] understanding directing self-consciously a power and an implicit wisdom deeper than consciousness.[11]

1930

6. Outer covering of part of a plant.
7. Plural of "Zoilus," who in classical times was the standard example of a bad critic.
8. **Voltaire (1694–1778) wrote critiques treating Shakespeare as a barbarous, irregular, and sometimes indecent natural genius.**

9. **August Wilhelm Schlegel, German critic and literary historian, whose *Lectures on Dramatic Art and Literature* (1808–9) present many of the ideas Coleridge develops in this lecture.**
10. The adjectival form of "genius."
11. I.e., the organic process of the imagination is in part unconscious.

From The Statesman's Manual

[*On Symbol and Allegory*][1]

The histories and political economy[2] of the present and preceding century partake in the general contagion of its mechanic philosophy, and are the *product* of an unenlivened generalizing Understanding. In the Scriptures they are the living *educts*[3] of the Imagination; of that reconciling and mediatory power, which incorporating the Reason in Images of the Sense, and organizing (as it were) the flux of the Senses by the permanence and self-circling energies of the Reason, gives birth to a system of symbols, harmonious in themselves, and consubstantial with the truths, of which they are the *conductors.* These are the Wheels which Ezekiel beheld, when the hand of the Lord was upon him, and he saw visions of God as he sate among the captives by the river of Chebar. *Whithersoever the Spirit was to go, the wheels went, and thither was their spirit to go: for the spirit of the living creature was in the wheels also.*[4] The truths and the symbols that represent them move in conjunction and form the living chariot that bears up (for *us*) the throne of the Divine Humanity. Hence, by a derivative, indeed, but not a divided, influence, and though in a secondary yet in more than a metaphorical sense, the Sacred Book is worthily intitled *the* WORD OF GOD. Hence too, its contents present to us the stream of time continuous as Life and a symbol of Eternity, inasmuch as the Past and the Future are virtually contained in the Present. According therefore to our relative position on its banks the Sacred History becomes prophetic, the Sacred Prophecies historical, while the power and substance of both inhere in its Laws, its Promises, and its Comminations.[5] In the Scriptures therefore both Facts and Persons must of necessity have a twofold significance, a past and a future, a temporary and a perpetual, a particular and a universal application. They must be at once Portraits and Ideals.

1. Coleridge published *The Statesman's Manual, or The Bible the Best Guide to Political Skill and Foresight* in 1816; it was intended to show that the Scriptures, properly interpreted, provide the universal principles that should guide lawmakers in meeting the political and economic emergencies of that troubled era. His discussion there of symbol, in contradistinction both to allegory and metaphor, has been often cited and elaborated in recent discussions of symbolism in poetry. Coleridge's analysis, however, is specifically directed not to poetry, but to his view that the persons and events in Biblical history signify timeless and universal, as well as particular and local truths; and that in God's created nature, each element and power is in essential interrelation with the whole which is manifested within that part.

2. Economic theory.

3. Those things which are educed—i.e., brought forth, evolved.

4. Slightly altered from the prophet Ezekiel's vision of the Chariot of God, when he had been "among the captives by the river of Chebar" (Ezekiel i.1–20). Ezekiel was among the Jews who had been taken into captivity in Babylonia by King Nebuchadnezzar in 597 B.C.; he was put in a community of Jewish captives at Tel-Abib on the banks of the Chebar canal.

5. Divine threats of punishment for sins.

Eheu! paupertina philosophia in paupertinam religionem ducit:[6] —A hunger-bitten and idea-less philosophy naturally produces a starveling and comfortless religion. It is among the miseries of the present age that it recognizes no medium between *Literal* and *Metaphorical.* Faith is either to be buried in the dead letter,[7] or its name and honors usurped by a counterfeit product of the mechanical understanding, which in the blindness of self-complacency confounds SYMBOLS with ALLEGORIES. Now an Allegory is but a translation of abstract notions into a picture-language which is itself nothing but an abstraction from objects of the senses; the principal being more worthless even than its phantom proxy, both alike unsubstantial, and the former shapeless to boot. On the other hand a Symbol (*ὁ ἔστιν ἀεὶ ταυτηγόρικον*)[8] is characterized by a translucence of the Special in the Individual or of the General in the Especial or of the Universal in the General. Above all by the translucence of the Eternal through and in the Temporal. It always partakes of the Reality which it renders intelligible; and while it enunciates the whole, abides itself as a living part in that Unity, of which it is the representative. The other are but empty echoes which the fancy arbitrarily associates with apparitions of matter, less beautiful but not less shadowy than the sloping orchard or hillside pasture-field seen in the transparent lake below. Alas! for the flocks that are to be led forth to such pastures! "*It shall even be as when the hungry dreameth, and behold! he eateth; but he waketh and his soul is empty: or as when the thirsty dreameth, and behold he drinketh; but he awaketh and is faint!*"[9] * * *

* * * The fact therefore, that the mind of man in its own primary and constituent forms represents the laws of nature, is a mystery which of itself should suffice to make us religious:[1] for it is a problem of which God is the only solution, God, the one before all, and of all, and through all!—True natural philosophy is comprized in the study of the science and language of *symbols*. The power delegated to nature is all in every part: and by a symbol I mean, not a metaphor or allegory or any other figure of speech or form of fancy, but an actual and essential part of that, the whole of which it represents. Thus our Lord speaks symbolically when he says that "the eye is the light of the body."[2] The genuine naturalist is a dramatic poet in his own line: and such as our myriad-minded Shakespeare is,

6. "Alas! a poverty-stricken philosophy leads to a poverty-stricken religion."
7. I.e., the Scriptures read entirely literally.
8. "Which is always tautegorical." Coleridge coined this word, and elsewhere defined "*tau*tegorical" as "expressing the *same* subject but with a difference, in contradistinction from metaphors and similitudes, that are always *alleg*orical" (Coleridge's italics). The root

meaning of *tau-* is "the same," and of *alle-* is "other"; the root meaning of *-gorical* is "speak."
9. Slightly altered from Isaiah xxix.8.
1. This paragraph is from Appendix C of *The Statesman's Manual*.
2. Matthew vi.22: "The light of the body is the eye." "Naturalist" (in the next sentence): one who studies natural science; a physicist.

compared with the Racines and Metastasios,[3] such and by a similar process of self-transformation would the man be, compared with the Doctors of the mechanic school,[4] who should construct his physiology on the heaven-descended, Know Thyself.[5]

[The Satanic Hero][6]

* * * In its state of immanence (or indwelling) in reason and religion, the WILL appears indifferently, as wisdom or as love: two names of the same power, the former more intelligential,[7] the latter more spiritual, the former more frequent in the Old, the latter in the New Testament. But in its utmost abstraction and consequent state of reprobation,[8] the Will becomes satanic pride and rebellious self-idolatry in the relations of the spirit to itself, and remorseless despotism relatively to others; the more hopeless as the more obdurate by its subjugation of sensual impulses, by its superiority to toil and pain and pleasure; in short, by the fearful resolve to find in itself alone the one absolute motive of action, under which all other motives from within and from without must be either subordinated or crushed.

This is the character which Milton has so philosophically as well as sublimely embodied in the Satan of his Paradise Lost. Alas! too often has it been embodied in *real* life! Too often has it given a dark and savage grandeur to the historic page! And wherever it has appeared, under whatever circumstances of time and country, the same ingredients have gone to its composition; and it has been identified by the same attributes. Hope in which there is no Cheerfulness; Steadfastness within and immovable Resolve, with outward Restlessness and whirling Activity; Violence with Guile; Temerity with Cunning; and, as the result of all, Interminableness of Object with perfect Indifference of Means; these are the qualities that have constituted the COMMANDING GENIUS! these are the Marks that have characterized the Masters of Mischief, the Liberticides, and mighty Hunters of Mankind, from NIMROD[9] to NAPOLEON. And

---

3. Jean Racine (1639–99), the great French author of verse tragedies. Pietro Metastasio (1698–1782), a minor Italian poet and author of opera librettos. Coleridge delighted in derogating French philosophy and culture, venting what he called his "Gall contra Gallois"—his gall against the Gauls.
4. I.e., learned men who hold a mechanistic philosophy of nature.
5. The Roman Juvenal, in *Satires* xi.27, had said that "From Heaven it descends, 'Know Thyself'." The original saying, "Know Thyself," was attributed by classical authors to the Delphic oracle.
6. From *The Statesman's Manual*, Appendix C. Coleridge analyzes the

character of Milton's Satan and goes on to recognize, and to warn his age against, the appeal of that type of Romantic hero (exemplified above all by the protagonists in Byron's romances and in his drama, *Manfred*) which was in large part modeled on the Satan of *Paradise Lost*.
7. Intellectual.
8. In its theological sense: rejection by God.
9. In Genesis x.9, Nimrod is described as "a mighty hunter before the Lord." The passage was traditionally interpreted to signify that Nimrod hunted down men, hence that he was the prototype of all tyrants and bloody conquerors.

from inattention to the possibility of such a character as well as from ignorance of its elements, even men of honest intentions too frequently become fascinated. Nay, whole nations have been so far duped by this want of insight and reflection as to regard with palliative admiration, instead of wonder and abhorrence, the Molochs[1] of human nature, who are indebted, for the far larger portion of their meteoric success, to their total want of principle, and who surpass the generality of their fellow creatures in one act of courage only, that of daring to say with their whole heart, "Evil, be thou my good!"—[2] All *system* so far is power; and a *systematic* criminal, self-consistent and entire in wickedness, who entrenches villainy within villainy, and barricadoes crime by crime, has removed a world of obstacles by the mere decision, that he will have no obstacles, but those of force and brute matter.

1816

1. Molochs, monsters of evil. In the Old Testament, Moloch is an idol to whom firstborn children are sacrificed. Milton adopted the name for the war-like fallen angel; see *Paradise Lost* II.43–107.
2. Spoken by Satan, *Paradise Lost* IV.110.

CHARLES LAMB
(1775–1834)

1782–89: At Christ's Hospital school; Coleridge a fellow student.
1820–25: Contributes "Essays of Elia" to the *London Magazine.*

Lamb was almost the exact contemporary of Wordsworth and Coleridge; he numbered these two poets, as well as Keats, among his close friends, published his own early poems in combination with those of Coleridge in 1796 and 1797, and supported the *Lyrical Ballads* and some of the other avant-garde poetry of his time. Yet Lamb lacks almost all the traits and convictions we think of as characteristically "Romantic." He happily lived all his life in the city and its environs, sharing Dr. Johnson's opinion that he who tires of London tires of life. He could not abide Shelley or his poetry and he distrusted Coleridge's supernaturalism and Wordsworth's oracular sublimities and religion of nature, preferring those elements in their poems which were human and realistic. In an age when many of the important writers were fervent radicals and some became equally fervent reactionaries, Lamb remained uncommitted in both politics and religion; and although on intimate terms with such dedicated reformers as Hazlitt, William Godwin, Thomas Holcroft, and Leigh Hunt, he chose them, as he said, not for their opinions, but "for some individuality of character which they manifested." In his own writings, the one attribute he shared with his great contemporaries was that of *l'étalage du moi,* "the display of one's own personality": many of his best familiar essays, like Wordsworth's poems, are made up of his early experiences and feelings, recollected in tranquility. But it must be remembered that, although personal poetry was a new and distinctive Romantic form, the personal essay was already a well-established genre which had been developed by Montaigne as early as the 16th century.

Lamb was born in the Inner Temple, an ancient section of London where his father was clerk and assistant to a lawyer. At the age of 7 he entered Christ's Hospital, the "Bluecoat School" of his essay *Christ's Hospital Five and Thirty Years Ago.* He left the school before he was 15 and soon thereafter became a clerk in the accounting department of the huge commercial house, The East India Company, where he remained for 33 years. His adult life was quiet and unadventurous, but under its calm surface, as Walter Pater said, lay "something of the fateful domestic horror, of the beautiful heroism and devotedness too, of old Greek tragedy." When he was 22 his beloved sister Mary, ten years his senior, broke under the strain of caring for her invalid parents and in an insane paroxysm stabbed her mother to the heart. Lamb wrote to Coleridge:

My dearest friend—
　　* * * My poor dear dearest sister in a fit of insanity has been the death of her own mother. I was at hand only time enough to snatch the knife out of her grasp. She is at present in a madhouse, from whence I fear she must be moved to an hospital. God has preserved to me my senses. * * * My poor father was slightly wounded, and I am left to take care of him and my aunt. * * * Write—as religious a letter as possible—but no mention of what is gone and done with—with me former things are passed away, and I have something more to do than to feel—
　　God Almighty have us all in his keeping.—

　　　　　　　　　　　　　　　　　　　　C. Lamb

Upon her recovery Mary was released to the care of her brother, who devoted to her and to their common household the rest of his life. Mary's attacks recurred, briefly but periodically, and when the terribly familiar symptoms began to manifest themselves, Lamb and Mary would walk arm in arm and weeping to the asylum, carrying a strait jacket with them.

Most of the time, however, Mary was her normally serene and gracious self, and she shared her brother's delight in old books, the theater, art galleries, and the inexhaustible variousness of the great city. She shared also his gregariousness and genius for friendship. The Wednesday (sometimes Thursday) night gatherings at the Lambs attracted a varied company which included many of the leading writers and artists of England. Among his guests Lamb moved with his peculiar shuffling gait, dressed invariably in old-fashioned black of clerical cut, his body fragile, but surmounted by a fine head; everyone remarked on the sad sweetness of his smile. He drew furiously upon a pipe of strong tobacco and drank copiously; as the alcohol eased his habitual stammer, his puns and practical jokes grew ever more outrageous. Occasionally an evening ended with Lamb drunk under the table. But his friends invariably applied to him the epithet "gentle"—to his great indignation. "For God's sake," he exploded to Coleridge, "don't make me ridiculous any more by terming me gentle-hearted in print, or do it in better verses." "Substitute drunken dog, ragged-head, seld-shaven, odd-eyed, stuttering, or any other epithet which truly and properly belongs to the gentleman in question." Lamb had, in fact, a complex temperament, in which the playfulness overlay a somber melancholy and the freakishness sometimes manifested a touch of malice. To requests from Wordsworth and Coleridge for criticism of their poems he replied with a caustic candor not entirely appreciated by its beneficiaries. This charming egotist cherished his prejudices and distastes—he called them his "imperfect sympathies"— no less than he did his sympathies and enjoyments, and he never encountered pretentiousness, complacency, or a solemnity too profound and sustained without puncturing it by a well-honed witticism. "What choice venom!" exclaimed his friend Hazlitt, an expert on the subject—but while Hazlitt managed to antagonize almost everyone by his outspokenness, few could take offense, and none could long sustain it, at Lamb's antic speech and behavior.

To supplement his salary at the East India House, Lamb had early turned to writing in a variety of forms. When in 1818, at the age of 43, he published his *Works*, he apparently thought his major writing had already been accomplished. He had produced a good deal of minor verse; a sentimental novel, *Rosamund Gray*; a blank verse tragedy in the Elizabethan manner, *John Woodvil*; a farce, *Mr. H——*, which was hissed by many (including the honest author) when it was produced at Drury Lane; and, in collaboration with his sister Mary, the excellent children's book, *Tales from Shakespeare*. His most impressive achievements were the brilliant comments incorporated in his anthology, important in the Elizabethan revival of that period, *Specimens of English Dramatic Poets Who Lived About the Time of Shakespeare*, together with two fine critical essays, *The Tragedies of Shakespeare* and *On the Genius and Character of Hogarth*. But not until two years after the appearance of his *Works* did Lamb begin to contribute to the *London Magazine* the *Essays of Elia*, which have elevated him to the rank of a major author.

Lamb's earlier attempts in the fictional forms show that he lacked the power of inventing characters and events, but in the familiar essay (in which he had, in effect, served a long apprenticeship in his letters to his friends) he was able to exploit his one great subject: himself, his connoisseurship of literature and of people, and his strong local attachments— "old chairs, old tables, streets, squares, where I have sunned myself, my old school." Under the pseudonym of an Italian clerk named Elia, whom he had known while briefly employed in the South Sea House, Lamb projects in his essays the character of a man who is whimsical but strongwilled, self-deprecating yet self-absorbed, a specialist in nostalgia and in that humor which balances delicately on the verge of pathos. So engaging is the literary persona which pervades his work that it has attracted a host of devotees who have established what has been called "the Elia industry." But the critical preoccupation with Lamb's seemingly ingenuous self-revelation has obscured the actual cunning of a deliberate and dedicated artist in prose. Lamb's style was not in any contemporary tradition. He wrote, as he said, "for antiquity"; his prose style, like that of Edmund Spenser's in verse, is an invented style. Although its basis is plain modern English, it is colored throughout by archaic words, expressions, and turns of syntax. In the conduct of his essays Lamb is capricious, droll, and (in the manner of earlier literary eccentrics such as Robert Burton and Laurence Sterne) he delights in tricks of words and thought and in the elaborate exploration of a literary conceit. Close imitators of Lamb's style invariably fall into archness and sentimentality. Lamb's inimitable feat was to transform whimsy into a classic type of the personal essay, uttered in one of the distinctive voices in English prose.

Christ's Hospital Five-and-Thirty Years Ago[1]

In Mr. Lamb's *Works*, published a year or two since, I find a magnificent eulogy on my old school, such as it was, or now appears to him to have been, between the years 1782 and 1789. It happens very oddly that my own standing at Christ's was nearly corresponding with his; and, with all gratitude to him for his enthusiasm for the cloisters, I think he has contrived to bring together whatever can be said in praise of them, dropping all the other side of the argument most ingeniously.

I remember L. at school, and can well recollect that he had some peculiar advantages, which I and others of his schoolfellows had not. His friends lived in town, and were near at hand; and he had the privilege of going to see them almost as often as he wished, through some invidious distinction, which was denied to us. The present worthy subtreasurer to the Inner Temple[2] can explain how that happened. He had his tea and hot rolls in a morning, while we were battening upon our quarter of a penny loaf—our *crug*—moistened with attenuated small beer, in wooden piggins,[3] smacking of the pitched leathern jack it was poured from. Our Monday's milk porritch, blue and tasteless, and the pease soup of Saturday, coarse and choking, were enriched for him with a slice of "extraordinary bread and butter," from the hot loaf of the Temple. The Wednesday's mess of millet,[4] somewhat less repugnant—(we had three banyan to four meat days in the week[5])—was endeared to his palate with a lump of double-refined, and a smack of ginger (to make it go down the more glibly) or the fragrant cinnamon. In lieu of our *half-pickled* Sundays, or *quite fresh* boiled beef on

1. Christ's Hospital, London (founded in 1552 by Edward VI), was run as a free boarding school for the sons of middle-class parents in straitened financial circumstances. Its students were known as "Bluecoat Boys," from their uniforms of a long blue gown and yellow stockings. Lamb had in 1813 published a magazine article, *Recollections of Christ's Hospital*, which the present essay undertakes to supplement by presenting the less formal side of school life. The "I" or narrator of the essay is Elia—a device which allows Lamb to combine his own circumstances and experiences with those of Coleridge, his older contemporary at the school.
2. Randal Norris, who had befriended young Charles Lamb. The Inner Temple is one of the four Inns of Court, the center of the English legal profession.
3. Small wooden pails. The "jack" is a leather vessel coated on the outside with pitch. "Small beer" is low in alcoholic content. "Crug": slang for bread.
4. Cereal.
5. "Banyan days" is a nautical term for days when no meat is served; it derives from "banian," a member of a Hindu caste to whom meat is forbidden.

Thursdays (strong as *caro equina*[6]), with detestable marigolds floating in the pail to poison the broth—our scanty mutton scrags[7] on Friday—and rather more savory, but grudging, portions of the same flesh, rotten-roasted[8] or rare, on the Tuesdays (the only dish which excited our appetites, and disappointed our stomachs, in almost equal proportion)—he had his hot plate of roast veal, or the more tempting griskin[9] (exotics unknown to our palates), cooked in the paternal kitchen (a great thing), and brought him daily by his maid or aunt! I remember the good old relative (in whom love forbade pride) squatting down upon some odd stone in a by-nook of the cloisters, disclosing the viands (of higher regale than those cates which the ravens ministered to the Tishbite[1]); and the contending passions of L. at the unfolding. There was love for the bringer; shame for the thing brought, and the manner of its bringing; sympathy for those who were too many to share in it; and, at top of all, hunger (eldest, strongest of the passions!) predominant, breaking down the stony fences of shame, and awkwardness, and a troubling over-consciousness.

I was a poor friendless boy. My parents, and those who should care for me, were far away. Those few acquaintances of theirs, which they could reckon upon being kind to me in the great city, after a little forced notice, which they had the grace to take of me on my first arrival in town, soon grew tired of my holiday visits. They seemed to them to recur too often, though I thought them few enough; and, one after another, they all failed me, and I felt myself alone among six hundred playmates.

O the cruelty of separating a poor lad from his early homestead! The yearnings which I used to have towards it in those unfledged years! How, in my dreams, would my native town (far in the west) come back, with its church, and trees, and faces! How I would wake weeping, and in the anguish of my heart exclaim upon sweet Calne in Wiltshire![2]

To this late hour of my life, I trace impressions left by the recollections of those friendless holidays. The long warm days of summer never return but they bring with them a gloom from the haunting memory of those *whole-day leaves*, when, by some strange arrangement, we were turned out for the livelong day, upon our own hands, whether we had friends to go to or none. I remember those bathing excursions to the New River which L. recalls with such relish, better, I think, than he can—for he was a home-seeking lad, and did not much care for such water pastimes: How merrily

---

6. Horsemeat.
7. Necks.
8. Overdone.
9. The lean part of a loin of pork.
1. The prophet Elijah, fed by the ravens

in I Kings xvii. "Cates": delicacies.
2. Coleridge had come to school from Ottery St. Mary, Devonshire, in the southwest of England.

we would sally forth into the fields; and strip under the first warmth of the sun; and wanton like young dace[3] in the streams; getting us appetites for noon, which those of us that were penniless (our scanty morning crust long since exhausted) had not the means of allaying—while the cattle, and the birds, and the fishes were at feed about us and we had nothing to satisfy our cravings—the very beauty of the day, and the exercise of the pastime, and the sense of liberty, setting a keener edge upon them! How faint and languid, finally, we would return, towards nightfall, to our desired morsel, half-rejoicing, half-reluctant that the hours of our uneasy liberty had expired!

It was worse in the days of winter, to go prowling about the streets objectless—shivering at cold windows of print shops, to extract a little amusement; or haply, as a last resort in the hopes of a little novelty, to pay a fifty-times repeated visit (where our individual faces should be as well known to the warden as those of his own charges) to the Lions in the Tower—to whose levee, by courtesy immemorial, we had a prescriptive title to admission.[1]

L.'s governor (so we called the patron who presented us to the foundation[2]) lived in a manner under his paternal roof. Any complaint which he had to make was sure of being attended to. This was understood at Christ's, and was an effectual screen to him against the severity of masters, or worse tyranny of the monitors. The oppressions of these young brutes are heart-sickening to call to recollection. I have been called out of my bed, and *waked for the purpose*, in the coldest winter nights—and this not once, but night after night—in my shirt, to receive the discipline of a leathern thong and eleven other sufferers, because it pleased my callow overseer, when there has been any talking heard after we were gone to bed, to make the six last beds in the dormitory, where the youngest children of us slept, answerable for an offense they neither dared to commit nor had the power to hinder. The same execrable tyranny drove the younger part of us from the fires, when our feet were perishing with snow; and, under the cruelest penalties, forbade the indulgence of a drink of water when we lay in sleepless summer nights fevered with the season and the day's sports.

There was one H——, who, I learned, in after days was seen expiating some maturer offense in the hulks.[3] (Do I flatter myself

---

3. A small quick-darting fish.
1. The Bluecoat Boys had the right of free admission to the royal menagerie, then housed in the Tower of London. A "levee" is a formal morning reception.
2. I.e., who vouched for a candidate for entrance to Christ's Hospital. Lamb's patron was Samuel Salt, a lawyer and Member of Parliament, for whom Lamb's father served as clerk.
3. Prison ship. (In Lamb's time the plural "hulks" had come to be used for the singular.) Nevis and St. Kitts are islands in the West Indies.

in fancying that this might be the planter of that name, who suffered—at Nevis, I think, or St. Kitts—some few years since? My friend Tobin was the benevolent instrument of bringing him to the gallows.) This petty Nero actually branded a boy who had offended him with a red-hot iron; and nearly starved forty of us with exacting contributions, to the one-half of our bread, to pamper a young ass, which, incredible as it may seem, with the connivance of the nurse's daughter (a young flame of his) he had contrived to smuggle in, and keep upon the leads[4] of the *ward*, as they called our dormitories. This game went on for better than a week, till the foolish beast, not able to fare well but he must cry roast meat—happier than Caligula's minion,[5] could he have kept his own counsel—but foolisher, alas! than any of his species in the fables—waxing fat, and kicking, in the fullness of bread, one unlucky minute would needs proclaim his good fortune to the world below; and, laying out his simple throat, blew such a ram's-horn blast, as (toppling down the walls of his own Jericho[6]) set concealment any longer at defiance. The client was dismissed, with certain attentions, to Smithfield; but I never understood that the patron underwent any censure on the occasion. This was in the stewardship of L.'s admired Perry.[7]

Under the same *facile* administration, can L. have forgotten the cool impunity with which the nurses used to carry away openly, in open platters, for their own tables, one out of two of every hot joint, which the careful matron had been seeing scrupulously weighed out for our dinners? These things were daily practiced in that magnificent apartment which L. (grown connoisseur since, we presume) praises so highly for the grand paintings "by Verrio,[8] and others," with which it is "hung round and adorned." But the sight of sleek, well-fed bluecoat boys in pictures was, at that time, I believe, little consolatory to him, or us, the living ones, who saw the better part of our provisions carried away before our faces by harpies; and ourselves reduced (with the Trojan in the hall of Dido)

To feed our mind with idle portraiture.[9]

L. has recorded the repugnance of the school to *gags*, or the fat of fresh beef boiled; and sets it down to some superstition. But these unctuous morsels are never grateful to young palates (chil-

---

4. A flat roof.
5. The favorite horse of the Emperor Caligula, who was fed gilded oats and appointed to the post of chief consul.
6. Joshua toppled the walls of Jericho by trumpet blasts (Joshua vi.16–20). "Smithfield": a market for horses and cattle.
7. John Perry, steward of the school,
described in Lamb's earlier essay.
8. Antonio Verrio, Italian painter of the 17th century. While living in England, he painted a large picture of the mathematics students of Christ's Hospital being received by James II.
9. In Virgil's *Aeneid* I.464; Aeneas is inspecting the paintings in Dido's temple to Juno.

dren are universally fat-haters), and in strong, coarse, boiled meats, *unsalted*, are detestable. A *gag-eater* in our time was equivalent to a *ghoul*, and held in equal detestation.——— suffered under the imputation.

> . . . . 'Twas said
> He ate strange flesh.[1]

He was observed, after dinner, carefully to gather up the remnants left at his table (not many nor very choice fragments, you may credit me)—and, in an especial manner, these disreputable morsels, which he would convey away and secretly stow in the settle that stood at his bedside. None saw when he ate them. It was rumored that he privately devoured them in the night. He was watched, but no traces of such midnight practices were discoverable. Some reported that on leave-days he had been seen to carry out of the bounds a large blue check handkerchief, full of something. This then must be the accursed thing. Conjecture next was at work to imagine how he could dispose of it. Some said he sold it to the beggars. This belief generally prevailed. He went about moping. None spake to him. No one would play with him. He was excommunicated; put out of the pale of the school. He was too powerful a boy to be beaten, but he underwent every mode of that negative punishment which is more grievous than many stripes. Still he persevered. At length he was observed by two of his schoolfellows, who were determined to get at the secret, and had traced him one leave-day for the purpose, to enter a large worn-out building, such as there exist specimens of in Chancery Lane, which are let out to various scales of pauperism, with open door and a common staircase. After him they silently slunk in, and followed by stealth up four flights, and saw him tap at a poor wicket, which was opened by an aged woman, meanly clad. Suspicion was now ripened into certainty. The informers had secured their victim. They had him in their toils. Accusation was formally preferred, and retribution most signal was looked for. Mr. Hathaway, the then steward (for this happened a little after my time), with that patient sagacity which tempered all his conduct, determined to investigate the matter before he proceeded to sentence. The result was that the supposed mendicants, the receivers or purchasers of the mysterious scraps, turned out to be the parents of ———, an honest couple come to decay—whom this seasonable supply had, in all probability, saved from mendicancy; and that this young stork, at the expense of his own good name, had all this while been only feeding the old birds!—The governors on this occasion,

1. Loosely quoted from Shakespeare's *Antony and Cleopatra* I.iv.67.

much to their honor, voted a present relief to the family of ———, and presented him with a silver medal. The lesson which the steward read upon RASH JUDGMENT, on the occasion of publicly delivering the medal to ———, I believe would not be lost upon his auditory.—I had left school then, but I well remember ———. He was a tall, shambling youth, with a cast in his eye, not at all calculated to conciliate hostile prejudices. I have since seen him carrying a baker's basket. I think I heard he did not do quite so well by himself as he had done by the old folks.

I was a hypochondriac lad;[2] and the sight of a boy in fetters, upon the day of my first putting on the blue clothes, was not exactly fitted to assuage the natural terrors of initiation. I was of tender years, barely turned of seven; and had only read of such things in books, or seen them but in dreams. I was told he had *run away.* This was the punishment for the first offense.—As a novice I was soon after taken to see the dungeons. These were little, square, Bedlam[3] cells, where a boy could just lie at his length upon straw and a blanket—a mattress, I think, was afterwards substituted —with a peep of light, let in askance, from a prison orifice at top, barely enough to read by. Here the poor boy was locked in by himself all day, without sight of any but the porter who brought him his bread and water—who *might not speak to him*—or of the beadle, who came twice a week to call him out to receive his periodical chastisement, which was almost welcome, because it separated him for a brief interval from solitude—and here he was shut up by himself *of nights* out of the reach of any sound, to suffer whatever horrors the weak nerves, and superstition incident to his time of life, might subject him to. This was the penalty for the second offense. Wouldst thou like, reader, to see what became of him in the next degree?

The culprit, who had been a third time an offender, and whose expulsion was at this time deemed irreversible, was brought forth, as at some solemn auto da fé,[4] arrayed in uncouth and most appalling attire—all trace of his late "watchet weeds"[5] carefully effaced, he was exposed in a jacket resembling those which London lamplighters formerly delighted in, with a cap of the same. The effect of this divestiture was such as the ingenious devisers of it could have anticipated. With his pale and frighted features, it was as if some of those disfigurements in Dante[6] had seized upon him. In this disguisement he was brought into the hall (*L.'s favorite state room*), where awaited him the whole number of his school-

---

2. From now on Elia speaks as Lamb, rather than as Coleridge.
3. St. Mary of Bethlehem, an insane asylum in London.
4. The ceremony prior to the execution

of heretics under the Spanish Inquisition (literally, "act of faith").
5. Blue clothes.
6. I.e., of the sinners in Dante's *Inferno;* see Canto XX.

fellows, whose joint lessons and sports he was thenceforth to share
no more; the awful presence of the steward, to be seen for the last
time; of the executioner beadle, clad in his state robe for the occasion; and of two faces more, of direr import, because never but in
these extremities visible. These were governors; two of whom by
choice, or charter, were always accustomed to officiate at these
Ultima Supplicia;[7] not to mitigate (so at least we understood it),
but to enforce the uttermost stripe. Old Bamber Gascoigne, and
Peter Aubert, I remember, were colleagues on one occasion, when
the beadle turning rather pale, a glass of brandy was ordered to
prepare him for the mysteries. The scourging was, after the old
Roman fashion, long and stately. The lictor[8] accompanied the
criminal quite round the hall. We were generally too faint, with
attending to the previous disgusting circumstances, to make accurate report with our eyes of the degree of corporal suffering inflicted. Report, of course, gave out the back knotty and livid. After
scourging, he was made over, in his *San Benito,*[9] to his friends, if
he had any (but commonly such poor runagates were friendless),
or to his parish officer, who, to enhance the effect of the scene, had
his station allotted to him on the outside of the hall gate.

These solemn pageantries were not played off so often as to spoil
the general mirth of the community. We had plenty of exercise
and recreation *after* school hours; and, for myself, I must confess
that I was never happier than *in* them. The Upper and the Lower
Grammar Schools were held in the same room; and an imaginary
line only divided their bounds. Their character was as different as
that of the inhabitants on the two sides of the Pyrenees. The Rev.
James Boyer[1] was the Upper Master; but the Rev. Matthew Field
presided over that portion of the apartment of which I had the
good fortune to be a member. We lived a life as careless as birds.
We talked and did just what we pleased, and nobody molested
us. We carried an accidence,[2] or a grammar, for form; but, for
any trouble it gave us, we might take two years in getting through
the verbs deponent, and another two in forgetting all that we had
learned about them. There was now and then the formality of saying a lesson, but if you had not learned it, a brush across the shoulders (just enough to disturb a fly) was the sole remonstrance. Field
never used the rod; and in truth he wielded the cane with no great
good will—holding it "like a dancer." It looked in his hands rather
like an emblem than an instrument of authority; and an emblem,
too, he was ashamed of. He was a good, easy man, that did not
care to ruffle his own peace, nor perhaps set any great consideration

---

7. Extreme punishments.
8. A Roman officer who cleared the
way for the chief magistrates.
9. The yellow robe worn by the condemned heretic at an auto da fé
1. This teacher is also described by

Coleridge in *Biographia Literaria,* Chapter I.
2. A table of the declension of nouns
and conjugation of verbs in Greek and
Latin. "Verbs deponent": verbs with an
active meaning but passive form.

upon the value of juvenile time. He came among us, now and then, but often stayed away whole days from us; and when he came it made no difference to us—he had his private room to retire to, the short time he stayed, to be out of the sound of our noise. Our mirth and uproar went on. We had classics of our own, without being beholden to "insolent Greece or haughty Rome,"[3] that passed current among us—*Peter Wilkins*—the *Adventures of the Hon. Captain Robert Boyle*—the *Fortunate Bluecoat Boy*[4]—and the like. Or we cultivated a turn for mechanic and scientific operations; making little sundials of paper; or weaving those ingenious parentheses called *cat cradles*; or making dry peas to dance upon the end of a tin pipe; or studying the art military over that laudable game "French and English,"[4a] and a hundred other such devices to pass away the time—mixing the useful with the agreeable—as would have made the souls of Rousseau and John Locke chuckle to have seen us.[5]

Matthew Field belonged to that class of modest divines who affect to mix in equal proportion the *gentleman*, the *scholar*, and the *Christian*; but, I know not how, the first ingredient is generally found to be the predominating dose in the composition. He was engaged in gay parties, or with his courtly bow at some episcopal levee, when he should have been attending upon us. He had for many years the classical charge of a hundred children, during the four or five first years of their education, and his very highest form seldom proceeded further than two or three of the introductory fables of Phaedrus.[6] How things were suffered to go on thus, I cannot guess. Boyer, who was the proper person to have remedied these abuses, always affected, perhaps felt, a delicacy in interfering in a province not strictly his own. I have not been without my suspicions, that he was not altogether displeased at the contrast we presented to his end of the school. We were a sort of Helots to his young Spartans.[7] He would sometimes, with ironic deference, send to borrow a rod of the Under Master, and then, with sardonic grin, observe to one of his upper boys, "how neat and fresh the twigs looked." While his pale students were battering their brains over Xenophon and Plato, with a silence as deep as that enjoined by the Samite,[8] we were enjoying ourselves at our ease in our little

3. Ben Jonson's *To the Memory of * * * William Shakespeare*, line 39.
4. All three were popular adventure stories or romances of the day.
4a. A page is covered with dots and the contestants, with eyes closed, try to draw a line which will cover the maximum number of the dots.
5. These two philosophers recommended systems of education which combined theory with practical experience.
6. A Roman author of the 1st century

A.D., author of a collection of beast fables, including such children's favorites as "The Fox and the Sour Grapes" and "King Log and King Watersnake."
7. The Spartans exhibited drunken Helots (slaves) as a warning example to their children.
8. Pythogoras of Samos, Greek mathematician and philosopher of the 6th century B.C., forbade his pupils to speak until they had studied with him five years.

Goshen.[9] We saw a little into the secrets of his discipline, and the prospect did but the more reconcile us to our lot. His thunders rolled innocuous for us: his storms came near, but never touched us; contrary to Gideon's miracle, while all around were drenched, our fleece was dry.[1] His boys turned out the better scholars; we, I suspect, have the advantage in temper. His pupils cannot speak of him without something of terror allaying their gratitude; the remembrance of Field comes back with all the soothing images of indolence, and summer slumbers, and work like play, and innocent idleness, and Elysian exemptions, and life itself a "playing holiday."

Though sufficiently removed from the jurisdiction of Boyer, we were near enough (as I have said) to understand a little of his system. We occasionally heard sounds of the *Ululantes*, and caught glances of Tartarus.[2] B. was a rabid pedant. His English style was cramped to barbarism. His Easter anthems (for his duty obliged him to those periodical flights) were grating as scrannel pipes.[3]— He would laugh, aye, and heartily, but then it must be at Flaccus's quibble about *Rex*[4]—or at the *tristis serveritas in vultu*, or *inspicere in patinas*, of Terence[5]—thin jests, which at their first broaching could hardly have had *vis*[6] enough to move a Roman muscle.— He had two wigs, both pedantic, but of different omen. The one serene, smiling, fresh powdered, betokening a mild day. The other, an old, discolored, unkempt, angry caxon,[7] denoting frequent and bloody execution. Woe to the school, when he made his morning appearance in his *passy*, or *passionate wig*. No comet expounded surer.[8]—J. B. had a heavy hand. I have known him double his knotty fist at a poor trembling child (the maternal milk hardly dry upon its lips) with a "Sirrah, do you presume to set your wits at me?"—Nothing was more common than to see him make a headlong entry into the schoolroom, from his inner recess, or library, and, with turbulent eye, singling out a lad, roar out, "Od's my life, sirrah" (his favorite adjuration), "I have a great mind to whip you"—then, with as sudden a retracting impulse, fling back into his lair—and, after a cooling lapse of some minutes

---

9. Where the Jews dwelt, protected from the swarms of flies with which the Lord plagued the Egyptians in Exodus viii.22.
1. Judges vi.37–38. As a sign to Gideon, the Lord soaked his sheepskin while leaving the earth around it dry.
2. In the *Aeneid* VI.557–58, Aeneas hears the groans and the sound of the lash from Tartarus, the infernal place of punishment for the wicked. "*Ululantes*" means "howling sufferers."
3. "Harsh pipes," an echo of Milton's *Lycidas*, line 124.
4. In *Satires* I.vii of Horace (Quintus

Horatius Flaccus), there is a pun on *Rex* as both a surname and the word for "king."
5. In Terence's *Andrea* V.ii one character says of a notorious liar that he has "a sober severity in his countenance." In his *Adelphi* III.iii, after a father has advised his son to look into the lives of men as a mirror, the slave advises the kitchen scullions "to look into the stew pans" as a mirror.
6. Force; a term in rhetorical theory.
7. A type of wig.
8. Comets were superstitiously regarded as omens of disaster.

(during which all but the culprit had totally forgotten the context) drive headlong out again, piecing out his imperfect sense, as if it had been some Devil's Litany, with the expletory yell—"*and I* WILL, *too.*"—In his gentler moods, when the *rabidus furor*[9] was assuaged, he had resort to an ingenious method, peculiar, for what I have heard, to himself, of whipping the boy, and reading the Debates,[1] at the same time; a paragraph, and a lash between; which in those times, when parliamentary oratory was most at a height and flourishing in these realms, was not calculated to impress the patient with a veneration for the diffuser graces of rhetoric.

Once, and but once, the uplifted rod was known to fall ineffectual from his hand—when droll squinting W—— having been caught putting the inside of the master's desk to a use for which the architect had clearly not designed it, to justify himself, with great simplicity averred, that *he did not know that the thing had been forewarned.* This exquisite irrecognition of any law antecedent to the *oral* or *declaratory* struck so irresistibly upon the fancy of all who heard it (the pedagogue himself not excepted)—that remission was unavoidable.

L. has given credit to B.'s great merits as an instructor. Coleridge, in his literary life, has pronounced a more intelligible and ample encomium on them. The author of the *Country Spectator*[2] doubts not to compare him with the ablest teachers of antiquity. Perhaps we cannot dismiss him better than with the pious ejaculation of C.—when he heard that his old master was on his deathbed: "Poor J. B.!—may all his faults be forgiven; and may he be wafted to bliss by little cherub boys all head and wings, with no *bottoms* to reproach his sublunary infirmities."

Under him were many good and sound scholars bred.—First Grecian[3] of my time was Lancelot Pepys Stevens, kindest of boys and men, since Co-grammar-master (and inseparable companion) with Dr. T——e. What an edifying spectacle did this brace of friends present to those who remembered the antisocialities of their predecessors!—You never met the one by chance in the street without a wonder, which was quickly dissipated by the almost immediate sub-appearance of the other. Generally arm-in-arm, these kindly coadjutors lightened for each other the toilsome duties of their profession, and when, in advanced age, one found it convenient to retire, the other was not long in discovering that it suited him to lay down the fasces[4] also. Oh, it is pleasant, as it is rare, to find

---

9. Mad rage.
1. The record of debates in Parliament.
2. Thomas Middleton, who was at school with Lamb and Coleridge, edited the magazine *Country Spectator* (1792–93) and later became Bishop of Calcutta.

3. The Grecians were the small group of superior scholars selected to be sent to a university (usually Cambridge) on a Christ's Hospital scholarship.
4. The bundle of rods, serving as the handle of an ax, carried before the Roman magistrates as a symbol of office.

the same arm linked in yours at forty, which at thirteen helped it to turn over the *Cicero De Amicitia*,[5] or some tale of Antique Friendship, which the young heart even then was burning to anticipate!—Co-Grecian with S. was Th——, who has since executed with ability various diplomatic functions at the Northern courts. Th—— was a tall, dark, saturnine youth, sparing of speech, with raven locks.—Thomas Fanshaw Middleton followed him (now Bishop of Calcutta), a scholar and a gentleman in his teens. He has the reputation of an excellent critic; and is author (besides the *Country Spectator*) of a *Treatise on the Greek Article*, against Sharpe. M. is said to bear his miter high in India, where the *regni novitas*[6] (I dare say) sufficiently justifies the bearing. A humility quite as primitive as that of Jewel or Hooker[7] might not be exactly fitted to impress the minds of those Anglo-Asiatic diocesans with a reverence for home institutions, and the church which those fathers watered. The manners of M. at school, though firm, were mild and unassuming.—Next to M. (if not senior to him) was Richards, author of the *Aboriginal Britons*, the most spirited of the Oxford Prize Poems; a pale, studious Grecian.—Then followed poor S——, ill-fated M——! of these the Muse is silent.[8]

> Finding some of Edward's race
> Unhappy, pass their annals by.[9]

Come back into memory, like as thou wert in the dayspring of thy fancies, with hope like a fiery column before thee—the dark pillar not yet turned—Samuel Taylor Coleridge—Logician, Metaphysician, Bard!—How have I seen the casual passer through the cloisters stand still, entranced with admiration (while he weighed the disproportion between the *speech* and the *garb* of the young Mirandola[1]), to hear thee unfold, in thy deep and sweet intonations, the mysteries of Jamblichus, or Plotinus[2] (for even in those years thou waxedst not pale at such philosophic draughts), or reciting Homer in his Greek, or Pindar—while the walls of the old Grey Friars[3] re-echoed to the accents of the *inspired charity-boy!* —Many were the "wit combats" (to dally awhile with the words of old Fuller) between him and C. V. Le G——, "which two I behold like a Spanish great galleon, and an English man-of-war; Master Coleridge, like the former, was built far higher in learning,

5. Cicero's essay "On Friendship."
6. Newness of the reign.
7. Famous divines in the 16th century, during the early period of the Anglican Church
8. Lamb identified these students as Scott, who died insane, and Maunde, who was expelled from the school.
9. Altered from Matthew Prior's *Carmen Seculare* (1700). "Edward's race" is applied to the students of Christ's hospital, founded by Edward VI.
1. Pico della Mirandola, the brilliant and charming humanist and philosopher of the Italian Renaissance, who died in 1494 at the age of 31.
2. Neo-Platonic philosophers.
3. Christ's Hospital was located in buildings that had once belonged to the Grey Friars (i.e., Franciscans).

solid, but slow in his perfromances. C. V. L., with the English man-of-war, lesser in bulk, but lighter in sailing, could turn with all tides, tack about, and take advantage of all winds, by the quickness of his wit and invention."[4]

Nor shalt thou, their compeer, be quickly forgotten, Allen, with the cordial smile, and still more cordial laugh, with which thou wert the *Nireus formosus*[5] of the school), in the days of thy maturer poignant jest of theirs; or the anticipation of some more material, and, peradventure practical one, of thine own. Extinct are those smiles, with that beautiful countenance, with which (for thou wert the *Nireus formosus*[4] of the school), in the days of thy maturer waggery, thou didst disarm the wrath of infuriated town-damsel, who, incensed by provoking pinch, turning tigress-like round, suddenly converted by thy angel look, exchanged the half-formed terrible *"bl——,"* for a gentler greeting—*"bless thy handsome face!"*

Next follow two, who ought to be now alive, and the friends of Elia—the junior Le G—— and F——;[6] who impelled, the former by a roving temper, the latter by too quick a sense of neglect—ill capable of enduring the slights poor Sizars[7] are sometimes subject to in our seats of learning—exchanged their Alma Mater for the camp; perishing, one by climate, and one on the plains of Salamanca: Le G——, sanguine, volatile, sweet-natured; F——, dogged, faithful, anticipative of insult, warmhearted, with something of the old Roman height about him.

Fine, frank-hearted Fr——, the present master of Hertford, with Marmaduke T——,[8] mildest of missionaries—and both my good friends still—close the catalogue of Grecians in my time.

1820, 1823

The Two Races of Men[1]

The human species, according to the best theory I can form of it, is composed of two distinct races, *the men who borrow*, and *the men*

4. Lamb adapts to Coleridge and Charles Valentine Le Grice the famous description of the wit combats between Shakespeare (the "man-of-war") and Ben Jonson (the "great galleon") in Thomas Fuller's *Worthies of England* (1662).
5. "The handsome Nireus," a Greek warrior in Homer's *Iliad* II.
6. Samuel Le Grice became an army officer and died in the West Indies; "F——" was Joseph Favell.
7. An undergraduate at Cambridge University who receives an allowance toward his expenses.
8. Frederick William Franklin and Marmaduke Thompson.
1. A small masterpiece in the tradition of the mock encomium, or ironic praise of the unpraiseworthy, such as Erasmus's *The Praise of Folly*. Lamb's oldest and closest friend, Coleridge, figures twice in the essay. In the role of heroic borrower of books almost never returned, he is Comberbatch—a private joke, for the name was identifiable only by Coleridge and a few initiates; in his second role, in which he returns books with the lavish interest of his extraordinary marginalia, he is S. T. C.—initials by which he was already known to many readers.

who lend. To these two original diversities may be reduced all those impertinent classifications of Gothic and Celtic tribes, white men, black men, red men. All the dwellers upon earth, "Parthians, and Medes, and Elamites," [2] flock hither, and do naturally fall in with one or other of these primary distinctions. The infinite superiority of the former, which I choose to designate as the *great race*, is discernible in their figure, port, and a certain instinctive sovereignty. The latter are born degraded. "He shall serve his brethren." [3] There is something in the air of one of this cast, lean and suspicious; contrasting with the open, trusting, generous manners of the other.

Observe who have been the greatest borrowers of all ages—Alcibiades—Falstaff—Sir Richard Steele—our late incomparable Brinsley [4]—what a family likeness in all four!

What a careless, even deportment hath your borrower! what rosy gills! what a beautiful reliance on Providence doth he manifest—taking no more thought than lilies! [5] What contempt for money—accounting it (yours and mine especially) no better than dross! What a liberal confounding of those pedantic distinctions of *meum* and *tuum*! [6] or rather, what a noble simplification of language (beyond Tooke [7]), resolving these supposed opposites into one clear, intelligible pronoun adjective! What near approaches doth he make to the primitive *community* [8]—to the extent of one half of the principle at least!

He is the true taxer who "calleth all the world up to be taxed"; [9] and the distance is as vast between him and *one of us*, as subsisted betwixt the Augustan Majesty and the poorest obolary [1] Jew that paid it tribute pittance at Jerusalem! His exactions, too, have such a cheerful, voluntary air! So far removed from your sour parochial or state-gatherers—those ink-horn varlets, who carry their want of welcome in their faces! He cometh to you with a smile, and troubleth you with no receipt; confining himself to no set season. Every day is his Candlemas, or his Feast of Holy Michael.[2] He applieth the *lene tormentum* [3] of a pleasant look to your purse—which to that gentle warmth expands her silken leaves, as naturally as the cloak of the traveler, for which sun and wind contended! He is the

2. Acts ii.9.
3. Noah's curse upon his youngest son, Ham, in Genesis ix.25.
4. Richard Brinsley Sheridan (1751–1816), dramatist, producer, and statesman.
5. I.e., than "the lilies of the field," in Matthew vi.28 and Luke xii.26–7.
6. Mine and thine.
7. John Horne Tooke, author of *The Diversions of Purley* (1786–98), a book on philology.
8. The community of the Apostles, who held all their possessions in common, Acts ii.44–5.
9. See Luke ii.1; this is the call that brought Joseph and Mary to Bethlehem.
1. Possessing an obolus, a Greek penny.
2. Feb. 2 and Sept. 29—English quarter-days, when rents fall due.
3. "The gentle spur"; said by Horace about wine, *Odes* III.xxi.13.

true Propontic which never ebbeth![4] The sea which taketh handsomely at each man's hand. In vain the victim, whom he delighteth to honor, struggles with destiny; he is in the net. Lend therefore cheerfully, O man ordained to lend—that thou lose not in the end, with thy worldly penny, the reversion [5] promised. Combine not preposterously in thine own person the penalties of Lazarus and of Dives! [6]—but, when thou seest the proper authority coming, meet it smilingly, as it were half-way. Come, a handsome sacrifice! See how light *he* makes of it! Strain not courtesies with a noble enemy.

Reflections like the foregoing were forced upon my mind by the death of my old friend, Ralph Bigod, Esq.,[7] who departed this life on Wednesday evening; dying, as he had lived, without much trouble. He boasted himself a descendant from mighty ancestors of that name, who heretofore held ducal dignities in this realm. In his actions and sentiments he belied not the stock to which he pretended. Early in life he found himself invested with ample revenues; which, with that noble disinterestedness which I have noticed as inherent in men of the *great race*, he took almost immediate measures entirely to dissipate and bring to nothing: for there is something revolting in the idea of a king holding a private purse; and the thoughts of Bigod were all regal. Thus furnished, by the very act of disfurnishment; getting rid of the cumbersome luggage of riches, more apt (as one sings)

> To slacken virtue, and abate her edge,
> Than prompt her to do aught may merit praise,[8]

he set forth, like some Alexander, upon his great enterprise, "Borrowing and to borrow!" [9]

In his periegesis,[1] or triumphant progress throughout this island, it has been calculated that he laid a tithe [2] part of the inhabitants under contribution. I reject this estimate as greatly exaggerated— but having had the honor of accompanying my friend, divers times, in his perambulations about this vast city, I own I was greatly struck at first with the prodigious number of faces we met, who claimed a sort of respectful acquaintance with us. He was one day so obliging as to explain the phenomenon. It seems, these were his tributaries; feeders of his exchequer; gentlemen, his good friends

---

4. See *Othello* III.iii.453–56.
5. The right of future possession— "promised," if you cast your bread upon the waters, Ecclesiastes xi.1, or lend to the poor, Proverbs xix.17.
6. Dives, the "rich man," finds when he dies that he is in hell, while Lazarus, who had been a beggar on earth, after death goes to dwell in "Abraham's bosom"; Luke xvi.19–26.
7. He has been identified as John Fenwick, editor of a newspaper, *Albion*.
8. Milton, *Paradise Regained* II.455–56.
9. Playing upon Revelation vi.2, "and he went forth conquering, and to conquer."
1. Tour.
2. One-tenth.

(as he was pleased to express himself), to whom he had occasionally been beholden for a loan. Their multitudes did no way disconcert him. He rather took a pride in numbering them; and, with Comus, seemed pleased to be "stocked with so fair a herd." [3]

With such sources, it was a wonder how he contrived to keep his treasury always empty. He did it by force of an aphorism, which he had often in his mouth, that "money kept longer than three days stinks." So he made use of it while it was fresh. A good part he drank away (for he was an excellent tosspot), some he gave away, the rest he threw away, literally tossing and hurling it violently from him —as boys do burrs, or as if it had been infectious—into ponds, or ditches, or deep holes—inscrutable cavities of the earth; or he would bury it (where he would never seek it again) by a river's side under some bank, which (he would facetiously observe) paid no interest—but out away from him it must go peremptorily, as Hagar's offspring [4] into the wilderness, while it was sweet. He never missed it. The streams were perennial which fed his fisc.[5] When new supplies became necessary, the first person that had the felicity to fall in with him, friend or stranger, was sure to contribute to the deficiency. For Bigod had an *undeniable* way with him. He had a cheerful, open exterior, a quick jovial eye, a bald forehead, just touched with gray (*cana fides*).[6] He anticipated no excuse, and found none. And, waiving for a while my theory as to the *great race*, I would put it to the most untheorizing reader, who may at times have disposable coin in his pocket, whether it is not more repugnant to the kindliness of his nature to refuse such a one as I am describing, than to say *no* to a poor petitionary rogue (your bastard borrower), who, by his mumping visnomy [7] tells you, that he expects nothing better; and, therefore, whose preconceived notions and expectations you do in reality so much less shock in the refusal.

When I think of this man; his fiery glow of heart; his swell of feeling; how magnificent, how *ideal* he was; how great at the midnight hour; and when I compare with him the companions with whom I have associated since, I grudge the saving of a few idle ducats, and think that I am fallen into the society of *lenders*, and *little men*.

To one like Elia, whose treasures are rather cased in leather covers than closed in iron coffers, there is a class of alienators [8] more formidable than that which I have touched upon; I mean your *borrowers of books*—those mutilators of collections, spoilers of the

3. Adapted from Milton's *Comus* 152.
4. Ishmael, the son of Hagar, in Genesis xxi.9 ff.
5. Public treasury.
6. "Hoary trustworthiness," i.e., of his

gray hair; the phrase is in Virgil's *Aeneid* I.292.
7. Dialect for "mumbling physiognomy."
8. Those who alienate property—i.e., transfer it to another.

symmetry of shelves, and creators of odd volumes. There is Comberbatch,[9] matchless in his depredations!

That foul gap in the bottom shelf facing you, like a great eye-tooth knocked out—(you are now with me in my little back study in Bloomsbury, reader!)—with the huge Switzerlike[1] tomes on each side (like the Guildhall giants, in their reformed posture, guardant of nothing) once held the tallest of my folios, *Opera Bonaventurae*,[2] choice and massy divinity, to which its two supporters (school divinity also, but of a lesser caliber—Bellarmine, and Holy Thomas), showed but as dwarfs—itself an Ascapart![3] *that* Comberbatch abstracted upon the faith of a theory he holds, which is more easy, I confess, for me to suffer by than to refute, namely, that "the title to property in a book (my Bonaventure, for instance), is in exact ratio to the claimant's powers of understanding and appreciating the same." Should he go on acting upon this theory, which of our shelves is safe?

The slight vacuum in the left-hand case—two shelves from the ceiling—scarcely distinguishable but by the quick eye of a loser—was whilom the commodious resting place of Browne on Urn Burial. C. will hardly allege that he knows more about that treatise than I do, who introduced it to him, and was indeed the first (of the moderns) to discover its beauties—but so have I known a foolish lover to praise his mistress in the presence of a rival more qualified to carry her off than himself. Just below, Dodsley's dramas want their fourth volume, where Vittoria Corombona is! The remainder nine are as distasteful as Priam's refuse sons, when the Fates *borrowed* Hector.[4] Here stood the Anatomy of Melancholy, in sober state. There loitered the Complete Angler; quiet as in life, by some stream side. In yonder nook, John Buncle, a widower-volume, with "eyes closed," mourns his ravished mate.[5]

One justice I must do my friend, that if he sometimes, like the sea, sweeps away a treasure, at another time, sealike, he throws up as rich an equivalent to match it. I have a small under-collection of this nature (my friend's gatherings in his various calls), picked up, he

9. Coleridge had left college for a brief and disastrous career as a cavalryman in the Light Dragoons, under the alias of Silas Tomkyn Comberbacke.
1. "Switzers" are Swiss guardsmen, selected for their imposing stature.
2. The theological *Works* of St. Bona-venture (1221–74); the "supporters" are St. Robert Bellarmine (1542–1621) and St. Thomas Aquinas (ca. 1225–74).
3. A giant, in the 14th-century verse romance, *Bevis of Hampton*.
4. I.e., the remaining nine volumes of Dodsley's *Collection* are rated as low by the lender as (in Homer's *Iliad*) Priam's remaining sons were rated by the Trojan king, after his greatest son, Hector, had been killed in battle.
5. The books in this paragraph: Sir Thomas Browne, *Hydriotaphia, or Urn Burial* (1658); Robert Dodsley's *Select Collection of Old Plays* (1744); John Webster's tragedy, *The White Devil, or Vittoria Corombona* (ca. 1608); Robert Burton, *The Anatomy of Melancholy* (1621); Izaak Walton, *The Compleat Angler* (1653); Thomas Amory, *John Buncle, Esq.* (1756–66)—a novel about a man who successively married seven wives, each of whom died within a few years.

has forgotten at what odd places, and deposited with as little memory as mine. I take in these orphans, the twice-deserted. These proselytes of the gate are welcome as the true Hebrews. There they stand in conjunction; natives, and naturalized. The latter seem as little disposed to inquire out their true lineage as I am. I charge no warehouse-room for these deodands,[6] nor shall ever put myself to the ungentlemanly trouble of advertising a sale of them to pay expenses.

To lose a volume to C. carries some sense and meaning in it. You are sure that he will make one hearty meal on your viands, if he can give no account of the platter after it. But what moved thee, wayward, spiteful K,[7] to be so importunate to carry off with thee, in spite of tears and adjurations to thee to forbear, the Letters of that princely woman, the thrice noble Margaret Newcastle?—knowing at the time, and knowing that I knew also, thou most assuredly wouldst never turn over one leaf of the illustrious folio—what but the mere spirit of contradiction, and childish love of getting the better of thy friend? Then, worst cut of all! to transport it with thee to the Gallican land—

> Unworthy land to harbor such a sweetness,
> A virtue in which all ennobling thoughts dwelt,
> Pure thoughts, kind thoughts, high thoughts, her sex's wonder![8]

——hadst thou not thy playbooks, and books of jests and fancies, about thee, to keep thee merry, even as thou keepest all companies with thy quips and mirthful tales? Child of the Greenroom,[9] it was unkindly done of thee. Thy wife, too, that part-French, better-part Englishwoman!—that *she* could fix upon no other treatise to bear away, in kindly token of remembering us, than the works of Fulke Greville, Lord Brook[10]—of which no Frenchman, nor woman of France, Italy, or England, was ever by nature constituted to comprehend a tittle! *Was there not Zimmerman on Solitude?*

Reader, if haply thou art blessed with a moderate collection, be shy of showing it; or if thy heart overfloweth to lend them, lend thy books; but let it be to such a one as S. T. C.—he will return them (generally anticipating the time appointed) with usury; enriched with annotations, tripling their value. I have had experience. Many are these precious MSS. of his (in *matter* oftentimes, and almost in *quantity* not unfrequently, vying with the originals) in no very

---

6. In English law, objects that are forfeited to the crown (because they have caused a human death).
7. James Kenney (1780–1849), an actor, who has borrowed and taken to France the *Sociable Letters* (1664) of Margaret Cavendish, Duchess of Newcastle.
8. Possibly composed by Lamb himself.
9. The room where actors await their cues.
10. Sir Fulke Greville, Baron Brooke (1554–1628). J. G. von Zimmerman's *Solitude* was translated into English about 1791.

clerkly hand—legible in my Daniel; [11] in old Burton; in Sir Thomas Browne; and those abstruser cogitations of the Greville, now, alas! wandering in Pagan lands. I counsel thee, shut not thy heart, nor thy library, against S. T. C.

1820, 1823

Witches, and Other Night Fears

We are too hasty when we set down our ancestors in the gross[1] for fools, for the monstrous inconsistencies (as they seem to us) involved in their creed of witchcraft. In the relations of this visible world we find them to have been as rational, and shrewd to detect an historic anomaly, as ourselves. But when once the invisible world was supposed to be opened, and the lawless agency of bad spirits assumed, what measures of probability, of decency,[2] of fitness, or proportion—of that which distinguishes the likely from the palpable absurd—could they have to guide them in the rejection or admission of any particular testimony?—That maidens pined away, wasting inwardly as their waxen images consumed before a fire—that corn was lodged,[3] and cattle lamed—that whirlwinds uptore in diabolic revelry the oaks of the forest—or that spits and kettles only danced a fearful-innocent vagary about some rustic's kitchen when no wind was stirring—were all equally probable where no law of agency was understood. That the prince of the powers of darkness, passing by the flower and pomp of the earth, should lay preposterous siege to the weak fantasy of indigent eld[4]—has neither likelihood nor unlikelihood *a priori* to us, who have no measure to guess at his policy, or standard to estimate what rate those anile[5] souls may fetch in the devil's market. Nor, when the wicked are expressly symbolized by a goat, was it to be wondered at so much, that *he* should come sometimes in that body, and assert his metaphor.—That the intercourse was opened at all between both worlds was perhaps the mistake—but that once assumed, I see no reason for disbelieving one attested story of this nature more than another on the score of absurdity. There is no law to judge of the lawless, or canon by which a dream may be criticized.

I have sometimes thought that I could not have existed in the days of received witchcraft; that I could not have slept in a village where one of those reputed hags dwelt. Our ancestors were bolder or more obtuse. Amidst the universal belief that these wretches

11. Samuel Daniel, the poet (1562–1619).
1. Wholesale; without exception.
2. I.e., appropriateness to the circumstances.
3. Beaten down.
4. Old age (archaic term).
5. Old-womanish.

were in league with the author of all evil, holding hell tributary to their muttering, no simple Justice of the Peace seems to have scrupled issuing, or silly Headborough[6] serving, a warrant upon them— as if they should subpoena Satan!—Prospero in his boat, with his books and wand about him, suffers himself to be conveyed away at the mercy of his enemies to an unknown island.[7] He might have raised a storm or two, we think, on the passage. His acquiescence is in exact analogy to the nonresistance of witches to the constituted powers.—What stops the Fiend in Spenser from tearing Guyon to pieces—or who had made it a condition of his prey, that Guyon must take assay of the glorious bait[8]—we have no guess. We do not know the laws of that country.

From my childhood I was extremely inquisitive about witches and witch stories. My maid, and more legendary[9] aunt, supplied me with good store. But I shall mention the accident which directed my curiosity originally into this channel. In my father's book-closet, the History of the Bible, by Stackhouse,[1] occupied a distinguished station. The pictures with which it abounds—one of the ark, in particular, and another of Solomon's temple, delineated with all the fidelity of ocular admeasurement, as if the artist had been upon the spot—attracted my childish attention. There was a picture, too, of the Witch raising up Samuel,[2] which I wish that I had never seen. We shall come to that hereafter. Stackhouse is in two huge tomes —and there was a pleasure in removing folios of that magnitude, which, with infinite straining, was as much as I could manage, from the situation which they occupied upon an upper shelf. I have not met with the work from that time to this, but I remember it consisted of Old Testament stories, orderly set down, with the *objection* appended to each story, and the *solution* of the objection regularly tacked to that. The *objection* was a summary of whatever difficulties had been opposed to the credibility of the history, by the shrewdness of ancient or modern infidelity, drawn up with an almost complimentary excess of candor. The *solution* was brief, modest, and satisfactory. The bane and antidote were both before you. To doubts so put, and so quashed, there seemed to be an end forever. The dragon lay dead, for the foot of the veriest babe to trample on. But—like as was rather feared than realized from that

6. Village constable.
7. Prospero, Duke of Milan, who possessed magical powers, had been abandoned at sea in a decrepit boat by his traitorous brother, Sebastian, in Shakespeare's *The Tempest* (I.ii.144–51).
8. The fiend, Mammon, tempts Sir Guyon to pluck golden apples from a tree in the Garden of Proserpina, "To which if he inclyned had at all, / That dreadfil feend, which did behind him wayt, / Would him have rent in thousand peeces strayt" (*Faerie Queene*

II.vii.63–64).
9. I.e., devoted to legends and superstitions.
1. Thomas Stackhouse's *New History of the Holy Bible from the Beginning of the World to the Establishment of Christianity* (1737).
2. At King Saul's request, the Witch of Endor called up the dead prophet Samuel, that Saul might question him about an impending battle with the Philistines (I Samuel xxviii).

slain monster in Spenser—from the womb of those crushed errors young dragonets would creep, exceeding the prowess of so tender a Saint George as myself to vanquish.[3] The habit of expecting objections to every passage, set me upon starting more objections, for the glory of finding a solution of my own for them. I became staggered and perplexed, a skeptic in long coats.[4] The pretty Bible stories which I had read, or heard read in church, lost their purity and sincerity of impression, and were turned into so many historic or chronologic theses to be defended against whatever impugners. I was not to disbelieve them, but—the next thing to that—I was to be quite sure that someone or other would or had disbelieved them. Next to making a child an infidel, is the letting him know that there are infidels at all. Credulity is the man's weakness, but the child's strength. O, how ugly sound scriptural doubts from the mouth of a babe and a suckling!—I should have lost myself in these mazes, and have pined away, I think, with such unfit sustenance as these husks afforded, but for a fortunate piece of ill fortune, which about this time befell me. Turning over the picture of the ark with too much haste, I unhappily made a breach in its ingenious fabric —driving my inconsiderate fingers right through the two larger quadrupeds—the elephant, and the camel—that stare (as well they might) out of the two last windows next the steerage in that unique piece of naval architecture. Stackhouse was henceforth locked up, and became an interdicted treasure. With the book, the *objections* and *solutions* gradually cleared out of my head, and have seldom returned since in any force to trouble me.—But there was one impression which I had imbibed from Stackhouse, which no lock or bar could shut out, and which was destined to try my childish nerves rather more seriously.—That detestable picture!

I was dreadfully alive to nervous terrors. The nighttime solitude, and the dark, were my hell. The sufferings I endured in this nature would justify the expression. I never laid my head on my pillow, I suppose, from the fourth to the seventh or eighth year of my life— so far as memory serves in things so long ago—without an assurance, which realized its own prophecy, of seeing some frightful specter. Be old Stackhouse then acquitted in part, if I say, that to his picture of the Witch raising up Samuel—(O that old man covered with a mantle!) I owe—not my midnight terrors, the hell of my infancy—but the shape and manner of their visitation. It was he who dressed up for me a hag that nightly sate upon my pillow—a sure bed-fellow, when my aunt or my maid was far from me. All day long, while the book was permitted me, I dreamed waking over his

3. Saint George, the dragon-slayer, patron saint of England, was the prototype of Spenser's Redcrosse Knight in *The Faerie Queene*. After the Redcrosse Knight has slain the dragon, some onlookers fear that dragonets may issue from the dead dragon's womb (I.xii.10).

4. I.e., in an infant's clothes.

delineation, and at night (if I may use so bold an expression) awoke into sleep, and found the vision true. I durst not, even in the daylight, once enter the chamber where I slept, without my face turned to the window, aversely from the bed where my witch-ridden pillow was.—Parents do not know what they do when they leave tender babes alone to go to sleep in the dark. The feeling about for a friendly arm—the hoping for a familiar voice—when they wake screaming—and find none to soothe them—what a terrible shaking it is to their poor nerves! The keeping them up till midnight, through candlelight and the unwholesome hours, as they are called —would, I am satisfied, in a medical point of view, prove the better caution.—That detestable picture, as I have said, gave the fashion to my dreams—if dreams they were—for the scene of them was invariably the room in which I lay. Had I never met with the picture, the fears would have come self-pictured in some shape or other—

Headless bear, black man, or ape[5]—

but, as it was, my imaginations took that form.—It is not book, or picture, or the stories of foolish servants, which create these terrors in children. They can at most but give them a direction. Dear little T.H.[6] who of all children has been brought up with the most scrupulous exclusion of every taint of superstition—who was never allowed to hear of goblin or apparition, or scarcely to be told of bad men, or to read or hear of any distressing story—finds all this world of fear, from which he has been so rigidly excluded *ab extra*, in his own "thick-coming fancies;"[7] and from his little midnight pillow, this nurse-child of optimism will start at shapes, unborrowed of tradition, in sweats to which the reveries of the cell-damned murderer are tranquility.

Gorgons, and Hydras, and Chimeras—dire stories of Celaeno and the Harpies[8]—may reproduce themselves in the brain of superstition—but they were there before. They are transcripts, types—the archetypes are in us, and eternal. How else should the recital of that, which we know in a waking sense to be false, come to affect us at all?—or

---

5. From the verse *Abstract of Melancholy* prefaced to Robert Burton's *The Anatomy of Melancholy* (1621): "my fantasy / Presents a thousand ugly shapes, / Headless bears, black men, and apes."

6. Thornton Hunt, oldest son of the essayist and critic Leigh Hunt, whom Lamb elsewhere called his "favorite child."

7. Lady Macbeth "is troubled with thick-coming fancies" in *Macbeth* V.iii.38. "*Ab extra*": from outside (Latin).

8. "Gorgons, Hydras, and Chimeras dire" (*Paradise Lost* II.628.) "Gorgons" were snaky-haired women, the sight of whom turned beholders to stone; "hydras" were poisonous water-snakes with multiple heads; "chimeras" had a lion's head, a goat's body, and a dragon's tail. When Aeneas and his followers sat down to feast, Celaeno and the other Harpies plundered and befouled their food (*Aeneid* III.209 ff.) (harpies were filthy, malign creatures, part woman and part bird).

———Names, whose sense we see not,
Fray us with things that be not?[9]

Is it that we naturally conceive terror from such objects, considered
in their capacity of being able to inflict upon us bodily injury?—O,
least of all! These terrors are of older standing. They date beyond
body—or, without the body, they would have been the same. All
the cruel, tormenting, defined devils in Dante—tearing, mangling,
choking, stifling, scorching demons—are they one half so fearful to
the spirit of a man, as the simple idea of a spirit unembodied following him—

> Like one that on a lonesome road
> Doth walk in fear and dread,
> And having once turned round, walks on,
> And turns no more his head;
> Because he knows a frightful fiend
> Doth close behind him tread.[1]

That the kind of fear here treated of is purely spiritual—that it is
strong in proportion as it is objectless upon earth—that it predominates in the period of sinless infancy—are difficulties, the solution
of which might afford some probable insight into our ante-mundane
condition,[2] and a peep at least into the shadow-land of pre-
existence.

My night fancies have long ceased to be afflictive. I confess an
occasional nightmare; but I do not, as in early youth, keep a stud[3]
of them. Fiendish faces, with the extinguished taper, will come and
look at me; but I know them for mockeries, even while I cannot
elude their presence, and I fight and grapple with them. For the
credit of my imagination, I am almost ashamed to say how tame
and prosaic my dreams are grown. They are never romantic, seldom
even rural. They are of architecture and of buildings—cities
abroad, which I have never seen, and hardly have hope to see. I
have traversed, for the seeming length of a natural day, Rome,
Amsterdam, Paris, Lisbon—their churches, palaces, squares, market-
places, shops, suburbs, ruins, with an inexpressible sense of delight
—a maplike distinctness of trace—and a daylight vividness of
vision, that was all but being awake.—I have formerly traveled
among the Westmoreland fells[4]—my highest Alps—but they are
objects too mighty for the grasp of my dreaming recognition; and
I have again and again awoke with ineffectual struggles of the inner

9. Spenser, *Epithalamion*, lines 343–
44: "Ne let hob Goblins, names whose
sence we see not, / Fray us with things
that be not." "Fray": Frighten.
1. "Mr. Coleridge's *Ancient Mariner*"
[Lamb's note]; lines 446–51.
2. I.e., our condition before we were
born into this world.
3. A group of breeding-horses (with a
pun on "night*mare*").

4. Hills. Lamb had visited Wordsworth's Westmoreland county, in the
Lake District, in 1802, and "Helvellyn" (below) was one of Wordsworth's
favorite mountains. Lamb pays quiet
tribute to his friend by alluding in his
phrase "the inner eye" to Wordsworth's
I Wandered Lonely as a Cloud: "They
flash upon that inward eye / Which is
the bliss of solitude."

eye, to make out a shape in any way whatever, of Helvellyn. Methought I was in that country, but the mountains were gone. The poverty of my dreams mortifies me. There is Coleridge, at his will can conjure up icy domes, and pleasure-houses for Kubla Khan, and Abyssinian maids, and songs of Abara, and caverns,

> Where Alph, the sacred river, runs,[5]

to solace his night solitudes—when I cannot muster a fiddle. Barry Cornwall has his tritons and his nereids gamboling before him in nocturnal visions, and proclaiming sons born to Neptune[6]—when my stretch of imaginative activity can hardly, in the night season, raise up the ghost of a fishwife. To set my failures in somewhat a mortifying light—it was after reading the noble *Dream* of this poet, that my fancy ran strong upon these marine spectra;[7] and the poor plastic power, such as it is, within me set to work, to humor my folly in a sort of dream that very night. Methought I was upon the ocean billows at some sea nuptials, riding and mounted high, with the customary train sounding their conchs before me, (I myself, you may be sure, the *leading god*) and jollily we went careering over the main, till just where Ino Leucothea[8] should have greeted me (I think it was Ino) with a white embrace, the billows gradually subsiding, fell from a sea-roughness to a sea-calm, and thence to a river-motion, and that river (as happens in the familiarization of dreams) was no other than the gentle Thames, which landed me, in the wafture of a placid wave or two, alone, safe and inglorious, somewhere at the foot of Lambeth palace.[9]

The degree of the soul's creativeness in sleep might furnish no whimsical criterion of the quantum[10] of poetical faculty resident in the same soul waking. An old gentleman, a friend of mine, and a humorist,[11] used to carry this notion so far, that when he saw any stripling of his acquaintance ambitious of becoming a poet, his first question would be—"Young man, what sort of dreams have you?" I have so much faith in my old friend's theory, that when I feel that idle vein returning upon me, I presently subside into my proper element of prose, remembering those eluding nereids, and that inauspicious inland landing.

1821, 1823

---

5. *Kubla Khan*, line 3; Lamb altered "ran" to "runs."

6. "Barry Cornwall" was the pen name of Bryan Waller Procter (1787–1874), poet and dramatist, who was Lamb's friend. Lamb's reference is to Cornwall's poem *A Dream* (1819), in which the narrator fantasies the appearance of various mythological figures from the ocean depths; the dreamer is awakened by a noisy celebration of the birth of a son to Neptune. "Tritons": sea gods, represented with a man's body and fish's tail, and carrying a trident (three-pronged fish-spear) and a shell trumpet; "nereids": sea nymphs.

7. Ocular images. "Plastic": formative, creative.

8. Ino threw herself into the sea to escape her maddened husband, and was transformed by Neptune into a sea goddess with the name Leucothea, "the white goddess."

9. London residence of the Archbishop of Canterbury on the southern bank of the Thames.

10. Amount.

11. In the old sense: whimsical.

Old China

I have an almost feminine partiality for old china. When I go to see any great house, I inquire for the china closet, and next for the picture gallery. I cannot defend the order of preference, but by saying that we have all some taste or other, of too ancient a date to admit of our remembering distinctly that it was an acquired one. I can call to mind the first play, and the first exhibition, that I was taken to; but I am not conscious of a time when china jars and saucers were introduced into my imagination.

I had no repugnance then—why should I now have?—to those little, lawless, azure-tinctured grotesques, that under the notion of men and women float about, uncircumscribed by any element, in that world before perspective—a china teacup.

I like to see my old friends—whom distance cannot diminish—figuring up in the air (so they appear to our optics), yet on terra firma still—for so we must in courtesy interpret that speck of deeper blue, which the decorous artist, to present absurdity, had made to spring up beneath their sandals.

I love the men with women's faces, and the women, if possible, with still more womanish expressions.

Here is a young and courtly mandarin, handing tea to a lady from a salver—two miles off. See how distance seems to set off respect! And here the same lady, or another—for likeness is identity on teacups—is stepping into a little fairy boat, moored on the hither side of this calm garden river, with a dainty mincing foot, which in a right angle of incidence (as angles go in our world) must infallibly land her in the midst of a flowery mead—a furlong off on the other side of the same strange stream!

Farther on—if far or near can be predicated of their world—see horses, trees, pagodas, dancing the hays.[1]

Here—a cow and rabbit couchant,[2] and coextensive—so objects show, seen through the lucid atmosphere of fine Cathay.[3]

I was pointing out to my cousin last evening, over our Hyson[4] (which we are old-fashioned enough to drink unmixed still of an afternoon), some of these *speciosa miracula*[5] upon a set of extraordinary old blue china (a recent purchase) which we were now for the first time using; and could not help remarking how favorable circumstances had been to us of late years that we could afford to please the eye sometimes with trifles of this sort—when a passing

---

1. An English country dance with a serpentining movement.
2. Heraldic term: lying down with the head raised.
3. The old European name for China.
4. A Chinese green tea.
5. "Shining wonders."

sentiment seemed to overshade the brows of my companion. I am quick at detecting these summer clouds in Bridget.[6]

"I wish the good old times would come again," she said, "when we were not quite so rich. I do not mean that I want to be poor; but there was a middle state"—so she was pleased to ramble on— "in which I am sure we were a great deal happier. A purchase is but a purchase, now that you have money enough and to spare. Formerly it used to be a triumph. When we coveted a cheap luxury (and, O! how much ado I had to get you to consent in those times!)—we were used to have a debate two or three days before, and to weigh the *for* and *against*, and think what we might spare it out of, and what saving we could hit upon, that should be an equivalent. A thing was worth buying then, when we felt the money that we paid for it.

"Do you remember the brown suit, which you made to hang upon you, till all your friends cried shame upon you, it grew so threadbare—and all because of that folio Beaumont and Fletcher,[7] which you dragged home late at night from Barker's in Covent Garden? Do you remember how we eyed it for weeks before we could make up our minds to the purchase, and had not come to a determination till it was near ten o'clock of the Saturday night, when you set off from Islington,[8] fearing you should be too late—and when the old bookseller with some grumbling opened his shop, and by the twinkling taper (for he was setting bedwards) lighted out the relic from his dusty treasures—and when you lugged it home, wishing it were twice as cumbersome—and when you presented it to me—and when we were exploring the perfectness of it (*collating,* you called it)—and while I was repairing some of the loose leaves with paste, which your impatience would not suffer to be left till daybreak—was there no pleasure in being a poor man? or can those neat black clothes which you wear now, and are so careful to keep brushed, since we have become rich and finical, give you half the honest vanity with which you flaunted it about in that overworn suit—your old corbeau[9]—for four or five weeks longer than you should have done, to pacify your conscience for the mighty sum of fifteen—or sixteen shillings was it?—a great affair we thought it then—which you had lavished on the old folio. Now you can afford to buy any book that pleases you, but I do not see that you ever bring me home any nice old purchases now.

"When you came home with twenty apologies for laying out a less number of shillings upon that print after Leonardo,[1] which we

6. In Lamb's essays, his name for his sister, Mary.
7. The Elizabethan dramatic collaborators, whose plays were first collected in a large folio volume in 1647.
8. In the north of London, where the Lambs had been living.

9. A dark green cloth, almost black (hence its name, the French for "raven").
1. Leonardo da Vinci (1452–1519), the great Italian painter. The painting is the one known as "Modesty and Vanity."

christened the 'Lady Blanch'; when you looked at the purchase, and thought of the money—and thought of the money, and looked again at the picture—was there no pleasure in being a poor man? Now, you have nothing to do but to walk into Colnaghi's, and buy a wilderness of Leonardos. Yet do you?

"Then, do you remember our pleasant walks to Enfield, and Potter's Bar, and Waltham,[2] when we had a holiday—holidays, and all other fun, are gone now we are rich—and the little hand-basket in which I used to deposit our day's fare of savory cold lamb and salad —and how you would pry about at noontide for some decent house, where we might go in and produce our store—only paying for the ale that you must call for—and speculate upon the looks of the landlady, and whether she was likely to allow us a tablecloth— and wish for such another honest hostess as Izaak Walton has described many a one on the pleasant banks of the Lea, when he went a-fishing—and sometimes they would prove obliging enough, and sometimes they would look grudgingly upon us—but we had cheerful looks still for one another, and would eat our plain food savorily, scarcely grudging Piscator[3] his Trout Hall? Now—when we go out a day's pleasuring, which is seldom, moreover, we *ride* part of the way—and go into a fine inn, and order the best of dinners, never debating the expense—which, after all, never has half the relish of those chance country snaps,[3a] when we were at the mercy of uncertain usage, and a precarious welcome.

"You are too proud to see a play anywhere now but in the pit. Do you remember where it was we used to sit, when we saw the *Battle of Hexham*, and the *Surrender of Calais*,[4] and Bannister and Mrs. Bland in the *Children in the Wood*[5]—when we squeezed out our shillings apiece to sit three or four times in a season in the one-shilling gallery—where you felt all the time that you ought not to have brought me—and more strongly I felt obligation to you for having brought me—and the pleasure was the better for a little shame—and when the curtain drew up, what cared we for our place in the house, or what mattered it where we were sitting, when our thoughts were with Rosalind in Arden, or with Viola at the Court of Illyria.[6] You used to say that the gallery was the best place of all for enjoying a play socially—that the relish of such exhibitions must be in proportion to the infrequency of going—that the company we met there, not being in general readers of plays, were obliged to attend the more, and did attend, to what was going on, on the stage—because a word lost would have been a chasm, which it was impossible for them to fill up. With such reflections we

---

2. All three are suburbs to the north of London.
3. The fisherman in Izaak Walton's *Complete Angler* (1653).
3a. Snacks.

4. Comedies by George Colman (1762–1836).
5. By Thomas Morton (1764–1838).
6. Rosalind in *As You Like It* and Viola in *Twelfth Night*.

consoled our pride then—and I appeal to you whether, as a woman, I met generally with less attention and accommodation than I have done since in more expensive situations in the house? The getting in indeed, and the crowding up those inconvenient stair-cases, was bad enough—but there was still a law of civility to woman recognized to quite as great an extent as we ever found in the other passages—and how a little difficulty overcome heightened the snug seat and the play, afterwards! Now we can only pay our money and walk in. You cannot see, you say, in the galleries now. I am sure we saw, and heard too, well enough then—but sight, and all, I think, is gone with our poverty.

"There was pleasure in eating strawberries, before they became quite common—in the first dish of peas, while they were yet dear— to have them for a nice supper, a treat. What treat can we have now? If we were to treat ourselves now—that is, to have dainties a little above our means, it would be selfish and wicked. It is the very little more that we allow ourselves beyond what the actual poor can get at that makes what I call a treat—when two people living to-gether, as we have done, now and then indulge themselves in a cheap luxury, which both like; while each apologizes, and is willing to take both halves of the blame to his single share. I see no harm in people making much of themselves, in that sense of the word. It may give them a hint how to make much of others. But now— what I mean by the word—we never do make much of ourselves. None but the poor can do it. I do not mean the veriest poor of all, but persons as we were, just above poverty.

"I know what you were going to say, that it is mighty pleasant at the end of the year to make all meet—and much ado we used to have every Thirty-first Night of December to account for our ex-ceedings—many a long face did you make over your puzzled ac-counts, and in contriving to make it out how we had spent so much—or that we had not spent so much—or that it was im-possible we should spend so much next year—and still we found our slender capital decreasing—but then, betwixt ways, and projects, and compromises of one sort or another, and talk of curtailing this charge, and doing without that for the future—and the hope that youth brings, and laughing spirits (in which you were never poor till now), we pocketed up our loss, and in conclusion, with 'lusty brimmers' (as you used to quote it out of *hearty cheerful Mr. Cot-ton*,[7] as you called him), we used to welcome in 'the coming guest.' Now we have no reckoning at all at the end of the old year—no flat-tering promises about the new year doing better for us."

Bridget is so sparing of her speech on most occasions that when she gets into a rhetorical vein, I am careful how I interrupt it. I

---

7. Charles Cotton, the 17th-century poet, a favorite of Lamb's; the quotations are from his poem *The New Year*.

could not help, however, smiling at the phantom of wealth which her dear imagination had conjured up out of a clear income of poor ——— hundred pounds a year. "It is true we were happier when we were poorer, but we were also younger, my cousin. I am afraid we must put up with the excess, for if we were to shake the superflux into the sea, we should not much mend ourselves. That we had much to struggle with, as we grew up together, we have reason to be most thankful. It strengthened and knit our compact closer. We could never have been what we have been to each other, if we had always had the sufficiency which you now complain of. The resisting power—those natural dilations of the youthful spirit, which circumstances cannot straiten—with us are long since passed away. Competence to age is supplementary youth, a sorry supplement indeed, but I fear the best that is to be had. We must ride where we formerly walked: live better and lie softer—and shall be wise to do so—than we had means to do in those good old days you speak of. Yet could those days return—could you and I once more walk our thirty miles a day—could Bannister and Mrs. Bland again be young, and you and I be young to see them—could the good old one-shilling gallery days return—they are dreams, my cousin, now—but could you and I at this moment, instead of this quiet argument, by our well-carpeted fireside, sitting on this luxurious sofa—be once more struggling up those inconvenient staircases, pushed about, and squeezed, and elbowed by the poorest rabble of poor gallery scramblers—could I once more hear those anxious shrieks of yours—and the delicious *Thank God, we are safe,* which always followed when the topmost stair, conquered, let in the first light of the whole cheerful theater down beneath us—I know not the fathom line that ever touched a descent so deep as I would be willing to bury more wealth in than Croesus had, or the great Jew R———[8] is supposed to have, to purchase it. And now do just look at that merry little Chinese waiter holding an umbrella, big enough for a bed-tester, over the head of that pretty insipid half Madonnaish chit of a lady in that very blue summerhouse."

1823, 1833

8. Nathan Meyer Rothschild (1777–1836) founded the English branch of the great European banking house.

WILLIAM HAZLITT
(1778–1830)

1813–14: Begins writing dramatic criticism and general essays.
1815–22: The height of his powers as essayist and as lecturer
on English poetry and drama.

"I started in life," Hazlitt wrote, "with the French Revolution, and I have lived, alas! to see the end of it. * * * Since then, I confess, I have no longer felt myself young, for with that my hopes fell." He was born into a radical circle, for the elder William Hazlitt, his father, was a Unitarian minister who declared from the pulpit his advocacy both of American independence and of the French Revolution. When young William was 5 years old, his father took the family to America in search of liberty and founded the first Unitarian Church in Boston; but four years later he returned to settle at Wem, in Shropshire. Despite the persistent attacks of reviewers and the backsliding of his once-radical friends, Hazlitt himself never wavered in his loyalty to liberty, equality, and the principles behind the overthrow of the monarchy in France. His first literary production, at the age of 13, was a letter to a newspaper in indignant protest against the mob which sacked Joseph Priestley's house, when the scientist and preacher had celebrated publicly the second anniversary of the fall of the Bastille. His last book, published in the year he died, was a four-volume life of Napoleon, in whom Hazlitt stubbornly insisted on seeing a noble-intentioned champion of the emancipation of mankind.

Hazlitt was a long time finding his vocation. When he attended the Hackney College, London, between the age of 15 and 18, he plunged into philosophical studies with such zeal that he ruined his health. In 1799 he took up the study of painting, and did not give up the ambition to become a portraitist until 1812. Hazlitt's first books dealt with philosophy, economics, and politics, and his first job as a journalist was as Parliamentary reporter for the *Morning Chronicle*. It was not until 1813, at the age of 36, that he began contributing dramatic criticism and miscellaneous essays to various periodicals, and so discovered what he had been born to do. Years of wide reading and hard thinking had made him thoroughly ready: within the next decade Hazlitt demonstrated himself to be a highly popular lecturer on Shakespeare, Elizabethan drama, and English poetry; a superb connoisseur of the theater and of painting; one of the two most important literary critics of the day (Coleridge is the other); and a master of the familiar essay.

Unlike his contemporaries, Coleridge, Lamb, and De Quincey, whose writings look back to the elaborate prose stylists of the earlier 17th century, Hazlitt developed a fast-moving, hard-hitting prose in what has been aptly called a "literary-colloquial English": it gives the effect of good talk, but heightened. He wrote, indeed, almost as fast as he talked, turning out at a single sitting enough text to fill ten or fifteen printed pages, almost without correction and (despite the density of literary quotations) without reference to books or notes. This rapidity was possible only because his essays are relatively planless. Hazlitt characteristically lays down a topic and then expands upon it by piling up relevant observations and instances, expressed in a sequence of forthright and relatively uncomplicated sentences; the essay accumulates instead of developing, and it does not round to a conclusion, but simply stops. Hazlitt's prose is unfailingly energetic; but his most satisfying essays, considered as integral works of literary art, are those which, like *My First Acquaintance with Poets*, have a narrative subject matter to give them a principle of organization.

In his demeanor Hazlitt was excessively bashful, suspicious, and gauche. Coleridge described him in 1803 as "brow-hanging, shoe-contemplative, strange. He is, I verily believe, kindly-natured * * * but he is jealous, gloomy, and of an irritable pride." Hazlitt's gracelessness and lack of talent for domesticity doomed him to be unlucky in love. At the age of 30 he married Sarah Stoddart, three years his senior, separated from her after ten inharmonious years, and several years later secured her consent to a Scottish divorce, in the hope he could marry Sarah Walker, the young daughter of his landlord in London. But the girl was a cold and faithless coquette, who (as Hazlitt himself relates in his confessional *Liber Amoris*) mercilessly teased and then jilted her infatuated lover. When in 1824 he married a widow with a substantial income, she too left him within three years, in part because of the antagonism of young William, Hazlitt's son by his first wife.

Hazlitt, it must be remembered, had grown up as a member of a highly unpopular minority, both in religion and politics; he found his friends deserting to the side of reaction; and his naturally combative disposition was exacerbated by the abuse directed against him in the periodicals of that day. In the course of his life he managed to quarrel violently, in private and in print, with almost all the people he had once most admired and liked, including Coleridge, Wordsworth, and Leigh Hunt; even Charles Lamb, with whom his friendship was the most intimate and enduring, was not always safe from Hazlitt's rasping tongue. But we may let the tolerant Lamb speak for the admirable qualities which emerged when Hazlitt relaxed in company he felt he could trust: "I think W.H. to be, in his natural state, one of the wisest and finest spirits breathing. * * * I think I shall go to my grave without finding, or expecting to find, such another companion."

What appealed to Hazlitt's personal admirers, as to the readers of his essays, was his courage and uncompromising honesty, and above all, his ardor, and his zest for life in all its variety—including even, as he announced in the title of a characteristic essay, *The Pleasure of Hating*. Hazlitt intensely relished, and could matchlessly communicate, the particular qualities of diverse things—whether a passage of poetry, a painting, a natural prospect, a person, or a well-directed blow in a prize fight. Despite the recurrent frustrations of his 52 years of existence, he was able, on looking back, to say with his last breath: "Well, I've had a happy life."

My First Acquaintance with Poets[1]

My father was a Dissenting Minister, at Wem, in Shropshire; and in the year 1798 (the figures that compose that date are to me like the "dreaded name of Demogorgon"[2]) Mr. Coleridge came to Shrewsbury, to succeed Mr. Rowe in the spiritual charge of a Unitarian congregation there. He did not come till late on the Saturday afternoon before he was to preach; and Mr. Rowe, who himself went down to the coach, in a state of anxiety and expectation, to look for the arrival of his successor, could find no one at all answering the description but a round-faced man, in a short black coat (like a shooting jacket) which hardly seemed to have been made for him, but who seemed to be talking at a great rate to his fellow passengers. Mr. Rowe had scarce returned to give an account of his disappointment, when the round-faced man in black entered, and dissipated all doubts on the subject, by beginning to talk. He did not cease while he stayed; nor has he since, that I know of. He held the good town of Shrewsbury in delightful suspense for three weeks that he remained there, "fluttering the *proud Salopians*, like an eagle in a dovecote";[3] and the Welsh mountains that skirt the horizon with their tempestuous confusion, agree to have heard no such mystic sounds since the days of

High-born Hoel's harp or soft Llewellyn's lay![4]

As we passed along between Wem and Shrewsbury, and I eyed their blue tops seen through the wintry branches, or the red rustling leaves of the sturdy oak trees by the roadside, a sound was in my ears as of a Siren's song; I was stunned, startled with it, as from deep sleep; but I had no notion then that I should ever be able to express my admiration to others in motley imagery or quaint allusion, till the light of his genius shone into my soul, like the

1. This essay was written a quarter century after the events it describes. Coleridge and Wordsworth had long given up their early radicalism, and both men had since quarreled violently with Hazlitt—hence the essay's elegiac note in dealing with the genius of the two poets. Nevertheless Hazlitt communicates the intense excitement he had felt when Coleridge awakened him to the sense of his own literary possibilities, and the essay remains an incomparable portrait of Wordsworth and Coleridge early in 1798, the period of their closest collaboration.
2. *Paradise Lost* II.964–65. To mythographers of the Renaissance, Demogorgon was a mysterious and terrifying demon, sometimes described as ancestor of all the gods. He plays a central role in Shelley's *Prometheus Unbound*.
3. Adapted from Shakespeare's *Coriolanus* V.vi.114–15. "Salopians" are inhabitants of Shropshire.
4. Gray's *The Bard*, line 28.

sun's rays glittering in the puddles of the road. I was at that time dumb, inarticulate, helpless, like a worm by the wayside, crushed, bleeding, lifeless; but now, bursting from the deadly bands that bound them,

> With Styx nine times round them,[5]

my ideas float on winged words, and as they expand their plumes, catch the golden light of other years. My soul has indeed remained in its original bondage, dark, obscure, with longings infinite and unsatisfied; my heart, shut up in the prison house of this rude clay, has never found, nor will it ever find, a heart to speak to; but that my understanding also did not remain dumb and brutish, or at length found a language to express itself, I owe to Coleridge. But this is not to my purpose.

My father lived ten miles from Shrewsbury, and was in the habit of exchanging visits with Mr. Rowe, and with Mr. Jenkins of White-church (nine miles farther on) according to the custom of Dissent-ing Ministers in each other's neighborhood. A line of communica-tion is thus established, by which the flame of civil and religious liberty is kept alive, and nourishes its smoldering fire unquenchable, like the fires in the *Agamemnon* of Aeschylus, placed at different stations, that waited for ten long years to announce with their blaz-ing pyramids the destruction of Troy. Coleridge had agreed to come over to see my father, according to the courtesy of the country, as Mr. Rowe's probable successor; but in the meantime, I had gone to hear him preach the Sunday after his arrival. A poet and a phi-losopher getting up into a Unitarian pulpit to preach the Gospel was a romance in these degenerate days, a sort of revival of the primitive spirit of Christianity, which was not to be resisted.

It was in January of 1798, that I rose one morning before day-light, to walk ten miles in the mud, and went to hear this cele-brated person preach. Never, the longest day I have to live, shall I have such another walk as this cold, raw, comfortless one, in the winter of the year 1798. *Il y a des impressions que ni le temps ni les circonstances peuvent effacer. Dusse-je vivre des siècles entiers, le doux temps de ma jeunesse ne peut renaître pour moi, ni s'effacer jamais dans ma mémoire.*[6] When I got there, the organ was playing the 100th psalm, and when it was done, Mr. Coleridge rose and gave out his text, "And he went up into the mountain to pray, *himself, alone.*"[7] As he gave out this text, his voice "rose like a steam of rich distilled perfume,"[8] and when he

---

5. Adapted from Pope's *Ode on St. Ce-cilia's Day,* lines 90–91.
6. "There are some impressions which neither time nor circumstances can ef-face. Might I live whole centuries, the sweet time of my youth could not be reborn for me, nor ever erased from my memory." Based on Rousseau's epis-tolary novel, *La Nouvelle Héloise* (1761), Part VI, Letter 7.
7. Cf. Matthew xiv.23; John vi.15.
8. Milton's *Comus,* line 556.

came to the two last words, which he pronounced loud, deep, and distinct, it seemed to me, who was then young, as if the sounds had echoed from the bottom of the human heart, and as if that prayer might have floated in solemn silence through the universe. The idea of St. John came into my mind, "of one crying in the wilderness, who had his loins girt about, and whose food was locusts and wild honey."[9] The preacher then launched into his subject, like an eagle dallying with the wind. The sermon was upon peace and war; upon church and state—not their alliance but their separation—on the spirit of the world and the spirit of Christianity, not as the same, but as opposed to one another. He talked of those who had "inscribed the cross of Christ on banners dripping with human gore." He made a poetical and pastoral excursion—and to show the fatal effects of war, drew a striking contrast between the simple shepherd boy, driving his team afield, or sitting under the hawthorn, piping to his flock, "as though he should never be old,"[1] and the same poor country lad, crimped,[2] kidnapped, brought into town, made drunk, at an alehouse, turned into a wretched drummer boy, with his hair sticking on end with powder and pomatum, a long cue at his back, and tricked out in the loathsome finery of the profession of blood.

> Such were the notes our once-loved poet sung.[3]

And for myself, I could not have been more delighted if I had heard the music of the spheres. Poetry and Philosophy had met together. Truth and Genius had embraced, under the eye and with the sanction of Religion. This was even beyond my hopes. I returned home well satisfied. The sun that was still laboring pale and wan through the sky, obscured by thick mists, seemed an emblem of the *good cause;*[4] and the cold dank drops of dew, that hung half melted on the beard of the thistle, had something genial and refreshing in them; for there was a spirit of hope and youth in all nature, that turned everything into good. The face of nature had not then the brand of *Jus Divinum*[5] on it:

> Like to that sanguine flower inscribed with woe.[6]

On the Tuesday following, the half-inspired speaker came. I was called down into the room where he was, and went half-hoping, half-afraid. He received me very graciously, and I listened for a long time without uttering a word. I did not suffer in his opinion by my silence. "For those two hours," he afterwards was pleased to say, "he was conversing with W. H.'s forehead!" His appearance

9. See Matthew iii. 3–4 and Mark i.3–6.
1. Sir Philip Sidney's *Arcadia* I.ii.
2. Trapped into enlisting in military service.
3. The first line of Pope's *Epistle to Robert, Earl of Oxford.*

4. The cause of liberty, i.e., the French Revolution.
5. The divine right (of kings).
6. I.e., the hyacinth, believed to be marked with the Greek lament "AI AI"; the line is from Milton's *Lycidas* (106).

was different from what I had anticipated from seeing him before. At a distance, and in the dim light of the chapel, there was to me a strange wildness in his aspect, a dusky obscurity, and I thought him pitted with the smallpox. His complexion was at that time clear, and even bright—

As are the children of yon azure sheen.[7]

His forehead was broad and high, light as if built of ivory, with large projecting eyebrows, and his eyes rolling beneath them, like a sea with darkened luster. "A certain tender bloom his face o'erspread,"[8] a purple tinge as we see it in the pale thoughtful complexions of the Spanish portrait painters, Murillo and Velasquez. His mouth was gross, voluptuous, open, eloquent; his chin good-humored and round; but his nose, the rudder of the face, the index of the will, was small, feeble, nothing—like what he has done. It might seem that the genius of his face as from a height surveyed and projected him (with sufficient capacity and huge aspiration) into the world unknown of thought and imagination, with nothing to support or guide his veering purpose, as if Columbus had launched his adventurous course for the New World in a scallop,[9] without oars or compass. So at least I comment on it after the event. Coleridge in his person was rather above the common size, inclining to the corpulent, or like Lord Hamlet, "somewhat fat and pursy."[1] His hair (now, alas! gray) was then black and glossy as the raven's, and fell in smooth masses over his forehead. This long pendulous hair is peculiar to enthusiasts, to those whose minds tend heavenward; and is traditionally inseparable (though of a different color) from the pictures of Christ. It ought to belong, as a character, to all who preach *Christ crucified*, and Coleridge was at that time one of those!

It was curious to observe the contrast between him and my father, who was a veteran in the cause, and then declining into the vale of years. He had been a poor Irish lad, carefully brought up by his parents, and sent to the University of Glasgow (where he studied under Adam Smith[2]) to prepare him for his future destination. It was his mother's proudest wish to see her son a Dissenting Minister. So if we look back to past generations (as far as eye can reach) we see the same hopes, fears, wishes, followed by the same disappointments, throbbing in the human heart; and so we may see them (if we look forward) rising up forever, and disappearing, like vaporish bubbles, in the human breast! After being tossed about from congregation to congregation in the heats of the Unitarian

7. See James Thomson, *The Castle of Indolence* II.xxxiii.
8. See *ibid.* I.lvii.
9. Probably for "shallop," a small boat.

1. Cf. *Hamlet* V.ii.298.
2. Scottish philosopher and author of the great economic treatise, *The Wealth of Nations* (1776).

controversy, and squabbles about the American war,[3] he had been relegated to an obscure village, where he was to spend the last thirty years of his life, far from the only converse that he loved, the talk about disputed texts of Scripture and the cause of civil and religious liberty. Here he passed his days, repining but resigned, in the study of the Bible, and the perusal of the Commentators— huge folios, not easily got through, one of which would outlast a winter! Why did he pore on these from morn to night (with the exception of a walk in the fields or a turn in the garden to gather broccoli plants or kidney beans of his own rearing, with no small degree of pride and pleasure)? Here were "no figures nor no fantasies"[4]—neither poetry nor philosophy—nothing to dazzle, nothing to excite modern curiosity; but to his lackluster eyes there appeared, within the pages of the ponderous, unwieldy, neglected tomes, the sacred name of JEHOVAH in Hebrew capitals: pressed down by the weight of the style, worn to the last fading thinness of the understanding, there were glimpses, glimmering notions of the patriarchal wanderings, with palm trees hovering in the horizon, and processions of camels at the distance of three thousand years; there was Moses with the Burning Bush, the number of the Twelve Tribes, types, shadows,[5] glosses on the law and the prophets; there were discussions (dull enough) on the age of Methuselah, a mighty speculation! there were outlines, rude guesses at the shape of Noah's Ark and of the riches of Solomon's Temple; questions as to the date of the creation, predictions of the end of all things; the great lapses of time, the strange mutations of the globe were unfolded with the voluminous leaf, as it turned over; and though the soul might slumber with an hieroglyphic veil of inscrutable mysteries drawn over it, yet it was in a slumber ill-exchanged for all the sharpened realities of sense, wit, fancy, or reason. My father's life was comparatively a dream; but it was a dream of infinity and eternity, of death, the resurrection, and a judgment to come!

No two individuals were ever more unlike than were the host and his guest. A poet was to my father a sort of nondescript: yet whatever added grace to the Unitarian cause was to him welcome. He could hardly have been more surprised or pleased if our visitor had worn wings. Indeed, his thoughts had wings; and as the silken sounds rustled round our little wainscoted parlor, my father threw back his spectacles over his forehead, his white hairs mixing with its sanguine hue; and a smile of delight beamed across his rugged cordial face, to think that Truth had found a new ally in Fancy! Besides, Coleridge seemed to take considerable notice of me, and

3. The American Revolution, with which a number of radical Unitarian preachers were in sympathy.
4. *Julius Caesar* II.i.231.
5. "Types" were characters and events in the Old Testament believed to prefigure analogous matters in the New Testament. "Shadows" were Old Testament foreshadowings of later events, or symbols of moral and theological truths.

that of itself was enough. He talked very familiarly, but agreeably, and glanced over a variety of subjects. At dinner time he grew more animated, and dilated in a very edifying manner on Mary Wollstonecraft and Mackintosh.[6] The last, he said, he considered (on my father's speaking of his *Vindiciae Gallicae* as a capital performance) as a clever scholastic[7] man—a master of the topics—or as the ready warehouseman of letters, who knew exactly where to lay his hand on what he wanted, though the goods were not his own. He thought him no match for Burke, either in style or matter. Burke was a metaphysician, Mackintosh a mere logician. Burke was an orator (almost a poet) who reasoned in figures, because he had an eye for nature: Mackintosh, on the other hand, was a rhetorician, who had only an eye to commonplaces. On this I ventured to say that I had always entertained a great opinion of Burke, and that (as far as I could find) the speaking of him with contempt might be made the test of a vulgar democratical mind. This was the first observation I ever made to Coleridge, and he said it was a very just and striking one. I remember the leg of Welsh mutton and the turnips on the table that day had the finest flavor imaginable. Coleridge added that Mackintosh and Tom Wedgwood[8] (of whom, however, he spoke highly) had expressed a very indifferent opinion of his friend Mr. Wordsworth, on which he remarked to them— "He strides on so far before you that he dwindles in the distance!" Godwin[9] had once boasted to him of having carried on an argument with Mackintosh for three hours with dubious success; Coleridge told him—"If there had been a man of genius in the room, he would have settled the question in five minutes." He asked me if I had ever seen Mary Wollstonecraft, and I said I had once for a few moments, and that she seemed to me to turn off Godwin's objections to something she advanced with quite a playful, easy air. He replied, that "this was only one instance of the ascendancy which people of imagination exercised over those of mere intellect." He did not rate Godwin very high (this was caprice or prejudice, real or affected) but he had a great idea of Mrs. Wollstonecraft's powers of conversation, none at all of her talent for book-making. We talked a little about Holcroft.[1] He had been asked if he was not much struck *with* him, and he said, he thought himself in more danger of being struck *by* him. I complained that he would

6. Mary Wollstonecraft's *A Vindication of the Rights of Men* (1790) and the Scottish philosopher James Mackintosh's *Vindiciae Gallicae* ("Defense of France," 1791) were both written in opposition to Edmund Burke's *Reflections on the French Revolution* (1790).
7. The Scholastics, medieval philosophers and theologians, organized their thought systematically, often under various "topics"—standard headings, or "commonplaces" (see the third

sentence following).
8. Son of Josiah Wedgwood (1730–95), who founded the great pottery firm which still exists.
9. William Godwin (1756–1836), radical philosopher and didactic novelist, author of the influential *Inquiry Concerning Political Justice* (1793).
1. Thomas Holcroft, another radical contemporary, author of plays and novels.

not let me get on at all, for he required a definition of even the commonest word, exclaiming, "What do you mean by a *sensation*, sir? What do you mean by an *idea?*" This, Coleridge said, was barricadoing the road to truth: it was setting up a turnpike gate at every step we took. I forget a great number of things, many more than I remember; but the day passed off pleasantly, and the next morning Mr. Coleridge was to return to Shrewsbury. When I came down to breakfast, I found that he had just received a letter from his friend, T. Wedgwood, making him an offer of £150 a year if he chose to waive his present pursuit, and devote himself entirely to the study of poetry and philosophy. Coleridge seemed to make up his mind to close with this proposal in the act of tying on one of his shoes. It threw an additional damp on his departure. It took the wayward enthusiast quite from us to cast him into Deva's winding vales,[2] or by the shores of old romance. Instead of living at ten miles' distance, of being the pastor of a Dissenting congregation at Shrewsbury, he was henceforth to inhabit the Hill of Parnassus, to be a Shepherd on the Delectable Mountains.[3] Alas! I knew not the way thither, and felt very little gratitude for Mr. Wedgwood's bounty. I was presently relieved from this dilemma; for Mr. Coleridge, asking for a pen and ink, and going to a table to write something on a bit of card, advanced towards me with undulating step, and giving me the precious document, said that that was his address, *Mr. Coleridge, Nether Stowey, Somersetshire*; and that he should be glad to see me there in a few weeks' time, and, if I chose, would come half-way to meet me. I was not less surprised than the shepherd boy (this simile is to be found in *Cassandra*[4]) when he sees a thunderbolt fall close at his feet. I stammered out my acknowledgments and acceptance of this offer (I thought Mr. Wedgwood's annuity a trifle to it) as well as I could; and this mighty business being settled, the poet-preacher took leave, and I accompanied him six miles on the road. It was a fine morning in the middle of winter, and he talked the whole way. The scholar in Chaucer is described as going

——sounding on his way.[5]

So Coleridge went on his. In digressing, in dilating, in passing from subject to subject, he appeared to me to float in air, to slide on ice. He told me in confidence (going along) that he should have preached two sermons before he accepted the situation at Shrews-

2. Milton, *Lycidas*, line 55: "Nor yet where Deva spreads her wizard stream" ("Deva" is the river Dee, in Wales). Since Milton speaks in that passage of "Druid bards," Hazlitt means that Coleridge will devote himself to imaginative writing.
3. An allegorical locale in Bunyan's *Pilgrim's Progress*, here used as another periphrasis for the occupation of poetry.
4. A romance by the 17th-century French writer La Calprenède.
5. *The Canterbury Tales*, General Prologue, line 309: "Souning in moral vertu was his speeche" (in Chaucer, the meaning of "souning in" is either "resounding in" or "consonant with").

bury, one on Infant Baptism, the other on the Lord's Supper, showing that he could not administer either, which would have effectually disqualified him for the object in view. I observed that he
continually crossed me on the way by shifting from one side of
the footpath to the other. This struck me as an odd movement;
but I did not at that time connect it with any instability of purpose or involuntary change of principle, as I have done since. He
seemed unable to keep on in a straight line. He spoke slightingly
of Hume[6] (whose *Essay on Miracles* he said was stolen from an
objection started in one of South's[7] sermons—*Credat Judaeus Ap-
pella!*) I was not very much pleased at this account of Hume, for
I had just been reading, with infinite relish, that completest of all
metaphysical *choke-pears*,[8] his *Treatise on Human Nature*, to which
the *Essays*, in point of scholastic subtlety and close reasoning, are
mere elegant trifling, light summer reading. Coleridge even denied
the excellence of Hume's general style, which I think betrayed a
want of taste or candor. He however made me amends by the manner in which he spoke of Berkeley.[9] He dwelt particularly on his
Essay on Vision as a masterpiece of analytical reasoning. So it undoubtedly is. He was exceedingly angry with Dr. Johnson for striking the stone with his foot, in allusion to this author's theory of
matter and spirit, and saying, "Thus I confute him, sir."[1] Coleridge drew a parallel (I don't know how he brought about the
connection) between Bishop Berkeley and Tom Paine.[2] He said
the one was an instance of a subtle, the other of an acute mind,
than which no two things could be more distinct. The one was
a shop-boy's quality, the other the characteristic of a philosopher.
He considered Bishop Butler[3] as a true philosopher, a profound
and conscientious thinker, a genuine reader of nature and of his
own mind. He did not speak of his *Analogy*, but of his *Sermons
at the Rolls' Chapel*, of which I had never heard. Coleridge somehow always contrived to prefer the *unknown* to the *known*. In this
instance he was right. The *Analogy* is a tissue of sophistry, of wire-
drawn, theological special-pleading; the *Sermons* (with the Preface
to them) are in a fine vein of deep, matured reflection, a candid
appeal to our observation of human nature, without pedantry and
without bias. I told Coleridge I had written a few remarks, and
was sometimes foolish enough to believe that I had made a discovery on the same subject (the *Natural Disinterestedness of the*

6. David Hume, 18th-century Scottish
philosopher.
7. Robert South (1634–1716), Anglican divine. The Latin phrase, from
Horace, *Satires* I.v.100, means, "Let
Apella the Jew believe it"—implying
that he himself does not.
8. A very sour variety of pear; hence,
anything hard to take in.
9. Bishop George Berkeley, 18th-cen-
tury idealist philosopher, and author of

an *Essay Toward a New Theory of
Vision* (1709).
1. See Boswell's *Life of Johnson* for
the year 1763.
2. Philosophical supporter of the American and French Revolutions and author of *Common Sense* and *The Rights
of Man.*
3. Joseph Butler. 18th-century theologian and moral philosopher, author of
the *Analogy of Religion* (1736).

Human Mind[4])—and I tried to explain my view of it to Coleridge, who listened with great willingness, but I did not succeed in making myself understood. I sat down to the task shortly afterwards for the twentieth time, got new pens and paper, determined to make clear work of it, wrote a few meager sentences in the skeleton-style of a mathematical demonstration, stopped halfway down the second page; and, after trying in vain to pump up any words, images, notions, apprehensions, facts, or observations, from that gulf of abstraction in which I had plunged myself for four or five years preceding, gave up the attempt as labor in vain, and shed tears of helpless despondency on the blank unfinished paper. I can write fast enough now. Am I better than I was then? Oh no! One truth discovered, one pang of regret at not being able to express it, is better than all the fluency and flippancy in the world. Would that I could go back to what I then was! Why can we not revive past times as we can revisit old places? If I had the quaint Muse of Sir Philip Sidney to assist me, I would write a *Sonnet to the Road between Wem and Shrewsbury,* and immortalize every step of it by some fond enigmatical conceit. I would swear that the very milestones had ears, and that Harmer Hill stooped with all its pines, to listen to a poet, as he passed! I remember but one other topic of discourse in this walk. He mentioned Paley,[5] praised the naturalness and clearness of his style, but condemned his sentiments, thought him a mere time-serving casuist, and said that "the fact of his work on Moral and Political Philosophy being made a text-book in our universities was a disgrace to the national character." We parted at the six-mile stone; and I returned homeward pensive but much pleased. I had met with unexpected notice from a person whom I believed to have been prejudiced against me. "Kind and affable to me had been his condescension, and should be honored ever with suitable regard."[6] He was the first poet I had known, and he certainly answered to that inspired name. I had heard a great deal of his powers of conversation, and was not disappointed. In fact, I never met with anything at all like them, either before or since. I could easily credit the accounts which were circulated of his holding forth to a large party of ladies and gentlemen, an evening or two before, on the Berkeleian Theory, when he made the whole material universe look like a transparency of fine words; and another story (which I believe he has somewhere told himself)[7] of his being asked to a party at Birmingham, of his smoking tobacco and going to sleep after dinner on a sofa, where the company found him, to their no small surprise, which was in-

---

4. Published as *An Essay on the Principles of Human Action* (1805).
5. William Paley, author of *Evidences of Christianity* (1794), and supporter of a utilitarian theology and morality.

6. Paraphrasing Adam's words about the angel Raphael in *Paradise Lost* VIII.648–50.
7. See *Biographia Literaria,* Chapter X.

creased to wonder when he started up of a sudden, and rubbing his eyes, looked about him, and launched into a three hours' description of the third heaven, of which he had had a dream, very different from Mr. Southey's *Vision of Judgment*,[8] and also from that other *Vision of Judgment*, which Mr. Murray, the secretary of the Bridge Street Junto, has taken into his especial keeping!

On my way back, I had a sound in my ears, it was the voice of Fancy: I had a light before me, it was the face of Poetry. The one still lingers there, the other has not quitted my side! Coleridge in truth met me half-way on the ground of philosophy, or I should not have been won over to his imaginative creed. I had an uneasy, pleasurable sensation all the time, till I was to visit him. During those months the chill breath of winter gave me a welcoming; the vernal air was balm and inspiration to me. The golden sunsets, the silver star of evening, lighted me on my way to new hopes and prospects. *I was to visit Coleridge in the spring*. This circumstance was never absent from my thoughts, and mingled with all my feelings. I wrote to him at the time proposed, and received an answer postponing my intended visit for a week or two, but very cordially urging me to complete my promise then. This delay did not damp, but rather increased my ardor. In the meantime, I went to Llangollen Vale,[9] by way of initiating myself in the mysteries of natural scenery; and I must say I was enchanted with it. I had been reading Coleridge's description of England in his fine *Ode on the Departing Year*, and I applied it, *con amore*,[1] to the objects before me. That valley was to me (in a manner) the cradle of a new existence: in the river that winds through it, my spirit was baptized in the waters of Helicon![2]

I returned home, and soon after set out on my journey with unworn heart and untired feet. My way lay through Worcester and Gloucester, and by Upton, where I thought of Tom Jones and the adventure of the muff.[3] I remember getting completely wet through one day, and stopping at an inn (I think it was at Tewkesbury) where I sat up all night to read *Paul and Virginia*.[4] Sweet were the showers in early youth that drenched my body, and sweet the drops of pity that fell upon the books I read! I recollect a remark of Coleridge's upon this very book that nothing could show the gross indelicacy of French manners and the entire corruption of their imagination more strongly than the behavior of the heroine in the

8. Robert Southey's sycophantic memorial poem describing the entrance into heaven of George III. "Mr. Murray" was Charles Murray, solicitor to an Association, located at New Bridge Street, for "Opposing Disloyal and Seditious Principles"; he prosecuted John Hunt for publishing Byron's *Vision of Judgment*, a brilliant parody of Southey's poem. Hazlitt derisively refers to the Association as a "junto"—

i.e., a group formed for political intrigue.
9. In north Wales (about 35 miles from Wem).
1. "With love," fervently.
2. A mountain sacred to Apollo and the Muses.
3. Henry Fielding's *Tom Jones* X.v. ff.
4. A sentimental love idyll (1788) by Bernardin de Saint-Pierre.

last fatal scene, who turns away from a person on board the sinking vessel, that offers to save her life, because he has thrown off his clothes to assist him in swimming. Was this a time to think of such a circumstance? I once hinted to Wordsworth, as we were sailing in his boat on Grasmere lake, that I thought he had borrowed the idea of his *Poems on the Naming of Places* from the local inscriptions of the same kind in *Paul and Virginia*. He did not own the obligation, and stated some distinction without a difference in defense to his claim to originality. Any the slightest variation would be sufficient for this purpose in his mind; for whatever *he* added or omitted would inevitably be worth all that any one else had done, and contain the marrow of the sentiment. I was still two days before the time fixed for my arrival, for I had taken care to set out early enough. I stopped these two days at Bridgewater, and when I was tired of sauntering on the banks of its muddy river, returned to the inn and read *Camilla*.[5] So have I loitered my life away, reading books, looking at pictures, going to plays, hearing, thinking, writing on what pleased me best. I have wanted only one thing to make me happy; but wanting that, have wanted everything![6]

I arrived, and was well received. The country about Nether Stowey is beautiful, green and hilly, and near the seashore. I saw it but the other day, after an interval of twenty years, from a hill near Taunton. How was the map of my life spread out before me, as the map of the country lay at my feet! In the afternoon, Coleridge took me over to Alfoxden, a romantic old family mansion of the St. Aubins, where Wordsworth lived. It was then in the possession of a friend of the poet's, who gave him the free use of it.[7] Somehow, that period (the time just after the French Revolution) was not a time when *nothing was given for nothing*. The mind opened and a softness might be perceived coming over the heart of individuals, beneath "the scales that fence" our self-interest. Wordsworth himself was from home, but his sister kept house, and set before us a frugal repast; and we had free access to her brother's poems, the *Lyrical Ballads*, which were still in manuscript, or in the form of *Sybilline Leaves*.[8] I dipped into a few of these with great satisfaction, and with the faith of a novice. I slept that night in an old room wth blue hangings, and covered with the round-faced family portraits of the age of George I and II and from the wooded declivity of the adjoining park that overlooked my window, at the dawn of day, could

———hear the loud stag speak.[9]

5. A novel by Fanny Burney, published 1796.
6. The love of Sarah Walker; see the introduction to Hazlitt, above.
7. A mistake; Wordsworth paid rent.

8. I.e., "prophetic writings"; used by Coleridge as the title for his published poems in 1817.
9. From Ben Jonson's poem *To Sir Robert Wroth*, line 22.

In the outset of life (and particularly at this time I felt it so) our imagination has a body to it. We are in a state between sleeping and waking, and have indistinct but glorious glimpses of strange shapes, and there is always something to come better than what we see. As in our dreams the fullness of the blood gives warmth and reality to the coinage of the brain, so in youth our ideas are clothed, and fed, and pampered with our good spirits; we breathe thick with thoughtless happiness, the weight of future years presses on the strong pulses of the heart, and we repose with undisturbed faith in truth and good. As we advance, we exhaust our fund of enjoyment and of hope. We are no longer wrapped in *lamb's wool*, lulled in Elysium. As we taste the pleasures of life, their spirit evaporates, the sense palls; and nothing is left but the phantoms, the lifeless shadows of what *has been!*

That morning, as soon as breakfast was over, we strolled out into the park, and seating ourselves on the trunk of an old ash tree that stretched along the ground, Coleridge read aloud with a sonorous and musical voice, the ballad of *Betty Foy*.[1] I was not critically or skeptically inclined. I saw touches of truth and nature, and took the rest for granted. But in the *Thorn*, the *Mad Mother*, and the *Complaint of a Poor Indian Woman*, I felt that deeper power and pathos which have been since acknowledged,

> In spite of pride, in erring reason's spite,[2]

as the characteristics of this author; and the sense of a new style and a new spirit in poetry came over me. It had to me something of the effect that arises from the turning up of the fresh soil, or of the first welcome breath of spring,

> While yet the trembling year is unconfirmed.[3]

Coleridge and myself walked back to Stowey that evening, and his voice sounded high

> Of Providence, foreknowledge, will, and fate,
> Fixed fate, free will, foreknowledge absolute,[4]

as we passed through echoing grove, by fairy stream or waterfall, gleaming in the summer moonlight! He lamented that Wordsworth was not prone enough to believe in the traditional superstitions of the place, and that there was a something corporeal, a *matter-of-fact-ness*, a clinging to the palpable, or often to the petty, in his poetry, in consequence. His genius was not a spirit that descended to him through the air; it sprung out of the ground like a flower, or unfolded itself from a green spray, on which the goldfinch sang.

1. Wordsworth's *Idiot Boy;* like the other poems mentioned, it was included in *Lyrical Ballads.*
2. Pope's *Essay on Man* I.293.
3. James Thomson, *The Seasons,* "Spring," line 18.
4. *Paradise Lost* II.559–60.

He said, however (if I remember right) that this objection must be confined to his descriptive pieces, that his philosophic poetry had a grand and comprehensive spirit in it, so that his soul seemed to inhabit the universe like a palace, and to discover truth by intuition, rather than by deduction. The next day Wordsworth arrived from Bristol at Coleridge's cottage. I think I see him now. He answered in some degree to his friend's description of him, but was more gaunt and Don Quixote-like. He was quaintly dressed (according to the *costume* of that unconstrained period) in a brown fustian[5] jacket and striped pantaloons. There was something of a roll, a lounge in his gait, not unlike his own Peter Bell.[6] There was a severe, worn pressure of thought about his temples, a fire in his eye (as if he saw something in objects more than the outward appearance), an intense high narrow forehead, a Roman nose, cheeks furrowed by strong purpose and feeling, and a convulsive inclination to laughter about the mouth, a good deal at variance with the solemn, stately expression of the rest of his face. Chantry's bust wants the marking traits; but he was teased into making it regular and heavy; Haydon's head of him, introduced into the *Entrance of Christ into Jerusalem*, is the most like his drooping weight of thought and expression.[7] He sat down and talked very naturally and freely, with a mixture of clear gushing accents in his voice, a deep guttural intonation, and a strong tincture of the northern *burr*, like the crust on wine. He instantly began to make havoc of the half of a Cheshire cheese on the table, and said triumphantly that "his marriage with experience had not been so unproductive as Mr. Southey's in teaching him a knowledge of the good things of this life." He had been to see the *Castle Specter* by Monk Lewis,[8] while at Bristol, and described it very well. He said "it fitted the taste of the audience like a glove." This *ad captandum*[9] merit was, however, by no means a recommendation of it, according to the severe principles of the new school, which reject rather than court popular effect. Wordsworth, looking out of the low, latticed window, said, "How beautifully the sun sets on that yellow bank!" I thought within myself, "With what eyes these poets see nature!" and ever after, when I saw the sunset stream upon the objects facing it, conceived I had made a discovery, or thanked Mr. Wordsworth for having made one for me! We went over to Alfoxden again the day following, and Wordsworth read us the story of *Peter Bell* in the open air; and the comment made upon it by his face and voice was very different from that of

---

5. A coarse and heavy cotton cloth.
6. The protagonist in Wordsworth's *Peter Bell*.
7. Sir Francis Chantrey, a sculptor; Benjamin Robert Haydon, painter of grandiose historical and religious pictures.

8. Matthew Gregory Lewis (1775–1818), called "Monk" Lewis from his horror tale, *The Monk* (1795). The *Castle Specter* was a play, also in the Gothic terror-mode.
9. "For the sake of captivating" an audience.

some later critics! Whatever might be thought of the poem, "his
face was as a book where men might read strange matters,"[1] and
he announced the fate of his hero in prophetic tones. There is a
chaunt in the recitation both of Coleridge and Wordsworth, which
acts as a spell upon the hearer, and disarms the judgment. Perhaps
they have deceived themselves by making habitual use of this ambiguous accompaniment. Coleridge's manner is more full, animated,
and varied; Wordsworth's more equable, sustained, and internal.
The one might be termed more *dramatic*, the other more *lyrical*.
Coleridge has told me that he himself liked to compose in walking
over uneven ground, or breaking through the straggling branches
of a copse wood; whereas Wordsworth always wrote (if he could)
walking up and down a straight gravel walk, or in some spot where
the continuity of his verse met with no collateral interruption. Returning that same evening, I got into a metaphysical argument with
Wordsworth, while Coleridge was explaining the different notes of
the nightingale to his sister, in which we neither of us succeeded
in making ourselves perfectly clear and intelligible. Thus I passed
three weeks at Nether Stowey and in the neighborhood, generally
devoting the afternoons to a delightful chat in an arbor made of
bark by the poet's friend Tom Poole, sitting under two fine elm
trees, and listening to the bees humming round us while we quaffed
our flip.[2] It was agreed, among other things, that we should make
a jaunt down the Bristol Channel, as far as Linton. We set off
together on foot, Coleridge, John Chester, and I. This Chester
was a native of Nether Stowey, one of those who were attracted to
Coleridge's discourse as flies are to honey, or bees in swarming-time
to the sound of a brass pan. He "followed in the chase like a dog
who hunts, not like one that made up the cry."[3] He had on a
brown cloth coat, boots, and corduroy breeches, was low in stature,
bowlegged, had a drag in his walk like a drover, which he assisted
by a hazel switch, and kept on a sort of trot by the side of Coleridge, like a running footman by a state coach, that he might not
lose a syllable or sound that fell from Coleridge's lips. He told me
his private opinion, that Coleridge was a wonderful man. He
scarcely opened his lips, much less offered an opinion the whole
way; yet of the three, had I to choose during that journey, I would
be John Chester. He afterwards followed Coleridge into Germany,
where the Kantean philosophers were puzzled how to bring him
under any of their categories. When he sat down at table with his
idol, John's felicity was complete; Sir Walter Scott's, or Mr. Blackwood's, when they sat down at the same table with the King,[4] was
not more so. We passed Dunster on our right, a small town be-

1. See *Macbeth* I.v.63–64.
2. Spiced and sweetened ale.
3. Cf. *Othello* II.iii.369–70.
4. At a banquet given to George IV
at Edinburgh, in 1822. William Blackwood, publisher of *Blackwood's Magazine*, was, like Scott, a Tory; hence
the irony.

tween the brow of a hill and the sea. I remember eying it wistfully as it lay below us: contrasted with the woody scene around, it looked as clear, as pure, as *embrowned* and ideal as any landscape I have seen since, of Gaspar Poussin's or Domenichino's. We had a long day's march—(our feet kept time to the echoes of Coleridge's tongue)—through Minehead and by the Blue Anchor, and on to Linton, which we did not reach till near midnight, and where we had some difficulty in making a lodgment. We however knocked the people of the house up at last, and we were repaid for our apprehensions and fatigue by some excellent rashers of fried bacon and eggs. The view in coming along had been splendid. We walked for miles and miles on dark brown heaths overlooking the channel, with the Welsh hills beyond, and at times descended into little sheltered valleys close by the seaside, with a smuggler's face scowling by us, and then had to ascend conical hills with a path winding up through a coppice to a barren top, like a monk's shaven crown, from one of which I pointed out to Coleridge's notice the bare masts of a vessel on the very edge of the horizon and within the red-orbed disk of the setting sun, like his own specter-ship in the *Ancient Mariner*. At Linton the character of the seacoast becomes more marked and rugged. There is a place called the Valley of Rocks (I suspect this was only the poetical name for it) bedded among precipices overhanging the sea, with rocky caverns beneath, into which the waves dash, and where the seagull forever wheels its screaming flight. On the tops of these are huge stones thrown transverse, as if an earthquake had tossed them there, and behind these is a fretwork of perpendicular rocks, something like the Giant's Causeway.[5] A thunderstorm came on while we were at the inn, and Coleridge was running out bareheaded to enjoy the commotion of the elements in the Valley of Rocks, but as if in spite, the clouds only muttered a few angry sounds, and let fall a few refreshing drops. Coleridge told me that he and Wordsworth were to have made this place the scene of a prose tale,[6] which was to have been in the manner of, but far superior to, the *Death of Abel*, but they had relinquished the design. In the morning of the second day, we breakfasted luxuriously in an old-fashioned parlor, on tea, toast, eggs, and honey, in the very sight of the beehives from which it had been taken, and a garden full of thyme and wild flowers that had produced it. On this occasion Coleridge spoke of Virgil's *Georgics*, but not well. I do not think he had much feeling for the classical or elegant. It was in this room that we found a little worn-out copy of the *Seasons*,[7] lying in a window seat, on which Coleridge exclaimed, "*That* is true fame!" He said Thomson was

5. A mass of rocks on the northern Irish coast.
6. The "prose tale" exists as a fragment, *The Wanderings of Cain*. The *Death of Abel* (1758) is by the once celebrated Swiss poet, Salomon Gessner.
7. By James Thomson, published 1726–30.

a great poet, rather than a good one; his style was as meretricious as his thoughts were natural. He spoke of Cowper as the best modern poet. He said the *Lyrical Ballads* were an experiment about to be tried by him and Wordsworth, to see how far the public taste would endure poetry written in a more natural and simple style than had hitherto been attempted; totally discarding the artifices of poetical diction, and making use only of such words as had probably been common in the most ordinary language since the days of Henry II. Some comparison was introduced between Shakespeare and Milton. He said "he hardly knew which to prefer. Shakespeare appeared to him a mere stripling in the art; he was as tall and as strong, with infinitely more activity than Milton, but he never appeared to have come to man's estate; or if he had, he would not have been a man, but a monster." He spoke with contempt of Gray, and with intolerance of Pope. He did not like the versification of the latter. He observed that "the ears of these couplet-writers might be charged with having short memories, that could not retain the harmony of whole passages." He thought little of Junius[8] as a writer; he had a dislike of Dr. Johnson; and a much higher opinion of Burke as an orator and politician, than of Fox or Pitt. He however thought him very inferior in richness of style and imagery to some of our elder prose writers, particularly Jeremy Taylor.[9] He liked Richardson, but not Fielding; nor could I get him to enter into the merits of *Caleb Williams*.[1] In short, he was profound and discriminating with respect to those authors whom he liked, and where he gave his judgment fair play; capricious, perverse, and prejudiced in his antipathies and distastes. We loitered on the "ribbed sea-sands,"[2] in such talk as this, a whole morning, and I recollect met with a curious seaweed, of which John Chester told us the country name! A fisherman gave Coleridge an account of a boy that had been drowned the day before, and that they had tried to save him at the risk of their own lives. He said "he did not know how it was that they ventured, but, sir, we have a *nature* towards one another." This expression, Coleridge remarked to me, was a fine illustration of that theory of disinterestedness which I (in common with Butler) had adopted. I broached to him an argument of mine to prove that *likeness* was not mere association of ideas. I said that the mark in the sand put one in mind of a man's foot, not because it was part of a former impression of a man's foot (for it was quite new) but because it was like the shape of a man's foot. He assented to the justness of this distinction (which

8. The pseudonym of an author (his identity is still unknown) of a series of attacks on George III and various politicians, 1769–72.
9. The 17th-century divine, author of *Holy Living* (1650) and *Holy Dying* (1651).

1. Samuel Richardson and Henry Fielding, the great 18th-century novelists. *Caleb Williams* (1794) was a novel by William Godwin.
2. Echoing *The Ancient Mariner*, line 227.

I have explained at length elsewhere, for the benefit of the curious)
and John Chester listened; not from any interest in the subject,
but because he was astonished that I should be able to suggest
anything to Coleridge that he did not already know. We returned
on the third morning, and Coleridge remarked the silent cottage-
smoke curling up the valleys where, a few evenings before, we had
seen the lights gleaming through the dark.

In a day or two after we arrived at Stowey, we set out, I on my
return home, and he for Germany. It was a Sunday morning, and
he was to preach that day for Dr. Toulmin of Taunton. I asked
him if he had prepared anything for the occasion? He said he had
not even thought of the text, but should as soon as we parted. I
did not go to hear him,—this was a fault—but we met in the
evening at Bridgewater. The next day we had a long day's walk
to Bristol, and sat down, I recollect, by a well-side on the road,
to cool ourselves and satisfy our thirst, when Coleridge repeated
to me some descriptive lines from his tragedy of *Remorse*; which
I must say became his mouth and that occasion better than they,
some years after, did Mr. Elliston's and the Drury Lane boards,[3]

> Oh memory! shield me from the world's poor strife,
> And give those scenes thine everlasting life.

I saw no more of him for a year or two, during which period
he had been wandering in the Hartz Forest in Germany; and his
return was cometary, meteorous, unlike his setting out. It was
not till some time after that I knew his friends Lamb and Southey.
The last always appears to me (as I first saw him) with a common-
place-book under his arm, and the first with a bon mot in his
mouth. It was at Godwin's that I met him with Holcroft and
Coleridge, where they were disputing fiercely which was the best
—*Man as he was, or man as he is to be.* "Give me," says Lamb,
"man as he is *not* to be." This saying was the beginning of a friendship between us, which I believe still continues.—Enough of this
for the present.

> But there is matter for another rhyme,
> And I to this may add a second tale.[4]

1823

3. Robert William Elliston, a well-
known actor. Coleridge's *Remorse* was
produced at Drury Lane Theatre in

1813.
4. Wordsworth, *Hart-Leap Well*, lines
95–96.

From Mr. Wordsworth[1]

Mr. Wordsworth's genius is a pure emanation of the Spirit of the Age. Had he lived in any other period of the world, he would never have been heard of. As it is, he has some difficulty to contend with the hebetude[2] of his intellect, and the meanness of his subject. With him "lowliness is young ambition's ladder":[3] but he finds it a toil to climb in this way the steep of Fame. His homely Muse can hardly raise her wing from the ground, nor spread her hidden glories to the sun. He has "no figures nor no fantasies, which busy *passion* draws in the brains of men":[4] neither the gorgeous machinery of mythologic lore, nor the splendid colors of poetic diction. His style is vernacular: he delivers household truths. He sees nothing loftier than human hopes; nothing deeper than the human heart. This he probes, this he tampers with, this he poises, with all its incalculable weight of thought and feeling, in his hands; and at the same time calms the throbbing pulses of his own heart, by keeping his eye ever fixed on the face of nature. If he can make the life-blood flow from the wounded breast, this is the living coloring with which he paints his verse: if he can assuage the pain or close up the wound with the balm of solitary musing, or the healing power of plants and herbs and "skyey influences,"[5] this is the sole triumph of his art. He takes the simplest elements of nature and of the human mind, the mere abstract conditions inseparable from our being, and tries to compound a new system of poetry from them; and has perhaps succeeded as well as any one could. "*Nihil humani a me alienum puto*"[6]—is the motto of his works. He thinks nothing low or indifferent of which this can be affirmed: every thing that professes to be more than this, that is not an absolute essence of truth and feeling, he holds to be vitiated, false, and spurious. In a word, his poetry is founded on setting up an opposition (and pushing it to the utmost length) between the natural and the artificial; between the spirit of humanity, and the spirit of fashion and of the world!

1. This was one of a series of essays on contemporary philosophers, poets, and statesmen which Hazlitt published in 1825 with the title *The Spirit of the Age: or Contemporary Portraits*. Like Shelley, Hazlitt attributed what was most distinctive in the intellectual and literary enterprise of his era to the impact on imagination of the French Revolution. See, e.g., the concluding page of Shelley's *Defence of Poetry*.

In this essay Hazlitt deals with Wordsworth's *Lyrical Ballads* and other early poems. With notable insight Hazlitt, alone among contemporary critics, writes a sociological study of Wordsworth's in-novations in poetry and criticism. He recognizes that the traditional hierarchy of poetic genres, subjects, and diction had reflected the class-structure of society, and that, by "leveling" this hierarchy, Wordsworth had effected a literary equivalent of the political and social revolution in France.

2. Dullness, lethargy.
3. Said by Brutus in *Julius Caesar* II.i.22.
4. *Ibid.*, II.i.231; Hazlitt substitutes "passion" for Brutus' word "care."
5. *Measure for Measure* III.i.9.
6. From the Roman writer of comedy, Terence: "Nothing that is human do I consider alien to me."

It is one of the innovations of the time. It partakes of, and is carried along with, the revolutionary movement of our age: the political changes of the day were the model on which he formed and conducted his poetical experiments. His Muse (it cannot be denied, and without this we cannot explain its character at all) is a leveling one. It proceeds on a principle of equality, and strives to reduce all things to the same standard. It is distinguished by a proud humility. It relies upon its own resources, and disdains external show and relief. It takes the commonest events and objects, as a test to prove that nature is always interesting from its inherent truth and beauty, without any of the ornaments of dress or pomp of circumstances to set it off. Hence the unaccountable mixture of seeming simplicity and real abstruseness in the *Lyrical Ballads*. Fools have laughed at, wise men scarcely understand them. He takes a subject or a story merely as pegs or loops to hang thought and feeling on; the incidents are trifling, in proportion to his contempt for imposing appearances; the reflections are profound, according to the gravity and the aspiring pretensions of his mind.

His popular, inartificial style gets rid (at a blow) of all the trappings of verse, of all the high places of poetry: "the cloud-capped towers, the solemn temples, the gorgeous palaces," are swept to the ground, and "like the baseless fabric of a vision, leave not a wreck behind."[7] All the traditions of learning, all the superstitions of age, are obliterated and effaced. We begin *de novo*, on a *tabula rasa*[8] of poetry. The purple pall, the nodding plume of tragedy are exploded as mere pantomime and trick, to return to the simplicity of truth and nature. Kings, queens, priests, nobles, the altar and the throne, the distinctions of rank, birth, wealth, power, "the judge's robe, the marshal's truncheon, the ceremony that to great ones 'longs,"[9] are not to be found here. The author tramples on the pride of art with greater pride. The Ode and Epode, the Strophe and the Antistrophe, he laughs to scorn. The harp of Homer, the trump of Pindar and of Alcaeus[1] are still. The decencies of costume, the decorations of vanity are stripped off without mercy as barbarous, idle, and Gothic.[2] The jewels in the crisped hair,[3] the diadem on the polished brow are thought meretricious, theatrical, vulgar; and nothing contents his fastidious taste beyond a simple garland of flowers. Neither does he avail himself of the advantages which nature or accident holds out to him. He chooses to have his subject a foil to his invention, to owe nothing but to himself. He gathers manna in the wilderness, he strikes the barren rock for the gushing moisture. He elevates the mean by the strength of his own aspirations; he

7. Altered from Prospero's speech in *The Tempest* IV.i.151–156.
8. "We begin anew, on a clean slate."
9. Altered from *Measure for Measure* II.ii.59–61.
1. Pindar and Alcaeus were Greek writers of odes.
2. I.e., uncouth; belonging to the Dark Ages.
3. From William Collins' ode, *The Manners*, line 55: "Whose jewels in his crisped ["curly"] hair."

clothes the naked with beauty and grandeur from the stores of his own recollections. No cypress grove loads his verse with funeral pomp: but his imagination lends "a sense of joy"

> To the bare trees and mountains bare,
> And grass in the green field.[4]

No storm, no shipwreck startles us by its horrors: but the rainbow lifts its head in the cloud, and the breeze sighs through the withered fern. No sad vicissitude of fate, no overwhelming catastrophe in nature deforms his page: but the dew-drop glitters on the bending flower, the tear collects in the glistening eye.

> Beneath the hills, along the flowery vales,
> The generations are prepared; the pangs,
> The internal pangs are ready; the dread strife
> Of poor humanity's afflicted will,
> Struggling in vain with ruthless destiny.[5]

As the lark ascends from its low bed on fluttering wing, and salutes the morning skies; so Mr. Wordsworth's unpretending Muse, in russet[6] guise, scales the summits of reflection, while it makes the round earth its footstool, and its home!

Possibly a good deal of this may be regarded as the effect of disappointed views and an inverted ambition. Prevented by native pride and indolence from climbing the ascent of learning or greatness, taught by political opinions to say to the vain pomp and glory of the world, "I hate ye,"[7] seeing the path of classical and artificial poetry blocked up by the cumbrous ornaments of style and turgid *commonplaces*, so that nothing more could be achieved in that direction but by the most ridiculous bombast or the tamest servility; he has turned back partly from the bias of his mind, partly perhaps from a judicious policy—has struck into the sequestered vale of humble life, sought out the Muse among sheep-cotes and hamlets and the peasant's mountain-haunts, has discarded all the tinsel pageantry of verse, and endeavored (not in vain) to aggrandize the trivial and add the charm of novelty to the familiar. No one has shown the same imagination in raising trifles into importance: no one has displayed the same pathos in treating of the simplest feelings of the heart. Reserved, yet haughty, having no unruly or violent passions, (or those passions having been early suppressed,) Mr. Wordsworth has passed his life in solitary musing, or in daily converse with the face of nature. He exemplifies in an eminent degree the power of *association*; for his poetry has no other source or character. He has dwelt among pastoral scenes, till each object has

---

4. Wordsworth, *To My Sister*, lines 6–9.
5. Wordsworth, *The Excursion* VI.53 ff. The first line is misquoted: "Amid the groves, under the shadowy hills. . . ."
6. A coarse homespun cloth, worn by country people.
7. Shakespeare and John Fletcher, *King Henry the Eighth* III.ii.365: "Vain pomp and glory of this world, I hate ye!"

become connected with a thousand feelings, a link in the chain of thought, a fiber of his own heart. Everyone is by habit and familiarity strongly attached to the place of his birth, or to objects that recall the most pleasing and eventful circumstances of his life. But to the author of the *Lyrical Ballads,* nature is a kind of home; and he may be said to take a personal interest in the universe. There is no image so insignificant that it has not in some mood or other found the way into his heart: no sound that does not awaken the memory of other years.——

> To him the meanest flower that blows can give
> Thoughts that do often lie too deep for tears.[8]

The daisy looks up to him with sparkling eye as an old acquaintance: the cuckoo haunts him with sounds of early youth not to be expressed: a linnet's nest startles him with boyish delight: an old withered thorn is weighed down with a heap of recollections: a grey cloak, seen on some wild moor, torn by the wind, or drenched in the rain, afterwards becomes an object of imagination to him: even the lichens on the rock have a life and being in his thoughts. He has described all these objects in a way and with an intensity of feeling that no one else had done before him, and has given a new view or aspect of nature. He is in this sense the most original poet now living, and the one whose writings could the least be spared: for they have no substitute elsewhere. The vulgar do not read them, the learned, who see all things through books, do not understand them, the great despise, the fashionable may ridicule them: but the author has created himself an interest in the heart of the retired and lonely student of nature, which can never die. Persons of this class will still continue to feel what he has felt: he has expressed what they might in vain wish to express, except with glistening eye and faltering tongue! There's a lofty philosophic tone, a thoughtful humanity, infused into his pastoral vein. Remote from the passions and events of the great world, he has communicated interest and dignity to the primal movements of the heart of man, and ingrafted his own conscious reflections on the casual thoughts of hinds and shepherds. Nursed amidst the grandeur of mountain scenery, he has stooped to have a nearer view of the daisy under his feet, or plucked a branch of white-thorn from the spray: but in describing it, his mind seems imbued with the majesty and solemnity of the objects around him—the tall rock lifts its head in the erectness of his spirit; the cataract roars in the sound of his verse; and in its dim and mysterious meaning, the mists seem to gather in the hollows of Helvellyn, and the forked Skiddaw[9] hovers in the distance. There is little mention of mountainous scenery in Mr.

8. Adapted from the conclusion of Wordsworth's *Ode: Intimations of Im-* *mortality.*
9. Mountains in the Lake District.

Wordsworth's poetry; but by internal evidence one might be almost sure that it was written in a mountainous country, from its bareness, its simplicity, its loftiness and its depth!

* * *

1825

On Going a Journey

One of the pleasantest things in the world is going a journey; but I like to go by myself. I can enjoy society in a room; but out of doors, nature is company enough for me. I am then never less alone than when alone.

> The fields his study, nature was his book.[1]

I cannot see the wit of walking and talking at the same time. When I am in the country, I wish to vegetate like the country. I am not for criticizing hedgerows and black cattle. I go out of town in order to forget the town and all that is in it. There are those who for this purpose go to watering places;[2] and carry the metropolis with them. I like more elbowroom, and fewer encumbrances. I like solitude, when I give myself up to it, for the sake of solitude; nor do I ask for

> —— a friend in my retreat,
> Whom I may whisper solitude is sweet.[3]

The soul of a journey is liberty, perfect liberty, to think, feel, do just as one pleases. We go a journey chiefly to be free of all impediments and of all inconveniences; to leave ourselves behind, much more to get rid of others. It is because I want a little breathing space to muse on indifferent matters, where Contemplation

> May plume her feathers and let grow her wings,
> That in the various bustle of resort
> Were all too ruffled, and sometimes impaired,[4]

that I absent myself from the town for awhile, without feeling at a loss the moment I am left by myself. Instead of a friend in a post chaise or in a tilbury,[5] to exchange good things with, and vary the same stale topics over again, for once let me have a truce with impertinence. Give me the clear blue sky over my head, and the green turf beneath my feet, a winding road before me, and a three hours' march to dinner—and then to thinking! It is hard if I

---

1. *Spring*, line 32, in *The Farmer's Boy* (1800) by Robert Bloomfield, a peasant poet.
2. Bathing resorts.
3. William Cowper, *Retirement* (1782), lines 741–42.
4. Milton's *Comus*, lines 378–80.
5. Lightweight, open, two-wheeled carriage; "post chaise": hired carriage.

cannot start some game on these lone heaths. I laugh, I run, I leap, I sing for joy. From the point of yonder rolling cloud, I plunge into my past being, and revel there, as the sunburnt Indian plunges headlong into the wave that wafts him to his native shore. Then long-forgotten things, like "sunken wrack and sumless treasuries,"[6] burst upon my eager sight, and I begin to feel, think, and be myself again. Instead of an awkward silence, broken by attempts at wit or dull commonplaces, mine is that undisturbed silence of the heart which alone is perfect eloquence. No one likes puns, alliterations, antitheses, argument, and analysis better than I do; but I sometimes had rather be without them. "Leave, oh, leave me to my repose!"[7] I have just now other business in hand, which would seem idle to you, but is with me "the very stuff of the conscience."[8] Is not this wild rose sweet without a comment? Does not this daisy leap to my heart, set in its coat of emerald? Yet if I were to explain to you the circumstance that has so endeared it to me, you would only smile. Had I not better then keep it to myself, and let it serve me to brood over, from here to yonder craggy point, and from thence onward to the far distant horizon? I should be but bad company all that way, and therefore prefer being alone. I have heard it said that you may, when the moody fit comes on, walk or ride on by yourself, and indulge your reveries. But this looks like a breach of manners, a neglect of others, and you are thinking all the time that you ought to rejoin your party. "Out upon such half-faced fellowship,"[9] say I. I like to be either entirely to myself, or entirely at the disposal of others; to talk or be silent, to walk or sit still, to be sociable or solitary. I was pleased with an observation of Mr. Cobbett's,[1] that "he thought it a bad French custom to drink our wine with our meals, and that an Englishman ought to do only one thing at a time." So I cannot talk and think, or indulge in melancholy musing and lively conversation by fits and starts. "Let me have a companion of my way," says Sterne, "were it but to remark how the shadows lengthen as the sun goes down."[2] It is beautifully said: but in my opinion, this continual comparing of notes interferes with the involuntary impression of things upon the mind, and hurts the sentiment. If you only hint what you feel in a kind of dumb show,[3] it is insipid; if you have to explain it, it is making a toil of a pleasure. You cannot read the book of nature, without being perpetually put to the trouble of translating it for the benefit of others. I am for the synthetical method on a journey, in preference to the analytical. I

6. Shakespeare's *Henry V* I.ii.165.
7. A refrain in Thomas Gray's *The Descent of Odin: An Ode* (1768).
8. Shakespeare's *Othello* I.ii.2.
9. Shakespeare's *1 Henry IV* I.iii.208.
1. William Cobbett (1763–1835), author of *Rural Rides* (1830), in which he comments upon the conditions

he observed while on an inspection tour of rural England.
2. Altered from Laurence Sterne, *The Sermons of Mr. Yorick* (1760–69), Vol. III.
3. An episode of pantomime in early English dramas.

am content to lay in a stock of ideas then, and to examine and anatomize them afterwards. I want to see my vague notions float like the down of the thistle before the breeze, and not to have them entangled in the briars and thorns of controversy. For once, I like to have it all my own way; and this is impossible unless you are alone, or in such company as I do not covet. I have no objection to argue a point with any one for twenty miles of measured road, but not for pleasure. If you remark the scent of a beanfield crossing the road, perhaps your fellow traveler has no smell. If you point to a distant object, perhaps he is shortsighted, and has to take out his glass to look at it. There is a feeling in the air, a tone in the color of a cloud which hits your fancy, but the effect of which you are unprepared to account for. There is then no sympathy, but an uneasy craving after it, and a dissatisfaction which pursues you on the way, and in the end probably produces ill humor. Now I never quarrel with myself, and take all my own conclusions for granted till I find it necessary to defend them against objections. It is not merely that you may not be of accord on the objects and circumstances that present themselves before you—they may recall a number of ideas, and lead to associations too delicate and refined to be possibly communicated to others. Yet these I love to cherish, and sometimes still fondly clutch them, when I can escape from the throng to do so. To give way to our feelings before company seems extravagance or affectation; on the other hand, to have to unravel this mystery of our being at every turn, and to make others take an equal interest in it (otherwise the end is not answered) is a task to which few are competent. We must "give it an understanding, but no tongue."[4] My old friend C——,[5] however, could do both. He could go on in the most delightful explanatory way over hill and dale, a summer's day, and convert a landscape into a didactic poem or a Pindaric ode. "He talked far above singing."[6] If I could so clothe my ideas in sounding and flowing words, I might perhaps wish to have someone with me to admire the swelling theme; or I could be more content, were it possible for me still to hear his echoing voice in the woods of All-Foxden.[7] They had "that fine madness in them which our first poets had";[8] and if they could have been caught by some rare instrument, would have breathed such strains as the following.

> —Here be woods as green
> As any, air likewise as fresh and sweet
> As when smooth Zephyrus plays on the fleet
> Face of the curled stream, with flow'rs as many

4. *Hamlet* I.ii.250.
5. Coleridge.
6. Beaumont and Fletcher's tragicomedy, *Philaster* (1611), V.v.165–66: "I did hear you talk, / Far above singing."
7. Hazlitt had visited Coleridge and

Wordsworth at Alfoxden, Somersetshire, in 1798; see *My First Acquaintance with Poets.*
8. Altered from Michael Drayton's *Elegy to * * * Henery Reynolds Esquire* (1627), lines 109–10.

As the young spring gives, and as choice as any;
Here be all new delights, cool streams and wells,
Arbors o'ergrown with woodbine, caves, and dells:
Choose where thou wilt, while I sit by and sing,
Or gather rushes to make many a ring
For thy long fingers; tell thee tales of love,
How the pale Phoebe, hunting in a grove,
First saw the boy Endymion, from whose eyes
She took eternal fire that never dies;
How she conveyed him softly in a sleep,
His temples bound with poppy, to the steep
Head of old Latmos, where she stoops each night,
Gilding the mountain with her brother's light,
To kiss her sweetest.—

FAITHFUL SHEPHERDESS.[9]

Had I words and images at command like these, I would attempt to wake the thoughts that lie slumbering on golden ridges in the evening clouds: but at the sight of nature my fancy, poor as it is, droops and closes up its leaves, like flowers at sunset. I can make nothing out on the spot: I must have time to collect myself.

In general, a good thing spoils out-of-door prospects: it should be reserved for table talk. L——[1] is for this reason, I take it, the worst company in the world out of doors; because he is the best within. I grant, there is one subject on which it is pleasant to talk on a journey; and that is, what one shall have for supper when we get to our inn at night. The open air improves this sort of conversation or friendly altercation, by setting a keener edge on appetite. Every mile of the road heightens the flavor of the viands we expect at the end of it. How fine it is to enter some old town, walled and turreted, just at the approach of nightfall, or to come to some straggling village, with the lights streaming through the surrounding gloom; and then after inquiring for the best entertainment that the place affords, to "take one's ease at one's inn!"[2] These eventful moments in our lives are in fact too precious, too full of solid, heartfelt happiness to be frittered and dribbled away in imperfect sympathy. I would have them all to myself, and drain them to the last drop: they will do to talk of or to write about afterwards. What a delicate speculation it is, after drinking whole goblets of tea,

The cups that cheer, but not inebriate,[3]

9. John Fletcher, *The Faithful Shepherdess* (a pastoral drama, 1610), I.iii. Phoebe (also known as Diana) is the moon goddess who fell in love with the handsome young shepherd, Endymion, on Mount Latmus, in southwestern Asia Minor. "Her brother's light" is that of Apollo, the sun god.
1. Charles Lamb. "Table talk": mealtime conversation.
2. Altered from *1 Henry IV* III.iii.68–69.
3. William Cowper, *The Task* IV.39–40.

and letting the fumes ascend into the brain, to sit considering what we shall have for supper—eggs and a rasher,[4] a rabbit smothered in onions, or an excellent veal cutlet! Sancho in such a situation once fixed upon cow-heel;[5] and his choice, though he could not help it, is not to be disparaged. Then in the intervals of pictured scenery and Shandean contemplation,[6] to catch the preparation and the stir in the kitchen—*Procul, O procul este profani!*[7] These hours are sacred to silence and to musing, to be treasured up in the memory, and to feed the source of smiling thoughts hereafter. I would not waste them in idle talk; or if I must have the integrity of fancy broken in upon, I would rather it were by a stranger than a friend. A stranger takes his hue and character from the time and place; he is a part of the furniture and costume of an inn. If he is a Quaker, or from the West Riding[8] of Yorkshire, so much the better. I do not even try to sympathize with him, and he *breaks no squares*.[9] I associate nothing with my traveling companion but present objects and passing events. In his ignorance of me and my affairs, I in a manner forget myself. But a friend reminds one of other things, rips up old grievances, and destroys the abstraction of the scene. He comes in ungraciously between us and our imaginary character. Something is dropped in the course of conversation that gives a hint of your profession and pursuits; or from having someone with you that knows the less sublime portions of your history, it seems that other people do. You are no longer a citizen of the world: but your "unhoused free condition is put into circumscription and confine."[1] The *incognito* of an inn is one of its striking privileges—"lord of oneself, uncumbered with a name."[2] Oh! it is great to shake off the trammels of the world and of public opinion—to lose our importunate, tormenting, everlasting personal identity in the elements of nature, and become the creature of the moment, clear of all ties— to hold to the universe only by a dish of sweetbreads, and to owe nothing but the score[3] of the evening—and no longer seeking for applause and meeting with contempt, to be known by no other title than *the Gentleman in the parlor!* One may take one's choice of all characters in this romantic state of uncertainty as to one's real pretensions, and become indefinitely respectable and negatively right-

4. A thin slice of bacon or ham.
5. The foot of a cow stewed so as to make a jelly. The episode occurs in Cervantes' *Don Quixote*, Part II (1615), Chapter 49.
6. An allusion to the seemingly random associations of ideas in the speech and thought of the characters in Laurence Sterne's *Tristram Shandy* (1760–67).
7. "Away! away! ye unhallowed ones!" Cried out by the priestess as she calls up Hecate, goddess of the underworld

(Virgil, *Aeneid* VI.258).
8. The western division.
9. I.e., doesn't change the circumstances. ("To break squares" meant to violate the regular order of doing something.)
1. Shakespeare's *Othello* I.ii.26–27.
2. Dryden, *To My Honored Kinsman, John Driden* (1700), line 18. "Incognito": anonymity; with one's name undivulged.
3. Bill for food and drink.

worshipful. We baffle prejudice and disappoint conjecture; and from being so to others, begin to be objects of curiosity and wonder even to ourselves. We are no more those hackneyed commonplaces that we appear in the world: an inn restores us to the level of nature, and quits scores[4] with society! I have certainly spent some enviable hours at inns—sometimes when I have been left entirely to myself, and have tried to solve some metaphysical problem, as once at Witham Common,[5] where I found out the proof that likeness is not a case of the association of ideas—at other times, when there have been pictures in the room, as at St. Neot's (I think it was), where I first met with Gribelin's engravings of the Cartoons,[6] into which I entered at once; and at a little inn on the borders of Wales, where there happened to be hanging some of Westall's drawings,[7] which I compared triumphantly (for a theory that I had, not for the admired artist) with the figure of a girl who had ferried me over the Severn, standing up in the boat between me and the fading twilight—at other times I might mention luxuriating in books, with a peculiar interest in this way, as I remember sitting up half the night to read *Paul and Virginia*,[8] which I picked up at an inn at Bridgewater, after being drenched in the rain all day; and at the same place I got through two volumes of Madame D'Arblay's *Camilla*.[9] It was on the tenth of April, 1798, that I sat down to a volume of the *New Eloise*, at the inn at Llangollen,[1] over a bottle of sherry and a cold chicken. The letter I chose was that in which St. Preux describes his feelings as he first caught a glimpse from the heights of the Jura of the Pays de Vaud, which I had brought with me as a *bonne bouche*[2] to crown the evening with. It was my birthday, and I had for the first time come from a place in the neighborhood to visit this delightful spot. The road to Llangollen turns off between Chirk and Wrexham; and on passing a certain point, you come all at once upon the valley, which opens like an amphitheater, broad, barren hills rising in majestic state on either side, with "green upland swells that echo to the bleat of flocks"[3] below, and the river Dee

---

4. Clears off debts.
5. In Somersetshire.
6. Simon Gribelin (1661–1733), who made engraved copies of the cartoons (i.e., full-scale drawings) that Raphael had designed for tapestries to be hung on the walls of the Sistine Chapel, in the Vatican. "St. Neot's": a town in Huntingdonshire.
7. Richard Westall (1765–1838), an English painter. The Severn is a river flowing through Wales and western England.
8. *Paul et Virginie* was a widely read novel of sentiment published by the French author, Bernardin de St. Pierre, in 1787.

9. *Camilla, or a Picture of Youth* (1796), a novel by Madame D'Arblay, whose maiden name had been Fanny Burney.
1. A town in Wales. *La Nouvelle Héloïse* is a novel by Rousseau published in 1761; the hero is St. Preux. The "Jura" is a mountain range on the French-Swiss border; the "Pays de Vaud" is a canton in Switzerland.
2. A sweetmeat, eaten after a meal.
3. Coleridge, *Ode to the Departing Year* (1796), lines 125–26; the quotation that follows ("glittered green * * *") is from the same poem, line 124.

babbling over its stony bed in the midst of them. The valley at this time "glittered green with sunny showers," and a budding ash tree dipped its tender branches in the chiding stream. How proud, how glad I was to walk along the high road that commanded the delicious prospect, repeating the lines which I have just quoted from Mr. Coleridge's poems! But besides the prospect which opened beneath my feet, another also opened to my inward sight, a heavenly vision, on which were written, in letters large as Hope could make them, these four words, LIBERTY, GENIUS, LOVE, VIRTUE; which have since faded into the light of common day, or mock my idle gaze.

The beautiful is vanished, and returns not.[4]

Still I would return some time or other to this enchanted spot; but I would return to it alone. What other self could I find to share that influx of thoughts, of regret, and delight, the traces of which I could hardly conjure up to myself, so much have they been broken and defaced! I could stand on some tall rock, and overlook the precipice of years that separates me from what I then was. I was at that time going shortly to visit the poet whom I have above named. Where is he now? Not only I myself have changed; the world, which was then new to me, has become old and incorrigible. Yet will I turn to thee in thought, O sylvan Dee, as then thou wert, in joy, in youth and gladness; and thou shalt always be to me the river of Paradise, where I will drink of the waters of life freely![5]

There is hardly any thing that shows the shortsightedness or capriciousness of the imagination more than traveling does. With change of place we change our ideas; nay, our opinions and feelings. We can by an effort indeed transport ourselves to old and long-forgotten scenes, and then the picture of the mind revives again;[6] but we forget those that we have just left. It seems that we can think but of one place at a time. The canvas of the fancy has only a certain extent, and if we paint one set of objects upon it, they immediately efface every other. We cannot enlarge our conceptions; we only shift our point of view. The landscape bares its bosom to the enraptured eye; we take our fill of it; and seem as if we could form no other image of beauty or grandeur. We pass on, and think no more of it: the horizon that shuts it from our sight also blots it from our memory like a dream. In traveling through a wild barren country, I can form no idea of a woody and cultivated one. It appears to me that all the world must be barren, like what I see of

4. From Coleridge's translation of Schiller's drama, *The Death of Wallenstein* (1799–1800), V.i.68. "Faded into the light of common day" is a reminiscence of Wordsworth's *Ode: Intimations of Immortality,* line 77.
5. See the description of the Garden of Eden, Genesis ii.8–10.
6. A reminiscence of Wordsworth's *Tintern Abbey,* line 61.

it. In the country we forget the town, and in town we despise the country. "Beyond Hyde Park," says Sir Fopling Flutter, "all is a desert."[7] All that part of the map that we do not see before us is a blank. The world in our conceit of it is not much bigger than a nut-shell. It is not one prospect expanded into another, county joined to county; kingdom to kingdom, lands to seas, making an image voluminous and vast—the mind can form no larger idea of space than the eye can take in at a single glance. The rest is a name written on a map, a calculation of arithmetic. For instance, what is the true signification of that immense mass of territory and population, known by the name of China to us? An inch of pasteboard on a wooden globe, of no more account than a China orange! Things near us are seen of the size of life: things at a distance are diminished to the size of the understanding. We measure the universe by ourselves, and even comprehend the texture of our own being only piecemeal. In this way, however, we remember an infinity of things and places. The mind is like a mechanical instrument that plays a great variety of tunes, but it must play them in succession. One idea recalls another, but it at the same time excludes all others. In trying to renew old recollections, we cannot as it were unfold the whole web of our existence; we must pick out the single threads. So in coming to a place where we have formerly lived and with which we have intimate associations, everyone must have found that the feeling grows more vivid the nearer we approach the spot, from the mere anticipation of the actual impression: we remember circumstances, feelings, persons, faces, names, that we had not thought of for years; but for the time all the rest of the world is forgotten!— To return to the question I have quitted above.

I have no objection to go to see ruins, aqueducts, pictures, in company with a friend or a party, but rather the contrary, for the former reason reversed. They are intelligible matters, and will bear talking about. The sentiment here is not tacit, but communicable and overt. Salisbury Plain is barren of criticism, but Stonehenge[8] will bear a discussion antiquarian, picturesque, and philosophical. In setting out on a party of pleasure, the first consideration always is where we shall go: in taking a solitary ramble, the question is what we shall meet with by the way. "The mind then is its own place";[9] nor are we anxious to arrive at the end of our journey. I can myself do the honors indifferently well to works of art and curiosity. I once took a party to Oxford with no mean *éclat*—showed them the seat of the Muses at a distance,

7. The line is in fact spoken by Harriet, the heroine of George Etheredge's Restoration comedy, *The Man of Mode, or Sir Fopling Flutter* (1676), V.ii. Hyde Park, in London, was favored by people of fashion.
8. The prehistoric circle of huge upright slabs of stone, on Salisbury Plain.
9. *Paradise Lost* I.254.

With glistering spires and pinnacles adorned[1]—

descanted on the learned air that breathes from the grassy quadran-
gles and stone walls of halls and colleges—was at home in the
Bodleian; and at Blenheim quite superseded the powdered Ciceroni
that attended us,[2] and that pointed in vain with his wand to commonplace beauties in matchless pictures.—As another exception to
the above reasoning, I should not feel confident in venturing on a
journey in a foreign country without a companion. I should want at
intervals to hear the sound of my own language. There is an involuntary antipathy in the mind of an Englishman to foreign manners
and notions that requires the assistance of social sympathy to carry
it off. As the distance from home increases, this relief, which was at
first a luxury, becomes a passion and an appetite. A person would
almost feel stifled to find himself in the deserts of Arabia without
friends and countrymen: there must be allowed to be something in
the view of Athens or old Rome that claims the utterance of
speech; and I own that the Pyramids are too mighty for any single
contemplation. In such situations, so opposite to all one's ordinary
train of ideas, one seems a species by oneself, a limb torn off from
society, unless one can meet with instant fellowship and support.—
Yet I did not feel this want or craving very pressing once, when I
first set my foot on the laughing shores of France. Calais was peopled with novelty and delight. The confused, busy murmur of the
place was like oil and wine poured into my ears; nor did the mariners' hymn, which was sung from the top of an old crazy vessel in
the harbor, as the sun went down, send an alien sound into my
soul. I breathed the air of general humanity. I walked over "the
vine-covered hills and gay regions of France,"[3] erect and satisfied;
for the image of man was not cast down and chained to the foot of
arbitrary thrones. I was at no loss for language, for that of all the
great schools of painting was open to me. The whole is vanished
like a shade. Pictures, heroes, glory, freedom, all are fled: nothing
remains but the Bourbons[4] and the French people!—There is
undoubtedly a sensation in traveling into foreign parts that is to be
had nowhere else: but it is more pleasing at the time than lasting.
It is too remote from our habitual associations to be a common
topic of discourse or reference, and, like a dream or another state of
existence, does not piece into our daily modes of life. It is an ani-

1. *Paradise Lost* III.550. *"Eclat"*:
pomp. The "party" consisted of Charles
and Mary Lamb.
2. *Cicerone* is Italian for a guide. The
Bodleian is the central library at
Oxford. Blenheim Palace, at Wood-
stock, near Oxford, was built for the
Duke of Marlborough in 1704.
3. From William Roscoe's *Song Writ-*

ten for * * * *the Anniversary of 14th
August, 1791.* Hazlitt had visited
France in 1802–3 in order to make
copies of paintings in the Louvre.
4. The French royal family, which had
been deposed during the Revolution,
was restored in 1814 after the fall of
Napoleon.

mated but a momentary hallucination. It demands an effort to exchange our actual for our ideal identity; and to feel the pulse of our old transports revive very keenly, we must "jump"[5] all our present comforts and connexions. Our romantic and itinerant character is not to be domesticated. Dr. Johnson remarked how little foreign travel added to the facilities of conversation in those who had been abroad.[6] In fact, the time we have spent there is both delightful and in one sense instructive; but it appears to be cut out of our substantial, downright existence, and never to join kindly on to it. We are not the same, but another, and perhaps more enviable individual, all the time we are out of our own country. We are lost to ourselves, as well as to our friends. So the poet somewhat quaintly sings,

> Out of my country and myself I go.

Those who wish to forget painful thoughts, do well to absent themselves for a while from the ties and objects that recall them: but we can be said only to fulfill our destiny in the place that gave us birth. I should on this account like well enough to spend the whole of my life in traveling abroad, if I could any where borrow another life to spend afterwards at home!

1822, 1825

5. Abandon, leave behind.
6. In Boswell's *Life of Johnson*, entry for May 13, 1778.

THOMAS DE QUINCEY
(1785–1859)

1821: Begins literary career with *Confessions of an English Opium-Eater*.
1853–60: "Collective Edition" of his writings.

De Quincey's father was a wealthy merchant, who died when Thomas was 7 years old. The boy was a precocious scholar, especially in Latin and Greek, and a gentle and bookish introvert; he found it difficult to adapt himself to discipline and routine, and was thrown into panic by any emergency that called for decisive action. He ran away from Manchester Grammar School and after a summer spent tramping through Wales, broke off completely from his family and guardians and went to London in the hope that he could obtain from moneylenders an advance on his prospective inheritance. There at the age of 17 he spent a terrible winter of loneliness and destitution, befriended only by some kindly streetwalkers. These early experiences with the sinister part of city life later became persistent elements in his dreams of terror.

After a reconciliation with his guardians he entered Worcester College, Oxford, on an inadequate allowance. He spent the years 1803–8 in sporadic attendance, isolated as usual, and devoting himself especially to two subjects not then part of the university curriculum: English literature and the German language. He left abruptly in the middle of his examination for the B.A. with honors because he could not face the ordeal of the oral part of the examination.

De Quincey had been an early and fervent admirer of Wordsworth and Coleridge. No sooner did he come of age and into his inheritance than, with his usual combination of generosity and improvidence, he made Coleridge an anonymous gift of £300. He visited with the Wordsworths at Grasmere, became an intimate friend, and when they left Dove Cottage for Allan Bank, took up his own residence at Dove Cottage in order to be near them. Here he built up a fine library and for a time lived the life of a rural scholar, trying to decide how to eke out his dwindling resources. In the meantime he fell in love with Margaret Simpson, the daughter of a small local landholder and farmer and, after she had borne him an illegitimate son, married her in February, 1817. This affair led to an estrangement from the Wordsworths and increased the drain on his resources. Worse still, De Quincey at this time became completely enslaved to opium. He had been taking the drug regularly since 1804, when, in accordance with the medical practice of the time, he had turned to it for relief from rheumatic pains in his face. A variety of physical ailments had led to increasingly large and frequent doses; now, driven by pain, poverty, and despair, he indulged in huge quantities of laudanum (opium dissolved in alcohol). From this time on, although he struggled intermittently to break the habit and often succeeded in reducing the dosage, he was never able to free himself from "the pleasures and pains of opium." It was during his periods of maximum addiction, and especially in the recurrent agonies of cutting down his opium allowance, that he had the grotesque and terrifying reveries and dreams which he wove into the pattern of his literary fantasies.

In desperation De Quincey at last, at the age of 36, turned to writing for a livelihood. The *Confessions of an English Opium-Eater*, which he contributed in two installments to the *London Magazine*, scored an immediate success and was at once reprinted as a book, but it earned De Quincey very little money. After frequent visits to London, and a number of varied contributions to the *London Magazine*, he moved his family to Edinburgh in 1828, in order to write for *Blackwood's Magazine*. For almost all the rest of his life De Quincey led a frantic existence, beset by rheumatism, toothache, stomach trouble, erysipelas, and finally gout, struggling with his native irresolution and melancholia and the horrors of the opium habit, dodging his creditors and the constant threat of imprisonment for debt. All the while he ground out articles on any salable subject in a ceaseless struggle to keep his eight children from starving to death. Only after his mother died and left him a small income was he able, in his 60's, to live in comparative ease and freedom under the care of his loyal and practical-minded daughters. The last decade of his life De Quincey spent mainly in gathering, revising, and expanding his essays for his "Collective Edition"; the final volume appeared in 1860, the year after his death.

Although De Quincey's life, in its externals, was disorderly, and his best-known writings were sensational in their matter, he was not a Bohemian dabbler in drugs and abnormality, but staunchly conventional and conservative—a rigid moralist, a sturdy Tory, and a faithful champion of the Church of England. Everybody who knew this shy and elusive little man has testified to his gentleness, his courteous and musical speech, and his elaborate and exquisite manners. Less obvious, under the surface timidity and irresolution, were the toughness and courage which sustained him through a long life of seemingly hopeless struggle.

Although more than 150 of De Quincey's anonymous essays have been identified, the great bulk of them were pieces of hasty journalism which are now read only by scholars. These range over history, political economy, and philosophy; in his commentaries on recent and contemporary German writers and thinkers, together with his translations from the German, De Quincey served for a time as an important avenue of access for Englishmen to the great new literature of the late 18th-century German renaissance. As a literary critic De Quincey was capable of a fine essay in critical impressionism, *On the Knocking at the Gate in Macbeth*, but he was too whimsical and unsystematic to rank with his greater contemporaries, Coleridge and Hazlitt; his best theoretical contributions are essays on "Style" and "Rhetoric." He wrote a number of vivid and candid biographical sketches of writers he knew personally, especially Wordsworth, Coleridge, Southey, and Lamb. His most distinctive and impressive achievements, however, are the writings which start with fact and move into macabre fantasy (*On Murder Considered as One of the Fine Arts*), and especially those that begin as quiet autobiography and develop into an elaborate and lurid construction made up from the materials of his dreams (*Confessions of an English Opium-Eater, Autobiographic Sketches, Suspiria de Profundis*, and *The English Mail Coach*). In these last pieces De Quincey revived the ornate prose style of the 17th-century writers, Sir Thomas Browne, Jeremy Taylor, and John Milton. To the modern reader De Quincey's slowly evolving sentences and paragraphs often seem too contrived, in their elaborate patterning of phrases, clauses, and sound sequences, to sustain his earlier reputation as one of the supreme prose stylists. What interests us more today in these fantasies is their subject matter and the novel principles which govern their over-all structure. He opened up to English literature the night-side of human consciousness, with all its grotesque strangeness, its *Angst* (anxiety), and its pervasive sense of guilt and alienation. "In dreams," De Quincey wrote, long before Sigmund Freud, "perhaps under some secret conflict of the midnight sleeper, lighted up to the consciousness at the time, but darkened to the memory as soon as all is finished, each several child of our mysterious race completes for himself the treason of the aboriginal fall." And for these dream writings De Quincey developed a mode of organization which is not based on chronological narrative, or exposition, or argument, but on the statement, variation, development, and counterpoint of thematic imagery, in a pattern derived from the art of music, in which he had a deep and abiding interest. For although by temperament a conservative, De Quincey was in his writings a radical innovator, whose experiments look ahead to the materials and methods of such modern masters in prose and verse as James Joyce, Franz Kafka, and T. S. Eliot.

Confessions of an English Opium-Eater The *Confessions* were published anonymously in two issues of the *London Magazine*, September and October, 1821, and were reprinted as a book the following year. In 1856 De Quincey revised the book for a collected edition of his writings, expanding it to well over twice its original length. The author was over 70 years old at the time, and privately expressed the judgment—shared by all readers since—that the expanded edition lacks the immediacy and artistic economy of the original. The selections below are from the first version of the *Confessions*, as printed in 1822.

The book is divided into three parts. The first part, "Preliminary Confessions," deals with De Quincey's early experiences—at school, in Wales, and in London—prior to taking opium. Part Two, "The Pleasures of Opium" (omitted here), describes the effects of his early moderate and occasional indulgence in the drug on his perceptions and reveries. Part Three, "The Pains of Opium," is an elaborate reconstruction of his fantastic nightmares; these, in modern medical opinion, are in part withdrawal symptoms, during periods when he tried to cut down his use of opium.

In De Quincey's own lifetime, and ever since, the charge has been brought that the reports of these dreams were largely fabricated by the author. But De Quincey himself always insisted that they were substantially accurate; and both the fact and the content of such anguished nightmares are corroborated by the testimony of another laudanum addict, Samuel Taylor Coleridge, in his poem *The Pains of Sleep* (1803).

From Confessions of an English Opium-Eater

From *Preliminary Confessions*[1]

* * * Another person there was at that time, whom I have since sought to trace with far deeper earnestness, and with far deeper sorrow at my failure. This person was a young woman, and one of that unhappy class who subsist upon the wages of prostitution. I feel no shame, nor have any reason to feel it, in avowing, that I was then on familiar and friendly terms with many women in that unfortunate condition. The reader needs neither smile at this avowal, nor frown. For, not to remind my classical readers of the old Latin proverb—"*Sine Cerere*," &c.,[2] it may well be supposed that in the existing state of my purse, my connection with such women could not have been an impure one. But the truth is, that at no time of my life have I been a person to hold myself polluted

1. The 17-year-old De Quincey, unhappy at Manchester Grammar School, had run away and taken refuge in London, his whereabouts unknown to his mother and his guardians. He had slept outdoors for two months, but has now been permitted, by a disreputable and seedy lawyer, to sleep in an unoccupied, unfurnished, and rat-infested house. There he and a 10-year-old girl, nameless and of uncertain parentage, huddle together for warmth, eking out a famished existence on whatever scraps De Quincey can scavenge from his landlord's frugal breakfast. He goes on to describe his friendship with a young prostitute, Ann.
2. *Sine Cerere et Baccho friget Venus*—"without Ceres and Bacchus [food and wine], love grows cold."

by the touch or approach of any creature that wore a human shape:
on the contrary, from my very earliest youth it has been my pride to
converse familiarly, *more Socratico*,[3] with all human beings, man,
woman, and child, that chance might fling in my way: a practice
which is friendly to the knowledge of human nature, to good feelings, and to that frrankness of address which becomes a man who
would be thought a philosopher. For a philosopher should not see
with the eyes of the poor limitary[4] creature, calling himself a man
of the world, and filled with narrow and self-regarding prejudices of
birth and education, but should look upon himself as a Catholic[5]
creature, and as standing in an equal relation to high and low—to
educated and uneducated, to the guilty and the innocent. Being
myself at that time of necessity a peripatetic, or a walker of the
street, I naturally fell in more frequently with those female peripa-
tetics who are technically called street-walkers. Many of these
women had occasionally taken my part against watchmen who
wished to drive me off the steps of houses where I was sitting. But
one amongst them, the one on whose account I have at all introduced this subject—yet no! let me not class thee, oh noble-minded
Ann——, with that order of women; let me find, if it be possible,
some gentler name to designate the condition of her to whose
bounty and compassion, ministering to my necessities when all the
world had forsaken me, I owe it that I am at this time alive.—For
many weeks I had walked at nights with this poor friendless girl up
and down Oxford Street, or had rested with her on steps and under
the shelter of porticos. She could not be so old as myself: she told
me, indeed, that she had not completed her sixteenth year. By such
questions as my interest about her prompted, I had gradually drawn
forth her simple history. Hers was a case of ordinary occurrence (as
I have since had reason to think), and one in which, if London
beneficence had better adapted its arrangements to meet it, the
power of the law might oftener be interposed to protect, and to
avenge. But the stream of London charity flows in a channel which,
though deep and mighty, is yet noiseless and underground; not
obvious or readily accessible to poor houseless wanderers: and it
cannot be denied that the outside air and framework of London
society is harsh, cruel, and repulsive. In any case, however, I saw
that part of her injuries might easily have been redressed; and I
urged her often and earnestly to lay her complaint before a magistrate: friendless as she was, I assured her that she would meet with
immediate attention; and that English justice, which was no respect-
er of persons, would speedily and amply avenge her on the brutal

3. "In the manner of Socrates"; i.e., by
a dialogue of questions and answers.
4. Limited.

5. In the sense of "inclusive in tastes
and understanding."

ruffian who had plundered her little property. She promised me often that she would; but she delayed taking the steps I pointed out from time to time: for she was timid and dejected to a degree which showed how deeply sorrow had taken hold of her young heart: and perhaps she thought justly that the most upright judge, and the most righteous tribunals, could do nothing to repair her heaviest wrongs. Something, however, would perhaps have been done: for it had been settled between us at length, but unhappily on the very last time but one that I was ever to see her, that in a day or two we should go together before a magistrate, and that I should speak on her behalf. This little service it was destined, however, that I should never realize. Meantime, that which she rendered to me, and which was greater than I could ever have repaid her, was this:—One night, when we were pacing slowly along Oxford Street, and after a day when I had felt more than usually ill and faint, I requested her to turn off with me into Soho Square: thither we went; and we sat down on the steps of a house, which, to this hour, I never pass without a pang of grief, and an inner act of homage to the spirit of that unhappy girl, in memory of the noble action which she there performed. Suddenly, as we sat, I grew much worse: I had been leaning my head against her bosom; and all at once I sank from her arms and fell backwards on the steps. From the sensations I then had, I felt an inner conviction of the liveliest kind that without some powerful and reviving stimulus, I should either have died on the spot—or should at least have sunk to a point of exhaustion from which all re-ascent under my friendless circumstances would soon have become hopeless. Then it was, at this crisis of my fate, that my poor orphan companion—who had herself met with little but injuries in this world—stretched out a saving hand to me. Uttering a cry of terror, but without a moment's delay, she ran off into Oxford Street, and in less time than could be imagined, returned to me with a glass of port wine and spices, that acted upon my empty stomach (which at that time would have rejected all solid food) with an instantaneous power of restoration: and for this glass the generous girl without a murmur paid out of her own humble purse at a time—be it remembered!—when she had scarcely wherewithal to purchase the bare necessaries of life, and when she could have no reason to expect that I should ever be able to reimburse her.——Oh! youthful benefactress! how often in succeeding years, standing in solitary places, and thinking of thee with grief of heart and perfect love, how often have I wished that, as in ancient times the curse of a father was believed to have a supernatural power, and to pursue its object with a fatal necessity of self-fulfillment,—even so the benediction of a heart oppressed with gratitude, might have a like prerogative; might have power given to it from above to chase—to haunt—to waylay[6]—to overtake—to pursue thee into the central darkness of a London brothel, or (if it were possible) into the darkness of the grave—there to awaken thee with an authentic message of peace and forgiveness, and of final reconciliation!

I do not often weep: for not only do my thoughts on subjects connected with the chief interests of man daily, nay hourly, descend a thousand fathoms "too deep for tears";[7] not only does the sternness of my habits of thought present an antagonism to the feelings which prompt tears—wanting of necessity to those who, being protected usually by their levity from any tendency to meditative sorrow, would by that same levity be made incapable of resisting it on any casual access of such feelings:—but also, I believe that all minds which have contemplated such objects as deeply as I have done, must, for their own protection from utter despondency, have early encouraged and cherished some tranquilizing belief as to the future balances and the hieroglyphic meanings of human sufferings. On these accounts, I am cheerful to this hour; and, as I have said, I do not often weep. Yet some feelings, though not deeper or more passionate, are more tender than others; and often, when I walk at this time in Oxford Street by dreamy lamplight, and hear those airs played on a barrel-organ which years ago solaced me and my dear companion (as I must always call her), I shed tears, and muse with myself at the mysterious dispensation which so suddenly and so critically separated us for ever.[8] * * *

From *Introduction to the Pains of Opium*[9]

* * * I remember, about this time, a little incident, which I mention, because, trifling as it was, the reader will soon meet it again in my dreams, which it influenced more fearfully than could be imagined. One day a Malay knocked at my door. What business a Malay could have to transact amongst English mountains, I cannot conjecture: but possibly he was on his road to a seaport about forty miles distant.

The servant who opened the door to him was a young girl born and bred amongst the mountains,[1] who had never seen an Asiatic

6. From Wordsworth's *She Was a Phantom of Delight*, line 10: "To haunt, to startle, and way-lay." De Quincey was an early and enthusiastic admirer of Wordsworth's poetry.
7. From the last line of Wordsworth's *Ode: Intimations of Immortality*.
8. De Quincey goes on to narrate that, having been given some money by a family friend who recognized him in the street, he had traveled to Eton to ask a young nobleman whom he knew to stand security for a loan that De Quincey was soliciting from a money-lender. When he

returned to London three days later, Ann had disappeared.
9. It is 1816; De Quincey is living at Dove Cottage, Grasmere, and for three years has been addicted to laudanum—i.e., opium dissolved in alcohol. At this time, he has succeeded in reducing his daily dosage from 8,000 to 1,000 drops, with a consequent improvement in health and energy.
1. The lovely Barbara Lewthwaite, whom Wordsworth had described as a "child of beauty rare" in his poem *The Pet Lamb*.

dress of any sort: his turban, therefore, confounded her not a little: and, as it turned out, that his attainments in English were exactly of the same extent as hers in the Malay, there seemed to be an impassable gulf fixed between all communication of ideas, if either party had happened to possess any. In this dilemma, the girl, recollecting the reputed learning of her master (and, doubtless, giving me credit for a knowledge of all the languages of the earth, besides, perhaps, a few of the lunar ones), came and gave me to understand that there was a sort of demon below, whom she clearly imagined that my art could exorcise from the house. I did not immediately go down: but, when I did, the group which presented itself, arranged as it was by accident, though not very elaborate, took hold of my fancy and my eye in a way that none of the statu-esque attitudes exhibited in the ballets at the Opera House, though so ostentatiously complex, had ever done. In a cottage kitchen, but paneled on the wall with dark wood that from age and rubbing resembled oak, and looking more like a rustic hall of entrance than a kitchen, stood the Malay—his turban and loose trousers of dingy white relieved upon the dark paneling: he had placed himself nearer to the girl than she seemed to relish; though her native spirit of mountain intrepidity contended with the feeling of simple awe which her countenance expressed as she gazed upon the tiger-cat before her. And a more striking picture there could not be imag-ined, than the beautiful English face of the girl, and its exquisite fairness, together with her erect and independent attitude, con-trasted with the sallow and bilious skin of the Malay, enameled or veneered with mahogany, by marine air, his small, fierce, restless eyes, thin lips, slavish gestures and adorations. Half-hidden by the ferocious looking Malay, was a little girl from a neighboring cottage who had crept in after him, and was now in the act of reverting its head, and gazing upwards at the turban and the fiery eyes beneath it, whilst with one hand he caught at the dress of the young woman for protection. My knowledge of the Oriental tongues is not remark-ably extensive, being indeed confined to two words—the Arabic word for barley, and the Turkish for opium (madjoon), which I have learnt from Anastasius.[2] And, as I had neither a Malay dic-tionary, nor even Adelung's *Mithridates*,[3] which might have helped me to a few words, I addressed him in some lines from the Iliad; considering that, of such languages as I possessed, Greek, in point of longitude, came geographically nearest to an Oriental one. He worshiped[4] me in a most devout manner, and replied in what I sup-

---

2. *Anastasius, or Memoirs of a Greek*, was a novel published anonymously by Thomas Hope in 1819. It included a de-scription of the physical effects of opium which De Quincey considered a "griev-ous misrepresentation."
3. *Mithridates* was a book on Oriental languages by the German philologist J. C. Adelung (1732–1806).
4. Bowed down to.

pose was Malay. In this way I saved my reputation with my neighbors: for the Malay had no means of betraying the secret. He lay down upon the floor for about an hour, and then pursued his journey. On his departure, I presented him with a piece of opium. To him, as an Orientalist, I concluded that opium must be familiar: and the expression of his face convinced me that it was. Nevertheless, I was struck with some little consternation when I saw him suddenly raise his hand to his mouth, and (in the schoolboy phrase) bolt the whole, divided into three pieces, at one mouthful. The quantity was enough to kill three dragoons and their horses: and I felt some alarm for the poor creature: but what could be done? I had given him the opium in compassion for his solitary life, on recollecting that if he had traveled on foot from London, it must be nearly three weeks since he could have exchanged a thought with any human being. I could not think of violating the laws of hospitality, by having him seized and drenched with an emetic, and thus frightening him into a notion that we were going to sacrifice him to some English idol. No: there was clearly no help for it:—he took his leave: and for some days I felt anxious: but as I never heard of any Malay being found dead, I became convinced that he was used[5] to opium: and that I must have done him the service I designed, by giving him one night of respite from the pains of wandering.

This incident I have digressed to mention, because this Malay (partly from the picturesque exhibition he assisted to frame, partly from the anxiety I connected with his image for some days) fastened afterwards upon my dreams, and brought other Malays with him worse than himself, that ran "amuck" at me, and led me into a world of troubles. * * *

From *The Pains of Opium*
* * *

I have thus described and illustrated my intellectual torpor, in terms that apply, more or less, to every part of the four years during which I was under the Circean[6] spells of opium. But for misery and suffering, I might, indeed, be said to have existed in a dormant state. I seldom could prevail on myself to write a letter; an answer of a few words, to any that I received, was the utmost that I could accomplish; and often *that* not until the letter had lain weeks, or even months, on my writing table. Without the aid of M.[7] all records of bills paid, or *to be* paid, must have perished: and my whole domestic economy, whatever became of Political Economy,[8]

5. "This, however, is not a necessary conclusion: the varieties of effect produced by opium on different constitutions are infinite" [De Quincey's note].
6. Like those of Circe (the enchantress in the *Odyssey* who turned Odysseus' men into swine).
7. Margaret Simpson, whom De Quincey

had married in 1817.
8. Inspired by David Ricardo's *Principles of Political Economy* (1817), De Quincey had begun to write, but never completed, a work he called *Prolegomena to All Future Systems of Political Economy*.

must have gone into irretrievable confusion.—I shall not afterwards allude to this part of the case: it is one, however, which the opium-eater will find, in the end, as oppressive and tormenting as any other, from the sense of incapacity and feebleness, from the direct embarrassments incident to the neglect or procrastination of each day's appropriate duties, and from the remorse which must often exasperate the stings of these evils to a reflective and conscientious mind. The opium-eater loses none of his moral sensibilities, or aspirations: he wishes and longs, as earnestly as ever, to realize what he believes possible, and feels to be exacted by duty; but his intellectual apprehension of what is possible infinitely outruns his power, not of execution only, but even of power to attempt. He lies under the weight of incubus and nightmare: he lies in sight of all that he would fain perform, just as a man forcibly confined to his bed by the mortal languor of a relaxing disease, who is compelled to witness injury or outrage offered to some object of his tenderest love: —he curses the spells which chain him down from motion:—he would lay down his life if he might get up and walk; but he is powerless as an infant, and cannot even attempt to rise.

I now pass to what is the main subject of these latter confessions, to the history and journal of what took place in my dreams; for these were the immediate and proximate cause of my acutest suffering.

The first notice I had of any important change going on in this part of my physical economy, was from the re-awakening of a state of eye generally incident to childhood, or exalted states of irritability. I know not whether my reader is aware that many children, perhaps most, have a power of painting, as it were, upon the darkness, all sorts of phantoms; in some, that power is simply a mechanic affection of the eye; others have a voluntary, or a semi-voluntary power to dismiss or to summon them; or, as a child once said to me when I questioned him on this matter, "I can tell them to go, and they go; but sometimes they come, when I don't tell them to come." Whereupon I told him that he had almost as unlimited a command over apparitions, as a Roman centurion[9] over his soldiers. —In the middle of 1817, I think it was, that this faculty became positively distressing to me: at night, when I lay awake in bed, vast processions passed along in mournful pomp; friezes of never-ending stories, that to my feelings were as sad and solemn as if they were stories drawn from times before Oedipus or Priam—before Tyre— before Memphis.[1] And, at the same time, a corresponding change took place in my dreams; a theater seemed suddenly opened and lighted up within my brain, which presented nightly spectacles of

9. A Roman officer commanding a troop of 100 soldiers (a "century").
1. Oedipus, king of Thebes; Priam, king of Troy; Tyre, the chief city of Phoeni-cia; Memphis, the capital of ancient Egypt. De Quincey is calling the roll of great civilizations in the past.

more than earthly splendor. And the four following facts may be mentioned, as noticeable at this time:

1. That, as the creative state of the eye increased, a sympathy seemed to arise between the waking and the dreaming states of the brain in one point—that whatsoever I happened to call up and to trace by a voluntary act upon the darkness was very apt to transfer itself to my dreams; so that I feared to exercise this faculty; for, as Midas turned all things to gold, that yet baffled his hopes and defrauded his human desires,[2] so whatsoever things capable of being visually represented I did but think of in the darkness, immediately shaped themselves into phantoms of the eye; and, by a process apparently no less inevitable, when thus once traced in faint and visionary colors, like writings in sympathetic ink,[3] they were drawn out by the fierce chemistry of my dreams, into insufferable splendor that fretted my heart.

2. For this, and all other changes in my dreams, were accompanied by deep-seated anxiety and gloomy melancholy, such as are wholly incommunicable by words. I seemed every night to descend, not metaphorically, but literally to descend, into chasms and sunless abysses, depths below depths, from which it seemed hopeless that I could ever reascend. Nor did I, by waking, feel that I *had* re-ascended. This I do not dwell upon; because the state of gloom which attended these gorgeous spectacles, amounting at least to utter darkness, as of some suicidal despondency, cannot be approached by words.

3. The sense of space, and in the end, the sense of time, were both powerfully affected. Buildings, landscapes, &c. were exhibited in proportions so vast as the bodily eye is not fitted to receive. Space swelled, and was amplified to an extent of unutterable infinity. This, however, did not disturb me so much as the vast expansion of time; I sometimes seemed to have lived for 70 or 100 years in one night; nay, sometimes had feelings representative of a millennium passed in that time, or, however, of a duration far beyond the limits of any human experience.

4. The minutest incidents of childhood, or forgotten scenes of later years, were often revived: I could not be said to recollect them; for if I had been told of them when waking, I should not have been able to acknowledge them as parts of my past experience. But placed as they were before me, in dreams like intuitions, and clothed in all their evanescent circumstances and accompanying feelings, I *recognized* them instantaneously. I was once told by a near relative of mine,[4] that having in her childhood fallen into a

---

2. When granted his rash wish that all he touched should turn to gold, King Midas was horrified to discover that his food, drink, and beloved daughter all became gold at his touch.

3. Invisible ink.

4. According to family report, the "near relative" was De Quincey's mother.

river, and being on the very verge of death but for the critical assistance which reached her, she saw in a moment her whole life, in its minutest incidents, arrayed before her simultaneously as in a mirror; and she had a faculty developed as suddenly for comprehending the whole and every part. This, from some opium experiences of mine, I can believe; I have, indeed, seen the same thing asserted twice in modern books, and accompanied by a remark which I am convinced is true; viz. that the dread book of account, which the Scriptures speak of,[5] is, in fact, the mind itself of each individual. Of this, at least, I feel assured, that there is no such thing as *forgetting* possible to the mind; a thousand accidents may, and will interpose a veil between our present consciousness and the secret inscriptions on the mind; accidents of the same sort will also rend away this veil; but alike, whether veiled or unveiled, the inscription remains forever; just as the stars seem to withdraw before the common light of day, whereas, in fact, we all know that it is the light which is drawn over them as a veil—and that they are waiting to be revealed, when the obscuring daylight shall have withdrawn.

Having noticed these four facts as memorably distinguishing my dreams from those of health, I shall now cite a case illustrative of the first fact; and shall then cite any others that I remember, either in their chronological order, or any other that may give them more effect as pictures to the reader.

I had been in youth, and even since, for occasional amusement, a great reader of Livy,[6] whom, I confess, that I prefer, both for style and matter, to any other of the Roman historians; and I had often felt as most solemn and appalling sounds, and most emphatically representative of the majesty of the Roman people, the two words so often occurring in Livy—*Consul Romanus*;[7] especially when the consul is introduced in his military character. I mean to say, that the words king—sultan—regent, &c. or any other titles of those who embody in their own persons the collective majesty of a great people, had less power over my reverential feelings. I had also, though no great reader of history, made myself minutely and critically familiar with one period of English history, viz. the period of the Parliamentary War, having been attracted by the moral grandeur of some who figured in that day, and by the many interesting memoirs which survive those unquiet times. Both these parts of my lighter reading, having furnished me often with matter of reflection, now furnished me with matter for my dreams. Often I used to see, after painting upon the blank darkness a sort of rehearsal whilst waking, a crowd of ladies, and perhaps a festival, and dances. And I

5. The books listing everyone's name at the Last Judgment (Revelation xx.12).
6. Titus Livius (59 B.C.–A.D. 17), author of a huge history of Rome in 142 books.

7. "Roman consul," one of two officials, elected annually, who wielded the chief military and judicial authority in Republican Rome.

heard it said, or I said to myself, "These are English ladies from the unhappy times of Charles I. These are the wives and the daughters of those who met in peace, and sat at the same tables, and were allied by marriage or by blood; and yet, after a certain day in August, 1642,[8] never smiled upon each other again, nor met but in the field of battle; and at Marston Moor, at Newbury, or at Naseby,[9] cut asunder all ties of love by the cruel saber, and washed away in blood the memory of ancient friendship."—The ladies danced, and looked as lovely as the court of George IV.[1] Yet I knew, even in my dream, that they had been in the grave for nearly two centuries.—This pageant would suddenly dissolve: and, at a clapping of hands, would be heard the heart-quaking sound of *Consul Romanus;* and immediately came "sweeping by," in gorgeous paludaments, Paulus or Marius,[2] girt round by a company of centurions, with the crimson tunic hoisted on a spear,[3] and followed by the *alalagmos*[3] of the Roman legions.

Many years ago, when I was looking over Piranesi's Antiquities of Rome, Mr. Coleridge, who was standing by, described to me a set of plates by that artist, called his *Dreams*,[4] and which record the scenery of his own visions during the delirium of a fever. Some of them (I describe only from memory of Mr. Coleridge's account) represented vast Gothic halls: on the floor of which stood all sorts of engines and machinery, wheels, cables, pulleys, levers, catapults, &c. &c. expressive of enormous power put forth, and resistance overcome. Creeping along the sides of the walls, you perceived a staircase; and upon it, groping his way upwards, was Piranesi himself: follow the stairs a little further, and you perceive it come to a sudden abrupt termination, without any balustrade, and allowing no step onwards to him who had reached the extremity, except into the depths below. Whatever is to become of poor Piranesi, you suppose, at least, that his labors must in some way terminate here. But raise your eyes, and behold a second flight of stairs still higher: on which again Piranesi is perceived, but this time standing on the very brink of the abyss. Again elevate your eye, and a still more aerial flight of stairs is beheld: and again is poor Piranesi busy on his aspiring labors: and so on, until the unfinished stairs and Piranesi

---

8. The raising of the king's banner on Castle Hill, Nottingham, on August 22, 1642, signaled the beginning of the English Civil War.
9. Scenes of the defeat of King Charles's forces in the Civil War.
1. The reigning monarch at the time the *Confessions* were written.
2. Lucius Paulus (d. 160 B.C.) and Caius Marius (d. 86 B.C.) were Roman generals who won famous victories. "Paludaments": the cloaks worn by Roman generals.
3. "The signal which announced a day of battle" [De Quincey's note to the re-

vised edition]. "*Alalagmos*": "A word expressing collectively the gathering of the Roman war-cries" [De Quincey's note to the revised edition]. The word is Greek.
4. Giovanni Piranesi (1720–78), a Venetian especially famed for his many etchings of ancient and modern Rome. He did not publish prints called *Dreams*; De Quincey doubtless refers to his series called *Carceri d'Invenzione*, "Imaginary Prisons." The description which De Quincey recalls from Coleridge's conversation is remarkably apt for these terrifying architectural fantasies.

both are lost in the upper gloom of the hall.—With the same power of endless growth and self-reproduction did my architecture proceed in dreams. In the early stage of my malady, the splendors of my dreams were indeed chiefly architectural: and I beheld such pomp of cities and palaces as was never yet beheld by the waking eye, unless in the clouds. From a great modern poet[5] I cite part of a passage which describes, as an appearance actually beheld in the clouds, what in many of its circumstances I saw frequently in sleep:

> The appearance, instantaneously disclosed,
> Was of a mighty city—boldly say
> A wilderness of building, sinking far
> And self-withdrawn into a wondrous depth,
> Far sinking into splendor—without end!
> Fabric it seem'd of diamond, and of gold,
> With alabaster domes, and silver spires,
> And blazing terrace upon terrace, high
> Uplifted; here, serene pavilions bright
> In avenues disposed; there towers begirt
> With battlements that on their restless fronts
> Bore stars—illumination of all gems!
> By earthly nature had the effect been wrought
> Upon the dark materials of the storm
> Now pacified: on them, and on the coves,
> And mountain-steeps and summits, whereunto
> The vapors had receded,—taking there
> Their station under a cerulean sky, &c. &c.

The sublime circumstance—"battlements that on their *restless* fronts bore stars,"—might have been copied from my architectural dreams, for it often occurred.—We hear it reported of Dryden, and of Fuseli[6] in modern times, that they thought proper to eat raw meat for the sake of obtaining splendid dreams: how much better for such a purpose to have eaten opium, which yet I do not remember that any poet is recorded to have done, except the dramatist Shadwell:[7] and in ancient days, Homer is, I think, rightly reputed to have known the virtues of opium.[8]

To my architecture succeeded dreams of lakes—and silvery expanses of water:—these haunted me so much, that I feared (though possibly it will appear ludicrous to a medical man) that some dropsical[9] state or tendency of the brain might thus be making

5. The quotation is from Wordsworth's *The Excursion*, Book II, lines 834 ff.; they describe a cloud structure after a storm.
6. John Henry Fuseli (1741–1825) was born in Switzerland and painted in England. He was a friend of William Blake, and was noted for his paintings of nightmarish fantasies.
7. Thomas Shadwell was a Restoration dramatist and poet; he is now better known as caricatured by Dryden (in *Mac Flecknoe* and other satires) than for his own writings.
8. In the *Odyssey*, Book IV, Homer lauded nepenthe (which is probably opium) as a "drug to heal all pain and anger, and bring forgetfulness of every sorrow."
9. Afflicted with dropsy—an accumulation of fluid in the bodily tissues and cavities.

itself (to use a metaphysical word) *objective;* and the sentient organ *project* itself as its own object.—For two months I suffered greatly in my head—a part of my bodily structure which had hitherto been so clear from all touch or taint of weakness (physically, I mean), that I used to say of it, as the last Lord Orford[1] said of his stomach, that it seemed likely to survive the rest of my person.—Till now I had never felt a headache even, or any the slightest pain, except rheumatic pains caused by my own folly. However, I got over this attack, though it must have been verging on something very dangerous.

The waters now changed their character,—from translucent lakes, shining like mirrors, they now became seas and oceans. And now came a tremendous change, which, unfolding itself slowly like a scroll, through many months, promised an abiding torment; and, in fact, it never left me until the winding up of my case. Hitherto the human face had mixed often in my dreams, but not despotically, nor with any special power of tormenting. But now that which I have called the tyranny of the human face began to unfold itself. Perhaps some part of my London life might be answerable for this. Be that as it may, now it was that upon the rocking waters of the ocean the human face began to appear: the sea appeared paved with innumerable faces, upturned to the heavens: faces, imploring, wrathful, despairing, surged upwards by thousands, by myriads, by generations, by centuries:—my agitation was infinite,—my mind tossed—and surged with the ocean.

May, 1818

The Malay has been a fearful enemy for months. I have been every night, through his means, transported into Asiatic scenes. I know not whether others share in my feelings on this point; but I have often thought that if I were compelled to forego England, and to live in China, and among Chinese manners and modes of life and scenery, I should go mad. The causes of my horror lie deep; and some of them must be common to others. Southern Asia, in general, is the seat of awful images and associations. As the cradle of the human race, it would alone have a dim and reverential feeling connected with it. But there are other reasons. No man can pretend that the wild, barbarous, and capricious superstitions of Africa, or of savage tribes elsewhere, affect him in the way that he is affected by the ancient, monumental, cruel, and elaborate religions of Indostan, &c. The mere antiquity of Asiatic things, of their institutions, histories, modes of faith, &c. is so impressive, that to me the vast age of the race and name overpowers the sense of youth in the individual. A young Chinese seems to me an antediluvian man

1. Horace Walpole, the 18th-century wit and letter-writer, author of the Gothic novel *The Castle of Otranto* (1764).

renewed. Even Englishmen, though not bred in any knowledge of such institutions, cannot but shudder at the mystic sublimity of *castes*[2] that have flowed apart, and refused to mix, through such immemorial tracts of time; nor can any man fail to be awed by the names of the Ganges, or the Euphrates. It contributes much to these feelings, that southern Asia is, and has been for thousands of years, the part of the earth most swarming with human life; the great *officina gentium*.[3] Man is a weed in those regions. The vast empires also, into which the enormous population of Asia has always been cast, give a further sublimity to the feelings associated with all Oriental names or images. In China, over and above what it has in common with the rest of southern Asia, I am terrified by the modes of life, by the manners, and the barrier of utter abhorrence, and want of sympathy, placed between us by feelings deeper than I can analyze. I could sooner live with lunatics, or brute animals. All this, and much more than I can say, or have time to say, the reader must enter into before he can comprehend the unimaginable horror which these dreams of Oriental imagery, and mythological tortures, impressed upon me. Under the connecting feeling of tropical heat and vertical sunlights, I brought together all creatures, birds, beasts, reptiles, all trees and plants, usages and appearances, that are found in all tropical regions, and assembled them together in China or Indostan. From kindred feelings, I soon brought Egypt and all her gods under the same law. I was stared at, hooted at, grinned at, chattered at, by monkeys, by paroquets, by cockatoos. I ran into pagodas: and was fixed, for centuries, at the summit, or in secret rooms; I was the idol; I was the priest; I was worshiped; I was sacrificed. I fled from the wrath of Brama through all the forests of Asia: Vishnu hated me: Seeva laid wait for me.[4] I came suddenly upon Isis and Osiris: I had done a deed, they said, which the ibis and the crocodile trembled at.[5] I was buried, for a thousand years, in stone coffins, with mummies and sphinxes, in narrow chambers at the heart of eternal pyramids. I was kissed, with cancerous kisses, by crocodiles; and laid, confounded with all unutterable slimy things, amongst reeds and Nilotic mud.

I thus give the reader some slight abstraction of my Oriental dreams, which always filled me with such amazement at the monstrous scenery, that horror seemed absorbed, for a while, in sheer astonishment. Sooner or later, came a reflux of feeling that swallowed up the astonishment, and left me, not so much in terror, as

2. The reference is to the Hindu caste system, with its sharp division between four hereditary social classes.
3. "Manufactory of populations."
4. In the Hindu triad, Brahma is the creative aspect of divine reality, Vishnu is its maintainer, and Shiva its destroyer.

5. Isis was the ancient Egyptian goddess of fertility; she was the sister and wife of Osiris, whose annual death and rebirth represented the seasonal cycle of nature. The ibis (a long-legged wading bird) and the crocodile were sacred animals in ancient Egypt.

in hatred and abomination of what I saw. Over every form, and threat, and punishment, and dim sightless incarceration, brooded a sense of eternity and infinity that drove me into an oppression as of madness. Into these dreams only, it was, with one or two slight exceptions, that any circumstances of physical horror entered. All before had been moral and spiritual terrors. But here the main agents were ugly birds, or snakes, or crocodiles; especially the last. The cursed crocodile became to me the object of more horror than almost all the rest. I was compelled to live with him; and (as was always the case almost in my dreams) for centuries. I escaped some-times, and found myself in Chinese houses, with cane tables, &c. All the feet of the tables, sofas, &c. soon became instinct with life: the abominable head of the crocodile, and his leering eyes, looked out at me, multiplied into a thousand repetitions: and I stood loath-ing and fascinated. And so often did this hideous reptile haunt my dreams, that many times the very same dream was broken up in the very same way: I heard gentle voices speaking to me (I hear every thing when I am sleeping); and instantly I awoke: it was broad noon; and my children were standing, hand in hand, at my bedside; come to show me their colored shoes, or new frocks, or to let me see them dressed for going out. I protest that so awful was the transition from the damned crocodile, and the other unuttera-ble monsters and abortions of my dreams, to the sight of innocent *human* natures and of infancy, that, in the mighty and sudden revulsion of mind, I wept, and could not forbear it, as I kissed their faces.

June, 1819

I have had occasion to remark, at various periods of my life, that the deaths of those whom we love, and indeed the contemplation of death generally, is (*ceteris paribus*)[6] more affecting in summer than in any other season of the year. And the reasons are these three, I think: first, that the visible heavens in summer appear far higher, more distant, and (if such a solecism may be excused) more infinite; the clouds, by which chiefly the eye expounds the dis-tance of the blue pavilion stretched over our heads, are in summer more voluminous, massed, and accumulated in far grander and more towering piles: secondly, the light and the appearances of the declining and the setting sun are much more fitted to be types and characters of the Infinite: and, thirdly, (which is the main reason) the exuberant and riotous prodigality of life naturally forces the mind more powerfully upon the antagonist thought of death, and the wintry sterility of the grave. For it may be observed, generally, that wherever two thoughts stand related to each other by a law of antagonism, and exist, as it were, by mutual repulsion, they are apt

6. "Other things being the same."

to suggest each other. On these accounts it is that I find it impossible to banish the thought of death when I am walking alone in the endless days of summer; and any particular death, if not more affecting, at least haunts my mind more obstinately and besiegingly in that season. Perhaps this cause, and a slight incident which I omit, might have been the immediate occasions of the following dream; to which, however, a predisposition must always have existed in my mind; but having been once roused, it never left me, and split into a thousand fantastic varieties, which often suddenly reunited, and composed again the original dream.

I thought that it was a Sunday morning in May, that it was Easter Sunday, and as yet very early in the morning. I was standing, as it seemed to me, at the door of my own cottage. Right before me lay the very scene which could really be commanded from that situation, but exalted, as was usual, and solemnized by the power of dreams. There were the same mountains, and the same lovely valley at their feet; but the mountains were raised to more than Alpine height, and there was interspace far larger between them of meadows and forest lawns; the hedges were rich with white roses; and no living creature was to be seen, excepting that in the green churchyard there were cattle tranquilly reposing upon the verdant graves, and particularly round about the grave of a child whom I had tenderly loved,[7] just as I had really beheld them, a little before sunrise in the same summer, when that child died. I gazed upon the well-known scene, and I said aloud (as I thought) to myself, "It yet wants much of sunrise; and it is Easter Sunday; and that is the day on which they celebrate the first-fruits of resurrection. I will walk abroad; old griefs shall be forgotten today; for the air is cool and still, and the hills are high, and stretch away to heaven; and the forest-glades are as quiet as the churchyard; and, with the dew, I can wash the fever from my forehead, and then I shall be unhappy no longer." And I turned, as if to open my garden gate; and immediately I saw upon the left a scene far different; but which yet the power of dreams had reconciled into harmony with the other. The scene was an Oriental one; and there also it was Easter Sunday, and very early in the morning. And at a vast distance were visible, as a stain upon the horizon, the domes and cupolas of a great city—an image or faint abstraction, caught perhaps in childhood from some picture of Jerusalem. And not a bow-shot from me, upon a stone, and shaded by Judean palms, there sat a woman; and I looked; and it was—Ann! She fixed her eyes upon me earnestly; and I said to her at length: "So then I have found you at last." I waited: but she answered me not a word. Her face was the same as when I saw it

7. The child was Wordsworth's daughter, Catherine, to whom De Quincey had been devoted; she died at the age of four. She is the subject of Wordsworth's moving sonnet *Surprised by Joy*.

last, and yet again how different! Seventeen years ago, when the lamplight fell upon her face, as for the last time I kissed her lips (lips, Ann, that to me were not polluted), her eyes were streaming with tears: the tears were now wiped away; she seemed more beautiful than she was at that time, but in all other points the same, and not older. Her looks were tranquil, but with unusual solemnity of expression; and I now gazed upon her with some awe, but suddenly her countenance grew dim, and, turning to the mountains, I perceived vapors rolling between us; in a moment, all had vanished; thick darkness came on; and, in the twinkling of an eye, I was far away from mountains, and by lamplight in Oxford Street, walking again with Ann—just as we walked seventeen years before, when we were both children.

As a final specimen, I cite one of a different character, from 1820.

The dream commenced with a music which now I often heard in dreams—a music of preparation and of awakening suspense; a music like the opening of the Coronation Anthem,[8] and which, like *that*, gave the feeling of a vast march—of infinite cavalcades filing off— and the tread of innumerable armies. The morning was come of a mighty day—a day of crisis and of final hope for human nature, then suffering some mysterious eclipse, and laboring in some dread extremity. Somewhere, I knew not where—somehow, I knew not how—by some beings, I knew not whom—a battle, a strife, an agony, was conducting,—was evolving like a great drama, or piece of music; with which my sympathy was the more insupportable from my confusion as to its place, its cause, its nature, and its possible issue. I, as is usual in dreams (where, of necessity, we make ourselves central to every movement), had the power, and yet had not the power, to decide it. I had the power, if I could raise myself, to will it; and yet again had not the power, for the weight of twenty Atlantics was upon me, or the oppression of inexpiable guilt. "Deeper than ever plummet sounded,"[9] I lay inactive. Then, like a chorus, the passion deepened. Some greater interest was at stake; some mightier cause than ever yet the sword had pleaded, or trumpet had proclaimed. Then came sudden alarms: hurryings to and fro: trepidations of innumerable fugitives, I knew not whether from the good cause or the bad: darkness and lights: tempest and human faces: and at last, with the sense that all was lost, female forms, and the features that were worth all the world to me, and but a moment allowed,—and clasped hands, and heart-breaking partings, and then —everlasting farewells! and with a sigh, such as the caves of hell sighed when the incestuous mother uttered the abhorred name of

8. Composed by Handel for the coronation   9. From Shakespeare's *The Tempest* of George II, 1727.   III.iii.101.

death,[10] the sound was reverberated—everlasting farewells! and again, and yet again reverberated—everlasting farewells!

And I awoke in struggles, and cried aloud—"I will sleep no more!"[11]

* * *

1821   1821; 1822

On the Knocking at the Gate in *Macbeth*[1]

From my boyish days I had always felt a great perplexity on one point in *Macbeth*. It was this: The knocking at the gate which succeeds to the murder of Duncan produced to my feelings an effect for which I never could account. The effect was that it reflected back upon the murderer a peculiar awfulness and a depth of solemnity; yet, however obstinately I endeavored with my understanding to comprehend this, for many years I never could see *why* it should produce such an effect.

Here I pause for one moment, to exhort the reader never to pay any attention to his understanding when it stands in opposition to any other faculty of his mind. The mere understanding, however useful and indispensable, is the meanest faculty in the human mind, and the most to be distrusted; and yet the great majority of people trust to nothing else—which may do for ordinary life, but not for philosophical purposes. Of this out of ten thousand instances that I might produce I will cite one. Ask of any person whatsoever who is not previously prepared for the demand by a knowledge of the perspective to draw in the rudest way the commonest appearance which depends upon the laws of that science—as, for instance, to represent the effect of two walls standing at right angles to each other, or the appearance of the houses on each side of a street as seen by a person looking down the street from one extremity. Now, in all cases, unless the person has happened to observe in pictures how it is that artists produce these effects, he will be utterly un-

10. The reference is to Milton's *Paradise Lost*, Book II, lines 777 ff. The "incestuous mother" is Sin, who is doubly incestuous: she is the daughter of Satan, who begot Death upon her, and she was in turn raped by her son and gave birth to a pack of "yelling Monsters."
11. Macbeth says (II.ii.35–36): "Methought I heard a voice cry 'Sleep no more! / Macbeth does murder sleep.' "
1. This essay, one of the best-known critiques of Shakespeare, deals with the scene in *Macbeth* (II.ii–iii) in which, just after they have murdered Duncan, Macbeth and his wife are startled by a loud knocking at the gate. De Quincey exhibits the procedure in Romantic criticism of making, as he says, the "understanding" wait upon the "feelings." Instead of judging the success or failure of a passage by its conformity to prior critical theory, De Quincey brings in theory only to explain his impression or immediate emotional response to the passage. The final paragraph demonstrates a weakness of this Romantic position when it is driven to an extreme, for it converts the reasonable view that Shakespeare must be presumed right until shown to be wrong into the untenable view that Shakespeare is an artistic deity who can do no wrong.

able to make the smallest approximation to it. Yet why? For he has actually seen the effect every day of his life. The reason is that he allows his understanding to overrule his eyes. His understanding, which includes no intuitive knowledge of the laws of vision, can furnish him with no reason why a line which is known and can be proved to be a horizontal line should not *appear* a horizontal line: a line that made any angle with the perpendicular less than a right angle would seem to him to indicate that his houses were all tumbling down together. Accordingly, he makes the line of his houses a horizontal line, and fails, of course, to produce the effect demanded. Here, then, is one instance out of many in which not only the understanding is allowed to overrule the eyes, but where the understanding is positively allowed to obliterate the eyes, as it were; for not only does the man believe the evidence of his understanding in opposition to that of his eyes, but (what is monstrous) the idiot is not aware that his eyes ever gave such evidence. He does not know that he has seen (and therefore *quoad* his consciousness[2] has *not* seen) that which he *has* seen every day of his life.

But to return from this digression. My understanding could furnish no reason why the knocking at the gate in *Macbeth* should produce any effect, direct or reflected. In fact, my understanding said positively that it could *not* produce any effect. But I knew better; I felt that it did; and I waited and clung to the problem until further knowledge should enable me to solve it. At length, in 1812, Mr. Williams made his debut on the stage of Ratcliffe Highway, and executed those unparalleled murders which have procured for him such a brilliant and undying reputation.[3] On which murders, by the way, I must observe that in one respect they have had an ill effect, by making the connoisseur in murder very fastidious in his taste, and dissatisfied by anything that has been since done in that line. All other murders look pale by the deep crimson of his; and, as an amateur[4] once said to me in a querulous tone, "There has been absolutely nothing *doing* since his time, or nothing that's worth speaking of." But this is wrong; for it is unreasonable to expect all men to be great artists, and born with the genius of Mr. Williams. Now, it will be remembered that in the first of these murders (that of the Marrs) the same incident (of a knocking at the door[5] soon after the work of extermination was complete) did actually occur which the genius of Shakespeare has invented; and

---

2. I.e., so far as his consciousness is concerned.
3. John Williams, a sailor, had thrown London into a panic (the date was actually December, 1811) by murdering the Marr family and, twelve days later, the Williamson family. De Quincey described these murders at length in the Postscript to his two essays *On Murder Considered as One of the Fine Arts*.
4. Here, a fancier or follower of an art or sport.
5. By a maidservant of the Marrs, returning from the purchase of oysters for supper.

all good judges, and the most eminent dilettanti,[6] acknowledged the felicity of Shakespeare's suggestion as soon as it was actually realized. Here, then, was a fresh proof that I was right in relying on my own feeling, in opposition to my understanding; and I again set myself to study the problem. At length I solved it to my own satisfaction; and my solution is this: Murder, in ordinary cases, where the sympathy is wholly directed to the case of the murdered person, is an incident of coarse and vulgar horror; and for this reason—that it flings the interest exclusively upon the natural but ignoble instinct by which we cleave to life: an instinct which, as being indispensable to the primal law of self-preservation, is the same in kind (though different in degree) amongst all living creatures. This instinct, therefore, because it annihilates all distinctions, and degrades the greatest of men to the level of "the poor beetle that we tread on,"[7] exhibits human nature in its most abject and humiliating attitude. Such an attitude would little suit the purposes of the poet. What then must he do? He must throw the interest on the murderer. Our sympathy must be with *him* (of course I mean a sympathy of comprehension, a sympathy by which we enter into his feelings, and are made to understand them—not a sympathy of pity or approbation).[8] In the murdered person, all strife of thought, all flux and reflux of passion and of purpose, are crushed by one overwhelming panic; the fear of instant death smites him "with its petrific[9] mace." But in the murderer, such a murderer as a poet will condescend to, there must be raging some great storm of passion—jealousy, ambition, vengeance, hatred—which will create a hell within him; and into this hell we are to look.

In *Macbeth*, for the sake of gratifying his own enormous and teeming faculty of creation, Shakespeare has introduced two murderers: and, as usual in his hands, they are remarkably discriminated; but—though in Macbeth the strife of mind is greater than in his wife, the tiger spirit not so awake, and his feelings caught chiefly by contagion from her—yet, as both were finally involved in the guilt of murder, the murderous mind of necessity is finally to be presumed in both. This was to be expressed; and, on its own account, as well as to make it a more proportionable antagonist to the unoffending nature of their victim, "the gracious Duncan," and adequately to expound "the deep damnation of his taking off,"[1] this was to be expressed with peculiar energy. We were to be made

---

6. Lovers of the fine arts.
7. Shakespeare's *Measure for Measure* III.i.79.
8. In a note De Quincey decries "the unscholarlike use of the word sympathy, at present so general, by which, instead of taking it in its proper sense, as the act of reproducing in our minds the feelings of another, whether for hatred, indignation, love, pity, or approbation, it is made a mere synonym of the word *pity* * * *"
9. Petrifying, turning to stone (from *Paradise Lost* X.294).
1. *Macbeth* III.i.66 and I.vii.20.

to feel that the human nature—i.e., the divine nature of love and mercy, spread through the hearts of all creatures, and seldom utterly withdrawn from man—was gone, vanished, extinct, and that the fiendish nature had taken its place. And, as this effect is marvelously accomplished in the *dialogues* and *soliloquies* themselves, so it is finally consummated by the expedient under consideration; and it is to this that I now solicit the reader's attention. If the reader has ever witnessed a wife, daughter, or sister in a fainting fit, he may chance to have observed that the most affecting moment in such a spectacle is *that* in which a sigh and a stirring announce the recommencement of suspended life. Or, if the reader has ever been present in a vast metropolis on the day when some great national idol was carried in funeral pomp to his grave, and, chancing to walk near the course through which it passed, has felt powerfully, in the silence and desertion of the streets, and in the stagnation of ordinary business, the deep interest which at that moment was possessing the heart of man—if all at once he should hear the death-like stillness broken up by the sound of wheels rattling away from the scene, and making known that the transitory vision was dissolved, he will be aware that at no moment was his sense of the complete suspension and pause in ordinary human concerns so full and affecting as at that moment when the suspension ceases, and the goings-on of human life are suddenly resumed. All action in any direction is best expounded, measured, and made apprehensible, by reaction. Now, apply this to the case in *Macbeth*. Here, as I have said, the retiring of the human heart and the entrance of the fiendish heart was to be expressed and made sensible. Another world has stepped in; and the murderers are taken out of the region of human things, human purposes, human desires. They are transfigured: Lady Macbeth is "unsexed";[2] Macbeth has forgot that he was born of woman; both are conformed to the image of devils; and the world of devils is suddenly revealed. But how shall this be conveyed and made palpable? In order that a new world may step in, this world must for a time disappear. The murderers and the murder must be insulated—cut off by an immeasurable gulf from the ordinary tide and succession of human affairs—locked up and sequestered in some deep recess; we must be made sensible that the world of ordinary life is suddenly arrested, laid asleep, tranced, racked into a dread armistice; time must be annihilated, relation to things without abolished; and all must pass self-withdrawn into a deep syncope[3] and suspension of earthly passion. Hence it is that, when the deed is done, when the work of darkness is perfect, then the world of darkness passes away like a pageantry in the clouds: the

2. Steeling herself to the murder, Lady Macbeth calls on the spirits of hell to "unsex me here" (I.v.42).

3. Fainting spell.

knocking at the gate is heard, and it makes known audibly that the reaction has commenced; the human has made its reflux upon the fiendish; the pulses of life are beginning to beat again; and the re-establishment of the goings-on of the world in which we live first makes us profoundly sensible of the awful parenthesis that had suspended them.

O mighty poet! Thy works are not as those of other men, simply and merely great works of art, but are also like the phenomena of nature, like the sun and the sea, the stars and the flowers, like frost and snow, rain and dew, hailstorm and thunder, which are to be studied with entire submission of our own faculties, and in the perfect faith that in them there can be no too much or too little, nothing useless or inert, but that, the farther we press in our discoveries, the more we shall see proofs of design and self-supporting arrangement where the careless eye had seen nothing but accident!

1823

[The Literature of Knowledge and the Literature of Power][1]

What is it that we mean by *literature*? Popularly, and amongst the thoughtless, it is held to include everything that is printed in a book. Little logic is required to disturb *that* definition. The most thoughtless person is easily made aware that in the idea of *literature* one essential element is some relation to a general and common interest of man—so that what applies only to a local, or professional, or merely personal interest, even though presenting itself in the shape of a book, will not belong to Literature. So far the definition is easily narrowed; and it is as easily expanded. For not only is much that takes a station in books not literature; but inversely, much that really *is* literature never reaches a station in books. The weekly sermons of Christendom, that vast pulpit literature which acts so extensively upon the popular mind—to warn, to uphold, to renew, to comfort, to alarm—does not attain the sanctuary of libraries in the ten-thousandth part of its extent. The Drama again—as, for instance, the finest of Shakespeare's plays in England, and all leading Athenian plays in the noontide of the Attic stage—operated

---

1. This, a section of an essay on Alexander Pope (written in 1848, revised in 1858), has achieved independent status as a contribution to literary theory. In an earlier treatment of this topic in *Letters to a Young Man* (1823), De Quincey wrote that "the true antithesis to knowledge," in defining the effects of literature, "is not *pleasure,* but *power*"; then added in a footnote that he owed this distinction "to many years' conversation with Mr. Wordsworth." In his "Essay Supplementary" to the Preface to his *Poems* (1815), Wordsworth had written that "every great poet * * * has to call forth and communicate *power*," and that for an original writer "to create taste is to call forth and bestow power, of which knowledge is the effect."

as a literature on the public mind, and were (according to the strictest letter of that term) *published* through the audiences that witnessed[2] their representation some time before they were published as things to be read; and they were published in this scenical mode of publication with much more effect than they could have had as books during ages of costly copying or of costly printing.

Books, therefore, do not suggest an idea coextensive and interchangeable with the idea of Literature; since much literature, scenic, forensic, or didactic[3] (as from lecturers and public orators), may never come into books, and much that *does* come into books may connect itself with no literary interest.[4] But a far more important correction, applicable to the common vague idea of literature, is to be sought not so much in a better definition of literature as in a sharper distinction of the two functions which it fulfills. In that great social organ which, collectively, we call literature, there may be distinguished two separate offices that may blend and often *do* so, but capable, severally, of a severe insulation, and naturally fitted for reciprocal repulsion. There is, first, the literature of *knowledge*; and, secondly, the literature of *power*. The function of the first is —to *teach*; the function of the second is—to *move*:[5] the first is a rudder; the second, an oar or a sail. The first speaks to the *mere* discursive[6] understanding; the second speaks ultimately, it may happen, to the higher understanding or reason, but always *through* affections of pleasure and sympathy. Remotely, it may travel towards an object seated in what Lord Bacon calls *dry* light;[7] but, proximately, it does and must operate—else it ceases to be a literature of *power*—on and through that *humid* light which clothes itself in the mists and glittering *iris*[8] of human passions, desires, and genial emotions. Men have so little reflected on the higher

2. "Charles I, for example, when Prince of Wales, and many others in his father's court, gained their known familiarity with Shakespeare not through the original quartos, so slenderly diffused, nor through the first folio of 1623, but through the court representations of his chief dramas at Whitehall" [De Quincey's note]. Whitehall was a royal palace in London; it was destroyed by fire in 1698.

3. "Scenic": dramatic. "Forensic": argumentative, designed to persuade; especially in legal proceedings. "Didactic": expository, designed to instruct.

4. "What are called *The Blue Books* —by which title are understood the folio reports issued every session of Parliament by committees of the two Houses, and stitched into blue covers —though often sneered at by the ignorant as so much wastepaper, will be acknowledged gratefully by those who have used them diligently as the main wellheads of all accurate information as to the Great Britain of this day. As an immense depository of faithful (*and not superannuated*) statistics, they are indispensable to the honest student. But no man would therefore class the *Blue Books* as literature" [De Quincey's note].

5. Through the 18th century many critical theorists, following classical precedent, asserted that the aims of poetry are to teach, to please, and to move the reader.

6. Ordered in a rational or logical way.

7. In his essay *Of Friendship*, Francis Bacon quotes Heraclitus, the early Greek philosopher, as saying "Dry light is ever the best," then goes on to distinguish between dry light and the light of an understanding which is "ever infused and drenched" in an individual's own "affections and customs."

8. Rainbow colors. "Genial": pertaining to genius; creative.

functions of literature as to find it a paradox if one should describe it as a mean or subordinate purpose of books to give information. But this is a paradox only in the sense which makes it honorable to be paradoxical. Whenever we talk in ordinary language of seeking information or gaining knowledge, we understand the words as connected with something of absolute novelty. But it is the grandeur of all truth which *can* occupy a very high place in human interests that it is never absolutely novel to the meanest of minds: it exists eternally by way of germ or latent principle in the lowest as in the highest, needing to be developed, but never to be planted. To be capable of transplantation is the immediate criterion of a truth that ranges on a lower scale. Besides which, there is a rarer thing than truth—namely, *power*, or deep sympathy with truth. What is the effect, for instance, upon society, of children? By the pity, by the tenderness, and by the peculiar modes of admiration, which connect themselves with the helplessness, with the innocence, and with the simplicity of children, not only are the primal affections strengthened and continually renewed, but the qualities which are dearest in the sight of heaven—the frailty, for instance, which appeals to forbearance, the innocence which symbolizes the heavenly, and the simplicity which is most alien from the worldly—are kept up in perpetual remembrance, and their ideals are continually refreshed. A purpose of the same nature is answered by the higher literature, viz. the literature of power. What do you learn from *Paradise Lost*? Nothing at all. What do you learn from a cookery book? Something new, something that you did not know before, in every paragraph. But would you therefore put the wretched cookery book on a higher level of estimation than the divine poem? What you owe to Milton is not any knowledge, of which a million separate items are still but a million of advancing steps on the same earthly level; what you owe is *power*—that is, exercise and expansion to your own latent capacity of sympathy with the infinite, where every pulse and each separate influx is a step upwards, a step ascending as upon a Jacob's ladder from earth to mysterious altitudes above the earth.[9] *All* the steps of knowledge, from first to last, carry you further on the same plane, but could never raise you one foot above your ancient level of earth: whereas the very *first* step in power is a flight—is an ascending movement into another element where earth is forgotten.

Were it not that human sensibilities are ventilated and continually called out into exercise by the great phenomena of infancy, or of real life as it moves through chance and change, or of literature as it recombines these elements in the mimicries of poetry,

9. The ladder which the patriarch Jacob saw in a dream, reaching from earth to heaven, on which angels were ascending and descending (Genesis xxviii.11–12).

romance, etc., it is certain that, like any animal power or muscular energy falling into disuse, all such sensibilities would gradually droop and dwindle. It is in relation to these great *moral* capacities of man that the literature of power, as contradistinguished from that of knowledge, lives and has its field of action. It is concerned with what is highest in man; for the Scriptures themselves never condescended to deal by suggestion or cooperation with the mere discursive understanding: when speaking of man in his intellectual capacity, the Scriptures speak not of the understanding, but of *"the understanding heart,"*[1]—making the heart, *i.e.* the great *intuitive* (or nondiscursive) organ, to be the interchangeable formula for man in his highest state of capacity for the infinite. Tragedy, romance, fairy tale, or epopee,[2] all alike restore to man's mind the ideals of justice, of hope, of truth, of mercy, of retribution, which else (left to the support of daily life in its realities) would languish for want of sufficient illustration. What is meant, for instance, by *poetic justice?*[3]—It does not mean a justice that differs by its object from the ordinary justice of human jurisprudence; for then it must be confessedly a very bad kind of justice; but it means a justice that differs from common forensic justice by the degree in which it *attains* its object, a justice that is more omnipotent over its own ends, as dealing—not with the refractory elements of earthly life, but with the elements of its own creation, and with materials flexible to its own purest preconceptions. It is certain that, were it not for the Literature of Power, these ideals would often remain amongst us as mere arid notional forms; whereas, by the creative forces of man put forth in literature, they gain a vernal life of restoration, and germinate into vital activities. The commonest novel, by moving in alliance with human fears and hopes, with human instincts of wrong and right, sustains and quickens those affections. Calling them into action, it rescues them from torpor. And hence the preeminency over all authors that merely *teach* of the meanest that *moves*, or that teaches, if at all, indirectly *by* moving. The very highest work that has ever existed in the Literature of Knowledge is but a *provisional* work: a book upon trial and sufferance, and *quamdiu bene se gesserit.*[4] Let its teaching be even partially revised, let it be but expanded—nay, even let its teaching be but placed in a better order—and instantly it is superseded. Whereas the feeblest works in the Literature of Power, surviving at all, survive as finished and unalterable amongst men. For instance, the *Principia* of Sir

1. In I Kings iii.9, King Solomon asks the Lord for "an understanding heart to judge thy people."
2. Epic poem (French).
3. A term in literary criticism for the distribution of earthly rewards and punishments, at the end of a work of literature, in proportion to the virtues and vices of the various characters.
4. "As long as it shall conduct itself well."

Isaac Newton[5] was a book *militant* on earth from the first. In all
stages of its progress it would have to fight for its existence: 1st, as
regards absolute truth; 2dly, when that combat was over, as regards
its form or mode of presenting the truth. And as soon as a La
Place,[6] or anybody else, builds higher upon the foundations laid by
this book, effectually he throws it out of the sunshine into decay
and darkness; by weapons won from this book he superannuates and
destroys this book, so that soon the name of Newton remains as a
mere *nominis umbra*,[7] but his book, as a living power, has transmi-
grated into other forms. Now, on the contrary, the *Iliad*, the *Prometheus* of Aeschylus, the *Othello* or *King Lear*, the *Hamlet* or *Macbeth*, and the *Paradise Lost*, are not militant, but triumphant
forever as long as the languages exist in which they speak or can be
taught to speak. They never *can* transmigrate into new incarnations.
To reproduce *these* in new forms, or variations, even if in some
things they should be improved, would be to plagiarize. A good
steam engine is properly superseded by a better. But one lovely pastoral valley is not superseded by another, nor a statute of Praxiteles
by a statue of Michael Angelo.[8] These things are separated not by
imparity, but by disparity. They are not thought of as unequal
under the same standard, but as different in *kind*, and, if otherwise
equal, as equal under a different standard. Human works of immortal beauty and works of nature in one respect stand on the same
footing: they never absolutely repeat each other, never approach so
near as not to differ; and they differ not as better and worse, or
simply by more and less: they differ by undecipherable and incommunicable differences, that cannot be caught by mimicries, that
cannot be reflected in the mirror of copies, that cannot become
ponderable in the scales of vulgar comparison.

Applying these principles to Pope as a representative of fine literature in general, we would wish to remark the claim which he has,
or which any equal writer has, to the attention and jealous winnowing of those critics in particular who watch over public morals. Clergymen, and all organs of public criticism put in motion by clergymen, are more especially concerned in the just appreciation of such
writers, if the two canons are remembered which we have endeavoured to illustrate, viz. that all works in this class, as opposed to
those in the literature of knowledge, 1st, work by far deeper agen-

---

5. Isaac Newton's great *Philosophiae
Naturalis Principia Mathematica*
("Mathematical Principles of Natural
Philosophy"), published 1687, set forth
the laws of motion and the principle of
universal gravitation. "Militant": combative.
6. Pierre-Simon, Marquis de Laplace,
mathematician and astronomer, author
of *A Treatise on Celestial Mechanics*
(1799–1825), was known as "the
Newton of France."
7. "Shadow of a name."
8. Praxiteles was a Greek sculptor, 4th
century B.C.; Michelangelo Buonarroti
(1475–1564) was the Renaissance
sculptor, painter, architect, and poet.

cies, and, 2dly, are more permanent; in the strictest sense they are κτήματα ἐς ἀεἰ:[9] and what evil they do, or what good they do, is commensurate with the national language, sometimes long after the nation has departed. At this hour, five hundred years since their creation, the tales of Chaucer,[1] never equaled on this earth for their tenderness, and for life of picturesqueness, are read familiarly by many in the charming language of their natal day, and by others in the modernizations of Dryden, of Pope, and Wordsworth.[2] At this hour, one thousand eight hundred years since their creation, the Pagan tales of Ovid,[3] never equaled on this earth for the gaiety of their movement and the capricious graces of their narrative, are read by all Christendom. This man's people and their monuments are dust; but *he* is alive: he has survived them, as he told us that he had it in his commission to do, by a thousand years; "and *shall* a thousand more.

All the literature of knowledge builds only ground-nests,[4] that are swept away by floods, or confounded by the plow; but the literature of power builds nests in aerial altitudes of temples sacred from violation, or of forests inaccessible to fraud. *This* is a great prerogative of the *power* literature; and it is a greater which lies in the mode of its influence. The *knowledge* literature, like the fashion of this world, passeth away. An Encyclopedia is its abstract; and, in this respect, it may be taken for its speaking symbol—that before one generation has passed an Encyclopedia is superannuated; for it speaks through the dead memory and unimpassioned understanding, which have not the repose of higher faculties, but are continually enlarging and varying their phylacteries.[5] But all literature properly so called—literature κατ᾽ ἐξοχην[6]—for the very same reason that it is so much more durable than the literature of knowledge, is (and by the very same proportion it is) more intense and electrically searching in its impressions. The directions in which the tragedy of this planet has trained our human feelings to play, and the combinations into which the poetry of this planet has thrown our human passions of love and hatred, of admiration and contempt, exercise a power for bad or good over human life that cannot be contemplated, when stretching through many generations, with-

9. "Everlasting possessions."
1. "The *Canterbury Tales* were not made public until 1380 or thereabouts; but the composition must have cost thirty or more years; not to mention that the work had probably been finished for some years before it was divulged" [De Quincey's note].
2. Following the example of various earlier poets who wrote modernized versions of Chaucer, Wordsworth had translated *The Prioress's Tale* and a section of *Troilus and Criseyde*.
3. The Latin poet (43 B.C.–A.D. 18), author of *Metamorphoses* and other books of verse narratives.
4. Nests built on the ground.
5. I.e., preestablished texts. "Phylacteries" are leather boxes, inscribed with quotations from the Hebrew Scriptures, worn by orthodox Jews during morning prayer.
6. In the highest degree.

out a sentiment allied to awe.[7] And of this let everyone be assured —that he owes to the impassioned books which he has read many a thousand more of emotions than he can consciously trace back to them. Dim by their origination, these emotions yet arise in him, and mould him through life, like forgotten incidents of his childhood.

1848, 1858

7. "The reason why the broad distinctions between the two literatures of power and knowledge so little fix the attention lies in the fact that a vast proportion of books—history, biography, travels, miscellaneous essays, etc. —lying in a middle zone, confound these distinctions by interblending them. All that we call 'amusement' or 'entertainment' is a diluted form of the power belonging to passion, and also a mixed form; and, where threads of direct *instruction* intermingle in the texture with these threads of *power*, this absorption of the duality into one representative *nuance* neutralizes the separate perception of either. Fused into a *tertium quid* [a third thing], or neutral state, they disappear to the popular eye as the repelling forces which, in fact, they are" [De Quincey's note].

GEORGE GORDON, LORD BYRON
(1788–1824)

1812:   *Childe Harold*, Cantos I and II.
1813–14: The Oriental tales, including *The Giaour, The Corsair, Lara.*
1816:   Separation from Lady Byron; leaves England, never to return.
1818:   Begins *Don Juan.*
1823:   Joins the Greek war for liberation from the Turks.

In his *History of English Literature*, written in the late 1850's, the French critic Hippolyte Taine gave only a few condescending pages to Wordsworth, Coleridge, Shelley, and Keats, and then devoted a long enthusiastic chapter to Lord Byron, "the greatest and most English of these artists; he is so great and so English that from him alone we shall learn more truths of his country and of his age than from all the rest together." Byron had achieved an immense European reputation during his own lifetime, while his English contemporaries were admired only by small coteries in England and America, and through much of the 19th century he continued to be rated as one of the greatest of English poets and the very prototype of literary Romanticism. His influence was felt everywhere, not only among minor writers—in the two or three decades after his death, most European poets struck Byronic attitudes—but among the major poets and novelists (including Goethe in Germany, Balzac and Stendhal in France, Pushkin and Dostoevsky in Russia, and Melville in America), painters (especially Delacroix), and composers (especially Beethoven and Berlioz).

These facts may surprise the student who is aware of the modern estimate of Byron as the least consequential of the five great poets of his day, whose poems have little in common with the distinctive innovations of Wordsworth, Coleridge, Keats, or Shelley. Only Shelley, among these writers, thought highly of either Byron or his work; while Byron spoke slightingly of all of them except Shelley, and in fact insisted that, measured against the poetic practice of Pope, he and his contemporaries were "all in the wrong, one as much as another * * * we are upon a wrong revolutionary poetical system, or systems, not worth a damn in itself." Byron's masterpiece, *Don Juan*, is an instance of that favorite neoclassic type, a satire against modern civilization, which has much more in common with the methods and aims of Pope, Swift, Voltaire, or Sterne than with those of his own contemporaries. Even Byron's lyrics are old-fashioned: many are in the 18th-century gentlemanly mode of witty extemporization and epigram (*Written after Swimming from Sestos to Abydos*) or continue the Cavalier tradition of the elaborate development of a compliment to a lady (*She Walks in Beauty* or *There Be None of Beauty's Daughters*).

Byron's chief claim to be called an arch-Romantic is that he provided his age with what Taine called its "ruling personage; that is, the model that contemporaries invest with their admiration and sympathy." This personage is the "Byronic hero." He occurs in various guises in Byron's writings, but from the first sketch in the opening Canto of *Childe Harold*, and in the verse romances and dramas that follow, his persistent character is that of a moody, passionate, and remorse-torn but unrepentant wanderer. In his developed form, as we find it in *Manfred*, he is an alien, mysterious, and gloomy spirit, immensely superior in his passions and powers to the common run of mankind, whom he regards with disdain. He harbors the torturing memory of an enormous, nameless guilt which drives him toward an inevitable doom. He is in his isolation absolutely self-reliant, inflexibly pursuing his own ends according to his self-generated moral code against any opposition, human or supernatural. And he exerts an attraction on other characters which is the more irresistible because it involves their terror at his obliviousness to ordinary human concerns and values. This figure, infusing the archrebel in a nonpolitical form with a strong erotic interest, gathered together and embodied the implicit yearnings of Byron's time, was imitated in life as well as in art, and helped shape the intellectual as well as the cultural history of the later 19th century. The literary descendants of the Byronic hero include Heathcliff in *Wuthering Heights*, Captain Ahab in *Moby Dick*, and the hero of Pushkin's great poem, *Eugene Onegin*. Bertrand Russell, in his *History of Western Philosophy*, gives a chapter to Byron—not because he was a systematic thinker, but because "Byronism," the attitude of "Titanic cosmic self-assertion," established an outlook and way of feeling that entered 19th-century philosophy and eventually helped to form Nietzsche's concept of the Superman, the great hero who stands outside the jurisdiction of the ordinary criteria of good and evil.

Byron's contemporaries insisted on identifying the author with his fictional characters. But Byron's letters and the testimony of his friends show that, except for recurrent moods of black depression, his own temperament was in many respects the antithesis to that of his heroes. He was passionate and willful, but when in good humor he could be very much a man of the world in the 18th-century style—gregarious, lively, tolerant, and a witty conversationalist capable of taking an ironic attitude toward his own activities as well as those of other men. The aloof hauteur he exhibited in public was largely a mask to hide his diffidence when in a strange company; he possessed devoted friends, both men and women, and among them he was usually unassuming, companionable, sometimes even exuberant, and tactful; to his household dependents he was unfailingly generous and tenaciously loyal. But if Byronism was largely a fiction, produced by a collaboration between Byron's imagination and that of his public, then the fiction was historically more important than the poet in his actual person.

Byron was descended from two aristocratic families, both of them colorful, violent, and dissolute. His grandfather was an admiral known as "Foulweather Jack"; his great-uncle was the fifth Baron Byron, known to his rural neighbors as the "Wicked Lord," who was tried by his peers for killing his kinsman, William Chaworth, in a drunken duel; his father, Captain John Byron, was a rake and fortune-hunter who rapidly dissipated the patrimony of two wealthy wives. Byron's mother was a Scotswoman, Catherine Gordon of Gight, the last descendant of a line of lawless Scottish lairds. After her husband died (Byron was then 3), she brought up her son in near poverty in Aberdeen, where he was indoctrinated with the Calvinistic morality of Scottish Presbyterianism. Mrs. Byron was an ill-educated and almost pathologically irascible woman, who nevertheless had an abiding love for her son; they fought violently when together, but corresponded affectionately enough when apart, until her death in 1811.

When Byron was 10, the death of his great-uncle, preceded by that of more immediate heirs to the title, made him the sixth Lord Byron. In a fashion suitable to his new eminence he was sent to Harrow School, then to Trinity College, Cambridge. Byron had been born with a clubfoot, which was made worse by inept medical treatment, and this defect all his life caused him physical suffering and agonized embarrassment. His lameness increased his avidity for athletic prowess, and he played cricket and made himself an expert boxer, fencer, and horseman, and a powerful swimmer. He was also sexually precocious; when only 7, he fell in love with a little cousin, Mary Duff, and so violently that ten years later news of her marriage threw him into convulsions. Both at Cambridge and at his ancestral estate of Newstead, he engaged with more than ordinary vigor in the expensive pursuits and fashionable dissipations of a young Regency lord. As a result, despite a sizeable and increasing income, Byron got into financial difficulties from which he did not entirely extricate himself until late in his life. In the course of his schooling he formed many close friendships, the most important with John Cam Hobhouse, a sturdy political liberal and commonsense moralist who exerted a steadying influence throughout Byron's turbulent life.

Despite his distractions at the university, Byron found time to try his hand at lyric verse, which was published in 1807 in a slim and conventional volume entitled *Hours of Idleness*. This was treated with unmerited harshness by the pontifical *Edinburgh Review*, and Byron was provoked to write in reply his first important poem, *English Bards and Scotch Reviewers*, a vigorous satire in the couplet style of the late 18th-century followers of Pope, in which he incorporated skillful but tactless ridicule of all his major poetic contemporaries, including Scott, Wordsworth, and Coleridge.

After attaining his M.A. degree and his majority, Byron set out with Hobhouse in 1809 on a tour through Portugal and Spain to Malta, and then to little-known Albania, Greece, and Asia Minor. In this adventurous two-year excursion, Byron accumulated materials which he wove into most of his important poems, including his last work, *Don Juan*. The first literary product was *Childe Harold*; he wrote the opening two cantos while on the tour which the poem describes, published them in 1812 soon after his return to England, and, in his own oft-quoted phrase, "awoke one morning and found myself famous." He became the literary and social celebrity of fashionable London, enjoying an unprecedented success, which he at once increased by his series of highly readable Near-Eastern verse tales; in these the Byronic hero, in various embodiments, flaunts his misanthropy and undergoes a variety of violent and romantic adventures which current gossip attributed to the author himself. In his chronic shortage of money, Byron could well have used the huge income from these publications, but instead maintained his status as an aristocratic amateur by giving the royalties away. Occupying his inherited seat in the House of Lords, Byron also became briefly active on the extreme liberal side of the Whig party and spoke courageously in defense of the Nottingham weavers who, made desperate by technological unemployment, had resorted to destroying the new textile machines; he also supported other liberal measures, including that of Catholic Emancipation.

In the meantime Byron found himself besieged by women. He was extraordinarily handsome—"so beautiful a countenance," Coleridge wrote, "I scarcely ever saw. * * * his eyes the open portals of the sun—things of light, and for light." Because of a constitutional tendency to obesity, however, Byron was able to maintain his beauty only by recurring again and again to a starvation diet of biscuits, soda water, and strong cathartics. Often as a result of female initiative rather than his own, Byron incurred a sequence of liaisons with ladies of fashion. One of these, the flamboyant, eccentric, and hysterical young Lady Caroline Lamb, caused him so much distress by her frenzied pursuit and public tantrums that Byron turned for relief to marriage with Annabella Milbanke, who was in every way Lady Caroline's opposite, for she was naïve, unworldly, intellectual (with a special passion for mathematics), and not a little priggish; she persuaded herself that she could make Byron over in her own image. This ill-starred marriage produced a daughter (Augusta Ada) and many scenes in which Byron, goaded by financial difficulties, behaved so frantically that his wife suspected his sanity; after only one year, the union ended in a legal separation. The final blow came when Lady Byron discovered her husband's incestuous relations with his half sister, Augusta Leigh. The two had been raised apart, so that they were almost strangers when they met as adults; also, Byron seems to have had one attribute in common with the Byronic hero—a compulsion to try forbidden experience (including, as we now know, homosexual love affairs), joined with a tendency to court his own destruction. Byron's affection for his sister, however guilty, was genuine, and endured all through his life. This affair proved a delicious morsel even to the jaded palate of the dissolute Regency society; Byron was ostracized by all but a few friends, and finally forced to leave England forever on April 25, 1816.

Byron now resumed the travels incorporated in the third and fourth cantos of *Childe Harold.* At Geneva he lived for several months in close and intellectually fruitful relation to Shelley, who was accompanied by his wife, Mary Godwin, and by his wife's stepsister, Claire Clairmont—a misguided girl of 17 who had forced herself upon Byron while he was still in England and who in January, 1817, bore him a daughter, Allegra. In the fall of 1817 Byron established himself in Venice, where he inaugurated various affairs that culminated in a period of frenzied debauchery which, Byron estimated, involved more than 200 women, mainly of the lower classes. This period was nevertheless one of great literary creativity: often working through the later hours of the night, he finished his tragedy *Manfred,* wrote the fourth canto of *Childe Harold,* and after turning out *Beppo,* a short rehearsal in the narrative style and stanza of *Don Juan,* began the composition of *Don Juan* itself. In the colloquial ottava rima, Byron finally learned to write poetry as well as he had written prose.

Exhausted and bored by promiscuity, Byron in 1819 settled into a placid and relatively faithful relationship with Teresa Guiccioli, the young wife of the elderly Count Alessandro Guiccioli; according to the Italian upper-class mores of the times, having contracted a marriage of convenience, she could now with propriety attach Byron to herself as a *cavalier servente.* Through Teresa's nationalistic family, the Gambas, Byron became involved in the Carbonari plot against Austrian control over northern Italy. When the Gambas were forced by the authorities to move to Pisa, Byron followed them there, and for the second time joined Shelley. There grew up about the two friends the "Pisan Circle," which in addition to the Gambas included Shelley's friends Thomas Medwin and Edward and Jane Williams, as well as the Greek nationalist leader Prince Mavrocordatos, the picturesque Irish Count Taaffe, and the flamboyant and mendacious adventurer Edward Trelawny, who seems to have stepped out of one of Byron's romances. The circle was gradually broken up, first by Shelley's anger over Byron's treatment of his daughter Allegra (Byron had sent the child to be brought up as a Catholic in an Italian convent, where she died of a fever in 1822); then by the expulsion of the Gambas, whom Byron followed to Genoa; and finally by the drowning of Shelley and Williams in July, 1822.

Byron meanwhile had been steadily at work on a series of closet tragedies (including *Cain, Sardanapalus,* and *Marino Faliero*) and on his superb satire, *The Vision of Judgment.* He also continued writing his incomparable series of vivid, informative, and witty letters to his friends in England. But increasingly Byron devoted himself to the continuation of *Don Juan.* He had always been diffident in his self-judgments and easily swayed by literary advice. But now, confident that he had at last found his métier and was accomplishing a masterpiece, Byron kept on, in spite of persistent objections against the supposed immorality of the poem by the English public, by his publisher, John Murray, by his friends and well-wishers, and by his extremely decorous mistress, the Countess Guiccioli—by almost everyone, in fact, except the idealist, Shelley, who thought *Juan* incomparably better than anything he himself could write, and insisted "that every word of it is pregnant with immortality."

Byron finally broke off literature for action: he organized an expedition to assist in the Greek war for independence from the Turks. He knew too well the conditions in Greece, and had too skeptical an estimate of human nature, to entertain hope of success; but he was bored with love, with the domesticity of his relations to Teresa, and in some moods, with life itself. He had, in addition, by his own writings helped to kindle European enthusiasm for the Greek cause, and now felt honor-bound to try what could be done. In the dismal, marshy town of Missolonghi he lived a Spartan existence, undertaking to train troops whom he had himself subsidized and exhibiting great practical grasp and power of leadership amid an incredible confusion of factionalism, intrigue, and military ineptitude, and despite an unhappy passion for his Greek page boy, Loukas. Worn out, he succumbed to a series of feverish attacks and died just after he had reached his 36th birthday. To this day Byron is revered by the Greek people as a national hero.

Students of Byron still feel, as his friends had felt, the magnetic attraction of his antithetic and variable temperament. As Mary Shelley wrote six years after his death, when she read Thomas Moore's edition of his *Letters and Journals:* "The Lord Byron I find there is our Lord Byron—the fascinating—faulty—childish—philosophical being—daring the world—docile to a private circle—impetuous and indolent—gloomy and yet more gay than any other. * * * [I become] reconciled (as I used to in his lifetime) to those waywardnesses which annoyed me when he was away, through the delightful and buoyant tone of his conversation and manners." Of his inner discordances, Byron himself was well aware; he told his friend Lady Blessington: "I am so changeable, being everything by turns and nothing long—I am such a strange *mélange* of good and evil, that it would be difficult to describe me." Yet he remained faithful to his own code: a determination always to tell the truth as he saw it about the world and about himself—his refusal, unlike most of us, to suppress or conceal any of his moods is what made him seem so contradictory—and a dedication to the freedom of nations and individuals. As he went on to say to Lady Blessington: "There are but two sentiments to which I am constant—a strong love of liberty, and a detestation of cant."

Written after Swimming from Sestos to Abydos[1]

1

If, in the month of dark December,
Leander, who was nightly wont
(What maid will not the tale remember?)
To cross thy stream, broad Hellespont!

1. The Hellespont (now called the Dardanelles) is the narrow strait between Europe and Asia. In the ancient story, retold in Christopher Marlowe's *Hero and Leander,* young Leander of Abydos, on the Asian side, swam nightly to visit Hero, a priestess of the goddess Venus at Sestos, until he was drowned when he made the attempt in a storm. Byron and a young Lt. Ekenhead swam the Hellespont in the reverse direction on May 3, 1810. Byron alternated between complacency and humor in his many references to the event. In a note to the poem, Byron mentions that the distance was "upwards of four English miles, though the actual breadth is barely one. The rapidity of the current is such that no boat can row directly across. * * * The water was extremely cold, from the melting of the mountain snows."

2

If, when the wintry tempest roared,   5
    He sped to Hero, nothing loath,
And thus of old thy current poured,
    Fair Venus! how I pity both!

3

For *me*, degenerate modern wretch,
    Though in the genial month of May,   10
My dripping limbs I faintly stretch,
    And think I've done a feat today.

4

But since he crossed the rapid tide,
    According to the doubtful story,
To woo—and—Lord knows what beside,   15
    And swam for Love, as I for Glory;

5

'Twere hard to say who fared the best:
    Sad mortals! thus the gods still plague you!
He lost his labor, I my jest;
    For he was drowned, and I've the ague.   20

1810   1812

When We Two Parted

When we two parted
    In silence and tears,
Half broken-hearted
    To sever for years,
Pale grew thy cheek and cold,   5
    Colder thy kiss;
Truly that hour foretold
    Sorrow to this.

The dew of the morning
    Sunk chill on my brow—   10
It felt like the warning
    Of what I feel now.
Thy vows are all broken,
    And light is thy fame;
I hear thy name spoken,   15
    And share in its shame.

They name thee before me,
    A knell to mine ear;
A shudder comes o'er me—
    Why wert thou so dear?   20
They know not I knew thee,
    Who knew thee too well—
Long, long shall I rue thee,
    Too deeply to tell.

In secret we met—
  In silence I grieve,   25
That thy heart could forget,
  Thy spirit deceive.
If I should meet thee
  After long years,   30
How should I greet thee?—
  With silence and tears.

1813   1816

She Walks in Beauty[1]

1

She walks in beauty, like the night
  Of cloudless climes and starry skies;
And all that's best of dark and bright
  Meet in her aspect and her eyes:
Thus mellowed to that tender light   5
  Which heaven to gaudy day denies.

2

One shade the more, one ray the less,
  Had half impaired the nameless grace
Which waves in every raven tress,
  Or softly lightens o'er her face;   10
Where thoughts serenely sweet express
  How pure, how dear their dwelling place.

3

And on that cheek, and o'er that brow,
  So soft, so calm, yet eloquent,
The smiles that win, the tints that glow,   15
  But tell of days in goodness spent,
A mind at peace with all below,
  A heart whose love is innocent!

June 12, 1814   1815

Stanzas for Music

There Be None of Beauty's Daughters

1

There be none of Beauty's daughters
  With a magic like thee;
And like music on the waters
  Is thy sweet voice to me:
When, as if its sound were causing   5
  The charméd ocean's pausing,
The waves lie still and gleaming,
  And the lulled winds seem dreaming;

1. One of the lyrics in *Hebrew Melodies* (1815), written to be set to adaptations of traditional Jewish tunes by the young musician Isaac Nathan. Byron wrote the lines the morning after he had met his beautiful young cousin by marriage, Mrs. Robert John Wilmot, who wore a black mourning gown brightened with spangles.

2

And the midnight moon is weaving
   Her bright chain o'er the deep;   10
Whose breast is gently heaving,
   As an infant's asleep:
So the spirit bows before thee,
   To listen and adore thee;
With a full but soft emotion,   15
   Like the swell of summer's ocean.

1816   1816

They Say That Hope Is Happiness

1

They say that Hope is happiness;
   But genuine Love must prize the past,
And Memory wakes the thoughts that bless:
   They rose the first—they set the last;

2

And all that Memory loves the most   5
   Was once our only Hope to be,
And all that Hope adored and lost
   Hath melted into Memory.

3

Alas! it is delusion all;
   The future cheats us from afar,   10
Nor can we be what we recall,
   Nor dare we think on what we are.

1816   1829

Darkness[1]

I had a dream, which was not all a dream.
The bright sun was extinguished, and the stars
Did wander darkling[2] in the eternal space,
Rayless, and pathless, and the icy earth
Swung blind and blackening in the moonless air;   5
Morn came and went—and came, and brought no day,
And men forgot their passions in the dread
Of this their desolation; and all hearts
Were chilled into a selfish prayer for light:
And they did live by watchfires—and the thrones,   10
The palaces of crownéd kings—the huts,
The habitations of all things which dwell,
Were burnt for beacons; cities were consumed,
And men were gathered round their blazing homes
To look once more into each other's face;   15
Happy were those who dwelt within the eye
Of the volcanoes, and their mountain torch:

1. A powerfully imagined blank-verse description of the end of life on earth—a speculation hardly less common in Byron's time than in ours.
2. In the dark.

A fearful hope was all the world contained;
Forests were set on fire—but hour by hour
They fell and faded—and the crackling trunks   20
Extinguished with a crash—and all was black.
The brows of men by the despairing light
Wore an unearthly aspect, as by fits
The flashes fell upon them; some lay down
And hid their eyes and wept; and some did rest   25
Their chins upon their clenchéd hands, and smiled;
And others hurried to and fro, and fed
Their funeral piles with fuel, and looked up
With mad disquietude on the dull sky,
The pall of a past world; and then again   30
With curses cast them down upon the dust,
And gnashed their teeth and howled: the wild birds shrieked
And, terrified, did flutter on the ground,
And flap their useless wings; the wildest brutes
Came tame and tremulous; and vipers crawled   35
And twined themselves among the multitude,
Hissing, but stingless—they were slain for food;
And War, which for a moment was no more,
Did glut himself again—a meal was bought
With blood, and each sate sullenly apart   40
Gorging himself in gloom: no love was left;
All earth was but one thought—and that was death
Immediate and inglorious; and the pang
Of famine fed upon all entrails—men
Died, and their bones were tombless as their flesh;   45
The meager by the meager were devoured,
Even dogs assailed their masters, all save one,
And he was faithful to a corse, and kept
The birds and beasts and famished men at bay,
Till hunger clung them, or the dropping dead   50
Lured their lank jaws; himself sought out no food,
But with a piteous and perpetual moan,
And a quick desolate cry, licking the hand
Which answered not with a caress—he died.
The crowd was famished by degrees; but two   55
Of an enormous city did survive,
And they were enemies: they met beside
The dying embers of an altar place,
Where had been heaped a mass of holy things
For an unholy usage; they raked up,   60
And shivering scraped with their cold skeleton hands
The feeble ashes, and their feeble breath
Blew for a little life, and made a flame
Which was a mockery; then they lifted up
Their eyes as it grew lighter, and beheld   65
Each other's aspects—saw, and shrieked, and died—

Even of their mutual hideousness they died,
Unknowing who he was upon whose brow
Famine had written Fiend. The world was void,
The populous and the powerful was a lump   70
Seasonless, herbless, treeless, manless, lifeless—
A lump of death—a chaos of hard clay.
The rivers, lakes, and ocean all stood still,
And nothing stirred within their silent depths;
Ships sailorless lay rotting on the sea,   75
And their masts fell down piecemeal: as they dropped
They slept on the abyss without a surge—
The waves were dead; the tides were in their grave,
The Moon, their mistress, had expired before;
The winds were withered in the stagnant air,   80
And the clouds perished; Darkness had no need
Of aid from them—She was the Universe.

1816   1816

So We'll Go No More A-Roving[1]

1

So we'll go no more a-roving
    So late into the night,
Though the heart be still as loving,
    And the moon be still as bright.

2

For the sword outwears its sheath,   5
    And the soul wears out the breast,
And the heart must pause to breathe,
    And Love itself have rest.

3

Though the night was made for loving,
    And the day returns too soon,   10
Yet we'll go no more a-roving
    By the light of the moon.

1817   1836

Stanzas to the Po[2]

River, that rollest by the ancient walls,
    Where dwells the Lady of my love, when she

1. Included in a letter to Thomas
Moore, February 28, 1817, and written
in the Lenten aftermath of a spell of
feverish dissipation in the Carnival
season at Venice. Byron wrote, "I
find 'the sword wearing out the scabbard,' though I have but just turned
the corner of twenty-nine." The poem
is based on the refrain of a Scottish
song, *The Jolly Beggar:* "And we'll
gang nae mair a roving / Sae late into
the nicht * * * "
2. This powerful lyric was written a
month or two after Byron had fallen in
love with the 19-year-old Italian Teresa
Guiccioli. The Po is a river in northern
Italy that flows into the Adriatic.

Walks by thy brink, and there perchance recalls
    A faint and fleeting memory of me;

What if thy deep and ample stream should be   5
    A mirror of my heart, where she may read
The thousand thoughts I now betray to thee,
    Wild as thy wave, and headlong as thy speed!

What do I say—a mirror of my heart?
    Are not thy waters sweeping, dark, and strong?   10
Such as my feelings were and are, thou art;
    And such as thou art were my passions long.

Time may have somewhat tamed them—not forever;
    Thou overflow'st thy banks, and not for aye
Thy bosom overboils, congenial river!   15
    Thy floods subside, and mine have sunk away—

But left long wrecks behind: and now again,
    Borne in our old unchanged career, we move:
Thou tendest wildly onwards to the main.
    And I—to loving *one* I should not love.   20

The current I behold will sweep beneath
    Her native walls, and murmur at her feet;
Her eyes will look on thee, when she shall breathe
    The twilight air, unharmed by summer's heat.

She will look on thee—I have looked on thee,   25
    Full of that thought; and, from that moment, ne'er
Thy waters could I dream of, name, or see,
    Without the inseparable sigh for her!

Her bright eyes will be imaged in thy stream—
    Yes! they will meet the wave I gaze on now: 30
Mine cannot witness, even in a dream,
    That happy wave repass me in its flow!

The wave that bears my tears returns no more:
    Will she return by whom that wave shall sweep?
Both tread thy banks, both wander on thy shore,   35
    I by thy source, she by the dark-blue deep.

But that which keepeth us apart is not
    Distance, nor depth of wave, nor space of earth,
But the distraction of a various lot,
    As various as the climates of our birth.   40

A stranger loves the Lady of the land,
    Born far beyond the mountains, but his blood
Is all meridian,[3] as if never fanned
    By the black wind that chills the polar flood.

---

3. Southern.

My blood is all meridian; were it not, 45
    I had not left my clime, nor should I be,
In spite of tortures, ne'er to be forgot,
    A slave again of love—at least of thee.

'Tis vain to struggle—let me perish young—
    Live as I lived, and love as I have loved; 50
To dust if I return, from dust I sprung,
    And then, at least, my heart can ne'er be moved.

1819   1824

When a Man Hath No Freedom
to Fight for at Home[4]

When a man hath no freedom to fight for at home,
    Let him combat for that of his neighbors;
Let him think of the glories of Greece and of Rome,
    And get knocked on his head for his labors.

To do good to mankind is the chivalrous plan, 5
    And is always as nobly requited;
Then battle for freedom wherever you can,
    And, if not shot or hanged, you'll get knighted.

November 5, 1820   1824

Stanzas Written on the Road Between
Florence and Pisa

Oh, talk not to me of a name great in story—
The days of our youth are the days of our glory;
And the myrtle and ivy of sweet two-and-twenty
Are worth all your laurels,[1] though ever so plenty.

What are garlands and crowns to the brow that is wrinkled? 5
'Tis but as a dead-flower with May-dew besprinkled:
Then away with all such from the head that is hoary!
What care I for the wreaths that can *only* give glory?

Oh FAME!—if I e'er took delight in thy praises,
'Twas less for the sake of thy high-sounding phrases, 10

---

4. The ironist's attitude toward gratuitous enlistment in a foreign war for national freedom—a cause to which Byron gave his own life less than four years later.

1. Myrtle was sacred to Venus, goddess of love, and ivy to Bacchus, god of wine and revelry; a laurel crown was awarded by the Greeks as a mark of high honor.

Than to see the bright eyes of the dear one discover
She thought that I was not unworthy to love her.

There chiefly I sought thee, *there* only I found thee;
Her glance was the best of the rays that surround thee;
When it sparkled o'er aught that was bright in my story, 15
I knew it was love, and I felt it was glory.
November, 1821   1830

From Childe Harold's Pilgrimage[1]

A ROMAUNT[2]

From *Canto I*

1

Oh, thou! in Hellas deemed of heavenly birth,
Muse! formed or fabled at the minstrel's will!
Since shamed full oft by later lyres on earth,
Mine dares not call thee from thy sacred hill:
Yet there I've wandered by thy vaunted rill;
Yes! sighed o'er Delphi's long-deserted shrine,   5
Where, save that feeble fountain, all is still;

1. *Childe Harold* is a travelogue, narrated by a melancholy, passionate, well-read, and very eloquent tourist. Byron wrote most of the first two cantos while on the tour through Spain, Portugal, Albania, and Greece which these cantos describe; when he published them, in 1812, they made him at one stroke the best known and most talked about English poet. Byron took up *Childe Harold* again in 1816, during the European tour he made after the breakup of his marriage. Canto III, published in 1816, moves through Belgium, up the Rhine, then to Switzerland and the Alps. Canto IV, published in 1818, describes the great cities and monuments of Italy.

Byron chose for his poem the Spenserian stanza, and like James Thomson (in the *Castle of Indolence*) and other 18th-century predecessors, he attempted in the first canto to imitate, in a serio-comic fashion, the archaic language of his Elizabethan model. (The word "Childe" itself is the ancient term for a young noble awaiting knighthood.) But Byron soon dropped the archaisms; and in the last two cantos, he adapts Spenser's mellifluous stanza to his own assured and brassy magniloquence.

In the Preface to his first two cantos, Byron had insisted that the narrator,

Childe Harold, was "a fictitious character," merely "the child of imagination." But in the manuscript version of these cantos, he had himself called his hero "Childe Burun," the early form of his own family name; the world insisted on identifying the character as well as the travels of the protagonist with those of the author; and in the fourth canto Byron, abandoning the third-person *dramatis persona,* spoke out frankly in the first person.

In its shock tactics of apostrophes, imperatives, exclamations, hyperbole, and abrupt changes in subject, pace, and mood, the style of *Childe Harold* is without close parallel in English; to it Goethe applied the terms *Keckheit, Kühnheit, und Grandiosität:* "daring, dash, and grandiosity." It is no small feat in the author to have converted a meticulously accurate tourist's record of scenes, memorials, and museums into a dramatic and passionate experience. The result is like seeing Europe by flashes of lightning, for everything is presented, not as it is in itself, but as it affects the violent sensibility of that new cultural phenomenon, the Romantic Man of Feeling.

2. A romance, or narrative of adventure.

Nor mote my shell awake the weary Nine[3]
To grace so plain a tale—this lowly lay of mine.

2

Whilome[4] in Albion's isle there dwelt a youth,   10
Who ne in virtue's ways did take delight;
But spent his days in riot most uncouth,
And vexed with mirth the drowsy ear of Night.
Ah, me! in sooth he was a shameless wight,
Sore given to revel and ungodly glee;   15
Few earthly things found favor in his sight
Save concubines and carnal companie,
And flaunting wassailers[5] of high and low degree.

3

Childe Harold was he hight—but whence his name
And lineage long, it suits me not to say;   20
Suffice it that perchance they were of fame,
And had been glorious in another day:
But one sad loscl[6] soils a name for aye,
However mighty in the olden time;
Nor all that heralds rake from coffined clay,   25
Nor florid prose, nor honeyed lies of rhyme,
Can blazon evil deeds, or consecrate a crime.

4

Childe Harold basked him in the noontide sun,
Disporting there like any other fly;
Nor deemed before his little day was done   30
One blast might chill him into misery.
But long ere scarce a third of his passed by,
Worse than adversity the Childe befell;
He felt the fullness of satiety:
Then loathed he in his native land to dwell,   35
Which seemed to him more lone than eremite's[7] sad cell.

5

For he through Sin's long labyrinth had run,
Nor made atonement when he did amiss;
Had sighed to many though he loved but one,
And that loved one, alas! could ne'er be his.   40
Ah, happy she! to 'scape from him whose kiss
Had been pollution unto aught so chaste;
Who soon had left her charms for vulgar bliss,
And spoiled her goodly lands to gild his waste,
Nor calm domestic peace had ever deigned to taste.   45

---

3. The "shell" is a lyre (Hermes is fabled to have invented the lyre by stretching strings over the hollow of a tortoise shell); the "Nine" are the Muses, whose "vaunted rill," (line 5) was the Castalian spring. "Mote": may.

4. Once upon a time.
5. Brazen topers.
6. Rascal. Byron's great-uncle, the 5th Lord Byron, had killed a kinsman in a drunken duel.
7. A religious hermit.

6

And now Childe Harold was sore sick at heart,
And from his fellow bacchanals would flee;
'Tis said, at times the sullen tear would start,
But Pride congealed the drop within his ee:[8]
Apart he stalked in joyless reverie,   50
And from his native land resolved to go,
And visit scorching climes beyond the sea;
With pleasure drugged, he almost longed for woe,
And e'en for change of scene would seek the shades below.

* * *

From *Canto III*

1

Is thy face like thy mother's, my fair child!
Ada![1] sole daughter of my house and heart?
When last I saw thy young blue eyes they smiled,
And then we parted—not as now we part,
But with a hope.—
                              Awaking with a start,   5
The waters heave around me; and on high
The winds lift up their voices: I depart,
Whither I know not; but the hour's gone by,
When Albion's[2] lessening shores could grieve or glad mine eye.

2

Once more upon the waters! yet once more!   10
And the waves bound beneath me as a steed
That knows his rider. Welcome to their roar!
Swift be their guidance, wheresoe'er it lead!
Though the strained mast should quiver as a reed,
And the rent canvas fluttering strew the gale,   15
Still must I on; for I am as a weed,
Flung from the rock on Ocean's foam, to sail
Where'er the surge may sweep, the tempest's breath prevail.

3

In my youth's summer[3] I did sing of One,
The wandering outlaw of his own dark mind;   20
Again I seize the theme, then but begun,
And bear it with me, as the rushing wind
Bears the cloud onwards: in that tale I find
The furrows of long thought, and dried-up tears,
Which, ebbing, leave a sterile track behind,   25
O'er which all heavily the journeying years
Plod the last sands of life—where not a flower appears.

---

8. Eye.
1. Byron's daughter, Augusta Ada, born
December, 1816, a month before her
parents separated. Byron's "hope" (line
5) had been for a reconciliation, but

he was never to see Ada again.
2. England's.
3. Byron wrote Canto I at 21; he is
now 28.

4

Since my young days of passion—joy, or pain—
Perchance my heart and harp have lost a string,
And both may jar:[4] it may be that in vain   30
I would essay as I have sung to sing.
Yet, though a dreary strain, to this I cling,
So that it wean me from the weary dream
Of selfish grief or gladness—so it fling
Forgetfulness around me—it shall seem   35
To me, though to none else, a not ungrateful theme.

5

He, who grown aged in this world of woe,
In deeds, not years, piercing the depths of life,
So that no wonder waits him—nor below
Can love, or sorrow, fame, ambition, strife,   40
Cut to his heart again with the keen knife
Of silent, sharp endurance—he can tell
Why thought seeks refuge in lone caves, yet rife
With airy images, and shapes which dwell
Still unimpaired, though old, in the soul's haunted cell.   45

6

'Tis to create, and in creating live
A being more intense, that we endow
With form our fancy, gaining as we give
The life we image, even as I do now.
What am I? Nothing: but not so art thou,   50
Soul of my thought![5] with whom I traverse earth,
Invisible but gazing, as I glow
Mixed with thy spirit, blended with thy birth,
And feeling still with thee in my crushed feelings' dearth.

7

Yet must I think less wildly—I *have* thought   55
Too long and darkly, till my brain became,
In its own eddy boiling and o'erwrought,
A whirling gulf of phantasy and flame:
And thus, untaught in youth my heart to tame,
My springs of life were poisoned. 'Tis too late!   60
Yet am I changed; though still enough the same
In strength to bear what time can not abate,
And feed on bitter fruits without accusing Fate.

8

Something too much of this—but now 'tis past,
And the spell closes with its silent seal.[6]   65
Long absent HAROLD reappears at last;
He of the breast which fain no more would feel,
Wrung with the wounds which kill not but ne'er heal;
Yet Time, who changes all, had altered him
In soul and aspect as in age: years steal   70

4. Sound discordant.
5. I.e., Childe Harold, his literary creation.

6. I.e., he sets the seal of silence on his
personal tale ("spell").

Fire from the mind as vigor from the limb,
And life's enchanted cup but sparkles near the brim.

9

His had been quaffed too quickly, and he found
The dregs were wormwood; but he filled again,
And from a purer fount, on holier ground,
And deemed its spring perpetual; but in vain!   75
Still round him clung invisibly a chain
Which galled forever, fettering though unseen,
And heavy though it clanked not; worn with pain,
Which pined although it spoke not, and grew keen,   80
Entering with every step he took through many a scene.

10

Secure in guarded coldness, he had mixed
Again in fancied safety with his kind,
And deemed his spirit now so firmly fixed
And sheathed with an invulnerable mind,   85
That, if no joy, no sorrow lurked behind;
And he, as one, might 'midst the many stand
Unheeded, searching through the crowd to find
Fit speculation—such as in strange land
He found in wonderworks of God and Nature's hand.   90

11

But who can view the ripened rose, nor seek
To wear it? who can curiously behold
The smoothness and the sheen of beauty's cheek,
Nor feel the heart can never all grow old?
Who can contemplate Fame through clouds unfold   95
The star which rises o'er her steep, nor climb?
Harold, once more within the vortex, rolled
On with the giddy circle, chasing Time,
Yet with a nobler aim than in his youth's fond[7] prime.

12

But soon he knew himself the most unfit   100
Of men to herd with Man, with whom he held
Little in common; untaught to submit
His thoughts to others, though his soul was quelled
In youth by his own thoughts; still uncompelled,
He would not yield dominion of his mind   105
To spirits against whom his own rebelled,
Proud though in desolation; which could find
A life within itself, to breathe without mankind.

13

Where rose the mountains, there to him were friends;
Where rolled the ocean, thereon was his home;   110
Where a blue sky, and glowing clime, extends,
He had the passion and the power to roam;
The desert, forest, cavern, breaker's foam,
Were unto him companionship; they spake
A mutual language, clearer than the tome   115

7. Foolish.

Of his land's tongue, which he would oft forsake
For Nature's pages glassed[8] by sunbeams on the lake.

14

Like the Chaldean,[9] he could watch the stars,
Till he had peopled them with beings bright
As their own beams; and earth, and earth-born jars,   120
And human frailties, were forgotten quite:
Could he have kept his spirit to that flight
He had been happy; but this clay will sink
Its spark immortal, envying it the light
To which it mounts, as if to break the link   125
That keeps us from yon heaven which woos us to its brink.

15

But in Man's dwellings he became a thing
Restless and worn, and stern and wearisome,
Drooped as a wild-born falcon with clipped wing,
To whom the boundless air alone were home: 130
Then came his fit again, which to o'ercome,
As eagerly the barred-up bird will beat
His breast and beak against his wiry dome
Till the blood tinge his plumage, so the heat
Of his impeded soul would through his bosom eat.   135

16

Self-exiled Harold wanders forth again,
With nought of hope left—but with less of gloom;
The very knowledge that he lived in vain,
That all was over on this side the tomb,
Had made Despair a smilingness assume,   140
Which, though 'twere wild—as on the plundered wreck
When mariners would madly meet their doom
With draughts intemperate on the sinking deck—
Did yet inspire a cheer which he forebore to check.

17

Stop!—for thy tread is on an Empire's dust!   145
An Earthquake's spoil is sepulchered below!
Is the spot marked with no colossal bust,
Nor column trophied for triumphal show?
None;[1] but the moral's truth tells simpler so,
As the ground was before, thus let it be—   150
How that red rain hath made the harvest grow!
And is this all the world has gained by thee,
Thou first and last of fields, king-making Victory?

18

And Harold stands upon this place of skulls,
The grave of France, the deadly Waterloo!   155
How in an hour the power which gave annuls
Its gifts, transferring fame as fleeting too!

8. Made glassy.
9. A people of ancient Babylonia, expert in astronomy.

1. Napoleon's defeat at Waterloo, near Brussels, had occurred only the year before, on June 18, 1815.

In "pride of place" here last the eagle flew,[2]
Then tore with bloody talon the rent plain,
Pierced by the shaft of banded nations through;   160
Ambition's life and labors all were vain;
He wears the shattered links of the world's broken chain.[3]

19

Fit retribution! Gaul[4] may champ the bit
And foam in fetters—but is Earth more free?
Did nations combat to make *One* submit;   165
Or league to teach all kings true sovereignty?
What! shall reviving Thralldom again be
The patched-up idol of enlightened days?
Shall we, who struck the Lion down, shall we
Pay the Wolf homage? proffering lowly gaze   170
And servile knees to thrones? No; *prove*[5] before ye praise!

20

If not, o'er one fallen despot boast no more!
In vain fair checks were furrowed with hot tears
For Europe's flowers long rooted up before
The trampler of her vineyards; in vain years   175
Of death, depopulation, bondage, fears,
Have all been borne, and broken by the accord
Of roused-up millions: all that most endears
Glory is when the myrtle wreathes a sword
Such as Harmodius drew on Athens' tyrant lord.[6]   180

21

There was a sound of revelry by night,
And Belgium's capital had gathered then
Her Beauty and her Chivalry, and bright
The lamps shone o'er fair women and brave men;[7]
A thousand hearts beat happily; and when   185
Music arose with its voluptuous swell,
Soft eyes looked love to eyes which spake again,
And all went merry as a marriage bell—
But hush! hark! a deep sound strikes like a rising knell!

22

Did ye not hear it?—No; 'twas but the wind,   190
Or the car rattling o'er the stony street;
On with the dance! let joy be unconfined;
No sleep till morn, when Youth and Pleasure meet
To chase the glowing Hours with flying feet—
But hark!—that heavy sound breaks in once more,   195

---

2. The eagle was the standard of Napoleon. "Pride of place" is a term from falconry, meaning the highest point of flight (cf. *Macbeth* II.iv.12).
3. Napoleon was then a prisoner at St. Helena.
4. France. Byron, like Shelley and other liberals, saw the defeat of the Napoleonic tyranny as at the same time a victory for tyrannous kings and the forces of extreme reaction throughout Europe.

5. Await the test (proof) of experience.
6. In 514 B.C. Harmodius and Aristogeiton, hiding their daggers in myrtle (symbol of love), killed Hipparchus, tyrant of Athens.
7. This famous ball, given by the Duchess of Richmond on the eve of the battle of Quatre Bras, which opened the conflict at Waterloo, is also described in Thackeray's *Vanity Fair*, Chapters 29–30.

As if the clouds its echo would repeat;
And nearer, clearer, deadlier than before!
Arm! Arm! it is—it is—the cannon's opening roar!

23

Within a windowed niche of that high hall
Sate Brunswick's fated chieftain;[8] he did hear   200
That sound the first amidst the festival,
And caught its tone with Death's prophetic ear;
And when they smiled because he deemed it near,
His heart more truly knew that peal too well
Which stretched his father on a bloody bier,   205
And roused the vengeance blood alone could quell:
He rushed into the field, and, foremost fighting, fell.

24

Ah! then and there was hurrying to and fro,
And gathering tears, and tremblings of distress,
And cheeks all pale, which but an hour ago   210
Blushed at the praise of their own loveliness;
And there were sudden partings, such as press
The life from out young hearts, and choking sighs
Which ne'er might be repeated; who could guess
If ever more should meet those mutual eyes,   215
Since upon night so sweet such awful morn could rise!

25

And there was mounting in hot haste: the steed,
The mustering squadron, and the clattering car,
Went pouring forward with impetuous speed,
And swiftly forming in the ranks of war;   220
And the deep thunder peal on peal afar;
And near, the beat of the alarming drum
Roused up the soldier ere the morning star;
While thronged the citizens with terror dumb,
Or whispering, with white lips—"The foe! They come! they come!"

26

And wild and high the "Cameron's gathering"[9] rose!   226
The war-note of Lochiel, which Albyn's hills
Have heard, and heard, too, have her Saxon foes—
How in the noon of night that pibroch[1] thrills,
Savage and shrill! But with the breath which fills   230
Their mountain pipe, so fill the mountaineers
With the fierce native daring which instills
The stirring memory of a thousand years,
And Evan's, Donald's fame[2] rings in each clansman's ears!

8. The Duke of Brunswick, nephew of George III of England, was killed in the battle of Quatre Bras, just as his father, commanding the Prussian army against Napoleon, had been killed at Auerstedt in 1806 (line 205).
9. The clan song of the Camerons, whose chief was called "Lochiel," after his estate. "Albyn's": Scotland's.
1. Bagpipe music, usually warlike in character.
2. Sir Evan and Donald Cameron, famous warriors in the Stuart cause in the 17th and 18th centuries.

27

And Ardennes[3] waves above them her green leaves,   235
Dewy with nature's teardrops, as they pass,
Grieving, if aught inanimate e'er grieves,
Over the unreturning brave—alas!
Ere evening to be trodden like the grass
Which now beneath them, but above shall grow   240
In its next verdure, when this fiery mass
Of living valor, rolling on the foe
And burning with high hope, shall molder cold and low.

28

Last noon beheld them full of lusty life,
Last eve in Beauty's circle proudly gay,
The midnight brought the signal-sound of strife,   245
The morn the marshaling in arms—the day
Battle's magnificently-stern array!
The thunderclouds close o'er it, which when rent
The earth is covered thick with other clay,   250
Which her own clay shall cover, heaped and pent,
Rider and horse—friend, foe—in one red burial blent!

* * *
36

There sunk the greatest, nor the worst of men,[4]
Whose spirit antithetically mixed
One moment of the mightiest, and again
On little objects with like firmness fixed,
Extreme in all things! hadst thou been betwixt,   320
Thy throne had still been thine, or never been;
For daring made thy rise as fall: thou seek'st
Even now to reassume the imperial mien,
And shake again the world, the Thunderer of the scene!

37

Conqueror and captive of the earth art thou!   325
She trembles at thee still, and thy wild name
Was ne'er more bruited in men's minds than now
That thou are nothing, save the jest of Fame,
Who wooed thee once, thy vassal, and became
The flatterer of thy fierceness, till thou wert   330
A god unto thyself; nor less the same
To the astounded kingdoms all inert,
Who deemed thee for a time whate'er thou didst assert.

38

Oh, more or less than man—in high or low,
Battling with nations, flying from the field;   335
Now making monarchs' necks thy footstool, now
More than thy meanest soldier taught to yield;
An empire thou couldst crush, command, rebuild,

3. A forested region covering parts of
Belgium, France, and Luxembourg,
which became a battlefield again in
both World Wars.
4. I.e., Napoleon. The description that
follows indicates the extent to which
Byron modeled the Byronic hero,
including Childe Harold himself, on his
conception of Napoleon.

But govern not thy petticst passion, nor,
However deeply in men's spirits skilled,   340
Look through thine own, nor curb the lust of war,
Nor learn that tempted Fate will leave the loftiest star.

39

Yet well thy soul hath brooked the turning tide
With that untaught innate philosophy,
Which, be it wisdom, coldness, or deep pride,   345
Is gall and wormwood to an enemy.
When the whole host of hatred stood hard by,
To watch and mock thee shrinking, thou hast smiled
With a sedate and all-enduring eye—
When Fortune fled her spoiled and favorite child,   350
He stood unbowed beneath the ills upon him piled.

40

Sager than in thy fortunes; for in them
Ambition steeled thee on too far to show
That just habitual scorn, which could contemn
Men and their thoughts; 'twas wise to feel, not so   355
To wear it ever on thy lip and brow,
And spurn the instruments thou wert to use
Till they were turned unto thine overthrow:
'Tis but a worthless world to win or lose;
So hath it proved to thee and all such lot⁵ who choose.   360

41

If, like a tower upon a headlong rock,
Thou hadst been made to stand or fall alone,
Such scorn of man had helped to brave the shock;
But men's thoughts were the steps which paved thy throne,
Their admiration thy best weapon shone;   365
The part of Philip's son⁶ was thine, not then
(Unless aside thy purple had been thrown)
Like stern Diogenes⁷ to mock at men;
For sceptered cynics earth were far too wide a den.

42

But quiet to quick bosoms is a hell,   370
And *there* hath been thy bane; there is a fire
And motion of the soul which will not dwell
In its own narrow being, but aspire
Beyond the fitting medium of desire;
And, but once kindled, quenchless evermore,   375
Preys upon high adventure, nor can tire
Of aught but rest; a fever at the core,
Fatal to him who bears, to all who ever bore.

43

This makes the madmen who have made men mad
By their contagion; Conquerors and Kings,   380

5. Hazard.
6. Alexander the Great, son of Philip of Macedon.
7. The Greek philosopher of Cynicism, contemporary of Alexander. It is related that Alexander was so struck by his independence of mind that he said, "If I were not Alexander, I should wish to be Diogenes"; hence the allusion in lines 367 and 369.

Founders of sects and systems, to whom add
Sophists, Bards, Statesmen, all unquiet things
Which stir too strongly the soul's secret springs,
And are themselves the fools to those they fool;
Envied, yet how unenviable! what stings   385
Are theirs! One breast laid open were a school
Which would unteach mankind the lust to shine or rule.

44

Their breath is agitation, and their life
A storm whereon they ride, to sink at last;
And yet so nursed and bigoted to strife,   390
That should their days, surviving perils past,
Melt to calm twilight, they feel overcast
With sorrow and supineness, and so die;
Even as a flame unfed which runs to waste
With its own flickering, or a sword laid by,   395
Which eats into itself and rusts ingloriously.

45

He who ascends to mountain tops, shall find
The loftiest peaks most wrapped in clouds and snow;
He who surpasses or subdues mankind,
Must look down on the hate of those below.   400
Though high *above* the sun of glory glow,
And far *beneath* the earth and ocean spread,
Round him are icy rocks, and loudly blow
Contending tempests on his naked head,
And thus reward the toils which to those summits led.[8]   405

* * *

52

Thus Harold inly said, and passed along,   460
Yet not insensibly to all which here
Awoke the jocund birds to early song
In glens which might have made even exile dear:
Though on his brow were graven lines austere,
And tranquil sternness which had ta'en the place   465
Of feelings fiercer far but less severe,
Joy was not always absent from his face,
But o'er it in such scenes would steal with transient trace.

53

Nor was all love shut from him, though his days
Of passion had consumed themselves to dust.   470
It is in vain that we would coldly gaze
On such as smile upon us; the heart must
Leap kindly back to kindness, though disgust
Hath weaned it from all wordlings: thus he felt,
For there was soft remembrance, and sweet trust   475
In one fond breast,[3] to which his own would melt,
And in its tenderer hour on that his bosom dwelt.

8. In the stanzas here omitted, Harold
is abruptly sent sailing up the Rhine,
meditating on the "thousand battles"
that "have assailed thy banks."

3. Commentators agree that the reference is to Byron's half sister, Augusta
Leigh.

54

And he had learned to love—I know not why,
For this in such as him seems strange of mood—
The helpless looks of blooming infancy,   480
Even in its earliest nurture; what subdued,
To change like this, a mind so far imbued
With scorn of man, it little boots to know;
But thus it was; and though in solitude
Small power the nipped affections have to grow,   485
In him this glowed when all beside had ceased to glow.

55

And there was one soft breast, as hath been said,
Which unto his was bound by stronger ties
Than the church links withal; and, though unwed,
That love was pure, and, far above disguise,   490
Had stood the test of mortal enmities
Still undivided, and cemented more
By peril, dreaded most in female eyes;
But this was firm, and from a foreign shore
Well to that heart might his these absent greetings pour! 495

* * *

68

Lake Leman[4] woos me with its crystal face,
The mirror where the stars and mountains view   645
The stillness of their aspect in each trace
Its clear depth yields of their far height and hue:
There is too much of man here, to look through
With a fit mind the might which I behold;
But soon in me shall Loneliness renew   650
Thoughts hid, but not less cherished than of old,
Ere mingling with the herd had penned me in their fold.

69

To fly from, need not be to hate, mankind:
All are not fit with them to stir and toil,
Nor is it discontent to keep the mind   655
Deep in its fountain, lest it overboil
In the hot throng, where we become the spoil
Of our infection, till too late and long
We may deplore and struggle with the coil,[5]
In wretched interchange of wrong for wrong   660
Midst a contentious world, striving where none are strong.

70

There, in a moment, we may plunge our years
In fatal penitence, and in the blight
Of our own soul turn all our blood to tears,
And color things to come with hues of night;   665
The race of life becomes a hopeless flight
To those that walk in darkness: on the sea,
The boldest steer but where their ports invite,

4. Harold has traveled across the Alps   5. Tumult.
to the Lake of Geneva, Switzerland.

But there are wanderers o'er Eternity
Whose bark drives on and on, and anchored ne'er shall be.   670

71

Is it not better, then, to be alone,
And love earth only for its earthly sake?
By the blue rushing of the arrowy Rhone,
Or the pure bosom of its nursing lake,
Which feeds it as a mother who doth make   675
A fair but froward infant her own care,
Kissing its cries away as these awake—
Is it not better thus our lives to wear,
Than join the crushing crowd, doomed to inflict or bear?

72

I live not in myself, but I become   680
Portion of that around me; and to me
High mountains are a feeling, but the hum
Of human cities torture: I can see
Nothing to loathe in nature, save to be
A link reluctant in a fleshly chain,   685
Classed among creatures, when the soul can flee,
And with the sky, the peak, the heaving plain
Of ocean, or the stars, mingle, and not in vain.[6]

73

And thus I am absorbed, and this is life:
I look upon the peopled desert past,   690
As on a place of agony and strife,
Where, for some sin, to sorrow I was cast,
To act and suffer, but remount at last
With a fresh pinion; which I feel to spring,
Though young, yet waxing vigorous, as the blast   695
Which it would cope with, on delighted wing,
Spurning the clay-cold bonds which round our being cling.

74

And when, at length, the mind shall be all free
From what it hates in this degraded form,
Reft of its carnal life, save what shall be   700
Existent happier in the fly and worm—
When elements to elements conform,
And dust is as it should be, shall I not
Feel all I see, less dazzling, but more warm?
The bodiless thought? the Spirit of each spot?   705
Of which, even now, I share at times the immortal lot?

75

Are not the mountains, waves, and skies a part
Of me and of my soul, as I of them?

6. Byron had lived in close contact with
Shelley at Geneva and had toured the
lake with him. At the time, he was
introduced to concepts of nature in the
poetry of Wordsworth, whom Shelley
had pressed on Byron's attention; these
ideas are reflected in Canto III, but the
voice is Byron's. Byron said of this
canto: "I was half mad during the time
of its composition, between metaphysics,
mountains, lakes, love unextinguishable,
thoughts unutterable, and the nightmare
of my own delinquencies."

Is not the love of these deep in my heart
With a pure passion? should I not contemn   710
All objects, if compared with these? and stem
A tide of suffering, rather than forego
Such feelings for the hard and worldly phlegm
Of those whose eyes are only turned below,
Gazing upon the ground, with thoughts which dare not glow?   715

76

But this is not my theme; and I return
To that which is immediate, and require
Those who find contemplation in the urn,[7]
To look on One, whose dust was once all fire,
A native of the land where I respire   720
The clear air for a while—a passing guest,
Where he became a being—whose desire
Was to be glorious; 'twas a foolish quest,
The which to gain and keep he sacrificed all rest.[8]

77

Here the self-torturing sophist, wild Rousseau,   725
The apostle of affliction, he who threw
Enchantment over passion, and from woe
Wrung overwhelming eloquence, first drew
The breath which made him wretched; yet he knew
How to make madness beautiful, and cast   730
O'er erring deeds and thoughts a heavenly hue
Of words, like sunbeams, dazzling as they past
The eyes, which o'er them shed tears feelingly and fast.

78

His love was passion's essence—as a tree
On fire by lightning; with ethereal flame   735
Kindled he was, and blasted; for to be
Thus, and enamored, were in him the same.
But his was not the love of living dame,
Nor of the dead who rise upon our dreams,
But of ideal beauty, which became   740
In him existence, and o'erflowing teems
Along his burning page, distempered though it seems.

* * *

85

Clear, placid Leman! thy contrasted lake,
With the wild world I dwelt in, is a thing
Which warns me with its stillness to forsake
Earth's troubled waters for a purer spring.   800
This quiet sail is as a noiseless wing
To waft me from distraction; once I loved

---

7. I.e., those who find matter for meditation in an urn containing the ashes of the dead.
8. Jean-Jacques Rousseau, who had been born in Geneva in 1712. Byron's characterization is based on Rousseau's novel, *La Nouvelle Héloïse*, as well as on his *Confessions*. It clearly influenced Shelley's representation of Rousseau six years later in his *Triumph of Life* (1822), lines 180 ff., below.

Torn ocean's roar, but thy soft murmuring
Sounds sweet as if a sister's voice reproved,
That I with stern delights should e'er have been so moved.   805

86

It is the hush of night, and all between
Thy margin and the mountains, dusk, yet clear,
Mellowed and mingling, yet distinctly seen,
Save darkened Jura,[9] whose capped heights appear
Precipitously steep; and drawing near,   810
There breathes a living fragrance from the shore,
Of flowers yet fresh with childhood; on the ear
Drops the light drip of the suspended oar,
Or chirps the grasshopper one good-night carol more.

87

He is an evening reveler, who makes   815
His life an infancy, and sings his fill;
At intervals, some bird from out the brakes[1]
Starts into voice a moment, then is still.
There seems a floating whisper on the hill,
But that is fancy, for the starlight dews   820
All silently their tears of love instill,
Weeping themselves away, till they infuse
Deep into Nature's breast the spirit of her hues.

88

Ye stars! which are the poetry of heaven!
If in your bright leaves we would read the fate   825
Of men and empires—'tis to be forgiven,
That in our aspirations to be great,
Our destinies o'erleap their mortal state,
And claim a kindred with you; for ye are
A beauty and a mystery, and create   830
In us such love and reverence from afar
That fortune—fame—power—life have named themselves a Star.

89

All heaven and earth are still—though not in sleep,
But breathless, as we grow when feeling most;
And silent, as we stand in thoughts too deep—   835
All heaven and earth are still. From the high host
Of stars to the lulled lake and mountain coast,
All is concentered in a life intense,
Where not a beam, nor air, nor leaf is lost,
But hath a part of being, and a sense   840
Of that which is of all Creator and defense.

90

Then stirs the feeling infinite, so felt
In solitude, where we are *least* alone;
A truth, which through our being then doth melt
And purifies from self: it is a tone,   845

9. The mountain range between Swit-   Lake of Geneva.
zerland and France, visible from the   1. Thickets.

The soul and source of music, which makes known
Eternal harmony, and sheds a charm,
Like to the fabled Cytherea's zone,[2]
Binding all things with beauty—'twould disarm
The specter Death, had he substantial power to harm.   850

91

Not vainly did the early Persian make
His altar the high places and the peak
Of earth-o'ergazing mountains, and thus take
A fit and unwalled temple, there to seek
The Spirit, in whose honor shrines are weak   855
Upreared of human hands. Come, and compare
Columns and idol-dwellings, Goth or Greek,
With Nature's realms of worship, earth and air,
Nor fix on fond abodes to circumscribe thy prayer!

92

The sky is changed!—and such a change! Oh night,   860
And storm, and darkness, ye are wondrous strong,
Yet lovely in your strength, as is the light
Of a dark eye in woman! Far along,
From peak to peak, the rattling crags among,
Leaps the live thunder! Not from one lone cloud,   865
But every mountain now hath found a tongue,
And Jura answers, through her misty shroud,
Back to the joyous Alps, who call to her aloud!

93

And this is in the night—Most glorious night!
Thou wert not sent for slumber! let me be   870
A sharer in thy fierce and far delight—
A portion of the tempest and of thee!
How the lit lake shines, a phosphoric sea,
And the big rain comes dancing to the earth!
And now again 'tis black—and now, the glee   875
Of the loud hills shakes with its mountain mirth,
As if they did rejoice o'er a young earthquake's birth.

94

Now, where the swift Rhone cleaves his way between
Heights which appear as lovers who have parted
In hate, whose mining depths so intervene   880
That they can meet no more, though brokenhearted!
Though in their souls, which thus each other thwarted,
Love was the very root of the fond rage
Which blighted their life's bloom, and then departed—
Itself expired, but leaving them an age   885
Of years all winters—war within themselves to wage:

95

Now, where the quick Rhone thus hath cleft his way,
The mightiest of the storms hath ta'en his stand:
For here, not one, but many, make their play,

2. The sash of Venus, which conferred the power to attract love.

And fling their thunderbolts from hand to hand,   890
Flashing and cast around: of all the band,
The brightest through these parted hills hath forked
His lightnings—as if he did understand,
That in such gaps as desolation worked,
There the hot shaft should blast whatever therein lurked.   895

96

Sky—mountains—river—winds—lake—lightnings! ye,
With night, and clouds, and thunder, and a soul
To make these felt and feeling, well may be
Things that have made me watchful; the far roll
Of your departing voices, is the knoll[3]   900
Of what in me is sleepless—if I rest.
But where of ye, oh tempests! is the goal?
Are ye like those within the human breast?
Or do ye find at length, like eagles, some high nest?

97

Could I embody and unbosom now   905
That which is most within me—could I wreak
My thoughts upon expression, and thus throw
Soul, heart, mind, passions, feelings, strong or weak,
All that I would have sought, and all I seek,
Bear, know, feel—and yet breathe—into *one* word,   910
And that one word were lightning, I would speak;
But as it is, I live and die unheard,
With a most voiceless thought, sheathing it as a sword.

98

The morn is up again, the dewy morn,
With breath all incense and with cheek all bloom,   915
Laughing the clouds away with playful scorn,
And living as if earth contained no tomb—
And glowing into day; we may resume
The march of our existence; and thus I,
Still on thy shores, fair Leman! may find room   920
And food for meditation, nor pass by
Much, that may give us pause, if pondered fittingly.

* * *

113[4]

I have not loved the world, nor the world me;
I have not flattered its rank breath, nor bowed
To its idolatries a patient knee—   1050
Nor coined my cheek to smiles—nor cried aloud
In worship of an echo; in the crowd
They could not deem me one of such; I stood
Among them, but not of them; in a shroud
Of thoughts which were not their thoughts, and still could,   1055
Had I not filed[5] my mind, which thus itself subdued.

---

3. Knell (old form).
4. Harold utters the following soliloquy as he stands at the summit of an Alpine pass, looking southward upon

Italy.
5. Defiled. In a note Byron refers to *Macbeth* III.i.65 ("For Banquo's issue have I filed my mind").

114

I have not loved the world, nor the world me—
But let us part fair foes; I do believe,
Though I have found them not, that there may be   1060
Words which are things, hopes which will not deceive,
And virtues which are merciful nor weave
Snares for the failing: I would also deem
O'er others' griefs that some sincerely grieve;
That two, or one, are almost what they seem—   1065
That goodness is no name, and happiness no dream.

115

My daughter! with thy name this song begun—
My daughter! with thy name thus much shall end!—
I see thee not—I hear thee not—but none
Can be so wrapped in thee; thou art the friend   1070
To whom the shadows of far years extend:
Albeit my brow thou never shouldst behold,
My voice shall with thy future visions blend,
And reach into thy heart—when mine is cold—
A token and a tone even from thy father's mold.   1075

116

To aid thy mind's development—to watch
Thy dawn of little joys—to sit and see
Almost thy very growth—to view thee catch
Knowledge of objects—wonders yet to thee!
To hold thee lightly on a gentle knee,   1080
And print on thy soft cheek a parent's kiss—
This, it should seem, was not reserved for me;
Yet this was in my nature—as it is,
I know not what is there, yet something like to this.

117

Yet, though dull Hate as duty should be taught,   1085
I know that thou wilt love me; though my name
Should be shut from thee, as a spell still fraught
With desolation, and a broken claim;
Though the grave closed between us—'twere the same;
I know that thou wilt love me; though to drain   1090
My blood from out thy being were an aim
And an attainment—all would be in vain—
Still thou wouldst love me, still that more than life retain.

118

The child of love—though born in bitterness
And nurtured in convulsion! Of thy sire   1095
These were the elements, and thine no less.
As yet such are around thee, but thy fire
Shall be more tempered and thy hope far higher.
Sweet be thy cradled slumbers! O'er the sea,
And from the mountains where I now respire,   1100
Fain would I waft such blessing upon thee,
As, with a sigh, I deem thou mightst have been to me!

From *Canto IV*

1

I stood in Venice, on the Bridge of Sighs,[1]
A palace and a prison on each hand:
I saw from out the wave her structures rise
As from the stroke of the enchanter's wand:
A thousand years their cloudy wings expand   5
Around me, and a dying Glory smiles
O'er the far times, when many a subject land
Looked to the wingéd Lion's[2] marble piles,
Where Venice sate in state, throned on her hundred isles!

2

She looks a sea Cybele,[3] fresh from ocean,   10
Rising with her tiara of proud towers
At airy distance, with majestic motion,
A ruler of the waters and their powers:
And such she was—her daughters had their dowers
From spoils of nations, and the exhaustless East   15
Poured in her lap all gems in sparkling showers:
In purple was she robed, and of her feast
Monarchs partook, and deemed their dignity increased.

3

In Venice Tasso's echoes are no more,
And silent rows the songless gondolier;[4]   20
Her palaces are crumbling to the shore,
And music meets not always now the ear:
Those days are gone—but Beauty still is here;
States fall, arts fade—but Nature doth not die,
Nor yet forget how Venice once was dear,   25
The pleasant place of all festivity,
The revel of the earth, the masque of Italy![5]

4

But unto us she hath a spell beyond
Her name in story, and her long array
Of mighty shadows, whose dim forms despond   30
Above the dogeless city's[6] vanished sway:
Ours is a trophy which will not decay
With the Rialto;[7] Shylock and the Moor
And Pierre cannot be swept or worn away—

1. A covered bridge between the Doge's Palace and the prison of San Marco.
2. The emblem of St. Mark, patron saint of Venice.
3. A nature goddess, sometimes represented wearing a crown ("tiara") of towers.
4. The gondoliers once had the custom of chanting stanzas of Tasso's *Jerusalem Delivered*.
5. "Masques" were lavish dramatic entertainments popular in the courts of the Renaissance, involving songs, dances, and elaborate costumes and staging.
6. The last duke ("doge") of Venice was deposed by Napoleon in 1797.
7. The business district in Venice, a setting in *The Merchant of Venice* and *Othello* ("the Moor"), and also in Thomas Otway's tragedy, *Venice Preserved* (1682), in which Pierre (line 34) is a leading character.

The keystones of the arch! though all were o'er,   35
For us repeopled were[8] the solitary shore.

* * *

132[9]

And thou, who never yet of human wrong   1180
Left the unbalanced scale, great Nemesis!
Here, where the ancient paid thee homage long—
Thou, who didst call the Furies from the abyss,
And round Orestes[1] bade them howl and hiss
For that unnatural retribution—just,   1185
Had it but been from hands less near—in this
Thy former realm, I call thee from the dust!
Dost thou not hear my heart?—Awake! thou shalt, and must.

133

It is not that I may not have incurred,
For my ancestral faults or mine, the wound   1190
I bleed withal, and, had it been conferred
With a just weapon, it had flowed unbound;
But now my blood shall not sink in the ground;
To thee I do devote it—*thou* shalt take
The vengeance, which shall yet be sought and found,[2]   1195
Which if *I* have not taken for the sake—
But let that pass—I sleep, but thou shalt yet awake.

134

And if my voice break forth, 'tis not that now
I shrink from what is suffered: let him speak
Who hath beheld decline upon my brow,   1200
Or seen my mind's convulsion leave it weak:
But in this page a record will I seek.
Not in the air shall these my words disperse,
Though I be ashes; a far hour shall wreak
The deep prophetic fullness of this verse,   1205
And pile on human heads the mountain of my curse!

135

That curse shall be Forgiveness.—Have I not—
Hear me, my mother Earth! behold it, Heaven!—
Have I not had to wrestle with my lot?
Have I not suffered things to be forgiven?   1210
Have I not had my brain seared, my heart riven,
Hopes sapped, name blighted, Life's life lied away?
And only not to desperation driven,
Because not altogether of such clay
As rots into the souls of those whom I survey.   1215

8. Would be.
9. Harold has journeyed from Venice
through Ferrara and Florence to Rome.
In this city he invokes (line 1181) the
Greek and Roman goddess Nemesis,
who represented divine retribution for
human transgressions, especially for
presumption against the gods.

1. The Furies pursued Orestes for killing his mother Clytemnestra, in order
to avenge her murder of his father
Agamemnon when he had returned from
the Trojan war.
2. Harold calls on Nemesis to avenge
the injustices which have driven him
into his exiled wandering.

136

From mighty wrongs to petty perfidy
Have I not seen what human things could do?
From the loud roar of foaming calumny
To the small whisper of the as paltry few,
And subtler venom of the reptile crew,   1220
The Janus glance[3] of whose significant eye,
Learning to lie with silence, would *seem* true,
And without utterance, save the shrug or sigh,
Deal round to happy fools its speechless obloquy.

137

But I have lived, and have not lived in vain: 1225
My mind may lose its force, my blood its fire,
And my frame perish even in conquering pain;
But there is that within me which shall tire
Torture and Time, and breathe when I expire;
Something unearthly which they deem not of,   1230
Like the remembered tone of a mute lyre,
Shall on their softened spirits sink, and move
In hearts all rocky now the late remorse of love.

*   *   *

175

But I forget.—My Pilgrim's shrine is won,[4]
And he and I must part—so let it be—
His task and mine alike are nearly done;
Yet once more let us look upon the sea;   1570
The midland ocean breaks on him and me,
And from the Alban Mount we now behold
Our friend of youth, that ocean,[5] which when we
Beheld it last by Calpe's rock[6] unfold
Those waves, we followed on till the dark Euxine rolled   1575

176

Upon the blue Symplegades.[7] Long years—
Long, though not very many—since have done
Their work on both; some suffering and some tears
Have left us nearly where we had begun:
Yet not in vain our mortal race hath run;   1580
We have had our reward, and it is here—
That we can yet feel gladdened by the sun,
And reap from earth, sea, joy almost as dear
As if there were no man to trouble what is clear.

3. I.e., facing both ways. In Roman mythology Janus was represented with two faces, looking both before and behind.
4. I.e., Harold has reached the goal of his religious pilgrimage.
5. Harold is standing on an Alban hill, looking over the Roman Campagna to the Mediterranean. In its concluding

passage (lines 1573 ff.) the poem thus rounds back to Harold's initial voyage, when he had first looked upon that sea.
6. The Rock of Gibraltar.
7. Two islands situated at the place where the Black Sea flows into the Bosphorus Strait. "Euxine": Greek name for the Black Sea.

177

Oh! that the Desert were my dwelling place,   1585
With one fair Spirit for my minister,
That I might all forget the human race,
And, hating no one, love but only her!
Ye Elements!—in whose ennobling stir
I feel myself exalted—Can ye not   1590
Accord me such a being?   Do I err
In deeming such inhabit many a spot?
Though with them to converse can rarely be our lot.

178

There is a pleasure in the pathless woods,
There is a rapture on the lonely shore,
There is society where none intrudes,   1595
By the deep sea, and music in its roar:
I love not Man the less, but Nature more,
From these our interviews, in which I steal
From all I may be, or have been before,   1600
To mingle with the Universe, and feel
What I can ne'er express, yet can not all conceal.

179

Roll on, thou deep and dark blue Ocean—roll!
Ten thousand fleets sweep over thee in vain;
Man marks the earth with ruin—his control   1605
Stops with the shore; upon the watery plain
The wrecks are all thy deed, nor doth remain
A shadow of man's ravage, save his own,
When, for a moment, like a drop of rain,
He sinks into thy depths with bubbling groan,   1610
Without a grave, unknelled, uncoffined, and unknown.

180

His steps are not upon thy paths—thy fields
Are not a spoil for him—thou dost arise
And shake him from thee; the vile strength he wields
For earth's destruction thou dost all despise,   1615
Spurning him from thy bosom to the skies,
And send'st him, shivering in thy playful spray
And howling, to his Gods, where haply lies
His petty hope in some near port or bay,
And dashest him again to earth—there let him lay.[8]   1620

181

The armaments which thunderstrike the walls
Of rock-built cities, bidding nations quake
And monarchs tremble in their capitals,
The oak leviathans,[1] whose huge ribs make

---

8. For "lie." Denounced by many critics, this has been called the most notorious solecism in English poetry. But
Byron, like other English aristocrats of
the time, deliberately affected a cavalier
indifference to commonplace grammar.
1. Warships.

Their clay creator the vain title take 1625
Of lord of thee, and arbiter of war—
These are thy toys, and, as the snowy flake,
They melt into thy yeast of waves, which mar
Alike the Armada's pride or spoils of Trafalgar.[2]

182

Thy shores are empires, changed in all save thee— 1630
Assyria, Greece, Rome, Carthage, what are they?
Thy waters washed them power while they were free,
And many a tyrant since; their shores obey
The stranger, slave, or savage; their decay
Has dried up realms to deserts—not so thou, 1635
Unchangeable save to thy wild waves' play;
Time writes no wrinkle on thine azure brow—
Such as creation's dawn beheld, thou rollest now.

183

Thou glorious mirror, where the Almighty's form
Glasses[3] itself in tempests; in all time, 1640
Calm or convulsed—in breeze, or gale, or storm,
Icing the pole, or in the torrid clime
Dark-heaving—boundless, endless, and sublime—
The image of Eternity—the throne
Of the Invisible; even from out thy slime 1645
The monsters of the deep are made; each zone
Obeys thee; thou goest forth, dread, fathomless, alone.

184

And I have loved thee, Ocean! and my joy
Of youthful sports was on thy breast to be
Borne, like thy bubbles, onward: from a boy 1650
I wantoned with thy breakers—they to me
Were a delight; and if the freshening sea
Made them a terror—'twas a pleasing fear,
For I was as it were a child of thee,
And trusted to thy billows far and near, 1655
And laid my hand upon thy mane—as I do here.

185

My task is done—my song hath ceased—my theme
Has died into an echo; it is fit
The spell should break of this protracted dream.
The torch shall be extinguished which hath lit 1660
My midnight lamp—and what is writ, is writ—
Would it were worthier! but I am not now
That which I have been—and my visions flit
Less palpably before me—and the glow
Which in my spirit dwelt is fluttering, faint, and low. 1665

2. The Spanish Armada, defeated by the English in 1588, lost many ships in a storm; another storm was responsible for the loss of a number of French ships that Nelson had captured at Trafalgar (1805).
3. Mirrors.

186
Farewell! a word that must be, and hath been—
A sound which makes us linger—yet—farewell!
Ye! who have traced the Pilgrim to the scene
Which is his last, if in your memories dwell
A thought which once was his, if on ye swell   1670
A single recollection, not in vain
He wore his sandal shoon and scallop shell;[4]
Farewell! with *him* alone may rest the pain,
If such there were—with *you*, the moral of his strain!

1812, 1816, 1818

4. Sandals and a scallop shell (worn on the hat) were traditional emblems of pilgrims to holy shrines.

Manfred   *Manfred* is Byron's first dramatic work. As its subtitle, "A Dramatic Poem," indicates, it was not intended to be produced on the stage; Byron also referred to it as a "metaphysical" drama—i.e., a drama of ideas. He began writing it in the autumn of 1816 while living in the Swiss Alps, whose austere grandeur stimulated his imagination; he finished the drama the following year in Italy.

Manfred's literary forebears include the villains of Gothic fiction and melodrama; the Greek Titan Prometheus, rebel against the deity; Milton's fallen angel, Satan; Ahasuerus, the legendary Wandering Jew who, having ridiculed Christ as he bore the Cross to Calvary, is doomed to live until Christ's Second Coming; and the story of Faust, who yielded his soul to the devil in order to gain superhuman powers. Byron denied that he had ever heard of Marlowe's *Doctor Faustus*, and since he knew no German, he had not read Goethe's *Faust*, of which Part I had been published in 1808. But Byron's friend, M. G. Lewis (author of the Gothic novel *The Monk*), had read parts of *Faust* to Byron in extempore translation during the summer of 1816, just before Byron composed *Manfred*, and Byron worked his memories of this oral translation into his own drama in a way which evoked Goethe's admiration.

Like Byron's earlier heroes, *Childe Harold* and the protagonists of some of his verse romances, Manfred is hounded by remorse for a transgression which (it is hinted but never quite specified) is incest with his sister Astarte; it is also hinted that Astarte has taken her own life. While this element in the drama is often regarded as Byron's veiled confession of his incestuous relations with his half sister, Augusta Leigh, we should take into account that the theme of incest was a common one in Gothic fiction and in the writings of major Romantic authors such as Goethe, Chateaubriand, Scott, and Shelley.

The character of Manfred is its author's supreme representation of the Byronic Hero. Byron's great invention is to have Manfred, unlike Faust, disdainfully reject the offer of a pact with the powers of darkness. He thereby sets himself up as the totally autonomous man, independent of the authority of society or any external power, whose own mind, as he says in the concluding scene (III.iv.127–40), generates the values by which he lives "in sufferance or in joy," and by reference to which he judges, requites, and finally destroys himself. In his book *Ecce Homo* Nietzsche, recognizing Byron's anticipation of his own *Uebermensch* (who posits for himself a moral code beyond the inherited standards of good and evil), asserted that the character of Manfred is greater than that of Goethe's Faust.

Manfred

A DRAMATIC POEM

"There are more things in heaven and earth, Horatio,
Than are dreamt of in your philosophy."[1]

Dramatis Personae

MANFRED	WITCH OF THE ALPS
CHAMOIS HUNTER	ARIMANES
ABBOT OF ST. MAURICE	NEMESIS
MANUEL	THE DESTINIES
HERMAN	SPIRITS, ETC.

The scene of the Drama is amongst the Higher Alps—partly in the Castle of Manfred, and partly in the Mountains.

Act I

SCENE I. MANFRED *alone.—Scene, a Gothic Gallery.*[2]*—Time, Midnight.*

MANFRED. The lamp must be replenished, but even then
    It will not burn so long as I must watch:
    My slumbers—if I slumber—are not sleep,
    But a continuance of enduring thought,
    Which then I can resist not: in my heart   5
    There is a vigil, and these eyes but close
    To look within; and yet I live, and bear
    The aspect and the form of breathing men.
    But grief should be the instructor of the wise;
    Sorrow is knowledge: they who know the most   10
    Must mourn the deepest o'er the fatal truth,
    The Tree of Knowledge is not that of Life.
    Philosophy and science, and the springs
    Of wonder, and the wisdom of the world,
    I have essayed, and in my mind there is   15
    A power to make these subject to itself—
    But they avail not: I have done men good,
    And I have met with good even among men—
    But this availed not: I have had my foes,
    And none have baffled, many fallen before me—   20

1. *Hamlet* I.v. 166–67.
2. I.e., a large chamber built in the medieval Gothic style with high, pointed arches.

But this availed not:—Good, or evil, life,
Powers, passions, all I see in other beings,
Have been to me as rain unto the sands,
Since that all-nameless hour. I have no dread,   *It is different from other men.*
And feel the curse to have no natural fear,   25
Nor fluttering throb, that beats with hopes or wishes,
Or lurking love of something on the earth.
Now to my task.—
               Mysterious Agency!
Ye spirits of the unbounded Universe,
Whom I have sought in darkness and in light—
Ye, who do compass earth about, and dwell   30
In subtler essence—ye, to whom the tops   *He conjures.*
Of mountains inaccessible are haunts,
And earth's and ocean's caves familiar things—
I call upon ye by the written charm   35
Which gives me power upon you—Rise! appear!   [*A pause.*]
They come not yet.—Now by the voice of him
Who is the first among you[3]—by this sign,
Which makes you tremble—by the claims of him
Who is undying[4]—Rise! appear!—Appear!   [*A pause.*]
If it be so.—Spirits of earth and air,
Ye shall not thus elude me: by a power,
Deeper than all yet urged, a tyrant-spell,
Which had its birthplace in a star condemned,
The burning wreck of a demolished world,   45
A wandering hell in the eternal space;
By the strong curse which is upon my soul,
The thought which is within me and around me,
I do compel ye to my will.—Appear!

    [*A star is seen at the darker end of the gallery: it is stationary; and a voice is heard singing.*]

               FIRST SPIRIT[5] *See note.*

      Mortal! to thy bidding bowed,   50
      From my mansion in the cloud,
      Which the breath of twilight builds,
      And the summer's sunset gilds
      With the azure and vermilion
      Which is mixed for my pavilion;   55
      Though thy quest may be forbidden,
      On a star-beam I have ridden;
      To thine adjuration bowed;
      Mortal—be thy wish avowed!

3. Arimanes, who appears in II.iv, below.
4. Probably God, to whom traditional magic conjurations often allude.
5. The Spirits, successively, are those of the Air, Mountain, Ocean, Earth, Winds, Night, and Manfred's guiding Star.

Voice of the SECOND SPIRIT

Mont Blanc is the monarch of mountains;   60
   They crowned him long ago
On a throne of rocks, in a robe of clouds,
   With a diadem of snow.
Around his waist are forests braced,
   The Avalanche in his hand;   65
But ere it fall, that thundering ball
   Must pause for my command.
The Glacier's cold and restless mass
   Moves onward day by day;
But I am he who bids it pass,   70
   Or with its ice delay.
I am the spirit of the place,
   Could make the mountain bow
And quiver to his caverned base—
   And what with me wouldst *Thou?*   75

Voice of the THIRD SPIRIT

In the blue depth of the waters,
   Where the wave hath no strife,
Where the wind is a stranger,
   And the sea-snake hath life,
Where the Mermaid is decking   80
   Her green hair with shells;
Like the storm on the surface
   Came the sound of thy spells;
O'er my calm Hall of Coral
   The deep echo rolled—   85
To the Spirit of Ocean
   Thy wishes unfold!

FOURTH SPIRIT

Where the slumbering earthquake
   Lies pillowed on fire,
And the lakes of bitumen   90
   Rise boilingly higher;
Where the roots of the Andes
   Strike deep in the earth,
As their summits to heaven
   Shoot soaringly forth;   95
I have quitted my birthplace,
   Thy bidding to bide—
Thy spell hath subdued me,
   Thy will be my guide!

FIFTH SPIRIT

I am the Rider of the wind,   100
   The Stirrer of the storm;
The hurricane I left behind

Is yet with lightning warm;
To speed to thee, o'er shore and sea
  I swept upon the blast: 105
The fleet I met sailed well, and yet
'Twill sink ere night be past.

SIXTH SPIRIT

My dwelling is the shadow of the night,
Why doth thy magic torture me with light?

SEVENTH SPIRIT

The star which rules thy destiny   110
Was ruled, ere earth began, by me:
It was a world as fresh and fair
As e'er revolved round sun in air;
Its course was free and regular,
Space bosomed not a lovelier star.   115
The hour arrived—and it became
A wandering mass of shapeless flame,
A pathless comet, and a curse,
The menace of the universe;
Still rolling on with innate force,   120
Without a sphere, without a course,
A bright deformity on high,
The monster of the upper sky!
And thou! beneath its influence born—
Thou worm! whom I obey and scorn—   125
Forced by a power (which is not thine,
And lent thee but to make thee mine)
For this brief moment to descend,
Where these weak spirits round thee bend
And parley with a thing like thee—   130
What wouldst thou, Child of Clay! with me?

THE SEVEN SPIRITS

Earth, ocean, air, night, mountains, winds, thy star,
  Are at thy beck and bidding, Child of Clay!
Before thee at thy quest their spirits are—
  What wouldst thou with us, son of mortals—say?   135

MANFRED. Forgetfulness—
FIRST SPIRIT. Of what—of whom—and why?
MANFRED. Of that which is within me; read it there—
  Ye know it, and I cannot utter it.
SPIRIT. We can but give thee that which we possess:
  Ask of us subjects, sovereignty, the power   140
O'er earth, the whole, or portion, or a sign
Which shall control the elements, whereof
We are the dominators—each and all,
These shall be thine.

MANFRED.   Oblivion, self-oblivion—
  Can ye not wring from out the hidden realms   145
  Ye offer so profusely what I ask?
SPIRIT. It is not in our essence, in our skill;
  But—thou mayst die.
MANFRED.   Will death bestow it on me?
SPIRIT. We are immortal, and do not forget;
  We are eternal; and to us the past   150
  Is as the future, present. Art thou answered?
MANFRED. Ye mock me—but the power which brought ye here
  Hath made you mine. Slaves, scoff not at my will!
  The mind, the spirit, the Promethean spark,[6]
  The lightning of my being, is as bright,   155
  Pervading, and far darting as your own,
  And shall not yield to yours, though cooped in clay!
  Answer, or I will teach you what I am.
SPIRIT. We answer as we answered; our reply
  Is even in thine own words.
MANFRED.   Why say ye so?   160
SPIRIT. If, as thou say'st, thine essence be as ours,
  We have replied in telling thee, the thing
  Mortals call death hath naught to do with us.
MANFRED. I then have called ye from your realms in vain;
  Ye cannot, or ye will not, aid me.
SPIRIT.   Say;   165
  What we possess we offer; it is thine:
  Bethink ere thou dismiss us, ask again—
  Kingdom, and sway, and strength, and length of days—
MANFRED. Accurséd! what have I to do with days?
  They are too long already.—Hence—begone!   170
SPIRIT.   Yet pause: being here, our will would do thee service;
  Bethink thee, is there then no other gift
  Which we can make not worthless in thine eyes?
MANFRED. No, none: yet stay—one moment, ere we part—
  I would behold ye face to face. I hear   175
  Your voices, sweet and melancholy sounds,
  As music on the waters; and I see
  The steady aspect of a clear large star;
  But nothing more. Approach me as ye are,
  Or one, or all, in your accustomed forms.   180
SPIRIT. We have no forms, beyond the elements
  Of which we are the mind and principle:
  But choose a form—in that we will appear.
MANFRED. I have no choice; there is no form on earth
  Hideous or beautiful to me. Let him,   185
  Who is most powerful of ye, take such aspect
  As unto him may seem most fitting—Come!

6. In Greek myth, Prometheus molded man from clay, and stole fire from
heaven in order to give it to men.

SEVENTH SPIRIT [*appearing in the shape of a beautiful female figure*].[7] Behold!

MANFRED.   Oh God! if it be thus, and *thou*
Art not a madness and a mockery,
I yet might be most happy. I will clasp thee,   190
And we again will be—   [*The figure vanishes.*]
         My heart is crushed!
             [MANFRED *falls senseless.*]

[*A Voice is heard in the Incantation[8] which follows.*]
     When the moon is on the wave,
       And the glowworm in the grass,
     And the meteor on the grave,
       And the wisp on the morass;   195
     When the falling stars are shooting,
     And the answered owls are hooting,
     And the silent leaves are still
     In the shadow of the hill,
     Shall my soul be upon thine,   200
     With a power and with a sign.

[handwritten margin note: Is this a catalogue of the cond'/ion of the guilty man?]

     Though thy slumber may be deep,
     Yet thy spirit shall not sleep;
     There are shades which will not vanish,
     There are thoughts thou canst not banish;   205
     By a power to thee unknown,
     Thou canst never be alone;
     Thou art wrapt as with a shroud,
     Thou art gathered in a cloud;
     And forever shalt thou dwell   210
     In the spirit of this spell.

[handwritten margin note: Manfred's curse.]

     Though thou seest me not pass by,
     Thou shalt feel me with thine eye
     As a thing that, though unseen,
     Must be near thee, and hath been;   215
     And when in that secret dread
     Thou hast turned around thy head,
     Thou shalt marvel I am not
     As thy shadow on the spot,
     And the power which thou dost feel   220
     Shall be what thou must conceal.

     And a magic voice and verse
     Hath baptized thee with a curse;

---

7. This shape may be a simulacrum of Astarte, whose phantom appears in II.iii.97; it probably represents, however, the ideal of the beautiful and good that Manfred had pursued in his uncorrupted youth.

8. Byron had published this "Incantation" as a separate poem, six months before *Manfred*.

And a spirit of the air
Hath begirt thee with a snare;   225
In the wind there is a voice
Shall forbid thee to rejoice;
And to thee shall Night deny
All the quiet of her sky;
And the day shall have a sun,   230
Which shall make thee wish it done.

From thy false tears I did distill
An essence which hath strength to kill;
From thy own heart I then did wring
The black blood in its blackest spring;   235
From thy own smile I snatched the snake,
For there it coiled as in a brake;[9]
From thy own lip I drew the charm
Which gave all these their chiefest harm;
In proving every poison known,   240
I found the strongest was thine own.

By thy cold breast and serpent smile,
By thy unfathomed gulfs of guile,
By that most seeming virtuous eye,
By thy shut soul's hypocrisy;   245
By the perfection of thine art
Which passed for human thine own heart;
By thy delight in others' pain,
And by thy brotherhood of Cain,[1]
I call upon thee! and compel   250
Thyself to be thy proper Hell!

And on thy head I pour the vial
Which doth devote thee to this trial;
Nor to slumber, nor to die,
Shall be in thy destiny;   255
Though thy death shall still seem near
To thy wish, but as a fear;
Lo! the spell now works around thee,
And the clankless chain hath bound thee;
O'er thy heart and brain together   260
Hath the word been passed—now wither!

SCENE II. *The Mountain of the Jungfrau.*[2]—*Time, Morning.*—
       MANFRED *alone upon the Cliffs.*

MANFRED. The spirits I have raised abandon me,
    The spells which I have studied baffle me,
    The remedy I recked of tortured me;

9. Thicket.
1. I.e., by your kinship with Cain, who murdered his brother Abel.
2. A high Alpine mountain in south-central Switzerland.

I lean no more on superhuman aid,
It hath no power upon the past, and for   5
The future, till the past be gulfed in darkness,
It is not of my search.—My mother Earth!
And thou fresh breaking Day, and you, ye Mountains,
Why are ye beautiful? I cannot love ye.
And thou, the bright eye of the universe,   10
That openest over all, and unto all
Art a delight—thou shin'st not on my heart.
And you, ye crags, upon whose extreme edge
I stand, and on the torrent's brink beneath
Behold the tall pines dwindled as to shrubs   15
In dizziness of distance; when a leap,
A stir, a motion, even a breath, would bring
My breast upon its rocky bosom's bed
To rest forever—wherefore do I pause?
I feel the impulse—yet I do not plunge;   20
I see the peril—yet do not recede;
And my brain reels—and yet my foot is firm.
There is a power upon me which withholds,
And makes it my fatality to live;
If it be life to wear within myself   25
This barrenness of spirit, and to be
My own soul's sepulcher, for I have ceased
To justify my deeds unto myself—
The last infirmity of evil. Ay,
Thou wingéd and cloud-cleaving minister,   [*An eagle passes.*]
Whose happy flight is highest into heaven,   31
Well may'st thou swoop so near me—I should be
Thy prey, and gorge thine eaglets; thou art gone
Where the eye cannot follow thee; but thine
Yet pierces downward, onward, or above,   35
With a pervading vision.—Beautiful!
How beautiful is all this visible world!
How glorious in its action and itself!
But we, who name ourselves its sovereigns, we,
Half dust, half deity, alike unfit   40
To sink or soar, with our mixed essence make
A conflict of its elements, and breathe
The breath of degradation and of pride,
Contending with low wants and lofty will,
Till our mortality predominates,   45
And men are—what they name not to themselves,
And trust not to each other. Hark! the note,
          [*The Shepherd's pipe in the distance is heard.*]
The natural music of the mountain reed—
For here the patriarchal days[3] are not
A pastoral fable—pipes in the liberal[4] air,   50

(margin annotation: Manfred can see but not really appreciate beauty.)

(margin annotation: Manfred's view of mankind.)

---

3. I.e., the days of the Old Testament   4. Free-moving.
patriarchs, who were shepherds.

Mixed with the sweet bells of the sauntering herd;
My soul would drink those echoes.—Oh, that I were
The viewless[5] spirit of a lovely sound,
A living voice, a breathing harmony,
A bodiless enjoyment—born and dying   55
With the blessed tone which made me!

Enter from below a CHAMOIS[6] HUNTER.

CHAMOIS HUNTER.   Even so
This way the chamois leaped: her nimble feet
Have baffled me; my gains today will scarce
Repay my breakneck travail.—What is here?
Who seems not of my trade, and yet hath reached   60
A height which none even of our mountaineers,
Save our best hunters, may attain: his garb
Is goodly, his mien manly, and his air
Proud as a freeborn peasant's, at this distance—
I will approach him nearer.

MANFRED [*not perceiving the other*]. To be thus—   65
Gray-haired with anguish, like these blasted pines,
Wrecks of a single winter, barkless, branchless,
A blighted trunk upon a curséd root,
Which but supplies a feeling to decay—
And to be thus, eternally but thus,   70
Having been otherwise! Now furrowed o'er
With wrinkles, plowed by moments, not by years
And hours—all tortured into ages—hours
Which I outlive!—Ye toppling crags of ice!
Ye avalanches, whom a breath draws down   75
In mountainous o'erwhelming, come and crush me!
I hear ye momently above, beneath,
Crash with a frequent conflict; but ye pass,
And only fall on things that still would live;
On the young flourishing forest, or the hut   80
And hamlet of the harmless villager.

CHAMOIS HUNTER. The mists begin to rise from up the valley;
I'll warn him to descend, or he may chance
To lose at once his way and life together.

MANFRED. The mists boil up around the glaciers; clouds   85
Rise curling fast beneath me, white and sulphury,
Like foam from the roused ocean of deep Hell,
Whose every wave breaks on a living shore
Heaped with the damned like pebbles.—I am giddy.

CHAMOIS HUNTER. I must approach him cautiously; if near,   90
A sudden step will startle him, and he
Seems tottering already.

MANFRED.   Mountains have fallen,
Leaping a gap in the clouds, and with the shock

---

5. Invisible.
6. A goatlike antelope, found in the high regions of European mountains.

Rocking their Alpine brethren; filling up
The ripe green valleys with destruction's splinters;   95
Damming the rivers with a sudden dash,
Which crushed the waters into mist, and made
Their fountains find another channel—thus,
Thus, in its old age, did Mount Rosenberg[7]—
Why stood I not beneath it?
CHAMOIS HUNTER.   Friend! have a care,   100
Your next step may be fatal!—for the love   *Good, God-fearing man,*
Of him who made you, stand not on that brink!
MANFRED [*not hearing him*]. Such would have been for me a
    fitting tomb;
My bones had then been quiet in their depth;
They had not then been strewn upon the rocks   105
For the wind's pastime—as thus—thus they shall be—
In this one plunge.—Farewell, ye opening heavens!
Look not upon me thus reproachfully—
Ye were not meant for me—Earth! take these atoms!
    [*As* MANFRED *is in act to spring from the cliff, the* CHAM-
    OIS HUNTER *seizes and retains him with a sudden grasp.*]
CHAMOIS HUNTER. Hold, madman!—though aweary of thy life,
Stain not our pure vales with thy guilty blood!   *Chamois Hunter has*
Away with me—I will not quit my hold.   *reverence for life.*
MANFRED. I am most sick at heart—nay, grasp me not—
I am all feebleness—the mountains whirl
Spinning around me—I grow blind—What art thou?   115
CHAMOIS HUNTER. I'll answer that anon.—Away with me!   *Leads Manfred*
The clouds grow thicker—there—now lean on me—   *to safety.*
Place your foot here—here, take this staff, and cling
A moment to that shrub—now give me your hand,
And hold fast by my girdle—softly—well—   120
The Chalet will be gained within an hour—
Come on, we'll quickly find a surer footing,
And something like a pathway, which the torrent
Hath washed since winter.—Come, 'tis bravely done;
You should have been a hunter.—Follow me.   125
    [*As they descend the rocks with difficulty, the scene
    closes.*]

Act II

SCENE I. *A Cottage amongst the Bernese Alps.*[8] MANFRED *and
    the* CHAMOIS HUNTER.

CHAMOIS HUNTER. No, no—yet pause—thou must not yet go
    forth:
Thy mind and body are alike unfit

7. In 1806, ten years before the composition of *Manfred*, a huge landslide
on Mount Rossberg, which Byron calls
"Rosenberg", had destroyed four villages and killed 457 people.
8. A mountain range in south-central
Switzerland.

To trust each other, for some hours, at least;
When thou art better, I will be thy guide—
But whither?

MANFRED.　　It imports not; I do know　　5
My route full well and need no further guidance.

CHAMOIS HUNTER. Thy garb and gait bespeak thee of high
　　lineage—
One of the many chiefs, whose castled crags
Look o'er the lower valleys—which of these
May call thee lord? I only know their portals;　　10
My way of life leads me but rarely down
To bask by the huge hearths of those old halls,
Carousing with the vassals; but the paths,
Which step from out our mountains to their doors,
I know from childhood—which of these is thine?　　15

MANFRED. No matter.

CHAMOIS HUNTER.　　Well, sir, pardon me the question,
And be of better cheer. Come, taste my wine;
'Tis of an ancient vintage; many a day
'T has thawed my veins among our glaciers, now
Let it do thus for thine—Come, pledge me fairly.　　20

MANFRED. Away, away! there's blood upon the brim!
Will it then never—never sink in the earth?

CHAMOIS HUNTER. What dost thou mean? thy senses wander
　　from thee.

MANFRED. I say 'tis blood—my blood! the pure warm stream
Which ran in the veins of my fathers, and in ours　　25
When we were in our youth, and had one heart,
And loved each other as we should not love,
And this was shed: but still it rises up,
Coloring the clouds, that shut me out from heaven,
Where thou art not—and I shall never be.　　30

CHAMOIS HUNTER. Man of strange words, and some half-mad-
　　dening sin,
Which makes thee people vacancy, whate'er
Thy dread and sufferance be, there's comfort yet—
The aid of holy men, and heavenly patience—

MANFRED. Patience and patience! Hence—that word was made
For brutes of burthen, not for birds of prey;
Preach it to mortals of a dust like thine,—
I am not of thine order.

CHAMOIS HUNTER.　　Thanks to heaven!
I would not be of thine for the free fame
Of William Tell;[9] but whatsoe'er thine ill,　　40
It must be borne, and these wild starts are useless.

MANFRED. Do I not bear it?—Look on me—I live.

CHAMOIS HUNTER. This is convulsion, and no healthful life.

---

9. William Tell was the hero who, according to legend, liberated Switzer-land from Austrian oppression in the 14th century.

MANFRED. I tell thee, man! I have lived many years,
Many long years, but they are nothing now   45
To those which I must number: ages—ages—
Space and eternity—and consciousness,
With the fierce thirst of death—and still unslaked!
CHAMOIS HUNTER. Why, on thy brow the seal of middle age
Hath scarce been set; I am thine elder far.   50
MANFRED. Think'st thou existence doth depend on time?
It doth; but actions are our epochs: mine
Have made my days and nights imperishable,
Endless, and all alike, as sands on the shore,
Innumerable atoms, and one desert,   55
Barren and cold, on which the wild waves break,
But nothing rests, save carcasses and wrecks,
Rocks, and the salt-surf weeds of bitterness.
CHAMOIS HUNTER. Alas! he's mad—but yet I must not leave him.
MANFRED. I would I were—for then the things I see   60
Would be but a distempered dream.
CHAMOIS HUNTER.   What is it
That thou dost see, or think thou look'st upon?
MANFRED. Myself, and thee—a peasant of the Alps,
Thy humble virtues, hospitable home,
And spirit patient, pious, proud and free;   65
Thy self-respect, grafted on innocent thoughts;
Thy days of health, and nights of sleep; thy toils,
By danger dignified, yet guiltless; hopes
Of cheerful old age and a quiet grave,
With cross and garland over its green turf,   70
And thy grandchildren's love for epitaph;
This do I see—and then I look within—
It matters not—my soul was scorched already!
CHAMOIS HUNTER. And wouldst thou then exchange thy lot for
     mine?
MANFRED. No, friend! I would not wrong thee, nor exchange   75
My lot with living being: I can bear—
However wretchedly, 'tis still to bear—
In life what others could not brook to dream,
But perish in their slumber.
CHAMOIS HUNTER.   And with this—
This cautious feeling for another's pain,   80
Canst thou be black with evil?—say not so.
Can one of gentle thoughts have wreak'd revenge
Upon his enemies?
MANFRED.   Oh! no, no, no!
My injuries came down on those who loved me—
On those whom I best loved: I never quelled[1]   85
An enemy, save in my just defense—
But my embrace was fatal.

1. Killed.

CHAMOIS HUNTER.   Heaven give thee rest!
And penitence restore thee to thyself;
My prayers shall be for thee.

MANFRED.   I need them not,
But can endure thy pity. I depart—   90
'Tis time—farewell!—Here's gold, and thanks for thee;
No words—it is thy due. Follow me not;
I know my path—the mountain peril's past:
And once again, I charge thee, follow not!   [*Exit* MANFRED.]

SCENE II. *A lower Valley in the Alps.—A Cataract.*

Enter MANFRED.

It is not noon; the sunbow's rays still arch
The torrent with the many hues of heaven,
And roll the sheeted silver's waving column
O'er the crag's headlong perpendicular,
And fling its lines of foaming light along,   5
And to and fro, like the pale courser's tail,
The Giant steed, to be bestrode by Death,
As told in the Apocalypse.[2] No eyes
But mine now drink this sight of loveliness;
I should be sole in this sweet solitude,   10
And with the Spirit of the place divide
The homage of these waters.—I will call her.

[MANFRED *takes some of the water into the palm of his*
hand, and flings it in the air, muttering the adjuration.
After a pause, the WITCH OF THE ALPS *rises beneath the*
arch of the sunbow of the torrent.]

Beautiful Spirit! with thy hair of light,
And dazzling eyes of glory, in whose form
The charms of earth's least mortal daughters grow   15
To an unearthly stature, in an essence
Of purer elements; while the hues of youth
—Carnationed like a sleeping infant's cheek
Rocked by the beating of her mother's heart,
Or the rose tints, which summer's twilight leaves   20
Upon the lofty glacier's virgin snow,
The blush of earth embracing with her heaven—
Tinge thy celestial aspect, and make tame
The beauties of the sunbow which bends o'er thee.
Beautiful Spirit! in thy calm clear brow,   25
Wherein is glassed[3] serenity of soul,
Which of itself shows immortality,
I read that thou wilt pardon to a Son
Of Earth, whom the abstruser powers permit
At times to commune with them—if that he   30

2. "And I looked, and behold a pale   him" (Revelation vi.8).
horse: and his name that sat on him   3. Reflected.
was Death, and Hell followed with

Avail him of his spells—to call thee thus,
And gaze on thee a moment.

WITCH.   Son of Earth!
I know thee, and the powers which give thee power;
I know thee for a man of many thoughts,
And deeds of good and ill, extreme in both,   35
Fatal and fated in thy sufferings.
I have expected this—what wouldst thou with me?

MANFRED. To look upon thy beauty—nothing further.
The face of the earth hath maddened me, and I
Take refuge in her mysteries, and pierce   40
To the abodes of those who govern her—
But they can nothing aid me. I have sought
From them what they could not bestow, and now
I search no further.

WITCH.   What could be the quest
Which is not in the power of the most powerful,   45
The rulers of the invisible?

MANFRED.   A boon;
But why should I repeat it? 'twere in vain.

WITCH. I know not that; let thy lips utter it.

MANFRED. Well, though it torture me, 'tis but the same;
My pang shall find a voice. From my youth upwards   50
My spirit walked not with the souls of men,
Nor looked upon the earth with human eyes;
The thirst of their ambition was not mine,
The aim of their existence was not mine;
My joys, my griefs, my passions, and my powers,   55
Made me a stranger; though I wore the form,
I had no sympathy with breathing flesh,
Nor midst the creatures of clay that girded me
Was there but one who—but of her anon.
I said, with men, and with the thoughts of men,   60
I held but slight communion; but instead,
My joy was in the Wilderness, to breathe
The difficult air of the iced mountain's top,
Where the birds dare not build, nor insect's wing
Flit o'er the herbless granite; or to plunge   65
Into the torrent, and to roll along
On the swift whirl of the new breaking wave
Of river-stream, or ocean, in their flow.
In these my early strength exulted; or
To follow through the night the moving moon,   70
The stars and their development; or catch
The dazzling lightnings till my eyes grew dim;
Or to look, list'ning, on the scattered leaves,
While Autumn winds were at their evening song.
These were my pastimes, and to be alone;   75
For if the beings, of whom I was one,—
Hating to be so—crossed me in my path,

[handwritten annotation:] Manfred views himself as apart from men.

I felt myself degraded back to them,
And was all clay again. And then I dived,
In my lone wanderings, to the caves of death,   80
Searching its cause in its effect; and drew
From withered bones, and skulls, and heaped up dust,
Conclusions most forbidden. Then I passed
The nights of years in sciences, untaught
Save in the old time; and with time and toil,   85
And terrible ordeal, and such penance
As in itself hath power upon the air
And spirits that do compass air and earth,
Space, and the peopled infinite, I made
Mine eyes familiar with Eternity,   90
Such as, before me, did the Magi,[4] and
He who from out their fountain dwellings raised
Eros and Anteros, at Gadara,[5]
As I do thee—and with my knowledge grew
The thirst of knowledge, and the power and joy   95
Of this most bright intelligence, until—
WITCH. Proceed.
MANFRED.   Oh! I but thus prolonged my words,
Boasting these idle attributes, because
As I approach the core of my heart's grief—
But to my task. I have not named to thee   100
Father or mother, mistress, friend, or being,
With whom I wore the chain of human ties;
If I had such, they seemed not such to me—
Yet there was one—
WITCH.   Spare not thyself—proceed.
MANFRED. She was like me in lineaments—her eyes,   105
Her hair, her features, all, to the very tone
Even of her voice, they said were like to mine;
But softened all, and tempered into beauty;
She had the same lone thoughts and wanderings,
The quest of hidden knowledge, and a mind   110
To comprehend the universe; nor these
Alone, but with them gentler powers than mine,
Pity, and smiles, and tears—which I had not;
And tenderness—but that I had for her;
Humility—and that I never had.   115
Her faults were mine—her virtues were her own—
I loved her, and destroyed her!
WITCH.   With thy hand?
MANFRED. Not with my hand, but heart—which broke her heart;
It gazed on mine, and withered. I have shed
Blood, but not hers—and yet her blood was shed—   120

---

4. Plural of "magus": a master of occult knowledge.
5. Iamblicus, the 4th-century Neoplatonic philosopher, called up Eros, god of love, and Anteros, god of unrequited love, from the hot springs named after them at Gadara, in Syria.

I saw—and could not stanch it.

WITCH.   And for this—
A being of the race thou dost despise,
The order which thine own would rise above,
Mingling with us and ours, thou dost forego
The gifts of our great knowledge, and shrink'st back   125
To recreant mortality—Away!

MANFRED. Daughter of Air! I tell thee, since that hour—
But words are breath—look on me in my sleep,
Or watch my watchings—Come and sit by me!
My solitude is solitude no more,   130
But peopled with the Furies—I have gnashed
My teeth in darkness till returning morn,
Then cursed myself till sunset—I have prayed
For madness as a blessing—'tis denied me.
I have affronted death—but in the war   135
Of elements the waters shrunk from me,
And fatal things passed harmless—the cold hand
Of an all-pitiless demon held me back,
Back by a single hair, which would not break.
In fantasy, imagination, all   140
The affluence of my soul—which one day was
A Croesus in creation[6]—I plunged deep,
But, like an ebbing wave, it dashed me back
Into the gulf of my unfathomed thought.
I plunged amidst mankind—Forgetfulness   145
I sought in all, save where 'tis to be found,
And that I have to learn—my sciences,[7]
My long pursued and superhuman art,
Is mortal here; I dwell in my despair—
And live—and live forever.

WITCH.   It may be   150
That I can aid thee.

MANFRED.   To do this thy power
Must wake the dead, or lay me low with them.
Do so—in any shape—in any hour—
With any torture—so it be the last.

WITCH. That is not in my province; but if thou   155
Wilt swear obedience to my will, and do
My bidding, it may help thee to thy wishes.

MANFRED. I will not swear—Obey! and whom? the spirits
Whose presence I command, and be the slave
Of those who served me—Never!

WITCH.   Is this all?   160
Hast thou no gentler answer?—Yet bethink thee,
And pause ere thou rejectest.

6. I.e., my imagination had at one time been as rich as King Croesus in its creative powers. Manfred's self-description in this passage, as longing for a death which is denied him, is modeled on the legend, often treated in Romantic literature, of the Wandering Jew.
7. Occult bodies of knowledge.

MANFRED.   I have said it.
WITCH. Enough!—I may retire then—say!
MANFRED.   Retire!
                                    [*The* WITCH *disappears.*]
MANFRED [*alone*]. We are the fools of time and terror: Days
   Steal on us and steal from us; yet we live,   165
   Loathing our life, and dreading still to die.
   In all the days of this detested yoke—
   This vital weight upon the struggling heart,
   Which sinks with sorrow, or beats quick with pain,
   Or joy that ends in agony or faintness—   170
   In all the days of past and future, for
   In life there is no present, we can number
   How few—how less than few—wherein the soul
   Forbears to pant for death, and yet draws back
   As from a stream in winter, though the chill   175
   Be but a moment's. I have one resource
   Still in my science—I can call the dead,
   And ask them what it is we dread to be:
   The sternest answer can but be the Grave,
   And that is nothing—if they answer not—   180
   The buried Prophet answered to the Hag
   Of Endor;[8] and the Spartan Monarch drew
   From the Byzantine maid's unsleeping spirit
   An answer and his destiny—he slew
   That which he loved, unknowing what he slew,   185
   And died unpardoned—though he called in aid
   The Phyxian Jove, and in Phigalia roused
   The Arcadian Evocators to compel
   The indignant shadow to depose her wrath,
   Or fix her term of vengeance—she replied   190
   In words of dubious import, but fulfilled.[9]
   If I had never lived, that which I love
   Had still been living; had I never loved,
   That which I love would still be beautiful—
   Happy and giving happiness. What is she?   195
   What is she now?—a sufferer for my sins—
   A thing I dare not think upon—or nothing.
   Within few hours I shall not call in vain—
   Yet in this hour I dread the thing I dare:

8. The Woman of Endor, at the behest of King Saul, summoned up the spirit of the dead prophet Samuel, who foretold that in an impending battle the Philistines would conquer the Israelites and kill Saul and his sons (I Samuel xxviii.7–19).

9. Plutarch relates that King Pausanias ("the Spartan Monarch") had accidentally killed Cleonice ("the Byzantine maid"), whom he desired as his mistress. Her ghost haunted him, until he called up her spirit to beg her forgiveness. She told him, enigmatically, that he would quickly be freed from his troubles; soon after that, he was killed. Another Pausanias, author of the *Description of Greece*, adds the details that King Pausanias, in the vain attempt to purge his guilt, had called for aid from Jupiter Phyxius and consulted the Evocators at Phigalia, in Arcadia, who had the power to call up the souls of the dead.

Until this hour I never shrunk to gaze   200
On spirit, good or evil—now I tremble,
And feel a strange cold thaw upon my heart.
But I can act even what I most abhor,
And champion human fears.—The night approaches. [*Exit.*]

SCENE III. *The Summit of the Jungfrau Mountain.*

Enter FIRST DESTINY.

The moon is rising broad, and round, and bright;
And here on snows, where never human foot
Of common mortal trod, we nightly tread,
And leave no traces; o'er the savage sea,
The glassy ocean of the mountain ice,   5
We skim its rugged breakers, which put on
The aspect of a tumbling tempest's foam,
Frozen in a moment—a dead whirlpool's image.
And this most steep fantastic pinnacle,
The fretwork of some earthquake—where the clouds   10
Pause to repose themselves in passing by—
Is sacred to our revels, or our vigils.
Here do I wait my sisters, on our way
To the Hall of Arimanes, for tonight
Is our great festival—'tis strange they come not.   15

A *Voice without, singing*
The Captive Usurper,[1]
Hurled down from the throne,
Lay buried in torpor,
Forgotten and lone;
I broke through his slumbers,   20
I shivered his chain,
I leagued him with numbers—
He's Tyrant again!
With the blood of a million he'll answer my care,
With a nation's destruction—his flight and despair.   25

Second Voice, without
The ship sailed on, the ship sailed fast,
But I left not a sail, and I left not a mast;
There is not a plank of the hull or the deck,
And there is not a wretch to lament o'er his wreck;
Save one, whom I held, as he swam, by the hair,   30
And he was a subject well worthy my care;
A traitor on land, and a pirate at sea—
But I saved him to wreak further havoc for me!

1. I.e., Napoleon. The song of the first Voice alludes to Napoleon's escape from his captivity on the island of Elba in March, 1815. After his defeat at the Battle of Waterloo, Napoleon was interned on another island, St. Helena, in October, 1815.

FIRST DESTINY, *answering*
  The city lies sleeping;
    The morn, to deplore it,
  May dawn on it weeping: 35
    Sullenly, slowly,
  The black plague flew o'er it—
    Thousands lie lowly;
  Tens of thousands shall perish—   40
    The living shall fly from
  The sick they should cherish;
    But nothing can vanquish
  The touch that they die from.
    Sorrow and anguish,   45
  And evil and dread,
    Envelope a nation—
  The blessed are the dead,
    Who see not the sight
    Of their own desolation;   50
  This work of a night—
This wreck of a realm—this deed of my doing—
For ages I've done, and shall still be renewing!

[*Enter the* SECOND *and* THIRD DESTINIES.]

THE THREE
  Our hands contain the hearts of men,
    Our footsteps are their graves;   55
  We only give to take again
    The spirits of our slaves!

FIRST DESTINY. Welcome!—Where's Nemesis?[2]
SECOND DESTINY.   At some great work;
  But what I know not, for my hands were full.
THIRD DESTINY. Behold she cometh.
    [*Enter* NEMESIS.]
FIRST DESTINY.   Say, where hast thou been?   60
  My sisters and thyself are slow tonight.
NEMESIS. I was detained repairing shattered thrones,
  Marrying fools, restoring dynasties,
  Avenging men upon their enemies,
  And making them repent their own revenge;   65
  Goading the wise to madness; from the dull
  Shaping out oracles to rule the world
  Afresh, for they were waxing out of date,
  And mortals dared to ponder for themselves,
  To weigh kings in the balance, and to speak   70
  Of freedom, the forbidden fruit.—Away!
  We have outstayed the hour—mount we our clouds! [*Exeunt.*]

---

2. The Greek and Roman goddess of
retribution, particularly of the sin of
hubris, overweening presumption
against the gods.

SCENE IV. *The Hall of* ARIMANES[3]—ARIMANES *on his Throne, a Globe of Fire, surrounded by the Spirits.*

Hymn of the SPIRITS

Hail to our Master!—Prince of Earth and Air!
  Who walks the clouds and waters—in his hand
The scepter of the elements which tear
  Themselves to chaos at his high command!
He breatheth—and a tempest shakes the sea;   5
  He speaketh—and the clouds reply in thunder;
He gazeth—from his glance the sunbeams flee;
  He moveth—earthquakes rend the world asunder.
Beneath his footsteps the volcanoes rise;
  His shadow is the Pestilence; his path   10
The comets herald through the crackling skies;
  And planets turn to ashes at his wrath.
To him War offers daily sacrifice;
  To him Death pays his tribute; Life is his,
With all its infinite of agonies—   15
  And his the spirit of whatever is!

Enter the DESTINIES and NEMESIS.

FIRST DESTINY. Glory to Arimanes! on the earth
  His power increaseth—both my sisters did
  His bidding, nor did I neglect my duty!
SECOND DESTINY. Glory to Arimanes! we who bow   20
  The necks of men, bow down before his throne!
THIRD DESTINY. Glory to Arimanes! we await
  His nod!
NEMESIS.   Sovereign of Sovereigns! we are thine,
  And all that liveth, more or less, is ours,
  And most things wholly so; still to increase   25
  Our power, increasing thine, demands our care,
  And we are vigilant.—Thy late commands
  Have been fulfilled to the utmost.

Enter MANFRED.

A SPIRIT.   What is here?
  A mortal!—Thou most rash and fatal wretch,
  Bow down and worship!
SECOND SPIRIT.   I do know the man—   30
  A Magian[4] of great power and fearful skill!
THIRD SPIRIT. Bow down and worship, slave!—What, know'st
  thou not
  Thine and our Sovereign?—Tremble, and obey!
ALL THE SPIRITS. Prostrate thyself, and thy condemnéd clay,
  Child of the Earth! or dread the worst.
MANFRED.   I know it;   35
  And yet ye see I kneel not. *Manfred will not be ruled by anyone.*

---

3. The name is derived from Ahriman, who in the dualistic Zoroastrian religion was the principle of darkness and evil.

4. A magus, master of occult knowledge.

FOURTH SPIRIT.   'Twill be taught thee.
MANFRED. 'Tis taught already—many a night on the earth,
  On the bare ground, have I bowed down my face,
  And strewed my head with ashes; I have known
  The fullness of humiliation, for   40
  I sunk before my vain despair, and knelt
  To my own desolation.
FIFTH SPIRIT.   Dost thou dare
  Refuse to Arimanes on his throne
  What the whole earth accords, beholding not
  The terror of his Glory?—Crouch! I say.   45
MANFRED. Bid *him* bow down to that which is above him,
  The overruling Infinite, the Maker
  Who made him not for worship—let him kneel,
  And we will kneel together.
THE SPIRITS.   Crush the worm!
  Tear him in pieces!—
FIRST DESTINY.   Hence! Avaunt!—he's mine.   50
  Prince of the Powers invisible! This man
  Is of no common order, as his port
  And presence here denote; his sufferings
  Have been of an immortal nature, like
  Our own; his knowledge and his powers and will,   55
  As far as is compatible with clay,
  Which clogs the ethereal essence, have been such
  As clay hath seldom borne; his aspirations
  Have been beyond the dwellers of the earth,
  And they have only taught him what we know—   60
  That knowledge is not happiness, and science
  But an exchange of ignorance for that
  Which is another kind of ignorance.
  This is not all; the passions, attributes
  Of earth and heaven, from which no power, nor being,   65
  Nor breath from the worm upwards is exempt,
  Have pierced his heart; and in their consequence
  Made him a thing, which I, who pity not,
  Yet pardon those who pity. He is mine,
  And thine, it may be—be it so, or not,   70
  No other Spirit in this region hath
  A soul like his—or power upon his soul.
NEMESIS. What doth he here then?
FIRST DESTINY.   Let him answer that.
MANFRED. Ye know what I have known; and without power
  I could not be amongst ye: but there are   75
  Powers deeper still beyond—I come in quest
  Of such, to answer unto what I seek.
NEMESIS. What wouldst thou?
MANFRED.   Thou canst not reply to me.
  Call up the dead—my question is for them.

NEMESIS. Great Arimanes, doth thy will avouch   80
   The wishes of this mortal?
ARIMANES.   Yea.
NEMESIS.   Whom wouldst thou
   Uncharnel?
MANFRED.   One without a tomb—call up
   Astarte.[5]

NEMESIS

Shadow! or Spirit!
   Whatever thou art,   85
Which still doth inherit
   The whole or a part
Of the form of thy birth,
   Of the mold of thy clay
Which returned to the earth—   90
   Reappear to the day!
Bear what thou borest,
   The heart and the form,
And the aspect thou worest
   Redeem from the worm.   95
Appear!—Appear!—Appear!
Who sent thee there requires thee here!

[The phantom of ASTARTE *rises and stands in the midst.]*

MANFRED. Can this be death? there's bloom upon her cheek;
   But now I see it is no living hue,
   But a strange hectic[6]—like the unnatural red   100
   Which Autumn plants upon the perished leaf.
   It is the same! Oh, God! that I should dread
   To look upon the same—Astarte!—No,
   I cannot speak to her—but bid her speak—
   Forgive me or condemn me.   105

NEMESIS

By the power which hath broken
   The grave which enthralled thee,
Speak to him who hath spoken,
   Or those who have called thee!

MANFRED.   She is silent,
   And in that silence I am more than answered.   110
NEMESIS. My power extends no further. Prince of air!
   It rests with thee alone—command her voice.
ARIMANES. Spirit—obey this scepter!

---

5. Byron applies to Manfred's beloved the name of Astarte (also known as Ashtoreth), goddess of love and fertility, the eastern equivalent of the Greek Goddess Aphrodite.
6. A feverish flush.

NEMESIS.   Silent still!
   She is not of our order, but belongs
   To the other powers. Mortal! thy quest is vain,   115
   And we are baffled also.
MANFRED.   Hear me, hear me—
   Astarte! my belovéd! speak to me:
   I have so much endured, so much endure—
   Look on me! the grave hath not changed thee more
   Than I am changed for thee. Thou lovedst me   120
   Too much, as I loved thee: we were not made
   To torture thus each other, though it were
   The deadliest sin to love as we have loved.
   Say that thou loath'st me not—that I do bear
   This punishment for both—that thou wilt be   125
   One of the blesséd—and that I shall die;
   For hitherto all hateful things conspire
   To bind me in existence—in a life
   Which makes me shrink from immortality—
   A future like the past. I cannot rest.   130
   I know not what I ask, nor what I seek:
   I feel but what thou art—and what I am;
   And I would hear yet once before I perish
   The voice which was my music—Speak to me!
   For I have called on thee in the still night,   135
   Startled the slumbering birds from the hushed boughs,
   And woke the mountain wolves, and made the caves
   Acquainted with thy vainly echoed name,
   Which answered me—many things answered me—
   Spirits and men—but thou wert silent all.   140
   Yet speak to me! I have outwatched the stars,
   And gazed o'er heaven in vain in search of thee.
   Speak to me! I have wandered o'er the earth,
   And never found thy likeness—Speak to me!
   Look on the fiends around—they feel for me: 145
   I fear them not, and feel for thee alone—
   Speak to me! though it be in wrath—but say—
   I reck not what—but let me hear thee once—
   This once—once more!
PHANTOM OF ASTARTE.   Manfred!
MANFRED.   Say on, say on—
   I live but in the sound—it is thy voice!   150
PHANTOM. Manfred! Tomorrow ends thine earthly ills.
   Farewell!
MANFRED. Yet one word more—am I forgiven?
PHANTOM. Farewell!
MANFRED.   Say, shall we meet again?
PHANTOM.   Farewell!
MANFRED. One word for mercy! Say, thou lovest me.
PHANTOM. Manfred!   [*The Spirit of* ASTARTE *disappears.*]

NEMESIS.   She's gone, and will not be recalled;   155
   Her words will be fulfilled. Return to the earth.

A SPIRIT.   He is convulsed—This is to be a mortal
   And seek the things beyond mortality.

ANOTHER SPIRIT.   Yet, see, he mastereth himself, and makes
   His torture tributary to his will.   160
   Had he been one of us, he would have made
   An awful spirit.

NEMESIS.   Hast thou further question
   Of our great sovereign, or his worshipers?

MANFRED.   None.

NEMESIS.   Then for a time farewell.

MANFRED.   We meet then! Where? On the earth?—   165
   Even as thou wilt: and for the grace accorded
   I now depart a debtor. Fare ye well!   [*Exit* MANFRED.]
     [*Scene closes.*]

Act III

SCENE 1. A *Hall in the Castle of* MANFRED. MANFRED *and*
HERMAN.

MANFRED.   What is the hour?

HERMAN.   It wants but one till sunset,
   And promises a lovely twilight.

MANFRED.   Say,
   Are all things so disposed of in the tower
   As I directed?

HERMAN.   All, my lord, are ready:
   Here is the key and casket.

MANFRED.   It is well: 5
   Thou may'st retire.   [*Exit* HERMAN.]

MANFRED [*alone*]. There is a calm upon me—
   Inexplicable stillness! which till now
   Did not belong to what I knew of life.
   If that I did not know philosophy
   To be of all our vanities the motliest,[7]   10
   The merest word that ever fooled the ear
   From out the schoolman's jargon, I should deem
   The golden secret, the sought "Kalon,"[8] found,
   And seated in my soul. It will not last,
   But it is well to have known it, though but once: 15
   It hath enlarged my thoughts with a new sense,
   And I within my tablets would note down
   That there is such a feeling. Who is there?
     Re-enter HERMAN.

---

7. "The most diverse"; or possibly, "the most foolish" ("motley" was the multicolored suit worn by a court jester).

8. The Greek word signified both "the Beautiful" and "the Good."

HERMAN. My lord, the abbot of St. Maurice[9] craves
　To greet your presence.
　　　　　　Enter the ABBOT OF ST. MAURICE.
ABBOT. 　　　　　　　　Peace be with Count Manfred! 　　20
MANFRED. Thanks, holy father! welcome to these walls;
　Thy presence honors them, and blesseth those
　Who dwell within them.
ABBOT.

　　　　　　　　　　Would it were so, Count!—
　But I would fain confer with thee alone.
MANFRED. Herman, retire.—What would my reverend guest? 　25
ABBOT. Thus, without prelude:—Age and zeal, my office,[1]
　And good intent, must plead my privilege;
　Our near, though not acquainted neighborhood,
　May also be my herald. Rumors strange,
　And of unholy nature, are abroad, 　　30
　And busy with thy name; a noble name
　For centuries: may he who bears it now
　Transmit it unimpaired!
MANFRED. 　　　　　　　Proceed—I listen.
ABBOT. 'Tis said thou holdest converse with the things
　Which are forbidden to the search of man; 　　35
　That with the dwellers of the dark abodes,
　The many evil and unheavenly spirits
　Which walk the valley of the shade of death,
　Thou communest. I know that with mankind,
　Thy fellows in creation, thou dost rarely 　　40
　Exchange thy thoughts, and that thy solitude
　Is as an anchorite's,[2] were it but holy.
MANFRED. And what are they who do avouch these things?
ABBOT. My pious brethren—the scared peasantry—
　Even thy own vassals—who do look on thee 　　45
　With most unquiet eyes. Thy life's in peril.
MANFRED. Take it.
ABBOT. 　　　　I come to save, and not destroy—
　I would not pry into thy secret soul;
　But if these things be sooth, there still is time
　For penitence and pity: reconcile thee 　　50
　With the true church, and through the church to heaven.
MANFRED. I hear thee. This is my reply: whate'er
　I may have been, or am, doth rest between
　Heaven and myself.—I shall not choose a mortal
　To be my mediator. Have I sinned 　　55
　Against your ordinances? prove and punish!
ABBOT. My son! I did not speak of punishment,
　But penitence and pardon; with thyself
　The choice of such remains—and for the last,

9. The Abbey of St. Maurice is in the　　2. An anchorite is a person who, for
Rhone Valley, in Switzerland.　　　　religious reasons, lives in seclusion.
1. Religious vocation.

Our institutions and our strong belief   60
Have given me power to smooth the path from sin
To higher hope and better thoughts; the first
I leave to heaven,—"Vengeance is mine alone!"
So saith the Lord,[3] and with all humbleness
His servant echoes back the awful word.   65

MANFRED. Old man! there is no power in holy men,
Nor charm in prayer—nor purifying form
Of penitence—nor outward look—nor fast—
Nor agony—nor, greater than all these,
The innate tortures of that deep despair,   70
Which is remorse without the fear of hell,
But all in all sufficient to itself
Would make a hell of heaven—can exorcise
From out the unbounded spirit the quick sense
Of its own sins, wrongs, sufferance, and revenge   75
Upon itself; there is no future pang
Can deal that justice on the self-condemned
He deals on his own soul.

ABBOT.   All this is well;
For this will pass away, and be succeeded
By an auspicious hope, which shall look up   80
With calm assurance to that blessèd place
Which all who seek may win, whatever be
Their earthly errors, so they be atoned:
And the commencement of atonement is
The sense of its necessity.—Say on—   85
And all our church can teach thee shall be taught;
And all we can absolve thee shall be pardoned.

MANFRED. When Rome's sixth emperor was near his last,
The victim of a self-inflicted wound,
To shun the torments of a public death   90
From senates once his slaves, a certain soldier,
With show of loyal pity, would have stanched
The gushing throat with his officious robe;
The dying Roman thrust him back, and said—
Some empire still in his expiring glance—   95
"It is too late—is this fidelity?"[4]

ABBOT. And what of this?

MANFRED.   I answer with the Roman,
"It is too late!"

ABBOT.   It never can be so,
To reconcile thyself with thy own soul,
And thy own soul with heaven. Hast thou no hope?   100
'Tis strange—even those who do despair above,
Yet shape themselves some fantasy on earth,

3. "Vengeance is mine; I will repay, saith the Lord" (Romans xii.19).
4. The "sixth Emperor" was Otho; Byron attaches to his suicide a story that Suetonius tells about the death of an earlier emperor, Nero.

To which frail twig they cling like drowning men.
MANFRED. Ay—father! I have had those earthly visions
    And noble aspirations in my youth, 105
    To make my own the mind of other men,
    The enlightener of nations; and to rise
    I knew not whither—it might be to fall;
    But fall, even as the mountain-cataract,
    Which, having leaped from its more dazzling height, 110
    Even in the foaming strength of its abyss
    (Which casts up misty columns that become
    Clouds raining from the reascended skies)
    Lies low but mighty still.—But this is past,
    My thoughts mistook themselves.
ABBOT.   And wherefore so? 115
MANFRED. I could not tame my nature down: for he
    Must serve who fain would sway—and soothe—and sue—
    And watch all time—and pry into all place—
    And be a living lie—who would become
    A mighty thing amongst the mean, and such 120
    The mass are; I disdained to mingle with
    A herd, though to be leader—and of wolves.
    The lion is alone, and so am I.
ABBOT. And why not live and act with other men?
MANFRED. Because my nature was averse from life; 125
    And yet not cruel; for I would not make,
    But find a desolation: like the wind,
    The red-hot breath of the most lone Simoom,[5]
    Which dwells but in the desert and sweeps o'er
    The barren sands which bear no shrubs to blast, 130
    And revels o'er their wild and arid waves,
    And seeketh not, so that it is not sought,
    But being met is deadly—such hath been
    The course of my existence; but there came
    Things in my path which are no more.
ABBOT.   Alas! 135
    I 'gin to fear that thou art past all aid
    From me and from my calling; yet so young,
    I still would—
MANFRED.   Look on me! there is an order
    Of mortals on the earth, who do become
    Old in their youth, and die ere middle age, 140
    Without the violence of warlike death;
    Some perishing of pleasure—some of study—
    Some worn with toil—some of mere weariness—
    Some of disease—and some insanity—
    And some of withered or of broken hearts; 145
    For this last is a malady which slays
    More than are numbered in the lists of Fate,

Manfred restates his aloofness.

5. A hot, wind-laden sand in the Sahara and Arabian deserts.

Taking all shapes and bearing many names.
Look upon me! for even of all these things
Have I partaken; and of all these things,   150
One were enough; then wonder not that I
Am what I am, but that I ever was,
Or having been, that I am still on earth.

ABBOT. Yet, hear me still—

MANFRED.   Old man! I do respect
Thine order, and revere thine years; I deem   155
Thy purpose pious, but it is in vain.
Think me not churlish; I would spare thyself,
Far more than me, in shunning at this time
All further colloquy; and so—farewell.   [*Exit* MANFRED.]

ABBOT. This should have been a noble creature: he   160
Hath all the energy which would have made
A goodly frame of glorious elements,
Had they been wisely mingled; as it is,
It is an awful chaos—light and darkness—
And mind and dust—and passions and pure thoughts,   165
Mixed, and contending without end or order,
All dormant or destructive. He will perish,
And yet he must not; I will try once more,
For such are worth redemption; and my duty
Is to dare all things for a righteous end.   170
I'll follow him—but cautiously, though surely. [*Exit* ABBOT.]

SCENE II. *Another Chamber.* MANFRED *and* HERMAN.

HERMAN. My lord, you bade me wait on you at sunset:
He sinks beyond the mountain.

MANFRED.   Doth he so?
I will look on him.
           [MANFRED *advances to the Window of the Hall.*]
                          Glorious Orb! the idol
Of early nature, and the vigorous race
Of undiseased mankind, the giant sons   5
Of the embrace of angels with a sex
More beautiful than they, which did draw down
The erring spirits who can ne'er return[6]—
Most glorious orb! that wert a worship, ere
The mystery of thy making was revealed!   10
Thou earliest minister of the Almighty,
Which gladdened, on their mountaintops, the hearts
Of the Chaldean shepherds, till they poured
Themselves in orisons![7] Thou material God!

6. "There were giants in the earth in those days; and also after that, when the sons of God came in unto the daughters of men, and they bare children to them, the same became mighty men which were of old, men of renown" (Genesis vi.4). Byron interprets "the sons of God" as denoting errant angels.

7. Prayers.

And representative of the Unknown,   15
Who chose thee for his shadow! Thou chief star!
Center of many stars! which mak'st our earth
Endurable, and temperest the hues
And hearts of all who walk within thy rays!
Sire of the seasons! Monarch of the climes,   20
And those who dwell in them! for near or far,
Our inborn spirits have a tint of thee,
Even as our outward aspects—thou dost rise,
And shine, and set in glory. Fare thee well!
I ne'er shall see thee more. As my first glance   25
Of love and wonder was for thee, then take
My latest look: thou wilt not beam on one
To whom the gifts of life and warmth have been
Of a more fatal nature. He is gone;
I follow.

                                                    [*Exit* MANFRED.]

SCENE III. *The Mountains—The Castle of* MANFRED *at some
distance—A Terrace before a Tower.—Time, Twilight.*
HERMAN, MANUEL, *and other Dependants of* MANFRED.

HERMAN. 'Tis strange enough; night after night, for years,
He hath pursued long vigils in this tower,
Without a witness. I have been within it—
So have we all been ofttimes; but from it,
Or its contents, it were impossible   5
To draw conclusions absolute of aught
His studies tend to. To be sure, there is
One chamber where none enter: I would give
The fee[8] of what I have to come these three years,
To pore upon its mysteries.
MANUEL.   'Twere dangerous;   10
Content thyself with what thou know'st already.
HERMAN. Ah, Manuel! thou art elderly and wise,
And couldst say much; thou hast dwelt within the castle—
How many years is 't?
MANUEL.   Ere Count Manfred's birth,
I served his father, whom he naught resembles.   15
HERMAN. There be more sons in like predicament.
But wherein do they differ?
MANUEL.   I speak not
Of features or of form, but mind and habits;
Count Sigismund was proud—but gay and free—
A warrior and a reveller; he dwelt not   20
With books and solitude, nor made the night
A gloomy vigil, but a festal time,
Merrier than day; he did not walk the rocks

8. Ownership.

And forests like a wolf, nor turn aside
From men and their delights.
HERMAN.   Beshrew[9] the hour,   25
But those were jocund times! I would that such
Would visit the old walls again; they look
As if they had forgotten them.
MANUEL.   These walls
Must change their chieftain first. Oh! I have seen
Some strange things in them, Herman.
HERMAN.   Come, be friendly;   30
Relate me some to while away our watch:
I've heard thee darkly speak of an event
Which happened hereabouts, by this same tower.
MANUEL. That was a night indeed! I do remember
'Twas twilight, as it may be now, and such   35
Another evening—yon red cloud, which rests
On Eigher's[1] pinnacle, so rested then—
So like that it might be the same; the wind
Was faint and gusty, and the mountain snows
Began to glitter with the climbing moon.   40
Count Manfred was, as now, within his tower—
How occupied, we knew not, but with him
The sole companion of his wanderings
And watchings—her, whom of all earthly things
That lived, the only one he seemed to love—   45
As he, indeed, by blood was bound to do,
The Lady Astarte, his—
                            Hush! who comes here?
        Enter the ABBOT.
ABBOT. Where is your master?
HERMAN.   Yonder in the tower.
ABBOT. I must speak with him.
MANUEL.   'Tis impossible;
He is most private, and must not be thus   50
Intruded on.
ABBOT.   Upon myself I take
The forfeit of my fault, if fault there be—
But I must see him.
HERMAN.   Thou hast seen him once
This eve already.
ABBOT.   Herman! I command thee,
Knock, and apprise the Count of my approach.   55
HERMAN. We dare not.
ABBOT.   Then it seems I must be herald
Of my own purpose.
MANUEL.   Reverend father, stop—
I pray you pause.
ABBOT.   Why so?

9. Curse (used jocularly).   1. A peak east of the Jungfrau.

MANUEL.   But step this way,
And I will tell you further.   [*Exeunt.*]

SCENE IV. *Interior of the Tower.*

MANFRED *alone*

The stars are forth, the moon above the tops
Of the snow-shining mountains.—Beautiful!
I linger yet with Nature, for the night
Hath been to me a more familiar face
Than that of man; and in her starry shade   5
Of dim and solitary loveliness,
I learned the language of another world.
I do remember me, that in my youth,
When I was wandering—upon such a night
I stood within the Coliseum's wall,   10
Midst the chief relics of almighty Rome.
The trees which grew along the broken arches
Waved dark in the blue midnight, and the stars
Shone through the rents of ruin; from afar
The watchdog bayed beyond the Tiber;[2] and   15
More near from out the Caesars' palace came
The owl's long cry, and, interruptedly,
Of distant sentinels the fitful song
Begun and died upon the gentle wind.
Some cypresses beyond the timeworn breach   20
Appeared to skirt the horizon, yet they stood
Within a bowshot. Where the Caesars dwelt,
And dwell the tuneless birds of night, amidst
A grove which springs through leveled battlements
And twines its roots with the imperial hearths,   25
Ivy usurps the laurel's place of growth—
But the gladiators' bloody Circus[3] stands,
A noble wreck in ruinous perfection!
While Caesar's chambers, and the Augustan halls,
Grovel on earth in indistinct decay.—   30
And thou didst shine, thou rolling moon, upon
All this, and cast a wide and tender light,
Which softened down the hoar austerity
Of rugged desolation, and filled up,
As 'twere anew, the gaps of centuries;   35
Leaving that beautiful which still was so,
And making that which was not, till the place
Became religion, and the heart ran o'er
With silent worship of the great of old—

---

2. The river Tiber flows through Rome. The palace (line 16) is that of the Roman emperors ("Caesars"); it stands on the Palatine hill, immediately southwest of the Coliseum.

3. The circular arena within the Coliseum where professional gladiators fought to the death as public entertainment.

The dead, but sceptered sovereigns, who still rule   40
Our spirits from their urns.—
                          'Twas such a night!
'Tis strange that I recall it at this time;
But I have found our thoughts take wildest flight
Even at the moment when they should array
Themselves in pensive order.
                    Enter the ABBOT.

ABBOT.   My good lord!   45
I crave a second grace for this approach;
But yet let not my humble zeal offend
By its abruptness—all it hath of ill
Recoils on me; its good in the effect
May light upon your head—could I say *heart*—   50
Could I touch *that*, with words or prayers, I should
Recall a noble spirit which hath wandered
But is not yet all lost.
MANFRED.   Thou know'st me not;
My days are numbered, and my deeds recorded:
Retire, or 'twill be dangerous—Away!   55
ABBOT. Thou dost not mean to menace me?
MANFRED.   Not I;
I simply tell thee peril is at hand,
And would preserve thee.
ABBOT.   What dost thou mean?
MANFRED.   Look there!
What dost thou see?
ABBOT.   Nothing.
MANFRED.   Look there, I say,
And steadfastly—now tell me what thou seest.   60
ABBOT. That which should shake me—but I fear it not:
I see a dusk and awful figure rise,
Like an infernal god, from out the earth;
His face wrapt in a mantle, and his form
Robed as with angry clouds: he stands between   65
Thyself and me—but I do fear him not.
MANFRED. Thou hast no cause; he shall not harm thee, but
His sight may shock thine old limbs into palsy.
I say to thee—Retire!
ABBOT.   And I reply—
Never—till I have battled with this fiend: 70
What doth he here?
MANFRED.   Why—ay—what doth he here?—
I did not send for him—he is unbidden.
ABBOT. Alas! lost mortal! what with guests like these
Hast thou to do? I tremble for thy sake:
Why doth he gaze on thee, and thou on him?   75
Ah! he unveils his aspect: on his brow

The thunder-scars are graven; from his eye
Glares forth the immortality of hell—
Avaunt!—
MANFRED. Pronounce—what is thy mission?
SPIRIT.   Come!
ABBOT. What art thou, unknown being? answer!—speak!   80
SPIRIT. The genius[4] of this mortal.—Come! 'tis time.
MANFRED. I am prepared for all things, but deny
The power which summons me. Who sent thee here?
SPIRIT. Thou'lt know anon—Come! Come!
MANFRED.   I have commanded
Things of an essence greater far than thine,   85
And striven with thy masters. Get thee hence!
SPIRIT. Mortal! thine hour is come—Away! I say.
MANFRED. I knew, and know my hour is come, but not
To render up my soul to such as thee:
Away! I'll die as I have lived—alone.   90
SPIRIT. Then I must summon up my brethren.—Rise!
                    [*Other Spirits rise up.*]
ABBOT. Avaunt! ye evil ones!—Avaunt! I say—
Ye have no power where piety hath power,
And I do charge ye in the name—
SPIRIT.   Old man!
We know ourselves, our mission, and thine order;   95
Waste not thy holy words on idle uses,
It were in vain: this man is forfeited.
Once more I summon him—Away! away!
MANFRED. I do defy ye—though I feel my soul
Is ebbing from me, yet I do defy ye;   100
Nor will I hence, while I have earthly breath
To breathe my scorn upon ye—earthly strength
To wrestle, though with spirits; what ye take
Shall be ta'en limb by limb.
SPIRIT.   Reluctant mortal!
Is this the Magian who would so pervade   105
The world invisible, and make himself
Almost our equal?—Can it be that thou
Art thus in love with life? the very life
Which made thee wretched!
MANFRED.   Thou false fiend, thou liest!
My life is in its last hour—*that* I know,   110
Nor would redeem a moment of that hour.
I do not combat against death, but thee
And thy surrounding angels; my past power
Was purchased by no compact with thy crew,
But by superior science—penance—daring—   115
And length of watching—strength of mind—and skill

4. The spirit or deity presiding over a human being from birth.

In knowledge of our fathers—when the earth
Saw men and spirits walking side by side
And gave ye no supremacy: I stand
Upon my strength—I do defy—deny—   120
Spurn back, and scorn ye!—

SPIRIT.   But thy many crimes
Have made thee—

MANFRED.   What are they to such as thee?
Must crimes be punished but by other crimes,
And greater criminals?—Back to thy hell!
Thou hast no power upon me, *that* I feel;   125
Thou never shalt possess me, *that* I know:
What I have done is done; I bear within
A torture which could nothing gain from thine:
The mind which is immortal makes itself
Requital for its good or evil thoughts,   130
Is its own origin of ill and end,
And its own place and time[5]—its innate sense,
When stripped of this mortality, derives
No color from the fleeting things without,
But is absorbed in sufferance or in joy,   135
Born from the knowledge of its own desert.
Thou didst not tempt me, and thou couldst not tempt me;
I have not been thy dupe nor am thy prey—
But was my own destroyer, and will be
My own hereafter.—Back, ye baffled fiends!   140
The hand of death is on me—but not yours!

                     [*The Demons disappear.*]

ABBOT. Alas! how pale thou art—thy lips are white—
And thy breast heaves—and in thy gasping throat
The accents rattle. Give thy prayers to Heaven—
Pray—albeit but in thought—but die not thus.   145

MANFRED. 'Tis over—my dull eyes can fix thee not;
But all things swim around me, and the earth
Heaves as it were beneath me. Fare thee well—
Give me thy hand.

ABBOTT.   Cold—cold—even to the heart—
But yet one prayer—Alas! how fares it with thee?   150

MANFRED. Old man! 'tis not so difficult to die.[6]

                     [MANFRED *expires.*]

ABBOT. He's gone—his soul hath ta'en its earthless flight—
Whither? I dread to think—but he is gone.

1816–17   1817

5. The last of several echoes by Manfred of Satan's claim that "The mind is its own place, and in itself / Can Make a Heaven of Hell, and a Hell of Heaven" (*Paradise Lost* I.254–55). See also above, I.i.252 and III.i.73.

6. When this line was omitted in the printing of the first edition, Byron wrote angrily to his publisher: "You have destroyed the whole effect and moral of the poem."

The Vision of Judgment[1]

By Quevedo Redivivus[2]

SUGGESTED BY THE COMPOSITION SO ENTITLED BY THE AUTHOR OF
Wat Tyler

"A Daniel come to judgment! yea, a Daniel!
I thank thee, Jew, for teaching me that word."[3]

1

Saint Peter sat by the celestial gate:
   His keys were rusty, and the lock was dull,
So little trouble had been given of late;
   Not that the place by any means was full,
But since the Gallic era "eighty-eight"[4]   5
   The devils had ta'en a longer, stronger pull,
And "a pull altogether," as they say
At sea—which drew most souls another way.

2

The angels all were singing out of tune,
   And hoarse with having little else to do,   10
Excepting to wind up the sun and moon,
   Or curb a runaway young star or two,
Or wild colt of a comet, which too soon
   Broke out of bounds o'er th' ethereal blue,

1. Although originally an ardent supporter of the French Revolution, Robert Southey soon turned a Tory and in 1813 was appointed poet laureate. Four years after the appointment he was dismayed by the unauthorized publication of his radical poetical drama *Wat Tyler*, which he had written in 1794 but had prudently left in manuscript. Byron reminds him of it in the subtitle. When King George III died in 1820—Shelley in his *Sonnet: England in 1819* had called him, accurately enough, "an old, mad, blind, despised, and dying king"— Southey did his official duty by writing *A Vision of Judgment* (1821). In this fulsome eulogy George III goes to heaven, confounds such detractors as John Wilkes and Junius, and obtains a testimonial of noble character from his old enemy, George Washington. The vision ends with the King, beatified, ceremoniously admitted to heaven.

Byron, responding to reports that Southey was vilifying him, had ridiculed the poet in his "Dedication" to Canto I of *Don Juan*. In the Preface to his *Vision of Judgment*, Southey then exhibited his bad judgment by denouncing Byron as head of the "Satanic School" of poetry, combining "lascivious" passages with "a satanic spirit of pride and audacious impiety." Byron immediately responded with *The Vision of Judgment*, in which he purports to tell the true story of how, with the unwitting help of Southey, King George had really managed to get into heaven. The poem is in the genre of the satiric attack on literary "dunces" by Dryden and Pope, but is written in the ottava rima stanza and the easy colloquial manner of Byron's *Don Juan*. In its quick, sure characterization, the pace and economy of its narrative, its inventiveness in detail, above all in the high spirits and unfailing good humor with which the author demolishes his opponent, this poem represents Byron the satirist at his masterful best.

2. "Quevedo Revived." Quevedo was a 17th-century Spanish author of *Sueños*, "Visions," written in prose and predominantly satirical in tone.

3. Quoted, not quite accurately, from *The Merchant of Venice*, IV.i.340–41.

4. The last year of the old régime in France, before the outbreak of the Revolution in 1789.

Splitting some planet with its playful tail,   15
As boats are sometimes by a wanton whale.

3

The guardian seraphs had retired on high,
    Finding their charges past all care below;
Terrestrial business filled nought in the sky
    Save the recording angel's black bureau;   20
Who found, indeed, the facts to multiply
    With such rapidity of vice and woe,
That he had stripped off both his wings in quills,
And yet was in arrear of human ills.

4

His business so augmented of late years,   25
    That he was forced, against his will no doubt
(Just like those cherubs, earthly ministers),
    For some resource to turn himself about,
And claim the help of his celestial peers,
    To aid him ere he should be quite worn out   30
By the increased demand for his remarks;
Six angels and twelve saints were named his clerks.

5

This was a handsome board—at least for heaven;
    And yet they had even then enough to do,
So many conquerors' cars were daily driven,   35
    So many kingdoms fitted up anew;
Each day too slew its thousands six or seven,
    Till at the crowning carnage, Waterloo,
They threw their pens down in divine disgust—
The page was so besmeared with blood and dust.   40

6

This by the way; 'tis not mine to record
    What angels shrink from: even the very devil
On this occasion his own work abhorred,
    So surfeited with the infernal revel:
Though he himself had sharpened every sword,   45
    It almost quenched his innate thirst of evil.
(Here Satan's sole good work deserves insertion—
'Tis, that he has both generals in reversion.[5])

7

Let's skip a few short years of hollow peace,
    Which peopled earth no better, hell as wont,   50
And heaven none—they form the tyrant's lease,
    With nothing but new names subscribed upon 't;
'Twill one day finish: meantime they increase,
    "With seven heads and ten horns," and all in front,

---

5. I.e., Satan has the legal right to the possession, after their deaths, of both Napoleon and Wellington, the commanding officers at the Battle of Waterloo.

Like Saint John's foretold beast;[6] but ours are born   55
Less formidable in the head than horn.

8

In the first year of freedom's second dawn[7]
    Died George the Third; although no tyrant, one
Who shielded tyrants, till each sense withdrawn
    Left him nor mental nor external sun: 60
A better farmer ne'er brushed dew from lawn,
    A worse king never left a realm undone!
He died—but left his subjects still behind,
One half as mad—and t'other no less blind.

9

He died! his death made no great stir on earth;   65
    His burial made some pomp; there was profusion
Of velvet, gilding, brass, and no great dearth
    Of aught but tears—save those shed by collusion.
For these things may be bought at their true worth;
    Of elegy there was the due infusion—   70
Bought also; and the torches, cloaks, and banners,
Heralds, and relics of old Gothic manners,

10

Formed a sepulchral melodrame. Of all
    The fools who flocked to swell or see the show,
Who cared about the corpse? The funeral   75
    Made the attraction, and the black the woe.
There throbbed not there a thought which pierced the pall;
    And when the gorgeous coffin was laid low,
It seemed the mockery of hell to fold
The rottenness of eighty years in gold.   80

11

So mix his body with the dust! It might
    Return to what it *must* far sooner, were
The natural compound left alone to fight
    Its way back into earth, and fire, and air;
But the unnatural balsams[8] merely blight   85
    What nature made him at his birth, as bare
As the mere million's base unmummied clay—
Yet all his spices but prolong decay.

12

He's dead—and upper earth with him has done;
    He's buried; save the undertaker's bill,   90
Or lapidary scrawl,[9] the world is gone
    For him, unless he left a German will;
But where's the proctor who will ask his son?[1]

6. The Book of Revelation describes such a beast, xiii.1.
7. 1820 was a year of new revolutionary movements in Italy and other countries of southern Europe.
8. I.e., embalming fluids.
9. Inscription cut into a stone monument.

1. A King's Proctor is an official who intervenes in the probate of a will, when chicanery is suspected. Byron alludes to the scandal that the will of George I, of the German House of Hanover, had been hidden by his son, George II, who was the grandfather of the late George III.

In whom his qualities are reigning still,
Except that household virtue, most uncommon,   95
Of constancy to a bad, ugly woman.

13

"God save the king!" It is a large economy
   In God to save the like; but if he will
Be saving, all the better; for not one am I
   Of those who think damnation better still: 100
I hardly know too if not quite alone am I
   In this small hope of bettering future ill
By circumscribing, with some slight restriction,
The eternity of hell's hot jurisdiction.

14

I know this is unpopular; I know   105
   'Tis blasphemous; I know one may be damned
For hoping no one else may e'er be so;
   I know my catechism; I know we're crammed
With the best doctrines till we quite o'erflow;
   I know that all save England's church have shammed,   110
And that the other twice two hundred churches
And synagogues have made a *damned* bad purchase.

15

God help us all! God help me too! I am,
   God knows, as helpless as the devil can wish,
And not a whit more difficult to damn,   115
   Than is to bring to land a late-hooked fish,
Or to the butcher to purvey the lamb;
   Not that I'm fit for such a noble dish,
As one day will be that immortal fry
Of almost everybody born to die.   120

16

Saint Peter sat by the celestial gate,
   And nodded o'er his keys; when, lo! there came
A wondrous noise he had not heard of late—
   A rushing sound of wind, and stream, and flame;
In short, a roar of things extremely great,   125
   Which would have made aught save a saint exclaim;
But he, with first a start and then a wink,
Said, "There's another star gone out, I think!"

17

But ere he could return to his repose,
   A cherub flapped his right wing o'er his eyes—   130
At which St. Peter yawned, and rubbed his nose:
   "Saint porter," said the angel, "prithee rise!"
Waving a goodly wing, which glowed, as glows
   An earthly peacock's tail, with heavenly dyes:
To which the saint replied, "Well, what's the matter?   135
"Is Lucifer come back with all this clatter?"

18

"No," quoth the cherub; "George the Third is dead."
    "And who *is* George the Third?" replied the apostle:
"*What George? what Third?*" "The king of England," said
    The angel. "Well! he won't find kings to jostle   140
Him on his way; but does he wear his head;
    Because the last we saw here had a tustle,
And ne'er would have got into heaven's good graces,
Had he not flung his head in all our faces.[2]

19

"He was, if I remember, king of France;   145
    That head of his, which could not keep a crown
On earth, yet ventured in my face to advance
    A claim to those of martyrs—like my own:
If I had had my sword, as I had once
    When I cut ears off, I had cut him down;[3]   150
But having but my *keys*, and not my brand,
I only knocked his head from out his hand.

20

"And then he set up such a headless howl,
    That all the saints came out and took him in;
And there he sits by St. Paul, cheek by jowl;   155
    That fellow Paul—the parvenu! The skin
Of St. Bartholomew,[4] which makes his cowl
    In heaven, and upon earth redeemed his sin
So as to make a martyr, never sped
Better than did this weak and wooden head.   160

21

"But had it come up here upon its shoulders,
    There would have been a different tale to tell:
The fellow-feeling in the saint's beholders
    Seems to have acted on them like a spell;
And so this very foolish head heaven solders   165
    Back on its trunk: it may be very well,
And seems the custom here to overthrow
Whatever has been wisely done below."

22

The angel answered, "Peter! do not pout:
    The king who comes has head and all entire,   170
And never knew much what it was about—
    He did as doth the puppet—by its wire,
And will be judged like all the rest, no doubt:
    My business and your own is not to inquire
Into such matters, but to mind our cue—   175
    Which is to act as we are bid to do."

2. Louis XVI, who had been guillotined in January, 1793.
3. When the officers came to take Jesus, "Simon Peter having a sword drew it, and smote the high priest's servant, and cut off his right ear" (John xviii.10). "Brand," line 151, is archaic for "sword."
4. According to tradition, the martyred St. Bartholomew was flayed alive.

23

While thus they spake, the angelic caravan,
    Arriving like a rush of mighty wind,
Cleaving the fields of space, as doth the swan
    Some silver stream (say Ganges, Nile, or Inde,   180
Or Thames, or Tweed), and 'midst them an old man
    With an old soul, and both extremely blind,
Halted before the gate, and in his shroud
Seated their fellow traveler on a cloud.

24

But bringing up the rear of this bright host   185
    A Spirit of a different aspect waved
His wings, like thunder clouds above some coast
    Whose barren beach with frequent wrecks is paved;
His brow was like the deep when tempest-tossed;
    Fierce and unfathomable thoughts engraved   190
Eternal wrath on his immortal face,
And *where* he gazed a gloom pervaded space.

25

As he drew near, he gazed upon the gate
    Ne'er to be entered more by him or Sin,
With such a glance of supernatural hate,   195
    As made Saint Peter wish himself within;
He pattered with his keys at a great rate,
    And sweated through his apostolic skin:
Of course his perspiration was but ichor,[5]
Or some such other spiritual liquor.   200

26

The very cherubs huddled all together,
    Like birds when soars the falcon; and they felt
A tingling to the tip of every feather,
    And formed a circle like Orion's belt
Around their poor old charge; who scarce knew whither   205
    His guards had led him, though they gently dealt
With royal manes[6] (for by many stories,
And true, we learn the angels all are Tories).

27

As things were in this posture, the gate flew
    Asunder, and the flashing of its hinges   210
Flung over space an universal hue
    Of many-colored flame, until its tinges
Reached even our speck of earth, and made a new
    Aurora borealis spread its fringes
O'er the North Pole; the same seen, when ice-bound,   215
    By Captain Parry's[7] crew, in "Melville's Sound."

28

And from the gate thrown open issued beaming
    A beautiful and mighty Thing of Light,

---

5. The fluid in the veins of the gods.
6. In Roman religion, spirits of the dead (pronounced *mā'nēz*).

7. Captain William Edward Parry, in his account of his *Voyage in 1819–20*, in search of a northwest passage.

Radiant with glory, like a banner streaming
 Victorious from some world-o'erthrowing fight: 220
My poor comparisons must needs be teeming
 With earthly likenesses, for here the night
Of clay obscures our best conceptions, saving
Johanna Southcote,[8] or Bob Southey raving.

29

'Twas the archangel Michael: all men know   225
 The make of angels and archangels, since
There's scarce a scribbler has not one to show,
 From the fiends' leader to the angels' prince.
There also are some altarpieces, though
 I really can't say that they much evince   230
One's inner notions of immortal spirits;
But let the connoisseurs explain *their* merits.

30

Michael flew forth in glory and in good;
 A goodly work of him from whom all glory
And good arise; the portal past—he stood;   235
 Before him the young cherubs and saints hoary—
(I say *young*, begging to be understood
 By looks, not years; and should be very sorry
To state, they were not older than St. Peter,
But merely that they seemed a little sweeter).   240

31

The cherubs and the saints bowed down before
 That arch-angelic hierarch, the first
Of essences angelical, who wore
 The aspect of a god; but this ne'er nursed
Pride in his heavenly bosom, in whose core   245
 No thought, save for his Master's service, durst
Intrude, however glorified and high;
He knew him but the viceroy of the sky.

32

He and the somber silent Spirit met—
 They knew each other both for good and ill;   250
Such was their power, that neither could forget
 His former friend and future foe; but still
There was a high, immortal, proud regret
 In either's eye, as if 'twere less their will
Than destiny to make the eternal years   255
Their date of war, and their "champ clos"[9] the spheres.

33

But here they were in neutral space: we know
 From Job, that Satan hath the power to pay
A heavenly visit thrice a year or so;

---

8. Joanna Southcott (1750–1814) was
a servant girl who, claiming direct com-
munications from the Almighty, became
head of a religious sect. In 1813 she
proclaimed that she was about to give
birth to a son, Shiloh, who would redeem
the world. The pregnancy turned out to
be a tumor, of which she died the following year.
9. "Enclosed field," the arena for
knightly tournaments.

And that the "sons of God," like those of clay,   260
Must keep him company;[1] and we might show
    From the same book, in how polite a way
    The dialogue is held between the Powers
Of Good and Evil—but 'twould take up hours.

34

And this is not a theologic tract,   265
    To prove with Hebrew and with Arabic
If Job be allegory or a fact,
    But a true narrative; and thus I pick
From out the whole but such and such an act
    As sets aside the slightest thought of trick.   270
'Tis every tittle true, beyond suspicion,
And accurate as any other vision.

35

The spirits were in neutral space, before
    The gate of heaven; like eastern thresholds is
The place where Death's grand cause is argued o'er,[2]   275
    And souls despatched to that world or to this;
And therefore Michael and the other wore
    A civil aspect: though they did not kiss,
Yet still between his Darkness and his Brightness
There passed a mutual glance of great politeness.   280

36

The Archangel bowed, not like a modern beau,
    But with a graceful oriental bend,
Pressing one radiant arm just where below
    The heart in good men is supposed to tend.
He turned as to an equal, not too low,   285
    But kindly; Satan met his ancient friend
With more hauteur, as might an old Castilian
Poor noble meet a mushroom rich civilian.[3]

37

He merely bent his diabolic brow
    An instant; and then raising it, he stood   290
In act to assert his right or wrong, and show
    Cause why King George by no means could or should
Make out a case to be exempt from woe
    Eternal, more than other kings, endued
With better sense and hearts, whom history mentions,   295
Who long have "paved hell with their good intentions."[4]

38

Michael began: "What wouldst thou with this man,
    Now dead, and brought before the Lord? What ill
Hath he wrought since his mortal race began,
    That thou canst claim him? Speak! and do thy will,   300

---

1. Job 1.6. "There was a day when the sons of God came to present themselves before the Lord, and Satan came also among them."
2. The gateways of walled cities in the Middle East were sometimes used for public debates and to administer justice.
3. Byron contrasts ancient Spanish noblemen with *nouveaux riches* who spring up as rapidly as mushrooms.
4. An old English proverb.

If it be just: if in this earthly span
  He hath been greatly failing to fulfil
His duties as a king and mortal, say,
And he is thine; if not, let him have way."

39

"Michael!" replied the Prince of Air, "even here,   305
  Before the Gate of him thou servest, must
I claim my subject: and will make appear
  That as he was my worshiper in dust,
So shall he be in spirit, although dear
  To thee and thine, because nor wine nor lust   310
Were of his weaknesses; yet on the throne
He reigned o'er millions to serve me alone.

40

"Look to *our* earth, or rather *mine*; it was,
  Once, *more* thy master's: but I triumph not
In this poor planet's conquest; nor, alas!   315
  Need he thou servest envy me my lot:
With all the myriads of bright worlds which pass
  In worship round him, he may have forgot
Yon weak creation of such paltry things:
I think few worth damnation save their kings—   320

41

"And these but as a kind of quitrent,[5] to
  Assert my right as lord: and even had
I such an inclination, 'twere (as you
  Well know) superfluous; they are grown so bad,
That hell has nothing better left to do   325
  Than leave them to themselves: so much more mad
And evil by their own internal curse,
Heaven cannot make them better, nor I worse.

42

"Look to the earth, I said, and say again:
  When this old, blind, mad, helpless, weak, poor worm   330
Began in youth's first bloom and flush to reign,
  The world and he both wore a different form,
And much of earth and all the watery plain
  Of ocean called him king: through many a storm
His isles had floated on the abyss of time;   335
For the rough virtues chose them for their clime.

43

"He came to his scepter young; he leaves it old:
  Look to the state in which he found his realm,
And left it; and his annals too behold,
  How to a minion first he gave the helm,[6]   340
How grew upon his heart a thirst for gold,
  The beggar's vice, which can but overwhelm
The meanest hearts; and for the rest, but glance
Thine eye along America and France.

5. A fixed rent, paid in place of services   George III made Prime Minister in
to a feudal lord.   1802.
6. The unpopular Earl of Bute, whom

44

" 'Tis true, he was a tool from first to last   345
   (I have the workmen safe); but as a tool
So let him be consumed. From out the past
   Of ages, since mankind have known the rule
Of monarchs—from the bloody rolls amassed
   Of sin and slaughter—from the Caesar's school,   350
Take the worst pupil; and produce a reign
More drenched with gore, more cumbered with the slain.

45

"He ever warred with freedom and the free:
   Nations as men, home subjects, foreign foes,
So that[7] they uttered the word 'Liberty!'   355
   Found George the Third their first opponent. Whose
History was ever stained as his will be
   With national and individual woes?
I grant his household abstinence; I grant
His neutral virtues, which most monarchs want;   360

46

"I know he was a constant consort; own
   He was a decent sire, and middling lord.
All this is much, and most upon a throne;
   As temperance, if at Apicius' board,[8]
Is more than at an anchorite's[9] supper shown.   365
   I grant him all the kindest can accord;
And this was well for him, but not for those
Millions who found him what oppression chose.

47

"The New World shook him off; the Old yet groans
   Beneath what he and his prepared, if not   370
Completed: he leaves heirs on many thrones
   To all his vices, without what begot
Compassion for him—his tame virtues; drones
   Who sleep, or despots who have now forgot
A lesson which shall be re-taught them, wake   375
Upon the thrones of earth; but let them quake!

48

"Five millions of the primitive,[1] who hold
   The faith which makes ye great on earth, implored
A *part* of that vast *all* they held of old—
   Freedom to worship—not alone your Lord,   380
Michael, but you, and you, Saint Peter! Cold
   Must be your souls, if you have not abhorred
The foe to Catholic participation
In all the license of a Christian nation.

49

"True! he allowed them to pray God; but as   385
   A consequence of prayer, refused the law

---

7. "Provided that."
8. I.e., At the table of Apicius (a famed Roman gourmet in the time of Augustus).
9. A religious hermit's.

1. The Irish Catholics. In 1795 George had opposed the Catholic Emancipation Bill, which gave Roman Catholics the right to hold public offices (line 383).

Which would have placed them upon the same base
    With those who did not hold the saints in awe."
But here Saint Peter started from his place,
    And cried, "You may the prisoner withdraw: 390
Ere heaven shall ope her portals to this Guelph,[2]
While I am guard, may I be damned myself!

50

"Sooner will I with Cerberus[3] exchange
    My office (and *his* is no sinecure)
Than see this royal Bedlam bigot range   395
    The azure fields of heaven, of that be sure!"
"Saint!" replied Satan, "you do well to avenge
    The wrongs he made your satellites endure;
And if to this exchange you should be given,
I'll try to coax *our* Cerberus up to heaven."   400

51

Here Michael interposed: "Good saint! and devil!
    Pray, not so fast; you both outrun discretion.
Saint Peter! you were wont to be more civil!
    Satan! excuse this warmth of his expression,
And condescension to the vulgar's level: 405
    Even saints sometimes forget themselves in session.
Have you got more to say?"—"No."—"If you please,
I'll trouble you to call your witnesses."

52

Then Satan turned and waved his swarthy hand,
    Which stirred with its electric qualities
Clouds farther off than we can understand,   410
    Although we find him sometimes in our skies;
Infernal thunder shook both sea and land
    In all the planets, and hell's batteries
Let off the artillery, which Milton mentions
As one of Satan's most sublime inventions.[4]   415

53

This was a signal unto such damned souls
    As have the privilege of their damnation
Extended far beyond the mere controls
    Of worlds past, present, or to come; no station   420
Is theirs particularly in the rolls
    Of hell assigned; but where their inclination
Or business carries them in search of game,
They may range freely—being damned the same.

54

They're proud of this—as very well they may,   425
    It being a sort of knighthood, or gilt key
Stuck in their loins;[5] or like an "entré"

---

2. The House of Hanover was descended from the German Guelphs.
3. The three-headed dog guarding the entrance to Hades.
4. In *Paradise Lost* VI. 469 ff., Satan announced his invention of the cannon for use in the war in heaven.
5. A gold key hung from the belt betokens certain official positions at the English court.

Up the back stairs, or such freemasonry.
I borrow my comparisons from clay,
    Being clay myself. Let not those spirits be   430
Offended with such base low likenesses;
We know their posts are nobler far than these.

55

When the great signal ran from heaven to hell—
    About ten million times the distance reckoned
From our sun to its earth, as we can tell   435
    How much time it takes up, even to a second,
For every ray that travels to dispel
    The fogs of London, through which, dimly beaconed,
The weathercocks are gilt some thrice a year,
If that the *summer* is not too severe—   440

56

I say that I can tell—'twas half a minute:
    I know the solar beams take up more time
Ere, packed up for their journey, they begin it;
    But then their telegraph[6] is less sublime,
And if they ran a race, they would not win it   445
    'Gainst Satan's couriers bound for their own clime.
The sun takes up some years for every ray
To reach its goal—the devil not half a day.

57

Upon the verge of space, about the size
    Of half-a-crown, a little speck appeared   450
(I've seen a something like it in the skies
    In the Aegean, ere a squall); it neared,
And, growing bigger, took another guise;
    Like an aërial ship it tacked, and steered,
Or *was* steered (I am doubtful of the grammar   455
Of the last phrase, which makes the stanza stammer—

58

But take your choice); and then it grew a cloud;
    And so it was—a cloud of witnesses.
But such a cloud! No land e'er saw a crowd
    Of locusts numerous as the heavens saw these;   460
They shadowed with their myriads space; their loud
    And varied cries were like those of wild geese
(If nations may be likened to a goose),
And realized the phrase of "hell broke loose."[7]

59

Here crashed a sturdy oath of stout John Bull,   465
    Who damned away his eyes as heretofore:
There Paddy brogued "By Jasus!"—"What's your wull?"
    The temperate Scot exclaimed: the French ghost swore
In certain terms I shan't translate in full,
    As the first coachman will; and 'midst the war,   470

6. In its original sense, any apparatus   7. *Paradise Lost* IV. 918.
for transmitting signals at a distance.

The voice of Jonathan was heard to express,
"*Our* president is going to war, I guess."[8]

60

Besides there were the Spaniard, Dutch, and Dane;
   In short, an universal shoal of shades,
From Otaheite's isle[9] to Salisbury Plain,   475
   Of all climes and professions, years and trades,
Ready to swear against the good king's reign,
   Bitter as clubs in cards are against spades;
All summoned by this grand "subpoena," to
Try if kings mayn't be damned like me or you.   480

61

When Michael saw this host, he first grew pale,
   As angels can; next, like Italian twilight,
He turned all colors—as a peacock's tail,
   Or sunset streaming through a Gothic skylight
In some old abbey, or a trout not stale,   485
   Or distant lightning on the horizon *by* night,
Or a fresh rainbow, or a grand review
Of thirty regiments in red, green, and blue.

62

Then he addressed himself to Satan: "Why—
   My good old friend, for such I deem you, though   490
Our different parties make us fight so shy,
   I ne'er mistake you for a *personal* foe;
Our difference is *political*, and I
   Trust that, whatever may occur below,
You know my great respect for you: and this   495
Makes me regret whate'er you do amiss—

63

"Why, my dear Lucifer, would you abuse
   My call for witnesses? I did not mean
That you should half of earth and hell produce;
   'Tis even superfluous, since two honest, clean,   500
True testimonies are enough: we lose
   Our time, nay, our eternity, between
The accusation and defense: if we
Hear both, 'twill stretch our immortality."

64

Satan replied, "To me the matter is   505
   Indifferent, in a personal point of view:
I can have fifty better souls than this
   With far less trouble than we have gone through
Already; and I merely argued his
   Late majesty of Britain's case with you   510
Upon a point of form: you may dispose
Of him; I've kings enough below, God knows!"

---

8. "Brother Jonathan" was the name applied to America and Americans, now replaced by "Uncle Sam"; the "I guess" was used by Byron as an obvious Americanism. This was written during the troubled Anglo-American relations after the War of 1812.
9. The old name for Tahiti.

65

Thus spoke the Demon (late called "multifaced"
    By multo-scribbling Southey[1]). "Then we'll call
One or two persons of the myriads placed   515
    Around our congress, and dispense with all
The rest," quoth Michael: "Who may be so graced
    As to speak first? there's choice enough—who shall
It be?" Then Satan answered, "There are many;
But you may choose Jack Wilkes[2] as well as any."   520

66

A merry, cock-eyed, curious-looking sprite
    Upon the instant started from the throng,
Dressed in a fashion now forgotten quite;
    For all the fashions of the flesh stick long
By people in the next world; where unite   525
    All the costumes since Adam's, right or wrong,
From Eve's fig leaf down to the petticoat,
Almost as scanty, of days less remote.

67

The spirit looked around upon the crowds
    Assembled, and exclaimed, "My friends of all   530
The spheres, we shall catch cold amongst these clouds;
    So let's to business: why this general call?
If those are freeholders I see in shrouds,
    And 'tis for an election that they bawl,
Behold a candidate with unturned coat!   535
Saint Peter, may I count upon your vote?"

68

"Sir," replied Michael, "you mistake; these things
    Are of a former life, and what we do
Above is more august; to judge of kings
    Is the tribunal met: so now you know."   540
"Then I presume those gentlemen with wings,"
    Said Wilkes, "are cherubs; and that soul below
Looks much like George the Third, but to my mind
A good deal older—Bless me! is he blind?"

69

"He is what you behold him, and his doom   545
    Depends upon his deeds," the Angel said.
"If you have aught to arraign in him, the tomb
    Gives license to the humblest beggar's head
To lift itself against the loftiest."—"Some,"
    Said Wilkes, "don't wait to see them laid in lead,   550
For such a liberty—and I, for one,
Have told them what I thought beneath the sun."

1. In *A Vision of Judgment* V. 70.
2. John Wilkes (1727–97), notorious libertine, wit, and courageous political radical, who in 1764 was expelled from the House of Commons and driven into exile for his libelous attack on George III in his weekly periodical, *The North Briton*. He later came back to England, became Lord Mayor of London, and was triumphantly returned to Parliament. For a supreme example of the wit and aplomb for which Byron admired Wilkes, see Boswell's account of Dr. Johnson's dinner with him in Volume 1.

70

"*Above* the sun repeat, then, what thou hast
    To urge against him," said the Archangel. "Why,"
Replied the spirit, "since old scores are past,   555
    Must I turn evidence? In faith, not I.
Besides, I beat him hollow at the last,
    With all his Lords and Commons:[3] in the sky
I don't like ripping up old stories, since
His conduct was but natural in a prince.   560

71

"Foolish, no doubt, and wicked, to oppress
    A poor unlucky devil without a shilling;
But then I blame the man himself much less
    Than Bute and Grafton,[4] and shall be unwilling
To see him punished here for their excess,   565
    Since they were both damned long ago, and still in
Their place below: for me, I have forgiven,
And vote his 'habeas corpus' into heaven."

72

"Wilkes," said the Devil, "I understand all this;
    You turned to half a courtier ere you died,[5]   570
And seem to think it would not be amiss
    To grow a whole one on the other side
Of Charon's ferry;[6] you forget that *his*
    Reign is concluded; whatsoe'er betide,
He won't be sovereign more: you've lost your labor   575
For at the best he will but be your neighbor.

73

"However, I knew what to think of it,
    When I beheld you in your jesting way
Flitting and whispering round about the spit
    Where Belial, upon duty for the day,   580
With Fox's lard was basting William Pitt,[7]
    His pupil; I knew what to think, I say:
That fellow even in hell breeds farther ills;
I'll have him *gagged*—'twas one of his own bills.[8]

74

"Call Junius!"[9] From the crowd a shadow stalked,   585

3. In 1782 Wilkes succeeded in getting the House of Commons to expunge the record of his expulsion.
4. The Duke of Grafton, like the Earl of Bute, was a minister subservient to George III.
5. Wilkes in his latter years softened his opposition and moved in higher social circles.
6. In Greek mythology, Charon ferried the dead to the underworld across the river Styx.
7. Charles James Fox, statesman and political opponent of William Pitt, prime minister under George III, was notably corpulent.
8. The Alien and Sedition Bills of 1795 severely restricted freedom of speech and of the press.
9. Pseudonym of the writer of a brilliant series of letters (1769–71), attacking supporters of George III and the King himself. His identity is an unsolved political mystery; among more than fifty possibilities proposed are Edmund Burke, John Horne Tooke, and Sir Philip Francis, mentioned in lines 631–32. When the letters were published as a book, the title-page read: *Letters of Junius, Stat Nominis Umbra* ("he stands, the shadow of a name"); hence the allusions, lines 593 ff., 667. The Latin phrase is from Lucan's *Pharsalia* I.135.

And at the name there was a general squeeze,
So that the very ghosts no longer walked
   In comfort, at their own aërial ease,
But were all rammed, and jammed (but to be balked,
   As we shall see), and jostled hands and knees,   590
Like wind compressed and pent within a bladder,
Or like a human colic, which is sadder.

75

The shadow came—a tall, thin, gray-haired figure,
   That looked as it had been a shade on earth;
Quick in its motions, with an air of vigor,   595
   But nought to mark its breeding or its birth:
Now it waxed little, then again grew bigger,
   With now an air of gloom, or savage mirth;
But as you gazed upon its features, they
Changed every instant—to *what*, none could say.   600

76

The more intently the ghosts gazed, the less
   Could they distinguish whose the features were;
The Devil himself seemed puzzled even to guess;
   They varied like a dream—now here, now there;
And several people swore from out the press,   605
   They knew him perfectly; and one could swear
He was his father: upon which another
Was sure he was his mother's cousin's brother:

77

Another, that he was a duke, or knight,
   An orator, a lawyer, or a priest,   610
A nabob,[1] a man-midwife; but the wight
   Mysterious changed his countenance at least
As oft as they their minds: though in full sight
   He stood, the puzzle only was increased;
The man was a phantasmagoria in   615
Himself—he was so volatile and thin.

78

The moment that you had pronounced him *one*,
   Presto! his face changed, and he was another;
And when that change was hardly well put on,
   It varied, till I don't think his own mother   620
(If that he had a mother) would her son
   Have known, he shifted so from one to t'other;
Till guessing from a pleasure grew a task,
At this epistolary "Iron Mask."[2]

79

For sometimes he like Cerberus would seem—   625
   "Three gentlemen at once" (as sagely says
Good Mrs. Malaprop[3]); then you might deem

---

1. A man of great wealth, especially one who has returned to England with a fortune acquired in India.
2. "The Man in the Iron Mask" was a state prisoner in the reign of Louis XIV, whose identity was thus concealed.
3. A character in R. B. Sheridan's *The Rivals*, who comically misused words; the word "malapropism" derives from her name.

That he was not even *one*; now many rays
   Were flashing round him; and now a thick steam
     Hid him from sight—like fogs on London days: 630
Now Burke, now Tooke, he grew to people's fancies,
And certes often like Sir Philip Francis.

80

I've an hypothesis—'tis quite my own;
   I never let it out till now, for fear
Of doing people harm about the throne,   635
   And injuring some minister or peer,
On whom the stigma might perhaps be blown;
   It is—my gentle public, lend thine ear!
'Tis, that what Junius we are wont to call
Was *really, truly*, nobody at all.   640

81

I don't see wherefore letters should not be
   Written without hands, since we daily view
Them written without heads; and books, we see,
   Are filled as well without the latter too:
And really till we fix on somebody   645
   For certain sure to claim them as his due,
Their author, like the Niger's mouth,[4] will bother
The world to say if *there* be mouth or author.

82

"And who and what art thou?" the Archangel said.
   "For *that* you may consult my title page,"   650
Replied this mighty shadow of a shade:
   "If I have kept my secret half an age,
I scarce shall tell it now."—"Canst thou upbraid,"
   Continued Michael, "George Rex, or allege
Aught further?" Junius answered, "You had better   655
First ask him for *his* answer to my letter:

83

"My charges upon record will outlast
   The brass of both his epitaph and tomb."
"Repent'st thou not," said Michael, "of some past
   Exaggeration? something which may doom   660
Thyself if false, as him if true? Thou wast
   Too bitter—is it not so?—in thy gloom
Of passion?"—"Passion!" cried the phantom dim,
"I loved my country, and I hated him.

84

"What I have written, I have written:[5] let   665
   The rest be on his head or mine!" So spoke
Old "Nominis Umbra"; and while speaking yet,
   Away he melted in celestial smoke.
Then Satan said to Michael, "Don't forget
   To call George Washington, and John Horne Tooke,[6]   670

---

4. Several recent British expeditio   [ ]   prominent English opponent of the
explore the course of the river N[ ] ,   war against the American colonies; see
in western Africa, had ended in failure.   note to line 585.
5. Said by Pilate, John xix.22.

And Franklin"—but at this time there was heard
A cry for room, though not a phantom stirred.

85

At length with jostling, elbowing, and the aid
    Of cherubim appointed to that post,
The devil Asmodeus[7] to the circle made   675
    His way, and looked as if his journey cost
Some trouble. When his burden down he laid,
    "What's this?" cried Michael; "why, 'tis not a ghost?"
"I know it," quoth the incubus; "but he
Shall be one, if you leave the affair to me.   680

86

"Confound the renegado! I have sprained
    My left wing, he's so heavy; one would think
Some of his works about his neck were chained.
    But to the point; while hovering o'er the brink
Of Skiddaw (where as usual it still rained),[8]   685
    I saw a taper, far below me, wink,
And stooping, caught this fellow at a libel—
No less on history than the Holy Bible.

87

"The former is the devil's scripture, and
    The latter yours, good Michael: so the affair   690
Belongs to all of us, you understand.
    I snatched him up just as you see him there,
And brought him off for sentence out of hand:
    I've scarcely been ten minutes in the air—
At least a quarter it can hardly be: 695
I dare say that his wife is still at tea."

88

Here Satan said, "I know this man of old,
    And have expected him for some time here;
A sillier fellow you will scarce behold,
    Or more conceited in his petty sphere: 700
But surely it was not worth while to fold
    Such trash below your wing, Asmodeus dear:
We had the poor wretch safe (without being bored
With carriage) coming of his own accord.

89

"But since he's here, let's see what he has done."   705
    "Done!" cried Asmodeus, "he anticipates
The very business you are now upon,
    And scribbles as if head clerk to the Fates.
Who knows to what his ribaldry may run,
    When such an ass as this, like Balaam's,[9] prates?"   710
"Let's hear," quoth Michael, "what he has to say:
You know we're bound to that in every way."

---

7. The devil in Le Sage's *Le Diable Boiteux* ("The Lame Devil"), published 1707, who carries Don Cleofas to the summit of San Salvador.

8. Mount Skiddaw, near Southey's home in the Lake Country.

9. Balaam's ass was granted speech in Numbers xxii.28 ff.

90

Now the bard, glad to get an audience, which
    By no means often was his case below,
Began to cough, and hawk, and hem, and pitch   715
    His voice into that awful note of woe
To all unhappy hearers within reach
    Of poets when the tide of rhyme's in flow;
But stuck fast with his first hexameter,
    Not one of all whose gouty feet would stir.   720

91

But ere the spavined dactyls[1] could be spurred
    Into recitative, in great dismay
Both cherubim and seraphim were heard
    To murmur loudly through their long array;
And Michael rose ere he could get a word   725
    Of all his foundered verses under way,
And cried, "For God's sake stop, my friend! 'twere best—
Non Di, non homines[2]—you know the rest."

92

A general bustle spread throughout the throng,
    Which seemed to hold all verse in detestation;   730
The angels had of course enough of song
    When upon service; and the generation
Of ghosts had heard too much in life, not long
    Before, to profit by a new occasion:
The monarch, mute till then, exclaimed, "What! what!   735
Pye[3] come again? No more—no more of that!"

93

The tumult grew; an universal cough
    Convulsed the skies, as during a debate,
When Castlereagh[4] has been up long enough
    (Before he was first minister of state,   740
I mean—the slaves hear now); some cried "Off, off!"
    As at a farce; till, grown quite desperate,
The bard Saint Peter prayed to interpose
(Himself an author)[5] only for his prose.

94

The varlet was not an ill-favored knave;   745
    A good deal like a vulture in the face,
With a hook nose and a hawk's eye, which gave
    A smart and sharper-looking sort of grace
To his whole aspect, which, though rather grave,

1. Southey's *A Vision of Judgment* was written in dactylic hexameters, a very awkward measure in English. A "spavined" horse is a lame one.
2. Horace, *Art of Poetry*, 372–73: "mediocribus esse poetis / Non homines, non di, non concessere columnae" ("mediocrity in poets has never been tolerated by either men, or gods, or booksellers").
3. Henry James Pye, an inept and much ridiculed poet, Southey's predecessor as poet laureate.
4. Viscount Castlereagh was foreign secretary when Byron wrote his poem. "The slaves hear now": i.e., now that he is Prime Minister members of the House of Commons listen obsequiously.
5. The reference is to the first and second epistles of Peter, very short books in the New Testament.

Was by no means so ugly as his case;   750
But that, indeed, was hopeless as can be,
Quite a poetic felony *"de se."*[6]

95

Then Michael blew his trump, and stilled the noise
    With one still greater, as is yet the mode
On earth besides; except some grumbling voice,   755
    Which now and then will make a slight inroad
Upon decorous silence, few will twice
    Lift up their lungs when fairly overcrowed;
And now the bard could plead his own bad cause,
With all the attitudes of self-applause.   760

96

He said—(I only give the heads)—he said,
    He meant no harm in scribbling; 'twas his way
Upon all topics; 'twas, besides, his bread,
    Of which he buttered both sides; 'twould delay
Too long the assembly (he was pleased to dread),   765
    And take up rather more time than a day,
To name his works—he would but cite a few—
"Wat Tyler"—"Rhymes on Blenheim"—"Waterloo."

97

He had written praises of a regicide;[7]
    He had written praises of all kings what ever;   770
He had written for republics far and wide,
    And then against them bitterer than ever:
For pantisocracy[8] he once had cried
    Aloud, a scheme less moral than 'twas clever;
Then grew a hearty anti-jacobin—   775
Had turned his coat—and would have turned his skin.

98

He had sung against all battles, and again
    In their high praise and glory; he had called
Reviewing "the ungentle craft,"[9] and then
    Become as base a critic as e'er crawled—   780
Fed, paid, and pampered by the very men
    By whom his muse and morals had been mauled:
He had written much blank verse, and blanker prose,
And more of both than anybody knows.

99

He had written Wesley's life—here turning round   785
    To Satan, "Sir, I'm ready to write yours,
In two octavo volumes, nicely bound,
    With notes and preface, all that most allures
The pious purchaser; and there's no ground
    For fear, for I can choose my own reviewers: 790

6. A felony "upon himself"; that is, suicide.
7. In an early poem on Henry Martin, one of the judges who had condemned Charles I to be beheaded.
8. An ideal community that Southey and Coleridge, in 1794–95, had planned to set up in America on the banks of the Susquehanna. The scheme was utopian, but in no way immoral.
9. In Southey's *The Remains of Henry Kirke White*, Vol. I (1808).

So let me have the proper documents,
That I may add you to my other saints."

100

Satan bowed, and was silent. "Well, if you,
    With amiable modesty, decline
My offer, what says Michael? There are few   795
    Whose memoirs could be rendered more divine.
Mine is a pen of all work; not so new
    As it was once, but I would make you shine
Like your own trumpet. By the way, my own
Has more of brass in it, and is as well blown.   800

101

"But talking about trumpets, here's my Vision!
    Now you shall judge, all people; yes, you shall
Judge with my judgment, and by my decision
    Be guided who shall enter heaven or fall.
I settle all these things by intuition,   805
    Times present, past, to come, heaven, hell, and all,
Like King Alfonso.[1] When I thus see double,
I save the Deity some worlds of trouble."

102

He ceased, and drew forth an MS.; and no
    Persuasion on the part of devils, saints,   810
Or angels, now could stop the torrent; so
    He read the first three lines of the contents;
But at the fourth, the whole spiritual show
    Had vanished, with variety of scents,
Ambrosial and sulphureous, as they sprang,   815
Like lightning, off from his "melodious twang."[2]

103

Those grand heroics acted as a spell:
    The angels stopped their ears and plied their pinions;
The devils ran howling, deafened, down to hell;
    The ghosts fled, gibbering, for their own dominions—   820
(For 'tis not yet decided where they dwell,
    And I leave every man to his opinions);
Michael took refuge in his trump—but, lo!
His teeth were set on edge, he could not blow!

104

Saint Peter, who has hitherto been known   825
    For an impetuous saint, upraised his keys,
And at the fifth line knocked the poet down;
    Who fell like Phaëton,[3] but more at ease,

---

1. "King Alphonso [of Castile, in the 13th century] speaking of the Ptolemean system, said that had he been consulted at the creation of the world, he would have spared the Maker some absurdities" [Byron's note].
2. John Aubrey in his *Miscellanies upon Various Subjects* (1696) had described

a ghost that vanished "with a curious perfume, and most melodious twang."
3. Phaethon, son of Apollo, tried to drive his father's chariot, the sun. He could not control the horses and was struck down into the sea by a thunderbolt of Zeus. The satiric point is that Apollo is the god of poetry as well as of the sun.

Into his lake, for there he did not drown;
   A different web being by the Destinies   830
Woven for the Laureate's final wreath, whene'er
   Reform shall happen either here or there.

105

He first sank to the bottom—like his works,
   But soon rose to the surface—like himself;
For all corrupted things are buoyed like corks,   835
   By their own rottenness, light as an elf,
Or wisp that flits o'er a morass: he lurks,
   It may be, still, like dull books on a shelf,
In his own den, to scrawl some "Life" or "Vision,"
As Welborn says—"the devil turned precisian."[4]   840

106

As for the rest, to come to the conclusion
   Of this true dream, the telescope is gone
Which kept my optics free from all delusion,
   And showed me what I in my turn have shown;
All I saw farther, in the last confusion,   845
   Was, that King George slipped into heaven for one;
And when the tumult dwindled to a calm,
I left him practicing the hundredth psalm.[5]

1821   1822

4. A "precisian" is a Puritan. Spoken by Welborn in Massinger's play, *A New Way to Pay Old Debts* (1626), I.i.6.

5. Which contains the relevant line, "Enter into his gates with thanksgiving."

Don Juan

Byron began his masterpiece (pronounced in the English fashion, *Don Joó-un*) in July of 1818, published it in installments, beginning with Cantos I and II in 1819, and continued working on it almost until his death. He extemporized the poem from episode to episode; "I *have* no plan," he said, "I *had* no plan; but I had or have materials." The work was composed with remarkable speed (the 888 lines of Canto XIII, for example, were accomplished within a week), and it seeks to give the effect of improvisation and comprehensiveness rather than of compression; it asks to be read rapidly, at a conversational pace.

The poem breaks off with the sixteenth canto, but even in its unfinished state *Don Juan* is the longest satire, and one of the longest of all poems, written in English. Its hero, the Spanish libertine, had in the original legend been superhuman in his sexual energy and wickedness. Throughout Byron's version the unspoken but persistent joke is that this violent and archetypal *homme fatal* of European legend is in fact more acted upon than active. Unfailingly amiable and well-intentioned, he is guilty largely of youth, charm, and a courteous and compliant spirit. The ladies do all the rest.

The chief models for the poem were the Italian seriocomic versions of medieval chivalric romances; the genre had been introduced by Pulci in the 15th century and achieved its greatest success in Ariosto's *Orlando Furioso* (1516). From these writers Byron caught the mixed moods and violent oscillations between the sublime and the ridiculous, as well as the easy, colloquial management of the complex ottava rima—an eight-line stanza in which the initial interlaced rhymes (*ababab*) build up to the comic turn in the final pat couplet (*cc*). Byron was influenced in the English use of this Italian form by a mildly amusing poem published in 1817, under the pseudonym of "Whistlecraft," by his friend John Hookham Frere. Other recognizable antecedents of *Don Juan* are Swift's *Gulliver's Travels* and Johnson's *Rasselas*, which also employed the naïve traveler as a satiric device, and Laurence Sterne's novel, *Tristram Shandy*, with its comic exploitation of a narrative medium blatantly subject to the whimsy of the author. But even the most original literary works play variations upon inherited conventions. Shelley at once recognized his friend's poem for what it was, "something wholly new and relative to the age."

Byron's most trusted literary advisers thought the poem disgracefully immoral, and John Murray took the precaution of printing the first two installments without identifying either Byron as the author or himself as the publisher. In our own day, however, the most common complaint is not that *Don Juan* is immoral, but that it is morally nihilistic—that the poem is destructive without limit, since it proposes no positive values as a base for the satire, but sees life, in the words of one critic, as "a strange meaningless pageant." Yet Byron insisted that *Don Juan* is "a *satire* on *abuses* of the present state of society," and "the most moral of poems." Though the final phrase exaggerates, it has a foundation of truth. What the poem most frequently attacks, in love, religion, and social relations, are very considerable vices—sham, hypocrisy, complacency, oppression, greed, and lust. Furthermore, the satire constantly, though silently, assumes as moral positives the qualities of courage, loyalty, generosity, and, above all, total candor; it merely implies that these virtues are excessively rare, and that the modern world is not constituted to reward, to encourage, or even to recognize them when they make their appearance. And *Don Juan* is zestfully on the side of life, in its abundant variety. "As to *Don Juan*," Byron wrote elatedly to a friend, "confess—confess, you dog and be candid. * * * It may be profligate, but is it not *life*, is it not *the thing?*"

It is a mistake to look to *Don Juan* primarily for the story. The controlling element is not the narrative but the narrator, and his temperament gives the work its unity. The poem is really an incessant monologue, in the course of which a story manages to be told. It opens with the first-person pronoun and immediately lets us into the story-teller's predicament: "I want a hero * * * " The voice then goes on, for almost two thousand stanzas, with effortless volubility and bewildering shifts of mood and perspective, using the occasion of Juan's misadventures to confide to us the speaker's thoughts and devastating judgments upon all the major institutions, activities, and values of Western society.

What Byron discovered in *Don Juan* was how to give literary expression to that aspect of his temperament which, in real life, his self-consciousness and reserve permitted him to display only in the security of a circle of intimate friends or in his wonderfully vivacious letters to people he trusted. The poet who in his brilliantly successful youth created the gloomy and misanthropic Byronic hero, in his later and sadder life created a character (not the hero, but the narrator of *Don Juan*) who is one of the great, and one of the most complex, comic inventions in literature.

From Don Juan
Fragment[1]

I would to heaven that I were so much clay,
    As I am blood, bone, marrow, passion, feeling—
Because at least the past were passed away—
    And for the future—(but I write this reeling,
Having got drunk exceedingly today,   5
    So that I seem to stand upon the ceiling)
I say—the future is a serious matter—
And so—for God's sake—hock[2] and soda water!

From *Canto I*

1

I want a hero: an uncommon want,
    When every year and month sends forth a new one,
Till, after cloying the gazettes with cant,
    The age discovers he is not the true one;
Of such as these I should not care to vaunt,   5
    I'll therefore take our ancient friend Don Juan—
We all have seen him, in the pantomime,[1]
Sent to the devil somewhat ere his time.

* * *

5

Brave men were living before Agamemnon[2]
    And since, exceeding valorous and sage,
A good deal like him too, though quite the same none;   35
    But then they shone not on the poet's page,
And so have been forgotten—I condemn none,
    But can't find any in the present age

---

1. This stanza was written on the back of part of the MS. of Canto I.
2. A white Rhine wine, from the German *Hochheimer*.
1. The Juan legend was a popular sub-ject in English pantomime.
2. In Homer's *Iliad*, the king commanding the Greeks in the siege of Troy. This line is translated from an ode by Horace.

Fit for my poem (that is, for my new one);
So, as I said, I'll take my friend Don Juan. 40

6

Most epic poets plunge *"in medias res"*[3]
   (Horace makes this the heroic turnpike road),
And then your hero tells, whene'er you please,
   What went before—by way of episode,
While seated after dinner at his ease, 45
   Beside his mistress in some soft abode,
Palace, or garden, paradise, or cavern,
Which serves the happy couple for a tavern.

7

That is the usual method, but not mine—
   My way is to begin with the beginning;
The regularity of my design 50
   Forbids all wandering as the worst of sinning,
And therefore I shall open with a line
   (Although it cost me half an hour in spinning)
Narrating somewhat of Don Juan's father, 55
And also of his mother, if you'd rather.

8

In Seville was he born, a pleasant city,
   Famous for oranges and women—he
Who has not seen it will be much to pity,
   So says the proverb—and I quite agree; 60
Of all the Spanish towns is none more pretty,
   Cadiz perhaps—but that you soon may see—
Don Juan's parents lived beside the river,
A noble stream, and called the Guadalquivir.

9

His father's name was Jóse[4]—*Don*, of course, 65
   A true Hidalgo, free from every stain
Of Moor or Hebrew blood, he traced his source
   Through the most Gothic gentlemen of Spain;
A better cavalier ne'er mounted horse,
   Or, being mounted, e'er got down again, 70
Than Jóse, who begot our hero, who
Begot—but that's to come—Well, to renew:

10

His mother was a learned lady, famed
   For every branch of every science known—
In every Christian language ever named, 75
   With virtues equaled by her wit alone:
She made the cleverest people quite ashamed,
   And even the good with inward envy groan,
Finding themselves so very much exceeded
In their own way by all the things that she did. 80

3. "Into the middle of things" (Horace, *Ars Poetica* 148).   4. Normally "José," of course; Byron transferred the accent for his meter.

11

Her memory was a mine: she knew by heart
    All Calderon and greater part of Lopé,[5]
So that if any actor missed his part
    She could have served him for the prompter's copy;
For her Feinagle's[6] were an useless art,   85
    And he himself obliged to shut up shop—he
Could never make a memory so fine as
That which adorned the brain of Donna Inez.

12

Her favorite science was the mathematical,
    Her noblest virtue was her magnanimity,   90
Her wit (she sometimes tried at wit) was Attic[7] all,
    Her serious sayings darkened to sublimity;
In short, in all things she was fairly what I call
    A prodigy—her morning dress was dimity,
Her evening silk, or, in the summer, muslin,   95
And other stuffs, with which I won't stay puzzling.

13

She knew the Latin—that is, "the Lord's prayer,"
    And Greek—the alphabet—I'm nearly sure;
She read some French romances here and there,
    Although her mode of speaking was not pure;   100
For native Spanish she had no great care,
    At least her conversation was obscure;
Her thoughts were theorems, her words a problem,
As if she deemed that mystery would ennoble 'em.

* * *

22

'Tis pity learned virgins ever wed
    With persons of no sort of education,
Or gentlemen, who, though well born and bred,   170
    Grow tired of scientific conversation:
I don't choose to say much upon this head,
    I'm a plain man, and in a single station,
But—Oh! ye lords of ladies intellectual.   175
Inform us truly, have they not henpecked you all?

23

Don Jóse and his lady quarrelled—*why*,
    Not any of the many could divine,
Though several thousand people chose to try,
    'Twas surely no concern of theirs nor mine;   180
I loathe that low vice, curiosity;
    But if there's anything in which I shine,

5. Lope de Vega and Calderón de la
Barca, the great Spanish dramatists of
the early 17th century.
6. Gregor von Feinagle, a German expert on mnemonics, who had lectured in
England in 1811.
7. Athenian. The common phrase "Attic
salt" signifies the famed wit of the
Athenians.

'Tis in arranging all my friends' affairs,
Not having, of my own, domestic cares.

24

And so I interfered, and with the best   185
  Intentions, but their treatment was not kind;
I think the foolish people were possessed,
  For neither of them could I ever find,
Although their porter afterwards confessed—
  But that's no matter, and the worst's behind,   190
For little Juan o'er me threw, downstairs,
A pail of housemaid's water unawares.

25

A little curly-headed, good-for-nothing,
  And mischief-making monkey from his birth;
His parents ne'er agreed except in doting   195
  Upon the most unquiet imp on earth;
Instead of quarreling, had they been but both in
  Their senses, they'd have sent young master forth
To school, or had him soundly whipped at home,
To teach him manners for the time to come.   200

26

Don Jóse and the Donna Inez led
  For some time an unhappy sort of life,
Wishing each other, not divorced, but dead;
  They lived respectably as man and wife,
Their conduct was exceedingly well-bred,   205
  And gave no outward signs of inward strife,
Until at length the smothered fire broke out,
And put the business past all kind of doubt.

27

For Inez called some druggists and physicians,
  And tried to prove her loving lord was *mad*,[8]   210
But as he had some lucid intermissions,
  She next decided he was only *bad*;
Yet when they asked her for her depositions,
  No sort of explanation could be had,
Save that her duty both to man and God   215
Required this conduct—which seemed very odd.

28

She kept a journal, where his faults were noted,
  And opened certain trunks of books and letters,
All which might, if occasion served, be quoted;
  And then she had all Seville for abettors,   220
Besides her good old grandmother (who doted);
  The hearers of her case became repeaters,
Then advocates, inquisitors, and judges,
Some for amusement, others for old grudges.

8. Lady Byron had thought her husband might be insane, and sought medical advice on the matter. This and other passages obviously allude to his wife, although Byron insisted that Donna Inez was not intended to be a caricature of Lady Byron.

29

And then this best and meekest woman bore   225
  With such serenity her husband's woes,
Just as the Spartan ladies did of yore,
  Who saw their spouses killed, and nobly chose
Never to say a word about them more—
  Calmly she heard each calumny that rose,   230
And saw *his* agonies with such sublimity,
That all the world exclaimed, "What magnanimity!"

* * *

32

Their friends had tried at reconciliation,
  Then their relations, who made matters worse   250
('Twere hard to tell upon a like occasion
  To whom it may be best to have recourse—
I can't say much for friend or yet relation);
  The lawyers did their utmost for divorce,
But scarce a fee was paid on either side   255
Before, unluckily, Don Jóse died.

33

He died: and most unluckily, because
  According to all hints I could collect
From counsel learned in those kinds of laws
  (Although their talk's obscure and circumspect),   260
His death contrived to spoil a charming cause;
  A thousand pities also with respect
To public feeling, which on this occasion
Was manifested in a great sensation.

* * *

37

Dying intestate, Juan was sole heir
  To a chancery suit,[9] and messuages, and lands,   290
Which, with a long minority and care,
  Promised to turn out well in proper hands:
Inez became sole guardian, which was fair,
  And answered but to nature's just demands;
An only son left with an only mother   295
Is brought up much more wisely than another.

38

Sagest of women, even of widows, she
  Resolved that Juan should be quite a paragon,
And worthy of the noblest pedigree
  (His sire was of Castile, his dam from Aragon).   300
Then for accomplishments of chivalry,
  In case our lord the king should go to war again,
He learned the arts of riding, fencing, gunnery,
And how to scale a fortress—or a nunnery.

9. A suit in what was then the highest   "Messuages": houses and the adjoining
English court, notorious for its delays.   lands.

39

But that which Donna Inez most desired,   305
   And saw into herself each day before all
The learned tutors whom for him she hired,
   Was that his breeding should be strictly moral:
Much into all his studies she inquired,
   And so they were submitted first to her, all,   310
Arts, sciences, no branch was made a mystery
To Juan's eyes, excepting natural history.[1]

40

The languages, especially the dead,
   The sciences, and most of all the abstruse,
The arts, at least all such as could be said   315
   To be the most remote from common use,
In all these he was much and deeply read;
   But not a page of anything that's loose,
Or hints continuation of the species,
Was ever suffered, lest he should grow vicious.   320

41

His classic studies made a little puzzle,
   Because of filthy loves of gods and goddesses,
Who in the earlier ages raised a bustle,
   But never put on pantaloons or bodices;
His reverend tutors had at times a tussle,   325
   And for their *Aeneids*, *Iliads*, and *Odysseys*,
Were forced to make an odd sort of apology,
For Donna Inez dreaded the mythology.

42

Ovid's a rake, as half his verses show him,
   Anacreon's morals are a still worse sample,   330
Catullus scarcely has a decent poem,
   I don't think Sappho's *Ode* a good example,
Although Longinus tells us there is no hymn
   Where the sublime soars forth on wings more ample;[2]
But Virgil's songs are pure, except that horrid one   335
Beginning with "*Formosum Pastor Corydon*."[3]

43

Lucretius' irreligion[4] is too strong
   For early stomachs, to prove wholesome food;
I can't help thinking Juvenal[5] was wrong,
   Although no doubt his real intent was good,   340
For speaking out so plainly in his song,
   So much indeed as to be downright rude;

---

1. Which includes biology and physiology.
2. The Greek rhetorician Longinus praises a passage from Sappho in *On the Sublime* X.
3. Virgil's *Eclogue II* begins: "The shepherd, Corydon, burned with love for the handsome Alexis."
4. In *De rerum natura* ("On the Nature of Things") Lucretius sets out to show that the universe can be explained without reference to any god.
5. The Latin satires of Juvenal attacked the corruption of Roman society in the first century A.D.

And then what proper person can be partial
To all those nauseous epigrams of Martial?

44

Juan was taught from out the best edition,   345
   Expurgated by learned men, who place,
Judiciously, from out the schoolboy's vision,
   The grosser parts; but fearful to deface
Too much their modest bard by this omission,
   And pitying sore his mutilated case,   350
They only add them all in an appendix,[6]
Which saves, in fact, the trouble of an index.

* * *

52

For my part I say nothing—nothing—but
   This I will say—my reasons are my own—   410
That if I had an only son to put
   To school (as God be praised that I have none)
'Tis not with Donna Inez I would shut
   Him up to learn his catechism alone,
No—no—I'd send him out betimes to college,   415
For there it was I picked up my own knowledge.

53

For there one learns—'tis not for me to boast,
   Though I acquired—but I pass over *that*,
As well as all the Greek I since have lost:
   I say that there's the place—but *"Verbum sat,"*[7]   420
I think I picked up too, as well as most,
   Knowledge of matters—but no matter *what*—
I never married—but, I think, I know
That sons should not be educated so.

54

Young Juan now was sixteen years of age,   425
   Tall, handsome, slender, but well knit: he seemed
Active, though not so sprightly, as a page;
   And everybody but his mother deemed
Him almost man; but she flew in a rage
   And bit her lips (for else she might have screamed)   430
If any said so, for to be precocious
Was in her eyes a thing the most atrocious.

55

Amongst her numerous acquaintance, all
   Selected for discretion and devotion,
There was the Donna Julia, whom to call   435
   Pretty were but to give a feeble notion
Of many charms in her as natural
   As sweetness to the flower, or salt to ocean,
Her zone[8] to Venus, or his bow to Cupid
(But this last simile is trite and stupid).   440

6. "Fact! There is, or was, such an edition, with all the obnoxious epigrams of Martial placed by themselves at the end" [Byron's note].

7. A word [to the wise] is sufficient.

8. Girdle.

56

The darkness of her Oriental eye
   Accorded with her Moorish origin
(Her blood was not all Spanish, by the by;
   In Spain, you know, this is a sort of sin).
When proud Granada fell, and, forced to fly,   445
   Boabdil wept,[9] of Donna Julia's kin
Some went to Africa, some stayed in Spain,
Her great-great-grandmamma chose to remain.

57

She married (I forget the pedigree)
   With an hidalgo,[1] who transmitted down   450
His blood less noble than such blood should be;
   At such alliances his sires would frown,
In that point so precise in each degree
   That they bred *in and in*, as might be shown,
Marrying their cousins—nay, their aunts, and nieces,   455
Which always spoils the breed, if it increases.

58

This heathenish cross restored the breed again,
   Ruined its blood, but much improved its flesh;
For from a root the ugliest in old Spain
   Sprung up a branch as beautiful as fresh;   460
The sons no more were short, the daughters plain:
   But there's a rumor which I fain would hush,
'Tis said that Donna Julia's grandmamma
Produced her Don more heirs at love than law.

59

However this might be, the race went on   465
   Improving still through every generation,
Until it centered in an only son,
   Who left an only daughter; my narration
May have suggested that this single one
   Could be but Julia (whom on this occasion   470
I shall have much to speak about), and she
Was married, charming, chaste, and twenty-three.

60

Her eye (I'm very fond of handsome eyes)
   Was large and dark, suppressing half its fire
Until she spoke, then through its soft disguise   475
   Flashed an expression more of pride than ire,
And love than either; and there would arise
   A something in them which was not desire,
But would have been, perhaps, but for the soul
Which struggled through and chastened down the whole.   480

61

Her glossy hair was clustered o'er a brow
   Bright with intelligence, and fair, and smooth;

9. The last Moorish king of Granada
(then a province in Spain) wept when
his capital fell to the Spaniards (1492).

1. A Spanish nobleman of the lower
class.

Her eyebrow's shape was like the aërial bow,
    Her cheek all purple with the beam of youth,
Mounting, at times, to a transparent glow,   485
    As if her veins ran lightning; she, in sooth,
Possessed an air and grace by no means common:
    Her stature tall—I hate a dumpy woman.

                    62
Wedded she was some years, and to a man
    Of fifty, and such husbands are in plenty;   490
And yet, I think, instead of such a ONE
    'Twere better to have TWO of five-and-twenty,
Especially in countries near the sun:
    And now I think on't, "*mi vien in mente*,"[2]
Ladies even of the most uneasy virtue   495
Prefer a spouse whose age is short of thirty.

                    63
'Tis a sad thing, I cannot choose but say,
    And all the fault of that indecent sun,
Who cannot leave alone our helpless clay,
    But will keep baking, broiling, burning on,   500
That howsoever people fast and pray,
    The flesh is frail, and so the soul undone:
What men call gallantry, and gods adultery,
Is much more common where the climate's sultry.

                    64
Happy the nations of the moral North!   505
    Where all is virtue, and the winter season
Sends sin, without a rag on, shivering forth
    ('Twas snow that brought St. Anthony to reason);[3]
Where juries cast up what a wife is worth
    By laying whate'er sum, in mulct,[4] they please on   510
The lover, who must pay a handsome price,
Because it is a marketable vice.

                    65
Alfonso was the name of Julia's lord,
    A man well looking for his years, and who
Was neither much beloved nor yet abhorred: 515
    They lived together as most people do,
Suffering each other's foibles by accord,
    And not exactly either *one* or *two*;
Yet he was jealous, though he did not show it,
For jealousy dislikes the world to know it.

                    * * *

                    69
Juan she saw, and, as a pretty child,   545
    Caressed him often—such a thing might be
Quite innocently done, and harmless styled,

---

2. "It comes to my mind."
3. "For the particulars of St. Anthony's recipe for hot blood in cold weather,
see Mr. **Alban Butler's** *Lives of the Saints*" [Byron's note].
4. By way of a fine or legal penalty.

When she had twenty years, and thirteen he;
But I am not so sure I should have smiled
   When he was sixteen, Julia twenty-three;   550
These few short years make wondrous alterations,
Particularly amongst sunburnt nations.

70

Whate'er the cause might be, they had become
   Changed; for the dame grew distant, the youth shy,
Their looks cast down, their greetings almost dumb,   555
   And much embarrassment in either eye;
There surely will be little doubt with some
   That Donna Julia knew the reason why,
But as for Juan, he had no more notion
Than he who never saw the sea, of ocean.   560

71

Yet Julia's very coldness still was kind,
   And tremulously gentle her small hand
Withdrew itself from his, but left behind
   A little pressure, thrilling, and so bland
And slight, so very slight, that to the mind   565
   'Twas but a doubt; but ne'er magician's wand
Wrought change with all Armida's[5] fairy art
Like what this light touch left on Juan's heart.

72

And if she met him, though she smiled no more,
   She looked a sadness sweeter than her smile,   570
As if her heart had deeper thoughts in store
   She must not own, but cherished more the while,
For that compression in its burning core;
   Even innocence itself has many a wile,
And will not dare to trust itself with truth,   575
And love is taught hypocrisy from youth.

* * *

76

She vowed she never would see Juan more,
   And next day paid a visit to his mother,
And looked extremely at the opening door,
   Which, by the Virgin's grace, let in another;
Grateful she was, and yet a little sore—   605
   Again it opens, it can be no other,
'Tis surely Juan now—No! I'm afraid
That night the Virgin was no further prayed.

77

She now determined that a virtuous woman
   Should rather face and overcome temptation,
That flight was base and dastardly, and no man   610
   Should ever give her heart the least sensation;
That is to say, a thought beyond the common

5. The sorceress who seduces Rinaldo in Tasso's *Jerusalem Delivered*.

Preference, that we must feel upon occasion,
For people who are pleasanter than others,   615
But then they only seem so many brothers.

78

And even if by chance—and who can tell?
  The devil's so very sly—she should discover
That all within was not so very well,
  And, if still free, that such or such a lover   620
Might please perhaps, a virtuous wife can quell
  Such thoughts, and be the better when they're over;
And if the man should ask, 'tis but denial:
I recommend young ladies to make trial.

79

And then there are such things as love divine,   625
  Bright and immaculate, unmixed and pure,
Such as the angels think so very fine,
  And matrons, who would be no less secure,
Platonic, perfect, "just such love as mine":
  Thus Julia said—and thought so, to be sure,   630
And so I'd have her think, were I the man
On whom her reveries celestial ran.

* * *

86

So much for Julia. Now we'll turn to Juan.
  Poor little fellow! he had no idea
Of his own case, and never hit the true one;
  In feelings quick as Ovid's Miss Medea,[6]
He puzzled over what he found a new one,   685
  But not as yet imagined it could be a
Thing quite in course, and not at all alarming,
Which, with a little patience, might grow charming.

* * *

90

Young Juan wandered by the glassy brooks,
  Thinking unutterable things; he threw
Himself at length within the leafy nooks   715
  Where the wild branch of the cork forest grew;
There poets find materials for their books,
  And every now and then we read them through,
So that their plan and prosody are eligible,
Unless, like Wordsworth, they prove unintelligible. 720

91

He, Juan (and not Wordsworth), so pursued
  His self-communion with his own high soul,
Until his mighty heart, in its great mood,
  Had mitigated part, though not the whole
Of its disease; he did the best he could   725

6. In *Metamorphoses* VII, Ovid tells the story of Medea's mad infatuation for Jason.

With things not very subject to control,
And turned, without perceiving his condition,
Like Coleridge, into a metaphysician.

92

He thought about himself, and the whole earth,
  Of man the wonderful, and of the stars,   730
And how the deuce they ever could have birth;
  And then he thought of earthquakes, and of wars,
How many miles the moon might have in girth,
  Of air-balloons, and of the many bars
To perfect knowledge of the boundless skies—   735
And then he thought of Donna Julia's eyes.

93

In thoughts like these true wisdom may discern
  Longings sublime, and aspirations high,
Which some are born with, but the most part learn
  To plague themselves withal, they know not why: 740
'Twas strange that one so young should thus concern
  His brain about the action of the sky;
If *you* think 'twas philosophy that this did,
I can't help thinking puberty assisted.

94

He pored upon the leaves, and on the flowers,   745
  And heard a voice in all the winds; and then
He thought of wood nymphs and immortal bowers,
  And how the goddesses came down to men:
He missed the pathway, he forgot the hours,
  And when he looked upon his watch again,   750
He found how much old Time had been a winner—
He also found that he had lost his dinner.

* * *

103

'Twas on a summer's day—the sixth of June—
  I like to be particular in dates,
Not only of the age, and year, but moon;
  They are a sort of post house, where the Fates   820
Change horses, making history change its tune,
  Then spur away o'er empires and o'er states,
Leaving at last not much besides chronology,
Excepting the post-obits[7] of theology.

104

'Twas on the sixth of June, about the hour   825
  Of half-past six—perhaps still nearer seven—
When Julia sate within as pretty a bower
  As e'er held houri in that heathenish heaven
Described by Mahomet, and Anacreon Moore,[8]

---

7. I.e., post-obit bonds (*post obitum*, "after death"): loans to an heir which fall due after the death of the person whose estate he is to inherit. Byron's meaning is probably that only theology purports to tell us what rewards are due in heaven.
8. Byron's friend, the poet Thomas Moore, who had translated the *Odes* of Anacreon; Byron is alluding to the

To whom the lyre and laurels have been given, 830
With all the trophies of triumphant song—
He won them well, and may he wear them long!

105

She sate, but not alone; I know not well
　How this same interview had taken place,
And even if I knew, I should not tell— 835
　People should hold their tongues in any case;
No matter how or why the thing befell,
　But there she and Juan, face to face—
When two such faces are so, 'twould be wise,
But very difficult, to shut their eyes. 840

106

How beautiful she looked! her conscious[9] heart
　Glowed in her cheek, and yet she felt no wrong.
Oh Love! how perfect is thy mystic art,
　Strengthening the weak, and trampling on the strong,
How self-deceitful is the sagest part 845
　Of mortals whom thy lure hath led along—
The precipice she stood on was immense,
So was her creed[1] in her own innocence.

107

She thought of her own strength, and Juan's youth,
　And of the folly of all prudish fears,
Victorious virtue, and domestic truth, 850
　And then of Don Alfonso's fifty years:
I wish these last had not occurred, in sooth,
　Because that number rarely much endears,
And through all climes, the snowy and the sunny, 855
Sounds ill in love, whate'er it may in money.

* * *

113

The sun set, and up rose the yellow moon:
　The devil's in the moon for mischief; they
Who called her CHASTE, methinks, began too soon
　Their nomenclature; there is not a day, 900
The longest, not the twenty-first of June,
　Sees half the business in a wicked way
On which three single hours of moonshine smile—
And then she looks so modest all the while.

114

There is a dangerous silence in that hour, 905
　A stillness, which leaves room for the full soul
To open all itself, without the power
　Of calling wholly back its self-control;
The silver light which, hallowing tree and tower,
　Sheds beauty and deep softness o'er the whole, 910

---

tale of *Paradise and the Peri* in 　9. Feelingful.
Moore's Oriental poem *Lalla Rookh*. 　1. Belief.

Breathes also to the heart, and o'er it throws
A loving languor, which is not repose.

115

And Julia sate with Juan, half embraced
    And half retiring from the glowing arm,
Which trembled like the bosom where 'twas placed;   915
    Yet still she must have thought there was no harm,
Or else 'twere easy to withdraw her waist;
    But then the situation had its charm,
And then——God knows what next—I can't go on;
I'm almost sorry that I e'er begun.   920

116

Oh Plato! Plato! you have paved the way,
    With your confounded fantasies, to more
Immoral conduct by the fancied sway
    Your system feigns o'er the controlless core   925
Of human hearts, than all the long array
    Of poets and romancers: You're a bore,
A charlatan, a coxcomb—and have been,
At best, no better than a go-between.

117

And Julia's voice was lost, except in sighs,
    Until too late for useful conversation;   930
The tears were gushing from her gentle eyes,
    I wish, indeed, they had not had occasion,
But who, alas! can love, and then be wise?
    Not that remorse did not oppose temptation;
A little still she strove, and much repented,   935
And whispering "I will ne'er consent"—consented.

* * *

126

'Tis sweet to win, no matter how, one's laurels
    By blood or ink; 'tis sweet to put an end
To strife; 'tis sometimes sweet to have our quarrels,
    Particularly with a tiresome friend:
Sweet is old wine in bottles, ale in barrels;   1005
    Dear is the helpless creature we defend
Against the world; and dear the schoolboy spot
We ne'er forget, though there we are forgot.

127

But sweeter still than this, than these, than all,
    Is first and passionate love—it stands alone,   1010
Like Adam's recollection of his fall;
    The tree of knowledge has been plucked—all's known—
And life yields nothing further to recall
    Worthy of this ambrosial sin, so shown,
No doubt in fable, as the unforgiven   1015
Fire which Prometheus[2] filched for us from heaven.

* * *

2. The Titan Prometheus incurred the wrath of Jupiter by stealing fire for mankind from heaven.

133

Man's a phenomenon, one knows not what,
    And wonderful beyond all wondrous measure;
'Tis pity though, in this sublime world, that
    Pleasure's a sin, and sometimes sin's a pleasure;   1060
Few mortals know what end they would be at,
    But whether glory, power, or love, or treasure,
The path is through perplexing ways, and when
The goal is gained, we die, you know—and then——

134

What then?—I do not know, no more do you—   1065
    And so good night.—Return we to our story:
'Twas in November, when fine days are few,
    And the far mountains wax a little hoary,
And clap a white cape on their mantles blue;
    And the sea dashes round the promontory,   1070
And the loud breaker boils against the rock,
And sober suns must set at five o'clock.

135

'Twas, as the watchmen say, a cloudy night;
    No moon, no stars, the wind was low or loud
By gusts, and many a sparkling hearth was bright   1075
    With the piled wood, round which the family crowd;
There's something cheerful in that sort of light,
    Even as a summer sky's without a cloud:
I'm fond of fire, and crickets, and all that,
A lobster salad, and champagne, and chat.   1080

136

'Twas midnight—Donna Julia was in bed,
    Sleeping, most probably—when at her door
Arose a clatter might awake the dead,
    If they had never been awoke before,
And that they have been so we all have read,   1085
    And are to be so, at the least, once more;
The door was fastened, but with voice and fist
First knocks were heard, then "Madam—Madam—hist!

137

"For God's sake, Madam—Madam—here's my master,
    With more than half the city at his back—   1090
Was ever heard of such a cursed disaster!
    'Tis not my fault—I kept good watch—Alack!
Do, pray, undo the bolt a little faster—
    They're on the stair just now, and in a crack
Will all be here; perhaps he yet may fly—   1095
Surely the window's not so *very* high!"

138

By this time Don Alfonso was arrived,
    With torches, friends, and servants in great number;
The major part of them had long been wived,
    And therefore paused not to disturb the slumber   1100
Of any wicked woman, who contrived

By stealth her husband's temples to encumber:[3]
Examples of this kind are so contagious,
Were *one* not punished, *all* would be outrageous.

139

I can't tell how, or why, or what suspicion   1105
　　Could enter into Don Alfonso's head;
But for a cavalier of his condition[4]
　　It surely was exceedingly ill-bred,
Without a word of previous admonition,
　　To hold a levee[5] round his lady's bed,   1110
And summon lackeys, armed with fire and sword,
To prove himself the thing he most abhorred.

140

Poor Donna Julia! starting as from sleep
　　(Mind that I do not say she had not slept),
Began at once to scream, and yawn, and weep;   1115
　　Her maid, Antonia, who was an adept,
Contrived to fling the bedclothes in a heap,
　　As if she had just now from out them crept:
I can't tell why she should take all this trouble
To prove her mistress had been sleeping double.   1120

141

But Julia mistress, and Antonia maid,
　　Appeared like two poor harmless women, who
Of goblins, but still more of men, afraid,
　　Had thought one man might be deterred by two,
And therefore side by side were gently laid,   1125
　　Until the hours of absence should run through,
And truant husband should return, and say,
"My dear, I was the first who came away."

142

Now Julia found at length a voice, and cried,
　　"In heaven's name, Don Alfonso, what d'ye mean?   1130
Has madness seized you? would that I had died
　　Ere such a monster's victim I had been!
What may this midnight violence betide,
　　A sudden fit of drunkenness or spleen?
Dare you suspect me, whom the thought would kill!   1135
Search, then, the room!"—Alfonso said, "I will."

143

He searched, they searched, and rummaged everywhere,
　　Closet and clothes-press, chest and window seat,
And found much linen, lace, and several pair
　　Of stockings, slippers, brushes, combs, complete,   1140
With other articles of ladies fair,
　　To keep them beautiful, or leave them neat:
Arrass they pricked and curtains with their swords,
And wounded several shutters, and some boards.

3. Horns growing on the forehead were
the traditional emblem of the cuckolded
husband.

4. Rank.
5. Morning reception.

144

Under the bed they searched, and there they found—   1145
    No matter what—it was not that they sought;
They opened windows, gazing if the ground
    Had signs or footmarks, but the earth said nought;
And then they stared each other's faces round:
    'Tis odd, not one of all these seekers thought,   1150
And seems to me almost a sort of blunder,
Of looking *in* the bed as well as under.

145

During this inquisition Julia's tongue
    Was not asleep—"Yes, search and search," she cried,
"Insult on insult heap, and wrong on wrong!   1155
    It was for this that I became a bride!
For this in silence I have suffered long
    A husband like Alfonso at my side;
But now I'll bear no more, nor here remain,
If there be law or lawyers in all Spain.   1160

146

"Yes, Don Alfonso! husband now no more,
    If ever you indeed deserved the name,
Is't worthy of your years?—you have threescore—
    Fifty, or sixty, it is all the same—
Is't wise or fitting, causeless to explore   1165
    For facts against a virtuous woman's fame?
Ungrateful, perjured, barbarous Don Alfonso,
How dare you think your lady would go on so?"

* * *

159

The Senhor Don Alfonso stood confused;   1265
    Antonia bustled round the ransacked room,
And, turning up her nose, with looks abused
    Her master, and his myrmidons, of whom
Not one, except the attorney, was amused;
    He, like Achates,[6] faithful to the tomb,   1270
So there were quarrels, cared not for the cause,
Knowing they must be settled by the laws.

160

With prying snub nose, and small eyes, he stood,
    Following Antonia's motions here and there,
With much suspicion in his attitude;   1275
    For reputations he had little care;
So that a suit or action were made good,
    Small pity had he for the young and fair,
And ne'er believed in negatives, till these
Were proved by competent false witnesses.   1280

6. The *fidus Achates* ("faithful Achates") of Virgil's *Aeneid*, whose loyalty to Aeneas has become proverbial.

161

But Don Alfonso stood with downcast looks,
    And, truth to say, he made a foolish figure;
When, after searching in five hundred nooks,
    And treating a young wife with so much rigor,
He gained no point, except some self-rebukes,   1285
    Added to those his lady with such vigor
Had poured upon him for the last half hour,
Quick, thick, and heavy—as a thundershower.

162

At first he tried to hammer an excuse,
    To which the sole reply was tears, and sobs,   1290
And indications of hysterics, whose
    Prologue is always certain throes, and throbs,
Gasps, and whatever else the owners choose—
    Alfonso saw his wife, and thought of Job's;[7]
He saw too, in perspective, her relations,   1295
And then he tried to muster all his patience.

163

He stood in act to speak, or rather stammer,
    But sage Antonia cut him short before
The anvil of his speech received the hammer,
    With "Pray, sir, leave the room, and say no more,   1300
Or madam dies."—Alfonso muttered, "D—n her."
    But nothing else, the time of words was o'er;
He cast a rueful look or two, and did,
He knew not wherefore, that which he was bid.

164

With him retired his "posse comitatus,"[8]   1305
    The attorney last, who lingered near the door
Reluctantly, still tarrying there as late as
    Antonia let him—not a little sore
At this most strange and unexplained "hiatus"
    In Don Alfonso's facts, which just now wore   1310
An awkward look; as he revolved the case,
The door was fastened in his legal face.

165

No sooner was it bolted, than—Oh shame!
    Oh sin! Oh sorrow! and Oh womankind!
How can you do such things and keep your fame,   1315
    Unless this world, and t'other too, be blind?
Nothing so dear as an unfilched good name!
    But to proceed—for there is more behind:
With much heartfelt reluctance be it said,
Young Juan slipped, half-smothered, from the bed.   1320

7. Job's wife had advised her afflicted husband to "curse God, and die" (Job ii.9).
8. The complete form of the modern word "posse" (posse comitatus means literally "power of the county," i.e., the body of citizens summoned by a sheriff to preserve order in the county).

166

He had been hid—I don't pretend to say
   How, nor can I indeed describe the where—
Young, slender, and packed easily, he lay,
   No doubt, in little compass, round or square;
But pity him I neither must nor may   1325
   His suffocation by that pretty pair;
'Twere better, sure, to die so, than be shut
With maudlin Clarence in his malmsey butt.[9]

* * *

169

What's to be done? Alfonso will be back   1345
   The moment he has sent his fools away.
Antonia's skill was put upon the rack,
   But no device could be brought into play—
And how to parry the renewed attack?
   Besides, it wanted but few hours of day: 1350
Antonia puzzled; Julia did not speak,
But pressed her bloodless lip to Juan's cheek.

170

He turned his lip to hers, and with his hand
   Called back the tangles of her wandering hair;
Even then their love they could not all command,   1355
   And half forgot their danger and despair:
Antonia's patience now was at a stand—
   "Come, come, 'tis no time now for fooling there,"
She whispered, in great wrath—"I must deposit
This pretty gentleman within the closet."   1360

* * *

173

Now, Don Alfonso entering, but alone,
   Closed the oration of the trusty maid:
She loitered, and he told her to be gone,
   An order somewhat sullenly obeyed;   1380
However, present remedy was none,
   And no great good seemed answered if she stayed:
Regarding both with slow and sidelong view,
She snuffed the candle, curtsied, and withdrew.

174

Alfonso paused a minute—then begun   1385
   Some strange excuses for his late proceeding;
He would not justify what he had done,
   To say the best, it was extreme ill-breeding;
But there were ample reasons for it, none
   Of which he specified in this his pleading: 1390

9. The Duke of Clarence, brother of Richard III, was reputed to have been assassinated by being drowned in a cask ("butt") of malmsey, a sweet and aromatic wine.

His speech was a fine sample, on the whole,
Of rhetoric, which the learned call *"rigmarole."*[1]

* * *

180

Alfonso closed his speech, and begged her pardon,
    Which Julia half withheld, and then half granted,
And laid conditions, he thought very hard on,
    Denying several little things he wanted: 1435
He stood like Adam lingering near his garden,
    With useless penitence perplexed and haunted,
Beseeching she no further would refuse,
When, lo! he stumbled o'er a pair of shoes.   1440

181

A pair of shoes!—what then? not much, if they
    Are such as fit with ladies' feet, but these
(No one can tell how much I grieve to say)
    Were masculine; to see them, and to seize,
Was but a moment's act.—Ah! well-a-day!   1445
    My teeth begin to chatter, my veins freeze—
Alfonso first examined well their fashion,
And then flew out into another passion.

182

He left the room for his relinquished sword,
    And Julia instant to the closet flew.
"Fly, Juan, fly! for heaven's sake—not a word—   1450
    The door is open—you may yet slip through
The passage you so often have explored—
    Here is the garden key—Fly—fly—Adieu!
Haste—haste! I hear Alfonso's hurrying feet—   1455
Day has not broke—there's no one in the street."

183

None can say that this was not good advice,
    The only mischief was, it came too late;
Of all experience 'tis the usual price,
    A sort of income tax laid on by fate: 1460
Juan had reached the room door in a trice,
    And might have done so by the garden gate,
But met Alfonso in his dressing gown,
Who threatened death—so Juan knocked him down.

184

Dire was the scuffle, and out went the light;   1465
    Antonia cried out "Rape!" and Julia "Fire!"
But not a servant stirred to aid the fight.
    Alfonso, pommeled to his heart's desire,
Swore lustily he'd be revenged this night;
    And Juan, too, blasphemed an octave higher;   1470
His blood was up: though young, he was a Tartar,[2]
And not at all disposed to prove a martyr.

---

1. Illogical sequence of vague statements.

2. "To catch a Tartar" is to tackle someone too strong for his assailant.

185

Alfonso's sword had dropped ere he could draw it,
    And they continued battling hand to hand.
For Juan very luckily ne'er saw it;
    His temper not being under great command,
If at that moment he had chanced to claw it,
    Alfonso's days had not been in the land
Much longer.—Think of husbands', lover's lives!
And how ye may be doubly widows—wives!

186

Alfonso grappled to detain the foe,
    And Juan throttled him to get away,
And blood ('twas from the nose) began to flow;
    At last, as they more faintly wrestling lay,
Juan contrived to give an awkward blow,
    And then his only garment quite gave way;
He fled, like Joseph,³ leaving it; but there,
I doubt, all likeness ends between the pair.

187

Lights came at length, and men, and maids, who found
    An awkward spectacle their eyes before;
Antonia in hysterics, Julia swooned,
    Alfonso leaning, breathless, by the door;
Some half-torn drapery scattered on the ground,
    Some blood, and several footsteps, but no more:
Juan the gate gained, turned the key about,
And liking not the inside, locked the out.

188

Here ends this canto.—Need I sing, or say,
    How Juan, naked, favored by the night,
Who favors what she should not, found his way,
    And reached his home in an unseemly plight?
The pleasant scandal which arose next day,
    The nine days' wonder which was brought to light,
And how Alfonso sued for a divorce,
Were in the English newspapers, of course.

189

If you would like to see the whole proceedings,
    The depositions, and the cause at full,
The names of all the witnesses, the pleadings
    Of counsel to nonsuit,⁴ or to annul,
There's more than one edition, and the readings
    Are various, but they none of them are dull;
The best is that in shorthand ta'en by Gurney,⁵
Who to Madrid on purpose made a journey.

---

3. In Genesis xxxix.7 ff. the chaste
Joseph flees from the advances of Poti-
phar's wife, leaving "his garment in
her hand."
4. Judgment against the plaintiff for
failure to establish his case.
5. William B. Gurney, official shorthand
writer for the Houses of Parliament and
a famous court reporter.

190

But Donna Inez, to divert the train
  Of one of the most circulating scandals
That had for centuries been known in Spain,   1515
  At least since the retirement of the Vandals,[6]
First vowed (and never had she vowed in vain)
  To Virgin Mary several pounds of candles;
And then, by the advice of some old ladies,
She sent her son to be shipped off from Cadiz.   1520

191

She had resolved that he should travel through
  All European climes, by land or sea,
To mend his former morals, and get new,
  Especially in France and Italy
(At least this is the thing most people do).   1525
  Julia was sent into a convent; she
Grieved, but, perhaps, her feelings may be better
Shown in the following copy of her letter:

192

"They tell me 'tis decided; you depart:
  'Tis wise—'tis well, but not the less a pain;   1530
I have no further claim on your young heart,
  Mine is the victim, and would be again;
To love too much has been the only art
  I used—I write in haste, and if a stain
Be on this sheet, 'tis not what it appears;   1535
My eyeballs burn and throb, but have no tears.

193

"I loved, I love you, for this love have lost
  State, station, heaven, mankind's, my own esteem,
And yet cannot regret what it hath cost,
  So dear is still the memory of that dream;   1540
Yet, if I name my guilt, 'tis not to boast,
  None can deem harshlier of me than I deem:
I trace this scrawl because I cannot rest—
I've nothing to reproach, or to request.

194

"Man's love is of man's life a thing apart,   1545
  'Tis woman's whole existence; man may range
The court, camp, church, the vessel, and the mart;
  Sword, gown, gain, glory, offer in exchange
Pride, fame, ambition, to fill up his heart,
  And few there are whom these cannot estrange;   1550
Men have all these resources, we but one,
To love again, and be again undone."

* * *

6. The Germanic tribe which overran Spain and other parts of southern Europe in the 4th and 5th centuries; notorious for rape and violence.

198

This note was written upon gilt-edged paper
    With a neat little crow-quill, slight and new;
Her small white hand could hardly reach the taper,[7]
    It trembled as magnetic needles do,   1580
And yet she did not let one tear escape her;
    The seal a sunflower; "*Elle vous suit partout*,"[8]
The motto, cut upon a white cornelian;
The wax was superfine, its hue vermilion.

199

This was Don Juan's earliest scrape; but whether   1585
    I shall proceed with his adventures is
Dependent on the public altogether;
    We'll see, however, what they say to this,
Their favor in an author's cap's a feather,
    And no great mischief's done by their caprice;   1590
And if their approbation we experience,
Perhaps they'll have some more about a year hence.

200

My poem's epic, and is meant to be
    Divided in twelve books; each book containing,
With love, and war, a heavy gale at sea,   1595
    A list of ships, and captains, and kings reigning,
New characters; the episodes are three;
    A panoramic view of hell's in training,
After the style of Virgil and of Homer,
So that my name of Epic's no misnomer.   1600

201

All these things will be specified in time,
    With strict regard to Aristotle's rules,
The *Vade Mecum*[9] of the true sublime,
    Which makes so many poets, and some fools:
Prose poets like blank verse, I'm fond of rhyme,   1605
    Good workmen never quarrel with their tools;
I've got new mythological machinery,
And very handsome supernatural scenery.

202

There's only one slight difference between
    Me and my epic brethren gone before,   1610
And here the advantage is my own, I ween
    (Not that I have not several merits more,
But this will more peculiarly be seen):
    They so embellish that 'tis quite a bore
Their labyrinth of fables to thread through,   1615
Whereas this story's actually true.

7. The candle (in order to melt wax to seal the letter).
8. "She follows you everywhere."
9. Handbook (Latin, "go with me");

Byron is deriding the interpretation of Aristotle's *Poetics* ("rules") as a guide for writing epic and tragedy.

203

If any person doubt it, I appeal
  To history, tradition, and to facts,
To newspapers, whose truth all know and feel,
  To plays in five, and operas in three acts;   1620
All these confirm my statement a good deal,
  But that which more completely faith exacts
Is that myself, and several now in Seville,
Saw Juan's last elopement with the devil.[1]

204

If ever I should condescend to prose,   1625
  I'll write poetical commandments, which
Shall supersede beyond all doubt all those
  That went before; in these I shall enrich
My text with many things that no one knows,
  And carry precept to the highest pitch: 1630
I'll call the work "Longinus o'er a Bottle,
Or Every Poet his *own* Aristotle."

205

Thou shalt believe in Milton, Dryden, Pope;[2]
  Thou shalt not set up Wordsworth, Coleridge, Southey;
Because the first is crazed beyond all hope,   1635
  The second drunk, the third so quaint and mouthy:
With Crabbe it may be difficult to cope,
  And Campbell's Hippocrene[3] is somewhat drouthy:
Thou shalt not steal from Samuel Rogers, nor
Commit—flirtation with the muse of Moore.[4]   1640

206

Thou shalt not covet Mr. Sotheby's Muse,[5]
  His Pegasus, nor anything that's his;
Thou shalt not bear false witness like "the Blues"[6]
  (There's one, at least, is very fond of this);
Thou shalt not write, in short, but what I choose: 1645
  This is true criticism, and you may kiss—
Exactly as you please, or not,—the rod;
But if you don't, I'll lay it on, by G—d!

207

If any person should presume to assert
  This story is not moral, first I pray   1650
That they will not cry out before they're hurt,
  Then that they'll read it o'er again, and say

---

1. The usual plays on the Juan legend ended with Juan in hell; a recent version is George Bernard Shaw's *Man and Superman*.
2. This is one of many passages, in prose and verse, in which Byron vigorously defended Dryden and Pope against his Romantic contemporaries.
3. Fountain on Mt. Helicon whose waters supposedly gave inspiration.
4. George Crabbe, whom Byron admired, was the author of *The Village* (1783) and other realistic poems of rural life. Thomas Campbell, Samuel Rogers, and Thomas Moore were minor poets of the Romantic period; the last two were close friends of Byron's (cf. line 829 and note).
5. William Sotheby, contemporary poet and translator, was a wealthy man (see line 1642). Pegasus was the winged horse, symbolizing poetic inspiration.
6. I.e., "bluestockings," a contemporary term for pedantic lady intellectuals, among whom Byron numbered his wife (line 1644).

(But, doubtless, nobody will be so pert)
    That this is not a moral tale, though gay;
Besides, in Canto Twelfth, I mean to show   1655
The very place where wicked people go.

* * *

213

But now at thirty years my hair is gray
    (I wonder what it will be like at forty?
I thought of a peruke[7] the other day)—
    My heart is not much greener; and, in short, I   1700
Have squandered my whole summer while 'twas May,
    And feel no more the spirit to retort; I
Have spent my life, both interest and principal,
And deem not, what I deemed, my soul invincible.

214

No more—no more—Oh! never more on me   1705
    The freshness of the heart can fall like dew,
Which out of all the lovely things we see
    Extracts emotions beautiful and new,
Hived in our bosoms like the bag o' the bee:
    Think'st thou the honey with those objects grew?   1710
Alas! 'twas not in them, but in thy power
To double even the sweetness of a flower.

215

No more—no more—Oh! never more, my heart,
    Canst thou be my sole world, my universe!
Once all in all, but now a thing apart,   1715
    Thou canst not be my blessing or my curse:
The illusion's gone forever, and thou art
    Insensible, I trust, but none the worse,
And in thy stead I've got a deal of judgment,
Though heaven knows how it ever found a lodgment.   1720

216

My days of love are over; me no more
    The charms of maid, wife, and still less of widow
Can make the fool of which they made before—
    In short, I must not lead the life I did do;
The credulous hope of mutual minds is o'er,   1725
    The copious use of claret is forbid too,
So for a good old-gentlemanly vice,
I think I must take up with avarice.

* * *

219

What are the hopes of man? Old Egypt's King   1745
    Cheops erected the first pyramid
And largest, thinking it was just the thing
    To keep his memory whole, and mummy hid:
But somebody or other rummaging

7. Wig.

Burglariously broke his coffin's lid: 1750
Let not a monument give you or me hopes,
Since not a pinch of dust remains of Cheops.

220

But I, being fond of true philosophy,
  Say very often to myself, "Alas!
All things that have been born were born to die,   1755
  And flesh (which Death mows down to hay) is grass;
You've passed your youth not so unpleasantly,
  And if you had it o'er again—'twould pass—
So thank your stars that matters are no worse,
And read your Bible, sir, and mind your purse."   1760

221

But for the present, gentle reader! and
  Still gentler purchaser! the bard—that's I—
Must, with permission, shake you by the hand,
  And so your humble servant, and good-by!
We meet again, if we should understand   1765
  Each other; and if not, I shall not try
Your patience further than by this short sample—
'Twere well if others followed my example.

222

"Go, little book, from this my solitude!
  I cast thee on the waters—go thy ways!
And if, as I believe, thy vein be good,   1770
  The world will find thee after many days."
When Southey's read, and Wordsworth understood,
  I can't help putting in my claim to praise—
The four first rhymes are Southey's, every line:[8]   1775
For God's sake, reader! take them not for mine!

From *Canto II*

8

But to our tale: the Donna Inez sent
  Her son to Cadiz only to embark;
To stay there had not answered her intent,
  But why?—we leave the reader in the dark—   60
'Twas for a voyage the young man was meant,
  As if a Spanish ship were Noah's ark,
To wean him from the wickedness of earth,
And send him like a dove of promise forth.

9

Don Juan bade his valet pack his things   65
  According to direction, then received
A lecture and some money: for four springs
  He was to travel; and though Inez grieved
(As every kind of parting has its stings),
  She hoped he would improve—perhaps believed: 70

8. The lines occur in the last stanza of Southey's *Epilogue to the Lay of the Laureate.*

A letter, too, she gave (he never read it)
Of good advice—and two or three of credit.

* * *

11

Juan embarked—the ship got under way,
    The wind was fair, the water passing rough;
A devil of a sea rolls in that bay,
    As I, who've crossed it oft, know well enough;
And, standing upon deck, the dashing spray   85
    Flies in one's face, and makes it weather-tough:
And there he stood to take, and take again,
His first—perhaps his last—farewell of Spain.

12

I can't but say it is an awkward sight
    To see one's native land receding through
The growing waters; it unmans one quite,   90
    Especially when life is rather new:
I recollect Great Britain's coast looks white,
    But almost every other country's blue,
When gazing on them, mystified by distance,   95
We enter on our nautical existence.

* * *

17

And Juan wept, and much he sighed and thought,
    While his salt tears dropped into the salt sea,   130
"Sweets to the sweet" (I like so much to quote;
    You must excuse this extract—'tis where she,
The Queen of Denmark, for Ophelia brought
    Flowers to the grave);[1] and, sobbing often, he
Reflected on his present situation,   135
And seriously resolved on reformation.

18

"Farewell, my Spain! a long farewell!" he cried,
    "Perhaps I may revisit thee no more,
But die, as many an exiled heart hath died,
    Of its own thirst to see again thy shore: 140
Farewell, where Guadalquiver's waters glide!
    Farewell, my mother! and, since all is o'er,
Farewell, too, dearest Julia!—(here he drew
Her letter out again, and read it through).

19

"And oh! if e'er I should forget, I swear—   145
    But that's impossible, and cannot be—
Sooner shall this blue ocean melt to air,
    Sooner shall earth resolve itself to sea,
Than I resign thine image, oh, my fair!
    Or think of anything, excepting thee;   150

---

1. Hamlet V.i.266.

A mind diseased no remedy can physic—
(Here the ship gave a lurch, and he grew seasick.)

20

"Sooner shall heaven kiss earth—(here he fell sicker)
    Oh, Julia! what is every other woe?—
(For God's sake let me have a glass of liquor;   155
    Pedro, Battista, help me down below.)
Julia, my love—(you rascal, Pedro, quicker)—
    Oh, Julia!—(this cursed vessel pitches so)—
Beloved Julia, hear me still beseeching!"
(Here he grew inarticulate with retching.)   160

21

He felt that chilling heaviness of heart,
    Or rather stomach, which, alas! attends,
Beyond the best apothecary's art,
    The loss of love, the treachery of friends,
Or death of those we dote on, when a part   165
    Of us dies with them as each fond hope ends:
No doubt he would have been much more pathetic,
But the sea acted as a strong emetic.[2]

* * *

49

'Twas twilight, and the sunless day went down   385
    Over the waste of waters; like a veil,
Which, if withdrawn, would but disclose the frown
    Of one whose hate is masked but to assail.
Thus to their hopeless eyes the night was shown,
    And grimly darkled o'er the faces pale,   390
And the dim desolate deep: twelve days had Fear
Been their familiar, and now Death was here.

50

Some trial had been making at a raft,
    With little hope in such a rolling sea,
A sort of thing at which one would have laughed,   395
    If any laughter at such times could be,
Unless with people who too much have quaffed,
    And have a kind of wild and horrid glee,
Half epileptical, and half hysterical—
Their preservation would have been a miracle.   400

51

At half-past eight o'clock, booms, hencoops, spars,
    And all things, for a chance, had been cast loose
That still could keep afloat the struggling tars,
    For yet they strove, although of no great use:
There was no light in heaven but a few stars,   405
    The boats put off o'ercrowded with their crews;
She gave a heel, and then a lurch to port,
And, going down head foremost—sunk, in short.

2. In stanzas 22–48 (here omitted) the ship, bound for Leghorn, runs into a violent storm, which leaves her a helpless, sinking wreck.

52

Then rose from sea to sky the wild farewell—
　　Then shrieked the timid, and stood still the brave— 410
Then some leaped overboard with dreadful yell,
　　As eager to anticipate their grave;
And the sea yawned around her like a hell,
　　And down she sucked with her the whirling wave,
Like one who grapples with his enemy, 415
And strives to strangle him before he die.

53

And first one universal shriek there rushed,
　　Louder than the loud ocean, like a crash
Of echoing thunder; and then all was hushed,
　　Save the wild wind and the remorseless dash 420
Of billows; but at intervals there gushed,
　　Accompanied with a convulsive splash,
A solitary shriek, the bubbling cry
Of some strong swimmer in his agony.

* * *

56

Juan got into the longboat, and there
　　Contrived to help Pedrillo[3] to a place;
It seemed as if they had exchanged their care,
　　For Juan wore the magisterial face
Which courage gives, while poor Pedrillo's pair 445
　　Of eyes were crying for their owner's case:
Battista, though (a name called shortly Tita),
Was lost by getting at some aqua-vita.[4]

57

Pedro, his valet, too, he tried to save,
　　But the same cause, conducive to his loss, 450
Left him so drunk, he jumped into the wave
　　As o'er the cutter's edge he tried to cross,
And so he found a wine-and-watery grave;
　　They could not rescue him although so close,
Because the sea ran higher every minute, 455
And for the boat—the crew kept crowding in it.

* * *

66

'Tis thus with people in an open boat,
　　They live upon the love of life, and bear
More than can be believed, or even thought,
　　And stand like rocks the tempest's wear and tear;
And hardship still has been the sailor's lot, 525
　　Since Noah's ark went cruising here and there;
She had a curious crew as well as cargo,
Like the first old Greek privateer, the *Argo*.[5]

3. Juan's tutor.
4. Brandy.
5. In the Greek myth, the *Argo* is the ship on which Jason set out in quest of the Golden Fleece. Byron ironically calls it a "privateer" (a private ship licensed by a government in wartime to attack and pillage enemy vessels).

67

But man is a carnivorous production,
　And must have meals, at least one meal a day;　　　530
He cannot live, like woodcocks, upon suction,[6]
　But, like the shark and tiger, must have prey;
Although his anatomical construction
　Bears vegetables, in a grumbling way,
Your laboring people think beyond all question　　535
Beef, veal, and mutton, better for digestion.

68

And thus it was with this our hapless crew;
　For on the third day there came on a calm,
And though at first their strength it might renew,
　And lying on their weariness like balm,　　　540
Lulled them like turtles sleeping on the blue
　Of ocean, when they woke they felt a qualm,
And fell all ravenously on their provision,
Instead of hoarding it with due precision.

* * *

72

The seventh day,[7] and no wind—the burning sun
　Blistered and scorched, and, stagnant on the sea,　570
They lay like carcasses; and hope was none,
　Save in the breeze that came not; savagely
They glared upon each other—all was done,
　Water, and wine, and food—and you might see
The longings of the cannibal arise　　　575
(Although they spoke not) in their wolfish eyes.

73

At length one whispered his companion, who
　Whispered another, and thus it went round,
And then into a hoarser murmur grew,
　An ominous, and wild, and desperate sound;　580
And when his comrade's thought each sufferer knew,
　'Twas but his own, suppressed till now, he found:
And out they spoke of lots for flesh and blood,
And who should die to be his fellow's food.

74

But ere they came to this, they that day shared　585
　Some leathern caps, and what remained of shoes;
And then they looked around them, and despaired,
　And none to be the sacrifice would choose;
At length the lots were torn up, and prepared,
　But of materials that must shock the Muse—　590
Having no paper, for the want of better,
They took by force from Juan Julia's letter.

6. Woodcocks probe the turf with long flexible bills, seeming to suck air as they feed.
7. On the fourth day the crew had killed and eaten Juan's pet spaniel. Byron based the episode of cannibalism that follows on various historical accounts of disasters at sea.

75

Then lots were made, and marked, and mixed, and handed
  In silent horror, and their distribution
Lulled even the savage hunger which demanded,   595
  Like the Promethean vulture,[8] this pollution;
None in particular had sought or planned it,
  'Twas nature gnawed them to this resolution,
By which none were permitted to be neuter—
And the lot fell on Juan's luckless tutor.   600

76

He but requested to be bled to death:
  The surgeon had his instruments, and bled
Pedrillo, and so gently ebbed his breath,
  You hardly could perceive when he was dead.
He died as born, a Catholic in faith,   605
  Like most in the belief in which they're bred,
And first a little crucifix he kissed,
And then held out his jugular and wrist.

77

The surgeon, as there was no other fee,
  Had his first choice of morsels for his pains;   610
But being thirstiest at the moment, he
  Preferred a draft from the fast-flowing veins:
Part was divided, part thrown in the sea,
  And such things as the entrails and the brains
Regaled two sharks, who followed o'er the billow—   615
The sailors ate the rest of poor Pedrillo.

78

The sailors ate him, all save three or four,
  Who were not quite so fond of animal food;
To these was added Juan, who, before
  Refusing his own spaniel, hardly could   620
Feel now his appetite increased much more;
  'Twas not to be expected that he should,
Even in extremity of their disaster,
Dine with them on his pastor and his master.

79   625

'Twas better that he did not; for, in fact,
  The consequence was awful in the extreme;
For they, who were most ravenous in the act,
  Went raging mad—Lord! how they did blaspheme!
And foam and roll, with strange convulsions racked,   630
  Drinking salt water like a mountain stream,
Tearing, and grinning, howling, screeching, swearing,
And, with hyena laughter, died despairing.

* * *

8. Because Prometheus had stolen fire from heaven to give to men, Zeus punished him by nailing him to a mountain peak, where an eagle fed on his ever-renewing liver.

103

As they drew nigh the land, which now was seen
    Unequal in its aspect here and there,
They felt the freshness of its growing green,
    That waved in forest tops, and smoothed the air,   820
And fell upon their glazed eyes like a screen
    From glistening waves, and skies so hot and bare—
Lovely seemed any object that should sweep
Away the vast, salt, dread, eternal deep.

104

The shore looked wild, without a trace of man,   825
    And girt by formidable waves; but they
Were mad for land, and thus their course they ran,
    Though right ahead the roaring breakers lay:
A reef between them also now began
    To show its boiling surf and bounding spray,   830
But finding no place for their landing better,
They ran the boat for shore—and overset her.

105

But in his native stream, the Guadalquiver,
    Juan to lave his youthful limbs was wont;
And having learnt to swim in that sweet river,   835
    Had often turned the art to some account:
A better swimmer you could scarce see ever,
    He could, perhaps, have passed the Hellespont,
As once (a feat on which ourselves we prided)
Leander, Mr. Ekenhead, and I did.[1]   840

106

So, here, though faint, emaciated, and stark,
    He buoyed his boyish limbs, and strove to ply
With the quick wave, and gain, ere it was dark,
    The beach which lay before him, high and dry:
The greatest danger here was from a shark,   845
    That carried off his neighbor by the thigh;
As for the other two, they could not swim,
So nobody arrived on shore but him.

107

Nor yet had he arrived but for the oar,
    Which, providentially for him, was washed   850
Just as his feeble arms could strike no more,
    And the hard wave o'erwhelmed him as 'twas dashed
Within his grasp; he clung to it, and sore
    The waters beat while he thereto was lashed;
At last, with swimming, wading, scrambling, he   855
Rolled on the beach, half senseless, from the sea:

108

There, breathless, with his digging nails he clung
    Fast to the sand, lest the returning wave,
From whose reluctant roar his life he wrung,

---

1. Like Leander in the myth, Byron and Lt. Ekenhead had swum the Helles- pont on May 3, 1810. See *Written After Swimming from Sestos to Abydos.*

Should suck him back to her insatiate grave: 860
And there he lay, full length, where he was flung,
    Before the entrance of a cliff-worn cave,
With just enough of life to feel its pain,
And deem that it was saved, perhaps, in vain.

109

With slow and staggering effort he arose,   865
    But sunk again upon his bleeding knee
And quivering hand; and then he looked for those
    Who long had been his mates upon the sea;
But none of them appeared to share his woes,
    Save one, a corpse, from out the famished three,   870
Who died two days before, and now had found
An unknown barren beach for burial ground.

110

And as he gazed, his dizzy brain spun fast,
    And down he sunk; and as he sunk, the sand
Swam round and round, and all his senses passed: 875
    He fell upon his side, and his stretched hand
Drooped dripping on the oar (their jurymast),
    And, like a withered lily, on the land
His slender frame and pallid aspect lay,
As fair a thing as e'er was formed of clay.   880

111

How long in his damp trance young Juan lay
    He knew not, for the earth was gone for him,
And time had nothing more of night nor day
    For his congealing blood, and senses dim;
And how this heavy faintness passed away   885
    He knew not, till each painful pulse and limb,
And tingling vein seemed throbbing back to life,
For Death, though vanquished, still retired with strife.

112

His eyes he opened, shut, again unclosed,
    For all was doubt and dizziness; he thought   890
He still was in the boat, and had but dozed,
    And felt again with his despair o'erwrought,
And wished it death in which he had reposed,
    And then once more his feelings back were brought,
And slowly by his swimming eyes was seen   895
A lovely female face of seventeen.

113

'Twas bending close o'er his, and the small mouth
    Seemed almost prying into his for breath;
And chafing him, the soft warm hand of youth
    Recalled his answering spirits back from death;   900
And, bathing his chill temples, tried to soothe
    Each pulse to animation, till beneath
Its gentle touch and trembling care, a sigh
To these kind efforts made a low reply.

114

Then was the cordial poured, and mantle flung   905
   Around his scarce-clad limbs; and the fair arm
Raised higher the faint head which o'er it hung;
   And her transparent cheek, all pure and warm,
Pillowed his deathlike forehead; then she wrung
   His dewy curls, long drenched by every storm;   910
And watched with eagerness each throb that drew
A sigh from his heaved bosom—and hers, too.

115

And lifting him with care into the cave,
   The gentle girl, and her attendant—one
Young, yet her elder, and of brow less grave,   915
   And more robust of figure—then begun
To kindle fire, and as the new flames gave
   Light to the rocks that roofed them, which the sun
Had never seen, the maid, or whatsoe'er
She was, appeared distinct, and tall, and fair.   920

116

Her brow was overhung with coins of gold,
   That sparkled o'er the auburn of her hair,
Her clustering hair, whose longer locks were rolled
   In braids behind; and though her stature were
Even of the highest for a female mold,   925
   They nearly reached her heel; and in her air
There was a something which bespoke command,
As one who was a lady in the land.

117

Her hair, I said, was auburn; but her eyes
   Were black as death, their lashes the same hue,   930
Of downcast length, in whose silk shadow lies
   Deepest attraction; for when to the view
Forth from its raven fringe the full glance flies,
   Ne'er with such force the swiftest arrow flew;
'Tis as the snake late coiled, who pours his length,   935
And hurls at once his venom and his strength.

* * *

123

And these two tended him, and cheered him both
   With food and raiment, and those soft attentions,
Which are (as I must own) of female growth,
   And have ten thousand delicate inventions: 980
They made a most superior mess of broth,
   A thing which poesy but seldom mentions,
But the best dish that e'er was cooked since Homer's
Achilles ordered dinner for newcomers.[2]

---

2. A reference to the lavish feast with which Achilles entertained Ajax, Phoenix, and Ulysses (*Iliad* IX.193 ff.).

124

I'll tell you who they were, this female pair,   985
   Lest they should seem princesses in disguise;
Besides, I hate all mystery, and that air
   Of claptrap, which your recent poets prize;
And so, in short, the girls they really were
   They shall appear before your curious eyes,   990
Mistress and maid; the first was only daughter
Of an old man, who lived upon the water.

125

A fisherman he had been in his youth,
   And still a sort of fisherman was he;
But other speculations were, in sooth,   995
   Added to his connection with the sea,
Perhaps not so respectable, in truth:
   A little smuggling, and some piracy,
Left him, at last, the sole of many masters
Of an ill-gotten million of piasters.[3]   1000

126

A fisher, therefore, was he—though of men,
   Like Peter the Apostle[4]—and he fished
For wandering merchant vessels, now and then,
   And sometimes caught as many as he wished;
The cargoes he confiscated, and gain   1005
   He sought in the slave market too, and dished
Full many a morsel for that Turkish trade,
By which, no doubt, a good deal may be made.

127

He was a Greek, and on his isle had built
   (One of the wild and smaller Cyclades[5])   1010
A very handsome house from out his guilt,
   And there he lived exceedingly at ease;
Heaven knows what cash he got or blood he spilt,
   A sad[1] old fellow was he, if you please;
But this I know, it was a spacious building,   1015
Full of barbaric carving, paint, and gilding.

128

He had an only daughter, called Haidée,
   The greatest heiress of the Eastern Isles;
Besides, so very beautiful was she,
   Her dowry was as nothing to her smiles: 1020
Still in her teens, and like a lovely tree
   She grew to womanhood, and between whiles
Rejected several suitors, just to learn
How to accept a better in his turn.

3. Near Eastern coins.
4. Christ's words to Peter and Andrew, both fishermen: "Follow me, and I will make you fishers of men" (Matthew iv.19).
5. A group of islands in the Aegean Sea.
1. In the playful sense: "wicked."

129

And walking out upon the beach, below   1025
   The cliff, towards sunset, on that day she found,
Insensible—not dead, but nearly so—
   Don Juan, almost famished, and half drowned;
But being naked, she was shocked, you know,
   Yet deemed herself in common pity bound,   1030
As far as in her lay, "to take him in,
A stranger"[2] dying, with so white a skin.

130

But taking him into her father's house
   Was not exactly the best way to save,
But like conveying to the cat the mouse,   1035
   Or people in a trance into their grave;
Because the good old man had so much "*νους*,"[3]
   Unlike the honest Arab thieves so brave,
He would have hospitably cured the stranger
And sold him instantly when out of danger.   1040

131

And therefore, with her maid, she thought it best
   (A virgin always on her maid relies)
To place him in the cave for present rest:
   And when, at last, he opened his black eyes,
Their charity increased about their guest;   1045
   And their compassion grew to such a size,
It opened half the turnpike gates to heaven
(St. Paul says 'tis the toll which must be given).[4]

* * *

141

And Haidée met the morning face to face;
   Her own was freshest, though a feverish flush
Had dyed it with the headlong blood, whose race
   From heart to cheek is curbed into a blush,
Like to a torrent which a mountain's base,   1125
   That overpowers some Alpine river's rush,
Checks to a lake, whose waves in circles spread;
Or the Red Sea—but the sea is not red.

142

And down the cliff the island virgin came,
   And near the cave her quick light footsteps drew,   1130
While the sun smiled on her with his first flame,
   And young Aurora[5] kissed her lips with dew,
Taking her for a sister; just the same
   Mistake you would have made on seeing the two,
Although the mortal, quite as fresh and fair,   1135
Had all the advantage, too, of not being air.

---

2. Cf. Matthew xxv.35: "I was a stranger, and ye took me in."
3. Nous, "intelligence"; in England, pronounced so as to rhyme with "mouse."
4. I Corinthians xiii.13.
5. The dawn.

143

And when into the cavern Haidée stepped
    All timidly, yet rapidly, she saw
That like an infant Juan sweetly slept;
    And then she stopped, and stood as if in awe   1140
(For sleep is awful), and on tiptoe crept
    And wrapped him closer, lest the air, too raw,
Should reach his blood, then o'er him still as death
Bent, with hushed lips, that drank his scarce-drawn breath.

* * *

148

And she bent o'er him, and he lay beneath,
    Hushed as the babe upon its mother's breast,
Drooped as the willow when no winds can breathe,
    Lulled like the depth of ocean when at rest,   1180
Fair as the crowning rose of the whole wreath,
    Soft as the callow cygnet[6] in its nest;
In short, he was a very pretty fellow,
Although his woes had turned him rather yellow.

149

He woke and gazed, and would have slept again,   1185
    But the fair face which met his eyes forbade
Those eyes to close, though weariness and pain
    Had further sleep a further pleasure made;
For woman's face was never formed in vain
    For Juan, so that even when he prayed   1190
He turned from grisly saints, and martyrs hairy,
To the sweet portraits of the Virgin Mary.

150

And thus upon his elbow he arose,
    And looked upon the lady, in whose cheek
The pale contended with the purple rose,   1195
    As with an effort she began to speak;
Her eyes were eloquent, her words would pose,
    Although she told him, in good modern Greek,
With an Ionian accent, low and sweet,
That he was faint, and must not talk, but eat.   1200

* * *

168

And every day by daybreak—rather early
    For Juan, who was somewhat fond of rest—
She came into the cave, but it was merely
    To see her bird reposing in his nest;   1340
And she would softly stir his locks so curly,
    Without disturbing her yet slumbering guest,
Breathing all gently o'er his cheek and mouth,
As o'er a bed of roses the sweet South.[7]

6. Young swan.   7. The south wind.

169

And every morn his color freshlier came,   1345
   And every day helped on his convalescence;
'Twas well, because health in the human frame
   Is pleasant, besides being true love's essence,
For health and idleness to passion's flame
   Are oil and gunpowder; and some good lessons   1350
Are also learnt from Ceres[8] and from Bacchus,
Without whom Venus will not long attack us.

170

While Venus fills the heart (without heart really
   Love, though good always, is not quite so good),
Ceres presents a plate of vermicelli—   1355
   For love must be sustained like flesh and blood—
While Bacchus pours out wine, or hands a jelly:
   Eggs, oysters, too, are amatory food;
But who is their purveyor from above
Heaven knows—it may be Neptune, Pan, or Jove.   1360

171

When Juan woke he found some good things ready,
   A bath, a breakfast, and the finest eyes
That ever made a youthful heart less steady,
   Besides her maid's, as pretty for their size;
But I have spoken of all this already—   1365
   And repetition's tiresome and unwise—
Well—Juan, after bathing in the sea,
Came always back to coffee and Haidée.

172

Both were so young, and one so innocent,
   That bathing passed for nothing; Juan seemed   1370
To her, as 'twere, the kind of being sent,
   Of whom these two years she had nightly dreamed,
A something to be loved, a creature meant
   To be her happiness, and whom she deemed
To render happy; all who joy would win   1375
Must share it—Happiness was born a twin.

173

It was such pleasure to behold him, such
   Enlargement of existence to partake
Nature with him, to thrill beneath his touch,
   To watch him slumbering, and to see him wake: 1380
To live with him forever were too much;
   But then the thought of parting made her quake:
He was her own, her ocean-treasure, cast
Like a rich wreck—her first love, and her last.

174

And thus a moon rolled on, and fair Haidée   1385
   Paid daily visits to her boy, and took
Such plentiful precautions, that still he

8. Goddess of the grain.

Remained unknown within his craggy nook;
At last her father's prows put out to sea,
  For certain merchantmen upon the look, 1390
Not as of yore to carry off an Io,[9]
But three Ragusan vessels, bound for Scio.[1]

175

Then came her freedom, for she had no mother,
  So that, her father being at sea, she was
Free as a married woman, or such other 1395
  Female, as where she likes may freely pass,
Without even the encumbrance of a brother,
  The freest she that ever gazed on glass:
I speak of Christian lands in this comparison,
Where wives, at least, are seldom kept in garrison. 1400

176

Now she prolonged her visits and her talk
  (For they must talk), and he had learnt to say
So much as to propose to take a walk—
  For little had he wandered since the day
On which, like a young flower snapped from the stalk, 1405
  Drooping and dewy on the beach he lay—
And thus they walked out in the afternoon,
And saw the sun set opposite the moon.

177

It was a wild and breaker-beaten coast,
  With cliffs above, and a broad sandy shore, 1410
Guarded by shoals and rocks as by an host,
  With here and there a creek, whose aspect wore
A better welcome to the tempest-tossed;
  And rarely ceased the haughty billow's roar,
Save on the dead long summer days, which make 1415
The outstretched ocean glitter like a lake.

178

And the small ripple split upon the beach
  Scarcely o'erpass'd the cream of your champagne,
When o'er the brim the sparkling bumpers reach,
  That spring dew of the spirit! the heart's rain! 1420
Few things surpass old wine; and they may preach
  Who please—the more because they preach in vain—
Let us have wine and woman, mirth and laughter,
Sermons and soda water the day after.

179

Man, being reasonable, must get drunk; 1425
  The best of life is but intoxication:
Glory, the grape, love, gold, in these are sunk
  The hopes of all men, and of every nation;
Without their sap, how branchless were the trunk
  Of life's strange tree, so fruitful on occasion: 1430

9. Io, a mistress of Zeus persecuted by
his jealous wife Hera, was kidnaped by
Phoenician merchants.

1. Ragusa (or Dubrovnik), is an Adriatic port; Scio is the Italian name for
Chios, an island near Turkey.

But to return—Get very drunk; and when
You wake with headache, you shall see what then.

180

Ring for your valet—bid him quickly bring
   Some hock and soda water, then you'll know
A pleasure worthy Xerxes the great king;[2]
   For not the blest sherbet, sublimed with snow,   1435
Nor the first sparkle of the desert spring,
   Nor Burgundy in all its sunset glow,
After long travel, ennui, love, or slaughter,
Vie with that draught of hock and soda water.   1440

181

The coast—I think it was the coast that I
   Was just describing—Yes, it *was* the coast—
Lay at this period quiet as the sky,
   The sands untumbled, the blue waves untossed,
And all was stillness, save the sea bird's cry,   1445
   And dolphin's leap, and little billow crossed
By some low rock or shelve, that made it fret
Against the boundary it scarcely wet.

182

And forth they wandered, her sire being gone,
   As I have said, upon an expedition;
And mother, brother, guardian, she had none,   1450
   Save Zoë, who, although with due precision
She waited on her lady with the sun,
   Thought daily service was her only mission,
Bringing warm water, wreathing her long tresses,   1455
And asking now and then for cast-off dresses.

183

It was the cooling hour, just when the rounded
   Red sun sinks down behind the azure hill,
Which then seems as if the whole earth it bounded,
   Circling all nature, hushed, and dim, and still,   1460
With the far mountain crescent half surrounded
   On one side, and the deep sea calm and chill
Upon the other, and the rosy sky,
With one star sparkling through it like an eye.

184

And thus they wandered forth, and hand in hand,   1465
   Over the shining pebbles and the shells,
Glided along the smooth and hardened sand,
   And in the worn and wild receptacles
Worked by the storms, yet worked as it were planned,
   In hollow halls, with sparry roofs and cells,   1470
They turned to rest; and, each clasped by an arm,
Yielded to the deep twilight's purple charm.

2. Xerxes, 5th-century Persian king, was said to have offered a reward to anyone who could discover a new kind of pleasure.

185

They looked up to the sky, whose floating glow
   Spread like a rosy ocean, vast and bright;
They gazed upon the glittering sea below,   1475
   Whence the broad moon rose circling into sight;
They heard the waves splash, and the wind so low,
   And saw each other's dark eyes darting light
Into each other—and, beholding this,
Their lips drew near, and clung into a kiss;   1480

186

A long, long kiss, a kiss of youth, and love,
   And beauty, all concéntrating like rays
Into one focus, kindled from above;
   Such kisses as belong to early days,
Where heart, and soul, and sense, in concert move,   1485
   And the blood's lava, and the pulse a blaze,
Each kiss a heart-quake—for a kiss's strength,
I think, it must be reckoned by its length.

187

By length I mean duration; theirs endured
   Heaven knows how long—no doubt they never reckoned;   1490
And if they had, they could not have secured
   The sum of their sensations to a second:
They had not spoken; but they felt allured,
   As if their souls and lips each other beckoned,
Which, being joined, like swarming bees they clung—   1495
Their hearts the flowers from whence the honey sprung.

188

They were alone, but not alone as they
   Who shut in chambers think it loneliness;
The silent ocean, and the starlight bay,
   The twilight glow, which momently grew less,   1500
The voiceless sands, and dropping caves, that lay
   Around them, made them to each other press,
As if there were no life beneath the sky
Save theirs, and that their life could never die.

189

They feared no eyes nor ears on that lone beach,   1505
   They felt no terrors from the night, they were
All in all to each other: though their speech
   Was broken words, they *thought* a language there—
And all the burning tongues the passions teach
   Found in one sigh the best interpreter   1510
Of nature's oracle—first love—that all
Which Eve has left her daughters since her fall.

190

Haidée spoke not of scruples, asked no vows,
   Nor offered any; she had never heard
Of plight and promises to be a spouse,   1515
   Or perils by a loving maid incurred;

She was all which pure ignorance allows,
  And flew to her young mate like a young bird;
And never having dreamt of falsehood, she
  Had not one word to say of constancy.[3]   1520

191

She loved, and was belovéd—she adored,
  And she was worshiped; after nature's fashion,
Their intense souls, into each other poured,
  If souls could die, had perished in that passion—
But by degrees their senses were restored,   1525
  Again to be o'ercome, again to dash on;
And, beating 'gainst *his* bosom, Haidée's heart
Felt as if never more to beat apart.

192

Alas! they were so young, so beautiful,
  So lonely, loving, helpless, and the hour   1530
Was that in which the heart is always full,
  And, having o'er itself no further power,
Prompts deeds eternity cannot annul,
  But pays off moments in an endless shower
Of hell-fire—all prepared for people giving   1535
Pleasure or pain to one another living.

193

Alas! for Juan and Haidée! they were
  So loving and so lovely—till then never,
Excepting our first parents, such a pair
  Had run the risk of being damned forever;   1540
And Haidée, being devout as well as fair,
  Had, doubtless, heard about the Stygian river,[4]
And hell and purgatory—but forgot
Just in the very crisis she should not.

194

They look upon each other, and their eyes   1545
  Gleam in the moonlight; and her white arm clasps
Round Juan's head, and his around hers lies
  Half buried in the tresses which it grasps;
She sits upon his knee, and drinks his sighs,
  He hers, until they end in broken gasps;   1550
And thus they form a group that's quite antique,
Half naked, loving, natural, and Greek.

195

And when those deep and burning moments passed,
  And Juan sunk to sleep within her arms,
She slept not, but all tenderly, though fast,   1555
  Sustained his head upon her bosom's charms;
And now and then her eye to heaven is cast,
  And then on the pale cheek her breast now warms,

3. Byron said, with reference to Haidée: "I was, and am, penetrated with the conviction that women only know evil from men, whereas men have no criterion to judge of purity or goodness but woman."
4. The Styx, which flows through Hades.

Pillowed on her o'erflowing heart, which pants
With all it granted, and with all it grants.   1560

196

An infant when it gazes on a light,
    A child the moment when it drains the breast,
A devotee when soars the Host[5] in sight,
    An Arab with a stranger for a guest,
A sailor when the prize has struck[6] in fight,   1565
    A miser filling his most hoarded chest,
Feel rapture; but not such true joy are reaping
As they who watch o'er what they love while sleeping.

197

For there it lies so tranquil, so beloved,
    All that it hath of life with us is living;   1570
So gentle, stirless, helpless, and unmoved,
    And all unconscious of the joy 'tis giving;
All it hath felt, inflicted, passed, and proved,
    Hushed into depths beyond the watcher's diving;
There lies the thing we love with all its errors   1575
And all its charms, like death without its terrors.

198

The lady watched her lover—and that hour
    Of Love's, and Night's, and Ocean's solitude,
O'erflowed her soul with their united power;
    Amidst the barren sand and rocks so rude   1580
She and her wave-worn love had made their bower,
    Where nought upon their passion could intrude,
And all the stars that crowded the blue space
Saw nothing happier than her glowing face.

199

Alas! the love of women! it is known   1585
    To be a lovely and a fearful thing;
For all of theirs upon that die is thrown,
    And if 'tis lost, life hath no more to bring
To them but mockeries of the past alone,
    And their revenge is as the tiger's spring,   1590
Deadly, and quick, and crushing; yet, as real
Torture is theirs, what they inflict they feel.

200

They are right; for man, to man so oft unjust,
    Is always so to women; one sole bond
Awaits them, treachery is all their trust;   1595
    Taught to conceal, their bursting hearts despond
Over their idol, till some wealthier lust
    Buys them in marriage—and what rests beyond?
A thankless husband, next a faithless lover,
Then dressing, nursing, praying, and all's over.   1600

5. The Eucharistic wafer.
6. Has lowered its flag in token of surrender.

201

Some take a lover, some take drams or prayers,
  Some mind their household, others dissipation,
Some run away, and but exchange their cares,
  Losing the advantage of a virtuous station;
Few changes e'er can better their affairs,   1605
  Theirs being an unnatural situation,
From the dull palace to the dirty hovel:
Some play the devil, and then write a novel.[7]

202

Haidée was Nature's bride, and knew not this;
  Haidée was Passion's child, born where the sun   1610
Showers triple light, and scorches even the kiss
  Of his gazelle-eyed daughters; she was one
Made but to love, to feel that she was his
  Who was her chosen: what was said or done
Elsewhere was nothing. She had nought to fear,   1615
Hope, care, nor love beyond, her heart beat *here*.

203

And oh! that quickening of the heart, that beat!
  How much it costs us! yet each rising throb
Is in its cause as its effect so sweet,
  That Wisdom, ever on the watch to rob   1620
Joy of its alchemy, and to repeat
  Fine truths; even Conscience, too, has a tough job
To make us understand each good old maxim,
So good—I wonder Castlereagh[8] don't tax 'em.

204

And now 'twas done—on the lone shore were plighted   1625
  Their hearts; the stars, their nuptial torches, shed
Beauty upon the beautiful they lighted:
  Ocean their witness, and the cave their bed,
By their own feelings hallowed and united,
  Their priest was Solitude, and they were wed: 1630
And they were happy, for to their young eyes
Each was an angel, and earth paradise.

* * *

208

But Juan! had he quite forgotten Julia?
  And should he have forgotten her so soon?
I can't but say it seems to me mostly truly a
  Perplexing question; but, no doubt, the moon   1660
Does these things for us, and whenever newly a
  Strong palpitation rises, 'tis her boon,
Else how the devil is it that fresh features
Have such a charm for us poor human creatures?

---

7. The impetuous and hysterical Lady
Caroline Lamb, having thrown herself
at Byron and been after a time rejected, incorporated incidents from the
affair in her novel, *Glenarvon* (1816).
8. Robert Stewart, Viscount Castlereagh,
British Foreign Secretary from 1812 to
1822.

209

I hate inconstancy—I loathe, detest,
   Abhor, condemn, abjure the mortal made
Of such quicksilver clay that in his breast
   No permanent foundation can be laid;
Love, constant love, has been my constant guest—
   And yet last night, being at a masquerade,
I saw the prettiest creature, fresh from Milan,
Which gave me some sensations like a villain.

210

But soon Philosophy came to my aid,
   And whispered, "Think of every sacred tie!"
"I will, my dear Philosophy!" I said,
   "But then her teeth, and then, oh, Heaven! her eye!
I'll just inquire if she be wife or maid,
   Or neither—out of curiosity."
"Stop!" cried Philosophy, with air so Grecian
(Though she was masked then as a fair Venetian);

211

"Stop!" so I stopped.—But to return: that which
   Men call inconstancy is nothing more
Than admiration due where nature's rich
   Profusion with young beauty covers o'er
Some favored object; and as in the niche
   A lovely statue we almost adore,
This sort of adoration of the real
Is but a heightening of the "beau ideal."[9]

212

'Tis the perception of the beautiful,
   A fine extension of the faculties,
Platonic, universal, wonderful,
   Drawn from the stars, and filtered through the skies,
Without which life would be extremely dull;
   In short, it is the use of our own eyes,
With one or two small senses added, just
To hint that flesh is formed of fiery dust.

213

Yet 'tis a painful feeling, and unwilling,
   For surely if we always could perceive
In the same object graces quite as killing
   As when she rose upon us like an Eve,
'Twould save us many a heartache, many a shilling
   (For we must get them anyhow, or grieve),
Whereas, if one sole lady pleased forever,
How pleasant for the heart, as well as liver!

* * *

216

In the meantime, without proceeding more
   In this anatomy, I've finished now

9. Ideal beauty.

Two hundred and odd stanzas as before,
   That being about the number I'll allow
Each canto of the twelve, or twenty-four;
   And, laying down my pen, I make my bow,   1725
Leaving Don Juan and Haidée to plead
For them and theirs with all who deign to read.

From *Canto III*

1

Hail, Muse! et cetera.—We left Juan sleeping,
   Pillowed upon a fair and happy breast,
And watched by eyes that never yet knew weeping,
   And loved by a young heart, too deeply blest
To feel the poison through her spirit creeping,   5
   Or know who rested there, a foe to rest,
Had soiled the current of her sinless years,
And turned her pure heart's purest blood to tears!

2

Oh, Love! what is it in this world of ours
   Which makes it fatal to be loved? Ah why   10
With cypress branches[1] hast thou wreathed thy bowers,
   And made thy best interpreter a sigh?
As those who dote on odors pluck the flowers,
   And place them on their breast—but place to die—
Thus the frail beings we would fondly cherish   15
Are laid within our bosoms but to perish.

3

In her first passion woman loves her lover,
   In all the others all she loves is love,
Which grows a habit she can ne'er get over,
   And fits her loosely—like an easy glove,
As you may find, whene'er you like to prove her: 20
   One man alone at first her heart can move;
She then prefers him in the plural number,
Not finding that the additions much encumber.

4

I know not if the fault be men's or theirs;
   But one thing's pretty sure; a woman planted[2]   25
(Unless at once she plunge for life in prayers)
   After a decent time must be gallánted;
Although, no doubt, her first of love affairs
   Is that to which her heart is wholly granted;
Yet there are some, they say, who have had *none*,   30
But those who have ne'er end with only *one*.

5

'Tis melancholy, and a fearful sign
   Of human frailty, folly, also crime,

---

1. **Signifying sorrow.**

2. Abandoned (from the French *planter
là*, to leave in the lurch).

That love and marriage rarely can combine,   35
   Although they both are born in the same clime;
Marriage from love, like vinegar from wine—
   A sad, sour, sober beverage—by time
Is sharpened from its high celestial flavor,
Down to a very homely household savor.   40

6

There's something of antipathy, as 'twere,
   Between their present and their future state;
A kind of flattery that's hardly fair
   Is used until the truth arrives too late—
Yet what can people do, except despair?   45
   The same things change their names at such a rate;
For instance—passion in a lover's glorious,
But in a husband is pronounced uxorious.

7

Men grow ashamed of being so very fond;
   They sometimes also get a little tired   50
(But that, of course, is rare), and then despond:
   The same things cannot always be admired,
Yet 'tis "so nominated in the bond,"[3]
   That both are tied till one shall have expired.
Sad thought! to lose the spouse that was adorning   55
Our days, and put one's servants into mourning.

8

There's doubtless something in domestic doings
   Which forms, in fact, true love's antithesis;
Romances paint at full length people's wooings,
   But only give a bust of marriages;   60
For no one cares for matrimonial cooings,
   There's nothing wrong in a connubial kiss:
Think you, if Laura had been Petrarch's wife,
He would have written sonnets all his life?

9

All tragedies are finished by a death,   65
   All comedies are ended by a marriage;
The future states of both are left to faith,
   For authors fear description might disparage
The worlds to come of both, or fall beneath,
   And then both worlds would punish their miscarriage;   70
So leaving each their priest and prayer book ready,
They say no more of Death or of the Lady.[4]

10

The only two that in my recollection
   Have sung of heaven and hell, or marriage, are
Dante and Milton, and of both the affection   75
   Was hapless in their nuptials, for some bar

3. Shylock: "Is it so nominated in the bond?" *The Merchant of Venice* IV.i.254.   4. Alluding to a popular ballad, *Death and the Lady*.

Of fault or temper ruined the connection
    (Such things, in fact, it don't ask much to mar);
But Dante's Beatrice and Milton's Eve
Were not drawn from their spouses, you conceive.   80

11

Some persons say that Dante meant theology
    By Beatrice, and not a mistress—I,
Although my opinion may require apology,
    Deem this a commentator's phantasy,
Unless indeed it was from his own knowledge he   85
    Decided thus, and showed good reason why;
I think that Dante's more abstruse ecstatics
Meant to personify the mathematics.

12

Haidée and Juan were not married, but
    The fault was theirs, not mine: it is not fair,
Chaste reader, then, in any way to put   90
    The blame on me, unless you wish they were;
Then if you'd have them wedded, please to shut
    The book which treats of this erroneous pair,
Before the consequences grow too awful;   95
'Tis dangerous to read of loves unlawful.

13

Yet they were happy—happy in the illicit
    Indulgence of their innocent desires;
But more imprudent grown with every visit,
    Haidée forgot the island was her sire's;   100
When we have what we like, 'tis hard to miss it,
    At least in the beginning, ere one tires;
Thus she came often, not a moment losing,
Whilst her piratical papa was cruising.

14

Let not his mode of raising cash seem strange,   105
    Although he fleeced the flags of every nation,
For into a prime minister but change
    His title, and 'tis nothing but taxation;
But he, more modest, took an humbler range
    Of life, and in an honester vocation   110
Pursued o'er the high seas his watery journey,
And merely practiced as a sea attorney.

15

The good old gentleman had been detained
    By winds and waves, and some important captures;
And, in the hope of more, at sea remained,   115
    Although a squall or two had damped his raptures,
By swamping one of the prizes; he had chained
    His prisoners, dividing them like chapters
In numbered lots; they all had cuffs and collars,
And averaged each from ten to a hundred dollars.   120

* * *

19

Then having settled his marine affairs,   145
    Despatching single cruisers here and there,
His vessel having need of some repairs,
    He shaped his course to where his daughter fair
Continued still her hospitable cares;
    But that part of the coast being shoal and bare,   150
And rough with reefs which ran out many a mile,
His port lay on the other side o' the isle.

20

And there he went ashore without delay,
    Having no customhouse nor quarantine
To ask him awkward questions on the way   155
    About the time and place where he had been:
He left his ship to be hove down next day,
    With orders to the people to careen;[5]
So that all hands were busy beyond measure,
In getting out goods, ballast, guns, and treasure.   160

* * *

27

He saw his white walls shining in the sun,
    His garden trees all shadowy and green;   210
He heard his rivulet's light bubbling run,
    The distant dog-bark; and perceived between
The umbrage of the wood so cool and dun,
    The moving figures, and the sparkling sheen
Of arms (in the East all arm)—and various dyes   215
Of colored garbs, as bright as butterflies.

28

And as the spot where they appear he nears,
    Surprised at these unwonted signs of idling,
He hears—alas! no music of the spheres,
    But an unhallowed, earthly sound of fiddling!   220
A melody which made him doubt his ears,
    The cause being past his guessing or unriddling;
A pipe, too, and a drum, and shortly after,
A most unoriental roar of laughter.

* * *

38

He did not know (alas! how men will lie)
    That a report (especially the Greeks)
Avouched his death (such people never die),
    And put his house in mourning several weeks—   300
But now their eyes and also lips were dry;
    The bloom, too, had returned to Haidée's cheeks.
Her tears, too, being returned into their fount,
She now kept house upon her own account.

5. To tip a vessel on its side in order to clean and repair its hull.

39

Hence all this rice, meat, dancing, wine, and fiddling,   305
    Which turned the isle into a place of pleasure;
The servants all were getting drunk or idling,
    A life which made them happy beyond measure.
Her father's hospitality seemed middling,
    Compared with what Haidée did with his treasure;   310
'Twas wonderful how things went on improving,
While she had not one hour to spare from loving.

40

Perhaps you think in stumbling on this feast,
    He flew into a passion, and in fact
There was no mighty reason to be pleased;   315
    Perhaps you prophesy some sudden act,
The whip, the rack, or dungeon at the least,
    To teach his people to be more exact,
And that, proceeding at a very high rate,
He showed the royal penchants of a pirate.   320

41

You're wrong.—He was the mildest mannered man
    That ever scuttled ship or cut a throat;
With such true breeding of a gentleman,
    You never could divine his real thought,
No courtier could, and scarcely woman can   325
    Gird more deceit within a petticoat;
Pity he loved adventurous life's variety,
He was so great a loss to good society.

* * *

48

Not that he was not sometimes rash or so,
    But never in his real and serious mood;
Then calm, concéntrated, and still, and slow,
    He lay coiled like the boa in the wood;   380
With him it never was a word and blow,
    His angry word once o'er, he shed no blood,
But in his silence there was much to rue,
And his *one* blow left little work for *two*.

49

He asked no further questions, and proceeded   385
    On to the house, but by a private way,
So that the few who met him hardly heeded,
    So little they expected him that day;
If love paternal in his bosom pleaded
    For Haidée's sake is more than I can say,   390
But certainly to one deemed dead returning,
This revel seemed a curious mode of mourning.

50

If all the dead could now return to life
    (Which God forbid!), or some, or a great many,

For instance, if a husband or his wife   395
   (Nuptial examples are as good as any),
No doubt whate'er might be their former strife,
   The present weather would be much more rainy—
Tears shed into the grave of the connection
Would share most probably its resurrection.   400

51

He entered in the house no more his home,
   A thing to human feelings the most trying,
And harder for the heart to overcome,
   Perhaps, than even the mental pangs of dying;
To find our hearthstone turned into a tomb,   405
   And round its once warm precincts palely lying
The ashes of our hopes, is a deep grief,
Beyond a single gentleman's belief.

52

He entered in the house—his home no more,
   For without hearts there is no home—and felt   410
The solitude of passing his own door
   Without a welcome: *there* he long had dwelt,
There his few peaceful days Time had swept o'er,
   There his warm bosom and keen eye would melt
Over the innocence of that sweet child,   415
His only shrine of feelings undefiled.

53

He was a man of a strange temperament,
   Of mild demeanor though of savage mood,
Moderate in all his habits, and content
   With temperance in pleasure, as in food,   420
Quick to perceive, and strong to bear, and meant
   For something better, if not wholly good;
His country's wrongs and his despair to save her
Had stung him from a slave to an enslaver.

* * *

96

But let me to my story: I must own,
   If I have any fault, it is digression—
Leaving my people to proceed alone,
   While I soliloquize beyond expression;   860
But these are my addresses from the throne,
   Which put off business to the ensuing session:
Forgetting each omission is a loss to
The world, not quite so great as Ariosto.[6]

97

I know that what our neighbors call *"longueurs,"*[7]   865
   (We've not so good a *word*, but have the *thing*,

6. Byron warmly admired this poet, author of *Orlando Furioso* (1532), the greatest of the Italian chivalric romances.

7. Boringly wordy passages of verse or prose (French).

In that complete perfection which insures
   An epic from Bob Southey[8] every Spring—)
Form not the true temptation which allures
   The reader; but 'twould not be hard to bring   870
Some fine examples of the *epopée*,[9]
To prove its grand ingredient is *ennui*.

98

We learn from Horace, "Homer sometimes sleeps";[1]
   We feel without him, Wordsworth sometimes wakes—
To show with what complacency he creeps,   875
   With his dear "Wagoners,"[2] around his lakes.
He wishes for "a boat" to sail the deeps—
   Of ocean?—No, of air; and then he makes
Another outcry for "a little boat,"
And drivels seas to set it well afloat.[3]   880

99

If he must fain sweep o'er the ethereal plain,
   And Pegasus[4] runs restive in his "Wagon,"
Could he not beg the loan of Charles's Wain?[5]
   Or pray Medea for a single dragon?[6]
Or if, too classic for his vulgar brain,   885
   He feared his neck to venture such a nag on,
And he must needs mount nearer to the moon,
Could not the blockhead ask for a balloon?

100

"Peddlers,"[7] and "Boats," and "Wagons!" Oh! ye shades
   Of Pope and Dryden, are we come to this?   890
That trash of such sort not alone evades,
   Contempt, but from the bathos' vast abyss
Floats scumlike uppermost, and these Jack Cades[8]
   Of sense and song above your graves may hiss—
The "little boatman" and his "Peter Bell"   895
Can sneer at him who drew "Achitophel!"[9]

8. Robert Southey (1774–1843), poet laureate and author of a number of epic-length narrative poems.
9. Epic poem (French); "*ennui*": boredom.
1. Horace, *Ars Poetica*, line 359: "Sometimes great Homer nods."
2. In 1819 Wordsworth had published a long narrative poem, *The Wagoner*.
3. In the Prologue to his poem *Peter Bell* (1819), Wordsworth wishes for "a little boat, / In shape a very crescent-moon: / Fast through the clouds my boat can sail * * *"
4. In Greek myth, the winged horse; he was said to have produced the fountain Hippocrene, sacred to the Muses, by stamping his hoof.
5. The constellation known in America as the Big Dipper.
6. When the Argonaut Jason abandoned Medea in order to take a new wife, she murdered their sons to punish her husband, then escaped in a chariot drawn by winged dragons.
7. Wordsworth's Peddler narrates the story of Margaret (reprinted above from the early manuscript, *The Ruined Cottage*). Byron knew this story in the later form which Wordsworth incorporated into Book I of *The Excursion* (1814).
8. Jack Cade was an adventurer who led an uprising against Henry VI in 1450.
9. I.e., John Dryden, author of *Absalom and Achitophel* (1681), whom Byron greatly admired. Wordsworth had derogated Dryden's poetry in the *Essay, Supplementary to the Preface* of his *Poems* (1815).

101

T' our tale.—The feast was over, the slaves gone,
   The dwarfs and dancing girls had all retired;
The Arab lore and poet's song were done,
   And every sound of revelry expired;   900
The lady and her lover, left alone,
   The rosy flood of twilight's sky admired—
Ave Maria![10] o'er the earth and sea,
That heavenliest hour of Heaven is worthiest thee!

102

Ave Maria! blessed be the hour!   905
   The time, the clime, the spot, where I so oft
Have felt that moment in its fullest power
   Sink o'er the earth so beautiful and soft,
While swung the deep bell in the distant tower,
   Or the faint dying day-hymn stole aloft,   910
And not a breath crept through the rosy air,
And yet the forest leaves seemed stirred with prayer.

103

Ave Maria! 'tis the hour of prayer!
   Ave Maria! 'tis the hour of love!
Ave Maria! may our spirits dare   915
   Look up to thine and to thy Son's above!
Ave Maria! oh that face so fair!
   Those downcast eyes beneath the Almighty dove—
What though 'tis but a pictured image strike—
That painting is no idol—'tis too like.   920

104

Some kinder casuists are pleased to say,
   In nameless print—that I have no devotion;
But set those persons down with me to pray,
   And you shall see who has the properest notion
Of getting into heaven the shortest way;   925
   My altars are the mountains and the ocean,
Earth, air, stars—all that springs from the great Whole,
Who hath produced, and will receive the soul.

* * *

From *Canto IV*

3

As boy, I thought myself a clever fellow,
   And wished that others held the same opinion;
They took it up when my days grew more mellow,
   And other minds acknowledged my dominion:
Now my sere fancy "falls into the yellow   20
   Leaf,"[1] and Imagination droops her pinion,

---

10. "Hail, Mary": these words open a Roman Catholic prayer. *Ave Maria* is sometimes used to refer to evening (or morning), since the prayer is part of the service at these times.

1. Cf. *Macbeth* V.iii.22–23: "My way of life / Is fallen into the sere, the yellow leaf."

And the sad truth which hovers o'er my desk
Turns what was once romantic to burlesque.

4

And if I laugh at any mortal thing,   25
    'Tis that I may not weep; and if I weep,
'Tis that our nature cannot always bring
    Itself to apathy, for we must steep
Our hearts first in the depths of Lethe's spring,
    Ere what we least wish to behold will sleep: 30
Thetis baptized her mortal son in Styx:[2]
A mortal mother would on Lethe fix.

5

Some have accused me of a strange design
    Against the creed and morals of the land,
And trace it in this poem every line: 35
    I don't pretend that I quite understand
My own meaning when I would be *very* fine;
    But the fact is that I have nothing planned,
Unless it were to be a moment merry,
A novel word in my vocabulary.   40

6

To the kind reader of our sober clime
    This way of writing will appear exotic;
Pulci[3] was sire of the half-serious rhyme,
    Who sang when chivalry was more Quixotic,
And reveled in the fancies of the time,   45
    True knights, chaste dames, huge giants, kings despotic;
But all these, save the last, being obsolete,
I chose a modern subject as more meet.

7

How I have treated it, I do not know;
    Perhaps no better than they have treated me   50
Who have imputed such designs as show
    Not what they saw, but what they wished to see:
But if it gives them pleasure, be it so;
    This is a liberal age, and thoughts are free:
Meantime Apollo plucks me by the ear,   55
And tells me to resume my story here.

* * *

26

Juan and Haidée gazed upon each other
    With swimming looks of speechless tenderness,
Which mixed all feelings, friend, child, lover, brother,
    All that the best can mingle and express

2. The river in Hades into which the nymph Thetis dipped Achilles, to make him invulnerable. Lethe, another river in Hades, brings oblivion of life.
3. Author of the *Morgante Maggiore*, prototype of the Italian seriocomic romance from which Byron derived the stanza and manner of *Don Juan*. See the introduction to *Don Juan*.

When two pure hearts are poured in one another,   205
    And love too much, and yet cannot love less;
But almost sanctify the sweet excess
By the immortal wish and power to bless.

27
Mixed in each other's arms, and heart in heart,
    Why did they not then die?—they had lived too long   210
Should an hour come to bid them breathe apart;
    Years could but bring them cruel things or wrong;
The world was not for them, nor the world's art
    For beings passionate as Sappho's song;
Love was born *with* them, *in* them, so intense,   215
It was their very spirit—not a sense.

28
They should have lived together deep in woods,
    Unseen as sings the nightingale; they were
Unfit to mix in these thick solitudes
    Called social, haunts of Hate, and Vice, and Care: 220
How lonely every freeborn creature broods!
    The sweetest songbirds nestle in a pair;
The eagle soars alone; the gull and crow
Flock o'er their carrion, just like men below.

29
Now pillowed cheek to cheek, in loving sleep,   225
    Haidée and Juan their siesta took,
A gentle slumber, but it was not deep,
    Forever and anon a something shook
Juan, and shuddering o'er his frame would creep;
    And Haidée's sweet lips murmured like a brook   230
A wordless music, and her face so fair
Stirred with her dream, as rose-leaves with the air;

30
Or as the stirring of a deep clear stream
    Within an Alpine hollow, when the wind
Walks o'er it, was 'she shaken by the dream,   235
    The mystical usurper of the mind—
O'erpowering us to be whate'er may seem
    Good to the soul which we no more can bind;
Strange state of being! (for 'tis still to be)
Senseless to feel, and with scaled eyes to see.   240

31
She dreamed of being alone on the seashore,
    Chained to a rock; she knew not how, but stir
She could not from the spot, and the loud roar
    Grew, and each wave rose roughly, threatening her;
And o'er her upper lip they seemed to pour,   245
    Until she sobbed for breath, and soon they were
Foaming o'er her lone head, so fierce and high—
Each broke to drown her, yet she could not die.

32

Anon—she was released, and then she strayed
   O'er the sharp shingles[4] with her bleeding feet,   250
And stumbled almost every step she made;
   And something rolled before her in a sheet,
Which she must still pursue howe'er afraid;
   'Twas white and indistinct, nor stopped to meet
Her glance nor grasp, for still she gazed and grasped,   255
And ran, but it escaped her as she clasped.

33

The dream changed—in a cave she stood, its walls
   Were hung with marble icicles; the work
Of ages on its water-fretted halls,
   Where waves might wash, and seals might breed and lurk;
Her hair was dripping, and the very balls   261
   Of her black eyes seemed turned to tears, and murk
The sharp rocks looked below each drop they caught,
Which froze to marble as it fell, she thought.

34

And wet, and cold, and lifeless at her feet,   265
   Pale as the foam that frothed on his dead brow,
Which she essayed in vain to clear (how sweet
   Were once her cares, how idle seemed they now!),
Lay Juan, nor could aught renew the beat
   Of his quenched heart; and the sea dirges low   270
Rang in her sad ears like a mermaid's song,
And that brief dream appeared a life too long.

35

And gazing on the dead, she thought his face
   Faded, or altered into something new—
Like to her father's features, till each trace   275
   More like and like to Lambro's aspect grew—
With all his keen worn look and Grecian grace;
   And starting, she awoke, and what to view?
Oh! Powers of Heaven! what dark eye meets she there?
'Tis—'tis her father's—fixed upon the pair!   280

36

Then shrieking, she arose, and shrieking fell,
   With joy and sorrow, hope and fear, to see
Him whom she deemed a habitant where dwell
   The ocean-buried, risen from death, to be
Perchance the death of one she loved too well: 285
   Dear as her father had been to Haidée,
It was a moment of that awful kind—
I have seen such—but must not call to mind.

37

Up Juan sprung to Haidée's bitter shriek,
   And caught her falling, and from off the wall   290
Snatched down his saber, in hot haste to wreak
   Vengeance on him who was the cause of all:

4. Loose pebbles.

Then Lambro, who till now forebore to speak,
  Smiled scornfully, and said, "Within my call,
A thousand scimitars await the word;   295
Put up, young man, put up your silly sword."

                        38
And Haidée clung around him; "Juan, 'tis—
  'Tis Lambro—'tis my father! Kneel with me—
He will forgive us—yes—it must be—yes.
  Oh! dearest father, in this agony   300
Of pleasure and of pain—even while I kiss
  Thy garment's hem with transport, can it be
That doubt should mingle with my filial joy?
Deal with me as thou wilt, but spare this boy."

                        39
High and inscrutable the old man stood,   305
  Calm in his voice, and calm within his eye—
Not always signs with him of calmest mood:
  He looked upon her, but gave no reply;
Then turned to Juan, in whose cheek the blood
  Oft came and went, as there resolved to die;   310
In arms, at least, he stood, in act to spring
On the first foe whom Lambro's call might bring.

                        40
"Young man, your sword"; so Lambro once more said:
  Juan replied, "Not while this arm is free."
The old man's cheek grew pale, but not with dread,   315
  And drawing from his belt a pistol, he
Replied, "Your blood be then on your own head."
  Then looked close at the flint, as if to see
'Twas fresh—for he had lately used the lock[5]—
And next proceeded quietly to cock.   320

                        41
It has a strange quick jar upon the ear,
  That cocking of a pistol, when you know
A moment more will bring the sight to bear
  Upon your person, twelve yards off, or so;
A gentlemanly distance,[6] not too near,   325
  If you have got a former friend for foe;
But after being fired at once or twice,
The ear becomes more Irish, and less nice.[7]

                        42
Lambro presented, and one instant more
  Had stopped this Canto, and Don Juan's breath,   330
When Haidée threw herself her boy before;
  Stern as her sire: "On me," she cried, "let death
Descend—the fault is mine; this fatal shore
  He found—but sought not. I have pledged my faith;

---

5. That part of the gun which explodes
the charge.
6. I.e., dueling distance.

7. Finicky. Byron alludes to the propensity of hotheaded young Irishmen
to fight duels.

I love him—I will die with him: I knew   335
Your nature's firmness—know your daughter's too."

43
A minute past, and she had been all tears,
   And tenderness, and infancy; but now
She stood as one who championed human fears—
   Pale, statue-like, and stern, she wooed the blow;   340
And tall beyond her sex, and their compeers,[8]
   She drew up to her height, as if to show
A fairer mark; and with a fixed eye scanned
Her father's face—but never stopped his hand.

44
He gazed on her, and she on him: 'twas strange   345
   How like they looked! the expression was the same;
Serenely savage, with a little change
   In the large dark eye's mutual-darted flame;
For she, too, was as one who could avenge,
   If cause should be—a lioness, though tame;   350
Her father's blood before her father's face
Boiled up, and proved her truly of his race.

45
I said they were alike, their features and
   Their stature differing but in sex and years;
Even to the delicacy of their hand   355
   There was resemblance, such as true blood wears;
And now to see them, thus divided, stand
   In fixed ferocity, when joyous tears,
And sweet sensations, should have welcomed both,
Show what the passions are in their full growth.   360

46
The father paused a moment, then withdrew
   His weapon, and replaced it; but stood still,
And looking on her, as to look her through,
   "Not I," he said, "have sought this stranger's ill;
Not I have made this desolation: few   365
   Would bear such outrage, and forbear to kill;
But I must do my duty—how thou hast
Done thine, the present vouches for the past.

47
"Let him disarm; or, by my father's head,
   His own shall roll before you like a ball!"   370
He raised his whistle as the word he said,
   And blew; another answered to the call,
And rushing in disorderly, though led,
   And armed from boot to turban, one and all,
Some twenty of his train came, rank on rank;   375
He gave the word, "Arrest or slay the Frank."[9]

---

8. I.e., she was the match in height of   9. Term used in the Near East to
Lambro and Juan.   designate a western European.

48

Then, with a sudden movement, he withdrew
  His daughter; while compressed within his clasp,
'Twixt her and Juan interposed the crew;
  In vain she struggled in her father's grasp—   380
His arms were like a serpent's coil: then flew
  Upon their prey, as darts an angry asp,
The file of pirates; save the foremost, who
Had fallen, with his right shoulder half cut through.

49

The second had his cheek laid open; but   385
  The third, a wary, cool old sworder, took
The blows upon his cutlass, and then put
  His own well in; so well, ere you could look,
His man was floored, and helpless at his foot,
  With the blood running like a little brook   390
From two smart saber gashes, deep and red—
Once on the arm, the other on the head.

50

And then they bound him where he fell, and bore
  Juan from the apartment: with a sign
Old Lambro bade them take him to the shore,   395
  Where lay some ships which were to sail at nine.
They laid him in a boat, and plied the oar
  Until they reached some galliots,[1] placed in line;
On board of one of these, and under hatches,
They stowed him, with strict orders to the watches.   400

51

The world is full of strange vicissitudes,
  And here was one exceedingly unpleasant:
A gentleman so rich in the world's goods,
  Handsome and young, enjoying all the present,
Just at the very time when he least broods   405
  On such a thing is suddenly to sea sent,
Wounded and chained, so that he cannot move,
And all because a lady fell in love.

* * *

56

Afric is all the sun's, and as her earth
  Her human clay is kindled; full of power
For good or evil, burning from its birth,
  The Moorish blood partakes the planet's hour,
And like the soil beneath it will bring forth: 445
  Beauty and love were Haidée's mother's dower;
But her large dark eye showed deep Passion's force,
Though sleeping like a lion near a source.

57

Her daughter, tempered with a milder ray,
  Like summer clouds all silvery, smooth, and fair,   450

---

1. A small, fast galley, propelled both by oars and sails.

Till slowly charged with thunder they display
   Terror to earth, and tempest to the air,
Had held till now her soft and milky way;
   But overwrought with passion and despair,
The fire burst forth from her Numidian[2] veins,   455
Even as the simoom[3] sweeps the blasted plains.

58

The last sight which she saw was Juan's gore,
   And he himself o'ermastered and cut down;
His blood was running on the very floor
   Where late he trod, her beautiful, her own;   460
Thus much she viewed an instant and no more—
   Her struggles ceased with one convulsive groan;
On her sire's arm, which until now scarce held
Her writhing, fell she like a cedar felled.

59

A vein had burst, and her sweet lips' pure dyes   465
   Were dabbled with the deep blood which ran o'er;
And her head drooped, as when the lily lies
   O'ercharged with rain: her summoned handmaids bore
Their lady to her couch with gushing eyes;
   Of herbs and cordials they produced their store,   470
But she defied all means they could employ,
Like one life could not hold, nor death destroy.

60

Days lay she in that state unchanged, though chill—
   With nothing livid,[4] still her lips were red;
She had no pulse, but death seemed absent still;   475
   No hideous sign proclaimed her surely dead;
Corruption came not in each mind to kill
   All hope; to look upon her sweet face bred
New thoughts of life, for it seemed full of soul—
She had so much, earth could not claim the whole.   480

* * *

69

Twelve days and nights she withered thus; at last,   545
   Without a groan, or sigh, or glance, to show
A parting pang, the spirit from her passed:
   And they who watched her nearest could not know
The very instant, till the change that cast
   Her sweet face into shadow, dull and slow,   550
Glazed o'er her eyes—the beautiful, the black—
Oh! to possess such luster—and then lack!

70

She died, but not alone; she held within
   A second principle of life, which might
Have dawned a fair and sinless child of sin;   555
   But closed its little being without light,

2. North African.   wind.
3. A violent, hot, dust-laden desert   4. I.e., she was ashen pale.

And went down to the grave unborn, wherein
    Blossom and bough lie withered with one blight;
In vain the dews of Heaven descend above
The bleeding flower and blasted fruit of love.   560

71

Thus lived—thus died she; never more on her
    Shall sorrow light, or shame. She was not made
Through years or moons the inner weight to bear,
    Which colder hearts endure till they are laid
By age in earth; her days and pleasures were   565
    Brief, but delightful—such as had not stayed
Long with her destiny; but she sleeps well
By the seashore, whereon she loved to dwell.

72

That isle is now all desolate and bare,
    Its dwellings down, its tenants passed away;   570
None but her own and father's grave is there,
    And nothing outward tells of human clay;
Ye could not know where lies a thing so fair,
    No stone is there to show, no tongue to say
What was; no dirge, except the hollow sea's,   575
Mourns o'er the beauty of the Cyclades.

73

But many a Greek maid in a loving song
    Sighs o'er her name; and many an islander
With her sire's story makes the night less long;
    Valor was his, and beauty dwelt with her: 580
If she loved rashly, her life paid for wrong—
    A heavy price must all pay who thus err,
In some shape; let none think to fly the danger,
For soon or late Love is his own avenger.[5]

* * *

1818–23   1819–24

5. Juan's adventures continue. He is sold as a slave in Constantinople to an enamored Sultana; she disguises him as a girl and adds him to her husband's harem for convenience of access. Juan escapes, joins the Russian army which is besieging Ismail, and so distinguishes himself in the capture of the town that he is sent with despatches to St. Petersburg. There he becomes "man-mistress" to the insatiable Catherine the Great; as the result of her assiduous attentions, he falls into a physical decline and, for a salutary change of scene and climate, is sent on a diplomatic mission to England. In Canto XVI, the last that Byron finished, he is in the middle of an amorous adventure while a guest at the medieval country mansion of an English nobleman, Lord Henry Amundeville, and his very beautiful wife.

PERCY BYSSHE SHELLEY
(1792–1822)

1811: Is expelled from Oxford and elopes with Harriet Westbrook.
1818: Leaves England for Italy, never to return.
1819: The great year: *Prometheus Unbound, The Cenci, Ode
to the West Wind*, and some of his best lyrics.
1820: Settles in Pisa and its vicinity; the "Pisan Circle."

Although he was an extreme heretic and nonconformist in all his life and
thought, Shelley emerged from a solidly conservative background. His
ancestors had been Sussex aristocrats since early in the 17th century; his
grandfather, Sir Bysshe Shelley, made himself the richest man in Horsham,
Sussex; his father, Timothy Shelley, was a hardheaded and conventional
member of Parliament. Percy Shelley himself was in line for a baronetcy,
and as befitted his station, was sent to be educated at Eton and at Oxford.
He was slight of build, eccentric in manner, and unskilled in sports or
fighting, and as a consequence, was mercilessly baited by older and
stronger boys. Even then he saw the petty tyranny of schoolmasters and
schoolmates as representative of man's general inhumanity to man, and
dedicated his life to a war against all injustice and oppression. He describes
the experience in the Dedication to *The Revolt of Islam*:

> So without shame, I spoke: "I will be wise,
> And just, and free, and mild, if in me lies
> Such power, for I grow weary to behold
> The selfish and the strong still tyrannize
> Without reproach or check." I then controlled
> My tears, my heart grew calm, and I was meek and bold.

At Oxford in the autumn of 1810 Shelley's closest friend was Thomas
Jefferson Hogg, a self-centered and self-confident young man who shared
Shelley's love of philosophy and scorn of orthodoxy. The two collaborated on a pamphlet, *The Necessity of Atheism*, which claimed that God's
existence cannot be proved on empirical grounds. Shelley refused to repudiate the document before the authorities and, to his great shock and
grief, was peremptorily expelled, terminating a university career that had
lasted only six months. This event opened a breach between Shelley
and his father that widened over the years.

Shelley went to London where, eager for a test of his zeal for social
justice, he took up the cause of Harriet Westbrook, the pretty and warm-
hearted daughter of a well-to-do tavern keeper, whose father, Shelley
wrote to Hogg, "has persecuted her in a most horrible way by endeavoring
to compel her to go to school." Harriet threw herself on Shelley's protection, and "gratitude and admiration," he wrote, "all demand that I shall
love her *forever*." He eloped with Harriet to Edinburgh and married her,
though against his firm conviction that marriage was a tyrannical and degrading social institution. He was then 18 years of age, and his bride 16.

The young couple moved restlessly from place to place, living on a small allowance granted reluctantly by their families. In February of 1812, accompanied by Harriet's sister Eliza, they traveled to Dublin to distribute Shelley's *Address to the Irish People* and otherwise take part in the movement for Catholic emancipation and for the amelioration of the oppressed and poverty-stricken people.

Back in London, Shelley became a disciple of the radical social philosopher William Godwin, author of the *Inquiry Concerning Political Justice*. In 1813 he printed privately his first important work, *Queen Mab*, a long prophetic poem set in the fantastic frame of the journey of a disembodied soul through space, to whom the fairy Mab reveals in visions the woeful past, the dreadful present, and the utopian future. Announcing that "there is no God!" Mab decries institutional religion and codified morality as the causes of social evil. She prophesies that, under the rule of the goddess Necessity, all institutions will wither away, and humanity will return to its natural condition of goodness and felicity.

In the following spring Shelley, who had drifted apart from Harriet, fell in love with the beautiful Mary Wollstonecraft Godwin. Acting according to his conviction that cohabitation without love is immoral, he abandoned Harriet, fled to France with Mary (taking along her half sister, Claire Clairmont), and—still acting in accordance with his belief in nonexclusive love—invited Harriet to come live with them in the relationship of a sister. Shelley's elopement with Mary outraged even her father, though his theoretical views of marriage had been no less liberal than Shelley's, and despite the fact that Shelley, himself in financial difficulties, had earlier taken over Godwin's very substantial debts. When he returned to London, Shelley found that the general public, his family, and most of his friends regarded him not only as an atheist and revolutionary, but also as a gross immoralist. When two years later, Harriet, pregnant by an unknown lover, drowned herself in a fit of despair, the courts denied Shelley the custody of their two children. Shelley married Mary Godwin and, in 1818, moved to Italy; thereafter he saw himself in the role of an alien and outcast, scorned and rejected by the mankind to whose welfare he had dedicated his powers and his life.

In Italy he resumed his restless existence, moving from town to town and house to house. His health was usually bad. Although the death of his grandfather in 1815 had provided a substantial income, he dissipated so much of it by his warmhearted but improvident support of William Godwin, Leigh Hunt, and other indigent pensioners that he was constantly short of money and harried by creditors. Within nine months, in 1818–19, Clara and William, the beloved children of Percy and Mary Shelley, both died. This tragedy threw Mary into a state of apathy and self-absorption which destroyed the earlier harmony of her relationship with her husband, and from which even the birth of another son, Percy Florence, could not entirely rescue her.

In these desperate circumstances, in a state sometimes verging on despair, and knowing that he almost entirely lacked an audience, Shelley wrote his greatest works. In 1819 he completed his masterpiece, *Prometheus Unbound*, and wrote a fine tragedy, *The Cenci*, as well as numerous lyric poems; a visionary call for a proletarian revolution, *The Mask of Anarchy*; a discerning and witty satire on Wordsworth, *Peter Bell the Third;* and a penetrating political essay, *A Philosophical View of Reform.* His works of the next two years include *A Defence of Poetry; Epipsychidion,* a rhapsodic vision of love as a union, beyond earthly limits, with what the title identifies as "the soul out of my soul"; *Adonais,* his noble elegy on the death of Keats; and *Hellas,* a lyrical drama evoked by the Greek war for liberation from the Turks, in which he again projected his vision of a new golden age. These writings, unlike the early *Queen Mab,* are the products of a mind enlarged and chastened by tragic experience, deepened by incessant philosophical speculation, and richly stored with the harvest of his reading—which Shelley carried on, as his friend Hogg said, "in season and out of season, at table, in bed, and especially during a walk," until he became one of the most erudite of poets. His delight in scientific discoveries and speculations continued, but his earlier zest for Gothic terrors and the social theories of the radical 18th-century optimists had given way to an absorption in Greek tragedy, Milton's *Paradise Lost,* and the Bible. While he did not give up his hopes for a millennial future (he wore a ring with the motto *Il buon tempo verrà*—"the good time will come"), he now attributed the evils of present society to man's own moral failures, and grounded the possibility of radical social reform upon a prior reform of man's moral nature through the redeeming power of love. Though often thought of as a simple-minded doctrinaire, Shelley in fact possessed a complex and energetically inquisitive intelligence which never halted at a fixed mental position; all his writings represent, not final solutions, but stages in a ceaseless exploration.

The poems of Shelley's maturity also show the influence of his study of Plato and the Neo-Platonists. Shelley found congenial the Platonic division of the cosmos into two worlds—the ordinary world of change, mortality, evil, and suffering, and the criterion world of perfect and eternal Forms, of which the world of sense-experience is only a distant and illusory reflection. The earlier interpretations of Shelley as a downright Platonic idealist, however, have been drastically modified by recent investigations of his reading and writings. Shelley was a close student of English empirical philosophy, which limits knowledge to valid reasoning upon what is given in sense-experience, and within this tradition he felt a special affinity to the radical skepticism of David Hume. Shelley was indeed an idealist, but as C. E. Pulos has shown in *The Deep Truth: A Study of Shelley's Scepticism,* his was "a qualified idealism," holding provisionally to the ideas envisioned by an imagination which transcends experience, but refusing to assert that these ideas are anything more than high possibilities. As Shelley wrote, we quickly reach "the verge where words abandon us, and what wonder if we grow dizzy to look down the dark abyss of how little we know." Many of his major poems express his sense of the limits of certain knowledge, and his refusal to let his intuitions and hopes harden into a philosophical or religious creed. To the skeptical idealism of the mature Shelley (see, e.g., the notes to his great lyrics from *Hellas*), the hope in the ultimate redemption of life by love and imagination is not a certainty, but a moral obligation. We must cling to hope because its contrary, despair about human possibility, is self-fulfilling, by ensuring the permanence of the conditions before which the mind has surrendered its aspirations. Hope does not guarantee achievement, but it keeps open the possibility of achievement, and so releases man's imaginative and creative powers, which are its only available means.

When in 1820 the Shelleys settled finally at Pisa, he came closer to finding contentment than at any time in his adult life. A group of friends, Shelley's "Pisan Circle," gathered around them, including for a while Lord Byron and the swashbuckling young Cornishman, Edward Trelawny. Chief in Shelley's affections, however, were Edward Williams, a retired lieutenant of a cavalry regiment serving in India, and his charming common-law wife, Jane, with whom Shelley carried on a flirtation and to whom he addressed some of his best lyrics and verse letters. The end came suddenly, and in a fashion pre-visioned in the ecstatic last stanza of *Adonais*, where Shelley had described his spirit as a ship driven by a violent storm out into the dark unknown. On July 8, 1822, Shelley and Edward Williams were sailing their open boat, the *Don Juan*, from Leghorn to their summer house near Lerici, on the Gulf of Spezia. A violent squall blew up and swamped the boat. When several days later the bodies were washed ashore they were cremated, and Shelley's ashes were buried in the Protestant Cemetery at Rome, near the graves of John Keats and of William Shelley, the poet's young son. He left unfinished *The Triumph of Life*, which was a new departure for Shelley and, in the estimation of many readers, promised to be his greatest poem. Byron, who did not pay moral compliments lightly, wrote to John Murray at the time of Shelley's death: "You were all brutally mistaken about Shelley, who was, without exception, the *best* and least selfish man I ever knew. I never knew one who was not a beast in comparison."

To many critics of the mid-20th century (and despite the reverence toward him of W. B. Yeats, an admitted master of the poetry these critics most admired), Shelley was a favorite resort for supposed examples of intellectual and emotional immaturity, shoddy workmanship, and incoherent imagery. In recent years, however, Shelley has been the subject of many sympathetic critics, whose studies have clarified the complex and coherent structure of his symbolism and have increasingly confirmed Wordsworth's recognition that "Shelley is one of the best *artists* of us all: I mean in workmanship of style." Shelley's expansion of the metrical and sonantal resources of verse is without recent parallel in the history of English literature. Furthermore, his successful poems show an astonishing range of voice, from the sovereign order in rage of *Ode to the West Wind*, through the calm and heroic dignity of the utterances of Prometheus, to the near approximation to the inexpressible in the description of Asia's transfiguration and in the visionary conclusion of *Adonais*. Most surprising, in a poet who almost entirely lacked an audience, is the assured urbanity, the effortless command of the tone and language of a cultivated man of the world, which is exemplified in passages that Shelley wrote all through his mature career, and most sustainedly in the narrative *Julian and Maddalo* and in the lyrics and verse letters that he composed during the last year of his life.

TEXTUAL NOTE

The printing of Shelley's writings has had a tangled history. Shelley had no chance to correct proofs for many of the poems published during his lifetime, especially those that appeared in periodicals, while a number of his poems were not printed until after his death. We know by reference to Shelley's manuscripts that his various editors and printers made many errors and introduced many changes. As a result the standard editions of Shelley's collected poems—and the selections and anthologies that have been based on these editions—have hitherto included important deviations from the poet's probable intentions.

The texts below are those prepared by Donald H. Reiman and Sharon B. Powers for *Shelley's Poetry and Prose*, A Norton Critical Edition (1977); Reiman has also edited for this anthology a few poems not included in that edition. The texts are based on Shelley's extant holograph manuscripts and transcripts, on first editions of the various works, and on any later editions that may have incorporated the author's own changes; they also take advantage of specialized editions and textual studies by various Shelley scholars.

The detailed rationale for these texts is provided in Reiman and Powers's Textual Introduction. Shelley's spellings have been kept (though in part regularized according to the poet's own preferred forms), as well as Shelley's punctuation of those texts that he himself prepared for printing. The modern reader should remember that Shelley's punctuation, in the common fashion of his time, was primarily rhetorical rather than syntactical. That is, a punctuation mark indicates a phrasal pause in the reading; there is an increasingly longer pause in the sequence: comma, semicolon, colon, period, and dash. Also, Shelley often relied on the natural pause at the end of a line of verse, where modern usage would call for a comma or other mark of punctuation.

Mutability

We are as clouds that veil the midnight moon;
    How restlessly they speed, and gleam, and quiver,
Streaking the darkness radiantly!—yet soon
    Night closes round, and they are lost for ever:

Or like forgotten lyres,[1] whose dissonant strings   5
    Give various response to each varying blast,
To whose frail frame no second motion brings
    One mood or modulation like the last.

We rest.—A dream has power to poison sleep;
    We rise.—One wandering thought pollutes the day;   10
We feel, conceive or reason, laugh or weep;
    Embrace fond woe, or cast our cares away:

It is the same!—For, be it joy or sorrow,
    The path of its departure still is free:
Man's yesterday may ne'er be like his morrow;   15
    Nought may endure but Mutability.

1816

1. Wind harps.

To Wordsworth[2]

Poet of Nature, thou hast wept to know
That things depart which never may return:
Childhood and youth, friendship and love's first glow,
Have fled like sweet dreams, leaving thee to mourn.
These common woes I feel. One loss is mine   5
Which thou too feel'st, yet I alone deplore.
Thou wert as a lone star, whose light did shine
On some frail bark in winter's midnight roar:
Thou hast like to a rock-built refuge stood
Above the blind and battling multitude: 10
In honoured poverty thy voice did weave
Songs consecrate to truth and liberty,—
Deserting these, thou leavest me to grieve,
Thus having been, that thou shouldst cease to be.

                                        1816

2. Shelley's grieved comment on the poet   his views had become conservative.
of nature and of social radicalism after

Alastor; or, The Spirit of Solitude According to Shelley's friend
Thomas Love Peacock, the poet was "at a loss for a title, and I proposed
that which he adopted: Alastor, or the Spirit of Solitude. The Greek word
Alastor is an evil genius. . . . I mention the true meaning of the word because
many have supposed *Alastor* to be the name of the hero" (*Memoirs of Shelley*). Peacock's definition of an *alastor* as "an *evil* genius" has compounded
the problems that many readers have found in interpreting this work: the
term "evil" does not seem to fit the attitude to the poet's solitary quest
expressed within the poem; the poem seems to clash with some statements
in Shelley's Preface; and the first and second paragraphs within the Preface
seem inconsistent with each other. These problems, however, are largely
resolved if we recognize that, in his first major achievement (he was only
23 when he wrote *Alastor*), Shelley established his characteristic procedure
of working with multiple perspectives. Both Preface and poem explore alternative and conflicting possibilities in what Shelley calls "doubtful knowledge"—matters which are humanly essential, but in which no certainty is
humanly possible.

The first paragraph of the Preface explains the "allegorical" plot. By
"allegorical" Shelley means that the poem, like Medieval and Renaissance
allegories such as Dante's *Divine Comedy* and Spenser's *Faerie Queene*, represents a spiritual need and aspiration in the vehicle of a journey and quest
in the physical world. At the time of his full sexual awakening, Shelley's
protagonist ceases to be "self-possessed"; that is, the natural objects within
the world "cease to suffice," for he envisions a "Being," a female Other,
who will answer to all that is best in his own self and will fulfill not only
the requirements of his "intellectual faculties" and "imagination," but also
his sexual needs, "the functions of sense." He commits himself to the
search for "a prototype" of this vision in the real world, but since his
desires are infinite and the world's possibilities are limited, his quest is
doomed to end in his early death.

The second paragraph proceeds to pass judgment upon such a Poet in terms of the values of "actual men"—the requirements of human and social life in this world. Since the visionary Poet turned away from both human and natural community in search of the projected demands of his own psyche, his lot can be said to have been "avenged" by the *alastor*, the spirit of solitude, in the sense of "solitude" as alienation from both nature and humanity. The Preface goes on, however, passionately to elevate the moral status of such a visionary over the status of a second class of "meaner spirits" who also "keep aloof from sympathies with their kind," but only because they ignobly lack any capacity to project their imagination beyond their own narrow selves, and so are "morally dead." The Preface leaves open a possibility which Shelley proceeded to explore in *Prometheus Unbound* and other poems—the possibility that there exists a third class of men who sustain an imaginative vision, but undertake to realize it, not in self-centered solitude, but by effecting a transformation in human nature, society, and milieu.

Diverse attitudes expressed within the poem itself are clarified, once we realize that the story is narrated—as the many echoes from Wordsworth in the opening invocation suggest—in the persona of a Wordsworthian poet for whom nature suffices both to the demands of his imagination and to his need for community. This narrator-poet proceeds to tell, with insight and compassion, but from his own perspective, the history of a nameless visionary Poet who, having himself passed through a Wordsworthian phase, then gives up everything for a goal beyond possibility.

In this early poem Shelley established a form, conceptual frame, and imagery for the Romantic quest which not only shaped his own later poems, but also served as a paradigm for the writings of many other poets, from Byron's *Manfred* and Keats's *Endymion* and Invocation to *The Fall of Hyperion* to the quest-poems of Shelley's later admirer William Butler Yeats.

Alastor; or, The Spirit of Solitude

Preface

The poem entitled "ALASTOR," may be considered as allegorical of one of the most interesting situations of the human mind. It represents a youth of uncorrupted feelings and adventurous genius led forth by an imagination inflamed and purified through familiarity with all that is excellent and majestic, to the contemplation of the universe. He drinks deep of the fountains of knowledge, and is still insatiate. The magnificence and beauty of the external world sinks profoundly into the frame of his conceptions, and affords to their modifications a variety not to be exhausted. So long as it is possible for his desires to point towards objects thus infinite and unmeasured, he is joyous, and tranquil, and self-possessed. But the period arrives when these objects cease to suffice. His mind is at length suddenly awakened and thirsts for intercourse with an intelligence similar to itself. He images to himself the Being whom he loves. Conversant with speculations of the sublimest and most perfect natures, the vision in which he embodies his own imaginations unites all of wonderful, or wise, or beautiful, which the poet, the philosopher, or the lover could depicture. The intellectual faculties, the imagination, the functions of sense, have their respective requisitions on the sympathy of corresponding powers in other human beings. The Poet is represented as uniting these requisitions, and attaching them to a single image.[1] He seeks in vain for a prototype of his conception. Blasted by his disappointment, he descends to an untimely grave.

The picture is not barren of instruction to actual men. The Poet's self-centred seclusion was avenged by the furies of an irresistible passion pursuing him to speedy ruin. But that Power which strikes the luminaries of the world with sudden darkness and extinction, by awakening them to too exquisite a perception of its influences, dooms to a slow and poisonous decay those meaner spirits that dare to abjure its dominion. Their destiny is more abject and inglorious as their delinquency is more contemptible and pernicious. They who, deluded by no generous error, instigated by no sacred thirst of doubtful knowledge, duped by no illustrious superstition, loving nothing on this earth, and cherishing no hopes beyond, yet keep aloof from sympathies with their kind, rejoicing neither in human joy nor mourning with human grief; these, and such as they, have their apportioned curse. They languish, because none feel with them their common nature. They are morally dead. They are neither friends, nor lovers, nor fathers, nor citizens of the world, nor benefactors of their country. Among those who attempt to exist without human sympathy, the pure and tender-hearted perish through the intensity and passion of their search after its communities, when the vacancy of their spirit suddenly makes itself felt. All else, selfish, blind, and torpid, are those unforeseeing multitudes who constitute, together with their own, the lasting misery and loneliness of the world. Those who love not their fellow-beings live unfruitful lives, and prepare for their old age a miserable grave.

> "The good die first,
> And those whose hearts are dry as summer dust,
> Burn to the socket!"[2]

December 14, 1815.

---

1. Shelley's view that the object of love is an idealized antitype to all that is best within the self is clarified by a passage in his *Essay on Love*, which may have been written at about the time of *Alastor*: "We dimly see within our intellectual nature . . . the ideal prototype of every thing excellent or lovely that we are capable of conceiving as belonging to the nature of men * * * [This is] a soul within our soul * * *. The discovery of its anti-type * * * in such proportion as the type within demands; this is the invisible and unattainable point to which Love tends; and * * * without the possession of which there is no rest nor respite to the heart over which it rules."

2. Quoted from Wordsworth's *The Excursion* I.519–21; the passage occurs in *The Ruined Cottage* (above, lines 96–98), which Wordsworth reworked into the first Book of *The Excursion* (1814).

Alastor; or, The Spirit of Solitude

Nondum amabam, et amare amabam, quærebam quid amarem, amans
amare.—*Confess. St. August.*[3]

Earth, ocean, air, beloved brotherhood!
If our great Mother[4] has imbued my soul
With aught of natural piety[5] to feel
Your love, and recompense the boon with mine;[6]
If dewy morn, and odorous noon, and even,   5
With sunset and its gorgeous ministers,[7]
And solemn midnight's tingling silentness;
If autumn's hollow sighs in the sere wood,
And winter robing with pure snow and crowns
Of starry ice the grey grass and bare boughs;   10
If spring's voluptuous pantings when she breathes
Her first sweet kisses, have been dear to me;
If no bright bird, insect, or gentle beast
I consciously have injured, but still loved
And cherished these my kindred; then forgive   15
This boast, beloved brethren, and withdraw
No portion of your wonted favour now!

Mother of this unfathomable world!
Favour my solemn song, for I have loved
Thee ever, and thee only; I have watched   20
Thy shadow, and the darkness of thy steps,
And my heart ever gazes on the depth
Of thy deep mysteries. I have made my bed
In charnels and on coffins, where black death
Keeps record of the trophies won from thee,   25
Hoping to still these obstinate questionings[8]
Of thee and thine, by forcing some lone ghost,
Thy messenger, to render up the tale
Of what we are. In lone and silent hours,
When night makes a weird sound of its own stillness,   30
Like an inspired and desperate alchymist
Staking his very life on some dark hope,

3. Condensed from a passage in St. Augustine, *Confessions* III.i: "Not yet did I
love, though I loved to love, seeking
what I might love, loving to love." Augustine thus describes his state of mind
when he was addicted to illicit sexual
love; the true object of his desire, which
compels the tortuous spiritual journey of
his life, he later discovered to be the infinite and transcendant God.
4. Nature, invoked as the common
mother of the elements and of the poet.

5. Wordsworth, *My Heart Leaps Up*
(above, lines 9–10): "And I could wish
my days to be / Bound each to each by
natural piety." Wordsworth also used
these lines as the epigraph to his *Ode:
Intimations of Immortality*.
6. I.e., with my love.
7. The sunset colors.
8. *Ode: Intimations of Immortality*, line
143: ". . . those obstinate questionings /
Of sense and outward things. . . ."

Have I mixed awful talk and asking looks
With my most innocent love, until strange tears
Uniting with those breathless kisses, made   35
Such magic as compels the charmed night
To render up thy charge: . . . and, though ne'er yet
Thou hast unveil'd thy inmost sanctuary,
Enough from incommunicable dream,
And twilight phantasms, and deep noonday thought,   40
Has shone within me, that serenely now
And moveless, as a long-forgotten lyre
Suspended in the solitary dome
Of some mysterious and deserted fane,[9]
I wait thy breath, Great Parent, that my strain   45
May modulate with murmurs of the air,
And motions of the forests and the sea,
And voice of living beings, and woven hymns
Of night and day, and the deep heart of man.[1]

There was a Poet whose untimely tomb   50
No human hands with pious reverence reared,
But the charmed eddies of autumnal winds
Built o'er his mouldering bones a pyramid
Of mouldering leaves in the waste wilderness:—
A lovely youth,—no mourning maiden decked   55
With weeping flowers, or votive cypress wreath,[2]
The lone couch of his everlasting sleep:—
Gentle, and brave, and generous,—no lorn[3] bard
Breathed o'er his dark fate one melodious sigh:
He lived, he died, he sung, in solitude.   60
Strangers have wept to hear his passionate notes,
And virgins, as unknown he past, have pined
And wasted for fond love of his wild eyes.
The fire of those soft orbs has ceased to burn,
And Silence, too enamoured of that voice,   65
Locks its mute music in her rugged cell.

By solemn vision, and bright silver dream,
His infancy was nutured. Every sight
And sound from the vast earth and ambient air,
Sent to his heart its choicest impulses.   70
The fountains of divine philosophy
Fled not his thirsting lips, and all of great
Or good, or lovely, which the sacred past
In truth or fable consecrates, he felt

9. Temple. The narrator calls on the Mother, his natural muse, to make him her wind-harp. Cf. the opening passage of Wordsworth's *Prelude*, Coleridge's *Dejection: An Ode*, and the conclusion of Shelley's *Ode to the West Wind* and of *Adonais*.
1. Cf. Wordsworth, *Tintern Abbey*, lines 95 ff.: "A presence . . . / Whose dwelling is . . . / the round ocean and the living air / And the blue sky, and in the mind of man; / A motion and a spirit. . . ."

2. "Votive": offered to fulfill a vow to the gods. The cypress represented mourning.
3. Abandoned.

And knew. When early youth had past, he left   75
His cold fireside and alienated home
To seek strange truths in undiscovered lands.
Many a wide waste and tangled wilderness
Has lured his fearless steps; and he has bought
With his sweet voice and eyes, from savage men,   80
His rest and food. Nature's most secret steps
He like her shadow has pursued, where'er
The red volcano overcanopies
Its fields of snow and pinnacles of ice
With burning smoke, or where bitumen lakes[4]   85
On black bare pointed islets ever beat
With sluggish surge, or where the secret caves
Rugged and dark, winding among the springs
Of fire and poison, inaccessible
To avarice or pride, their starry domes   90
Of diamond and of gold expand above
Numberless and immeasurable halls,
Frequent[5] with crystal column, and clear shrines
Of pearl, and thrones radiant with chrysolite.[6]
Nor had that scene of ampler majesty   95
Than gems or gold, the varying roof of heaven
And the green earth lost in his heart its claims
To love and wonder; he would linger long
In lonesome vales, making the wild his home,
Until the doves and squirrels would partake   100
From his innocuous hand his bloodless food,[7]
Lured by the gentle meaning of his looks,
And the wild antelope, that starts whene'er
The dry leaf rustles in the brake,[8] suspend
Her timid steps to gaze upon a form   105
More graceful than her own.

                                          His wandering step
Obedient to high thoughts, has visited
The awful ruins of the days of old:
Athens, and Tyre, and Balbec,[9] and the waste
Where stood Jerusalem, the fallen towers   110
Of Babylon, the eternal pyramids,
Memphis and Thebes,[1] and whatsoe'er of strange
Sculptured on alabaster obelisk,
Or jasper tomb, or mutilated sphynx,
Dark Æthiopia in her desert hills   115
Conceals. Among the ruined temples there,
Stupendous columns, and wild images

---

4. Lakes of pitch, flowing from a volcano.
5. Crowded.
6. An olive-green stone.
7. Shelley was himself a vegetarian.
8. Thicket.

9. Tyre: once an important commercial city on the Phoenician coast; Balbec: an ancient city in Syria.
1. Memphis: the ruined capital of Lower Egypt; Thebes: the ancient capital of Upper Egypt.

Of more than man, where marble dæmons watch
The Zodiac's brazen mystery,[2] and dead men
Hang their mute thoughts on the mute walls around,[3]   120
He lingered, poring on memorials
Of the world's youth, through the long burning day
Gazed on those speechless shapes, nor, when the moon
Filled the mysterious halls with floating shades
Suspended he that task, but ever gazed   125
And gazed, till meaning on his vacant mind
Flashed like strong inspiration, and he saw
The thrilling secrets of the birth of time.

Meanwhile an Arab maiden brought his food,
Her daily portion, from her father's tent,   130
And spread her matting for his couch, and stole
From duties and repose to tend his steps:—
Enamoured, yet not daring for deep awe
To speak her love:—and watched his nightly sleep,
Sleepless herself, to gaze upon his lips   135
Parted in slumber, whence the regular breath
Of innocent dreams arose: then, when red morn
Made paler the pale moon, to her cold home
Wildered,[4] and wan, and panting, she returned.

The Poet wandering on, through Arabie   140
And Persia, and the wild Carmanian waste,[5]
And o'er the aërial mountains which pour down
Indus and Oxus[6] from their icy caves,
In joy and exultation held his way;
Till in the vale of Cashmire, far within   145
Its loneliest dell, where odorous plants entwine
Beneath the hollow rocks a natural bower,
Beside a sparkling rivulet he stretched
His languid limbs. A vision on his sleep
There came, a dream of hopes that never yet   150
Had flushed his cheek. He dreamed a veiled maid
Sate near him, talking in low solemn tones.
Her voice was like the voice of his own soul
Heard in the calm of thought; its music long,
Like woven sounds of streams and breezes, held   155
His inmost sense suspended in its web
Of many-coloured woof and shifting hues.
Knowledge and truth and virtue were her theme,
And lofty hopes of divine liberty,
Thoughts the most dear to him, and poesy,   160

2. In the temple of Isis at Denderah, Egypt, the Zodiac is represented on the ceiling. Dæmons: in Greek mythology demons were not evil spirits but minor deities, or attendant spirits.

3. I.e., by quotations inscribed in the stone.
4. Astray, bewildered.
5. A desert in southern Persia.
6. Rivers in Asia.

Herself a poet.[7] Soon the solemn mood
Of her pure mind kindled through all her frame
A permeating fire: wild numbers then
She raised, with voice stifled in tremulous sobs
Subdued by its own pathos: her fair hands   165
Were bare alone, sweeping from some strange harp
Strange symphony, and in their branching veins
The eloquent blood told an ineffable tale.
The beating of her heart was heard to fill
The pauses of her music, and her breath   170
Tumultuously accorded with those fits
Of intermitted song. Sudden she rose,
As if her heart impatiently endured
Its bursting burthen: at the sound he turned,
And saw by the warm light of their own life   175
Her glowing limbs beneath the sinuous veil
Of woven wind, her outspread arms now bare,
Her dark locks floating in the breath of night,
Her beamy bending eyes, her parted lips
Outstretched, and pale, and quivering eagerly.   180
His strong heart sunk and sickened with excess
Of love. He reared his shuddering limbs and quelled
His gasping breath, and spread his arms to meet
Her panting bosom: . . . she drew back a while,
Then, yielding to the irresistible joy,   185
With frantic gesture and short breathless cry
Folded his frame in her dissolving arms.
Now blackness veiled his dizzy eyes, and night
Involved and swallowed up the vision; sleep,
Like a dark flood suspended in its course,   190
Rolled back its impulse on his vacant brain.

Roused by the shock he started from his trance—
The cold white light of morning, the blue moon
Low in the west, the clear and garish hills,
The distinct valley and the vacant woods,   195
Spread round him where he stood. Whither have fled
The hues of heaven that canopied his bower
Of yesternight? The sounds that soothed his sleep,
The mystery and the majesty of Earth,
The joy, the exultation? His wan eyes   200
Gaze on the empty scene as vacantly
As ocean's moon looks on the moon in heaven.
The spirit of sweet human love has sent
A vision to the sleep of him who spurned
Her choicest gifts. He eagerly pursues   205
Beyond the realms of dream that fleeting shade;
He overleaps the bounds. Alas! alas!

---

7. The envisioned maiden embodies all three qualities specified in the Preface: intellect (line 158), imagination (lines 160–61), and sexuality (lines 176 ff.).

Were limbs, and breath, and being intertwined
Thus treacherously? Lost, lost, for ever lost,
In the wide pathless desart of dim sleep,   210
That beautiful shape! Does the dark gate of death
Conduct to thy mysterious paradise,
O Sleep?[8] Does the bright arch of rainbow clouds,
And pendent mountains seen in the calm lake,
Lead only to a black and watery depth,   215
While death's blue vault, with loathliest vapours hung,
Where every shade which the foul grave exhales
Hides its dead eye from the detested day,
Conduct[9], O Sleep, to thy delightful realms?
This doubt with sudden tide flowed on his heart,   220
The insatiate hope which it awakened, stung
His brain even like despair.
               While day-light held
The sky, the Poet kept mute conference
With his still soul. At night the passion came,
Like the fierce fiend of a distempered dream,   225
And shook him from his rest, and led him forth
Into the darkness.—As an eagle grasped
In folds of the green serpent, feels her breast
Burn with the poison, and precipitates[1]
Through night and day, tempest, and calm, and cloud,   230
Frantic with dizzying anguish, her blind flight
O'er the wide aëry wilderness:[2] thus driven
By the bright shadow of that lovely dream,
Beneath the cold glare of the desolate night,
Through tangled swamps and deep precipitous dells,   235
Startling with careless step the moon-light snake,
He fled. Red morning dawned upon his flight,
Shedding the mockery of its vital hues
Upon his cheek of death. He wandered on
Till vast Aornos seen from Petra's steep[3]   240
Hung o'er the low horizon like a cloud;
Through Balk,[4] and where the desolated tombs
Of Parthian kings scatter to every wind
Their wasting dust, wildly he wandered on,
Day after day, a weary waste of hours,   245
Bearing within his life the brooding care
That ever fed on its decaying flame.
And now his limbs were lean; his scattered hair
Sered by the autumn of strange suffering
Sung dirges in the wind; his listless hand   250
Hung like dead bone within its withered skin;

8. I.e., is death the only access to this maiden of his dream?
9. "Conduct" is a singular subjunctive verb; its subject is "vault" (line 216).
1. Hastens.
2. The eagle and serpent locked in mortal combat is a recurrent image in Shelley's poems.

3. Aornos is a high mountain and Petra ("the rock") a mountain stronghold in the northern part of Ancient Arabia.
4. Balk is the ancient Bactria; it is now part of Afghanistan, but in ancient times was Persian. The Parthians (line 243) inhabited northern Persia.

Life, and the lustre that consumed it, shone
As in a furnace burning secretly
From his dark eyes alone. The cottagers,
Who ministered with human charity   255
His human wants, beheld with wondering awe
Their fleeting visitant. The mountaineer,
Encountering on some dizzy precipice
That spectral form, deemed that the Spirit of wind
With lightning eyes, and eager breath, and feet   260
Disturbing not the drifted snow, had paused
In its career: the infant would conceal
His troubled visage in his mother's robe
In terror at the glare of those wild eyes,
To remember their strange light in many a dream   265
Of after-times; but youthful maidens, taught
By nature, would interpret half the woe
That wasted him, would call him with false names
Brother, and friend,[5] would press his pallid hand
At parting, and watch, dim through tears, the path   270
Of his departure from their father's door.

    At length upon the lone Chorasmian shore[6]
He paused, a wide and melancholy waste
Of putrid marshes. A strong impulse urged
His steps to the sea-shore. A swan was there,   275
Beside a sluggish stream among the reeds.
It rose as he approached, and with strong wings
Scaling the upward sky, bent its bright course
High over the immeasurable main.
His eyes pursued its flight.—"Thou hast a home,   280
Beautiful bird; thou voyagest to thine home,
Where thy sweet mate will twine her downy neck
With thine, and welcome thy return with eyes
Bright in the lustre of their own fond joy.
And what am I that I should linger here,   285
With voice far sweeter than thy dying notes,
Spirit more vast than thine, frame more attuned
To beauty, wasting these surpassing powers
In the deaf air, to the blind earth, and heaven
That echoes not my thoughts?" A gloomy smile   290
Of desperate hope wrinkled his quivering lips.
For sleep, he knew, kept most relentlessly
Its precious charge,[7] and silent death exposed,
Faithless perhaps as sleep, a shadowy lure,
With doubtful smile mocking its own strange charms.   295

---

5. The maidens call him "false" (i.e., mistaken) names signifying a shared human affection instead of his unearthly love.
6. The shore of Lake Aral in modern Russia, about 175 miles east of the Caspian Sea.
7. I.e., the maiden in the sleeper's dream. The passage goes on to express the skeptical fear that neither sleep nor death may yield the Poet his desire.

Startled by his own thoughts he looked around.
There was no fair fiend[8] near him, not a sight
Or sound of awe but in his own deep mind.
A little shallop[9] floating near the shore
Caught the impatient wandering of his gaze.   300
It had been long abandoned, for its sides
Gaped wide with many a rift, and its frail joints
Swayed with the undulations of the tide.
A restless impulse urged him to embark
And meet lone Death on the drear ocean's waste;   305
For well he knew that mighty Shadow loves
The slimy caverns of the populous deep.

The day was fair and sunny, sea and sky
Drank its inspiring radiance, and the wind
Swept strongly from the shore, blackening the waves.   310
Following his eager soul, the wanderer
Leaped in the boat, he spread his cloak aloft
On the bare mast, and took his lonely seat,
And felt the boat speed o'er the tranquil sea
Like a torn cloud before the hurricane.   315

As one that in a silver vision floats
Obedient to the sweep of odorous winds
Upon resplendent clouds, so rapidly
Along the dark and ruffled waters fled
The straining boat.—A whirlwind swept it on,   320
With fierce gusts and precipitating force,
Through the white ridges of the chafed sea.
The waves arose. Higher and higher still
Their fierce necks writhed beneath the tempest's scourge
Like serpents struggling in a vulture's grasp.   325
Calm and rejoicing in the fearful war
Of wave running on wave, and blast on blast
Descending, and black flood on whirlpool driven
With dark obliterating course, he sate:
As if their genii were the ministers   330
Appointed to conduct him to the light
Of those beloved eyes, the Poet sate
Holding the steady helm. Evening came on,
The beams of sunset hung their rainbow hues
High 'mid the shifting domes of sheeted spray   335
That canopied his path o'er the waste deep;
Twilight, ascending slowly from the east,
Entwin'd in duskier wreaths her braided locks
O'er the fair front and radiant eyes of day;
Night followed, clad with stars. On every side   340
More horribly the multitudinous streams

8. Apparently, he suspects there may
have been an external agent luring him
to the death described in the preceding
lines.
9. A light, open boat.

Of ocean's mountainous waste to mutual war
Rushed in dark tumult thundering, as to mock
The calm and spangled sky. The little boat
Still fled before the storm; still fled, like foam   345
Down the steep cataract of a wintry river;
Now pausing on the edge of the riven wave;
Now leaving far behind the bursting mass
That fell, convulsing ocean. Safely fled—
As if that frail and wasted human form,   350
Had been an elemental god.[1]
                    At midnight
The moon arose: and lo! the etherial cliffs[2]
Of Caucasus, whose icy summits shone
Among the stars like sunlight, and around
Whose cavern'd base the whirlpools and the waves   355
Bursting and eddying irresistibly
Rage and resound for ever.—Who shall save?—
The boat fled on,—the boiling torrent drove,—
The crags closed round with black and jagged arms,
The shattered mountain overhung the sea,   360
And faster still, beyond all human speed,
Suspended on the sweep of the smooth wave,
The little boat was driven. A cavern there
Yawned, and amid its slant and winding depths
Ingulphed the rushing sea. The boat fled on   365
With unrelaxing speed.—"Vision and Love!"
The Poet cried aloud, "I have beheld
The path of thy departure. Sleep and death
Shall not divide us long!"

                    The boat pursued
The winding of the cavern.[3] Day-light shone   370
At length upon that gloomy river's flow;
Now, where the fiercest war among the waves
Is calm, on the unfathomable stream
The boat moved slowly. Where the mountain, riven,
Exposed those black depths to the azure sky,   375
Ere yet the flood's enormous volume fell
Even to the base of Caucasus, with sound
That shook the everlasting rocks, the mass
Filled with one whirlpool all that ample chasm;
Stair above stair the eddying waters rose,   380
Circling immeasurably fast, and laved
With alternating dash the knarled roots
Of mighty trees, that stretched their giant arms
In darkness over it. I' the midst was left,
Reflecting, yet distorting every cloud,   385

---

1. A god of one of the natural elements; cf. line 1.
2. I.e., cliffs high in the air.
3. A boat beating upstream within a cave, like the eagle and serpent, is a recurrent Shelleyan image.

A pool of treacherous and tremendous calm.
Seized by the sway of the ascending stream,
With dizzy swiftness, round, and round, and round,
Ridge after ridge the straining boat arose,
Till on the verge of the extremest curve,   390
Where, through an opening of the rocky bank,
The waters overflow, and a smooth spot
Of glassy quiet mid those battling tides
Is left, the boat paused shuddering.—Shall it sink
Down the abyss? Shall the reverting stress   395
Of that resistless gulph embosom it?
Now shall it fall?—A wandering stream of wind,
Breathed from the west, has caught the expanded sail,
And, lo! with gentle motion, between banks
Of mossy slope, and on a placid stream,   400
Beneath a woven grove it sails, and, hark!
The ghastly torrent mingles its far roar,
With the breeze murmuring in the musical woods.
Where the embowering trees recede, and leave
A little space of green expanse, the cove   405
Is closed by meeting banks, whose yellow flowers
For ever gaze on their own drooping eyes,
Reflected in the crystal calm.[4] The wave
Of the boat's motion marred their pensive task,
Which nought but vagrant bird, or wanton wind,   410
Or falling spear-grass, or their own decay
Had e'er disturbed before. The Poet longed
To deck with their bright hues his withered hair,
But on his heart its solitude returned,
And he forbore. Not the strong impulse hid   415
In those flushed cheeks, bent eyes, and shadowy frame,
Had yet performed its ministry: it hung
Upon his life, as lightning in a cloud
Gleams, hovering ere it vanish, ere the floods
Of night close over it.   420
                                    The noonday sun
Now shone upon the forest, one vast mass
Of mingling shade, whose brown magnificence
A narrow vale embosoms. There, huge caves,
Scooped in the dark base of their aëry rocks
Mocking[5] its moans, respond and roar for ever.   425
The meeting boughs and implicated[6] leaves
Wove twilight o'er the Poet's path, as led
By love, or dream, or god, or mightier Death,
He sought in Nature's dearest haunt, some bank,

---

4. Another recurrent image: flowers overhanging their own reflection. It signifies here that, within the limits of the natural world, the correspondent Other satisfies the need of the Self for community. The Poet (lines 412 ff.) is momentarily tempted to let this realm of experience suffice, but his unsatisfiable need revives, and he is once more driven on in solitude by "the strong impulse," his *alastor*.

5. As often in Shelley, "mocking" has a double sense: mimicking, as well as ridiculing, the sounds of the forest (line 421).

6. Intertwined.

Her cradle, and his sepulchre. More dark   430
And dark the shades accumulate. The oak,
Expanding its immense and knotty arms,
Embraces the light beech. The pyramids
Of the tall cedar overarching, frame
Most solemn domes within, and far below.   435
Like clouds suspended in an emerald sky,
The ash and the acacia floating hang
Tremulous and pale. Like restless serpents, clothed
In rainbow and in fire, the parasites,
Starred with ten thousand blossoms, flow around   440
The grey trunks, and, as gamesome infants' eyes,
With gentle meanings, and most innocent wiles,
Fold their beams round the hearts of those that love,
These twine their tendrils with the wedded boughs
Uniting their close union;[7] the woven leaves   445
Make net-work of the dark blue light of day,
And the night's noontide clearness, mutable
As shapes in the weird clouds. Soft mossy lawns
Beneath these canopies extend their swells,
Fragrant with perfumed herbs, and eyed with blooms   450
Minute yet beautiful. One darkest glen
Sends from its woods of musk-rose, twined with jasmine,
A soul-dissolving odour, to invite
To some more lovely mystery. Through the dell,
Silence and Twilight here, twin-sisters, keep   455
Their noonday watch, and sail among the shades,
Like vaporous shapes half seen; beyond, a well,
Dark, gleaming, and of most translucent wave,
Images all the woven boughs above,
And each depending leaf, and every speck   460
Of azure sky, darting between their chasms;
Nor aught else in the liquid mirror laves
Its portraiture, but some inconstant star
Between one foliaged lattice twinkling fair,
Or, painted bird, sleeping beneath the moon,   465
Or gorgeous insect floating motionless,
Unconscious of the day, ere yet his wings
Have spread their glories to the gaze of noon.

      Hither the Poet came. His eyes beheld
Their own wan light through the reflected lines   470
Of his thin hair, distinct in the dark depth
Of that still fountain; as the human heart,
Gazing in dreams over the gloomy grave,
Sees its own treacherous likeness there. He heard
The motion of the leaves, the grass that sprung   475
Startled and glanced and trembled even to feel

---

7. All these embracements and diverse
modes of "union" exemplify the communion of things within the natural
world.

An unaccustomed presence, and the sound
Of the sweet brook that from the secret springs
Of that dark fountain rose. A Spirit seemed
To stand beside him[8]—clothed in no bright robes   480
Of shadowy silver or enshrining light,
Borrowed from aught the visible world affords
Of grace, or majesty, or mystery;—
But, undulating woods, and silent well,
And leaping rivulet, and evening gloom   485
Now deepening the dark shades, for speech assuming
Held commune with him, as if he and it
Were all that was,—only . . . when his regard
Was raised by intense pensiveness, . . . two eyes,
Two starry eyes, hung in the gloom of thought,   490
And seemed with their serene and azure smiles
To beckon him.

           Obedient to the light
That shone within his soul, he went, pursuing
The windings of the dell.—The rivulet
Wanton and wild, through many a green ravine   495
Beneath the forest flowed. Sometimes it fell
Among the moss with hollow harmony
Dark and profound. Now on the polished stones
It danced; like childhood laughing as it went:
Then, through the plain in tranquil wanderings crept,   500
Reflecting every herb and drooping bud
That overhung its quietness.—"O stream!
Whose source is inaccessibly profound,
Whither do thy mysterious waters tend?
Thou imagest my life. Thy darksome stillness,   505
Thy dazzling waves, thy loud and hollow gulphs,
Thy searchless[9] fountain, and invisible course
Have each their type in me: and the wide sky,
And measureless ocean may declare as soon
What oozy cavern or what wandering cloud   510
Contains thy waters, as the universe
Tell where these living thoughts reside, when stretched
Upon thy flowers my bloodless limbs shall waste
I' the passing wind!"

           Beside the grassy shore
Of the small stream he went; he did impress   515
On the green moss his tremulous step, that caught

---

8. This difficult passage describes another temptation to let Nature suffice, parallel to that in lines 412 ff. The "Spirit" is Nature, which assumes a form—clothed in natural things and attributes, but lacking "light" (line 481) —that seems to allow communication (and communion) with the poet, and gives him the momentary impression that there is no ideal beyond itself (lines 486–88). But when (lines 488 ff.) the Poet raises his eyes above the natural scene, he sees the beckoning eyes of the maiden of his vision and moves on (lines 491–92), obedient to an inner light which has no counterpart in Nature.
9. Undiscoverable.

Strong shuddering from his burning limbs. As one
Roused by some joyous madness from the couch
Of fever, he did move; yet, not like him,
Forgetful of the grave, where, when the flame   520
Of his frail exultation shall be spent,
He must descend. With rapid steps he went
Beneath the shade of trees, beside the flow
Of the wild babbling rivulet; and now
The forest's solemn canopies were changed   525
For the uniform and lightsome[1] evening sky.
Grey rocks did peep from the spare moss, and stemmed
The struggling brook: tall spires of windlestrae[2]
Threw their thin shadows down the rugged slope,
And nought but knarled roots[3] of antient pines   530
Branchless and blasted, clenched with grasping roots
The unwilling soil. A gradual change was here,
Yet ghastly. For, as fast years flow away,
The smooth brow gathers, and the hair grows thin
And white, and where irradiate[4] dewy eyes   535
Had shone, gleam stony orbs:—so from his steps
Bright flowers departed, and the beautiful shade
Of the green groves, with all their odorous winds
And musical motions. Calm, he still pursued
The stream, that with a larger volume now   540
Rolled through the labyrinthine dell; and there
Fretted a path through its descending curves
With its wintry speed. On every side now rose
Rocks, which, in unimaginable forms,
Lifted their black and barren pinnacles   545
In the light of evening, and its precipice[5]
Obscuring the ravine, disclosed above,
Mid toppling stones, black gulphs and yawning caves,
Whose windings gave ten thousand various tongues
To the loud stream. Lo! where the pass expands   550
Its stony jaws, the abrupt mountain breaks,
And seems, with its accumulated crags,
To overhang the world: for wide expand
Beneath the wan stars and descending moon
Islanded seas, blue mountains, mighty streams,   555
Dim tracts and vast, robed in the lustrous gloom
Of leaden-coloured even, and fiery hills
Mingling their flames with twilight, on the verge
Of the remote horizon. The near scene,
In naked and severe simplicity,   560
Made contrast with the universe. A pine,[6]

1. Illuminated.
2. Scottish dialect for "windlestraw"—tall, dried stalks of grass.
3. Apparently an error for "trunks."
4. Used adjectivally: illumined, brilliant.
5. Headlong fall (of the stream, line 540).
6. Pine trees in Shelley often signify persistence and steadfastness amid change and vicissitudes.

Rock-rooted, stretched athwart the vacancy
Its swinging boughs, to each inconstant blast
Yielding one only response, at each pause
In most familiar cadence, with the howl   565
The thunder and the hiss of homeless streams
Mingling its solemn song, whilst the broad river,
Foaming and hurrying o'er its rugged path,
Fell into that immeasurable void
Scattering its waters to the passing winds.   570

Yet the grey precipice and solemn pine
And torrent, were not all;—one silent nook
Was there. Even on the edge of that vast mountain,
Upheld by knotty roots and fallen rocks,
It overlooked in its serenity   575
The dark earth, and the bending vault of stars.
It was a tranquil spot, that seemed to smile
Even in the lap of horror. Ivy clasped
The fissured stones with its entwining arms,
And did embower with leaves for ever green,   580
And berries dark, the smooth and even space
Of its inviolated floor, and here
The children of the autumnal whirlwind bore,
In wanton sport, those bright leaves, whose decay,
Red, yellow, or etherially pale,   585
Rivals the pride of summer. 'Tis the haunt
Of every gentle wind, whose breath can teach
The wilds to love tranquillity. One step,
One human step alone, has ever broken
The stillness of its solitude:—one voice   590
Alone inspired its echoes,—even that voice
Which hither came, floating among the winds,
And led the loveliest among human forms
To make their wild haunts the depository
Of all the grace and beauty that endued   595
Its motions, render up its majesty,
Scatter its music on the unfeeling storm,
And to the damp leaves and blue cavern mould,
Nurses of rainbow flowers and branching moss,
Commit the colours of that varying cheek,   600
That snowy breast, those dark and drooping eyes.

The dim and hornéd moon[7] hung low, and poured
A sea of lustre on the horizon's verge
That overflowed its mountains. Yellow mist
Filled the unbounded atmosphere, and drank   605
Wan moonlight even to fulness: not a star
Shone, not a sound was heard; the very winds,

7. Crescent-shaped, with the points curved in.

Danger's grim playmates, on that precipice
Slept, clasped in his embrace.—O, storm of death!
Whose sightless[8] speed divides this sullen night: 610
And thou, colossal Skeleton, that, still
Guiding its irresistible career
In thy devastating omnipotence,
Art king of this frail world, from the red field
Of slaughter, from the reeking hospital,   615
The patriot's sacred couch, the snowy bed
Of innocence, the scaffold and the throne,
A mighty voice invokes thee. Ruin calls
His brother Death. A rare and regal prey
He hath prepared, prowling around the world;   620
Glutted with which thou mayst repose, and men
Go to their graves like flowers or creeping worms,
Nor ever more offer at thy dark shrine
The unheeded tribute of a broken heart.

　　When on the threshold of the green recess   625
The wanderer's footsteps fell, he knew that death
Was on him. Yet a little, ere it fled,
Did he resign his high and holy soul
To images of the majestic past,
That paused within his passive being now,   630
Like winds that bear sweet music, when they breathe
Through some dim latticed chamber. He did place
His pale lean hand upon the rugged trunk
Of the old pine. Upon an ivied stone
Reclined his languid head, his limbs did rest,   635
Diffused and motionless, on the smooth brink
Of that obscurest chasm;—and thus he lay,
Surrendering to their final impulses
The hovering powers of life. Hope and despair,
The torturers, slept; no mortal pain or fear   640
Marred his repose, the influxes of sense,
And his own being unalloyed by pain,
Yet feebler and more feeble, calmly fed
The stream of thought, till he lay breathing there
At peace, and faintly smiling:—his last sight   645
Was the great moon, which o'er the western line
Of the wide world her mighty horn suspended,
With whose dun[9] beams inwoven darkness seemed
To mingle. Now upon the jagged hills
It rests, and still as the divided frame   650
Of the vast meteor[1] sunk, the Poet's blood,
That ever beat in mystic sympathy
With nature's ebb and flow, grew feebler still:

8. Invisible; or perhaps "unseeing."
9. Darkened, dimmed.
1. I.e., the moon; "meteor" was once
used for any phenomenon within the
earth's atmosphere.

And when two lessening points of light alone
Gleamed through the darkness, the alternate gasp   655
Of his faint respiration scarce did stir
The stagnate night:[2]—till the minutest ray
Was quenched, the pulse yet lingered in his heart.
It paused—it fluttered. But when heaven remained
Utterly black, the murky shades involved   660
An image, silent, cold, and motionless,
As their own voiceless earth and vacant air.
Even as a vapour[3] fed with golden beams
That ministered on sunlight, ere the west
Eclipses it, was now that wonderous frame—   665
No sense, no motion, no divinity—
A fragile lute, on whose harmonious strings
The breath of heaven did wander—a bright stream
Once fed with many-voiced waves—a dream
Of youth, which night and time have quenched for ever,   670
Still, dark, and dry, and unremembered now.

O, for Medea's wondrous alchemy,[4]
Which wheresoe'er it fell made the earth gleam
With bright flowers, and the wintry boughs exhale
From vernal blooms fresh fragrance! O, that God,   675
Profuse of poisons, would concede the chalice
Which but one living man has drained,[5] who now,
Vessel of deathless wrath, a slave that feels
No proud exemption in the blighting curse
He bears, over the world wanders for ever,   680
Lone as incarnate death! O, that the dream
Of dark magician in his visioned cave,[6]
Raking the cinders of a crucible
For life and power, even when his feeble hand
Shakes in its last decay, were the true law   685
Of this so lovely world! But thou art fled
Like some frail exhalation; which the dawn
Robes in its golden beams,—ah! thou hast fled!
The brave, the gentle, and the beautiful,
The child of grace and genius. Heartless things   690
Are done and said i' the world, and many worms
And beasts and men live on, and mighty Earth
From sea and mountain, city and wilderness,

2. The Poet's life ebbs in consonance with the descent of the "hornéd moon," to the moment when only the two "points of light"—its horns—show above the hills.
3. I.e., a cloud. "Ministered on": attended, acted as a servant to.
4. Medea brewed a magic potion to rejuvenate the dying Aeson; where some of the potion spilled on the ground, flowers sprang up (Ovid, *Metamorphoses* vii.275 ff.).
5. The Wandering Jew; according to a medieval legend, he had taunted Christ on the way to His crucifixion and was condemned to wander the world, deathless, until Christ's second coming.
6. Cave in which he has visions. The "dark magician" is an alchemist attempting to produce the elixir of enduring life.

In vesper low or joyous orison,[7]
Lifts still its solemn voice:—but thou art fled—   695
Thou canst no longer know or love the shapes
Of this phantasmal scene, who have to thee
Been purest ministers, who are, alas!
Now thou art not. Upon those pallid lips
So sweet even in their silence, on those eyes   700
That image sleep in death, upon that form
Yet safe from the worm's outrage, let no tear
Be shed—not even in thought. Nor, when those hues
Are gone, and those divinest lineaments,
Worn by the senseless[8] wind, shall live alone   705
In the frail pauses of this simple strain,
Let not high verse, mourning the memory
Of that which is no more, or painting's woe
Or sculpture, speak in feeble imagery
Their own cold powers. Art and eloquence,   710
And all the shews o' the world are frail and vain
To weep a loss that turns their lights to shade.
It is a woe too "deep for tears,"[9] when all
Is reft at once, when some surpassing Spirit,
Whose light adorned the world around it, leaves   715
Those who remain behind, not sobs or groans,
The passionate tumult of a clinging hope;
But pale despair and cold tranquillity,
Nature's vast frame, the web of human things,
Birth and the grave, that are not as they were.   720

1815   1816

Mont Blanc[1]

LINES WRITTEN IN THE VALE OF CHAMOUNI

I

The everlasting universe of things
Flows through the mind, and rolls its rapid waves,

7. Prayer; vesper: evening prayer.
8. Unfeeling.
9. From the last line of Wordsworth's *Ode: Intimations of Immortality*: "Thoughts that do often lie too deep for tears."
1. Mont Blanc, near the French border with Italy, is the highest mountain in the Alps. When he conceived the poem, Shelley was standing on a bridge over the Arve River in the Valley of Chamonix, in what is now southeastern France.
   Shelley wrote of this poem: "It was composed under the immediate impression of the deep and powerful feelings excited by the objects which it attempts to describe; and, as an indisciplined overflowing of the soul, rests its claim to approbation on an attempt to imitate the untamable wildness and inaccessible solemnity from which those feelings sprang."
   Shelley's comment points to two important attributes of *Mont Blanc*. First, he attempts, as in other poems (supremely in *Ode to the West Wind*), to make the poem iconic, or directly imitative of the alternating "wildness" and "solemnity" of the scene and the consonant thought and feelings it evokes. Second, this work belongs to the genre of the "local" poem, a descriptive-meditative presentation of a precisely identified landscape. In this respect it resembles Wordsworth's *Tintern Abbey*, the major influence on *Mont Blanc*. Shelley's poem, like Wordsworth's, poses the question of the significance of the interchange between nature and the human mind; he

Now dark—now glittering—now reflecting gloom—
Now lending splendour, where from secret springs
The source of human thought its tribute brings   5
Of waters,—with a sound but half its own.
Such as a feeble brook will oft assume
In the wild woods, among the mountains lone,
Where waterfalls around it leap forever,
Where woods and winds contend, and a vast river   10
Over its rocks ceaselessly bursts and raves.

II

Thus thou, Ravine of Arve—dark, deep Ravine—
Thou many-coloured, many-voiced vale,
Over whose pines, and crags, and caverns sail
Fast cloud shadows and sunbeams: awful[2] scene,   15
Where Power in likeness of the Arve comes down
From the ice gulphs that gird his secret throne,
Bursting through these dark mountains like the flame
Of lightning through the tempest;—thou dost lie,
Thy giant brood of pines around thee clinging,   20
Children of elder time, in whose devotion
The chainless winds still come and ever came
To drink their odours, and their mighty swinging
To hear—an old and solemn harmony;
Thine earthly rainbows stretched across the sweep   25
Of the etherial waterfall, whose veil
Robes some unsculptured[3] image; the strange sleep
Which when the voices of the desart fail
Wraps all in its own deep eternity;—
Thy caverns echoing to the Arve's commotion,   30
A loud, lone sound no other sound can tame;
Thou art pervaded with that ceaseless motion,
Thou art the path of that unresting sound—
Dizzy Ravine! and when I gaze on thee
I seem as in a trance sublime and strange   35

proposes, however, a very different answer to that question.

The poem raises the central problem about the nature of "Power," the ultimate principle behind all natural and mental process. The symbol of this Power is the river Arve (lines 16–17), which has its "secret throne" at the summit of Mont Blanc, the highest peak in Europe, and beyond human access. The process of the Arve begins with the unseen fall of snow and the unheard play of winds at the far height of the mountain, becomes the Mer de Glace glacier, moves down the mountain, and melts into the river which runs through its ravine into the valley of Chamonix in southeastern France. Shelley's answer is austerely skeptical. He postulates only that "the power is there," at the inaccessible peak of Mont Blanc, but refuses to invest it with anthropomorphic intentions or values.

What we do know is that this Power, as it descends from its secret throne into the human ken, remorselessly destroys all things, animal and human (lines 100–20); yet in its simultaneous form as a river (lines 120–26), it with equal moral indifference is the "breath and blood of distant lands," and the source of life-giving rain. It is the enlightened human will alone which can convert this purposeless destroyer and preserver to its own human ends, even to the revolutionary end of total reform (lines 80–83). The poem ends like *Ode to the West Wind*, with a rhetorical question; the implication is that phenomenal nature is in itself but a universal blank, except as it is invested with significance by the imagination of man.

2. Awe-inspiring.
3. I.e., not formed by man.

To muse on my own separate phantasy,
My own, my human mind, which passively
Now renders and receives fast influencings,
Holding an unremitting interchange
With the clear universe of things around;[4]   40
One legion of wild thoughts, whose wandering wings
Now float above thy darkness, and now rest
Where that or thou art no unbidden guest,
In the still cave of the witch Poesy,[5]
Seeking among the shadows that pass by   45
Ghosts of all things that are, some shade of thee,
Some phantom, some faint image; till the breast
From which they fled recalls them, thou art there![6]

III

Some say that gleams of a remoter world
Visit the soul in sleep,—that death is slumber,   50
And that its shapes the busy thoughts outnumber
Of those who wake and live.—I look on high;
Has some unknown omnipotence unfurled
The veil of life and death? or do I lie
In dream, and does the mightier world of sleep   55
Spread far around and inaccessibly
Its circles? For the very spirit fails,
Driven like a homeless cloud from steep to steep
That vanishes among the viewless[7] gales!
Far, far above, piercing the infinite sky,   60
Mont Blanc appears,—still, snowy, and serene—
Its subject mountains their unearthly forms
Pile around it, ice and rock; broad vales between
Of frozen floods, unfathomable deeps,
Blue as the overhanging heaven, that spread   65
And wind among the accumulated steeps;
A desart peopled by the storms alone,
Save when the eagle brings some hunter's bone,
And the wolf tracts[8] her there—how hideously
Its shapes are heaped around! rude, bare, and high,   70
Ghastly, and scarred, and riven.—Is this the scene
Where the old Earthquake-dæmon[9] taught her young
Ruin? Were these their toys? or did a sea
Of fire, envelope once this silent snow?
None can reply—all seems eternal now.   75

4. This passage is remarkably parallel to a passage Shelley could not have read in *The Prelude*, published in 1850, in which Wordsworth discovers, in the landscape viewed from Mount Snowdon, the "type" or "emblem" of the human mind in its interchange with nature. See *The Prelude*, above, XIV.63 ff.
5. I.e., in that part of the mind which creates poetry.
6. I.e., the thoughts (line 41) seek, in the poet's creative faculty, some shade, phantom, or image of the Arve; and when the breast, which has forgotten these images, recalls them again—there, suddenly, does the Arve exist.
7. Invisible.
8. Tracks, traces.
9. A "daemon" is a supernatural being, halfway between men and the gods; here, it represents the force that makes earthquakes.

The wilderness has a mysterious tongue
Which teaches awful doubt, or faith so mild,
So solemn, so serene, that man may be
But for such faith with nature reconciled;[1]
Thou hast a voice, great Mountain, to repeal   80
Large codes of fraud and woe; not understood
By all, but which[2] the wise, and great, and good
Interpret, or make felt, or deeply feel.

IV

The fields, the lakes, the forests, and the streams,
Ocean, and all the living things that dwell   85
Within the dædal[3] earth; lightning, and rain,
Earthquake, and fiery flood, and hurricane,
The torpor of the year when feeble dreams
Visit the hidden buds, or dreamless sleep
Holds every future leaf and flower;—the bound   90
With which from that detested trance they leap;
The works and ways of man, their death and birth,
And that of him and all that his may be;
All things that move and breathe with toil and sound
Are born and die; revolve, subside and swell.   95
Power dwells apart in its tranquillity
Remote, serene, and inaccessible:
And *this*, the naked countenance of earth,
On which I gaze, even these primæval mountains
Teach the adverting mind. The glaciers creep   100
Like snakes that watch their prey, from their far fountains,
Slow rolling on; there, many a precipice,
Frost and the Sun in scorn of mortal power
Have piled: dome, pyramid, and pinnacle,
A city of death, distinct with many a tower   105
And wall impregnable of beaming ice.
Yet not a city, but a flood of ruin
Is there, that from the boundaries of the sky
Rolls its perpetual stream; vast pines are strewing
Its destined path, or in the mangled soil   110
Branchless and shattered stand: the rocks, drawn down
From yon remotest waste, have overthrown
The limits of the dead and living world,
Never to be reclaimed. The dwelling-place
Of insects, beasts, and birds, becomes its spoil;   115
Their food and their retreat forever gone,
So much of life and joy is lost. The race
Of man, flies far in dread; his work and dwelling

---

1. "Simply by holding such a faith"—such as Wordsworth's "cheerful faith" (lines 133–34) in *Tintern Abbey* "that all which we behold / Is full of blessings." In Shelley's balance of possibilities, the landscape is equally capable of teaching this faith and the "awful [i.e., awesome] doubt" that nature is indifferent to human ends and values.
2. The reference is to "voice," line 80.
3. Intricately formed; derived from Daedalus, builder of the labyrinth in Crete.

Vanish, like smoke before the tempest's stream,
And their place is not known. Below, vast caves   120
Shine in the rushing torrents' restless gleam,
Which from those secret chasms in tumult welling[4]
Meet in the vale, and one majestic River,
The breath and blood of distant lands, for ever
Rolls its loud waters to the ocean waves,   125
Breathes its swift vapours to the circling air.

V

Mont Blanc yet gleams on high:—the power is there,
The still and solemn power of many sights,
And many sounds, and much of life and death.
In the calm darkness of the moonless nights,   130
In the lone glare of day, the snows descend
Upon that Mountain; none beholds them there,
Nor when the flakes burn in the sinking sun,
Or the star-beams dart through them:—Winds contend
Silently there, and heap the snow with breath   135
Rapid and strong, but silently! Its home
The voiceless lightning in these solitudes
Keeps innocently, and like vapour broods
Over the snow. The secret strength of things
Which governs thought, and to the infinite dome   140
Of heaven is as a law, inhabits thee!
And what were thou,[5] and earth, and stars, and sea,
If to the human mind's imaginings
Silence and solitude were vacancy?

1816   1817

Hymn to Intellectual Beauty[1]

1

The awful shadow of some unseen Power
   Floats though unseen amongst us,—visiting
   This various world with as inconstant wing
As summer winds that creep from flower to flower.—
Like moonbeams that behind some piny mountain shower,   5
   It visits with inconstant glance
   Each human heart and countenance;
Like hues and harmonies of evening,—
   Like clouds in starlight widely spread,—
   Like memory of music fled,—   10

---

4. Like lines 9–11, an echo of Coleridge's description of the chasm and sacred river in *Kubla Khan*, lines 12–24. The "majestic River" (line 123) is the Arve, which flows into Lake Geneva.
5. Mont Blanc.
1. "Intellectual" means "non-sensible." "Intellectual Beauty" is beyond access

by sense experience; it is postulated to account for occasional states of awareness which lend splendor, grace, and truth both to the natural world and to man's moral consciousness. To this mystery (stanzas 5–7) Shelley had, at its early visitation, dedicated his powers, and to it he now prays as he passes the noon of life (stanza 7).

Like aught that for its grace may be
Dear, and yet dearer for its mystery.

2

Spirit of BEAUTY, that dost consecrate
　With thine own hues all thou dost shine upon
　Of human thought or form,—where art thou gone? 15
Why dost thou pass away and leave our state,
This dim vast vale of tears, vacant and desolate?
　　Ask why the sunlight not forever
　　Weaves rainbows o'er yon mountain river,
Why aught should fail and fade that once is shewn, 20
　　Why fear and dream and death and birth
　　Cast on the daylight of this earth
　　Such gloom,—why man has such a scope
For love and hate, despondency and hope?

3

No voice from some sublimer world hath ever 25
　　To sage or poet these responses given—
　　Therefore the name of God and ghosts and Heaven,
Remain the records of their vain endeavour,[2]
Frail spells—whose uttered charm might not avail to sever,
　　From all we hear and all we see, 30
　　Doubt, chance, and mutability.
Thy light alone—like mist o'er mountains driven,
　　Or music by the night wind sent
　　Through strings of some still instrument,[3]
　　Or moonlight on a midnight stream, 35
Gives grace and truth to life's unquiet dream.

4

Love, Hope, and Self-esteem, like clouds depart
　And come, for some uncertain moments lent.
　Man were immortal, and omnipotent,
Didst thou, unknown and awful as thou art, 40
Keep with thy glorious train firm state within his heart.[4]
　　Thou messenger of sympathies,
　　That wax and wane in lovers' eyes—
Thou—that to human thought art nourishment,
　　Like darkness to a dying flame! 45
　　Depart not as thy shadow came,
　　Depart not—lest the grave should be,
Like life and fear, a dark reality.

5

While yet a boy I sought for ghosts, and sped
　　Through many a listening chamber, cave and ruin, 50
　　And starlight wood, with fearful steps pursuing
Hopes of high talk with the departed dead.

---

2. The names (line 28) are groundless guesses at identifying the mystery by religious philosophers and poets (line 26).
3. A wind harp.
4. I.e., "man would be immortal * * * if thou didst keep * * *"

I called on poisonous names with which our youth is fed;[5]
   I was not heard—I saw them not—
   When musing deeply on the lot   55
Of life, at that sweet time when winds are wooing
   All vital things that wake to bring
   News of buds and blossoming,—
   Sudden, thy shadow fell on me;
I shrieked, and clasped my hands in extacy!   60

6

I vowed that I would dedicate my powers
   To thee and thine—have I not kept the vow?
   With beating heart and streaming eyes, even now
I call the phantoms of a thousand hours
Each from his voiceless grave: they have in visioned bowers   65
   Of studious zeal or love's delight
   Outwatched with me the envious night[6]—
They know that never joy illumed my brow
   Unlinked with hope that thou wouldst free
   This world from its dark slavery,   70
   That thou—O awful LOVELINESS,
Wouldst give whate'er these words cannot express.

7

The day becomes more solemn and serene
   When noon is past—there is a harmony
   In autumn, and a lustre in its sky,   75
Which through the summer is not heard or seen,
As if it could not be, as if it had not been!
   Thus let thy power, which like the truth
   Of nature on my passive youth
Descended, to my onward life supply   80
   Its calm—to one who worships thee,
   And every form containing thee,
   Whom, SPIRIT fair, thy spells did bind
To fear[7] himself, and love all human kind.

1816   1817

Ozymandias[8]

I met a traveller from an antique land,
Who said—"Two vast and trunkless legs of stone
Stand in the desert. . . . Near them, on the sand,
Half sunk a shattered visage lies, whose frown,
And wrinkled lip, and sneer of cold command,   5

5. Lines 49–52 refer to Shelley's youthful experiments with magic. The "poisonous names" in line 53 are those in the prayers he had been taught as a child.
6. I.e., watched until the night, envious of their delight, had reluctantly departed.
7. Probably in the old sense: to stand in awe of.
8. According to Diodorus Siculus, the Greek historian of the 1st century B.C., the largest statue in Egypt had the inscription: "I am Ozymandias, king of kings; if anyone wishes to know what I am and where I lie, let him surpass me in some of my exploits." Ozymandias was the Greek name for Ramses II of Egypt, 13th century B.C.

Tell that its sculptor well those passions read
Which yet survive, stamped on these lifeless things,
The hand that mocked them, and the heart that fed;[9]
And on the pedestal, these words appear:
My name is Ozymandias, King of Kings,   10
Look on my Works, ye Mighty, and despair!
Nothing beside remains. Round the decay
Of that colossal Wreck, boundless and bare
The lone and level sands stretch far away."

1817   1818

Stanzas Written in Dejection— December 1818, Near Naples[1]

The Sun is warm, the sky is clear,
The waves are dancing fast and bright,
Blue isles and snowy mountains wear
The purple noon's transparent might,
The breath of the moist earth is light   5
Around its unexpanded buds;
Like many a voice of one delight
The winds, the birds, the Ocean-floods;
The City's voice itself is soft, like Solitude's.

I see the Deep's untrampled floor   10
With green and purple seaweeds strown;
I see the waves upon the shore
Like light dissolved in star-showers, thrown;
I sit upon the sands alone;
The lightning of the noontide Ocean   15
Is flashing round me, and a tone
Arises from its measured motion,
How sweet! did any heart now share in my emotion.

Alas, I have nor hope nor health
Nor peace within nor calm around,   20
Nor that content surpassing wealth
The sage[2] in meditation found,
And walked with inward glory crowned;
Nor fame nor power nor love nor leisure—
Others I see whom these surround,   25
Smiling they live and call life pleasure:
To me that cup has been dealt in another measure.

9. "The hand" is the sculptor's, who had "mocked" (both imitated and derided) the sculptured passions; "the heart" is the king's, which has "fed" his passions.
1. Shelley's first wife, Harriet, had drowned herself; Clara, his baby daughter by Mary Shelley, had just died; and Shelley himself was plagued by ill health, pain, financial worries, and the sense that he had failed as a poet.
2. Probably the Roman emperor Marcus Aurelius (2nd century A.D.), Stoic philosopher who wrote twelve books of *Meditations*.

Yet now despair itself is mild,
Even as the winds and waters are;
I could lie down like a tired child   30
And weep away the life of care
Which I have borne and yet must bear
Till Death like Sleep might steal on me,
And I might feel in the warm air
My cheek grow cold, and hear the Sea   35
Breathe o'er my dying brain its last monotony.

Some might lament that I were cold,
As I, when this sweet day is gone,[3]
Which my lost heart, too soon grown old,
Insults with this untimely moan—   40
They might lament,—for I am one
Whom men love not, and yet regret;
Unlike this day, which, when the Sun
Shall on its stainless glory set,
Will linger though enjoyed, like joy in Memory yet.   45

1818   1824

Julian and Maddalo;

A Conversation[1]

The meadows with fresh streams, the bees with thyme,
The goats with the green leaves of budding spring,
Are saturated not—nor Love with tears.
                                                    VIRGIL'S *Gallus*.[2]

Count Maddalo is a Venetian nobleman of antient family and of
great fortune, who, without mixing much in the society of his
countrymen, resides chiefly at his magnificent palace in that city.
He is a person of the most consummate genius, and capable, if he

---

3. I.e., as I will lament this sweet day
when it has gone.

1. Shelley undertook this poem in the
autumn of 1818 while living at Este,
near Venice, in a villa that had been
put at his disposal by Lord Byron; he
completed it the following summer at
Leghorn, Italy. It was not published,
however, until 1824, two years after
his death. The poem had its origin in a
projected drama about Torquato Tasso
(1544–95), the Italian author of an
epic about a medieval Crusade, *Jerusalem Delivered*. Tasso, who suffered
from paranoid delusions of persecution,
was confined for seven years in a madhouse by Alphonso II, Duke of Este; a
legend (now known to be groundless)
had developed that he had been imprisoned because of his passion for Leonora
d'Este, the Duke's sister. Shelley soon
abandoned the drama, however, and
instead wrote a dialogue between himself (Julian) and Byron (Maddalo)

which culminates in a visit to a nameless maniac who is confined in an
asylum, where the two friends overhear
his ravings about an unhappy love
affair which has caused his mental
breakdown.

The conversation between Julian and
Maddalo demonstrates the range of
Shelley's mastery of poetic idiom and
tone. In a letter to his publisher
Charles Ollier (May 14, 1820), Shelley
contrasted this poem to the elevated
mode of his *Prometheus Unbound* as a
deliberate "attempt in a different style,
in which I am not yet sure of myself, a
sermo pedestris [plain talk] way of
treating human nature." In the dialogue
Shelley sets forth sharply the opposition between his own stubborn idealism
and Byron's sardonic view of the
narrow limits of human nature and
possibilities; yet he sustains (in the
preface as well as the poem) an ironic
stance toward himself and his own

would direct his energies to such an end, of becoming the redeemer of his degraded country. But it is his weakness to be proud: he derives, from a comparison of his own extraordinary mind with the dwarfish intellects that surround him, an intense apprehension of the nothingness of human life. His passions and his powers are incomparably greater than those of other men; and, instead of the latter having been employed in curbing the former, they have mutually lent each other strength. His ambition preys upon itself, for want of objects which it can consider worthy of exertion. I say that Maddalo is proud, because I can find no other word to express the concentered and impatient feelings which consume him; but it is on his own hopes and affections only that he seems to trample, for in social life no human being can be more gentle, patient, and unassuming than Maddalo. He is cheerful, frank, and witty. His more serious conversation is a sort of intoxication; men are held by it as by a spell. He has travelled much; and there is an inexpressible charm in his relation of his adventures in different countries.

Julian is an Englishman of good family, passionately attached to those philosophical notions which assert the power of man over his own mind, and the immense improvements of which, by the extinction of certain moral superstitions, human society may be yet susceptible. Without concealing the evil in the world, he is for ever speculating how good may be made superior. He is a complete infidel, and a scoffer at all things reputed holy; and Maddalo takes a wicked pleasure in drawing out his taunts against religion. What Maddalo thinks on these matters is not exactly known. Julian, in spite of his heterodox opinions, is conjectured by his friends to possess some good qualities. How far this is possible the pious reader will determine. Julian is rather serious.

Of the Maniac I can give no information. He seems by his own account to have been disappointed in love. He was evidently a very cultivated and amiable person when in his right senses. His story, told at length, might be like many other stories of the same kind: the unconnected exclamations of his agony will perhaps be found a sufficient comment for the text of every heart.

> I rode one evening with Count Maddalo
> Upon the bank of land which breaks the flow
> Of Adria towards Venice:[3]—a bare strand
> Of hillocks, heaped from ever-shifting sand,

beliefs, while capturing the ease, urbanity, and rallying good humor of familiar discourse between friends.

2. Virgil, *Eclogues* X.29–30. The eclogue (i.e., pastoral poem) describes the love of Virgil's friend and fellow poet, Gaius Cornelius Gallus (1st century B.C.), for a mistress who has left him.

3. I.e., along the sands of a narrow island, the Lido, across the lagoon from Venice; "Adria" is the Adriatic Sea. Shelley describes his actual conversation with Byron on this occasion in a letter to Mary Shelley, August 23, 1818.

Matted with thistles and amphibious weeds,   5
Such as from earth's embrace the salt ooze breeds,
Is this;—an uninhabitable sea-side
Which the lone fisher, when his nets are dried,
Abandons; and no other object breaks
The waste, but one dwarf tree and some few stakes   10
Broken and unrepaired, and the tide makes
A narrow space of level sand thereon,—
Where 'twas our wont[4] to ride while day went down.
This ride was my delight.—I love all waste
And solitary places; where we taste   15
The pleasure of believing what we see
Is boundless, as we wish our souls to be:
And such was this wide ocean, and this shore
More barren than its billows;—and yet more
Than all, with a remembered friend I love   20
To ride as then I rode;—for the winds drove
The living spray along the sunny air
Into our faces; the blue heavens were bare,
Stripped to their depths by the awakening North;
And, from the waves, sound like delight broke forth 25
Harmonizing with solitude, and sent
Into our hearts aërial merriment . . .
So, as we rode, we talked; and the swift thought,
Winging itself with laughter, lingered not,
But flew from brain to brain,—such glee was ours—   30
Charged with light memories of remembered hours,
None slow enough for sadness: till we came
Homeward, which always makes the spirit tame.
This day had been cheerful but cold, and now
The sun was sinking, and the wind also.   35
Our talk grew somewhat serious, as may be
Talk interrupted with such raillery
As mocks itself, because it cannot scorn
The thoughts it would extinguish:—'twas forlorn
Yet pleasing, such as once, so poets tell,   40
The devils held within the dales of Hell
Concerning God, freewill and destiny:[5]
Of all that earth has been or yet may be,
All that vain men imagine or believe,
Or hope can paint or suffering may atchieve,   45
We descanted,[6] and I (for ever still
Is it not wise to make the best of ill?)
Argued against despondency, but pride
Made my companion take the darker side.
The sense that he was greater than his kind   50

4. Custom.
5. An allusion to *Paradise Lost*
II.555–61, where the fallen angels
"reasoned high / Of Providence, Foreknowledge, Will, and Fate."
6. Talked at length.

Had struck, methinks, his eagle spirit blind
By gazing on its own exceeding light.[7]
—Meanwhile the sun paused ere it should alight,
Over the horizon of the mountains;—Oh,
How beautiful is sunset, when the glow   55
Of Heaven descends upon a land like thee,
Thou Paradise of exiles, Italy!
Thy mountains, seas and vineyards and the towers
Of cities they encircle!—it was ours
To stand on thee, beholding it; and then   60
Just where we had dismounted, the Count's men
Were waiting for us with the gondola.—
As those who pause on some delightful way
Though bent on pleasant pilgrimage, we stood
Looking upon the evening and the flood   65
Which lay between the city and the shore
Paved with the image of the sky . . . the hoar
And aery Alps towards the North appeared
Through mist, an heaven-sustaining bulwark reared
Between the East and West; and half the sky   70
Was roofed with clouds of rich emblazonry[8]
Dark purple at the zenith, which still grew
Down the steep West into a wondrous hue
Brighter than burning gold, even to the rent
Where the swift sun yet paused in his descent   75
Among the many folded hills: they were
Those famous Euganean hills,[9] which bear
As seen from Lido through the harbour piles
The likeness of a clump of peaked isles—
And then—as if the Earth and Sea had been   80
Dissolved into one lake of fire, were seen
Those mountains towering as from waves of flame
Around the vaporous sun, from which there came
The inmost purple spirit of light, and made
Their very peaks transparent. "Ere it fade,"   85
Said my Companion, "I will shew you soon
A better station"—so, o'er the lagune
We glided, and from that funereal bark[1]
I leaned, and saw the City, and could mark
How from their many isles, in evening's gleam,   90
Its temples and its palaces did seem
Like fabrics of enchantment piled to Heaven.
I was about to speak, when—"We are even

---

7. According to legend, the eagle has the keenest vision of all living things; an aged eagle, by flying toward the sun, burns away the scales from its eyes. The passage also echoes Milton's description of God: "Dark with excessive light thy skirts appear" (*Paradise Lost* III.380).

8. Brilliant colors, as on a banner or heraldic device.
9. A range of hills west of Venice.
1. Boat appropriate for a funeral. Shelley wrote in his letter to Mary (note 3, above) that gondolas are "furnished with black & painted black."

Now at the point I meant," said Maddalo,
And bade the gondolieri cease to row. 95
"Look, Julian, on the West, and listen well
If you hear not a deep and heavy bell."
I looked, and saw between us and the sun
A building on an island; such a one
As age to age might add, for uses vile, 100
A windowless, deformed and dreary pile;[2]
And on the top an open tower, where hung
A bell, which in the radiance swayed and swung;
We could just hear its hoarse and iron tongue:
The broad sun sunk behind it, and it tolled 105
In strong and black relief.—"What we behold
Shall be the madhouse and its belfry tower,"
Said Maddalo, "and ever at this hour
Those who may cross the water, hear that bell
Which calls the maniacs each one from his cell 110
To vespers."—"As much skill as need to pray
In thanks or hope for their dark lot have they
To their stern maker,"[3] I replied. "O ho!
You talk as in years past," said Maddalo.
" 'Tis strange men change not. You were ever still 115
Among Christ's flock a perilous infidel,
A wolf for the meek lambs—if you can't swim
Beware of Providence." I looked on him,
But the gay smile had faded in his eye.
"And such,"—he cried, "is our mortality 120
And this must be the emblem and the sign
Of what should be eternal and divine!—
And like that black and dreary bell, the soul,
Hung in a heaven-illumined tower, must toll
Our thoughts and our desires to meet below 125
Round the rent heart and pray—as madmen do
For what? they know not,—till the night of death
As sunset that strange vision, severeth
Our memory from itself,[4] and us from all
We sought and yet were baffled!" I recall 130
The sense of what he said, although I mar
The force of his expressions. The broad star
Of day meanwhile had sunk behind the hill
And the black bell became invisible
And the red tower looked grey, and all between 135
The churches, ships and palaces were seen
Huddled in gloom;—into the purple sea
The orange hues of heaven sunk silently.

2. I.e., a large building.
3. I.e., it takes a madman to thank
God for making him mad.
4. I.e., death's darkness cuts us off
from memory of ourselves, as the setting of the sun cut off the strange scene described in lines 70 ff.

We hardly spoke, and soon the gondola
Conveyed me to my lodging by the way.   140

    The following morn was rainy, cold and dim:
Ere Maddalo arose, I called on him,
And whilst I waited with his child[5] I played;
A lovelier toy sweet Nature never made,
A serious, subtle, wild, yet gentle being,   145
Graceful without design and unforeseeing,[6]
With eyes—oh speak not of her eyes!—which seem
Twin mirrors of Italian Heaven, yet gleam
With such deep meaning, as we never see
But in the human countenance: with me   150
She was a special favourite: I had nursed
Her fine and feeble limbs when she came first
To this bleak world; and she yet seemed to know
On second sight her antient[7] playfellow,
Less changed than she was by six months or so;   155
For after her first shyness was worn out
We sate there, rolling billiard balls about.
When the Count entered—salutations past[8]—
"The word you spoke last night might well have cast
A darkness on my spirit—if man be   160
The passive thing you say, I should not see
Much harm in the religions and old saws[9]
(Though I may never own such leaden laws)
Which break a teachless nature to the yoke:[1]
Mine is another faith"—thus much I spoke   165
And noting he replied not, added: "See
This lovely child, blithe, innocent and free;
She spends a happy time with little care
While we to such sick thoughts subjected are
As came on you last night—it is our will   170
That thus enchains us to permitted ill—
We might be otherwise—we might be all
We dream of happy, high, majestical.
Where is the love, beauty and truth we seek
But in our mind? and if we were not weak   175
Should we be less in deed than in desire?"
"Ay, if we were not weak—and we aspire
How vainly to be strong!" said Maddalo;
"You talk Utopia." "It remains to know,"[2]

5. Allegra, Byron's natural child by
Claire Clermont (Mary Shelley's stepsister). Claire had raised Allegra in
Shelley's household, then sent the 15-
month-old child to Byron on April 28,
1818—some "six months or so" (line
155) before the time represented in this
poem.
6. I.e., without awareness of the fact.
7. Former.

8. After greetings had been exchanged.
9. Proverbial sayings. "Own" (line
163): Acknowledge.
1. I.e., which teach an unteachable
nature to submit to the yoke.
2. I.e., it is still to be discovered—
whether, i.e., I talk an impossibly ideal
condition of mankind ("Utopia"), or a
condition that mankind will actually
achieve.

I then rejoined, "and those who try may find 180
How strong the chains are which our spirit bind;
Brittle perchance as straw . . . We are assured
Much may be conquered, much may be endured
Of what degrades and crushes us. We know
That we have power over ourselves to do 185
And suffer—what, we know not till we try;
But something nobler than to live and die—
So taught those kings of old philosophy
Who reigned, before Religion made men blind;[3]
And those who suffer with their suffering kind 190
Yet feel their faith, religion."[4] "My dear friend,"
Said Maddalo, "my judgement will not bend
To your opinion, though I think you might
Make such a system refutation-tight
As far as words go. I knew one like you 195
Who to this city came some months ago
With whom I argued in this sort, and he
Is now gone mad,—and so he answered me,—
Poor fellow! but if you would like to go
We'll visit him, and his wild talk will show 200
How vain are such aspiring theories."
"I hope to prove the induction otherwise,[5]
And that a want of that true theory, still,
Which seeks a 'soul of goodness' in things ill[6]
Or in himself or others has thus bowed 205
His being—there are some by nature proud,
Who patient in all else demand but this:
To love and be beloved with gentleness;
And being scorned, what wonder if they die
Some living death? this is not destiny 210
But man's own wilful ill." As thus I spoke
Servants announced the gondola, and we
Through the fast-falling rain and high-wrought sea
Sailed to the island where the madhouse stands.
We disembarked. The clap of tortured hands, 215
Fierce yells and howlings and lamentings keen,
And laughter where complaint had merrier been,[7]
Moans, shrieks and curses and blaspheming prayers
Accosted us.[8] * * *

3. I.e., so taught the classical philosophers, who lived before Christianity darkened people's vision.
4. I.e., those non-Christian thinkers who sympathize with the suffering of the human race ("their * * * kind"), and feel that their humanism is itself a religion.
5. I.e., I hope that reasoning from experience will lead to a different conclusion.
6. "There is some soul of goodness in things evil" (Shakespeare's *Henry V* IV.1.4).
7. I.e., would have been merrier.

8. In the omitted passage, Julian and Maddalo listen, unobserved, to the maniac's broken and obscure ravings. From these it appears that he had a passionate love affair with a woman who, in a physical revulsion, had rejected his embraces, reviled him, and deserted him. Most biographers agree that Shelley wrote into these recollections his own emotional turmoil when Mary Shelley became estranged from him after the deaths of their daughter Clara (September, 1818) and their son William (June, 1819).

He ceased, and overcome leant back awhile,
Then rising, with a melancholy smile
Went to a sofa, and lay down, and slept
A heavy sleep, and in his dreams he wept
And muttered some familiar name, and we   515
Wept without shame in his society.
I think I never was impressed so much;
The man who were not, must have lacked a touch
Of human nature . . . then we lingered not,
Although our argument was quite forgot,   520
But calling the attendants, went to dine
At Maddalo's; yet neither cheer nor wine
Could give us spirits, for we talked of him
And nothing else, till daylight made stars dim;
And we agreed his was some dreadful ill   525
Wrought on him boldly, yet unspeakable
By a dear friend; some deadly change in love
Of one vowed deeply which he dreamed not of;
For whose sake he, it seemed, had fixed a blot
Of falshood on his mind which flourished not   530
But in the light of all-beholding truth;
And having stamped this canker[9] on his youth
She had abandoned him—and how much more
Might be his woe, we guessed not—he had store
Of friends and fortune once, as we could guess   535
From his nice[1] habits and his gentleness;
These were now lost . . . it were a grief indeed
If he had changed one unsustaining reed
For all that such a man might else adorn.
The colours of his mind seemed yet unworn;[2]   540
For the wild language of his grief was high,
Such as in measure were called poetry;
And I remember one remark which then
Maddalo made. He said: "Most wretched men
Are cradled into poetry by wrong,   545
They learn in suffering what they teach in song."
    If I had been an unconnected man[3]
I, from this moment, should have formed some plan
Never to leave sweet Venice,—for to me
It was delight to ride by the lone sea;   550
And then, the town is silent—one may write
Or read in gondolas by day or night,
Having the little brazen[4] lamp alight,
Unseen, uninterrupted; books are there,
Pictures, and casts from all those statues fair   555
Which were twin-born with poetry,[5] and all

9. An ulcer or spreading sore.
1. Agreeable, cultivated.
2. I.e., his ability to express himself seemed yet unaffected. "Colours" is apparently used, in an archaic sense, for varieties of verbal expression.
3. Free from family relationships.
4. Brass.
5. I.e., plaster casts of all those fair statues which sprang from the imagination at the same time as poetry.

We seek in towns, with little to recall
Regrets for the green country. I might sit
In Maddalo's great palace, and his wit
And subtle talk would cheer the winter night   560
And make me know myself, and the firelight
Would flash upon our faces, till the day
Might dawn and make me wonder at my stay:
But I had friends in London too: the chief
Attraction here, was that I sought relief   565
From the deep tenderness that maniac wrought
Within me—'twas perhaps an idle thought,
But I imagined that if day by day
I watched him, and but seldom went away,
And studied all the beatings of his heart   570
With zeal, as men study some stubborn art
For their own good, and could by patience find
An entrance to the caverns of his mind,
I might reclaim him from his dark estate:
In friendships I had been most fortunate—   575
Yet never saw I one whom I would call
More willingly my friend; and this was all
Accomplished not; such dreams of baseless[6] good
Oft come and go in crowds or solitude
And leave no trace—but what I now designed   580
Made for long years impression on my mind.
The following morning, urged by my affairs,
I left bright Venice.

                    After many years
And many changes I returned; the name
Of Venice, and its aspect, was the same;   585
But Maddalo was travelling far away
Among the mountains of Armenia.
His dog was dead. His child had now become
A woman; such as it has been my doom[7]
To meet with few, a wonder of this earth,   590
Where there is little of transcendent worth,
Like one of Shakespeare's women: kindly she
And with a manner beyond courtesy
Received her father's friend; and when I asked
Of the lorn[8] maniac, she her memory tasked   595
And told as she had heard the mournful tale:
"That the poor sufferer's health began to fail
Two years from my departure, but that then
The Lady who had left him, came again.
Her mien[9] had been imperious, but she now   600
Looked meek—perhaps remorse had brought her low.
Her coming made him better, and they stayed
Together at my father's—for I played

---

6. Without foundation.   8. Abandoned.
7. Fortune, fate.   9. Look, bearing.

As I remember with the lady's shawl—
I might be six years old—but after all   605
She left him" . . . "Why, her heart must have been tough:
How did it end?" "And was not this enough?
They met—they parted"—"Child, is there no more?"
"Something within that interval which bore
The stamp of *why* they parted, *how* they met: 610
Yet if thine aged eyes disdain to wet
Those wrinkled cheeks with youth's remembered tears,
Ask me no more, but let the silent years
Be closed and ceared[1] over their memory
As yon mute marble where their corpses lie."   615
I urged and questioned still, she told me how
All happened—but the cold world shall not know.

1818–19   1824

A Song: "Men of England"[2]

Men of England, wherefore plough
For the lords who lay ye low?
Wherefore weave with toil and care
The rich robes your tyrants wear?

Wherefore feed and clothe and save   5
From the cradle to the grave
Those ungrateful drones who would
Drain your sweat—nay, drink your blood?

Wherefore, Bees of England, forge
Many a weapon, chain, and scourge,   10
That these stingless drones may spoil
The forced produce of your toil?

Have ye leisure, comfort, calm,
Shelter, food, love's gentle balm?
Or what is it ye buy so dear   15
With your pain and with your fear?

The seed ye sow, another reaps;
The wealth ye find, another keeps;
The robes ye weave, another wears;
The arms ye forge, another bears.   20

---

1. I.e., cered: saturated with wax, as is cerecloth, the winding-sheet for the dead.
2. This and the two following poems were written at a time of turbulent unrest, after the return of troops from the Napoleonic Wars had precipitated a great economic depression. The *Song*, expressing Shelley's hope for a proletarian revolution, was originally planned as one of a series for workingmen; it has become, as the poet wished, a hymn of the British labor movement.

Sow seed—but let no tyrant reap:
Find wealth—let no impostor heap:
Weave robes—let not the idle wear:
Forge arms—in your defence to bear.

Shrink to your cellars, holes, and cells—   25
In halls ye deck another dwells.
Why shake the chains ye wrought? when see
The steel ye tempered glance on ye.

With plough and spade and hoe and loom
Trace your grave and build your tomb   30
And weave your winding-sheet—till fair
England be your Sepulchre.

1819   1839

England in 1819

An old, mad, blind, despised, and dying King;[3]
Princes, the dregs of their dull race, who flow
Through public scorn,—mud from a muddy spring;
Rulers who neither see nor feel nor know,
But leechlike to their fainting country cling   5
Till they drop, blind in blood, without a blow.
A people starved and stabbed in th'untilled field;[4]
An army, whom liberticide and prey
Makes as a two-edged sword to all who wield;
Golden and sanguine laws[5] which tempt and slay;   10
Religion Christless, Godless—a book sealed;
A senate, Time's worst statute, unrepealed[6]—
Are graves from which a glorious Phantom[7] may
Burst, to illumine our tempestuous day.

1819   1839

To Sidmouth and Castlereagh[1]

As from their ancestral oak
   Two empty ravens wind their clarion,
Yell by yell, and croak by croak,

3. George III, who had been declared insane in 1811; he died in 1820.
4. Alluding to the "Peterloo Massacre" on August 16, 1819; in St. Peter's field, near Manchester, a troop of cavalry had charged into a crowd attending a peaceful rally in support of Parliamentary reform. "Peterloo" is an ironic combination of "Waterloo" and "St. Peter's."
5. Laws bought with gold, and leading to bloodshed.
6. The law imposing disabilities upon Dissenters and Roman Catholics.
7. I.e., a revolution.

1. Shelley's powerful satire is directed against Viscount Castlereagh, foreign secretary 1812–22, who took a leading part in the European settlement after the Battle of Waterloo, and Viscount Sidmouth (1757–1844), the home secretary, whose cruelly coercive measures (supported by Castlereagh) against unrest in the laboring classes were in large part responsible for the "Peterloo massacre."
   When this poem was printed by Mrs. Shelley in 1839, it was given the title *Similes for Two Political Characters of 1819.*

When they scent the noonday smoke
Of fresh human carrion:—   5

As two gibbering night-birds flit
From their bowers of deadly yew
Through the night to frighten it—
When the moon is in a fit,
And the stars are none, or few:—   10

As a shark and dogfish wait
Under an Atlantic isle
For the Negro-ship, whose freight
Is the theme of their debate,
Wrinkling their red gills the while—   15

Are ye—two vultures sick for battle,
Two scorpions under one wet stone,
Two bloodless wolves whose dry throats rattle,
Two crows perched on the murrained[2] cattle,
Two vipers tangled into one.   20

1819   1832; 1839

The Indian Girl's Song[3] [The Indian Serenade]

I arise from dreams of thee
In the first sleep of night—
The winds are breathing low
And the stars are burning bright.
I arise from dreams of thee—   5
And a spirit in my feet
Has borne me—Who knows how?
To thy chamber window, sweet!—

The wandering airs they faint
On the dark silent stream—   10
The champak[4] odours fail
Like sweet thoughts in a dream;
The nightingale's complaint—
It dies upon her heart—
As I must die on thine   15
O beloved as thou art!

O lift me from the grass!
I die, I faint, I fail!
Let thy love in kisses rain
On my lips and eyelids pale.   20

2. A "murrain" is a malignant disease of domestic animals.

3. Usually entitled *The Indian Serenade*, this poem is not a personal utterance but a dramatic lyric, sung by an imagined East Indian girl and manifesting the conventional extravagance of an Oriental love poem.

4. An Indian species of magnolia, bearing fragrant orange flowers.

My cheek is cold and white, alas!
My heart beats loud and fast.
Oh press it close to thine again
Where it will break at last.

1819   1822

Ode to the West Wind[1]

I

O wild West Wind, thou breath of Autumn's being,
Thou, from whose unseen presence the leaves dead
Are driven, like ghosts from an enchanter fleeing,

Yellow, and black, and pale, and hectic[2] red,
Pestilence-stricken multitudes: O Thou,   5
Who chariotest to their dark wintry bed

The winged seeds, where they lie cold and low,
Each like a corpse within its grave, until
Thine azure sister of the Spring[3] shall blow

Her clarion[4] o'er the dreaming earth, and fill   10
(Driving sweet buds like flocks to feed in air)
With living hues and odours plain and hill:

Wild Spirit, which art moving everywhere;
Destroyer and Preserver; hear, O hear!

II

Thou on whose stream, 'mid the steep sky's commotion,   15
Loose clouds like Earth's decaying leaves are shed,
Shook from the tangled boughs of Heaven and Ocean,[5]

1. "This poem was conceived and chiefly written in a wood that skirts the Arno, near Florence, and on a day when that tempestuous wind, whose temperature is at once mild and animating, was collecting the vapors which pour down the autumnal rains" [Shelley's note]. As in other major Romantic poems—for example, the opening of Wordsworth's *Prelude*, Coleridge's *Dejection*, and the conclusion to Shelley's *Adonais*—the rising wind, linked with the cycle of the seasons, is presented as the outer correspondent to an inner change from apathy to spiritual vitality, and from imaginative sterility to a burst of creative power which is paralleled to the inspiration of the Biblical prophets. In Hebrew, Latin, Greek, and many other languages, the words for wind, breath, soul, and inspiration are all identical or related. Thus Shelley's west wind is a "spirit" (the Latin *spiritus*: wind, breath, soul, and the root word in "inspiration"), the "breath of Autumn's being," which on earth, sky, and sea destroys in the au-

tumn in order to revive in the spring. Around this central image the poem weaves various cycles of death and regeneration—vegetational, human, and divine.

The stanza used in this ode was developed by Shelley from the interlaced three-line units of the Italian *terza rima: aba bcb cdc*, etc. Shelley's stanza consists of a set of four such tercets, closed by a couplet rhyming with the middle line of the preceding tercet: *aba bcb cdc ded ee*.

2. The kind of fever which occurs in tuberculosis.
3. The west wind that will blow in the spring.
4. A high, shrill trumpet.
5. I.e., the fragmentary clouds ("leaves") are torn by the wind from the larger and higher clouds ("boughs"), which are formed by a union of air with vapor drawn up by the sun from the ocean. "Angels" (line 18) suggests the old sense: messengers, harbingers.

Angels of rain and lightning: there are spread
On the blue surface of thine aery surge,
Like the bright hair uplifted from the head   20

Of some fierce Mænad,[6] even from the dim verge
Of the horizon to the zenith's height,
The locks of the approaching storm. Thou Dirge

Of the dying year, to which this closing night
Will be the dome of a vast sepulchre,   25
Vaulted with all thy congregated might

Of vapours,[7] from whose solid atmosphere
Black rain and fire and hail will burst: O hear!

III

Thou who didst waken from his summer dreams
The blue Mediterranean, where he lay,   30
Lulled by the coil of his chrystalline streams,[8]

Beside a pumice isle in Baiæ's bay,[9]
And saw in sleep old palaces and towers
Quivering within the wave's intenser day,[1]

All overgrown with azure moss and flowers   35
So sweet, the sense faints picturing them! Thou
For whose path the Atlantic's level powers

Cleave themselves into chasms, while far below
The sea-blooms and the oozy woods which wear
The sapless foliage of the ocean, know   40

Thy voice, and suddenly grow grey with fear,
And tremble and despoil themselves:[2] O hear!

IV

If I were a dead leaf thou mightest bear;
If I were a swift cloud to fly with thee;
A wave to pant beneath thy power, and share   45

The impulse of thy strength, only less free
Than thou, O Uncontrollable! If even
I were as in my boyhood, and could be

6. A female votary who danced frenziedly in the worship of Dionysus (Bacchus), the Greek god of wine and vegetation. As vegetation god, he was fabled
to die in the fall and to be resurrected
in the spring.
7. Clouds.
8. The currents that flow in the Mediterranean Sea, sometimes with a visible difference in color.
9. "Pumice": a porous volcanic stone.

"Baiæ's bay," west of Naples was the
locale of imposing villas erected by
Roman emperors.
1. Shelley once observed that, when reflected in water, colors are "more vivid
yet blended with more harmony."
2. "The vegetation at the bottom of the
sea * * * sympathizes with that of the
land in the change of seasons" [Shelley's
note].

The comrade of thy wanderings over Heaven,
As then, when to outstrip thy skiey speed   50
Scarce seemed a vision; I would ne'er have striven

As thus with thee in prayer in my sore need.
Oh! lift me as a wave, a leaf, a cloud!
I fall upon the thorns of life! I bleed!

A heavy weight of hours has chained and bowed   55
One too like thee: tameless, and swift, and proud.

                    V

Make me thy lyre,[3] even as the forest is:
What if my leaves are falling like its own!
The tumult of thy mighty harmonies

Will take from both a deep, autumnal tone,   60
Sweet though in sadness. Be thou, Spirit fierce,
My spirit! Be thou me, impetuous one!

Drive my dead thoughts over the universe
Like withered leaves to quicken a new birth!
And, by the incantation of this verse,   65

Scatter, as from an unextinguished hearth
Ashes and sparks, my words among mankind!
Be through my lips to unawakened Earth

The trumpet of a prophecy![4] O Wind,
If Winter comes, can Spring be far behind?   70

1819   1820

3. The Eolian lyre, which responds to   10, as well as an allusion to the last
the wind with alternating musical chords. trump of the apocalypse in Revelation
4. A reference to the "clarion" of line   xi.15.

Prometheus Unbound   Shelley composed this work in Italy between the autumn of 1818 and the close of 1819 and published it the following summer. Upon its completion he wrote in a letter, "It is a drama, with characters and mechanism of a kind yet unattempted; and I think the execution is better than any of my former attempts." It is based upon the *Prometheus Bound* of Aeschylus, which dramatizes the sufferings of Prometheus, unrepentant champion of mankind, who, because he had stolen fire from heaven, was condemned by Zeus to be chained to Mt. Caucasus and to be tortured by a vulture feeding upon his liver; in a lost sequel, Aeschylus reconciled Prometheus with his oppressor. Shelley continued Aeschylus' story, but transformed it into a symbolic drama about the origin of evil and its elimination. In such earlier writings as *Queen Mab* Shelley had expressed his belief that injustice and suffering can be eliminated by an external revolution which will wipe out or radically reform the sole causes of evil, existing social, political, and religious institutions. Implicit in *Prometheus*

Unbound, on the other hand, is the view that both the origin of evil and the possibility of reform are the moral responsibility of man himself. Social chaos and wars are a gigantic projection of man's moral disorder and inner division and conflict; tyrants are the outer representatives of the tyranny of man's baser over his better elements; hatred for others is an expression of self-contempt; and successful political reform is impossible unless man has first reformed his own nature at its roots, by substituting selfless love for divisive hate. Shelley thus incorporates into his secular myth of universal regeneration by an apocalypse of man's moral imagination, the ethical teaching of Christ on the Mount, as well as the highest classical morality represented in the *Prometheus* of Aeschylus. And Shelley warns (IV.562 ff.) that even should such a victory take place—the reintegration of splintered man, with a consequent restoration of moral and political order and a release of all man's creative powers in art and science—the price of its continuation is an unremitting vigilance lest the serpent deep in human nature should break loose and start the cycle all over again.

Shelley wrote in his Preface that Prometheus is, "as it were, the type of the highest perfection of moral and intellectual nature." But he also warned that it is a mistake to suppose that the poem contains "a reasoned system on the theory of human life. Didactic poetry is my abhorrence." *Prometheus Unbound* is not a dramatized philosophical essay, nor a moral allegory, but a large and intricate imaginative construction which involves premises about the nature of man and the springs of morality and creativity. The non-Christian poet, Yeats, called it one of "the sacred books of the world," and the Christian critic, C. S. Lewis, found in it many of the powers of Dante.

From Prometheus Unbound

A LYRICAL DRAMA

Dramatis Personae

PROMETHEUS	HERCULES
DEMOGORGON	THE PHANTASM OF JUPITER
JUPITER	THE SPIRIT OF THE EARTH
THE EARTH	THE SPIRIT OF THE MOON
OCEAN	SPIRITS OF THE HOURS
APOLLO	SPIRITS
MERCURY	ECHOES
ASIA	FAUNS
PANTHEA } *Oceanides*	FURIES
IONE	

From *Act I*

SCENE—A *Ravine of Icy Rocks in the Indian Caucasus.*[1] PRO-METHEUS *is discovered bound to the Precipice.* PANTHEA *and* IONE *are seated at his feet. Time, night. During the Scene, morning slowly breaks.*

1. The Himalayan mountains.

PROMETHEUS. Monarch of Gods and Dæmons,[2] and all Spirits
But One, who throng those bright and rolling Worlds
Which Thou and I alone of living things
Behold with sleepless eyes! regard this Earth
Made multitudinous with thy slaves, whom thou   5
Requitest for knee-worship, prayer and praise,
And toil, and hecatombs[3] of broken hearts,
With fear and self-contempt and barren hope;
Whilst me, who am thy foe, eyeless in hate,[4]
Hast thou made reign and triumph, to thy scorn,   10
O'er mine own misery and thy vain revenge.—
Three thousand years of sleep-unsheltered hours
And moments—aye[5] divided by keen pangs
Till they seemed years, torture and solitude,
Scorn and despair,—these are mine empire:—   15
More glorious far than that which thou surveyest
From thine unenvied throne, O Mighty God!
Almighty, had I deigned[6] to share the shame
Of thine ill tyranny, and hung not here
Nailed to this wall of eagle-baffling mountain,   20
Black, wintry, dead, unmeasured; without herb,
Insect, or beast, or shape or sound of life.
Ah me, alas, pain, pain ever, forever!

No change, no pause, no hope!—Yet I endure.
I ask the Earth, have not the mountains felt?   25
I ask yon Heaven—the all-beholding Sun,
Has it not seen? The Sea, in storm or calm,
Heaven's ever-changing Shadow, spread below—
Have its deaf waves not heard my agony?
Ah me, alas, pain, pain ever, forever!   30

The crawling glaciers pierce me with the spears·
Of their moon-freezing chrystals; the bright chains
Eat with their burning cold into my bones.
Heaven's winged hound, polluting from thy lips
His beak in poison not his own, tears up   35
My heart;[7] and shapeless sights come wandering by,
The ghastly people of the realm of dream,
Mocking me: and the Earthquake-fiends are charged
To wrench the rivets from my quivering wounds
When the rocks split and close again behind;   40
While from their loud abysses howling throng
The genii of the storm, urging the rage
Of whirlwind, and afflict me with keen hail.
And yet to me welcome is Day and Night,

---

2. Prometheus is addressing Jupiter.
"Daemons" are supernatural beings,
intermediary between gods and men.
The "One" in the next line is Demogorgon; see II.iv, below.
3. Large sacrificial offerings.
4. Blinded by hate.

5. Always.
6. I.e., you would have been all-powerful, if I had deigned.
7. The vulture, tearing daily at Prometheus' heart, was kissed by Jupiter by
way of reward.

Whether one breaks the hoar frost of the morn,   45
Or starry, dim, and slow, the other climbs
The leaden-coloured East; for then they lead·
The wingless, crawling Hours,[8] one among whom
—As some dark Priest hales the reluctant victim—
Shall drag thee, cruel King, to kiss the blood   50
From these pale feet,[9] which then might trample thee
If they disdained not such a prostrate slave.
Disdain? Ah no! I pity thee.[1]—What Ruin
Will hunt thee undefended through wide Heaven!
How will thy soul, cloven to its depth with terror,   55
Gape like a Hell within! I speak in grief,
Not exultation, for I hate no more,
As then, ere misery made me wise.—The Curse
Once breathed on thee I would recall. Ye Mountains,
Whose many-voiced Echoes, through the mist   60
Of cataracts, flung the thunder of that spell!
Ye icy Springs, stagnant with wrinkling frost,
Which vibrated to hear me, and then crept
Shuddering through India! Thou serenest Air,
Through which the Sun walks burning without beams!   65
And ye swift Whirlwinds, who on poised wings
Hung mute and moveless o'er yon hushed abyss,
As thunder louder than your own made rock
The orbed world! If then my words had power
—Though I am changed so that aught evil wish   70
Is dead within, although no memory be
Of what is hate—let them not lose it now![2]
What was that curse? for ye all heard me speak.[3]

* * *

PHANTASM

Fiend, I defy thee! with a calm, fixed mind,
    All that thou canst inflict I bid thee do;
Foul Tyrant both of Gods and Humankind,
    One only being shalt thou not subdue.   265
        Rain then thy plagues upon me here,
        Ghastly disease and frenzying fear;
        And let alternate frost and fire
            Eat into me, and be thine ire
Lightning and cutting hail and legioned forms   270
Of furies, driving by upon the wounding storms.

8. The Hours were represented in Greek myth and art by human figures with wings. "Hales" (line 49): drags.
9. One of a number of implied parallels between the agony of Prometheus and the passion of Christ.
1. At this early point occurs the crisis of the action: the beginning of Prometheus' change of heart from hate to compassion, which is consummated in lines 303–5. The rest of the symbolic drama gradually unfolds the consequences of this moral triumph—of which Prometheus himself is unaware.
2. I.e., let my words not lose their power now.
3. In the passage here omitted, none dares to repeat the curse Prometheus had proclaimed against Jupiter for fear of that god's vengeance. Prometheus is finally forced to call up the Phantasm of Jupiter himself who, in the next excerpt, repeats the words of Prometheus' curse.

Aye, do thy worst. Thou art Omnipotent.
  O'er all things but thyself I gave thee power,
And my own will. Be thy swift mischiefs sent
    To blast mankind, from yon etherial tower.   275
      Let thy malignant spirit move
      Its darkness over those I love:
      On me and mine I imprecate[4]
      The utmost torture of thy hate
And thus devote to sleepless agony   280
This undeclining head while thou must reign on high.

But thou who art the God and Lord—O thou
  Who fillest with thy soul this world of woe,
To whom all things of Earth and Heaven do bow
  In fear and worship—all-prevailing foe!
      I curse thee! let a sufferer's curse   285
      Clasp thee, his torturer, like remorse,
      Till thine Infinity shall be
      A robe of envenomed agony;
And thine Omnipotence a crown of pain
To cling like burning gold round thy dissolving brain.[5]   290

Heap on thy soul by virtue of this Curse
  Ill deeds, then be thou damned, beholding good,
Both infinite as is the Universe,
  And thou, and thy self-torturing solitude.
      An awful Image of calm power   295
      Though now thou sittest, let the hour
      Come, when thou must appear to be
      That which thou art internally.
And after many a false and fruitless crime
Scorn track thy lagging fall through boundless space and time. 300
                    [*The Phantasm vanishes.*]

PROMETHEUS. Were these my words, O Parent?
THE EARTH.   They were thine.
PROMETHEUS. It doth repent me: words are quick and vain;
  Grief for awhile is blind, and so was mine.
  I wish no living thing to suffer pain.   305

THE EARTH

Misery, O misery to me,
That Jove at length should vanquish thee.[6]
Wail, howl aloud, Land and Sea,
The Earth's rent heart shall answer ye.
Howl, Spirits of the living and the dead,   310
Your refuge, your defence lies fallen and vanquished.

4. Invoke, pray for.
5. Like the poisoned shirt of the centaur Nessus, which consumed Hercules' flesh when he put it on. The following lines allude to the mock crowning of Christ with a crown of thorns.
6. Earth mistakes mercy for submission, and therefore interprets Prometheus' victory as his defeat.

FIRST ECHO
Lies fallen and vanquished?

SECOND ECHO
Fallen and vanquished!

IONE[7]
Fear not—'tis but some passing spasm,
The Titan is unvanquished still.[8]   315

* * *

FURY. Behold, an emblem—those who do endure
Deep wrongs for man, and scorn and chains, but heap   595
Thousand-fold torment on themselves and him.
PROMETHEUS. Remit the anguish of that lighted stare—
Close those wan lips—let that thorn-wounded brow
Stream not with blood—it mingles with thy tears!
Fix, fix those tortured orbs in peace and death   600
So thy sick throes shake not that crucifix,
So those pale fingers play not with thy gore.—
O horrible! Thy name I will not speak,
It hath become a curse.[9] I see, I see
The wise, the mild, the lofty and the just,   605
Whom thy slaves hate for being like to thee,
Some hunted by foul lies from their heart's home,
An early-chosen, late-lamented home,
As hooded ounces cling to the driven hind,[1]
Some linked to corpses in unwholesome cells: 610
Some—hear I not the multitude laugh loud?—
Impaled in lingering fire: and mighty realms
Float by my feet like sea-uprooted isles
Whose sons are kneaded down in common blood
By the red light of their own burning homes.   615
FURY. Blood thou canst see, and fire; and canst hear groans;
Worse things, unheard, unseen, remain behind.
PROMETHEUS. Worse?
FURY. In each human heart terror survives
The ravin it has gorged[2]: the loftiest fear
All that they would disdain to think were true: 620

---

7. Ione, Panthea, and Asia (in the following scene) are sisters and Oceanids —i.e., daughters of Oceanus.
8. In the omitted passage the herald Mercury, at Jupiter's command, brings a group of Furies (in Greek myth, avengers of crimes against the gods) who tempt Prometheus to despair by revealing the loathsome potentialities for evil in mankind's conscious and unconscious mind. In the climactic temptation, a Fury tears aside a veil to reveal a representation ("emblem," line 594) of the suffering Christ on the cross.
9. I.e., the name "Christ" has become, literally, a curse-word, and metaphorically, a curse to mankind, in that His religion of love is used to justify religious wars and bloody oppression.
1. Female deer. "Ounces" are cheetahs, or leopards used in hunting (hoods were sometimes placed over their eyes to make them easier to control).
2. I.e., the prey that it has greedily devoured.

Hypocrisy and custom make their minds
The fanes³ of many a worship, now outworn.
They dare not devise good for man's estate
And yet they know not that they do not dare.
The good want power, but to weep barren tears.   625
The powerful goodness want: worse need for them.
The wise want love, and those who love want wisdom;
And all best things are thus confused to ill.
Many are strong and rich,—and would be just,—
But live among their suffering fellow men   630
As if none felt: they know not what they do.⁴
PROMETHEUS. Thy words are like a cloud of winged snakes
  And yet, I pity those they torture not.
FURY. Thou pitiest them? I speak no more!   [*Vanishes.*]
PROMETHEUS.   Ah woe!
  Ah woe! Alas! pain, pain ever, forever!   635
  I close my tearless eyes, but see more clear
  Thy works within my woe-illumed mind,
  Thou subtle Tyrant!⁵ . . . Peace is in the grave—
  The grave hides all things beautiful and good—
  I am a God and cannot find it there,   640
  Nor would I seek it: for, though dread revenge,
  This is defeat, fierce King, not victory.
  The sights with which thou torturest gird my soul
  With new endurance, till the hour arrives
  When they shall be no types of things which are.   645
PANTHEA. Alas! what sawest thou?
PROMETHEUS. There are two woes:
  To speak and to behold; thou spare me one.⁶
  Names are there, Nature's sacred watchwords—they
  Were borne aloft in bright emblazonry.⁷
  The nations thronged around, and cried aloud   650
  As with one voice, "Truth, liberty and love!"
  Suddenly fierce confusion fell from Heaven
  Among them—there was strife, deceit and fear;
  Tyrants rushed in, and did divide the spoil.
  This was the shadow of the truth I saw.   655
THE EARTH. I felt thy torture, Son, with such mixed joy
  As pain and Virtue give.—To cheer thy state
  I bid ascend those subtle and fair spirits
  Whose homes are the dim caves of human thought

---

3. Temples.
4. The Fury ironically echoes Christ's plea for forgiveness of his crucifiers: "Father, forgive them; for they know not what they do" (Luke xxiii.24). Lines 625–28 are Shelley's comment on his own age of political reaction and oppression. This passage underlies

Yeats's description of the troubled era after World War I in *The Second Coming* (below), lines 3–8.
5. I.e., Jupiter (also addressed as "fierce King," line 642).
6. I.e., spare me the woe of speaking (about what I have beheld).
7. As in a brilliant display of banners.

And who inhabit, as birds wing the wind,   660
Its world-surrounding ether;[8] they behold
Beyond that twilight realm, as in a glass,
The future—may they speak comfort to thee![9]

* * *

From *Act II*[1]

SCENE IV—*The Cave of* DEMOGORGON, ASIA *and* PANTHEA.
PANTHEA. What veiled form sits on that ebon throne?
ASIA. The veil has fallen! . . .
PANTHEA.   I see a mighty Darkness
   Filling the seat of power; and rays of gloom
   Dart round, as light from the meridian Sun,
   Ungazed upon and shapeless—neither limb   5
   Nor form—nor outline;[2] yet we feel it is
   A living Spirit.
DEMOGORGON. Ask what thou wouldst know.
ASIA. What canst thou tell?
DEMOGORGON.   All things thou dar'st demand.
ASIA. Who made the living world?
DEMOGORGON.   God.
ASIA.   Who made all
   That it contains—thought, passion, reason, will,   10
   Imagination?
DEMOGORGON. God, Almighty God.
ASIA. Who made that sense[3] which, when the winds of Spring

8. A medium, weightless and infinitely elastic, once supposed to permeate the universe.
9. The speech of the Earth ushers in a troop of spirits representing the noble and virtuous potentialities of the mind, on which rests the hope of a future felicity for humanity. "Glass": mirror.
1. Act II has opened with Asia—the feminine principle and embodiment of love, who was separated from Prometheus at the moment of his fall into divisive hate—in a lovely Indian valley at the first hour of the dawn of the spring season of redemption. Asia and her sister Panthea have been led, by a sweet and irresistible compulsion, first to the portal and then down into the depths of the cave of Demogorgon—the central enigma of Shelley's poem.
Commentators have usually equated Demogorgon with *necessity*, but the interpretation, though pertinent, is too neat and confining. More flexibly, he can be thought of as *process*, the inexorable way in which things evolve. But the ultimate mover of that process—the ultimate reason for things—must remain, Shelley skeptically insists, a mystery beyond the limits of accessible knowledge. Demogorgon, like the inaccessible Power represented by the Arve in *Mont Blanc* (above), is implacable, neutral, and the more terrifying because he himself is ignorant of the principle that controls him. He serves merely to stimulate Asia to ask once more the ultimate and persistent questions about the "why" of creation, good, and evil. But "the deep truth is imageless" (line 116). Demogorgon can give merely riddling answers, which in fact stimulate Asia to bring to full awareness what she had obscurely known already (lines 121–23). The one question he can answer unequivocally is not "why," but "when": the hour in the process when Prometheus shall arise. That hour (line 128) is now.
2. Echoing Milton's description of Death, *Paradise Lost* II.666–73.
3. Presumably the sense by which one is aware of the "unseen Power" which Shelley calls "Intellectual Beauty"; see *Hymn to Intellectual Beauty*, stanza 2.

In rarest visitation, or the voice
Of one beloved heard in youth alone,
Fills the faint eyes with falling tears, which dim   15
The radiant looks of unbewailing flowers,
And leaves this peopled earth a solitude
When it returns no more?

DEMOGORGON.   Merciful God.

ASIA. And who made terror, madness, crime, remorse,
Which from the links of the great chain of things   20
To every thought within the mind of man
Sway and drag heavily—and each one reels
Under the load towards the pit of death;
Abandoned hope, and love that turns to hate;
And self-contempt, bitterer to drink than blood;   25
Pain, whose unheeded and familiar speech
Is howling and keen shrieks, day after day;
And Hell, or the sharp fear of Hell?[4]

DEMOGORGON.   He reigns.

ASIA. Utter his name—a world pining in pain
Asks but his name; curses shall drag him down.   30

DEMOGORGON. He reigns.

ASIA.   I feel, I know it—who?

DEMOGORGON.   He reigns.

ASIA. Who reigns? There was the Heaven and Earth at first
And Light and Love;—then Saturn,[5] from whose throne
Time fell, an envious shadow; such the state
Of the earth's primal spirits beneath his sway   35
As the calm joy of flowers and living leaves
Before the wind or sun has withered them
And semivital worms; but he refused
The birthright of their being, knowledge, power,
The skill which wields the elements, the thought   40
Which pierces this dim Universe like light,
Self-empire and the majesty of love,
For thirst of which they fainted. Then Prometheus
Gave wisdom, which is strength, to Jupiter
And with this law alone: "Let man be free,"   45
Clothed him with the dominion of wide Heaven.
To know nor faith nor love nor law, to be
Omnipotent but friendless, is to reign;
And Jove now reigned; for on the race of man
First famine, and then toil, and then disease,   50
Strife, wounds, and ghastly death unseen before,
Fell; and the unseasonable seasons drove,
With alternating shafts of frost and fire,
Their shelterless, pale tribes to mountain caves;

---

4. The nouns "hope," "love," etc. (lines 24–28), are all objects of the verb "made" (line 19).
5. In Greek myth, Saturn's reign was the golden age. In Shelley's version, Saturn refused to grant men knowledge and science, so that it was an age of ignorant innocence in which man's deepest needs were unfulfilled.

And in their desart[6] hearts fierce wants he sent   55
And mad disquietudes, and shadows idle
Of unreal good, which levied mutual war,
So ruining the lair wherein they raged.
Prometheus saw, and waked the legioned hopes
Which sleep within folded Elysian flowers,   60
Nepenthe, Moly, Amaranth,[7] fadeless blooms;
That they might hide with thin and rainbow wings
The shape of Death; and Love he sent to bind
The disunited tendrils of that vine
Which bears the wine of life, the human heart;   65
And he tamed fire which, like some beast of prey,
Most terrible, but lovely, played beneath
The frown of man, and tortured to his will
Iron and gold, the slaves and signs of power,
And gems and poisons, and all subtlest forms   70
Hidden beneath the mountains and the waves.
He gave man speech, and speech created thought,
Which is the measure of the Universe;
And Science struck the thrones of Earth and Heaven
Which shook, but fell not; and the harmonious mind   75
Poured itself forth in all-prophetic song,
And music lifted up the listening spirit
Until it walked, exempt from mortal care,
Godlike, o'er the clear billows of sweet sound;
And human hands first mimicked and then mocked[8]   80
With moulded limbs more lovely than its own
The human form, till marble grew divine,
And mothers, gazing, drank the love men see
Reflected in their race, behold, and perish.[9] —
He told the hidden power of herbs and springs,   85
And Disease drank and slept—Death grew like sleep.—
He taught the implicated[1] orbits woven
Of the wide-wandering stars, and how the Sun
Changes his lair, and by what secret spell
The pale moon is transformed, when her broad eye   90
Gazes not on the interlunar[2] sea;
He taught to rule, as life directs the limbs,
The tempest-winged chariots of the Ocean,
And the Celt knew the Indian.[3] Cities then
Were built, and through their snow-like columns flowed   95
The warm winds, and the azure æther shone,
And the blue sea and shadowy hills were seen . . .

6. Empty, forsaken.
7. These are medicinal drugs and flowers in Greek myth. Asia (lines 59–97) is describing the various sciences and arts given to man by Prometheus, the culture-bringer.
8. I.e., sculptors first merely reproduced, but later improved upon ("mocked"), the beauty of the human form.
9. Expectant mothers looked at the beautiful statues so that their children might, by prenatal influence, be born with that beauty which makes beholders die of love.
1. Inter-involved.
2. The phase between old and new moon, when the moon is invisible.
3. The reference is to the ships in which the Celtic (here, non-Graeco-Roman) races of Europe were able to sail to India.

Such the alleviations of his state
Prometheus gave to man—for which he hangs
Withering in destined pain—but who rains down   100
Evil, the immedicable plague, which while
Man looks on his creation like a God
And sees that it is glorious, drives him on,
The wreck of his own will, the scorn of Earth,
The outcast, the abandoned, the alone?—   105
Not Jove: while yet his frown shook Heaven, aye when
His adversary from adamantine chains
Cursed him, he trembled like a slave. Declare
Who is his master? Is he too a slave?
DEMOGORGON. All spirits are enslaved which serve things evil: 110
    Thou knowest if Jupiter be such or no.
ASIA. Whom calledst thou God?
DEMOGORGON.   I spoke but as ye speak—
    For Jove is the supreme of living things.
ASIA. Who is the master of the slave?
DEMOGORGON.   —If the Abysm
    Could vomit forth its secrets:—but a voice   115
    Is wanting, the deep truth is imageless;[4]
    For what would it avail to bid thee gaze
    On the revolving world? what to bid speak
    Fate, Time, Occasion, Chance and Change? To these
    All things are subject but eternal Love.   120
ASIA. So much I asked before, and my heart gave
    The response thou hast given; and of such truths
    Each to itself must be the oracle.—
    One more demand . . . and do thou answer me
    As my own soul would answer, did it know   125
    That which I ask.—Prometheus shall arise
    Henceforth the Sun of this rejoicing world:
    When shall the destined hour arrive?
DEMOGORGON.   Behold![5]
ASIA. The rocks are cloven, and through the purple night
    I see Cars drawn by rainbow-winged steeds   130
    Which trample the dim winds—in each there stands
    A wild-eyed charioteer, urging their flight.
    Some look behind, as fiends pursued them there
    And yet I see no shapes but the keen stars:
    Others with burning eyes lean forth, and drink   135
    With eager lips the wind of their own speed,
    As if the thing they loved fled on before,
    And now—even now they clasped it; their bright locks
    Stream like a comet's flashing hair: they all
    Sweep onward.—
DEMOGORGON. These are the immortal Hours   140
    Of whom thou didst demand.—One waits for thee.

---

4. I.e., ultimate truths can be neither
known nor expressed.
5. Demogorgon's answer is a gesture: he
points to the approaching chariots
("cars").

ASIA. A Spirit with a dreadful countenance
    Checks its dark chariot by the craggy gulph.
    Unlike thy brethren, ghastly charioteer,
    Who art thou? whither wouldst thou bear me? Speak!   145
SPIRIT. I am the shadow of a destiny
    More dread than is my aspect—ere yon planet
    Has set, the Darkness[6] which ascends with me
    Shall wrap in lasting night Heaven's kingless throne.
ASIA. What meanest thou?
PANTHEA.   That terrible shadow floats   150
    Up from its throne, as may the lurid[7] smoke
    Of earthquake-ruined cities o'er the sea.—
    Lo! it ascends the Car . . . the coursers fly
    Terrified; watch its path among the stars
    Blackening the night!
ASIA.   Thus I am answered—strange!   155
PANTHEA. See, near the verge[8] another chariot stays;
    An ivory shell inlaid with crimson fire
    Which comes and goes within its sculptured rim
    Of delicate strange tracery—the young Spirit
    That guides it, has the dove-like eyes of hope.   160
    How its soft smiles attract the soul!—as light[9]
    Lures winged insects through the lampless air.

                            SPIRIT
My coursers are fed with the lightning,
    They drink of the whirlwind's stream
And when the red morning is brightning   165
    They bathe in the fresh sunbeam;
    They have strength for their swiftness I deem:
Then ascend with me, daughter of Ocean.

I desire—and their speed makes night kindle;
    I fear—they outstrip the Typhoon;   170
Ere the cloud piled on Atlas[1] can dwindle
    We encircle the earth and the moon:
    We shall rest from long labours at noon:
Then ascend with me, daughter of Ocean.

SCENE V—*The Car pauses within a Cloud on the top of a snowy
Mountain.* ASIA, PANTHEA, *and the* SPIRIT OF THE HOUR.

                            SPIRIT
On the brink of the night and the morning
    My coursers are wont to respire,[2]
But the Earth has just whispered a warning
    That their flight must be swifter than fire:
    They shall drink the hot speed of desire!   5

6. I.e., Demogorgon, who is ascending (lines 150–55) to effect the dethronement of Jupiter.
7. Red-glaring.
8. Horizon.
9. The ancient image of the soul, "psyche," was a moth. The chariot described here will carry Asia to a reunion with Prometheus.
1. The mountains of North Africa, which the Greeks regarded as so high they supported the heavens.
2. Catch their breath.

ASIA. Thou breathest on their nostrils—but my breath
  Would give them swifter speed.
SPIRIT.   Alas, it could not.
PANTHEA. Oh Spirit! pause and tell whence is the light
  Which fills the cloud? the sun is yet unrisen.
SPIRIT. The sun will rise not until noon[3]—Apollo   10
  Is held in Heaven by wonder—and the light
  Which fills this vapour, as the aerial hue
  Of fountain-gazing roses fills the water,
  Flows from thy mighty sister.
PANTHEA.   Yes, I feel . . .
ASIA. What is it with thee, sister? Thou art pale.   15
PANTHEA. How thou art changed! I dare not look on thee;
  I feel, but see thee not. I scarce endure
  The radiance of thy beauty.[4] Some good change
  Is working in the elements which suffer
  Thy presence thus unveiled.—The Nereids tell   20
  That on the day when the clear hyaline
  Was cloven at thy uprise, and thou didst stand
  Within a veined shell,[5] which floated on
  Over the calm floor of the chrystal sea,
  Among the Ægean isles, and by the shores   25
  Which bear thy name, love, like the atmosphere
  Of the sun's fire filling the living world,
  Burst from thee, and illumined Earth and Heaven
  And the deep ocean and the sunless caves
  And all that dwells within them; till grief cast   30
  Eclipse upon the soul from which it came:
  Such art thou now, nor is it I alone,
  Thy sister, thy companion, thine own chosen one,
  But the whole world which seeks thy sympathy.
  Hearest thou not sounds i' the air which speak the love   35
  Of all articulate beings? Feelest thou not
  The inanimate winds enamoured of thee?—List!   [*Music*.]
ASIA. Thy words are sweeter than aught else but his
  Whose echoes they are—yet all love is sweet,
  Given or returned; common as light is love   40
  And its familiar voice wearies not ever.
  Like the wide Heaven, the all-sustaining air,
  It makes the reptile equal to the God . . .
  They who inspire it most are fortunate
  As I am now; but those who feel it most   45

---

3. Noon will be the time of the reunion
between Prometheus and Asia.
4. In an earlier scene, Panthea had envisioned in a dream the radiant and eternal inner form of Prometheus emerging
through his "wound-worn limbs." The
corresponding transfiguration of Asia,
prepared for by her descent to the un-

derworld, now takes place.
5. The story told by the Nereids (sea
nymphs) serves to associate Asia with
Aphrodite, goddess of love, emerging (as
in Botticelli's painting) from the Mediterranean on a seashell. "Hyaline": the
glassy sea.

Are happier still, after long sufferings
As I shall soon become.

PANTHEA.   List! Spirits speak.

VOICE (*in the air, singing*)[6]

Life of Life! thy lips enkindle
    With their love the breath between them
And thy smiles before they dwindle   50
    Make the cold air fire; then screen them
In those looks where whoso gazes
Faints, entangled in their mazes.

Child of Light! thy limbs are burning
    Through the vest which seems to hide them   55
As the radiant lines of morning
    Through the clouds ere they divide them,
And this atmosphere divinest
Shrouds thee wheresoe'er thou shinest.

Fair are others;—none beholds thee   60
    But thy voice sounds low and tender
Like the fairest, for it folds thee
    From the sight, that liquid splendour,
And all feel, yet see thee never
As I feel now, lost forever!   65

Lamp of Earth! where'er thou movest
    Its dim shapes are clad with brightness
And the souls of whom thou lovest
    Walk upon the winds with lightness
Till they fail, as I am failing,   70
Dizzy, lost . . . yet unbewailing!

ASIA

My soul is an enchanted Boat
    Which, like a sleeping swan, doth float
Upon the silver waves of thy sweet singing,
    And thine doth like an Angel sit   75
    Beside the helm conducting it
Whilst all the winds with melody are ringing.
    It seems to float ever—forever—
    Upon that many winding River
    Between mountains, woods, abysses,   80
    A Paradise of wildernesses,
Till like one in slumber bound
Borne to the Ocean, I float down, around,
Into a Sea profound, of ever-spreading sound.

6. The voice attempts to describe, in a dizzying whirl of optical paradoxes, what it feels like to look upon the naked essence of love and beauty.

Meanwhile thy Spirit lifts its pinions[7]   85
In Music's most serene dominions,
Catching the winds that fan that happy Heaven.
And we sail on, away, afar,
Without a course—without a star—
But by the instinct of sweet Music driven   90
Till through Elysian garden islets
By thee, most beautiful of pilots,
Where never mortal pinnace[8] glided,
The boat of my desire is guided—
Realms where the air we breathe is Love   95
Which in the winds and on the waves doth move,
Harmonizing this Earth with what we feel above.

We have past Age's icy caves,
And Manhood's dark and tossing waves
And Youth's smooth ocean, smiling to betray;   100
Beyond the glassy gulphs we flee
Of shadow-peopled Infancy,
Through Death and Birth to a diviner day,[9]
A Paradise of vaulted bowers
Lit by downward-gazing flowers   105
And watery paths that wind between
Wildernesses calm and green,
Peopled by shapes too bright to see,
And rest, having beheld—somewhat like thee,
Which walk upon the sea, and chaunt melodiously!   110

From *Act III*

SCENE I—*Heaven.* JUPITER *on his Throne;* THETIS *and the other Deities assembled.*

JUPITER. Ye congregated Powers of Heaven who share
    The glory and the strength of him ye serve,
    Rejoice! henceforth I am omnipotent.
    All else had been subdued to me—alone
    The soul of man, like unextinguished fire,   5
    Yet burns towards Heaven with fierce reproach and doubt
    And lamentation and reluctant prayer,
    Hurling up insurrection, which might make
    Our antique empire insecure, though built
    On eldest faith, and Hell's coeval,[1] fear.   10
    And though my curses through the pendulous[2] air
    Like snow on herbless peaks, fall flake by flake
    And cling to it[3]—though under my wrath's night

7. Wings.
8. Small boat.
9. Asia is describing what it feels like to be transfigured—in the image of moving backward down the stream of time, through youth and infancy and birth it-self, in order to die to this life and be born again to a "diviner" existence.
1. Of the same age.
2. Suspending.
3. "It" is "the soul of man," line 5 (as also in lines 14 and 16).

It climb the crags of life, step after step,
Which wound it, as ice wounds unsandalled feet,   15
It yet remains supreme o'er misery,
Aspiring . . . unrepressed; yet soon to fall:
Even now have I begotten a strange wonder,
That fatal Child,[4] the terror of the Earth,
Who waits but till the destined Hour arrive,   20
Bearing from Demogorgon's vacant throne
The dreadful might of ever living limbs
Which clothed that awful spirit unbeheld—
To redescend, and trample out the spark . . .[5]

Pour forth Heaven's wine, Idæan Ganymede,[6]   25
And let it fill the dædal cups like fire
And from the flower-inwoven soil divine
Ye all triumphant harmonies arise
As dew from Earth under the twilight stars;
Drink! be the nectar circling through your veins   30
The soul of joy, ye ever-living Gods,
Till exultation burst in one wide voice
Like music from Elysian winds.—
                              And thou
Ascend beside me, veiled in the light
Of the desire which makes thee one with me,   35
Thetis, bright Image of Eternity!—
When thou didst cry, "Insufferable might![7]
God! spare me! I sustain not the quick flames,
The penetrating presence; all my being,
Like him whom the Numidian seps[8] did thaw   40
Into a dew with poison, is dissolved,
Sinking through its foundations"—even then
Two mighty spirits, mingling, made a third
Mightier than either—which unbodied now
Between us, floats, felt, although unbeheld,   45
Waiting the incarnation, which ascends—
Hear ye the thunder of the fiery wheels
Griding[9] the winds?—from Demogorgon's throne.—
Victory! victory! Feel'st thou not, O World,
The Earthquake of his chariot thundering up   50
Olympus?
           [*The Car of the* HOUR *arrives.* DEMOGORGON *descends and
           moves towards the Throne of* JUPITER.]
           Awful Shape, what art thou? Speak!
DEMOGORGON. Eternity—demand no direr name.

---

4. The son of Jupiter and Thetis; Jupiter
believes that he has begotten a child
who will assume the bodily form of the
conquered Demogorgon and then return
to announce his victory and to trample
out the resistance of Prometheus.
5. The "spark" of Prometheus' defiance.
6. Ganymede had been seized on Mt.
Ida by an eagle and carried to heaven to
be Jupiter's cupbearer. "dædal": skill-

fully wrought (from the name of the
Greek craftsman, Dædalus).
7. This description of the sexual union
of Jupiter and Thetis is a grotesque
parody of the reunion of Prometheus
and Asia.
8. A serpent of Numidia (North Africa)
whose bite was thought to cause putrefaction.
9. Cutting with a rasping sound.

Descend, and follow me down the abyss.
I am thy child,[1] as thou wert Saturn's child,
Mightier than thee; and we must dwell together   55
Henceforth in darkness.—Lift thy lightnings not.
The tyranny of Heaven none may retain,
Or reassume, or hold succeeding thee . . .
Yet if thou wilt—as 'tis the destiny
Of trodden worms to writhe till they are dead—   60
Put forth thy might.

JUPITER.   Detested prodigy!
Even thus beneath the deep Titanian prisons[2]
I trample thee! . . . thou lingerest?

                                   Mercy! mercy!
No pity—no release, no respite! . . . Oh,
That thou wouldst make mine enemy my judge.   65
Even where he hangs, seared by my long revenge
On Caucasus—he would not doom me thus.—
Gentle and just and dreadless, is he not
The monarch of the world?[3] what then art thou? . . .
No refuge! no appeal— . . .

                         Sink with me then—   70
We two will sink on the wide waves of ruin
Even as a vulture and a snake outspent
Drop, twisted in inextricable fight,[4]
Into a shoreless sea.—Let Hell unlock
Its mounded Oceans of tempestuous fire,   75
And whelm on them into the bottomless void
This desolated world and thee and me,
The conqueror and the conquered, and the wreck
Of that for which they combated.

                               Ai! Ai!
The elements obey me not . . . I sink . . .   80
Dizzily down—ever, forever, down—
And, like a cloud, mine enemy above
Darkens my fall with victory!—Ai, Ai![5]

From SCENE IV—*A Forest. In the Background a Cave.*
PROMETHEUS, ASIA, PANTHEA, IONE, *and the* SPIRIT OF THE EARTH.[6]

*　*　*

1. Ironically, and in a figurative sense:
Demogorgon's function follows from Jupiter's actions.
2. After they overthrew the Titans,
Jupiter and the Olympian gods had
imprisoned them in Tartarus, deep
beneath the earth.
3. The ultimate irony: Jupiter appeals to
those very qualities of Prometheus for
which he has hitherto persecuted him,
begging for a mercy which Prometheus
has already granted him; but Prometheus' change from vengefulness to
mercy is in fact the cause of Jupiter's
present downfall.

4. The eagle (or vulture) and the snake
locked in equal combat—a favorite Shelleyan image.
5. Jupiter's scream is to be imagined
diminishing to silence.
6. After Jupiter's annihilation (described
in Scene ii), Hercules unbinds Prometheus, who is reunited with Asia and retires to a cave "where we will sit and
talk of time and change / * * * ourselves unchanged." In the speech which
concludes the act (reprinted here) the
Spirit of the Hour describes what happened in the human world when he
sounded the apocalyptic trumpet.

[*The* SPIRIT OF THE HOUR *enters.*]

PROMETHEUS. We feel what thou hast heard and seen—yet speak.

SPIRIT OF THE HOUR. Soon as the sound had ceased whose thunder filled
The abysses of the sky, and the wide earth,
There was a change . . . the impalpable thin air 100
And the all-circling sunlight were transformed
As if the sense of love dissolved in them
Had folded itself round the sphered world.
My vision then grew clear and I could see
Into the mysteries of the Universe.[7] 105
Dizzy as with delight I floated down,
Winnowing the lightsome air with languid plumes,
My coursers sought their birthplace in the sun
Where they henceforth will live exempt from toil,
Pasturing flowers of vegetable fire— 110
And where my moonlike car will stand within
A temple, gazed upon by Phidian forms,[8]
Of thee, and Asia and the Earth, and me
And you fair nymphs, looking the love we feel,
In memory of the tidings it has borne, 115
Beneath a dome fretted with graven flowers,
Poised on twelve columns of resplendent stone
And open to the bright and liquid sky.
Yoked to it by an amphisbænic snake[9]
The likeness of those winged steeds will mock[1] 120
The flight from which they find repose.—Alas,
Whither has wandered now my partial[2] tongue
When all remains untold which ye would hear!—
As I have said, I floated to the Earth:
It was, as it is still, the pain of bliss 125
To move, to breathe, to be; I wandering went
Among the haunts and dwellings of mankind
And first was disappointed not to see
Such mighty change as I had felt within
Expressed in outward things; but soon I looked, 130
And behold! thrones were kingless, and men walked
One with the other even as spirits do,
None fawned, none trampled; hate, disdain or fear,
Self-love or self-contempt on human brows
No more inscribed, as o'er the gate of hell, 135
"All hope abandon, ye who enter here";[3]
None frowned, none trembled, none with eager fear

7. I.e., the earth's atmosphere clarifies, no longer refracting the sunlight, and so allows the Spirit of the Hour to see what was happening on earth.
8. The crescent-shaped ("moonlike") chariot, its apocalytpic mission accomplished, will be frozen to stone, and will be surrounded by the sculptured forms of other agents in the drama. Phidias (5th century B.C.) was the noblest of Greek sculptors.

9. A mythical snake with a head at either end; it serves here as a symbolic warning that a reversal of the process is always possible. Cf. IV.561–69.
1. "Imitate" and also, in their immobility, "mock at" the flight they represent.
2. "Biased," or, possibly, "telling only part of the story."
3. The inscription over the gate of hell in Dante's *Inferno* III.9.

Gazed on another's eye of cold command
Until the subject of a tyrant's will
Became, worse fate, the abject of his own[4]   140
Which spurred him, like an outspent horse, to death.
None wrought his lips in truth-entangling lines
Which smiled the lie his tongue disdained to speak;
None with firm sneer trod out in his own heart
The sparks of love and hope, till there remained   145
Those bitter ashes, a soul self-consumed,
And the wretch crept, a vampire among men,
Infecting all with his own hideous ill.
None talked that common, false, cold, hollow talk
Which makes the heart deny the yes it breathes   150
Yet question that unmeant hypocrisy
With such a self-mistrust as has no name.
And women, too, frank, beautiful and kind
As the free Heaven which rains fresh light and dew
On the wide earth, past: gentle radiant forms,   155
From custom's evil taint exempt and pure;
Speaking the wisdom once they could not think,
Looking emotions once they feared to feel
And changed to all which once they dared not be,
Yet being now, made Earth like Heaven—nor pride   160
Nor jealousy nor envy nor ill shame,
The bitterest of those drops of treasured gall,
Spoilt the sweet taste of the nepenthe,[5] love.

Thrones, altars, judgement-seats and prisons; wherein
And beside which, by wretched men were borne   165
Sceptres, tiaras, swords and chains, and tomes
Of reasoned wrong, glozed on[6] by ignorance,
Were like those monstrous and barbaric shapes,
The ghosts of a no more remembered fame,
Which from their unworn obelisks[7] look forth   170
In triumph o'er the palaces and tombs
Of those who were their conquerors, mouldering round.
Those imaged to the pride of Kings and Priests
A dark yet mighty faith, a power as wide
As is the world it wasted, and are now   175
But an astonishment; even so the tools
And emblems of its last captivity
Amid the dwellings of the peopled Earth,
Stand, not o'erthrown, but unregarded now.
And those foul shapes, abhorred by God and man—   180
Which under many a name and many a form
Strange, savage, ghastly, dark and execrable

4. I.e., he was so abjectly enslaved that
his own will accorded with the tyrants's
will.
5. A drug (probably opium) that brings
forgetfulness of pain and sorrow.
6. Annotated, explained.
7. The Egyptian obelisks (tapering
shafts of stone), brought to Rome by
its conquering armies, included hieroglyphs which—since they were still
undeciphered in Shelley's time—seemed
"monstrous and barbaric shapes" (line
170).

Were Jupiter,[8] the tyrant of the world;
And which the nations panic-stricken served
With blood, and hearts broken by long hope, and love   185
Dragged to his altars soiled and garlandless
And slain amid men's unreclaiming tears,
Flattering the thing they feared, which fear was hate—
Frown, mouldering fast, o'er their abandoned shrines.
The painted veil, by those who were, called life,[9]   190
Which mimicked, as with colours idly spread,
All men believed and hoped, is torn aside—
The loathsome mask has fallen, the man remains
Sceptreless, free, uncircumscribed—but man:
Equal, unclassed, tribeless, and nationless,   195
Exempt from awe, worship, degree,—the King
Over himself; just, gentle, wise—but man:
Passionless? no—yet free from guilt or pain
Which were, for his will made, or suffered them,
Nor yet exempt, though ruling them like slaves,   200
From chance and death and mutability,
The clogs of that which else might oversoar
The loftiest star of unascended Heaven
Pinnacled dim in the intense inane.[10]

From Act IV[1]

SCENE—*A Part of the Forest near the Cave of* PROMETHEUS.

* * *

IONE.   Even whilst we speak
New notes arise . . . What is that awful sound?   185

---

8. The "foul shapes" (line 180) were statues of the gods who, whatever their names, were all really manifestations of Jupiter.

9. I.e., which was thought to be life by men as they were before their regeneration.

10. I.e., a dim point in the extreme of empty space. The sense of lines 198–204 is: if regenerate man were to be released from all earthly and biological impediments ("clogs"), he would become what even the stars are not—a pure ideal.

1. The original drama, completed in the spring of 1819, consisted of three acts. Later that year Shelley added a jubilant fourth act. In Revelation xxi, the apocalyptic replacement of the old world by "a new heaven and new earth" had been symbolized by the marriage of the Lamb with the New Jerusalem. Shelley's fourth act, somewhat like the conclusion of Blake's *Jerusalem,* expands this figure into a cosmic epithalamion, representing a union of divided elements which enacts everywhere the reunion of Prometheus and Asia that is taking place off-stage.

Shelley's model is the Renaissance masque, which combines song and dance with spectacular displays. Panthea and Ione serve as commentators on the action, which is divided into three episodes. In the first episode, omitted here, the purified "Spirits of the human mind" unite in a ritual dance with the Hours of the glad new day. In the second episode (below, lines 194–318), there appear emblematic representations of the moon and the earth, each bearing an infant whose hour has come round at last; Shelley based this description in part on Chapter 1 of Ezekiel, the vision of the chariot of divine glory, which had traditionally been interpreted as a portent of apocalypse. The third episode (lines 319–502) is the bacchanalian dance of the love-intoxicated moon around her brother and paramour, the rejuvenescent earth. By way of coda (lines 549 to the end), Demogorgon calls upon all beings to hear his proclamation of the moral significance of this great drama of man's self-betrayal and self-redemption.

PANTHEA. 'Tis the deep music of the rolling world
   Kindling within the strings of the waved air
   Æolian modulations.[2]
IONE.   Listen too,
   How every pause is filled with under-notes,
   Clear, silver, icy, keen, awakening tones   190
   Which pierce the sense and live within the soul
   As the sharp stars pierce Winter's chrystal air
   And gaze upon themselves within the sea.
PANTHEA. But see, where through two openings in the forest
   Which hanging branches overcanopy,   195
   And where two runnels of a rivulet
   Between the close moss violet-inwoven
   Have made their path of melody, like sisters
   Who part with sighs that they may meet in smiles,
   Turning their dear disunion to an isle   200
   Of lovely grief, a wood of sweet sad thoughts;
   Two visions of strange radiance float upon
   The Ocean-like inchantment of strong sound
   Which flows intenser, keener, deeper yet
   Under the ground and through the windless air.   205
IONE. I see a chariot like that thinnest boat
   In which the Mother of the Months is borne
   By ebbing light into her western cave
   When she upsprings from interlunar dreams,[3]
   O'er which is curved an orblike canopy   210
   Of gentle darkness, and the hills and woods
   Distinctly seen through that dusk aery veil
   Regard[4] like shapes in an enchanter's glass;
   Its wheels are solid clouds, azure and gold,
   Such as the genii of the thunderstorm   215
   Pile on the floor of the illumined sea
   When the Sun rushes under it; they roll
   And move and grow as with an inward wind.
   Within it sits a winged Infant, white
   Its countenance like the whiteness of bright snow,   220
   Its plumes are as feathers of sunny frost,
   Its limbs gleam white, through the wind-flowing folds
   Of its white robe, woof of ætherial pearl.
   Its hair is white,—the brightness of white light
   Scattered in strings,[5] yet its two eyes are Heavens   225
   Of liquid darkness, which the Deity
   Within, seems pouring, as a storm is poured
   From jagged clouds, out of their arrowy lashes,

2. I.e., evoking music like that of the Eolian harp.

3. I.e., the chariot is a thin crescent-shape, like the new moon, when it carries within it the outline of the old moon ("Mother of the Months") to the cave where she is reborn during the "interlunar" period—i.e., when the moon is entirely invisible.

4. Appear.

5. The infant resembles "one like unto the Son of man" in Revelation i.13–14: "His head and his hairs were white like wool, as white as snow." The description that follows, of the light radiated from the infant's eyes, echoes the description in Ezekiel's vision, i.27–8, of the "brightness round about" that "was the appearance of the likeness of the glory of the Lord."

Tempering the cold and radiant air around
With fire that is not brightness;[6] in its hand   230
It sways a quivering moonbeam, from whose point
A guiding power directs the chariot's prow
Over its wheeled clouds which as they roll
Over the grass and flowers and waves, wake sounds
Sweet as a singing rain of silver dew.   235
PANTHEA. And from the other opening in the wood
Rushes with loud and whirlwind harmony
A sphere, which is as many thousand spheres,
Solid as chrystal, yet through all its mass
Flow, as through empty space, music and light: 240
Ten thousand orbs involving and involved,[7]
Purple and azure, white and green and golden,
Sphere within sphere, and every space between
Peopled with unimaginable shapes
Such as ghosts dream dwell in·the lampless deep   245
Yet each intertranspicuous,[8] and they whirl
Over each other with a thousand motions
Upon a thousand sightless[9] axles spinning
And with the force of self-destroying swiftness,
Intensely, slowly, solemnly roll on—   250
Kindling with mingled sounds, and many tones.
Intelligible words and music wild.—
With mighty whirl the multitudinous Orb
Grinds the bright brook into an azure mist
Of elemental subtlety, like light,   255
And the wild odour of the forest flowers,
The music of the living grass and air,
The emerald light of leaf-entangled beams
Round its intense, yet self-conflicting[1] speed,
Seem kneaded into one aerial mass   260
Which drowns the sense. Within the Orb itself,
Pillowed upon its alabaster arms
Like to a child o'erwearied with sweet toil,
On its own folded wings and wavy hair
The Spirit of the Earth is laid asleep,   265
And you can see its little lips are moving
Amid the changing light of their own smiles
Like one who talks of what he loves in dream—
IONE. 'Tis only mocking[2] the Orb's harmony. . .

6. Shelley knew, from the account by Sir Humphry Davy, Herschel's discovery (1800) that there are what Herschel called "dark rays"—i.e., infrared radiation; Davy suggested that the moon gave off such rays.
7. The transparent sphere is an emblem of earth. The description of its spinning and that of its interior orbs echoes both Ezekiel i.15–17–"the appearance of the wheels and their work . . . was as it were a wheel in the middle of a wheel" —and *Paradise Lost* V.620–24, which de-scribes the "mystical dance" of the angels in heaven, whose movements resemble the revolving spheres of the planets: "mazes intricate, / Eccentric, intervolved, yet regular / Then most, when most irregular they seem."
8. I.e., transparent, so that each can be seen through the others.
9. Invisible.
1. Because its component spheres are spinning in opposed directions.
2. Imitating.

PANTHEA. And from a star upon its forehead, shoot,   270
   Like swords of azure fire, or golden spears
With tyrant-quelling myrtle[3] overtwined,
Embleming Heaven and Earth united now,
Vast beams like spokes of some invisible wheel
Which whirl as the Orb whirls, swifter than thought,   275
Filling the abyss with sunlike lightenings,
And perpendicular now, and now transverse,
Pierce the dark soil, and as they pierce and pass
Make bare the secrets of the Earth's deep heart,[4]
Infinite mine of adamant[5] and gold,   280
Valueless[6] stones and unimagined gems,
And caverns on chrystalline columns poised
With vegetable silver overspread,
Wells of unfathomed fire, and watersprings
Whence the great Sea, even as a child, is fed   285
Whose vapours clothe Earth's monarch mountain-tops
With kingly, ermine snow; the beams flash on
And make appear the melancholy ruins
Of cancelled cycles;[7] anchors, beaks of ships,
Planks turned to marble, quivers, helms and spears   290
And gorgon-headed targes,[8] and the wheels
Of scythed chariots,[9] and the emblazonry
Of trophies, standards and armorial beasts[1]
Round which Death laughed, sepulchred emblems
Of dead Destruction, ruin within ruin!   295
The wrecks beside of many a city vast,
Whose population which the Earth grew over
Was mortal but not human;[2] see, they lie,
Their monstrous works and uncouth skeletons,
Their statues, homes, and fanes;[3] prodigious shapes   300
Huddled in grey annihilation, split,
Jammed in the hard black deep; and over these
The anatomies[4] of unknown winged things,
And fishes which were isles of living scale,
And serpents, bony chains, twisted around   305
The iron crags, or within heaps of dust
To which the tortuous strength of their last pangs
Had crushed the iron crags;—and over these
The jagged alligator and the might
Of earth-convulsing behemoth,[5] which once   310
Were monarch beasts, and on the slimy shores

3. The myrtle, sacred to Venus, symbolizes love.
4. I.e., the star on the infant's forehead radiates penetrating beams which (like modern x-rays) reveal what lies beneath the surface of the earth.
5. Very hard rock.
6. Priceless.
7. I.e., of civilizations that flourished, then disappeared.
8. Shields embossed with a gorgon's head. "Helms": helmets.

9. Ancient war-chariots sometimes had steel blades fastened to the revolving wheels.
1. Animals in heraldic insignia.
2. I.e., a pre-human race of beings which once overspread the earth.
3. Temples.
4. Skeletons.
5. The huge land-animal described in Job xl.15–24. Shelley apparently identifies the Leviathan, the sea-beast in Job, as a huge, extinct alligator (line 309).

And weed-overgrown continents of Earth
Increased and multiplied like summer worms
On an abandoned corpse, till the blue globe
Wrapt Deluge round it like a cloak, and they   315
Yelled, gaspt and were abolished; or some God
Whose throne was in a Comet, past, and cried—
"Be not!"—And like my words they were no more.[6]

THE EARTH

The joy, the triumph, the delight, the madness,
The boundless, overflowing, bursting gladness,
The vaporous exultation, not to be confined![7]   320
Ha! ha! the animation of delight
Which wraps me, like an atmosphere of light,
And bears me as a cloud is borne by its own wind!

THE MOON

Brother mine, calm wanderer,   325
Happy globe of land and air,
Some Spirit[8] is darted like a beam from thee,
Which penetrates my frozen frame
And passes with the warmth of flame—
With love and odour and deep melody   330
Through me, through me!—

THE EARTH

Ha! ha! the caverns of my hollow mountains,
My cloven fire-crags, sound-exulting fountains
Laugh with a vast and inextinguishable laughter.
The Oceans and the Desarts and the Abysses   335
And the deep air's unmeasured wildernesses
Answer from all their clouds and billows, echoing after.

They cry aloud as I do—"Sceptred Curse,[9]
Who all our green and azure Universe
Threatenedst to muffle round with black destruction, sending   340
A solid cloud to rain hot thunderstones,
And splinter and knead down my children's bones,
All I bring forth, to one void mass battering and blending,

"Until each craglike tower and storied column,
Palace and Obelisk and Temple solemn,   345

6. According to the theory of "Catastrophism" proposed by G. F. Cuvier, *Researches on Fossil Bones* (1812), successive geologic layers of fossils are evidence of a sequence of catastrophes—volcanic upheavals and gigantic floods—each of which wiped out the forms of life that then existed. Shelley proposes two hypotheses (lines 314–18): either the floods originated from some cataclysm on earth, or else they were prodigious tides caused by the gravitational pull of a passing comet.

In writing this passage, Shelley recalled Keats's *Endymion* III.123–36, which described the remains on the ocean floor of extinct cultures and animal species.
7. Literally, the earth's gases are bursting out through its volcanoes.
8. Physically, the gravitational force exerted by the earth on the satellite moon.
9. Jupiter.

My imperial mountains crowned with cloud and snow and fire,
  My sea-like forests, every blade and blossom
  Which finds a grave or cradle in my bosom,
Were stamped by thy strong hate into a lifeless mire,

    "How art thou sunk, withdrawn, cover'd—drunk up   350
    By thirsty nothing, as the brackish [1] cup
Drained by a Desart-troop, a little drop for all;
    And from beneath, around, within, above,
    Filling thy void annihilation, Love
Bursts in like light on caves cloven by thunderball."   355

THE MOON

  The snow upon my lifeless mountains
  Is loosened into living fountains,
My solid Oceans flow and sing and shine
  A spirit from my heart bursts forth,
  It clothes with unexpected birth   360
My cold bare bosom: Oh! it must be thine
      On mine, on mine!

  Gazing on thee I feel, I know,
  Green stalks burst forth, and bright flowers grow
And living shapes upon my bosom move: 365
  Music is in the sea and air,
  Winged clouds soar here and there,
Dark with the rain new buds are dreaming of:
      'Tis Love, all Love!

THE EARTH

  It interpenetrates my granite mass,   370
  Through tangled roots and trodden clay doth pass
Into the utmost leaves and delicatest flowers;
  Upon the winds, among the clouds 'tis spread,
  It wakes a life in the forgotten dead,
They breathe a spirit up from their obscurest bowers,   375

  And like a storm, bursting its cloudy prison
  With thunder and with whirlwind, has arisen
Out of the lampless caves of unimagined being,
  With earthquake shock and swiftness making shiver
  Thought's stagnant chaos, unremoved forever,   380
Till Hate and Fear and Pain, light-vanquished shadows, fleeing,

  Leave Man, who was a many-sided mirror
  Which could distort to many a shape of error
This true fair world of things—a Sea reflecting Love;
  Which over all his kind, as the Sun's Heaven   385
  Gliding o'er Ocean, smooth, serene and even,
Darting from starry depths radiance and light, doth move,

---

1. Slightly salty.

Leave Man, even as a leprous child is left
Who follows a sick beast to some warm cleft
Of rocks, through which the might of healing springs is poured;
  Then when it wanders home with rosy smile   391
  Unconscious, and its mother fears awhile
It is a Spirit—then, weeps on her child restored.[2]

Man, oh, not men[3]! a chain of linked thought,
Of love and might to be divided not,   395
Compelling the elements with adamantine stress—
  As the Sun rules,[4] even with a tyrant's gaze,
  The unquiet Republic of the maze
Of Planets, struggling fierce towards Heaven's free wilderness.

Man, one harmonious Soul of many a soul   400
  Whose nature is its own divine controul
Where all things flow to all, as rivers to the sea;
  Familiar acts are beautiful through love;
  Labour and Pain and Grief in life's green grove
Sport like tame beasts—none knew how gentle they could be! 405

His Will, with all mean passions, bad delights,
And selfish cares, its trembling satellites,
A spirit ill to guide, but mighty to obey,
  Is as a tempest-winged ship, whose helm
  Love rules, through waves which dare not overwhelm,   410
Forcing Life's wildest shores to own its sovereign sway.

All things confess his strength.—Through the cold mass
Of marble and of colour his dreams pass;
Bright threads, whence mothers weave the robes their children
    wear;
  Language is a perpetual Orphic song,[5]   415
  Which rules with Dædal harmony a throng
Of thoughts and forms, which else senseless and shapeless were.

The Lightning is his slave;[6] Heaven's utmost deep
Gives up her stars, and like a flock of sheep
They pass before his eye, are numbered, and roll on!   420
  The Tempest is his steed,—he strides the air;
  And the abyss shouts from her depth laid bare,
"Heaven, hast thou secrets? Man unveils me; I have none."

THE MOON
The shadow of white Death has past

2. A reminiscence of the legend of King Bladud of Britain who, a banished leper, was following a lost swine and stumbled upon the hot springs (now in the town of Bath), which cured him.
3. Human society, once splintered by hate, is now united by love into a single macrocosmic Man.
4. By gravitational force.
5. Like the music of Orpheus, which attracted and controlled beasts, rocks, and trees. "dædal": skillful, intricate.
6. The Earth describes regenerate man's scientific and technological triumphs.

From my path in Heaven at last,   425
A clinging shroud of solid frost and sleep—
And through my newly-woven bowers
Wander happy paramours
Less mighty, but as mild as those who keep
          Thy vales more deep.   430

THE EARTH

As the dissolving warmth of Dawn may fold
A half-unfrozen dewglobe, green and gold
And chrystalline, till it becomes a winged mist
    And wanders up the vault of the blue Day,
    Outlives the noon, and on the Sun's last ray   435
Hang o'er the Sea—a fleece of fire and amethyst—

THE MOON

Thou art folded, thou art lying
In the light which is undying
Of thine own joy and Heaven's smile divine;
    All suns and constellations shower   440
    On thee a light, a life, a power
Which doth array thy sphere—thou pourest thine
          On mine, on mine!

THE EARTH

I spin beneath my pyramid of night[7]
Which points into the Heavens, dreaming delight,   445
Murmuring victorious joy in my enchanted sleep;
    As a youth lulled in love-dreams, faintly sighing,
    Under the shadow of his beauty lying
Which round his rest a watch of light and warmth doth keep.

THE MOON

As in the soft and sweet eclipse   450
When soul meets soul on lovers' lips,
High hearts are calm and brightest eyes are dull;
    So when thy shadow falls on me[8]
    Then am I mute and still,—by thee
Covered; of thy love, Orb most beautiful,   455
          Full, oh, too full!—

Thou art speeding round the Sun
Brightest World of many a one,
Green and azure sphere, which shinest
    With a light which is divinest   460
    Among all the lamps of Heaven
To whom life and light is given;
    I, thy chrystal paramour,

---

7. The conical shadow cast by the earth
as it intercepts the sun's light.

8. In the eclipse of the moon, when it
enters the earth's shadow.

Borne beside thee by a power
Like the polar Paradise,
Magnet-like, of lovers' eyes;[9]   465
I, a most enamoured maiden
Whose weak brain is overladen
With the pleasure of her love—
Maniac-like around thee move,
Gazing, an insatiate bride,   470
On thy form from every side
Like a Mænad round the cup
Which Agave lifted up
In the weird Cadmæan forest.—[1]
Brother, wheresoe'er thou soarest   475
I must hurry, whirl and follow
Through the Heavens wide and hollow,
Sheltered by the warm embrace
Of thy soul, from hungry space,
Drinking, from thy sense and sight   480
Beauty, majesty, and might,
As a lover or a chameleon
Grows like what it looks upon,
As a violet's gentle eye
Gazes on the azure sky   485
Until its hue grows like what it beholds,
As a grey and watery mist
Glows like solid amethyst
Athwart the western mountain it enfolds,   490
When the sunset sleeps
      Upon its snow—

THE EARTH

And the weak day weeps[2]
      That it should be so.
O gentle Moon, the voice of thy delight   495
Falls on me like thy clear and tender light
Soothing the seaman, borne the summer night
      Through isles forever calm;
O gentle Moon, thy chrystal accents pierce
The caverns of my Pride's deep Universe,   500
Charming the tyger Joy, whose tramplings fierce
      Made wounds, which need thy balm.

* * *

DEMOGORGON

Man, who wert once a despot and a slave,—
A dupe and a deceiver,—a Decay,   550

---

9. As it circles the earth, the moon spins so as to keep the same side constantly toward it.
1. The Mænads were female participants in the ecstatic worship of Dionysus (Bacchus). Agave, daughter of King Cadmus, in a blind frenzy tore her own son Pentheus to bits when he was caught spying on the Dionysiac rites.
2. I.e., with the dew at nightfall.

A Traveller from the cradle to the grave
  Through the dim night of this immortal Day:

ALL

Speak—thy strong words may never pass away.

DEMOGORGON

This is the Day which down the void Abysm
At the Earth-born's spell[3] yawns for Heaven's Despotism,   555
  And Conquest is dragged Captive through the deep;[4]
Love from its awful throne of patient power
In the wise heart, from the last giddy hour
  Of dread endurance, from the slippery, steep,
And narrow verge of crag-like Agony, springs   560
And folds over the world its healing wings.

Gentleness, Virtue, Wisdom and Endurance,—
These are the seals of that most firm assurance
  Which bars the pit over Destruction's strength;
And if, with infirm hand, Eternity,   565
Mother of many acts and hours, should free
  The serpent that would clasp her with his length[5]—
These are the spells by which to reassume
An empire o'er the disentangled Doom.[6]

To suffer woes which Hope thinks infinite;   570
To forgive wrongs darker than Death or Night;
  To defy Power, which seems Omnipotent;
To love, and bear; to hope, till Hope creates
From its own wreck the thing it contemplates;
  Neither to change nor falter nor repent: 575
This, like thy glory, Titan! is to be
Good, great and joyous, beautiful and free;
This is alone Life, Joy, Empire and Victory.

1818–19   1820

The Cloud

I bring fresh showers for the thirsting flowers,
  From the seas and the streams;
I bear light shade for the leaves when laid

---

3. Prometheus' spell—i.e., his magical words of pity, in place of vengefulness.
4. Ephesians iv.8: "When [Christ] ascended up on high, he led captivity captive."
5. A final reminder that the serpent incessantly struggles to break loose and start the cycle all over again. Felicity must continue to be earned.
6. Shelley's four cardinal virtues (line 562), which seal the serpent in the pit, also constitute the formulas ("spells") by which to remaster him, should he again break loose. These virtues are expanded upon in the concluding lines (570–75).

In their noon-day dreams.
From my wings are shaken the dews that waken   5
    The sweet buds every one,
When rocked to rest on their mother's [1] breast,
    As she dances about the Sun.
I wield the flail of the lashing hail,
    And whiten the green plains under,   10
And then again I dissolve it in rain,
    And laugh as I pass in thunder.

I sift the snow on the mountains below,
    And their great pines groan aghast;
And all the night 'tis my pillow white,   15
    While I sleep in the arms of the blast.
Sublime on the towers of my skiey bowers,
    Lightning my pilot sits;
In a cavern under is fettered the thunder,
    It struggles and howls at fits;[2]   20
Over Earth and Ocean, with gentle motion,
    This pilot is guiding me,
Lured by the love of the genii that move
    In the depths of the purple sea;[3]
Over the rills, and the crags, and the hills,   25
    Over the lakes and the plains,
Wherever he dream, under mountain or stream,
    The Spirit he loves remains;
And I all the while bask in Heaven's blue smile,[4]
    Whilst he is dissolving in rains.   30

The sanguine Sunrise, with his meteor eyes,[5]
    And his burning plumes outspread,
Leaps on the back of my sailing rack,[6]
    When the morning star shines dead;
As on the jag of a mountain crag,   35
    Which an earthquake rocks and swings,
An eagle alit one moment may sit
    In the light of its golden wings.
And when Sunset may breathe, from the lit Sea beneath,
    Its ardours of rest and of love,   40
And the crimson pall[7] of eve may fall
    From the depth of Heaven above,
With wings folded I rest, on mine aëry nest,
    As still as a brooding dove.

1. I.e., the earth's.
2. Fitfully.
3. I.e., atmospheric electricity, guiding the cloud (line 17), discharges as lightning when "lured" by the attraction of an opposite charge.
4. The upper part of the cloud remains exposed to the sun.
5. I.e., bright as a burning meteor. The following line refers to the sun's corona.
6. High, broken clouds, driven by the wind.
7. Coverlet of rich material.

That orbed maiden with white fire laden 45
 Whom mortals call the Moon,
Glides glimmering o'er my fleece-like floor,
 By the midnight breezes strewn;
And wherever the beat of her unseen feet,
 Which only the angels hear, 50
May have broken the woof,[8] of my tent's thin roof,
 The stars peep behind her, and peer;
And I laugh to see them whirl and flee,
 Like a swarm of golden bees,
When I widen the rent in my wind-built tent, 55
 Till the calm rivers, lakes, and seas,
Like strips of the sky fallen through me on high,
 Are each paved with the moon and these.[9]

I bind the Sun's throne with a burning zone[1]
 And the Moon's with a girdle of pearl; 60
The volcanos are dim and the stars reel and swim
 When the whirlwinds my banner unfurl.
From cape to cape, with a bridge-like shape,
 Over a torrent sea,
Sunbeam-proof, I hang like a roof— 65
 The mountains its columns be!
The triumphal arch, through which I march
 With hurricane, fire, and snow,
When the Powers of the Air, are chained to my chair,
 Is the million-coloured Bow; 70
The sphere-fire[2] above its soft colours wove
 While the moist Earth was laughing below.

I am the daughter of Earth and Water,
 And the nursling of the Sky;
I pass through the pores, of the ocean and shores; 75
 I change, but I cannot die—
For after the rain, when with never a stain
 The pavilion of Heaven is bare,
And the winds and sunbeams, with their convex gleams,
 Build up the blue dome of Air[3]— 80
I silently laugh at my own cenotaph,[4]
 And out of the caverns of rain,
Like a child from the womb, like a ghost from the tomb,
 I arise, and unbuild it again.—

1820   1820

8. Texture.
9. I.e., the stars reflected in the water.
1. Girdle, belt.
2. The sunlight.
3. The blue color of the sky; the phenomenon, as Shelley indicates, results from the way "sunbeams" are filtered by the earth's atmosphere.
4. The memorial monument ("cenotaph") of the dead cloud is the cloudless blue dome of the sky.

To a Sky-Lark[1]

Hail to thee, blithe Spirit!
   Bird thou never wert—
That from Heaven, or near it,
   Pourest thy full heart
In profuse strains of unpremeditated art.   5

Higher still and higher
   From the earth thou springest
Like a cloud of fire;
   The blue deep thou wingest,
And singing still dost soar, and soaring ever singest.   10

In the golden lightning
   Of the sunken Sun—
O'er which clouds are brightning,
   Thou dost float and run;
Like an unbodied joy whose race is just begun.   15

The pale purple even
   Melts around thy flight,
Like a star of Heaven
   In the broad day-light
Thou art unseen,—but yet I hear thy shrill delight,   20

Keen as are the arrows
   Of that silver sphere,[2]
Whose intense lamp narrows
   In the white dawn clear
Until we hardly see—we feel that it is there.   25

All the earth and air
   With thy voice is loud,
As when Night is bare
   From one lonely cloud
The moon rains out her beams—and Heaven is overflowed.   30

What thou art we know not;
   What is most like thee?
From rainbow clouds there flow not
   Drops so bright to see
As from thy presence showers a rain of melody.   35

1. The European skylark is a small bird that sings only in flight, usually when it is too high to be visible.
   The bird, freed from the bonds of earth and soaring beyond the reach of all the physical senses except hearing, is made the emblem of a non-material spirit of pure joy, beyond the possibility of empirical knowledge; see lines 15, 31.
2. The morning star.

Like a Poet hidden
  In the light of thought,
Singing hymns unbidden,
  Till the world is wrought
To sympathy with hopes and fears it heeded not: 40

Like a high-born maiden
  In a palace-tower,
Soothing her love-laden
  Soul in secret hour,
With music sweet as love—which overflows her bower: 45

Like a glow-worm golden
  In a dell of dew,
Scattering unbeholden
  Its aerial hue
Among the flowers and grass which screen it from the view: 50

Like a rose embowered
  In its own green leaves—
By warm winds deflowered—
  Till the scent it gives
Makes faint with too much sweet heavy-winged thieves:[3]   55

Sound of vernal showers
  On the twinkling grass,
Rain-awakened flowers,
  All that ever was
Joyous, and clear and fresh, thy music doth surpass.   60

Teach us, Sprite[4] or Bird,
  What sweet thoughts are thine;
I have never heard
  Praise of love or wine
That panted forth a flood of rapture so divine: 65

Chorus Hymeneal[5]
  Or triumphal chaunt
Matched with thine would be all
  But an empty vaunt,
A thing wherein we feel there is some hidden want.   70

What objects are the fountains
  Of thy happy strain?
What fields or waves or mountains?
  What shapes of sky or plain?
What love of thine own kind? what ignorance of pain?   75

3. I.e., the "warm winds," line 53.   5. Marital (from Hymen, Greek god of
4. Spirit.   marriage).

With thy clear keen joyance
    Languor cannot be—
Shadow of annoyance
    Never came near thee;
Thou lovest—but ne'er knew love's sad satiety.   80

Waking or asleep,
    Thou of death must deem
Things more true and deep
    Than we mortals dream,
Or how could thy notes flow in such a chrystal stream?   85

We look before and after,
    And pine for what is not—
Our sincerest laughter
    With some pain is fraught—
Our sweetest songs are those that tell of saddest thought.   90

Yet if we could scorn
    Hate and pride and fear;
If we were things born
    Not to shed a tear,
I know not how thy joy we ever should come near.   95

Better than all measures
    Of delightful sound—
Better than all treasures
    That in books are found—
Thy skill to poet were, thou Scorner of the ground!   100

Teach me half the gladness
    That thy brain must know,
Such harmonious madness
    From my lips would flow
The world should listen then—as I am listening now.   105

1820   1820

Song of Apollo[1]

The sleepless Hours who watch me as I lie
    Curtained with star-enwoven tapestries
From the broad moonlight of the open sky;
    Fanning the busy dreams from my dim eyes,

1. Written, with the companion piece that follows, for the opening scene in Mary Shelley's verse drama *Midas*. Apollo, god of the sun, of healing, and of poetry and the other arts, sings this serenely Olympian hymn in a contest with Pan, the goatlike deity of flocks, forests, and wild life. In the play, old Tmolus, a mountain god who judges the contest, awards the prize to Apollo; when Midas, a mortal, objects, preferring Pan's song of earthly desire, passions, and suffering, Apollo affixes on him asses' ears.

Waken me when their mother, the grey Dawn,   5
Tells them that Dreams and that the moon is gone.

Then I arise; and climbing Heaven's blue dome,
    I walk over the mountains and the waves,
Leaving my robe upon the Ocean foam.
    My footsteps pave the clouds with fire; the caves   10
Are filled with my bright presence, and the air
Leaves the green Earth to my embraces bare.

The sunbeams are my shafts with which I kill
    Deceit, that loves the night and fears the day.
All men who do, or even imagine ill   15
    Fly[2] me; and from the glory of my ray
Good minds, and open actions take new might
Until diminished, by the reign of night.

I feed the clouds, the rainbows and the flowers
    With their ætherial colours; the moon's globe   20
And the pure stars in their eternal bowers
    Are cinctured[3] with my power as with a robe;
Whatever lamps on Earth or Heaven may shine
Are portions of one spirit; which is mine.

I stand at noon upon the peak of Heaven;   25
    Then with unwilling steps, I linger down
Into the clouds of the Atlantic even.
    For grief that I depart they weep and frown—
What look is more delightful, than the smile
With which I soothe them from the Western isle?   30

I am the eye with which the Universe
    Beholds itself, and knows it is divine.
All harmony of instrument and verse,
    All prophecy and medicine are mine;
All light of art or nature—to my song   35
Victory and praise, in its own right, belong.

1820   1824

Song of Pan[1]

From the forests and highlands
    We come, we come,
From the river-girt islands
    Where loud waves were dumb
Listening my sweet pipings.   5
        The wind in the reeds and the rushes,
        The bees on the bells of thyme,
        The birds in the myrtle bushes,
        The cicadæ[2] above in the lime,

2. Flee from.
3. Girdled.
1. Pan's reply to Apollo in his singing
contest. As against Apollo's divine

imperturbability, the god of the natural
world expresses quasi-human experiences
of desire, loss, and disillusionment.
2. Locusts.

And the lizards below in the grass,   10
Were silent as even old Tmolus was,
    Listening my sweet pipings.

Liquid Peneus[3] was flowing—
And all dark Tempe lay
In Olympus' shadow, outgrowing   15
    The light of the dying day,
    Speeded with my sweet pipings.
        The sileni and sylvans and fauns[4]
        And the nymphs of the woods and the waves,
    To the edge of the moist river-lawns   20
    And the brink of the dewy caves,
        And all that did then attend and follow
Were as silent for love, as you now, Apollo,
    For envy of my sweet pipings.

I sang of the dancing stars,   25
    I sang of the dædal[5] Earth,
And of Heaven, and the giant wars,[6]
    And Love and Death and Birth;
        And then I changed my pipings,
        Singing how, down the vales of Mænalus   30
    I pursued a maiden and clasped a reed.[7]
    Gods and men, we are all deluded thus!—
    It breaks in our bosom and then we bleed;
        They wept as, I think, both ye now would,
If envy or age had not frozen your blood,   35
    At the sorrow of my sweet pipings.

1820   1824

To Night[1]

Swiftly walk o'er the western wave,
        Spirit of Night!
Out of the misty eastern cave
Where, all the long and lone daylight
Thou wovest dreams of joy and fear,   5
Which make thee terrible and dear,
        Swift be thy flight!

Wrap thy form in a mantle grey,
        Star-inwrought!

---

3. The river Peneus flows through the lovely valley of Tempe, in northeastern Greece.
4. The male sileni, sylvans, and fauns, and the female nymphs, are all minor rural or woodland deities.
5. Intricately formed.
6. The wars of the Titans, sons of Earth, against the gods of Olympus.

7. Pan pursued the nymph, Syrinx, but as he caught her, she turned into a reed. From it he made Pan's pipe, the "syrinx."
1. Night and darkness, as opposed to daylight, are often for Shelley symbols of the primordial powers and revelations of the poetic imagination. See, e.g., the opening of *The Triumph of Life*, below.

Blind with thine hair the eyes of day,   10
Kiss her until she be wearied out—
Then wander o'er City and sea and land,
Touching all with thine opiate wand—
        Come, long-sought!

When I arose and saw the dawn   15
        I sighed for thee;
When Light rode high, and the dew was gone,
And noon lay heavy on flower and tree,
And the weary Day turned to his rest,[2]
Lingering like an unloved guest,   20
        I sighed for thee.

Thy brother Death came, and cried,
        Wouldst thou me?
Thy sweet child Sleep, the filmy-eyed,
Murmured like a noontide bee,   25
Shall I nestle near thy side?
Wouldst thou me? and I replied,
        No, not thee!

Death will come when thou art dead,
        Soon, too soon—   30
Sleep will come when thou art fled;
Of neither would I ask the boon
I ask of thee, beloved Night—
Swift be thine approaching flight,
        Come soon, soon!   35

1820   1824

To ——— [Music, When Soft Voices Die]

Music, when soft voices die,
Vibrates in the memory.—
Odours, when sweet violets sicken,
Live within the sense they quicken.—

Rose leaves, when the rose is dead,   5
Are heaped for the beloved's bed[3] —
And so thy thoughts,[4] when thou art gone,
Love itself shall slumber on. . . .

1821   1824

O World, O Life, O Time

O World, O Life, O Time,
On whose last steps I climb,

---

2. Here the "Day" is the male sun, not
the female "day" with whom the Spirit
of Night dallies in stanza 2.

3. I.e., the fallen petals form a bed for
the dead rose.
4. I.e., my thoughts of thee.

Trembling at that where I had stood before,
When will return the glory of your prime?
No more, O never more!   5

Out of the day and night
A joy has taken flight—
Fresh spring and summer [   ] and winter hoar
Move my faint heart with grief, but with delight
No more, O never more!   10

1824

Choruses from Hellas[1]

Worlds on Worlds[2]

Worlds on worlds are rolling ever
From creation to decay,
Like the bubbles on a river
Sparkling, bursting, borne away.
But *they*[3] are still immortal   5
Who through Birth's orient[4] portal
And Death's dark chasm hurrying to and fro,
Clothe their unceasing flight
In the brief dust and light
Gathered around their chariots as they go;   10
New shapes they still may weave,
New Gods, new Laws receive,
Bright or dim are they as the robes they last
On Death's bare ribs had cast.

A Power from the unknown God,   15
A Promethean Conqueror,[5] came;
Like a triumphal path he trod
The thorns of death and shame.
A mortal shape to him

1. *Hellas*, a closet drama written in the autumn of 1821, was inspired by the Greek war for independence against the Turks. In his Preface Shelley declared that he viewed this revolution as auguring the final overthrow of all tyranny. The choruses below are sung by Greek captive women. The first chorus describes the emergence of Christ into the revolving cycle of history; the second chorus concludes the drama.
2. "The popular notions of Christianity are represented in this chorus as true in their relation to the worship they superseded . . . without considering their merits in a relation more universal. . . . The concluding verses indicate a progressive state of more or less exalted existence. . . . Let it not be supposed that I mean to dogmatise upon a subject [i.e., the problem of evil, and the possibility

of its future elimination] upon which all men are equally ignorant. . . . That there is a true solution to the riddle, and that in our present state that solution is unattainable by us, are propositions that may be regarded as equally certain: meanwhile, as it is the province of the poet to attach himself to those ideas which exalt and ennoble humanity, let him be permitted to have conjectured the condition of that futurity towards which we are all impelled by an inextinguishable thirst for immortality . . ." [Shelley's note].
3. The immortal "beings which inhabit the planets and . . . clothe themselves in matter" [Shelley's note].
4. Eastern.
5. Christ, whom Shelley compares to Prometheus, who brought fire and the arts of civilization to mankind.

Was like the vapour dim 20
Which the orient planet animates with light;
Hell, Sin, and Slavery came
Like bloodhounds mild and tame,
Nor preyed, until their Lord had taken flight;
The moon of Mahomet[6] 25
Arose, and it shall set,
While blazoned as on Heaven's immortal noon
The cross leads generations on.[7]

Swift as the radiant shapes of sleep
From one whose dreams are Paradise 30
Fly, when the fond wretch wakes to weep,
And Day peers forth with her blank eyes;
So fleet, so faint, so fair,
The Powers of earth and air
Fled from the folding star[8] of Bethlehem: 35
Apollo, Pan, and Love,
And even Olympian Jove
Grew weak, for killing Truth had glared on them;
Our hills and seas and streams,
Dispeopled of their dreams, 40
Their waters turned to blood, their dew to tears,
Wailed for the golden years.

The World's Great Age[1]

The world's great age begins anew,
The golden years return,[2]
The earth doth like a snake renew
Her winter weeds[3] outworn;
Heaven smiles, and faiths and empires gleam
Like wrecks of a dissolving dream. 5

A brighter Hellas rears its mountains
From waves serener far,

---

6. The crescent, emblem of Mohammedanism, which was founded six centuries
after the birth of Christ.
7. The Roman emperor Constantine
was converted to Christianity when he
saw a bright cross imposed on the sun
at noon.
8. The star of evening, the time when
sheep are driven into the sheepfold.
Shelley goes on to describe the pagan
gods of earth and Olympus fleeing before the star of Bethlehem.
1. "Prophecies of wars, and rumours of
wars, etc., may safely be made by poet
or prophet in any age, but to anticipate
however darkly a period of regeneration
and happiness is a more hazardous exercise of the faculty which bards possess
or fain. It will remind the reader . . . of
Isaiah and Virgil, whose ardent spirits

. . . saw the possible and perhaps approaching state of society in which the
'lion shall lie down with the lamb,' and
'omnis feret omnia tellus.' Let these great
names be my authority and excuse"
[Shelley's note]. The quotations are
from Isaiah's millennial prophecy (e.g.,
Chapters xxv, lxv), and Vergil's prediction, in Eclogue IV, of a return of the
golden age, when "all the earth will produce all things." Shelley's comments
here, and in the title-footnote to *Worlds
on Worlds,* are cogent expressions of the
skeptical idealism of his maturity.
2. In Greek myth, the first period of history, when Saturn reigned, was the
golden age.
3. Clothes (especially mourning garments) as well as dead vegetation.

A new Peneus[4] rolls his fountains
   Against the morning-star,   10
Where fairer Tempes bloom, there sleep
Young Cyclads[5] on a sunnier deep.

A loftier Argo[6] cleaves the main,
   Fraught with a later prize;
Another Orpheus[7] sings again,   15
   And loves, and weeps, and dies;
A new Ulysses leaves once more
Calypso[8] for his native shore.

O, write no more the tale of Troy,
   If earth Death's scroll must be!   20
Nor mix with Laian[9] rage the joy
   Which dawns upon the free;
Although a subtler Sphinx renew
Riddles of death Thebes never knew.

Another Athens shall arise,   25
   And to remoter time
Bequeath, like sunset to the skies,
   The splendour of its prime,
And leave, if nought so bright may live,
All earth can take or Heaven can give.   30

Saturn and Love their long repose
   Shall burst, more bright and good
Than all who fell, than One who rose,
   Than many unsubdued;[1]
Not gold, not blood their altar dowers   35
But votive tears and symbol flowers.

O cease! must hate and death return?
   Cease! must men kill and die?
Cease! drain not to its dregs the urn
   Of bitter prophecy.
The world is weary of the past,   40
O, might it die or rest at last!

1821   1822

4. The river that flows through the beautiful vale of Tempe (line 11).
5. The Cyclades, islands in the Aegean Sea.
6. On which Jason sailed in his quest for the Golden Fleece.
7. The legendary player on the lyre who was torn to pieces by the frenzied Thracian women while he was mourning the death of his wife, Eurydice.
8. The nymph deserted by Ulysses on his voyage back from the Trojan War to his native Ithaca.
9. King Laius of Thebes was killed in a quarrel by his son Oedipus, who did not recognize his father. Shortly thereafter, Oedipus delivered Thebes from the ravages of the Sphinx by answering its riddle (lines 23–24):

1. "Saturn and Love were among the deities of a real or imaginary state of innocence and happiness. 'All' those 'who fell' [are] the Gods of Greece, Asia, and Egypt; the 'One who rose' [is] Jesus Christ ... and the 'many unsubdued' [are] the monstrous objects of the idolatry of China, India, the Antarctic islands, and the native tribes of America" [Shelley's note].

Adonais

An Elegy on the Death of John Keats, Author of Endymion, Hyperion, Etc.[1]

[Thou wert the morning star among the living,
Ere thy fair light had fled—
Now, having died, thou art as Hesperus, giving
New splendour to the dead.][2]

1

I weep for Adonais—he is dead!
O, weep for Adonais! though our tears
Thaw not the frost which binds so dear a head!
And thou, sad Hour,[3] selected from all years
To mourn our loss, rouse thy obscure compeers,   5
And teach them thine own sorrow, say: with me
Died Adonais; till the Future dares
Forget the Past, his fate and fame shall be
An echo and a light unto eternity!

2

Where wert thou mighty Mother,[4] when he lay,   10
When thy Son lay, pierced by the shaft which flies
In darkness?[5] where was lorn Urania

---

1. John Keats died in Rome February 23, 1821, and was buried there in the Protestant Cemetery. Shelley had met Keats, had invited him to be his guest at Pisa, and had gradually come to recognize him as "among the writers of the highest genius who have adorned our age" (Preface to *Adonais*). The name "Adonais" is derived from Adonis, the handsome youth who had been loved by the goddess Venus and slain by a wild boar; the function of the beast in this poem is attributed to the anonymous author of a vituperative review of Keats's *Endymion* in the *Quarterly Review*, April, 1818 (now known to be John Wilson Croker), whom Shelley mistakenly believed to be responsible for Keats's illness and death.

Shelley described *Adonais* in a letter as a "highly wrought piece of art." Its artistry consists in part in the care with which it follows the conventions of the pastoral elegy, established more than two thousand years earlier by the Greek Sicilian poets Theocritus, Bion, and Moschus—Shelley had himself translated into English Bion's *Lament for Adonis* and Moschus' *Lament for Bion*. We recognize the centuries-old poetic ritual in many verbal echoes, and in such devices as the mournful and accusing invocation to a muse (stanzas 2–4), the sympathetic participation of nature in the death of the poet (stanzas 14–17), the procession of appropriate mourners (stanzas 30–35), the denunciation of unworthy practitioners of the pastoral or literary art (stan-

zas 17, 27–29, 36–37); and above all in the shift from despair at the finality of human death (lines 64, 190: "*He* will awake no more, oh, never more!") to consolation in the sudden and contradictory discovery that the grave is a gate to a higher existence (line 343: "Peace, peace! he is not dead, he doth not sleep"). These familiar elements Shelley transforms into a densely symbolic poetic construction; *Adonais* ranks with Milton's *Lycidas* among the supreme examples of the exacting form of the pastoral elegy.

2. Shelley prefixed to *Adonais* a Greek epigram, attributed to Plato; this is Shelley's own translation of the Greek. (See also *The Triumph of Life*, below, line 256 and footnote.) The planet Venus appears both as the morning star, Lucifer, and the evening star, Hesperus or Vesper. Shelley makes of this phenomenon a key symbol for Adonais' triumph over death, in stanzas 44–46.

3. Shelley follows the classical mode of personifying the hours, which mark the passage of time and turn of the seasons.

4. Urania. She had originally been the Muse of astronomy, but the name was also an epithet for Venus. Shelley converts Venus Urania, who in Greek myth had been the lover of Adonis, into the mother of Adonais.

5. The allusion is to the anonymity of the review of *Endymion*. "Lorn": abandoned.

When Adonais died? With veiled eyes,
'Mid listening Echoes, in her Paradise
She sate, while one,[6] with soft enamoured breath,   15
Rekindled all the fading melodies,
With which, like flowers that mock the corse[7] beneath,
He had adorned and hid the coming bulk of death.

3

O, weep for Adonais—he is dead!
Wake, melancholy Mother, wake and weep!   20
Yet wherefore? Quench within their burning bed
Thy fiery tears, and let thy loud heart keep
Like his, a mute and uncomplaining sleep;
For he is gone, where all things wise and fair
Descend;—oh, dream not that the amorous Deep[8]   25
Will yet restore him to the vital air;
Death feeds on his mute voice, and laughs at our despair.

4

Most musical of mourners, weep again!
Lament anew, Urania!—He[9] died,
Who was the Sire of an immortal strain,   30
Blind, old, and lonely, when his country's pride,
The priest, the slave, and the liberticide,
Trampled and mocked with many a loathed rite
Of lust and blood; he went, unterrified,
Into the gulph of death; but his clear Sprite[1]   35
Yet reigns o'er earth; the third among the sons of light.[2]

5

Most musical of mourners, weep anew!
Not all to that bright station dared to climb;
And happier they their happiness who knew,
Whose tapers yet burn through that night of time   40
In which suns perished; others more sublime,
Struck by the envious wrath of man or God,
Have sunk, extinct in their refulgent prime;
And some yet live, treading the thorny road,
Which leads, through toil and hate, to Fame's serene abode.   45

6

But now, thy youngest, dearest one, has perished
The nursling of thy widowhood, who grew,
Like a pale flower by some sad maiden cherished,
And fed with true love tears, instead of dew;[3]
Most musical of mourners, weep anew!   50
Thy extreme[4] hope, the loveliest and the last,

6. I.e., the echo of Keats's voice in his poems.
7. Corpse.
8. Abyss.
9. Milton, regarded as precursor of the great poetic tradition in which Keats wrote: he had adopted Urania as the muse of *Paradise Lost*. Lines 31–35 describe Milton's life during the restoration of the Stuart monarchy.

1. Spirit.
2. The three are Milton and his great predecessors in epic poetry, Homer and Dante. The stanza following describes the lot of other poets, to Shelley's own time.
3. An allusion to an incident in Keats's *Isabella*.
4. Last, as well as highest.

The bloom, whose petals nipt before they blew[5]
Died on the promise of the fruit, is waste;
The broken lily lies—the storm is overpast.

7

To that high Capital,[6] where kingly Death   55
Keeps his pale court in beauty and decay,
He came; and bought, with price of purest breath,
A grave among the eternal.—Come away!
Haste, while the vault of blue Italian day
Is yet his fitting charnel-roof! while still   60
He lies, as if in dewy sleep he lay;
Awake him not! surely he takes his fill
Of deep and liquid rest, forgetful of all ill.

8

He will awake no more, oh, never more!—
Within the twilight chamber spreads apace,   65
The shadow of white Death, and at the door
Invisible Corruption waits to trace
His extreme way to her dim dwelling-place;
The eternal Hunger sits, but pity and awe
Soothe her pale rage, nor dares she to deface   70
So fair a prey, till darkness, and the law
Of change, shall o'er his sleep the mortal curtain draw.

9

O, weep for Adonais!—The quick[7] Dreams,
The passion-winged Ministers of thought,
Who were his flocks,[8] whom near the living streams   75
Of his young spirit he fed, and whom he taught
The love which was its music, wander not,—
Wander no more, from kindling brain to brain,
But droop there, whence they sprung; and mourn their lot
Round the cold heart, where, after their sweet pain,   80
They ne'er will gather strength, or find a home again.

10

And one[9] with trembling hands clasps his cold head,
And fans him with her moonlight wings, and cries:
"Our love, our hope, our sorrow, is not dead;
See, on the silken fringe of his faint eyes,   85
Like dew upon a sleeping flower, there lies
A tear some Dream has loosened from his brain."
Lost Angel of a ruined Paradise!
She knew not 'twas her own; as with no stain
She faded, like a cloud which had outwept its rain.   90

11

One from a lucid[1] urn of starry dew
Washed his light limbs as if embalming them;
Another clipt her profuse locks, and threw

---

5. Bloomed.
6. I.e., Rome.
7. Living.
8. The products of Keats's imagination,

figuratively represented (according to pastoral convention) as his sheep.
9. I.e., one of the Dreams (line 73).
1. Luminous.

The wreath upon him, like an anadem,[2]
Which frozen tears instead of pearls begem;   95
Another in her wilful grief would break
Her bow and winged reeds, as if to stem
A greater loss with one which was more weak;
And dull the barbed fire against his frozen cheek.

12

Another Splendour on his mouth alit,   100
That mouth, whence it was wont to draw the breath
Which gave it strength to pierce the guarded wit,[3]
And pass into the panting heart beneath
With lightning and with music: the damp death
Quenched its caress upon his icy lips;   105
And, as a dying meteor stains a wreath
Of moonlight vapour, which the cold night clips,[4]
It flushed through his pale limbs, and past to its eclipse.

13

And others came . . . Desires and Adorations,
Winged Persuasions and veiled Destinies,   110
Splendours, and Glooms, and glimmering Incarnations
Of hopes and fears, and twilight Phantasies;
And Sorrow, with her family of Sighs,
And Pleasure, blind with tears, led by the gleam
Of her own dying smile instead of eyes,   115
Came in slow pomp;—the moving pomp might seem
Like pageantry of mist on an autumnal stream.

14

All he had loved, and moulded into thought,
From shape, and hue, and odour, and sweet sound,
Lamented Adonais. Morning sought   120
Her eastern watchtower, and her hair unbound,
Wet with the tears which should adorn the ground,
Dimmed the aerial eyes that kindle day;
Afar the melancholy thunder moaned,
Pale Ocean in unquiet slumber lay,   125
And the wild winds flew round, sobbing in their dismay.

15

Lost Echo sits amid the voiceless mountains,
And feeds her grief with his remembered lay,
And will no more reply to winds or fountains,
Or amorous birds perched on the young green spray,   130
Or herdsman's horn, or bell at closing day;
Since she can mimic not his lips, more dear
Than those for whose disdain she pined away
Into a shadow of all sounds:[5]—a drear
Murmur, between their songs, is all the woodmen hear.   135

---

2. A rich garland.
3. The cautious intellect of the listener.
4. Embraces.
5. Because of her unrequited love for Narcissus, who was enamored of his own reflection (line 141), the nymph Echo pined away until she was only a reflected sound.

16

Grief made the young Spring wild, and she threw down
Her kindling buds, as if she Autumn were,
Or they dead leaves; since her delight is flown
For whom should she have waked the sullen year?
To Phœbus was not Hyacinth so dear[6]   140
Nor to himself Narcissus, as to both
Thou Adonais: wan they stand and sere[7]
Amid the faint companions of their youth,
With dew all turned to tears; odour, to sighing ruth.[8]

17

Thy spirit's sister, the lorn nightingale[9]   145
Mourns not her mate with such melodious pain;
Not so the eagle, who like thee could scale
Heaven, and could nourish in the sun's domain
Her mighty youth with morning,[10] doth complain,
Soaring and screaming round her empty nest,   150
As Albion[1] wails for thee: the curse of Cain
Light on his[2] head who pierced thy innocent breast,
And scared the angel soul that was its earthly guest!

18

Ah woe is me! Winter is come and gone,
But grief returns with the revolving year;   155
The airs and streams renew their joyous tone;
The ants, the bees, the swallows reappear;
Fresh leaves and flowers deck the dead Seasons' bier;
The amorous birds now pair in every brake,
And build their mossy homes in field and brere;[3]   160
And the green lizard, and the golden snake,
Like unimprisoned flames, out of their trance awake.

19

Through wood and stream and field and hill and Ocean
A quickening life from the Earth's heart has burst
As it has ever done, with change and motion,   165
From the great morning of the world when first
God dawned on Chaos; in its stream immersed
The lamps of Heaven flash with a softer light;
All baser things pant with life's sacred thirst;
Diffuse themselves; and spend in love's delight,   170
The beauty and the joy of their renewed might.

20

The leprous corpse touched by this spirit tender
Exhales itself in flowers of gentle breath;
Like incarnations of the stars, when splendour

6. Young Hyacinthus was loved by
Phoebus Apollo, who accidentally killed
him in a game of quoits. Apollo made
the hyacinth flower spring from his blood.
7. Dried, withered.
8. Pity.
9. To whom Keats had written *Ode to a
Nightingale*.

10. In the legend, the aged eagle, to
renew his youth, flies toward the sun
until his old plumage is burned off and
the film cleared from his eyes.
1. England.
2. I.e., of the reviewer of *Endymion*.
3. Briar. "Brake": thicket.

Is changed to fragrance, they illumine death 175
And mock the merry worm that wakes beneath;
Nought we know, dies. Shall that alone which knows
Be as a sword consumed before the sheath
By sightless lightning?[4]—th'intense atom glows
A moment, then is quenched in a most cold repose. 180

21

Alas! that all we loved of him should be,
But for our grief, as if it had not been,
And grief itself be mortal! Woe is me!
Whence are we, and why are we? of what scene
The actors or spectators? Great and mean 185
Meet massed in death, who lends what life must borrow.
As long as skies are blue, and fields are green,
Evening must usher night, night urge the morrow,
Month follow month with woe, and year wake year to sorrow.

22

He will awake no more, oh, never more! 190
"Wake thou," cried Misery, "childless Mother, rise
Out of thy sleep, and slake,[5] in thy heart's core,
A wound more fierce than his with tears and sighs."
And all the Dreams that watched Urania's eyes,
And all the Echoes whom their sister's song[6] 195
Had held in holy silence, cried: "Arise!"
Swift as a Thought by the snake Memory stung,
From her ambrosial rest the fading Splendour[7] sprung.

23

She rose like an autumnal Night, that springs
Out of the East, and follows wild and drear 200
The golden Day, which, on eternal wings,
Even as a ghost abandoning a bier,
Had left the Earth a corpse. Sorrow and fear
So struck, so roused, so rapt Urania;
So saddened round her like an atmosphere 205
Of stormy mist; so swept her on her way
Even to the mournful place where Adonais lay.

24

Out of her secret Paradise she sped,
Through camps and cities rough with stone, and steel,
And human hearts, which to her aery tread 210
Yielding not, wounded the invisible
Palms of her tender feet where'er they fell:
And barbed tongues, and thoughts more sharp than they
Rent the soft Form they never could repel,
Whose sacred blood, like the young tears of May, 215
Paved with eternal flowers that undeserving way.

---

4. The sword is the mind which knows;
the sheath is its vehicle, the material
body. "Sightless": invisible.

5. Assuage.
6. I.e., the Echo in line 127.
7. Urania.

25

In the death chamber for a moment Death
Shamed by the presence of that living Might
Blushed to annihilation, and the breath
Revisited those lips, and life's pale light   220
Flashed through those limbs, so late her dear delight.
"Leave me not wild and drear and comfortless,
As silent lightning leaves the starless night!
Leave me not!" cried Urania: her distress
Roused Death: Death rose and smiled, and met her vain caress. 225

26

"Stay yet awhile! speak to me once again;
Kiss me, so long but as a kiss may live;
And in my heartless[8] breast and burning brain
That word, that kiss shall all thoughts else survive
With food of saddest memory kept alive,   230
Now thou art dead, as if it were a part
Of thee, my Adonais! I would give
All that I am to be as thou now art!
But I am chained to Time, and cannot thence depart!

27

"Oh gentle child, beautiful as thou wert,   235
Why didst thou leave the trodden paths of men
Too soon, and with weak hands though mighty heart
Dare the unpastured dragon in his den?[9]
Defenceless as thou wert, oh where was then
Wisdom the mirrored shield, or scorn the spear?[1]   240
Or hadst thou waited the full cycle, when
Thy spirit should have filled its crescent sphere,[2]
The monsters of life's waste had fled from thee like deer.

28

"The herded wolves, bold only to pursue;
The obscene ravens, clamorous o'er the dead;   245
The vultures to the conqueror's banner true
Who feed where Desolation first has fed,
And whose wings rain contagion;—how they fled,
When like Apollo, from his golden bow,
The Pythian of the age[3] one arrow sped   250
And smiled!—The spoilers tempt no second blow,
They fawn on the proud feet that spurn them lying low.

29

"The sun comes forth, and many reptiles spawn;
He sets, and each ephemeral insect then
Is gathered into death without a dawn,   255

8. Because her heart had been given to
Adonais.
9. I.e., the hostile reviewers.
1. The allusion is to Perseus, who had
cut off Medusa's head while avoiding the
direct sight of her · (which would have
turned him to stone) by looking only at
her reflection in his shield.

2. I.e., when thy spirit, like the full
moon, should have reached its maturity.
3. Byron, who had directed against critics of the age his satiric poem, *English
Bards and Scotch Reviewers* (1809). The
allusion is to Apollo, called "the
Pythian" because he had slain the
dragon Python.

And the immortal stars awake again;
So is it in the world of living men:
A godlike mind soars forth, in its delight
Making earth bare and veiling heaven,[4] and when
It sinks, the swarms that dimmed or shared its light   260
Leave to its kindred lamps[5] the spirit's awful night."

30

Thus ceased she: and the mountain shepherds came
Their garlands sere, their magic mantles rent;
The Pilgrim of Eternity,[6] whose fame
Over his living head like Heaven is bent,   265
An early but enduring monument,
Came, veiling all the lightnings of his song
In sorrow; from her wilds Ierne sent
The sweetest lyrist of her saddest wrong,[7]
And love taught grief to fall like music from his tongue.   270

31

Midst others of less note, came one frail Form,[8]
A phantom among men; companionless
As the last cloud of an expiring storm
Whose thunder is its knell; he, as I guess,
Had gazed on Nature's naked loveliness,   275
Actæon-like, and now he fled astray
With feeble steps o'er the world's wilderness,
And his own thoughts, along that rugged way,
Pursued, like raging hounds, their father and their prey.[9]

32

A pardlike[1] Spirit beautiful and swift—   280
A Love in desolation masked;—a Power
Girt round with weakness;—it can scarce uplift
The weight of the superincumbent hour;[2]
It is a dying lamp, a falling shower,
A breaking billow;—even whilst we speak   285
Is it not broken? On the withering flower
The killing sun smiles brightly: on a cheek
The life can burn in blood, even while the heart may break.

33

His head was bound with pansies overblown,
And faded violets, white, and pied, and blue;   290
And a light spear topped with a cypress cone,
Round whose rude shaft dark ivy tresses grew[3]

4. As the sun reveals the earth but veils the other stars.
5. The other stars (i.e., creative minds), of lesser brilliance than the sun.
6. Byron, who had referred to his Childe Harold as one of the "wanderers o'er eternity" (III.669).
7. Thomas Moore (1779–1852) from Ireland ("Ierne"), who had written poems about the oppression of his native land.
8. Shelley himself, represented in one of his aspects—like the Poet in *Alastor*, rather than the author of *Prometheus Unbound*.
9. Actaeon, while hunting, came upon the naked Diana bathing, and in punishment was turned into a stag and torn to pieces by his own hounds.
1. Leopard-like.
2. I.e., the heavy, overhanging hour of Keats's death.
3. Like the thyrsus, the leaf-entwined and cone-topped staff carried by Dionysus. The pansies are emblems of sorrowful thought; the cypress is an emblem of mourning.

Yet dripping with the forest's noonday dew,
Vibrated, as the ever-beating heart
Shook the weak hand that grasped it; of that crew   295
He came the last, neglected and apart;
A herd-abandoned deer struck by the hunter's dart.

34

All stood aloof, and at his partial⁴ moan
Smiled through their tears; well knew that gentle band
Who in another's fate now wept his own;   300
As in the accents of an unknown land,
He sung new sorrow; sad Urania scanned
The Stranger's mien, and murmured: "who art thou?"
He answered not, but with a sudden hand
Made bare his branded and ensanguined brow,   305
Which was like Cain's or Christ's⁵—Oh! that it should be so!

35

What softer voice is hushed over the dead?
Athwart what brow is that dark mantle thrown?
What form leans sadly o'er the white death-bed,
In mockery of monumental stone,⁶   310
The heavy heart heaving without a moan?
If it be He,⁷ who, gentlest of the wise,
Taught, soothed, loved, honoured the departed one;
Let me not vex, with inharmonious sighs
The silence of that heart's accepted sacrifice.   315

36

Our Adonais has drunk poison—oh!
What deaf and viperous murderer could crown
Life's early cup with such a draught of woe?
The nameless worm⁸ would now itself disown:
It felt, yet could escape the magic tone   320
Whose prelude held all envy, hate, and wrong,
But what was howling in one breast alone,
Silent with expectation of the song,⁹
Whose master's hand is cold, whose silver lyre unstrung.

37

Live thou, whose infamy is not thy fame!   325
Live! fear no heavier chastisement from me,
Thou noteless blot on a remembered name!
But be thyself, and know thyself to be!
And ever at thy season be thou free
To spill the venom when thy fangs o'erflow: 330
Remorse and Self-contempt shall cling to thee;
Hot Shame shall burn upon thy secret brow,
And like a beaten hound tremble thou shalt—as now.

4. I.e., with reference to himself.
5. His bloody ("ensanguined") brow bore a mark like that with which God had branded Cain for murdering Abel—or like that left by Christ's crown of thorns.
6. I.e., in imitation of a memorial statue.

7. Leigh Hunt, close friend both of Keats and Shelley.
8. Snake; i.e., the anonymous reviewer.
9. I.e., the promise of later greatness in Keats's early poems "held . . . silent" the expression of all malignant feelings except the reviewer's.

38

Nor let us weep that our delight is fled
Far from these carrion kites[10] that scream below;   335
He wakes or sleeps with the enduring dead;
Thou canst not soar where he is sitting now.—
Dust to the dust! but the pure spirit shall flow
Back to the burning fountain whence it came,
A portion of the Eternal,[11] which must glow   340
Through time and change, unquenchably the same,
Whilst thy cold embers choke the sordid hearth of shame.

39

Peace, peace! he is not dead, he doth not sleep—
He hath awakened from the dream of life—
'Tis we, who lost in stormy visions, keep   345
With phantoms an unprofitable strife,
And in mad trance, strike with our spirit's knife
Invulnerable nothings.—*We* decay
Like corpses in a charnel; fear and grief
Convulse us and consume us day by day,   350
And cold hopes swarm like worms within our living clay.

40

He has outsoared the shadow of our night;[1]
Envy and calumny and hate and pain,
And that unrest which men miscall delight,
Can touch him not and torture not again;   355
From the contagion of the world's slow stain
He is secure, and now can never mourn
A heart grown cold, a head grown grey in vain;
Nor, when the spirit's self has ceased to burn,
With sparkless ashes load an unlamented urn.   360

41

He lives, he wakes—'tis Death is dead, not he;
Mourn not for Adonais.—Thou young Dawn
Turn all thy dew to splendour, for from thee
The spirit thou lamentest is not gone;
Ye caverns and ye forests, cease to moan!   365
Cease ye faint flowers and fountains, and thou Air
Which like a mourning veil thy scarf hadst thrown
O'er the abandoned Earth, now leave it bare
Even to the joyous stars which smile on its despair![2]

42

He is made one with Nature: there is heard   370
His voice in all her music, from the moan
Of thunder, to the song of night's sweet bird;[3]

10. Large birds of prey; a species of hawk.
11. Shelley adopts for this poem the Neo-Platonic view that all life and all forms emanate from the Absolute, the eternal One. The Absolute is imaged as a radiant light-source and an overflowing fountain, which circulates continuously through the dross of matter (stanza 43) and back to its source.

1. He has soared beyond the shadow cast by the earth as it intercepts the sun's light.
2. Shelley's science is as usual, accurate: it is the envelope of air around the earth which, by diffusing and reflecting sunlight, veils the stars.
3. The nightingale, in allusion to Keats's *Ode to a Nightingale*.

He is a presence to be felt and known
In darkness and in light, from herb and stone,
Spreading itself where'er that Power may move   375
Which has withdrawn his being to its own;
Which wields the world with never wearied love,
Sustains it from beneath, and kindles it above.

43

He is a portion of the loveliness
Which once he made more lovely: he doth bear   380
His part, while the one Spirit's plastic[4] stress
Sweeps through the dull dense world, compelling there,
All new successions to the forms they wear;
Torturing th'unwilling dross that checks its flight
To its own likeness, as each mass may bear;[5]   385
And bursting in its beauty and its might
From trees and beasts and men into the Heaven's light.

44

The splendours of the firmament of time
May be eclipsed, but are extinguished not;
Like stars to their appointed height they climb   390
And death is a low mist which cannot blot
The brightness it may veil.[6] When lofty thought
Lifts a young heart above its mortal lair,
And love and life contend in it, for what
Shall be its earthly doom, the dead live there[7]   395
And move like winds of light on dark and stormy air.

45

The inheritors of unfulfilled renown[8]
Rose from their thrones, built beyond mortal thought,
Far in the Unapparent. Chatterton
Rose pale, his solemn agony had not   400
Yet faded from him; Sidney, as he fought
And as he fell and as he lived and loved
Sublimely mild, a Spirit without spot,
Arose; and Lucan, by his death approved:[9]
Oblivion as they rose shrank like a thing reproved.   405

46

And many more, whose names on Earth are dark
But whose transmitted effluence cannot die
So long as fire outlives the parent spark,
Rose, robed in dazzling immortality.

---

4. Formative, shaping.
5. I.e., to the degree that a particular substance will permit. Different kinds of matter offer variable resistance to the attempts of the "one Spirit" to realize itself. The stars (line 387) are of such a refined matter that they permit an approximation to the radiance of the spirit itself.
6. The radiance of stars (i.e., of poets) persists, even when they are temporarily "eclipsed" by another heavenly body, or obscured by the veil of the earth's at-

mosphere.
7. I.e., in the thought of the "young heart" (line 393). "Doom": destiny.
8. Poets who (like Keats) died young, before achieving their full measure of fame. Thomas Chatterton (1752–70) committed suicide at 17; Sir Philip Sidney (1554–86) died in battle at 32; and the Roman poet Lucan (A.D. 39–65) killed himself at 26 to escape a sentence of death for having plotted against Nero.
9. Justified, proved worthy.

"Thou art become as one of us," they cry,   410
"It was for thee yon kingless sphere has long
Swung blind in unascended majesty,
Silent alone amid an Heaven of song.
Assume thy winged throne, thou Vesper of our throng!"[1]

47

Who mourns for Adonais? oh come forth   415
Fond wretch! and know thyself and him aright.
Clasp with thy panting soul the pendulous[2] Earth;
As from a centre, dart thy spirit's light
Beyond all worlds, until its spacious might
Satiate the void circumference: then shrink   420
Even to a point within our day and night;[3]
And keep thy heart light lest it make thee sink
When hope has kindled hope, and lured thee to the brink.

48

Or go to Rome, which is the sepulchre
O, not of him, but of our joy: 'tis nought   425
That ages, empires, and religions there
Lie buried in the ravage they have wrought;
For such as he can lend,—they[4] borrow not
Glory from those who made the world their prey;
And he is gathered to the kings of thought   430
Who waged contention with their time's decay,
And of the past are all that cannot pass away.

49

Go thou to Rome,—at once the Paradise,
The grave, the city, and the wilderness;
And where its wrecks like shattered mountains rise,   435
And flowering weeds, and fragrant copses[5] dress
The bones of Desolation's nakedness
Pass, till the Spirit of the spot shall lead
Thy footsteps to a slope of green access[6]
Where, like an infant's smile, over the dead,   440
A light of laughing flowers along the grass is spread.

50

And grey walls moulder round,[7] on which dull Time
Feeds, like slow fire upon a hoary brand;[8]
And one keen pyramid with wedge sublime,[9]

1. Adonais assumes his place in the sphere of Vesper, the evening star, hitherto unoccupied ("kingless"), hence also "silent" amid the music of the other spheres.
2. Suspended, floating in space.
3. The poet bids the wretch so foolish ("fond") as to mourn Adonais to stretch his imagination so as to reach the poet's own cosmic viewpoint, and then allow it to contract ("shrink") back to its ordinary vantage-point on earth—where, unlike Adonais in his heavenly place, we have an alternation of day and night (line 421).
4. I.e., poets like Keats, who can bestow ("lend") glory, as opposed to the Roman conquerors, who borrowed glory from those they conquered.
5. Undergrowth. In Shelley's time the ruins of ancient Rome were overgrown with weeds and shrubbery.
6. The Protestant Cemetery, Keats's burial place. The next line is a glancing allusion to Shelley's 3-year-old son William, also buried there.
7. The wall of ancient Rome formed one boundary of the cemetery.
8. A burning log.
9. The tomb of Gaius Cestius, a Roman tribune, just outside the cemetery.

Pavilioning the dust of him who planned   445
This refuge for his memory, doth stand
Like flame transformed to marble; and beneath,
A field is spread, on which a newer band
Have pitched in Heaven's smile their camp of death
Welcoming him we lose with scarce extinguished breath.   450

51

Here pause: these graves are all too young as yet
To have outgrown the sorrow which consigned
Its charge to each; and if the seal is set,
Here, on one fountain of a mourning mind,[1]
Break it not thou! too surely shalt thou find   455
Thine own well full, if thou returnest home,
Of tears and gall. From the world's bitter wind
Seek shelter in the shadow of the tomb.
What Adonais is, why fear we to become?

52

The One remains, the many change and pass;   460
Heaven's light forever shines, Earth's shadows fly;
Life, like a dome of many-coloured glass,
Stains the white radiance of Eternity,
Until Death tramples it to fragments.[2]—Die,
If thou wouldst be with that which thou dost seek!   465
Follow where all is fled!—Rome's azure sky,
Flowers, ruins, statues, music, words, are weak
The glory they transfuse with fitting truth to speak.

53

Why linger, why turn back, why shrink, my Heart?
Thy hopes are gone before; from all things here   470
They have departed; thou shouldst now depart!
A light is past from the revolving year,
And man, and woman; and what still is dear
Attracts to crush, repels to make thee wither.
The soft sky smiles,—the low wind whispers near: 475
'Tis Adonais calls! oh, hasten thither,
No more let Life divide what Death can join together.

54

That Light whose smile kindles the Universe,
That Beauty in which all things work and move,
That Benediction which the eclipsing Curse   480
Of birth can quench not, that sustaining Love
Which through the web of being blindly wove
By man and beast and earth and air and sea,
Burns bright or dim, as each are mirrors of[3]

---

1. Shelley's mourning for his son.
2. Earthly life colors ("stains") the pure white light of the One, which is the source of all light (see lines 339–40 and note). The azure sky, flowers, etc., of lines 466–68 exemplify earthly colors which, however beautiful, fall far short of the "glory" of the pure Light which they transmit, but refract ("transfuse").
3. I.e., according to the degree that each reflects.

The fire for which all thirst;[4] now beams on me, 485
Consuming the last clouds of cold mortality.

55

The breath whose might I have invoked in song[5]
Descends on me; my spirit's bark is driven,
Far from the shore, far from the trembling throng
Whose sails were never to the tempest given; 490
The massy earth and sphered skies are riven!
I am borne darkly, fearfully, afar;
Whilst burning through the inmost veil of Heaven,
The soul of Adonais, like a star,
Beacons from the abode where the Eternal are. 495

1821   1821

A Dirge

Rough wind, that moanest loud
  Grief too sad for song;
Wild wind, when sullen cloud
  Knells all the night long;
Sad storm, whose tears are vain, 5
Bare woods, whose branches strain,
Deep caves and dreary main,—
  Wail, for the world's wrong!

1821   1824

When the Lamp Is Shattered

When the lamp is shattered
The light in the dust lies dead—
  When the cloud is scattered
The rainbow's glory is shed—
  When the lute is broken 5
Sweet tones are remembered not—
  When the lips have spoken
Loved accents are soon forgot.

  As music and splendour
Survive not the lamp and the lute, 10
  The heart's echoes render
No song when the spirit is mute—
  No song—but sad dirges
Like the wind through a ruined cell

4. The "thirst" of the human spirit is to return to the fountain and fire (the "burning fountain," line 339) which is its source.

5. Two years earlier, Shelley had "invoked" (prayed to, and also asked for) "the breath of Autumn's being" in his *Ode to the West Wind*.

Or the mournful surges 15
That ring the dead seaman's knell.

When hearts have once mingled
Love first leaves the well-built nest[1]—
The weak one is singled
To endure what it once possest.
  O Love! who bewailest
The frailty of all things here,
  Why choose you the frailest[2]
For your cradle, your home and your bier?

Its passions will rock thee 25
As the storms rock the ravens on high—
  Bright Reason will mock thee
Like the Sun from a wintry sky—
  From thy nest every rafter
Will rot, and thine eagle home[3] 30
  Leave thee naked to laughter
When leaves fall and cold winds come.

1822   1824

To Jane. The Invitation[1]

Best and brightest, come away—
Fairer far than this fair day
Which like thee to those in sorrow
Comes to bid a sweet good-morrow
To the rough year just awake
In its cradle on the brake.[2]— 5
The brightest hour of unborn spring
Through the winter wandering
Found, it seems, this halcyon[3] morn
To hoar February born;
Bending from Heaven in azure mirth 10
It kissed the forehead of the earth
And smiled upon the silent sea,
And bade the frozen streams be free
And waked to music all their fountains,
And breathed upon the frozen mountains, 15
And like a prophetess of May
Strewed flowers upon the barren way,

1. Love first flies off from the sturdier
heart.
2. I.e., the human heart.
3. Like the lofty, and therefore exposed,
nest of the eagle.
1. "Jane" is Jane Williams, the common-law wife of Edward Williams, Shel-

ley's close friend. This invitation to an
outdoor excursion exemplifies Shelley's
grace and urbanity, writing in the ancient tradition of the verse letter.
2. Thicket.
3. Calm and peaceful.

Making the wintry world appear
Like one on whom thou smilest, dear.   20

Away, away from men and towns
To the wild wood and the downs,
To the silent wilderness
Where the soul need not repress
Its music lest it should not find   25
An echo in another's mind,
While the touch of Nature's art
Harmonizes heart to heart.—
I leave this notice on my door
For each accustomed visitor—   30
"I am gone into the fields
To take what this sweet hour yields.
Reflexion, you may come tomorrow,
Sit by the fireside with Sorrow—
You, with the unpaid bill, Despair,   35
You, tiresome verse-reciter Care,
I will pay you in the grave,
Death will listen to your stave[4]—
Expectation too, be off!—
To-day is for itself enough—   40
Hope, in pity mock not woe
With smiles, nor follow where I go;
Long having lived on thy sweet food,
At length I find one moment's good
After long pain—with all your love   45
This you never told me of."

Radiant Sister of the day,
Awake, arise and come away
To the wild woods and the plains
And the pools where winter-rains   50
Image all their roof of leaves,
Where the pine its garland weaves
Of sapless green and ivy dun
Round stems that never kiss the Sun—
Where the lawns and pastures be   55
And the sandhills of the sea—
Where the melting hoar-frost wets
The daisy-star that never sets,
And wind-flowers, and violets
Which yet join not scent to hue   60
Crown the pale year weak and new,
When the night is left behind
In the deep east dun and blind
And the blue noon is over us,

4. Stanza, set of verses.

And the multitudinous   65
Billows murmur at our feet
Where the earth and ocean meet,
And all things seem only one
In the universal Sun.—

1822   1824

To Jane (The Keen Stars Were Twinkling)

The keen stars were twinkling
And the fair moon was rising among them,
        Dear Jane.
    The guitar was tinkling
But the notes were not sweet 'till you sung them   5
        Again.—
    As the moon's soft splendour
O'er the faint cold starlight of Heaven
        Is thrown—
    So your voice most tender   10
To the strings without soul had then given
        Its own.

    The stars will awaken,
Though the moon sleep a full hour later,
        Tonight;   15
    No leaf will be shaken
While the dews of your melody scatter
        Delight.
    Though the sound overpowers
Sing again, with your dear voice revealing   20
        A tone
    Of some world far from ours,
Where music and moonlight and feeling
        Are one.

1822   1832; 1839

Lines Written in the Bay of Lerici[1]

Bright wanderer,[2] fair coquette of Heaven,
To whom alone it has been given
To change and be adored for ever. . . .
Envy not this dim world, for never
But once within its shadow grew   5
One fair as [thou], but far more true.
She left me at the silent time
When the moon had ceased to climb
The azure dome of Heaven's steep,
And like an albatross asleep,   10
Balanced on her wings of light,

1. Another of Shelley's last lyrics, inspired   2. I.e., the moon.
by Jane Williams.

Hovered in the purple night,
Ere she sought her Ocean nest
In the chambers of the west.—
She left me, and I staid alone   15
Thinking over every tone,
Which though now silent to the ear
The enchanted heart could hear
Like notes which die when born, but still
Haunt the echoes of the hill: 20
And feeling ever—O too much—
The soft vibrations of her touch
As if her gentle hand even now
Lightly trembled on my brow;
And thus although she absent were   25
Memory gave me all of her
That even fancy dares to claim.—
Her presence had made weak and tame
All passions, and I lived alone,
In the time which is our own;   30
The past and future were forgot
As they had been, and would be, not.—
But soon, the guardian angel gone,
The demon³ reassumed his throne
In my faint heart . . . I dare not speak   35
My thoughts; but thus disturbed and weak
I sate and watched the vessels glide
Along the ocean bright and wide,
Like spirit-winged chariots sent
O'er some serenest element   40
To ministrations strange and far;
As if to some Elysian star
They sailed for drink to medicine
Such sweet and bitter pain as mine.
And the wind that winged their flight   45
From the land came fresh and light,
And the scent of sleeping flowers
And the coolness of the hours
Of dew, and the sweet warmth of day
Was scattered o'er the twinkling bay;   50
And the fisher with his lamp
And spear, about the low rocks damp
Crept, and struck the fish who came
To worship the delusive flame:
Too happy, they whose pleasure sought   55
Extinguishes all sense and thought
Of the regret that pleasure [leaves]⁴
Destroying life alone not peace.

1822   1862, 1961

---

3. I.e., the passions, with their compul-   4. This word has been suggested by
sion to look before and after (lines 29–   earlier editors; Shelley left a blank space.
32).

The Triumph of Life

Shelley left this poem in process when he died in early July, 1822. He took its central event from Petrarch's six *Trionfi*, "triumph" having the meaning of the Latin *triumphus*, the ceremonial entrance of a victorious general into ancient Rome in a procession which included his prisoners of war. The poem is strongly influenced by Dante's *Divine Comedy*, not only in its *terza rima* (the verse form also of Petrarch's *Trionfi*) but also in over-all conception, in a number of narrative details, and in style. It is notable that Shelley, like Keats in *The Fall of Hyperion*, left unfinished at his death a long poem in the form of a Dantean dream-vision, in which the poet faces up to the discovery that human history has been a continuous process of human suffering and defeat—and in Shelley's version, an almost unrelieved narrative of human weakness and evil-doing.

We ought to be wary, however, of a tendency to dramatize Shelley's career by imposing on it the form of a tragic plot, moving inexorably to *The Triumph of Life*, from which there was no exit except the poet's own death. The vision in the poem of the frantic, quiescent, or despairing captives in the procession of Life—including all who have in the least degree compromised in spirit or aspiration with the passions, temptations, or values of fleshly life and the material world—is a desolate one, but its darkness is not unrelieved. There are the "sacred few" among humanity who have not compromised at all. The band of "mighty captives" chained to Life's car represent a full spectrum of relative worth, from mighty villains to mighty heroes. And although we lack Shelley's answer to the question posed at the end of the fragment—"then, what is Life?"—there is no determinative evidence that he planned to depart from the precedent of all his other long poems, in which he allowed some scope of possibility for redeeming life by the cardinal Shelleyan virtues; and above all by that love which, as he says near the close of *The Triumph of Life* (lines 472–76), led Dante safely "from the lowest depths of Hell" through Purgatory to Heaven and back to earth.

But any statement of how Shelley would have ended this fragment is speculative. What is certain is the vitality and the timbre of the poetic voice in the portion before us. No other narrative poem quite matches in its opening the assurance of Shelley's forty-line induction, as the sun springs forth like a bridegroom coming out of his chamber, to be greeted with the quiet ceremonies of natural worship by the revolving world, to whom it brings light, heat, and joyous reawakening—to all except the poet who composes himself to sleep as the world awakes, to undergo, in the transparent darkness of a trance, the crisis of his vision. And the promise of this extraordinary opening is fulfilled in the unflagging narrative drive, and in the ease and precision of language, of the rest of the poem, which expresses an *élan* even in its grimmest passages.

The Triumph of Life does not sound like the voice of a defeated poet, but of a poet who, just attaining the height of his powers, was making a masterful new beginning.

The Triumph of Life

Swift as a spirit hastening to his task
   Of glory and of good, the Sun sprang forth
Rejoicing in his splendour, and the mask

   Of darkness fell from the awakened Earth.
The smokeless altars of the mountain snows   5
   Flamed above crimson clouds, and at the birth

Of light, the Ocean's orison[1] arose
   To which the birds tempered their matin lay.
All flowers in field or forest which unclose

   Their trembling eyelids to the kiss of day,   10
Swinging their censers in the element,
   With orient[2] incense lit by the new ray

Burned slow and inconsumably, and sent
   Their odorous sighs up to the smiling air,
And in succession due, did Continent,   15

   Isle, Ocean, and all things that in them wear
The form and character of mortal mould
   Rise as the Sun their father rose, to bear

Their portion of the toil which he of old
   Took as his own and then imposed on them;   20
But I, whom thoughts which must remain untold

   Had kept as wakeful as the stars that gem
The cone of night,[3] now they were laid asleep,
   Stretched my faint limbs beneath the hoary stem

Which an old chestnut flung athwart the steep   25
   Of a green Apennine:[4] before me fled
The night; behind me rose the day; the Deep

   Was at my feet, and Heaven above my head
When a strange trance over my fancy grew
   Which was not slumber, for the shade it spread   30

1. Prayer: to which (in the next line) the birds tuned their chanted morning prayer ("matin lay").
2. Eastern, morning.
3. The conical shadow cast by the earth as it intercepts the light of the sun.
4. The Apennines are a chain of mountains extending down the peninsula of Italy.

Was so transparent that the scene came through
　As clear as when a veil of light is drawn
O'er evening hills they glimmer;[5] and I knew

　That I had felt the freshness of that dawn,
Bathed in the same cold dew my brow and hair　　　35
　And sate as thus upon that slope of lawn

Under the self same bough, and heard as there
　The birds, the fountains and the Ocean hold
Sweet talk in music through the enamoured air.
　And then a Vision on my brain was rolled....　　　40

———————————

As in that trance of wondrous thought I lay
　This was the tenour of my waking dream.
Methought I sate beside a public way

　Thick strewn with summer dust, and a great stream
Of people there was hurrying to and fro　　　45
　Numerous as gnats upon the evening gleam,

All hastening onward, yet none seemed to know
　Whither he went, or whence he came, or why
He made one of the multitude, yet so

　Was borne amid the crowd as through the sky　50
One of the million leaves of summer's bier.—
　Old age and youth, manhood and infancy,

Mixed in one mighty torrent did appear,
　Some flying from the thing they feared and some
Seeking the object of another's fear,　　　55

　And others as with steps towards the tomb
Pored on the trodden worms that crawled beneath,
　And others mournfully within the gloom

Of their own shadow walked, and called it death ...
　And some fled from it[6] as it were a ghost,　60
Half fainting in the affliction of vain breath.

　But more with motions which each other crost
Pursued or shunned the shadows the clouds threw
　Or birds within the noonday ether lost,

5. Apparently, "[so that] they glimmer."　6. I.e., from their own shadow, death (line 59).

Upon that path where flowers never grew;　　　　　　65
　　And weary with vain toil and faint for thirst
Heard not the fountains whose melodious dew

　　　Out of their mossy cells forever burst
Nor felt the breeze which from the forest told
　　Of grassy paths, and wood lawns interspersed　　　70

With overarching elms and caverns cold,
　　And violet banks where sweet dreams brood, but they
Pursued their serious folly as of old. . . .

　　　And as I gazed methought that in the way
The throng grew wilder, as the woods of June　　　75
　　When the South wind shakes the extinguished day.—

And a cold glare, intenser than the noon
　　But icy cold, obscured with [blinding][7] light
The Sun as he the stars. Like the young Moon

　　　When on the sunlit limits of the night　　　80
Her white shell trembles amid crimson air
　　And whilst the sleeping tempest gathers might

Doth, as a herald of its coming, bear
　　The ghost of her dead Mother, whose dim form
Bends in dark ether from her infant's chair,[8]　　　85

　　　So came a chariot on the silent storm
Of its own rushing splendour, and a Shape
　　So sate within as one whom years deform

Beneath a dusky hood and double cape
　　Crouching within the shadow of a tomb,　　　90
And o'er what seemed the head a cloud like crape

　　Was bent,[9] a dun and faint etherial gloom
Tempering the light; upon the chariot's beam
　　A Janus-visaged[1] Shadow did assume

7. Mary Shelley filled in a blank space in the manuscript with "blinding."
8. The crescent new moon bearing the faint outline of the full moon in its arms—the omen of a coming storm, as in Coleridge's *Dejection: An Ode*, epigraph, and lines 9–14. The parallel is to the crescent-formed chariot bearing the dark Shape of Life.
9. "Cloud" is the subject of "was bent"; "crape": black cloth, worn in mourning; "dun": dark.
1. The Roman god Janus was represented with two faces, looking before and after. The shadowy charioteer guiding his team (which is invisible in the glare), however, has four faces, all of them blindfolded ("banded," line 100). Harold Bloom points out that this description of the chariot of Life is a parodic version of Ezekiel's vision of a divine chariot in the likeness of four living creatures, each having four faces, and in their progress forming rings which "were full of eyes" (Ezekiel i. 4–28); echoed in *Paradise Lost* VI. 749–72.

The guidance of that wonder-winged team.   95
  The Shapes which drew it in thick lightnings
Were lost: I heard alone on the air's soft stream

  The music of their ever moving wings.
All the four faces of that charioteer
  Had their eyes banded . . . little profit brings   100

Speed in the van and blindness in the rear,
  Nor then avail the beams that quench the Sun[2]
Or that these banded eyes could pierce the sphere

  Of all that is, has been, or will be done.—
So ill was the car guided, but it past   105
  With solemn speed majestically on . . .

The crowd gave way, and I arose aghast,
  Or seemed to rise, so mighty was the trance,
And saw like clouds upon the thunder blast

  The million with fierce song and maniac dance   110
Raging around; such seemed the jubilee
  As when to greet some conqueror's advance

Imperial Rome poured forth her living sea
  From senatehouse and prison and theatre
When Freedom left those who upon the free   115

  Had bound a yoke which soon they stooped to bear.[3]
Nor wanted here the just similitude
  Of a triumphal pageant, for where'er

The chariot rolled a captive multitude
  Was driven; all those who had grown old in power   120
Or misery,—all who have their age subdued,

  By action or by suffering, and whose hour
Was drained to its last sand in weal or woe,
  So that the trunk survived both fruit and flower;

All those whose fame or infamy must grow   125
  Till the great winter lay the form and name
Of their own earth with them forever low[4]—

  All but the sacred few who could not tame
Their spirits to the Conqueror, but as soon
  As they had touched the world with living flame   130

2. As described in lines 77–79.
3. I.e., when those free men who had enslaved other free men soon lost their own freedom, bearing the yoke they had imposed on others.
4. Until the world shall end in ice.

Fled back like eagles to their native noon,[5]
  Or those who put aside the diadem
Of earthly thrones or gems, till the last one

  Were there; for they of Athens and Jerusalem[6]
Were neither mid the mighty captives seen   135
  Nor mid the ribald crowd that followed them

Or fled before.... Swift, fierce and obscene
  The wild dance maddens in the van, and those
Who lead it, fleet as shadows on the green,

  Outspeed the chariot and without repose   140
Mix with each other in tempestuous measure
  To savage music.... Wilder as it grows,

They, tortured by the agonizing pleasure,
  Convulsed and on the rapid whirlwinds spun
Of that fierce spirit, whose unholy leisure   145

  Was soothed by mischief since the world begun,
Throw back their heads and loose their streaming hair,
  And in their dance round her who dims the Sun

Maidens and youths fling their wild arms in air
  As their feet twinkle; now recede and now   150
Bending within each other's atmosphere

  Kindle invisibly; and as they glow
Like moths by light attracted and repelled,
  Oft to new bright destruction come and go,

Till like two clouds into one vale impelled   155
  That shake the mountains when their lightnings mingle
And die in rain,—the fiery band which held

  Their natures, snaps ... ere the shock cease to tingle
One falls and then another in the path
  Senseless, nor is the desolation single,   160

Yet ere I can say *where* the chariot hath
  Past over them; nor other trace I find
But as of foam after the Ocean's wrath

5. Alluding to the legend that aged eagles renew their youth by flying toward
the sun.
6. In the Roman triumphs, the conquered chieftains were chained to the
conqueror's chariot, in order to heighten
their dishonor. In Shelley's version, this
"captive multitude" bound to the chariot
(lines 118–20) includes all the men
whose exceptional power or talent had
made them famous or infamous (line
125), except the "sacred few." The latter
are divided into two classes: those who
had died young, and those who, having
lived into older age, had resisted the corrupting influence of "earthly thrones or
gems" (line 133). These few included,
doubtless, Socrates and Jesus ("of Athens and Jerusalem," line 134).

Is spent upon the desert shore.—Behind,
Old men, and women foully disarrayed   165
   Shake their grey hair in the insulting wind,

Limp in the dance and strain with limbs decayed
   To reach the car of light which leaves them still
Farther behind and deeper in the shade.

   But not the less with impotence of will   170
They wheel, though ghastly shadows interpose
   Round them and round each other, and fulfill

Their work and to the dust whence they arose
   Sink and corruption veils them as they lie—
And frost in these performs what fire in those.[7]   175

   Struck to the heart by this sad pageantry,
Half to myself I said, "And what is this?
   Whose shape is that within the car? & why"—

I would have added—"is all here amiss?"
   But a voice answered . . "Life" . . . I turned and knew   180
(O Heaven have mercy on such wretchedness!)

   That what I thought was an old root which grew
To strange distortion out of the hill side
   Was indeed one of that deluded crew,

And that the grass which methought hung so wide   185
   And white, was but his thin discoloured hair,
And that the holes it vainly sought to hide

   Were or had been eyes.—"If thou canst forbear
To join the dance, which I had well forborne,"[8]
   Said the grim Feature, of my thought aware,   190

"I will tell all that which to this deep scorn
   Led me and my companions, and relate
The progress of the pageant since the morn;

   "If thirst of knowledge doth not thus abate,
Follow it even to the night, but I   195
   Am weary" . . . Then like one who with the weight

7. In addition to the "mighty captives" described in lines 118–27, there are two other groups: (1) the young men and women in front of the chariot who, in an erotic frenzy, dance, couple, fall senseless, and are crushed, leaving as their only trace a sexual foam (lines 137–64); and (2) the old men and women at the rear of the procession, attempting impotently to catch up with the chariot and to imitate the young in their bacchanalian dance (lines 164–75). Line 175: i.e., "frost destroys these old people, as fire had destroyed those young people."

8. I.e., "which I would have done well to avoid." "Feature": in the old sense, form, shape.

Of his own words is staggered, wearily
   He paused, and ere he could resume, I cried,
"First who art thou?" . . . "Before thy memory

   "I feared, loved, hated, suffered, did, and died,[9]   200
And if the spark with which Heaven lit my spirit
   Earth had with purer nutriment supplied

"Corruption would not now thus much inherit
   Of what was once Rousseau—nor this disguise
Stain that within which still disdains to wear it.—   205

   "If I have been extinguished, yet there rise
A thousand beacons from the spark I bore."[1]—
   "And who are those chained to the car?" "The Wise,

"The great, the unforgotten: they who wore
   Mitres and helms and crowns, or wreathes of light,[2]   210
Signs of thought's empire over thought; their lore

   "Taught them not this—to know themselves; their might
Could not repress the mutiny within,
   And for the morn of truth they feigned, deep night

"Caught them ere evening." "Who is he with chin   215
   Upon his breast and hands crost on his chain?"
"The Child of a fierce hour; he sought to win

   "The world, and lost all it did contain
Of greatness, in its hope destroyed; and more
   Of fame and peace than Virtue's self can gain   220

"Without the opportunity which bore
   Him on its eagle's pinion to the peak
From which a thousand climbers have before

   "Fall'n as Napoleon fell."—I felt my cheek
Alter to see the great form pass away   225
   Whose grasp had left the giant world so weak

That every pigmy kicked it as it lay—
   And much I grieved to think how power and will
In opposition rule our mortal day—

---

9. I.e., Rousseau (1712–78) had lived
and died before Shelley was born.
1. The sparks of Rousseau's writings had
kindled a thousand signal fires—including that of the French Revolution, of
which one child was Napoleon, who is
described in lines 215–27.

2. I.e., mitred churchmen, helmeted soldiers, crowned kings, and haloed sages.
With line 208 Rousseau begins to identify some of the "mighty captives"
whom the narrator had noted earlier
(lines 118 ff.).

And why God made irreconcilable   230
Good and the means of good;[3] and for despair
  I half disdained mine eye's desire to fill

With the spent vision of the times that were
And scarce have ceased to be . . . "Dost thou behold,"
Said then my guide, "those spoilers spoiled, Voltaire,   235

  "Frederic, and Kant, Catherine, and Leopold,[4]
Chained hoary anarchs,[5] demagogue and sage
  Whose name the fresh world thinks already old—

"For in the battle Life and they did wage
  She remained conqueror—I was overcome   240
By my own heart alone, which neither age

  "Nor tears nor infamy nor now the tomb
Could temper to its object."[6]—"Let them pass"—
  I cried—"the world and its mysterious doom

"Is not so much more glorious than it was   245
  That I desire to worship those who drew
New figures on its false and fragile glass

  "As the old faded."—"Figures ever new
Rise on the bubble, paint them how you may;
  We have but thrown, as those before us threw,   250

"Our shadows on it as it past away.
  But mark, how chained to the triumphal chair
The mighty phantoms of an elder day—

  "All that is mortal of great Plato there
Expiates the joy and woe his master knew not;   255
  That star that ruled his doom was far too fair—

"And Life, where long that flower of Heaven grew not,
  Conquered the heart by love which gold or pain
Or age or sloth or slavery could subdue not[7]—

---

3. I.e., the desire as against the means to do good.
4. Presumably Voltaire (the immensely influential thinker of the 18th-century Enlightenment) is the "demagogue"; Frederick the Great of Prussia, Catherine the Great of Russia, and Leopold II of the Holy Roman Empire, all influenced by Voltaire's ideas, are the "anarchs"; and Immanuel Kant (the great philosopher of the German Enlightenment) is the "sage."
5. Leaders who bring about anarchy.
6. While the nationalists of the Enlightenment were conquered by Life, Rousseau was self-conquered by his own heart's limitless desires, which no experience could moderate ("temper") to be content with an achievable object.
7. I.e., all of Plato except his immortal philosophy is expiating the passions of life which Socrates, "his master," escaped, but to which Plato succumbed because of his love for the boy Aster, who died young (line 257). The name "Aster" designates a flower, but also means "star" in Greek—the two meanings are joined in the figure "flower of heaven" (line 256). Aster is the subject of the epigram attributed to Plato, which Shelley used as the motto for *Adonais*, above.

"And near [him] walk the [Macedonian][8] twain,   260
The tutor and his pupil,[9] whom Dominion
Followed as tame as vulture in a chain.—

"The world was darkened beneath either pinion
Of him whom from the flock of conquerors
Fame singled as her thunderbearing minion;   265

"The other long outlived both woes and wars,
Throned in new thoughts of men, and still had kept
The jealous keys of truth's eternal doors

"If Bacon's spirit [eagle][1] had not leapt
Like lightning out of darkness; he compelled   270
The Proteus shape of Nature's as it slept

"To wake and to unbar the caves that held
The treasure of the secrets of its reign[2]—
See the great bards of old who inly quelled

"The passions which they sung, as by their strain   275
May well be known: their living melody
Tempers its own contagion to the vein

"Of those who are infected with it[3]—I
Have suffered what I wrote, or viler pain![4]—

"And so my words were seeds of misery—   280
Even as the deeds of others."—"Not as theirs,"[5]
I said—he pointed to a company

In which I recognized amid the heirs
Of Cæsar's crime from him to Constantine.[6]
The Anarchs old whose force and murderous snares   285

Had founded many a sceptre bearing line
And spread the plague of blood and gold abroad,
And Gregory and John[7] and men divine

8. Conjectural words for blank spaces in the manuscript.
9. Aristotle and his pupil, Alexander the Great of Macedonia, a kingdom north of Greece.
1. Conjectural.
2. Shelley represents Aristotle, because of the authority long exerted by his philosophy on the minds of men, to have been no less a tyrant than Alexander; he would even now bar us from truth, had not Francis Bacon, the Renaissance thinker, reopened the way by his new method of scientific inquiry. "Proteus": a sea god who could assume various shapes.
3. I.e., moderates the disease (of passion) with which it infects the veins of those who hear it.

4. I.e., Rousseau, unlike the classical poets (lines 274–75), had himself suffered the passions he expresses in his writings.
5. I.e., "not the seeds of such misery as were the deeds of those men." "Theirs" refers to the evil "company," to whom Rousseau has pointed (line 282), just before the narrator speaks.
6. Cæsar's "crime" had been to destroy the Roman Republic and to become the first of a line of emperors, his "heirs" extending to Constantine, who established Christianity as the religion of Rome early in the 4th century.
7. Pope Gregory the Great established the independent political power of the papacy; "John" is a name frequently assumed by Popes.

Who rose like shadows between Man and god
   Till that eclipse, still hanging under Heaven,   290
Was worshipped by the world o'er which they strode

   For the true Sun it quenched.[8]—"Their power was given
But to destroy," replied the leader—"I
   Am one of those who have created, even

   "If it be but a world of agony."—   295
   "Whence camest thou and whither goest thou?
How did thy course begin," I said, "and why?

   "Mine eyes are sick of this perpetual flow
Of people, and my heart of one sad thought.—
   Speak."[9] "Whence I came, partly I seem to know,   300

"And how and by what paths I have been brought
   To this dread pass, methinks even thou mayst guess;
Why this should be my mind can compass not;

   "Whither the conqueror hurries me still less.
But follow thou, and from spectator turn   305
   Actor or victim in this wretchedness,

"And what thou wouldst be taught I then may learn
   From thee.—Now listen . . . In the April prime[1]
When all the forest tops began to burn

   "With kindling green, touched by the azure clime   310
Of the young year, I found myself asleep
   Under a mountain, which from unknown time

"Had yawned into a cavern high and deep,
   And from it came a gentle rivulet
Whose water like clear air in its calm sweep   315

   "Bent the soft grass and kept for ever wet
The stems of the sweet flowers, and filled the grove
   With sound which all who hear must needs forget

"All pleasure and all pain, all hate and love,
   Which they had known before that hour of rest: 320
A sleeping mother then would dream not of

   "The only child who died upon her breast
At eventide, a king would mourn no more
   The crown of which his brow was dispossest

---

8. I.e., institutional Christianity has eclipsed the true God.
9. The rest of the fragment consists of Rousseau's allegorical account of his own life, in response to the only two of the narrator's four questions (lines 296–97) which, he says, the limitations of his knowledge permit him partially to answer.
1. Spring, the first season of the year.

"When the sun lingered o'er the Ocean floor   325
    To gild his rival's new prosperity.—
Thou wouldst forget thus vainly to deplore

"Ills, which if ills, can find no cure from thee,
The thought of which no other sleep will quell
    Nor other music blot from memory—   330

"So sweet and deep is the oblivious[2] spell.—
    Whether my life had been before that sleep
The Heaven which I imagine, or a Hell

"Like this harsh world in which I wake to weep,
I know not. I arose and for a space   335
    The scene of woods and waters seemed to keep,

"Though it was now broad day, a gentle trace
    Of light diviner than the common Sun
Sheds on the common Earth, but all the place

"Was filled with many sounds woven into one   340
Oblivious melody, confusing sense
    Amid the gliding waves and shadows dun;

"And as I looked the bright omnipresence
    Of morning through the orient[3] cavern flowed,
And the Sun's image radiantly intense   345

"Burned on the waters of the well that glowed
Like gold, and threaded all the forest maze
    With winding paths of emerald fire—there stood

"Amid the sun, as he amid the blaze
    Of his own glory, on the vibrating   350
Floor of the fountain, paved with flashing rays,

"A shape all light,[4] which with one hand did fling
Dew on the earth, as if she were the Dawn
    Whose invisible rain forever seemed to sing

2. Causing forgetfulness. Shelley models Rousseau's account of his life in part on Rousseau's own confessional writings and in part (as numerous verbal echoes indicate) on Wordsworth's *Ode: Intimations of Immortality* and its account of the westward course of man's life. Shelley, however, substitutes his own interpretations and evaluations for those expressed by Wordsworth.

3. Facing the east. The cavern runs from east to west through the mountain, and as Rousseau grows older, he follows the course of its rivulet westward.

4. "The shape all light," whose significance has been much disputed, seems to represent the Rousseauistic and Wordsworthean ideal of nature and of trust in the natural human instincts. The description of the shape echoes Wordsworth's description, in the *Intimations Ode*, of the celestial light, glory, and splendor which in his youth had invested the common earth. In Shelley's poem the enchanting feminine shape, formed by a reflection of the sun's light from the material medium of water, apparently leads Rousseau on only to betray him (382 ff., 400 ff.)

"A silver music on the mossy lawn,   355
   And still before her on the dusky grass
Iris[5] her many coloured scarf had drawn.—

"In her right hand she bore a chrystal glass
Mantling with bright Nepenthe;[6]—the fierce splendour
   Fell from her as she moved under the mass   360

"Of the deep cavern, and with palms so tender
   Their tread broke not the mirror of its billow,
Glided along the river, and did bend her

"Head under the dark boughs, till like a willow
Her fair hair swept the bosom of the stream   365
   That whispered with delight to be their pillow.—

"As one enamoured is upborne in dream
   O'er lily-paven lakes mid silver mist
To wondrous music, so this shape might seem

"Partly to tread the waves with feet which kist   370
The dancing foam, partly to glide along
   The airs that roughened the moist amethyst,

"Or the slant morning beams that fell among
   The trees, or the soft shadows of the trees;
And her feet ever to the ceaseless song   375

"Of leaves and winds and waves and birds and bees
And falling drops moved in a measure new
   Yet sweet, as on the summer evening breeze

"Up from the lake a shape of golden dew
   Between two rocks, athwart the rising moon,   380
Dances i' the wind where eagle never flew.—

"And still her feet, no less than the sweet tune
To which they moved, seemed as they moved, to blot
   The thoughts of him who gazed on them, and soon

"All that was seemed as if it had been not,   385
   As if the gazer's mind was strewn beneath
Her feet like embers, and she, thought by thought,

"Trampled its fires into the dust of death,
   As Day upon the threshold of the east
Treads out the lamps of night, until the breath   390

5. The rainbow.
6. A drug causing total forgetfulness.
The sinister suggestion subtly introduced
in the description of the shape ("the
fierce splendor," line 359) is heightened
by echoes from Milton's *Comus*, lines
672 ff., in which the enchanter Comus
(born of Circe, "daughter of the Sun")
tries to seduce the Lady by a beverage
which Milton compared to Nepenthe.

"Of darkness reillumines even the least
  Of heaven's living eyes[7]—like day she came,
Making the night a dream; and ere she ceased

"To move, as one between desire and shame
Suspended, I said—'If, as it doth seem,   395
  Thou comest from the realm without a name,

"'Into this valley of perpetual dream,
  Shew whence I came, and where I am, and why—
Pass not away upon the passing stream.'

"'Arise and quench thy thirst,' was her reply.   400
And as a shut lily, stricken by the wand
  Of dewy morning's vital alchemy,

"I rose; and, bending at her sweet command,
  Touched with faint lips the cup she raised,
And suddenly my brain became as sand   405

"Where the first wave had more than half erased
The track of deer on desert Labrador,
  Whilst the fierce wolf from which they fled amazed

"Leaves his stamp visibly upon the shore
  Until the second bursts—so on my sight   410
Burst a new Vision never seen before.—

"And the fair shape waned in the coming light
As veil by veil the silent splendour drops
  From Lucifer, amid the chrysolite[8]

"Of sunrise ere it strike the mountain tops—   415
  And as the presence of that fairest planet
Although unseen is felt by one who hopes

"That his day's path may end as he began it
In that star's smile,[9] whose light is like the scent
  Of a jonquil when evening breezes fan it,   420

"Or the soft notes in which his dear lament
  The Brescian shepherd breathes,[1] or the caress
That turned his weary slumber to content.—

"So knew I in that light's severe excess
The presence of that shape which on the stream   425
  Moved, as I moved along the wilderness,

7. The stars.
8. A greenish gem.
9. I.e., of the star which is both the
morning star, Lucifer (line 414) and the
evening star, Venus.
1. "The favorite song, *Stanco di pascolar*

le pecorelle, is a Brescian national air"
[Mary Shelley's note]. The title translates, "I am tired of pasturing the
sheep." Brescia is a province in northern Italy.

"More dimly than a day appearing dream,
  The ghost of a forgotten form of sleep,
A light from Heaven whose half extinguished beam

"Through the sick day in which we wake to weep   430
Glimmers, forever sought, forever lost.—
  So did that shape its obscure tenour keep

"Beside my path, as silent as a ghost;[2]
  But the new Vision, and its cold bright car,
With savage music, stunning music, crost   435

  "The forest, and as if from some dread war
Triumphantly returning, the loud million
  Fiercely extolled the fortune of her star.—

"A moving arch of victory the vermilion
  And green and azure plumes of Iris[3] had   440
Built high over her wind-winged pavilion,

  "And underneath ætherial glory clad
The wilderness, and far before her flew
  The tempest of the splendour which forbade

"Shadow to fall from leaf or stone;—the crew   445
  Seemed in that light like atomies[4] that dance
Within a sunbeam.—Some upon the new

  "Embroidery of flowers that did enhance
The grassy vesture of the desart, played,
  Forgetful of the chariot's swift advance;   450

"Others stood gazing till within the shade
  Of the great mountain its light left them dim.—
Others outspeeded it, and others made

  "Circles around it like the clouds that swim
Round the high moon in a bright sea of air,   455
  And more did follow, with exulting hymn,

"The chariot and the captives fettered there,
  But all like bubbles on an eddying flood
Fell into the same track at last and were

  "Borne onward.—I among the multitude   460
Was swept; me sweetest flowers delayed not long,
  Me not the shadow nor the solitude,

2. In lines 410–33 the brilliance of the
chariot of Life makes the fair shape fade
until, like the morning star, Lucifer (line
414) in the daytime, its presence is felt.

although no longer seen.
3. Goddess of the rainbow.
4. Particles of dust.

"Me not the falling stream's Lethean[5] song,
  Me, not the phantom of that early form
Which moved upon its motion,—but among   465

"The thickest billows of the living storm
  I plunged, and bared my bosom to the clime
Of that cold light, whose airs too soon deform.—

"Before the chariot had begun to climb
  The opposing steep of that mysterious dell,
Behold a wonder worthy of the rhyme   470

"Of him[6] who from the lowest depths of Hell
Through every Paradise and through all glory
Love led serene, and who returned to tell

"In words of hate and awe the wondrous story   475
  How all things are transfigured, except Love;
For deaf as is a sea which wrath makes hoary

"The world can hear not the sweet notes that move
The sphere whose light is melody to lovers[7]—
  A wonder worthy of his rhyme—the grove   480

"Grew dense with shadows to its inmost covers,
  The earth was grey with phantoms,[8] and the air
Was peopled with dim forms, as when there hovers

"A flock of vampire-bats before the glare
Of the tropic sun, bringing ere evening   485
  Strange night upon some Indian isle,—thus were

"Phantoms diffused around, and some did fling
  Shadows of shadows, yet unlike themselves,
Behind them, some like eaglets on the wing

"Were lost in white blaze, others like elves   490
Danced in a thousand unimagined shapes
  Upon the sunny streams and grassy shelves;

"And others sate chattering like restless apes
  On vulgar paws and voluble like fire.
Some made a cradle of the ermined capes   495

---

5. Causing forgetfulness, like the river Lethe in Hades.
6. Dante, who describes this pilgrimage in *The Divine Comedy;* "Love" is embodied in that poem by Beatrice.
7. The third sphere of the planet Venus (Love), in Dante's Ptolemaic universe.

8. Lucretius, *De rerum natura*, Book IV, says that ideas, superstitions, and passions peel off of men as *simulacra* (semblances, phantoms) and float about in space.

"Of kingly mantles, some upon the tiar
Of pontiffs[9] sate like vultures, others played
    Within the crown which girt with empire

"A baby's or an idiot's brow, and made
    Their nests in it; the old anatomies[1]   500
Sate hatching their bare brood under the shade

    "Of demon wings, and laughed from their dead eyes
To reassume the delegated power
    Arrayed in which these worms did monarchize

"Who make this earth their charnel.[2]—Others more   505
    Humble, like falcons sate upon the fist
Of common men, and round their heads did soar,

    "Or like small gnats and flies, as thick as mist
On evening marshes, thronged about the brow
    Of lawyer, statesman, priest and theorist,   510

"And others like discoloured flakes of snow
    On fairest bosoms and the sunniest hair
Fell, and were melted by the youthful glow

    "Which they extinguished; for like tears, they were
A veil to those from whose faint lids they rained   515
    In drops of sorrow.—I became aware

"Of whence those forms proceeded which thus stained
    The track in which we moved; after brief space
From every form the beauty slowly waned,

    "From every firmest limb and fairest face   520
The strength and freshness fell like dust, and left
    The action and the shape without the grace

"Of life; the marble brow of youth was cleft
    With care, and in the eyes where once hope shone
Desire like a lioness bereft   525

    "Of its last cub, glared ere it died; each one
Of that great crowd sent forth incessantly
    These shadows, numerous as the dead leaves blown

"In Autumn evening from a poplar tree—
    Each, like himself and like each other were,   530
At first, but soon distorted, seemed to be

---

9. The tiara, or triple crown of the popes.
1. Skeletonlike monsters.
2. The monarchs who had made the earth one great cemetery ("charnel") were like grave-worms, for they fed upon the corpses they had slaughtered.

"Obscure clouds moulded by the casual air;
And of this stuff the car's creative ray
Wrought all the busy phantoms that were there

"As the sun shapes the clouds[3]—thus, on the way   535
Mask after mask fell from the countenance
And form of all, and long before the day

"Was old, the joy which waked like Heaven's glance
The sleepers in the oblivious valley, died,
And some grew weary of the ghastly dance   540

"And fell, as I have fallen by the way side,
Those soonest from whose forms most shadows past
And least of strength and beauty did abide."—

"Then, what is Life?" I said . . . the cripple cast
His eye upon the car which now had rolled   545
Onward, as if that look must be the last,

And answered . . . . . "Happy those for whom the fold
Of

1822   1824

3. The shadows and phantoms of lines 480 ff. originate (lines 516 ff.) in the qualities of beauty, strength, and freshness, which fall like masks away from the men and women in the procession, as their hope degenerates into mere desire. These shadows of lost physical qualities at first (line 530) resembled the person from whom they originated, and the other shadows from that person; but they were distorted by the currents of the air and miscreated into phantoms by the light from the car of Life (lines 531–35).

From A *Defence of Poetry*   In 1820 Shelley's good friend Thomas Love Peacock published an ironic essay, *The Four Ages of Poetry*, implicitly directed against the towering claims for poetry and the poetic imagination by his Romantic contemporaries. Peacock adopted the premise of Wordsworth and other Romantic critics—that poetry in its origin was a primitive use of language and mind—but from this premise, Peacock proceeded to draw the conclusion that it has become a useless anachronism in this age of science and technology. Peacock was himself a poet, as well as the best contemporary prose satirist, and Shelley saw the joke; but he also recognized that the position which Peacock, as a satirist, had only half-humorously assumed was very close to that actually held in his day by Utilitarian philosophers and material-minded laymen who either attacked or contemptuously ignored the imaginative faculty and its achievements. He therefore undertook, as he good-humoredly wrote to Peacock, "to break a lance with you * * * in honor of my mistress Urania," even though he was only "the knight of the shield of shadow and the lance of gossamere." The result was *The Defence of Poetry*, planned to consist of three parts. The last two parts were never written, and even the existing section, written in 1821, remained unpublished until 1840, eighteen years after Shelley's death.

For many decades Shelley's *Defence* was regarded as one of the classic essays in literary criticism. Its reputation, however, diminished in the era of the New Criticism, during the middle decades of the present century, when the chief interest was in applied commentary and the kind of critical theory that will provide useful distinctions for the close analysis of particular literary texts. But Shelley's main enterprise, although different, is no less valid, and a rarer achievement in the history of critical writings. His emphasis is on the universal and permanent forms, qualities, and values that all great poems, as products of imagination, possess in common—on those aspects, as he puts it, in which time, person, and place "are convertible with respect to the highest poetry without injuring it as poetry." Shelley's position thus parallels that of William Blake, and has analogues to that of "archetypal" criticism in our own time. More than this: Shelley extends the term "poet" to comprehend all the creative minds that break out of the limitations of their age and place to approximate the enduring and general forms of value—including not only writers in verse and prose, but artists, legislators, and prophets, as well as the founders of a new organization of society, morality, or religion.

The very range of the *Defence* gives it unequaled importance as a ringing claim for the validity and indispensability of the visionary and creative imagination in all the great human concerns. And no later writer has exceeded the cogency of the attack, which Shelley includes, on our acquisitive society and its narrowly material concept of utility and progress. This bias has permitted man to make enormous progress in science and in his material well-being without a proportionate development of his "poetical faculty," the moral imagination; with the grotesque result, as Shelley says, that "man, having enslaved the elements, remains himself a slave."

From A Defence of Poetry

Part I

According to one mode of regarding those two classes of mental action, which are called reason and imagination, the former may be considered as mind contemplating the relations borne by one thought to another, however produced; and the latter, as mind acting upon those thoughts so as to colour them with its own light, and composing from them, as from elements, other thoughts, each containing within itself the principle of its own integrity. The one[1] is the τὸ ποιεῖν,[2] or the principle of synthesis, and has for its objects those forms which are common to universal nature and existence itself; the other is the τὸ λογιζειν,[3] or principle of analysis, and its action regards the relations of things, simply as relations; considering thoughts, not in their integral unity, but as the algebrai-

---

1. "The one" is the imagination; "the other" (in the same sentence) is the reason.

2. *To poiein,* "making." The Greek word from which "poet" derives means "maker," and the term "maker" had

been adopted as a name for poets by Renaissance critics such as Sir Philip Sidney, in his *Apology for Poetry* (1595), which Shelley had carefully studied.

3. *To logizein,* "calculating, reasoning."

cal representations which conduct to certain general results. Reason is the enumeration of quantities already known; imagination is the perception of the value of those quantities, both separately and as a whole. Reason respects the differences, and imagination the similitudes of things. Reason is to Imagination as the instrument to the agent, as the body to the spirit, as the shadow to the substance.[4]

* * *

In the youth of the world, men dance and sing and imitate natural objects, observing[5] in these actions, as in all others, a certain rhythm or order. And, although all men observe a similar, they observe not the same order, in the motions of the dance, in the melody of the song, in the combinations of language, in the series of their imitations of natural objects. For there is a certain order or rhythm belonging to each of these classes of mimetic representation, from which the hearer and the spectator receive an intenser and purer pleasure than from any other: the sense of an approximation to this order has been called taste, by modern writers. Every man in the infancy of art, observes an order which approximates more or less closely to that from which this highest delight results: but the diversity is not sufficiently marked, as that its gradations should be sensible, except in those instances where the predominance of this faculty of approximation to the beautiful (for so we may be permitted to name the relation between this highest pleasure and its cause) is very great. Those in whom it exists in excess are poets, in the most universal sense of the word; and the pleasure resulting from the manner in which they express the influence of society or nature upon their own minds, communicates itself to others, and gathers a sort of reduplication from that community. Their language is vitally metaphorical; that is, it marks the before unapprehended relations of things, and perpetuates their apprehension, until the words which represent them, become through time signs for portions or classes of thoughts[6] instead of pictures of integral thoughts; and then if no new poets should arise to create afresh the associations which have been thus disorganised, language will be dead to all the nobler purposes of human intercourse. These similitudes or relations are finely said by Lord Bacon to be "the same footsteps of nature impressed upon the various subjects of the world"[7]—and he considers the faculty which perceives them as the storehouse of axioms common to all knowledge. In the infancy of society every author is necessarily a poet, because language itself is poetry; and to be a poet is to apprehend the true and the beautiful,

---

4. In the paragraph here omitted, Shelley defines poetry as "the expression of the imagination" and asserts that it is "connate with the origin of man."
5. Following.

6. I.e., abstract concepts.
7. In Bacon's *De Augmentis Scientiarum* (On the Enlargement of the Sciences). I.iii.

in a word the good which exists in the relation, subsisting, first between existence and perception, and secondly between perception and expression. Every original language near to its source is in itself the chaos of a cyclic poem:[8] the copiousness of lexicography[9] and the distinctions of grammar are the works of a later age, and are merely the catalogue and the form of the creations of Poetry.

But Poets, or those who imagine and express this indestructible order, are not only the authors of language and of music, of the dance and architecture and statuary and painting; they are the institutors of laws, and the founders of civil society and the inventors of the arts of life and the teachers, who draw into a certain propinquity with the beautiful and the true that partial apprehension of the agencies of the invisible world which is called religion.[1] Hence all original religions are allegorical, or susceptible of allegory, and, like Janus[2] have a double face of false and true. Poets, according to the circumstances of the age and nation in which they appeared, were called in the earlier epochs of the world legislators, or prophets:[3] a poet essentially comprises and unites both these characters. For he not only beholds intensely the present as it is, and discovers those laws according to which present things ought to be ordered, but he beholds the future in the present, and his thoughts are the germs of the flower and the fruit of latest time. Not that I assert poets to be prophets in the gross sense of the word, or that they can foretell the form as surely as they foreknow the spirit of events: such is the pretence of superstition which would make poetry an attribute of prophecy, rather than prophecy an attribute of poetry. A Poet participates in the eternal, the infinite, and the one; as far as relates to his conceptions, time and place and number are not. The grammatical forms which express the moods of time, and the difference of persons and the distinction of place are convertible with respect to the highest poetry without injuring it as poetry; and the choruses of Æschylus, and the book of Job, and Dante's Paradise would afford, more than any other writings, examples of this fact, if the limits of this essay did not forbid citation. The creations of sculpture, painting, and music, are illustrations still more decisive.

* * *

A poem is the very image of life expressed in its eternal truth. There is this difference between a story and a poem, that a story is a catalogue of detached facts, which have no other bond of connex-

8. A set of poems (e.g., "the Arthurian cycle") which deal with the same subject.

9. The making of a dictionary.

1. Shelley thus e.. rges the discussion to include all creative insights, or imao:- tive break-throughs, of mankind in v

ever area they may occur, includ:- non-institutional religion.

2. Roman god of beginnings and endings, represented with two heads whic face in opposite directions.

3. The Roman *vates* signified both p. et and poet.

ion than time, place, circumstance, cause and effect; the other is the creation of actions according to the unchangeable forms of human nature, as existing in the mind of the creator, which is itself the image of all other minds. The one is partial, and applies only to a definite period of time, and a certain combination of events which can never again recur; the other is universal, and contains within itself the germ of a relation to whatever motives or actions have place in the possible varieties of human nature. Time, which destroys the beauty and the use of the story of particular facts, stript of the poetry which should invest them, augments that of Poetry, and for ever develops new and wonderful applications of the eternal truth which it contains. Hence epitomes have been called the moths of just history;[4] they eat out the poetry of it. The story of particular facts is as a mirror which obscures and distorts that which should be beautiful: Poetry is a mirror which makes beautiful that which is distorted.

The parts of a composition may be poetical, without the composition as a whole being a poem. A single sentence may be considered as a whole though it be found in a series of unassimilated portions; a single word even may be a spark of inextinguishable thought. And thus all the great historians, Herodotus, Plutarch, Livy,[5] were poets; and although the plan of these writers, especially that of Livy, restrained them from developing this faculty in its highest degree, they make copious and ample amends for their subjection, by filling all the interstices of their subjects with living images.

Having determined what is poetry, and who are poets, let us proceed to estimate its effects upon society.

Poetry is ever accompanied with pleasure: all spirits on which it falls, open themselves to receive the wisdom which is mingled with its delight. In the infancy of the world, neither poets themselves nor their auditors are fully aware of the excellence of poetry: for it acts in a divine and unapprehended manner, beyond and above consciousness; and it is reserved for future generations to contemplate and measure the mighty cause and effect in all the strength and splendour of their union. Even in modern times, no living poet ever arrived at the fulness of his fame; the jury which sits in judgment upon a poet, belonging as he does to all time, must be composed of his peers: it must be impanneled by Time from the selectest of the wise of many generations. A Poet is a nightingale, who sits in darkness and sings to cheer its own solitude with sweet sounds; his auditors are as men entranced by the melody of an unseen musician, who feel that they are moved and softened, yet know not whence or

4. By Bacon in *The Advancement of Learning* II.ii.4. "Epitomes": abstracts, summaries.
5. Herodotus (ca. 480–ca. 425 B.C.) wrote the first systematic history of Greece; Plutarch (ca. 46–ca. 120 A.D.) wrote *Parallel Lives* of eminent Greeks and Romans; Titus Livius (59 B.C.– A.D. 17) wrote an immense history of Rome.

why. The poems of Homer and his contemporaries were the delight of infant Greece; they were the elements of that social system which is the column upon which all succeeding civilization has reposed. Homer embodied the ideal perfection of his age in human character; nor can we doubt that those who read his verses were awakened to an ambition of becoming like to Achilles, Hector and Ulysses: the truth and beauty of friendship, patriotism and persevering devotion to an object, were unveiled to the depths in these immortal creations: the sentiments of the auditors must have been refined and enlarged by a sympathy with such great and lovely impersonations, until from admiring they imitated, and from imitation they identified themselves with the objects of their admiration. Nor let it be objected, that these characters are remote from moral perfection, and that they can by no means be considered as edifying patterns for general imitation. Every epoch under names more or less specious has deified its peculiar errors; Revenge is the naked Idol of the worship of a semi-barbarous age; and Self-deceit is the veiled Image of unknown evil before which luxury and satiety lie prostrate. But a poet considers the vices of his contemporaries as the temporary dress in which his creations must be arrayed, and which cover without concealing the eternal proportions of their beauty. An epic or dramatic personage is understood to wear them around his soul, as he may the antient armour or the modern uniform around his body; whilst it is easy to conceive a dress more graceful than either. The beauty of the internal nature cannot be so far concealed by its accidental vesture, but that the spirit of its form shall communicate itself to the very disguise, and indicate the shape it hides from the manner in which it is worn. A majestic form and graceful motions will express themselves through the most barbarous and tasteless costume. Few poets of the highest class have chosen to exhibit the beauty of their conceptions in its naked truth and splendour; and it is doubtful whether the alloy of costume, habit, &c., be not necessary to temper this planetary music[6] for mortal ears.

The whole objection, however, of the immorality of poetry[7] rests upon a misconception of the manner in which poetry acts to produce the moral improvement of man. Ethical science[8] arranges the elements which poetry has created, and propounds schemes and proposes examples of civil and domestic life: nor is it for want of admirable doctrines that men hate, and despise, and censure, and deceive, and subjugate one another. But Poetry acts in another and diviner manner. It awakens and enlarges the mind itself by render-

6. The music made by the revolving crystalline spheres of the planets, inaudible to human ears.
7. In the preceding paragraph Shelley has been implicitly dealing with the charge, voiced by Plato in his *Republic*, that poetry is immoral because it represents evil characters acting evilly.
8. Moral philosophy.

ing it the receptacle of a thousand unapprehended combinations of thought. Poetry lifts the veil from the hidden beauty of the world, and makes familiar objects be as if they were not familiar; it reproduces[9] all that it represents, and the impersonations clothed in its Elysian light stand thenceforward in the minds of those who have once contemplated them, as memorials of that gentle and exalted content[1] which extends itself over all thoughts and actions with which it coexists. The great secret of morals is Love; or a going out of our own nature, and an identification of ourselves with the beautiful which exists in thought, action, or person, not our own. A man, to be greatly good, must imagine intensely and comprehensively; he must put himself in the place of another and of many others; the pains and pleasures of his species must become his own. The great instrument of moral good is the imagination;[2] and poetry administers to the effect by acting upon the cause. Poetry enlarges the circumference of the imagination by replenishing it with thoughts of ever new delight, which have the power of attracting and assimilating to their own nature all other thoughts, and which form new intervals and interstices whose void for ever craves fresh food. Poetry strengthens that faculty which is the organ of the moral nature of man, in the same manner as exercise strengthens a limb. A Poet therefore would do ill to embody his own conceptions of right and wrong, which are usually those of his place and time, in his poetical creations, which participate in neither. By this assumption of the inferior office of interpreting the effect, in which perhaps after all he might acquit himself but imperfectly, he would resign the glory in a participation in the cause.[3] There was little danger that Homer, or any of the eternal Poets, should have so far misunderstood themselves as to have abdicated this throne of their widest dominion. Those in whom the poetical faculty, though great, is less intense, as Euripides, Lucan, Tasso,[4] Spenser, have frequently affected a moral aim, and the effect of their poetry is diminished in exact proportion to the degree in which they compel us to advert to this purpose.[5]

* * *

9. Produces anew, recreates.

1. Contentment (pronounced con-tént).

2. Central to Shelley's theory is the concept (developed by 18th-century philosophers) of the sympathetic imagination—the faculty by which an individual is enabled to identify himself with the thoughts and feelings of other men. Shelley claims that the faculty which in poetry enables us to share the joys and sufferings of invented characters is also the basis of all morality, for it compels us to feel for others as we feel for ourselves.

3. The "effect," or the explicit moral standards into which imaginative insights are translated at a particular time or place, is contrasted to the "cause" of all morality, the imagination itself.

4. Euripides, Greek writer of tragedies, 5th century B.C.; Lucan, Roman poet, 1st century A.D., author of the *Pharsalia*; Tasso, Italian poet of the 16th century, author of *Jerusalem Delivered*, an epic poem about a crusade. "Affected": assumed, adopted.

5. In the omitted passage Shelley reviews the history of drama and poetry in relation to civilization and morality, and proceeds to refute the charge that poets are less useful than "reasoners and merchants." He begins by defining utility in terms of pleasure, and then distinguishes between the lower (physical and material) and the higher (imaginative) pleasures.

It is difficult to define pleasure in its highest sense; the definition involving a number of apparent paradoxes. For, from an inexplicable defect of harmony in the constitution of human nature, the pain of the inferior is frequently connected with the pleasures of the superior portions of our being. Sorrow, terror, anguish, despair itself are often the chosen expressions of an approximation to the highest good. Our sympathy in tragic fiction depends on this principle; tragedy delights by affording a shadow of the pleasure which exists in pain. This is the source also of the melancholy which is inseparable from the sweetest melody. The pleasure that is in sorrow is sweeter than the pleasure of pleasure itself. And hence the saying, "It is better to go to the house of mourning, than to the house of mirth."[6] Not that this highest species of pleasure is necessarily linked with pain. The delight of love and friendship, the ecstasy of the admiration of nature, the joy of the perception and still more of the creation of poetry is often wholly unalloyed.

The production and assurance of pleasure in this highest sense is true utility. Those who produce and preserve this pleasure are Poets or poetical philosophers.

The exertions of Locke, Hume, Gibbon, Voltaire, Rousseau,[7] and their disciples, in favour of oppressed and deluded humanity, are entitled to the gratitude of mankind. Yet it is easy to calculate the degree of moral and intellectual improvement which the world would have exhibited, had they never lived. A little more nonsense would have been talked for a century or two; and perhaps a few more men, women, and children, burnt as heretics. We might not at this moment have been congratulating each other on the abolition of the Inquisition in Spain.[8] But it exceeds all imagination to conceive what would have been the moral condition of the world if neither Dante, Petrarch, Boccaccio, Chaucer, Shakespeare, Calderon, Lord Bacon, nor Milton, had ever existed; if Raphael and Michael Angelo had never been born; if the Hebrew poetry had never been translated; if a revival of the study of Greek literature had never taken place; if no monuments of antient sculpture had been handed down to us; and if the poetry of the religion of the antient world had been extinguished together with its belief. The human mind could never, except by the intervention of these excitements, have been awakened to the invention of the grosser sciences, and that application of analytical reasoning to the aberrations of society, which it is now attempted to exalt over the direct expression of the inventive and creative faculty itself.

We have more moral, political and historical wisdom, than we know how to reduce into practice; we have more scientific and eco-

6. Ecclesiastes vii.2.
7. In a note Shelley says that although Peacock had classified Rousseau with these other thinkers, "he was essentially a poet. The others, even Voltaire, were mere reasoners."
8. The Inquisition had been suspended in 1820, the year before Shelley wrote this essay; it was not abolished permanently until 1834.

nomical knowledge than can be accommodated to the just distribution of the produce which it multiplies. The poetry in these systems of thought, is concealed by the accumulation of facts and calculating processes. There is no want of knowledge respecting what is wisest and best in morals, government, and political economy, or at least, what is wiser and better than what men now practise and endure. But we let *"I dare not* wait upon *I would,* like the poor cat i' the adage."[9] We want the creative faculty to imagine that which we know; we want the generous impulse to act that which we imagine; we want the poetry of life: our calculations have outrun conception; we have eaten more than we can digest. The cultivation of those sciences which have enlarged the limits of the empire of man over the external world, has, for want of the poetical faculty, proportionally circumscribed those of the internal world; and man, having enslaved the elements, remains himself a slave. To what but a cultivation of the mechanical arts in a degree disproportioned to the presence of the creative faculty, which is the basis of all knowledge, is to be attributed the abuse of all invention for abridging and combining labour, to the exasperation of the inequality of mankind? From what other cause has it arisen that these inventions which should have lightened, have added a weight to the curse imposed on Adam? **Poetry, and the principle of Self, of which money is the visible incarnation, are the God and Mammon of the world.**[10]

The functions of the poetical faculty are two-fold; by one it creates new materials of knowledge, and power and pleasure; by the other it engenders in the mind a desire to reproduce and arrange them according to a certain rhythm and order which may be called the beautiful and the good. The cultivation of poetry is never more to be desired than at periods when, from an excess of the selfish and calculating principle, the accumulation of the materials of external life exceed the quantity of the power of assimilating them to the internal laws of human nature. The body has then become too unwieldy for that which animates it.

Poetry is indeed something divine. It is at once the centre and circumference of knowledge; it is that which comprehends all science, and that to which all science must be referred. It is at the same time the root and blossom of all other systems of thought; it is that from which all spring, and that which adorns all; and that which, if blighted, denies the fruit and the seed, and withholds from the barren world the nourishment and the succession of the scions of the tree of life. It is the perfect and consummate surface and bloom of things; it is as the odour and the colour of the rose to the texture of the elements which compose it, as the form and the splendour of unfaded beauty to the secrets of anatomy and corrup-

9. *Macbeth* I.vii.44–45.
10. "Ye cannot serve God and Mammon" (Matthew vi.24).

tion. What were Virtue, Love, Patriotism, Friendship etc.—what were the scenery of this beautiful Universe which we inhabit—what were our consolations on this side of the grave—and what were our aspirations beyond it—if Poetry did not ascend to bring light and fire from those eternal regions where the owl-winged faculty of calculation dare not ever soar? Poetry is not like reasoning, a power to be exerted according to the determination of the will. A man cannot say, "I will compose poetry." The greatest poet even cannot say it: for the mind in creation is as a fading coal which some invisible influence, like an inconstant wind, awakens to transitory brightness: this power arises from within, like the colour of a flower which fades and changes as it is developed, and the conscious portions of our natures are unprophetic either of its approach or its departure.[11] Could this influence be durable in its original purity and force, it is impossible to predict the greatness of the results; but when composition begins, inspiration is already on the decline, and the most glorious poetry that has ever been communicated to the world is probably a feeble shadow of the original conception of the poet. I appeal to the greatest Poets of the present day, whether it be not an error to assert that the finest passages of poetry are produced by labour and study. The toil and the delay recommended by critics can be justly interpreted to mean no more than a careful observation of the inspired moments, and an artificial connexion of the spaces between their suggestions by the intertexture of conventional expressions; a necessity only imposed by the limitedness of the poetical faculty itself. For Milton conceived the Paradise Lost as a whole before he executed it in portions. We have his own authority also for the Muse having "dictated" to him the "unpremeditated song,"[1] and let this be an answer to those who would allege the fifty-six various readings of the first line of the Orlando Furioso.[2] Compositions so produced are to poetry what mosaic is to painting. This instinct and intuition of the poetical faculty is still more observable in the plastic and pictorial arts: a great statue or picture grows under the power of the artist as a child in the mother's womb; and the very mind which directs the hands in formation is incapable of accounting to itself for the origin, the gradations, or the media of the process.

Poetry is the record of the best and happiest[3] moments of the happiest and best minds. We are aware of evanescent visitations of thought and feeling sometimes associated with place or person, sometimes regarding our own mind alone, and always arising unfore-

---

11. This passage reiterates the ancient belief that the highest poetry is "inspired," and therefore occurs independently of the intention, effort, or consciousness of the poet. Unlike earlier critics, however, Shelley attributes such poetry not to a god or muse but to the unconscious depths within the poet's own mind.

1. *Paradise Lost* IX.21–24.
2. The epic poem by the 16th-century Italian poet Ariosto, noted for his care in composition.
3. In the double sense of "most joyous" and "most apt or felicitous in invention."

seen and departing unbidden, but elevating and delightful beyond all expression: so that even in the desire and the regret they leave, there cannot but be pleasure, participating as it does in the nature of its object. It is as it were the interpenetration of a diviner nature through our own; but its footsteps are like those of a wind over a sea, where the coming calm erases, and whose traces remain only as on the wrinkled sand which paves it. These and corresponding conditions of being are experienced principally by those of the most delicate sensibility and the most enlarged imagination; and the state of mind produced by them is at war with every base desire. The enthusiasm of virtue, love, patriotism, and friendship is essentially linked with these emotions; and whilst they last, self appears as what it is, an atom to a Universe. Poets are not only subject to these experiences as spirits of the most refined organization, but they can colour all that they combine with the evanescent hues of this etherial world; a word, or a trait in the representation of a scene or a passion, will touch the enchanted chord, and reanimate, in those who have ever experienced these emotions, the sleeping, the cold, the buried image of the past. Poetry thus makes immortal all that is best and most beautiful in the world; it arrests the vanishing apparitions which haunt the interlunations[4] of life, and veiling them or in language or in form sends them forth among mankind, bearing sweet news of kindred joy to those with whom their sisters abide—abide, because there is no portal of expression from the caverns of the spirit which they inhabit into the universe of things. Poetry redeems from decay the visitations of the divinity in man.

Poetry turns all things to loveliness; it exalts the beauty of that which is most beautiful, and it adds beauty to that which is most deformed; it marries exultation and horror, grief and pleasure, eternity and change; it subdues to union under its light yoke all irreconcilable things. It transmutes all that it touches, and every form moving within the radiance of its presence is changed by wondrous sympathy to an incarnation of the spirit which it breathes; its secret alchemy turns to potable gold[5] the poisonous waters which flow from death through life; it strips the veil of familiarity from the world, and lays bare the naked and sleeping beauty which is the spirit of its forms.

All things exist as they are perceived: at least in relation to the percipient. "The mind is its own place, and of itself can make a heaven of hell, a hell of heaven."[6] But poetry defeats the curse which binds us to be subjected to the accident of surrounding impressions. And whether it spreads its own figured curtain or withdraws life's dark veil from before the scene of things, it equally cre-

---

4. The dark intervals between the old and new moon.
5. Alchemists aimed to produce a drinkable form of gold that would be an elixir of life, curing all diseases.
6. Satan's speech, *Paradise Lost* I.254–55.

ates for us a being within our being. It makes us the inhabitants of a world to which the familiar world is a chaos. It reproduces the common universe of which we are portions and percipients, and it purges from our inward sight the film of familiarity which obscures from us the wonder of our being. It compels us to feel that which we perceive, and to imagine that which we know. It creates anew the universe after it has been annihilated in our minds by the recurrence of impressions blunted by reiteration.[7] It justifies that bold and true word of Tasso: *Non merita nome di creatore, se non Iddio ed il Poeta*.[8]

A Poet, as he is the author to others of the highest wisdom, pleasure, virtue and glory, so he ought personally to be the happiest, the best, the wisest, and the most illustrious of men. As to his glory, let Time be challenged to declare whether the fame of any other institutor of human life be comparable to that of a poet. That he is the wisest, the happiest, and the best, inasmuch as he is a poet, is equally incontrovertible: the greatest poets have been men of the most spotless virtue, of the most consummate prudence, and, if we could look into the interior of their lives, the most fortunate of men: and the exceptions, as they regard those who possessed the poetic faculty in a high yet inferior degree, will be found on consideration to confirm rather than destroy the rule. Let us for a moment stoop to the arbitration of popular breath, and usurping and uniting in our own persons the incompatible characters of accuser, witness, judge and executioner, let us decide without trial, testimony, or form that certain motives of those who are "there sitting where we dare not soar"[9] are reprehensible. Let us assume that Homer was a drunkard, that Virgil was a flatterer, that Horace was a coward, that Tasso was a madman, that Lord Bacon was a peculator, that Raphael was a libertine, that Spenser was a poet laureate.[1] It is inconsistent with his division of our subject to cite living poets, but Posterity has done ample justice to the great names now referred to. Their errors have been weighed and found to have been dust in the balance; if their sins "were as scarlet, they are now white as snow";[2] they have been washed in the blood of the mediator and the redeemer Time. Observe in what a ludicrous chaos the imputations of real or fictitious crime have been confused in the contemporary calumnies against poetry and poets;[3] consider how little is, as it

7. Shelley's version of a widespread Romantic doctrine that the poetic imagination transforms the familiar into the miraculous and recreates the old world into a new world. See, e.g., Coleridge's *Biographia Literaria*, above, Chap. IV, on "freshness of sensation"; and Carlyle's *Sartor Resartus*, below, Bk. III, Chap. 8, "Natural Supernaturalism."
8. "No one merits the name of Creator except God and the Poet." Quoted by Pierantonio Serassi in his *Life of Torquato Tasso* (1785).

9. *Paradise Lost* IV.829.
1. Charges, some of them valid, which had in fact been made against these men. Raphael is the 16th-century Italian painter. The ironic use of "poet laureate" as a derogatory term was a dig at Robert Southey, who held that honor at the time of writing.
2. Isaiah i.18.
3. Shelley alludes especially to the charges of immorality by contemporary reviewers against Lord Byron and himself.

appears—or appears, as it is; look to your own motives, and judge not, lest ye be judged.

Poetry, as has been said, in this respect differs from logic, that it is not subject to the controul of the active powers of the mind, and that its birth and recurrence has no necessary connexion with consciousness or will. It is presumptuous to determine that these[4] are the necessary conditions of all mental causation, when mental effects are experienced insusceptible of being referred to them. The frequent recurrence of the poetical power, it is obvious to suppose, may produce in the mind an habit of order and harmony correlative with its own nature and with its effects upon other minds. But in the intervals of inspiration, and they may be frequent without being durable, a poet becomes a man, and is abandoned to the sudden reflux of the influences under which others habitually live. But as he is more delicately organized than other men, and sensible to pain and pleasure, both his own and that of others, in a degree unknown to them, he will avoid the one and pursue the other with an ardour proportioned to this difference. And he renders himself obnoxious to calumny,[5] when he neglects to observe the circumstances under which these objects of universal pursuit and flight have disguised themselves in one another's garments.

But there is nothing necessarily evil in this error, and thus cruelty, envy, revenge, avarice, and the passions purely evil, have never formed any portion of the popular imputations on the lives of poets.

I have thought it most favourable to the cause of truth to set down these remarks according to the order in which they were suggested to my mind, by a consideration of the subject itself, instead of following that of the treatise that excited me to make them public.[6] Thus although devoid of the formality of a polemical reply; if the view they contain be just, they will be found to involve a refutation of the doctrines of the Four Ages of Poetry, so far at least as regards the first division of the subject. I can readily conjecture what should have moved the gall of the learned and intelligent author of that paper; I confess myself, like him, unwilling to be stunned by the Theseids[7] of the hoarse Codri of the day. Bavius and Mævius undoubtedly are, as they ever were, insufferable persons. But it belongs to a philosophical critic to distinguish rather than confound.

The first part of these remarks has related to Poetry in its elements and principles; and it has been shewn, as well as the narrow limits assigned them would permit, that what is called poetry, in a

---

4. I.e., consciousness or will. Shelley again proposes that some mental processes are unconscious—outside our control or awareness.
5. Exposed to slander.
6. Peacock's *Four Ages of Poetry*.

7. Epic poems about Theseus. Codrus (plural "Codri") was the Roman author of a long, dull *Theseid*, attacked by Juvenal and others; "Bavius and Maevius" were would-be poets satirized by Virgil and Horace.

restricted sense, has a common source with all other forms of order and of beauty according to which the materials of human life are susceptible of being arranged, and which is poetry in an universal sense.

The second part[8] will have for its object an application of these principles to the present state of the cultivation of Poetry, and a defence of the attempt to idealize the modern forms of manners and opinions, and compel them into a subordination to the imaginative and creative faculty. For the literature of England, an energetic development of which has ever preceded or accompanied a great and free development of the national will, has arisen as it were from a new birth. In spite of the low-thoughted envy which would undervalue contemporary merit, our own will be a memorable age in intellectual achievements, and we live among such philosophers and poets as surpass beyond comparison any who have appeared since the last national struggle for civil and religious liberty.[9] The most unfailing herald, companion, and follower of the awakening of a great people to work a beneficial change in opinion or institution, is Poetry. At such periods there is an accumulation of the power of communicating and receiving intense and impassioned conceptions respecting man and nature. The persons in whom this power resides, may often, as far as regards many portions of their nature, have little apparent correspondence with that spirit of good of which they are the ministers. But even whilst they deny and abjure, they are yet compelled to serve, the Power which is seated upon the throne of their own soul. It is impossible to read the compositions of the most celebrated writers of the present day without being startled with the electric life which burns within their words. They measure the circumference and sound the depths of human nature with a comprehensive and all-penetrating spirit, and they are themselves perhaps the most sincerely astonished at its manifestations, for it is less their spirit than the spirit of the age.[1] Poets are the hierophants[2] of an unapprehended inspiration, the mirrors of the gigantic shadows which futurity casts upon the present, the words which express what they understand not; the trumpets which sing to battle, and feel not what they inspire; the influence which is moved not, but moves.[3] Poets are the unacknowledged legislators of the World.

1821   1840

8. Shelley, however, completed only the first part of his *Defence*.
9. In the age of Milton and the English Civil War.
1. By "the spirit of the age" Shelley identifies what was later to be called "the Romantic movement" in contemporary literature and philosophy; he recognized its greatness, as well as its relation to the ferment of ideas and aspirations effected by the French Revolution. See also below, Hazlitt's *Mr. Wordsworth*, from his book *The Spirit of the Age*.
2. Priests who are expositors of sacred mysteries.
3. Aristotle had said that God is the "Unmoved Mover" of the universe.

JOHN KEATS

(1795–1821)

1817: *Poems*, Keats's first book.
1818: *Endymion*.
1819: Keats's *annus mirabilis*, in which he writes almost all
     his greatest poems.
1820: Publishes the volume *Lamia, Isabella, The Eve of St.*
     Agnes, and Other Poems.

No major poet has had a less propitious origin. Keats's father was head
ostler at a London livery stable; he married his employer's daughter and
inherited the business. Mrs. Keats, by all reports, was a strongly sensuous
woman, and a rather casual but affectionate mother to her four children
—John (the first-born), his two brothers, and a sister. Keats was sent to
the Reverend John Clarke's private school at Enfield, where he was a
noisy, high-spirited boy; despite his small physique (when full-grown, he
was barely over five feet in height), he distinguished himself in skylarking
and fist-fights. Here Keats had the good fortune to have as a teacher
Charles Cowden Clarke, son of the headmaster, who later became himself
a man of letters; he encouraged Keats's passion for reading and, both at
school and in the course of their later friendship, introduced him to
Spenser and other poets, to music, and to the theater.

When Keats was 8 his father was killed by a fall from a horse, and
when he was 14, his mother died of tuberculosis. Although the livery
stable had prospered, and £8,000 had been left in trust to the children
by Keats's grandmother, the estate remained tied up in a Chancery suit
for all of Keats's lifetime. The children's guardian, Richard Abbey, was
an unimaginative and practical-minded businessman; he took Keats out
of school at the age of 15 and bound him apprentice to Thomas Hammond, a surgeon and apothecary at Edmonton. In 1815 Keats carried on
his medical studies at Guy's Hospital, London, and the next year qualified
to practice as an apothecary—but almost immediately, over his guardian's
protests, he abandoned medicine for poetry.

This decision was influenced by Keats's friendship with Leigh Hunt,
then editor of the *Examiner* and a leading political radical, a minor poet,
and a prolific writer of criticism and periodical essays. Hunt, the first
successful author of Keats's acquaintance, added his enthusiastic encouragement of Keats's poetic efforts to that of Clarke. More important, he
introduced Keats to writers greater than Hunt himself, Hazlitt, Lamb, and
Shelley, as well as to Benjamin Robert Haydon, painter of grandiose historical and religious canvases. Through Hunt Keats also met John Hamilton
Reynolds, and then Charles Wentworth Dilke and Charles Brown, men
who became his intimate friends and provided him with an essential circumstance for a fledgling poet, a sympathetic and appreciative audience.

The rapidity and sureness of Keats's development has no match. He
did not even undertake poetry until his 18th year, and for the next few

years produced album verse which was at best merely competent and at times exhibited a labored vulgarity of sentiment and phrasing. Suddenly, in 1816, he spoke out loud and bold in *On First Looking into Chapman's Homer*, a major sonnet in the grand style. Later that same year he wrote *Sleep and Poetry*, in which he laid out for himself a poetic program deliberately modeled on the careers of the greatest poets, asking only

> for ten years, that I may overwhelm
> Myself in poesy; so I may do the deed
> That my own soul has to itself decreed.

For even while his health was good, Keats felt a foreboding of early death, and applied himself to his art with a desperate urgency. In 1817 Keats went on to compose *Endymion*, an ambitious undertaking of more than 4,000 lines. It is a profuse and often obscure allegory of the poet's quest for an ideal feminine counterpart and a flawless happiness beyond earthly possibility; in a number of passages, however, it already exhibits the sure movement and phrasing of his mature poetic style. But Keats's critical judgment and aspiration exceeded his achievement: long before he completed it, he declared impatiently that he carried on with the "slipshod" *Endymion* only as a poetic exercise and "trial of invention" and began to block out the more ambitious *Hyperion*, conceived on the model of Milton's *Paradise Lost* in that most demanding of forms, the epic poem. The extent of his success in achieving the Miltonic manner is one of the reasons why Keats left off before *Hyperion* was finished, for he recognized that he was uncommonly susceptible to poetic influences, and regarded this as a threat to his poetic individuality. "I will write independently," he insisted. "The Genius of Poetry must work out its own salvation in a man." He had refused the chance of intimacy with Shelley "that I might have my own unfettered scope"; he had broken away from Leigh Hunt's influence lest he get "the reputation of Hunt's *élève*"; now he shied away from domination by Milton's idiosyncratic and powerfully infectious style.

With the year 1818 began a series of disappointments and disasters which culminated in Keats's mortal illness. Sentimental legend used to fix the blame upon two anonymous articles: a scurrilous attack on Keats as a member of the "Cockney School" (that is, Leigh Hunt's radical literary circle in London) which appeared in the heavily Tory *Blackwood's Magazine*, and a savage mauling of *Endymion* in the *Quarterly Review*. Shelley gave impetus to this myth by his description of Keats as "a pale flower" in *Adonais*, and Byron, who knew even less about Keats, asserted that he was "snuffed out by an article." But in fact, Keats had the good sense to recognize that the attacks were motivated by Tory bias and class snobbery, and he has already passed his own severe judgment on *Endymion*: "My own domestic criticism," he said, "has given me pain without comparison beyond what *Blackwood* or the *Quarterly* could possibly inflict." More important was the financial distress of his brother George and his young bride, who had just emigrated to Kentucky and lost their money in an ill-advised investment; Keats, himself always short of funds, had now to turn to literary journey-work to eke out the family income. His younger brother Tom contracted tuberculosis, and the poet, in constant attendance upon him through the later months of 1818, helplessly watched him waste away until his death that December. In the spring and summer of that year

Keats had taken a strenuous walking tour in the English Lake Country, Scotland, and Ireland; it was a glorious adventure, but a totally exhausting one in wet, cold weather, and Keats returned in August with a chronically ulcerated throat made increasingly ominous by the shadow of the tuberculosis which had killed his mother and brother. And in the late fall of 1818 Keats fell desperately, unwillingly, helplessly in love with Fanny Brawne. This pretty, vivacious, and mildly flirtatious girl of 18 had little interest in poetry, but she possessed an alert and sensible mind and loved Keats sincerely, and might well have made him an excellent wife. They became engaged, but Keats's dedication to poetry, his poverty, and his growing illness made marriage impossible and love a torment.

In this period of acute distress and emotional turmoil, within five years of his first trying his hand at poetry, Keats achieved the culmination of his brief poetic career. Between January and September of 1819, masterpiece followed masterpiece in astonishing succession: *The Eve of St. Agnes*, *La Belle Dame sans Merci*, all six of the great *Odes*, *Lamia*, and a sufficient number of fine sonnets to make him, with Wordsworth, the major Romantic craftsman in that form. All of these poems possess the distinctive qualities of the work of Keats's maturity: a slow-paced, gracious movement; a concreteness of description in which all the senses—tactile, gustatory, kinetic, organic, as well as visual and auditory—combine to give the total apprehension of an experience; an intense delight at the sheer existence of things outside himself, the poet seeming to lose his own identity in the fullness of identification with the object he contemplates; and a concentrated felicity of phrasing which reminded Keats's friends, as it has so many critics since, of the language of Shakespeare. And under the rich sensuous surface we find Keats's characteristic presentation of all experience as a tangle of inseparable but irreconcilable opposites. He finds melancholy in delight, and pleasure in pain; he feels the highest intensity of love as an approximation to death; he inclines equally toward a life of indolence and "sensation" and toward a life of thought; he is aware both of the attraction of an imaginative dream world without "disagreeables" and the remorseless pressure of the actual; he aspires at the same time for aesthetic detachment and for social responsibility.

His letters, no less remarkable than his poetry, show that Keats felt on his pulses the conflicts he dramatized in his major poems. Above all, they reveal him wrestling with the problem of evil and suffering in the world—what to make of our lives in the discovery that "the world is full of misery and heartbreak, pain, sickness and oppression." To the end of his life Keats, with stubborn courage, refused to seek comfort by substituting for the complexity and contradictions of experience in this world either the simplicity of inherited philosophical doctrines or the absolutes of a religious creed. At the close of his poetic career, in the latter part of 1819, Keats began to rework the epic *Hyperion* into the form of a dream vision which he called *The Fall of Hyperion*. In the introductory section of this fragment the poet is told by the prophetess Moneta that he has hitherto been merely a dreamer; he must know that

> The poet and the dreamer are distinct,
> Diverse, sheer opposite, antipodes,

and that the height of poetry can only be reached by

those to whom the miseries of the world
Are misery, and will not let them rest.

Keats was seemingly planning to undertake a new direction and subject matter, when death intervened.

On the night of February 3, 1820, he coughed up some blood. He refused to evade the truth: "I cannot be deceived in that color; that drop of blood is my death warrant. I must die." That spring and summer a series of hemorrhages rapidly weakened him. In the autumn he allowed himself to be persuaded to seek a milder climate in Italy in the company of Joseph Severn, a young painter; but these last months were only what he called "a posthumous existence." He died in Rome on February 23, 1821, and was buried in the Protestant Cemetery. At times the agony of his disease, the apparent frustration of his hopes for great poetic achievement, and the despair of his passion for Fanny Brawne combined to compel even Keats's brave spirit to bitterness, resentment, and jealousy, but he always recovered his gallantry. His last letter, written to Charles Brown, concludes: "I can scarcely bid you good-bye, even in a letter. I always made an awkward bow. God bless you! John Keats."

No one can read Keats's poems and letters without an undersense of the immense waste of so extraordinary an intellect and genius cut off so early. What he might have accomplished is beyond conjecture; what we do know is that his achievement, when he stopped writing at the age of 24, greatly exceeds that at the corresponding age of Chaucer, Shakespeare, or Milton.

The texts of the poems are those newly prepared by Jack Stillinger, on the basis both of printed versions and manuscript materials, for his edition of *The Poems of John Keats* (Cambridge, Mass., 1978). The editors are grateful to Professor Stillinger, and to Harvard University Press, for making available to us proofs of these superbly edited texts prior to their publication.

On First Looking into Chapman's Homer[1]

Much have I travell'd in the realms of gold,
    And many goodly states and kingdoms seen;
    Round many western islands have I been
Which bards in fealty to Apollo hold.
Oft of one wide expanse had I been told   5
    That deep-brow'd Homer ruled as his demesne;[2]
    Yet did I never breathe its pure serene[3]
Till I heard Chapman speak out loud and bold:
Then felt I like some watcher of the skies

1. Keats's former schoolteacher, Charles Cowden Clarke, introduced him to Homer in the robust translation of the Elizabethan poet George Chapman. They read through the night, and Keats walked home at dawn; this sonnet, his first great poem, reached Clarke by the ten o'clock mail that same morning. That it was Balboa, not Cortez, who caught his first sight of the Pacific from the heights of Darien, in Panama, matters to history but not to poetry.
2. Realm, feudal possession.
3. Clear expanse of air.

When a new planet swims into his ken;   10
Or like stout Cortez when with eagle eyes
    He star'd at the Pacific—and all his men
Look'd at each other with a wild surmise—
    Silent, upon a peak in Darien.

October, 1816   1816

From Sleep and Poetry[1]

* * *

O for ten years, that I may overwhelm
Myself in poesy; so I may do the deed
That my own soul has to itself decreed.
Then will I pass the countries that I see
In long perspective, and continually   100
Taste their pure fountains. First the realm I'll pass
Of Flora, and old Pan:[2] sleep in the grass,
Feed upon apples red, and strawberries,
And choose each pleasure that my fancy sees;
Catch the white-handed nymphs in shady places,   105
To woo sweet kisses from averted faces,—
Play with their fingers, touch their shoulders white
Into a pretty shrinking with a bite
As hard as lips can make it: till agreed,
A lovely tale of human life we'll read.   110
And one will teach a tame dove how it best
May fan the cool air gently o'er my rest;
Another, bending o'er her nimble tread,
Will set a green robe floating round her head,
And still will dance with ever varied ease,   115
Smiling upon the flowers and the trees:
Another will entice me on, and on
Through almond blossoms and rich cinnamon;
Till in the bosom of a leafy world
We rest in silence, like two gems upcurl'd   120
In the recesses of a pearly shell.

---

1. At the early age of 21, Keats set himself a rigorous regimen of poetic training modeled on the course followed by the greatest poets. Virgil had established the pattern of beginning with pastoral writing and proceeding gradually to the point at which he was ready to undertake the epic, and this pattern had been deliberately followed by Spenser and Milton. Keats's version of this program, as he describes it here, is to begin with the realm of "Flora, and old Pan" (line 102) and, within ten years, to climb up to the level of poetry dealing with "the agonies, the strife / Of human hearts" (lines 124–25). The latter achievement Keats found best represented among his contemporaries by Wordsworth and, less successfully, by Shelley—Keats's vision of the chariot of poesy (lines 125–154) echoes Shelley's allegorical visions. The program Keats set himself is illuminated by his analysis of Wordsworth's progress in his letter to J. H. Reynolds of May 3, 1818, below.
2. I.e., the carefree pastoral world. Flora was the Roman goddess of flowers, and Pan the Greek god of pastures, woods, and animal life.

And can I ever bid these joys farewell?
Yes, I must pass them for a nobler life,
Where I may find the agonies, the strife
Of human hearts: for lo! I see afar,   125
O'er sailing the blue cragginess, a car[3]
And steeds with streamy manes—the charioteer
Looks out upon the winds with glorious fear:
And now the numerous tramplings quiver lightly
Along a huge cloud's ridge; and now with sprightly   130
Wheel downward come they into fresher skies,
Tipt round with silver from the sun's bright eyes.
Still downward with capacious whirl they glide;
And now I see them on a green-hill's side
In breezy rest among the nodding stalks.   135
The charioteer with wond'rous gesture talks
To the trees and mountains; and there soon appear
Shapes of delight, of mystery, and fear,
Passing along before a dusky space
Made by some mighty oaks: as they would chase   140
Some ever-fleeting music on they sweep.
Lo! how they murmur, laugh, and smile, and weep:
Some with upholden hand and mouth severe;
Some with their faces muffled to the ear
Between their arms; some, clear in youthful bloom,   145
Go glad and smilingly athwart the gloom;
Some looking back, and some with upward gaze;
Yes, thousands in a thousand different ways
Flit onward—now a lovely wreath of girls
Dancing their sleek hair into tangled curls;   150
And now broad wings. Most awfully intent,
The driver of those steeds is forward bent,
And seems to listen: O that I might know
All that he writes with such a hurrying glow.

   The visions all are fled—the car is fled   155
Into the light of heaven, and in their stead
A sense of real things comes doubly strong,
And, like a muddy stream, would bear along
My soul to nothingness: but I will strive
Against all doubtings, and will keep alive   160
The thought of that same chariot, and the strange
Journey it went.

          *   *   *

Nov.–Dec., 1816   1817

---

3. This chariot, with its "charioteer" (line 127), represents the higher poetic imagination, which bodies forth (line 138), the matters "of delight, of mystery, and fear" that characterize the grander poetic forms.

On Seeing the Elgin Marbles[4]

My spirit is too weak—mortality
  Weighs heavily on me like unwilling sleep,
  And each imagined pinnacle and steep
Of godlike hardship tells me I must die
Like a sick eagle looking at the sky.   5
  Yet 'tis a gentle luxury to weep
  That I have not the cloudy winds to keep
Fresh for the opening of the morning's eye.
Such dim-conceived glories of the brain
  Bring round the heart an undescribable feud;   10
So do these wonders a most dizzy pain,
  That mingles Grecian grandeur with the rude
Wasting of old time—with a billowy main—
  A sun—a shadow of a magnitude.

1817

On the Sea

It keeps eternal whisperings around
  Desolate shores, and with its mighty swell
  Gluts twice ten thousand caverns; till the spell
Of Hecate leaves them their old shadowy sound.
Often 'tis in such gentle temper found   5
  That scarcely will the very smallest shell
  Be moved for days from whence it sometime fell,
When last the winds of heaven were unbound.
O ye who have your eyeballs vext and tir'd,
  Feast them upon the wideness of the sea;   10
    O ye whose ears are dinned with uproar rude,
    Or fed too much with cloying melody—
    Sit ye near some old cavern's mouth and brood
Until ye start, as if the sea nymphs quired.

1817   1817

4. Lord Elgin had brought to England in 1806 the marble statues and friezes which adorned the Parthenon at Athens; in 1816 they were purchased by the government for the British Museum. Keats's response to his first sight of these time-worn memorials of Grecian artistry is characteristically intense, mixed, and subtly analyzed.

From Endymion: A Poetic Romance[1]

"The stretched metre of an antique song"

INSCRIBED TO THE MEMORY OF THOMAS CHATTERTON

Preface

Knowing within myself the manner in which this Poem has been produced, it is not without a feeling of regret that I make it public. What manner I mean, will be quite clear to the reader, who must soon perceive great inexperience, immaturity, and every error denoting a feverish attempt, rather than a deed accomplished. The two first books, and indeed the two last, I feel sensible are not of such completion as to warrant their passing the press; nor should they if I thought a year's castigation would do them any good;—it will not: the foundations are too sandy. It is just that this youngster should die away: a sad thought for me, if I had not some hope that while it is dwindling I may be plotting, and fitting myself for verses fit to live.

This may be speaking too presumptuously, and may deserve a punishment: but no feeling man will be forward to inflict it: he will leave me alone, with the conviction that there is not a fiercer hell than the failure in a great object. This is not written with the least atom of purpose to forestall criticisms of course, but from the desire I have to conciliate men who are competent to look, and who do look with a zealous eye, to the honour of English literature. The imagination of a boy is healthy, and the mature imagination

---

1. This poem of more than 4,000 lines (based on the classical myth of a mortal beloved by the goddess of the moon) tells of Endymion's long and agonized search for an immortal goddess whom he had seen in several visions. In the course of his wanderings he comes upon an Indian maid who had been abandoned by the followers of Bacchus, and to his utter despair succumbs to a sensual passion for her, in apparent betrayal of his love for his heavenly ideal. In the resolution, the Indian maid reveals that she is herself Cynthia (Diana), goddess of the moon, and also the celestial goddess of his earlier visions.

Keats set himself to writing a long poem before he was entirely ready in range of knowledge, clarity of thought, or stylistic assurance; the poem reaches a high level only in single passages. The interpretation which seems best to fit the text is that ideal love and imaginative beauty are to be found only by way of instinctual impulses and earthly sexuality, which the ideal repeats, in one of Keats's phrases, "in a finer tone." The poem's constitution is so cloudy, however, that its purport is disputed. But Keats has disarmed all external criticism by his self-criticism in the candid and insightful Preface, which has become a classic statement of the characteristics of unripe genius.

The verse epigraph is adapted from Shakespeare's Sonnet 17, line 12: "And stretchéd meter of an antique song." Thomas Chatterton (1752-70), to whom *Endymion* is inscribed, wrote a number of brilliant pseudo-archaic poems which he attributed to an imaginary 15th-century poet, Thomas Rowley. Reduced to despair by neglect and poverty, Chatterton poisoned himself with arsenic when he was only 17. He came to be greatly admired in the Romantic period. Wordsworth, in *Resolution and Independence*, lines 43-44, called him "the marvelous Boy,/the sleepless Soul that perished in his pride," and Keats described him as "the most English of poets except Shakespeare."

of a man is healthy; but there is a space of life between, in which the soul is in a ferment, the character undecided, the way of life uncertain, the ambition thick-sighted: thence proceeds mawkishness, and all the thousand bitters which those men I speak of must necessarily taste in going over the following pages.

I hope I have not in too late a day touched the beautiful mythology of Greece, and dulled its brightness: for I wish to try once more,[2] before I bid it farewel.

Teignmouth, April 10, 1818

From *Book I*
[A THING OF BEAUTY]

A thing of beauty is a joy for ever:
Its loveliness increases; it will never
Pass into nothingness; but still will keep
A bower quiet for us, and a sleep
Full of sweet dreams, and health, and quiet breathing.   5
Therefore, on every morrow, are we wreathing
A flowery band to bind us to the earth,
Spite of despondence, of the inhuman dearth
Of noble natures, of the gloomy days,
Of all the unhealthy and o'er-darkened ways   10
Made for our searching: yes, in spite of all,
Some shape of beauty moves away the pall
From our dark spirits. Such the sun, the moon,
Trees old, and young sprouting a shady boon
For simple sheep; and such are daffodils   15
With the green world they live in; and clear rills
That for themselves a cooling covert make
'Gainst the hot season; the mid forest brake,[3]
Rich with a sprinkling of fair musk-rose blooms:
And such too is the grandeur of the dooms[4]   20
We have imagined for the mighty dead;
All lovely tales that we have heard or read:
An endless fountain of immortal drink,
Pouring unto us from the heaven's brink.[5]

Nor do we merely feel these essences   25
For one short hour; no, even as the trees
That whisper round a temple become soon
Dear as the temple's self, so does the moon,
The passion poesy, glories infinite,

2. In *Hyperion*, which Keats was already planning.
3. Thicket.
4. Judgments.
5. The poet sets up, and searches to resolve, the basic opposition between the inevitably "mortal" pleasures in this life and the conceived possibility of "immortal" delight. Thus "essences" (line 25) seem to be the things of beauty in this world, purged of the mutability that is inescapable in ordinary experience. The central passage dealing with this theme is below, Book I, lines 777 ff.

Haunt us till they become a cheering light 30
Unto our souls, and bound to us so fast,
That, whether there be shine, or gloom o'ercast,
They alway must be with us, or we die.

Therefore, 'tis with full happiness that I
Will trace the story of Endymion. 35
The very music of the name has gone
Into my being, and each pleasant scene
Is growing fresh before me as the green
Of our own vallies * * *

[THE "PLEASURE THERMOMETER"]

"Peona![6] ever have I long'd to slake
My thirst for the world's praises: nothing base, 770
No merely slumberous phantasm, could unlace
The stubborn canvas for my voyage prepar'd—
Though now 'tis tatter'd; leaving my bark bar'd
And sullenly drifting: yet my higher hope
Is of too wide, too rainbow-large a scope, 775
To fret at myriads of earthly wrecks.
Wherein lies happiness?[7] In that which becks
Our ready minds to fellowship divine,
A fellowship with essence; till we shine,
Full alchemiz'd,[8] and free of space. Behold 780
The clear religion of heaven! Fold
A rose leaf round thy finger's taperness,
And soothe thy lips: hist, when the airy stress
Of music's kiss impregnates the free winds,
And with a sympathetic touch unbinds 785
Eolian[9] magic from their lucid wombs:
Then old songs waken from enclouded tombs;
Old ditties sigh above their father's grave;
Ghosts of melodious prophecyings rave

6. The sister to whom Endymion confides his troubles.
7. Of lines 777–857, Keats wrote to his publisher, John Taylor: "When I wrote it, it was the regular stepping of the Imagination towards a Truth. My having written that Argument will perhaps be of the greatest Service to me of anything I ever did—It set before me at once the gradations of Happiness even like a kind of Pleasure Thermometer, and is my first step towards the chief attempt in the Drama—the playing of different Natures with Joy and Sorrow." The gradations on this "Pleasure Thermometer" mark the stages on the way to what Keats calls "happiness" (line 777)—his secular version of the religious concept of "felicity" which, in the orthodox view, is to be achieved by a surrender of one-self to God. For Keats the way to happiness lies through a fusion of ourselves, first sensuously, with the lovely objects of nature and art (lines 781–97), then on a higher level, with other human beings through "love and friendship" (line 801) but in the final degree, only through sexual love. By this "self-destroying," or total loss of personal identity through our imaginative identification with a beloved person outside ourselves, we escape from the material and spatial limits, and from the self-centered condition, of ordinary experience, to achieve a "fellowship with essence," which is a kind of immortality within our mortal existence (line 844).
8. Transformed by alchemy from a base to a precious metal.
9. From Aeolus, god of winds.

Round every spot where trod Apollo's foot;⠀⠀⠀⠀⠀⠀790
Bronze clarions awake, and faintly bruit,[1]
Where long ago a giant battle was;
And, from the turf, a lullaby doth pass
In every place where infant Orpheus slept.
Feel we these things?—that moment have we stept⠀⠀⠀795
Into a sort of oneness, and our state
Is like a floating spirit's. But there are
Richer entanglements, enthralments far
More self-destroying, leading, by degrees,
To the chief intensity: the crown of these⠀⠀⠀⠀800
Is made of love and friendship, and sits high
Upon the forehead of humanity.
All its more ponderous and bulky worth
Is friendship, whence there ever issues forth
A steady splendour; but at the tip-top,⠀⠀⠀⠀⠀805
There hangs by unseen film, an orbed drop
Of light, and that is love: its influence,
Thrown in our eyes, genders a novel sense,
At which we start and fret; till in the end,
Melting into its radiance, we blend,⠀⠀⠀⠀⠀⠀810
Mingle, and so become a part of it,—
Nor with aught else can our souls interknit
So wingedly: when we combine therewith,
Life's self is nourish'd by its proper pith,[2]
And we are nurtured like a pelican brood.[3]⠀⠀⠀815
Aye, so delicious is the unsating food,
That men, who might have tower'd in the van
Of all the congregated world, to fan
And winnow from the coming step of time
All chaff of custom, wipe away all slime⠀⠀⠀⠀820
Left by men-slugs and human serpentry,
Have been content to let occasion die,
Whilst they did sleep in love's elysium.
And, truly, I would rather be struck dumb,
Than speak against this ardent listlessness:⠀⠀⠀825
For I have ever thought that it might bless
The world which benefits unknowingly;
As does the nightingale, upperched high,
And cloister'd among cool and bunched leaves—
She sings but to her love, nor e'er conceives⠀⠀⠀830
How tiptoe Night holds back her dark-grey hood.[4]
Just so may love, although 'tis understood
The mere commingling of passionate breath,
Produce more than our searching witnesseth:

1. Make a sound.
2. Its own elemental substance.
3. Young pelicans were once thought to feed on their mother's flesh; so our life is nourished by another's life, with which it fuses in love.
4. I.e., in order better to hear.

What I know not: but who, of men, can tell   835
That flowers would bloom, or that green fruit would swell
To melting pulp, that fish would have bright mail,
The earth its dower of river, wood, and vale,
The meadows runnels, runnels pebble-stones,
The seed its harvest, or the lute its tones,   840
Tones ravishment, or ravishment its sweet,
If human souls did never kiss and greet?

   "Now, if this earthly love has power to make
Men's being mortal, immortal; to shake
Ambition from their memories, and brim   845
Their measure of content; what merest whim,
Seems all this poor endeavour after fame,
To one, who keeps within his stedfast aim
A love immortal, an immortal too.
Look not so wilder'd; for these things are true,   850
And never can be born of atomies[5]
That buzz about our slumbers, like brain-flies,
Leaving us fancy-sick. No, no, I'm sure,
My restless spirit never could endure
To brood so long upon one luxury,   855
Unless it did, though fearfully, espy
A hope beyond the shadow of a dream."
Apr.–Nov., 1817   1818

On Sitting Down to Read *King Lear* Once Again[1]

      O golden-tongued Romance, with serene lute!
         Fair plumed syren, queen of far-away!
         Leave melodizing on this wintry day,
      Shut up thine olden pages, and be mute.
      Adieu! for, once again, the fierce dispute   5
         Betwixt damnation and impassion'd clay
         Must I burn through; once more humbly assay
      The bitter-sweet of this Shaksperean fruit.
      Chief Poet! and ye clouds of Albion,[2]
         Begetters of our deep eternal theme!   10
      When through the old oak forest I am gone,
         Let me not wander in a barren dream:

---

5. Mites, tiny flying insects.
1. Keats pauses in revising *Endymion: A Poetic Romance* to read again Shakespeare's great tragedy. The word "syren" (line 2) indicates Keats's feeling that Romance was enticing him from the poet's prime duty, to deal with "the agonies, the strife / Of human hearts" (*Sleep and Poetry*, lines 124–125).
2. Albion is the old Celtic name for England; *King Lear* is set in Celtic Britain. The "oak forest" of line 11 refers either to *King Lear* or (more likely) to the romance, *Endymion*.

But, when I am consumed in the fire,
Give me new phoenix[3] wings to fly at my desire.

January, 1818   1838, 1848

When I Have Fears That I May Cease to Be[4]

When I have fears that I may cease to be
  Before my pen has glean'd my teeming brain,
Before high piled books, in charactry,[5]
  Hold like rich garners the full ripen'd grain;
When I behold, upon the night's starr'd face,   5
  Huge cloudy symbols of a high romance,
And think that I may never live to trace
  Their shadows, with the magic hand of chance;
And when I feel, fair creature of an hour,
  That I shall never look upon thee more,   10
Never have relish in the fairy power
  Of unreflecting love;—then on the shore
Of the wide world I stand alone, and think
Till love and fame to nothingness do sink.

January, 1818   1848

To Homer

Standing aloof in giant ignorance,
  Of thee I hear and of the Cyclades,[6]
As one who sits ashore and longs perchance
  To visit dolphin-coral in deep seas.
So wast thou blind;—but then the veil was rent,   5
  For Jove uncurtain'd heaven to let thee live,
And Neptune made for thee a spumy tent,
  And Pan made sing for thee his forest-hive;
Aye on the shores of darkness there is light,
  And precipices show untrodden green,   10
There is a budding morrow in midnight,
  There is a triple sight in blindness keen;
Such seeing hadst thou, as it once befel
To Dian, Queen of Earth, and Heaven, and Hell.[7]

1818   1848

---

3. The fabulous bird which periodically burns itself to death in order to rise anew from the ashes.
4. The first, and one of the most successful, of Keats's attempts at the sonnet in the Shakespearean rhyme scheme.
5. Characters; written or printed letters of the alphabet.
6. A group of islands in the Aegean Sea, off Greece; Keats's allusion is to his ignorance of the Greek language.
7. In later cults Diana was worshiped as a three-figured goddess, the deity of nature and of the moon, as well as queen of hell. The "triple sight" which blind Homer paradoxically commands is of these three regions, and also of heaven, sea, and earth (the realms of Jove, Neptune, and Pan, lines 6–8).

The Eve of St. Agnes[1]

1

St. Agnes' Eve—Ah, bitter chill it was!
The owl, for all his feathers, was a-cold;
The hare limp'd trembling through the frozen grass,
And silent was the flock in woolly fold:
Numb were the Beadsman's[2] fingers, while he told   5
His rosary, and while his frosted breath,
Like pious incense from a censer old,
Seem'd taking flight for heaven, without a death,
Past the sweet Virgin's picture, while his prayer he saith.

2

His prayer he saith, this patient, holy man;   10
Then he takes his lamp, and riseth from his knees,
And back returneth, meagre, barefoot, wan,
Along the chapel aisle by slow degrees:
The sculptur'd dead, on each side, seem to freeze,
Emprison'd in black, purgatorial rails: 15
Knights, ladies, praying in dumb orat'ries,[3]
He passeth by; and his weak spirit fails
To think[4] how they may ache in icy hoods and mails.

3

Northward he turneth through a little door,
And scarce three steps, ere Music's golden tongue   20
Flatter'd[5] to tears this aged man and poor;
But no—already had his deathbell rung;
The joys of all his life were said and sung:
His was harsh penance on St. Agnes' Eve:
Another way he went, and soon among   25
Rough ashes sat he for his soul's reprieve,
And all night kept awake, for sinners' sake to grieve.

4

That ancient Beadsman heard the prelude soft;
And so it chanc'd, for many a door was wide,

1. St. Agnes, martyred ca. 303 at the age of 13, is the patron saint of virgins. Legend has it that if a virtuous young girl performs the proper ritual, she will dream of her future husband on the evening before St. Agnes' Day, which falls on January 21. Keats combined this superstition with the Romeo and Juliet theme of young love thwarted by feuding families and told the story in a sequence of sensuously evolving Spenserian stanzas. The luxurious product has been called "a colored dream," but it is a complexly meaningful dream, in which the strong contrasts of heat and cold, crimson and silver, youth and age, revelry and austere penance, sensuality and chastity, life and death, hell and heaven, assume symbolic values. They are used to figure forth the extremes of spirituality and of grossness that are involved in sexuality, the difference between the dream and the reality of passion, and the ambivalences at the center of human love. The poem is Keats's first complete success in sustained narrative.
2. A "beadsman" is paid to pray for his benefactor. He "tells" (counts) the beads of his rosary, to keep track of his prayers.
3. Silent chapels.
4. I.e., when he thinks.
5. Beguiled, charmed.

From hurry to and fro. Soon, up aloft, 30
The silver, snarling trumpets 'gan to chide:
The level chambers, ready with their pride,[6]
Were glowing to receive a thousand guests:
The carved angels, ever eager-eyed,
Star'd, where upon their heads the cornice rests, 35
With hair blown back, and wings put cross-wise on their breasts.

5

At length burst in the argent revelry,[7]
With plume, tiara, and all rich array,
Numerous as shadows haunting fairily
The brain, new stuff'd, in youth, with triumphs gay 40
Of old romance. These let us wish away,
And turn, sole-thoughted, to one Lady there,
Whose heart had brooded, all that wintry day,
On love, and wing'd St. Agnes' saintly care,
As she had heard old dames full many times declare. 45

6

They told her how, upon St. Agnes' Eve,
Young virgins might have visions of delight,
And soft adorings from their loves receive
Upon the honey'd middle of the night,
If ceremonies due they did aright; 50
As, supperless to bed they must retire,
And couch supine their beauties, lily white;
Nor look behind, nor sideways, but require
Of heaven with upward eyes for all that they desire.

7

Full of this whim was thoughtful Madeline: 55
The music, yearning like a god in pain,
She scarcely heard: her maiden eyes divine,
Fix'd on the floor, saw many a sweeping train
Pass by—she heeded not at all: in vain
Came many a tiptoe, amorous cavalier, 60
And back retir'd, not cool'd by high disdain;
But she saw not: her heart was otherwhere:
She sigh'd for Agnes' dreams, the sweetest of the year.

8

She danc'd along with vague, regardless eyes,
Anxious her lips, her breathing quick and short: 65
The hallow'd hour was near at hand: she sighs
Amid the timbrels,[8] and the throng'd resort
Of whisperers in anger, or in sport;
'Mid looks of love, defiance, hate, and scorn,
Hoodwink'd with faery fancy;[9] all amort, 70

6. Ostentation.
7. Silver-clad revelers.
8. Small drums.
9. She was blinded ("hoodwink'd"—as though the eyes were covered by a hood) by her charmed imagination; "all amort": as though dead.

Save to St. Agnes and her lambs unshorn,[1]
And all the bliss to be before to-morrow morn.

9

So, purposing each moment to retire,
She linger'd still. Meantime, across the moors,
Had come young Porphyro, with heart on fire   75
For Madeline. Beside the portal doors,
Buttress'd from moonlight,[2] stands he, and implores
All saints to give him sight of Madeline,
But for one moment in the tedious hours,
That he might gaze and worship all unseen;   80
Perchance speak, kneel, touch, kiss—in sooth such things have been.

10

He ventures in: let no buzz'd whisper tell:
All eyes be muffled, or a hundred swords
Will storm his heart, Love's fev'rous citadel:
For him, those chambers held barbarian hordes,   85
Hyena foemen, and hot-blooded lords,
Whose very dogs would execrations howl
Against his lineage: not one breast affords
Him any mercy, in that mansion foul,
Save one old beldame,[3] weak in body and in soul.   90

11

Ah, happy chance! the aged creature came,
Shuffling along with ivory-headed wand,[4]
To where he stood, hid from the torch's flame,
Behind a broad hall-pillar, far beyond
The sound of merriment and chorus bland:[5]   95
He startled her; but soon she knew his face,
And grasp'd his fingers in her palsied hand,
Saying, "Mercy, Porphyro! hie thee from this place;
They are all here to-night, the whole blood-thirsty race!

12

"Get hence! get hence! there's dwarfish Hildebrand;   100
He had a fever late, and in the fit
He cursed thee and thine, both house and land:
Then there's that old Lord Maurice, not a whit
More tame for his gray hairs—Alas me! flit!
Flit like a ghost away."—"Ah, Gossip[6] dear,   105
We're safe enough; here in this arm-chair sit,
And tell me how"—"Good Saints! not here, not here;
Follow me, child, or else these stones will be thy bier."

---

1. On St. Agnes' Day it was the custom to offer lambs' wool at the altar, to
be made into cloth by nuns.
2. Sheltered from the moonlight by the
buttresses (the supports projecting
from the wall).
3. Old (and usually, homely) woman;

an ironic development in English from
the French meaning, "lovely lady."
4. Staff.
5. Soft.
6. In the old sense: godmother, or old
friend.

13

He follow'd through a lowly arched way,
Brushing the cobwebs with his lofty plume,   110
And as she mutter'd "Well-a—well-a-day!"
He found him in a little moonlight room,
Pale, lattic'd, chill, and silent as a tomb.
"Now tell me where is Madeline," said he,
"O tell me, Angela, by the holy loom   115
Which none but secret sisterhood may see,
When they St. Agnes' wool are weaving piously."

14

"St. Agnes! Ah! it is St. Agnes' Eve—
Yet men will murder upon holy days:
Thou must hold water in a witch's sieve,[7]   120
And be liege-lord of all the Elves and Fays,
To venture so: it fills me with amaze
To see thee, Porphyro!—St. Agnes' Eve!
God's help! my lady fair the conjuror plays[8]
This very night: good angels her deceive!   125
But let me laugh awhile, I've mickle[9] time to grieve."

15

Feebly she laugheth in the languid moon,
While Porphyro upon her face doth look,
Like puzzled urchin on an aged crone
Who keepeth clos'd a wond'rous riddle-book,   130
As spectacled she sits in chimney nook.
But soon his eyes grew brilliant, when she told
His lady's purpose; and he scarce could brook[1]
Tears, at the thought of those enchantments cold,
And Madeline asleep in lap of legends old.   135

16

Sudden a thought came like a full-blown rose,
Flushing his brow, and in his pained heart
Made purple riot: then doth he propose
A stratagem, that makes the beldame start:
"A cruel man and impious thou art: 140
Sweet lady, let her pray, and sleep, and dream
Alone with her good angels, far apart
From wicked men like thee. Go, go!—I deem
Thou canst not surely be the same that thou didst seem."

17

"I will not harm her, by all saints I swear,"   145
Quoth Porphyro: "O may I ne'er find grace
When my weak voice shall whisper its last prayer,
If one of her soft ringlets I displace,

---

7. A sieve made to hold water by witchcraft.
8. I.e., in her attempt to evoke the vision of her lover.
9. Much.
1. "Brook" ordinarily means "endure," although Keats apparently uses it for "restrain."

Or look with ruffian passion in her face:
Good Angela, believe me by these tears;   150
Or I will, even in a moment's space,
Awake, with horrid shout, my foemen's ears,
And beard them, though they be more fang'd than wolves and
    bears."

18
"Ah! why wilt thou affright a feeble soul?
A poor, weak, palsy-stricken, churchyard thing,   155
Whose passing-bell[2] may ere the midnight toll;
Whose prayers for thee, each morn and evening,
Were never miss'd."—Thus plaining,[3] doth she bring
A gentler speech from burning Porphyro;
So woful, and of such deep sorrowing,   160
That Angela gives promise she will do
Whatever he shall wish, betide her weal or woe.

19
Which was, to lead him, in close secrecy,
Even to Madeline's chamber, and there hide
Him in a closet, of such privacy   165
That he might see her beauty unespied,
And win perhaps that night a peerless bride,
While legion'd fairies pac'd the coverlet,
And pale enchantment held her sleepy-eyed.
Never on such a night have lovers met,   170
Since Merlin paid his Demon all the monstrous debt.[4]

20
"It shall be as thou wishest," said the Dame:
"All cates[5] and dainties shall be stored there
Quickly on this feast-night: by the tambour frame[6]
Her own lute thou wilt see: no time to spare,   175
For I am slow and feeble, and scarce dare
On such a catering trust my dizzy head.
Wait here, my child, with patience; kneel in prayer
The while: Ah! thou must needs the lady wed,
Or may I never leave my grave among the dead."   180

21
So saying, she hobbled off with busy fear.
The lover's endless minutes slowly pass'd;
The dame return'd, and whisper'd in his ear
To follow her; with aged eyes aghast
From fright of dim espial. Safe at last,   185
Through many a dusky gallery, they gain
The maiden's chamber, silken, hush'd, and chaste;
Where Porphyro took covert, pleas'd amain.[7]
His poor guide hurried back with agues in her brain.

2. Death knell.
3. Complaining.
4. Probably the episode in the Arthurian legends in which Merlin, the magician, lost his life when the wily Vivien turned one of his spells against him.
5. Delicacies.
6. A drum-shaped embroidery frame.
7. Mightily.

22

Her falt'ring hand upon the balustrade,   190
Old Angela was feeling for the stair,
When Madeline, St. Agnes' charmed maid,
Rose, like a mission'd spirit,[8] unaware:
With silver taper's light, and pious care,
She turn'd, and down the aged gossip led   195
To a safe level matting. Now prepare,
Young Porphyro, for gazing on that bed;
She comes, she comes again, like ring-dove fray'd[9] and fled.

23

Out went the taper as she hurried in;
Its little smoke, in pallid moonshine, died: 200
She clos'd the door, she panted, all akin
To spirits of the air, and visions wide:
No uttered syllable, or, woe betide!
But to her heart, her heart was voluble,
Paining with eloquence her balmy side;   205
As though a tongueless nightingale should swell
Her throat in vain, and die, heart-stifled, in her dell.

24

A casement high and triple-arch'd there was,
All garlanded with carven imag'ries
Of fruits, and flowers, and bunches of knot-grass,   210
And diamonded with panes of quaint device,
Innumerable of stains and splendid dyes,
As are the tiger-moth's deep-damask'd wings;
And in the midst, 'mong thousand heraldries,
And twilight saints, and dim emblazonings,   215
A shielded scutcheon blush'd with blood of queens and kings.[1]

25

Full on this casement shone the wintry moon,
And threw warm gules[2] on Madeline's fair breast,
As down she knelt for heaven's grace and boon;[3]
Rose-bloom fell on her hands, together prest,   220
And on her silver cross soft amethyst,
And on her hair a glory, like a saint:
She seem'd a splendid angel, newly drest,
Save wings, for heaven:—Porphyro grew faint:
She knelt, so pure a thing, so free from mortal taint.   225

26

Anon his heart revives: her vespers done,
Of all its wreathed pearls her hair she frees;
Unclasps her warmed jewels one by one;
Loosens her fragrant boddice; by degrees

8. Like an angel sent on a mission.
9. Frightened.
1. I.e., among the genealogical emblems ("heraldries") and other devices ("emblazonings"), a heraldic shield sig-nified by its colors that the family was of royal blood.
2. In heraldry, the color red.
3. Gift, blessing.

Her rich attire creeps rustling to her knees: 230
Half-hidden, like a mermaid in sea-weed,
Pensive awhile she dreams awake, and sees,
In fancy, fair St. Agnes in her bed,
But dares not look behind, or all the charm is fled.

27

Soon, trembling in her soft and chilly nest,   235
In sort of wakeful swoon, perplex'd[4] she lay,
Until the poppied warmth of sleep oppress'd
Her soothed limbs, and soul fatigued away;
Flown, like a thought, until the morrow-day;
Blissfully haven'd both from joy and pain;   240
Clasp'd like a missal where swart Paynims pray;[5]
Blinded alike from sunshine and from rain,
As though a rose should shut, and be a bud again.

28

Stol'n to this paradise, and so entranced,
Porphyro gazed upon her empty dress,   245
And listen'd to her breathing, if it chanced
To wake into a slumberous tenderness;
Which when he heard, that minute did he bless,
And breath'd himself: then from the closet crept,
Noiseless as fear in a wide wilderness,   250
And over the hush'd carpet, silent, stept,
And 'tween the curtains peep'd, where, lo!—how fast she slept.

29

Then by the bed-side, where the faded moon
Made a dim, silver twilight, soft he set
A table, and, half anguish'd, threw thereon   255
A cloth of woven crimson, gold, and jet:—
O for some drowsy Morphean amulet![6]
The boisterous, midnight, festive clarion,[7]
The kettle-drum, and far-heard clarionet,
Affray his ears, though but in dying tone:—   260
The hall door shuts again, and all the noise is gone.

30

And still she slept an azure-lidded sleep,
In blanched linen, smooth, and lavender'd,
While he from forth the closet brought a heap
Of candied apple, quince, and plum, and gourd;[8]   265
With jellies soother than the creamy curd,
And lucent syrops, tinct with cinnamon;
Manna and dates, in argosy transferr'd

4. In a confused state between waking and sleeping.
5. Variously interpreted; perhaps: held tightly, cherished, like a Christian prayer book ("missal") in a land where the religion is that of dark-skinned pagans ("swart Paynims").
6. Sleep-producing charm.
7. High-pitched trumpet.
8. Melon. According to the legend, the dream lover would bring the virgin a feast of delicacies.

From Fez;[9] and spiced dainties, every one,
From silken Samarcand to cedar'd Lebanon.   270

31

These delicates he heap'd with glowing hand
On golden dishes and in baskets bright
Of wreathed silver: sumptuous they stand
In the retired quiet of the night,
Filling the chilly room with perfume light.—   275
"And now, my love, my seraph[1] fair, awake!
Thou art my heaven, and I thine eremite:[2]
Open thine eyes, for meek St. Agnes' sake,
Or I shall drowse beside thee, so my soul doth ache."

32

Thus whispering, his warm, unnerved arm   280
Sank in her pillow. Shaded was her dream
By the dusk curtains:—'twas a midnight charm
Impossible to melt as iced stream:
The lustrous salvers in the moonlight gleam;
Broad golden fringe upon the carpet lies: 285
It seem'd he never, never could redeem
From such a stedfast spell his lady's eyes;
So mus'd awhile, entoil'd in woofed phantasies.[3]

33

Awakening up, he took her hollow lute,—
Tumultuous,—and, in chords that tenderest be,   290
He play'd an ancient ditty, long since mute,
In Provence call'd, "La belle dame sans mercy":[4]
Close to her ear touching the melody;—
Wherewith disturb'd, she utter'd a soft moan:
He ceased—she panted quick—and suddenly   295
Her blue affrayed eyes wide open shone:
Upon his knees he sank, pale as smooth-sculptured stone.

34

Her eyes were open, but she still beheld,
Now wide awake, the vision of her sleep:
There was a painful change, that nigh expell'd   300
The blisses of her dream so pure and deep:
At which fair Madeline began to weep,
And moan forth witless words with many a sigh;
While still her gaze on Porphyro would keep;
Who knelt, with joined hands and piteous eye,   305
Fearing to move or speak, she look'd so dreamingly.

9. I.e., jellies softer ("soother") than
the curds of cream, clear ("lucent")
syrups tinged with cinnamon, and sweet
gums ("manna") and dates transported
in a great merchant ship ("argosy")
from Fez.
1. One of the highest order of angels.

2. A religious hermit.
3. Entangled in a weave of fantasies.
4. "The Lovely Lady Without Pity,"
by the medieval poet, Alain Chartier.
Keats later used the title for his own
ballad.

35

"Ah, Porphyro!" said she, "but even now
Thy voice was at sweet tremble in mine ear,
Made tuneable with every sweetest vow;
And those sad eyes were spiritual and clear: 310
How chang'd thou art! how pallid, chill, and drear!
Give me that voice again, my Porphyro,
Those looks immortal, those complainings dear!
Oh leave me not in this eternal woe,
For if thou diest, my love, I know not where to go."   315

36

Beyond a mortal man impassion'd far
At these voluptuous accents, he arose,
Ethereal, flush'd, and like a throbbing star
Seen mid the sapphire heaven's deep repose;
Into her dream he melted, as the rose   320
Blendeth its odour with the violet,—
Solution sweet: meantime the frost-wind blows
Like Love's alarum pattering the sharp sleet
Against the window-panes; St. Agnes' moon hath set.

37

'Tis dark: quick patbereth the flaw-blown[5] sleet: 325
"This is no dream, my bride, my Madeline!"
'Tis dark: the iced gusts still rave and beat:
"No dream, alas! alas! and woe is mine!
Porphyro will leave me here to fade and pine.—
Cruel! what traitor could thee hither bring?   330
I curse not, for my heart is lost in thine,
Though thou forsakest a deceived thing;—
A dove forlorn and lost with sick unpruned wing."

38

"My Madeline! sweet dreamer! lovely bride!
Say, may I be for aye thy vassal blest?   335
Thy beauty's shield, heart-shap'd and vermeil[6] dyed?
Ah, silver shrine, here will I take my rest
After so many hours of toil and quest,
A famish'd pilgrim,—saved by miracle.
Though I have found, I will not rob thy nest   340
Saving of thy sweet self; if thou think'st well
To trust, fair Madeline, to no rude infidel.

39

"Hark! 'tis an elfin-storm from faery land,
Of haggard[7] seeming, but a boon indeed:
Arise—arise! the morning is at hand;—   345
The bloated wassaillers[8] will never heed:—
Let us away, my love, with happy speed;
There are no ears to hear, or eyes to see,—

5. Gust-blown.   hawk).
6. Vermilion.   8. Drunken carousers.
7. Wild, untamed (originally, a wild

Drown'd all in Rhenish and the sleepy mead:[9]
Awake! arise! my love, and fearless be,   350
For o'er the southern moors I have a home for thee."

40

She hurried at his words, beset with fears,
For there were sleeping dragons all around,
At glaring watch, perhaps, with ready spears—
Down the wide stairs a darkling[1] way they found.—   355
In all the house was heard no human sound.
A chain-droop'd lamp was flickering by each door;
The arras, rich with horseman, hawk, and hound,
Flutter'd in the besieging wind's uproar;
And the long carpets rose along the gusty floor.   360

41

They glide, like phantoms, into the wide hall;
Like phantoms, to the iron porch, they glide;
Where lay the Porter, in uneasy sprawl,
With a huge empty flaggon by his side:
The wakeful bloodhound rose, and shook his hide,   365
But his sagacious eye an inmate owns:[2]
By one, and one, the bolts full easy slide:—
The chains lie silent on the footworn stones;—
The key turns, and the door upon its hinges groans.

42

And they are gone: ay, ages long ago   370
These lovers fled away into the storm.
That night the Baron dreamt of many a woe,
And all his warrior-guests, with shade and form
Of witch, and demon, and large coffin-worm,
Were long be-nightmar'd. Angela the old   375
Died palsy-twitch'd, with meagre face deform;
The Beadsman, after thousand aves[3] told,
For aye unsought for slept among his ashes cold.
Jan.–Feb., 1819   1820

Why Did I Laugh Tonight? No Voice Will Tell[4]

Why did I laugh tonight? No voice will tell:
    No god, no demon of severe response,
    Deigns to reply from heaven or from hell.
        Then to my human heart I turn at once—

9. Rhine wine and the sleep-producing mead (a heavy fermented drink made with honey).
1. In the dark.
2. Acknowledges a member of the household.
3. The prayers beginning *Ave Maria* ("Hail Mary").
4. In the letter to his brother and sister-in-law, George and Georgiana

Keats, into which he copied this sonnet, March 19, 1819, Keats wrote: "Though the first steps to it were through my human passions, they went away, and I wrote with my Mind—and perhaps I must confess a little bit of my heart. * * * I went to bed, and enjoyed an uninterrupted sleep. Sane I went to bed and sane I arose."

Heart! thou and I are here sad and alone; 5
  Say, wherefore did I laugh? O mortal pain!
O darkness! darkness! ever must I moan,
  To question heaven and hell and heart in vain!
Why did I laugh? I know this being's lease—
  My fancy to its utmost blisses spreads: 10
Yet could I on this very midnight cease,
  And the world's gaudy ensigns[5] see in shreds.
Verse, fame, and beauty are intense indeed,
But death intenser—death is life's high meed.

March, 1819   1848

Bright Star, Would I Were Stedfast as Thou Art[6]

Bright star, would I were stedfast as thou art—
  Not in lone splendor hung aloft the night,
And watching, with eternal lids apart,
  Like nature's patient, sleepless eremite,[7]
The moving waters at their priestlike task 5
  Of pure ablution[8] round earth's human shores,
Or gazing on the new soft-fallen mask
  Of snow upon the mountains and the moors;
No—yet still stedfast, still unchangeable,
  Pillow'd upon my fair love's ripening breast, 10
To feel for ever its soft swell and fall,
  Awake for ever in a sweet unrest,
Still, still to hear her tender-taken breath,
And so live ever—or else swoon to death.[9]

1819–20   1838

La Belle Dame sans Merci: A Ballad[1]

1

O what can ail thee, knight at arms,
  Alone and palely loitering?
The sedge has wither'd from the lake,
  And no birds sing.

5. Banners.
6. While on a tour of the Lake Country in 1818, Keats had said that the austere scenes "refine one's sensual vision into a sort of north star which can never cease to be open lidded and steadfast over the wonders of the great Power"; the thought developed into this sonnet. Keats drafted this poem in 1819, then copied it into his volume of Shakespeare's poems, while on the way to his death in Italy in September, 1820.
7. Hermit, religious solitary.
8. Washing, as part of a religious rite.
9. In the earlier version: "Half pas-sionless, and so swoon on to death."
1. The title, though not the subject matter, was taken from a medieval poem by Alain Chartier and means "The Lovely Lady Without Pity." The story of a mortal destroyed by his love for a supernatural *femme fatale* has been told repeatedly in myth, fairy tale, and ballad, but never so hauntingly. The metrical key to its effect is the poignant and richly suggestive suspension achieved by shortening to two stresses the final line of each stanza. We print here Keats's first version, written in a letter to his brother and sister-in-law. The version published in

2

O what can ail thee, knight at arms,
　　So haggard and so woe-begone?
The squirrel's granary is full,
　　And the harvest's done.

3

I see a lily on thy brow
　　With anguish moist and fever dew,
And on thy cheeks a fading rose
　　Fast withereth too.

4

I met a lady in the meads,
　　Full beautiful, a fairy's child;
Her hair was long, her foot was light,
　　And her eyes were wild.

5

I made a garland for her head,
　　And bracelets too, and fragrant zone;[2]
She look'd at me as she did love,
　　And made sweet moan.

6

I set her on my pacing steed,
　　And nothing else saw all day long,
For sidelong would she bend, and sing
　　A fairy's song.

7

She found me roots of relish sweet,
　　And honey wild, and manna dew,
And sure in language strange she said—
　　I love thee true.

8

She took me to her elfin grot,
　　And there she wept, and sigh'd full sore,
And there I shut her wild wild eyes
　　With kisses four.

9

And there she lulled me asleep,
　　And there I dream'd—Ah! woe betide!
The latest[3] dream I ever dream'd
　　On the cold hill's side.

10

I saw pale kings, and princes too,
　　Pale warriors, death pale were they all;
They cried—"La belle dame sans merci
　　Hath thee in thrall!"

5

10

15

20

25

30

35

40

1820, "Ah, what can ail thee, wretched
wight," is a rare instance in which
Keats weakened a poem by revision.
　Keats imitates a frequent procedure
of folk ballads by casting the poem
into the dialogue form. The first three
stanzas are addressed to the knight,
and the rest of the poem is his reply.
2. Girdle.
3. Last.

11

I saw their starv'd lips in the gloam
   With horrid warning gaped wide,
And I awoke and found me here
   On the cold hill's side.

12

And this is why I sojourn here,   45
   Alone and palely loitering,
Though the sedge is wither'd from the lake,
   And no birds sing.

April, 1819   1820

Sonnet to Sleep

O soft embalmer of the still midnight,
   Shutting with careful fingers and benign
Our gloom-pleas'd eyes, embower'd from the light,
   Enshaded in forgetfulness divine:
O soothest[1] Sleep! if so it please thee, close,   5
   In midst of this thine hymn, my willing eyes,
Or wait the Amen ere thy poppy[2] throws
   Around my bed its lulling charities.
Then save me or the passed day will shine
   Upon my pillow, breeding many woes: 10
Save me from curious[3] conscience, that still hoards
   Its strength for darkness, burrowing like the mole;
Turn the key deftly in the oiled wards,[4]
   And seal the hushed casket of my soul.

April, 1819   1838, 1848

Ode to Psyche[1]

O Goddess! hear these tuneless numbers, wrung
   By sweet enforcement and remembrance dear,
And pardon that thy secrets should be sung

1. Softest.
2. Opium is made from the dried juice of the opium poppy.
3. Scrupulous.
4. The ridges in a lock which determine the pattern of the key.
1. This poem initiated the sequence of five great odes that Keats wrote in late April and in May, 1819. Since it is copied into the same journal-letter which included the sonnet *If by Dull Rhymes Our English Must be Chain'd*, it is likely that Keats's experiments with sonnet schemes led to the development of the intricate and varied stanzas of his odes, and also that Keats abandoned the sonnet upon discovering the richer possibilities of the more spacious form. In a letter of April 30, 1819, Keats said that of all his poems up to that time, *Psyche* "is the first and the only one with which I have taken even moderate pains. I have for the most part dashed off my lines in a hurry. This I have done leisurely—I think it reads the more richly for it and will I hope encourage me to write other things in even a more peaceable and healthy spirit." In the story told by the Roman author Apuleius in the 2nd century A.D., Psyche was a lovely mortal beloved by Cupid, "the winged boy," son of Venus. After various tribulations, imposed by Venus because she

Even into thine own soft-conched[2] ear:
Surely I dreamt to-day, or did I see   5
    The winged Psyche with awaken'd eyes?[3]
I wander'd in a forest thoughtlessly,
    And, on the sudden, fainting with surprise,
Saw two fair creatures, couched side by side
    In deepest grass, beneath the whisp'ring roof   10
    Of leaves and trembled blossoms, where there ran
        A brooklet, scarce espied:
'Mid hush'd, cool-rooted flowers, fragrant-eyed,
    Blue, silver-white, and budded Tyrian,[4]
They lay calm-breathing on the bedded grass;   15
    Their arms embraced, and their pinions[5] too;
    Their lips touch'd not, but had not bade adieu,
As if disjoined by soft-handed slumber,
And ready still past kisses to outnumber
    At tender eye-dawn of aurorean love:[6]   20
        The winged boy I knew;
    But who wast thou, O happy, happy dove?
        His Psyche true!

O latest born and loveliest vision far
    Of all Olympus' faded hierarchy![7]   25
Fairer than Phoebe's sapphire-region'd star,[8]
    Or Vesper, amorous glow-worm of the sky;
Fairer than these, though temple thou hast none,
    Nor altar heap'd with flowers;
Nor virgin-choir to make delicious moan   30
    Upon the midnight hours;
No voice, no lute, no pipe, no incense sweet
    From chain-swung censer teeming;
No shrine, no grove, no oracle, no heat
    Of pale-mouth'd prophet dreaming.   35

---

was jealous of Psyche's beauty, Psyche was wedded to Cupid and translated to heaven as an immortal.

The tendency in recent criticism of Keats is to read the *Ode* as a quasi-allegory, in which Psyche (in Greek: soul, or mind) represents "the human-soul-in-love" (Harold Bloom) or else the modern inward-oriented poetry of the mind (W. J. Bate). To this latter-day goddess, Keats in the last two stanzas promises to establish a place of worship within "some untrodden region" of his own mind, with himself as poet-priest and prophet.

2. Soft and shaped like a seashell.
3. Another of Keats's inquiries into the relation of dreams to poetic vision; see, e.g., *Sleep and Poetry*, the concluding line of *Ode to a Nightingale*, the open-

ing section of *The Fall of Hyperion: A Dream.*
4. The purple dye anciently made in Tyre.
5. Wings.
6. Aurora was the goddess of the dawn.
7. The ranks of the classic gods of Mt. Olympus. "You must recollect that Psyche was not embodied as a goddess before the time of Apuleius the Platonist who lived after the Augustan age, and consequently the goddess was never worshiped or sacrificed to with any of the ancient fervor—and perhaps never thought of in the old religion" (Keats, letter of April 30, 1819).
8. The moon, supervised by the goddess Phoebe (Diana). "Vesper": the evening star.

O brightest! though too late for antique vows,
    Too, too late for the fond believing lyre,
When holy were the haunted forest boughs,
    Holy the air, the water, and the fire;
Yet even in these days so far retir'd   40
    From happy pieties, thy lucent fans,⁹
    Fluttering among the faint Olympians,
I see, and sing, by my own eyes inspired.
So let me be thy choir, and make a moan
    Upon the midnight hours;   45
Thy voice, thy lute, thy pipe, thy incense sweet
    From swinged censer teeming;
Thy shrine, thy grove, thy oracle, thy heat
    Of pale-mouth'd prophet dreaming.

Yes, I will be thy priest, and build a fane¹   50
    In some untrodden region of my mind,
Where branched thoughts, new grown with pleasant pain,
    Instead of pines shall murmur in the wind:
Far, far around shall those dark-cluster'd trees
    Fledge² the wild-ridged mountains steep by steep;   55
And there by zephyrs, streams, and birds, and bees,
    The moss-lain Dryads³ shall be lull'd to sleep;
And in the midst of this wide quietness
A rosy sanctuary will I dress
With the wreath'd trellis of a working brain,   60
    With buds, and bells, and stars without a name,
With all the gardener Fancy e'er could feign,
    Who breeding flowers, will never breed the same:
And there shall be for thee all soft delight
    That shadowy thought can win,   65
A bright torch, and a casement ope at night,
    To let the warm Love⁴ in!
April, 1819   1820

If by Dull Rhymes Our English Must Be Chain'd¹

If by dull rhymes our English must be chain'd,
    And, like Andromeda,² the sonnet sweet
        Fetter'd, in spite of pained loveliness;
    Let us find out, if we must be constrain'd,

---

9. Shining wings.
1. Temple.
2. I.e., the trees shall stand, rank against rank, like layers of feathers.
3. Wood nymphs.
4. I.e., Cupid, god of love.
1. In a letter including this sonnet, Keats wrote that "I have been endeavoring to discover a better sonnet stanza than we have," objecting especially to the "pouncing rhymes" of the Petrarchan form and the inevitable tick of the closing couplet in the Shakespearean stanza.
2. Andromeda was chained to a rock in order to placate a sea monster, but was rescued by Perseus.

Sandals more interwoven and complete   5
To fit the naked foot of Poesy;
    Let us inspect the lyre, and weigh the stress
Of every chord,[3] and see what may be gain'd
By ear industrious, and attention meet;
    Misers of sound and syllable, no less   10
Than Midas[4] of his coinage, let us be
Jealous of dead leaves in the bay wreath crown;
So, if we may not let the muse be free,
    She will be bound with garlands of her own.

April, 1819   1848

Ode to a Nightingale[1]

1

My heart aches, and a drowsy numbness pains
    My sense, as though of hemlock[2] I had drunk,
Or emptied some dull opiate to the drains
    One minute past, and Lethe-wards[3] had sunk:
'Tis not through envy of thy happy lot,   5
    But being too happy in thine happiness,—
        That thou, light-winged Dryad of the trees,
          In some melodious plot
Of beechen green, and shadows numberless,
    Singest of summer in full-throated ease.   10

2

O, for a draught of vintage! that hath been
    Cool'd a long age in the deep-delved earth,
Tasting of Flora[4] and the country green,
    Dance, and Provençal song,[5] and sunburnt mirth!
O for a beaker full of the warm South,   15
    Full of the true, the blushful Hippocrene,[6]
        With beaded bubbles winking at the brim,
          And purple-stained mouth;
That I might drink, and leave the world unseen,
    And with thee fade away into the forest dim: 20

---

3. Lyre-string.
4. King Midas was granted his wish that all he touched should turn to gold.
1. Charles Brown, with whom Keats was then living in Hampstead, wrote: "In the spring of 1819 a nightingale had built her nest near my house. Keats felt a tranquil and continual joy in her song; and one morning he took his chair from the breakfast table to the grass plot under a plum tree, where he sat for two or three hours. When he came into the house, I perceived he had some scraps of paper in his hand, and these he was quietly thrusting behind the books. On inquiry, I found those scraps, four or five in number, con-tained his poetic feeling on the song of our nightingale."
2. A poisonous herb, not the North American evergreen tree.
3. Toward Lethe, the river in Hades whose waters cause forgetfulness.
4. Roman goddess of flowers, or the flowers themselves.
5. Provence, in southern France, was in the late Middle Ages renowned for its troubadours, the writers and singers of love songs.
6. Pronounced *Hip'-ocreen*: fountain of the Muses on Mt. Helicon; hence, the waters of inspiration, here applied met-aphorically to a beaker of wine.

3

Fade far away, dissolve, and quite forget
   What thou among the leaves hast never known,
The weariness, the fever, and the fret
   Here, where men sit and hear each other groan;
Where palsy shakes a few, sad, last gray hairs,   25
   Where youth grows pale, and spectre-thin, and dies;[7]
     Where but to think is to be full of sorrow
       And leaden-eyed despairs,
Where Beauty cannot keep her lustrous eyes,
   Or new Love pine at them beyond to-morrow.   30

4

Away! away! for I will fly to thee,
   Not charioted by Bacchus and his pards,
But on the viewless wings of Poesy,[8]
   Though the dull brain perplexes and retards:
Already with thee! tender is the night,   35
   And haply the Queen-Moon is on her throne,
     Cluster'd around by all her starry Fays;[9]
       But here there is no light,
Save what from heaven is with the breezes blown
   Through verdurous[1] glooms and winding mossy ways. 40

5

I cannot see what flowers are at my feet,
   Nor what soft incense hangs upon the boughs,
But, in embalmed[2] darkness, guess each sweet
   Wherewith the seasonable month endows
The grass, the thicket, and the fruit-tree wild;   45
   White hawthorn, and the pastoral eglantine;[3]
     Fast fading violets cover'd up in leaves;
       And mid-May's eldest child,
The coming musk-rose, full of dewy wine,
   The murmurous haunt of flies on summer eves.   50

6

Darkling[4] I listen; and, for many a time
   I have been half in love with easeful Death,
Call'd him soft names in many a mused[5] rhyme,
   To take into the air my quiet breath;
Now more than ever seems it rich to die,   55
   To cease upon the midnight with no pain,
     While thou art pouring forth thy soul abroad
       In such an ecstasy!

7. Keats's brother, Tom, wasted by tuberculosis, had died the previous winter.
8. I.e., not by getting drunk on wine (the "vintage" of stanza two), but on the invisible ("viewless") wings of the poetic fancy. (Bacchus, god of wine, was sometimes represented in a chariot drawn by "pards"—leopards.)
9. Fairies.

1. Green-foliaged.
2. Perfumed.
3. Sweetbrier, or honeysuckle.
4. In the dark.
5. Meditated. Two earlier poems ("rhymes") by Keats which called on "easeful Death" are the sonnets *Why Did I Laugh Tonight? No Voice Will Tell* and *Bright Star, Would I Were Stedfast As Thou Art.*

Still wouldst thou sing, and I have ears in vain—
    To thy high requiem become a sod.   60

7

Thou wast not born for death, immortal Bird!
    No hungry generations tread thee down;
The voice I hear this passing night was heard
    In ancient days by emperor and clown:
Perhaps the self-same song that found a path   65
    Through the sad heart of Ruth,⁶ when, sick for home,
        She stood in tears amid the alien corn;
            The same that oft-times hath
    Charm'd magic casements, opening on the foam
        Of perilous seas, in faery lands forlorn.   70

8

Forlorn!⁷ the very word is like a bell
    To toll me back from thee to my sole self!
Adieu! the fancy⁸ cannot cheat so well
    As she is fam'd to do, deceiving elf.
Adieu! adieu! thy plaintive anthem⁹ fades   75
    Past the near meadows, over the still stream,
        Up the hill-side; and now 'tis buried deep
            In the next valley-glades:
    Was it a vision, or a waking dream?
        Fled is that music:—Do I wake or sleep?¹⁰   80

May, 1819   1819, 1820

Ode on a Grecian Urn¹

1

Thou still unravish'd bride of quietness,
    Thou foster-child of silence and slow time,
Sylvan² historian, who canst thus express

6. The young widow in the Biblical Book of Ruth. "Corn": i.e., wheat.
7. One critic has said that "forlorn"—which means "long past" as well as "sorrowful"—"has its feet in two worlds," the faeryland of imagination and the woe of reality to which the word reawakens the lyric speaker.
8. I.e., "the viewless wings of Poesy" of line 33.
9. Hymn.
10. See *Ode to Psyche*, note to line 6.
1. This urn, with its sculptured reliefs of Dionysian ecstasies, panting young lovers in flight and pursuit, a pastoral piper under spring foliage, and the quiet celebration of communal pieties, resembles parts of various vases, sculptures, and paintings; but it existed in all its particulars only in Keats's imagination. In the urn—which captures moments of intense experience in attitudes of grace and freezes them into marble immobility—Keats found the perfect correlative for his persistent concern with the longing for permanence in a world of change. The interpretation of the details with which Keats develops this concept, however, is hotly disputed, all the way from the opening phrase—is "still" an adverb ("as yet") or an adjective ("motionless")?—to the two concluding lines, an ending which has already accumulated as much critical discussion as the "two-handed engine" in Milton's *Lycidas* or the cruxes in Shakespeare's plays. But these disputes testify to the enigmatic richness of meaning in the five short stanzas, and show that the ode has become a central point of reference in the criticism of the English lyric.
2. Rustic, representing a woodland scene.

A flowery tale more sweetly than our rhyme:
What leaf-fring'd legend haunts about thy shape   5
  Of deities or mortals, or of both,
    In Tempe or the dales of Arcady?[3]
  What men or gods are these? What maidens loth?
What mad pursuit? What struggle to escape?
    What pipes and timbrels? What wild ecstasy?   10

2

Heard melodies are sweet, but those unheard
  Are sweeter; therefore, ye soft pipes, play on;
Not to the sensual ear,[4] but, more endear'd,
  Pipe to the spirit ditties of no tone:
Fair youth, beneath the trees, thou canst not leave   15
  Thy song, nor ever can those trees be bare;
    Bold lover, never, never canst thou kiss,
Though winning near the goal—yet, do not grieve;
    She cannot fade, though thou hast not thy bliss,
  For ever wilt thou love, and she be fair!   20

3

Ah, happy, happy boughs! that cannot shed
  Your leaves, nor ever bid the spring adieu;
And, happy melodist, unwearied,
  For ever piping songs for ever new;
More happy love! more happy, happy love!   25
  For ever warm and still to be enjoy'd,
    For ever panting, and for ever young;
All breathing human passion far above,
    That leaves a heart high-sorrowful and cloy'd,
  A burning forehead, and a parching tongue.   30

4

Who are these coming to the sacrifice?
  To what green altar, O mysterious priest,
Lead'st thou that heifer lowing at the skies,
  And all her silken flanks with garlands drest?
What little town by river or sea shore,   35
  Or mountain-built with peaceful citadel,
    Is emptied of this folk, this pious morn?
And, little town, thy streets for evermore
  Will silent be; and not a soul to tell
    Why thou art desolate, can e'er return.   40

5

O Attic[5] shape! Fair attitude! with brede
  Of marble men and maidens overwrought,[6]
With forest branches and the trodden weed;

---

3. Tempe is a beautiful valley in Greece, which has come to represent supreme rural beauty. The "dales of Arcady" are the valleys of Arcadia, a state in ancient Greece often used as a symbol of the pastoral ideal.
4. The ear of sense (as opposed to that of the "spirit," or imagination).
5. Greek. Attica was the region of Greece in which Athens was located.
6. Ornamented all over ("overwrought") with an interwoven pattern ("brede").

Thou, silent form, dost tease us out of thought
As doth eternity: Cold Pastoral!   45
When old age shall this generation waste,
Thou shalt remain, in midst of other woe
Than ours, a friend to man, to whom thou say'st,
"Beauty is truth, truth beauty,"[7]—that is all
Ye know on earth, and all ye need to know.   50

May, 1819   1820

Ode on Melancholy   This is Keats's best-known statement of his
recurrent theme of the inextricable contrarieties of life. The remarkable last
stanza, in which Melancholy becomes a veiled goddess in a mystery religion,
implies that it is the tragic human destiny that beauty, joy, and life itself
take their quality and value from the very fact that they are transitory,
and turn into their opposites.

The poem originally included the following stanza, which Keats canceled
in MS:

Though you should build a bark of dead men's bones,
    And rear a phantom gibbet for a mast,
Stitch creeds together for a sail, with groans
    To fill it out, bloodstained and aghast;
Although your rudder be a Dragon's tail,
    Long sever'd, yet still hard with agony,
    Your cordage large uprootings from the skull
Of bald Medusa: certes you would fail
    To find the Melancholy, whether she
    Dreameth in any isle of Lethe dull.

Ode on Melancholy

1

No, no, go not to Lethe,[1] neither twist
    Wolf's-bane, tight-rooted, for its poisonous wine;
Nor suffer thy pale forehead to be kiss'd
    By nightshade,[2] ruby grape of Proserpine;

---

7. The quotation marks around this
phrase are found in the volume of
poems Keats published in 1820; but
there are no quotation marks in the
version printed in *Annals of the Fine
Arts* that same year, or in the four
transcripts of the poem made by
Keats's friends. This discrepancy has
encouraged the diversity of critical
interpretations of the last two lines.
Leading critics disagree whether the
whole of these lines is said by the urn,
or "Beauty is truth, truth beauty" by
the urn and the rest by Keats or else
by an invented lyric speaker; whether
the "ye" in the last line is addressed to
the lyric speaker, to the readers, to the
urn, or to the figures on the urn;
whether, "all ye know" is that beauty
is truth, or this plus the statement in
lines 46–48; and whether "beauty is
truth" is a universal and profound
metaphysical proposition, or an over-
statement uttered in the course of a
dramatic dialogue, or simply nonsense.
(The various commentaries are collected in *Keats's Well-Read Urn*, ed.
H. T. Lyon, 1958).
1. The waters of forgetfulness in
Hades.
2. "Nightshade" and "wolfsbane" (line
2) are poisonous plants. Proserpine is
the wife of Pluto and queen of the
infernal regions.

Make not your rosary of yew-berries,[3]   5
  Nor let the beetle, nor the death-moth be
Your mournful Psyche,[4] nor the downy owl
A partner in your sorrow's mysteries;[5]
  For shade to shade will come too drowsily,
    And drown the wakeful anguish of the soul.[6]   10

2

But when the melancholy fit shall fall
  Sudden from heaven like a weeping cloud,
That fosters the droop-headed flowers all,
  And hides the green hill in an April shroud;
Then glut thy sorrow on a morning rose,   15
  Or on the rainbow of the salt sand-wave,
    Or on the wealth of globed peonies;
Or if thy mistress some rich anger shows,
  Emprison her soft hand, and let her rave,
    And feed deep, deep upon her peerless eyes.   20

3

She dwells[7] with Beauty—Beauty that must die;
  And Joy, whose hand is ever at his lips
Bidding adieu; and aching Pleasure nigh,
  Turning to poison while the bee-mouth sips:
Ay, in the very temple of Delight   25
  Veil'd Melancholy has her sovran shrine,
    Though seen of none save him whose strenuous tongue
Can burst Joy's grape against his palate fine;[8]
His soul shall taste the sadness of her might,
    And be among her cloudy trophies hung.[9]   30
May, 1819   1820

Ode on Indolence[1]

"They toil not, neither do they spin."[2]

1

One morn before me were three figures seen,
  With bowed necks, and joined hands, side-faced;
And one behind the other stepp'd serene,

---

3. A symbol of death.
4. In ancient times Psyche (the soul) was sometimes represented as a butterfly or moth, fluttering out of the mouth of a dying man. The allusion may also be to the death's-head moth, which has skull-like markings on its back. The "beetle" of line 6 refers to replicas of the large black beetle, the scarab, which were often placed by Egyptians in their tombs as a symbol of resurrection.
5. Secret religious rites.
6. I.e., sorrow needs contrast to sustain its intensity.

7. I.e., Melancholy, personified as a goddess whose chief place of worship ("shrine," line 26) is located "in the very temple of Delight" (line 25).
8. Sensitive, subtly discriminative.
9. A reference to the Greek and Roman practice of hanging trophies in the temples of the gods.
1. On March 19, 1819, Keats wrote to George and Georgiana Keats: "This morning I am in a sort of temper indolent and supremely careless * * * Neither Poetry, nor Ambition, nor Love have any alertness of countenance as they pass by me: they seem rather like

In placid sandals, and in white robes graced:
They pass'd, like figures on a marble urn, 5
    When shifted round to see the other side;
        They came again: as when the urn once more
Is shifted round, the first seen shades return;
    And they were strange to me, as may betide
        With vases, to one deep in Phidian[3] lore. 10

2

How is it, shadows, that I knew ye not?
    How came ye muffled in so hush a masque?
Was it a silent deep-disguised plot
    To steal away, and leave without a task
My idle days? Ripe was the drowsy hour; 15
    The blissful cloud of summer-indolence
        Benumb'd my eyes; my pulse grew less and less;
Pain had no sting, and pleasure's wreath no flower.
    O, why did ye not melt, and leave my sense
        Unhaunted quite of all but—nothingness? 20

3

A third time pass'd they by, and, passing, turn'd
    Each one the face a moment whiles to me;
Then faded, and to follow them I burn'd
    And ached for wings, because I knew the three:
The first was a fair maid, and Love her name; 25
    The second was Ambition, pale of cheek,
        And ever watchful with fatigued eye;
The last, whom I love more, the more of blame
    Is heap'd upon her, maiden most unmeek,—
        I knew to be my demon Poesy. 30

4

They faded, and, forsooth! I wanted wings:
    O folly! What is Love? and where is it?
And for that poor Ambition—it springs
    From a man's little heart's short fever-fit;
For Poesy!—no,—she has not a joy,— 35
    At least for me,—so sweet as drowsy noons,
        And evenings steep'd in honied indolence;
O, for an age so shelter'd from annoy,
    That I may never know how change the moons,
        Or hear the voice of busy common-sense! 40

5

A third time came they by;—alas! wherefore?
    My sleep had been embroider'd with dim dreams;
My soul had been a lawn besprinkled o'er

three figures on a greek vase—a Man
and two women—whom no one but
myself could distinguish in their disguisement. This is the only happiness;
and is a rare instance of advantage in
the body overpowering the Mind." The
Ode was probably written soon after
this time, but was not published until
long after the poet's death, in 1848.
2. Matthew vi.28.
3. Phidias was the great Athenian
sculptor of the 5th century B.C. who
designed the marble sculptures for the
Parthenon.

With flowers, and stirring shades, and baffled beams:
The morn was clouded, but no shower fell, 45
Though in her lids hung the sweet tears of May;
The open casement press'd a new-leaved vine,
Let in the budding warmth and throstle's lay;
O shadows! 'twas a time to bid farewell!
Upon your skirts had fallen no tears of mine. 50

6

So, ye three ghosts, adieu! Ye cannot raise
My head cool-bedded in the flowery grass;
For I would not be dieted with praise,
A pet-lamb in a sentimental farce!⁴
Fade softly from my eyes, and be once more 55
In masque-like figures on the dreamy urn;
Farewell! I yet have visions for the night,
And for the day faint visions there is store;
Vanish, ye phantoms, from my idle spright,⁵
Into the clouds, and never more return! 60

1819　　　　　　　　　　　　　　　　　　　　1848

4. In a letter of June 9, 1819, Keats wrote: "I have been very idle lately, very averse to writing; both from the overpowering idea of our dead poets and from abatement of my love of fame. I hope I am a little more of a Philosopher than I was, consequently a little less of a versifying Pet-lamb * * * You will judge of my 1819 temper when I tell you that the thing I have most enjoyed this year has been writing an ode to Indolence."
5. Spirit.

Lamia Keats himself cited, as the source of his plot, a story in Robert Burton's *Anatomy of Melancholy* (1621): "One Menippus Lycius, a young man twenty-five years of age, that going betwixt Cenchreas and Corinth, met such a phantasm in the habit of a fair gentlewoman, which, taking him by the hand, carried him home to her house, in the suburbs of Corinth. * * * The young man, a philosopher, otherwise staid and discreet, able to moderate his passions, though not this of love, tarried with her a while to his great content, and at last married her, to whose wedding, amongst other guests, came Apollonius; who, by some probable conjectures, found her out to be a serpent, a lamia; and that all her furniture was, like Tantalus' gold, described by Homer, no substance but mere illusions. When she saw herself descried, she wept, and desired Apollonius to be silent, but he would not be moved, and thereupon she, plate, house, and all that was in it, vanished in an instant: many thousands took notice of this fact, for it was done in the midst of Greece."

In ancient demonology, a "lamia"—pronounced *lā´-mĭ-a*—was a monster in woman's form who preyed on human beings. There are various clues (see especially Part II, 229–38) that Keats invested the ancient legend with allegorical significance. Its interpretation, however, and even the inclination of Keats's own sympathies in the contest between Lamia and Apollonius, have been disputed. It is possible that Keats failed to make up his mind, or wavered in the course of composition. What seems to be Keats's indecision, however, may in fact indicate that he intended to present an inevitably fatal situation, in which no one is entirely blameless or blameworthy, and no character is meant to monopolize either our sympathy or antipathy. Lamia is an enchantress, a liar, and a calculating expert in *amour*; but she apparently intends no harm, is genuinely in love, and is very beautiful. And both male protagonists exhibit culpable extremes which alienate our sympathy. Lycius, though an attractive young lover, is gullible, a slave to his passions, and capable of gratuitous cruelty; while Apollonius, though realistically clear-sighted, is rigid, puritanical, and inhumane.

The poem, written between late June and early September, 1819, is a return, after the Spenserian stanzas of *The Eve of St. Agnes,* to the pentameter couplets Keats had used in *Endymion* and other early narrative poems. But Keats had in the meantime been studying Dryden's closed and strong-paced couplets. The initial lines of Dryden's version of Boccaccio's story *Cymon and Iphigenia* will show the kind of narrative model which helped Keats make the technical transition from the fluent but sprawling gracefulness of the opening of *Endymion* to the vigor and economy of the opening of *Lamia*:

> In that sweet isle where Venus keeps her court,
> And every grace, and all the loves, resort;
> Where either sex is formed of softer earth,
> And takes the bent of pleasure from their birth;
> There lived a Cyprian lord, above the rest
> Wise, wealthy, with a numerous issue blessed; * * *

Lamia

Part I

Upon a time, before the faery broods
Drove Nymph and Satyr from the prosperous woods,[1]
Before King Oberon's bright diadem,
Sceptre, and mantle, clasp'd with dewy gem,
Frighted away the Dryads and the Fauns   5
From rushes green, and brakes,[2] and cowslip'd lawns,
The ever-smitten Hermes empty left
His golden throne, bent warm on amorous theft:[3]
From high Olympus had he stolen light,
On this side of Jove's clouds, to escape the sight   10
Of his great summoner, and made retreat
Into a forest on the shores of Crete.
For somewhere in that sacred island dwelt
A nymph, to whom all hoofed Satyrs knelt;
At whose white feet the languid Tritons[4] poured   15

1. Nymphs and satyrs—like the dryads and fauns in line 5—were all minor classical deities of the woods and fields, said here to have been driven off by Oberon, king of the fairies, who were supernatural beings of the postclassical era.
2. Thickets.
3. Hermes (or Mercury), wing-footed messenger at the summons of Jove (line 11), was notoriously amorous.
4. Minor sea gods.

Pearls, while on land they wither'd and adored.
Fast by the springs where she to bathe was wont,
And in those meads where sometime she might haunt,
Were strewn rich gifts, unknown to any Muse,
Though Fancy's casket were unlock'd to choose.   20
Ah, what a world of love was at her feet!
So Hermes thought, and a celestial heat
Burnt from his winged heels to either ear,
That from a whiteness, as the lily clear,
Blush'd into roses 'mid his golden hair,   25
Fallen in jealous curls about his shoulders bare.[5]

From vale to vale, from wood to wood, he flew,
Breathing upon the flowers his passion new,
And wound with many a river to its head,
To find where this sweet nymph prepar'd her secret bed: 30
In vain; the sweet nymph might nowhere be found,
And so he rested, on the lonely ground,
Pensive, and full of painful jealousies
Of the Wood-Gods, and even the very trees.
There as he stood, he heard a mournful voice,   35
Such as once heard, in gentle heart, destroys
All pain but pity: thus the lone voice spake:
"When from this wreathed tomb shall I awake!
When move in a sweet body fit for life,
And love, and pleasure, and the ruddy strife   40
Of hearts and lips! Ah, miserable me!"
The God, dove-footed,[6] glided silently
Round bush and tree, soft-brushing, in his speed,
The taller grasses and full-flowering weed,
Until he found a palpitating snake,   45
Bright, and cirque-couchant[7] in a dusky brake.

She was a gordian[8] shape of dazzling hue,
Vermilion-spotted, golden, green, and blue;
Striped like a zebra, freckled like a pard,
Eyed like a peacock,[9] and all crimson barr'd;   50
And full of silver moons, that, as she breathed,
Dissolv'd, or brighter shone, or interwreathed
Their lustres with the gloomier tapestries—
So rainbow-sided, touch'd with miseries,
She seem'd, at once, some penanced lady elf,   55
Some demon's mistress, or the demon's self.

5. The curls clung jealously to his bare
shoulders. This line is the first of a
number of Alexandrines—a six-foot
line, used to introduce variety of metric
movement—that Keats learned from
Dryden. Another such device is the trip-
let in lines 61–63.
6. Quietly as a dove.

7. Lying in a circular coil.
8. Intricately twisted, like the knot
tied by King Gordius, which no one
could undo.
9. Having multicolored spots, like the
"eyes" in a peacock's tail. "Pard":
leopard.

Upon her crest she wore a wannish[1] fire
Sprinkled with stars, like Ariadne's tiar:[2]
Her head was serpent, but ah, bitter-sweet!
She had a woman's mouth with all its pearls[3] complete: 60
And for her eyes: what could such eyes do there
But weep, and weep, that they were born so fair?
As Proserpine still weeps for her Sicilian air.[4]
Her throat was serpent, but the words she spake
Came, as through bubbling honey, for Love's sake.   65
And thus; while Hermes on his pinions lay,
Like a stoop'd falcon[5] ere he takes his prey.

"Fair Hermes, crown'd with feathers, fluttering light,
I had a splendid dream of thee last night:
I saw thee sitting, on a throne of gold,   70
Among the Gods, upon Olympus old,
The only sad one; for thou didst not hear
The soft, lute-finger'd Muses chaunting clear,
Nor even Apollo when he sang alone,
Deaf to his throbbing throat's long, long melodious moan.   75
I dreamt I saw thee, robed in purple flakes,
Break amorous through the clouds, as morning breaks,
And, swiftly as a bright Phœbean dart,[6]
Strike for the Cretan isle; and here thou art!
Too gentle Hermes, hast thou found the maid?"   80
Whereat the star of Lethe[7] not delay'd
His rosy eloquence, and thus inquired:
"Thou smooth-lipp'd serpent, surely high inspired!
Thou beauteous wreath, with melancholy eyes,
Possess whatever bliss thou canst devise,   85
Telling me only where my nymph is fled,—
Where she doth breathe!" "Bright planet, thou hast said,"
Return'd the snake, "but seal with oaths, fair God!"
"I swear," said Hermes, "by my serpent rod,
And by thine eyes, and by thy starry crown!"   90
Light flew his earnest words, among the blossoms blown.
Then thus again the brilliance feminine:
"Too frail of heart! for this lost nymph of thine,
Free as the air, invisibly, she strays
About these thornless wilds; her pleasant days   95
She tastes unseen; unseen her nimble feet
Leave traces in the grass and flowers sweet;

1. Rather dark.
2. Ariadne, who was transformed into a constellation, had been represented in a painting by Titian wearing a symbolic crown, or tiara ("tiar"), of stars.
3. "Pearls" had become almost a synonym for teeth in Elizabethan poetry.
4. Proserpine had been carried off to Hades by Pluto from the field of Enna, in Sicily.

5. "Stoop" is the term for the plunge of a falcon upon his prey.
6. A ray of Phoebus Apollo, god of the sun.
7. Hermes, when he appeared like a star on the banks of Lethe, in the darkness of Hades. (One of Hermes' offices was to guide the souls of the dead to the lower regions.)

From weary tendrils, and bow'd branches green,
She plucks the fruit unseen, she bathes unseen:
And by my power is her beauty veil'd   100
To keep it unaffronted, unassail'd
By the love-glances of unlovely eyes,
Of Satyrs, Fauns, and blear'd Silenus'[8] sighs.
Pale grew her immortality, for woe
Of all these lovers, and she grieved so   105
I took compassion on her, bade her steep
Her hair in weïrd[9] syrops, that would keep
Her loveliness invisible, yet free
To wander as she loves, in liberty.
Thou shalt behold her, Hermes, thou alone,   110
If thou wilt, as thou swearest, grant my boon!"
Then, once again, the charmed God began
An oath, and through the serpent's ears it ran
Warm, tremulous, devout, psalterian.[1]
Ravish'd, she lifted her Circean[2] head,   115
Blush'd a live damask, and swift-lisping said,
"I was a woman, let me have once more
A woman's shape, and charming as before.
I love a youth of Corinth—O the bliss!
Give me my woman's form, and place me where he is.   120
Stoop, Hermes, let me breathe upon thy brow,
And thou shalt see thy sweet nymph even now."
The God on half-shut feathers sank serene,
She breath'd upon his eyes, and swift was seen
Of both the guarded nymph near-smiling on the green.   125
It was no dream; or say a dream it was,
Real are the dreams of Gods, and smoothly pass
Their pleasures in a long immortal dream.
One warm, flush'd moment, hovering, it might seem
Dash'd by the wood-nymph's beauty, so he burn'd;   130
Then, lighting on the printless verdure, turn'd
To the swoon'd serpent, and with languid arm,
Delicate, put to proof the lythe Caducean charm.[3]
So done, upon the nymph his eyes he bent
Full of adoring tears and blandishment,   135
And towards her stept: she, like a moon in wane,
Faded before him, cower'd, nor could restrain
Her fearful sobs, self-folding like a flower
That faints into itself at evening hour:
But the God fostering her chilled hand,   140
She felt the warmth, her eyelids open'd bland,[4]

8. Silenus was a satyr, tutor of Bacchus, and always drunk.
9. Magical: Keats makes the word a dissyllable.
1. Either "like a psalm" or "like the sound of the psaltery" (an ancient stringed instrument).
2. Like that of Circe. the enchantress in the *Odyssey*. "Live damask": a living damask rose (large and fragrant pink rose).
3. I.e., put to the test the magic of the flexible Caduceus (Hermes' official staff).
4. Softly.

And, like new flowers at morning song of bees,
Bloom'd, and gave up her honey to the lees.[5]
Into the green-recessed woods they flew;
Nor grew they pale, as mortal lovers do.   145

    Left to herself, the serpent now began
To change; her elfin blood in madness ran,
Her mouth foam'd, and the grass, therewith besprent,[6]
Wither'd at dew so sweet and virulent;
Her eyes in torture fix'd, and anguish drear,   150
Hot, glaz'd, and wide, with lid-lashes all sear,
Flash'd phosphor and sharp sparks, without one cooling tear.
The colours all inflam'd throughout her train,
She writh'd about, convuls'd with scarlet pain:
A deep volcanian[7] yellow took the place   155
Of all her milder-mooned body's grace;
And, as the lava ravishes the mead,
Spoilt all her silver mail, and golden brede;[8]
Made gloom of all her frecklings, streaks and bars,
Eclips'd her crescents, and lick'd up her stars: 160
So that, in moments few, she was undrest
Of all her sapphires, greens, and amethyst,
And rubious-argent:[9] of all these bereft,
Nothing but pain and ugliness were left.
Still shone her crown; that vanish'd, also she   165
Melted and disappear'd as suddenly;
And in the air, her new voice luting soft,
Cried, "Lycius! gentle Lycius!"—Borne aloft
With the bright mists about the mountains hoar
These words dissolv'd: Crete's forests heard no more.   170

    Whither fled Lamia, now a lady bright,
A full-born beauty new and exquisite?
She fled into that valley they pass o'er
Who go to Corinth from Cenchreas' shore;[1]
And rested at the foot of those wild hills,   175
The rugged founts of the Peræan rills,
And of that other ridge whose barren back
Stretches, with all its mist and cloudy rack,
South-westward to Cleone. There she stood
About a young bird's flutter from a wood,   180
Fair, on a sloping green of mossy tread,
By a clear pool, wherein she passioned[2]
To see herself escap'd from so sore ills,
While her robes flaunted with the daffodils.

5. Dregs.
6. Sprinkled.
7. The color of sulphur (thrown up by a volcano), in contrast to her former silvery moon color.
8. "Mail": interlinked rings, as in a coat of armor; "brede": embroidery,

interwoven pattern.
9. Silvery red.
1. Cenchrea (Keats's "Cenchreas") was a harbor of Corinth, in southern Greece.
2. Felt intense excitement.

Ah, happy Lycius!—for she was a maid   185
More beautiful than ever twisted braid,
Or sigh'd, or blush'd, or on spring-flowered lea[3]
Spread a green kirtle to the minstrelsy:
A virgin purest lipp'd, yet in the lore
Of love deep learned to the red heart's core: 190
Not one hour old, yet of sciential brain
To unperplex bliss from its neighbour pain;[4]
Define their pettish limits, and estrange
Their points of contact, and swift counterchange;
Intrigue with the specious chaos,[5] and dispart   195
Its most ambiguous atoms with sure art;
As though in Cupid's college she had spent
Sweet days a lovely graduate, still unshent,[6]
And kept his rosy terms in idle languishment.

Why this fair creature chose so fairily   200
By the wayside to linger, we shall see;
But first 'tis fit to tell how she could muse
And dream, when in the serpent prison-house,
Of all she list,[7] strange or magnificent:
How, ever, where she will'd, her spirit went;   205
Whether to faint Elysium, or where
Down through tress-lifting waves the Nereids[8] fair
Wind into Thetis' bower by many a pearly stair;
Or where God Bacchus drains his cups divine,
Stretch'd out, at ease, beneath a glutinous pine;   210
Or where in Pluto's gardens palatine
Mulciber's columns gleam in far piazzian line.[9]
And sometimes into cities she would send
Her dream, with feast and rioting to blend;
And once, while among mortals dreaming thus,   215
She saw the young Corinthian Lycius
Charioting foremost in the envious race,
Like a young Jove with calm uneager face,
And fell into a swooning love of him.
Now on the moth-time of that evening dim   220
He would return that way, as well she knew,
To Corinth from the shore; for freshly blew
The eastern soft wind, and his galley now

3. Meadow: "kirtle": gown.
4. I.e., of knowledgeable ("sciential") brain to disentangle ("unperplex") bliss from its closely-related pain, to define their quarreled-over ("pettish") limits, and to separate out ("estrange") their points of contact and the swift changes of each condition into its opposite. Cf. Keats's *Ode on Melancholy*, lines 25–26.
5. I.e., turn to her own artful purpose
the seeming ("specious") chaos.
6. Unspoiled. "Rosy terms": the terms spent studying in "Cupid's college."
7. Wished.
8. Sea nymphs, of whom Thetis (the mother of Achilles) was one.
9. I.e., columns made by Mulciber (Vulcan, god of fire and metalworking) gleam in long lines around open courts (piazzas). "Palatine": palatial.

Grated the quaystones with her brazen prow
In port Cenchreas, from Egina isle   225
Fresh anchor'd; whither he had been awhile
To sacrifice to Jove, whose temple there
Waits with high marble doors for blood and incense rare.
Jove heard his vows, and better'd his desire;
For by some freakful chance he made retire   230
From his companions, and set forth to walk,
Perhaps grown wearied of their Corinth talk:
Over the solitary hills he fared,
Thoughtless at first, but ere eve's star appeared
His phantasy was lost, where reason fades,   235
In the calm'd twilight of Platonic shades.[1]
Lamia beheld him coming, near, more near—
Close to her passing, in indifference drear,
His silent sandals swept the mossy green;
So neighbour'd to him, and yet so unseen   240
She stood: he pass'd, shut up in mysteries,
His mind wrapp'd like his mantle, while her eyes
Follow'd his steps, and her neck regal white
Turn'd—syllabling thus, "Ah, Lycius bright,
And will you leave me on the hills alone?   245
Lycius, look back! and be some pity shown."
He did; not with cold wonder fearingly,
But Orpheus-like at an Eurydice;[2]
For so delicious were the words she sung,
It seem'd he had lov'd them a whole summer long: 250
And soon his eyes had drunk her beauty up,
Leaving no drop in the bewildering cup,
And still the cup was full,—while he, afraid
Lest she should vanish ere his lip had paid
Due adoration, thus began to adore;   255
Her soft look growing coy, she saw his chain so sure:
"Leave thee alone! Look back! Ah, Goddess, see
Whether my eyes can ever turn from thee!
For pity do not this sad heart belie[3]—
Even as thou vanishest so I shall die.   260
Stay! though a Naiad of the rivers, stay!
To thy far wishes will thy streams obey:
Stay! though the greenest woods be thy domain,
Alone they can drink up the morning rain:
Though a descended Pleiad,[4] will not one   265
Of thine harmonious sisters keep in tune
Thy spheres, and as thy silver proxy shine?

1. I.e., he was absorbed in musing about
the obscurities of Plato's philosophy.
2. As Orpheus looked at Eurydice in
Hades. Orpheus was allowed by Pluto
to lead Eurydice back to earth on condition that he not look back at her, but
he could not resist doing so, hence
lost her once more.
3. Be false to.
4. One of the seven sisters composing
the constellation Pleiades.

So sweetly to these ravish'd ears of mine
Came thy sweet greeting, that if thou shouldst fade
Thy memory will waste me to a shade:—   270
For pity do not melt!"—"If I should stay,"
Said Lamia, "here, upon this floor of clay,
And pain my steps upon these flowers too rough,
What canst thou say or do of charm enough
To dull the nice⁵ remembrance of my home?   275
Thou canst not ask me with thee here to roam
Over these hills and vales, where no joy is,—
Empty of immortality and bliss!
Thou art a scholar, Lycius, and must know
That finer spirits cannot breathe below   280
In human climes, and live: Alas! poor youth,
What taste of purer air hast thou to soothe
My essence? What serener palaces,
Where I may all my many senses please,
And by mysterious sleights a hundred thirsts appease?   285
It cannot be—Adieu!" So said, she rose
Tiptoe with white arms spread. He, sick to lose
The amorous promise of her lone complain,
Swoon'd, murmuring of love, and pale with pain.
The cruel lady, without any show   290
Of sorrow for her tender favourite's woe,
But rather, if her eyes could brighter be,
With brighter eyes and slow amenity,
Put her new lips to his, and gave afresh
The life she had so tangled in her mesh: 295
And as he from one trance was wakening
Into another, she began to sing,
Happy in beauty, life, and love, and every thing,
A song of love, too sweet for earthly lyres,
While, like held breath, the stars drew in their panting fires. 300
And then she whisper'd in such trembling tone,
As those who, safe together met alone
For the first time through many anguish'd days,
Use other speech than looks; bidding him raise
His drooping head, and clear his soul of doubt,   305
For that she was a woman, and without
Any more subtle fluid in her veins
Than throbbing blood, and that the self-same pains
Inhabited her frail-strung heart as his.
And next she wonder'd how his eyes could miss   310
Her face so long in Corinth, where, she said,
She dwelt but half retir'd, and there had led
Days happy as the gold coin could invent
Without the aid of love; yet in content
Till she saw him, as once she pass'd him by,   315

5. Detailed, minutely accurate.

Where 'gainst a column he leant thoughtfully
At Venus' temple porch, 'mid baskets heap'd
Of amorous herbs and flowers, newly reap'd
Late on that eve, as 'twas the night before
The Adonian feast;[6] whereof she saw no more,   320
But wept alone those days, for why should she adore?
Lycius from death awoke into amaze,
To see her still, and singing so sweet lays;
Then from amaze into delight he fell
To hear her whisper woman's lore so well;   325
And every word she spake entic'd him on
To unperplex'd delight[7] and pleasure known.
Let the mad poets say whate'er they please
Of the sweets of Fairies, Peris,[8] Goddesses,
There is not such a treat among them all,   330
Haunters of cavern, lake, and waterfall,
As a real woman, lineal indeed
From Pyrrha's pebbles[9] or old Adam's seed.
Thus gentle Lamia judg'd, and judg'd aright,
That Lycius could not love in half a fright,   335
So threw the goddess off, and won his heart
More pleasantly by playing woman's part,
With no more awe than what her beauty gave,
That, while it smote, still guaranteed to save.
Lycius to all made eloquent reply,   340
Marrying to every word a twinborn sigh;
And last, pointing to Corinth, ask'd her sweet,
If 'twas too far that night for her soft feet.
The way was short, for Lamia's eagerness
Made, by a spell, the triple league decrease   345
To a few paces; not at all surmised
By blinded Lycius, so in her comprized.[1]
They pass'd the city gates, he knew not how,
So noiseless, and he never thought to know.

As men talk in a dream, so Corinth all,   350
Throughout her palaces imperial,
And all her populous streets and temples lewd,[2]
Mutter'd, like tempest in the distance brew'd,
To the wide-spreaded night above her towers.
Men, women, rich and poor, in the cool hours,   355
Shuffled their sandals o'er the pavement white,
Companion'd or alone; while many a light
Flared, here and there, from wealthy festivals,

6. The feast of Adonis, beloved by Venus.
7. I.e., delight not mixed with its neighbor, pain; see line 192.
8. Fairylike creatures in Persian mythology.
9. Descended from the pebbles with which, in Greek myth, Pyrrha and Deucalion repeopled the earth after the flood.
1. Bound up.
2. Temples of Venus, whose worship sometimes involved ritual prostitution.

And threw their moving shadows on the walls,
Or found them cluster'd in the corniced shade   360
Of some arch'd temple door, or dusky colonnade.

   Muffling his face, of greeting friends in fear,
Her fingers he press'd hard, as one came near
With curl'd gray beard, sharp eyes, and smooth bald crown,
Slow-stepp'd, and robed in philosophic gown: 365
Lycius shrank closer, as they met and past,
Into his mantle, adding wings to haste,
While hurried Lamia trembled: "Ah," said he,
"Why do you shudder, love, so ruefully?
Why does your tender palm dissolve in dew?"—   370
"I'm wearied," said fair Lamia: "tell me who
Is that old man? I cannot bring to mind
His features:—Lycius! wherefore did you blind
Yourself from his quick eyes?" Lycius replied,
" 'Tis Apollonius sage, my trusty guide   375
And good instructor; but to-night he seems
The ghost of folly haunting my sweet dreams."

   While yet he spake they had arrived before
A pillar'd porch, with lofty portal door,
Where hung a silver lamp, whose phosphor glow   380
Reflected in the slabbed steps below,
Mild as a star in water; for so new,
And so unsullied was the marble hue,
So through the crystal polish, liquid fine,
Ran the dark veins, that none but feet divine   385
Could e'er have touch'd there. Sounds Æolian[3]
Breath'd from the hinges, as the ample span
Of the wide doors disclos'd a place unknown
Some time to any, but those two alone,
And a few Persian mutes, who that same year   390
Were seen about the markets: none knew where
They could inhabit; the most curious
Were foil'd, who watch'd to trace them to their house:
And but the flitter-winged verse must tell,
For truth's sake, what woe afterwards befel,   395
'Twould humour many a heart to leave them thus,
Shut from the busy world of more incredulous.

Part II

Love in a hut, with water and a crust,
Is—Love, forgive us!—cinders, ashes, dust;
Love in a palace is perhaps at last
More grievous torment than a hermit's fast:—

---

3. Like sounds from the wind harp (Aeolus is god of winds), which
responds musically to a current of air.

That is a doubtful tale from faery land, 5
Hard for the non-elect to understand.
Had Lycius liv'd to hand his story down,
He might have given the moral a fresh frown,
Or clench'd it quite: but too short was their bliss
To breed distrust and hate, that make the soft voice hiss 10
Besides, there, nightly, with terrific glare,
Love, jealous grown of so complete a pair,
Hover'd and buzz'd his wings, with fearful roar,
Above the lintel of their chamber door,
And down the passage cast a glow upon the floor. 15

For all this came a ruin: side by side
They were enthroned, in the even tide,
Upon a couch, near to a curtaining
Whose airy texture, from a golden string,
Floated into the room, and let appear 20
Unveil'd the summer heaven, blue and clear,
Betwixt two marble shafts:—there they reposed,
Where use had made it sweet, with eyelids closed,
Saving a tythe which love still open kept,
That they might see each other while they almost slept; 25
When from the slope side of a suburb hill,
Deafening the swallow's twitter, came a thrill
Of trumpets—Lycius started—the sounds fled,
But left a thought, a buzzing in his head.
For the first time, since first he harbour'd in 30
That purple-lined palace of sweet sin,
His spirit pass'd beyond its golden bourn
Into the noisy world almost forsworn.
The lady, ever watchful, penetrant,
Saw this with pain, so arguing a want 35
Of something more, more than her empery[4]
Of joys; and she began to moan and sigh
Because he mused beyond her, knowing well
That but a moment's thought is passion's passing bell.[5]
"Why do you sigh, fair creature?" whisper'd he: 40
"Why do you think?" return'd she tenderly:
"You have deserted me;—where am I now?
Not in your heart while care weighs on your brow:
No, no, you have dismiss'd me; and I go
From your breast houseless: ay, it must be so." 45
He answer'd, bending to her open eyes,
Where he was mirror'd small in paradise,
"My silver planet, both of eve and morn![6]
Why will you plead yourself so sad forlorn,
While I am striving how to fill my heart 50

4. Empire.
5. Death knell.

6. The planet Venus, which is both the
morning and the evening star.

With deeper crimson, and a double smart?
How to entangle, trammel up and snare
Your soul in mine, and labyrinth you there
Like the hid scent in an unbudded rose?
Ay, a sweet kiss—you see your mighty woes.[7]   55
My thoughts! shall I unveil them? Listen then!
What mortal hath a prize, that other men
May be confounded and abash'd withal,
But lets it sometimes pace abroad majestical,
And triumph, as in thee I should rejoice   60
Amid the hoarse alarm of Corinth's voice.
Let my foes choke, and my friends shout afar,
While through the thronged streets your bridal car
Wheels round its dazzling spokes."—The lady's cheek
Trembled; she nothing said, but, pale and meek,   65
Arose and knelt before him, wept a rain
Of sorrows at his words; at last with pain
Beseeching him, the while his hand she wrung,
To change his purpose. He thereat was stung,
Perverse, with stronger fancy to reclaim   70
Her wild and timid nature to his aim:
Besides, for all his love, in self despite,
Against his better self, he took delight
Luxurious in her sorrows, soft and new.
His passion, cruel grown, took on a hue   75
Fierce and sanguineous as 'twas possible
In one whose brow had no dark veins to swell.
Fine was the mitigated fury, like
Apollo's presence when in act to strike
The serpent—Ha, the serpent! certes, she   80
Was none. She burnt, she lov'd the tyranny,
And, all subdued, consented to the hour
When to the bridal he should lead his paramour.
Whispering in midnight silence, said the youth,
"Sure some sweet name thou hast, though, by my truth,   85
I have not ask'd it, ever thinking thee
Not mortal, but of heavenly progeny,
As still I do. Hast any mortal name,
Fit appellation for this dazzling frame?
Or friends or kinsfolk on the citied earth,   90
To share our marriage feast and nuptial mirth?"
"I have no friends," said Lamia, "no, not one;
My presence in wide Corinth hardly known:
My parents' bones are in their dusty urns
Sepulchred, where no kindled incense burns,   95
Seeing all their luckless race are dead, save me,
And I neglect the holy rite for thee.
Even as you list invite your many guests;

7. Playfully: "You see how great your troubles were!"

But if, as now it seems, your vision rests
With any pleasure on me, do not bid   100
Old Apollonius—from him keep me hid."
Lycius, perplex'd at words so blind and blank,
Made close inquiry; from whose touch she shrank,
Feigning a sleep; and he to the dull shade
Of deep sleep in a moment was betray'd.   105

    It was the custom then to bring away,
The bride from home at blushing shut of day,
Veil'd, in a chariot, heralded along
By strewn flowers, torches, and a marriage song,
With other pageants: but this fair unknown   110
Had not a friend. So being left alone,
(Lycius was gone to summon all his kin)
And knowing surely she could never win
His foolish heart from its mad pompousness,
She set herself, high-thoughted, how to dress   115
The misery in fit magnificence.
She did so, but 'tis doubtful how and whence
Came, and who were her subtle servitors.
About the halls, and to and from the doors,
There was a noise of wings, till in short space   120
The glowing banquet-room shone with wide-arched grace.
A haunting music, sole perhaps and lone
Supportress of the faery-roof, made moan
Throughout, as fearful the whole charm might fade.
Fresh carved cedar, mimicking a glade   125
Of palm and plantain, met from either side,
High in the midst, in honour of the bride:
Two palms and then two plantains, and so on,
From either side their stems branch'd one to one
All down the aisled place; and beneath all   130
There ran a stream of lamps straight on from wall to wall.
So canopied, lay an untasted feast
Teeming with odours. Lamia, regal drest,
Silently paced about, and as she went,
In pale contented sort of discontent,   135
Mission'd her viewless servants to enrich
The fretted[8] splendour of each nook and niche.
Between the tree-stems, marbled plain at first,
Came jasper pannels; then, anon, there burst
Forth creeping imagery of slighter trees,   140
And with the larger wove in small intricacies.
Approving all, she faded at self-will,
And shut the chamber up, close, hush'd and still,
Complete and ready for the revels rude,
When dreadful[9] guests would come to spoil her solitude.   145

8. Adorned with fretwork (interlaced   9. Terrifying.
patterns).

The day appear'd, and all the gossip rout.
O senseless Lycius! Madman! wherefore flout
The silent-blessing fate, warm cloister'd hours,
And show to common eyes these secret bowers?
The herd approach'd; each guest, with busy brain,   150
Arriving at the portal, gaz'd amain,[1]
And enter'd marveling: for they knew the street,
Remember'd it from childhood all complete
Without a gap, yet ne'er before had seen
That royal porch, that high-built fair demesne;[2]   155
So in they hurried all, maz'd, curious and keen:
Save one, who look'd thereon with eye severe,
And with calm-planted steps walk'd in austere;
'Twas Apollonius: something too he laugh'd,
As though some knotty problem, that had daft[3]   160
His patient thought, had now begun to thaw,
And solve and melt:—'twas just as he foresaw.

He met within the murmurous vestibule
His young disciple. " 'Tis no common rule,
Lycius," said he, "for uninvited guest   165
To force himself upon you, and infest
With an unbidden presence the bright throng
Of younger friends; yet must I do this wrong,
And you forgive me." Lycius blush'd, and led
The old man through the inner doors broad-spread;   170
With reconciling words and courteous mien
Turning into sweet milk the sophist's spleen.

Of wealthy lustre was the banquet-room,
Fill'd with pervading brilliance and perfume:
Before each lucid pannel fuming stood   175
A censer fed with myrrh and spiced wood,
Each by a sacred tripod held aloft,
Whose slender feet wide-swerv'd upon the soft
Wool-woofed[4] carpets: fifty wreaths of smoke
From fifty censers their light voyage took   180
To the high roof, still mimick'd as they rose
Along the mirror'd walls by twin-clouds odorous.
Twelve sphered tables, by silk seats insphered,
High as the level of a man's breast rear'd
On libbard's[5] paws, upheld the heavy gold   185
Of cups and goblets, and the store thrice told
Of Ceres' horn,[6] and, in huge vessels, wine
Come from the gloomy tun with merry shine.
Thus loaded with a feast the tables stood,
Each shrining in the midst the image of a God.   190

1. Intently.   5. Leopard's.
2. Estate.   6. The horn of plenty, overflowing with
3. Baffled, bewildered.   the products of Ceres, goddess of vege-
4. Woven.   tation.

When in an antichamber every guest
Had felt the cold full sponge to pleasure press'd,
By minist'ring slaves, upon his hands and feet,
And fragrant oils with ceremony meet
Pour'd on his hair, they all mov'd to the feast   195
In white robes, and themselves in order placed
Around the silken couches, wondering
Whence all this mighty cost and blaze of wealth could spring.

    Soft went the music the soft air along,
While fluent Greek a vowel'd undersong   200
Kept up among the guests, discoursing low
At first, for scarcely was the wine at flow;
But when the happy vintage touch'd their brains,
Louder they talk, and louder come the strains
Of powerful instruments:—the gorgeous dyes,   205
The space, the splendour of the draperies,
The roof of awful richness, nectarous cheer,
Beautiful slaves, and Lamia's self, appear,
Now, when the wine has done its rosy deed,
And every soul from human trammels freed,   210
No more so strange; for merry wine, sweet wine,
Will make Elysian shades not too fair, too divine.

    Soon was God Bacchus at meridian height;
Flush'd were their cheeks, and bright eyes double bright:
Garlands of every green, and every scent   215
From vales deflower'd, or forest-trees branch-rent,
In baskets of bright osier'd[7] gold were brought
High as the handles heap'd, to suit the thought
Of every guest; that each, as he did please,
Might fancy-fit his brows, silk-pillow'd at his ease.   220

    What wreath for Lamia? What for Lycius?
What for the sage, old Apollonius?
Upon her aching forehead be there hung
The leaves of willow and of adder's tongue;[8]
And for the youth, quick, let us strip for him   225
The thyrsus,[9] that his watching eyes may swim
Into forgetfulness; and, for the sage,
Let spear-grass and the spiteful thistle wage
War on his temples. Do not all charms fly
At the mere touch of cold philosophy?[1]   230
There was an awful[2] rainbow once in heaven:

---

7. Plaited. An "osier" is a willow rod used in weaving baskets.
8. A fern whose spikes resemble a serpent's tongue.
9. The vine-covered staff of Bacchus, used to signify drunkenness.
1. "Philosophy" in the sense of "natural philosophy," or science. Benajmin

Haydon tells in his *Autobiography* how, at a hard-drinking and high-spirited dinner party, Keats had agreed with Charles Lamb (to what extent jokingly, is not clear) that Newton's *Optics* "had destroyed all the poetry of the rainbow by reducing it to the prismatic colors."
2. Awe-inspiring.

We know her woof, her texture; she is given
In the dull catalogue of common things.
Philosophy will clip an Angel's wings,
Conquer all mysteries by rule and line,   235
Empty the haunted air, and gnomed mine[3]—
Unweave a rainbow, as it erewhile made
The tender-person'd Lamia melt into a shade.

    By her glad Lycius sitting, in chief place,
Scarce saw in all the room another face,   240
Till, checking his love trance, a cup he took
Full brimm'd, and opposite sent forth a look
'Cross the broad table, to beseech a glance
From his old teacher's wrinkled countenance,
And pledge him.[4] The bald-head philosopher   245
Had fix'd his eye, without a twinkle or stir
Full on the alarmed beauty of the bride,
Brow-beating her fair form, and troubling her sweet pride.
Lycius then press'd her hand, with devout touch,
As pale it lay upon the rosy couch: 250
'Twas icy, and the cold ran through his veins;
Then sudden it grew hot, and all the pains
Of an unnatural heat shot to his heart.
"Lamia, what means this? Wherefore dost thou start?
Know'st thou that man?" Poor Lamia answer'd not.   255
He gaz'd into her eyes, and not a jot
Own'd[5] they the lovelorn piteous appeal:
More, more he gaz'd: his human senses reel:
Some hungry spell that loveliness absorbs;
There was no recognition in those orbs.   260
"Lamia!" he cried—and no soft-toned reply.
The many heard, and the loud revelry
Grew hush; the stately music no more breathes;
The myrtle[6] sicken'd in a thousand wreaths:
By faint degrees, voice, lute, and pleasure ceased;   265
A deadly silence step by step increased,
Until it seem'd a horrid presence there,
And not a man but felt the terror in his hair.
"Lamia!" he shriek'd; and nothing but the shriek
With its sad echo did the silence break.   270
"Begone, foul dream!" he cried, gazing again
In the bride's face, where now no azure vein
Wander'd on fair-spaced temples; no soft bloom
Misted the cheek; no passion to illume
The deep-recessed vision:—all was blight;   275
Lamia, no longer fair, there sat a deadly white.
"Shut, shut those juggling[7] eyes, thou ruthless man!

3. Gnomes were guardians of mines.
4. Drink a toast to him.
5. Acknowledged.

6. Sacred to Venus, hence an emblem of love.
7. Deceiving, full of trickery.

Turn them aside, wretch! or the righteous ban
Of all the Gods, whose dreadful images
Here represent their shadowy presences,   280
May pierce them on the sudden with the thorn
Of painful blindness; leaving thee forlorn,
In trembling dotage to the feeblest fright
Of conscience, for their long offended might,
For all thine impious proud-heart sophistries,   285
Unlawful magic, and enticing lies.
Corinthians! look upon that gray-beard wretch!
Mark how, possess'd, his lashless eyelids stretch
Around his demon eyes! Corinthians, see!
My sweet bride withers at their potency."   290
"Fool!" said the sophist, in an under-tone
Gruff with contempt; which a death-nighing moan
From Lycius answer'd, as heart-struck and lost,
He sank supine beside the aching ghost.
"Fool! Fool!" repeated he, while his eyes still   295
Relented not, nor mov'd; "from every ill
Of life have I preserv'd thee to this day,
And shall I see thee made a serpent's prey?"
Then Lamia breath'd death breath; the sophist's eye,
Like a sharp spear, went through her utterly,   300
Keen, cruel, perceant,[8] stinging: she, as well
As her weak hand could any meaning tell,
Motion'd him to be silent; vainly so,
He look'd and look'd again a level—No!
"A Serpent!" echoed he; no sooner said,   305
Than with a frightful scream she vanished:
And Lycius' arms were empty of delight,
As were his limbs of life, from that same night.
On the high couch he lay!—his friends came round—
Supported him—no pulse, or breath they found,   310
And, in its marriage robe, the heavy body wound.
July–Aug., 1819   1820

To Autumn[1]

1

Season of mists and mellow fruitfulness,
    Close bosom-friend of the maturing sun;
Conspiring with him how to load and bless
    With fruit the vines that round the thatch-eves run;
To bend with apples the moss'd cottage-trees,   5

8. Piercing.
1. Two days after this serene and gracious ode was composed, Keats wrote to J. H. Reynolds: "I never liked stubble fields so much as now—Aye, better than the chilly green of the spring. Somehow a stubble plain looks warm —in the same way that some pictures look warm—this struck me so much in my Sunday's walk that I composed upon it."

And fill all fruit with ripeness to the core;
  To swell the gourd, and plump the hazel shells
With a sweet kernel; to set budding more,
And still more, later flowers for the bees,
Until they think warm days will never cease,   10
  For summer has o'er-brimm'd their clammy cells.

2

Who hath not seen thee oft amid thy store?
  Sometimes whoever seeks abroad may find
Thee sitting careless on a granary floor,
  Thy hair soft-lifted by the winnowing[2] wind;   15
Or on a half-reap'd furrow sound asleep,
  Drows'd with the fume of poppies, while thy hook[3]
    Spares the next swath and all its twined flowers:
And sometimes like a gleaner thou dost keep
  Steady thy laden head across a brook;   20
  Or by a cyder-press, with patient look,
    Thou watchest the last oozings hours by hours.

3

Where are the songs of spring? Ay, where are they?
  Think not of them, thou hast thy music too,—
While barred clouds bloom the soft-dying day,   25
  And touch the stubble-plains with rosy hue;
Then in a wailful choir the small gnats mourn
  Among the river sallows,[4] borne aloft
    Or sinking as the light wind lives or dies;
And full-grown lambs loud bleat from hilly bourn;[5]   30
  Hedge-crickets sing; and now with treble soft
  The red-breast whistles from a garden-croft;[6]
    And gathering swallows twitter in the skies.

September 19, 1819   1820

2. To "winnow" is to fan the chaff   5. Region.
from the grain.   6. A "croft" is an enclosed plot of
3. Scythe.   farm land.
4. Willows.

The Fall of Hyperion: A Dream

In September of 1818, at the close of his 23rd year and while he was serving as nurse to his dying brother Tom, Keats undertook an epic poem, modeled on *Paradise Lost*, which he called *Hyperion*. Its subject, the displacement of Saturn and his fellow Titans by Zeus and the other Olympians, was taken from Greek mythology, but the primary epic question, like that in *Paradise Lost*, was *unde malum?*—whence and why evil? Keats set out to represent an answer, not in terms of the Christian or any other religious creed, but in humanistic terms, delimited to man and his natural milieu. The Titans had been equable and benign gods, ruling in the Saturnian, or golden, age of general felicity. Yet at the beginning of the poem all the Titans except Hyperion, god of the sun, have been dethroned; and the uncomprehending Saturn again and again raises the question, Who? Why? How? Is there blank unreason and injustice at the heart of the universe? Oceanus, god of the sea, offers a valid but incomplete solution: the gods, though themselves blameless, have fallen in the natural progression of things, according to which each stage of development is fated to give place to a higher excellence, "for 'tis the eternal law / That first in beauty should be first in might." And it is the part of wisdom and virtue among the Titans to accept this truth uncomplainingly,

> for to bear all naked truths,
> And to envisage circumstance, all calm,
> That is the top of sovereignty.

In Book III of the original *Hyperion* this is supplemented by the experience of Apollo, still a youth on earth but destined to displace Hyperion among the heavenly powers. He lives in "aching ignorance" of the universe and its processes, but he is aware of his ignorance and avid for knowledge. To him appears Mnemosyne, herself a Titan, but one who has deserted her fellow gods "For prophecies of thee, and for the sake / Of loveliness new born." Suddenly Apollo reads in the face of Mnemosyne—goddess of memory, who will be mother of the muses, and so of all the arts—the silent record of the defeat of the Titans and at once soars to the knowledge that he seeks: the deep understanding, at once intoxicating and agonizing, that life involves process, and process entails change and suffering, and that there can be no creative progress except by the defeat and destruction of the preceding stage. Apollo cries out:

> Knowledge enormous makes a god of me.
> Names, deeds, gray legends, dire events, rebellions,
> Majesties, sovran voices, agonies,
> Creations and destroyings, all at once
> Pour into the wide hollows of my brain
> And deify me, as if of some blithe wine
> Or elixir peerless I had drunk,
> And so become immortal.

This is an enlargement of Apollo's awareness to encompass the sense of the tragic nature of life which it has been the Titans' deficiency to lack. As the fragment breaks off Apollo is transfigured, like one who should "with fierce convulse / Die into life," not only into the god of the sun, who has earned the right to displace Hyperion, but also into the god of the highest poetry.

This extraordinary fragment Keats wrote mainly in the two months between late September and December, 1818, and he abandoned it entirely by April of 1819. Late that summer, however, he took up the theme again, under the title *The Fall of Hyperion: A Dream*. This time his primary model is Dante, especially the *Purgatorio*, which he had been carefully studying in Cary's translation. In *The Divine Comedy* all the narrated events had been represented as a vision granted to Dante at the beginning of the poem. In similar fashion Keats begins his new poem with a long induction in which the poet, in a dream, earns the right to a vision finally granted him by Moneta (her Latin name suggests "the Admonisher"), who replaces Mnemosyne; this vision incorporates the epic events narrated in the first *Hyperion*. The induction, in effect, shifts the center of poetic concern from the epic action to the evolving consciousness of the narrative poet himself, as he seeks his identity and status; it serves also to displace the earlier ordeal through which Apollo had become god of poetry by the ordeal of this particular poet.

As early as *Sleep and Poetry* (1816), Keats had begun to explore the baffling relation of dreams to insight, of wishful fantasies and illusions to imaginative truth, of the life of actuality and of humane action to the contemplative vision of the poet; and he had worked these matters into his poetic program to move from the realm of "Flora, and old Pan" to the "nobler life" of "the agonies, the strife / Of human hearts." He continued to widen these speculations in *Endymion* and a number of his shorter poems; and his letters show his ceaseless effort to assimilate his ever-enlarging experience, his sharpening sense of suffering humanity, and his awareness of the need for some equivalent of the "salvation" offered by a religious creed he could not accept, into his theory and program of poetry. (See especially the letters, included here, on "The Chambers of Human Life" and on "The Vale of Soul-Making.") Into the induction to the long "Dream" which constitutes *The Fall of Hyperion*, Keats works the results of his sustained attempts to differentiate escapist dreams, as well as the creeds of the religious "fanatic," from the imaginative vision of the poet; he presents these results as progressive discoveries which he had made at the various stages of his own development as a poet. The induction, therefore, is Keats's equivalent of a poem he never saw, Wordsworth's *Prelude*, the account of "the Growth of a Poet's Mind." But whereas Wordsworth had represented his evolution of mind, up to and through the crisis in which he discovered his poetic identity, in the mode of literal autobiography, Keats instead employs the pattern of a ritual initiation. In the course of this agonizing rite of passage the poet progresses, in quantum leaps of expanding awareness of what it is to be human, and a poet of humanity, to the stage at which, having passed through and beyond the sufferings of ordinary experience to achieve aesthetic insight and distance—the power (line 304) "To see as a god sees"—he has defined the kind of poet he is and earned the right to essay his epic poem of tragic suffering.

A number of reasons impelled Keats to abandon *The Fall of Hyperion* at the 61st line of the second Canto. Keats wrote to Reynolds on September 21, 1819:

I have given up Hyperion * * * Miltonic verse cannot be written but in an artful or rather artist's humour. I wish to give myself up to other sensations. English ought to be kept up. It may be interesting to you to pick out some lines from Hyperion and put a mark X to the false beauty proceeding from art, and one || to the true voice of feeling.

The two *Hyperions* are astonishing achievements; but they are achievements, as Keats, with his matchless acumen in self-criticism recognized, which have the air of artistic *tours de force*, written in an age in which the high artifice of the epic matter and style had ceased to be the natural voice of the poet. In the same letter Keats mentions having composed two days earlier the ode *To Autumn*; in this, his last and most flawless major poem, the poet had envisaged the circumstance of the cycle of life and death, all calm, and had uttered his experience in the true voice of feeling.

The Fall of Hyperion: A Dream

Canto I

Fanatics have their dreams, wherewith they weave
A paradise for a sect; the savage too
From forth the loftiest fashion of his sleep
Guesses at heaven: pity these have not
Trac'd upon vellum or wild Indian leaf   5
The shadows of melodious utterance.
But bare of laurel they live, dream, and die;
For Poesy alone can tell her dreams,
With the fine spell of words alone can save
Imagination from the sable charm   10
And dumb enchantment. Who alive can say
"Thou art no poet; may'st not tell thy dreams"?
Since every man whose soul is not a clod
Hath visions, and would speak, if he had lov'd
And been well nurtured in his mother tongue.   15
Whether the dream now purposed to rehearse
Be poet's or fanatic's will be known
When this warm scribe my hand is in the grave.

Methought I stood where trees of every clime,
Palm, myrtle, oak, and sycamore, and beech,   20
With plantane, and spice blossoms, made a screen;
In neighbourhood of fountains, by the noise
Soft showering in mine ears, and, by the touch
Of scent, not far from roses. Turning round,
I saw an arbour with a drooping roof   25
Of trellis vines, and bells, and larger blooms,
Like floral-censers swinging light in air;
Before its wreathed doorway, on a mound
Of moss, was spread a feast of summer fruits,
Which, nearer seen, seem'd refuse of a meal   30
By angel tasted, or our mother Eve;[1]
For empty shells were scattered on the grass,
And grape stalks but half bare, and remnants more,
Sweet smelling, whose pure kinds I could not know.
Still was more plenty than the fabled horn[2]   35
Thrice emptied could pour forth, at banqueting
For Proserpine return'd to her own fields,[3]
Where the white heifers low. And appetite
More yearning than on earth I ever felt
Growing within, I ate deliciously;   40

1. In *Paradise Lost* V.321 ff., Eve serves the visiting angel, Raphael, with a meal of fruits and fruit juices. Keats thus adapts Milton's Eden to represent the early stage of his own experience and poetry.

2. The cornucopia, or horn of plenty.
3. When Proserpine each year is released by her husband, Pluto, god of the underworld, for a sojourn on earth, it is the beginning of spring.

And, after not long, thirsted, for thereby
Stood a cool vessel of transparent juice,
Sipp'd by the wander'd bee, the which I took,
And, pledging all the mortals of the world,
And all the dead whose names are in our lips,   45
Drank. That full draught is parent of my theme.[4]
No Asian poppy, nor elixir fine
Of the soon fading jealous caliphat;[5]
No poison gender'd in close monkish cell
To thin the scarlet conclave of old men,[6]   50
Could so have rapt unwilling life away.
Among the fragrant husks and berries crush'd,
Upon the grass I struggled hard against
The domineering potion; but in vain:
The cloudy swoon came on, and down I sunk   55
Like a Silenus[7] on an antique vase.
How long I slumber'd 'tis a chance to guess.
When sense of life return'd, I started up
As if with wings; but the fair trees were gone,
The mossy mound and arbour were no more;   60
I look'd around upon the carved sides
Of an old sanctuary with roof august,
Builded so high, it seem'd that filmed clouds
Might spread beneath, as o'er the stars of heaven;
So old the place was, I remembered none   65
The like upon the earth; what I had seen
Of grey cathedrals, buttress'd walls, rent towers,
The superannuations of sunk realms,
Or nature's rocks toil'd hard in waves and winds,
Seem'd but the faulture[8] of decrepit things   70
T. that eternal domed monument.
Upon the marble at my feet there lay
Store of strange vessels, and large draperies,
Which needs had been of dyed asbestus wove,
Or in that place the moth could not corrupt,[9]   75
So white the linen; so, in some, distinct
Ran imageries from a sombre loom.
All in a mingled heap confus'd there lay
Robes, golden tongs, censer, and chafing dish,
Girdles, and chains, and holy jewelries.[10]   80

Turning from these with awe, once more I rais'd
My eyes to fathom the space every way;

---

4. The drink puts the poet to sleep and effects the dream within a dream which constitutes the rest of his poem.
5. A council of caliphs, Mohammedan rulers, who plot to kill each other with a poisonous draft ("elixir").
6. The College of Cardinals.
7. An elderly satyr, usually represented as dead drunk.
8. Defects. "To" (1.71): compared to.
9. Matthew vi.20. "Lay up for yourselves treasures in heaven, where neither moth nor rust doth corrupt."
10. Offerings to the gods were spread on the floor of Greek temples.

The embossed roof, the silent massy range
Of columns north and south, ending in mist
Of nothing, then to eastward, where black gates   85
Were shut against the sunrise evermore.[1]
Then to the west I look'd, and saw far off
An image, huge of feature as a cloud,
At level of whose feet an altar slept,
To be approach'd on either side by steps,   90
And marble balustrade, and patient travail
To count with toil the innumerable degrees.
Towards the altar sober-pac'd I went,
Repressing haste, as too unholy there;
And, coming nearer, saw beside the shrine   95
One minist'ring[2]; and there arose a flame.
When in mid-May the sickening east wind
Shifts sudden to the south, the small warm rain
Melts out the frozen incense from all flowers,
And fills the air with so much pleasant health   100
That even the dying man forgets his shroud;
Even so that lofty sacrificial fire,
Sending forth Maian[3] incense, spread around
Forgetfulness of every thing but bliss,
And clouded all the altar with soft smoke,   105
From whose white fragrant curtains thus I heard
Language pronounc'd. "If thou canst not ascend
These steps,[4] die on that marble where thou art.
Thy flesh, near cousin to the common dust,
Will parch for lack of nutriment—thy bones   110
Will wither in few years, and vanish so
That not the quickest eye could find a grain
Of what thou now art on that pavement cold.
The sands of thy short life are spent this hour,
And no hand in the universe can turn   115
Thy hour glass, if these gummed leaves be burnt
Ere thou canst mount up these immortal steps."
I heard, I look'd: two senses both at once
So fine, so subtle, felt the tyranny
Of that fierce threat, and the hard task proposed.   120
Prodigious seem'd the toil; the leaves were yet
Burning,—when suddenly a palsied chill
Struck from the paved level up my limbs,
And was ascending quick to put cold grasp
Upon those streams that pulse beside the throat: 125

1. The poet cannot turn back to his
origin in the east, and the ways north
and south lead nowhere; he must travel
the way of mortal life toward the
sunset. Cf. the westering course of the
sun in Wordsworth's *Ode: Intimations
of Immortality.*
2. Who identifies herself, line 226, as
Moneta.

3. Maia was one of the Pleiades, a
daughter of Atlas and (by Zeus) the
mother of Hermes.
4. These steps which the poet must
ascend to knowledge were probably
suggested by the stairs going up the
steep side of the Purgatorial Mount, in
Dante's *Purgatorio.*

I shriek'd; and the sharp anguish of my shriek
Stung my own ears—I strove hard to escape
The numbness; strove to gain the lowest step.
Slow, heavy, deadly was my pace: the cold
Grew stifling, suffocating, at the heart;   130
And when I clasp'd my hands I felt them not.
One minute before death, my iced foot touch'd
The lowest stair; and as it touch'd, life seem'd
To pour in at the toes: I mounted up,
As once fair angels on a ladder flew   135
From the green turf to heaven.[5]—"Holy Power,"
Cried I, approaching near the horned shrine,[6]
"What am I that should so be sav'd from death?
What am I that another death come not
To choak my utterance sacrilegious here?"   140
Then said the veiled shadow—"Thou hast felt
What 'tis to die and live again before
Thy fated hour. That thou hadst power to do so
Is thy own safety; thou hast dated on
Thy doom."[7]—"High Prophetess," said I, "purge off   145
Benign, if so it please thee, my mind's film."
"None can usurp this height," return'd that shade,
"But those to whom the miseries of the world
Are misery, and will not let them rest.
All else who find a haven in the world,   150
Where they may thoughtless sleep away their days,
If by a chance into this fane[8] they come,
Rot on the pavement where thou rotted'st half."[9]—
"Are there not thousands in the world," said I,
Encourag'd by the sooth voice of the shade,   155
"Who love their fellows even to the death;
Who feel the giant agony of the world;
And more, like slaves to poor humanity,
Labour for mortal good? I sure should see
Other men here: but I am here alone."   160
"They whom thou spak'st of are no vision'ries,"
Rejoin'd that voice—"They are no dreamers weak,
They seek no wonder but the human face;
No music but a happy-noted voice—
They come not here, they have no thought to come—   165
And thou art here, for thou art less than they.
What benefit canst thou do, or all thy tribe,

---

5. The ladder by which, in a dream, Jacob saw angels passing between heaven and earth; Genesis xxviii.12 and *Paradise Lost* III.510–15.
6. As e.g., in Exodus xxvii.2, "And thou shalt make the horns of [the altar] upon the four corners thereof." In his description of the temple and its accouterments, Keats deliberately mingles Hebrew, Christian, and pagan ele-

ments, to represent the poet's passage through the stage represented by all religions, which are "dreams" made into the creed for "a sect" (lines 1–18).
7. I.e., you have postponed the time when you will be judged.
8. Temple.
9. I.e., "where you halfway rotted."

To the great world? Thou art a dreaming thing;
A fever of thyself—think of the earth;
What bliss even in hope is there for thee?   170
What haven? Every creature hath its home;
Every sole man hath days of joy and pain,
Whether his labours be sublime or low—
The pain alone; the joy alone; distinct:
Only the dreamer venoms all his days,   175
Bearing more woe than all his sins deserve.
Therefore, that happiness be somewhat shar'd,
Such things as thou art are admitted oft
Into like gardens thou didst pass erewhile,
And suffer'd in these temples; for that cause   180
Thou standest safe beneath this statue's knees."
"That I am favored for unworthiness,
By such propitious parley medicin'd
In sickness not ignoble, I rejoice,
Aye, and could weep for love of such award."   185
So answer'd I, continuing, "If it please,
[1]Majestic shadow, tell me: sure not all
Those melodies sung into the world's ear
Are useless: sure a poet is a sage;
A humanist, physician to all men.   190
That I am none I feel, as vultures feel
They are no birds when eagles are abroad.
What am I then? Thou spakest of my tribe:
What tribe?"—The tall shade veil'd in drooping white
Then spake, so much more earnest, that the breath   195
Mov'd the thin linen folds that drooping hung
About a golden censer from the hand
Pendent.—"Art thou not of the dreamer tribe?
The poet and the dreamer are distinct,
Diverse, sheer opposite, antipodes.   200
The one pours out a balm upon the world,
The other vexes it." Then shouted I
Spite of myself, and with a Pythia's spleen,[2]
"Apollo! faded, far flown Apollo!
Where is thy misty pestilence[3] to creep   205
Into the dwellings, through the door crannies,
Of all mock lyrists, large self worshipers,
And careless hectorers in proud bad verse.[4]

1. Keats's friend, Richard Woodhouse, crossed out lines 187–210 in a manuscript of the poem, with the marginal comment next to lines 197–99: "K. seems to have intended to erase this & the next 21 lines." Perhaps his ground for this opinion is the repetition between lines 187 and 211, and between lines 194–98 and 216–20.
2. With the anger ("spleen") of the Pythia, the priestess who served at Delphi as the oracle of Apollo, the god of poetry.
3. Apollo was a sender of plagues, as well as the inspirer of prophecy and poetry.
4. This has been conjectured as referring to Byron, or else to several contemporaries, including Shelley and Wordsworth. But the poetic types, not individuals, are all that matter to Keats's argument.

Though I breathe death with them it will be life
To see them sprawl before me into graves.[5]　　210
Majestic shadow, tell me where I am:
Whose altar this; for whom this incense curls:
What image this, whose face I cannot see,
For the broad marble knees; and who thou art,
Of accent feminine, so courteous."　　215
Then the tall shade in drooping linens veil'd
Spake out, so much more earnest, that her breath
Stirr'd the thin folds of gauze that drooping hung
About a golden censer from her hand
Pendent; and by her voice I knew she shed　　220
Long treasured tears. "This temple sad and lone
Is all spar'd from the thunder of a war
Foughten long since by giant hierarchy
Against rebellion: this old image here,
Whose carved features wrinkled as he fell,　　225
Is Saturn's; I, Moneta, left supreme
Sole priestess of his desolation."—
I had no words to answer; for my tongue,
Useless, could find about its roofed home
No syllable of a fit majesty　　230
To make rejoinder to Moneta's mourn.
There was a silence while the altar's blaze
Was fainting for sweet food: I look'd thereon
And on the paved floor, where nigh were pil'd
Faggots of cinnamon, and many heaps　　235
Of other crisped spice-wood—then again
I look'd upon the altar and its horns
Whiten'd with ashes, and its lang'rous flame,
And then upon the offerings again;
And so by turns—till sad Moneta cried,　　240
"The sacrifice is done, but not the less

5. In lines 147–210, we find a series of progressive distinctions: (1) between humanitarians who feel for "the miseries of the world" and those men who are "thoughtless" sleepers (lines 147–53); (2) within the class of humanitarians, between those who actively "benefit * * * the great world" and the poets who are "visionaries" and "dreamers" (lines 161–69); (3) and within the class of poets, between those who are merely dreamers and those who are sages and healers (lines 187–202). As in the colloquy between Asia and Demogorgon (see above, Shelley's *Prometheus Unbound*, II.1–128), the interchange here represents, in dramatized form, a process of inner analysis and self-discovery on the part of the questing poet. Moneta's charges should not be read as final judgments but as tests to determine the "tribe" to which the narrating poet belongs—tests he passes by the nature of the responses he makes. The fact that Moneta continuously alters the categories by which she judges him signifies that, in the very course of his self-investigation, he changes and grows into what he is at the end of the process. At this point, the fact that the narrator himself proceeds to bring charges against self-indulgent and irresponsible poets distinguishes him from the class of poets he denounces and thus shows that he is ready for the final stage of his ordeal, his initiation into the realm of the highest poetry, through the revelation of the "high tragedy" (line 277) of what it means to be human. This ultimate enlightenment, which begins with line 291 and which was intended to constitute the remainder of the poem, is a vision in a dream within a dream (see line 46 and footnote).

Will I be kind to thee for thy good will.
My power, which to me is still a curse,
Shall be to thee a wonder; for the scenes
Still swooning vivid through my globed brain   245
With an electral changing misery
Thou shalt with those dull mortal eyes behold,
Free from all pain, if wonder pain thee not."
As near as an immortal's sphered words
Could to a mother's soften, were these last: 250
But yet I had a terror of her robes,
And chiefly of the veils, that from her brow
Hung pale, and curtain'd her in mysteries
That made my heart too small to hold its blood.
This saw that Goddess, and with sacred hand   255
Parted the veils. Then saw I a wan face,
Not pin'd by human sorrows, but bright blanch'd
By an immortal sickness which kills not;
It works a constant change, which happy death
Can put no end to; deathwards progressing   260
To no death was that visage; it had pass'd
The lily and the snow; and beyond these
I must not think now, though I saw that face—
But for her eyes I should have fled away.
They held me back, with a benignant light,   265
Soft mitigated by divinest lids
Half closed, and visionless entire they seem'd
Of all external things—they saw me not,
But in blank splendor beam'd like the mild moon,
Who comforts those she sees not, who knows not   270
What eyes are upward cast. As I had found
A grain of gold upon a mountain's side,
And twing'd with avarice strain'd out my eyes
To search its sullen entrails rich with ore,
So at the view of sad Moneta's brow,   275
I ached to see what things the hollow brain
Behind enwombed: what high tragedy
In the dark secret chambers of her skull
Was acting, that could give so dread a stress
To her cold lips, and fill with such a light   280
Her planetary eyes; and touch her voice
With such a sorrow. "Shade of Memory!"
Cried I, with act adorant at her feet,
"By all the gloom hung round thy fallen house,
By this last temple, by the golden age,   285
By great Apollo, thy dear foster child,
And by thy self, forlorn divinity,
The pale Omega[6] of a wither'd race,
Let me behold, according as thou said'st,
What in thy brain so ferments to and fro."—   290

6. The long *O*, final letter of the Greek alphabet; hence, "last member."

No sooner had this conjuration pass'd
My devout lips, than side by side we stood,
(Like a stunt bramble by a solemn pine)
Deep in the shady sadness of a vale,[7]
Far sunken from the healthy breath of morn,   295
Far from the fiery noon, and eve's one star.
Onward I look'd beneath the gloomy boughs,
And saw, what first I thought an image huge,
Like to the image pedestal'd so high
In Saturn's temple. Then Moneta's voice   300
Came brief upon mine ear,—"So Saturn sat
When he had lost his realms."—Whereon there grew
A power within me of enormous ken,
To see as a God sees, and take the depth
Of things as nimbly as the outward eye   305
Can size and shape pervade. The lofty theme
At those few words hung vast before my mind,
With half unravel'd web. I set myself
Upon an eagle's watch, that I might see,
And seeing ne'er forget. No stir of life   310
Was in this shrouded vale, not so much air
As in the zoning[8] of a summer's day
Robs not one light seed from the feather'd grass,
But where the dead leaf fell there did it rest:
A stream went voiceless by, still deaden'd more   315
By reason of the fallen divinity
Spreading more shade: the Naiad[9] mid her reeds
Press'd her cold finger closer to her lips.
Along the margin sand large footmarks went
No farther than to where old Saturn's feet   320
Had rested, and there slept, how long a sleep!
Degraded, cold, upon the sodden ground
His old right hand lay nerveless, listless, dead,
Unsceptred; and his realmless[1] eyes were clos'd,
While his bow'd head seem'd listening to the Earth,   325
His antient mother,[2] for some comfort yet.

It seem'd no force could wake him from his place;
But there came one who with a kindred hand
Touch'd his wide shoulders, after bending low
With reverence, though to one who knew it not.   330
Then came the griev'd voice of Mnemosyne,[3]

7. This was the opening line of the
original *Hyperion.* The rest of the
poem is a revised version of part of
that first text, with the poet now represented as allowed to envision the course
of events which Moneta remembers
(lines 282, 289–90).
8. Course.
9. Water nymph.
1. Saturn's eyes, when open, express

the fact that he has lost his realm.
2. Saturn and the other Titans were the
children of Heaven and Earth.
3. As in II.50 below, Keats substitutes
for "Moneta" the "Mnemosyne" of the
first *Hyperion.* This may be a slip, but
more likely indicates an alternative
name for Moneta, in her role as partic-
ipant in, and commentator on, the
tragic action.

And griev'd I hearken'd. "That divinity
Whom thou saw'st step from yon forlornest wood,
And with slow pace approach our fallen King,
Is Thea,[4] softest-natur'd of our brood."   335
I mark'd the goddess in fair statuary
Surpassing wan Moneta by the head,[5]
And in her sorrow nearer woman's tears.
There was a listening fear in her regard,
As if calamity had but begun;   340
As if the vanward clouds[6] of evil days
Had spent their malice, and the sullen rear
Was with its stored thunder labouring up.
One hand she press'd upon that aching spot
Where beats the human heart; as if just there,   345
Though an immortal, she felt cruel pain;
The other upon Saturn's bended neck
She laid, and to the level of his hollow ear
Leaning, with parted lips, some words she spake
In solemn tenor and deep organ tune;   350
Some mourning words, which in our feeble tongue
Would come in this-like accenting; how frail
To that large utterance of the early Gods!—
"Saturn! look up—and for what, poor lost King?[7]
I have no comfort for thee, no—not one: 355
I cannot cry, *Wherefore thus sleepest thou?*
For heaven is parted from thee, and the earth
Knows thee not, so afflicted, for a God;
And ocean too, with all its solemn noise,
Has from thy sceptre pass'd, and all the air   360
Is emptied of thine hoary majesty.
Thy thunder, captious at the new command,
Rumbles reluctant o'er our fallen house;
And thy sharp lightning in unpracticed hands
Scorches and burns our once serene domain.   365
With such remorseless speed still come new woes
That unbelief has not a space to breathe.[8]
Saturn, sleep on:—Me thoughtless,[9] why should I
Thus violate thy slumbrous solitude?
Why should I ope thy melancholy eyes?   370
Saturn, sleep on, while at thy feet I weep."

    As when, upon a tranced summer night,
Forests, branch-charmed by the earnest stars,[1]

---

4. Sister and wife of Hyperion.
5. I.e., Thea was a head taller than
Moneta.
6. The front line of clouds.
7. Keats several times recalls *King
Lear*, in representing the condition of
Saturn.
8. I.e., that disbelief has not an instant
to catch its breath.

9. I.e., how thoughtless I am!
1. Keats here sacrifices to epic severity
a notable figure in the first *Hyperion* I,
72 ff., "As when, upon a tranced sum-
mer-night / Those green-robed senators
of mighty woods, / Tall oaks, branch-
charmed by the earnest stars, /
Dream * * *.

Dream, and so dream all night, without a noise,
Save from one gradual solitary gust,   375
Swelling upon the silence; dying off;
As if the ebbing air had but one wave;
So came these words, and went; the while in tears
She press'd her fair large forehead to the earth,
Just where her fallen hair might spread in curls,   380
A soft and silken mat for Saturn's feet.
Long, long, those two were postured motionless,
Like sculpture builded up upon the grave
Of their own power. A long awful time
I look'd upon them; still they were the same;   385
The frozen God still bending to the earth,
And the sad Goddess weeping at his feet;
Moneta silent. Without stay or prop
But my own weak mortality, I bore
The load of this eternal quietude,   390
The unchanging gloom, and the three fixed shapes
Ponderous upon my senses a whole moon.
For by my burning brain I measured sure
Her silver seasons shedded on the night,
And every day by day methought I grew   395
More gaunt and ghostly. Oftentimes I pray'd
Intense, that death would take me from the vale
And all its burthens. Gasping with despair
Of change, hour after hour I curs'd myself:
Until old Saturn rais'd his faded eyes,   400
And look'd around, and saw his kingdom gone,
And all the gloom and sorrow of the place,
And that fair kneeling Goddess at his feet.
As the moist scent of flowers, and grass, and leaves
Fills forest dells with a pervading air   405
Known to the woodland nostril, so the words
Of Saturn fill'd the mossy glooms around,
Even to the hollows of time-eaten oaks,
And to the windings in the foxes' hole,
With sad low tones, while thus he spake, and sent   410
Strange musings to the solitary Pan.

  "Moan, brethren, moan; for we are swallow'd up
And buried from all godlike exercise
Of influence benign on planets pale,
And peaceful sway above man's harvesting,   415
And all those acts which deity supreme
Doth ease its heart of love in. Moan and wail.
Moan, brethren, moan; for lo! the rebel spheres
Spin round, the stars their antient courses keep,
Clouds still with shadowy moisture haunt the earth,   420
Still suck their fill of light from sun and moon,
Still buds the tree, and still the sea-shores murmur.

There is no death in all the universe,
No smell of death—there shall be death[2]—Moan, moan,
Moan, Cybele,[3] moan, for thy pernicious babes   425
Have chang'd a God into a shaking palsy.
Moan, brethren, moan; for I have no strength left,
Weak as the reed—weak—feeble as my voice—
O, O, the pain, the pain of feebleness.
Moan, moan; for still I thaw—or give me help: 430
Throw down those imps[4] and give me victory.
Let me hear other groans, and trumpets blown
Of triumph calm, and hymns of festival
From the gold peaks of heaven's high piled clouds;
Voices of soft proclaim,[5] and silver stir   435
Of strings in hollow shells; and let there be
Beautiful things made new for the surprize
Of the sky children."—So he feebly ceas'd,
With such a poor and sickly sounding pause,
Methought I heard some old man of the earth   440
Bewailing earthly loss; nor could my eyes
And ears act with that pleasant unison of sense
Which marries sweet sound with the grace of form,
And dolorous accent from a tragic harp
With large limb'd visions.[6] More I scrutinized: 445
Still fix'd he sat beneath the sable trees,
Whose arms spread straggling in wild serpent forms,
With leaves all hush'd: his awful presence there
(Now all was silent) gave a deadly lie
To what I erewhile heard: only his lips   450
Trembled amid the white curls of his beard.
They told the truth, though, round, the snowy locks
Hung nobly, as upon the face of heaven
A midday fleece of clouds. Thea arose
And stretch'd her white arm through the hollow dark,   455
Pointing some whither: whereat he too rose
Like a vast giant seen by men at sea
To grow pale from the waves at dull midnight.[7]
They melted from my sight into the woods:
Ere I could turn, Moneta cried—"These twain   460
Are speeding to the families of grief,
Where roof'd in by black rocks they waste in pain
And darkness for no hope."—And she spake on,
As ye may read who can unwearied pass
Onward from the antichamber of this dream,   465

2. The passing of the Saturnian golden age (paralleled by Keats with the fable of the loss of Eden) has introduced suffering, and will also introduce death.
3. Pronounced *Sĭb'elē*, the wife of Saturn and mother of the Olympian gods, who have overthrown their parents.
4. I.e., his rebellious children.
5. Used as a noun, "proclamation."
6. I.e., he could not attach this speech, like that of a feebly complaining old mortal, to the visible form of the large-limbed god who uttered it.
7. I.e., like a giant who is seen by men at sea to emerge, pale, from the waves.

Where even at the open doors awhile
I must delay, and glean my memory
Of her high phrase: perhaps no further dare.

Canto II

"Mortal, that thou may'st understand aright,
I humanize my sayings to thine ear,
Making comparisons of earthly things;
Or thou might'st better listen to the wind,
Whose language is to thee a barren noise,   5
Though it blows legend-laden through the trees.
In melancholy realms big tears are shed,
More sorrow like to this, and such-like woe,
Too huge for mortal tongue, or pen of scribe.
The Titans fierce, self-hid, or prison-bound,   10
Groan for the old allegiance[1] once more,
Listening in their doom for Saturn's voice.
But one of our whole eagle-brood still keeps
His sov'reignty, and rule, and majesty;
Blazing Hyperion on his orbed fire   15
Still sits, still snuffs the incense teeming up
From man to the Sun's God: yet unsecure;
For as upon the earth dire prodigies[2]
Fright and perplex, so also shudders he;
Nor at dog's howl, or gloom-bird's even screech,   20
Or the familiar visitings of one
Upon the first toll of his passing bell:[3]
But horrors portion'd to a giant nerve
Make great Hyperion ache. His palace bright,
Bastion'd with pyramids of glowing gold,   25
And touch'd with shade of bronzed obelisks,
Glares a blood red through all the thousand courts,
Arches, and domes, and fiery galeries:
And all its curtains of Aurorian clouds
Flush angerly: when he would taste the wreaths   30
Of incense breath'd aloft from sacred hills,
Instead of sweets, his ample palate takes
Savour of poisonous brass and metals sick.
Wherefore when harbour'd in the sleepy west,
After the full completion of fair day,   35
For rest divine upon exalted couch
And slumber in the arms of melody,
He paces through the pleasant hours of ease,

1. The meter requires four syllables: *al-lĕ'gi-ánce.*
2. Terrifying omens.
3. Lines 20–22 might be paraphrased: "Not, however, at such portents as a dog's howl or the evening screech of the owl, nor with the well-known feelings ["visitings"] of someone when he hears the first stroke of his own death knell * * *" It had been the English custom to ring the church bell when a person was close to death, to invite hearers to pray for his departing soul. See, e.g., Shakespeare, *Venus and Adonis*, lines 701–2; and for "visitings," *Macbeth* I.v.46.

With strides colossal, on from hall to hall;
While, far within each aisle and deep recess,   40
His winged minions in close clusters stand
Amaz'd, and full of fear; like anxious men
Who on a wide plain gather in sad troops,
When earthquakes jar their battlements and towers.
Even now, while Saturn, rous'd from icy trance,   45
Goes, step for step, with Thea from yon woods,
Hyperion, leaving twilight in the rear,
Is sloping to the threshold of the west.
Thither we tend."—Now in clear light I stood,
Reliev'd from the dusk vale. Mnemosyne   50
Was sitting on a square edg'd polish'd stone,
That in its lucid depth reflected pure
Her priestess-garments. My quick eyes ran on
From stately nave to nave, from vault to vault,
Through bowers of fragrant and enwreathed light,   55
And diamond paved lustrous long arcades.
Anon rush'd by the bright Hyperion;
His flaming robes stream'd out beyond his heels,
And gave a roar, as if of earthly fire,
That scar'd away the meek ethereal hours   60
And made their dove-wings tremble: on he flared

1819   1856

This Living Hand, Now Warm and Capable[1]

This living hand, now warm and capable
Of earnest grasping, would, if it were cold
And in the icy silence of the tomb,
So haunt thy days and chill thy dreaming nights
That thou would wish thine own heart dry of blood,   5
So in my veins red life might stream again,
And thou be conscience-calm'd. See, here it is—
I hold it towards you.

Late 1819?   1856

1. Found written in the margin of a page of Keats's unfinished satire, *The Cap and Bells*, and commonly assumed, although without evidence, to have been addressed to Fanny Brawne. It has been suggested that Keats sketched this passage for a drama he was planning to write.

Letters   Keats's letters constitute a running commentary on his life, reading, thinking, and writing. They demonstrate an extraordinary intelligence, whose very lack of academic or technical training gives its expression a freedom from jargon and standard categories that is equally challenging and rewarding to the reader. Keats's early reputation as a poet of pure luxury, sensation, and art for art's sake has been revolutionized since, early this century, critics began to pay close attention to his letters. For Keats thought hard and persistently about life and art, and any seed of an ethical or critical idea that he picked up from his intellectual contemporaries (Hazlitt, Coleridge, Wordsworth) instantly germinated and flourished in the rich soil of his imagination. What T. S. Eliot said about the metaphysical poets applies equally to Keats in his letters: his "mode of feeling was directly and freshly altered by [his] reading and thought." And like Donne, he looked not only into the heart, but literally, "into the cerebral cortex, the nervous system, and the digestive tract." A number of Keats's casual comments on the poet and on poetry included below—especially those dealing with what we now call empathy, and with "negative capability"—have become standard points of reference in aesthetic theory. But nothing that Keats said did he himself regard as ultimate; each statement constituted only a stage in his continuing exploration into what he called "the mystery."

The text below is that of the edition of the *Letters* by Hyder E. Rollins (1958), which reproduces the original MSS. precisely, so that the reader may follow Keats's pen as, throwing spelling and grammar to the winds, it strains to keep up with the rush of his thoughts.

To Benjamin Bailey[1]
[*The Authenticity of the Imagination*]

[November 22, 1817]

My dear Bailey,

    * * * O I wish I was as certain of the end of all your troubles as that of your momentary start about the authenticity of the Imagination. I am certain of nothing but of the holiness of the Heart's affections and the truth of Imagination—What the imagination seizes as Beauty must be truth[2]—whether it existed before or not—for I have the same Idea of all our Passions as of Love they are all in their sublime, creative of essential Beauty—In a Word, you may know my favorite Speculation by my first Book and the little song I sent in my last[3]—which is a representation from the fancy of the probable mode of operating in these Matters—The Imagination may be compared to Adam's dream[4]—he awoke and found it truth. I am the more zealous in this affair, because I have never yet been able to perceive how any thing can be known for truth by consequitive reasoning[5]—and yet it must be—Can it be that even the greatest Philosopher ever ~~when~~ arrived at his goal without putting aside numerous objections—However it may be, O for a Life of Sensations[6] rather than of Thoughts! It is "a Vision in the form of

---

1. Bailey was one of Keats's closest friends. Keats had stayed with him the month before at Oxford, where Bailey was an undergraduate.
2. The phrase occurs in a poetic context at the close of *Ode on a Grecian Urn*. Try substituting "real," or "reality," where Keats uses the word "truth."
3. The song was "O Sorrow," from *Endymion*.
4. In *Paradise Lost* VIII.452–90, Adam dreams that Eve has been created, and awakes to find her real.
5. Consecutive reasoning—reasoning which moves by logical steps.
6. Not only sense experiences, but also the intuitive perceptions of truths, as opposed to truth achieved by consecutive reasoning.

Youth" a Shadow of reality to come—and this consideration has further conv[i]nced me for it has come as auxiliary to another favorite Speculation of mine, that we shall enjoy ourselves here after by having what we called happiness on Earth repeated in a finer tone and so repeated[7]—And yet such a fate can only befall those who delight in sensation rather than hunger as you do after Truth— Adam's dream will do here and seems to be a conviction that Imagination and its empyreal reflection is the same as human Life and its spiritual repetition. But as I was saying—the simple imaginative Mind may have its rewards in the repeti[ti]on of its own silent Working coming continually on the spirit with a fine suddenness— to compare great things with small—have you never by being surprised with an old Melody—in a delicious place—by a delicious voice, fe[l]t over again your very speculations and surmises at the time it first operated on your soul—do you not remember forming to yourself the singer's face more beautiful that[8] it was possible and yet with the elevation of the Moment you did not think so—even then you were mounted on the Wings of Imagination so high—that the Prototype must be here after—that delicious face you will see— What a time! I am continually running away from the subject— sure this cannot be exactly the case with a complex Mind—one that is imaginative and at the same time careful of its fruits—who would exist partly on sensation partly on thought—to whom it is necessary that years should bring the philosophic Mind[9]—such an one I consider your's and therefore it is necessary to your eternal Happiness that you not only ~~have~~ drink this old Wine of Heaven which I shall call the redigestion of our most ethereal Musings on Earth; but also increase in knowledge and know all things. I am glad to hear you are in a fair Way for Easter—you will soon get through your unpleasant reading and then!—but the world is full of troubles and I have not much reason to think myself pesterd with many—I think Jane or Marianne has a better opinion of me than I deserve—for really and truly I do not think my Brothers illness connected with mine—you know more of the real Cause than they do—nor have I any chance of being rack'd as you have been[1]—you perhaps at one time thought there was such a thing as Worldly Happiness to be arrived at, at certain periods of time marked out—you have of necessity from your disposition been thus led away—I scarcely remember counting upon any Happiness—I look not for it if it be not in the present hour—nothing startles me beyond the Moment. The setting sun will always set me to rights—or if a Sparrow come before my

7. Cf. the "Pleasure Thermometer" in *Endymion*, Book I, lines 777 ff.
8. For "than."
9. An echo of Wordsworth, *Ode: Intimations of Immortality*, line 187.
1. Keats's friends Jane and Marianne

Reynolds feared that Keats's ill health at this time threatened tuberculosis, from which his brother Tom was suffering. Bailey had recently suffered pain (been "racked") because of an unsuccessful love affair.

Window I take part in its existince and pick about the Gravel. The first thing that strikes me on hea[r]ing a Misfortune having befalled another is this. Well it cannot be helped.—he will have the pleasure of trying the resources of his spirit, and I beg now my dear Bailey that hereafter should you observe any thing cold in me not to but[2] it to the account of heartlessness but abstraction—for I assure you I sometimes feel not the influence of a Passion or Affection during a whole week—and so long this sometimes continues I begin to suspect myself and the genuiness of my feelings at other times—thinking them a few barren Tragedy-tears * * *

Your affectionate friend
John Keats—

To George and Thomas Keats
[Negative Capability]

[December 21, 27 (?), 1817]

My dear Brothers

I must crave your pardon for not having written ere this * * * I spent Friday evening with Wells[1] & went the next morning to see *Death on the Pale horse.* It is a wonderful picture, when West's age is considered;[2] But there is nothing to be intense upon; no women one feels mad to kiss; no face swelling into reality. the excellence of every Art is its intensity, capable of making all disagreeables evaporate, from their being in close relationship with Beauty & Truth[3]— Examine King Lear & you will find this examplified throughout; but in this picture we have unpleasantness without any momentous depth of speculation excited, in which to bury its repulsiveness— The picture is larger than Christ rejected—I dined with Haydon[4] the sunday after you left, & had a very pleasant day, I dined too (for I have been out too much lately) with Horace Smith & met his two Brothers with Hill & Kingston & one Du Bois,[5] they only served to convince me, how superior humour is to wit in respect to enjoyment—These men say things which make one start, without making one feel, they are all alike; their manners are alike; they all know fashionables; they have a mannerism in their very eating & drinking, in their mere handling a Decanter—They talked of Kean[6] & his

2. For "put."
1. Charles Wells, a former schoolmate of Tom Keats and, for a time, a friend of John Keats.
2. Benjamin West (1738–1820), painter of historical pictures, was an American who moved to England and became president of the Royal Academy. The "Christ Rejected" mentioned a few sentences farther on is also by West.
3. Keats's solution to a problem at least as old as Aristotle: why do we enjoy the aesthetic representation of a subject which in real life would be ugly or painful?
4. Keats's close friend, Benjamin Haydon, painter of grandiose historical and religious pictures.
5. Horace Smith was one of the best known literary wits of the day; the others mentioned were men of letters or of literary interests.
6. Edmund Kean, the noted Shakespearean actor of the early 19th century.

low company—Would I were with that company instead of yours said I to myself! I know such like acquaintance will never do for me & yet I am going to Reynolds, on wednesday—Brown & Dilke[7] walked with me & back from the Christmas pantomime.[8] I had not a dispute but a disquisition with Dilke, on various subjects; several things dovetailed in my mind, & at once it struck me, what quality went to form a Man of Achievement especially in Literature & which Shakespeare posessed so enormously—I mean *Negative Capability*,[9] that is when man is capable of being in uncertainties, Mysteries, doubts, without any irritable reaching after fact & reason—Coleridge, for instance, would let go by a fine isolated verisimilitude caught from the Penetralium[1] of mystery, from being incapable of remaining content with half knowledge. This pursued through Volumes would perhaps take us no further than this, that with a great poet the sense of Beauty overcomes every other consideration, or rather obliterates all consideration.

Shelley's poem[2] is out & there are words about its being objected too, as much as Queen Mab was. Poor Shelley I think he has his Quota of good qualities, in sooth la!! Write soon to your most sincere friend & affectionate Brother

John

To John Hamilton Reynolds[1]
[*Wordsworth's Poetry*]

[February 3, 1818]

My dear Reynolds,

     * * * It may be said that we ought to read our Contemporaries.

---

7. John Hamilton Reynolds, 'Charles Armitage Brown, and Charles Wentworth Dilke were all writers and friends of Keats.

8. Christmas pantomimes were performed each year at Drury Lane and Covent Garden.

9. This famous and elusive phrase has accumulated a heavy body of commentary. Two points may here suffice: (1) Keats is concerned with a central aesthetic question of his day: to distinguish between what was called the "objective" poet, who simply and impersonally presents his material, and the "subjective" or "sentimental" poet, who presents his material as it appears when viewed through his personal interests, beliefs, and feelings. The poet of "negative capability" is the objective poet. (See the letter to Reynolds, Feb. 3, 1818, below.) (2) Keats goes on to propose that, within a poem, the presentation of matter in an artistic form that appeals to our "sense of Beauty" is enough, independently of its truth or falsity when considered outside the poem according to nonartistic logical criteria. T. S. Eliot illuminated an important aspect of Keats's meaning when he observed that a theory "which has entered into poetry is established, for its truth or falsity in one sense ceases to matter, and its truth in another sense is proved" (*The Metaphysical Poets*).

1. The Latin *penetralia* signified the innermost and most secret parts of a temple.

2. *Laon and Cythna* (1817), which dealt with incest, and had to be recalled by the author; it was revised and republished as *The Revolt of Islam* (1818). *Queen Mab* (1813) was a youthful poem in which Shelley presented his radical program for the achievement of the millennium by the elimination of "kings, priests, and statesmen," and the reform of human institutions.

1. Reynolds, a close friend, was at this time an insurance clerk and also an able, though minor, poet and man of letters.

that Wordsworth &c should have their due from us. but for the sake of a few fine imaginative or domestic passages, are we to be bullied into a certain Philosophy engendered in the whims of an Egotist[2]— Every man has his speculations, but every man does not brood and peacock over them till he makes a false coinage and deceives himself—Many a man can travel to the very bourne[2a] of Heaven, and yet want confidence to put down his halfseeing. Sancho[3] will invent a Journey heavenward as well as any body. We hate poetry that has a palpable design upon us—and if we do not agree, seems to put its hand in its breeches pocket. Poetry should be great & unobtrusive, a thing which enters into one's soul, and does not startle it or amaze it with itself but with its subject.—How beautiful are the retired flowers! how would they lose their beauty were they to throng into the highway crying out, admire me I am a violet! dote upon me I am a primrose! Modern poets differ from the Elizabethans in this. Each of the moderns like an Elector of Hanover governs his petty state, & knows how many straws are swept daily from the Causeways in all his dominions & has a continual itching that all the Housewives should have their coppers well scoured: the antients were ~~Emperors of large~~ Emperors of vast Provinces, they had only heard of the remote ones and scarcely cared to visit them.—I will cut all this—I will have no more of Wordsworth or Hunt[4] in particular—Why should we be of the tribe of Manasseh, when we can wander with Esau?[5] why should we kick against the Pricks, when we can walk on Roses? Why should we be owls, when we can be Eagles? Why be teased with "nice Eyed wagtails," when we have in sight "the Cherub Contemplation"?[6]—Why with Wordsworths "Matthew with a bough of wilding in his hand" when we can have Jacques "under an oak &c"[7]—The secret of the Bough of Wilding will run through your head faster than I can write it—Old Matthew spoke to him some years ago on some nothing, & because he happens in an Evening Walk to imagine the figure of the old man—he must stamp it down in black & white, and it is henceforth sacred—I don't mean to deny Wordsworth's grandeur & Hunt's merit, but I mean to say we need not be teazed with grandeur & merit—when we can

2. Keats immensely admired Wordsworth, as succeeding letters will show, and learned more from him than from any poetic contemporary. He had reservations, however, about the subjective and didactic qualities of Wordsworth's poetry (see the letter to George and Thomas Keats, above)—reservations which, in some moods, he stated in unflattering terms.
2a. Boundary.
3. Sancho Panza, the earthy squire in *Don Quixote*.
4. Leigh Hunt, a poet who earlier had strongly influenced Keats's style.
5. I.e., why should we remain in a conventional way of life (as did the tribe of Manasseh, which followed the conventional paths of Old Testament history) when we can become adventurers (like Esau, who sold his birthright in Genesis xxv.29–34 and became a domestic outlaw).
6. The first phrase is from Hunt's *Nymphs*, the second from Milton's *Il Penseroso* (line 54).
7. The Wordsworth phrase is from his poem *The Two April Mornings* (a "wilding" is an uncultivated tree or plant, especially the wild apple tree). For Jacques "under an oak," see *As You Like It*, II.i.31.

have them uncontaminated & unobtrusive. Let us have the old Poets, & robin Hood[8] Your letter and its sonnets gave me more pleasure than will the 4th Book of Childe Harold[9] & the whole of any body's life & opinions. * * *

Y[r] sincere friend and Coscribbler
John Keats.

To John Taylor[1]
[Keats's Axioms in Poetry]

[February 27, 1818]

My dear Taylor,

Your alteration strikes me as being a great improvement—the page looks much better. * * * It is a sorry thing for me that any one should have to overcome Prejudices in reading my Verses—that affects me more than any hypercriticism on any particular Passage. In *Endymion* I have most likely but moved into the Go-cart from the leading strings. In Poetry I have a few Axioms, and you will see how far I am from their Centre. 1st I think Poetry should surprise by a fine excess and not by Singularity—it should strike the Reader as a wording of his own highest thoughts, and appear almost a Remembrance—2nd Its touches of Beauty should never be half way therby making the reader breathless instead of content: the rise, the progress, the setting of imagery should like the Sun come natural natural too him—shine over him and set soberly although in magnificence leaving him in the Luxury of twilight—but it is easier to think what Poetry should be than to write it—and this leads me on to another axiom. That if Poetry comes not as naturally as the Leaves to a tree it had better not come at all. However it may be with me I cannot help looking into new countries with "O for a Muse of fire to ascend!"[2]—If Endymion serves me as a Pioneer perhaps I ought to be content. I have great reason to be content, for thank God I can read and perhaps understand Shakspeare to his depths, and I have I am sure many friends, who, if I fail, will attribute any change in my Life and Temper to Humbleness rather than to Pride—to a cowering under the Wings of great Poets rather than to a Bitterness that I am not appreciated. I am anxious to get Endymion printed that I may forget it and proceed. * * *

Your sincere and oblig[d] friend
John Keats—

P.S. You shall have a sho[r]t *Preface* in good time—

---

8. A reference to two sonnets on Robin Hood by Reynolds which he had sent to Keats.
9. Canto IV of Byron's *Childe Harold* was being eagerly awaited by English readers.

1. Member of the publishing firm of Taylor and Hessey, to whom Keats wrote this letter while *Endymion* was being put through the press.
2. Altered from Shakespeare's *Henry V*, Prologue, line 1.

To John Hamilton Reynolds

[*Milton, Wordsworth, and the Chambers of Human Life*]

[May 3, 1818]

My dear Reynolds.

* * * Were I to study physic or rather Medicine again,—I feel it would not make the least difference in my Poetry; when the Mind is in its infancy a Bias in is in reality a Bias, but when we have acquired more strength, a Bias becomes no Bias. Every department of knowledge we see excellent and calculated towards a great whole. I am so convinced of this, that I am glad at not having given away my medical Books, which I shall again look over to keep alive the little I know thitherwards; and moreover intend through you and Rice to become a sort of Pip-civilian.[1] An extensive knowledge is needful to thinking people—it takes away the heat and fever; and helps, by widening speculation, to ease the Burden of the Mystery:[2] a thing I begin to understand a little, and which weighed upon you in the most gloomy and true sentence in your Letter. The difference of high Sensations with and without knowledge appears to me this —in the latter case we are falling continually ten thousand fathoms deep and being blown up again without wings and with all [the] horror of a Case bare shoulderd Creature—in the former case, our shoulders are fledged,[3] and we go thro' the same Fir air and space without fear. * * *

You say "I fear there is little chance of any thing else in this life." You seem by that to have been going through with a more painful and acute test zest the same labyrinth that I have—I have come to the same conclusion thus far. My Branchings out therefrom have been numerous: one of them is the consideration of Wordsworth's genius and as a help, in the manner of gold being the meridian Line of worldly wealth,—how he differs from Milton.[4]—And here I have nothing but surmises, from an uncertainty whether Miltons apparently less anxiety for Humanity proceeds from his seeing further or no than Wordsworth: And whether Wordsworth has in truth epic passions, and martyrs himself to the human heart, the main region of his song[5]—In regard to his genius alone—we find what he says true as far as we have experienced and we can judge no further but by larger experience—for axioms in philosophy are

---

1. Apparently, "a small-scale layman." James Rice, a lawyer, was one of Keats's favorite friends.
2. *Tintern Abbey*, line 38. Here begins Keats's wonderfully insightful expansion of the significance of this and other phrases and passages in Wordsworth.
3. Grow wings.

4. I.e., as gold is the standard of material wealth (in the way that the meridian line of Greenwich Observatory, England, is the reference for measuring degrees of longitude), so Milton is the standard of poetic value, by which we may measure Wordsworth.
5. Cf. "Prospectus" to *The Recluse*, line 41.

not axioms until they are proved upon our pulses: We read fine——
things but never feel them to thee[6] full until we have gone the same
steps as the Author.—I know this is not plain; you will know exactly
my meaning when I say, that now I shall relish Hamlet more than
I ever have done—Or, better—You are sensible no man can set
down Venery[7] as a bestial or joyless thing until he is sick of it and
therefore all philosophizing on it would be mere wording. Until we
are sick, we understand not;—in fine, as Byron says, "Knowledge
is Sorrow";[8] and I go on to say that "Sorrow is Wisdom"—and further for aught we can know for certainty! "Wisdom is folly" * * *
  I will return to Wordsworth—whether or no he has an extended
vision or a circumscribed grandeur—whether he is an eagle in his
nest, or on the wing—And to be more explicit and to show you how
tall I stand by the giant, I will put down a simile of human life as
far as I now perceive it; that is, to the point to which I say we both
have arrived at—Well—I compare human life to a large Mansion
of Many Apartments, two of which I can only describe, the doors
of the rest being as yet shut upon me—The first we step into we
call the infant or thoughtless Chamber, in which we remain as long
as we do not think—We remain there a long while, and notwithstanding the doors of the second Chamber remain wide open, showing a bright appearance, we care not to hasten to it; but are at length
imperceptibly impelled by the awakening of the thinking principle
—within us—we no sooner get into the second Chamber, which I
shall call the Chamber of Maiden-Thought,[9] than we become intoxicated with the light and the atmosphere, we see nothing but
pleasant wonders, and think of delaying there for ever in delight:
However among the effects this breathing is father of is that tremendous one of sharpening one's vision into the ~~head~~ heart and
nature of Man—of convincing ones nerves that the World is full
of Misery and Heartbreak, Pain, Sickness and oppression—whereby
This Chamber of Maiden Thought becomes gradually darken'd and
at the same time on all sides of it many doors are set open—but all
dark—all leading to dark passages—We see not the ballance of
good and evil. We are in a Mist—We are now in that state—We
feel the "burden of the Mystery," To this point was Wordsworth
come, as far as I can conceive when he wrote "Tintern Abbey" and
it seems to me that his Genius is explorative of those dark Passages.
Now if we live, and go on thinking, we too shall explore them. he
is a Genius and superior [to] us, in so far as he can, more than we,
make discoveries, and shed a light in them—Here I must think
Wordsworth is deeper than Milton—though I think it has depended

6. For "the."
7. Sexual indulgence.
8. *Manfred* I.i.10: "Sorrow is knowledge."

9. I.e., innocent thought, with the implication (as in "maiden voyage") of a
first undertaking.

more upon the general and gregarious advance of intellect, than individual greatness of Mind—From the Paradise Lost and the other Works of Milton, I hope it is not too presuming, even between ourselves to say, his Philosophy, human and divine, may be tolerably understood by one not much advanced in years, In his time englishmen were just emancipated from a great superstition—and Men had got hold of certain points and resting places in reasoning which were too newly born to be doubted, and too much ~~oppressed~~ opposed by the Mass of Europe not to be thought etherial and authentically divine—who could gainsay his ideas on virtue, vice, and Chastity in Comus, just at the time of the dismissal of Cod-pieces[1] and a hundred other disgraces? who would not rest satisfied with his hintings at good and evil in the Paradise Lost, when just free from the inquisition and burning in Smithfield?[2] The Reformation produced such immediate and ~~great~~ benefits, that Protestantism was considered under the immediate eye of heaven, and its own remaining Dogmas and superstitions, then, as it were, regenerated, constituted those resting places and seeming sure points of Reasoning—from that I have mentioned, Milton, whatever he may have thought in the sequel,[3] appears to have been content with these by his writings—He did not think into the human heart, as Wordsworth has done—Yet Milton as a Philosop[h]er, had sure as great powers as Wordsworth—What is then to be inferr'd? O many things—It proves there is really a grand march of intellect—, It proves that a mighty providence subdues the mightiest Minds to the service of the time being, whether it be in human Knowledge or Religion— * * *

Your affectionate friend
John Keats.

To Richard Woodhouse[1]

[A Poet Has No Identity]

[October 27, 1818]

My dear Woodhouse,

  Your Letter gave me a great satisfaction; more on account of its friendliness, than any relish of that matter in it which is accounted so acceptable in the "genus irritabile"[2] The best answer I can give you is in a clerklike manner to make some observations on two

---

1. In the 15th and 16th centuries the codpiece was a flap, often ornamental, which covered an opening in the front of men's breeches.
2. An open place northwest of the walls of the City of London where, in the 16th century, heretics were burned.
3. I.e., later on.

1. Woodhouse was a young lawyer with literary interests who recognized Keats's talents and prepared, or preserved, manuscript copies of many of his poems and letters.
2. "The irritable race," a phrase Horace had applied to poets (Epistles II.ii.102).

principle points, which seem to point like indices into the midst of the whole pro and con, about genius, and views and atchievements and ambition and cœtera. 1ˢᵗ As to the poetical Character itself, (I mean that sort of which, if I am any thing, I am a Member; that sort distinguished from the wordsworthian or egotistical sublime; which is a thing per se and stands alone) it is not itself—it has no self—it is every thing and nothing—It has no character—it enjoys light and shade; it lives in gusto, be it foul or fair, high or low, rich or poor, mean or elevated—It has as much delight in conceiving an Iago as an Imogen.[3] What shocks the virtuous philosop[h]er, delights the camelion[4] Poet. It does no harm from its relish of the dark side of things any more than from its taste for the bright one; because they both end in speculation.[5] A Poet is the most unpoetical of any thing in existence; because he has no Identity—he is continually in for[6]—and filling some other Body—The Sun, the Moon, the Sea and Men and Women who are creatures of impulse are poetical and have about them an unchangeable attribute—the poet has none; no identity—he is certainly the most unpoetical of all God's Creatures. If then he has no self, and if I am a Poet, where is the Wonder that I should say I would ~~right~~ write no more? Might I not at that very instant [have] been cogitating on the Characters of saturn and Ops?[7] It is a wretched thing to confess; but is a very fact that not one word I ever utter can be taken for granted as an opinion growing out of my identical nature—how can it, when I have no nature? When I am in a room with People if I ever am free from speculating on creations of my own brain, then not myself goes home to myself: but the identity of every one in the room begins to to press upon me[8] that, I am in a very little time an[ni]hilated—not only among Men; it would be the same in a Nursery of children: I know not whether I make myself wholly understood: I hope enough so to let you see that no dependence is to be placed on what I said that day.

In the second place I will speak of my views, and of the life I purpose to myself—I am ambitious of doing the world some good: if I should be spared that may be the work of maturer years—in the interval I will assay to reach to as high a summit in Poetry as the nerve[9] bestowed upon me will suffer. The faint conceptions I have of Poems to come brings the blood frequently into my forehead—

3. Iago is the villain in Shakespeare's *Othello* and Imogen the virtuous heroine of his *Cymbeline*.
4. The chameleon is a lizard which camouflages itself by matching its color to its surroundings.
5. "In speculation" here means "in contemplation"—i.e., without affecting our practical judgment or actions.
6. Instead of "in for," Keats may have intended to write "informing."
7. Characters in Keats's *Hyperion*. Woodhouse had written Keats a letter, expressing concern at a remark by Keats that, since former writers had preempted the best poetic materials and styles, there was nothing new left for the modern poet.
8. Perhaps "*so* to press upon me."
9. Sinew.

All I hope is that I may not lose all interest in human affairs—that the solitary indifference I feel for applause even from the finest Spirits, will not blunt any acuteness of vision I may have. I do not think it will—I feel assured I should write from the mere yearning and fondness I have for the Beautiful even if my night's labours should be burnt every morning and no eye ever shine upon them. But even now I am perhaps not speaking from myself; but from some character in whose soul I now live. I am sure however that this next sentence is from myself. I feel your anxiety, good opinion and friendliness in the highest degree, and am

Your's most sincerely
John Keats

To George and Georgiana Keats[1]
["The Vale of Soul-Making"]

[February 14–May 3, 1819]

My Dear Brother & Sister——

* * * I have this moment received a note from Haslam[2] in which he expects the death of his Father who has been for some time in a state of insensibility—his mother bears up he says very well—I shall go to twon[3] tommorrow to see him. This is the world —thus we cannot expect to give way many hours to pleasure—Circumstances are like Clouds continually gathering and bursting— While we are laughing the seed of some trouble is put into he the wide arable land of events—while we are laughing it sprouts is[4] grows and suddenly bears a poison fruit which we must pluck— Even so we have leisure to reason on the misfortunes of our friends; our own touch us too nearly for words. Very few men have ever arrived at a complete disinterestedness of Mind: very few have been influenced by a pure desire of the benefit of others—in the greater part of the Benefactors of & to Humanity some meretricious motive has sullied their greatness—some melodramatic scenery has facinated them—From the manner in which I feel Haslam's misfortune I perceive how far I am from any humble standard of disinterestedness—Yet this feeling ought to be carried to its highest pitch, as there is no fear of its ever injuring society—which it would do I fear pushed to an extremity—For in wild nature the Hawk would loose his Breakfast of Robins and the Robin his of Worms The Lion must starve as well as the swallow—The greater part of

---

1. Keats's younger brother and his wife, who had emigrated to Louisville, Kentucky, in 1818. This is part of a long letter, which Keats wrote over a period of several months.

2. William Haslam, a young businessman and intimate friend.
3. For "town."
4. For "it."

Men make their way with the same instinctiveness, the same un-
wandering eye from their purposes, the same animal eagerness as
the Hawk—The Hawk wants a Mate, so does the Man—look at
them both they set about it and procure on[e] in the same manner
—They want both a nest and they both set about one in the same
manner—they get their food in the same manner—The noble animal Man for his amusement smokes his pipe—the Hawk balances
about the Clouds—that is the only difference of their leisures. This
it is that makes the Amusement of Life—to a speculative Mind. I
go among the Feilds and catch a glimpse of a stoat[5] or a fieldmouse
peeping out of the withered grass—the creature hath a purpose and
its eyes are bright with it—I go amongst the buildings of a city and
I see a Man hurrying along—to what? The Creature has a purpose
and his eyes are bright with it. But then as Wordsworth says, "we
have all one human heart"[6]—there is an ellectric fire in human nature tending to purify—so that among these human creature[s] there
is continully some birth of new heroism—The pity is that we must
wonder at it: as we should at finding a pearl in rubbish—I have no
doubt that thousands of people never heard of have had hearts
comp[l]etely disinterested: I can remember but two—Socrates and
Jesus—their Histories evince it—What I heard a little time ago,
Taylor observe with respect to Socrates, may be said of Jesus—
That he was so great as man that though he transmitted no writing
of his own to posterity, we have his Mind and his sayings and his
greatness handed to us by others. It is to be lamented that the history of the latter was written and revised by Men interested in the
pious frauds of Religion. Yet through all this I see his splendour.
Even here though I myself am pursueing the same instinctive course
as the veriest human animal you can think of—I am however young
writing at random—straining at particles of light in the midst of
a great darkness—without knowing the bearing of any one assertion
of any one opinion. Yet may I not in this be free from sin?[7] May
there not be superior beings amused with any graceful, though instinctive attitude my mind my[8] fall into, as I am entertained with
the alertness of a Stoat or the anxiety of a Deer? Though a quarrel
in the streets is a thing to be hated, the energies displayed in it are
fine; the commonest Man shows a grace in his quarrel—By a superior being our reasoning[s] may take the same tone—though er-

5. A weasel.
6. *The Old Cumberland Beggar*, line
153.
7. Keats speculates that though his instinctive course is not, any more than
an animal's, "disinterested" (free from
selfish interests), it may still be, like an
animal's, natural, hence innocent and
possessed of an innate grace and beauty.

He further supposes that this may be
the nature of poetry, also, as distinguished from the deliberate and self-
conscious process of philosophical reasoning. Compare the letter on
"Negative Capability," Dec. 21, 1817,
above.
8. For "may."

roneous they may be fine—This is the very thing in which consists poetry; and if so it is not so fine a thing as philosophy—For the same reason that an eagle is not so fine a thing as a truth—Give me this credit—Do you not think I strive—to know myself? Give me this credit—and you will not think that on my own accou[n]t I repeat Milton's lines

> "How charming is divine Philosophy
> Not harsh and crabbed as dull fools suppose
> But musical as is Apollo's lute"—[9]

No—no for myself—feeling grateful as I do to have got into a state of mind to relish them properly—Nothing ever becomes real till it is experienced—Even a Proverb is no proverb to you till your Life has illustrated it— * * *

The common cognomen of this world among the misguided and superstitious is "a vale of tears" from which we are to be redeemed by a certain arbitary interposition of God and taken to Heaven— What a little circumscribe[d] straightened notion! Call the world if you Please "The vale of Soul-making" Then you will find out the use of the world (I am speaking now in the highest terms for human nature admitting it to be immortal which I will here take for granted for the purpose of showing a thought which has struck me concerning it) I say "*Soul making*" Soul as distinguished from an Intelligence—There may be intelligences or sparks of the divinity in millions—but they are not Souls ~~the~~ till they acquire identities, till each one is personally itself. I[n]telligences are atoms of perception —they know and they see and they are pure, in short they are God —how then are Souls to be made? How then are these sparks which are God to have identity given them—so as ever to possess a bliss peculiar to each ones individual existence? How, but by the medium of a world like this? This point I sincerely wish to consider because I think it a grander system of salvation than the chrysteain religion —or rather it is a system of Spirit-creation[1]—This is effected by three grand materials acting the one upon the other for a series of years—These three Materials are the *Intelligence*—the *human heart* (as distinguished from intelligence or Mind) and the *World* or *Elemental space* suited for the proper action of *Mind and Heart* on each

9. *Comus*, lines 475–77.

1. Keats is struggling magnificently for an analogy which will embody his solution to the ancient riddle of evil, as an alternative to what he understands to be the Christian view: evil exists as a test of man's merit of salvation in heaven, and this world is only a proving ground for a later and better life. Keats proposes that the function of the human experience of sorrow and pain is to feed and discipline the form-less and unstocked "intelligence" that a man possesses at birth, and thus to shape it into a rich and coherent "identity," or "soul." This result provides a justification ("salvation") for our suffering life on its own terms; that is, experience is its own reward, and not in heaven, but on earth. The passage is Keats's version of what Wordsworth says in the last two stanzas of his *Ode: Intimations of Immortality*.

other for the purpose of forming the *Soul* or *Intelligence destined to possess the sense of Identity*. I can scarcely express what I but dimly perceive—and yet I think I perceive it—that you may judge the more clearly I will put it in the most homely form possible—I will call the *world* a School instituted for the purpose of teaching little children to read—I will call the *human heart* the *horn Book*[2] used in that School—and I will call the *Child able to read, the Soul* made from that *school* and its *hornbook*. Do you not see how necessary a World of Pains and troubles is to school an Intelligence and make it a soul? A Place where the heart must feel and suffer in a thousand diverse ways! Not merely is the Heart a Hornbook, It is the Minds Bible, it is the Minds experience, it is the teat from which the Mind or intelligence sucks its identity—As various as the Lives of Men are—so various become their souls, and thus does God make individual beings, Souls, Identical Souls of the sparks of his own essence—This appears to me a faint sketch of a system of Salvation which does not affront our reason and humanity—I am convinced that many difficulties which christians labour under would vanish before it—There is one wh[i]ch even now Strikes me—the Salvation of Children—In them the Spark or intelligence returns to God without any identity—it having had no time to learn of, and be altered by, the heart—or seat of the human Passions—It is pretty generally suspected that the chr[i]stian scheme has been coppied from the ancient persian and greek Philosophers. Why may they not have made this simple thing even more simple for common apprehension by introducing Mediators and Personages in the same manner as in the hethen mythology abstractions are personified—Seriously I think it probable that this System of Soul-making—may have been the Parent of all the more palpable and personal Schemes of Redemption, among the Zoroastrians the Christians and the Hindoos. For as one part of the human species must have their carved Jupiter; so another part must have the palpable and named Mediatior and saviour, their Christ their Oromanes and their Vishnu[2a]—If what I have said should not be plain enough, as I fear it may not be, I will but[3] you in the place where I began in this series of thoughts—I mean, I began by seeing how man was formed by circumstances—and what are circumstances?—but touchstones of his heart—? and what are touch stones?—but proovings of his hearrt?—and what are proovings of his heart but fortifiers or alterers of his nature? and what is his altered nature but his soul?—and what was his soul before it came into the world and had These provings and

2. A child's primer, which used to consist of a sheet of paper mounted on thin wood, protected by a sheet of transparent horn.
2a. Oromanes (Ahriman) was the principle of evil, locked in a persisting struggle with Ormazd, the principle of good, in the Zoroastrian religion. Vishnu was the deity who creates and preserves the world, in Hindu belief.
3. For "put."

alterations and perfectionings?—An intelligences—without Identity
—and how is this Identity to be made? Through the medium of
the Heart? And how is the heart to become this Medium but in a
world of Circumstances?—There now I think what with Poetry
and Theology you may thank your Stars that my pen is not very
long winded— * * *

This is the 3ᵈ of May & every thing is in delightful forwardness:
the violets are not withered, before the peeping of the first rose;
You must let me know every thing, how parcels go & come, what
papers you have, & what Newspapers you want, & other things—
God bless you my dear Brother & Sister

Your ever Affectionate Brother
John Keats—

To Percy Bysshe Shelley[1]
["*Load Every Rift with Ore*"]

[August 16, 1820]

My dear Shelley,

I am very much gratified that you, in a foreign country, and with
a mind almost over occupied, should write to me in the strain of
the Letter beside me. If I do not take advantage of your invitation
it will be prevented by a circumstance I have very much at heart to
prophesy[2]—There is no doubt that an english winter would put an
end to me, and do so in a lingering hateful manner, therefore I must
either voyage or journey to Italy as a soldier marches up to a battery. My nerves at present are the worst part of me, yet they feel
soothed when I think that come what extreme may, I shall not be
destined to remain in one spot long enough to take a hatred of any
four particular bed-posts. I am glad you take any pleasure in my
poor Poem;[3]—which I would willingly take the trouble to unwrite,
if possible, did I care so much as I have done about Reputation. I
received a copy of the Cenci,[4] as from yourself from Hunt. There
is only one part of it I am judge of; the Poetry, and dramatic effect,
which by many spirits now a days is considered the mammon. A
modern work it is said must have a purpose,[5] which may be the God
—*an artist* must serve Mammon—he must have "self concentration" selfishness perhaps. You I am sure will forgive me for sincerely
remarking that you might curb your magnanimity and be more of
an artist, and "load every rift"[6] of your subject with ore. The thought

---

1. Written in reply to a letter urging
Keats (who was ill) to spend the winter with the Shelleys in Pisa.
2. His own death.
3. Keats's *Endymion*, Shelley had written, contains treasures, "though treasures poured forth with indistinct profusion." Keats here responds with advice in kind.

4. Shelley's blank-verse tragedy, *The
Cenci*, had been published in the spring
of 1820.
5. Wordsworth had said this in his Preface to *Lyrical Ballads*. For "Mammon"
see Matthew vi.24, and Luke xvi.13: "Ye
cannot serve God and mammon."
6. Spenser, *Faerie Queene* II.vii.28:
"With rich metall loaded every rifte."

of such discipline must fall like cold chains upon you, who perhaps
never sat with your wings furl'd for six Months together. And is not
this extraordina[r]y talk for the writer of Endymion? whose mind
was like a pack of scattered cards—I am pick'd up and sorted to a
pip.[7] My Imagination is a Monastry and I am its Monk—you must
explain my metap°'[8] to yourself. I am in expectation of Prometheus[9]
every day. Could I have my own wish for its interest effected you
would have it still in manuscript—or be but now putting an end
to the second act. I remember you advising me not to publish my
first-blights, on Hampstead heath—I am returning advice upon your
hands. Most of the Poems in the volume I send you[1] have been
written above two years, and would never have been publish'd but
from a hope of gain; so you see I am inclined enough to take your
advice now. I must exp[r]ess once more my deep sense of your kindness, adding my sincere thanks and respects for M⁰⁰ Shelley. In the
hope of soon seeing you I remain

most sincerely yours,
John Keats—

7. Perfectly ordered; all the suits in
the deck matched up ("pips" are the
conventional spots on playing cards).
8. I.e., "metaphysics."
9. *Prometheus Unbound*, of which Shelley had promised Keats a copy.
1. Keats's volume of 1820, including
Lamia, The Eve of St. Agnes, and the
Odes. When Shelley drowned, he had
this small book open in his pocket.

MARY WOLLSTONECRAFT SHELLEY
(1797–1851)
1818: *Frankenstein*

Shelley wrote of his young wife, in the Dedication to *The Revolt of Islam*:

> They say that thou wert lovely from thy birth,
> Of glorious parents, thou aspiring Child.

The "glorious parents" were William Godwin, the leading reformer and
radical philosopher of that time, and Mary Wollstonecraft, famed as the
author of *A Vindication of the Rights of Woman*; Wollstonecraft had died
as the result of childbed fever incurred when she gave birth to Mary. Four
years later Godwin married a widow, Mary Jane Clairmont, who soon had
more than she could cope with trying to manage a family in increasing
financial difficulties, and composed of five children of diverse parentage.
Mary bitterly resented her stepmother but adored her father who, she later
said, "was my God—and I remember many childish instances of the excess
of attachment I bore for him."

To ease the situation, Mary was sent at the age of 14 to live in Dundee,
Scotland, with the family of William Baxter, an admirer of Godwin. After
two pleasant years roaming the countryside, daydreaming, and writing stories (which have been lost), she returned in 1814 to her father's house in
London. There at the age of 16 she encountered the 21-year-old poet Shel-

ley, a devotee of Godwin's and almost a daily visitor, who had become estranged from his wife Harriet. The young people fell in love and met secretly; within a few months Mary was pregnant. On July 28 Shelley and Mary ran off to Europe, taking with them Mary's stepsister Jane Clairmont, who later changed her name to Claire. Mary described their happy feckless wanderings through France, Switzerland, and Germany in her first book, *History of a Six Week's Tour*, published anonymously in 1817.

Back in England, Mary gave premature birth to a daughter who lived only a few weeks; only a year later, in 1816, she bore a son, William. Shelley was usually in financial difficulties, and often had to hide from his creditors to avoid arrest. Nonetheless, he contributed substantial sums (borrowed against his expectations as heir to his father, Sir Timothy) to Godwin's support, even though Godwin, despite his earlier advocacy of free love, refused to countenance Shelley's liaison with his daughter. Claire Clairmont meanwhile sought out and had a brief affair with a rather reluctant Byron, who left her pregnant. In the spring of 1816 Shelley and Mary went abroad again with Claire, and at Claire's behest settled in Geneva, where Byron, accompanied by his physician and friend John William Polidori, set up residence in the nearby Villa Diodati. Mary tells us, in an Introduction to *Frankenstein*, that on one of their many animated evenings together, when the group had been reading ghost stories, Byron suggested that each one write a tale of the supernatural. Further conversations among Byron, Shelley, and Polidori about the principle of life, and about contemporary experiments with galvanic electricity on dead tissue, fired Mary's invention. Encouraged and assisted by Shelley, she wrote *Frankenstein; or, the Modern Prometheus*, and published it anonymously in 1818.

Frankenstein caused something of a literary sensation in London. As its double origin in terror tales and science indicates, it was on the one side a product of the 18th-century vogue for Gothic novels of horror and the macabre, on the other an innovative work in its introduction as protagonist of a synthetic human character. This novel by an author not yet 20, however, transcends in literary interest both its antecedents and successors, for it is artfully structured, exploits powerfully analogues to the biblical and Miltonic accounts of the newly created Adam and of Satan, and deals critically with two central Romantic themes. The scientist Frankenstein instances the Faustian and Promethean spirit of overweening creative ambition which, in Mary's rendering, dehumanizes the protagonist and leads to his destruction and the death of all he loves. The being that Frankenstein creates, on the other hand, represents the Romantic (and post-Romantic) concern with human isolation and alienation. He profoundly needs sympathy and relationship, but is cut off from humanity by his origin and monstrosity; since his overtures to human beings evoke only horror and disgust, his love, rejected, turns into murderous hate. *Frankenstein* is not only a major Romantic achievement; its account of the monstrous potentiality of human creative power when severed from moral concerns and social affiliation has made it a modern myth which recurs persistently in fiction, melodrama, and film, and haunts the popular consciousness.

The last six years of Mary's life with Shelley, spent first in England and then in Italy, were filled with personal disasters. In October, 1816, Mary's sensitive but moody half sister, Fanny Imlay, feeling herself an unloved burden on the Godwin household, committed suicide by an overdose of laudanum. Two months later Shelley's abandoned wife, Harriet, pregnant by an unknown lover, drowned herself in the Serpentine lake at Hyde Park. Shelley at once married Mary, but the courts denied him custody of Harriet's two children on the grounds that he was morally unfit to rear them. In September of 1818 came the death of Mary's third baby, Clara, followed less than nine months later by the death of her adored son, William; so that Mary at 22 had been three times a mother and three times bereaved. These tragedies and her own ill health threw her into a state of depression, which was only partly relieved by the birth of a second son, Florence Percy, in November of 1819, and was deepened again the next spring by a miscarriage, and by the death of Claire's daughter, Allegra, whom Byron had placed in an Italian convent. Mary's habitual reserve, which masked the depth of her feelings, now became an absorption in her own sorrows which caused her to withdraw, emotionally, from her husband. When Shelley was drowned on the Gulf of Spezia in July, 1822, Mary was left with a lifelong sense that she had failed her husband when he most needed her.

An impoverished widow of 24, Mary returned to England with two ambitions. One was to disseminate Shelley's poetry and to rescue from obloquy the character of Shelley, whom she idolized in memory; the other was to support by her writings her surviving son. Her only financial assistance was a small allowance given her by Sir Timothy Shelley, which he threatened to cut off if she wrote a biography of his radical and scandal-haunted son, whom he wished to be forgotten by the world. In the remaining quarter-century of her life Mary published a great variety of works, and was a notable success as a professional woman of letters. She wrote five more novels, of which the first two are by far the best. *The Last Man* (1826), a narrative of the decimation of mankind by a plague until there is only a single survivor, almost equals *Frankenstein* as a powerful analysis of human isolation; while *Valperga* (1823), set in the Italian middle ages, is a very readable romance about a quasi-Napoleonic figure who sacrifices his love and his humanity to a lust for political power. She wrote also some 25 short tales—including *The Transformation*, an insightful study of a dual personality—and left in manuscript a novella, *Mathilda* (written in 1819, but not published until 1959), which deals with the disastrous results of a father's incestuous passion for a daughter who resembles his dead wife. In 1835–39 Mary contributed to the *Cabinet Cyclopedia* five volumes of admirable biographical and critical studies of Continental authors. She also published several separate editions of her husband's writings in verse and prose. In accordance with what was then standard editorial procedure, she altered and emended Shelley's texts; she also, however, added prefaces and notes, relating Shelley's writings to the circumstances of his life and mind, which have remained an important resource for all scholars of Romantic literature.

Not until old Sir Timothy died in 1844, leaving his title and estate to Mary's son, did she find herself in comfortable circumstances. Her latter days were cheered by the devotion of her son—who was an amiable man, but entirely lacked the genius of his parents—and by her close friendship with Jane St. John, an admirer of Shelley's poetry, whom Sir Percy Florence married in 1848. Mary Shelley died three years later, at the age of 53.

During her widowhood Mary craved social acceptance and status, and although she maintained liberal opinions, tried hard, by adapting herself to conventional standards both in her writings and her social life, to work free of the onus she had inherited from what her contemporaries regarded as the scandalous opinions and careers of her mother, father, and husband. In later life she wrote an apologia in her journal, dated October 21, 1838, which reveals the burden of a life spent trying to measure up to the example set by her famous parents:

> In the first place, with regard to "the good cause"—the cause of the advancement of freedom and knowledge, of the rights of women, etc.—I am not a person of opinions. * * * Some have a passion for reforming the world; others do not cling to particular opinions. That my parents and Shelley were of the former class, makes me respect it. * * * For myself, I earnestly desire the good and enlightenment of my fellow creatures, and see all, in the present course, tending to the same, and rejoice; but I am not for violent extremes, which only brings on an injurious reaction. * * *
>
> To hang back, as I do, brings a penalty. I was nursed and fed with a love of glory. To be something great and good was the precept given me by my father; Shelley reiterated it. * * * But Shelley died, and I was alone. * * * My total friendlessness, my horror of pushing, and inability to put myself forward unless led, cherished and supported—all this has sunk me in a state of loneliness no other human being ever before, I believe, endured—except Robinson Crusoe. * * *
>
> But I have never crouched to society—never sought it unworthily. If I have never written to vindicate the rights of women, I have ever defended women when oppressed. At every risk I have befriended and supported victims to the social system; but I make no boast, for in truth it is simple justice I perform; and so am I still reviled for being worldly. * * *
>
> Such as I have written appears to me the exact truth.

Introduction to *Frankenstein*[1]

The Publishers of the Standard Novels, in selecting 'Frankenstein' for one of their series, expressed a wish that I should furnish them with some account of the origin of the story. I am the more willing to comply, because I shall thus give a general answer to the question, so very frequently asked me—'How I, then a young girl, came to think of, and to dilate upon, so very hideous an idea?' It is true that I am very averse to bringing myself forward in print; but

1. Mary Shelley wrote this Introduction for the third edition of *Frankenstein* published in a series, "Standard Novels," 1831; it is thus 15 years later than the events of 1816 that it recalls. In it she undertakes to explain—in terms of outer events that engage with her fantasy life to effect an obsessive visionary experience—how it is that an author in her late teens could write a work which, as we now recognize, is a classic in the genre of terror tales, and which has become an enduring myth.

The text is reprinted from *Frankenstein; or, The Modern Prometheus*, A Norton Critical Edition, edited by J. Paul Hunter (in preparation).

as my account will only appear as an appendage to a former production, and as it will be confined to such topics as have connection with my authorship alone, I can scarcely accuse myself of a personal intrusion.

It is not singular that, as the daughter of two persons of distinguished literary celebrity,[2] I should very early in life have thought of writing. As a child I scribbled; and my favourite pastime, during the hours given me for recreation, was to 'write stories.' Still I had a dearer pleasure than this, which was the formation of castles in the air—the indulging in waking dreams—the following up trains of thought, which had for their subject the formation of a succession of imaginary incidents. My dreams were at once more fantastic and agreeable than my writings. In the latter I was a close imitator—rather doing as others had done, than putting down the suggestions of my own mind. What I wrote was intended at least for one other eye—my childhood's companion and friend;[3] but my dreams were all my own; I accounted for them to nobody; they were my refuge when annoyed—my dearest pleasure when free.

I lived principally in the country as a girl, and passed a considerable time in Scotland. I made occasional visits to the more picturesque parts; but my habitual residence was on the blank and dreary northern shores of the Tay, near Dundee. Blank and dreary on retrospection I call them; they were not so to me then. They were the eyry of freedom, and the pleasant region where unheeded I could commune with the creatures of my fancy. I wrote then—but in a most common-place style. It was beneath the trees of the grounds belonging to our house, or on the bleak sides of the woodless mountains near, that my true compositions, the airy flights of my imagination, were born and fostered. I did not make myself the heroine of my tales. Life appeared to me too common-place an affair as regarded myself. I could not figure to myself that romantic woes or wonderful events would ever be my lot; but I was not confined to my own identity, and I could people the hours with creations far more interesting to me at that age, than my own sensations.

After this my life became busier, and reality stood in place of fiction. My husband,[4] however, was, from the first, very anxious that I should prove myself worthy of my parentage, and enrol myself on the page of fame. He was for ever inciting me to obtain literary reputation, which even on my own part I cared for then, though since I have become infinitely indifferent to it. At this time he desired that I should write, not so much with the idea that I

2. Mary Wollstonecraft and William Godwin.
3. Isabel Baxter, the daughter of William Baxter, with whom Mary had lived in Dundee, Scotland, in 1812–14.
4. Mary and Percy Shelley did not in fact marry until December, some six months after the events described in the Introduction.

could produce any thing worthy of notice, but that he might himself judge how far I possessed the promise of better things hereafter. Still I did nothing. Travelling, and the cares of a family, occupied my time; and study, in the way of reading, or improving my ideas in communication with his far more cultivated mind, was all of literary employment that engaged my attention.

In the summer of 1816, we visited Switzerland, and became the neighbours of Lord Byron. At first we spent our pleasant hours on the lake, or wandering on its shores; and Lord Byron, who was writing the third canto of Childe Harold, was the only one among us who put his thoughts upon paper. These, as he brought them successively to us, clothed in all the light and harmony of poetry, seemed to stamp as divine the glories of heaven and earth, whose influences we partook with him.

But it proved a wet, ungenial summer, and incessant rain often confined us for days to the house. Some volumes of ghost stories, translated from the German into French, fell into our hands.[5] There was the History of the Inconstant Lover, who, when he thought to clasp the bride to whom he had pledged his vows, found himself in the arms of the pale ghost of her whom he had deserted. There was the tale of the sinful founder of his race, whose miserable doom it was to bestow the kiss of death on all the younger sons of his fated house, just when they reached the age of promise. His gigantic, shadowy form, clothed like the ghost in Hamlet, in complete armour, but with the beaver[6] up, was seen at midnight, by the moon's fitful beams, to advance slowly along the gloomy avenue. The shape was lost beneath the shadow of the castle walls; but soon a gate swung back, a step was heard, the door of the chamber opened, and he advanced to the couch of the blooming youths, cradled in healthy sleep. Eternal sorrow sat upon his face as he bent down and kissed the forehead of the boys, who from that hour withered like flowers snapt upon the stalk. I have not seen these stories since then; but their incidents are as fresh in my mind as if I had read them yesterday.

'We will each write a ghost story,' said Lord Byron; and his proposition was acceded to. There were four of us.[7] The noble author began a tale, a fragment of which he printed at the end of his poem of Mazeppa. Shelley, more apt to embody ideas and sentiments in

---

5. The French translation, published anonymously in 1812, was called *Fantasmagoriana, or Collected Stories of Apparitions of Specters, Ghosts, Phantoms, Etc.* The stories she goes on to describe, somewhat inaccurately, are *The Dead Fiancée* and *Family Portraits*.

6. The hinged piece of armor that covers the face. Cf. *Hamlet* I.ii.226–30.
7. Byron, Shelley, Mary Shelley, and John William Polidori, Byron's physician and friend. Mary omits Claire Clairmont, her stepsister and Byron's former mistress, who was staying with the Shelleys at Geneva.

the radiance of brilliant imagery, and in the music of the most melodious verse that adorns our language, than to invent the machinery of a story, commenced one founded on the experiences of his early life. Poor Polidori had some terrible idea about a skull-headed lady, who was so punished for peeping through a key-hole—what to see I forget—something very shocking and wrong of course; but when she was reduced to a worse condition than the renowned Tom of Coventry,[8] he did not know what to do with her, and was obliged to despatch her to the tomb of the Capulets,[9] the only place for which she was fitted. The illustrious poets also, annoyed by the platitude of prose, speedily relinquished their uncongenial task.

I busied myself *to think of a story,*—a story to rival those which had excited us to this task. One which would speak to the mysterious fears of our nature, and awaken thrilling horror—one to make the reader dread to look round, to curdle the blood, and quicken the beatings of the heart. If I did not accomplish these things, my ghost story would be unworthy of its name. I thought and pondered —vainly. I felt that blank incapability of invention which is the greatest misery of authorship, when dull Nothing replies to our anxious invocations. *Have you thought of a story?* I was asked each morning, and each morning I was forced to reply with a mortifying negative.

Every thing must have a beginning, to speak in Sanchean[1] phrase, and that beginning must be linked to something that went before. The Hindoos give the world an elephant to support it, but they make the elephant stand upon a tortoise. Invention, it must be humbly admitted, does not consist in creating out of void, but out of chaos; the materials must, in the first place, be afforded: it can give form to dark, shapeless substances, but cannot bring into being the substance itself. In all matters of discovery and invention, even of those that appertain to the imagination, we are continually reminded of the story of Columbus and his egg.[2] Invention consists in the capacity of seizing on the capabilities of a subject, and in the power of moulding and fashioning ideas suggested to it.

Many and long were the conversations between Lord Byron and Shelley, to which I was a devout but nearly silent listener. During one of these, various philosophical doctrines were discussed, and among others the nature of the principle of life, and whether there

8. "Peeping Tom" who, according to the legend, was struck blind when he looked at Lady Godiva as she rode naked through Coventry.
9. Where Romeo and Juliet died.
1. I.e., of Sancho Panza, the literal-minded squire in Cervantes' novel, *Don Quixote* (1605).
2. According to popular legend, Christopher Columbus boasted that he could accomplish the impossible feat of making an egg stand on end. When challenged to do so, he lightly cracked one end and stood the egg upright.

was any probability of its ever being discovered and communicated.[3] They talked of the experiments of Dr. Darwin,[4] (I speak not of what the Doctor really did, or said that he did, but, as more to my purpose, of what was then spoken of as having been done by him,) who preserved a piece of vermicelli[5] in a glass case, till by some extraordinary means it began to move with voluntary motion. Not thus, after all, would life be given. Perhaps a corpse would be re-animated; galvanism[6] had given token of such things: perhaps the component parts of a creature might be manufactured, brought together, and endued with vital warmth.

Night waned upon this talk, and even the witching hour had gone by, before we retired to rest. When I placed my head on my pillow, I did not sleep, nor could I be said to think. My imagination, unbidden, possessed and guided me, gifting the successive images that arose in my mind with a vividness far beyond the usual bounds of reverie. I saw—with shut eyes, but acute mental vision, —I saw the pale student of unhallowed arts kneeling beside the thing he had put together. I saw the hideous phantasm of a man stretched out, and then, on the working of some powerful engine, show signs of life, and stir with an uneasy, half vital motion. Frightful must it be; for supremely frightful would be the effect of any human endeavour to mock the stupendous mechanism of the Creator of the world. His success would terrify the artist; he would rush away from his odious handywork, horror-stricken. He would hope that, left to itself, the slight spark of life which he had communicated would fade; that this thing, which had received such imperfect animation, would subside into dead matter; and he might sleep in the belief that the silence of the grave would quench for ever the transient existence of the hideous corpse which he had looked upon as the cradle of life. He sleeps; but he is awakened; he opens his eyes; behold the horrid thing stands at his bedside, opening his curtains, and looking on him with yellow, watery, but speculative eyes.

I opened mine in terror. The idea so possessed my mind, that a thrill of fear ran through me, and I wished to exchange the ghastly image of my fancy for the realities around. I see them still; the very

---

3. James Rieger conjectures that Mary may in fact be remembering a conversation between Polidori and Shelley, which apparently took place a day before Byron suggested writing ghost stories, and which, as Polidori records in his diary for June 15, 1816, was "about principles—whether man was to be thought merely an instrument." Polidori had recently published a thesis on sleepwalking.

4. Erasmus Darwin (1731–1802), physician, natural scientist, and widely read author of the long poems, *The Botanic Garden* and *The Loves of the Plants*; he was the grandfather of Charles Darwin.

5. A thin spaghetti.

6. The use of electric current to induce muscle twitches in dead tissue. Mary Shelley probably has in mind a widely discussed experiment of 1803, in which Giovanni Aldini had effected spasmodic contractions in the corpse of a criminal executed at Newgate prison.

room, the dark *parquet*,[7] the closed shutters, with the moonlight struggling through, and the sense I had that the glassy lake and white high Alps were beyond. I could not so easily get rid of my hideous phantom; still it haunted me. I must try to think of something else. I recurred to my ghost story,—my tiresome unlucky ghost story! O! if I could only contrive one which would frighten my reader as I myself had been frightened that night!

Swift as light and as cheering was the idea that broke in upon me. 'I have found it! What terrified me will terrify others; and I need only describe the spectre which had haunted my midnight pillow.' On the morrow I announced that I had *thought of a story.* I began that day with the words, *It was on a dreary night of November,* making only a transcript of the grim terrors of my waking dream.

At first I thought but of a few pages—of a short tale; but Shelley urged me to develope the idea at greater length. I certainly did not owe the suggestion of one incident, nor scarcely of one train of feeling, to my husband, and yet but for his incitement, it would never have taken the form in which it was presented to the world.[8] From this declaration I must except the preface. As far as I can recollect, it was entirely written by him.

And now, once again, I bid my hideous progeny go forth and prosper. I have an affection for it, for it was the offspring of happy days, when death and grief were but words, which found no true echo in my heart. Its several pages speak of many a walk, many a drive, and many a conversation, when I was not alone; and my companion was one who, in this world, I shall never see more. But this is for myself; my readers have nothing to do with these associations.

I will add but one word as to the alterations I have made. They are principally those of style. I have changed no portion of the story, nor introduced any new ideas or circumstances. I have mended the language where it was so bald as to interfere with the interest of the narrative; and these changes occur almost exclusively in the beginning of the first volume. Throughout they are entirely confined to such parts as are mere adjuncts to the story, leaving the core and substance of it untouched.

M.W.S.

London, October 15, 1831

7. A floor made of wooden pieces arranged in a pattern.
8. Mary Shelley understates both her husband's help in writing *Frankenstein* and (in the last paragraph) the extent of the changes she made in the third edition. For details, see the editorial matter in Hunter's edition. Shelley had written a Preface for the first, anonymously published edition of *Frankenstein* (1818).

Transformation[1]

Forthwith this frame of mine was wrench'd
  With a woful agony,
Which forced me to begin my tale,
  And then it set me free.
Since then, at an uncertain hour,
  That agony returns;
And till my ghastly tale is told
  This heart within me burns.
—COLERIDGE'S ANCIENT MARINER

I have heard it said, that, when any strange, supernatural, and necromantic adventure has occurred to a human being, that being, however desirous he may be to conceal the same, feels at certain periods torn up as it were by an intellectual earthquake, and is forced to bare the inner depths of his spirit to another. I am a witness of the truth of this. I have dearly sworn to myself never to reveal to human ears the horrors to which I once, in excess of fiendly pride, delivered myself over. The holy man who heard my confession, and reconciled me to the church, is dead. None knows that once——

Why should it not be thus? Why tell a tale of impious tempting of Providence, and soul-subduing humiliation? Why? answer me, ye who are wise in the secrets of human nature! I only know that so it is; and in spite of strong resolve—of a pride that too much masters me—of shame, and even of fear, so to render myself odious to my species—I must speak.

Genoa! my birth-place—proud city! looking upon the blue waves of the Mediterranean sea—dost thou remember me in my boyhood, when thy cliffs and promontories, thy bright sky and gay vineyards, were my world? Happy time! when to the young heart the narrow-bounded universe, which leaves, by its very limitation, free scope to the imagination, enchains our physical energies, and, sole period in our lives, innocence and enjoyment are united. Yet, who can look back to childhood, and not remember its sorrows and its harrowing

---

1. *Transformation*, like most of Mary Shelley's tales and short stories, was written for *The Keepsake*, one of the most popular of the English literary annuals—lavishly bound and illustrated collections of fiction and poems designed to be used as gift books, or for display on drawing-room tables. Its central incident was suggested to the author by Byron's unfinished drama, *The Deformed Transformed* (1824), but she had earlier employed a version of the diabolical double—the projection of a split personality—in the division between the scientist-creator and his monstrous creature in *Frankenstein* (1818). Among the many successors to Mary Shelley's stories of the *Doppelgänger* are Robert Louis Stevenson's *Dr. Jekyll and Mr. Hyde*, Oscar Wilde's *The Picture of Dorian Gray*, and Joseph Conrad's *The Secret Sharer* (included in this volume, below).

This text is reprinted from *Mary Shelley, Collected Tales and Stories*, edited by Charles E. Robinson (1976).

fears? I was born with the most imperious, haughty, tameless spirit, with which ever mortal was gifted. I quailed before my father only; and he, generous and noble, but capricious and tyrannical, at once fostered and checked the wild impetuosity of my character, making obedience necessary, but inspiring no respect for the motives which guided his commands. To be a man, free, independent; or, in better words, insolent and domineering, was the hope and prayer of my rebel heart.

My father had one friend, a wealthy Genoese noble, who in a political tumult was suddenly sentenced to banishment, and his property confiscated. The Marchese Torella went into exile alone. Like my father, he was a widower: he had one child, the almost infant Juliet, who was left under my father's guardianship. I should certainly have been an unkind master to the lovely girl, but that I was forced by my position to become her protector. A variety of childish incidents all tended to one point,—to make Juliet see in me a rock of refuge; I in her, one, who must perish through the soft sensibility of her nature too rudely visited, but for my guardian care. We grew up together. The opening rose in May was not more sweet than this dear girl. An irradiation of beauty was spread over her face. Her form, her step, her voice—my heart weeps even now, to think of all of relying, gentle, loving, and pure, that was enshrined in that celestial tenement. When I was eleven and Juliet eight years of age, a cousin of mine, much older than either—he seemed to us a man—took great notice of my playmate; he called her his bride, and asked her to marry him. She refused, and he insisted, drawing her unwillingly towards him. With the countenance and emotions of a maniac I threw myself on him—I strove to draw his sword—I clung to his neck with the ferocious resolve to strangle him: he was obliged to call for assistance to disengage himself from me. On that night I led Juliet to the chapel of our house: I made her touch the sacred relics—I harrowed her child's heart, and profaned her child's lips with an oath, that she would be mine, and mine only.

Well, those days passed away. Torella returned in a few years, and became wealthier and more prosperous than ever. When I was seventeen, my father died; he had been magnificent to prodigality; Torella rejoiced that my minority would afford an opportunity for repairing my fortunes. Juliet and I had been affianced beside my father's deathbed—Torella was to be a second parent to me.

I desired to see the world, and I was indulged. I went to Florence, to Rome, to Naples; thence I passed to Toulon, and at length reached what had long been the bourne[2] of my wishes, Paris. There was wild work in Paris then. The poor king, Charles the Sixth,[3]

2. Limit, goal.
3. Charles VI was king of France, 1380–1422.

now sane, now mad, now a monarch, now an abject slave, was the very mockery of humanity. The queen, the dauphin,[4] the Duke of Burgundy, alternately friends and foes—now meeting in prodigal feasts, now shedding blood in rivalry—were blind to the miserable state of their country, and the dangers that impended over it, and gave themselves wholly up to dissolute enjoyment or savage strife. My character still followed me. I was arrogant and self-willed; I loved display, and above all, I threw all control far from me. Who could control me in Paris? My young friends were eager to foster passions which furnished them with pleasures. I was deemed handsome—I was master of every knightly accomplishment. I was disconnected with any political party. I grew a favourite with all: my presumption and arrogance were pardoned in one so young: I became a spoiled child. Who could control me? not the letters and advice of Torella—only strong necessity visiting me in the abhorred shape of an empty purse. But there were means to refill this void. Acre after acre, estate after estate, I sold. My dress, my jewels, my horses and their caparisons, were almost unrivalled in gorgeous Paris, while the lands of my inheritance passed into possession of others.

The Duke of Orleans was waylaid and murdered by the Duke of Burgundy. Fear and terror possessed all Paris. The dauphin and the queen shut themselves up; every pleasure was suspended. I grew weary of this state of things, and my heart yearned for my boyhood's haunts. I was nearly a beggar, yet still I would go there, claim my bride, and rebuild my fortunes. A few happy ventures as a merchant would make me rich again. Nevertheless, I would not return in humble guise. My last act was to dispose of my remaining estate near Albaro for half its worth, for ready money. Then I despatched all kinds of artificers, arras,[5] furniture of regal splendour, to fit up the last relic of my inheritance, my palace in Genoa. I lingered a little longer yet, ashamed at the part of the prodigal returned, which I feared I should play. I sent my horses. One matchless Spanish jennet[6] I despatched to my promised bride; its caparisons flamed with jewels and cloth of gold. In every part I caused to be entwined the initials of Juliet and her Guido. My present found favour in hers and in her father's eyes.

Still to return a proclaimed spendthrift, the mark of impertinent wonder, perhaps of scorn, and to encounter singly the reproaches or taunts of my fellow-citizens, was no alluring prospect. As a shield between me and censure, I invited some few of the most reckless of my comrades to accompany me: thus I went armed against the world, hiding a rankling feeling, half fear and half penitence, by bravado and an insolent display of satisfied vanity.

---

4. The title given to the oldest son of the kings of France.

5. Rich tapestries.

6. Small Spanish horse.

I arrived in Genoa. I trod the pavement of my ancestral palace. My proud step was no interpreter of my heart, for I deeply felt that, though surrounded by every luxury, I was a beggar. The first step I took in claiming Juliet must widely declare me such. I read contempt or pity in the looks of all. I fancied, so apt is conscience to imagine what it deserves, that rich and poor, young and old, all regarded me with derision. Torella came not near me. No wonder that my second father should expect a son's deference from me in waiting first on him. But, galled and stung by a sense of my follies and demerit, I strove to throw the blame on others. We kept nightly orgies in Palazzo Carega. To sleepless, riotous nights, followed listless, supine mornings. At the Ave Maria[7] we showed our dainty persons in the streets, scoffing at the sober citizens, casting insolent glances on the shrinking women. Juliet was not among them—no, no; if she had been there, shame would have driven me away, if love had not brought me to her feet.

I grew tired of this. Suddenly I paid the Marchese a visit. He was at his villa, one among the many which deck the suburb of San Pietro d'Arena. It was the month of May—a month of May in that garden of the world—the blossoms of the fruit trees were fading among thick, green foliage; the vines were shooting forth; the ground strewed with the fallen olive blooms; the fire-fly was in the myrtle hedge; heaven and earth wore a mantle of surpassing beauty. Torella welcomed me kindly, though seriously; and even his shade of displeasure soon wore away. Some resemblance to my father— some look and tone of youthful ingenuousness, lurking still in spite of my misdeeds, softened the good old man's heart. He sent for his daughter—he presented me to her as her betrothed. The chamber became hallowed by a holy light as she entered. Hers was that cherub look, those large, soft eyes, full dimpled cheeks, and mouth of infantine sweetness, that expresses the rare union of happiness and love. Admiration first possessed me; she is mine! was the second proud emotion, and my lips curled with haughty triumph. I had not been the *enfant gâté*[8] of the beauties of France not to have learnt the art of pleasing the soft heart of woman. If towards men I was overbearing, the deference I paid to them was the more in contrast. I commenced my courtship by the display of a thousand gallantries to Juliet, who, vowed to me from infancy, had never admitted the devotion of others; and who, though accustomed to expressions of admiration, was uninitiated in the language of lovers.

For a few days all went well. Torella never alluded to my extravagance; he treated me as a favourite son. But the time came, as we discussed the preliminaries to my union with his daughter, when this fair face of things should be overcast. A contract had been

---

7. The sunset hour, when the Catholic prayer "Hail Mary" is recited.   8. Spoiled child.

drawn up in my father's lifetime. I had rendered this, in fact, void, by having squandered the whole of the wealth which was to have been shared by Juliet and myself. Torella, in consequence, chose to consider this bond as cancelled, and proposed another, in which, though the wealth he bestowed was immeasurably increased, there were so many restrictions as to the mode of spending it, that I, who saw independence only in free career being given to my own imperious will, taunted him as taking advantage of my situation, and refused utterly to subscribe to his conditions. The old man mildly strove to recall me to reason. Roused pride became the tyrant of my thought: I listened with indignation—I repelled him with disdain.

"Juliet, thou art mine! Did we not interchange vows in our innocent childhood? are we not one in the sight of God? and shall thy cold-hearted, cold-blooded father divide us? Be generous, my love, be just; take not away a gift, last treasure of thy Guido—retract not thy vows—let us defy the world, and setting at nought the calculations of age, find in our mutual affection a refuge from every ill."

Fiend I must have been, with such sophistry to endeavour to poison that sanctuary of holy thought and tender love. Juliet shrank from me affrighted. Her father was the best and kindest of men, and she strove to show me how, in obeying him, every good would follow. He would receive my tardy submission with warm affection; and generous pardon would follow my repentance. Profitless words for a young and gentle daughter to use to a man accustomed to make his will, law; and to feel in his own heart a despot so terrible and stern, that he could yield obedience to nought save his own imperious desires! My resentment grew with resistance; my wild companions were ready to add fuel to the flame. We laid a plan to carry off Juliet. At first it appeared to be crowned with success. Midway, on our return, we were overtaken by the agonized father and his attendants. A conflict ensued. Before the city guard came to decide the victory in favour of our antagonists, two of Torella's servitors were dangerously wounded.

This portion of my history weighs most heavily with me. Changed man as I am, I abhor myself in the recollection. May none who hear this tale ever have felt as I. A horse driven to fury by a rider armed with barbed spurs, was not more a slave than I, to the violent tyranny of my temper. A fiend possessed my soul, irritating it to madness. I felt the voice of conscience within me; but if I yielded to it for a brief interval, it was only to be a moment after torn, as by a whirlwind, away—borne along on the stream of desperate rage—the plaything of the storms engendered by pride. I was imprisoned, and, at the instance of Torella, set free. Again I returned to carry off both him and his child to France; which hapless country, then preyed on by freebooters and gangs of lawless soldiery, offered a grateful refuge to a criminal like me. Our plots were discovered. I was sentenced to banishment; and, as my debts were already enormous, my remaining property was put in the hands of commissioners for their payment. Torella again offered his mediation, requiring only my promise not to renew my abortive attempts on himself and his daughter. I spurned his offers, and fancied that I triumphed when I was thrust out from Genoa, a solitary and penniless exile. My companions were gone: they had been dismissed the city some weeks before, and were already in France. I was alone —friendless; with nor sword at my side, nor ducat in my purse.

I wandered along the sea-shore, a whirlwind of passion possessing and tearing my soul. It was as if a live coal had been set burning in my breast. At first I meditated on what I *should do*. I would join a band of freebooters. Revenge!—the word seemed balm to me:—I hugged it—caressed it—till, like a serpent, it stung me. Then again I would abjure and despise Genoa, that little corner of the world. I would return to Paris, where so many of my friends swarmed; where my services would be eagerly accepted; where I would carve out fortune with my sword, and might, through success, make my paltry birth-place, and the false Torella, rue the day when they drove me, a new Coriolanus,[9] from her walls. I would return to Paris—thus, on foot—a beggar—and present myself in my poverty to those I had formerly entertained sumptuously? There was gall in the mere thought of it.

The reality of things began to dawn upon my mind, bringing despair in its train. For several months I had been a prisoner: the evils of my dungeon had whipped my soul to madness, but they had subdued my corporeal frame. I was weak and wan. Torella had used a thousand artifices to administer to my comfort; I had detected and scorned them all—and I reaped the harvest of my obduracy. What was to be done?—Should I crouch before my foe, and sue for forgiveness?—Die rather ten thousand deaths!—Never should they obtain that victory! Hate—I swore eternal hate! Hate from whom?—to whom?—From a wandering outcast—to a mighty noble. I and my feelings were nothing to them: already had they forgotten one so unworthy. And Juliet!—her angel-face and sylph-like form gleamed among the clouds of my despair with vain beauty; for I had lost her—the glory and flower of the world! Another will call her his!—that smile of paradise will bless another!

Even now my heart fails within me when I recur to this rout of grim-visaged ideas. Now subdued almost to tears, now raving in my agony, still I wandered along the rocky shore, which grew at each

---

9. Gaius Marcus Coriolanus, a Roman general, 5th century B.C. He was banished on the charge of aspiring to become a tyrant, then led a rebellion against his native Rome. He is the protagonist of Shakespeare's play *Coriolanus*.

step wilder and more desolate. Hanging rocks and hoar precipices overlooked the tideless ocean; black caverns yawned; and for ever, among the seaworn recesses, murmured and dashed the unfruitful waters. Now my way was almost barred by an abrupt promontory, now rendered nearly impracticable by fragments fallen from the cliff. Evening was at hand, when, seaward, arose, as if on the waving of a wizard's wand, a murky web of clouds, blotting the late azure sky, and darkening and disturbing the till now placid deep. The clouds had strange fantastic shapes; and they changed, and mingled, and seemed to be driven about by a mighty spell. The waves raised their white crests; the thunder first muttered, then roared from across the waste of waters, which took a deep purple dye, flecked with foam. The spot where I stood, looked, on one side, to the wide-spread ocean; on the other, it was barred by a rugged promontory. Round this cape suddenly came, driven by the wind, a vessel. In vain the mariners tried to force a path for her to the open sea— the gale drove her on the rocks. It will perish!—all on board will perish!—Would I were among them! And to my young heart the idea of death came for the first time blended with that of joy. It was an awful sight to behold that vessel struggling with her fate. Hardly could I discern the sailors, but I heard them. It was soon all over!—A rock, just covered by the tossing waves, and so unperceived, lay in wait for its prey. A crash of thunder broke over my head at the moment that, with a frightful shock, the skiff dashed upon her unseen enemy. In a brief space of time she went to pieces. There I stood in safety; and there were my fellow-creatures, battling, how hopelessly, with annihilation. Methought I saw them struggling—too truly did I hear their shrieks, conquering the barking surges in their shrill agony. The dark breakers threw hither and thither the fragments of the wreck: soon it disappeared. I had been fascinated to gaze till the end: at last I sank on my knees—I covered my face with my hands: I again looked up; something was floating on the billows towards the shore. It neared and neared. Was that a human form?—It grew more distinct; and at last a mighty wave, lifting the whole freight, lodged it upon a rock. A human being bestriding a sea-chest!—A human being!—Yet was it one? Surely never such had existed before—a misshapen dwarf, with squinting eyes, distorted features, and body deformed, till it became a horror to behold. My blood, lately warming towards a fellow-being so snatched from a watery tomb, froze in my heart. The dwarf got off his chest; he tossed his straight, straggling hair from his odious visage:

"By St. Beelzebub!"[1] he exclaimed, "I have been well bested." He looked round and saw me. "Oh, by the fiend! here is another

1. The devil.

ally of the mighty one. To what saint did you offer prayers, friend
—if not to mine? Yet I remember you not on board."

I shrank from the monster and his blasphemy. Again he questioned me, and I muttered some inaudible reply. He continued:—

"Your voice is drowned by this dissonant roar. What a noise the
big ocean makes! Schoolboys bursting from their prison are not
louder than these waves set free to play. They disturb me. I will no
more of their ill-timed brawling.—Silence, hoary One!—Winds,
avaunt!—to your homes!—Clouds, fly to the antipodes,[2] and leave
our heaven clear!"

As he spoke, he stretched out his two long lank arms, that looked
like spider's claws, and seemed to embrace with them the expanse
before him. Was it a miracle? The clouds became broken, and fled;
the azure sky first peeped out, and then was spread a calm field of
blue above us; the stormy gale was exchanged to the softly breathing west; the sea grew calm; the waves dwindled to riplets.

"I like obedience even in these stupid elements," said the dwarf.
"How much more in the tameless mind of man! It was a well got
up storm, you must allow—and all of my own making."

It was tempting Providence to interchange talk with this magician. But *Power*, in all its shapes, is venerable to man. Awe, curiosity, a clinging fascination, drew me towards him.

"Come, don't be frightened, friend," said the wretch: "I am
good-humoured when pleased; and something does please me in
your well-proportioned body and handsome face, though you look a
little woe-begone. You have suffered a land—I, a sea wreck. Perhaps
I can allay the tempest of your fortunes as I did my own. Shall we
be friends?"—And he held out his hand; I could not touch it.
"Well, then, companions—that will do as well. And now, while I
rest after the buffeting I underwent just now, tell me why, young
and gallant as you seem, you wander thus alone and downcast on
this wild sea-shore."

The voice of the wretch was screeching and horrid, and his con-
tortions as he spoke were frightful to behold. Yet he did gain a kind
of influence over me, which I could not master, and I told him my
tale. When it was ended, he laughed long and loud: the rocks
echoed back the sound: hell seemed yelling around me.

"Oh, thou cousin of Lucifer!" said he; "so thou too hast fallen
through thy pride; and, though bright as the son of Morning,[3] thou
art ready to give up thy good looks, thy bride, and thy well-being,
rather than submit thee to the tyranny of good. I honour thy

---

2. Diametrically opposite sides of the globe.
3. Lucifer (Latin, "light-bringing") is the morning star. The name had been applied to Satan, through a mistaken interpretation of Isaiah xiv.12 as a refer-
ence to the rebel angel who was hurled
from heaven: "How art thou fallen from
heaven, O Lucifer, son of the morning."

choice, by my soul!—So thou hast fled, and yield the day; and mean to starve on these rocks, and to let the birds peck out thy dead eyes, while thy enemy and thy betrothed rejoice in thy ruin. Thy pride is strangely akin to humility, methinks."

As he spoke, a thousand fanged thoughts stung me to the heart.

"What would you that I should do?" I cried.

"I!—Oh, nothing, but lie down and say your prayers before you die. But, were I you, I know the deed that should be done."

I drew near him. His supernatural powers made him an oracle in my eyes; yet a strange unearthly thrill quivered through my frame as I said—"Speak!—teach me—what act do you advise?"

"Revenge thyself, man!—humble thy enemies!—set thy foot on the old man's neck, and possess thyself of his daughter!"

"To the east and west I turn," cried I, "and see no means! Had I gold, much could I achieve; but, poor and single, I am powerless."

The dwarf had been seated on his chest as he listened to my story. Now he got off; he touched a spring; it flew open!—What a mine of wealth—of blazing jewels, beaming gold, and pale silver—was displayed therein. A mad desire to possess this treasure was born within me.

"Doubtless," I said, "one so powerful as you could do all things."

"Nay," said the monster, humbly, "I am less omnipotent than I seem. Some things I possess which you may covet; but I would give them all for a small share, or even for a loan of what is yours."

"My possessions are at your service," I replied, bitterly—"my poverty, my exile, my disgrace—I make a free gift of them all."

"Good! I thank you. Add one other thing to your gift, and my treasure is yours."

"As nothing is my sole inheritance, what besides nothing would you have?"

"Your comely face and well-made limbs."

I shivered. Would this all-powerful monster murder me? I had no dagger. I forgot to pray—but I grew pale.

"I ask for a loan, not a gift," said the frightful thing: "lend me your body for three days—you shall have mine to cage your soul the while, and, in payment, my chest. What say you to the bargain? —Three short days."

We are told that it is dangerous to hold unlawful talk; and well do I prove the same. Tamely written down, it may seem incredible that I should lend any ear to this proposition; but, in spite of his unnatural ugliness, there was something fascinating in a being whose voice could govern earth, air, and sea. I felt a keen desire to comply; for with that chest I could command the world. My only hesitation resulted from a fear that he would not be true to his bargain. Then, I thought, I shall soon die here on these lonely sands, and the limbs he covets will be mine no more:—it is worth the chance. And, besides, I knew that, by all the rules of art-magic, there were formula and oaths which none of its practisers dared break. I hesitated to reply; and he went on, now displaying his wealth, now speaking of the petty price he demanded, till it seemed madness to refuse. Thus is it: place our bark in the current of the stream, and down, over fall and cataract it is hurried; give up our conduct to the wild torrent of passion, and we are away, we know not whither.

He swore many an oath, and I adjured him by many a sacred name; till I saw this wonder of power, this ruler of the elements, shiver like an autumn leaf before my words; and as if the spirit spake unwillingly and per force within him, at last, he, with broken voice, revealed the spell whereby he might be obliged, did he wish to play me false, to render up the unlawful spoil. Our warm life-blood must mingle to make and to mar the charm.

Enough of this unholy theme. I was persuaded—the thing was done. The morrow dawned upon me as I lay upon the shingles,[4] and I knew not my own shadow as it fell from me. I felt myself changed to a shape of horror, and cursed my easy faith and blind credulity. The chest was there—there the gold and precious stones for which I had sold the frame of flesh which nature had given me. The sight a little stilled my emotions: three days would soon be gone.

They did pass. The dwarf had supplied me with a plenteous store of food. At first I could hardly walk, so strange and out of joint were all my limbs; and my voice—it was that of the fiend. But I kept silent, and turned my face to the sun, that I might not see my shadow, and counted the hours, and ruminated on my future conduct. To bring Torella to my feet—to possess my Juliet in spite of him—all this my wealth could easily achieve. During dark night I slept, and dreamt of the accomplishment of my desires. Two suns had set—the third dawned. I was agitated, fearful. Oh expectation, what a frightful thing art thou, when kindled more by fear than hope! How dost thou twist thyself round the heart, torturing its pulsations! How dost thou dart unknown pangs all through our feeble mechanism, now seeming to shiver us like broken glass, to nothingness—now giving us a fresh strength, which can *do* nothing, and so torments us by a sensation, such as the strong man must feel who cannot break his fetters, though they bend in his grasp. Slowly paced the bright, bright orb up the eastern sky; long it lingered in the zenith, and still more slowly wandered down the west: it touched the horizon's verge—it was lost! Its glories were on the

4. Beach pebbles.

summits of the cliff—they grew dun and gray. The evening star shone bright. He will soon be here.

He came not!—By the living heavens, he came not!—and night dragged out its weary length, and, in its decaying age, "day began to grizzle its dark hair,"[5] and the sun rose again on the most miserable wretch that ever upbraided its light. Three days thus I passed. The jewels and the gold—oh, how I abhorred them!

Well, well—I will not blacken these pages with demoniac ravings. All too terrible were the thoughts, the raging tumult of ideas that filled my soul. At the end of that time I slept; I had not before since the third sunset; and I dreamt that I was at Juliet's feet, and she smiled, and then she shrieked—for she saw my transformation —and again she smiled, for still her beautiful lover knelt before her. But it was not I—it was he, the fiend, arrayed in my limbs, speaking with my voice, winning her with my looks of love. I strove to warn her, but my tongue refused its office; I strove to tear him from her, but I was rooted to the ground—I awoke with the agony. There were the solitary hoar precipices—there the plashing sea, the quiet strand, and the blue sky over all. What did it mean? was my dream but a mirror of the truth? was he wooing and winning my betrothed? I would on the instant back to Genoa—but I was banished. I laughed—the dwarf's yell burst from my lips—*I* banished! O, no! they had not exiled the foul limbs I wore; I might with these enter, without fear of incurrring the threatened penalty of death, my own, my native city.

I began to walk towards Genoa. I was somewhat accustomed to my distorted limbs; none were ever so ill adapted for a straight-forward movement; it was with infinite difficulty that I proceeded. Then, too, I desired to avoid all the hamlets strewed here and there on the sea-beach, for I was unwilling to make a display of my hid-eousness. I was not quite sure that, if seen, the mere boys would not stone me to death as I passed, for a monster: some ungentle saluta-tions I did receive from the few peasants or fishermen I chanced to meet. But it was dark night before I approached Genoa. The weather was so balmy and sweet that it struck me that the Mar-chese and his daughter would very probably have quitted the city for their country retreat. It was from Villa Torella that I had attempted to carry off Juliet; I had spent many an hour reconnoi-tring the spot, and knew each inch of ground in its vicinity. It was beautifully situated, embosomed in trees, on the margin of a stream. As I drew near, it became evident that my conjecture was right; nay, moreover, that the hours were being then devoted to feasting and merriment. For the house was lighted up; strains of soft and

5. Misquoted from Byron's play, *Werner* (III.iv.152–53): "the gray / Begins to grizzle the black hair of night."

gay music were wafted towards me by the breeze. My heart sank within me. Such was the generous kindness of Torella's heart that I felt sure that he would not have indulged in public manifestations of rejoicing just after my unfortunate banishment, but for a cause I dared not dwell upon.

The country people were all alive and flocking about; it became necessary that I should study to conceal myself; and yet I longed to address some one, or to hear others discourse, or in any way to gain intelligence of what was really going on. At length, entering the walks that were in immediate vicinity to the mansion, I found one dark enough to veil my excessive frightfulness; and yet others as well as I were loitering in its shade. I soon gathered all I wanted to know—all that first made my very heart die with horror, and then boil with indignation. To-morrow Juliet was to be given to the peni-tent, reformed, beloved Guido—to-morrow my bride was to pledge her vows to a fiend from hell! And I did this!—my accursed pride —my demoniac violence and wicked self-idolatry had caused this act. For if I had acted as the wretch who had stolen my form had acted—if, with a mien at once yielding and dignified, I had pre-sented myself to Torella, saying, I have done wrong, forgive me; I am unworthy of your angel-child, but permit me to claim her here-after, when my altered conduct shall manifest that I abjure my vices, and endeavour to become in some sort worthy of her. I go to serve against the infidels;[6] and when my zeal for religion and my true penitence for the past shall appear to you to cancel my crimes, permit me again to call myself your son. Thus had he spoken; and the penitent was welcomed even as the prodigal son of scripture:[7] the fatted calf was killed for him; and he, still pursuing the same path, displayed such open-hearted regret for his follies, so humble a concession of all his rights, and so ardent a resolve to reacquire them by a life of contrition and virtue, that he quickly conquered the kind, old man; and full pardon, and the gift of his lovely child, followed in swift succession.

O! had an angel from Paradise whispered to me to act thus! But now, what would be the innocent Juliet's fate? Would God permit the foul union—or, some prodigy destroying it, link the dishon-oured name of Carega with the worst of crimes? To-morrow at dawn they were to be married: there was but one way to prevent this—to meet mine enemy, and to enforce the ratification of our agreement. I felt that this could only be done by a mortal struggle. I had no sword—if indeed my distorted arms could wield a soldier's weapon—but I had a dagger, and in that lay my every hope. There was no time for pondering or balancing nicely the question: I might

6. I.e., in a Crusade.
7. Christ tells the parable of the prodigal son in Luke xv.11–32.

die in the attempt; but besides the burning jealousy and despair of my own heart, honour, mere humanity, demanded that I should fall rather than not destroy the machinations of the fiend.

The guests departed—the lights began to disappear; it was evident that the inhabitants of the villa were seeking repose. I hid myself among the trees—the garden grew desert—the gates were closed—I wandered round and came under a window—ah! well did I know the same!—a soft twilight glimmered in the room—the curtains were half withdrawn. It was the temple of innocence and beauty. Its magnificence was tempered, as it were, by the slight disarrangements occasioned by its being dwelt in, and all the objects scattered around displayed the taste of her who hallowed it by her presence. I saw her enter with a quick light step—I saw her approach the window—she drew back the curtain yet further, and looked out into the night. Its breezy freshness played among her ringlets, and wafted them from the transparent marble of her brow. She clasped her hands, she raised her eyes to Heaven. I heard her voice. Guido! she softly murmured, Mine own Guido! and then, as if overcome by the fulness of her own heart, she sank on her knees: —her upraised eyes—her negligent but graceful attitude—the beaming thankfulness that lighted up her face—oh, these are tame words! Heart of mine, thou imagest ever, though thou canst not portray, the celestial beauty of that child of light and love.

I heard a step—a quick firm step along the shady avenue. Soon I saw a cavalier, richly dressed, young and, methought, graceful to look on, advance.—I hid myself yet closer.—The youth approached; he paused beneath the window. She arose, and again looking out she saw him, and said—I cannot, no, at this distant time I cannot record her terms of soft silver tenderness; to me they were spoken, but they were replied to by him.

"I will not go," he cried: "here where you have been, where your memory glides like some Heaven-visiting ghost, I will pass the long hours till we meet, never, my Juliet, again, day or night, to part. But do thou, my love, retire; the cold morn and fitful breeze will make thy cheek pale, and fill with languor thy love-lighted eyes. Ah, sweetest! could I press one kiss upon them, I could, methinks, repose."

And then he approached still nearer, and methought he was about to clamber into her chamber. I had hesitated, not to terrify her; now I was no longer master of myself. I rushed forward—I threw myself on him—I tore him away—I cried, "O loathsome and foul-shaped wretch!"

I need not repeat epithets, all tending, as it appeared, to rail at a person I at present feel some partiality for. A shriek rose from Juliet's lips. I neither heard nor saw—I *felt* only mine enemy, whose throat I grasped, and my dagger's hilt; he struggled, but could not escape: at length hoarsely he breathed these words: "Do! —strike home! destroy this body—you will still live: may your life be long and merry!"

The descending dagger was arrested at the word, and he, feeling my hold relax, extricated himself and drew his sword, while the uproar in the house, and flying of torches from one room to the other, showed that soon we should be separated—and I—oh! far better die: so that he did not survive, I cared not. In the midst of my frenzy there was much calculation:—fall I might, and so that he did not survive, I cared not for the death-blow I might deal against myself. While still, therefore, he thought I paused, and while I saw the villanous resolve to take advantage of my hesitation, in the sudden thrust he made at me, I threw myself on his sword, and at the same moment plunged my dagger, with a true desperate aim, in his side. We fell together, rolling over each other, and the tide of blood that flowed from the gaping wound of each mingled on the grass. More I know not—I fainted.

Again I returned to life: weak almost to death, I found myself stretched upon a bed—Juliet was kneeling beside it. Strange! my first broken request was for a mirror. I was so wan and ghastly, that my poor girl hesitated, as she told me afterwards; but, by the mass! I thought myself a right proper youth when I saw the dear reflection of my own well-known features. I confess it is a weakness, but I avow it, I do entertain a considerable affection for the countenance and limbs I behold, whenever I look at a glass; and have more mirrors in my house, and consult them oftener than any beauty in Venice. Before you too much condemn me, permit me to say that no one better knows than I the value of his own body; no one, probably, except myself, ever having had it stolen from him.

Incoherently I at first talked of the dwarf and his crimes, and reproached Juliet for her too easy admission of his love. She thought me raving, as well she might, and yet it was some time before I could prevail on myself to admit that the Guido whose penitence had won her back for me was myself; and while I cursed bitterly the monstrous dwarf, and blest the well-directed blow that had deprived him of life, I suddenly checked myself when I heard her say—Amen! knowing that him whom she reviled was my very self. A little reflection taught me silence—a little practice enabled me to speak of that frightful night without any very excessive blunder. The wound I had given myself was no mockery of one—it was long before I recovered—and as the benevolent and generous Torella sat beside me, talking such wisdom as might win friends to repentance, and mine own dear Juliet hovered near me, administering to my wants, and cheering me by her smiles, the work of my bodily cure and mental reform went on together. I have never, indeed, wholly recovered my strength—my cheek is paler since—my person a little bent. Juliet sometimes ventures to allude bitterly to the malice that caused this change, but I kiss her on the moment, and tell her all is for the best. I am a fonder and more faithful husband—and true is this—but for that wound, never had I called her mine.

I did not revisit the sea-shore, nor seek for the fiend's treasure; yet, while I ponder on the past, I often think, and my confessor was not backward in favouring the idea, that it might be a good rather than an evil spirit, sent by my guardian angel, to show me the folly and misery of pride. So well at least did I learn this lesson, roughly taught as I was, that I am known now by all my friends and fellow-citizens by the name of Guido il Cortese.[8]

1831

8. "Guido the Courteous."

Romantic Lyric Poets

In the variety and magnitude of the lyric achievement by its major poets, the Romantic period ranks with Elizabethan and Jacobean times as one of the two greatest ages of the English lyric. It cannot approach the earlier period, however, in the number of second-order poets, many of them anonymous, who wrote excellent songs. The late 16th and early 17th centuries had been a great age of English vocal music, when there had been a pressing demand for poetic texts to match to the many exquisite airs and madrigals. In the Romantic period, however, lyric poems were mainly "art lyrics," written not to be sung but to be read, and no doubt the decline in the number of gifted amateurs who turned their hand to this form is related to the decline of England, through the 18th and 19th centuries, as a great singing nation.

This section represents Romantic poets good enough to have kept their places in all representative anthologies of lyric poems. It will be noted that there is no single, identifiable type of "Romantic lyric." The scope of these writers is very wide; it includes Thomas Moore's tinkling echoes of Cavalier gallantries, W. S. Landor's revitalization of the tradition of classic epigram, John Clare's achievement of Wordsworth's early aim (poems on common things, written in language really spoken by the peasant class), Scott's brilliant imitations of the popular ballad and George Darley's of Elizabethan song, Thomas Love Peacock's parody of the contemporary verse romance, the grotesque fantasy of Leigh Hunt's *The Fish, the Man, and the Spirit*, and the crossing of the Jacobean macabre with Gothic horror in the extraordinary songs of Thomas Lovell Beddoes.

WILLIAM LISLE BOWLES
(1762–1850)

Bowles was a clergyman who is noted in literature less for what he wrote than for his effect on other writers. In 1789 he published *Fourteen Sonnets*, which did much to revive that important poetic form, and also influenced the longer Romantic poems of the meditative description of a natural scene. And in 1806 he brought out an edition of Pope which derogated Pope's merits, starting a literary controversy in which Byron eloquently supported the virtues of the neoclassic poet.

In the first chapter of *Biographia Literaria*, Coleridge testifies to the extraordinary impact on his poetic sensibility and practice of Bowles's *Sonnets* of 1789; his enthusiasm was in considerable part shared by Wordsworth and Southey. Like *Frost at Midnight* and *Tintern Abbey*, Bowles's sonnets present a determinate speaker in a particular place; his opening description of the natural scene evokes a process of memory, meditation, and feeling, expressed in ordinary language, correlative with details of the scene, and sustained to the end of the poem.

To the River Itchin, Near Winton[1]

Itchin, when I behold thy banks again,
  Thy crumbling margin, and thy silver breast,
  On which the self-same tints still seem'd to rest,
Why feels my heart the shivering sense of pain?
Is it—that many a summer's day has past   5
  Since, in life's morn, I carolled on thy side?
  Is it—that oft, since then, my heart has sighed,
As Youth, and Hope's delusive gleams, flew fast?
  Is it—that those, who circled on thy shore,
  Companions of my youth, now meet no more?   10
Whate'er the cause, upon thy banks I bend,
  Sorrowing, yet feel such solace at my heart,
As at the meeting of some long-lost friend,
  From whom, in happier hours, we wept to part.

1789

1. Compare Coleridge's Sonnet *to the River Otter*.

SIR WALTER SCOTT
(1771–1832)

Sir Walter Scott (he was made a baronet in 1820) spent a great part of his childhood in the valley of the Tweed River, and at that time and in many later rides along the Border and in the Highlands he absorbed Scottish gossip, history, legend, song, and folklore. He was an inordinate reader with a capacious memory, and even while he was studying law in Edinburgh he spent a great deal of time reading medieval romances, history, travel books, and other documents, which provided him with the anti-quarian learning he later poured into his novels. In 1802–3 he published an important three-volume collection of popular ballads, *Minstrelsy of the Scottish Border*, sometimes piecing out the missing parts of the ballads from his own invention. Between 1805 and 1813 he wrote a series of metrical romances loosely modeled on medieval narrative forms—including *The Lay of the Last Minstrel, Marmion, The Lady of the Lake*—which made him for a time the most widely read of English poets. When his public was won over by Byron's more brilliant narrative romances, Scott turned to writing (until 1827, anonymously) his great series of historical novels. He made a large fortune, but went deeply into debt by building up the huge, pseudo-medieval estate of Abbotsford on the banks of the Tweed, where he attempted to live the antique life of a lord of the manor. In 1826 the failure of the printing firm of James Ballantyne (in which Scott was a silent partner) and of his publisher, Archibald Constable, plunged him into financial disaster, from which he struggled heroically all the rest of his life to extricate himself. Only after his death were his debts finally paid off, with money realized by the sale of his copyrights.

The Dreary Change is Scott's quiet and controlled version of the Wordsworthian theme of an apparent loss of glory in the landscape which is in fact a change in the mind of the observer. And in some of his lyrics deriving from the popular ballad and folk song, Scott (like Keats in *La Belle Dame Sans Merci*) captured from his originals the artistic values of understatement and terse suggestiveness.

The Dreary Change

> The sun upon the Weirdlaw Hill,
>   In Ettrick's vale, is sinking sweet;
> The westland wind is hush and still,
>   The lake lies sleeping at my feet.
> Yet not the landscape to mine eye   5
>   Bears those bright hues that once it bore;
> Though evening, with her richest dye,
>   Flames o'er the hills of Ettrick's shore.
>
> With listless look along the plain,
>   I see Tweed's silver current glide,   10
> And coldly mark the holy fane
>   Of Melrose rise in ruined pride.
> The quiet lake, the balmy air,
>   The hill, the stream, the tower, the tree—
> Are they still such as once they were?   15
>   Or is the dreary change in me?
>
> Alas, the warped and broken board,
>   How can it bear the painter's dye!
> The harp of strained and tuneless chord,
>   How to the minstrel's skill reply!   20
> To aching eyes each landscape lowers,
>   To feverish pulse each gale blows chill;
> And Araby's or Eden's bowers
>   Were barren as this moorland hill.

1817

Jock of Hazeldean[4]

> "Why weep ye by the tide, ladie?
>   Why weep ye by the tide?
> I'll wed ye to my youngest son,
>   And ye sall be his bride:

4. The first stanza is from a traditional Scottish ballad.

And ye sall be his bride, ladie,   5
    Sae comely to be seen"—
But ay she loot the tears down fa'
    For Jock of Hazeldean.

"Now let this willfu' grief be done,
    And dry that cheek so pale;   10
Young Frank is chief of Errington
    And lord of Langley Dale;
His step is first in peaceful ha',
    His sword in battle keen"—
But ay she loot the tears down fa'   15
    For Jock of Hazeldean.

"A chain of gold ye sall not lack,
    Nor braid to bind your hair;
Nor mettled hound, nor managed[5] hawk,
    Nor palfrey fresh and fair;   20
And you, the foremost o' them a',
    Shall ride our forest queen"—
But ay she loot the tears down fa'
    For Jock of Hazeldean.

The kirk was decked at morningtide,   25
    The tapers glimmered fair;
The priest and bridegroom wait the bride,
    And dame and knight are there.
They sought her baith by bower and ha';
    The ladie was not seen!   30
She's o'er the Border and awa'
    Wi' Jock of Hazeldean.

                                                    1816

Proud Maisie[6]

Proud Maisie is in the wood
    Walking so early;
Sweet Robin sits on the bush,
    Singing so rarely.

"Tell me, thou bonny bird,   5
    When shall I marry me?"—
"When six braw[7] gentlemen
    Kirkward shall carry ye."

"Who makes the bridal bed,
    Birdie, say truly?"—   10

5. Trained.   (Chapter 40).
6. Sung by crazy Madge Wildfire on her   7. Fine.
   deathbed in *The Heart of Midlothian*

"The gray-headed sexton
    That delves the grave duly.

"The glowworm o'er grave and stone
    Shall light thee steady,
The owl from the steeple sing,   15
    'Welcome, proud lady.' "

                          1818

ROBERT SOUTHEY
(1774–1843)

Time has dealt harshly with Robert Southey, for he is remembered mainly for his close association with poets greater than himself and for Byron's brilliant lampoons in *Don Juan* and *The Vision of Judgment*. He attended Oxford, was for a short time a fervent supporter of the French Revolution, and wrote an epic and two dramas inspired by that event. With Coleridge (who became his brother-in-law) he planned the frustrated "Pantisocracy" on the banks of the Susquehanna and collaborated on several poems. In 1803 he settled at Keswick in the Lake Country, within long walking distance of his friend Wordsworth; with advancing age, he settled into a Tory viewpoint more conservative than either Wordsworth's or Coleridge's. All his life a learned and hard-working professional writer, he produced thousands of pages of epic and shorter poems, history, essays, biographies, and anything else for which there was a market; he was awarded the laureateship in 1813.

The only Southey writings still widely read are a few lyrics, a beautifully lucid short *Life of Nelson* (1813), and—a piece so widely loved and often retold that it has lost its connection with its author and acquired the status of an anonymous "fairy tale"—the story of *The Three Bears*.

My Days Among the Dead Are Passed

My days among the dead are passed;
    Around me I behold,
Where'er these casual eyes are cast,
    The mighty minds of old;
My never-failing friends are they,   5
With whom I converse day by day.

With them I take delight in weal,
    And seek relief in woe;
And while I understand and feel
    How much to them I owe,   10
My cheeks have often been bedewed
With tears of thoughtful gratitude.

My thoughts are with the dead, with them
    I live in long-past years,
Their virtues love, their faults condemn,   15
    Partake their hopes and fears,
And from their lessons seek and find
Instruction with an humble mind.

My hopes are with the dead, anon
    My place with them will be,   20
And I with them shall travel on
    Through all futurity;
Yet leaving here a name, I trust,
That will not perish in the dust.

1818   1823

WALTER SAVAGE LANDOR
(1775–1864)

Landor was born well-to-do, and with a violently independent and combative temper: he quarreled with the authorities at Rugby and at Oxford,
with his wife and family, with servants and officials, with the governments of Europe (he was a Revolutionary sympathizer, and unlike most
of his literary contemporaries never wavered in his republicanism), and
with his neighbors, first in Wales and then in Italy; he was constantly
embroiled in expensive litigation. But in the course of his long life the
generous-hearted and outspoken poet also acquired many friends and admirers, ranging from Southey and Hazlitt in the Romantic generation to
Robert Browning, Charles Dickens, and Algernon Charles Swinburne
among the Victorians. He lived in Italy from 1815 to 1835. When he
returned to England he was lionized for a time as an active Romantic poet
when all the others were dead or silent, but a notorious outburst, which
led to court action, forced him in 1857 to take up once more his exile in
Italy, where he died in his 90th year.

Most of the writings of this greatly irascible man, whether in prose or
verse, have characteristics to which critics apply the terms "serene" and
"marmoreal." His best-known prose works are the numerous *Imaginary
Conversations* (1824–53), mainly between historical figures, and on literary, philosophic, and political topics. These have their strong admirers,
but they are written in a style which is so elevated and remote that they
sometimes suggest dialogues between heroic-sized Greek statues. He wrote
many long narrative and dramatic poems, of which the most durable is
the epic *Gebir*, published in the same year as *Lyrical Ballads* (1798). But
Landor's supreme achievement, in which he emulated Greek and Roman
models, is in the short lyric, usually an elegy or a courtly compliment
which is stripped down until it approximates an epigram. He is the master
of a form of verse very rare in English—the spare, elegant, and severely
formal utterance of lyric passion.

Mother, I Cannot Mind My Wheel

Mother, I cannot mind my wheel;
   My fingers ache, my lips are dry:
Oh! if you felt the pain I feel!
   But oh, who ever felt as I!

No longer could I doubt him true,   5
   All other men may use deceit;
He always said my eyes were blue,
   And often swore my lips were sweet.

1806

Rose Aylmer[1]

Ah, what avails the sceptered race,
   Ah, what the form divine!
What every virtue, every grace!
   Rose Aylmer, all were thine.

Rose Aylmer, whom these wakeful eyes   5
   May weep, but never see,
A night of memories and of sighs
   I consecrate to thee.

1806

The Three Roses[2]

When the buds began to burst,
Long ago, with Rose the First
I was walking; joyous then
Far above all other men,
Till before us up there stood   5
Britonferry's[3] oaken wood,
Whispering, *"Happy as thou art,*
Happiness and thou must part."
Many summers have gone by
Since a Second Rose and I   10
(Rose from that same stem) have told
This and other tales of old.
She upon her wedding day
Carried home my tenderest lay:[4]
From her lap I now have heard   15
Gleeful, chirping, Rose the Third.

1. Rose Aylmer was the daughter of the fourth Baron Aylmer (hence "the sceptered race," line 1). She became a friend of Landor's in 1794 at the age of 17, and died suddenly in Calcutta, six years later.

2. The first Rose was Rose Aylmer, the second her niece, and the third her grandniece.
3. In Wales.
4. Landor's epithalamion, *To a Bride.*

Not for *her* this hand of mine
Rhyme with nuptial wreath shall twine;
Cold and torpid it must lie,
Mute the tongue, and closed the eye.

20

1855

Past Ruined Ilion

Past ruined Ilion Helen lives,
    Alcestis rises from the shades;[5]
Verse calls them forth; 'tis verse that gives
    Immortal youth to mortal maids.

Soon shall oblivion's deepening veil   5
    Hide all the peopled hills you see,
The gay, the proud, while lovers hail
    These many summers you and me.

The tear for fading beauty check,
    For passing glory cease to sigh;   10
One form shall rise above the wreck,
    One name, Ianthe, shall not die.

1831

Dirce

Stand close around, ye Stygian set,[6]
    With Dirce in one boat conveyed!
Or Charon, seeing, may forget
    That he is old and she a shade.

1831

Twenty Years Hence

Twenty years hence my eyes may grow
If not quite dim, yet rather so,
Still yours from others they shall know
    Twenty years hence.

Twenty years hence though it may hap   5
That I be called to take a nap
In a cool cell where thunderclap
    Was never heard,

There breathe but o'er my arch of grass
A not too sadly sighed *Alas*,   10
And I shall catch, ere you can pass,
    That wingéd word.

1846

5. Helen of Troy ("Ilion"). Alcestis
gave her own life in exchange for that of
her husband, but was rescued from
Hades ("the shades") by Hercules.
6. I.e., the shades of the dead, ferried
by Charon over the river Styx to Hades.

Well I Remember How You Smiled

Well I remember how you smiled
  To see me write your name upon
The soft sea-sand. . . "O! *what a child!*
  You think you're writing upon stone!"
I have since written what no tide   5
  Shall ever wash away, what men
Unborn shall read o'er ocean wide
  And find Ianthe's name again.

1863

THOMAS MOORE
(1779–1852)

Although he was the Irish Catholic son of a Dublin grocer, Tom Moore became the fashionable versifier of Regency England. His *Irish Melodies*, published between 1807 and 1834 with accompanying music (some of the tunes were by Moore himself), were an immense success, and for many years his Irish wit, charm, liberalism, and singing voice made him a brilliant figure in literary and social circles, especially among the aristocratic Whig reformers. The same qualities made him one of Byron's closest friends. He wrote numerous satires, lampoons, and prose pieces. He is chiefly remembered, however, for *Lalla Rookh* (1817), written during the vogue for Oriental verse romances, which achieved a great European success; his fine *Life of Byron* (1830); and a handful of songs—most of them in the tradition of amatory gallantry that goes back to the 17th-century Cavaliers—which transcend the triviality, prettiness, and easy pathos of his lyric standard, and have won their way into that repertory which is sung on a social evening around the piano.

Believe Me, If All Those Endearing Young Charms

Believe me, if all those endearing young charms,
  Which I gaze on so fondly today,
Were to change by tomorrow, and fleet in my arms,
  Like fairy-gifts fading away,
Thou wouldst still be adored, as this moment thou art,   5
  Let thy loveliness fade as it will,
And around the dear ruin each wish of my heart
  Would entwine itself verdantly still.

It is not while beauty and youth are thine own,
    And thy checks unprofaned by a tear   10
That the fervor and faith of a soul can be known,
    To which time will but make thee more dear;
No, the heart that has truly loved never forgets,
    But as truly loves on to the close,
As the sunflower turns on her god, when he sets,   15
    The same look which she turned when he rose.

                                 1808

The Harp That Once Through Tara's Halls[1]

The harp that once through Tara's halls
    The soul of music shed,
Now hangs as mute on Tara's walls
    As if that soul were fled.—
So sleeps the pride of former days,   5
    So glory's thrill is o'er,
And hearts that once beat high for praise
    Now feel that pulse no more.

No more to chiefs and ladies bright
    The harp of Tara swells;   10
The chord alone that breaks at night
    Its tale of ruin tells.
Thus Freedom now so seldom wakes,
    The only throb she gives,
Is when some heart indignant breaks,   15
    To show that still she lives.

                                 1834

The Time I've Lost in Wooing

The time I've lost in wooing,
In watching and pursuing
    The light that lies
    In woman's eyes,
Has been my heart's undoing.   5
Though Wisdom oft has sought me,
I scorned the lore she brought me,
    My only books
    Were woman's looks,
And folly's all they've taught me.   10

---

1. Tara, northwest of Dublin, was capital of Ireland during the Middle Ages, when that country was a great center of European civilization and learning.

Her smile when Beauty granted,
I hung with gaze enchanted,
    Like him, the sprite,[2]
    Whom maids by night
Oft meet in glen that's haunted.   15
Like him, too, Beauty won me,
But while her eyes were on me;
    If once their ray
    Was turned away,
Oh! winds could not outrun me.   20

And are those follies going?
And is my proud heart growing
    Too cold or wise
    For brilliant eyes
Again to set it glowing?   25
No, vain, alas! th' endeavor
From bonds so sweet to sever;
    Poor Wisdom's chance
    Against a glance
Is now as weak as ever.   30

                                          1834

2. The Irish fairy; he can be controlled by mortals only when their eyes are
fixed on him.

LEIGH HUNT
(1784–1859)

James Henry Leigh Hunt was an impulsive, warm-hearted, but improvident man, who begot a large family, was in constant financial difficulties,
and often fell back on the charity of his friends. But however inept in
managing his personal affairs, Hunt was a fighting liberal journalist. With
his brother John he began the *Examiner*, a weekly periodical which ran
for fourteen years as the most formidable opponent of the oppressive
Tory government. In 1812 the brothers were fined and imprisoned for denouncing the Prince Regent (later George IV) as a liar and "a fat
Adonis of fifty." Leigh Hunt spent two rather comfortable years in jail,
living with his family and free to write and receive visits from his friends
and political admirers. In 1822 he took his family to Pisa to join Shelley
and Byron in establishing a quarterly, the *Liberal*, but the drowning of
Shelley and Byron's impatience with his collaborator brought the periodical to a close after only four issues. Back in England, Hunt carried on a
great variety of activities through a long literary career, and before he died
gained the friendship and somewhat qualified esteem of Browning, Thomas
Carlyle, and Dickens.

As an informal essayist Hunt is copious, relaxed, and often engaging; but
he was overshadowed by his great prose contemporaries, Lamb, Hazlitt, and

De Quincey. He was a voluminous reviewer and critic. His theatrical criticism is the best surviving record of the day-to-day popular theater; his literary criticism, while admirable for the sensitive taste and generosity with which he recognized and championed unpopular new poets, especially Shelley and Keats, lacks the theoretical penetration and the distinction which characterized the critical writings of Coleridge and Hazlitt. Hunt also undertook a variety of poems, many of them on Italian and classical themes; the most ambitious, *The Story of Rimini* (1816), is written in loose and freely running couplets, and treats a serious theme in an incongruously arch and familiar style. For a short time this poem strongly influenced Hunt's young disciple, John Keats, who caught from it the relaxed meter and lush sensuousness that mar his early poems and thus gave some grounds for John Gibson Lockhart's grouping of Keats with Hunt in his brutal attack on the lower-class vulgarity of the "Cockney School of Poetry" in *Blackwood's Magazine* (1817).

The Fish, the Man, and the Spirit

TO A FISH

You strange, astonished-looking, angle-faced,
Dreary-mouthed, gaping wretches of the sea,
Gulping salt-water everlastingly,
Cold-blooded, though with red your blood be graced,
And mute, though dwellers in the roaring waste;   5
And you, all shapes beside, that fishy be—
Some round, some flat, some long, all devilry,
Legless, unloving, infamously chaste—

O scaly, slippery, wet, swift, staring wights,
What is't ye do? what life lead? eh, dull goggles?   10
How do ye vary your vile days and nights?
How pass your Sundays? Are ye still but joggles
In ceaseless wash? Still nought but gapes, and bites,
And drinks, and stares, diversified with boggles?[1]

A FISH ANSWERS

Amazing monster! that, for aught I know,   15
With the first sight of thee didst make our race
Forever stare! Oh flat and shocking face,
Grimly divided from the breast below!
Thou that on dry land horribly dost go
With a split body and most ridiculous pace,   20
Prong after prong, disgracer of all grace,
Long-useless-finned, haired, upright, unwet, slow!

O breather of unbreathable, sword-sharp air,
How canst exist? How bear thyself, thou dry
And dreary sloth? What particle canst share   25

1. Sudden movements of alarm.

Of the only blessed life, the watery?
I sometimes see of ye an actual *pair*
Go by! linked fin by fin! most odiously.

THE FISH TURNS INTO A MAN, AND THEN INTO A
SPIRIT, AND AGAIN SPEAKS

Indulge thy smiling scorn, if smiling still,
O man! and loathe, but with a sort of love;   30
For difference must its use by difference prove,
And, in sweet clang, the spheres with music fill.
One of the spirits am I, that at his will
Live in whate'er has life—fish, eagle, dove—
No hate, no pride, beneath nought, nor above,   35
A visitor of the rounds of God's sweet skill.

Man's life is warm, glad, sad, 'twixt loves and graves,
Boundless in hope, honored with pangs austere,
Heaven-gazing; and his angel-wings he craves:
The fish is swift, small-needing, vague yet clear,   40
A cold, sweet, silver life, wrapped in round waves,
Quickened with touches of transporting fear.

                                                 1836

Rondeau[2]

Jenny kissed me when we met,
    Jumping from the chair she sat in;
Time, you thief, who love to get
    Sweets into your list, put that in:
Say I'm weary, say I'm sad,   5
    Say that health and wealth have missed me,
Say I'm growing old, but add,
    Jenny kissed me.

                                                 1838

2. Jenny is said to be Mrs. Jane Welsh   the rondeau, an elaborate French verse
Carlyle. This is a shortened form of   form which normally has fifteen lines.

THOMAS LOVE PEACOCK
(1785–1866)

Peacock, the son of a London businessman, had a position with the East
India Company which allowed him leisure to devote to his writing. Although he was himself a poet, his *Four Ages of Poetry* (1820) was a sly
comment on the excesses of his Romantic contemporaries in the ironic
guise of a history of the decline of poetry from its golden past; it evoked

from his close friend Shelley *The Defense of Poetry* by way of refutation. Peacock's finest achievements are his inimitable novels—including *Headlong Hall* (1816), *Melincourt* (1817), *Nightmare Abbey* (1818), and *Crotchet Castle* (1831)—in which he gathers a group of argumentative eccentrics in a country house and sets them to talking. His protagonists represent extreme or bigoted or visionary points of view on all sides of the important topics of the day; among them are caricatures of his great contemporaries, Wordsworth, Coleridge, Southey, Byron, as well as his friend Shelley—who took no offense. The novels also included satiric songs. The one reprinted here is taken from *The Misfortunes of Elphin* (1829); it explodes the Romantic vogue of the long, pseudohistorical metrical romance in forty devastating lines.

The War Song of Dinas Vawr

The mountain sheep are sweeter,
But the valley sheep are fatter;
We therefore deemed it meeter
To carry off the latter.
We made an expedition;   5
We met a host, and quelled it;
We forced a strong position,
And killed the men who held it.

On Dyfed's richest valley,
Where herds of kine were browsing,   10
We made a mighty sally,
To furnish our carousing.
Fierce warriors rushed to meet us;
We met them, and o'erthrew them:
They struggled hard to beat us;   15
But we conquered them, and slew them.

As we drove our prize at leisure,
The king marched forth to catch us:
His rage surpassed all measure,
But his people could not match us.   20
He fled to his hall pillars;
And, ere our force we led off,
Some sacked his house and cellars,
While others cut his head off.

We there, in strife bewild'ring,   25
Spilt blood enough to swim in:
We orphaned many children,
And widowed many women.
The eagles and the ravens

We glutted with our foemen;   30
The heroes and the cravens,
The spearmen and the bowmen.

We brought away from battle,
And much their land bemoaned them,
Two thousand head of cattle,   35
And the head of him who owned them:
Ednyfed, king of Dyfed,
His head was borne before us;
His wine and beasts supplied our feasts,
And his overthrow, our chorus.   40

                                                         1829

JOHN CLARE
(1793–1864)

John Clare was the nearest thing to the artless "natural poet" for whom primitivists had been searching ever since the mid-18th century. An earlier and far greater peasant poet, Robert Burns, had managed to acquire a solid liberal education; Clare, however, was born at Helpston, a Northamptonshire village, of a field laborer who was barely literate and a mother who was entirely illiterate, and himself obtained only sufficient schooling to enable him to read and write. Although he was a sickly and fearful child, he had to work hard in the field, where he found himself composing verse "for downright pleasure in giving vent to my feelings." In 1820 publication of his *Poems Descriptive of Rural Life* attracted critical attention, and on a trip to London he was made much of by leading writers of the day. But his celebrity soon dimmed, and his three later books of verse were failures. Under these and other disappointments his mind gave way in 1837, and he spent almost all the rest of his life in an asylum. The place was for him a refuge as well as a confinement, for he was treated kindly, allowed to wander about the countryside, and encouraged to go on writing his verses; some of his best achievements are the poems composed in his madness.

Clare did not, of course, write independently of a poetic tradition, for he had studied the poetry of James Thomson, Milton, Wordsworth, and Coleridge. But he managed to stay true to his own experience of unspectacular country sights and customs and to capture in his verse the country idiom. Clare's homely mouse, in the poem below, is a bit of pure rustic impressionism in a way that even Robert Burns's moralized mouse is not. And a small proportion of Clare's introspective asylum-poems achieve so haunting a poignancy and are spoken in so quietly distinctive a voice that they have made the great mass of mainly humdrum manuscripts he left at his death an exciting place of discovery for recent editors.

Mouse's Nest

I found a ball of grass among the hay
And progged[1] it as I passed and went away;
And when I looked I fancied something stirred,
And turned again and hoped to catch the bird—
When out an old mouse bolted in the wheats   5
With all her young ones hanging at her teats;
She looked so odd and so grotesque to me,
I ran and wondered what the thing could be,
And pushed the knapweed[2] bunches where I stood;
Then the mouse hurried from the craking[3] brood.   10
The young ones squeaked, and as I went away
She found her nest again among the hay.
The water o'er the pebbles scarce could run
And broad old cesspools[4] glittered in the sun.

ca. 1835–37   1935

I Am

I am—yet what I am, none cares or knows;
    My friends forsake me like a memory lost:
I am the self-consumer of my woes—
    They rise and vanish in oblivions host,
Like shadows in love frenzied stifled throes   5
    And yet I am, and live—like vapours tossed

Into the nothingness of scorn and noise,
    Into the living sea of waking dreams,
Where there is neither sense of life or joys,
    But the vast shipwreck of my life's esteems;   10
Even the dearest that I love the best
    Are strange—nay, rather, stranger than the rest.

I long for scenes where man hath never trod
    A place where woman never smiled or wept
There to abide with my Creator God,   15
    And sleep as I in childhood sweetly slept,
Untroubling and untroubled where I lie
    The grass below, above, the vaulted sky.

1842–64   1848

1. Prodded.
2. A plant with knobs of purple flowers.
3. Squawking.
4. Low spots where water has collected.

Clock a Clay[1]

In the cowslip's peeps[2] I lie
Hidden from the buzzing fly
While green grass beneath me lies
Pearled wi' dew like fishes' eyes
Here I lie a Clock a clay   5
Waiting for the time o' day

While grassy forests quake surprise
And the wild wind sobs and sighs
My gold home rocks as like to fall
On its pillar green and tall   10
When the pattering rain drives by
Clock a Clay keeps warm and dry

Day by day and night by night
All the week I hide from sight
In the cowslips peeps I lie   15
In rain and dew still warm and dry
Day and night and night and day
Red black spotted clock a clay

My home it shakes in wind and showers
Pale green pillar topped wi' flowers   20
Bending at the wild wind's breath
Till I touch the grass beneath
Here still I live lone clock a clay
Watching for the time of day

ca. 1848   1873

Song

I peeled bits of straw and I got switches too
From the gray peeling willow as idlers do,
And I switched at the flies as I sat all alone
Till my flesh, blood, and marrow was turned to dry bone.
My illness was love, though I knew not the smart,   5
But the beauty of love was the blood of my heart.
Crowded places, I shunned them as noises too rude

---

1. The ladybird, or ladybug. The sixth and last lines allude to the children's game of telling the hour by the number of taps it takes to make the ladybird fly away home.
2. Cf. the opening lines of Ariel's song in Act V of Shakespeare's *Tempest*: "Where the bee sucks, there suck I: / In a cowslip's bell I lie." "Peeps": i.e., pips —single blossoms of flowers growing in a cluster. The cowslip is a yellow primrose.

And fled to the silence of sweet solitude,
Where the flower in green darkness buds, blossoms, and fades,
Unseen of all shepherds and flower-loving maids—   10
The hermit bees find them but once and away;
There I'll bury alive and in silence decay.

I looked on the eyes of fair woman too long,
Till silence and shame stole the use of my tongue:
When I tried to speak to her I'd nothing to say,   15
So I turned myself round and she wandered away.
When she got too far off, why, I'd something to tell,
So I sent sighs behind her and walked to my cell.
Willow switches I broke and peeled bits of straws,
Ever lonely in crowds, in nature's own laws—   20
My ballroom the pasture, my music the bees,
My drink was the fountain, my church the tall trees.
Who ever would love or be tied to a wife
When it makes a man mad all the days of his life?

1842–64   1920

Song [Secret Love]

    I hid my love when young while I
    Couldn't bear the buzzing of a fly
    I hid my love to my despite
    Till I could not bear to look at light
    I dare not gaze upon her face   5
    But left her memory in each place
    Where ere I saw a wild flower lie
    I kissed and bade my love goodbye

    I met her in the greenest dells
    Where dew drops pearl the wood bluebells   10
    The lost breeze kissed her bright blue eye
    The bee kissed and went singing by
    A sunbeam found a passage there
    A gold chain round her neck so fair
    As secret as the wild bee's song   15
    She lay there all the summer long

    I hid my love in field and town
    Till e'en the breeze would knock me down
    The bees seemed singing ballads o'er
    The fly's buss[1] turned a Lion's roar   20
    And even silence found a tongue
    To haunt me all the summer long
    The riddle nature could not prove
    Was nothing else but secret love

1842–64   1920

1. Buzz; it may also mean "kiss."

An Invite to Eternity

Wilt thou go with me sweet maid
Say maiden wilt thou go with me
Through the valley depths of shade
Of night and dark obscurity
Where the path hath lost its way   5
Where the sun forgets the day
Where there's nor life nor light to see
Sweet maiden wilt thou go with me

Where stones will turn to flooding streams
Where plains will rise like ocean waves   10
Where life will fade like visioned dreams
And mountains darken into caves
Say maiden wilt thou go with me
Through this sad non-identity
Where parents live and are forgot   15
And sisters live and know us not

Say maiden wilt thou go with me
In this strange death of life to be
To live in death and be the same
Without this life or home or name   20
At once to be and not to be
That was and is not—yet to see
Things pass like shadows—and the sky
Above, below, around us lie.

The land of shadows wilt thou trace   25
And look nor know each other's face
The present mixed with reasons gone
And past and present all as one
Say maiden can thy life be led
To join the living with the dead   30
Then trace thy footsteps on with me
We're wed to one eternity
1842–64   1920

A Vision

I lost the love of heaven above
I spurned the lust of earth below
I felt the sweets of fancied love
And hell itself my only foe

I lost earth's joys but felt the glow   5
Of heaven's flame abound in me

Till loveliness and I did grow
The bard of immortality

I loved but woman fell away   10
I hid me from her faded fame
I snatched the sun's eternal ray
And wrote till earth was but a name

In every language upon earth
On every shore, o'er every sea,
I gave my name immortal birth,   15
And kept my spirit with the free

1844   1924

GEORGE DARLEY
(1795–1846)

Darley, an Irish mathematician, was one of the poets who figured in the
"Elizabethan revival" of the later Romantic period. He wrote prose tales,
dramatic criticism, and various dramas in the style of Shakespeare's contemporaries. His long work, *Nepenthe* (1835), includes most of his best
lyrics, from which the first of the following poems has been selected; the
last poem is from *Syren Songs* (1837). The distinctive charm of Darley's
lyrics is that they recall, without merely mimicking, their Elizabethan and
17th-century originals. The stately lyric *It Is Not Beauty I Demand* was for
years printed in Palgrave's *Golden Treasury* as a poem of the Caroline
period.

The Phoenix[1]

O blest unfabled Incense Tree,
That burns in glorious Araby,
With red scent chalicing the air,
Till earth-life grow Elysian there!

Half-buried to her flaming breast   5
In this bright tree, she makes her nest,
Hundred-sunned Phoenix! when she must
Crumble at length to hoary dust!

Her gorgeous deathbed! her rich pyre
Burnt up with aromatic fire!   10
Her urn, sight high from spoiler men!
Her birthplace when self-born again!

---

1. A legendary bird: only one exists at a time; it dies periodically, singing, in aromatic flames, and is reborn from the ashes.

The mountainless green wilds among,
Here ends she her unechoing song!
With amber tears and odorous sighs   15
Mourned by the desert where she dies!

                                                      1835

It Is Not Beauty I Demand

It is not Beauty I demand,
    A crystal brow, the moon's despair,
Nor the snow's daughter, a white hand,
    Nor mermaid's yellow pride of hair.

Tell me not of your starry eyes,   5
    Your lips that seem on roses fed,
Your breasts where Cupid trembling lies,
    Nor sleeps for kissing of his bed.

A bloomy pair of vermeil cheeks,
    Like Hebe's in her ruddiest hours,   10
A breath that softer music speaks
    Than summer winds a-wooing flowers.

These are but gauds; nay, what are lips?
    Coral beneath the ocean-stream,
Whose brink when your adventurer sips   15
    Full oft he perisheth on them.

And what are cheeks but ensigns oft
    That wave hot youth to fields of blood?
Did Helen's breast though ne'er so soft,
    Do Greece or Ilium any good?   20

Eyes can with baleful ardor burn,
    Poison can breath that erst perfumed,
There's many a white hand holds an urn
    With lovers' hearts to dust consumed.

For crystal brows—there's naught within,   25
    They are but empty cells for pride;
He who the Syren's hair would win
    Is mostly strangled in the tide.

Give me, instead of beauty's bust,
    A tender heart, a loyal mind,   30
Which with temptation I could trust,
    Yet never linked with error find.

One in whose gentle bosom I
    Could pour my secret heart of woes,
Like the care-burdened honey-fly   35
    That hides his murmurs in the rose.

My earthly comforter! whose love
So indefeasible might be,
That when my spirit won above
Hers could not stay for sympathy.

40

1828

The Mermaidens' Vesper Hymn

Troop home to silent grots and caves!
Troop home! and mimic as you go
The mournful winding of the waves
Which to their dark abysses flow.

At this sweet hour, all things beside
In amorous pairs to covert creep;
The swans that brush the evening tide
Homeward in snowy couples keep.

5

In his green den the murmuring seal
Close by his sleek companion lies;
While singly we to bedward steal,
And close in fruitless sleep our eyes.

10

In bowers of love men take their rest,
In loveless bowers we sigh alone,
With bosom friends are others blest—
But we have none! but we have none!

15

1837

THOMAS LOVELL BEDDOES
(1803–1849)

Beddoes was the most gifted poet of the late Romantic "Elizabethan revival." By profession a physician and anatomist, he studied at Oxford and Göttingen, then spent most of his mature life as a solitary wanderer among the universities of Germany and Switzerland, involving himself in various radical movements. His letters contain shrewd and caustic criticism of his own and others' writings, but also reveal an eccentricity and a despondency that sometimes verge on madness. His only two published volumes, *The Improvisatore* (1821) and *The Bride's Tragedy* (1822), he wrote while still an undergraduate at Oxford. His later writings consist mainly of massive fragments of drama and romance. The major work was *Death's Jest-Book, or The Fool's Tragedy*, begun in the later 1820's, incessantly patched and revised for the next quarter century, and left still unfinished at his death. A nightmarish drama of murder, disguise, revenge, and ghosts, it reveals that his chief models were Jacobean tragedy, English and German terror tales of the "Gothic" vogue, and the more fantastic among

the writings of Shelley. Beddoes' lyrics, many of which were incorporated
in his dramas, specialize in the sinister and the grotesquely comic effect,
and at their best achieve an exquisite movement and a thrilling felicity
of unexpected phrasing. Beddoes, like his Jacobean masters, John Webster
and Cyril Tourneur—and his contemporary master, Shelley—was much
obsessed by death, as a thing at once terrible and dear. He ended his own
life, after several unsuccessful attempts, by taking poison.

Song

How many times do I love thee, dear?
　　Tell me how many thoughts there be
　　　　In the atmosphere
　　　　Of a new-fall'n year,
　　Whose white and sable hours appear　　　　　　5
　　The latest flake of Eternity—
So many times do I love thee, dear.

How many times do I love again?
　　Tell me how many beads there are
　　　　In a silver chain
　　　　Of evening rain,　　　　　　　　　　10
　　Unraveled from the tumbling main,
　　　And threading the eye of a yellow star—
So many times do I love again.

1824　　　　　　　　　　　　　　　　　　　　1851

Song

Old Adam, the carrion crow,
　　The old crow of Cairo;
He sat in the shower, and let it flow
　　Under his tail and over his crest;
　　　And through every feather　　　　　　5
　　Leaked the wet weather;
And the bough swung under his nest;
　　For his beak it was heavy with marrow.
　　　Is that the wind dying? O no;
　　　It's only two devils, that blow　　　　　10
　　Through a murderer's bones, to and fro,
　　　In the ghosts' moonshine.

Ho! Eve, my gray carrion wife,
　　When we have supped on kings' marrow,
Where shall we drink and make merry our life?　　15
　　Our nest it is queen Cleopatra's skull,

'Tis cloven and cracked,
And battered and hacked,
But with tears of blue eyes it is full:
Let us drink then, my raven of Cairo.   20
    Is that the wind dying? O no;
    It's only two devils, that blow
    Through a murderer's bones, to and fro,
        In the ghosts' moonshine.

1825–28   1849–50

The Phantom Wooer

A ghost, that loved a lady fair,
Ever in the starry air
    Of midnight at her pillow stood;
And, with a sweetness skies above
The luring words of human love,   5
    Her soul the phantom wooed.
Sweet and sweet is their poisoned note,
The little snakes of silver throat,
In mossy skulls that nest and lie,
Ever singing, "Die, oh! die."   10

Young soul put off your flesh, and come
With me into the quiet tomb,
    Our bed is lovely, dark, and sweet;
The earth will swing us, as she goes,
Beneath our coverlid of snows,   15
    And the warm leaden sheet.
Dear and dear is their poisoned note,
The little snakes of silver throat,
In mossy skulls that nest and lie,
Ever singing, "Die, oh! die."   20

1844–48   1849–50

The Victorian Age

(1832-1901)

1832:   The First Reform Bill.
1837:   Victoria becomes queen.
1846:   The Corn Laws repealed.
1851:   The Great Exhibition in London.
1859:   Charles Darwin's *Origin of Species* published.
1870–71: Franco-Prussian War.
1901:   Death of Victoria.

AN AGE OF EXPANSION

In 1897 Mark Twain was visiting London during the Diamond Jubilee celebrations honoring the 60th anniversary of Queen Victoria's coming to the throne. "British history is two thousand years old," Twain observed, "and yet in a good many ways the world has moved farther ahead since the Queen was born than it moved in all the rest of the two thousand put together." And if the whole world had "moved" during that long lifetime and reign of Victoria's, it was in her own country itself that the expansionist movement was most marked and dramatic, a movement that brought England to its highest point of development as a world power.

In the 18th century the pivotal city of Western civilization had been Paris; by the second half of the 19th century this center of influence had shifted to London, a city which expanded from about 2 million inhabitants when Victoria came to the throne to 6.5 million at the time of her death. The rapid growth of London is one of the many indications of the most important development of the age: the shift from a way of life based on the ownership of land to a modern urban economy based on trade and manufacturing. "We have been living, as it were, the life of three hundred years in thirty" was the impression formed by Dr. Thomas Arnold during the early stages of England's industrialization. By the end of the century—after the resources of steam power had been more fully exploited for fast railways and iron ships, for looms, printing presses, and farmers' combines, and after the introduction of the telegraph, intercontinental cable, anesthetics, and universal compulsory education—a late Victorian could look back with astonishment on these developments during his lifetime. Walter Besant, one of these late Victorians, observed that so completely transformed were "the mind and habits of the ordinary Englishman" by 1897, "that he would not, could he see him, recognize his own grandfather."

Because England was the first country to become industrialized, her transformation was an especially painful one, but being first had a compensation: it was profitable. An early start enabled England to capture markets all over the globe. Her cotton and other manufactured products were exported in English ships, a merchant fleet whose size was without parallel in other countries. The profits gained from her trade led also to extensive capital investments in all continents (especially in the underdeveloped sections of her own Empire) so that after England had become the world's workshop, London became, from 1870 on, the world's banker.

The effect of these developments on Victorian character has been described by the historian David Thomson. The period, he says in *England and the Nineteenth Century* (1950), "is one of strenuous activity and dynamic change, of ferment of ideas and recurrent social unrest, of great inventiveness and expansion." And he adds:

> The whole meaning of Victorian England is lost if it is thought of as a country of stuffy complacency and black top-hatted moral priggery. Its frowsty crinolines and dingy hansom cabs, its gas-lit houses and overornate draperies, concealed a people engaged in a tremendously exciting adventure—the daring experiment of fitting industrial man into a democratic society. Their failures, faults, and ludicrous shortcomings are all too apparent: but the days when Mr. Lytton Strachey could afford to laugh at the foibles of the "Eminent Victorians" have passed, and we must ask ourselves the question of whether we *can* laugh at our great-grandfathers' attempts to solve problems to which we have so far failed to find an answer. At least the Victorians found greatness, stability, and peace and the whole world, marveling, envied them for it.

The reactions of Victorian writers to the fast-paced expansion of England were various. Thomas Babington Macaulay (1800–59) relished the spectacle as wholly delightful. During the prosperous 1850's Macaulay's essays and histories, with their recitations of the statistics of industrial growth, constituted a Hymn to Progress as well as a celebration of the superior qualities of the English people—"the greatest and most highly civilized people that ever the world saw." And later in the century there were lesser jingoists whose writings confidently pointed out the reasons for further national self-congratulation. More representative, perhaps, was Tennyson, whose capacity to relish industrial change was only sporadic. Much of the time he felt instead that leadership in commerce and industry was being paid for at a terrible price in human happiness. In their experience a so-called "progress" had been gained only by abandoning the traditional rhythms of life and traditional patterns of human relationships which had sustained mankind for centuries. In the melancholy poetry of Matthew Arnold this note is often struck:

> For what wears out the life of mortal men?
> 'Tis that from change to change their being rolls;
> 'Tis that repeated shocks, again, again,
> Exhaust the energy of strongest souls.

An occasional ride on a roller coaster may be exhilarating, but to be chained aboard for a lifetime is a nightmare.

Accounts of the Victorian state of mind can be wildly contradictory when interpreters focus on one side of this set of attitudes and exclude the other. Thus Betty Askwith could assert in *The Lyttletons: A Family Chronicle* (1975) that during the period from 1830 to 1880 "the educated classes of England believed that they had the answer to everything * * * It was an age of certainty and of faith only paralleled by the great cathedral-building epoch of the Middle Ages." But according to Carol T. Christ (*The Finer Optic*, also 1975), this same period was one of "agony and confusion. The Victorians felt * * * a desperate pessimism based on the fear of * * * experience with no meaning beyond itself." To restore focus, it can be said that although most perceptive Victorians did share a sense of satisfaction in the industrial and political preeminence of England during the period, they also suffered from an anxious sense of something lost, a sense too of being displaced persons in a world made alien by technological changes which had been exploited too quickly for the adaptive powers of the human psyche. In this respect, as in many others, the Victorians may remind us of their English-speaking counterparts in America during the second half of the 20th century who have taken over a leading position in the Western world with similar mixed feelings of satisfaction and anxiety.

DIFFERENT CRITICAL REACTIONS TO THE VICTORIAN AGE

To suggest a similarity between the Victorians and ourselves (a similarity, not an identity) seems a necessary preliminary for a reading of their writings. In the earlier decades of the 20th century such an understanding perspective was conspicuously absent. It was then the fashion for most literary critics to treat their Victorian predecessors as somewhat absurd creatures with whose way of life they had little in common. Lytton Strachey's skillful puncturing of over-inflated Victorian balloons is characteristic of the attitudes of the Georgian period (1911–36). A subtler example occurs in Virginia Woolf's *Orlando*, a delightful fictionalized survey of English literature from Elizabethan times to 1928, in which the Victorians are presented in terms of dampness, rain, and proliferating vegetation:

> Ivy grew in unparalleled profusion. Houses that had been of bare stone were smothered in greenery. * * * And just as the ivy and the evergreen rioted in the damp earth outside, so did the same fertility show itself within. The life of the average woman was a succession of childbirths. * * * Giant cauliflowers towered deck above deck till they rivaled * * * the elm trees themselves. Hens laid incessantly eggs of no special tint. * * * The whole sky itself as it spread wide above the British Isles was nothing but a vast feather bed.

This witty description not only identifies a distinguishing quality of Victorian life and literature—creative energy—but it reveals that the author of the passage did not admire such creative energy. In fact, she felt terrified by it as if it might smother her. Woolf was the daughter of Sir Leslie Stephen (1832–1904), himself an eminent Victorian. Growing up under such towering shadows, she and her generation had to mock their predecessors.

The Georgian reaction against the Victorians is now only a matter of the history of taste, but its aftereffects still sometimes crop up when the term "Victorian" is employed in an exclusively pejorative sense. Most of us would rather be called a thief than a prude, and if the connotation of "Victorian" is narrowed down to suggest "prude" and nothing else, we remain seriously hampered in enjoying to the full what the Victorian writers accomplished. Sympathy may not be essential, but condescension is fatal to understanding. Happily, the note of condescension has all but disappeared from critical studies of more recent date. Indeed the pendulum has swung far to the other side. In *In Bluebeard's Castle* (1971) the critic George Steiner notes how most of us are affected by images of the past which are "often as highly structured and selective as myths," in particular an image of a lost garden of Eden. For Steiner, the lost Eden is located in the golden age of Victoria, "that great summer" of human civilization. "Our sensibility locates that garden in England and western Europe between ca. the 1820's and 1915." Steiner's evaluation would have astounded earlier 20th-century critics to whom Victorian England seemed not Eden but Hell.

But to revert from image and myth to history leads to a second difficulty about the term "Victorian." For a period almost 70 years in length we can hardly expect our generalizations to be uniformly applicable. As a preliminary corrective it is helpful to subdivide the age into three phases: Early Victorian (1832–48); Mid-Victorian (1848–70); Late Victorian (1870–1901). It may also be convenient to subdivide the Late phase by considering the final decade, the 90's, as a bridge between two centuries.

THE EARLY PERIOD (1832–48): A TIME OF TROUBLES

The early phase has been sometimes characterized as the Time of Troubles. In 1832 the passing of a Reform Bill had seemed to satisfy many of the demands of the middle classes, who were gradually taking over control of England's economy. The bill extended the right to vote to all men owning property worth ten pounds or more in annual rent. In effect the voting public hereafter included the lower middle classes but not the working classes (the latter had to wait their turn until 1867 when a second Reform Bill was passed). Even more important than the extension of the franchise was the abolition in 1832 of an archaic electoral system whereby some of the new industrial cities were unrepresented in Parliament while "rotten boroughs" (communities which had become depopulated) elected the nominees of the local squire. Because it broke up the monopoly of power that the conservative landowners had so long enjoyed (the Tory party had been in office almost continuously from 1783 until 1830), the Reform Bill represents the beginning of a new age. Yet this celebrated piece of legislation could hardly be expected to solve all the economic, social, and political problems that had been building up while England was developing into a modern democratic and industrialized state. In the early 1840's a severe depression, with widespread unemployment, led to rioting. Even without the provocation of unemployment, conditions in the new industrial and coal-mining areas were sufficiently inflammatory to create fears of revolution. Workers and their families in the slums of such cities as Manchester lived like packs of rats in a sewer, and the conditions under which women and children toiled in mines and factories were unimaginably brutal. Elizabeth Barrett's poem *The Cry of the Children* (1843) may strike us as hysterical exaggeration, but it was based upon reliable evidence concerning children of five years of age who dragged heavy tubs of coal through low-ceilinged mine-passages for 16 hours a day. Life in early Victorian mines and factories was much like Thomas Hobbes's "state of nature"—"poor, nasty, brutish, and short."

The owners of mines and factories regarded themselves as innocent of blame for such conditions, for they were wedded to an economic theory of laissez faire, which assumed that unregulated working conditions would ultimately benefit everyone. A sense of the seemingly hopeless complexity of the situation during the Hungry 1840's is provided by an entry for 1842 in the diary of the statesman Charles Greville, an entry written at the same time that Carlyle was making his contribution to the "Condition of England Question," *Past and Present*. Conditions in the north of England, Greville reports, were "appalling."

> There is an immense and continually increasing population, no adequate demand for labor, * * * no confidence, but a universal alarm, disquietude, and discontent. Nobody can sell anything. * * * Certainly I have never seen * * * so serious a state of things as that which now stares us in the face; and this after thirty years of uninterrupted peace, and the most ample scope afforded for the development of all our resources. * * * One remarkable feature in the present condition of affairs is that nobody can account for it, and nobody pretends to be able to point out any remedy.

In reality many remedies were being pointed out. One of the most striking was put forward by the Chartists, a large organization of workingmen. In 1838 the organization drew up a "People's Charter" advocating the extension of the right to vote, the use of secret balloting, and other legislative reforms. For ten years the Chartist leaders engaged in agitation to have their program adopted by Parliament. Their fiery speeches, addressed to large mobs of discontented people, alarmed those who were not themselves suffering from hunger. In *Locksley Hall*, Tennyson seems to have had the Chartist mobs in mind when he pictured the threat posed by this time of troubles: "Slowly comes a hungry people, as a lion, creeping nigher, / Glares at one that nods and winks behind a slowly-dying fire." Although in the eyes of posterity the Chartist program seems an eminently reasonable one, it was premature in the 1840's. More immediately feasible was the agitation to abolish the high tariffs on imported grains, tariffs known as the Corn Laws (the word "corn" in England refers to wheat and other grains). These high tariffs had been established to protect English farm products from having to compete with low-priced products imported from abroad. Landowners and farmers fought to keep these tariffs in force so that high prices for their wheat would be assured, but the rest of the population suffered severely from the exorbitant price of bread or, in years of bad crops, from scarcity of food. In 1845 serious crop failures in England and the outbreak of potato blight in Ireland, convinced Sir Robert Peel, the Tory Prime Minister, that traditional protectionism must be abandoned. In 1846 the Corn Laws were repealed by Parliament, and the way was paved for the introduction of a system of Free Trade whereby goods could be imported with the payment of only minimal tariff duties. Although Free Trade did not eradicate the slums of Manchester, it worked well for many years and helped to relieve the major crisis of the Victorian economy. In 1848, when armed revolutions were exploding violently in every country in Europe, England was relatively unaffected. A monster Chartist demonstration fizzled out harmlessly in London, and Englishmen settled down to enjoy two decades of prosperity.

This Time of Troubles left its mark on some early Victorian literature. "Insurrection is a most sad necessity," Carlyle writes in his *Past and Present*, "and governors who wait for that to instruct them are surely getting into the fatalest courses." A similar refrain runs through Carlyle's history *The French Revolution* (1837). Memories of the French Reign of Terror lasted longer than memories of Trafalgar and Waterloo, memories freshened by later outbreaks of civil strife, "the red fool-fury of the Seine" as Tennyson described one of the violent overturnings of government in France. It is the novelists of the 1840's and early 1850's, however, who show the most marked response to the industrial and political scene. Vivid records of these conditions are to be found in the fiction of Charles Kingsley (1819–75), Elizabeth Gaskell (1810–65), and Benjamin Disraeli (1804–81), a novelist who became Prime Minister. For his novel *Sybil* (1845) Disraeli chose an appropriate subtitle, *The Two Nations*—a phrase that pointed up the line dividing the England of the rich from the other nation, the England of the poor.

THE MID-VICTORIAN PERIOD (1848–70): ECONOMIC PROSPERITY AND RELIGIOUS CONTROVERSY

In the decades following the Time of Troubles some Victorian writers, such as Dickens, continued to make critical attacks on the shortcomings of the Victorian social scene. Even more critical and indignant than Dickens was John Ruskin, who abandoned the criticism of art during this period in order to expose the faults of Victorian industry and commerce, as in his prophetic history of architecture, *The Stones of Venice* (1853) or in his attacks upon laissez-faire economics in *Unto This Last* (1862). Generally speaking, however, the comfortable and commonsensical novels of Anthony Trollope (1815–82) are a more characteristic reflection of the mid-Victorian attitude towards the social and political scene. The second phase of the Victorian age had many harassing problems, but it was a time of prosperity. On the whole its institutions worked well. Even the badly-bungled war against Russia in the Crimea (1854–56) did not seriously affect the growing sense of satisfaction that the challenging difficulties of the 1840's had been solved or would be solved by English wisdom and energy. The monarchy was proving its worth in a modern setting. The queen and her husband, Prince Albert, were themselves models of middle-class domesticity and devotion to duty. The aristocracy was discovering that Free Trade was enriching rather than impoverishing their estates; agriculture flourished together with trade and industry. And through a succession of Factory Acts in Parliament, which restricted child labor and limited hours of employment, the condition of the working classes was also being gradually improved. When we speak of Victorian complacency or stability or optimism, we are usually referring to this mid-Victorian phase—"The Age of Improvement," as the historian Asa Briggs has called it. "Of all the decades in our history," writes G. M. Young, "a wise man would choose the eighteen-fifties to be young in."

In 1851 Prince Albert opened the Great Exhibition in Hyde Park where a gigantic glass greenhouse, the Crystal Palace, had been erected to display the exhibits of modern industry and science. The Crystal Palace was one of the first buildings constructed according to modern architectural principles in which materials such as glass and iron are employed for purely functional ends (much late Victorian furniture, on the other hand, with its fantastic and irrelevant ornamentation, was constructed according to the opposite principle). The building itself, as well as the exhibits, symbolized the triumphant feats of Victorian technology. As Benjamin Disraeli wrote to a friend in 1862: "It is a privilege to live in this age of rapid and brilliant events. What an error to consider it a utilitarian age. It is one of infinite romance."

In the strenuous assertiveness of some of Robert Browning's poetry one might detect parallels to the confident mood inspired by the Great Exhibition. Generally, however, most mid-Victorian poetry and critical prose was less preoccupied with technology, economics, and politics than with the conflict between religion and science. This conflict was not, of course, altogether a new one. Tennyson's *In Memoriam* (1850), like much mid-Victorian literature, carries on the religious debates of earlier decades. These debates, in their earlier form, had been generally between the Utilitarians, the followers of Jeremy Bentham (1772–1832) and the philosophical conservatives, the followers of Samuel Taylor Coleridge. As John Stuart Mill demonstrates in his excellent essays on Bentham and Coleridge, these two writers divided between them the allegiance of all thoughtful people in England. Bentham and his disciples were reformers of a distinctive cast of mind. Their aim was to test all institutions in the light of human reason in order to determine whether such institutions were useful—that is, whether they contributed to the greatest happiness of the greatest numbers. This "Utilitarian" test was an extremely effective method of correcting inefficiencies in government administration: the drastic remodeling of the Civil Service in Victorian England was a tribute to Benthamite thinking. But such a test, if applied to a long-established institution like the Church of England, or to religious belief in general, could have, and did have, disruptive effects. Was religious belief useful for the needs of a reasonable person? To the Benthamites the answer was evident: religious belief was merely an outmoded superstition. This answer was emphatically stated in a letter by Harriet Martineau (1802–76), a Utilitarian writer and freethinker: "There is no *theory* of a God, of an author of Nature, of an origin of the universe, which is not utterly repugnant to my faculties; which is not (to my feelings) so irreverent as to make me blush; so misleading as to make me mourn."

Opponents of Utilitarianism, including Coleridge, argued that Bentham's view of human nature was unrealistically narrow, that man had always needed a faith as profoundly as he had needed food, and that if reason seemed to demonstrate the irrelevance of religion then reason must be an inadequate mode of arriving at truth. These anti-Utilitarians were of two types. The first were those such as Carlyle, who abandoned institutional Christianity yet sought to retain some sort of substitute religious belief—a quest that is vividly described in his spiritual autobiography, *Sartor Resartus*. Others, led by John Henry Newman, argued that only a powerful, dogmatic, and traditional religious institution could withstand the attacks of irreverent thinkers of the Benthamite stamp. In the 1830's and 1840's (before he was converted to Roman Catholicism), Newman became the leader of an impressive crusade to strengthen the Church of England. The movement he headed is known under various names including "The Oxford

Movement," because it originated at Oxford University, or as "Tractarianism," because Newman and his conservative followers developed their arguments in defense of a High Church in a series of pamphlets or tracts. Whatever name it went by, Newman's campaign produced a lively controversy. When Arthur Hugh Clough and Matthew Arnold were at Oxford in the early 1840's, the university was seething with religious debates, debates that were to have a marked effect on the poetry written by both men in the 1850's.

In mid-Victorian England these controversies continued, but with an added intensification. Leadership in the anticlerical position passed gradually from the Utilitarians to some of the leaders of science, in particular to Thomas Henry Huxley, who popularized the theories of Charles Darwin. Although many English scientists were themselves men of strong religious convictions, the impact of their scientific discoveries seemed consistently damaging to established faiths. Complaining about the "flimsiness" of his own religious faith in 1851, Ruskin exclaimed: "If only the Geologists would let me alone, I could do very well, but those dreadful hammers! I hear the clink of them at the end of every cadence of the Bible verses."

The damage lamented by Ruskin was effected in two ways. First the scientific attitude of mind was applied towards a study of the Bible itself. This kind of investigation, developed especially in Germany, was known as the "Higher Criticism." Instead of treating the Bible as a sacredly infallible document, scientifically-minded scholars examined it as a mere text of history and presented evidence about its composition that believers, especially in Protestant countries, found disconcerting, to say the least. The second kind of damage was effected by the view of man implicit in the discoveries of Geology and Astronomy, the new and "Terrible Muses" of literature, as Tennyson called them in a late poem. Geology, by extending the history of the earth backwards millions of years, reduced the stature of man in time. John Tyndall, an eminent physicist, said in an address at Belfast in 1874 that in the 18th century, men had an "unwavering trust" in the "chronology of the Old Testament," but in Victorian times men have had to become accustomed to "the idea that not for six thousand, nor for sixty thousand, nor for six thousand thousand, but for aeons embracing untold millions of years, this earth has been the theater of life and death. The riddle of the rocks has been read by the geologist and paleontologist, from sub-Cambrian depths to the deposits thickening over the sea bottoms of today. And upon the leaves of that stone book are * * * stamped the characters, plainer and surer than those formed by the ink of history, which carry the mind back into abysses of past time." The discoveries of astronomers, by extending a knowledge of stellar distances to dizzying expanses, were likewise disconcerting. Carlyle's friend, John Sterling, remarked in a letter of 1837 how geology "gives one the same sort of bewildering view of the abysmal extent of Time that Astronomy does of Space." To Tennyson's speaker in *Maud* (1855) the stars are "innumerable" tyrants of "iron skies." They are "Cold fires, yet with power to burn and brand / His nothingness into man."

In the mid-Victorian period Biology reduced mankind even further into "nothingness." Darwin's great treatise, *The Origin of Species* (1859), was interpreted by the nonscientific public in a variety of ways. Some chose to assume that evolution was synonymous with progress, but most readers recognized that Darwin's theory of natural selection conflicted not only with the concept of creation derived from the Bible but also with long-established assumptions of the values attached to man's special role in the world. Darwin's later treatise, *The Descent of Man* (1871), raised more explicitly the haunting question of man's identification with the animal kingdom. If the principle of survival of the fittest was accepted as the key to conduct, there remained the inquiry: fittest for what? As John Fowles noted in 1968, Darwin's theories made the Victorians feel "infinitely isolated." "By the 1860's the great iron structures of their philosophies, religions, and social stratifications were already beginning to look dangerously corroded to the more perspicacious."

Disputes about evolutionary science, like the disputes about the Oxford Movement, are a reminder that beneath the placidly prosperous surface of the mid-Victorian age there were serious conflicts and anxieties. In the same year as the Great Exhibition, with its celebration of the triumphs of trade and industry, Charles Kingsley wrote, "The young men and women of our day are fast parting from their parents and each other; the more thoughtful are wandering either towards Rome, towards sheer materialism, or towards an unchristian and unphilosophic spiritualism."

THE LATE PERIOD (1870–1901): DECAY OF VICTORIAN VALUES

The third phase of the Victorian age is more difficult to categorize. At first glance its point of view seems merely an extension of mid-Victorianism whose golden glow lingered on through the Jubilee years of 1887 and 1897 (years celebrating the 50th and 60th anniversaries of the queen's accession) down to 1914. For many Victorians, this final phase of the century was a time of serenity and security, the age of house parties and long weekends in the country. In the amber of Henry James's prose is immortalized a sense of the comfortable pace of these pleasant, well-fed gatherings. Life in London, too, was for many an exhilarating heyday. In *My Life and Loves*, the Irish-American Frank Harris, often a severe critic of the English scene, records his recollections of the gaiety of London in the 1880's: "London: who would give even an idea of its varied delights: London, the center of civilization, the queen city of the world without a peer in the multitude of its attractions, as superior to Paris as Paris is to New York." Yet as the leading social critic of the 1860's, Matthew Arnold, had tried to show, there were anomalies in the seemingly smooth-working institutions of mid-Victorian England, and after 1870 flaws became evident. The sudden emergence of Bismarck's Germany after the defeat of France in 1871 was progressively to confront England with powerful threats to her naval and military position and also to her exclusive preeminence in trade and industry. The recovery of the United States after the Civil War likewise provided new and serious competition. In 1873 and 1874 such severe economic depressions occurred that the rate of emigration rose to an alarming degree. Another threat to the domestic balance of power was the growth of labor as a political and economic force. In 1867, under Disraeli's guidance, a second Reform Bill had been passed which extended the right to vote to sections of the working classes, and this, together with the subsequent development of trade unions, made labor a political force to be reckoned with. The Labor Party represented a wide variety of shades of socialism. Some labor leaders were disciples of the Tory-Socialism of John Ruskin and shared his idealistic conviction that the middle-class economic and political system, with its distrust of state interference, was irresponsible and immoral. Other labor leaders had been infected instead by the revolutionary theories of Karl Marx and Friedrich Engels as expounded in their *Communist Manifesto* of 1847 and in Marx's *Capital* (1867, 1885, 1895). Perhaps the first English author of note to be connected with Marxism was the poet and painter William Morris. Morris, himself a man of some independent means, was too much of an individualist to follow consistently an orthodox Marxist line, but he did share with Marx a conviction that utopia could be achieved only after the working classes had, by revolution, taken control of government and industry.

In much of the literature of this final phase of Victorianism we can sense an over-all change of attitudes. Some of the late Victorian writers expressed the change openly by simply attacking the major mid-Victorian idols. Samuel Butler (1835–1902), for example, set about demolishing Darwin, Tennyson, and Prime Minister Gladstone, figures whose aura of authority reminded him of his own father. For the more worldly and casual-mannered Prime Minister Disraeli, on the other hand, Butler could express considerable admiration: "Earnestness was his greatest danger, but if he did not quite overcome it (as who indeed can? it is the last enemy that shall be subdued), he managed to veil it with a fair amount of success." In his novel, *The Way of All Flesh*, much of which was written in the 1870's, Butler satirized family life, in particular the tyrannical self-righteousness of a Victorian father, his own father (a clergyman) serving as his model. Butler's open revolt was perhaps premature. More typical were Walter Pater and his followers, writers who concluded that the striving of their predecessors was ultimately pointless, that the answers to man's problems are not to be found, and that our role is to enjoy the fleeting moments of beauty in "this short day of frost and sun." It is symptomatic of this shift in point of view that Edward FitzGerald's beautiful translation of the *Rubáiyát of Omar Khayyám* (1859), with its melancholy theme that life's problems are insoluble, went virtually unnoticed in the 1860's but became a popular favorite in subsequent decades.

THE NINETIES

The changes in attitude that had begun cropping up in the 1870's became much more conspicuous in the final decade of the century and give the 90's a special aura of notoriety. Of course the changes were not in evidence everywhere. Throughout the Empire at its outposts in India and Africa—an Empire which by 1890 comprised more than a quarter of all the territory on the surface of the world—Englishmen were building railways and administering governments with the same strenuous dedication to duty as in the mid-Victorian period. The stories of Kipling and Conrad variously record the struggles of such men. But back in England, Victorian standards were breaking down on several fronts. One colorful embodiment of changing values was Victoria's son and heir, Edward Prince of Wales, who was entering his 50th year as the 90's began. A pleasure-seeking, easy-going person, Edward was the antithesis of his father, Prince Albert, an earnest-minded intellectual who had devoted his life to hard work and to administrative responsibilities. Edward's carryings-on were a favorite topic for newspaper articles, one of which noted how this father of five children "openly maintained scandalous relations with ballet dancers and chorus singers." The familiar epithet "Gay Nineties," however inadequate to characterize the decade, evokes the rakish life style of Victoria's son.

Much of the writing of the decade illustrates a breakdown of a different sort. Melancholy, not gaiety, is characteristic of its spirit. Artists of the 90's, representing the aesthetic movement, were very much aware of living at the end of a great century, and often cultivated a deliberately *fin-de-siècle* ("end-of-century") pose. A studied languor, a weary sophistication, a search for new ways of titillating jaded palates can be found in both the poetry and the prose of the period. *The Yellow Book*, a periodical which ran from 1894 to 1897, is generally taken to represent the aestheticism of the 90's. The startling black-and-white drawings and designs of its art editor, Aubrey Beardsley (1872–98), the prose of George Moore and Max Beerbohm, and the poetry of Ernest Dowson illustrate different aspects of the movement. In 1893, an Austrian critic, Max Nordau, summed up what seemed to him to be happening, in a book that was as sensational as its title: *Degeneration*.

From a different perspective, an evaluation of the 90's directly contrary to Nordau's could be argued for, perhaps entitled "Regeneration." The final decade can be viewed, that is, as either the beginning of a great future movement in literature or as the ending and death of another great movement in literature. Possibly it may be more fruitful to see this transitional decade as both a beginning and an ending. Herbert Gerber, a literary historian, offers a useful generalization (applicable to the 1790's as well as to the 1890's) on this point. According to Gerber, it seems to be "that at the end of centuries * * * human beings, but artists in particular, are infected by a sense of death, decay, agony, old gods falling, cultural decline, on the one hand, or by a sense of regeneration * * * on the other."

In Dickens's *David Copperfield* (1850), the hero affirms: "I have always been thoroughly in earnest." Forty-five years later, Wilde's comedy, *The Importance of Being Earnest*, turns this typical mid-Victorian word, "earnest," into a pun, a key joke in this comic spectacle of earlier Victorian values being turned upside down. As Richard Le Galliene (a novelist of the 90's) remarked in *The Romantic Nineties* (1926): "Wilde made dying Victorianism laugh at itself, and it may be said to have died of the laughter."

EARNESTNESS, RESPECTABILITY, AND THE EVANGELICALS

Wilde's decades, the 1880's and 1890's, when being earnest was apparently not important, can be legitimately overlooked if we are trying to categorize the Victorian age as a whole instead of distinguishing the stages of its development. Why has the term "earnest" been so often applied to the typical Victorian writers? It should be noted that the quality of earnestness (or as some historians call it, more appropriately, "eagerness") was not strained. It did not exclude high spirits and humor. An age which relished the comic genius of Dickens and Thackeray, the grotesque humor of Browning and Carlyle, the nonsensical whimsy of Edward Lear and Lewis Carroll, was not exclusively dedicated to mere solemnity. Nevertheless the general Victorian preference for earnestness of spirit was firmly rooted and can best be accounted for by distinguishing it not from what came after but from what went before it.

The connection between literature in the Romantic and Victorian ages are close. Victorian poets as different as Browning and Swinburne both derive from Shelley. Tennyson is a follower of Keats, Arnold is a follower of Wordsworth, and many other instances of such continuity and influence may be cited. Most Victorian writers, both in poems and in essays, grappled with the same religious issues that had been a central concern for Wordsworth, Blake, and Shelley. As M. H. Abrams demonstrates in *Natural Supernaturalism* (1971), the post-Romantics from Tennyson through Yeats continued the Romantic endeavor to salvage "the cardinal values of their religious heritage by reconstituting them in a way that would make them intellectually acceptable, as well as emotionally pertinent, for the time being."

A dividing point, however, may be observed in Carlyle's well-known advice to his contemporaries in 1834: "Close thy *Byron*; open thy *Goethe*." Carlyle's advice could be interpreted in two ways. The first is with reference to literary forms. A Victorian writer might avoid the wild excesses, the lack of controlled form of much Romantic writing, Byron himself foresaw that such a reformation was necessary. "We are all on a wrong tack ('Lakers' and all)," he wrote. "Our successors will have to go back to the riding school * * * and learn to ride the great horse." Some of Byron's Victorian successors ignored his prediction; they too rode Pegasus bareback as casually as he had done. Yet several Victorian poets, Tennyson in particular, do fulfill Byron's prediction. The energy of Romantic literature persists, but it is channeled into a stricter concern for disciplined forms. It is significant that the Romantic poet most influential in the Victorian age was Keats, the most form-conscious of the Romantics, rather than Byron.

Carlyle himself was not primarily concerned with a chastening of literary forms. He was saying, in effect: "Stop moping. There is work to be done, work that requires the earnest efforts of all of us." Byronism, in this context, meant the easygoing aristocratic code of the Regency, with its preference for a happy-go-lucky enjoyment of the physical pleasures of life, for hunting and hard drinking and lounging. Lord Melbourne, Victoria's first Prime Minister, embodied such a view of life and found himself out of place under the new dispensation—an "autumn rose" as Strachey called him. Carlyle's gospel, on the other hand, was soon to be extremely timely for the new generation. From 1830 on there developed what the historian Arnold Toynbee calls a "challenge." The earnest strivings of the Victorians provided the needed "response." A speech made by the heroine of *Jane Eyre* sums up these developments. After she refuses to accept a proposal by the Byronic-style Mr. Rochester to live with him and he is bewailing his lonely lot, Jane Eyre advises him sternly: "Mr. Rochester * * * we are born to strive and endure—you as well as I: do so."

A further indication of the timeliness of Carlyle's call to action in *Sartor Resartus* is its Evangelical tone. In its strictest sense "Evangelical" refers to part of a branch of the Church of England called the Low Church. Zealously dedicated to good causes (they were responsible for the emancipation of all the slaves in the British Empire as early as 1833), advocates of a strict puritan code of morality, and righteously censorious of worldliness in others, the Evangelicals became a powerful and active minority in the early part of the 19th century. Much of their power depended on the fact that their view of life and religion was virtually identical with that of a much larger group, the Nonconformists—that is, the Baptists, Methodists, Congregationalists, and other Protestant sects outside the Church of England. When united for action with this large group of sects, whose membership included a generous proportion of successful businessmen, the Evangelicals were a formidable force.

Finally, the term "Evangelical" has been loosely applied to cover any kind of enthusiastic concern for reform. It is thus used to describe anyone infected with the *spirit* of the Evangelical movement even though he does not subscribe to its ethical code or its beliefs. Victorian earnestness may therefore be explained partly as a response to a challenging situation and partly as rooted in an active religious movement that left its stamp on agnostics as well as on believers. George Eliot is an example of this Evangelical legacy. After having abandoned Christianity and having flouted convention by living for years with a married man, she devoted her novels to painstaking analyses of problems of conscience and moral choice. It would be difficult to name a Victorian writer of any consequence who remained an Evangelical in the true sense of the term; it would be equally difficult to name one who was not affected by what Evangelicalism had stood for.

The code of puritanism and respectability advocated by the Nonconformists and Evangelicals is symbolized by the joyless Victorian Sunday. In 1837, a new Sunday Observance Bill was introduced into Parliament. Although the Bill did not quite pass, the Sober Sunday ritual became established by custom if not by law. To later generations, even more repressive was the puritans' standard of sexual behavior, with its intense concern for female innocence—or, as its opponents contended, for female ignorance. The history of Victorian asceticism is nevertheless much more complex than common supposition allows, as may be suggested by the fact that in 1850 8,000 prostitutes were known by the police to be operating in London. In the city of Leeds, a few years earlier, statistics indicate that there were two churches and 39 chapels or meeting houses to compete with 451 taverns and 98 brothels. For a striking corrective to the commonly accepted suppositions about Victorian asceticism, Steven Marcus' study of the sexual habits of different classes of mid-19th-century English society, *The Other Victorians* (1966), may be consulted.

The middle-class puritan code was largely derived from the Old Testament, but it also reflected commercial experience in which sobriety, hard work, and a joyless abstention from worldly pleasures paid off, paradoxically enough, in worldly success. Intermixed with this ascetic code was an insistence upon respectability—an insistence reflecting the insecurity of a newly powerful class in a fluid society, a class anxious to have a fixed set of manners by which to live and to measure themselves and the families of others. Hence developed the phenomenon of "Mrs. Grundyism": conformity in its worst sense—that is, external conformity.

It is against this background that John Stuart Mill's essay *On Liberty* (1859) should be read. The status of liberty in Victorian England was actually one of the most outstanding achievements of the age. For continental agitators of Left, Right, or Center in politics, Victorian England was the land of freedom, an asylum where the policeman (who was unarmed) was a friendly protector instead of an instrument of tyranny. To this asylum flocked General Torrijos (whose plot against the Spanish monarchy involved Tennyson); Mazzini, the Italian nationalist; Louis Napoleon of France; Kossuth, the Hungarian patriot; Prince Metternich of Austria; and Karl Marx himself, whose major work, *Capital*, was conceived in the Reading Room of the British Museum. The Victorian achievement in religious as well as political freedom is also impressive. Atheist orators such as Charles Bradlaugh enjoyed the privilege of addressing large audiences. In 1844, Friedrich Engels (not usually friendly towards the English scene) observed: "England is unquestionably the freest—that is, the least unfree —country in the world, North America not excepted."

Under such circumstances, why did Mill consider liberty a problem? Mill was inspired by his experience that individuality is threatened not merely by political tyrannies or entrenched religions. It is threatened also by the less tangible pressures exerted by society itself, in particular by the middle-class conventions which weighed upon the nonconformist in society rather than upon the Nonconformist in religion. In Hardy's late-Victorian novel, *Jude the Obscure*, a novel which contributed to the breakdown of the puritan code in literature, it is revealing that when the heroine resolves to leave her husband she justifies her action by citing a passage from Mill's *On Liberty*.

THE ROLE OF WOMEN IN VICTORIAN LIFE AND LITERATURE

Hardy's heroine might also have cited a later treatise by Mill on a different aspect of liberty: *The Subjection of Women* (1869) in which he boldly challenged long-established assumptions about women's roles in society. Although Mill's treatise, like Mary Wollstonecraft's *A Vindication of the Rights of Woman* (1792) was ahead of its time (he was subjected to a barrage of ridicule from such magazines as *Punch*), what he said brought into focus a number of issues that had been under discussion in earlier Victorian debates. The Woman Question, as it was called, was concerned with issues of sexual inequality in politics, economic life, education, and social intercourse. In the political sphere it was abundantly evident that women continued to rank as second-class citizens. Like millions of working-class men, they could not vote or hold office except the highest office of queen (and Victoria was in general an anti-feminist). Petitions to Parliament advocating women's suffrage were introduced as early as the 1840's, but they did not become law until 1918. Less prolonged was the agitation to allow married women the right to own and handle their own property instead of being exclusively dependent upon the wishes of their husbands, agitation which culminated successfully in the passing of the Married Women's Property Acts (1870–1908). Previous legislation, the Factory Acts, corrected some of the worst aspects of women's employment in mines and factories, including the 16-hour day, although here the argument for reform was based not on women's equality but rather on the earlier chivalric view of their comparative frailty of physique.

To review these instances of gross inequality should not obscure how important a part women did play in shaping the life of the age. *De jure*, they seemed powerless dependents; *de facto* they often wielded a great deal of power. In Mill's view the drive for power derived from the very conditions of sexual inequality. "Where liberty cannot be hoped for, and power can, power becomes the grand object of human desire." On the domestic scene one of the ways such power could be manifested, as writers of Victorian comedy and farce often showed, was simple shrewishness. Thus when Dickens' Mr. Bumble, after being browbeaten by his formidable wife, learns that "the law supposes that your wife acts under your direction," he is astounded. " 'If the law supposes that,' said Mr. Bumble * * * 'the law is a ass—a idiot. If that's the eye of the law, the law is a bachelor.' " On a more serious level, as many a Victorian biography can show, women of character had other ways of making their wills prevail, a control extending beyond the household. Although a Victorian grandmother was unable to vote, she might exert a much more decisive influence on events than her husband did in exercising his ballot.

Issues of the legal status of women, issues that could be settled by legislation, are rarely featured in Victorian novels or poems. When novelists and poets dealt with feminist topics, they commonly portrayed women's domestic and social roles as educated companions of men or as doll-like subordinates. Tennyson's long poem *The Princess* (1847), with its fantasy of a college being established for women from whose precincts all males are excluded, was inspired by contemporary discussions of the need for women to obtain an education more advanced than what had been provided by the popular finishing schools such as Miss Pinkerton's academy in Thackeray's *Vanity Fair*. Such discussions led, in the following year, to the establishment of the first college for women in London, an experiment later recommended by Thomas Henry Huxley, a strong advocate of advanced education for women. By the end of the century these efforts began to bear fruit as higher education for women became grudgingly accepted as a fact of life. And coincident with changes in education were overall changes in attitudes towards how a woman of the middle or upper classes should spend her time. Early Victorians treasured a role of elegant idleness for women; in the later period the need for "something to do," as the novelist Dinah Maria Mulock called it, came to be recognized, within the home and without.

Ultimately, as Victorian novels illustrate, the basic problem in the Woman Question was not political, economic, or even educational. It was how women were regarded, and regarded themselves, as members of a society. In the final pages of our section, this basic problem is dramatized under the title "The Woman Question" as one of three issues with which Victorian writers were most keenly concerned. Selections from the writings of Florence Nightingale, George Eliot, and others reveal how the roles of women were diversely regarded over the 60-year period.

THE DIVERSITY OF VICTORIAN LITERATURE

The weight of the puritan code on the literature of early and mid-Victorian England was, as we might expect, considerable. It was most evident in the novels, for novels were commonly read aloud in family gatherings, and the need to avoid topics which might cause embarrassment to young girls established taboos that the novelist could not dare ignore, although he might sometimes skillfully circumvent them. Thackeray and others offered protests, but it was not until near the end of the century or later that the novelists broke clear of those restrictions. The poets and essayists fared better. When Browning was writing *The Ring and the Book* he was obviously unconcerned about whether his poem might raise blushes on prudish cheeks, and Swinburne's *Poems and Ballads* flouts the taboos in the manner of the French poets whom he admired (of his Victorian contemporaries Swinburne remarked that "their ears are the chastest part about them"). Both volumes appeared in the 1860's at the same time as the essays of Matthew Arnold with their attacks on the narrowness of the puritan middle-class mind.

Too much can be made of the importance of these taboos as literary conventions in the Victorian age. A much more significant kind of pressure from the Victorian audience on its writers, one that they were themselves inclined to comply with, was the desire on the part of readers to be guided and edified. The newly expanding reading public, despite its air of solid confidence, wanted help from its authors, and its authors were understandably flattered by the request. Only a few, such as Dante Gabriel Rossetti, ignored it; the others all exhibit, in varying degrees, an air of prophecy and mission. Carlyle in his lectures *On Heroes* identifies the writer or "Poet" such as Shakespeare with the great prophets such as Mahomet, and in his own writings it is evident that he sought to make his mark as a seer rather than as a mere man of letters. The very high status that even Matthew Arnold claimed for literature is evident in his statement that "most of what now passes with us for religion and philosophy will be replaced by poetry." Perhaps the most extreme example of a Victorian writer with a sense of mission is, however, John Ruskin, a writer who had opinions on every topic. Tennyson, here as in most instances, is more representative. To provide firm guidance in problems of science and religion, the destiny of nations and daily life, was a task that sometimes appealed to Tennyson and sometimes appalled him. As we might expect, several of his poems are concerned with the dilemma of a writer's divided duty towards his public and his art —a dilemma that has become even more acute in the 20th century as the reading public has further expanded.

The existence of this dilemma may help to explain another characteristic of Victorian literature: its variety both in style and in subject matter. Variety is in part a symptom of the Victorian writers' bold independence and their zest for literary experiment for its own sake, but it is also a symptom of an absence of any final general agreement concerning the function of literature and art in a democratic society. Writers and their audiences might usually agree that instruction was a desirable attribute of a work of literature, but what was to constitute the insruction and what was the appropriate mode in which to convey it?

It is among the poets that the search for appropriate modes is most evident. All of them seem driven to experiment in a variety of ways. In versification, although making considerable use of traditional forms such as the sonnet, most of them preferred experimenting with new or unusual metrical patterns, as did Swinburne, Gerard Manley Hopkins, and, later, Thomas Hardy. In line with their metrical experiments are their experiments in the art of narrative poetry. During an age which witnessed the emergence of the novel as one of the dominant forms of literature, the poets sought new ways of telling stories in verse, as Tennyson's *Maud* or Browning's *The Ring and the Book* will illustrate. Some of them, such as George Meredith, Morris, and Emily Brontë, novelists as well as poets, were especially aware that poetry can offer unusual resources for the writer of narratives, as demonstrated by the compression and intensification of Morris's early poems or Meredith's *Modern Love*. Others, in particular Clough, sought to write narrative poems as if they were novels, poems that are long, casual in tone, and usually prosaic in style.

To illustrate the diversity of styles in Victorian writing, two poems, published within the space of three years, may be compared. Tennyson's *The Lotos-Eaters* (1842) is in the grand manner of English poetry, the culmination of a poetic tradition emphasizing beautiful cadences and vowel sounds: "To watch the crisping ripples on the beach, / And tender curving lines of creamy spray." In Browning's *The Bishop Orders his Tomb* (1845), the colloquial tone of the speaker, as he hisses his hatred of a rival, seems to belong to a different century: "Shrewd was that snatch from out the corner south / He graced his carrion with, God curse the same!" And if we ignore the stylistic differences here and concentrate upon a possible similarity— that both poems, like many Victorian writings, evoke the past of myth and history—what is to be done to align these works with other works of the same period? What resemblance is there to Dickens' *Oliver Twist* (1838) for example, with its realistic scenes of a sordid workhouse, or to Carlyle's *Past and Present* (1843) with its idiosyncratic manner of exposing the sufferings of the Victorian poor, or to John Ruskin's *Modern Painters* (1843) with its rhapsodic celebrations of alpine scenery and romantic sunsets? As a result, most candid literary historians admit that while we may confidently identify the distinguishing characteristics of individual Victorian writers, of a Browning, a Dickens, or a Newman, it is extremely difficult to devise satisfactory statements about Victorian literature that are generally applicable to most or all of these writers. This admission is distressing to tidy minds, but in itself it tells us something distinctive about Victorian literature as a whole.

What we can perhaps isolate is what Jerome Buckley calls the "temper" of Victorian literature, a state of mind and emotion already described in this introduction as an eager or earnest response to the expanding horizons of 19th-century life. We also encounter some frequently recurring subjects in Victorian literature, including a preoccupation with man's relationship to God, and also an acute awareness of time, past, present, and future. Among the poets (and the novelists as well) one topic that links their writings together is love, for love, despite the reputed strain of puritanism in the age, is as prominent in Victorian poetry as it had been in the time of John Donne and his followers. Although the Victorian poets, unlike their 17th-century predecessors, rarely made witty proposals for gathering rosebuds, they explored other aspects of love relationships, such as the timeless equilibrium of lovers pictured by D. G. Rossetti, or the poignant experience of isolation by Arnold and Christina Rossetti, or the hostility of partners of a shattered marriage in Meredith's *Modern Love*. All these aspects, and more, are present in the poetry of Robert Browning, and his comprehensive exploration of such relationships links him to his contemporaries. In reviewing Browning's volume, *Men and Women*, William Morris (himself a fine love poet) praised some of the monologues dealing with religious issues, but added that these, "as it is in all art, in all life," however fine, were "but a supplement to the love-poems."

If Victorian poets and novelists write extensively of love and personal relationships, there is also a large body of writings in which these subjects are relatively subordinate, writings categorized as nonfictional prose. Although the term is clumsy and also not quite exact (for practitioners of nonfictional prose such as Carlyle and Pater resorted, on occasion, to fictional narratives), it has its uses to distinguish these prose writers from the novelists. The seven writers featured in our selections are Carlyle, Newman, Mill, Ruskin, Arnold, Huxley, and Pater.

On behalf of their kinds of writing, Pater argued, in his essay on *Style* (1889), that prose was "the special and opportune art of the modern world." His contention was not that prose is superior to verse but that it more readily conveys the "chaotic variety and complexity" of modern life, the "incalculable" intellectual diversity of the "master currents of the present time." Whether prose is a more appropriate medium than verse to communicate the "chaotic variety" of an age remains a matter of dispute, but what Pater says of the age itself would be much more generally agreed upon. Toward this condition of their age the Victorian writers of nonfictional prose responded in a variety of ways and in a variety of styles. All sought in their distinctive manners to create some sort of order out of the chaos. Pater himself, coming to maturity late in the century, differs from the others in his distaste for controversy. By writing critical essays celebrating a beautifully ordered world of art and literature, Pater sought to rise above the flux and chaos which he saw as characteristic of his century. His predecessors were more engaged in shaping and reconstructing the social order. All of them use prose primarily as an instrument of persuasion and argument. On a wide range of controversial topics—religious, political, or aesthetic—they seek to convince a reader to share their convictions and values. Their modes of persuasion differ. Mill and Huxley rely on clear reasoning, logical argument, and the kind of lucid style favored by essayists of the 18th century, uncolored by the emotional heightening of romanticism. Carlyle and Ruskin, in much of their writing, seem closer to the 17th century than to the 18th. Their "polyphonic" style, as it has been called, has affinities with the prose rhythms of Sir Thomas Browne and Robert Burton. It is a style that also appeals to the eye as well as the ear, and, by a combination of vivid effects, plays upon the feelings of the reader. Poetic passages in Newman and Arnold also play upon our feelings, but much of their writing is less mannered and more in the relatively prosaic vein of Mill and Huxley.

However various their styles, all of these Victorian prose writers were linked by a common concern for the fate of man in an industrial, democratic, and increasingly secularized society. Of their interlocking debates on education, leadership, and the role of science and religion, C. F. Harrold aptly says: "What they wrote constitutes a fascinating chapter in the history of the English mind, and also provides a perspective for viewing much that continues to perplex the world. Above all, a survey of their beliefs and assumptions will illuminate the richness of their prose, a prose which is often highly allusive, sometimes deceptively simple, and always susceptible to fresh and profitable interpretation as the symbol of their thought and the eloquent expression of their convictions."

If the Victorian age can lay claim to greatness for its poetry, its prose, and its novels, no such claim can be made for its plays, at least until the final decade of the century. Here we must distinguish between playwriting on the one hand and theatrical activity on the other. For the theater itself, throughout the period, was a flourishing and popular institution. As Robert Corrigan notes: "In the decade between 1850 and 1860 the number of theaters built throughout the country was doubled, and in the middle of the sixties, in London alone, 150,000 would be attending the theater on any given day." But while the theater flourished, playwriting languished. The state of Victorian music was similar, for while there was a great demand for symphony concerts, operas, and oratorios, there was a dearth of great composers. Plays were written and produced, often domestic melodramas and farces, but they were not plays of lasting interest (except for the remarkable comic operas of W. S. Gilbert and Arthur Sullivan). And when major writers like Tennyson, Browning, and Henry James were lured by the popular impact of stage performances to try their hand at drama, the results were disappointing. Only as the century drew to its close did significant writing for the stage re-emerge after long absence, in the lively dramas of Oscar Wilde and George Bernard Shaw.

It will be obvious that any estimate of Victorian literature has to take into account the outstanding achievements of the Victorian novelists. From the time of Charles Dickens (1812–70), early in the period (his first novel, *Pickwick Papers*, was published in the same year as Victoria became queen), to the final decade when the late novels of Thomas Hardy (1840–1928) such as his *Tess of the D'Urbervilles* (1891) appeared, a long line of novelists continued to turn out monumental masterpieces that delighted their contemporaries and that continue to delight readers today as is evident by their being among the most readily available books in English.

After Dickens's epoch-making early novels had appeared on the scene in the 1830's, each subsequent decade featured the emergence of new novelists of stature such as Charlotte Brontë (1816–55) and Emily Brontë (1818–48) in the 1840's, and William Makepeace Thackeray (1811–63) whose prominence in the 1850's was a challenge to Dickens's continued preeminence and popularity. In the 1860's, Anthony Trollope (1815–82) established himself as a portraitist of mid-Victorian society, and in the 1870's, George Eliot (1819–80) published what is generally regarded as her finest novel, *Middlemarch* (1872), although she had already established her reputation earlier with *Adam Bede* (1859) and *The Mill on the Floss* (1860). In the 1880's, George Meredith (1828–1909)—a less well-known novelist today—finally began to receive adequate attention from the critics and public for novels he had published earlier such as *The Ordeal of Richard Feverel* (1859). In addition to these major novelists from Dickens to Hardy, several noteworthy names could be cited of writers who contributed to the rich variety of the Victorian novel, such as Elizabeth Gaskell (1810–65), Wilkie Collins (1824–89), George Gissing (1857–1903), and others.

Often these novelists confront the same issues and employ similar styles as their contemporaries among the poets and essayists (the stylistic affinities between Browning and Dickens, for example, are striking). One significant difference, however, is that the novelists for the most part do not share the preoccupation of the Victorian poets and essayists with man's relationship to God. Like their greatest predecessors—Fielding, Richardson, and Jane Austen—most of the Victorian novelists were primarily concerned with man in society and with those aspects of experience categorized by the title of Lionel Trilling's essay: "Manners, Morals and the Novel," to which we can add an additional topic—Money. Typically these stories center on the struggles of a protagonist, male or female, to find himself in relation to other men and women, in love or marriage, with family or neighbors, or with associates in his working career. Occasionally such a search may take on quasi-religious dimensions, as in the later novels of Thomas Hardy or in that unclassifiable sport among Victorian novels, Emily Brontë's *Wuthering Heights* (1847), and more indirectly, in George Eliot's novels, with their persistent concern with the role of free will and fate in the lives of their characters. On the whole, however, the Victorian novelists were less occupied with man's relation to God than with his relation to other people.

And for the most part, the other people were the reader's contemporaries. The historical novel, as established by Sir Walter Scott, remained popular throughout the post-Romantic period, but it was a form especially congenial to the lesser novelists, such as Bulwer Lytton (*The Last Days of Pompeii*, 1834) or Charles Reade (*The Cloister and the Hearth*, 1861). While the major novelists occasionally tried their hand at historical fiction, their preference was for the contemporary. Whether the story was set in the rural landscapes of Eliot's Warwickshire and Hardy's Wessex, Trollope's cathedral towns, or Dickens's fogbound London, readers expected a representation of daily 19th-century life that would be recognizably familiar to them.

To satisfy such expectations they were provided with a rich fare. Dickens was praised by Walter Bagehot for having described London "like a special correspondent for posterity." His contemporaries and successors among the novelists were also skillful reporters, and most of them were more scrupulously concerned with detailed realism than he had been. Disputes about the degree of Dickens's realism have persisted among critical readers from his day to ours, but what is now generally recognized is that he was much more than a brilliant reporter, and that the heightening and stylization of his novels produce effects like poetic drama that are very different from straightforward realism. "Every writer of fiction," he said, "although he may not adopt the dramatic form, writes, in effect, for the stage." The attitude to this aspect of his writing by other novelists is of crucial importance in understanding how the Victorian novel developed. Among Dickens's rivals and successors there was a common agreement that the stagey aspect of his novels was his most glaring fault, and each novelist in turn set out to correct that fault by his own example of what he believed was a more realistic representation of life. Thackeray's masterpiece, *Vanity Fair* (1848), has to a modern reader many mannerisms of its own, but is much less blatantly mannered than a characteristic Dickens novel. "The Art of Novels," Thackeray affirmed in a letter, "*is* to represent Nature: to convey as strongly as possible the sentiment of reality." In Thackeray's disciple,

Anthony Trollope, and later in the drab narratives of George Gissing, a lesser figure, there is a similar reduction of stagelike scenes and effects. In George Eliot this reaction against novelistic theatricalism took a more influential turn: she set out to explore what the theatrical writer rarely explores —the inner lives of her characters. Early in the 20th century, the young D. H. Lawrence, beginning his career as a novelist, remarked to a friend: "You see, it was really George Eliot who started it all, and how wild they all were with her for doing it. It was she who started putting all the action inside. Before, you know, with Fielding and the others, it had been outside. Now I wonder which is right?" Lawrence himself decided, as a practicing novelist, that Fielding and his Victorian followers could be as right as George Eliot, but most early 20th-century novelists preferred to follow Eliot's example and concentrate on the inner lives of their characters; and critical readers, adapting their tastes to the new mode, were disposed to undervalue Victorian novels which had portrayed people acting rather than people recollecting, or reflecting, or trying to come to a decision.

Contributing to this underevaluation of the Victorian achievement was the assumption that novels published in serial form (as Victorian novels had usually been published) must be slapdash productions altogether deficient in art, or as Henry James characterized them, "large loose baggy monsters." James's affectionate derogation is applicable to such a novel as Dickens's early *Pickwick Papers*, but it does not apply at all to some of Dickens's later novels such as *Bleak House* (a masterpiece of narrative construction). Eliot's *Middlemarch* (1872), Hardy's *Jude the Obscure* (1895), or the tight and intricate plotting of Wilkie Collins' detective novel, *The Moonstone* (1868). Serial publication, as later critics have come to recognize, did not necessarily preclude artful storytelling, and it had advantages to offset the possible disadvantages of fragmentation. Publication by installments challenged the novelists to sustain the interest of their readers; in every single number they had to entertain them or, to use the traditional critical term, to provide delight. Like an actor or public speaker, the Victorian novelists had a sense, during the very process of writing their books, of how their audience was responding to their performance. And it was an audience that offered a special challenge because of its exceptional diversity; Victorian readers ranged from the sophisticated and well-read lawyer to the semiliterate household servant. The present-day division of the novel-reading public into highbrow, middlebrow, and lowbrow existed only in embryonic form in the Victorian age, and did not become a significant controlling influence on the novelist until late in the century.

This popular genre is thus especially representative of all but the religious attitudes that have been emphasized in this account of the Victorian period: the earnest sense of responsibility, the occasional lapses of taste, and the overflowing creative energy of its writers. Near the end of his life Thackeray drew a comparison between himself and Dickens: "I am played out. All I can do now is to bring out my old puppets. * * * But, if he live to be ninety, Dickens will still be creating new characters. In his art that man is marvelous." Wrung from a novelist whose own writings occupy more than twenty thick volumes, this compliment is quintessentially Victorian.

THOMAS CARLYLE
(1795–1881)

1833: *Sartor Resartus* published in *Fraser's Magazine*.
1834: Moves to London from Craigenputtock in Scotland.
1837: *The French Revolution* published.
1843: *Past and Present* published.
1866: Death of Jane Carlyle.

W. B. Yeats once asked William Morris what writers had inspired the socialist movement of the 1880's, and Morris replied: "Oh, Ruskin and Carlyle, but somebody should have been beside Carlyle and punched his head every five minutes." Morris's mixed feelings of admiration and exasperation are typical of the response Carlyle evokes in many readers. Anyone approaching his prose for the first time should expect to be sometimes bewildered. Like George Bernard Shaw, Carlyle discovered, early in life, that exaggeration can be a highly effective way of gaining the attention of an audience. But it can also be a way of distracting an audience unfamiliar with the idiosyncrasies of his rhetoric and unprepared for the distinctive enjoyments his writings can provide.

One of the idiosyncrasies of his prose is that it is meant to be read aloud. "His paragraphs," as Emerson observed, "are all a sort of splendid conversation." As a talker Carlyle was as famous in his day as Dr. Johnson in his. Charles Darwin testified that he was "the best worth listening to of any man I know." No Boswell has adequately recorded this talk, but no Boswell was needed, for Carlyle has contrived to get the sound of his own spoken voice into his writings. It is a noisy and emphatic voice, startling upon first acquaintance. To become familiar with its unusual sounds and rhythms, one can best begin by reading aloud from some of Carlyle's portraits of his contemporaries which are included in the following selections. Many of these colorful portraits are from his letters, and it becomes evident that the mannerisms of the author were simply the mannerisms of the man and were congenial and appropriate for the author's purposes.

Carlyle was 41 years old when Victoria became queen of England. He had been born in the same year as Keats, yet he is rarely grouped with his contemporaries among the Romantic writers. Instead his name is linked with younger men such as Dickens, Browning, and Ruskin, the early generation of Victorian writers. The classification is fitting, for it was Carlyle's role to foresee the problems that were to preoccupy the Victorians and early to report upon his experiences in confronting these problems. After 1837 his loud voice began to attract an audience, and he soon became one of the most influential figures of the age, affecting the attitudes of scientists, statesmen, and especially of men of letters. His wife once complained that Ralph Waldo Emerson had no ideas (except mad ones) that he had not derived from Carlyle. "But pray, Mrs. Carlyle," replied a friend, "*who has?*' "

Before attaining such prestige among the Victorians, however, Carlyle had a long wait. His early career is the dramatic story of struggles against narrowness of background, poverty, ill-health, and religious uncertainties.

Carlyle was born in Ecclefechan, a village in Scotland, the eldest child of a large family. His mother, at the time of her marriage, had been illiterate. His father, James Carlyle, a stonemason and later a farmer, was proudly characterized by his son as a peasant. The key to the character of James Carlyle was the Scottish Calvinism which he instilled into the members of his household. Frugality, hard work, a tender but undemonstrative family loyalty, and a peculiar blend of self-denial and self-righteousness were characteristic features of Carlyle's childhood home. The stamp of its discipline, imprinted upon him for life, can be detected even in Carlyle's sense of humor, which was highly developed yet limited. The trivial banter of London's bohemia did not merely bore him; it drove him to furious repudiations. His incapacity to enjoy the fun of Charles Lamb is comparable to his father's stern rejection of workmen who wasted time.

With his father's aid the young Carlyle was educated at Annan Academy and at Edinburgh University, the subject of his special interest being mathematics; he left without taking a degree. It was his parents' hope that their son would become a clergyman, but in this respect Thomas made a severe break with his ancestry. He was a prodigious reader, and his exposure to such skeptical writers as Hume, Voltaire, and Gibbon had undermined his faith. Gibbon's *Decline and Fall of the Roman Empire*, he told Emerson, was "the splendid bridge from the old world to the new." By the time he was 23, Carlyle had crossed the bridge and had abandoned his Christian faith and his proposed career as a clergyman. During the period in which he was thinking through his religious position, he supported himself by teaching school in Scotland, and later by tutoring private pupils, but from 1824 to the end of his life he relied exclusively upon his writings for his livelihood. His early writings consisted of translations, biographies, and critical studies of Goethe and other German authors, to whose view of life he was deeply attracted. The German Romantics (loosely grouped by Carlyle under the label "Mystics") were the second most important influence on his life and character, exceeded only by his early family experiences. Aided by the writings of these German poets and philosophers, he arrived finally at a faith in life that served as a substitute for the Christian faith he had lost.

His most significant early essay, *Characteristics*, appeared in *The Edinburgh Review* in 1831. A year earlier he had begun writing his full-length autobiographical novel, *Sartor Resartus*, a work which he had great difficulty in persuading anyone to publish. In book form *Sartor* first appeared in America in 1836, where Carlyle's follower, Emerson, had prepared an enthusiastic audience for this unusual work. His American following (which was later to become a vast one) did little at first, however, to relieve the poverty in which he still found himself after fifteen years of writing. In 1837 the tide at last turned when he published *The French Revolution*. "O it has been a great success, dear," his wife assured him, but her husband, embittered by the long struggle, was incredulous that the sought-for recognition had at last come to him.

It was in character for his wife, Jane Welsh Carlyle, to be less surprised by his success than he was. That Thomas Carlyle was a genius had been an article of faith to her from her first meeting with him in 1821. A clever girl, the daughter of a doctor of good family, Jane Welsh had many suitors. When in 1826 she finally accepted Carlyle, her family and friends were shocked. This peasant's son, of no fixed employment, seemed a fantastic choice. Subsequent events seemed to confirm her family's verdict. Not long after marriage, Carlyle insisted upon their retiring to a remote farm at Craigenputtock where for six years (1828–34) this sociable woman was obliged to live in isolation and loneliness. After they moved to London in 1834 and settled in a house on Cheyne Walk in Chelsea, Jane Carlyle was considerably happier and enjoyed her role as hostess. Her husband, however, remained a difficult man to live with. His stomach ailments, irascible nerves, and preoccupation with his writings, as well as the lionizing to which he was subjected, left him with little inclination for domestic amenities.

This marriage of the Carlyles has aroused almost as much interest as that of the Brownings. Their friend the Reverend W. H. Brookfield (whose marriage was an unhappy one) once said cynically that marrying is "dipping into a pitcher of snakes for the chance of an eel," and partisan biographers have argued that Jane Welsh drew a snake instead of an eel. Even without such partisanship, it is easy to be sorry for the wife. Yet if we study her letters, before and after her marriage, it is evident that she got what she asked for. She wanted a man of genius who would change the world. She paid for what she wanted by years of comparative poverty, ill health, and loneliness. Just before her death in 1866, she had the satisfaction of enjoying to the full a high point of her husband's triumph when the peasant's son she had chosen returned to Scotland to deliver his inaugural address as Lord Rector of Edinburgh University.

During the first thirty years of Carlyle's residence in London he wrote extensive historical works and many pamphlets concerning contemporary issues. After *The French Revolution* he edited, in 1845, the *Letters and Speeches of Oliver Cromwell*, a Puritan leader of heroic dimensions in Carlyle's eyes, and later wrote a full-length biography, *The History of Friedrich II of Prussia, Called Frederick the Great* (1858–65). Carlyle's pamphleteering is seen at its best in *Past and Present* (1843) and in its most violent phase in his *Latter-Day Pamphlets* (1850). Following the death of his wife, he wrote very little. For the remaining fifteen years of his life he confined himself to reading, or to talking to the stream of visitors who called at Cheyne Walk to listen to the "Sage of Chelsea," as he came to be called. In 1874 he accepted the Prussian Order of Merit from Bismarck but declined an English baronetcy offered by Disraeli. In 1881 he died and was buried near his family in Ecclefechan churchyard.

To understand Carlyle's role as historian, biographer, and social critic, it is essential to understand his attitude towards religion. The qualities of his prose style as well as his mature evaluation of past and present are ultimately attributable to religious experiences undergone in his earlier years. By the time he was 23, he had been shorn of his faith in Christianity. At this stage, as Carlyle observed with dismay, many men seemed content simply to stop. A Utilitarian such as James Mill or some of his common-sensical professors at the University of Edinburgh regarded society and the universe itself as machines. To such men the machines might sometimes seem complex, but they were not mysterious, for machines are subject to man's control and understanding through reason and observation. To Carlyle, and to many others, life without a sense of the divine was a mean-ingless nightmare. In the first part of "The Everlasting No," a chapter of *Sartor Resartus*, he gives a memorable picture of the horrors of such a soulless world that drove him in 1822 to thoughts of suicide. The 18th-century Enlightenment had left him not in light but in darkness. As William Barrett says of modern man, in his study of 20th-century Ex-istentialism: "The individual is thrust out of the sheltered nest that society has provided. He can no longer hide his nakedness by the old disguises."

Barrett's choice of terms here is identical with Carlyle's metaphor of the "Clothes Philosophy." The naked man seeks clothing for protection. One solution, represented by Coleridge and his followers, was to repudiate the skepticism of Voltaire and Hume and to return to the protective be-liefs and rituals of the Christian church. To Carlyle such a return was pointless. The traditional Christian coverings were worn out—"Hebrew Old Clothes" he called them. His own solution, described in "The Ever-lasting Yea," was to tailor a new suit of beliefs from German philosophy, shreds of Scottish Calvinism, and his own observations. The following sum-marizes his basic religious attitude: "Gods die with the men who have con-ceived them. But the god-stuff roars eternally, like the sea. * * * Even the gods must be born again. We must be born again." Although this passage is from *The Plumed Serpent*, by D. H. Lawrence (a writer who resembles Carlyle at almost every point), it might have come from any one of Car-lyle's own books—most especially from *Sartor Resartus*, in which he de-scribes his being born again—his "Fire-baptism"—into a new secular faith.

On what evidence was the new faith based? Carlyle and Lawrence might contend that the word "evidence" is irrelevant here. Or Carlyle might cite the religious experience itself, the moment of insight when he saw the realities behind the appearances. He might also cite his realization that all the sciences he had studied had failed to answer the important ques-tions confronting man, which remain what he called "mysteries." From this latter realization there derives what seems an anti-intellectual strain in Carlyle. He speaks often of the limitations of the conscious analytic intellect and praises instead the instinctive responses of the unconsciously healthy soul, responses which include a sense of religious awe.

The most appropriate term to describe Carlyle's central position is *vi-talism*. The presence of energy in the world was, in itself, for him, a sign of the godhead. Carlyle therefore judges everything in terms of the pres-ence or absence of some vital spark. The minds of men, books, societies, churches, or even landscapes, are rated as alive or dead, dynamic or merely mechanical. The government of Louis XVI, for example, was obviously moribund, doomed to be swept away by the dynamic forces of the French Revolution. The government of Victorian England seemed likewise to be doomed unless infused with vital energies of leadership and an awareness of the real needs of mankind. When an editor complained that his essay *Characteristics* was "inscrutable," Carlyle remarked: "My own fear was that it might be too *scrutable;* for it indicates decisively enough that Society (in my view) is utterly condemned to destruction, and even now beginning its long travail-throes of Newbirth."

This preoccupation with revolution and the destruction of the old orders suggests that Carlyle's politics were radical, but his position is bewilderingly difficult to classify. During the Hungry 1840's, he was one of the most outspoken critics of middle-class bunglings and of the economic theory of laissez faire which, in his opinion, was ultimately responsible for these bunglings. On behalf of the millions of people suffering from the miseries attendant upon a major breakdown of industry and agriculture he did strenuous work. At other times, because of his insistence upon strong and heroic leadership, Carlyle appears to be a violent conservative, or, as some have argued, virtually a fascist. That some aspects of his political position are similar to fascism is beyond dispute. The theory of democracy seemed to him to be based on an unrealistic premise about the basic needs of mankind, and he had no confidence that democratic institutions could work efficiently. A few men in every age are, in his view, leaders; the rest are followers and are happy only as followers. Society should be organized so that these gifted leaders can have scope to govern effectively. Such leaders are, for Carlyle, heroes. George Bernard Shaw, who learned much from Carlyle, would call them supermen. Liberals and democrats, however, might call them dictators. Although Carlyle was aware that the Western world was committed to a faith in a system of balloting and of legislative debate, he was confident that the system would eventually break down. The democratic assumption that all voters are equally capable of choice and the assumption that men value liberty more than they value order seemed to him nonsense. To all of us nurtured in presuppositions about the virtues of the democratic system of politics, it is instructive to confront this potent Victorian critic of democracy. But it is also instructive to observe how his political authoritarianism became intensified as he grew older. In his earlier writings Carlyle was arguing, in effect, that in politics, as well as in religion, men need the guiding hand of some kind of father. In his later writings, on the other hand, he seems to be arguing for the need of some kind of ruthless commander. His opinions about how governors should treat Negro workers on the Jamaica plantations make painful reading. As he himself said, these fierce *Latter-Day Pamphlets* had "divided me altogether from the mob of 'Progress-of-the-Species' and other vulgar." One distinction should, however, be noted. Concerning the English and Irish laborers thrown out of work by economic circumstances Carlyle writes with affectionate compassion. But toward anyone who does not *want* to work (as he had been informed was the case in Jamaica), he writes with the savage contempt of the hard-working northerner. Once more the test remains for Carlyle the presence or absence of energy.

The effect of vitalism on Carlyle's prose style will also be evident. At the time he began to write, the essayists of the 18th century, Samuel Johnson in particular, were the models of good prose. Carlyle recognized that their style, however admirable an instrument for reasoning, analysis, and generalized exposition, did not suit his purposes. Like a poet, he wanted to convey the sense of experience itself. Like a preacher or prophet, he wanted to exhort or inspire his readers rather than to develop a chain of logical argument. Like a psychoanalyst, he wanted to explore the unconscious and irrational levels of human life, the hidden nine tenths of the iceberg rather than the conscious and rational fraction above the surface. To this end he developed his highly individual manner of writing, with its vivid imagery of fire and barnyard and zoo, its mixture of Biblical rhythms and explosive talk, and its inverted and unorthodox syntax. Classicists may complain, as Landor did, that the result is not English. Carlyle would reply that it is not 18th-century English, but that his style was appropriate for a Victorian who reports of revolutions in society and in thought. In reply to a friend who had protested about his stylistic experiments Carlyle exclaimed: "Do you reckon this really a time for Purism of Style? I do not: with whole ragged battalions of Scott's Novel Scotch, with Irish, German, French, and even Newspaper Cockney * * * storming in on us, and the whole structure of our Johnsonian English breaking up from its foundations—revolution *there* as visible as anywhere else!" Carlyle's defense of his style can be tested by his history, *The French Revolution*. One may agree or disagree with the historian's explanations of how the fire started or how it was extinguished. But the fire itself is unquestionably there before us, roaring, palpable, giving off a heat of its own.

In 1847 Emerson made his second visit to Carlyle in England and recorded his impressions of his writings and talk: "In Carlyle, as in Byron, one is more struck with the rhetoric than with the matter. He has manly superiority rather than intellectuality, and so makes good hard hits all the time. There is more character than intellect in every sentence, herein strongly resembling Samuel Johnson." We should misunderstand Emerson if we took this verdict to be unkind. What he says has the virtue of putting Carlyle into the appropriate company of Byron and Dr. Johnson instead of Immanuel Kant and St. Thomas Aquinas. There are readers in the 20th century, of whom D. H. Lawrence was one, who find Carlyle's religious position, even his political position, worthy of imitation. But most readers today would instead share George Eliot's opinion (in an essay of 1855) that Carlyle was "more of an artist than a philosopher." As she said: "No novelist has made his creations live for us more thoroughly." Carlyle is best regarded, that is, as a man of letters, the inventor of a distinctive and extremely effective prose medium which can bring to life for us the very texture of events in scenes such as when a king confronts a guillotine, a young agnostic confronts the devil, or a talker such as Coleridge stupefies an audience of admiring disciples.

[Carlyle's Portraits of His Contemporaries][1]

[KING WILLIAM IV AT 69]

The old King came driving to the ground, near where I was standing: he was in regimentals [2] with a most copious plume of feathers, so that while he sat all shrunk together in the open carriage, you saw little else but a lock of feathers, and might have taken our Defender of the Faith for some singular species of *Clocker* [3] coming thither. On dismounting, he showed an innocent respectable old face; straddled out his legs greatly (which seemed weak), rested on his heels, *stiddering* [4] himself, and looked round with much simplicity what they wanted next with him. The Review itself was a wheeling and marching of foot and horse, several thousands; a flaring and a blaring from trumpet and drum, with artillery-vollies, sham-charges, and then a continued explosion of musketry and cannon from the whole posse of them, like a long explosion of Mount Ætna: all very grand.

[From a letter to his mother, July 19, 1835]

[QUEEN VICTORIA AT 18]

Yesterday, going through one of the Parks, I saw the poor little Queen. She was in an open carriage, preceded by three or four swift red-coated troopers; all off for Windsor just as I happened to pass. Another carriage or carriages followed with maids-of-honour, etc.: the whole drove very fast. It seemed to me the poor little Queen was a bit modest, nice sonsy [5] little lassie; blue eyes, light hair, fine white skin; of extremely small stature: she looked timid, anxious, almost frightened; for the people looked at her in perfect silence; one old liveryman alone touched his hat to her: I was heartily sorry for the poor bairn,—tho' perhaps she might have said as Parson Swan did, "*Greet* [6] not for me brethren; for verily, yea verily, I

---

1. Carlyle once said that "human Portraits, faithfully drawn, are of all pictures the welcomest on human walls." With his pen, rather than with brush, he himself has created a strikingly colorful gallery of his contemporaries.
  A few of the following selections (all of them excerpted by the present editor) were written for publication, in particular the elaborate portrait of Coleridge; ; the majority of them, however, are sketches from his letters, sometimes in the vein of caricature. As Charles Sanders notes, all of them—like most of the portraits by Chaucer, Browning, and Yeats—are "appraisal portraits." Carlyle has been called the Victorian Rembrandt. But with his sharp eye for absurdities he is often the Victorian Daumier or Rowlandson. This element of caricature can be partly explained in terms of difference of age. It will be noted that most of the celebrities described were men older than Carlyle, and he had the customary determination of youth to make fun of the pretensions of an older and established generation. In Carlyle's case there was the additional urge to be irreverent in that he was a provincial in a great metropolis with the provincial's need to assert his independence of judgment.
  The portraits are not presented chronologically. The first two are sketches of royalty; the others are of English writers. Titles for each portrait have been assigned by the editor.
2. I.e., in military uniform.
3. Clucking hen (Scottish).
4. Steadying (Scottish).
5. Sweet (Scottish).
6. Weep.

greet not for mysel'." It is a strange thing to look at the fashion of this world!

[From a letter to his mother, April 12, 1838]

[CHARLES LAMB AT 56]

Charles Lamb I sincerely believe to be in some considerable degree *insane*. A more pitiful, rickety, gasping, staggering, stammering Tom fool I do not know. He is witty by denying truisms, and abjuring good manners. His speech wriggles hither and thither with an incessant painful fluctuation; not an opinion in it or a fact or even a phrase that you can thank him for: more like a convulsion fit than natural systole and diastole.—Besides he is now a confirmed shameless drunkard: *asks* vehemently for gin-and-water in strangers' houses; tipples until he is utterly mad, and is only not thrown out of doors because he is too much despised for taking such trouble with him. Poor Lamb! Poor England where such a despicable abortion is named genius!—He said: There are just two things I regret in English History; first that Guy Faux's plot did not take effect (there would have been so glorious an *explosion*); second that the Royalists did not hang Milton (then we might have laughed at them); etc., etc.

[From *Notebooks*, November 2, 1831]

[SAMUEL TAYLOR COLERIDGE AT 53] [7]

Coleridge sat on the brow of Highgate Hill, in those years, looking down on London and its smoke-tumult, like a sage escaped from the inanity of life's battle; attracting towards him the thoughts of innumerable brave souls still engaged there. His express contributions to poetry, philosophy, or any specific province of human literature or enlightenment, had been small and sadly intermittent; but he had, especially among young inquiring men, a higher than literary, a kind of prophetic or magician character. He was thought to hold, he alone in England, the key of German and other Transcendentalisms; knew the sublime secret of believing by "the reason" what "the understanding" had been obliged to fling out as incredible; and could still, after Hume and Voltaire had done their best and worst with him, profess himself an orthodox Christian, and say and print to the Church of England, with its singular old rubrics and surplices at Allhallowtide,[8] *Esto perpetua*. A sublime man; who, alone in those dark days, had saved his crown of spiritual

7. In 1816 Coleridge moved to a London suburb as a permanent guest in the home of James Gillman. Here he received visits from admirers of his philosophy such as Carlyle's friend, John Sterling, from whose biography, by Carlyle, this selection has been taken. Carlyle's visits were made during his first residence in London in 1824–25.

8. November 1, a festival in honor of all the saints, celebrated by the Roman Catholic and Angelican Churches. The Latin means, "Be thou everlasting"— the last words of Paolo Sarpi (1552–1623), theologian and historian, addressed to the city of Venice.

manhood; escaping from the black materialisms, and revolutionary deluges, with "God, Freedom, Immortality" still his: a king of men. The practical intellects of the world did not much heed him, or carelessly reckoned him a metaphysical dreamer: but to the rising spirits of the young generation he had this dusky sublime character; and sat there as a kind of *Magus*,[9] girt in mystery and enigma; his Dodona [1] oak-grove (Mr. Gillman's house at Highgate) whispering strange things, uncertain whether oracles or jargon.

The Gillmans did not encourage much company, or excitation of any sort, round their sage; nevertheless access to him, if a youth did reverently wish it, was not difficult. He would stroll about the pleasant garden with you, sit in the pleasant rooms of the place,— perhaps take you to his own peculiar room, high up, with a rearward view, which was the chief view of all. A really charming outlook, in fine weather. Close at hand, wide sweep of flowery leafy gardens, their few houses mostly hidden, the very chimney-pots veiled under blossomy umbrage, flowed gloriously down hill, gloriously issuing in wide-tufted undulating plain-country, rich in all charms of field and town. Waving blooming country of the brightest green; dotted all over with handsome villas, handsome groves; crossed by roads and human traffic, here inaudible or heard only as a musical hum: and behind all swam, under olive-tinted haze, the illimitable limitary ocean of London, with its domes and steeples definite in the sun, big Paul's and the many memories attached to it hanging high over all. Nowhere, of its kind, could you see a grander prospect on a bright summer day, with the set of the air going southward,—southward, and so draping with the city-smoke not *you* but the city. Here for hours would Coleridge talk, concerning all conceivable or inconceivable things; and liked nothing better than to have an intelligent, or failing that, even a silent and patient human listener. He distinguished himself to all that ever heard him as at least the most surprising talker extant in this world,— and to some small minority, by no means to all, as the most excellent.

The good man, he was now getting old, towards sixty perhaps; and gave you the idea of a life that had been full of sufferings; a life heavy-laden, half-vanquished, still swimming painfully in seas of manifold physical and other bewilderment. Brow and head were round, and of massive weight, but the face was flabby and irresolute. The deep eyes, of a light hazel, were as full of sorrow as of inspiration; confused pain looked mildly from them, as in a kind of mild astonishment. The whole figure and air, good and amiable otherwise, might be called flabby and irresolute; expressive of weakness

9. An oriental magician or sorcerer.
1. An oracle in Greece. Prophecies were voiced by priests who interpreted the rustling sounds made by oak leaves stirred by the wind.

under possibility of strength. He hung loosely on his limbs, with knees bent, and stooping attitude; in walking, he rather shuffled than decisively stept; and a lady once remarked, he never could fix which side of the garden walk would suit him best, but continually shifted, in corkscrew fashion, and kept trying both. A heavy-laden, high-aspiring and surely much-suffering man. His voice, naturally soft and good, had contracted itself into a plaintive snuffle and singsong; he spoke as if preaching,—you would have said, preaching earnestly and also hopelessly the weightiest things. I still recollect his "object" and "subject," terms of continual recurrence in the Kantean province; and how he sang and snuffled them into "om-m-mject" and "sum-m-mject," with a kind of solemn shake or quaver, as he rolled along. No talk, in his century or in any other, could be more surprising. * * *

Nothing could be more copious than his talk; and furthermore it was always, virtually or literally, of the nature of a monologue; suffering no interruption, however reverent; hastily putting aside all foreign additions, annotations, or most ingenuous desires for elucidation, as well-meant superfluities which would never do. Besides, it was talk not flowing anywhither like a river, but spreading everywhither in inextricable currents and regurgitations like a lake or sea; terribly deficient in definite goal or aim, nay often in logical intelligibility; *what* you were to believe or do, on any earthly or heavenly thing, obstinately refusing to appear from it. So that, most times, you felt logically lost; swamped near to drowning in this tide of ingenious vocables, spreading out boundless as if to submerge the world.

To sit as a passive bucket and be pumped into, whether you consent or not, can in the long-run be exhilarating to no creature; how eloquent soever the flood of utterance that is descending. But if it be withal a confused unintelligible flood of utterance, threatening to submerge all known landmarks of thought, and drown the world and you!—I have heard Coleridge talk, with eager musical energy, two stricken hours, his face radiant and moist, and communicate no meaning whatsoever to any individual of his hearers,—certain of whom, I for one, still kept eagerly listening in hope; the most had long before given up, and formed (if the room were large enough) secondary humming groups of their own. He began anywhere: you put some question to him, made some suggestive observation: instead of answering this, or decidedly setting out towards answer of it, he would accumulate formidable apparatus, logical swim-bladders, transcendental life-preservers and other precautionary and vehiculatory gear, for setting out; perhaps did at last get under way, —but was swiftly solicited, turned aside by the glance of some radiant new game on this hand or that, into new courses; and ever

into new; and before long into all the Universe, where it was uncertain what game you would catch, or whether any.

His talk, alas, was distinguished, like himself, by irresolution: it
disliked to be troubled with conditions, abstinences, definite fulfil-
ments;—loved to wander at its own sweet will, and make its auditor and his claims and humble wishes a mere passive bucket for itself! He had knowledge about many things and topics, much curious
reading; but generally all topics led him, after a pass or two, into
the high seas of theosophic philosophy, the hazy infinitude of
Kantean transcendentalism, with its "sum-m-mjects" and "om-m-
mjects." Sad enough; for with such indolent impatience of the
claims and ignorances of others, he had not the least talent for
explaining this or anything unknown to them; and you swam and
fluttered in the mistiest wide unintelligible deluge of things, for
most part in a rather profitless uncomfortable manner.

Glorious islets, too, I have seen rise out of the haze; but they
were few, and soon swallowed in the general element again. Balmy
sunny islets, islets of the blest and the intelligible:—on which occasions those secondary humming groups would all cease humming,
and hang breathless upon the eloquent words; till once your islet
got wrapt in the mist again, and they could recommence humming.
* * * Coleridge was not without what talkers call wit, and there
were touches of prickly sarcasm in him, contemptuous enough of
the world and its idols and popular dignitaries; he had traits even
of poetic humour: but in general he seemed deficient in laughter;
or indeed in sympathy for concrete human things either on the
sunny or on the stormy side. One right peal of concrete laughter
at some convicted flesh-and-blood absurdity, one burst of noble indignation at some injustice or depravity, rubbing elbows with us
on this solid Earth, how strange would it have been in that Kantean
haze-world, and how infinitely cheering amid its vacant air-castles
and dim-melting ghosts and shadows! None such ever came. His
life had been an abstract thinking and dreaming, idealistic, passed
amid the ghosts of defunct bodies and of unborn ones. The meaning singsong of that theosophico-metaphysical monotony left on
you, at last, a very dreary feeling. * * *

But indeed, to the young ardent mind, instinct with pious nobleness, yet driven to the grim deserts of Radicalism for a faith, his
speculations had a charm much more than literary, a charm almost
religious and prophetic. The constant gist of his discourse was lamentation over the sunk condition of the world; which he recognised to be given-up to Atheism and Materialism, full of mere
sordid misbeliefs, mispursuits and misresults. All Science had become mechanical; the science not of men, but of a kind of human
beavers. Churches themselves had died away into a godless mechan-

ical condition; and stood there as mere Cases of Articles, mere
Forms of Churches; like the dried carcasses of once-swift camels,
which you find left withering in the thirst of the universal desert,
—ghastly portents for the present, beneficent ships of the desert
no more. Men's souls were blinded, hebetated,[2] and sunk under the
influence of Atheism and Materialism, and Hume and Voltaire:
the world for the present was as an extinct world, deserted of God,
and incapable of welldoing till it changed its heart and spirit. This,
expressed I think with less of indignation and with more of long-
drawn querulousness, was always recognisable as the ground-tone:
—in which truly a pious young heart, driven into Radicalism and
the opposition party, could not but recognise a too sorrowful truth;
and ask of the Oracle, with all earnestness, What remedy, then?

The remedy, though Coleridge himself professed to see it as in
sunbeams, could not, except by processes unspeakably difficult, be
described to you at all. On the whole, those dead Churches, this
dead English Church especially, must be brought to life again.
Why not? It was not dead; the soul of it, in this parched-up body,
was tragically asleep only. Atheistic Philosophy was true on its side,
and Hume and Voltaire could on their own ground speak irrefrag-
ably for themselves against any Church: but lift the Church and
them into a higher sphere of argument, *they* died into inanition,
the Church revivified itself into pristine florid vigour,—became once
more a living ship of the desert, and invincibly bore you over stock
and stone. But how, but how! By attending to the "reason" of man,
said Coleridge, and duly chaining-up the "understanding" of man:
the *Vernunft* (Reason) and *Verstand* (Understanding) of the Germans, it all turned upon these, if you could well understand them,
—which you couldn't. For the rest, Mr. Coleridge had on the anvil
various Books, especially was about to write one grand Book *On
the Logos*, which would help to bridge the chasm for us. So much
appeared, however: Churches, though proved false (as you had imagined), were still true (as you were to imagine): here was an Artist
who could burn you up an old Church, root and branch; and then
as the Alchymists professed to do with organic substances in general, distil you an "Astral Spirit" from the ashes, which was the
very image of the old burnt article, its airdrawn counterpart,—
this you still had, or might get, and draw uses from, if you could.
Wait till the Book on the Logos were done;—alas, till your own
terrene eyes, blind with conceit and the dust of logic, were purged,
subtilised and spiritualised into the sharpness of vision requisite
for discerning such an "om-m-mject."—The ingenuous young English head, of those days, stood strangely puzzled by such revelations;
uncertain whether it were getting inspired, or getting infatuated

2. Dulled.

into flat imbecility; and strange effulgence, of new day or else of deeper meteoric night, coloured the horizon of the future for it.

[From *Life of John Sterling*, 1851]

[WILLIAM WORDSWORTH IN HIS SEVENTIES]

On a summer morning (let us call it 1840 then) I was apprised by Taylor[3] that Wordsworth had come to town, and would meet a small party of us at a certain tavern in St. James's Street, at breakfast, to which I was invited for the given day and hour. We had a pretty little room, quiet though looking street-ward (tavern's name is quite lost to me); the morning sun was pleasantly tinting the opposite houses, a balmy, calm and sunlight morning. Wordsworth, I think, arrived just along with me; we had still five minutes of sauntering and miscellaneous talking before the whole were assembled. I do not positively remember any of them, except that James Spedding[1] was there, and that the others, not above five or six in whole, were polite intelligent quiet persons, and, except Taylor and Wordsworth, not of any special distinction in the world. Breakfast was pleasant, fairly beyond the common of such things. Wordsworth seemed in good tone, and, much to Taylor's satisfaction, talked a great deal; about "poetic" correspondents of his own (i.e. correspondents for the sake of his poetry; especially one such who had sent him, from Canton, an excellent chest of tea; correspondent grinningly applauded by us all); then about ruralities and miscellanies. * * * These were the first topics. Then finally about literature, literary laws, practices, observances, at considerable length, and turning wholly on the mechanical part, including even a good deal of shallow enough etymology, from me and others, which was well received. On all this Wordsworth enlarged with evident satisfaction, and was joyfully reverent of the "wells of English undefiled";[2] though stone dumb as to the deeper rules and wells of Eternal Truth and Harmony, which you were to try and set forth by said undefiled wells of English or what other speech you had! To me a little disappointing, but not much; though it would have given me pleasure had the robust veteran man emerged a little out of vocables into things, now and then, as he never once chanced to do. For the rest, he talked well in his way; with veracity, easy brevity and force, as a wise tradesman would of his tools and workshop,—and as no unwise one could. His voice was good, frank and sonorous, though practically clear distinct and forcible rather than melodious; the tone of him businesslike, sedately confident; no discourtesy, yet no anxiety about being courteous. A fine whole-

3. Henry Taylor, contemporary playwright.
1. Editor of the works of Francis Bacon.
2. Spenser, *Faerie Queene* IV.ii.32—referring to Chaucer.

some rusticity, fresh as his mountain breezes, sat well on the stalwart veteran, and on all he said and did. You would have said he was a usually taciturn man; glad to unlock himself to audience sympathetic and intelligent, when such offered itself. His face bore marks of much, not always peaceful, meditation; the look of it not bland or benevolent so much as close impregnable and hard: a man *multa tacere loquive paratus*,[3] in a world where he had experienced no lack of contradictions as he strode along! The eyes were not very brilliant, but they had a quiet clearness; there was enough of brow and well shaped; rather too much of cheek ("horse face" I have heard satirists say); face of squarish shape and decidedly longish, as I think the head itself was (its "length" going horizontal); he was large-boned, lean, but still firm-knit tall and strong-looking when he stood, a right good old steel-grey figure, with rustic simplicity and dignity about him, and a vivacious strength looking through him which might have suited one of those old steel-grey markgrafs[4] whom Henry the Fowler set up to ward the "marches" and do battle with the intrusive heathen in a stalwart and judicious manner.

On this and other occasional visits of his, I saw Wordsworth a number of times, at dinner, in evening parties; and we grew a little more familiar, but without much increase of real intimacy or affection springing up between us. He was willing to talk with me in a corner, in noisy extensive circles, having weak eyes, and little loving the general babble current in such places. One evening, probably about this time, I got him upon the subject of great poets, who I thought might be admirable equally to us both; but was rather mistaken, as I gradually found. Pope's partial failure I was prepared for; less for the narrowish limits visible in Milton and others. I tried him with Burns, of whom he had sung tender recognition; but Burns also turned out to be a limited inferior creature, any genius he had a theme for one's pathos rather; even Shakespeare himself had his blind sides, his limitations; gradually it became apparent to me that of transcendent unlimited there was, to this critic, probably but one specimen known, Wordsworth himself! He by no means said so, or hinted so, in words; but on the whole it was all I gathered from him in this considerable *tête-à-tête* of ours; and it was not an agreeable conquest. New notion as to poetry or poet I had not in the smallest degree got; but my insight into the depths of Wordsworth's pride in himself had considerably augmented; and it did not increase my love of him; though I did not in the least hate it either, so quiet was it, so fixed, unappealing, like a dim old lichened crag on the wayside, the private meaning of which, in con-

---

3. "Prepared to speak out or to pass over much in silence."
4. Governors appointed by Henry I of Germany, "the Fowler" (876–936), to guard the borders ("marches") of his kingdom.

trast with any public meaning it had, you recognised with a kind of not wholly melancholy grin. * * *

During the last seven or ten years of his life, Wordsworth felt himself to be a recognised lion, in certain considerable London circles, and was in the habit of coming up to town with his wife for a month or two every season, to enjoy his quiet triumph and collect his bits of tribute *tales quales*.[5] * * * Wordsworth took his bit of lionism very quietly, with a smile sardonic rather than triumphant, and certainly got no harm by it, if he got or expected little good. His wife, a small, withered, puckered, winking lady, who never spoke, seemed to be more in earnest about the affair, and was visibly and sometimes ridiculously assiduous to secure her proper place of precedence at table. * * * The light was always afflictive to his eyes; he carried in his pocket something like a skeleton brass candlestick, in which, setting it on the dinner-table, between him and the most afflictive or nearest of the chief lights, he touched a little spring, and there flirted out, at the top of his brass implement, a small vertical green circle which prettily enough threw his eyes into shade, and screened him from that sorrow. In proof of his equanimity as lion I remember, in connection with this green shade, one little glimpse. * * * Dinner was large, luminous, sumptuous; I sat a long way from Wordsworth; dessert I think had come in, and certainly there reigned in all quarters a cackle as of Babel (only politer perhaps), which far up in Wordsworth's quarter (who was leftward on my side of the table) seemed to have taken a sententious, rather louder, logical and quasi-scientific turn, heartily unimportant to gods and men, so far as I could judge of it and of the other babble reigning. I looked upwards, leftwards, the coast being luckily for a moment clear; there, far off, beautifully screened in the shadow of his vertical green circle, which was on the farther side of him, sate Wordsworth, silent, slowly but steadily gnawing some portion of what I judged to be raisins, with his eye and attention placidly fixed on these and these alone. The sight of whom, and of his rock-like indifference to the babble, quasi-scientific and other, with attention turned on the small practical alone, was comfortable and amusing to me, who felt like him but could not eat raisins. This little glimpse I could still paint, so clear and bright is it, and this shall be symbolical of all.

In a few years, I forget in how many and when, these Wordsworth appearances in London ceased; we heard, not of ill-health perhaps, but of increasing love of rest; at length of the long sleep's coming; and never saw Wordsworth more. One felt his death as the extinction of a public light, but not otherwise.

[From *Reminiscences*, 1867, 1881]

5. Of such a sort.

[ALFRED TENNYSON AT 34]

Alfred is one of the few British or Foreign Figures (a not increasing number I think!) who are and remain beautiful to me;—a true human soul, or some authentic approximation thereto, to whom your own soul can say, Brother!—However, I doubt he will not come; he often skips me, in these brief visits to Town; skips everybody indeed; being a man solitary and sad, as certain men are, dwelling in an element of gloom,—carrying a bit of Chaos about him, in short, which he is manufacturing into Cosmos!

Alfred is the son of a Lincolnshire Gentleman Farmer, I think; indeed, you see in his verses that he is a native of "moated granges," and green, fat pastures, not of mountains and their torrents and storms. He had his breeding at Cambridge, as if for the Law or Church; being master of a small annuity on his Father's decease, he preferred clubbing with his Mother and some Sisters, to live unpromoted and write Poems. In this way he lives still, now here, now there; the family always within reach of London, never in it; he himself making rare and brief visits, lodging in some old comrade's rooms. I think he must be under forty, not much under it. One of the finest-looking men in the world. A great shock of rough dusty-dark hair; bright-laughing hazel eyes; massive aquiline face, most massive yet most delicate; of sallow-brown complexion, almost Indian-looking; clothes cynically loose, free-and-easy;—smokes infinite tobacco. His voice is musical metallic,—fit for loud laughter and piercing wail, and all that may lie between; speech and speculation free and plenteous: I do not meet, in these late decades, such company over a pipe!—We shall see what he will grow to. He is often unwell; very chaotic,—his way is through Chaos and the Bottomless and Pathless; not handy for making out many miles upon.

[From a letter to Emerson, August 5, 1844]

[WILLIAM MAKEPEACE THACKERAY AT 42]

Thackeray has very rarely come athwart me since his return: he is a big fellow, soul and body; of many gifts and qualities (particularly in the Hogarth[6] line, with a dash of Sterne[7] superadded), of enormous *appetite* withal, and very uncertain and chaotic in all points except his *outer breeding*, which is fixed enough, and *perfect* according to the modern English style. I rather dread explosions in his history. A *big*, fierce, weeping, hungry man; not a strong one.

[From a letter to Emerson, September 9, 1853]

---

6. William Hogarth (1697–1764), a realistic and satirical painter of English life.

7. Laurence Sterne (1713–68), whose novels are often sentimental.

From Characteristics[1]

The healthy know not of their health, but only the sick: this is the Physician's Aphorism; and applicable in a far wider sense than he gives it. We may say, it holds no less in moral, intellectual, political, poetical, than in merely corporeal therapeutics; that wherever, or in what shape soever, powers of the sort which can be named *vital* are at work, herein lies the test of their working right or working wrong.

In the Body, for example, as all doctors are agreed, the first condition of complete health is, that each organ perform its function unconsciously, unheeded; let but any organ announce its separate existence, were it even boastfully, and for pleasure, not for pain, then already has one of those unfortunate "false centres of sensibility" established itself, already is derangement there. The perfection of bodily well-being is, that the collective bodily activities seem one; and be manifested, moreover, not in themselves, but in the action they accomplish. * * *

However, without venturing into the abstruse, or too eagerly asking Why and How, in things where our answer must needs prove, in great part, an echo of the question, let us be content to remark farther, in the merely historical way, how that Aphorism of the bodily Physician holds good in quite other departments. Of the Soul, with her activities, we shall find it no less true than of the Body: nay, cry the Spiritualists, is not that very division of the unity, Man, into a dualism of Soul and Body, itself the symptom of disease; as, perhaps, your frightful theory of Materialism, of his being but a Body, and therefore, at least, once more a unity, may be the paroxysm which was critical, and the beginning of cure! But omitting this, we observe, with confidence enough, that the truly strong mind, view it as Intellect, as Morality, or under any other aspect, is nowise the mind acquainted with its strength; that here

1. First published in the *Edinburgh Review*, ostensibly as a review of two books of philosophy which had appeared in 1830 and 1831: *An Essay on the Origin and Prospects of Man* by Thomas Hope, and *Philosophical Lectures* by Friedrich von Schlegel. Hope was a Utilitarian writer, and his analytical treatise may have inspired the first half of the essay, in which Carlyle exposes what seems to him the most characteristic symptom of modern man's diseased state of mind and spirit: self-consciousness. Schlegel's book, an example of the German transcendental philosophy which Carlyle admired, may have inspired the second half of his essay, in which he points out the encouraging prospects for the future if mankind can find a new religious faith. Yet it is only near the end of *Characteristics* that Carlyle finally refers directly to these two books as such, for his real object, as his title suggests, is not to write a mere book review but to describe the state of mind and society characteristic of the age. This early essay, even in the necessarily abridged form adopted here, contains in embryo all the basic religious and political ideas that Carlyle was to develop in his later writings.

as before the sign of health is Unconsciousness. In our inward, as in our outward world, what is mechanical lies open to us; not what is dynamical and has vitality. Of our Thinking, we might say, it is but the mere upper surface that we shape into articulate Thoughts; —underneath the region of argument and conscious discourse, lies the region of meditation; here, in its quiet mysterious depths, dwells what vital force is in us; here, if aught is to be created, and not merely manufactured and communicated, must the work go on. Manufacture is intelligible, but trivial; Creation is great, and cannot be understood. Thus if the Debater and Demonstrator, whom we may rank as the lowest of true thinkers, knows what he has done, and how he did it, the Artist, whom we rank as the highest, knows not; must speak of Inspiration, and in one or the other dialect, call his work the gift of a divinity.

But on the whole "genius is ever a secret to itself";[2] of this old truth we have, on all sides, daily evidence. The Shakespeare takes no airs for writing *Hamlet* and the *Tempest*, understands not that it is anything surprising: Milton, again, is more conscious of his faculty, which accordingly is an inferior one. On the other hand, what cackling and strutting must we not often hear and see, when, in some shape of academical prolusion, maiden speech, review article, this or the other well-fledged goose has produced its goose-egg, of quite measurable value, were it the pink of its whole kind; and wonders why all mortals do not wonder!

Foolish enough, too, was the College Tutor's surprise at Walter Shandy:[3] how, though unread in Aristotle, he could nevertheless argue; and not knowing the name of any dialectic tool, handled them all to perfection. Is it the skilfulest anatomist that cuts the best figure[4] at Sadler's Wells? or does the boxer hit better for knowing that he has a *flexor longus* and a *flexor brevis*?[5] But indeed, as in the higher case of the Poet, so here in that of the Speaker and Inquirer, the true force is an unconscious one. The healthy Understanding, we should say, is not the Logical, argumentative, but the Intuitive; for the end of Understanding is not to prove and find reasons, but to know and believe. Of logic, and its limits, and uses and abuses, there were much to be said and examined; one fact, however, which chiefly concerns us here, has long been familiar: that the man of logic and the man of insight; the Reasoner and the Discoverer, or even Knower, are quite separable, —indeed, for most part, quite separate characters. In practical matters, for example, has it not become almost proverbial that the man of logic cannot prosper? This is he whom business-people call Sys-

2. From an essay by the German poet J. C. F. von Schiller (1759–1805).
3. Laurence Sterne, *Tristram Shandy* I.xix.

4. Makes the most striking appearance. "Sadler's Wells" refers to a London theater.
5. Technical terms for bodily muscles.

tematic and Theoriser and Word-monger; his *vital* intellectual force lies dormant or extinct, his whole force is mechanical, conscious: of such a one it is foreseen that, when once confronted with the infinite complexities of the real world, his little compact theorem of the world will be found wanting; that unless he can throw it overboard and become a new creature, he will necessarily founder. * * * Never since the beginning of Time was there, that we hear or read of, so intensely self-conscious a Society. Our whole relations to the Universe and to our fellow-man have become an Inquiry, a Doubt; nothing will go on of its own accord, and do its function quietly; but all things must be probed into, the whole working of man's world be anatomically studied. Alas, anatomically studied, that it may be medically aided! Till at length indeed, we have come to such a pass, that except in this same *medicine*, with its artifices and appliances, few can so much as imagine any strength or hope to remain for us. The whole Life of Society must now be carried on by drugs: doctor after doctor appears with his nostrum, of Co-operative Societies, Universal Suffrage, Cottage-and-Cow systems, Repression of Population, Vote by Ballot. To such height has the dyspepsia of Society reached; as indeed the constant grinding internal pain, or from time to time the mad spasmodic throes, of all Society do otherwise too mournfully indicate.

Far be it from us to attribute, as some unwise persons do, the disease itself to this unhappy sensation that there is a disease! The Encyclopedists[6] did not produce the troubles of France; but the troubles of France produced the Encyclopedists, and much else. The Self-consciousness is the symptom merely; nay, it is also the attempt towards cure. We record the fact, without special censure; not wondering that Society should feel itself, and in all ways complain of aches and twinges, for it has suffered enough. * * *

But leaving this, let us rather look within, into the Spiritual condition of Society, and see what aspects and prospects offer themselves there. * * * To begin with our highest Spiritual function, with Religion, we might ask, Whither has Religion now fled? Of Churches and their establishments we here say nothing; nor of the unhappy domains of Unbelief, and how innumerable men, blinded in their minds, have grown to "live without God in the world";[7] but, taking the fairest side of the matter, we ask, What is the nature of that same Religion, which still lingers in the hearts of the few who are called, and call themselves, specially the Religious? Is it a healthy religion, vital, unconscious of itself; that shines forth spontaneously in doing of the Work, or even in preaching of the Word? Unhappily, no. Instead of heroic martyr Conduct, and in-

---

6. Diderot, Voltaire, and other critics of the established order in France who were contributors to the *Encyclopédie* (1751–52, 1776–80).
7. Cf. Ephesians ii.12.

spired and soul-inspiring Eloquence, whereby Religion itself were brought home to our living bosoms, to live and reign there, we have "Discourses on the Evidences,"[8] endeavouring, with smallest result, to make it probable that such a thing as Religion exists. The most enthusiastic Evangelicals do not preach a Gospel, but keep describing how it should and might be preached: to awaken the sacred fire of faith, as by a sacred contagion, is not their endeavour; but, at most, to describe how Faith shows and acts, and scientifically distinguish true Faith from false. Religion, like all else, is conscious of itself, listens to itself; it becomes less and less creative, vital; more and more mechanical. Considered as a whole, the Christian Religion of late ages has been continually dissipating itself into Metaphysics; and threatens now to disappear, as some rivers do, in deserts of barren sand.

Of Literature, and its deep-seated, wide-spread maladies, why speak? Literature is but a branch of Religion, and always participates in its character: however, in our time, it is the only branch that still shows any greenness; and, as some think, must one day become the main stem. * * * Nay, is not the diseased self-conscious state of Literature disclosed in this one fact, which lies so near us here, the prevalence of Reviewing! Sterne's wish for a reader "that would give-up the reins of his imagination into his author's hands, and be pleased he knew not why, and cared not wherefore,"[9] might lead him a long journey now. Indeed, for our best class of readers, the chief pleasure, a very stinted one, is this same knowing of the Why; which many a Kames and Bossu[1] has been, ineffectually enough, endeavouring to teach us: till at last these also have laid down their trade; and now your Reviewer is a mere *taster*; who tastes, and says, by the evidence of such palate, such tongue, as he has got, It is good, It is bad. Was it thus that the French carried out certain inferior creatures on their Algerine Expedition, to taste the wells for them, and try whether they were poisoned? Far be it from us to disparage our own craft, whereby we have our living! Only we must note these things: that Reviewing spreads with strange vigour; that such a man as Byron reckons the Reviewer and the Poet equal; that at the last Leipzig Fair, there was advertised a Review of Reviews. By and by it will be found that all Literature has become one boundless self-devouring Review; and, as in London routs,[2] we have to *do* nothing, but only to *see* others do nothing.—Thus does Literature also, like a sick thing, superabundantly "listen to itself."

No less is this unhealthy symptom manifest, if we cast a glance

---

8. *Evidences of Christianity* (1794) by William Paley, a Utilitarian theologian.
9. Sterne's *Tristram Shandy* (III.xii).
1. Henry Home, Lord Kames (1696–

1782), author of *Elements of Criticism;* René le Bossu (1631–80), French literary critic.
2. Fashionable gatherings.

on our Philosophy, on the character of our speculative Thinking. Nay already, as above hinted, the mere existence and necessity of a Philosophy is an evil. Man is sent hither not to question, but to work: "the end of man," it was long ago written, "is an Action, not a Thought."[3] In the perfect state, all Thought were but the picture and inspiring symbol of Action; Philosophy, except as Poetry and Religion, would have no being. And yet how, in this imperfect state, can it be avoided, can it be dispensed with? Man stands as in the centre of Nature; his fraction of Time encircled by Eternity, his handbreadth of Space encircled by Infinitude: how shall he forbear asking himself, What am I; and Whence; and Whither? How too, except in slight partial hints, in kind asseverations and assurances, such as a mother quiets her fretfully inquisitive child with, shall he get answer to such inquiries?

The disease of Metaphysics, accordingly, is a perennial one. In all ages, those questions of Death and Immortality, Origin of Evil, Freedom and Necessity, must, under new forms, anew make their appearance; ever, from time to time, must the attempt to shape for ourselves some Theorem of the Universe be repeated. And ever unsuccessfully: for what Theorem of the Infinite can the Finite render complete? We, the whole species of Mankind, and our whole existence and history, are but a floating speck in the illimitable ocean of the All; yet *in* that ocean; indissoluble portion thereof; partaking of its infinite tendencies: borne this way and that by its deep-swelling tides, and grand ocean currents;—of which what faintest chance is there that we should ever exhaust the significance, ascertain the goings and comings? A region of Doubt, therefore, hovers forever in the background; in Action alone can we have certainty. Nay properly Doubt is the indispensable inexhaustible material whereon Action works, which Action has to fashion into Certainty and Reality; only on a canvas of Darkness, such is man's way of being, could the many-coloured picture of our Life paint itself and shine. * * *

Now this is specially the misery which has fallen on man in our Era. Belief, Faith has well-nigh vanished from the world. The youth on awakening in this wondrous Universe no longer finds a competent theory of its wonders. Time was, when if he asked himself, What is man, What are the duties of man? the answer stood ready written for him. But now the ancient "ground-plan of the All" belies itself when brought into contact with reality; Mother Church has, to the most, become a superannuated Step-mother, whose lessons go disregarded; or are spurned at, and scornfully gainsaid. For young Valour and thirst of Action no ideal Chivalry invites to heroism, prescribes what is heroic: the old ideal of Man-

3. Aristotle, *Ethics* I.iii.

hood has grown obsolete, and the new is still invisible to us, and we grope after it in darkness, one clutching this phantom, another that; Werterism,[4] Byronism, even Brummelism, each has its day. For Contemplation and love of Wisdom, no Cloister now opens its religious shades; the Thinker must, in all senses, wander homeless, too often aimless, looking up to a Heaven which is dead for him, round to an Earth which is deaf. Action, in those old days, was easy, was voluntary, for the divine worth of human things lay acknowledged; Speculation was wholesome, for it ranged itself as the handmaid of Action; what could not so range itself died out by its natural death, by neglect. Loyalty still hallowed obedience, and made rule noble; there was still something to be loyal to: the Godlike stood embodied under many a symbol in men's interests and business; the Finite shadowed forth the Infinite; Eternity looked through Time. The Life of man was encompassed and overcanopied by a glory of Heaven, even as his dwelling-place by the azure vault.

How changed in these new days! Truly may it be said, the Divinity has withdrawn from the Earth; or veils himself in that widewasting Whirlwind of a departing Era, wherein the fewest can discern his goings. Not Godhead, but an iron, ignoble circle of Necessity embraces all things; binds the youth of these times into a sluggish thrall, or else exasperates him into a rebel. Heroic Action is paralysed; for what worth now remains unquestionable with him? At the fervid period when his whole nature cries aloud for Action, there is nothing sacred under whose banner he can act; the course and kind and conditions of free Action are all but undiscoverable. Doubt storms-in on him through every avenue; inquiries of the deepest, painfulest sort must be engaged with; and the invincible energy of young years waste itself in sceptical, suicidal cavillings; in passionate "questionings of Destiny," whereto no answer will be returned.

For men, in whom the old perennial principle of Hunger (be it Hunger of the poor Day-drudge who stills it with eighteenpence a-day, or of the ambitious Place-hunter who can nowise still it with so little) suffices to fill-up existence, the case is bad; but not the worst. These men have an aim, such as it is; and can steer towards it, with chagrin enough truly; yet, as their hands are kept full, without desperation. Unhappier are they to whom a higher instinct has been given; who struggle to be persons, not machines; to whom the Universe is not a warehouse, or at best a fancy-bazaar, but a mystic temple and hall of doom. For such men there lie properly two courses open. The lower, yet still an estimable class, take up with worn-out Symbols of the Godlike; keep trimming and trucking be-

---

4. The cultivation of melancholy based on the model of Goethe's novel, *The Sorrows of Young Werther*. "Brum-melism": a fad for wearing elegant clothes in the manner of Beau Brummel, a dandy of George IV's time.

tween these and Hypocrisy, purblindly enough, miserably enough.
A numerous intermediate class end in Denial; and form a theory
that there is no theory; that nothing is certain in the world, except
this fact of Pleasure being pleasant; so they try to realise what trifling
modicum of Pleasure they can come at, and to live contented therewith, winking hard. Of these we speak not here; but only of the
second nobler class, who also have dared to say No and cannot yet
say Yea; but feel that in the No they dwell as in a Golgotha, where
life enters not, where peace is not appointed them.

Hard, for most part, is the fate of such men; the harder the
nobler they are. In dim forecastings, wrestles within them the "Divine Idea of the World" yet will nowhere visibly reveal itself. They
have to realise a Worship for themselves, or live unworshipping.
The Godlike has vanished from the world; and they, by the strong
cry of their soul's agony, like true wonder-workers, must again evoke
its presence. This miracle is their appointed task; which they must
accomplish, or die wretchedly: this miracle has been accomplished
by such; but not in our land; our land yet knows not of it. Behold
a Byron, in melodious tones, "cursing his day": he mistakes earth-
born passionate Desire for heaven-inspired Freewill; without heavenly load-star, rushes madly into the dance of meteoric lights that
hover on the mad Mahlstrom; and goes down among its eddies.
Hear a Shelley filling the earth with inarticulate wail; like the infinite, inarticulate grief and weeping of forsaken infants. A noble
Friedrich Schlegel,[5] stupefied in that fearful loneliness, as of a silenced battle-field, flies back to Catholicism; as a child might to
its slain mother's bosom, and cling there. In lower regions, how
many a poor Hazlitt must wander on God's verdant earth, like the
Unblest on burning deserts; passionately dig wells, and draw up
only the dry quicksand; believe that he is seeking Truth, yet only
wrestle among endless Sophisms, doing desperate battle as with
spectre-hosts; and die and make no sign!

To the better order of such minds any mad joy of Denial has
long since ceased: the problem is not now to deny, but to ascertain and perform. Once in destroying the False, there was a certain
inspiration; but now the genius of Destruction has done its work,
there is now nothing more to destroy. The doom of the Old has
long been pronounced, and irrevocable; the Old has passed away:
but, alas, the New appears not in its stead; the Time is still in
pangs of travail with the New. Man has walked by the light of
conflagrations, and amid the sound of falling cities; and now there
is darkness, and long watching till it be morning. The voice even
of the faithful can but exclaim: "As yet struggles the twelfth hour
of the Night: birds of darkness are on the wing, spectres uproar,

5. German literary critic and leader of   1808 he joined the Roman Catholic
the Romantic school (1772–1829). In   Church.

the dead walk, the living dream.—Thou, Eternal Providence, wilt cause the day to dawn!"[6]

Such being the condition, temporal and spiritual, of the world at our Epoch, can we wonder that the world "listens to itself," and struggles and writhes, everywhere externally and internally, like a thing in pain? Nay, is not even this unhealthy action of the world's Organisation, if the symptom of universal disease, yet also the symptom and sole means of restoration and cure? The effort of Nature, exerting her medicative force to cast-out foreign impediments, and once more become One, become whole? In Practice, still more in Opinion, which is the precursor and prototype of Practice, there must needs be collision, convulsion; much has to be ground away. Thought must needs be Doubt and Inquiry before it can again be Affirmation and Sacred Precept. Innumerable "Philosophies of Man," contending in boundless hubbub, must annihilate each other, before an inspired Poesy and Faith for Man can fashion itself together. * * *

For ourselves, the loud discord which jars in these two Works,[7] in innumerable works of the like import, and generally in all the Thought and Action of this period, does not any longer utterly confuse us. Unhappy who, in such a time, felt not, at all conjunctures, ineradicably in his heart the knowledge that a God made this Universe, and a Demon not! And shall Evil always prosper, then? Out of all Evil comes Good; and no Good that is possible but shall one day be real. Deep and sad as is our feeling that we stand yet in the bodeful Night; equally deep, indestructible is our assurance that the Morning also will not fail. Nay already, as we look round, streaks of a dayspring are in the east; it is dawning; when the time shall be fulfilled, it will be day. The progress of man towards higher and nobler developments of whatever is highest and noblest in him, lies not only prophesied to Faith, but now written to the eye of Observation, so that he who runs may read.

One great step of progress, for example, we should say, in actual circumstances, was this same; the clear ascertainment that we are in progress. About the grand Course of Providence, and his final Purposes with us, we can know nothing, or almost nothing: man begins in darkness, ends in darkness; mystery is everywhere around us and in us, under our feet, among our hands. Nevertheless so much has become evident to every one, that this wondrous Mankind is advancing somewhither; that at least all human things are, have been and forever will be, in Movement and Change;—as, indeed, for beings that exist in Time, by virtue of Time, and are made

6. "Jean Paul's *Hesperus*" [Carlyle's note]. Jean Paul Richter (1763–1825) was a German humorist.

7. Books by Hope and Schlegel. See the title note.

of Time, might have been long since understood. In some provinces, it is true, as in Experimental Science, this discovery is an old one; but in most others it belongs wholly to these latter days. How often, in former ages, by eternal Creeds, eternal Forms of Government and the like, has it been attempted, fiercely enough, and with destructive violence, to chain the Future under the Past; and say to the Providence, whose ways with man are mysterious, and through the great deep: Hitherto shalt thou come, but no farther! A wholly insane attempt; and for man himself, could it prosper, the frightfulest of all enchantments, a very Life-in-Death. Man's task here below, the destiny of every individual man, is to be in turns Apprentice and Workman; or say rather, Scholar, Teacher, Discoverer: by nature he has a strength for learning, for imitating; but also a strength for acting, for knowing on his own account. Are we not in a world seen to be Infinite; the relations lying closest together modified by those latest discovered and lying farthest asunder? Could you ever spell-bind man into a Scholar merely, so that he had nothing to discover, to correct; could you ever establish a Theory of the Universe that were entire, unimprovable, and which needed only to be got by heart; man then were spiritually defunct, the Species we now name Man had ceased to exist. But the gods, kinder to us than we are to ourselves, have forbidden such suicidal acts. As Phlogiston[8] is displaced by Oxygen, and the Epicycles of Ptolemy by the Ellipses of Kepler,[9] so does Paganism give place to Catholicism, Tyranny to Monarchy, and Feudalism to Representative Government,—where also the process does not stop. Perfection of Practice, like completeness of Opinion, is always approaching, never arrived; Truth, in the words of Schiller, *immer wird, nie ist*; never *is*, always *is a-being*.

Sad, truly, were our condition did we know but this, that Change is universal and inevitable. Launched into a dark shoreless sea of Pyrrhonism, what would remain for us but to sail aimless, hopeless; or make madly merry, while the devouring Death had not yet ingulfed us? As indeed, we have seen many, and still see many do. Nevertheless so stands it not. The venerator of the Past (and to what pure heart is the Past, in that "moonlight of memory," other than sad and holy?) sorrows not over its departure, as one utterly bereaved. The true Past departs not, nothing that was worthy in the Past departs; no Truth or Goodness realised by man ever dies, or can die; but is all still here, and, recognised or not, lives and works through endless changes. If all things, to speak in the German dialect, are discerned by us, and exist for us, in an element of

8. A hypothetical substance which, according to older theories of chemistry, was part of all combustible objects and was released in burning.
9. Ptolemy, an astronomer of Alexandria, 2nd century A.D. Johannes Kep-

ler (1571–1630), German astronomer whose theories of planetary orbits (together with the earlier discoveries of Copernicus) supplanted the Ptolemaic theories.

Time, and therefore of Mortality and Mutability; yet Time itself reposes on Eternity: the truly Great and Transcendental has its basis and substance in Eternity; stands revealed to us as Eternity in a vesture of Time. Thus in all Poetry, Worship, Art, Society, as one form passes into another, nothing is lost: it is but the superficial, as it were the *body* only, that grows obsolete and dies; under the mortal body lies a *soul* which is immortal; which anew incarnates itself in fairer revelation; and the Present is the living sumtotal of the whole Past.

In Change, therefore, there is nothing terrible, nothing supernatural: on the contrary, it lies in the very essence of our lot and life in this world. To-day is not yesterday: we ourselves change; how can our Works and Thoughts, if they are always to be the fittest, continue always the same? Change, indeed, is painful; yet ever needful; and if Memory have its force and worth, so also has Hope. Nay, if we look well to it, what is all Derangement, and necessity of great Change, in itself such an evil, but the product simply of *increased resources* which the old *methods* can no longer administer; of new wealth which the old coffers will no longer contain? What is it, for example, that in our own day bursts asunder the bonds of ancient Political Systems, and perplexes all Europe with the fear of Change, but even this: the increase of social resources, which the old social methods will no longer sufficiently administer? The new omnipotence of the Steam-engine is hewing asunder quite other mountains than the physical. Have not our economical distresses, those barnyard Conflagrations[1] themselves, the frightfulest madness of our mad epoch, their rise also in what is a real increase: increase of Men; of human Force; properly, in such a Planet as ours, the most precious of all increases? It is true again, the ancient methods of administration will no longer suffice. Must the indomitable millions, full of old Saxon energy and fire, lie cooped-up in this Western Nook, choking one another, as in a Blackhole of Calcutta,[2] while a whole fertile untenanted Earth, desolate for want of the ploughshare, cries: Come and till me, come and reap me?[3] If the ancient Captains can no longer yield guidance, new must be sought after: for the difficulty lies not in nature, but in artifice; the European Calcutta-Blackhole has no walls but air ones and paper ones. —So too, Scepticism itself, with its innumerable mischiefs, what is it but the sour fruit of a most blessed increase, that of Knowledge; a fruit too that will not always continue *sour?*

In fact, much as we have said and mourned about the unproduc-

---

1. Rick-burning in the 1820's and 1830's by disgruntled farm laborers in England.
2. A small room in which 146 European men and women were imprisoned by the Indians in 1756. After one night, only 23 remained alive.
3. Carlyle often urged emigration to America as a solution to the over-crowding of Europe. One of his brothers did emigrate, and became a farmer in Ontario, Canada.

tive prevalence of Metaphysics, it was not without some insight into the use that lies in them. Metaphysical Speculation, if a necessary evil, is the forerunner of much good. The fever of Scepticism must needs burn itself out, and burn out thereby the Impurities that caused it; then again will there be clearness, health. The principle of life, which now struggles painfully, in the outer, thin and barren domain of the Conscious or Mechanical, may then withdraw into its inner sanctuaries, its abysses of mystery and miracle; withdraw deeper than ever into that domain of the Unconscious, by nature infinite and inexhaustible; and creatively work there. From that mystic region, and from that alone, all wonders, all Poesies, and Religions, and Social Systems have proceeded: the like wonders, and greater and higher, lie slumbering there; and, brooded on by the spirit of the waters, will evolve themselves, and rise like exhalations from the Deep. * * *

Remarkable it is, truly, how everywhere the eternal fact begins again to be recognised, that there is a Godlike in human affairs; that God not only made us and beholds us, but is in us and around us; that the Age of Miracles, as it ever was, now is. Such recognition we discern on all hands and in all countries: in each country after its own fashion. In France, among the younger nobler minds, strangely enough; where, in their loud contention with the Actual and Conscious, the Ideal or Unconscious is, for the time, without exponent; where Religion means not the parent of Polity, as of all that is highest, but Polity itself; and this and the other earnest man has not been wanting, who could audibly whisper to himself: "Go to, I will make religion." In England still more strangely; as in all things, worthy England will have its way: by the shrieking of hysterical women,[4] casting out of devils, and other "gifts of the Holy Ghost." Well might Jean Paul say, in this his twelfth hour of the Night, "the living dream"; well might he say, "the dead walk."[5] Meanwhile let us rejoice rather that so much has been seen into, were it through never so diffracting media, and never so madly distorted; that in all dialects, though but half-articulately, this high Gospel begins to be preached: Man is still Man. The genius of Mechanism, as was once before predicted, will not always sit like a choking incubus on our soul; but at length, when by a new magic Word the old spell is broken, become our slave, and as familiar-spirit do all our bidding. "We are near awakening when we dream that we dream."[6]

He that has an eye and a heart can even now say: Why should I falter? Light has come into the world; to such as love Light, so

4. An allusion to followers of Carlyle's friend, the preacher Edward Irving. Women in Irving's congregation asserted that they had acquired the gift of tongues.

5. See note 6 above, Jean Paul's *Hesperus.*
6. Quoted from a work by the German poet Novalis (1772–1801).

as Light must be loved, with a boundless all-doing, all-enduring love. For the rest, let that vain struggle to read the mystery of the Infinite cease to harass us. It is a mystery which, through all ages, we shall only read here a line of, there another line of. Do we not already know that the name of the Infinite is GOOD, is GOD? Here on Earth we are as Soldiers, fighting in a foreign land; that understand not the plan of the campaign, and have no need to understand it; seeing well what is at our hand to be done. Let us do it like Soldiers; with submission, with courage, with a heroic joy. "Whatsoever thy hand findeth to do, do it with all thy might."[7] Behind us, behind each one of us, lie Six Thousand Years of human effort, human conquest: before us is the boundless Time, with its as yet uncreated and unconquered Continents and Eldorados, which we, even we, have to conquer, to create; and from the bosom of Eternity there shine for us celestial guiding stars.

> "My inheritance how wide and fair!
> Time is my fair seed-field, of Time I'm heir."[8]

1831   1831

From Sartor Resartus[1]
The Everlasting No

Under the strange nebulous envelopment, wherein our Professor has now shrouded himself, no doubt but his spiritual nature is nevertheless progressive, and growing: for how can the "Son of

---

7. Ecclesiastes ix.10.
8. From Goethe's romance, *Wilhelm Meisters Wanderjahre* (1821).
1. *Sartor Resartus* is a combination of novel, autobiography, and essay. To present some of his own experiences, Carlyle invented a hero, Professor Diogenes Teufelsdröckh of Germany, whose name itself (meaning "God-Begotten Devil's Dung") suggests the grotesque and fantastic humor which Carlyle used to expound a serious treatise. Teufelsdröckh tells the story of his unhappiness in love and of his difficulties in religion. He also airs his opinions on a variety of subjects. Interspersed between the Professor's words (which are in quotation marks) are the remarks of an editor, also imaginary, who has the task of putting together the story from assorted documents written by Teufelsdröckh. The title, meaning "The Tailor Re-Tailored," refers to the editor's role of patching the story together. The title also refers to Carlyle's so-called "Clothes Philosophy," which is expounded by the hero in many chap-

ters of *Sartor*. In effect this Clothes Philosophy is an attempt to demonstrate the difference between the appearances of things and their reality. The appearance of a man depends upon the costume he wears; the reality of a man is the body underneath the costume. By analogy, Carlyle suggests that institutions, such as churches or governments, are like clothes. They may be useful "visible emblems" of the spiritual forces which they cover, but they wear out and have to be replaced by new clothes. The Christian church, for example, which once expressed man's permanent religious desires, is, in Carlyle's terms, worn out and must be discarded. But the underlying religious spirit must be recognized and kept alive at all costs. In this respect, the Clothes Philosophy has much in common with the theory of archetypal experiences developed in the 20th century by the psychiatrist Carl Jung. Carlyle extends his analogy, however, into many other areas. Clothes hide the body just as the world of nature cloaks

Time," in any case, stand still? We behold him, through those dim years, in a state of crisis, of transition: his mad Pilgrimings, and general solution into aimless Discontinuity, what is all this but a mad Fermentation; wherefrom, the fiercer it is, the clearer product will one day evolve itself?

Such transitions are ever full of pain: thus the Eagle when he moults is sickly; and, to attain his new beak, must harshly dash-off the old one upon rocks. What Stoicism soever our Wanderer, in his individual acts and motions, may affect, it is clear that there is a hot fever of anarchy and misery raging within: coruscations of which flash out: as, indeed, how could there be other? Have we not seen him disappointed, bemocked of Destiny, through long years? All that the young heart might desire and pray for has been denied; nay, as in the last worst instance, offered and then snatched away. Ever an "excellent Passivity"; but of useful, reasonable Activity, essential to the former as Food to Hunger, nothing granted: till at length, in this wild Pilgrimage, he must forcibly seize for himself an Activity, though useless, unreasonable. Alas, his cup of bitterness, which had been filling drop by drop, ever since that first "ruddy morning" in the Hinterschlag Gymnasium,[2] was at the very lip; and then with that poison-drop, of the Towgood-and-Blumine business,[3] it runs over, and even hisses over in a deluge of foam.

He himself says once, with more justice than originality: "Man is, properly speaking, based upon Hope, he has no other possession but Hope; this world of his is emphatically the Place of Hope." What, then, was our Professor's possession? We see him, for the present, quite shut-out from Hope; looking not into the golden orient, but vaguely all round into a dim copper firmament, pregnant with earthquake and tornado.

Alas, shut-out from Hope, in a deeper sense than we yet dream of! For, as he wanders wearisomely through this world, he has now lost all tidings of another and higher. Full of religion, or at least of religiosity, as our Friend has since exhibited himself, he hides not that, in those days, he was wholly irreligious: "Doubt had darkened into Unbelief," says he; "shade after shade goes grimly over your soul, till you have the fixed, starless, Tartarean black." To such readers as have reflected, what can be called reflecting, on man's life, and happily discovered, in contradiction to much Profit-

---

the reality of God and as the body itself cloaks the reality of man's soul. The discovery of these realities behind the appearances is, for Carlyle and for his hero, the initial stage of a solution to the dilemmas of life.

Teufelsdröckh's religious development, as described in the following chapters, may be contrasted with J. S. Mill's account of his own crisis of spirit in his *Autobiography*. Our

three selections are Chapters VII–IX of Book II.
2. "Smite-Behind Grammar School"; Teufelsdröckh's unhappiness had begun with his loneliness at this school.
3. Blumine, a girl loved by Teufelsdröckh, had married his friend Towgood. His distress is pictured in the preceding chapter, entitled "Sorrows of Teufelsdröckh."

and-loss Philosophy,[4] speculative and practical, that Soul is *not* synonymous with Stomach; who understand, therefore, in our Friend's words, "that, for man's well-being, Faith is properly the one thing needful; how, with it, Martyrs, otherwise weak, can cheerfully endure the shame and the cross; and without it, Worldlings puke-up their sick existence, by suicide, in the midst of luxury": to such it will be clear that, for a pure moral nature, the loss of his religious Belief was the loss of everything. Unhappy young man! All wounds, the crush of long-continued Destitution, the stab of false Friendship and of false Love, all wounds in thy so genial heart, would have healed again, had not its life-warmth been withdrawn. Well might he exclaim, in his wild way: "Is there no God, then; but at best an absentee God, sitting idle, ever since the first Sabbath, at the outside of his Universe, and *seeing* it go? Has the word Duty no meaning; is what we call Duty no divine Messenger and Guide, but a false earthly Fantasm, made-up of Desire and Fear, of emanations from the Gallows and from Dr. Graham's Celestial-Bed?[5] Happiness of an approving Conscience! Did not Paul of Tarsus, whom admiring men have since named Saint, feel that *he* was 'the chief of sinners';[6] and Nero of Rome, jocund in spirit (*wohlgemuth*), spend much of his time in fiddling? Foolish Word-monger and Motive-grinder, who in thy Logic-mill hast an earthly mechanism for the Godlike itself, and wouldst fain grind me out Virtue from the husks of Pleasure,—I tell thee, Nay! To the unregenerate Prometheus Vinctus[7] of a man, it is ever the bitterest aggravation of his wretchedness that he is conscious of Virtue, that he feels himself the victim not of suffering only, but of injustice. What then? Is the heroic inspiration we name Virtue but some Passion; some bubble of the blood, bubbling in the direction others *profit* by? I know not: only this I know, If what thou namest Happiness be our true aim, then are we all astray. With Stupidity and sound Digestion man may front much. But what, in these dull unimaginative days, are the terrors of Conscience to the diseases of the Liver! Not on Morality, but on Cookery, let us build our stronghold: there brandishing our frying-pan, as censer, let us offer sweet incense to the Devil, and live at ease on the fat things *he* has provided for his Elect!"

Thus has the bewildered Wanderer to stand, as so many have done, shouting question after question into the Sibyl-cave of Destiny,[8]

4. Utilitarian theory of ethics that our actions should be based on calculating the sum of pleasures and pains which would result from such actions. This "hedonistic calculus" horrified Carlyle because it left out of account man's religious instincts.
5. James Graham (1745–94), a quack doctor, had invented an elaborate bed which was supposed to cure sterility in couples using it. In this passage the bed is apparently a symbol of sexual desires.
6. See I Timothy i.15.
7. I.e., Prometheus Bound; this is also the title of a play by Aeschylus depicting the sufferings of a hero who defied Zeus.
8. An allusion to Virgil's *Aeneid* VI.

and receive no Answer but an Echo. It is all a grim Desert, this once-fair world of his; wherein is heard only the howling of wild-beasts, or the shrieks of despairing, hate-filled men; and no Pillar of Cloud by day, and no Pillar of Fire by night,[9] any longer guides the Pilgrim. To such length has the spirit of Inquiry carried him. "But what boots it (*was thut's*)?" cries he: "it is but the common lot in this era. Not having come to spiritual majority prior to the *Siècle de Louis Quinze*,[1] and not being born purely a Loghead (*Dummkopf*), thou hast no other outlook. The whole world is, like thee, sold to Unbelief, their old Temples of the Godhead, which for long have not been rainproof, crumble down; and men ask now: Where is the Godhead; our eyes never saw him?"

Pitiful enough were it, for all these wild utterances, to call our Diogenes wicked. Unprofitable servants as we all are, perhaps at no era of his life was he more decisively the Servant of Goodness, the Servant of God, than even now when doubting God's existence. "One circumstance I note," says he: "after all the nameless woe that Inquiry, which for me, what it is not always, was genuine Love of Truth, had wrought me, I nevertheless still loved Truth, and would bate no jot of my allegiance to her. 'Truth'! I cried, 'though the Heavens crush me for following her: no Falsehood! though a whole celestial Lubberland[2] were the price of Apostasy.' In conduct it was the same. Had a divine Messenger from the clouds, or miraculous Handwriting on the wall, convincingly proclaimed to me *This thou shalt do*, with what passionate readiness, as I often thought, would I have done it, had it been leaping into the infernal Fire. Thus, in spite of all Motive-grinders, and Mechanical Profit-and-Loss Philosophies, with the sick ophthalmia and hallucination they had brought on, was the Infinite nature of Duty still dimly present to me: living without God in the world, of God's light I was not utterly bereft; if my as yet sealed eyes, with their unspeakable longing, could nowhere see Him, nevertheless in my heart He was present, and His heaven-written Law still stood legible and sacred there."

Meanwhile, under all these tribulations, and temporal and spiritual destitutions, what must the Wanderer, in his silent soul, have endured! "The painfullest feeling," writes he, "is that of your own Feebleness (*Unkraft*); ever, as the English Milton says, to be weak is the true misery.[3] And yet of your Strength there is and can be no clear feeling, save by what you have prospered in, by what you have done. Between vague wavering Capability and fixed indubitable Performance, what a difference! A certain inarticulate Self-conscious-

36 ff., where Aeneas questions the Cumaean sibyl.
9. Exodus xiii.21.
1. "The Century of Louis XV," an allusion to Voltaire's history of the skeptical and enquiring spirit of 18th-

century France during the reign of Louis XV (1710–74): *Précis du Siècle de Louis XV*.
2. Land of Plenty.
3. *Paradise Lost* I.157: "Fallen cherub, to be weak is miserable."

ness dwells dimly in us; which only our Works can render articulate and decisively discernible. Our Works are the mirror wherein the spirit first sees its natural lineaments. Hence, too, the folly of that impossible Precept, *Know thyself;*[4] till it be translated into this partially possible one, *Know what thou canst work-at.*

"But for.me, so strangely unprosperous had I been, the net-result of my Workings amounted as yet simply to—Nothing. How then could I believe in my Strength, when there was as yet no mirror to see it in? Ever did this agitating, yet, as I now perceive, quite frivolous question, remain to me insoluble: Hast thou a certain Faculty, a certain Worth, such even as the most have not; or art thou the completest Dullard of these modern times? Alas! the fearful Unbelief is unbelief in yourself; and how could I believe? Had not my first, last Faith in myself, when even to me the Heavens seemed laid open, and I dared to love, been all-too cruelly belied? The speculative Mystery of Life grew ever more mysterious to me: neither in the practical Mystery[5] had I made the slightest progress, but been everywhere buffeted, foiled, and contemptuously cast-out. A feeble unit in the middle of a threatening Infinitude, I seemed to have nothing given me but eyes, whereby to discern my own wretchedness. Invisible yet impenetrable walls, as of Enchantment, divided me from all living: was there, in the wide world, any true bosom I could press trustfully to mine? O Heaven, No, there was none! I kept a lock upon my lips: why should I speak much with that shifting variety of so-called Friends, in whose withered, vain and too-hungry souls Friendship was but an incredible tradition? In such cases, your resource is to talk little, and that little mostly from the Newspapers. Now when I look back, it was a strange isolation I then lived in. The men and women around me, even speaking with me, were but Figures; I had, practically, forgotten that they were alive, that they were not merely automatic. In.midst of their crowded streets and assemblages, I walked solitary; and (except as it was my own heart, not another's, that I kept devouring) savage also, as the tiger in his jungle. Some comfort it would have been, could I, like a Faust,[6] have fancied myself tempted and tormented of the Devil; for a Hell, as I imagine, without Life, though only diabolic Life, were more frightful: but in our age of Down-pulling and Disbelief, the very Devil has been pulled down, you cannot so much as believe in a Devil. To me the Universe was all void of Life, of Purpose, of Volition, even of Hostility: it was one huge, dead, immeasurable Steam-engine, rolling on, in its dead indifference, to grind me limb from limb. O, the vast, gloomy, solitary Golgotha,[7] and Mill of

4. This maxim was inscribed in gold letters over the portico of the temple at Delphi.
5. A profession or practical occupation.

6. Faust, the hero of a drama by Goethe, was tempted by the Devil.
7. Calvary, the place where Christ was crucified.

Death! Why was the Living banished thither companionless, conscious? Why, if there is no Devil; nay, unless the Devil is your God?"

A prey incessantly to such corrosions, might not, moreover, as the worst aggravation to them, the iron constitution even of a Teufelsdröckh threaten to fail? We conjecture that he has known sickness; and, in spite of his locomotive habits, perhaps sickness of the chronic sort. Hear this, for example: "How beautiful to die of broken-heart, on Paper! Quite another thing in practice; every window of your Feeling, even of your Intellect, as it were, begrimed and mud-bespattered, so that no pure ray can enter; a whole Drugshop in your inwards; the fordone soul drowning slowly in quagmires of Disgust!"

Putting all which external and internal miseries together, may we not find in the following sentences, quite in our Professor's still vein, significance enough? "From Suicide a certain aftershine (*Nachschein*) of Christianity withheld me: perhaps also a certain indolence of character; for, was not that a remedy I had at any time within reach? Often, however, was there a question present to me: Should some one now, at the turning of that corner, blow thee suddenly out of Space, into the other World, or other No-World, by pistol-shot,—how were it? On which ground, too, I have often, in sea-storms and sieged cities and other death-scenes, exhibited an imperturbability, which passed, falsely enough, for courage.

"So had it lasted," concludes the Wanderer, "so had it lasted, as in bitter protracted Death-agony, through long years. The heart within me, unvisited by any heavenly dewdrop, was smouldering in sulphurous, slow-consuming fire. Almost since earliest memory I had shed no tear; or once only when I, murmuring half-audibly, recited Faust's Deathsong, that wild *Selig der den er im Siegesglanze findet* (Happy whom *he* finds in Battle's splendour),[8] and thought that of this last Friend[9] even I was not forsaken, that Destiny itself could not doom me not to die. Having no hope, neither had I any definite fear, were it of Man or of Devil: nay, I often felt as if it might be solacing, could the Arch-Devil himself, though in Tartarean terrors, but rise to me, that I might tell him a little of my mind. And yet, strangely enough, I lived in a continual, indefinite, pining fear; tremulous, pusillanimous, apprehensive of I knew not what: it seemed as if all things in the Heavens above and the Earth beneath would hurt me; as if the Heavens and the Earth were but boundless jaws of a devouring monster, wherein I, palpitating, waited to be devoured.

"Full of such humour, and perhaps the miserablest man in the

---

8. Adapted from Goethe's *Faust* I.iv.   9. Death.
1573–76.

whole French Capital or Suburbs, was I, one sultry Dogday,[1] after much perambulation, toiling along the dirty little *Rue Saint-Thomas de l'Enfer*,[2] among civic rubbish enough, in a close atmosphere, and over pavements hot as Nebuchadnezzar's Furnace; whereby doubtless my spirits were little cheered; when, all at once, there rose a Thought in me, and I asked myself: 'What *art* thou afraid of? Wherefore, like a coward, dost thou forever pip and whimper, and go cowering and trembling? Despicable biped! what is the sumtotal of the worst that lies before thee? Death? Well, Death; and say the pangs of Tophet[3] too, and all that the Devil and Man may, will or can do against thee! Hast thou not a heart; canst thou not suffer whatsoever it be; and, as a Child of Freedom, though outcast, trample Tophet itself under thy feet, while it consumes thee? Let it come, then; I will meet it and defy it!' And as I so thought, there rushed like a stream of fire over my whole soul; and I shook base Fear away from me forever. I was strong, of unknown strength; a spirit, almost a god. Ever from that time, the temper of my misery was changed: not Fear or whining Sorrow was it, but Indignation and grim fire-eyed Defiance.

"Thus had the Everlasting No[4] (*das ewige Nein*) pealed authoritatively through all the recesses of my Being, of my Me; and then was it that my whole Me stood up, in native God-created majesty, and with emphasis recorded its Protest. Such a Protest, the most important transaction in Life, may that same Indignation and Defiance, in a psychological point of view, be fitly called. The Everlasting No had said: 'Behold, thou art fatherless, outcast, and the Universe is mine (the Devil's)'; to which my whole Me now made answer: '*I am not thine, but Free, and forever hate thee!*'

"It is from this hour that I incline to date my Spiritual Newbirth, or Baphometic Fire-baptism;[5] perhaps I directly thereupon began to be a Man."

Centre of Indifference

Though, after this "Baphometic Fire-baptism" of his, our Wanderer signifies that his Unrest was but increased; as indeed, "Indignation and Defiance," especially against things in general, are not the most peaceable inmates; yet can the Psychologist surmise that it was no longer a quite hopeless Unrest; that henceforth it had at least a

1. A hot and unwholesome summer period, coinciding with the prominence of Sirius, the Dog Star, is called the season of the dog days.
2. "St. Thomas-of-Hell Street." In later life Carlyle admitted that this incident was based upon his own experience during a walk in Edinburgh (rather than in Paris) when he was 26 or 27 years of age. For a period of three weeks, he said, he had been suffering from "total sleeplessness."

3. Hell.
4. This phrase does not signify the hero's protest. It represents the sum of all the forces that had denied meaning to life. These negative forces, which had hitherto held the hero in bondage, are repudiated by his saying, "No!" to the "Everlasting No."
5. A transformation by a flash of spiritual illumination. The term may derive from Baphomet, an idol that inspired such spiritual experiences.

fixed centre to revolve round. For the fire-baptised soul, long so scathed and thunder-riven, here feels its own Freedom, which feeling is its Baphometic Baptism: the citadel of its whole kingdom it has thus gained by assault, and will keep inexpugnable; outwards from which the remaining dominions, not indeed without hard battling, will doubtless by degrees be conquered and pacificated. Under another figure, we might say, if in that great moment, in the *Rue Saint-Thomas de l'Enfer*, the old inward Satanic School[1] was not yet thrown out of doors, it received peremptory judicial notice to quit; —whereby, for the rest, its howl-chantings, Ernulphus-cursings,[2] and rebellious gnashings of teeth, might, in the meanwhile, become only the more tumultuous, and difficult to keep secret.

Accordingly, if we scrutinise these Pilgrimings well, there is perhaps discernible henceforth a certain incipient method in their madness. Not wholly as a Spectre does Teufelsdröckh now storm through the world; at worst as a spectre-fighting Man, nay who will one day be a Spectre-queller. If pilgriming restlessly to so many "Saints' Wells,"[3] and ever without quenching of his thirst, he nevertheless finds little secular wells, whereby from time to time some alleviation is ministered. In a word, he is now, if not ceasing, yet intermitting to "eat his own heart"; and clutches round him outwardly on the NOT-ME for wholesomer food. Does not the following glimpse exhibit him in a much more natural state?

"Towns also and Cities, especially the ancient, I failed not to look upon with interest. How beautiful to see thereby, as through a long vista, into the remote Time; to have as it were, an actual section of almost the earliest Past brought safe into the Present, and set before your eyes! There, in that old City, was a live ember of Culinary Fire put down, say only two-thousand years ago; and there, burning more or less triumphantly, with such fuel as the region yielded, it has burnt, and still burns, and thou thyself seest the very smoke thereof. Ah! and the far more mysterious live ember of Vital Fire was then also put down there; and still miraculously burns and spreads; and the smoke and ashes thereof (in these Judgment-Halls and Church-yards), and its bellows-engines (in these Churches), thou still seest; and its flame, looking out from every kind countenance, and every hateful one, still warms thee or scorches thee.

"Of Man's Activity and Attainment the chief results are aeriform, mystic, and preserved in Tradition only: such are his Forms of Government, with the Authority they rest on; his Customs, or Fashions both of Cloth-habits and of Soul-habits; much more his collec-

---

1. A term coined by Robert Southey to characterize the self-assertive and rebellious temper of the poetry of Byron and Shelley.
2. A curse devised by Ernulf (1040–1124), Bishop of Rochester, when sentencing persons to excommunication. See

Sterne's *Tristram Shandy* III.xi.
3. Holy fountains or wells whose waters were reputed to restore health. Here a figurative allusion to Teufelsdröckh's unsuccessful search, at this time, for a religious solution to his problems.

tive stock of Handicrafts, the whole Faculty he has acquired of manipulating Nature: all these things, as indispensable and priceless as they are, cannot in any way be fixed under lock and key, but must flit, spirit-like, on impalpable vehicles, from Father to Son; if you demand sight of them, they are nowhere to be met with. Visible Plowmen and Hammermen there have been, ever from Cain and Tubalcain downwards:[4] but where does your accumulated Agricultural, Metallurgic, and other Manufacturing SKILL lie warehoused? It transmits itself on the atmospheric air, on the sun's rays (by Hearing and by Vision); it is a thing aeriform, impalpable, of quite spiritual sort. In like manner, ask me not, Where are the LAWS where is the GOVERNMENT? In vain wilt thou go to Schönbrunn, to Downing Street, to the Palais Bourbon:[5] thou findest nothing there but brick or stone houses, and some bundles of Papers tied with tape. Where, then, is that same cunningly-devised almighty Government of theirs to be laid hands on? Everywhere, yet nowhere: seen only in its works, this too is a thing aeriform, invisible; or if you will, mystic and miraculous. So spiritual (*geistig*) is our whole daily Life: all that we do springs out of Mystery, Spirit, invisible Force; only like a little Cloud-image, or Armida's Palace,[6] air-built, does the Actual body itself forth from the great mystic Deep.

"Visible and tangible products of the Past, again, I reckon-up to the extent of three. Cities, with their Cabinets and Arsenals; then tilled Fields, to either or to both of which divisions Roads with their Bridges, may belong; and thirdly—Books. In which third truly, the last invented, lies a worth far surpassing that of the two others. Wondrous indeed is the virtue of a true Book. Not like a dead city of stones, yearly crumbling, yearly needing repair; more like a tilled field, but then a spiritual field: like a spiritual tree, let me rather say, it stands from year to year, and from age to age (we have Books that already number some hundred-and-fifty human ages); and yearly comes its new produce of leaves (Commentaries, Deductions, Philosophical, Political Systems; or were it only Sermons, Pamphlets, Journalistic Essays), every one of which is talismanic and thaumaturgic,[7] for it can persuade men. O thou who art able to write a Book, which once in the two centuries or oftener there is a man gifted to do, envy not him whom they name City-builder, and inexpressibly pity him whom they name Conqueror or City-burner! Thou too art a Conqueror and Victor; but of the true sort, namely over the Devil: thou too hast built what will outlast all marble and metal, and be a wonder-bringing City of the Mind, a Temple and Seminary and Prophetic Mount, whereto all kindreds of the Earth will pilgrim. —Fool! why journeyest thou wearisomely, in thy antiquarian fervour, to gaze on the stone pyramids of Geeza, or the clay ones of

4. See Genesis, iv.1–22.
5. Headquarters of government in Vienna, London, and Paris, respectively.
6. The magic palace of a beautiful enchantress in Tasso's *Jerusalem Delivered*.
7. Miracle-working.

Sacchara?[8] These stand there, as I can tell thee, idle and inert, looking over the Desert, foolishly enough, for the last three-thousand years: but canst thou not open thy Hebrew BIBLE, then, or even Luther's Version thereof?"

No less satisfactory is his sudden appearance not in Battle, yet on some Battle-field; which, we soon gather, must be that of Wagram;[9] so that here, for once, is a certain approximation to distinctiveness of date. Omitting much, let us impart what follows:

"Horrible enough! A whole Marchfeld[1] strewed with shell-splinters, cannon-shot, ruined tumbrils, and dead men and horses; stragglers still remaining not so much as buried. And those red mould heaps: ay, there lie the Shells of Men, out of which all the Life and Virtue has been blown; and now are they swept together, and crammed-down out of sight, like blown Egg-shells!—Did Nature, when she bade the Donau bring down his mould-cargoes from the Carinthian and Carpathian Heights, and spread them out here into the softest, richest level,—intend thee, O Marchfeld, for a corn-bearing Nursery, whereon her children might be nursed; or for a Cockpit, wherein they might the more commodiously be throttled and tattered? Were thy three broad Highways, meeting here from the ends of Europe, made for Ammunition-wagons, then? Were thy Wagrams and Stillfrieds[2] but so many ready-built Casemates,[3] wherein the house of Hapsburg might batter with artillery, and with artillery be battered? König Ottokar, amid yonder hillocks, dies under Rodolf's truncheon; here Kaiser Franz falls a-swoon under Napoleon's: within which five centuries, to omit the others, how has thy breast, fair Plain, been defaced and defiled! The greensward is torn-up and trampled-down; man's fond care of it, his fruit-trees, hedge-rows, and pleasant dwellings, blown away with gunpowder; and the kind seedfield lies a desolate, hideous Place of Sculls.—Nevertheless, Nature is at work; neither shall these Powder-Devilkins with their utmost devilry gainsay her: but all that gore and carnage will be shrouded-in, absorbed into manure; and next year the Marchfeld will be green, nay greener. Thrifty unwearied Nature, ever out of our great waste educing some little profit of thy own,—how dost thou, from the very carcass of the Killer, bring Life for the Living![4]

"What, speaking in quite unofficial language, is the net-purport and upshot of war? To my own knowledge, for example, there dwell

8. Pyramids at Ghizeh and Sakkara near Cairo.
9. A village in Austria; site of Napoleon's victory over the Austrians, July, 1809.
1. A fertile plain in Austria whose soil (according to Teufelsdröckh) was brought down from the Carpathian mountains by the Danube (Donau) River.
2. Stillfried was the site of a battle in which Ottokar, King ("könig") of Bohemia, was killed by the forces of Rudolph of Hapsburg in 1278. In 1809 the Hapsburg armies, under Emperor Francis ("Franz") I, were in turn defeated by Napoleon at nearby Wagram.
3. Fortified chambers.
4. Cf. Byron's reflections on the battlefield at Waterloo: "How that red rain hath made the harvest grow!"—*Childe Harold's Pilgrimage*, III.xvii.150.

and toil, in the British village of Dumdrudge, usually some five-hundred souls. From these, by certain 'Natural Enemies' [5] of the French, there are successively selected, during the French war, say thirty able-bodied men: Dumdrudge, at her own expense, has suckled and nursed them: she has, not without difficulty and sorrow, fed them up to manhood, and even trained them to crafts, so that one can weave, another build, another hammer, and the weakest can stand under thirty stone avoirdupois. Nevertheless, amid much weeping and swearing, they are selected; all dressed in red; and shipped away, at the public charges, some two-thousand miles, or say only to the south of Spain;[6] and fed there till wanted. And now to that same spot, in the south of Spain, are thirty similar French artisans, from a French Dumdrudge, in like manner wending: till at length, after infinite effort, the two parties come into actual juxtaposition; and Thirty stands fronting Thirty, each with a gun in his hand. Straightway the word 'Fire!' is given: and they blow the souls out of one another; and in place of sixty brisk useful craftsmen, the world has sixty dead carcasses, which it must bury, and anew shed tears for. Had these men any quarrel? Busy as the Devil is, not the smallest! They lived far enough apart; were the entirest strangers; nay, in so wide a Universe, there was even, unconsciously, by Commerce, some mutual helpfulness between them. How then? Simpleton! their Governors had fallen-out; and, instead of shooting one another, had the cunning to make these poor blockheads shoot.— Alas, so is it in Deutschland, and hitherto in all other lands; still as of old, 'what devilry soever Kings do, the Greeks must pay the piper!'[7]—In that fiction of the English Smollet,[8] it is true, the final Cessation of War is perhaps prophetically shadowed forth; where the two Natural Enemies, in person, take each a Tobacco-pipe, filled with Brimstone; light the same, and smoke in one another's faces, till the weaker gives in: but from such predicted Peace-Era, what blood-filled trenches, and contentious centuries, may still divide us!"

Thus can the Professor, at least in lucid intervals, look away from his own sorrows, over the many-coloured world, and pertinently enough note what is passing there. We may remark, indeed, that for the matter of spiritual culture, if for nothing else, perhaps few periods of his life were richer than this. Internally, there is the most momentous instructive Course of Practical Philosophy, with Experiments, going on; towards the right comprehension of which his Peripatetic[9] habits, favourable to Meditation, might help him rather than hinder. Externally, again, as he wanders to and fro, there are, if for the longing heart little substance, yet for the seeing eye

---

5. Term often used in English newspapers to account for the frequency of wars between the English and French.
6. Where British armies fought against Napoleon, 1808–14.
7. Cf. Horace, *Epistles*, I.ii.14.

8. See Chapter XLI of *The Adventures of Ferdinand Count Fathom* by Tobias Smollett (1721–71).
9. Walking about, after the manner of Aristotle who delivered his lectures while walking in the Lyceum.

sights enough: in these so boundless Travels of his, granting that the Satanic School was even partially kept down, what an incredible knowledge of our Planet, and its Inhabitants and their Works, that is to say, of all knowable things, might not Teufelsdröckh acquire!

"I have read in most Public Libraries," says he, "including those of Constantinople and Samarcand: in most Colleges, except the Chinese Mandarin ones, I have studied, or seen that there was no studying. Unknown Languages have I oftenest gathered from their natural repertory, the Air, by my organ of Hearing; Statistics, Geographics, Topographics came, through the Eye, almost of their own accord. The ways of Man, how he seeks food, and warmth, and protection for himself, in most regions, are ocularly known to me. Like the great Hadrian,[1] I meted-out much of the terraqueous Globe with a pair of Compasses[2] that belonged to myself only.

"Of great Scenes why speak? Three summer days, I lingered reflecting, and even composing (*dichtete*), by the Pine-chasms of Vaucluse; and in that clear Lakelet [3] moistened my bread. I have sat under the Palm-trees of Tadmor; [4] smoked a pipe among the ruins of Babylon. The great Wall of China I have seen; and can testify that it is of gray brick, coped and covered with granite, and shows only second-rate masonry.—Great Events, also, have not I witnessed? Kings sweated-down (*ausgemergelt*) into Berlin-and-Milan Customhouse-Officers; [5] the World well won, and the World well lost; [6] oftener than once a hundred-thousand individuals shot (by each other) in one day. All kindreds and peoples and nations dashed together, and shifted and shovelled into heaps, that they might ferment there, and in time unite. The birth-pangs of Democracy,[7] wherewith convulsed Europe was groaning in cries that reached Heaven, could not escape me.

"For great Men I have ever had the warmest predilection; and can perhaps boast that few such in this era have wholly escaped me. Great Men are the inspired (speaking and acting) Texts of that divine BOOK OF REVELATION, whereof a Chapter is completed from epoch to epoch, and by some named HISTORY; to which inspired Texts your numerous talented men, and your innumerable untalented men, are the better or worse exegetic Commentaries, and wagonload of too-stupid, heretical or orthodox, weekly Sermons. For my study, the inspired Texts themselves! Thus did not I, in very early days, having disguised me as tavern-waiter, stand behind

---

1. Roman emperor (76–138) who traveled extensively throughout his empire.
2. I.e., legs.
3. A pool at the base of a mountain in Vaucluse in southern France. The adjacent "Pine-chasms" were one of Petrarch's favorite haunts. For Teufelsdröckh the area served as one of the "secular wells" that helped to restore him to spiritual health.

4. Palmyra in Syria.
5. Napoleon reduced some of Europe's kings to the status of mere tax collectors for his regime.
6. Cf. the title of Dryden's play *All for Love, or the World Well Lost.*
7. As manifested in the revolutionary outbreaks in France (1789 and 1830) and in the agitations in England preceding the Reform Bill of 1832.

the field-chairs, under that shady Tree at Treisnitz by the Jena Highway; [8] waiting upon the great Schiller and greater Goethe; and hearing what I have not forgotten. For—"

—But at this point the Editor recalls his principle of caution, some time ago laid down, and must suppress much. Let not the sacredness of Laurelled, still more, of Crowned Heads, be tampered with. Should we, at a future day, find circumstances altered, and the time come for Publication, then may these glimpses into the privacy of the Illustrious be conceded; which for the present were little better than treacherous, perhaps traitorous Eavesdroppings. Of Lord Byron, therefore, of Pope Pius, Emperor Tarakwang, and the "White Water-roses" [9] (Chinese Carbonari) with their mysteries, no notice here! Of Napoleon himself we shall only, glancing from afar, remark that Teufelsdröckh's relation to him seems to have been of very varied character. At first we find our poor Professor on the point of being shot as a spy; then taken into private conversation, even pinched on the ear, yet presented with no money; at last indignantly dismissed, almost thrown out of doors, as an "Ideologist." "He himself," says the Professor, "was among the completest Ideologists, at least Ideopraxists: [1] in the Idea (*in der Idee*) he lived, moved and fought. The man was a Divine Missionary, though unconscious of it; and preached, through the cannon's throat, that great doctrine, *La carrière ouverte aux talens* (The Tools to him that can handle them), which is our ultimate Political Evangel, wherein alone can liberty lie. Madly enough he preached, it is true, as Enthusiasts [2] and first Missionaries are wont, with imperfect utterance, amid much frothy rant; yet as articulately perhaps as the case admitted. Or call him, of you will, an American Backwoodsman, who had to fell unpenetrated forests, and battle with innumerable wolves, and did not entirely forbear strong liquor, rioting, and even theft; whom, notwithstanding, the peaceful Sower will follow, and, as he cuts the boundless harvest, bless."

More legitimate and decisively authentic is Teufelsdröckh's appearance and emergence (we know not well whence) in the solitude of the North Cape, on that June Midnight. He has a "light-blue Spanish cloak" hanging round him, as his "most commodious, principal, indeed sole upper-garment"; and stands there, on the World-promontory, looking over the infinite Brine, like a little blue Belfry (as we figure), now motionless indeed, yet ready, if stirred, to ring quaintest changes.

"Silence as of death," writes he; "for Midnight, even in the Arctic latitudes, has its character: nothing but the granite cliffs ruddytinged, the peaceable gurgle of that slow-heaving Polar Ocean, over

8. Where Goethe and Schiller met during the 1790's when they were collaborating on their writings.
9. Like the Carbonari in Italy, a secret revolutionary society in China during the regime of Emperor "Tarakwang" (Tao Kuang, 1821–50).
1. Those who put ideas into practice.
2. Religious fanatics.

which in the utmost North the great Sun hangs low and lazy, as if he too were slumbering. Yet is his cloud-couch wrought of crimson and cloth-of-gold; yet does his light stream over the mirror of waters, like a tremulous fire-pillar, shooting downwards to the abyss, and hide itself under my feet. In such moments, Solitude also is invaluable; for who would speak, or be looked on, when behind him lies all Europe and Africa, fast asleep, except the watchmen; and before him the silent Immensity, and Palace of the Eternal, whereof our Sun is but a porch-lamp?

"Nevertheless, in this solemn moment comes a man, or monster, scrambling from among the rock-hollows; and, shaggy, huge as the Hyperborean [3] Bear, hails me in Russian speech: most probably, therefore, a Russian Smuggler. With courteous brevity, I signify my indifference to contraband trade, my humane intentions, yet strong wish to be private. In vain: the monster, counting doubtless on his superior stature, and minded to make sport for himself, or perhaps profit, were it with murder, continues to advance; ever assailing me with his importunate train-oil[4] breath; and now has advanced, till we stand both on the verge of the rock, the deep Sea rippling greedily down below. What argument will avail? On the thick Hyperborean, cherubic reasoning, seraphic eloquence were lost. Prepared for such extremity, I, deftly enough, whisk aside one step; draw out, from my interior reservoirs, a sufficient Birmingham Horse-pistol, and say, 'Be so obliging as retire, Friend (*Er ziehe sich zurück, Freund*), and with promptitude!' This logic even the Hyperborean understands: fast enough, with apologetic, petitionary growl, he sidles off; and, except for suicidal as well as homicidal purposes, need not return.

"Such I hold to be the genuine use of Gunpowder: that it makes all men alike tall. Nay, if thou be cooler, cleverer than I, if thou have more *Mind*, though all but no *Body* whatever, then canst thou kill me first, and are the taller. Hereby, at last, is the Goliath powerless, and the David resistless; savage Animalism is nothing, inventive Spiritualism is all.

"With respect to Duels, indeed, I have my own ideas. Few things, in this so surprising world, strike me with more surprise. Two little visual Spectra of men, hovering with insecure enough cohesion in the midst of the UNFATHOMABLE, and to dissolve therein, at any rate, very soon,—make pause at the distance of twelve paces asunder; whirl round; and, simultaneously by the cunningest mechanism, explode one another into Dissolution; and off-hand become Air, and Nonextant! Deuce on it (*verdammt*), the little spitfires!—Nay, I think with old Hugo von Trimberg:[5] 'God must needs laugh outright, could such a thing be, to see his wondrous Manikins here below.' "

3. From the far North.
4. Whale oil.

5. Medieval poet (1260–1309).

But amid these specialties, let us not forget the great generality, which is our Chief guest here: How prospered the inner man of Teufelsdröckh under so much outward shifting? Does Legion [6] still lurk in him, though repressed; or has he exorcised that Devil's Brood? We can answer that the symptoms continue promising. Experience is the grand spiritual Doctor; and with him Teufelsdröckh has been long a patient, swallowing many a bitter bolus.[7] Unless our poor Friend belong to the numerous class of Incurables, which seems not likely, some cure will doubtless be effected. We should rather say that Legion, or the Satanic School, was now pretty well extirpated and cast out, but next to nothing introduced in its room; whereby the heart remains, for the while, in a quiet but no comfortable state.

"At length, after so much roasting," thus writes our Autobiographer, "I was what you might name calcined. Pray only that it be not rather, as is the more frequent issue, reduced to a *caput-mortuum!*[8] But in any case, by mere dint of practice, I had grown familiar with many things. Wretchedness was still wretched; but I could now partly see through it, and despise it. Which highest mortal, in this inane Existence, had I not found a Shadow-hunter, or Shadow-hunted; and, when I looked through his brave garnitures, miserable enough? Thy wishes have all been sniffed aside, thought I: but what, had they ever been all granted! Did not the Boy Alexander weep because he had not two Planets to conquer; or a whole Solar System; or after that, a whole Universe? *Ach Gott*, when I gazed into these Stars, have they not looked-down on me as if with pity, from their serene spaces; like Eyes glistening with heavenly tears over the little lot of man! Thousands of human generations, all as noisy as our own, have been swallowed-up of Time, and there remains no wreck of them any more; and Arcturus and Orion and Sirius and the Pleiades are still shining in their courses, clear and young, as when the Shepherd first noted them in the plain of Shinar.[9] Pshaw! what is this paltry little Dog-cage[1] of an Earth; what art thou that sittest whining there? Thou art still Nothing, Nobody: true; but who, then, is Something, Somebody? For thee the Family of Man has no use; it rejects thee; thou art wholly as a dissevered limb: so be it; perhaps it is better so!"

Too-heavy-laden Teufelsdröckh! Yet surely his bands are loosen-

6. Unclean spirits as described in Mark v.9.
7. Large pill.
8. Death's head.
9. The shepherd is probably Abraham, who was commanded by the Lord to "tell the stars, if thou be able to number them" (Genesis xv.5). Shinar was a plain in the Sumerian region (in mod-ern times, Iraq). Abraham migrated from the Sumerian city of Ur (Genesis x.10; xi.31).
1. A drum-shaped cage that turns when a dog runs inside the cylinder. This dog-powered device, attached to a kitchen spit, was used for turning joints of meat during roasting.

ing: one day he will hurl the burden far from him, and bound forth free and with a second youth.

The Everlasting Yea

"Temptations in the Wilderness!"[2] exclaims Teufelsdröckh: "Have we not all to be tried with such? Not so easily can the old Adam, lodged in us by birth, be dispossessed. Our Life is compassed round with Necessity; yet is the meaning of Life itself no other than Freedom, than Voluntary Force: thus have we a warfare; in the beginning, especially, a hard-fought battle. For the God-given mandate, *Work thou in Welldoing*, lies mysteriously written, in Promethean[3] Prophetic Characters, in our hearts; and leaves us no rest, night or day, till it be deciphered and obeyed; till it burn forth, in our conduct, a visible, acted Gospel of Freedom. And as the clay-given mandate, *Eat thou and be filled*, at the same time persuasively proclaims itself through every nerve,—must not there be a confusion, a contest, before the better Influence can become the upper?

"To me nothing seems more natural than that the Son of Man, when such God-given mandate first prophetically stirs within him, and the Clay must now be vanquished, or vanquish,—should be carried of the spirit into grim Solitudes, and there fronting the Tempter do grimmest battle with him; defiantly setting him at naught, till he yield and fly. Name it as we choose: with or without visible Devil, whether in the natural Desert of rocks and sands, or in the populous moral Desert of selfishness and baseness,—to such Temptation are we all called. Unhappy if we are not! Unhappy if we are but Half-men, in whom that divine handwriting has never blazed forth, all-subduing, in true sun-splendour; but quivers dubiously amid meaner lights: or smoulders, in dull pain, in darkness, under earthly vapours!—Our Wilderness is the wide World in an Atheistic Century; our Forty Days are long years of suffering and fasting: nevertheless, to these also comes an end. Yes, to me also was given, if not Victory, yet the consciousness of Battle, and the resolve to persevere therein while life or faculty is left. To me also, entangled in the enchanted forests, demon-peopled, doleful of sight and of sound, it was given, after weariest wanderings, to work out my way into the higher sunlit slopes—of that Mountain which has no summit, or whose summit is in Heaven only!"

He says elsewhere, under a less ambitious figure; as figures are, once for all, natural to him: "Has not thy Life been that of most sufficient men (*tüchtigen Männer*) thou hast known in this generation? An outflush of foolish young Enthusiasm, like the first

2. Matthew iv.1.
3. Fiery or fiery-spirited, an allusion to Prometheus, the defiant Titan who brought the secret of fire-making to man.

fallow-crop, wherein are as many weeds as valuable herbs: this all parched away, under the Droughts of practical and spiritual Unbelief, as Disappointment, in thought and act, often-repeated gave rise to Doubt, and Doubt gradually settled into Denial! If I have had a second-crop, and now see the perennial greensward, and sit under umbrageous[4] cedars, which defy all Drought (and Doubt); herein too, be the Heavens praised, I am not without examples, and even exemplars."

So that, for Teufelsdröckh also, there has been a "glorious revolution":[5] these mad shadow-hunting and shadow-hunted Pilgrimings of his were but some purifying "Temptation in the Wilderness," before his Apostolic work (such as it was) could begin; which Temptation is now happily over, and the Devil once more worsted! Was "that high moment in the *Rue de l'Enfer*," then, properly the turning-point of the battle; when the Fiend said, *Worship me or be torn in shreds*; and was answered valiantly with an *Apage Satana*?[6] —Singular Teufelsdröckh, would thou hadst told thy singular story in plain words! But it is fruitless to look there, in those Paper-bags,[7] for such. Nothing but innuendoes, figurative crotchets: a typical Shadow, fitfully wavering, prophetico-satiric; no clear logical Picture. "How paint to the sensual eye," asks he once, "what passes in the Holy-of-Holies of Man's Soul; in what words, known to these profane times, speak even afar-off of the unspeakable?" We ask in turn: Why perplex these times, profane as they are, with needless obscurity, by omission and by commission? Not mystical only is our Professor, but whimsical; and involves himself, now more than ever, in eye-bewildering *chiaroscuro*.[8] Successive glimpses, here faithfully imparted, our more gifted readers must endeavour to combine for their own behoof.

He says: "The hot Harmattan wind[9] had raged itself out; its howl went silent within me; and the long-deafened soul could now hear. I paused in my wild wanderings; and sat me down to wait, and consider; for it was as if the hour of change drew nigh. I seemed to surrender, to renounce utterly, and say: Fly, then, false shadows of Hope; I will chase you no more, I will believe you no more. And ye too, haggard spectres of Fear, I care not for you; ye too are all shadows and a lie. Let me rest here: for I am way-weary and life-weary; I will rest here, were it but to die: to die or to live is alike to me; alike insignificant."—And again: "Here, then, as I lay in that CENTRE OF INDIFFERENCE; cast, doubtless by benignant upper Influence, into a healing sleep, the heavy dreams rolled gradually away, and I awoke to a new Heaven and a new Earth.[1] The first

---

4. Shady.
5. The overthrow of James II of England in 1688.
6. "Get thee hence, Satan!" (Matthew iv.8–10).

7. Bags containing documents and writings by Teufelsdröckh.
8. Light and shade.
9. A hot dry wind in Africa.
1. Revelation xxi.1.

preliminary moral Act, Annihilation of Self (*Selbsttödtung*), had been happily accomplished; and my mind's eyes were now unsealed, and its hands ungyved."[2]

Might we not also conjecture that the following passage refers to his Locality, during this same "healing sleep"; that his Pilgrim-staff lies cast aside here, on "the high table-land"; and indeed that the repose is already taking wholesome effect on him? If it were not that the tone, in some parts, has more of riancy,[3] even of levity, than we could have expected! However, in Teufelsdröckh, there is always the strangest Dualism: light dancing, with guitar-music, will be going on in the fore-court, while by fits from within comes the faint whimpering of woe and wail. We transcribe the piece entire:

"Beautiful it was to sit there, as in my skyey Tent, musing and meditating; on the high table-land, in front of the Mountains; over me, as roof, the azure Dome, and around me, for walls, four azure-flowing curtains,—namely, of the Four azure winds, on whose bottom-fringes also I have seen gilding. And then to fancy the fair Castles that stood sheltered in these Mountain hollows; with their green flower-lawns, and white dames and damosels, lovely enough: or better still, the straw-roofed Cottages, wherein stood many a Mother baking bread, with her children round her:—all hidden and protectingly folded-up in the valley-folds; yet there and alive, as sure as if I beheld them. Or to see, as well as fancy, the nine Towns and Villages, that lay round my mountain-seat, which, in still weather, were wont to speak to me (by their steeple-bells) with metal tongue; and, in almost all weather, proclaimed their vitality by repeated Smoke-clouds; whereon, as on a culinary horologe,[4] I might read the hour of the day. For it was the smoke of cookery, as kind housewives at morning, midday, eventide, were boiling their husbands' kettles; and ever a blue pillar rose up into the air, successively or simultaneously, from each of the nine, saying, as plainly as smoke could say: Such and such a meal is getting ready here. Not uninteresting! For you have the whole Borough, with all its love-makings and scandal-mongeries, contentions and content-ments, as in miniature, and could cover it all with your hat.—If, in my wide Wayfarings, I had learned to look into the business of the World in its details, here perhaps was the place for combining it into general propositions, and deducing inferences therefrom.

"Often also could I see the black Tempest marching in anger through the Distance: round some Schreckhorn,[5] as yet grim-blue, would the eddying vapour gather, and there tumultuously eddy, and flow down like a mad witch's hair; till, after a space, it vanished, and, in the clear sunbeam, your Schreckhorn stood smiling grim-

2. Unfettered.
3. Gaiety.
4. Clock.

5. "Peak of Terror." A mountain in Switzerland.

white, for the vapour had held snow. How thou fermentest and elaboratest, in thy great fermenting-vat and laboratory of an Atmosphere, of a World, O Nature!—Or what is Nature? Ha! why do I not name thee GOD? Art not thou the 'Living Garment of God'? O Heavens, is it, in very deed, HE, then, that ever speaks through thee; that lives and loves in thee, that lives and loves in me?

"Fore-shadows, call them rather fore-splendours, of that Truth, and Beginning of Truths, fell mysteriously over my soul. Sweeter than Dayspring to the Shipwrecked in Nova Zembla;[6] ah, like the mother's voice to her little child that strays bewildered, weeping, in unknown tumults; like soft streamings of celestial music to my too-exasperated heart, came that Evangel. The Universe is not dead and demoniacal, a charnel-house with spectres; but godlike, and my Father's!

"With other eyes, too, could I now look upon my fellow man; with an infinite Love, an infinite Pity. Poor, wandering, wayward man! Art thou not tired, and beaten with stripes, even as I am? Ever, whether thou bear the royal mantle or the beggar's gabardine, art thou not so weary, so heavy-laden; and thy Bed of Rest is but a Grave. O my Brother, my Brother, why cannot I shelter thee in my bosom, and wipe away all tears from thy eyes! Truly, the din of many-voiced Life, which, in this solitude, with the mind's organ, I could hear, was no longer a maddening discord, but a melting one; like inarticulate cries, and sobbings of a dumb creature, which in the ear of Heaven are prayers. The poor Earth, with her poor joys, was now my needy Mother, not my cruel Stepdame; man, with his so mad Wants and so mean Endeavours, had become the dearer to me; and even for his sufferings and his sins, I now first named him Brother. Thus I was standing in the porch of that '*Sanctuary of Sorrow*';[7] by strange, steep ways had I too been guided thither; and ere long its sacred gates would open, and the '*Divine Depth of Sorrow*' lie disclosed to me."

The Professor says, he here first got eye on the Knot that had been strangling him, and straightway could unfasten it, and was free. "A vain interminable controversy," writes he, "touching what is at present called Origin of Evil, or some such thing, arises in every soul, since the beginning of the world; and in every soul, that would pass from idle Suffering into actual Endeavouring, must first be put an end to. The most, in our time, have to go content with a simple, incomplete enough Suppression of this controversy; to a few some Solution of it is indispensable. In every new era, too, such Solution comes-out in different terms; and ever the Solution

6. A Dutch sea captain, whose ship was wrecked off the island of Nova Zembla in the Arctic in 1596, recorded in his journal his thankfulness at the coming of daylight.
7. Adapted from Goethe's *Wilhelm Meister*.

of the last era has become obsolete, and is found unserviceable. For it is man's nature to change his Dialect from century to century; he cannot help it though he would. The authentic *Church-Catechism* of our present century has not yet fallen into my hands: meanwhile, for my own private behoof, I attempt to elucidate the matter so. Man's Unhappiness, as I construe, comes of his Greatness; it is because there is an Infinite in him, which with all his cunning he cannot quite bury under the Finite. Will the whole Finance Ministers and Upholsterers and Confectioners of modern Europe undertake, in joint-stock company, to make one Shoeblack HAPPY? They cannot accomplish it, above an hour or two; for the Shoeblack also has a Soul quite other than his Stomach; and would require, if you consider it, for his permanent satisfaction and saturation, simply this allotment, no more, and no less: *God's infinite Universe altogether to himself*, therein to enjoy infinitely, and fill every wish as fast as it rose. Oceans of Hochheimer,[8] a Throat like that of Ophiuchus:[9] speak not of them; to the infinite Shoeblack they are as nothing. No sooner is your ocean filled, than he grumbles that it might have been of better vintage. Try him with half of a Universe, of an Omnipotence, he sets to quarrelling with the proprietor of the other half, and declares himself the most maltreated of men.—Always there is a black spot in our sunshine: it is even as I said, the *Shadow of Ourselves*.

"But the whim we have of Happiness is somewhat thus. By certain valuations, and averages, of our own striking, we come upon some sort of average terrestrial lot; this we fancy belongs to us by nature, and of indefeasible right. It is simple payment of our wages, of our deserts; requires neither thanks nor complaint; only such *overplus* as there may be do we account Happiness; any *deficit* again is Misery. Now consider that we have the valuation of our own deserts ourselves, and what a fund of Self-conceit there is in each of us,—do you wonder that the balance should so often dip the wrong way, and many a Blockhead cry: See there, what a payment; was ever worthy gentleman so used!—I tell thee, Blockhead, it all comes of thy Vanity; of what thou *fanciest* those same deserts of thine to be. Fancy that thou deservest to be hanged (as is most likely), thou wilt feel it happiness to be only shot: fancy that thou deservest to be hanged in a hair-halter, it will be a luxury to die in hemp.

"So true is it, what I then say, that *the Fraction of Life can be increased in value not so much by increasing your Numerator as by lessening your Denominator*. Nay, unless my Algebra deceive me, *Unity* itself divided by *Zero* will give *Infinity*. Make thy claim of wages a zero, then; thou hast the world under thy feet. Well did

---

8. Rhine wine or hock from Hochheim.   9. The serpent in the constellation Serpentarius.

the Wisest of our time write: 'It is only with Renunciation (*Entsagen*) that Life, properly speaking, can be said to begin.'[1]

"I asked myself: What is this that, ever since earliest years, thou hast been fretting and fuming, and lamenting and self-tormenting, on account of? Say it in a word: is it not because thou art not HAPPY? Because the THOU (sweet gentleman) is not sufficiently honoured, nourished, soft-bedded, and lovingly cared for? Foolish soul! What Act of Legislature was there that *thou* shouldst be Happy? A little while ago thou hadst no right to *be* at all. What if thou wert born and predestined not to be Happy, but to be Unhappy! Art thou nothing other than a Vulture, then, that fliest through the Universe seeking after somewhat to *eat*; and shrieking dolefully because carrion enough is not given thee? Close thy *Byron*; open thy *Goethe*."

"*Es leuchtet mir ein,*[2] I see a glimpse of it!" cries he elsewhere: "there is in man a HIGHER than Love of Happiness: he can do without Happiness, and instead thereof find Blessedness! Was it not to preach-forth this same HIGHER that sages and martyrs, the Poet and the Priest, in all times, have spoken and suffered; bearing testimony, through life and through death, of the Godlike that is in Man, and how in the Godlike only has he Strength and Freedom? Which God-inspired Doctrine art thou also honoured to be taught; O Heavens! and broken with manifold merciful Afflictions, even till thou become contrite, and learn it! O, thank thy Destiny for these; thankfully bear what yet remain: thou hadst need of them; the Self in thee needed to be annihilated. By benignant fever-paroxysms is Life rooting out the deep-seated chronic Diseases, and triumphs over Death. On the roaring billows of Time, thou art not engulfed, but borne aloft into the azure of Eternity. Love not Pleasure; love God.[3] This is the EVERLASTING YEA, wherein all contradiction is solved: wherein whoso walks and works, it is well with him."

And again: "Small is it that thou canst trample the Earth with its injuries under thy feet, as old Greek Zeno[4] trained thee: thou canst love the Earth while it injures thee, and even because it injures thee; for this a Greater than Zeno was needed, and he too was sent. Knowest thou that '*Worship of Sorrow*'?[5] The Temple thereof, founded some eighteen centuries ago, now lies in ruins, overgrown with jungle, the habitation of doleful creatures: nevertheless, venture forward; in a low crypt, arched out of falling fragments, thou findest the Altar still there, and its sacred Lamp perennially burning."

1. Adapted from *Wilhelm Meister;* "the wisest of our time" is Goethe.
2. An exclamation of Wilhelm Meister's.
3. II Timothy iii.4.
4. Greek Stoic philosopher of the 3rd century B.C. After being injured in a fall Zeno is reputed to have struck the earth with his hand as if the earth were responsible for his injury. Afterwards he committed suicide. Hence he is said to "trample the Earth."
5. Christianity.

Without pretending to comment on which strange utterances, the Editor will only remark, that there lies beside them much of a still more questionable character; unsuited to the general apprehension; nay wherein he himself does not see his way. Nebulous disquisitions on Religion, yet not without bursts of splendour; on the "perennial continuance of Inspiration"; on Prophecy; that there are "true Priests, as well as Baal-Priests,[6] in our own day": with more of the like sort. We select some fractions, by way of finish to this farrago.

"Cease, my much-respected Herr von Voltaire," thus apostrophises the Professor: "shut thy sweet voice; for the task appointed thee seems finished. Sufficiently hast thou demonstrated this proposition, considerable or otherwise: That the Mythus of the Christian Religion looks not in the eighteenth century as it did in the eighth. Alas, were thy six-and-thirty quartos, and the six-and-thirty thousand other quartos and folios, and flying sheets or reams, printed before and since on the same subject, all needed to convince us of so little! But what next? Wilt thou help us to embody the divine Spirit of that Religion in a new Mythus, in a new vehicle and vesture, that our Souls, otherwise too like perishing, may live? What! thou hast no faculty in that kind? Only a torch for burning, no hammer for building? Take our thanks, then, and —— thyself away.

"Meanwhile what are antiquated Mythuses to me? Or is the God present, felt in my own heart, a thing which Herr von Voltaire will dispute out of me; or dispute into me? To the '*Worship of Sorrow*' ascribe what origin and genesis thou pleasest, *has* not that Worship originated, and been generated; is it not *here*? Feel it in thy heart, and then say whether it is of God! This is Belief; all else is Opinion, —for which latter whoso will let him worry and be worried."

"Neither," observes he elsewhere, "shall ye tear-out one another's eyes, struggling over 'Plenary Inspiration,'[7] and suchlike: try rather to get a little even Partial Inspiration, each of you for himself. One BIBLE I know, of whose Plenary Inspiration doubt is not so much as possible; nay with my own eyes I saw the God's-Hand writing it: thereof all other Bibles are but leaves,—say, in Picture-Writing to assist the weaker faculty."

Or, to give the wearied reader relief, and bring it to an end, let him take the following perhaps more intelligible passage:

"To me, in this our life," says the Professor, "which is an internecine warfare with the Time-spirit, other warfare seems questionable. Hast thou in any way a Contention with thy brother, I advise thee, think well what the meaning thereof is. If thou gauge

---

6. False priests. See I Kings xviii.17-40.
7. Doctrine that all statements in the Bible are supernaturally inspired and authoritative. Voltaire had sought to demonstrate that this doctrine was absurd.

it to the bottom, it is simply this: 'Fellow, see! thou art taking more than thy share of Happiness in the world, something from *my* share: which, by the Heavens, thou shalt not; nay I will fight thee rather.'—Alas, and the whole lot to be divided is such a beggarly matter, truly a 'feast of shells,'[8] for the substance has been spilled out: not enough to quench one Appetite; and the collective human species clutching at them!—Can we not, in all such cases, rather say: 'Take it, thou too-ravenous individual; take that pitiful additional fraction of a share, which I reckoned mine, but which thou so wantest; take it with a blessing: would to Heaven I had enough for thee!'—If Fichte's *Wissenschaftslehre*[9] be, 'to a certain extent, Applied Christianity,' surely to a still greater extent, so is this. We have here not a Whole Duty of Man,[1] yet a Half Duty, namely the Passive half: could we but do it, as we can demonstrate it!

"But indeed Conviction, were it never so excellent, is worthless till it convert itself into Conduct. Nay properly Conviction is not possible till then; inasmuch as all Speculation is by nature endless, formless, a vortex amid vortices: only by a felt indubitable certainty of Experience does it find any centre to revolve round, and so fashion itself into a system. Most true is it, as a wise man teaches us, that 'Doubt of any sort cannot be removed except by Action.'[2] On which ground, too, let him who gropes painfully in darkness or uncertain light, and prays vehemently that the dawn may ripen into day, lay this other precept well to heart, which to me was of invaluable service: '*Do the Duty which lies nearest thee*,' which thou knowest to be a Duty! Thy second Duty will already have become clearer.

"May we not say, however, that the hour of Spiritual Enfranchisement is even this: When your Ideal World, wherein the whole man has been dimly struggling and inexpressibly languishing to work, becomes revealed, and thrown open; and you discover, with amazement enough, like the Lothario in *Wilhelm Meister*, that your 'America is here or nowhere'? The Situation that has not its Duty, its Ideal, was never yet occupied by man. Yes here, in this poor, miserable, hampered, despicable Actual, wherein thou even now standest, here or nowhere is thy Ideal: work it out therefrom; and working, believe, live, be free. Fool! the Ideal is in thyself, the impediment too is in thyself: thy Condition is but the stuff thou art to shape that same Ideal out of: what matters whether such stuff be of this sort or that, so the Form thou give it be heroic, be poetic? O thou that pinest in the imprisonment of the Actual, and criest bitterly to the gods for a kingdom wherein to rule and create, know

8. Empty eggshells.
9. "The Doctrine of Knowledge"; by the German philosopher Johann Gottlieb Fichte (1762–1814).
1. Title of an anonymous book of reli-
gious instruction first published in 1659.
2. This and the following quotation are from Goethe's *Wilhelm Meister*.

this of a truth: the thing thou seekest is already with thee, 'here or nowhere,' couldst thou only see!

"But it is with man's Soul as it was with Nature: the beginning of Creation is—Light.[3] Till the eye have vision, the whole members are in bonds.[4] Divine moment, when over the tempest-tost Soul, as once over the wild-weltering Chaos, it is spoken: Let there be Light! Ever to the greatest that has felt such moment, is it not miraculous and God-announcing; even as, under simpler figures, to the simplest and least. The mad primeval Discord is hushed; the rudely-jumbled conflicting elements bind themselves into separate Firmaments: deep silent rock-foundations are built beneath; and the skyey vault with its everlasting Luminaries above: instead of a dark wasteful Chaos, we have a blooming, fertile, heaven-encompassed World.

"I too could now say to myself: Be no longer a Chaos, but a World, or even Worldkin. Produce! Produce! Were it but the pitifullest infinitesimal fraction of a Product, produce it, in God's name! 'Tis the utmost thou hast in thee: out with it, then. Up, up! Whatsoever thy hand findeth to do, do it with thy whole might. Work while it is called Today; for the Night cometh, wherein no man can work."[5]

Natural Supernaturalism[1]

It is in his stupendous Section, headed *Natural Supernaturalism*, that the Professor first becomes a Seer; and, after long effort, such as we have witnessed, finally subdues under his feet this refractory Clothes-Philosophy, and takes victorious possession thereof. Phantasms enough he has had to struggle with; "Cloth-webs and Cobwebs," of Imperial Mantles, Superannuated Symbols, and what not:

3. Cf. Genesis i.3.
4. Cf. Matthew vi.22–23.
5. Adapted from Ecclesiastes ix. 10 and John ix. 4.
1. Book III, Chapter 8. The characteristically paradoxical title of this chapter can best be understood by reference to the chapter on miracles in David Hume's *An Enquiry Concerning Human Understanding* (1748), to which Carlyle makes several direct and indirect allusions in his own exposition of the nature of the miraculous. In his skeptical analysis of miracles (Christian miracles in particular), Hume asserts: "A miracle is a violation of the laws of nature. * * * It is no miracle that a man, seemingly in good health, should die on a sudden. * * * But it is a miracle that a dead man should come to life, because that

has never been observed in any age or country." The young Carlyle seems to have been impressed by Hume's arguments, as he had also been impressed (and depressed) by Gibbon's relentless exposure of traditional Christianity in *The Decline and Fall of the Roman Empire*. In his later resolution of his dilemma, he bypassed Hume's arguments. Instead of arguing whether miracles in the traditional sense (such as the resurrection of Christ) have occurred, he contends that *everything* in our experience is a miracle of a supernatural and inexplicable order, hence an appropriate cause for wonder and joy. The natural *is* supernatural. "To me," said Wordsworth, "the meanest flower that blows can give / Thoughts that do often lie too deep for tears."

yet still did he courageously pierce through. Nay, worst of all, two quite mysterious, world-embracing Phantasms, TIME and SPACE, have ever hovered round him, perplexing and bewildering: but with these also he now resolutely grapples, these also he victoriously rends asunder. In a word, he has looked fixedly on Existence, till one after the other, its earthly hulls and garnitures have all melted away; and now, to his rapt vision, the interior celestial Holy of Holies lies disclosed.

Here, therefore, properly it is that the Philosophy of Clothes attains to Transcendentalism;[2] this last leap, can we but clear it, takes us safe into the promised land, where *Palingenesia*,[3] in all senses, may be considered as beginning. "Courage, then!" may our Diogenes exclaim, with better right than Diogenes the First once did.[4] This stupendous Section we, after long painful meditation, have found not to be unintelligible; but, on the contrary, to grow clear, nay radiant, and all-illuminating. Let the reader, turning on it what utmost force of speculative intellect is in him, do his part; as we, by judicious selection and adjustment, shall study to do ours:

"Deep has been, and is, the significance of Miracles," thus quietly begins the Professor; "far deeper perhaps than we imagine. Meanwhile, the question of questions were: What specially is a Miracle? To that Dutch King of Siam, an icicle had been a miracle; whoso had carried with him an air-pump, and vial of vitriolic ether, might have worked a miracle.[5] To my Horse, again, who unhappily is still more unscientific, do not I work a miracle, and magical '*Open sesame!*'[6] every time I please to pay twopence, and open for him an impassable *Schlagbaum*, or shut Turnpike?

" 'But is not a real Miracle simply a violation of the Laws of Nature?' ask several. Whom I answer by this new question: What are the Laws of Nature? To me perhaps the rising of one from the dead were no violation of these Laws, but a confirmation; were some far deeper Law, now first penetrated into, and by Spiritual Force, even as the rest have all been, brought to bear on us with its Material Force.

"Here too may some inquire, not without astonishment: On what ground shall one, that can make Iron swim,[7] come and declare that therefore he can teach Religion? To us, truly, of the Nineteenth Century, such declaration were inept enough; which

2. A term loosely used here to refer to any philosophy which opposes materialism or empiricism, and which asserts the domination of the intuitive or spiritual over the material [C. F. Harrold].

3. Rebirth.

4. Near the end of a dull lecture, Diogenes ("the First"), a philosopher of the Cynic school, called out to his fellow listeners: "Courage, friends! I see land."

5. In his chapter on miracles, Hume cites an incident of an Indian prince refusing to believe that water can be turned into ice. Carlyle notes that anybody could do so by treating a flask of sulphuric ether with an air pump.

6. The magic password for opening a door in the cavern in the story *Ali Baba and the Forty Thieves*, in *The Arabian Nights*.

7. Elisha's miracle of causing an axehead to float in water (II Kings i.17).

nevertheless to our fathers, of the First Century, was full of meaning.

" 'But is it not the deepest Law of Nature that she be constant?' cries an illuminated class: 'Is not the Machine of the Universe fixed to move by unalterable rules?' Probable enough, good friends: nay I, too, must believe that the God, whom ancient inspired men assert to be 'without variableness or shadow of turning,'[8] does indeed never change; that Nature, that the Universe, which no one whom it so pleases can be prevented from calling a Machine, does move by the most unalterable rules. And now of you, too, I make the old inquiry: What those same unalterable rules, forming the complete Statute-Book of Nature, may possibly be?

"They stand written in our Works of Science, say you; in the accumulated records of Man's Experience?—Was Man with his Experience present at the Creation, then, to see how it all went on? Have any deepest scientific individuals yet dived down to the foundations of the Universe, and gauged everything there? Did the Maker take them into His counsel; that they read His groundplan of the incomprehensible All; and can say, This stands marked therein, and no more than this? Alas, not in anywise! These scientific individuals have been nowhere but where we also are; have seen some handbreadths deeper than we see into the Deep that is infinite, without bottom as without shore.

"Laplace's Book on the Stars,[9] wherein he exhibits that certain Planets, with their Satellites, gyrate round our worthy Sun, at a rate and in a course, which, by greatest good fortune, he and the like of him have succeeded in detecting,—is to me as precious as to another. But is this what thou namest 'Mechanism of the Heavens,' and 'System of the World'; this, wherein Sirius and the Pleiades, and all Herschel's[1] Fifteen-thousand Suns per minute, being left out, some paltry handful of Moons, and inert Balls, had been—looked at, nicknamed, and marked in the Zodiacal Way-bill;[2] so that we can now prate of their Whereabout; their How, their Why, their What, being hid from us, as in the signless Inane?

"System of Nature! To the wisest man, wide as is his vision, Nature remains of quite *infinite* depth, of quite infinite expansion; and all Experience thereof limits itself to some few computed centuries and measured square-miles. The course of Nature's phases, on this our little fraction of a Planet, is partially known to us: but who knows what deeper courses these depend on; what infinitely larger

---

8. James i.17.
9. Pierre Laplace (1749–1827) wrote *A Treatise on Celestial Mechanics* (1799–1825) and other astronomical studies.
1. Sir William Herschel (1738–1832) was an astronomer credited with discovering

thousands of stars and other celestial bodies.
2. A way-bill was a document issued with freight shipments, providing complete information about contents and routes.

Cycle (of causes) our little Epicycle[3] revolves on? To the Minnow
every cranny and pebble, and quality and accident, of its little
native Creek may have become familiar: but does the Minnow
understand the Ocean Tides and periodic Currents, the Trade-
winds, and Monsoons, and Moon's Eclipses; by all which the condition of its little Creek is regulated, and may, from time to time
(*un*miraculously enough), be quite overset and reversed? Such a
minnow is Man; his Creek this Planet Earth; his Ocean the
immeasurable All; his Monsoons and periodic Currents the mysterious Course of Providence through Æons of Æons.

"We speak of the Volume of Nature: and truly a Volume it is,
—whose Author and Writer is God. To read it! Dost thou, does
man, so much as well know the Alphabet thereof? With its Words,
Sentences, and grand descriptive Pages, poetical and philosophical,
spread out through Solar Systems, and Thousands of Years, we shall
not try thee. It is a Volume written in celestial hieroglyphs, in the
true Sacred-writing; of which even Prophets are happy that they can
read here a line and there a line. As for your Institutes, and Acade-
mies of Science, they strive bravely; and, from amid the thick-
crowded, inextricably intertwisted hieroglyphic writing, pick out, by
dextrous combination, some Letters in the vulgar Character, and
therefrom put together this and the other economic Recipe,[4] of
high avail in Practice. That Nature is more than some boundless
Volume of such Recipes, or huge, well-nigh inexhaustible Domes-
tic-Cookery Book, of which the whole secret will in this manner one
day evolve itself, the fewest dream.

"Custom," continues the Professor, "doth make dotards of us
all.[5] Consider well, thou wilt find that Custom is the greatest of
Weavers; and weaves air-raiment for all the Spirits of the Universe;
whereby indeed these dwell with us visibly, as ministering servants,
in our houses and workshops; but their spiritual nature becomes, to
the most, forever hidden. Philosophy complains that Custom has
hoodwinked us, from the first; that we do everything by Custom,
even Believe by it; that our very Axioms, let us boast of Free-thinking as we may, are oftenest simply such Beliefs as we have never
heard questioned. Nay, what is Philosophy throughout but a continual battle against Custom; an ever-renewed effort to *transcend* the
sphere of blind Custom, and so become Transcendental?

"Innumerable are the illusions and legerdemain-tricks of Custom:
but of all these, perhaps the cleverest is her knack of persuading us
that the Miraculous, by simple repetition, ceases to be Miraculous.
True, it is by this means we live; for man must work as well as

---

3. In Ptolemaic astronomy, a circle in
which a planet moves, the center of this
circle being carried round on the circumference of a larger circle (the "infinitely
larger Cycle").

4. I.e., a law in Economics, such as the
Law of Supply and Demand.
5. Cf. *Hamlet* I.iii.83: "Thus conscience
does make cowards of us all."

wonder: and herein is Custom so far a kind nurse, guiding him to his true benefit. But she is a fond foolish nurse, or rather we are false foolish nurselings, when, in our resting and reflecting hours, we prolong the same deception. Am I to view the Stupendous with stupid indifference, because I have seen it twice, or two-hundred, or two-million times? There is no reason in Nature or in Art why I should: unless, indeed, I am a mere Work-Machine, for whom the divine gift of Thought were no other than the terrestrial gift of Steam is to the Steam-engine; a power whereby cotton might be spun, and money and money's worth realised.

"Notable enough too, here as elsewhere, wilt thou find the potency of Names; which indeed are but one kind of such custom-woven, wonder-hiding Garments. Witchcraft, and all manner of Spectre-work, and Demonology, we have now named Madness and Diseases of the Nerves. Seldom reflecting that still the new question comes upon us: What is Madness, what are Nerves? Ever, as before, does Madness remain a mysterious-terrific, altogether *infernal* boiling-up of the Nether Chaotic Deep, through this fair-painted Vision of Creation; which swims thereon, which we name the Real. Was Luther's Picture of the Devil[6] less a Reality, whether it were formed within the bodily eye, or without it? In every the wisest Soul lies a whole world of internal Madness, an authentic Demon-Empire; out of which, indeed, his world of Wisdom has been creatively built together, and now rests there, as on its dark foundations does a habitable flowery Earth-rind.

"But deepest of all illusory Appearances, for hiding Wonder, as for many other ends, are your two grand fundamental world-enveloping Appearances, SPACE and TIME. These, as spun and woven for us from before Birth itself, to clothe our celestial ME for dwelling here, and yet to blind it,—lie all-embracing, as the universal canvas, or warp and woof, whereby all minor Illusions, in this Phantasm Existence, weave and paint themselves. In vain, while here on Earth, shall you endeavour to strip them off; you can, at best, but rend them asunder for moments, and look through.

"Fortunatus had a wishing Hat, which when he put on, and wished himself Anywhere, behold he was There.[7] By this means had Fortunatus triumphed over Space, he had annihilated Space; for him there was no Where, but all was Here. Were a Hatter to establish himself, in the Wahngasse of Weissnichtwo, and make felts of this sort for all mankind, what a world we should have of it! Still stranger, should, on the opposite side of the street, another

6. Martin Luther threw his inkstand at an apparition of the Devil which visited his study when he was translating the Psalms.
7. In the legend on which Thomas Dek-ker based his play *Old Fortunatus* (1600), a magic hat enabled the owner instantaneously to be anywhere he wished.

Hatter establish himself; and, as his fellow-craftsman made Space-annihilating Hats, make Time-annihilating! Of both would I purchase, were it with my last groschen;[8] but chiefly of this latter. To clap-on your felt, and, simply by wishing that you were Any*where*, straightway to be *There*! Next to clap-on your other felt, and, simply by wishing that you were Any*when*, straightway to be *Then*! This were indeed the grander: shooting at will from the Fire-Creation of the World to its Fire-Consummation; here historically present in the First Century, conversing face to face with Paul and Seneca;[9] there prophetically in the Thirty-first, conversing also face to face with other Pauls and Senecas, who as yet stand hidden in the depth of that late Time!

"Or thinkest thou it were impossible, unimaginable? Is the Past annihilated, then, or only past; is the Future non-extant, or only future? Those mystic faculties of thine, Memory and Hope, already answer: already through those mystic avenues, thou the Earth-blinded summonest both Past and Future, and communest with them, though as yet darkly, and with mute beckonings. The curtains of Yesterday drop down, the curtains of Tomorrow roll up; but Yesterday and Tomorrow both *are*. Pierce through the Time-element, glance into the Eternal. Believe what thou findest written in the sanctuaries of Man's Soul, even as all Thinkers, in all ages, have devoutly read it there: that Time and Space are not God, but creations of God; that with God as it is a universal HERE, so is it an everlasting Now.

"And seest thou therein any glimpse of IMMORTALITY?—O Heaven! Is the white Tomb of our Loved One, who died from our arms, and had to be left behind us there, which rises in the distance, like a pale, mournfully receding Milestone, to tell how many toilsome uncheered miles we have journeyed on alone,—but a pale spectral Illusion! Is the lost Friend still mysteriously Here, even as we are Here mysteriously, with God!—Know of a truth that only the Time-shadows have perished, or are perishable; that the real Being of whatever was, and whatever is, and whatever will be, *is* even now and forever. This, should it unhappily seem new, thou mayest ponder at thy leisure; for the next twenty years, or the next twenty centuries: believe it thou must; understand it thou canst not.

"That the Thought-forms, Space and Time, wherein, once for all, we are sent into this Earth to live, should condition and determine our whole Practical reasonings, conceptions, and imagings or imaginings, seems altogether fit, just, and unavoidable. But that they should, furthermore, usurp such sway over pure spiritual Medita-

---

8. Small German coins.
9. There is a legend that the Roman philosopher Seneca (4 B.C.–A.D. 65) had
conversed with St. Paul.

tion, and blind us to the wonder everywhere lying close on us, seems nowise so. Admit Space and Time to their due rank as Forms of Thought;[1] nay even, if thou wilt, to their quite undue rank of Realities: and consider, then, with thyself how their thin disguises hide from us the brightest God-effulgences! Thus, were it not miraculous, could I stretch forth my hand and clutch the Sun? Yet thou seest me daily stretch forth my hand and therewith clutch many a thing, and swing it hither and thither. Art thou a grown baby, then, to fancy that the Miracle lies in miles of distance, or in pounds avoirdupois of weight; and not to see that the true inexplicable God-revealing Miracle lies in this, that I can stretch forth my hand at all; that I have free Force to clutch aught therewith? Innumerable other of this sort are the deceptions, and wonder-hiding stupefactions, which Space practices on us.

"Still worse is it with regard to Time. Your grand antimagician, and universal wonder-hider, is this same lying Time. Had we but the Time-annihilating Hat, to put on for once only, we should see ourselves in a World of Miracles, wherein all fabled or authentic Thaumaturgy,[2] and feats of Magic, were outdone. But unhappily we have not such a Hat; and man, poor fool that he is, can seldom and scantily help himself without one.

"Were it not wonderful, for instance, had Orpheus, or Amphion, built the walls of Thebes by the mere sound of his Lyre?[3] Yet tell me, Who built these walls of Weissnichtwo; summoning out all the sandstone rocks, to dance along from the *Steinbruch* (now a huge Troglodyte Chasm,[4] with frightful green-mantled pools), and shape themselves into Doric and Ionic pillars, squared ashlar houses[5] and noble streets? Was it not the still higher Orpheus, or Orpheuses, who, in past centuries, by the divine Music of Wisdom, succeeded in civilising Man? Our highest Orpheus walked in Judea, eighteen-hundred years ago: his sphere-melody, flowing in wild native tones, took captive the ravished souls of men; and, being of a true sphere-melody, still flows and sounds, though now with thousandfold accompaniments, and rich symphonies, through all our hearts; and modulates, and divinely leads them. Is that a wonder, which happens in two hours; and does it cease to be wonderful if happening in two million? Not only was Thebes built by the music of an Orpheus; but without the music of some inspired Orpheus was no city ever built, no work that man glories in ever done.

1. The idea that time and space are modes of perception rather than realities is derived from the philosophy of Immanuel Kant (1724–1804), author of *A Critique of Pure Reason* (1781).
2. The working of miracles and magical occurrences.
3. The musicians Orpheus and Amphion effected miracles: Orpheus, with his lyre,

could spellbind wild beasts; Amphion's playing, during the building of Thebes, caused the stones for the walls to be drawn into place.
4. The emptied stone-quarry (*Steinbruch*) looks now like the site of primitive cave-dwellers (Troglodytes).
5. Houses made of squared blocks of hewn stone.

"Sweep away the Illusion of Time; glance, if thou have eyes, from the near moving-cause to its far-distant Mover: The stroke that came transmitted through a whole galaxy of elastic balls, was it less a stroke than if the last ball only had been struck, and sent flying? O, could I (with the Time-annihilating Hat) transport thee direct from the Beginnings to the Endings, how were thy eyesight unsealed, and thy heart set flaming in the Light-sea of celestial wonder! Then sawest thou that this fair Universe, were it in the meanest province thereof, is in very deed the star-domed City of God;[6] that through every star, through every grass-blade, and most through every Living Soul, the glory of a present God still beams. But Nature, which is the Time-vesture of God, and reveals Him to the wise, hides Him from the foolish.

"Again, could anything be more miraculous than an actual authentic Ghost? The English Johnson longed, all his life, to see one; but could not, though he went to Cock Lane, and thence to the church-vaults, and tapped on coffins.[7] Foolish Doctor! Did he never, with the mind's eye as well as with the body's, look round him into that full tide of human Life he so loved; did he never so much as look into Himself? The good Doctor was a Ghost, as actual and authentic as heart could wish; well-nigh a million of Ghosts were travelling the streets by his side. Once more I say, sweep away the illusion of Time; compress the threescore years into three minutes: what else was he, what else are we? Are we not Spirits, that are shaped into a body, into an Appearance; and that fade away again into air and Invisibility? This is no metaphor, it is a simple scientific *fact*; we start out of Nothingness, take figure, and are Apparitions; round us, as round the veriest spectre, is Eternity; and to Eternity minutes are as years and æons. Come there not tones of Love and Faith, as from celestial harp-strings, like the Song of beatified Souls? And again, do not we squeak and jibber (in our discordant, screech-owlish debatings and recriminatings); and glide bodeful, and feeble, and fearful; or uproar (*poltern*), and revel in our mad Dance of the Dead,—till the scent of the morning air[8] summons us to our still Home; and dreamy Night becomes awake and Day? Where now is Alexander of Macedon: does the steel Host, that yelled in fierce battle-shouts at Issus and Arbela,[9] remain behind him; or have they all vanished utterly, even as perturbed Goblins must? Napoleon too, and his Moscow Retreats and Austerlitz Campaigns! Was it all other than the veriest Spectre-hunt; which has now, with its howling tumult that made Night hideous, flitted away?—Ghosts! There are nigh a thousand-million walking

6. Title of St. Augustine's famous work.
7. The Cock Lane ghost in London, which proved to be a fraud, was investigated by Dr. Johnson. See Boswell for the year 1763.

8. Cf. *Hamlet* I.i.148–56 and v.58.
9. Sites of two victories won by the army of Alexander the Great against the Persians under Darius (333–31 B.C.).

the Earth openly at noon-tide; some half-hundred have vanished from it, some half-hundred have arisen in it, ere thy watch ticks once.

"O Heaven, it is mysterious, it is awful to consider that we not only carry each a future Ghost within Him; but are, in very deed, Ghosts! These Limbs, whence had we them; this stormy Force; this life-blood with its burning Passion? They are dust and shadow, a Shadow-system gathered round our ME; wherein, through some moments or years, the Divine Essence is to be revealed in the Flesh. That warrior on his strong war-horse, fire flashes through his eyes; force dwells in his arm and heart: but warrior and war-horse are a vision; a revealed Force, nothing more. Stately they tread the Earth, as if it were a firm substance: fool! the Earth is but a film; it cracks in twain, and warrior and war-horse sink beyond plummet's sounding.[1] Plummet's? Fantasy herself will not follow them. A little while ago, they were not; a little while, and they are not, their very ashes are not.

"So has it been from the beginning, so will it be to the end. Generation after generation takes to itself the Form of a Body; and forth-issuing from Cimmerian[2] Night, on Heaven's mission APPEARS. What Force and Fire is in each he expends: one grinding in the mill of Industry; one hunter-like climbing the giddy Alpine heights of Science; one madly dashed in pieces on the rocks of Strife, in war with his fellow:—and then the Heaven-sent is recalled; his earthly Vesture falls away, and soon even to sense becomes a vanished Shadow. Thus, like some wild-flaming, wild-thundering train of Heaven's Artillery, does this mysterious MANKIND thunder and flame, in long-drawn, quick-succeeding grandeur, through the unknown Deep. Thus, like a God-created, fire-breathing Spirit-host, we emerge from the Inane;[3] haste stormfully across the astonished Earth; then plunge again into the Inane. Earth's mountains are levelled, and her seas filled up, in our passage: can the Earth, which is but dead and a vision, resist Spirits which have reality and are alive? On the hardest adamant some footprint of us is stamped-in; the last Rear of the host will read traces of the earliest Van. But whence? —O Heaven, whither? Sense knows not; Faith knows not; only that it is through Mystery to Mystery, from God and to God.

> We *are such stuff*
> As dreams are made of, and our little Life
> Is rounded with a sleep![4]

1830–31   1833–34

1. *The Tempest* V.i.56. A plummet is a weight at the end of a line used to sound the depth of water under a ship.
2. I.e., a people living in perpetual darkness. See *Odyssey* XI.14.

3. The formless void of infinite space [NED].
4. *The Tempest* IV.i.156–58, a favorite passage for Carlyle, here slightly misquoted (Shakespeare wrote: "dreams are made on").

From The French Revolution[1]
September in Paris[2]

The tocsin is pealing its loudest, the clocks inaudibly striking *Three*, when poor Abbé Sicard,[3] with some thirty other Nonjurant Priests,[4] in six carriages, fare along the streets, from their preliminary House of Detention at the Townhall, westward towards the Prison of the Abbaye. Carriages enough stand deserted on the streets; these six move on,—through angry multitudes, cursing as they move. Accursed Aristocrat Tartuffes,[5] this is the pass ye have brought us to! And now ye will break the Prisons, and set Capet Veto[6] on horseback to ride over us? Out upon you, Priests of Beelzebub and Moloch; of Tartuffery, Mammon and the Prussian Gallows,—which ye name Mother-Church and God!—Such reproaches have the poor Nonjurants to endure, and worse; spoken in on them by frantic Patriots, who mount even on the carriage-steps; the very Guards hardly refraining. Pull up your carriage-blinds?—No! answers Patriotism, clapping its horny paw on the carriage-blind, and crushing it down again. Patience in oppression has limits: we are close on the Abbaye, it has lasted long: a poor Nonjurant, of quicker temper, smites the horny paw with his cane; nay, finding solacement in it, smites the unkempt head, sharply and again more sharply, twice over,—seen clearly of us and of the

---

world. It is the last that we see clearly. Alas, next moment, the carriages are locked and blocked in endless raging tumults; in yells deaf to the cry for mercy, which answer the cry for mercy with sabre-thrusts through the heart. The thirty Priests are torn out, are massacred about the Prison-Gate, one after one,—only the poor Abbé Sicard, whom one Moton a watchmaker, knowing him, heroically tried to save and secrete in the Prison, escapes to tell;—and it is Night and Orcus,[7] and Murder's snaky-sparkling head *has* risen in the murk!—

From Sunday afternoon (exclusive of intervals and pauses not final) till Thursday evening, there follow consecutively a Hundred Hours. Which hundred hours are to be reckoned with the hours of the Bartholomew Butchery, of the Armagnac Massacres, Sicilian Vespers, or whatsoever is savagest in the annals of this world. Horrible the hour when man's soul, in its paroxysm, spurns asunder the barriers and rules; and shows what dens and depths are in it! For Night and Orcus, as we say, as was long prophesied, have burst forth, here in this Paris, from their subterranean imprisonment: hideous, dim-confused; which it is painful to look on; and yet which cannot, and indeed which should not, be forgotten.

The Reader, who looks earnestly through this dim Phantasmagory of the Pit, will discern few fixed certain objects; and yet still a few. He will observe, in this Abbaye Prison, the sudden massacre of the Priests being once over, a strange Court of Justice, or call it Court of Revenge and Wild-Justice, swiftly fashion itself, and take seat round a table, with the Prison-Registers spread before it;—Stanislas Maillard, Bastille-hero, famed Leader of the Menads,[8] presiding. O Stanislas, one hoped to meet thee elsewhere than here; thou shifty Riding-Usher, with an inkling of Law! This work also thou hadst to do; and then—to depart for ever from our eyes. At *La Force*, at the *Châtelet*, the *Conciergerie*, the like Court forms itself, with the like accompaniments: the thing that one man does, other men can do. There are some Seven Prisons in Paris, full of Aristocrats with conspiracies;—nay not even *Bicêtre* and *Salpêtrière* shall escape, with their Forgers of Assignats:[9] and there are seventy times seven hundred Patriot hearts in a state of frenzy. Scoundrel hearts also there are; as perfect, say, as the Earth holds,—if such are needed. To whom, in this mood, law is as no-law; and killing, by what name soever called, is but work to be done.

So sit these sudden Courts of Wild-Justice, with the Prison-Registers before them; unwonted wild tumult howling all round; the Prisoners in dread expectancy within. Swift: a name is called; bolts

---

7. Hades, the underworld of the dead.
8. Frenzied women of Greece, followers of Dionysus. Maillard had led a mob of women in the march to Versailles in October, 1789.

9. Paper money issued by the French revolutionary government. Royalists accused of forging such currency had been imprisoned.

jingle, a Prisoner is there. A few questions are put; swiftly this sudden Jury decides: Royalist Plotter or not? Clearly not; in that case, Let the Prisoner be enlarged with *Vive la Nation*. Probably yea; then still, Let the Prisoner be enlarged, but without *Vive la Nation*; or else it may run. Let the Prisoner be conducted to La Force. At La Force again their formula is, Let the Prisoner be conducted to the Abbaye.—"To La Force then!" Volunteer bailiffs seize the doomed man; he is at the outer gate; "enlarged," or "conducted," not into La Force, but into a howling sea; forth, under an arch of wild sabres, axes and pikes; and sinks, hewn asunder. And another sinks, and another; and there forms itself a piled heap of corpses, and the kennels begin to run red. Fancy the yells of these men, their faces of sweat and blood; the crueller shrieks of these women, for there are women too; and a fellow-mortal hurled naked into it all! Jourgniac de Saint-Méard has seen battle, has seen an effervescent Regiment du Roi in mutiny; but the bravest heart may quail at this. The Swiss Prisoners, remnants of the Tenth of August,[1] "clasped each other spasmodically, and hung back; grey veterans crying: 'Mercy, Messieuers; ah, mercy!' But there was no mercy. Suddenly, however, one of these men steps forward. He had on a blue frock coat; he seemed about thirty, his stature was above common, his look noble and martial. 'I go first,' said he, 'since it must be so: adieu!' Then dashing his hat sharply behind him: 'Which way?' cried he to the Brigands: 'Show it me, then.' They open the folding gate; he is announced to the multitude. He stands a moment motionless; then plunges forth among the pikes, and dies of a thousand wounds."

Man after man is cut down; the sabres need sharpening, the killers refresh themselves from wine-jugs. Onward and onward goes the butchery; the loud yells wearying down into bass growls. A sombre-faced shifting multitude looks on; in dull approval, or dull disapproval; in dull recognition that it is Necessity. "An *Anglais* in drab greatcoat" was seen, or seemed to be seen, serving liquor from his own drambottle;—for what purpose, "if not set on by Pitt," Satan and himself know best! Witty Dr. Moore grew sick on approaching, and turned into another street.—Quick enough goes this Jury-Court; and rigorous. The brave are not spared, nor the beautiful, nor the weak. Old M. de Montmorin, the Minister's Brother, was acquitted by the Tribunal of the Seventeenth; and conducted back, elbowed by howling galleries; but is not acquitted here. Princess de Lamballe[2] has lain down on bed: "Madame, you are to be removed to the Abbaye." "I do not wish to remove; I

---

1. Remnants of the Swiss Guards, most of whom had been massacred on August 10, 1792, when defending the king's palace from a mob.
2. Great-granddaughter of the King of Sardinia; she had married a Bourbon, was early widowed, and later became a close friend of Queen Marie Antoinette, with whom she had been imprisoned.

am well enough here." There is a need-be for removing. She will arrange her dress a little, then; rude voices answer, "You have not far to go." She too is led to the hell-gate; a manifest Queen's-Friend. She shivers back, at the sight of bloody sabres; but there is no return: Onwards! That fair hind head is cleft with the axe; the neck is severed. That fair body is cut in fragments; with indignities, and obscene horrors of moustachio *grands-lèvres*,[3] which human nature would fain find incredible,—which shall be read in the original language only. She was beautiful, she was good, she had known no happiness. Young hearts, generation after generation, will think with themselves: O worthy of worship, thou king-descended, god-descended, and poor sister-woman! why was not I there; and some Sword Balmung[4] or Thor's Hammer in my hand? Her head is fixed on a pike; paraded under the windows of the Temple; that a still more hated, a Marie Antoinette, may see. One Municipal, in the Temple with the Royal Prisoners at the moment, said, "Look out." Another eagerly whispered, "Do not look." The circuit of the Temple is guarded, in these hours, by a long stretched tricolor riband: terror enters, and the clangour of infinite tumult; hitherto not regicide, though that too may come.

But it is more edifying to note what thrillings of affection, what fragments of wild virtues turn up in this shaking asunder of man's existence; for of these too there is a proportion. Note old Marquis Cazotte: he is doomed to die; but his young Daughter clasps him in her arms, with an inspiration of eloquence, with a love which is stronger than very death: the heart of the killers themselves is touched by it; the old man is spared. Yet he was guilty, if plotting for his King is guilt: in ten days more, a Court of Law condemned him, and he had to die elsewhere; bequeathing his Daughter a lock of his old grey hair. Or note old M. de Sombreuil, who also had a Daughter:—My Father is not an Aristocrat: O good gentlemen, I will swear it, and testify it, and in all ways prove it; we are not; we hate Aristocrats! "Wilt thou drink Aristocrats' blood?" The man lifts blood (if universal Rumour can be credited); the poor maiden does drink. "This Sombreuil is innocent then!" Yes, indeed,—and now note, most of all, how the bloody pikes, at this news, do rattle to the ground; and the tiger-yells become bursts of jubilee over a brother saved; and the old man and his daughter are clasped to bloody bosoms, with hot tears; and borne home in triumph of *Vive la Nation*, the killers refusing even money! Does it seem strange, this temper of theirs? It seems very certain, well proved by Royalist testimony in other instances; and very significant.

---

3. "Thick lips"—a figure of speech to characterize the mob.

4. The sharp sword of Siegfried, hero of the *Nibelungenlied*.

Place de la Révolution[1]

To this conclusion, then, hast thou come, O hapless Louis! The Son of Sixty Kings is to die on the Scaffold by form of Law. Under Sixty Kings this same form of Law, form of Society, has been fashioning itself together, these thousand years; and has become, one way and other, a most strange Machine. Surely, if needful, it is also frightful, this Machine; dead, blind; not what it should be; which, with swift stroke, or by cold slow torture, has wasted the lives and souls of innumerable men. And behold now a King himself, or say rather Kinghood in his person, is to expire here in cruel tortures;—like a Phalaris[2] shut in the belly of his own red-heated Brazen Bull! It is ever so; and thou shouldst know it, O haughty tyrannous man: injustice breeds injustice; curses and falsehoods do verily return "always *home*," wide as they may wander. Innocent Louis bears the sins of many generations: he too experiences that man's tribunal is not in this Earth; that if he had no Higher one, it were not well with him.

A King dying by such violence appeals impressively to the imagination; as the like must do, and ought to do. And yet at bottom it is not the King dying, but the man! Kingship is a coat: the grand loss is of the skin. The man from whom you take his Life, to him can the whole combined world do *more*? Lally[3] went on his hurdle; his mouth filled with a gag. Miserablest mortals, doomed for picking pockets, have a whole five-act Tragedy in them, in that dumb pain, as they go to the gallows, unregarded; they consume the cup of trembling down to the lees. For Kings and for Beggars, for the justly doomed and the unjustly, it is a hard thing to die. Pity them all: thy utmost pity, with all aids and appliances and throne-and-scaffold contrasts, how far short is it of the thing pitied!

A Confessor has come; Abbé Edgeworth, of Irish extraction, whom the King knew by good report, has come promptly on this solemn mission. Leave the Earth alone, then, thou hapless King; it with its malice will go its way, thou also canst go thine. A hard scene yet remains: the parting with our loved ones. Kind hearts, environed in the same grim peril with us; to be left *here*! Let the Reader look with the eyes of Valet Cléry,[4] through these glass-doors, where also the Municipality watches; and see the cruellest of scenes:

---

1. Part III, Book 2, Chapter viii. On January 20, 1793, by a small majority, the Convention of Delegates in Paris had voted for the death of the king.
2. A Sicilian tyrant whose victims were roasted alive by being confined inside the brass figure of a bull under which a fire was lit.
3. A French general who was accused unjustly of treachery and executed in 1766. The gag in his mouth was presumably to prevent his protesting his innocence.
4. The valet who attended the king during his imprisonment and who later published a journal.

"At half-past eight, the door of the ante-room opened: the Queen appeared first, leading her Son by the hand; then Madame Royale[5] and Madame Elizabeth: they all flung themselves into the arms of the King. Silence reigned for some minutes; interrupted only by sobs. The Queen made a movement to lead his Majesty towards the inner room, where M. Edgeworth was waiting unknown to them: 'No,' said the King, 'let us go into the dining-room, it is there only that I can see you.' They entered there; I shut the door of it, which was of glass. The King sat down, the Queen on his left hand, Madame Elizabeth on his right, Madame Royale almost in front; the young Prince remained standing between his Father's legs. They all leaned towards him, and often held him embraced. This scene of woe lasted an hour and three quarters; during which we could hear nothing; we could see only that always when the King spoke, the sobbings of the Princesses redoubled, continued for some minutes; and that then the King began again to speak." —And so our meetings and our partings do now end! The sorrows we gave each other; the poor joys we faithfully shared, and all our lovings and our sufferings, and confused toilings under the earthly Sun, are over. Thou good soul, I shall never, never through all ages of Time, see thee any more!—NEVER! O Reader, knowest thou that hard word?

For nearly two hours this agony lasts; then they tear themselves asunder. "Promise that you will see us on the morrow." He promises:—Ah yes, yes; yet once; and go now, ye loved ones; cry to God for yourselves and me!—It was a hard scene, but it is over. He will not see them on the morrow. The Queen, in passing through the ante-room, glanced at the Cerberus Municipals;[6] and, with woman's vehemence, said through her tears, "*Vous êtes tous des scélérats.*"[7]

King Louis slept sound, till five in the morning, when Cléry, as he had been ordered, awoke him. Cléry dressed his hair: while this went forward, Louis took a ring from his watch, and kept trying it on his finger; it was his wedding-ring, which he is now to return to the Queen as a mute farewell. At half-past six, he took the Sacrament; and continued in devotion, and conference with Abbé Edgeworth. He will not see his Family: it were too hard to bear.

At eight, the Municipals enter: the King gives them his Will, and messages and effects; which they, at first, brutally refuse to take charge of: he gives them a roll of gold pieces, a hundred and

5. The king's daughter, the Duchesse d'Angoulême (1778–1851); Madame Elizabeth was the king's sister, guillotined a year later.

6. Municipal officers, likened to Cerberus, the three-headed dog that guarded the entrance to Hades.

7. "You are all scoundrels."

twenty-five louis; these are to be returned to Malesherbes,[8] who had lent them. At nine, Santerre[9] says the hour is come. The King begs yet to retire for three minutes. At the end of three minutes, Santerre again says the hour is come. "Stamping on the ground with his right foot, Louis answers: '*Partons*, Let us go.' "—How the rolling of those drums comes in, through the Temple bastions and bulwarks, on the heart of a queenly wife; soon to be a widow! He is gone, then, and has not seen us? A Queen weeps bitterly; a King's Sister and Children. Over all these Four does Death also hover: all shall perish miserably save one; she, as Duchesse d'Angoulême, will live,—not happily.

At the Temple Gate were some faint cries, perhaps from voices of Pitiful women: "*Grâce!*[1] *Grâce!*" Through the rest of the streets there is silence as of the grave. No man not armed is allowed to be there: the armed, did any even pity, dare not express it, each man overawed by all his neighbours. All windows are down, none seen looking through them. All shops are shut. No wheel-carriage rolls, this morning, in these streets but one only. Eighty-thousand armed men stand ranked, like armed statues of men; cannons bristle, cannoneers with match burning, but no word or movement: it is as a city enchanted into silence and stone: one carriage with its escort, slowly rumbling, is the only sound. Louis reads, in his Book of Devotion, the Prayers of the Dying: clatter of this death-march falls sharp on the ear, in the great silence; but the thought would fain struggle heavenward, and forget the Earth.

As the clocks strike ten, behold the Place de la Révolution, once Place de Louis Quinze: the Guillotine, mounted near the old Pedestal where once stood the Statue of that Louis! Far round, all bristles with cannons and armed men: spectators crowding in the rear; D'Orléans Égalité[2] there in cabriolet. Swift messengers, *hoquetons*, speed to the Townhall, every three minutes: near by is the Convention sitting,—vengeful for Lepelletier.[3] Heedless of all, Louis reads his Prayers of the Dying; not till five minutes yet has he finished; then the Carriage opens. What temper he is in? Ten different witnesses will give ten different accounts of it. He is in the collision of all tempers; arrived now at the black Mahlstrom and descent of Death: in sorrow, in indignation, in resignation struggling to be resigned. "Take care of M. Edgeworth," he straitly

8. A delegate who had defended the king. He was guillotined a year later.
9. A Jacobin leader who commanded the troops in Paris.
1. "Mercy!"
2. The Duc d'Orléans, a Royalist who had become a revolutionary leader, was called Égalité (Equality). Despite his having voted for the king's death, he was himself executed in 1793.
3. A delegate who had voted for the king's death and was killed by a Royalist sympathizer.

charges the Lieutenant who is sitting with them: then they two descend.

The drums are beating: "*Taisez-vous*, Silence!" he cries "in a terrible voice, *d'une voix terrible*." He mounts the scaffold, not without delay; he is in puce[4] coat, breeches of grey, white stockings. He strips off the coat; stands disclosed in a sleeve-waistcoat of white flannel. The Executioners approach to bind him: he spurns, resists; Abbé Edgeworth has to remind him how the Saviour, in whom men trust, submitted to be bound. His hands are tied, his head bare; the fatal moment is come. He advances to the edge of the Scaffold, "his face very red," and says: "Frenchmen, I die innocent: it is from the Scaffold and near appearing before God that I tell you so. I pardon my enemies; I desire that France——" A General on horseback, Santerre or another, prances out, with uplifted hand: "*Tambours!*" The drums drown the voice. "Executioners, do your duty!" The Executioners, desperate lest themselves be murdered (for Santerre and his Armed Ranks will strike, if they do not), seize the hapless Louis: six of them desperate, him singly desperate, struggling there; and bind him to their plank. Abbé Edgeworth, stooping, bespeaks him: "Son of Saint Louis,[5] ascend to Heaven." The Axe clanks down; a King's Life is shorn away. It is Monday the 21st of January 1793. He was aged Thirty-eight years four months and twenty-eight days.

Executioner Samson shows the Head: fierce shout of *Vive la République* rises, and swells; caps raised on bayonets, hats waving: students of the College of Four Nations take it up, on the far Quais; fling it over Paris. D'Orléans drives off in his cabriôlet: the Townhall Councillors rub their hands, saying, "It is done, It is done." There is dipping of handkerchiefs, of pike-points in the blood. Headsman Samson, though he afterwards denied it, sells locks of the hair: fractions of the puce coat are long after worn in rings.—And so, in some half-hour it is done; and the multitude has all departed. Pastry-cooks, coffee-sellers, milkmen sing out their trivial quotidian cries: the world wags on, as if this were a common day. In the coffee-houses that evening, says Prudhomme, Patriot shook hands with Patriot in a more cordial manner than usual. Not till some days after, according to Mercier, did public men see what a grave thing it was.

From *Cause and Effect*[1]

* * * Yes, Reader, here is the miracle. Out of that putrescent rubbish of Scepticism, Sensualism, Sentimentalism, hollow Ma-

4. Dull red.
5. Louis IX, king of France (reigned 1226–70).
1. Part III, Book 3, Chapter i. Be-
tween the execution of the king and the advent of Napoleon, the revolutionary movement in France suffered from dissension and counterrevolu-

chiavelism, such a Faith has verily risen; flaming in the heart of a People. A whole People, awakening as it were to consciousness in deep misery, believes that it is within reach of a Fraternal Heaven-on-Earth. With longing arms, it struggles to embrace the Unspeakable; cannot embrace it, owing to certain causes.—Seldom do we find that a whole People can be said to have any Faith at all; except in things which it can eat and handle. Whensoever it gets any Faith, its history becomes spirit-stirring, noteworthy. But since the time when steel Europe shook itself simultaneously at the word of Hermit Peter,[2] and rushed towards the Sepulchre where God had lain, there was no universal impulse of Faith that one could note. Since Protestantism went silent, no Luther's voice, no Zisca's[3] drum any longer proclaiming that God's truth was *not* the Devil's Lie; and the Last of the Cameronians[4] (Renwick was the name of him; honour to the name of the brave!) sank, shot, on the Castle-hill of Edinburgh, there was no partial impulse of Faith among Nations. Till now, behold, once more, this French Nation believes! Herein, we say, in that astonishing Faith of theirs, lies the miracle. It is a Faith undoubtedly of the more prodigious sort, even among Faiths; and will embody itself in prodigies. It is the soul of that world-prodigy named French Revolution; whereat the world still gazes and shudders.

But, for the rest, let no man ask History to explain by cause and effect how the business proceeded henceforth. This battle of Mountain and Gironde,[5] and what follows, is the battle of Fanaticisms and Miracles; unsuitable for cause and effect. The sound of it, to the mind, is as a hubbub of voices in distraction; little of articulate is to be gathered by long listening and studying; only battle-tumult, shouts of triumph, shrieks of despair. The Mountain has left no Memoirs; the Girondins have left Memoirs, which are too often little other than long-drawn Interjections, of *Woe is me*, and *Cursed be ye*. So soon as History can philosophically delineate the conflagration of a kindled Fireship,[6] she may try this other task. Here lay the bitumen-stratum, there the brimstone one; so ran the

tionary outbreaks which led to the Reign of Terror (1793–94). During this period most of the political leaders and thousands of their followers lost their lives. Before recommencing his narrative, Carlyle pauses, in this chapter, to consider some of the forces underlying these developments.

2. Leader of the First Crusade to Palestine in the late 11th century.

3. Ca. 1360–1424; successful general and leader of the Hussites, a religious sect in Bohemia.

4. A 17th-century Scottish sect. See Sir Walter Scott's novel, *The Heart of Midlothian.*

5. The Girondists were a party of moderate revolutionaries, often of middle-class backgrounds. They were liquidated (as the Marxists say) by their opponents, the Jacobins, who were more adept in controlling the populace. Because the Jacobin delegates in the National Assembly sat in the most elevated place, the party was sometimes called the "Mountain."

6. A ship filled with combustibles (such as gunpowder and brimstone) which is set adrift among enemy shipping to create havoc.

vein of gunpowder, of nitre, terebinth[7] and foul grease: this, were she inquisitive enough, History might partly know. But how they acted and reacted below decks, one fire-stratum playing into the other, by its nature and the art of man, now when all hands ran raging, and the flames lashed high over shrouds and topmast: this let not History attempt.

The Fireship is old France, the old French Form of Life; her crew a Generation of men. Wild are their cries and their ragings there, like spirits tormented in that flame. But, on the whole, are they not *gone*, O Reader? Their Fireship and they, frightening the world, have sailed away; its flames and its thunders quite away, into the Deep of Time. One thing therefore History will do: pity them all; for it went hard with them all. Not even the seagreen Incorruptible[8] but shall have some pity, some human love, though it takes an effort. And now, so much once thoroughly attained, the rest will become easier. To the eye of equal brotherly pity, innumerable perversions dissipate themselves; exaggerations and execrations fall off, of their own accord. Standing wistfully on the safe shore, we will look, and see, what is of interest to us, what is adapted to us.

1834–37   1837

From Past and Present[1]

From *Democracy*

If the Serene Highnesses and Majesties do not take note of that,[2] then, as I perceive, *that* will take note of itself! The time for levity, insincerity, and idle babble and play-acting, in all kinds, is gone

---

7. Turpentine.
8. Maximilien Robespierre, "the Incorruptible"; chief of the Jacobin party and principal instigator of the Reign of Terror.
1. In 1842 there were reputedly 1.5 million unemployed in England (out of a population of 18 million). The closing of factories and the reduction of wages led to severe rioting in the manufacturing districts. Bread-hungry mobs (as well as the Chartist mobs who demanded political reforms) caused many observers to dread that a large-scale revolution was imminent. Carlyle was himself so appalled by the plight of the industrial workers that he postponed his researches into the life and times of Cromwell in order to air his views on the contemporary crisis. *Past and Present*, a book written in seven weeks, was a call for heroic leadership. Cromwell and other historic leaders are cited, but the principal example from

the past is Abbot Samson, a medieval monk who established order in the monasteries under his charge. Carlyle hoped that the "Captains of Industry" might provide a comparable leadership in 1843. He was aware that the spread of democracy was inevitable, but he had little confidence in it as a method of producing leaders. Nor did he have any confidence, at this time, in the landed aristocracy who seemed to him preoccupied with fox-hunting, preserving their game, and upholding the tariffs on grain (the Corn Laws). In place of a "Do nothing Aristocracy" there was need for a "Working Aristocracy." The first selection here printed is from Book III, Chapter 13.
2. The previous chapter, "Reward," had urged that English manufacturers needed the help of everyone, and that Parliament should remove the tariffs (Corn Laws) restricting the growth of trade and industry.

by; it is a serious, grave time. Old long-vexed questions, not yet solved in logical words or parliamentary laws, are fast solving themselves in facts, somewhat unblessed to behold! This largest of questions, this question of Work and Wages, which ought, had we heeded Heaven's voice, to have begun two generations ago or more, cannot be delayed longer without hearing Earth's voice. "Làbour" will verily need to be somewhat "organized," as they say,—God knows with what difficulty. Man will actually need to have his debts and earnings a little better paid by man; which, let Parliaments speak of them, or be silent of them, are eternally his due from man, and cannot, without penalty and at length not without death-penalty,[3] be withheld. How much ought to cease among us straightway; how much ought to begin straightway, while the hours yet are!

Truly they are strange results to which this of leaving all to "Cash"; of quietly shutting up the God's Temple, and gradually opening wide-open the Mammon's Temple, with "Laissez-faire, and Every man for himself,"—have led us in these days! We have Upper, speaking Classes, who indeed do "speak" as never man spake before; the withered flimsiness, godless baseness and barrenness of whose Speech might of itself indicate what kind of Doing and practical Governing went on under it! For Speech is the gaseous element out of which most kinds of Practice and Performance, especially all kinds of moral Performance, condense themselves, and take shape; as the one is, so will the other be. Descending, accordingly, into the Dumb Class in its Stockport Cellars[4] and Poor-Law Bastilles,[5] have we not to announce that they are hitherto unexampled in the History of Adam's Posterity?

Life was never a May-game for men: in all times the lot of the dumb millions born to toil was defaced with manifold sufferings, injustices, heavy burdens, avoidable and unavoidable; not play at all, but hard work that made the sinews sore and the heart sore. As bond-slaves, *villani, bordarii, sochemanni,* nay indeed as dukes, earls and kings, men were oftentimes made weary of their life; and had to say, in the sweat of their brow and of their soul, Behold, it is not sport, it is grim earnest, and our back can bear no more! Who knows not what massacrings and harryings there have been; grinding, long-continuing, unbearable injustices,—till the heart had to rise in madness, and some "*Eu Sachsen, nimith euer sachses,* You Saxons, out with your gully-knives, then!" You Saxons, some "arrestment," partial "arrestment of the Knaves and Dastards" has

3. I.e., by the outbreak of a revolution, as in France.
4. In a cellar in the slum district of Stockport, an industrial town near Manchester, three children were poisoned by their starving parents in order to collect insurance benefits from a burial society.
5. I.e. workhouse for the unemployed.

become indispensable!—The page of Dryasdust[6] is heavy with such details.

And yet I will venture to believe that in no time, since the beginnings of Society, was the lot of those same dumb millions of toilers so entirely unbearable as it is even in the days now passing over us. It is not to die, or even to die of hunger, that makes a man wretched; many men have died; all men must die,—the last exit of us all is in a Fire-Chariot of Pain.[7] But it is to live miserable we know not why; to work sore and yet gain nothing; to be heartworn, weary, yet isolated, unrelated, girt-in with a cold universal Laissez-faire: it is to die slowly all our life long, imprisoned in a deaf, dead, Infinite Injustice, as in the accursed iron belly of a Phalaris' Bull![8] This is and remains for ever intolerable to all men whom God has made. Do we wonder at French Revolutions, Chartisms, Revolts of Three Days? The times, if we will consider them, are really unexampled.

Never before did I hear of an Irish Widow reduced to "prove her sisterhood by dying of typhus-fever and infecting seventeen persons,"—saying in such undeniable way, "You *see*, I was your sister!"[9] Sisterhood, brotherhood, was often forgotten; but not till the rise of these ultimate Mammon and Shotbelt Gospels[1] did I ever see it so expressly denied. If no pious Lord or *Law-ward* would remember it, always some pious Lady ("*Hlaf dig,*" Benefactress, "*Loaf-giveress,*" they say she is,—blessings on her beautiful heart!) was there, with mild mother-voice and hand, to remember it; some pious thoughtful *Elder*, what we now call "Prester," *Presbyter* or "Priest," was there to put all men in mind of it, in the name of the God who had made all.

Not even in Black Dahomey[2] was it ever, I think, forgotten to the typhus-fever length. Mungo Park,[3] resourceless, had sunk down to die under the Negro Village-Tree, a horrible White object in the eyes of all. But in the poor Black Woman, and her daughter who stood aghast at him, whose earthly wealth and funded capital consisted of one small calabash of rice, there lived a heart richer

---

6. An imaginary author of dull histories.
7. Cf. II Kings ii.11–12.
8. Phalaris was a Sicilian tyrant whose victims were roasted alive by being confined inside the brass figure of a bull under which a fire was lit.
9. An incident referred to several times in *Past and Present.* Dickens in *Bleak House* also showed how indifference to the lack of sanitation in London slums led to the spread of disease to other parts of the city.
1. "Mammon Gospel" signifies the pursuit of wealth according to the economic code of laissez faire, whereby no one took the responsibility of caring for the starving widow. "Shotbelt Gospel": the attitudes of land-owning aristocracy who were committed to preserving their exclusive right to shoot game birds and animals.
2. A state in west Africa where savage customs, such as human sacrifice and cannibalism, persisted.
3. Explorer and author of *Travels in the Interior of Africa* (1799). In 1806 he was killed by Africans.

than "*Laissez-faire*": they, with a royal munificence, boiled their rice for him; they sang all night to him, spinning assiduous on their cotton distaffs, as he lay to sleep: "Let us pity the poor white man; no mother has he to fetch him milk, no sister to grind him corn!" Thou poor black Noble One,—thou *Lady* too: did not a God make thee too; was there not in thee too something of a God!—

Gurth,[4] born thrall of Cedric the Saxon, has been greatly pitied by Dryasdust and others. Gurth, with the brass collar round his neck, tending Cedric's pigs in the glades of the wood, is not what I call an exemplar of human felicity: but Gurth, with the sky above him, with the free air and tinted boscage and umbrage round him, and in him at least the certainty of supper and social lodging when he came home; Gurth to me seems happy, in comparison with many a Lancashire and Buckinghamshire man, of these days, not born thrall of anybody! Gurth's brass collar did not gall him: Cedric *deserved* to be his Master. The pigs were Cedric's, but Gurth too would get his parings of them. Gurth had the inexpressible satisfaction of feeling himself related indissolubly, though in a rude brass-collar way, to his fellow-mortals in this Earth. He had superiors, inferiors, equals.—Gurth is now "emancipated" long since; has what we call "Liberty." Liberty, I am told, is a Divine thing. Liberty when it becomes the "Liberty to die by starvation" is not so divine!

Liberty? The true liberty of a man, you would say, consisted in his finding out, or being forced to find out, the right path, and to walk thereon. To learn, or to be taught, what work he actually was able for; and then by permission, persuasion, and even compulsion, to set about doing of the same! That is his true blessedness, honour, "liberty" and maximum of wellbeing: if liberty be not that, I for one have small care about liberty. You do not allow a palpable madman to leap over precipices; you violate his liberty, you that are wise; and keep him, were it in strait-waistcoats, away from the precipices! Every stupid, every cowardly and foolish man is but a less palpable madman: his true liberty were that a wiser man, that any and every wiser man, could, by brass collars, or in whatever milder or sharper way, lay hold of him when he was going wrong, and order and compel him to go a little righter. O, if thou really art my *Senior*, Seigneur, my *Elder*, Presbyter or Priest, —if thou art in very deed my *Wiser*, may a beneficent instinct lead and impel thee to "conquer" me, to command me! If thou do know better than I what is good and right, I conjure thee in the name of God, force me to do it; were it by never such brass collars, whips and handcuffs, leave me not to walk over precipices! That I have

4. A swineherd described in Scott's *Ivanhoe*.

been called, by all the Newspapers, a "free man" will avail me little, if my pilgrimage have ended in death and wreck. O that the Newspapers had called me slave, coward, fool, or what it pleased their sweet voices to name me, and I had attained not death, but life!—Liberty requires new definitions.

A conscious abhorrence and intolerance of Folly, of Baseness, Stupidity, Poltroonery and all that brood of things, dwells deep in some men: still deeper in others an *un*conscious abhorrence and intolerance, clothed moreover by the beneficent Supreme Powers in what stout appetites, energies, egoisms so-called, are suitable to it;—these latter are your Conquerors, Romans, Normans, Russians, Indo-English; Founders of what we call Aristocracies. Which indeed have they not the most "divine right" to found;—being themselves very truly Ἄριστοι, BRAVEST, BEST; and conquering generally a confused rabble of WORST, or at lowest, clearly enough, of WORSE? I think their divine right, tried, with affirmatory verdict, in the greatest Law-Court known to me, was good! A class of men who are dreadfully exclaimed against by Dryasdust; of whom nevertheless beneficent Nature has oftentimes had need; and may, alas, again have need.

When, across the hundredfold poor scepticisms, trivialisms, and constitutional cobwebberies of Dryasdust, you catch any glimpse of a William the Conqueror,[5] a Tancred of Hauteville[6] or such like,—do you not discern veritably some rude outline of a true God-made King; whom not the Champion of England[7] cased in tin, but all Nature and the Universe were calling to the throne? It is absolutely necessary that he get thither. Nature does not mean her poor Saxon children to perish, of obesity, stupor or other malady, as yet: a stern Ruler and Line of Rulers therefore is called in, —a stern but most beneficent *perpetual House-Surgeon* is by Nature herself called in, and even the appropriate *fees* are provided for him! Dryasdust talks lamentably about Hereward[8] and the Fen Counties; fate of Earl Waltheof;[9] Yorkshire and the North reduced to ashes; all of which is undoubtedly lamentable. But even Dryas-

---

5. King William I of England (reigned 1066–87), surnamed the Conqueror after the Battle of Hastings in 1066. Being an illegitimate son, he also bore the surname of William the Bastard. Although some historians condemn William as a ruthless ruler, he is ranked by Carlyle as a hero because of his strong and efficient government. William fulfilled the requirements of the kingly hero described by Carlyle in his lectures *On Heroes:* a man fittest "to *command* over us * * * to tell us what we are to *do*."
6. Norman hero of the First Crusade.

7. An official who goes through a formality, at coronation ceremonies, of demanding whether anyone challenges the right of the monarch to ascend the throne. He wears full armor ("cased in tin"). A symbol for Carlyle of outworn feudal customs.
8. Hereward the Wake, an outlaw whose exploits against William the Conqueror made him seem a romantic figure like Robin Hood.
9. His execution in 1075, on a supposedly trumped-up charge, is cited as a blot on William's record as king.

dust apprises me of one fact: "A child, in this William's reign, might have carried a purse of gold from end to end of England." My erudite friend, it is a fact which outweighs a thousand! Sweep away thy constitutional, sentimental, and other cobwebberies; look eye to eye, if thou still have any eye, in the face of this big burly William Bastard: thou wilt see a fellow of most flashing discernment, of most strong lion-heart;—in whom, as it were, within a frame of oak and iron, the gods have planted the soul of "a man of genius"! Dost thou call that nothing? I call it an immense thing! —Rage enough was in this Willelmus Conquaestor, rage enough for his occasions;—and yet the essential element of him, as of all such men, is not scorching *fire*, but shining illuminative *light*. Fire and light are strangely interchangeable; nay, at bottom, I have found them different forms of the same most godlike "elementary substance" in our world: a thing worth stating in these days. The essential element of this Conquaestor is, first of all, the most sun-eyed perception of what *is* really what on this God's-Earth;—which, thou wilt find, does mean at bottom "Justice," and "Virtues" not a few: *Conformity* to what the Maker has seen good to make; that, I suppose, will mean Justice and a Virtue or two?—

Dost thou think Willelmus Conquaestor would have tolerated ten years' jargon, one hour's jargon, on the propriety of killing Cotton-manufactures by partridge Corn-Laws?[1] I fancy, this was not the man to knock out of his night's-rest with nothing but a noisy bedlamism in your mouth! "Assist us still better to bush the partridges; strangle Plugson who spins the shirts?"[2]—"*Par la Splendeur de Dieu!*"[3]—Dost thou think Willelmus Conquaestor, in this new time, with Steam-engine Captains of Industry on one hand of him, and Joe-Manton Captains of Idleness[4] on the other, would have doubted which *was* really the BEST; which did deserve strangling, and which not?

I have a certain indestructible regard for Willelmus Conquaestor. A resident House-Surgeon, provided by Nature for her beloved English People, and even furnished with the requisite fees, as I said; for he by no means felt himself doing Nature's work, this Willelmus, but his own work exclusively! And his own work withal it was; informed "*par la Splendeur de Dieu.*"—I say, it is necessary to get the work out of such a man, however harsh that be! When

---

1. See the title note.
2. This speech sums up the pleas of the High Tariff lobby in Parliament. "Keep the Corn Laws intact so that the aristocratic landlords may continue to enjoy shooting partridges on their estates; subdue the manufacturing leaders by preventing trade." ("Plugson of Undershot" was Carlyle's term to describe the new class of industrial leaders.)
3. "By the splendor of God!"—one of William's oaths.
4. The idle aristocracy who wasted time shooting partridges with guns made by Joseph Manton, a London gunsmith.

a world, not yet doomed for death, is rushing down to ever-deeper Baseness and Confusion, it is a dire necessity of Nature's to bring in her ARISTOCRACIES, her BEST, even by forcible methods. When their descendants or representatives cease entirely to *be* the Best, Nature's poor world will very soon rush down again to Baseness; and it becomes a dire necessity of Nature's to cast them out. Hence French Revolutions, Five-point Charters, Democracies, and a mournful list of *Etceteras*, in these our afflicted times. * * *

Democracy, the chase of Liberty in that direction, shall go its full course; unrestrained by him of Pferdefuss-Quacksalber, or any of *his* household. The Toiling Millions of Mankind, in most vital need and passionate instinctive desire of Guidance, shall cast away False-Guidance; and hope, for an hour, that No-Guidance will suffice them: but it can be for an hour only. The smallest item of human Slavery is the oppression of man by his Mock-Superiors; the palpablest, but I say at bottom the smallest. Let him shake off such oppression, trample it indignantly under his feet; I blame him not, I pity and commend him. But oppression by your Mock-Superiors well shaken off, the grand problem yet remains to solve: That of finding government by your Real-Superiors! Alas, how shall we ever learn the solution of that, benighted, bewildered, sniffing, sneering, godforgetting unfortunates as we are? It is a work for centuries; to be taught us by tribulations, confusions, insurrections, obstructions; who knows if not by conflagration and despair! It is a lesson inclusive of all other lessons; the hardest of all lessons to learn. * * *

Captains of Industry[1]

If I believed that Mammonism with its adjuncts was to continue henceforth the one serious principle of our existence, I should reckon it idle to solicit remedial measures from any Government, the disease being insusceptible of remedy. Government can do much, but it can in no wise do all. Government, as the most conspicuous object in Society, is called upon to give signal of what shall be done; and, in many ways, to preside over, further, and command the doing of it. But the Government cannot do, by all its signalling and commanding, what the Society is radically indisposed to do. In the long-run every Government is the exact symbol of its People, with their wisdom and unwisdom; we have to say, Like People like Government.—The main substance of this immense Problem of Organizing Labour, and first of all of Managing the Working Classes, will, it is very clear, have to be solved by those who stand practically in the middle of it; by those who themselves work and preside over work. Of all that can be enacted

1. From Book IV, Chapter 4.

by any Parliament in regard to it, the germs must already lie potentially extant in those two Classes, who are to obey such enactment. A Human Chaos *in* which there is no light, you vainly attempt to irradiate by light shed *on* it: order never can arise there.

But it is my firm conviction that the "Hell of England" will *cease* to be that of "not making money"; that we shall get a nobler Hell and a nobler Heaven! I anticipate light *in* the Human Chaos, glimmering, shining more and more; under manifold true signals from without That light shall shine. Our deity no longer being Mammon,—O Heavens, each man will then say to himself: "Why such deadly haste to make money? I shall not go to Hell, even if I do not make money! There is another Hell, I am told!" Competition, at railway-speed, in all branches of commerce and work will then abate:—good felt-hats for the head, in every sense, instead of seven-feet lath-and-plaster hats on wheels,[2] will then be discoverable! Bubble-periods,[3] with their panics and commercial crises, will again become infrequent; steady modest industry will take the place of gambling speculation. To be a noble Master, among noble Workers, will again be the first ambition with some few; to be a rich Master only the second. How the Inventive Genius of England, with the whirr of its bobbins and billy-rollers[4] shoved somewhat into the backgrounds of the brain, will contrive and devise, not cheaper produce exclusively, but fairer distribution of the produce at its present cheapness! By degrees, we shall again have a Society with something of Heroism in it, something of Heaven's Blessing on it; we shall again have, as my German friend[5] asserts, "instead of Mammon-Feudalism with unsold cotton-shirts and Preservation of the Game, noble just Industrialism and Government by the Wisest!"

It is with the hope of awakening here and there a British man to know himself for a man and divine soul, that a few words of parting admonition, to all persons to whom the Heavenly Powers have lent power of any kind in this land, may now be addressed. And first to those same Master-Workers, Leaders of Industry; who stand nearest, and in fact powerfullest, though not most prominent, being as yet in too many senses a Virtuality rather than an Actuality.

The Leaders of Industry, if Industry is ever to be led, are virtually the Captains of the World; if there be no nobleness in them, there will never be an Aristocracy more. But let the Captains of Industry

2. A London hatter's mode of advertising. Carlyle considered most advertisements to be wasteful.
3. Periods of violent fluctuation in the stock market caused by unsound speculating.
4. Machines used to prepare cotton or wool for spinning.
5. Teufelsdröckh, the hero of *Sartor Resartus*.

consider: once again, are they born of other clay than the old Captains of Slaughter; doomed for ever to be not Chivalry, but a mere gold-plated *Doggery*,—what the French well name *Canaille*, "Doggery" with more or less gold carrion at its disposal? Captains of Industry are the true Fighters, henceforth recognizable as the only true ones: Fighters against Chaos, Necessity and the Devils and Jötuns;[6] and lead on Mankind in that great, and alone true, and universal warfare; the stars in their courses fighting for them, and all Heaven and all Earth saying audibly, Well done! Let the Captains of Industry retire into their own hearts, and ask solemnly, If there is nothing but vulturous hunger for fine wines, valet reputation and gilt carriages, discoverable there? Of hearts made by the Almighty God I will not believe such a thing. Deep-hidden under wretchedest god-forgetting Cants, Epicurisms, Dead-Sea Apisms;[7] forgotten as under foullest fat Lethe mud and weeds, there is yet, in all hearts born into this God's-World, a spark of the Godlike slumbering. Awake, O nightmare sleepers; awake, arise, or be for ever fallen! This is not playhouse poetry; it is sober fact. Our England, our world cannot live as it is. It will connect itself with a God again, or go down with nameless throes and fire-consummation to the Devils. Thou who feelest aught of such a Godlike stirring in thee, any faintest intimation of it as through heavy-laden dreams, follow *it*, I conjure thee. Arise, save thyself, be one of those that save thy country.

Bucaniers,[8] Chactaw Indians, whose supreme aim in fighting is that they may get the scalps, the money, that they may amass scalps and money; out of such came no Chivalry, and never will! Out of such came only gore and wreck, infernal rage and misery; desperation quenched in annihilation. Behold it, I bid thee, behold there, and consider! What is it that thou have a hundred thousand-pound bills laid up in thy strong-room, a hundred scalps hung up in thy wigwam? I value not them or thee. Thy scalps and thy thousand-pound bills are as yet nothing, if no nobleness from within irradiate them; if no Chivalry, in action, or in embryo ever struggling towards birth and action, be there.

Love of men cannot be bought by cash-payment; and without love, men cannot endure to be together. You cannot lead a Fighting World without having it regimented, chivalried: the thing, in a day, becomes impossible; all men in it, the highest at first, the very lowest at last, discern consciously, or by a noble instinct, this necessity. And can you any more continue to lead a Working World

6. Giants of Scandinavian mythology.
7. A tribe of men living near the Dead Sea were transformed into apes because they had ignored the prophecies of Moses. This story, of Mohammedan origin, is used by Carlyle to represent the possible fate of nations which are indifferent to their social problems.
8. Buccaneers.

unregimented, anarchic? I answer, and the Heavens and Earth are now answering, No! The thing becomes not "in a day" impossible; but in some two generations it does. Yes, when fathers and mothers, in Stockport hunger-cellars, begin to eat their children, and Irish widows have to prove their relationship by dying of typhus-fever; and amid Governing "Corporations of the Best and Bravest," busy to preserve their game by "bushing," dark millions of God's human creatures start up in mad Chartisms, impracticable Sacred-Months, and Manchester Insurrections;[9]—and there is a virtual Industrial Aristocracy as yet only half-alive, spell-bound amid money-bags and ledgers; and an actual Idle Aristocracy seemingly near dead in somnolent delusions, in trespasses and double-barrels;[1] "sliding," as on inclined-planes, which every new year they *soap* with new Hansard's-jargon[2] under God's sky, and so are "sliding" ever faster, towards a "scale" and balance-scale whereon is written *Thou art found Wanting:*—in such days, after a generation or two, I say, it does become, even to the low and simple, very palpably impossible! No Working World, any more than a Fighting World, can be led on without a noble Chivalry of Work, and laws and fixed rules which follow out of that,—far nobler than any Chivalry of Fighting was. As an anarchic multitude on mere Supply-and-demand, it is becoming inevitable that we dwindle in horrid suicidal convulsion, and self-abrasion, frightful to the imagination, into *Chactaw* Workers. With wigwams and scalps,—with palaces and thousand-pound bills; with savagery, depopulation, chaotic desolation! Good Heavens, will not one French Revolution and Reign of Terror suffice us, but must there be two? There will be two if needed; there will be twenty if needed; there will be precisely as many as are needed. The Laws of Nature will have themselves fulfilled. That is a thing certain to me.

Your gallant battle-hosts and work-hosts, as the others did, will need to be made loyally yours; they must and will be regulated, methodically secured in their just share of conquest under you;—joined with you in veritable brotherhood, sonhood, by quite other and deeper ties than those of temporary day's wages! How would mere redcoated regiments, to say nothing of chivalries, fight for you, if you could discharge them on the evening of the battle, on payment of the stipulated shillings,—and they discharge you on the morning of it! Chelsea Hospitals,[3] pensions, promotions, rigorous lasting covenant on the one side and on the other, are indis-

9. In 1819 a large open-air labor meeting in Manchester was broken up by charging cavalry. Thirteen men and women were massacred, and many others were wounded.
1. Carlyle is suggesting that the only concern of the landed aristocrats is to keep trespassers off their game preserves and reserve shooting rights to themselves.
2. Parliamentary oratory, as in Hansard's printed record of debates in the House of Commons.
3. Home for disabled veterans.

pensable even for a hired fighter. The Feudal Baron, much more,
—how could he subsist with mere temporary mercenaries round
him, at sixpence a day; ready to go over to the other side, if seven-
pence were offered? He could not have subsisted;—and his noble
instinct saved him from the necessity of even trying! The Feudal
Baron had a Man's Soul in him; to which anarchy, mutiny, and
the other fruits of temporary mercenaries, were intolerable: he had
never been a Baron otherwise, but had continued a Chactaw and
Bucanier. He felt it precious, and at last it became habitual, and
his fruitful enlarged existence included it as a necessity, to have
men round him who in heart loved him; whose life he watched
over with rigour yet with love; who were prepared to give their life
for him, if need came. It was beautiful; it was human! Man lives
not otherwise, nor can live contented, anywhere or anywhen. Isolation is the sum-total of wretchedness to man. To be cut off, to be
left solitary: to have a world alien, not your world; all a hostile
camp for you; not a home at all, of hearts and faces who are yours,
whose you are! It is the frightfullest enchantment; too truly a work
of the Evil One. To have neither superior, nor inferior, nor equal,
united manlike to you. Without father, without child, without
brother. Man knows no sadder destiny. "How is each of us," exclaims Jean Paul,[4] "so lonely in the wide bosom of the All!" En-
cased each as in his transparent "ice-palace"; our brother visible
in his, making signals and gesticulations to us;—visible, but for
ever unattainable: on his bosom we shall never rest, nor he on ours.
It was not a God that did this; no!

Awake, ye noble Workers, warriors in the one true war: all this
must be remedied. It is you who are already half-alive, whom I will
welcome into life; whom I will conjure in God's name to shake off
your enchanted sleep, and live wholly! Cease to count scalps, gold-
purses; not in these lies your or our salvation. Even these, if you
count only these, will not be left. Let bucaniering be put far from
you; alter, speedily abrogate all laws of the bucaniers, if you would
gain any victory that shall endure. Let God's justice, let pity, nobleness and manly valour, with more gold-purses or with fewer, testify
themselves in this your brief Life-transit to all the Eternities, the
Gods and Silences. It is to you I call; for ye are not dead, ye
are already half-alive: there is in you a sleepless dauntless energy, the prime-matter of all nobleness in man. Honour to you
in your kind. It is to you I call: ye know at least this, That the
mandate of God to His creature man is: Work! The future Epic
of the World rests not with those that are near dead, but with those
that are alive, and those that are coming into life.

Look around you. Your world-hosts are all in mutiny, in con-

4. Jean Paul Richter (1763–1825), German humorist.

fusion, destitution; on the eve of fiery wreck and madness! They will not march farther for you, on the sixpence a day and supply-and-demand principle: they will not; nor ought they, nor can they. Ye shall reduce them to order, begin reducing them. To order, to just subordination; noble loyalty in return for noble guidance. Their souls are driven nigh mad; let yours be sane and ever saner. Not as a bewildered bewildering mob; but as a firm regimented mass, with real captains over them, will these men march any more. All human interests, combined human endeavours, and social growths in this world, have, at a certain stage of their development, required organizing: and Work, the grandest of human interests, does now require it.

God knows, the task will be hard: but no noble task was ever easy. This task will wear away your lives, and the lives of your sons and grandsons: but for what purpose, if not for tasks like this, were lives given to men? Ye shall cease to count your thousand-pound scalps, the noble of you shall cease! Nay, the very scalps, as I say, will not long be left if you count on these. Ye shall cease wholly to be barbarous vulturous Chactaws, and become noble European Nineteenth-Century Men. Ye shall know that Mammon, in never such gigs[5] and flunkey "respectabilities," is not the alone God; that of himself he is but a Devil, and even a Brute-god.

Difficult? Yes, it will be difficult. The short-fibre cotton; that too was difficult. The waste cotton-shrub, long useless, disobedient, as the thistle by the wayside,—have ye not conquered it; made it into beautiful bandana webs; white woven shirts for men; bright-tinted air-garments wherein flit goddesses? Ye have shivered mountains asunder, made the hard iron pliant to you as soft putty: the Forest-giants, Marsh-jötuns bear sheaves of golden grain; Aegir the Sea-demon[6] himself stretches his back for a sleek highway to you, and on Firehorses and Windhorses ye career. Ye are most strong. Thor red-bearded, with his blue sun-eyes, with his cheery heart and strong thunder-hammer, he and you have prevailed. Ye are most strong, ye Sons of the icy North, of the far East,—far marching from your rugged Eastern Wildernesses, hitherward from the grey Dawn of Time! Ye are Sons of the *Jötun*-land; the land of Difficulties Conquered. Difficult? You must try this thing. Once try it with the understanding that it will and shall have to be done. Try it as ye try the paltrier thing, making of money! I will bet on you once more, against all Jötuns, Tailor-gods,[7] Double-barrelled Law-wards, and Denizens of Chaos whatsoever!

1843   1843

5. To own a gig (a light carriage) was a sign of respectable status comparable to owning certain kinds of automobiles today. Carlyle ridiculed the passion for respectability as "gigmanity."
6. From Scandinavian mythology.
7. False gods.

JOHN HENRY CARDINAL NEWMAN
(1801–1890)

Like Carlyle, John Henry Newman powerfully affected the thinking of his contemporaries, whether they agreed with him or disagreed. Even today, according to Martin Svaglic, Newman attracts both "apotheosizers" and "calumniators" who praise or blame him "as an unusually compelling spokesman for what some consider eternal verities and others regressive myths." During his long lifetime, Newman frequently found himself at the center of some of the most intense disputes that stirred Victorian England, disputes in which he himself emerged as a controversialist of great skill—engagingly persuasive in defense of his position and devastatingly effective in disposing of opponents. Thomas Hardy, whose position was at the opposite extreme from Newman's, paid him a high compliment when he noted in his diary: "Worked at J. H. Newman's *Apologia* which we have all been talking about lately. * * * Style charming and his logic really human, being based not on syllogisms but on converging probabilities. Only—and here comes the fatal catastrophe—there is no first link to his excellent chain of reasoning, and down you come headlong."

Newman was born in London, the son (like Browning) of a banker. In his spiritual autobiography, *Apologia Pro Vita Sua* (in effect, his vindication of his life), he traces the principal stages of his religious development from the strongly Protestant period of his youth to his conversion to Roman Catholicism in 1845. Along the way, after being elected to a fellowship at Oriel College in Oxford and becoming an Anglican clergyman, he was attracted briefly into the orbit of religious liberalism. Gradually coming to realize, however, that liberalism, with its reliance upon human reason, would be powerless to defend traditional religion from attack, Newman shifted over into the new High Church wing of the Anglican Church and soon was recognized as the leading figure of the Oxford Movement. During the 1830's he attracted a large and influential following by his sermons at Oxford and his writing of tracts. His efforts to demonstrate the dogmatic and authoritative tradition of Anglicanism finally provoked so much opposition that he was reduced to silence. After much reflection he took the final step. At the age of 44 he entered the Roman Catholic priesthood and moved to Birmingham where he spent the rest of his life. In 1879 he was created Cardinal.

Despite his mastery of prose style, Newman found the act of composition to be even more painfully difficult than most of us do. During his years at Birmingham he was nevertheless prompted to write several books including works of religious poetry and fiction. Most celebrated is the series of articles, published as his *Apologia* in 1864, in which he replied to an attack upon his intellectual honesty made by Charles Kingsley. Although parts of the *Apologia*, being devoted to fine points of theological doctrine and church history, are difficult for the ordinary reader to follow, the main argument is clearly and persuasively developed. The dignity and candor with which Newman reviewed the stages of his religious development, the repeated appeals to his fellow countrymen's sense of honesty and fair play, the unobtrusively beautiful prose style, gained for his masterpiece a sympathetic audience even among those who had been least disposed to listen to his side of the dispute with Kingsley.

Seemingly less controversial than the *Apologia* are Newman's lectures on the aims of education which were delivered in Dublin at the newly-founded Catholic University of Ireland, a university of which he was for a few years the rector. These lectures, published in 1852 and later entitled *The Idea of a University*, are a classic statement of the value of "the disciplined intellect" which can be developed by a liberal education rather than by a technical training. The lectures may be compared with the later lectures of Matthew Arnold and T. H. Huxley.

It should be noted that Newman's view of a liberal education is largely independent of his religious position. Such an education, he said, could form the minds of profligates and anticlericals as well as of saints and priests of the church. In considerable measure his view reflects his admiration for the kind of intellectual enlargement he had himself enjoyed as an undergraduate at Trinity College, Oxford. One of the most touching passages in the *Apologia* is Newman's account of his farewell to an Oxford friend, in February, 1846, as he was preparing his final departure from the precincts of the university he loved:

> In him I took leave of my first College, Trinity, which was so dear to me. * * * There used to be much snapdragon growing on the walls opposite my freshman's rooms there, and I had taken it as the emblem of my perpetual residence even unto death in my University.
> On the morning of the 23rd I left the Observatory. I have never seen Oxford since, excepting its spires, as they are seen from the railway.

From The Idea of a University
From *Discourse* V. *Knowledge Its Own End*

6

Now bear with me, Gentlemen, if what I am about to say has at first sight a fanciful appearance. Philosophy, then, or Science, is related to Knowledge in this way: Knowledge is called by the name of Science or Philosophy, when it is acted upon, informed, or if I may use a strong figure, impregnated by Reason. Reason is the principle of that intrinsic fecundity of Knowledge, which, to those who possess it, is its especial value, and which dispenses with the necessity of their looking abroad for any end to rest upon external to itself. Knowledge, indeed, when thus exalted into a scientific form, is also power; not only is it excellent in itself, but whatever such excellence may be, it is something more, it has a result beyond itself. Doubtless; but that is a further consideration, with which I am not concerned. I only say that, prior to its being a power, it is a good; that it is, not only an instrument, but an end. I know well it may resolve itself into an art, and terminate in a mechanical process, and in tangible fruit; but it also may fall back upon that Reason which informs it, and resolve itself into Philosophy. In one case it is called Useful Knowledge, in the other Liberal. The same person may cultivate it in both ways at once; but this again is a matter foreign to my subject; here I do but say that there are two ways of using Knowledge, and in matter of fact those who use it in one way are not likely to use it in the other, or at least in a very limited measure. You see, then, here are two methods of Education; the end of the one is to be philosophical, of the other to be mechanical; the one rises towards general ideas, the other is exhausted upon what is particular and external. Let me not be thought to deny the necessity, or to decry the benefit, of such attention to what is particular and practical, as belongs to the useful or mechanical arts; life could not go on without them; we owe our daily welfare to them; their exercise is the duty of the many, and we owe to the many a debt of gratitude for fulfilling that duty. I only say that Knowledge, in proportion as it tends more and more to be particular, ceases to be Knowledge. It is a question whether Knowledge can in any proper sense be predicated of the brute creation; without pretending to metaphysical exactness of phraseology, which would be unsuitable to an occasion like this, I say, it seems to me improper to call that passive sensation, or perception of things, which brutes seem to possess, by the name of Knowledge. When I speak of Knowledge, I mean something intellectual, something which grasps what it perceives through the senses; something which takes a view of things; which sees more than the senses convey; which reasons upon what it sees, and while it sees; which invests it with an idea. It expresses itself, not in a mere enunciation, but by an enthymeme:[1] it is of the nature of science from the first, and in this consists its dignity. The principle of real dignity in Knowledge, its worth, its desirableness, considered irrespectively of its results, is this germ within it of a scientific or a philosophical process. This is how it comes to be an end in itself; this is why it admits of being called Liberal. Not to know the relative disposition of things is the state of slaves or children; to have mapped out the Universe is the boast, or at least the ambition, of Philosophy.

Moreover, such knowledge is not a mere extrinsic or accidental advantage, which is ours today and another's tomorrow, which may be got up from a book, and easily forgotten again, which we can command or communicate at our pleasure, which we can borrow for the occasion, carry about in our hand, and take into the market; it is an acquired illumination, it is a habit, a personal possession, and an inward endowment. And this is the reason why it is more correct, as well as more usual, to speak of a University as a place of education than of instruction, though, when knowledge is concerned, instruction would at first sight have seemed the more appropriate word. We are instructed, for instance, in manual exercises,

1. A syllogism in which one of the premises is understood but not stated.

in the fine and useful arts, in trades, and in ways of business; for these are methods, which have little or no effect upon the mind itself, are contained in rules committed to memory, to tradition, or to use, and bear upon an end external to themselves. But education is a higher word; it implies an action upon our mental nature, and the formation of a character; it is something individual and permanent, and is commonly spoken of in connection with religion and virtue. When, then, we speak of the communication of Knowledge as being Education, we thereby really imply that that Knowledge is a state or condition of mind; and since cultivation of mind is surely worth seeking for its own sake, we are thus brought once more to the conclusion, which the word "Liberal" and the word "Philosophy" have already suggested, that there is a Knowledge, which is desirable, though nothing come of it, as being of itself a treasure, and a sufficient remuneration of years of labor. * * *

From *Discourse VII. Knowledge Viewed in Relation to Professional Skill*

1

I have been insisting, in my two preceding Discourses, first, on the cultivation of the intellect, as an end which may reasonably be pursued for its own sake; and next, on the nature of that cultivation, or what that cultivation consists in. Truth of whatever kind is the proper object of the intellect; its cultivation then lies in fitting it to apprehend and contemplate truth. Now the intellect in its present state, with exceptions which need not here be specified, does not discern truth intuitively, or as a whole. We know, not by a direct and simple vision, not at a glance, but, as it were, by piecemeal and accumulation, by a mental process, by going round an object, by the comparison, the combination, the mutual correction, the continual adaptation, of many partial notions, by the employment, concentration, and joint action of many faculties and exercises of mind. Such a union and concert of the intellectual powers, such an enlargement and development, such a comprehensiveness, is necessarily a matter of training. And again, such a training is a matter of rule; it is not mere application, however exemplary, which introduces the mind to truth, nor the reading many books, nor the getting up many subjects, nor the witnessing many experiments, nor the attending many lectures. All this is short of enough; a man may have done it all, yet be lingering in the vestibule of knowledge: he may not realize what his mouth utters; he may not see with his mental eye what confronts him; he may have no grasp of things as they are; or at least he may have no power at all of advancing one step forward of himself, in consequence of what he has already acquired, no power of discriminating between truth and falsehood, of sifting out the grains of truth from the mass, of arranging things according to their real value, and, if I may use the phrase, of building up ideas. Such a power is the result of a scientific formation of mind; it is an acquired faculty of judgment, of clearsightedness, of sagacity, of wisdom, of philosophical reach of mind, and of intellectual self-possession and repose—qualities which do not come of mere acquirement. The bodily eye, the organ for apprehending material objects, is provided by nature; the eye of the mind, of which the object is truth, is the work of discipline and habit.

This process of training, by which the intellect, instead of being formed or sacrificed to some particular or accidental purpose, some specific trade or profession, or study or science, is disciplined for its own sake, for the perception of its own proper object, and for its own highest culture, is called Liberal Education; and though there is no one in whom it is carried as far as is conceivable, or whose intellect would be a pattern of what intellects should be made, yet there is scarcely anyone but may gain an idea of what real training is, and at least look towards it, and make its true scope and result, not something else, his standard of excellence; and numbers there are who may submit themselves to it, and secure it to themselves in good measure. And to set forth the right standard, and to train according to it, and to help forward all students toward it according to their various capacities, this I conceive to be the business of a University.

2

Now this is what some great men are very slow to allow; they insist that Education should be confined to some particular and narrow end, and should issue in some definite work, which can be weighed and measured. They argue as if every thing, as well as every person, had its price; and that where there has been a great outlay, they have a right to expect a return in kind. This they call making Education and Instruction "useful," and "Utility" becomes their watchword. With a fundamental principle of this nature, they very naturally go on to ask what there is to show for the expense of a University; what is the real worth in the market of the article called "a Liberal Education," on the supposition that it does not teach us definitely how to advance our manufactures, or to improve our lands, or to better our civil economy; or again, if it does not at once make this man a lawyer, that an engineer, and that a surgeon; or at least if it does not lead to discoveries in chemistry, astronomy, geology, magnetism, and science of every kind. * * *

5

* * * This is the obvious answer which may be made to those who urge upon us the claims of Utility in our plans of Education;[2]

2. The Utilitarians argued that a useful education would be one which trained the mind in the "habit of pushing things up to their first principles." Newman had earlier pointed out that a liberal education does exactly that and is hence useful.

but I am not going to leave the subject here: I mean to take a wider view of it. Let us take "useful," as Locke[3] takes it, in its proper and popular sense, and then we enter upon a large field of thought, to which I cannot do justice in one Discourse, though today's is all the space that I can give to it. I say, let us take "useful" to mean, not what is simply good, but what *tends* to good, or is the *instrument* of good; and in this sense also, Gentlemen, I will show you how a liberal education is truly and fully a useful, though it be not a professional, education. "Good" indeed means one thing, and "useful" means another; but I lay it down as a principle, which will save us a great deal of anxiety, that, though the useful is not always good, the good is always useful. Good is not only good, but reproductive of good; this is one of its attributes; nothing is excellent, beautiful, perfect, desirable for its own sake, but it overflows, and spreads the likeness of itself all around it. Good is prolific; it is not only good to the eye, but to the taste; it not only attracts us, but it communicates itself; it excites first our admiration and love, then our desire and our gratitude, and that, in proportion to its intenseness and fullness in particular instances. A great good will impart great good. If then the intellect is so excellent a portion of us, and its cultivation so excellent, it is not only beautiful, perfect, admirable, and noble in itself, but in a true and high sense it must be useful to the possessor and to all around him; not useful in any low, mechanical, mercantile sense, but as diffusing good, or as a blessing, or a gift, or power, or a treasure, first to the owner, then through him to the world. I say then, if a liberal education be good, it must necessarily be useful too.

6

You will see what I mean by the parallel of bodily health. Health is a good in itself, though nothing came of it, and is especially worth seeking and cherishing; yet, after all, the blessings which attend its presence are so great, while they are so close to it and so redound back upon it and encircle it, that we never think of it except as useful as well as good, and praise and prize it for what it does, as well as for what it is, though at the same time we cannot point out any definite and distinct work or production which it can be said to effect. And so as regards intellectual culture, I am far from denying utility in this large sense as the end of Education, when I lay it down that the culture of the intellect is a good in itself and its own end; I do not exclude from the idea of intellectual culture what it cannot but be, from the very nature of things; I only deny that we must be able to point out, before we have any right to call it useful, some art, or business, or profession, or trade, or work, as resulting from it, and as its real and complete end. The parallel is

---

3. John Locke (1632–1704), whose treatise *Of Education* advocated a utilitarian concept of education.

exact: As the body may be sacrificed to some manual or other toil, whether moderate or oppressive, so may the intellect be devoted to some specific profession; and I do not call *this* the culture of the intellect. Again, as some member or organ of the body may be inordinately used and developed, so may memory, or imagination, or the reasoning faculty; and *this* again is not intellectual culture. On the other hand, as the body may be tended, cherished, and exercised with a simple view to its general health, so may the intellect also be generally exercised in order to its perfect state; and this *is* its cultivation.

Again, as health ought to precede labor of the body, and as a man in health can do what an unhealthy man cannot do, and as of this health the properties are strength, energy, agility, graceful carriage and action, manual dexterity, and endurance of fatigue, so in like manner general culture of mind is the best aid to professional and scientific study, and educated men can do what illiterate cannot; and the man who has learned to think and to reason and to compare and to discriminate and to analyze, who has refined his taste, and formed his judgment, and sharpened his mental vision, will not indeed at once be a lawyer, or a pleader, or an orator, or a statesman, or a physician, or a good landlord, or a man of business, or a soldier, or an engineer, or a chemist, or a geologist, or an antiquarian, but he will be placed in that state of intellect in which he can take up any one of the sciences or callings I have referred to, or any other for which he has a taste or special talent, with an ease, a grace, a versatility, and a success, to which another is a stranger. In this sense then, and as yet I have said but a very few words on a large subject, mental culture is emphatically *useful*.

If then I am arguing, and shall argue, against Professional or Scientific knowledge as the sufficient end of a University Education, let me not be supposed, Gentlemen, to be disrespectful towards particular studies, or arts, or vocations, and those who are engaged in them. In saying that Law or Medicine is not the end of a University course, I do not mean to imply that the University does not teach Law or Medicine. What indeed can it teach at all, if it does not teach something particular? It teaches *all* knowledge by teaching all *branches* of knowledge, and in no other way. I do but say that there will be this distinction as regards a Professor of Law, or of Medicine, or of Geology, or of Political Economy, in a University and out of it, that out of a University he is in danger of being absorbed and narrowed by his pursuit, and of giving Lectures which are the Lectures of nothing more than a lawyer, physician, geologist, or political economist; whereas in a University he will just know where he and his science stand, he has come to it, as it were, from a height, he has taken a survey of all knowledge, he is kept from extravagance by the very rivalry of other studies, he has gained from them a special illumination and largeness of mind and freedom and self-possession, and he treats his own in consequence with a philosophy and a resource, which belongs not to the study itself, but to his liberal education.

This then is how I should solve the fallacy, for so I must call it, by which Locke and his disciples would frighten us from cultivating the intellect, under the notion that no education is useful which does not teach us some temporal calling, or some mechanical art, or some physical secret. I say that a cultivated intellect, because it is a good in itself, brings with it a power and a grace to every work and occupation which it undertakes, and enables us to be more useful, and to a greater number. There is a duty we owe to human society as such, to the state to which we belong, to the sphere in which we move, to the individuals towards whom we are variously related, and whom we successively encounter in life; and that philosophical or liberal education, as I have called it, which is the proper function of a University, if it refuses the foremost place to professional interests, does but postpone them to the formation of the citizen, and, while it subserves the larger interests of philanthropy, prepares also for the successful prosecution of those merely personal objects which at first sight it seems to disparage. * * *

10

But I must bring these extracts[4] to an end. Today I have confined myself to saying that that training of the intellect, which is best for the individual himself, best enables him to discharge his duties to society. The Philosopher, indeed, and the man of the world differ in their very notion, but the methods, by which they are respectively formed, are pretty much the same. The Philosopher has the same command of matters of thought, which the true citizen and gentleman has of matters of business and conduct. If then a practical end must be assigned to a University course, I say it is that of training good members of society. Its art is the art of social life, and its end is fitness for the world. It neither confines its views to particular professions on the one hand, nor creates heroes or inspires genius on the other. Works indeed of genius fall under no art; heroic minds come under no rule; a University is not a birthplace of poets or of immortal authors, of founders of schools, leaders of colonies, or conquerors of nations. It does not promise a generation of Aristotles or Newtons, of Napoleons or Washingtons, or Raphaels or Shakespeares, though such miracles of nature it has before now contained within its precincts. Nor is it content on the other hand with forming the critic or the experimentalist, the economist or the engineer, though such too it includes within its scope. But a University training is the great ordinary means to a great but ordinary

4. Quotations cited from other authorities on education.

end; it aims at raising the intellectual tone of society, at cultivating the public mind, at purifying the national taste, at supplying true principles to popular enthusiasm and fixed aims to popular aspiration, at giving enlargement and sobriety to the ideas of the age, at facilitating the exercise of political power, and refining the intercourse of private life. It is the education which gives a man a clear conscious view of his own opinions and judgments, a truth in developing them, an eloquence in expressing them, and a force in urging them. It teaches him to see things as they are, to go right to the point, to disentangle a skein of thought, to detect what is sophistical, and to discard what is irrelevant. It prepares him to fill any post with credit, and to master any subject with facility. It shows him how to accommodate himself to others, how to throw himself into their state of mind, how to bring before them his own, how to influence them, how to come to an understanding with them, how to bear with them. He is at home in any society, he has common ground with every class; he knows when to speak and when to be silent; he is able to converse, he is able to listen; he can ask a question pertinently, and gain a lesson seasonably, when he has nothing to impart himself; he is ever ready, yet never in the way; he is a pleasant companion, and a comrade you can depend upon; he knows when to be serious and when to trifle, and he has a sure tact which enables him to trifle with gracefulness and to be serious with effect. He has the repose of a mind which lives in itself, while it lives in the world, and which has resources for its happiness at home when it cannot go abroad. He has a gift which serves him in public, and supports him in retirement,[5] without which good fortune is but vulgar, and with which failure and disappointment have a charm. The art which tends to make a man all this is in the object which it pursues as useful as the art of wealth or the art of health, though it is less susceptible of method, and less tangible, less certain, less complete in its result.

1852, 1873

---

5. In one of his later works, *The Grammar of Assent* (1870), Newman enlarges upon this aspect of his subject in a passage describing the impact that classical literature may have on us at different ages of our lives, a passage admired by James Joyce. "Let us consider, too, how differently young and old are affected by the words of some classic author, such as Homer or Horace. Passages, which to a boy are but rhetorical commonplaces, neither better nor worse than a hundred others which any clever writer might supply, which he gets by heart and thinks very fine, and imitates, as he thinks, successfully, in his own flowing versification, at length come home to him, when long years have passed, and he has had experience of life, and pierce him, as if he had never before known them, with their sad earnestness and vivid exactness. Then he comes to understand how it is that lines, the birth of some chance morning or evening at an Ionian festival, or among the Sabine hills, have lasted generation after generation, for thousands of years, with a power over the mind, and a charm, which the current literature of his own day, with all its obvious advantages, is utterly unable to rival. Perhaps this is the reason of the medieval opinion about Virgil, as if a prophet or magician; his single words and phrases, his pathetic half lines, giving utterance, as the voice of Nature herself, to that pain and weariness, yet hope of better things, which is the experience of her children in every time."

From Apologia Pro Vita Sua

From *Chapter III. History of My Religious Opinions from 1839 to 1841*

And now that I am about to trace, as far as I can, the course of that great revolution of mind, which led me to leave my own home, to which I was bound by so many strong and tender ties, I feel overcome with the difficulty of satisfying myself in my account of it, and have recoiled from the attempt, till the near approach of the day, on which these lines must be given to the world, forces me to set about the task. For who can know himself, and the multitude of subtle influences which act upon him? And who can recollect, at the distance of twenty-five years, all that he once knew about his thoughts and his deeds, and that, during a portion of his life, when, even at the time, his observation, whether of himself or of the external world, was less than before or after, by very reason of the perplexity and dismay which weighed upon him, when, in spite of the light given to him according to his need amid his darkness, yet a darkness it emphatically was? And who can suddenly gird himself to a new and anxious undertaking, which he might be able indeed to perform well, were full and calm leisure allowed him to look through every thing that he had written, whether in published works or private letters? yet again, granting that calm contemplation of the past, in itself so desirable, who could afford to be leisurely and deliberate, while he practices on himself a cruel operation, the ripping up of old griefs, and the venturing again upon the *infandum dolorem* [1] of years, in which the stars of this lower heaven were one by one going out? I could not in cool blood, nor except upon the imperious call of duty, attempt what I have set myself to do. It is both to head and heart an extreme trial, thus to analyze what has so long gone by, and to bring out the results of that examination. I have done various bold things in my life; this is the boldest, and, were I not sure I should after all succeed in my object, it would be madness to set about it.

In the spring of 1839 my position in the Anglican Church was at its height. I had supreme confidence in my controversial *status*, and I had a great and still growing success, in recommending it to others. I had in the foregoing autumn been somewhat sore at the Bishop's Charge,[2] but I have a letter which shows that all annoyance had passed from my mind. In January, if I recollect aright, in order to meet the popular clamor against myself and others, and to satisfy the Bishop, I had collected into one all the strong things

---

1. "Grief beyond words" (*Aeneid* II.3).
2. In 1838 Newman had been hurt when his Bishop, Richard Bagot of Oxford (whom he admired), criticized some of the Tracts published by the Anglo-Catholic group.

which they, and especially I, had said against the Church of Rome, in order to their insertion among the advertisements appended to our publications.[3] Conscious as I was that my opinions in religion were not gained, as the world said, from Roman sources, but were, on the contrary, the birth of my own mind and of the circumstances in which I had been placed, I had a scorn of the imputations which were heaped upon me. It was true that I held a large bold system of religion, very unlike the Protestantism of the day, but it was the concentration and adjustment of the statements of great Anglican authorities, and I had as much right to hold it, as the Evangelical, and more right than the Liberal party could show, for asserting their own respective doctrines. As I declared on occasion of Tract 90,[4] I claimed, in behalf of who would in the Anglican Church, the right of holding with Bramhall a comprecation with the Saints, and the Mass all but Transubstantiation with Andrewes, or with Hooker that Transubstantiation itself is not a point for Churches to part communion upon, or with Hammond that a General Council, truly such, never did, never shall err in a matter of faith, or with Bull that man had in paradise and lost on the fall, a supernatural habit of grace, or with Thorndike that penance is a propitiation for post-baptismal sin, or with Pearson [5] that the all-powerful name of Jesus is no otherwise given than in the Catholic Church. "Two can play at that," was often in my mouth, when men of Protestant sentiments appealed to the Articles, Homilies, or Reformers; in the sense that, if they had a right to speak loud, I had the liberty to speak out as well as they, and had the means, by the same or parallel appeals, of giving them tit for tat. I thought that the Anglican Church was tyrannized over by a mere party, and I aimed at bringing into effect the promise contained in the motto to the *Lyra*, "They shall know the difference now." [6] I only asked to be allowed to show them the difference.

What will best describe my state of mind at the early part of 1839 is an Article in the *British Critic* for that April. I have looked over it now, for the first time since it was published; and have been struck by it for this reason: it contains the last words which I ever spoke as an Anglican to Anglicans. It may now be

3. Tracts and articles written by High Church Anglican clergymen who made up the Tractarian Anglo-Catholic party or Oxford Movement. Their opponents, the Evangelicals and also the Broad Church liberals, accused them of favoring Roman Catholic doctrines.

4. An interpretation of Anglicanism by Newman, published in 1841, which provoked an acrimonious controversy.

5. All the names here are those of Anglican clergymen of the 16th and 17th centuries. Newman and his Anglo-Catholic party frequently reinforced their theological arguments by drawing from the writings of these earlier divines, especially from Richard Hooker's *The Laws of Ecclesiastical Polity* (1593), a defense of the Anglican position as a *via media* (middle way) between Roman Catholicism and Protestantism. See Vol. 1 of the present anthology.

6. On returning to battle the Trojans Achilles had boasted: "You shall know the difference now that I am back again." (*Iliad* XXVIII.125). His words served as the motto for *Lyra Apostolica*, a series of Anglo-Catholic articles published in the *British Magazine* of which Newman served as editor.

read as my parting address and valediction, made to my friends. I little knew it at the time. It reviews the actual state of things, and it ends by looking toward the future. It is not altogether mine; for my memory goes to this, that I had asked a friend to do the work; that then, the thought came on me, that I would do it myself; and that he was good enough to put into my hands what he had with great appositeness written, and that I embodied it in my Article. Every one, I think, will recognize the greater part of it as mine. It was published two years before the affair of Tract 90, and was entitled "The State of Religious Parties."

In this Article, I begin by bringing together testimonies from our enemies to the remarkable success of our exertions. One writer said: "Opinions and views of a theology of a very marked and peculiar kind have been extensively adopted and strenuously upheld, and are daily gaining ground among a considerable and influential portion of the members, as well as ministers of the Established Church." * * *

After thus stating the phenomenon of the time, as it presented itself to those who did not sympathize in it, the Article proceeds to account for it; and this it does by considering it as a reaction from the dry and superficial character of the religious teaching and the literature of the last generation, or century, and as a result of the need which was felt both by the hearts and the intellects of the nation for a deeper philosophy, and as the evidence and as the partial fulfillment of that need, to which even the chief authors of the then generation had borne witness. First, I mentioned the literary influence of Walter Scott, who turned men's minds in the direction of the middle ages. "The general need," I said, "of something deeper and more attractive, than what had offered itself elsewhere, may be considered to have led to his popularity; and by means of his popularity he reacted on his readers, stimulating their mental thirst, feeding their hopes, setting before them visions, which, when once seen, are not easily forgotten, and silently indoctrinating them with nobler ideas, which might afterwards be appealed to as first principles."

Then I spoke of Coleridge, thus: "While history in prose and verse was thus made the instrument of Church feelings and opinions, a philosophical basis for the same was laid in England by a very original thinker, who, while he indulged a liberty of speculation, which no Christian can tolerate, and advocated conclusions which were often heathen rather than Christian, yet after all installed a higher philosophy into inquiring minds, than they had hitherto been accustomed to accept. In this way he made trial of his age, and succeeded in interesting its genius in the cause of Catholic truth."

Then come Southey and Wordsworth, "two living poets, one of

whom in the department of fantastic fiction, the other in that of philosophical meditation, have addressed themselves to the same high principles and feelings, and carried forward their readers in the same direction."

* * *

These being the circumstances under which the Movement began and progressed, it was absurd to refer it to the act of two or three individuals. It was not so much a movement as a "spirit afloat"; it was within us, "rising up in hearts where it was least suspected, and working itself, though not in secret, yet so subtly and impalpably, as hardly to admit of precaution or encounter on any ordinary human rules of opposition. It is," I continued, "an adversary in the air, a something one and entire, a whole wherever it is, unapproachable and incapable of being grasped, as being the result of causes far deeper than political or other visible agencies, the spiritual awakening of spiritual wants."

* * *

Lastly, I proceeded to the question of that future of the Anglican Church, which was to be a new birth of the Ancient Religion. And I did not venture to pronounce upon it. "About the future, we have no prospect before our minds whatever, good or bad. Ever since that great luminary, Augustine, proved to be the last bishop of Hippo, Christians have had a lesson against attempting to foretell, *how* Providence will prosper and" [or?] "bring to an end, what it begins." Perhaps the lately revived principles would prevail in the Anglican Church; perhaps they would be lost in some miserable schism, or some more miserable compromise; but there was nothing rash in venturing to predict that "neither Puritanism nor Liberalism had any permanent inheritance within her."

Then I went on: "As to Liberalism, we think the formularies of the Church will ever, with the aid of a good Providence, keep it from making any serious inroads upon the clergy. Besides, it is too cold a principle to prevail with the multitude." But as regarded what was called Evangelical Religion or Puritanism, there was more to cause alarm. I observed upon its organization; but on the other hand it had no intellectual basis; no internal idea, no principle of unity, no theology. "Its adherents," I said, "are already separating from each other; they will melt away like a snowdrift. It has no straightforward view on any one point, on which it professes to teach, and to hide its poverty, it has dressed itself out in a maze of words. We have no dread of it at all; we only fear what it may lead to. It does not stand on intrenched ground, or make any pretense to a position; it does but occupy the space between contending powers, Catholic Truth and Rationalism. Then indeed will be the stern encounter, when two real and living principles, simple, entire, and consistent, one in the Church, the other out of it, at length rush upon each other, contending not for names and words, or half-views, but for elementary notions and distinctive moral characters."

Whether the ideas of the coming age upon religion were true or false, at least they would be real. "In the present day," I said, "mistiness is the mother of wisdom. A man who can set down a half-a-dozen general propositions, which escape from destroying one another only by being diluted into truisms, who can hold the balance between opposites so skillfully as to do without fulcrum or beam, who never enunciates a truth without guarding himself against being supposed to exclude the contradictory—who holds that Scripture is the only authority, yet that the Church is to be deferred to, that faith only justifies, yet that it does not justify without works, that grace does not depend on the sacraments, yet is not given without them, that bishops are a divine ordinance, yet those who have them not are in the same religious condition as those who have—this is your safe man and the hope of the Church; this is what the Church is said to want, not party men, but sensible, temperate, sober, well-judging persons, to guide it through the channel of no-meaning, between the Scylla and Charybdis of Aye and No."

This state of things, however, I said, could not last, if men were to read and think. They "will not keep in that very attitude which you call sound Church-of-Englandism or orthodox Protestantism. They cannot go on forever standing on one leg, or sitting without a chair, or walking with their feet tied, or like Tityrus's stags grazing in the air.[7] They will take one view or another, but it will be a consistent view. It may be Liberalism, or Erastianism, or Popery, or Catholicity; but it will be real."

I concluded the Article by saying, that all who did not wish to be "democratic, or pantheistic, or popish," must "look out for *some* Via Media which will perserve us from what threatens, though it cannot restore the dead. The spirit of Luther is dead; but Hildebrand and Loyola are alive.[8] Is it sensible, sober, judicious, to be so very angry with those writers of the day, who point to the fact, that our divines of the seventeenth century have occupied a ground which is the true and intelligible mean between extremes? Is it wise to quarrel with this ground, because it is not exactly what we should choose, had we the power of choice? Is it true moderation, instead of trying to fortify a middle doctrine, to fling stones at those who do? . . . Would you rather have your sons and daughters members of the Church of England or of the Church of Rome?"

And thus I left the matter. But, while I was thus speaking of the future of the Movement, I was in truth winding up my accounts

7. Virgil, *Eclogues* I.59.
8. Hildebrand (Pope Gregory VII) and St. Ignatius of Loyola, representing medieval and modern Catholicism.

with it, little dreaming that it was so to be; while I was still, in some way or other, feeling about for an available *Via Media*, I was soon to receive a shock which was to cast out of my imagination all middle courses and compromises forever.[1] As I have said, this Article appeared in the April number of the *British Critic*; in the July number, I cannot tell why, there is no Article of mine; before the number for October, the event had happened to which I have alluded.

But before I proceed to describe what happened to me in the summer of 1839, I must detain the reader for a while, in order to describe the *issue* of the controversy between Rome and the Anglican Church, as I viewed it. This will involve some dry discussion; but it is as necessary for my narrative, as plans of buildings and homesteads are at times needed in the proceedings of our law courts.

* * *

From *Chapter V. Position of My Mind Since 1845*

Starting then with the being of a God (which, as I have said, is as certain to me as the certainty of my own existence, though when I try to put the grounds of that certainty into logical shape I find a difficulty in doing so in mood and figure to my satisfaction), I look out of myself into the world of men, and there I see a sight which fills me with unspeakable distress. The world seems simply to give the lie to that great truth, of which my whole being is so full; and the effect upon me is, in consequence, as a matter of necessity, as confusing as if it denied that I am in existence myself. If I looked into a mirror, and did not see my face, I should have the sort of feeling which actually comes upon me, when I look into this living busy world, and see no reflection of its Creator. This is, to me, one of the great difficulties of this absolute primary truth, to which I referred just now. Were it not for this voice, speaking so clearly in my conscience and my heart, I should be an atheist, or a pantheist, or a polytheist when I looked into the world. I am speaking for myself only; and I am far from denying the real force of the arguments in proof of a God, drawn from the general facts of human society, but these do not warm me or enlighten me; they do not take away the winter of my desolation, or make the buds unfold and the leaves grow within me, and my moral being rejoice. The sight of the world is nothing else than the prophet's scroll, full of "lamentations, and mourning, and woe."[2]

To consider the world in its length and breadth, its various history, the many races of man, their starts, their fortunes, their

---

1. The "shock" was prompted by his discovery in 1839, in the course of studying church history, that the Anglican position seemed to be identical with that of a heretical movement of the 5th century.
2. Ezekiel ii.9–10.

mutual alienation, their conflicts; and then their ways, habits, governments, forms of worship; their enterprises, their aimless courses, their random achievements and acquirements, the impotent conclusion of long-standing facts, the tokens so faint and broken, of a superintending design, the blind evolution of what turn out to be great powers or truth, the progress of things, as if from unreasoning elements, not towards final causes, the greatness and littleness of man, his far-reaching aims, his short duration, the curtain hung over his futurity, the disappoinments of life, the defeat of good, the success of evil, physical pain, mental anguish, the prevalence and intensity of sin, the pervading idolatries, the corruptions, the dreary hopeless irreligion, that condition of the whole race, so fearfully yet exactly described in the Apostle's words, "having no hope and without God in the world"[3]—all this is a vision to dizzy and appall; and inflicts upon the mind the sense of a profound mystery which is absolutely beyond human solution.

What shall be said to this heart-piercing, reason-bewildering fact? I can only answer that either there is no Creator, or this living society of men is in a true sense discarded from His presence. Did I see a boy of good make and mind, with the tokens on him of a refined nature, cast upon the world without provision, unable to say whence he came, his birthplace or his family connections, I should conclude that there was some mystery connected with his history, and that he was one, of whom, from one cause or other, his parents were ashamed. Thus only should I be able to account for the contrast between the promise and condition of his being. And so I argue about the world—*if* there be a God, *since* there is a God, the human race is implicated in some terrible aboriginal calamity. It is out of joint with the purposes of its Creator. This is a fact, a fact as true as the fact of its existence; and thus the doctrine of what is theologically called original sin becomes to me almost as certain as that the world exists, and as the existence of God.

And now, supposing it were the blessed and loving will of the Creator to interfere in this anarchical condition of things, what are we to suppose would be the methods which might be necessarily or naturally involved in His object of mercy? Since the world is in so abnormal a state, surely it would be no surprise to me if the interposition were of necessity equally extraordinary—or what is called miraculous. But that subject does not directly come into the scope of my present remarks. Miracles as evidence involve an argument; and of course I am thinking of some means which does not immediately run into argument. I am rather asking what must be the face-to-face antagonist, by which to withstand and baffle the fierce energy of passion and the all-corroding, all-dissolving skepticism of the intellect in religious inquiries? I have no intention at

3. Ephesians ii.12.

all to deny that truth is the real object of our reason, and that, if it does not attain to truth, either the premise or the process is in fault; but I am not speaking of right reason, but of reason as it acts in fact and concretely in fallen man. I know that even the unaided reason, when correctly exercised, leads to a belief in God, in the immortality of the soul, and in a future retribution; but I am considering it actually and historically; and in this point of view, I do not think I am wrong in saying that its tendency is towards a simple unbelief in matters of religion. No truth, however sacred, can stand against it, in the long run; and hence it is that in the pagan world, when our Lord came, the last traces of the religious knowledge of former times were all but disappearing from those portions of the world in which the intellect had been active and had had a career.

And in these latter days, in like manner, outside the Catholic Church things are tending, with far greater rapidity than in that old time from the circumstance of the age, to atheism in one shape or other. What a scene, what a prospect, does the whole of Europe present at this day! and not only Europe, but every government and every civilization through the world, which is under the influence of the European mind! Especially, for it most concerns us, how sorrowful, in the view of religion, even taken in its most elementary, most attenuated form, is the spectacle presented to us by the educated intellect of England, France, and Germany! Lovers of their country and of their race, religious men, external to the Catholic Church, have attempted various expedients to arrest fierce willful human nature in its onward course, and to bring it into subjection. The necessity of some form of religion for the interests of humanity has been generally acknowledged: but where was the concrete representative of things invisible, which would have the force and the toughness necessary to be a breakwater against the deluge? Three centuries ago the establishment of religion, material, legal, and social was generally adopted as the best expedient for the purpose, in those countries which separated from the Catholic Church; and for a long time it was successful; but now the crevices of those establishments are admitting the enemy. Thirty years ago, education was relied upon: ten years ago there was a hope that wars would cease forever, under the influence of commercial enterprise and the reign of the useful and fine arts;[4] but will anyone venture to say that there is anything anywhere on this earth, which will afford a fulcrum for us, whereby to keep the earth from moving onwards?

The judgment, which experience passes on establishments or

4. A reference to the optimism generated at the time of the Great Exhibition of 1851, a mood which was sobered by the sufferings endured during the Crimean War (1854–56).

education, as a means of maintaining religious truth in this anarchical world, must be extended even to Scripture, though Scripture be divine. Experience proves surely that the Bible does not answer a purpose, for which it was never intended. It may be accidentally the means of the conversion of individuals; but a book, after all, cannot make a stand against the wild living intellect of man, and in this day it begins to testify, as regards its own structure and contents, to the power of that universal solvent,[5] which is so successfully acting upon religious establishments.

Supposing then it to be the Will of the Creator to interfere in human affairs, and to make provisions for retaining in the world a knowledge of Himself, so definite and distinct as to be proof against the energy of human skepticism, in such a case—I am far from saying that there was no other way—but there is nothing to surprise the mind, if He should think fit to introduce a power into the world, invested with the prerogative of infallibility in religious matters. Such a provision would be a direct, immediate, active, and prompt means of withstanding the difficulty; it would be an instrument suited to the need; and, when I find that this is the very claim of the Catholic Church, not only do I feel no difficulty in admitting the idea, but there is a fitness in it, which recommends it to my mind. And thus I am brought to speak of the Church's infallibility, as a provision, adapted by the mercy of the Creator, to preserve religion in the world, and to restrain that freedom of thought, which of course in itself is one of the greatest of our natural gifts, and to rescue it from its own suicidal excesses. And let it be observed that, neither here nor in what follows, shall I have occasion to speak directly of the revealed body of truths, but only as they bear upon the defense of natural religion. I say that a power, possessed of infallibility in religious teaching, is happily adapted to be a working instrument, in the course of human affairs, for smiting hard and throwing back the immense energy of the aggressive intellect—and in saying this, as in the other things that I have to say, it must still be recollected that I am all along bearing in mind my main purpose, which is a defense of myself.

I am defending myself here from a plausible charge brought against Catholics, as will be seen better as I proceed. The charge is this: that I, as a Catholic, not only make profession to hold doctrines which I cannot possibly believe in my heart, but that I also believe in the existence of a power on earth, which at its own will imposes upon men any new set of *credenda*,[6] when it pleases, by a claim to infallibility; in consequence, that my own thoughts are not my own property; that I cannot tell that tomorrow I may not have to give up what I hold today, and that the necessary effect of

5. Allusion to the Higher Criticism, a method of analyzing the Bible as history. 6. Beliefs.

such a condition of mind must be a degrading bondage, or a bitter inward rebellion relieving itself in secret infidelity, or the necessity of ignoring the whole subject of religion in a sort of disgust, and of mechanically saying everything that the Church says, and leaving to others the defense of it. As then I have above spoken of the relation of my mind towards the Catholic Creed, so now I shall speak of the attitude which it takes up in the view of the Church's infallibility.

And first, the initial doctrine of the infallible teacher must be an emphatic protest against the existing state of mankind. Man had rebelled against his Maker. It was this that caused the divine interposition: and the first act of the divinely accredited messenger must be to proclaim it. The Church must denounce rebellion as of all possible evils the greatest. She must have no terms with it; if she would be true to her Master, she must ban and anathematize it. This is the meaning of a statement which has furnished matter for one of those special accusations to which I am at present replying: I have, however, no fault at all to confess in regard to it; I have nothing to withdraw, and in consequence I here deliberately repeat it. I said, "The Catholic Church holds it better for the sun and moon to drop from heaven, for the earth to fail, and for all the many millions on it to die of starvation in extremest agony, as far as temporal affliction goes, than that one soul, I will not say, should be lost, but should commit one single venial sin, should tell one willful untruth, or should steal one poor farthing without excuse." I think the principle here enunciated to be the mere preamble in the formal credentials of the Catholic Church, as an Act of Parliament might begin with a "*Whereas*." It is because of the intensity of the evil which has possession of mankind that a suitable antagonist has been provided against it; and the initial act of that divinely-commissioned power is of course to deliver her challenge and to defy the enemy. Such a preamble then gives a meaning to her position in the world, and an interpretation to her whole course of teaching and action.

From *Liberalism*

I have been asked to explain more fully what it is I mean by "Liberalism," because merely to call it the Antidogmatic Principle is to tell very little about it. * * * Now by Liberalism I mean false liberty of thought, or the exercise of thought upon matters, in which, from the constitution of the human mind, thought cannot be brought to any successful issue, and therefore is out of place. Among such matters are first principles of whatever kind; and of these the most sacred and momentous are especially to be reckoned the truths of Revelation. Liberalism then is the mistake of subjecting to human judgment those revealed doctrines which are in their nature beyond and independent of it, and of claiming to determine on intrinsic grounds the truth and value of propositions which rest for their reception simply on the external authority of the Divine Word. * * *

I conclude this notice of Liberalism in Oxford, and the party which was antagonistic to it,[7] with some propositions in detail, which, as a member of the latter, and together with the High Church, I earnestly denounced and abjured.

1. No religious tenet is important, unless reason shows it to be so.

Therefore, e.g., the doctrine of the Athanasian Creed[8] is not to be insisted on, unless it tends to convert the soul; and the doctrine of the Atonement is to be insisted on, if it does convert the soul.

2. No one can believe what he does not understand.

Therefore, e.g., there are no mysteries in true religion.

3. No theological doctrine is anything more than an opinion which happens to be held by bodies of men.

Therefore, e.g., no creed, as such, is necessary for salvation.

4. It is dishonest in a man to make an act of faith in what he has not had brought home to him by actual proof.

Therefore, e.g., the mass of men ought not absolutely to believe in the divine authority of the Bible.

5. It is immoral in a man to believe more than he can spontaneously receive as being congenial to his moral and mental nature.

Therefore, e.g., a given individual is not bound to believe in eternal punishment.

6. No revealed doctrines or precepts may reasonably stand in the way of scientific conclusions.

Therefore, e.g., Political Economy may reverse our Lord's declarations about poverty and riches, or a system of Ethics may teach that the highest condition of body is ordinarily essential to the highest state of mind.

7. Christianity is necessarily modified by the growth of civilization, and the exigencies of times.

Therefore, e.g., the Catholic priesthood, though necessary in the Middle Ages, may be superseded now.

8. There is a system of religion more simply true than Christianity as it has ever been received.

Therefore, e.g., we may advance that Christianity is the "corn of wheat" which has been dead for 1800 years, but at length will bear fruit; and that Mahometanism is the manly religion, and existing Christianity the womanish.

9. There is a right of Private Judgment: that is, there is no existing authority on earth competent to interfere with the liberty of individuals in reasoning and judging for themselves about the Bible

---

7. The Tractarians or Party of the Oxford Movement.   8. Belief in the Trinity.

and its contents, as they severally please.

Therefore, e.g., religious establishments requiring subscription are Antichristian.

10. There are rights of conscience such that everyone may lawfully advance a claim to profess and teach what is false and wrong in matters, religious, social, and moral, provided that to his private conscience it seems absolutely true and right.

Therefore, e.g., individuals have a right to preach and practice fornication and polygamy.

11. There is no such thing as a national or state conscience.

Therefore, e.g., no judgments can fall upon a sinful or infidel nation.

12. The civil power has no positive duty, in a normal state of things, to maintain religious truth.

Therefore, e.g., blasphemy and sabbath-breaking are not rightly punishable by law.

13. Utility and expedience are the measure of political duty.

Therefore, e.g., no punishment may be enacted, on the ground that God commands it: e.g., on the text, "Whoso sheddeth man's blood, by man shall his blood be shed." [9]

14. The Civil Power may dispose of Church property without sacrilege.

Therefore, e.g., Henry VIII committed no sin in his spoliations.[1]

15. The Civil Power has the right of ecclesiastical jurisdiction and administration.

Therefore, e.g., Parliament may impose articles of faith on the Church or suppress Dioceses.[2]

16. It is lawful to rise in arms against legitimate princes.

Therefore, e.g., the Puritans in the seventeenth century, and the French in the eighteenth, were justified in their Rebellion and Revolution respectively.

17. The people are the legitimate source of power.

Therefore, e.g., Universal Suffrage is among the natural rights of man.

18. Virtue is the child of knowledge, and vice of ignorance.

Therefore, e.g., education, periodical literature, railroad traveling, ventilation, drainage, and the arts of life, when fully carried out, serve to make a population moral and happy.

All of these propositions, and many others too, were familiar to me thirty years ago, as in the number of the tenets of Liberalism, and, while I gave in to none of them except No. 12, and perhaps No. 11, and partly No. 1, before I began to publish, so afterwards

---

9. Genesis ix.6.
1. The dissolution of the monasteries by Henry VIII.
2. Allusion to the abolishing of ten Irish bishoprics by liberal reformers in Parliament in 1833. This instance of interference by the state in affairs of the church had prompted Newman and his associates into organizing a "party of opposition": the Oxford Movement.

I wrote against most of them in some part or other of my Anglican works. * * *

I need hardly say that the above Note is mainly historical. How far the Liberal party of 1830–40 really held the above eighteen Theses, which I attributed to them, and how far and in what sense I should oppose those Theses now, could scarcely be explained without a separate Dissertation.

                                                    1864–65

JOHN STUART MILL
(1806–1873)

In many American colleges the writings of J. S. Mill are studied in courses in government or in philosophy, and it may therefore be asked why they should also have a place in the study of literature. It is evident that Mill is the least literary of the important Victorian prose writers. His analytic mind, preoccupied with abstractions rather than with the concrete details that are the concern of the more typical man of letters, his self-effacing manner, and his relatively colorless style are the marks of a writer whose value lies in his generalizations from experience rather than in the rendering of particular experiences for their own sake. Yet a knowledge of Mill's writings is essential to our understanding of Victorian literature. He is one of the leading figures in the intellectual history of his century, a thinker whose honest grappling with the political and religious problems of his age was to have a profound influence on writers as diverse as Arnold, Swinburne, and Hardy.

Mill was educated at home in London under the direction of his father, James Mill, a leader of the Utilitarians. James Mill believed that ordinary schooling fails to develop our intellectual capacities early enough, and he demonstrated his point by the extraordinary results he achieved in training his son. As a child John Stuart Mill read Greek and Latin, and as a boy he could carry on intelligent discussions of problems in mathematics, philosophy, and economics. By the time he was 14, as he reports in his *Autobiography,* his intensive education enabled him to start his career "with an advantage of a quarter of a century" over his contemporaries.

Mill worked in the office of the East India Company for many years and also served a term in Parliament in the 1860's, but his principal energies were devoted to his writings on such subjects as logic and philosophy, political principles, and economics. He began as a disciple of the Utilitarian theories of his father and of Jeremy Bentham but became gradually dissatisfied with the narrowness of their conception of human motives. His honesty and open-mindedness enabled him to appreciate the values of such anti-Utilitarians as Coleridge and Carlyle, and, whenever possible, to incorporate some of these values into the Utilitarian system. His essay on Coleridge's enlightened conservatism in politics and religion is a striking example of Mill's capacity for sympathetic understanding. In part this sympathy was gained by the lesson he learned through experiencing a nervous breakdown during his early 20's. This painful event, described in the chapter of his *Autobiography* included below, taught him that the lack of concern for the affections and emotions of men, characteristic of the Utilitarian system of thought (and typified by his own education), was a fatal flaw in that system. His tribute to the therapeutic value of art (because of its effect on human emotions), both in his *Autobiography* and in his early essay *What Is Poetry*, would have astonished Mill's master, Bentham, who had equated poetry with pushpin, a trifling game.

Mill's emotional life was also broadened by his love for Harriet Taylor, a married woman who shared his intellectual interests and eventually became his wife, in 1851, after the death of her husband. Mill later described her as "the inspirer, and in part the author, of all that is best in my writings." Under her influence he became an advocate for the cause of female emancipation, one of several unpopular movements to which he was dedicated. Throughout human history, as Mill saw it, the role of a husband has always been legally that of a tyrant, and the object of his far-seeing essay *The Subjection of Women* (1869) was to change law and public opinion so that half the human race might be liberated from slavery into the status of individuals. The subjection of women was, however, only one aspect of the tyranny against which he fought. His fundamental concern was to prevent the subjection of individuals in a democracy. His classic treatise *On Liberty* (1859) is not a traditional liberal attack against tyrannical kings or dictators; it is an attack against tyrannical majorities. Mill foresaw that in democracies such as America, the pressure toward conformity might crush all individualists (intellectual individualists in particular) to the level of what he called a "collective mediocrity." Throughout all of his writings, even in his discussions of the advantages of socialism, Mill is concerned with demonstrating that the individual is more important than institutions such as church or state. In *On Liberty* we find a characteristic example of the process of his reasoning, but here, where the theme of individualism is central, his logic is charged with eloquence.

A similar eloquence is evident in a passage from his *Principles of Political Economy* (1848), a prophetic comment on the fate of the individual in an overpopulated world:

> There is room in the world, no doubt, and even in old countries, for a great increase of population, supposing the arts of life go on improving, and capital to increase. But even if innocuous, I confess I see very little reason for desiring it. * * * It is not good for a man to be kept perforce at all times in the presence of his species. A world from which solitude is extirpated, is a very poor ideal. Solitude, in the sense of being often alone, is essential to any depth of meditation or of character: and solitude in the presence of natural beauty and grandeur, is the cradle of thoughts and aspirations which are not only good for the individual, but which society could ill do without. Nor is there much satisfaction in contemplating the world with nothing left to the spontaneous activity of nature; with every rood of land brought into cultivation, which is capable of growing food for human beings; every flowery waste or natural pasture ploughed up, all quadrupeds or birds which are not domesticated for man's use exterminated as his rivals for food, every hedgerow or superfluous tree rooted out, and scarcely a place left where a wild shrub or flower could grow without being eradicated as a weed in the name of improved agriculture. If the earth must lose that great portion of its pleasantness which it owes to things that the unlimited increase of wealth and population would ex-

tirpate from it, for the mere purpose of enabling it to support a larger, but not a better or a happier population, I sincerely hope, for the sake of posterity, that they will be content to be stationary, long before necessity compels them to it.

What Is Poetry?

It has often been asked, What Is Poetry? And many and various are the answers which have been returned. The vulgarest of all—one with which no person possessed of the faculties to which poetry addresses itself can ever have been satisfied—is that which confounds poetry with metrical composition; yet to this wretched mockery of a definition many have been led back by the failure of all their attempts to find any other that would distinguish what they have been accustomed to call poetry from much which they have known only under other names.

That, however, the word "poetry" imports something quite peculiar in its nature; something which may exist in what is called prose as well as in verse; something which does not even require the instrument of words, but can speak through the other audible symbols called musical sounds, and even through the visible ones which are the language of sculpture, painting, and architecture—all this, we believe, is and must be felt, though perhaps indistinctly, by all upon whom poetry in any of its shapes produces any impression beyond that of tickling the ear. The distinction between poetry and what is not poetry, whether explained or not, is felt to be fundamental; and, where every one feels a difference, a difference there must be. All other appearances may be fallacious; but the appearance of a difference is a real difference. Appearances too, like other things, must have a cause; and that which can cause anything, even an illusion, must be a reality. And hence, while a half-philosophy disdains the classifications and distinctions indicated by popular language, philosophy carried to its highest point frames new ones, but rarely sets aside the old, content with correcting and regularizing them. It cuts fresh channels for thought, but does not fill up such as it finds ready-made: it traces, on the countrary, more deeply, broadly, and distinctly, those into which the current has spontaneously flowed.

Let us then attempt, in the way of modest inquiry, not to coerce and confine Nature within the bounds of an arbitrary definition, but rather to find the boundaries which she herself has set, and erect a barrier round them; not calling mankind to account for having misapplied the word "poetry," but attempting to clear up the conception which they already attach to it, and to bring forward as a distinct principle that which, as a vague feeling, has really guided them in their employment of the term.

The object of poetry is confessedly to act upon the emotions; and therein is poetry sufficiently distinguished from what Wordsworth affirms to be its logical opposite; namely, not prose. but matter of fact, or science.[1] The one addresses itself to the belief; the other, to the feelings. The one does its work by convincing or persuading; the other, by moving. The one acts by presenting a proposition to the understanding; the other, by offering interesting objects of contemplation to the sensibilities.

This, however, leaves us very far from a definition of poetry. This distinguishes it from one thing; but we are bound to distinguish it from everything. To bring thoughts or images before the mind, for the purpose of acting upon the emotions, does not belong to poetry alone. It is equally the province (for example) of the novelist: and yet the faculty of the poet and that of the novelist are as distinct as any other two faculties; as the faculties of the novelist and of the orator, or of the poet and the metaphysician. The two characters may be united, as characters the most disparate may; but they have no natural connection.

Many of the greatest poems are in the form of fictitious narratives; and, in almost all good serious fictions, there is true poetry. But there is a radical distinction between the interest felt in a story as such, and the interest excited by poetry; for the one is derived from incident, the other from the representation of feeling. In one, the source of the emotion excited is the exhibition of a state or states of human sensibility; in the other, of a series of states of mere outward circumstances. Now, all minds are capable of being affected more or less by representations of the latter kind, and all, or almost all, by those of the former; yet the two sources of interest correspond to two distinct and (as respects their greatest development) mutually exclusive characters of mind.

At what age is the passion for a story, for almost any kind of story, merely as a story, the most intense? In childhood. But that also is the age at which poetry, even of the simplest description, is least relished and least understood; because the feelings with which it is especially conversant are yet undeveloped, and, not having been even in the slightest degree experienced, cannot be sympathized with. In what stage of the progress of society, again, is storytelling most valued, and the storyteller in greatest request and honor? In a rude state like that of the Tartars and Arabs at this day, and of almost all nations in the earliest ages. But, in this state of society, there is little poetry except ballads, which are mostly narrative—that is, essentially stories—and derive their principal interest from the incidents. Considered as poetry, they are of the lowest and most elementary kind: the feelings depicted, or rather indicated, are the simplest our nature has; such joys and griefs as the immediate pressure of some outward event excites in rude minds, which live wholly immersed in outward things, and have never, either from choice or a force they could not resist,

---

1. See above, Wordsworth's Preface to *Lyrical Ballads.*

turned themselves to the contemplation of the world within. Passing now from childhood, and from the childhood of society, to the grown-up men and women of this most grown-up and unchildlike age, the minds and hearts of greatest depth and elevation are commonly those which take greatest delight in poetry: the shallowest and emptiest, on the contrary, are, at all events, not those least addicted to novel-reading. This accords, too, with all analogous experience of human nature. The sort of persons whom not merely in books, but in their lives, we find perpetually engaged in hunting for excitement from without, are invariably those who do not possess, either in the vigor of their intellectual powers or in the depth of their sensibilities, that which would enable them to find ample excitement nearer home. The most idle and frivolous persons take a natural delight in fictitious narrative: the excitement it affords is of the kind which comes from without. Such persons are rarely lovers of poetry, though they may fancy themselves so because they relish novels in verse. But poetry, which is the delineation of the deeper and more secret workings of human emotion, is interesting only to those to whom it recalls what they have felt, or whose imagination it stirs up to conceive what they could feel, or what they might have been able to feel, had their outward circumstances been different.

Poetry, when it is really such, is truth; and fiction also, if it is good for anything, is truth: but they are different truths. The truth of poetry is to paint the human soul truly: the truth of fiction is to give a true picture of life. The two kinds of knowledge are different, and come by different ways, come mostly to different persons. Great poets are often proverbially ignorant of life. What they know has come by observation of themselves: they have found within them one highly delicate and sensitive specimen of human nature, on which the laws of emotion are written in large characters, such as can be read off without much study. Other knowledge of mankind, such as comes to men of the world by outward experience, is not indispensable to them as poets: but, to the novelist, such knowledge is all in all; he has to describe outward things, not the inward man; actions and events, not feelings; and it will not do for him to be numbered among those, who, as Madame Roland said of Brissot, know man, but not *men*.[2]

All this is no bar to the possibility of combining both elements, poetry and narrative or incident, in the same work, and calling it either a novel or a poem; but so may red and white combine on the same human features or on the same canvas. There is one order of composition which requires the union of poetry and incident, each in its highest kind—the dramatic. Even there, the two elements are perfectly distinguishable, and may exist of un-

2. Jacques Pierre Brissot (1754–93), a leading reformer during the French Revolution, is characterized in the *Mém-* *oires* of Jeanne Manon Roland (1754–93).

equal quality and in the most various proportion. The incidents of a dramatic poem may be scanty and ineffective, though the delineation of passion and character may be of the highest order, as in Goethe's admirable "Torquato Tasso"; or, again, the story as a mere story may be well got up for effect, as is the case with some of the most trashy productions of the Minerva Press: [3] it may even be, what those are not, a coherent and probable series of events, though there be scarcely a feeling exhibited which is not represented falsely, or in a manner absolutely commonplace. The combination of the two excellences is what renders Shakespeare so generally acceptable, each sort of readers finding in him what is suitable to their faculties. To the many, he is great as a storyteller; to the few, as a poet.

In limiting poetry to the delineation of states of feeling, and denying the name where nothing is delineated but outward objects, we may be thought to have done what we promised to avoid—to have not found, but made, a definition in opposition to the usage of language, since it is established by common consent that there is a poetry called descriptive. We deny the charge. Description is not poetry because there is descriptive poetry, no more than science is poetry because there is such a thing as a didactic poem. But an object which admits of being described, or a truth which may fill a place in a scientific treatise, may also furnish an occasion for the generation of poetry, which we thereupon choose to call descriptive or didactic. The poetry is not in the object itself, nor in the scientific truth itself, but in the state of mind in which the one and the other may be contemplated. The mere delineation of the dimensions and colors of external objects is not poetry, no more than a geometrical ground-plan of St. Peter's or Westminster Abbey is painting. Descriptive poetry consists, no doubt, in description, but in description of things as they appear, not as they are; and it paints them, not in their bare and natural lineaments, but seen through the medium and arrayed in the colors of the imagination set in action by the feelings. If a poet describes a lion, he does not describe him as a naturalist would, nor even as a traveler would, who was intent upon stating the truth, the whole truth, and nothing but the truth. He describes him by imagery, that is, by suggesting the most striking likenesses and contrasts which might occur to a mind contemplating a lion, in the state of awe, wonder, or terror, which the spectacle naturally excites, or is, on the occasion, supposed to excite. Now, this is describing the lion professedly, but the state of excitement of the spectator really. The lion may be described falsely or with exaggeration and the poetry be all the better: but, if the human emotion be not painted with scrupulous truth, the poetry is bad poetry; i.e., is not poetry at all, but a failure.

Thus far, our progress towards a clear view of the essentials of

3. Early 19th-century publishing house that fostered the production of sentimental novels.

poetry has brought us very close to the last two attempts at a definition of poetry which we happen to have seen in print, both of them by poets, and men of genius. The one is by Ebenezer Elliott, the author of "Corn-law Rhymes," and other poems of still greater merit. "Poetry," says he, "is impassioned truth." [4] The other is by a writer in "Blackwood's Magazine," and comes, we think, still nearer the mark. He defines poetry, "man's thoughts tinged by his feelings." There is in either definition a near approximation to what we are in search of. Every truth which a human being can enunciate, every thought, even every outward impression, which can enter into his consciousness, may become poetry, when shown through any impassioned medium; when invested with the coloring of joy, or grief, or pity, or affection, or admiration, or reverence, or awe, or even hatred or terror; and, unless so colored, nothing, be it as interesting as it may, is poetry. But both these definitions fail to discriminate between poetry and eloquence. Eloquence, as well as poetry, is impassioned truth; eloquence, as well as poetry, is thoughts colored by the feelings. Yet common apprehension and philosophic criticism alike recognize a distinction between the two: there is much that everyone would call eloquence, which no one would think of classing as poetry. A question will sometimes arise, whether some particular author is a poet; and those who maintain the negative commonly allow, that, though not a poet, he is a highly eloquent writer. The distinction between poetry and eloquence appears to us to be equally fundamental with the distinction between poetry and narrative, or between poetry and description, while it is still farther from having been satisfactorily cleared up than either of the others.

Poetry and eloquence are both alike the expression or utterance of feeling: but, if we may be excused the antithesis, we should say that eloquence is *heard*; poetry is *over*heard. Eloquence supposes an audience. The peculiarity of poetry appears to us to lie in the poet's utter unconsciousness of a listener. Poetry is feeling confessing itself to itself in moments of solitude, and embodying itself in symbols which are the nearest possible representations of the feeling in the exact shape in which it exists in the poet's mind. Eloquence is feeling pouring itself out to other minds, courting their sympathy, or endeavoring to influence their belief, or move them to passion or to action.

All poetry is of the nature of soliloquy. It may be said that poetry which is printed on hot-pressed paper, and sold at a bookseller's shop, is a soliloquy in full dress and on the stage. It is so; but there is nothing absurd in the idea of such a mode of soliloquizing. What we have said to ourselves we may tell to others afterwards; what we have said or done in solitude we may voluntarily reproduce when we know that other eyes are upon us. But

4. Preface to *Corn-Law Rhymes* (1828) by Ebenezer Elliot (1781–1849).

no trace of consciousness that any eyes are upon us must be visible in the work itself. The actor knows that there is an audience present: but, if he act as though he knew it, he acts ill. A poet may write poetry, not only with the intention of printing it, but for the express purpose of being paid for it. That it should *be* poetry, being written under such influences, is less probable, not, however, impossible; but no otherwise possible than if he can succeed in excluding from his work every vestige of such lookings-forth into the outward and every-day world, and can express his emotions exactly as he has felt them in solitude, or as he is conscious that he should feel them, though they were to remain for ever unuttered, or (at the lowest) as he knows that others feel them in similar circumstances of solitude. But when he turns round, and addresses himself to another person; when the act of utterance is not itself the end, but a means to an end—viz., by the feelings he himself expresses, to work upon the feelings, or upon the belief or the will of another; when the expression of his emotions, or of his thoughts tinged by his emotions, is tinged also by that purpose, by that desire of making an impression upon another mind—then it ceases to be poetry, and becomes eloquence.

Poetry, accordingly, is the natural fruit of solitude and meditation; eloquence, of intercourse with the world. The persons who have most feeling of their own, if intellectual culture has given them a language in which to express it, have the highest faculty of poetry: those who best understand the feelings of others are the most eloquent. The persons and the nations who commonly excel in poetry are those whose character and tastes render them least dependent upon the applause or sympathy or concurrence of the world in general. Those to whom that applause, that sympathy, that concurrence, are most necessary, generally excel most in eloquence. And hence, perhaps, the French, who are the least poetical of all great and intellectual nations, are among the most eloquent; the French also being the most sociable, the vainest, and the least self-dependent.

If the above be, as we believe, the true theory of the distinction commonly admitted between eloquence and poetry, or even though it be not so, yet if, as we cannot doubt, the distinction above stated be a real bona fide distinction, it will be found to hold, not merely in the language of words, but in all other language, and to intersect the whole domain of art.

Take, for example, music. We shall find in that art, so peculiarly the expression of passion, two perfectly distinct styles—one of which may be called the poetry, the other the oratory, of music. This difference, being seized, would put an end to much musical sectarianism. There has been much contention whether the music of the modern Italian school, that of Rossini,[5] and his suc-

5. G. A. Rossini (1792–1868), composer of operas.

cessors, be impassioned or not. Without doubt, the passion it expresses is not the musing, meditative tenderness or pathos or grief of Mozart or Beethoven; yet it is passion, but garrulous passion, the passion which pours itself into other ears, and therein the better calculated for dramatic effect, having a natural adaptation for dialogue. Mozart also is great in musical oratory; but his most touching compositions are in the opposite style, that of soliloquy. Who can imagine "Dove sono" [6] *heard?* We imagine it *overheard.*

Purely pathetic music commonly partakes of soliloquy. The soul is absorbed in its distress and, though there may be bystanders, it is not thinking of them. When the mind is looking within, and not without, its state does not often or rapidly vary; and hence the even, uninterrupted flow, approaching almost to monotony, which a good reader or a good singer will give to words or music of a pensive or melancholy cast. But grief, taking the form of a prayer or of a complaint, becomes oratorical: no longer low and even and subdued, it assumes a more emphatic rhythm, a more rapidly returning accent; instead of a few slow, equal notes, following one after another at regular intervals, it crowds note upon note, and often assumes a hurry and bustle like joy. Those who are familiar with some of the best of Rossini's serious compositions, such as the air "Tu che i miseri conforti," [7] in the opera of "Tancredi," or the duet "Ebben per mia memoria," [8] in "La Gazza Ladra," will at once understand and feel our meaning. Both are highly tragic and passionate: the passion of both is that of oratory, not poetry. The like may be said of that most moving invocation in Beethoven's "Fidelio,"

> "Komm, Hoffnung, lass das letzte Stern
> Der Müde nicht erbleichen "—[9]

in which Madame Schröder Devrient exhibited such consummate powers of pathetic expression. How different from Winter's beautiful "Paga fui," [1] the very soul of melancholy exhaling itself in solitude! fuller of meaning, and therefore more profoundly poetical, than the words for which it was composed; for it seems to express, not simple melancholy, but the melancholy of remorse.

If from vocal music we now pass to instrumental, we may have a specimen of musical oratory in any fine military symphony or march; while the poetry of music seems to have attained its consummation in Beethoven's "Overture to Egmont," so wonderful in its mixed expression of grandeur and melancholy.

6. "Where are fled [the lovely moments?]"—soprano aria from Act III of Mozart's opera *The Marriage of Figaro.*
7. "You, who give comfort to the wretched," soprano aria from Rossini's *Tancredi* (1813).
8. "Indeed according to my memory," soprano aria from Rossini's *La Gazza Ladra* (1817).
9. "Come, Hope, let not the weary person's last star fade out." Aria from *Fidelio* (1805). Mill seems to be quoting from memory. The passage should read: "Komm, Hoffnung, lass den letzten Stern / Der Müden nicht erbleichen."
1. "I have been contented." Aria from the once-popular opera *Il Ratto di Proserpina* by Peter Winter (1775–1825), first performed in London in 1804.

In the arts which speak to the eye, the same distinctions will be found to hold, not only between poetry and oratory, but between poetry, oratory, narrative, and simple imitation or description.

Pure description is exemplified in a mere portrait or a mere landscape, productions of art, it is true, but of the mechanical rather than of the fine arts; being works of simple imitation, not creation. We say, a mere portrait or a mere landscape; because it is possible for a portrait or a landscape, without ceasing to be such, to be also a picture, like Turner's [2] landscapes, and the great portraits by Titian or Vandyke.

Whatever in painting or sculpture expresses human feeling— or character, which is only a certain state of feeling grown habitual —may be called, according to circumstances, the poetry or the eloquence of the painter's or the sculptor's art: the poetry, if the feeling declares itself by such signs as escape from us when we are unconscious of being seen; the oratory, if the signs are those we use for the purpose of voluntary communication.

The narrative style answers to what is called historical painting, which it is the fashion among connoisseurs to treat as the climax of the pictorial art. That it is the most difficult branch of the art, we do not doubt, because, in its perfection, it includes the perfection of all the other branches; as, in like manner, an epic poem, though, in so far as it is epic (i.e., narrative), it is not poetry at all, is yet esteemed the greatest effort of poetic genius, because there is no kind whatever of poetry which may not appropriately find a place in it. But an historical picture as such, that is, as the representation of an incident, must necessarily, as it seems to us, be poor and ineffective. The narrative powers of painting are extremely limited. Scarcely any picture, scarcely even any series of pictures, tells its own story without the aid of an interpreter. But it is the single figures, which, to us, are the great charm even of an historical picture. It is in these that the power of the art is really seen. In the attempt to narrate, visible and permanent signs are too far behind the fugitive audible ones, which follow so fast one after another; while the faces and figures in a narrative picture, even though they be Titian's, stand still. Who would not prefer one "Virgin and Child" of Raphael to all the pictures which Rubens, with his fat, frouzy Dutch Venuses, ever painted?—though Rubens, besides excelling almost everyone in his mastery over the mechanical parts of his art, often shows real genius in *grouping* his figures, the peculiar problem of historical painting. But then, who, except a mere student of drawing and coloring, ever cared to look twice at any of the figures themselves? The power of painting lies in poetry, of which Rubens had not the slightest tincture, not in narrative, wherein he might have excelled.

2. J. W. M. Turner (1775–1851), English landscape painter.

The single figures, however, in an historical picture, are rather the eloquence of painting than the poetry. They mostly (unless they are quite out of place in the picture) express the feelings of one person as modified by the presence of others. Accordingly, the minds whose bent leads them rather to eloquence than to poetry rush to historical painting. The French painters, for instance, seldom attempt, because they could make nothing of, single heads, like those glorious ones of the Italian masters with which they might feed themselves day after day in their own Louvre. They must all be historical; and they are, almost to a man, attitudinizers. If we wished to give any young artist the most impressive warning our imagination could devise against that kind of vice in the pictorial which corresponds to rant in the histrionic art, we would advise him to walk once up and once down the gallery of the Luxembourg.[3] Every figure in French painting or statuary seems to be showing itself off before spectators. They are not poetical, but in the worst style of corrupted eloquence.

1833, 1859

From Coleridge[1]

The name of Coleridge is one of the few English names of our time which are likely to be oftener pronounced, and to become symbolical of more important things, in proportion as the inward workings of the age manifest themselves more and more in outward facts. Bentham[2] excepted, no Englishman of recent date has left his impress so deeply in the opinions and mental tendencies of those among us who attempt to enlighten their practice by philosophical meditation. If it be true, as Lord Bacon affirms, that a knowledge of the speculative opinions of the men between twenty and thirty years of age is the great source of political prophecy, the existence of Coleridge will show itself by no slight or ambiguous traces in the coming history of our country; for no one has contributed more to shape the opinions of those among its younger men, who can be said to have opinions at all.

The influence of Coleridge, like that of Bentham, extends far beyond those who share in the peculiarities of his religious or philosophical creed. He has been the great awakener in this country of the spirit of philosophy, within the bounds of traditional opinions. He has been, almost as truly as Bentham, "the great questioner of things established";[3] for a questioner needs not necessarily

3. A palace in Paris, where paintings of scenes from French history were exhibited.
1. In his *Autobiography* Mill discusses Samuel Taylor Coleridge as a poet. In the present essay he discusses Coleridge as a political and religious philosopher whose conversation and writings on conservatism had a profound influence on Mill's contemporaries in the 1820's and 1830's.
2. Jeremy Bentham (1748–1832), originator of Utilitarian theories of politics and ethics. In 1838 Mill had published an important essay assessing Bentham's influence as a philosopher for which the essay on Coleridge is a companion piece.
3. A quotation from Mill's essay on Bentham.

be an enemy. By Bentham, beyond all others, men have been led to ask themselves, in regard to any ancient or received opinion, Is it true? and by Coleridge, What is the meaning of it? The one took his stand *outside* the received opinion, and surveyed it as an entire stranger to it: the other looked at it from within, and endeavored to see it with the eyes of a believer in it; to discover by what apparent facts it was at first suggested, and by what appearances it has ever since been rendered continually credible— has seemed, to a succession of persons, to be a faithful interpretation of their experience. Bentham judged a proposition true or false as it accorded or not with the result of his own inquiries; and did not search very curiously into what might be meant by the proposition, when it obviously did not mean what he thought true. With Coleridge, on the contrary, the very fact that any doctrine had been believed by thoughtful men, and received by whole nations or generations of mankind, was part of the problem to be solved; was one of the phenomena to be accounted for. And, as Bentham's short and easy method of referring all to the selfish interests of aristocracies or priests or lawyers, or some other species of imposters, could not satisfy a man who saw so much farther into the complexities of the human intellect and feelings, he considered the long or extensive prevalence of any opinion as a presumption that it was not altogether a fallacy; that, to its first authors at least, it was the result of a struggle to express in words something which had a reality to them, though perhaps not to many of those who have since received the doctrine by mere tradition. The long duration of a belief, he thought, is at least proof of an adaptation in it to some portion or other of the human mind: and if, on digging down to the root, we do not find, as is generally the case, some truth, we shall find some natural want or requirement of human nature which the doctrine in question is fitted to satisfy; among which wants the instincts of selfishness and of credulity have a place, but by no means an exclusive one. From this difference in the points of view of the two philosophers, and from the too rigid adherence of each to his own, it was to be expected that Bentham should continually miss the truth which is in the traditional opinions, and Coleridge that which is out of them and at variance with them. But it was also likely that each would find, or show the way to finding, much of what the other missed.

It is hardly possible to speak of Coleridge, and his position among his contemporaries, without reverting to Bentham: they are connected by two of the closest bonds of association—resemblance and contrast. It would be difficult to find two persons of philosophic eminence more exactly the contrary of one another. Compare their modes of treatment of any subject, and you might fancy them inhabitants of different worlds. They seem to have scarcely a principle or a premise in common. Each of them sees scarcely any thing but what the other does not see. Bentham would have regarded Coleridge with a peculiar measure of the good-humored contempt with which he was accustomed to regard all modes of philosophizing different from his own. Coleridge would probably have made Bentham one of the exceptions to the enlarged and liberal appreciation which (to the credit of *his* mode of philosophizing) he extended to most thinkers of any eminence from whom he differed. But contraries, as logicians say, are but *quae in eodem genere maxime distant*—the things which are farthest from one another in the same kind. These two agreed in being the men, who, in their age and country, did most to enforce, by precept and example, the necessity of a philosophy. They agreed in making it their occupation to recall opinions to first principles; taking no proposition for granted without examining into the grounds of it, and ascertaining that it possessed the kind and degree of evidence suitable to its nature. They agreed in recognizing that sound theory is the only foundation for sound practice; and that whoever despises theory, let him give himself what airs of wisdom he may, is self-convicted of being a quack. If a book were to be compiled containing all the best things ever said on the rule-of-thumb school of political craftsmanship, and on the insufficiency for practical purposes of what the mere practical man calls experience, it is difficult to say whether the collection would be more indebted to the writings of Bentham or of Coleridge. They agreed, too, in perceiving that the groundwork of all other philosophy must be laid in the philosophy of the mind. To lay this foundation deeply and strongly, and to raise a superstructure in accordance with it, were the objects to which their lives were devoted. They employed, indeed, for the most part, different materials; but as the materials of both were real observations, the genuine product of experience, the results will, in the end, be found, not hostile, but supplementary, to one another. Of their methods of philosophizing, the same thing may be said: they were different, yet both were legitimate logical processes. In every respect, the two men are each other's "completing counterpart": the strong points of each correspond to the weak points of the other. Whoever could master the premises and combine the methods of both would possess the entire English philosophy of his age. Coleridge used to say that every one is born either a Platonist or an Aristotelian: it may be similarly affirmed that every Englishman of the present day is by implication either a Benthamite or a Coleridgian; holds views of human affairs which can only be proved true on the principles either of Bentham or of Coleridge. * * *

From On·Liberty

From *Chapter III. Of Individuality as One of the Elements of Well-Being*

* * * Few persons, out of Germany, even comprehend the meaning of the doctrine which Wilhelm von Humboldt, so eminent both as a savant and as a politician, made the text of a treatise— that "the end of man, or that which is prescribed by the eternal or immutable dictates of reason, and not suggested by vague and transient desires, is the highest and most harmonious development of his powers to a complete and consistent whole"; that, therefore, the object "towards which every human being must ceaselessly direct his efforts, and on which especially those who design to in- fluence their fellow men must ever keep their eyes, is the indi- viduality of power and development"; that for this there are two requisites, "freedom, and variety of situations"; and that from the union of these arise "individual vigor and manifold diversity," which combine themselves in "originality."[1]

Little, however, as people are accustomed to a doctrine like that of Von Humboldt, and surprising as it may be to them to find so high a value attached to individuality, the question, one must nevertheless think, can only be one of degree. No one's idea of ex- cellence in conduct is that people should do absolutely nothing but copy one another. No one would assert that people ought not to put into their mode of life, and into the conduct of their concerns, any impress whatever of their own judgment, or of their own indi- vidual character. On the other hand, it would be absurd to pretend that people ought to live as if nothing whatever had been known in the world before they came into it; as if experience had as yet done nothing towards showing that one mode of existence, or conduct, is preferable to another. Nobody denies that people should be so taught and trained in youth, as to know and benefit by the ascer- tained results of human experience. But it is the privilege and proper condition of a human being, arrived at the maturity of his faculties, to use and interpret experience in his own way. It is for him to find out what part of recorded experience is properly ap- plicable to his own circumstances and character. The traditions and customs of other people are, to a certain extent, evidence of what their experience has taught *them*; presumptive evidence, and as such, have a claim to his deference: but, in the first place, their experience may be too narrow; or they may not have interpreted it rightly. Secondly, their interpretation of experience may be

1. From *The Sphere and Duties of Government*, by Baron Wilhelm von Humboldt (1767–1835), Prussian statesman and man of letters. Orig- inally written in 1791, this treatise was first published in Germany in 1852 and was translated into English in 1854.

correct, but unsuitable to him. Customs are made for customary circumstances, and customary characters; and his circumstances or his character may be uncustomary. Thirdly, though the customs be both good as customs, and suitable to him, yet to conform to custom, merely *as* custom, does not educate or develop in him any of the qualities which are the distinctive endowment of a human being. The human faculties of perception, judgment, discriminative feeling, mental activity, and even moral preference are exercised only in making a choice. He who does anything because it is the custom makes no choice. He gains no practice either in discerning or in desiring what is best. The mental and moral, like the muscular powers, are improved only by being used. The faculties are called into no exercise by doing a thing merely because others do it, no more than by believing a thing only because others believe it. If the grounds of an opinion are not conclusive to the person's own reason, his reason cannot be strengthened, but is likely to be weakened, by his adopting it: and if the inducements to an act are not such as are consentaneous[2] to his own feelings and character (where affection, or the rights of others, are not concerned) it is so much done towards rendering his feelings and character inert and torpid, instead of active and energetic.

He who lets the world, or his own portion of it, choose his plan of life for him has no need of any other faculty than the apelike one of imitation. He who chooses his plan for himself employs all his faculties. He must use observation to see, reasoning and judgment to foresee, activity to gather materials for decision, discrimination to decide, and when he has decided, firmness and self-control to hold to his deliberate decision. And these qualities he requires and exercises exactly in proportion as the part of his conduct which he determines according to his own judgment and feelings is a large one. It is possible that he might be guided in some good path, and kept out of harm's way, without any of these things. But what will be his comparative worth as a human being? It really is of importance, not only what men do, but also what manner of men they are that do it. Among the works of man, which human life is rightly employed in perfecting and beautifying, the first in importance surely is man himself. Supposing it were possible to get houses built, corn grown, battles fought, causes tried, and even churches erected and prayers said, by machinery—by automatons in human form—it would be a considerable loss to exchange for these automatons even the men and women who at present inhabit the more civilized parts of the world, and who assuredly are but starved specimens of what nature can and will produce. Human nature is not a machine to be built after a model, and set to do exactly the work prescribed for it, but a tree, which requires to grow and develop itself on all sides, according to the tendency of the inward forces

2. Agreeable.

which make it a living thing.

It will probably be conceded that it is desirable people should exercise their understandings, and that an intelligent following of custom, or even occasionally an intelligent deviation from custom, is better than a blind and simply mechanical adhesion to it. To a certain extent it is admitted that our understanding should be our own: but there is not the same willingness to admit that our desires and impulses should be our own likewise; or that to possess impulses of our own, and of any strength, is anything but a peril and a snare. Yet desires and impulses are as much a part of a perfect human being, as beliefs and restraints: and strong impulses are only perilous when not properly balanced; when one set of aims and inclinations is developed into strength, while others, which ought to coexist with them, remain weak and inactive. It is not because men's desires are strong that they act ill; it is because their consciences are weak. There is no natural connection between strong impulses and a weak conscience. The natural connection is the other way. To say that one person's desires and feelings are stronger and more various than those of another is merely to say that he has more of the raw material of human nature, and is therefore capable, perhaps of more evil, but certainly of more good. Strong impulses are but another name for energy. Energy may be turned to bad uses; but more good may always be made of an energetic nature than of an indolent and impassive one. Those who have most natural feeling are always those whose cultivated feelings may be made the strongest. The same strong susceptibilities which make the personal impulses vivid and powerful are also the source from whence are generated the most passionate love of virture, and the sternest self-control. It is through the cultivation of these that society both does its duty and protects its interests: not by rejecting the stuff of which heroes are made, because it knows not how to make them. A person whose desires and impulses are his own—are the expression of his own nature, as it has been developed and modified by his own culture—is said to have a character. One whose desires and impulses are not his own, has no character, no more than a steam engine has a character. If, in addition to being his own, his impulses are strong, and are under the government of a strong will, he has an energetic character. Whoever thinks that individuality of desires and impulses should not be encouraged to unfold itself must maintain that society has no need of strong natures—is not the better for containing many persons who have much character—and that a high general average of energy is not desirable.

In some early states of society, these forces might be, and were, too much ahead of the power which society then possessed of disciplining and controlling them. There has been a time when the element of spontaneity and individuality was in excess, and the social principle had a hard struggle with it. The difficulty then was to induce men of strong bodies or minds to pay obedience to any rules which required them to control their impulses. To overcome this difficulty, law and discipline, like the Popes struggling against the Emperors, asserted a power over the whole man, claiming to control all his life in order to control his character—which society had not found any other sufficient means of binding. But society has now fairly got the better of individuality; and the danger which threatens human nature is not the excess, but the deficiency, of personal impulses and preferences. Things are vastly changed, since the passions of those who were strong by station or by personal endowment were in a state of habitual rebellion against laws and ordinances, and required to be rigorously chained up to enable the persons within their reach to enjoy any particle of security. In our times, from the highest class of society down to the lowest, everyone lives as under the eye of a hostile and dreaded censorship. Not only in what concerns others, but in what concerns only themselves, the individual or the family do not ask themselves—what do I prefer? or, what would suit my character and disposition? or, what would allow the best and highest in me to have fair play, and enable it to grow and thrive? They ask themselves, what is suitable to my position? what is usually done by persons of my station and pecuniary circumstances? or (worse still) what is usually done by persons of a station and circumstances superior to mine? I do not mean that they choose what is customary, in preference to what suits their own inclination. It does not occur to them to have any inclination, except for what is customary. Thus the mind itself is bowed to the yoke: even in what people do for pleasure, conformity is the first thing thought of; they like in crowds; they exercise choice only among things commonly done: peculiarity of taste, eccentricity of conduct, are shunned equally with crimes: until by dint of not following their own nature, they have no nature to follow: their human capacities are withered and starved: they become incapable of any strong wishes or native pleasures, and are generally without either opinions or feelings of home growth, or properly their own. Now is this, or is it not, the desirable condition of human nature?

It is so, on the Calvinistic theory. According to that, the one great offense of man is self-will. All the good of which humanity is capable is comprised in obedience. You have no choice; thus you must do, and no otherwise: "whatever is not a duty is a sin." Human nature being radically corrupt, there is no redemption for anyone until human nature is killed within him. To one holding this theory of life, crushing out any of the human faculties, capacities, and susceptibilities is no evil: man needs no capacity but that of surrendering himself to the will of God: and if he uses any of his faculties for any other purpose but to do that supposed will more effectually, he is better without them. This is the theory of Calvinism; and it is held, in a mitigated form, by many who do not consider themselves Calvinists; the mitigation consisting in giving a less ascetic interpretation to the alleged will of God; asserting it to be his will that mankind should gratify some of their inclinations; of course not in the manner they themselves prefer, but in the way of obedience, that is, in a way prescribed to them by authority; and, therefore, by the necessary conditions of the case, the same for all.

In some such insidious form there is at present a strong tendency to this narrow theory of life, and to the pinched and hidebound type of human character which it patronizes. Many persons, no doubt, sincerely think that human beings thus cramped and dwarfed are as their Maker designed them to be; just as many have thought that trees are a much finer thing when clipped into pollards,[3] or cut out into figures of animals, than as nature made them. But if it be any part of religion to believe that man was made by a good Being, it is more consistent with that faith to believe that this Being gave all human faculties that they might be cultivated and unfolded, not rooted out and consumed, and that he takes delight in every nearer approach made by his creatures to the ideal conception embodied in them, every increase in any of their capabilities of comprehension, of action, or of enjoyment. There is a different type of human excellence from the Calvinistic; a conception of humanity as having its nature bestowed on it for other purposes than merely to be abnegated. "Pagan self-assertion" is one of the elements of human worth, as well as "Christian self-denial."[4] There is a Greek ideal of self-development, which the Platonic and Christian ideal of self-government blends with, but does not supersede. It may be better to be a John Knox than an Alcibiades, but it is better to be a Pericles than either;[5] nor would a Pericles, if we had one in these days, be without anything good which belonged to John Knox.

It is not by wearing down into uniformity all that is individual in themselves, but by cultivating it and calling it forth, within the limits imposed by the rights and interests of others, that human beings become a noble and beautiful object of contemplation; and as the works partake the character of those who do them, by the same process human life also becomes rich, diversified, and animating, furnishing more abundant aliment to high thoughts and elevating feelings, and strengthening the tie which binds every individual to the race, by making the race infinitely better worth belonging to. In proportion to the development of his individuality, each person becomes more valuable to himself, and is therefore capable of being more valuable to others. There is a greater fullness

3. Trees that acquire an artificial shape by being cut back so as to produce a mass of dense foliage.
4. From the *Essays* (1848) of John Sterling, a minor writer and friend of Thomas Carlyle's.
5. John Knox (1505–72) was the stern Scottish Calvinist reformer; Alcibiades (450–404 B.C.) was a dissolute Athenian commander, and Pericles (500–429 B.C.) was a model statesman in Athens.

of life about his own existence, and when there is more life in the units there is more in the mass which is composed of them. As much compression as is necessary to prevent the stronger specimens of human nature from encroaching on the rights of others cannot be dispensed with; but for this there is ample compensation even in the point of view of human development. The means of development which the individual loses by being prevented from gratifying his inclinations to the injury of others are chiefly obtained at the expense of the development of other people. And even to himself there is a full equivalent in the better development of the social part of his nature, rendered possible by the restraint put upon the selfish part. To be held to rigid rules of justice for the sake of others develops the feelings and capacities which have the good of others for their object. But to be restrained in things not affecting their good, by their mere displeasure, develops nothing valuable, except such force of character as may unfold itself in resisting the restraint. If acquiesced in, it dulls and blunts the whole nature. To give any fair play to the nature of each, it is essential that different persons should be allowed to lead different lives. In proportion as this latitude has been exercised in any age, has that age been noteworthy to posterity. Even despotism does not produce its worst effects, so long as individuality exists under it; and whatever crushes individuality is despotism, by whatever name it may be called, and whether it professes to be enforcing the will of God or the injunctions of men.

Having said that Individuality is the same thing with development, and that it is only the cultivation of individuality which produces, or can produce, well-developed human beings, I might here close the argument: for what more or better can be said of any condition of human affairs than that it brings human beings themselves nearer to the best thing they can be? or what worse can be said of any obstruction to good than that it prevents this? Doubtless, however, these considerations will not suffice to convince those who most need convincing; and it is necessary further to show that these developed human beings are of some use to the undeveloped—to point out to those who do not desire liberty, and would not avail themselves of it, that they may be in some intelligible manner rewarded for allowing other people to make use of it without hindrance.

In the first place, then, I would suggest that they might possibly learn something from them. It will not be denied by anybody, that originality is a valuable element in human affairs. There is always need of persons not only to discover new truths, and point out when what were once truths are true no longer, but also to commence new practices, and set the example of more enlightened conduct, and better taste and sense in human life. This cannot well be gainsaid by anybody who does not believe that the world has already attained perfection in all its ways and practices. It is true that this benefit is not capable of being rendered by everybody alike: there are but few persons, in comparison with the whole of mankind, whose experiments, if adopted by others, would be likely to be any improvement on established practice. But these few are the salt of the earth; without them, human life would become a stagnant pool. Not only is it they who introduce good things which did not before exist; it is they who keep the life in those which already existed. If there were nothing new to be done, would human intellect cease to be necessary? Would it be a reason why those who do the old things should forget why they are done, and do them like cattle, not like human beings? There is only too great a tendency in the best beliefs and practices to degenerate into the mechanical; and unless there were a succession of persons whose ever-recurring originality prevents the grounds of those beliefs and practices from becoming merely traditional, such dead matter would not resist the smallest shock from anything really alive, and there would be no reason why civilization should not die out, as in the Byzantine Empire. Persons of genius, it is true, are, and are always likely to be, a small minority; but in order to have them, it is necessary to preserve the soil in which they grow. Genius can only breathe freely in an *atmosphere* of freedom. Persons of genius are, *ex vi termini*,[6] *more* individual than any other people—less capable, consequently, of fitting themselves, without hurtful compression, into any of the small number of molds which society provides in order to save its members the trouble of forming their own character. If from timidity they consent to be forced into one of these molds, and to let all that part of themselves which cannot expand under the pressure remain unexpanded, society will be little the better for their genius. If they are of a strong character, and break their fetters, they become a mark for the society which has not succeeded in reducing them to commonplace, to point at with solemn warning as "wild," "erratic," and the like; much as if one should complain of the Niagara River for not flowing smoothly between its banks like a Dutch canal.

I insist thus emphatically on the importance of genius, and the necessity of allowing it to unfold itself freely both in thought and in practice, being well aware that no one will deny the position in theory, but knowing also that almost everyone, in reality, is totally indifferent to it. People think genius a fine thing if it enables a man to write an exciting poem, or paint a picture. But in its true sense, that of originality in thought and action, though no one says that it is not a thing to be admired, nearly all, at heart, think that they can do very well without it. Unhappily this is too natural to be wondered at. Originality is the one thing which unoriginal minds cannot feel the use of. They cannot see what it is to do for

6. Latin for "by force of the term," i.e., by definition.

them: how should they? If they could see what it would do for them, it would not be originality. The first service which originality has to render them is that of opening their eyes: which being once fully done, they would have a chance of being themselves original. Meanwhile, recollecting that nothing was ever yet done which some-one was not the first to do, and that all good things which exist are the fruits of originality, let them be modest enough to believe that there is something still left for it to accomplish, and assure them-selves that they are more in need of originality, the less they are conscious of the want.

In sober truth, whatever homage may be professed, or even paid, to real or supposed mental superiority, the general tendency of things throughout the world is to render mediocrity the ascendant power among mankind. In ancient history, in the middle ages, and in a diminishing degree through the long transition from feudality to the present time, the individual was a power in himself; and if he had either great talents or a high social position, he was a con-siderable power. At present individuals are lost in the crowd. In politics it is almost a triviality to say that public opinion now rules the world. The only power deserving the name is that of masses, and of governments while they make themselves the organ of the tend-encies and instincts of masses. This is as true in the moral and social relations of private life as in public transactions. Those whose opinions go by the name of public opinion, are not always the same sort of public: in America they are the whole white population; in England, chiefly the middle class. But they are always a mass, that is to say, collective mediocrity. And what is a still greater novelty, the mass do not now take their opinions from dignitaries in Church or State, from ostensible leaders, or from books. Their thinking is done for them by men much like themselves, addressing them or speaking in their name, on the spur of the moment, through the newspapers. I am not complaining of all this. I do not assert that anything better is compatible, as a general rule, with the present low state of the human mind. But that does not hinder the govern-ment of mediocrity from being mediocre government. No govern-ment by a democracy or a numerous aristocracy, either in its political acts or in the opinions, qualities, and tone of mind which it fosters, ever did or could rise above mediocrity, except in so far as the sovereign Many have let themselves be guided (which in their best times they always have done) by the counsels and influence of a more highly gifted and instructed One or Few. The initiation of all wise or noble things, comes and must come from individuals; generally at first from some one individual. The honor and glory of the average man is that he is capable of following that initiative; that he can respond internally to wise and noble things, and be led to them with his eyes open. I am not countenancing the sort of "hero worship" which applauds the strong man of genius for forcibly seizing on the government of the world and making it do his bidding in spite of itself. All he can claim is freedom to point out the way. The power of compelling others into it is not only inconsistent with the freedom and development of all the rest, but corrupting to the strong man himself. It does seem, however, that when the opinions of masses of merely average men are everywhere become or becoming the dominant power, the counterpoise and corrective to that tendency would be the more and more pronounced individuality of those who stand on the higher eminences of thought. It is in these circumstances most especially that exceptional individuals, instead of being deterred, should be encouraged in acting differently from the mass. In other times there was no advantage in their doing so, unless they acted not only differently, but better. In this age, the mere example of nonconformity, the mere refusal to bend the knee to custom, is itself a service. Precisely because the tyranny of opinion is such as to make eccentricity a reproach, it is desirable, in order to break through that tyranny, that people should be eccentric. Eccentricity has always abounded when and where strength of character has abounded; and the amount of eccentricity in a society has generally been proportional to the amount of genius, mental vigor, and moral courage which it contained. That so few now dare to be eccentric marks the chief danger of the time. * * *

There is one characteristic of the present direction of public opinion, peculiarly calculated to make it intolerant of any marked demonstration of individuality. The general average of mankind are not only moderate in intellect, but also moderate in inclinations: they have no tastes or wishes strong enough to incline them to do anything unusual, and they consequently do not understand those who have, and class all such with the wild and intemperate whom they are accustomed to look down upon. Now, in addition to this fact which is general, we have only to suppose that a strong movement has set in towards the improvement of morals, and it is evident what we have to expect. In these days such a movement has set in; much has actually been effected in the way of increased regularity of conduct, and discouragement of excesses; and there is a philanthropic spirit abroad, for the exercise of which there is no more inviting field than the moral and prudential improvement of our fellow creatures. These tendencies of the times cause the public to be more disposed than at most former periods to prescribe general rules of conduct, and endeavor to make everyone conform to the approved standard. And that standard, express or tacit, is to desire nothing strongly. Its ideal of character is to be without any marked character; to maim by compression, like a Chinese lady's foot, every part of human nature which stands out prominently, and tends to make the person markedly dissimilar in outline to commonplace humanity.

As is usually the case with ideals which exclude one half of what is desirable, the present standard of approbation produces only an inferior imitation of the other half. Instead of great energies guided by vigorous reason, and strong feelings strongly controlled by a conscientious will, its result is weak feelings and weak energies, which therefore can be kept in outward conformity to rule without any strength either of will or reason. Already energetic characters on any large scale are becoming merely traditional. There is now scarcely any outlet for energy in this country except business. The energy expended in this may still be regarded as considerable. What little is left from that employment, is expended on some hobby; which may be a useful, even a philanthropic hobby, but is always some one thing, and generally a thing of small dimensions. The greatness of England is now all collective: individually small, we only appear capable of anything great by our habit of combining; and with this our moral and religious philanthropies are perfectly contented. But it was men of another stamp than this that made England what it has been; and men of another stamp will be needed to prevent its decline.

The despotism of custom is everywhere the standing hindrance to human advancement, being in unceasing antagonism to that disposition to aim at something better than customary, which is called, according to circumstances, the spirit of liberty, or that of progress or improvement. The spirit of improvement is not always a spirit of liberty, for it may aim at forcing improvements on an unwilling people; and the spirit of liberty, in so far as it resists such attempts, may ally itself locally and temporarily with the opponents of improvement; but the only unfailing and permanent source of improvement is liberty, since by it there are as many possible independent centers of improvement as there are individuals. The progressive principle, however, in either shape, whether as the love of liberty or of improvement, is antagonistic to the sway of Custom, involving at least emancipation from that yoke; and the contest between the two constitutes the chief interest of the history of mankind. The greater part of the world has, properly speaking, no history, because the depotism of Custom is complete. This is the case over the whole East. Custom is there, in all things, the final appeal; justice and right mean conformity to custom; the argument of custom no one, unless some tyrant intoxicated with power, thinks of resisting. And we see the result. Those nations must once have had originality; they did not start out of the ground populous, lettered, and versed in many of the arts of life; they made themselves all this, and were then the greatest and most powerful nations of the world. What are they now? The subjects or dependants of tribes whose forefathers wandered in the forests when theirs had magnificent palaces and gorgeous temples, but over whom custom exercised only a divided rule with liberty and progress. A people, it appears, may be progressive for a certain length of time, and then stop: when does it stop? When it ceases to possess individuality. If a similar change should befall the nations of Europe, it will not be in exactly the same shape: the despotism of custom with which these nations are threatened is not precisely stationariness. It proscribes singularity, but it does not preclude change, provided all change together. We have discarded the fixed costumes of our forefathers; everyone must still dress like other people, but the fashion may change once or twice a year. We thus take care that when there is change it shall be for change's sake, and not from any idea of beauty or convenience; for the same idea of beauty or convenience would not strike all the world at the same moment, and be simultaneously thrown aside by all at another moment. But we are progressive as well as changeable: we continually make new inventions in mechanical things, and keep them until they are again superseded by better; we are eager for improvement in politics, in education, even in morals, though in this last our idea of improvement chiefly consists in persuading or forcing other people to be as good as ourselves. It is not progress that we object to; on the contrary, we flatter ourselves that we are the most progressive people who ever lived. It is individuality that we war against: we should think we had done wonders if we had made ourselves all alike; forgetting that the unlikeness of one person to another is generally the first thing which draws the attention of either to the imperfection of his own type, and the superiority of another, or the possibility, by combining the advantages of both, of producing something better than either. We have a warning example in China—a nation of much talent, and, in some respects, even wisdom, owing to the rare good fortune of having been provided at an early period with a particularly good set of customs, the work, in some measure, of men to whom even the most enlightened European must accord, under certain limitations, the title of sages and philosophers. They are remarkable, too, in the excellence of their apparatus for impressing, as far as possible, the best wisdom they possess upon every mind in the community, and securing that those who have appropriated most of it shall occupy the posts of honor and power. Surely the people who did this have discovered the secret of human progressiveness, and must have kept themselves steadily at the head of the movement of the world. On the contrary, they have become stationary—have remained so for thousands of years; and if they are ever to be farther improved, it must be by foreigners. They have succeeded beyond all hope in what English philanthropists are so industriously working at—in making a people all alike, all governing their thoughts and conduct by the same maxims and rules; and these are the fruits. The modern regime of public opinion is, in an unorganized form, what the Chinese educational and political systems are in an organized; and unless individuality shall be able successfully to assert itself against this yoke, Europe, notwithstanding its noble antecedents and its professed Christianity, will tend to become another China. * * *

1859

From The Subjection of Women

The object of this Essay is to explain as clearly as I am able, the grounds of an opinion which I have held from the very earliest period when I had formed an opinion at all on social or political matters, and which, instead of being weakened or modified, has been constantly growing stronger by the progress of reflection and the experience of life: That the principle which regulates the existing social relations between the two sexes—the legal subordination of one sex to the other—is wrong in itself, and now one of the chief hindrances to human improvement; and that it ought to be replaced by a principle of perfect equality, admitting no power or privilege on the one side, nor disability on the other.

* * *

Some will object, that a comparison cannot fairly be made between the government of the male sex and the forms of unjust power[1] which I have adduced in illustration of it, since these are arbitrary, and the effect of mere usurpation, while it on the contrary is natural. But was there ever any domination which did not appear natural to those who possessed it? There was a time when the division of mankind into two classes, a small one of masters and a numerous one of slaves, appeared, even to the most cultivated minds, to be a natural, and the only natural, condition of the human race. No less an intellect, and one which contributed no less to the progress of human thought, than Aristotle, held this opinion without doubt or misgiving; and rested it on the same premises on which the same assertion in regard to the dominion of men over women is usually based, namely that there are different natures among mankind, free natures, and slave natures; that the Greeks were of a free nature, the barbarian races of Thracians and Asiatics of a slave nature. But why need I go back to Aristotle? Did not the slaveowners of the Southern United States maintain the same doctrine, with all the fanaticism with which men cling to the theories that justify their passions and legitimate their personal interests? Did they not call heaven and earth to witness that the dominion of the white man over the black is natural, that the black race is by nature incapable of freedom, and marked out for slavery? some even going so far as to say that the freedom of manual laborers is an

---

1. As examples of unjust power Mill had cited the forceful control of slaves by slave-owners or of nations by military despots.

unnatural order of things anywhere. Again, the theorists of absolute monarchy have always affirmed it to be the only natural form of government; issuing from the patriarchal, which was the primitive and spontaneous form of society, framed on the model of the paternal, which is anterior to society itself, and, as they contend, the most natural authority of all. * * * So true is it that unnatural generally means only uncustomary, and that everything which is usual appears natural. The subjection of women to men being a universal custom, any departure from it quite naturally appears unnatural. But how entirely, even in this case, the feeling is dependent on custom, appears by ample experience. Nothing so much astonishes the people of distant parts of the world, when they first learn anything about England, as to be told that it is under a queen: the thing seems to them so unnatural as to be almost incredible. To Englishmen this does not seem in the least degree unnatural, because they are used to it; but they do feel it unnatural that women should be soldiers or members of parliament. In the feudal ages, on the contrary, war and politics were not thought unnatural to women, because not unusual; it seemed natural that women of the privileged classes should be of manly character, inferior in nothing but bodily strength to their husbands and fathers. The independence of women seemed rather less unnatural to the Greeks than to other ancients, on account of the fabulous Amazons (whom they believed to be historical), and the partial example afforded by the Spartan women; who, though no less subordinate by law than in other Greek states, were more free in fact, and being trained to bodily exercises in the same manner with men, gave ample proof that they were not naturally disqualified for them. There can be little doubt that Spartan experience suggested to Plato, among many other of his doctrines, that of the social and political equality of the two sexes.[2]

But, it will be said, the rule of men over women differs from all these others in not being a rule of force: it is accepted voluntarily; women make no complaint, and are consenting parties to it. In the first place, a great number of women do not accept it. Ever since there have been women able to make their sentiments known by their writings (the only mode of publicity which society permits to them), an increasing number of them have recorded protests against their present social condition: and recently many thousands of them, headed by the most eminent women known to the public, have petitioned Parliament for their admission to the Parliamentary Suffrage. The claim of women to be educated as solidly, and in the same branches of knowledge, as men, is urged with growing intensity, and with a great prospect of success; while the demand for their admission into professions and occupations hitherto closed against

2. See Plato, *The Republic*, V.

them, becomes every year more urgent. Though there are not in this country, as there are in the United States, periodical Conventions and an organized party to agitate for the Rights of Women,[3] there is a numerous and active Society organized and managed by women, for the more limited object of obtaining the political franchise. Nor is it only in our own country and in America that women are beginning to protest, more or less collectively, against the disabilities under which they labor. France, and Italy, and Switzerland, and Russia now afford examples of the same thing. How many more women there are who silently cherish similar aspirations, no one can possibly know; but there are abundant tokens how many *would* cherish them, were they not so strenuously taught to repress them as contrary to the proprieties of their sex. * * *

All causes, social and natural, combine to make it unlikely that women should be collectively rebellious to the power of men. They are so far in a position different from all other subject classes, that their masters require something more from them than actual service. Men do not want solely the obedience of women, they want their sentiments. All men, except the most brutish, desire to have, in the woman most nearly connected with them, not a forced slave but a willing one, not a slave merely, but a favorite. They have therefore put everything in practice to enslave their minds. The masters of all other slaves rely, for maintaining obedience, on fear; either fear of themselves, or religious fears. The masters of women wanted more than simple obedience, and they turned the whole force of education to effect their purpose. All women are brought up from the very earliest years in the belief that their ideal of character is the very opposite to that of men; not self-will, and government by self-control, but submission, and yielding to the control of others. All the moralities tell them that it is the duty of women, and all the current sentimentalities that it is their nature, to live for others; to make complete abnegation of themselves, and to have no life but in their affections. And by their affections are meant the only ones they are allowed to have—those to the men with whom they are connected, or to the children who constitute an additional and indefeasible tie between them and a man. When we put together three things—first, the natural attraction between opposite sexes; secondly, the wife's entire dependence on the husband, every privilege or pleasure she has being either his gift, or depending entirely on his will; and lastly, that the principal object of human pursuit, consideration, and all objects of social ambition, can in general be sought or obtained by her only through him, it would be a miracle if the object of being attractive to men had not become the polar star of feminine education and formation of character. And,

3. Such as the Women's Rights Convention held at Worcester, Massachusetts in October, 1850, which had occasioned an essay by Mill's wife entitled *Enfranchisement of Women* (1851).

this great means of influence over the minds of women having been acquired, an instinct of selfishness made men avail themselves of it to the utmost as a means of holding women in subjection, by representing to them meekness, submissiveness, and resignation of all individual will into the hands of a man, as an essential part of sexual attractiveness. Can it be doubted that any of the other yokes which mankind have succeeded in breaking, would have subsisted till now if the same means had existed, and had been as sedulously used, to bow down their minds to it? If it had been made the object of the life of every young plebeian to find personal favor in the eyes of some patrician, of every young serf with some seigneur; if domestication with him, and a share of his personal affections, had been held out as the prize which they all should look out for, the most gifted and aspiring being able to reckon on the most desirable prizes; and if, when this prize had been obtained, they had been shut out by a wall of brass from all interests not centering in him, all feelings and desires but those which he shared or inculcated; would not serfs and seigneurs, plebeians and patricians, have been as broadly distinguished at this day as men and women are? and would not all but a thinker here and there, have believed the distinction to be a fundamental and unalterable fact in human nature?

The preceding considerations are amply sufficient to show that custom, however universal it may be, affords in this case no presumption, and ought not to create any prejudice, in favor of the arrangements which place women in social and political subjection to men. But I may go farther, and maintain that the course of history, and the tendencies of progressive human society, afford not only no presumption in favor of this system of inequality of rights, but a strong one against it; and that, so far as the whole course of human improvement up to this time, the whole stream of modern tendencies, warrants any inference on the subject, it is, that this relic of the past is discordant with the future, and must necessarily disappear.

For, what is the peculiar character of the modern world—the difference which chiefly distinguishes modern institutions, modern social ideas, modern life itself, from those of times long past? It is, that human beings are no longer born to their place in life, and chained down by an inexorable bond to the place they are born to, but are free to employ their faculties, and such favorable chances as offer, to achieve the lot which may appear to them most desirable. * * *

On the other point which is involved in the just equality of women, their admissibility to all the functions and occupations hitherto retained as the monopoly of the stronger sex, I should anticipate no difficulty in convincing anyone who has gone with me on the subject of the equality of women in the family. I believe that their disabilities elsewhere are only clung to in order to maintain their subordination in domestic life; because the generality of the male sex cannot yet tolerate the idea of living with an equal. Were it not for that, I think that almost everyone, in the existing state of opinion in politics and political economy, would admit the injustice of excluding half the human race from the greater number of lucrative occupations, and from almost all high social functions; ordaining from their birth either that they are not, and cannot by any possibility become, fit for employments which are legally open to the stupidest and basest of the other sex, or else that however fit they may be, those employments shall be interdicted to them, in order to be preserved for the exclusive benefit of males. In the last two centuries, when (which was seldom the case) any reason beyond the mere existence of the fact was thought to be required to justify the disabilities of women, people seldom assigned as a reason their inferior mental capacity; which, in times when there was a real trial of personal faculties (from which all women were not excluded) in the struggles of public life, no one really believed in. The reason given in those days was not women's unfitness, but the interest of society, by which was meant the interest of men: just as the *raison d'état*, meaning the convenience of the government, and the support of existing authority, was deemed a sufficient explanation and excuse for the most flagitious crimes. In the present day, power holds a smoother language, and whomsoever it oppresses, always pretends to do so for their own good: accordingly, when anything is forbidden to women, it is thought necessary to say, and desirable to believe, that they are incapable of doing it, and that they depart from their real path of success and happiness when they aspire to it. But to make this reason plausible (I do not say valid), those by whom it is urged must be prepared to carry it to a much greater length than anyone ventures to do in the face of present experience. It is not sufficient to maintain that women on the average are less gifted than men on the average, with certain of the higher mental faculties, or that a smaller number of women than of men are fit for occupations and functions of the highest intellectual character. It is necessary to maintain that no women at all are fit for them, and that the most eminent women are inferior in mental faculties to the most mediocre of the men on whom those functions at present devolve. For if the performance of the function is decided either by competition, or by any mode of choice which secures regard to the public interest, there needs to be no apprehension that any important employments will fall into the hands of women inferior to average men, or to the average of their male competitors. The only result would be that there would be fewer women than men in such employments; a result certain to happen in any case, if only from the preference always likely to be felt by the majority of women for the one vocation in which there is

nobody to compete with them. Now, the most determined deprecia-
tor of women will not venture to deny, that when we add the experience of recent times to that of ages past, women, and not a few
merely, but many women, have proved themselves capable of everything, perhaps without a single exception, which is done by men,
and of doing it successfully and creditably. The utmost that can be
said is, that there are many things which none of them have succeeded in doing as well as they have been done by some men—
many in which they have not reached the very highest rank. But
there are extremely few, dependent only on mental faculties, in
which they have not attained the rank next to the highest. Is not
this enough, and much more than enough, to make it a tyranny to
them, and a detriment to society, that they should not be allowed
to compete with men for the exercise of these functions? Is it not a
mere truism to say, that such functions are often filled by men far
less fit for them than numbers of women, and who would be beaten
by women in any fair field of competition? What difference does it
make that there may be men somewhere, fully employed about
other things, who may be still better qualified for the things in
question than these women? Does not this take place in all compe-
titions? Is there so great a superfluity of men fit for high duties,
that society can afford to reject the service of any competent
person? Are we so certain of always finding a man made to our
hands for any duty or function of social importance which falls
vacant, that we lose nothing by putting a ban upon one-half of
mankind, and refusing beforehand to make their faculties available,
however distinguished they may be? And even if we could do without them, would it be consistent with justice to refuse to them their
fair share of honor and distinction, or to deny to them the equal
moral right of all human beings to choose their occupation (short
of injury to others) according to their own preferences, at their own
risk? Nor is the injustice confined to them: it is shared by those
who are in a position to benefit by their services. To ordain that any
kind of persons shall not be physicians, or shall not be advocates, or
shall not be members of parliament, is to injure not them only, but
all who employ physicians or advocates, or elect members of parliament, and who are deprived of the stimulating effect of greater
competition on the exertions of the competitors, as well as
restricted to a narrower range of individual choice.

* * *

There remains a question, not of less importance than those
already discussed, and which will be asked the most importunately
by those opponents whose conviction is somewhat shaken on the
main point. What good are we to expect from the changes proposed in our customs and institutions? Would mankind be at all
better off if women were free? If not, why disturb their minds, and

attempt to make a social revolution in the name of an abstract right?

* * *

To which let me first answer, the advantage of having the most universal and pervading of all human relations regulated by justice instead of injustice. The vast amount of this gain to human nature, it is hardly possible, by any explanation or illustration, to place in a stronger light than it is placed by the bare statement, to anyone who attaches a moral meaning to words. All the selfish propensities, the self-worship, the unjust self-preference, which exist among mankind, have their source and root in, and derive their principal nourishment from, the present constitution of the relation between men and women. Think what it is to a boy, to grow up to manhood in the belief that without any merit or any exertion of his own, though he may be the most frivolous and empty or the most ignorant and stolid of mankind, by the mere fact of being born a male he is by right the superior of all and every one of an entire half of the human race: including probably some whose real superiority to himself he has daily or hourly occasion to feel; but even if in his whole conduct he habitually follows a woman's guidance, still, if he is a fool, she thinks that of course she is not, and cannot be, equal in ability and judgment to himself; and if he is not a fool, he does worse—he sees that she is superior to him, and believes that, notwithstanding her superiority, he is entitled to command and she is bound to obey. What must be the effect on his character, of this lesson?[4] And men of the cultivated classes are often not aware how deeply it sinks into the immense majority of male minds. For, among right-feeling and well-bred people, the inequality is kept as much as possible out of sight; above all, out of sight of the children. As much obedience is required from boys to their mother as to their father: they are not permitted to domineer over their sisters, nor are they accustomed to see these postponed to them, but the contrary; the compensations of the chivalrous feeling being made prominent, while the servitude which requires them is kept in the background. Well brought-up youths in the higher classes thus often escape the bad influences of the situation in their early years, and only experience them when, arrived at manhood, they fall under the dominion of facts as they really exist. Such people are little aware, when a boy is differently brought up, how early the notion of his inherent superiority to a girl arises in his mind; how it grows with his growth and strengthens with his strength; how it is inoculated by one schoolboy upon another; how early the youth thinks himself superior to his mother, owing her perhaps forbearance, but no real respect; and

---

4. Cf. Thackeray on such marriages: "it is worse still, for the man himself perhaps, whenever in his dim comprehension the idea dawns that his slave and drudge yonder is, in truth, his superior." —*Henry Esmond*, I.xi.

how sublime and sultan-like a sense of superiority he feels, above all, over the woman whom he honors by admitting her to a partnership of his life. Is it imagined that all this does not pervert the whole manner of existence of the man, both as an individual and as a social being? It is an exact parallel to the feeling of a hereditary king that he is excellent above others by being born a king, or a noble by being born a noble. The relation between husband and wife is very like that between lord and vassal, except that the wife is held to more unlimited obedience than the vassal was. However the vassal's character may have been affected, for better and for worse, by his subordination, who can help seeing that the lord's was affected greatly for the worse? whether he was led to believe that his vassals were really superior to himself, or to feel that he was placed in command over people as good as himself, for no merits of labors of his own, but merely for having, as Figaro says, taken the trouble to be born. The self-worship of the monarch, or of the feudal superior, is matched by the self-worship of the male. Human beings do not grow up from childhood in the possession of unearned distinctions, without pluming themselves upon them. Those whom privileges not acquired by their merit, and which they feel to be disproportioned to it, inspire with additional humility, are always the few, and the best few. The rest are only inspired with pride, and the worst sort of pride, that which values itself upon accidental advantages, not of its own achieving. Above all, when the feeling of being raised above the whole of the other sex is combined with personal authority over one individual among them; the situation, if a school of conscientious and affectionate forbearance to those whose strongest points of character are conscience and affection, is to men of another quality a regularly constituted Academy or Gymnasium for training them in arrogance and overbearingness; which vices, if curbed by the certainty of resistance in their intercourse with other men, their equals, break out towards all who are in a position to be obliged to tolerate them, and often revenge themselves upon the unfortunate wife for the involuntary restraint which they are obliged to submit to elsewhere.

The example afforded, and the education given to the sentiments, by laying the foundation of domestic existence upon a relation contradictory to the first principles of social justice, must, from the very nature of man, have a perverting influence of such magnitude, that it is hardly possible with our present experience to raise our imaginations to the conception of so great a change for the better as would be made by its removal. All that education and civilization are doing to efface the influences on character of the law of force, and replace them by those of justice, remains merely on the surface, as long as the citadel of the enemy is not attacked. The principle of the modern movement in morals and politics, is that conduct, and conduct alone, entitles to respect: that not what men are, but what they do, constitutes their claim to deference; that, above all, merit, and not birth, is the only rightful claim to power and authority. If no authority, not in its nature temporary, were allowed to one human being over another, society would not be employed in building up propensities with one hand which it has to curb with the other. The child would really, for the first time in man's existence on earth, be trained in the way he should go, and when he was old there would be a chance that he would not depart from it. But so long as the right of the strong to power over the weak rules in the very heart of society, the attempt to make the equal right of the weak the principle of its outward actions will always be an uphill struggle; for the law of justice, which is also that of Christianity, will never get possession of men's inmost sentiments; they will be working against it, even when bending to it.

The second benefit to be expected from giving to women the free use of their faculties, by leaving them the free choice of their employments, and opening to them the same field of occupation and the same prizes and encouragements as to other human beings, would be that of doubling the mass of mental faculties available for the higher service of humanity. Where there is now one person qualified to benefit mankind and promote the general improvement, as a public teacher, or an administrator of some branch of public or social affairs, there would then be a chance of two. Mental superiority of any kind is at present everywhere so much below the demand; there is such a deficiency of persons competent to do excellently anything which it requires any considerable amount of ability to do; that the loss to the world, by refusing to make use of one-half of the whole quantity of talent it possesses, is extremely serious. It is true that this amount of mental power is not totally lost. Much of it is employed, and would in any case be employed, in domestic management, and in the few other occupations open to women and from the remainder indirect benefit is in many individual cases obtained, through the personal influence of individual women over individual men. But these benefits are partial; their range is extremely circumscribed; and if they must be admitted, on the one hand, as a deduction from the amount of fresh social power that would be acquired by giving freedom to one-half of the whole sum of human intellect, there must be added, on the other, the benefit of the stimulus that would be given to the intellect of men by the competition; or (to use a more true expression) by the necessity that would be imposed on them of deserving precedency before they could expect to obtain it.

* * *

When we consider the positive evil caused to the disqualified half of the human race by their disqualification—first in the loss of the most inspiriting and elevating kind of personal enjoyment, and next in the weariness, disappointment, and profound dissatisfaction with life, which are so often the substitute for it; one feels that among all the lessons which men require for carrying on the struggle against the inevitable imperfections of their lot on earth, there is no lesson which they more need, than not to add to the evils which nature inflicts, by their jealous and prejudiced restrictions on one another. Their vain fears only substitute other and worse evils for those which they are idly apprehensive of: while every restraint on the freedom of conduct of any of their human fellow creatures, (otherwise than by making them responsible for any evil actually caused by it), dries up *pro tanto*[5] the principal fountain of human happiness, and leaves the species less rich, to an inappreciable degree, in all that makes life valuable to the individual human being.

From Autobiography

From *Chapter* V. A Crisis in My Mental History.
One Stage Onward

For some years after this time[1] I wrote very little, and nothing regularly, for publication: and great were the advantages which I derived from the intermission. It was of no common importance to me, at this period, to be able to digest and mature my thoughts for my own mind only, without any immediate call for giving them out in print. Had I gone on writing, it would have much disturbed the important transformation in my opinions and character, which took place during those years. The origin of this transformation, or at least the process by which I was prepared for it, can only be explained by turning some distance back.

From the winter of 1821, when I first read Bentham, and especially from the commencement of the *Westminster Review*, I had what might truly be called an object in life; to be a reformer of the world. My conception of my own happiness was entirely identified with this object. The personal sympathies I wished for were those of fellow laborers in this enterprise. I endeavored to pick up as many flowers as I could by the way; but as a serious and permanent personal satisfaction to rest upon, my whole reliance was placed on this; and I was accustomed to felicitate myself on the certainty of a happy life which I enjoyed, through placing my happiness in something durable and distant, in which some progress might be always making, while it could never be exhausted by complete attainment. This did very well for several years, during which the general improvement going on in the world and the idea of myself as engaged with others in struggling to promote it, seemed enough to fill up an interesting and animated existence. But the time came

5. By so much.
1. 1828. Mill had been contributing articles to the *Westminster Review*.

when I awakened from this as from a dream. It was in the autumn of 1826. I was in a dull state of nerves, such as everybody is occasionally liable to; unsusceptible to enjoyment or pleasurable excitement; one of those moods when what is pleasure at other times becomes insipid or indifferent; the state, I should think, in which converts to Methodism usually are, when smitten by their first "conviction of sin." In this frame of mind it occurred to me to put the question directly to myself: "Suppose that all your objects in life were realized; that all the changes in institutions and opinions which you are looking forward to could be completely effected at this very instant: would this be a great joy and happiness to you?" And an irrepressible self-consciousness distinctly answered, "No!" At this my heart sank within me: the whole foundation on which my life was constructed fell down. All my happiness was to have been found in the continual pursuit of this end. The end had ceased to charm, and how could there ever again be any interest in the means? I seemed to have nothing left to live for.

At first I hoped that the cloud would pass away of itself; but it did not. A night's sleep, the sovereign remedy for the smaller vexations of life, had no effect on it. I awoke to a renewed consciousness of the woeful fact. I carried it with me into all companies, into all occupations. Hardly anything had power to cause me even a few minutes' oblivion of it. For some months the cloud seemed to grow thicker and thicker. The lines in Coleridge's *Dejection*—I was not then acquainted with them—exactly describe my case:

> A grief without a pang, void, dark and drear,
> A drowsy, stifled, unimpassioned grief,
> Which finds no natural outlet or relief
> In word, or sigh, or tear.[2]

In vain I sought relief from my favorite books; those memorials of past nobleness and greatness from which I had always hitherto drawn strength and animation. I read them now without feeling, or with the accustomed feeling minus all its charm; and I became persuaded that my love of mankind, and of excellence for its own sake, had worn itself out. I sought no comfort by speaking to others of what I felt. If I had loved anyone sufficiently to make confiding my griefs a necessity, I should not have been in the condition I was. I felt, too, that mine was not an interesting, or in any way respectable distress. There was nothing in it to attract sympathy. Advice, if I had known where to seek it, would have been most precious. The words of Macbeth to the physician[3] often occurred to my thoughts. But there was no one on whom I could build the faintest hope of such assistance. My father, to whom it would have been natural to me to have recourse in any practical difficulties, was the last person to whom, in such a case as this, I

2. *Dejection: An Ode*, lines 21–24.
3. "Canst thou not minister to a

mind   diseas'd * * * ?"   (*Macbeth*
V.iii.40–44).

looked for help. Everything convinced me that he had no knowledge of any such mental state as I was suffering from, and that even if he could be made to understand it, he was not the physician who could heal it. My education, which was wholly his work, had been conducted without any regard to the possibility of its ending in this result; and I saw no use in giving him the pain of thinking that his plans had failed, when the failure was probably irremediable, and, at all events, beyond the power of *his* remedies. Of other friends, I had at that time none to whom I had any hope of making my condition intelligible. It was however abundantly intelligible to myself; and the more I dwelt upon it, the more hopeless it appeared.

My course of study had led me to believe that all mental and moral feelings and qualities, whether of a good or of a bad kind, were the results of association; that we love one thing, and hate another, take pleasure in one sort of action or contemplation, and pain in another sort, through the clinging of pleasurable or painful ideas to those things, from the effect of education or of experience. As a corollary from this, I had always heard it maintained by my father, and was myself convinced, that the object of education should be to form the strongest possible associations of the salutary class; associations of pleasure with all things beneficial to the great whole, and of pain with all things hurtful to it. This doctrine appeared inexpugnable; but it now seemed to me, on retrospect, that my teachers had occupied themselves but superficially with the means of forming and keeping up these salutary associations. They seemed to have trusted altogether to the old familiar instruments, praise and blame, reward and punishment. Now, I did not doubt that by these means, begun early, and applied unremittingly, intense associations of pain and pleasure, especially of pain, might be created, and might produce desires and aversions capable of lasting undiminished to the end of life. But there must always be something artificial and casual in associations thus produced. The pains and pleasures thus forcibly associated with things are not connected with them by any natural tie; and it is therefore, I thought, essential to the durability of these associations that they should have beome so intense and inveterate as to be practically indissoluble, before the habitual exercise of the power of analysis had commenced. For I now saw, or thought I saw, what I had always before received with incredulity—that the habit of analysis has a tendency to wear away the feelings: as indeed it has, when no other mental habit is cultivated, and the analyzing spirit remains without its natural complements and correctives. The very excellence of analysis (I argued) is that it tends to weaken and undermine whatever is the result of prejudice; that it enables us mentally to separate ideas which have only casually clung together: and no associations whatever could ultimately resist this dissolving force, were it not that we owe to analysis our clearest knowledge of the permanent sequences in nature; the real connections between Things, not dependent on our will and feelings; natural laws, by virtue of which, in many cases, one thing is inseparable from another in fact; which laws, in proportion as they are clearly perceived and imaginatively realized, cause our ideas of things which are always joined together in Nature to cohere more and more closely in our thoughts. Analytic habits may thus even strengthen the associations between causes and effects, means and ends, but tend altogether to weaken those which are, to speak familiarly, a *mere* matter of feeling. They are therefore (I thought) favorable to prudence and clear-sightedness, but a perpetual worm at the root both of the passions and of the virtues; and, above all, fearfully undermine all desires, and all pleasures, which are the effects of association, that is, according to the theory I held, all except the purely physical and organic; of the entire insufficiency of which to make life desirable, no one had a stronger conviction than I had. These were the laws of human nature, by which, as it seemed to me, I had been brought to my present state. All those to whom I looked up were of opinion that the pleasure of sympathy with human beings, and the feelings which made the good of others, and especially of mankind on a large scale, the object of existence, were the greatest and surest sources of happiness. Of the truth of this I was convinced, but to know that a feeling would make me happy if I had it, did not give me the feeling. My education, I thought, had failed to create these feelings in sufficient strength to resist the dissolving influence of analysis, while the whole course of my intellectual cultivation had made precocious and premature analysis the inveterate habit of my mind. I was thus, as I said to myself, left stranded at the commencement of my voyage, with a well-equipped ship and a rudder, but no sail; without any real desire for the ends which I had been so carefully fitted out to work for: no delight in virtue, or the general good, but also just as little in anything else. The fountains of vanity and ambition seemed to have dried up within me, as completely as those of benevolence. I had had (as I reflected) some gratification of vanity at too early an age: I had obtained some distinction, and felt myself of some importance, before the desire of distinction and of importance had grown into a passion: and little as it was which I had attained, yet having been attained too early, like all pleasures enjoyed too soon, it had made me *blasé* and indifferent to the pursuit. Thus neither selfish nor unselfish pleasures were pleasures to me. And there seemed no power in nature sufficient to begin the formation of my character anew, and create in a mind now irretrievably analytic, fresh associations of pleasure with any of the objects of human desire.

These were the thoughts which mingled with the dry heavy dejection of the melancholy winter of 1826–7. During this time I was not incapable of my usual occupations. I went on with them mechanically, by the mere force of habit. I had been so drilled in a certain sort of mental exercise that I could still carry it on when all the spirit had gone out of it. I even composed and spoke several speeches at the debating society, how, or with what degree of success, I know not. Of four years continual speaking at that society, this is the only year of which I remember next to nothing. Two lines of Coleridge, in whom alone of all writers I have found a true description of what I felt, were often in my thoughts, not at this time (for I had never read them), but in a later period of the same mental malady:

> Work without hope draws nectar in a sieve,
> And hope without an object cannot live.[4]

In all probability my case was by no means so peculiar as I fancied it, and I doubt not that many others have passed through a similar state; but the idiosyncrasies of my education had given to the general phenomenon a special character, which made it seem the natural effect of causes that it was hardly possible for time to remove. I frequently asked myself if I could, or if I was bound to go on living, when life must be passed in this manner. I generally answered to myself, that I did not think I could possibly bear it beyond a year. When, however, not more than half that duration of time had elapsed, a small ray of light broke in upon my gloom. I was reading, accidentally, Marmontel's *Mémoires*,[5] and came to the passage which relates his father's death, the distressed position of the family, and the sudden inspiration by which he, then a mere boy, felt and made them feel that he would be everything to them—would supply the place of all that they had lost. A vivid conception of that scene and its feelings came over me, and I was moved to tears. From this moment my burden grew lighter. The oppression of the thought that all feeling was dead within me was gone. I was no longer hopeless: I was not a stock or a stone. I had still, it seemed, some of the material out of which all worth of character, and all capacity for happiness, are made. Relieved from my ever present sense of irremediable wretchedness, I gradually found that the ordinary incidents of life could again give me some pleasure; that I could again find enjoyment, not intense, but sufficient for cheerfulness, in sunshine and sky, in books, in conversation, in public affairs; and that there was, once more, excitement, though of a moderate kind, in exerting myself for my opinions, and for the public good. Thus the cloud gradually drew off, and I again enjoyed life: and though I had several relapses, some of which lasted many months, I never again was as miserable as I had been.

The experiences of this period had two very marked effects on

---

4. From Coleridge's short poem *Work Without Hope.*   5. J. F. Marmontel (1723–99), whose *Mémoires* were published in 1804.

my opinions and character. In the first place, they led me to adopt a theory of life, very unlike that on which I had before acted, and having much in common with what at that time I certainly had never heard of, the anti-self-consciousness theory of Carlyle.[6] I never, indeed, wavered in the conviction that happiness is the test of all rules of conduct, and the end of life. But I now thought that this end was only to be attained by not making it the direct end. Those only are happy (I thought) who have their minds fixed on some object other than their own happiness; on the happiness of others, on the improvement of mankind, even on some art or pursuit, followed not as a means, but as itself an ideal end. Aiming thus at something else, they find happiness by the way. The enjoyments of life (such was now my theory) are sufficient to make it a pleasant thing, when they are taken *en passant*, without being made a principal object. Once make them so, and they are immediately felt to be insufficient. They will not bear a scrutinizing examination. Ask yourself whether you are happy, and you cease to be so. The only chance is to treat, not happiness, but some end external to it, as the purpose of life. Let your self-consciousness, your scrutiny, your self-interrogation exhaust themselves on that; and if otherwise fortunately circumstanced you will inhale happiness with the air you breathe, without dwelling on it or thinking about it, without either forestalling it in imagination, or putting it to flight by fatal questioning. This theory now became the basis of my philosophy of life. And I still hold to it as the best theory for all those who have but a moderate degree of sensibility and of capacity for enjoyment, that is, for the great majority of mankind.

The other important change which my opinions at this time underwent was that I, for the first time, gave its proper place, among the prime necessities of human well-being, to the internal culture of the individual. I ceased to attach almost exclusive importance to the ordering of outward circumstances, and the training of the human being for speculation and for action.

I had now learnt by experience that the passive susceptibilities needed to be cultivated as well as the active capacities, and required to be nourished and enriched as well as guided. I did not, for an instant, lose sight of, or undervalue, that part of the truth which I had seen before; I never turned recreant to intellectual culture, or ceased to consider the power and practice of analysis as an essential condition both of individual and of social improvement. But I thought that it had consequences which required to be corrected, by joining other kinds of cultivation with it. The maintenance of a due balance among the faculties now seemed to me of primary importance. The cultivation of the feelings became one of the cardinal points in my ethical and philosophical creed. And my thoughts and inclinations turned in an increasing degree toward

6. See Carlyle's *Characteristics* and Chapter IX of *Sartor Resartus*, "The Everlasting Yea."

whatever seemed capable of being instrumental to that object.

I now began to find meaning in the things which I had read or heard about the importance of poetry and art as instruments of human culture. But it was some time longer before I began to know this by personal experience. The only one of the imaginative arts in which I had from childhood taken great pleasure was music; the best effect of which (and in this it surpasses perhaps every other art) consists in exciting enthusiasm; in winding up to a high pitch those feelings of an elevated kind which are already in the character, but to which this excitement gives a glow and a fervor, which, though transitory at its utmost height, is precious for sustaining them at other times. This effect of music I had often experienced; but like all my pleasurable susceptibilities it was suspended during the gloomy period. I had sought relief again and again from this quarter, but found none. After the tide had turned, and I was in process of recovery, I had been helped forward by music, but in a much less elevated manner. I at this time first became acquainted with Weber's *Oberon*,[7] and the extreme pleasure which I drew from its delicious melodies did me good, by showing me a source of pleasure to which I was as susceptible as ever. The good, however, was much impaired by the thought that the pleasure of music (as is quite true of such pleasure as this was, that of mere tune) fades with familiarity, and requires either to be revived by intermittence, or fed by continual novelty. And it is very characteristic both of my then state, and of the general tone of my mind at this period of my life, that I was seriously tormented by the thought of the exhaustibility of musical combinations. The octave consists only of five tones and two semitones, which can be put together in only a limited number of ways, of which but a small proportion are beautiful: most of these, it seemed to me, must have been already discovered, and there could not be room for a long succession of Mozarts and Webers, to strike out, as these had done, entirely new and surpassingly rich veins of musical beauty. This source of anxiety may, perhaps, be thought to resemble that of the philosophers of Laputa,[8] who feared lest the sun should be burnt out. It was, however, connected with the best feature in my character, and the only good point to be found in my very unromantic and in no way honorable distress. For though my dejection, honestly looked at, could not be called other than egotistical, produced by the ruin, as I thought, of my fabric of happiness, yet the destiny of mankind in general was ever in my thoughts, and could not be separated from my own. I felt that the flaw in my life must be a flaw in life itself; that the question was whether, if the reformers of society and government could succeed in their objects, and every person in the

7. A romantic opera composed by Carl Maria von Weber (1786–1826).   8. See *Gulliver's Travels*, Part III.

community were free and in a state of physical comfort, the pleasures of life, being no longer kept up by struggle and privation, would cease to be pleasures. And I felt that unless I could see my way to some better hope than this for human happiness in general, my dejection must continue; but that if I could see such an outlet, I should then look on the world with pleasure; content as far as I was myself concerned, with any fair share of the general lot.

This state of my thoughts and feelings made the fact of my reading Wordsworth for the first time (in the autumn of 1828), an important event in my life. I took up the collection of his poems from curiosity, with no expectation of mental relief from it, though I had before resorted to poetry with that hope. In the worst period of my depression, I had read through the whole of Byron (then new to me), to try whether a poet, whose peculiar department was supposed to be that of the intenser feelings, could rouse any feeling in me. As might be expected, I got no good from this reading, but the reverse. The poet's state of mind was too like my own. His was the lament of a man who had worn out all pleasures, and who seemed to think that life, to all who possess the good things of it, must necessarily be the vapid, uninteresting thing which I found it. His Harold and Manfred had the same burden on them which I had; and I was not in a frame of mind to desire any comfort from the vehement sensual passion of his Giaours, or the sullenness of his Laras.[9] But while Byron was exactly what did not suit my condition, Wordsworth was exactly what did. I had looked into *The Excursion*[1] two or three years before, and found little in it; and I should probably have found as little had I read it at this time. But the miscellaneous poems, in the two-volume edition of 1815 (to which little of value was added in the latter part of the author's life), proved to be the precise thing for my mental wants at that particular juncture.

In the first place, these poems addressed themselves powerfully to one of the strongest of my pleasurable susceptibilities, the love of rural objects and natural scenery; to which I had been indebted not only for much of the pleasure of my life, but quite recently for relief from one of my longest relapses into depression. In this power of rural beauty over me, there was a foundation laid for taking pleasure in Wordsworth's poetry; the more so, as his scenery lies mostly among mountains, which, owing to my early Pyrenean excursion,[2] were my ideal of natural beauty. But Wordsworth would never have had any great effect on me, if he had merely placed

9. The heroes of some of Byron's early poems were usually gloomy and self-preoccupied. Mill refers here to *Childe Harold's Pilgrimage* (1812–18), *Manfred* (1817), *The Giaour* (1813) and *Lara* (1814).
1. A long meditative poem by Words-

worth, published in 1814.
2. At 15 Mill had been deeply affected by the landscape of the Pyrenees in Spain, a mountainous region which also made a strong impression upon Tennyson.

before me beautiful pictures of natural scenery. Scott does this still better than Wordsworth, and a very second-rate landscape does it more effectually than any poet. What made Wordsworth's poems a medicine for my state of mind, was that they expressed, not mere outward beauty, but states of feeling, and of thought colored by feeling, under the excitement of beauty. They seemed to be the very culture of the feelings, which I was in quest of. In them I seemed to draw from a source of inward joy, of sympathetic and imaginative pleasure, which could be shared in by all human beings; which had no connection with struggle or imperfection, but would be made richer by every improvement in the physical or social condition of mankind. From them I seemed to learn what would be the perennial sources of happiness, when all the greater evils of life shall have been removed. And I felt myself at once better and happier as I came under their influence. There have certainly been, even in our own age, greater poets than Wordsworth; but poetry of deeper and loftier feeling could not have done for me at that time what his did. I needed to be made to feel that there was real, permanent happiness in tranquil contemplation. Wordsworth taught me this, not only without turning away from, but with a greatly increased interest in the common feelings and common destiny of human beings. And the delight which these poems gave me proved that with culture of this sort, there was nothing to dread from the most confirmed habit of analysis. At the conclusion of the Poems came the famous *Ode*, falsely called Platonic, *Intimations of Immortality*: in which, along with more than his usual sweetness of melody and rhythm, and along with the two passages of grand imagery but bad philosophy so often quoted, I found that he too had had similar experience to mine; that he also had felt that the first freshness of youthful enjoyment of life was not lasting; but that he had sought for compensation, and found it, in the way in which he was now teaching me to find it. The result was that I gradually, but completely, emerged from my habitual depression, and was never again subject to it. I long continued to value Wordsworth less according to his intrinsic merits than by the measure of what he had done for me. Compared with the greatest poets, he may be said to be the poet of unpoetical natures, possessed of quiet and contemplative tastes. But unpoetical natures are precisely those which require poetic cultivation. This cultivation Wordsworth is much more fitted to give than poets who are intrinsically far more poets than he. * * *

1873

ELIZABETH BARRETT BROWNING
(1806–1861)

Until her marriage to Robert Browning when she was 40, Elizabeth Barrett lived at home with her family, where she received a remarkable education, having been tutored in Greek and in classical philosophy. At an early age she began writing poetry (her first volume was printed when she was 13), and by her 30's she had attracted a considerable following among the reading public. Her long poem, *Aurora Leigh* (1857), was a best seller. This story of the experiences of a woman writer, set in Victorian times, is told in a variety of blank verse that makes for fluid narrative, and the poem reads like a novel. Parts of *Aurora Leigh* show the influence of two French women writers admired by the poet, Madame de Staël and George Sand, but overall the poem had distinctive originality. As Cora Kaplan observed in 1978, this poem is the first work in English by a woman author in which the heroine is herself an author.

Most of Elizabeth Barrett's poetry expressed an ardent concern for liberal causes of her day. For example, in 1843, when government investigations had exposed the exploitation of children employed in coal mines and factories, she wrote *The Cry of the Children*, of which the following stanza is typical:

> "For oh," say the children, "we are weary,
>   And we cannot run or leap;
> If we cared for any meadows, it were merely
>   To drop down in them and sleep.
> Our knees tremble sorely in the stooping,
>   We fall upon our faces, trying to go;
> And underneath our heavy eyelids drooping
>   The reddest flower would look as pale as snow.
> For, all day, we drag our burden tiring
>   Through the coal-dark, underground;
>
> Or, all day, we drive the wheels of iron
>   In the factories, round and round."

In later poems she took up the cause of Italian nationalism. Her topical poems, of great reputation in the Victorian age, are now read more for their historical than for their poetic interest. This reservation in no way applies, however, to her *Sonnets from the Portuguese*, a sequence of 44 sonnets in which she recorded the stages of her love for Robert Browning, a sequence she presented under the guise of a translation from the Portuguese language. This volume remains one of the best-known and best-liked love poems in the language.

From Sonnets from the Portuguese

21

Say over again, and yet once over again,
That thou dost love me. Though the word repeated

Should seem "a cuckoo song," as thou dost treat it,
Remember, never to the hill or plain,
Valley and wood, without her cuckoo strain   5
Comes the fresh Spring in all her green completed.
Belovéd, I, amid the darkness greeted
By a doubtful spirit voice, in that doubt's pain
Cry, "Speak once more—thou lovest!" Who can fear
Too many stars, though each in heaven shall roll,   10
Too many flowers, though each shall crown the year?
Say thou dost love me, love me, love me—toll
The silver iterance!—only minding, Dear,
To love me also in silence with thy soul.

22

When our two souls stand up erect and strong,
Face to face, silent, drawing nigh and nigher,
Until the lengthening wings break into fire
At either curvéd point—what bitter wrong
Can the earth do to us, that we should not long   5
Be here contented? Think. In mounting higher,
The angels would press on us and aspire
To drop some golden orb of perfect song
Into our deep, dear silence. Let us stay
Rather on earth, Belovéd—where the unfit   10
Contrarious moods of men recoil away
And isolate pure spirits, and permit
A place to stand and love in for a day,
With darkness and the death-hour rounding it.

32

The first time that the sun rose on thine oath
To love me, I looked forward to the moon
To slacken all those bonds which seemed too soon
And quickly tied to make a lasting troth.
Quick-loving hearts, I thought, may quickly loathe;   5
And, looking on myself, I seemed not one
For such man's love!—more like an out-of-tune
Worn viol, a good singer would be wroth
To spoil his song with, and which, snatched in haste,
Is laid down at the first ill-sounding note.   10
I did not wrong myself so, but I placed
A wrong on *thee*. For perfect strains may float
'Neath master-hands, from instruments defaced—
And great souls, at one stroke, may do and dote.

43

How do I love thee? Let me count the ways.
I love thee to the depth and breadth and height
My soul can reach, when feeling out of sight
For the ends of Being and ideal Grace.
I love thee to the level of everyday's   5
Most quiet need, by sun and candlelight.
I love thee freely, as men strive for Right;

I love thee purely, as they turn from Praise.
I love thee with the passion put to use
In my old griefs, and with my childhood's faith.   10
I love thee with a love I seemed to lose
With my lost saints—I love thee with the breath,
Smiles, tears, of all my life!—and, if God choose,
I shall but love thee better after death.

1850

ALFRED, LORD TENNYSON

(1809–1892)

1830: *Poems, Chiefly Lyrical*.
1833: Death of Arthur Hallam.
1842: *Poems*.
1850: *In Memoriam*. Tennyson appointed poet laureate.
1859: *Idylls of the King* (first four books).

Whether or not Alfred Tennyson was the greatest of the Victorian poets, as affirmed by many critics today, there is no doubt that in his own lifetime he was the most popular of poets. On the bookshelves of almost every family of readers in England and the United States, from 1850 onwards, were the works of a man who had incontestably gained the title that Walt Whitman longed for: "The Poet of the People." Popularity inevitably provided provocation for a reaction in the decades following his death. In the course of repudiating their Victorian predecessors, the Edwardians and Georgians established the fashion of making fun of Tennyson's great achievements. Samuel Butler (1835–1902), who anticipated early 20th-century tastes, has a characteristic entry in his *Notebooks*: "Talking it over, we agreed that Blake was no good because he learnt Italian at 60 in order to study Dante, and we knew Dante was no good because he was so fond of Virgil, and Virgil was no good because Tennyson ran him, and as for Tennyson—well, Tennyson goes without saying." In the second half of the 20th century, Butler's confident assumption that Tennyson's poetry was simply contemptible no longer "goes without saying." The delights to be found in this superb "lord of language"—as Tennyson himself addresses his favorite predecessor, Virgil—have been rediscovered, and Tennyson's stature as one of the major poets of any age has been re-established. In 1892, the year of his death, he himself had made an accurate prophecy of his changing status in his lines on *Poets and Critics*:

> What is true at last will tell:
> Few at first will place thee well;
> Some too low would have thee shine,
> Some too high—no fault of thine—
> Hold thine own, and work thy will!

Like his poetry, Tennyson's life and character have been reassessed in the 20th century. To many of his contemporaries he seemed a remote wizard, secure in his laureate's robes, a man whose life had been sheltered, marred only by the loss of his best friend in youth. During much of his career Tennyson may have been isolated, but his was not a sheltered life in the real sense of the word. Although he grew up in a parsonage, it was not the kind of parsonage one encounters in the novels of Jane Austen. It was a household dominated by frictions and loyalties and broodings over ancestral inheritances, in which the children showed marked strains of instability and eccentricity.

Alfred was the fourth son in a family of twelve children. One of his brothers had to be confined to an insane asylum for life; another was long a victim of the opium habit; another had violent quarrels with his father, who had become a drunkard. This father, the Reverend Dr. George Tennyson, was the eldest son of a wealthy landowner. He had been obliged to become a clergyman, a profession he disliked, because he had been disinherited in favor of his younger brother. George Tennyson therefore settled in a small rectory at Somersby in Lincolnshire where he tutored his sons in classical and modern languages to prepare them for entering the university.

Before leaving this strange household for Cambridge, Alfred had already demonstrated a flair for writing verse—precocious exercises in the manner of Milton or Byron or the Elizabethan dramatists. He had even published a volume in 1827, in collaboration with his brother Charles, *Poems by Two Brothers*. This feat drew him to the attention of a group of gifted undergraduates at Cambridge, the "Apostles," who encouraged him to devote his life to poetry. Up until this time, the young man had known scarcely anyone outside the circle of his own family. Despite his massive frame and powerful physique, he was painfully shy, and the friendships he found at Cambridge, as well as the intellectual and political discussions in which he participated, served to give him confidence and to widen his horizons as a poet. The most important of these friendships was with Arthur Hallam, a leader of the Apostles, who later became engaged to Tennyson's sister. Hallam's sudden death, in 1833, seemed an overwhelming calamity to his friend. Not only the long elegy *In Memoriam* but many of Tennyson's other poems are tributes to this early friendship.

Alfred's career at Cambridge was interrupted and finally broken off in 1831 by family dissensions and financial need, and he returned home to study and practice the craft of poetry. His early volumes (1830 and 1832) were attacked as "obscure" or "affected" by some of the reviewers. Tennyson suffered acutely under hostile criticism, but he also profited from it. His volume of 1842 demonstrated a remarkable advance in taste and technical excellence, and in 1850 he at last attained fame and full critical recognition with *In Memoriam*. In the same year he became poet laureate in succession to Wordsworth. The struggle during the previous twenty years had been made especially painful by the long postponement of his marriage to Emily Sellwood, with whom he had fallen in love in 1836 but could not marry, because of poverty, until 1850.

His life thereafter was a comfortable one. He was as popular as Byron had been, and his fame lasted for much longer. The earnings from his poetry (sometimes exceeding £10,000 a year) enabled him to purchase a house in the country and to enjoy the kind of seclusion he liked. His notoriety was enhanced, like that of G. B. Shaw and Walt Whitman, by his colorful appearance. Huge and shaggy, in cloak and broadbrimmed hat, gruff in manner as a farmer, he impressed everyone as what is called a "character." The pioneer photographer, Julia Cameron, who took magnificent portraits of him, called him "the most beautiful old man on earth." He also had a booming voice, when reading his poetry, that electrified listeners much as Dylan Thomas electrified audiences in the 20th century: "mouthing out his hollow o's and a's, / Deep-chested music." Moreover, for many Victorian readers, he seemed not only a great poetical phrasemaker and a striking individual but also a wise man whose occasional pronouncements on politics or world affairs represented the national voice itself. In 1884 he accepted a peerage. In 1892 he died and was buried in Westminster Abbey.

It is often said that success was bad for Tennyson, and that after *In Memoriam* his poetic power seriously declined. That in his last 42 years certain of his mannerisms became accentuated is true. One of the difficulties of his dignified blank verse was, as he said himself, that it is hard to describe commonplace objects and "at the same time to retain poetical elevation." This difficulty is evident, for example, in *Enoch Arden* (1864), a long blank verse narrative of everyday life in a fishing village, in which a basketful of fish is ornately described as "Enoch's ocean spoil / In ocean-smelling osier." In others of his later poems, those dealing with national affairs, there is also an increased shrillness of tone—a mannerism accentuated by Tennyson's realizing that like Dickens he had a vast public behind him to back up his pronouncements.

It is foolish, however, to try to shelve all of Tennyson's later productions. In 1855 he published his experimental monologue *Maud*, perhaps his finest long poem. In 1859 he published four books of his *Idylls of the King*, a large-scale epic which occupied most of his energies in the second half of his career. About this late poem, completed in twelve books, in 1888, there is less agreement. Some readers consider it to be complacent—mere "lollipops," as Carlyle called it. Yet *Idylls of the King* is not simply a hymn to progress. It records, instead, a cycle of change from a society that has emerged from a wasteland into civilization but which may revert to a wasteland once more. In any event, even if this ambitious epic does not always show Tennyson in his best vein, there is no sign of decline in his late lyrics. The 80-year-old poet who wrote *Crossing the Bar* had certainly not lost his touch.

The problem of Tennyson's development is really of more significance for the period before 1850 rather than afterwards. W. H. Auden has stated that Tennyson had "the finest ear, perhaps, of any English poet." The interesting point is that Tennyson did not "have" such an ear: he developed it. Studies of the original versions of his poems in the 1830 and 1832 volumes demonstrate that not only was his taste uncertain at the outset of his career but that his sense of meter was originally unreliable. The harmonics he was to achieve from 1842 onwards had to be learned just as a pianist with a weak left hand has to overcome his weakness by constant exercise. Like Chaucer or Keats or Pope, Tennyson studied his predecessors assiduously to perfect his technique. Anyone wanting to learn the traditional craft of English verse can study with profit the various stages of revision that such poems as *The Lotos-Eaters* were subjected to by this painstaking and artful poet.

If the early Tennyson was uncertain of meter, he had other skills that were immediately in evidence. One of these was a capacity for linking scenery to states of mind. As early as 1835, J. S. Mill identified the special kind of scene-painting to be found in early poems such as *Mariana*: "* * * not the power of producing that rather vapid species of composition usually termed descriptive poetry * * * but the power of *creating* scenery, in keeping with some state of human feeling so fitted to it as to be the embodied symbol of it, and to summon up the state of feeling itself, with a force not to be surpassed by anything but reality."

A second aspect of Tennyson's early development was his increased preoccupation with problems of his day. If Mill praised his capacity to render landscape, he also urged, in his review, Tennyson's further responsibilities—to "cultivate, and with no half devotion, philosophy as well as poetry." Advice of this kind Tennyson was already predisposed to heed. The death of Hallam, the religious uncertainties which he had himself experienced, together with his own extensive study of writings by geologists, astronomers, and biologists, led him to confront many of the religious issues that bewildered his generation and later generations. The result was *In Memoriam* (1850), a long elegy written over a period of seventeen years, embodying the poet's reflections on man's relation to God and to nature.

Was Tennyson intellectually equipped to deal with the great questions raised in *In Memoriam*? The answer may depend on a reader's religious and philosophical presuppositions. Some, such as T. H. Huxley, considered Tennyson an intellectual giant, a thinker who had mastered the scientific thought of his century and fully confronted the issues it raised. Others dismissed Tennyson, in this phase, as a lightweight. Auden went so far as to call him the "stupidest" of English poets. We might say more accurately that his mind was slow, ponderous, brooding, and we should add that for the composition of *In Memoriam* such qualities of mind were assets, not liabilities. In these terms we can understand when Tennyson's poetry really fails to measure up: it is when he writes of events of the moment over which his thoughts and feelings have had no time to brood. Several of his poems are essentially newspaper pieces. They are Letters to the Editor, in effect, with the ephemeral heat and simplicity we expect of such productions. *The Charge of the Light Brigade*, inspired by a report in *The Times* of a cavalry charge at Balaclava during the Crimean War, is one of the best of his productions in this category.

Tennyson's poems of contemporary events were inevitably popular in his own day. So too were those poems where, as in *Locksley Hall*, he dipped into the future. The technological changes wrought by Victorian inventors and engineers fascinated him. Sometimes they gave him an assurance of human progress as swaggeringly exultant as that of Macaulay. At other times the horrors of industrialism's by-products in the slums, the bloodshed of war, the greed of the newly rich, destroyed his hopes that man was evolving upwards. Such a late poem as *The Dawn* embodies an attitude which he found in Virgil: "Thou majestic in thy sadness at the doubtful doom of human kind."

For despite Tennyson's fascination with technological developments, he was essentially a poet of the countryside, a man whose whole being was conditioned by the recurring rhythms of rural rather than urban life. He had the countryman's awareness of traditional roots and his sense of the past. It is appropriate that most of his best poems are about the past, not about the present or future. The past is his great theme: his own past (as in *In the Valley of Cauteretz*), his country's past (as in *The Revenge*), the past of mankind, the past of the world itself:

> There rolls the deep where grew the tree.
> O earth, what changes hast thou seen!
> There where the long street roars hath been
> The stillness of the central sea.

Tennyson is the first major writer to express this awareness of the vast extent of geological time that has haunted human consciousness since Victorian scientists exposed the history of the earth's crust. In his more usual vein, however, it is the recorded past of mankind that inspires him, the classical past in particular. Classical themes, as Douglas Bush has noted, "generally banished from his mind what was timid, parochial, sentimental * * * and evoked his special gifts and most authentic emotions, his rich and wistful sense of the past, his love of nature, and his power of style."

One returns, finally then, to the question of language. At the time of his death, a critic complained that Tennyson was merely "a discoverer of words rather than of ideas." The same complaint has been made by George Bernard Shaw and others—not about Tennyson but about Shakespeare.

Mariana[1]

"Mariana in the moated grange."
Measure for Measure

With blackest moss the flower plots
    Were thickly crusted, one and all;
The rusted nails fell from the knots
    That held the pear to the gable wall.
The broken sheds looked sad and strange: 5
    Unlifted was the clinking latch;
    Weeded and worn the ancient thatch
Upon the lonely moated grange.
        She only said, "My life is dreary,
            He cometh not," she said;   10
        She said, "I am aweary, aweary,
            I would that I were dead!"

Her tears fell with the dews at even;
    Her tears fell ere the dews were dried;
She could not look on the sweet heaven,   15
    Either at morn or eventide.
After the flitting of the bats,
        When thickest dark did trance[2] the sky,

1. Mariana, in Shakespeare's *Measure for Measure* (III.i.277), waits in a grange (an outlying farmhouse) for her lover who has deserted her.
2. Traverse (noted by R. W. Hill).

She drew her casement curtain by,
And glanced athwart the glooming flats.   20
    She only said, "The night is dreary,
        He cometh not," she said;
    She said, "I am aweary, aweary,
        I would that I were dead!"

Upon the middle of the night,   25
    Waking she heard the nightfowl crow;
The cock sung out an hour ere light;
    From the dark fen the oxen's low
Came to her; without hope of change,
    In sleep she seemed to walk forlorn,   30
    Till cold winds woke the gray-eyed morn
About the lonely moated grange.
    She only said, "The day is dreary,
        He cometh not," she said;
    She said, "I am aweary, aweary,   35
        I would that I were dead!"

About a stonecast from the wall
    A sluice with blackened waters slept,
And o'er it many, round and small,
    The clustered marish-mosses[3] crept.   40
Hard by a poplar shook alway,
    All silver-green with gnarlèd bark:
For leagues no other tree did mark
The level waste, the rounding gray.
    She only said, "My life is dreary,   45
        He cometh not," she said;
    She said, "I am aweary, aweary,
        I would that I were dead!"

And ever when the moon was low,
    And the shrill winds were up and away,   50
In the white curtain, to and fro,
    She saw the gusty shadow sway.
But when the moon was very low,
    And wild winds bound within their cell,[4]
    The shadow of the poplar fell   55
Upon her bed, across her brow.
    She only said, "The night is dreary,
        He cometh not," she said;
    She said, "I am aweary, aweary,
        I would that I were dead!"   60

All day within the dreamy house,
    The doors upon their hinges creaked;
The blue fly sung in the pane; the mouse

---

3. "The little marsh-moss lumps that float on the surface of water" [Tennyson's comment].

4. According to Virgil, Aeolus, god of winds, kept the winds imprisoned in a cave. See *Aeneid*, I, 50–59.

Behind the moldering wainscot shrieked,[5]
Or from the crevice peered about.   65
   Old faces glimmered through the doors,
   Old footsteps trod the upper floors,
Old voices called her from without.
      She only said, "My life is dreary,
         He cometh not," she said;   70
      She said, "I am aweary, aweary,
         I would that I were dead!"

The sparrow's chirrup on the roof,
   The slow clock ticking, and the sound
Which to the wooing wind aloof   75
   The poplar made, did all confound
Her sense; but most she loathed the hour
   When the thick-moted sunbeam lay
   Athwart the chambers, and the day
Was sloping toward his western bower.   80
      Then, said she, "I am very dreary,
         He will not come," she said;
      She wept, "I am aweary, aweary,
         Oh God, that I were dead!"

1830

Sonnet

She took the dappled partridge flecked with blood,
   And in her hand the drooping pheasant bare,
   And by his feet she held the woolly hare,
And like a master painting where she stood,
Looked some new goddess of an English wood.   5
   Nor could I find an imperfection there,
   Nor blame the wanton act that showed so fair—
To me whatever freak[6] she plays is good.
Hers is the fairest Life that breathes with breath,
   And *their* still plumes and azure eyelids closed   10
      Made quiet Death so beautiful to see
That Death lent grace to Life and Life to Death
   And in one image Life and Death reposed,
      To make my love an Immortality.

ca. 1830   1931

The Lady of Shalott

Part I

On either side the river lie
Long fields of barley and of rye,
That clothe the wold[1] and meet the sky;

---

5. Cf. "And a time for the wind * * *
to shake the wainscot where the fieldmouse trots / And to shake the tattered
arras. * * * " (T. S. Eliot, *Four Quar-*

tets: East Coker, lines 11–13).
6. Prank.
1. Rolling plains.

And through the field the road runs by
    To many-towered Camelot;[2]   5
And up and down the people go,
Gazing where the lilies blow[3]
Round an island there below,
    The island of Shalott.

Willows whiten, aspens quiver,   10
Little breezes dusk and shiver
Through the wave that runs forever
By the island in the river
    Flowing down to Camelot.
Four gray walls, and four gray towers,   15
Overlook a space of flowers,
And the silent isle imbowers
    The Lady of Shalott.

By the margin, willow-veiled,
Slide the heavy barges trailed   20
By slow horses; and unhailed
The shallop[4] flitteth silken-sailed
    Skimming down to Camelot:
But who hath seen her wave her hand?
Or at the casement seen her stand?   25
Or is she known in all the land,
    The Lady of Shalott?

Only reapers, reaping early
In among the bearded barley,
Hear a song that echoes cheerly   30
From the river winding clearly,
    Down to towered Camelot;
And by the moon the reaper weary,
Piling sheaves in uplands airy,
Listening, whispers " 'Tis the fairy   35
    Lady of Shalott."

Part II

There she weaves by night and day
A magic web with colors gay.
She has heard a whisper say,
A curse is on her if she stay   40
    To look down to Camelot.
She knows not what the curse may be,
And so she weaveth steadily,
And little other care hath she,
    The Lady of Shalott.   45

2. Legendary city in which King
Arthur's palace was located.
3. Bloom.
4. A light open boat.

And moving through a mirror clear[5]
That hangs before her all the year,
Shadows of the world appear.
There she sees the highway near
     Winding down to Camelot;   50
There the river eddy whirls,
And there the surly village churls,
And the red cloaks of market girls,
     Pass onward from Shalott.

Sometimes a troop of damsels glad,   55
An abbot on an ambling pad,[6]
Sometimes a curly shepherd lad,
Or long-haired page in crimson clad,
     Goes by to towered Camelot;
And sometimes through the mirror blue   60
The knights come riding two and two:
She hath no loyal knight and true,
     The Lady of Shalott.

But in her web she still delights
To weave the mirror's magic sights,   65
For often through the silent nights
A funeral, with plumes and lights
     And music, went to Camelot;
Or when the moon was overhead,
Came two young lovers lately wed: 70
"I am half sick of shadows," said
     The Lady of Shalott.

Part III

A bowshot from her bower eaves,
He rode between the barley sheaves,
The sun came dazzling through the leaves,   75
And flamed upon the brazen greaves[7]
     Of bold Sir Lancelot.
A red-cross knight[8] forever kneeled
To a lady in his shield,
That sparkled on the yellow field,   80
     Beside remote Shalott.

The gemmy bridle glittered free,
Like to some branch of stars we see
Hung in the golden Galaxy.
The bridle bells rang merrily   85
     As he rode down to Camelot;

---

5. Weavers used mirrors, placed facing their looms, in order to see the progress of their work.
6. Easy-paced horse.
7. Armor protecting the leg below the knee.
8. Cf. Spenser's *Faerie Queen* I and III.ii.17–25.

And from his blazoned baldric⁹ slung
A mighty silver bugle hung,
And as he rode his armor rung,
    Beside remote Shalott.   90

All in the blue unclouded weather
Thick-jeweled shone the saddle leather,
The helmet and the helmet-feather
Burned like one burning flame together,
    As he rode down to Camelot;   95
As often through the purple night,
Below the starry clusters bright,
Some bearded meteor, trailing light,
    Moves over still Shalott.

His broad clear brow in sunlight glowed;   100
On burnished hooves his war horse trode;
From underneath his helmet flowed
His coal-black curls as on he rode,
    As he rode down to Camelot.
From the bank and from the river   105
He flashed into the crystal mirror,
"Tirra lirra," by the river
    Sang Sir Lancelot.

She left the web, she left the loom,
She made three paces through the room,   110
She saw the water lily bloom,
She saw the helmet and the plume,
    She looked down to Camelot.
Out flew the web and floated wide;
The mirror cracked from side to side;   115
"The curse is come upon me," cried
    The Lady of Shalott.

Part IV

In the stormy east wind straining,
The pale yellow woods were waning,
The broad stream in his banks complaining,   120
Heavily the low sky raining
    Over towered Camelot;
Down she came and found a boat
Beneath a willow left afloat,
And round about the prow she wrote   125
    The Lady of Shalott.

And down the river's dim expanse
Like some bold seër in a trance,

9. A richly decorated sash worn diagonally across the breast.

Seeing all his own mischance—
With a glassy countenance
    Did she look to Camelot.   130
And at the closing of the day
She loosed the chain, and down she lay;
The broad stream bore her far away,
    The Lady of Shalott.   135

Lying, robed in snowy white
That loosely flew to left and right—
The leaves upon her falling light—
Through the noises of the night
    She floated down to Camelot;   140
And as the boat-head wound along
The willowy hills and fields among,
They heard her singing her last song,
    The Lady of Shalott.

Heard a carol, mournful, holy,   145
Chanted loudly, chanted lowly,
Till her blood was frozen slowly,
And her eyes were darkened wholly,
    Turned to towered Camelot.
For ere she reached upon the tide   150
The first house by the waterside,
Singing in her song she died,
    The Lady of Shalott.

Under tower and balcony,
By garden wall and gallery,
A gleaming shape she floated by,   155
Dead-pale between the houses high,
    Silent into Camelot.
Out upon the wharfs they came,
Knight and burgher, lord and dame,
And round the prow they read her name, 160
    The Lady of Shalott.

Who is this? and what is here?
And in the lighted palace near
Died the sound of royal cheer;
And they crossed themselves for fear,   165
    All the knights at Camelot:
But Lancelot mused a little space;
He said, "She has a lovely face;
God in his mercy lend her grace,
    The Lady of Shalott."   170

1832   1832, 1842

The Lotos-Eaters[1]

"Courage!" he[2] said, and pointed toward the land,
"This mounting wave will roll us shoreward soon."
In the afternoon they came unto a land[3]
In which it seeméd always afternoon.
All round the coast the languid air did swoon,   5
Breathing like one that hath a weary dream.
Full-faced above the valley stood the moon;
And, like a downward smoke, the slender stream
Along the cliff to fall and pause and fall did seem.

A land of streams! some, like a downward smoke,   10
Slow-dropping veils of thinnest lawn,[4] did go;
And some through wavering lights and shadows broke,
Rolling a slumbrous sheet of foam below.
They saw the gleaming river seaward flow
From the inner land; far off, three mountaintops   15
Three silent pinnacles of aged snow,
Stood sunset-flushed; and, dewed with showery drops,
Up-clomb the shadowy pine above the woven copse.

The charméd sunset lingered low adown
In the red West; through mountain clefts the dale   20
Was seen far inland, and the yellow down[5]
Bordered with palm, and many a winding vale
And meadow, set with slender galingale;[6]
A land where all things always seemed the same!
And round about the keel with faces pale,   25
Dark faces pale against that rosy flame,
The mild-eyed melancholy Lotos-eaters came.

Branches they bore of that enchanted stem,
Laden with flower and fruit, whereof they gave
To each, but whoso did receive of them   30
And taste, to him the gushing of the wave
Far far away did seem to mourn and rave
On alien shores; and if his fellow spake,

1. Based on a short episode from the *Odyssey* (IX.82–97) in which the weary Greek veterans of the Trojan War are tempted by a desire to abandon their long voyage homeward. As Odysseus later reported: "On the tenth day we set foot on the land of the lotos-eaters who eat a flowering food. * * * I sent forth certain of my company [who] * * * mixed with the men of the lotos-eaters who * * * gave them of the lotos to taste. Now whosoever of them did eat the honey-sweet fruit of the lotos had no more wish to bring tidings nor to come back, but there he chose to abide * * * forgetful of his homeward way."
Tennyson expands Homer's brief account into an elaborate picture of weariness and the desire for rest and death. The descriptions in the first stanzas are similar to Spenser's *Faerie Queene* (II.vi). The final section derives, in part, from Lucretius' conception of the gods in *De rerum natura*.
2. Odysseus (or Ulysses).
3. The repetition of "land" from line 1 was deliberate; Tennyson said that this "no rhyme" was "lazier" in its effect. Compare "afternoon" (lines 3–4) and the rhyming of "adown" and "down" (lines 19, 21).
4. A fine, thin linen.
5. An open plain on high ground.
6. A plant resembling tall coarse grass.

His voice was thin, as voices from the grave;
And deep-asleep he seemed, yet all awake,　　　　35
And music in his ears his beating heart did make.

They sat them down upon the yellow sand,
Between the sun and moon upon the shore;
And sweet it was to dream of Fatherland,
Of child, and wife, and slave; but evermore　　　　40
Most weary seemed the sea, weary the oar,
Weary the wandering fields of barren foam.
Then some one said, "We will return no more";
And all at once they sang, "Our island home[7]
Is far beyond the wave; we will no longer roam."　　　　45

Choric Song[8]

1

There is sweet music here that softer falls
Than petals from blown roses on the grass,
Or night-dews on still waters between walls
Of shadowy granite, in a gleaming pass;
Music that gentlier on the spirit lies,　　　　50
Than tired eyelids upon tired eyes;[9]
Music that brings sweet sleep down from the blissful skies.
Here are cool mosses deep,
And through the moss the ivies creep,
And in the stream the long-leaved flowers weep,　　　　55
And from the craggy ledge the poppy hangs in sleep.

2

Why are we weighed upon with heaviness,
And utterly consumed with sharp distress,
While all things else have rest from weariness?
All things have rest: why should we toil alone,　　　　60
We only toil, who are the first of things,
And make perpetual moan,
Still from one sorrow to another thrown;
Nor ever fold our wings,
And cease from wanderings,　　　　65
Nor steep our brows in slumber's holy balm;
Nor harken what the inner spirit sings,
"There is no joy but calm!"—
Why should we only toil, the roof and crown of things?[1]

3

Lo! in the middle of the wood,　　　　70
The folded leaf is wooed from out the bud
With winds upon the branch, and there
Grows green and broad, and takes no care,

---

7. Ithaca.
8. Sung by the mariners.
9. Tennyson wanted the word to be pronounced as *tie-yerd* rather than *tier'd* or *tire-èd*, thus "making the word neither monosyllabic or disyllabic, but a dreamy child of the two."

1. Cf.: "Why then dost thou, O man, that of them all / Art Lord, and eke of nature Soveraine, / Wilfully * * * wast thy joyous houres in needlesse paine * * * ?" (Spenser's *Faerie Queene*, II.vi.17).

Sun-steeped at noon, and in the moon
Nightly dew-fed; and turning yellow   75
Falls, and floats adown the air.
Lo! sweetened with the summer light,
The full-juiced apple, waxing over-mellow,
Drops in a silent autumn night.
All its allotted length of days   80
The flower ripens in its place,
Ripens and fades, and falls, and hath no toil,
Fast-rooted in the fruitful soil.

4

Hateful is the dark blue sky,
Vaulted o'er the dark blue sea.
Death is the end of life; ah, why   85
Should life all labor be?
Let us alone. Time driveth onward fast,
And in a little while our lips are dumb.
Let us alone. What is it that will last?   90
All things are taken from us, and become
Portions and parcels of the dreadful past.
Let us alone. What pleasure can we have
To war with evil? Is there any peace
In ever climbing up the climbing wave?   95
All things have rest, and ripen toward the grave
In silence—ripen, fall, and cease:
Give us long rest or death, dark death, or dreamful ease.[2]

5

How sweet it were, hearing the downward stream,
With half-shut eyes ever to seem
Falling asleep in a half-dream!   100
To dream and dream, like yonder amber light,
Which will not leave the myrrh-bush on the height;
To hear each other's whispered speech;
Eating the Lotos day by day,   105
To watch the crisping[3] ripples on the beach,
And tender curving lines of creamy spray;
To lend our hearts and spirits wholly
To the influence of mild-minded melancholy;
To muse and brood and live again in memory,   110
With those old faces of our infancy
Heaped over with a mound of grass,
Two handfuls of white dust, shut in an urn of brass!

6

Dear is the memory of our wedded lives,
And dear the last embraces of our wives   115
And their warm tears; but all hath suffered change;
For surely now our household hearths are cold,
Our sons inherit us, our looks are strange,

---

2. Cf.: "Sleepe after toyle, port after
stormie seas, / Ease after warre, death
after life does greatly please." (*Faerie*
Queene, I.ix.40).
3. Curling.

And we should come like ghosts to trouble joy.
Or else the island princes[4] overbold   120
Have eat our substance, and the minstrel sings
Before them of the ten years' war in Troy,
And our great deeds, as half-forgotten things.
Is there confusion in the little isle?
Let what is broken so remain.   125
The Gods are hard to reconcile;
'Tis hard to settle order once again.
There *is* confusion worse than death,
Trouble on trouble, pain on pain,
Long labor unto aged breath,   130
Sore tasks to hearts worn out by many wars
And eyes grown dim with gazing on the pilot-stars.

7

But, propped on beds of amaranth[5] and moly,
How sweet—while warm airs lull us, blowing lowly—
With half-dropped eyelid still,   135
Beneath a heaven dark and holy,
To watch the long bright river drawing slowly
His waters from the purple hill—
To hear the dewy echoes calling
From cave to cave through the thick-twined vine—   140
To watch the emerald-colored water falling
Through many a woven acanthus[6] wreath divine!
Only to hear and see the far-off sparkling brine,
Only to hear were sweet, stretched out beneath the pine.

8

The Lotos blooms below the barren peak,   145
The Lotos blows by every winding creek;
All day the wind breathes low with mellower tone;
Through every hollow cave and alley lone
Round and round the spicy downs the yellow Lotos dust is blown.
We have had enough of action, and of motion we,   150
Rolled to starboard, rolled to larboard, when the surge was seething
    free,
Where the wallowing monster spouted his foam-fountains in the sea.
Let us swear an oath, and keep it with an equal mind,
In the hollow Lotos land to live and lie reclined
On the hills like Gods together, careless of mankind.   155
For they lie beside their nectar, and the bolts[7] are hurled
Far below them in the valleys, and the clouds are lightly curled
Round their golden houses, girdled with the gleaming world;
Where they smile in secret, looking over wasted lands,
Blight and famine, plague and earthquake, roaring deeps and fiery
    sands,   160
Clanging fights, and flaming towns, and sinking ships, and praying
    hands.

---

4. Penelope's suitors.
5. A legendary unfading flower; "moly": a flower with magical properties mentioned by Homer.

6. A plant resembling a thistle. Its leaves were the model for ornaments on Corinthian columns.
7. Thunderbolts.

But they smile, they find a music centered in a doleful song
Steaming up, a lamentation and an ancient tale of wrong,
Like a tale of little meaning though the words are strong;
Chanted from an ill-used race of men that cleave the soil,   165
Sow the seed, and reap the harvest with enduring toil,
Storing yearly little dues of wheat, and wine and oil;
Till they perish and they suffer—some, 'tis whispered—down in hell
Suffer endless anguish, others in Elysian valleys dwell,
Resting weary limbs at last on beds of asphodel.[8]   170
Surely, surely, slumber is more sweet than toil, the shore
Than labor in the deep mid-ocean, wind and wave and oar;
O, rest ye, brother mariners, we will not wander more.

                                                          1832, 1842

St. Agnes' Eve[9]

Deep on the convent roof the snows
    Are sparkling to the moon;
My breath to heaven like vapor goes;
    May my soul follow soon!
The shadows of the convent towers   5
    Slant down the snowy sward,
Still creeping with the creeping hours
    That lead me to my Lord.
Make Thou my spirit pure and clear
    As are the frosty skies,   10
Or this first snowdrop of the year
    That in my bosom lies.

As these white robes are soiled and dark,
    To yonder shining ground;
As this pale taper's earthly spark,   15
    To yonder argent round;
So shows my soul before the Lamb,
    My spirit before Thee;
So in mine earthly house I am,
    To that I hope to be.   20
Break up the heavens, O Lord! and far,
    Through all yon starlight keen,
Draw me, thy bride, a glittering star,
    In raiment white and clean.

He lifts me to the golden doors;   25
    The flashes come and go;
All heaven bursts her starry floors,

8. A yellow lilylike flower supposed to
grow in the Elysian valleys.
9. The evening preceding January 21,
St. Agnes's Day, honoring the patron
saint of virgins. According to a legend
(which Keats also used), a young girl
might have a vision of her future
bridegroom if she performed certain rituals on this wintry evening. As Tennyson said, "Here the legend is told by a
nun," and the "Heavenly Bridegroom"
is Christ.

And strows her lights below,
And deepens on and up! the gates
   Roll back, and far within   30
For me the Heavenly Bridegroom waits,
   To make me pure of sin.
The Sabbaths of Eternity,
   One Sabbath deep and wide—
A light upon the shining sea—   35
   The Bridegroom with his bride!

1833   1836, 1842

You Ask Me, Why, Though Ill at Ease[1]

You ask me, why, though ill at ease,
   Within this region I subsist,
   Whose spirits falter in the mist,
And languish for the purple seas.

It is the land that freemen till,   5
   That sober-suited Freedom chose,
   The land, where girt with friends or foes
A man may speak the thing he will;

A land of settled government,
   A land of just and old renown,   10
   Where Freedom slowly broadens down
From precedent to precedent;

Where faction seldom gathers head,
   But, by degrees to fullness wrought,
   The strength of some diffusive thought   15
Hath time and space to work and spread.

Should banded unions[2] persecute
   Opinion, and induce a time
   When single thought is civil crime,
And individual freedom mute,   20

Though power should make from land to land
   The name of Britain trebly great—
   Though every channel of the State
Should fill and choke with golden sand—

Yet waft me from the harbor-mouth,   25
   Wild wind! I seek a warmer sky,
   And I will see before I die
The palms and temples of the South.

1833   1842

1. Written at the time of the disturbances during and after the passing of the Reform Bill of 1832.

2. Any organized political groups, not necessarily trade unions.

Lines

Here[3] often, when a child I lay reclined,
   I took delight in this locality.
Here stood the infant Ilion of the mind,
   And here the Grecian ships did seem to be.
The drain-cut levels of the marshy lea—
Gray sea banks and pale sunsets—dreary wind,
   Dim shores, dense rains, and heavy-clouded sea!

1833   1850

Ulysses[1]

It little profits that an idle king,
By this still hearth, among these barren crags,
Matched with an aged wife, I mete and dole
Unequal laws[2] unto a savage race,
That hoard, and sleep, and feed, and know not me.   5

   I cannot rest fròm travel; I will drink
Life to the lees. All times I have enjoyed
Greatly, have suffered greatly, both with those
That loved me, and alone; on shore, and when
Through scudding drifts[3] the rainy Hyades   10
Vexed the dim sea. I am become a name;
For always roaming with a hungry heart
Much have I seen and known—cities of men
And manners, climates, councils, governments,
Myself not least, but honored of them all—   15
And drunk delight of battle with my peers,
Far on the ringing plains of windy Troy.
I am a part of all that I have met;
Yet all experience is an arch wherethrough
Gleams that untraveled world whose margin fades   20
Forever and forever when I move.
How dull it is to pause, to make an end,
To rust unburnished, not to shine in use!
As though to breathe were life! Life piled on life
Were all too little, and of one to me   25

---

3. At Mablethorpe, on the Lincolnshire coast.

1. According to Dante, after Ulysses had returned home to Ithaca and had settled down to rule his island kingdom, he became restless and desired to set out on another voyage of exploration to the west. In old age he persuaded a band of his followers to accompany him on such a voyage. "Consider your origin," he addressed them, "ye were not formed to live like brutes, but to follow virtue and knowledge" (*Inferno* XXVI).

   The contrast between the conscientious administrator, Telemachus, and the energetic quester, his father, has been variously interpreted. A few readers argue that Ulysses is not represented in the monologue as a great hero but as irresponsible. Tennyson himself stated that the poem expressed his own "need of going forward and braving the struggle of life" after the death of Hallam.

2. Measure out rewards and punishments.

3. Driving showers of spray and rain; the "Hyades" are a group of stars whose rising was assumed to be followed by rain.

Little remains; but every hour is saved
From that eternal silence, something more,
A bringer of new things; and vile it were
For some three suns to store and hoard myself,
And this gray spirit yearning in desire   30
To follow knowledge like a sinking star,
Beyond the utmost bound of human thought.

    This is my son, mine own Telemachus,
To whom I leave the scepter and the isle—
Well-loved of me, discerning to fulfill   35
This labor, by slow prudence to make mild
A rugged people, and through soft degrees
Subdue them to the useful and the good.
Most blameless is he, centered in the sphere
Of common duties, decent not to fail   40
In offices of tenderness, and pay
Meet adoration to my household gods,
When I am gone. He works his work, I mine.

    There lies the port; the vessel puffs her sail;
There gloom the dark, broad seas. My mariners,   45
Souls that have toiled, and wrought, and thought with me—
That ever with a frolic welcome took
The thunder and the sunshine, and opposed
Free hearts, free foreheads—you and I are old;
Old age hath yet his honor and his toil.   50
Death closes all; but something ere the end,
Some work of noble note, may yet be done,
Not unbecoming men that strove with Gods.
The lights begin to twinkle from the rocks;
The long day wanes; the slow moon climbs; the deep   55
Moans round with many voices. Come, my friends,
'Tis not too late to seek a newer world.
Push off, and sitting well in order smite
The sounding furrows; for my purpose holds
To sail beyond the sunset, and the baths   60
Of all the western stars,[4] until I die.
It may be that the gulfs will wash us down;
It may be we shall touch the Happy Isles,[5]
And see the great Achilles, whom we knew.
Though much is taken, much abides; and though   65
We are not now that strength which in old days
Moved earth and heaven, that which we are, we are—
One equal temper of heroic hearts,
Made weak by time and fate, but strong in will
To strive, to seek, to find, and not to yield.   70

1833   1842

4. The outer ocean or river which, in Greek cosmology, surrounded the flat circle of the earth, and into which the stars descended.
5. Elysium, or the Islands of the Blessed, where heroes such as Achilles were supposed to enjoy life after death. These islands were thought to be in the far-western ocean.

Tithonus[1]

The woods decay, the woods decay and fall,
The vapors weep their burthen to the ground,
Man comes and tills the field and lies beneath,
And after many a summer dies the swan.[2]
Me only cruel immortality   5
Consumes; I wither slowly in thine arms,[3]
Here at the quiet limit of the world,
A white-haired shadow roaming like a dream
The ever-silent spaces of the East,
Far-folded mists, and gleaming halls of morn.   10

    Alas! for this gray shadow, once a man—
So glorious in his beauty and thy choice,
Who madest him thy chosen, that he seemed
To his great heart none other than a God!
I asked thee, "Give me immortality."   15
Then didst thou grant mine asking with a smile,
Like wealthy men who care not how they give.
But thy strong Hours indignant worked their wills,
And beat me down and marred and wasted me,
And though they could not end me, left me maimed   20
To dwell in presence of immortal youth,
Immortal age beside immortal youth,
And all I was in ashes. Can thy love,
Thy beauty, make amends, though even now,
Close over us, the silver star,[4] thy guide,   25
Shines in those tremulous eyes that fill with tears
To hear me? Let me go; take back thy gift.
Why should a man desire in any way
To vary from the kindly race of men,
Or pass beyond the goal of ordinance[5]   30
Where all should pause, as is most meet for all?

    A soft air fans the cloud apart; there comes
A glimpse of that dark world where I was born.
Once more the old mysterious glimmer steals
From thy pure brows, and from thy shoulders pure,   35
And bosom beating with a heart renewed.
Thy cheek begins to redden through the gloom,
Thy sweet eyes brighten slowly close to mine,
Ere yet they blind the stars, and the wild team[6]

---

1. Tithonus, a Trojan prince, was loved by the goddess of the dawn, Eos or Aurora, who obtained for him the gift of living forever but neglected to obtain for him the gift of everlasting youth. In the monologue, Tithonus appears as an aged man, dwelling still in the palace of the goddess, and cut off by his frustrating predicament from the normal cycle of human life which culminates in death. To him immortality, not death, is "cruel."
2. Some species of swans live for at least fifty years.
3. I.e., the arms of Eos.
4. The morning star that precedes the dawn.
5. What is decreed or ordained as human destiny.
6. The horses that draw Eos' chariot into the sky at daybreak.

Which love thee, yearning for thy yoke, arise,   40
And shake the darkness from their loosened manes,
And beat the twilight into flakes of fire.
    Lo! ever thus thou growest beautiful
In silence, then before thine answer given
Departest, and thy tears are on my cheek.   45
    Why wilt thou ever scare me with thy tears,
And make me tremble lest a saying learnt,
In days far-off, on that dark earth, be true?
"The Gods themselves cannot recall their gifts."
    Ay me! ay me! with what another heart   50
In days far-off, and with what other eyes
I used to watch—if I be he that watched—
The lucid outline forming round thee; saw
The dim curls kindle into sunny rings;
Changed with thy mystic change, and felt my blood   55
Glow with the glow that slowly crimsoned all
Thy presence and thy portals, while I lay,
Mouth, forehead, eyelids, growing dewy-warm
With kisses balmier than half-opening buds
Of April, and could hear the lips that kissed   60
Whispering I knew not what of wild and sweet,
Like that strange song I heard Apollo sing,
While Ilion like a mist rose into towers.[7]
    Yet hold me not forever in thine East;
How can my nature longer mix with thine?   65
Coldly thy rosy shadows bathe me, cold
Are all thy lights, and cold my wrinkled feet
Upon thy glimmering thresholds, when the steam
Floats up from those dim fields about the homes
Of happy men that have the power to die,   70
And grassy barrows of the happier dead.
Release me, and restore me to the ground.
Thou seest all things, thou wilt see my grave;
Thou wilt renew thy beauty morn by morn,
I earth in earth forget these empty courts,   75
And thee returning on thy silver wheels.

1833, 1859   1860

Break, Break, Break

Break, break, break,
   On thy cold gray stones, O Sea!
And I would that my tongue could utter
   The thoughts that arise in me.

O, well for the fisherman's boy,   5
   That he shouts with his sister at play!
O, well for the sailor lad,
   That he sings in his boat on the bay!

7. The walls of Troy (Ilion) were supposed to have been built to the strains of Apollo's music.

And the stately ships go on
   To their haven under the hill;
But O for the touch of a vanished hand,   10
   And the sound of a voice that is still!

Break, break, break,
   At the foot of thy crags, O Sea!
But the tender grace of a day that is dead   15
   Will never come back to me.

1834   1842

The Epic [Morte d'Arthur][1]

At Francis Allen's on the Christmas eve—
The game of forfeits done—the girls all kissed
Beneath the sacred bush[2] and passed away—
The parson Holmes, the poet Everard Hall,
The host, and I sat round the wassail-bowl,   5
Then halfway ebbed; and there we held a talk,
How all the old honor had from Christmas gone,
Or gone or dwindled down to some odd games
In some odd nooks like this; till I, tired out
With cutting eights that day upon the pond,   10
Where, three times slipping from the outer edge,
I bumped the ice into three several stars,
Fell in a doze; and half-awake I heard
The parson taking wide and wider sweeps,
Now harping on the church-commissioners,[3]   15
Now hawking at geology and schism;
Until I woke, and found him settled down
Upon the general decay of faith
Right through the world: "at home was little left,
And none abroad; there was no anchor, none,   20
To hold by." Francis, laughing, clapped his hand
On Everard's shoulder, with "I hold by him."
"And I," quoth Everard, "by the wassail-bowl."
"Why yes," I said, "we knew your gift that way
At college; but another which you had—   25
I mean of verse (for so we held it then),
What came of that?" "You know," said Frank, "he burnt
His epic, his King Arthur, some twelve books"—

1. At age 24, Tennyson proposed to write a long epic on King Arthur. Five years later he had completed one book of the twelve, the story of Arthur's death, which he published in 1842 under the title *Morte d'Arthur*. In this early version, the story is given a framework entitled *The Epic*, which consists of a short introductory section (51 lines) and an epilogue (30 lines), describing a party on Christmas Eve in modern times, at which the poet reads *Morte d'Arthur* to his friends. In 1869, Tennyson incorporated *Morte d'Arthur* into his long narrative poem, *Idylls of the King*; it appears there as the twelfth book, under the new title, *The Passing of Arthur*. At this time *The Epic* framework was discarded and some lines added. The 1842 version can be reconstructed (only two lines are modified) by reading *The Passing of Arthur*, lines 170–440.
2. Mistletoe.
3. Commissioners appointed by the government in 1835 to regulate finances of the Anglican Church.

And then to me demanding why: "O, sir,
He thought that nothing new was said, or else 30
Something so said 'twas nothing—that a truth
Looks freshest in the fashion of the day;
God knows; he has a mint of reasons; ask.
It pleased *me* well enough." "Nay, nay," said Hall,
"Why take the style of those heroic times? 35
For nature brings not back the mastodon,
Nor we those times; and why should any man
Remodel models? these twelve books of mine
Were faint Homeric echoes,[4] nothing-worth,
Mere chaff and draff, much better burnt." "But I," 40
Said Francis, "picked the eleventh from this hearth,
And have it; keep a thing, its use will come.
I hoard it as a sugarplum for Holmes."
He laughed, and I, though sleepy, like a horse
That hears the corn-bin open, pricked my ears; 45
For I remembered Everard's college fame
When we were Freshmen. Then at my request
He brought it; and the poet, little urged,
But with some prelude of disparagement,
Read, mouthing out his hollow o's and a's, 50
Deep-chested music, and to this result.[5]

* * *

  Here ended Hall, and our last light, that long
Had winked and threatened darkness, flared and fell; 325
At which the parson, sent to sleep with sound,
And waked with silence, grunted "Good!" but we
Sat rapt: it was the tone with which he read—
Perhaps some modern touches here and there
Redeemed it from the charge of nothingness— 330
Or else we loved the man, and prized his work;
I know not; but we sitting, as I said,
The cock crew loud, as at that time of year
The lusty bird takes every hour for dawn.[6]
Then Francis, muttering, like a man ill-used, 335
"There now—that's nothing!" drew a little back,
And drove his heel into the smoldered log,
That sent a blast of sparkles up the flue.
And so to bed, where yet in sleep I seemed
To sail with Arthur under looming shores, 340
Point after point; till on to dawn, when dreams
Begin to feel the truth and stir of day,
To me, methought, who waited with the crowd,
There came a bark that, blowing forward, bore
King Arthur, like a modern gentleman 345
Of stateliest port; and all the people cried,

4. Cf. Walter Savage Landor's comment
after reading *Morte d'Arthur* in manuscript: "It is more Homeric than any
poem of our time, and rivals some of
the noblest parts of the Odyssey."
5. Here followed the 271 lines of *Morte*

d'Arthur in 1842 (see below, *The Passing of Arthur*, lines 170–440). *The Epic*
then continued as follows.
6. See *Hamlet* I.i.157–60 on the legend
of the cock's crowing "all night long"
on Christmas Eve.

"Arthur is come again: he cannot die."
Then those that stood upon the hills behind
Repeated—"Come again, and thrice as fair";
And, further inland, voices echoed—"Come   350
With all good things, and war shall be no more."
At this a hundred bells began to peal,
That with the sound I woke, and heard indeed
The clear church bells ring in the Christmas morn.

1833–38   1842

Sonnet [1]

How thought you that this thing could captivate?
    What are those graces that could make her dear,
    Who is not worth the notice of a sneer
To rouse the vapid devil of her hate?
A speech conventional, so void of weight   5
    That after it has buzzed about one's ear,
    'Twere rich refreshment for a week to hear
The dentist babble or the barber prate;

A hand displayed with many a little art;
    An eye that glances on her neighbor's dress;   10
    A foot too often shown for my regard;
An angel's form—a waiting-woman's[2] heart;
    A perfect-featured face, expressionless,
        Insipid, as the Queen upon a card.

1836   1931

Move Eastward, Happy Earth

Move eastward, happy earth, and leave
    Yon orange sunset waning slow;
From fringes of the faded eve,
    O happy planet, eastward go,
Till over thy dark shoulder glow   5
    Thy silver sister-world,[3] and rise
    To glass herself in dewy eyes
That watch me from the glen below.

Ah, bear me with thee, smoothly borne,
    Dip forward under starry light,   10

1. Perhaps inspired by Tennyson's disillusioned feelings toward Rosa Baring, a
beautiful girl of high social station in
Somersby, for whom he had a short-
lived infatuation.

2. Female servant's.
3. The planet Venus, or perhaps the
moon, which will be reflected in the eyes
of the speaker's beloved.

And move me to my marriage morn,
    And round again to happy night.

ca. 1836   1842

The Eagle: A Fragment

He clasps the crag with crooked hands;
Close to the sun in lonely lands,
Ringed with the azure world, he stands.

The wrinkled sea beneath him crawls:
He watches from his mountain walls,   5
And like a thunderbolt he falls.

                                      1851

Locksley Hall[1]

Comrades, leave me here a little, while as yet 'tis early morn;
Leave me here, and when you want me, sound upon the bugle horn.

'Tis the place, and all around it, as of old, the curlews call,
Dreary gleams[2] about the moorland flying over Locksley Hall;

Locksley Hall, that in the distance overlooks the sandy tracts,   5
And the hollow ocean-ridges roaring into cataracts.

Many a night from yonder ivied casement, ere I went to rest,
Did I look on great Orion sloping slowly to the west.

Many a night I saw the Pleiads,[3] rising through the mellow shade,
Glitter like a swarm of fireflies tangled in a silver braid.   10

Here about the beach I wandered, nourishing a youth sublime
With the fairy tales of science, and the long result of time;

When the centuries behind me like a fruitful land reposed;
When I clung to all the present for the promise that it closed;[4]

When I dipped into the future far as human eye could see,   15
Saw the vision of the world and all the wonder that would be.—

1. The situation in this poem—of a young man's being jilted by a girl who chose to marry a wealthy landowner—may have been suggested to Tennyson by the experience of his brother. Frederick Tennyson, a hot-tempered man, had fallen in love with his cousin, Julia Tennyson, and was similarly unsuccessful. It may also have been inspired by Tennyson's own frustrated courtship of Rosa Baring, who rejected the young poet in favor of a wealthy suitor. Concerning the ranting tone of the speaker (a tone accentuated by the heavily marked trochaic meter), Tennyson himself said: "The whole poem represents young life, its good side, its deficiencies, and its yearnings."

2. Tennyson stated that "gleams" does not refer to "curlews" flying but to streaks of light.

3. The Pleiades, a seven-starred constellation.

4. Enclosed.

In the spring a fuller crimson comes upon the robin's breast;
In the spring the wanton lapwing gets himself another crest;

In the spring a livelier iris changes on the burnished dove;[5]
In the spring a young man's fancy lightly turns to thoughts of love. 20

Then her cheek was pale and thinner than should be for one so young,
And her eyes on all my motions with a mute observance hung.

And I said, "My cousin Amy, speak, and speak the truth to me,
Trust me, cousin, all the current of my being sets to thee."

On her pallid cheek and forehead came a color and a light, 25
As I have seen the rosy red flushing in the northern night.

And she turned—her bosom shaken with a sudden storm of sighs—
All the spirit deeply dawning in the dark of hazel eyes—

Saying, "I have hid my feelings, fearing they should do me wrong";
Saying, "Dost thou love me, cousin?" weeping, "I have loved thee
   long." 30

Love took up the glass of Time, and turned it in his glowing hands;
Every moment, lightly shaken, ran itself in golden sands.

Love took up the harp of Life, and smote on all the chords with
   might;
Smote the chord of Self, that, trembling, passed in music out of
   sight.

Many a morning on the moorland did we hear the copses ring, 35
And her whisper thronged my pulses with the fullness of the spring.

Many an evening by the waters did we watch the stately ships,
And our spirits rushed together at the touching of the lips.

O my cousin, shallow-hearted! O my Amy, mine no more!
O the dreary, dreary moorland! O the barren, barren shore! 40

Falser than all fancy fathoms, falser than all songs have sung,
Puppet to a father's threat, and servile to a shrewish tongue!

Is it well to wish thee happy?—having known me—to decline
On a range of lower feelings and a narrower heart than mine!

Yet it shall be; thou shalt lower to his level day by day, 45
What is fine within thee growing coarse to sympathize with clay.

As the husband is, the wife is; thou art mated with a clown,[6]
And the grossness of his nature will have weight to drag thee down.

He will hold thee, when his passion shall have spent its novel force,
Something better than his dog, a little dearer than his horse. 50

What is this? his eyes are heavy; think not they are glazed with wine.
Go to him, it is thy duty; kiss him, take his hand in thine.

---

5. Rainbow-like colors of a dove's throat   season.
plumage are intensified in the mating   6. Boor.

It may be my lord is weary, that his brain is overwrought;
Soothe him with thy finer fancies, touch him with thy lighter
 thought.

He will answer to the purpose, easy things to understand—   55
Better thou wert dead before me, though I slew thee with my hand!

Better thou and I were lying, hidden from the heart's disgrace,
Rolled in one another's arms, and silent in a last embrace.

Cursed be the social wants that sin against the strength of youth!
Cursed be the social lies that warp us from the living truth!   60

Cursed be the sickly forms that err from honest Nature's rule!
Cursed be the gold that gilds the straitened[7] forehead of the fool!

Well—'tis well that I should bluster!—Hadst thou less unworthy
 proved—
Would to God—for I had loved thee more than ever wife was loved.

Am I mad, that I should cherish that which bears but bitter fruit? 65
I will pluck it from my bosom, though my heart be at the root.

Never, though my mortal summers to such length of years should
 come
As the many-wintered crow[8] that leads the clanging rookery home.

Where is comfort? in division of the records of the mind?
Can I part her from herself, and love her, as I knew her, kind?   70

I remember one that perished; sweetly did she speak and move;
Such a one do I remember, whom to look at was to love.

Can I think of her as dead, and love her for the love she bore?
No—she never loved me truly; love is love for evermore.

Comfort? comfort scorned of devils! this is truth the poet[9] sings, 75
That a sorrow's crown of sorrow is remembering happier things.

Drug thy memories, lest thou learn it, lest thy heart be put to proof,
In the dead unhappy night, and when the rain is on the roof.

Like a dog, he hunts in dreams, and thou art staring at the wall,
Where the dying night-lamp flickers, and the shadows rise and
 fall.   80

Then a hand shall pass before thee, pointing to his drunken sleep,
To thy widowed[1] marriage-pillows, to the tears that thou wilt weep.

Thou shalt hear the "Never, never," whispered by the phantom years.
And a song from out the distance in the ringing of thine ears;

And an eye shall vex thee, looking ancient kindness on thy pain.   85
Turn thee, turn thee on thy pillow; get thee to thy rest again.

Nay, but Nature brings thee solace; for a tender voice will cry.
'Tis a purer life than thine, a lip to drain thy trouble dry.

---

7. Narrowed.
8. A rook, a long-lived bird.
9. Dante (*Inferno* V.121–23).

1. Presumably figurative. Her marriage
having become a mockery, she is widowed.

Baby lips will laugh me down; my latest rival brings thee rest.
Baby fingers, waxen touches, press me from the mother's breast.   90

O, the child too clothes the father with a dearness not his due.
Half is thine and half is his; it will be worthy of the two.

O, I see thee old and formal, fitted to thy petty part,
With a little hoard of maxims preaching down a daughter's heart.

"They were dangerous guides the feelings—she herself was not ex-
     empt—   95
Truly, she herself had suffered"—Perish in thy self-contempt!

Overlive it—lower yet—be happy! wherefore should I care?
I myself must mix with action, lest I wither by despair.

What is that which I should turn to, lighting upon days like these?
Every door is barred with gold, and opens but to golden keys.   100

Every gate is thronged with suitors, all the markets overflow.
I have but an angry fancy; what is that which I should do?

I had been content to perish, falling on the foeman's ground,
When the ranks are rolled in vapor, and the winds are laid with
     sound.[2]

But the jingling of the guinea helps the hurt that Honor feels,   105
And the nations do but murmur, snarling at each other's heels.

Can I but relive in sadness? I will turn that earlier page.
Hide me from my deep emotion, O thou wondrous Mother-Age![3]

Make me feel the wild pulsation that I felt before the strife,
When I heard my days before me, and the tumult of my life;   110

Yearning for the large excitement that the coming years would yield,
Eager-hearted as a boy when first he leaves his father's field,

And at night along the dusky highway near and nearer drawn,
Sees in heaven the light of London flaring like a dreary dawn;

And his spirit leaps within him to be gone before him then,   115
Underneath the light he looks at, in among the throngs of men;

Men, my brothers, men the workers, ever reaping something new;
That which they have done but earnest[4] of the things that they
     shall do.

For I dipped into the future, far as human eye could see,
Saw the Vision of the world, and all the wonder that would be;   120

Saw the heavens fill with commerce, argosies of magic sails,[5]
Pilots of the purple twilight, dropping down with costly bales;

---

2. It was once believed that the firing of
artillery stilled the winds.
3. Perhaps signifying the consolations of
a future age of progress. See also line
185.
4. A pledge.
5. Probably airships, such as balloons.

Heard the heavens fill with shouting, and there rained a ghastly dew
From the nations' airy navies grappling in the central blue;

Far along the world-wide whisper of the south wind rushing
    warm,   125
With the standards of the peoples plunging through the thunder-
    storm;

Till the war drum throbbed no longer, and the battle flags were
    furled
In the Parliament of man, the Federation of the world.

There the common sense of most shall hold a fretful realm in awe,
And the kindly earth shall slumber, lapped in universal law.   130

So I triumphed ere my passion sweeping through me left me dry,
Left me with the palsied heart, and left me with the jaundiced eye;

Eye, to which all order festers, all things here are out of joint.
Science moves, but slowly, slowly, creeping on from point to point;

Slowly comes a hungry people, as a lion, creeping nigher,   135
Glares at one that nods and winks behind a slowly-dying fire.

Yet I doubt not through the ages one increasing purpose runs,
And the thoughts of men are widened with the process of the suns.

What is that to him that reaps not harvest of his youthful joys,
Though the deep heart of existence beat forever like a boy's?   140

Knowledge comes, but wisdom lingers, and I linger on the shore,
And the individual withers, and the world is more and more.

Knowledge comes, but wisdom lingers, and he bears a laden breast,
Full of sad experience, moving toward the stillness of his rest.

Hark, my merry comrades call me, sounding on the bugle horn,   145
They to whom my foolish passion were a target for their scorn.

Shall it not be scorn to me to harp on such a moldered string?
I am shamed through all my nature to have loved so slight a thing.

Weakness to be wroth with weakness! woman's pleasure, woman's
    pain—
Nature made them blinder motions bounded in a shallower brain.   150

Woman is the lesser man, and all thy passions, matched with mine,
Are as moonlight unto sunlight, and as water unto wine—

Here at least, where nature sickens, nothing. Ah, for some retreat
Deep in yonder shining Orient, where my life began to beat,

Where in wild Mahratta-battle[6] fell my father evil-starred—   155
I was left a trampled orphan, and a selfish uncle's ward.

Or to burst all links of habit—there to wander far away,
On from island unto island at the gateways of the day.

6. A reference to wars waged by a   in India (1803 and 1817).
Hindu people against the British forces

Larger constellations burning, mellow moons and happy skies,
Breadths of tropic shade and palms in cluster, knots of Paradise. 160

Never comes the trader, never floats an European flag,
Slides the bird o'er lustrous woodland, swings the trailer[7] from the
 crag;

Droops the heavy-blossomed bower, hangs the heavy-fruited tree—
Summer isles of Eden lying in dark purple spheres of sea.

There methinks would be enjoyment more than in this march of
 mind, 165
In the steamship, in the railway, in the thoughts that shake mankind.

There the passions cramped no longer shall have scope and breathing space;
I will take some savage woman, she shall rear my dusky race.

Iron-jointed, supple-sinewed, they shall dive, and they shall run,
Catch the wild goat by the hair, and hurl their lances in the sun; 170

Whistle back the parrot's call, and leap the rainbows of the brooks,
Not with blinded eyesight poring over miserable books—

Fool, again the dream, the fancy! but I *know* my words are wild,
But I count the gray barbarian lower than the Christian child.

I, to herd with narrow foreheads, vacant of our glorious gains. 175
Like a beast with lower pleasures, like a beast with lower pains!

Mated with a squalid savage—what to me were sun or clime?
I the heir of all the ages, in the foremost files of time—

I that rather held it better men should perish one by one,
Than that earth should stand at gaze like Joshua's moon in
 Ajalon![8] 180

Not in vain the distance beacons. Forward, forward let us range,
Let the great world spin forever down the ringing grooves[9] of change.

Through the shadow of the globe we sweep into the younger day;
Better fifty years of Europe than a cycle of Cathay.[1]

Mother-Age—for mine I knew not—help me as when life begun; 185
Rift the hills, and roll the waters, flash the lightnings, weigh the sun.

O, I see the crescent promise of my spirit hath not set.
Ancient founts of inspiration well through all my fancy yet.

Howsoever these things be, a long farewell to Locksley Hall!
Now for me the woods may wither, now for me the roof-tree fall. 190

7. A vine.
8. At the command of Joshua, the sun
and moon stood still while the Israelites
completed the slaughter of their enemies
in the valley of Ajalon (Joshua x.12–
13).

9. Railroad tracks. Tennyson at one
time had the impression that train
wheels ran in grooved rails.
1. China, regarded in the 19th century as a static, unprogressive country.

Comes a vapor from the margin, blackening over heath and holt,
Cramming all the blast before it, in its breast a thunderbolt.

Let it fall on Locksley Hall, with rain or hail, or fire or snow;
For the mighty wind arises, roaring seaward, and I go.
1837–38   1842

From THE PRINCESS[1]

Sweet and Low

Sweet and low, sweet and low,
   Wind of the western sea,
Low, low, breathe and blow,
   Wind of the western sea!
Over the rolling waters go,   5
Come from the dying moon, and blow,
   Blow him again to me;
While my little one, while my pretty one, sleeps.

Sleep and rest, sleep and rest,
   Father will come to thee soon;   10
Rest, rest, on mother's breast,
   Father will come to thee soon;
Father will come to his babe in the nest,
Silver sails all out of the west
   Under the silver moon;
Sleep, my little one, sleep, my pretty one, sleep.   15

1850

The Splendor Falls

The splendor falls on castle walls
   And snowy summits old in story;
The long light shakes across the lakes,
   And the wild cataract leaps in glory.
Blow, bugle, blow, set the wild echoes flying,   5
Blow, bugle; answer, echoes, dying, dying, dying.

O, hark, O, hear! how thin and clear,
   And thinner, clearer, farther going!
O, sweet and far from cliff and scar[2]
   The horns of Elfland faintly blowing!   10
Blow, let us hear the purple glens replying,
Blow, bugle; answer, echoes, dying, dying, dying.

1. *The Princess* (1847), a long narrative poem, contains interludes in which
occasional songs are sung. The six of
these in our selection, some of which
first appeared in later editions of the
poem, rank among the finest of Tennyson's lyrics, and various 19th- and
20th-century composers have set them
to music.
2. Mountainside.

O love, they die in yon rich sky,
    They faint on hill or field or river;
Our echoes roll from soul to soul,   15
    And grow forever and forever.
Blow, bugle, blow, set the wild echoes flying,
And answer, echoes, answer, dying, dying, dying.

                              1850

Tears, Idle Tears[3]

    Tears, idle tears, I know not what they mean,
Tears from the depth of some divine despair
Rise in the heart, and gather to the eyes,
In looking on the happy autumn-fields,
And thinking of the days that are no more.   5

    Fresh as the first beam glittering on a sail,
That brings our friends up from the underworld,
Sad as the last which reddens over one
That sinks with all we love below the verge;
So sad, so fresh, the days that are no more.   10

    Ah, sad and strange as in dark summer dawns
The earliest pipe of half-awakened birds
To dying ears, when unto dying eyes
The casement slowly grows a glimmering square;
So sad, so strange, the days that are no more.   15

    Dear as remembered kisses after death,
And sweet as those by hopeless fancy feigned
On lips that are for others; deep as love,
Deep as first love, and wild with all regret;
O Death in Life, the days that are no more!   20

                              1847

Ask Me No More

Ask me no more: the moon may draw the sea;
    The cloud may stoop from heaven and take the shape,
    With fold to fold, of mountain or of cape;
But O too fond, when have I answered thee?
            Ask me no more.   5

Ask me no more: what answer should I give?
    I love not hollow cheek or faded eye:

3. Tennyson commented: "This song came to me on the yellowing autumn-tide at Tintern Abbey, full for me of its bygone memories." This locale would be for him associated both with Wordsworth's *Tintern Abbey* and with memories of Hallam, who was buried across the Bristol Channel in this area. "It is what I have always felt even from a boy, and what as a boy I called the 'passion of the past.' And it is so always with me now; it is the distance that charms me in the landscape, the picture and the past, and not the immediate today in which I move."

Yet, O my friend, I will not have thee die!
Ask me no more, lest I should bid thee live;
            Ask me no more.   10

Ask me no more: thy fate and mine are sealed;
  I strove against the stream and all in vain;
  Let the great river take me to the main.
No more, dear love, for at a touch I yield;
            Ask me no more.   15
                     1850

Now Sleeps the Crimson Petal

Now sleeps the crimson petal, now the white;
Nor waves the cypress in the palace walk;
Nor winks the gold fin in the porphyry font.
The firefly wakens; waken thou with me.

Now droops the milk-white peacock like a ghost,   5
And like a ghost she glimmers on to me.

Now lies the Earth all Danaë[4] to the stars,
And all thy heart lies open unto me.

Now slides the silent meteor on, and leaves
A shining furrow, as thy thoughts in me.   10

Now folds the lily all her sweetness up,
And slips into the bosom of the lake.
So fold thyself, my dearest, thou, and slip
Into my bosom and be lost in me.
                     1847

Come Down, O Maid[5]

Come down, O maid, from yonder mountain height.
What pleasure lives in height (the shepherd sang),
In height and cold, the splendor of the hills?
But cease to move so near the heavens, and cease
To glide a sunbeam by the blasted pine,   5
To sit a star upon the sparkling spire;
And come, for Love is of the valley, come,
For Love is of the valley, come thou down
And find him; by the happy threshold, he,
Or hand in hand with Plenty in the maize,   10
Or red with spirted purple of the vats,
Or foxlike in the vine;[6] nor cares to walk

4. Danaë, a Greek princess, was confined in a metal tower by her father to prevent suitors from coming near her. Zeus, however, succeeded in visiting her in the form of a shower of gold. Their offspring was the hero Perseus.

5. Written during Tennyson's visit to the Swiss alps in 1846, after he had seen Mount Jungfrau ("The Maiden").
6. This image comes from the Song of Solomon ii.15.

With Death and Morning on the Silver Horns,[7]
Nor wilt thou snare him in the white ravine,
Nor find him dropped upon the firths of ice,[8]   15
That huddling slant in furrow-cloven falls
To roll the torrent out of dusky doors.[9]
But follow; let the torrent dance thee down
To find him in the valley; let the wild
Lean-headed eagles yelp alone, and leave   20
The monstrous ledges there to slope, and spill
Their thousand wreaths of dangling water-smoke,
That like a broken purpose waste in air.
So waste not thou, but come; for all the vales
Await thee; azure pillars of the hearth[10]   25
Arise to thee; the children call, and I
Thy shepherd pipe, and sweet is every sound,
Sweeter thy voice, but every sound is sweet;
Myriads of rivulets hurrying through the lawn,
The moan of doves in immemorial elms,   30
And murmuring of innumerable bees.

                                                        1847

["The Woman's Cause Is Man's"][1]

"Blame not thyself too much," I said, "nor blame
Too much the sons of men and barbarous laws;   240
These were the rough ways of the world till now.
Henceforth thou hast a helper, me, that know
The woman's cause is man's: they rise or sink
Together, dwarfed or godlike, bond or free:
For she that out of Lethe scales with man   245
The shining steps of Nature, shares with man
His nights, his days, moves with him to one goal,
Stays all the fair young planet in her hands—
If she be small, slight-natured, miserable,
How shall men grow? but work no more alone!   250
Our place is much: as far as in us lies
We two will serve them both in aiding her—
Will clear away the parasitic forms
That seem to keep her up but drag her down—
Will leave her space to burgeon out of all   255
Within her—let her make herself her own
To give or keep, to live and learn and be
All that not harms distinctive womanhood.

---

7. Mountain peaks.
8. Glaciers.
9. Heaps of rock and refuse at the base of a glacier through which the mountain torrent forces its way down to the valley below.
10. Columns of smoke from the houses in the valley.
1. *The Princess* tells the story of a prince who courts the young and beautiful Princess Ida, who has established a university from which men are excluded; she has also vowed she will never marry. At the end she is persuaded that her feminist experiment was a failure, but the prince assures her that ideal relations between men and women may be achieved in the future. Our selection, covering the prince's key speech, is from book VII, lines 239–91.

For woman is not undevelopt man,
But diverse: could we make her as the man,   260
Sweet Love were slain: his dearest bond is this,
Not like to like, but like in difference.
Yet in the long years liker must they grow;
The man be more of woman, she of man;
He gain in sweetness and in moral height,   265
Nor lose the wrestling thews that throw the world;
She mental breadth, nor fail in childward care,
Nor lose the childlike in the larger mind;
Till at the last she set herself to man,
Like perfect music unto noble words;   270
And so these twain, upon the skirts of Time,
Sit side by side, full-summed in all their powers,
Dispensing harvest, sowing the To-be,
Self-reverent each and reverencing each,
Distinct in individualities,   275
But like each other even as those who love.
Then comes the statelier Eden back to men:
Then reign the world's great bridals, chaste and calm:
Then springs the crowning race of humankind.
May these things be!"
                    Sighing she spoke "I fear
They will not."   280
                "Dear, but let us type them now
In our own lives, and this proud watchword rest
Of equal; seeing either sex alone
Is half itself, and in true marriage lies
Nor equal, nor unequal: each fulfils   285
Defect in each, and always thought in thought,
Purpose in purpose, will in will, they grow,
The single pure and perfect animal,
The two-celled heart beating, with one full stroke,
Life."
        And again sighing she spoke: "A dream   290
That once was mine! what woman taught you this?"
1839–47   1847

In Memoriam A. H. H.

Like most of Tennyson's writings, *In Memoriam* shows his debt to earlier poetry. In its celebration of male friendship, as Christopher Ricks has shown, the poem has many affinities with Shakespeare's *Sonnets,* and as an elegy it is of course in the tradition of Milton's *Lycidas* and Shelley's *Adonais.* Its structure, however, is strikingly different. Resembling a song cycle more than a symphony, it is made up of individual lyric units, seemingly self-sustaining, that may be enjoyed by themselves even though the full pleasure to be derived from each component depends upon its relationship to the poem as a whole. The circumstances of the poem's composition help to explain how this new kind of elegy was evolved. The sudden death of Arthur Hallam at the age of 22 had a profound effect on Tennyson. The young poet had cherished Hallam not only as his closest friend and the fiancé of his sister but as an all-wise counselor upon whose judgment he depended for guidance. This fatherly prop having been pulled away, Tennyson was overwhelmed with doubts about the meaning of life and man's role in the universe, doubts reinforced by his own study of geology and other sciences. As a kind of poetic diary recording the variety of his feelings and reflections he began to compose a series of lyrics. These "short swallow-flights of song," as he calls them, written at intervals over a period of seventeen years, were later grouped into one long elegy in which a progressive development from despair to some sort of hope, as in section 95, is recorded.

Some of the early sections of the poem resemble traditional pastoral elegies, including those portraying the voyage during which Hallam's body was brought to England for burial (sections 9–15 and 19). Other early sections portraying the speaker's loneliness, in which even Christmas festivities seem joyless (sections 28–30), are more distinctive. With the passage of time, indicated by anniversaries and by recurring changes of the seasons, the speaker comes to accept the loss and to assert his belief in life and in an afterlife. In particular the recurring Christmases (sections 28, 78, 104) indicate the stages of his development, yet the pattern of progress in the poem is not a simple unimpeded movement upwards. Dramatic conflicts recur throughout. Thus the most intense expression of doubt occurs not at the beginning of *In Memoriam* but as late as sections 54, 55, and 56.

The quatrain form in which the whole poem is written is usually called the *"In Memoriam* stanza," although it had been occasionally used by earlier poets. So rigid a form taxed Tennyson's ingenuity in achieving variety, but it is one of several means by which the diverse parts of the poem are knitted together.

The introductory section, consisting of 11 stanzas, is commonly referred to as the "Prologue," although Tennyson did not assign a title to it. It was written in 1849 after the rest of the poem was complete.

From In Memoriam A. H. H.

OBIIT MDCCCXXXIII

Strong Son of God, immortal Love,
    Whom we, that have not seen thy face,
    By faith, and faith alone, embrace,
Believing where we cannot prove;[1]

Thine are these orbs[2] of light and shade;   5
    Thou madest Life in man and brute;
    Thou madest Death; and lo, thy foot
Is on the skull which thou hast made.

Thou wilt not leave us in the dust:
    Thou madest man, he knows not why,   10

1. See John xx.24–29, in which Jesus rebukes Thomas for his doubts concerning the Resurrection: "Blessed are they that have not seen, and yet have believed." For first line of poem, cf. *Love*, by George Herbert: "Immortal Love, Author of this great frame, / Sprung from that beauty which can never fade, How hath Man parceled out Thy glorious name, / And thrown it on the dust which Thou hast made?" [noted by R. W. Hill].

2. Planets.

He thinks he was not made to die;
And thou hast made him: thou art just.

Thou seemest human and divine,
　　The highest, holiest manhood, thou.
　　Our wills are ours, we know not how;   15
Our wills are ours, to make them thine.

Our little systems[3] have their day;
　　They have their day and cease to be;
　　They are but broken lights of thee,
And thou, O Lord, art more than they.   20

We have but faith: we cannot know,
　　For knowledge is of things we see;
　　And yet we trust it comes from thee,
A beam in darkness: let it grow.

Let knowledge grow from more to more,   25
　　But more of reverence in us dwell;
　　That mind and soul, according well,
May make one music as before,[4]

But vaster. We are fools and slight;
　　We mock thee when we do not fear: 30
　　But help thy foolish ones to bear;
Help thy vain worlds to bear thy light.

Forgive what seemed my sin in me,
　　What seemed my worth since I began;
　　For merit lives from man to man,   35
And not from man, O Lord, to thee.

Forgive my grief for one removed,
　　Thy creature, whom I found so fair.
　　I trust he lives in thee, and there
I find him worthier to be loved.   40

Forgive these wild and wandering cries,
　　Confusions of a wasted[5] youth;
　　Forgive them where they fail in truth,
And in thy wisdom make me wise.

1849

1

I held it truth, with him who sings
　　To one clear harp in divers tones,[6]
　　That men may rise on stepping stones
Of their dead selves to higher things.

---

3. Systems of religion and philosophy.
4. As in the days of fixed religious faith.
5. Desolated.
6. Identified by Tennyson as Goethe.

But who shall so forecast the years   5
   And find in loss a gain to match?
   Or reach a hand through time to catch
The far-off interest of tears?

Let Love clasp Grief lest both be drowned,
   Let darkness keep her raven gloss.   10
   Ah, sweeter to be drunk with loss,
To dance with Death, to beat the ground,

Than that the victor Hours should scorn
   The long result of love, and boast,
   "Behold the man that loved and lost,   15
But all he was is overworn."

2

Old yew, which graspest at the stones
   That name the underlying dead,
   Thy fibers net the dreamless head,
Thy roots are wrapped about the bones.

The seasons bring the flower again,   5
   And bring the firstling to the flock;
   And in the dusk of thee the clock
Beats out the little lives of men.

O, not for thee the glow, the bloom,
   Who changest not in any gale,   10
   Nor branding summer suns avail
To touch thy thousand years of gloom;[7]

And gazing on thee, sullen tree,
   Sick for[8] thy stubborn hardihood,
   I seem to fail from out my blood   15
And grow incorporate into thee.

3

O Sorrow, cruel fellowship,
   O Priestess in the vaults of Death,
   O sweet and bitter in a breath,
What whispers from thy lying lip?

"The stars," she whispers, "blindly run;   5
   A web is woven across the sky;
   From out waste places comes a cry,
And murmurs from the dying sun;

"And all the phantom, Nature, stands—
   With all the music in her tone,   10
   A hollow echo of my own—
A hollow form with empty hands."

7. The ancient yew tree, growing in the grounds near the clock tower and church where Hallam was to be buried, seems neither to blossom in spring nor change from its dark mournful color in summer.
8. Envying or longing to share.

And shall I take a thing so blind,
　　Embrace her[9] as my natural good;
　　Or crush her, like a vice of blood,   15
Upon the threshold of the mind?

4

To Sleep I give my powers away;
　　My will is bondsman to the dark;
　　I sit within a helmless bark,
And with my heart I muse and say:

O heart, how fares it with thee now,   5
　　That thou should fail from thy desire,
　　Who scarcely darest to inquire,
"What is it makes me beat so low?"

Something it is which thou hast lost,
　　Some pleasure from thine early years.   10
　　Break thou deep vase of chilling tears,
That grief hath shaken into frost![1]

Such clouds of nameless trouble cross
　　All night below the darkened eyes;
　　With morning wakes the will, and cries,   15
"Thou shalt not be the fool of loss."

5

I sometimes hold it half a sin
　　To put in words the grief I feel;
　　For words, like Nature, half reveal
And half conceal the Soul within.

But, for the unquiet heart and brain,   5
　　A use in measured language lies;
　　The sad mechanic exercise,
Like dull narcotics, numbing pain.

In words, like weeds,[2] I'll wrap me o'er,
　　Like coarsest clothes against the cold;   10
　　But that large grief which these enfold
Is given in outline and no more.

6

One writes, that "Other friends remain,"
　　That "Loss is common to the race"—
　　And common is the commonplace,
And vacant chaff well meant for grain.

That loss is common would not make   5
　　My own less bitter, rather more:

9. I.e., sorrow.
1. Tennyson comments: "Water can be brought below freezing-point and not turn into ice—if it be kept still; but if it be moved suddenly it turns into ice and may break a vase."
2. Garments.

Too common! Never morning wore
To evening, but some heart did break.

O father, wheresoe'er thou be,
    Who pledgest[3] now thy gallant son;   10
    A shot, ere half thy draft be done,
Hath stilled the life that beat from thee.

O mother, praying God will save
    Thy sailor—while thy head is bowed,
    His heavy-shotted hammock-shroud   15
Drops in his vast and wandering grave.

Ye know no more than I who wrought
    At that last hour to please him well;[4]
    Who mused on all I had to tell,
And something written, something thought;   20

Expecting still his advent home;
    And ever met him on his way
    With wishes, thinking, "here today,"
Or "here tomorrow will he come."

O somewhere, meek, the unconscious dove,   25
    That sittest ranging[5] golden hair;
    And glad to find thyself so fair,
Poor child, that waitest for thy love!

For now her father's chimney glows
    In expectation of a guest;   30
    And thinking "this will please him best,"
She takes a riband or a rose;

For he will see them on tonight;
    And with the thought her color burns;
    And, having left the glass, she turns   35
Once more to set a ringlet right;

And, even when she turned, the curse
    Had fallen, and her future Lord
    Was drowned in passing through the ford,
Or killed in falling from his horse.   40

O what to her shall be the end?
    And what to me remains of good?
    To her, perpetual maidenhood,
And unto me no second friend.

3. Toasts.
4. According to Tennyson's son, his father had discovered that he had been writing a letter to Hallam during the very hour when his friend died.
5. Arranging.

7

Dark house,[6] by which once more I stand
  Here in the long unlovely street,
  Doors, where my heart was used to beat
So quickly, waiting for a hand,

A hand that can be clasped no more—   5
  Behold me, for I cannot sleep,
  And like a guilty thing I creep
At earliest morning to the door.

He is not here; but far away
  The noise of life begins again,   10
  And ghastly through the drizzling rain
On the bald street breaks the blank day.

8

A happy lover who has come
  To look on her that loves him well,
  Who 'lights and rings the gateway bell,
And learns her gone and far from home;

He saddens, all the magic light   5
  Dies off at once from bower and hall,
  And all the place is dark, and all
The chambers emptied of delight:

So find I every pleasant spot
  In which we two were wont to meet,
  The field, the chamber, and the street,   10
For all is dark where thou art not.

Yet as that other, wandering there
  In those deserted walks, may find
  A flower beat with rain and wind,   15
Which once she fostered up with care;

So seems it in my deep regret,
  O my forsaken heart, with thee
  And this poor flower of poesy
Which little cared for fades not yet.   20

But since it pleased a vanished eye,
  I go to plant it on his tomb,
  That if it can it there may bloom,
Or dying, there at least may die.

9

Fair ship, that from the Italian shore
  Sailest the placid ocean-plains

6. House on Wimpole Street, in London, where Hallam had lived.

With my lost Arthur's loved remains,
Spread thy full wings, and waft him o'er.

So draw him home to those that mourn   5
  In vain; a favorable speed
  Ruffle thy mirrored mast, and lead
Through prosperous floods his holy urn.

All night no ruder air perplex
  Thy sliding keel, till Phosphor,[7] bright   10
  As our pure love, through early light
Shall glimmer on the dewey decks.

Sphere all your lights around, above;
  Sleep, gentle heavens, before the prow;
  Sleep, gentle winds, as he sleeps now,   15
My friend, the brother of my love;

My Arthur, whom I shall not see
  Till all my widowed race be run;
  Dear as the mother to the son,
More than my brothers are to me.   20

                        10
I hear the noise about thy keel;
  I hear the bell struck in the night;
  I see the cabin window bright;
I see the sailor at the wheel.

Thou bring'st the sailor to his wife,   5
  And traveled men from foreign lands;
  And letters unto trembling hands:
And, thy dark freight, a vanished life.

So bring him; we have idle dreams;
  This look of quiet flatters thus   10
  Our home-bred fancies. O, to us,
The fools of habit, sweeter seems

To rest beneath the clover sod,
  That takes the sunshine and the rains,
  Or where the kneeling hamlet drains   15
The chalice of the grapes of God;[8]

Than if with thee the roaring wells
  Should gulf him fathom-deep in brine,
  And hands so often clasped in mine,
Should toss with tangle[9] and with shells.   20

7. The morning star.   building rather than in the churchyard.
8. Referring to a burial inside a church   9. Seaweed.

11

Calm is the morn without a sound,
   Calm as to suit a calmer grief,
   And only through the faded leaf
The chestnut pattering to the ground;

Calm and deep peace on this high wold,[1]   5
   And on these dews that drench the furze,
   And all the silvery gossamers
That twinkle into green and gold;

Calm and still light on yon great plain
   That sweeps with all its autumn bowers,   10
   And crowded farms and lessening towers,
To mingle with the bounding main;

Calm and deep peace in this wide air,
   These leaves that redden to the fall,
   And in my heart, if calm at all,   15
If any calm, a calm despair;

Calm on the seas, and silver sleep,
   And waves that sway themselves in rest,
   And dead calm in that noble breast
Which heaves but with the heaving deep.[2]   20

12

Lo, as a dove when up she springs
   To bear through Heaven a tale of woe,
   Some dolorous message knit below
The wild pulsation of her wings;

Like her I go; I cannot stay;   5
   I leave this mortal ark behind,[3]
   A weight of nerves without a mind,
And leave the cliffs, and haste away

O'er ocean-mirrors rounded large,
   And reach the glow of southern skies,   10
   And see the sails at distance rise,
And linger weeping on the marge,

And saying; "Comes he thus, my friend?
   Is this the end of all my care?"

---

1. High and open countryside.
2. It is now the autumn of 1833, and the poet imagines that Hallam's body was already being brought back by ship to England. The date of the actual voyage seems to have been later in the year.
3. According to Christopher Ricks, the account of the imagined flight of the soul refers to Genesis viii.8, when Noah first sends a dove from the ark to discover whether the flood has subsided, "but the dove found no rest for the sole of her foot, and she returned unto him into the ark, for the waters were on the face of the earth."

And circle moaning in the air: 15
"Is this the end? Is this the end?"

And forward dart again, and play
   About the prow, and back return
   To where the body sits, and learn
That I have been an hour away.   20

13

Tears of the widower, when he sees
   A late-lost form that sleep reveals,
   And moves his doubtful arms, and feels
Her place is empty,[4] fall like these;

Which weep a loss forever new,   5
   A void where heart on heart reposed;
   And, where warm hands have pressed and closed,
Silence, till I be silent too;

Which weep the comrade of my choice,
   An awful thought, a life removed,   10
   The human-hearted man I loved,
A Spirit, not a breathing voice.

Come, Time, and teach me, many years,
   I do not suffer in a dream;
   For now so strange do these things seem,   15
Mine eyes have leisure for their tears,

My fancies time to rise on wing,
   And glance about the approaching sails,
   As though they brought but merchants' bales,
And not the burthen that they bring.[5]   20

14

If one should bring me this report,
   That thou[1] hadst touched the land today,
   And I went down unto the quay,
And found thee lying in the port;

And standing, muffled round with woe,   5
   Should see thy passengers in rank
   Come stepping lightly down the plank
And beckoning unto those they know;

And if along with these should come
   The man I held as half divine,   10

---

4. Cf. Milton's sonnet: *Methought I Saw My Late Espoused Saint*: "But O, as to embrace me she inclined, / I waked, she fled, and day brought back my night" [noted by Christopher Ricks].
5. The speaker asks Time to teach him to confront the awesome fact of what has happened (line 10) so that he will not delude himself by fancying the ship is bearing only merchandise and not the body of his friend.
1. I.e., the ship.

Should strike a sudden hand in mine,
    And ask a thousand things of home;

And I should tell him all my pain,
    And how my life had drooped of late,
    And he should sorrow o'er my state   15
And marvel what possessed my brain;

And I perceived no touch of change,
    No hint of death in all his frame,
    But found him all in all the same,
I should not feel it to be strange.   20

15

Tonight the winds begin to rise
    And roar from yonder dropping day;
    The last red leaf is whirled away,
The rooks are blown about the skies;

The forest cracked, the waters curled,   5
    The cattle huddled on the lea;
    And wildly dashed on tower and tree
The sunbeam strikes along the world:

And but for fancies, which aver
    That all thy motions gently pass   10
    Athwart a plane of molten glass,
I scarce could brook the strain and stir

That makes the barren branches loud;
    And but for fear it is not so,
    The wild unrest that lives in woe   15
Would dote and pore on yonder cloud

That rises upward always higher,
    And onward drags a laboring breast,
    And topples round the dreary west,
A looming bastion fringed with fire.   20

* * *

19

The Danube to the Severn[2] gave
    The darkened heart that beat no more;
    They laid him by the pleasant shore,
And in the hearing of the wave.

There twice a day the Severn fills;   5
    The salt sea water passes by,

---

2. Hallam died at Vienna on the Danube. His burial place is on the banks of the Severn, a tidal river in the southwest of England.

And hushes half the babbling Wye,[3]
And makes a silence in the hills.

The Wye is hushed nor moved along,
    And hushed my deepest grief of all,   10
    When filled with tears that cannot fall,
I brim with sorrow drowning song.

The tide flows down, the wave again
    Is vocal in its wooded walls;
    My deeper anguish also falls,   15
And I can speak a little then.

                    * * *

                    21
I sing to him that rests below,
    And, since the grasses round me wave,
    I take the grasses of the grave,[4]
And make them pipes whereon to blow.

The traveler hears me now and then,   5
    And sometimes harshly will he speak:
    "This fellow would make weakness weak,
And melt the waxen hearts of men."

Another answers: "Let him be,
    He loves to make parade of pain,   10
    That with his piping he may gain
The praise that comes to constancy."

A third is wroth: "Is this an hour
    For private sorrow's barren song,
    When more and more the people throng   15
The chairs and thrones of civil power?

"A time to sicken and to swoon,
    When Science reaches forth her arms[5]
    To feel from world to world, and charms
Her secret from the latest moon?"[6]   20

Behold, ye speak an idle thing;
    Ye never knew the sacred dust.
    I do but sing because I must,
And pipe but as the linnets sing;

---

3. The water of the Wye River, a tributary of the Severn, is dammed up as the
tide flows in, and its sound is silenced
until, with the turn of the tide, its
"wave" once more becomes "vocal"
(lines 13–14); these stanzas were written
at Tintern Abbey in the Wye River
country.
4. The speaker assumes that the burial
was in the churchyard; in fact, Hal-

lam's body was interred in a vault inside St. Andrews church at Clevedon,
Somersetshire, on January 3, 1834. See
section 10, lines 11–16.
5. Astronomical instruments such as tel-
escopes.
6. Probably alluding to the discovery,
in 1846, of the planet Neptune and its
moon.

And one is glad; her note is gay,   25
    For now her little ones have ranged;
    And one is sad; her note is changed,
Because her brood is stolen away.

22

The path by which we twain did go,
    Which led by tracts that pleased us well,
    Through four sweet years arose and fell,
From flower to flower, from snow to snow;

And we with singing cheered the way,   5
    And, crowned with all the season lent,
    From April on to April went,
And glad at heart from May to May.

But where the path we walked began
    To slant the fifth autumnal slope,[7]   10
    As we descended following Hope,
There sat the Shadow feared of man;

Who broke our fair companionship,
    And spread his mantle dark and cold,
    And wrapped thee formless in the fold,   15
And dulled the murmur on thy lip,

And bore thee where I could not see
    Nor follow, though I walk in haste,
    And think that somewhere in the waste
The Shadow sits and waits for me.   20

23

Now, sometimes in my sorrow shut,
    Or breaking into song by fits,
    Alone, alone, to where he sits,
The Shadow cloaked from head to foot,

Who keeps the keys of all the creeds,   5
    I wander, often falling lame,
    And looking back to whence I came,
Or on to where the pathway leads;

And crying, How changed from where it ran
    Through lands where not a leaf was dumb,
    But all the lavish hills would hum   10
The murmur of a happy Pan;

When each by turns was guide to each,
    And Fancy light from Fancy caught,
    And Thought leapt out to wed with Thought   15
Ere Thought could wed itself with Speech;

7. Hallam died in early autumn (September 15, 1833) in the fifth year of
the friendship.

And all we met was fair and good,
　　And all was good that Time could bring,
　　And all the secret of the Spring
Moved in the chambers of the blood;　　　　　20

And many an old philosophy
　　On Argive heights divinely sang,[8]
　　And round us all the thicket rang
To many a flute of Arcady.[9]

24

And was the day of my delight
　　As pure and perfect as I say?
　　The very source and fount of day
Is dashed with wandering isles of night.[1]

If all was good and fair we met,　　　　　5
　　This earth had been the Paradise
　　It never looked to human eyes
Since our first sun arose and set.

And is it that the haze of grief
　　Makes former gladness loom so great?　　　10
　　The lowness of the present state,
That sets the past in this relief?

Or that the past will always win
　　A glory from its being far,
　　And orb into the perfect star　　　　　15
We saw not when we moved therein?[2]

25

I know that this was Life—the track
　　Whereon with equal feet we fared;
　　And then, as now, the day prepared
The daily burden for the back.

But this it was that made me move　　　　　5
　　As light as carrier birds in air;
　　I loved the weight I had to bear,
Because it needed help of Love;

Nor could I weary, heart or limb,
　　When mighty Love would cleave in twain　　10
　　The lading of a single pain,
And part it, giving half to him.

---

8. In classical times the Greek city of Argos was renowned for its music.
9. Sheep-raising region in Greece associated with pastoral poetry.
1. Moving spots on the sun.
2. The speaker speculates whether past experiences seem so much more "pure and perfect" (line 2) than present ones because they are far distant from us in time just as our planet Earth would have the deceptive appearance of being a perfect orb if we viewed it from a great distance in space, as from another planet. See *Locksley Hall Sixty Years After*, lines 187–92.

26

Still onward winds the dreary way;
    I with it, for I long to prove
    No lapse of moons can canker Love,
Whatever fickle tongues may say.

And if that eye which watches guilt   5
    And goodness, and hath power to see
    Within the green the mouldered tree,
And towers fallen as soon as built—

O, if indeed that eye foresee
    Or see—in Him is no before—   10
    In more of life true life no more
And Love the indifference to be,

Then might I find, ere yet the morn
    Breaks hither over Indian seas,
    That Shadow waiting with the keys,   15
To shroud me from my proper scorn.[3]

27

I envy not in any moods
    The captive void of noble rage,
    The linnet born within the cage,
That never knew the summer woods;

I envy not the beast that takes   5
    His license in the field of time,
    Unfettered by the sense of crime,
To whom a conscience never wakes;

Nor, what may count itself as blest,
    The heart that never plighted troth   10
    But stagnates in the weeds of sloth;
Nor any want-begotten rest.[4]

I hold it true, whate'er befall;
    I feel it, when I sorrow most;
    'Tis better to have loved and lost   15
Than never to have loved at all.

28

The time draws near the birth of Christ.[5]
    The moon is hid, the night is still;
    The Christmas bells from hill to hill
Answer each other in the mist.

Four voices of four hamlets round,   5
    From far and near, on mead and moor,

3. The Deity, being outside time, sees
(rather than foresees) whether or not
the rest of life ("more of life," line 11)
will be pointless. If pointless then the
way for the speaker to deal with his
self-scorn ("proper scorn") might be
to seek death.
4. Complacency resulting from some
deficiency or "want."
5. The first Christmas after Hallam's
death (1833); the setting is Tennyson's
family home in Lincolnshire.

Swell out and fail, as if a door
Were shut between me and the sound;

Each voice four changes [6] on the wind,
  That now dilate, and now decrease,
  Peace and goodwill, goodwill and peace,   10
Peace and goodwill, to all mankind.

This year I slept and woke with pain,
  I almost wished no more to wake,
  And that my hold on life would break   15
Before I heard those bells again;

But they my troubled spirit rule,
  For they controlled me when a boy;
  They bring me sorrow touched with joy,
The merry, merry bells of Yule.   20

29

With such compelling cause to grieve
  As daily vexes household peace,
  And chains regret to his decease,
How dare we keep our Christmas eve;

Which brings no more a welcome guest   5
  To enrich the threshold of the night
  With showered largess of delight
In dance and song and game and jest?

Yet go, and while the holly boughs
  Entwine the cold baptismal font,
  Make one wreath more for Use and Wont,[7]   10
That guard the portals of the house;

Old sisters of a day gone by,
  Gray nurses, loving nothing new;
  Why should they miss their yearly due   15
Before their time? They too will die.

30

With trembling fingers did we weave
  The holly round the Christmas hearth;
  A rainy cloud possessed the earth,
And sadly fell our Christmas eve.

At our old pastimes in the hall   5
  We gamboled, making vain pretense
  Of gladness, with an awful sense
Of one mute Shadow watching all.

---

6. Different sequences in which church bells are pealed.
7. Personifying the spirits who expect customary observances of the Christmas season to be followed.

We paused: the winds were in the beech;
   We heard them sweep the winter land;   10
   And in a circle hand-in-hand
Sat silent, looking each at each.

Then echo-like our voices rang;
   We sung, though every eye was dim,
   A merry song we sang with him   15
Last year; impetuously we sang.

We ceased; a gentler feeling crept
   Upon us: surely rest is meet.[8]
   "They rest," we said, "their sleep is sweet,"
And silence followed, and we wept.   20

Our voices took a higher range;
   Once more we sang: "They do not die
   Nor lose their mortal sympathy,
Nor change to us, although they change;

"Rapt [9] from the fickle and the frail   25
   With gathered power, yet the same,
   Pierces the keen seraphic flame
From orb to orb,[10] from veil to veil."

Rise, happy morn, rise, holy morn,
   Draw forth the cheerful day from night: 30
   O Father, touch the east, and light
The light that shone when Hope was born.

* * *

34

My own dim life should teach me this,
   That life shall live forevermore,
   Else earth is darkness at the core,
And dust and ashes all that is;

This round of green, this orb of flame,   5
   Fantastic beauty; such as lurks
   In some wild poet, when he works
Without a conscience or an aim.[1]

What then were God to such as I?
   'Twere hardly worth my while to choose   10
   Of things all mortal, or to use
A little patience ere I die;

'Twere best at once to sink to peace,
   Like birds the charming serpent draws,[2]

---

8. Proper or appropriate.
9. Carried away from.
10. The angelic spirit ("flame") of the dead moves from star to star.
1. Perhaps Thomas Lovell Beddoes, a brilliantly promising but erratic poet, admired by Tennyson, who committed suicide in 1849.
2. Some snakes are reputed to capture their prey by casting a charm.

To drop head-foremost in the jaws 15
Of vacant darkness and to cease.

35

Yet if some voice that man could trust
Should murmur from the narrow house,
"The cheeks drop in, the body bows;
Man dies, nor is there hope in dust";

Might I not say? "Yet even here, 5
But for one hour, O Love, I strive
To keep so sweet a thing alive."
But I should turn mine ears and hear

The moanings of the homeless sea,
The sound of streams that swift or slow 10
Draw down Aeonian hills,[3] and sow
The dust of continents to be;

And Love would answer with a sigh,
"The sound of that forgetful shore
Will change my sweetness more and more, 15
Half-dead to know that I shall die."

O me, what profits it to put
An idle case? If Death were seen
At first as Death, Love had not been,
Or been in narrowest working shut, 20

Mere fellowship of sluggish moods,
Or in his coarsest Satyr-shape
Had bruised the herb and crushed the grape,
And basked and battened in the woods.[4]

* * *

39

Old warder of these buried bones,
And answering now my random stroke
With fruitful cloud and living smoke,
Dark yew, that graspest at the stones

And dippest toward the dreamless head, 5
To thee too comes the golden hour
When flower is feeling after flower;[5]
But Sorrow—fixed upon the dead,

And darkening the dark graves of men—
What whispered from her lying lips? 10

---

3. Hills that are aeons old, seemingly everlasting.
4. Lines 18 ff. may be paraphrased: if we knew death to be final and that no afterlife were possible, love could not exist except on a primitive or bestial level.

5. The ancient yew tree in the graveyard was described in section 2 as never changing. Now the speaker discovers that in the flowering season, if the tree is struck ("my random stroke," line 2), it gives off a cloud of golden pollen.

Thy gloom is kindled at the tips,[6]
And passes into gloom again.

* * *

44

How fares it with the happy dead?
  For here the man is more and more;
  But he forgets the days before
God closed the doorways of his head.[7]

The days have vanished, tone and tint,   5
  And yet perhaps the hoarding sense [8]
  Gives out at times (he knows not whence)
A little flash, a mystic hint;

And in the long harmonious years
  (If Death so taste Lethean springs [9])   10
  May some dim touch of earthly things
Surprise thee ranging with thy peers.

If such a dreamy touch should fall,
  O turn thee round, resolve the doubt;
  My guardian angel will speak out   15
In that high place, and tell thee all.

* * *

47

That each, who seems a separate whole,
  Should move his rounds,[1] and fusing all
  The skirts [2] of self again, should fall
Remerging in the general Soul,

Is faith as vague as all unsweet.   5
  Eternal form shall still divide
  The eternal soul from all beside;
And I shall know him when we meet;

And we shall sit at endless feast,
  Enjoying each the other's good.   10
  What vaster dream can hit the mood
Of Love on earth? He seeks at least

Upon the last and sharpest height,
  Before the spirits fade away,
  Some landing place, to clasp and say,   15
"Farewell! We lose ourselves in light."

6. Only the tips of the yew-branches
are in flower.
7. This difficult stanza has been variously interpreted. If "man" (line 2)
refers to the dead, the passage means
that in our living world the dead man
is more and more remembered, but that
he, in the afterworld, is shut off through
death from remembering past experiences on earth. Alternatively if "man"
refers to living mankind rather than to
the "happy dead," the passage means
that as man grows up (line 2) he forgets his earliest infancy, especially the
two-year period before the sutures of
his skull are closed.
8. Memory.
9. I.e., springs of forgetfulness.
1. I.e., go through the customary circuit
of life.
2. Outer edges or fringes.

48

If these brief lays, of Sorrow born,
　　Were taken to be such as closed
　　Grave doubts and answers here proposed,
Then these were such as men might scorn.

Her [3] care is not to part and prove;　　　　　5
　　She takes, when harsher moods remit,
　　What slender shade of doubt may flit,
And makes it vassal unto love;

And hence, indeed, she sports with words,
　　But better serves a wholesome law,　　　　10
　　And holds it sin and shame to draw
The deepest measure from the chords;

Nor dare she trust a larger lay,
　　But rather loosens from the lip
　　Short swallow-flights of song, that dip　　15
Their wings in tears, and skim away.

* * *

50

Be near me when my light is low,
　　When the blood creeps, and the nerves prick
　　And tingle; and the heart is sick,
And all the wheels of being slow.

Be near me when the sensuous frame　　　　5
　　Is racked with pangs that conquer trust;
　　And Time, a maniac scattering dust,
And Life, a Fury slinging flame.

Be near me when my faith is dry,
　　And men the flies of latter spring,　　　　10
　　That lay their eggs, and sting and sing
And weave their petty cells and die.

Be near me when I fade away,
　　To point the term of human strife,
　　And on the low dark verge of life　　　　15
The twilight of eternal day.

* * *

54

O, yet we trust that somehow good
　　Will be the final goal of ill,
　　To pangs of nature, sins of will,
Defects of doubt, and taints of blood;

That nothing walks with aimless feet;　　　　5
　　That not one life shall be destroyed,

---

3. I.e., sorrow's.

Or cast as rubbish to the void,
When God hath made the pile complete;

That not a worm is cloven in vain;
    That not a moth with vain desire   10
    Is shriveled in a fruitless fire,
Or but subserves another's gain.

Behold, we know not anything;
    I can but trust that good shall fall
    At last—far off—at last, to all,   15
And every winter change to spring.

So runs my dream; but what am I?
    An infant crying in the night;
    An infant crying for the light,
And with no language but a cry.   20

55

The wish, that of the living whole
    No life may fail beyond the grave,
    Derives it not from what we have
The likest God within the soul?

Are God and Nature then at strife,   5
    That Nature lends such evil dreams?
    So careful of the type [4] she seems,
So careless of the single life,

That I, considering everywhere
    Her secret meaning in her deeds,
    And finding that of fifty seeds   10
She often brings but one to bear,

I falter where I firmly trod,
    And falling with my weight of cares
    Upon the great world's altar-stairs   15
That slope through darkness up to God,

I stretch lame hands of faith, and grope,
    And gather dust and chaff, and call
    To what I feel is Lord of all,
And faintly trust the larger hope.[5]   20

56

"So careful of the type?" but no.
    From scarpéd [6] cliff and quarried stone
    She [7] cries, "A thousand types are gone;
I care for nothing, all shall go.

"Thou makest thine appeal to me: 5
    I bring to life, I bring to death;
    The spirit does but mean the breath:
I know no more." And he, shall he,

---

4. Species.
5. As expressed in lines 1–2 of this section.
6. Cut away so that the strata are exposed.
7. Nature.

Man, her last work, who seemed so fair,
   Such splendid purpose in his eyes, 10
   Who rolled the psalm to wintry skies,
Who built him fanes [8] of fruitless prayer,

Who trusted God was love indeed
   And love Creation's final law—
   Though Nature, red in tooth and claw 15
With ravine, shrieked against his creed—

Who loved, who suffered countless ills,
   Who battled for the True, the Just,
   Be blown about the desert dust,
Or sealed within the iron hills? [9] 20

No more? A monster then, a dream,
   A discord. Dragons of the prime,
   That tare [1] each other in their slime,
Were mellow music matched with [2] him.

O life as futile, then, as frail!
   O for thy voice to soothe and bless! 25
   What hope of answer, or redress?
Behind the veil, behind the veil.

57

Peace; come away: [3] the song of woe
   Is after all an earthly song.
   Peace; come away: we do him wrong
To sing so wildly: let us go.

Come; let us go: your cheeks are pale; 5
   But half my life I leave behind.
   Methinks my friend is richly shrined;
But I shall pass, my work will fail.

Yet in these ears, till hearing dies,
   One set slow bell will seem to toll 10
   The passing of the sweetest soul
That ever looked with human eyes.

I hear it now, and o'er and o'er,
   Eternal greetings to the dead;
   And "Ave,[4] Ave, Ave," said, 15
"Adieu, adieu," forevermore.

58

In those sad words I took farewell.
   Like echoes in sepulchral halls,
   As drop by drop the water falls
In vaults and catacombs, they fell;

---

8. Temples.
9. Preserved like fossils in rock.
1. Tore (archaic).
2. In comparison with.

3. Perhaps addressed to Emily Tennyson, the poet's sister and Hallam's fiancée.
4. Hail.

And, falling, idly broke the peace 5
    Of hearts that beat from day to day,
    Half-conscious of their dying clay,
And those cold crypts where they shall cease.

The high Muse answered: "Wherefore grieve
    Thy brethren with a fruitless tear? 10
    Abide a little longer here,
And thou shalt take a nobler leave."

59

O Sorrow, wilt thou live with me
    No casual mistress, but a wife,[5]
    My bosom friend and half of life;
As I confess it needs must be?

O Sorrow, wilt thou rule my blood, 5
    Be sometimes lovely like a bride,
    And put thy harsher moods aside,
If thou wilt have me wise and good?

My centered passion cannot move,
    Nor will it lessen from today; 10
    But I'll have leave at times to play
As with the creature of my love;

And set thee forth, for thou art mine,
    With so much hope for years to come,
    That, howsoe'er I know thee, some 15
Could hardly tell what name were thine.

* * *

64

Dost thou[6] look back on what hath been,
    As some divinely gifted man,
    Whose life in low estate began
And on a simple village green;

Who breaks his birth's invidious bar, 5
    And grasps the skirts of happy chance,
    And breasts the blows of circumstance,
And grapples with his evil star;

Who makes by force his merit known
    And lives to clutch the golden keys,[7] 10
    To mold a mighty state's decrees,
And shape the whisper of the throne;

And moving up from high to higher,
    Becomes on Fortune's crowning slope

---

5. Cf. *Richard II*, V.i.93–94: "Come, come, in wooing sorrow let's be brief, / Since, wedding it, there is such length in grief" [noted by Christopher Ricks].
6. I.e., Hallam.
7. Badges of high public office.

The pillar of a people's hope,   15
The center of a world's desire;

Yet feels, as in a pensive dream,
    When all his active powers are still,
    A distant dearness in the hill,
A secret sweetness in the stream,   20

The limit of his narrower fate,
    While yet beside its vocal springs
    He played at counselors and kings,
With one that was his earliest mate;

Who plows with pain his native lea   25
    And reaps the labor of his hands,
    Or in the furrow musing stands:
"Does my old friend remember me?"

* * *

67

When on my bed the moonlight falls,
    I know that in thy place of rest
    By that broad water of the west[8]
There comes a glory on the walls:

Thy marble bright in dark appears,   5
    As slowly steals a silver flame
    Along the letters of thy name,
And o'er the number of thy years.

The mystic glory swims away,
    From off my bed the moonlight dies;   10
    And closing eaves of wearied eyes
I sleep till dusk is dipped in gray;

And then I know the mist is drawn
    A lucid veil from coast to coast,
    And in the dark church like a ghost   15
Thy tablet glimmers to the dawn.

* * *

70

I cannot see the features right,
    When on the gloom I strive to paint
    The face I know; the hues are faint
And mix with hollow masks of night;

Cloud-towers by ghostly masons wrought,   5
    A gulf that ever shuts and gapes,
    A hand that points, and palléd shapes
In shadowy thoroughfares of thought;

8. The Severn River.

And crowds that stream from yawning doors,
  And shoals of puckered faces drive;   10
  Dark bulks that tumble half alive,
And lazy lengths on boundless shores;

Till all at once beyond the will
  I hear a wizard music roll,
  And through a lattice on the soul   15
Looks thy fair face and makes it still.

71

Sleep, kinsman thou to death and trance
  And madness, thou [9] has forged at last
  A night-long present of the past
In which we went through summer France.[1]

Hadst thou such credit with the soul?   5
  Then bring an opiate trebly strong,
  Drug down the blindfold sense of wrong,
That so my pleasure may be whole;

While now we talk as once we talked
  Of men and minds, the dust of change,   10
  The days that grow to something strange,
In walking as of old we walked

Beside the river's wooded reach,
  The fortress, and the mountain ridge,
  The cataract flashing from the bridge,   15
The breaker breaking on the beach.

72

Risest thou thus, dim dawn, again,[2]
  And howlest, issuing out of night,
  With blasts that blow the poplar white,
And lash with storm the streaming pane?

Day, when my crowned estate [3] begun   5
  To pine in that reverse of doom,[4]
  Which sickened every living bloom,
And blurred the splendor of the sun;

Who usherest in the dolorous hour
  With thy quick tears that make the rose   10
  Pull sideways, and the daisy close
Her crimson fringes to the shower;

Who mightst have heaved a windless flame
  Up the deep East, or, whispering, played

---

9. I.e., sleep.
1. In the summer of 1830, Hallam and Tennyson went through southern France en route to Spain.
2. September 15, 1834, the first anniversary of Hallam's death.
3. State of happiness.
4. The reversal or disaster which doom brought upon him when Hallam died.

A checker-work of beam and shade   15
Along the hills, yet looked the same,

As wan, as chill, as wild as now;
   Day, marked as with some hideous crime,
   When the dark hand struck down through time,
And canceled nature's best: but thou,   20

Lift as thou mayst thy burthened brows
   Through clouds that drench the morning star,
   And whirl the ungarnered sheaf afar,
And sow the sky with flying boughs,

And up thy vault with roaring sound   25
   Climb thy thick noon, disastrous day;
   Touch thy dull goal of joyless gray,
And hide thy shame beneath the ground.

* * *
75
I leave thy praises unexpressed
   In verse that brings myself relief,
   And by the measure of my grief
I leave thy greatness to be guessed.

What practice howsoe'er expert   5
   In fitting aptest words to things,
   Or voice the richest-toned that sings,
Hath power to give thee as thou wert?

I care not in these fading days
   To raise a cry that lasts not long,   10
   And round thee with the breeze of song
To stir a little dust of praise.

Thy leaf has perished in the green,
   And, while we breathe beneath the sun,
   The world which credits what is done   15
Is cold to all that might have been.

So here shall silence guard thy fame;
   But somewhere, out of human view,
   Whate'er thy hands are set to do
Is wrought with tumult of acclaim.   20

* * *
78
Again at Christmas [5] did we weave
   The holly round the Christmas hearth;
   The silent snow possessed the earth,
And calmly fell our Christmas eve.

5. The second Christmas (1834) after Hallam's death.

The yule clog [6] sparkled keen with frost,   5
    No wing of wind the region swept,
    But over all things brooding slept
The quiet sense of something lost.

As in the winters left behind,
    Again our ancient games had place,   10
    The mimic picture's [7] breathing grace,
And dance and song and hoodman-blind.

Who showed a token of distress?
    No single tear, no mark of pain—
    O sorrow, then can sorrow wane?   15
O grief, can grief be changed to less?

O last regret, regret can die!
    No—mixed with all this mystic frame,
    Her [8] deep relations are the same,
But with long use her tears are dry.   20

* * *

82

I wage not any feud with Death
    For changes wrought on form and face;
    No lower life that earth's embrace
May breed with him can fright my faith.

Eternal process moving on,   5
    From state to state the spirit walks;
    And these are but the shattered stalks,
Or ruined chrysalis of one.

Nor blame I Death, because he bare
    The use of virtue out of earth;   10
    I know transplanted human worth
Will bloom to profit, otherwhere.

For this alone on Death I wreak
    The wrath that garners in my heart:
    He put our lives so far apart   15
We cannot hear each other speak.

83

Dip down upon the northern shore,
    O sweet new-year [9] delaying long;
Thou doest expectant Nature wrong;
Delaying long, delay no more.

What stays thee from the clouded noons,   5
    Thy sweetness from its proper place?
    Can trouble live with April days,
Or sadness in the summer moons?

6. Log.
7. A game in which the participants
pose in the manner of some famous
statue or painting and the spectators
try to guess what work of art is being
mimicked.
8. I.e., sorrow's.
9. Spring of 1835.

Bring orchis, bring the foxglove spire,
  The little speedwell's [1] darling blue,   10
  Deep tulips dashed with fiery dew,
Laburnums, dropping-wells of fire.

O thou, new-year, delaying long,
  Delayest the sorrow in my blood,
  That longs to burst a frozen bud   15
And flood a fresher throat with song.

84

When I contemplate all alone
  The life that had been thine below,
  And fix my thoughts on all the glow
To which thy crescent would have grown,

I see thee sitting crowned with good,   5
  A central warmth diffusing bliss
  In glance and smile, and clasp and kiss,
On all the branches of thy blood;

Thy blood, my friend, and partly mine;
  For now the day was drawing on,   10
  When thou shouldst link thy life with one
Of mine own house, and boys of thine

Had babbled "Uncle" on my knee;
  But that remorseless iron hour
  Made cypress of her orange flower,[2]   15
Despair of hope, and earth of thee.

I seem to meet their least desire,
  To clap their cheeks, to call them mine.
  I see their unborn faces shine
Beside the never-lighted fire.   20

I see myself an honored guest,
  Thy partner in the flowery walk
  Of letters, genial table talk,
Or deep dispute, and graceful jest;

While now thy prosperous labor fills   25
  The lips of men with honest praise,
  And sun by sun the happy days
Descend below the golden hills

With promise of a morn as fair;
  And all the train of bounteous hours   30
  Conduct, by paths of growing powers,
To reverence and the silver hair;

Till slowly worn her earthly robe,
  Her lavish mission richly wrought,

---

1. A blue spring flower.
2. Orange blossoms are associated with brides—here the poet's sister, Emily Tennyson, to whom Hallam had been engaged.

Leaving great legacies of thought,   35
Thy spirit should fail from off the globe;

What time mine own might also flee,
    As linked with thine in love and fate,
    And, hovering o'er the dolorous strait
To the other shore, involved in thee,   40

Arrive at last the blessed goal,
    And He that died in Holy Land
    Would reach us out the shining hand,
And take us as a single soul.

What reed was that on which I leant?   45
    Ah, backward fancy, wherefore wake
    The old bitterness again, and break
The low beginnings of content?

* * *

86

Sweet after showers, ambrosial air,
    That rollest from the gorgeous gloom
    Of evening over brake and bloom
And meadow, slowly breathing bare

The round of space,[3] and rapt below   5
    Through all the dewy-tasseled wood,
    And shadowing down the hornéd flood[4]
In ripples, fan my brows and blow

The fever from my cheek, and sigh
    The full new life that feeds thy breath   10
    Throughout my frame, till Doubt and Death,
Ill brethren, let the fancy fly

From belt to belt of crimson seas
    On leagues of odor streaming far,
    To where in yonder orient star   15
A hundred spirits whisper "Peace."

87

I passed beside the reverend walls[5]
    In which of old I wore the gown;
    I roved at random through the town,
And saw the tumult of the halls;

And heard once more in college fanes   5
    The storm their high-built organs make,
    And thunder-music, rolling, shake
The prophet blazoned on the panes;

3. Air that is slowly clearing the clouds
from the sky.
4. "Between two promontories." [Tenny-
son's comment].
5. Of Trinity College, Cambridge University.

And caught once more the distant shout,
　　The measured pulse of racing oars　　　　　　10
　　Among the willows; paced the shores
And many a bridge, and all about

The same gray flats again, and felt
　　The same, but not the same; and last
　　Up that long walk of limes I passed　　　　　　15
To see the rooms in which he dwelt.

Another name was on the door.
　　I lingered; all within was noise
　　Of songs, and clapping hands, and boys
That crashed the glass and beat the floor;　　　　20

Where once we held debate, a band
　　Of youthful friends,[6] on mind and art,
　　And labor, and the changing mart,
And all the framework of the land;

When one would aim an arrow fair,　　　　　　25
　　But send it slackly from the string;
　　And one would pierce an outer ring,
And one an inner, here and there;

And last the master bowman, he,
　　Would cleave the mark. A willing ear　　　　　30
　　We lent him. Who but hung to hear
The rapt oration flowing free

From point to point, with power and grace
　　And music in the bounds of law,[7]
　　To those conclusions when we saw　　　　　　35
The God within him light his face,

And seem to lift the form, and glow
　　In azure orbits heavenly-wise;
　　And over those ethereal eyes
The bar of Michael Angelo?[8]　　　　　　40

88

Wild bird, whose warble, liquid sweet,
　　Rings Eden through the budded quicks,[9]

---

6. The "Apostles," an undergraduate club to which Tennyson and Hallam had belonged.
7. An essay presented by Hallam at Cambridge in 1831 provides an example of his skill in theological argument (see *The Writings of Arthur Hallam*, edited by T. H. V. Motter, 1943, pp. 198–213). This essay, much admired by Tennyson, may have influenced the main argument of *In Memoriam*. In his essay Hallam develops an idea he had stated in a letter to Tennyson's sister: "It is by the heart, not by the head, that we must all be convinced of the two great fundamental truths, the reality of Love, and the reality of Evil." See also *In Memoriam*, section 109, lines 1–8 below.
8. Hallam, like Michelangelo, had a prominent ridge of bone above his eyes.
9. Hawthorn hedges. The "wild bird" is presumably a nightingale.

O tell me where the senses mix,
O tell me where the passions meet,

Whence radiate: fierce extremes employ   45
   Thy spirits in the darkening leaf,[1]
   And in the midmost heart of grief
Thy passion clasps a secret joy;

And I—my harp would prelude woe—
   I cannot all command the strings;   50
   The glory of the sum of things
Will flash along the chords and go.

89

Witch elms that counterchange the floor
Of this flat lawn with dusk and bright;[2]
   And thou, with all thy breadth and height
Of foliage, towering sycamore;

How often, hither wandering down,   5
   My Arthur found your shadows fair,
   And shook to all the liberal air
The dust and din and steam of town!

He brought an eye for all he saw;
   He mixed in all our simple sports;   10
   They pleased him, fresh from brawling courts
And dusty purlieus of the law.[3]

O joy to him in this retreat,
   Immantled in ambrosial dark,
   To drink the cooler air, and mark   15
The landscape winking through the heat!

O sound to rout the brood of cares,
   The sweep of scythe in morning dew,
   The gust that round the garden flew,
And tumbled half the mellowing pears!   20

O bliss, when all in circle drawn
   About him, heart and ear were fed
   To hear him, as he lay and read
The Tuscan poets[4] on the lawn!

Or in the all-golden afternoon   25
   A guest, or happy sister, sung,
   Or here she brought the harp and flung
A ballad to the brightening moon.

Nor less it pleased in livelier moods,
   Beyond the bounding hill to stray,   30

---

1. Cf. Keats' *Ode to a Nightingale* (lines 10 and 60) and his sonnet on *King Lear*, line 5.
2. Shadows of the elm tree checker the lawn at Somersby, the Tennysons' country home.
3. Hallam became a law student in London after leaving Cambridge.
4. Petrarch and Dante.

And break the livelong summer day
With banquet in the distant woods;

Whereat we glanced from theme to theme,
    Discussed the books to love or hate,
    Or touched the changes of the state,
Or threaded some Socratic dream;[5]   35

But if I praised the busy town,
    He loved to rail against it still,
    For "ground in yonder social mill
We rub each other's angles down,   40

"And merge," he said, "in form and gloss
    The picturesque of man and man."
    We talked: the stream beneath us ran,
The wine-flask lying couched in moss,

Or cooled within the glooming wave;   45
    And last, returning from afar,
    Before the crimson-circled star [6]
Had fallen into her father's grave,

And brushing ankle-deep in flowers,
    We heard behind the woodbine veil   50
    The milk that bubbled in [7] the pail,
And buzzings of the honeyed hours.

* * *

91

When rosy plumelets tuft the larch,
    And rarely [8] pipes the mounted thrush,
    Or underneath the barren bush
Flits by the sea-blue bird [9] of March;

Come, wear the form by which I know   5
    Thy spirit in time among thy peers;
    The hope of unaccomplished years
Be large and lucid round thy brow.

When summer's hourly-mellowing change
    May breathe, with many roses sweet,   10
    Upon the thousand waves of wheat
That ripple round the lowly grange,

Come; not in watches of the night,
    But where the sunbeam broodeth warm,
    Come, beauteous in thine after form,
And like a finer light in light.   15

* * *

5. I.e., worked our way through some discourse of Socrates (as recorded by Plato).
6. Venus, which will sink into the west as the sun has done. According to the nebular hypothesis, planets were flung from the sun into the outer spaces of our solar system; in this sense the sun is the "father" of planets.
7. Into.
8. Exquisitely.
9. Kingfisher.

93

I shall not see thee. Dare I say
   No spirit ever brake the band
   That stays him from the native land
Where first he walked when clasped in clay?[1]

No visual shade of someone lost,   5
   But he, the Spirit himself, may come
   Where all the nerve of sense is numb,
Spirit to Spirit, Ghost to Ghost.

Oh, therefore from thy sightless[2] range
   With gods in unconjectured bliss,   10
   Oh, from the distance of the abyss
Of tenfold-complicated change,

Descend, and touch, and enter; hear
   The wish too strong for words to name,
   That in this blindness of the frame[3]   15
My Ghost may feel that thine is near.

94

How pure at heart and sound in head,
   With what divine affections bold
   Should be the man whose thought would hold
An hour's communion with the dead.

In vain shalt thou, or any, call   5
   The spirits from their golden day,
   Except, like them, thou too canst say,
My spirit is at peace with all.

They haunt the silence of the breast,
   Imaginations calm and fair,   10
   The memory like a cloudless air,
The conscience as a sea at rest;

But when the heart is full of din,
   And doubt beside the portal waits,
   They can but listen at the gates,   15
And hear the household jar within.

95

By night we lingered on the lawn,
   For underfoot the herb was dry;
   And genial warmth; and o'er the sky
The silvery haze of summer drawn;

And calm that let the tapers burn   5
   Unwavering: not a cricket chirred;

---

1. I.e., when he was alive and clothed in flesh.
2. Invisible.
3. The living body.

The brook alone far off was heard,
And on the board the fluttering urn.[4]

And bats went round in fragrant skies,
   And wheeled or lit the filmy shapes[5]   10
   That haunt the dusk, with ermine capes
And woolly breasts and beaded eyes;

While now we sang old songs that pealed
   From knoll to knoll, where, couched at ease,
   The white kine[6] glimmered, and the trees   15
Laid their dark arms[7] about the field.

But when those others, one by one,
   Withdrew themselves from me and night,
   And in the house light after light
Went out, and I was all alone,   20

A hunger seized my heart; I read
   Of that glad year which once had been,
   In those fallen leaves which kept their green,
The noble letters of the dead.

And strangely on the silence broke   25
   The silent-speaking words, and strange
   Was love's dumb cry defying change
To test his worth; and strangely spoke

The faith, the vigor, bold to dwell
   On doubts that drive the coward back,   30
   And keen through wordy snares to track
Suggestion to her inmost cell.

So word by word, and line by line,
   The dead man touched me from the past,
   And all at once it seemed at last   35
The[8] living soul was flashed on mine,

And mine in this was wound, and whirled
   About empyreal heights of thought,
   And came on that which is, and caught
The deep pulsations of the world,   40

Aeonian music[9] measuring out
   The steps of Time—the shocks of Chance—

---

4. Urn to boil water for tea or coffee, heated by a fluttering flame.
5. The white-winged night moths called ermine moths.
6. Cows.
7. Cast the shadows of their branches.

8. Printed "His" in the first edition; and line 37 read, in the first edition, "And mine in his was wound."
9. The music of the universe which has pulsated for aeons of time.

The blows of Death. At length my trance
Was canceled, stricken through with doubt.[10]

Vague words! but ah, how hard to frame   45
    In matter-molded forms of speech,
    Or even for intellect to reach
Through memory that which I became.

Till now the doubtful dusk revealed
    The knolls once more where, couched at ease,   50
    The white kine glimmered, and the trees
Laid their dark arms about the field;

And sucked from out the distant gloom
    A breeze began to tremble o'er
    The large leaves of the sycamore,   55
And fluctuate all the still perfume,

And gathering freshlier overhead,
    Rocked the full-foliaged elms, and swung
    The heavy-folded rose, and flung
The lilies to and fro, and said,   60

"The dawn, the dawn," and died away;
    And East and West, without a breath,
    Mixed their dim lights, like life and death,
To broaden into boundless day.

96

You say, but with no touch of scorn,
    Sweet-hearted, you,[1] whose light blue eyes
    Are tender over drowning flies,
You tell me, doubt is Devil-born.

I know not: one[2] indeed I knew   5
    In many a subtle question versed,
    Who touched a jarring lyre at first,
But ever strove to make it true;

10. In a letter of 1874 replying to an inquiry about his experience of mystical trances, Tennyson wrote: "A kind of waking trance I have frequently had, quite up from boyhood, when I have been all alone. This has generally come upon me through repeating my own name two or three times to myself silently, till all at once, as if were out of the intensity of the consciousness of individuality, the individuality itself seemed to dissolve and fade away into boundless being, and this not a confused state, but the clearest of the clearest, the surest of the surest, the weirdest of the weirdest, utterly beyond words, where death was an almost laughable impossibility, the loss of personality (if so it were) seeming no extinction but the only true life. * * * This might * * * be the state which St. Paul describes, 'Whether in the body I cannot tell, or whether out of the body I cannot tell.' * * * I am ashamed of my feeble description. Have I not said the state is utterly beyond words? But in a moment, when I come back to my normal state of 'sanity,' I am ready to fight for *mein liebes Ich* [my dear self], and hold that it will last for aeons of aeons."—*Alfred Lord Tennyson, A Memoir*, 1897, I, 320.
1. A woman of simple faith, perhaps Emily Sellwood.
2. Hallam.

Perplexed in faith, but pure in deeds,
   At last he beat his music out.   10
   There lives more faith in honest doubt,
Believe me, than in half the creeds.

He fought his doubts and gathered strength,
   He would not make his judgment blind,
   He faced the specters of the mind   15
And laid them; thus he came at length

To find a stronger faith his own,
   And Power was with him in the night,
   Which makes the darkness and the light,
And dwells not in the light alone,   20

But in the darkness and the cloud,[3]
   As over Sinaï's peaks of old,
   While Israel made their gods of gold,
Although the trumpet blew so loud.

* * *

99

Risest thou thus, dim dawn, again,[4]
   So loud with voices of the birds,
   So thick with lowings of the herds,
Day, when I lost the flower of men;

Who tremblest through thy darkling red   5
   On yon swollen brook that bubbles fast[5]
   By meadows breathing of the past,
And woodlands holy to the dead;

Who murmurest in the foliage eaves
   A song that slights the coming care,[6]   10
   And Autumn laying here and there
A fiery finger on the leaves;

Who wakenest with thy balmy breath
   To myriads on the genial earth,
   Memories of bridal, or of birth,[7]   15
And unto myriads more, of death.

Oh, wheresoever those[8] may be,
   Betwixt the slumber of the poles,

3. See Exodus xix.16–25. After veiling Mount Sinai in a "cloud" of smoke, God addressed Moses from the darkness.
4. September 15, 1835, the second anniversary of Hallam's death.
5. Reflections of the clouded red light of dawn quiver on the surface of the fast-moving water. Cf. Shakespeare's *Sonnets* (33): "Full many a glorious morning have I seen * * * Gilding pale streams with heavenly alchemy."
6. I.e., disregards future events such as death or the coming of autumn. Cf. Shelley's *Ode to the West Wind*.
7. Cf. *Epilogue*, below, lines 117–28.
8. I.e., the "myriads" who remember death.

Today they count as kindred souls;
  They know me not, but mourn with me.   20

* * *
103

On that last night before we went
  From out the doors where I was bred,[9]
  I dreamed a vision of the dead,
Which left my after-morn content.

Methought I dwelt within a hall,   5
  And maidens with me; distant hills
  From hidden summits fed with rills
A river sliding by the wall.

The hall with harp and carol rang.
  They sang of what is wise and good   10
  And graceful. In the center stood
A statue veiled, to which they sang;

And which, though veiled, was known to me,
  The shape of him I loved, and love
  Forever. Then flew in a dove   15
And brought a summons from the sea;[1]

And when they learnt that I must go,
  They wept and wailed, but led the way
  To where the little shallop[2] lay
At anchor in the flood below;   20

And on by many a level mead,
  And shadowing bluff that made the banks,
  We glided winding under ranks
Of iris and the golden reed;

And still as vaster grew the shore   25
  And rolled the floods in grander space,
  The maidens gathered strength and grace
And presence, lordlier than before;

And I myself, who sat apart
  And watched them, waxed in every limb;   30
  I felt the thews of Anakim,[3]
The pulses of a Titan's heart;

As one would sing the death of war,
  And one would chant the history
  Of that great race which is to be,[4]   35
And one the shaping of a star;

---

9. In 1837 Tennyson and his family moved away from their home in Lincolnshire, which had been closely associated with his friendship with Hallam. In section 104 the move seems to occur in 1835, the year of the third Christmas after Hallam's death.
1. Cf. *Crossing the Bar:* "And one clear call for me."
2. A light open boat.
3. Plural of *Anak;* i.e., a reference to the giant sons of Anak. See Numbers xiii.33. The Titans (line 32) were giants of Greek mythology.
4. See the account of the "crowning race" in *Epilogue,* below, lines 128–44.

Until the forward-creeping tides
 Began to foam, and we to draw
 From deep to deep, to where we saw
A great ship lift her shining sides.[5]   40

The man we loved was there on deck,
 But thrice as large as man he bent
 To greet us. Up the side I went,
And fell in silence on his neck;

Whereat those maidens with one mind   45
 Bewailed their lot; I did them wrong:
 "We served thee here," they said, "so long,
And wilt thou leave us now behind?"

So rapt [6] I was, they could not win
 An answer from my lips, but he   50
 Replying, "Enter likewise ye
And go with us:" they entered in.

And while the wind began to sweep
 A music out of sheet and shroud,
 We steered her toward a crimson cloud   55
That landlike slept along the deep.

104

The time draws near the birth of Christ; [7]
 The moon is hid, the night is still;
 A single church below the hill
Is pealing, folded in the mist.

A single peal of bells below,   5
 That wakens at this hour of rest
 A single murmur in the breast,
That these are not the bells I know.

Like strangers' voices here they sound,
 In lands where not a memory strays,   10
 Nor landmark breathes of other days,
But all is new unhallowed ground.

105

Tonight ungathered let us leave
 This laurel, let this holly stand:[8]
 We live within the stranger's land,
And strangely falls our Christmas eve.

---

5. Cf. *Morte d'Arthur*, lines 255–322, in which Bedivere is left behind as Arthur's barge, the ship of death, sails away. In the present dream vision, not only is the speaker taken aboard but also his companions, who represent the creative arts of this world—"all the human powers and talents that do not pass with life but go along with it,"

as Tennyson said of this passage.
6. Entranced.
7. See note 9 to section 103.
8. Cf. section 29 in which the family in their former home still continued to gather holly. In the new home, in "stranger's land," the customary observances lapse.

Our father's dust is left alone   5
   And silent under other snows:
   There in due time the woodbine blows,
The violet comes, but we are gone.

No more shall wayward grief abuse
   The genial hour with mask and mime;   10
   For change of place, like growth of time,
Has broke the bond of dying use.

Let cares that petty shadows cast,
   By which our lives are chiefly proved,
   A little spare the night I loved,   15
And hold it solemn to the past.

But let no footstep beat the floor,
   Nor bowl of wassail mantle warm;[9]
   For who would keep an ancient form
Through which the spirit breathes no more?   20

Be neither song, nor game, nor feast;
   Nor harp be touched, nor flute be blown;
   No dance, no motion, save alone
What lightens in the lucid east

Of rising worlds[10] by yonder wood.   25
   Long sleeps the summer in the seed;
   Run out your measured arcs, and lead
The closing cycle rich in good.

106

Ring out, wild bells, to the wild sky,
   The flying cloud, the frosty light:
   The year is dying in the night;
Ring out, wild bells, and let him die.

Ring out the old, ring in the new,   5
   Ring, happy bells, across the snow:
   The year is going, let him go;
Ring out the false, ring in the true.

Ring out the grief that saps the mind,
   For those that here we see no more;   10
   Ring out the feud of rich and poor,
Ring in redress to all mankind.

Ring out a slowly dying cause,
   And ancient forms of party strife;
   Ring in the nobler modes of life,   15
With sweeter manners, purer laws.

9. I.e., no bowl of hot punch warm the mantelpiece.

10. "The scintillating motion of the stars that rise" [Tennyson's note].

Ring out the want, the care, the sin,
   The faithless coldness of the times;
   Ring out, ring out my mournful rhymes,
But ring the fuller minstrel in.   20

Ring out false pride in place and blood,
   The civic slander and the spite;
   Ring in the love of truth and right,
Ring in the common love of good.

Ring out old shapes of foul disease;   25
   Ring out the narrowing lust of gold;
   Ring out the thousand wars of old,
Ring in the thousand years of peace.

Ring in the valiant man and free,
   The larger heart, the kindlier hand;   30
   Ring out the darkness of the land,
Ring in the Christ that is to be.[11]

107

It is the day when he was born.[12]
   A bitter day that early sank
   Behind a purple-frosty bank
Of vapor, leaving night forlorn.

The time admits not flowers or leaves   5
   To deck the banquet. Fiercely flies
   The blast of North and East, and ice
Makes daggers at the sharpened eaves,

And bristles all the brakes and thorns
   To yon hard crescent, as she hangs   10
   Above the wood which grides[1] and clangs
Its leafless ribs and iron horns

Together, in the drifts[2] that pass
   To darken on the rolling brine
   That breaks the coast. But fetch the wine,   15
Arrange the board and brim the glass;

Bring in great logs and let them lie,
   To make a solid core of heat;
   Be cheerful-minded, talk and treat
Of all things even as he were by;   20

We keep the day. With festal cheer,
   With books and music, surely we

---

11. These allusions to the second coming of Christ and to the millennium are derived from Revelation xx, but Tennyson has interpreted the Biblical account in his own way. He once told his son of his conviction that "the forms of Christian religion would alter; but that the spirit of Christ would still grow from more to more."
12. February 1.
1. Clashes with a strident noise.
2. Either cloud-drifts or clouds of snow.

Will drink to him, whate'er he be,
And sing the songs he loved to hear.

* * *

109

Heart-affluence in discursive talk
From household fountains never dry;
The critic clearness of an eye
That saw through all the Muses' walk; [3]

Seraphic intellect and force   5
To seize and throw the doubts of man;
Impassioned logic, which outran
The hearer in its fiery course;

High nature amorous of the good,
But touched with no ascetic gloom;   10
And passion pure in snowy bloom
Through all the years of April blood;

A love of freedom rarely felt,
Of freedom in her regal seat
Of England; not the schoolboy heat,   15
The blind hysterics of the Celt; [4]

And manhood fused with female grace
In such a sort, the child would twine
A trustful hand, unasked, in thine,
And find his comfort in thy face;   20

All these have been, and thee mine eyes
Have looked on: if they looked in vain,
My shame is greater who remain,
Nor let thy wisdom make me wise.

* * *

113

'Tis held that sorrow makes us wise;
Yet how much wisdom sleeps with thee
Which not alone had guided me,
But served the seasons that may rise;[5]

For can I doubt, who knew thee keen   5
In intellect, with force and skill
To strive, to fashion, to fulfill—
I doubt not what thou wouldst have been:

A life in civic action warm,
A soul on highest mission sent,   10

---

3. The realm of art and literature.
4. In particular the French at the time of the Revolution of 1789. See also section 127, lines 7–8.

5. I.e., Hallam's wisdom, had he lived, would have been of service to other men than the speaker.

A potent voice of Parliament,
A pillar steadfast in the storm,

Should licensed boldness gather force,
   Becoming, when the time has birth,
   A lever to uplift the earth   15
And roll it in another course,

With thousand shocks that come and go,
   With agonies, with energies,
   With overthrowings, and with cries,
And undulations to and fro.   20
       * * *

115

Now fades the last long streak of snow,
   Now burgeons every maze of quick [6]
   About the flowering squares, and thick
By ashen roots the violets blow.

Now rings the woodland loud and long,   5
   The distance takes a lovelier hue,
   And drowned in yonder living blue
The lark becomes a sightless song.

Now dance the lights on lawn and lea,
   The flocks are whiter down the vale,   10
   And milkier every milky sail
On winding stream or distant sea;

Where now the seamew pipes, or dives
   In yonder greening gleam, and fly
   The happy birds, that change their sky   15
To build and brood, that live their lives

From land to land; and in my breast
   Spring wakens too, and my regret
   Becomes an April violet,
And buds and blossoms like the rest.   20
       * * *

118

Contémplate all this work of Time,
   The giant laboring in his youth;
   Nor dream of human love and truth,
As dying Nature's earth and lime;

But trust that those we call the dead   5
   Are breathers of an ampler day
   For ever nobler ends. They[7] say,
The solid earth whereon we tread

6. In hawthorn hedges; "squares":   7. Geologists and astronomers.
fields.

In tracts of fluent heat began,
    And grew to seeming-random forms,   10
    The seeming prey of cyclic storms,
Till at the last arose the man;

Who throve and branched from clime to clime,
    The herald of a higher race,
    And of himself in higher place,   15
If so he type[8] this work of time

Within himself, from more to more;
    Or, crowned with attributes of woe
    Like glories, move his course, and show
That life is not as idle ore,   20

But iron dug from central gloom,
    And heated hot with burning fears,
    And dipped in baths of hissing tears,
And battered with the shocks of doom

To shape and use. Arise and fly   25
    The reeling Faun, the sensual feast;
    Move upward, working out the beast,
And let the ape and tiger die.

119

Doors, where my heart was used to beat
    So quickly, not as one that weeps
    I come once more; the city sleeps;
I smell the meadow in the street;

I hear a chirp of birds; I see   5
    Betwixt the black fronts long-withdrawn
    A light blue lane of early dawn,
And think of early days and thee,

And bless thee, for thy lips are bland,
    And bright the friendship of thine eye;   10
    And in my thoughts with scarce a sigh
I take the pressure of thine hand.

120

I trust I have not wasted breath:
    I think we are not wholly brain,
    Magnetic mockeries;[9] not in vain,
Like Paul[1] with beasts, I fought with Death;

Not only cunning casts in clay: 5
    Let Science prove we are, and then

8. Emulate, prefigure as a type.
9. Mechanisms operated by responses to electrical forces.
1. I Corinthians xv.32.

What matters Science unto men,
At least to me? I would not stay.

Let him, the wiser man who springs
   Hereafter, up from childhood shape   10
   His action like the greater ape,
But I was *born* to other things.

121

Sad Hesper[2] o'er the buried sun
   And ready, thou, to die with him,
   Thou watchest all things ever dim
And dimmer, and a glory done.

The team is loosened from the wain,[3]   5
   The boat is drawn upon the shore;
   Thou listenest to the closing door,
And life is darkened in the brain.

Bright Phosphor,[4] fresher for the night,
   By thee the world's great work is heard   10
   Beginning, and the wakeful bird;
Behind thee comes the greater light.[5]

The market boat is on the stream,
   And voices hail it from the brink;
   Thou hear'st the village hammer clink,   15
And see'st the moving of the team.

Sweet Hesper-Phosphor, double name[6]
   For what is one, the first, the last,
   Thou, like my present and my past,
Thy place is changed; thou art the same.   20

* * *

123

There rolls the deep where grew the tree.
   O earth, what changes hast thou seen!
   There where the long street roars hath been
The stillness of the central sea.[7]

The hills are shadows, and they flow   5
   From form to form, and nothing stands;
   They melt like mist, the solid lands,
Like clouds they shape themselves and go.

---

2. Evening star.
3. Hay wagon.
4. Morning star.
5. Cf. Genesis i.16: "The greater light to rule the day."
6. The same planet, Venus, is both evening star and morning star.
7. Cf. a passage from Sir Charles Lyell's *The Principles of Geology* (1832), a book well-known to Tennyson. In discussing the "interchange of sea and land" that has occurred "on the surface of our globe" Lyell remarks: "In the Mediterranean alone, many flourishing inland towns and a still greater number of ports now stand where the sea rolled its waves since the era when civilized nations first grew in Europe."

But in my spirit will I dwell,
    And dream my dream, and hold it true;   10
    For though my lips may breathe adieu,
I cannot think the thing farewell.

124

That which we dare invoke to bless;
    Our dearest faith; our ghastliest doubt;
    He, They, One, All; within, without;
The Power in darkness whom we guess—

I found Him not in world or sun,   5
    Or eagle's wing, or insect's eye,[8]
    Nor through the questions men may try,
The petty cobwebs we have spun.

If e'er when faith had fallen asleep,
    I heard a voice, "believe no more,"   10
    And heard an ever-breaking shore
That tumbled in the Godless deep,

A warmth within the breast would melt
    The freezing reason's colder part,
    And like a man in wrath the heart   15
Stood up and answered, "I have felt."

No, like a child in doubt and fear:
    But that blind clamor made me wise;
    Then was I as a child that cries,
But, crying, knows his father near;   20

And what I am beheld again
    What is, and no man understands;
    And out of darkness came the hands
That reach through nature, molding men.

       * * *

126

Love is and was my lord and king,
    And in his presence I attend
    To hear the tidings of my friend,
Which every hour his couriers bring.

Love is and was my king and lord,   5
    And will be, though as yet I keep
    Within the court on earth, and sleep
Encompassed by his faithful guard,

---

8. He does not discover satisfactory proof of God's existence in the 18th-century argument that because objects in nature are designed there must exist a designer.

And hear at times a sentinel
   Who moves about from place to place,   10
   And whispers to the worlds of space,
In the deep night, that all is well.

127

And all is well, though faith and form[9]
   Be sundered in the night of fear;
   Well roars the storm to those that hear
A deeper voice across the storm,

Proclaiming social truth shall spread,   5
   And justice, even though thrice again
   The red fool-fury of the Seine
Should pile her barricades with dead.[1]

But ill for him that wears a crown,[2]
   And him, the lazar, in his rags!   10
   They tremble, the sustaining crags;
The spires of ice are toppled down,

And molten up, and roar in flood;
   The fortress crashes from on high,
   The brute earth lightens[3] to the sky,   15
And the great Aeon[4] sinks in blood,

And compassed by the fires of hell,
   While thou, dear spirit, happy star,
   O'erlook'st the tumult from afar,
And smilest, knowing all is well.   20

       * * *

129

Dear friend, far off, my lost desire,
   So far, so near in woe and weal,
   O loved the most, when most I feel
There is a lower and a higher;

Known and unknown, human, divine;   5
   Sweet human hand and lips and eye;
   Dear heavenly friend that canst not die,
Mine, mine, forever, ever mine;

Strange friend, past, present, and to be;
   Loved deeplier, darklier understood;   10

9. Traditional institutions through which faith was formerly expressed, such as the Church. See Carlyle's essay, *Characteristics*, above.
1. Revolutionary uprisings in France, in each of which a king lost his throne (line 9): in 1789 against Louis XVI, in 1830 against Charles X, and in 1848 against Louis Philippe. The third (line 6) would have been a prophecy if, as Tennyson recollected, section 126 was finished at a date earlier than 1848.
2. See 2 *Henry IV*, III.i.31: "Uneasy lies the head that wears a crown." "Lazar": pauper suffering from disease.
3. Is lit up by fire.
4. A vast tract of time, here perhaps modern western civilization.

Behold, I dream a dream of good,
And mingle all the world with thee.

130

Thy voice is on the rolling air;[5]
   I hear thee where the waters run;
   Thou standest in the rising sun,[6]
And in the setting thou art fair.

What art thou then? I cannot guess;   5
   But though I seem in star and flower
   To feel thee some diffusive power,
I do not therefore love thee less.

My love involves the love before;
   My love is vaster passion now;   10
   Tho' mix'd with God and Nature thou,
I seem to love thee more and more.

Far off thou art, but ever nigh;
   I have thee still, and I rejoice;
   I prosper, circled with thy voice;   15
I shall not lose thee tho' I die.

131

O living will[7] that shalt endure
   When all that seems shall suffer shock,
   Rise in the spiritual rock,[8]
Flow through our deeds and make them pure,

That we may lift from out of dust   5
   A voice as unto him that hears,
   A cry above the conquered years
To one that with us works, and trust,

With faith that comes of self-control,
   The truths that never can be proved   10
   Until we close with all we loved,
And all we flow from, soul in soul.

From *Epilogue*[9]

* * *

And rise, O moon, from yonder down,
   Till over down and over dale   110

---

5. Cf. Shelley, *Adonais*, 370 ff.: "He is made one with Nature: there is heard / His voice in all her music" [noted by Christopher Ricks].
6. "And I saw an angel standing in the sun." Revelation xix.17.
7. Tennyson later commented that he meant here the moral will of mankind.

8. Christ (see I Corinthians x.4).
9. The *Epilogue* describes the wedding day of Tennyson's sister Cecilia to Edmund Lushington. At the conclusion (reprinted here) the speaker reflects upon their moonlit wedding night and the kind of offspring which will result from their union.

All night the shining vapor sail
And pass the silent-lighted town,

The white-faced halls, the glancing rills,
    And catch at every mountain head,
    And o'er the friths[1] that branch and spread   115
Their sleeping silver through the hills;

And touch with shade the bridal doors,
    With tender gloom the roof, the wall;
    And breaking let the splendor fall
To spangle all the happy shores   120

By which they rest, and ocean sounds,
    And, star and system rolling past,
    A soul shall draw from out the vast
And strike his being into bounds,

And, moved through life of lower phase,   125
    Result in man,[2] be born and think,
    And act and love, a closer link
Betwixt us and the crowning race

Of those that, eye to eye, shall look
    On knowledge; under whose command   130
    Is Earth and Earth's, and in their hand
Is Nature like an open book;

No longer half-akin to brute,
    For all we thought and loved and did,
    And hoped, and suffered, is but seed   135
Of what in them is flower and fruit;

Whereof the man that with me trod
    This planet was a noble type
    Appearing ere the times were ripe,
That friend of mine who lives in God,   140

That God, which ever lives and loves,
    One God, one law, one element,
    And one far-off divine event,
To which the whole creation moves.

1833–50   1850

1. Inlets of the sea.
2. A child will be conceived and will develop in embryo through various stages. This development is similar to the evolution of man from the animal to the human level and perhaps to a future higher stage of development.

The Charge of the Light Brigade[1]

1

Half a league, half a league,
Half a league onward,
All in the valley of Death
    Rode the six hundred.
"Forward the Light Brigade!   5
Charge for the guns!" he said.
Into the valley of Death
    Rode the six hundred.

2

"Forward, the Light Brigade!"
Was there a man dismayed?   10
Not though the soldier knew
    Someone had blundered.
Theirs not to make reply,
Theirs not to reason why,
Theirs but to do and die.   15
Into the valley of Death
    Rode the six hundred.

3

Cannon to right of them,
Cannon to left of them,
Cannon in front of them   20
    Volleyed and thundered;
Stormed at with shot and shell,
Boldly they rode and well,
Into the jaws of Death,
Into the mouth of hell   25
    Rode the six hundred.

4

Flashed all their sabers bare,
Flashed as they turned in air
Sab'ring the gunners there,
Charging an army, while   30
    All the world wondered.
Plunged in the battery smoke
Right through the line they broke;
Cossack and Russian
Reeled from the saber stroke   35
    Shattered and sundered.
Then they rode back, but not,
    Not the six hundred.

1. During the Crimean War, owing to confusion of orders, a brigade of British cavalry charged some entrenched batteries of Russian artillery. This blunder cost the lives of three fourths of the 600 horsemen engaged (see Cecil Woodham-Smith, *The Reason Why*, 1954). Tennyson rapidly composed his "ballad" (as he called the poem) after reading an account of the battle in a newspaper.

5

Cannon to right of them,
Cannon to left of them,   40
Cannon behind them
   Volleyed and thundered;
Stormed at with shot and shell,
While horse and hero fell,
They that had fought so well   45
Came through the jaws of Death,
Back from the mouth of hell,
All that was left of them,
   Left of six hundred.

6

When can their glory fade?   50
O the wild charge they made!
   All the world wondered.
Honor the charge they made!
Honor the Light Brigade,
   Noble six hundred!   55

1854   1854

From Maud[1]

Part I

VI

* * *

5

Ah, what shall I be at fifty
Should Nature keep me alive,   220
If I find the world so bitter
When I am but twenty-five?
Yet, if she were not a cheat,
If Maud were all that she seemed,

---

1. Tennyson described this experimental long poem as a "monodrama," in which a speaker tells his story in a sequence of short lyrics, in varying meters—a method which requires the reader to fill in the events of the action on the evidence of the speaker's shifting emotional states. The speaker is a young man, living alone in the country, whose disillusionment after his father's suicide has left him full of a bitterness that borders on madness. He is restored to sanity and intense happiness when he discovers that Maud, the beautiful daughter of a local landowner, accepts his love for her. Our selections focus on the stages of this love affair. In the early sections he is fearful of love itself ("And most of all would I flee from the cruel madness of love"), and he is suspicious that Maud is stony-hearted and will make a fool of him. When she accepts his proposal, he is, at first, deliriously exultant, but, later, serene and secure. Subsequent sections of the poem (not represented here) show how the resolution of his problems is shattered when he loses Maud after killing her brother in a duel. Eventually he finds a fresh resolution by enlisting to fight against Russia in the Crimean war.

Maud was the poem that Tennyson most enjoyed reading aloud. He called it "a little *Hamlet*," but it is closer to *Romeo and Juliet* in its picture of love in the midst of family feuds.

And her smile were all that I dreamed,[2]   225
Then the world were not so bitter
But a smile could make it sweet.

* * *

8

Perhaps the smile and tender tone
Came out of her pitying womanhood,
For am I not, am I not, here alone
So many a summer since she died,   255
My mother, who was so gentle and good?
Living alone in an empty house,
Here half-hid in the gleaming wood,
Where I hear the dead at midday moan,
And the shrieking rush of the wainscot mouse,   260
And my own sad name in corners cried,
When the shiver of dancing leaves is thrown
About its echoing chambers wide,
Till a morbid hate and horror have grown
Of a world in which I have hardly mixed,   265
And a morbid eating lichen fixed
On a heart half turned to stone.

* * *

10

I have played with her when a child;
She remembers it now we meet.
Ah, well, well, well, I *may* be beguiled
By some coquettish deceit.
Yet, if she were not a cheat,   280
And Maud were all that she seemed,
And her smile had all that I dreamed,
Then the world were not so bitter
But a smile could make it sweet.

VIII

She came to the village church,
And sat by a pillar alone;
An angel watching an urn
Wept over her, carved in stone;
And once, but once, she lifted her eyes,   305
And suddenly, sweetly, strangely blushed
To find they were met by my own;
And suddenly, sweetly, my heart beat stronger
And thicker, until I heard no longer
The snowy-banded, dilettante,   310
Delicate-handed priest intone;
And thought, is it pride? and mused and sighed,
"No surely, now it cannot be pride."

2. On a previous day he had encountered Maud and was surprised by her smiling at him.

XI

1

O let the solid ground
   Not fail beneath my feet
Before my life has found   400
   What some have found so sweet;
Then let come what come may,
What matter if I go mad,
I shall have had my day.

2

Let the sweet heavens endure,   405
   Not close and darken above me
Before I am quite quite sure
   That there is one to love me;
Then let come what come may
To a life that has been so sad,   410
I shall have had my day.

XII

1

Birds in the high Hall-garden
   When twilight was falling,
Maud, Maud, Maud, Maud,
   They were crying and calling.   415

2

Where was Maud? in our wood;
   And I, who else, was with her,
Gathering woodland lilies,
   Myriads blow together.

3

Birds in our wood[3] sang   420
   Ringing through the valleys,
Maud is here, here, here
   In among the lilies.

4

I kissed her slender hand,
   She took the kiss sedately;   425
Maud is not seventeen,
   But she is tall and stately.

5

I to cry out on pride
   Who have won her favor!
O Maud were sure of Heaven   430
   If lowliness[4] could save her.

---

3. The wood in the valley of the speaker's small country estate. Here the "little birds" (as Tennyson called them in a note) are responding, in a sort of duet, to the caws of the rooks in the garden of Maud's family estate.
4. Meekness.

6

I know the way she went
   Home with her maiden posy,
For her feet have touched the meadows
   And left the daisies rosy.[5]   435

7

Birds in the high Hall-garden
   Were crying and calling to her,
Where is Maud, Maud, Maud?
   One is come to woo her.

8

Look, a horse at the door,   440
   And little King Charley snarling,[6]
Go back, my lord, across the moor,
   You are not her darling.

XVI

*   *   *

3

Catch not my breath, O clamorous heart,
   Let not my tongue be a thrall to my eye,
For I must tell her before we part,
   I must tell her, or die.[7]   570

XVIII

1

I have led her home, my love, my only friend.
There is none like her, none.   600
And never yet so warmly ran my blood
And sweetly, on and on
Calming itself to the long-wished-for end.
Full to the banks, close on the promised good.

2

None like her, none.   605
Just now the dry-tongued laurels' pattering talk
Seemed her light foot along the garden walk,
And shook my heart to think she comes once more.
But even then I heard her close the door;
The gates of heaven are closed, and she is gone.   610

3

There is none like her, none,
Nor will be when our summers have deceased.
O, art thou[8] sighing for Lebanon

---

5. As Tennyson explained: "If you tread on the daisy [English variety], it turns up a rosy underside."
6. Maud's dog snarls at the aristocratic visitor who is the speaker's rival for Maud's hand.
7. He is about to propose to Maud, who will accept him.
8. The vast old cedar tree in Maud's garden, addressed in a 14-line question about its ancestry on Mount Lebanon in Syria and its ultimate ancestry in Eden. See Song of Solomon v.15.

In the long breeze that streams to thy delicious East,
Sighing for Lebanon,   615
Dark cedar, though thy limbs have here increased,
Upon a pastoral slope as fair,
And looking to the South and fed
With honeyed rain and delicate air,
And haunted by the starry head   620
Of her whose gentle will has changed my fate,
And made my life a perfumed altar-flame;
And over whom thy darkness must have spread
With such delight as theirs of old, thy great
Forefathers of the thornless garden, there   625
Shadowing the snow-limbed Eve from whom she came?

4

Here will I lie, while these long branches sway,
And you fair stars that crown a happy day
Go in and out as if at merry play,
Who am no more so all forlorn   630
As when it seemed far better to be born
To labor and the mattock-hardened hand
Than nursed at ease and brought to understand
A sad astrology,[9] the boundless plan
That makes you tyrants in your iron skies,   635
Innumerable, pitiless, passionless eyes,
Cold fires, yet with power to burn and brand
His nothingness into man.

5

But now shine on, and what care I,
Who in this stormy gulf have found a pearl   640
The countercharm of space and hollow sky,[1]
And do accept my madness, and would die
To save from some slight shame one simple girl?—

6

Would die, for sullen-seeming Death may give
More life to Love than is or ever was   645
In our low world, where yet 'tis sweet to live.
Let no one ask me how it came to pass;
It seems that I am happy, that to me
A livelier emerald twinkles in the grass,
A purer sapphire melts into the sea.   650

7

Not die, but live a life of truest breath,
And teach true life to fight with mortal wrongs.
O, why should Love, like men in drinking songs,
Spice his fair banquet with the dust of death?[2]
Make answer, Maud my bliss,   655

9. Astronomy.
1. Something that calms his former
fears of the vastness of space revealed
by modern astronomy.

2. I.e., why do we try to intensify the
experience of love by linking it with
death?

Maud made my Maud by that long loving kiss,
Life of my life, wilt thou not answer this?
"The dusky strand of Death inwoven here
With dear Love's tie, makes Love himself more dear."

8

Is that enchanted moan only the swell   660
Of the long waves that roll in yonder bay?
And hark the clock within, the silver knell
Of twelve sweet hours that passed in bridal white,
And died to live, long as my pulses play;
But now by this my love has closed her sight   665
And given false death[3] her hand, and stolen away
To dreamful wastes where footless fancies dwell
Among the fragments of the golden day.
May nothing there her maiden grace affright!
Dear heart, I feel with thee the drowsy spell.   670
My bride to be, my evermore delight,
My own heart's heart, my ownest own, farewell;
It is but for a little space I go.
And ye[4] meanwhile far over moor and fell
Beat to the noiseless music of the night!   675
Has our whole earth gone nearer to the glow
Of your soft splendors that you look so bright?
I have climbed nearer out of lonely hell.
Beat, happy stars, timing with things below,
Beat with my heart more blest than heart can tell,   680
Blest, but for some dark undercurrent woe
That seems to draw—but it shall not be so;
Let all be well, be well.

* * *   1855

In the Valley of Cauteretz[5]

All along the valley, stream that flashest white,
Deepening thy voice with the deepening of the night,
All along the valley, where thy waters flow,
I walked with one I loved two and thirty years ago.
All along the valley, while I walked today,   5
The two and thirty years were a mist that rolls away;
For all along the valley, down thy rocky bed,
Thy living voice to me was as the voice of the dead,
And all along the valley, by rock and cave and tree,
The voice of the dead was a living voice to me.   10

1861   1864

---

3. I.e., sleep.
4. The stars.
5. A valley in the French Pyrenees

visited by Tennyson and Hallam in
1830 and revisited by Tennyson in
1861.

Idylls of the King When John Milton was considering subjects suitable for an epic poem, one of those he entertained was the story of the Christian British king, Arthur, a semi-legendary leader of about 500 A.D. who fought off the heathen Saxon invaders who had swarmed into Britain after the withdrawal of the Roman legions. Tennyson likewise saw that the Arthurian story had epic potential and selected it for his life-work as "the greatest of all poetical subjects." At intervals, over a period of 50 years, he labored over the 12 books that make up his *Idylls of the King,* completing the work in 1888.

The principal source of Tennyson's stories of Arthur and his knights was Sir Thomas Malory's *Morte Darthur,* a version which Malory translated into English prose from French sources in 1470. As Talbot Donaldson has suggested, one basis of the appeal of the Arthurian stories, like the legends of Robin Hood and stories of the American West, is that all three represent the struggle of individuals to restore order in situations of chaos and anarchy, a task performed in the face of "seemingly overwhelming odds." The individual stories in Tennyson's *Idylls* have the same basic appeal, but the overall design of the whole poem is more ambitious and impressive. The *Idylls of the King* represent the rise and fall of a civilization. They imply that after 2000 years of Christianity, Western civilization may be going through a cycle in which it must confront the possibilities of a renewal in the future or an apocalyptic extinction. The first book, *The Coming of Arthur,* introduces the basic myth of a springtime hero transforming a wasteland and inspiring faith and hope in the highest values of civilized life among his devoted followers. Succeeding books move through summer and autumn and culminate in the bleak wintry scene of Arthur's last battle in which his order perishes in a civil war; the leader of the enemy forces is his own nephew, Sir Modred.

Throughout the later books of the *Idylls* the forces of opposition grow in strength, and disaffections infect leading figures of the Round Table itself. The most glaring example is the adulterous relationship between Guinevere, Arthur's "sumptuous" queen (as Tennyson once described her), and the king's chief lieutenant and friend, Sir Launcelot. Many other fallings away subsequently come to light, such as the perfidious betrayal by Sir Gawain in *Pelleas and Ettarre,* and the cynical conduct of Sir Tristram, whose story is told in the bitter tenth book, *The Last Tournament.* Even Merlin, Arthur's trusted magician and counselor, becomes corrupted and can perform no further offices for the king (*Merlin and Vivien*). These accumulating signs of decline and fall figure prominently in the two late idylls that make up the following selections.

From Idylls of the King

Pelleas and Ettarre[1]

King Arthur made new knights to fill the gap
Left by the Holy Quest;[2] and as he sat

---

1. The ninth book of the *Idylls.* Most of the story, except the ending, is based on Malory's *Morte Darthur* (IV. 21–24). Tennyson said of it: "Almost the sad-

In hall at old Caerleon,[3] the high doors
Were softly sundered, and through these a youth,
Pelleas, and the sweet smell of the fields   5
Passed, and the sunshine came along with him.

   "Make me thy knight, because I know, Sir King,
All that belongs to knighthood, and I love."
Such was his cry: for having heard the King
Had let proclaim a tournament—the prize   10
A golden circlet and a knightly sword,
Full fain had Pelleas for his lady won
The golden circlet, for himself the sword:
And there were those who knew him near the King,
And promised for him: and Arthur made him knight.   15

   And this new knight, Sir Pelleas of the isles—
But lately come to his inheritance,
And lord of many a barren isle was he—
Riding at noon, a day or twain before,
Across the forest called of Dean,[4] to find   20
Caerleon and the King, had felt the sun
Beat like a strong knight on his helm, and reeled
Almost to falling from his horse; but saw
Near him a mound of even-sloping side,
Whereon a hundred stately beeches grew,   25
And here and there great hollies under them;
But for a mile all round was open space,
And fern and heath: and slowly Pelleas drew
To that dim day, then binding his good horse
To a tree, cast himself down; and as he lay   30
At random looking over the brown earth
Through that green-glooming twilight of the grove,
It seemed to Pelleas that the fern without
Burned as a living fire of emeralds,
So that his eyes were dazzled looking at it.   35
Then o'er it crossed the dimness of a cloud
Floating, and once the shadow of a bird
Flying, and then a fawn; and his eyes closed.
And since he loved all maidens, but no maid
In special, half-awake he whispered, "Where?   40
O where? I love thee, though I know thee not.
For fair thou art and pure as Guinevere,
And I will make thee with my spear and sword
As famous—O my Queen, my Guinevere,
For I will be thine Arthur when we meet."   45

---

dest of the Idylls. The breaking of the storm."
2. In the preceding idyll, *The Holy Grail*, many knights had misguidedly deserted the Round Table to seek the Holy Grail.

3. Ancient village in Monmouthshire, near Wales, where Arthur often held his court.
4. Extensive tract in the river Wye region adjacent to Monmouthshire.

Suddenly wakened with a sound of talk
And laughter at the limit of the wood,
And glancing through the hoary boles, he saw,
Strange as to some old prophet might have seemed
A vision hovering on a sea of fire,   50
Damsels in divers colors like the cloud
Of sunset and sunrise, and all of them
On horses, and the horses richly trapped
Breast-high in that bright line of bracken stood:
And all the damsels talked confusedly,   55
And one was pointing this way, and one that,
Because the way was lost.

          And Pelleas rose,
And loosed his horse, and led him to the light,
There she that seemed the chief among them said,
"In happy time behold our pilot-star!   60
Youth, we are damsels-errant, and we ride,
Armed as ye see, to tilt against the knights
There at Caerleon, but have lost our way:
To right? to left? straight forward? back again?
Which? tell us quickly."

          Pelleas gazing thought,   65
"Is Guinevere herself so beautiful?"
For large her violet eyes looked, and her bloom
A rosy dawn kindled in stainless heavens,
And round her limbs, mature in womanhood;
And slender was her hand and small her shape;   70
And but for those large eyes, the haunts of scorn,
She might have seemed a toy to trifle with,
And pass and care no more. But while he gazed
The beauty of her flesh abashed the boy,
As though it were the beauty of her soul: 75
For as the base man, judging of the good,
Puts his own baseness in him by default
Of will and nature, so did Pelleas lend
All the young beauty of his own soul to hers,
Believing her; and when she spake to him,   80
Stammered, and could not make her a reply.
For out of the waste islands had he come,
Where saving his own sisters he had known
Scarce any but the women of his isles,
Rough wives, that laughed and screamed against the gulls,   85
Makers of nets, and living from the sea.

Then with a slow smile turned the lady round
And looked upon her people; and as when
A stone is flung into some sleeping tarn,

The circle widens till it lip the marge,   90
Spread the slow smile through all her company.
Three knights were thereamong; and they too smiled,
Scorning him; for the lady was Ettarre,
And she was a great lady in her land.

   Again she said, "O wild and of the woods,   95
Knowest thou not the fashion of our speech?
Or have the Heavens but given thee a fair face,
Lacking a tongue?"

                     "O damsel," answered he,
"I woke from dreams; and coming out of gloom
Was dazzled by the sudden light, and crave   100
Pardon: but will ye to Caerleon? I
Go likewise: shall I lead you to the King?"

   "Lead then," she said; and through the woods they went.
And while they rode, the meaning in his eyes,
His tenderness of manner, and chaste awe,   105
His broken utterances and bashfulness,
Were all a burthen to her, and in her heart
She muttered, "I have lighted on a fool,
Raw, yet so stale!" But since her mind was bent
On hearing, after trumpet blown, her name   110
And title, "Queen of Beauty," in the lists
Cried—and beholding him so strong, she thought
That peradventure he will fight for me,
And win the circlet: therefore flattered him,
Being so gracious, that he wellnigh deemed   115
His wish by hers was echoed; and her knights
And all her damsels too were gracious to him,
For she was a great lady.

                          And when they reached
Caerleon, ere they passed to lodging, she,
Taking his hand, "O the strong hand," she said,   120
"See! look at mine! but wilt thou fight for me,
And win me this fine circlet, Pelleas,
That I may love thee?"

                       Then his helpless heart
Leaped, and he cried, "Ay! wilt thou if I win?"
'Ay, that will I," she answered, and she laughed,   125
And straitly nipped the hand, and flung it from her;
Then glanced askew at those three knights of hers,
Till all her ladies laughed along with her.

   "O happy world," thought Pelleas, "all, meseems,
Are happy; I the happiest of them all."   130

Nor slept that night for pleasure in his blood,
And green wood-ways, and eyes among the leaves;
Then being on the morrow knighted, sware
To love one only. And as he came away,
The men who met him rounded on their heels   135
And wondered after him, because his face
Shone like the countenance of a priest of old
Against the flame about a sacrifice
Kindled by fire from heaven: so glad was he.

Then Arthur made vast banquets, and strange knights   140
From the four winds came in: and each one sat,
Though served with choice from air, land, stream, and sea,
Oft in mid-banquet measuring with his eyes
His neighbor's make and might: and Pelleas looked
Noble among the noble, for he dreamed   145
His lady loved him, and he knew himself
Loved of the King: and him his new-made knight
Worshipped, whose lightest whisper moved him more
Than all the ranged reasons of the world.

Then blushed and brake the morning of the jousts,   150
And this was called "The Tournament of Youth":
For Arthur, loving his young knight, withheld
His older and his mightier from the lists,
That Pelleas might obtain his lady's love,
According to her promise. and remain   155
Lord of the tourney. And Arthur had the jousts
Down in the flat field by the shore of Usk[5]
Holden: the gilded parapets were crowned
With faces, and the great tower filled with eyes
Up to the summit, and the trumpets blew.   160
There all day long Sir Pelleas kept the field
With honor: so by that strong hand of his
The sword and golden circlet were achieved.

Then rang the shout his lady loved: the heat
Of pride and glory fired her face; her eye   165
Sparkled; she caught the circlet from his lance,
And there before the people crowned herself:
So for the last time she was gracious to him.

Then at Caerleon for a space—her look
Bright for all others, cloudier on her knight—   170
Lingered Ettarre: and seeing Pelleas droop,
Said Guinevere, "We marvel at thee much,
O damsel, wearing this unsunny face
To him who won thee glory!" And she said,

5. River near Caerleon.

"Had ye not held your Lancelot in your bower,   175
My Queen, he had not won." Whereat the Queen,
As one whose foot is bitten by an ant,
Glanced down upon her, turned and went her way.

      But after, when her damsels, and herself,
And those three knights all set their faces home,   180
Sir Pelleas followed. She that saw him cried,
"Damsels—and yet I should be shamed to say it—
I cannot bide Sir Baby. Keep him back
Among yourselves. Would rather that we had
Some rough old knight who knew the worldly way,   185
Albeit grizzlier than a bear, to ride
And jest with: take him to you, keep him off,
And pamper him with papmeat, if ye will,
Old milky fables of the wolf and sheep,
Such as the wholesome mothers tell their boys.   190
Nay, should ye try him with a merry one
To find his mettle, good: and if he fly us,
Small matter! let him." This her damsels heard,
And mindful of her small and cruel hand,
They, closing round him through the journey home,   195
Acted her hest,[6] and always from her side
Restrained him with all manner of device,
So that he could not come to speech with her.
And when she gained her castle, upsprang the bridge,
Down rang the grate of iron through the groove,   200
And he was left alone in open field.
      "These be the ways of ladies," Pelleas thought,
"To those who love them, trials of our faith.
Yea, let her prove me to the uttermost,
For loyal to the uttermost am I."   205
So made his moan; and, darkness falling, sought
A priory not far off, there lodges, but rose
With morning every day, and, moist or dry,
Full-armed upon his charger all day long.
Sat by the walls, and no one opened to him.   210

      And this persistence turned her scorn to wrath.
Then calling her three knights, she charged them, "Out!
And drive him from the walls." And out they came,
But Pelleas overthrew them as they dashed
Against him one by one; and these returned,   215
But still he kept his watch beneath the wall.

      Thereon her wrath became a hate; and once,
A week beyond, while walking on the walls
With her three knights, she pointed downward, "Look,

6. Command.

He haunts me—I cannot breathe—besieges me; 220
Down! strike him! put my hate into your strokes,
And drive him from my walls." And down they went,
And Pelleas overthrew them one by one;
And from the tower above him cried Ettarre,
"Bind him, and bring him in."

                He heard her voice; 225
Then let the strong hand, which had overthrown
Her minion-knights,[7] by those he overthrew
Be bounden straight, and so they brought him in.

Then when he came before Ettarre, the sight
Of her rich beauty made him at once glance 230
More bondsman in his heart than in his bonds.
Yet with good cheer he spake, "Behold me, Lady,
A prisoner, and the vassal of thy will;
And if thou keep me in thy donjon here,
Content am I so that I see thy face 235
But once a day: for I have sworn my vows,
And thou hast given thy promise, and I know
That all these pains are trials of my faith,
And that thyself, when thou hast seen me strained
And sifted to the utmost, wilt at length 240
Yield me thy love and know me for thy knight."

Then she began to rail so bitterly,
With all her damsels, he was stricken mute;
But when she mocked his vows and the great King,
Lighted on words: "For pity of thine own self, 245
Peace, Lady, peace: is he not thine and mine?"
"Thou fool," she said, "I never heard his voice
But longed to break away. Unbind him now,
And thrust him out of doors; for save he be
Fool to the midmost marrow of his bones, 250
He will return no more." And those, her three,
Laughed, and unbound, and thrust him from the gate.

And after this, a week beyond, again
She called them, saying, "There he watches yet,
There like a dog before his master's door! 255
Kicked, he returns: do ye not hate him, ye?
Ye know yourselves: how can ye bide at peace,
Affronted with his fulsome innocence?
Are ye but creatures of the board and bed,
No men to strike? Fall on him all at once, 260
And if ye slay him I reck not: if ye fail,
Give ye the slave mine order to be bound,
Bind him as heretofore, and bring him in:
It may be ye shall slay him in his bonds."
    She spake; and at her will they couched their spears, 265

7. Minion: compliant and obsequious dependent of a ruler.

Three against one: and Gawain[8] passing by,
Bound upon solitary adventure, saw
Low down beneath the shadow of those towers
A villainy, three to one: and through his heart
The fire of honor and all noble deeds   270
Flashed, and he called, "I strike upon thy side—
The caitiffs!" "Nay," said Pelleas, "but forbear;
He needs no aid who doth his lady's will."

   So Gawain, looking at the villainy done,
Forbore, but in his heat and eagerness   275
Trembled and quivered, as the dog, withheld
A moment from the vermin that he sees
Before him, shivers, ere he springs and kills.

   And Pelleas overthrew them, one to three;
And they rose up, and bound, and brought him in.   280
Then first her anger, leaving Pelleas, burned
Full on her knights in many an evil name
Of craven, weakling, and thrice-beaten hound:
"Yet, take him, ye that scarce are fit to touch,
Far less to bind, your victor, and thrust him out,   285
And let who will release him from his bonds.
And if he comes again"—there she brake short;
And Pelleas answered, "Lady, for indeed
I loved you and I deemed you beautiful,
I cannot brook to see your beauty marred   290
Through evil spite: and if ye love me not,
I cannot bear to dream you so forsworn:
I had liefer ye were worthy of my love,
Than to be loved again of you—farewell;
And though ye kill my hope, not yet my love,   295
Vex not yourself: ye will not see me more."

   While thus he spake, she gazed upon the man
Of princely bearing, though in bonds, and thought,
"Why have I pushed him from me? this man loves,
If love there be: yet him I loved not. Why?   300
I deemed him fool? yea, so? or that in him
A something—was it nobler than myself?—
Seemed my reproach? He is not of my kind.
He could not love me, did he know me well.
Nay, let him go— and quickly." And her knights   305
Laughed not, but thrust him bounden out of door.

   Forth sprang Gawain, and loosed him from his bonds,
And flung them o'er the walls; and afterward,
Shaking his hands, as from a lazar's[9] rag,
"Faith of my body," he said, "and art thou not—   310

---

8. A nephew of King Arthur and one of
his chief knights.   9. Leper's.

Yea thou art he, whom late our Arthur made
Knight of his table; yea and he that won
The circlet? wherefore hast thou so defamed
Thy brotherhood in me and all the rest,
As let these caitiffs on thee work their will?"   315

    And Pelleas answered, "O, their wills are hers
For whom I won the circlet; and mine, hers,
Thus to be bounden, so to see her face,
Marred though it be with spite and mockery now,
Other than when I found her in the woods;   320
And though she hath me bounden but in spite,
And all to flout me, when they bring me in,
Let me be bounden, I shall see her face;
Else must I die through mine unhappiness."

    And Gawain answered kindly though in scorn,   325
"Why, let my lady bind me if she will,
And let my lady beat me if she will:
But an[1] she send her delegate to thrall
These fighting hands of mine—Christ kill me then
But I will slice him handless by the wrist,   330
And let my lady sear the stump for him,
Howl as he may. But hold me for your friend:
Come, ye know nothing: here I pledge my troth,
Yea, by the honor of the Table Round,
I will be leal[2] to thee and work thy work,   335
And tame thy jailing princess to thine hand.
Lend me thine horse and arms, and I will say
That I have slain thee. She will let me in
To hear the manner of thy fight and fall;
Then, when I come within her counsels, then   340
From prime to vespers will I chant thy praise
As prowest[3] knight and truest lover, more
Than any have sung thee living, till she long
To have thee back in lusty life again,
Not to be bound, save by white bonds and warm,   345
Dearer than freedom. Wherefore now thy horse
And armor: let me go: be comforted:
Give me three days to melt her fancy, and hope
The third night hence will bring thee news of gold."

    Then Pelleas lent his horse and all his arms,   350
Saving the goodly sword, his prize, and took
Gawain's, and said, "Betray me not, but help—
Art thou not he whom men call light-of-love?"

    "Ay," said Gawain, "for women be so light."
Then bounded forward to the castle walls,   355

1. If.   3. Bravest or noblest.
2. Loyal.

And raised a bugle hanging from his neck,
And winded it, and that so musically
That all the old echoes hidden in the wall
Rang out like hollow woods at hunting-tide.

Up ran a score of damsels to the tower;   360
"Avaunt," they cried, "our lady loves thee not."
But Gawain lifting up his vizor said,
"Gawain am I, Gawain of Arthur's court,
And I have slain this Pelleas whom ye hate:
Behold his horse and armor. Open gates,   365
And I will make you merry."

                              And down they ran,
Her damsels, crying to their lady, "Lo!
Pelleas is dead—he told us—he that hath
His horse and armor: will ye let him in?
He slew him! Gawain, Gawain of the court,   370
Sir Gawain—there he waits below the wall,
Blowing his bugle as who should say him nay."

And so, leave given, straight on through open door
Rode Gawain, whom she greeted courteously.
"Dead, is it so?" she asked. "Ay, ay," said he,   375
"And oft in dying cried upon your name."
"Pity on him," she answered, "a good knight,
But never let me bide one hour at peace."
"Ay," thought Gawain, "and you be fair enow:
But I to your dead man have given my troth,   380
That whom ye loathe, him will I make you love."

So those three days, aimless about the land,
Lost in a doubt, Pelleas wandering
Waited, until the third night brought a moon
With promise of large light on woods and ways.   385

Hot was the night and silent; but a sound
Of Gawain ever coming, and this lay—
Which Pelleas had heard sung before the Queen,
And seen her sadden listening—vexed his heart,
And marred his rest—"A worm within the rose."   390

"A rose, but one, none other rose had I,
A rose, one rose, and this was wondrous fair,
One rose, a rose that gladdened earth and sky,
One rose, my rose, that sweetened all mine air—
I cared not for the thorns; the thorns were there.   395

"One rose, a rose to gather by and by,
One rose, a rose, to gather and to wear,
No rose but one—what other rose had I?

One rose, my rose; a rose that will not die,—
He dies who loves it,—if the worm be there."   400

This tender rhyme, and evermore the doubt,
"Why lingers Gawain with his golden news?"
So shook him that he could not rest, but rode
Ere midnight to her walls, and bound his horse
Hard by the gates. Wide open were the gates,   405
And no watch kept; and in through these he passed,
And heard but his own steps, and his own heart
Beating, for nothing moved but his own self,
And his own shadow. Then he crossed the court,
And spied not any light in hall or bower,   410
But saw the postern portal also wide
Yawning; and up a slope of garden, all
Of roses white and red, and brambles mixed
And overgrowing them, went on, and found,
Here too, all hushed below the mellow moon,   415
Save that one rivulet from a tiny cave
Came lightening downward, and so spilled itself
Among the roses, and was lost again.

Then was he ware of three pavilions reared
Above the bushes, gilden-peaked: in one,   420
Red after revel, droned her lurdane[4] knights
Slumbering, and their three squires across their feet:
In one, their malice on the placid lip
Frozen by sweet sleep, four of her damsels lay:
And in the third, the circlet of the jousts   425
Bound on her brow, were Gawain and Ettarre.[5]

Back, as a hand that pushes through the leaf
To find a nest and feels a snake, he drew:
Back, as a coward slinks from what he fears
To cope with, or a traitor proven, or hound   430
Beaten, did Pelleas in an utter shame
Creep with his shadow through the court again,
Fingering at his sword-handle until he stood
There on the castle-bridge once more, and thought,
"I will go back, and slay them where they lie."   435

And so went back, and seeing them yet in sleep
Said, "Ye, that so dishallow the holy sleep,

4. Heavy and stupid.
5. Cf. Malory IV. 23: "And then it was in the month of May, that she and sir Gawaine went out of the castle and supped in a pavilion, and there was a bed made, and there sir Gawaine and the lady Ettarre went to bed together; and in another pavilion she laid her damsels; and in the third pavilion she laid part of her knights: for then she had no dread nor fear of sir Pelles. And there sir Gawaine lay with her, doing his pleasure in that pavilion, two days and two nights, against the faithful promise that he made to sir Pelles."

Your sleep is death," and drew the sword, and thought,
"What! slay a sleeping knight? the King hath bound
And sworn me to this brotherhood"; again,   440
"Alas that ever a knight should be so false."
Then turned, and so returned, and groaning laid
The naked sword athwart their naked throats,
There left it, and them sleeping; and she lay,
The circlet of the tourney round her brows,   445
And the sword of the tourney across her throat.

And forth he passed, and mounting on his horse
Stared at her towers that, larger than themselves
In their own darkness, thronged into the moon.
Then crushed the saddle with his thighs, and clenched   450
His hands, and maddened with himself and moaned:

"Would they have risen against me in their blood
At the last day? I might have answered them
Even before high God. O towers so strong,
Huge, solid, would that even while I gaze   455
The crack of earthquake shivering to your base
Split you, and Hell burst up your harlot roofs
Bellowing, and charred you through and through within,
Black as the harlot's heart—hollow as a skull!
Let the fierce east scream through your eyelet-holes,   460
And whirl the dust of harlots round and round
In dung and nettles! hiss, snake—I saw him there—
Let the fox bark, let the wolf yell. Who yells
Here in the still sweet summer night, but I—
I, the poor Pelleas whom she called her fool?   465
Fool, beast—he, she, or I? myself most fool;
Beast too, as lacking human wit—disgraced,
Dishonored all for trial of true love—
Love?—we be all alike: only the King
Hath made us fools and liars. O noble vows!   470
O great and sane and simple race of brutes
That own[6] no lust because they have no law!
For why should I have loved her to my shame?
I loathe her, as I loved her to my shame.
I never loved her, I but lusted for her—   475
Away—"
          He dashed the rowel into his horse,
And bounded forth and vanished through the night.

Then she, that felt the cold touch on her throat,
Awaking knew the sword, and turned herself
To Gawain: "Liar, for thou hast not slain   480
This Pelleas! here he stood, and might have slain

___

6. Acknowledge.

Me and thyself." And he that tells the tale
Says that her ever-veering fancy turned
To Pelleas, as the one true knight on earth,
And only lover; and through her love her life   485
Wasted and pined, desiring him in vain.

But he by wild and way, for half the night,
And over hard and soft, striking the sod
From out the soft, the spark from off the hard,
Rode till the star above the wakening sun,   490
Beside that tower where Percivale was cowled,[7]
Glanced from the rosy forehead of the dawn.
For so the words were flashed into his heart
He knew not whence or wherefore: "O sweet star,
Pure on the virgin forehead of the dawn!"   495
And there he would have wept, but felt his eyes
Harder and drier than a fountain bed
In summer: thither came the village girls
And lingered talking, and they come no more
Till the sweet heavens have filled it from the heights   500
Again with living waters in the change
Of seasons: hard his eyes; harder his heart
Seemed; but so weary were his limbs, that he,
Gasping, "Of Arthur's hall am I, but here,
Here let me rest and die," cast himself down,   505
And gulfed his griefs in inmost sleep; so lay,
Till shaken by a dream, that Gawain fired
The hall of Merlin, and the morning star
Reeled in the smoke, brake into flame, and fell.

He woke, and being ware of someone nigh,   510
Sent hands upon him, as to tear him, crying,
"False! and I held thee pure as Guinevere."

But Percivale stood near him and replied,
"Am I but false as Guinevere is pure?
Or art thou mazed with dreams? or being one   515
Of our free-spoken Table hast not heard
That Lancelot"—there he checked himself and paused.

Then fared it with Sir Pelleas as with one
Who gets a wound in battle, and the sword
That made it plunges through the wound again,   520
And pricks it deeper: and he shrank and wailed,
"Is the Queen false?" and Percivale was mute.
"Have any of our Round Table held their vows?"
And Percivale made answer not a word.
"Is the King true?" "The King!" said Percivale.   525

7. Percivale, one of the most devout of   Table to become a monk in a priory.
Arthur's knights, had left the Round

"Why then let man couple at once with wolves.
What! art thou mad?"

                   But Pelleas, leaping up,
Ran through the doors and vaulted on his horse
And fled: small pity upon his horse had he,
Or on himself, or any, and when he met   530
A cripple, one that held a hand for alms—
Hunched as he was, and like an old dwarf-elm
That turns its back on the salt blast, the boy
Paused not, but overrode him, shouting, "False,
And false with Gawain!" and so left him bruised   535
And battered, and fled on, and hill and wood
Went ever streaming by him till the gloom,
That follows on the turning of the world,
Darkened the common path: he twitched the reins,
And made his beast that better knew it, swerve   540
Now off it and now on; but when he saw
High up in heaven the hall that Merlin built,
Blackening against the dead-green stripes of even,
"Black nest of rats," he groaned, "ye build too high."

    Not long thereafter from the city gates   545
Issued Sir Lancelot riding airily,
Warm with a gracious parting from the Queen,
Peace at his heart, and gazing at a star
And marveling what it was: on whom the boy,
Across the silent seeded meadow-grass   550
Borne, clashed: and Lancelot, saying, "What name hast thou
That ridest here so blindly and so hard?"
"No name, no name," he shouted, "a scourge am I
To lash the treasons of the Table Round."
"Yea, but thy name?" "I have many names," he cried: 555
"I am wrath and shame and hate and evil fame,
And like a poisonous wind I pass to blast
And blaze the crime of Lancelot and the Queen."
"First over me," said Lancelot, "shalt thou pass."
"Fight therefore," yelled the youth, and either knight   560
Drew back a space, and when they closed, at once
The weary steed of Pelleas floundering flung
His rider, who called out from the dark field,
"Thou art false as Hell: slay me: I have no sword."
Then Lancelot, "Yea, between thy lips—and sharp;   565
But here will I disedge[8] it by thy death."
"Slay then," he shrieked, "my will is to be slain,"
And Lancelot, with his heel upon the fallen,
Rolling his eyes, a moment stood, then spake:
"Rise, weakling; I am Lancelot; say thy say."   570

---

8. I.e., blunt your sharp tongue.

And Lancelot slowly rode his warhorse back
To Camelot, and Sir Pelleas in brief while
Caught his unbroken limbs from the dark field,
And followed to the city. It chanced that both
Brake into hall together, worn and pale. 575
There with her knights and dames was Guinevere.
Full wonderingly she gazed on Lancelot
So soon returned, and then on Pelleas, him
Who had not greeted her, but cast himself
Down on a bench, hard-breathing. "Have ye fought?" 580
She asked of Lancelot. "Ay, my Queen," he said.
"And thou hast overthrown him?" "Ay, my Queen."
Then she, turning to Pelleas, "O young knight,
Hath the great heart of knighthood in thee failed
So far thou canst not bide, unfrowardly, 585
A fall from *him*?" Then, for he answered not,
"Or hast thou other griefs? If I, the Queen,
May help them, loose thy tongue, and let me know."
But Pelleas lifted up an eye so fierce
She quailed; and he, hissing "I have no sword," 590
Sprang from the door into the dark.[9] The Queen
Looked hard upon her lover, he on her;
And each foresaw the dolorous day to be:
And all talk died, as in a grove all song
Beneath the shadow of some bird of prey: 595
Then a long silence came upon the hall,
And Modred[10] thought, "The time is hard at hand."
1869   1869

The Passing of Arthur[1]

That story which the bold Sir Bedivere,[2]
First made and latest left of all the knights,
Told, when the man was no more than a voice

9. Malory's version ends differently. His Pelleas is rescued from despair by a damsel of the Lake who, by enchantment, contrives a punishment for the haughty Ettarre. "So the lady Ettarre died for sorrow, and the damsel of the lake rejoiced sir Pelleas and loved together during their lives." Tennyson's Pelleas, as we learn in *The Last Tournament* (the idyll following *Pelleas and Ettarre*) is so disillusioned by the corruptions he has discovered that he establishes a mock court of his own where his followers indulge in drunken revelry. Through a messenger he reports to Arthur: "Tell thou the King * * * / My tower is full of harlots, like his court, / But mine are worthier, seeing they profess / To be none other than themselves."
10. Arthur's nephew, who leads the

forces that revolt against the king.
1. On the composition of this final Idyll and its relation to Tennyson's *Morte d'Arthur* of 1842, see note to *The Epic*. The principal source was Sir Thomas Malory's *Morte Darthur* XXI.4–5. Preceding the action of this Idyll, Arthur had been in France with his nephew Gawain fighting against the forces of Lancelot. Learning at that time of the gathering of an army against him in England, under the leadership of his nephew Modred, Arthur returned there to engage in his last battle. Upon landing at Dover, Gawain was slain.
2. A knight who had long been close to the king, described in *The Coming of Arthur*: "Bedivere, the first of all his knights / knighted by Arthur at his crowning."

In the white winter of his age, to those
With whom he dwelt, new faces, other minds.   5

    For on their march to westward, Bedivere,
Who slowly paced among the slumbering host,
Heard in his tent the moanings of the King:

    "I found Him in the shining of the stars,
I marked Him in the flowering of His fields,   10
But in His ways with men I find Him not.
I waged His wars, and now I pass and die.
O me! for why is all around us here
As if some lesser god had made the world,
But had not force to shape it as he would,   15
Till the High God behold it from beyond,
And enter it, and make it beautiful?
Or else as if the world were wholly fair,
But that these eyes of men are dense and dim,
And have not power to see it as it is: 20
Perchance, because we see not to the close;—
For I, being simple, thought to work His will,
And have but stricken with the sword in vain;
And all whereon I learned in wife and friend
Is traitor to my peace, and all my realm   25
Reels back into the beast, and is no more.
My God, thou has forgotten me in my death:[3]
Nay—God my Christ—I pass but shall not die."

    Then, ere that last weird battle in the west,
There came on Arthur sleeping, Gawain killed   30
In Lancelot's war, the ghost of Gawain blown
Along a wandering wind, and past his ear
Went shrilling, "Hollow, hollow all delight!
Hail, King! tomorrow thou shalt pass away.
Farewell! there is an isle of rest for thee.   35
And I am blown along a wandering wind,
And hollow, hollow, hollow all delight."
And fainter onward, like wild birds that change
Their season in the night and wail their way
From cloud to cloud, down the long wind the dream   40
Shrilled; but in going mingled with dim cries
Far in the moonlit haze among the hills,
As of some lonely city sacked by night,
When all is lost, and wife and child with wail
Pass to new lords; and Arthur woke and called,   45
"Who spake? A dream. O light upon the wind,
Thine, Gawain, was the voice—are these dim cries
Thine? or doth all that haunts the waste and wild
Mourn, knowing it will go along with me?"

3. Cf. "My God, my God, why hast thou forsaken me?" Matthew xxvii.46.

This heard the bold Sir Bedivere and spake: 50
"O me, my King, let pass whatever will,
Elves, and the harmless glamor of the field;⁴
But in their stead thy name and glory cling
To all high places like a golden cloud
Forever: but as yet thou shalt not pass. 55
Light was Gawain in life, and light in death
Is Gawain, for the ghost is as the man;
And care not thou for dreams from him, but rise—
I hear the steps of Modred in the west,
And with him many of thy people, and knights 60
Once thine, whom thou hast loved, but grosser grown
Than heathen, spitting at their vows and thee.
Right well in heart they know thee for the King.
Arise, go forth and conquer as of old."

Then spake King Arthur to Sir Bedivere: 65
"Far other is this battle in the west
Whereto we move, than when we strove in youth,
And brake the petty kings, and fought with Rome,
Or thrust the heathen from the Roman wall,
And shook him through the north. Ill doom is mine 70
To war against my people and my knights.
The king who fights his people fights himself.
And they thy knights, who loved me once, the stroke
That strikes them dead is as my death to me.
Yet let us hence, and find or feel a way 75
Through this blind haze, which ever since I saw
One lying in the dust at Almesbury,⁵
Hath folded in the passes of the world."

Then rose the King and moved his host by night,
And ever pushed Sir Modred, league by league, 80
Back to the sunset bound of Lyonnesse—⁶
A land of old upheaven from the abyss
By fire, to sink into the abyss again;
Where fragments of forgotten peoples dwelled,
And the long mountains ended in a coast 85
Of ever-shifting sand, and far away
The phantom circle of a moaning sea.
There the pursuer could pursue no more,
And he that fled no further fly the King;
And there, that day when the great light of heaven 90
Burned at his lowest in the rolling year,
On the waste sand by the waste sea they closed.
Nor ever yet had Arthur fought a fight

4. Tennyson said the reference is to "the legends which cluster round the King's name." One legend told of the elves' bestowing gifts on Arthur as a child.
5. The convent to which Guinevere had withdrawn; during the king's farewell visit to her there, she had lain in the dust at his feet.
6. Legendary land extending west from Cornwall which sank into the sea.

Like this last, dim, weird battle of the west.
A deathwhite mist slept over sand and sea: 95
Whereof the chill, to him who breathed it, drew
Down with his blood, till all his heart was cold
With formless fear; and even on Arthur fell
Confusion, since he saw not whom he fought.
For friend and foe were shadows in the mist,   100
And friend slew friend not knowing whom he slew;
And some had visions out of golden youth,
And some beheld the faces of old ghosts
Look in upon the battle; and in the mist
Was many a noble deed, many a base,   105
And chance and craft and strength in single fights,
And ever and anon with host to host
Shocks, and the splintering spear, the hard mail hewn,
Shield-breakings, and the clash of brands, the crash
Of battleaxes on shattered helms, and shrieks   110
After the Christ, of those who falling down
Looked up for heaven, and only saw the mist;
And shouts of heathen and the traitor knights,
Oaths, insult, filth, and monstrous blasphemies,
Sweat, writhings, anguish, laboring of the lungs   115
In that close mist, and cryings for the light,
Moans of the dying, and voices of the dead.

Last, as by some one deathbed after wail
Of suffering, silence follows, or through death
Or deathlike swoon, thus over all that shore,   120
Save for some whisper of the seething seas,
A dead hush fell; but when the dolorous day
Grew drearier toward twilight falling, came
A bitter wind, clear from the North, and blew
The mist aside, and with that wind the tide   125
Rose, and the pale King glanced across the field
Of battle: but no man was moving there;
Nor any cry of Christian heard thereon,
Nor yet of heathen; only the wan wave
Brake in among dead faces, to and fro   130
Swaying the helpless hands, and up and down
Tumbling the hollow helmets of the fallen,
And shivered brands that once had fought with Rome,
And rolling far along the gloomy shores
The voice of days of old and days to be.   135

Then spake King Arthur to Sir Bedivere,
And whiter than the mist that all day long
Had held the field of battle was the King:

"Hearest thou this great voice that shakes the world,
And wastes the narrow realm whereon we move,   140
And beats upon the faces of the dead,

My dead, as though they had not died for me?—
O Bedivere, for on my heart hath fallen
Confusion, till I know not what I am,
Nor whence I am, nor whether I be King.   145
Behold, I seem but King among the dead."

    Then spake the bold Sir Bedivere: "My King,
King everywhere! and so the dead have kings,
There also will I worship thee as King.
Yet still thy life is whole, and still I live   150
Who love thee; but who hates thee, he that brought
The heathen back among us, yonder stands,
Modred, unharmed, the traitor of thine house."

    Then spake the King: "My house hath been my doom.
But call not thou this traitor of my house   155
Who hath but dwelled beneath one roof with me.
My house are rather they who sware my vows,
Yea, even while they brake them, owned me King.
And well for thee, saying in my dark hour,
When all the purport of my throne hath failed,   160
That quick or dead thou holdest me for King.
King am I, whatsoever be their cry;
And one last act of kinghood shalt thou see
Yet, ere I pass." And uttering this the King
Made at the man: then Modred smote his liege   165
Hard on that helm which many a heathen sword
Had beaten thin; while Arthur at one blow,
Striking the last stroke with Excalibur,
Slew him, and all but slain himself, he fell.

    So all day long the noise of battle rolled   170
Among the mountains by the winter sea;
Until King Arthur's Table, man by man,
Had fallen in Lyonnesse about their lord,
King Arthur. Then, because his wound was deep,
The bold Sir Bedivere uplifted him,   175
And bore him to a chapel nigh the field,
A broken chancel with a broken cross,
That stood on a dark strait of barren land:
On one side lay the Ocean, and on one
Lay a great water, and the moon was full.   180

    Then spake King Arthur to Sir Bedivere:
"The sequel of today unsolders all
The goodliest fellowship of famous knights
Whereof this world holds record. Such a sleep
They sleep—the men I loved. I think that we   185
Shall never more, at any future time,
Delight our souls with talk of knightly deeds,

Walking about the gardens and the halls
Of Camelot, as in the days that were.
I perish by this people which I made,—   190
Though Merlin sware that I should come again
To rule once more;[7] but, let what will be, be,
I am so deeply smitten through the helm
That without help I cannot last till morn.
Thou therefore take my brand[8] Excalibur,   195
Which was my pride: for thou rememberest how
In those old days, one summer noon, an arm
Rose up from out the bosom of the lake,
Clothed in white samite,[9] mystic, wonderful,
Holding the sword—and how I rowed across   200
And took it, and have worn it, like a king;
And, wheresoever I am sung or told
In aftertime, this also shall be known:
But now delay not: take Excalibur,
And fling him far into the middle mere:[1]   205
Watch what thou seëst, and lightly[2] bring me word."

    To him replied the bold Sir Bedivere:
"It is not meet, Sir King, to leave thee thus,
Aidless, alone, and smitten through the helm—
A little thing may harm a wounded man;   210
Yet I thy hest will all perform at full,
Watch what I see, and lightly bring thee word."

    So saying, from the ruined shrine he stepped,
And in the moon athwart the place of tombs,
Where lay the mighty bones of ancient men,   215
Old knights, and over them the sea-wind sang
Shrill, chill, with flakes of foam, He, stepping down
By zigzag paths, and juts of pointed rock,
Came on the shining levels of the lake.

    There drew he forth the brand Excalibur,   220
And o'er him, drawing it, the winter moon,
Brightening the skirts of a long cloud, ran forth
And sparkled keen with frost against the hilt:
For all the haft twinkled with diamond sparks,
Myriads of topaz-lights, and jacinth-work[3]   225
Of subtlest jewelry. He gazed so long
That both his eyes were dazzled as he stood,
This way and that dividing the swift mind,
In act to throw: but at the last it seemed

7. Cf. Malory XXI.7: "Some men yet say in many parts of England that King Arthur is not dead, but by the will of our Lord in another place. And men say that he will come again."
8. Sword.
9. A rich, heavy silk.
1. Middle of the lake.
2. Quickly.
3. A "jacinth" is a red gem.

Better to leave Excalibur concealed   230
There in the many-knotted waterflags,
That whistled stiff and dry about the marge.
So strode he back slow to the wounded King.

    Then spake King Arthur to Sir Bedivere:
"Hast thou performed my mission which I gave?   235
What is it thou hast seen? or what hast heard?"

    And answer made the bold Sir Bedivere:
"I heard the ripple washing in the reeds,
And the wild water lapping on the crag."

    To whom replied King Arthur, faint and pale: 240
"Thou hast betrayed thy nature and thy name,
Not rendering true answer, as beseemed
Thy fëalty, nor like a noble knight:
For surer sign had followed, either hand,
Or voice, or else a motion of the mere.   245
This is a shameful thing for men to lie.
Yet now, I charge thee, quickly go again,
As thou art lief⁴ and dear, and do the thing
I bade thee, watch, and lightly bring me word."

    Then went Sir Bedivere the second time   250
Across the ridge, and paced beside the mere,
Counting the dewy pebbles, fixed in thought;
But when he saw the wonder of the hilt,
How curiously⁵ and strangely chased, he smote
His palms together, and he cried aloud: 255

    "And if indeed I cast the brand away,
Surely a precious thing, one worthy note,
Should thus be lost forever from the earth,
Which might have pleased the eyes of many men.
What good should follow this, if this were done?   260
What harm, undone? Deep harm to disobey,
Seeing obedience is the bond of rule.
Were it well to obey then, if a king demand
An act unprofitable, against himself?
The King is sick, and knows not what he does.   265
What record, or what relic of my lord
Should be to aftertime, but empty breath
And rumors of a doubt? But were this kept,
Stored in some treasure-house of mighty kings,
Some one might show it at a joust of arms,   270
Saying, 'King Arthur's sword, Excalibur,
Wrought by the lonely maiden of the Lake.

---

4. Beloved.   5. Skillfully; "chased": adorned.

Nine years she wrought it, sitting in the deeps
Upon the hidden bases of the hills.'
So might some old man speak in the aftertime   275
To all the people, winning reverence.
But now much honor and much fame were lost."

So spake he, clouded with his own conceit,[6]
And hid Excalibur the second time,
And so strode back slow to the wounded king.   280

Then spoke King Arthur, breathing heavily:
"What is it thou hast seen? or what hast heard?"

And answer made the bold Sir Bedivere:
"I heard the water lapping on the crag,
And the long ripple washing in the reeds."   285

To whom replied King Arthur, much in wrath:
"Ah, miserable and unkind, untrue,
Unknightly, traitor-hearted! Woe is me!
Authority forgets a dying king,
Laid widowed of the power in his eye   290
That bowed the will. I see thee what thou art,
For thou, the latest-left of all my knights,
In whom should meet the offices of all,
Thou wouldst betray me for the precious hilt;
Either from lust of gold, or like a girl   295
Valuing the giddy pleasure of the eyes.
Yet, for a man may fail in duty twice,
And the third time may prosper, get thee hence:
But, if thou spare to fling Excalibur,
I will arise and slay thee with my hands."   300

Then quickly rose Sir Bedivere, and ran,
And, leaping down the ridges lightly, plunged
Among the bullrush beds, and clutched the sword,
And strongly wheeled and threw it. The great brand
Made lightnings in the splendor of the moon,   305
And flashing round and round, and whirled in an arch,
Shot like a streamer of the northern morn,
Seen where the moving isles of winter shock[7]
By night, with noises of the Northern Sea.
So flashed and fell the brand Excalibur: 310
But ere he dipped the surface, rose an arm
Clothed in white samite, mystic, wonderful,
And caught him by the hilt, and brandished him
Three times, and drew him under in the mere.
And lightly went the other to the King.   315

6. Vain and foolish fancies.   "northern morn": the northern lights.
7. I.e., where the icebergs collide;

Then spoke King Arthur, drawing thicker breath:
"Now see I by thine eyes that this is done.
Speak out: what is it thou hast heard, or seen?"

And answer made the bold Sir Bedivere:
"Sir King, I closed mine eyelids, lest the gems   320
Should blind my purpose, for I never saw,
Nor shall see, here or elsewhere, till I die,
Not though I live three lives of mortal men,
So great a miracle as yonder hilt.
Then with both hands I flung him, wheeling him;   325
But when I looked again, behold an arm,
Clothed in white samite, mystic, wonderful,
That caught him by the hilt, and brandished him
Three times, and drew him under in the mere."

And answer made King Arthur, breathing hard: 330
"My end draws nigh; 'tis time that I were gone.
Make broad thy shoulders to receive my weight,
And bear me to the margin; yet I fear
My wound hath taken cold, and I shall die."

So saying, from the pavement he half rose,   335
Slowly, with pain, reclining on his arm,
And looking wistfully with wide blue eyes
As in a picture. Him Sir Bedivere
Remorsefully regarded through his tears,
And would have spoken, but he found not words;   340
Then took with care, and kneeling on one knee,
O'er both his shoulders drew the languid hands,
And rising bore him through the place of tombs.

But, as he walked, King Arthur panted hard,
Like one that feels a nightmare on his bed
When all the house is mute. So sighed the King,   345
Muttering and murmuring at his ear, "Quick, quick!
I fear it is too late, and I shall die."
But the other swiftly strode from ridge to ridge,
Clothed with his breath, and looking, as he walked,
Larger than human on the frozen hills.   350
He heard the deep behind him, and a cry
Before. His own thought drove him like a goad.
Dry clashed his harness in the icy caves
And barren chasms, and all to left and right
The bare black cliff clanged round him, as he based   355
His feet on juts of slippery crag that rang
Sharp-smitten with the dint of armèd heels—
And on a sudden, lo! the level lake,
And the long glories of the winter moon.   360

Then saw they how there hove a dusky barge,
Dark as a funeral scarf from stem to stern,
Beneath them; and descending they were ware
That all the decks were dense with stately forms,
Black-stoled, black-hooded, like a dream—by these   365
Three Queens with crowns of gold: and from them rose
A cry that shivered to the tingling stars,
And, as it were one voice, an agony
Of lamentation, like a wind that shrills
All night in a waste land, where no one comes,   370
Or hath come, since the making of the world.

Then murmured Arthur, "Place me in the barge."
So to the barge they came. There those three Queens
Put forth their hands, and took the King, and wept.
But she, that rose the tallest of them all   375
And fairest, laid his head upon her lap,
And loosed the shattered casque,[8] and chafed his hands,
And called him by his name, complaining loud,
And dropping bitter tears against a brow
Striped with dark blood: for all his face was white   380
And colorless, and like the withered moon
Smote by the fresh beam of the springing east;
And all his greaves and cuisses dashed with drops
Of onset;[9] and the light and lustrous curls—
That made his forehead like a rising sun   385
High from the daïs-throne—were parched with dust;
Or, clotted into points and hanging loose,
Mixed with the knightly growth that fringed his lips.
So like a shattered column lay the King;
Not like that Arthur who, with lance in rest,   390
From spur to plume a star of tournament,
Shot through the lists at Camelot, and charged
Before the eyes of ladies and of kings.

Then loudly cried the bold Sir Bedivere:
"Ah! my Lord Arthur, whither shall I go?   395
Where shall I hide my forehead and my eyes?
For now I see the true old times are dead,
When every morning brought a noble chance,
And every chance brought out a noble knight.
Such times have been not since the light that led   400
The holy Elders with the gift of myrrh.[1]
But now the whole Round Table is dissolved
Which was an image of the mighty world,

---

8. Helmet.
9. "Greaves": armor to protect the leg
below the knee; "cuisses": armor to protect the front of the thighs; "onset":

blood from battle.
1. I.e., the star that guided the three
kings ("Elders") to the Christ Child at
Bethlehem.

And I, the last, go forth companionless,
And the days darken round me, and the years,   405
Among new men, strange faces, other minds."

    And slowly answered Arthur from the barge:
"The old order changeth, yielding place to new,
And God fulfills himself in many ways,
Lest one good custom should corrupt the world.   410
Comfort thyself: what comfort is in me?
I have lived my life, and that which I have done
May He within himself make pure! but thou,
If thou shouldst never see my face again,
Pray for my soul. More things are wrought by prayer   415
Than this world dreams of. Wherefore, let thy voice
Rise like a fountain for me night and day.
For what are men better than sheep or goats
That nourish a blind life within the brain,
If, knowing God, they lift not hands of prayer   420
Both for themselves and those who call them friend?
For so the whole round earth is every way
Bound by gold chains about the feet of God.
But now farewell. I am going a long way
With these thou seëst—if indeed I go   425
(For all my mind is clouded with a doubt)—
To the island-valley of Avilion;[2]
Where falls not hail, or rain, or any snow,
Nor ever wind blows loudly; but it lies
Deep-meadowed, happy, fair with orchard lawns   430
And bowery hollows crowned with summer sea,
Where I will heal me of my grievous wound."

    So said he, and the barge with oar and sail
Moved from the brink, like some full-breasted swan
That, fluting a wild carol ere her death,   435
Ruffles her pure cold plume, and takes the flood
With swarthy webs. Long stood Sir Bedivere
Revolving many memories, till the hull
Looked one black dot against the verge of dawn,
And on the mere the wailing died away.   440

    But when that moan had passed for evermore,
The stillness of the dead world's winter dawn
Amazed him, and he groaned, "The King is gone."
And therewithal came on him the weird rhyme,
"From the great deep to the great deep he goes."   445

    Whereat he slowly turned and slowly clomb
The last hard footstep of that iron crag;
Thence marked the black hull moving yet, and cried,

---

2. Avalon, in Celtic mythology and me-   where heroes enjoyed life after death.
dieval romance, the Vale of the Blessed

"He passes to be King among the dead,
And after healing of his grievous wound   450
He comes again; but—if he come no more—
O me, be yon dark Queens in yon black boat,
Who shrieked and wailed, the three whereat we gazed
On that high day, when, clothed with living light,
They stood before his throne in silence, friends   455
Of Arthur, who should help him at his need?"

    Then from the dawn it seemed there came, but faint
As from beyond the limit of the world,
Like the last echo born of a great cry,
Sounds, as if some fair city were one voice   460
Around a king returning from his wars.

    Thereat once more he moved about, and clomb
Even to the highest he could climb, and saw,
Straining his eyes beneath an arch of hand,
Or thought he saw, the speck that bare the King,   465
Down that long water opening on the deep
Somewhere far off, pass on and on, and go
From less to less and vanish into light.
And the new sun rose bringing the new year.

1833–69   1869

Northern Farmer[1]

NEW STYLE

1

Dosn't thou 'ear my 'erse's[2] legs, as they canters awaäy?
Proputty,[3] proputty, proputty—that's what I 'ears 'em saäy.
Proputty, proputty, proputty—Sam, thou's an ass for thy paaïns;
Theer's moor sense i' one o' 'is legs, nor in all thy braaïns.

2

Whoä—theer's a craw[4] to pluck wi' tha, Sam: youn's Parson's
    'ouse—   5
Dosn't thou knaw that a man mun be eäther a man or a mouse?
Time to think on it then; for thou'll be twenty to weeäk.[5]
Proputty, proputty—woä then, woä—let ma 'ear mysén[6] speäk.

---

1. This monologue exemplifies the diversity of Tennyson's talents. A passionate attachment to land and property, which was portrayed sympathetically by Wordsworth in *Michael*, is here represented humorously. The harsh common sense of the farmer's attitude towards love and marriage is reinforced by his jaw-breaking north-English dialect.
    This is the second of a pair of monologues in dialect. In the first, *Northern* *Farmer: Old Style*, the speaker is a bailiff who has spent his life supervising the farmlands of a wealthy squire. In the second, the "new style" farmer is himself an independent landowner.
2. Horse's.
3. Property.
4. Crow.
5. This week.
6. Myself.

3

Me an' thy muther, Sammy, 'as beän a-talkin' o' thee;
Thou's beän talkin' to muther, an' she beän a-tellin' it me.
Thou'll not marry for munny—thou's sweet upo' Parson's lass—   10
Noä—thou'll marry for luvv—an' we boäth on us thinks tha an ass.

4

Seeäed her todaäy goä by—Saäint's-daäy—they was ringing the
   bells.
She's a beauty, thou thinks—an' soä is scoors o' gells,[7]
Them as 'as munny an' all—wot's a beauty!—the flower as blaws.   15
But proputty, proputty sticks, an' proputty, proputty graws.

5

Do'ant be stunt;[8] taäke time. I knaws what maäkes tha sa mad.
Warn't I craäzed fur the lasses mysén when I wur a lad?
But I knawed a Quaäker feller as often 'as towd[9] ma this:
"Doänt thou marry for munny, but goä wheer munny is!"   20

6

An' I went wheer munny war; an' thy muther coom to 'and,
Wi' lots o' munny laaïd by, an' a nicetish bit o' land.
Maäybe she warn't a beauty—I niver giv it a thowt—
But warn't she as good to cuddle an' kiss as a lass as 'ant nowt?[1]

7

Parson's lass 'ant nowt, an she weänt 'a nowt[2] when 'e's deäd,   25
Mun be a guvness, lad, or summut, and addle[3] her breäd.
Why? fur 'e's nobbut[4] a curate, an' weänt niver get hissén clear,
An' 'e maäde the bed as 'e ligs[5] on afoor 'e coomed to the shere.

8

An' thin 'e coomed to the parish wi' lots o' Varsity debt,
Stook to his taaïl they did, an' 'e 'ant got shut on 'em[6] yet.   30
An' 'e ligs on 'is back i' the grip,[7] wi' noän to lend 'im a shuvv,
Woorse nor a far-weltered yowe;[8] fur, Sammy, 'e married fur luvv.

9

Luvv? what's luvv? thou can luvv thy lass an' 'er munny too,
Mäukin' 'em goä togither, as they've good right to do.
Couldn' I luvv thy muther by cause o' 'er munny laaïd by?   35
Naäy—fur I luvved 'er a vast sight moor fur it; reäson why.

10

Aye, an' thy muther says thou wants to marry the lass,
Cooms of a gentleman burn;[9] an' we boäth on us thinks tha an ass.

7. Scores of girls.   4. Only.
8. Stubborn.   5. Lies; "shere": shire.
9. Told.   6. Rid of them.
1. Has nothing.   7. Ditch.
2. Won't have anything.   8. Ewe lying on her back.
3. Earn.   9. Born.

Woä then, proputty, wiltha?—an ass as near as mays nowt[1]—
Woä then, wiltha? dangtha!—the bees is as fell as owt.[2]   40

11

Breäk me a bit o' the esh[3] for his 'eäd, lad, out o' the fence!
Gentleman burn! what's gentleman burn? is it shillins an' pence?
Proputty, proputty's ivrything 'ere, an', Sammy, I'm blest
If it isn't the saäme oop younder, fur them as 'as it's the best.

12

Tis'n them as 'as munny as breäks into 'cuses an' steäls,   45
Them as 'as coäts to their backs an' taäkes their regular meäls.
Noä, but it's them as niver knaws wheer a meäl's to be 'ad.
Taäke my word for it, Sammy, the poor in a loomp is bad.

13

Them or thir feythers, tha sees, mun 'a beän a laäzy lot,
Fur work mun 'a gone to the gittin' whiniver munny was got.   50
Feyther 'ad ammost nowt; leästways 'is munny was 'id.
But 'e tued an' moiled[4] issén deäd, an' 'e died a good un, 'e did.

14

Looök thou theer wheer Wrigglesby beck[5] cooms out by the 'ill!
Feyther run oop[6] to the farm, an' I runs oop to the mill;
An' I'll run oop to the brig,[7] an' that thou'll live to see;   55
And if thou marries a good un I'll leäve the land to thee.

15

Thim's my noätions, Sammy, wheerby I meäns to stick;
But if thou marries a bad un, I'll leäve the land to Dick.—
Coom oop, proputty, proputty—that's what I 'ears 'im saäy—
Proputty, proputty, proputty—canter an' canter awaäy.   60
                                                              1869

Flower in the Crannied Wall

Flower in the crannied wall,
I pluck you out of the crannies,
I hold you here, root and all, in my hand,
Little flower—but if I could understand
What you are, root and all, and all in all,   5
I should know what God and man is.
                                                              1869

---

1. Makes nothing.
2. The flies are as mean as anything.
3. A branch of ash leaves (to keep the flies off the horse's head).
4. Toiled and drudged.
5. Brook.
6. I.e., father's property ran up.
7. Bridge.

The Revenge[1]

A BALLAD OF THE FLEET

1

At Flores in the Azores Sir Richard Grenville lay,
And a pinnace, like a fluttered bird, came flying from far away:
"Spanish ships of war at sea! we have sighted fifty-three!"
Then sware Lord Thomas Howard: " 'Fore God I am no coward;
But I cannot meet them here, for my ships are out of gear,
And the half my men are sick. I must fly, but follow quick.   5
We are six ships of the line; can we fight with fifty-three?"

2

Then spake Sir Richard Grenville: "I know you are no coward;
You fly them for a moment to fight with them again.
But I've ninety men and more that are lying sick ashore.   10
I should count myself the coward if I left them, my Lord Howard,
To these Inquisition dogs and the devildoms of Spain."

3

So Lord Howard passed away with five ships of war that day,
Till he melted like a cloud in the silent summer heaven;
But Sir Richard bore in hand all his sick men from the land   15
Very carefully and slow,
Men of Bideford in Devon,
And we laid them on the ballast down below;
For we brought them all aboard,
And they blessed him in their pain, that they were not left to
Spain,   20
To the thumbscrew and the stake, for the glory of the Lord.

4

He had only a hundred seamen to work the ship and to fight,
And he sailed away from Flores till the Spaniard came in sight,
With his huge sea-castles heaving upon the weather bow.
"Shall we fight or shall we fly?
Good Sir Richard, tell us now,   25
For to fight is but to die!
There'll be little of us left by the time this sun be set."
And Sir Richard said again: "We be all good English men.
Let us bang these dogs of Seville, the children of the devil,
For I never turned my back upon Don or devil yet."   30

5

Sir Richard spoke and he laughed, and we roared a hurrah, and so
The little Revenge ran on sheer into the heart of the foe,

1. Based on Sir Walter Ralegh's account of an engagement in 1591 off the coast of Flores, one of the islands of the Azores, in which five Spanish ships were sunk by the *Revenge* during a fifteen-hour battle.

With her hundred fighters on deck, and her ninety sick below;
For half of their fleet to the right and half to the left were seen,   35
And the little Revenge ran on through the long sea lane between.

6

Thousands of their soldiers looked down from their decks and
    laughed,
Thousands of their seamen made mock at the mad little craft
Running on and on, till delayed
By their mountain-like San Philip that, of fifteen hundred tons,   40
And up-shadowing high above us with her yawning tiers of guns,
Took the breath from our sails, and we stayed.

7

And while now the great San Philip hung above us like a cloud
Whence the thunderbolt will fall
Long and loud,   45
Four galleons drew away
From the Spanish fleet that day,
And two upon the larboard and two upon the starboard lay,
And the battle thunder broke from them all.

8

But anon the great San Philip, she bethought herself and went,   50
Having that within her womb that had left her ill content;
For a dozen times they came with their pikes and musqueteers,
And the rest they came aboard us, and they fought us hand to hand,
And a dozen times we shook 'em off as a dog that shakes his ears
When he leaps from the water to the land.   55

9

And the sun went down, and the stars came out far over the
    summer sea,
But never a moment ceased the fight of the one and the fifty-three.
Ship after ship, the whole night long, their high-built galleons came,
Ship after ship, the whole night long, with her battle thunder and
    flame;
Ship after ship, the whole night long, drew back with her dead and
    her shame.   60
For some were sunk and many were shattered, and so could fight us
    no more—
God of battles, was ever a battle like this in the world before?

10

For he said, "Fight on! fight on!"
Though his vessel was all but a wreck;
And it chanced that, when half of the short summer night was
    gone,   65
With a grisly wound to be dressed he had left the deck,
But a bullet struck him that was dressing it suddenly dead,

And himself he was wounded again in the side and the head,
And he said, "Fight on! fight on!"

11

And the night went down, and the sun smiled out far over the
    summer sea,   70
And the Spanish fleet with broken sides lay round us all in a ring;
But they dared not touch us again, for they feared that we still
    could sting,
So they watched what the end would be.
And we had not fought them in vain,
But in perilous plight were we,   75
Seeing forty of our poor hundred were slain,
And half of the rest of us maimed for life
In the crash of the cannonades and the desperate strife;
And the sick men down in the hold were most of them stark and
    cold,
And the pikes were all broken or bent, and the powder was all of
    it spent;   80
And the masts and the rigging were lying over the side;
But Sir Richard cried in his English pride:
"We have fought such a fight for a day and a night
As may never be fought again!
We have won great glory, my men!   85
And a day less or more
At sea or ashore,
We die—does it matter when?
Sink me the ship, Master Gunner—sink her, split her in twain!
Fall into the hands of God, not into the hands of Spain!"   90

12

And the gunner said, "Aye, aye," but the seamen made reply:
"We have children, we have wives,
And the Lord hath spared our lives.
We will make the Spaniard promise, if we yield, to let us go;
We shall live to fight again and to strike another blow."   95
And the lion there lay dying, and they yielded to the foe.

13

And the stately Spanish men to their flagship bore him then,
Where they laid him by the mast, old Sir Richard caught at last,
And they praised him to his face with their courtly foreign grace;
But he rose upon their decks, and he cried: 100
"I have fought for Queen and Faith like a valiant man and true;
I have only done my duty as a man is bound to do.
With a joyful spirit I Sir Richard Grenville die!"
And he fell upon their decks, and he died.

14

And they stared at the dead that had been so valiant and true,   105
And had holden the power and glory of Spain so cheap

That he dared her with one little ship and his English few;
Was he devil or man? He was devil for aught they knew,
But they sank his body with honor down into the deep,
And they manned the Revenge with a swarthier alien crew,   110
And away she sailed with her loss and longed for her own;
When a wind from the lands they had ruined awoke from sleep,
And the water began to heave and the weather to moan,
And or ever that evening ended a great gale blew,
And a wave like the wave that is raised by an earthquake grew,   115
Till it smote on their hulls and their sails and their masts and their
    flags,
And the whole sea plunged and fell on the shot-shattered navy of
    Spain,
And the little Revenge herself went down by the island crags
To be lost evermore in the main.

                                                  1878

To Virgil

WRITTEN AT THE REQUEST OF THE MANTUANS[1] FOR THE
NINETEENTH CENTENARY OF VIRGIL'S DEATH

1

Roman Virgil, thou that singest
    Ilion's lofty temples robed in fire,
Ilion falling, Rome arising,
    wars, and filial faith, and Dido's pyre;[2]

2

Landscape-lover, lord of language
    more than he that sang the "Works and Days,"[3]
All the chosen coin of fancy
    flashing out from many a golden phrase;

3

Thou that singest wheat and woodland,
    tilth and vineyard, hive and horse and herd;   5
All the charm of all the Muses
    often flowering in a lonely word;

4

Poet of the happy Tityrus[4]
    piping underneath his beechen bowers;
Poet of the poet-satyr[5]
    whom the laughing shepherd bound with flowers;

1. Inhabitants of Mantua, the city near
which Virgil was born.
2. The allusions in this stanza are to incidents in Virgil's *Aeneid*, especially the
fall of Troy (Ilion).

3. Hesiod, a Greek poet, whose *Works
and Days* anticipated Virgil's *Georgics* in
its pictures of farm life.
4. A shepherd in Virgil's *Eclogue* I.
5. Silenus, in *Eclogue* VI.

5

Chanter of the Pollio,[6] glorying
　　　　in the blissful years again to be,
Summers of the snakeless meadow,
　　　　unlaborious earth and oarless sea;　　　　　　10

6

Thou that seest Universal
　　　　Nature moved by Universal Mind;
Thou majestic in thy sadness
　　　　at the doubtful doom of human kind;

7

Light among the vanished ages;
　　　　star that gildest yet this phantom shore;
Golden branch[7] amid the shadows,
　　　　kings and realms that pass to rise no more;

8

Now thy Forum roars no longer,
　　　　fallen every purple Caesar's dome—
Though thine ocean-roll of rhythm　　　　　　　　15
　　　　sound forever of Imperial Rome—

9

Now the Rome of slaves hath perished,
　　　　and the Rome of freemen[8] holds her place,
I, from out the Northern Island
　　　　sundered once from all the human race,

10

I salute thee, Mantovano,[9]
　　　　I that loved thee since my day began,
Wielder of the stateliest measure
　　　　ever molded by the lips of man.
1882　　　　　　　　　　　　　　　　　　　　　　　　　1882　　20

"Frater Ave atque Vale"[1]

Row us out from Desenzano,[2] to your Sirmione row!
So they rowed, and there we landed—"O venusta Sirmio!"
There to me through all the groves of olive in the summer glow,
There beneath the Roman ruin where the purple flowers grow,

---

6. A friend of Virgil's who is celebrated
in *Eclogue* IV.
7. A golden bough enabled Aeneas to
enter the world of the shades. See *Aeneid*
VI.208 ff.
8. Italy had only recently been liberated
and unified.
9. Mantuan.
1. "Brother, hail and farewell," a line
from an elegy by the Roman poet Catullus on the death of his brother (CI.10).

Tennyson himself had recently lost his
brother Charles.
2. A town on Lake Garda in Italy,
which Tennyson visited in 1880. Sirmione is a beautiful peninsula jutting
into the lake, on which Catullus had his
summer home. Catullus' poem in
honor of the locality includes the phrase
"*O venusta Sirmio!*" ("O lovely Sirmio!").

Came that "Ave atque Vale" of the Poet's hopeless woe,   5
Tenderest of Roman poets nineteen hundred years ago,
"Frater Ave atque Vale"—as we wandered to and fro
Gazing at the Lydian[3] laughter of the Garda Lake below
Sweet Catullus's all-but-island, olive-silvery Sirmio!

1880   1883

The Dawn

"You are but children."
—EGYPTIAN PRIEST TO SOLON

Red of the Dawn!
Screams of a babe in the red-hot palms of a Moloch[1] of Tyre,
    Man with his brotherless dinner on man in the tropical wood,
    Priests in the name of the Lord passing souls through fire to the
        fire,
Head-hunters and boats of Dahomey[2] that float upon human
    blood!   5

Red of the Dawn!
Godless fury of peoples, and Christless frolic of kings,
    And the bolt of war dashing down upon cities and blazing farms,
    For Babylon was a child newborn, and Rome was a babe in arms,
And London and Paris and all the rest are as yet but in leading
    strings.   10

Dawn not Day,
While scandal is mouthing a bloodless name at *her* cannibal feast,
    And rake-ruined bodies and souls go down in a common wreck,
    And the Press of a thousand cities is prized for it smells of the
        beast,
Or easily violates virgin Truth for a coin or a check.   15

Dawn not Day!
Is it Shame, so few should have climbed from the dens in the level
    below,
    Men, with a heart and a soul, no slaves of a four-footed will?
    But if twenty million of summers are stored in the sunlight still,
We are far from the noon of man, there is time for the race to
    grow.   20

Red of the Dawn!
Is it turning a fainter red? So be it, but when shall we lay
    The Ghost of the Brute that is walking and haunting us yet, and
        be free?
    In a hundred, a thousand winters? Ah, what will *our* children be?
The men of a hundred thousand, a million summers away?   25

1892

3. The Etruscans, who settled near Lake Garda, were thought to be descended from the Lydians of Asia Minor.
1. A god to whom children were sacrificed as burnt offerings.

2. West African country in which the custom of human sacrifice persisted in the 19th century. In 1892, after a war, Dahomey became a French colony.

Crossing the Bar[1]

Sunset and evening star,
   And one clear call for me!
And may there be no moaning of the bar,[2]
   When I put out to sea,

But such a tide as moving seems asleep,   5
   Too full for sound and foam,
When that which drew from out the boundless deep
   Turns again home.

Twilight and evening bell,
   And after that the dark!
And may there be no sadness of farewell,   10
   When I embark;

For though from out our bourne[3] of Time and Place
   The flood may bear me far,
I hope to see my Pilot face to face   15
   When I have crossed the bar.

1889   1889

1. Although not the last poem written by Tennyson, *Crossing the Bar* appears, at his request, as the final poem in all collections of his work.

2. Mournful sound of the ocean beating on a sand bar at the mouth of a harbor.
3. Boundary.

EDWARD FITZGERALD
(1809–1883)

Omar Khayyám was a 12th-century mathematician, astronomer, and teacher, from Nishapur in Persia. He was also the author of numerous rhymed quatrains, a verse form called *rubāʿi* in Persian. Omar's four-lined epigrams were subsequently brought together in collections called *Rubáiyát* and recorded in various manuscripts.

Over 700 years later, in 1857, one such Omar manuscript came into the hands of Edward FitzGerald, a Victorian man of letters, who made from it one of the most popular poems in the English language. FitzGerald was a scholar of comfortable means who lived in the country reading the classics and cultivating his garden. He also cultivated his friendships with writers like Tennyson, Thackeray, and Carlyle, to whom he wrote charming letters. His translations from Greek and Latin were largely ignored, and so too, at first, was his translation of Omar's Persian verses, which he published anonymously. In 1859, only two reviewers noticed the appearance of the *Rubáiyát*, and the edition was soon remaindered. Two years later the volume was discovered by D. G. Rossetti, and enthusiasm for it gradually spread, until edition after edition was called for. The demand for the poem led FitzGerald to revise his translation considerably by further polishing his already finely polished stanzas (the fifth version of these revisions appears below).

The Italians have a witty saying that translations are like spouses: a beautiful translation is apt to be unfaithful, and a faithful translation is apt to be ugly. Experts have argued at great length whether FitzGerald's adaptation of Omar's poem is a faithful translation, but no one argues its beauty.

One reader said of FitzGerald's witty and melancholy masterpiece: "It reads like the latest and freshest expression of the perplexity and of the doubt of the generation to which we ourselves belong." This comment was made by the American Charles Eliot Norton writing in 1869. Norton's favorable opinion has been endorsed by later generations as well. The *Rubáiyát* has much in common with another late Victorian volume, *The Shropshire Lad* by A. E. Housman, and the remarkable popularity of these two collections of nostalgic lyrics is a reminder that to be popular, especially among young readers, poetry does not have to offer optimistic edification. As George Moore said, "The sadness of life is the joy of art."

The Rubáiyát of Omar Khayyám

1

Wake! For the Sun, who scattered into flight
The Stars before him from the Field of Night,
　　Drives Night along with them from Heav'n and strikes
The Sultán's Turret with a Shaft of Light.

2

Before the phantom of False morning[1] died,　　　　　　5
Methought a Voice within the Tavern cried,
　　"When all the Temple is prepared within,
Why nods the drowsy Worshiper outside?"

3

And, as the Cock crew, those who stood before
The Tavern shouted—"Open, then, the Door!　　　　　10
　　You know how little while we have to stay,
And, once departed, may return no more."

4

Now the New Year[2] reviving old Desires,
The thoughtful Soul to Solitude retires,
　　Where the WHITE HAND OF MOSES on the Bough
Puts out, and Jesus from the Ground suspires.[3]　　　　15

5

Iram[4] indeed is gone with all his Rose,
And Jamshyd's[5] Sev'n-ringed Cup where no one knows;
　　But still a Ruby kindles in the Vine,
And many a Garden by the Water blows.　　　　　　20

6

And David's lips are locked; but in divine
High-piping Pehleví,[6] with "Wine! Wine! Wine!

---

1. "A transient Light on the Horizon about an hour before the * * * True Dawn" [FitzGerald's note].
2. In Persia, the beginning of spring.
3. Breathes. "Moses" and "Jesus": plants named in honor of prophets who came before Mohammed. The Persians believed that the healing power of Jesus was in his breath.
4. "A royal Garden now sunk somewhere in the Sands of Arabia" [FitzGerald's note].
5. Legendary king.
6. The classical language of Persia.

Red Wine!"—the Nightingale cries to the Rose
That sallow cheek of hers to incarnadine.

7

Come, fill the Cup, and in the fire of Spring   25
Your Winter-garment of Repentance fling;
    The Bird of Time has but a little way
To flutter—and the Bird is on the Wing.

8

Whether at Naishápur or Babylon,
Whether the Cup with sweet or bitter run,   30
    The Wine of Life keeps oozing drop by drop,
The Leaves of Life keep falling one by one.

9

Each Morn a thousand Roses brings, you say;
Yes, but where leaves the Rose of Yesterday?
    And this first Summer month that brings the Rose   35
Shall take Jamshyd and Kaikobád[7] away.

10

Well, let it take them! What have we to do
With Kaikobád the Great, or Kaikhosrú?
    Let Zál and Rustum bluster as they will,[8]
Or Hátim[9] call to Supper—heed not you.   40

11

With me along the strip of Herbage strown
That just divides the desert from the sown,
    Where name of Slave and Sultán is forgot—
And Peace to Mahmúd[1] on his golden Throne!

12

A Book of Verses underneath the Bough,   45
A Jug of Wine, a Loaf of Bread—and Thou
    Beside me singing in the Wilderness—
Oh, Wilderness were Paradise enow!

13

Some for the Glories of This World; and some
Sigh for the Prophet's[2] Paradise to come;
    Ah, take the Cash, and let the Credit go,   50
Nor heed the rumble of a distant Drum!

14

Look to the blowing Rose about us—"Lo,
Laughing," she says, "into the world I blow,
    At once the silken tassel of my Purse
Tear, and its Treasure on the Garden throw."   55

15

And those who husbanded the Golden Grain,
And those who flung it to the winds like Rain,
    Alike to no such aureate Earth are turned
As, buried once, Men want dug up again.   60

---

7. Founder of a line of Persian kings.   9. A generous host.
8. Kaikhosrú: a king; Zál and Rustum: 1. A sultan who conquered India.
son and father who were warriors.   2. Mohammed's.

16

The Worldly Hope men set their Hearts upon
Turns Ashes—or it prospers; and anon,
   Like Snow upon the Desert's dusty Face,
Lighting a little hour or two—is gone.

17

Think, in this battered Caravanserai[3]
Whose Portals are alternate Night and Day,
   How Sultán after Sultán with his Pomp
Abode his destined Hour, and went his way.

18

They say the Lion and the Lizard keep
The Courts where Jamshyd gloried and drank deep;
   And Bahrám,[4] that great Hunter—the Wild Ass
Stamps o'er his Head, but cannot break his Sleep.

19

I sometimes think that never blows so red
The Rose as where some buried Caesar bled;
   That every Hyacinth[5] the Garden wears
Dropped in her Lap from some once lovely Head.

20

And this reviving Herb whose tender Green
Fledges the River-Lip on which we lean—
   Ah, lean upon it lightly! for who knows
From what once lovely Lip it springs unseen!

21

Ah, my Belovéd, fill the Cup that clears
TODAY of past Regrets and future Fears:
   Tomorrow!—Why, Tomorrow I may be
Myself with Yesterday's Sev'n thousand Years.

22

For some we loved, the loveliest and the best
That from his Vintage rolling Time hath pressed,
   Have drunk their Cup a Round or two before,
And one by one crept silently to rest.

23

And we, that now make merry in the Room
They left, and Summer dresses in new bloom,
   Ourselves must we beneath the Couch of Earth
Descend—ourselves to make a Couch—for whom?

24

Ah, make the most of what we yet may spend,
Before we too into the Dust descend;
   Dust into Dust, and under Dust to lie,
Sans Wine, sans Song, sans Singer, and—sans End!

65

70

75

80

85

90

95

3. Inn.
4. A king who was lost while hunting a wild ass.
5. In classical myth, the hyacinth had associations of sadness because the plant was supposed to have sprung from the blood of Hyacinthus, a beautiful youth who was killed in an accident. Its petals were marked AI, meaning "alas." FitzGerald, however, seems to be referring more particularly to the shape of the flower, as in Homer's *Odyssey* VI.231, where locks of hair are likened to hyacinth clusters.

25

Alike for those who for TODAY prepare,
And those that after some TOMORROW stare,
   A Muezzín[6] from the Tower of Darkness cries,
"Fools, your Reward is neither Here nor There."   100

26

Why, all the Saints and Sages who discussed
Of the Two Worlds so wisely—they are thrust
   Like foolish Prophets forth; their Words to Scorn
Are scattered, and their Mouths are stopped with Dust.

27

Myself when young did eagerly frequent   105
Doctor and Saint, and heard great argument
   About it and about; but evermore
Came out by the same door where in I went.

28

With them the seed of Wisdom did I sow,
And with mine own hand wrought to make it grow;   110
   And this was all the Harvest that I reaped—
"I came like Water, and like Wind I go."

29

Into this Universe, and *Why* not knowing
Nor *Whence*, like Water willy-nilly flowing;
   And out of it, as Wind along the Waste,   115
I know not *Whither*, willy-nilly blowing.

30

What, without asking, hither hurried *Whence?*
And, without asking, *Whither* hurried hence!
   Oh, many a Cup of this forbidden Wine[7]
Must drown the memory of that insolence!   120

31

Up from the Earth's Center through the Seventh Gate
I rose, and on the Throne of Saturn[8] sate,
   And many a Knot unraveled by the Road;
But not the Master-knot of Human Fate.

32

There was the Door to which I found no Key;   125
There was the Veil through which I might not see;
   Some little talk awhile of ME and THEE
There was—and then no more of THEE and ME.

33

Earth could not answer; nor the Seas that mourn
In flowing Purple, of their Lord forlorn;   130
   Nor rolling Heaven, with all his Signs[9] revealed
And hidden by the sleeve of Night and Morn.

34

Then of the THEE IN ME who works behind
The Veil, I lifted up my hands to find

---

6. One who calls the hour of prayer
from the tower of a mosque.
7. Alcohol is forbidden to strict Moslems.

8. The seat of knowledge. According to
a note by FitzGerald, Saturn was lord
of the seventh heaven.
9. I.e., of the zodiac.

A lamp amid the Darkness; and I heard,
As from Without—"The Me within Thee blind!" 135

35

Then to the Lip of this poor earthen Urn
I leaned, the Secret of my Life to learn;
    And Lip to Lip it murmured—"While you live,
Drink!—for, once dead, you never shall return." 140

36

I think the Vessel, that with fugitive
Articulation answered, once did live,
    And drink; and Ah! the passive Lip I kissed,
How many Kisses might it take—and give!

37

For I remember stopping by the way 145
To watch a Potter thumping his wet Clay;
    And with its all-obliterated Tongue
It murmured—"Gently, Brother, gently, pray!"

38

And has not such a Story from of Old
Down Man's successive generations rolled 150
    Of such a clod of saturated Earth
Cast by the Maker into Human mold?

39

And not a drop that from our Cups we throw
For Earth to drink of,[1] but may steal below
    To quench the fire of Anguish in some Eye 155
There hidden—far beneath, and long ago.

40

As then the Tulip, for her morning sup
Of Heav'nly Vintage, from the soil looks up,
    Do you devoutly do the like, till Heav'n
To Earth invert you—like an empty Cup. 160

41

Perplexed no more with Human or Divine,
Tomorrow's tangle to the winds resign,
    And lose your fingers in the tresses of
The Cypress-slender Minister of Wine.[2]

42

And if the Wine you drink, the Lip you press, 165
End in what All begins and ends in—Yes;
    Think then you are Today what Yesterday
You were—Tomorrow you shall not be less.

43

So when that Angel of the darker Drink
At last shall find you by the river brink, 170
    And offering his Cup, invite your Soul
Forth to your Lips to quaff—you shall not shrink.

44

Why, if the Soul can fling the Dust aside,

1. A reference to the custom of pouring some wine on the ground before
drinking in order to refresh some dead
and buried wine-drinker.
2. Maiden who serves the wine.

And naked on the Air of Heaven ride,
    Were 't not a Shame—were 't not a Shame for him   175
In this clay carcass crippled to abide?

45

'Tis but a Tent where takes his one day's rest
A Sultán to the realm of Death addressed;
    The Sultán rises, and the dark Ferrásh[3]
Strikes, and prepares it for another Guest.   180

46

And fear not lest Existence closing your
Account, and mine, should know the like no more;
    The Eternal Sakí[4] from that Bowl has poured
Millions of Bubbles like us, and will pour.

47

When You and I behind the Veil are past,   185
Oh, but the long, long while the World shall last,
    Which of our Coming and Departure heeds
As the Sea's self should heed a pebble-cast.

48

A Moment's Halt—a momentary taste
Of BEING from the Well amid the Waste—   190
    And Lo!—the phantom Caravan has reached
The NOTHING it set out from—Oh, make haste!

49

Would you that spangle of Existence spend
About THE SECRET—quick about it, Friend!
    A Hair perhaps divides the False and True—   195
And upon what, prithee, may life depend?

50

A Hair perhaps divides the False and True—
Yes; and a single Alif[5] were the clue—
    Could you but find it—to the Treasure-house,
And peradventure to THE MASTER too;   200

51

Whose secret Presence, through Creation's veins
Running Quicksilver-like, eludes your pains;
    Taking all shapes from Máh to Máhi;[6] and
They change and perish all—but He remains;

52

A moment guessed—then back behind the Fold
Immersed of Darkness round the Drama rolled   205
    Which, for the Pastime of Eternity,
He doth Himself contrive, enact, behold.

53

But if in vain, down on the stubborn floor
Of Earth, and up to Heav'n's unopening Door,
    You gaze TODAY, while You are You—how then   210
TOMORROW, You when shall be You no more?

---

3. Servant who takes down ("strikes")
a tent.
4. Servant who passes the wine.

5. The first letter of the Arabic alphabet, represented by a single vertical line.
6. I.e., from lowest to highest.

54

Waste not your Hour, nor in the vain pursuit
Of This and That endeavor and dispute;
   Better be jocund with the fruitful Grape
Than sadden after none, or bitter, Fruit.

55

You know, my Friends, with what a brave Carouse
I made a Second Marriage in my house;
   Divorced old barren Reason from my Bed,
And took the Daughter of the Vine to Spouse.

56

For "Is" and "Is-not" though with Rule and Line,
And "Up-and-down" by Logic, I define,
   Of all that one should care to fathom, I
Was never deep in anything but—Wine.

57

Ah, but my Computations, People say,
Reduced the Year to better reckoning?[7]—Nay,
   'Twas only striking from the Calendar
Unborn Tomorrow, and dead Yesterday.

58

And lately, by the Tavern Door agape,
Came shining through the Dusk an Angel Shape
   Bearing a Vessel on his Shoulder; and
He bid me taste of it; and 'twas—the Grape!

59

The Grape that can with Logic absolute
The Two-and-Seventy jarring Sects[8] confute;
   The sovereign Alchemist that in a trice
Life's leaden metal into Gold transmute;

60

The mighty Mahmúd, Allah-breathing Lord,
That all the misbelieving and black Horde[9]
   Of Fears and Sorrows that infest the Soul
Scatters before him with his whirlwind Sword.

61

Why, be this Juice the growth of God, who dare
Blaspheme the twisted tendril as a Snare?
   A Blessing, we should use it, should we not?
And if a Curse—why, then, Who set it there?

62

I must abjure the Balm of Life, I must,
Scared by some After-reckoning ta'en on trust
   Or lured with Hope of some Diviner Drink,
To fill the Cup—when crumbled into Dust!

---

7. As a mathematician, Omar had devised an improved calendar.
8. "The 72 religions supposed to divide the world" [FitzGerald's note].

9. "Alluding to Sultan Mahmúd's Conquest of India and its dark people" [FitzGerald's note].

63

Oh threats of Hell and Hopes of Paradise!
One thing at least is certain—*This* Life flies;   250
    One thing is certain and the rest is Lies—
The Flower that once has blown forever dies.

64

Strange, is it not? that of the myriads who
Before us passed the door of Darkness through,
    Not one returns to tell us of the Road,   255
Which to discover we must travel too.

65

The Revelations of Devout and Learn'd
Who rose before us, and as Prophets burned,[1]
    Are all but Stories, which, awoke from Sleep,
They told their comrades, and to Sleep returned.   260

66

I sent my Soul through the Invisible,
Some letter of that After-life to spell;
    And by and by my Soul returned to me,
And answered, "I Myself am Heav'n and Hell"—

67

Heaven but the Vision of fulfilled Desire,   265
And Hell the Shadow from a Soul on fire
    Cast on the Darkness into which Ourselves,
So late emerged from, shall so soon expire.

68

We are no other than a moving row
Of Magic Shadow-shapes that come and go   270
    Round with the Sun-illumined Lantern held
In Midnight by the Master of the Show;

69

But helpless Pieces of the Game He plays
Upon this Checkerboard of Nights and Days;
    Hither and thither moves, and checks, and slays,   275
And one by one back in the Closet lays.

70

The Ball no question makes of Ayes and Noes,
But Here or There as strikes the Player[2] goes;
    And He that tossed you down into the Field,
He knows about it all—HE knows—HE knows!   280

71

The Moving Finger writes, and, having writ,
Moves on; nor all your Piety nor Wit
    Shall lure it back to cancel half a Line,
Nor all your Tears wash out a Word of it.

72

And that inverted Bowl they call the Sky,   285
Whereunder crawling cooped we live and die,

---

1. Inspired by burning zeal to spread   2. Polo player.
their prophecies.

Lift not your hands to *It* for help—for It
As impotently moves as you or I.

73

With Earth's first Clay They did the Last Man knead,
And there of the Last Harvest sowed the Seed;   290
   And the first Morning of Creation wrote
What the Last Dawn of Reckoning shall read.

74

YESTERDAY *This* Day's Madness did prepare;
TOMORROW's Silence, Triumph, or Despair.
   Drink! for you know not whence you came, nor why;   295
Drink, for you know not why you go, nor where.

75

I tell you this—When, started from the Goal,
Over the flaming shoulders of the Foal
   Of Heav'n Parwín and Mushtarí they flung,
In my predestined Plot of Dust and Soul[3]   300

76

The Vine had struck a fiber; which about
If clings my Being—let the Dervish[4] flout;
   Of my Base metal may be filed a Key,
That shall unlock the Door he howls without.

77

And this I know: whether the one True Light   305
Kindle to Love, or Wrath—consume me quite,
   One Flash of It within the Tavern caught
Better than in the Temple lost outright.

78

What! out of senseless Nothing to provoke
A conscious Something to resent the yoke   310
   Of unpermitted Pleasure, under pain
Of Everlasting Penalties, if broke!

79

What! from his helpless Creature be repaid
Pure Gold for what he lent him dross-allayed—
   Sue for a Debt he never did contract,   315
And cannot answer—Oh, the sorry trade!

80

O Thou, who didst with pitfall and with gin[5]
Beset the Road I was to wander in,
   Thou wilt not with Predestined Evil round
Enmesh, and then impute my Fall to Sin!   320

---

3. The speaker asserts that his fate was predestined in accordance with the relationship of the stars and planets at the moment of his birth when he "started from the Goal." In his horoscope, the particular relationship involved the Pleiades ("Parwín") and the planet Jupiter ("Mushtarí") which were "flung" by the gods into a special position in relation to the place in the sky of the constellation Equuleus ("the Foal" or Colt).
4. Ascetic, who would despise ("flout") wine as a means of discovering truth.
5. Trap.

81

O Thou, who Man of Baser Earth didst make,
And ev'n with Paradise devise the Snake,
  For all the Sin wherewith the Face of Man
Is blackened—Man's forgiveness give—and take!

———————

82

As under cover of departing Day   325
Slunk hunger-stricken Ramazán[6] away,
  Once more within the Potter's house alone
I stood, surrounded by the Shapes of Clay—

83

Shapes of all Sorts and Sizes, great and small,
That stood along the floor and by the wall;   330
  And some loquacious Vessels were; and some
Listened perhaps, but never talked at all.

84

Said one among them—"Surely not in vain
My substance of the common Earth was ta'en
  And to this Figure molded, to be broke,   335
Or trampled back to shapeless Earth again."

85

Then said a Second—"Ne'er a peevish Boy
Would break the Bowl from which he drank in joy;
  And He that with his hand the Vessel made
Will surely not in after Wrath destroy."   340

86

After a momentary silence spake
Some Vessel of a more ungainly Make:
  "They sneer at me for leaning all awry;
What! did the Hand, then, of the Potter shake?"

87

Whereat someone of the loquacious Lot—   345
I think a Súfi[7] pipkin—waxing hot—
  "All this of Pot and Potter—Tell me then,
Who is the Potter, pray, and who the Pot?"

88

"Why," said another, "Some there are who tell
Of one who threatens he will toss to Hell   350
  The luckless Pots he marred in making—Pish!
He's a Good Fellow, and 'twill all be well."

89

"Well," murmured one, "Let whoso make or buy,
My Clay with long Oblivion is gone dry;
  But fill me with the old familiar Juice,   355
Methinks I might recover by and by."

———

6. The month of fasting—during which   7. Mystic.
no food is eaten from sunrise to sunset.

90

So while the Vessels one by one were speaking
The little Moon looked in that all were seeking;[8]
    And then they jogged each other, "Brother! Brother!
Now for the Porter's shoulder-knot[9] a-creaking!"   360

91

Ah, with the Grape my fading Life provide,
And wash the Body whence the Life has died,
    And lay me, shrouded in the living Leaf,
By some not unfrequented Garden-side—

92

That ev'n my buried Ashes such a snare   365
Of Vintage shall fling up into the Air
    As not a True-believer passing by
But shall be overtaken unaware.

93

Indeed the Idols I have loved so long
Have done my credit in this World much wrong,   370
    Have drowned my Glory in a shallow Cup,
And sold my Reputation for a Song.

94

Indeed, indeed, Repentance oft before
I swore—but was I sober when I swore?
    And then and then came Spring, and Rose-in-hand   375
My threadbare Penitence apieces tore.

95

And much as Wine has played the Infidel,
And robbed me of my Robe of Honor—Well,
    I wonder often what the Vintners buy
One-half so precious as the stuff they sell.   380

96

Yet Ah, that Spring should vanish with the Rose!
That Youth's sweet-scented manuscript should close!
    The Nightingale that in the branches sang,
Ah whence, and whither flown again, who knows!

97

Would but the Desert of the Fountain yield   385
One glimpse—if dimly, yet indeed, revealed,
    To which the fainting Traveler might spring,
As springs the trampled herbage of the field.

98

Would but some wingéd Angel ere too late
Arrest the yet unfolded Roll of Fate,   390
    And make the stern Recorder otherwise
Enregister, or quite obliterate!

8. "At the close of the Fasting Month, Ramazán * * * the first Glimpse of the New Moon * * * is looked for with the utmost Anxiety and hailed with all Acclamation" [FitzGerald's note].

9. The rope or strap on which were hung the wine jars carried by the porter.

99

Ah, Love! could you and I with Him conspire
To grasp this sorry Scheme of Things entire,
    Would not we shatter it to bits—and then
Remold it nearer to the Heart's Desire!   395

100

Yon rising Moon that looks for us again—
How oft hereafter will she wax and wane;
    How oft hereafter rising look for us
Through this same Garden—and for *one* in vain!   400

101

And when like her, O Sákí, you shall pass
Among the Guests Star-scattered on the Grass,
    And in your joyous errand reach the spot
Where I made One—turn down an empty Glass!

TAMÁM[1]

1857   1859, 1889
1. "It is ended."

ROBERT BROWNING

(1812–1889)

1846: Marriage to Elizabeth Barrett and residence in Italy.
1855: *Men and Women* published.
1861: Death of Elizabeth Barrett Browning.
1868–69: *The Ring and the Book* published.

During the years of his marriage Robert Browning was sometimes referred to as "Mrs. Browning's husband." Elizabeth Barrett, who seems to us now a minor figure, was at that time a famous poet while her husband was a relatively unknown experimenter whose poems were greeted with misunderstanding or indifference. Not until the 1860's did he at last gain a public and become recognized as the rival or equal of Tennyson. In the 20th century his reputation has persisted, but in an unusual way: his poetry is admired by two groups of readers widely different in tastes. To one group his work is a moral tonic. Such readers appreciate him as a man who lived bravely and as a writer who showed life to be a joyful battle, the imperfections of this world being remedied, under the dispensations of an all-loving God, by the perfections of the next. Typical of this group are the Browning Societies which have flourished in England and America. Members of these societies usually regard their poet as a wise philosopher and religious teacher who resolved the doubts which had troubled Arnold and Tennyson and which have continued to trouble later generations of less confident writers.

A second group of readers enjoy Browning less for his attempt to solve problems of religious doubt than for his attempt to solve the problems of how poetry should be written. Such poets as Ezra Pound and Robert Lowell have valued him as a major artist; they have recognized that more than any other 19th-century poet (even including Hopkins), it was Browning who energetically hacked through a trail that has subsequently become the main road of 20th-century poetry. In *Poetry and the Age* (1953) Randall Jarrell remarked how "the dramatic monologue, which once had depended for its effect upon being a departure from the norm of poetry, now became in one form or another the norm." Later poets such as Edward Lucie-Smith in England and Richard Howard in America are especially close to Browning's mode. In 1969, Howard dedicated a volume of monologues to Browning: "to the great poet of otherness * * * who said, as I should like to say, 'I'll tell my state as though 'twere none of mine.'"

The dramatic monologue, as Browning uses it, enables the reader, speaker, and poet to be located at an appropriate distance from each other, aligned in such a way that the reader must work *through* the words of the speaker toward the meaning of the poet himself. For example, in the well-known early monologue *My Last Duchess*, we listen to the Duke as he speaks of his dead wife, and it is almost as if we were overhearing a man talking into the telephone of a booth adjacent to ours. From his one-sided conversation we piece together the situation, both past and present, and we infer what sort of woman the Duchess really was, and what sort of man is the Duke. Ultimately we may also infer what the poet himself thinks of the speaker he has created. In this instance, from evidence outside the poem we know that Browning had a special aversion for domestic tyrants. His own father-in-law was to provide him with a striking example of the breed, and it is revealing that in his longest poem, *The Ring and the Book*, he once more explored the story of another domestic tyrant who, like the Duke, was irritated by his wife's virtues. Yet from *My Last Duchess* itself, if we exclude external evidence, it is interesting to note how persuasive is the Duke's own side of the story:

> She had
> A heart—how shall I say?—too soon made glad,
> Too easily impressed; she liked whate'er
> She looked on, and her looks went everywhere.

Although Browning contrives that our verdict as jurymen will be a just one, he does allow us a considerable amount of latitude. And in some of his later monologues we are really obliged to grope toward a choice. In reading *A Grammarian's Funeral*, for example, can we be sure that the central character is a hero? Or is he merely a fool? Browning has not made the answer easy for us.

In addition to his experiments with the dramatic monologue Browning also made experiments with language and syntax. The grotesque rhymes and jaw-breaking diction which he often employs have been repugnant to some critics; George Santayana, for instance, dismissed him as a clumsy barbarian. But to those who understand Browning's aims, the incongruities of language are not literally incongruous but functional, a humorous and appropriate counterpart to an imperfect world. Ezra Pound's tribute to "Old Hippety-Hop o' the accents," as he addresses Browning, is both affectionate and memorable:

Heart that was big as the bowels of Vesuvius
Words that were winged as her sparks in eruption,
Eagled and thundered as Jupiter Pluvius
Sound in your wind past all signs o' corruption.

This capacity to attract the admiration of such a diversity of readers, sophisticated and unsophisticated, is one of several ways in which Browning's writings can be likened to those of Dickens and Shakespeare.

The personal life of Robert Browning falls into three phases: his years as a child and young bachelor, as a husband, and as a widower. Each of these phases is most appropriately considered in relation to his development as a poet.

He was born in Camberwell, a London suburb, within a few months of the births of Dickens and Thackeray. His father, a bank clerk, was a learned man with an extensive library. His mother was a kindly, religious-minded woman, interested in music, whose love for her brilliant son was warmly reciprocated. Until the time of his marriage at the age of 34 Browning was rarely absent from his parents' home. He attended a boarding school near Camberwell, traveled a little (to Russia and Italy), and was a student at the University of London for a short period, but he preferred to pursue his education at home where he was tutored in foreign languages, music, boxing, and horsemanship, and where he read omnivorously. From this unusual education he acquired a store of knowledge upon which to draw for the background of his poems.

The "obscurity" of which his contemporaries complained in his earlier poetry may be partly accounted for by the circumstances of Browning's education. He was inclined to assume that his out-of-the-ordinary learning was generally shared by educated readers. Often it was not. But the obscurity of such poems as *Sordello* (1840) is attributable not only to the nature of Browning's learning but to the poet's anxious desire to avoid exposing himself too explicitly before his readers. His first poem, *Pauline*, published when he was 21, had been modeled on the example of Shelley, the most personal of poets. When a review by John Stuart Mill pointed out that the young author was parading a "morbid state" of self-worship, Browning was overwhelmed with embarrassment. He resolved to avoid confessional writings thereafter.

One way of reducing the personal element in his poetry was to write plays instead of soul-searching narratives or lyrics. In 1836, encouraged by the actor W. C. Macready, Browning began work on his first play, *Strafford*, a historical tragedy that lasted only four nights when it was produced at a London theater in 1837. For ten years the young writer struggled to produce other plays that would better hold the attention of an audience, but as stage productions they all remained failures. Browning nevertheless profited from this otherwise disheartening experience. Writing dialogue for actors led him to explore another form more congenial to his genius, the dramatic monologue, a form that enabled him through imaginary speakers to avoid explicit autobiography and yet did not demand that these speakers act out their story with the speed or the simplifications that stage production demands. As William Irvine notes: "In Browning's monologues, murderers recollect, but do not commit, their murders." His first collection of such monologues, *Dramatic Lyrics*, appeared in 1842. Unlike Tennyson's volume, appearing the same year, *Dramatic Lyrics* was as poorly received by reviewers and public as Browning's plays had been.

Browning's resolution to avoid the subjective manner of Shelley did not preclude his being influenced by the earlier poet in other ways. At 14, when he first discovered Shelley's works, he became an atheist and liberal. Although he outgrew the atheism, after a struggle, and also the extreme phases of his liberalism, he retained from Shelley's influence something permanent and more difficult to define: an ardent dedication to ideals (often undefined ideals) and an energetic striving toward goals (often undefined goals). This quality of aspiration is much more mixed with earthiness—even worldliness—in Browning's character than in Shelley's. To soar upwards on a skylark's wing was not to Browning's taste. He is more like Robert Frost's swinger of birches who climbs a tree toward heaven but is anxious to swing down to earth again before getting too far away.

Yet the element of worldliness should not obscure from us Browning's ardent romanticism. His love affair with Elizabeth Barrett was romantic in several of the senses of that hard-worked adjective. It is easy to see why the well-known story of their courtship has been retold by novelists, dramatists, and movie-producers, for the situation had the dramatic ingredients of Browning's own favorite story of St. George rescuing the maiden from the dragon. Almost everything seemed unpropitious when Browning met Elizabeth Barrett in 1845. She was six years older than he was, a semi-invalid, jealously guarded by her possessively tyrannical father. But love, as the poet was to say later, is best, and love swept aside all obstacles. After their elopement to Italy, the former semi-invalid was soon enjoying good health and a full life. The husband likewise seemed to thrive during the years of this remarkable marriage. Like many English poets he was especially at ease in the warm lands of the Mediterranean. His most memorable volume of poems, *Men and Women* (1855), reflects his enjoyment of Italy: its picturesque landscapes and lively street scenes as well as its monuments from the past—its Renaissance past in particular, a period of expanding energies which was congenial to his own expansive temperament.

The happy fifteen-year sojourn in Italy ended in 1861 with Elizabeth's death. The widower returned to London with his son. During the 28 years remaining to him, the quantity of verse he produced did not diminish. Nor, during the first decade, did it decrease in quality. *Dramatis Personae* (1864) is a volume containing some of his finest monologues, such as *Caliban upon Setebos*. And in 1868 he published his greatest single poem, *The Ring and the Book*, which was inspired by his discovery of an old book of legal records concerning a murder trial in 17th-century Rome. His poem tells the story of a brutally sadistic husband, Count Guido Francheschini (who has much in common with the duke in *My Last Duchess*). The middle-aged Guido grows dissatisfied with his young wife, Pompilia, and accuses her of having adulterous relations with a handsome priest who, like St. George, had tried to rescue her from the dragon's den in which her husband confined her. Eventually Guido stabs his wife to death and is himself executed. In a series of 12 books Browning retells this tale of violence, presenting it from the contrasting points of view of participants and spectators. Because of its vast scale, *The Ring and the Book* is like a Victorian novel, but in its experiments with multiple points of view it anticipates later novels such as Conrad's *Lord Jim*. (Unlike Tennyson's major long poem, *The Idylls of the King*, Browning's 12 monologues do not lend themselves to excerpting, and we have therefore restricted our selection from *The Ring and the Book* to a brief lyric passage in which he dedicates his poem to his dead wife.)

After *The Ring and the Book* several more volumes appeared. In general Browning's writings during the last two decades of his life suffer from a certain mechanical repetition of mannerism and an excess of argumentation—faults into which he may have been led by the unqualified enthusiasm of his admirers, for it was during this period that he gained his great following. When he died, in 1889, he was buried in Westminster Abbey.

During these London years Browning became abundantly fond of social life. He dined at the homes of friends and at clubs, where he enjoyed port wine and conversation. He would talk loudly and emphatically about many topics—except his own poetry, about which he was usually reticent. His reticence bothered many of his admirers. American women visiting in London, after having looked forward to meeting the author whose poems had inspired them to higher things, were disappointed—almost appalled—when they met the man at a dinner party. He did not "look like a poet." His late poem *House* may show why he gave such an impression. Behind the façade of the hearty diner-out, Browning could live and think as he pleased, just as he had discovered in writing his monologues the advantage, for him, of indirect speaking. Each speaker of monologue provides a mask for the poet.

Despite his bursts of outspokenness, Browning's character is thus not so clearly known to us as that of Tennyson or Arnold or Carlyle. Hardy once said that Browning's character seemed to him "*the* literary puzzle of the 19th century." To solve the puzzle one biographer, Betty Miller, has tried to show that Browning was not such a happy and confident person as he is usually represented to have been, an impression that can be reinforced by the note of desperation in such poems as *Childe Roland*. And although later biographies correct the eccentricities of this interpretation they also demonstrate that Browning was a complex figure. Like Yeats, he was a poet preoccupied with masks. On the occasion of his burial in Westminster Abbey, his friend Henry James reflected that many oddities and many great writers have been buried there, "but none of the odd ones have been so great and none of the great ones been so odd."

Just as Browning's character is harder to identify than that of Tennyson, so also are his poems more difficult to relate to the age in which they were written than are the sometimes topical poems of Tennyson. Our first impression may be that there is no connection whatever. Bishops and painters of the Renaissance, physicians of the Roman Empire, musicians of 18th-century Germany—as we explore this gallery of talking portraits we seem to be in a world of time long past, remote from the world of steam engines and disputes about man's descent from the ape.

Yet our first impression is misleading. Many of these portraits explore problems that confronted Browning's contemporaries, especially problems of faith and doubt, good and evil, and problems of the function of the artist in modern life. *Caliban upon Setebos*, for example, is a highly topical critique of Darwinism and of natural (as opposed to supernatural) religions.

Browning's own attitude towards these topics is partially concealed because of his use of speakers and of settings from earlier ages, yet we do encounter certain recurrent religious assumptions that we can safely assign to the poet himself. The most recurrent is that God has created an imperfect world as a kind of testing-ground, a "vale of soul-making," as Keats had said. It followed, for Browning's purposes, that man's soul must be immortal and that heaven itself be perfect. As Abt Vogler affirms: "On the earth the broken arcs; in the heaven, a perfect round." Armed with such a faith, Browning gives the impression that he was himself untroubled by the doubts that gnawed at the hearts of Arnold and Clough and Tennyson. The "evidence" presented by historical criticism of the Bible he could dismiss as simply irrelevant, just as D. H. Lawrence, a later romantic, disposed of evolution by contending that he did not feel the evidence for it in his solar plexus.

This kind of religious conviction attracts many readers who expect poetry to provide uplift and reassurances. Other readers find it an insurmountable obstacle, as fatuous as Macaulay's faith in progress. To what extent our capacity to enjoy the writings of an author is hindered if his religious position seems repellent to us is one of the most important problems in modern criticism. The problem is much too vast to explore here, but there is at least room to insert a qualifying clause to modify the indictment that Browning's critics too hastily draw up against his cheerful religious position. A blind optimist might be simply unreadable, but Browning's optimism was not blind. Few writers, in fact, seem to have been more aware of the existence of evil. His gallery of villains—murderers, sadistic husbands, mean and petty manipulators—is an extraordinary one. Nothing is more essential to a fair-minded study of his poetry than our recognition that his apparent optimism is consistently being tested by his bringing to light the evils of man's nature. Readers who prefer to dispose of his writings by pinning them down in a formulated phrase, instead of reading them with attention, invariably cite the following lines as summing up all of Browning:

> God's in his heaven—
> All's right with the world!

But if we turn to the poem in which these lines appear, we have to modify our formulation. *Pippa Passes* is a collection of sordid tales such as one encounters on the front page of the most lurid style of newspaper. The heroine, who works in a sweatshop 364 days a year, is about to be sent to Rome as a prostitute; a man and woman living in adultery have just murdered the woman's husband; a waspish set of Bohemians have tricked a youth into marriage. Because Pippa's innocence seems to counteract the sordidness of the other scenes, we may say afterwards that God is in his heaven. But that all's right with the world is merely affirmed by the girl; the poem does not show it.

A second aspect of Browning's poetry that separates it from the Victorian age is its style. The most representative Victorian poets such as Tennyson or Dante Gabriel Rossetti write in the manner of Keats, Milton, Spenser, and of classical poets such as Virgil. Theirs is the central stylistic tradition in English poetry, one which favors smoothly polished texture and pleasing liquidity of sound. Browning draws from a different tradition, more colloquial and discordant, a tradition which includes the poetry of John Donne, the soliloquies of Shakespeare, the comic verse of the early 19th-century poet Thomas Hood, and certain features of the narrative style of Chaucer. Of most significance are Browning's affinities with Donne. Both poets sacrifice, on occasion, the pleasures of harmony and of a consistent elevation of tone by using a harshly discordant style and unexpected juxtapositions that startle us into an awareness of a world of everyday realities and trivialities. Browning's late poem, *The Householder*, is an excellent example of this Donne-like vein. Readers who dislike this kind of poetry in Browning or in Donne argue that it suffers from prosiness. Oscar Wilde once described the novelist George Meredith as "a prose Browning." And so, he added, was Browning. Wilde's joke may help us to relate Browning to his contemporaries. For if Browning seems out of step with his fellow Victorian poets, he is by no means out of step with his contemporaries in prose. The grotesque, which plays such a prominent role in the style and subject matter of Carlyle and Dickens, and in the aesthetic theories of John Ruskin, is equally prominent in Browning's verse:

> Fee, faw, fum! bubble and squeak!
> Blessedest Thursday's the fat of the week.
> Rumble and tumble, sleek and rough,
> Stinking and savory, smug and gruff.

These opening lines of *Holy-Cross Day* display a kind of noisy jocularity in presenting a situation of grave seriousness similar to that used by Carlyle in his *Sartor Resartus*. It was fitting that Browning and Carlyle remained good friends, even though the elder writer kept urging Browning to give up verse in favor of prose.

The link between Browning and the Victorian prose writers is not limited to style. With the later generation of Victorian novelists, George Eliot, George Meredith, and Henry James, Browning shares a central preoccupation. Like Eliot in particular, he was interested in exposing the devious ways in which our minds work and the complexity of our motives. "My stress lay on incidents in the development of a human soul," he wrote; "little else is worth study." His psychological insights can be illustrated in such poems as *The Bishop Orders His Tomb* or *Dîs Aliter Visum*. Although these are spoken monologues, not inner monologues in the manner of James Joyce, yet the insight into the workings of the minds of men is similarly acute. As in reading Joyce, we must be on our guard to follow the rapid shifts of the speaker's mental processes as jumps are made from one cluster of associations to another.

But Browning's role as a forerunner of 20th-century literature should not blind us to his essential Victorianism. Energy is the most characteristic aspect of his writing, and energy is perhaps the most characteristic aspect of Victorian literature in general. Often, of course, such energy was misdirected. Gerard Manley Hopkins identified this failing precisely when he complained of Browning's "Broad Church" way of talking, like "a man bouncing up from table with his mouth full of bread and cheese and saying that he meant to stand no blasted nonsense." At its best, however, such buoyancy is a virtue imparting a creative vitality to all of Browning's writings.

Porphyria's Lover[1]

The rain set early in tonight,
    The sullen wind was soon awake,
It tore the elm-tops down for spite,
    And did its worst to vex the lake:
    I listened with heart fit to break.   5
When glided in Porphyria; straight
    She shut the cold out and the storm,
And kneeled and made the cheerless grate
    Blaze up, and all the cottage warm;
    Which done, she rose, and from her form   10
Withdrew the dripping cloak and shawl,
    And laid her soiled gloves by, untied
Her hat and let the damp hair fall,
    And, last, she sat down by my side
    And called me. When no voice replied,   15
She put my arm about her waist,
    And made her smooth white shoulder bare,
And all her yellow hair displaced,
    And, stooping, made my cheek lie there,
    And spread, o'er all, her yellow hair,   20
Murmuring how she loved me—she
    Too weak, for all her heart's endeavor,
To set its struggling passion free
    From pride, and vainer ties dissever,
    And give herself to me forever.   25
But passion sometimes would prevail,
    Nor could tonight's gay feast restrain
A sudden thought of one so pale
    For love of her, and all in vain:
    So, she was come through wind and rain.   30
Be sure I looked up at her eyes
    Happy and proud; at last I knew
Porphyria worshiped me: surprise
    Made my heart swell, and still it grew
    While I debated what to do.   35
That moment she was mine, mine, fair,
    Perfectly pure and good: I found
A thing to do, and all her hair
    In one long yellow string I wound
    Three times her little throat around,   40
And strangled her. No pain felt she;
    I am quite sure she felt no pain.
As a shut bud that holds a bee,

1. One of a pair of monologues originally published under the title *Madhouse Cells*, a title that emphasized the abnormal state of mind of the speaker.

I warily oped her lids: again
    Laughed the blue eyes without a stain.   45
And I untightened next the tress
    About her neck; her cheek once more
Blushed bright beneath my burning kiss:
    I propped her head up as before,
    Only, this time my shoulder bore   50
Her head, which droops upon it still:
    The smiling rosy little head,
So glad it has its utmost will,
    That all it scorned at once is fled,
    And I, its love, am gained instead!   55
Porphyria's love: she guessed not how
    Her darling one wish would be heard.
And thus we sit together now,
    And all night long we have not stirred,
    And yet God has not said a word!   60

1834   1836, 1842

Soliloquy of the Spanish Cloister[1]

1

Gr-r-r—there go, my heart's abhorrence!
    Water your damned flowerpots, do!
If hate killed men, Brother Lawrence,
    God's blood, would not mine kill you!
What? your myrtle bush wants trimming?   5
    Oh, that rose has prior claims—
Needs its leaden vase filled brimming?
    Hell dry you up with its flames!

2

At the meal we sit together:
    Salve tibi![2] I must hear   10
Wise talk of the kind of weather,
    Sort of season, time of year:
Not a plenteous cork crop: scarcely
    Dare we hope oak-galls,[3] *I doubt:*
What's the Latin name for "parsley"?   15
    What's the Greek name for Swine's Snout?

3

Whew! We'll have our platter burnished,
    Laid with care on our own shelf!
With a fire-new spoon we're furnished,
    And a goblet for ourself,   20

1. No period of history is specified in this poem. The monastery setting is timeless and serves to intensify the pressure of meanness and hatred that is boiling up in the speaker.
2. "Hail to thee!" This and other speeches in italics in this stanza are supposed to be the words of Brother Lawrence.
3. Abnormal outgrowths on oak trees, used for tanning.

Rinsed like something sacrificial
　　Ere 'tis fit to touch our chaps[4]—
Marked with L. for our initial!
　　(He-he! There his lily snaps!)

4

Saint, forsooth! While brown Dolores　　　　　　25
　　Squats outside the Convent bank
With Sanchicha, telling stories,
　　Steeping tresses in the tank,
Blue-black, lustrous, thick like horsehairs,
　　—Can't I see his dead eye glow,　　　　　　30
Bright as 'twere a Barbary corsair's?[5]
　　(That is, if he'd let it show!)

5

When he finishes refection,[6]
　　Knife and fork he never lays
Cross-wise, to my recollection,　　　　　　35
　　As do I, in Jesu's praise.
I the Trinity illustrate,
　　Drinking watered orange pulp—
In three sips the Arian[7] frustrate;
　　While he drains his at one gulp.　　　　　　40

6

Oh, those melons? If he's able
　　We're to have a feast! so nice!
One goes to the Abbot's table,
　　All of us get each a slice.
How go on your flowers? None double?　　　　　　45
　　Not one fruit-sort can you spy?
Strange!—And I, too, at such trouble,
　　Keep them close-nipped on the sly!

7

There's a great text in Galatians,[8]
　　Once you trip on it, entails　　　　　　50
Twenty-nine distinct damnations,
　　One sure, if another fails:
If I trip him just a-dying,
　　Sure of heaven as sure can be,
Spin him round and send him flying
　　Off to hell, a Manichee?[9]　　　　　　55

8

Or, my scrofulous French novel
　　On gray paper with blunt type!

---

4. Jaws.
5. Pirate of the Barbary Coast of northern Africa, renowned for fierceness and
lechery.
6. Dinner.
7. Heretical followers of Arius (256–
336), who denied the doctrine of the
Trinity.
8. The speaker hopes to obtain Lawrence's damnation by luring him into a

heresy, this to be accomplished by exposing him to the difficult task of interpreting "Galatians" in an unswervingly orthodox way. In Galatians v.15–
23, St. Paul specifies an assortment of
"works of the flesh" that lead to damnation, which could make up a total of
"twenty-nine."
9. A heretic, a follower of the Persian
prophet of the 3rd century, Mani.

Simply glance at it, you grovel
      Hand and foot in Belial's gripe: 60
If I double down its pages
      At the woeful sixteenth print,
When he gathers his greengages,
      Ope a sieve and slip it in't?

                        9

Or, there's Satan!—one might venture   65
      Pledge one's soul to him,[1] yet leave
Such a flaw in the indenture
      As he'd miss till, past retrieve,
Blasted lay that rose-acacia
      We're so proud of! *Hy, Zy, Hine* . . .[2]   70
'St, there's Vespers! *Plena gratiá*
      Ave, Virgo![3] Gr-r-r—you swine!

ca. 1839   1842

My Last Duchess[1]

FERRARA

That's my last Duchess painted on the wall,
Looking as if she were alive. I call
That piece a wonder, now: Frà Pandolf's[2] hands
Worked busily a day, and there she stands.
Will't please you sit and look at her? I said   5
"Frà Pandolf" by design, for never read
Strangers like you that pictured countenance,
The depth and passion of its earnest glance,
But to myself they turned (since none puts by
The curtain I have drawn for you, but I)   10
And seemed as they would ask me, if they durst,
How such a glance came there; so, not the first
Are you to turn and ask thus Sir, 'twas not
Her husband's presence only, called that spot
Of joy into the Duchess' cheek: perhaps   15
Frà Pandolf chanced to say "Her mantle laps
Over my lady's wrist too much," or "Paint
Must never hope to reproduce the faint
Half-flush that dies along her throat": such stuff
Was courtesy, she thought, and cause enough   20

1. The speaker would pledge his own soul to Satan in return for blasting Lawrence and his "rose-acacia," but the pledge would be so cleverly worded that the speaker would not have to pay, himself, his debt to Satan. There would be an escape-clause, a "flaw in the indenture," for himself.
2. Perhaps the opening of a mysterious curse against Lawrence.
3. "Full of grace, Hail, Virgin!" The speaker's twisted state of mind may be reflected in his mixed-up version of the prayer to Mary: "Ave, Maria, gratia plena."
1. The poem is based on incidents in the life of Alfonso II, Duke of Ferrara in Italy, whose first wife, Lucrezia, a young girl, died in 1561 after three years of marriage. Following her death, the Duke negotiated through an agent to marry a niece of the Count of Tyrol. Browning represents the Duke as addressing this agent.
2. Brother Pandolf, an imaginary painter.

For calling up that spot of joy. She had
A heart—how shall I say?—too soon made glad,
Too easily impressed; she liked whate'er
She looked on, and her looks went everywhere.
Sir, 'twas all one! My favor at her breast,   25
The dropping of the daylight in the West,
The bough of cherries some officious fool
Broke in the orchard for her, the white mule
She rode with round the terrace—all and each
Would draw from her alike the approving speech,   30
Or blush, at least. She thanked men—good! but thanked
Somehow—I know not how—as if she ranked
My gift of a nine-hundred-years-old name
With anybody's gift. Who'd stoop to blame
This sort of trifling? Even had you skill   35
In speech—(which I have not)—to make your will
Quite clear to such an one, and say, "Just this
Or that in you disgusts me; here you miss,
Or there exceed the mark"—and if she let
Herself be lessoned so, nor plainly set   40
Her wits to yours, forsooth, and made excuse
—E'en then would be some stooping; and I choose
Never to stoop. Oh sir, she smiled, no doubt,
Whene'er I passed her; but who passed without
Much the same smile? This grew; I gave commands;   45
Then all smiles stopped together. There she stands
As if alive. Will't please you rise? We'll meet
The company below, then. I repeat,
The Count your master's known munificence
Is ample warrant that no just pretense   50
Of mine for dowry will be disallowed;
Though his fair daughter's self, as I avowed
At starting, is my object. Nay, we'll go
Together down, sir. Notice Neptune, though,
Taming a sea horse, thought a rarity,   55
Which Claus of Innsbruck[3] cast in bronze for me!

1842   1842

The Laboratory
Ancien Régime

1

Now that I, tying thy glass mask tightly,
May gaze thro' these faint smokes curling whitely,
As thou pliest thy trade in this devil's-smithy—
Which is the poison to poison her, prithee?

2

He is with her, and they know that I know   5
Where they are, what they do: they believe my tears flow
While they laugh, laugh at me, at me fled to the drear
Empty church, to pray God in, for them!—I am here.

3. An unidentified or imaginary sculptor. The Count of Tyrol had his capital at Innsbruck.

3

Grind away, moisten and mash up thy paste,
Pound at thy powder—I am not in haste!
Better sit thus, and observe thy strange things,
Than go where men wait me and dance at the King's.

4

That in the mortar—you call it a gum?
Ah, the brave tree whence such gold oozings come!
And yonder soft phial, the exquisite blue,
Sure to taste sweetly, is that poison too?

5

Had I but all of them, thee and thy treasures,
What a wild crowd of invisible pleasures!
To carry pure death in an earring, a casket,
A signet, a fan-mount, a filigree basket!

6

Soon, at the King's,[1] a mere lozenge to give,
And Pauline should have just thirty minutes to live!
But to light a pastile, and Elise, with her head
And her breast and her arms and her hands, should drop dead!

7

Quick—is it finished? The color's too grim!
Why not soft like the phial's, enticing and dim?
Let it brighten her drink, let her turn it and stir,
And try it and taste, ere she fix and prefer!

8

What a drop! She's not little, no minion [2] like me!
That's why she ensnared him: this never will free
The soul from those masculine eyes—say, "no!"
To that pulse's magnificent come-and-go.

9

For only last night, as they whispered, I brought
My own eyes to bear on her so, that I thought
Could I keep them one half minute fixed, she would fall
Shriveled; she fell not; yet this does it all!

10

Not that I bid you spare her the pain;
Let death be felt and the proof remain:
Brand, burn up, bite into its grace—
He is sure to remember her dying face!

11

Is it done? Take my mask off! Nay, be not morose;
It kills her, and this prevents seeing it close:
The delicate droplet, my whole fortune's fee!
If it hurts her, beside, can it ever hurt me?

10

15

20

25

30

35

40

---

1. Probably King Louis XIV of France (1643–1715). In the 1670's a police investigation disclosed that an extraordinary number of women and men attached to the King's court had been disposing of rivals and enemies by poisonings. Some 36 of the accused courtiers and the dealers from whom they had purchased poisons were punished by torture and burnt to death.
2. A dainty and delicate person.

12

Now, take all my jewels, gorge gold to your fill,   45
You may kiss me, old man, on my mouth if you will!
But brush this dust off me, lest horror it brings
Ere I know it—next moment I dance at the King's!
ca. 1844   1844

The Lost Leader[1]

1

Just for a handful of silver he left us,
    Just for a riband to stick in his coat—
Found the one gift of which fortune bereft us,
    Lost all the others she lets us devote;
They, with the gold to give, doled him out silver,   5
    So much was theirs who so little allowed:
How all our copper had gone for his service!
    Rags—were they purple, his heart had been proud!
We that had loved him so, followed him, honored him,
    Lived in his mild and magnificent eye,   10
Learned his great language, caught his clear accents,
    Made him our pattern to live and to die!
Shakespeare was of us, Milton was for us,
    Burns, Shelley, were with us—they watch from their graves!
He alone breaks from the van[2] and the freemen   15
    —He alone sinks to the rear and the slaves!

2

We shall march prospering—not through his presence;
    Songs may inspirit us—not from his lyre;
Deeds will be done—while he boasts his quiescence,
    Still bidding crouch whom the rest bade aspire: 20
Blot out his name, then, record one lost soul more,
    One task more declined, one more footpath untrod,
One more devils'-triumph and sorrow for angels,
    One wrong more to man, one more insult to God!
Life's night begins: let him never come back to us!   25
    There would be doubt, hesitation and pain,
Forced praise on our part—the glimmer of twilight,
    Never glad confident morning again!
Best fight on well, for we taught him—strike gallantly,
    Menace our heart ere we master his own;   30
Then let him receive the new knowledge and wait us,
    Pardoned in heaven, the first by the throne!
1843   1845

1. William Wordsworth, who had been
an ardent liberal in his youth, had become a political conservative in later
years. In old age, when he accepted a
grant of money from the government
("a handful of silver") and also the
office of poet laureate ("a riband to stick
in his coat"), he alienated some of his
young admirers such as Browning, whose
liberalism was then as ardent as Wordsworth's had once been.
    Cf. J. G. Whittier's poem *Ichabod*,
which embodies a similar sense of sorrowful indignation over the apostasy of
Daniel Webster, a great leader formerly
admired by the poet.
2. Vanguard of the army of liberalism.

How They Brought the Good News from Ghent to Aix[1]

(16—)

1

I sprang to the stirrup, and Joris, and he;
I galloped, Dirck galloped, we galloped all three;
"Good speed!" cried the watch, as the gate-bolts undrew;
"Speed!" echoed the wall to us galloping through;
Behind shut the postern, the lights sank to rest,   5
And into the midnight we galloped abreast.

2

Not a word to each other; we kept the great pace
Neck by neck, stride by stride, never changing our place;
I turned in my saddle and made its girths tight,
Then shortened each stirrup, and set the pique[2] right,   10
Rebuckled the cheek-strap, chained slacker the bit,
Nor galloped less steadily Roland a whit.

3

'Twas moonset at starting; but while we drew near
Lokeren, the cocks crew and twilight dawned clear;
At Boom, a great yellow star came out to see;   15
At Düffeld, 'twas morning as plain as could be;
And from Mecheln church-steeple we heard the half-chime,
So, Joris broke silence with, "Yet there is time!"

4

At Aershot, up leaped of a sudden the sun,
And against him the cattle stood black every one,   20
To stare through the mist at us galloping past,
And I saw my stout galloper Roland at last,
With resolute shoulders, each butting away
The haze, as some bluff river headland its spray:

5

And his low head and crest, just one sharp ear bent back   25
For my voice, and the other pricked out on his track;
And one eye's black intelligence—ever that glance
O'er its white edge at me, his own master, askance!
And the thick heavy spume-flakes which ay and anon
His fierce lips shook upwards in galloping on.   30

6

By Hasselt, Dirck groaned; and cried Joris, "Stay spur!
Your Roos galloped bravely, the fault's not in her,
We'll remember at Aix"—for one heard the quick wheeze
Of her chest, saw the stretched neck and staggering knees,
And sunk tail, and horrible heave of the flank,   35
As down on her haunches she shuddered and sank.

1. The distance between Ghent, in Flanders, and Aix-la-Chapelle is about one hundred miles. Browning said that the incident, occurring during the wars between Flanders and Spain, was an imaginary one.
2. Spur or pommel.

7

So, we were left galloping, Joris and I,
Past Looz and past Tongres, no cloud in the sky;
The broad sun above laughed a pitiless laugh,
'Neath our feet broke the brittle bright stubble like chaff;   40
Till over by Dalhem a dome-spire sprang white,
And "Gallop," gasped Joris, "for Aix is in sight!"

8

"How they'll greet us!"—and all in a moment his roan
Rolled neck and croup over, lay dead as a stone;
And there was my Roland to bear the whole weight   45
Of the news which alone could save Aix from her fate,
With his nostrils like pits full of blood to the brim,
And with circles of red for his eye-sockets' rim.

9

Then I cast loose my buffcoat, each holster let fall,
Shook off both my jack boots, let go belt and all,   50
Stood up in the stirrup, leaned, patted his ear,
Called my Roland his pet name, my horse without peer;
Clapped my hands, laughed and sang, any noise, bad or good,
Till at length into Aix Roland galloped and stood.

10

And all I remember is—friends flocking round   55
As I sat with his head 'twixt my knees on the ground;
And no voice but was praising this Roland of mine,
As I poured down his throat our last measure of wine,
Which (the burgesses voted by common consent)
Was no more than his due who brought good news from Ghent.   60
ca. 1844   1845

Home-Thoughts, from Abroad

1

Oh, to be in England
Now that April's there,
And whoever wakes in England
Sees, some morning, unaware,
That the lowest boughs and the brushwood sheaf   5
Round the elm-tree bole are in tiny leaf,
While the chaffinch sings on the orchard bough
In England—now!

2

And after April, when May follows,
And the whitethroat builds, and all the swallows!   10
Hark, where my blossomed peartree in the hedge
Leans to the field and scatters on the clover
Blossoms and dewdrops—at the bent spray's edge—
That's the wise thrush; he sings each song twice over,

Lest you should think he never could recapture   15
The first fine careless rapture!
And though the fields look rough with hoary dew,
All will be gay when noontide wakes anew
The buttercups, the little children's dower
—Far brighter than this gaudy melon-flower!   20

ca. 1845   1845

Home-Thoughts, from the Sea

Nobly, nobly Cape Saint Vincent[1] to the northwest died away;
Sunset ran, one glorious blood-red, reeking into Cadiz Bay;
Bluish 'mid the burning water, full in face Trafalgar[2] lay;
In the dimmest northeast distance dawned Gibraltar grand and gray;
"Here and here did England help me: how can I help England?"—
    say,   5
Whoso turns as I, this evening, turn to God to praise and pray,
While Jove's planet[3] rises yonder, silent over Africa.

1844   1845

The Bishop Orders His Tomb at Saint Praxed's Church[1]

ROME, 15—

Vanity, saith the preacher, vanity![2]
Draw round my bed: is Anselm keeping back?
Nephews—sons mine . . . ah God, I know not! Well—
She, men would have to be your mother once,
Old Gandolf envied me, so fair she was!   5
What's done is done, and she is dead beside,
Dead long ago, and I am Bishop since,
And as she died so must we die ourselves,
And thence ye may perceive the world's a dream.
Life, how and what is it? As here I lie   10

1. Off the coast of Portugal, scene of British naval victory under Admiral Nelson (1797).
2. A cape in Spain, where Nelson won his great victory over Napoleon's fleets (1805).
3. Jupiter.
1. In *Fra Lippo Lippi* Browning represents the dawn of the Renaissance in Italy, with its fresh zest for "the beauty and the wonder and the power" of man's experiences in this world. In the present monologue he portrays a later stage of the Renaissance when such worldliness, full-blown, had infected even some of the leading churchmen of Italy. Browning's portrait of the dying bishop is, however, not primarily a satire against corruption in the church. It is a brilliant exposition of the workings of a mind, a mind that has been conditioned by special historical circumstances. The Victorian historian of art, John Ruskin, said of this poem: "I know of no other piece of modern English, prose or poetry, in which there is so much told, as in these lines, of the Renaissance spirit—its worldliness, inconsistency, pride, hypocrisy, ignorance of itself, love of art, of luxury, and of good Latin. It is nearly all that I have said of the central Renaissance in thirty pages of the *Stones of Venice,* put into as many lines, Browning's also being the antecedent work."

St. Praxed's Church was named in honor of St. Praxedes, a Roman virgin of the 2nd century who gave her riches to poor Christians. Both the bishop and his predecessor, Gandolf, are imaginary persons.
2. Cf. Ecclesiastes i.2.

In this state chamber, dying by degrees,
Hours and long hours in the dead night, I ask
"Do I live, am I dead?" Peace, peace seems all.
Saint Praxed's ever was the church for peace;
And so, about this tomb of mine. I fought   15
With tooth and nail to save my niche, ye know:
—Old Gandolf cozened[3] me, despite my care;
Shrewd was that snatch from out the corner south
He graced his carrion with, God curse the same!
Yet still my niche is not so cramped but thence   20
One sees the pulpit o' the epistle side,[4]
And somewhat of the choir, those silent seats,
And up into the aery dome where live
The angels, and a sunbeam's sure to lurk:
And I shall fill my slab of basalt[5] there,   25
And 'neath my tabernacle[6] take my rest,
With those nine columns round me, two and two,
The odd one at my feet where Anselm stands:
Peach-blossom marble all, the rare, the ripe
As fresh-poured red wine of a mighty pulse.[7]   30
—Old Gandolf with his paltry onion-stone,[8]
Put me where I may look at him! True peach,
Rosy and flawless: how I earned the prize!
Draw close: that conflagration of my church
—What then? So much was saved if aught were missed!   35
My sons, ye would not be my death? Go dig
The white-grape vineyard where the oil-press stood,
Drop water gently till the surface sink,
And if ye find . . . Ah God, I know not, I! . . .
Bedded in store of rotten fig leaves soft,   40
And corded up in a tight olive-frail,[9]
Some lump, ah God, of *lapis lazuli*,[1]
Big as a Jew's head cut off at the nape,
Blue as a vein o'er the Madonna's breast . . .
Sons, all have I bequeathed you, villas, all,   45
That brave Frascati[2] villa with its bath,
So, let the blue lump poise between my knees,
Like God the Father's globe on both his hands
Ye worship in the Jesu Church[3] so gay,
For Gandolf shall not choose but see and burst!   50
Swift as a weaver's shuttle fleet our years:[4]
Man goeth to the grave, and where is he?

3. Cheated.
4. The Epistles of the New Testament are read from the right-hand side of the altar (as one faces it).
5. Dark-colored igneous rock.
6. Stone canopy or tentlike roof, presumably supported by the "nine columns" under which the sculptured effigy of the Bishop would lie on the slab of basalt.
7. Browning uses "pulse" in the special sense of a pulpy mash of fermented grapes from which a strong wine might be poured off. In a later poem, the *Epilogue* to *Pacchiarotto*, he likens such wine to "viscous blood" that has been "squeezed gold" from the "pulp" of the grapes.
8. An inferior marble that peels in layers.
9. Basket for holding olives.
1. Valuable bright blue stone.
2. Suburb of Rome, used as a resort by wealthy Italians.
3. Il Gesù, a Jesuit church in Rome.
4. Cf. Job vii.6.

Did I say basalt for my slab, sons? Black[5]—
'Twas ever antique-black I meant! How else
Shall ye contrast my frieze[6] to come beneath?   55
The bas-relief in bronze ye promised me,
Those Pans and Nymphs ye wot of, and perchance
Some tripod, thyrsus, with a vase or so,
The Saviour at his sermon on the mount,
Saint Praxed in a glory, and one Pan   60
Ready to twitch the Nymph's last garment off,
And Moses with the tables[7] . . . but I know
Ye mark me not! What do they whisper thee,
Child of my bowels, Anselm? Ah, ye hope
To revel down my villas while I gasp   65
Bricked o'er with beggar's moldy travertine[8]
Which Gandolf from his tomb-top chuckles at!
Nay, boys, ye love me—all of jasper, then!
'Tis jasper ye stand pledged to, lest I grieve
My bath must needs be left behind, alas!   70
One block, pure green as a pistachio nut,
There's plenty jasper somewhere in the world—
And have I not Saint Praxed's ear to pray
Horses for ye, and brown Greek manuscripts,
And mistresses with great smooth marbly limbs?   75
—That's if ye carve my epitaph aright,
Choice Latin, picked phrase, Tully's[9] every word,
No gaudy ware like Gandolf's second line—
Tully, my masters? Ulpian[1] serves his need!
And then how I shall lie through centuries,   80
And hear the blessed mutter of the mass,
And see God made and eaten all day long,[2]
And feel the steady candle flame, and taste
Good strong thick stupefying incense-smoke!
For as I lie here, hours of the dead night,   85
Dying in state and by such slow degrees,
I fold my arms as if they clasped a crook,[3]
And stretch my feet forth straight as stone can point,
And let the bedclothes, for a mortcloth,[4] drop
Into great laps and folds of sculptor's-work: 90
And as yon tapers dwindle, and strange thoughts

5. Black marble.
6. Continuous band of sculpture.
7. The "bas-relief" (or sculpture in which the figures do not project far from the background surface) would consist of a mixture of pagan and religious scenes (lines 57–62). Among the former would be a "tripod," on which priestesses at the oracle of Delphi sat to make their prophecies, and a "thyrsus," a long staff carried in processions in honor of Bacchus, the god of wine. The religious scenes would include St. Praxed with her halo ("a glory") and Moses with the stone tablets ("tables") on which the Ten Commandments were written. Such intermingling of pagan and Christian traditions, characteristic of the Renaissance, had been attacked in 1841 in *Contrasts*, a book on architecture by A. W. Pugin, a Roman Catholic.
8. Italian limestone.
9. A familiar name for Marcus Tullius Cicero, whose writing was the model, during the Renaissance, of classical Latin prose.
1. Late Latin prose-writer, not considered a model of good style.
2. Reference to the doctrine of transubstantiation.
3. Bishop's staff or crozier.
4. Rich cloth spread over a dead body or coffin.

Grow, with a certain humming in my ears,
About the life before I lived this life,
And this life too, popes, cardinals, and priests,
Saint Praxed at his sermon on the mount,[5]
Your tall pale mother with her talking eyes,   95
And new-found agate urns as fresh as day,
And marble's language, Latin pure, discreet
—Aha, ELUCESCEBAT[6] quoth our friend?
No Tully, said I, Ulpian at the best!   100
Evil and brief hath been my pilgrimage.[7]
All *lapis*, all, sons! Else I give the Pope
My villas! Will ye ever eat my heart?
Ever your eyes were as a lizard's quick,
They glitter like your mother's for my soul,   105
Or ye would heighten my impoverished frieze,
Pierce out its starved design, and fill my vase
With grapes, and add a vizor and a Term,[8]
And to the tripod ye would tie a lynx
That in his struggle throws the thyrsus down,   110
To comfort me on my entablature[9]
Whereon I am to lie till I must ask
"Do I live, am I dead?" There, leave me, there!
For ye have stabbed me with ingratitude
To death—ye wish it—God, ye wish it! Stone—   115
Gritstone,[10] a-crumble! Clammy squares which sweat
As if the corpse they keep were oozing through—
And no more *lapis* to delight the world!
Well go! I bless ye. Fewer tapers there,
But in a row: and, going, turn your backs   120
—Aye, like departing altar-ministrants,
And leave me in my church, the church for peace,
That I may watch at leisure if he leers—
Old Gandolf, at me, from his onion-stone,
As still he envied me, so fair she was!   125
1844   1845

Meeting at Night[1]

1

The gray sea and the long black land;
And the yellow half-moon large and low;
And the startled little waves that leap

5. The bishop is confusing St. Praxed (a woman) with Christ—an indication that his mind is wandering.
6. Word from Gandolf's epitaph meaning "he was illustrious." The bishop considers the form of the verb to be in "gaudy" bad taste. If the epitaph had been copied from Cicero instead of from Ulpian, the word would have been *elucebat*.
7. Cf. Genesis xlvii.9.
8. "Vizor": part of a helmet, often rep-

resented in sculpture. "Term": statue of Terminus, the Roman god of boundaries, usually represented without arms.
9. Horizontal platform supporting a statue or effigy.
10. Coarse sandstone such as that used for grindstones.
1. This poem and the one which follows it appeared originally under the single title *Night and Morning*. The speaker in both is a man.

In fiery ringlets from their sleep,
As I gain the cove with pushing prow,   5
And quench its speed i' the slushy sand.

2

Then a mile of warm sea-scented beach;
Three fields to cross till a farm appears;
A tap at the pane, the quick sharp scratch
And blue spurt of a lighted match,   10
And a voice less loud, through its joys and fears,
Than the two hearts beating each to each!

1845

Parting at Morning

Round the cape of a sudden came the sea,
And the sun looked over the mountain's rim:
And straight was a path of gold for him,[2]
And the need of a world of men for me.

1845

A Toccata of Galuppi's[1]

1

Oh, Galuppi, Baldassaro, this is very sad to find!
I can hardly misconceive you; it would prove me deaf and blind;
But although I take your meaning, 'tis with such a heavy mind!

2

Here you come with your old music, and here's all the good it brings.
What, they lived once thus at Venice where the merchants were
    the kings,
Where Saint Mark's is, where the Doges used to wed the sea with   5
    rings?[2]

2. The sun.
1. There are three speakers in this short poem. The first is a 19th-century scientist in England who is listening to a musical composition by Baldassaro Galuppi (1706–85), a Venetian. The music evokes for this scientist the voice of the dead composer (the third speaker) who comments upon the pointless and butterfly-like frivolity of his 18th-century contemporaries. The second group of voices is made up of comments by members of Galuppi's audience as they respond to the different moods of his clavichord-playing during a party which the scientist imagines to have taken place in Venice.

    A "toccata" is defined in Grove's *Dictionary of Music* as a "touch-piece,

or a composition intended to exhibit the touch and execution of the performer." The same authority states that "no particular composition was taken as the basis of the poem," but Browning is known to have himself played on the organ some unpublished compositions by Galuppi, and one of these, not yet identified, may have occasioned the poem. Browning's interest in music was keen, and his knowledge of the art was more extensive than that of most English poets.

2. An annual ceremony in which the Doge, the Venetian chief magistrate, threw a ring into the water to symbolize the bond between his city, with its maritime empire, and the sea.

3

Aye, because the sea's the street there; and 'tis arched by . . . what
you call
. . . Shylock's bridge[3] with houses on it, where they kept the carnival:
I was never out of England—it's as if I saw it all.

4

Did young people take their pleasure when the sea was warm in
May?   10
Balls and masks[4] begun at midnight, burning ever to midday,
When they made up fresh adventures for the morrow, do you say?

5

Was a lady such a lady, cheeks so round and lips so red—
On her neck the small face buoyant, like a bellflower on its bed,
O'er the breast's superb abundance where a man might base his
head?   15

6

Well, and it was graceful of them—they'd break talk off and afford
—She, to bite her mask's black velvet—he, to finger on his sword,
While you sat and played toccatas, stately at the clavichord?[5]

7

What? Those lesser thirds so plaintive, sixths diminished, sigh on
sigh,
Told them something? Those suspensions, those solutions—"Must
we die?"   20
Those commiserating sevenths[6]—"Life might last! we can but
try!"

8

"Were you happy?"—"Yes."—"And are you still as happy?"—
"Yes. And you?"
—"Then, more kisses!"—"Did *I* stop them, when a million seemed
so few?"
Hark, the dominant's persistence till it must be answered to!

9

So, an octave struck the answer. Oh, they praised you, I dare say!   25
"Brave Galuppi! that was music; good alike at grave and gay!
I can always leave off talking when I hear a master play!"

10

Then they left you for their pleasure: till in due time, one by one,
Some with lives that came to nothing, some with deeds as well un-
done,   29
Death stepped tacitly and took them where they never see the sun.

3. The Rialto, a bridge over the Grand
Canal.
4. Masquerades.
5. A keyboard instrument in which the
strings are struck by metal hammers.
As a mechanism it resembles a piano,
but the sound is more like that of a
harpsichord.
6. This term and others in these lines
all refer to the technical devices used
by Galuppi to produce alternating moods
in his music, conflict in each instance
being resolved into harmony. Thus the
"dominant" (the fifth note of the
scale), after being persistently sounded,
is answered by a resolving chord (lines
24–25).

11

But when I sit down to reason, think to take my stand nor swerve,
While I triumph o'er a secret wrung from nature's close reserve,
In you come with your cold music till I creep through every nerve.

12

Yes, you, like a ghostly cricket, creaking where a house was burned:
"Dust and ashes, dead and done with, Venice spent what Venice
    earned.
The soul, doubtless, is immortal—where a soul can be discerned.

13

"Yours for instance: you know physics, something of geology,
Mathematics are your pastime; souls shall rise in their degree;
Butterflies may dread extinction—you'll not die, it cannot be!

14

"As for Venice and her people, merely born to bloom and drop,
Here on earth they bore their fruitage, mirth and folly were the
    crop:
What of soul was left, I wonder, when the kissing had to stop?

15

"Dust and ashes!" So you creak it, and I want the heart to scold.
Dear dead women, with such hair, too—what's become of all the
    gold
Used to hang and brush their bosoms? I feel chilly and grown old.
ca. 1847   1855

Memorabilia[1]

1

Ah, did you once see Shelley plain,
    And did he stop and speak to you
And did you speak to him again?
    How strange it seems and new!

2

But you were living before that,
    And also you are living after;
And the memory I started at—
    My starting moves your laughter.

3

I crossed a moor, with a name of its own
    And a certain use in the world no doubt,
Yet a hand's-breadth of it shines alone
    'Mid the blank miles round about:

1. The title means "things worth remembering." Browning reports that he once met a stranger in a bookstore who mentioned having talked with Shelley. "Suddenly the stranger paused, and burst into laughter as he observed me staring at him with blanched face. * * * I still vividly remember how strangely the presence of a man who had seen and spoken with Shelley affected me."

4
For there I picked up on the heather
And there I put inside my breast
A molted feather, an eagle feather!   15
Well, I forget the rest.

ca. 1851   1855

Love Among the Ruins[1]

1

Where the quiet-colored end of evening smiles,
    Miles and miles
On the solitary pastures where our sheep
    Half-asleep
Tinkle homeward through the twilight, stray or stop   5
    As they crop—
Was the site once of a city great and gay
    (So they say),
Of our country's very capital, its prince
    Ages since   10
Held his court in, gathered councils, wielding far
    Peace or war.

2

Now—the country does not even boast a tree,
    As you see,
To distinguish slopes of verdure, certain rills   15
    From the hills
Intersect and give a name to (else they run
    Into one),
Where the domed and daring palace shot its spires
    Up like fires   20
O'er the hundred-gated circuit of a wall
    Bounding all,
Made of marble, men might march on nor be pressed,
    Twelve abreast.

3

And such plenty and perfection, see, of grass   25
    Never was!
Such a carpet as, this summertime, o'erspreads
    And embeds
Every vestige of the city, guessed alone,
    Stock or stone—   30
Where a multitude of men breathed joy and woe
    Long ago;
Lust of glory pricked their hearts up, dread of shame
    Struck them tame;

1. The ruins may be those of such cities as Babylon or Nineveh or one of the Etruscan cities of Italy.
    The unusual stanza used in this poem was invented by Browning. The contrast between past and present, which is the core of the poem, is reinforced by devoting one half of each stanza to the past and the other half to the present.

And that glory and that shame alike, the gold   35
    Bought and sold.

4

Now—the single little turret that remains
    On the plains,
By the caper overrooted, by the gourd
    Overscored,   40
While the patching houseleek's[2] head of blossom winks
    Through the chinks—
Marks the basement whence a tower in ancient time
    Sprang sublime,
And a burning ring, all round, the chariots traced   45
    As they raced,
And the monarch and his minions and his dames
    Viewed the games.

5

And I know, while thus the quiet-colored eve
    Smiles to leave
To their folding, all our many-tinkling fleece   50
    In such peace,
And the slopes and rills in undistinguished gray
    Melt away—
That a girl with eager eyes and yellow hair
    Waits me there   55
In the turret whence the charioteers caught soul
    For the goal,
When the king looked, where she locks now, breathless, dumb
    Till I come.   60

6

But he looked upon the city, every side,
    Far and wide,
All the mountains topped with temples, all the glades'
    Colonnades,
All the causeys,[3] bridges, aqueducts—and then,   65
    All the men!
When I do come, she will speak not, she will stand,
    Either hand
On my shoulder, give her eyes the first embrace
    Of my face,   70
Ere we rush, ere we extinguish sight and speech
    Each on each.

7

In one year they sent a million fighters forth
    South and north,
And they built their gods a brazen pillar high   75
    As the sky,
Yet reserved a thousand chariots in full force—
    Gold, of course,

---

2. Common European plant, with petals clustered in the shape of rosettes.

3. Causeways or roads raised above low ground.

Oh heart! oh blood that freezes, blood that burns!
    Earth's returns   80
For whole centuries of folly, noise, and sin!
    Shut them in,
With their triumphs and their glories and the rest!
    Love is best.

1852   1855

Women and Roses[1]

1

I dream of a red-rose tree.
And which of its roses three
Is the dearest rose to me?

2

Round and round, like a dance of snow
In a dazzling drift, as its guardians, go   5
Floating the women faded for ages,
Sculptured in stone, on the poet's pages.
Then follow women fresh and gay,
Living and loving and loved today.
Last, in the rear, flee the multitude of maidens,   10
Beauties yet unborn. And all, to one cadence,
They circle their rose on my rose tree.

3

Dear rose, thy term is reached,
Thy leaf hangs loose and bleached:
Bees pass it unimpeached.[2]   15

4

Stay then, stoop, since I cannot climb,
You, great shapes of the antique time!
How shall I fix you, fire you, freeze you,
Break my heart at your feet to please you?
Oh, to possess and be possessed!   20
Hearts that beat 'neath each pallid breast!
Once but of love, the poesy, the passion,
Drink but once and die!—In vain, the same fashion,
They circle their rose on my rose tree.

5

Dear rose, thy joy's undimmed,   25
Thy cup is ruby-rimmed,
Thy cup's heart nectar-brimmed.

6

Deep, as drops from a statue's plinth[3]
The bee sucked in by the hyacinth,

1. Like Chaucer in the *Romaunt of the Rose* and also like Tennyson in *Maud*, the speaker in the following dream lyric associates roses with fair women and a garden of roses with the garden of love. The beautiful women of the past are first evoked (stanzas 3, 4); then those of the present (stanzas 5, 6); and finally those of the future (stanzas 7, 8). All, however, elude him. William Morris noted in 1855 that the poem's "concentrated thought" cannot be paraphrased because in such poems "there are so many exquisitely small and delicate turns of thought running through the music and along with it."
2. Unhindered.
3. Base.

So will I bury me while burning,   30
Quench like him at a plunge my yearning,
Eyes in your eyes, lips on your lips!
Fold me fast where the cincture[4] slips,
Prison all my soul in eternities of pleasure,
Girdle me for once! But no—the old measure,   35
They circle their rose on my rose tree.

7

Dear rose without a thorn,
Thy bud's the babe unborn:
First streak of a new morn.

8

Wings, lend wings for the cold, the clear!   40
What is far conquers what is near.
Roses will bloom nor want beholders,
Sprung from the dust where our flesh molders.
What shall arrive with the cycle's change?
A novel grace and a beauty strange.   45
I will make an Eve, be the artist that began her,
Shaped her to his mind!—Alas! in like manner
They circle their rose on my rose tree.

1852   1855

"Childe Roland to the Dark Tower Came"[1]

(SEE EDGAR'S SONG IN "LEAR")

1

My first thought was, he lied in every word,
That hoary cripple, with malicious eye
Askance[2] to watch the working of his lie
On mine, and mouth scarce able to afford

4. Ornamental belt worn by women, usually across the hips.
1. Browning stated that this poem "came upon me as a kind of dream," and that it was written in one day. Although the poem was among those of his own writings that pleased him most, he was reluctant to explain what the dream (or nightmare) signified. He once agreed with a friend's suggestion that the meaning might be expressed in the statement: "He that endureth to the end shall be saved." Most readers have responded to the poem in this way, finding in the story of Roland's quest an inspiring expression of defiance and courage. Other readers find the poem to be more expressive of despair than of enduring hope, and it is at least true that the landscape is as grim and nightmarelike as in such 20th-century writings as T. S. Eliot's

Hollow Men or Franz Kafka's *Penal Colony*. It has been said of *Childe Roland* that every reader can be his own allegorist, and such a poem thus poses a further large question of whether or not total comprehension of a work is always essential for appreciation of literature.

The lines from Shakespeare's *King Lear* (III.iv.187–90), from which the title is taken, are spoken when Lear is about to enter a hovel on the heath, and Edgar, feigning madness, chants the fragment of a song reminiscent of quests and challenges in fairy tales: "Child Rowland to the dark tower came; / His word was still / 'Fie, foh, and fum! / I smell the blood of a British man.' " A "childe" is a youth of gentle birth, usually a candidate for knighthood.
2. Squinting sidewise.

Suppression of the glee, that pursed and scored   5
    Its edge, at one more victim gained thereby.

2

What else should he be set for, with his staff?
    What, save to waylay with his lies, ensnare
    All travelers who might find him posted there,
And ask the road? I guessed what skull-like laugh   10
Would break, what crutch 'gin write my epitaph
    For pastime in the dusty thoroughfare,

3

If at his counsel I should turn aside
    Into that ominous tract which, all agree,
    Hides the Dark Tower. Yet acquiescingly   15
I did turn as he pointed: neither pride
Nor hope rekindling at the end descried,
    So much as gladness that some end might be.

4

For, what with my whole world-wide wandering,
    What with my search drawn out through years, my hope   20
    Dwindled into a ghost not fit to cope
With that obstreperous joy success would bring,
I hardly tried now to rebuke the spring
    My heart made, finding failure in its scope.

5

As when a sick man very near to death[3]   25
    Seems dead indeed, and feels begin and end
    The tears and takes the farewell of each friend,
And hears one bid the other go, draw breath
Freelier outside ("since all is o'er," he saith,
    "And the blow fallen no grieving can amend"),   30

6

While some discuss if near the other graves
    Be room enough for this, and when a day
    Suits best for carrying the corpse away,
With care about the banners, scarves and staves:
And still the man hears all, and only craves   35
    He may not shame such tender love and stay.

7

Thus, I had so long suffered in this quest,
    Heard failure prophesied so oft, been writ
    So many times among "The Band"—to wit,
The knights who to the Dark Tower's search addressed   40
Their steps—that just to fail as they, seemed best,
    And all the doubt was now—should I be fit?

8

So, quiet as despair, I turned from him,
    That hateful cripple, out of his highway
    Into the path he pointed. All the day   45

3. Cf. *A Valediction: Forbidding Mourning*, lines 1–4, by John Donne, a poet much admired by Browning.

Had been a dreary one at best, and dim
Was settling to its close, yet shot one grim
    Red leer to see the plain catch its estray.[4]

9
For mark! no sooner was I fairly found
    Pledged to the plain, after a pace or two,   50
    Than, pausing to throw backward a last view
O'er the safe road, 'twas gone; gray plain all round:
Nothing but plain to the horizon's bound.
    I might go on; naught else remained to do.

10
So, on I went. I think I never saw   55
    Such starved ignoble nature; nothing throve:
    For flowers—as well expect a cedar grove!
But cockle,[5] spurge, according to their law
Might propagate their kind, with none to awe,
    You'd think; a burr had been a treasure trove.   60

11
No! penury, inertness and grimace,
    In some strange sort, were the land's portion. "See
    Or shut your eyes," said Nature peevishly,
"It nothing skills: I cannot help my case;
'Tis the Last Judgment's fire must cure this place,   65
    Calcine[6] its clods and set my prisoners free."

12
If there pushed any ragged thistle stalk
    Above its mates, the head was chopped; the bents[7]
    Were jealous else. What made those holes and rents
In the dock's[8] harsh swarth leaves, bruised as to balk   70
All hope of greenness? 'tis a brute must walk
    Pashing their life out, with a brute's intents.

13
As for the grass, it grew as scant as hair
    In leprosy; thin dry blades pricked the mud
    Which underneath looked kneaded up with blood.   75
One stiff blind horse, his every bone a-stare,
Stood stupefied, however he came there:
    Thrust out past service from the devil's stud!

14
Alive? he might be dead for aught I know,
    With that red gaunt and colloped[9] neck a-strain,   80
    And shut eyes underneath the rusty mane;
Seldom went such grotesqueness with such woe;
I never saw a brute I hated so;
    He must be wicked to deserve such pain.

---

4. Literally, a domestic animal that has strayed away from its home.
5. A weed that bears burrs. "Spurge" is a bitter-juiced weed.
6. Turn to powder by heat.
7. Coarse, stiff grasses.
8. Coarse plant.
9. Ridged.

15

I shut my eyes and turned them on my heart.   85
    As a man calls for wine before he fights,
    I asked one draught of earlier, happier sights,
Ere fitly I could hope to play my part.
Think first, fight afterwards—the soldier's art:
    One taste of the old time sets all to rights.   90

16

Not it! I fancied Cuthbert's reddening face
    Beneath its garniture of curly gold,
    Dear fellow, till I almost felt him fold
An arm in mine to fix me to the place,
That way he used. Alas, one night's disgrace!   95
    Out went my heart's new fire and left it cold.

17

Giles then, the soul of honor—there he stands
    Frank as ten years ago when knighted first.
    What honest man should dare (he said) he durst.
Good—but the scene shifts—faugh! what hangman hands   100
Pin to his breast a parchment? His own bands
    Read it. Poor traitor, spit upon and cursed!

18

Better this present than a past like that;
    Back therefore to my darkening path again!
    No sound, no sight as far as eye could strain.   105
Will the night send a howlet[1] or a bat?
I asked: when something on the dismal flat
    Came to arrest my thoughts and change their train.

19

A sudden little river crossed my path
    As unexpected as a serpent comes.   110
    No sluggish tide congenial to the glooms;
This, as it frothed by, might have been a bath
For the fiend's glowing hoof—to see the wrath
    Of its black eddy bespate[2] with flakes and spumes.

20

So petty yet so spiteful! All along,   115
    Low scrubby alders kneeled down over it;
    Drenched willows flung them headlong in a fit
Of mute despair, a suicidal throng:
The river which had done them all the wrong,
    Whate'er that was, rolled by, deterred no whit.   120

21

Which, while I forded—good saints, how I feared
    To set my foot upon a dead man's cheek,
    Each step, or feel the spear I thrust to seek
For hollows, tangled in his hair or beard!
—It may have been a water rat I speared,   125
    But, ugh! it sounded like a baby's shriek.

1. Owl.   2. Bespattered.

22

Glad was I when I reached the other bank.
   Now for a better country. Vain presage!
   Who were the strugglers, what war did they wage,
Whose savage trample thus could pad the dank   130
Soil to a plash? Toads in a poisoned tank,
   Or wild cats in a red-hot iron cage—

23

The fight must so have seemed in that fell cirque.[3]
   What penned them there, with all the plain to choose?
   No footprint leading to that horrid mews,[4]   135
None out of it. Mad brewage set to work
Their brains, no doubt, like galley slaves the Turk
   Pits for his pastime, Christians against Jews.

24

And more than that—a furlong on—why, there!
   What bad use was that engine for, that wheel,   140
   Or brake,[5] not wheel—that harrow fit to reel
Men's bodies out like silk? with all the air
Of Tophet's[6] tool, on earth left unaware,
   Or brought to sharpen its rusty teeth of steel.

25

Then came a bit of stubbed ground, once a wood,   145
   Next a marsh, it would seem, and now mere earth
   Desperate and done with; (so a fool finds mirth,
Makes a thing and then mars it, till his mood
Changes and off he goes!) within a rood[7]—
   Bog, clay and rubble, sand and stark black dearth.   150

26

Now blotches rankling, colored gay and grim,
   Now patches where some leanness of the soil's
   Broke into moss or substances like boils;
Then came some palsied oak, a cleft in him
Like a distorted mouth that splits its rim   155
   Gaping at death, and dies while it recoils.

27

And just as far as ever from the end!
   Naught in the distance but the evening, naught
   To point my footstep further! At the thought,
A great black bird, Apollyon's[8] bosom friend,   160
Sailed past, nor beat his wide wing dragon-penned[9]
   That brushed my cap—perchance the guide I sought.

---

3. Dreadful arena.
4. Enclosed stable yard.
5. A toothed machine used for separating the fibers of flax or hemp. Here an instrument of torture.
6. Hell's. See also Jeremiah xix.4–5.
7. Quarter acre of land.

8. In Revelation ix.11, Apollyon is "an angel of the bottomless pit." In Bunyan's *Pilgrim's Progress*, he is a hideous "monster"; "he had wings like a dragon."
9. With wings or pinions like those of a dragon.

28

For, looking up, aware I somehow grew,
　　'Spite of the dusk, the plain had given place
　　All round to mountains—with such name to grace　　165
Mere ugly heights and heaps now stolen in view.
How thus they had surprised me—solve it, you!
　　How to get from them was no clearer case.

29

Yet half I seemed to recognize some trick
　　Of mischief happened to me, God knows when—　　170
　　In a bad dream perhaps. Here ended, then,
Progress this way. When, in the very nick
Of giving up, one time more, came a click
　　As when a trap shuts—you're inside the den!

30

Burningly it came on me all at once,　　175
　　This was the place! those two hills on the right,
　　Crouched like two bulls locked horn in horn in fight;
While to the left, a tall scalped mountain . . . Dunce,
Dotard, a-dozing at the very nonce,[1]
　　After a life spent training for the sight!　　180

31

What in the midst lay but the Tower itself?
　　The round squat turret, blind as the fool's heart,[2]
　　Built of brown stone, without a counterpart
In the whole world. The tempest's mocking elf
Points to the shipman thus the unseen shelf　　185
　　He strikes on, only when the timbers start.

32

Not see? because of night perhaps?—why, day
　　Came back again for that! before it left,
　　The dying sunset kindled through a cleft:
The hills, like giants at a hunting, lay,　　190
Chin upon hand, to see the game at bay—
　　"Now stab and end the creature—to the heft!"[3]

33

Not hear? when noise was everywhere! it tolled
　　Increasing like a bell. Names in my ears
　　Of all the lost adventurers my peers—　　195
How such a one was strong, and such was bold,
And such was fortunate, yet each of old
　　Lost, lost! one moment knelled the woe of years.

34

There they stood, ranged along the hillsides, met
　　To view the last of me, a living frame　　200

---

1. Moment.
2. Cf. "The fool hath said in his heart,
There is no God" (Psalms xiv.1).
3. Handle of dagger or sword.

For one more picture! in a sheet of flame
I saw them and I knew them all. And yet
Dauntless the slug-horn[4] to my lips I set,
   And blew. *"Childe Roland to the Dark Tower came."*

1852   1855

Respectability

1

Dear, had the world in its caprice
   Deigned to proclaim "I know you both,
   Have recognized your plighted troth,
Am sponsor for you: live in peace!"—
How many precious months and years   5
   Of youth had passed, that speed so fast,
   Before we found it out at last,
The world, and what it fears?

2

How much of priceless life were spent
   With men that every virtue decks,   10
   And women models of their sex,
Society's true ornament—
Ere we dared wander, nights like this,
   Through wind and rain, and watch the Seine,
   And feel the Boulevard break again   15
To warmth and light and bliss?

3

I know! the world proscribes not love;
   Allows my fingers to caress
   Your lips' contour and downiness,
Provided it supply a glove.   20
   The world's good word!—the Institute![1]
   Guizot receives Montalembert!
Eh? Down the court three lampions[2] flare:
Put forward your best foot!

ca. 1852   1855

---

4. This Scottish word meant the war cry or slogan (*slug-horn*) of a clan about to engage in battle, but in 1770 the poet Chatterton was misled into using it to mean a kind of trumpet or horn. Browning followed Chatterton's example, although the original meaning would also be relevant here.

1. A building in Paris, which the lovers are approaching in their walk. The speaker is reminded that at a meeting of the French Academy, held in the Institute, occurred a glaring instance of the hypocrisy which he thinks is characteristic of all social relations. In 1852, François Guizot had delivered a flowery speech of welcome in honor of Charles Montalembert, an author whom Guizot at heart despised.

2. Ornamental lamps illuminating the courtyard of the Institute.

Fra Lippo Lippi[1]

I am poor brother Lippo, by your leave!
You need not clap your torches to my face.
Zooks,[2] what's to blame? you think you see a monk!
What, 'tis past midnight, and you go the rounds,
And here you catch me at an alley's end   5
Where sportive ladies leave their doors ajar?
The Carmine's[3] my cloister: hunt it up,
Do—harry out, if you must show your zeal,
Whatever rat, there, haps on his wrong hole,
And nip each softling of a wee white mouse,   10
Weke, weke, that's crept to keep him company!
Aha, you know your betters! Then, you'll take
Your hand away that's fiddling on my throat,
And please to know me likewise. Who am I?
Why, one, sir, who is lodging with a friend   15
Three streets off—he's a certain . . . how d'ye call?
Master—a . . . Cosimo of the Medici,[4]
I' the house that caps the corner. Boh! you were best!
Remember and tell me, the day you're hanged,
How you affected such a gullet's gripe![5]   20
But you,[6] sir, it concerns you that your knaves
Pick up a manner nor discredit you:
Zooks, are we pilchards,[7] that they sweep the streets
And count fair prize what comes into their net?
He's Judas to a tittle, that man is![8]   25
Just such a face! Why, sir, you make amends.
Lord, I'm not angry! Bid your hangdogs go
Drink out this quarter-florin to the health
Of the munificent House that harbors me
(And many more beside, lads! more beside!)   30
And all's come square again. I'd like his face—
His, elbowing on his comrade in the door

1. This monologue portrays the dawn of the Renaissance in Italy at a point when the medieval attitude towards life and art was about to be displaced by a fresh appreciation of earthly pleasures. It was from Giorgio Vasari's *Lives of the Painters* that Browning derived most of his information about the life of the Florentine painter and friar, Lippi (1406–69), but the theory of art propounded by Lippi in the poem was developed by the poet himself. Browning's own partiality for this poem may be attributed, in part, to his having identified himself with his hero, an artist whose aesthetic principles made him a misfit among his more pharisaical contemporaries.

2. A shortened version of "Gadzooks," a mild oath now obscure in meaning but perhaps resembling a phrase still in use: "God's truth."
3. Santa Maria del Carmine, a church and cloister of the Carmelite order of friars to which Lippi belonged.
4. Lippi's patron, banker and virtual ruler of Florence.
5. I.e., how you had the arrogance to choke the gullet of someone with my connections.
6. The officer in charge of the patrol of policemen or watchmen.
7. Small fish.
8. I.e., one of the watchmen has a face that would serve as a model for a painting of Judas.

With the pike and lantern—for the slave that holds
John Baptist's head a-dangle by the hair
With one hand ("Look you, now," as who should say)   35
And his weapon in the other, yet unwiped!
It's not your chance to have a bit of chalk,
A wood-coal or the like? or you should see!
Yes, I'm the painter, since you style me so.
What, brother Lippo's doings, up and down,   40
You know them and they take you? like enough!
I saw the proper twinkle in your eye—
'Tell you, I liked your looks at very first.
Let's sit and set things straight now, hip to haunch.
Here's spring come, and the nights one makes up bands   45
To roam the town and sing out carnival,[9]
And I've been three weeks shut within my mew,[1]
A-painting for the great man, saints and saints
And saints again. I could not paint all night—
Ouf! I leaned out of window for fresh air.   50
There came a hurry of feet and little feet,
A sweep of lute-strings, laughs, and whifts of song—
Flower o' the broom,
Take away love, and our earth is a tomb!
Flower o' the quince,   55
I let Lisa go, and what good in life since?[2]
Flower o' the thyme—and so on. Round they went.
Scarce had they turned the corner when a titter
Like the skipping of rabbits by moonlight—three slim shapes,
And a face that looked up . . . zooks, sir, flesh and blood,   60
That's all I'm made of! Into shreds it went,
Curtain and counterpane and coverlet,
All the bed-furniture—a dozen knots,
There was a ladder! Down I let myself,
Hands and feet, scrambling somehow, and so dropped,   65
And after them. I came up with the fun
Hard by Saint Laurence,[3] hail fellow, well met—
Flower o' the rose,
If I've been merry, what matter who knows?
And so as I was stealing back again   70
To get to bed and have a bit of sleep
Ere I rise up tomorrow and go work
On Jerome knocking at his poor old breast
With his great round stone to subdue the flesh,[4]
You snap me of the sudden. Ah, I see!   75
Though your eye twinkles still, you shake your head—
Mine's shaved—a monk, you say—the sting's in that!
If Master Cosimo announced himself,

9. Season of revelry before the commencement of Lent.
1. Private den.
2. This and other interspersed flower-
songs are called *stornelli* in Italy.

3. San Lorenzo, a church in Florence.
4. A picture of St. Jerome (ca. 340–
420), whose ascetic observances were
hardly a congenial subject for such a
painter as Lippi.

Mum's the word naturally; but a monk!
Come, what am I a beast for? tell us, now!   80
I was a baby when my mother died
And father died and left me in the street.
I starved there, God knows how, a year or two
On fig skins, melon parings, rinds and shucks,
Refuse and rubbish. One fine frosty day,   85
My stomach being empty as your hat,
The wind doubled me up and down I went.
Old Aunt Lapaccia trussed me with one hand
(Its fellow was a stinger as I knew),
And so along the wall, over the bridge,   90
By the straight cut to the convent. Six words there,
While I stood munching my first bread that month:
"So, boy, you're minded," quoth the good fat father
Wiping his own mouth, 'twas refection time[5]—
"To quit this very miserable world?   95
Will you renounce" . . . "the mouthful of bread?" thought I;
By no means! Brief, they made a monk of me;
I did renounce the world, its pride and greed,
Palace, farm, villa, shop, and banking house,
Trash, such as these poor devils of Medici   100
Have given their hearts to—all at eight years old.
Well, sir, I found in time, you may be sure,
'Twas not for nothing—the good bellyful,
The warm serge and the rope that goes all round,
And day-long blessed idleness beside!   105
"Let's see what the urchin's fit for"—that came next.
Not overmuch their way, I must confess.
Such a to-do! They tried me with their books:
Lord, they'd have taught me Latin in pure waste!
Flower o' the clove,   110
All the Latin I construe is "amo," I love!
But, mind you, when a boy starves in the streets
Eight years together, as my fortune was,
Watching folk's faces to know who will fling
The bit of half-stripped grape bunch he desires,   115
And who will curse or kick him for his pains—
Which gentleman processional and fine,
Holding a candle to the Sacrament,
Will wink and let him lift a plate and catch
The droppings of the wax to sell again,   120
Or holla for the Eight[6] and have him whipped—
How say I?—nay, which dog bites, which lets drop
His bone from the heap of offal in the street—
Why, soul and sense of him grow sharp alike,
He learns the look of things, and none the less   125
For admonition from the hunger-pinch.
I had a store of such remarks, be sure,

5. Mealtime.   6. Florentine magistrates.

Which, after I found leisure, turned to use.
I drew men's faces on my copybooks,
Scrawled them within the antiphonary's marge,[7]   130
Joined legs and arms to the long music-notes,
Found eyes and nose and chin for A's and B's,
And made a string of pictures of the world
Betwixt the ins and outs of verb and noun,
On the wall, the bench, the door. The monks looked black.   135
"Nay," quoth the Prior,[8] "turn him out, d' ye say?
In no wise. Lose a crow and catch a lark.
What if at last we get our man of parts,
We Carmelites, like those Camaldolese
And Preaching Friars,[9] to do our church up fine   140
And put the front on it that ought to be!"
And hereupon he bade me daub away.
Thank you! my head being crammed, the walls a blank,
Never was such prompt disemburdening.
First, every sort of monk, the black and white,   145
I drew them, fat and lean: then, folk at church,
From good old gossips waiting to confess
Their cribs of barrel droppings, candle ends—
To the breathless fellow at the altar-foot,
Fresh from his murder, safe and sitting there   150
With the little children round him in a row
Of admiration, half for his beard and half
For that white anger of his victim's son
Shaking a fist at him with one fierce arm,
Signing himself with the other because of Christ   155
(Whose sad face on the cross sees only this
After the passion[1] of a thousand years)
Till some poor girl, her apron o'er her head
(Which the intense eyes looked through), came at eve
On tiptoe, said a word, dropped in a loaf,   160
Her pair of earrings and a bunch of flowers
(The brute took growling), prayed, and so was gone.
I painted all, then cried " 'Tis ask and have;
Choose, for more's ready!"—laid the ladder flat,
And showed my covered bit of cloister wall.   165
The monks closed in a circle and praised loud
Till checked, taught what to see and not to see,
Being simple bodies—"That's the very man!
Look at the boy who stoops to pat the dog!
That woman's like the Prior's niece who comes   170
To care about his asthma: it's the life!"
But there my triumph's straw-fire flared and funked;[2]
Their betters took their turn to see and say:
The Prior and the learned pulled a face

7. Margin of music book used for
choral singing.
8. Head of a Carmelite convent.
9. Benedictine and Dominican religious orders, respectively.
1. Sufferings.
2. Went up in smoke.

And stopped all that in no time. "How? what's here? 175
Quite from the mark of painting, bless us all!
Faces, arms, legs and bodies like the true
As much as pea and pea! it's devil's game!
Your business is not to catch men with show,
With homage to the perishable clay, 180
But lift them over it, ignore it all,
Make them forget there's such a thing as flesh.
Your business is to paint the souls of men—
Man's soul, and it's a fire, smoke . . . no, it's not . . .
It's vapor done up like a newborn babe— 185
(In that shape when you die it leaves your mouth)
It's . . . well, what matters talking, it's the soul!
Give us no more of body than shows soul!
Here's Giotto,[3] with his Saint a-praising God,
That sets us praising—why not stop with him? 190
Why put all thoughts of praise out of our head
With wonder at lines, colors, and what not?
Paint the soul, never mind the legs and arms!
Rub all out, try at it a second time.
Oh, that white smallish female with the breasts, 195
She's just my niece . . . Herodias,[4] I would say—
Who went and danced and got men's heads cut off!
Have it all out!" Now, is this sense, I ask?
A fine way to paint soul, by painting body
So ill, the eye can't stop there, must go further 200
And can't fare worse! Thus, yellow does for white
When what you put for yellow's simply black,
And any sort of meaning looks intense
When all beside itself means and looks naught.
Why can't a painter lift each foot in turn, 205
Left foot and right foot, go a double step,
Make his flesh liker and his soul more like,
Both in their order? Take the prettiest face,
The Prior's niece . . . patron-saint—is it so pretty
You can't discover if it means hope, fear, 210
Sorrow or joy? won't beauty go with these?
Suppose I've made her eyes all right and blue,
Can't I take breath and try to add life's flash,
And then add soul and heighten them threefold?
Or say there's beauty with no soul at all— 215
(I never saw it—put the case the same—)
If you get simple beauty and naught else,
You get about the best thing God invents:
That's somewhat: and you'll find the soul you have missed,
Within yourself, when you return him thanks. 220

3. Great Florentine painter (1276–
1337), whose stylized pictures of religious subjects were admired as models
of pre-Renaissance art.
4. Herodias, also called Salome, had
the same name as her mother, Herodias,
sister-in-law of King Herod. The daughter's dance coincided with the beheading
of John the Baptist, who had aroused
her mother's displeasure. See Matthew
xiv.1–2.

"Rub all out!" Well, well, there's my life, in short,
And so the thing has gone on ever since.
I'm grown a man no doubt, I've broken bounds:
You should not take a fellow eight years old
And make him swear to never kiss the girls. 225
I'm my own master, paint now as I please—
Having a friend, you see, in the Corner-house![5]
Lord, it's fast holding by the rings in front—
Those great rings serve more purposes than just
To plant a flag in, or tie up a horse! 230
And yet the old schooling sticks, the old grave eyes
Are peeping o'er my shoulder as I work,
The heads shake still—"It's art's decline, my son!
You're not of the true painters, great and old;
Brother Angelico's the man, you'll find; 235
Brother Lorenzo stands his single peer:[6]
Fag on at flesh, you'll never make the third!"
Flower o' the pine,
You keep your mistr . . . manners, and I'll stick to mine!
I'm not the third, then: bless us, they must know! 240
Don't you think they're the likeliest to know,
They with their Latin? So, I swallow my rage,
Clench my teeth, suck my lips in tight, and paint
To please them—sometimes do and sometimes don't;
For, doing most, there's pretty sure to come 245
A turn, some warm eve finds me at my saints—
A laugh, a cry, the business of the world—
(*Flower o' the peach,*
Death for us all, and his own life for each!)
And my whole soul revolves, the cup runs over, 250
The world and life's too big to pass for a dream,
And I do these wild things in sheer despite,
And play the fooleries you catch me at,
In pure rage! The old mill-horse, out at grass
After hard years, throws up his stiff heels so, 255
Although the miller does not preach to him
The only good of grass is to make chaff.[7]
What would men have? Do they like grass or no—
May they or mayn't they? all I want's the thing
Settled forever one way. As it is, 260
You tell too many lies and hurt yourself:
You don't like what you only like too much,
You do like what, if given you at your word,
You find abundantly detestable.
For me, I think I speak as I was taught; 265
I always see the garden and God there
A-making man's wife: and, my lesson learned,

5. The Medici palace.
6. Fra Angelico (1387–1455) and Lorenzo Monaco (1370–1425), whose paintings were in the approved traditional manner.
7. Straw.

The value and significance of flesh,
I can't unlearn ten minutes afterwards.

  You understand me: I'm a beast, I know. 270
But see, now—why, I see as certainly
As that the morning star's about to shine,
What will hap some day. We've a youngster here
Comes to our convent, studies what I do,
Slouches and stares and lets no atom drop: 275
His name is Guidi[8]—he'll not mind the monks—
They call him Hulking Tom, he lets them talk—
He picks my practice up—he'll paint apace,
I hope so—though I never live so long,
I know what's sure to follow. You be judge! 280
You speak no Latin more than I, belike;
However, you're my man, you've seen the world
—The beauty and the wonder and the power,
The shapes of things, their colors, lights and shades,
Changes, surprises—and God made it all! 285
—For what? Do you feel thankful, aye or no,
For this fair town's face, yonder river's line,
The mountain round it and the sky above,
Much more the figures of man, woman, child,
These are the frame to? What's it all about? 290
To be passed over, despised? or dwelt upon,
Wondered at? oh, this last of course!—you say.
But why not do as well as say—paint these
Just as they are, careless what comes of it?
God's works—paint any one, and count it crime 295
To let a truth slip. Don't object, "His works
Are here already; nature is complete:
Suppose you reproduce her—(which you can't)
There's no advantage! You must beat her, then."
For, don't you mark? we're made so that we love 300
First when we see them painted, things we have passed
Perhaps a hundred times nor cared to see;
And so they are better, painted—better to us,
Which is the same thing. Art was given for that;
God uses us to help each other so, 305
Lending our minds out. Have you noticed, now,
Your cullion's[9] hanging face? A bit of chalk,
And trust me but you should, though! How much more,
If I drew higher things with the same truth!
That were to take the Prior's pulpit-place, 310
Interpret God to all of you! Oh, oh,
It makes me mad to see what men shall do
And we in our graves! This world's no blot for us,

8. Guidi or Masaccio (1401–28), a painter who may have been Lippi's master rather than his pupil, although Browning, in a letter to the press in 1870, argued that Lippi had been born earlier. Like Lippi, Masaccio was in revolt against the medieval theory of art. His frescoes in the chapel of Santa Maria del Carmine (Fra Lippo's church) are considered his masterpiece.
9. Rascal's.

Nor blank; it means intensely, and means good:
To find its meaning is my meat and drink.   315
"Aye, but you don't so instigate to prayer!"
Strikes in the Prior: "when your meaning's plain
It does not say to folk—remember matins,
Or, mind you fast next Friday!" Why, for this
What need of art at all? A skull and bones,   320
Two bits of stick nailed crosswise, or, what's best,
A bell to chime the hour with, does as well.
I painted a Saint Laurence[1] six months since
At Prato, splashed the fresco in fine style:
"How looks my painting, now the scaffold's down?"   325
I ask a brother: "Hugely," he returns—
"Already not one phiz of your three slaves
Who turn the Deacon off his toasted side,
But it's scratched and prodded to our heart's content,
The pious people have so eased their own   330
With coming to say prayers there in a rage:
We get on fast to see the bricks beneath.
Expect another job this time next year,
For pity and religion grow i' the crowd—
Your painting serves its purpose!" Hang the fools!   335

  —That is—you'll not mistake an idle word
Spoke in a huff by a poor monk, God wot,
Tasting the air this spicy night which turns
The unaccustomed head like Chianti wine!
Oh, the church knows! don't misreport me, now!   340
It's natural a poor monk out of bounds
Should have his apt word to excuse himself:
And hearken how I plot to make amends.
I have bethought me: I shall paint a piece
. . . There's for you! Give me six months, then go, see   345
Something in Sant' Ambrogio's![2] Bless the nuns!
They want a cast o' my office.[3] I shall paint
God in the midst, Madonna and her babe,
Ringed by a bowery flowery angel brood,
Lilies and vestments and white faces, sweet   350
As puff on puff of grated orris-root[4]
When ladies crowd to Church at midsummer.
And then i' the front, of course a saint or two—
Saint John, because he saves the Florentines,
Saint Ambrose, who puts down in black and white   355
The convent's friends and gives them a long day,
And Job, I must have him there past mistake,
The man of Uz (and Us without the z,
Painters who need his patience). Well, all these

1. A scene representing the fiery martyrdom of Saint Laurence; a "fresco" is
painted quickly on fresh plaster over a
surface of bricks. Prato is a town near
Florence.
2. A convent church in Florence.

3. Sample of my work. The completed
painting, which Browning saw in Florence, is Lippi's "Coronation of the Virgin."
4. Powder (like talcum) made from
sweet-smelling roots of a flower.

Secured at their devotion, up shall come 360
Out of a corner when you least expect,
As one by a dark stair into a great light,
Music and talking, who but Lippo! I!—
Mazed, motionless and moonstruck—I'm the man!
Back I shrink—what is this I see and hear? 365
I, caught up with my monk's things by mistake,
My old serge gown and rope that goes all round,
I, in this presence, this pure company!
Where's a hole, where's a corner for escape?
Then steps a sweet angelic slip of a thing 370
Forward, puts out a soft palm—"Not so fast!"
—Addresses the celestial presence, "nay—
He made you and devised you, after all,
Though he's none of you! Could Saint John there draw—
His camel-hair⁵ make up a painting-brush? 375
We come to brother Lippo for all that,
Iste perfecit opus!"⁶ So, all smile—
I shuffle sideways with my blushing face
Under the cover of a hundred wings
Thrown like a spread of kirtles when you're gay 380
And play hot cockles,⁷ all the doors being shut,
Till, wholly unexpected, in there pops
The hothead husband! Thus I scuttle off
To some safe bench behind, not letting go
The palm of her, the little lily thing 385
That spoke the good word for me in the nick,
Like the Prior's niece . . . Saint Lucy, I would say.
And so all's saved for me, and for the church
A pretty picture gained. Go, six months hence!
Your hand, sir, and good-by: no lights, no lights! 390
The street's hushed, and I know my own way back,
Don't fear me! There's the gray beginning. Zooks!

ca. 1853   1855

The Last Ride Together

1

I said—Then, dearest, since 'tis so,
Since now at length my fate I know,
Since nothing all my love avails,
Since all, my life seemed meant for, fails,
    Since this was written and needs must be— 5
My whole heart rises up to bless
Your name in pride and thankfulness!
Take back the hope you gave—I claim
Only a memory of the same,

---

5. "And John was clothed with camel's hair" (Mark i.6).
6. "This man made the work." In this painting, as later completed, these words appear beside a figure which Browning took to be Lippi's self-portrait.
7. A game in which a player wears a blindfold. "Kirtles": skirts.

  —And this beside, if you will not blame, 10
   Your leave for one more last ride with me.

     2

My mistress bent that brow of hers;
Those deep dark eyes where pride demurs
When pity would be softening through,
Fixed me a breathing-while or two 15
  With life or death in the balance: right!
The blood replenished me again;
My last thought was at least not vain:
I and my mistress, side by side
Shall be together, breathe and ride, 20
So, one day more am I deified.
  Who knows but the world may end tonight?

     3

Hush! if you saw some western cloud
All billowy-bosomed, over-bowed
By many benedictions—sun's 25
And moon's and evening star's at once—
  And so, you, looking and loving best,
Conscious grew, your passion drew
Cloud, sunset, moonrise, star-shine too,
Down on you, near and yet more near, 30
Till flesh must fade for heaven was here!—
Thus leant she and lingered[1]—joy and fear!
  Thus lay she a moment on my breast.

     4

Then we began to ride. My soul
Smoothed itself out, a long-cramped scroll 35
Freshening and fluttering in the wind.
Past hopes already lay behind.
  What need to strive with a life awry?
Had I said that, had I done this,
So might I gain, so might I miss. 40
Might she have loved me? just as well
She might have hated, who can tell!
Where had I been now if the worst befell?
  And here we are riding, she and I.

     5

Fail I alone, in words and deeds? 45
Why, all men strive and who succeeds?
We rode; it seemed my spirit flew,
Saw other regions, cities new,
  As the world rushed by on either side.
I thought—All labor, yet no less 50
Bear up beneath their unsuccess.
Look at the end of work, contrast
The petty done, the undone vast,
This present of theirs with the hopeful past!
  I hoped she would love me; here we ride. 55

1. Before she mounts her horse.

6

What hand and brain went ever paired?
What heart alike conceived and dared?
What act proved all its thought had been?
What will but felt the fleshly screen?
    We ride and I see her bosom heave.   60
There's many a crown for who can reach.
Ten lines, a statesman's life in each![2]
The flag stuck on a heap of bones,
A soldier's doing! what atones?
They scratch his name on the Abbey stones.   65
    My riding is better, by their leave.

7

What does it all mean, poet? Well,
Your brains beat into rhythm, you tell
What we felt only; you expressed
You hold things beautiful the best,   70
    And pace them in rhyme so, side by side.
'Tis something, nay 'tis much: but then,
Have you yourself what's best for men?
Are you—poor, sick, old ere your time—
Nearer one whit your own sublime   75
Than we who never have turned a rhyme?
    Sing, riding's a joy! For me, I ride.

8

And you, great sculptor—so, you gave
A score of years to Art, her slave,
And that's your Venus, whence we turn   80
To yonder girl that fords the burn![3]
    You acquiesce, and shall I repine?
What, man of music, you grown gray
With notes and nothing else to say,
Is this your sole praise from a friend,   85
"Greatly his opera's strains intend,
But in music we know how fashions end!"
    I gave my youth; but we ride, in fine.[4]

9

Who knows what's fit for us? Had fate
Proposed bliss here should sublimate   90
My being—had I signed the bond—
Still one must lead some life beyond,
    Have a bliss to die with, dim-descried.
This foot once planted on the goal,
This glory-garland round my soul,   95
Could I descry such? Try and test!
I sink back shuddering from the quest.

---

2. If a man tries hard enough, he may be crowned with what seems to be success. He might become, for example, an eminent "statesman." Yet his only memorial would be a short sketch of his career ("ten lines") in some history or biographical dictionary.
3. Crosses the brook.
4. In short.

Earth being so good, would Heaven seem best?[5]
    Now, Heaven and she are beyond this ride.

10

And yet—she has not spoke so long!   100
What if heaven be that, fair and strong
At life's best, with our eyes upturned
Whither life's flower is first discerned,
    We, fixed so, ever should so abide?
What if we still ride on, we two   105
With life forever old yet new,
Changed not in kind but in degree,
The instant made eternity—
And heaven just prove that I and she
    Ride, ride together, forever ride?   110

                                                 1855

Andrea del Sarto[1]

(CALLED "THE FAULTLESS PAINTER")

But do not let us quarrel any more,
No, my Lucrezia; bear with me for once:
Sit down and all shall happen as you wish.
You turn your face, but does it bring your heart?
I'll work then for your friend's friend, never fear,   5
Treat his own subject after his own way,
Fix his own time, accept too his own price,
And shut the money into this small hand
When next it takes mine. Will it? tenderly?
Oh, I'll content him—but tomorrow, Love!   10
I often am much wearier than you think,

---

5. If fate had decreed that he could possess his mistress fully, life on earth would have been so blissful that heaven could offer nothing for him to look forward to after death. Hence (he argues) to preserve "a bliss to die with" (line 93), it is better that she never really became his on earth.

1. This portrait of Andrea del Sarto (1486–1531) was derived from a biography written by his pupil, Giorgio Vasari, author of *The Lives of the Painters*. Vasari's account seeks to explain why his Florentine master, one of the most skillful painters of the Renaissance, never altogether fulfilled the promise he had shown early in his career and why he had never arrived (in Vasari's opinion) at the level of such artists as Raphael. Vasari noted that Andrea suffered from "a certain timidity of mind * * * which rendered it impossible that those evidences of ardor and animation, which are proper to the more exalted character, should ever appear in him."

Browning also follows Vasari's account of Andrea's marriage to a beautiful widow, Lucrezia, "an artful woman who made him do as she pleased in all things." Vasari reports that Andrea's "immoderate love for her soon caused him to neglect the studies demanded by his art," and that this infatuation had "more influence over him than the glory and honor towards which he had begun to make such hopeful advances."

Browning's poem has often been praised for its exposition of a paradoxical theory of success and failure, but it has other qualities as well. Its slow-paced, enervated blank-verse line, its setting of a quiet evening in autumn, its comparative lack of the movement and noise that we expect in Browning's energetic verse create a unity of impression that is unobtrusive yet effective. Richard Altick has noted how the atmosphere of this monologue resembles Shakespeare's Sonnet 23: "In me thou see'st the twilight of such day / As after sunset fadeth in the west."

This evening more than usual, and it seems
As if—forgive now—should you let me sit
Here by the window with your hand in mine
And look a half-hour forth on Fiesole,[2]   15
Both of one mind, as married people use,
Quietly, quietly the evening through,
I might get up tomorrow to my work
Cheerful and fresh as ever. Let us try.
Tomorrow, how you shall be glad for this!   20
Your soft hand is a woman of itself,
And mine the man's bared breast she curls inside.
Don't count the time lost, neither; you must serve
For each of the five pictures we require:
It saves a model. So! keep looking so—   25
My serpentining beauty, rounds on rounds![3]
—How could you ever prick those perfect ears,
Even to put the pearl there! oh, so sweet—
My face, my moon, my everybody's moon,
Which everybody looks on and calls his,   30
And, I suppose, is looked on by in turn,
While she looks—no one's: very dear, no less.[4]
You smile? why, there's my picture ready made,
There's what we painters call our harmony!
A common grayness silvers everything[5]—   35
All in a twilight, you and I alike
—You, at the point of your first pride in me
(That's gone you know)—but I, at every point;
My youth, my hope, my art, being all toned down
To yonder sober pleasant Fiesole.   40
There's the bell clinking from the chapel top;
That length of convent wall across the way
Holds the trees safer, huddled more inside;
The last monk leaves the garden; days decrease,
And autumn grows, autumn in everything.   45
Eh? the whole seems to fall into a shape
As if I saw alike my work and self
And all that I was born to be and do,
A twilight-piece. Love, we are in God's hand.
How strange now, looks the life he makes us lead;   50
So free we seem, so fettered fast we are!
I feel he laid the fetter: let it lie!
This chamber for example—turn your head—
All that's behind us! You don't understand
Nor care to understand about my art,   55
But you can hear at least when people speak:
And that cartoon,[6] the second from the door

2. A suburb on the hills overlooking Florence.
3. Coils of hair like the coils of a serpent.
4. Her affections are centered upon no one person, not even upon her husband, yet she is nevertheless dear to him. Cf. *My Last Duchess*, lines 23–24.
5. The predominant color in many of Andrea's paintings is silver gray.
6. Drawing.

—It is the thing, Love! so such things should be—
Behold Madonna!—I am bold to say.
I can do with my pencil what I know,   60
What I see, what at bottom of my heart
I wish for, if I ever wish so deep—
Do easily, too—when I say, perfectly,
I do not boast, perhaps: yourself are judge,
Who listened to the Legate's[7] talk last week,   65
And just as much they used to say in France.
At any rate 'tis easy, all of it!
No sketches first, no studies, that's long past:
I do what many dream of, all their lives,
—Dream? strive to do, and agonize to do,   70
And fail in doing. I could count twenty such
On twice your fingers, and not leave this town,
Who strive—you don't know how the others strive
To paint a little thing like that you smeared
Carelessly passing with your robes afloat—   75
Yet do much less, so much less, Someone[8] says
(I know his name, no matter)—so much less!
Well, less is more, Lucrezia: I am judged.
There burns a truer light of God in them,
In their vexed beating stuffed and stopped-up brain,   80
Heart, or whate'er else, than goes on to prompt
This low-pulsed forthright craftsman's hand of mine.
Their works drop groundward, but themselves, I know,
Reach many a time a heaven that's shut to me,
Enter and take their place there sure enough,   85
Though they come back and cannot tell the world.
My works are nearer heaven, but I sit here.
The sudden blood of these men! at a word—
Praise them, it boils, or blame them, it boils too.
I, painting from myself and to myself,   90
Know what I do, am unmoved by men's blame
Or their praise either. Somebody remarks
Morello's[9] outline there is wrongly traced,
His hue mistaken; what of that? or else,
Rightly traced and well ordered; what of that?   95
Speak as they please, what does the mountain care?
Ah, but a man's reach should exceed his grasp,
Or what's a heaven for? All is silver-gray
Placid and perfect with my art: the worse!
I know both what I want and what might gain,   100
And yet how profitless to know, to sigh
"Had I been two, another and myself,
Our head would have o'erlooked the world!"[1] No doubt.
Yonder's a work now, of that famous youth

---

7. A deputy of the Pope.
8. Probably Michelangelo (1475–1564).
9. A mountain peak outside Florence.
1. I.e., if I had been both an aspiring,

dedicated, and soul-conscious artist as
well as a faultless craftsman, the combination would have been unsurpassable.
See also line 140 ("we half-men").

The Urbinate[2] who died five years ago.   105
('Tis copied, George Vasari sent it me.)[3]
Well, I can fancy how he did it all,
Pouring his soul, with kings and popes to see,
Reaching, that heaven might so replenish him,
Above and through his art—for it gives way;   110
That arm is wrongly put—and there again—
A fault to pardon in the drawing's lines,
Its body, so to speak: its soul is right,
He means right—that, a child may understand.
Still, what an arm! and I could alter it: 115
But all the play, the insight and the stretch—
Out of me, out of me! And wherefore out?
Had you enjoined them on me, given me soul,
We might have risen to Rafael, I and you!
Nay, Love, you did give all I asked, I think—   120
More than I merit, yes, by many times.
But had you—oh, with the same perfect brow,
And perfect eyes, and more than perfect mouth,
And the low voice my soul hears, as a bird
The fowler's pipe,[4] and follows to the snare—   125
Had you, with these the same, but brought a mind!
Some women do so. Had the mouth there urged
"God and the glory! never care for gain.
The present by the future, what is that?
Live for fame, side by side with Agnolo![5]   130
Rafael is waiting: up to God, all three!"
I might have done it for you. So it seems:
Perhaps not. All is as God overrules.
Beside, incentives come from the soul's self;
The rest avail not. Why do I need you?   135
What wife had Rafael, or has Agnolo?
In this world, who can do a thing, will not;
And who would do it, cannot, I perceive:
Yet the will's somewhat—somewhat, too, the power—
And thus we half-men struggle. At the end,   140
God, I conclude, compensates, punishes.
'Tis safer for me, if the award be strict,
That I am something underrated here.
Poor this long while, despised, to speak the truth.
I dared not, do you know, leave home all day,   145
For fear of chancing on the Paris lords.
The best is when they pass and look aside;
But they speak sometimes; I must bear it all.
Well may they speak! That Francis,[6] that first time,

2. Raphael (1483–1520), born at Urbino.
3. In saying that the painting is a copy, Andrea may perhaps be concerned to prevent Lucrezia from selling it.
4. Whistle or call used by hunters to lure wildfowl into range.

5. Michelangelo.
6. King Francis I of France had invited Andrea to his court at Fontainebleau and warmly encouraged him in his painting. On returning to Florence, however, Andrea is reputed to have stolen some funds entrusted to him by

And that long festal year at Fontainebleau! 150
I surely then could sometimes leave the ground,
Put on the glory, Rafael's daily wear,
In that humane great monarch's golden look—
One finger in his beard or twisted curl
Over his mouth's good mark that made the smile, 155
One arm about my shoulder, round my neck,
The jingle of his gold chain in my ear,
I painting proudly with his breath on me,
All his court round him, seeing with his eyes,
Such frank French eyes, and such a fire of souls 160
Profuse, my hand kept plying by those hearts—
And, best of all, this, this, this face beyond,
This in the background, waiting on my work,
To crown the issue with a last reward!
A good time, was it not, my kingly days? 165
And had you not grown restless . . . but I know—
'Tis done and past; 'twas right, my instinct said;
Too live the life grew, golden and not gray,
And I'm the weak-eyed bat no sun should tempt
Out of the grange whose four walls make his world.[7] 170
How could it end in any other way?
You called me, and I came home to your heart.
The triumph was—to reach and stay there; since
I reached it ere the triumph, what is lost?
Let my hands frame your face in your hair's gold, 175
You beautiful Lucrezia that are mine!
"Rafael did this, Andrea painted that;
The Roman's is the better when you pray,
But still the other's Virgin was his wife—"
Men will excuse me. I am glad to judge 180
Both pictures in your presence; clearer grows
My better fortune, I resolve to think.
For, do you know, Lucrezia, as God lives,
Said one day Agnolo, his very self,
To Rafael . . . I have known it all these years . . . 185
(When the young man was flaming out his thoughts
Upon a palace wall for Rome to see,
Too lifted up in heart because of it)
"Friend, there's a certain sorry little scrub
Goes up and down our Florence, none cares how, 190
Who, were he set to plan and execute
As you are, pricked on by your popes and kings,
Would bring the sweat into that brow of yours!"
To Rafael's—And indeed the arm is wrong.
I hardly dare . . . yet, only you to see, 195

Francis, and to please Lucrezia he built
a house with the money. Now he is
afraid of being insulted by "Paris lords"
on the streets.
7. The bat, a creature of evening,
thrives best in the confines of the
"four walls" of a farm building
("grange"). See also line 261 in which
Andrea thinks of heaven as a place of
four walls.

Give the chalk here—quick, thus the line should go!
Aye, but the soul! he's Rafael! rub it out!
Still, all I care for, if he spoke the truth,
(What he? why, who but Michel Agnolo?
Do you forget already words like those?)   200
If really there was such a chance, so lost—
Is, whether you're—not grateful—but more pleased.
Well, let me think so. And you smile indeed!
This hour has been an hour! Another smile?
If you would sit thus by me every night   205
I should work better, do you comprehend?
I mean that I should earn more, give you more.
See, it is settled dusk now; there's a star;
Morello's gone, the watch-lights show the wall,
The cue-owls[8] speak the name we call them by.   210
Come from the window, love—come in, at last,
Inside the melancholy little house
We built to be so gay with. God is just.
King Francis may forgive me: oft at nights
When I look up from painting, eyes tired out,   215
The walls become illumined, brick from brick
Distinct, instead of mortar, fierce bright gold,
That gold of his I did cement them with!
Let us but love each other. Must you go?
That Cousin here again? he waits outside?   220
Must see you—you, and not with me? Those loans?
More gaming debts to pay?[9] you smiled for that?
Well, let smiles buy me! have you more to spend?
While hand and eye and something of a heart
Are left me, work's my ware, and what's it worth? 225
I'll pay my fancy. Only let me sit
The gray remainder of the evening out,
Idle, you call it, and muse perfectly
How I could paint, were I but back in France,
One picture, just one more—the Virgin's face,   230
Not yours this time! I want you at my side
To hear them—that is, Michel Agnolo—
Judge all I do and tell you of its worth.
Will you? Tomorrow, satisfy your friend.
I take the subjects for his corridor,   235
Finish the portrait out of hand—there, there,
And throw him in another thing or two
If he demurs; the whole should prove enough
To pay for this same Cousin's freak. Beside,
What's better and what's all I care about,   240
Get you the thirteen scudi[1] for the ruff!

---

8. An owl whose cry sounds like the Italian word *ciù*.
9. Lucrezia's "Cousin" (or lover or "friend") owes gambling debts to a creditor. Andrea has already contracted (lines 5–10) to pay off these debts by painting some pictures according to the creditor's specifications. Now he agrees to pay off further debts.
1. Italian coins.

Love, does that please you? Ah, but what does he,
The Cousin! What does he to please you more?

I am grown peaceful as old age tonight.
I regret little, I would change still less.   245
Since there my past life lies, why alter it?
The very wrong to Francis!—it is true
I took his coin, was tempted and complied,
And built this house and sinned, and all is said.
My father and my mother died of want.[2]   250
Well, had I riches of my own? you see
How one gets rich! Let each one bear his lot.
They were born poor, lived poor, and poor they died:
And I have labored somewhat in my time
And not been paid profusely. Some good son   255
Paint my two hundred pictures—let him try!
No doubt, there's something strikes a balance. Yes,
You loved me quite enough, it seems tonight.
This must suffice me here. What would one have?
In heaven, perhaps, new chances, one more chance—   260
Four great walls in the New Jerusalem,
Meted on each side by the angel's reed,[3]
For Leonard,[4] Rafael, Agnolo and me
To cover—the three first without a wife,
While I have mine! So—still they overcome   265
Because there's still Lucrezia—as I choose.

Again the Cousin's whistle! Go, my Love.

ca. 1853   1855

Two in the Campagna[1]

1

I wonder do you feel today
    As I have felt since, hand in hand,
We sat down on the grass, to stray
    In spirit better through the land,
This morn of Rome and May?   5

2

For me, I touched a thought, I know,
    Has tantalized me many times,
(Like turns of thread the spiders throw
    Mocking across our path) for rhymes
To catch at and let go.   10

2. According to Vasari, Andrea's infatuation for Lucrezia prompted him
to stop supporting his poverty-stricken
parents.
3. Measuring rod. For "New Jerusalem," see Revelation xxi.10–21.

4. Leonardo da Vinci (1452–1519).
1. The Campagna is the name for the
level plains and pasture lands near
Rome where the ruins of ancient cities
are overrun with wild flowers.

3

Help me to hold it! First it left
    The yellowing fennel,[2] run to seed
There, branching from the brickwork's cleft,
    Some old tomb's ruin: yonder weed
Took up the floating weft,[3]   15

4

Where one small orange cup amassed
    Five beetles—blind and green they grope
Among the honey-meal: and last,
    Everywhere on the grassy slope
I traced it. Hold it fast!   20

5

The champaign[4] with its endless fleece
    Of feathery grasses everywhere!
Silence and passion, joy and peace,
    An everlasting wash of air—
Rome's ghost since her decease.   25

6

Such life here, through such lengths of hours,
    Such miracles performed in play,
Such primal naked forms of flowers,
    Such letting nature have her way
While heaven looks from its towers!   30

7

How say you? Let us, O my dove,
    Let us be unashamed of soul,
As earth lies bare to heaven above!
    How is it under our control
To love or not to love?   35

8

I would that you were all to me,
    You that are just so much, no more.
Nor yours nor mine, nor slave nor free!
    Where does the fault lie? What the core
O' the wound, since wound must be?   40

9

I would I could adopt your will,
    See with your eyes, and set my heart
Beating by yours, and drink my fill
    At your soul's springs—your part my part
In life, for good and ill.   45

10

No. I yearn upward, touch you close,
    Then stand away. I kiss your cheek,
Catch your soul's warmth—I pluck the rose
    And love it more than tongue can speak—
Then the good minute goes.   50

2. A yellow-flowered plant from which
a pungent spice is derived.
3. Threads crossing from side to side
of a web.
4. Here, the Campagna.

11

Already how am I so far
    Out of that minute? Must I go
Still like the thistle-ball, no bar,
    Onward, whenever light winds blow,
Fixed by no friendly star?   55

12

Just when I seemed about to learn!
    Where is the thread now? Off again!
The old trick! Only I discern—
    Infinite passion, and the pain
Of finite hearts that yearn.   60

1854   1855

A Grammarian's Funeral[1]

SHORTLY AFTER THE REVIVAL OF LEARNING IN EUROPE

Let us begin and carry up this corpse,
    Singing together.
Leave we the common crofts, the vulgar thorpes[2]
    Each in its tether[3]
Sleeping safe on the bosom of the plain,   5
    Cared for till cock-crow:
Look out if yonder be not day again
    Rimming the rock-row!
That's the appropriate country; there, man's thought,
    Rarer, intenser,   10
Self-gathered for an outbreak, as it ought,
    Chafes in the censer.
Leave we the unlettered plain its herd and crop;[4]
    Seek we sepulture
On a tall mountain, citied to the top,   15
    Crowded with culture!
All the peaks soar, but one the rest excels;
    Clouds overcome it;
No! yonder sparkle is the citadel's
    Circling its summit.   20

1. The speaker is one of the students who are bearing the body of their scholarly master to the mountaintop for burial. The student's defense of the dead grammarian's idealistic dedication to knowledge and faith in a future life is expressed in some of the harshest-sounding and most laborious verse ever written by Browning. It is this grotesque combination of opposites (soaring idealism in conjunction with harsh or petty realities) that gives *A Grammarian's Funeral* its distinctive tone.

No model for the grammarian has been specifically identified. Browning seems to have had in mind the kind of early Renaissance scholar whose devotion to the Greek language made it possible for others to enjoy the more recognizably significant aspects of the revival of learning.
2. "Crofts" are small tracts of land farmed by peasants; "thorpes" are villages.
3. Restricted to a narrow sphere like an animal tied to a stake.
4. Flatlands at the base of the mountain which are populated by illiterate shepherds and peasants. "Sepulture": burial place.

Thither our path lies; wind we up the heights:
　　Wait ye the warning?
Our low life was the level's and the night's;
　　He's for the morning.
Step to a tune, square chests, erect each head,　　　25
　　'Ware[5] the beholders!
This is our master, famous, calm, and dead,
　　Borne on our shoulders.

Sleep, crop and herd! sleep, darkling thorpe and croft,
　　Safe from the weather!　　　　　　　　　　　30
He, whom we convoy to his grave aloft,
　　Singing together,
He was a man born with thy face and throat,
　　Lyric Apollo![6]
Long he lived nameless: how should spring take note　　35
　　Winter would follow?
Till lo, the little touch, and youth was gone!
　　Cramped and diminished,
Moaned he, "New measures, other feet anon!
　　My dance is finished?"　　　　　　　　　　40
No, that's the world's way: (keep the mountain-side,
　　Make for the city!)
He knew the signal, and stepped on with pride
　　Over men's pity;
Left play for work, and grappled with the world　　　45
　　Bent on escaping:
"What's in the scroll," quoth he, "thou keepest furled?
　　Show me their shaping,
Theirs who most studied man, the bard and sage—
　　Give!"—So, he gowned him,[7]　　　　　　　50
Straight got by heart that book to its last page:
　　Learned, we found him.
Yea, but we found him bald too, eyes like lead,
　　Accents uncertain:
"Time to taste life," another would have said,　　　55
　　"Up with the curtain!"
This man said rather, "Actual life comes next?
　　Patience a moment!
Grant I have mastered learning's crabbed text,
　　Still there's the comment.[8]　　　　　　　60
Let me know all! Prate not of most or least,
　　Painful or easy!
Even to the crumbs I'd fain eat up the feast,
　　Aye, nor feel queasy."
Oh, such a life as he resolved to live,　　　　　65
　　When he had learned it,

---

5. Look out for!
6. God of music and embodiment of male beauty.
7. Dressed in academic gown; became a scholar.
8. Commentaries or annotations upon a text.

When he had gathered all books had to give!
    Sooner, he spurned it.
Image the whole, then execute the parts—
    Fancy the fabric   70
Quite, ere you build, ere steel strike fire from quartz,
    Ere mortar dab brick!

(Here's the town gate reached: there's the market place
    Gaping before us.)
Yea, this in him was the peculiar grace   75
    (Hearten our chorus!)
That before living he'd learn how to live—
    No end to learning:
Earn the means first—God surely will contrive
    Use for our earning.   80
Others mistrust and say, "But time escapes:
    Live now or never!"
He said, "What's time? Leave Now for dogs and apes!
    Man has Forever."
Back to his book then: deeper drooped his head: 85
    Calculus[9] racked him:
Leaden before, his eyes grew dross of lead:
    Tussis[1] attacked him.
"Now, master, take a little rest!"—not he!
    (Caution redoubled,   90
Step two abreast, the way winds narrowly!)
    Not a whit troubled
Back to his studies, fresher than at first,
    Fierce as a dragon
He (soul-hydroptic[2] with a sacred thirst)   95
    Sucked at the flagon.
Oh, if we draw a circle premature,
    Heedless of far gain,
Greedy for quick returns of profit, sure
    Bad is our bargain!   100
Was it not great? did not he throw on God
    (He loves the burthen)—
God's task to make the heavenly period
    Perfect the earthen?
Did not he magnify the mind, show clear   105
    Just what it all meant?
He would not discount life, as fools do here,
    Paid by installment.
He ventured neck or nothing—heaven's success
    Found, or earth's failure: 110
"Wilt thou trust death or not?" He answered "Yes:
    Hence with life's pale lure!"
That low man seeks a little thing to do,
    Sees it and does it:

9. A stone such as a gallstone.   2. Insatiably soul-thirsty.
1. A cough.

This high man, with a great thing to pursue, 115
    Dies ere he knows it.
That low man goes on adding one to one,
    His hundred's soon hit:
This high man, aiming at a million,
    Misses an unit.[3] 120
That, has the world here—should he need the next,
    Let the world mind him!
This, throws himself on God, and unperplexed
    Seeking shall find him.
So, with the throttling hands of death at strife, 125
    Ground he at grammar;
Still, through the rattle, parts of speech were rife:
    While he could stammer
He settled *Hoti's* business—let it be!—
    Properly based *Oun*— 130
Gave us the doctrine of the enclitic *De*,[4]
    Dead from the waist down.
Well, here's the platform, here's the proper place:
    Hail to your purlieus,
All ye highfliers of the feathered race, 135
    Swallows and curlews!
Here's the top peak; the multitude below
    Live, for they can, there:
This man decided not to Live but Know—
    Bury this man there? 140
Here—here's his place, where meteors shoot, clouds form,
    Lightnings are loosened,
Stars come and go! Let joy break with the storm,
    Peace let the dew send!
Lofty designs must close in like effects: 145
    Loftily lying,
Leave him—still loftier than the world suspects,
    Living and dying.

ca. 1854   1855

Confessions

1

What is he buzzing in my ears?
    "Now that I come to die,
Do I view the world as a vale of tears?"
    Ah, reverend sir, not I!

2

What I viewed there once, what I view again 5
    Where the physic bottles stand

---

3. A small item such as some trifling worldly pleasure.
4. *"Hoti," "Oun,"* and *"De"* are Greek particles meaning "that," "then," and "towards." An unaccented word such as *de* is "enclitic" when it affects the accentuation of a word adjacent to it.

On the table's edge—is a suburb lane,
    With a wall to my bedside hand.

3

That lane sloped, much as the bottles do,
    From a house you could descry   10
O'er the garden wall: is the curtain blue
    Or green to a healthy eye?

4

To mine, it serves for the old June weather
    Blue above lane and wall;
And that farthest bottle labeled "Ether"   15
    Is the house o'ertopping all.

5

At a terrace, somewhere near the stopper,
    There watched for me, one June,
A girl: I know, sir, it's improper,
    My poor mind's out of tune.   20

6

Only, there was a way . . . you crept
    Close by the side to dodge
Eyes in the house, two eyes except:
    They styled their house "The Lodge."

7

What right had a lounger up their lane?   25
    But, by creeping very close,
With the good wall's help—their eyes might strain
    And stretch themselves to O's,

8

Yet never catch her and me together,
    As she left the attic, there,   30
By the rim of the bottle labeled "Ether,"
    And stole from stair to stair,

9

And stood by the rose-wreathed gate. Alas,
    We loved, sir—used to meet:
How sad and bad and mad it was—   35
    But then, how it was sweet!

ca. 1859   1864

Youth and Art

1

It once might have been, once only:
    We lodged in a street together,
You, a sparrow on the housetop lonely,
    I, a lone she-bird of his feather.

2

Your trade was with sticks and clay, 5
    You thumbed, thrust, patted, and polished,
Then laughed, "They will see some day
    Smith made, and Gibson[1] demolished."

3

My business was song, song, song;
    I chirped, cheeped, trilled, and twittered, 10
"Kate Brown's on the boards ere long,
    And Grisi's[2] existence embittered!"

4

I earned no more by a warble
    Than you by a sketch in plaster;
You wanted a piece of marble, 15
    I needed a music master.

5

We studied hard in our styles,
    Chipped each at a crust like Hindoos,
For air looked out on the tiles,
    For fun watched each other's windows. 20

6

You lounged, like a boy of the South,
    Cap and blouse—nay, a bit of beard, too;
Or you got it, rubbing your mouth
    With fingers the clay adhered to.

7

And I—soon managed to find 25
    Weak points in the flower-fence facing,
Was forced to put up a blind
    And be safe in my corset lacing.

8

No harm! It was not my fault
    If you never turned your eye's tail up, 30
As I shook upon E *in alt*,[3]
    Or ran the chromatic scale up:

9

For spring bade the sparrows pair,
    And the boys and girls gave guesses,
And stalls in our street looked rare 35
    With bulrush and watercresses.

10

Why did not you pinch a flower
    In a pellet of clay and fling it?
Why did not I put a power
    Of thanks in a look, or sing it? 40

11

I did look, sharp as a lynx,
    (And yet the memory rankles)

1. John Gibson (1790–1866), English sculptor.
2. Giulia Grisi (1811–69), a famous Italian soprano.
3. High E.

When models arrived, some minx
    Tripped upstairs, she and her ankles.

12

But I think I gave you as good!   45
    "That foreign fellow—who can know
How she pays, in a playful mood,
    For his tuning her that piano?"

13

Could you say so, and never say
    "Suppose we join hands and fortunes,   50
And I fetch her from over the way,
    Her, piano, and long tunes and short tunes"?

14

No, no: you would not be rash,
    Nor I rasher and something over:
You've to settle yet Gibson's hash,   55
    And Grisi yet lives in clover.

15

But you meet the Prince[4] at the Board,
    I'm queen myself at *bals-paré*,[5]
I've married a rich old lord,
    And you're dubbed knight and an R. A.   60

16

Each life unfulfilled, you see;
    It hangs still, patchy and scrappy:
We have not sighed deep, laughed free,
    Starved, feasted, despaired—been happy.

17

And nobody calls you a dunce,   65
    And people suppose me clever:
This could but have happened once,
    And we missed it, lost it forever.

ca. 1860   1864

4. Perhaps Prince Albert, a patron of the arts. Now that the sculptor has acquired a title and is an "R. A." (a member of the respectable Royal Academy of Arts), he serves on committees or boards with the prince.
5. Fancy-dress balls.

Caliban upon Setebos Two closely related controversies of the Victorian period led Browning to write this poem (whose title means "Caliban's thoughts about Setebos"). The first, stimulated by Darwin, was concerned with man's origins and his relation to other animals (the poem teems with animal life; in 295 lines, as Park Honan has shown, there are 63 references to animals). Caliban, the half-man and half-monster of Shakespeare's *Tempest*, provided the poet with a model of how the mind of a primitive creature may operate. The second controversy concerned the nature of God and God's responsibility for the existence of suffering in the world. Like many men, Caliban thinks of God's nature as similar to his own. His anthropomorphic conception of the deity, whom he calls Setebos, is confined to what he has observed of life on his island and to what he has observed of himself. From the former derives his "natural theology," that is, his identifying the character of God from evidences provided by nature rather than from the evidence of supernatural revelation. From the latter, his observation of his own character, derives Caliban's conception of God's willful power. Caliban himself admires power and thinks of God in Calvinistic terms as a being who selects at random some creatures who are to be saved and others who are to be condemned to suffer. One critic, Patricia Ball, has ingeniously likened Caliban's views of the deity to those of the characters in *Waiting for Godot* by Samuel Beckett.

An obstacle for the reader is Caliban's use of the third person pronoun. He says that he "never speaks his mind save housed as now"—that is, he thinks if he is adequately hidden under the slush in his cave, the deity will not catch him thinking; he may remind us of the hero of George Orwell's 1984 trying to evade the Thought Police. But to make especially sure of not being caught, Caliban refers to himself in the third person. Thus " 'Will sprawl" means "Caliban will sprawl" (an apostrophe before the verb usually indicates that Caliban himself is the implied subject). When he feels that Setebos will not hear him, he then slips into the first person (e.g., line 56 or 68). The deity is also referred to in the third person but with an initial capital letter ("He").

Caliban upon Setebos

OR NATURAL THEOLOGY IN THE ISLAND

"Thou thoughtest that I was altogether such a one as thyself."[1]

> ['Will sprawl, now that the heat of day is best,
> Flat on his belly in the pit's much mire,
> With elbows wide, fists clenched to prop his chin.
> And, while he kicks both feet in the cool slush,
> And feels about his spine small eft-things[2] course,   5
> Run in and out each arm, and make him laugh:
> And while above his head a pompion plant,[3]
> Coating the cave-top as a brow its eye,
> Creeps down to touch and tickle hair and beard,
> And now a flower drops with a bee inside,   10
> And now a fruit to snap at, catch and crunch—
> He looks out o'er yon sea which sunbeams cross
> And recross till they weave a spider web
> (Meshes of fire, some great fish breaks at times)
> And talks to his own self, howe'er he please,   15
> Touching that other, whom his dam[4] called God.
> Because to talk about Him, vexes—ha,
> Could He but know! and time to vex is now,
> When talk is safer than in wintertime.
> Moreover Prosper[5] and Miranda sleep   20

1. Psalms 50:21. The speaker is God.
2. Water lizards.
3. Pumpkin plant.
4. Caliban's mother, Sycorax.

5. Prospero the magician, who is Caliban's master in *The Tempest*. Miranda is Prospero's daughter.

In confidence he drudges at their task,
And it is good to cheat the pair, and gibe,
Letting the rank tongue blossom into speech.]

Setebos, Setebos, and Setebos!
'Thinketh, He dwelleth i' the cold o' the moon.   25

'Thinketh He made it, with the sun to match,
But not the stars; the stars came otherwise;
Only made clouds, winds, meteors, such as that:
Also this isle, what lives and grows thereon,
And snaky sea which rounds and ends the same.   30

'Thinketh, it came of being ill at ease:
He hated that He cannot change His cold,
Nor cure its ache. 'Hath spied an icy fish
That longed to 'scape the rock-stream where she lived,
And thaw herself within the lukewarm brine   35
O' the lazy sea her stream thrusts far amid,
A crystal spike 'twixt two warm walls of wave;[6]
Only, she ever sickened, found repulse
At the other kind of water, not her life,
(Green-dense and dim-delicious, bred o' the sun)   40
Flounced back from bliss she was not born to breathe,
And in her old bounds buried her despair,
Hating and loving warmth alike: so He.

'Thinketh, He made thereat the sun, this isle,
Trees and the fowls here, beast and creeping thing.   45
Yon otter, sleek-wet, black, lithe as a leech;
Yon auk,[7] one fire-eye in a ball of foam,
That floats and feeds; a certain badger brown
He hath watched hunt with that slant white-wedge eye
By moonlight; and the pie[8] with the long tongue   50
That pricks deep into oakwarts for a worm,
And says a plain word when she finds her prize,
But will not eat the ants; the ants themselves
That build a wall of seeds and settled stalks
About their hole—He made all these and more,   55
Made all we see, and us, in spite: how else?
He could not, Himself, make a second self
To be His mate; as well have made Himself:
He would not make what he mislikes or slights,
An eyesore to Him, or not worth His pains: 60
But did, in envy, listlessness, or sport,
Make what Himself would fain, in a manner, be—
Weaker in most points, stronger in a few,
Worthy, and yet mere playthings all the while,
Things He admires and mocks too—that is it.   65

6. I.e., the thin stream of cold water   7. Sea bird.
which is driven into the warm ocean   8. Magpie.
like a spike between walls.

Because, so brave, so better though they be,
It nothing skills if He begin to plague.[9]
Look now, I melt a gourd-fruit into mash,
Add honeycomb and pods, I have perceived,
Which bite like finches when they bill and kiss— 70
Then, when froth rises bladdery,[1] drink up all,
Quick, quick, till maggots scamper through my brain;
Last, throw me on my back i' the seeded thyme,
And wanton, wishing I were born a bird.
Put case, unable to be what I wish, 75
I yet could make a live bird out of clay:
Would not I take clay, pinch my Caliban
Able to fly?—for, there, see, he hath wings,
And great comb like the hoopoe's[2] to admire,
And there, a sting to do his foes offense, 80
There, and I will that he begin to live,
Fly to yon rock-top, nip me off the horns
Of grigs[3] high up that make the merry din,
Saucy through their veined wings, and mind me not.
In which feat, if his leg snapped, brittle clay, 85
And he lay stupid-like—why, I should laugh;
And if he, spying me, should fall to weep,
Beseech me to be good, repair his wrong,
Bid his poor leg smart less or grow again—
Well, as the chance were, this might take or else 90
Not take my fancy: I might hear his cry,
And give the mankin three sound legs for one,
Or pluck the other off, leave him like an egg,
And lessoned he was mine and merely clay.
Were this no pleasure, lying in the thyme, 95
Drinking the mash, with brain become alive,
Making and marring clay at will? So He.

'Thinketh, such shows nor right nor wrong in Him,
Nor kind, nor cruel: He is strong and Lord.
'Am strong myself compared to yonder crabs 100
That march now from the mountain to the sea;
'Let twenty pass, and stone the twenty-first,
Loving not, hating not, just choosing so.
'Say, the first straggler that boasts purple spots
Shall join the file, one pincer twisted off; 105
'Say, this bruised fellow shall receive a worm,
And two worms he whose nippers end in red;
As it likes me each time, I do: so He.

Well then, 'supposeth He is good i' the main,
Placable if His mind and ways were guessed, 110
But rougher than His handiwork, be sure!

---

9. I.e., our superior virtues are of no
help to us if God elects to inflict plagues
upon us.

1. Bubbly.
2. Bird with bright plumage.
3. Grasshoppers.

Oh, He hath made things worthier than Himself,
And envieth that, so helped, such things do more
Than He who made them! What consoles but this?
That they, unless through Him, do naught at all,   115
And must submit: what other use in things?
'Hath cut a pipe of pithless elder-joint
That, blown through, gives exact the scream o' the jay
When from her wing you twitch the feathers blue:
Sound this, and little birds that hate the jay   120
Flock within stone's throw, glad their foe is hurt:
Put case such pipe could prattle and boast forsooth,
"I catch the birds, I am the crafty thing,
I make the cry my maker cannot make
With his great round mouth; he must blow through mine!"   125
Would not I smash it with my foot? So He.

But wherefore rough, why cold and ill at ease?
Aha, that is a question! Ask, for that,
What knows—the something over Setebos
That made Him, or He, may be, found and fought,   130
Worsted, drove off and did to nothing,[4] perchance.
There may be something quiet o'er His head,
Out of His reach, that feels nor joy nor grief,
Since both derive from weakness in some way.
I joy because the quails come; would not joy   135
Could I bring quails here when I have a mind:
This Quiet, all it hath a mind to, doth.
'Esteemeth stars the outposts of its couch,
But never spends much thought nor care that way.
It may look up, work up—the worse for those   140
It works on! 'Careth but for Setebos[5]
The many-handed as a cuttlefish,
Who, making Himself feared through what He does,
Looks up, first, and perceives he cannot soar
To what is quiet and hath happy life;   145
Next looks down here, and out of very spite
Makes this a bauble-world to ape yon real,
These good things to match those as hips[6] do grapes.
'Tis solace making baubles, aye, and sport.
Himself peeped late, eyed Prosper at his books   150
Careless and lofty, lord now of the isle:
Vexed, 'stitched a book of broad leaves, arrow-shaped,
Wrote thereon, he knows what, prodigious words;
Has peeled a wand and called it by a name;
Weareth at whiles for an enchanter's robe   155
The eyed skin of a supple oncelot;[7]

---

4. Completely overcame.
5. Caliban is concerned to appease only Setebos, not the other deity—the Quiet.
6. Hard fruits produced by wild roses.

7. Browning may have invented this term from the Spanish *oncela* or from the French *ocelot*. Both words signify a leopard or spotted wildcat.

And hath an ounce[8] sleeker than youngling mole,
A four-legged serpent he makes cower and couch,
Now snarl, now hold its breath and mind his eye,
And saith she is Miranda and my wife: 160
'Keeps for his Ariel[9] a tall pouch-bill crane
He bids go wade for fish and straight disgorge;
Also a sea beast, lumpish, which he snared,
Blinded the eyes of, and brought somewhat tame,
And split its toe-webs, and now pens the drudge   165
In a hole o' the rock and calls him Caliban;
A bitter heart that bides its time and bites.
'Plays thus at being Prosper in a way,
Taketh his mirth with make-believes: so He.

His dam held that the Quiet made all things   170
Which Setebos vexed only: 'holds not so.
Who made them weak, meant weakness He might vex.
Had He meant other, while His hand was in,
Why not make horny eyes no thorn could prick,
Or plate my scalp with bone against the snow,   175
Or overscale my flesh 'neath joint and joint,
Like an orc's[1] armor? Aye—so spoil His sport!
He is the One now: only He doth all.

'Saith, He may like, perchance, what profits Him.
Aye, himself loves what does him good; but why?   180
'Gets good no otherwise. This blinded beast
Loves whoso places flesh-meat on his nose,
But, had he eyes, would want no help, but hate
Or love, just as it liked him: He hath eyes.
Also it pleaseth Setebos to work,   185
Use all His hands, and exercise much craft,
By no means for the love of what is worked.
'Tasteth, himself, no finer good i' the world
When all goes right, in this safe summertime,
And he wants little, hungers, aches not much,   190
Than trying what to do with wit and strength.
'Falls to make something: 'piled yon pile of turfs,
And squared and stuck there squares of soft white chalk,
And, with a fish-tooth, scratched a moon on each,
And set up endwise certain spikes of tree,   195
And crowned the whole with a sloth's skull a-top,
Found dead i' the woods, too hard for one to kill.
No use at all i' the work, for work's sole sake;
'Shall some day knock it down again: so He.

'Saith He is terrible: watch His feats in proof!   200
One hurricane will spoil six good months' hope.
He hath a spite against me, that I know,

8. A large, ferocious leopard, six or
seven feet in length.
9. In *The Tempest*, a spirit who serves

Prospero.
1. Killer whale's.

Just as He favors Prosper, who knows why?
So it is, all the same, as well I find.
'Wove wattles half the winter, fenced them firm   205
With stone and stake to stop she-tortoises
Crawling to lay their eggs here: well, one wave,
Feeling the foot of Him upon its neck,
Gaped as a snake does, lolled out its large tongue,
And licked the whole labor flat; so much for spite.   210
'Saw a ball[2] flame down late (yonder it lies)
Where, half an hour before, I slept i' the shade:
Often they scatter sparkles: there is force!
'Dug up a newt He may have envied once
And turned to stone, shut up inside a stone.   215
Please Him and hinder this?—What Prosper does?[3]
Aha, if He would tell me how! Not He!
There is the sport: discover how or die!
All need not die, for of the things o' the isle
Some flee afar, some dive, some run up trees;   220
Those at His mercy—why, they please Him most
When . . . when . . . well, never try the same way twice!
Repeat what act has pleased, He may grow wroth.
You must not know His ways, and play Him off,
Sure of the issue. 'Doth the like himself: 225
'Spareth a squirrel that it nothing fears
But steals the nut from underneath my thumb,
And when I threat, bites stoutly in defense:
'Spareth an urchin[4] that contrariwise
Curls up into a ball, pretending death   230
For fright at my approach: the two ways please.
But what would move my choler more than this,
That either creature counted on its life
Tomorrow and next day and all days to come,
Saying, forsooth, in the inmost of its heart,   235
"Because he did so yesterday with me,
And otherwise with such another brute,
So must he do henceforth and always."—Aye?
Would teach the reasoning couple what "must" means!
'Doth as he likes, or wherefore Lord? So He.   240

'Conceiveth all things will continue thus,
And we shall have to live in fear of Him
So long as He lives, keeps His strength: no change,
If He have done His best, make no new world
To please Him more, so leave off watching this—   245
If He surprise not even the Quiet's self
Some strange day—or, suppose, grow into it
As grubs grow butterflies: else, here are we,
And there is He, and nowhere help at all.

2. Meteorite.
3. I.e., shall I please Setebos, as
Prospero does, and thus prevent my
being punished as the newt was punished?
4. Hedgehog.

'Believeth with the life, the pain shall stop.   250
His dam held different, that after death
He both plagued enemies and feasted friends:
Idly!⁵ He doth His worst in this our life,
Giving just respite lest we die through pain,
Saving last pain for worst—with which, an end.   255
Meanwhile, the best way to escape His ire
Is, not to seem too happy. 'Sees, himself,
Yonder two flies, with purple films and pink,
Bask on the pompion-bell above: kills both.
'Sees two black painful beetles roll their ball   260
On head and tail as if to save their lives:
Moves them the stick away they strive to clear.

Even so, 'would have Him misconceive, suppose
This Caliban strives hard and ails no less,
And always, above all else, envies Him;   265
Wherefore he mainly dances on dark nights,
Moans in the sun, gets under holes to laugh,
And never speaks his mind save housed as now:
Outside, 'groans, curses. If He caught me here,
O'erheard this speech, and asked "What chucklest at?"   270
'Would, to appease Him, cut a finger off,
Or of my three kid yearlings burn the best,
Or let the toothsome apples rot on tree,
Or push my tame beast for the orc to taste:
While myself lit a fire, and made a song   275
And sung it, *"What I hate, be consecrate*
To celebrate Thee and Thy state, no mate
For Thee; what see for envy in poor me?"
Hoping the while, since evils sometimes mend,
Warts rub away and sores are cured with slime,   280
That some strange day, will either the Quiet catch
And conquer Setebos, or likelier He
Decrepit may doze, doze, as good as die.

———————

[What, what? A curtain o'er the world at once!
Crickets stop hissing; not a bird—or, yes,   285
There scuds His raven that has told Him all!
It was fool's play this prattling! Ha! The wind
Shoulders the pillared dust, death's house o' the move,
And fast invading fires begin! White blaze—
A tree's head snaps—and there, there, there, there, there,   290
His thunder follows! Fool to gibe at Him!
Lo! 'Lieth flat and loveth Setebos!
'Maketh his teeth meet through his upper lip,

---

5. I.e., Caliban thinks his mother's   with man is confined to this world;
opinion was wrong or idle. God's sport   there is no afterlife.

Will let those quails fly, will not eat this month
    One little mess of whelks,[6] so he may 'scape!]   295
ca. 1860   1864

Prospice[7]

Fear death?—to feel the fog in my throat,
    The mist in my face,
When the snows begin, and the blasts denote
    I am nearing the place,
The power of the night, the press of the storm,   5
    The post of the foe;
Where he stands, the Arch Fear in a visible form,
    Yet the strong man must go:
For the journey is done and the summit attained,
    And the barriers fall,   10
Though a battle's to fight ere the guerdon be gained,
    The reward of it all.
I was ever a fighter, so—one fight more,
    The best and the last!
I would hate that death bandaged my eyes, and forbore,   15
    And bade me creep past.
No! let me taste the whole of it, fare like my peers
    The heroes of old,
Bear the brunt, in a minute pay glad life's arrears
    Of pain, darkness, and cold.   20
For sudden the worst turns the best to the brave,
    The black minute's at end,
And the elements' rage, the fiend-voices that rave,
    Shall dwindle, shall blend,
Shall change, shall become first a peace out of pain,   25
    Then a light, then thy breast,
O thou soul of my soul![8] I shall clasp thee again,
    And with God be the rest!
ca. 1861   1864

Abt Vogler[1]

(AFTER HE HAS BEEN EXTEMPORIZING UPON THE MUSICAL INSTRUMENT OF HIS INVENTION)

1

Would that the structure brave, the manifold music I build,
    Bidding my organ obey, calling its keys to their work,

6. Shellfish.
7. The title means "Look forward."
8. Browning's wife.
1. Georg Joseph Vogler (1749–1814),

a German priest and musician, held the honorary title of *Abbé* or *Abt*. As a composer, teacher, and designer of musical instruments he was well known

Claiming each slave of the sound, at a touch, as when Solomon
    willed
    Armies of angels that soar, legions of demons that lurk,
Man, brute, reptile, fly—alien of end and of aim,   5
    Adverse, each from the other heaven-high, hell-deep removed—
Should rush into sight at once as he named the ineffable Name,[2]
    And pile him a palace straight, to pleasure the princess he
    loved!

2

Would it might tarry like his, the beautiful building of mine,
    This which my keys in a crowd pressed and importuned to
    raise!   10
Ah, one and all, how they helped, would dispart now and now com-
    bine,
    Zealous to hasten the work, heighten their master his praise!
And one would bury his brow with a blind plunge down to hell,
    Burrow awhile and build, broad on the roots of things,
Then up again swim into sight, having based me my palace well,   15
    Founded it, fearless of flame, flat on the nether springs.

3

And another would mount and march, like the excellent minion he
    was,
    Aye, another and yet another, one crowd but with many a crest,
Raising my rampired walls of gold as transparent as glass,
    Eager to do and die, yield each his place to the rest: 20
For higher still and higher (as a runner tips with fire,
    When a great illumination surprises a festal night—
Outlining round and round Rome's dome from space to spire)[3]
    Up, the pinnacled glory reached, and the pride of my soul was
    in sight.

4

In sight? Not half! for it seemed, it was certain, to match man's
    birth,   25
    Nature in turn conceived, obeying an impulse as I;
And the emulous heaven yearned down, made effort to reach the
    earth,
    As the earth had done her best, in my passion, to scale the sky:

---

in his own day, but he was most famous
as an extemporizer at the organ. Browning's soliloquy represents Vogler at
the organ joyfully improvising a piece
of music and then reflecting upon the
ephemeral existence of such a unique
work of art and of its possible relation
to God's purposes in heaven and on
earth. In this connection, a suggestive
comparison can be made between Browning's conception of a palace of music
inhabited by the "wonderful Dead" and
W. B. Yeats's conception of a heaven
of art in his Byzantium poems.

    A characteristic feature of *Abt Vogler*
is the use of exceptionally long sentences, densely packed with details,
which may evoke for us the effects of
rolling organ music. The resulting movement is markedly different from the brisk
staccato rhythms of *A Toccata of
Galuppi's*.
    The "musical instrument of his in-
vention" is a compact organ called the
Orchestrion.
2. According to Jewish legend, King
Solomon (because he possessed a seal
inscribed with the "ineffable Name" of
God) had the power of compelling the
demons of earth and air to perform his
bidding.
3. On festival nights the dome of St.
Peter's in Rome is illuminated by a series
of lights ignited by a torchbearer.

Novel splendors burst forth, grew familiar and dwelt with mine,
    Not a point nor peak but found and fixed its wandering star; 30
Meteor-moons, balls of blaze: and they did not pale nor pine,
    For earth had attained to heaven, there was no more near nor
      far.

5

Nay more; for there wanted not who walked in the glare and glow,
    Presences plain in the place; or, fresh from the Protoplast,[4]
Furnished for ages to come, when a kindlier wind should blow, 35
    Lured now to begin and live, in a house to their liking at last;
Or else the wonderful Dead who have passed through the body and
      gone,
    But were back once more to breathe in an old world worth
      their new:
What never had been, was now; what was, as it shall be anon;
    And what is—shall I say, matched both? for I was made per-
      fect too.
        40

6

All through my keys that gave their sounds to a wish of my soul,
    All through my soul that praised as its wish flowed visibly forth,
All through music and me! For think, had I painted the whole,
    Why, there it had stood, to see, nor the process so wonder-
      worth:
Had I written the same, made verse—still, effect proceeds from
      cause,
        45
    Ye know why the forms are fair, ye hear how the tale is told;
It is all triumphant art, but art in obedience to laws,
    Painter and poet are proud in the artist-list enrolled—

7

But here is the finger of God, a flash of the will that can,
    Existent behind all laws, that made them and, lo, they are! 50
And I know not if, save in this, such gift be allowed to man,
    That out of three sounds he frame, not a fourth sound, but a
      star.[5]
Consider it well: each tone of our scale in itself is naught;
    It is everywhere in the world—loud, soft, and all is said:
Give it to me to use! I mix it with two in my thought:
        55
    And, there! Ye have heard and seen: consider and bow the
      head!

8

Well, it is gone at last, the palace of music I reared;
    Gone! and the good tears start, the praises that come too slow;
For one is assured at first, one scarce can say that he feared,
    That he even gave it a thought, the gone thing was to go. 60
Never to be again! But many more of the kind
    As good, nay, better perchance: is this your comfort to me?

---

4. The original or archetypal form of
a species. The "presences" from this
source are beings of the future, not
yet existing, who are "lured" into life
by the music. Cf. *Women and Roses*,
stanzas 7 and 8.

5. I.e., the musician's combining of
three notes into a new harmonic unit
is a creative act as miraculous as the
creation of a star.

To me, who must be saved because I cling with my mind
  To the same, same self, same love, same God: aye, what was,
    shall be.

                                   9
Therefore to whom turn I but to thee, the ineffable Name?   65
  Builder and maker, thou, of houses not made with hands![6]
What, have fear of change from thee who art ever the same?
  Doubt that thy power can fill the heart that thy power expands?
There shall never be one lost good! What was, shall live as before;
  The evil is null, is naught, is silence implying sound;   70
What was good shall be good, with, for evil, so much good more;
  On the earth the broken arcs; in the heaven, a perfect round.

                                  10
All we have willed or hoped or dreamed of good shall exist;
  Not its semblance, but itself; no beauty, nor good, nor power
Whose voice has gone forth, but each survives for the melodist   75
  When eternity affirms the conception of an hour.
The high that proved too high, the heroic for earth too hard,
  The passion that left the ground to lose itself in the sky,
Are music sent up to God by the lover and the bard;
  Enough that he heard it once: we shall hear it by-and-by.   80

                                  11
And what is our failure here but a triumph's evidence
  For the fullness of the days? Have we withered or agonized?
Why else was the pause prolonged but that singing might issue
    thence?
  Why rushed the discords in but that harmony should be
    prized?
Sorrow is hard to bear, and doubt is slow to clear,   85
  Each sufferer says his say, his scheme of the weal and woe:
But God has a few of us whom he whispers in the ear;
  The rest may reason and welcome: 'tis we musicians know.

                                  12
Well, it is earth with me; silence resumes her reign:
  I will be patient and proud, and soberly acquiesce.   90
Give me the keys. I feel for the common chord again,
  Sliding by semitones, till I sink to the minor—yes,
And I blunt it into a ninth, and I stand on alien ground,
  Surveying awhile the heights I rolled from into the deep;
Which, hark, I have dared and done, for my resting place is
    found,   95
  The C Major of this life:[7] so, now I will try to sleep.

                                                          1864

6. See II Corinthians v.1, in which St.
Paul speaks of "a building of God, an
house not made with hands, eternal in the
heavens."
7. Vogler's last moments of playing express first his sadness that he cannot
remain forever among the "heights" of
the music he has temporarily created,
and afterwards his acceptance of this
return to man's ordinary existence.
Thus he plays in a "minor" key, pauses
for a short space on the "alien ground"
of a "ninth" (a discord which requires
a resolution), and finally concludes in
"C Major," a key without sharps or
flats and representing the plane of ordinary life.

Dis Aliter Visum; Or, Le Byron de Nos Jours[1]

I

Stop, let me have the truth of that!
  Is that all true? I say, the day
Ten years ago when both of us
    Met on a morning, friends—as thus
We meet this evening, friends or what?—   5

II

Did you—because I took your arm
  And sillily smiled, "A mass of brass
That sea looks, blazing underneath!"
    While up the cliff-road edged with heath,
We took the turns nor came to harm—   10

III

Did you consider "Now makes twice
  That I have seen her, walked and talked
With this poor pretty thoughtful thing,
    Whose worth I weigh: she tries to sing;
Draws, hopes in time the eye grows nice;[2]   15

IV

"Reads verse and thinks she understands;
  Loves all, at any rate, that's great,
Good, beautiful; but much as we
    Down at the bath-house love the sea,
Who breathe its salt and bruise its sands: 20

V

"While . . . do but follow the fishing-gull
  That flaps and floats from wave to cave!

1. The first half of the title, from Virgil's *Aeneid* II.428, is a comment on the slaying of a good man who seemingly deserved a better fate but "the gods willed it otherwise." The second half of the title presumably points up the difference between Byron's impetuous conduct as a lover and the timid behavior of the poet who is his latter-day successor, the Byron of *our* days. At least two 19th-century French poets had been called the French Byron (Alphonse Lamartine and Alfred de Musset), but Browning does not seem to have had a special model in mind.
This monologue is Browning's most complex treatment of a situation frequently recurrent in his poems: that of a person, late in life, who looks back on a lost opportunity of establishing a love-relationship. The speaker, a woman in her early thirties, encounters an elderly French poet with whom she had fallen in love ten years earlier. At the hotel on the coast of France where they meet, as the poem opens, the poet has been reminding her of their previous acquaintance. She stops his narrative to offer her own vehemently expressed version of why he had rejected the chance of loving her as a young girl. Her analysis of his motives involves her imagining what his thoughts had been ten years earlier, and these imagined thoughts include speeches that he supposes *she* might make. The woman not only recreates the situation but passes judgment on the poet's failure. Because her indictment of him is expressed in terms that echo ideas of love and heaven frequently expressed in other poems by Browning, we get the impression that she is the author's spokeswoman, but this impression is complicated by our judgment of the distortion imposed by the intensity of her hatred. Was she incipiently this shrewish ten years earlier, we wonder, or was her present character shaped by that disillusioning experience and by the incompatible marriage she has made in the interval?
2. Discriminating.

There's the sea-lover, fair my friend![3]
   What then? Be patient, mark and mend!
Had you the making of your skull?"   25

VI

And did you, when we faced the church
   With spire and sad slate roof, aloof
From human fellowship so far,
   Where a few graveyard crosses are,
And garlands for the swallows' perch,—   30

VII

Did you determine, as we stepped
   O'er the lone stone fence, "Let me get
Her for myself, and what's the earth
   With all its art, verse, music, worth—
Compared with love, found, gained, and kept?   35

VIII

"Schumann's our music-maker now;
   Has his march-movement youth and mouth?
Ingres's the modern man that paints;
   Which will lean on me, of his saints?
Heine[4] for songs; for kisses, how?"   40

IX

And did you, when we entered, reached
   The votive frigate,[5] soft aloft
Riding on air this hundred years,
   Safe-smiling at old hopes and fears,—
Did you draw profit while she preached?   45

X

Resolving, "Fools we wise men grow!
   Yes, I could easily blurt out curt
Some question that might find reply
   As prompt in her stopped lips, dropped eye,
And rush of red to cheek and brow: 50

XI

"Thus were a match made, sure and fast,
   'Mid the blue weed-flowers round the mound
Where, issuing, we shall stand and stay
   For one more look at baths and bay,
Sands, seagulls, and the old church last—   55

XII

"A match 'twixt me, bent, wigged and lamed,
   Famous, however, for verse and worse,

---

3. The poet thinks that the amateurish quality of the girl's involvement with art and literature is similar to the bathers' relative ignorance of the true nature of the sea. The bathers are acquainted only with the sea's fringes, as contrasted with the gull, who is fully immersed in his element.
4. Heinrich Heine (1800–1856), poet; Robert Schumann (1810–1856) com-
poser; Jean August Ingres (1780–1867), painter. Cf. *The Last Ride Together*, stanzas 7 and 8.
5. Model of a ship hanging in the church as a thanksgiving offering for the safe return of sailors from a stormy voyage. The ship "preached" assurances to the man about the possible risks involved in a relationship with the girl.

Sure of the Fortieth spare Armchair[6]
  When gout and glory seat me there,
So, one whose love-freaks pass unblamed,—   60
          XIII

"And this young beauty, round and sound
  As a mountain-apple, youth and truth
With loves and doves, at all events
  With money in the Three per Cents;[7]
Whose choice of me would seem profound:—   65
          XIV

"She might take me as I take her.
  Perfect the hour would pass, alas!
Climb high, love high, what matter? Still,
  Feet, feelings, must descend the hill:
An hour's perfection can't recur.   70
          XV

"Then follows Paris and full time
  For both to reason: 'Thus with us!'[8]
She'll sigh, 'Thus girls give body and soul
  At first word, think they gain the goal,
When 'tis the starting-place they climb!   75
          XVI

" 'My friend makes verse and gets renown;
  Have they all fifty years, his peers?
He knows the world, firm, quiet and gay;
  Boys will become as much one day:
They're fools; he cheats, with beard less brown.   80
          XVII

" 'For boys say, *Love me or I die!*
  He did not say, *The truth is, youth
I want, who am old and know too much;*
  I'd catch youth: lend me sight and touch!
Drop heart's blood where life's wheels grate dry!'   85
          XVIII

"While I should make rejoinder"—(then
  It was, no doubt, you ceased that least
Light pressure of my arm in yours)
  " 'I can conceive of cheaper cures
For a yawning-fit o'er books and men.   90
          XIX

" 'What? All I am, was, and might be,
  All, books taught, art brought, life's whole strife,

---

6. One of the 40 seats in the French Academy to which famous writers are elected when a vacancy occurs through death of a member.
7. Her private income is from safe investments in government bonds.
8. The man imagines what they would say or think of each other if, after their "hour's perfection," they descended to the everyday realities of living in Paris together. What she *might* have said (stanzas 15–18) leads to his resolution to break off the relationship.

Painful results since precious, just
   Were fitly exchanged, in wise disgust,
For two cheeks freshened by youth and sea?   95

XX

" 'All for a nosegay!—what came first;
   With fields on flower, untried each side;
I rally, need my books and men,
   And find a nosegay': drop it, then,
No match yet made for best or worst!"   100

XXI

That ended me. You judged the porch
   We left by, Norman; took our look
At sea and sky; wondered so few
   Find out the place for air and view;
Remarked the sun began to scorch;   105

XXII

Descended, soon regained the baths,
   And then, good-bye! Years ten since then:
Ten years! We meet: you tell me, now,
   By a window-seat for that cliff-brow,
On carpet-stripes for those sand-paths.   110

XXIII

Now I may speak: you fool, for all
   Your lore! WHO made things plain in vain?
What was the sea for? What, the gray
   Sad church, that solitary day,
Crosses and graves and swallows' call?   115

XXIV

Was there naught better than to enjoy?
   No feat which, done, would make time break,
And let us pent-up creatures through
   Into eternity, our due?
No forcing earth teach heaven's employ?   120

XXV

No wise beginning, here and now,
   What cannot grow complete (earth's feat)
And heaven must finish,[9] there and then?
   No tasting earth's true food for men,
Its sweet in sad, its sad in sweet?   125

XXVI

No grasping at love, gaining a share
   O' the sole spark from God's life at strife
With death, so, sure of range above
   The limits here? For us and love,
Failure; but, when God fails, despair.[1]   130

---

9. Cf. *Abt Vogler*, line 72: "On the earth the broken arcs; in the heaven, a perfect round."
1. To believe that love, because imper-fect, is not worth the risk is a denial of God's role, a blasphemy. Cf. *A Grammarian's Funeral*, line 10.

XXVII

This you call wisdom? Thus you add
  Good unto good again, in vain?
You loved, with body worn and weak;
  I loved, with faculties to seek:
Were both loves worthless since ill-clad?   135

XXVIII

Let the mere starfish in his vault
  Crawl in a wash of weed, indeed,
Rose-jacynth to the fingertips:
  He, whole in body and soul, outstrips
Man, found with either in default.[2]   140

XXIX

But what's whole, can increase no more,
  Is dwarfed and dies, since here's its sphere.
The devil laughed at you in his sleeve!
  You knew not? That I well believe;
Or you had saved two souls: nay, four.   145

XXX

For Stephanie sprained last night her wrist,
  Ankle or something. "Pooh," cry you?
At any rate she danced, all say,
  Vilely; her vogue has had its day.
Here comes my husband from his whist.   150

ca. 1862   1864

Rabbi Ben Ezra[1]

1

Grow old along with me!
  The best is yet to be,
The last of life, for which the first was made:
  Our times are in His hand
  Who saith, "A whole I planned,   5
Youth shows but half; trust God: see all nor be afraid!"

2

Not that, amassing flowers,
  Youth sighed, "Which rose make ours,
Which lily leave and then as best recall?"

2. In its perfect adaptation to a limited earthly environment the starfish "outstrips" man. Man's distinctive role, by contrast, is to aspire to the unobtainable.
1. The speaker, Abraham Ibn Ezra (ca. 1092–1167), was an eminent Biblical scholar of Spain, but Browning makes little attempt to present him as a distinct individual or to relate him to the age in which he lived. Unlike the more characteristic monologues, *Rabbi Ben Ezra* is not dramatic but declamatory.

Not that, admiring stars,   10
  It yearned, "Nor Jove, nor Mars;
Mine be some figured flame which blends, transcends them all!"

3

  Not for such hopes and fears
  Annulling youth's brief years,
Do I remonstrate: folly wide the mark!   15
  Rather I prize the doubt
  Low kinds exist without,
Finished and finite clods, untroubled by a spark.

4

  Poor vaunt of life indeed,
  Were man but formed to feed   20
On joy, to solely seek and find and feast:
  Such feasting ended, then
  As sure an end to men;
Irks care the crop-full bird? Frets doubt the maw-crammed beast?[2]

5

  Rejoice we are allied   25
  To That which doth provide
And not partake, effect and not receive!
  A spark disturbs our clod;
  Nearer we hold of God
Who gives, than of His tribes that take, I must believe.   30

6

  Then, welcome each rebuff
  That turns earth's smoothness rough,
Each sting that bids nor sit nor stand but go!
  Be our joys three parts pain!
  Strive, and hold cheap the strain;   35
Learn, nor account the pang; dare, never grudge the throe![3]

7

  For thence—a paradox
  Which comforts while it mocks—
Shall life succeed in that it seems to fail:
  What I aspired to be,   40
  And was not, comforts me:
A brute I might have been, but would not sink i' the scale.

8

  What is he but a brute
  Whose flesh has soul to suit,
Whose spirit works lest arms and legs want play?   45
  To man, propose this test—
  Thy body at its best,
How far can that project thy soul on its lone way?

---

2. I.e., does care disturb a bird whose gullet ("crop") is full of food? does doubt trouble an animal whose stomach ("maw") is full?
3. Anguish.

9

Yet gifts should prove their use:
I own the Past profuse
Of power each side, perfection every turn:
Eyes, ears took in their dole,
Brain treasured up the whole;
Should not the heart beat once, "How good to live and learn"?   50

10

Not once beat, "Praise be Thine!
I see the whole design,   55
I, who saw power, see now love perfect too:
Perfect I call Thy plan:
Thanks that I was a man!
Maker, remake, complete—I trust what Thou shalt do!"   60

11

For pleasant is this flesh;
Our soul, in its rose-mesh[4]
Pulled ever to the earth, still yearns for rest;
Would we some prize might hold
To match those manifold   65
Possessions of the brute—gain most, as we did best!

12

Let us not always say,
"Spite of this flesh today
I strove, made head, gained ground upon the whole!"
As the bird wings and sings,   70
Let us cry, "All good things
Are ours, nor soul helps flesh more, now, than flesh helps soul!"

13

Therefore I summon age
To grant youth's heritage,
Life's struggle having so far reached its term: 75
Thence shall I pass, approved
A man, for aye removed
From the developed brute; a god though in the germ.

14

And I shall thereupon
Take rest, ere I be gone   80
Once more on my adventure brave and new:[5]
Fearless and unperplexed,
When I wage battle next,
What weapons to select, what armor to indue.[6]

15

Youth ended, I shall try   85
My gain or loss thereby;

4. The body, which holds the soul in
its net.

5. In the next life.
6. Put on.

Leave the fire ashes,[7] what survives is gold:
    And I shall weigh the same,
    Give life its praise or blame:
Young, all lay in dispute; I shall know, being old.   90

16

    For note, when evening shuts,
    A certain moment cuts
The deed off, calls the glory from the gray:
    A whisper from the west
    Shoots—"Add this to the rest,   95
Take it and try its worth: here dies another day."

17

    So, still within this life,
    Though lifted o'er its strife,
Let me discern, compare, pronounce at last,
    "This rage was right i' the main,
    That acquiescence vain: 100
The Future I may face now I have proved the Past."

18

    For more is not reserved
    To man, with soul just nerved
To act tomorrow what he learns today: 105
    Here, work enough to watch
    The Master work, and catch
Hints of the proper craft, tricks of the tool's true play.

19

    As it was better, youth
    Should strive, through acts uncouth,   110
Toward making, than repose on aught found made:
    So, better, age, exempt
    From strife, should know, than tempt[8]
Further. Thou waitedst age: wait death nor be afraid!

20

    Enough now, if the Right   115
    And Good and Infinite
Be named here, as thou callest thy hand thine own,
    With knowledge absolute,
    Subject to no dispute
From fools that crowded youth, nor let thee feel alone.[9]   120

21

    Be there, for once and all,
    Severed great minds from small,
Announced to each his station in the Past!
    Was I, the world arraigned,[1]

---

7. If the fire leaves ashes.
8. Attempt.
9. Stanzas 20 and 21 affirm that in age we can more readily think independently than in youth. Maturity enables us to ignore the pressure of having to conform to the thinking of the crowd of small-minded people.
1. Was I, whom the world arraigned.

Were they, my soul disdained,
Right? Let age speak the truth and give us peace at last!

22

Now, who shall arbitrate?
Ten men love what I hate,
Shun what I follow, slight what I receive;
Ten, who in ears and eyes
Match me: we all surmise,
They this thing, and I that: whom shall my soul believe?

23

Not on the vulgar mass
Called "work," must sentence pass,
Things done, that took the eye and had the price;
O'er which, from level stand,
The low world laid its hand,
Found straightway to its mind, could value in a trice:

24

But all, the world's coarse thumb
And finger failed to plumb,
So passed in making up the main account;
All instincts immature,
All purposes unsure,
That weighed not as his work, yet swelled the man's amount:

25

Thoughts hardly to be packed
Into a narrow act,
Fancies that broke through language and escaped;
All I could never be,
All, men ignored in me,
This, I was worth to God, whose wheel[2] the pitcher shaped.

26

Aye, note that Potter's wheel,
That metaphor! and feel
Why time spins fast, why passive lies our clay—
Thou, to whom fools propound,[3]
When the wine makes its round,
"Since life fleets, all is change; the Past gone, seize today!"

27

Fool! All that is, at all,
Lasts ever, past recall;
Earth changes, but thy soul and God stand sure:
What entered into thee,
That was, is, and shall be:
Time's wheel runs back or stops: Potter and clay endure.

125

130

135

140

145

150

155

160

---

2. The potting-wheel on which the
speaker's highest qualities of soul were
shaped into an enduring "pitcher" by
God. See Isaiah lxiv.8.
3. Perhaps addressed to Omar Khay-

yám, whose poem, *The Rubáiyát*, urged
men to eat, drink, and be merry. Edward FitzGerald's translation of Omar's
poem had appeared in 1859.

28

He fixed thee 'mid this dance
 Of plastic circumstance,
This Present, thou, forsooth, wouldst fain arrest:[4]   165
 Machinery just meant
 To give thy soul its bent,
Try thee and turn thee forth, sufficiently impressed.

29

 What though the earlier grooves
 Which ran the laughing loves   170
Around thy base,[5] no longer pause and press?
 What though, about thy rim,
 Skull-things in order grim
Grow out, in graver mood, obey the sterner stress?

30

 Look not thou down but up!   175
 To uses of a cup,
The festal board, lamp's flash, and trumpet's peal,
 The new wine's foaming flow,
 The Master's lips a-glow!
Thou, heaven's consummate cup, what need'st thou with earth's
   wheel?   180

31

 But I need, now as then,
 Thee, God, who moldest men;
And since, not even while the whirl was worst,
 Did I—to the wheel of life
 With shapes and colors rife,   185
Bound dizzily—mistake my end, to slake Thy thirst:

32

 So, take and use Thy work:
 Amend what flaws may lurk,
What strain o' the stuff, what warpings past the aim!
 My times be in Thy hand!   190
 Perfect the cup as planned!
Let age approve of youth, and death complete the same!
ca. 1862   1864

Apparent Failure

"We shall soon lose a celebrated building."
    PARIS NEWSPAPER

1

No, for I'll save it! Seven years since,
 I passed through Paris, stopped a day
 To see the baptism of your Prince;[1]

4. I.e., you would be glad to stop ("arrest") time at this present point of your life.
5. Base of the clay pitcher.

1. Prince Louis, son of Napoleon III, was baptized in June, 1856. Browning had witnessed the event.

Saw, made my bow, and went my way:
Walking the heat and headache off,   5
    I took the Seine-side, you surmise,
Thought of the Congress, Gortschakoff,
    Cavour's appeal and Buol's replies,[2]
So sauntered till—what met my eyes?

2

Only the Doric little Morgue!   10
    The dead-house where you show your drowned:
Petrarch's Vaucluse makes proud the Sorgue,[3]
    Your Morgue has made the Seine renowned.
One pays one's debt in such a case;
    I plucked up heart and entered—stalked,   15
Keeping a tolerable face
    Compared with some whose cheeks were chalked:
Let them! No Briton's to be balked!

3

First came the silent gazers; next,
    A screen of glass, we're thankful for;   20
Last, the sight's self, the sermon's text,
    The three men who did most abhor
Their life in Paris yesterday,
    So killed themselves: and now, enthroned
Each on his copper couch, they lay   25
    Fronting me, waiting to be owned.
I thought, and think, their sin's atoned.

4

Poor men, God made, and all for that!
    The reverence struck me; o'er each head
Religiously was hung its hat,   30
    Each coat dripped by the owner's bed,
Sacred from touch: each had his berth,
    His bounds, his proper place of rest,
Who last night tenanted on earth
    Some arch, where twelve such slept abreast—   35
Unless the plain asphalt seemed best.

5

How did it happen, my poor boy?
    You wanted to be Buonaparte
And have the Tuileries[4] for toy,
    And could not, so it broke your heart?   40
You, old one by his side, I judge,
    Were, red as blood, a socialist,
A leveler! Does the Empire grudge
    You've gained what no Republic missed?
Be quiet, and unclench your fist!   45

2. The Congress of Paris which met in 1856 to establish peace terms after the Crimean War. Russia was represented by Prince Alexander Gortschakoff, Piedmont by Count Cavour, and Austria by Count von Buol-Schauenstein.
3. The Sorgue River is renowned because the poet Petrarch lived in Vaucluse, a village on its banks.
4. The palace in Paris where the kings of France had resided.

6

And this—why, he was red in vain,
  Or black[5]—poor fellow that is blue!
What fancy was it turned your brain?
  Oh, women were the prize for you!
Money gets women, cards and dice   50
  Get money, and ill luck gets just
The copper couch and one clear nice
  Cool squirt of water o'er your bust,
The right thing to extinguish lust!

7

It's wiser being good than bad;   55
  It's safer being meek than fierce:
It's fitter being sane than mad.
  My own hope is, a sun will pierce
The thickest cloud earth ever stretched;
  That, after Last, returns the First,   60
Though a wide compass round be fetched;
  That what began best, can't end worst,
Nor what God blessed once, prove accursed.

1863   1864

O Lyric Love[1]

O lyric Love, half angel and half bird
And all a wonder and a wild desire—
Boldest of hearts that ever braved the sun,
Took sanctuary within the holier blue,
And sang a kindred soul out to his face—   5
Yet human at the red-ripe of the heart—
When the first summons from the darkling earth
Reached thee amid thy chambers, blanched their blue,
And bared them of the glory—to drop down,
To toil for man, to suffer or to die—   10
This is the same voice: can thy soul know change?
Hail then, and hearken from the realms of help!
Never may I commence my song, my due
To God who best taught song by gift of thee,
Except with bent head and beseeching hand—   15
That still, despite the distance and the dark,
What was, again may be; some interchange
Of grace, some splendor once thy very thought,
Some benediction anciently thy smile:
—Never conclude, but raising hand and head   20
Thither where eyes, that cannot reach, yet yearn

5. Reference to a gambling game, *rouge-et-noir*, in which red or black may win the stakes.
1. These lines, which conclude Book I of *The Ring and the Book*, are addressed to the poet's wife, who had died in 1861. Ten out of the twelve books of this long poem are dramatic monologues, each speaker commenting upon the murder of Pompilia Franceschini by her husband, Guido. In Books I and XII, however, Browning usually speaks, as in this dedicatory passage, in his own person.

For all hope, all sustainment, all reward,
Their utmost up and on—so blessing back
In those thy realms of help, that heaven thy home,
Some whiteness which, I judge, thy face makes proud,   25
Some wanness where, I think, thy foot may fall!

1868

The Householder [1]

[*Epilogue to* Fifine *at the Fair*]

1

Savage I was sitting in my house, late, lone:
    Dreary, weary with the long day's work:
Head of me, heart of me, stupid as a stone:
    Tongue-tied now, now blaspheming like a Turk;
When, in a moment, just a knock, call, cry,   5
    Half a pang and all a rapture, there again were we!—
"What, and is it really you again?" quoth I:
    "I again, what else did you expect?" quoth She.

2

"Never mind, hie away from this old house—
    Every crumbling brick embrowned with sin and shame!   10
Quick, in its corners ere certain shapes arouse!
    Let them—every devil of the night—lay claim,
Make and mend, or rap and rend, for me! Good-by!
    God be their guard from disturbance at their glee,
Till, crash, comes down the carcass in a heap!" quoth I: 15
    "Nay, but there's a decency required!" quoth She.

3

"Ah, but if you knew how time has dragged, days, nights!
    All the neighbor-talk with man and maid—such men!
All the fuss and trouble of street sounds, window sights:
    All the worry of flapping door and echoing roof; and then,   20
All the fancies . . . Who were they had leave, dared try
    Darker arts that almost struck despair in me?
If you knew but how I dwelt down here!" quoth I:
    "And was I so better off up there?" quoth She.

4

"Help and get it over! *Reunited to his wife*   25
    (How draw up the paper lets the parish-people know?)
Lies M., or N., departed from this life,
    Day the this or that, month and year the so and so.
What i' the way of final flourish? Prose, verse? Try!
    Affliction sore long time he bore, or, what is it to be?   30
Till God did please to grant him ease. Do end!" quoth I:
    "I end with—Love is all and Death is naught!" quoth She.

1872   1872

1. This dialogue with the spirit of Browning's dead wife can be compared with Dante Gabriel Rossetti's *The Blessed Damozel.* The "neighbor-talk" in stanza 3 probably refers to the gossip in London in 1869 over the fact that Browning was turned down when he proposed marriage to Lady Ashburton, a bewitching and wealthy widow.

House

1

Shall I sonnet-sing you about myself?
  Do I live in a house you would like to see?
Is it scant of gear, has it store of pelf?
  "Unlock my heart with a sonnet-key?"

2

Invite the world, as my betters have done?   5
  "Take notice: this building remains on view,
Its suites of reception every one,
  Its private apartment and bedroom too;

3

"For a ticket, apply to the Publisher."
  No: thanking the public, I must decline.   10
A peep through my window, if folk prefer;
  But, please you, not foot over threshold of mine!

4

I have mixed with a crowd and heard free talk
  In a foreign land where an earthquake chanced:
And a house stood gaping, naught to balk   15
  Man's eye wherever he gazed or glanced.

5

The whole of the frontage shaven sheer,
  The inside gaped: exposed to day,
Right and wrong and common and queer,
  Bare, as the palm of your hand, it lay.   20

6

The owner? Oh, he had been crushed, no doubt!
  "Odd tables and chairs for a man of wealth!
What a parcel of musty old books about!
  He smoked—no wonder he lost his health!

7

"I doubt if he bathed before he dressed.   25
  A brazier?—the pagan, he burned perfumes!
You see it is proved, what the neighbors guessed:
  His wife and himself had separate rooms."

8

Friends, the goodman of the house at least
  Kept house to himself till an earthquake came: 30
'Tis the fall of its frontage permits you feast
  On the inside arrangement you praise or blame.

9

Outside should suffice for evidence:
  And whoso desires to penetrate
Deeper, must dive by the spirit-sense—   35
  No optics like yours, at any rate!

10

"Hoity toity! A street to explore,
 Your house the exception! '*With this same key
Shakespeare unlocked his heart*,' once more!" [2]
 Did Shakespeare? If so, the less Shakespeare he!

40
1876

To Edward FitzGerald[1]

I chanced upon a new book yesterday;
I opened it, and, where my finger lay
 'Twixt page and uncut page, these words I read—
Some six or seven at most—and learned thereby
That you, FitzGerald, whom by ear and eye
 She never knew, "thanked God my wife was dead."
Aye, dead! and were yourself alive, good Fitz,
How to return you thanks would task my wits.
 Kicking you seems the common lot of curs—
While more appropriate greeting lends you grace,
Surely to spit there glorifies your face—
 Spitting from lips once sanctified by hers.

5

10

1889

1889

Epilogue to *Asolando*[2]

At the midnight in the silence of the sleep-time,
 When you[3] set your fancies free,
Will they pass to where—by death, fools think, imprisoned—

2. The quotation is from Wordsworth's
Scorn Not the Sonnet, which praises the
sonnet form as the one in which Shakespeare had revealed his true self. In
theory, if not in practice, Browning
strongly disapproved of a poet who "unlocked his heart" in public. A striking
example of this failing was *The House
of Life*, a sonnet sequence by D. G. Rossetti, published in 1870. It has been
conjectured that the glimpses into the
intimacies of domestic life and love relations, featured in Rossetti's sonnets,
probably prompted Browning to present
his case on behalf of an artist's right to
privacy and need for reticence.
1. In 1861 FitzGerald wrote to a friend:
"Mrs. Browning's death is rather a relief
to me, I must say: no more *Aurora Leighs*
[title of a popular poem by Mrs. Brown-
ing], thank God! * * * She and her sex

had better mind the kitchen and the children." Browning discovered the passage
among FitzGerald's posthumously published letters and in white heat wrote this
rejoinder which was published in the
Athenaeum. In defense of his poem,
Browning wrote a long and eloquent
letter to the Tennysons (who had been
close friends of FitzGerald), which has
been published in the *Times Literary
Supplement* (June 3, 1965), 464.
2. The final poem in *Asolando*, a volume published on the day of Browning's
death. Browning is said to have recognized that because the third stanza
sounded "like bragging" he ought to consider canceling it. "But it's the simple
truth," he added, "and as it's true, it
shall stand."
3. Any loved person who survives the
speaker.

Low he lies who once so loved you, whom you loved so,
  —Pity me?   5
Oh to love so, be so loved, yet so mistaken!
  What had I on earth to do
With the slothful, with the mawkish, the unmanly?
Like the aimless, helpless, hopeless, did I drivel
  —Being—who?   10

One who never turned his back but marched breast forward,
  Never doubted clouds would break,
Never dreamed, though right were worsted, wrong would triumph,
Held we fall to rise, are baffled to fight better,
  Sleep to wake.   15

No, at noonday in the bustle of man's work-time
  Greet the unseen[4] with a cheer!
Bid him forward, breast and back as either should be,
"Strive and thrive!" cry, "Speed—fight on, fare ever
  There as here!"   20
1889   1890

4. The speaker, after he is dead.

EMILY BRONTË
(1818–1848)

Before completing her famous novel, *Wuthering Heights*, Emily Brontë
wrote a number of poems recording experiences of love which often seem
similar to the strange passion of Heathcliff and Catherine Earnshaw in
her novel. Such lyrics were part of a long narrative concerning Gondal,
an imaginary kingdom the scenery of which resembled the locality in
Yorkshire where Emily had grown up with her two sisters, Charlotte and
Anne. Various pairs of lovers are the speakers in the poems. At the time
of their first publication in 1846 these unsual poems, with their hymnlike
stanzas, were ignored. In the 20th century, however, their haunting picture
of a love that defies death has aroused considerable interest.

Remembrance

Cold in the earth—and the deep snow piled above thee,
Far, far removed, cold in the dreary grave!
Have I forgot, my only Love, to love thee,
Severed at last by Time's all-severing wave?

Now, when alone, do my thoughts no longer hover   5
Over the mountains, on that northern shore,
Resting their wings where heath and fern leaves cover
Thy noble heart forever, ever more?

Cold in the earth—and fifteen wild Decembers,
From those brown hills, have melted into spring;
Faithful, indeed, is the spirit that remembers
After such years of change and suffering!   10

Sweet Love of youth, forgive, if I forget thee,
While the world's tide is bearing me along;
Other desires and other hopes beset me,
Hopes which obscure, but cannot do thee wrong!   15

No later light has lightened up my heaven,
No second morn has ever shone for me;
All my life's bliss from thy dear life was given,
All my life's bliss is in the grave with thee.   20

But, when the days of golden dreams had perished,
And even Despair was powerless to destroy,
Then did I learn how existence could be cherished,
Strengthened, and fed without the aid of joy.

Then did I check the tears of useless passion—   25
Weaned my young soul from yearning after thine;
Sternly denied its burning wish to hasten
Down to that tomb already more than mine.

And, even yet, I dare not let it languish,
Dare not indulge in memory's rapturous pain;   30
Once drinking deep of that divinest anguish,
How could I seek the empty world again?

1846

The Prisoner

A FRAGMENT

In the dungeon crypts idly did I stray,[1]
Reckless of the lives wasting there away;
"Draw the ponderous bars! open, Warder stern!"
He dared not say me nay—the hinges harshly turn.

"Our guests are darkly lodged," I whispered, gazing through   5
The vault, whose grated eye showed heaven more gray than blue
(This was when glad Spring laughed in awaking pride);
"Aye, darkly lodged enough!" returned my sullen guide.

Then, God forgive my youth! forgive my careless tongue!
I scoffed, as the chill chains on the damp flagstones rung: 10
"Confined in triple walls, art thou so much to fear,
That we must bind thee down and clench thy fetters here?"

---

1. The speaker, a man, is visiting a dungeon in his father's castle.

The captive raised her face; it was as soft and mild
As sculptured marble saint; or slumbering unweaned child;
It was so soft and mild, it was so sweet and fair,   15
Pain could not trace a line, or grief a shadow there!

The captive raised her hand and pressed it to her brow;
"I have been struck," she said, "and I am suffering now;
Yet these are little worth, your bolts and irons strong:
And, were they forged in steel, they could not hold me long."   20

Hoarse laughed the jailor grim: "Shall I be won to hear;
Dost think, fond,[2] dreaming wretch, that *I* shall grant thy prayer?
Or, better still, wilt melt my master's heart with groans?
Ah! sooner might the sun thaw down these granite stones.

"My master's voice is low, his aspect bland and kind,   25
But hard as hardest flint the soul that lurks behind;
And I am rough and rude, yet not more rough to see
Than is the hidden ghost that has its home in me."

About her lips there played a smile of almost scorn.
"My friend," she gently said, "you have not heard me mourn;   30
When you my kindred's lives, *my* lost life can restore,
Then may I weep and sue—but never, friend, before!

"Still, let my tyrants know, I am not doomed to wear
Year after year in gloom, and desolate despair;
A messenger of Hope comes every night to me,   35
And offers for short life, eternal liberty.

"He comes with western winds, with evening's wandering airs,
With that clear dusk of heaven that brings the thickest stars,
Winds take a pensive tone, and stars a tender fire,
And visions rise, and change, that kill me with desire.   40

"Desire for nothing known in my maturer years,
When Joy grew mad with awe, at counting future tears.
When, if my spirit's sky was full of flashes warm,
I knew not whence they came, from sun or thunderstorm.

"But, first, a hush of peace—a soundless calm descends;   45
The struggle of distress and fierce impatience ends;
Mute music soothes my breast—unuttered harmony,
That I could never dream, till Earth was lost to me.

"Then dawns the Invisible; the Unseen its truth reveals;
My outward sense is gone, my inward essence feels;   50
Its wings are almost free—its home, its harbor found,
Measuring the gulf, it stoops—and dares the final bound.

2. Foolish.

"Oh! dreadful is the check—intense the agony—
When the ear begins to hear, and the eye begins to see;
When the pulse begins to throb, the brain to think again;   55
The soul to feel the flesh, and the flesh to feel the chain.

"Yet I would lose no sting, would wish no torture less;
The more that anguish racks, the earlier it will bless;
And robed in fires of hell, or bright with heavenly shine,
If it but herald death, the vision is divine!"[3]   60

She ceased to speak, and we, unanswering, turned to go—
We had no further power to work the captive woe:
Her cheek, her gleaming eye, declared that man had given
A sentence, unapproved, and overruled by Heaven.

1846

No Coward Soul Is Mine[4]

No coward soul is mine,
No trembler in the world's storm-troubled sphere;
   I see Heaven's glories shine,
And faith shines equal, arming me from fear.

   O God within my breast,   5
Almighty, ever-present Deity!
   Life—that in me has rest,
As I—undying Life—have power in Thee!

   Vain are the thousand creeds
That move men's hearts—unutterably vain;   10
   Worthless as withered weeds,
Or idlest froth amid the boundless main,

   To waken doubt in one
Holding so fast by Thine infinity;
   So surely anchored on   15
The steadfast rock of immortality.

   With wide-embracing love
Thy spirit animates eternal years
   Pervades and broods above,
Changes, sustains, dissolves, creates, and rears.   20

   Though earth and man were gone,
And suns and universes ceased to be,
   And Thou were left alone,
Every existence would exist in Thee.

3. Cf. the words of the dying Catherine in *Wuthering Heights*: "The thing that irks me most is this shattered prison [my body]. * * * I'm tired of being enclosed here. I'm wearying to escape into that glorious world, and to be always there. * * * I shall be incomparably beyond and above you all."
4. According to Charlotte Brontë, these are the last lines written by her sister.

> There is not room for Death, 25
> Nor atom that his might could render void;
> Thou—Thou art Being and Breath,
> And what Thou art may never be destroyed.

> 1850

JOHN RUSKIN

(1819–1900)

1843:   Publication of first volume of *Modern Painters.*
1851–53: *The Stones of Venice.*
1860:   *Unto This Last.*

John Ruskin was both the leading Victorian critic of art and an important critic of society. These two roles can be traced back to two important influences of his childhood. His father, a wealthy wine merchant, was fond of travel, and on tours of the Continent he introduced his son to landscape, architecture, and art. From this exposure John Ruskin acquired a zest for beauty that animates even the most theoretical of his discussions of aesthetics. In his autobiography he describes his first view of the Swiss Alps at sunset: "the seen walls of lost Eden could not have been more beautiful" (he was 14 at the time):

> It is not possible to imagine, in any time of the world, a more blessed entrance into life, for a child of such a temperament as mine. True, the temperament belonged to the age: a very few years,—within the hundred,—before that, no child could have been born to care for mountains, or for the men that lived among them, in that way. Till Rousseau's time, there had been no "sentimental" love of nature; and till Scott's, no such apprehensive love of "all sorts and conditions of men," not in the soul merely, but in the flesh. * * * I went down that evening from the garden-terrace of Schaffhausen with my destiny fixed in all of it that was to be sacred and useful.

Ruskin's choice of phrase in evoking this dedication scene reflects the second influence in his life, often at variance with the first: his daily Bible-readings under the direction of his mother. From this Biblical indoctrination, Ruskin derived some elements of his lush and highly rhythmical prose style, but more especially his sense of prophecy and mission as a critic of modern society.

Ruskin's life was spent in traveling, lecturing, and writing. His prodigious literary output can be roughly divided into three phases. At first he was preoccupied with problems of art. *Modern Painters,* which he began writing at the age of 23 after his graduation from Oxford, was a defense of the English landscape painter J. M. W. Turner (1775–1851). This defense (which was to extend to five volumes) involved Ruskin in problems of truth in art (as in his chapter on the "Pathetic Fallacy") and in the ultimate importance of imagination (as in his discussion of Turner's painting, "The Slave Ship").

During the 1850's Ruskin's principal interest shifted from art to architecture, especially to the problem of determining what kind of society is capable of producing great buildings. His enthusiasm for Gothic architecture was infectious, and he has sometimes been blamed for the prevalence of Gothic buildings on college campuses in America. A study of *The Stones of Venice* (1851–53), however (especially the chapter included below), will show that merely to revive the Gothic style was not his concern. What he wanted to revive was the kind of society that had produced such architecture, a society in which the individual workman could express himself and enjoy what Ruskin's disciple, William Morris, called "work-pleasure." A mechanized production-line society, such as Ruskin's or our own, could not produce Gothic architecture but only imitations of its mannerisms. Ruskin's concern was to change industrial society, not to decorate concrete towers with gargoyles.

This interest in the stultifying effects of industrialism led Ruskin gradually into economics. After 1860 the critic of art became (like his master, Carlyle) an outspoken critic of laissez-faire economics. His conception of the responsibilities of employers towards their workmen, as expounded in *Unto this Last* (1860), was dismissed by his contemporaries as an absurdity. What he was laboring to show was that self-seeking business relationships might be made over on the principle of dedicated service, taking as a model the learned professions and also the military. The soldier, however crude, is more highly regarded by society than the capitalist, Ruskin said, "for the soldier's trade * * * is not slaying, but being slain." Although his position was essentially conservative in the proper sense of the word (he styled himself "a violent Tory of the old school;—Walter Scott's school"), he was regarded as a radical eccentric. It was many years before his social criticism gained a following among writers as diverse as William Morris, George Bernard Shaw, and D. H. Lawrence; and in particular among the founders of the British Labour Party his influence was to be profound and lasting.

Ruskin's realization, after 1860, that despite his fame he was becoming isolated and that the world was continuing to move in directions opposite from those to which he pointed may have contributed to the recurrent mental breakdowns from which he suffered between 1870 and 1900. As he reports in *Fors Clavigera* (1880): "The doctors said I went mad, this time two years ago, from overwork," but he had not then been working harder than usual. "I went mad because nothing came of my work * * * because after I got [my manuscripts] published, nobody believed a word of them." Also contributing to his breakdowns may have been his unhappiness in his relations with women. His marriage to Effie Gray in 1848 was a disaster. After six years of living together an annulment was arranged on the grounds that the marriage had not been consummated. Ruskin testified that he had not found his wife's person physically attractive, although by others she was considered a great beauty. One of these admirers was the Pre-Raphaelite painter John Millais, who fell in love with her at a time when he was painting her husband's portrait; shortly after the annulment he married her. In later years Ruskin fell pathetically in love with a young Irish girl, Rose La Touche, whom he first met when he was nearly forty and she was a child of nine. They were divided not only by the gap of age but by religious differences. She was an intensely pious believer, and for several years after Ruskin proposed marriage to her, when she was 18, she tried unsuccessfully to persuade him to return to the Evangelical faith that he had abandoned. In 1875, after herself suffering attacks of mental illness, Rose La Touche died at the age of 25. In his autobiography Ruskin commented: "I wonder mightily what sort of creature I should have turned out, if instead of the distracting and useless pain, I had had the joy of approved love, and the untellable, incalculable motive of its sympathy and praise. It seems to me such things are not allowed in the world. The men capable of the highest imaginative passion are always tossed on fiery waves by it." During the last thirty years of his life, in spite of his despair following Rose's death and recurring attacks of mental illness, Ruskin remained active and productive. His publications during this period include six volumes of his lectures on art which he had delivered as Slade Professor of Fine Arts at Oxford, as well as his letters to workmen, *Fors Clavigera* (1871–84), and his delightful autobiography, *Praeterita* (1885–89). One topic that becomes especially prominent in these later writings is pollution of air and water—an ideal subject for Ruskin's eloquence. In discussing it he combines his lifelong love for beautiful landscape and landscape-painting with his later acquired conviction that modern industrial leadership was woefully irresponsible. A letter of A. E. Housman, who was an undergraduate at Oxford in 1877, provides a vivid record of how effective Ruskin could be:

This afternoon Ruskin gave us a great outburst against modern times. He had got a picture of Turner's, framed and glassed, representing Leicester and the Abbey in the distance at sunset, over a river. He read the account of Wolsey's death out of *Henry VIII*. Then he pointed to the picture as representing Leicester when Turner had drawn it. Then he said, "You, if you like, may go to Leicester to see what it is like now. I never shall. But I can make a pretty good guess." Then he caught up a paintbrush. "These stepping-stones of course have been done away with, and are replaced by a be-au-ti-ful iron bridge." Then he dashed in the iron bridge on the glass of the picture. "The colour of the stream is supplied on one side by the indigo factory." Forthwith one side of the stream became indigo. "On the other side by the soap factory." Soap dashed in. "They mix in the middle—like curds," he said, working them together with a sort of malicious deliberation. "This field, over which you see the sun setting behind the abbey, is now occupied in a *proper* manner." Then there went a flame of scarlet across the picture, which developed itself into windows and roofs and red brick, and rushed up into a chimney. "The atmosphere is supplied—thus!" A puff and cloud of smoke all over Turner's sky: and then the brush thrown down, and Ruskin confronting modern civilization amidst a tempest of applause, which he always elicits now, as he has this term become immensely popular, his lectures being crowded, whereas of old he used to prophesy to empty benches.

From Modern Painters

[A Definition of Greatness in Art][1]

Painting, or art generally, as such, with all its technicalities, difficulties, and particular ends, is nothing but a noble and expressive language, invaluable as the vehicle of thought, but by itself nothing. He who has learned what is commonly considered the whole art of painting, that is, the art of representing any natural object faithfully, has as yet only learned the language by which his thoughts are to be expressed. He has done just as much towards being that which we ought to respect as a great painter, as a man who has learnt how to express himself grammatically and melodiously has towards being a great poet. The language is, indeed, more difficult of acquirement in the one case than in the other, and possesses more power of delighting the sense, while it speaks to the intellect; but it is, nevertheless, nothing more than language, and all those excellences which are peculiar to the painter as such, are merely what rhythm, melody, precision, and force are in the words of the orator and the poet, necessary to their greatness, but not the tests of their greatness. It is not by the mode of representing and saying, but by what is represented and said, that the respective greatness either of the painter or the writer is to be finally determined. * * *

* * * So that, if I say that the greatest picture is that which conveys to the mind of the spectator the greatest number of the greatest ideas, I have a definition which will include as subjects of comparison every pleasure which art is capable of conveying. If I were to say, on the contrary, that the best picture was that which most closely imitated nature, I should assume that art could only please by imitating nature; and I should cast out of the pale of criticism those parts of works of art which are not imitative, that is to say, intrinsic beauties of color and form, and those works of art wholly, which, like the Arabesques of Raffaelle in the Loggias,[2] are not imitative at all. Now, I want a definition of art wide enough to include all its varieties of aim. I do not say, therefore, that the art is greatest which gives most pleasure, because perhaps there is some art whose end is to teach, and not to please. I do not say that the art is greatest which teaches us most, because perhaps there is some art whose end is to please, and not to teach. I do not say that the art is greatest which imitates best, because perhaps there is some art whose end is to create and not to imitate. But I say that the art is greatest which conveys to the mind of the spectator, by any

1. From Volume I, Part I, Section i, Chapter 2.
2. The arabesques in the Loggia of the Vatican, designed by Raphael, were decorative wall-paintings which feature a complex pattern of leaves, animals, and human figures.

means whatsoever, the greatest number of the greatest ideas; and I call an idea great in proportion as it is received by a higher faculty of the mind, and as it more fully occupies, and in occupying, exercises and exalts, the faculty by which it is received.

If this, then, be the definition of great art, that of a great artist naturally follows. He is the greatest artist who has embodied, in the sum of his works, the greatest number of the greatest ideas.

["The Slave Ship"][1]

But I think the noblest sea that Turner has ever painted, and, if so, the noblest certainly ever painted by man, is that of "The Slave Ship," the chief Academy picture of the exhibition of 1840.[2] It is a sunset on the Atlantic after prolonged storm; but the storm is partially lulled, and the torn and streaming rain clouds are moving in scarlet lines to lose themselves in the hollow of the night. The whole surface of sea included in the picture is divided into two ridges of enormous swell, not high, nor local, but a low, broad heaving of the whole ocean, like the lifting of its bosom by deep-drawn breath after the torture of the storm. Between these two ridges the fire of the sunset falls along the trough of the sea, dyeing it with an awful but glorious light, the intense and lurid splendor which burns like gold and bathes like blood. Along this fiery path and valley the tossing waves by which the swell of the sea is restlessly divided lift themselves in dark, indefinite, fantastic forms, each casting a faint and ghastly shadow behind it along the illumined foam. They do not rise everywhere, but three or four together in wild groups, fitfully and furiously, as the under-strength of the swell compels or permits them; leaving between them treacherous spaces of level and whirling water, now lighted with green and lamplike fire, now flashing back the gold of the declining sun, now fearfully shed from above with the indistinguishable images of the burning clouds, which fall upon them in flakes of crimson and scarlet and give to the reckless waves the added motion of their own fiery being. Purple and blue, the lurid shadows of the hollow breakers are cast upon the mist of night, which gathers cold and low, advancing like the shadow of death upon the guilty ship as it labors amidst the lightning of the sea, its thin masts written upon the sky in lines of blood, girded with condemnation in that fearful hue which signs the sky with horror, and mixes its flaming flood with the sunlight, and, cast far along the desolate heave of the sepulchral waves, incarnadines the multitudinous sea.[3]

1. From Volume I, Part II, Section v, Chapter 3.
2. The painting is of a ship in which slaves are being transported. Victims who have died during the passage are being thrown overboard at sunset: as Ruskin noted, "the near sea is encumbered with corpses." The "Academy" is the Royal Academy of Arts, founded in London in 1768.
3. See *Macbeth* II.ii.62.

I believe, if I were reduced to rest Turner's immortality upon any single work, I should choose this. Its daring conception—ideal in the highest sense of the word—is based on the purest truth, and wrought out with the concentrated knowledge of a life; its color is absolutely perfect, not one false or morbid hue in any part or line, and so modulated that every square inch of canvas is a perfect composition; its drawing as accurate as fearless; the ship buoyant, bending, and full of motion; its tones as true as they are wonderful; and the whole picture dedicated to the most sublime of subjects and impressions—completing thus the perfect system of all truth which we have shown to be formed by Turner's works—the power, majesty, and deathfulness of the open, deep, illimitable Sea.

1843

From *Of the Pathetic Fallacy*[4]

* * * Now, therefore, putting these tiresome and absurd words[5] quite out of our way, we may go on at our ease to examine the point in question—namely, the difference between the ordinary, proper, and true appearances of things to us; and the extraordinary, or false appearances, when we are under the influence of emotion, or contemplative fancy; false appearances, I say, as being entirely unconnected with any real power of character in the object, and only imputed to it by us.

For instance—

> The spendthrift crocus, bursting through the mold
> Naked and shivering, with his cup of gold.[6]

This is very beautiful, and yet very untrue. The crocus is not a spendthrift, but a hardy plant; its yellow is not gold, but saffron. How is it that we enjoy so much the having it put into our heads that it is anything else than a plain crocus?

It is an important question. For, throughout our past reasonings about art, we have always found that nothing could be good or useful, or ultimately pleasurable, which was untrue. But here is something pleasurable in written poetry, which is nevertheless *un*true. And what is more, if we think over our favorite poetry, we

4. From Volume III, Part IV, Chapter 12. In this celebrated chapter Ruskin shifts from discussing problems of truth and realism in art to the same problems in literature. The term *pathetic* refers not to something feebly ineffective but to the emotion (pathos) with which a writer invests his descriptions of objects, and of the distortion (fallacy) that may result. Poets such as Tennyson protested that Ruskin was being unfairly rigorous

in pointing up the fallacy, and it may be noted that Ruskin himself falls into it often. See, e.g., his reference to the "guilty ship" in his discussion of Turner above.
5. The metaphysical terms "objective" and "subjective" as applied to kinds of truth.
6. From a poem by Oliver Wendell Holmes.

shall find it full of this kind of fallacy, and that we like it all the more for being so.

It will appear also, on consideration of the matter, that this fallacy is of two principal kinds. Either, as in this case of the crocus, it is the fallacy of willful fancy, which involves no real expectation that it will be believed; or else it is a fallacy caused by an excited state of the feelings, making us, for the time, more or less irrational. Of the cheating of the fancy we shall have to speak presently; but, in this chapter, I want to examine the nature of the other error, that which the mind admits when affected strongly by emotion. Thus, for instance, in *Alton Locke*—

> They rowed her in across the rolling foam—
> The cruel, crawling foam.[7]

The foam is not cruel, neither does it crawl. The state of mind which attributes to it these characters of a living creature is one in which the reason is unhinged by grief. All violent feelings have the same effect. They produce in us a falseness in all our impressions of external things, which I would generally characterize as the "pathetic fallacy."

Now we are in the habit of considering this fallacy as eminently a character of poetical description, and the temper of mind in which we allow it, as one eminently poetical, because passionate. But, I believe, if we look well into the matter, that we shall find the greatest poets do not often admit this kind of falseness—that it is only the second order of poets who much delight in it.

Thus, when Dante describes the spirits falling from the bank of Acheron "as dead leaves flutter from a bough," [8] he gives the most perfect image possible of their utter lightness, feebleness, passiveness, and scattering agony of despair, without, however, for an instant losing his own clear perception that *these* are souls, and *those* are leaves: he makes no confusion of one with the other. But when Coleridge speaks of

> The one red leaf, the last of its clan,
> That dances as often as dance it can,[9]

he has a morbid, that is to say, a so far false, idea about the leaf: he fancies a life in it, and will, which there are not; confuses its powerlessness with choice, its fading death with merriment, and the wind that shakes it with music. Here, however, there is some beauty, even in the morbid passage; but take an instance in Homer and Pope. Without the knowledge of Ulysses, Elpenor, his young-

---

7. From Charles Kingsley's novel *Alton Locke* (1850).   8. Dante, *Inferno* III.112.
9. *Christabel*, lines 49–50.

est follower, has fallen from an upper chamber in the Circean palace,
and has been left dead, unmissed by his leader or companions, in
the haste of their departure. They cross the sea to the Cimmerian
land; and Ulysses summons the shades from Tartarus. The first
which appears is that of the lost Elpenor. Ulysses, amazed, and in
exactly the spirit of bitter and terrified lightness which is seen in
Hamlet, addresses the spirit with the simple, startled words: "Elpenor! How camest thou under the shadowy darkness? Hast thou
come faster on foot than I in my black ship?"[1] Which Pope renders
thus:

> O, say, what angry power Elpenor led
> To glide in shades, and wander with the dead?
> How could thy soul, by realms and seas disjoined,
> Outfly the nimble sail, and leave the lagging wind?

I sincerely hope the reader finds no pleasure here, either in the
nimbleness of the sail, or the laziness of the wind! And yet how
is it that these conceits are so painful now, when they have been
pleasant to us in the other instances?

For a very simple reason. They are not a *pathetic* fallacy at all,
for they are put into the mouth of the wrong passion—a passion
which never could possibly have spoken them—agonized curiosity.
Ulysses wants to know the facts of the matter; and the very last
thing his mind could do at the moment would be to pause, or suggest in anywise what was *not* a fact. The delay in the first three
lines, and conceit in the last, jar upon us instantly, like the most
frightful discord in music. No poet of true imaginative power could
possibly have written the passage.

Therefore, we see that the spirit of truth must guide us in some
sort, even in our enjoyment of fallacy. Coleridge's fallacy has no
discord in it, but Pope's has set our teeth on edge. * * *

1856

From The Stones of Venice
[*The Savageness of Gothic Architecture*][2]

* * * I am not sure when the word "Gothic" was first generically applied to the architecture of the North; but I presume
that, whatever the date of its original usage, it was intended to imply
reproach, and express the barbaric character of the nations among
whom that architecture arose. It never implied that they were literally of Gothic lineage, far less that their architecture had been
originally invented by the Goths themselves; but it did imply that

1. *Odyssey* XI.57.   2. From Volume II, Chapter 6.

they and their buildings together exhibited a degree of sternness and rudeness, which, in contradistinction to the character of Southern and Eastern nations, appeared like a perpetual reflection of the contrast between the Goth and the Roman in their first encounter. And when that fallen Roman, in the utmost impotence of his luxury, and insolence of his guilt, became the model for the imitation of civilized Europe,[3] at the close of the so-called Dark Ages, the word Gothic became a term of unmitigated contempt, not unmixed with aversion. From that contempt, by the exertion of the antiquaries and architects of this century, Gothic architecture has been sufficiently vindicated; and perhaps some among us, in our admiration of the magnificent science of its structure, and sacredness of its expression, might desire that the term of ancient reproach should be withdrawn, and some other, of more apparent honorableness, adopted in its place. There is no chance, as there is no need, of such a substitution. As far as the epithet was used scornfully, it was used falsely; but there is no reproach in the word, rightly understood; on the contrary, there is a profound truth, which the instinct of mankind almost unconsciously recognizes. It is true, greatly and deeply true, that the architecture of the North is rude and wild; but it is not true that, for this reason, we are to condemn it, or despise. Far otherwise: I believe it is in this very character that it deserves our profoundest reverence.

The charts of the world which have been drawn up by modern science have thrown into a narrow space the expression of a vast amount of knowledge, but I have never yet seen any one pictorial enough to enable the spectator to imagine the kind of contrast in physical character which exists between Northern and Southern countries. We know the differences in detail, but we have not that broad glance and grasp which would enable us to feel them in their fullness. We know that gentians grow on the Alps, and olives on the Apennines; but we do not enough conceive for ourselves that variegated mosaic of the world's surface which a bird sees in its migration, that difference between the district of the gentian and of the olive which the stork and the swallow see far off, as they lean upon the sirocco wind.[4] Let us, for a moment, try to raise ourselves even above the level of their flight, and imagine the Mediterranean lying beneath us like an irregular lake, and all its ancient promontories sleeping in the sun: here and there an angry spot of thunder, a gray stain of storm, moving upon the burning field; and here and

3. Renaissance architecture, based on imitating classical buildings, was distasteful to Ruskin. He later stated that his aim in *The Stones of Venice* had been "to show that the Gothic architecture of Venice had risen out of * * * a state of pure national faith and domestic virtue; and that its Renaissance architecture had arisen out of * * * a state of concealed national infidelity and domestic corruption."

4. Hot wind from the southern Mediterranean.

there a fixed wreath of white volcano smoke, surrounded by its circle of ashes; but for the most part a great peacefulness of light, Syria and Greece, Italy and Spain, laid like pieces of a golden pavement into the sea-blue, chased, as we stoop nearer to them, with bossy beaten work of mountain chains, and glowing softly with terraced gardens, and flowers heavy with frankincense, mixed among masses of laurel, and orange, and plumy palm, that abate with their gray-green shadows the burning of the marble rocks, and of the ledges of porphyry sloping under lucent sand. Then let us pass farther towards the north, until we see the orient colors change gradually into a vast belt of rainy green, where the pastures of Switzerland, and poplar valleys of France, and dark forests of the Danube and Carpathians stretch from the mouths of the Loire to those of the Volga, seen through clefts in gray swirls of rain cloud and flaky veils of the mist of the brooks, spreading low along the pasture lands: and then, farther north still, to see the earth heave into mighty masses of leaden rock and heathy moor, bordering with a broad waste of gloomy purple that belt of field and wood, and splintering into irregular and grisly islands amidst the northern seas, beaten by storm, and chilled by ice drift, and tormented by furious pulses of contending tide, until the roots of the last forests fail from among the hill ravines, and the hunger of the north wind bites their peaks into barrenness; and, at last, the wall of ice, durable like iron, sets, deathlike, its white teeth against us out of the polar twilight. And, having once traversed in thought this gradation of the zoned iris of the earth in all its material vastness, let us go down nearer to it, and watch the parallel change in the belt of animal life: the multitudes of swift and brilliant creatures that glance in the air and sea, or tread the sands of the southern zone; striped zebras and spotted leopards, glistening serpents, and birds arrayed in purple and scarlet. Let us contrast their delicacy and brilliancy of color, and swiftness of motion, with the frost-cramped strength, and shaggy covering, and dusky plumage of the northern tribes; contrast the Arabian horse with the Shetland, the tiger and leopard with the wolf and bear, the antelope with the elk, the bird of paradise with the osprey: and then, submissively acknowledging the great laws by which the earth and all that it bears are ruled throughout their being, let us not condemn, but rejoice in the expression by man of his own rest in the statutes of the lands that gave him birth. Let us watch him with reverence as he sets side by side the burning gems, and smooths with soft sculpture the jasper pillars, that are to reflect a ceaseless sunshine, and rise into a cloud-less sky: but not with less reverence let us stand by him, when, with rough strength and hurried stroke, he smites an uncouth animation out of the rocks which he has torn from among the moss of the moorland, and heaves into the darkened air the pile of iron buttress and rugged wall, instinct with work of an imagination as wild and wayward as the northern sea; creations of ungainly shape and rigid limb, but full of wolfish life; fierce as the winds that beat, and changeful as the clouds that shade them.

There is, I repeat, no degradation, no reproach in this, but all dignity and honorableness: and we should err grievously in refusing either to recognize as an essential character of the existing architecture of the North, or to admit as a desirable character in that which it yet may be, this wildness of thought, and roughness of work; this look of mountain brotherhood between the cathedral and the Alp; this magnificence of sturdy power, put forth only the more energetically because the fine finger-touch was chilled away by the frosty wind, and the eye dimmed by the moor mist, or blinded by the hail; this outspeaking of the strong spirit of men who may not gather redundant fruitage from the earth, nor bask in dreamy benignity of sunshine, but must break the rock for bread, and cleave the forest for fire, and show, even in what they did for their delight, some of the hard habits of the arm and heart that grew on them as they swung the ax or pressed the plow.

If, however, the savageness of Gothic architecture, merely as an expression of its origin among Northern nations, may be considered, in some sort, a noble character, it possesses a higher nobility still, when considered as an index, not of climate, but of religious principle.

In the 13th and 14th paragraphs of Chapter XXI of the first volume of this work, it was noticed that the systems of architectural ornament, properly so called, might be divided into three: (1) Servile ornament, in which the execution or power of the inferior workman is entirely subjected to the intellect of the higher; (2) Constitutional ornament, in which the executive inferior power is, to a certain point, emancipated and independent, having a will of its own, yet confessing its inferiority and rendering obedience to higher powers; and (3) Revolutionary ornament, in which no executive inferiority is admitted at all. I must here explain the nature of these divisions at somewhat greater length.

Of Servile ornament, the principal schools are the Greek, Ninevite, and Egyptian; but their servility is of different kinds. The Greek master-workman was far advanced in knowledge and power above the Assyrian or Egyptian. Neither he nor those for whom he worked could endure the appearance of imperfection in anything; and, therefore, what ornament he appointed to be done by those beneath him was composed of mere geometrical forms—balls, ridges, and perfectly symmetrical foliage—which could be executed with absolute precision by line and rule, and were as perfect in their way, when completed, as his own figure sculpture. The Assyrian and Egyptian, on the contrary, less cognizant of accurate form in anything, were content to allow their figure sculpture to be executed by inferior workmen, but lowered the method of its treatment to a standard which every workman could reach, and then trained him by discipline so rigid that there was no chance of his falling beneath the standard appointed. The Greek gave to the lower workman no subject which he could not perfectly execute. The Assyrian gave him subjects which he could only execute imperfectly, but fixed a legal standard for his imperfection. The workman was, in both systems, a slave.

But in the medieval, or especially Christian, system of ornament, this slavery is done away with altogether; Christianity having recognized, in small things as well as great, the individual value of every soul. But it not only recognizes its value; it confesses its imperfection, in only bestowing dignity upon the acknowledgment of unworthiness. That admission of lost power and fallen nature, which the Greek or Ninevite felt to be intensely painful, and, as far as might be, altogether refused, the Christian makes daily and hourly, contemplating the fact of it without fear, as tending, in the end, to God's greater glory. Therefore, to every spirit which Christianity summons to her service, her exhortation is: Do what you can, and confess frankly what you are unable to do; neither let your effort be shortened for fear of failure, nor your confession silenced for fear of shame. And it is, perhaps, the principal admirableness of the Gothic schools of architecture, that they thus receive the results of the labor of inferior minds; and out of fragments full of imperfection, and betraying that imperfection in every touch, indulgently raise up a stately and unaccusable whole.

But the modern English mind has this much in common with that of the Greek, that it intensely desires, in all things, the utmost completion or perfection compatible with their nature. This is a noble character in the abstract, but becomes ignoble when it causes us to forget the relative dignities of that nature itself, and to prefer the perfectness of the lower nature to the imperfection of the higher; not considering that as, judged by such a rule, all the brute animals would be preferable to man, because more perfect in their functions and kind, and yet are always held inferior to him, so also in the works of man, those which are more perfect in their kind are always inferior to those which are, in their nature, liable to more faults and shortcomings. For the finer the nature, the more flaws it will show through the clearness of it; and it is a law of this universe that the best things shall be seldomest seen in their best form. The wild grass grows well and strongly, one year with another; but the wheat is, according to the greater nobleness of its nature, liable to the bitterer blight. And therefore, while in all things that we see, or do, we are to desire perfection, and strive for it, we are nevertheless not to set the meaner thing, in its narrow accomplishment, above the nobler thing, in its mighty progress; not to esteem smooth minuteness above shattered majesty; not to prefer mean victory to honorable defeat; not to lower the level of our aim, that we may the more surely enjoy the complacency of success. But above all, in our dealings with the souls of other men, we are to take care how we check, by severe requirement or narrow caution, efforts which might otherwise lead to a noble issue; and, still more, how we withhold our admiration from great excellencies, because they are mingled with rough faults. Now, in the make and nature of every man, however rude or simple, whom we employ in manual labor, there are some powers for better things: some tardy imagination, torpid capacity of emotion, tottering steps of thought, there are, even at the worst; and in most cases it is all our own fault that they *are* tardy or torpid. But they cannot be strengthened, unless we are content to take them in their feebleness, and unless we prize and honor them in their imperfection above the best and most perfect manual skill. And this is what we have to do with all our laborers; to look for the *thoughtful* part of them, and get that out of them, whatever we lose for it, whatever faults and errors we are obliged to take with it. For the best that is in them cannot manifest itself, but in company with much error. Understand this clearly: You can teach a man to draw a straight line, and to cut one; to strike a curved line, and to carve it; and to copy and carve any number of given lines or forms, with admirable speed and perfect precision; and you find his work perfect of its kind: but if you ask him to think about any of those forms, to consider if he cannot find any better in his own head, he stops; his execution becomes hesitating; he thinks, and ten to one he thinks wrong; ten to one he makes a mistake in the first touch he gives to his work as a thinking being. But you have made a man of him for all that. He was only a machine before, an animated tool.

And observe, you are put to stern choice in this matter. You must either make a tool of the creature, or a man of him. You cannot make both. Men were not intended to work with the accuracy of tools, to be precise and perfect in all their actions. If you will have that precision out of them, and make their fingers measure degrees like cogwheels, and their arms strike curves like compasses, you must unhumanize them. All the energy of their spirits must be given to make cogs and compasses of themselves. All their attention and strength must go to the accomplishment of the mean act. The eye of the soul must be bent upon the finger point, and the soul's force must fill all the invisible nerves that guide it, ten hours a day, that it may not err from its steely precision, and so soul and sight be worn away, and the whole human being be lost at last—a heap of sawdust, so far as its intellectual work in this world is concerned; saved only by its Heart, which cannot go into the form of cogs and compasses, but expands, after the ten hours are over, into fireside humanity. On the other hand, if you will make a man of the working creature, you cannot make a tool. Let him but begin to imagine, to think, to try to do anything worth doing; and the engine-turned precision is lost at once. Out come all his roughness, all his dullness, all his incapability; shame upon shame, failure upon failure, pause after pause: but out comes the whole majesty of him also; and we know the height of it only, when we see the clouds settling upon him. And, whether the clouds be bright or dark, there will be transfiguration behind and within them.

And now, reader, look round this English room of yours, about which you have been proud so often, because the work of it was so good and strong, and the ornaments of it so finished. Examine again all those accurate moldings, and perfect polishings, and unerring adjustments of the seasoned wood and tempered steel. Many a time you have exulted over them, and thought how great England was, because her slightest work was done so thoroughly. Alas! if read rightly, these perfectnesses are signs of a slavery in our England a thousand times more bitter and more degrading than that of the scourged African, or helot[5] Greek. Men may be beaten, chained, tormented, yoked like cattle, slaughtered like summer flies, and yet remain in one sense, and the best sense, free. But to smother their souls within them, to blight and hew into rotting pollards[6] the suckling branches of their human intelligence, to make the flesh and skin which, after the worm's work on it, is to see God, into leathern thongs to yoke machinery with—this is to be slave-masters indeed; and there might be more freedom in England, though her feudal lords' lightest words were worth men's lives, and though the blood of the vexed husbandman dropped in the furrows of her fields, than there is while the animation of her multitudes is sent like fuel to feed the factory smoke, and the strength of them is given daily to be wasted into the fineness of a web, or racked into the exactness of a line.

And, on the other hand, go forth again to gaze upon the old cathedral front, where you have smiled so often at the fantastic ignorance of the old sculptors: examine once more those ugly goblins, and formless monsters, and stern statues, anatomiless and rigid; but do not mock at them, for they are signs of the life and liberty of every workman who struck the stone; a freedom of thought, and rank in scale of being, such as no laws, no charters, no charities can secure; but which it must be the first aim of all Europe at this day to regain for her children.

Let me not be thought to speak wildly or extravagantly. It is verily this degradation of the operative into a machine, which, more

5. A class of serfs in Sparta.   6. Trees with top branches cut back to the trunk.

than any other evil of the times, is leading the mass of the nations everywhere into vain, incoherent, destructive struggling for a freedom of which they cannot explain the nature to themselves. Their universal outcry against wealth, and against nobility, is not forced from them either by the pressure of famine, or the sting of mortified pride. These do much, and have done much in all ages; but the foundations of society were never yet shaken as they are at this day. It is not that men are ill fed, but that they have no pleasure in the work by which they make their bread, and therefore look to wealth as the only means of pleasure. It is not that men are pained by the scorn of the upper classes, but they cannot endure their own; for they feel that the kind of labor to which they are condemned is verily a degrading one, and makes them less than men. Never had the upper classes so much sympathy with the lower, or charity for them, as they have at this day, and yet never were they so much hated by them: for, of old, the separation between the noble and the poor was merely a wall built by law; now it is a veritable difference in level of standing, a precipice between upper and lower grounds in the field of humanity, and there is pestilential air at the bottom of it. I know not if a day is ever to come when the nature of right freedom will be understood, and when men will see that to obey another man, to labor for him, yield reverence to him or to his place, is not slavery. It is often the best kind of liberty—liberty from care. The man who says to one, Go, and he goeth, and to another, Come, and he cometh, has, in most cases, more sense of restraint and difficulty than the man who obeys him. The movements of the one are hindered by the burden on his shoulder; of the other, by the bridle on his lips: there is no way by which the burden may be lightened; but we need not suffer from the bridle if we do not champ at it. To yield reverence to another, to hold ourselves and our lives at his disposal, is not slavery; often, it is the noblest state in which a man can live in this world. There is, indeed, a reverence which is servile, that is to say irrational or selfish: but there is also noble reverence, that is to say, reasonable and loving; and a man is never so noble as when he is reverent in this kind; nay, even if the feeling pass the bounds of mere reason, so that it be loving, a man is raised by it. Which had, in reality, most of the serf nature in him—the Irish peasant who was lying in wait yesterday for his landlord, with his musket muzzle thrust through the ragged hedge; or that old mountain servant, who, 200 years ago, at Inverkeithing, gave up his own life and the lives of his seven sons for his chief?[7]—as each fell, calling forth his brother to the death, "Another for Hector!" And therefore, in all ages and all countries, reverence has been paid and sacrifice made by men to each other, not only without com-

7. An incident described in the Preface to Walter Scott's novel *The Fair Maid of Perth.*

plaint, but rejoicingly; and famine, and peril, and sword, and all evil, and all shame, have been borne willingly in the causes of masters and kings; for all these gifts of the heart ennobled the men who gave not less than the men who received them, and nature prompted, and God rewarded the sacrifice. But to feel their souls withering within them, unthanked, to find their whole being sunk into an unrecognized abyss, to be counted off into a heap of mechanism, numbered with its wheels, and weighed with its hammer strokes—this nature bade not—this God blesses not—this humanity for no long time is able to endure.

We have much studied and much perfected, of late, the great civilized invention of the division of labor; only we give it a false name. It is not, truly speaking, the labor that is divided; but the men: Divided into mere segments of men—broken into small fragments and crumbs of life; so that all the little piece of intelligence that is left in a man is not enough to make a pin, or a nail, but exhausts itself in making the point of a pin, or the head of a nail. Now it is a good and desirable thing, truly, to make many pins in a day; but if we could only see with what crystal sand their points were polished—sand of human soul, much to be magnified before it can be discerned for what it is—we should think there might be some loss in it also. And the great cry that rises from all our manufacturing cities, louder than their furnace blast, is all in very deed for this—that we manufacture everything there except men; we blanch cotton, and strengthen steel, and refine sugar, and shape pottery; but to brighten, to strengthen, to refine, or to form a single living spirit, never enters into our estimate of advantages. And all the evil to which that cry is urging our myriads can be met only in one way: not by teaching nor preaching, for to teach them is but to show them their misery, and to preach to them, if we do nothing more than preach, is to mock at it. It can be met only by a right understanding, on the part of all classes, of what kinds of labor are good for men, raising them, and making them happy; by a determined sacrifice of such convenience, or beauty, or cheapness as is to be got only by the degradation of the workman; and by equally determined demand for the products and results of healthy and ennobling labor.

And how, it will be asked, are these products to be recognized, and this demand to be regulated? Easily: by the observance of three broad and simple rules:

1. Never encourage the manufacture of any article not absolutely necessary, in the production of which *Invention* has no share.

2. Never demand an exact finish for its own sake, but only for some practical or noble end.

3. Never encourage imitation or copying of any kind, except for the sake of preserving record of great works.

The second of these principles is the only one which directly rises out of the consideration of our immediate subject; but I shall briefly explain the meaning and extent of the first also, reserving the enforcement of the third for another place.

1. Never encourage the manufacture of anything not necessary, in the production of which invention has no share.

For instance. Glass beads are utterly unnecessary, and there is no design or thought employed in their manufacture. They are formed by first drawing out the glass into rods; these rods are chopped up into fragments of the size of beads by the human hand, and the fragments are then rounded in the furnace. The men who chop up the rods sit at their work all day, their hands vibrating with a perpetual and exquisitely timed palsy, and the beads dropping beneath their vibration like hail. Neither they, nor the men who draw out the rods or fuse the fragments, have the smallest occasion for the use of any single human faculty; and every young lady, therefore, who buys glass beads is engaged in the slave trade, and in a much more cruel one than that which we have so long been endeavoring to put down.

But glass cups and vessels may become the subjects of exquisite invention; and if in buying these we pay for the invention, that is to say for the beautiful form, or color, or engraving, and not for mere finish of execution, we are doing good to humanity.

So, again, the cutting of precious stones, in all ordinary cases, requires little exertion of any mental faculty; some tact and judgment in avoiding flaws, and so on, but nothing to bring out the whole mind. Every person who wears cut jewels merely for the sake of their value is, therefore, a slave driver.

But the working of the goldsmith, and the various designing of grouped jewelry and enamel-work, may become the subject of the most noble human intelligence. Therefore, money spent in the purchase of well-designed plate, of precious engraved vases, cameos, or enamels, does good to humanity; and, in work of this kind, jewels may be employed to heighten its splendor; and their cutting is then a price paid for the attainment of a noble end, and thus perfectly allowable.

I shall perhaps press this law farther elsewhere, but our immediate concern is chiefly with the second, namely, never to demand an exact finish, when it does not lead to a noble end. For observe, I have only dwelt upon the rudeness of Gothic, or any other kind of imperfectness, as admirable, where it was impossible to get design or thought without it. If you are to have the thought of a rough and untaught man, you must have it in a rough and untaught way; but from an educated man, who can without effort express his thoughts in an educated way, take the graceful expression, and be thankful. Only *get* the thought, and do not silence the peasant because he cannot speak good grammar, or until you have taught him his grammar. Grammar and refinement are good things, both, only be sure of the better thing first. And thus in art, delicate finish is desirable from the greatest masters, and is always given by them. In some places Michael Angelo, Leonardo, Phidias, Perugino, Turner all finished with the most exquisite care; and the finish they give always leads to the fuller accomplishment of their noble purposes. But lower men than these cannot finish, for it requires consummate knowledge to finish consummately, and then we must take their thoughts as they are able to give them. So the rule is simple: Always look for invention first, and after that, for such execution as will help the invention, and as the inventor is capable of without painful effort, and *no more*. Above all, demand no refinement of execution where there is no thought, for that is slaves' work, unredeemed. Rather choose rough work than smooth work, so only that the practical purpose be answered, and never imagine there is reason to be proud of anything that may be accomplished by patience and sandpaper.

I shall only give one example, which however will show the reader what I mean, from the manufacture already alluded to, that of glass. Our modern glass is exquisitely clear in its substance, true in its form, accurate in its cutting. We are proud of this. We ought to be ashamed of it. The old Venice glass was muddy, inaccurate in all its forms, and clumsily cut, if at all. And the old Venetian was justly proud of it. For there is this difference between the English and Venetian workman, that the former thinks only of accurately matching his patterns, and getting his curves perfectly true and his edges perfectly sharp, and becomes a mere machine for rounding curves and sharpening edges, while the old Venetian cared not a whit whether his edges were sharp or not, but he invented a new design for every glass that he made, and never molded a handle or a lip without a new fancy in it. And therefore, though some Venetian glass is ugly and clumsy enough, when made by clumsy and uninventive workmen, other Venetian glass is so lovely in its forms that no price is too great for it; and we never see the same form in it twice. Now you cannot have the finish and the varied form too. If the workman is thinking about his edges, he cannot be thinking of his design; if of his design, he cannot think of his edges. Choose whether you will pay for the lovely form or the perfect finish, and choose at the same moment whether you will make the worker a man or a grindstone.

Nay, but the reader interrupts me—"If the workman can design beautifully, I would not have him kept at the furnace. Let him be taken away and made a gentleman, and have a studio, and design his glass there, and I will have it blown and cut for him by common workmen, and so I will have my design and my finish too."

All ideas of this kind are founded upon two mistaken suppositions: the first, that one man's thoughts can be, or ought to be, executed by another man's hands; the second, that manual labor is a degradation, when it is governed by intellect.

On a large scale, and in work determinable by line and rule, it is indeed both possible and necessary that the thoughts of one man should be carried out by the labor of others; in this sense I have already defined the best architecture to be the expression of the mind of manhood by the hands of childhood. But on a smaller scale, and in a design which cannot be mathematically defined, one man's thoughts can never be expressed by another: and the difference between the spirit of touch of the man who is inventing, and of the man who is obeying directions, is often all the difference between a great and a common work of art. How wide the separation is between original and secondhand execution, I shall endeavor to show elsewhere; it is not so much to our purpose here as to mark the other and more fatal error of despising manual labor when governed by intellect; for it is no less fatal an error to despise it when thus regulated by intellect, than to value it for its own sake. We are always in these days endeavoring to separate the two; we want one man to be always thinking, and another to be always working, and we call one a gentleman, and the other an operative; whereas the workman ought often to be thinking, and the thinker often to be working, and both should be gentlemen, in the best sense. As it is, we make both ungentle, the one envying, the other despising, his brother; and the mass of society is made up of morbid thinkers, and miserable workers. Now it is only by labor that thought can be made healthy, and only by thought that labor can be made happy, and the two cannot be separated with impunity. It would be well if all of us were good handicraftsmen in some kind, and the dishonor of manual labor done away with altogether; so that though there should still be a trenchant distinction of race between nobles and commoners, there should not, among the latter, be a trenchant distinction of employment, as between idle and working men, or between men of liberal and illiberal professions. All professions should be liberal, and there should be less pride felt in peculiarity of employment, and more in excellence of achievement. And yet more, in each several profession, no master should be too proud to do its hardest work. The painter should grind his own colors; the architect work in the mason's yard with his men; the master manufacturer be himself a more skillful operative than any man in his mills; and the distinction between one man and another be only in experience and skill, and the authority and wealth which these must naturally and justly obtain.

I should be led far from the matter in hand, if I were to pursue this interesting subject. Enough, I trust, has been said to show the reader that the rudeness or imperfection which at first rendered the term "Gothic" one of reproach is indeed, when rightly understood, one of the most noble characters of Christian architecture, and not only a noble but an *essential* one. It seems a fantastic paradox, but it is nevertheless a most important truth, that no architecture can be truly noble which is *not* imperfect. And this is easily demonstrable. For since the architect, whom we will suppose capable of doing all in perfection, cannot execute the whole with his own hands, he must either make slaves of his workmen in the old Greek, and present English fashion, and level his work to a slave's capacities, which is to degrade it; or else he must take his workmen as he finds them, and let them show their weaknesses together with their strength, which will involve the Gothic imperfection, but render the whole work as noble as the intellect of the age can make it.

But the principle may be stated more broadly still. I have confined the illustration of it to architecture, but I must not leave it as if true of architecture only. Hitherto I have used the words imperfect and perfect merely to distinguish between work grossly unskillful, and work executed with average precision and science; and I have been pleading that any degree of unskillfulness should be admitted, so only that the laborer's mind had room for expression. But, accurately speaking, no good work whatever can be perfect, and *the demand for perfection is always a sign of a misunderstanding of the ends of art.*

This for two reasons, both based on everlasting laws. The first, that no great man ever stops working till he has reached his point of failure; that is to say, his mind is always far in advance of his powers of execution, and the latter will now and then give way in trying to follow it; besides that he will always give to the inferior portions of his work only such inferior attention as they require; and according to his greatness he becomes so accustomed to the feeling of dissatisfaction with the best he can do, that in moments of lassitude or anger with himself he will not care though the beholder be dissatisfied also. I believe there has only been one man who would not acknowledge this necessity, and strove always to reach perfection, Leonardo; the end of his vain effort being merely that he would take ten years to a picture, and leave it unfinished. And therefore, if we are to have great men working at all, or less men doing their best, the work will be imperfect, however beautiful. Of human work none but what is bad can be perfect, in its own bad way.[8]

8. "The Elgin marbles are supposed by many persons to be 'perfect.' In the most important portions they indeed approach perfection, but only there. The draperies are unfinished, the hair and wool of the animals are unfinished, and the entire bas-reliefs of the frieze are roughly cut" [Ruskin's note]. Ruskin is referring to the collection of statues brought from Athens to England by Lord Elgin, statues which were considered models of perfect realism.

The second reason is that imperfection is in some sort essential to all that we know of life. It is the sign of life in a mortal body, that is to say, of a state of progress and change. Nothing that lives is, or can be, rigidly perfect; part of it is decaying, part nascent. The foxglove blossom—a third part bud, a third part past, a third part in full bloom—is a type of the life of this world. And in all things that live there are certain irregularities and deficiencies which are not only signs of life, but sources of beauty. No human face is exactly the same in its lines on each side, no leaf perfect in its lobes, no branch in its symmetry. All admit irregularity as they imply change; and to banish imperfection is to destroy expression, to check exertion, to paralyze vitality. All things are literally better, lovelier, and more beloved for the imperfections which have been divinely appointed, that the law of human life may be Effort, and the law of human judgment, Mercy.

Accept this then for a universal law, that neither architecture nor any other noble work of man can be good unless it be imperfect; and let us be prepared for the otherwise strange fact, which we shall discern clearly as we approach the period of the Renaissance, that the first cause of the fall of the arts of Europe was a relentless requirement of perfection, incapable alike either of being silenced by veneration for greatness, or softened into forgiveness of simplicity.

Thus far then of the Rudeness or Savageness, which is the first mental element of Gothic architecture. It is an element in many other healthy architectures also, as in Byzantine and Romanesque; but true Gothic cannot exist without it. * * *

1851–53

The Storm-Cloud of the Nineteenth Century

Lecture I[1]

Let me first assure my audience that I have no *arrière pensée*[2] in the title chosen for this lecture. I might, indeed, have meant, and it

1. Delivered February 4, 1884, at the London Institution. Some newspapers complained that the lecture seemed merely to blame air pollution on the Devil; however, what Ruskin was blaming was the devil of industrialism, the source of the "Manchester devil's darkness" and of the "dense manufacturing mist." As E. T. Cook noted: "industrial statistics fully bear out the date which Ruskin fixes for the growth of the phenomena in question: the storm-cloud thickened just when the consumption of coal went up by leaps and bounds, both in this country [England] and in the industrialized parts of central Europe."

Much of the evidence cited in the lecture derives from diaries and sketchbooks in which, over a period of 50 years, Ruskin had recorded observations of sunsets and storms, a record that enabled him to point up the changes. As he stated in his second lecture: "Had the weather when I was young been such as it is now, no book such as *Modern Painters* ever would or *could* have been written; for every argument, and every sentiment in that book, was founded on the personal experience of the beauty and blessing of nature, all spring and summer long; and on the then demonstrable fact that over a great portion of the world's surface the air and the earth were fitted to the education of the spirit of man as closely as a schoolboy's primer is to his labor, and as gloriously as a lover's mistress is to his eyes.

"That harmony is now broken, and broken the world round. * * *"

2. Afterthought or hidden meaning.

would have been only too like me to mean, any number of things by such a title;—but, tonight, I mean simply what I have said, and propose to bring to your notice a series of cloud phenomena, which, so far as I can weigh existing evidence, are peculiar to our own times; yet which have not hitherto received any special notice or description from meteorologists.

So far as the existing evidence, I say, of former literature can be interpreted, the storm-cloud—or more accurately plague-cloud, for it is not always stormy—which I am about to describe to you, never was seen but by now living, or *lately* living eyes. It is not yet twenty years that this—I may well call it, wonderful—cloud has been, in its essence, recognizable. There is no description of it, so far as I have read, or by any ancient observer. Neither Homer nor Virgil, neither Aristophanes nor Horace, acknowledge any such clouds among those compelled by Jove. Chaucer has no word of them, nor Dante; Milton none, nor Thomson. In modern times, Scott, Wordsworth, and Byron are alike unconscious of them; and the most observant and descriptive of scientific men, De Saussure,[3] is utterly silent concerning them. Taking up the traditions of air from the year before Scott's death, I am able, by my own constant and close observation, to certify you that in the forty following years (1831 to 1871 approximately—for the phenomena in question came on gradually)—no such clouds as these are, and are now often for months without intermission, were ever seen in the skies of England, France, or Italy.

In those old days, when weather was fine, it was luxuriously fine; when it was bad—it was often abominably bad, but it had its fit of temper and was done with it—it didn't sulk for three months without letting you see the sun,—nor send you one cyclone inside out, every Saturday afternoon, and another outside in, every Monday morning.

In fine weather the sky was either blue or clear in its light; the clouds, either white or golden, adding to, not abating, the luster of the sky. In wet weather, there were two different species of clouds, —those of beneficent rain, which for distinction's sake I will call the non-electric rain-cloud, and those of storm, usually charged highly with electricity. The beneficent rain-cloud was indeed often extremely dull and gray for days together, but gracious nevertheless, felt to be doing good, and often to be delightful after drought; capable also of the most exquisite coloring, under certain conditions; and continually traversed in clearing by the rainbow:—and, secondly, the storm-cloud, always majestic, often dazzlingly beautiful, and felt also to be beneficent in its own way, affecting the mass of

---

3. Horace Bénédict de Saussure (1740–99), Swiss geologist and alpinist.

the air with vital agitation, and purging it from the impurity of all morbific elements.

In the entire system of the Firmament, thus seen and understood, there appeared to be, to all the thinkers of those ages, the incontrovertible and unmistakable evidence of a Divine Power in creation, which had fitted, as the air for human breath, so the clouds for human sight and nourishment;—the Father who was in heaven feeding day by day the souls of His children with marvels, and satisfying them with bread, and so filling their hearts with food and gladness.[4]

* * *

Thus far then of clouds that were once familiar; now at last, entering on my immediate subject, I shall best introduce it to you by reading an entry in my diary which gives progressive description of the most gentle aspect of the modern plague-cloud.

Bolton Abbey, 4th July, 1875.

Half-past eight, morning; the first bright morning for the last fortnight.

At half-past five it was entirely clear, and entirely calm; the moorlands glowing, and the Wharfe[5] glittering in sacred light, and even the thin-stemmed field-flowers quiet as stars, in the peace in which—

> All trees and simples, great and small,
>   That balmy leaf do bear,
> Than they were painted on a wall,
>   No more do move, nor steir.[6]

But, an hour ago, the leaves at my window first shook slightly. They are now trembling *continuously*, as those of all the trees, under a gradually rising wind, of which the tremulous action sacrcely permits the direction to be defined,—but which falls and returns in fits of varying force, like those which precede a thunderstorm—never wholly ceasing: the direction of its upper current is shown by a few ragged white clouds, moving fast from the north, which rose, at the time of the first leaf-shaking, behind the edge of the moors in the east.

This wind is the plague-wind of the eighth decade of years in the nineteenth century; a period which will assuredly be recognized in future meteorological history as one of phenomena hitherto unrecorded in the courses of nature, and characterized preeminently by the almost ceaseless action of this calamitous wind. While I have been writing these sentences, the white clouds above specified have increased to twice the size they had when I

---

4. Acts xiv.17.
5. River near Bolton Abbey in Yorkshire.

6. Stir. From a hymn by a Scottish clergyman, Alexander Herne (1560–1609).

began to write; and in about two hours from this time—say by eleven o'clock, if the wind continue,—the whole sky will be dark with them, as it was yesterday, and has been through prolonged periods during the last five years. I first noticed the definite character of this wind, and of the clouds it brings with it, in the year 1871, describing it then in the July number of *Fors Clavigera;* but little, at that time, apprehending either its universality, or any probability of its annual continuance. I am able now to state positively that its range of power extends from the North of England to Sicily; and that it blows more or less during the whole of the year, except the early autumn. This autumnal abdication is, I hope, beginning: it blew but feebly yesterday, though without intermission, from the north, making every shady place cold, while the sun was burning; its effect on the sky being only to dim the blue of it between masses of ragged cumulus. Today it has entirely fallen; and there seems hope of bright weather, the first for me since the end of May, when I had two fine days at Aylesbury; the third, May 28th, being black again from morning to evening. There seems to be some reference to the blackness caused by the prevalence of this wind in the old French name of Bise, "*grey* wind"; and, indeed, one of the darkest and bitterest days of it I ever saw was at Vevay in 1872.

The first time I recognized the clouds brought by the plaguewind as distinct in character was in walking back from Oxford, after a hard day's work, to Abingdon, in the early spring of 1871: it would take too long to give you any account this evening of the particulars which drew my attention to them; but during the following months I had too frequent opportunities of verifying my first thoughts of them, and on the first of July in that year wrote the description of them which begins the *Fors Clavigera* of August, thus:—

It is the first of July, and I sit down to write by the dismalest light that ever yet I wrote by; namely, the light of this midsummer morning, in mid-England (Matlock, Derbyshire), in the year 1871.

For the sky is covered with gray cloud;—not rain-cloud, but a dry black veil, which no ray of sunshine can pierce; partly diffused in mist, feeble mist, enough to make distant objects unintelligible, yet without any substance, or wreathing, or color of its own. And everywhere the leaves of the trees are shaking fitfully, as they do before a thunderstorm; only not violently, but enough to show the passing to and fro of a strange, bitter, blighting wind. Dismal enough, had it been the first morning of its kind that summer had sent. But during all this spring, in London, and at Oxford, through meager March, through changelessly sullen

April, through despondent May, and darkened June, morning after morning has come gray-shrouded thus.

And it is a new thing to me, and a very dreadful one. I am fifty years old, and more; and since I was five, have gleaned the best hours of my life in the sun of spring and summer mornings; and I never saw such as these, till now.

And the scientific men are busy as ants, examining the sun and the moon, and the seven stars, and can tell me all about *them*, I believe, by this time; and how they move, and what they are made of.

And I do not care, for my part, two copper spangles how they move, nor what they are made of. I can't move them any other way than they go, nor make them of anything else, better than they are made. But I would care much and give much, if I could be told where this bitter wind comes from, and what *it* is made of.

For, perhaps, with forethought, and fine laboratory science, one might make it of something else.

It looks partly as if it were made of poisonous smoke; very possibly it may be: there are at least two hundred furnace chimneys in a square of two miles on every side of me. But mere smoke would not blow to and fro in that wild way. It looks more to me as if it were made of dead men's souls—such of them as are not gone yet where they have to go, and may be flitting hither and thither, doubting, themselves, of the fittest place for them.

You know, if there *are* such things as souls, and if ever any of them haunt places where they have been hurt, there must be many above us, just now, displeased enough!

The last sentence refers of course to the battles of the Franco-German campaign, which was especially horrible to me, in its digging, as the Germans should have known, a moat flooded with waters of death between the two nations for a century to come.

Since that Midsummer day, my attention, however otherwise occupied, has never relaxed in its record of the phenomena characteristic of the plague-wind; and I now define for you, as briefly as possible, the essential signs of it.

(1.) It is a wind of darkness,—all the former conditions of tormenting winds, whether from the north or east, were more or less capable of co-existing with sunlight, and often with steady and bright sunlight; but whenever, and wherever the plague-wind blows, be it but for ten minutes, the sky is darkened instantly.

(2.) It is a malignant *quality* of wind, unconnected with any one quarter of the compass; it blows indifferently from all, attaching its own bitterness and malice to the worst characters of the proper winds of each quarter. It will blow either with drenching rain, or dry rage, from the south,—with ruinous blasts from the west,—with bitterest chills from the north,—and with venomous blight from the east.

Its own favorite quarter, however, is the southwest, so that it is distinguished in its malignity equally from the Bise of Provence, which is a north wind always, and from our own old friend, the east.

(3.) It always blows *tremulously*, making the leaves of the trees shudder as if they were all aspens, but with a peculiar fitfulness which gives them—and I watch them this moment as I write—an expression of anger as well as of fear and distress. You may see the kind of quivering, and hear the ominous whimpering, in the gusts that precede a great thunderstorm; but plague-wind is more panic-struck, and feverish; and its sound is a hiss instead of a wail.

When I was last at Avallon, in South France, I went to see *Faust*[7] played at the little country theater: it was done with scarcely any means of pictorial effect, except a few old curtains, and a blue light or two. But the night on the Brocken was nevertheless extremely appalling to me,—a strange ghastliness being obtained in some of the witch scenes merely by fine management of gesture and drapery; and in the phantom scenes, by the half-palsied, half-furious, faltering or fluttering past of phantoms stumbling as into graves; as if of not only soulless, but senseless, Dead, moving with the very action, the rage, the decrepitude, and the trembling of the plague-wind.

(4.) Not only tremulous at every moment, it is also *intermittent* with a rapidity quite unexampled in former weather. There are, indeed, days—and weeks, on which it blows without cessation, and is as inevitable as the Gulf Stream; but also there are days when it is contending with healthy weather, and on such days it will remit for half an hour, and the sun will begin to show itself, and then the wind will come back and cover the whole sky with clouds in ten minutes; and so on, every half-hour, through the whole day; so that it is often impossible to go on with any kind of drawing in color, the light being never for two seconds the same from morning till evening.

(5.) It degrades, while it intensifies, ordinary storm; but before I read you any description of its efforts in this kind, I must correct an impression which has got abroad through the papers, that I speak as if the plague-wind blew now always, and there were no more any natural weather. On the contrary, the winter of 1787–9 was one of the most healthy and lovely I ever saw ice in;—Coniston lake[8]

---

7. Goethe's drama, which Ruskin saw in 1882.
8. In the Lake District of North Lanca-

shire where Ruskin's house, Brantwood, was located.

shone under the calm clear frost in one marble field, as strong as the floor of Milan Cathedral, half a mile across and four miles down; and the first entries in my diary which I read you shall be from the 22nd to 26th June, 1876, of perfectly lovely and natural weather:—

Sunday, 25th June, 1876

Yesterday, an entirely glorious sunset, unmatched in beauty since that at Abbeville,[9]—deep scarlet, and purest rose, on purple gray, in bars; and stationary, plumy, sweeping filaments above in upper sky, like *"using up the brush,"* said Joanie; remaining in glory, every moment best, changing from one good into another, (but only in color or light—*form steady,*) for half an hour full, and the clouds afterwards fading into the gray against amber twilight, *stationary in the same form for about two hours,* at least. The darkening rose tint remained till half-past ten, the grand time being at nine.

The day had been fine,—exquisite green light on afternoon hills.

Monday, 26th June, 1876.

Yesterday an entirely perfect summer light on the Old Man;[1] Lancaster Bay all clear; Ingleborough and the great Pennine fault as on a map. Divine beauty of western color on thyme and rose, —then twilight of clearest *warm* amber far into night, of *pale* amber all night long; hills dark-clear against it.

And so it continued, only growing more intense in blue and sunlight, all day. After breakfast, I came in from the well under strawberry bed, to say I had never seen anything like it, so pure or intense, in Italy; and so it went glowing on, cloudless, with soft north wind, all day.

16th July.

The sunset almost too bright *through the blinds* for me to read Humboldt at tea by,—finally, new moon like a lime-light, reflected on breeze-struck water; traces, across dark calm, of reflected hills.

These extracts are, I hope, enough to guard you against the absurdity of supposing that it all only means that I am myself soured, or doting, in my old age, and always in an ill humor. Depend upon it, when old men are worth anything, they are better-humored than young ones; and have learned to see what good there is, and pleasantness, in the world they are likely so soon to have orders to quit.

Now then—take the following sequences of accurate description of thunderstorm, *with* plague-wind.

---

9. Ruskin had made a sketch of this sunset, in October 1868, and described it as "a beautiful example of what * * * a sunset could then be, in the districts of Kent and Picardy unaffected by smoke."
1. Mountain near Ruskin's home.

22nd June, 1876.

Thunderstorm; pitch dark, with no *blackness*,—but deep, high, *filthiness* of lurid, yet not sublimely lurid, smoke-cloud; dense manufacturing mist; fearful squalls of shivery wind, making Mr. Severn's sails[2] quiver like a man in a fever fit—all about four, afternoon—but only two or three claps of thunder, and feeble, though near, flashes. I never saw such a dirty, weak, foul storm. It cleared suddenly after raining all afternoon, at half-past eight to nine, into pure, natural weather,—low rain-clouds on quite clear, green, wet hills.

Brantwood, 13th August, 1879.

The most terrific and horrible thunderstorm, this morning, I ever remember. It waked me at six, or a little before—then rolling incessantly, like railway luggage trains, quite ghastly in its mockery of them—the air one loathsome mass of sultry and foul fog, like smoke; scarcely raining at all, but increasing to heavier rollings, with flashes quivering vaguely through all the air, and at last terrific double streams of reddish-violet fire, not forked or zigzag, but rippled rivulets—two at the same instant some twenty to thirty degrees apart, and lasting on the eye at least half a second, with grand artillery-peals following; not rattling crashes, or irregular cracklings, but delivered volleys. It lasted an hour, then passed off, clearing a little, without rain to speak of,—not a glimpse of blue,—and now, half-past seven, seems settling down again into Manchester devil's darkness.

Quarter to eight, morning.—Thunder returned, all the air collapsed into one black fog, the hills invisible, and scarcely visible the opposite shore; heavy rain in short fits, and frequent, though less formidable, flashes, and shorter thunder. While I have written this sentence the cloud has again dissolved itself, like a nasty solution in a bottle, with miraculous and unnatural rapidity, and the hills are in sight again; a double-forked flash—rippled, I mean, like the others—starts into its frightful ladder of light between me and Wetherlam, as I raise my eyes. All black above, a rugged spray cloud on the Eaglet. The "Eaglet" is my own name for the bold and elevated crag to the west of the little lake above Coniston mines. It had no name among the country people, and is one of the most conspicuous features of the mountain chain, as seen from Brantwood.)

Half-past eight.—Three times light and three times dark since last I wrote, and the darkness seeming each time as it settles more loathsome, at last stopping my reading in mere blindness. One lurid gleam of white cumulus in upper lead-blue sky, seen for half a minute through the sulphurous chimney-pot vomit of blackguardly cloud beneath, where its rags were thinnest.

---

2. A neighbor's sailboat on Coniston Lake.

Thursday, 22nd Feb. 1883.

Yesterday a fearfully dark mist all afternoon, with steady, south plague-wind of the bitterest, nastiest, poisonous blight, and fretful flutter. I could scarcely stay in the wood for the horror of it. Today, really rather bright blue, and bright semi-cumuli, with the frantic Old Man blowing sheaves of lancets and chisels across the lake—not in strength enough, or whirl enough, to raise it in spray, but tracing every squall's outline in black on the silver grey waves, and whistling meanly, and as if on a flute made of a file.

Sunday, 17th August, 1879.

Raining in foul drizzle, slow and steady; sky pitch-dark, and I just get a little light by sitting in the bow-window; diabolic clouds over everything: and looking over my kitchen garden yesterday, I found it one miserable mass of weeds gone to seed, the roses in the higher garden putrefied into brown sponges, feeling like dead snails; and the half-ripe strawberries all rotten at the stalks.

And now I come to the most important sign of the plague-wind and the plague-cloud: that in bringing on their peculiar darkness, they *blanch* the sun instead of reddening it. And here I must note briefly to you the uselessness of observation by instruments, or machines, instead of eyes. In the first year when I had begun to notice the specialty of the plague-wind, I went of course to the Oxford observatory to consult its registrars. They have their anemometer always on the twirl, and can tell you the force, or at least the pace, of a gale, by day or night. But the anemometer can only record for you how often it has been driven round, not at all whether it went round *steadily*, or went round *trembling*. And on that point depends the entire question whether it is a plague breeze or a healthy one: and what's the use of telling you whether the wind's strong or not, when it can't tell you whether it's a strong medicine, or a strong poison?

But again—you have your *sun*-measure, and can tell exactly at any moment how strong, or how weak, or how wanting, the sun is. But the sun-measurer can't tell you whether the rays are stopped by a dense *shallow* cloud, or a thin *deep* one. In healthy weather, the sun is hidden behind a cloud, as it is behind a tree; and, when the cloud is past, it comes out again, as bright as before. But in plague-wind, the sun is choked out of the whole heaven, all day long, by a cloud which may be a thousand miles square and five miles deep.

And yet observe: that thin, scraggy, filthy, mangy, miserable cloud, for all the depth of it, can't turn the sun red, as a good, business-like fog does with a hundred feet or so of itself. By the plague-wind every breath of air you draw is polluted, half round the world;

in a London fog the air itself is pure, though you choose to mix up dirt with it, and choke yourself with your own nastiness.

Now I'm going to show you a diagram of a sunset in entirely pure weather, above London smoke.[3] I saw it and sketched it from my old post of observation—the top garret of my father's house at Herne Hill. There, when the wind is south, we are outside of the smoke and above it; and this diagram, admirably enlarged from my own drawing by my, now in all things best aide-de-camp, Mr. Collingwood, shows you an old-fashioned sunset—the sort of thing Turner and I used to have to look at,—(nobody else ever would) constantly. Every sunset and every dawn, in fine weather, had something of the sort to show us. This is one of the last pure sunsets I ever saw, about the year 1876,—and the point I want you to note in it is, that the air being pure, the smoke on the horizon, though at last it hides the sun, yet hides it through gold and vermilion. Now, don't go away fancying there's any exaggeration in that study. The *prismatic* colors, I told you, were simply impossible to paint; these, which are transmitted colors, can indeed be suggested, but no more. The brightest pigment we have would look dim beside the truth.

I should have liked to have blotted down for you a bit of plague-cloud to put beside this; but Heaven knows, you can see enough of it nowadays without any trouble of mine; and if you want, in a hurry, to see what the sun looks like through it, you've only to throw a bad half-crown into a basin of soap and water.

Blanched Sun,—blighted grass,—blinded man.—If, in conclusion, you ask me for any conceivable cause or meaning of these things—I can tell you none, according to your modern beliefs; but I can tell you what meaning it would have borne to the men of old time. Remember, for the last twenty years, England, and all foreign nations, either tempting her, or following her, have blasphemed[4] the name of God deliberately and openly; and have done iniquity by proclamation, every man doing as much injustice to his brother as it is in his power to do. Of states in such moral gloom every seer of old predicted the physical gloom, saying, "The light shall be darkened in the heavens thereof, and the stars shall withdraw their shining."[5] All Greek, all Christian, all Jewish prophecy insists on the same truth through a thousand myths; but of all the chief, to former thought, was the fable of the Jewish warrior and prophet, for whom the sun hasted not to go down,[6] with which I leave you

---

3. The illustration shown at the lecture was entitled "An Old-Fashioned Sunset, 1876."
4. Ruskin, in a note, defined blasphemy as " 'harmful speaking'–not against God only, but against man, and against all the good works and purposes of Nature. The word is accurately opposed to 'Euphemy,' the right or well-speaking of God and His world. * * * And the universal instinct of blasphemy in the modern scientific mind is above all manifested in its love of what is ugly, and natural enthrallment by the abominable."
5. Joel ii.10.
6. On Joshua's commanding the sun to stand still, see Joshua x.13.

to compare at leisure the physical result of your own wars and prophecies, as declared by your own elect journal not fourteen days ago,—that the Empire of England, on which formerly the sun never set, has become one on which he never rises.[7]

What is best to be done, do you ask me? The answer is plain. Whether you can affect the signs of the sky or not, you *can* the signs of the times. Whether you can bring the *sun* back or not, you can assuredly bring back your own cheerfulness, and your own honesty. You may not be able to say to the winds, "Peace; be still,"[8] but you can cease from the insolence of your own lips, and the troubling of your own passions. And all *that* it would be extremely well to do, even though the day *were* coming when the sun should be as darkness, and the moon as blood.[9] But, the paths of rectitude and piety once regained, who shall say that the promise of old time would not be found to hold for us also?—"Bring ye all the tithes into my storehouse, and prove me now herewith, saith the Lord God, if I will not open you the windows of heaven, and pour you out a blessing, that there shall not be room enough to receive it."[1]

1884

7. In January, 1884, after weeks of sun-less weather, the *Pall Mall Gazette* had made joking references to the popular boast about the sun never setting on the British dominions, for the good reason that it never rises.

8. Mark iv.39.
9. Cf. the prophecy in Revelation vi.12: "the sun became black as sackcloth of hair, and the moon became as blood."
1. Malachi iii.10.

ARTHUR HUGH CLOUGH
(1819–1861)

The writings of Clough (whose name is pronounced so as to rhyme with *rough*) are usually treated as a kind of footnote to those of his friend Matthew Arnold. Read in this way they can indeed add to our understanding of Arnold's early poems written during the phase of religious stress shared by both young men. Some of Clough's admirers argue, however, that such a reading is to be deplored because Clough, despite his frequent clumsiness in versification, is a poet of considerable stature in his own right. What is beyond dispute is that he provides exceptional insights into the intellectual history of his century.

Like many Victorians (including John Ruskin, his exact contemporary), Clough was permanently influenced by his mother's pious religious convictions, her influence being reinforced by his years at Rugby School, where he was the prize pupil of Dr. Thomas Arnold. Later, at Oxford, his earnest preoccupation with religious duty was undermined by a number of different intellectual developments. He was forced to think through questions of High Church authoritarianism and traditionalism—provoked by John Henry Newman's presence at Oxford—and to confront the evidence of scientific critics who challenged the authority and authenticity of the Scriptures. Clough emerged as a skeptic in the real sense of the word. In a letter to his sister in 1847, speaking of the Atonement as an article of Christian faith, he remarks: "I think others are more right who say boldly. We don't understand it, and therefore we *won't* fall down and worship it. Though there is no occasion for adding—'there *is* nothing in it—' I should say, Until I know, I will wait: and if I am not born with the power to discover, I will do what I can * * * and neither pretend to know, nor without knowing, pretend to embrace: nor yet oppose those who by whatever means are increasing or trying to increase knowledge." A year later, reflections of this kind led Clough to resign his fellowship at Oxford where he was expected to subscribe to the doctrines of the Church of England. For the rest of his life he held various educational posts and also traveled extensively—to the United States, where his early childhood had been spent, and in Italy, a country which served as the setting of several of his poems.

Much of Clough's poetry was published posthumously. His first volume, *The Bothie of Tober-na-Vuolich* (1848), is a delightful novel in verse, an undergraduate love story exhibiting aspects of his character omitted in Arnold's picture of him in *Thyrsis*. For despite his painful exposure to religious uncertainties, Clough had a strain of high spirits and fun that gives flavor to his best poems. In his later poems, including *Dipsychus* (1850), the strains of earnestness, uncertainty, and humor are blended into an ironic point of view different from Matthew Arnold's and, in fact, different from the characteristic tone of most of his contemporaries. Perhaps one of the reasons that Clough's poetry has been inadequately appreciated is that this distinctive tone of his is most evident in his full-length poems rather than in the short hymnlike verses by which he is usually represented in anthologies.

Epi-strauss-ium[1]

Matthew and Mark and Luke and holy John
Evanished all and gone!
Yea, he[2] that erst, his dusky curtains quitting,
Through Eastern pictured panes his level beams transmitting,
With gorgeous portraits blent,   5
On them his glories intercepted spent,
Southwestering now, through windows plainly glassed,
On the inside face his radiance keen hath cast,
And in the luster lost, invisible, and gone,
Are, say you, Matthew, Mark, and Luke and holy John?   10
Lost, is it? lost, to be recovered never?
However,
The place of worship the meantime with light

---

1. The title is a play on *epi-thalamium*, which means "concerning the bridal chamber." The word usually refers to a song in honor of a bride and bridegroom (as in Spenser's poem). Clough's title means "concerning Strauss-ism," a reference to D. F. Strauss, a German Biblical scholar whose *Life of Jesus* was translated into English by George Eliot in 1846. The "light" of Strauss's analysis reputedly showed up the historical inaccuracy of parts of the Gospels in the Bible.

2. The sun. Cf. lines 13–16 of *Say Not the Struggle*, below.

Is, if less richly, more sincerely bright,
And in blue skies the Orb is manifest to sight.   15
1847   1869

The Latest Decalogue

Thou shalt have one God only; who
Would be at the expense of two?
No graven images may be
Worshiped, except the currency.
Swear not at all; for, for thy curse   5
Thine enemy is none the worse.
At church on Sunday to attend
Will serve to keep the world thy friend.
Honor thy parents; that is, all
From whom advancement may befall.   10
Thou shalt not kill; but need'st not strive
Officiously to keep alive.
Do not adultery commit;
Advantage rarely comes of it.
Thou shalt not steal; an empty feat,   15
When it's so lucrative to cheat.
Bear not false witness; let the lie
Have time on its own wings to fly.
Thou shalt not covet, but tradition
Approves all forms of competition.   20

The sum of all is, thou shalt love,
If anybody, God above:
At any rate shall never labor
More than thyself to love thy neighbor.[3]

                                                                   1862

Say Not the Struggle Nought Availeth

Say not the struggle nought availeth,
    The labor and the wounds are vain,
The enemy faints not, nor faileth,
    And as things have been they remain.

If hopes were dupes, fears may be liars;   5
    It may be, in yon smoke concealed,
Your comrades chase e'en now the fliers,
    And, but for you, possess the field.

For while the tired waves, vainly breaking,
    Seem here no painful inch to gain,   10
Far back, through creeks and inlets making,
    Comes silent, flooding in, the main.

3. Lines 21–24 were discovered in one   originally included in published versions
of Clough's manuscripts and were not   of the poem.

And not by eastern windows only,
　　When daylight comes, comes in the light,
In front, the sun climbs slow, how slowly,
　　But westward, look, the land is bright.

1849   1862

From Dipsychus
I Dreamt a Dream[4]

I dreamt a dream; till morning light
A bell rang in my head all night,
Tinkling and tinkling first, and then
Tolling; and tinkling; tolling again.
So brisk and gay, and then so slow!　　　　　　　　　5
O joy, and terror! mirth, and woe!
Ting, ting, there is no God; ting, ting—
Dong, there is no God; dong,
There is no God; dong, dong!

Ting, ting, there is no God; ting, ting;　　　　　　10
Come dance and play, and merrily sing—
Ting, ting a ding; ting, ting a ding!
O pretty girl who trippest along,
Come to my bed—it isn't wrong.
Uncork the bottle, sing the song!　　　　　　　　　15
Ting, ting a ding: dong, dong.
Wine has dregs; the song an end;
A silly girl is a poor friend
And age and weakness who shall mend?
Dong, there is no God; Dong!　　　　　　　　　　20

Ting, ting a ding! Come dance and sing!
Staid Englishmen, who toil and slave
From your first breeching[5] to your grave,
And seldom spend and always save,
And do your duty all your life　　　　　　　　　　25
By your young family and wife;
Come, be 't not said you ne'er had known
What earth can furnish you alone.
The Italian, Frenchman, German even,
Have given up all thoughts of heaven;　　　　　　30
And you still linger—oh, you fool!
Because of what you learnt at school.
You should have gone at least to college,

---

4. Dipsychus, the Faust-like hero of
Clough's long poem, is in Venice, a
city of many bells, where he reports
observations and reflections to a companion. The hero's name means "two-
souled," a reference to the split be-

tween his worldliness and his idealism.
This selection is from Scene V, lines
7–92 and 120–29.
5. First wearing of trousers or breeches
by a boy.

And got a little ampler knowledge.
Ah well, and yet—dong, dong, dong: 35
Do, if you like, as now you do;
If work's a cheat, so's pleasure too;
And nothing's new and nothing's true;
Dong, there is no God; dong!

O Rosalie, my precious maid,   40
I think thou thinkest love is true;
And on thy fragrant bosom laid
I almost could believe it too.
O in our nook, unknown, unseen,
We'll hold our fancy like a screen,   45
Us and the dreadful fact between.
And it shall yet be long, aye, long,
The quiet notes of our low song
Shall keep us from that sad dong, dong.
Hark, hark, hark! O voice of fear![6]   50
It reaches us here, even here!
Dong, there is no God; dong!

Ring ding, ring ding, tara, tara,
To battle, to battle—haste, haste—
To battle, to battle—aha, aha!   55
On, on, to the conqueror's feast.
From east and west, and south and north,
Ye men of valor and of worth,
Ye mighty men of arms, come forth,
And work your will, for that is just;   60
And in your impulse put your trust,
Beneath your feet the fools are dust.
Alas, alas! O grief and wrong,
The good are weak, the wicked strong;
And O my God, how long, how long?   65
Dong, there is no God; dong!

Ring, ting; to bow before the strong,
There is a rapture too in this;
Speak, outraged maiden, in thy wrong
Did terror bring no secret bliss?   70
Were boys' shy lips worth half a song
Compared to the hot soldier's kiss?
Work for thy master, work, thou slave
He is not merciful, but brave.
Be 't joy to serve, who free and proud   75
Scorns thee and all the ignoble crowd;
Take that, 'tis all thou art allowed,
Except the snaky hope that they
May sometime serve, who rule today,
When, by hell-demons, shan't they pay?   80

6. Cf. *Love's Labour's Lost* (V.ii.911–12): " 'Cuckoo, cuckoo!' O word of
fear, / Unpleasing to a married ear!"

O wickedness, O shame and grief,
And heavy load, and no relief!
O God, O God! and which is worst,
To be the curser or the cursed,
The victim or the murderer? Dong   85
Dong, there is no God; dong!

* * *

I had a dream, from eve to light
A bell went sounding all the night.
Gay mirth, black woe, thin joys, huge pain:
I tried to stop it, but in vain.   90
It ran right on, and never broke;
Only when day began to stream
Through the white curtains to my bed,
And like an angel at my head
Light stood and touched me—I awoke,   95
And looked, and said, "It is a dream."

"*There Is No God,*" *the Wicked Saith*[7]

"There is no God," the wicked saith,
  "And truly it's a blessing,
For what he might have done with us
  It's better only guessing."

"There is no God," a youngster thinks,   5
  "Or really, if there may be,
He surely didn't mean a man
  Always to be a baby."

"There is no God, or if there is,"
  The tradesman thinks, "'twere funny   10
If he should take it ill in me
  To make a little money."

"Whether there be," the rich man says,
  "It matters very little,
For I and mine, thank somebody,   15
  Are not in want of victual."

Some others, also, to themselves
  Who scarce so much as doubt it,
Think there is none, when they are well,
  And do not think about it.   20

But country folks who live beneath
  The shadow of the steeple;
The parson and the parson's wife,
  And mostly married people;

7. From *Dipsychus* V.152 ff.

Youths green and happy in first love,   25
So thankful for illusion;
And men caught out in what the world
Calls guilt, in first confusion;

And almost everyone when age,
Disease, or sorrows strike him,   30
Inclines to think there is a God,
Or something very like Him.

1850   1865

MATTHEW ARNOLD
(1822–1888)

1853: *Poems* (with Preface) published.
1857: Elected Professor of Poetry at Oxford.
1869: *Culture and Anarchy* published.

How is a full and enjoyable life to be lived in a modern industrial society? This was the recurrent topic in the poetry and prose of Matthew Arnold. In his poetry the question itself is raised; in his prose some answers are attempted. Arnold's mode of posing such questions may not always satisfy us, and his answers may sometimes be simply wrong. What is less excusable, as he himself said of Ruskin, is that he could be not only wrong but dogmatic when he was wrong. On the whole, however, his writings have fared well with posterity. "The misapprehensiveness of his age is exactly what a poet is sent to remedy," wrote Browning. Oddly enough it is to Arnold's work rather than to Browning's that the statement seems more appropriate. And its applicability to Arnold has persisted from Victorian times to ours, in part because the "misapprehensiveness" has also persisted. Of all the major Victorian writers, as F. R. Leavis has said, it is Arnold who, "because of the peculiar quality of his intelligence and the peculiar nature of his relation to his time, will repay special study in a way no others will."

Matthew Arnold was born in Laleham, a village in the valley of the Thames. That his childhood was spent in the vicinity of a river seems appropriate, for clear-flowing streams were later to appear in his poems as symbols of serenity. At 6, Arnold was moved to Rugby School, where his father, Dr. Thomas Arnold, had become headmaster. As a clergyman Dr. Arnold was a leader of the liberal or Broad Church and hence one of the principal opponents of John Henry Newman. As a headmaster he became famous as an educational reformer, a teacher who instilled into his pupils an earnest preoccupation with moral and social issues and also an awareness of the connection between liberal studies and modern life. At Rugby his eldest son, Matthew, was directly exposed to the powerful force of the father's mind and character. The son's attitude towards this force was a mixture of attraction and repulsion. That he was permanently influenced by his father is evident in his poems and in his writings on religion and politics, but like many sons of clergymen, he made a determined effort in his youth to be different. At Oxford he behaved like a character from one of Evelyn Waugh's early novels. Elegantly and colorfully dressed, alternately languid or merry in manner, he attracted attention as a dandy whose irreverent jokes irritated his more solemn undergraduate friends and acquaintances. With Rugby standards he appeared to have no connection. Even his studies did not seem to occupy him seriously. By a session of cramming, he managed to earn second-class honors in his final examinations, a near disaster that was redeemed by his election to a fellowship at Oriel College.

Arnold's biographers usually dismiss his youthful frivolity of spirit as a temporary pose or mask, but it was more. It remained to color his prose style, brightening his most serious criticism with geniality and wit. For most readers the jauntiness of his prose is a virtue, although for others it is offensive. Anyone suspicious of urbanity and irony would applaud Whitman's sour comment that Arnold is "one of the dudes of literature." A more appropriate estimate of his manner is provided by Arnold's own description of Sainte-Beuve as a critic: "a critic of measure, not exuberant; of the center, not provincial * * * with gay and amiable temper, his manner as good as his matter—the '*critique souriant*' [smiling critic]."

Unlike Tennyson or Carlyle, Arnold had to confine his writing and reading to his spare time. In 1847 he took the post of private secretary to Lord Lansdowne, and in 1851, the year of his marriage, he became an inspector of schools, a position which he held for 35 years. Although his work as an inspector may have reduced his output as a writer, it had several advantages. His extensive traveling in England took him to the homes of the more ardently Protestant middle classes, and when he criticized the dullness of middle-class life (as he often did), Arnold knew his subject intimately. His position also led to travel on the Continent to study the schools of Europe. As a critic of English education he was thus able to make helpful comparisons and to draw on a stock of fresh ideas in the same way as in his literary criticism he used his knowledge of French, German, Italian, and classical literatures to measure the achievements of English writers. Despite the monotony of much of his work as an inspector, Arnold became convinced of its importance. It was work that contributed to what he regarded as the most important need of his century: the development of a satisfactory system of education for the middle classes.

In 1849 Arnold published *The Strayed Reveler*, the first of his volumes of poetry. Eight years later, as a tribute to his poetic achievement, he was elected to the Professorship of Poetry at Oxford, a part-time position which he held for ten years. Later, like Dickens and Thackeray before him, Arnold toured America in order to make money by lecturing. For his two visits (1883 and 1886) there was the further inducement of seeing his daughter Lucy, who had married an American. Two years after his second visit to the United States, Arnold died of a sudden heart attack.

Arnold's career as a writer can be divided roughly into four periods. In the 1850's appeared most of his poems; in the 1860's, his literary criticism and social criticism; in the 1870's, his religious and educational writings, and in the 1880's, his second set of essays in literary criticism.

About his career as a poet, two questions are repeatedly asked. The first is whether his poetry is as effective or better than his prose; the second is why he virtually stopped writing poetry after 1860. The first has, of course, been variously answered. Many would endorse Tennyson's request in a letter: "Tell Mat not to write any more of those prose things like *Literature and Dogma*, but to give us something like his *Thyrsis, Scholar Gypsy*, or *Forsaken Merman*." At the opposite extreme is a recent critic, J. D. Jump, who has a high regard for Arnold's prose but considers only one of the poems to have merit: *Dover Beach*. Such readers complain, and with good cause, of Arnold's bad habits as a poet: for example, his excessive reliance upon italics instead of upon meter as a method of emphasizing the meaning of a line. Or they cite the prosy flatness with which he opens his fine sonnet *To a Friend*: "Who prop, thou ask'st, in these bad days, my mind?" Contrariwise, when Arnold leaves the flat plane of versified reflections and attempts to scale the heights of what he called "the grand style," there is a different kind of uncertainty which becomes evident, as in *Sohrab and Rustum*, in the over-elaborated similes. Yet the success of such lovely poems as *Thyrsis* is more than enough to overcome the indictments of the critics. Often, as in *Thyrsis*, he is at his best as a poet of nature. Settings of seashore or river or mountaintop provide something more than picturesque backdrops for these poems; they function to draw the meaning together. A concern for rendering outdoor nature may seem a curious accomplishment for so sophisticated a writer, but as his contemporaries noted, Arnold is in this respect, as in several others, similar to Thomas Gray.

Arnold's own verdict on the qualities of his poetry is a reasonable one. In a letter to his mother, in 1869, he writes: "My poems represent, on the whole, the main movement of mind of the last quarter of a century, and thus they will probably have their day as people become conscious to themselves of what that movement of mind is, and interested in the literary productions which reflect it. It might be fairly urged that I have less poetical sentiment than Tennyson, and less intellectual vigor and abundance than Browning; yet, because I have perhaps more of a fusion of the two than either of them, and have more regularly applied that fusion to the main line of modern development, I am likely enough to have my turn, as they have had theirs."

The emphasis in the letter upon "movement of mind" suggests that Arnold's poetry and prose should be studied together. Such an approach can be fruitful provided that it does not obscure the important difference between Arnold the poet and Arnold the critic. T. S. Eliot once said of his own writings that "in one's prose reflections one may be legitimately occupied with ideals, whereas in the writing of verse, one can deal only with actuality." Arnold's writings provide a nice verification of Eliot's seeming paradox. As a poet he usually records his own experiences, his own feelings of loneliness and isolation as a lover, his longing for a serenity that he cannot find, his melancholy sense of the passing of youth (more than for many men, Arnold's thirtieth birthday was an awesome landmark after which he felt, he said, "three parts iced over"). Above all he records his despair in a universe in which man's role seemed as incongruous as it was later to seem to Thomas Hardy. In a memorable passage of his *Stanzas from the Grande Chartreuse* he describes himself as "wandering between two worlds, one dead, / The other powerless to be born." And addressing the representatives of a faith which seems to him dead, he cries: "Take me, cowled forms, and fence me round, / Till I possess my soul again."

As a poet, then, like T. S. Eliot and W. H. Auden, Arnold provides a record of a sick individual in a sick society. This was "actuality" as he experienced it. As a prose-writer, a formulator of "ideals," he seeks a different role. It is the role of what Auden calls the "healer" of a sick society, or as he himself called Goethe, the "Physician of the iron age." And in this difference we have a clue to the question previously raised: why did Arnold virtually abandon the writing of poetry and shift into criticism? Among other reasons he abandoned it because he was dissatisfied with the kind of poetry he himself was writing.

In one of his excellent letters to his friend Arthur Hugh Clough in the 1850's (letters which provide the best insight we have into Arnold's mind and tastes) this note of dissatisfaction is struck: "I am glad you like the *Gypsy Scholar*—but what does it *do* for you? Homer *animates*—Shakespeare *animates*—in its poor way I think *Sohrab and Rustum animates*—the *Gypsy Scholar* at best awakens a pleasing melancholy. But this is not what we want." It is evident that early in his career Arnold had evolved a theory of what poetry should do for its readers, a theory based, in part, on his impression of what classical poetry had achieved. To help make life bearable, poetry, in Arnold's view, must bring joy. As he says in the Preface to his *Poems* in 1853, it must "inspirit and rejoice the reader"; it must "convey a charm, and infuse delight." Such a demand does not exclude tragic poetry but does exclude works "in which suffering finds no vent in action; in which a continual state of mental distress is prolonged." Of Charlotte Brontë's novel *Villette* he says witheringly: "The writer's mind contains nothing but hunger, rebellion, and rage. * * * No fine writing can hide this thoroughly, and it will be fatal to her in the long run." Judged by such a standard, most 19th-century poems, including *Empedocles on Etna* and others by Arnold, were unsatisfactory. And when Arnold tried himself to write poems which would meet his own requirements—*Sohrab and Rustum* or *Balder Dead*—he was not at his best. By the late 1850's he thus found himself at a dead end. By turning aside to literary criticism he was able partially to escape the dilemma. In his prose his melancholy and "morbid" personality was subordinated to the resolutely cheerful and purposeful character he had created for himself by an effort of will.

Arnold's two volumes of *Essays in Criticism* (1865 and 1888) repeatedly show how authors as different as Marcus Aurelius, Tolstoy, Homer, and Wordsworth provide the virtues he sought in his reading. Among these virtues was plainness of style. Although he could on occasion recommend the richness of language of such poets as Keats or Tennyson— their "natural magic" as he himself called it—Arnold's usual preference was for literature that was unadorned. And beyond stylistic excellences the principal virtue he admired as a critic was what he called the quality of "high seriousness." Given a world in which formal religion appeared to be of subordinate importance, it became increasingly important to Arnold that the poet must be a serious thinker who could offer guidance for his readers. Arnold's attitude towards religion helps to account for his finally asking perhaps too much from literature. Excessive expectations underlie his most glaring blunder as a critic: his solemnly inadequate discussion of Chaucer's lack of high seriousness in *The Study of Poetry*.

In *The Function of Criticism* it is apparent that Arnold regarded good literary criticism, as he regarded literature itself, as a potent force in producing a civilized society. From a close study of this basic essay one could forecast the third stage of his career: his excursion into the criticism of society which was to culminate in *Culture and Anarchy* (1869) and *Friendship's Garland* (1871).

Arnold's starting point as a critic of society is different from that of Carlyle and John Ruskin. The older prophets attacked the Victorian middle classes on the grounds of their materialism, their selfish indifference to the sufferings of the poor—their immorality, in effect. Arnold argued instead that the "Philistines," as he called them, were not so much wicked as ignorant, narrow-minded, and suffering from the dullness of their private lives. This novel analysis was reinforced by Arnold's conviction that the world of the future would be a middle-class world, a world dominated therefore by a class inadequately equipped for leadership and inadequately equipped to enjoy civilized living.

To establish this point, Arnold employed cajolery, satire, and even quotations from the newspapers with considerable effect. He also employed catchwords (such as "sweetness and light") which have remained useful slogans even though they are an obstacle to understanding the complexities of his position. His view of civilization, for example, was pared down to a four-point formula of the four "powers": conduct, intellect and knowledge, beauty, social life and manners. The formula was simple and workable. Applying it to French or American civilizations, he had a scale by which to show up the virtues of different countries as well as their inadequacies. Applying the formula to his own country, Arnold usually awarded the Victorian middle classes an "A" in the first category (of conduct) but a failing grade in the other three categories.

Arnold's relentless exposure of middle-class narrow-mindedness eventually led him into the arena of religious controversy. As a critic of religious institutions he was arguing, in effect, that just as the middle classes did not know how to lead full lives, so also did they not know how to read the Bible intelligently or attend church intelligently. Of the Christian religion he remarked that there are two things "that surely must be clear to anybody with eyes in his head. One is, that men cannot do without it; the other that they cannot do with it as it is." His three full-length studies of the Bible, including *Literature and Dogma* (1873), are best considered in this way as a postscript to his social criticism. The Bible, to Arnold, was a great work of literature like the *Odyssey*, and the Church of England was a great national institution like Parliament. Both Bible and church must be preserved not because historical Christianity was credible but because both, when properly understood, were agents of what he called "culture"—they contributed to making mankind more civilized.

The term *culture* is perhaps Arnold's most familiar catchword, although what he meant by it has sometimes been misunderstood. For him the term connotes the qualities of an open-minded intelligence (as described in *The Function of Criticism*)—a refusal to take things on authority. In this respect, Arnold appears close to T. H. Huxley and J. S. Mill. But the word also connotes a full awareness of man's past and a capacity to enjoy the best works of art, literature, history, and philosophy that have come down to us from that past. As a way of viewing life in all its aspects, including the social, political, and religious, culture represents for Arnold the most effective way of curing the ills of a sick society. It is his principal prescription.

To attempt to define culture brings one to a final aspect of Arnold's career as a critic: his writings on education, in which he sought to make cultural values, as he said, "prevail." Most obviously these writings comprise his reply to Huxley in his admirably reasoned essay, *Literature and Science*, as well as his volumes of official reports written as an inspector of schools. Less obviously they comprise all of his prose. At the core of these writings is his belief that good education is the crucial need for modern man. Arnold was essentially a great teacher raised to the nth degree. He has the faults of a teacher: a tendency to repeat himself, to lean too hard on formulated phrases, and he displays something of the lectern manner at times. He also has the great teacher's virtues, in particular the virtue of skillfully conveying to us the conviction on which all his arguments are based. This conviction is that the humanist tradition of which he is the expositor can enable the individual man or woman to live life more fully as well as to change the course of society. For these values Arnold fought. He boxed with the gloves on—kid gloves, his opponents used to say—and he provided a lively exhibition of footwork that is a pleasure in itself for us to witness. Yet the gracefulness of the display should not obscure the fact that he is landing hard blows squarely on what Carlyle called the vast blockheadism.

Although his lifelong attacks against the inadequacies of puritanism make Arnold one of the most anti-Victorian figures of the Victorian age, there is an assumption behind his attacks that is itself characteristically Victorian. This assumption is that the puritan middle classes *can* be changed, that they are, as we would more clumsily say, educable. In 1852, writing to Clough on the subject of equality (a political objective in which he believed by conviction if not by instinct), he observed: "I am more and more convinced that the world tends to become more comfortable for the mass, and more uncomfortable for those of any natural gift or distinction—and it is as well perhaps that it should be so—for hitherto the gifted have astonished and delighted the world, but not trained or inspired or in any real way changed it." Arnold's gifts as a poet and critic enabled him to do both: to delight the world and also to change it.

Shakespeare

Others abide our question. Thou art free.
We ask and ask—Thou smilest and art still,
Out-topping knowledge. For the loftiest hill,
Who to the stars uncrowns his majesty,

Planting his steadfast footsteps in the sea,[1]
Making the heaven of heavens his dwelling place,

---

1. Cf. William Cowper's Olney Hymn 35: "God moves in a mysterious way / His wonders to perform; / He plants his footsteps in the sea, / And rides upon the storm."

Spares but the cloudy border of his base
To the foiled searching of mortality;

And thou, who didst the stars and sunbeams know,
Self-schooled, self-scanned, self-honored, self-secure,   10
Didst tread on earth unguessed at.—Better so!

All pains the immortal spirit must endure,
All weakness which impairs, all griefs which bow,
Find their sole speech in that victorious brow.

1844   1849

In Harmony with Nature [2]

TO A PREACHER

"In harmony with Nature?" Restless fool,
Who with such heat dost preach what were to thee,
When true, the last impossibility—
To be like Nature strong, like Nature cool!

Know, man hath all which Nature hath, but more,   5
And in that *more* lie all his hopes of good.
Nature is cruel, man is sick of blood;
Nature is stubborn, man would fain adore;

Nature is fickle, man hath need of rest;
Nature forgives no debt, and fears no grave;   10
Man would be mild, and with safe conscience blest.

Man must begin, know this, where Nature ends;
Nature and man can never be fast friends.
Fool, if thou canst not pass her, rest her slave!

1844(?)   1849

To a Friend

Who prop, thou ask'st, in these bad days, my mind?—
He much, the old man,[3] who, clearest-souled of men,
Saw The Wide Prospect, and the Asian Fen,
And Tmolus hill, and Smyrna bay, though blind.

Much he, whose friendship I not long since won,   5
That halting slave, who in Nicopolis [4]

2. Originally entitled: "To an Independent Preacher, who preached that we should be 'In Harmony with Nature.'"
3. Homer, who was reputed to have been born in Smyrna, a seaport of what is now Turkey. From Smyrna he saw across the sea to Europe ("The Wide Prospect") as well as to the nearby marshes ("Fen") and mountain ranges ("Tmolus hill") of Asia Minor.
4. Epictetus, a lame philosopher who was exiled to Nicopolis where he taught Stoicism to Arrian, a Greek historian.

Taught Arrian, when Vespasian's brutal son [5]
Cleared Rome of what most shamed him. But be his

My special thanks, whose even-balanced soul,
From first youth tested up to extreme old age,   10
Business could not make dull, nor passion wild;

Who saw life steadily, and saw it whole;
The mellow glory of the Attic stage,
Singer of sweet Colonus,[6] and its child.

                                                        1849

The Forsaken Merman[1]

Come, dear children, let us away;
Down and away below!
Now my brothers call from the bay,
Now the great winds shoreward blow,
Now the salt tides seaward flow;
Now the wild white horses play,   5
Champ and chafe and toss in the spray.
Children dear, let us away!
This way, this way!

Call her once before you go—
Call once yet!   10
In a voice that she will know:
"Margaret! Margaret!"
Children's voices should be dear
(Call once more) to a mother's ear;
Children's voices, wild with pain—   15
Surely she will come again!
Call her once and come away;
This way, this way!
"Mother dear, we cannot stay!
The wild white horses foam and fret."   20
Margaret! Margaret!

Come, dear children, come away down;
Call no more!
One last look at the white-walled town,
And the little gray church on the windy shore,   25
Then come down!
She will not come though you call all day;
Come away, come away!

5. I.e., the Emperor Domitian (81–
96). Because the philosophers had
"shamed" him, he had ordered their
expulsion from Rome.
6. Sophocles (496–406 B.C.), a native
of Colonus, sang of his town in his
Oedipus at Colonus.

1. For a comparison of Arnold's skillful telling of this story with the Danish
version from which he derived it, see
C. B. Tinker and H. F. Lowry: *The
Poetry of Arnold: A Commentary*
(1940), pp. 129–132.

Children dear, was it yesterday   30
We heard the sweet bells over the bay?
In the caverns where we lay,
Through the surf and through the swell,
The far-off sound of a silver bell?
Sand-strewn caverns, cool and deep,   35
Where the winds are all asleep;
Where the spent lights quiver and gleam,
Where the salt weed sways in the stream,
Where the sea beasts, ranged all round,
Feed in the ooze of their pasture ground;   40
Where the sea snakes coil and twine,
Dry their mail and bask in the brine;
Where great whales come sailing by,
Sail and sail, with unshut eye,
Round the world for ever and aye?   45
When did music come this way?
Children dear, was it yesterday?

Children dear, was it yesterday
(Call yet once) that she went away?
Once she sate with you and me,   50
On a red gold throne in the heart of the sea,
And the youngest sate on her knee.
She combed its bright hair, and she tended it well,
When down swung the sound of a far-off bell.
She sighed, she looked up through the clear green sea;   55
She said: "I must go, for my kinsfolk pray
In the little gray church on the shore today.
'Twill be Easter time in the world—ah me!
And I lose my poor soul, Merman! here with thee."
I said: "Go up, dear heart, through the waves;   60
Say thy prayer, and come back to the kind sea caves!"
She smiled, she went up through the surf in the bay.
Children dear, was it yesterday?

  Children dear, were we long alone?
"The sea grows stormy, the little ones moan;   65
Long prayers," I said, "in the world they say;
Come!" I said; and we rose through the surf in the bay.
We went up the beach, by the sandy down
Where the sea stocks bloom, to the white-walled town;
Through the narrow paved streets, where all was still,   70
To the little gray church on the windy hill.
From the church came a murmur of folk at their prayers,
But we stood without in the cold blowing airs.
We climbed on the graves, on the stones worn with rains,
And we gazed up the aisle through the small leaded panes.   75
She sate by the pillar; we saw her clear:
"Margaret, hist! come quick, we are here!
Dear heart," I said, "we are long alone;

The sea grows stormy, the little ones moan."
But, ah, she gave me never a look,   80
For her eyes were sealed to the holy book!
Loud prays the priest; shut stands the door.
Come away, children, call no more!
Come away, come down, call no more!

Down, down, down!   85
Down to the depths of the sea!
She sits at her wheel in the humming town,
Singing most joyfully.
Hark what she sings: "O joy, O joy,
For the humming street, and the child with its toy!   90
For the priest, and the bell, and the holy well;
For the wheel where I spun,
And the blessed light of the sun!"
And so she sings her fill,
Singing most joyfully,   95
Till the spindle drops from her hand,
And the whizzing wheel stands still.
She steals to the window, and looks at the sand,
And over the sand at the sea;
And her eyes are set in a stare;   100
And anon there breaks a sigh,
And anon there drops a tear,
From a sorrow-clouded eye,
And a heart sorrow-laden,
A long, long sigh;   105
For the cold strange eyes of a little Mermaiden
And the gleam of her golden hair.

Come away, away children;
Come children, come down!
The hoarse wind blows coldly;
Lights shine in the town.   110
She will start from her slumber
When gusts shake the door;
She will hear the winds howling,
Will hear the waves roar.   115
We shall see, while above us
The waves roar and whirl,
A ceiling of amber,
A pavement of pearl.
Singing: "Here came a mortal,   120
But faithless was she!
And alone dwell forever
The kings of the sea."

But, children, at midnight,
When soft the winds blow,
When clear falls the moonlight,   125

When spring tides are low;
When sweet airs come seaward
From heaths starred with broom,
And high rocks throw mildly   130
On the blanched sands a gloom;
Up the still, glistening beaches,
Up the creek we will hie,
Over the banks of bright seaweed
The ebb tide leaves dry.   135
We will gaze, from the sand hills,
At the white, sleeping town;
At the church on the hillside—
And then come back down.
Singing: "There dwells a loved one,   140
But cruel is she!
She left lonely forever
The kings of the sea."

                                                              1849

Isolation. To Marguerite[1]

We were apart; yet, day by day,
I bade my heart more constant be.
I bade it keep the world away,
And grow a home for only thee;
Nor feared but thy love likewise grew,   5
Like mine, each day, more tried, more true.

The fault was grave! I might have known,
What far too soon, alas! I learned—
The heart can bind itself alone,
And faith may oft be unreturned.   10
Self-swayed our feelings ebb and swell—
Thou lov'st no more—Farewell! Farewell!

Farewell!—and thou, thou lonely heart,[2]
Which never yet without remorse
Even for a moment didst depart   15
From thy remote and spheréd course
To haunt the place where passions reign—
Back to thy solitude again!

Back! with the conscious thrill of shame
Which Luna[3] felt, that summer night,   20

1. Addressed to a girl Arnold is reputed
to have met in Switzerland in the 1840's.
It has been commonly assumed that she
was French or Swiss, but some recent
biographies speculate she might have
been Mary Claude, a girl Arnold knew
in England at this same period, who, although English, had connections with
Germany and had translated German
prose and verse.
2. Presumably the speaker's heart, not
Marguerite's.
3. Luna (or Diana), the goddess of
chastity and of the moon, fell in love
with Endymion, a handsome shepherd,
whom she discovered asleep on Mt.
Latmos.

Flash through her pure immortal frame,
When she forsook the starry height
To hang over Endymion's sleep
Upon the pine-grown Latmian steep.

Yet she, chaste queen, had never proved   25
How vain a thing is mortal love,
Wandering in Heaven, far removed.
But thou hast long had place to prove
This truth—to prove, and make thine own:
"Thou hast been, shalt be, art, alone."   30

Or, if not quite alone, yet they
Which touch thee are unmating things—
Ocean and clouds and night and day;
Lorn autumns and triumphant springs;
And life, and others' joy and pain,   35
And love, if love, of happier men.

Of happier men—for they, at least,
Have *dreamed* two human hearts might blend
In one, and were through faith released
From isolation without end   40
Prolonged; nor knew, although not less
Alone than thou, their loneliness.

1857

To Marguerite—Continued

Yes! in the sea of life enisled,
With echoing straits between us thrown,
Dotting the shoreless watery wild,
We mortal millions live *alone*.
The islands feel the enclasping flow,   5
And then their endless bounds they know.

But when the moon their hollows lights,
And they are swept by balms of spring,
And in their glens, on starry nights,
The nightingales divinely sing;
And lovely notes, from shore to shore,   10
Across the sounds and channels pour—

Oh! then a longing like despair
Is to their farthest caverns sent;
For surely once, they feel, we were   15
Parts of a single continent!
Now round us spreads the watery plain—
Oh might our marges meet again!

Who ordered that their longing's fire
Should be, as soon as kindled, cooled?   20

Who renders vain their deep desire?—
A God, a God their severance ruled!
And bade betwixt their shores to be
The unplumbed, salt, estranging sea.

ca. 1849   1852

The Buried Life

Light flows our war of mocking words, and yet,
Behold, with tears mine eyes are wet!
I feel a nameless sadness o'er me roll.
Yes, yes, we know that we can jest,
We know, we know that we can smile!   5
But there's a something in this breast,
To which thy light words bring no rest,
And thy gay smiles no anodyne.
Give me thy hand, and hush awhile,
And turn those limpid eyes on mine,   10
And let me read there, love! thy inmost soul.

Alas! is even love too weak
To unlock the heart, and let it speak?
Are even lovers powerless to reveal
To one another what indeed they feel?   15
I knew the mass of men concealed
Their thoughts, for fear that if revealed
They would by other men be met
With blank indifference, or with blame reproved;
I knew they lived and moved   20
Tricked in disguises, alien to the rest
Of men, and alien to themselves—and yet
The same heart beats in every human breast!
But we, my love!—doth a like spell benumb
Our hearts, our voices?—must we too be dumb?   25

Ah! well for us, if even we,
Even for a moment, can get free
Our heart, and have our lips unchained;
For that which seals them hath been deep-ordained!

Fate, which foresaw   30
How frivolous a baby man would be—
By what distractions he would be possessed,
How he would pour himself in every strife,
And well-nigh change his own identity—
That it might keep from his capricious play   35
His genuine self, and force him to obey
Even in his own despite his being's law,
Bade through the deep recesses of our breast
The unregarded river of our life
Pursue with indiscernible flow its way;   40

And that we should not see
The buried stream, and seem to be
Eddying at large in blind uncertainty,
Though driving on with it eternally.

But often, in the world's most crowded streets,[1]   45
But often, in the din of strife,
There rises an unspeakable desire
After the knowledge of our buried life;
A thirst to spend our fire and restless force
In tracking out our true, original course;   50
A longing to inquire
Into the mystery of this heart which beats
So wild, so deep in us—to know
Whence our lives come and where they go.
And many a man in his own breast then delves,   55
But deep enough, alas! none ever mines.
And we have been on many thousand lines,
And we have shown, on each, spirit and power;
But hardly have we, for one little hour,
Been on our own line, have we been ourselves—   60
Hardly had skill to utter one of all
The nameless feelings that course through our breast,
But they course on forever unexpressed.
And long we try in vain to speak and act
Our hidden self, and what we say and do   65
Is eloquent, is well—but 'tis not true!
And then we will no more be racked
With inward striving, and demand
Of all the thousand nothings of the hour
Their stupefying power;   70
Ah yes, and they benumb us at our call!
Yet still, from time to time, vague and forlorn,
From the soul's subterranean depth upborne
As from an infinitely distant land,
Come airs, and floating echoes, and convey   75
A melancholy into all our day.[2]

Only—but this is rare—
When a beloved hand is laid in ours,
When, jaded with the rush and glare
Of the interminable hours,   80
Our eyes can in another's eyes read clear,
When our world-deafened ear
Is by the tones of a loved voice caressed—

---

1. This passage, like many others in
Arnold's poetry, illustrates the impact
on his writings of Wordsworth. In this
instance cf. Wordsworth's *Tintern Abbey*, lines 25–27: "But oft, in lonely
rooms, and 'mid the din / Of towns
and cities, I have owed to them, / In
hours of weariness, sensations sweet."
2. Cf. Wordsworth's *Ode: Intimations
of Immortality*, lines 151–53: "Those
shadowy recollections, / Which, be they
what they may, / Are yet the fountain
light of all our day."

A bolt is shot back somewhere in our breast,
And a lost pulse of feeling stirs again. 85
The eye sinks inward, and the heart lies plain,
And what we mean, we say, and what we would, we know.
A man becomes aware of his life's flow,
And hears its winding murmur; and he sees
The meadows where it glides, the sun, the breeze. 90

And there arrives a lull in the hot race
Wherein he doth forever chase
That flying and elusive shadow, rest.
An air of coolness plays upon his face,
And an unwonted calm pervades his breast. 95
And then he thinks he knows
The hills where his life rose,
And the sea where it goes.

1852

Memorial Verses[1]

APRIL, 1850

Goethe in Weimar sleeps, and Greece,
Long since, saw Byron's struggle cease.
But one such death remained to come;
The last poetic voice is dumb—
We stand today by Wordsworth's tomb. 5

When Byron's eyes were shut in death,
We bowed our head and held our breath.
He taught us little; but our soul
Had *felt* him like the thunder's roll.
With shivering heart the strife we saw 10
Of passion with eternal law;
And yet with reverential awe
We watched the fount of fiery life
Which served for that Titanic strife.

When Goethe's death was told, we said: 15
Sunk, then, is Europe's sagest head.
Physician of the iron age,
Goethe has done his pilgrimage.
He took the suffering human race,
He read each wound, each weakness clear; 20

1. This elegy was written shortly after Wordsworth had died in April, 1850, at the age of 80. Arnold had known the poet as a man and deeply admired his writings—as is evident not only in this poem but in his late essay, *Wordsworth*. Byron, who died in Greece in 1824, had affected Arnold profoundly in his youth, but later that strenuous "Titanic" po-etry seemed to him less satisfactory, its value limited by its lack of serenity. His final verdict on Byron can be en-countered in his essay in *Essays in Criticism: Second Series*. Goethe, who died in 1832, was regarded by Arnold as a great philosophical poet and the most significant man of letters of the early 19th century.

And struck his finger on the place,
And said: *Thou ailest here, and here!*
He looked on Europe's dying hour
Of fitful dream and feverish power;
His eye plunged down the weltering strife,   25
The turmoil of expiring life—
He said: *The end is everywhere,*
Art still has truth, take refuge there!
And he was happy, if to know
Causes of things, and far below   30
His feet to see the lurid flow
Of terror, and insane distress,
And headlong fate, be happiness.

    And Wordsworth!—Ah, pale ghosts, rejoice!
For never has such soothing voice   35
Been to your shadowy world conveyed,
Since erst, a morn, some wandering shade
Heard the clear song of Orpheus[2] come
Through Hades, and the mournful gloom.
Wordsworth has gone from us—and ye,   40
Ah, may ye feel his voice as we!
He too upon a wintry clime
Had fallen—on this iron time
Of doubts, disputes, distractions, fears.
He found us when the age had bound   45
Our souls in its benumbing round;
He spoke, and loosed our heart in tears.
He laid us as we lay at birth
On the cool flowery lap of earth,
Smiles broke from us and we had ease;   50
The hills were round us, and the breeze
Went o'er the sunlit fields again;
Our foreheads felt the wind and rain.
Our youth returned; for there was shed
On spirits that had long been dead,   55
Spirits dried up and closely furled,
The freshness of the early world.

    Ah! since dark days still bring to light
Man's prudence and man's fiery might,
Time may restore us in his course   60
Goethe's sage mind and Byron's force;
But where will Europe's latter hour
Again find Wordsworth's healing power?
Others will teach us how to dare,
And against fear our breast to steel;   65
Others will strengthen us to bear—

2. By means of his beautiful music,   in his search for the shade of his dead
Orpheus won his way through Hades   wife, Eurydice.

But who, ah! who, will make us feel?
The cloud of mortal destiny,
Others will front it fearlessly—
But who, like him, will put it by?   70

    Keep fresh the grass upon his grave
O Rotha,[3] with thy living wave!
Sing him thy best! for few or none
Hears thy voice right, now he is gone.

1850   1850

Lines Written in Kensington Gardens[4]

In this lone, open glade I lie,
Screened by deep boughs on either hand;
And at its end, to stay the eye,
Those black-crowned, red-boled pine trees stand!

Birds here make song, each bird has his,   5
Across the girdling city's hum.
How green under the boughs it is!
How thick the tremulous sheep-cries come![5]

Sometimes a child will cross the glade
To take his nurse his broken toy;   10
Sometimes a thrush flit overhead
Deep in her unknown day's employ.

Here at my feet what wonders pass,
What endless, active life is here!
What blowing daisies, fragrant grass!   15
An air-stirred forest, fresh and clear.

Scarce fresher is the mountain sod
Where the tired angler lies, stretched out,
And, eased of basket and of rod,
Counts his day's spoil, the spotted trout.   20

In the huge world, which roars hard by,
Be others happy if they can!
But in my helpless cradle I
Was breathed on by the rural Pan.

I, on men's impious uproar hurled,   25
Think often, as I hear them rave,
That peace has left the upper world
And now keeps only in the grave.

Yet here is peace forever new!
When I who watch them am away,   30

3. A river near Wordsworth's burial
place.
4. A park in the heart of London.

5. Sheep are sometimes grazed in London parks.

Still all things in this glade go through
The changes of their quiet day.

Then to their happy rest they pass!
The flowers upclose, the birds are fed,
The night comes down upon the grass,   35
The child sleeps warmly in his bed.

Calm soul of all things! make it mine
To feel, amid the city's jar,
That there abides a peace of thine,
Man did not make, and cannot mar.   40

The will to neither strive nor cry,
The power to feel with others give!
Calm, calm me more! nor let me die
Before I have begun to live.

                                                        1852

Philomela[1]

Hark! ah, the nightingale—
The tawny-throated!
Hark, from that moonlit cedar what a burst!
What triumph! hark!—what pain!

O wanderer from a Grecian shore,   5
Still, after many years, in distant lands,
Still nourishing in thy bewildered brain
That wild, unquenched, deep-sunken, old-world pain—
Say, will it never heal?
And can this fragrant lawn   10
With its cool trees, and night,
And the sweet, tranquil Thames,
And moonshine, and the dew,
To thy racked heart and brain
Afford no balm?   15

Dost thou tonight behold,
Here, through the moonlight on this English grass,
The unfriendly palace in the Thracian wild?
Dost thou again peruse
With hot cheeks and seared eyes   20
The too clear web,[2] and thy dumb sister's shame?
Dost thou once more assay
Thy flight, and feel come over thee,
Poor fugitive, the feathery change

1. The Greek tale of violence evoked by the song of the nightingale concerned two sisters, Philomela and Procne. In Arnold's version, Philomela was married to a king of Thrace. After learning that her husband had raped Procne and cut out her tongue to prevent the outrage being discovered, Philomela was transformed into a nightingale.
2. A picture in needlework made by Procne to tell what had happened to her.

Once more, and once more seem to make resound   25
With love and hate, triumph and agony,
Lone Daulis, and the high Cephissian vale?[3]
Listen, Eugenia[4]—
How thick the bursts come crowding through the leaves!
Again—thou hearest?   30
Eternal passion!
Eternal pain!

1848   1853

3. Daulis, a city in Phocis, where   ley in Phocis.
Philomela's transformation took place;   4. Unidentified listener.
the "Cephissian vale" was a river val-

The Scholar Gypsy

The story of a 17th-century student who left Oxford and joined a band of gypsies had made a strong impression on Arnold. In the poem he wistfully imagines that the spirit of this scholar is still to be encountered in the Cumner countryside near Oxford, having achieved immortality by a serene pursuit of the secret of human existence. Like Keats's nightingale, the scholar has escaped "the weariness, the fever, and the fret" of modern life.

At the outset, the poet addresses a shepherd who has been helping him in his search for traces of the scholar. The shepherd is addressed as "you." After line 61, with the shift to "thou" and "thy," the person addressed is the scholar himself, and the poet thereafter sometimes uses the pronoun "we" to indicate he is speaking for all mankind of later generations.

About the setting Arnold wrote to his brother Tom on May 15, 1857: "You alone of my brothers are associated with that life at Oxford, the *freest* and most delightful part, perhaps, of my life, when with you and Clough and Walrond I shook off all the bonds and formalities of the place, and enjoyed the spring of life and that unforgotten Oxfordshire and Berkshire country. Do you remember a poem of mine called 'The Scholar Gipsy'? It was meant to fix the remembrance of those delightful wanderings of ours in the Cumner Hills."

The passage from Joseph Glanvill's *Vanity of Dogmatizing* (1661) which inspired the poem was included by Arnold as a note:

There was very lately a lad in the University of Oxford, who was by his poverty forced to leave his studies there; and at last to join himself to a company of vagabond gypsies. Among these extravagant people, by the insinuating subtilty of his carriage, he quickly got so much of their love and esteem as that they discovered to him their mystery. After he had been a pretty while exercised in the trade, there chanced to ride by a couple of scholars, who had formerly been of his acquaintance. They quickly spied out their old friend among the gypsies; and he gave them an account of the necessity which drove him to that kind of life, and told them that the people he went with were not such imposters as they were taken for, but that they had a traditional kind of learning among them, and could do wonders by the power of imagination, their fancy binding that of others: that himself had learned much of their art, and when he had compassed the whole secret, he intended, he said, to leave their company, and give the world an account of what he had learned.

The Scholar Gypsy

Go, for they call you, shepherd, from the hill;
  Go, shepherd, and untie the wattled cotes![1]
    No longer leave thy wistful flock unfed,
    Nor let thy bawling fellows rack their throats,
      Nor the cropped herbage shoot another head.   5
        But when the fields are still,
        And the tired men and dogs all gone to rest,
        And only the white sheep are sometimes seen
        Cross and recross the strips of moon-blanched green,
  Come, shepherd, and again begin the quest!   10

Here, where the reaper was at work of late—
  In this high field's dark corner, where he leaves
    His coat, his basket, and his earthen cruse,[2]
    And in the sun all morning binds the sheaves,
      Then here, at noon, comes back his stores to use—   15
        Here will I sit and wait,
        While to my ear from uplands far away
        The bleating of the folded[3] flocks is borne,
        With distant cries of reapers in the corn[4]—
  All the live murmur of a summer's day.   20

Screened is this nook o'er the high, half-reaped field,
  And here till sundown, shepherd! will I be.
    Through the thick corn the scarlet poppies peep,
    And round green roots and yellowing stalks I see
      Pale pink convolvulus in tendrils creep;   25
        And air-swept lindens yield
        Their scent, and rustle down their perfumed showers
        Of bloom on the bent grass[5] where I am laid,
        And bower me from the August sun with shade;
  And the eye travels down to Oxford's towers.   30

And near me on the grass lies Glanvill's book—
  Come, let me read the oft-read tale again!
    The story of the Oxford scholar poor,
    Of pregnant parts[6] and quick inventive brain,
      Who, tired of knocking at preferment's door,   35
        One summer morn forsook
        His friends, and went to learn the gypsy lore,
        And roamed the world with that wild brotherhood,
        And came, as most men deemed, to little good,
  But came to Oxford and his friends no more.   40

But once, years after, in the country lanes,
  Two scholars, whom at college erst he knew,

---

1. Sheepfolds woven from sticks.
2. Pot or jug for carrying his drink.
3. Penned up.

4. Grain or wheat.
5. A stiff kind of grass.
6. Teeming with ideas.

Met him, and of his way of life inquired;
  Whereat he answered, that the gypsy crew,
    His mates, had arts to rule as they desired 45
      The workings of men's brains,
And they can bind them to what thoughts they will.
  "And I," he said, "the secret of their art,
    When fully learned, will to the world impart;
But it needs heaven-sent moments for this skill." 50

This said, he left them, and returned no more.—
  But rumors hung about the countryside,
    That the lost Scholar long was seen to stray,
    Seen by rare glimpses, pensive and tongue-tied,
      In hat of antique shape, and cloak of gray, 55
      The same the gypsies wore.
Shepherds had met him on the Hurst [7] in spring;
  At some lone alehouse in the Berkshire moors,
  On the warm ingle-bench, [8] the smock-frocked boors
Had found him seated at their entering, 60

But, 'mid their drink and clatter, he would fly.
  And I myself seem half to know thy looks,
    And put the shepherds, wanderer! on thy trace;
And boys who in lone wheatfields scare the rooks[9]
    I ask if thou hast passed their quiet place; 65
      Or in my boat I lie
Moored to the cool bank in the summer heats,
  'Mid wide grass meadows which the sunshine fills,
  And watch the warm, green-muffled Cumner hills,
And wonder if thou haunt'st their shy retreats. 70

For most, I know, thou lov'st retired ground!
  Thee at the ferry Oxford riders blithe,
    Returning home on summer nights, have met
Crossing the stripling Thames[1] at Bab-lock-hithe,
    Trailing in the cool stream thy fingers wet, 75
      As the punt's rope chops round;[2]
And leaning backward in a pensive dream,
  And fostering in thy lap a heap of flowers
  Plucked in shy fields and distant Wychwood bowers,
And thine eyes resting on the moonlit stream. 80

And then they land, and thou art seen no more!—

---

7. A hill near Oxford. All the place names in the poem (except those in the final two stanzas) refer to the countryside near Oxford.
8. Fireside bench. "Boors," here, are rustics.
9. Boys hired to frighten crows away from eating wheat grains. See Hardy's novel *Jude the Obscure*, I.ii.
1. I.e., the narrow upper reaches of the river before it broadens out to its full width.
2. The scholar's flat-bottomed boat ("punt") is tied up by a rope at the river bank near the ferry-crossing like the speaker's boat (in the previous stanza), which was "moored to the cool bank." The motion of the boat as it is stirred by the current of the river causes the chopping sound of the rope in the water.

Maidens, who from the distant hamlets come
  To dance around the Fyfield elm in May,
Oft through the darkening fields have seen thee roam,
  Or cross a stile into the public way.   85
    Oft thou hast given them store
Of flowers—the frail-leafed, white anemone,
  Dark bluebells drenched with dews of summer eves,
  And purple orchises with spotted leaves—
But none hath words she can report of thee.   90

And, above Godstow Bridge, when hay time's here
  In June, and many a scythe in sunshine flames,
  Men who through those wide fields of breezy grass
Where black-winged swallows haunt the glittering Thames,
  To bathe in the abandoned lasher pass,[3]   95
    Have often passed thee near
Sitting upon the river bank o'ergrown;
  Marked thine outlandish garb, thy figure spare,
  Thy dark vague eyes, and soft abstracted air—
But, when they came from bathing, thou wast gone!   100

At some lone homestead in the Cumner hills,
  Where at her open door the housewife darns,
  Thou hast been seen, or hanging on a gate
To watch the threshers in the mossy barns.
  Children, who early range these slopes and late   105
    For cresses from the rills,
Have known thee eying, all an April day,
  The springing pastures and the feeding kine;
  And marked thee, when the stars come out and shine,
Through the long dewy grass move slow away.   110

In autumn, on the skirts of Bagley Wood—
  Where most the gypsies by the turf-edged way
  Pitch their smoked tents, and every bush you see
With scarlet patches tagged and shreds of gray,
  Above the forest ground called Thessaly—   115
    The blackbird, picking food,
Sees thee, nor stops his meal, nor fears at all;
  So often has he known thee past him stray,
  Rapt, twirling in thy hand a withered spray,
And waiting for the spark from heaven to fall.   120

And once, in winter, on the causeway chill
  Where home through flooded fields foot-travelers go,
  Have I not passed thee on the wooden bridge,
Wrapped in thy cloak and battling with the snow,
  Thy face tow'rd Hinksey and its wintry ridge?   125
    And thou hast climbed the hill,
And gained the white brow of the Cumner range;

3. Water that spills over a dam or weir.

Turned once to watch, while thick the snowflakes fall,
The line of festal light in Christ Church hall[4]—
   Then sought thy straw in some sequestered grange.   130

But what—I dream! Two hundred years are flown
Since first thy story ran through Oxford halls,
   And the grave Glanvill did the tale inscribe
That thou wert wandered from the studious walls
     To learn strange arts, and join a gypsy tribe;   135
     And thou from earth art gone
Long since, and in some quiet churchyard laid—
   Some country nook, where o'er thy unknown grave
   Tall grasses and white flowering nettles wave,
Under a dark, red-fruited yew tree's shade.   140

—No, no, thou hast not felt the lapse of hours!
For what wears out the life of mortal men?
   'Tis that from change to change their being rolls;
'Tis that repeated shocks, again, again,
     Exhaust the energy of strongest souls   145
     And numb the elastic powers.
Till having used our nerves with bliss and teen,[5]
   And tired upon a thousand schemes our wit,
   To the just-pausing Genius[6] we remit
Our worn-out life, and are—what we have been.   150

Thou hast not lived, why should'st thou perish, so?
Thou hadst *one* aim, *one* business, *one* desire;
   Else wert thou long since numbered with the dead!
Else hadst thou spent, like other men, thy fire!
     The generations of thy peers are fled,   155
     And we ourselves shall go;
But thou possessest an immortal lot,
   And we imagine thee exempt from age
   And living as thou liv'st on Glanvill's page,
Because thou hadst—what we, alas! have not.   160

For early didst thou leave the world, with powers
Fresh, undiverted to the world without,
   Firm to their mark, not spent on other things;
Free from the sick fatigue, the languid doubt,
     Which much to have tried, in much been baffled, brings. 165
     O life unlike to ours!
Who fluctuate idly without term or scope,
   Of whom each strives, nor knows for what he strives,
   And each half[7] lives a hundred different lives;
Who wait like thee, but not, like thee, in hope.   170

Thou waitest for the spark from heaven! and we,
   Light half-believers of our casual creeds,
     Who never deeply felt, nor clearly willed,

---

4. The dining hall of an Oxford college.
5. Vexation.
6. Perhaps the spirit of the universe, which pauses briefly to receive back the life given to us.
7. An adverb modifying "lives."

Whose insight never has borne fruit in deeds,
  Whose vague resolves never have been fulfilled;   175
   For whom each year we see
Breeds new beginnings, disappointments new;
  Who hesitate and falter life away,
  And lose tomorrow the ground won today—
Ah! do not we, wanderer! await it too?   180
Yes, we await it!—but it still delays,
  And then we suffer! and amongst us one,[8]
   Who most has suffered, takes dejectedly
His seat upon the intellectual throne;
   And all his store of sad experience he   185
    Lays bare of wretched days;
Tells us his misery's birth and growth and signs,
  And how the dying spark of hope was fed,
  And how the breast was soothed, and how the head,
  And all his hourly varied anodynes.   190

This for our wisest! and we others pine,
  And wish the long unhappy dream would end,
  And waive all claim to bliss, and try to bear;
With close-lipped patience for our only friend,
  Sad patience, too near neighbor to despair—   195
   But none has hope like thine!
Thou through the fields and through the woods dost stray,
  Roaming the countryside, a truant boy,
  Nursing thy project in unclouded joy,
And every doubt long blown by time away.   200

O born in days when wits were fresh and clear,
  And life ran gaily as the sparkling Thames;
   Before this strange disease of modern life,
With its sick hurry, its divided aims,
  Its heads o'ertaxed, its palsied hearts, was rife—   205
   Fly hence, our contact fear!
Still fly, plunge deeper in the bowering wood!
  Averse, as Dido[9] did with gesture stern
  From her false friend's approach in Hades turn,
Wave us away, and keep thy solitude!   210

Still nursing the unconquerable hope,
  Still clutching the inviolable shade,
   With a free, onward impulse brushing through,
By night, the silvered branches of the glade—
  Far on the forest skirts, where none pursue.   215
   On some mild pastoral slope
Emerge, and resting on the moonlit pales
  Freshen thy flowers as in former years
  With dew, or listen with enchanted ears,

8. Probably Tennyson, whose *In Memoriam* had appeared in 1850, or perhaps Goethe.
9. Dido committed suicide after her lover, Aeneas, deserted her. When he later encountered her in Hades, she turned sternly away from him.

From the dark dingles,[10] to the nightingales! 220
But fly our paths, our feverish contact fly!
  For strong the infection of our mental strife,
    Which, though it gives no bliss, yet spoils for rest;
  And we should win thee from thy own fair life,
    Like us distracted, and like us unblest. 225
      Soon, soon thy cheer would die,
  Thy hopes grow timorous, and unfixed thy powers,
  And thy clear aims be cross and shifting made;
  And then thy glad perennial youth would fade,
  Fade, and grow old at last, and die like ours. 230

Then fly our greetings, fly our speech and smiles!
  —As some grave Tyrian trader, from the sea,
    Descried at sunrise an emerging prow
  Lifting the cool-haired creepers stealthily,
    The fringes of a southward-facing brow 235
      Among the Aegean isles;
  And saw the merry Grecian coaster come,
    Freighted with amber grapes, and Chian wine,
    Green, bursting figs, and tunnies[1] steeped in brine—
  And knew the intruders on his ancient home, 240

The young lighthearted masters of the waves—
  And snatched his rudder, and shook out more sail;
    And day and night held on indignantly
  O'er the blue Midland waters with the gale,
    Betwixt the Syrtes[2] and soft Sicily, 245
      To where the Atlantic raves
  Outside the western straits; and unbent sails
    There, where down cloudy cliffs, through sheets of foam,
    Shy traffickers, the dark Iberians[3] come;
  And on the beach undid his corded bales.[4] 250

1853

10. Small deep valleys.
1. Tuna fish.
2. Shoals off the coast of North Africa.
3. Dark inhabitants of Spain and Portugal—perhaps associated with gypsies.
4. The elaborate simile of the final two stanzas has been variously interpreted and misinterpreted. The trader from Tyre is disconcerted when, peering out through the foliage ("fringes") that screens his hiding place, he sees noisy intruders entering his harbor. Like the Scholar Gypsy, when similarly intruded upon by hearty extroverts, he resolves to flee and seek a new home. The reference (line 249) to the Iberians as "*shy* traffickers" (traders) is explained by Kenneth Allott as having been derived from Herodotus' *History* (IV.196). Herodotus describes a distinctive method of selling goods established by Carthaginian merchants who used to sail through the straits of Gibraltar to trade with the inhabitants of the coast of West Africa.

The Carthaginians would leave bales of their merchandise on display along the beaches and, without having seen their prospective customers, would return to their ships. The shy natives would then come down from their inland hiding places and set gold beside the bales they wished to buy. When the natives withdrew in their turn, the Carthaginians would return to the beach and decide whether payments were adequate, a process repeated until agreement was reached. On the Atlantic coasts this method of bargaining persisted into the 19th century. As William Beloe, a translator of Herodotus, noted in 1844: "In this manner they transact their exchange without seeing one another, or without the least instance of dishonesty * * * on either side." For the solitary Tyrian trader such a procedure, with its avoidance of *contact* (line 221), would have been especially appropriate.

Dover Beach

The sea is calm tonight.
The tide is full, the moon lies fair
Upon the straits—on the French coast the light
Gleams and is gone; the cliffs of England stand,
Glimmering and vast, out in the tranquil bay.   5
Come to the window, sweet is the night air!
Only, from the long line of spray
Where the sea meets the moon-blanched land,
Listen! you hear the grating roar[1]
Of pebbles which the waves draw back, and fling,   10
At their return, up the high strand,
Begin, and cease, and then again begin,
With tremulous cadence slow, and bring
The eternal note of sadness in.

Sophocles long ago   15
Heard it on the Aegean, and it brought
Into his mind the turbid ebb and flow
Of human misery;[2] we
Find also in the sound a thought,
Hearing it by this distant northern sea.   20

The Sea of Faith
Was once, too, at the full, and round earth's shore
Lay like the folds of a bright girdle furled.[3]
But now I only hear
Its melancholy, long, withdrawing roar,   25
Retreating, to the breath
Of the night wind, down the vast edges drear
And naked shingles[4] of the world.

Ah, love, let us be true
To one another! for the world, which seems   30
To lie before us like a land of dreams,
So various, so beautiful, so new,
Hath really neither joy, nor love, nor light,
Nor certitude, nor peace, nor help for pain;
And we are here as on a darkling plain   35

1. Cf. Wordsworth's *It Is a Beauteous Evening:* "Listen! the mighty Being is awake, / And doth with his eternal motion make / A sound like thunder—everlastingly."
2. See Sophocles' *Antigone*, lines 583 ff.
3. This difficult line means, in general, that at high tide the sea envelops the land closely. Its forces are "gathered" up (to use Wordsworth's term for it) like the "folds" of bright clothing ("girdle") which have been compressed ("furled"). At ebb tide, as the sea retreats, it is unfurled and spread out. It still surrounds the shoreline but not as an "enclasping flow" (as Arnold speaks of the sea in *To Marguerite, Continued*). See also *2 Henry IV*, III.i.49–51: "to see / The beachy girdle of the ocean / Too wide for Neptune's hips."
4. Beaches covered with pebbles.

Swept with confused alarms of struggle and flight,
Where ignorant armies [5] clash by night.

ca. 1851   1867

Stanzas from the Grande Chartreuse[1]

Through Alpine meadows soft-suffused
With rain, where thick the crocus blows,
Past the dark forges long disused,
The mule track from Saint Laurent goes.
The bridge is crossed, and slow we ride,   5
Through forest, up the mountainside.

The autumnal evening darkens round,
The wind is up, and drives the rain;
While, hark! far down, with strangled sound
Doth the Dead Guier's[2] stream complain,   10
Where that wet smoke, among the woods,
Over his boiling cauldron broods.

Swift rush the spectral vapors white
Past limestone scars [3] with ragged pines,
Showing—then blotting from our sight!—   15
Halt—through the cloud-drift something shines!
High in the valley, wet and drear,
The huts of Courrerie appear.

Strike leftward! cries our guide; and higher
Mounts up the stony forest way.   20
At last the encircling trees retire;
Look! through the showery twilight gray
What pointed roofs are these advance?—
A palace of the Kings of France?

Approach, for what we seek is here!   25
Alight, and sparely sup, and wait
For rest in this outbuilding near;
Then cross the sward and reach that gate.
Knock; pass the wicket! Thou art come
To the Carthusians' world-famed home.   30

---

5. Perhaps the revolutions of 1848 or
a reference to the siege of Rome by the
French in 1849. The date of composition
of the poem is unknown, although generally assumed to be 1851.
1. A monastery situated high in the
French Alps. It was established in 1084
by St. Bruno, founder of the Carthusians
(line 30), whose austere regimen of
solitary contemplation, fasting, and religious exercises (lines 37–44) had remained virtually unchanged for centuries.

Arnold visited the site September 7,
1851, accompanied by his bride. His account may be compared with that by
Wordsworth (*Prelude* VI. 416–88) who
had made a similar visit in 1790.
2. The Guiers Mort river flows down
from the monastery and joins the Guiers
Vif in the valley below. Wordsworth
speaks of the two rivers as "the sister
streams of Life and Death."
3. Precipices.

The silent courts, where night and day
Into their stone-carved basins cold
The splashing icy fountains play—
The humid corridors behold!
Where, ghostlike in the deepening night,   35
Cowled forms brush by in gleaming white.

The chapel, where no organ's peal
Invests the stern and naked prayer—
With penitential cries they kneel
And wrestle; rising then, with bare   40
And white uplifted faces stand,
Passing the Host from hand to hand;[4]

Each takes, and then his visage wan
Is buried in his cowl once more.
The cells!—the suffering Son of Man   45
Upon the wall—the knee-worn floor—
And where they sleep, that wooden bed,
Which shall their coffin be, when dead![5]

The library, where tract and tome
Not to feed priestly pride are there,   50
To hymn the conquering march of Rome,
Nor yet to amuse, as ours are!
They paint of souls the inner strife,
Their drops of blood, their death in life.

The garden, overgrown—yet mild,   55
See, fragrant herbs[6] are flowering there!
Strong children of the Alpine wild
Whose culture is the brethren's care;
Of human tasks their only one,
And cheerful works beneath the sun.   60

Those halls, too, destined to contain
Each its own pilgrim-host of old,
From England, Germany, or Spain—
All are before me! I behold
The House, the Brotherhood austere!   65
—And what am I, that I am here?

For rigorous teachers seized my youth,
And purged its faith, and trimmed its fire,
Showed me the high, white star of Truth,

---

4. Arnold, during his short visit, may not
actually have witnessed the service of
the Mass in the monastery. The consecrated wafer (the Host) is not passed
from the hand of the officiating priest
to the hands of the communicant (as is
the practice in Arnold's own Anglican
church) but placed, instead, on the
tongue of the communicant (who kneels
rather than stands). See Tinker and
Lowry, *The Poetry of Matthew Arnold:
A Commentary*, pp. 249–51.
5. A Carthusian is buried on a wooden
plank but does not sleep in a coffin.
6. From which the liqueur, Chartreuse,
is manufactured. Sales of this liqueur
provide the principal revenues for up-
keep of the monastery.

There bade me gaze, and there aspire.   70
Even now their whispers pierce the gloom:
What dost thou in this living tomb?

Forgive me, masters of the mind![7]
At whose behest I long ago
So much unlearnt, so much resigned—   75
I come not here to be your foe!
I seek these anchorites, not in ruth,[8]
To curse and to deny your truth;

Not as their friend, or child, I speak!
But as, on some far northern strand,   80
Thinking of his own Gods, a Greek
In pity and mournful awe might stand
Before some fallen Runic stone—[9]
For both were faiths, and both are gone.

Wandering between two worlds, one dead,   85
The other powerless to be born,
With nowhere yet to rest my head,
Like these, on earth I wait forlorn.
Their faith, my tears, the world deride—
I come to shed them at their side.   90

Oh, hide me in your gloom profound,
Ye solemn seats of holy pain!
Take me, cowled forms, and fence me round,
Till I possess my soul again;
Till free my thoughts before me roll,   95
Not chafed by hourly false control!

For the world cries your faith is now
But a dead time's exploded dream;
My melancholy, sciolists[1] say,
Is a passed mode, an outworn theme—   100
As if the world had ever had
A faith, or sciolists been sad!

Ah, if it *be* passed, take away,
At least, the restlessness, the pain;
Be man henceforth no more a prey   105
To these out-dated stings again!
The nobleness of grief is gone—
Ah, leave us not the fret alone!

7. Writers whose insistence upon testing religious beliefs in the light of fact and reason persuaded Arnold that faith in Christianity (especially in the Roman Catholic or Anglo Catholic forms) was no longer tenable in the modern world.
8. Remorse for having adopted the rationalist view of Christianity.
9. A monument inscribed in Teutonic letters (runes), emblematic of a Nordic religion that has become extinct. The relic reminds the Greek that his own religion is likewise dying and will soon be extinct. See Arnold's *Preface* of 1853, second paragraph.
1. Superficial-minded persons who pretend to know the answers to all questions.

But—if you[2] cannot give us ease—
Last of the race of them who grieve   110
Here leave us to die out with these
Last of the people who believe!
Silent, while years engrave the brow;
Silent—the best are silent now.

Achilles[3] ponders in his tent,   115
The kings of modern thought[4] are dumb;
Silent they are, though not content,
And wait to see the future come.
They have the grief men had of yore,
But they contend and cry no more.   120

Our fathers[5] watered with their tears
This sea of time whereon we sail,
Their voices were in all men's ears
Who passed within their puissant hail.
Still the same ocean round us raves,   125
But we stand mute, and watch the waves.

For what availed it, all the noise
And outcry of the former men?—
Say, have their sons achieved more joys,
Say, is life lighter now than then?   130
The sufferers died, they left their pain—
The pangs which tortured them remain.

What helps it now, that Byron bore,
With haughty scorn which mocked the smart,
Through Europe to the Aetolian shore[6]   135
The pageant of his bleeding heart?
That thousands counted every groan,
And Europe made his woe her own?

What boots it, Shelley! that the breeze
Carried thy lovely wail away,   140
Musical through Italian trees
Which fringe thy soft blue Spezzian bay?[7]
Inheritors of thy distress
Have restless hearts one throb the less?

2. It is not clear whether the speaker has resumed addressing his "rigorous teachers" (line 67) or (as would seem more likely) a combination of the sciolists, who scorn the speaker's melancholy and the worldly, who scorn the faith of the monks. See his address to the "sons of the world" (lines 160–68).
3. Achilles, after the death of Patroclus, refused to participate in the Trojan war; hence similar to modern intellectual leaders who refuse to speak out about their frustrated sense of alienation.
4. Variously but never satisfactorily identified as Newman or Carlyle (the latter was said to have preached the gospel of silence in 40 volumes). Another advocate of stoical silence was the French poet, Alfred de Vigny (1797–1863).
5. Predecessors among the Romantic writers such as Byron.
6. Region in Greece where Byron died.
7. The Gulf of Spezzia in Italy, where Shelley was drowned.

Or are we easier, to have read,   145
O Obermann![8] the sad, stern page,
Which tells us how thou hidd'st thy head
From the fierce tempest of thine age
In the lone brakes of Fontainebleau,
Or chalets near the Alpine snow?   150

Ye slumber in your silent grave!—
The world, which for an idle day
Grace to your mood of sadness gave,
Long since hath flung her weeds[9] away.
The eternal trifler[1] breaks your spell;   155
But we—we learnt your lore too well!

Years hence, perhaps, may dawn an age,
More fortunate, alas! than we,
Which without hardness will be sage,
And gay without frivolity.   160
Sons of the world, oh, speed those years;
But, while we wait, allow our tears!

Allow them! We admire with awe
The exulting thunder of your race;
You give the universe your law,   165
You triumph over time and space!
Your pride of life, your tireless powers,
We laud them, but they are not ours.

We are like children reared in shade
Beneath some old-world abbey wall,   170
Forgotten in a forest glade,
And secret from the eyes of all.
Deep, deep the greenwood round them waves,
Their abbey, and its close[2] of graves!

But, where the road runs near the stream,   175
Oft through the trees they catch a glance
Of passing troops in the sun's beam—
Pennon, and plume, and flashing lance!
Forth to the world those soldiers fare,
To life, to cities, and to war!   180

And through the wood, another way,
Faint bugle notes from far are borne,
Where hunters gather, staghounds bay,[3]
Round some fair forest-lodge at morn.
Gay dames are there, in sylvan green;   185
Laughter and cries—those notes between!

8. Melancholy hero of *Obermann* (1804),
a novel by Senancour.
9. Mourning clothes.
1. The sciolist, as in line 99.

2. Enclosure.
3. Cf. the contrast between recluses and
hunters in *The Scholar Gypsy*, lines 71–
81.

The banners flashing through the trees
Make their blood dance and chain their eyes;
That bugle music on the breeze
Arrests them with a charmed surprise.   190
Banner by turns and bugle woo:
Ye shy recluses, follow too!

O children, what do ye reply?—
"Action and pleasure, will ye roam
Through these secluded dells to cry   195
And call us?—but too late ye come!
Too late for us your call ye blow,
Whose bent was taken long ago.

"Long since we pace this shadowed nave;
We watch those yellow tapers shine,   200
Emblems of hope over the grave,
In the high altar's depth divine;
The organ carries to our ear
Its accents of another sphere.

"Fenced early in this cloistral round   205
Of reverie, of shade, of prayer,
How should we grow in other ground?
How can we flower in foreign air?
—Pass, banners, pass, and bugles, cease;
And leave our desert to its peace!"   210

1852(?)   1855

Thyrsis[1]

A MONODY, TO COMMEMORATE THE AUTHOR'S FRIEND,
ARTHUR HUGH CLOUGH, WHO DIED AT FLORENCE, 1861

How changed is here each spot man makes or fills!
In the two Hinkseys[2] nothing keeps the same;

1. In the 1840's, at Oxford, Clough had been one of Arnold's closest friends. After the death of this fellow poet, twenty years later, Arnold revisited the Thames-valley countryside which they had explored together. The familiar scenes prompted him to review the changes wrought by time on the ideals shared in his Oxford days with Clough, ideals symbolized, in part, by a distant elm and by the story of the Scholar Gypsy. The survival of these ideals in the face of the difficulties of modern life is the subject of this elegy. Unlike Tennyson in such elegies as *In Memoriam*, Arnold rarely touches here upon other kinds of immortality.

As a framework for his elegy, Arnold draws on the same Greek and Latin pastoral tradition from which Milton's *Lycidas* and Shelley's *Adonais* were derived. Hence Clough is referred to by one of the traditional names for a shepherd-poet, Thyrsis, and Arnold himself as Corydon. The sense of distancing which results from this traditional elegiac mode is reduced considerably by the realism of the setting with its bleak wintry landscape at twilight, a landscape which is brightened, in turn, by evocations of the return of hopeful springtime.

2. The villages of North Hinksey and South Hinksey.

The village street its haunted mansion lacks,
And from the sign is gone Sibylla's name,[3]
   And from the roofs the twisted chimney stacks—   5
      Are ye too changed, ye hills?
See, 'tis no foot of unfamiliar men
   Tonight from Oxford up your pathway strays!
   Here came I often, often, in old days—
      Thyrsis and I; we still had Thyrsis then.   10

Runs it not here, the track by Childsworth Farm,
   Past the high wood, to where the elm tree crowns
     The hill behind whose ridge the sunset flames?
The signal-elm, that looks on Ilsley Downs,
     The Vale, the three lone weirs, the youthful Thames?—   15
      This winter eve is warm,
Humid the air! leafless, yet soft as spring,
   The tender purple spray on copse and briers!
   And that sweet city with her dreaming spires,
      She needs not June for beauty's heightening,   20

Lovely all times she lies, lovely tonight!—
   Only, methinks, some loss of habit's power
     Befalls me wandering through this upland dim.
Once passed I blindfold here, at any hour;
     Now seldom come I, since I came with him.   25
      That single elm tree bright
Against the west—I miss it! is it gone?
   We prized it dearly; while it stood, we said,
   Our friend, the Gypsy Scholar, was not dead;
      While the tree lived, he in these fields lived on.   30

Too rare, too rare, grow now my visits here,
   But once I knew each field, each flower, each stick;
     And with the countryfolk acquaintance made
By barn in threshing time, by new-built rick.
     Here, too, our shepherd pipes we first assayed.   35
      Ah me! this many a year
My pipe is lost, my shepherd's holiday!
   Needs must I lose them, needs with heavy heart
   Into the world and wave of men depart;
      But Thyrsis of his own will went away.[4]   40

It irked him to be here, he could not rest.
   He loved each simple joy the country yields,
     He loved his mates; but yet he could not keep,[5]
For that a shadow loured on the fields,
     Here with the shepherds and the silly[6] sheep.   45
      Some life of men unblest

3. Sibylla Kerr had been the proprietress of a tavern in South Hinksey.
4. Arnold left Oxford out of the necessity for earning a living; Clough left as a matter of principle when in 1848 he resigned a fellowship rather than subscribe to the creed of the Anglican Church.
5. Stay.
6. Innocent.

He knew, which made him droop, and filled his head.
He went; his piping took a troubled sound
Of storms[7] that rage outside our happy ground;
He could not wait their passing, he is dead.   50

So, some tempestuous morn in early June,
When the year's primal burst of bloom is o'er,
Before the roses and the longest day—
When garden walks and all the grassy floor
With blossoms red and white of fallen May   55
And chestnut flowers are strewn—
So have I heard the cuckoo's parting cry,
From the wet field, through the vexed garden trees,
Come with the volleying rain and tossing breeze:
The bloom is gone, and with the bloom go I!   60

Too quick despairer, wherefore wilt thou go?
Soon will the high Midsummer pomps come on,
Soon will the musk carnations break and swell,
Soon shall we have gold-dusted snapdragon,
Sweet-william with his homely cottage smell,   65
And stocks in fragrant blow;
Roses that down the alleys shine afar,
And open, jasmine-muffled lattices,
And groups under the dreaming garden trees,
And the full moon, and the white evening star.   70

He hearkens not! light comer, he is flown!
What matters it? next year he will return,
And we shall have him in the sweet spring days,
With whitening hedges, and uncrumpling fern,
And bluebells trembling by the forest ways,   75
And scent of hay new-mown.
But Thyrsis never more we swains shall see,
See him come back, and cut a smoother reed,
And blow a strain the world at last shall heed—
For Time, not Corydon, hath conquered thee!   80

Alack, for Corydon no rival now!—
But when Sicilian shepherds lost a mate,
Some good survivor with his flute would go,
Piping a ditty sad for Bion's fate;[8]
And cross the unpermitted ferry's flow,[9]   85
And relax Pluto's brow,
And make leap up with joy the beauteous head
Of Proserpine, among whose crownéd hair
Are flowers first opened on Sicilian air,
And flute his friend, like Orpheus, from the dead.[1]   90

7. Religious and political controversies.
8. Moschus, a Greek poet, composed a pastoral elegy upon the death of the poet Bion in Sicily.
9. The river Styx across which the dead were ferried to the underworld where Pluto ruled with his queen, Proserpine.

In spring, Proserpine's returning above ground in Sicily would cause the flowers to blossom.
1. Orpheus' music enabled him to enter the "unpermitted" realms of the dead and to bring his wife, Eurydice, back with him to the land of the living.

O easy access to the hearer's grace
   When Dorian shepherds[2] sang to Proserpine!
     For she herself had trod Sicilian fields,
    She knew the Dorian water's gush divine,
      She knew each lily white which Enna yields,[3]   95
       Each rose with blushing face;
    She loved the Dorian pipe, the Dorian strain.
     But ah, of our poor Thames she never heard!
     Her foot the Cummer cowslips never stirred;
   And we should tease her with our plaint in vain!   100

Well! wind-dispersed and vain the words will be,
   Yet, Thyrsis, let me give my grief its hour
    In the old haunt, and find our tree-topped hill!
    Who, if not I, for questing here hath power?
     I know the wood which hides the daffodil,   105
      I know the Fyfield tree,
    I know what white, what purple fritillaries[4]
     The grassy harvest of the river fields,
     Above by Ensham, down by Sandford, yields,
   And what sedged brooks are Thames's tributaries;   110

I know these slopes; who knows them if not I?—
   But many a dingle[5] on the loved hillside,
     With thorns once studded, old, white-blossomed trees,
    Where thick the cowslips grew, and far descried
      High towered the spikes of purple orchises,   115
       Hath since our day put by
    The coronals of that forgotten time;
     Down each green bank hath gone the plowboy's team,
     And only in the hidden brookside gleam
   Primroses, orphans of the flowery prime.   120

Where is the girl, who by the boatman's door,
   Above the locks, above the boating throng,
     Unmoored our skiff when through the Wytham flats,
    Red loosestrife[6] and blond meadowsweet among
      And darting swallows and light water-gnats,   125
       We tracked the shy Thames shore?
    Where are the mowers, who, as the tiny swell
     Of our boat passing heaved the river grass,
     Stood with suspended scythe to see us pass?—
   They all are gone, and thou art gone as well!   130

Yes, thou art gone! and round me too the night
   In ever-nearing circle weaves her shade.
    I see her veil draw soft across the day,

2. The Dorian Greeks had colonized Sicily, the home of pastoral poetry.
3. From a meadow near Enna, a Sicilian town, Proserpine had been carried off to the underworld by Pluto (or Dis). Cf. the touchstone lines admired by Arnold in *Paradise Lost* (IV.268–71): "that fair field / Of Enna, where Proserpine gathering flowers, / Herself a fairer flower, by gloomy Dis / Was gathered * * * "
4. Flowers commonly found in moist meadows.
5. Small deep valley.
6. Flowers which grow on banks of streams.

I feel her slowly chilling breath invade
    The cheek grown thin, the brown hair sprent[7] with gray; 135
      I feel her finger light
Laid pausefully upon life's headless train;
    The foot less prompt to meet the morning dew,
    The heart less bounding at emotion new,
And hope, once crushed, less quick to spring again. 140

And long the way appears, which seemed so short
    To the less practiced eye of sanguine youth;
    And high the mountaintops, in cloudy air,
The mountaintops where is the throne of Truth,[8]
    Tops in life's morning sun so bright and bare! 145
      Unbreachable the fort
Of the long-battered world uplifts its wall;
    And strange and vain the earthly turmoil grows,
    And near and real the charm of thy repose,
And night as welcome as a friend would fall. 150

But hush! the upland hath a sudden loss
    Of quiet!—Look, adown the dusk hillside,
    A troop of Oxford hunters going home,
As in old days, jovial and talking, ride!
    From hunting with the Berkshire hounds they come. 155
      Quick! let me fly, and cross
Into yon farther field!—'Tis done; and see,
    Backed by the sunset, which doth glorify
    The orange and pale violet evening sky,
Bare on its lonely ridge, the Tree! the Tree! 160

I take the omen! Eve lets down her veil,
    The white fog creeps from bush to bush about,
    The west unflushes, the high stars grow bright,
And in the scattered farms the lights come out.
    I cannot reach the signal-tree tonight, 165
      Yet, happy omen, hail!
Hear it from thy broad lucent Arno vale[9]
    (For there thine earth-forgetting eyelids keep
    The morningless and unawakening sleep
Under the flowery oleanders pale), 170

Hear it, O Thyrsis, still our tree is there!—
    Ah, vain! These English fields, this upland dim,
    These brambles pale with mist engarlanded,
That lone, sky-pointing tree, are not for him;
    To a boon southern country he is fled, 175
      And now in happier air,
Wandering with the great Mother's[1] train divine

---

7. Sprinkled.
8. Cf. Pope's *Essay on Criticism*, II.220–32.
9. Clough was buried in Florence, which is situated in the valley of the Arno River.

1. Demeter (whose name may mean Earth Mother) was worshiped as the goddess of agriculture. The "immortal chants" (line 181) would be sung in her honor by her followers, members of the "train divine" (line 176).

(And purer or more subtle soul than thee,
I trow, the mighty Mother doth not see)
  Within a folding of the Apennine,[2]   180

Thou hearest the immortal chants of old!—
Putting his sickle to the perilous grain
  In the hot cornfield of the Phrygian king,[3]
For thee the Lityerses song again
  Young Daphnis with his silver voice doth sing;   185
    Sings his Sicilian fold,
His sheep, his hapless love, his blinded eyes—
And how a call celestial round him rang,
And heavenward from the fountain brink he sprang,
  And all the marvel of the golden skies.   190

There thou art gone, and me thou leavest here
Sole in these fields! yet will I not despair.
  Despair I will not, while I yet descry
'Neath the mild canopy of English air
  That lonely tree against the western sky.   195
    Still, still these slopes, 'tis clear,
Our Gypsy Scholar haunts, outliving thee!
  Fields where soft sheep from cages pull the hay,
  Woods with anemones in flower till May,
Know him a wanderer still; then why not me?   200

A fugitive and gracious light he seeks,
Shy to illumine; and I seek it too.
  This does not come with houses or with gold,
With place, with honor, and a flattering crew;
  'Tis not in the world's market bought and sold—   205
    But the smooth-slipping weeks
Drop by, and leave its seeker still untired;
  Out of the heed of mortals he is gone,
  He wends unfollowed, he must house alone;
Yet on he fares, by his own heart inspired.   210

Thou too, O Thyrsis, on like quest wast bound;
Thou wanderedst with me for a little hour!
  Men gave thee nothing; but this happy quest,
If men esteemed thee feeble, gave thee power,

---

2. Mountains near Florence.
3. Arnold includes a note from Servius'
commentary on Virgil's *Eclogues:*
"Daphnis, the ideal Sicilian shepherd
of Greek pastoral poetry, was said to
have followed into Phrygia his mistress Piplea, who had been carried off by
robbers, and to have found her in the
power of the king of Phrygia, Lityerses.
Lityerses used to make strangers try a
contest with him in reaping corn, and to
put them to death if he overcame them.
Hercules arrived in time to save Daphnis, took upon himself the reaping
contest with Lityerses, overcame him,
and slew him. The Lityerses song connected with this tradition was, like the
Linus song, one of the early plaintive
strains of Greek popular poetry, and
used to be sung by corn reapers. Other
traditions represented Daphnis as beloved by a nymph who exacted from
him an oath to love no one else. He fell
in love with a princess, and was struck
blind by the jealous nymph. Mercury,
who was his father, raised him to
heaven, and made a fountain spring up
in the place from which he ascended. At
this fountain the Sicilians offered yearly
sacrifices."

If men procured thee trouble, gave thee rest.   215
    And this rude Cumner ground,
Its fir-topped Hurst, its farms, its quiet fields,
    Here cam'st thou in thy jocund youthful time,
    Here was thine height of strength, thy golden prime!
And still the haunt beloved a virtue yields.   220

What though the music of thy rustic flute
    Kept not for long its happy, country tone;
    Lost it too soon, and learnt a stormy note[4]
Of men contention-tossed, of men who groan,
    Which tasked thy pipe too sore, and tired thy throat—   225
    It failed, and thou wast mute!
Yet hadst thou alway visions of our light,
    And long with men of care thou couldst not stay,
    And soon thy foot resumed its wandering way,
Left human haunt, and on alone till night.   230

Too rare, too rare, grow now my visits here!
    'Mid city noise, not, as with thee of yore,
    Thyrsis! in reach of sheep-bells is my home.
—Then through the great town's harsh, heart-wearying roar,
    Let in thy voice a whisper often come,   235
        To chase fatigue and fear:
Why faintest thou? I wandered till I died.
Roam on! The light we sought is shining still.
Dost thou ask proof? Our tree yet crowns the hill,
Our Scholar travels yet the loved hillside.   240
                        1866

Growing Old[1]

What is it to grow old?
Is it to lose the glory of the form,
    The luster of the eye?
Is it for beauty to forego her wreath?
    —Yes, but not this alone.   5

Is it to feel our strength—
Not our bloom only, but our strength—decay?
    Is it to feel each limb
Grow stiffer, every function less exact,
    Each nerve more loosely strung?   10

Yes, this, and more; but not
Ah, 'tis not what in youth we dreamed 'twould be!
    'Tis not to have our life

---

4. Clough's poetry often dealt with contemporary religious problems
1. Arnold's poem may have been prompted as a rejoinder to Browning's enthusiastic picture of old age in *Rabbi Ben Ezra* (1864).

Mellowed and softened as with sunset glow,
A golden day's decline.   15

'Tis not to see the world
As from a height, with rapt prophetic eyes,
And heart profoundly stirred;
And weep, and feel the fullness of the past,[2]
The years that are no more.   20

It is to spend long days
And not once feel that we were ever young;
It is to add, immured
In the hot prison of the present, month
To month with weary pain.   25

It is to suffer this,
And feel but half, and feebly, what we feel.
Deep in our hidden heart
Festers the dull remembrance of a change,
But no emotion—none.   30

It is—last stage of all—
When we are frozen up within, and quite
The phantom of ourselves,
To hear the world applaud the hollow ghost
Which blamed the living man.   35

1867

The Last Word

Creep into thy narrow bed,
Creep, and let no more be said!
Vain thy onset! all stands fast.
Thou thyself must break at last.

Let the long contention cease!   5
Geese are swans, and swans are geese.
Let them have it how they will!
Thou art tired; best be still.

They out-talked thee, hissed thee, tore thee?
Better men fared thus before thee;   10
Fired their ringing shot and passed,
Hotly charged—and sank at last.

Charge once more, then, and be dumb!
Let the victors, when they come,
When the forts of folly fall,
Find thy body by the wall!

1867

2. Cf. Tennyson's *Tears, Idle Tears.*

Preface to *Poems* (1853)

In two small volumes of poems, published anonymously, one in 1849, the other in 1852, many of the poems which compose the present volume have already appeared. The rest are now published for the first time.

I have, in the present collection, omitted the poem from which the volume published in 1852 took its title.[1] I have done so, not because the subject of it was a Sicilian Greek born between two and three thousand years ago, although many persons would think this a sufficient reason. Neither have I done so because I had, in my own opinion, failed in the delineation which I intended to effect. I intended to delineate the feelings of one of the last of the Greek religious philosophers, one of the family of Orpheus and Musaeus,[2] having survived his fellows, living on into a time when the habits of Greek thought and feeling had begun fast to change, character to dwindle, the influence of the Sophists[3] to prevail. Into the feelings of a man so situated there entered much that we are accustomed to consider as exclusively modern; how much, the fragments[4] of Empedocles himself which remain to us are sufficient at least to indicate. What those who are familiar only with the great monuments of early Greek genius suppose to be its exclusive characteristics, have disappeared; the calm, the cheerfulness, the disinterested objectivity have disappeared; the dialogue of the mind with itself has commenced; modern problems have presented themselves, we hear already the doubts, we witness the discouragement, of Hamlet and of Faust.

The representation of such a man's feelings must be interesting, if consistently drawn. We all naturally take pleasure, says Aristotle, in any imitation or representation whatever;[5] this is the basis of our

1. *Empedocles on Etna*, the long poem that supplied the title for Arnold's second collection of poems, portrays the disillusioned reflections of the Greek philosopher and scientist Empedocles and culminates in the speaker's suicide on Mount Etna in Sicily, in the 5th century B.C. Because of his dissatisfaction with what he calls the "morbid" tone of *Empedocles on Etna* Arnold continued to exclude it from his volumes of poetry until 1867 when he reprinted it at the request, he said, "of a man of genius, whom it had the honor and good fortune to interest—Mr. Robert Browning." It should be noted that in the arguments developed in the *Preface* against his own poem (and against 19th-century poetry in general) Arnold is exclusively concerned with narrative and dramatic poetry. The *Preface,* as he himself remarked

in 1854, "leaves * * * untouched the question, how far, and in what manner, the opinions there expressed respecting the choice of subjects apply to lyric poetry; that region of the poetical field which is chiefly cultivated at present."
2. Pupil of the poet and musician Orpheus. The latter was the legendary founder of the Orphic religion that flourished in 6th-century Greece and later declined.
3. Greek rhetoricians, often criticized because of their reputed concern for niceties of expression over substance of knowledge.
4. Empedocles' writings (medical and scientific treatises in verse) have survived only in fragments.
5. See Aristotle, *Poetics*, especially 1, 2, 4, 7, 14.

love of poetry; and we take pleasure in them, he adds, because all knowledge is naturally agreeable to us; not to the philosopher only, but to mankind at large. Every representation therefore which is consistently drawn may be supposed to be interesting, inasmuch as it gratifies this natural interest in knowledge of all kinds. What is *not* interesting is that which does not add to our knowledge of any kind; that which is vaguely conceived and loosely drawn; a representation which is general, indeterminate, and faint, instead of being particular, precise, and firm.

Any accurate representation may therefore be expected to be interesting; but, if the representation be a poetical one, more than this is demanded. It is demanded, not only that it shall interest, but also that it shall inspirit and rejoice the reader; that it shall convey a charm, and infuse delight. For the Muses, as Hesiod says, were born that they might be "a forgetfulness of evils, and a truce from cares":[6] and it is not enough that the poet should add to the knowledge of men, it is required of him also that he should add to their happiness. "All art," says Schiller, "is dedicated to Joy, and there is no higher and no more serious problem, than how to make men happy. The right art is that alone, which creates the highest enjoyment."[7]

A poetical work, therefore, is not yet justified when it has been shown to be an accurate, and therefore interesting representation; it has to be shown also that it is a representation from which men can derive enjoyment. In presence of the most tragic circumstances, represented in a work of Art, the feeling of enjoyment, as is well known, may still subsist; the representation of the most utter calamity, of the liveliest anguish, is not sufficient to destroy it; the more tragic the situation, the deeper becomes the enjoyment; and the situation is more tragic in proportion as it becomes more terrible.

What then are the situations, from the representation of which, though accurate, no poetical enjoyment can be derived? They are those in which the suffering finds no vent in action; in which a continuous state of mental distress is prolonged, unrelieved by incident, hope, or resistance; in which there is everything to be endured, nothing to be done. In such situations there is inevitably something morbid, in the description of them something monotonous. When they occur in actual life, they are painful, not tragic; the representation of them in poetry is painful also.

To this class of situations, poetically faulty as it appears to me, that of Empedocles, as I have endeavored to represent him, belongs; and I have therefore excluded the poem from the present collection.

6. From *Theogony* 52–56, by the early Greek poet Hesiod.
7. J. C. F. von Schiller, *On the Use of the Chorus in Tragedy*, prefatory essay to *The Bride of Messina* (1803). See *Friedrich Schiller's Works* (1903), VIII, 224.

And why, it may be asked, have I entered into this explanation respecting a matter so unimportant as the admission or exclusion of the poem in question? I have done so, because I was anxious to avow that the sole reason for its exclusion was that which has been stated above; and that it has not been excluded in deference to the opinion which many critics of the present day appear to entertain against subjects chosen from distant times and countries: against the choice, in short, of any subjects but modern ones.

"The poet," it is said, and by an intelligent critic, "the poet who would really fix the public attention must leave the exhausted past, and draw his subjects from matters of present import, and *therefore* both of interest and novelty."[8]

Now this view I believe to be completely false. It is worth examining, inasmuch as it is a fair sample of a class of critical dicta everywhere current at the present day, having a philosophical form and air, but no real basis in fact; and which are calculated to vitiate the judgment of readers of poetry, while they exert, so far as they are adopted, a misleading influence on the practice of those who write it.

What are the eternal objects of poetry, among all nations and at all times? They are actions; human actions; possessing an inherent interest in themselves, and which are to be communicated in an interesting manner by the art of the poet.[9] Vainly will the latter imagine that he has everything in his own power; that he can make an intrinsically inferior action equally delightful with a more excellent one by his treatment of it; he may indeed compel us to admire his skill, but his work will possess, within itself, an incurable defect.

The poet, then, has in the first place to select an excellent action; and what actions are the most excellent? Those, certainly, which most powerfully appeal to the great primary human affections: to those elementary feelings which subsist permanently in the race, and which are independent of time. These feelings are permanent and the same; that which interests them is permanent and the same also. The modernness or antiquity of an action, therefore, has nothing to do with its fitness for poetical representation; this depends upon its inherent qualities. To the elementary part of our nature, to our passions, that which is great and passionate is eternally interesting; and interesting solely in proportion to its greatness and to its passion. A great human action of a thousand years ago is more interesting to it than a smaller human action of today, even though upon the representation of this last the most consummate skill may have been expended, and though it has the advantage of

8. In the *Spectator* of April 2nd, 1853. The words quoted were not used with reference to poems of mine [Arnold's note]. According to Arnold the "intel-ligent critic" was R. S. Rintoul, editor of the *Spectator*.
9. Cf. Aristotle, *Poetics* 6.

appealing by its modern language, familiar manners, and contemporary allusions, to all our transient feelings and interests. These, however, have no right to demand of a poetical work that it shall satisfy them; their claims are to be directed elsewhere. Poetical works belong to the domain of our permanent passions; let them interest these, and the voice of all subordinate claims upon them is at once silenced.

Achilles, Prometheus, Clytemnestra, Dido—what modern poem presents personages as interesting, even to us moderns, as these personages of an "exhausted past"? We have the domestic epic dealing with the details of modern life which pass daily under our eyes;[1] we have poems representing modern personages in contact with the problems of modern life, morel, intellectual, and social; these works have been produced by poets the most distinguished of their nation and time; yet I fearlessly assert that *Hermann and Dorothea, Childe Harold, Jocelyn, The Excursion,*[2] leave the reader cold in comparison with the effect produced upon him by the latter books of the *Iliad,* by the *Oresteia,*[3] or by the episode of Dido.[4] And why is this? Simply because in the three last-named cases the action is greater, the personages nobler, the situations more intense: and this is the true basis of the interest in a poetical work, and this alone.

It may be urged, however, that past actions may be interesting in themselves, but that they are not to be adopted by the modern poet, because it is impossible for him to have them clearly present to his own mind, and he cannot therefore feel them deeply, nor represent them forcibly. But this is not necessarily the case. The externals of a past action, indeed, he cannot know with the precision of a contemporary; but his business is with its essentials. The outward man of Oedipus or of Macbeth, the houses in which they lived, the ceremonies of their courts, he cannot accurately figure to himself; but neither do they essentially concern him. His business is with their inward man; with their feelings and behavior in certain tragic situations, which engage their passions as men; these have in them nothing local and casual; they are as accessible to the modern poet as to a contemporary.

The date of an action, then, signifies nothing: the action itself, its selection and construction, this is what is all-important. This the Greeks understood far more clearly than we do. The radical difference between their poetical theory and ours consists, as it appears to me, in this: that, with them, the poetical character of the action

1. Perhaps alluding to such poems as Tennyson's *The Princess* (1847) and Alexander Smith's *Life Drama* (1853).
2. Long poems by Goethe (1797), Byron (1818), Lamartine (1836), and Wordsworth (1814), respectively.
3. A trilogy of plays by Aeschylus concerned with the stories of Agamemnon, Clytemnestra, and their son, Orestes.
4. See Virgil's *Aeneid* IV.

in itself, and the conduct of it, was the first consideration; with us, attention is fixed mainly on the value of the separate thoughts and images which occur in the treatment of an action. They regarded the whole; we regard the parts. With them, the action predominated over the expression of it; with us, the expression predominates over the action. Not that they failed in expression, or were inattentive to it; on the contrary, they are the highest models of expression, the unapproached masters of the *grand style:* but their expression is so excellent because it is so admirably kept in its right degree of prominence; because it is so simple and so well subordinated; because it draws its force directly from the pregnancy of the matter which it conveys. For what reason was the Greek tragic poet confined to so limited a range of subjects? Because there are so few actions which unite in themselves, in the highest degree, the conditions of excellence: and it was not thought that on any but an excellent subject could an excellent poem be constructed. A few actions, therefore, eminently adapted for tragedy, maintained almost exclusive possession of the Greek tragic stage; their significance appeared inexhaustible; they were as permanent problems, perpetually offered to the genius of every fresh poet. This too is the reason of what appears to us moderns a certain baldness of expression in Greek tragedy; of the triviality with which we often reproach the remarks of the chorus, where it takes part in the dialogue: that the action itself, the situation of Orestes, or Merope, or Alcmaeon,[5] was to stand the central point of interest, unforgotten, absorbing, principal; that no accessories were for a moment to distract the spectator's attention from this; that the tone of the parts was to be perpetually kept down, in order not to impair the grandiose effect of the whole. The terrible old mythic story on which the drama was founded stood, before he entered the theater, traced in its bare outlines upon the spectator's mind; it stood in his memory, as a group of statuary, faintly seen, at the end of a long and dark vista: then came the poet, embodying outlines, developing situations, not a word wasted, not a sentiment capriciously thrown in: stroke upon stroke, the drama proceeded: the light deepened upon the group; more and more it revealed itself to the riveted gaze of the spectator: until at last, when the final words were spoken, it stood before him in broad sunlight, a model of immortal beauty.

This was what a Greek critic demanded; this was what a Greek poet endeavored to effect. It signified nothing to what time an action belonged; we do not find that the *Persae* occupied a particularly high rank among the dramas of Aeschylus, because it represented a

---

5. Merope, queen of Messene in Greece, appears in plays by Euripides and in Arnold's own play *Merope* (1858). Alcmaeon was the son of a legendary Greek hero, who like Orestes, avenged his father's death by killing his mother. He was the subject of several Greek plays now lost.

matter of contemporary interest:[6] this was not what a cultivated Athenian required, he required that the permanent elements of his nature should be moved; and dramas of which the action, though taken from a long-distant mythic time, yet was calculated to accomplish this in a higher degree than that of the *Persae,* stood higher in his estimation accordingly. The Greeks felt, no doubt, with their exquisite sagacity of taste, that an action of present times was too near them, too much mixed up with what was accidental and passing, to form a sufficiently grand, detached, and self-subsistent object for a tragic poem: such objects belonged to the domain of the comic poet, and of the lighter kinds of poetry. For the more serious kinds, for *pragmatic* poetry, to use an excellent expression of Polybius,[7] they were more difficult and severe in the range of subjects which they permitted. Their theory and practice alike, the admirable treatise of Aristotle, and the unrivaled works of their poets, exclaim with a thousand tongues—"All depends upon the subject; choose a fitting action, penetrate yourself with the feeling of its situations; this done, everything else will follow."

But for all kinds of poetry alike there was one point on which they were rigidly exacting; the adaptability of the subject to the kind of poetry selected, and the careful construction of the poem.

How different a way of thinking from this is ours! We can hardly at the present day understand what Menander[8] meant when he told a man who inquired as to the progress of his comedy that he had finished it, not having yet written a single line, because he had constructed the action of it in his mind. A modern critic would have assured him that the merit of his piece depended on the brilliant things which arose under his pen as he went along. We have poems which seem to exist merely for the sake of single lines and passages; not for the sake of producing any total impression. We have critics who seem to direct their attention merely to detached expressions, to the language about the action, not to the action itself. I verily think that the majority of them do not in their hearts believe that there is such a thing as a total impression to be derived from a poem at all, or to be demanded from a poet; they think the term a commonplace of metaphysical criticism. They will permit the poet to select any action he pleases, and to suffer that action to go as it will, provided he gratifies them with occasional bursts of fine writing, and with a shower of isolated thoughts and images. That is, they permit him to leave their poetical sense ungratified, provided that he gratifies their rhetorical sense and their curiosity. Of his neglecting to gratify these, there is little

6. Aeschylus' *Persians* (472 B.C.) portrays the Greek victory over the Persian invaders, which had occurred only a few years before the play was produced.

7. Greek historian (202–120 B.C.).
8. Greek writer of comedies (342–292 B.C.).

danger. He needs rather to be warned against the danger of attempting to gratify these alone; he needs rather to be perpetually reminded to prefer his action to everything else; so to treat this, as to permit its inherent excellences to develop themselves, without interruption from the intrusion of his personal peculiarities; most fortunate, when he most entirely succeeds in effecting himself, and in enabling a noble action to subsist as it did in nature.

But the modern critic not only permits a false practice; he absolutely prescribes false aims.—"A true allegory of the state of one's own mind in a representative history," the poet is told, "is perhaps the highest thing that one can attempt in the way of poetry." [9] And accordingly he attempts it. An allegory of the state of one's own mind, the highest problem of an art which imitates actions! No assuredly, it is not, it never can be so: no great poetical work has ever been produced with such an aim. *Faust* itself, in which something of the kind is attempted, wonderful passages as it contains, and in spite of the unsurpassed beauty of the scenes which relate to Margaret, *Faust* itself, judged as a whole, and judged strictly as a poetical work, is defective: its illustrious author, the greatest poet of modern times, the greatest critic of all times, would have been the first to acknowledge it; he only defended his work, indeed, by asserting it to be "something incommensurable."[1]

The confusion of the present times is great, the multitude of voices counseling different things bewildering, the number of existing works capable of attracting a young writer's attention and of becoming his models, immense. What he wants is a hand to guide him through the confusion, a voice to prescribe to him the aim which he should keep in view, and to explain to him that the value of the literary works which offer themselves to his attention is relative to their power of helping him forward on his road towards this aim. Such a guide the English writer at the present day will nowhere find. Failing this, all that can be looked for, all indeed that can be desired is, that his attention should be fixed on excellent models; that he may reproduce, at any rate, something of their excellence, by penetrating himself with their works and by catching their spirit, if he cannot be taught to produce what is excellent independently.

Foremost among these models for the English writer stands Shakespeare: a name the greatest perhaps of all poetical names; a name never to be mentioned without reverence. I will venture, however, to express a doubt, whether the influence of his works,

9. *North British Review*, XIX (August, 1853), 180 (U.S. edition). Arnold seems not to have noticed that Goethe (a critic he revered) had been cited earlier in the article as the authority for this critical generalization.
1. J. Eckermann, *Conversations with Goethe*, Jan. 3, 1830.

excellent and fruitful for the readers of poetry, for the great majority, has been of unmixed advantage to the writers of it. Shakespeare indeed chose excellent subjects; the world could afford no better than Macbeth, or Romeo and Juliet, or Othello: he had no theory respecting the necessity of choosing subjects of present import, or the paramount interest attaching to allegories of the state of one's own mind; like all great poets, he knew well what constituted a poetical action; like them, wherever he found such an action, he took it; like them, too, he found his best in past times. But to these general characteristics of all great poets he added a special one of his own; a gift, namely, of happy, abundant, and ingenious expression, eminent and unrivaled: so eminent as irresistibly to strike the attention first in him, and even to throw into comparative shade his other excellences as a poet. Here has been the mischief. These other excellences were his fundamental excellences *as a poet*; what distinguishes the artist from the mere amateur, says Goethe, is *Architectonicè* in the highest sense;[2] that power of execution, which creates, forms, and constitutes: not the profoundness of single thoughts, not the richness of imagery, not the abundance of illustration. But these attractive accessories of a poetical work being more easily seized than the spirit of the whole, and these accessories being possessed by Shakespeare in an unequaled degree, a young writer having recourse to Shakespeare as his model runs great risk of being vanquished and absorbed by them, and, in consequence, of reproducing, according to the measure of his power, these, and these alone.[3] Of this preponderating quality of Shakespeare's genius, accordingly almost the whole of modern English poetry has, it appears to me, felt the influence. To the exclusive attention on the part of his imitators to this it is in a great degree owing, that of the majority of modern poetical works the details alone are valuable, the composition worthless. In reading them one is perpetually reminded of that terrible sentence on a modern French poet: *Il dit tout ce qu'il veut, mais malheureusement il n'a rien à dire.*[4]

Let me give an instance of what I mean. I will take it from the works of the very chief among those who seem to have been formed in the school of Shakespeare: of one whose exquisite

---

2. In Goethe's essay *Concerning the So-called Dilettantism* (1799) in his *Werke*, 1851, XXV, 322.

3. Cf. Arnold's letter to Clough (Oct. 28, 1852): "More and more I feel that the difference between a mature and a youthful age of the world compels the poetry of the former to use great plainness of speech * * * and that Keats and Shelley were on a false track when they set themselves to reproduce the exuberance of expression, the charm, the richness of images, and the felicity, of the Elizabethan poets."

4. "He says everything he wishes to, but unfortunately he has nothing to say"— a comment on Théophile Gautier (1811–72) whose emphasis on style was severely criticized by Arnold in his late essay *Wordsworth* (see below).

genius and pathetic death render him forever interesting. I will take the poem of *Isabella, or the Pot of Basil,* by Keats. I choose this rather than the *Endymion,* because the latter work (which a modern critic has classed with the *Fairy Queen!* [5]) although undoubtedly there blows through it the breath of genius, is yet as a whole so utterly incoherent, as not strictly to merit the name of a poem at all. The poem of *Isabella,* then, is a perfect treasure-house of graceful and felicitous words and images: almost in every stanza there occurs one of those vivid and picturesque turns of expression, by which the object is made to flash upon the eye of the mind, and which thrill the reader with a sudden delight. This one short poem contains, perhaps, a greater number of happy single expressions which one could quote than all the extant tragedies of Sophocles. But the action, the story? The action in itself is an excellent one; but so feebly is it conceived by the poet, so loosely constructed, that the effect produced by it, in and for itself, is absolutely null. Let the reader, after he has finished the poem of Keats, turn to the same story in the *Decameron:*[6] he will then feel how pregnant and interesting the same action has become in the hands of a great artist, who above all things delineates his object; who subordinates expression to that which it is designed to express.

I have said that the imitators of Shakespeare, fixing their attention on his wonderful gift of expression, have directed their imitation to this, neglecting his other excellences. These excellences, the fundamental excellences of poetical art, Shakespeare no doubt possessed them—possessed many of them in a splendid degree; but it may perhaps be doubted whether even he himself did not sometimes give scope to his faculty of expression to the prejudice of a higher poetical duty. For we must never forget that Shakespeare is the great poet he is from his skill in discerning and firmly conceiving an excellent action, from his power of intensely feeling a situation, of intimately associating himself with a character; not from his gift of expression, which rather even leads him astray, degenerating sometimes into a fondness for curiosity of expression, into an irritability of fancy, which seems to make it impossible for him to say a thing plainly, even when the press of the action demands the very directest language, or its level character the very simplest. Mr. Hallam, than whom it is impossible to find a saner and more judicious critic, has had the courage (for at the present day it needs courage) to remark, how extremely and faultily difficult Shakespeare's language often is.[7] It is so: you may find main scenes in some of his greatest tragedies, *King Lear* for instance, where the language is so artificial, so curiously tortured,

5. In the *North British Review,* XIX (Aug., 1853), 172, 74, Keats' *Endymion* is twice linked with Spenser's *Faerie Queene* as "leisurely compositions of the sweet sensuous order."

6. Boccaccio's *Decameron,* 4th day, 5th novel.
7. Henry Hallam, historian (1779–1859), *Introduction to the Literature of Europe* (1838–39), Ch. 23.

and so difficult, that every speech has to be read two or three times before its meaning can be comprehended. This over-curiousness of expression is indeed but the excessive employment of a wonderful gift—of the power of saying a thing in a happier way than any other man; nevertheless, it is carried so far that one understands what M. Guizot meant, when he said that Shake-speare appears in his language to have tried all styles except that of simplicity.[8] He has not the severe and scrupulous self-restraint of the ancients, partly no doubt, because he had a far less culti-vated and exacting audience. He has indeed a far wider range than they had, a far richer fertility of thought; in this respect he rises above them. In his strong conception of his subject, in the genuine way in which he is penetrated with it, he resembles them, and is unlike the moderns. But in the accurate limitation of it, the conscientious rejection of superfluities, the simple and rigorous development of it from the first line of his work to the last, he falls below them, and comes nearer to the moderns. In his chief works, besides what he has of his own, he has the ele-mentary soundness of the ancients; he has their important action and their large and broad manner; but he has not their purity of method. He is therefore a less safe model; for what he has of his own is personal, and inseparable from his own rich nature; it may be imitated and exaggerated, it cannot be learned or applied as an art. He is above all suggestive; more valuable, therefore, to young writers as men than as artists. But clearness of arrangement, rigor of development, simplicity of style—these may to a certain extent be learned; and these may, I am convinced, be learned best from the ancients, who although infinitely less suggestive than Shakespeare, are thus, to the artist, more instructive.

What, then, it will be asked, are the ancients to be our sole models? the ancients with their comparatively narrow range of experience, and their widely different circumstances? Not, cer-tainly, that which is narrow in the ancients, nor that in which we can no longer sympathize. An action like the action of the *Anti-gone* of Sophocles, which turns upon the conflict between the heroine's duty to her brother's corpse and that to the laws of her country, is no longer one in which it is possible that we should feel a deep interest. I am speaking too, it will be remembered, not of the best sources of intellectual stimulus for the general reader, but of the best models of instruction for the individual writer. This last may certainly learn of the ancients, better than anywhere else, three things which it is vitally important for him to know: the all-importance of the choice of a subject; the necessity of accurate construction; and the subordinate character of expression. He will learn from them how unspeakably superior

---

8. F. P. G. Guizot, French historian (1787–1874), discussing Shakespeare's   sonnets in his *Shakespeare et son Temps* (1852), p. 114.

is the effect of the one moral impression left by a great action treated as a whole, to the effect produced by the most striking single thought or by the happiest image. As he penetrates into the spirit of the great classical works, as he becomes gradually aware of their intense significance, their noble simplicity, and their calm pathos, he will be convinced that it is this effect, unity and profoundness of moral impression, at which the ancient poets aimed; that it is this which constitutes the grandeur of their works, and which makes them immortal. He will desire to direct his own efforts towards producing the same effect. Above all, he will deliver himself from the jargon of modern criticism, and escape the danger of producing poetical works conceived in the spirit of the passing time, and which partake of its transitoriness.

The present age makes great claims upon us; we owe it service, it will not be satisfied without our admiration. I know not how it is, but their commerce with the ancients appears to me to produce, in those who constantly practice it, a steadying and composing effect upon their judgment, not of literary works only, but of men and events in general. They are like persons who have had a very weighty and impressive experience; they are more truly than others under the empire of facts, and more independent of the language current among those with whom they live. They wish neither to applaud nor to revile their age; they wish to know what it is, what it can give them, and whether this is what they want. What they want, they know very well; they want to educe and cultivate what is best and noblest in themselves; they know, too, that this is no easy task—χαλεπὸν, as Pittacus said, χαλεπὸν ἐσθλὸν ἔμμεναι[9]—and they ask themselves sincerely whether their age and its literature can assist them in the attempt. If they are endeavoring to practice any art, they remember the plain and simple proceedings of the old artists, who attained their grand results by penetrating themselves with some noble and significant action, not by inflating themselves with a belief in the pre-eminent importance and greatness of their own times. They do not talk of their mission, nor of interpreting their age, nor of the coming poet; all this, they know, is the mere delirium of vanity; their business is not to praise their age, but to afford to the men who live in it the highest pleasure which they are capable of feeling. If asked to afford this by means of subjects drawn from the age itself, they ask what special fitness the present age has for supplying them. They are told that it is an era of progress, an age commissioned to carry out the great ideas of industrial development and social amelioration. They reply that with all this they can do nothing; that the elements they need for the exercise of their art are great actions, calculated powerfully and delightfully to affect what is permanent in the human soul;

9. "It is hard to be good." An aphorism of Pittacus, a Greek sage, 7th century B.C.

that so far as the present age can supply such actions, they will gladly make use of them; but that an age wanting in moral grandeur can with difficulty supply such, and an age of spiritual discomfort with difficulty be powerfully and delightfully affected by them.

A host of voices will indignantly rejoin that the present age is inferior to the past neither in moral grandeur nor in spiritual health. He who possesses the discipline I speak of will content himself with remembering the judgments passed upon the present age, in this respect, by the two men, the one of strongest head, the other of widest culture, whom it has produced; by Goethe and by Niebuhr.[1] It will be sufficient for him that he knows the opinions held by these two great men respecting the present age and its literature; and that he feels assured in his own mind that their aims and demands upon life were such as he would wish, at any rate, his own to be; and their judgment as to what is impeding and disabling such as he may safely follow. He will not, however, maintain a hostile attitude towards the false pretensions of his age: he will content himself with not being overwhelmed by them. He will esteem himself fortunate if he can succeed in banishing from his mind all feelings of contradiction, and irritation, and impatience; in order to delight himself with the contemplation of some noble action of a heroic time, and to enable others, through his representation of it, to delight in it also.

I am far indeed from making any claim, for myself, that I possess this discipline; or for the following poems, that they breathe its spirit. But I say, that in the sincere endeavor to learn and practice, amid the bewildering confusion of our times, what is sound and true in poetical art, I seemed to myself to find the only sure guidance, the only solid footing, among the ancients. They, at any rate, knew what they wanted in art, and we do not. It is this uncertainty which is disheartening, and not hostile criticism. How often have I felt this when reading words of disparagement or of cavil: that it is the uncertainty as to what is really to be aimed at which makes our difficulty, not the dissatisfaction of the critic, who himself suffers from the same uncertainty. *Non me tua fervida terrent Dicta; . . . Dii me terrent, et Jupiter hostis.*[2]

Two kinds of *dilettanti*, says Goethe, there are in poetry: he who neglects the indispensable mechanical part, and thinks he has done enough if he shows spirituality and feeling; and he who seeks to arrive at poetry merely by mechanism, in which he can acquire an artisan's readiness, and is without soul and matter.[3] And he adds, that the first does most harm to art, and the last to

1. B. G. Niebuhr (1776–1831), German historian.
2. Virgil, *Aeneid* XII. 894–95: "Your fiery speeches do not frighten me; it is the gods and the enmity of Jupiter that frighten me" (Turnus, a warrior abandoned by the gods, is replying to Aeneas who has taunted him with being afraid).
3. See note 2, Goethe's essay, above.

himself. If we must be *dilettanti*; if it is impossible for us, under the circumstances amidst which we live, to think clearly, to feel nobly, and to delineate firmly; if we cannot attain to the mastery of the great artists; let us, at least, have so much respect for our art as to prefer it to ourselves. Let us not bewilder our successors; let us transmit to them the practice of poetry, with its boundaries and wholesome regulative laws, under which excellent works may again, perhaps, at some future time, be produced, not yet fallen into oblivion through our neglect, not yet condemned and canceled by the influence of their eternal enemy, caprice.

From The Function of Criticism at the Present Time[1]

Many objections have been made to a proposition which, in some remarks of mine on translating Homer,[2] I ventured to put forth; a proposition about criticism, and its importance at the present day. I said: "Of the literature of France and Germany, as of the intellect of Europe in general, the main effort, for now many years, has been a critical effort; the endeavor, in all branches of knowledge, theology, philosophy, history, art, science, to see the object as in itself it really is." I added, that owing to the operation in English literature of certain causes, "almost the last thing for which one would come to English literature is just that very thing which now Europe most desires—criticism"; and that the power and value of English literature was thereby impaired. More than one rejoinder declared that the importance I here assigned to criticism was excessive, and asserted the inherent superiority of the creative effort of the human spirit over its critical effort. And the other day, having been led by a Mr. Shairp's excellent notice of Wordsworth[3] to turn again to his biography, I found, in the words of this great man, whom I, for one, must always listen to with the profoundest respect,

1. This essay served as an introduction to Arnold's volume of *Essays in Criticism* (1865). As a declaration of intentions, it can serve as a standard for measuring his total accomplishment in criticism. The essay makes us aware that criticism, for Arnold, meant a great deal more than casual book-reviewing or mere censoriousness. He was not a Utilitarian, yet his object in this essay is to show that good criticism is useful. Creative writers, he argues, can profit in a special way from good criticism, but all of us can also derive from it benefits of the greatest value. In particular, we may develop a civilized attitude of mind in which to examine the social, political, aesthetic, and religious problems which confront us.
2. *On Translating Homer* (1861).
3. J. C. Shairp's essay *Wordsworth:*

The Man and the Poet was published in 1864. Arnold comments in a footnote: "I cannot help thinking that a practice, common in England during the last century, and still followed in France, of printing a notice of this kind—a notice by a competent critic—to serve as an introduction to an eminent author's works, might be revived among us with advantage. To introduce all succeeding editions of Wordsworth, Mr. Shairp's notice might, it seems to me, excellently serve; it is written from the point of view of an admirer, nay, of a disciple, and that is right; but then the disciple must be also, as in this case he is, a critic, a man of letters, not, as too often happens, some relation or friend with no qualification for his task except affection for his author."

a sentence passed on the critic's business, which seems to justify every possible disparagement of it. Wordsworth says in one of his letters:

"The writers in these publications (the Reviews), while they prosecute their inglorious employment, cannot be supposed to be in a state of mind very favorable for being affected by the finer influences of a thing so pure as genuine poetry."

And a trustworthy reporter of his conversation quotes a more elaborate judgment to the same effect:

"Wordsworth holds the critical power very low, infinitely lower than the inventive; and he said today that if the quantity of time consumed in writing critiques on the works of others were given to original composition, of whatever kind it might be, it would be much better employed; it would make a man find out sooner his own level, and it would do infinitely less mischief. A false or malicious criticism may do much injury to the minds of others; a stupid invention, either in prose or verse, is quite harmless."

It is almost too much to expect of poor human nature, that a man capable of producing some effect in one line of literature, should, for the greater good of society, voluntarily doom himself to impotence and obscurity in another. Still less is this to be expected from men addicted to the composition of the "false or malicious criticism" of which Wordsworth speaks. However, everybody would admit that a false or malicious criticism had better never have been written. Everybody, too, would be willing to admit, as a general proposition, that the critical faculty is lower than the inventive. But is it true that criticism is really, in itself, a baneful and injurious employment; is it true that all time given to writing critiques on the works of others would be much better employed if it were given to original composition, of whatever kind this may be? Is it true that Johnson had better have gone on producing more *Irenes*[4] instead of writing his *Lives of the Poets*; nay, is it certain that Wordsworth himself was better employed in making his Ecclesiastical Sonnets[5] than when he made his celebrated Preface so full of criticism, and criticism of the works of others? Wordsworth was himself a great critic, and it is to be sincerely regretted that he has not left us more criticism; Goethe was one of the greatest of critics, and we may sincerely congratulate ourselves that he has left us so much criticism. Without wasting time over the exaggeration which Wordsworth's judgment on criticism clearly contains, or over an attempt to trace the causes—not difficult, I think, to be traced—which may have led Wordsworth to this exaggeration, a critic may

4. *Irene* is the name of a clumsy play by Samuel Johnson.
5. A sonnet sequence by Wordsworth, usually regarded as minor verse. The Preface is to his *Lyrical Ballads* of 1800.

with advantage seize an occasion for trying his own conscience, and for asking himself of what real service, at any given moment, the practice of criticism either is or may be made to his own mind and spirit, and to the minds and spirits of others.

The critical power is of lower rank than the creative. True; but in assenting to this proposition, one or two things are to be kept in mind. It is undeniable that the exercise of a creative power, that a free creative activity, is the highest function of man; it is proved to be so by man's finding in it his true happiness. But it is undeniable, also, that men may have the sense of exercising this free creative activity in other ways than in producing great works of literature or art; if it were not so, all but a very few men would be shut out from the true happiness of all men. They may have it in well-doing, they may have it in learning, they may have it even in criticizing. This is one thing to be kept in mind. Another is, that the exercise of the creative power in the production of great works of literature or art, however high this exercise of it may rank, is not at all epochs and under all conditions possible; and that therefore labor may be vainly spent in attempting it, which might with more fruit be used in preparing for it, in rendering it possible. This creative power works with elements, with materials; what if it has not those materials, those elements, ready for its use? In that case it must surely wait till they are ready. Now, in literature—I will limit myself to literature, for it is about literature that the question arises—the elements with which the creative power works are ideas; the best ideas on every matter which literature touches, current at the time. At any rate we may lay it down as certain that in modern literature no manifestation of the creative power not working with these can be very important or fruitful. And I say *current* at the time, not merely accessible at the time; for creative literary genius does not principally show itself in discovering new ideas, that is rather the business of the philosopher. The grand work of literary genius is a work of synthesis and exposition, not of analysis and discovery; its gift lies in the faculty of being happily inspired by a certain intellectual and spiritual atmosphere, by a certain order of ideas, when it finds itself in them; of dealing divinely with these ideas, presenting them in the most effective and attractive combinations—making beautiful works with them, in short. But it must have the atmosphere, it must find itself amidst the order of ideas, in order to work freely; and these it is not so easy to command. This is why great creative epochs in literature are so rare, this is why there is so much that is unsatisfactory in the productions of many men of real genius; because, for the creation of a masterwork of literature two powers must concur, the power of the man and the power of the moment, and the man is not enough without the moment; the creative power has, for its happy exercise, appointed elements, and those elements are not in its own control.

Nay, they are more within the control of the critical power. It is the business of the critical power, as I said in the words already quoted, "in all branches of knowledge, theology, philosophy, history, art, science, to see the object as in itself it really is." Thus it tends, at last, to make an intellectual situation of which the creative power can profitably avail itself. It tends to establish an order of ideas, if not absolutely true, yet true by comparison with that which it displaces; to make the best ideas prevail. Presently these new ideas reach society, the touch of truth is the touch of life, and there is a stir and growth everywhere; out of this stir and growth come the creative epochs of literature.

Or, to narrow our range, and quit these considerations of the general march of genius and of society—considerations which are apt to become too abstract and impalpable—everyone can see that a poet, for instance, ought to know life and the world before dealing with them in poetry; and life and the world being in modern times very complex things, the creation of a modern poet, to be worth much, implies a great critical effort behind it; else it must be a comparatively poor, barren, and short-lived affair. This is why Byron's poetry had so little endurance in it, and Goethe's so much; both Byron and Goethe had a great productive power, but Goethe's was nourished by a great critical effort providing the true materials for it, and Byron's was not; Goethe knew life and the world, the poet's necessary subjects, much more comprehensively and thoroughly than Byron. He knew a great deal more of them, and he knew them much more as they really are.

It has long seemed to me that the burst of creative activity in our literature, through the first quarter of this century, had about it in fact something premature; and that from this cause its productions are doomed, most of them, in spite of the sanguine hopes which accompanied and do still accompany them, to prove hardly more lasting than the productions of far less splendid epochs. And this prematureness comes from its having proceeded without having its proper data, without sufficient materials to work with. In other words, the English poetry of the first quarter of this century, with plenty of energy, plenty of creative force, did not know enough. This makes Byron so empty of matter, Shelley so incoherent, Wordsworth even, profound as he is, yet so wanting in completeness and variety. Wordsworth cared little for books, and disparaged Goethe. I admire Wordsworth, as he is, so much that I cannot wish him different; and it is vain, no doubt, to imagine such a man different from what he is, to suppose that he *could* have been different. But surely the one thing wanting to make Wordsworth an even greater poet than he is—his thought richer, and his influence of wider application—was that he should have read more books, among them, no doubt, those of that Goethe whom he disparaged without reading him.

But to speak of books and reading may easily lead to a misunderstanding here. It was not really books and reading that lacked to our poetry at this epoch: Shelley had plenty of reading, Coleridge had immense reading. Pindar and Sophocles—as we all say so glibly, and often with so little discernment of the real import of what we are saying—had not many books; Shakespeare was no deep reader. True; but in the Greece of Pindar and Sophocles, in the England of Shakespeare, the poet lived in a current of ideas in the highest degree animating and nourishing to the creative power; society was, in the fullest measure, permeated by fresh thought, intelligent and alive. And this state of things is the true basis for the creative power's exercise, in this it finds its data, its materials, truly ready for its hand; all the books and reading in the world are only valuable as they are helps to this. Even when this does not actually exist, books and reading may enable a man to construct a kind of semblance of it in his own mind, a world of knowledge and intelligence in which he may live and work. This is by no means an equivalent to the artist for the nationally diffused life and thought of the epochs of Sophocles or Shakespeare; but, besides that it may be a means of preparation for such epochs, it does really constitute, if many share in it, a quickening and sustaining atmosphere of great value. Such an atmosphere the many-sided learning and the long and widely combined critical effort of Germany formed for Goethe, when he lived and worked. There was no national glow of life and thought there as in the Athens of Pericles[6] or the England of Elizabeth. That was the poet's weakness. But there was a sort of equivalent for it in the complete culture and unfettered thinking of a large body of Germans. That was his strength. In the England of the first quarter of this century there was neither a national glow of life and thought, such as we had in the age of Elizabeth, nor yet a culture and a force of learning and criticism such as were to be found in Germany. Therefore the creative power of poetry wanted, for success in the highest sense, materials and a basis; a thorough interpretation of the world was necessarily denied to it.

At first sight it seems strange that out of the immense stir of the French Revolution and its age should not have come a crop of works of genius equal to that which came out of the stir of the great productive time of Greece, or out of that of the Renascence, with its powerful episode the Reformation. But the truth is that the stir of the French Revolution took a character which essentially distinguished it from such movements as these. These were, in the main, disinterestedly intellectual and spiritual movements; movements in which the human spirit looked for its satisfaction in itself

6. Pericles (d. 429 B.C.), the leading statesman of Athens during a period of the city's most outstanding achievements in art, literature, and politics.

and in the increased play of its own activity. The French Revolution took a political, practical character. The movement, which went on in France under the old *régime*, from 1700 to 1789, was far more really akin than that of the Revolution itself to the movement of the Renascence; the France of Voltaire and Rousseau told far more powerfully upon the mind of Europe than the France of the Revolution. Goethe reproached this last expressly with having "thrown quiet culture back." Nay, and the true key to how much in our Byron, even in our Wordsworth, is this!—that they had their source in a great movement of feeling, not in a great movement of mind. The French Revolution, however—that object of so much blind love and so much blind hatred—found undoubtedly its motive power in the intelligence of men, and not in their practical sense; this is what distinguishes it from the English Revolution of Charles the First's time. This is what makes it a more spiritual event than our Revolution, an event of much more powerful and worldwide interest, though practically less successful; it appeals to an order of ideas which are universal, certain, permanent. 1789 asked of a thing, Is it rational? 1642 asked of a thing, Is it legal? or, when it went furthest, Is it according to conscience? This is the English fashion, a fashion to be treated, within its own sphere, with the highest respect; for its success, within its own sphere, has been prodigious. But what is law in one place is not law in another; what is law here today is not law even here tomorrow; and as for conscience, what is binding on one man's conscience is not binding on another's. The old woman who threw her stool at the head of the surpliced minister in St. Giles's Church at Edinburgh[7] obeyed an impulse to which millions of the human race may be permitted to remain strangers. But the prescriptions of reason are absolute, unchanging, of universal validity; *to count by tens is the easiest way of counting*—that is a proposition of which everyone, from here to the Antipodes, feels the force; at least I should say so if we did not live in a country where it is not impossible that any morning we may find a letter in the *Times* declaring that a decimal coinage is an absurdity.[8] That a whole nation should have been penetrated with an enthusiasm for pure reason, and with an ardent zeal for making its prescriptions triumph, is a very remarkable thing, when we consider how little of mind, or anything so worthy and quickening as mind, comes into the motives which alone, in general, impel great masses of men. In spite of the extravagant direction given to this enthusiasm, in spite of the crimes and follies in which it lost itself, the French Revolution derives from the force, truth, and universality of the ideas which it took for its law, and from the passion

7. In 1637 rioting broke out in Scotland against a new kind of church service prescribed by Charles I. The riot was started by an old woman hurling a stool at a clergyman.
8. In 1863 a proposal in Parliament to introduce the French decimal system for weights and measures had provoked articles in the *Times* defending the English system (of ounces and pounds or inches and feet) as more practical.

with which it could inspire a multitude for these ideas, a unique and still living power; it is—it will probably long remain—the greatest, the most animating event in history. And as no sincere passion for the things of the mind, even though it turn out in many respects an unfortunate passion, is ever quite thrown away and quite barren of good, France has reaped from hers one fruit—the natural and legitimate fruit though not precisely the grand fruit she expected: she is the country in Europe where *the people* is most alive.

But the mania for giving an immediate political and practical application to all these fine ideas of the reason was fatal. Here an Englishman is in his element: on this theme we can all go on for hours. And all we are in the habit of saying on it has undoubtedly a great deal of truth. Ideas cannot be too much prized in and for themselves, cannot be too much lived with; but to transport them abruptly into the world of politics and practice, violently to revolutionize this world to their bidding—that is quite another thing. There is the world of ideas and there is the world of practice; the French are often for suppressing the one and the English the other; but neither is to be suppressed. A member of the House of Commons said to me the other day: "That a thing is an anomaly, I consider to be no objection to it whatever." I venture to think he was wrong; that a thing is an anomaly *is* an objection to it, but absolutely and in the sphere of ideas: it is not necessarily, under such and such circumstances, or at such and such a moment, an objection to it in the sphere of politics and practice. Joubert[9] has said beautifully: "*C'est la force et le droit qui règlent toutes choses dans le monde; la force en attendant le droit.*"—"Force and right are the governors of this world; force till right is ready." *Force till right is ready;* and till right is ready, force, the existing order of things, is justified, is the legitimate ruler. But right is something moral, and implies inward recognition, free assent of the will; we are not ready for right—*right*, so far as we are concerned, *is not ready*—until we have attained this sense of seeing it and willing it. The way in which for us it may change and transform force, the existing order of things, and become, in its turn, the legitimate ruler of the world, should depend on the way in which, when our time comes, we see it and will it. Therefore for other people enamored of their own newly discerned right, to attempt to impose it upon us as ours, and violently to substitute their right for our force, is an act of tyranny, and to be resisted. It sets at nought the second great half of our maxim, *force till right is ready*. This was the grand error of the French Revolution; and its movement of ideas, by quitting the intellectual sphere and rushing furiously into the political sphere, ran, indeed, a prodigious and memorable course, but produced no such intellectual fruit as the movement of ideas of the Renascence,

9. Joseph Joubert (1754–1824), French moralist about whom Arnold wrote one of his *Essays in Criticism.*

and created, in opposition to itself, what I may call an *epoch of concentration*. The great force of that epoch of concentration was England; and the great voice of that epoch of concentration was Burke.[10] It is the fashion to treat Burke's writings on the French Revolution as superannuated and conquered by the event; as the eloquent but unphilosophical tirades of bigotry and prejudice. I will not deny that they are often disfigured by the violence and passion of the moment, and that in some directions Burke's view was bounded, and his observation therefore at fault. But on the whole, and for those who can make the needful corrections, what distinguishes these writings is their profound, permanent, fruitful, philosophical truth. They contain the true philosophy of an epoch of concentration, dissipate the heavy atmosphere which its own nature is apt to engender round it, and make its resistance rational instead of mechanical.

But Burke is so great because, almost alone in England, he brings thought to bear upon politics, he saturates politics with thought. It is his accident that his ideas were at the service of an epoch of concentration, not of an epoch of expansion; it is his characteristic that he so lived by ideas, and had such a source of them welling up within him, that he could float even an epoch of concentration and English Tory politics with them. It does not hurt him that Dr. Price[11] and the Liberals were enraged with him; it does not even hurt him that George the Third and the Tories were enchanted with him. His greatness is that he lived in a world which neither English Liberalism nor English Toryism is apt to enter—the world of ideas, not the world of catchwords and party habits. So far is it from being really true of him that he "to party gave up what was meant for mankind,"[1] that at the very end of his fierce struggle with the French Revolution, after all his invectives against its false pretensions, hollowness, and madness, with his sincere convictions of its michievousness, he can close a memorandum on the best means of combating it, some of the last pages [2] he ever wrote—the *Thoughts on French Affairs*, in December 1791—with these striking words:

"The evil is stated, in my opinion, as it exists. The remedy must be where power, wisdom, and information, I hope, are more united with good intentions than they can be with me. I have done with this subject, I believe, forever. It has given me many anxious moments for the last two years. *If a great change is to be made in human affairs, the minds of men will be fitted to it; the general opinions and feelings will draw that way. Every fear, every hope will*

10. Edmund Burke (1729–97), prominent statesman and author of *Reflections on the French Revolution* (1790), which expressed the conservative opposition to revolutionary theories.
11. Richard Price (1723–91), a prorevolutionary clergyman who was an opponent of Burke's.

1. See Oliver Goldsmith's poem, *Retaliation* (1774).
2. Arnold was mistaken; Burke continued to write for another six years after 1791. According to Arnold's editor, R. H. Super, the mistake was caused by misunderstanding a passage in one of Burke's letters.

forward it; and then they who persist in opposing this mighty current in human affairs, will appear rather to resist the decrees of Providence itself, than the mere designs of men. They will not be resolute and firm, but perverse and obstinate."

That return of Burke upon himself has always seemed to me one of the finest things in English literature, or indeed in any literature. That is what I call living by ideas: when one side of a question has long had your earnest support, when all your feelings are engaged, when you hear all round you no language but one, when your party talks this language like a steam engine and can imagine no other— still to be able to think, still to be irresistibly carried, if so it be, by the current of thought to the opposite side of the question, and, like Balaam,[3] to be unable to speak anything *but what the Lord has put in your mouth.* I know nothing more striking, and I must add that I know nothing more un-English.

For the Englishman in general is like my friend the Member of Parliament, and believes, point-blank, that for a thing to be an anomaly is absolutely no objection to it whatever. He is like the Lord Auckland of Burke's day, who, in a memorandum on the French Revolution, talks of certain "miscreants, assuming the name of philosophers, who have presumed themselves capable of establishing a new system of society." The Englishman has been called a political animal, and he values what is political and practical so much that ideas easily become objects of dislike in his eyes, and thinkers, "miscreants," because ideas and thinkers have rashly meddled with politics and practice. This would be all very well if the dislike and neglect confined themselves to ideas transported out of their own sphere, and meddling rashly with practice; but they are inevitably extended to ideas as such, and to the whole life of intelligence; practice is everything, a free play of the mind is nothing. The notion of the free play of the mind upon all subjects being a pleasure in itself, being an object of desire, being an essential provider of elements without which a nation's spirit, whatever compensations it may have for them, must, in the long run, die of inanition, hardly enters into an Englishman's thoughts. It is noticeable that the word *curiosity*, which in other languages is used in a good sense, to mean, as a high and fine quality of man's nature, just this disinterested love of a free play of the mind on all subjects, for its own sake—it is noticeable, I say, that this word has in our language no sense of the kind, no sense but a rather bad and disparaging one. But criticism, real criticism, is essentially the exercise of this very quality. It obeys an instinct prompting it to try to know the best that is known and thought in the world, irrespectively of practice, politics, and everything of the kind; and to value knowledge and thought as they approach this best, without the intrusion

3. Cf. Numbers xxii.38.

of any other considerations whatever. This is an instinct for which there is, I think, little original sympathy in the practical English nature, and what there was of it has undergone a long benumbing period of blight and suppression in the epoch of concentration which followed the French Revolution.

But epochs of concentration cannot well endure forever; epochs of expansion, in the due course of things, follow them. Such an epoch of expansion seems to be opening in this country. In the first place all danger of a hostile forcible pressure of foreign ideas upon our practice has long disappeared; like the traveler in the fable, therefore, we begin to wear our cloak a little more loosely.[4] Then, with a long peace, the ideas of Europe steal gradually and amicably in, and mingle, though in infinitesimally small quantities at a time, with our own notions. Then, too, in spite of all that is said about the absorbing and brutalizing influence of our passionate material progress, it seems to me indisputable that this progress is likely, though not certain, to lead in the end to an apparition of intellectual life; and that man, after he has made himself perfectly comfortable and has now to determine what to do with himself next, may begin to remember that he has a mind, and that the mind may be made the source of great pleasure. I grant it is mainly the privilege of faith, at present, to discern this end to our railways, our business, and our fortune-making; but we shall see if, here as elsewhere, faith is not in the end the true prophet. Our ease, our traveling, and our unbounded liberty to hold just as hard and securely as we please to the practice to which our notions have given birth, all tend to beget an inclination to deal a little more freely with these notions themselves, to canvass them a little, to penetrate a little into their real nature. Flutterings of curiosity, in the foreign sense of the word, appear amongst us, and it is in these that criticism must look to find its account. Criticism first; a time of true creative activity, perhaps—which, as I have said, must inevitably be preceded amongst us by a time of criticism—hereafter, when criticism has done its work.

It is of the last importance that English criticism should clearly discern what rule for its course, in order to avail itself of the field now opening to it, and to produce fruit for the future, it ought to take. The rule may be summed up in one word—*disinterestedness*.[5] And how is criticism to show disinterestedness? By keeping aloof from what is called "the practical view of things"; by resolutely following the law of its own nature, which is to be a free play of the mind on all subjects which it touches. By steadily refusing to lend itself to any of those ulterior, political, practical considerations about ideas, which plenty of people will be sure to attach to them,

4. See Aesop's fable of the wind and the sun.
5. This key word in Arnold's argument connotes independence and objectivity of mind. It should not be confused, as it often is, with mere lack of interest.

which perhaps ought often to be attached to them, which in this country at any rate are certain to be attached to them quite sufficiently, but which criticism has really nothing to do with. Its business is, as I have said, simply to know the best that is known and thought in the world, and by in its turn making this known, to create a current of true and fresh ideas. Its business is to do this with inflexible honesty, with due ability; but its business is to do no more, and to leave alone all questions of practical consequences and applications, questions which will never fail to have due prominence given to them. Else criticism, besides being really false to its own nature, merely continues in the old rut which it has hitherto followed in this country, and will certainly miss the chance now given to it. For what is at present the bane of criticism in this country? It is that practical considerations cling to it and stifle it. It subserves interests not its own. Our organs of criticism are organs of men and parties having practical ends to serve, and with them those practical ends are the first thing and the play of mind the second; so much play of mind as is compatible with the prosecution of those practical ends is all that is wanted. An organ like the *Revue des Deux Mondes*,[6] having for its main function to understand and utter the best that is known and thought in the world, existing, it may be said, as just an organ for a free play of the mind, we have not. But we have the *Edinburgh Review*, existing as an organ of the old Whigs, and for as much play of mind as may suit its being that; we have the *Quarterly Review*, existing as an organ of the Tories, and for as much play of mind as may suit its being that; we have the *British Quarterly Review*, existing as an organ of the political Dissenters, and for as much play of mind as may suit its being that; we have the *Times*, existing as an organ of the common, satisfied, well-to-do Englishman, and for as much play of mind as may suit its being that. And so on through all the various fractions, political and religious, of our society; every fraction has, as such, its organ of criticism, but the notion of combining all fractions in the common pleasure of a free disinterested play of mind meets with no favor. Directly this play of mind wants to have more scope, and to forget the pressure of practical considerations a little, it is checked, it is made to feel the chain. We saw this the other day in the extinction, so much to be regretted, of the *Home and Foreign Review*.[6a] Perhaps in no organ of criticism in this country was there so much knowledge, so much play of mind; but these could not save it. The *Dublin Review* subordinates play of mind to the practical business of English and Irish Catholicism, and lives. It must needs be that men should act in sects and parties, that each of these sects and parties should have its organ, and should make

6. An international magazine of exceptionally high quality, founded in Paris in 1829.

6a. A liberal Catholic periodical, founded in 1862, which ceased publication in 1864.

this organ subserve the interests of its action; but it would be well, too, that there should be a criticism, not the minister of these interests, not their enemy, but absolutely and entirely independent of them. No other criticism will ever attain any real authority or make any real way towards its end—the creating a current of true and fresh ideas.

It is because criticism has so little kept in the pure intellectual sphere, has so little detached itself from practice, has been so directly polemical and controversial, that it has so ill accomplished, in this country, its best spiritual work, which is to keep man from a self-satisfaction which is retarding and vulgarizing, to lead him towards perfection, by making his mind dwell upon what is excellent in itself, and the absolute beauty and fitness of things. A polemical practical criticism makes men blind even to the ideal imperfection of their practice, makes them willingly assert its ideal perfection, in order the better to secure it against attack; and clearly this is narrowing and baneful for them. If they were reassured on the practical side, speculative considerations of ideal perfection they might be brought to entertain, and their spiritual horizon would thus gradually widen. Sir Charles Adderley[7] says to the Warwickshire farmers:

"Talk of the improvement of breed! Why, the race we ourselves represent, the men and women, the old Anglo-Saxon race, are the best breed in the whole world. . . . The absence of a too enervating climate, too unclouded skies, and a too luxurious nature, has produced so vigorous a race of people, and has rendered us so superior to all the world."

Mr. Roebuck[8] says to the Sheffield cutlers:

"I look around me and ask what is the state of England? Is not property safe? Is not every man able to say what he likes? Can you not walk from one end of England to the other in perfect security? I ask you whether, the world over or in past history, there is anything like it? Nothing. I pray that our unrivaled happiness may last."

Now obviously there is a peril for poor human nature in words and thoughts of such exuberant self-satisfaction, until we find ourselves safe in the streets of the Celestial City.

*Das wenige verschwindet leicht dem Blicke
Der vorwärts sieht, wie viel noch übrig bleibt—*[9]

says Goethe; "the little that is done seems nothing when we look forward and see how much we have yet to do." Clearly this is a

---

7. 1814–1905; conservative politician and wealthy landowner.
8. John Arthur Roebuck (1801–79), radical politician and representative in

Parliament for the industrial city of Sheffield.
9. Goethe's *Iphigenie auf Tauris* I.ii.91–92.

better line of reflection for weak humanity, so long as it remains on this earthly field of labor and trial.

But neither Sir Charles Adderley nor Mr. Roebuck is by nature inaccessible to considerations of this sort. They only lose sight of them owing to the controversial life we all lead, and the practical form which all speculation takes with us. They have in view opponents whose aim is not ideal, but practical; and in their zeal to uphold their own practice against these innovators, they go so far as even to attribute to this practice an ideal perfection. Somebody has been wanting to introduce a six-pound franchise,[10] or to abolish church-rates, or to collect agricultural statistics by force, or to diminish local self-government. How natural, in reply to such proposals, very likely improper or ill-timed, to go a little beyond the mark and to say stoutly, "Such a race of people as we stand, so superior to all the world! The old Anglo-Saxon race, the best breed in the whole world! I pray that our unrivaled happiness may last! I ask you whether, the world over or in past history, there is anything like it?" And so long as criticism answers this dithyramb by insisting that the old Anglo-Saxon race would be still more superior to all others if it had no church-rates, or that our unrivaled happiness would last yet longer with a six-pound franchise, so long will the strain, "The best breed in the whole world!" swell louder and louder, everything ideal and refining will be lost out of sight, and both the assailed and their critics will remain in a sphere, to say the truth, perfectly unvital, a sphere in which spiritual progression is impossible. But let criticism leave church-rates and the franchise alone, and in the most candid spirit, without a single lurking thought of practical innovation, confront with our dithyramb this paragraph on which I stumbled in a newspaper immediately after reading Mr. Roebuck:

"A shocking child murder has just been committed at Nottingham. A girl named Wragg left the workhouse there on Saturday morning with her young illegitimate child. The child was soon afterwards found dead on Mapperly Hills, having been strangled. Wragg is in custody."

Nothing but that; but, in juxtaposition with the absolute eulogies of Sir Charles Adderley and Mr. Roebuck, how eloquent, how suggestive are those few lines! "Our old Anglo-Saxon breed, the best in the whole world!"—how much that is harsh and ill-favored there is in this best! Wragg! If we are to talk of ideal perfection, of "the best in the whole world," has anyone reflected what a touch of grossness in our race, what an original shortcoming in the more delicate spiritual perceptions, is shown by the natural growth amongst us of such hideous names—Higginbottom, Stiggins, Bugg!

10. A radical proposal to extend the right to vote to anyone owning land worth £6 annual rent. "Church-rates": taxes supporting the Church of England.

In Ionia and Attica they were luckier in this respect than "the best race in the world"; by the Ilissus[1] there was no Wragg, poor thing! And "our unrivaled happiness"—what an element of grimness, bareness, and hideousness mixes with it and blurs it; the workhouse, the dismal Mapperly Hills[2]—how dismal those who have seen them will remember—the gloom, the smoke, the cold, the strangled illegitimate child! "I ask you whether, the world over or in past history, there is anything like it?" Perhaps not, one is inclined to answer; but at any rate, in that case, the world is very much to be pitied. And the final touch—short, bleak and inhuman: *Wragg is in custody*. The sex lost in the confusion of our unrivaled happiness; or (shall I say?) the superfluous Christian name lopped off by the straightforward vigor of our old Anglo-Saxon breed! There is profit for the spirit in such contrasts as this; criticism serves the cause of perfection by establishing them. By eluding sterile conflict, by refusing to remain in the sphere where alone narrow and relative conceptions have any worth and validity, criticism may diminish its momentary importance, but only in this way has it a chance of gaining admittance for those wider and more perfect conceptions to which all its duty is really owed. Mr. Roebuck will have a poor opinion of an adversary who replies to his defiant songs of triumph only by murmuring under his breath, *Wragg is in custody*; but in no other way will these songs of triumph be induced gradually to moderate themselves, to get rid of what in them is excessive and offensive, and to fall into a softer and truer key.

It will be said that it is a very subtle and indirect action which I am thus prescribing for criticism, and that, by embracing in this manner the Indian virtue of detachment and abandoning the sphere of practical life, it condemns itself to a slow and obscure work. Slow and obscure it may be, but it is the only proper work of criticism. The mass of mankind will never have any ardent zeal for seeing things as they are; very inadequate ideas will always satisfy them. On these inadequate ideas reposes, and must repose, the general practice of the world. That is as much as saying that whoever sets himself to see things as they are will find himself one of a very small circle; but it is only by this small circle resolutely doing its own work that adequate ideas will ever get current at all. The rush and roar of practical life will always have a dizzying and attracting effect upon the most collected spectator, and tend to draw him into its vortex; most of all will this be the case where that life is so powerful as it is in England. But it is only by remaining collected, and refusing to lend himself to the point of view of the practical man, that the critic can do the practical man any service; and it is only by the greatest sincerity in pursuing his own course, and by at last convincing even the practical man of his sin-

1. A stream in Attica, Greece.
2. Adjacent to the coal-mining and industrial area of Nottingham (later associated with the writings of D. H. Lawrence).

cerity, that he can escape misunderstandings which perpetually threaten him.

For the practical man is not apt for fine distinctions, and yet in these distinctions truth and the highest culture greatly find their account. But it is not easy to lead a practical man—unless you reassure him as to your practical intentions, you have no chance of leading him—to see that a thing which he has always been used to look at from one side only, which he greatly values, and which, looked at from that side, quite deserves, perhaps, all the prizing and admiring which he bestows upon it—that this thing, looked at from another side, may appear much less beneficent and beautiful, and yet retain all its claims to our practical allegiance. Where shall we find language innocent enough, how shall we make the spotless purity of our intentions evident enough, to enable us to say to the political Englishman that the British Constitution itself, which, seen from the practical side, looks such a magnificent organ of progress and virtue, seen from the speculative side—with its compromises, its love of facts, its horror of theory, its studied avoidance of clear thoughts—that, seen from this side, our august Constitution sometimes looks—forgive me, shade of Lord Somers![3]—a colossal machine for the manufacture of Philistines?[4] How is Cobbett[5] to say this and not be misunderstood, blackened as he is with the smoke of a lifelong conflict in the field of political practice? how is Mr. Carlyle to say it and not be misunderstood, after his furious raid into this field with his *Latter-day Pamphlets?* how is Mr. Ruskin, after his pugnacious political economy?[6] I say, the critic must keep out of the region of immediate practice in the political, social, humanitarian sphere if he wants to make a beginning for that more free speculative treatment of things, which may perhaps one day make its benefits felt even in this sphere, but in a natural and thence irresistible manner.

Do what he will, however, the critic will still remain exposed to frequent misunderstandings, and nowhere so much as in this country. For here people are particularly indisposed even to comprehend that without this free disinterested treatment of things, truth and the highest culture are out of the question. So immersed are they in practical life, so accustomed to take all their notions from this life and its processes, that they are apt to think that truth and culture themselves can be reached by the processes of this life, and that it is an impertinent singularity to think of reaching them in

---

3. John Somers (1651–1716), statesman responsible for formulating the Declaration of Rights.
4. The unenlightened middle classes whose opposition to the men of culture is parallel to the Biblical tribe which fought against the people of Israel, "the children of light." Arnold's repeated use of this parallel has established the term

in our language.
5. William Cobbett (1762–1835), vehement reformer whose political position anticipated that of Dickens.
6. Reference to *Unto this Last* (1862) in which Ruskin shifted from art criticism to an attack on traditional theories of economics.

any other. "We are all *terrae filii*,"[7] cries their eloquent advocate; "all Philistines together. Away with the notion of proceeding by any other course than the course dear to the Philistines; let us have a social movement, let us organize and combine a party to pursue truth and new thought, let us call it *the liberal party*, and let us all stick to each other, and back each other up. Let us have no nonsense about independent criticism, and intellectual delicacy, and the few and the many. Don't let us trouble ourselves about foreign thought; we shall invent the whole thing for ourselves as we go along. If one of us speaks well, applaud him; if one of us speaks ill, applaud him too; we are all in the same movement, we are all liberals, we are all in pursuit of truth." In this way the pursuit of truth becomes really a social, practical, pleasurable affair, almost requiring a chairman, a secretary, and advertisements; with the excitement of an occasional scandal, with a little resistance to give the happy sense of difficulty overcome; but, in general, plenty of bustle and very little thought. To act is so easy, as Goethe says; to think is so hard! It is true that the critic has many temptations to go with the stream, to make one of the party movement, one of these *terrae filii*; it seems ungracious to refuse to be a *terrae filius* when so many excellent people are; but the critic's duty is to refuse, or, if resistance is vain, at least to cry with Obermann: *Périssons en résistant.*[8] * * *

For criticism, these are elementary laws; but they never can be popular, and in this country they have been very little followed, and one meets with immense obstacles in following them. That is a reason for asserting them again and again. Criticism must maintain its independence of the practical spirit and its aims. Even with well-meant efforts of the practical spirit it must express dissatisfaction, if in the sphere of the ideal they seem impoverishing and limiting. It must not hurry on to the goal because of its practical importance. It must be patient, and know how to wait; and flexible, and know how to attach itself to things and how to withdraw from them. It must be apt to study and praise elements that for the fullness of spiritual perfection are wanted, even though they belong to a power which in the practical sphere may be maleficent. It must be apt to discern the spiritual shortcomings or illusions of powers that in the practical sphere may be beneficent. And this without any notion of favoring or injuring, in the practical sphere, one power or the other; without any notion of playing off, in this sphere, one power against the other. When one looks, for instance, at the English Divorce Court—an institution which perhaps has its practical conveniences, but which in the

---

7. "Sons of the earth."
8. "Let us die resisting." Three paragraphs are omitted here. They consist of a highly allusive account of a con-

troversy concerning Biblical history. The discussion further illustrates the difficulties of a critic's remaining impartial.

ideal sphere is so hideous; an institution which neither makes divorce impossible nor makes it decent, which allows a man to get rid of his wife, or a wife of her husband, but makes them drag one another first, for the public edification, through a mire of unutterable infamy—when one looks at this charming institution, I say, with its crowded trials, its newspaper reports, and its money compensations, this institution in which the gross unregenerate British Philistine has indeed stamped an image of himself—one may be permitted to find the marriage theory of Catholicism refreshing and elevating. Or when Protestantism, in virtue of its supposed rational and intellectual origin, gives the law to criticism too magisterially, criticism may and must remind it that its pretensions, in this respect, are illusive and do it harm; that the Reformation was a moral rather than an intellectual event; that Luther's theory of grace no more exactly reflects the mind of the spirit than Bossuet's philosophy of history[9] reflects it; and that there is no more antecedent probability of the Bishop of Durham's[1] stock of ideas being agreeable to perfect reason than of Pope Pius the Ninth's. But criticism will not on that account forget the achievements of Protestantism in the practical and moral sphere; nor that, even in the intellectual sphere, Protestantism, though in a blind and stumbling manner, carried forward the Renascence, while Catholicism threw itself violently across its path.

I lately heard a man of thought and energy contrasting the want of ardor and movement which he now found amongst young men in this country with what he remembered in his own youth, twenty years ago. "What reformers we were then!" he exclaimed; "What a zeal we had! how we canvassed every institution in Church and State, and were prepared to remodel them all on first principles!" He was inclined to regret, as a spiritual flagging, the lull which he saw. I am disposed rather to regard it as a pause in which the turn to a new mode of spiritual progress is being accomplished. Everything was long seen, by the young and ardent amongst us, in inseparable connection with politics and practical life. We have pretty well exhausted the benefits of seeing things in this connection, we have got all that can be got by so seeing them. Let us try a more disinterested mode of seeing them; let us betake ourselves more to the serener life of the mind and spirit. This life, too, may have its excesses and dangers; but they are not for us at present. Let us think of quietly enlarging our stock of true and fresh ideas, and not, as soon as we get an idea or half an idea, be running out with it into the street, and trying to make it rule there. Our ideas will, in the end, shape the world all the better for matur-

---

9. Bishop Jacques Bossuet (1627–1704) whose theory of history is limited by its Roman Catholic bias (in Arnold's view), just as Martin Luther's exclusive view of grace reflects the bias of extreme Protestantism.
1. An Anglican bishop.

ing a little. Perhaps in fifty years' time it will in the English House of Commons be an objection to an institution that it is an anomaly, and my friend the Member of Parliament will shudder in his grave. But let us in the meanwhile rather endeavor that in twenty years' time it may, in English literature, be an objection to a proposition that it is absurd. That will be a change so vast, that the imagination almost fails to grasp it. *Ab integro saeclorum nascitur ordo.*[2]

If I have insisted so much on the course which criticism must take where politics and religion are concerned, it is because, where these burning matters are in question, it is most likely to go astray. I have wished, above all, to insist on the attitude which criticism should adopt towards things in general; on its right tone and temper of mind. But then comes another question as to the subject matter which literary criticism should most seek. Here, in general, its course is determined for it by the idea which is the law of its being; the idea of a disinterested endeavor to learn and propagate the best that is known and thought in the world, and thus to establish a current of fresh and true ideas. By the very nature of things, as England is not all the world, much of the best that is known and thought in the world cannot be of English growth, must be foreign; by the nature of things, again, it is just this that we are least likely to know, while English thought is streaming in upon us from all sides, and takes excellent care that we shall not be ignorant of its existence. The English critic of literature, therefore, must dwell much on foreign thought, and with particular heed on any part of it, which, while significant and fruitful in itself, is for any reason specially likely to escape him. Again, judging is often spoken of as the critic's one business, and so in some sense it is; but the judgment which almost insensibly forms itself in a fair and clear mind, along with fresh knowledge, is the valuable one; and thus knowledge, and ever fresh knowledge, must be the critic's great concern for himself. And it is by communicating fresh knowledge, and letting his own judgment pass along with it—but insensibly, and in the second place, not the first, as a sort of companion and clue, not as an abstract lawgiver—that the critic will generally do most good to his readers. Sometimes, no doubt, for the sake of establishing an author's place in literature, and his relation to a central standard (and if this is not done, how are we to get at our *best in the world?*) criticism may have to deal with a subject matter so familiar that fresh knowledge is out of the question, and then it must be all judgment; an enunciation and detailed application of principles. Here the great safeguard is never to let oneself become abstract, always to retain an intimate and lively consciousness of the truth of what one is saying, and, the moment this fails us, to be sure that something is wrong. Still under all circumstances,

2. "Order is born from the renewal of the ages" (Virgil, *Eclogues* IV.5).

this mere judgment and application of principles is, in itself, not the most satisfactory work to the critic; like mathematics, it is tautological, and cannot well give us, like fresh learning, the sense of creative activity.

But stop, some one will say; all this talk is of no practical use to us whatever; this criticism of yours is not what we have in our minds when we speak of criticism; when we speak of critics and criticism, we mean critics and criticism of the current English literature of the day; when you offer to tell criticism its function, it is to this criticism that we expect you to address yourself. I am sorry for it, for I am afraid I must disappoint these expectations. I am bound by my own definition of criticism: *a disinterested endeavor to learn and propagate the best that is known and thought in the world.* How much of current English literature comes into this "best that is known and thought in the world"? Not very much I fear; certainly less, at this moment, than of the current literature of France or Germany. Well, then, am I to alter my definition of criticism, in order to meet the requirements of a number of practicing English critics, who, after all, are free in their choice of a business? That would be making criticism lend itself just to one of those alien practical considerations, which, I have said, are so fatal to it. One may say, indeed, to those who have to deal with the mass—so much better disregarded—of current English literature, that they may at all events endeavor, in dealing with this, to try it, so far as they can, by the standard of the best that is known and thought in the world; one may say, that to get anywhere near this standard, every critic should try and possess one great literature, at least, besides his own; and the more unlike his own, the better. But, after all, the criticism I am really concerned with—the criticism which alone can much help us for the future, the criticism which, throughout Europe, is at the present day meant, when so much stress is laid on the importance of criticism and the critical spirit—is a criticism which regards Europe as being, for intellectual and spiritual purposes, one great confederation, bound to a joint action and working to a common result; and whose members have, for their proper outfit, a knowledge of Greek, Roman, and Eastern antiquity, and of one another. Special, local, and temporary advantages being put out of account, that modern nation will in the intellectual and spiritual sphere make most progress, which most thoroughly carries out this program. And what is that but saying that we too, all of us, as individuals, the more thoroughly we carry it out, shall make the more progress?

There is so much inviting us!—what are we to take? what will nourish us in growth towards perfection? That is the question which, with the immense field of life and of literature lying before him, the critic has to answer; for himself first, and afterwards for others. In this idea of the critic's business the essays brought together in the following pages have had their origin; in this idea, widely different as are their subjects, they have, perhaps, their unity.

I conclude with what I said at the beginning: to have the sense of creative activity is the great happiness and the great proof of being alive, and it is not denied to criticism to have it; but then criticism must be sincere, simple, flexible, ardent, ever widening its knowledge. Then it may have, in no contemptible measure, a joyful sense of creative activity; a sense which a man of insight and conscience will prefer to what he might derive from a poor, starved, fragmentary, inadequate creation. And at some epochs no other creation is possible.

Still, in full measure, the sense of creative activity belongs only to genuine creation; in literature we must never forget that. But what true man of letters ever can forget it? It is no such common matter for a gifted nature to come into possession of a current of true and living ideas, and to produce amidst the inspiration of them, that we are likely to underrate it. The epochs of Aeschylus and Shakespeare make us feel their pre-eminence. In an epoch like those is, no doubt, the true life of literature; there is the promised land, towards which criticism can only beckon. That promised land it will not be ours to enter, and we shall die in the wilderness: but to have desired to enter it, to have saluted it from afar, is already, perhaps, the best distinction among contemporaries; it will certainly be the best title to esteem with posterity.

1864, 1865

From Maurice de Guérin[1]
[A *Definition of Poetry*]

The grand power of poetry is its interpretative power; by which I mean, not a power of drawing out in black and white an explanation of the mystery of the universe, but the power of so dealing with things as to awaken in us a wonderfully full, new, and intimate sense of them, and of our relations with them. When this sense is awakened in us, as to objects without us, we feel ourselves to be in contact with the essential nature of those objects, to be no longer bewildered and oppressed by them, but to have their secret, and to be in harmony with them; and this feeling calms and satisfies us as no other can. Poetry, indeed, interprets in another way besides this; but one of its two ways of interpreting, of exercising its highest power, is by awakening this sense in us. I will not now inquire whether this sense is illusive, whether it can be proved not to be

1. 1810–39; a minor French poet. The essay was included in *Essays in Criticism: First Series.*

illusive, whether it does absolutely make us possess the real nature of things; all I say is, that poetry can awaken it in us, and that to awaken it is one of the highest powers of poetry. The interpretations of science do not give us this intimate sense of objects as the interpretations of poetry give it; they appeal to a limited faculty, and not to the whole man. * * *

I have said that poetry interprets in two ways; it interprets by expressing, with magical felicity, the physiognomy and movement of the outward world, and it interprets by expressing, with inspired conviction, the ideas and laws of the inward world of man's moral and spiritual nature. In other words, poetry is interpretative both by having *natural magic* in it, and by having *moral profundity*. In both ways it illuminates man; it gives him a satisfying sense of reality; it reconciles him with himself and the universe. Thus Aeschylus's "δράσαντι παθεῖν"[2] and his "ἀνήριθμον γέλασμα"[3] are alike interpretative. Shakespeare interprets both when he says,

> Full many a glorious morning have I seen,
> Flatter the mountaintops with sovereign eye;[4]

and when he says,

> There's a divinity that shapes our ends,
> Rough-hew them as we will.[5]

These great poets unite in themselves the faculty of both kinds of interpretation, the naturalistic and the moral. But it is observable that in the poets who unite both kinds, the latter (the moral) usually ends by making itself the master. In Shakespeare the two kinds seem wonderfully to balance one another; but even in him the balance leans; his expression tends to become too little sensuous and simple, too much intellectualized. The same thing may be yet more strongly affirmed of Lucretius and of Wordsworth. In Shelley there is not a balance of the two gifts, nor even a coexistence of them, but there is a passionate straining after them both, and this is what makes Shelley, as a man, so interesting; I will not now inquire how much Shelley achieves as a poet, but whatever he achieves, he in general fails to achieve natural magic in his expression; in Mr. Palgrave's charming *Treasury*[6] may be seen a gallery of his failures.[7] But in Keats and Guérin, in whom the faculty of

---

2. "The doer must suffer." From Aeschylus' *Choephori* (line 313).
3. "Countless laughter." From Aeschylus' *Prometheus Bound* (line 90).
4. Shakespeare, *Sonnets* XXXIII.1–2.
5. *Hamlet* V.ii.10–11.
6. Francis Palgrave's anthology of poems, *The Golden Treasury*, was first published in 1861.
7. "Compare, for example, his *Lines Written in the Euganean Hills*, with Keats's *Ode to Autumn* . . . The latter

piece *renders* Nature; the former *tries to render* her. I will not deny, however, that Shelley has natural magic in his rhythm; what I deny is, that he has it in his language. It always seems to me that the right sphere for Shelley's genius was the sphere of music, not of poetry; the medium of sounds he can master, but to master the more difficult medium of words he has neither intellectual force enough nor sanity enough" [Arnold's note].

naturalistic interpretation is overpoweringly predominant, the natural magic is perfect; when they speak of the world they speak like Adam naming by divine inspiration the creatures; their expression corresponds with the thing's essential reality.

1863, 1865

From Culture and Anarchy[1]
From *Chapter I. Sweetness and Light*

[PURITANISM AND CULTURE]

The impulse of the English race towards moral development and self-conquest has nowhere so powerfully manifested itself as in Puritanism. Nowhere has Puritanism found so adequate an expression as in the religious organization of the Independents.[2] The modern Independents have a newspaper, the *Nonconformist*, written with great sincerity and ability. The motto, the standard, the profession of faith which this organ of theirs carries aloft, is: "The Dissidence of Dissent and the Protestantism of the Protestant religion." There is sweetness and light, and an ideal of complete harmonious human perfection! One need not go to culture and poetry to find language to judge it. Religion, with its instinct for perfection, supplies language to judge it, language, too, which is in our mouths every day. "Finally, be of one mind, united in feeling," says St. Peter.[3] There is an ideal which judges the Puritan ideal: "The Dissidence of Dissent and the Protestantism of the Protestant religion!" And religious organizations like this are what people believe in, rest in, would give their lives for! Such, I say, is the wonderful virtue of even the beginnings of perfection, of having conquered even the plain faults of our animality, that the religious organization which has helped us to do it can seem to us some-

1. As a critic of social life, Arnold sought to test Victorian institutions according to whether they seemed to him civilized. A characteristic quality of the civilized state of mind is summed up, for his purposes, in his formula "sweetness and light," a phrase suggesting reasonableness of temper and intellectual insight. Arnold derived the phrase from a fable contrasting the spider with the bee in Swift's *Battle of the Books*. The spider (representing a narrow, self-centered, and uncultured mind) spins out of itself "nothing at all but flybane and cobweb." The bee (representing a cultured mind that has drawn nourishment from the humanist tradition) ranges far and wide and brings to its hive honey and also wax out of which candles may be made. Therefore the bee, Swift says, furnishes mankind "with the two noblest of things, which are sweetness and light."

The three following excerpts illustrate aspects of Arnold's indictment of the middle classes for their lack of sweetness and light. The first and third expose the narrowness and dullness of middle-class Puritan religious institutions in both the 17th and 19th centuries. The second, "Doing As One Likes," shows the limitations of the middle-class political bias and the irresponsibility of *laissez faire*. Here Arnold is most close to Carlyle and Ruskin. These three extracts indicate why it has been said that Matthew Arnold discovered the foibles of Main Street fifty years before Sinclair Lewis exposed them in his novels of American life.

2. A 17th-century Puritan group (of which Cromwell was an adherent), allied with the Congregationalists.

3. Cf. I Peter iii.8.

thing precious, salutary, and to be propagated, even when it wears such a brand of imperfection on its forehead as this. And men have got such a habit of giving to the language of religion a special application, of making it a mere jargon, that for the condemnation which religion itself passes on the shortcomings of their religious organizations they have no ear; they are sure to cheat themselves and to explain this condemnation away. They can only be reached by the criticism which culture, like poetry, speaking a language not to be sophisticated, and resolutely testing these organizations by the ideal of a human perfection complete on all sides, applies to them.

But men of culture and poetry, it will be said, are again and again failing, and failing conspicuously, in the necessary first stage to a harmonious perfection, in the subduing of the great obvious faults of our animality, which it is the glory of these religious organizations to have helped us to subdue. True, they do often so fail. They have often been without the virtues as well as the faults of the Puritan; it has been one of their dangers that they so felt the Puritan's faults that they too much neglected the practice of his virtues. I will not, however, exculpate them at the Puritan's expense. They have often failed in morality, and morality is indispensable. And they have been punished for their failure, as the Puritan has been rewarded for his performance. They have been punished wherein they erred; but their ideal of beauty, of sweetness and light, and a human nature complete on all its sides, remains the true ideal of perfection still; just as the Puritan's ideal of perfection remains narrow and inadequate, although for what he did well he has been richly rewarded. Notwithstanding the mighty results of the Pilgrim Fathers' voyage, they and their standard of perfection are rightly judged when we figure to ourselves Shakespeare or Virgil—souls in whom sweetness and light, and all that in human nature is most humane, were eminent—accompanying them on their voyage, and think what intolerable company Shakespeare and Virgil would have found them! In the same way let us judge the religious organizations which we see all around us. Do not let us deny the good and the happiness which they have accomplished; but do not let us fail to see clearly that their idea of human perfection is narrow and inadequate, and that the Dissidence of Dissent and the Protestantism of the Protestant religion will never bring humanity to its true goal. As I said with regard to wealth: Let us look at the life of those who live in and for it—so I say with regard to the religious organizations. Look at the life imaged in such a newspaper as the *Nonconformist*—a life of jealousy of the Establishment,[4] disputes, tea-meetings, openings of chapels, sermons; and then think of it as an ideal of a human life completing

4. The Church of England or the Established Church.

itself on all sides, and aspiring with all its organs after sweetness, light, and perfection!

From *Chapter II. Doing As One Likes*

* * * When I began to speak of culture, I insisted on our bondage to machinery, on our proneness to value machinery as an end in itself, without looking beyond it to the end for which alone, in truth, it is valuable. Freedom, I said, was one of those things which we thus worshiped in itself, without enough regarding the ends for which freedom is to be desired. In our common notions and talk about freedom, we eminently show our idolatry of machinery. Our prevalent notion is—and I quoted a number of instances to prove it—that it is a most happy and important thing for a man merely to be able to do as he likes. On what he is to do when he is thus free to do as he likes, we do not lay so much stress. Our familiar praise of the British Constitution under which we live, is that it is a system of checks—a system which stops and paralyzes any power in interfering with the free action of individuals. To this effect Mr. Bright,[1] who loves to walk in the old ways of the Constitution, said forcibly in one of his great speeches, what many other people are every day saying less forcibly, that the central idea of English life and politics is *the assertion of personal liberty.* Evidently this is so; but evidently, also, as feudalism, which with its ideas, and habits of subordination was for many centuries silently behind the British Constitution, dies out, and we are left with nothing but our system of checks, and our notion of its being the great right and happiness of an Englishman to do as far as possible what he likes, we are in danger of drifting towards anarchy. We have not the notion, so familiar on the Continent and to antiquity, of *the State*—the nation in its collective and corporate character, entrusted with stringent powers for the general advantage, and controlling individual wills in the name of an interest wider than that of individuals. We say, what is very true, that this notion is often made instrumental to tyranny; we say that a State is in reality made up of the individuals who compose it, and that every individual is the best judge of his own interests. Our leading class is an aristocracy, and no aristocracy likes the notion of a State-authority greater than itself, with a stringent administrative machinery superseding the decorative inutilities of lord-lieutenancy, deputy-lieutenancy, and the *posse comitatus,*[2] which are all in its own hands. Our middle class, the great representative of trade and Dissent, with its maxims of every man for himself in business, every man for himself in religion, dreads

1. John Bright, 19th-century orator and reformer.
2. I.e., "power of the county"—a feudal method of enforcing law by local authorities instead of by agencies of the central government.

a powerful administration which might somehow interfere with it; and besides, it has its own decorative inutilities of vestrymanship and guardianship, which are to this class what lord-lieutenancy and the county magistracy are to the aristocratic class, and a stringent administration might either take these functions out of its hands, or prevent its exercising them in its own comfortable, independent manner, as at present.

Then as to our working class. This class, pressed constantly by the hard daily compulsion of material wants, is naturally the very center and stronghold of our national idea, that it is man's ideal right and felicity to do as he likes. I think I have somewhere related how M. Michelet[3] said to me of the people of France, that it was "a nation of barbarians civilized by the conscription." He meant that through their military service the idea of public duty and of discipline was brought to the mind of these masses, in other respects so raw and uncultivated. Our masses are quite as raw and uncultivated as the French; and so far from their having the idea of public duty and of discipline, superior to the individual's self-will, brought to their mind by a universal obligation of military service, such as that of the conscription—so far from their having this, the very idea of a conscription is so at variance with our English notion of the prime right and blessedness of doing as one likes, that I remember the manager of the Clay Cross works in Derbyshire told me during the Crimean war, when our want of soldiers was much felt and some people were talking of a conscription, that sooner than submit to a conscription the population of that district would flee to the mines, and lead a sort of Robin Hood life underground.

For a long time, as I have said, the strong feudal habits of subordination and deference continued to tell upon the working class. The modern spirit has now almost entirely dissolved those habits, and the anarchical tendency of our worship of freedom in and for itself, of our superstitious faith, as I say, in machinery, is becoming very manifest. More and more, because of this our blind faith in machinery, because of our want of light to enable us to look beyond machinery to the end for which machinery is valuable, this and that man, and this and that body of men, all over the country, are beginning to assert and put in practice an Englishman's right to do what he likes; his right to march where he likes, meet where he likes, enter where he likes, hoot as he likes, threaten as he likes, smash as he likes.[4] All this, I say, tends to anarchy; and though a number of excellent people, and particularly my friends of the Liberal or progressive party, as they call themselves, are kind enough to reassure us by saying that these are trifles, that a few

3. Jules Michelet (1798–1874), French historian.
4. Reference to the riots of 1866 in which a London mob demolished the iron railings enclosing Hyde Park.

transient outbreaks of rowdyism signify nothing, that our system of liberty is one which itself cures all the evils which it works, that the educated and intelligent classes stand in overwhelming strength and majestic repose, ready, like our military force in riots, to act at a moment's notice—yet one finds that one's Liberal friends generally say this because they have such faith in themselves and their nostrums, when they shall return, as the public welfare requires, to place and power. But this faith of theirs one cannot exactly share, when one has so long had them and their nostrums at work, and see that they have not prevented our coming to our present embarrassed condition. And one finds, also, that the outbreaks of rowdyism tend to become less and less of trifles, to become more frequent rather than less frequent; and that meanwhile our educated and intelligent classes remain in their majestic repose, and somehow or other, whatever happens, their overwhelming strength, like our military force in riots, never does act.

How, indeed, *should* their overwhelming strength act, when the man who gives an inflammatory lecture, or breaks down the park railings, or invades a Secretary of State's office, is only following an Englishman's impulse to do as he likes; and our own conscience tells us that we ourselves have always regarded this impulse as something primary and sacred? Mr. Murphy[5] lectures at Birmingham, and showers on the Catholic population of that town "words," says the Home Secretary, "only fit to be addressed to thieves or murderers." What then? Mr. Murphy has his own reasons of several kinds. He suspects the Roman Catholic Church of designs upon Mrs. Murphy; and he says if mayors and magistrates do not care for their wives and daughters, he does. But, above all, he is doing as he likes; or, in worthier language, asserting his personal liberty. "I will carry out my lectures if they walk over my body as a dead corpse, and I say to the Mayor of Birmingham that he is my servant while I am in Birmingham, and as my servant he must do his duty and protect me." Touching and beautiful words, which find a sympathetic chord in every British bosom! The moment it is plainly put before us that a man is asserting his personal liberty, we are half disarmed; because we are believers in freedom, and not in some dream of a right reason to which the assertion of our freedom is to be subordinated. Accordingly, the Secretary of State had to say that although the lecturer's language was "only fit to be addressed to thieves or murderers," yet, "I do not think he is to be deprived, I do not think that anything I have said could justify the inference that he is to be deprived, of the right of protection in a place built by him for the purpose of these lectures; because the language was not language which afforded grounds for a criminal

---

5. An orator whose inflammatory anti-Catholic public speech *The Errors of* *the Roman Church* led to rioting in Birmingham and other cities in 1867.

prosecution." No, nor to be silenced by Mayor, or Home Secretary, or any administrative authority on earth, simply on their notion of what is discreet and reasonable! This is in perfect consonance with our public opinion, and with our national love for the assertion of personal liberty. * * *

From *Chapter V. Porro Unum Est Necessarium* [1]

* * *Sweetness and light evidently have to do with the bent or side in humanity which we call Hellenic. Greek intelligence has obviously for its essence the instinct for what Plato calls the true, firm, intelligible law of things; the law of light, of seeing things as they are. Even in the natural sciences, where the Greeks had not time and means adequately to apply this instinct, and where we have gone a great deal further than they did, it is this instinct which is the root of the whole matter and the ground of all our success; and this instinct the world has mainly learnt of the Greeks, inasmuch as they are humanity's most signal manifestation of it. Greek art, again, Greek beauty, have their root in the same impulse to see things as they really are, inasmuch as Greek art and beauty rest on fidelity to nature—the *best* nature—and on a delicate discrimination of what this best nature is. To say we work for sweetness and light, then, is only another way of saying that we work for Hellenism. But, oh! cry many people, sweetness and light are not enough; you must put strength or energy along with them, and make a kind of trinity of strength, sweetness and light, and then, perhaps, you may do some good. That is to say, we are to join Hebraism, strictness of the moral conscience, and manful walking by the best light we have, together with Hellenism, inculcate both, and rehearse the praises of both.

Or, rather, we may praise both in conjunction, but we must be careful to praise Hebraism most. "Culture," says an acute, though somewhat rigid critic, Mr. Sidgwick,[2] "diffuses sweetness and light. I do not undervalue these blessings, but religion gives fire and strength, and the world wants fire and strength even more than sweetness and light." By religion, let me explain, Mr. Sidgwick here means particularly that Puritanism on the insufficiency of which I have been commenting and to which he says I am unfair. Now, no doubt, it is possible to be a fanatical partisan of light and the instincts which push us to it, a fanatical enemy of strict-

---

1. Luke x.42: "But one thing is needful." This chapter develops a contrast established in Ch. IV between *Hebraism* (Puritan morality and energetic devotion to work) and *Hellenism* (cultivation of the aesthetic and intellectual understanding of life). The Puritan middle classes, according to Arnold, think that the "one thing needful" is the Hebraic form of virtue.

2. Henry Sidgwick, philosopher (1838–1900), whose article on Arnold appeared in *Macmillan's Magazine*, Aug., 1867.

ness of moral conscience and the instincts which push us to it. A fanaticism of this sort deforms and vulgarizes the well-known work, in some respects so remarkable, of the late Mr. Buckle.[3] Such a fanaticism carries its own mark with it, in lacking sweetness; and its own penalty, in that, lacking sweetness, it comes in the end to lack light too. And the Greeks—the great exponents of humanity's bent for sweetness and light united, of its perception that the truth of things must be at the same time beauty—singularly escaped the fanaticism which we moderns, whether we Hellenize or whether we Hebraize, are so apt to show. They arrived—though failing, as has been said, to give adequate practical satisfaction to the claims of man's moral side—at the idea of a comprehensive adjustment of the claims of both the sides in man, the moral as well as the intellectual, of a full estimate of both, and of a reconciliation of both; an idea which is philosophically of the greatest value, and the best of lessons for us moderns. So we ought to have no difficulty in conceding to Mr. Sidgwick that manful walking by the best light one has—fire and strength as he calls it—has its high value as well as culture, the endeavor to see things in their truth and beauty, the pursuit of sweetness and light. But whether at this or that time, and to this or that set of persons, one ought to insist most on the praises of fire and strength, or on the praises of sweetness and light, must depend, one would think, on the circumstances and needs of that particular time and those particular persons. And all that we have been saying, and indeed any glance at the world around us, shows that with us, with the most respectable and strongest part of us, the ruling force is now, and long has been, a Puritan force—the care for fire and strength, strictness of conscience, Hebraism, rather than the care for sweetness and light, spontaneity of consciousness, Hellenism.

Well, then, what is the good of our now rehearsing the praises of fire and strength to ourselves, who dwell too exclusively on them already? When Mr. Sidgwick says so broadly, that the world wants fire and strength even more than sweetness and light, is he not carried away by a turn for broad generalization? does he not forget that the world is not all of one piece, and every piece with the same needs at the same time? It may be true that the Roman world at the beginning of our era, or Leo the Tenth's Court at the time of the Reformation, or French society in the eighteenth century,[4] needed fire and strength even more than sweetness and light. But can it be said that the Barbarians who overran the empire needed fire and strength even more than sweetness and light; or

3. Henry Thomas Buckle (1821–62), author of *A History of Civilization.*
4. Societies representing an excess of sophisticated worldliness as at the courts of such a Roman emperor as Nero (A.D. 54–68), or Pope Leo X (1513–21), or Louis XV (1715–74).

that the Puritans needed them more; or that Mr. Murphy, the Birmingham lecturer, and the Rev. W. Cattle[5] and his friends, need them more?

The Puritan's great danger is that he imagines himself in possession of a rule telling him the *unum necessarium*, or one thing needful, and that he then remains satisfied with a very crude conception of what this rule really is and what it tells him, thinks he has now knowledge and henceforth needs only to act, and, in this dangerous state of assurance and self-satisfaction, proceeds to give full swing to a number of the instincts of his ordinary self. Some of the instincts of his ordinary self he has, by the help of his rule of life, conquered; but others which he has not conquered by this help he is so far from perceiving to need subjugation, and to be instincts of an inferior self, that he even fancies it to be his right and duty, in virtue of having conquered a limited part of himself, to give unchecked swing to the remainder. He is, I say, a victim of Hebraism, of the tendency to cultivate strictness of conscience rather than spontaneity of consciousness. And what he wants is a larger conception of human nature, showing him the number of other points at which his nature must come to its best, besides the points which he himself knows and thinks of. There is no *unum necessarium*, or one thing needful, which can free human nature from the obligation of trying to come to its best at all these points. The real *unum necessarium* for us is to come to our best at all points. Instead of our "one thing needful," justifying in us vulgarity, hideousness, ignorance, violence— our vulgarity, hideousness, ignorance, violence, are really so many touchstones which try our one thing needful, and which prove that in the state, at any rate, in which we ourselves have it, it is not all we want. And as the force which encourages us to stand staunch and fast by the rule and ground we have is Hebraism, so the force which encourages us to go back upon this rule, and to try the very ground on which we appear to stand, is Hellenism —a turn for giving our consciousness free play and enlarging its range. And what I say is, not that Hellenism is always for everybody more wanted than Hebraism, but that for the Rev. W. Cattle at this particular moment, and for the great majority of us his fellow countrymen, it is more wanted.

* * *

The newspapers a short time ago contained an account of the suicide of a Mr. Smith, secretary to some insurance company, who, it was said, "labored under the apprehension that he would come

---

5. A Nonconformist clergyman who was chairman of the anti-Catholic meeting addressed by Murphy in 1867. See "Doing As One Likes," above.

to poverty, and that he was eternally lost." And when I read these words, it occurred to me that the poor man who came to such a mournful end was, in truth, a kind of type—by the selection of his two grand objects of concern, by their isolation from everything else, and their juxtaposition to one another—of all the strongest, most respectable, and most representative part of our nation. "He labored under the apprehension that he would come to poverty, and that he was eternally lost." The whole middle class have a conception of things—a conception which makes us call them Philistines—just like that of this poor man; though we are seldom, of course, shocked by seeing it take the distressing, violently morbid, and fatal turn, which it took with him. But how generally, with how many of us, are the main concerns of life limited to these two: the concern for making money, and the concern for saving our souls! And how entirely does the narrow and mechanical conception of our secular business proceed from a narrow and mechanical conception of our religious business! What havoc do the united conceptions make of our lives! It is because the second-named of these two master-concerns presents to us the one thing needful in so fixed, narrow, and mechanical a way, that so ignoble a fellow master-concern to it as the first-named becomes possible; and, having been once admitted, takes the same rigid and absolute character as the other.

Poor Mr. Smith had sincerely the nobler master-concern as well as the meaner—the concern for saving his soul (according to the narrow and mechanical conception which Puritanism has of what the salvation of the soul is), as well as the concern for making money. But let us remark how many people there are, especially outside the limits of the serious and conscientious middle class to which Mr. Smith belonged, who take up with a meaner master-concern—whether it be pleasure, or field sports, or bodily exercises, or business, or popular agitation—who take up with one of these exclusively, and neglect Mr. Smith's nobler master-concern, because of the mechanical form which Hebraism has given to this noble master-concern. Hebraism makes it stand, as we have said, as something talismanic, isolated, and all-sufficient, justifying our giving our ordinary selves free play in bodily exercises, or business, or popular agitation, if we have made our account square with this master-concern; and, if we have not, rendering other things indifferent, and our ordinary self all we have to follow, and to follow with all the energy that is in us, till we do. Whereas the idea of perfection at all points, the encouraging in ourselves spontaneity of consciousness, the letting a free play of thought live and flow around all our activity, the indisposition to allow one side of our activity to stand as so all-important and all-sufficing that it makes other sides indifferent—this bent of mind in us may not only check us in following unreservedly a mean master-concern of any kind, but may even, also, bring new life and movement into that side of us with which alone Hebraism concerns itself, and awaken a healthier and less mechanical activity there. Hellenism may thus actually serve to further the designs of Hebraism.

* * *

1868, 1869

From Wordsworth[1]

* * * Wordsworth has been in his grave for some thirty years, and certainly his lovers and admirers cannot flatter themselves that this great and steady light of glory as yet shines over him. He is not fully recognized at home; he is not recognized at all abroad. Yet I firmly believe that the poetical performance of Wordsworth is, after that of Shakespeare and Milton, of which all the world now recognizes the worth, undoubtedly the most considerable in our language from the Elizabethan age to the present time. Chaucer is anterior; and on other grounds, too, he cannot well be brought into the comparison. But taking the roll of our chief poetical names, besides Shakespeare and Milton, from the age of Elizabeth downwards, and going through it—Spenser, Dryden, Pope, Gray, Goldsmith, Cowper, Burns, Coleridge, Scott, Campbell, Moore, Byron, Shelley, Keats (I mention those only who are dead)—I think it certain that Wordsworth's name deserves to stand, and will finally stand, above them all. Several of the poets named have gifts and excellences which Wordsworth has not. But taking the performance of each as a whole, I say that Wordsworth seems to me to have left a body of poetical work superior in power, in interest, in the qualities which give enduring freshness, to that which any one of the others has left.

But this is not enough to say. I think it certain, further, that if we take the chief poetical names of the Continent since the death of Molière, and, omitting Goethe, confront the remaining names with that of Wordsworth, the result is the same. Let us take Klopstock, Lessing, Schiller, Uhland, Rückert, and Heine for Germany; Filicaia, Alfieri, Manzoni, and Leopardi for Italy; Racine, Boileau, Voltaire, André Chénier, Béranger, Lamartine, Musset, M. Victor

---

1. In one of his letters to Clough, Arnold remarked that those who cannot read Greek literature "should read nothing but Milton and parts of Wordsworth: the state should see to it." The following essay, which served as the introduction to a volume of Words-worth's poems selected by Arnold, demonstrates the reasons for this admiration. A further tribute to Wordsworth is expressed in Arnold's poem *Memorial Verses.* The opening paragraphs of the essay, which are omitted here, review the history of Wordsworth's reputation.

Hugo (he has been so long celebrated that although he still lives I may be permitted to name him) for France. Several of these, again, have evidently gifts and excellences to which Wordsworth can make no pretension. But in real poetical achievement it seems to me indubitable that to Wordsworth, here again, belongs the palm. * * *

This is a high claim to make for Wordsworth. But if it is a just claim, if Wordsworth's place among the poets who have appeared in the last two or three centuries is after Shakespeare, Molière, Milton, Goethe, indeed, but before all the rest, then in time Wordsworth will have his due. We shall recognize him in his place, as we recognize Shakespeare and Milton; and not only we ourselves shall recognize him, but he will be recognized by Europe also. Meanwhile, those who recognize him already may do well, perhaps, to ask themselves whether there are not in the case of Wordsworth certain special obstacles which hinder or delay his due recognition by others, and whether these obstacles are not in some measure removable.

The *Excursion* and the *Prelude,* his poems of greatest bulk, are by no means Wordsworth's best work. His best work is in his shorter pieces, and many indeed are there of these which are of first-rate excellence. But in his seven volumes the pieces of high merit are mingled with a mass of pieces very inferior to them; so inferior to them that it seems wonderful how the same poet should have produced both. Shakespeare frequently has lines and passages in a strain quite false, and which are entirely unworthy of him. But one can imagine him smiling if one could meet him in the Elysian Fields and tell him so; smiling and replying that he knew it perfectly well himself, and what did it matter? But with Wordsworth the case is different. Work altogether inferior, work quite uninspired, flat, and dull, is produced by him with evident unconsciousness of its defects, and he presents it to us with the same faith and seriousness as his best work. Now a drama or an epic fill the mind, and one does not look beyond them; but in a collection of short pieces the impression made by one piece requires to be continued and sustained by the piece following. In reading Wordsworth the impression made by one of his fine pieces is too often dulled and spoiled by a very inferior piece coming after it.

Wordsworth composed verses during a space of some sixty years; and it is no exaggeration to say that within one single decade of those years, between 1798 and 1808, almost all his really first-rate work was produced. A mass of inferior work remains, work done before and after this golden prime, imbedding the first-rate work and clogging it, obstructing our approach to it, chilling, not unfrequently, the high-wrought mood with which we leave it. To be recognized far and wide as a great poet, to be possible and receivable as a classic, Wordsworth needs to be relieved of a great deal of the poetical baggage which now encumbers him.[2] * * *

Disengaged from the quantity of inferior work which now obscures them, the best poems of Wordsworth, I hear many people say, would indeed stand out in great beauty, but they would prove to be very few in number, scarcely more than a half a dozen. I maintain, on the other hand, that what strikes me with admiration, what establishes in my opinion Wordsworth's superiority, is the great and ample body of powerful work which remains to him, even after all his inferior work has been cleared away. He gives us so much to rest upon, so much which communicates his spirit and engages ours!

This is of very great importance. If it were a comparison of single pieces, or of three or four pieces, by each poet, I do not say that Wordsworth would stand decisively above Gray, or Burns, or Coleridge, or Keats, or Manzoni, or Heine. It is in his ampler body of powerful work that I find his superiority. His good work itself, his work which counts, is not all of it, of course, of equal value. Some kinds of poetry are in themselves lower kinds than others. The ballad kind is a lower kind: the didactic kind, still more, is a lower kind. Poetry of this latter sort counts, too, sometimes, by its biographical interest partly, not by its poetical interest pure and simple; but then this can only be when the poet producing it has the power and importance of Wordsworth, a power and importance which he assuredly did not establish by such didactic poetry alone. Altogether, it is, I say, by the great body of powerful and significant work which remains to him, after every reduction and deduction has been made, that Wordsworth's superiority is proved.

To exhibit this body of Wordsworth's best work, to clear away obstructions from around it, and to let it speak for itself, is what every lover of Wordsworth should desire. Until this has been done, Wordsworth, whom we, to whom he is dear, all of us know and feel to be so great a poet, has not had a fair chance before the world. When once it has been done, he will make his way best, not by our advocacy of him, but by his own worth and power. * * * Yet at the outset, before he has been duly known and recognized, we may do Wordsworth a service, perhaps, by indicating in what his superior power and worth will be found to consist, and in what it will not.

Long ago, in speaking of Homer, I said that the noble and profound application of ideas to life is the most essential part of poetic greatness. I said that a great poet receives his distinctive character of superiority from his application, under the conditions immutably fixed by the laws of poetic beauty and poetic truth, from his application, I say, to his subject, whatever it may be, of the ideas

---

2. Two paragraphs, here omitted, criticize Wordsworth's system of classifying his poems.

On man, on nature, and on human life,[3]

which he has acquired for himself. The line quoted is Wordsworth's own; and his superiority arises from his powerful use, in his best pieces, his powerful application to his subject, of ideas "on man, on nature, and on human life."

Voltaire, with his signal acuteness, most truly remarked that "no nation has treated in poetry moral ideas with more energy and depth than the English nation." And he adds: "There, it seems to me, is the great merit of the English poets." Voltaire does not mean, by "treating in poetry moral ideas," the composing moral and didactic poems—that brings us but a very little way in poetry. He means just the same thing as was meant when I spoke above "of the noble and profound application of ideas to life"; and he means the application of these ideas under the conditions fixed for us by the laws of poetic beauty and poetic truth. If it is said that to call these ideas *moral* ideas is to introduce a strong and injurious limitation, I answer that it is to do nothing of the kind, because moral ideas are really so main a part of human life. The question, *how to live*, is itself a moral idea; and it is the question which most interests every man, and with which, in some way or other, he is perpetually occupied. A large sense is of course to be given to the term *moral*. Whatever bears upon the question, "how to live," comes under it.

> Nor love thy life, nor hate; but, what thou liv'st,
> Live well; how long or short, permit to heaven.[4]

In those fine lines Milton utters, as everyone at once perceives, a moral idea. Yes, but so too, when Keats consoles the forward-bending lover on the Grecian Urn, the lover arrested and presented in immortal relief by the sculptor's hand before he can kiss, with the line,

> Forever wilt thou love, and she be fair,[5]

he utters a moral idea. When Shakespeare says that

> We are such stuff
> As dreams are made on, and our little life
> Is rounded with a sleep,[6]

he utters a moral idea.

Voltaire was right in thinking that the energetic and profound treatment of moral ideas, in this large sense, is what distinguishes the English poetry. He sincerely meant praise, not dispraise or hint of limitation; and they err who suppose that poetic limitation is a necessary consequence of the fact, the fact being granted as Voltaire states it. If what distinguishes the greatest poets is their

3. *The Recluse*, line 754.
4. *Paradise Lost* XI.553–54.
5. *Ode on a Grecian Urn*, line 20.
6. *The Tempest* IV.i.156–58.

powerful and profound application of ideas to life, which surely no good critic will deny, then to prefix to the term ideas here the term moral makes hardly any difference, because human life itself is in so preponderating a degree moral.

It is important, therefore, to hold fast to this: that poetry is at bottom a criticism of life; that the greatness of a poet lies in his powerful and beautiful application of ideas to life—to the question: How to live. Morals are often treated in a narrow and false fashion; they are bound up with systems of thought and belief which have had their day; they are fallen into the hands of pedants and professional dealers; they grow tiresome to some of us. We find attraction, at times, even in a poetry of revolt against them; in a poetry which might take for its motto Omar Khayyám's words: "Let us make up in the tavern for the time which we have wasted in the mosque." Or we find attractions in a poetry indifferent to them: in a poetry where the contents may be what they will, but where the form is studied and exquisite. We delude ourselves in either case; and the best cure for our delusion is to let our minds rest upon that great and inexhaustible word *life*, until we learn to enter into its meaning. A poetry of revolt against moral ideas is a poetry of revolt against life; a poetry of indifference towards moral ideas is a poetry of indifference towards *life*.

Epictetus had a happy figure for things like the play of the senses, or literary form and finish, or argumentative ingenuity, in comparison with "the best and master thing" for us, as he called it, the concern, how to live. Some people were afraid of them, he said, or they disliked and undervalued them. Such people were wrong; they were unthankful or cowardly. But the things might also be overprized, and treated as final when they are not. They bear to life the relation which inns bear to home. "As if a man, journeying home, and finding a nice inn on the road, and liking it, were to stay forever at the inn! Man, thou hast forgotten thine object; thy journey was not *to* this, but *through* this. 'But this inn is taking.' And how many other inns, too, are taking, and how many fields and meadows! but as places of passage merely. You have an object, which is this: to get home, to do your duty to your family, friends, and fellow-countrymen, to attain inward freedom, serenity, happiness, contentment. Style takes your fancy, arguing takes your fancy, and you forget your home and want to make your abode with them and to stay with them, on the plea that they are taking. Who denies that they are taking? but as places of passage, as inns. And when I say this, you suppose me to be attacking the care for style, the care for argument. I am not; I attack the resting in them, the not looking to the end which is beyond them."

Now, when we come across a poet like Théophile Gautier[7] we have a poet who has taken up his abode at an inn, and never got farther. There may be inducements to this or that one of us, at this or that moment, to find delight in him, to cleave to him; but after all, we do not change the truth about him—we only stay ourselves in his inn along with him. And when we come across a poet like Wordsworth, who sings

> Of truth, of grandeur, beauty, love, and hope,
> And melancholy fear subdued by faith,
> Of blessed consolations in distress,
> Of moral strength and intellectual power,
> Of joy in widest commonalty spread—[8]

then we have a poet intent on "the best and master thing," and who prosecutes his journey home. We say, for brevity's sake, that he deals with *life*, because he deals with that in which life really consists. * * *

No Wordsworthian will doubt this. Nay, the fervent Wordsworthian will add, as Mr. Leslie Stephen does, that Wordsworth's poetry is precious because his philosophy is sound; that his "ethical system is as distinctive and capable of exposition as Bishop Butler's"; that his poetry is informed by ideas which "fall spontaneously into a scientific system of thought."[9] But we must be on our guard against the Wordsworthians, if we want to secure for Wordsworth his due rank as a poet. The Wordsworthians are apt to praise him for the wrong things, and to lay far too much stress upon what they call his philosophy. His poetry is the reality, his philosophy—so far, at least, as it may put on the form and habit of "a scientific system of thought," and the more that it puts them on—is the illusion. Perhaps we shall one day learn to make this proposition general, and to say: Poetry is the reality, philosophy the illusion. But in Wordsworth's case, at any rate, we cannot do him justice until we dismiss his formal philosophy.

The *Excursion* abounds with philosophy and therefore the *Excursion* is to the Wordsworthian what it never can be to the disinterested lover of poetry—a satisfactory work. "Duty exists," says Wordsworth, in the *Excursion*; and then he proceeds thus—

> . . . Immutably survive,
> For our support, the measures and the forms,

7. Théophile Gautier (1811–72), a poet whose preoccupation with "literary form and finish" and indifference towards edification in literature made him an important exponent of art for art's sake in France, like D. G. Rossetti in England. Arnold often deplored his fellow Victorians' fondness for the stunning phrasemaking of such poets as Tennyson, Keats, and Rossetti.
8. *The Recluse*, lines 767–71.
9. From an essay on "Wordsworth's Ethics" in *Hours in a Library* by Leslie Stephen (1832–1904).

Which an abstract Intelligence supplies,
Whose kingdom is, where time and space are not.[1]

And the Wordsworthian is delighted, and thinks that here is a
sweet union of philosophy and poetry. But the disinterested lover
of poetry will feel that the lines carry us really not a step farther
than the proposition which they would interpret; that they are a
tissue of elevated but abstract verbiage, alien to the very nature of
poetry.

* * *

Even the "intimations" of the famous *Ode*, those cornerstones
of the supposed philosophic system of Wordsworth—the idea of
the high instincts and affections coming out in childhood, testify-
ing of a divine home recently left, and fading away as our life
proceeds—this idea, of undeniable beauty as a play of fancy, has
itself not the character of poetic truth of the best kind; it has no
real solidity. The instinct of delight in Nature and her beauty had
no doubt extraordinary strength in Wordsworth himself as a child.
But to say that universally this instinct is mighty in childhood, and
tends to die away afterwards, is to say what is extremely doubtful.
In many people, perhaps with the majority of educated persons, the
love of nature is nearly imperceptible at ten years old, but strong
and operative at thirty. In general we may say of these high instincts
of early childhood, the base of the alleged systematic philosophy of
Wordsworth, what Thucydides says of the early achievements of
the Greek race: "It is impossible to speak with certainty of what is
so remote; but from all that we can really investigate, I should say
that they were no very great things."

Finally, the "scientific system of thought" in Wordsworth gives
us at least such poetry as this, which the devout Wordsworthian accepts—

O for the coming of that glorious time
When, prizing knowledge as her noblest wealth
And best protection, this Imperial Realm,
While she exacts allegiance, shall admit
An obligation, on her part, to *teach*
Them who are born to serve her and obey;
Binding herself by statute to secure,
For all the children whom her soil maintains,
The rudiments of letters, and inform
The mind with moral and religious truth.[2]

Wordsworth calls Voltaire dull, and surely the production of these
un-Voltairian lines must have been imposed on him as a judgment!
One can hear them being quoted at a Social Science Congress; one
can call up the whole scene. A great room in one of our dismal
provincial towns; dusty air and jaded afternoon daylight; benches

1. *The Excursion* IV.73–76.   2. *The Excursion* IX.293–302.

full of men with bald heads and women in spectacles; an orator lifting up his face from a manuscript written within and without to declaim these lines of Wordsworth; and in the soul of any poor child of nature who may have wandered in thither, an unutterable sense of lamentation, and mourning, and woe!

"But turn we," as Wordsworth says, "from these bold, bad men,"[3] the haunters of Social Science Congresses. And let us be on our guard, too, against the exhibitors and extollers of a "scientific system of thought" in Wordsworth's poetry. The poetry will never be seen aright while they thus exhibit it. The cause of its greatness is simple, and may be told quite simply. Wordsworth's poetry is great because of the extraordinary power with which Wordsworth feels the joy offered to us in nature, the joy offered to us in the simple primary affections and duties; and because of the extraordinary power with which, in case after case, he shows us this joy, and renders it so as to make us share it.

The source of joy from which he thus draws is the truest and most unfailing source of joy accessible to man. It is also accessible universally. Wordsworth brings us word, therefore, according to his own strong and characteristic line, he brings us word

Of joy in widest commonalty spread.[4]

Here is an immense advantage for a poet. Wordsworth tells of what all seek, and tells of it at its truest and best source, and yet a source where all may go and draw for it.

Nevertheless, we are not to suppose that everything is precious which Wordsworth, standing even at this perennial and beautiful source, may give us. Wordsworthians are apt to talk as if it must be. They will speak with the same reverence of *The Sailor's Mother*, for example, as of *Lucy Gray*. They do their master harm by such lack of discrimination. *Lucy Gray* is a beautiful success; *The Sailor's Mother* is a failure. To give aright what he wishes to give, to interpret and render successfully, is not always within Wordsworth's own command. It is within no poet's command; here is the part of the Muse, the inspiration, the God, the "not ourselves." In Wordsworth's case, the accident, for so it may almost be called, of inspiration, is of peculiar importance. No poet, perhaps, is so evidently filled with a new and sacred energy when the inspiration is upon him; no poet, when it fails him, is so left "weak as is a breaking wave."[5] I remember hearing him say that "Goethe's poetry was not inevitable enough." The remark is striking and true; no line in Goethe, as Goethe said himself, but its maker knew well how it came there. Wordsworth is right, Goethe's poetry is not inevitable; not inevitable enough. But Wordsworth's poetry, when

3. In Wordsworth's poem *To the Lady Fleming.*
4. *The Recluse*, line 771.

5. Wordsworth, *A Poet's Epitaph*, line 58.

he is at his best, is inevitable, as inevitable as Nature herself. It might seem that Nature not only gave him the matter for his poem, but wrote his poem for him. He has no style. He was too conversant with Milton not to catch at times his master's manner, and he has fine Miltonic lines; but he has no assured poetic style of his own, like Milton. When he seeks to have a style he falls into ponderosity and pomposity. In the *Excursion* we have his style, as an artistic product of his own creation; and although Jeffrey[6] completely failed to recognize Wordsworth's real greatness, he was yet not wrong in saying of the *Excursion*, as a work of poetic style: "This will never do." And yet magical as is that power, which Wordsworth has not, of assured and possessed poetic style, he has something which is an equivalent for it.

Everyone who has any sense for these things feels the subtle turn, the heightening, which is given to a poet's verse by his genius for style. We can feel it in the

> After life's fitful fever he sleeps well[7]—

of Shakespeare; in the

> . . . though fall'n on evil days,
> On evil days though fall'n, and evil tongues[8]—

of Milton. It is the incomparable charm of Milton's power of poetic style which gives such worth to *Paradise Regained*, and makes a great poem of a work in which Milton's imagination does not soar high. Wordsworth has in constant possession, and at command, no style of this kind; but he had too poetic a nature, and had read the great poets too well, not to catch, as I have already remarked, something of it occasionally. We find it not only in his Miltonic lines; we find it in such a phrase as this, where the manner is his own, not Milton's—

> the fierce confederate storm
> Of sorrow barricadoed evermore
> Within the walls of cities;[9]

although even here, perhaps, the power of style which is undeniable, is more properly that of eloquent prose than the subtle heightening and change wrought by genuine poetic style. It is style, again, and the elevation given by style, which chiefly makes the effectiveness of *Laodameia*. Still the right sort of verse to choose from Wordsworth, if we are to seize his true and most characteristic form of expression, is a line like this from *Michael*—

> And never lifted up a single stone.

6. Francis Jeffrey (1773–1850), contributor to the *Edinburgh Review*.
7. *Macbeth* III.ii.23.
8. *Paradise Lost* VII.25–26.
9. *The Recluse*, lines 831–33.

There is nothing subtle in it, no heightening, no study of poetic style, strictly so called, at all; yet it is expression of the highest and most truly expressive kind.

Wordsworth owed much to Burns, and a style of perfect plainness, relying for effect solely on the weight and force of that which with entire fidelity it utters, Burns could show him.

> The poor inhabitant below
> Was quick to learn and wise to know,
> And keenly felt the friendly glow
>   And softer flame;
> But thoughtless follies laid him low
>   And stained his name.[1]

Everyone will be conscious of a likeness here to Wordsworth; and if Wordsworth did great things with this nobly plain manner, we must remember, what indeed he himself would always have been forward to acknowledge, that Burns used it before him.

Still Wordsworth's use of it has something unique and unmatchable. Nature herself seems, I say, to take the pen out of his hand, and to write for him with her own bare, sheer, penetrating power. This arises from two causes: from the profound sincereness with which Wordsworth feels his subject, and also from the profoundly sincere and natural character of his subject itself. He can and will treat such a subject with nothing but the most plain, first-hand, almost austere naturalness. His expression may often be called bald, as, for instance, in the poem of *Resolution and Independence*; but it is bald as the bare mountaintops are bald, with a baldness which is full of grandeur.

Wherever we meet with the successful balance, in Wordsworth, of profound truth of subject with profound truth of execution, he is unique. His best poems are those which most perfectly exhibit this balance. I have a warm admiration for *Laodameia* and for the great *Ode*; but if I am to tell the very truth, I find *Laodameia* not wholly free from something artificial, and the great *Ode* not wholly free from something declamatory. If I had to pick out poems of a kind most perfectly to show Wordsworth's unique power, I should rather choose poems such as *Michael, The Fountain, The Highland Reaper*.[2] And poems with the peculiar and unique beauty which distinguishes these, Wordsworth produced in considerable number; besides very many other poems of which the worth, although not so rare as the worth of these, is still exceedingly high.

* * *

I have spoken lightly of Wordsworthians; and if we are to get Wordsworth recognized by the public and by the world, we must recommend him not in the spirit of a clique, but in the spirit of

---

1. From Burns's *A Bard's Epitaph*.   2. I.e., *The Solitary Reaper*.

disinterested lovers of poetry. But I am a Wordsworthian myself. I can read with pleasure and edification *Peter Bell*, and the whole series of *Ecclesiastical Sonnets*, and the address to Mr. Wilkinson's spade, and even the *Thanksgiving Ode*—everything of Wordsworth, I think, except *Vaudracour and Julia*. It is not for nothing that one has been brought up in the veneration of a man so truly worthy of homage; that one has seen him and heard him, lived in his neighborhood, and been familiar with his country. No Wordsworthian has a tenderer affection for this pure and sage master than I, or is less really offended by his defects. But Wordsworth is something more than the pure and sage master of a small band of devoted followers, and we ought not to rest satisfied until he is seen to be what he is. He is one of the very chief glories of English Poetry; and by nothing is England so glorious as by her poetry. Let us lay aside every weight which hinders our getting him recognized as this, and let our one study be to bring to pass, as widely as possible and as truly as possible, his own word concerning his poems: "They will co-operate with the benign tendencies in human nature and society, and will, in their degree, be efficacious in making men wiser, better, and happier."[3]

1879

The Study of Poetry[1]

"The future of poetry is immense, because in poetry, where it is worthy of its high destinies, our race, as time goes on, will find an ever surer and surer stay. There is not a creed which is not shaken, not an accredited dogma which is not shown to be questionable, not a received tradition which does not threaten to dissolve. Our religion has materialized itself in the fact, in the supposed fact; it has attached its emotion to the fact, and now the fact is failing it. But for poetry the idea is everything; the rest is a world of illusion, of divine illusion. Poetry attaches its emotion to the idea; the idea *is* the fact. The strongest part of our religion today is its unconscious poetry."

Let me be permitted to quote these words of my own, as uttering the thought which should, in my opinion, go with us and govern

3. Wordsworth's letter to Lady Beaumont, May 21, 1807.
1. Aside from its vindication of the importance of literature, this essay is an interesting example of the variety of Arnold's own reading. To know literature in only one language seemed to him not to know literature. His personal *Notebooks* show that throughout his active life he continued to read books in French, German, Italian, Latin, and Greek. His favorite authors in these languages are used by him as a means of testing English poetry. The testing is sometimes a severe one. Readers may also protest that despite Arnold's own wit, his essay is limited by an incomplete recognition of the values of comic literature, a shortcoming abundantly evident in the discussion of Chaucer. Nevertheless, whether we agree or disagree with some of Arnold's verdicts, we can be attracted by the combination of traditionalism and impressionism on which these verdicts are based, and we can enjoy the memorable phrasemaking in which the verdicts are expressed. *The Study of Poetry* has been extraordinarily potent in shaping literary tastes in England and in America.

us in all our study of poetry. In the present work[2] it is the course of one great contributory stream to the world-river of poetry that we are invited to follow. We are here invited to trace the stream of English poetry. But whether we set ourselves, as here, to follow only one of the several streams that make the mighty river of poetry, or whether we seek to know them all, our governing thought should be the same. We should conceive of poetry worthily, and more highly than it has been the custom to conceive of it. We should conceive of it as capable of higher uses, and called to higher destinies, than those which in general men have assigned to it hitherto. More and more mankind will discover that we have to turn to poetry to interpret life for us, to console us, to sustain us. Without poetry, our science will appear incomplete; and most of what now passes with us for religion and philosophy will be replaced by poetry. Science, I say, will appear incomplete without it. For finely and truly does Wordsworth call poetry "the impassioned expression which is in the countenance of all science";[3] and what is a countenance without its expression? Again, Wordsworth finely and truly calls poetry "the breath and finer spirit of all knowledge": our religion, parading evidences such as those on which the popular mind relies now; our philosophy, pluming itself on its reasonings about causation and finite and infinite being; what are they but the shadows and dreams and false shows of knowledge? The day will come when we shall wonder at ourselves for having trusted to them, for having taken them seriously; and the more we perceive their hollowness, the more we shall prize "the breath and finer spirit of knowledge" offered to us by poetry.

But if we conceive thus highly of the destinies of poetry, we must also set our standard for poetry high, since poetry, to be capable of fulfilling such high destinies, must be poetry of a high order of excellence. We must accustom ourselves to a high standard and to a strict judgment. Sainte-Beuve[4] relates that Napoleon one day said, when somebody was spoken of in his presence as a charlatan: "Charlatan as much as you please; but where is there *not* charlatanism?"—"Yes," answers Sainte-Beuve, "in politics, in the art of governing mankind, that is perhaps true. But in the order of thought, in art, the glory, the eternal honor is that charlatanism shall find no entrance; herein lies the inviolableness of that noble portion of man's being." It is admirably said, and let us hold fast to it. In poetry, which is thought and art in one, it is the glory, the eternal honor, that charlatanism shall find no entrance; that this noble sphere be kept inviolate and inviolable. Charlatanism is for confusing or obliterating the distinctions between excellent and in-

2. An anthology of English poetry for which Arnold's essay served as the introduction.
3. See Wordsworth's Preface to *Lyrical Ballads*.
4. Charles Augustin Sainte-Beuve (1804–69), French critic who influenced Arnold.

ferior, sound and unsound or only half-sound, true and untrue or only half-true. It is charlatanism, conscious or unconscious, whenever we confuse or obliterate these. And in poetry, more than anywhere else, it is unpermissible to confuse or obliterate them. For in poetry the distinction between excellent and inferior, sound and unsound or only half-sound, true and untrue or only half-true, is of paramount importance. It is of paramount importance because of the high destinies of poetry. In poetry, as a criticism of life under the conditions fixed for such a criticism by the laws of poetic truth and poetic beauty, the spirit of our race will find, we have said, as time goes on and as other helps fail, its consolation and stay. But the consolation and stay will be of power in proportion to the power of the criticism of life. And the criticism of life will be of power in proportion as the poetry conveying it is excellent rather than inferior, sound rather than unsound or half-sound, true rather than untrue or half-true.

The best poetry is what we want; the best poetry will be found to have a power of forming, sustaining, and delighting us, as nothing else can. A clearer, deeper sense of the best in poetry, and of the strength and joy to be drawn from it, is the most precious benefit which we can gather from a poetical collection such as the present. And yet in the very nature and conduct of such a collection there is inevitably something which tends to obscure in us the consciousness of what our benefit should be, and to distract us from the pursuit of it. We should therefore steadily set it before our minds at the outset, and should compel ourselves to revert constantly to the thought of it as we proceed.

Yes; constantly in reading poetry, a sense for the best, the really excellent, and of the strength and joy to be drawn from it, should be present in our minds and should govern our estimate of what we read. But this real estimate, the only true one, is liable to be superseded, if we are not watchful, by two other kinds of estimate, the historic estimate and the personal estimate, both of which are fallacious. A poet or a poem may count to us historically, they may count to us on grounds personal to ourselves, and they may count to us really. They may count to us historically. The course of development of a nation's language, thought, and poetry, is profoundly interesting; and by regarding a poet's work as a stage in this course of development we may easily bring ourselves to make it of more importance as poetry than in itself it really is, we may come to use a language of quite exaggerated praise in criticizing it; in short, to overrate it. So arises in our poetic judgments the fallacy caused by the estimate which we may call historic. Then, again, a poet or a poem may count to us on grounds personal to ourselves. Our personal affinities, likings, and circumstances, have great power to sway our estimate of this or that poet's work, and to make us attach more importance to it as poetry than in itself it really possesses, because to us it is, or has been, of high importance. Here also we overrate the object of our interest, and apply to it a language of praise which is quite exaggerated. And thus we get the source of a second fallacy in our poetic judgments—the fallacy caused by an estimate which we may call personal.

Both fallacies are natural. It is evident how naturally the study of the history and development of a poetry may incline a man to pause over reputations and works once conspicuous but now obscure, and to quarrel with a careless public for skipping, in obedience to mere tradition and habit, from one famous name or work in its national poetry to another, ignorant of what it misses, and of the reason for keeping what it keeps, and of the whole process of growth in its poetry. The French have become diligent students of their own early poetry, which they long neglected; the study makes many of them dissatisfied with their so-called classical poetry, the court-tragedy of the seventeenth century, a poetry which Pellisson[5] long ago reproached with its want of the true poetic stamp, with its *politesse stérile et rampante*,[6] but which nevertheless has reigned in France as absolutely as if it had been the perfection of classical poetry indeed. The dissatisfaction is natural; yet a lively and accomplished critic, M. Charles d'Héricault, the editor of Clément Marot,[7] goes too far when he says that "the cloud of glory playing round a classic is a mist as dangerous to the future of a literature as it is intolerable for the purposes of history." "It hinders," he goes on, "it hinders us from seeing more than one single point, the culminating and exceptional point; the summary, fictitious and arbitrary, of a thought and of a work. It substitutes a halo for a physiognomy, it puts a statue where there was once a man, and hiding from us all trace of the labor, the attempts, the weaknesses, the failures, it claims not study but veneration; it does not show us how the thing is done, it imposes upon us a model. Above all, for the historian this creation of classic personages is inadmissible; for it withdraws the poet from his time, from his proper life, it breaks historical relationships, it blinds criticism by conventional admiration, and renders the investigation of literary origins unacceptable. It gives us a human personage no longer, but a God seated immovable amidst His perfect work, like Jupiter on Olympus; and hardly will it be possible for the young student, to whom such work is exhibited at such a distance from him, to believe that it did not issue ready made from that divine head."

All this is brilliantly and tellingly said, but we must plead for a

5. Paul Pellison, 17th-century French critic.
6. "Conventionality that is barren and bombastic."
7. D'Héricault's edition of Marot was published in 1868. The graceful poetry of Clément Marot (ca. 1495–1544) was admired and imitated in late 19th-century England, sometimes at the expense of overlooking the excellences of the more severely classical 17th-century French poets such as Racine.

distinction. Everything depends on the reality of a poet's classic character. If he is a dubious classic, let us sift him; if he is a false classic, let us explode him. But if he is a real classic, if his work belongs to the class of the very best (for this is the true and right meaning of the word *classic, classical*), then the great thing for us is to feel and enjoy his work as deeply as ever we can, and to appreciate the wide difference between it and all work which has not the same high character. This is what is salutary, this is what is formative; this is the great benefit to be got from the study of poetry. Everything which interferes with it, which hinders it, is injurious. True, we must read our classic with open eyes, and not with eyes blinded with superstition; we must perceive when his work comes short, when it drops out of the class of the very best, and we must rate it, in such cases, at its proper value. But the use of this negative criticism is not in itself, it is entirely in its enabling us to have a clearer sense and a deeper enjoyment of what is truly excellent. To trace the labor, the attempts, the weaknesses, the failures of a genuine classic, to acquaint oneself with his time and his life and his historical relationships, is mere literary dilettantism unless it has that clear sense and deeper enjoyment for its end. It may be said that the more we know about a classic the better we shall enjoy him; and, if we lived as long as Methuselah and had all of us heads of perfect clearness and wills of perfect steadfastness, this might be true in fact as it is plausible in theory. But the case here is much the same as the case with the Greek and Latin studies of our schoolboys. The elaborate philological groundwork which we require them to lay is in theory an admirable preparation for appreciating the Greek and Latin authors worthily. The more thoroughly we lay the groundwork, the better we shall be able, it may be said, to enjoy the authors. True, if time were not so short, and schoolboys' wits not so soon tired and their power of attention exhausted; only, as it is, the elaborate philological preparation goes on, but the authors are little known and less enjoyed. So with the investigator of "historic origins" in poetry. He ought to enjoy the true classic all the better for his investigations; he often is distracted from the enjoyment of the best, and with the less good he overbusies himself, and is prone to overrate it in proportion to the trouble which it has cost him.

The idea of tracing historic origins and historical relationships cannot be absent from a compilation like the present. And naturally the poets to be exhibited in it will be assigned to those persons for exhibition who are known to prize them highly, rather than to those who have no special inclination towards them. Moreover the very occupation with an author, and the business of exhibiting him, disposes us to affirm and amplify his importance. In the present work, therefore, we are sure of frequent temptation to adopt the historic estimate, or the personal estimate, and to forget the real estimate; which latter, nevertheless, we must employ if we are to make poetry yield us its full benefit. So high is that benefit, the benefit of clearly feeling and of deeply enjoying the really excellent, the truly classic in poetry, that we do well, I say, to set it fixedly before our minds as our object in studying poets and poetry, and to make the desire of attaining it the one principle to which, as the *Imitation* says, whatever we may read or come to know, we always return. *Cum multa legeris et cognoveris, ad unum semper oportet redire principium.*[8]

The historic estimate is likely in especial to affect our judgment and our language when we are dealing with ancient poets; the personal estimate when we are dealing with poets our contemporaries, or at any rate modern. The exaggerations due to the historic estimate are not in themselves, perhaps, of very much gravity. Their report hardly enters the general ear; probably they do not always impose even on the literary men who adopt them. But they lead to a dangerous abuse of language. So we hear Cædmon,[9] amongst our own poets, compared to Milton. I have already noticed the enthusiasm of one accomplished French critic for "historic origins." Another eminent French critic, M. Vitet, comments upon that famous document of the early poetry of his nation, the *Chanson de Roland.*[1] It is indeed a most interesting document. The *joculator* or *jongleur*[2] Taillefer, who was with William the Conqueror's army at Hastings, marched before the Norman troops, so said the tradition, singing "of Charlemagne and of Roland and of Oliver, and of the vassals who died at Roncevaux"; and it is suggested that in the *Chanson de Roland* by one Turoldus or *Théroulde*, a poem preserved in a manuscript of the twelfth century in the Bodleian Library at Oxford, we have certainly the matter, perhaps even some of the words, of the chant which Taillefer sang. The poem has vigor and freshness; it is not without pathos. But M. Vitet is not satisfied with seeing in it a document of some poetic value, and of very high historic and linguistic value; he sees in it a grand and beautiful work, a monument of epic genius. In its general design he finds the grandiose conception, in its details he finds the constant union of simplicity with greatness, which are the marks, he truly says, of the genuine epic, and distinguish it from the artificial epic of literary ages. One thinks of Homer; this is the sort of praise which is given to Homer, and justly given. Higher praise there cannot well be, and it is the praise due to epic poetry of the highest order only, and to no other. Let us try, then, the *Chanson de Ro-*

8. "When you have read and learned many things, you ought always to return to the one principle" (*The Imitation of Christ* III.43, famous devotional work by Thomas à Kempis, 1380–1471).
9. 7th-century Old English poet.

1. 11th-century epic poem in Old French which tells of the wars of Charlemagne against the Moors in Spain, and of the bravery of the French leaders, Roland and Oliver.
2. I.e., minstrel.

land at its best. Roland, mortally wounded, lays himself down under
a pine tree, with his face turned towards Spain and the enemy—

> *De plusurs choses à remembrer li prist,*
> *De tantes teres cume li bers cunquist,*
> *De dulce France, des humes de sun lign,*
> *De Carlemagne sun seignor ki l'nurrit.*[3]

That is primitive work, I repeat, with an undeniable poetic quality
of its own. It deserves such praise, and such praise is sufficient for
it. But now turn to Homer—

> Ὣς φάτο τοὺς δ' ἤδη κάτεχεν φυσίζοος αἶα
> ἐν Λακεδαίμονι αὖθι, φίλῃ ἐν πατρίδι γαίῃ.[4]

We are here in another world, another order of poetry altogether;
here is rightly due such supreme praise as that which M. Vitet gives
to the *Chanson de Roland*. If our words are to have any meaning,
if our judgments are to have any solidity, we must not heap that
supreme praise upon poetry of an order immeasurably inferior.

Indeed there can be no more useful help for discovering what
poetry belongs to the class of the truly excellent, and can therefore do us most good, than to have always in one's mind lines and
expressions of the great masters, and to apply them as a touchstone
to other poetry. Of course we are not to require this other poetry
to resemble them; it may be very dissimilar. But if we have any tact
we shall find them, when we have lodged them well in our minds,
an infallible touchstone for detecting the presence or absence of
high poetic quality, and also the degree of this quality, in all other
poetry which we may place beside them. Short passages, even single
lines, will serve our turn quite sufficiently. Take the two lines which
I have just quoted from Homer, the poet's comment on Helen's
mention of her brothers—or take his

> Ἆ δειλώ, τί σφῶϊ δόμεν Πηληϊ ἄνακτι
> θνητῷ; ὑμεῖς δ' ἐστὸν ἀγήρω τ' ἀθανάτω τε.
> ἦ ἵνα δυστήνοισι μετ' ἀνδράσιν ἄλγε' ἔχητον;[5]

the address of Zeus to the horses of Peleus—or take finally his

> Καὶ σέ, γέρον, τὸ πρὶν μὲν ἀκούομεν ὄλβιον εἶναι·[6]

---

3. " 'Then began he to call many things
to remembrance—all the lands which his
valor conquered and pleasant France,
and the men of his lineage, and Charlemagne his liege lord who nourished
him.' *Chanson de Roland* III.939–42"
[Arnold's note].
4. " 'So said she; they long since in
Earth's soft arms were reposing, /
There, in their own dear land, their
fatherland, Lacedaemon.' *Iliad* III.243–

44 (translated by Dr. Hawtrey)" [Ar-
nold's note].
5. " 'Ah, unhappy pair, why gave we
you to King Peleus, to a mortal? but
ye are without old age, and immortal.
Was it that with men born to misery ye
might have sorrow?' *Iliad* XVII.443–
45" [Arnold's note].
6. " 'Nay, and thou too, old man, in
former days wast, as we hear, happy.'
Iliad XXIV.543" [Arnold's note].

the words of Achilles to Priam, a suppliant before him. Take that incomparable line and a half of Dante, Ugolino's tremendous words—

> Io no piangeva; sì dentro impietrai.
> Piangevan elli . . .[7]

take the lovely words of Beatrice to Virgil—

> Io son fatta da Dio, sua mercè, tale,
> Che la vostra miseria non mi tange,
> Nè fiamma d'esto incendio non m'assale . . .[8]

take the simple, but perfect, single line—

> In la sua volontade è nostra pace.[9]

Take of Shakespeare a line or two of Henry the Fourth's expostulation with sleep—

> Wilt thou upon the high and giddy mast
> Seal up the shipboy's eyes, and rock his brains
> In cradle of the rude imperious surge . . .[1]

and take, as well, Hamlet's dying request to Horatio—

> If thou didst ever hold me in thy heart,
> Absent thee from felicity awhile,
> And in this harsh world draw thy breath in pain,
> To tell my story . . .[2]

Take of Milton that Miltonic passage—

> Darkened so, yet shone
> Above them all the archangel; but his face
> Deep scars of thunder had intrenched, and care
> Sat on his faded cheek . . .[3]

add two such lines as—

> And courage never to submit or yield
> And what is else not to be overcome . . .[4]

and finish with the exquisite close to the loss of Proserpine, the loss

> . . . which cost Ceres all that pain
> To seek her through the world.[5]

7. " 'I wailed not, so of stone I grew within; *they* wailed.' *Inferno* XXXIII. 49–50" [Arnold's note].
8. " 'Of such sort hath God, thanked be His mercy, made me, that your misery toucheth me not, neither doth the flame of this fire strike me.' *Inferno* II.91–93" [Arnold's note].
9. " 'In His will is our peace.' *Paradiso* III.85" [Arnold's note].
1. *2 Henry IV* III.i.18–20.
2. *Hamlet* V.ii.357–60.
3. *Paradise Lost* I.599–602.
4. *Ibid.* I.108–9.
5. *Ibid.* IV.271–72.

These few lines, if we have tact and can use them, are enough even of themselves to keep clear and sound our judgments about poetry, to save us from fallacious estimates of it, to conduct us to a real estimate.

The specimens I have quoted differ widely from one another, but they have in common this: the possession of the very highest poetical quality. If we are thoroughly penetrated by their power, we shall find that we have acquired a sense enabling us, whatever poetry may be laid before us, to feel the degree in which a high poetical quality is present or wanting there. Critics give themselves great labor to draw out what in the abstract constitutes the characters of a high quality of poetry. It is much better simply to have recourse to concrete examples—to take specimens of poetry of the high, the very highest quality, and to say: The characters of a high quality of poetry are what is expressed *there*. They are far better recognized by being felt in the verse of the master, than by being perused in the prose of the critic. Nevertheless if we are urgently pressed to give some critical account of them, we may safely, perhaps, venture on laying down, not indeed how and why the characters arise, but where and in what they arise. They are in the matter and substance of the poetry, and they are in its manner and style. Both of these, the substance and matter on the one hand, the style and manner on the other, have a mark, an accent, of high beauty, worth, and power. But if we are asked to define this mark and accent in the abstract, our answer must be: No, for we should thereby be darkening the question, not clearing it. The mark and accent are as given by the substance and matter of that poetry, by the style and manner of that poetry, and of all other poetry which is akin to it in quality.

Only one thing we may add as to the substance and matter of poetry, guiding ourselves by Aristotle's profound observation that the superiority of poetry over history consists in its possessing a higher truth and a higher seriousness ($\phi\iota\lambda o\sigma o\phi\acute{\omega}\tau\epsilon\rho o\nu$ $\kappa\alpha\grave{\iota}$ $\sigma\pi o\upsilon\delta\alpha\iota\acute{o}\tau\epsilon\rho o\nu$).[6] Let us add, therefore, to what we have said, this: that the substance and matter of the best poetry acquire their special character from possessing, in an eminent degree, truth and seriousness. We may add yet further, what is in itself evident, that to the style and manner of the best poetry their special character, their accent, is given by their diction, and, even yet more, by their movement. And though we distinguish between the two characters, the two accents, of superiority, yet they are nevertheless vitally connected one with the other. The superior character of truth and seriousness, in the matter and substance of the best poetry, is inseparable from the superiority of diction and movement marking its style and manner. The two superiorities are closely related, and

6. Aristotle, *Poetics* IX.

are in steadfast proportion one to the other. So far as high poetic truth and seriousness are wanting to a poet's matter and substance, so far also, we may be sure, will a high poetic stamp of diction and movement be wanting to his style and manner. In proportion as this high stamp of diction and movement, again, is absent from a poet's style and manner, we shall find, also, that high poetic truth and seriousness are absent from his substance and matter.

So stated, these are but dry generalities; their whole force lies in their application. And I could wish every student of poetry to make the application of them for himself. Made by himself, the application would impress itself upon his mind far more deeply than made by me. Neither will my limits allow me to make any full application of the generalities above propounded; but in the hope of bringing out, at any rate, some significance in them, and of establishing an important principle more firmly by their means, I will, in the space which remains to me, follow rapidly from the commencement the course of our English poetry with them in my view.

Once more I return to the early poetry of France, with which our own poetry, in its origins, is indissolubly connected. In the twelfth and thirteenth centuries, that seed time of all modern language and literature, the poetry of France had a clear predominance in Europe. Of the two divisions of that poetry, its productions in the *langue d'oïl* and its productions in the *langue d'oc*,[7] the poetry of the *langue d'oc*, of southern France, of the troubadours, is of importance because of its effect on Italian literature—the first literature of modern Europe to strike the true and grand note, and to bring forth, as in Dante and Petrarch it brought forth, classics. But the predominance of French poetry in Europe, during the twelfth and thirteenth centuries, is due to its poetry of the *langue d'oïl*, the poetry of northern France and of the tongue which is now the French language. In the twelfth century the bloom of this romance poetry was earlier and stronger in England, at the court of our Anglo-Norman kings, than in France itself. But it was a bloom of French poetry; and as our native poetry formed itself, it formed itself out of this. The romance poems which took possession of the heart and imagination of Europe in the twelfth and thirteenth centuries are French; "they are," as Southey justly says, "the pride of French literature, nor have we anything which can be placed in competition with them." Themes were supplied from all quarters: but the romance setting which was common to them all, and which gained the ear of Europe, was French. This constituted for the French poetry, literature, and language, at the height of the Middle Age, an unchallenged predominance. The

7. Medieval dialects of France; in the northern dialect, from which modern French derives, the word *oui* ("yes") was pronounced *oïl;* in the southern dialect it was pronounced *oc.*

Italian Brunetto Latini, the master of Dante, wrote his *Treasure* in French because, he says, "*la parleure en est plus délitable et plus commune à toutes gens.*"[8] In the same century, the thirteenth, the French romance writer, Christian of Troyes, formulates the claims, in chivalry and letters, of France, his native country, as follows:

> *Or vous ert par ce livre apris,*
> *Que Gresse ot de chevalerie*
> *Le premier los et de clergie;*
> *Puis vint chevalerie à Rome,*
> *Et de la clergie la some,*
> *Qui ore est en France venue.*
> *Diex doinst qu'ele i soit retenue*
> *Et que li lius li abelisse*
> *Tant que de France n'isse*
> *L'onor qui s'i est arestée!*

"Now by this book you will learn that first Greece had the renown for chivalry and letters; then chivalry and the primacy in letters passed to Rome, and now it is come to France. God grant it may be kept there; and that the place may please it so well, that the honor which has come to make stay in France may never depart thence!"

Yet it is now all gone, this French romance poetry, of which the weight of substance and the power of style are not unfairly represented by this extract from Christian of Troyes. Only by means of the historic estimate can we persuade ourselves now to think that any of it is of poetical importance.

But in the fourteenth century there comes an Englishman nourished on this poetry; taught his trade by this poetry, getting words, rhyme, meter from this poetry; for even of that stanza which the Italians used, and which Chaucer derived immediately from the Italians, the basis and suggestion was probably given in France. Chaucer (I have already named him) fascinated his contemporaries, but so too did Christian of Troyes and Wolfram of Eschenbach.[9] Chaucer's power of fascination, however, is enduring; his poetical importance does not need the assistance of the historic estimate; it is real. He is a genuine source of joy and strength, which is flowing still for us and will flow always. He will be read, as time goes on, far more generally than he is read now. His language is a cause of difficulty for us; but so also, and I think in quite as great a degree, is the language of Burns. In Chaucer's case, as in that of Burns, it is a difficulty to be unhesitatingly accepted and overcome.

If we ask ourselves wherein consists the immense superiority of Chaucer's poetry over the romance poetry—why it is that in passing from this to Chaucer we suddenly feel ourselves to be in an-

8. "French speech is more delightful and more commonly known to all peo-   ples."
9. 12th-century German poet.

other world, we shall find that his superiority is both in the substance of his poetry and in the style of his poetry. His superiority
in substance is given by his large, free, simple, clear yet kindly view
of human life—so unlike the total want, in the romance poets, of
all intelligent command of it. Chaucer has not their helplessness;
he has gained the power to survey the world from a central, a
truly human point of view. We have only to call to mind the Prologue to *The Canterbury Tales*. The right comment upon it is Dryden's: "It is sufficient to say, according to the proverb, that *here
is God's plenty*." And again: "He is a perpetual fountain of good
sense."[1] It is by a large, free, sound representation of things, that
poetry, this high criticism of life, has truth of substance; and
Chaucer's poetry has truth of substance.

Of his style and manner, if we think first of the romance poetry
and then of Chaucer's divine liquidness of diction, his divine fluidity of movement, it is difficult to speak temperately. They are irresistible, and justify all the rapture with which his successors speak
of his "gold dewdrops of speech."[2] Johnson misses the point entirely when he finds fault with Dryden for ascribing to Chaucer
the first refinement of our numbers, and says that Gower[3] also can
show smooth numbers and easy rhymes. The refinement of our
numbers means something far more than this. A nation may have
versifiers with smooth numbers and easy rhymes, and yet may have
no real poetry at all. Chaucer is the father of our splendid English poetry; he is our "well of English undefiled,"[4] because by the
lovely charm of his diction, the lovely charm of his movement, he
makes an epoch and founds a tradition. In Spenser, Shakespeare,
Milton, Keats, we can follow the tradition of the liquid diction,
the fluid movement, of Chaucer; at one time it is his liquid diction
of which in these poets we feel the virtue, and at another time it
is his fluid movement. And the virtue is irresistible.

Bounded as is my space, I must yet find room for an example
of Chaucer's virtue, as I have given examples to show the virtue
of the great classics. I feel disposed to say that a single line is
enough to show the charm of Chaucer's verse; that merely one
line like this—

O martyr souded[5] in virginitee!

has a virtue of manner and movement such as we shall not find
in all the verse of romance poetry—but this is saying nothing. The

1. Both quotations are from Dryden's
Preface to his *Fables* (1700).
2. *The Life of Our Lady*, a poem by
John Lydgate (ca. 1370–ca. 1451).
3. John Gower (ca. 1325–1408), friend
of Chaucer and author of the *Con-
fessio Amantis*, a long poem in octo-
syllabic couplets.

4. Said of Chaucer by Spenser (*Faerie
Queene* IV.ii.32).
5. "The French *soudé*: soldered, fixed
fast" [Arnold's note]. The line is from
the Prioress's Tale (line 127): Chaucer
wrote "souded to" rather than "souded
in."

virtue is such as we shall not find, perhaps, in all English poetry, outside the poets whom I have named as the special inheritors of Chaucer's tradition. A single line, however, is too little if we have not the strain of Chaucer's verse well in our memory; let us take a stanza. It is from *The Prioress's Tale*, the story of the Christian child murdered in a Jewry—

> My throte is cut unto my nekke-bone
> Saidè this child, and as by way of kinde
> I should have deyd, yea, longè time agone;
> But Jesu Christ, as ye in bookès finde,
> Will that his glory last and be in minde,
> And for the worship of his mother dere
> Yet may I sing O *Alma* loud and clere.

Wordsworth has modernized this Tale, and to feel how delicate and evanescent is the charm of verse, we have only to read Wordsworth's first three lines of this stanza after Chaucer's—

> My throat is cut unto the bone, I trow,
> Said this young child, and by the law of kind
> I should have died, yea, many hours ago.

The charm is departed. It is often said that the power of liquidness and fluidity in Chaucer's verse was dependent upon a free, a licentious dealing with language, such as is now impossible; upon a liberty, such as Burns too enjoyed, of making words like *neck*, *bird*, into a dissyllable by adding to them, and words like *cause*, *rhyme*, into a dissyllable by sounding the *e* mute. It is true that Chaucer's fluidity is conjoined with this liberty, and is admirably served by it; but we ought not to say that it was dependent upon it. It was dependent upon his talent. Other poets with a like liberty do not attain to the fluidity of Chaucer; Burns himself does not attain to it. Poets, again, who have a talent akin to Chaucer's, such as Shakespeare or Keats, have known how to attain to his fluidity without the like liberty.

And yet Chaucer is not one of the great classics. His poetry transcends and effaces, easily and without effort, all the romance poetry of Catholic Christendom; it transcends and effaces all the English poetry contemporary with it, it transcends and effaces all the English poetry subsequent to it down to the age of Elizabeth. Of such avail is poetic truth of substance, in its natural and necessary union with poetic truth of style. And yet, I say, Chaucer is not one of the great classics. He has not their accent. What is wanting to him is suggested by the mere mention of the name of the first great classic of Christendom, the immortal poet who died eighty years before Chaucer—Dante. The accent of such verse as

In la sua volontade è nostra pace . . .

is altogether beyond Chaucer's reach; we praise him, but we feel that this accent is out of the question for him. It may be said that it was necessarily out of the reach of any poet in the England of that stage of growth. Possibly; but we are to adopt a real, not a historic, estimate of poetry. However we may account for its absence, something is wanting, then, to the poetry of Chaucer, which poetry must have before it can be placed in the glorious class of the best. And there is no doubt what that something is. It is the σπουδαιότης, the high and excellent seriousness, which Aristotle assigns as one of the grand virtues of poetry. The substance of Chaucer's poetry, his view of things and his criticism of life, has largeness, freedom, shrewdness, benignity; but it has not this high seriousness. Homer's criticism of life has it, Dante's has it, Shakespeare's has it. It is this chiefly which gives to our spirits what they can rest upon; and with the increasing demands of our modern ages upon poetry, this virtue of giving us what we can rest upon will be more and more highly esteemed. A voice from the slums of Paris, fifty or sixty years after Chaucer, the voice of poor Villon[6] out of his life of riot and crime, has at its happy moments (as, for instance, in the last stanza of *La Belle Heaulmière*[7]) more of this important poetic virtue of seriousness than all the productions of Chaucer. But its apparition in Villon, and in men like Villon, is fitful; the greatness of the great poets, the power of their criticism of life, is that their virtue is sustained.

To our praise, therefore, of Chaucer as a poet there must be this limitation: he lacks the high seriousness of the great classics, and therewith an important part of their virtue. Still, the main fact for us to bear in mind about Chaucer is his sterling value according to that real estimate which we firmly adopt for all poets. He has poetic truth of substance, though he has not high poetic seriousness, and corresponding to his truth of substance he has an exquisite virtue of style and manner. With him is born our real poetry.

For my present purpose I need not dwell on our Elizabethan poetry, or on the continuation and close of this poetry in Milton. We all of us profess to be agreed in the estimate of this poetry; we all of us recognize it as great poetry, our greatest, and Shake-

---

6. François Villon (1431–84), French poet and vagabond.

7. "The name *Heaulmière* is said to be derived from a headdress (helm) worn as a mask by courtesans. In Villon's ballad, a poor old creature of this class laments her days of youth and beauty. The last stanza of the ballad runs thus —'*Ainsi le bon temps regretons / Entre nous, pauvres vieilles sottes, / Assises bas, à croppetons, / Tout en ung tas comme pelottes; / A petit feu de chenevottes / Tost allumées, tost estainctes, / Et jadis fusmes si mignottes! / Ainsi en prend à maintz et maintes.*' [It may be translated:] 'Thus amongst ourselves we regret the good time, poor silly old things, low-seated on our heels, all in a heap like so many balls; by a little fire of hemp stalks, soon lighted, soon spent. And once we were such darlings! So fares it with many and many a one'" [Arnold's note].

speare and Milton as our poetical classics. The real estimate, here, has universal currency. With the next age of our poetry divergency and difficulty begin. An historic estimate of that poetry has established itself; and the question is, whether it will be found to coincide with the real estimate.

The age of Dryden, together with our whole eighteenth century which followed it, sincerely believed itself to have produced poetical classics of its own, and even to have made advance, in poetry, beyond all its predecessors. Dryden regards as not seriously disputable the opinion "that the sweetness of English verse was never understood or practiced by our fathers."[8] Cowley could see nothing at all in Chaucer's poetry. Dryden heartily admired it, and, as we have seen, praised its matter admirably; but of its exquisite manner and movement all he can find to say is that "there is the rude sweetness of a Scotch tune in it, which is natural and pleasing, though not perfect."[9] Addison, wishing to praise Chaucer's numbers, compares them with Dryden's own. And all through the eighteenth century, and down even into our own times, the stereotyped phrase of approbation for good verse found in our early poetry has been, that it even approached the verse of Dryden, Addison, Pope, and Johnson.

Are Dryden and Pope poetical classics? Is the historic estimate, which represents them as such, and which has been so long established that it cannot easily give way, the real estimate? Wordsworth and Coleridge, as is well known, denied it; but the authority of Wordsworth and Coleridge does not weigh much with the young generation, and there are many signs to show that the eighteenth century and its judgments are coming into favor again. Are the favorite poets of the eighteenth century classics?

It is impossible within my present limits to discuss the question fully. And what man of letters would not shrink from seeming to dispose dictatorially of the claims of two men who are, at any rate, such masters in letters as Dryden and Pope; two men of such admirable talent, both of them, and one of them, Dryden, a man, on all sides, of such energetic and genial power? And yet, if we are to gain the full benefit from poetry, we must have the real estimate of it. I cast about for some mode of arriving, in the present case, at such an estimate without offense. And perhaps the best way is to begin, as it is easy to begin, with cordial praise.

When we find Chapman, the Elizabethan translator of Homer, expressing himself in his preface thus: "Though truth in her very nakedness sits in so deep a pit, that from Gades to Aurora and Ganges few eyes can sound her, I hope yet those few here will so

8. Dryden's *Essay on Dramatic Poesy.* Cowley is the poet. Abraham Cowley (1618–67).
9. Dryden's Preface to his *Fables.*

discover and confirm that, the date being out of her darkness in this morning of our poet, he shall now gird his temples with the sun," we pronounce that such a prose is intolerable. When we find Milton writing: "And long it was not after, when I was confirmed in this opinion, that he, who would not be frustrate of his hope to write well hereafter in laudable things, ought himself to be a true poem"[1]—we pronounce that such a prose has its own grandeur, but that it is obsolete and inconvenient. But when we find Dryden telling us: "What Virgil wrote in the vigor of his age, in plenty and at ease, I have undertaken to translate in my declining years; struggling with wants, oppressed with sickness, curbed in my genius, liable to be misconstrued in all I write"[2]—then we exclaim that here at last we have the true English prose, a prose such as we would all gladly use if we only knew how. Yet Dryden was Milton's contemporary.

But after the Restoration the time had come when our nation felt the imperious need of a fit prose. So, too, the time had likewise come when our nation felt the imperious need of freeing itself from the absorbing preoccupation which religion in the Puritan age had exercised. It was impossible that this freedom should be brought about without some negative excess, without some neglect and impairment of the religious life of the soul; and the spiritual history of the eighteenth century shows us that the freedom was not achieved without them. Still, the freedom was achieved; the preoccupation, an undoubtedly baneful and retarding one if it had continued, was got rid of. And as with religion amongst us at that period, so it was also with letters. A fit prose was a necessity; but it was impossible that a fit prose should establish itself amongst us without some touch of frost to the imaginative life of the soul. The needful qualities for a fit prose are regularity, uniformity, precision, balance. The men of letters, whose destiny it may be to bring their nation to the attainment of a fit prose, must of necessity, whether they work in prose or in verse, give a predominating, an almost exclusive attention to the qualities of regularity, uniformity, precision, balance. But an almost exclusive attention to these qualities involves some repression and silencing of poetry.

We are to regard Dryden as the puissant and glorious founder, Pope as the splendid high priest, of our age of prose and reason, of our excellent and indispensable eighteenth century. For the purposes of their mission and destiny their poetry, like their prose, is admirable. Do you ask me whether Dryden's verse, take it almost where you will, is not good?

> A milk-white Hind, immortal and unchanged,
> Fed on the lawns and in the forest ranged.[3]

1. Milton's *Apology for Smectymnuus.* in his translation of Virgil.
2. Dryden's *Postscript to the Reader* 3. *The Hind and the Panther* I.1–2.

I answer: Admirable for the purposes of the inaugurator of an age of prose and reason. Do you ask me whether Pope's verse, take it almost where you will, is not good?

> To Hounslow Heath I point, and Banstead Down;
> Thence comes your mutton, and these chicks my own.[4]

I answer: Admirable for the purposes of the high priest of an age of prose and reason. But do you ask me whether such verse proceeds from men with an adequate poetic criticism of life, from men whose criticism of life has a high seriousness, or even, without that high seriousness, has poetic largeness, freedom, insight, benignity? Do you ask me whether the application of ideas to life in the verse of these men, often a powerful application, no doubt, is a powerful *poetic* application? Do you ask me whether the poetry of these men has either the matter or the inseparable manner of such an adequate poetic criticism; whether it has the accent of

> Absent thee from felicity awhile . . .

or of

> And what is else not to be overcome . . .

or of

> O martyr souded in virginitee!

I answer: It has not and cannot have them; it is the poetry of the builders of an age of prose and reason. Though they may write in verse, though they may in a certain sense be masters of the art of versification, Dryden and Pope are not classics of our poetry, they are classics of our prose.

Gray is our poetical classic of that literature and age; the position of Gray is singular, and demands a word of notice here. He has not the volume or the power of poets who, coming in times more favorable, have attained to an independent criticism of life. But he lived with the great poets, he lived, above all, with the Greeks, through perpetually studying and enjoying them; and he caught their poetic point of view for regarding life, caught their poetic manner. The point of view and the manner are not self-sprung in him, he caught them of others; and he had not the free and abundant use of them. But whereas Addison and Pope never had the use of them, Gray had the use of them at times. He is the scantiest and frailest of classics in our poetry, but he is a classic.

And now, after Gray, we are met, as we draw towards the end of the eighteenth century, we are met by the great name of Burns. We enter now on times where the personal estimate of poets begins to be rife, and where the real estimate of them is not reached

4. *Imitations of Horace,* Satire II.ii. 143–44.

without difficulty. But in spite of the disturbing pressures of personal partiality, of national partiality, let us try to reach a real estimate of the poetry of Burns.

By his English poetry Burns in general belongs to the eighteenth century, and has little importance for us.

> Mark ruffian Violence, distained with crimes,
> Rousing elate in these degenerate times;
> View unsuspecting Innocence a prey,
> As guileful Fraud points out the erring way;
> While subtle Litigation's pliant tongue
> The life-blood equal sucks of Right and Wrong![5]

Evidently this is not the real Burns, or his name and fame would have disappeared long ago. Nor is Clarinda's love-poet, Sylvander,[6] the real Burns either. But he tells us himself: "These English songs gravel me to death. I have not the command of the language that I have of my native tongue. In fact, I think that my ideas are more barren in English than in Scotch. I have been at *Duncan Gray* to dress it in English, but all I can do is desperately stupid."[7] We English turn naturally, in Burns, to the poems in our own language, because we can read them easily; but in those poems we have not the real Burns.

The real Burns is of course in his Scotch poems. Let us boldly say that of much of this poetry, a poetry dealing perpetually with Scotch drink, Scotch religion, and Scotch manners, a Scotchman's estimate is apt to be personal. A Scotchman is used to this world of Scotch drink, Scotch religion, and Scotch manners; he has a tenderness for it; he meets its poet half way. In this tender mood he reads pieces like the *Holy Fair* or *Halloween*. But this world of Scotch drink, Scotch religion, and Scotch manners is against a poet, not for him, when it is not a partial countryman who reads him; for in itself it is not a beautiful world, and no one can deny that it is of advantage to a poet to deal with a beautiful world. Burns's world of Scotch drink, Scotch religion, and Scotch manners, is often a harsh, a sordid, a repulsive world; even the world of his *Cotter's Saturday Night* is not a beautiful world. No doubt a poet's criticism of life may have such truth and power that it triumphs over its world and delights us. Burns may triumph over his world, often he does triumph over his world, but let us observe how and where. Burns is the first case we have had where the bias of the personal estimate tends to mislead; let us look at him closely, he can bear it.

Many of his admirers will tell us that we have Burns, convivial, genuine, delightful, here—

5. *On the Death of Lord President Dundas,* lines 25–30.
6. Burns, styling himself Sylvander, carried on an idyllic correspondence with a Mrs. Maclehose, addressing her as Clarinda.
7. Letter to George Thomson, October 19, 1794.

> Leeze me on drink! it gies us mair
>   Than either school or college;
> It kindles wit, it waukens lair,
>   It pangs us fou o' knowledge.
> Be't whisky gill or penny wheep
>   Or ony stronger potion,
> It never fails, on drinking deep,
>   To kittle up our notion
>   By night or day.[8]

There is a great deal of that sort of thing in Burns, and it is un-satisfactory, not because it is bacchanalian poetry, but because it has not that accent of sincerity which bacchanalian poetry, to do it justice, very often has. There is something in it of bravado, something which makes us feel that we have not the man speaking to us with his real voice; something, therefore, poetically unsound.

With still more confidence will his admirers tell us that we have the genuine Burns, the great poet, when his strain asserts the independence, equality, dignity, of men, as in the famous song *For A' That and A' That*—

> A prince can mak' a belted knight,
>   A marquis, duke, and a' that;
> But an honest man's aboon his might,
>   Guid faith he mauna fa' that!
>   For a' that, and a' that,
>   Their dignities, and a' that,
>   The pith o' sense, and pride o' worth,
>   Are higher rank than a' that.

Here they find his grand, genuine touches; and still more, when this puissant genius, who so often set morality at defiance, falls moralizing—

> The sacred lowe o' weel-placed love
>   Luxuriantly indulge it;
> But never tempt th' illicit rove,
>   Though naething should divulge it.
> I waive the quantum o' the sin,
>   The hazard o' concealing,
> But och! it hardens a' within,
>   And petrifies the feeling.[9]

Or in a higher strain—

> Who made the heart, 'tis He alone
>   Decidedly can try us;
> He knows each chord, its various tone;
>   Each spring, its various bias.
> Then at the balance let's be mute,

---

8. *The Holy Fair*, lines 163–71.   9. *Epistle to a Young Friend*, lines 41–48.

> We never can adjust it;
> What's *done* we partly may compute,
> But know not what's resisted.[1]

Or in a better strain yet, a strain, his admirers will say, unsurpassable—

> To make a happy fireside clime
> To weans and wife,
> That's the true pathos and sublime
> Of human life.[2]

There is criticism of life for you, the admirers of Burns will say to us; there is the application of ideas to life! There is, undoubtedly. The doctrine of the last-quoted lines coincides almost exactly with what was the aim and end, Xenophon tells us, of all the teaching of Socrates. And the application is a powerful one; made by a man of vigorous understanding, and (need I say?) a master of language.

But for supreme poetical success more is required than the powerful application of ideas to life; it must be an application under the conditions fixed by the laws of poetic truth and poetic beauty. Those laws fix as an essential condition, in the poet's treatment of such matters as are here in question, high seriousness—the high seriousness which comes from absolute sincerity. The accent of high seriousness, born of absolute sincerity, is what gives to such verse as

In la sua volontade è nostra pace . . .

to such criticism of life as Dante's, its power. Is this accent felt in the passages which I have been quoting from Burns? Surely not; surely, if our sense is quick, we must perceive that we have not in those passages a voice from the very inmost soul of the genuine Burns; he is not speaking to us from these depths, he is more or less preaching. And the compensation for admiring such passages less, for missing the perfect poetic accent in them, will be that we shall admire more the poetry where that accent is found.

No; Burns, like Chaucer, comes short of the high seriousness of the great classics, and the virtue of matter and manner which goes with that high seriousness is wanting to his work. At moments he touches it in a profound and passionate melancholy, as in those four immortal lines taken by Byron as a motto for *The Bride of Abydos*, but which have in them a depth of poetic quality such as resides in no verse of Byron's own—

> Had we never loved sae kindly,
> Had we never loved sae blindly,

1. *Address to the Unco Guid*, lines 57–64. 2. *Epistle to Dr. Blacklock*, lines 51–54.

> Never met, or never parted,
> We had ne'er been broken-hearted.[3]

But a whole poem of that quality Burns cannot make; the rest, in the *Farewell to Nancy*, is verbiage.

We arrive best at the real estimate of Burns, I think, by conceiving his work as having truth of matter and truth of manner, but not the accent or the poetic virtue of the highest masters. His genuine criticism of life, when the sheer poet in him speaks, is ironic; it is not—

> Thou Power Supreme, whose mighty scheme
> These woes of mine fulfill,
> Here firm I rest, they must be best
> Because they are Thy will![4]

It is far rather: "Whistle owre the lave o't!"[5] Yet we may say of him as of Chaucer, that of life and the world, as they come before him, his view is large, free, shrewd, benignant—truly poetic, therefore; and his manner of rendering what he sees is to match. But we must note, at the same time, his great difference from Chaucer. The freedom of Chaucer is heightened, in Burns, by a fiery, reckless energy; the benignity of Chaucer deepens, in Burns, into an overwhelming sense of the pathos of things—of the pathos of human nature, the pathos, also, of nonhuman nature. Instead of the fluidity of Chaucer's manner, the manner of Burns has spring, bounding swiftness. Burns is by far the greater force, though he has perhaps less charm. The world of Chaucer is fairer, richer, more significant than that of Burns; but when the largeness and freedom of Burns get full sweep, as in *Tam o' Shanter*, or still more in that puissant and splendid production, *The Jolly Beggars*, his world may be what it will, his poetic genius triumphs over it. In the world of *The Jolly Beggars* there is more than hideousness and squalor, there is bestiality; yet the piece is a superb poetic success. It has a breadth, truth, and power which make the famous scene in Auerbach's Cellar, of Goethe's *Faust*, seem artificial and tame beside it, and which are only matched by Shakespeare and Aristophanes.

Here, where his largeness and freedom serve him so admirably, and also in those poems and songs where to shrewdness he adds infinite archness and wit, and to benignity infinite pathos, where his manner is flawless, and a perfect poetic whole is the result—in things like the address to the mouse whose home he had ruined, in things like *Duncan Gray*, *Tam Glen*, *Whistle and I'll Come to You, My Lad*, *Auld Lang Syne* (this list might be made much longer)—here we have the genuine Burns, of whom the real esti-

---

3. *Ae Fond Kiss* (also called *A Farewell to Nancy*), lines 13–16.
4. *Winter: A Dirge*, lines 17–20.

5. "Whistle over what's left of it." The phrase is a refrain from one of Burns's poems.

mate must be high indeed. Not a classic, nor with the excellent
σπουδαιότης[6] of the great classics, nor with a verse rising to a criticism of life and a virtue like theirs; but a poet with thorough truth
of substance and an answering truth of style, giving us a poetry
sound to the core. We all of us have a leaning towards the pathetic,
and may be inclined perhaps to prize Burns most for his touches
of piercing, sometimes almost intolerable, pathos; for verse like—

> We twa hae paidl't i' the burn
> From mornin' sun till dine;
> But seas between us braid hae roared
> Sin auld lang syne . . .[7]

where he is as lovely as he is sound. But perhaps it is by the perfection of soundness of his lighter and archer masterpieces that
he is poetically most wholesome for us. For the votary misled by
a personal estimate of Shelley, as so many of us have been, are,
and will be—of that beautiful spirit building his many-colored haze
of words and images

> Pinnacled dim in the intense inane[8]—

no contact can be wholesomer than the contact with Burns at his
archest and soundest. Side by side with the

> On the brink of the night and the morning
> My coursers are wont to respire,
> But the Earth has just whispered a warning
> That their flight must be swifter than fire . . .[9]

of *Prometheus Unbound*, how salutary, how very salutary, to place
this from *Tam Glen*—

> My minnie does constantly deave me
> And bids me beware o' young men;
> They flatter, she says, to deceive me;
> But wha can think sae o' Tam Glen?

But we enter on burning ground as we approach the poetry of
times so near to us—poetry like that of Byron, Shelley, and Wordsworth—of which the estimates are so often not only personal, but
personal with passion. For my purpose, it is enough to have taken
the single case of Burns, the first poet we come to of whose work
the estimate formed is evidently apt to be personal, and to have
suggested how we may proceed, using the poetry of the great classics
as a sort of touchstone, to correct this estimate, as we had previously
corrected by the same means the historic estimate where we met
with it. A collection like the present, with its succession of cele-

---

6. "High seriousness."
7. *Auld Lang Syne*, lines 17–20.
8. Shelley, *Prometheus Unbound* III.

iv.204.
9. *Ibid.* II.v.1–4.

brated names and celebrated poems, offers a good opportunity to
us for resolutely endeavoring to make our estimates of poetry real.
I have sought to point out a method which will help us in making
them so, and to exhibit it in use so far as to put anyone who likes
in a way of applying it for himself.

At any rate the end to which the method and the estimate are
designed to lead, and from leading to which, if they do lead to it,
they get their whole value—the benefit of being able clearly to feel
and deeply to enjoy the best, the truly classic, in poetry—is an end,
let me say it once more at parting, of supreme importance. We are
often told that an era is opening in which we are to see multitudes
of a common sort of readers, and masses of a common sort of literature; that such readers do not want and could not relish anything better than such literature, and that to provide it is becoming a vast and profitable industry. Even if good literature entirely
lost currency with the world, it would still be abundantly worth
while to continue to enjoy it by oneself. But it never will lose currency with the world, in spite of momentary appearances; it never
will lose supremacy. Currency and supremacy are insured to it, not
indeed by the world's deliberate and conscious choice, but by something far deeper—by the instinct of self-preservation in humanity.

1880

Literature and Science[1]

Practical people talk with a smile of Plato and of his absolute
ideas: and it is impossible to deny that Plato's ideas do often seem
unpractical and unpracticable, and especially when one views them
in connection with the life of a great work-a-day world like the
United States. The necessary staple of the life of such a world
Plato regards with disdain; handicraft and trade and the working
professions he regards with disdain; but what becomes of the life
of an industrial modern community if you take handicraft and
trade and the working professions out of it? The base mechanic
arts and handicrafts, says Plato, bring about a natural weakness
in the principle of excellence in a man, so that he cannot govern
the ignoble growths in him, but nurses them, and cannot understand fostering any other. Those who exercise such arts and trades,
as they have their bodies, he says, marred by their vulgar businesses,

1. Delivered as a lecture during Arnold's tour of the United States in
1883, and published in *Discourses in
America* (1885), this essay has become
a classic contribution to a subject endlessly debated. Its main argument was
summed up by Stuart P. Sherman: "If
Arnold had said outright that the study
of letters helps us to *bear* the grand
results of science, he would not have
been guilty of a superficial epigram; he
would have spoken from the depths of
his experience."

so they have their souls, too, bowed and broken by them. And if one of these uncomely people has a mind to seek self-culture and philosophy, Plato compares him to a bald little tinker, who has scraped together money, and has got his release from service, and has had a bath, and bought a new coat, and is rigged out like a bridegroom about to marry the daughter of his master who has fallen into poor and helpless estate.

Nor do the working professions fare any better than trade at the hands of Plato. He draws for us an inimitable picture of the working lawyer, and of his life of bondage; he shows how this bondage from his youth up has stunted and warped him, and made him small and crooked of soul, encompassing him with difficulties which he is not man enough to rely on justice and truth as means to encounter, but has recourse, for help out of them, to falsehood and wrong. And so, says Plato, this poor creature is bent and broken, and grows up from boy to man without a particle of soundness in him, although exceedingly smart and clever in his own esteem.

One cannot refuse to admire the artist who draws these pictures. But we say to ourselves that his ideas show the influence of a primitive and obsolete order of things, when the warrior caste and the priestly caste were alone in honor, and the humble work of the world was done by slaves. We have now changed all that; the modern majesty consists in work, as Emerson declares; and in work, we may add, principally of such plain and dusty kind as the work of cultivators of the ground, handicraftsmen, men of trade and business, men of the working professions. Above all is this true in a great industrious community such as that of the United States.

Now education, many people go on to say, is still mainly governed by the ideas of men like Plato, who lived when the warrior caste and the priestly or philosophical class were alone in honor, and the really useful part of the community were slaves. It is an education fitted for persons of leisure in such a community. This education passed from Greece and Rome to the feudal communities of Europe, where also the warrior caste and the priestly caste were alone held in honor, and where the really useful and working part of the community, though not nominally slaves as in the pagan world, were practically not much better off than slaves, and not more seriously regarded. And how absurd it is, people end by saying, to inflict this education upon an industrious modern community, where very few indeed are persons of leisure, and the mass to be considered has not leisure, but is bound, for its own great good, and for the great good of the world at large, to plain labor and to industrial pursuits, and the education in question tends necessarily to make men dissatisfied with these pursuits and unfitted for them!

That is what is said. So far I must defend Plato, as to plead that his view of education and studies is in the general, as it seems to me, sound enough, and fitted for all sorts and conditions of men, whatever their pursuits may be. "An intelligent man," says Plato, "will prize those studies which result in his soul getting soberness, righteousness, and wisdom, and will less value the others."[2] I cannot consider *that* a bad description of the aim of education, and of the motives which should govern us in the choice of studies, whether we are preparing ourselves for a hereditary seat in the English House of Lords or for the pork trade in Chicago.

Still I admit that Plato's world was not ours, that his scorn of trade and handicraft is fantastic, that he had no conception of a great industrial community such as that of the United States, and that such a community must and will shape its education to suit its own needs. If the usual education handed down to it from the past does not suit it, it will certainly before long drop this and try another. The usual education in the past has been mainly literary. The question is whether the studies which were long supposed to be the best for all of us are practically the best now; whether others are not better. The tyranny of the past, many think, weighs on us injuriously in the predominance given to letters in education. The question is raised whether, to meet the needs of our modern life, the predominance ought not now to pass from letters to science; and naturally the question is nowhere raised with more energy than here in the United States. The design of abasing what is called "mere literary instruction and education," and of exalting what is called "sound, extensive, and practical scientific knowledge," is, in this intensely modern world of the United States, even more perhaps than in Europe, a very popular design, and makes great and rapid progress.

I am going to ask whether the present movement for ousting letters from their old predominance in education, and for transferring the predominance in education to the natural sciences, whether this brisk and flourishing movement ought to prevail, and whether it is likely that in the end it really will prevail. An objection may be raised which I will anticipate. My own studies have been almost wholly in letters, and my visits to the field of the natural sciences have been very slight and inadequate, although those sciences have always strongly moved my curiosity. A man of letters, it will perhaps be said, is not competent to discuss the comparative merits of letters and natural science as means of education. To this objection I reply, first of all, that his incompetence, if he attempts the discussion but is really incompetent for it, will be abundantly visible; nobody will be taken in; he will have plenty of sharp observers and critics to save mankind from that danger. But the line I am going to follow is, as you will soon discover, so extremely

2. Plato, *Republic* IX.591.

simple, that perhaps it may be followed without failure even by one who for a more ambitious line of discussion would be quite incompetent.

Some of you may possibly remember a phrase of mine which has been the object of a good deal of comment; an observation to the effect that in our culture, the aim being *to know ourselves and the world*, we have, as the means to this end, *to know the best which has been thought and said in the world*.[3] A man of science, who is also an excellent writer and the very prince of debaters, Professor Huxley, in a discourse at the opening of Sir Josiah Mason's college at Birmingham,[4] laying hold of this phrase, expanded it by quoting some more words of mine, which are these: "The civilized world is to be regarded as now being, for intellectual and spiritual purposes, one great confederation, bound to a joint action and working to a common result; and whose members have for their proper outfit a knowledge of Greek, Roman, and Eastern antiquity, and of one another. Special local and temporary advantages being put out of account, that modern nation will in the intellectual and spiritual sphere make most progress, which most thoroughly carries out this program."

Now on my phrase, thus enlarged, Professor Huxley remarks that when I speak of the above-mentioned knowledge as enabling us to know ourselves and the world, I assert *literature* to contain the materials which suffice for thus making us know ourselves and the world. But it is not by any means clear, says he, that after having learnt all which ancient and modern literatures have to tell us, we have laid a sufficiently broad and deep foundation for that criticism of life, that knowledge of ourselves and the world, which constitutes culture. On the contrary, Professor Huxley declares that he finds himself "wholly unable to admit that either nations or individuals will really advance, if their oufit draws nothing from the stores of physical science. An army without weapons of precision, and with no particular base of operations, might more hopefully enter upon a campaign on the Rhine, than a man, devoid of a knowledge of what physical science has done in the last century, upon a criticism of life."

This shows how needful it is for those who are to discuss any matter together, to have a common understanding as to the sense of the terms they employ—how needful, and how difficult. What Professor Huxley says, implies just the reproach which is so often brought against the study of belles-lettres, as they are called: that the study is an elegant one, but slight and ineffectual; a smattering of Greek and Latin and other ornamental things, of little use for anyone whose object is to get at truth, and to be a practical man.

3. See *The Function of Criticism at the Present Time.*

4. See T. H. Huxley's lecture *Science and Culture.*

So, too, M. Renan[5] talks of the "superficial humanism" of a school course which treats us as if we were all going to be poets, writers, preachers, orators, and he opposes this humanism to positive science, or the critical search after truth. And there is always a tendency in those who are remonstrating against the predominance of letters in education, to understand by letters belles-lettres, and by belles-lettres a superficial humanism, the opposite of science or true knowledge.

But when we talk of knowing Greek and Roman antiquity, for instance, which is the knowledge people have called the humanities, I for my part mean a knowledge which is something more than a superficial humanism, mainly decorative. "I call all teaching *scientific*," says Wolf,[6] the critic of Homer, "which is systematically laid out and followed up to its original sources. For example: a knowledge of classical antiquity is scientific when the remains of classical antiquity are correctly studied in the original languages." There can be no doubt that Wolf is perfectly right; that all learning is scientific which is systematically laid out and followed up to its original sources, and that a genuine humanism is scientific.

When I speak of knowing Greek and Roman antiquity, therefore, as a help to knowing ourselves and the world, I mean more than a knowledge of so much vocabulary, so much grammar, so many portions of authors in the Greek and Latin languages, I mean knowing the Greeks and Romans, and their life and genius, and what they were and did in the world; what we get from them, and what is its value. That, at least, is the ideal; and when we talk of endeavoring to know Greek and Roman antiquity, as a help to knowing ourselves and the world, we mean endeavoring so to know them as to satisfy this ideal, however much we may still fall short of it.

The same also as to knowing our own and other modern nations, with the like aim of getting to understand ourselves and the world. To know the best that has been thought and said by the modern nations, is to know, says Professor Huxley, "only what modern *literatures* have to tell us; it is the criticism of life contained in modern literature." And yet "the distinctive character of our times," he urges, "lies in the vast and constantly increasing part which is played by natural knowledge." And how, therefore, can a man, devoid of knowledge of what physical science has done in the last century, enter hopefully upon a criticism of modern life?

Let us, I say, be agreed about the meaning of the terms we are using. I talk of knowing the best which has been thought and uttered in the world; Professor Huxley says this means knowing *literature*. Literature is a large word; it may mean everything writ-

5. Ernest Renan (1823–92), French religious philosopher and author of *The Life of Jesus*.

6. Friedrich August Wolf (1759–1824), German scholar.

ten with letters or printed in a book. Euclid's *Elements* and Newton's *Principia* are thus literature. All knowledge that reaches us through books is literature. But by literature Professor Huxley means belles-lettres. He means to make me say, that knowing the best which has been thought and said by the modern nations is knowing their belles-lettres and no more. And this is no sufficient equipment, he argues, for a criticism of modern life. But as I do not mean, by knowing ancient Rome, knowing merely more or less of Latin belles-lettres, and taking no account of Rome's military, and political, and legal, and administrative work in the world; and as, by knowing ancient Greece, I understand knowing her as the giver of Greek art, and the guide to a free and right use of reason and to scientific method, and the founder of our mathematics and physics and astronomy and biology—I understand knowing her as all this, and not merely knowing certain Greek poems, and histories, and treatises, and speeches—so as to the knowledge of modern nations also. By knowing modern nations, I mean not merely knowing their belles-lettres, but knowing also what has been done by such men as Copernicus, Galileo, Newton, Darwin. "Our ancestors learned," says Professor Huxley, "that the earth is the center of the visible universe, and that man is the cynosure of things terrestrial; and more especially was it inculcated that the course of nature had no fixed order, but that it could be, and constantly was, altered." "But for us now," continues Professor Huxley, "the notions of the beginning and the end of the world entertained by our forefathers are no longer credible. It is very certain that the earth is not the chief body in the material universe, and that the world is not subordinated to man's use. It is even more certain that nature is the expression of a definite order, with which nothing interferes." "And yet," he cries, "the purely classical education advocated by the representatives of the humanists in our day gives no inkling of all this."

In due place and time I will just touch upon that vexed question of classical education; but at present the question is as to what is meant by knowing the best which modern nations have thought and said. It is not knowing their belles-lettres merely which is meant. To know Italian belles-lettres is not to know Italy, and to know English belles-lettres is not to know England. Into knowing Italy and England there comes a great deal more, Galileo and Newton amongst it. The reproach of being a superficial humanism, a tincture of belles-lettres, may attach rightly enough to some other disciplines; but to the particular discipline recommended when I proposed knowing the best that has been thought and said in the world, it does not apply. In that best I certainly include what in modern times has been thought and said by the great observers and knowers of nature.

There is, therefore, really no question between Professor Huxley and me as to whether knowing the great results of the modern scientific study of nature is not required as a part of our culture, as well as knowing the products of literature and art. But to follow the processes by which those results are reached, ought, say the friends of physical science, to be made the staple of education for the bulk of mankind. And here there does arise a question between those whom Professor Huxley calls with playful sarcasm "the Levites of culture," and those whom the poor humanist is sometimes apt to regard as its Nebuchadnezzars.[7]

The great results of the scientific investigation of nature we are agreed upon knowing, but how much of our study are we bound to give to the processes by which those results are reached? The results have their visible bearing on human life. But all the processes, too, all the items of fact, by which those results are reached and established, are interesting. All knowledge is interesting to a wise man, and the knowledge of nature is interesting to all men. It is very interesting to know, that, from the albuminous white of the egg, the chick in the egg gets the materials for its flesh, bones, blood, and feathers; while, from the fatty yolk of the egg, it gets the heat and energy which enable it at length to break its shell and begin the world. It is less interesting, perhaps, but still it is interesting, to know that when a taper burns, the wax is converted into carbonic acid and water. Moreover, it is quite true that the habit of dealing with facts, which is given by the study of nature, is, as the friends of physical science praise it for being, an excellent discipline. The appeal, in the study of nature, is constantly to observation and experiment; not only is it said that the thing is so, but we can be made to see that it is so. Not only does a man tell us that when a taper burns the wax is converted into carbonic acid and water, as a man may tell us, if he likes, that Charon[8] is punting his ferry boat on the river Styx, or that Victor Hugo is a sublime poet, or Mr. Gladstone the most admirable of statesmen; but we are made to see that the conversion into carbonic acid and water does actually happen. This reality of natural knowledge it is, which makes the friends of physical science contrast it, as a knowledge of things, with the humanist's knowledge, which is, say they, a knowledge of words. And hence Professor Huxley is moved to lay it down that, "for the purpose of attaining real culture, an exclusively scientific education is at least as effectual as an exclusively literary education." And a certain President of the Section for Mechanical Science in the British Association is, in Scripture phrase, "very bold," and de-

7. Huxley implied that the humanists are hidebound conservatives like the Levites, priests who were preoccupied with traditional ritual observances. Arnold implies that the scientists may be like Nebuchadnezzar, a Babylonian king who destroyed the temple of Jerusalem.
8. Boatman in Greek mythology who conducted the souls of the dead across the river Styx.

clares that if a man, in his mental training, "has substituted literature and history for natural science, he has chosen the less useful
alternative." But whether we go these lengths or not, we must all
admit that in natural science the habit gained of dealing with facts
is a most valuable discipline, and that everyone should have some
experience of it.

More than this, however, is demanded by the reformers. It is
proposed to make the training in natural science the main part of
education, for the great majority of mankind at any rate. And here,
I confess, I part company with the friends of physical science, with
whom up to this point I have been agreeing. In differing from
them, however, I wish to proceed with the utmost caution and diffidence. The smallness of my own acquaintance with the disciplines
of natural science is ever before my mind, and I am fearful of doing
these disciplines an injustice. The ability and pugnacity of the
partisans of natural science make them formidable persons to contradict. The tone of tentative inquiry, which befits a being of dim
faculties and bounded knowledge, is the tone I would wish to take
and not to depart from. At present it seems to me, that those who
are for giving to natural knowledge, as they call it, the chief place
in the education of the majority of mankind, leave one important
thing out of their account: the constitution of human nature. But
I put this forward on the strength of some facts not at all recondite,
very far from it; facts capable of being stated in the simplest possible fashion, and to which, if I so state them, the man of science
will, I am sure, be willing to allow their due weight.

Deny the facts altogether, I think, he hardly can. He can hardly
deny, that when we set ourselves to enumerate the powers which
go to the building up of human life, and say that they are the
power of conduct, the power of intellect and knowledge, the power
of beauty, and the power of social life and manners—he can hardly
deny that this scheme, though drawn in rough and plain lines
enough, and not pretending to scientific exactness, does yet give a
fairly true representation of the matter. Human nature is built up
by these powers; we have the need for them all. When we have
rightly met and adjusted the claims of them all, we shall then be in
a fair way for getting soberness and righteousness, with wisdom.
This is evident enough, and the friends of physical science would
admit it.

But perhaps they may not have sufficiently observed another
thing: namely, that the several powers just mentioned are not isolated, but there is, in the generality of mankind, a perpetual tendency to relate them one to another in divers ways. With one such
way of relating them I am particularly concerned now. Following
our instinct for intellect and knowledge, we acquire pieces of knowledge; and presently, in the generality of men, there arises the desire

to relate these pieces of knowledge to our sense for conduct, to our sense for beauty—and there is weariness and dissatisfaction if the desire is balked. Now in this desire lies, I think, the strength of that hold which letters have upon us.

All knowledge is, as I said just now, interesting; and even items of knowledge which from the nature of the case cannot well be related, but must stand isolated in our thoughts, have their interest. Even lists of exceptions have their interest. If we are studying Greek accents, it is interesting to know that *pais* and *pas*, and some other monosyllables of the same form of declension, do not take the circumflex upon the last syllable of the genitive plural, but vary, in this respect, from the common rule. If we are studying physiology, it is interesting to know that the pulmonary artery carries dark blood and the pulmonary vein carries bright blood, departing in this respect from the common rule for the division of labor between the veins and the arteries. But everyone knows how we seek naturally to combine the pieces of our knowledge together, to bring them under general rules, to relate them to principles; and how unsatisfactory and tiresome it would be to go on forever learning lists of exceptions, or accumulating items of fact which must stand isolated.

Well, that same need of relating our knowledge, which operates here within the sphere of our knowledge itself, we shall find operating, also, outside that sphere. We experience, as we go on learning and knowing—the vast majority of us experience—the need of relating what we have learnt and known to the sense which we have in us for conduct, to the sense which we have in us for beauty.

A certain Greek prophetess of Mantineia in Arcadia, Diotima by name, once explained to the philosopher Socrates that love, and impulse, and bent of all kinds, is, in fact, nothing else but the desire in men that good should forever be present to them. This desire for good, Diotima assured Socrates, is our fundamental desire, of which fundamental desire every impulse in us is only some one particular form.[9] And therefore this fundamental desire it is, I suppose—this desire in men that good should be forever present to them—which acts in us when we feel the impulse for relating our knowledge to our sense for conduct and to our sense for beauty. At any rate, with men in general the instinct exists. Such is human nature. And the instinct, it will be admitted, is innocent, and human nature is preserved by our following the lead of its innocent instincts. Therefore, in seeking to gratify this instinct in question, we are following the instinct of self-preservation in humanity.

But, no doubt, some kinds of knowledge cannot be made to directly serve the instinct in question, cannot be directly related to the sense for beauty, to the sense for conduct. These are instrument

9. Plato, *Symposium* 201–7.

knowledges; they lead on to other knowledges, which can. A man who passes his life in instrument knowledges is a specialist. They may be invaluable as instruments to something beyond, for those who have the gift thus to employ them; and they may be disciplines in themselves wherein it is useful for everyone to have some schooling. But it is inconceivable that the generality of men should pass all their mental life with Greek accents or with formal logic. My friend Professor Sylvester,[1] who is one of the first mathematicians in the world, holds transcendental doctrines as to the virtue of mathematics, but those doctrines are not for common men. In the very Senate House and heart of our English Cambridge[2] I once ventured, though not without an apology for my profaneness, to hazard the opinion that for the majority of mankind a little of mathematics, even, goes a long way. Of course this is quite consistent with their being of immense importance as an instrument to something else; but it is the few who have the aptitude for thus using them, not the bulk of mankind.

The natural sciences do not, however, stand on the same footing with these instrument knowledges. Experience shows us that the generality of men will find more interest in learning that, when a taper burns, the wax is converted into carbonic acid and water, or in learning the explanation of the phenomenon of dew, or in learning how the circulation of the blood is carried on, than they find in learning that the genitive plural of *pais* and *pas* does not take the circumflex on the termination. And one piece of natural knowledge is added to another, and others are added to that, and at last we come to propositions so interesting as Mr. Darwin's famous proposition that "our ancestor was a hairy quadruped furnished with a tail and pointed ears, probably arboreal in his habits." Or we come to propositions of such reach and magnitude as those which Professor Huxley delivers, when he says that the notions of our forefathers about the beginning and the end of the world were all wrong, and that nature is the expression of a definite order with which nothing interferes.

Interesting, indeed, these results of science are, important they are, and we should all of us be acquainted with them. But what I now wish you to mark is, that we are still, when they are propounded to us and we receive them, we are still in the sphere of intellect and knowledge. And for the generality of men there will be found, I say, to arise, when they have duly taken in the proposition that their ancestor was "a hairy quadruped furnished with a tail and pointed ears, probably arboreal in his habits," there will be found to arise an invincible desire to relate this proposition to

1. James T. Sylvester, professor of mathematics at Johns Hopkins University.
2. At Cambridge University, mathematics have been traditionally emphasized. In its original form, *Literature and Science* had been delivered as a lecture at Cambridge.

the sense in us for conduct, and to the sense in us for beauty. But this the men of science will not do for us, and will hardly even profess to do. They will give us other pieces of knowledge, other facts, about other animals and their ancestors, or about plants, or about stones, or about stars; and they may finally bring us to those great "general conceptions of the universe, which are forced upon us all," says Professor Huxley, "by the progress of physical science." But still it will be *knowledge* only which they give us; knowledge not put for us into relation with our sense for conduct, our sense for beauty, and touched with emotion by being so put; not thus put for us, and therefore, to the majority of mankind, after a certain while, unsatisfying, wearying.

Not to the born naturalist, I admit. But what do we mean by a born naturalist? We mean a man in whom the zeal for observing nature is so uncommonly strong and eminent, that it marks him off from the bulk of mankind. Such a man will pass his life happily in collecting natural knowledge and reasoning upon it, and will ask for nothing, or hardly anything, more. I have heard it said that the sagacious and admirable naturalist whom we lost not very long ago, Mr. Darwin, once owned to a friend that for his part he did not experience the necessity for two things which most men find so necessary to them—religion and poetry; science and the domestic affections, he thought, were enough. To a born naturalist, I can well understand that this should seem so. So absorbing is his occupation with nature, so strong his love for his occupation, that he goes on acquiring natural knowledge and reasoning upon it, and has little time or inclination for thinking about getting it related to the desire in man for conduct, the desire in man for beauty. He relates it to them for himself as he goes along, so far as he feels the need; and he draws from the domestic affections all the additional solace necessary. But then Darwins are extremely rare. Another great and admirable master of natural knowledge, Faraday,[3] was a Sandemanian. That is to say, he related his knowledge to his instinct for conduct and to his instinct for beauty, by the aid of that respectable Scottish sectary,[4] Robert Sandeman. And so strong, in general, is the demand of religion and poetry to have their share in a man, to associate themselves with his knowing, and to relieve and rejoice it, that, probably, for one man amongst us with the disposition to do as Darwin did in this respect, there are at least fifty with the disposition to do as Faraday.

Education lays hold upon us, in fact, by satisfying this demand. Professor Huxley holds up to scorn medieval education, with its neglect of the knowledge of nature, its poverty even of literary studies, its formal logic devoted to "showing how and why that

3. Michael Faraday (1791–1867), famous chemist.
4. I.e., a zealous member of a sect.

Robert Sandeman (1718–71) was the founder of a Scottish sect bearing his name.

which the Church said was true must be true." But the great medieval Universities were not brought into being, we may be sure, by the zeal for giving a jejune and contemptible education. Kings have been their nursing fathers, and queens have been their nursing mothers, but not for this. The medieval Universities came into being, because the supposed knowledge, delivered by Scripture and the Church, so deeply engaged men's hearts, by so simply, easily, and powerfully relating itself to their desire for conduct, their desire for beauty. All other knowledge was dominated by this supposed knowledge and was subordinated to it, because of the surpassing strength of the hold which it gained upon the affections of men, by allying itself profoundly with their sense for conduct, their sense for beauty.

But now, says Professor Huxley, conceptions of the universe fatal to the notions held by our forefathers have been forced upon us by physical science. Grant to him that they are thus fatal, that the new conceptions must and will soon become current everywhere, and that everyone will finally perceive them to be fatal to the beliefs of our forefathers. The need of humane letters, as they are truly called, because they serve the paramount desire in men that good should be forever present to them—the need of humane letters, to establish a relation between the new conceptions, and our instinct for beauty, our instinct for conduct, is only the more visible. The Middle Age could do without humane letters, as it could do without the study of nature, because its supposed knowledge was made to engage its emotions so powerfully. Grant that the supposed knowledge disappears, its power of being made to engage the emotions will of course disappear along with it—but the emotions themselves, and their claim to be engaged and satisfied, will remain. Now if we find by experience that humane letters have an undeniable power of engaging the emotions, the importance of humane letters in a man's training becomes not less, but greater, in proportion to the success of modern science in extirpating what it calls "medieval thinking."

Have humane letters, then, have poetry and eloquence, the power here attributed to them of engaging the emotions, and do they exercise it? And if they have it and exercise it, *how* do they exercise it, so as to exert an influence upon man's sense for conduct, his sense for beauty? Finally, even if they both can and do exert an influence upon the senses in question, how are they to relate to them the results—the modern results—of natural science? All these questions may be asked. First, have poetry and eloquence the power of calling out the emotions? The appeal is to experience. Experience shows that for the vast majority of men, for mankind in general, they have the power. Next, do they exercise it? They do. But then, *how* do they exercise it so as to affect man's sense for

conduct, his sense for beauty? And this is perhaps a case for applying the Preacher's words: "Though a man labor to seek it out, yet
he shall not find it; yea, farther, though a wise man think to know
it, yet shall he not be able to find it."[5] Why should it be one thing,
in its effect upon the emotions, to say, "Patience is a virtue," and
quite another thing, in its effect upon the emotions, to say with
Homer,

τλητὸν γὰρ Μοῖραι θυμὸν θέσαν ἀνθρώποισιν[6]—

"for an enduring heart have the destinies appointed to the children
of men"? Why should it be one thing, in its effect upon the emotions, to say with the philosopher Spinoza, *Felicitas in eo consistit
quod homo suum esse conservare potest*—"Man's happiness consists in his being able to preserve his own essence,"[7] and quite another thing, in its effect upon the emotions, to say with the Gospel,
"What is a man advantaged, if he gain the whole world, and lose
himself, forfeit himself?" [8] How does this difference of effect arise?
I cannot tell, and I am not much concerned to know; the important
thing is that it does arise, and that we can profit by it. But how,
finally, are poetry and eloquence to exercise the power of relating
the modern results of natural science to man's instinct for conduct,
his instinct for beauty? And here again I answer that I do not
know *how* they will exercise it, but that they can and will exercise
it I am sure. I do not mean that modern philosophical poets and
modern philosophical moralists are to come and relate for us, in
express terms, the results of modern scientific research to our instinct for conduct, our instinct for beauty. But I mean that we shall
find, as a matter of experience, if we know the best that has been
thought and uttered in the world, we shall find that the art and
poetry and eloquence of men who lived, perhaps, long ago, who
had the most limited natural knowledge, who had the most erroneous conceptions about many important matters, we shall find
that this art, and poetry, and eloquence, have in fact not only the
power of refreshing and delighting us, they have also the power—
such is the strength and worth, in essentials, of their authors' criticism of life—they have a fortifying, and elevating, and quickening,
and suggestive power, capable of wonderfully helping us to relate
the results of modern science to our need for conduct, our need
for beauty. Homer's conceptions of the physical universe were, I
imagine, grotesque; but really, under the shock of hearing from
modern science that "the world is not subordinated to man's use,
and that man is not the cynosure of things terrestrial," I could, for
my own part, desire no better comfort than Homer's line which I
quoted just now,

5. "Ecclesiastes viii.17" [Arnold's note].   7. Spinoza, *Ethics* IV.xviii.
6. "*Iliad* XXIV.49" [Arnold's note].   8. Cf. Luke ix.25.

τλητὸν γὰρ Μοῖραι θυμὸν θέσαν ἀνθρώποισιν—

"for an enduring heart have the destinies appointed to the children of men"!

And the more that men's minds are cleared, the more that the results of science are frankly accepted, the more that poetry and eloquence come to be received and studied as what in truth they really are—the criticism of life by gifted men, alive and active with extraordinary power at an unusual number of points—so much the more will the value of humane letters, and of art also, which is an utterance having a like kind of power with theirs, be felt and acknowledged, and their place in education be secured.

Let us therefore, all of us, avoid indeed as much as possible any invidious comparison between the merits of humane letters, as means of education, and the merits of the natural sciences. But when some President of a Section for Mechanical Science insists on making the comparison, and tells us that "he who in his training has substituted literature and history for natural science has chosen the less useful alternative," let us make answer to him that the student of humane letters only, will, at least, know also the great general conceptions brought in by modern physical science; for science, as Professor Huxley says, forces them upon us all. But the student of the natural sciences only, will, by our very hypothesis, know nothing of humane letters; not to mention that in setting himself to be perpetually accumulating natural knowledge, he sets himself to do what only specialists have in general the gift for doing genially. And so he will probably be unsatisfied, or at any rate incomplete, and even more incomplete than the student of humane letters only.

I once mentioned in a school report, how a young man in one of our English training colleges having to paraphrase the passage in *Macbeth* beginning,

Can'st thou not minister to a mind diseased?[9]

turned this line into, "Can you not wait upon the lunatic?" And I remarked what a curious state of things it would be, if every pupil of our national schools knew, let us say, that the moon is two thousand one hundred and sixty miles in diameter, and thought at the same time that a good paraphrase for

Can'st thou not minister to a mind diseased?

was, "Can you not wait upon the lunatic?" If one is driven to choose, I think I would rather have a young person ignorant about the moon's diameter, but aware that "Can you not wait upon the lunatic?" is bad, than a young person whose education had been

9. *Macbeth* V.iii.40.

such as to manage things the other way.

Or to go higher than the pupils of our national schools. I have in my mind's eye a member of our British Parliament who comes to travel here in America, who afterwards relates his travels, and who shows a really masterly knowledge of the geology of this great country and of its mining capabilities, but who ends by gravely suggesting that the United States should borrow a prince from our Royal Family, and should make him their king, and should create a House of Lords of great landed proprietors after the pattern of ours; and then America, he thinks, would have her future happily and perfectly secured. Surely, in this case, the President of the Section for Mechanical Science would himself hardly say that our member of Parliament, by concentrating himself upon geology and mineralogy, and so on, and not attending to literature and history, had "chosen the more useful alternative."

If then there is to be separation and option between humane letters on the one hand, and the natural sciences on the other, the great majority of mankind, all who have not exceptional and overpowering aptitudes for the study of nature, would do well, I cannot but think, to chose to be educated in humane letters rather than in the natural sciences. Letters will call out their being at more points, will make them live more.

I said that before I ended I would just touch on the question of classical education, and I will keep my word. Even if literature is to retain a large place in our education, yet Latin and Greek, say the friends of progress, will certainly have to go. Greek is the grand offender in the eyes of these gentlemen. The attackers of the established course of study think that against Greek, at any rate, they have irresistible arguments. Literature may perhaps be needed in education, they say; but why on earth should it be Greek literature? Why not French or German? Nay, "has not an Englishman models in his own literature of every kind of excellence?"[1] As before, it is not on any weak pleadings of my own that I rely for convincing the gainsayers; it is on the constitution of human nature itself, and on the instinct of self-preservation in humanity. The instinct for beauty is set in human nature, as surely as the instinct for knowledge is set there, or the instinct for conduct. If the instinct for beauty is served by Greek literature and art as it is served by no other literature and art, we may trust to the instinct of self-preservation in humanity for keeping Greek as part of our culture. We may trust to it for even making the study of Greek more prevalent than it is now. Greek will come, I hope, some day to be studied more rationally than at present; but it will be increasingly studied as men increasingly feel the need in them for beauty, and how powerfully Greek art and Greek literature can serve this need.

1. Quoted from Huxley's *Science and Culture.*

Women will again study Greek, as Lady Jane Grey[2] did; I believe that in that chain of forts, with which the fair host of the Amazons are now engirdling our English universities,[3] I find that here in America, in colleges like Smith College in Massachusetts, and Vassar College in the State of New York, and in the happy families of the mixed universities out West, they are studying it already.

Defuit una mihi symmetria prisca—"The antique symmetry was the one thing wanting to me," said Leonardo da Vinci; and he was an Italian. I will not presume to speak for the Americans, but I am sure that, in the Englishman, the want of this admirable symmetry of the Greeks is a thousand times more great and crying than in any Italian. The results of the want show themselves most glaringly, perhaps, in our architecture, but they show themselves, also, in all our art. *Fit details strictly combined, in view of a large general result nobly conceived*; that is just the beautiful *symmetria prisca* of the Greeks, and it is just where we English fail, where all our art fails. Striking ideas we have, and well-executed details we have; but that high symmetry which, with satisfying and delightful effect, combines them, we seldom or never have. The glorious beauty of the Acropolis at Athens did not come from single fine things stuck about on that hill, a statue here, a gateway there—no, it arose from all things being perfectly combined for a supreme total effect. What must not an Englishman feel about our deficiencies in this respect, as the sense for beauty, whereof this symmetry is an essential element, awakens and strengthens within him! what will not one day be his respect and desire for Greece and its *symmetria prisca*, when the scales drop from his eyes as he walks the London streets, and he sees such a lesson in meanness as the Strand, for instance, in its true deformity! But here we are coming to our friend Mr. Ruskin's province,[4] and I will not intrude upon it, for he is its very sufficient guardian.

And so we at last find, it seems, we find flowing in favor of the humanities the natural and necessary stream of things, which seemed against them when we started. The "hairy quadruped furnished with a tail and pointed ears, probably arboreal in his habits," this good fellow carried hidden in his nature, apparently, something destined to develop into a necessity for humane letters. Nay, more; we seem finally to be even led to the further conclusion that our hairy ancestor carried in his nature, also, a necessity for Greek.

And therefore, to say the truth, I cannot really think that humane letters are in much actual danger of being thrust out from their leading place in education, in spite of the array of authorities against

2. Lady Jane Grey (1537–54) was reputed to be a learned scholar in Greek. She was proclaimed Queen of England in 1553, but was forced to abdicate the throne nine days afterwards. Later she was executed by order of Queen Mary.

3. Colleges for women at Oxford and Cambridge.

4. In such books as *The Stones of Venice* John Ruskin (1819–1900) had criticized the "meanness" of Victorian architecture.

them at this moment. So long as human nature is what it is, their attractions will remain irresistible. As with Greek, so with letters generally: they will some day come, we may hope, to be studied more rationally, but they will not lose their place. What will happen will rather be that there will be crowded into education other matters besides, far too many; there will be, perhaps, a period of unsettlement and confusion and false tendency; but letters will not in the end lose their leading place. If they lose it for a time, they will get it back again. We shall be brought back to them by our wants and aspirations. And a poor humanist may possess his soul in patience, neither strive nor cry, admit the energy and brilliancy of the partisans of physical science, and their present favor with the public, to be far greater than his own, and still have a happy faith that the nature of things works silently on behalf of the studies which he loves, and that, while we shall all have to acquaint ourselves with the great results reached by modern science, and to give ourselves as much training in its disciplines as we can conveniently carry, yet the majority of men will always require humane letters; and so much the more, as they have the more and the greater results of science to relate to the need in man for conduct, and to the need in him for beauty.

1882, 1885

THOMAS HENRY HUXLEY
(1825–1895)

In Victorian controversies over religion and education, one of the most distinctive participants was Thomas Henry Huxley, a scientist who wrote clear, readable, and very persuasive English prose. Huxley's literary skill was responsible for his being lured out of his laboratory onto the platforms of public debate where his role was to champion, as he said, "the application of scientific methods of investigation to all the problems of life."

Huxley, a schoolmaster's son, was born in a London suburb. Until beginning the study of medicine, at 17, he had had little formal education, having taught himself classical and modern languages as well as the rudiments of scientific theory. In 1846, after receiving his degree in medicine, he embarked on a long voyage to the South Seas during which he studied the marine life of the tropical oceans and established a considerable reputation as a zoologist. Later he made investigations in geology and physiology, completing a total of 250 research papers during his lifetime. He also held teaching positions and served on public committees, but it was as a popularizer of science that he made his real mark. His popularizing was of two kinds. The first was to make the results of scientific investigations intelligi-

ble to a large audience. Such lectures as *On a Piece of Chalk* (too long
to include here) are models of clear, vivid exposition that can be studied
with profit by anyone interested in the art of teaching. His second kind
of popularizing consisted of expounding the values of scientific education
or of the application of scientific thinking to problems in religion. Here
Huxley excels not so much as a teacher as a debater. In 1860 he demonstrated his argumentative skill when, as Darwin's defender or "Bulldog,"
he demolished Bishop Wilberforce in a battle over *The Origin of Species*.
In the 1870's, in such lectures as *Science and Culture*, he engaged in more
genial fencing with Matthew Arnold concerning the relative importance of
the study of science or the humanities in education. And in the 1880's
he debated with Gladstone on the topic of interpreting the Bible. His
essay *Agnosticism and Christianity* indicates his premises in this controversy.

Summing up his own career in his *Autobiography*, Huxley noted that
he had subordinated his ambition for scientific fame to other ends: "to
the popularization of science; to the development and organization of scientific education; to the endless series of battles and skirmishes over evolution; and to untiring opposition to that ecclesiastical spirit, that clericalism,
which * * * to whatever denomination it may belong, is the deadly enemy of science." In fighting these "battles" Huxley operated from different
bases. Most of the time he wrote as a biologist engaged in assessing all
assumptions by the tests of laboratory science. In this role he argued that
man is merely an animal and that traditional religion is a tissue of superstitions and lies. At other times, however, Huxley wrote as a humanist and
even as a follower of Carlyle. As he stated in a letter: "*Sartor Resartus* led
me to know that a deep sense of religion was compatible with the entire
absence of theology." In this second role he argued that man is a very
special kind of animal whose great distinction is that he is endowed with
a moral sense and with freedom of the will, a creature who is admirable
not for following nature but for departing from nature. The humanistic
streak muddies the seemingly clear current of Huxley's thinking yet makes
him a more interesting figure than he might otherwise have been. It is
noteworthy that in the writings of his grandsons, Julian Huxley, the
biologist, and Aldous Huxley, the novelist, a similar division of mind
can once more be detected.

Even in his dying, T. H. Huxley continued his role as controversialist.
The words he asked to be engraved on his tomb are typical of his view of
life and typical, also, in the effect they had on his contemporaries, some
of whom found the epitaph to be shocking:

> Be not afraid, ye waiting hearts that weep
> For still he giveth His beloved sleep,
> And if an endless sleep He wills, so best.

From A Liberal Education[1]
[A *Game of Chess*]

Suppose it were perfectly certain that the life and fortune of every one of us would, one day or other, depend upon his winning or losing a game of chess. Don't you think that we should all consider it to be a primary duty to learn at least the names and the moves of the pieces; to have a notion of a gambit,[2] and a keen eye for all the means of giving and getting out of check? Do you not think that we should look with a disapprobation amounting to scorn, upon the father who allowed his son, or the state which allowed its members, to grow up without knowing a pawn from a knight?

Yet it is a very plain and elementary truth that the life, the fortune, and the happiness of every one of us, and, more or less, of those who are connected with us, do depend upon our knowing something of the rules of a game infinitely more difficult and complicated than chess. It is a game which has been played for untold ages, every man and woman of us being one of the two players in a game of his or her own. The chessboard is the world, the pieces are the phenomena of the universe, the rules of the game are what we call the laws of Nature. The player on the other side is hidden from us. We know that his play is always fair, just, and patient. But also we know, to our cost, that he never overlooks a mistake, or makes the smallest allowance for ignorance. To the man who plays well, the highest stakes are paid, with that sort of overflowing generosity with which the strong shows delight in strength. And one who plays ill is checkmated—without haste, but without remorse.

My metaphor will remind some of you of the famous picture in which Retzsch[3] has depicted Satan playing at chess with man for his soul. Substitute for the mocking fiend in that picture a calm, strong angel who is playing for love, as we say, and would rather lose than win—and I should accept it as an image of human life.

Well, what I mean by Education is learning the rules of this mighty game. In other words, education is the instruction of the intellect in the laws of Nature, under which name I include not merely things and their forces, but men and their ways; and the fashioning of the affections and of the will into an earnest and loving desire to move in harmony with those laws. For me, education means neither more nor less than this. Anything which professes to call itself education must be tried by this standard, and if it

---

1. Originally an address, delivered at the South London Working Men's College in 1868.
2. An opening move in chess in which a pawn or other pieces are sacrificed in order to gain a favorable position.
3. Friedrich A. M. Retzsch (1779–1857), German painter.

fails to stand the test, I will not call it education, whatever may be the force of authority, or of numbers, upon the other side.

It is important to remember that, in strictness, there is no such thing as an uneducated man. Take an extreme case. Suppose that an adult man, in the full vigor of his faculties, could be suddenly placed in the world, as Adam is said to have been, and then left to do as he best might. How long would he be left uneducated? Not five minutes. Nature would begin to teach him, through the eye, the ear, the touch, the properties of objects. Pain and pleasure would be at his elbow telling him to do this and avoid that; and by slow degrees the man would receive an education which, if narrow, would be thorough, real, and adequate to his circumstances, though there would be no extras and very few accomplishments.

And if to this solitary man entered a second Adam or, better still, an Eve, a new and greater world, that of social and moral phenomena, would be revealed. Joys and woes, compared with which all others might seem but faint shadows, would spring from the new relations. Happiness and sorrow would take the place of the coarser monitors, pleasure and pain; but conduct would still be shaped by the observation of the natural consequences of actions; or, in other words, by the laws of the nature of man.

To every one of us the world was once as fresh and new as to Adam. And then, long before we were susceptible of any other mode of instruction, Nature took us in hand, and every minute of waking life brought its educational influence, shaping our actions into rough accordance with Nature's laws, so that we might not be ended untimely by too gross disobedience. Nor should I speak of this process of education as past for anyone, be he as old as he may. For every man the world is as fresh as it was at the first day, and as full of untold novelties for him who has the eyes to see them. And Nature is still continuing her patient education of us in that great university, the universe, of which we are all members—Nature having no Test Acts.[4]

Those who take honors in Nature's university, who learn the laws which govern men and things and obey them, are the really great and successful men in this world. The great mass of mankind are the "Poll,"[5] who pick up just enough to get through without much discredit. Those who won't learn at all are plucked;[6] and then you can't come up again. Nature's pluck means extermination.

Thus the question of compulsory education is settled so far as Nature is concerned. Her bill on that question was framed and passed long ago. But, like all compulsory legislation, that of Nature

4. Legislation (repealed in 1854) which excluded from Oxford and Cambridge any student who would not profess faith in the 39 Articles of the Church of England.

5. English slang term describing the mass of students who get through college with very low (but passing) grades.
6. Failed.

is harsh and wasteful in its operation. Ignorance is visited as sharply as willful disobedience—incapacity meets with the same punishment as crime. Nature's discipline is not even a word and a blow, and the blow first; but the blow without the word. It is left to you to find out why your ears are boxed.

The object of what we commonly call education—that education in which man intervenes and which I shall distinguish as artificial education—is to make good these defects in Nature's methods; to prepare the child to receive Nature's education, neither incapably nor ignorantly, nor with willful disobedience; and to understand the preliminary symptoms of her pleasure, without waiting for the box on the ear. In short, all artificial education ought to be an anticipation of natural education. And a liberal education is an artificial education which has not only prepared a man to escape the great evils of disobedience to natural laws, but has trained him to appreciate and to seize upon the rewards which Nature scatters with as free a hand as her penalties.

That man, I think, has had a liberal education who has been so trained in youth that his body is the ready servant of his will, and does with ease and pleasure all the work that, as a mechanism, it is capable of; whose intellect is a clear, cold, logic engine, with all its parts of equal strength, and in smooth working order; ready, like a steam engine, to be turned to any kind of work, and spin the gossamers as well as forge the anchors of the mind; whose mind is stored with a knowledge of the great and fundamental truths of Nature and of the laws of her operations; one who, no stunted ascetic, is full of life and fire, but whose passions are trained to come to heel by a vigorous will, the servant of a tender conscience; who has learned to love all beauty, whether of Nature or of art, to hate all vileness, and to respect others as himself.

Such a one and no other, I conceive, has had a liberal education; for he is, as completely as a man can be, in harmony with Nature. He will make the best of her, and she of him. They will get on together rarely; she as his ever beneficent mother; he as her mouthpiece, her conscious self, her minister and interpreter. * * *

1868, 1870

From An Address on University Education[1]
[The Function of a Professor]

Up to this point I have considered only the teaching aspect of your great foundation, that function of the university in virtue of

1. During a visit to the United States in 1876 Huxley delivered an address in Baltimore on the occasion of the founding of the Johns Hopkins University, a newly endowed institution which encouraged research.

which it plays the part of a reservoir of ascertained truth, so far as our symbols can ever interpret nature. All can learn; all can drink of this lake. It is given to few to add to the store of knowledge, to strike new springs of thought, or to shape new forms of beauty. But so sure as it is that men live not by bread, but by ideas, so sure is it that the future of the world lies in the hands of those who are able to carry the interpretation of nature a step further than their predecessors; so certain is it that the highest function of a university is to seek out those men, cherish them, and give their ability to serve their kind full play.

I rejoice to observe that the encouragement of research occupies so prominent a place in your official documents, and in the wise and liberal inaugural address of your president. This subject of the encouragement, or, as it is sometimes called, the endowment of research, has of late years greatly exercised the minds of men in England. It was one of the main topics of discussion by the members of the Royal Commission of whom I was one, and who not long since issued their report, after five years' labor. Many seem to think that this question is mainly one of money; that you can go into the market and buy research, and that supply will follow demand, as in the ordinary course of commerce. This view does not commend itself to my mind. I know of no more difficult practical problem than the discovery of a method of encouraging and supporting the original investigator without opening the door to nepotism and jobbery. My own conviction is admirably summed up in the passage of your president's address, "that the best investigators are usually those who have also the responsibilities of instruction, gaining thus the incitement of colleagues, the encouragement of pupils, and the observation of the public." * * *

It appears to me that what I have ventured to lay down as the principles which should govern the relations of a university to education in general, are entirely in accordance with the measures you have adopted. You have set no restrictions upon access to the instruction you propose to give; you have provided that such instruction, either as given by the university or by associated institutions, should cover the field of human intellectual activity. You have recognized the importance of encouraging research. You propose to provide means by which young men, who may be full of zeal for a literary or for a scientific career, but who also may have mistaken aspiration for inspiration, may bring their capacities to a test, and give their powers a fair trial. If such a one fail, his endowment terminates and there is no harm done. If he succeed, you may give power of flight to the genius of a Davy or a Faraday,[2] a Carlyle or a Locke, whose influence on the future of his fellow

2. Sir Humphry Davy (1778–1829), English chemist and inventor; Michael Faraday (1791–1867), at one time Davy's laboratory assistant, who became famous for his discovery of the induction of electric currents.

men shall be absolutely incalculable.

You have enunciated the principle that "the glory of the university should rest upon the character of the teachers and scholars, and not upon their numbers of buildings constructed for their use." And I look upon it as an essential and most important feature of your plan that the income of the professors and teachers shall be independent of the number of students whom they can attract. In this way you provide against the danger, patent elsewhere, of finding attempts at improvement obstructed by vested interests; and, in the department of medical education especially, you are free of the temptation to set loose upon the world men utterly incompetent to perform the serious and responsible duties of their profession.

1876–77

From Science and Culture[1]

From the time that the first suggestion to introduce physical science into ordinary education was timidly whispered, until now, the advocates of scientific education have met with opposition of two kinds. On the one hand, they have been pooh-poohed by the men of business who pride themselves on being the representatives of practicality; while, on the other hand, they have been excommunicated by the classical scholars, in their capacity of Levites in charge of the ark of culture[2] and monopolists of liberal education.

The practical men believed that the idol whom they worship—rule of thumb—has been the source of the past prosperity, and will suffice for the future welfare of the arts and manufactures. They are of opinion that science is speculative rubbish; that theory and practice have nothing to do with one another; and that the scientific habit of mind is an impediment, rather than an aid, in the conduct of ordinary affairs.

I have used the past tense in speaking of the practical men—for although they were very formidable thirty years ago, I am not sure that the pure species has not been extirpated. In fact, so far as mere argument goes, they have been subjected to such a *feu d'enfer*[3] that it is a miracle if any have escaped. But I have remarked that your typical practical man has an unexpected resemblance to one of Milton's angels. His spiritual wounds, such as are inflicted by logical weapons, may be as deep as a well and as wide as a church

---

1. This essay was first delivered as an address in 1880. The occasion had been the opening of a new Scientific College at Birmingham which had been endowed by Sir Josiah Mason (1795–1881), a self-made businessman. For Matthew Arnold's reply to Huxley's argument see his essay *Literature and Science*.
2. In the Old Testament, the Levites were the priests preoccupied with traditional ritual observances (see Joshua vi).
3. Hell-fire.

door, but beyond shedding a few drops of ichor,[4] celestial or otherwise, he is no whit the worse. So, if any of these opponents be left, I will not waste time in vain repetition of the demonstrative evidence of the practical value of science; but knowing that a parable will sometimes penetrate where syllogisms fail to effect an entrance, I will offer a story for their consideration.

Once upon a time, a boy, with nothing to depend upon but his own vigorous nature, was thrown into the thick of the struggle for existence in the midst of a great manufacturing population. He seems to have had a hard fight, inasmuch as, by the time he was thirty years of age, his total disposable funds amounted to twenty pounds. Nevertheless, middle life found him giving proof of his comprehension of the practical problems he had been roughly called upon to solve, by a career of remarkable prosperity.

Finally, having reached old age with its well-earned surroundings of "honor, troops of friends,"[5] the hero of my story bethought himself of those who were making a like start in life, and how he could stretch out a helping hand to them.

After long and anxious reflection this successful practical man of business could devise nothing better than to provide them with the means of obtaining "sound, extensive, and practical scientific knowledge." And he devoted a large part of his wealth and five years of incessant work to this end.

I need not point the moral of a tale which, as the solid and spacious fabric of the Scientific College assures us, is no fable, nor can anything which I could say intensify the force of this practical answer to practical objections.

We may take it for granted then, that, in the opinion of those best qualified to judge, the diffusion of thorough scientific education is an absolutely essential condition of industrial progress; and that the College which has been opened today will confer an inestimable boon upon those whose livelihood is to be gained by the practice of the arts and manufactures of the district.

The only question worth discussion is whether the conditions under which the work of the College is to be carried out are such as to give it the best possible chance of achieving permanent success.

Sir Josiah Mason, without doubt most wisely, has left very large freedom of action to the trustees, to whom he proposes ultimately to commit the administration of the College, so that they may be able to adjust its arrangements in accordance with the changing conditions of the future. But, with respect to three points, he has laid most explicit injunctions upon both administrators and teachers.

---

4. Ethereal fluid which supposedly flows through the veins of the gods. 5. Cf. *Macbeth* V.iii.25.

Party politics are forbidden to enter into the minds of either, so far as the work of the College is concerned; theology is as sternly banished from its precincts; and finally, it is especially declared that the College shall make no provision for "mere literary instruction and education."

It does not concern me at present to dwell upon the first two injunctions any longer than may be needful to express my full conviction of their wisdom. But the third prohibition brings us face to face with those other opponents of scientific education, who are by no means in the moribund condition of the practical man, but alive, alert, and formidable.

It is not impossible that we shall hear this express exclusion of "literary instruction and education" from a College which, nevertheless, professes to give a high and efficient education, sharply criticized. Certainly the time was that the Levites of culture would have sounded their trumpets against its walls as against an educational Jericho.[6]

How often have we not been told that the study of physical science is incompetent to confer culture; that it touches none of the higher problems of life; and, what is worse, that the continual devotion to scientific studies tends to generate a narrow and bigoted belief in the applicability of scientific methods to the search after truth of all kinds? How frequently one has reason to observe that no reply to a troublesome argument tells so well as calling its author a "mere scientific specialist." And, as I am afraid it is not permissible to speak of this form of opposition to scientific education in the past tense; may we not expect to be told that this, not only omission, but prohibition, of "mere literary instruction and education" is a patent example of scientific narrow-mindedness?

I am not acquainted with Sir Josiah Mason's reasons for the action which he has taken; but if, as I apprehend is the case, he refers to the ordinary classical course of our schools and universities by the name of "mere literary instruction and education," I venture to offer sundry reasons of my own in support of that action.

For I hold very strongly by two convictions: The first is that neither the discipline nor the subject matter of classical education is of such direct value to the student of physical science as to justify the expenditure of valuable time upon either; and the second is that for the purpose of attaining real culture, an exclusively scientific education is at least as effectual as an exclusively literary education.

I need hardly point out to you that these opinions, especially the latter, are diametrically opposed to those of the great majority of educated Englishmen, influenced as they are by school and university traditions. In their belief, culture is obtainable only by a

6. See Joshua vi.

liberal education; and a liberal education is synonymous, not merely with education and instruction in literature, but in one particular form of literature, namely, that of Greek and Roman antiquity. They hold that the man who has learned Latin and Greek, however little, is educated; while he who is versed in other branches of knowledge, however deeply, is a more or less respectable specialist, not admissible into the cultured caste. The stamp of the educated man, the University degree, is not for him.

I am too well acquainted with the generous catholicity of spirit, the true sympathy with scientific thought, which pervades the writings of our chief apostle of culture[7] to identify him with these opinions; and yet one may cull from one and another of those epistles to the Philistines, which so much delight all who do not answer to that name, sentences which lend them some support.

Mr. Arnold tells us that the meaning of culture is "to know the best that has been thought and said in the world." It is the criticism of life contained in literature. That criticism regards "Europe as being, for intellectual and spiritual purposes, one great confederation, bound to a joint action and working to a common result; and whose members have, for their common outfit, a knowledge of Greek, Roman, and Eastern antiquity, and of one another. Special, local, and temporary advantages being put out of account, that modern nation will in the intellectual and spiritual sphere make most progress, which most thoroughly carries out this program. And what is that but saying that we too, all of us, as individuals, the more thoroughly we carry it out, shall make the more progress?"[8]

We have here to deal with two distinct propositions. The first, that a criticism of life is the essence of culture; the second, that literature contains the materials which suffice for the construction of such criticism.

I think that we must all assent to the first proposition. For culture certainly means something quite different from learning or technical skill. It implies the possession of an ideal, and the habit of critically estimating the value of things by comparison with a theoretic standard. Perfect culture should supply a complete theory of life, based upon a clear knowledge alike of its possibilities and of its limitations.

But we may agree to all this, and yet strongly dissent from the assumption that literature alone is competent to supply this knowledge. After having learnt all that Greek, Roman, and Eastern antiquity have thought and said, and all that modern literature have to tell us, it is not self-evident that we have laid a sufficiently broad and deep foundation for that criticism of life which constitutes culture.

7. I.e., Matthew Arnold. For his discussion of the Philistines, see *Culture and Anarchy*.

8. From Arnold's *Function of Criticism*, fourth paragraph from the end.

Indeed, to anyone acquainted with the scope of physical science, it is not at all evident. Considering progress only in the "intellectual and spiritual sphere," I find myself wholly unable to admit that either nations or individuals will really advance, if their common outfit draws nothing from the stores of physical science. I should say that an army, without weapons of precision and with no particular base of operations, might more hopefully enter upon a campaign on the Rhine than a man, devoid of a knowledge of what physical science has done in the last century, upon a criticism of life.

When a biologist meets with an anomaly, he instinctively turns to the study of development to clear it up. The rationale of contradictory opinions may with equal confidence be sought in history.

It is, happily, no new thing that Englishmen should employ their wealth in building and endowing institutions for educational purposes. But, five or six hundred years ago, deeds of foundation expressed or implied conditions as nearly as possible contrary to those which have been thought expedient by Sir Josiah Mason. That is to say, physical science was practically ignored, while a certain literary training was enjoined as a means to the acquirement of knowledge which was essentially theological.

The reason of this singular contradiction between the actions of men alike animated by a strong and disinterested desire to promote the welfare of their fellows, is easily discovered.

At that time, in fact, if anyone desired knowledge beyond such as could be obtained by his own observation, or by common conversation, his first necessity was to learn the Latin language, inasmuch as all the higher knowledge of the western world was contained in works written in that language. Hence, Latin grammar, with logic and rhetoric, studied through Latin, were the fundamentals of education. With respect to the substance of the knowledge imparted through this channel, the Jewish and Christian Scriptures, as interpreted and supplemented by the Romish Church, were held to contain a complete and infallibly true body of information.

Theological dicta were, to the thinkers of those days, that which the axioms and definitions of Euclid are to the geometers of these. The business of the philosophers of the Middle Ages was to deduce from the data furnished by the theologians, conclusions in accordance with ecclesiastical decrees. They were allowed the high privilege of showing, by logical process, how and why that which the Church said was true, must be true. And if their demonstrations fell short of or exceeded this limit, the Church was maternally ready to check their aberrations; if need were, by the help of the secular arm.

Between the two, our ancestors were furnished with a compact and complete criticism of life. They were told how the world began and how it would end; they learned that all material existence was but a base and insignificant blot upon the fair face of the spiritual world, and that nature was, to all intents and purposes, the playground of the devil; they learned that the earth is the center of the visible universe, and that man is the cynosure of things terrestrial, and more especially was it inculcated that the course of nature had no fixed order, but that it could be, and constantly was, altered by the agency of innumerable spiritual beings, good and bad, according as they were moved by the deeds and prayers of men. The sum and substance of the whole doctrine was to produce the conviction that the only thing really worth knowing in this world was how to secure that place in a better which, under certain conditions, the Church promised.

Our ancestors had a living belief in this theory of life, and acted upon it in their dealings with education, as in all other matters. Culture meant saintliness—after the fashion of the saints of those days; the education that led to it was, of necessity, theological; and the way to theology lay through Latin.

That the study of nature—further than was requisite for the satisfaction of everyday wants—should have any bearing on human life was far from the thoughts of men thus trained. Indeed, as nature had been cursed for man's sake, it was an obvious conclusion that those who meddled with nature were likely to come into pretty close contact with Satan. And, if any born scientific investigator followed his instincts, he might safely reckon upon earning the reputation, and probably upon suffering the fate, of a sorcerer.

Had the western world been left to itself in Chinese isolation, there is no saying how long this state of things might have endured. But, happily, it was not left to itself. Even earlier than the thirteenth century, the development of Moorish civilization in Spain and the great movement of the Crusades had introduced the leaven which, from that day to this, has never ceased to work. At first, through the intermediation of Arabic translations, afterwards by the study of the originals, the western nations of Europe became acquainted with the writings of the ancient philosophers and poets, and, in time, with the whole of the vast literature of antiquity.

Whatever there was of high intellectual aspiration or dominant capacity in Italy, France, Germany, and England, spent itself for centuries in taking possession of the rich inheritance left by the dead civilizations of Greece and Rome. Marvelously aided by the invention of printing,[9] classical learning spread and flourished. Those who possessed it prided themselves on having attained the

9. In the mid-15th century.

highest culture then within the reach of mankind.

And justly. For, saving Dante on his solitary pinnacle, there was no figure in modern literature at the time of the Renaissance to compare with the men of antiquity; there was no art to compete with their sculpture; there was no physical science but that which Greece had created. Above all, there was no other example of perfect intellectual freedom—of the unhesitating acceptance of reason as the sole guide to truth and the supreme arbiter of conduct.

The new learning necessarily soon exerted a profound influence upon education. The language of the monks and schoolmen[1] seemed little better than gibberish to scholars fresh from Virgil and Cicero, and the study of Latin was placed upon a new foundation. Moreover, Latin itself ceased to afford the sole key to knowledge. The student who sought the highest thought of antiquity found only a secondhand reflection of it in Roman literature, and turned his face to the full light of the Greeks. And after a battle, not altogether dissimilar to that which is at present being fought over the teaching of physical science, the study of Greek was recognized as an essential element of all higher education.

Then the Humanists, as they were called, won the day; and the great reform which they effected was of incalculable service to mankind. But the nemesis of all reformers is finality; and the reformers of education, like those of religion, fell into the profound, however common, error of mistaking the beginning for the end of the work of reformation.

The representatives of the Humanists, in the nineteenth century, take their stand upon classical education as the sole avenue to culture as firmly as if we were still in the age of Renaissance. Yet, surely, the present intellectual relations of the modern and the ancient worlds are profoundly different from those which obtained three centuries ago. Leaving aside the existence of a great and characteristically modern literature, of modern painting, and, especially, of modern music, there is one feature of the present state of the civilized world which separates it more widely from the Renaissance than the Renaissance was separated from the Middle Ages.

This distinctive character of our own times lies in the vast and constantly increasing part which is played by natural knowledge. Not only is our daily life shaped by it; not only does the prosperity of millions of men depend upon it, but our whole theory of life has long been influenced, consciously or unconsciously, by the general conceptions of the universe which have been forced upon us by physical science.

In fact, the most elementary acquaintance with the results of scientific investigation shows us that they offer a broad and striking

1. Exponents of the theology, philosophy, and logic of the medieval period in Europe.

contradiction to the opinion so implicitly credited and taught in the Middle Ages.

The notions of the beginning and the end of the world entertained by our forefathers are no longer credible. It is very certain that the earth is not the chief body in the material universe, and that the world is not subordinated to man's use. It is even more certain that nature is the expression of a definite order with which nothing interferes, and that the chief business of mankind is to learn that order and govern themselves accordingly. Moreover this scientific "criticism of life" presents itself to us with different credentials from any other. It appeals not to authority, nor to what anybody may have thought or said, but to nature. It admits that all our interpretations of natural fact are more or less imperfect and symbolic, and bids the learner seek for truth not among words but among things. It warns us that the assertion which outstrips evidence is not only a blunder but a crime.

The purely classical education advocated by the representatives of the Humanists in our day gives no inkling of all this. A man may be a better scholar than Erasmus,[2] and know no more of the chief causes of the present intellectual fermentation than Erasmus did. Scholarly and pious persons, worthy of all respect, favor us with allocutions upon the sadness of the antagonism of science to their medieval way of thinking, which betray an ignorance of the first principles of scientific investigation, an incapacity for understanding what a man of science means by veracity, and an unconsciousness of the weight of established scientific truths, which is almost comical. * * *

Thus I venture to think that the pretensions of our modern Humanists to the possession of the monopoly of culture and to the exclusive inheritance of the spirit of antiquity must be abated, if not abandoned. But I should be very sorry that anything I have said should be taken to imply a desire on my part to depreciate the value of classical education, as it might be and as it sometimes is. The native capacities of mankind vary no less than their opportunities; and while culture is one, the road by which one man may best reach it is widely different from that which is most advantageous to another. Again, while scientific education is yet inchoate and tentative, classical education is thoroughly well organized upon the practical experience of generations of teachers. So that, given ample time for learning and estimation for ordinary life, or for a literary career, I do not think that a young Englishman in search of culture can do better than follow the course usually marked out for him, supplementing its deficiencies by his own efforts.

But for those who mean to make science their serious occupation; or who intend to follow the profession of medicine; or who have to

2. Eminent Dutch humanist and scholar (1466–1536).

enter early upon the business of life; for all these, in my opinion, classical education is a mistake; and it is for this reason that I am glad to see "mere literary education and instruction" shut out from the curriculum of Sir Josiah Mason's College, seeing that its inclusion would probably lead to the introduction of the ordinary smattering of Latin and Greek.

Nevertheless, I am the last person to question the importance of genuine literary education, or to suppose that intellectual culture can be complete without it. An exclusively scientific training will bring about a mental twist as surely as an exclusively literary training. The value of the cargo does not compensate for a ship's being out of trim; and I should be very sorry to think that the Scientific College would turn out none but lopsided men.

There is no need, however, that such a catastrophe should happen. Instruction in English, French, and German is provided, and thus the three greatest literatures of the modern world are made accessible to the student.

French and German, and especially the latter language, are absolutely indispensable to those who desire full knowledge in any department of science. But even supposing that the knowledge of these languages acquired is not more than sufficient for purely scientific purposes, every Englishman has, in his native tongue, an almost perfect instrument of literary expression; and, in his own literature, models of every kind of literary excellence. If an Englishman cannot get literary culture out of his Bible, his Shakespeare, his Milton, neither, in my belief, will the profoundest study of Homer and Sophocles, Virgil and Horace, give it to him.

Thus, since the constitution of the College makes sufficient provision for literary as well as for scientific education, and since artistic instruction is also contemplated, it seems to me that a fairly complete culture is offered to all who are willing to take advantage of it. * * *

1880, 1881

From Agnosticism and Christianity[1]

Nemo ergo ex me scire quaerat, quod me nescire scio, nisi forte ut nescire discat.
—AUGUSTINUS, *De Civ. Dei,* XII.7.[2]

The present discussion has arisen out of the use, which has become general in the last few years, of the terms "Agnostic" and

1. This essay appeared in a magazine in 1889 as a reply to critics who had argued that agnostics were simply infidels under a new name. It was later included in Huxley's volume, *Essays on Some Controverted Questions*

(1892).
2. "No one, therefore, should seek to learn knowledge from me, for I know that I do not know—unless indeed he wishes to learn that he does not know." St. Augustine, *City of God* XII.7.

"Agnosticism."[3]

The people who call themselves "Agnostics" have been charged with doing so because they have not the courage to declare themselves "Infidels." It has been insinuated that they have adopted a new name in order to escape the unpleasantness which attaches to their proper denomination. To this wholly erroneous imputation I have replied by showing that the term "Agnostic" did, as a matter of fact, arise in a manner which negatives it; and my statement has not been, and cannot be, refuted. Moreover, speaking for myself, and without impugning the right of any other person to use the term in another sense, I further say that Agnosticism is not properly described as a "negative" creed, nor indeed as a creed of any kind, except in so far as it expresses absolute faith in the validity of a principle, which is as much ethical as intellectual. This principle may be stated in various ways, but they all amount to this: that it is wrong for a man to say that he is certain of the objective truth of any proposition unless he can produce evidence which logically justifies that certainty. This is what Agnosticism asserts; and, in my opinion, it is all that is essential to Agnosticism. That which Agnostics deny and repudiate, as immoral, is the contrary doctrine, that there are propositions which men ought to believe, without logically satisfactory evidence; and that reprobation ought to attach to the profession of disbelief in such inadequately supported propositions. The justification of the Agnostic principle lies in the success which follows upon its application, whether in the field of natural, or in that of civil, history; and in the fact that, so far as these topics are concerned, no sane man thinks of denying its validity.

Still speaking for myself, I add that though Agnosticism is not, and cannot be, a creed, except in so far as its general principle is concerned; yet that the application of that principle results in the denial of, or the suspension of judgment concerning, a number of propositions respecting which our contemporary ecclesiastical "gnostics" profess entire certainty. And, in so far as these ecclesiastical persons can be justified in their old-established custom (which many nowadays think more honored in the breach than the observance) of using opprobrious names to those who differ from them, I fully admit their right to call me and those who think with me "Infidels"; all I have ventured to urge is that they must not expect us to speak of ourselves by that title.

The extent of the region of the uncertain, the number of the problems the investigation of which ends in a verdict of not proven, will vary according to the knowledge and the intellectual habits of the individual Agnostic. I do not very much care to speak of anything as "unknowable." What I am sure about is that there are many topics about which I know nothing; and which, so far as I

3. The term "agnostic" was coined by Huxley.

can see, are out of reach of my faculties. But whether these things are knowable by anyone else is exactly one of those matters which is beyond my knowledge, though I may have a tolerably strong opinion as to the probabilities of the case. Relatively to myself, I am quite sure that the region of uncertainty—the nebulous country in which words play the part of realities—is far more extensive than I could wish. Materialism and Idealism; Theism and Atheism; the doctrine of the soul and its mortality or immortality—appear in the history of philosophy like the shades of Scandinavian heroes, eternally slaying one another and eternally coming to life again in a metaphysical "Nifelheim."[4] It is getting on for twenty-five centuries, at least, since mankind began seriously to give their minds to these topics. Generation after generation, philosophy has been doomed to roll the stone uphill; and, just as all the world swore it was at the top, down it has rolled to the bottom again.[5] All this is written in innumerable books; and he who will toil through them will discover that the stone is just where it was when the work began. Hume saw this; Kant saw it; since their time, more and more eyes have been cleansed of the films which prevented them from seeing it; until now the weight and number of those who refuse to be the prey of verbal mystifications has begun to tell in practical life.

It was inevitable that a conflict should arise between Agnosticism and Theology; or rather, I ought to say, between Agnosticism and Ecclesiasticism. For Theology, the science, is one thing; and Ecclesiasticism, the championship of a foregone conclusion[6] as to the truth of a particular form of Theology, is another. With scientific Theology, Agnosticism has no quarrel. On the contrary, the Agnostic, knowing too well the influence of prejudice and idiosyncrasy, even on those who desire most earnestly to be impartial, can wish for nothing more urgently than that the scientific theologian should not only be at perfect liberty to thresh out the matter in his own fashion; but that he should, if he can, find flaws in the Agnostic position; and, even if demonstration is not to be had, that he should put, in their full force, the grounds of the conclusions he thinks probable. The scientific theologian admits the Agnostic principle, however widely his results may differ from those reached by the majority of Agnostics.

But, as between Agnosticism and Ecclesiasticism, or, as our neighbors across the Channel call it, Clericalism, there can be neither peace nor truce. The Cleric asserts that it is morally wrong not to believe certain propositions, whatever the results of a strict

4: Realms of cold and darkness in Norse mythology.
5. Cf. the Greek story of Sisyphus in Hades, who was condemned to keep rolling a stone uphill which always rolled downhill again before it reached the summit.
6. "Let us maintain, before we have proved. This seeming paradox is the secret of happiness. (Dr. Newman, *Tract 85*)" [Huxley's note].

scientific investigation of the evidence of these propositions. He tells us "that religious error is, in itself, of an immoral nature."[7] He declares that he has prejudged certain conclusions, and looks upon those who show cause for arrest of judgment as emissaries of Satan. It necessarily follows that, for him, the attainment of faith, not the ascertainment of truth, is the highest aim of mental life. And, on careful analysis of the nature of this faith, it will too often be found to be, not the mystic process of unity with the Divine, understood by the religious enthusiast; but that which the candid simplicity of a Sunday scholar once defined it to be. "Faith," said this unconscious plagiarist of Tertullian,[8] "is the power of saying you believe things which are incredible."

Now I, and many other Agnostics, believe that faith, in this sense, is an abomination; and though we do not indulge in the luxury of self-righteousness so far as to call those who are not of our way of thinking hard names, we do feel that the disagreement between ourselves and those who hold this doctrine is even more moral than intellectual. It is desirable there should be an end of any mistakes on this topic. If our clerical opponents were clearly aware of the real state of the case, there would be an end of the curious delusion, which often appears between the lines of their writings, that those whom they are so fond of calling "Infidels" are people who not only ought to be, but in their hearts are, ashamed of themselves. It would be discourteous to do more than hint the antipodal opposition of this pleasant dream of theirs to facts.

The clerics and their lay allies commonly tell us that if we refuse to admit that there is good ground for expressing definite convictions about certain topics, the bonds of human society will dissolve and mankind lapse into savagery. There are several answers to this assertion. One is that the bonds of human society were formed without the aid of their theology; and, in the opinion of not a few competent judges, have been weakened rather than strengthened by a good deal of it. Greek science, Greek art, the ethics of old Israel, the social organization of old Rome, contrived to come into being, without the help of anyone who believed in a single distinctive article of the simplest of the Christian creeds. The science, the art, the jurisprudence, the chief political and social theories, of the modern world have grown out of those of Greece and Rome—not by favor of, but in the teeth of, the fundamental teachings of early Christianity, to which science, art, and any serious occupation with the things of this world, were alike despicable.

Again, all that is best in the ethics of the modern world, in so far as it has not grown out of Greek thought, or Barbarian manhood, is the direct development of the ethics of old Israel. There

7. "Dr Newman, *Essay on Development*" [Huxley's note].   8. Roman author and Church Father (ca. 155–ca. 222).

is no code of legislation, ancient or modern, at once so just and so merciful, so tender to the weak and poor, as the Jewish law; and, if the Gospels are to be trusted, Jesus of Nazareth himself declared that he taught nothing but that which lay implicitly, or explicitly, in the religious and ethical system of his people.

"And the scribe said unto him, Of a truth, Teacher, thou hast well said that he is one; and there is none other but he and to love him with all the heart, and with all the understanding, and with all the strength, and to love his neighbour as himself, is much more than all whole burnt offerings and sacrifices." (Mark xii.32–33)

Here is the briefest of summaries of the teaching of the prophets of Israel of the eighth century; does the Teacher, whose doctrine is thus set forth in his presence, repudiate the exposition? Nay; we are told, on the contrary, that Jesus saw that he "answered discreetly," and replied, "Thou art not far from the kingdom of God."

So that I think that even if the creeds,[9] from the so-called "Apostles'" to the so-called "Athanasian," were swept into oblivion; and even if the human race should arrive at the conclusion that, whether a bishop washes a cup or leaves it unwashed, is not a matter of the least consequence, it will get on very well. The causes which have led to the development of morality in mankind, which have guided or impelled us all the way from the savage to the civilized state, will not cease to operate because a number of ecclesiastical hypotheses turn out to be baseless. And, even if the absurd notion that morality is more the child of speculation than of practical necessity and inherited instinct, had any foundation; if all the world is going to thieve, murder, and otherwise misconduct itself as soon as it discovers that certain portions of ancient history are mythical; what is the relevance of such arguments to any one who holds by the Agnostic principle?

Surely, the attempt to cast out Beelzebub by the aid of Beelzebub is a hopeful procedure as compared to that of preserving morality by the aid of immorality. For I suppose it is admitted that an Agnostic may be perfectly sincere, may be competent, and may have studied the question at issue with as much care as his clerical opponents. But, if the Agnostic really believes what he says, the "dreadful consequence" argufier (consistently, I admit, with his own principles) virtually asks him to abstain from telling the truth, or to say what he believes to be untrue, because of the supposed injurious consequences to morality. "Beloved brethren, that we may be spotlessly moral, before all things let us lie," is the sum total of many an exhortation addressed to the "Infidel." Now, as I have already pointed out, we cannot oblige our exhorters. We leave the practical application of the convenient doctrines of "Reserve" and

9. Summaries of Christian doctrine.

"Non-natural interpretation" to those who invented them.

I trust that I have now made amends for any ambiguity, or want of fullness, in my previous exposition of that which I hold to be the essence of the Agnostic doctrine. Henceforward, I might hope to hear no more of the assertion that we are necessarily Materialists, Idealists, Atheists, Theists, or any other ists, if experience had led me to think that the proved falsity of a statement was any guarantee against its repetition. And those who appreciate the nature of our position will see, at once, that when Ecclesiasticism declares that we ought to believe this, that, and the other, and are very wicked if we don't, it is impossible for us to give any answer but this: We have not the slightest objection to believe anything you like, if you will give us good grounds for belief; but, if you cannot, we must respectfully refuse, even if that refusal should wreck morality and insure our own damnation several times over. We are quite content to leave that to the decision of the future. The course of the past has impressed us with the firm conviction that no good ever comes of falsehood, and we feel warranted in refusing even to experiment in that direction. * * *

1889, 1892

GEORGE MEREDITH
(1828–1909)

Like Thomas Hardy, George Meredith preferred writing poetry to writing novels, but it was as the author of *The Ordeal of Richard Feverel* (1859), *The Egoist* (1879), and other novels that he made his mark. His poems nevertheless deserve more attention than they have yet received, especially *Modern Love* (1862). This sequence of 50 16-line sonnets is a kind of novel in verse which analyzes the sufferings of a man and wife whose marriage is breaking up. The story is told, for the most part, by the husband speaking in the first person, but the opening and closing sections are in third person. *Modern Love* was probably derived, in part, from Meredith's own experiences. At 21, at the outset of his career as a writer in London, he married a daughter of the satirist Thomas Love Peacock. Nine years later, after a series of quarrels, his wife eloped to Europe with another artist. The Merediths were never reconciled, and in 1861 she died.

From Modern Love

1

By this he knew she wept with waking eyes:
That, at his hand's light quiver by her head,
The strange low sobs that shook their common bed

Were called into her with a sharp surprise,
And strangled mute, like little gaping snakes,   5
Dreadfully venomous to him. She lay
Stone-still, and the long darkness flowed away
With muffled pulses. Then, as midnight makes
Her giant heart of Memory and Tears
Drink the pale drug of silence, and so beat   10
Sleep's heavy measure, they from head to feet
Were moveless, looking through their dead black years
By vain regret scrawled over the blank wall.
Like sculptured effigies they might be seen
Upon their marriage tomb, the sword between;[1]   15
Each wishing for the sword that severs all.

2

It ended, and the morrow brought the task.
Her eyes were guilty gates, that let him in
By shutting all too zealous for their sin:
Each sucked a secret, and each wore a mask.
But, oh, the bitter taste her beauty had!   5
He sickened as at breath of poison-flowers:
A languid humor stole among the hours,
And if their smiles encountered, he went mad,
And raged deep inward, till the light was brown
Before his vision, and the world, forgot,   10
Looked wicked as some old dull murder spot.
A star with lurid beams, she seemed to crown
The pit of infamy: and then again
He fainted on his vengefulness, and strove
To ape the magnanimity of love,   15
And smote himself, a shuddering heap of pain.

3

This was the woman; what now of the man?[2]
But pass him. If he comes beneath a heel,
He shall be crushed until he cannot feel,
Or, being callous, haply till he can.
But he is nothing—nothing? Only mark   5
The rich light striking out from her on him!
Ha! what a sense it is when her eyes swim
Across the man she singles, leaving dark
All else! Lord God, who mad'st the thing so fair,
See that I am drawn to her even now!   10
It cannot be such harm on her cool brow
To put a kiss? Yet if I meet him there!
But she is mine! Ah, no! I know too well

1. The now silent couple are as motionless as recumbent stone statues on top
of a tomb. In medieval legend, a naked
sword between lovers ensured chastity.
2. I.e., a rival with whom the wife has
fallen in love.

I claim a star whose light is overcast:
I claim a phantom woman in the Past.   15
The hour has struck, though I heard not the bell!

15

I think she sleeps: it must be sleep, when low
Hangs that abandoned arm toward the floor;
The face turned with it. Now make fast the door.
Sleep on: it is your husband, not your foe.
The Poet's black stage-lion[3] of wronged love   5
Frights not our modern dames—well if he did!
Now will I pour new light upon that lid,
Full-sloping like the breasts beneath. "Sweet dove,
Your sleep is pure. Nay, pardon: I disturb.
I do not? good!" Her waking infant-stare   10
Grows woman to the burden[4] my hands bear:
Her own handwriting to me when no curb
Was left on Passion's tongue. She trembles through;
A woman's tremble—the whole instrument—
I show another letter[5] lately sent.   15
The words are very like: the name is new.

16

In our old shipwrecked days there was an hour,
When in the firelight steadily aglow,
Joined slackly, we beheld the red chasm grow
Among the clicking coals. Our library bower
That eve was left to us: and hushed we sat   5
As lovers to whom Time is whispering.
From sudden-opened doors we heard them sing:
The nodding elders mixed good wine with chat.
Well knew we that Life's greatest treasure lay
With us, and of it was our talk. "Ah, yes!   10
Love dies!" I said: I never thought it less.
She yearned to me that sentence to unsay.
Then when the fire domed blackening, I found
Her cheek was salt against my kiss, and swift
Up the sharp scale of sobs her breast did lift—   15
Now am I haunted by that taste! that sound!

17

At dinner, she is hostess, I am host.
Went the feast ever cheerfuller? She keeps
The Topic over intellectual deeps
In buoyancy afloat. They see no ghost.

---

3. Probably a reference to Shakespeare's portrait of a jealous husband in *Othello*.
4. A letter once written by the wife to the husband.
5. A letter she has recently written to the man she now loves.

With sparkling surface-eyes we ply the ball: 5
It is in truth a most contagious game:
HIDING THE SKELETON, shall be its name.
Such play as this the devils might appall!
But here's the greater wonder: in that we,
Enamored of an acting naught can tire,   10
Each other, like true hypocrites, admire;
Warm-lighted looks, Love's ephemeridae,[6]
Shoot gayly o'er the dishes and the wine.
We waken envy of our happy lot.
Fast, sweet, and golden, shows the marriage knot.   15
Dear guests, you now have seen Love's corpse-light[7] shine.

23

'Tis Christmas weather, and a country house
Receives us: rooms are full: we can but get
An attic crib.[8] Such lovers will not fret
At that, it is half-said. The great carouse
Knocks hard upon the midnight's hollow door,   5
But when I knock at hers, I see the pit.
Why did I come here in that dullard fit?
I enter, and lie couched upon the floor.
Passing, I caught the coverlet's quick beat:
Come, Shame, burn to my soul! and Pride, and Pain—   10
Foul demons that have tortured me, enchain!
Out in the freezing darkness the lambs bleat.
The small bird stiffens in the low starlight.
I know not how, but shuddering as I slept,
I dreamed a banished angel to me crept: 15
My feet were nourished on her breasts all night.

35

It is no vulgar[9] nature I have wived.
Secretive, sensitive, she takes a wound
Deep to her soul, as if the sense had swooned,
And not a thought of vengeance had survived.
No confidences has she: but relief   5
Must come to one whose suffering is acute.
O have a care of natures that are mute!
They punish you in acts: their steps are brief.
What is she doing? What does she demand
From Providence or me? She is not one   10
Long to endure this torpidly, and shun
The drugs[1] that crowd about a woman's hand.
At Forfeits[2] during snow we played, and I

---

6. Insects which live for one day only.
7. Phosphorescent light such as seen in marshes. When appearing in a cemetery it was believed to portend a funeral.
8. Small room.
9. Coarse or insensitive.
1. I.e., poison to be used for suicide.

2. A parlor game. Any player who broke one of the rules had to deposit something with the judge (in this instance, money). To win back this "forfeit," the player had to perform some act, on the orders of the judge, that would amuse the other players.

Must kiss her. "Well performed!" I said: then she:
"'Tis hardly worth the money, you agree?"   15
Save her? What for? To act this wedded lie!

42

I am to follow her.[3] There is much grace
In women when thus bent on martyrdom.
They think that dignity of soul may come,
Perchance, with dignity of body. Base!
But I was taken by that air of cold   5
And statuesque sedateness, when she said
"I'm going"; lit a taper, bowed her head,
And went, as with the stride of Pallas[4] bold.
Fleshly indifference horrible! The hands
Of Time now signal: O, she's safe from me!   10
Within those secret walls what do I see?
Where first she set the taper down she stands:
Not Pallas: Hebe shamed![5] Thoughts black as death
Like a stirred pool in sunshine break. Her wrists
I catch: she faltering, as she half resists,   15
"You love . . . ? love . . . ? love . . . ?" all on an indrawn breath.

43

Mark where the pressing wind shoots javelinlike
Its skeleton shadow on broad-backed wave!
Here is a fitting spot to dig Love's grave;
Here where the ponderous breakers plunge and strike,
And dart their hissing tongues high up the sand: 5
In hearing of the ocean, and in sight
Of those ribbed wind-streaks running into white.
If I the death of Love had deeply planned,
I never could have made it half so sure,
As by the unblessed kisses which upbraid   10
The full-waked sense: or failing that, degrade!
'Tis morning: but no morning can restore
What we have forfeited. I see no sin:
The wrong is mixed. In tragic life, God wot,
No villain need be! Passions spin the plot: 15
We are betrayed by what is false within.

48

Their sense is with their senses all mixed in,
Destroyed by subtleties these women are![6]

3. In an attempt to restore the marriage, the couple have resolved to try resuming marital relations. The experiment fails.
4. Pallas Athene, a goddess, usually pictured with the figure of a mature and powerful woman, bearing a shield and spear.
5. Hebe, goddess of youth, and, for a time, cupbearer to the gods. This office she gave up because of the shame she felt when she fell down while serving wine to the gods.
6. In a previous section, the couple had at last talked together about her affair and seemed reconciled. But when he discloses to her his own recent passing affair with a mistress (his "lost Lady," line 9), his wife resolves to give him up to the mistress. Her resolve is a noble one, but, in his view, without "sense" or "brain."

More brain, O Lord, more brain! or we shall mar
Utterly this fair garden we might win.
Behold! I looked for peace, and thought it near.   5
Our inmost hearts had opened, each to each.
We drank the pure daylight of honest speech.
Alas! that was the fatal draft, I fear.
For when of my lost Lady came the word,
This woman, O this agony of flesh!   10
Jealous devotion bade her break the mesh,
That I might seek that other like a bird.
I do adore the nobleness! despise
The act! She has gone forth, I know not where.
Will the hard world my sentience of her share?   15
I feel the truth; so let the world surmise.

49

He found her by the ocean's moaning verge,
Nor any wicked change in her discerned;
And she believed his old love had returned,
Which was her exultation, and her scourge.
She took his hand, and walked with him, and seemed   5
The wife he sought, though shadowlike and dry.
She had one terror, lest her heart should sigh,
And tell her loudly she no longer dreamed.
She dared not say, "This is my breast: look in."
But there's a strength to help the desperate weak.   10
That night he learned how silence best can speak
The awful things when Pity pleads for Sin.
About the middle of the night her call
Was heard, and he came wondering to the bed.
"Now kiss me, dear! it may be, now!" she said.   15
Lethe[7] had passed those lips, and he knew all.

50

Thus piteously Love closed what he begat:
The union of this ever diverse pair!
These two were rapid falcons in a snare,
Condemned to do the flitting of the bat.
Lovers beneath the singing sky of May,   5
They wandered once; clear as the dew on flowers:
But they fed not on the advancing hours:
Their hearts held cravings for the buried day.
Then each applied to each that fatal knife,
Deep questioning, which probes to endless dole.   10
Ah, what a dusty answer gets the soul
When hot for certainties in this our life!—
In tragic hints here see what evermore

---

7. River of forgetfulness in Hades, the Greek underworld.

Moves dark as yonder midnight ocean's force,
Thundering like ramping hosts of warrior horse,   15
To throw that faint thin line upon the shore!

                                                    1862

Dirge in Woods

A wind sways the pines,
            And below
Not a breath of wild air;
Still as the mosses that glow
On the flooring and over the lines   5
Of the roots here and there.
The pine tree drops its dead;
They are quiet, as under the sea.
Overhead, overhead
Rushes life in a race,   10
As the clouds the clouds chase;
            And we go,
And we drop like the fruits of the tree,
            Even we,
            Even so.   15

                                                    1870

Lucifer in Starlight

On a starred night Prince Lucifer uprose.
Tired of his dark dominion, swung the fiend
Above the rolling ball, in cloud part screened,
Where sinners hugged their specter of repose.
Poor prey to his hot fit of pride were those.   5
And now upon his western wing he leaned,
Now his huge bulk o'er Afric's sands careened,
Now the black planet shadowed Arctic snows.
Soaring through wider zones that pricked his scars[1]
With memory of the old revolt from Awe,   10
He reached a middle height, and at the stars,
Which are the brain of heaven, he looked, and sank.
Around the ancient track marched, rank on rank,
The army of unalterable law.

                                                    1883

1. The vast expanse of sky reminds Satan of the wounds he suffered when his revolt against God was crushed and he was hurled from heaven to hell.

DANTE GABRIEL ROSSETTI
(1828–1882)

Rossetti was the son of an Italian patriot whose political activities had led to his being exiled to England. The Rossetti household in London was one in which liberal politics and other controversial topics were hotly debated, but the son did not catch the infection. Displaying extraordinary early promise both as a painter and as a poet, Dante Gabriel Rossetti confined his interest to art. The beauty of colors and textures, above all the beauty of a woman's face and figure, made up for him a world isolated from the Victorian scene. His view of life and art, derived in part from his close study of Keats's poems and letters, anticipated by many years the aesthetic movement later to be represented by such men as Walter Pater, Oscar Wilde, and the painter James McNeill Whistler, who were to insist that art must be exclusively concerned with the beautiful, not with the useful or didactic.

The beauty that Rossetti admired in the faces of women was of a distinctive kind. In at least two of his models he found what he sought. The first was his wife, Elizabeth Siddal, whose suicide in 1862 haunted him with a sense of guilt for the rest of his life. The other was Jane Morris, the wife of his friend William Morris. In Rossetti's paintings both of these models are shown with dreamy stares, as if they were breathless from visions of heaven, but counteracting this impression is an emphasis on parted lips and fully rounded curves suggesting a more earthly kind of ecstasy. A similar combination is to be found in Rossetti's poems. *The Blessed Damozel*, first written when he was 18, portrays a heaven that is warm with physical bodies. And *The House of Life* (1870), his sonnet sequence, undertakes to explore the relationship of spirit to body in love. Some Victorian readers saw no Dante-like spirituality in *The House of Life*. Robert Buchanan saw in the poem nothing but lewd sensuality, and in 1871 he published a pamphlet, *The Fleshly School of Poetry*, which treated Rossetti's poetry to the most severe abuse. Buchanan's attack hurt the poet profoundly and contributed to the recurring seizures of nervous depression from which he suffered in the remaining years of his life.

Rossetti and his artist friends used to call such women as Jane Morris "stunners." The epithet can also be applied to Rossetti's own poetry, especially his later writings. In his maturity he used stunning polysyllabic diction to give an effect of opulence and density to his lines. His earlier poems such as *My Sister's Sleep* are usually much less elaborate in manner and can be related to the Pre-Raphaelite movement of which, in 1848, he became a founder and energetic leader.

This Pre-Raphaelite Brotherhood, as it was called, was a group of young artists and writers. The most prominent members were painters such as John Everett Millais, William Holman Hunt, and Rossetti himself. Their principal object was to reform English painting by repudiating the established academic style in favor of a revival of the simplicity and pure colors of pre-Renaissance art. Because each artist preferred to develop his own individual manner, the Brotherhood did not cohere for more than a few years. Rossetti himself grew away from the Pre-Raphaelite manner and cultivated a more richly ornate style of painting. In both the early and late phases of his writing and painting, however, it can be said that he remained a poet in his painting and a painter in his poetry. "Color and meter," he once said, "these are the true patents of nobility in painting and poetry, taking precedence of all intellectual claims."

The Blessed Damozel[1]

The blessed damozel leaned out
  From the gold bar of heaven;
Her eyes were deeper than the depth
  Of waters stilled at even;
She had three lilies in her hand,   5
  And the stars in her hair were seven.

Her robe, ungirt from clasp to hem,
  No wrought flowers did adorn,
But a white rose of Mary's gift,
  For service meetly worn;   10
Her hair that lay along her back
  Was yellow like ripe corn.[2]

Herseemed[3] she scarce had been a day
  One of God's choristers;
The wonder was not yet quite gone   15
  From that still look of hers;
Albeit, to them she left, her day
  Had counted as ten years.

(To one it is ten years of years.
  . . . Yet now, and in this place,   20
Surely she leaned o'er me—her hair
  Fell all about my face. . . .
Nothing: the autumn-fall of leaves.
  The whole year sets apace.)

It was the rampart of God's house   25
  That she was standing on;
By God built over the sheer depth
  The which is Space begun;
So high, that looking downward thence
  She scarce could see the sun.   30

1. "Damozel," a poetic version of the word "damsel," signifying a young unmarried lady. Rossetti once explained that *The Blessed Damozel* is related to Poe's *Raven*, a poem which he admired. "I saw that Poe had done the utmost it was possible to do with the grief of the lover on earth, and so I determined to reverse the conditions, and give utterance to the yearning of the loved one in heaven."
2. Grain.
3. It seemed to her.

It lies in heaven, across the flood
  Of ether, as a bridge.
Beneath the tides of day and night
  With flame and darkness ridge
The void, as low as where this earth   35
  Spins like a fretful midge.

Around her, lovers, newly met
  'Mid deathless love's acclaims,
Spoke evermore among themselves
  Their heart-remembered names;
And the souls mounting up to God   40
  Went by her like thin flames.

And still she bowed herself and stooped
  Out of the circling charm;
Until her bosom must have made
  The bar she leaned on warm,   45
And the lilies lay as if asleep
  Along her bended arm.

From the fixed place of heaven she saw
  Time like a pulse shake fierce   50
Through all the worlds. Her gaze still strove
  Within the gulf to pierce
Its path; and now she spoke as when
  The stars sang in their spheres.

The sun was gone now; the curled moon   55
  Was like a little feather
Fluttering far down the gulf; and now
  She spoke through the still weather.
Her voice was like the voice the stars
  Had when they sang together.   60

(Ah, sweet! Even now, in that bird's song,
  Strove not her accents there,
Fain to be harkened? When those bells
  Possessed the midday air,
Strove not her steps to reach my side   65
  Down all the echoing stair?)

"I wish that he were come to me,
  For he will come," she said.
"Have I not prayed in heaven?—on earth,
  Lord, Lord, has he not prayed?   70
Are not two prayers a perfect strength?
  And shall I feel afraid?

"When round his head the aureole clings,
  And he is clothed in white,
I'll take his hand and go with him   75
  To the deep wells of light;

As unto a stream we will step down,
  And bathe there in God's sight.

"We two will stand beside that shrine,
  Occult, withheld, untrod,   80
Whose lamps are stirred continually
  With prayer sent up to God;
And see our old prayers, granted, melt
  Each like a little cloud.

"We two will lie i' the shadow of   85
  That living mystic tree[4]
Within whose secret growth the Dove
  Is sometimes felt to be,
While every leaf that His plumes touch
  Saith His Name audibly.   90

"And I myself will teach to him,
  I myself, lying so,
The songs I sing here; which his voice
  Shall pause in, hushed and slow,
And find some knowledge at each pause,   95
  Or some new thing to know."

(Alas! We two, we two, thou say'st!
  Yea, one wast thou with me
That once of old. But shall God lift
  To endless unity   100
The soul whose likeness with thy soul
  Was but its love for thee?)

"We two," she said, "will seek the groves
  Where the lady Mary is,
With her five handmaidens, whose names   105
  Are five sweet symphonies,
Cecily, Gertrude, Magdalen,
  Margaret, and Rosalys.

"Circlewise sit they, with bound locks
  And foreheads garlanded;   110
Into the fine cloth white like flame
  Weaving the golden thread,
To fashion the birth-robes for them
  Who are just born, being dead.

"He shall fear, haply, and be dumb;   115
  Then will I lay my cheek
To his, and tell about our love,
  Not once abashed or weak;

4. See Revelation xxii.2.

And the dear Mother will approve
  My pride, and let me speak.   120

"Herself shall bring us, hand in hand,
  To Him round whom all souls
Kneel, the clear-ranged unnumbered heads
  Bowed with their aureoles;
And angels meeting us shall sing   125
  To their citherns and citoles.[5]

"There will I ask of Christ the Lord
  Thus much for him and me—
Only to live as once on earth
  With Love—only to be,   130
As then awhile, forever now,
  Together, I and he."

She gazed and listened and then said,
  Less sad of speech than mild—
"All this is when he comes." She ceased.   135
  The light thrilled toward her, filled
With angels in strong, level flight.
  Her eyes prayed, and she smiled.

(I saw her smile.) But soon their path
  Was vague in distant spheres;   140
And then she cast her arms along
  The golden barriers,
And laid her face between her hands,
  And wept. (I heard her tears.)

1846   1850

My Sister's Sleep[6]

She fell asleep on Christmas Eve.
  At length the long-ungranted shade
  Of weary eyelids overweighed
The pain nought else might yet relieve.

Our mother, who had leaned all day   5
  Over the bed from chime to chime,
  Then raised herself for the first time,
And as she sat her down, did pray.

Her little worktable was spread
  With work to finish. For the glare
  Made by her candle, she had care   10
To work some distance from the bed.

5. Guitar-like instruments.
6. The incident in this poem is imaginary, not autobiographical.

Without, there was a cold moon up,
  Of winter radiance sheer and thin;
  The hollow halo it was in   15
Was like an icy crystal cup.

Through the small room, with subtle sound
  Of flame, by vents the fireshine drove
  And reddened. In its dim alcove
The mirror shed a clearness round.   20

I had been sitting up some nights,
  And my tired mind felt weak and blank;
  Like a sharp strengthening wine it drank
The stillness and the broken lights.

Twelve struck. That sound, by dwindling years   25
  Heard in each hour, crept off; and then
  The ruffled silence spread again,
Like water that a pebble stirs.

Our mother rose from where she sat;
  Her needles, as she laid them down,   30
  Met lightly, and her silken gown
Settled—no other noise than that.

"Glory unto the Newly Born!"
  So, as said angels, she did say,   35
  Because we were in Christmas Day,
Though it would still be long till morn:

Just then in the room over us
  There was a pushing back of chairs,
  As some who had sat unawares
So late, now heard the hour, and rose.   40

With anxious softly-stepping haste
  Our mother went where Margaret lay,
  Fearing the sounds o'erhead—should they
Have broken her long watched-for rest!

She stooped an instant, calm, and turned,   45
  But suddenly turned back again;
  And all her features seemed in pain
With woe, and her eyes gazed and yearned.

For my part, I but hid my face,
  And held my breath, and spoke no word.   50
  There was none spoken; but I heard
The silence for a little space.

Our mother bowed herself and wept;
  And both my arms fell, and I said,
  "God knows I knew that she was dead."   55
And there, all white, my sister slept.

Then kneeling, upon Christmas morn
    A little after twelve o'clock,
    We said, ere the first quarter struck,
"Christ's blessing on the newly born!"   60

1847   1850

The Sea-Limits[7]

Consider the sea's listless chime:
    Time's self it is, made audible—
    The murmur of the earth's own shell.
Secret continuance sublime
    Is the sea's end: our sight may pass   5
    No furlong further. Since time was,
This sound hath told the lapse of time.

No quiet, which is death's—it hath
    The mournfulness of ancient life,
    Enduring always at dull strife.   10
As the world's heart of rest and wrath,
    Its painful pulse is in the sands.
    Last utterly, the whole sky stands,
Gray and not known, along its path.

Listen alone beside the sea,   15
    Listen alone among the woods;
    Those voices of twin solitudes
Shall have one sound alike to thee:
    Hark where the murmurs of thronged men
    Surge and sink back and surge again—   20
Still the one voice of wave and tree.

Gather a shell from the strown beach
    And listen at its lips: they sigh
    The same desire and mystery,
The echo of the whole sea's speech.   25
    And all mankind is thus at heart
    Not anything but what thou art:
And Earth, Sea, Man, are all in each.

1849   1870

The Woodspurge

The wind flapped loose, the wind was still,
Shaken out dead from tree and hill;
I had walked on at the wind's will—
I sat now, for the wind was still.

7. For other poems on the theme of time and the sea, see Arnold's *Dover Beach* and T. S. Eliot's *Four Quartets*.

Between my knees my forehead was— 5
My lips, drawn in, said not Alas!
My hair was over in the grass,
My naked ears heard the day pass.

My eyes, wide open, had the run
Of some ten weeds to fix upon; 10
Among those few, out of the sun,
The woodspurge flowered, three cups in one.

From perfect grief there need not be
Wisdom or even memory;
One thing then learned remains to me— 15
The woodspurge has a cup of three.

1856   1870

From The House of Life
The Sonnet

A Sonnet is a moment's monument—
  Memorial from the Soul's eternity
  To one dead deathless hour. Look that it be,
Whether for lustral[1] rite or dire portent,
Of its own arduous fullness reverent; 5
  Carve it in ivory or in ebony,
  As Day or Night may rule; and let Time see
Its flowering crest impearled and orient.

A Sonnet is a coin; its face reveals
  The soul—its converse, to what Power 'tis due— 10
Whether for tribute to the august appeals
  Of Life, or dower in Love's high retinue,
It serve; or, 'mid the dark wharf's cavernous breath,
In Charon's[2] palm it pay the toll to Death.

4. Lovesight

When do I see thee most, belovéd one?
  When in the light the spirits of mine eyes
  Before thy face, their altar, solemnize
The worship of that Love through thee made known?
Or when in the dusk hours (we two alone) 5
  Close-kissed and eloquent of still replies
  Thy twilight-hidden glimmering visage lies,
And my soul only sees thy soul its own?

O love, my love! if I no more should see
Thyself, nor on the earth the shadow of thee, 10
  Nor image of thine eyes in any spring—
How then should sound upon Life's darkening slope

---

1. Purification.
2. The ferryman who, for a fee, rowed the souls of the dead across the river Styx.

The ground-whirl of the perished leaves of Hope,
   The wind of Death's imperishable wing?

19. Silent Noon

Your hands lie open in the long fresh grass—
   The finger-points look through like rosy blooms;
    Your eyes smile peace. The pasture gleams and glooms
'Neath billowing skies that scatter and amass.
All round our nest, far as the eye can pass,
   Are golden kingcup-fields with silver edge
    Where the cow-parsley skirts the hawthorn hedge.
'Tis visible silence, still as the hourglass.

Deep in the sun-searched growths the dragonfly
Hangs like a blue thread loosened from the sky—
   So this winged hour is dropped to us from above.
Oh! clasp we to our hearts, for deathless dower,
This close-companioned inarticulate hour
   When twofold silence was the song of love.

49. Willowwood—I

I sat with Love upon a woodside well,
   Leaning across the water, I and he;
   Nor ever did he speak nor looked at me,
But touched his lute wherein was audible
The certain secret thing he had to tell.
   Only our mirrored eyes met silently
   In the low wave; and that sound came to be
The passionate voice I knew; and my tears fell.

And at their fall, his eyes beneath grew hers;
   And with his foot and with his wing feathers
   He swept the spring that watered my heart's drouth.
Then the dark ripples spread to waving hair,
And as I stooped, her own lips rising there
   Bubbled with brimming kisses at my mouth.

63. Inclusiveness

The changing guests, each in a different mood,
   Sit at the roadside table and arise;
   And every life among them in like wise
Is a soul's board set daily with new food.
What man has bent o'er his son's sleep, to brood
   How that face shall watch his when cold it lies?—
   Or thought, as his own mother kissed his eyes,
Of what her kiss was when his father wooed?

May not this ancient room thou sitt'st in dwell
   In separate living souls for joy or pain?
   Nay, all its corners may be painted plain

Where Heaven shows pictures of some life spent well;
    And may be stamped, a memory all in vain,
Upon the sight of lidless eyes in Hell.

71. *The Choice—I*

Eat thou and drink; tomorrow thou shalt die.
    Surely the earth, that's wise being very old,
    Needs not our help. Then loose me, love, and hold
Thy sultry hair up from my face; that I
May pour for thee this golden wine, brim-high,   5
    Till round the glass thy fingers glow like gold.
    We'll drown all hours: thy song, while hours are tolled,
Shall leap, as fountains veil the changing sky.

Now kiss, and think that there are really those,
    My own high-bosomed beauty, who increase   10
        Vain gold, vain lore, and yet might choose our way!
        Through many years they toil; then on a day
They die not—for their life was death—but cease;
And round their narrow lips the mold falls close.

72. *The Choice—II*

Watch thou and fear; tomorrow thou shalt die.
    Or art thou sure thou shalt have time for death?
    Is not the day which God's word promiseth
To come man knows not when? In yonder sky,
Now while we speak, the sun speeds forth; can I   5
    Or thou assure him of his goal? God's breath
    Even at this moment haply quickeneth
The air to a flame; till spirits, always nigh

Though screened and hid, shall walk the daylight here.
    And dost thou prate of all that man shall do?   10
        Canst thou, who hast but plagues, presume to be
        Glad in his gladness that comes after thee?
    Will *his* strength slay *thy* worm in Hell? Go to:
Cover thy countenance, and watch, and fear.

73. *The Choice—III*

Think thou and act; tomorrow thou shalt die.
    Outstretched in the sun's warmth upon the shore,
    Thou say'st: "Man's measured path is all gone o'er:
Up all his years, steeply, with strain and sigh,
Man clomb until he touched the truth; and I,   5
    Even I, am he whom it was destined for."
    How should this be? Art thou then so much more
Than they who sowed, that thou shouldst reap thereby?

Nay, come up hither. From this wave-washed mound
    Unto the furthest flood-brim look with me;   10

Then reach on with thy thought till it be drowned.
  Miles and miles distant though the last line be,
And though thy soul sail leagues and leagues beyond—
  Still, leagues beyond those leagues, there is more sea.

97. A Superscription

Look in my face; my name is Might-have-been;
  I am also called No-more, Too-late, Farewell;
  Unto thine ear I hold the dead-sea shell
Cast up thy Life's foam-fretted feet between;
Unto thine eyes the glass[3] where that is seen
  Which had Life's form and Love's, but by my spell
  Is now a shaken shadow intolerable,
Of ultimate things unuttered the frail screen.

Mark me, how still I am! But should there dart
  One moment through thy soul the soft surprise
  Of that winged Peace which lulls the breath of sighs—
Then shalt thou see me smile, and turn apart
Thy visage to mine ambush at thy heart
  Sleepless with cold commemorative eyes.

101. *The One Hope*

When vain desire at last and vain regret
  Go hand in hand to death, and all is vain,
  What shall assuage the unforgotten pain
And teach the unforgetful to forget?
Shall Peace be still a sunk stream long unmet—
  Or may the soul at once in a green plain
  Stoop through the spray of some sweet life-fountain
And cull the dew-drenched flowering amulet?[4]
Ah! when the wan soul in that golden air
  Between the scriptured petals softly blown
  Peers breathless for the gift of grace unknown,
Ah! let none other alien spell soe'er
But only the one Hope's one name be there—
  Not less nor more, but even that word alone.

1848–80
                                    1870, 1881

She Bound Her Green Sleeve

A FRAGMENT

She bound her green sleeve on my helm,
  Sweet pledge of love's sweet meed;[5]
Warm was her bared arm round my neck
  As well she bade me speed;

3. Mirror.
4. A charm to protect the wearer from   harm.
                                    5. Reward.

And her kiss clings still between my lips,   5
Heart's beat and strength at need.

1870   1886

The Orchard-Pit

A FRAGMENT

Piled deep below the screening apple branch
    They lie with bitter[6] apples in their hands:
And some are only ancient bones that blanch,
And some had ships that last year's wind did launch,
    And some were yesterday the lords of lands.   5

In the soft dell, among the apple trees,
    High up above the hidden pit she stands,[7]
And there forever sings, who gave to these,
That lie below, her magic hour of ease,
    And those her apples holden in their hands.   10

This in my dreams is shown me; and her hair
    Crosses my lips and draws my burning breath;
Her song spreads golden wings upon the air,
Life's eyes are gleaming from her forehead fair,
    And from her breasts the ravishing eyes of Death.   15

Men say to me that sleep hath many dreams,
    Yet I knew never but this dream alone:
There, from a dried-up channel, once the stream's,
The glen slopes up; even such in sleep it seems
    As to my waking sight the place well known.   20

My love I call her, and she loves me well:
    But I love her as in the maelstrom's cup
The whirled stone loves the leaf inseparable
That clings to it round all the circling swell,
    And that the same last eddy swallows up.   25

1869   1886

6. There is some evidence that Rossetti wrote "bitten" rather than "bitter"—a misprint that would affect our interpretation of the poem. See Oswald Doughty's edition of the *Poems* (1957), p. 307.

7. Cf. Swinburne's *Garden of Proserpine*, lines 49–50: "Pale, beyond porch and portal, / Crowned with calm leaves, she stands."

CHRISTINA ROSSETTI

(1830–1894)

Christina, the sister of Dante Gabriel Rossetti, was a devout High Church Anglican whose quiet life was dedicated to good works for church and charity and, until his death in 1854, to the care of her father, to whom she was keenly attached, and of her mother, who died in 1886. On two occasions her religious principles were responsible for breaking off plans for marriage. Her first fiancé reverted to Roman Catholicism, and her second lover seemed insufficiently concerned with religion. In both instances she suffered painfully, and most of her love lyrics are records of frustration and parting. Only rarely does she write of the happiness of union. Even her early poems focus on a painful sense of isolation. In *Heart's Chill Between*, written when she was 16, she records the haunting aftereffects following the break-up of a love relation:

> And often through the long long night,
> Waking when none are near,
> I feel my heart beat fast with fright,
> Yet know not what I fear:
> Oh how I long to see the light,
> And the sweet birds to hear.

Her volume of 1862, *Goblin Market and Other Poems*, was the first collection of poetry in the Pre-Raphaelite manner to gain recognition from the public. The long narrative poem providing the volume with its title became an early established favorite as a seemingly simple moral fable for children. Later readers have likened it to Coleridge's ballad *The Ancient Mariner* and detect in it a more complex representation of religious themes of temptation and sin redeemed by vicarious suffering, although the fruit that tempts Laura is clearly not from the Tree of Knowledge but from an orchard of sensual delights. In its deceptively simple style, *Goblin Market*, like most of her poems, demonstrates her affinity with the early aims of the Pre-Raphaelite group, but her lyric gift is distinctive enough to defy histori-cal classification. England, the birthplace of poets, has produced few women poets of note (as contrasted with the roll call of great novelists who were women). Of these few Christina Rossetti was described, in a letter by Vir-ginia Woolf, as "the first of our English poetesses." "She sings like a robin and sometimes like a nightingale," Woolf continued, and, in another letter, she affirmed: "Do you know she was about as good as poetesses are made, since Sappho jumped" (Sappho, the famous Greek lyricist, committed suicide).

Song

> When I am dead, my dearest,
> Sing no sad songs for me;
> Plant thou no roses at my head,
> Nor shady cypress tree.
> Be the green grass above me   5
> With showers and dewdrops wet;
> And if thou wilt, remember,
> And if thou wilt, forget.
>
> I shall not see the shadows,
> I shall not feel the rain;   10

I shall not hear the nightingale
   Sing on as if in pain.
And dreaming through the twilight
   That doth not rise nor set,
Haply I may remember,   15
   And haply may forget.

1848   1862

After Death

The curtains were half drawn; the floor was swept
   And strewn with rushes; rosemary and may
   Lay thick upon the bed on which I lay,
Where, through the lattice, ivy-shadows crept.
He leaned above me, thinking that I slept   5
   And could not hear him; but I heard him say,
   "Poor child, poor child"; and as he turned away
Came a deep silence, and I knew he wept.
He did not touch the shroud, or raise the fold
   That hid my face, or take my hand in his,   10
   Or ruffle the smooth pillows for my head.
   He did not love me living; but once dead
He pitied me; and very sweet it is
To know he still is warm though I am cold.

1849   1862

In an Artist's Studio[1]

One face looks out from all his canvases,
   One selfsame figure sits or walks or leans:
   We found her hidden just behind those screens,
That mirror gave back all her loveliness.
A queen in opal or in ruby dress,   5
   A nameless girl in freshest summer-greens,
   A saint, an angel—every canvas means
The same one meaning, neither more nor less.
He feeds upon her face by day and night,
   And she with true kind eyes looks back on him,   10
Fair as the moon and joyful as the light:
   Not wan with waiting, not with sorrow dim;
Not as she is, but was when hope shone bright;
   Not as she is, but as she fills his dream.

1856   1861

1. William Michael Rossetti, Christina's younger brother, noted, "The reference is apparently to our brother's studio, and to his constantly-repeated heads of the lady whom he afterwards married, Miss Siddal."

A Birthday

My heart is like a singing bird
  Whose nest is in a watered shoot:
My heart is like an apple tree
  Whose boughs are bent with thickset fruit;
My heart is like a rainbow shell   5
  That paddles in a halcyon sea;
My heart is gladder than all these
  Because my love is come to me.

Raise me a dais of silk and down;
  Hang it with vair[1] and purple dyes;   10
Carve it in doves and pomegranates,
  And peacocks with a hundred eyes;
Work it in gold and silver grapes,
  In leaves and silver fleurs-de-lys;
Because the birthday of my life   15
  Is come, my love is come to me.

1857   1861

An Apple Gathering

I plucked pink blossoms from mine apple tree
  And wore them all that evening in my hair:
Then in due season when I went to see
  I found no apples there.

With dangling basket all along the grass   5
  As I had come I went the selfsame track:
My neighbors mocked me while they saw me pass
  So empty-handed back.

Lilian and Lilias smiled in trudging by,
  Their heaped-up basket teased me like a jeer;   10
Sweet-voiced they sang beneath the sunset sky,
  Their mother's home was near.

Plump Gertrude passed me with her basket full,
  A stronger hand than hers helped it along;
A voice talked with her through the shadows cool   15
  More sweet to me than song.

Ah Willie, Willie, was my love less worth
  Than apples with their green leaves piled above?
I counted rosiest apples on the earth
  Of far less worth than love.   20

---

1. Squirrel fur.

So once it was with me you stooped to talk
   Laughing and listening in this very lane;
To think that by this way we used to walk
   We shall not walk again!

I let my neighbors pass me, ones and twos   25
   And groups; the latest said the night grew chill,
And hastened: but I loitered; while the dews
   Fell fast I loitered still.

1857   1861

Uphill

Does the road wind uphill all the way?
   Yes, to the very end.
Will the day's journey take the whole long day?
   From morn to night, my friend.

But is there for the night a resting place?   5
   A roof for when the slow dark hours begin.
May not the darkness hide it from my face?
   You cannot miss that inn.

Shall I meet other wayfarers at night?
   Those who have gone before.   10
Then must I knock, or call when just in sight?
   They will not keep you standing at that door.

Shall I find comfort, travel-sore and weak?
   Of labor you shall find the sum.
Will there be beds for me and all who seek?   15
   Yea, beds for all who come.

1858   1861

Goblin Market

Morning and evening
Maids heard the goblins cry:
"Come buy our orchard fruits,
Come buy, come buy:
Apples and quinces,   5
Lemons and oranges,
Plump unpecked cherries,
Melons and raspberries,
Bloom-down-cheeked peaches,
Swart-headed mulberries,   10
Wild free-born cranberries,
Crabapples, dewberries,
Pineapples, blackberries,
Apricots, strawberries;—
All ripe together   15

In summer weather,—
Morns that pass by,
Fair eyes that fly;
Come buy, come buy:
Our grapes fresh from the vine,   20
Pomegranates full and fine,
Dates and sharp bullaces,
Rare pears and greengages,
Damsons¹ and bilberries,
Taste them and try: 25
Currants and gooseberries,
Bright-fire-like barberries,
Figs to fill your mouth,
Citrons from the South,
Sweet to tongue and sound to eye;   30
Come buy, come buy."
Evening by evening
Among the brookside rushes,
Laura bowed her head to hear,
Lizzie veiled her blushes: 35
Crouching close together
In the cooling weather,
With clasping arms and cautioning lips,
With tingling cheeks and finger tips.
"Lie close," Laura said,   40
Pricking up her golden head:
"We must not look at goblin men,
We must not buy their fruits:
Who knows upon what soil they fed
Their hungry thirsty roots?"   45
"Come buy," call the goblins
Hobbling down the glen.
"Oh," cried Lizzie, "Laura, Laura,
You should not peep at goblin men."
Lizzie covered up her eyes,   50
Covered close lest they should look;
Laura reared her glossy head,
And whispered like the restless brook:
'Look, Lizzie, look, Lizzie,
Down the glen tramp little men.   55
One hauls a basket,
One bears a plate,
One lugs a golden dish
Of many pounds' weight.
How fair the vine must grow   60
Whose grapes are so luscious;
How warm the wind must blow
Through those fruit bushes."

---

1. Bullaces, greengages, and damsons are varieties of plums.

"No," said Lizzie: "No, no, no;
Their offers should not charm us,   65
Their evil gifts would harm us."
She thrust a dimpled finger
In each ear, shut eyes and ran:
Curious Laura chose to linger
Wondering at each merchant man.   70
One had a cat's face,
One whisked a tail,
One tramped at a rat's pace,
One crawled like a snail,
One like a wombat prowled obtuse and furry,   75
One like a ratel² tumbled hurry skurry.
She heard a voice like voice of doves
Cooing all together:
They sounded kind and full of loves
In the pleasant weather.   80

Laura stretched her gleaming neck
Like a rush-imbedded swan,
Like a lily from the beck,³
Like a moonlit poplar branch,
Like a vessel at the launch   85
When its last restraint is gone.

Backwards up the mossy glen
Turned and trooped the goblin men,
With their shrill repeated cry,
"Come buy, come buy."   90
When they reached where Laura was
They stood stock still upon the moss,
Leering at each other,
Brother with queer brother;
Signaling each other,   95
Brother with sly brother.
One set his basket down,
One reared his plate;
One began to weave a crown
Of tendrils, leaves, and rough nuts brown   100
(Men sell not such in any town);
One heaved the golden weight
Of dish and fruit to offer her:
"Come buy, come buy," was still their cry.
Laura stared but did not stir,   105
Longed but had no money.
The whisk-tailed merchant bade her taste
In tones as smooth as honey,

2. Ratel (pronounced ray-tell): South Af-   3. Small brook.
rican mammal resembling a badger.

The cat-faced purr'd,
The rat-paced spoke a word   110
Of welcome, and the snail-paced even was heard;
One parrot-voiced and jolly
Cried "Pretty Goblin" still for "Pretty Polly";
One whistled like a bird.

But sweet-tooth Laura spoke in haste: 115
"Good Folk, I have no coin;
To take were to purloin:
I have no copper in my purse,
I have no silver either,
And all my gold is on the furze   120
That shakes in windy weather
Above the rusty heather."
"You have much gold upon your head,"
They answered all together:
"Buy from us with a golden curl."   125
She clipped a precious golden lock,
She dropped a tear more rare than pearl,
Then sucked their fruit globes fair or red.
Sweeter than honey from the rock,
Stronger than man-rejoicing wine,   130
Clearer than water flowed that juice;
She never tasted such before,
How should it cloy with length of use?
She sucked and sucked and sucked the more
Fruits which that unknown orchard bore;   135
She sucked until her lips were sore;
Then flung the emptied rinds away
But gathered up one kernel stone,
And knew not was it night or day
As she turned home alone.   140

Lizzie met her at the gate
Full of wise upbraidings:
"Dear, you should not stay so late,
Twilight is not good for maidens;
Should not loiter in the glen   145
In the haunts of goblin men.
Do you not remember Jeanie,
How she met them in the moonlight,
Took their gifts both choice and many,
Ate their fruits and wore their flowers   150
Plucked from bowers
Where summer ripens at all hours?
But ever in the noonlight
She pined and pined away;
Sought them by night and day,   155
Found them no more, but dwindled and grew gray;
Then fell with the first snow,

While to this day no grass will grow
Where she lies low:
I planted daisies there a year ago   160
That never blow.
You should not loiter so."
"Nay, hush," said Laura:
"Nay, hush, my sister:
I ate and ate my fill,   165
Yet my mouth waters still:
Tomorrow night I will
Buy more"; and kissed her.
"Have done with sorrow;
I'll bring you plums tomorrow   170
Fresh on their mother twigs,
Cherries worth getting;
You cannot think what figs
My teeth have met in,
What melons icy-cold   175
Piled on a dish of gold
Too huge for me to hold,
What peaches with a velvet nap,
Pellucid grapes without one seed:
Odorous indeed must be the mead   180
Whereon they grow, and pure the wave they drink
With lilies at the brink,
And sugar-sweet their sap."

Golden head by golden head,
Like two pigeons in one nest   185
Folded in each other's wings,
They lay down in their curtained bed:
Like two blossoms on one stem,
Like two flakes of new-fallen snow,
Like two wands of ivory   190
Tipped with gold for awful⁴ kings.
Moon and stars gazed in at them,
Wind sang to them lullaby,
Lumbering owls forebore to fly,
Not a bat flapped to and fro   195
Round their nest:
Cheek to cheek and breast to breast
Locked together in one nest.

Early in the morning
When the first cock crowed his warning, 200
Neat like bees, as sweet and busy,
Laura rose with Lizzie:
Fetched in honey, milked the cows,
Aired and set to rights the house,
Kneaded cakes of whitest wheat,   205

4. Awe-inspiring.

Cakes for dainty mouths to eat,
Next churned butter, whipped up cream,
Fed their poultry, sat and sewed;
Talked as modest maidens should:
Lizzie with an open heart,   210
Laura in an absent dream,
One content, one sick in part;
One warbling for the mere bright day's delight,
One longing for the night.

At length slow evening came: 215
They went with pitchers to the reedy brook;
Lizzie most placid in her look,
Laura most like a leaping flame,
They drew the gurgling water from its deep.
Lizzie plucked purple and rich golden flags,   220
Then turning homeward said: "The sunset flushes
Those furthest loftiest crags;
Come, Laura, not another maiden lags.
No willful squirrel wags,
The beasts and birds are fast asleep."   225
But Laura loitered still among the rushes.
And said the bank was steep.

And said the hour was early still,
The dew not fallen, the wind not chill;
Listening ever, but not catching   230
The customary cry,
"Come buy, come buy,"
With its iterated jingle
Of sugar-baited words:
Not for all her watching   235
Once discerning even one goblin
Racing, whisking, tumbling, hobbling—
Let alone the herds
That used to tramp along the glen,
In groups or single,   240
Of brisk fruit-merchant men.
Till Lizzie urged, "O Laura, come;
I hear the fruit-call, but I dare not look:
You should not loiter longer at this brook:
Come with me home.   245
The stars rise, the moon bends her arc,
Each glow-worm winks her spark,
Let us get home before the night grows dark:
For clouds may gather
Though this is summer weather,   250
Put out the lights and drench us through;
Then if we lost our way what should we do?

Laura turned cold as stone
To find her sister heard that cry alone,
That goblin cry,   255
"Come buy our fruits, come buy."
Must she then buy no more such dainty fruit?
Must she no more such succous pasture find,
Gone deaf and blind?
Her tree of life dropped from the root: 260
She said not one word in her heart's sore ache:
But peering through the dimness, nought discerning,
Trudged home, her pitcher dripping all the way;
So crept to bed, and lay
Silent till Lizzie slept;   265
Then sat up in a passionate yearning.
And gnashed her teeth for balked desire, and wept
As if her heart would break.

Day after day, night after night,
Laura kept watch in vain   270
In sullen silence of exceeding pain.
She never caught again the goblin cry,
"Come buy, come buy";—
She never spied the goblin men
Hawking their fruits along the glen: 275
But when the noon waxed bright
Her hair grew thin and gray;
She dwindled, as the fair full moon doth turn
To swift decay and burn
Her fire away.   280

One day remembering her kernelstone
She set it by a wall that faced the south;
Dewed it with tears, hoped for a root,
Watched for a waxing shoot,
But there came none.   285
It never saw the sun,
It never felt the trickling moisture run:
While with sunk eyes and faded mouth
She dreamed of melons, as a traveler sees
False waves in desert drouth   290
With shade of leaf-crowned trees,
And burns the thirstier in the sandful breeze.

She no more swept the house,
Tended the fowls or cows,
Fetched honey, kneaded cakes of wheat,   295
Brought water from the brook:
But sat down listless in the chimneynook
And would not eat.

Tender Lizzie could not bear
To watch her sister's cankerous care,   300
Yet not to share.
She night and morning
Caught the goblins' cry:
"Come buy our orchard fruits,
Come buy, come buy":—   305
Beside the brook, along the glen,
She heard the tramp of goblin men,
The voice and stir
Poor Laura could not hear;
Longed to buy fruit to comfort her,   310
But feared to pay too dear.
She thought of Jeanie in her grave,
Who should have been a bride;
But who for joys brides hope to have
Fell sick and died   315
In her gay prime,
In earliest winter time,
With the first glazing rime,
With the first snow-fall of crisp winter time.

Till Laura dwindling   320
Seemed knocking at Death's door.
Then Lizzie weighed no more
Better and worse;
But put a silver penny in her purse,
Kissed Laura, crossed the heath with clumps of furze 325
At twilight, halted by the brook:
And for the first time in her life
Began to listen and look.

Laughed every goblin
When they spied her peeping: 330
Came towards her hobbling,
Flying, running, leaping,
Puffing and blowing,
Chuckling, clapping, crowing,
Cluckling and gobbling,   335
Mopping and mowing,
Full of airs and graces,
Pulling wry faces,
Demure grimaces,
Cat-like and rat-like,   340
Ratel- and wombat-like,
Snail-paced in a hurry,
Parrot-voiced and whistler,
Helter skelter, hurry skurry,
Chattering like magpies,   345
Fluttering like pigeons,

Gliding like fishes,—
Hugged her and kissed her:
Squeezed and caressed her:
Stretched up their dishes,   350
Panniers, and plates:
"Look at our apples
Russet and dun,
Bob at our cherries,
Bite at our peaches,   355
Citrons and dates,
Grapes for the asking,
Pears red with basking
Out in the sun,
Plums on their twigs;   360
Pluck them and suck them,—
Pomegranates, figs."

"Good folk," said Lizzie,
Mindful of Jeanie:
"Give me much and many":   365
Held out her apron,
Tossed them her penny
"Nay, take a seat with us,
Honor and eat with us,"
They answered grinning: 370
"Our feast is but beginning.
Night yet is early,
Warm and dew-pearly,
Wakeful and starry:
Such fruits as these   375
No man can carry;
Half their bloom would fly,
Half their dew would dry,
Half their flavor would pass by.
Sit down and feast with us,   380
Be welcome guest with us,
Cheer you and rest with us."—
"Thank you, said Lizzie: "But one waits
At home alone for me:
So without further parleying,   385
If you will not sell me any
Of your fruits though much and many,
Give me back my silver penny
I tossed you for a fee."—
The began to scratch their pates,   390
No longer wagging, purring,
But visibly demurring,
Grunting and snarling.
One called her proud,

Cross-grained, uncivil;   395
Their tones waxed loud,
Their looks were evil.
Lashing their tails
They trod and hustled her,
Elbowed and jostled her,   400
Clawed with their nails,
Barking, mewing, hissing, mocking,
Tore her gown and soiled her stocking,
Twitched her hair out by the roots,
Stamped upon her tender feet,   405
Held her hands and squeezed their fruits
Against her mouth to make her eat.

White and golden Lizzie stood,
Like a lily in a flood,—
Like a rock of blue-veined stone   410
Lashed by tides obstreperously,—
Like a beacon left alone
In a hoary roaring sea,
Sending up a golden fire,—
Like a fruit-crowned orange-tree   415
White with blossoms honey-sweet
Sore beset by wasp and bee,—
Like a royal virgin town
Topped with gilded dome and spire
Close beleaguered by a fleet   420
Mad to tug her standard down.

One may lead a horse to water,
Twenty cannot make him drink.
Though the goblins cuffed and caught her,
Coaxed and fought her,   425
Bullied and besought her,
Scratched her, pinched her black as ink,
Kicked and knocked her,
Mauled and mocked her,
Lizzie uttered not a word;   430
Would not open lip from lip
Lest they should cram a mouthful in:
But laughed in heart to feel the drip
Of juice that syruped all her face,
And lodged in dimples of her chin,   435
And streaked her neck which quaked like curd.
At last the evil people,
Worn out by her resistance,
Flung back her penny, kicked their fruit
Along whichever road they took,   440
Not leaving root or stone or shoot;
Some writhed into the ground,

Some dived into the brook
With ring and ripple,
Some scudded on the gale without a sound,
Some vanished in the distance.   445

In a smart, ache, tingle,
Lizzie went her way;
Knew not was it night or day;
Sprang up the bank, tore through the furze,   450
Threaded copse and dingle,
And heard her penny jingle
Bouncing in her purse,—
Its bounce was music to her ear.
She ran and ran   455
As if she feared some goblin man
Dogged her with gibe or curse
Or something worse:
But not one goblin skurried after,
Nor was she pricked by fear;   460
The kind heart made her windy-paced
That urged her home quite out of breath with haste
And inward laughter.

She cried, "Laura," up the garden,
"Did you miss me?   465
Come and kiss me.
Never mind my bruises,
Hug me, kiss me, suck my juices
Squeezed from goblin fruits for you,
Goblin pulp and goblin dew.   470
Eat me, drink me, love me;
Laura, make much of me;
For your sake I have braved the glen
And had to do with goblin merchant men."

Laura started from her chair,   475
Flung her arms up in the air,
Clutched her hair:
"Lizzie, Lizzie, have you tasted
For my sake the fruit forbidden?
Must your light like mine be hidden,   480
Your young life like mine be wasted,
Undone in mine undoing,
And ruined in my ruin,
Thirsty, cankered, goblin-ridden?"—
She clung about her sister,   485
Kissed and kissed and kissed her:
Tears once again
Refreshed her shrunken eyes,

Dropping like rain
After long sultry drouth;
Shaking with anguish, fear, and pain,   490
She kissed and kissed her with a hungry mouth.

Her lips began to scorch,
That juice was wormwood to her tongue,
She loathed the feast: 495
Writhing as one possessed she leaped and sung,
Rent all her robe, and wrung
Her hands in lamentable haste,
And beat her breast,
Her locks streamed like the torch   500
Borne by a racer at full speed,
Or like the mane of horses in their flight,
Or like an eagle when she stems[5] the light
Straight toward the sun,
Or like a caged thing freed,   505
Or like a flying flag when armies run.

Swift fire spread through her veins, knocked at her heart,
Met the fire smoldering there
And overbore its lesser flame;
She gorged on bitterness without a name: 510
Ah fool, to choose such part
Of soul-consuming care!
Sense failed in the mortal strife:
Like the watch-tower of a town
Which an earthquake shatters down,   515
Like a lightning-stricken mast,
Like a wind-uprooted tree
Spun about,
Like a foam-topped waterspout
Cast down headlong in the sea,   520
She fell at last;
Pleasure past and anguish past,
Is it death or is it life?

Life out of death.
That night long Lizzie watched by her,   525
Counted her pulse's flagging stir,
Felt for her breath,
Held water to her lips, and cooled her face
With tears and fanning leaves.
But when the first birds chirped about their eaves, 530
And early reapers plodded to the place
Of golden sheaves,
And dew-wet grass

5. Breasts or makes headway against.

Bowed in the morning winds so brisk to pass,
And new buds with new day   535
Opened of cup-like lilies on the stream,
Laura awoke as from a dream,
Laughed in the innocent old way,
Hugged Lizzie but not twice or thrice;
Her gleaming locks showed not one thread of gray,   540
Her breath was sweet as May,
And light danced in her eyes.

Days, weeks, months, years
Afterwards, when both were wives
With children of their own;   545
Their mother-hearts beset with fears,
Their lives bound up in tender lives;
Laura would call the little ones
And tell them of her early prime,
Those pleasant days long gone   550
Of not-returning time:
Would talk about the haunted glen,
The wicked quaint fruit-merchant men,
Their fruits like honey to the throat
But poison in the blood   555
(Men sell not such in any town):
Would tell them how her sister stood
In deadly peril to do her good,
And win the fiery antidote:
Then joining hands to little hands   560
Would bid them cling together,—
"For there is no friend like a sister
In calm or stormy weather;
To cheer one on the tedious way,
To fetch one if one goes astray,   565
To lift one if one totters down,
To strengthen whilst one stands."

1859   1862

A Life's Parallels

Never on this side of the grave again,
    On this side of the river,
On this side of the garner of the grain,
    Never.

Ever while time flows on and on and on,   5
    That narrow noiseless river,
Ever while corn bows heavy-headed, wan,
    Ever.

Never despairing, often fainting, ruing,
But looking back, ah never!
Faint yet pursuing, faint yet still pursuing
Ever.   10

ca. 1881   1893

Cardinal Newman[1]

In the grave whither thou goest.

O weary Champion of the Cross, lie still:
Sleep thou at length the all-embracing sleep;
Long was thy sowing day, rest now and reap:
Thy fast was long, feast now thy spirit's fill.
Yea take thy fill of love, because thy will   5
Chose love not in the shallows but the deep:
Thy tides were spring tides, set against the neap[2]
Of calmer souls: thy flood rebuked their rill.
Now night has come to thee—please God, of rest:
So some time must it come to every man;   10
To first and last, where many last are first.
Now fixed and finished thine eternal plan,
Thy best has done its best, thy worst its worst:
Thy best its best, please God, thy best its best.

1890   1893

Sleeping at Last

Sleeping at last, the trouble and tumult over,
Sleeping at last, the struggle and horror past,
Cold and white, out of sight of friend and of lover,
Sleeping at last.

No more a tired heart downcast or overcast,   5
No more pangs that wring or shifting fears that hover,
Sleeping at last in a dreamless sleep locked fast.

Fast asleep. Singing birds in their leafy cover
Cannot wake her, nor shake her the gusty blast.
Under the purple thyme and the purple clover   10
Sleeping at last.

1893   1896

1. Written on the occasion of the death of John Henry Newman. The epigraph is from Ecclesiastes ix.10.   2. Tides which do not rise to the high-water mark of the spring tides.

WILLIAM MORRIS
(1834–1896)

In his Apology to *The Earthly Paradise* Morris described himself as "the idle singer of an empty day," yet the word "idle," applied to him, seems incongruous or comic. Painter, businessman, poet, designer of furniture, printer, weaver, and political agitator, Morris was one of the most active men of his century.

Although anthologies usually feature his incidental lyrics, Morris was primarily, like Chaucer, a narrative poet. His early volume *The Defense of Guenevere* (1858) contains his most effective narratives: poems such as *The Haystack in the Floods* illustrate his flair for intense and concentrated storytelling. In his later volumes Morris abandons this promising vein and presents more diffuse and easily readable retellings of the sagas of Iceland as in *Sigurd the Volsung* (1876) or of classical legends as in *The Life and Death of Jason* (1867) and *The Earthly Paradise* (1868). The readability of these popular classical narratives is partly attributable to Morris's treatment of the rhymed couplet, a form he preferred to blank verse. In his hands the rhyming is so contrivedly unobtrusive that the narrative seems to flow without interruption. The following passage is representative (on a starlit night Medea first declares her love for Jason):

> "Upon the day thou weariest of me,
> I wish that thou mayst somewhat think of this,
> And 'twixt thy new-found kisses, and the bliss
> Of something sweeter than thine old delight,
> Remember thee a little of this night
> Of marvels, and this starlit, silent place,
> And these two lovers standing face to face."

Such poems had a marked influence on the early poetry of W. B. Yeats, who was honored when Morris said of his early volume of poems (*The Wanderings of Oisin*, 1889): "You write my kind of poetry."

Morris, in turn, was deeply attached to his own literary master, John Ruskin. Like Ruskin he became progressively dissatisfied with the drabness of the modern industrial world, and in later years became convinced that a political revolution was needed to restore mankind to a state in which work could once more be enjoyed, without the exploitation of workers that seemed to him prevalent in Victorian England. In his late poem, *The Pilgrim of Hope* (1885), Morris prophesies a changed society in which "Hope is awake in the faces angerless now no more, / Till the new peace dawn on the world, the fruit of the people's war." And in his prose narrative, *News from Nowhere* (1891), he spells out more explicitly his ideal of a communist (and machineless) state, an ideal derived partly from his study of Karl Marx but more from his lifelong love for the color and vitality of medieval life.

Christ Keep the Hollow Land[1]

Christ keep the Hollow Land
  All the summertide;
Still we cannot understand
  Where the waters glide:

Only dimly seeing them   5
  Coldly slipping through
Many green-lipped cavern mouths
  Where the hills are blue.

                                1856

1. From a song sung by the heroine of   was published in the *Oxford and Cam-*
a prose story, *The Hollow Land*, which   *bridge Magazine*.

The Defense of Guenevere   Several episodes in Thomas Malory's *Morte Darthur* (1470), one of Morris's favorite books, provided the materials on which he based this poem, although how he presents them is strikingly original. In Malory's narrative, Arthur's kingdom is eventually destroyed by dissensions among his followers; one chief focus of dissension concerned rumors of an adulterous relation between Queen Guenevere and Arthur's chief knight, Launcelot. On two occasions Guenevere had been discovered in apparently compromising circumstances, both of which led to public accusations of adultery. On the first occasion (lines 167–220), her accuser, Sir Mellyagraunce, was challenged by Launcelot to a trial by battle, in which Mellyagraunce was slain. The queen's honor was thereby restored, although, in the poem, the Mellyagraunce scandal is revived by Sir Gauwaine in his accusations against her. The second occasion, which occurred just before the poem opens, was more seriously incriminating. A band of 13 knights had plotted to trap Launcelot when he was enjoying a visit at night in the queen's chamber, at her invitation (lines 242–77). In making his escape, Launcelot killed all but one of the knights—an event which would later lead to civil war. In Malory's version there is no formal trial of the queen after this event; she is simply told of her sentence, which is to be burned to death at the stake, and is thereafter rescued by Launcelot who takes her away to safety in his castle. Morris's trial scene is hence his own invention, although he probably drew from another episode, in Chapter XVIII of Malory, which shows Guenevere being accused of treason by Sir Gauwaine in the presence of 24 of his knights.

According to Morris's daughter, this poem originally opened with a long introductory passage of description and background, which Morris wisely decided to omit. As a result we are plunged at once into a dramatic scene reminiscent of the openings of some of the dramatic monologues of Robert Browning (the Victorian poet whom Morris most admired). Also like Browning is the way Guenevere's speech keeps shifting back and forth from present to past events such as her recalling the spring day, early in her marriage to Arthur, when Launcelot first kissed her.

During the same year in which Morris's poem appeared, one of Tennyson's *Idylls of the King*, also focused on Guenevere, was published. It is interesting to compare the two portraits of the queen, especially in terms of their pictorial qualities. Actually, although Morris remarked in an interview that Shakespeare's plays had not affected his writing (because he preferred narrative and lyric over dramatic poetry), his portrait of Guenevere has more in common with Shakespeare's seductively eloquent queen in *Antony and Cleopatra* than it shares with Tennyson's subdued representation of a guilt-ridden wife in the *Idylls*.

The Defense of Guenevere

But, knowing now that they would have her speak,
She threw her wet hair backward from her brow,
Her hand close to her mouth touching her cheek,

As though she had had there a shameful blow,
And feeling it shameful to feel ought but shame   5
All through her heart, yet felt her cheek burned so,

She must a little touch it; like one lame
She walked away from Gauwaine, with her head
Still lifted up; and on her cheek of flame

The tears dried quick; she stopped at last and said: 10
"O knights and lords, it seems but little skill[1]
To talk of well-known things past now and dead.

"God wot I ought to say, I have done ill,
And pray you all forgiveness heartily!
Because you must be right such great lords—still   15

"Listen, suppose your time were come to die,
And you were quite alone and very weak;
Yea, laid a dying while very mightily

"The wind was ruffling up the narrow streak
Of river through your broad lands running well: 20
Suppose a hush should come, then someone speak:

" 'One of these cloths is heaven, and one is hell,
Now choose one cloth forever, which they be,
I will not tell you, you must somehow tell

" 'Of your own strength and mightiness; here, see!'   25
Yea, yea, my lord, and you to ope your eyes,
At foot of your familiar bed to see

1. Use.

"A great God's angel standing, with such dyes,
Not known on earth, on his great wings, and hands,
Held out two ways, light from the inner skies   30

"Showing him well, and making his commands
Seem to be God's commands, moreover, too,
Holding within his hands the cloths on wands;

"And one of these strange choosing cloths was blue,
Wavy and long, and one cut short and red;   35
No man could tell the better of the two.

"After a shivering half hour you said,
'God help! heaven's color, the blue'; and he said, 'hell.'[2]
Perhaps you then would roll upon your bed,

"And cry to all good men that loved you well,   40
'Ah Christ! if only I had known, known, known';
Launcelot went away, then I could tell,

"Like wisest man how all things would be, moan,
And roll and hurt myself, and long to die,
And yet fear much to die for what was sown.   45

"Nevertheless you, O Sir Gauwaine, lie,
Whatever may have happened through these years,
God knows I speak truth, saying that you lie."

Her voice was low at first, being full of tears,
But as it cleared, it grew full loud and shrill,   50
Growing a windy shriek in all men's ears,

A ringing in their startled brains, until
She said that Gauwaine lied, then her voice sunk,
And her great eyes began again to fill,

Though still she stood right up, and never shrunk,   55
But spoke on bravely, glorious lady fair!
Whatever tears her full lips may have drunk,

She stood, and seemed to think, and wrung her hair,
Spoke out at last with no more trace of shame,
With passionate twisting of her body there: 60

"It chanced upon a day that Launcelot came
To dwell at Arthur's court: at Christmas time
This happened; when the heralds sung his name,

---

2. According to one interpretation of
this passage, the blue cloth represents
Arthur. The contrary interpretation is
that it represents Launcelot.

" 'Son of King Ban[3] of Benwick,' seemed to chime
Along with all the bells that rang that day,   65
O'er the white roofs, with little change of rhyme.

"Christmas and whitened winter passed away,
And over me the April sunshine came,
Made very awful with black hail-clouds, yea.

"And in Summer I grew white with flame,   70
And bowed my head down—Autumn, and the sick
Sure knowledge things would never be the same,

"However often Spring might be most thick
Of blossoms and buds, smote on me, and I grew
Careless of most things, let the clock tick, tick,   75

"To my unhappy pulse, that beat right through
My eager body; while I laughed out loud,
And let my lips curl up at false or true,

"Seemed cold and shallow without any cloud.
Behold my judges, then the cloths were brought: 80
While I was dizzied thus, old thoughts would crowd,

"Belonging to the time ere I was bought
By Arthur's great name and his little love,
Must I give up forever then, I thought,

"That which I deemed would ever round me move   85
Glorifying all things; for a little word,[4]
Scarce ever meant at all, must I now prove

"Stone-cold for ever? Pray you, does the Lord
Will that all folks should be quite happy and good?
I love God now a little, if this cord[5]   90

"Were broken, once for all what striving could
Make me love anything in earth or heaven.
So day by day it grew, as if one should

"Slip slowly down some path worn smooth and even,
Down to a cool sea on a summer day;   95
Yet still in slipping there was some small leaven

"Of stretched hands catching small stones by the way,
Until one surely reached the sea at last,
And felt strange new joy as the worn head lay

3. Launcelot's father, a king of Brittany.

4. I.e., her marriage vow.

5. I.e., her ties with Launcelot.

"Back, with the hair like seaweed; yea all past   100
Sweat of the forehead, dryness of the lips,
Washed utterly out by the dear waves o'ercast,

"In the lone sea, far off from any ships!
Do I not know now of a day in Spring?
No minute of that wild day ever slips   105

"From out my memory; I hear thrushes sing,
And wheresoever I may be, straightway
Thoughts of it all come up with most fresh sting:

"I was half mad with beauty on that day,
And went without my ladies all alone,   110
In a quiet garden walled round every way;

"I was right joyful of that wall of stone,
That shut the flowers and trees up with the sky,
And trebled all the beauty: to the bone,

"Yea right through to my heart, grown very shy   115
With weary thoughts, it pierced, and made me glad;
Exceedingly glad, and I knew verily,

"A little thing just then had made me mad;
I dared not think, as I was wont to do,
Sometimes, upon my beauty; If I had   120

"Held out my long hand up against the blue,
And, looking on the tenderly darkened fingers,
Thought that by rights one ought to see quite through,

"There, see you, where the soft still light yet lingers,
Round by the edges; what should I have done,   125
If this had joined with yellow spotted singers,

"And startling green drawn upward by the sun?
But shouting, loosed out, see now! all my hair,
And trancedly stood watching the west wind run

"With faintest half-heard breathing sound—why there   130
I lose my head e'en now in doing this;
But shortly listen—In that garden fair

"Came Launcelot walking; this is true, the kiss
Wherewith we kissed in meeting that spring day,
I scarce dare talk of the remembered bliss,   135

"When both our mouths went wandering in one way,

And aching sorely, met among the leaves;
Our hands being left behind strained far away.

"Never within a yard of my bright sleeves
Had Launcelot come before—and now, so nigh!   140
After that day why is it Guenevere grieves?

"Nevertheless you, O Sir Gauwaine, lie,
Whatever happened on through all those years,
God knows I speak truth, saying that you lie.

"Being such a lady could I weep these tears   145
If this were true? A great queen such as I
Having sinned this way, straight her conscience sears;

"And afterwards she liveth hatefully,
Slaying and poisoning, certes never weeps—
Gauwaine be friends now, speak me lovingly.   150

"Do I not see how God's dear pity creeps
All through your frame, and trembles in your mouth?
Remember in what grave your mother sleeps,

"Buried in some place far down in the south,
Men are forgetting as I speak to you;   155
By her head severed in that awful drouth

"Of pity that drew Agravaine's fell blow,[6]
I pray your pity! let me not scream out
Forever after, when the shrill winds blow

"Through half your castle-locks! let me not shout   160
Forever after in the winter night
When you ride out alone! in battle rout

"Let not my rusting tears make your sword light![7]
Ah! God of mercy how he turns away!
So, ever must I dress me to the fight,   165

"So—let God's justice work! Gauwaine, I say,
See me hew down your proofs: yea all men know
Even as you said how Mellyagraunce one day,

"One bitter day in *la Fausse Garde*,[8] for so
All good knights held it after, saw—   170
Yea, sirs, by cursed unknightly outrage; though

6. Gauwaine's brother, Agravaine, had
beheaded their mother after she had
been accused of adultery.

7. Weak.
8. The False Castle—a term expressing
her contempt.

"You, Gauwaine, held his word without a flaw,
This Mellyagraunce saw blood upon my bed—[9]
Whose blood then pray you? is there any law

"To make a queen say why some spots of red   175
Lie on her coverlet? or will you say,
'Your hands are white, lady, as when you wed,

" 'Where did you bleed?' and must I stammer out—'Nay,
I blush indeed, fair lord, only to rend
My sleeve up to my shoulder, where there lay   180

" 'A knife-point last night': so must I defend
The honor of the lady Guenevere?
Not so, fair lords, even if the world should end

"This very day, and you were judges here
Instead of God. Did you see Mellyagraunce   185
When Launcelot stood by him? what white fear

"Curdled his blood, and how his teeth did dance,
His side sink in? as my knight cried and said,
'Slayer of unarmed men, here is a chance!

" 'Setter of traps,[1] I pray you guard your head,   190
By God I am so glad to fight with you,
Stripper of ladies, that my hand feels lead

" 'For driving weight; hurrah now! draw and do,
For all my wounds are moving in my breast,
And I am getting mad with waiting so.'   195

"He struck his hands together o'er the beast,
Who fell down flat, and groveled at his feet,
And groaned at being slain so young—'at least.'

"My knight said, 'Rise you, sir, who are so fleet
At catching ladies, half-armed will I fight,   200
My left side all uncovered!' then I weet,

"Up sprang Sir Mellyagraunce with great delight
Upon his knave's face; not until just then
Did I quite hate him, as I saw my knight

9. Guenevere, and some of her young knights who had been wounded in a skirmish, were confined for a night in a room in Mellyagraunce's castle. Discovering bloodstains on her bedclothes the following morning, Mellyagraunce accused her of adulterous relations with one of the wounded knights. Actually her visiting bedfellow had been Launcelot, who had cut his hand on the window-bars as he climbed into her room.
1. Mellyagraunce had tried to prevent Launcelot from coming to defend the Queen's honor by making him fall through a trapdoor into a dungeon.

"Along the lists look to my stake and pen   205
With such a joyous smile, it made me sigh
From agony beneath my waist-chain,[2] when

"The fight began, and to me they drew nigh;
Ever Sir Launcelot kept him on the right,
And traversed warily, and ever high   210

"And fast leaped caitiff's sword, until my knight
Sudden threw up his sword to his left hand,
Caught it, and swung it; that was all the fight.

"Except a spout of blood on the hot land;
For it was hottest summer; and I know   215
I wondered how the fire, while I should stand,

"And burn, against the heat, would quiver so,
Yards above my head; thus these matters went:
Which things were only warnings of the woe

"That fell on me. Yet Mellyagraunce was shent,[3]   220
For Mellyagraunce had fought against the Lord;
Therefore, my lords, take heed lest you be blent[4]

"With all this wickedness; say no rash word
Against me, being so beautiful; my eyes,
Wept all away the gray, may bring some sword   225

"To drown you in your blood; see my breast rise,
Like waves of purple sea, as here I stand;
And how my arms are moved in wonderful wise,

"Yea also at my full heart's strong command,
See through my long throat how the words go up   230
In ripples to my mouth; how in my hand

"The shadow lies like wine within a cup
Of marvelously colored gold; yea now
This little wind is rising, look you up,

"And wonder how the light is falling so   235
Within my moving tresses: will you dare,
When you have looked a little on my brow,

"To say this thing is vile? or will you care
For any plausible lies of cunning woof,
When you can see my face with no lie there   240

2. She is chained to a stake, at which   3. Destroyed.
she will be burned if Launcelot fails to 4. Blinded.
overcome her accuser.

"Forever? am I not a gracious proof—
'But in your chamber Launcelot was found'—
Is there a good knight then would stand aloof,

"When a queen says with gentle queenly sound:
'O true as steel come now and talk with me,   245
I love to see your step upon the ground

" 'Unwavering, also well I love to see
That gracious smile light up your face, and hear
Your wonderful words, that all mean verily

" 'The thing they seem to mean: good friend, so dear   250
To me in everything, come here tonight,
Or else the hours will pass most dull and drear;

" 'If you come not, I fear this time I might
Get thinking over much of times gone by,
When I was young, and green hope was in sight: 255

" 'For no man cares now to know why I sigh;
And no man comes to sing me pleasant songs,
Nor any brings me the sweet flowers that lie

" 'So thick in the gardens; therefore one so longs
To see you, Launcelot; that we may be   260
Like children once again, free from all wrongs

" 'Just for one night.' Did he not come to me?
What thing could keep true Launcelot away
If I said 'Come?' there was one less than three

"In my quiet room that night, and we were gay;   265
Till sudden I rose up, weak, pale, and sick,
Because a bawling broke our dream up, yea

"I looked at Launcelot's face and could not speak,
For he looked helpless too, for a little while;
Then I remember how I tried to shriek,   270

"And could not, but fell down; from tile to tile
The stones they threw up rattled o'er my head
And made me dizzier; till within a while

"My maids were all about me, and my head
On Launcelot's breast was being soothed away   275
From its white chattering, until Launcelot said—

"By God! I will not tell you more today,
Judge any way you will—what matters it?
You know quite well the story of that fray,

"How Launcelot stilled their bawling, the mad fit   280
That caught up Gauwaine—all, all, verily,
But just that which would save me; these things flit.

"Nevertheless you, O Sir Gauwaine, lie,
Whatever may have happened these long years,
God knows I speak truth, saying that you lie!   285

"All I have said is truth, by Christ's dear tears."
She would not speak another word, but stood.
Turned sideways; listening, like a man who hears

His brother's trumpet sounding through the wood
Of his foes' lances. She leaned eagerly,   290
And gave a slight spring sometimes, as she could

At last hear something really; joyfully
Her cheek grew crimson, as the headlong speed
Of the roan charger drew all men to see,
The knight who came was Launcelot at good need.   295

1859

The Haystack in the Floods[1]

Had she come all the way for this,
To part at last without a kiss?
Yea, had she borne the dirt and rain
That her own eyes might see him slain
Beside the haystack in the floods?   5

Along the dripping leafless woods,
The stirrup touching either shoe,
She rode astride as troopers do;
With kirtle[2] kilted to her knee,
To which the mud splashed wretchedly;   10
And the wet dripped from every tree
Upon her head and heavy hair,
And on her eyelids broad and fair;
The tears and rain ran down her face.
By fits and starts they rode apace,   15
And very often was his place
Far off from her; he had to ride
Ahead, to see what might betide
When the roads crossed; and sometimes, when
There rose a murmuring from his men,   20
Had to turn back with promises.
Ah me! she had but little ease;

1. After the defeat of the French at
Poitiers in 1356, an English knight, Sir
Robert de Marny, is riding with Jehane,
his mistress, to reach the frontier of
Gascony, which was in English hands.
2. Long skirt.

And often for pure doubt and dread
She sobbed, made giddy in the head
By the swift riding; while, for cold,
Her slender fingers scarce could hold   25
The wet reins; yea, and scarcely, too,
She felt the foot within her shoe
Against the stirrup: all for this,
To part at last without a kiss
Beside the haystack in the floods.   30

For when they neared that old soaked hay,
They saw across the only way
That Judas, Godmar, and the three
Red running lions dismally   35
Grinned from his pennon, under which
In one straight line along the ditch,
They counted thirty heads.

               So then
While Robert turned round to his men,
She saw at once the wretched end,   40
And, stooping down, tried hard to rend
Her coif the wrong way from her head,
And hid her eyes; while Robert said:
"Nay, love, 'tis scarcely two to one;
At Poictiers where we made them run   45
So fast—why, sweet my love, good cheer,
The Gascon frontier is so near,
Nought after this."

               But: "O!" she said,
"My God! my God! I have to tread
The long way back without you; then   50
The court at Paris; those six men;[3]
The gratings of the Chatelet;
The swift Seine on some rainy day
Like this, and people standing by,
And laughing, while my weak hands try   55
To recollect how strong men swim.[4]
All this, or else a life with him,
For which I should be damned at last,
Would God that this next hour were past!"

3. The judges. The "Chatelet" is a prison in Paris.
4. In trial by water, a woman accused of witchcraft or other crimes was thrown into the river to determine her guilt or innocence. For this ordeal, the accused would customarily have her hands tied. If she sank she was deemed innocent and thereafter spared by being hauled from the water. If she floated she was guilty and thereafter burned. In Morris' version Jehane would have no chance of escaping death; if she swam she would be burned, and if she sank she would be drowned. See line 107.

He answered not, but cried his cry,　　　　　60
"St. George for Marny!" cheerily;
And laid his hand upon her rein.
Alas! no man of all his train
Gave back that cheery cry again;
And, while for rage his thumb beat fast　　65
Upon his sword hilt, someone cast
About his neck a kerchief long,
And bound him.

　　　　　　　　Then they went along
To Godmar; who said: "Now, Jehane,
Your lover's life is on the wane　　　　　　70
So fast, that, if this very hour
You yield not as my paramour,
He will not see the rain leave off:
Nay, keep your tongue from gibe and scoff,
Sir Robert, or I slay you now."　　　　　　75

She laid her hand upon her brow,
Then gazed upon the palm, as though
She thought her forehead bled, and: "No!"
She said, and turned her head away,
As there was nothing else to say,　　　　　80
And everything were settled: red
Grew Godmar's face from chin to head:
"Jehane, on yonder hill there stands
My castle, guarding well my lands;
What hinders me from taking you,　　　　　85
And doing that I list to do
To your fair willful body, while
Your knight lies dead?"

　　　　　　　　A wicked smile
Wrinkled her face, her lips grew thin,
A long way out she thrust her chin:　　　　90
"You know that I should strangle you
While you were sleeping; or bite through
Your throat, by God's help: ah!" she said,
"Lord Jesus, pity your poor maid!
For in such wise they hem me in,　　　　　95
I cannot choose but sin and sin,
Whatever happens: yet I think
They could not make me eat or drink,
And so should I just reach my rest."
"Nay, if you do not my behest,　　　　　100
O Jehane! though I love you well,"
Said Godmar, "would I fail to tell
All that I know?" "Foul lies," she said.

"Eh? lies, my Jehane? by God's head,
At Paris folks would deem them true!   105
Do you know, Jehane, they cry for you:
'Jehane the brown! Jehane the brown!
Give us Jehane to burn or drown!'
Eh!—gag me Robert!—sweet my friend,
This were indeed a piteous end   110
For those long fingers, and long feet,
And long neck, and smooth shoulders sweet;
An end that few men would forget
That saw it. So, an hour yet:
Consider, Jehane, which to take   115
Of life or death!"

                        So, scarce awake,
Dismounting, did she leave that place,
And totter some yards: with her face
Turned upward to the sky she lay,
Her head on a wet heap of hay,   120
And fell asleep: and while she slept,
And did not dream, the minutes crept
Round to the twelve again; but she,
Being waked at last, sighed quietly,
And strangely childlike came, and said: 125
"I will not." Straightway Godmar's head,
As though it hung on strong wires, turned
Most sharply round, and his face burned.

For Robert, both his eyes were dry,
He could not weep, but gloomily   130
He seemed to watch the rain; yea, too,
His lips were firm; he tried once more
To touch her lips; she reached out, sore
And vain desire so tortured them,
The poor gray lips, and now the hem   135
Of his sleeve brushed them.

                        With a start
Up Godmar rose, thrust them apart;
From Robert's throat he loosed the bands
Of silk and mail; with empty hands
Held out, she stood and gazed, and saw,   140
The long bright blade without a flaw
Glide out from Godmar's sheath, his hand
In Robert's hair; she saw him bend
Back Robert's head; she saw him send
The thin steel down; the blow told well,   145
Right backward the knight Robert fell,
And moaned as dogs do, being half dead,
Unwitting, as I deem: so then

Godmar turned grinning to his men,
Who ran, some five or six, and beat   150
His head to pieces at their feet.

Then Godmar turned again and said:
"So, Jehane, the first fitte[5] is read!
Take note, my lady, that your way
Lies backward to the Chatelet!"   155
She shook her head and gazed awhile
At her cold hands with a rueful smile,
As though this thing had made her mad.

This was the parting that they had
Beside the haystack in the floods.   160

                                                       1858

From The Earthly Paradise

An Apology

Of Heaven or Hell I have no power to sing,
I cannot ease the burden of your fears,
Or make quick-coming death a little thing,
Or bring again the pleasure of past years,
Nor for my words shall ye forget your tears,   5
Or hope again for aught that I can say,
The idle singer of an empty day.

But rather, when, aweary of your mirth,
From full hearts still unsatisfied ye sigh,
And, feeling kindly unto all the earth,   10
Grudge every minute as it passes by,
Made the more mindful that the sweet days die—
Remember me a little then, I pray,
The idle singer of an empty day.

The heavy trouble, the bewildering care   15
That weighs us down who live and earn our bread,
These idle verses have no power to bear;
So let me sing of names rememberéd,
Because they, living not, can ne'er be dead,
Or long time take their memory quite away   20
From us poor singers of an empty day.

Dreamer of dreams, born out of my due time,
Why should I strive to set the crooked straight?[6]
Let it suffice me that my murmuring rhyme

---

5. Section or canto of a poem.
6. In 1856, when Morris was an undergraduate, he wrote in a letter: "I
can't enter into politico-social subjects
with any interest, for on the whole I
see that things are in a muddle, and
I have no power or vocation to set them
right in ever so little a degree. My work
is the embodiment of dreams in one form
or another."

Beats with light wing against the ivory gate,[7]   25
Telling a tale not too importunate
To those who in the sleepy region stay,
Lulled by the singer of an empty day.

    Folk say a wizard to a northern king
At Christmastide such wondrous things did show,   30
That through one window men beheld the spring,
And through another saw the summer glow,
And through a third the fruited vines a-row,
While still, unheard, but in its wonted way,
Piped the drear wind of that December day.   35

    So with this Earthly Paradise it is,
If ye will read aright, and pardon me,
Who strive to build a shadowy isle of bliss
Midmost the beating of the steely sea,
Where tossed about all hearts of men must be;   40
Whose ravening monsters mighty men shall slay,
Not the poor singer of an empty day.

1868–70

A Death Song[8]

What cometh here from west to east a-wending?
And who are these, the marchers stern and slow?
We bear the message that the rich are sending
Aback to those who bade them wake and know.
Not one, not one, nor thousands must they slay,   5
But one and all if they would dusk the day.

We asked them for a life of toilsome earning—
They bade us bide their leisure for our bread;
We craved to speak to tell our woeful learning—
We come back speechless, bearing back our dead.   10
Not one, not one, nor thousands must they slay,
But one and all if they would dusk the day.

They will not learn; they have no ears to hearken;
They turn their faces from the eyes of fate;
Their gay-lit halls shut out the skies that darken.   15
But, lo! this dead man knocking at the gate.
Not one, not one, nor thousands must they slay,
But one and all if they would dusk the day.

Here lies the sign that we shall break our prison;
Amidst the storm he won a prisoner's rest;   20

---

7. At the cave of Morpheus, god of dreams, were two gates: through the gate of horn came prophetic dreams, and through the ivory gate came fictitious dreams.
8. In a Socialist parade of 1887, in which Morris was one of the marchers, his friend Alfred Linnell was beaten by the police and died of injuries. Morris printed this poem as a penny pamphlet to raise money for Linnell's family.

But in the cloudy dawn the sun arisen
Brings us our day of work to win the best.
Not one, not one, nor thousands must they slay,
But one and all if they would dusk the day.

1891

For the Bed at Kelmscott[9]

The wind's on the wold
And the night is a-cold,
And Thames runs chill
'Twixt mead and hill;
But kind and dear   5
Is the old house here,
And my heart is warm
'Midst winter's harm.
Rest, then, and rest,
And think of the best   10
'Twixt summer and spring,
When all birds sing
In the town of the tree,
And ye lie in me
And scarce dare move,   15
Lest the earth and its love
Should fade away
Ere the full of the day.
I am old and have seen
Many things that have been—   20
Both grief and peace
And wane and increase.
No tale I tell
Of ill or well,
But this I say,   25
Night treadeth on day.
And for worst and best
Right good is rest.

1893

9. **Kelmscott Manor was owned by Morris. The bed itself is the speaker.**

ALGERNON CHARLES SWINBURNE

(1837–1909)

Swinburne's writings are of interest in their own right and also as evidence
of the breakdown of conventional Victorian standards during the latter part
of the 19th century. Like the fat boy in *Pickwick Papers* who terrified the
old lady by announcing: "I wants to make your flesh creep," Swinburne set

about shocking his elders by a variety of rebellious gestures. In religion he appeared to be a pagan; in politics, a liberal republican dedicated to the overthrow of established governments. And on the subject of love he was often preoccupied with the pleasures of the lover who inflicts pain or accepts pain, pleasures of which he had read in the writings of the Marquis de Sade. As Arnold Bennett said of *Anactoria*, Swinburne played "a rare trick" on England by "enshrining in the topmost heights of its literature a lovely poem that cannot be discussed."

To a more limited extent Swinburne also expressed his rebellion against established codes by his personal behavior. He came from a distinguished family and attended Eton and Oxford, but sought the company of the bohemians of Paris and of London where he became temporarily associated with D. G. Rossetti and other Pre-Raphaelites. By 1879 his dissipations had profoundly affected his frail physique, and he was obliged to put himself into the protective custody of a friend, Theodore Watts-Dunton, who removed him to the countryside and kept him alive although sobered and tamed.

Swinburne continued to write voluminously and sometimes memorably, as in his fine late poem, *The Lake of Gaube*, but most of his best poetry is in his early publications. His early play, *Atalanta in Calydon* (1865), was described by Swinburne himself as "pure Greek," and his command of classical allusions here, as well as in other poems, is indeed impressive. Yet the kind of spirit which he found in Greek literature was not the traditional quality of classic serenity admired by Matthew Arnold. Like Shelley (the poet he most closely resembles), Swinburne loved Greece as a land of liberty in which men had expressed themselves with the most complete unrestraint. To call such an ardently romantic poet "classical" requires a series of qualifying clauses that make the term meaningless.

In his play and in the volume which followed it, *Poems and Ballads* (1866), Swinburne demonstrated a metrical virtuosity which dazzled his early readers and is still dazzling. Those who demand that poetry should make sense, first and foremost, may find that much of his poetry is not to their taste. What he offers, instead, are heady rhythmical patterns in which words are relished primarily for sound rather than for sense.

> There lived a singer in France of old
> By the tideless dolorous midland sea.
> In a land of sand and ruin and gold
> There shone one woman, and none but she.

These lines from *The Triumph of Time* have often been cited to illustrate Swinburne's qualities. Like some of the poems of the later French Symbolists, such passages defy traditional kinds of critical analysis and oblige us to reconsider the variety of ways in which poetry may achieve its effects.

Another noteworthy aspect of these poems is their recurring preoccupation with death, as in the memorable recreations of the underworld garden of Proserpine, frozen in timelessness. And as the critic Jerome McGann notes: "No English poet has composed more elegies than Swinburne." The death of any prominent figure, such as Browning, almost always prompted Swinburne to compose a poem for the occasion. Some of these are merely competent editorials in verse; others, especially his moving *Ave Atque Vale* in honor of Charles Baudelaire, are of a different dimension. Swinburne modestly hoped that *Ave Atque Vale* might find its niche as a fourth in line among the major elegies in English, following Milton's *Lycidas*, Shelley's *Adonais*, and Arnold's *Thyrsis*. McGann argues that the "elusive beauty and enigmatic greatness" of Swinburne's elegy make his poem clearly superior to *Thyrsis* and assure *Ave Atque Vale* the third place (at least) in this distinguished quartet.

Choruses from Atalanta in Calydon

When the Hounds of Spring[1]

When the hounds of spring are on winter's traces,
    The mother of months in meadow or plain
Fills the shadows and windy places
    With lisp of leaves and ripple of rain;
And the brown bright nightingale[2] amorous   5
Is half assuaged for Itylus,
For the Thracian ships and the foreign faces,
    The tongueless vigil and all the pain.

Come with bows bent and with emptying of quivers,
    Maiden most perfect, lady of light,   10
With a noise of winds and many rivers,
    With a clamor of waters, and with might;
Bind on thy sandals, O thou most fleet,
Over the splendor and speed of thy feet;
For the faint east quickens, the wan west shivers,   15
    Round the feet of the day and the feet of the night.

Where shall we find her, how shall we sing to her,
    Fold our hands round her knees, and cling?
O that man's heart were as fire and could spring to her,
    Fire, or the strength of the streams that spring!   20
For the stars and the winds are unto her
As raiment, as songs of the harp player;
For the risen stars and the fallen cling to her,
    And the southwest wind and the west wind sing.

For winter's rains and ruins are over,   25
    And all the season of snows and sins;
The days dividing lover and lover,
    The light that loses, the night that wins;

1. This choral hymn, with which Swinburne's tragedy opens, is addressed to Artemis (or Diana), virgin goddess and huntress. Artemis was also goddess of the moon and hence, as affecting the seasons, the "mother of months" (line 2).

2. Philomela, after being raped by her brother-in-law and having her tongue cut out, was changed into a nightingale. To obtain revenge, her sister, Procne, killed her own son, Itylus, and fed the child's body to her husband, Tereus, a Thracian king.

And time remembered is grief forgotten,
And frosts are slain and flowers begotten,
And in green underwood and cover   30
    Blossom by blossom the spring begins.

The full streams feed on flower of rushes,
    Ripe grasses trammel a traveling foot,
The faint fresh flame of the young year flushes   35
    From leaf to flower and flower to fruit;
And fruit and leaf are as gold and fire,
And the oat[3] is heard above the lyre,
And the hoofèd heel of a satyr crushes
    The chestnut husk at the chestnut root.   40

And Pan by noon and Bacchus by night,
    Fleeter of foot than the fleet-foot kid,
Follows with dancing and fills with delight
    The Maenad and the Bassarid;[4]
And soft as lips that laugh and hide,   45
The laughing leaves of the trees divide,
And screen from seeing and leave in sight
    The god pursuing, the maiden hid.

The ivy falls with the Bacchanal's hair
    Over her eyebrows hiding her eyes;
The wild vine slipping down leaves bare   50
    Her bright breast shortening into sighs;
The wild vine slips with the weight of its leaves,
But the berried ivy catches and cleaves
To the limbs that glitter, the feet that scare   55
    The wolf that follows, the fawn that flies.

Before the Beginning of Years

Before the begining of years
    There came to the making of man
Time, with a gift of tears;
    Grief, with a glass that ran;
Pleasure, with pain for leaven;   5
    Summer, with flowers that fell;
Remembrance fallen from heaven,
    And madness risen from hell;
Strength without hands to smite;
    Love that endures for a breath;   10
Night, the shadow of light,
    And life, the shadow of death.

And the high gods took in hand
    Fire, and the falling of tears,

---

3. Musical pipe made from an oaten straw.
4. Participants in the spring festival honoring Dionysus (or Bacchus). Such festivals sometimes developed into frenzied sexual orgies.

And a measure of sliding sand   15
   From under the feet of the years;
And froth and drift of the sea;
   And dust of the laboring earth;
And bodies of things to be
   In the houses of death and of birth;   20
And wrought with weeping and laughter,
   And fashioned with loathing and love,
With life before and after
   And death beneath and above,
For a day and a night and a morrow,   25
   That his strength might endure for a span
With travail and heavy sorrow,
   The holy spirit of man.

From the winds of the north and the south
   They gathered as unto strife;   30
They breathed upon his mouth,
   They filled his body with life;
Eyesight and speech they wrought
   For the veils of the soul therein,
A time for labor and thought,   35
   A time to serve and to sin;
They gave him light in his ways,
   And love, and a space for delight,
And beauty and length of days,
   And night, and sleep in the night.   40
His speech is a burning fire;
   With his lips he travaileth;
In his heart is a blind desire,
   In his eyes foreknowledge of death;
He weaves, and is clothed with derision;   45
   Sows, and he shall not reap;
His life is a watch or a vision
   Between a sleep and a sleep.

                                             1865

From The Triumph of Time
I Will Go Back to the Great Sweet Mother

33
I will go back to the great sweet mother,
   Mother and lover of men, the sea.
I will go down to her, I and none other,
   Close with her, kiss her, and mix her with me;
Cling to her, strive with her, hold her fast.
O fair white mother, in days long past   5
Born without sister, born without brother,
   Set free my soul as thy soul is free.

34

O fair green-girdled mother of mine,
    Sea, that art clothed with the sun and the rain,   10
Thy sweet hard kisses are strong like wine,
    Thy large embraces are keen like pain.
Save me and hide me with all thy waves,
Find me one grave of thy thousand graves,
Those pure cold populous graves of thine   15
    Wrought without hand in a world without stain.

35

I shall sleep, and move with the moving ships,
    Change as the winds change, veer in the tide;
My lips will feast on the foam of thy lips,
    I shall rise with thy rising, with thee subside;   20
Sleep, and not know if she[1] be, if she were,
Filled full with life to the eyes and hair,
As a rose is fulfilled to the roseleaf tips
    With splendid summer and perfume and pride.

36

This woven raiment of nights and days,   25
    Were it once cast off and unwound from me,
Naked and glad would I walk in thy ways,
    Alive and aware of thy ways and thee;
Clear of the whole world, hidden at home,
Clothed with the green and crowned with the foam,   30
A pulse of the life of thy straits and bays,
    A vein in the heart of the streams of the sea.

37

Fair mother, fed with the lives of men,
    Thou art subtle and cruel of heart, men say.
Thou hast taken, and shalt not render again;   35
    Thou art full of thy dead, and cold as they.
But death is the worst that comes of thee;
Thou art fed with our dead, O mother, O sea,
But when hast thou fed on our hearts? or when,
    Having given us love, hast thou taken away?   40

38

O tender-hearted, O perfect lover,
    Thy lips are bitter, and sweet thine heart.
The hopes that hurt and the dreams that hover,
    Shall they not vanish away and apart?
But thou, thou art sure, thou art older than earth;   45
Thou art strong for death and fruitful of birth;
Thy depths conceal and thy gulfs discover;
    From the first thou wert; in the end thou art.

1862–66   1866

---

1. The woman to whom the poem is addressed. She had deserted the speaker for another man.

Hymn to Proserpine

(AFTER THE PROCLAMATION IN ROME OF THE CHRISTIAN FAITH)

Vicisti, Galilaee [1]

I have lived long enough, having seen one thing, that love hath an
    end;
Goddess and maiden and queen, be near me now and befriend.
Thou art more than the day or the morrow, the seasons that laugh
    or that weep;
For these give joy and sorrow; but thou, Proserpina, sleep.
Sweet is the treading of wine, and sweet the feet of the dove;   5
But a goodlier gift is thine than foam of the grapes or love.
Yea, is not even Apollo, with hair and harpstring of gold,
A bitter god to follow, a beautiful god to behold?
I am sick of singing; the bays[2] burn deep and chafe. I am fain
To rest a little from praise and grievous pleasure and pain.   10
For the gods we know not of, who give us our daily breath,
We know they are cruel as love or life, and lovely as death.

O gods dethroned and deceased, cast forth, wiped out in a day!
From your wrath is the world released, redeemed from your chains,
    men say.
New gods are crowned in the city; their flowers have broken your
    rods;   15
They are merciful, clothed with pity, the young compassionate gods.
But for me their new device is barren, the days are bare;
Things long past over suffice, and men forgotten that were.
Time and the gods are at strife; ye dwell in the midst thereof,
Draining a little life from the barren breasts of love.   20
I say to you, cease, take rest; yea, I say to you all, be at peace,
Till the bitter milk of her breast and the barren bosom shall cease.

Wilt thou yet take all, Galilean? But these thou shalt not take—
The laurel, the palms, and the paean, the breasts of the nymphs in
    the brake,
Breasts more soft than a dove's, that tremble with tenderer breath;
And all the wings of the Loves, and all the joy before death;   26
All the feet of the hours that sound as a single lyre,

---

1. "Thou hast conquered, O Galilean"
—words supposedly addressed to Christ
by the Roman emperor, Julian the
Apostate, on his deathbed in 363.
Julian had tried to revive paganism and
to discourage Christianity, which, after
a proclamation of 313, had been tolerated in Rome. His efforts, however,
were unsuccessful. The speaker of the
poem, a Roman patrician and also a
poet (line 9), is like the Emperor
Julian: he prefers the old order of
pagan gods. His hymn is addressed to
the goddess Proserpine, who was carried

off by Hades (or Pluto) to be queen
of the lower world. In this role she is
addressed in the poem as goddess of
death and of sleep. The speaker also
associates her with the earth itself
(line 93) because she was the daughter
of Demeter (or Ceres), goddess of agriculture, whose name means "earth-
mother." Swinburne may have derived
some details here from the 4th-century
Latin poet Claudian, whose long narrative *The Rape of Proserpine* provides
helpful background for this hymn.
2. Laurel leaves of a poet's crown.

Dropped and deep in the flowers, with strings that flicker like fire.
More than these wilt thou give, things fairer than all these things?
Nay, for a little we live, and life hath mutable wings. 30
A little while and we die; shall life not thrive as it may?
For no man under the sky lives twice, outliving his day.
And grief is a grievous thing, and a man hath enough of his tears;
Why should he labor, and bring fresh grief to blacken his years?

Thou hast conquered, O pale Galilean; the world has grown gray
    from thy breath; 35
We have drunken of things Lethean,[3] and fed on the fullness of
    death.
Laurel is green for a season, and love is sweet for a day;
But love grows bitter with treason, and laurel outlives not May.
Sleep, shall we sleep after all? for the world is not sweet in the end;
For the old faiths loosen and fall, the new years ruin and rend. 40
Fate is a sea without shore, and the soul is a rock that abides;
But her ears are vexed with the roar and her face with the foam of
    the tides.
O lips that the live blood faints in, the leavings of racks and rods!
O ghastly glories of saints, dead limbs of gibbeted gods!
Though all men abase them before you in spirit, and all knees bend,
I kneel not, neither adore you, but standing look to the end. 46

All delicate days and pleasant, all spirits and sorrows are cast
Far out with the foam of the present that sweeps to the surf of the
    past;
Where beyond the extreme sea wall, and between the remote sea
    gates,
Waste water washes, and tall ships founder, and deep death waits;
Where, mighty with deepening sides, clad about with the seas as
    with wings, 51
And impelled of invisible tides, and fulfilled of unspeakable things,
White-eyed and poisonous-finned, shark-toothed and serpentine-
    curled,
Rolls, under the whitening wind of the future, the wave of the
    world.
The depths stand naked in sunder behind it, the storms flee away;
In the hollow before it the thunder is taken and snared as a prey; 56
In its sides is the north wind bound; and its salt is of all men's tears,
With light of ruin, and sound of changes, and pulse of years;
With travail of day after day, and with trouble of hour upon hour.
And bitter as blood is the spray; and the crests are as fangs that de-
    vour; 60
And its vapor and storm of its steam as the sighing of spirits to be;
And its noise as the noise in a dream; and its depths as the roots of
    the sea;
And the height of its heads as the height of the utmost stars of the
    air;

3. I.e., of Lethe, a river in the lower world. By drinking its waters the dead forgot
the past.

And the ends of the earth at the might thereof tremble, and time
    is made bare.
Will ye bridle the deep sea with reins, will ye chasten the high sea
    with rods?   65
Will ye take her to chain her with chains, who is older than all ye
    gods?
All ye as a wind shall go by, as a fire shall ye pass and be past;
Ye are gods, and behold, ye shall die, and the waves be upon you
    at last.
In the darkness of time, in the deeps of the years, in the changes
    of things,
Ye shall sleep as a slain man sleeps, and the world shall forget you
    for kings.   70
Though the feet of thine high priests tread where thy lords and our
    forefathers trod,
Though these that were gods are dead, and thou being dead art a
    god,
Though before thee the throned Cytherean[4] be .fallen, and hidden
    her head,
Yet thy kingdom shall pass, Galilean, thy dead shall go down to
    thee dead.

Of the maiden thy mother men sing as a goddess with grace clad
    around;   75
Thou art throned where another was king; where another was queen
    she is crowned.
Yea, once we had sight of another; but now she is queen, say these.
Not as thine, not as thine was our mother, a blossom of flowering
    seas,
Clothed round with the world's desire as with raiment, and fair as
    the foam,
And fleeter than kindled fire, and a goddess, and mother of Rome.[5]
For thine came pale and a maiden, and sister to sorrow; but ours, 81
Her deep hair heavily laden with odor and color of flowers,
White rose of the rose-white water, a silver splendor, a flame,
Bent down unto us that besought her, and earth grew sweet with
    her name.
For thine came weeping, a slave among slaves, and rejected; but she
Came flushed from the full-flushed wave, and imperial, her foot on
    the sea.   86
And the wonderful waters knew her, the winds and the viewless
    ways,
And the roses grew rosier, and bluer the sea-blue stream of the bays.

Ye are fallen, our lords, by what token? we wist that ye should not
    fall.
Ye were all so fair that are broken; and one more fair than ye all. 90
But I turn to her[6] still, having seen she shall surely abide in the end;

4. Aphrodite (or Venus), who was
born from the waves near the island of
Cythera.

5. Aeneas, the founder of Rome, was
said to have been the son of Aphrodite.
6. Proserpine.

Goddess and maiden and queen, be near me now and befriend.
O daughter of earth, of my mother, her crown and blossom of birth,
I am also, I also, thy brother; I go as I came unto earth.
In the night where thine eyes are as moons are in heaven, the night
    where thou art, 95
Where the silence is more than all tunes, where sleep overflows
    from the heart,
Where the poppies are sweet as the rose in our world, and the red
    rose is white,
And the wind falls faint as it blows with the fume of the flowers of
    the night,
And the murmur of spirits that sleep in the shadow of gods from
    afar
Grows dim in thine ears and deep as the deep dim soul of a star, 100
In the sweet low light of thy face, under heavens untrod by the sun,
Let my soul with their souls find place, and forget what is done and
    undone.
Thou art more than the gods who number the days of our temporal
    breath;
For these give labor and slumber; but thou, Proserpina, death.
Therefore now at thy feet I abide for a season in silence. I know 105
I shall die as my fathers died, and sleep as they sleep; even so.
For the glass of the years is brittle wherein we gaze for a span.
A little soul for a little bears up this corpse which is man.
So long I endure, no longer; and laugh not again, neither weep. 109
For there is no god found stronger than death; and death is a sleep.

          1866

The Garden of Proserpine[1]

    Here, where the world is quiet;
      Here, where all trouble seems
    Dead winds' and spent waves' riot
      In doubtful dreams of dreams;
    I watch the green field growing 5
    For reaping folk and sowing,
    For harvest time and mowing,
      A sleepy world of streams.

    I am tired of tears and laughter,
      And men that laugh and weep; 10
    Of what may come hereafter
      For men that sow to reap;

1. Or Proserpina, the goddess who was carried off by Hades (or Pluto) to be queen of the lower world. According to some accounts, she had there a garden of ever-blooming flowers. The Greek and Roman festivals honoring her and her mother, Ceres, emphasized Proserpine's return to the upper world in spring. In Swinburne's poems, however, the emphasis is on her role as goddess of death and eternal sleep. Swinburne also associates her with the sea, which he usually represents as eternally unchanging despite its surface change-fulness.

I am weary of days and hours,
Blown buds of barren flowers,
Desires and dreams and powers
    And everything but sleep.   15

Here life has death for neighbor,
    And far from eye or ear
Wan waves and wet winds labor,
    Weak ships and spirits steer;   20
They drive adrift, and whither
They wot not who make thither;
But no such winds blow hither,
    And no such things grow here.

No growth of moor or coppice,   25
    No heather flower or vine,
But bloomless buds of poppies,
    Green grapes of Proserpine,
Pale beds of blowing rushes,
Where no leaf blooms or blushes   30
Save this whereout she crushes
    For dead men deadly wine.

Pale, without name or number,
    In fruitless fields of corn,[2]
They bow themselves and slumber   35
    All night till light is born;
And like a soul belated,
In hell and heaven unmated,
By cloud and mist abated
    Comes out of darkness morn.   40

Though one were strong as seven,
    He too with death shall dwell,
Nor wake with wings in heaven,
    Nor weep for pains in hell;
Though one were fair as roses,   45
His beauty clouds and closes;
And well though love reposes,
    In the end it is not well.

Pale, beyond porch and portal,
    Crowned with calm leaves, she stands   50
Who gathers all things mortal
    With cold immortal hands;
Her languid lips are sweeter
Than love's who fears to greet her
To men that mix and meet her   55
    From many times and lands.

She waits for each and other,
    She waits for all men born;

2. Wheat or grain.

Forgets the earth her mother,
   The life of fruits and corn;   60
And spring and seed and swallow
Take wing for her and follow
Where summer song rings hollow
   And flowers are put to scorn.

There go the loves that wither,   65
   The old loves with wearier wings;
And all dead years draw thither,
   And all disastrous things;
Dead dreams of days forsaken,
Blind buds that snows have shaken,   70
Wild leaves that winds have taken,
   Red strays of ruined springs.

We are not sure of sorrow,
   And joy was never sure;
Today will die tomorrow;   75
   Time stoops to no man's lure;
And love, grown faint and fretful,
With lips but half regretful
Sighs, and with eyes forgetful
   Weeps that no loves endure.   80

From too much love of living,
   From hope and fear set free,
We thank with brief thanksgiving
   Whatever gods may be
That no life lives forever;   85
That dead men rise up never;
That even the weariest river
   Winds somewhere safe to sea.

Then star nor sun shall waken,
   Nor any change of light: 90
Nor sound of waters shaken,
   Nor any sound or sight:
Nor wintry leaves nor vernal,
Nor days nor things diurnal;
Only the sleep eternal   95
   In an eternal night.

1866

Ave Atque Vale[1]

In Memory of Charles Baudelaire

Nous devrions pourtant lui porter quelques fleurs;
Les morts, les pauvres morts, ont de grandes douleurs,
Et quand Octobre souffle, émondeur des vieux arbres,
Son vent mélancolique à l'entour de leurs marbres,
Certe, ils doivent trouver les vivants bien ingrats.
　　　　　　　　　　—"Les Fleurs du Mal."

Shall I strew on thee rose or rue or laurel,[2]
　Brother, on this that was the veil[3] of thee?
Or quiet sea-flower molded by the sea,
Or simplest growth of meadow-sweet or sorrel,
　Such as the summer-sleepy Dryads[4] weave,　　　　5
　Waked up by snow-soft sudden rains at eve?
Or wilt thou rather, as on earth before,
　Half-faded fiery blossoms, pale with heat
　And full of bitter summer, but more sweet
To thee than gleanings of a northern shore　　　　10
　Trod by no tropic feet?[5]

II

For always thee the fervid languid glories
　Allured of heavier suns in mightier skies;
　Thine ears knew all the wandering watery sighs
Where the sea sobs round Lesbian promontories,　　　15
　The barren kiss of piteous wave to wave
　That knows not where is that Leucadian grave[6]
Which hides too deep the supreme head of song.
　Ah, salt and sterile as her kisses were,
　The wild sea winds her and the green gulfs bear　　20

1. "Hail and farewell"—a line from an elegy by Catullus occasioned by a farewell visit to the grave of his brother to whom he brought gifts, a situation closely echoed in Swinburne's final stanza. Charles Baudelaire (1821–1867) had impressed Swinburne as one of the "most perfect poets of the century." In 1861, in an essay on the second edition of Baudelaire's collection *Les Fleurs du Mal* ("Flowers of Evil," 1857), Swinburne had commented on the French poet's preoccupation with "sad and strange things"—"the sharp and cruel enjoyments of pain, the acrid relish of suffering felt or inflicted"; "it has the languid, lurid beauty of close and threatening weather—a heavy, heated temperature, with dangerous hothouse scents in it." These qualities are also celebrated in Swinburne's elegy into which are woven many allusions to Baudelaire's poems, especially his *Litanies de Satan*, which Swinburne regarded as the "keynote" poem of *Les Fleurs du Mal*. The epigraph, from *La servante au grand coeur* ("The great-hearted servant") may be translated: "We must nevertheless bring some flowers to her [or him]. The dead, the poor dead, have great sadnesses. And when October, the pruner of old trees, blows its melancholy wind in the vicinity of their marble tombs, then indeed they must find the living highly ungrateful."
2. Symbols of love, mourning, and poetic fame.
3. I.e., the body as a veil for the soul.
4. Wood-nymphs.
5. A voyage to the tropics in Baudelaire's youth made a lasting impact on his poetry.
6. According to legend the poetess Sappho, who was born on the island of Lesbos, destroyed herself by leaping from the rock of Leucas into the Ionian Sea. In this section Swinburne makes allusions to Baudelaire's *Lesbos*.

Hither and thither, and vex and work her wrong,
    Blind gods that cannot spare.

III

Thou sawest, in thine old singing season, brother,
    Secrets and sorrows unbeheld of us:
    Fierce loves, and lovely leaf-buds poisonous,   25
Bare to thy subtler eye, but for none other
    Blowing by night in some unbreathed-in clime;
    The hidden harvest of luxurious time,
Sin without shape, and pleasure without speech;
    And where strange dreams in a tumultuous sleep   30
    Make the shut eyes of stricken spirits weep;
And with each face thou sawest the shadow on each,
    Seeing as men sow men reap.[7]

IV

O sleepless heart and somber soul unsleeping,
    That were athirst for sleep and no more life   35
    And no more love, for peace and no more strife!
Now the dim gods of death have in their keeping
    Spirit and body and all the springs of song,
    Is it well now where love can do no wrong,
Where stingless pleasure has no foam or fang   40
    Behind the unopening closure of her lips?
    Is it not well where soul from body slips
And flesh from bone divides without a pang
    As dew from flower-bell drips?

V

It is enough; the end and the beginning   45
    Are one thing to thee, who art past the end.
    O hand unclasped of unbeholden friend,
For thee no fruits to pluck, no palms for winning,
    No triumph and no labor and no lust,
    Only dead yew-leaves and a little dust.   50
O quiet eyes wherein the light saith naught,
    Whereto the day is dumb, nor any night
    With obscure finger silences your sight,
Nor in your speech the sudden soul speaks thought,
    Sleep, and have sleep for light.   55

VI

Now all strange hours and all strange loves are over,
    Dreams and desires and somber songs and sweet,
    Hast thou found place at the great knees and feet
Of some pale Titan-woman like a lover,
    Such as thy vision here solicited,[8]   60
    Under the shadow of her fair vast head,
The deep division of prodigious breasts,
    The solemn slope of mighty limbs asleep,

---

7. See Galatians vi.7, "Whatsoever a man soweth, that shall he also reap."

8. An allusion to Baudelaire's *Le Géante* ("The Giantess").

The weight of awful tresses that still keep
The savor and shade of old-world pine forests   65
   Where the wet hill-winds weep?

           VII

Hast thou found any likeness for thy vision?
   O gardener of strange flowers, what bud, what bloom,
   Hast thou found sown, what gathered in the gloom?
What of despair, of rapture, of derision,   70
   What of life is there, what of ill or good?
   Are the fruits gray like dust or bright like blood?
Does the dim ground grow any seed of ours,
   The faint fields quicken any terrene root,
   In low lands where the sun and moon are mute   75
And all the stars keep silence? Are there flowers
   At all, or any fruit?

           VIII

Alas, but though my flying song flies after,
   O sweet strange elder singer, thy more fleet
   Singing, and footprints of thy fleeter feet,   80
Some dim derision of mysterious laughter
   From the blind tongueless warders of the dead,
   Some gainless glimpse of Proserpine's[9] veiled head,
Some little sound of unregarded tears
   Wept by effaced unprofitable eyes,   85
   And from pale mouths some cadence of dead sighs—
These only, these the hearkening spirit hears,
   Sees only such things rise.

           IX

Thou art far too far for wings of words to follow,
   Far too far off for thought or any prayer.   90
   What ails us with thee, who art wind and air?
What ails us gazing where all seen is hollow?
   Yet with some fancy, yet with some desire,
   Dreams pursue death as winds a flying fire,
Our dreams pursue our dead and do not find.   95
   Still, and more swift than they, the thin flame flies,
   The low light fails us in elusive skies,
Still the foiled earnest ear is deaf, and blind
   Are still the eluded eyes.

           X

Not thee, O never thee, in all time's changes,   100
   Not thee, but this the sound of thy sad soul,
   The shadow of thy swift spirit, this shut scroll
I lay my hand on, and not death estranges
   My spirit from communion of thy song—
   These memories and these melodies that throng   105

9. Queen of the underworld.

Veiled porches of a Muse funereal—[1]
    These I salute, these touch, these clasp and fold
    As though a hand were in my hand to hold,
Or through mine ears a mourning musical
    Of many mourners rolled.   110

XI

I among these, I also, in such station
    As when the pyre was charred, and piled the sods,
    And offering to the dead made, and their gods,
The old mourners had, standing to make libation,
    I stand, and to the gods and to the dead   115
    Do reverence without prayer or praise, and shed
Offering to these unknown, the gods of gloom,
    And what of honey and spice my seedlands bear,
    And what I may of fruits in this chilled air,
And lay, Orestes-like, across the tomb   120
    A curl of severed hair.[2]

XII

But by no hand nor any treason stricken,
    Not like the low-lying head of Him, the King,
    The flame that made of Troy a ruinous thing,
Thou liest, and on this dust no tears could quicken   125
    There fall no tears like theirs[3] that all men hear
    Fall tear by sweet imperishable tear
Down the opening leaves of holy poets' pages.
    Thee not Orestes, not Electra mourns;
    But bending us-ward with memorial urns   130
The most high Muses that fulfill all ages
    Weep, and our God's heart yearns.

XIII

For, sparing of his sacred strength, not often
    Among us darkling here the lord of light[4]
    Makes manifest his music and his might   135
In hearts that open and in lips that soften
    With the soft flame and heat of songs that shine.
    Thy lips indeed he touched with bitter wine,
And nourished them indeed with bitter bread;
    Yet surely from his hand thy soul's food came;   140
    The fire that scarred thy spirit at his flame
Was lighted, and thine hungering heart he fed
    Who feeds our hearts with fame.

---

1. According to Jerome McGann, Swinburne associates Baudelaire's distinctive kind of poetry with a tenth muse, one who inspires songs of lamentation ("funereal"). What is meant by this muse's "veiled porches" seems tantalizingly obscure.
2. For lines 120–29, see Aeschylus' *Choëphoroe*, 4–8. King Agamemnon, after returning from Troy, had been treacherously slain, an event that made "a ruinous thing" of the Greek victory. His son, Orestes, visits Agamemnon's grave and dedicates on it a lock of his own hair which is later discovered by his sister, Electra, who mournfully visits her father's grave to offer libations.
3. Referring to the muses and holy poets, not to Orestes and Electra (noted by Jerome McGann).
4. Apollo, god of light and poetry.

XIV

Therefore he too now at thy soul's sunsetting,
  God of all suns and songs he too bends down   145
    To mix his laurel with thy cypress crown.[5]
And save thy dust from blame and from forgetting.
  Therefore he too, seeing all thou wert and art,
  Compassionate, with sad and sacred heart,
Mourns thee of many his children the last dead,   150
  And hallows with strange tears and alien sighs
    Thine unmelodious mouth and sunless eyes,
And over thine irrevocable head
    Sheds light from the under skies.[6]

XV

And one weeps with him in the ways Lethean,[7]   155
  And stains with tears her changing bosom chill;
    That obscure Venus of the hollow hill,
That thing transformed which was the Cytherean,
  With lips that lost their Grecian laugh divine
  Long since, and face no more called Erycine;[8]   160
A ghost, a bitter and luxurious god.
  Thee also with fair flesh and singing spell
  Did she, a sad and second prey,[9] compel
Into the footless places once more trod,
    And shadows hot from hell.   165

XVI

And now no sacred staff shall break in blossom,[1]
  No choral salutation lure to light
    A spirit sick with perfume and sweet night
And love's tired eyes and hands and barren bosom.
  There is no help for these things; none to mend   170
  And none to mar; not all our songs, O friend,
Will make death clear or make life durable.
  Howbeit with rose and ivy and wild vine
  And with wild notes about this dust of thine
At least I fill the place where white dreams dwell[2]   175
    And wreathe an unseen shrine.

---

5. "Laurel": the crown of Apollo, a wreath honoring poets; "Cypress": associated with mourning.

6. Flickering flaming light of the underworld.

7. Lethe was the river of oblivion in Hades.

8. The Venus of medieval legends held her court inside a mountain in Germany (the Hörselberg). This later Venus is a transformed version of the joyous foamborn goddess associated wih the island of Cythera and also worshiped in Sicily at a shrine on Mt. Eryx (hence *Erycine*). Horace described her as "blithe goddess of Eryx, about whom hover mirth and desire" (*Odes*, I, ii, 33–34).

9. The first "prey" of Venus had been Tannhäuser, whom she had lured into the "footless places" of her cave; Baudelaire is her "second prey." Swinburne, after reading Baudelaire's pamphlet on Wagner's *Tannhäuser*, described this Venus as "the queen of evil, the lady of lust."

1. After Tannhäuser's pilgrimage to Rome to seek absolution for having lived in sin with Venus, a miraculous event occurred: the Pope's staff burst into blossom.

2. Presumably the abode of the ghosts of the dead.

XVII

Sleep; and if life was bitter to thee, pardon,
    If sweet, give thanks; thou hast no more to live;
    And to give thanks is good, and to forgive.
Out of the mystic and the mournful garden   180
    Where all day through thine hands in barren braid
    Wove the sick flowers of secrecy and shade,
Green buds of sorrow and sin, and remnants grey,
    Sweet-smelling, pale with poison, sanguine-hearted,
    Passions that sprang from sleep and thoughts that started, 185
Shall death not bring us all as thee one day
    Among the days departed?

XVIII

For thee, O now a silent soul, my brother,
    Take at my hands this garland, and farewell.
    Thin is the leaf, and chill the wintry smell,   190
And chill the solemn earth, a fatal mother,
    With sadder than the Niobean womb,[3]
    And in the hollow of her breasts a tomb.
Content thee, howsoe'er, whose days are done;
    There lies not any troublous thing before,
    Nor sight nor sound to war against thee more,   195
For whom all winds are quiet as the sun,
    All waters as the shore.

1866-67   1868

The Lake of Gaube[1]

The sun is lord and god, sublime, serene,
    And sovereign on the mountains: earth and air
Lie prone in passion, blind with bliss unseen
    By force of sight and might of rapture, fair
    As dreams that die and know not what they were.   5

3. Niobe's fourteen children were slain by Apollo and Artemis.

1. Gaube (rhyming with *robe*) is a deep glacier-fed lake high in the Pyrenees mountains of France, not far from the setting of Tennyson's *In the Valley of Cauteretz*. In the spring of 1862, when mountain flowers were in bloom, Swinburne had hiked up the steep path to the lake where he plunged into the water from a rock and swam across to the opposite bank, "to the horror of the natives," as Edmund Gosse remarked, "who had a tradition that to bathe in Gaube was to court certain death." More than 30 years later, Swinburne looked back on this ecstatic experience of being submerged in icy lake water as contrasted with being exposed to the hot life-giving sunlight —a contrast leading to meditations on life, death, art, and man's relation to the world of nature. Nature is variously represented in the poem but most strikingly by the little lizards (salamanders) Swinburne encountered in the area, one of which he tamed as a pet (hence he speaks of its "kindly trust in man"). In his critical essay on the Jacobean dramatist, John Ford, Swinburne likened Ford's poetry "to a mountain lake shut in by solitary highlands, without visible outlet or inlet, seen fitlier by starlight than by sunlight; much such a one as the Lac de Gaube above Cauteretz, steel-blue and somber, with a strange attraction for the swimmer in its cold smooth reticence and breathless calm."

The lawns, the gorges, and the peaks are one
Glad glory, thrilled with sense of unison
In strong compulsive silence of the sun.

Flowers dense and keen as midnight stars aflame
   And living things of light like flames in flower[2]   10
That glance and flash as though no hand might tame
   Lightnings whose life outshone their stormlit hour
   And played and laughed on earth, with all their power
Gone, and with all their joy of life made long
And harmless as the lightning life of song,   15
Shine sweet like stars when darkness feels them strong.

The deep mild purple flaked with moonbright gold
   That makes the scales seem flowers of hardened light,[3]
The flamelike tongue, the feet that noon leaves cold,
   The kindly trust in man, when once the sight   20
   Grew less than strange, and faith bade fear take flight,
Outlive the little harmless life that shone
And gladdened eyes that loved it, and was gone
Ere love might fear that fear had looked thereon.

Fear held the bright thing hateful, even as fear,   25
   Whose name is one with hate and horror, saith
That heaven, the dark deep heaven of water near,
   Is deadly deep as hell and dark as death.
   The rapturous plunge that quickens blood and breath
With pause more sweet than passion, ere they strive   30
To raise again the limbs that yet would dive
Deeper, should there have slain the soul alive.

As the bright salamander in fire of the noonshine exults and is glad
    of his day,
The spirit that quickens my body rejoices to pass from the sunlight
    away,
To pass from the glow of the mountainous flowerage, the high mul-
    titudinous bloom,   35
Far down through the fathomless night of the water, the gladness
    of silence and gloom.
Death-dark and delicious as death in the dream of a lover and drea-
    mer may be,
It clasps and encompasses body and soul with delight to be living
    and free:
Free utterly now, though the freedom endure but the space of a
    perilous breath,

2. I.e., salamanders, reputed in myth to be imperishable in fire.
3. In an essay, *Notes of Travel* (1894), Swinburne described the sala-mander he tamed at Gaube, "The quaintest of dumb four-footed friends," and spoke of "the beauty of its pur-ple-black coat of scaled armor inlaid with patches of dead-leaf gold, its shin-ing eyes, and its flashing tongue."

And living, though girdled about with the darkness and coldness
    and strangeness of death: 40
Each limb and each pulse of the body rejoicing, each nerve of the
    spirit at rest,
All sense of the soul's life rapture, a passionate peace in its blind-
    ness blessed.
So plunges the downward swimmer, embraced of the water unfath-
    omed of man,
The darkness unplummeted, icier than seas in midwinter, for bless-
    ing or ban;
And swiftly and sweetly, when strength and breath fall short, and
    the dive is done,   45
Shoots up as a shaft from the dark depth shot, sped straight into
    sight of the sun;
And sheer through the snow-soft water, more dark than the roof of
    the pines above,
Strikes forth, and is glad as a bird whose flight is impelled and sus-
    tained of love.
As a sea-mew's[4] love of the sea-wind breasted and ridden for rap-
    ture's sake
Is the love of his body and soul for the darkling delight of the sound-
    less lake: 50
As the silent speed of a dream too living to live for a thought's
    space more
Is the flight of his limbs through the still strong chill of the dark-
    ness from shore to shore.
Might life be as this is and death be as life that casts off time as a
    robe,
The likeness of infinite heaven were a symbol revealed of the lake of
    Gaube.

        Whose thought has fathomed and measured   55
            The darkness of life and of death,
        The secret within them treasured,
            The spirit that is not breath?
        Whose vision has yet beholden
            The splendor of death and of life?   60
        Though sunset as dawn be golden,
            Is the word of them peace, not strife?
        Deep silence answers: the glory
            We dream of may be but a dream,
        And the sun of the soul wax hoary   65
            As ashes that show not a gleam.
        But well shall it be with us ever
            Who drive through the darkness here,
        If the soul that we live by never,
            For aught that a lie saith, fear.   70

                                  1894, 1904

4. Sea gull's.

WALTER PATER
(1839–1894)

Studies in the History of the Renaissance, a collection of essays published in 1873, was the first of several volumes which established Walter Pater as the most important critical writer of the late Victorian period. His flair for critical writing may have first been sparked when he was an undergraduate at Oxford (1858–62) where he heard and enjoyed the lectures of Matthew Arnold, who was then Professor of Poetry. After graduation Pater remained at Oxford, a shy bachelor who spent his life as a tutor of classics (for the story of his earlier years see *The Child in the House* in the following selections, an autobiographical sketch that provides a helpful introduction to all of his writings). In view of his retiring disposition Pater was surprised and even alarmed by the impact made by his books on young readers of the 1870's and 1880's. Some of his younger followers such as Oscar Wilde and George Moore may have misread him. It can be demonstrated that Pater's writings (especially his historical novel *Marius the Epicurean*, 1885) have much in common with his earnest-minded mid-Victorian predecessors, but his disciples overlooked these similarities. To them, his work seemed strikingly different and, in its quiet way, more subversive than the head-on attacks against traditional Victorianism made by Swinburne or Samuel Butler. Instead of recommending a continuation of the painful quest for Truth that had dominated Oxford in the days of Newman, Pater assured his readers that the quest was pointless. Truth, he said, is relative. And instead of echoing Carlyle's call to duty and social responsibilities, Pater reminded his readers that life passes quickly and that our only responsibility is to enjoy fully "this short day of frost and sun," to relish its sensations, especially those sensations provoked by works of art.

This epicurean gospel was conveyed in a highly-wrought prose style that baffles anyone who likes to read quickly. Pater believed that prose was as difficult an art as poetry, and he expected his own elaborate sentences to be savored. Like Flaubert, the French novelist whom he admired, Pater painstakingly revised his sentences with special attention to their rhythms and seeking always the right word, *le mot juste*, as Flaubert had called it. For many years Pater's day would begin with his making a careful study of a dictionary. What Pater said of Dante is an apt description of his own polished style: "He is one of those artists whose general effect largely depends on vocabulary, on the minute particles of which his work is wrought, on the color and outline of single words and phrases."

Aside from his interest as a key figure in the transition from mid-Victorianism to the decadence of the 1890's, Pater's essays also command our attention as examples of impressionistic criticism at its best. In each of his essays he seeks to communicate what he called the "special unique impression of pleasure" made upon him by the works of some artist or writer. His range of subjects included the dialogues of Plato, the paintings of Leonardo da Vinci, the plays of Shakespeare, and the writings of the French Roman-

tic school of the 19th century. Of particular value to students of English
literature are his discriminating studies of Wordsworth, Coleridge, Lamb,
and Sir Thomas Browne in his volume of *Appreciations* (1889), and his
essay on the poetry of William Morris entitled *Aesthetic Poetry* (1868).
These and other essays by Pater were praised by Oscar Wilde in a review in
1890 as "absolutely modern, in the true meaning of the term modernity.
For he to whom the present is the only thing that is present, knows nothing of the age in which he lives. * * * The true critic is he who bears
within himself the dreams and ideas and feelings of myriad generations, and
to whom no form of thought is alien, no emotional impulse obscure."

The final sentences of his *Appreciations* volume are a revealing indication
of Pater's critical position. After having attempted to show the differences
between the classical and romantic schools of art, he concludes that most
great artists combine the qualities of both. "To discriminate schools, of art,
of literature," he writes, "is, of course, part of the obvious business of literary criticism: but, in the work of literary production, it is easy to be overmuch occupied concerning them. For, in truth, the legitimate contention
is, not of one age or school of literary art against another, but of all successive schools alike, against the stupidity which is dead to the substance, and
the vulgarity which is dead to form."

From The Renaissance
Preface

Many attempts have been made by writers on art and poetry to
define beauty in the abstract, to express it in the most general
terms, to find some universal formula for it. The value of these
attempts has most often been in the suggestive and penetrating
things said by the way. Such discussions help us very little to enjoy
what has been well done in art or poetry, to discriminate between
what is more and what is less excellent in them, or to use words
like beauty, excellence, art, poetry, with a more precise meaning
than they would otherwise have. Beauty, like all other qualities
presented to human experience, is relative; and the definition of it
becomes unmeaning and useless in proportion to its abstractness.
To define beauty, not in the most abstract but in the most concrete
terms possible, to find not its universal formula, but the formula
which expresses most adequately this or that special manifestation
of it, is the aim of the true student of aesthetics.

"To see the object as in itself it really is,"[1] has been justly said
to be the aim of all true criticism whatever; and in aesthetic criticism the first step towards seeing one's object as it really is, is to
know one's own impression as it really is, to discriminate it, to
realize it distinctly. The objects with which aesthetic criticism deals
—music, poetry, artistic and accomplished forms of human life—

---

1. See Matthew Arnold, *The Function of Criticism*, opening paragraph.

are indeed receptacles of so many powers or forces: they possess, like the products of nature, so many virtues or qualities. What is this song or picture, this engaging personality presented in life or in a book, to *me?* What effect does it really produce on me? Does it give me pleasure? and if so, what sort or degree of pleasure? How is my nature modified by its presence, and under its influence? The answers to these questions are the original facts with which the aesthetic critic has to do; and, as in the study of light, of morals, of number, one must realize such primary data for one's self, or not at all. And he who experiences these impressions strongly, and drives directly at the discrimination and analysis of them, has no need to trouble himself with the abstract question what beauty is in itself, or what its exact relation to truth or experience—metaphysical questions, as unprofitable as metaphysical questions elsewhere. He may pass them all by as being, answerable or not, of no interest to him.

The aesthetic critic, then, regards all the objects with which he has to do, all works of art, and the fairer forms of nature and human life, as powers or forces producing pleasurable sensations, each of a more or less peculiar or unique kind. This influence he feels, and wishes to explain, by analyzing and reducing it to its elements. To him, the picture, the landscape, the engaging personality in life or in a book, "La Gioconda," the hills of Carrara, Pico of Mirandola,[2] are valuable for their virtues, as we say, in speaking of a herb, a wine, a gem; for the property each has of affecting one with a special, a unique, impression of pleasure. Our education becomes complete in proportion as our susceptibility to these impressions increases in depth and variety. And the function of the aesthetic critic is to distinguish, to analyze, and separate from its adjuncts, the virtue by which a picture, a landscape, a fair personality in life or in a book, produces this special impression of beauty or pleasure, to indicate what the source of that impression is, and under what conditions it is experienced. His end is reached when he has disengaged that virtue, and noted it, as a chemist notes some natural element, for himself and others; and the rule for those who would reach this end is stated with great exactness in the words of a recent critic of Sainte-Beuve: *De se borner à connaître de près les belles choses, et à s'en nourrir en exquis amateurs, en humanistes accomplis.*[3]

What is important, then, is not that the critic should possess a

2. "La Gioconda" is Leonardo da Vinci's famous painting, the "Mona Lisa"; "the hills of Carrara" are marble quarries in Italy; Pico of Mirandola (or Pico della Mirandola) was an Italian philosopher and classical scholar (1463–94), subject of an es- say by Pater which was included in *The Renaissance.*

3. "To confine themselves to knowing beautiful things intimately, and to sustain themselves by these, as sensitive amateurs and accomplished humanists do."

correct abstract definition of beauty for the intellect, but a certain kind of temperament, the power of being deeply moved by the presence of beautiful objects. He will remember always that beauty exists in many forms. To him all periods, types, schools of taste, are in themselves equal. In all ages there have been some excellent workmen, and some excellent work done. The question he asks is always: In whom did the stir, the genius, the sentiment of the period find itself? where was the receptacle of its refinement, its elevation, its taste? "The ages are all equal," says William Blake, "but genius is always above its age."

Often it will require great nicety to disengage this virtue from the commoner elements with which it may be found in combination. Few artists, not Goethe or Byron even, work quite cleanly, casting off all debris, and leaving us only what the heat of their imagination has wholly fused and transformed. Take, for instance, the writings of Wordsworth. The heat of his genius, entering into the substance of his work, has crystallized a part, but only a part, of it; and in that great mass of verse there is much which might well be forgotten. But scattered up and down it, sometimes fusing and transforming entire compositions, like the stanzas on *Resolution and Independence*, or the *Ode on the Recollections of Childhood*,[4] sometimes, as if at random, depositing a fine crystal here or there, in a matter it does not wholly search through and transmute, we trace the action of his unique, incommunicable faculty, that strange, mystical sense of a life in natural things, and of man's life as a part of nature, drawing strength and color and character from local influences, from the hills and streams, and from natural sights and sounds. Well! that is the *virtue*, the active principle in Wordsworth's poetry; and then the function of the critic of Wordsworth is to follow up that active principle, to disengage it, to mark the degree in which it penetrates his verse.

The subjects of the following studies are taken from the history of the *Renaissance*, and touch what I think the chief points in that complex, many-sided movement. I have explained in the first of them what I understand by the word, giving it a much wider scope than was intended by those who originally used it to denote that revival of classical antiquity in the fifteenth century which was only one of many results of a general excitement and enlightening of the human mind, but of which the great aim and achievements of what, as Christian art, is often falsely opposed to the Renaissance, were another result. This outbreak of the human spirit may be traced far into the Middle Age itself, with its motives already clearly pro-

---

4. Wordsworth's *Ode* was entitled *Intimations of Immortality from Recollections of Early Childhood.*

nounced, the care for physical beauty, the worship of the body, the breaking down of those limits which the religious system of the Middle Age imposed on the heart and the imagination. I have taken as an example of this movement, this earlier Renaissance within the Middle Age itself, and as an expression of its qualities, two little compositions in early French; not because they constitute the best possible expression of them, but because they help the unity of my series, inasmuch as the Renaissance ends also in France, in French poetry, in a phase of which the writings of Joachim du Bellay[5] are in many ways the most perfect illustration. The Renaissance, in truth, put forth in France an aftermath, a wonderful later growth, the products of which have to the full that subtle and delicate sweetness which belongs to a refined and comely decadence, just as its earliest phases have the freshness which belongs to all periods of growth in art, the charm of *ascêsis*,[6] of the austere and serious girding of the loins in youth.

But it is in Italy, in the fifteenth century, that the interest of the Renaissance mainly lies—in that solemn fifteenth century which can hardly be studied too much, not merely for its positive results in the things of the intellect and the imagination, its concrete works of art, its special and prominent personalities, with their profound aesthetic charm, but for its general spirit and character, for the ethical qualities of which it is a consummate type.

The various forms of intellectual activity which together make up the culture of an age, move for the most part from different starting points, and by unconnected roads. As products of the same generation they partake indeed of a common character, and unconsciously illustrate each other; but of the producers themselves, each group is solitary, gaining what advantage or disadvantage there may be in intellectual isolation. Art and poetry, philosophy and the religious life, and that other life of refined pleasure and action in the conspicuous places of the world, are each of them confined to its own circle of ideas, and those who prosecute either of them are generally little curious of the thoughts of others. There come, however, from time to time, eras of more favorable conditions, in which the thoughts of men draw nearer together than is their wont, and the many interests of the intellectual world combine in one complete type of general culture. The fifteenth century in Italy is one of these happier eras, and what is sometimes said of the age of Pericles is true of that of Lorenzo: it is an age productive in personalities, many-sided, centralized, complete. Here, artists and philosophers and those whom the action of the world has elevated and made keen, do not live in isolation, but breathe a common air, and catch

5. French poet and critic (1524–60), subject of another essay in *The Ren-* *aissance*.
6. Asceticism.

light and heat from each other's thoughts. There is a spirit of general elevation and enlightenment in which all alike communicate. The unity of this spirit gives unity to all the various products of the Renaissance; and it is to this intimate alliance with mind, this participation in the best thoughts which that age produced, that the art of Italy in the fifteenth century owes much of its grave dignity and influence.

I have added an essay on Winckelmann,[7] as not incongruous with the studies which precede it, because Winckelmann, coming in the eighteenth century, really belongs in spirit to an earlier age. By his enthusiasm for the things of the intellect and the imagination for their own sake, by his Hellenism, his lifelong struggle to attain to the Greek spirit, he is in sympathy with the humanists of a previous century. He is the last fruit of the Renaissance, and explains in a striking way its motive and tendencies.

[*"La Gioconda"*][8]

"La Gioconda" is, in the truest sense, Leonardo's masterpiece, the revealing instance of his mode of thought and work. In suggestiveness, only the "Melancholia" of Dürer[9] is comparable to it; and no crude symbolism disturbs the effect of its subdued and graceful mystery. We all know the face and hands of the figure, set in its marble chair, in that circle of fantastic rocks, as in some faint light under sea. Perhaps of all ancient pictures time has chilled it least. As often happens with works in which invention seems to reach its limit, there is an element in it given to, not invented by, the master. In that inestimable folio of drawings, once in the possession of Vasari, were certain designs by Verrocchio,[1] faces of such impressive beauty that Leonardo in his boyhood copied them many times. It is hard not to connect with these designs of the elder, by-past master, as with its germinal principle, the unfathomable smile, always with a touch of something sinister in it, which plays over all Leonardo's work. Besides, the picture is a portrait. From childhood we see this image defining itself on the fabric of his dreams, and but for express historical testimony, we might fancy

7. Johann Joachim Winckelmann (1717–68), German classicist.
8. "La Gioconda" or "Mona Lisa," famous painting by Leonardo da Vinci which now hangs in the Louvre in Paris. The sitter for the portrait may have been Lisa, the third wife of the Florentine Francesco del Giocondo (to whom Pater refers as "Il Giocondo") —hence her title, La Gioconda. *Mona* (more correctly *Monna*) *Lisa* means "Madonna Lisa" or "My Lady Lisa."

This selection is drawn from the essay on Leonardo da Vinci.
9. Albrecht Dürer (1471–1528), German artist whose picture of the spirit of Melancholy is full of details which may stimulate reflection in the spectator.
1. Andrea del Verrocchio (1435–88), Florentine painter and sculptor. Giorgio Vasari, author of *Lives of the Most Excellent Italian Painters* (1550).

that this was but his ideal lady, embodied and beheld at last. What was the relationship of a living Florentine to this creature of his thought? By what strange affinities had the dream and the person grown up thus apart, and yet so closely together? Present from the first incorporeally in Leonardo's brain, dimly traced in the designs of Verrocchio, she is found present at last in Il Giocondo's house. That there is much of mere portraiture in the picture is attested by the legend that by artificial means, the presence of mimes[2] and flute-players, that subtle expression was protracted on the face. Again, was it in four years and by renewed labor never really completed, or in four months and as by stroke of magic, that the image was projected?

The presence that rose thus so strangely beside the waters, is expressive of what in the ways of a thousand years men had come to desire. Hers is the head upon which all "the ends of the world are come,"[3] and the eyelids are a little weary. It is a beauty wrought out from within upon the flesh, the deposit, little cell by cell, of strange thoughts and fantastic reveries and exquisite passions. Set it for a moment beside one of those white Greek goddesses or beautiful women of antiquity, and how would they be troubled by this beauty, into which the soul with all its maladies has passed! All the thoughts and experience of the world have etched and molded there, in that which they have of power to refine and make expressive the outward form, the animalism of Greece, the lust of Rome, the mysticism of the Middle Age with its spiritual ambition and imaginative loves, the return of the Pagan world, the sins of the Borgias.[4] She is older than the rocks among which she sits; like the vampire,[5] she has been dead many times, and learned the secrets of the grave; and has been a diver in deep seas, and keeps their fallen day about her; and trafficked for strange webs with Eastern merchants, and, as Leda, was the mother of Helen of Troy,[6] and, as Saint Anne, the mother of Mary; and all this has been to her but as the sound of lyres and flutes, and lives only in the delicacy with which it has molded the changing lineaments, and tinged the eyelids and the hands. The fancy of a perpetual life, sweeping together ten thousand experiences, is an old one; and modern philosophy has conceived the idea of humanity as wrought upon by, and summing up in itself, all modes of thought and life. Certainly Lady Lisa might stand as the embodiment of the old fancy, the symbol of the modern idea.

2. Mimics or clowns.
3. I Corinthians x.11.
4. The Borgias were an Italian family during the Renaissance whose reputation for scandalous conduct was notorious.

5. A dead body which, according to widespread legends, returns from the grave to prey upon the living.
6. Leda's union with Zeus (who approached her in the form of a swan) produced Helen of Troy.

Conclusion[7]

Λέγει που Ἡράκλειτος ὅτι πάντα χωρεῖ καὶ οὐδὲν μένει[8]

To regard all things and principles of things as inconstant modes or fashions has more and more become the tendency of modern thought. Let us begin with that which is without—our physical life. Fix upon it in one of its more exquisite intervals, the moment, for instance, of delicious recoil from the flood of water in summer heat. What is the whole physical life in that moment but a combination of natural elements to which science gives their names? But those elements, phosphorus and lime and delicate fibers, are present not in the human body alone: we detect them in places most remote from it. Our physical life is a perpetual motion of them—the passage of the blood, the waste and repairing of the lenses of the eye, the modification of the tissues of the brain under every ray of light and sound—processes which science reduces to simpler and more elementary forces. Like the elements of which we are composed, the action of these forces extends beyond us: it rusts iron and ripens corn. Far out on every side of us those elements are broadcast, driven in many currents; and birth and gesture and death and the springing of violets from the grave are but a few out of ten thousand resultant combinations. That clear, perpetual outline of face and limb is but an image of ours, under which we group them— a design in a web, the actual threads of which pass out beyond it. This at least of flamelike our life has, that it is but the concurrence, renewed from moment to moment, of forces parting sooner or later on their ways.

Or, if we begin with the inward world of thought and feeling, the whirlpool is still more rapid, the flame more eager and devouring. There it is no longer the gradual darkening of the eye, the gradual fading of color from the wall—movements of the shore-side, where the water flows down indeed, though in apparent rest—but the race of the midstream, a drift of momentary acts of sight and passion and thought. At first sight experience seems to bury us under a flood of external objects, pressing upon us with a sharp and importunate reality, calling us out of ourselves in a thousand forms of action. But when reflection begins to play upon those objects they are dissipated under its influence; the cohesive force seems suspended like some trick of magic; each object is loosed into a group of impressions—color, odor, texture—in the mind of the observer.

7. "This brief 'Conclusion' was omitted in the second edition of this book, as I conceived it might possibly mislead some of those young men into whose hands it might fall. On the whole, I have thought it best to reprint it here, with some slight changes which bring it closer to my original meaning. I have dealt more fully in *Marius the Epicurean* with the thoughts suggested by it" [Pater's note to the third edition, 1888].
8. "Heraclitus says, 'All things give way; nothing remaineth'" [Pater's translation].

And if we continue to dwell in thought on this world, not of objects in the solidity with which language invests them, but of impressions, unstable, flickering, inconsistent, which burn and are extinguished with our consciousness of them, it contracts still further: the whole scope of observation is dwarfed into the narrow chamber of the individual mind. Experience, already reduced to a group of impressions, is ringed round for each one of us by that thick wall of personality through which no real voice has ever pierced on its way to us, or from us to that which we can only conjecture to be without. Every one of those impressions is the impression of the individual in his isolation, each mind keeping as a solitary prisoner its own dream of a world. Analysis goes a step farther still, and assures us that those impressions of the individual mind to which, for each one of us, experience dwindles down, are in perpetual flight; that each of them is limited by time, and that as time is infinitely divisible, each of them is infinitely divisible also; all that is actual in it being a single moment, gone while we try to apprehend it, of which it may ever be more truly said that it has ceased to be than that it is. To such a tremulous wisp constantly reforming itself on the stream, to a single sharp impression, with a sense in it, a relic more or less fleeting, of such moments gone by, what is real in our life fines itself down. It is with this movement, with the passage and dissolution of impressions, images, sensations, that analysis leaves off—that continual vanishing away, that strange, perpetual weaving and unweaving of ourselves.

Philosophiren, says Novalis, *ist dephlegmatisiren, vivificiren.*[9] The service of philosophy, of speculative culture, towards the human spirit is to rouse, to startle it to a life of constant and eager observation. Every moment some form grows perfect in hand or face; some tone on the hills or the sea is choicer than the rest; some mood of passion or insight or intellectual excitement is irresistibly real and attractive to us—for that moment only. Not the fruit of experience, but experience itself, is the end. A counted number of pulses only is given to us of a variegated, dramatic life. How may we see in them all that is to be seen in them by the finest senses? How shall we pass most swiftly from point to point, and be present always at the focus where the greatest number of vital forces unite in their purest energy?

To burn always with this hard, gemlike flame, to maintain this ecstasy, is success in life. In a sense it might even be said that our failure is to form habits: for, after all, habit is relative to a stereotyped world, and meantime it is only the roughness of the eye that makes any two persons, things, situations, seem alike. While all

9. "To philosophize is to cast off inertia, to make oneself alive." "Novalis" was the pseudonym of Friedrich von Hardenberg (1772–1801), German Romantic writer.

melts under our feet, we may well grasp at any exquisite passion, or
any contribution to knowledge that seems by a lifted horizon to set
the spirit free for a moment, or any stirring of the senses, strange
dyes, strange colors, and curious odors, or work of the artist's hands,
or the face of one's friend. Not to discriminate every moment some
passionate attitude in those about us, and in the very brilliancy of
their gifts some tragic dividing of forces on their ways, is, on this
short day of frost and sun, to sleep before evening. With this sense
of the splendor of our experience and of its awful brevity, gathering
all we are into one desperate effort to see and touch, we shall hardly
have time to make theories about the things we see and touch.
What we have to do is to be forever curiously testing new opinions
and courting new impressions, never acquiescing in a facile orthodoxy of Comte, or of Hegel,[1] or of our own. Philosophical theories
or ideas, as points of view, instruments of criticism, may help us to
gather up what might otherwise pass unregarded by us. "Philosophy
is the microscope of thought." The theory or idea or system which
requires of us the sacrifice of any part of this experience, in consideration of some interest into which we cannot enter, or some
abstract theory we have not identified with ourselves, or of what is
only conventional, has no real claim upon us.

One of the most beautiful passages of Rousseau is that in the
sixth book of the *Confessions*, where he describes the awakening in
him of the literary sense. An undefinable taint of death had clung
always about him, and now in early manhood he believed himself
smitten by mortal disease. He asked himself how he might make
as much as possible of the interval that remained; and he was not
biased by anything in his previous life when he decided that it must
be by intellectual excitement, which he found just then in the
clear, fresh writings of Voltaire. Well! we are all *condamnés* as
Victor Hugo says: we are all under sentence of death but with a
sort of indefinite reprieve—*les hommes sont tous condamnés à mort
avec des sursis indéfinis*: we have an interval, and then our place
knows us no more. Some spend this interval in listlessness, some
in high passions, the wisest, at least among "the children of this
world," in art and song. For our one chance lies in expanding that
interval, in getting as many pulsations as possible into the given
time. Great passions may give us this quickened sense of life, ecstasy
and sorrow of love, the various forms of enthusiastic activity, disinterested or otherwise, which come naturally to many of us. Only
be sure it is passion—that it does yield you this fruit of a quickened,
multiplied consciousness. Of such wisdom, the poetic passion, the
desire of beauty, the love of art for its own sake, has most. For art
comes to you proposing frankly to give nothing but the highest

1. Auguste Comte (1798–1857), French
founder of positivism; Georg W. F.
Hegel (1770–1831), German idealistic
philosopher.

quality to your moments as they pass, and simply for those moments'
sake.

1868   1873

The Child in the House[1]

As Florian Deleal walked, one hot afternoon, he overtook by the
wayside a poor aged man, and, as he seemed weary with the road,
helped him on with the burden which he carried, a certain distance.
And as the man told his story, it chanced that he named the place,
a little place in the neighborhood of a great city, where Florian had
passed his earliest years, but which he had never since seen, and,
the story told, went forward on his journey comforted. And that
night, like a reward for his pity, a dream of that place came to
Florian, a dream which did for him the office of the finer sort of
memory, bringing its object to mind with a great clearness, yet, as
sometimes happens in dreams, raised a little above itself, and above
ordinary retrospect. The true aspect of the place, especially of the
house there in which he had lived as a child, the fashion of its
doors, its hearths, its windows, the very scent upon the air of it, was
with him in sleep for a season; only, with tints more musically blent
on wall and floor, and some finer light and shadow running in
and out along its curves and angles, and with all its little carvings

1. Pater was 41 when he wrote this
self-portrait, in the third person, of his
boyhood, 30 years earlier. Like Dickens
in *David Copperfield*, he modified some
of the circumstances of his growing up,
most particularly the death of his
father. Pater's father, a surgeon, died
when his son was an infant, and the
boy had no way of remembering him.
Florian's father, a soldier, dies in
India, but the boy remembers him vividly and is haunted by his ghost. In
most other respects the circumstances
of Pater's life seem similar to those of
Florian Deleal's. After the father's
death, the Pater family settled in a
modest house in Enfield, a village on
the north border of London; it was the
model for the house so fondly recollected in the story, although Pater's
memories of it seem to have combined
with memories of a large house in
Kent, south of London, where he had
visited relatives. The Pater children—
an older brother and two sisters, who
are briefly mentioned in the story—
were brought up by their mother and
an aunt, and also by a grandmother
who died in 1848 when Pater was
living in the Enfield house. In 1853 the
family moved to another house in the
vicinity of Canterbury, where Pater
attended King's School before going to
Oxford.

The "process of our brain-building"
—the plot line of Pater's story—culminates for Florian in the development of
his religious sensibilities at the age of
12 or so. The final pages here offer a
clue to Pater's own mature attitudes
towards religion, which some readers
find baffling. As a boy Pater himself
had always intended to become an
Anglican clergyman, but his studies at
Oxford of Darwin and other writers led
him to abandon his belief in Christianity. Unlike some other Victorians, however, this loss of belief did not stop
him from going to church. Instead he
attended services regularly throughout
most of his lifetime, loving "for their
own sakes," like the boy Florian,
"church lights, holy days, all that
belonged to the comely order of the
sanctuary."

Interesting comparisons may be made
between Pater's sketch of the process
of Florian's growing up and such first-
person autobiographies as John Stuart
Mill's or such fictional versions as
James Joyce's *Portrait of the Artist as
a Young Man*. Some of the stages of
Stephen Dedalus's religious experiences
seem reminiscent of Florian's, and in
view of Joyce's keen admiration for
Pater's writings, the resemblance is an
appropriate one.

daintier. He awoke with a sigh at the thought of almost thirty years which lay between him and that place, yet with a flutter of pleasure still within him at the fair light, as if it were a smile, upon it. And it happened that this accident of his dream was just the thing needed for the beginning of a certain design he then had in view, the noting, namely, of some things in the story of his spirit—in that process of brain-building by which we are, each one of us, what we are. With the image of the place so clear and favorable upon him, he fell to thinking of himself therein, and how his thoughts had grown up to him. In that half-spiritualized house he could watch the better, over again, the gradual expansion of the soul which had come to be there—of which indeed, through the law which makes the material objects about them so large an element in children's lives, it had actually become a part; inward and outward being woven through and through each other into one inextricable texture—half, tint and trace and accident of homely color and form, from the wood and the bricks; half, mere soul-stuff, floated thither from who knows how far.[2] In the house and garden of his dream he saw a child moving, and could divide the main streams at least of the winds that had played on him, and study so the first stage in that mental journey.

The *old house*, as when Florian talked of it afterwards he always called it (as all children do, who can recollect a change of home, soon enough but not too soon to mark a period in their lives), really was an old house; and an element of French descent in its inmates—descent from Watteau, the old court painter,[3] one of whose gallant pieces still hung in one of the rooms—might explain, together with some other things, a noticeable trimness and comely whiteness about everything there—the curtains, the couches, the paint on the walls with which the light and shadow played so delicately; might explain also the tolerance of the great poplar in the garden, a tree most often despised by English people, but which French people love, having observed a certain fresh way its leaves have of dealing with the wind, making it sound, in never so slight a stirring of the air, like running water.

The old-fashioned, low wainscoting went round the rooms, and up the staircase with carved balusters and shadowy angles, landing halfway up at a broad window, with a swallow's nest below the sill, and the blossom of an old pear tree showing across it in late April, against the blue, below which the perfumed juice of the find of fallen fruit in autumn was so fresh. At the next turning came the closet which held on its deep shelves the best china. Little angel

2. Cf. Wordsworth's *Ode: Intimations of Immortality* (lines 59–63): "The Soul that rises with us * * * cometh from afar."

3. Jean Antoine Watteau (1684–1721), a French painter about whom Pater wrote an essay which is included in his *Imaginary Portraits* (1887).

faces and reedy flutings stood out round the fireplace of the children's room. And on the top of the house, above the large attic, where the white mice ran in the twilight—an infinite, unexplored wonderland of childish treasures, glass beads, empty scent-bottles still sweet, thrum[4] of colored silks, among its lumber—a flat space of roof, railed round, gave a view of the neighboring steeples; for the house, as I said, stood near a great city, which sent up heavenwards, over the twisting weather vanes, not seldom, its beds of rolling cloud and smoke, touched with storm or sunshine. But the child of whom I am writing did not hate the fog because of the crimson lights which fell from it sometimes upon the chimneys, and the whites which gleamed through its openings, on summer mornings, on turret or pavement. For it is false to suppose that a child's sense of beauty is dependent on any choiceness or special fineness, in the objects which present themselves to it, though this indeed comes to be the rule with most of us in later life; earlier, in some degree, we see inwardly; and the child finds for itself, and with unstinted delight, a difference for the sense, in those whites and reds through the smoke on very homely buildings, and in the gold of the dandelions at the road-side, just beyond the houses, where not a handful of earth is virgin and untouched, in the lack of better ministries to its desire of beauty.

This house then stood not far beyond the gloom and rumors of the town, among high garden wall, bright all summer-time with goldenrod, and brown-and-golden wallflower—*Flos Parietis*, as the children's Latin-reading father taught them to call it, while he was with them. Tracing back the threads of his complex spiritual habit, as he was used in after years to do, Florian found that he owed to the place many tones of sentiment afterwards customary with him, certain inward lights under which things most naturally presented themselves to him. The coming and going of travelers to the town along the way, the shadow of the streets, the sudden breath of the neighboring gardens, the singular brightness of bright weather there, its singular darknesses which linked themselves in his mind to certain engraved illustrations in the old big Bible at home, the coolness of the dark, cavernous shops round the great church, with its giddy winding stair up to the pigeons and the bells—a citadel of peace in the heart of the trouble—all this acted on his childish fancy, so that ever afterwards the like aspects and incidents never failed to throw him into a well-recognized imaginative mood, seeming actually to have become a part of the texture of his mind. Also, Florian could trace home to this point a pervading preference in himself for a kind of comeliness and dignity, an *urbanity* literally, in modes of

---

4. Scraps. "Lumber": worn out or discarded household furnishings stored in the attic.

life, which he connected with the pale people of towns, and which made him susceptible to a kind of exquisite satisfaction in the trimness and well-considered grace of certain things and persons he afterwards met with, here and there, in his way through the world.

So the child of whom I am writing lived on there quietly; things without thus ministering to him, as he sat daily at the window with the birdcage hanging below it, and his mother taught him to read, wondering at the ease with which he learned, and at the quickness of his memory. The perfume of the little flowers of the lime tree fell through the air upon them like rain; while time seemed to move ever more slowly to the murmur of the bees in it, till it almost stood still on June afternoons. How insignificant, at the moment, seem the influences of the sensible[5] things which are tossed and fall and lie about us, so, or so, in the environment of early childhood. How indelibly, as we afterwards discover, they affect us; with what capricious attractions and associations they figure themselves on the white paper,[6] the smooth wax, of our ingenuous souls, as "with lead in the rock forever,"[7] giving form and feature, and as it were assigned house-room in our memory, to early experiences of feeling and thought, which abide with us ever afterwards, thus, and not otherwise. The realities and passions, the rumors of the greater world without, steal in upon us, each by its own special little passageway, through the wall of custom about us; and never afterwards quite detach themselves from this or that accident, or trick, in the mode of their first entrance to us. Our susceptibilities, the discovery of our powers, manifold experiences—our various experiences of the coming and going of bodily pain, for instance—belong to this or the other well-remembered place in the material habitation—that little white room with the window across which the heavy blossoms could beat so peevishly in the wind, with just that particular catch or throb, such a sense of teasing in it, on gusty mornings; and the early habitation thus gradually becomes a sort of material shrine or sanctuary of sentiment; a system of visible symbolism interweaves itself through all our thoughts and passions; and irresistibly, little shapes, voices, accidents—the angle at which the sun in the morning fell on the pillow—become parts of the great chain wherewith we are bound.

Thus far, for Florian, what all this had determined was a peculiarly strong sense of home—so forcible a motive with all of us—prompting to us our customary love of the earth, and the larger part of our fear of death, that revulsion we have from it, as from something strange, untried, unfriendly; though lifelong imprisonment,

5. Perceived by the senses.
6. An allusion to John Locke's theory in his *Essay on Human Understanding* (1690) that the mind, in its early stages, is a blank page, a *"tabula rasa,"* on which impressions from the outer world are written.
7. Job xix. 23–24.

they tell you, and final banishment from home is a thing bitterer still; the looking forward to but a short space, a mere childish *goûter*[8] and dessert of it, before the end, being so great a resource of effort to pilgrims and wayfarers, and the soldier in distant quarters, and lending, in lack of that, some power of solace to the thought of sleep in the home churchyard, at least—dead cheek by dead cheek, and with the rain soaking in upon one from above.

So powerful is this instinct, and yet accidents like those I have been speaking of so mechanically determine it; its essence being indeed the early familiar, as constituting our ideal, or typical conception, of rest and security. Out of so many possible conditions, just this for you and that for me, brings ever the unmistakeable realization of the delightful *chez soi*;[9] this for the Englishman, for me and you, with the closely drawn white curtain and the shaded lamp; that, quite other, for the wandering Arab, who folds his tent every morning, and makes his sleeping-place among haunted ruins, or in old tombs.

With Florian then the sense of home became singularly intense, his good fortune being that the special character of his home was in itself so essentially homelike. As after many wanderings I have come to fancy that some parts of Surrey and Kent are, for Englishmen, the true landscape, true home-counties, by right, partly, of a certain earthy warmth in the yellow of the sand below their gorse bushes, and of a certain gray-blue mist after rain, in the hollows of the hills there, welcome to fatigued eyes, and never seen farther south;[1] so I think that the sort of house I have described, with precisely those proportions of red-brick and green, and with a just perceptible monotony in the subdued order of it, for its distinguishing note, is for Englishmen at least typically home-life. And so for Florian that general human instinct was reinforced by this special home-likeness in the place his wandering soul had happened to light on, as, in the second degree, its body and earthly tabernacle; the sense of harmony between his soul and its physical environment became, for a time at least, like perfectly played music, and the life led there singularly tranquil and filled with a curious sense of self-possession. The love of security, of an habitually undisputed standing-ground or sleeping-place, came to count for much in the generation and correcting of his thoughts, and afterwards as a salutary principle of restraint in all his wanderings of spirit. The wistful yearning towards home, in absence from it, as the shadows of evening deepened, and he followed in thought what was doing there from hour to hour, interpreted to him much of a yearning and

8. Snack.
9. At home.
1. Presumably meaning southern land-
scapes outside of England such as in Mediterranean countries.

regret he experienced afterwards, towards he knew not what, out of strange ways of feeling and thought in which, from time to time, his spirit found itself alone; and in the tears shed in such absences there seemed always to be some soul-subduing foretaste of what his last tears might be.

And the sense of security could hardly have been deeper, the quiet of the child's soul being one with the quiet of its home, a place "enclosed" and "sealed." But upon this assured place, upon the child's assured soul which resembled it, there came floating in from the larger world without, as at windows left ajar unknowingly, or over the high garden walls, two streams of impressions, the sentiments of beauty and pain—recognitions of the visible, tangible, audible loveliness of things, as a very real and somewhat tyrannous element in them—and of the sorrow of the world, of grown people and children and animals, as a thing not to be put by in them. From this point he could trace two predominant processes of mental change in him—the growth of an almost diseased sensibility to the spectacle of suffering, and, parallel with this, the rapid growth of a certain capacity of fascination by bright color and choice form—the sweet curvings, for instance, of the lips of those who seemed to him comely persons, modulated in such delicate unison to the things they said or sang—marking early the activity in him of more than customary sensuousness, "the lust of the eye,"[2] as the Preacher says, which might lead him, one day, how far! Could he have foreseen the weariness of the way! In music sometimes the two sorts of impressions came together, and he would weep, to the surprise of older people. Tears of joy too the child knew, also to older people's surprise; real tears, once, of relief from long-strung, childish expectation, when he found returned at evening, with new roses in her cheeks, the little sister who had been to a place where there was a wood, and brought back for him a treasure of fallen acorns, and black crow's feathers, and his peace at finding her again near him mingled all night with some intimate sense of the distant forest, the rumor of its breezes, with the glossy blackbirds aslant and the branches lifted in them, and of the perfect nicety of the little cups that fell. So those two elementary apprehensions of the tenderness and of the color in things grew apace in him, and were seen by him afterwards to send their roots back into the beginnings of life.

Let me note first some of the occasions of his recognition of the element of pain in things—incidents, now and again, which seemed suddenly to awake in him the whole force of that sentiment which Goethe has called the *Weltschmerz*,[3] and in which the concentrated sorrow of the world seemed suddenly to lie heavy upon him.

2. John ii.16.　　　　3. World-weariness.

A book lay in an old bookcase, of which he cared to remember one picture—a woman sitting, with hands bound behind her, the dress, the cap, the hair, folded with a simplicity which touched him strangely, as if not by her own hands, but with some ambiguous care at the hands of others—Queen Marie Antoinette, on her way to execution—we all remember David's[4] drawing, meant merely to make her ridiculous. The face that had been so high had learned to be mute and resistless; but out of its very resistlessness, seemed now to call on men to have pity, and forbear; and he took note of that, as he closed the book, as a thing to look at again, if he should at any time find himself tempted to be cruel. Again, he would never quite forget the appeal in the small sister's face, in the garden under the lilacs, terrified at a spider lighted on her sleeve. He could trace back to the look then noted a certain mercy he conceived always for people in fear, even of little things, which seemed to make him, though but for a moment, capable of almost any sacrifice of himself. Impressible, susceptible persons, indeed, who had had their sorrows, lived about him; and this sensibility was due in part to the tacit influence of their presence, enforcing upon him habitually the fact that there are those who pass their days, as a matter of course, in a sort of "going quietly." Most poignantly of all he could recall, in unfading minutest circumstance, the cry on the stair, sounding bitterly through the house, and struck into his soul forever, of an aged woman, his father's sister, come now to announce his death in distant India; how it seemed to make the aged woman like a child again; and, he knew not why, but this fancy was full of pity to him. There were the little sorrows of the dumb animals too—of the white angora, with a dark tail like an ermine's, and a face like a flower, who fell into a lingering sickness, and became quite delicately human in its valetudinarianism,[5] and came to have a hundred different expressions of voice—how it grew worse and worse, till it began to feel the light too much for it, and at last, after one wild morning of pain, the little soul flickered away from the body, quite worn to death already, and now but feebly retaining it.

So he wanted another pet; and as there were starlings about the place, which could be taught to speak, one of them was caught, and he meant to treat it kindly; but in the night its young ones could be heard crying after it, and the responsive cry of the mother bird towards them; and at last, with the first light, though not till after some debate with himself, he went down and opened the cage, and saw a sharp bound of the prisoner up to her nestlings; and therewith came the sense of remorse—that he too was become an

4. Jacques Louis David (1748–1825), French painter.   5. Condition of being an invalid.

accomplice in moving, to the limit of his small power, the springs and handles of that great machine in things, constructed so ingeniously to play pain-fugues on the delicate nerve-work of living creatures.[6]

I have remarked how, in the process of our brain-building, as the house of thought in which we live gets itself together, like some airy bird's nest of floating thistledown and chance straws, compact at last, little accidents have their consequence; and thus it happened that, as he walked one evening, a garden gate, usually closed, stood open; and lo! within, a great red hawthorn in full flower, embossing heavily the bleached and twisted trunk and branches, so aged that there were but few green leaves thereon—a plumage of tender, crimson fire out of the heart of the dry wood. The perfume of the tree had now and again reached him, in the currents of the wind, over the wall, and he had wondered what might be behind it, and was now allowed to fill his arms with the flowers—flowers enough for all the old blue-china pots along the chimney-piece, making *fête* in the children's room. Was it some periodic moment in the expansion of soul within him, or mere trick of heat in the heavily-laden summer air? But the beauty of the thing struck home to him feverishly; and in dreams all night he loitered along a magic roadway of crimson flowers, which seemed to open ruddily in thick, fresh masses about his feet, and fill softly all the little hollows in the banks on either side. Always afterwards, summer by summer, as the flowers came on, the blossom of the red hawthorn still seemed to him absolutely the reddest of all things; and the goodly crimson, still alive in the works of old Venetian masters or old Flemish tapestries, called out always from afar the recollection of the flame in those perishing little petals, as it pulsed gradually out of them, kept long in the drawers of an old cabinet. Also then, for the first time, he seemed to experience a passionateness in his relation to fair outward objects, an inexplicable excitement in their presence, which disturbed him, and from which he half longed to be free. A touch of regret or desire mingled all night with the remembered presence of the red flowers, and their perfume in the darkness about him; and the longing for some undivined, entire possession of them was the beginning of a revelation to him, growing ever clearer, with the coming of the gracious summer guise of fields and trees and persons in each succeeding year, of a certain, at times seemingly exclusive, predominance in his interests, of beautiful physical things, a kind of tyranny of the senses over him.

In later years he came upon philosophies which occupied him much in the estimate of the proportion of the sensuous and the

---

6. This commentary on the pain-machine and the sufferings of birds and animals anticipates many passages in the poems and novels of Hardy.

ideal elements in human knowledge, the relative parts they bear in it; and, in his intellectual scheme, was led to assign very little to the abstract thought, and much to its sensible vehicle or occasion. Such metaphysical speculation did but reinforce what was instinctive in his way of receiving the world, and for him, everywhere, that sensible vehicle or occasion became, perhaps only too surely, the necessary concomitant of any perception of things, real enough to be of any weight or reckoning, in his house of thought. There were times when he could think of the necessity he was under of associating all thoughts to touch and sight, as a sympathetic link between himself and actual, feeling, living objects; a protest in favor of real men and women against mere gray, unreal abstractions; and he remembered gratefully how the Christian religion, hardly less than the religion of the ancient Greeks, translating so much of its spiritual verity into things that may be seen, condescends in part to sanction this infirmity, if so it be, of our human existence, wherein the world of sense is so much with us,[7] and welcomed this thought as a kind of keeper and sentinel over his soul therein. But certainly, he came more and more to be unable to care for, or think of, soul but as in an actual body, or of any world but that wherein are water and trees, and where men and women look, so or so, and press actual hands. It was the trick even his pity learned, fastening those who suffered in anywise to his affections by a kind of sensible attachments. He would think of Julian, fallen into incurable sickness, as spoiled in the sweet blossom of his skin like pale amber, and his honeylike hair; of Cecil, early dead, as cut off from the lilies, from golden summer days, from women's voices; and then what comforted him a little was the thought of the turning of the child's flesh to violets in the turf above him. And thinking of the very poor, it was not the things which most men care most for that he yearned to give them; but fairer roses, perhaps, and power to taste quite as they will, at their ease and not task-burdened, a certain desirable, clear light in the new morning, through which sometimes he had noticed them, quite unconscious of it, on their way to their early toil.

So he yielded himself to these things, to be played upon by them like a musical instrument, and began to note with deepening watchfulness, but always with some puzzled, unutterable longing in his enjoyment, the phases of the seasons and of the growing or waning day, down even to the shadowy changes wrought on bare wall or ceiling—the light cast up from the snow, bringing out their darkest angles; the brown light in the cloud, which meant rain; that almost too austere clearness, in the protracted light of the lengthening day, before warm weather began, as if it lingered but to make a severer

7. Cf. Wordsworth's sonnet, *The World Is Too Much with Us.*

workday, with the school books opened earlier and later; that beam of June sunshine, at last, as he lay awake before the time, a way of gold dust across the darkness; all the humming, the freshness, the perfume of the garden seemed to lie upon it—and coming in one afternoon in September, along the red gravel walk, to look for a basket of yellow crab apples left in the cool, old parlor, he remembered it the more, and how the colors struck upon him, because a wasp on one bitten apple stung him, and he felt the passion of sudden, severe pain. For this too brought its curious reflections; and, in relief from it, he would wonder over it—how it had then been with him—puzzled at the depth of the charm or spell over him, which lay, for a little while at least, in the mere absence of pain; once, especially, when an older boy taught him to make flowers of sealing wax, and he had burnt his hand badly at the lighted taper, and been unable to sleep. He remembered that also afterwards, as a sort of typical thing—a white vision of heat about him, clinging closely, through the languid scent of the ointments put upon the place to make it well.

Also, as he felt this pressure upon him of the sensible world, then, as often afterwards, there would come another sort of curious questioning how the last impressions of eye and ear might happen to him, how they would find him—the scent of the last flower, the soft yellowness of the last morning, the last recognition of some object of affection, hand or voice; it could not be but that the latest look of the eyes, before their final closing, would be strangely vivid; one would go with the hot tears, the cry, the touch of the wistful bystander, impressed how deeply on one! or would it be, perhaps, a mere frail retiring of all things, great or little, away from one, into a level distance?

For with this desire of physical beauty mingled itself early the fear of death—the fear of death intensified by the desire of beauty. Hitherto he had never gazed upon dead faces, as sometimes, afterwards, at the morgue in Paris,[8] or in that fair cemetery at Munich, where all the dead must go and lie in state before burial, behind glass windows, among the flowers and incense and holy candles—the aged clergy with their sacred ornaments, the young men in their dancing-shoes and spotless white linen—after which visits, those waxen, resistless faces would always live with him for many days, making the broadest sunshine sickly. The child had heard indeed of the death of his father, and how, in the Indian station, a fever had taken him, so that though not in action he had yet died as a soldier; and hearing of the "resurrection of the just,"[9] he could think of him as still abroad in the world, somehow, for his protec-

8. Concerning the Paris Morgue, where bodies of unidentified suicides were on public display, see Browning's poem, *Apparent Failure.*
9. Luke xiv.14.

tion—a grand, though perhaps rather terrible figure, in beautiful soldier's things, like the figure in the picture of Joshua's Vision in the
Bible[1]—and of that, round which the mourners moved so softly,
and afterwards with such solemn singing, as but a worn-out garment
left at a deserted lodging. So it was, until on a summer day he
walked with his mother through a fair churchyard. In a bright dress
he rambled among the graves, in the gay weather, and so came, in
one corner, upon an open grave for a child—a dark space on the
brilliant grass—the black mold lying heaped up round it, weighing
down the little jeweled branches of the dwarf rose bushes in
flower. And therewith came, full-grown, never wholly to leave him,
with the certainty that even children do sometimes die, the physical
horror of death, with its wholly selfish recoil from the association of
lower forms of life, and the suffocating weight above. No benign,
grave figure in beautiful soldier's things any longer abroad in the
world for his protection! only a few poor, piteous bones; and above
them, possibly, a certain sort of figure he hoped not to see. For sitting one day in the garden below an open window, he heard people
talking, and could not but listen, how, in a sleepless hour, a sick
woman had seen one of the dead sitting beside her, come to call her
hence; and from the broken talk evolved with much clearness the
notion that not all those dead people had really departed to the
churchyard, nor were quite so motionless as they looked, but led a
secret, half-fugitive life in their old homes, quite free by night,
though sometimes visible in the day, dodging from room to room,
with no great goodwill towards those who shared the place with
them. All night the figure sat beside him in the reveries of his
broken sleep, and was not quite gone in the morning—an odd, irreconcilable new member of the household, making the sweet familiar
chambers unfriendly and suspect by its uncertain presence. He
could have hated the dead he had pitied so, for being thus. Afterwards he came to think of those poor, home-returning ghosts, which
all men have fancied to themselves—the *revenants*[2]—pathetically,
as crying, or beating with vain hands at the doors, as the wind
came, their cries distinguishable in it as a wilder inner note. But,
always making death more unfamiliar still, that old experience
would ever, from time to time, return to him; even in the living he
sometimes caught its likeness; at any time or place, in a moment,
the faint atmosphere of the chamber of death would be breathed
around him, and the image with the bound chin, the quaint smile,
the straight, stiff feet, shed itself across the air upon the bright
carpet, amid the gayest company, or happiest communing with himself.

1. See Joshua v.13–15.
2. Ghosts of the dead who return to
haunt the living, like Cathy in Emily
Brontë's *Wuthering Heights* (a novel
admired by Pater), who beats on the
windowpanes beside Lockwood's bed.

To most children the somber questionings to which impressions like these attach themselves, if they come at all, are actually suggested by religious books, which therefore they often regard with much secret distaste, and dismiss, as far as possible, from their habitual thoughts as a too depressing element in life. To Florian such impressions, these misgivings as to the ultimate tendency of the years, of the relationship between life and death, had been suggested spontaneously in the natural course of his mental growth by a strong innate sense for the soberer tones in things, further strengthened by actual circumstances; and religious sentiment, that system of biblical ideas in which he had been brought up, presented itself to him as a thing that might soften and dignify, and light up as with a "lively hope,"[3] a melancholy already deeply settled in him. So he yielded himself easily to religious impressions, and with a kind of mystical appetite for sacred things; the more as they came to him through a saintly person[4] who loved him tenderly, and believed that this early preoccupation with them already marked the child out for a saint. He began to love, for their own sakes, church lights, holy days, all that belonged to the comely order of the sanctuary, the secrets of its white linen, and holy vessels, and fonts of pure water; and its hieratic purity and simplicity became the type of something he desired always to have about him in actual life. He pored over the pictures in religious books, and knew by heart the exact mode in which the wrestling angel grasped Jacob, how Jacob looked in his mysterious sleep, how the bells and pomegranates were attached to the hem of Aaron's vestment, sounding sweetly as he glided over the turf of the holy place.[5] His way of conceiving religion came then to be in effect what it ever afterwards remained—a sacred history indeed, but still more a sacred ideal, a transcendent version or representation, under intenser and more expressive light and shade, of human life and its familiar or exceptional incidents, birth, death, marriage, youth, age, tears, joy, rest, sleep, waking—a mirror, toward which men might turn away their eyes from vanity and dullness, and see themselves therein as angels, with their daily meat and drink, even, become a kind of sacred transaction—a complementary strain or burden,[6] applied to our everyday existence, whereby the stray snatches of music in it reset themselves, and fall into the scheme of some higher and more consistent harmony. A place adumbrated itself in his thoughts, wherein those sacred personalities, which are at once the reflex and the pattern of our nobler phases of life, housed themselves; and this region in his intellectual

---

3. I Peter i.3.
4. Probably referring to the Reverend John Keble (1792–1866), leader of the High Church movement, whom Pater met in 1854.

5. The allusions are, respectively, to Genesis xxxii.24, Genesis xxviii.11–15, and Exodus xxix.24–26.
6. Bass part in music.

scheme all subsequent experience did but tend still further to realize and define. Some ideal, hieratic persons he would always need to
occupy it and keep a warmth there. And he could hardly understand those who felt no such need at all, finding themselves quite
happy without such heavenly companionship, and sacred double of
their life, beside them.

Thus a constant substitution of the typical for the actual took
place in his thoughts. Angels might be met by the way, under English elm or beech tree; mere messengers seemed like angels, bound
on celestial errands; a deep mysticity brooded over real meetings
and partings; marriages were made in heaven; and deaths also, with
hands of angels thereupon, to bear soul and body quietly asunder,
each to its appointed rest. All the acts and accidents of daily life
borrowed a sacred color and significance; the very colors of things
became themselves weighty with meanings like the sacred stuffs of
Moses' tabernacle,[7] full of penitence or peace. Sentiment, con-
gruous in the first instance only with those divine transactions, the
deep, effusive unction of the House of Bethany,[8] was assumed as
the due attitude for the reception of our everyday existence; and for
a time he walked through the world in a sustained, not unpleasura-
ble awe, generated by the habitual recognition, beside every circumstance and event of life, of its celestial correspondent.

Sensibility—the desire of physical beauty—a strange biblical awe,
which made any reference to the unseen act on him like solemn
music—these qualities the child took away with him, when, at
about the age of twelve years, he left the old house, and was taken
to live in another place. He had never left home before, and, anticipating much from this change, had long dreamed over it, jealously
counting the days till the time fixed for departure should come; had
been a little careless about others even, in his strong desire for it—
when Lewis fell sick, for instance, and they must wait still two days
longer. At last the morning came, very fine; and all things—the very
pavement with its dust, at the roadside—seemed to have a white,
pearl-like luster in them. They were to travel by a favorite road on
which he had often walked a certain distance, and on one of those
two prisoner days, when Lewis was sick, had walked farther than
ever before, in his great desire to reach the new place. They had
started and gone a little way when a pet bird was found to have
been left behind, and must even now—so it presented itself to him
—have already all the appealing fierceness and wild self-pity at
heart of one left by others to perish of hunger in a closed house;

7. Exodus xxxix.25–27.
8. Matthew xxvi.6–13. The reference is
to a "very precious ointment" ("unction") that a woman poured on
Christ's head; when his disciples protested the expense of the ointment,
Christ rebuked them, saying "For in
that she hath poured this ointment on
my body, she did it for my burial."

and he returned to fetch it, himself in hardly less stormy distress. But as he passed in search of it from room to room, lying so pale, with a look of meekness in their denudation, and at last through that little, stripped white room, the aspect of the place touched him like the face of one dead; and a clinging back towards it came over him, so intense that he knew it would last long, and spoiling all his pleasure in the realization of a thing so eagerly anticipated. And so, with the bird found, but himself in an agony of homesickness, thus capriciously sprung up within him, he was driven quickly away, far into the rural distance, so fondly speculated on, of that favorite country road.

1878, 1895

From Appreciations
From *Style*

Since all progress of mind consists for the most part in differentiation, in the resolution of an obscure and complex object into its component aspects, it is surely the stupidest of losses to confuse things which right reason has put asunder, to lose the sense of achieved distinctions, the distinction between poetry and prose, for instance, or, to speak more exactly, between the laws and characteristic excellences of verse and prose composition. On the other hand, those who have dwelt most emphatically on the distinction between prose and verse, prose and poetry, may sometimes have been tempted to limit the proper functions of prose too narrowly; and this again is at least false economy, as being, in effect, the renunciation of a certain means or faculty, in a world where after all we must needs make the most of things. Critical efforts to limit art *a priori*,[1] by anticipations regarding the natural incapacity of the material with which this or that artist works, as the sculptor with solid form, or the prose-writer with the ordinary language of men, are always liable to be discredited by the facts of artistic production; and while prose is actually found to be a colored thing with Bacon, picturesque with Livy and Carlyle, musical with Cicero and Newman, mystical and intimate with Plato and Michelet[2] and Sir Thomas Browne, exalted or florid, it may be, with Milton and Taylor,[3] it will be useless to protest that it can be nothing at all, except something very tamely and narrowly confined to mainly practical ends—a kind of "good round hand"; as useless as the protest that poetry might not touch prosaic subjects as with Wordsworth, or an abstruse matter as with Browning, or treat contemporary life

---

1. Prior to experience.
2. Jules Michelet (1798–1874), French historian.

3. Jeremy Taylor (1613–67), famous for the elaborate style of his sermons.

nobly as with Tennyson. In subordination to one essential beauty in all good literary style, in all literature as a fine art, as there are many beauties of poetry so the beauties of prose are many, and it is the business of criticism to estimate them as such; as it is good in the criticism of verse to look for those hard, logical, and quasi-prosaic excellences which that too has, or needs. To find in the poem, amid the flowers, the allusions, the mixed perspectives, of *Lycidas* for instance, the thought, the logical structure: how wholesome! how delightful! as to identify in prose what we call the poetry, the imaginative power, not treating it as out of place and a kind of vagrant intruder, but by way of an estimate of its rights, that is, of its achieved powers, there.

Dryden, with the characteristic instinct of his age, loved to emphasize the distinction between poetry and prose, the protest against their confusion with each other, coming with somewhat diminished effect from one whose poetry was so prosaic. In truth, his sense of prosaic excellence affected his verse rather than his prose, which is not only fervid, richly figured, poetic, as we say, but vitiated, all unconsciously, by many a scanning line. Setting up correctness, that humble merit of prose, as the central literary excellence, he is really a less correct writer than he may seem, still with an imperfect mastery of the relative pronoun. It might have been foreseen that, in the rotations of mind, the province of poetry in prose would find its assertor; and, a century after Dryden, amid very different intellectual needs, and with the need therefore of great modifications in literary form, the range of the poetic force in literature was effectively enlarged by Wordsworth. The true distinction between prose and poetry he regarded as the almost technical or accidental one of the absence or presence of metrical beauty, or, say! metrical restraint; and for him the opposition came to be between verse and prose of course; but, as the essential dichotomy in this matter, between imaginative and unimaginative writing, parallel to De Quincey's distinction between "the literature of power and the literature of knowledge,"[4] in the former of which the composer gives us not fact, but his peculiar sense of fact, whether past or present.

Dismissing then, under sanction of Wordsworth, that harsher opposition of poetry to prose, as savoring in fact of the arbitrary psychology of the last century, and with it the prejudice that there can be but one only beauty of prose style, I propose here to point out certain qualities of all literature as a fine art, which, if they apply to the literature of fact, apply still more to the literature of the imaginative sense of fact, while they apply indifferently to verse and prose, so far as either is really imaginative—certain conditions of true art in both alike, which conditions may also contain in them

4. De Quincey's essay on this topic appeared in 1848.

the secret of the proper discrimination and guardianship of the peculiar excellences of either.

The line between fact and something quite different from external fact is, indeed, hard to draw. In Pascal,[5] for instance, in the persuasive writers generally, how difficult to define the point where, from time to time, argument which, if it is to be worth anything at all, must consist of facts or groups of facts, becomes a pleading—a theorem no longer, but essentially an appeal to the reader to catch the writer's spirit, to think with him, if one can or will—an expression no longer of fact but of his sense of it, his peculiar intuition of a world, prospective, or discerned below the faulty conditions of the present, in either case changed somewhat from the actual world. In science, on the other hand, in history so far as it conforms to scientific rule, we have a literary domain where the imagination may be thought to be always an intruder. And as, in all science, the functions of literature reduce themselves eventually to the transcribing of fact, so all the excellences of literary form in regard to science are reducible to various kinds of painstaking; this good quality being involved in all "skilled work" whatever, in the drafting of an act of parliament, as in sewing. Yet here again, the writer's sense of fact, in history especially, and in all those complex subjects which do but lie on the borders of science, will still take the place of fact, in various degrees. Your historian, for instance, with absolutely truthful intention, amid the multitude of facts presented to him must needs select, and in selecting assert something of his own humor, something that comes not of the world without but of a vision within. So Gibbon molds his unwieldy material to a preconceived view. Livy, Tacitus, Michelet, moving full of poignant sensibility amid the records of the past, each, after his own sense, modifies—who can tell where and to what degree?—and becomes something else than a transcriber; each, as he thus modifies, passing into the domain of art proper. For just in proportion as the writer's aim, consciously or unconsciously, comes to be the transcribing, not of the world, not of mere fact, but of his sense of it, he becomes an artist, his work *fine* art; and good art (as I hope ultimately to show) in proportion to the truth of his presentment of that sense; as in those humbler or plainer functions of literature also, truth—truth to bare fact, there—is the essence of such artistic quality as they may have. Truth! there can be no merit, no craft at all, without that. And further, all beauty is in the long run only *fineness* of truth, or what we call expression, the finer accommodation of speech to that vision within.

—The transcript of his sense of fact rather than the fact, as being preferable, pleasanter, more beautiful to the writer himself. In

---

5. Blaise Pascal (1623–62), French scientist, philosopher, and theologian.

literature, as in every other product of human skill, in the molding of a bell or a platter for instance, wherever this sense asserts itself, wherever the producer so modifies his work as, over and above its primary use or intention, to make it pleasing (to himself, of course, in the first instance) there, "fine" as opposed to merely serviceable art, exists. Literary art, that is, like all art which is in any way imitative or reproductive of fact—form, or color, or incident—is the representation of such fact as connected with soul, of a specific personality, in its preferences, its volition and power.

Such is the matter of imaginative or artistic literature—this transcript, not of mere fact, but of fact in its infinite variety, as modified by human preference in all its infinitely varied forms. It will be good literary art not because it is brilliant or sober, or rich, or impulsive, or severe, but just in proportion as its representation of that sense, that soul-fact, is true, verse being only one department of such literature, and imaginative prose, it may be thought, being the special art of the modern world. That imaginative prose should be the special and opportune art of the modern world results from two important facts about the latter: first, the chaotic variety and complexity of its interests, making the intellectual issue, the really master currents of the present time incalculable—a condition of mind little susceptible of the restraint proper to verse form, so that the most characteristic verse of the nineteenth century has been lawless verse; and secondly, an all-pervading naturalism, a curiosity about everything whatever as it really is, involving a certain humility of attitude, cognate to what must, after all, be the less ambitious form of literature. And prose thus asserting itself as the special and privileged artistic faculty of the present day, will be, however critics may try to narrow its scope, as varied in its excellence as humanity itself reflecting on the facts of its latest experience—an instrument of many stops, meditative, observant, descriptive, eloquent, analytic, plaintive, fervid. Its beauties will be not exclusively "pedestrian": it will exert, in due measure, all the varied charms of poetry, down to the rhythm which, as in Cicero, or Michelet, or Newman, at their best, gives its musical value to every syllable. * * *

If the style be the man, in all the color and intensity of a veritable apprehension, it will be in a real sense "impersonal."

I said, thinking of books like Victor Hugo's *Les Misérables*, that prose literature was the characteristic art of the nineteenth century, as others, thinking of its triumphs since the youth of Bach, have assigned that place to music. Music and prose literature are, in one sense, the opposite terms of art; the art of literature presenting to the imagination, through the intelligence, a range of interests, as free and various as those which music presents to it through sense. And certainly the tendency of what has been here said is to bring literature too under those conditions, by conformity to which music takes rank as the typically perfect art. If music be the ideal of all art whatever, precisely because in music it is impossible to distinguish the form from the substance or matter, the subject from the expression, then, literature, by finding its specific excellence in the absolute correspondence of the term to its import, will be but fulfilling the condition of all artistic quality in things everywhere, of all good art.

Good art, but not necessarily great art; the distinction between great art and good art depending immediately, as regards literature at all events, not on its form, but on the matter. Thackeray's *Esmond*, surely, is greater art than *Vanity Fair*, by the greater dignity of its interests. It is on the quality of the matter it informs or controls, its compass, its variety, its alliance to great ends, or the depth of the note of revolt, or the largeness of hope in it, that the greatness of literary art depends, as *The Divine Comedy, Paradise Lost, Les Misérables*, the English Bible, are great art. Given the conditions I have tried to explain as constituting good art—then, if it be devoted further to the increase of men's happiness, to the redemption of the oppressed, or the enlargement of our sympathies with each other, or to such presentment of new or old truth about ourselves and our relation to the world as may ennoble and fortify us in our sojourn here, or immediately, as with Dante, to the glory of God, it will be also great art; if, over and above those qualities I summed up as mind and soul—that color and mystic perfume, and that reasonable structure, it has something of the soul of humanity in it, and finds its logical, architectural place, in the great structure of human life.

1889

Light Verse

Despite its later reputation as an age of solemnity, the Victorian age produced a remarkable outburst of humorous prose and verse from the time of Dickens' *Pickwick Papers* at the beginning of the period to the operas of Gilbert and Sullivan near the end. The following selections provide examples of two varieties of Victorian light verse. One, represented by W. S. Gilbert, makes playful mockery of institutions such as the Court of Chancery and marriage. Gilbert's burlesque mode is also to be found, though managed by less inspired writers, in many pages of *Punch*, a humorous and satirical magazine which began publication in 1841. Although exaggeration and absurdities are important ingredients in these writings, the world of Gilbert is still recognizably related to the ordinary world.

The other variety is a more distinctive Victorian specialty—nonsense-writing—represented here by the verse of Edward Lear and Lewis Carroll. Nonsense-writing was occasionally used by Shakespeare and, in our own century, by James Joyce and James Thurber, but the period in which this genre had its finest flowering was, without question, the Victorian age. Freudian explanations can be devised to account for its appearance during this particular period, and indeed, if nonsense-writing does originate in a writer's repressions, we may have a clue to the undertone of melancholy that some readers detect in the verses of Lear and Carroll. The best nonsense-writing, however, raises its own less solemn problems. Lear and Carroll created a zany upside-down world full of puzzles; the attempt to solve such puzzles, even when they cannot be solved, is in itself a perennial satisfaction.

EDWARD LEAR
(1812–1888)

Edward Lear was a landscape painter who spent much of his life in Mediterranean countries. In 1846 he published his first *Book of Nonsense*, a collection of limericks for children. The form of the limerick was not invented by Lear, but his use of it served to establish its popularity. In later volumes of the *Book of Nonsense* he used other forms of verse, some of them modeled on rhythms which had been developed by his close friend Tennyson. All of his own poems were characteristically classified by Lear as "nonsense pure and absolute," yet it is as the author of *The Owl and the Pussy-Cat*, *The Jumblies*, and other poems that Lear is remembered. Evidently pure and absolute nonsense is a rare art.

How Pleasant to Know Mr. Lear

"How pleasant to know Mr. Lear!"
Who has written such volumes of stuff!

    Some think him ill-tempered and queer,
        But a few think him pleasant enough.

His mind is concrete and fastidious,   5
    His nose is remarkably big;
His visage is more or less hideous,
    His beard it resembles a wig.

He has ears, and two eyes, and ten fingers,
    Leastways if you reckon two thumbs;   10
Long ago he was one of the singers,
    But now he is one of the dumbs.

He sits in a beautiful parlor,
    With hundreds of books on the wall;
He drinks a great deal of Marsala,   15
    But never gets tipsy at all.

He has many friends, lay men and clerical,
    Old Foss is the name of his cat;
His body is perfectly spherical,
    He weareth a runcible[1] hat.   20

When he walks in waterproof white,
    The children run after him so!
Calling out, "He's come out in his night-
    Gown, that crazy old Englishman, oh!"

He weeps by the side of the ocean,   25
    He weeps on the top of the hill;
He purchases pancakes and lotion,
    And chocolate shrimps from the mill.

He reads, but he cannot speak, Spanish,
    He cannot abide ginger beer: 30
Ere the days of his pilgrimage vanish,
    How pleasant to know Mr. Lear!

                  1871

Limerick

There was a young man in Iowa
Who exclaimed, "Where on earth shall I stow her!"
Of his sister he spoke, who was felled by an Oak
      Which abound in the plains of Iowa.

                  1933

The Jumblies

    They went to sea in a sieve, they did;
      In a sieve they went to sea;

1. A runcible spoon is a spoon-shaped fork with a cutting edge.

In spite of all their friends could say,
On a winter's morn, on a stormy day,
  In a sieve they went to sea.   5
And when the sieve turned round and round,
And everyone cried, "You'll be drowned!"
They called aloud, "Our sieve ain't big,
But we don't care a button; we don't care a fig—
  In a sieve we'll go to sea!"   10
    Far and few, far and few,
      Are the lands where the Jumblies live.
      Their heads are green, and their hands are blue;
        And they went to sea in a sieve.

They sailed away in a sieve, they did,   15
  In a sieve they sailed so fast,
With only a beautiful pea-green veil
Tied with a ribbon, by way of a sail,
  To a small tobacco-pipe mast.
And everyone said who saw them go,   20
"Oh! won't they be soon upset, you know,
For the sky is dark, and the voyage is long;
And, happen what may, it's extremely wrong
  In a sieve to sail so fast."

The water it soon came in, it did;   25
  The water it soon came in.
So, to keep them dry, they wrapped their feet
In a pinky paper all folded neat;
  And they fastened it down with a pin.
And they passed the night in a crockery-jar;   30
And each of them said, "How wise we are!
Though the sky be dark, and the voyage be long,
Yet we never can think we were rash or wrong,
  While round in our sieve we spin."

And all night long they sailed away;   35
  And, when the sun went down,
They whistled and warbled a moony song
To the echoing sound of a coppery gong,
  In the shade of the mountains brown,
"O Timballoo! how happy we are   40
When we live in a sieve and a crockery-jar!
And all night long, in the moonlight pale,
We sail away with a pea-green sail
  In the shade of the mountains brown."

They sailed to the Western Sea, they did—   45
  To a land all covered with trees;
And they bought an owl, and a useful cart,
And a pound of rice, and a cranberry tart,
  And a hive of silvery bees;
And they bought a pig, and some green jackdaws,   50

And a lovely monkey with lollipop paws,
And seventeen bags of edelweiss tea,
And forty bottles of ring-bo-ree,
    And no end of Stilton cheese.

And in twenty years they all came back—   55
    In twenty years or more;
And everyone said, "How tall they've grown!
For they've been to the Lakes, and the Torrible Zone,
    And the hills of the Chankly Bore."
And they drank their health, and gave them a feast   60
Of dumplings made of beautiful yeast;
And everyone said, "If we only live,
We, too, will go to sea in a sieve,
    To the hills of the Chankly Bore."
        Far and few, far and few,   65
            Are the lands where the Jumblies live.
        Their heads are green, and their hands are blue;
            And they went to sea in a sieve.

            1871

Cold Are the Crabs

Cold are the crabs that crawl on yonder hills,
Colder the cucumbers that grow beneath,
And colder still the brazen chops that wreathe
    The tedious gloom of philosophic pills!
For when the tardy film of nectar fills   5
The ample bowls of demons and of men,
There lurks the feeble mouse, the homely hen,
    And there the porcupine with all her quills.
Yet much remains—to weave a solemn strain
That lingering sadly—slowly dies away,   10
Daily departing with departing day.
A pea-green gamut on a distant plain
When wily walruses in congress meet—
    Such such is life—

            1953

LEWIS CARROLL
(1832–1898)

Charles Lutwidge Dodgson was a deacon in the Anglican Church and a lecturer in mathematics at Oxford. Most of his publications were mathematical treatises, but his fame rests on the strange pair of books he wrote for children: *Alice in Wonderland* (1865) and *Through the Looking-Glass* (1871), both published under the pseudonym Lewis Carroll. Like *Gulliver's Travels* these narratives have long been enjoyed, at different levels, by both children and adults. The various songs scattered through the stories are sometimes parodies, as, for example, *The Aged, Aged Man*, but more often they are classic examples of nonsense verse. Poems such as *Jabberwocky* exhibit a mathematician's fondness for puzzles combined with a literary man's fondness for word games. At this level *Jabberwocky* can be enjoyed as a small-scale *Finnegans Wake*.

Carroll learned something of his art from Edward Lear, also an eccentric Victorian bachelor, but Carroll's nonsense, hovering often on the brink of satire, has more edge to it.

Jabberwocky[1]

'Twas brillig, and the slithy toves
    Did gyre and gimble in the wabe;
All mimsy were the borogoves,
    And the mome raths outgrabe.

"Beware the Jabberwock, my son!   5
    The jaws that bite, the claws that catch!
Beware the Jubjub bird, and shun
    The frumious Bandersnatch!"

He took his vorpal sword in hand;
    Long time the manxome foe he sought—   10
So rested he by the Tumtum tree,
    And stood awhile in thought.

And, as in uffish thought he stood,
    The Jabberwock, with eyes of flame,
Came whiffling through the tulgey wood,   15
    And burbled as it came!

One, two! One, two! And through and through
    The vorpal blade went snicker-snack!
He left it dead, and with its head
    He went galumphing back.   20

"And hast thou slain the Jabberwock?
    Come to my arms, my beamish boy!
O frabjous day! Callooh! Callay!"
    He chortled in his joy.

'Twas brillig, and the slithy toves   25
    Did gyre and gimble in the wabe;

1. From *Through the Looking-Glass*, Chapter I.

> All mimsy were the borogoves,
>   And the mome raths outgrabe.

1855   1871

[*Humpty Dumpty's Explication of* Jabberwocky][2]

"You seem very clever at explaining words, Sir," said Alice. "Would you kindly tell me the meaning of the poem *Jabberwocky*?"

"Let's hear it," said Humpty Dumpty. "I can explain all the poems that ever were invented—and a good many that haven't been invented just yet."

This sounded very hopeful, so Alice repeated the first verse:

> " 'Twas brillig, and the slithy toves
>   Did gyre and gimble in the wabe;
> All mimsy were the borogoves,
>   And the mome raths outgrabe."

"That's enough to begin with," Humpty Dumpty interrupted: "there are plenty of hard words there. 'Brillig' means four o'clock in the afternoon—the time when you begin *broiling* things for dinner."

"That'll do very well," said Alice: "and 'slithy'?"[3]

"Well, 'slithy' means 'lithe and slimy.' 'Lithe' is the same as 'active.' You see it's like a portmanteau—there are two meanings packed up into one word."

"I see it now," Alice remarked thoughtfully: "and what are 'toves'?"

"Well, 'toves' are something like badgers—they're something like lizards—and they're something like corkscrews."

"They must be very curious creatures."

"They are that," said Humpty Dumpty: "also they make their nests under sundials—also they live on cheese."

"And what's to 'gyre' and to 'gimble'?"

"To 'gyre' is to go round and round like a gyroscope. To 'gimble' is to make holes like a gimlet."

"And the 'wabe' is the grass plot round a sundial, I suppose?" said Alice, surprised at her own ingenuity.

"Of course it is. It's called 'wabe,' you know, because it goes a long way before it, and a long way behind it——"

"And a long way beyond it on each side," Alice added.

"Exactly so. Well then, 'mimsy' is 'flimsy and miserable' (there's another portmanteau for you). And a 'borogove' is a thin shabby-looking bird with its feathers sticking out all round—something like a live mop."

2. From *Through the Looking-Glass*, Chapter VI.
3. Concerning the pronunciation of these words, Carroll later said: "The 'i' in 'slithy' is long, as in 'writhe'; and 'toves' is pronounced so as to rhyme with 'groves.' Again, the first 'o' in 'borogroves' is pronounced like the 'o' in 'borrow.' I have heard people try to give it the sound of the 'o' in 'worry.' Such is Human Perversity."

"And then 'mome raths'?" said Alice. "If I'm not giving you too much trouble."

"Well, a 'rath' is a sort of green pig: but 'mome' I'm not certain about. I think it's short for 'from home'—meaning that they'd lost their way, you know."

"And what does 'outgrabe' mean?"

"Well, 'outgribing' is something between bellowing and whistling, with a kind of sneeze in the middle: however, you'll hear it done, maybe—down in the wood yonder—and when you've once heard it you'll be *quite* content. Who's been repeating all that hard stuff to you?"

"I read it in a book," said Alice.

1871

The White Knight's Song[4]

I'll tell thee everything I can;
    There's little to relate.
I saw an aged, aged man,
    A-sitting on a gate.
"Who are you, aged man?" I said.   5
    "And how is it you live?"
And his answer trickled through my head
    Like water through a sieve.

He said "I look for butterflies
    That sleep among the wheat: 10
I make them into mutton-pies,
    And sell them in the street.
I sell them unto men," he said,
    "Who sail on stormy seas;
And that's the way I get my bread—   15
    A trifle, if you please."

But I was thinking of a plan
    To dye one's whiskers green,
And always use so large a fan
    That they could not be seen.   20
So, having no reply to give
    To what the old man said,
I cried, "Come, tell me how you live!"
    And thumped him on the head.

His accents mild took up the tale;   25
    He said, "I go my ways,
And when I find a mountain-rill,

4. From Chapter VIII of *Through the Looking-Glass.* Cf. Wordsworth's poem concerning the aged leech-gatherer: *Resolution and Independence.*

I set it in a blaze;
And thence they make a stuff they call
   Rowland's Macassar Oil— 30
Yet twopence-halfpenny is all
   They give me for my toil."

But I was thinking of a way
   To feed oneself on batter,
And so go on from day to day 35
   Getting a little fatter.
I shook him well from side to side,
   Until his face was blue;
"Come, tell me how you live," I cried
   "And what it is you do!" 40

He said, "I hunt for haddocks' eyes
   Among the heather bright,
And work them into waistcoat-buttons
   In the silent night.
And these I do not sell for gold 45
   Or coin of silvery shine,
But for a copper halfpenny,
   And that will purchase nine.

"I sometimes dig for buttered rolls,
   Or set limed twigs for crabs; 50
I sometimes search the grassy knolls
   For wheels of hansom-cabs.
And that's the way" (he gave a wink)
   "By which I get my wealth—
And very gladly will I drink 55
   Your Honor's noble health."

I heard him then, for I had just
   Completed my design
To keep the Menai bridge[5] from rust
   By boiling it in wine. 60
I thanked him much for telling me
   The way he got his wealth,
But chiefly for his wish that he
   Might drink my noble health.

And now, if e'er by chance I put 65
   My fingers into glue,
Or madly squeeze a right-hand foot
   Into a left-hand shoe,
Or if I drop upon my toe
   A very heavy weight, 70
I weep, for it reminds me so
Of that old man I used to know—
Whose look was mild, whose speech was slow,

5. Railway bridge in Wales (completed in 1850).

Whose hair was whiter than the snow,
Whose face was very like a crow, 75
With eyes, like cinders, all aglow,
Who seemed distracted with his woe.
Who rocked his body to and fro,
And muttered mumblingly and low,
As if his mouth were full of dough, 80
Who snorted like a buffalo—
That summer evening long ago
        A-sitting on a gate.

1856   1871

The Walrus and the Carpenter[6]

The sun was shining on the sea,
    Shining with all his might;
He did his very best to make
    The billows smooth and bright—
And this was odd, because it was 5
    The middle of the night.

The moon was shining sulkily,
    Because she thought the sun
Had got no business to be there
    After the day was done— 10
"It's very rude of him," she said,
    "To come and spoil the fun!"

The sea was wet as wet could be,
    The sands were dry as dry.
You could not see a cloud, because 15
    No cloud was in the sky;
No birds were flying overhead—
    There were no birds to fly.

The Walrus and the Carpenter
    Were walking close at hand; 20
They wept like anything to see
    Such quantities of sand.
"If this were only cleared away,"
    They said, "it *would* be grand!"

"If seven maids with seven mops 25
    Swept it for half a year,
Do you suppose," the Walrus said,
    "That they could get it clear?"
"I doubt it," said the Carpenter,
    And shed a bitter tear. 30

6. Recited by Tweedledee in Chapter IV of *Through the Looking-Glass*.

"O Oysters, come and walk with us!"
   The Walrus did beseech.
"A pleasant walk, a pleasant talk,
   Along the briny beach;
We cannot do with more than four,   35
   To give a hand to each."

The eldest Oyster looked at him,
   But never a word he said;
The eldest Oyster winked his eye,
   And shook his heavy head—   40
Meaning to say he did not choose
   To leave the oyster-bed.

But four young Oysters hurried up,
   All eager for the treat;
Their coats were brushed, their faces washed,
   Their shoes were clean and neat—   45
And this was odd, because, you know,
   They hadn't any feet.

Four other Oysters followed them,
   And yet another four;
And thick and fast they came at last,   50
   And more, and more, and more—
All hopping through the frothy waves,
   And scrambling to the shore.

The Walrus and the Carpenter   55
   Walked on a mile or so,
And then they rested on a rock
   Conveniently low;
And all the little Oysters stood
   And waited in a row.   60

"The time has come," the Walrus said,
   "To talk of many things:
Of shoes—and ships—and sealing-wax—
   Of cabbages—and kings—
And why the sea is boiling hot—   65
   And whether pigs have wings."

"But wait a bit," the Oysters cried,
   "Before we have our chat;
For some of us are out of breath,
   And all of us are fat!"   70
"No hurry!" said the Carpenter.
   They thanked him much for that.

"A loaf of bread," the Walrus said,
   "Is what we chiefly need;
Pepper and vinegar besides   75
   Are very good indeed—

Now, if you're ready, Oysters dear,
  We can begin to feed."

"But not on us!" the Oysters cried,   80
  Turning a little blue.
"After such kindness, that would be
  A dismal thing to do!"
"The night is fine," the Walrus said,
  "Do you admire the view?

"It was so kind of you to come!   85
  And you are very nice!"
The Carpenter said nothing but
  "Cut us another slice.
I wish you were not quite so deaf—
  I've had to ask you twice!"   90

"It seems a shame," the Walrus said,
  "To play them such a trick,
After we've brought them out so far,
  And made them trot so quick!"
The Carpenter said nothing but   95
  "The butter's spread too thick!"

"I weep for you," the Walrus said;
  "I deeply sympathize."
With sobs and tears he sorted out
  Those of the largest size,   100
Holding his pocket-handkerchief
  Before his streaming eyes.

"O Oysters," said the Carpenter,
  "You've had a pleasant run!
Shall we be trotting home again?"   105
  But answer came there none—
And this was scarcely odd, because
  They'd eaten every one.

1871

From The Hunting of the Snark
The Baker's Tale

They roused him[7] with muffins—they roused him with ice—
  They roused him with mustard and cress—
They roused him with jam and judicious advice—
  They set him conundrums to guess.

7. I.e., the Baker, a member of the
Snark-hunting expedition. He had fainted
when the leader of the crew, the Bellman, had mentioned that one species
of Snark is called Boojum. The nameless Baker's fear of Boojums turns out
later to have been well founded: at the
end of the poem he encounters a Boojum and is never seen again.

When at length he sat up and was able to speak,   5
    His sad story he offered to tell;
And the Bellman cried, "Silence! Not even a shriek!"
    And excitedly tingled his bell.

There was silence supreme! Not a shriek, not a scream,
    Scarcely even a howl or a groan,   10
As the man they called "Ho!" told his story of woe
    In an antediluvian tone.

"My father and mother were honest though poor—"
    "Skip all that!" cried the Bellman in haste.
"If it once becomes dark, there's no chance of a Snark—   15
    We have hardly a minute to waste!"

"I skip forty years," said the Baker, in tears,
    "And proceed without further remark
To the day when you took me aboard of your ship
    To help you in hunting the Snark.   20

"A dear uncle of mine (after whom I was named)
    Remarked, when I bade him farewell—"
"Oh, skip your dear uncle!" the Bellman exclaimed,
    As he angrily tingled his bell.

"He remarked to me then," said that mildest of men,   25
    " 'If your Snark be a Snark, that is right;
Fetch it home by all means—you may serve it with greens,
    And it's handy for striking a light.

" 'You may seek it with thimbles—and seek it with care;
    You may hunt it with forks and hope;   30
You may threaten its life with a railway-share;
    You may charm it with smiles and soap—' "

("That's exactly the method," the Bellman bold
    In a hasty parenthesis cried,
"That's exactly the way I have always been told   35
    That the capture of Snarks should be tried!")

" 'But oh, beamish[8] nephew, beware of the day,
    If your Snark be a Boojum! For then
You will softly and suddenly vanish away,
    And never be met with again!'   40

"It is this, it is this that oppresses my soul,
    When I think of my uncle's last words;
And my heart is like nothing so much as a bowl
    Brimming over with quivering curds!

"It is this, it is this—" "We have had that before!"   45
    The Bellman indignantly said.
And the Baker replied, "Let me say it once more.
    It is this, it is this that I dread!

8. See *Jabberwocky*, line 22.

"I engage with the Snark—every night after dark—
  In a dreamy, delirious fight;
I serve it with greens in those shadowy scenes,
  And I use it for striking a light;   50

"But if ever I meet with a Boojum, that day,
  In a moment (of this I am sure),
I shall softly and suddenly vanish away—
  And the notion I cannot endure!"   55

1874–76   1876

W. S. GILBERT
(1836–1911)

Before becoming a full-time writer William Schwenck Gilbert had worked
in the civil service and as a lawyer. In 1869 he published *Bab Ballads*, a
collection of narrative verses he had contributed to a magazine called *Fun*.
These ballads are indeed funny but also curiously macabre in their imperturbable accounts of disasters, cannibalism, and murders. Gilbert's skills as a
writer of light verse, together with his experience in devising plays for the
London theater, were responsible for his triumphant success as a librettist
in a series of light operas which he composed in collaboration with the eminent musician, Sir Arthur Sullivan. For 25 years (1871–96) Gilbert and
Sullivan captivated audiences in London and New York with such delightfully entertaining productions as *H.M.S. Pinafore* and *The Mikado*. Most
of these operas exhibit Gilbert's satirical flair; good-hearted fun is made of
the pretentious ineffectuality of the House of Lords and of corner-cutting
lawyers and politicians, as well as of bumbling admirals and generals. The
good-hearted quality is especially evident in the happy endings of the
operas: the satire is usually blunted in the finales by a jovial-spirited acceptance as part of our common humanity of characters who in earlier scenes
were exposed as foolish or inept.

  Gilbert was knighted in 1907 (some 25 years after Sullivan had received
the same honor in token of Queen Victoria's interest in his "serious"
music). Gilbert died on May 29, 1911, while gallantly attempting to save a
young woman from drowning.

When I, Good Friends, Was Called to the Bar[1]

When I, good friends, was called to the bar,
  I'd an appetite fresh and hearty,
But I was, as many young barristers are,
  An impecunious party.
I'd a swallow-tail coat of a beautiful blue—   5

1. Before a breach of promise suit   the court "how I came to be a Judge"
begins in *Trial by Jury*, the Judge tells   in this song.

A brief which I bought of a booby[2]—
A couple of shirts and a collar or two,
And a ring that looked like a ruby!

CHORUS.   A couple of shirts, etc.

In Westminster Hall[3] I danced a dance,
    Like a semidespondent fury;   10
For I thought I should never hit on a chance
    Of addressing a British jury—
But I soon got tired of third-class journeys,
    And dinners of bread and water;
So I fell in love with a rich attorney's   15
    Elderly, ugly daughter.

CHORUS.   So he fell in love, etc.

The rich attorney, he jumped with joy,
    And replied to my fond professions:
"You shall reap the reward of your pluck, my boy
    At the Bailey and Middlesex Sessions.[4]   20
You'll soon get used to her looks," said he,
    "And a very nice girl you'll find her!
She may very well pass for forty-three
    In the dusk, with a light behind her!"

CHORUS.   She may very well, etc.

The rich attorney was good as his word;   25
    The briefs came trooping gaily,
And every day my voice was heard
    At the Sessions or Ancient Bailey.
All thieves who could my fees afford
    Relied on my orations,   30
And many a burglar I've restored
    To his friends and his relations.

CHORUS.   And many a burglar, etc.

At length I became as rich as the Gurneys[5]—
    An incubus then I thought her,
So I threw over that rich attorney's   35
    Elderly, ugly daughter.
The rich attorney my character high
    Tried vainly to disparage—

2. A fool or dunce. A "brief" is a summary of the facts of a case which is
prepared (usually by an attorney) to
assist a barrister in presenting the case
in court.
3. Courtrooms of the Court of Chancery in London.

4. Old Bailey was a court where criminals were tried; "sessions": meetings of
the county court of Middlesex (which
includes London).
5. A wealthy banking family. "Incubus": oppressive demon as encountered
in a nightmare.

And now, if you please, I'm ready to try
This Breach of Promise of Marriage!   40

1875

If You're Anxious for to Shine in the High Aesthetic Line[1]

> Am I alone,
>   And unobserved? I am!
> Then let me own
>   I'm an aesthetic sham!
>
> This air severe   5
>   Is but a mere
>   Veneer!
>
> This cynic smile
>   Is but a wile
>   Of guile!   10
>
> This costume chaste
>   Is but good taste
>   Misplaced!
>
>   Let me confess!
> A languid love for lilies does *not* blight me!   15
> Lank limbs and haggard cheeks do *not* delight me!
>   I do *not* care for dirty greens
>   By any means.
>   I do *not* long for all one sees
>   That's Japanese.[2]   20
> I am *not* fond of uttering platitudes
>   In stained-glass attitudes.
> In short, my medievalism's affectation,
> Born of a morbid love of admiration!

If you're anxious for to shine in the high aesthetic line as a man of
    culture rare,   25
You must get up all the germs of the transcendental terms, and
    plant them everywhere.
You must lie upon the daisies and discourse in novel phrases of
    your complicated state of mind,

1. Sung in *Patience* (Act I) by Reginald Bunthorne, a caricature of such poets of the "aesthetic school" as Oscar Wilde.
2. To admire Japanese vases and paintings had become a cult among aesthetes like the painter James McNeill Whistler (1834–1903). Bunthorne's other references are probably to Pre-Raphaelite paintings such as Rossetti's portraits of languidly-gazing women (sometimes in green dresses) in which the subject might be posed in a cramped posture like a figure in a stained-glass window.

The meaning doesn't matter if it's only idle chatter of a transcendental kind.

And everyone will say,
As you walk your mystic way,

"If this young man expresses himself in terms too deep for *me*,   30
Why, what a very singularly deep young man this deep young man
must be!"

Be eloquent in praise of the very dull old days which have long
since passed away,
And convince 'em, if you can, that the reign of good Queen Anne
was Culture's palmiest day.
Of course you will pooh-pooh whatever's fresh and new, and declare
it's crude and mean,   35
For Art stopped short in the cultivated court of the Empress
Josephine.[3]

And everyone will say,
As you walk your mystic way,

"If that's not good enough for him which is good enough for *me*,
Why, what a very cultivated kind of youth this kind of youth must
be!"   40

Then a sentimental passion of a vegetable fashion must excite your
languid spleen,
An attachment à *la* Plato[4] for a bashful young potato, or a not-too-
French French bean!
Though the Philistines[5] may jostle, you will rank as an apostle in
the high aesthetic band,
If you walk down Piccadilly with a poppy or a lily in your medieval
hand.

And everyone will say,   45
As you walk your flowery way,

"If he's content with a vegetable love which would certainly not
suit *me*,
Why, what a most particularly pure young man this pure young
man must be!"

1881

When Britain Really Ruled the Waves[1]

When Britain really ruled the waves
(In good Queen Bess's time)—

---

3. Napoleon's wife, and Empress of
France from 1804 to 1811.
4. Platonic love denotes a spiritual
relationship, devoid of sexual desire.
5. A term used by Matthew Arnold to
describe the respectable middle classes,
who predictably disapproved of the aesthetes' flamboyant behavior.
1. From *Iolanthe* (Act II), sung by
Lord Mountararat, following a discussion about whether or not members of
the House of Lords should obtain their
titles by competitive examination
instead of by inheritance. His Lordship
prefaces his song by affirming "that if
there is any institution in Great Britain
which is not susceptible of any
improvement at all, it is the House of
Peers!"

The House of Peers made no pretense
To intellectual eminence,
   Or scholarship sublime;   5
Yet Britain won her proudest bays[2]
In good Queen Bess's glorious days!

CHORUS.   Yes, Britain won, etc.

When Wellington thrashed Bonaparte,
   As every child can tell,
The House of Peers, throughout the war,   10
Did nothing in particular,
   And did it very well:
Yet Britain set the world ablaze
In good King George's glorious days![3]

CHORUS.   Yes, Britain set, etc.

And while the House of Peers withholds   15
   Its legislative hand,
And noble statesmen do not itch
To interfere with matters which
   They do not understand,
As bright will shine Great Britain's rays   20
As in King George's glorious days!

CHORUS.   As bright will shine, etc.

1882

2. I.e., honors.
3. At the time of the Battle of Water- loo (1815), Britain's king was George III (1760–1820).

Victorian Issues

EVOLUTION

One of the most dramatic controversies in the Victorian age concerned theories of evolution. This controversy exploded into prominence in 1859 when Charles Darwin's *Origin of Species* was published, but it had been rumbling for many years previously. Sir Charles Lyell's *Principles of Geology* (1830) and Robert Chambers' popular book, *Vestiges of Creation* (1843–46), had already raised issues which Tennyson aired in his *In Memoriam* (1850). It was Darwin, however, with his monumental marshaling of evidence to establish his theory of natural selection, who finally brought the topic fully into the open, and the public, as well as the experts, took sides.

The opposition aroused by Darwin's treatise came from two different quarters. The first consisted of some of his fellow scientists who affirmed that his theory was unsound. The second consisted of religious leaders who attacked his theory because it seemed to contradict a literal interpretation of the Bible. Sometimes the two kinds of opposition combined forces as in 1860 when his scientific opponents selected Bishop Wilberforce to be their spokesman in spearheading their attack on *The Origin of Species*. In replying to such attacks, Darwin had the good fortune to be supported by two of the ablest popularizers of science in his day, T. H. Huxley and John Tyndall. Moreover, although shy by temperament, Darwin was himself (as Tyndall affirms and the following selections will illustrate) an exceptionally effective expositor of his own theories.

CHARLES DARWIN: *From* The Descent of Man
[*Natural Selection and Sexual Selection*][1]

A brief summary will here be sufficient to recall to the reader's mind the more salient points in this work. Many of the views which have been advanced are highly speculative, and some no doubt will prove erroneous; but I have in every case given the reasons which

1. Charles Darwin (1809–82) developed an interest in geology and biology at Cambridge where he was studying to become a clergyman. Aided by a private income, he resolved to devote the rest of his life to scientific research.

The observations he made during a long voyage to the South Seas on H.M.S. *Beagle* (on which he served as a naturalist) led Darwin to construct hypotheses about evolution. In 1858, more than twenty years after his re-have led me to one view rather than to another. It seemed worth while to try how far the principle of evolution would throw light on some of the more complex problems in the natural history of man. False facts are highly injurious to the progress of science, for they often long endure; but false views, if supported by some evidence, do little harm, as everyone takes a salutary pleasure in proving their falseness; and when this is done, one path towards error is closed and the road to truth is often at the same time opened.

The main conclusion arrived at in this work, and now held by many naturalists who are well competent to form a sound judgment, is that man is descended from some less highly organized form. The grounds upon which this conclusion rests will never be shaken, for the close similarity between man and the lower animals in embryonic development, as well as in innumerable points of structure and constitution, both of high and of the most trifling importance—the rudiments which he retains, and the abnormal reversions to which he is occasionally liable—are facts which cannot be disputed. They have long been known, but until recently they told us nothing with respect to the origin of man. Now when viewed by the light of our knowledge of the whole organic world, their meaning is unmistakable. The great principle of evolution stands up clear and firm, when these groups of facts are considered in connection with others, such as the mutual affinities of the members of the same group, their geographical distribution in past and present times, and their geological succession. It is incredible that all these facts should speak falsely. He who is not content to look, like a savage, at the phenomena of nature as disconnected cannot any longer believe that man is the work of a separate act of creation. He will be forced to admit that the close resemblance of the embryo of man to that, for instance, of a dog—the construction of his skull, limbs, and whole frame, independently of the uses to which the parts may be put, on the same plan with that of other mammals— the occasional reappearance of various structures, for instance of several distinct muscles, which man does not normally possess, but which are common to the Quadrumana[2]—and a crowd of analogous facts—all point in the plainest manner to the conclusion that man is the codescendant with other mammals of a common pro-

---

turn to England from his voyage, he ventured to submit a paper developing his theory of the origin of species. A year later, when his theory appeared in book form, Darwin emerged as a famous and controversial figure. During the remainder of his life he published several treatises, some of which develop and clarify the theory of *The Origin of Species*. One of these works, *The Descent of Man* (1871) was espe-

cially provocative in its stress on the similarities between men and animals and in its naturalistic explanations of the beautiful colorings of birds, insects, and flowers. The present selection is from Chapter XXI of *The Descent of Man*.

2. Animals such as monkeys whose hind feet and forefeet can be used as hands—hence "four-handed."

genitor. * * *

By considering the embryological structure of man—the homologies which he presents with the lower animals, the rudiments which he retains, and the reversions to which he is liable—we can partly recall in imagination the former condition of our early progenitors; and can approximately place them in their proper position in the zoological series. We thus learn that man is descended from a hairy quadruped, furnished with a tail and pointed ears, probably arboreal in its habits, and an inhabitant of the Old World. This creature, if its whole structure had been examined by a naturalist, would have been classed amongst the Quadrumana, as surely as would the common and still more ancient progenitor of the Old and New World monkeys. The Quadrumana and all the higher mammals are probably derived from an ancient marsupial animal, and this through a long line of diversified forms, either from some reptile-like or some amphibianlike creature, and this again from some fishlike animal. In the dim obscurity of the past we can see that the early progenitor of all the Vertebrata must have been an aquatic animal, provided with branchae, with the two sexes united in the same individual, and with the most important organs of the body (such as the brain and heart) imperfectly developed. This animal seems to have been more like the larvae of our existing marine ascidians[3] than any other known form. * * *

Sexual selection has been treated at great length in these volumes; for, as I have attempted to show, it has played an important part in the history of the organic world. * * *

The belief in the power of sexual selection rests chiefly on the following considerations. The characters which we have the best reason for supposing to have been thus acquired are confined to one sex; and this alone renders it probable that they are in some way connected with the act of reproduction. These characters in innumerable instances are fully developed only at maturity; and often during only a part of the year, which is always the breeding season. The males (passing over a few exceptional cases) are the most active in courtship; they are the best armed, and are rendered the most attractive in various ways. It is to be especially observed that the males display their attractions with elaborate care in the presence of the females; and that they rarely or never display them excepting during the season of love. It is incredible that all this display should be purposeless. Lastly we have distinct evidence with some quadrupeds and birds that the individuals of the one sex are capable of feeling a strong antipathy or preference for certain individuals of the opposite sex.

Bearing these facts in mind, and not forgetting the marked re-

3. Part of a group of marine animals called Tunicata, or popularly "sea squirts," sometimes assumed to be ancestors of the vertebrate animals.

sults of man's unconscious selection, it seems to me almost certain that if the individuals of one sex were during a long series of generations to prefer pairing with certain individuals of the other sex, characterized in some peculiar manner, the offspring would slowly but surely become modified in this same manner. I have not attempted to conceal that, excepting when the males are more numerous than the females, or when polygamy prevails, it is doubtful how the more attractive males succeed in leaving a larger number of offspring to inherit their superiority in ornaments or other charms than the less attractive males; but I have shown that this would probably follow from the females—especially the more vigorous females which would be the first to breed, preferring not only the more attractive but at the same time the more vigorous and victorious males.

Although we have some positive evidence that birds appreciate bright and beautiful objects, as with the bowerbirds of Australia, and although they certainly appreciate the power of song, yet I fully admit that it is an astonishing fact that the females of many birds and some mammals should be endowed with sufficient taste for what has apparently been effected through sexual selection; and this is even more astonishing in the case of reptiles, fish, and insects. But we really know very little about the minds of the lower animals. It cannot be supposed that male birds of paradise or peacocks, for instance, should take so much pains in erecting, spreading, and vibrating their beautiful plumes before the females for no purpose. We should remember the fact given on excellent authority in a former chapter, namely that several peahens, when debarred from an admired male, remained widows during a whole season rather than pair with another bird.

Nevertheless I know of no fact in natural history more wonderful than that the female argus pheasant should be able to appreciate the exquisite shading of the ball-and-socket ornaments and the elegant patterns on the wing feathers of the male. He who thinks that the male was created as he now exists must admit that the great plumes, which prevent the wings from being used for flight, and which, as well as the primary feathers, are displayed in a manner quite peculiar to this one species during the act of courtship, and at no other time, were given to him as an ornament. If so, he must likewise admit that the female was created and endowed with the capacity of appreciating such ornaments. I differ only in the conviction that the male argus pheasant acquired his beauty gradually, through the females having preferred during many generations the more highly ornamented males; the aesthetic capacity of the females having been advanced through exercise or habit in the same manner as our own taste is gradually improved. In the male, through the fortunate chance of a few feathers not having been modified, we can distinctly see how simple spots with a little fulvous[4] shading on one side might have been developed by small and graduated steps into the wonderful ball-and-socket ornaments; and it is probable that they were actually thus developed. * * *

He who admits the principle of sexual selection will be led to the remarkable conclusion that the cerebral system not only regulates most of the existing functions of the body, but has indirectly influenced the progressive development of various bodily structures and of certain mental qualities. Courage, pugnacity, perseverance, strength and size of body, weapons of all kinds, musical organs, both vocal and instrumental, bright colors, stripes and marks, and ornamental appendages have all been indirectly gained by the one sex or the other, through the influence of love and jealousy, through the appreciation of the beautiful in sound, color or form, and through the exertion of a choice; and these powers of the mind manifestly depend on the development of the cerebral system. * * *

The main conclusion arrived at in this work, namely that man is descended from some lowly-organized form, will, I regret to think, be highly distasteful to many persons. But there can hardly be a doubt that we are descended from barbarians. The astonishment which I felt on first seeing a party of Fuegians[5] on a wild and broken shore will never be forgotten by me, for the reflection at once rushed into my mind—such were our ancestors. These men were absolutely naked and bedaubed with paint, their long hair was tangled, their mouths frothed with excitement, and their expression was wild, startled, and distrustful. They possessed hardly any arts, and like wild animals lived on what they could catch; they had no government, and were merciless to everyone not of their own small tribe. He who has seen a savage in his native land will not feel much shame, if forced to acknowledge that the blood of some more humble creature flows in his veins. For my own part I would as soon be descended from that heroic little monkey, who braved his dreaded enemy in order to save the life of his keeper; or from that old baboon, who, descending from the mountains, carried away in triumph his young comrade from a crowd of astonished dogs[6]— as from a savage who delights to torture his enemies, offers up bloody sacrifices, practices infanticide without remorse, treats his wives like slaves, knows no decency, and is haunted by the grossest superstitions.

Man may be excused for feeling some pride at having risen, though not through his own exertions, to the very summit of the

4. Dull yellow.
5. Savages inhabiting the islands off the southern tip of South America. Tierra del Fuego, which Darwin had visited in 1832. See his *Voyage of the*

Beagle. Chapter X.
6. Incidents described in Chapter IV of *The Descent of Man* to demonstrate that animals may be endowed with a moral sense.

organic scale; and the fact of his having thus risen, instead of having been aboriginally placed there, may give him hopes for a still higher destiny in the distant future. But we are not here concerned with hopes or fears, only with the truth as far as our reason allows us to discover it. I have given the evidence to the best of my ability; and we must acknowledge, as it seems to me, that man with all his noble qualities, with sympathy which feels for the most debased, with benevolence which extends not only to other men but to the humblest living creature, with his godlike intellect which has penetrated into the movements and constitution of the solar system—with all these exalted powers—Man still bears in his bodily frame the indelible stamp of his lowly origin.

JOHN TYNDALL: *From* The Belfast Address
[*Darwin's Method of Argument*][7]

Mr. Darwin shirks no difficulty; and, saturated as the subject was with his own thought, he must have known, better than his critics, the weakness as well as the strength of his theory. This of course would be of little avail were his object a temporary dialectic victory, instead of the establishment of a truth which he means to be everlasting. But he takes no pains to disguise the weakness he has discerned; nay, he takes every pains to bring it into the strongest light. His vast resources enable him to cope with objections started by himself and others, so as to leave the final impression upon the reader's mind that, if they be not completely answered, they certainly are not fatal. Their negative force being thus destroyed, you are free to be influenced by the vast positive mass of evidence he is able to bring before you. This largeness of knowledge, and readiness of resource, render Mr. Darwin the most terrible of antagonists. Accomplished naturalists have leveled heavy and sustained criticisms against him—not always with the view of fairly weighing his theory, but with the express intention of exposing its weak points only. This does not irritate him. He treats every objection with a soberness and thoroughness which even Bishop Butler [8] might be proud to imitate, surrounding each fact with its appropriate detail, placing it in its proper relations, and usually giving it a significance which, as long as it was kept isolated, failed to appear. This is done without a trace of ill temper. He moves over the subject with the passionless strength of a glacier; and the

7. John Tyndall (1820–93) was a physicist and popularizer of science. In 1874 he delivered an address on religion and science entitled *The Belfast Address,* later published in his collection of essays, *Fragments of Science* (1899).

8. Joseph Butler (1692–1752), Bishop of Durham. In his book *The Analogy of Religion* (1736), objections to religious faith are aired calmly and fully before being answered by the author.

grinding of the rocks is not always without a counterpart in the logical pulverization of the objector. But though in handling this mighty theme all passion has been stilled, there is an emotion of the intellect, incident to the discernment of new truth, which often colors and warms the pages of Mr. Darwin. His success has been great; and this implies not only the solidity of his work, but the preparedness of the public mind for such a revelation. On this head, a remark of Agassiz[9] impressed me more than anything else. Sprung from a race of theologians, this celebrated man combated to the last the theory of natural selection. One of the many times I had the pleasure of meeting him in the United States was at Mr. Winthrop's beautiful residence at Brookline, near Boston. Rising from luncheon, we all halted as if by common consent, in front of a window, and continued there a discussion which had been started at table. The maple was in its autumn glory, and the exquisite beauty of the scene outside seemed, in my case, to interpenetrate without disturbance the intellectual action. Earnestly, almost sadly, Agassiz turned, and said to the gentlemen standing round, "I confess that I was not prepared to see this theory received as it has been by the best intellects of our time. Its success is greater than I could have thought possible."

1874, 1899

LEONARD HUXLEY: *From* The Life and Letters of Thomas Henry Huxley

[*The Huxley-Wilberforce Debate at Oxford*][1]

The famous Oxford Meeting of 1860 was of no small importance in Huxley's career. It was not merely that he helped to save a great cause from being stifled under misrepresentation and ridicule—that he helped to extort for it a fair hearing; it was now that he first made himself known in popular estimation as a dangerous adversary in debate—a personal force in the world of science which

9. Louis Agassiz (1807–73), Swiss naturalist who became professor of zoology and geology at Harvard. He refused to accept the concept of evolution.
1. At meetings of the British Association for the Advancement of Science, the reading of a paper is followed by a discussion. In 1860, at Oxford, this discussion developed into a debate between Thomas Henry Huxley, a defender of Darwin's theories, and Bishop Samuel Wilberforce (1805–73). Although he had majored in mathematics as an undergraduate, Wilberforce could hardly lay claim to be a scientist. He was willing, nevertheless, to serve as a spokesman for those scientists who dis-

agreed with *The Origin of Species*, and he reportedly came to the meeting ready to "smash Darwin." The bishop's principal qualifications for this role were his great powers as a smoothly persuasive orator (he was commonly known by his detractors as "Soapy Sam"), but he met more than his match in Huxley.

Because no complete transcript of this celebrated debate was made at the time, Huxley's son Leonard, in writing his father's biography, had to reconstruct the scene by combining quotations from reports made by magazine writers and other witnesses. The account given here is from Chapter XIV.

could not be neglected. From this moment he entered the front fighting line in the most exposed quarter of the field. * * *

It was the merest chance, as I have already said, that Huxley attended the meeting of the section that morning. Dr. Draper of New York was to read a paper on the *Intellectual Development of Europe considered with reference to the views of Mr. Darwin.* "I can still hear," writes one who was present, "the American accents of Dr. Draper's opening address when he asked 'Air we a fortuitous concourse of atoms?' " However, it was not to hear him, but the eloquence of the Bishop, that the members of the Association crowded in such numbers into the Lecture Room of the Museum, that this, the appointed meeting place of the section, had to be abandoned for the long west room, since cut in two by a partition for the purposes of the library. It was not term time, nor were the general public admitted; nevertheless the room was crowded to suffocation long before the protagonists appeared on the scene, 700 persons or more managing to find places. The very windows by which the room was lighted down the length of its west side were packed with ladies, whose white handkerchiefs, waving and fluttering in the air at the end of the Bishop's speech, were an unforgettable factor in the acclamation of the crowd.

On the east side between the two doors was the platform. Professor Henslow, the President of the section, took his seat in the center; upon his right was the Bishop, and beyond him again Dr. Draper; on his extreme left was Mr. Dingle, a clergyman from Lanchester, near Durham, with Sir J. Hooker and Sir J. Lubbock in front of him, and nearer the center, Professor Beale of King's College, London, and Huxley.

The clergy, who shouted lustily for the Bishop, were massed in the middle of the room; behind them in the northwest corner a knot of undergraduates (one of these was T. H. Green, who listened but took no part in the cheering) had gathered together beside Professor Brodie, ready to lift their voices, poor minority though they were, for the opposite party. Close to them stood one of the few men among the audience already in Holy orders, who joined in—and indeed led—the cheers for the Darwinians.

So "Dr. Draper droned out his paper, turning first to the right hand and then to the left, of course bringing in a reference to the *Origin of Species* which set the ball rolling."

An hour or more that paper lasted, and then discussion began. The President "wisely announced *in limine*[2] that none who had not valid arguments to bring forward on one side or the other would be allowed to address the meeting; a caution that proved necessary, for no fewer than four combatants had their utterances burked by him, because of their indulgence in vague declamation."

2. As a starting point.

"First spoke" (writes Professor Farrar) "a layman from Brompton, who gave his name as being one of the Committee of the (newly formed) Economic section of the Association. He, in a stentorian voice, let off his theological venom. Then jumped up Richard Greswell with a thin voice, saying much the same, but speaking as a scholar; but we did not merely want any theological discussion, so we shouted them down. Then a Mr. Dingle got up and tried to show that Darwin would have done much better if he had taken him into consultation. He used the blackboard and began a mathematical demonstration on the question—'Let this point A be man, and let that point B be the mawnkey.' He got no further; he was shouted down with cries of 'mawnkey.' None of these had spoken more than three minutes. It was when these were shouted down that Henslow said he must demand that the discussion should rest on *scientific* grounds only.

"Then there were calls for the Bishop, but he rose and said he understood his friend Professor Beale had something to say first. Beale, who was an excellent histologist,[3] spoke to the effect that the new theory ought to meet with fair discussion, but added, with great modesty, that he himself had not sufficient knowledge to discuss the subject adequately. Then the Bishop spoke the speech that you know, and the question about his mother being an ape, or his grandmother."

From the scientific point of view, the speech was of small value. It was evident from his mode of handling the subject that he had been "crammed up to the throat," and knew nothing at first hand; he used no argument beyond those to be found in his *Quarterly* article, which appeared a few days later, and is now admitted to have been inspired by Owen.[4] "He ridiculed Darwin badly and Huxley savagely; but," confesses one of his strongest opponents, "all in such dulcet tones, so persuasive a manner, and in such well turned periods, that I who had been inclined to blame the President for allowing a discussion that could serve no scientific purpose, now forgave him from the bottom of my heart."

The Bishop spoke thus "for full half an hour with inimitable spirit, emptiness and unfairness." "In a light, scoffing tone, florid and fluent, he assured us there was nothing in the idea of evolution; rock pigeons were what rock pigeons had always been. Then, turning to his antagonist with a smiling insolence, he begged to know, was it through his grandfather or his grandmother that he claimed his descent from a monkey?"

This was the fatal mistake of his speech. Huxley instantly grasped the tactical advantage which the descent to personalities gave him. He turned to Sir Benjamin Brodie, who was sitting beside him, and emphatically striking his hand upon his knee, exclaimed, "The

3. Biologist specializing in the study of the minute structure of the tissues of plants and animals.

4. Sir Richard Owen (1804–92), a leading zoologist and paleontologist, was opposed to Darwin's theories.

Lord hath delivered him into mine hands." The bearing of the exclamation did not dawn upon Sir Benjamin until after Huxley had completed his "forcible and eloquent" answer to the scientific part of the Bishop's argument, and proceeded to make his famous retort.

"On this" (continues the writer in *Macmillan's Magazine*) "Mr. Huxley slowly and deliberately arose. A slight tall figure, stern and pale, very quiet and very grave, he stood before us and spoke those tremendous words—words which no one seems sure of now, nor, I think, could remember just after they were spoken, for their meaning took away our breath, though it left us in no doubt as to what it was. He was not ashamed to have a monkey for his ancestor; but he would be ashamed to be connected with a man who used great gifts to obscure the truth. No one doubted his meaning, and the effect was tremendous. One lady fainted and had to be carried out; I, for one, jumped out of my seat."

The fullest and probably most accurate account of these concluding words is the following, from a letter of the late John Richard Green, then an undergraduate, to his friend, afterwards Professor Boyd Dawkins:

"I asserted—and I repeat—that a man has no reason to be ashamed of having an ape for his grandfather. If there were an ancestor whom I should feel shame in recalling it would rather be a man—a man of restless and versatile intellect—who, not content with an equivocal success in his own sphere of activity, plunges into scientific questions with which he has no real acquaintance, only to obscure them by an aimless rhetoric, and distract the attention of his hearers from the real point at issue by eloquent digressions and skilled appeals to religious prejudice."

The result of this encounter, though a check to the other side, cannot, of course, be represented as an immediate and complete triumph for evolutionary doctrine. This was precluded by the character and temper of the audience, most of whom were less capable of being convinced by the arguments than shocked by the boldness of the retort, although, being gentlefolk, as Professor Farrar remarks, they were disposed to admit on reflection that the Bishop had erred on the score of taste and good manners. Nevertheless, it was a noticeable feature of the occasion, Sir M. Foster tells me, that when Huxley rose he was received coldly, just a cheer of encouragement from his friends, the audience as a whole not joining in it. But as he made his points the applause grew and widened, until, when he sat down, the cheering was not very much less than that given to the Bishop. To that extent he carried an unwilling audience with him by the force of his speech. The debate on the ape question, however, was continued elsewhere during the next two years, and the evidence was completed by the unanswerable demonstrations of Sir W. H. Flower at the Cambridge meeting of the Association in 1862.

The importance of the Oxford meeting lay in the open resistance that was made to authority, at a moment when even a drawn battle was hardly less effectual than acknowledged victory. Instead of being crushed under ridicule, the new theories secured a hearing, all the wider, indeed, for the startling nature of their defense.

1901

SIR EDMUND GOSSE: *From* Father and Son[5]
[*The Dilemma of the Fundamentalist and Scientist*]

So, through my Father's brain, in that year of scientific crisis, 1857, there rushed two kinds of thought, each absorbing, each convincing, yet totally irreconcilable. There is a peculiar agony in the paradox that truth has two forms, each of them indisputable, yet each antagonistic to the other. It was this discovery, that there were two theories of physical life, each of which was true, but the truth of each incompatible with the truth of the other, which shook the spirit of my Father with perturbation. It was not, really, a paradox, it was a fallacy, if he could only have known it, but he allowed the turbid volume of superstition to drown the delicate stream of reason. He took one step in the service of truth, and then he drew back in an agony, and accepted the servitude of error.

This was the great moment in the history of thought when the theory of the mutability of species was preparing to throw a flood of light upon all departments of human speculation and action. It was becoming necessary to stand emphatically in one army or the other. Lyell was surrounding himself with disciples, who were making strides in the direction of discovery. Darwin had long been collecting facts with regard to the variation of animals and plants. Hooker and Wallace, Asa Gray and even Agassiz, each in his own sphere, were coming closer and closer to a perception of that secret which was first to reveal itself clearly to the patient and humble genius of Darwin. In the year before, in 1856, Darwin, under pressure from Lyell, had begun that modest statement of the new revelation, that "abstract of an essay," which developed so mightily into *The Origin of Species.* Wollaston's *Variation of Species* had just appeared, and had been a nine days' wonder in the wilderness.

5. Philip Henry Gosse (1810–88) was a zoologist of some repute and also an ardent adherent of a strict Protestant sect, the Plymouth Brethren. To reconcile his scientific knowledge with his fundamentalist position in religion, Gosse published a book called *Omphalos* which pleased no one. His dilemma is described by his son, the literary critic Sir Edmund Gosse (1849–1928), in an autobiography published in 1907. The present selection is from Chapter V.

On the other side, the reactionaries, although never dreaming of the fate which hung over them, had not been idle. In 1857 the astounding question had for the first time been propounded with contumely, "What, then, did we come from orangoutang?" The famous *Vestiges of Creation* had been supplying a sugar-and-water panacea for those who could not escape from the trend of evidence, and who yet clung to revelation. Owen was encouraging reaction by resisting, with all the strength of his prestige, the theory of the mutability of species.

In this period of intellectual ferment, as when a great political revolution is being planned, many possible adherents were confidentially tested with hints and encouraged to reveal their bias in a whisper. It was the notion of Lyell, himself a great mover of men, that, before the doctrine of natural selection was given to a world which would be sure to lift up at it a howl of execration, a certain bodyguard of sound and experienced naturalists, expert in the description of species, should be privately made aware of its tenor. Among those who were thus initiated, or approached with a view towards possible illumination, was my Father. He was spoken to by Hooker, and later on by Darwin, after meetings of the Royal Society in the summer of 1857.

My Father's attitude towards the theory of natural selection was critical in his career, and oddly enough, it exercised an immense influence on my own experience as a child. Let it be admitted at once, mournful as the admission is, that every instinct in his intelligence went out at first to greet the new light. It had hardly done so, when a recollection of the opening chapter of Genesis checked it at the outset. He consulted with Carpenter, a great investigator, but one who was fully as incapable as himself of remodeling his ideas with regard to the old, accepted hypotheses. They both determined, on various grounds, to have nothing to do with the terrible theory, but to hold steadily to the law of the fixity of species. * * *

My Father had never admired Sir Charles Lyell. I think that the famous Lord Chancellor manner of the geologist intimidated him, and we undervalue the intelligence of those whose conversation puts us at a disadvantage. For Darwin and Hooker, on the other hand, he had a profound esteem, and I know not whether this had anything to do with the fact that he chose, for his impetuous experiment in reaction, the field of geology, rather than that of zoology or botany. Lyell had been threatening to publish a book on the geological history of Man, which was to be a bombshell flung into the camp of the catastrophists. My Father, after long reflection, prepared a theory of his own, which, as he fondly hoped, would take the wind out of Lyell's sails, and justify geology to godly readers of Genesis. It was, very briefly, that there had been no gradual modification of the surface of the earth, or slow development of organic forms, but that when the catastrophic act of creation took place, the world presented, instantly, the structural appearance of a planet on which life had long existed.

The theory, coarsely enough, and to my Father's great indignation, was defined by a hasty press as being this—that God hid the fossils in the rocks in order to tempt geologists into infidelity. In truth, it was the logical and inevitable conclusion of accepting, literally, the doctrine of a sudden act of creation; it emphasized the fact that any breach in the circular course of nature could be conceived only on the supposition that the object created bore false witness to past processes, which had never taken place.

Never was a book cast upon the waters with greater anticipations of success than was this curious, this obstinate, this fanatical volume. My Father lived in a fever of suspense, waiting for the tremendous issue. This *Omphalos* of his, he thought, was to bring all the turmoil of scientific speculation to a close, fling geology into the arms of Scripture, and make the lion eat grass with the lamb. It was not surprising, he admitted, that there had been experienced an ever-increasing discord between the facts which geology brings to light and the direct statements of the early chapters of Genesis. Nobody was to blame for that. My Father, and my Father alone, possessed the secret of the enigma; he alone held the key which could smoothly open the lock of geological mystery. He offered it, with a glowing gesture, to atheists and Christians alike. This was to be the universal panacea; this the system of intellectual therapeutics which could not but heal all the maladies of the age. But, alas! atheists and Christians alike looked at it, and laughed, and threw it away.

In the course of that dismal winter, as the post began to bring in private letters, few and chilly, and public reviews, many and scornful, my Father looked in vain for the approval of the churches, and in vain for the acquiescence of the scientific societies, and in vain for the gratitude of those "thousands of thinking persons," which he had rashly assured himself of receiving. As his reconciliation of Scripture statements and geological deductions was welcomed nowhere; as Darwin continued silent, and the youthful Huxley was scornful, and even Charles Kingsley,[6] from whom my Father had expected the most instant appreciation, wrote that he could not "give up the painful and slow conclusion of five and twenty years' study of geology, and believe that God has written on the rocks one enormous and superfluous lie"—as all this happened or failed to happen, a gloom, cold and dismal, descended upon our morning teacups. * * *

1907

6. Charles Kingsley (1819-75), clergyman and novelist.

INDUSTRIALISM: PROGRESS OR DECLINE?

Was the machine age a blessing or a curse? Was the middle-class economic system making mankind happier or more wretched? Was human progress probable, and how, in fact, is progress to be defined? In confronting these questions, Victorian writers were generally divided into two camps. The changes brought about by industrialism impressed one group of writers as an appalling retrogression. They pointed to the dreadful living and working conditions of the industrial classes, and they deplored the disappearance of what Karl Marx called the "feudal, patriarchal, idyllic relations" between employer and employee which, they believed, had existed in earlier economies. These critics are represented by essayists such as Carlyle, Ruskin, and Morris, and by novelists such as Charles Kingsley and Charles Dickens, whose *Hard Times* was praised by Ruskin as the greatest of his novels and one that "should be studied with close and earnest care by persons interested in social questions." Related to this essentially conservative group, although working from assumptions and to conclusions altogether different from theirs, are Karl Marx and Friedrich Engels, whose interest in the English industrial experiment was keen. Engels spent 20 months observing industrial conditions in Manchester, and his book *The Condition of the Working Class in England* (1845) prepared the ground for his collaborating with Marx in writing *The Communist Manifesto* of 1848, both works being exposures of what seemed to him to be the inadequacies and inequities of middle-class industrial society. In the opposite camp from Carlyle or Engels were writers who found the new society an unqualified improvement over societies of earlier ages. The historian Thomas Babington Macaulay was the most effective Victorian spokesman for this view. A masterful debater and a memorable prose stylist, Macaulay sought to show up the absurdity of anyone who did not share his satisfaction in the accomplishments of his own century. The popularity of his writings suggests that his position was shared by many of his contemporaries. One of these was the sociologist Herbert Spencer, an extreme example of a writer whose faith in the advantage of the new system was unbounded. The "advancement" of mankind toward a state of "perfection" was, according to Spencer, a "certainty." Basing his observations on the industrial development of England, Spencer argued that future human advancement would be accelerated by individual enterprise, whereas government control was almost invariably an obstacle to progress.

THOMAS BABINGTON MACAULAY: *From* A Review
of Southey's *Colloquies*[1]
[*Evidence of Progress*]

* * * Perhaps we could not select a better instance of the spirit which pervades the whole book than the passages in which Mr.

1. Published in the *Edinburgh Review* (1830). In a book entitled *Colloquies on the Progress and Prospects of So-* *ciety* (1829), the poet and man of letters Robert Southey (1774–1843) had sought to expose the evils of indus-

Southey gives his opinion of the manufacturing system. There is nothing which he hates so bitterly. It is, according to him, a system more tyrannical than that of the feudal ages, a system of actual servitude, a system which destroys the bodies and degrades the minds of those who are engaged in it. He expresses a hope that the competition of other nations may drive us out of the field; that our foreign trade may decline; and that we may thus enjoy a restoration of national sanity and strength. But he seems to think that the extermination of the whole manufacturing population would be a blessing, if the evil could be removed in no other way.

Mr. Southey does not bring forward a single fact in support of these views; and, as it seems to us, there are facts which lead to a very different conclusion. In the first place, the poor rate[2] is very decidedly lower in the manufacturing than in the agricultural districts. If Mr. Southey will look over the Parliamentary returns on this subject, he will find that the amount of parochial relief required by the laborers in the different counties of England is almost exactly in inverse proportion to the degree in which the manufacturing system has been introduced into those counties. The returns for the years ending in March, 1825, and in March, 1828, are now before us. In the former year we find the poor rate highest in Sussex,[3] about twenty shillings to every inhabitant. Then come Buckinghamshire, Essex, Suffolk, Bedfordshire, Huntingdonshire, Kent, and Norfolk. In all these the rate is above fifteen shillings a head. We will not go through the whole. Even in Westmoreland and the North Riding of Yorkshire, the rate is at more than eight shillings. In Cumberland and Monmouthshire, the most fortunate of all the agricultural districts, it is at six shillings. But in the West Riding of Yorkshire,[4] it is as low as five shillings: and when we come to Lancashire, we find it at four shillings, one-fifth of what it is in Sussex. The returns of the year ending in March, 1828, are a little, and but a little, more unfavorable to the manufacturing districts. Lancashire, even in that season of distress, required a smaller poor rate than any other district, and little more than one-fourth of the poor rate raised in Sussex. Cumberland alone, of the agricultural districts, was as well off as the West Riding of Yorkshire. These facts seem to indicate that the manufacturer is both in a more comfortable and in a less dependent situation than the agricultural laborer.

As to the effect of the manufacturing system on the bodily health,

trialism and to assert the superiority of the traditional feudal and agricultural way of life of England's past. His romantic Toryism provoked Macaulay (1800–59) to review the book in a long and characteristic essay. As in his popular *History of England* (1849–61), Macaulay seeks here to demolish his opponent with a bombardment of facts and figures demonstrating that industrialism and middle-class government have resulted in progress and increased comforts for mankind.

2. Taxes on property, to provide food and lodging for the unemployed or unemployable. The amount or rate of such taxes varied from district to district in England, depending upon local conditions of unemployment.

3. A predominantly agricultural district.

4. A manufacturing district.

we must beg leave to estimate it by a standard far too low and vulgar for a mind so imaginative as that of Mr. Southey, the proportion of births and deaths. We know that, during the growth of this atrocious system, this new misery, to use the phrases of Mr. Southey, this new enormity, this birth of a portentous age, this pest which no man can approve whose heart is not seared or whose understanding has not been darkened, there has been a great diminution of mortality, and that this diminution has been greater in the manufacturing towns than anywhere else. The mortality still is, as it always was, greater in towns than in the country. But the difference has diminished in an extraordinary degree. There is the best reason to believe that the annual mortality of Manchester, about the middle of the last century, was one in twenty-eight. It is now reckoned at one in forty-five. In Glasgow and Leeds a similar improvement has taken place. Nay, the rate of mortality in those three great capitals of the manufacturing districts is now considerably less than it was, fifty years ago, over England and Wales, taken together, open country and all. We might with some plausibility maintain that the people live longer because they are better fed, better lodged, better clothed, and better attended in sickness, and that these improvements are owing to that increase of national wealth which the manufacturing system has produced.

Much more might be said on this subject. But to what end? It is not from bills of mortality and statistical tables that Mr. Southey has learned his political creed. He cannot stoop to study the history of the system which he abuses, to strike the balance between the good and evil which it has produced, to compare district with district, or generation with generation. We will give his own reason for his opinion, the only reason which he gives for it, in his own words:

"We remained a while in silence looking upon the assemblage of dwellings below. Here, and in the adjoining hamlet of Millbeck, the effects of manufactures and of agriculture may be seen and compared. The old cottages are such as the poet and the painter equally delight in beholding. Substantially built of the native stone without mortar, dirtied with no white lime, and their long low roofs covered with slate, if they had been raised by the magic of some indigenous Amphion's[5] music, the materials could not have adjusted themselves more beautifully in accord with the surrounding scene; and time has still further harmonized them with weather stains, lichens, and moss, short grasses, and short fern, and stone-plants of various kinds. The ornamented chimneys, round or square, less adorned than those which, like little turrets, crest the houses of the Portuguese peasantry, and yet not less happily suited to their place; the hedge of clipped box beneath the windows, the rose bushes beside the door, the little patch of flower ground, with its

5. According to Greek mythology, Amphion's magical skill as a harp player caused the walls of Thebes to be erected without human aid.

tall hollyhocks in front; the garden beside, the beehives, and the orchard with its bank of daffodils and snowdrops, the earliest and the profusest in these parts, indicate in the owners some portion of ease and leisure, some regard to neatness and comfort, some sense of natural, and innocent, and healthful enjoyment. The new cottages of the manufacturers are upon the manufacturing pattern —naked, and in a row.

" 'How is it,' said I, 'that everything which is connected with manufactures presents such features of unqualified deformity? From the largest of Mammon's temples down to the poorest hovel in which his helotry are stalled, these edifices have all one character. Time will not mellow them; nature will neither clothe nor conceal them; and they will remain always as offensive to the eye as to the mind.' "

Here is wisdom. Here are the principles on which nations are to be governed. Rosebushes and poor rates, rather than steam engines and independence. Mortality and cottages with weather stains, rather than health and long life with edifices which time cannot mellow. We are told that our age has invented atrocities beyond the imagination of our fathers; that society has been brought into a state compared with which extermination would be a blessing; and all because the dwellings of cotton-spinners are naked and rectangular. Mr. Southey has found out a way, he tells us, in which the effects of manufactures and agriculture may be compared. And what is this way? To stand on a hill, to look at a cottage and a factory, and to see which is the prettier. Does Mr. Southey think that the body of the English peasantry live, or ever lived, in substantial or ornamented cottages, with boxhedges, flower gardens, beehives, and orchards? If not, what is his parallel worth? We despise those mock philosophers,[6] who think that they serve the cause of science by depreciating literature and the fine arts. But if anything could excuse their narrowness of mind, it would be such a book as this. It is not strange that, when one enthuisast makes the picturesque the test of political good, another should feel inclined to proscribe altogether the pleasures of taste and imagination. * * *

It is not strange that, differing so widely from Mr. Southey as to the past progress of society, we should differ from him also as to its probable destiny. He thinks, that to all outward appearance, the country is hastening to destruction; but he relies firmly on the goodness of God. We do not see either the piety or the rationality of thus confidently expecting that the Supreme Being will interfere to disturb the common succession of causes and effects. We, too, rely on his goodness, on his goodness as manifested, not in extraordinary interpositions, but in those general laws which it has pleased

---

6. Presumably such Utilitarian philosophers as Jeremy Bentham, who had equated poetry with pushpin, a trifling game. It should be noted, however, that although Macaulay often attacked the Utilitarians for their narrow preoccupation with theory, his own position has much in common with theirs.

him to establish in the physical and in the moral world. We rely on the natural tendency of the human intellect to truth, and on the natural tendency of society to improvement. We know no well-authenticated instance of a people which has decidedly retrograded in civilization and prosperity, except from the influence of violent and terrible calamities, such as those which laid the Roman Empire in ruins, or those which, about the beginning of the sixteenth century, desolated Italy. We know of no country which, at the end of fifty years of peace and tolerably good government, has been less prosperous than at the beginning of that period. The political importance of a state may decline, as the balance of power is disturbed by the introduction of new forces. Thus the influence of Holland and of Spain is much diminished. But are Holland and Spain poorer than formerly? We doubt it. Other countries have outrun them. But we suspect that they have been positively, though not relatively, advancing. We suspect that Holland is richer than when she sent her navies up the Thames,[7] that Spain is richer than when a French king was brought captive to the footstool of Charles the Fifth.[8]

History is full of the signs of this natural progress of society. We see in almost every part of the annals of mankind how the industry of individuals, struggling up against wars, taxes, famines, conflagrations, mischievous prohibitions, and more mischievous protections, creates faster than governments can squander, and repairs whatever invaders can destroy. We see the wealth of nations increasing, and all the arts of life approaching nearer and nearer to perfection, in spite of the grossest corruption and the wildest profusion on the part of rulers.

The present moment is one of great distress. But how small will that distress appear when we think over the history of the last forty years; a war,[9] compared with which all other wars sink into insignificance; taxation, such as the most heavily taxed people of former times could not have conceived; a debt larger than all the public debts that ever existed in the world added together; the food of the people studiously rendered dear; the currency imprudently debased, and imprudently restored. Yet is the country poorer than in 1790? We firmly believe that, in spite of all the misgovernment of her rulers, she has been almost constantly becoming richer and richer. Now and then there has been a stoppage, now and then a short retrogression; but as to the general tendency there can be no doubt. A single breaker may recede; but the tide is evidently coming in.

If we were to prophesy that in the year 1930 a population of

7. In 1667 a Dutch fleet displayed its power by sailing up the river Thames without being challenged by the English navy.
8. The Spanish king, Charles V, captured the king of France, Francis I, in the battle of Pavia (1525).
9. The wars against France and Napoleon, extending, with some interruptions, from 1792 to 1815.

fifty millions, better fed, clad, and lodged than the English of our
time, will cover these islands, that Sussex and Huntingdonshire will
be wealthier than the wealthiest parts of the West Riding of Yorkshire now are, that cultivation, rich as that of a flower garden, will
be carried up to the very tops of Ben Nevis and Helvellyn,[1] that
machines constructed on principles yet undiscovered will be in every
house, that there will be no highways but railroads, no traveling
but by steam, that our debt, vast as it seems to us, will appear to
our great-grandchildren a trifling encumbrance, which might easily
be paid off in a year or two, many people would think us insane.
We prophesy nothing; but this we say: If any person had told the
Parliament which met in perplexity and terror after the crash in
1720 that in 1830 the wealth of England would surpass all their
wildest dreams, that the annual revenue would equal the principal
of that debt which they considered as an intolerable burden, that
for one man of ten thousand pounds then living there would be
five men of fifty thousand pounds, that London would be twice as
large and twice as populous, and that nevertheless the rate of mortality would have diminished to one-half of what it then was, that
the post office would bring more into the exchequer than the excise
and customs had brought in together under Charles the Second,
that stage coaches would run from London to York in twenty-four
hours, that men would be in the habit of sailing without wind, and
would be beginning to ride without horses, our ancestors would
have given as much credit to the prediction as they gave to *Gulliver's
Travels.* Yet the prediction would have been true; and they would
have perceived that it was not altogether absurd, if they had considered that the country was then raising every year a sum which
would have purchased the fee-simple[2] of the revenue of the Plantag-
enets, ten times what supported the Government of Elizabeth, three
times what, in the time of Cromwell, had been thought intolerably
oppressive. To almost all men the state of things under which
they have been used to live seems to be the necessary state of
things. We have heard it said that five per cent is the natural interest
of money, that twelve is the natural number of a jury, that forty
shillings is the natural qualification of a county voter. Hence it is
that, though in every age everybody knows that up to his own time
progressive improvement has been taking place, nobody seems to
reckon on any improvement during the next generation. We cannot absolutely prove that those are in error who tell us that society
has reached a turning point, that we have seen our best days. But
so said all who came before us, and with just as much apparent
reason. "A million a year will beggar us," said the patriots of 1640.
"Two millions a year will grind the country to powder," was the

---

1. Mountains, in Scotland and in the
English Lake District, respectively.
2. Absolute ownership of their estates.

The Plantagenet family provided the
monarchs of England from 1145 to 1485.

cry in 1660. "Six millions a year, and a debt of fifty millions!" exclaimed Swift, "the high allies have been the ruin of us." "A hundred and forty millions of debt!" said Junius;[3] "well may we say that we owe Lord Chatham more than we shall ever pay, if we owe him such a load as this." "Two hundred and forty millions of debt!" cried all the statesmen of 1783 in chorus; "what abilities, or what economy on the part of a minister, can save a country so burdened?" We know that if, since 1783, no fresh debt had been incurred, the increased resources of the country would have enabled us to defray that debt at which Pitt, Fox, and Burke stood aghast, nay, to defray it over and over again, and that with much lighter taxation than what we have actually borne. On what principle is it that, when we see nothing but improvement behind us, we are to expect nothing but deterioration before us?

It is not by the intermeddling of Mr. Southey's idol, the omniscient and omnipotent State, but by the prudence and energy of the people, that England has hitherto been carried forward in civilization; and it is to the same prudence and the same energy that we now look with comfort and good hope. Our rulers will best promote the improvement of the nation by strictly confining themselves to their own legitimate duties, by leaving capital to find its most lucrative course, commodities their fair price, industry and intelligence their natural reward, idleness and folly their natural punishment, by maintaining peace, by defending property, by diminishing the price of law, and by observing strict economy in every department of the State. Let the Government do this: the People will assuredly do the rest.

1830

FRIEDRICH ENGELS: The Great Towns[4]

Industry and commerce attain their highest stage of development in the big towns, so that it is here that the effects of industrialization on the wage earners can be most clearly seen. It is in these big towns that the concentration of property has reached its highest point. Here the manners and customs of the good old days have been most effectively destroyed. Here the very name of "Merry

---

3. Pseudonym of a political commentator whose letters (1769–72) usually praised William Pitt, Earl of Chatham. Pitt, as leader of the war against France, which gained Canada for England, could have been blamed for running his country into debt.
4. From Chapter 3 of *The Condition of the Working Class in England* (1845)

translated from the German by W. O. Henderson and W. H. Chaloner (1958). The first two paragraphs are the conclusion of Chapter 2: "The Industrial Proletariat." These eyewitness accounts describe conditions of 1844 when Engels (1820–1895) had been living in England, chiefly in Manchester. The book was first translated into English in 1892.

England" has long since been forgotten, because the inhabitants of the great manufacturing centers have never even heard from their grandparents what life was like in those days. In these towns there are only rich and poor, because the lower middle classes are fast disappearing. At one time this section of the middle classes was the most stable social group, but now it has become the least stable. It is represented in the big factory towns today partly by a few survivors from a bygone age and partly by a group of people who are anxious to get rich as quickly as possible. Of these shady speculators and dubious traders one becomes rich while ninety-nine go bankrupt. Indeed, for more than half of those who have failed, bankruptcy has become a habit.

The vast majority of the inhabitants of these towns are the workers. We propose to discuss their condition and to discover how they have been influenced by life and work in the great factory towns.

* * *

London is unique, because it is a city in which one can roam for hours without leaving the built-up area and without seeing the slightest sign of the approach of open country. This enormous agglomeration of population on a single spot has multiplied a hundred-fold the economic strength of the two and a half million inhabitants concentrated there. This great population has made London the commercial capital of the world and has created the gigantic docks in which are assembled the thousands of ships which always cover the River Thames. I know nothing more imposing than the view one obtains of the river when sailing from the sea up to London Bridge. Especially above Woolwich the houses and docks are packed tightly together on both banks of the river. The further one goes up the river the thicker becomes the concentration of ships lying at anchor, so that eventually only a narrow shipping lane is left free in midstream. Here hundreds of steamships dart rapidly to and fro. All this is so magnificent and impressive that one is lost in admiration. The traveler has good reason to marvel at England's greatness even before he steps on English soil.

It is only later that the traveler appreciates the human suffering which has made all this possible. He can only realize the price that has been paid for all this magnificence after he has tramped the pavements of the main streets of London for some days and has tired himself out by jostling his way through the crowds and dodging the endless stream of coaches and carts which fills the streets. It is only when he has visited the slums of this great city that it dawns upon him that the inhabitants of modern London have had to sacrifice so much that is best in human nature in order to create those wonders of civilization with which their city teems. The vast majority of Londoners have had to let so many of their potential creative faculties lie dormant, stunted and unused in order that a small,

closely-knit group of their fellow citizens could develop to the full
the qualtities with which nature has endowed them. The restless
and noisy activity of the crowded streets is highly distasteful, and it
is surely abhorrent to human nature itself. Hundreds of thousands
of men and women drawn from all classes and ranks of society pack
the streets of London. Are they not all human beings with the same
innate characteristics and potentialities? Are they not all equally
interested in the pursuit of happiness? And do they not all aim at
happiness by following similar methods? Yet they rush past each
other as if they had nothing in common. They are tactily agreed on
one thing only—that everyone should keep to the right of the pavement so as not to collide with the stream of people moving in the
opposite direction. No one even thinks of sparing a glance for his
neighbor in the streets. The more that Londoners are packed into a
tiny space, the more repulsive and disgraceful becomes the brutal
indifference with which they ignore their neighbors and selfishly
concentrate upon their private affairs. We know well enough that
this isolation of the individual—this narrow-minded egotism—is
everywhere the fundamental principle of modern society. But
nowhere is this selfish egotism so blatantly evident as in the frantic bustle of the great city. The disintegration of society into individuals, each guided by his private principles and each pursuing his
own aims has been pushed to its furthest limits in London. Here
indeed human society has been split into its component atoms.

From this it follows that the social conflict—the war of all
against all—is fought in the open. * * * Here men regard their fellows not as human beings, but as pawns in the struggle for existence. Everyone exploits his neighbor with the result that the
stronger tramples the weaker under foot. The strongest of all, a tiny
group of capitalists, monopolize everything, while the weakest, who
are in the vast majority, succumb to the most abject poverty.

What is true of London is true also of all the great towns, such
as Manchester, Birmingham, and Leeds. Everywhere one finds on
the one hand the most barbarous indifference and selfish egotism
and on the other the most distressing scenes of misery and poverty.
Signs of social conflict are to be found everywhere. Everyone turns
his house into a fortress to defend himself—under the protection of
the law—from the depredations of his neighbors. Class warfare is
so open and shameless that it has to be seen to be believed. The
observer of such an appalling state of affairs must shudder at the
consequences of such feverish activity and can only marvel that so
crazy a social and economic structure should survive at all. * * *

Every great town has one or more slum areas into which the
working classes are packed. Sometimes, of course, poverty is to be
found hidden away in alleys close to the stately homes of the
wealthy. Generally, however, the workers are segregated in separate

districts where they struggle through life as best they can out of sight of the more fortunate classes of society. The slums of the English towns have much in common—the worst houses in a town being found in the worst districts. They are generally unplanned wildernesses of one- or two-storied terrace houses built of brick. Wherever possible these have cellars which are also used as dwellings. These little houses of three or four rooms and a kitchen are called cottages, and throughout England, except for some parts of London, are where the working classes normally live. These streets themselves are usually unpaved and full of holes. They are filthy and strewn with animal and vegetable refuse. Since they have neither gutters nor drains the refuse accumulates in stagnant, stinking puddles. Ventilation in the slums is inadequate owing to the hopelessly unplanned nature of these areas. A great many people live huddled together in a very small area, and so it is easy to imagine the nature of the air in these workers' quarters. However, in fine weather the streets are used for the drying of washing, and clothes lines are stretched across the streets from house to house and wet garments are hung out on them.

We propose to describe some of these slums in detail. * * *

If we cross Blackstone Edge on foot or take the train we reach Manchester, the regional capital of South Lancashire, and enter the classic home of English industry. This is the masterpiece of the Industrial Revolution and at the same time the mainspring of all the workers' movements. Once more we are in a beautiful hilly countryside. The land slopes gently down toward the Irish Sea, intersected by the charming green valleys of the Ribble, the Irwell, the Mersey, and their tributaries. A hundred years ago this region was to a great extent thinly populated marshland. Now it is covered with towns and villages and is the most densely populated part of England. In Lancashire—particularly in Manchester—is to be found not only the origin but the heart of the industry of the United Kingdom. Manchester Exchange is the thermometer which records all the fluctuations of industrial and commercial activity. The evolution of the modern system of manufacture has reached its climax in Manchester. It was in the South Lancashire cotton industry that water and steam power first replaced hand machines. It was here that such machines as the power-loom and the self-acting mule replaced the old hand-loom and spinning wheel. It is here that the division of labor has been pushed to its furthest limits. These three factors are the essence of modern industry. In all three of them the cotton industry was the pioneer and remains ahead in all branches of industry. In the circumstances it is to be expected that it is in this region that the inevitable consequences of industrialization in so far as they affect the working classes are most strikingly evident. Nowhere else can the life and conditions of the industrial proletariat be studied in all their aspects as in South Lancashire. Here can be seen most clearly the degradation into which the worker sinks owing to the introduction of steam power, machinery, and the division of labor. Here, too, can be seen most the strenuous efforts of the proletariat to raise themselves from their degraded situation. I propose to examine conditions in Manchester in greater detail for two reasons. In the first place, Manchester is the classic type of modern industrial town. Secondly, I know Manchester as well as I know my native town and I know more about it than most of its inhabitants. * * *

Owing to the curious lay-out of the town it is quite possible for someone to live for years in Manchester and to travel daily to and from his work without ever seeing a working-class quarter or coming into contact with an artisan. He who visits Manchester simply on business or for pleasure need never see the slums, mainly because the working-class districts and the middle-class districts are quite distinct. This division is due partly to deliberate policy and partly to instinctive and tacit agreement between the two social groups. In those areas where the two social groups happen to come into contact with each other the middle classes sanctimoniously ignore the existence of their less fortunate neighbors. In the center of Manchester there is a fairly large commercial district, which is about half a mile long and half a mile broad. This district is almost entirely given over to offices and warehouses. Nearly the whole of this district has no permanent residents and is deserted at night, when only policemen patrol its dark, narrow thoroughfares with their bull's-eye lanterns. This district is intersected by certain main streets which carry an enormous volume of traffic. The lower floors of the buildings are occupied by shops of dazzling splendor. A few of the upper stories on these premises are used as dwellings and the streets present a relatively busy appearance until late in the evening. Around this commercial quarter there is a belt of built-up areas on the average one and a half miles in width, which is occupied entirely by working-class dwellings. This area of workers' houses includes all Manchester proper, except the center, all Salford and Hulme, an important part of Pendleton and Chorlton, two-thirds of Ardwick, and certain small areas of Cheetham Hill and Broughton. Beyond this belt of working-class houses or dwellings lie the districts inhabited by the middle classes and the upper classes. The former are to be found in regularly laid out streets near the working-class districts —in Chorlton and in the remoter parts of Cheetham Hill. The villas of the upper classes are surrounded by gardens and lie in the higher and remoter parts of Chorlton and Ardwick or on the breezy heights of Cheetham Hill, Broughton, and Pendleton. The upper class enjoy healthy country air and live in luxurious and comfortable dwellings which are linked to the center of Manchester by omnibuses which run every fifteen or thirty minutes. To such an extent has the convenience of the rich been considered in the planning of Manchester that these plutocrats can travel from their houses to their places of business in the center of the town by the shortest routes, which run entirely through working-class districts, without even realizing how close they are to the misery and filth which lie on both sides of the road. * * *

I will now give a description of the working-class districts of Manchester. The first of them is the Old Town, which lies between the northern limit of the commercial quarter and the River Irk. Here even the better streets, such Todd Street, Long Millgate, Withy Grove, and Shudehill are narrow and tortuous. The houses are dirty, old, and tumble-down. The sidestreets have been built in a disgraceful fashion. If one enters the district near the "Old Church" and goes down Long Millgate, one sees immediately on the right hand side a row of antiquated houses where not a single front wall is standing upright. This is a remnant of the old Manchester of the days before the town became industrialized. The original inhabitants and their children have left for better houses in other districts, while the houses in Long Millgate, which no longer satisfied them, were left to a tribe of workers containing a strong Irish element. Here one is really and truly in a district which is quite obviously given over entirely to the working classes, because even the shopkeepers and the publicans of Long Millgate make no effort to give their establishments a semblance of cleanliness. The condition of this street may be deplorable, but it is by no means as bad as the alleys and courts which lie behind it, and which can be approached only by covered passages so narrow that two people cannot pass. Anyone who has never visited these courts and alleys can have no idea of the fantastic way in which the houses have been packed together in disorderly confusion in impudent defiance of all reasonable principles of town planning. And the fault lies not merely in the survival of old property from earlier periods in Manchester's history. Only in quite modern times has the policy of cramming as many houses as possible on to such space as was not utilized in earlier periods reached its climax. The result is that today not an inch of space remains between the houses and any further building is now physically impossible. To prove my point I reproduce a small section of a plan of Manchester.[5] It is by no means the

5. Not reproduced in the present version.

worst slum in Manchester and it does not cover one-tenth of the area of Manchester.

This sketch will be sufficient to illustrate the crazy layout of the whole district lying near the River Irk. There is a very sharp drop of some 15 to 30 feet down to the south bank of the Irk at this point. As many as three rows of houses have generally been squeezed onto this precipitous slope. The lowest row of houses stands directly on the bank of the river while the front walls of the highest row stand on the crest of the ridge in Long Millgate. Moreover, factory buildings are also to be found on the banks of the river. In short the layout of the upper part of Long Millgate at the top of the rise is just as disorderly and congested as the lower part of the street. To the right and left a number of covered passages from Long Millgate give access to several courts. On reaching them one meets with a degree of dirt and revolting filth the like of which is not to be found elsewhere. The worst courts are those leading down to the Irk, which contain unquestionably the most dreadful dwellings I have ever seen. In one of these courts, just at the entrance where the covered passage ends, there is a privy without a door. This privy is so dirty that the inhabitants of the court can only enter or leave the court if they are prepared to wade through puddles of stale urine and excrement. Anyone who wishes to confirm this description should go to the first court on the bank of the Irk above Ducie Bridge. Several tanneries are situated on the bank of the river and they fill the neighborhood with the stench of animal putrefaction. The only way of getting to the courts below Ducie Bridge is by going down flights of narrow dirty steps and one can only reach the houses by treading over heaps of dirt and filth. The first court below Ducie Bridge is called Allen's Court. At the time of the cholera [1832] this court was in such a disgraceful state that the sanitary inspectors [of the local Board of Health] evacuated the inhabitants. The court was then swept and fumigated with chlorine. In his pamphlet Dr. Kay gives a horrifying description of conditions in this court at that time. Since Kay wrote this pamphlet, this court appears to have been at any rate partly demolished and rebuilt. If one looks down the river from Ducie Bridge one does at least see several ruined walls and high piles of rubble, side by side with some recently built houses. The view from this bridge, which is mercifully concealed by a high parapet from all but the tallest mortals, is quite characteristic of the whole district. At the bottom the Irk flows, or rather, stagnates. It is a narrow, coal-black, stinking river full of filth and rubbish which it deposits on the more low-lying right bank. In dry weather this bank presents the spectacle of a series of the most revolting blackish-green puddles of slime from the depths of which bubbles of miasmatic gases constantly rise and create a stench which is unbearable even to those standing on the bridge forty or fifty feet above the level of the water. Moreover, the flow of the river is continually interrupted by numerous high weirs, behind which large quantities of slime and refuse collect and putrefy. Above Ducie Bridge there are some tall tannery buildings, and further up there are dye-works, bone mills, and gasworks. All the filth, both liquid and solid, discharged by these works finds its way into the River Irk, which also receives the contents of the adjacent sewers and privies. The nature of the filth deposited by this river may well be imagined. If one looks at the heaps of garbage below Ducie Bridge one can gauge the extent to which accumulated dirt, filth, and decay permeate the courts on the steep left bank of the river. The houses are packed very closely together and since the bank of the river is very steep it is possible to see a part of every house. All of them have been blackened by soot, all of them are crumbling with age and all have broken window panes and window frames. In the background there are old factory buildings which look like barracks. On the opposite, low-lying bank of the river, one sees a long row of houses and factories. The second house is a roofless ruin, filled with refuse, and the third is built in such a low situation that the ground floor is uninhabitable and has neither doors nor windows. In the background one sees the paupers' cemetery, and the stations of the railways to Liverpool and Leeds. Behind these buildings is situated the workhouse, Manchester's "Poor Law Bastille."[6] The workhouse is built on a hill and from behind its high walls and battlements seems to threaten the whole adjacent working-class quarter like a fortress.

Above Ducie Bridge the left bank of the Irk becomes flatter and the right bank of the Irk becomes steeper and so the condition of the houses on both sides of the river becomes worse rather than better. Turning left from the main street which is still Long Mill-gate, the visitor can easily lose his way. He wanders aimlessly from one court to another. He turns one corner after another through innumerable narrow dirty alleyways and passages, and in only a few minutes he has lost all sense of direction and does not know which way to turn. The area is full of ruined or half-ruined buildings. Some of them are actually uninhabited and that means a great deal in this quarter of the town. In the houses one seldom sees a wooden or a stone floor, while the doors and windows are nearly always broken and badly fitting. And as for the dirt! Everywhere one sees

6. The workhouses established by the Poor Laws of the 1830's, because of the strict regimens enforced on inmates, were commonly likened to prisons such as the Bastille in Paris.

heaps of refuse, garbage, and filth. There are stagnant pools instead of gutters and the stench alone is so overpowering that no human being, even partially civilized, would find it bearable to live in such a district.[7] The recently constructed extension of the Leeds railway which crosses the Irk at this point has swept away some of these courts and alleys, but it has thrown open to public gaze some of the others. So it comes about that there is to be found immediately under the railway bridge a court which is even filthier and more revolting than all the others. This is simply because it was formerly so hidden and secluded that it could only be reached with considerable difficulty, [but is now exposed to the human eye]. I thought I knew this district well, but even I would never have found it had not the railway viaduct made a breach in the slums at this point. One walks along a very rough path on the river bank, in between clothes-posts and washing lines to reach a chaotic group of little, one-storied, one-roomed cabins. Most of them have earth floors, and working, living, and sleeping all take place in the one room. In such a hole, barely six feet long and five feet wide, I saw two beds—and what beds and bedding!—which filled the room, except for the fireplace and the doorstep. Several of these huts, as far as I could see, were completely empty, although the door was open and the inhabitants were leaning against the door posts. In front of the doors filth and garbage abounded. I could not see the pavement, but from time to time, I felt it was there because my feet scraped it. This whole collection of cattle sheds for human beings was surrounded on two sides by houses and a factory and on a third side by the river. [It was possible to get to this slum by only two routes]. One was the narrow path along the river bank, while the other was a narrow gateway which led to another human rabbit warren which was nearly as badly built and was nearly in such a bad condition as the one I have just described.

Enough of this! All along the Irk slums of this type abound. There is an unplanned and chaotic conglomeration of houses, most

---

7. Cf. another account of Manchester slums of the same decade in Elizabeth Gaskell's novel *Mary Barton* (1848), Chapter 6: "Women from their doors tossed household slops of *every* description into the gutter; they ran into the next pool, which overflowed and stagnated. Heaps of ashes were stepping-stones, on which the passer-by, who cared in the least for cleanliness, took care not to put his foot. Our friends [two factory workers] were not dainty, but even they picked their way, till they got to some steps leading down . . . into the cellar in which a family of human beings lived. . . . After the account I have given of the state of the street, no one can be surprised that on going into the cellar inhabited by Davenport, the smell was so foetid as almost to knock the two men down. Quickly recovering themselves, as those inured to such things do, they began to penetrate the thick darkness of the place, and to see three or four children rolling on the damp, nay wet brick floor, through which the stagnant, filthy moisture of the street oozed up; the fireplace was empty and black; the wife sat on her husband's lair [couch], and cried in the dank loneliness."

of which are more or less unhabitable. The dirtiness of the interiors of these premises is fully in keeping with the filth that surrounds them. How can people dwelling in such places keep clean! There are not even adequate facilities for satisfying the most natural daily needs. There are so few privies that they are either filled up every day or are too far away for those who need to use them. How can these people wash when all that is available is the dirty water of the Irk? Pumps and piped water are to be found only in the better-class districts of the town. Indeed no one can blame these helots of modern civilization if their homes are no cleaner than the occasional pigsties which are a feature of these slums. There are actually some property owners who are not ashamed to let dwellings such as those which are to be found below Scotland Bridge. Here on the quayside a mere six feet from the water's edge is to be found a row of six or seven cellars, the bottoms of which are at least two feet beneath the low-water level of the Irk. [What can one say of the owner of] the corner house—situated on the opposite bank of the river above Scotland Bridge—who actually lets the upper floor although the premises downstairs are quite·uninhabitable, and no attempt has been made to·board up the gaps left by the disappearance of doors and windows? This sort of thing is by no means uncommon in this part of Manchester, where, owing to the lack of conveniences, such deserted ground floors are often used by the whole neighborhood as privies.

1845

CHARLES KINGSLEY: *From* Alton Locke[8]
[*A London Slum*]

It was a foul, chilly, foggy Saturday night. From the butchers' and greengrocers' shops the gaslights flared and flickered, wild and ghastly, over haggard groups of slipshod dirty women, bargaining for scraps of stale meat and frostbitten vegetables, wrangling about short weight and bad quality. Fish stalls and fruit stalls lined the edge of the greasy pavement, sending up odors as foul as the language of sellers and buyers. Blood and sewer water crawled from under doors and out of spouts, and reeked down the gutters among offal, animal and vegetable, in every stage of putrefaction. Foul vapors rose from cow sheds and slaughterhouses, and the doorways of undrained alleys, where the inhabitants carried the filth out on

8. From Chapter VIII of *Alton Locke*, a novel by Charles Kingsley (1819–75). Under the influence of Carlyle's writings and also as a result of his own observations, Kingsley, a clergy- man, became deeply concerned with the sufferings of the working classes. The speaker here is a young tailor who is accompanied by an elderly Scottish bookseller, Sandy Mackaye.

their shoes from the backyard into the court, and from the court up into the main street; while above, hanging like cliffs over the streets—those narrow, brawling torrents of filth, and poverty, and sin—the houses with their teeming load of life were piled up into the dingy, choking night. A ghastly, deafening, sickening sight it was. Go, scented Belgravian![9] and see what London is! and then go to the library which God has given thee—one often fears in vain—and see what science says this London might be! * * *

We went on through a back street or two, and then into a huge, miserable house, which, a hundred years ago, perhaps, had witnessed the luxury, and rung to the laughter of some one great fashionable family, alone there in their glory. Now every room of it held its family, or its group of families—a phalanstery[1] of all the fiends—its grand staircase, with the carved balustrades rotting and crumbling away piecemeal, converted into a common sewer for all its inmates. Up stair after stair we went, while wails of children, and curses of men, steamed out upon the hot stifling rush of air from every doorway, till, at the topmost story, we knocked at a garret door. We entered. Bare it was of furniture, comfortless, and freezing cold; but, with the exception of the plaster dropping from the roof, and the broken windows, patched with rags and paper, there was a scrupulous neatness about the whole, which contrasted strangely with the filth and slovenliness outside. There was no bed in the room—no table. On a broken chair by the chimney sat a miserable old woman, fancying that she was warming her hands over embers which had long been cold, shaking her head, and muttering to herself, with palsied lips, about the guardians and the workhouse; while upon a few rags on the floor lay a girl, ugly, small-pox-marked, hollow-eyed, emaciated, her only bedclothes the skirt of a large handsome new riding habit, at which two other girls, wan and tawdry, were stitching busily, as they sat right and left of her on the floor. The old woman took no notice of us as we entered; but one of the girls looked up, and, with a pleased gesture of recognition, put her finger up to her lips, and whispered, "Ellen's asleep."

"I'm not asleep, dears," answered a faint unearthly voice; "I was only praying. Is that Mr. Mackaye?"

"Aye, my lassies; but ha' ye gotten na fire the nicht?"

"No," said one of them, bitterly, "we've earned no fire tonight, by fair trade or foul either."

1850

9. Inhabitant of Belgravia, a wealthy residential district of London.
1. A kind of model housing develop-

ment proposed by the French socialist François Fourier (1772–1830).

CHARLES DICKENS: *From* Hard Times[2]
[*Coketown*]

It was a town of red brick, or of brick that would have been red
if the smoke and ashes had allowed it; but as matters stood it was a
town of unnatural red and black like the painted face of a savage. It
was a town of machinery and tall chimneys, out of which interminable serpents of smoke trailed themselves forever and ever, and
never got uncoiled. It had a black canal in it, and a river that ran
purple with ill-smelling dye, and vast piles of buildings full of windows where there was a rattling and a trembling all day long, and
where the piston of the steam engine worked monotonously up and
down like the head of an elephant in a state of melancholy madness. It contained several large streets all very like one another, and
many small streets still more like one another, inhabited by people
equally like one another, who all went in and out at the same
hours, with the same sound upon the same pavements, to do the
same work, and to whom every day was the same as yesterday and
tomorrow, and every year the counterpart of the last and the next.

These attributes of Coketown were in the main inseparable from
the work by which it was sustained; against them were to be set off,
comforts of life which found their way all over the world, and ele-
gancies of life which made, we will not ask how much of the fine
lady, who could scarcely bear to hear the place mentioned. The rest
of its features were voluntary, and they were these.

You saw nothing in Coketown but what was severely workful. If
the members of a religious persuasion built a chapel there—as the
members of eighteen religious persuasions had done—they made it
a pious warehouse of red brick, with sometimes (but this is only in
highly ornamented examples) a bell in a birdcage on the top of it.
The solitary exception was the New Church; a stuccoed edifice with
a square steeple over the door terminating in four short pinnacles
like florid wooden legs. All the public inscriptions in the town were
painted alike, in severe characters of black and white. The jail
might have been the infirmary, the infirmary might have been the
jail, the town hall might have been either, or both, or anything else,
for anything that appeared to the contrary in the graces of their
construction. Fact, fact, fact, everywhere in the material aspect of
the town; fact, fact, fact, everywhere in the immaterial. The
M'Choakumchild school was all fact, and the school of design was
all fact, and the relations between master and man were all fact,
and everything was fact between the lying-in hospital and the cemetery, and what you couldn't state in figures, or show to be purchasa-

---

2. From Chapter V of *Hard Times*, a
novel by Charles Dickens (1812–70).
The picture of Coketown was based on
Dickens's impressions of the raw industrial towns of central and northern England such as Manchester and,
in particular, Preston, a cotton-manu-
facturing center in Lancashire.

ble in the cheapest market and salable in the dearest, was not, and
never should be, world without end, Amen.

1854

HERBERT SPENCER: *From* Social Statics[1]
[*Progress Through Individual Enterprise*]

* * * Under the natural order of things, the unfolding of an
intelligent, self-helping character, must keep pace with the amelioration of physical circumstances—the advance of the one with
the exertions put forth to achieve the other; so that in establishing
arrangements conducive to robustness of body, robustness of mind
must be insensibly acquired. Contrariwise, to whatever extent activity of thought and firmness of purpose are made less needful by an
artificial performance of their work, to that same extent must their
increase, and the dependent social improvements be retarded.

Should proof of this be asked for, it may be found in the contrast
between English energy and Continental helplessness. English engineers (Manby, Wilson, and Co.) established the first gasworks in
Paris, after the failure of a French company;[2] and many of the gasworks throughout Europe have been constructed by Englishmen.
An English engineer (Miller) introduced steam navigation on the
Rhône; another English engineer (Pritchard) succeeded in ascending the Danube by steam, after the French and Germans had failed.
The first steamboats on the Loire were built by Englishmen (Faw-
cett and Preston); the great suspension bridge at Pesth[3] has been
built by an Englishman (Tierney Clarke); and an Englishman
(Vignolles) is now building a still greater suspension bridge over
the Dnieper; many continental railways have had Englishmen as
consulting engineers; and in spite of the celebrated Mining College
at Freyburg, several of the mineral fields along the Rhine have
been opened up by English capital employing English skill. Now
why is this? Why were our coaches so superior to the diligences and
eilwagen[4] of our neighbours? Why did our railway system develop
so much faster? Why are our towns better drained, better paved,
and better supplied with water? There was originally no greater
mechanical aptitude, and no greater desire to progress in us than
in the connate nations of northern Europe. If anything, we were
comparatively deficient in these respects. Early improvements in
the arts of life were imported. The germs of our silk and woolen

1. From Chapter XXVIII. Herbert
Spencer (1820–1903) was a philosopher
and sociologist.
2. A demonstration of the commercial
possibilities of gas for lighting was
first made by a Frenchman, Philippe
Lebon (1767–1804), but it was in
England that his discoveries were first
exploited successfully. By 1812 a gas
company was chartered in London, and
miles of pipes were soon laid down.
English companies thereafter were frequently employed to install gas lines
and fixtures in Europe and in America.
3. In Hungary.
4. Stage coaches.

manufactures came from abroad. The first waterworks in London were erected by a Dutchman. How happens it, then, that we have now reversed the relationship? How happens it, that instead of being dependent on continental skill and enterprise, our skill and enterprise are at a premuim on the Continent? Manifestly the change is due to difference of discipline. Having been left in a greater degree than others to manage their own affairs, the English people have become self-helping, and have acquired great practical ability. Whilst conversely that comparative helplessness of the paternally-governed nations of Europe, illustrated in the above facts, and commented upon by Laing, in his *Notes of a Traveler*, and by other observers, is a natural result of the state-superintendence policy—is the reaction attendant on the action of official mechanisms —is the atrophy corresponding to some artificial hypertrophy.

1850

THE WOMAN QUESTION

"The greatest social difficulty in England today is the relationship between men and women. The principal difference between ourselves and our ancestors is that they took society as they found it while we are self-conscious and perplexed. The institution of marriage might almost seem just now to be upon trial." This assertion by Justin M'Carthy (1830–1912), appearing in an essay on novels in the *Westminster Review* (July, 1864), could be further extended, for on trial throughout the Victorian period was not only the institution of marriage but the family itself, and, most particularly, the traditional roles of women as wives, mothers, and daughters. "The Woman Question," as it was called, was no less prominent an issue for debate than evolution or industrialism.

As indicated in a section of the introduction, "The Role of Women in Victorian Life and Literature," the Woman Question was not one but many. The mixed opinions of Queen Victoria herself make an interesting illustration of some of its different aspects. Believing in education for her sex, she gave support and encouragement to the founding of a college for women in 1847. On the other hand, she opposed the movement to give women the right to vote, which she described in a letter as "this mad folly." But most interesting, for our purposes, is another letter in which she comments on women and marriage. In 1858, writing to her recently married daughter, Victoria remarks: "There is great happiness * * * in devoting oneself to another who is worthy of one's affection; still, men are very selfish and the woman's devotion is always one of submission which makes our poor sex so very unenviable. This you will feel hereafter—I know; though it cannot be otherwise as God has willed it so."

Many of the queen's female subjects shared her assumptions that woman's role was to be accepted as divinely willed—as illustrated in our selections from Mrs. Ellis's popular guidebook, *The Women of England*

(1839). The required "submission" of which the queen wrote was justified
in many quarters on the grounds of the supposed intellectual inferiority of
women. As popularly accepted lore expressed it: "Average Weight of
Man's Brain 3½ lbs; Woman's 2 lbs, 11 ozs." In such quarters it would
follow that a woman who tried to cultivate her intellect beyond drawing-
room accomplishments was violating the order of Nature and of religious
tradition. Woman was to be valued, instead, for other qualities considered
to be especially characteristic of her sex: tenderness of understanding,
unworldliness and innocence, domestic affection, and, in various degrees,
submissiveness. Another early Victorian guidebook, *The Female Instructor*,
in reminding wives of their dependent roles, recommended always wearing
one's wedding ring so that whenever a wife felt "ruffled" she might "cast
your eyes upon it, and call to mind who gave it you." Indeed, as George
Eliot maintained in her essay on Mary Wollstonecraft, the exalted pedestal
on which women had been placed by men was one of the principal obstacles to their achieving any change of status.

It is commonly said that, as a result, Victorian women, married or
unmarried, suffered painfully from boredom. The experiences of Caroline
Helstone in Charlotte Brontë's *Shirley* (1849) would illustrate. Living in
the home of her uncle, a clergyman, she finds no outlet for her energies,
and her boredom becomes so intense that she longs for death—a situation
repeated, 70 years later, in D. H. Lawrence's story of a clergyman's daughter, *The Virgin and the Gipsy*. A reviewer of *Shirley* commented:

> The author is very bitter against *men* * * * she speaks as one outraged
> and aggrieved by their contemptuous treatment of her sex. We discern
> symptoms of a bitterness * * * almost a fierceness—for which there is
> probably some good cause. But there are few women of strong powers of
> mind, such as the author of this book unquestionably is, who do not feel
> that the social position of women is not at all what it should be, and
> hence she speaks in her angry and indignant tone.

Yet generalizations about bored Victorian females need to be severely
qualified. In the same year *Shirley* appeared, Harriet Martineau noted that
"nineteen-twentieths of the women in England earn their bread." Although
the millions of women employed as domestics, or as seamstresses, or factory
workers, or farm laborers, had many problems, excessive leisure was not one
of them. To be bored was the privilege of wives and daughters in upper
and middle-class families in which feminine idleness was treasured as a
status symbol. It was only among this small and important segment of the
population, as the novelist Dinah Maria Mulock emphasizes, that there was
"nothing to do" for these comfortably well-off wives and daughters,
because in such households the servants ran everything, even taking over
the principal role in the rearing of children. Another group in which frusta-
tion was common consisted of women from the same classes whose families
had lost their fortunes, thereby obliging their daughters to seek employment as governesses. Charlotte Brontë's governess-heroine, Jane Eyre,
reflecting that among both men and women, "millions are in silent revolt
against their lot" adds:

> Women are supposed to be very calm generally: but women feel just as
> men feel; they need exercise for their faculties and a field for their efforts
> as much as their brothers do; they suffer from too rigid a restraint, too

absolute a stagnation, precisely as men would suffer; and it is narrow-minded in their more privileged fellow-creatures to say that they ought to confine themselves to making puddings and knitting stockings, to playing on the piano and embroidering bags. It is thoughtless to condemn them, or laugh at them, if they seek to do more or learn more than custom has pronounced necessary for their sex.

George Meredith, in his *Essay on Comedy* (1873), develops the same argu-ment; the test of a civilization, he writes, is whether men "consent to talk on equal terms with their women, and to listen to them." Yet at least two reviewers of *Jane Eyre*, both women, regarded such proposals as virtually seditious. Margaret Oliphant called the novel "a wild declaration of the 'Rights of Women' in a new aspect." And Elizabeth Rigby attacked its "pervading tone of ungodly discontent."

In some households such discontent, whether godly or ungodly, led to a daughter's open rebellion. A remarkable instance was Florence Nightin-gale, who found family life in the 1850's intolerably pointless, and, despite parental opposition, cut loose from home to carve out a career for herself in nursing and hospital administration.

According to Sir Walter Besant, similar drives for independence pro-duced an extraordinary change in the status of women during the late Vic-torian period, opening up for them a wide variety of professional opportuni-ties. Many women became successful novelists. Inevitably some of them were hacks, of whom George Eliot made fun in her essay *Silly Novels by Lady Novelists* (1855), but others such as the Brontë sisters were major artists, and Eliot herself was one of the great novelists of the language.

Eliot's judicious essay on the Women Question, inspired by her rereading of Mary Wollstonecraft, is included in our selections. It should be noted, however, that it was not only as an essayist but as a novelist that the Woman Question engaged her attention, as in her highly complex portrait of the frustrations of Maggie Tulliver, the bookish early-Victorian heroine of *The Mill on the Floss*. And her portraits of women were not restricted to the frustrated and discontented. As a realist Eliot recognized that many upper- and middle-class women apparently found their leisurely lives fully enjoyable. In *Middlemarch*, for example, she portrays one of these in Celia Brooke Chetham, who rejoices in her comfortable life as wife and mother on a country estate. Her sister Dorothea, however (whom Celia regards with affectionate indulgence as an eccentric misfit) finds the traditional womanly dispensation as painfully frustrating as Florence Nightingale had found it. And it was on behalf of such women as Dorothea that Mill devel-oped his argument in *The Subjection of Women* (1869), a classic essay (included above) that should be read in conjunction with the following selections.

SARAH STICKNEY ELLIS: *From* The Women of
England: Their Social Duties and Domestic Habits[1]

[Disinterested Kindness]

To men belongs the potent—(I had almost said the *omnipotent*)
consideration of worldly aggrandizement; and it is constantly misleading their steps, closing their ears against the voice of conscience,
and beguiling them with the promise of peace, where peace was
never found. * * * How often has man returned to his home with a
mind confused by the many voices, which in the mart, the
exchange, or the public assembly, have addressed themselves to his
inborn selfishness, or his worldly pride; and while his integrity was
shaken, and his resolution gave way beneath the pressure of apparent necessity, or the insidious pretenses of expediency, he has stood
corrected before the clear eye of woman, as it looked directly to the
naked truth, and detected the lurking evil of the specious act he
was about to commit. Nay, so potent may have become this secret
influence, that he may have borne it about with him like a kind of
second conscience, for mental reference, and spiritual counsel, in
moments of trial; and when the snares of the world were around
him, and temptations from within and without have bribed over the
witness in his own bosom, he has thought of the humble monitress
who sat alone, guarding the fireside comforts of his distant home;
and the remembrance of her character, clothed in moral beauty, has
scattered the clouds before his mental vision, and sent him back to
that beloved home, a wiser and a better man.

The women of England, possessing the grand privilege of being
better instructed than those of any other country, in the minutiae
of domestic comfort, have obtained a degree of importance in
society far beyond what their unobtrusive virtues would appear to
claim. The long-established customs of their country have placed in
their hands the high and holy duty of cherishing and protecting the
minor morals of life, from whence springs all that is elevated in purpose, and glorious in action. The sphere of their direct personal
influence is central, and consequently small; but its extreme operations are as widely extended as the range of human feeling. They
may be less striking in society than some of the women of other
countries, and may feel themselves, on brilliant and stirring occasions, as simple, rude, and unsophisticated in the popular science of

---

1. Sarah Stickney (died 1872), an
essayist, married in 1837 William Ellis,
a missionary, and worked with him for
the temperance movement and other
Evangelical causes. Mrs. Ellis's book
on women's education and domestic
roles (1839) became a best seller and
went through 16 editions in two years.
In the 1840's she founded a school for
girls which sought to inculcate her
theories that feminine education should
cultivate what she called "the heart"
rather than the intellectual faculties of
her pupils.

excitement; but as far as the noble daring of Britain has sent forth her adventurous sons, and that is to every point of danger on the habitable globe, they have borne along with them a generosity, a disinterestedness, and a moral courage, derived in no small measure from the female influence of their native country.

It is a fact well worthy of our most serious attention, and one which bears immediately upon the subject under consideration, that the present state of our national affairs is such as to indicate that the influence of woman in counteracting the growing evils of society is about to be more needed than ever.

* * *

In order to ascertain what kind of education is most effective in making woman what she ought to be, the best method is to inquire into the character, station, and peculiar duties of woman throughout the largest portion of her earthly career; and then ask, for what she is most valued, admired, and beloved?

In answer to this, I have little hesitation in saying—for her disinterested kindness. Look at all the heroines, whether of romance or reality—at all the female characters that are held up to universal admiration—at all who have gone down to honored graves, amongst the tears and lamentations of their survivors. Have these been the learned, the accomplished women; the women who could solve problems, and elucidate systems of philosophy? No: or if they have, they have also been women who were dignified with the majesty of moral greatness. * * *

Let us single out from any particular seminary a child who has been there from the years of ten to fifteen, and reckon, if it can be reckoned, the pains that have been spent in making that child proficient in Latin. Have the same pains been spent in making her disinterestedly kind? And yet what man is there in existence who would not rather his wife should be free from selfishness, than be able to read Virgil without the use of a dictionary? * * * I still cling fondly to the hope that some system of female instruction will be discovered, by which the young women of England may be sent from school to the homes of their parents, habituated to be on the watch for every opportunity of doing good to others; making it the first and the last inquiry of every day, "What can I do to make my parents, my brothers, or my sisters, more happy? I am but a feeble instrument in the hands of Providence, but as He will give me strength, I hope to pursue the plan to which I have been accustomed, of seeking my own happiness only in the happiness of others."

1839

GEORGE ELIOT: Margaret Fuller and Mary Wollstonecraft[1]

The death of new books just now gives us time to recur to less recent ones which we have hitherto noticed but slightly; and among these we choose the late edition of Margaret Fuller's *Woman in the Nineteenth Century*, because we think it has been unduly thrust into the background by less comprehensive and candid productions on the same subject. Notwithstanding certain defects of taste and a sort of vague spiritualism and grandiloquence which belong to all but the very best American writers, the book is a valuable one; it has the enthusiasm of a noble and sympathetic nature, with the moderation and breadth and large allowance of a vigorous and culti- vated understanding. There is no exaggeration of woman's moral excellence or intellectual capabilities; no injudicious insistence on her fitness for this or that function hitherto engrossed by men; but a calm plea for the removal of unjust laws and artificial restrictions, so that the possibilities of her nature may have room for full devel- opment, a wisely stated demand to disencumber her of the

> Parasitic forms
> That seem to keep her up, but drag her down—
> And leave her field to burgeon and to bloom
> From all within her, make herself her own
> To give or keep, to live and learn and be
> All that not harms distinctive womanhood.[2]

It is interesting to compare this essay of Margaret Fuller's pub-

1. Before beginning her career as a novelist, George Eliot (1819–80; her real name was Marian Evans) contrib- uted essays to the *Westminster Review*, a learned journal at one time edited by John Stuart Mill. Eliot's brilliant mind and breadth of knowledge led to her appointment as assistant editor after she settled in London in 1851. The pres- ent essay was published in another journal, *The Leader*, in October, 1855. It is a retrospective book-review essay on two important feminist publications —Mary Wollstonecraft's *A Vindication of the Rights of Woman* (1792; see above) and *Woman in the Nineteenth Century* (1855; published originally as *The Great Lawsuit*, 1843), by Mar- garet Fuller (1810–50), an American essayist and editor whom Eliot warmly admired.

As Barbara Hardy notes, despite "her generous sympathy with Victorian feminism," George Eliot "played no active part in the movement." Eliot seems to have shared the view of women's relation to men expressed by the Prince in Tennyson's *Princess*, whose speeches she cites in this essay. As she herself wrote in 1854, in another essay, *Women in France*: "Women became superior in France by being admitted to a common fund of ideas, to common objects of interest with men; and this must ever be the essential condition at once of true womanly culture and of true social well-being. * * * Let the whole field of reality be laid open to woman as well as to man, and then that which is pecu- liar in the mental modification, instead of being, as it is now, a source of dis- cord and repulsion between the sexes, will be found to be a necessary comple- ment to the truth and beauty of life."
2. Tennyson, *The Princess* VII.253–58. As noted by Thomas Pinney, the quota- tion, slightly inaccurate, is from the un- revised 1847 text of the poem.

lished in its earliest form in 1843,[3] with a work on the position of woman, written between sixty and seventy years ago—we mean Mary Wollstonecraft's *Rights of Woman*. The latter work was not continued beyond the first volume; but so far as this carries the subject, the comparison, at least in relation to strong sense and loftiness of moral tone, is not at all disadvantageous to the woman of the last century. There is in some quarters a vague prejudice against the *Rights of Woman* as in some way or other a reprehensible book, but readers who go to it with this impression will be surprised to find it eminently serious, severely moral, and withal rather heavy —the true reason, perhaps, that no edition has been published since 1796, and that it is now rather scarce. There are several points of resemblance, as well as of striking difference, between the two books. A strong understanding is present in both; but Margaret Fuller's mind was like some regions of her own American continent, where you are constantly stepping from the sunny "clearings" into the mysterious twilight of the tangled forest—she often passes in one breath from forcible reasoning to dreamy vagueness; moreover, her unusually varied culture gives her great command of illustration. Mary Wollstonecraft, on the other hand, is nothing if not rational; she has no erudition, and her grave pages are lit up by no ray of fancy. In both writers we discern, under the brave bearing of a strong and truthful nature, the beating of a loving woman's heart, which teaches them not to undervalue the smallest offices of domestic care or kindliness. But Margaret Fuller, with all her passionate sensibility, is more of the literary woman, who would not have been satisfied without intellectual production; Mary Wollstonecraft, we imagine, wrote not at all for writing's sake, but from the pressure of other motives. So far as the difference of date allows, there is a striking coincidence in their trains of thought; indeed, every important idea in the *Rights of Woman*, except the combination of home education with a common day-school for boys and girls, reappears in Margaret Fuller's essay.

One point on which they both write forcibly is the fact that, while men have a horror of such faculty or culture in the other sex as tends to place it on a level with their own, they are really in a state of subjection to ignorant and feeble-minded women. Margaret Fuller says:

> Wherever man is sufficiently raised above extreme poverty or brutal stupidity, to care for the comforts of the fireside, or the bloom and ornament of life, woman has always power enough, if she chooses to exert it, and is usually disposed to do so, in proportion to her ignorance and childish vanity. Unacquainted with the importance of life and its purposes, trained to a selfish coquetry

---

3. Original version published in *The Dial*; revised and expanded in 1855.

and love of petty power, she does not look beyond the pleasure of making herself felt at the moment, and governments are shaken and commerce broken up to gratify the pique of a female favorite. The English shopkeeper's wife does not vote, but it is for her interest that the politician canvasses by the coarsest flattery.

Again:

All wives, bad or good, loved or unloved, inevitably influence their husbands from the power their position not merely gives, but necessitates of coloring evidence and infusing feelings in hours when the—patient, shall I call him?—is off his guard.

Hear now what Mary Wollstonecraft says on the same subject:

Women have been allowed to remain in ignorance and slavish dependence many, very many years, and still we hear of nothing but their fondness of pleasure and sway, their preference of rakes and soldiers, their childish attachment to toys, and the vanity that makes them value accomplishments more than virtues. History brings forward a fearful catalogue of the crimes which their cunning has produced, when the weak slaves have had sufficient address to overreach their masters. . . . When, therefore, I call women slaves, I mean in a political and civil sense; for indirectly they obtain too much power, and are debased by their exertions to obtain illicit sway. . . . The libertinism, and even the virtues of superior men, will always give women of some description great power over them; and these weak women, under the influence of childish passions and selfish vanity, *will throw a false light over the objects which the very men view with their eyes who ought to enlighten their judgment.* Men of fancy, and those sanguine characters who mostly hold the helm of human affairs in general, relax in the society of women; and surely I need not cite to the most superficial reader of history the numerous examples of vice and oppression which the private intrigues of female favorites have produced; not to dwell on the mischief that naturally arises from the blundering interposition of well-meaning folly. *For in the transactions of business it is much better to have to deal with a knave than a fool, because a knave adheres to some plan, and any plan of reason may be seen through sooner than a sudden flight of folly.* The power which vile and foolish women have had over wise men who possessed sensibility is notorious.

There is a notion commonly entertained among men that an instructed woman, capable of having opinions, is likely to prove an unpracticable yoke-fellow, always pulling one way when her husband wants to go the other, oracular in tone, and prone to give curtain lectures[4] on metaphysics. But surely, so far as obstinacy is con-

---

4. See Douglas Jerrold's comic sketches of a wife who delivers nightly lectures to her husband from behind their bed-cur-tains, *Mrs. Caudle's Curtain Lectures* (1846).

cerned, your unreasoning animal is the most unmanageable of creatures, where you are not allowed to settle the question by a cudgel,
a whip and bridle, or even a string to the leg. For our own parts, we
see no consistent or commodious medium between the old plan of
corporal discipline and that thorough education of women which
will make them rational beings in the highest sense of the word.
Wherever weakness is not harshly controlled it must *govern*, as you
may see when a strong man holds a little child by the hand, how he
is pulled hither and thither, and wearied in his walk by his submission to the whims and feeble movements of his companion. A really
cultured woman, like a really cultured man, will be ready to yield in
trifles. So far as we see, there is no indissoluble connection between
infirmity of logic and infirmity of will, and a woman quite innocent
of an opinion in philosophy, is as likely as not to have an indomitable opinion about the kitchen. As to airs of superiority, no woman
ever had them in consequence of true culture, but only because her
culture was shallow or unreal, only as a result of what Mrs. Malaprop well calls "the ineffectual qualities in a woman"[5]—mere
acquisitions carried about, and not knowledge thoroughly assimilated so as to enter into the growth of the character.

To return to Margaret Fuller, some of the best things she says are
on the folly of absolute definitions of woman's nature and absolute
demarcations of woman's mission. "Nature," she says, "seems to
delight in varying the arrangements, as if to show that she will be
fettered by no rule; and we must admit the same varieties that she
admits." Again: "If nature is never bound down, nor the voice of
inspiration stifled, that is enough. We are pleased that women
should write and speak, if they feel need of it, from having something to tell; but silence for ages would be no misfortune, if that
silence be from divine command, and not from man's tradition."
And here is a passage, the beginning of which has been often
quoted:

> If you ask me what offices they [women] may fill, I reply—
> any. I do not care what case you put; let them be sea-captains if
> you will. I do not doubt there are women well fitted for such an
> office, and, if so, I should be as glad as to welcome the Maid of
> Saragossa, or the Maid of Missolonghi, or the Suliote heroine, or
> Emily Plater.[6] I think women need, especially at this juncture, a

5. In response to compliments about her
"intellectual accomplishments," Mrs.
Malaprop exclaims: "Ah! few gentlemen, nowadays, know how to value the
ineffectual qualities in a woman!" See *The
Rivals* III.ii (1775), by Richard Brinsley
Sheridan.
6. The Maid of Saragossa was Maria
Agustin, who fought against the French
at the seige of Saragossa, in Spain, in
1808 (see Byron's *Childe Harold's Pil-

grimage I.liv–lvi); the Maid of Missolonghi, an unidentified Greek, must have
made some heroic exploit during the
Turkish seiges of that town in 1822 or
1826; the Suliote heroine was probably
Moscha, who led a band of 300 women
to rout the Turks during the seige of
Souli, in Albania, in 1803; Emily Plater,
a Polish patriot, became a captain in
command of a company in the insurgent
army fighting the Russians in 1831.

much greater range of occupation than they have, to rouse their latent powers. . . . In families that I know, some little girls like to saw wood, others to use carpenter's tools. Where these tastes are indulged, cheerfulness and good-humor are promoted. Where they are forbidden, because "such things are not proper for girls," they grow sullen and mischievous. Fourier had observed these wants of women, as no one can fail to do who watches the desires of. little girls, or knows the *ennui* that haunts grown women, except where they make to themselves a serene little world by art of some kind. He, therefore, in proposing a great variety of employments, in manufactures or the care of plants and animals, allows for one-third of women as likely to have a taste for masculine pursuits, one-third of men for feminine.[7] . . . I have no doubt, however, that a large proportion of women would give themselves to the same employments as now, because there are circumstances that must lead them. Mothers will delight to make the nest soft and warm. Nature would take care of that; no need to clip the wings of any bird that wants to soar and sing, or finds in itself the strength of pinion for a migratory flight unusual to its kind. The difference would be that *all* need not be constrained to employments for which *some* are unfit.

Apropos of the same subject, we find Mary Wollstonecraft offering a suggestion which the women of the United States have already begun to carry out. She says:

Women, in particular, all want to be ladies, which is simply to have nothing to do, but listlessly to go they scarcely care where, for they cannot tell what. But what have women to do in society? I may be asked, but to loiter with easy grace; surely you would not condemn them all to suckle fools and chronicle small beer.[8] No. *Women might certainly study the art of healing, and be physicians as well as nurses.* . . . Business of various kinds they might likewise pursue, if they were educated in a more orderly manner. . . . Women would not then marry for a support, as men accept of places under government, and neglect the implied duties.

Men pay a heavy price for their reluctance to encourage self-help and independent resources in women. The precious meridian years of many a man of genius have to be spent in the toil of routine, that an "establishment" may be kept up for a woman who can understand none of his secret yearnings,[9] who is fit for nothing but to sit in her drawing-room like a doll-Madonna in her shrine. No matter. Anything is more endurable than to change our established formulae about women, or to run the risk of looking up to our wives instead of looking down on them. *Sit divus, dummodo non sit vivus*

7. Charles Fourier (1772–1837), in his utopian treatise *The New Industrial World* (1829–30), develops these theories in his discussion of "The Little Hordes."
8. Iago on the role of women (*Othello* II.i.160).
9. Cf. Eliot's fictional representation of such a situation in her account of Dr. Lydgate's married life in *Middlemarch*.

(let him be a god, provided he be not living), said the Roman magnates of Romulus;[1] and so men say of women, let them be idols,
useless absorbents of previous things, provided we are not obliged to
admit them to be strictly fellow-beings, to be treated, one and all,
with justice and sober reverence.

On one side we hear that woman's position can never be
improved until women themselves are better; and, on the other,
that women can never become better until their position is
improved—until the laws are made more just, and a wider field
opened to feminine activity. But we constantly hear the same
difficulty stated about the human race in general. There is a perpetual action and reaction between individuals and institutions; we
must try and mend both by little and little—the only way in which
human things can be mended. Unfortunately, many over-zealous
champions of women assert their actual equality with men—nay,
even their moral superiority to men—as a ground for their release
from oppressive laws and restrictions. They lose strength immensely
by this false position. If it were true, then there would be a case in
which slavery and ignorance nourished virtue, and so far we should
have an argument for the continuance of bondage. But we want
freedom and culture for woman, because subjection and ignorance
have debased her, and with her, Man; for—

> If she be small, slight-natured, miserable,
> How shall men grow?[2]

Both Margaret Fuller and Mary Wollstonecraft have too much
sagacity to fall into this sentimental exaggeration. Their ardent
hopes of what women may become do not prevent them from
seeing and painting women as they are. On the relative moral
excellence of men and women Mary Wollstonecraft speaks with the
most decision:

> Women are supposed to possess more sensibility, and even
> humanity, than men, and their strong attachments and instanta-
> neous emotions of compassion are given as proofs; but the clinging
> affection of ignorance has seldom anything noble in it, and may
> mostly be resolved into selfishness, as well as the affection of chil-
> dren and brutes. I have known many weak women whose sensibil-
> ity was entirely engrossed by their husbands; and as for their
> humanity, it was very faint indeed, or rather it was only a tran-
> sient emotion of compassion. Humanity does not consist "in a
> squeamish ear," says an eminent orator.[3] "It belongs to the mind
> as well as to the nerves." But this kind of exclusive affection,
> though it degrades the individual, should not be brought forward

---

1. Cf. *Historia Augusta*, "Geta" II, in
which the same cynical comment is
made on a proposal to have a man deified.

2. Tennyson, *The Princess* VII.249–50.
3. Unidentified, perhaps Edmund Burke
(1729–97).

as a proof of the inferiority of the sex, because it is the natural consequence of confined views; for even women of superior sense, having their attention turned to little employments and private plans, rarely rise to heroism, unless when spurred on by love! and love, as an heroic passion, like genius, appears but once in an age. I therefore agree with the moralist who asserts "that women have seldom so much generosity as men"; and that their narrow affections, to which justice and humanity are often sacrificed, render the sex apparently inferior, especially as they are commonly inspired by men; but I contend that the heart would expand as the understanding gained strength, if women were not depressed from their cradles.

We had marked several other passages of Margaret Fuller's for extract, but as we do not aim at an exhaustive treatment of our subject, and are only touching a few of its points, we have, perhaps, already claimed as much of the reader's attention as he will be willing to give to such desultory material.

1855

DINAH MARIA MULOCK: *From* A Woman's Thoughts About Women[1]

[Something to Do]

Man and woman were made for, and not like one another. Only one "right" we have to assert in common with mankind—and that is as much in our hands as theirs—the right of having something to do. * * * But how few parents ever consider this? Tom, Dick, and Harry, aforesaid, leave school and plunge into life; "the girls" likewise finish their education, come home, and stay at home. That is enough. Nobody thinks it needful to waste a care upon them. Bless them, pretty dears, how sweet they are! papa's nosegay of beauty to adorn his drawing-room. He delights to give them all they can desire—clothes, amusements, society; he and mamma together take every domestic care off their hands; they have abundance of time and nothing to occupy it; plenty of money, and little use for it; pleasure without end, but not one definite object of interest or employment; flattery and flummery enough, but no solid food whatever to satisfy mind or heart—if they happen to possess either—at the very emptiest and most craving season of both. They have literally nothing whatever to do. * * *

And so their whole energies are devoted to the massacre of old Time. They prick him to death with crochet and embroidery nee-

1. In 1857, a year earlier than her book on women, Dinah Mulock (1826–87) had published her best-known novel, a Victorian best-seller, *John Halifax, Gentleman*. In 1864 she married George Craik.

dles; strum him deaf with piano and harp playing—*not* music; cut him up with morning visitors, or leave his carcass in ten-minute parcels at every "friend's" house they can think of. Finally, they dance him defunct at all sort of unnatural hours; and then, rejoicing in the excellent excuse, smother him in sleep for a third of the following day. Thus he dies, a slow, inoffensive, perfectly natural death; and they will never recognize his murder till, on the confines of this world, or from the unknown shores of the next, the question meets them: "What have you done with Time?"—Time, the only mortal gift bestowed equally on every living soul, and excepting the soul, the only mortal loss which is totally irretrievable. * * *

But "what am I to do with my life?" as once asked me one girl out of the numbers who begin to feel aware that, whether marrying or not, each possesses an individual life, to spend, to use, or to lose. And herein lies the momentous question. A definite answer to this question is simply impossible. Generally—and this is the best and safest guide—she will find her work lying very near at hand: some desultory tastes to condense into regular studies, some faulty household quietly to remodel, some child to teach, or parent to watch over. All these being needless or unattainable, she may extend her service out of the home into the world, which perhaps never at any time so much needed the help of us women. And hardly one of its charities and duties can be done so thoroughly as by a wise and tender woman's hand.

These are they who are little spoken of in the world at large. * * * They have made for themselves a place in the world: the harsh, practical, yet not ill-meaning world, where all find their level soon or late, and where a frivolous young maid sunk into a helpless old one, can no more expect to keep her pristine position than a last year's leaf to flutter upon a spring bough. But an old maid who deserves well of this same world, by her ceaseless work therein, having won her position, keeps it to the end.

Not an ill position either, or unkindly; often higher and more honorable than that of many a mother of ten sons. In households, where "Auntie" is the universal referee, nurse, playmate, comforter, and counselor: in society, where "that nice Miss So-and-so," though neither clever, handsome, nor young, is yet such a person as can neither be omitted nor overlooked: in charitable works, where she is "such a practical body—always knows exactly what to do, and how to do it": or perhaps, in her own house, solitary indeed, as every single woman's home must be, yet neither dull nor unhappy in itself, and the nucleus of cheerfulness and happiness to many another home besides.

Published or unpublished, this woman's life is a goodly chronicle, the title page of which you may read in her quiet countenance; her manner, settled, cheerful, and at ease; her unfailing interest in all things and all people. You will rarely find she thinks much about herself; she has never had time for it. And this her life-chronicle, which, out of its very fullness, has taught her that the more one does, the more one finds to do—she will never flourish in your face, or the face of Heaven, as something uncommonly virtuous and extraordinary. She knows that, after all, she has simply done what it was her duty to do.

But—and when her place is vacant on earth, this will be said of her assuredly, both here and Otherwhere—"*She hath done what she could.*"

1858

FLORENCE NIGHTINGALE: *From* Cassandra[1]

[Nothing to Do]

Why have women passion, intellect, moral activity—these three —and a place in society where no one of the three can be exercised? Men say that God punishes for complaining. No, but men are angry with misery. They are irritated with women for not being happy. They take it as a personal offense. To God alone may women complain without insulting Him! * * *

Is discontent a privilege?

Yes, it is a privilege for you to suffer for your race—a privilege not reserved to the Redeemer, and the martyrs alone, but one enjoyed by numbers in every age.

The commonplace life of thousands; and in that is its only interest—its only merit as a history; viz., that it *is* the type of common sufferings—the story of one who has not the courage to resist nor to submit to the civilization of her time—is this.

Poetry and imagination begin life. A child will fall on its knees on the gravel walk at the sight of a pink hawthorn in full flower, when it is by itself, to praise God for it.

Then comes intellect. It wishes to satisfy the wants which intel-

1. Florence Nightingale (1820–1910) was in 1854 to become world famous for organizing a contingent of nurses to take care of sick and wounded soldiers in the Crimean War, an event that provided an outlet for her passionate desire to change the world of hospital treatments. At the time she was writing *Cassandra*, however, she had not yet been able to realize her aims; at 32 she was still living at home, unmarried (having declined several proposals), with her well-to-do family. Some members of her family, in particular her mother, strongly opposed her nursing ambitions and kept pressure on her to remain at home. In 1852, so bored with family and social life that she had thoughts of suicide, she began writing *Cassandra*, which she called her "family manuscript"; it is a record of her frustrations before she escaped into a professional world where there was "something to do." In 1859 she revised the manuscript and a few copies were privately printed that year, but it was not published until 1928. The title refers to the Trojan princess whose true prophecies went unheeded by those around her.

lect creates for it. But there is a physical, not moral, impossibility of supplying the wants of the intellect in the sate of civilization at which we have arrived. The stimulus, the training, the time, are all three wanting to us; or, in other words, the means and inducements are not there.

Look at the poor lives we lead. It is a wonder that we are so good as we are, not that we are so bad. In looking round we are struck with the power of the organizations we see, not with their want of power. Now and then, it is true, we are conscious that *there* is an inferior organization, but, in general, just the contrary. Mrs A. has the imagination, the poetry of a Murillo,[2] and has sufficient power of execution to show that she might have had a great deal more. Why is she not a Murillo? From a material difficulty, not a mental one. If she has a knife and fork in her hands for three hours of the day, she cannot have a pencil or brush. Dinner is the great sacred ceremony of this day, the great sacrament. To be absent from dinner is equivalent to being ill. Nothing else will excuse us from it. Bodily incapacity is the only apology valid. If she has a pen and ink in her hands during other three hours, writing answers for the penny post, again, she cannot have her pencil, and so *ad infinitum* through life. People have no type before them in their lives, neither fathers nor mothers, nor the children themselves. They look at things in detail. They say, "It is very desirable that A., my daughter, should go to such a party, should know such a lady, should sit by such a person." It is true. But what standard have they before them of the nature and destination of man? The very words are rejected as pedantic. But might they not, at least, have a type in their minds that such an one might be a discoverer through her intellect, such another through her art, a third through her moral power?

Women often try one branch of intellect after another in their youth, e.g., mathematics. But that, least of all, is compatible with the life of "society." It is impossible to follow up anything systematically. Women often long to enter some man's profession where they would find direction, competition (or rather opportunity of measuring the intellect with others) and, above all, time.

In those wise institutions, mixed as they are with many follies, which will last as long as the human race lasts, because they are adapted to the wants of the human race; those institutions which we call monasteries, and which, embracing much that is contrary to the laws of nature, are yet better adapted to the union of the life of action and that of thought than any other mode of life with which we are acquainted; in many such, four and a half hours, at least, are daily set aside for thought, rules are given for thought, training and

2. Bartolomé Murillo (1618–82), Spanish painter.

opportunity afforded. Among us there is *no* time appointed for this purpose, and the difficulty is that, in our social life, we must be always doubtful whether we ought not to be with somebody else or be doing something else.

Are men better off than women in this?

If one calls upon a friend in London and sees her son in the drawing room, it strikes one as odd to find a young man sitting idle in his mother's drawing room in the morning. For men, who are seen much in those haunts, there is no end of the epithets we have: "knights of the carpet," "drawing-room heroes," "ladies' men." But suppose we were to see a number of men in the morning sitting round a table in the drawing-room, looking at prints, doing worsted work, and reading little books, how we should laugh! A member of the House of Commons was once known to do worsted work. Of another man was said, "His only fault is that he is too good; he drives out with his mother every day in the carriage, and if he is asked anywhere he answers that he must dine with his mother, but, if she can spare him, he will come in to tea, and he does not come."

Now, why is it more ridiculous for a man than for a woman to do worsted work and drive out every day in the carriage? Why should we laugh if we were to see a parcel of men sitting round a drawing room table in the morning, and think it all right if they were women?

Is man's time more valuable than woman's? or is the difference between man and woman this, that woman has confessedly nothing to do?

Women are never supposed to have any occupation of sufficient importance *not* to be interrupted, except "suckling their fools";[3] and women themselves have accepted this, have written books to support it, and have trained themselves so as to consider whatever they do as *not* of such value to the world or to others, but that they can throw it up at the first "claim of social life." They have accustomed themselves to consider intellectual occupation as a merely selfish amusement, which it is their "duty" to give up for every trifler more selfish than themselves.

* * *

Women have no means given them, whereby they *can* resist the "claims of social life." They are taught from their infancy upwards that it is a wrong, ill-tempered, and a misunderstanding of "woman's mission" (with a great M) if they do not allow themselves *willingly* to be interrupted at all hours. If a woman has once put in a claim to be treated as a man by some work of science or art

3. See Iago's cynical comments on women's role: "To suckle fools, and chronicle small beer." (*Othello* II.i.160).

or literature, which she can *show* as the "fruit of her leisure," then she will be considered justified in *having* leisure (hardly, perhaps, even then). But if not, not. If she has nothing to show, she must resign herself to her fate.

"I like riding about this beautiful place, why don't you? I like walking about the garden, why don't you?" is the common expostulation—as if we were children, whose spirits rise during a fortnight's holiday, who think that they will last forever—and look neither backwards nor forwards.

Society triumphs over many. They wish to regenerate the world with their institutions, with their moral philosophy, with their love. Then they sink to living from breakfast till dinner, from dinner till tea, with a little worsted work, and to looking forward to nothing but bed.

When shall we see a life full of steady enthusiasm, walking straight to its aim, flying home, as that bird is now, against the wind—with the calmness and the confidence of one who knows the laws of God and can apply them?

* * *

When shall we see a woman making a *study* of what she does? Married women cannot; for a man would think, if his wife undertook any great work with the intention of carrying it out—of making anything but a sham of it—that she would "suckle his fools and chronicle his small beer" less well for it—that he would not have so good a dinner—that she would destroy, as it is called, his domestic life.

The intercourse of man and woman—how frivolous, how unworthy it is! Can we call *that* the true vocation of woman—her high career? Look round at the marriages which you know. The true marriage—that noble union, by which a man and woman become together the one perfect being—probably does not exist at present upon earth.

It is not surprising that husbands and wives seem so little part of one another. It is surprising that there is so much love as there is. For there is no food for it. What does it live upon—what nourishes it? Husbands and wives never seem to have anything to say to one another. What do they talk about? Not about any great religious, social, political questions or feelings. They talk about who shall come to dinner, who is to live in this lodge and who in that, about the improvement of the place, or when they shall go to London. If there are children, they form a common subject of some nourishment. But, even then, the case is oftenest thus—the husband is to think of how they are to get on in life; the wife of bringing them up at home.

But any real communion between husband and wife—any

descending into the depths of their being, and drawing out thence what they find and comparing it—do we ever dream of such a thing? Yes, we may dream of it during the season of "passion," but we shall not find it afterwards. We even expect it to go off, and lay our account that it will. If the husband has, by chance, gone into the depths of *his* being, and found there anything unorthodox, he, oftenest, conceals it carefully from his wife—he is afraid of "unsettling her opinions." * * * For woman is "by birth a Tory"—has often been said—by education a "Tory," we mean.

Women dream till they have no longer the strength to dream; those dreams against which they so struggle, so honestly, vigorously, and conscientiously, and so in vain, yet which are their life, without which they could not have lived; those dreams go at last. All their plans and visions seem vanished, and they know not where; gone, and they cannot recall them. They do not even remember them. And they are left without the food of reality or of hope.

Later in life, they neither desire nor dream, neither of activity, nor of love, nor of intellect. The last often survives the longest. They wish, if their experiences would benefit anybody, to give them to someone. But they never find an hour free in which to collect their thoughts, and so discouragement becomes ever deeper and deeper, and they less and less capable of undertaking anything.

It seems as if the female spirit of the world were mourning everlastingly over blessings, not *lost*, but which she has never had, and which, in her discouragement she feels that she never will have, they are so far off.

The more complete a woman's organization, the more she will feel it, till at last there shall arise a woman, who will resume, in her own soul, all the sufferings of her race, and that women will be the Saviour of her race.

1852–59   1928

WALTER BESANT: *From* The Queen's Reign[1]

[*The Transformation of Women's Status between 1837 and 1897*]

Let me present to you, first, an early Victorian girl, born about the Waterloo year; next, her granddaughter, born about 1875. * * *

The young lady of 1837 * * * cannot reason on any subject whatever because of her ignorance—as she herself would say, because she is a woman. In her presence, and indeed in the presence of ladies generally, men talk trivialities. * * * It has often

1. Walter Besant (1836–1901), literary critic, historian, and novelist. His history, *The Queen's Reign* (1897) celebrated the improvements which he thought had occurred during his lifetime.

been charged against Thackeray[2] that his good women were insipid. Thackeray, like most artists, could only draw the women of his own time, and at that time they were undoubtedly insipid. Men, I suppose, liked them so. To be childishly ignorant; to carry shrinking modesty so far as to find the point of a shoe projecting beyond the folds of a frock indelicate; to confess that serious subjects were beyond a woman's grasp; never even to pretend to form an independent judgment; to know nothing of Art, History, Science, Literature, Politics, Sociology, Manners—men liked these things; women yielded to please the men; her very ignorance formed a subject of laudable pride with the Englishwoman of the Forties. * * * There was something Oriental in the seclusion of women in the home, and their exclusion from active and practical life. * * *

Let us turn to the Englishwoman—the young Englishwoman—of 1897. She is educated. Whatever things are taught to the young man are taught to the young woman. If she wants to explore the wickedness of the world she can do so, for it is all in the books. The secrets of Nature are not closed to her; she can learn the structure of the body if she wishes. At school, at college, she studies just as the young man studies, but harder and with greater concentration. * * * She has invaded the professions. She cannot become a priest, because the Oriental prejudice against women still prevails, so that women in High Church places are not allowed to sing in the choir, or to play the organ, not to speak of preaching. * * * In the same way she cannot enter the Law. Some day she will get over this restriction, but not yet. For a long time she was kept out of medicine. That restriction is now removed; she can, and she does, practice as a physician or a surgeon, generally the former. I believe that she has shown in this profession, as in her university studies, she can stand, *inter pares*,[3] among her equals and her peers, not her superiors. There is no branch of literature in which women have not distinguished themselves. * * * In music they compose, but not greatly; they play and sing divinely. The acting of the best among them is equal to that of any living man. They have become journalists, in some cases of remarkable ability; in fact, there are thousands of women who now make their livelihood by writing in all its branches. As for the less common professions—the accountants, architects, actuaries, agents—they are rapidly being taken over by women.

It is no longer a question of necessity; women do not ask themselves whether they must earn their own bread, or live a life of dependence. Necessity or no necessity they demand work, with

2. The novelist William Makepeace Thackeray (1811–63). The character of Amelia Sedley, in his novel, *Vanity Fair* (1848), is cited by Besant as typical of the "insipid" women of the 1840's.
3. Between equals.

independence and personal liberty. Whether they will take upon them the duties and responsibilities of marriage, they postpone for further consideration. I believe that, although in the first eager running there are many who profess to despise marriage, the voice of nature and the instinctive yearning for love will prevail.

Personal independence: that is the keynote of the situation. Mothers no longer attempt the old control over their daughters: they would find it impossible. The girls go off by themselves on their bicycles; they go about as they please; they neither compromise themselves nor get talked about. For the first time in man's history it is regarded as a right and proper thing to trust a girl as a boy insists upon being trusted. Out of this personal freedom will come, I daresay, a change in the old feelings of young man to maiden. He will not see in her a frail, tender plant which must be protected from cold winds; she can protect herself perfectly well. He will not see in her any longer a creature of sweet emotions and pure aspirations, coupled with a complete ignorance of the world, because she already knows all that she wants to know. Nor will he see in her a companion whose mind is a blank, and whose conversation is insipid, because she already knows as much as he knows himself. Nor, again, will he see in her a housewife whose whole time will be occupied in superintending servants or in making, brewing, confecting things with her own hand.

1897

The Nineties

The state of mind prevailing during the final decade of the 19th century was characterized previously (in the introduction to the Victorian Age) as typical neither of the earlier Victorians nor of the 20th century. As a result of their between-centuries role, writers of the 1890's are sometimes styled "Late Victorians"—a perfectly legitimate label in chronological terms—and sometimes (more ambiguously) "the first of the 'Moderns.'" In our anthology we retain as "Late Victorians" those writers who made their chief contribution before 1900. And we reserve for the 20th century a number of writers—already on the scene in the 1890's—whose work achieved particular prominence in the 20th century: these are William Butler Yeats, George Bernard Shaw, Joseph Conrad, A. E. Housman, and Thomas Hardy. Hardy's writings offer an example of our principle. He was born 15 or 20 years before most of the writers of the 90's, and his last two great novels, *Tess of the D'Urbervilles* and *Jude the Obscure*, were both published during that decade. But since it was only after 1900 that Hardy made his name as a poet, we include him in the 20th century, even though many of the attitudes towards life and literature in his poetry are recognizably Victorian, and his writings can be considered as having contributed, in part, to the overall accomplishments of Victorian literature. (The same generalizations may be made about Gerald Manley Hopkins, whose work was not, however, published until 1918.) The problem of placing Hardy or Hopkins in one age or another is a striking reminder that literary history, as is sometimes said of all history, is a seamless web, resistant to the divisive time categories that we set up for ease of reference.

Of the two groups of writers of the 90's represented in the following selections of late Victorians, the first—including Oscar Wilde, Ernest Dowson, and perhaps peripherally, Francis Thompson—were proponents of "art for art's sake": they believed that art should be unconcerned with controversial issues, such as politics, and that it should be restricted to celebrating beauty in a highly polished style. The "aesthetes," as these writers and artists were called, included in their group painters such as James McNeill Whistler, critics such as Arthur Symons, and the young Yeats. In 1936, when Yeats in old age was compiling an anthology of "modern verse," he looked back, as he often did, to the group of poets of the 1890's to which he himself had once been attached, a group styling itself The Rhymers' Club, whose members used to meet at a restaurant to read their poems aloud to each other. Among this coterie, an admiration for the writings of Walter Pater was, according to Yeats, a badge of membership. Indeed the first "poem" in Yeats's anthology is a passage of Pater's prose which Yeats prints as verse—the passage about the Mona Lisa in *The Renaissance* which begins: "She is older than the rocks among which she sits."

The Rhymers' Club poets liked to think of themselves as anti-Victorians, and had some cause to do so in view of their revolt against the moral earnestness of such early Victorian prophets as Carlyle and against a whole set of middle-class opinions which they enjoyed mocking. Even Matthew Arnold, although appreciated for his ridicule of middle-class Philistines, was somewhat suspect in the eyes of the aesthetes because he had attacked, in his essay on Wordsworth, the French poet Théophile Gautier, who was regarded as a chief progenitor of the aesthetic movement. In this respect there are similarities betwen England in the 1890's and England in the 1660's, for in the earlier period French literature had been similarly reverenced. What Tennyson called in 1873 "the poisonous honey stolen from France" was, in the 1890's, the favored fare. Nevertheless it can be shown that the aesthetes' credo of art for art's sake was also rooted in the writings of some of their 19th-century predecessors in England. The poets of the aesthetic movement were in a sense the last heirs of the Romantics; the appeal to sensation in their imagery goes back through Rossetti and Tennyson to Keats. They developed this sensationalism, however, much more histrionically than their predecessors, seeking compensation for the drabness of ordinary life in melancholy suggestiveness, antibourgeois sensationalism, heady ritualism, world-weariness, or mere emotional debauchery. What makes the 90's important as a period of English literary history is not, however, its writers' sensationalism and desire to shock. It is their strongly held belief in the independence of art, their view that a work of art has its own unique kind of value—that, in T. S. Eliot's phrase, poetry must be judged "as poetry and not another thing"—which has most strongly influenced later generations. Not only did the aesthetic movement nurse the young Yeats and provide him with his lifelong belief in poetry as poetry rather than as a means to some moral or other end; it is also provided modern criticism with its basic assumptions. "Art for art's sake" was in the 90's a provocative slogan; today it is a commonplace, and there are few significant critics who would not accept some version of it. The whole modern movement in criticism, as well as the new poetic techniques associated with it, has been largely concerned with demonstrating the uniqueness of the literary use of language and with training us to see works of literary art as possessing their special kind of form, their special kind of meaning, and hence their special kind of value. In this it is the heir of the 90's, however much it may have modified or enriched the legacy. It was the poets of the 90's, too, who first absorbed the influence of the French *symboliste* poets, an influence which has proved pervasive in the 20th century and is especially strong (though in different ways) in the poetry of Yeats and Eliot.

Our second group of 90's writers is represented by two poets, William Ernest Henley and Rudyard Kipling, who have been labeled "the Hearties" of the period. Such a term is a perky simplification, but it dramatizes the contrast between these two poets and their contemporaries. Although both Henley and Kipling were acquainted with grief and wrote about it, the predominant note in their late Victorian poems is strenuously affirmative, especially of the values of a life of action. Another characteristic quality shared by the two poets is realism—also evident in some of the novels of the period such as George Moore's *Esther Waters* (1894). Henley's strain of realism appears in his grim sketches of hospital experiences, and Kipling's in his distinctive recreation of the lives of common soldiers in the British army in India and Africa. And finally both poets are linked in their shared belief in the civilizing mission of British imperial power and the responsbilities called for in exercising that power—what Kipling called "The White Man's Burden." Today's readers generally find such poems as Henley's *England, My England* sheer jingo, but it is evident that for millions of late Victorians, this poem would strike a sympathetic response, one that accorded well with the shrill tone of the popular press during the war against the Boers in South Africa, with which the century closed.

Ironically, perhaps, it was Kipling who in 1897 wrote, in his hymn, *Recessional*, not a jingoistic celebration of 60 years of Victoria's reign, but, instead, a haunting elegy that evokes the achievement of his country and his century, but also, from the vaster perspectives of human history, the fragility of that achievement.

WILLIAM ERNEST HENLEY
(1849–1903)

During the 1880's and 1890's William Ernest Henley edited the *National Observer* and other periodicals in London, where he became a powerful figure in literary circles. The affectionate regard in which he was held by his contemporaries was enhanced by his courageous confrontation of long years of crippling physical pain caused by tuberculosis of the bone. Yeats said of him: "I disagreed with him about everything, but I admired him beyond words."

Most of Henley's poems, such as his vivid accounts of his hospital experiences, are realistic sketches of city life, often in free verse. Also characteristic, but in a different vein, are his hearty affirmations of faith in man's indomitable spirit, as in *Invictus*, and his patriotic verses expressing his pride in England's imperial role and her shoulderng the responsibility for a world order. In *England, my England* he writes:

> They call you proud and hard,
>   England, my England:
> You with worlds to watch and ward,
>   England, my own!
> You whose mailed hand keeps the keys
>   Of such teeming destinies
> You could know nor dread nor ease
>   Were the Song on your bugles blown,
>   England
>   Round the Pit on your bugles blown!

The spirit in poems such as these links Henley's writings to the poetry of his friend, Rudyard Kipling, another writer of the "hearty" school.

In Hospital

Waiting

A square, squat room (a cellar on promotion),
Drab to the soul, drab to the very daylight;
Plasters astray in unnatural-looking tinware;
Scissors and lint and apothecary's jars.

Here, on a bench a skeleton would writhe from,   5
Angry and sore, I wait to be admitted;
Wait till my heart is lead upon my stomach,
While at their ease two dressers do their chores.

One has a probe—it feels to me a crowbar.
A small boy sniffs and shudders after bluestone.[1]   10
A poor old tramp explains his poor old ulcers.
Life is (I think) a blunder and a shame.

Discharged

Carry me out
Into the wind and the sunshine,
Into the beautiful world.

O, the wonder, the spell of the streets!
The stature and strength of the horses,   5
The rustle and echo of footfalls,
The flat roar and rattle of wheels!
A swift tram floats huge on us . . .
It's a dream?
The smell of the mud in my nostrils   10
Blows brave—like a breath of the sea!

As of old,
Ambulant, undulant drapery,
Vaguely and strangely provocative,
Flutters and beckons. O, yonder—   15
Is it?—the gleam of a stocking!
Sudden, a spire
Wedged in the mist! O, the houses,
The long lines of lofty, gray houses,
Crosshatched with shadow and light!   20
These are the streets. . . .
Each is an avenue leading
Whither I will!

1. Or copper sulphate, commonly used in emergency wards as an emetic for
patients who have taken poison.

Free . . . !
Dizzy, hysterical, faint,
I sit, and the carriage rolls on with me   25
Into the wonderful world.

1875/88

Invictus[2]

Out of the night that covers me,
    Black as the Pit from pole to pole,
I thank whatever gods may be
    For my unconquerable soul.

In the fell clutch of circumstance   5
    I have not winced nor cried aloud.
Under the bludgeonings of chance
    My head is bloody, but unbowed.

Beyond this place of wrath and tears
    Looms but the Horror of the shade,   10
And yet the menace of the years
    Finds, and shall find, me unafraid.

It matters not how strait the gate,
    How charged with punishments the scroll,
I am the master of my fate;   15
    I am the captain of my soul.

1875   1888

Madam Life's a Piece in Bloom

Madam Life's a piece in bloom
    Death goes dogging everywhere:
She's the tenant of the room,
    He's the ruffian on the stair.

You shall see her as a friend,   5
    You shall bilk him once or twice;
But he'll trap you in the end,
    And he'll stick you for her price.

With his kneebones at your chest,
    And his knuckles in your throat,   10
You would reason—plead—protest!
    Clutching at her petticoat;

2. Unconquered.

> But she's heard it all before,
>> Well she knows you've had your fun,
> Gingerly she gains the door,   15
>> And your little job is done.

1877   1888

Barmaid[3]

Though, if you ask her name, she says ELISE,
Being plain Elizabeth, e'en let it pass,
And own that, if her aspirates take their ease,
She ever makes a point, in washing glass,
Handling the engine,[4] turning taps for tots,
And countering change, and scorning what men say,
Of posing as a dove among the pots,[5]
Nor often gives her dignity away.
Her head's a work of art; and, if her eyes
Be tired and ignorant, she has a waist;
Cheaply the mode she shadows; and she tries
From penny novels to amend her taste;
    And, having mopped the zinc[6] for certain years,
    And faced the gas, she fades and disappears.

1898

3. From *London Types*. This poem (in quatorzains) accompanied a picture of a barmaid by William Nicholson. Cf. Tennyson's sonnet, *She Took the Dappled Partridge*, in which the woman's posing is likened to a "master painting" (line 4).

4. Handle of the pump for drawing up beer from casks to the bar. "Tots": small drinks of whiskey or other hard liquors.
5. Pewter beer mugs.
6. Bar counters made of zinc.

OSCAR WILDE
(1854–1900)

In Oscar Wilde's comedy *The Importance of Being Earnest* (1895) there is an account of a rakish character, Ernest Worthing, who dies in a Paris hotel attended by the manager. Five years later, Wilde himself died in Paris (where he was living in exile) attended by a hotel manager. The coincidence seems a curious paradigm of Wilde's whole career, for with him the connections between his life and his art were unusually close. Indeed, in his last years, he told André Gide that he seemed to have put his genius into his life and only his talent into his writings.

His father, Sir William, was a distinguished surgeon in Dublin where Wilde was born and grew up. After majoring in classical studies at Trinity College, Dublin, he won a scholarship to Oxford and there established a brilliant academic record. At Oxford he came under the influence of the aesthetic theories of John Ruskin (who was at the time Professor of Fine

Arts), and, more importantly, of Walter Pater. With characteristic hyperbole Wilde affirmed of Pater's *Renaissance*: "It is my golden book; I never travel anywhere without it. But it is the very flower of decadence; the last trumpet should have sounded the moment it was written."

After graduating in 1878 Wilde settled in London, where his fellow Irishmen, George Bernard Shaw and William Butler Yeats, were also to settle. Here Wilde quickly established himself both as a writer and as a spokesman for the school of "Art for Art's Sake." In Wilde's view this school included not only French poets and critics but also a line of English poets going back through Rossetti and the Pre-Raphaelites to Keats. In 1882 he visited America for a lengthy (and successful) lecture tour during which he startled audiences by airing the gospel of the "aesthetic movement." In one of these lectures he asserted that "to disagree with three-fourths of all England on all points of view is one of the first elements of sanity."

For his role as a spokesman for Aestheticism Wilde had many gifts. From all accounts he was a dazzling conversationalist. Yeats reported, after first listening to him: "I never before heard a man talking with perfect sentences, as if he had written them all overnight with labor and yet all spontaneous." Wilde delighted his listeners not only by his polished wordplay but also by uttering opinions that were both outrageous and incongruous, as for example, his solemn affirmation that Queen Victoria was one of the three women he most admired and whom he would have married "with pleasure" (the other two were Sarah Bernhardt, the actress, and Lily Langtry, reputedly a mistress of Victoria's son, Edward, Prince of Wales).

In addition to his mastery of witty conversation Wilde had the gifts of an actor who delights in gaining attention. Pater had been a most shy and reticent man, but there was nothing reticent about his disciple who had discovered, early, that a flamboyant style of dress was one of the most effective means of gaining attention. Like the dandies of the earlier decades of the 19th century (including Disraeli and Dickens), Wilde favored colorful costumes in marked contrast to the sober black suits of the late-Victorian middle classes. A green carnation in his buttonhole and velvet knee breeches became for Wilde badges of his youthful iconoclasm, and even when he approached middle age, he continued to emphasize the gap between generations. In a letter written when he was 42 years old, he remarked: "The opinions of the old on matters of Art are, of course, of no value whatever."

Wilde's campaign early prompted an amused response from middle-class quarters. In 1881, Gilbert and Sullivan staged their comic opera, *Patience*, which mocked the affectations of the aesthetes in the character of Bunthorne, especially in his song *If You're Anxious for to Shine in the High Aesthetic Line*.

Wilde's successes for 17 years in England and America were of course not limited to his self-advertising stunts as a dandy. In his writings he excelled in a variety of genres: as a critic of literature and of society (*The Decay of Lying*, 1889, and *The Soul of Man Under Socialism*, 1891), and also as a novelist, poet, and dramatist. His novel, *The Portrait of Dorian Gray*, created a sensation when it was published in 1891. It is a strikingly ingenious story of a handsome young man and his selfish pursuit of sensual pleasures. Until the end of the book he himself remains fresh and healthy in appearance while his portrait mysteriously changes into a horrible image of his corrupted soul. Although the Preface to the novel (which we include) emphasizes that art and morality are totally separate, in the novel itself, at least in its later chapters, Wilde seems to be expounding a moral lesson on the evils of self-regarding hedonism.

As a poet Wilde felt overshadowed by the Victorian predecessors whom he admired: Browning, Rossetti, and Swinburne, and had trouble finding his own voice. Many of the poems in his first volume (1881) are highly derivative, but such pieces as *The Harlot's House* and *Impression du Matin* offer a distinctive perspective on city streets that seems to anticipate early poems by T. S. Eliot. His most outstanding success, however, was as a writer of comedies, which were staged in London and New York from 1892 through 1895, including *Lady Windermere's Fan, A Woman of No Importance, An Ideal Husband,* and *The Importance of Being Earnest.*

By the spring of 1895 this triumphant success suddenly crumbled when Wilde was arrested and sentenced to jail, with hard labor, for two years. Wilde had been married for several years and was the father of two children at the time of his meeting, in 1891, with a handsome young poet, Lord Alfred Douglas, with whom he established a homosexual relationship, which was to prove a disaster for him. In 1895, Lord Alfred's father, the Marquis of Queensberry, accused Wilde of homosexuality; Wilde recklessly sued for libel, lost the case, and was thereupon arrested and convicted for what was then on the statute books a serious criminal offense. The revulsion of feeling against him in England and in America was violent, and the aesthetic movement itself suffered a severe setback not only with the public but among writers as well.

His two years in jail led Wilde to write two sober and emotionally high-pitched works, his poem, *The Ballad of Reading Gaol* (1898), and his prose confession, *De Profoundis* (1905) in which he said:

> The gods had given me almost everything. I had a genius, a distinguished name, high social position, brilliancy, intellectual daring * * * I treated art as the supreme reality and life as a mere mode of fiction * * * But I let myself be lured into long spells of senseless and sensual ease * * * Tired of being on the heights, I deliberately went to the depths in the search for new sensation. What the paradox was to me in the sphere of thought, perversity became to me in the sphere of passion * * * I ended in horrible disgrace. There is only one thing for me now, absolute humility.

James Joyce, another exile from Ireland, had mixed feelings about Wilde's literary accomplishments (especially of his strange play, *Salomé,* 1893), but in this final phase of Wilde's life Joyce saw in him something of the figure of the martyred artist.

After leaving jail Wilde, a ruined man, emigrated to France, where he lived out the last three years of his life under an assumed name. Before his departure from England he had been divorced and declared a bankrupt, and in France he had to rely on friends for financial support. Wilde is buried in Paris in the same cemetery as the poet, Charles Baudelaire, whose *Fleurs du Mal* had profoundly affected his attitudes towards life and literature.

Impression du Matin[1]

The Thames nocturne of blue and gold[2]
    Changed to a harmony in gray;
    A barge with ocher-colored hay
Dropped from the wharf:[3] and chill and cold

The yellow fog came creeping down   5
    The bridges, till the houses' walls
    Seemed changed to shadows, and St. Paul's
Loomed like a bubble o'er the town.

Then suddenly arose the clang
    Of waking life; the streets were stirred   10
    With country wagons; and a bird
Flew to the glistening roofs and sang.

But one pale woman all alone,
    The daylight kissing her wan hair,
    Loitered beneath the gas lamps' flare,   15
With lips of flame and heart of stone.

1881

Hélas[4]

To drift with every passion till my soul
Is a stringed lute on which all winds can play,
Is it for this that I have given away
Mine ancient wisdom, and austere control?
Methinks my life is a twice-written scroll   5
Scrawled over on some boyish holiday
With idle songs for pipe and virelay,[5]
Which do but mar the secret of the whole.
Surely there was a time I might have trod
The sunlit heights, and from life's dissonance   10
Struck one clear chord to reach the ears of God.
Is that time dead? lo! with a little rod
I did but touch the honey of romance—
And must I lose a soul's inheritance?[6]

1881

---

1. "Impression of the Morning."
2. Cf. the "Nocturnes" (paintings of nighttime scenes) done by James McNeill Whistler in the 1870's. *Nocturne in Blue and Gold: Old Battersea Bridge* (on the cover of this volume) was one of this series; it was painted by 1875 but given its present title in 1892. An earlier painting by Whistler, *Harmony in Gray*, may be referred to in the next line.
3. I.e., left the wharf and went down river with the ebb tide.
4. "Alas!"
5. A song or short lyric in stanzas.
6. Perhaps referring to Numbers xx.10–13. After Moses had obtained water for his people by striking a rock with his rod, he was denied the privilege of entering the Promised Land.

E Tenebris[7]

Come down, O Christ, and help me! reach thy hand,
    For I am drowning in a stormier sea
    Than Simon on thy lake of Galilee:[8]
The wine of life is spilt upon the sand,
My heart is as some famine-murdered land   5
    Whence all good things have perished utterly,
    And well I know my soul in Hell must lie
If I this night before God's throne should stand.
"He sleeps perchance, or rideth to the chase,
    Like Baal, when his prophets howled that name   10
    From morn to noon on Carmel's smitten height."[9]
Nay, peace, I shall behold, before the night,
    The feet of brass,[1] the robe more white than flame,
The wounded hands, the weary human face.

                                  1881

The Harlot's House

We caught the tread of dancing feet,
We loitered down the moonlit street,
And stopped beneath the harlot's house.

Inside, above the din and fray,
We hard the loud musicians play
The *Treues Liebes Herz* of Strauss.[2]

Like strange mechanical grotesques,
Making fantastic arabesques,
The shadows raced across the blind.

We watched the ghostly dancers spin
To sound of horn and violin,
Like black leaves wheeling in the wind.

Like wire-pulled automatons,
Slim silhouetted skeletons
Went sidling through the slow quadrille.[3]

7. "Out of Darkness."
8. Simon Peter, one of the 12 apostles, came close to drowning in a storm until rescued by Christ (see Matthew xiv.28).
9. The poet imagines an ironic voice discouraging him; it uses the language of Elijah when he mocked the priests of Baal for their god's impotence by suggesting that perhaps Baal was on a journey or asleep (see I Kings xviii.19–40).

1. Cf. Revelation i ff., where the "Son of man" is seen in a vision, "his feet like unto fine brass, as if they burned in a furnace."
2. *Heart of True Love*, a waltz by the Austrian composer and "Waltz King," Johann Strauss (1825–99).
3. Intricate dance involving four couples facing each other in a square.

They took each other by the hand,
And danced a stately saraband;[4]
Their laughter echoed thin and shrill.

Sometimes a clockwork puppet pressed
A phantom lover to her breast,
Sometimes they seemed to try to sing.

Sometimes a horrible marionette
Came out, and smoked its cigarette
Upon the steps like a live thing.[5]

Then, turning to my love, I said,
"The dead are dancing with the dead,
The dust is whirling with the dust."

But she—she heard the violin,
And left my side, and entered in:
Love passed into the house of lust.

Then suddenly the tune went false,
The dancers wearied of the waltz,
The shadows ceased to wheel and whirl.

And down the long and silent street,
The dawn, with silver-sandaled feet,
Crept like a frightened girl.

1885, 1908

Sonnet: On the Sale by Auction of Keats' Love Letters

These are the letters which Endymion[6] wrote
To one he loved in secret and apart,
And now the brawlers of the auction-mart
Bargain and bid for each tear-blotted note,
Aye! for each separate pulse of passion quote
The merchant's price! I think they love not art
Who break the crystal of a poet's heart,
That small and sickly eyes may glare or gloat.

Is it not said, that many years ago,
In a far Eastern town some soldiers ran
With torches through the midnight, and began
To wrangle for mean raiment, and to throw

---

4. A slow and stately dance, originating in Spain.
5. In an illustration for the poem by Althea Gyles (approved by Wilde) the marionette is pictured as a man in evening dress.
6. Young hero of Keats's long poem *Endymion* (1817). The letters were to Fanny Brawne; most of them had been published in 1878.

Dice for the garments of a wretched man,
Not knowing the God's wonder, or His woe?

1886

Symphony in Yellow[7]

An omnibus across the bridge
    Crawls like a yellow butterfly,
    And, here and there, a passerby
Shows like a little restless midge.

Big barges full of yellow hay   5
    Are moored against the shadowy wharf,
    And, like a yellow silken scarf,
The thick fog hangs along the quay.

The yellow leaves begin to fade
    And flutter from the Temple[8] elms,   10
    And at my feet the pale green Thames
Lies like a rod of rippled jade.

1889

Preface to *The Picture of Dorian Gray*

The artist is the creator of beautiful things.

To reveal art and conceal the artist is art's aim.

The critic is he who can translate into another manner or a new
material his impression of beautiful things.

    The highest, as the lowest, form of criticism is a mode
    of autobiography.

Those who find ugly meaning in beautiful things are corrupt without being charming. This is a fault.

    Those who find beautiful meanings in beautiful
    things are the cultivated. For these there is hope.

They are the elect to whom beautiful things mean only
    Beauty.

    There is no such thing as a moral or an immoral book.

    Books are well written, or badly written. That is all.

The nineteenth-century dislike of Realism is the rage of Caliban[9]
seeing his own face in a glass.

    The nineteenth-century dislike of Romanticism is
    the rage of Caliban not seeking his own face in a
    glass.

7. Cf. the titles of Whistler's paintings
Symphony in White (1862) and *Symphony in Gray and Green* (1867).
8. Site of two of the Inns of Court,
formerly occupied by the Knights Templars.
9. The character in Shakespeare's *Tempest* is half-man, half-monster.

The moral life of man forms part of the subject matter of the artist, but the morality of art consists in the perfect use of an imperfect medium. No artist desires to prove anything. Even things that are true can be proved.

No artist has ethical sympathies. An ethical sympathy in an artist is an unpardonable mannerism of style.

No artist is ever morbid. The artist can express everything.

Thought and language are to the artist instruments of an art.

Vice and Virtue are to the artist materials for an art.

From the point of view of form, the type of all the arts is the art of the musician. From the point of view of feeling, the actor's craft is the type.

All art is at once surface and symbol.

Those who go beneath the surface do so at their peril.

Those who read the symbol do so at their peril.

It is the spectator, and not life, that art really mirrors.

Diversity of opinion about a work of art shows that the work is new, complex, and vital.

When critics disagree the artist is in accord with himself. We can forgive a man for making a useful thing as long as he does not admire it. The only excuse for making a useless thing is that one admires it intensely.

All art is quite useless.

1891

The Importance of Being Earnest

Of the four stage comedies by Wilde, his last, *The Importance of Being Earnest*, is generally regarded as his masterpiece. It was first staged in February, 1895, and was an immediate hit. Only one critic failed to find it delightful; curiously, this was Wilde's fellow playwright from Ireland, George Bernard Shaw, who was not amused. He found Wilde's wit "hateful" and "sinister," and thought the play exhibited "real degeneracy." Despite Shaw's complaints, the first London production ran for 86 performances, but when Wilde was sentenced to prison, production ceased for several years. Shortly before his death it was revived in London and New York, and has subsequently become a classic of the theater.

In its original version the play was in four acts. At the request of the stage-producer, Wilde reduced it to three acts—the version almost always used in performances and therefore the version we reprint. A few of the notes in the present text cite passages from the four-act version.

The play was first published in 1899. Earlier, in an interview, Wilde had described his overall aim in writing it: "It has as its philosophy * * * that we should treat all the trivial things of life seriously, and all the serious things of life with sincere and studied triviality." Just before his death he remarked that although he was pleased with the "bright and happy" tone and temper of his play, he wished it might have had a "higher seriousness of intent." A strain of solemnity would have been inappropriate, but *The Importance of Being Earnest* has its own serious qualities—the seriousness of a unified work of art. As Ian Gregor has shown, Wilde combines the resources of paradox in language and of farce in plot to create a fantasy world, "a completely realized idyll, offering itself as something irrecoverably *other* than life, not a wish-fulfillment of life as it might be lived."

The literary ancestry of Wilde's play has been variously identified. In its witty wordplay and worldly attitudes it has been likened to comedies of the Restoration period such as Congreve's *Love for Love.* In its genial and light-hearted tone, it has some affinities with the festive comedies of Shakespeare, such as *Twelfth Night,* and with Goldsmith's *She Stoops to Conquer.* A more immediate predecessor was *Engaged* (1877), a comic play by W. S. Gilbert which anticipated some of the burlesque effects exploited by Wilde, such as the interrupting of sentimental scenes by the consumption of food, and the inviolable imperturbability of the speakers. Gilbert's advice to the actors who were putting on his *Engaged* is worth citing, as a clue to how *The Importance of Being Earnest* may be most effectively imagined as a stage-representation:

> It is absolutely essential to the success of this piece that it should be played with the most perfect earnestness and gravity throughout. * * * Directly the actors show that they are conscious of the absurdity of their utterances the piece begins to drag.

The Importance of Being Earnest

First Act

SCENE—*Morning room in* ALGERNON'S *flat in Half-Moon Street.*[1] *The room is luxuriously and artistically furnished. The sound of a piano is heard in the adjoining room.*

> [LANE *is arranging afternoon tea on the table, and after the music has ceased,* ALGERNON *enters.*]

ALGERNON. Did you hear what I was playing, Lane?

LANE. I didn't think it polite to listen, sir.

ALGERNON. I'm sorry for that, for your sake. I don't play accurately —anyone can play accurately—but I play with wonderful expression. As far as the piano is concerned, sentiment is my forte. I keep science for Life.

LANE. Yes, sir.

ALGERNON. And, speaking of the science of Life, have you got the cucumber sandwiches cut for Lady Bracknell?[2]

LANE. Yes, sir. [*Hands them on a salver.*]

ALGERNON. [*inspects them, takes two, and sits down on the sofa*] Oh! . . . by the way, Lane, I see from your book[3] that on Thurs-

---

1. A highly fashionable location (at the time of the play) in the west end of London.
2. The name of a place in Berkshire where the mother of Lord Alfred Douglas had her summer home, which Wilde had visited.
3. "Cellar book," in which records were kept of wines.

day night, when Lord Shoreman and Mr. Worthing were dining with me, eight bottles of champagne are entered as having been consumed.

LANE. Yes, sir; eight bottles and a pint.

ALGERNON. Why is it that at a bachelor's establishment the servants invariably drink the champagne? I ask merely for information.

LANE. I attribute it to the superior quality of the wine, sir. I have often observed that in married households the champagne is rarely of a first-rate brand.

ALGERNON. Good Heavens! Is marriage so demoralizing as that?

LANE. I believe it *is* a very pleasant state, sir. I have had very little experience of it myself up to the present. I have only been married once. That was in consequence of a misunderstanding between myself and a young person.

ALGERNON. [*languidly*] I don't know that I am much interested in your family life, Lane.

LANE. No, sir; it is not a very interesting subject. I never think of it myself.

ALGERNON. Very natural, I am sure. That will do, Lane, thank you.

LANE. Thank you, sir. [LANE *goes out.*]

ALGERNON. Lane's views on marriage seem somewhat lax. Really, if the lower orders don't set us a good example, what on earth is the use of them? They seem, as a class, to have absolutely no sense of moral responsibility.

[*Enter* LANE.]

LANE. Mr. Ernest Worthing.

[*Enter* JACK.] [LANE *goes out.*]

ALGERNON. How are you, my dear Ernest? What brings you up to town?

JACK. Oh, pleasure, pleasure! What else should bring one anywhere? Eating as usual, I see, Algy!

ALGERNON. [*stiffy*] I believe it is customary in good society to take some slight refreshment at five o'clock. Where have you been since last Thursday?

JACK. [*sitting down on the sofa*] In the country.

ALGERNON. What on earth do you do there?

JACK. [*pulling off his gloves*] When one is in town one amuses oneself. When one is in the country one amuses other people. It is excessively boring.

ALGERNON. And who are the people you amuse?

JACK. [*airily*] Oh, neighbors, neighbors.

ALGERNON. Got nice neighbors in your part of Shropshire?

JACK. Perfectly horrid! Never speak to one of them.

ALGERNON. How immensely you must amuse them! [*Goes over and takes sandwich.*] By the way, Shropshire is your county, is it not?

JACK. Eh? Shropshire?[4] Yes, of course. Hallo! Why all these cups? Why cucumber sandwiches? Why such reckless extravagance in one so young? Who is coming to tea?

ALGERNON. Oh! merely Aunt Augusta and Gwendolen.

JACK. How perfectly delightful!

ALGERNON. Yes, that is all very well; but I am afraid Aunt Augusta won't quite approve of your being here.

JACK. May I ask why?

ALGERNON. My dear fellow, the way you flirt with Gwendolen is perfectly disgraceful. It is almost as bad as the way Gwendolen flirts with you.

JACK. I am in love with Gwendolen. I have come up to town expressly to propose to her.

ALGERNON. I thought you had come up for pleasure? . . . I call that business.

JACK. How utterly unromantic you are!

ALGERNON. I really don't see anything romantic in proposing. It is very romantic to be in love. But there is nothing romantic about a definite proposal. Why, one may be accepted. One usually is, I believe. Then the excitement is all over. The very essence of romance is uncertainty. If ever I get married, I'll certainly try to forget the fact.

JACK. I have no doubt about that, dear Algy. The Divorce Court was specially invented for people whose memories are so curiously constituted.

ALGERNON. Oh! there is no use speculating on that subject. Divorces are made in Heaven——[JACK *puts out his hand to take a sandwich.* ALGERNON *at once interferes.*] Please don't touch the cucumber sandwiches. They are ordered specially for Aunt Augusta. [*Takes one and eats it.*]

JACK. Well, you have been eating them all the time.

ALGERNON. That is quite a different matter. She is my aunt. [*Takes plate from below.*] Have some bread and butter. The bread and butter is for Gwendolen. Gwendolen is devoted to bread and butter.

JACK. [*advancing to table and helping himself*] And very good bread and butter it is too.

ALGERNON. Well, my dear fellow, you need not eat as if you were going to eat it all. You behave as if you were married to her already. You are not married to her already, and I don't think you ever will be.

JACK. Why on earth do you say that?

ALGERNON. Well, in the first place girls never marry the men they

4. As we learn later, the estate is in Hertfordshire, a very long distance from Shropshire. In the four-act version of the play, when this discrepancy is pointed out by Algernon, Jack replies: "My dear fellow! Surely you don't expect me to be accurate about geography? No gentleman is accurate about geography. Why, I got a prize for geography when I was at school. I can't be expected to know anything about it now."

flirt with. Girls don't think it right.

JACK. Oh, that is nonsense!

ALGERNON. It isn't. It is a great truth. It accounts for the extraordinary number of bachelors that one sees all over the place. In the second place, I don't give my consent.

JACK. Your consent!

ALGERNON. My dear fellow, Gwendolen is my first cousin. And before I allow you to marry her, you will have to clear up the whole question of Cecily. [*Rings bell.*]

JACK. Cecily! What on earth do you mean? What do you mean, Algy, by Cecily? I don't know anyone of the name of Cecily.
    [*Enter* LANE.]

ALGERNON. Bring me that cigarette case Mr. Worthing left in the smoking-room the last time he dined here.

LANE. Yes, sir.   [LANE *goes out.*]

JACK. Do you mean to say you have had my cigarette case all this time? I wish to goodness you had let me know. I have been writing frantic letters to Scotland Yard[5] about it. I was very nearly offering a large reward.

ALGERNON. Well, I wish you would offer one. I happen to be more than usually hard up.

JACK. There is no good offering a large reward now that the thing is found.

    [*Enter* LANE *with the cigarette case on a salver.* ALGERNON *takes it at once.* LANE *goes out.*]

ALGERNON. I think that is rather mean of you, Ernest, I must say. [*Opens case and examines it.*] However, it makes no matter, for, now that I look at the inscription inside, I find that the thing isn't yours after all.

JACK. Of course it's mine. [*Moving to him.*] You have seen me with it a hundred times, and you have no right whatsoever to read what is written inside. It is a very ungentlemanly thing to read a private cigarette case.

ALGERNON. Oh! it is absurd to have a hard-and-fast rule about what one should read and what one shouldn't. More than half of modern culture depends on what one shouldn't read.

JACK. I am quite aware of the fact, and I don't propose to discuss modern culture. It isn't the sort of thing one should talk of in private. I simply want my cigarette case back.

ALGERNON. Yes; but this isn't your cigarette case. This cigarette case is a present from someone of the name of Cecily, and you said you didn't know anyone of that name.

JACK. Well, if you want to know, Cecily happens to be my aunt.

ALGERNON. Your aunt!

JACK. Yes. Charming old lady she is, too. Lives at Tunbridge Wells.[6] Just give it back to me, Algy.

5. Police headquarters in London.
6. A fashionable resort town south of London.

ALGERNON. [*retreating to back of sofa*] But why does she call herself Cecily if she is your aunt and lives at Tunbridge Wells? [*Reading.*] "From little Cecily with her fondest love."

JACK. [*moving to sofa and kneeling upon it*] My dear fellow, what on earth is there in that? Some aunts are tall, some aunts are not tall. That is a matter that surely an aunt may be allowed to decide for herself. You seem to think that every aunt should be exactly like your aunt! That is absurd! For Heaven's sake give me back my cigarette case. [*Follows Algy round the room.*]

ALGERNON. Yes. But why does your aunt call you her uncle? "From little Cecily, with her fondest love to her dear Uncle Jack." There is no objection, I admit, to an aunt being a small aunt, but why an aunt, no matter what her size may be, should call her own nephew her uncle, I can't quite make out. Besides, your name isn't Jack at all; it is Ernest.

JACK. It isn't Ernest; it's Jack.

ALGERNON. You have always told me it was Ernest. I have introduced you to everyone as Ernest. You answer to the name of Ernest. You look as if your name was Ernest. You are the most earnest looking person I ever saw in my life. It is perfectly absurd your saying that your name isn't Ernest. It's on your cards. Here is one of them. [*Taking it from case.*] "Mr. Ernest Worthing, B. 4, The Albany."[7] I'll keep this as a proof that your name is Ernest if ever you attempt to deny it to me, or to Gwendolen, or to anyone else. [*Puts the card in his pocket.*]

JACK. Well, my name is Ernest in town and Jack in the country, and the cigarette case was given to me in the country.

ALGERNON. Yes, but that does not account for the fact that your small Aunt Cecily, who lives at Tunbridge Wells, calls you her dear uncle. Come, old boy, you had much better have the thing out at once.

JACK. My dear Algy, you talk exactly as if you were a dentist. It is very vulgar to talk like a dentist when one isn't a dentist. It produces a false impression.

ALGERNON. Well, that is exactly what dentists always do. Now, go on! Tell me the whole thing. I may mention that I have always suspected you of being a confirmed and secret Bunburyist; and I am quite sure of it now.

JACK. Bunburyist? What on earth do you mean by a Bunburyist?

ALGERNON. I'll reveal to you the meaning of that incomparable expression as soon as you are kind enough to inform me why you are Ernest in town and Jack in the country.

JACK. Well, produce my cigarette case first.

ALGERNON. Here it is. [*Hands cigarette case.*] Now produce your explanation, and pray make it improbable. [*Sits on sofa.*]

JACK. My dear fellow, there is nothing improbable about my explanation at all. In fact it's perfectly ordinary. Old Mr. Thomas

7. A former residence of the Duke of Albany (brother of George IV) near Piccadilly which had been converted into elegant apartments often rented by country gentry for visits to London.

Cardew, who adopted me when I was a little boy, made me in his will guardian to his granddaughter, Miss Cecily Cardew. Cecily, who addresses me as her uncle from motives of respect that you could not possibly appreciate, lives at my place in the country under the charge of her admirable governess, Miss Prism.

ALGERNON. Where is that place in the country, by the way?

JACK. That is nothing to you, dear boy. You are not going to be invited. . . . I may tell you candidly that the place is not in Shropshire.

ALGERNON. I suspected that, my dear fellow! I have Bunburyed all over Shropshire on two separate occasions. Now, go on. Why are you Earnest in town and Jack in the country?

JACK. My dear Algy, I don't know whether you will be able to understand my real motives. You are hardly serious enough. When one is placed in the position of guardian, one has to adopt a very high moral tone on all subjects. It's one's duty to do so. And as a high moral tone can hardly be said to conduce very much to either one's health or one's happiness, in order to get up to town I have always pretended to have a younger brother of the name of Ernest, who lives in the Albany, and gets into the most dreadful scrapes. That, my dear Algy, is the whole truth pure and simple.

ALGERNON. The truth is rarely pure and never simple. Modern life would be very tedious if it were either, and modern literature a complete impossibility!

JACK That wouldn't be at all a bad thing.

ALGERNON. Literary criticism is not your forte, my dear fellow. Don't try it. You should leave that to people who haven't been at a University. They do it so well in the daily papers. What you really are is a Bunburyist. I was quite right in saying you were a Bunburyist. You are one of the most advanced Bunburyists I know.

JACK. What on earth do you mean?

ALGERNON. You have invented a very useful young brother called Ernest, in order that you may be able to come up to town as often as you like. I have invented an invaluable permanent invalid called Bunbury, in order that I may be able to go down into the country whenever I choose. Bunbury is perfectly invaluable. If it wasn't for Bunbury's extraordinary bad health, for instance, I wouldn't be able to dine with you at Willis's[8] tonight, for I have been really engaged[9] to Aunt Augusta for more than a week.

JACK. I haven't asked you to dine with me anywhere tonight.

ALGERNON. I know. You are absurdly careless about sending out invitations. It is very foolish of you. Nothing annoys people so much as not receiving invitations.

JACK. You had much better dine with your Aunt Augusta.

8. A first-class restaurant in the vicinity of St. James's Street.

9. I.e., committed to attend her dinner party.

ALGERNON. I haven't the smallest intention of doing anything of
the kind. To begin with, I dined there on Monday, and once a
week is quite enough to dine with one's own relations. In the
second place, whenever I do dine there I am always treated as a
member of the family, and sent down with[1] either no woman at
all, or two. In the third place, I know perfectly well whom she
will place me next to, tonight. She will place me next Mary Farquhar, who always flirts with her own husband across the dinner
table. That is not very pleasant. Indeed, it is not even decent . . .
and that sort of thing is enormously on the increase. The amount
of women in London who flirt with their own husbands is perfectly scandalous. It looks so bad. It is simply washing one's clean
linen in public. Besides, now that I know you to be a confirmed
Bunburyist, I naturally want to talk to you about Bunburying. I
want to tell you the rules.

JACK. I'm not a Bunburyist at all. If Gwendolen accepts me, I am
going to kill my brother, indeed I think I'll kill him in any case.
Cecily is a little too much interested in him. It is rather a bore.
So I am going to get rid of Ernest. And I strongly advise you to
do the same with Mr. . . . with your invalid friend who has the
absurd name.

ALGERNON. Nothing will induce me to part with Bunbury, and if
you ever get married, which seems to me extremely problematic,
you will be very glad to know Bunbury. A man who marries without knowing Bunbury has a very tedious time of it.

JACK. That is nonsense. If I marry a charming girl like Gwendolen,
and she is the only girl I ever saw in my life that I would marry,
I certainly won't want to know Bunbury.

ALGERNON. Then your wife will. You don't seem to realize, that in
married life three is company and two is none.

JACK. [*sententiously*] That, my dear young friend, is the theory
that the corrupt French Drama has been propounding for the last
fifty years.[2]

ALGERNON. Yes; and that the happy English home has proved in
half the time.

JACK. For heaven's sake, don't try to be cynical. It's perfectly easy
to be cynical.

ALGERNON. My dear fellow, it isn't easy to be anything nowadays.
There's such a lot of beastly competition about. [*The sound of
an electric bell is heard.*] Ah! that must be Aunt Augusta. Only
relatives, or creditors, ever ring in that Wagnerian manner.[3]
Now, if I get her out of the way for ten minutes, so that you can
have an opportunity for proposing to Gwendolen, may I dine

---

1. I.e., required to escort, as a dinner
partner.
2. Almost all the plays by the leading
French playwrights of the second half
of the 19th century (Alexandre Dumas
fils, Émile Augier, and Victorien
Sardou) focus on the topic of marital
infidelity. As Brander Matthews, an
American critic noted in 1882, "the
trio—husband, wife, and lover" had
become "almost universal" in the
French theater.
3. Insistently loud, like some of the
music in Richard Wagner's large-scaled
operas.

with you tonight at Willis's?

JACK. I suppose so, if you want to.

ALGERNON. Yes, but you must be serious about it. I hate people who are not serious about meals. It is so shallow of them.

[*Enter* LANE.]

LANE. Lady Bracknell and Miss Fairfax.

[ALGERNON *goes forward to meet them. Enter* LADY BRACK-NELL *and* GWENDOLEN.]

LADY BRACKNELL. Good afternoon, dear Algernon, I hope you are behaving very well.

ALGERNON. I'm feeling very well, Aunt Augusta.

LADY BRACKNELL. That's not quite the same thing. In fact the two things rarely go together. [*Sees* JACK *and bows to him with icy coldness.*]

ALGERNON. [*to* GWENDOLEN] Dear me, you are smart![4]

GWENDOLEN. I am always smart! Aren't I, Mr. Worthing?

JACK. You're quite perfect, Miss Fairfax.

GWENDOLEN. Oh! I hope I am not that. It would leave no room for developments, and I intend to develop in many directions. [GWENDOLEN *and* JACK *sit down together in the corner.*]

LADY BRACKNELL. I'm sorry if we are a little late, Algernon, but I was obliged to call on dear Lady Harbury. I hadn't been there since her poor husband's death. I never saw a woman so altered; she looks quite twenty years younger. And now I'll have a cup of tea, and one of those nice cucumber sandwiches you promised me.

ALGERNON. Certainly, Aunt Augusta. [*Goes over to teatable.*]

LADY BRACKNELL. Won't you come and sit here, Gwendolen?

GWENDOLEN. Thanks, mamma,[5] I'm quite comfortable where I am.

ALGERNON. [*picking up empty plate in horror*] Good heavens! Lane! Why are there no cucumber sandwiches? I ordered them specially.

LANE. [*gravely*] There were no cucumbers in the market this morning, sir. I went down twice.

ALGERNON. No cucumbers!

LANE. No, sir. Not even for ready money.

ALGERNON. That will do, Lane, thank you.

LANE. Thank you, sir.

ALGERNON. I am greatly distressed, Aunt Augusta, about there being no cucumbers, not even for ready money.

LADY BRACKNELL. It really makes no matter, Algernon. I had some crumpets[6] with Lady Harbury, who seems to me to be living entirely for pleasure now.

ALGERNON. I hear her hair has turned quite gold from grief.

LADY BRACKNELL. It certainly has changed its color. From what cause I, of course, cannot say. [ALGERNON *crosses and hands tea.*] Thank you. I've quite a treat for you tonight, Algernon. I

---

4. Elegantly fashionable.
5. Pronounced with accent on second syllable.
6. A kind of toasted muffin.

am going to send you down with Mary Farquhar. She is such a nice woman, and so attentive to her husband. It's delightful to watch them.

ALGERNON. I am afraid, Aunt Augusta, I shall have to give up the pleasure of dining with you tonight after all.

LADY BRACKNELL. [*frowning*] I hope not, Algernon. It would put my table completely out. Your uncle would have to dine upstairs. Fortunately he is accustomed to that.

ALGERNON. It is a great bore, and, I need hardly say, a terrible disappointment to me, but the fact is I have just had a telegram to say that my poor friend Bunbury is very ill again. [*Exchanges glances with* JACK.] They seem to think I should be with him.

LADY BRACKNELL. It is very strange. This Mr. Bunbury seems to suffer from curiously bad health.

ALGERNON. Yes; poor Bunbury is a dreadful invalid.

LADY BRACKNELL. Well, I must say, Algernon, that I think it is high time that Mr. Bunbury made up his mind whether he was going to live or to die. This shilly-shallying with the question is absurd. Nor do I in any way approve of the modern sympathy with invalids. I consider it morbid. Illness of any kind is hardly a thing to be encouraged in others. Health is the primary duty of life. I am always telling that to your poor uncle, but he never seems to take much notice . . . as far as any improvement in his ailments goes. I should be obliged if you would ask Mr. Bunbury, from me, to be kind enough not to have a relapse on Saturday, for I rely on you to arrange my music for me. It is my last reception, and one wants something that will encourage conversation, particularly at the end of the season[7] when everyone has practically said whatever they had to say, which, in most cases, was probably not much.

ALGERNON. I'll speak to Bunbury, Aunt Augusta, if he is still conscious, and I think I can promise you he'll be all right by Saturday. Of course the music is a great difficulty. You see, if one plays good music, people don't listen, and if one plays bad music, people don't talk. But I'll run over the program I've drawn out, if you will kindly come into the next room for a moment.

LADY BRACKNELL. Thank you, Algernon. It is very thoughtful of you. [*Rising, and following* ALGERNON.] I'm sure the program will be delightful, after a few expurgations. French songs I cannot possibly allow. People always seem to think that they are improper, and either look shocked, which is vulgar, or laugh, which is worse. But German sounds a thoroughly respectable language, and indeed, I believe is so. Gwendolen, you will accompany me.

GWENDOLEN. Certainly, mamma.

[LADY BRACKNELL *and* ALGERNON *go into the music room,* GWENDOLEN *remains behind.*]

7. The social season, extending from May through July, when people of fashion came into London from their country estates for entertainments and parties.

JACK. Charming day it has been, Miss Fairfax.

GWENDOLEN. Pray don't talk to me about the weather, Mr. Worthing. Whenever people talk to me about the weather, I always feel quite certain that they mean something else. And that makes me so nervous.

JACK. I do mean something else.

GWENDOLEN. I thought so. In fact, I am never wrong.

JACK. And I would like to be allowed to take advantage of Lady Bracknell's temporary absence . . .

GWENDOLEN. I would certainly advise you to do so. Mamma has a way of coming back suddenly into a room that I have often had to speak to her about.

JACK. [*nervously*] Miss Fairfax, ever since I met you I have admired you more than any girl . . . I have ever met since . . . I met you.

GWENDOLEN. Yes, I am quite aware of the fact. And I often wish that in public, at any rate, you had been more demonstrative. For me you have always had an irresistible fascination. Even before I met you I was far from indifferent to you. [JACK *looks at her in amazement.*] We live, as I hope you know, Mr. Worthing, in an age of ideals. The fact is constantly mentioned in the more expensive monthly magazines, and has reached the provincial pulpits, I am told: and my ideal has always been to love someone of the name of Ernest. There is something in that name that inspires absolute confidence. The moment Algernon first mentioned to me that he had a friend called Ernest, I knew I was destined to love you.

JACK. You really love me, Gwendolen?

GWENDOLEN. Passionately!

JACK. Darling! You don't know how happy you've made me.

GWENDOLEN. My own Ernest!

JACK. But you don't really mean to say that you couldn't love me if my name wasn't Ernest?

GWENDOLEN. But your name is Ernest.

JACK. Yes, I know it is. But supposing it was something else? Do you mean to say you couldn't love me then?

GWENDOLEN. [*glibly*] Ah! that is clearly a metaphysical speculation, and like most metaphysical speculations has very little reference at all to the actual facts of real life, as we know them.

JACK. Personally, darling, to speak quite candidly, I don't much care about the name of Ernest . . . I don't think the name suits me at all.

GWENDOLEN. It suits you perfectly. It is a divine name. It has a music of its own. It produces vibrations.

JACK. Well, really, Gwendolen, I must say that I think there are lots of other much nicer names. I think Jack, for instance, a charming name.

GWENDOLEN. Jack? . . . No, there is very little music in the name Jack, if any at all, indeed. It does not thrill. It produces absolutely no vibrations. . . . I have known several Jacks, and they all, without exception, were more than usually plain. Besides, Jack is a notorious domesticity for John! And I pity any woman who is married to a man called John. She would probably never be allowed to know the entrancing pleasure of a single moment's solitude. The only really safe name is Ernest.

JACK. Gwendolen, I must get christened at once—I mean we must get married at once. There is no time to be lost.

GWENDOLEN. Married, Mr. Worthing?

JACK. [*astounded*] Well . . . surely. You know that I love you, and you led me to believe, Miss Fairfax, that you were not absolutely indifferent to me.

GWENDOLEN. I adore you. But you haven't proposed to me yet. Nothing has been said at all about marriage. The subject has not even been touched on.

JACK. Well . . . may I propose to you now?

GWENDOLEN. I think it would be an admirable opportunity. And to spare you any possible disappointment, Mr. Worthing, I think it only fair to tell you quite frankly beforehand that I am fully determined to accept you.

JACK. Gwendolen!

GWENDOLEN. Yes, Mr. Worthing, what have you got to say to me?

JACK. You know what I have got to say to you.

GWENDOLEN. Yes, but you don't say it.

JACK. Gwendolen, will you marry me? [*Goes on his knees.*]

GWENDOLEN. Of course I will, darling. How long you have been about it! I am afraid you have had very little experience in how to propose.

JACK. My own one, I have never loved anyone in the world but you.

GWENDOLEN. Yes, but men often propose for practice. I know my brother Gerald does. All my girlfriends tell me so. What wonderfully blue eyes you have, Ernest! They are quite, quite blue. I hope you will always look at me just like that, especially when there are other people present.

[*Enter* LADY BRACKNELL.]

LADY BRACKNELL. Mr. Worthing! Rise, sir, from this semi-recumbent posture. It is most indecorous.

GWENDOLEN. Mamma! [*He tries to rise; she restrains him.*] I must beg you to retire. This is no place for you. Besides, Mr. Worthing has not quite finished yet.

LADY BRACKNELL. Finished what, may I ask?

GWENDOLEN. I am engaged to Mr. Worthing, mamma.

[*They rise together.*]

LADY BRACKNELL. Pardon me, you are not engaged to anyone. When you do become engaged to someone, I, or your father, should his health permit him, will inform you of the fact. An engagement should come on a young girl as a surprise, pleasant or unpleasant, as the case may be. It is hardly a matter that she could be allowed to arrange for herself. . . . And now I have a few questions to put to you, Mr. Worthing. While I am making these inquiries, you, Gwendolen, will wait for me below in the carriage.

GWENDOLEN. [*reproachfully*] Mamma!

LADY BRACKNELL. In the carriage, Gwendolen! [GWENDOLEN *goes to the door. She and* JACK *blow kisses to each other behind* LADY BRACKNELL's *back.* LADY BRACKNELL *looks vaguely about as if she could not understand what the noise was. Finally turns round.*] Gwendolen, the carriage!

GWENDOLEN. Yes, mamma. [*Goes out, looking back at* JACK.]

LADY BRACKNELL. [*sitting down*] You can take a seat, Mr. Worthing.

[*Looks in her pocket for notebook and pencil.*]

JACK. Thank you, Lady Bracknell, I prefer standing.

LADY BRACKNELL. [*pencil and notebook in hand*] I feel bound to tell you that you are not down on my list of eligible young men, although I have the same list as the dear Duchess of Bolton has. We work together, in fact. However, I am quite ready to enter your name, should your answers be what a really affectionate mother requires. Do you smoke?

JACK. Well, yes, I must admit I smoke.

LADY BRACKNELL. I am glad to hear it. A man should always have an occupation of some kind. There are far too many idle men in London as it is. How old are you?

JACK. Twenty-nine.

LADY BRACKNELL. A very good age to be married at. I have always been of opinion that a man who desires to get married should know either everything or nothing. Which do you know?

JACK. [*after some hesitation*] I know nothing, Lady Bracknell.

LADY BRACKNELL. I am pleased to hear it. I do not approve of anything that tampers with natural ignorance. Ignorance is like a delicate exotic fruit; touch it and the bloom is gone. The whole theory of modern education is radically unsound. Fortunately in England, at any rate, education produces no effect whatsoever. If it did, it would prove a serious danger to the upper classes, and probably lead to acts of violence in Grosvenor Square.[8] What is your income?

JACK. Between seven and eight thousand a year.

LADY BRACKNELL. [*makes a note in her book*] In land, or in investments?

JACK. In investments, chiefly.

LADY BRACKNELL. That is satisfactory. What between the duties expected of one during one's lifetime, and the duties exacted from one after one's death,[9] land has ceased to be either a profit or a pleasure. It gives one position, and prevents one from keeping it up. That's all that can be said about land.

JACK. I have a country house with some land, of course, attached to it, about fifteen hundred acres, I believe; but I don't depend on

8. Fashionable residential area in the west end of London.　　9. The word play is on "death duties" —i.e., inheritance taxes.

that for my real income. In fact, as far as I can make out, the poachers are the only people who make anything out of it.

LADY BRACKNELL. A country house! How many bedrooms? Well, that point can be cleared up afterwards. You have a town house, I hope? A girl with a simple, unspoiled nature, like Gwendolen, could hardly be expected to reside in the country.

JACK. Well, I own a house in Belgrave Square,[1] but it is let by the year to Lady Bloxham. Of course, I can get it back whenever I like, at six months' notice.

LADY BRACKNELL. Lady Bloxham? I don't know her.

JACK. Oh, she goes about very little. She is a lady considerably advanced in years.,

LADY BRACKNELL. Ah, nowadays that is no guarantee of respectability of character. What number in Belgrave Square?

JACK. 149.

LADY BRACKNELL. [*shaking her head*] The unfashionable side. I thought there was something. However, that could easily be altered.

JACK. Do you mean the fashion, or the side?

LADY BRACKNELL. [*sternly*] Both, if necessary, I presume. What are your politics?

JACK. Well, I am afraid I really have none. I am a Liberal Unionist.[2]

LADY BRACKNELL. Oh, they count as Tories. They dine with us. Or come in the evening, at any rate. Now to minor matters. Are your parents living?

JACK. I have lost both my parents.

LADY BRACKNELL. Both? . . . That seems like carelessness. Who was your father? He was evidently a man of some wealth. Was he born in what the Radical papers call the purple of commerce, or did he rise from the ranks of aristocracy?

JACK. I am afraid I really don't know. The fact is, Lady Bracknell, I said I had lost my parents. It would be nearer the truth to say that my parents seem to have lost me. . . . I don't actually know who I am by birth. I was . . . well, I was found.

LADY BRACKNELL. Found!

JACK. The late Mr. Thomas Cardew, an old gentleman of a very charitable and kindly disposition, found me, and gave me the name of Worthing, because he happened to have a first-class ticket for Worthing in his pocket at the time. Worthing is a place in Sussex. It is a seaside resort.

LADY BRACKNELL. Where did the charitable gentleman who had a first-class ticket for this seaside resort find you?

JACK. [*gravely*] In a handbag.

LADY BRACKNELL. A handbag?

JACK. [*very seriously*] Yes, Lady Bracknell. I was in a handbag—a

1. Another fashionable residential area in the west end known as Belgravia.
2. A splinter group of members of the Liberal Party who, in 1886, led by Joseph Chamberlain, joined forces with the Conservative party (the "Tories") in opposing Home Rule for Ireland.

somewhat large, black leather handbag, with handles to it—an ordinary handbag, in fact.

LADY BRACKNELL. In what locality did this Mr. James, or Thomas, Cardew come across this ordinary handbag?

JACK. In the cloak room at Victoria Station. It was given to him in mistake for his own.[3]

LADY BRACKNELL. The cloak room at Victoria Station?

JACK. Yes. The Brighton line.

LADY BRACKNELL. The line is immaterial. Mr. Worthing, I confess I feel somewhat bewildered by what you have just told me. To be born, or at any rate, bred in a handbag, whether it had handles or not, seems to me to display a contempt for the ordinary decencies of family life that remind one of the worst excesses of the French Revolution. And I presume you know what that unfortunate movement led to? As for the particular locality in which the handbag was found, a cloak room at a railway station might serve to conceal a social indiscretion—has probably, indeed, been used for that purpose before now—but it could hardly be regarded as an assured basis for a recognized position in good society.

JACK. May I ask you then what you would advise me to do? I need hardly say I would do anything in the world to ensure Gwendolen's happiness.

LADY BRACKNELL. I would strongly advise you, Mr. Worthing, to try and acquire some relations as soon as possible, and to make a definite effort to produce at any rate one parent, of either sex, before the season is quite over.[4]

JACK. Well, I don't see how I could possibly manage to do that. I can produce the handbag at any moment. It is in my dressing room at home. I really think that should satisfy you, Lady Bracknell.

LADY BRACKNELL. Me, sir! What has it to do with me? You can hardly imagine that I and Lord Bracknell would dream of allowing our only daughter—a girl brought up with the utmost care—to marry into a clock room, and form an alliance with a parcel? Good morning, Mr. Worthing!

[LADY BRACKNELL *sweeps out in majestic indignation.*]

JACK. Good morning! [ALGERNON, *from the other room, strikes up the Wedding March.* JACK *looks perfectly furious, and goes to the door.*] For goodness' sake don't play that ghastly tune, Algy! How idiotic you are!

[*The music stops, and* ALGERNON *enters cheerily.*]

---

3. In the four-act version of the play Jack explains further what happened to Mr. Cardew: "He did not discover the error till he arrived at his own house. All subsequent efforts to ascertain who I was were unavailing."

4. In the four-act version of the play Jack later comments to Algernon about Lady Bracknell's demands about locating parents: "After all what does it matter whether a man has ever had a father and mother or not? Mothers, of course, are all right. They pay a chap's bills and don't bother him. But fathers bother a chap and never pay his bills. I don't know a single chap at the club who speaks to his father." And Algernon remarks: "Yes. Fathers are certainly not popular just at present. * * * They are like these chaps, the minor poets. They are never quoted."

ALGERNON. Didn't it go off all right, old boy? You don't mean to say Gwendolen refused you? I know it is a way she has. She is always refusing people. I think it is most ill-natured of her.

JACK. Oh, Gwendolen is as right as a trivet.[5] As far as she is concerned, we are engaged. Her mother is perfectly unbearable. Never met such a Gorgon[6] . . . I don't really know what a Gorgon is like, but I am quite sure that Lady Bracknell is one. In any case, she is a monster, without being a myth, which is rather unfair . . . I beg your pardon, Algy, I suppose I shouldn't talk about your own aunt in that way before you.

ALGERNON. My dear boy, I love hearing my relations abused. It is the only thing that makes me put up with them at all. Relations are simply a tedious pack of people who haven't got the remotest knowledge of how to live, nor the smallest instinct about when to die.

JACK. Oh, that is nonsense!

ALGERNON. It isn't!

JACK. Well, I won't argue about the matter. You always want to argue about things.

ALGERNON. That is exactly what things were originally made for.

JACK. Upon my word, if I thought that, I'd shoot myself . . . [*A pause.*] You don't think there is any chance of Gwendolen becoming like her mother in about a hundred and fifty years, do you, Algy?

ALGERNON. All women become like their mothers. That is their tragedy. No man does. That's his.

JACK. Is that clever?

ALGERNON. It is perfectly phrased! and quite as true as any observation in civilized life should be.

JACK. I am sick to death of cleverness. Everybody is clever nowadays. You can't go anywhere without meeting clever people. The thing has become an absolute public nuisance. I wish to goodness we had a few fools left.

ALGERNON. We have.

JACK. I should extremely like to meet them. What do they talk about?

ALGERNON. The fools? Oh! about the clever people, of course.

JACK. What fools!

ALGERNON. By the way, did you tell Gwendolen the truth about your being Ernest in town, and Jack in the country?

JACK. [*in a very patronizing manner*] My dear fellow, the truth isn't quite the sort of thing one tells to a nice sweet refined girl. What extraordinary ideas you have about the way to behave to a woman!

ALGERNON. The only way to behave to a woman is to make love to her, if she is pretty, and to someone else if she is plain.

---

5. Proverbial expression meaning reliably steady, like a tripod ("trivet") used to support pots over a fire.

6. A mythical female creature, like Medusa, whose look turned into stone anyone beholding her.

JACK. Oh, that is nonsense.

ALGERNON. What about your brother? What about the profligate Ernest?

JACK. Oh, before the end of the week I shall have got rid of him. I'll say he died in Paris of apoplexy. Lots of people die of apoplexy, quite suddenly, don't they?

ALGERNON. Yes, but it's hereditary, my dear fellow. It's a sort of thing that runs in families. You had much better say a severe chill.

JACK. You are sure a severe chill isn't hereditary, or anything of that kind?

ALGERNON. Of course it isn't!

JACK. Very well, then. My poor brother Ernest is carried off suddenly in Paris, by a severe chill. That gets rid of him.[7]

ALGERNON. But I thought you said that . . . Miss Cardew was a little too much interested in your poor brother Ernest? Won't she feel his loss a good deal?

JACK. Oh, that is all right. Cecily is not a silly romantic girl, I am glad to say. She has got a capital appetite, goes on long walks, and pays no attention at all to her lessons.

ALGERNON. I would rather like to see Cecily.

JACK. I will take very good care you never do. She is excessively pretty, and she is only just eighteen.

ALGERNON. Have you told Gwendolen yet that you have an excessively pretty ward who is only just eighteen?

JACK. Oh! one doesn't blurt these things out to people. Cecily and Gwendolen are perfectly certain to be extremely great friends. I'll bet you anything you like that half an hour after they have met, they will be calling each other sister.

ALGERNON. Women only do that when they have called each other a lot of other things first. Now, my dear boy, if we want to get a good table at Willis's, we really must go and dress. Do you know it is nearly seven?

JACK. [*irritably*] Oh! it always is nearly seven.

ALGERNON. Well, I'm hungry.

JACK. I never knew you when you weren't. . . .

ALGERNON. What shall we do after dinner? Go to the theater?

JACK. Oh no! I loathe listening.

ALGERNON. Well, let us go to the club?

JACK. Oh, no! I hate talking.

ALGERNON. Well, we might trot around to the Empire[8] at ten?

JACK. Oh no! I can't bear looking at things. It is so silly.

ALGERNON. Well, what shall we do?

JACK. Nothing!

ALGERNON. It is awfully hard work doing nothing. However, I don't

---

7. In the four-act version of the play Jack explains further: "I'll wear mourning for him, of course; that would be only decent. I don't at all mind wearing mourning. I think that all black, with a good pearl pin, rather smart. Then I'll go down home and break the news to my household."

8. A music hall in Leicester Square which featured light entertainment.

mind hard work where there is no definite object of any kind.

[*Enter* LANE.]

LANE. Miss Fairfax.

[*Enter* GWENDOLEN. LANE *goes out.*]

ALGERNON. Gwendolen, upon my word!

GWENDOLEN. Algy, kindly turn your back. I have something very particular to say to Mr. Worthing.

ALGERNON. Really, Gwendolen, I don't think I can allow this at all.

GWENDOLEN. Algy, you always adopt a strictly immoral attitude towards life. You are not quite old enough to do that. [ALGERNON *retires to the fireplace.*]

JACK. My own darling!

GWENDOLEN. Ernest, we may never be married. From the expression on mamma's face I fear we never shall. Few parents nowadays pay any regard to what their children say to them. The old-fashioned respect for the young is fast dying out. Whatever influence I ever had over mamma, I lost at the age of three. But although she may prevent us from becoming man and wife, and I may marry someone else, and marry often, nothing that she can possibly do can alter my eternal devotion to you.

JACK. Dear Gwendolen!

GWENDOLEN. The story of your romantic origin, as related to me by mamma, with unpleasing comments, has naturally stirred the deeper fibers of my nature. Your Christian name has an irresistible fascination. The simplicity of your character makes you exquisitely incomprehensible to me. Your town address at the Albany I have. What is your address in the country?

JACK. The Manor House, Woolton, Hertfordshire.

[ALGERNON, *who has been carefully listening, smiles to himself, and writes the address on his shirt-cuff.*[9] *Then picks up the Railway Guide.*]

GWENDOLEN. There is a good postal service, I suppose? It may be necessary to do something desperate. That of course will require serious consideration. I will communicate with you daily.

JACK. My own one!

GWENDOLEN. How long do you remain in town?

JACK. Till Monday.

GWENDOLEN. Good! Algy, you may turn round now.

ALGERNON. Thanks, I've turned round already.

GWENDOLEN. You may also ring the bell.

JACK. You will let me see you to your carriage, my own darling?

GWENDOLEN. Certainly.

JACK. [*to* LANE, *who now enters*] I will see Miss Fairfax out.

LANE. Yes, sir. [JACK *and* GWENDOLEN *go off.*]

[LANE *presents several letters on a salver to* ALGERNON. *It is to be surmised that they are bills, as* ALGERNON *after looking at the envelopes, tears them up.*]

---

9. Because shirt-cuffs were heavily starched they provided a good surface on which to make notes.

ALGERNON. A glass of sherry, Lane.

LANE. Yes, sir.

ALGERNON. Tomorrow, Lane, I'm going Bunburying.

LANE. Yes, sir.

ALGERNON. I shall probably not be back till Monday. You can put up my dress clothes, my smoking jacket,[1] and all the Bunbury suits . . .

LANE. Yes, sir. [*Handing sherry.*]

ALGERNON. I hope tomorrow will be a fine day, Lane.

LANE. It never is, sir.

ALGERNON. Lane, you're a perfect pessimist.

LANE. I do my best to give satisfaction, sir.

> [*Enter* JACK. LANE *goes off.*]

JACK. There's a sensible, intellectual girl! the only girl I ever cared for in my life. [ALGERNON *is laughing immoderately.*] What on earth are you so amused at?

ALGERNON. Oh, I'm a little anxious about poor Bunbury, that is all.

JACK. If you don't take care, your friend Bunbury will get you into a serious scrape some day.

ALGERNON. I love scrapes. They are the only things that are never serious.

JACK. Oh, that's nonsense, Algy. You never talk anything but nonsense.

ALGERNON. Nobody ever does.

> [JACK *looks indignantly at him, and leaves the room.* ALGERNON *lights a cigarette, reads his shirt-cuff, and smiles.*]

ACT-DROP[2]

Second Act

SCENE—*Garden at the Manor House. A flight of gray stone steps leads up to the house. The garden, an old-fashioned one, full of roses. Time of year, July. Basket chairs, and a table covered with books, are set under a large yew tree.*

> [MISS PRISM[3] *discovered seated at the table.* CECILY *is at the back watering flowers.*]

MISS PRISM. [*calling*] Cecily, Cecily! Surely such a utilitarian occupation as the watering of flowers is rather Moulton's duty than yours? Especially at a moment when intellectual pleasures await you. Your German grammar is on the table. Pray open it at page fifteen. We will repeat yesterday's lesson.

CECILY. [*coming over very slowly*] But I don't like German. It isn't at all a becoming language. I know perfectly well that I look

---

1. Coat worn when gentlemen assembled in a room designated for smoking. The object was to avoid contaminating their regular clothing with the smell of cigars or pipes, which was considered offensive to ladies.

2. A special curtain lowered during theatrical performances to denote intervals between acts or scenes.

3. The name has connotations with the expression "prunes and prism" from Dickens' *Little Dorrit* (XLI) in which Mrs. General, a prim and proper teacher of manners for young ladies, trains them to repeat "prunes and prism" aloud because this exercise "gives a pretty form to the lips."

quite plain after my German lesson.

MISS PRISM. Child, you know how anxious your guardian is that you should improve yourself in every way. He laid particular stress on your German, as he was leaving for town yesterday. Indeed, he always lays stress on your German when he is leaving for town.

CECILY. Dear Uncle Jack is so very serious! Sometime he is so serious that I think he cannot be quite well.

MISS PRISM. [*drawing herself up*] Your guardian enjoys the best of health, and his gravity of demeanor is especially to be commended in one so comparatively young as he is. I know no one who has a higher sense of duty and responsibility.

CECILY. I suppose that is why he often looks a little bored when we three are together.

MISS PRISM. Cecily! I am surprised at you. Mr. Worthing has many troubles in his life. Idle merriment and triviality would be out of place in his conversation. You must remember his constant anxiety about that unfortunate young man his brother.

CECILY. I wish Uncle Jack would allow that unfortunate young man, his brother, to come down here sometimes. We might have a good influence over him, Miss Prism. I am sure you certainly would. You know German, and geology, and things of that kind influence a man very much. [CECILY *begins to write in her diary.*]

MISS PRISM. [*shaking her head*] I do not think that even I could produce any effect on a character that according to his own brother's admission is irretrievably weak and vacillating. Indeed I am not sure that I would desire to reclaim him. I am not in favor of this modern mania for turning bad people into good people at a moment's notice. As a man sows so let him reap. You must put away your diary, Cecily. I really don't see why you should keep a diary at all.

CECILY. I keep a diary in order to enter the wonderful secrets of my life. If I didn't write them down I should probably forget all about them.

MISS PRISM. Memory, my dear Cecily, is the diary that we all carry about with us.

CECILY. Yes, but it usually chronicles the things that have never happened, and couldn't possibly have happened. I believe that Memory is responsible for nearly all the three-volume novels that Mudie sends us.[4]

MISS PRISM. Do not speak slightingly of the three-volume novel, Cecily. I wrote one myself in earlier days.

CECILY. Did you really, Miss Prism? How wonderfully clever you are! I hope it did not end happily? I don't like novels that end happily. They depress me so much.

4. Mudie's Circulating Library loaned copies of new three-volume novels (usually sentimental tales) to subscribers for a moderate fee. Mudie's power in controlling the book market, especially for novels, was on the wane by 1895.

MISS PRISM. The good ended happily, and the bad unhappily. That is what Fiction means.

CECILY. I suppose so. But it seems very unfair. And was your novel ever published?

MISS PRISM. Alas! no. The manuscript unfortunately was abandoned. I use the word in the sense of lost or mislaid. To your work, child, these speculations are profitless.

CECILY. [*smiling*] But I see dear Dr. Chasuble coming up through the garden.

MISS PRISM. [*rising and advancing*] Dr. Chasuble! This is indeed a pleasure.

[*Enter* CANON CHASUBLE.]

CHASUBLE. And how are we this morning? Miss Prism, you are, I trust, well?

CECILY. Miss Prism has just been complaining of a slight headache. I think it would do her so much good to have a short stroll with you in the Park, Dr. Chasuble.

MISS PRISM. Cecily, I have not mentioned anything about a headache.

CECILY. No, dear Miss Prism, I know that, but I felt instinctively that you had a headache. Indeed I was thinking about that, and not about my German lesson, when the Rector came in.

CHASUBLE. I hope Cecily, you are not inattentive.

CECILY. Oh, I am afraid I am.

CHASUBLE. That is strange. Were I fortunate enough to be Miss Prism's pupil, I would hang upon her lips. [MISS PRISM *glares*.] I spoke metaphorically.—My metaphor was drawn from bees. Ahem! Mr. Worthing I suppose, has not returned from town yet?

MISS PRISM. We do not expect him till Monday afternoon.

CHASUBLE. Ah yes, he usually likes to spend his Sunday in London. He is not one of those whose sole aim is enjoyment, as, by all accounts, that unfortunate young man his brother seems to be. But I must not disturb Egeria[5] and her pupil any longer.

MISS PRISM. Egeria? My name is Laetitia, Doctor.

CHASUBLE. [*bowing*] A classical allusion merely, drawn from the Pagan authors. I shall see you both no doubt at Evensong?[6]

MISS PRISM. I think, dear Doctor, I will have a stroll with you. I find I have a headache after all, and a walk might do it good.

CHASUBLE. With pleasure, Miss Prism, with pleasure. We might go as far as the schools and back.

MISS PRISM. That would be delightful. Cecily, you will read your Political Economy[7] in my absence. The chapter on the Fall of the Rupee you may omit. It is somewhat too sensational. Even these metallic problems have their melodramatic side.

[*Goes down the garden with* DR. CHASUBLE.]

5. Roman goddess of fountains. Her name was also used as an epithet for a woman who provides guidance for other women.
6. Evening church services.

7. I.e., book about economics. The "rupee" was the basic unit of currency in India. British civil servants who worked in India were paid in rupees, and would suffer from its fall in value.

CECILY. [*picks up books and throws them back on table*] Horrid
Political Economy! Horrid Geography! Horrid, horrid German!
    [*Enter* MERRIMAN *with a card on a salver.*]

MERRIMAN. Mr. Ernest Worthing has just driven over from the station. He has brought his luggage with him.

CECILY. [*takes the card and reads it.*] "Mr. Ernest Worthing, B.
4, The Albany, W." Uncle Jack's brother! Did you tell him Mr.
Worthing was in town?

MERRIMAN. Yes, Miss. He seemed very much disappointed. I mentioned that you and Miss Prism were in the garden. He said he
was anxious to speak to you privately for a moment.

CECILY. Ask Mr. Ernest Worthing to come here. I suppose you had
better talk to the housekeeper about a room for him.

MERRIMAN. Yes, Miss.   [MERRIMAN *goes off.*]

CECILY. I have never met any really wicked person before. I feel
rather frightened. I am so afraid he will look just like everyone
else.
    [*Enter* ALGERNON, *very gay and debonair.*] He does!

ALGERNON. [*raising his hat.*] You are my little cousin Cecily, I'm
sure.

CECILY. You are under some strange mistake. I am not little. In
fact, I believe I am more than usually tall for my age. [ALGER-
NON *is rather taken aback.*] But I am your cousin Cecily. You, I
see from your card, are Uncle Jack's brother, my cousin Ernest,
my wicked cousin Ernest.

ALGERNON. Oh! I am not really wicked at all, cousin Cecily. You
mustn't think that I am wicked.

CECILY. If you are not, then you have certainly been deceiving us
all in a very inexcusable manner. I hope you have not been leading a double life, pretending to be wicked and being really good
all the time. That would be hypocrisy.

ALGERNON. [*looks at her in amazement*] Oh! Of course I have
been rather reckless.

CECILY. I am glad to hear it.

ALGERNON. In fact, now you mention the subject, I have been very
bad in my own small way.

CECILY. I don't think you should be so proud of that, though I am
sure it must have been very pleasant.

ALGERNON. It is much pleasanter being here with you.

CECILY. I can't understand how you are here at all. Uncle Jack
won't be back till Monday afternoon.

ALGERNON. That is a great disappointment. I am obliged to go up
by the first train on Monday morning. I have a business appointment that I am anxious . . . to miss.

CECILY. Couldn't you miss it anywhere but in London?

ALGERNON. No: the appointment is in London.

CECILY. Well, I know, of course, how important it is not to keep a
business engagement, if one wants to retain any sense of the

beauty of life, but still I think you had better wait till Uncle Jack arrives. I know he wants to speak to you about your emigrating.

ALGERNON. About my what?

CECILY. Your emigrating. He has gone up to buy your outfit.

ALGERNON. I certainly wouldn't let Jack buy my outfit. He has no taste in neckties at all.

CECILY. I don't think you will require neckties. Uncle Jack is sending you to Australia.[8]

ALGERNON. Australia? I'd sooner die.

CECILY. Well, he said at dinner on Wednesday night, that you would have to choose between this world, the next world, and Australia.

ALGERNON. Oh, well! The accounts I have received of Australia and the next world are not particularly encouraging. This world is good enough for me, cousin Cecily.

CECILY. Yes, but are you good enough for it?

ALGERNON. I'm afraid I'm not that. That is why I want you to reform me. You might make that your mission, if you don't mind, cousin Cecily.

CECILY. I'm afraid I've no time, this afternoon.

ALGERNON. Well, would you mind my reforming myself this afternoon?

CECILY. It is rather Quixotic of you. But I think you should try.

ALGERNON. I will. I feel better already.

CECILY. You are looking a little worse.

ALGERNON. That is because I am hungry.

CECILY. How thoughtless of me. I should have remembered that when one is going to lead an entirely new life, one requires regular and wholesome meals. Won't you come in?

ALGERNON. Thank you. Might I have a buttonhole[9] first? I never have any appetite unless I have a buttonhole first.

CECILY. A Maréchale Niel?[1] [Picks up scissors.]

ALGERNON. No, I'd sooner have a pink rose.

CECILY. Why? [Cuts a flower.]

ALGERNON. Because you are like a pink rose, cousin Cecily.

CECILY. I don't think it can be right for you to talk to me like that. Miss Prism never says such things to me.

ALGERNON. Then Miss Prism is shortsighted old lady. [CECILY puts the rose in his buttonhole.] You are the prettiest girl I ever saw.

CECILY. Miss Prism says that all good looks are a snare.

ALGERNON. They are a snare that every sensible man would like to be caught in.

CECILY. Oh! I don't think I would care to catch a sensible man. I shouldn't know what to talk to him about.

8. Although Australia had originally been a place to which criminals were banished, it was, by this time, like Canada, a place to which families might send harmless but useless members, who would be paid an allowance to remain abroad.
9. I.e., a flower worn in the buttonhole of a man's coat lapel.
1. A chrome-yellow variety of rose named after one of the generals of Napoleon III.

[*They pass into the house.* MISS PRISM *and* DR. CHASUBLE *return.*]

MISS PRISM. You are too much alone, dear Dr. Chasuble. You should get married. A misanthrope I can understand—a woman-thrope, never!

CHASUBLE. [*with a scholar's shudder*][2] Believe me, I do not deserve so neologistic a phrase. The precept as well as the practice of the Primitive Church was distinctly against matrimony.

MISS PRISM. [*sententiously*] That is obviously the reason why the Primitive Church has not lasted up to the present day. And you do not seem to realize, dear Doctor, that by persistently remaining single, a man converts himself into a permanent public temptation. Men should be more careful; this very celibacy leads weaker vessels astray.

CHASUBLE. But is a man not equally attractive when married?

MISS PRISM. No married man is ever attractive except to his wife.

CHASUBLE. And often, I've been told, not even to her.

MISS PRISM. That depends on the intellectual sympathies of the woman. Maturity can always be depended on. Ripeness can be trusted. Young women are green. [DR. CHASUBLE *starts.*] I spoke horticulturally. My metaphor was drawn from fruits. But where is Cecily?

CHASUBLE. Perhaps she followed us to the schools.

[*Enter* JACK *slowly from the back of the garden. He is dressed in the deepest mourning, with crape hat-band and black gloves.*]

MISS PRISM. Mr. Worthing!

CHASUBLE. MR. WORTHING?

MISS PRISM. This is indeed a surprise. We did not look for you till Monday afternoon.

JACK. [*shakes* MISS PRISM'S *hand in a tragic manner*] I have returned sooner than I expected. Dr. Chasuble, I hope you are well?

CAHSUBLE. Dear Mr. Worthing, I trust this garb of woe does not betoken some terrible calamity?

JACK. My brother.

MISS PRISM. More shameful debts and extravagance?

CHASUBLE. Still leading his life of pleasure?

JACK. [*shaking his head*] Dead!

CHASUBLE. Your brother Ernest dead?

JACK. Quite dead.

MISS PRISM. What a lesson for him! I trust he will profit by it.

CHASUBLE. Mr. Worthing, I offer you my sincere condolence. You have at least the consolation of knowing that you were always the most generous and forgiving of brothers.

JACK. Poor Ernest! He had many faults, but it is a sad, sad blow.

CHASUBLE. Very sad indeed. Were you with him at the end?

2. He shudders because instead of using the correct word for woman-hater, "misogynist," she has coined her own expression.

JACK. No. He died abroad; in Paris, in fact. I had a telegram last night from the manager of the Grand Hotel.

CHASUBLE. Was the cause of death mentioned?

JACK. A severe chill, it seems.

MISS PRISM. As a man sows, so shall he reap.[3]

CHASUBLE. [*raising his hand*] Charity, dear Miss Prism, charity! None of us are perfect. I myself am peculiarly susceptible to drafts. Will the interment take place here?

JACK. No. He seemed to have expressed a desire to be buried in Paris.

CHASUBLE. In Paris! [*Shakes his head.*] I fear that hardly points to any very serious state of mind at the last. You would no doubt wish me to make some slight allusion to this tragic domestic affliction next Sunday. [JACK *presses his hand convulsively.*] My sermon on the meaning of the manna in the wilderness can be adapted to almost any occasion, joyful, or, as in the present case, distressing. [*All sigh.*] I have preached it at harvest celebrations, christenings, confirmations, on days of humiliation and festal days. The last time I delivered it was in the Cathedral, as a charity sermon on behalf of the Society for the Prevention of Discontent among the Upper Orders. The Bishop, who was present, was much struck by some of the analogies I drew.

JACK. Ah! That reminds me, you mentioned christenings, I think, Dr. Chasuble? I suppose you know how to christen all right? [DR. CHASUBLE *looks astounded.*] I mean, of course, you are continually christening, aren't you?

MISS PRISM. It is, I regret to say, one of the Rector's most constant duties in this parish. I have often spoken to the poorer classes on the subject. But they don't seem to know what thrift is.

CHASUBLE. But is there any particular infant in whom you are interested, Mr. Worthing? Your brother was, I believe, unmarried, was he not?

JACK. Oh yes.

MISS PRISM. [*bitterly*] People who live entirely for pleasure usually are.

JACK. But it is not for any child, dear Doctor. I am very fond of children. No! the fact is, I would like to be christened myself, this afternoon, if you have nothing better to do.

CHASUBLE. But surely, Mr. Worthing, you have been christened already?

JACK. I don't remember anything about it.

CHASUBLE. But have you any grave doubts on the subject?

JACK. I certainly intend to have. Of course I don't know if the thing would bother you in any way, or if you think I am a little too old now.

CHASUBLE. Not at all. The sprinkling, and, indeed, the immersion of adults is a perfectly canonical practice.

JACK. Immersion!

3. Cf. Galatians vi. 7.

CHASUBLE. You need have no apprehensions. Sprinkling is all that is necessary, or indeed I think advisable. Our weather is so changeable. At what hour would you wish the ceremony performed?

JACK. Oh, I might trot round about five if that would suit you.

CHASUBLE. Perfectly, perfectly! In fact I have two similar ceremonies to perform at that time. A case of twins that occurred recently in one of the outlying cottages on your own estate. Poor Jenkins the carter, a most hard-working man.

JACK. Oh! I don't see much fun in being christened along with other babies. It would be childish. Would half-past five do?

CHASUBLE. Admirably! Admirably! [*Takes out watch.*] And now, dear Mr. Worthing, I will not intrude any longer into a house of sorrow. I would merely beg you not to be too much bowed down by grief. What seem to us bitter trials are often blessings in disguise.

MISS PRISM. This seems to me a blessing of an extremely obvious kind.

[*Enter* CECILY *from the house.*]

CECILY. Uncle Jack! Oh, I am pleased to see you back. But what horrid clothes you have got on! Do go and change them.

MISS PRISM. Cecily!

CHASUBLE. My child! my child! [CECILY *goes towards* JACK; *he kisses her brow in a melancholy manner.*]

CECILY. What is the matter, Uncle Jack? Do look happy! You look as if you had toothache, and I have got such a surprise for you. Who do you think is in the dining room? Your brother!

JACK. Who?

CECILY. Your brother Ernest. He arrived about half an hour ago.

JACK. What nonsense! I haven't got a brother!

CECILY. Oh, don't say that. However badly he may have behaved to you in the past he is still your brother. You couldn't be so heartless as to disown him. I'll tell him to come out. And you will shake hands with him, won't you, Uncle Jack? [*Runs back into the house.*]

CHASUBLE. These are very joyful tidings.

MISS PRISM. After we had all been resigned to his loss, his sudden return seems to me peculiarly distressing.

JACK. My brother is in the dining room? I don't know what it all means. I think it is perfectly absurd.

[*Enter* ALGERNON *and* CECILY *hand in hand. They come slowly up to* JACK.]

JACK. Good heavens! [*Motions* ALGERNON *away*.]

ALGERNON. Brother John, I have come down from town to tell you that I am very sorry for all the trouble I have given you, and that I intend to lead a better life in the future. [JACK *glares at him and does not take his hand.*]

CECILY. Uncle Jack, you are not going to refuse your own brother's hand?

JACK. Nothing will induce me to take his hand. I think his coming down here disgraceful. He knows perfectly well why.

CECILY. Uncle Jack, do be nice. There is some good in everyone. Ernest has just been telling me about his poor invalid friend Mr. Bunbury whom he goes to visit so often. And surely there must be much good in one who is kind to an invalid, and leaves the pleasures of London to sit by a bed of pain.

JACK. Oh! he has been talking about Bunbury, has he?

CECILY. Yes, he has told me all about poor Mr. Bunbury, and his terrible state of health.

JACK. Bunbury! Well, I won't have him talk to you about Bunbury or about anything else. It is enough to drive one perfectly frantic.

ALGERNON. Of course I admit that the faults were all on my side. But I must say that I think that Brother John's coldness to me is peculiarly painful. I expected a more enthusiastric welcome, especially considering it is the first time I have come here.

CECILY. Uncle Jack, if you don't shake hands with Ernest, I will never forgive you.

JACK. Never forgive me?

CECILY. Never, never, never!

JACK. Well, this is the last time I shall ever do it. [*Shakes hands with Algernon and glares.*]

CHASUBLE. It's pleasant, is it not, to see so perfect a reconciliation? I think we might leave the two brothers together.

MISS PRISM. Cecily, you will come with us.

CECILY. Certainly, Miss Prism. My little task of reconciliation is over.

CHASUBLE. You have done a beautiful action today, dear child.

MISS PRISM. We must not be premature in our judgments.

CECILY. I feel very happy. [*They all go off.*]

JACK. You young scoundrel, Algy, you must get out of this place as soon as possible. I don't allow any Bunburying here.

[*Enter* MERRIMAN.]

MERRIMAN. I have put Mr. Ernest's things in the room next to yours, sir. I suppose that is all right?

JACK. What?

MERRIMAN. Mr. Ernest's luggage, sir. I have unpacked it and put it in the room next to your own.

JACK. His luggage?

MERRIMAN. Yes, sir. Three portmanteaus,[4] a dressing case, two hat-boxes, and a large luncheon basket.

ALGERNON. I am afraid I can't stay more than a week this time.

JACK. Merriman, order the dogcart[5] at once. Mr. Ernest has been suddenly called back to town.

MERRIMAN. Yes, sir.

[*Goes back into the house.*]

ALGERNON. What a fearful liar you are, Jack. I have not been called

---

4. Large leather suitcases.
5. Horse-drawn cart with seats, origi- nally designed to carry hunters and their hunting dogs.

back to town at all.

JACK. Yes, you have.

ALGERNON. I haven't heard anyone call me.

JACK. Your duty as a gentleman calls you back.

ALGERNON. My duty as a gentleman has never interfered with my pleasures in the smallest degree.

JACK. I can quite understand that.

ALGERNON. Well, Cecily is a darling.

JACK. You are not to talk of Miss Cardew like that. I don't like it.

ALGERNON. Well, I don't like your clothes. You look perfectly ridiculous in them. Why on earth don't you go up and change? It is perfectly childish to be in deep mourning for a man who is actually staying for a whole week with you in your house as a guest. I call it grotesque.

JACK. You are certainly not staying with me for a whole week as a guest or anything else. You have got to leave . . . by the four-five train.

ALGERNON. I certainly won't leave you so long as you are in mourning. It would be most unfriendly. If I were in mourning you would stay with me, I suppose. I should think it very unkind if you didn't.

JACK. Well, will you go if I change my clothes?

ALGERNON. Yes, if you are not too long. I never saw anybody take so long to dress, and with such little result.

JACK. Well, at any rate, that is better than being always overdressed as you are.

ALGERNON. If I am occasionally a little overdressed, I make up for it by being always immensely overeducated.

JACK. Your vanity is ridiculous, your conduct an outrage, and your presence in my garden utterly absurd. However, you have got to catch the four-five, and I hope you will have a pleasant journey back to town. This Bunburying, as you call it, has not been a great success for you. [*Goes into the house.*]

ALGERNON. I think it has been a great success. I'm in love with Cecily, and that is everything.

[*Enter* CECILY *at the back of the garden. She picks up the can and begins to water the flowers.*]

But I must see her before I go, and make arrangements for another Bunbury. Ah, there she is.

CECILY. Oh, I merely came back to water the roses. I thought you were with Uncle Jack.

ALGERNON. He's gone to order the dogcart for me.

CECILY. Oh, is he going to take you for a nice drive?

ALGERNON. He's going to send me away.

CECILY. Then have we got to part?

ALGERNON. I am afraid so. It's very painful parting.

CECILY. It is always painful to part from people whom one has known for a very brief space of time. The absence of old friends one can endure with equanimity. But even a momentary separation from anyone to whom one has just been introduced is almost unbearable.

ALGERNON. Thank you.

[*Enter* MERRIMAN.]

MERRIMAN. The dogcart is at the door, sir. [ALGERNON *looks appealingly at* CECILY.]

CECILY. It can wait, Merriman . . . for . . . five minutes.

MERRIMAN. Yes, Miss. [*Exit* MERRIMAN.]

ALGERNON. I hope, Cecily, I shall not offend you if I state quite frankly and openly that you seem to me to be in every way the visible personification of absolute perfection.

CECILY. I think your frankness does you great credit, Ernest. If you will allow me I will copy your remarks into my diary. [*Goes over to table and begins writing in diary.*]

ALGERNON. Do you really keep a diary? I'd give anything to look at it. May I?

CECILY. Oh no. [*Puts her hand over it.*] You see, it is simply a very young girl's record of her own thoughts and impressions, and consequently meant for publication. When it appears in volume form I hope you will order a copy. But pray, Ernest, don't stop. I delight in taking down from dictation. I have reached "absolute perfection." You can go on. I am quite ready for more.

ALGERNON. [*somewhat taken aback*] Ahem! Ahem!

CECILY. Oh, don't cough, Ernest. When one is dictating one should speak fluently and not cough. Besides, I don't know how to spell a cough. [*Writes as* ALGERNON *speaks.*]

ALGERNON. [*speaking very rapidly*] Cecily, ever since I first looked upon your wonderful and incomparable beauty, I have dared to love you wildly, passionately, devotedly, hopelessly.

CECILY. I don't think that you should tell me that you love me wildly, passionately, devotedly, hopelessly. Hopelessly doesn't seem to make much sense, does it?

ALGERNON. Cecily!

[*Enter* MERRIMAN.]

MERRIMAN. The dogcart is waiting, sir.

ALGERNON. Tell it to come round next week, at the same hour.

MERRIMAN. [*looks at* CECILY, *who makes no sign*] Yes, sir.

[MERRIMAN *retires.*]

CECILY. Uncle Jack would be very much annoyed if he knew you were staying on till next week, at the same hour.

ALGERNON. Oh, I don't care about Jack. I don't care for anybody in the whole world but you. I love you, Cecily. You will marry me, won't you?

CECILY. You silly boy! Of course. Why, we have been engaged for the last three months.

ALGERNON. For the last three months?

CECILY. Yes, it will be exactly three months on Thursday.

ALGERNON. But how did we become engaged?

CECILY. Well, ever since dear Uncle Jack first confessed to us that he had a younger brother who was very wicked and bad, you of course have formed the chief topic of conversation between myself and Miss Prism. And of course a man who is much talked about is always very attractive. One feels there must be something in him after all. I daresay it was foolish of me, but I fell in love with you, Ernest.

ALGERNON. Darling! And when was the engagement actually settled?

CECILY. On the 14th of February last. Worn out by your entire ignorance of my existence, I determined to end the matter one way or the other, and after a long struggle with myself I accepted you under this dear old tree here. The next day I bought this little ring in your name, and this is the little bangle with the true lovers' knot I promised you always to wear.

ALGERNON. Did I give you this? It's very pretty, isn't it?

CECILY. Yes, you've wonderfully good taste, Ernest. It's the excuse I've always given for your leading such a bad life. And this is the box in which I keep all your dear letters. [*Kneels at table, opens box, and produces letters tied up with blue ribbon.*]

ALGERNON. My letters! But my own sweet Cecily, I have never written you any letters.

CECILY. You need hardly remind me of that, Ernest. I remember only too well that I was forced to write your letters for you. I always wrote three times a week, and sometimes oftener.

ALGERNON. Oh, do let me read them, Cecily?

CECILY. Oh, I couldn't possibly. They would make you far too conceited. [*Replaces box.*] The three you wrote me after I had broken off the engagement are so beautiful, and so badly spelled, that even now I can hardly read them without crying a little.

ALGERNON. But was our engagement ever broken off?

CECILY. Of course it was. On the 22nd of last March. You can see the entry if you like. [*Shows diary.*] "Today I broke off my engagement with Ernest. I feel it is better to do so. The weather still continues charming."

ALGERNON. But why on earth did you break it off? What had I done? I had done nothing at all. Cecily, I am very much hurt indeed to hear you broke it off. Particularly when the weather was so charming.

CECILY. It would hardly have been a really serious engagement if it hadn't been broken off at least once. But I forgave you before the week was out.

ALGERNON. [*crossing to her, and kneeling*] What a perfect angel you are, Cecily.

CECILY. You dear romantic boy. [*He kisses her, she puts her fingers through his hair.*] I hope your hair curls naturally, does it?

ALGERNON. Yes, darling, with a little help from others.

CECILY. I am so glad.

ALGERNON. You'll never break off our engagement again, Cecily?

CECILY. I don't think I could break it off now that I have actually met you. Besides, of course, there is the question of your name.

ALGERNON. Yes, of course. [*Nervously.*]

CECILY. You must not laugh at me, darling, but it had always been a girlish dream of mine to love someone whose name was Ernest. [ALGERNON *rises*, CECILY *also.*] There is something in that name that seems to inspire absolute confidence. I pity any poor married woman whose husband is not called Ernest.

ALGERNON. But, my dear child, do you mean to say you could not love me if I had some other name?

CECILY. But what name?

ALGERNON. Oh, any name you like—Algernon—for instance . . .

CECILY. But I don't like the name of Algernon.

ALGERNON. Well, my own dear, sweet, loving little darling, I really can't see why you should object to the name of Algernon. It is not at all a bad name. In fact, it is rather an aristocratic name. Half of the chaps who get into the Bankruptcy Court are called Algernon. But seriously, Cecily . . . [*Moving to her*] . . . if my name was Algy, couldn't you love me?

CECILY. [*rising*] I might respect you, Ernest, I might admire your character, but I fear that I should not be able to give you my undivided attention.

ALGERNON. Ahem! Cecily! [*Picking up hat.*] Your Rector here is, I suppose, thoroughly experienced in the practice of all the rites and ceremonials of the Church?

CECILY. Oh, yes. Dr. Chasuble is a most learned man. He has never written a single book, so you can imagine how much he knows.

ALGERNON. I must see him at once on a most important christening —I mean on most important business.

CECILY. Oh!

ALGERNON. I shan't be away more than half an hour.

CECILY. Considering that we have been engaged since February the 14th, and that I only met you today for the first time, I think it is rather hard that you should leave me for so long a period as half an hour. Couldn't you make it twenty minutes?

ALGERNON. I'll be back in no time.

[*Kisses her and rushes down the garden.*]

CECILY. What an impetuous boy he is! I like his hair so much. I must enter his proposal in my diary.

[*Enter* MERRIMAN.]

MERRIMAN. A Miss Fairfax has just called to see Mr. Worthing. On very important business, Miss Fairfax states.

CECILY. Isn't Mr. Worthing in his library?

MERRIMAN. Mr. Worthing went over in the direction of the Rectory some time ago.

CECILY. Pray ask the lady to come out here; Mr. Worthing is sure to be back soon. And you can bring tea.

MERRIMAN. Yes, Miss. [*Goes out.*]

CECILY. Miss Fairfax! I suppose one of the many good elderly women who are associated with Uncle Jack in some of his philanthropic work in London. I don't quite like women who are interested in philanthropic work. I think it is so forward of them.

[*Enter* MERRIMAN.]

MERRIMAN. Miss Fairfax.

[*Enter* GWENDOLEN.] [*Exit* MERRIMAN.]

CECILY. [*advancing to meet her*] Pray let me introduce myself to you. My name is Cecily Cardew.

GWENDOLEN. Cecily Cardew? [*Moving to her and shaking hands.*] What a very sweet name! Something tells me that we are going to be great friends. I like you already more than I can say. My first impressions of people are never wrong.

CECILY. How nice of you to like me so much after we have known each other such a comparatively short time. Pray sit down.

GWENDOLEN. [*still standing up*] I may call you Cecily, may I not?

CECILY. With pleasure!

GWENDOLEN. And you will always call me Gwendolen, won't you?

CECILY. If you wish.

GWENDOLEN. Then that is all quite settled, is it not?

CECILY. I hope so. [*A pause. They both sit down together.*]

GWENDOLEN. Perhaps this might be a favorable opportunity for my mentioning who I am. My father is Lord Bracknell. You have never heard of papa, I suppose?

CECILY. I don't think so.

GWENDOLEN. Outside the family circle, papa, I am glad to say, is entirely unknown. I think that is quite as it should be. The home seems to me to be the proper sphere for the man. And certainly once a man begins to neglect his domestic duties he becomes painfully effeminate, does he not? And I don't like that. It makes men so very attractive. Cecily, mamma, whose views on education are remarkably strict, has brought me up to be extremely shortsighted; it is part of her system; so do you mind my looking at you through my glasses?

CECILY. Oh! not at all, Gwendolen. I am very fond of being looked at.

GWENDOLEN. [*after examining* CECILY *carefully through a lorgnette*] You are here on a short visit, I suppose.

CECILY. Oh no! I live here.

GWENDOLEN. [*severely*] Really? Your mother, no doubt, or some female relative of advanced years, resides here also?

CECILY. Oh no! I have no mother, nor, in fact, any relations.

GWENDOLEN. Indeed?

CECILY. My dear guardian, with the assistance of Miss Prism, has the arduous task of looking after me.

GWENDOLEN. Your guardian?

CECILY. Yes, I am Mr. Worthing's ward.

GWENDOLEN. Oh! It is strange he never mentioned to me that he had a ward. How secretive of him! He grows more interesting hourly. I am not sure, however, that the news inspires me with feelings of unmixed delight. [*Rising and going to her.*] I am very fond of you, Cecily; I have liked you ever since I met you! But I am bound to state that now that I know that you are Mr. Worthing's ward, I cannot help expressing a wish you were—well just a little older than you seem to be—and not quite so very alluring in appearance. In fact, if I may speak candidly——

CECILY. Pray do! I think that whenever one has anything unpleasant to say, one should always be quite candid.

GWENDOLEN. Well, to speak with perfect candor, Cecily, I wish that you were fully forty-two, and more than usually plain for your age. Ernest has a strong upright nature. He is the very soul of truth and honor. Disloyalty would be as impossible to him as deception. But even men of the noblest possible moral character are extremely susceptible to the influence of the physical charms of others. Modern, no less than Ancient History, supplies us with many most painful examples of what I refer to. If it were not so, indeed, History would be quite unreadable.

CECILY. I beg your pardon, Gwendolen, did you say Ernest?

GWENDOLEN. Yes.

CECILY. Oh, but it is not Mr. Ernest Worthing who is my guardian. It is his brother—his elder brother.

GWENDOLEN. [*sitting down again*] Ernest never mentioned to me that he had a brother.

CECILY. I am sorry to say they have not been on good terms for a long time.

GWENDOLEN. Ah! that accounts for it. And now that I think of it I have never heard any man mention his brother. The subject seems distasteful to most men. Cecily, you have lifted a load from my mind. I was growing almost anxious. It would have been terrible if any cloud had come across a friendship like ours, would it not? Of course you are quite, quite sure that it is not Mr. Ernest Worthing who is your guardian?

CECILY. Quite sure. [*A pause.*] In fact, I am going to be his.

GWENDOLEN. [*inquiringly*] I beg your pardon?

CECILY. [*rather shy and confidingly*] Dearest Gwendolen, there is no reason why I should make a secret of it to you. Our little county newspaper is sure to chronicle the fact next week. Mr. Ernest Worthing and I are engaged to be married.

GWENDOLEN. [*quite politely, rising*] My darling Cecily, I think there must be some slight error. Mr. Ernest Worthing is engaged to me. The announcement will appear in the *Morning Post* on Saturday at the latest.

CECILY. [*very politely, rising*] I am afraid you must be under some misconception. Ernest proposed to me exactly ten minutes ago. [*Shows diary.*]

GWENDOLEN. [*examines diary through her lorgnette carefully*] It is certainly very curious, for he asked me to be his wife yesterday afternoon at 5:30. If you would care to verify the incident, pray do so. [*Produces diary of her own.*] I never travel without my diary. One should always have something sensational to read in the train. I am so sorry, dear Cecily, if it is any disappointment to you, but I am afraid I have the prior claim.

CECILY. It would distress me more than I can tell you, dear Gwendolen, if it caused you any mental or physical anguish, but I feel bound to point out that since Ernest proposed to you he clearly has changed his mind.

GWENDOLEN. [*meditatively*] If the poor fellow has been entrapped into any foolish promise I shall consider it my duty to rescue him at once, and with a firm hand.

CECILY. [*thoughtfully and sadly*] Whatever unfortunate entanglement my dear boy may have got into, I will never reproach him with it after we are married.

GWENDOLEN. Do you allude to me, Miss Cardew, as an entanglement? You are presumptuous. On an occasion of this kind it becomes more than a moral duty to speak one's mind. It becomes a pleasure.

CECILY. Do you suggest, Miss Fairfax, that I entrapped Ernest into an engagement? How dare you? This is no time for wearing the shallow mask of manners. When I see a spade I call it a spade.

GWENDOLEN. [*satirically*] I am glad to say that I have never seen a spade. It is obvious that our social spheres have been widely different.

[*Enter* MERRIMAN, *followed by the footman. He carries a salver, tablecloth, and plate stand.* CECILY *is about to retort. The presence of the servants exercises a restraining influence, under which both girls chafe.*]

MERRIMAN. Shall I lay tea here as usual, Miss?

CECILY. [*sternly, in a calm voice*] Yes, as usual.

[MERRIMAN *begins to clear table and lay cloth. A long pause.* CECILY *and* GWENDOLEN *glare at each other.*]

GWENDOLEN. Are there many interesting walks in the vicinity, Miss Cardew?

CECILY. Oh! yes! a great many. From the top of one of the hills quite close one can see five counties.

GWENDOLEN. Five counties! I don't think I should like that. I hate crowds.

CECILY. [*sweetly*] I suppose that is why you live in town? [GWENDOLEN *bites her lip, and beats her foot nervously with her parasol.*]

GWENDOLEN. [*looking round*] Quite a well-kept garden this is, Miss Cardew.

CECILY. So glad you like it, Miss Fairfax.

GWENDOLEN. I had no idea there were any flowers in the country.

CECILY. Oh, flowers are as common here, Miss Fairfax, as people are in London.

GWENDOLEN. Personally I cannot understand how anybody manages to exist in the country, if anybody who is anybody does. The country always bores me to death.

CECILY. Ah! This is what the newspapers call agricultural depression, is it not? I believe the aristocracy are suffering very much from it just at present. It is almost an epidemic amongst them, I have been told. May I offer you some tea, Miss Fairfax?

GWENDOLEN. [*with elaborate politeness*] Thank you. [*Aside.*] Detestable girl! But I require tea!

CECILY. [*sweetly*] Sugar?

GWENDOLEN. [*superciliously*] No, thank you. Sugar is not fashionable any more. [CECILY *looks angrily at her, takes up the tongs and puts four lumps of sugar into the cup.*]

CECILY. [*severely*] Cake or bread and butter?

GWENDOLEN. [*in a bored manner*] Bread and butter, please. Cake is rarely seen at the best houses nowadays.

CECILY. [*cuts a very large slice of cake, and puts it on the tray*] Hand that to Miss Fairfax.

[MERRIMAN *does so, and goes out with footman.* GWENDOLEN *drinks the tea and makes a grimace. Puts down cup at once, reaches out her hand to the bread and butter, looks at it, and finds it is cake. Rises in indignation.*]

GWENDOLEN. You have filled my tea with lumps of sugar, and though I asked most distinctly for bread and butter, you have given me cake. I am known for the gentleness of my disposition, and the extraordinary sweetness of my nature, but I warn you, Miss Cardew, you may go too far.

CECILY. [*rising*] To save my poor, innocent, trusting boy from the machinations of any other girl there are no lengths to which I would not go.

GWENDOLEN. From the moment I saw you I distrusted you. I felt that you were false and deceitful. I am never deceived in such matters. My first impressions of people are invariably right.

CECILY. It seems to me, Miss Fairfax, that I am trespassing on your valuable time. No doubt you have many other calls of a similar character to make in the neighborhood.

[*Enter* JACK.]

GWENDOLEN. [*catching sight of him*] Ernest! My own Ernest!

JACK. Gwendolen! Darling! [*Offers to kiss her.*]

GWENDOLEN. [*drawing back*] A moment! May I ask if you are engaged to be married to this young lady? [*Points to* CECILY.]

JACK. [*laughing*] To dear little Cecily! Of course not! What could have put such an idea into your pretty little head?

GWENDOLEN. Thank you. You may! [*Offers her cheek.*]

CECILY. [*very sweetly*] I knew there must be some misunderstanding, Miss Fairfax. The gentleman whose arm is at present round your waist is my dear guardian, Mr. John Worthing.

GWENDOLEN. I beg your pardon?

CECILY. This is Uncle Jack.

GWENDOLEN. [*receding*] Jack! Oh!

[*Enter* ALGERNON.]

CECILY. Here is Ernest.

ALGERNON. [*goes straight over to* CECILY *without noticing anyone else*] My own love! [*Offers to kiss her.*]

CECILY. [*drawing back*] A moment, Ernest! May I ask you—are you engaged to be married to this young lady?

ALGERNON. [*looking round*] To what young lady? Good heavens! Gwendolen!

CECILY. Yes! to good heavens, Gwendolen, I mean to Gwendolen.

ALGERNON. [*laughing*] Of course not! What could have put such an idea into your pretty little head?

CECILY. Thank you. [*Presenting her cheek to be kissed.*] You may. [ALGERNON *kisses her.*]

GWENDOLEN. I felt there was some slight error, Miss Cardew. The gentleman who is now embracing you is my cousin, Mr. Algernon Moncrieff.

CECILY. [*breaking away from* ALGERNON] Algernon Moncrieff! Oh! [*The two girls move towards each other and put their arms round each other's waists as if for protection.*]

CECILY. Are you called Algernon?

ALGERNON. I cannot deny it.

CECILY. Oh!

GWENDOLEN. Is your name really John?

JACK. [*standing rather proudly*] I could deny it if I liked, I could deny anything if I liked. But my name certainly is John. It has been John for years.

CECILY. [*to* GWENDOLEN] A gross deception has been practiced on both of us.

GWENDOLEN. My poor wounded Cecily!

CECILY. My sweet wronged Gwendolen!

GWENDOLEN. [*slowly and seriously*] You will call me sister, will you not? [*They embrace.* JACK *and* ALGERNON *groan and walk up and down.*]

CECILY. [*rather brightly*] There is just one question I would like to be allowed to ask my guardian.

GWENDOLEN. An admirable idea! Mr. Worthing, there is just one question I would like to be permitted to put to you. Where is your brother Ernest? We are both engaged to be married to your brother Ernest, so it is a matter of some importance to us to know where your brother Ernest is at present.

JACK. [*slowly and hesitatingly*] Gwendolen—Cecily—it is very painful for me to be forced to speak the truth. It is the first time in my life that I have ever been reduced to such a painful position, and I am really quite inexperienced in doing anything of the kind. However I will tell you quite frankly that I have no brother Ernest. I have no brother at all. I never had a brother in my life, and I certainly have not the smallest intention of ever having one in the future.

CECILY. [*surprised*] No brother at all?

JACK. [*cheerily*] None!

GWENDOLEN. [*severely*] Had you never a brother of any kind?

JACK. [*pleasantly*] Never. Not even of any kind.

GWENDOLEN. I am afraid it is quite clear, Cecily, that neither of us is engaged to be married to anyone.

CECILY. It is not a very pleasant position for a young girl suddenly to find herself in. Is it?

GWENDOLEN. Let us go into the house. They will hardly venture to come after us there.

CECILY. No, men are so cowardly, aren't they?

[*They retire into the house with scornful looks.*]

JACK. This ghastly state of things is what you call Bunburying, I suppose?

ALGERNON. Yes, and a perfectly wonderful Bunbury it is. The most wonderful Bunbury I have ever had in my life.

JACK. Well, you've no right whatsoever to Bunbury here.

ALGERNON. That is absurd. One has a right to Bunbury anywhere one chooses. Every serious Bunburyist knows that.

JACK. Serious Bunburyist! Good heavens!

ALGERNON. Well, one must be serious about something, if one wants to have any amusement in life. I happen to be serious about Bunburying. What on earth you are serious about I haven't got the remotest idea. About everything, I should fancy. You have such an absolutely trivial nature.

JACK. Well, the only small satisfaction I have in the whole of this wretched business is that your friend Bunbury is quite exploded. You won't be able to run down to the country quite so often as you used to do, dear Algy. And a very good thing too.

ALGERNON. Your brother is a little off-color, isn't he, dear Jack? You won't be able to disappear to London quite so frequently as your wicked custom was. And not a bad thing either.

JACK. As for your conduct towards Miss Cardew, I must say that your taking in a sweet, simple, innocent girl like that is quite inexcusable. To say nothing of the fact that she is my ward.

ALGERNON. I can see no possible defense at all for your deceiving a brilliant, clever, thoroughly experienced young lady like Miss Fairfax. To say nothing of the fact that she is my cousin.

JACK. I wanted to be engaged to Gwendolen, that is all. I love her.

ALGERNON. Well, I simply wanted to be engaged to Cecily. I adore her.

JACK. There is certainly no chance of your marrying Miss Cardew.

ALGERNON. I don't think there is much likelihood, Jack, of you and Miss Fairfax being united.

JACK. Well, that is no business of yours.

ALGERNON. If it was my business, I wouldn't talk about it. [*Begins to eat muffins.*] It is very vulgar to talk about one's business. Only people like stockbrokers do that, and then merely at dinner parties.

JACK. How you can sit there, calmly eating muffins when we are in this horrible trouble, I can't make out. You seem to me to be perfectly heartless.

ALGERNON. Well, I can't eat muffins in an agitated manner. The butter would probably get on my cuffs. One should always eat muffins quite calmly. It is the only way to eat them.

JACK. I say it's perfectly heartless your eating muffins at all, under the circumstances.

ALGERNON. When I am in trouble, eating is the only thing that consoles me. Indeed, when I am in really great trouble, as anyone who knows me intimately will tell you, I refuse everything except food and drink. At the present moment I am eating muffins because I am unhappy. Besides, I am particularly fond of muffins. [*Rising.*]

JACK. [*rising*] Well, that is no reason why you should eat them all in that greedy way. [*Takes muffins from* ALGERNON.]

ALGERNON. [*offering tea cake*] I wish you would have tea cake instead. I don't like tea cake.

JACK. Good heavens! I suppose a man may eat his own muffins in his own garden.

ALGERNON. But you have just said it was perfectly heartless to eat muffins.

JACK. I said it was perfectly heartless of you, under the circumstances. That is a very different thing.

ALGERNON. That may be. But the muffins are the same. [*He seizes the muffin dish from* JACK.]

JACK. Algy, I wish to goodness you would go.

ALGERNON. You can't possibly ask me to go without having some dinner. It's absurd. I never go without my dinner. No one ever does, except vegetarians and people like that. Besides I have just made arrangements with Dr. Chasuble to be christened at a quarter to six under the name of Ernest.

JACK. My dear fellow, the sooner you give up that nonsense the better. I made arrangements this morning with Dr. Chasuble to be christened myself at 5:30, and I naturally will take the name of Ernest. Gwendolen would wish it. We can't both be christened Ernest. It's absurd. Besides, I have a perfect right to be christened if I like. There is no evidence at all that I ever have been christened by anybody. I should think it extremely probable I never was, and so does Dr. Chasuble. It is entirely different in your case. You have been christened already.

ALGERNON. Yes, but I have not been christened for years.

JACK. Yes, but you have been christened. That is the important thing.

ALGERNON. Quite so. So I know my constitution can stand it. If you are not quite sure about your ever having been christened, I must say I think it rather dangerous your venturing on it now. It might make you very unwell. You can hardly have forgotten that someone very closely connected with you was very nearly carried off this week in Paris by a severe chill.

JACK. Yes, but you said yourself that a severe chill was not hereditary.

ALGERNON. It usen't to be, I know—but I daresay it is now. Science
is always making wonderful improvements in things.

JACK. [*picking up the muffin dish*] Oh, that is nonsense; you are
always talking nonsense.

ALGERNON. Jack, you are at the muffins again! I wish you wouldn't.
There are only two left. [*Takes them.*] I told you I was particularly fond of muffins.

JACK. But I hate tea cake.

ALGERNON. Why on earth then do you allow tea cake to be served
up for your guests? What ideas you have of hospitality!

JACK. Algernon! I have already told you to go. I don't want you
here. Why don't you go!

ALGERNON. I haven't quite finished my tea yet! and there is still one
muffin left. [*Jack groans, and sinks into a chair.* ALGERNON *still
continues eating.*]

ACT-DROP

Third Act

SCENE—*Morning room at the Manor House.*

[GWENDOLEN *and* CECILY *are at the window, looking out
into the garden.*]

GWENDOLEN. The fact that they did not follow us at once into the
house, as anyone else would have done, seems to me to show that
they have some sense of shame left.

CECILY. They have been eating muffins. That looks like repentance.

GWENDOLEN. [*after a pause*] They don't seem to notice us at all.
Couldn't you cough?

CECILY. But I haven't got a cough.

GWENDOLEN. They're looking at us. What effrontery!

CECILY. They're approaching. That's very forward of them.

GWENDOLEN. Let us preserve a dignified silence.

CECILY. Certainly. It's the only thing to do now.

[*Enter* JACK *followed by* ALGERNON. *They whistle some
dreadful popular air from a British Opera.*][6]

GWENDOLEN. This dignified silence seems to produce an unpleasant effect.

CECILY. A most distasteful one.

GWENDOLEN. But we will not be the first to speak.

CECILY. Certainly not.

GWENDOLEN. Mr. Worthing, I have something very particular to
ask you. Much depends on your reply.

CECILY. Gwendolen, your common sense is invaluable. Mr. Moncrieff, kindly answer me the following question. Why did you
pretend to be my guardian's brother?

6. Probably a reference to one of the operas of Gilbert and Sullivan.

ALGERNON. In order that I might have an opportunity of meeting you.

CECILY. [*To* GWENDOLEN] That certainly seems a satisfactory explanation, does it not?

GWENDOLEN. Yes, dear, if you can believe him.

CECILY. I don't. But that does not affect the wonderful beauty of his answer.

GWENDOLEN. True. In matters of grave importance, style, not sincerity is the vital thing. Mr. Worthing, what explanation can you offer to me for pretending to have a brother? Was it in order that you might have an opportunity of coming up to town to see me as often as possible?

JACK. Can you doubt it, Miss Fairfax?

GWENDOLEN. I have the gravest doubts upon the subject. But I intend to crush them. This is not the moment for German skepticism.⁷ [*Moving to* CECILY.] Their explanations appear to be quite satisfactory, especially Mr. Worthing's. That seems to me to have the stamp of truth upon it.

CECILY. I am more than content with what Mr. Moncrieff said. His voice alone inspires one with absolute credulity.

GWENDOLEN. Then you think we should forgive them?

CECILY. Yes. I mean no.

GWENDOLEN. True! I had forgotten. There are principles at stake that one cannot surrender. Which of us should tell them? The task is not a pleasant one.

CECILY. Could we not both speak at the same time?

GWENDOLEN. An excellent idea! I nearly always speak at the same time as other people. Will you take the time from me?

CECILY. Certainly. [GWENDOLEN *beats time with uplifted finger.*]

GWENDOLEN AND CECILY. [*speaking together*] Your Christian names are still an insuperable barrier. That is all!

JACK AND ALGERNON. [*speaking together*] Our Christian names! Is that all? But we are going to be christened this afternoon.

GWENDOLEN. [*to* JACK] For my sake you are prepared to do this terrible thing?

JACK. I am.

CECILY. [*to* ALGERNON] To please me you are ready to face this fearful ordeal?

ALGERNON. I am!

GWENDOLEN. How absurd to talk of the equality of the sexes! Where questions of self-sacrifice are concerned, men are infinitely beyond us.

JACK. We are. [*Clasps hands with* ALGERNON.]

CECILY. They have moments of physical courage of which we women know absolutely nothing.

GWENDOLEN. [*to* JACK] Darling!

ALGERNON. [*to* CECILY] Darling. [*They fall into each other's arms.*]

7. Many 19th-century German scholars (D. F. Strauss, for example) seemed, in England, to be notoriously skeptical in their analyses of religious texts.

[*Enter* MERRIMAN. *When he enters he coughs loudly, seeing the situation.*]

MERRIMAN. Ahem! Ahem! Lady Bracknell!

JACK. Good heavens!

[*Enter* LADY BRACKNELL. *The couples separate in alarm. Exit* MERRIMAN.]

LADY BRACKNELL. Gwendolen! What does this mean?

GWENDOLEN. Merely that I am engaged to be married to Mr. Worthing, mamma.

LADY BRACKNELL. Come here. Sit down. Sit down immediately. Hesitation of any kind is a sign of mental decay in the young, of physical weakness in the old. [*Turns to* JACK.] Apprised, sir, of my daughter's sudden flight by her trusty maid, whose confidence I purchased by means of a small coin, I followed her at once by a luggage train. Her unhappy father is, I am glad to say, under the impression that she is attending a more than usually lengthy lecture by the University Extension Scheme on the Influence of a permanent income on Thought. I do not propose to undeceive him. Indeed I have never undeceived him on any question. I would consider it wrong. But of course, you will clearly understand that all communication between yourself and my daughter must cease immediately from this moment. On this point, as indeed on all points, I am firm.

JACK. I am engaged to be married to Gwendolen, Lady Bracknell!

LADY BRACKNELL. You are nothing of the kind, sir. And now, as regards Algernon! . . . Algernon!

ALGERNON. Yes, Aunt Augusta.

LADY BRACKNELL. May I ask if it is in this house that your invalid friend Mr. Bunbury resides?

ALGERNON. [*stammering*] Oh! No! Bunbury doesn't live here. Bunbury is somewhere else at present. In fact, Bunbury is dead.

LADY BRACKNELL. Dead! When did Mr. Bunbury die? His death must have been extremely sudden.

ALGERNON. [*airily*] Oh! I killed Bunbury this afternoon. I mean poor Bunbury died this afternoon.

LADY BRACKNELL. What did he die of?

ALGERNON. Bunbury? Oh, he was quite exploded.

LADY BRACKNELL. Exploded! Was he the victim of a revolutionary outrage? I was not aware that Mr. Bunbury was interested in social legislation. If so, he is well punished for his morbidity.

ALGERNON. My dear Aunt Augusta, I mean he was found out! The doctors found out that Bunbury could not live, that is what I mean—so Bunbury died.

LADY BRACKNELL. He seems to have had great confidence in the opinion of his physicians. I am glad, however, that he made up his mind at the last to some definite course of action, and acted under proper medical advice. And now that we have finally got rid of this Mr. Bunbury, may I ask, Mr. Worthing, who is that young person whose hand my nephew Algernon is now holding in what seems to me a peculiarly unnecessary manner?

JACK. That lady is Miss Cecily Cardew, my ward.

[LADY BRACKNELL *bows coldly to* CECILY.]

ALGERNON. I am engaged to be married to Cecily, Aunt Augusta.

LADY BRACKNELL. I beg your pardon?

CECILY. Mr. Moncrieff and I are engaged to be married, Lady Bracknell.

LADY BRACKNELL. [*with a shiver, crossing to the sofa and sitting down*] I do not know whether there is anything peculiarly exciting in the air of this particular part of Hertfordshire, but the number of engagements that go on seems to me considerably above the proper average that statistics have laid down for our guidance. I think some preliminary inquiry on my part would not be out of place. Mr. Worthing, is Miss Cardew at all connected with any of the larger railway stations in London? I merely desire information. Until yesterday I had no idea that there were any families or persons whose origin was a Terminus.[8]

[JACK *looks perfectly furious, but restrains himself.*]

JACK. [*in a clear, cold voice*] Miss Cardew is the granddaughter of the late Mr. Thomas Cardew of 149, Belgrave Square, S.W.; Gervase Park, Dorking, Surrey; and the Sporran, Fifeshire, N.B.[9]

LACY BRACKNELL. That sounds not unsatisfactory. Three addresses always inspire confidence, even in tradesmen. But what proof have I of their authenticity?

JACK. I have carefully preserved the Court Guides of the period. They are open to your inspection, Lady Bracknell.

LADY BRACKNELL. [*grimly*] I have known strange errors in that publication.

JACK. Miss Cardew's family solicitors are Messrs. Markby, Markby, and Markby.

LADY BRACKNELL. Markby, Markby, and Markby? A firm of the very highest position in their profession. Indeed I am told that one of the Mr. Markbys is occasionally to be seen at dinner parties. So far I am satisfied.

JACK. [*very irritably*] How extremely kind of you, Lady Bracknell! I have also in my possession, you will be pleased to hear, certificates of Miss Cardew's birth, baptism, whooping cough, registration, vaccination, confirmation, and the measles; both the German and the English variety.

LADY BRACKNELL. Ah! A life crowded with incident, I see; though perhaps somewhat too exciting for a young girl. I am not myself in favor of premature experiences. [*Rises, looks at her watch.*] Gwendolen! the time approaches for our departure. We have not a moment to lose. As a matter of form, Mr. Worthing, I had better ask you if Miss Cardew has any little fortune?

---

8. Station at the end of a railway line, and also the name of the Roman god of boundaries.

9. Presumably North Britain, i.e., Scotland.

JACK. Oh! about a hundred and thirty thousand pounds in the Funds.[1] That is all. Good-bye, Lady Bracknell. So pleased to have seen you.

LADY BRACKNELL. [*sitting down again*] A moment, Mr. Worthing. A hundred and thirty thousand pounds! And in the Funds! Miss Cardew seems to me a most attractive young lady, now that I look at her. Few girls of the present day have any really solid qualities, any of the qualities that last, and improve with time. We live, I regret to say, in an age of surfaces. [*To* CECILY.] Come over here, dear [CECILY *goes across.*] Pretty child! your dress is sadly simple, and your hair seems almost as Nature might have left it. But we can soon alter all that. A thoroughly experienced French maid produces a really marvelous result in a very brief space of time. I remember recommending one to young Lady Lancing, and after three months her own husband did not know her.

JACK. [*aside*] And after six months nobody knew her.

LADY BRACKNELL. [*glares at* JACK *for a few moments. Then bends, with a practiced smile, to* CECILY.] Kindly turn round, sweet child [CECILY *turns completely round.*] No, the side view is what I want. [CECILY *presents her profile.*] Yes, quite as I expected. There are distinct social possibilities in your profile. The two weak points in our age are its want of principle and its want of profile. The chin a little higher, dear. Style largely depends on the way the chin is worn. They are worn very high, just at present. Algernon!

ALGERNON. Yes, Aunt Augusta!

LADY BRACKNELL. There are distinct social possibilities in Miss Cardew's profile.

ALGERNON. Cecily is the sweetest, dearest, prettiest girl in the whole world. And I don't care twopence about social possibilities.

LADY BRACKNELL. Never speak disrespectfully of Society, Algernon. Only people who can't get into it do that. [*To* CECILY.] Dear child, of course you know that Algernon has nothing but his debts to depend upon. But I do not approve of mercenary marriages. When I married Lord Bracknell I had no fortune of any kind. But I never dreamed for a moment of allowing that to stand in my way. Well, I suppose I must give my consent.

ALGERNON. Thank you, Aunt Augusta.

LADY BRACKNELL. Cecily, you may kiss me!

CECILY. [*kisses her*] Thank you, Lady Bracknell.

LADY BRACKNELL. You may also address me as Aunt Augusta for the future.

CECILY. Thank you, Aunt Augusta.

LADY BRACKNELL. The marriage, I think, had better take place quite soon.

ALGERNON. Thank you, Aunt Augusta.

CECILY. Thank you, Aunt Augusta.

---

1. Interest-bearing government bonds.

LADY BRACKNELL. To speak frankly, I am not in favor of long engagements. They give people the opportunity of finding out each other's character before marriage, which I think is never advisable.

JACK. I beg your pardon for interrupting you, Lady Bracknell, but this engagement is quite out of the question. I am Miss Cardew's guardian, and she cannot marry without my consent until she comes of age. That consent I absolutely decline to give.

LADY BRACKNELL. Upon what grounds may I ask? Algernon is an extremely, I may almost say an ostentatiously, eligible young man. He has nothing, but he looks everything. What more can one desire?

JACK. It pains me very much to have to speak frankly to you, Lady Bracknell, about your nephew, but the fact is that I do not approve at all of his moral character. I suspect him of being untruthful. [ALGERNON *and* CECILY *look at him in indignant amazement.*]

LADY BRACKNELL. Untruthful! My nephew Algernon? Impossible! He is an Oxonian.[2]

JACK. I fear there can be no possible doubt about the matter. This afternoon, during my temporary absence in London on an important question of romance, he obtained admission to my house by means of the false pretense of being my brother. Under an assumed name he drank, I've just been informed by my butler, an entire pint bottle of my Perrier-Jouet, Brut, '89;[3] a wine I was specially reserving for myself. Continuing his disgraceful deception, he succeeded in the course of the afternoon in alienating the affections of my only ward. He subsequently stayed to tea, and devoured every single muffin. And what makes his conduct all the more heartless is, that he was perfectly well aware from the first that I have no brother, that I never had a brother, and that I don't intend to have a brother, not even of any kind. I distinctly told him so myself yesterday afternoon.

LADY BRACKNELL. Ahem! Mr. Worthing, after careful consideration I have decided entirely to overlook my nephew's conduct to you.

JACK. That is very generous of you, Lady Bracknell. My own decision, however, is unalterable. I decline to give my consent.

LADY BRACKNELL. [*to* CECILY] Come here, sweet child. [CECILY *goes over.*] How old are you, dear?

CECILY. Well, I am really only eighteen, but I always admit to twenty when I go to evening parties.

LADY BRACKNELL. You are perfectly right in making some slight alteration. Indeed, no woman should ever be quite accurate about her age. It looks so calculating. . . . [*In a meditative manner.*] Eighteen, but admitting to twenty at evening parties. Well, it will not be very long before you are of age and free from the restraints of tutelage. So I don't think your guardian's consent is,

---

2. I.e., he had been a student at Oxford (originally spelled *Oxenford*).

3. An outstanding brand and year of dry champagne.

after all, a matter of any importance.

JACK. Pray excuse me, Lady Bracknell, for interrupting you again, but it is only fair to tell you that according to the terms of her grandfather's will Miss Cardew does not come legally of age till she is thirty-five.

LADY BRACKNELL. That does not seem to me to be a grave objection. Thirty-five is a very attractive age. London society is full of women of the very highest birth who have, of their own free choice, remained thirty-five for years. Lady Dumbleton is an instance in point. To my own knowledge she has been thirty-five ever since she arrived at the age of forty, which was many years ago now. I see no reason why our dear Cecily should not be even still more attractive at the age you mention than she is at present. There will be a large accumulation of property.

CECILY. Algy, could you wait for me till I was thirty-five?

ALGERNON. Of course I could, Cecily. You know I could.

CECILY. Yes, I felt it instinctively, but I couldn't wait all that time. I hate waiting even five minutes for anybody. It always makes me rather cross. I am not punctual myself, I know, but I do like punctuality in others, and waiting, even to be married, is quite out of the question.

ALGERNON. Then what is to be done, Cecily?

CECILY. I don't know, Mr. Moncrieff.

LADY BRACKNELL. My dear Mr. Worthing, as Miss Cardew states positively that she cannot wait till she is thirty-five—a remark which I am bound to say seems to me to show a somewhat impatient nature—I would beg of you to reconsider your decision.

JACK. But my dear Lady Bracknell, the matter is entirely in your own hands. The moment you consent to my marriage with Gwendolen, I will most gladly allow your nephew to form an alliance with my ward.

LADY BRACKNELL. [*rising and drawing herself up.*] You must be quite aware that what you propose is out of the question.

JACK. Then a passionate celibacy is all that any of us can look forward to.

LADY BRACKNELL. This is not the destiny I propose for Gwendolen. Algernon, of course, can choose for himself. [*Pulls out her watch.*] Come, dear; [GWENDOLEN *rises.*] we have already missed five, if not six, trains. To miss any more might expose us to comment on the platform.

[*Enter* DR. CHASUBLE.]

CHASUBLE. Everything is quite ready for the christenings.

LADY BRACKNELL. The christenings, sir! Is not that somewhat premature!

CHASUBLE. [*looking rather puzzled, and pointing to* JACK *and* ALGERNON] Both these gentlemen have expressed a desire for immediate baptism.

LADY BRACKNELL. At their age? The idea is grotesque and irreligious! Algernon, I forbid you to be baptized. I will not hear of such excesses. Lord Bracknell would be highly displeased if he learned that that was the way in which you wasted your time and money.

CHASUBLE. Am I to understand then that there are to be no christenings at all this afternoon?

JACK. I don't think that, as things are now, it would be of much practical value to either of us, Dr. Chasuble.

CHASUBLE. I am grieved to hear such sentiments from you, Mr. Worthing. They savor of the heretical views of the Anabaptists,[4] views that I have completely refuted in four of my unpublished sermons. However, as your present mood seems to be one peculiarly secular, I will return to the church at once. Indeed, I have just been informed by the pew-opener[5] that for the last hour and a half Miss Prism has been waiting for me in the vestry.

LADY BRACKNELL. [*starting*] Miss Prism! Did I hear you mention a Miss Prism?

CHASUBLE. Yes, Lady Bracknell. I am on my way to join her.

LADY BRACKNELL. Pray allow me to detain you for a moment. This matter may prove to be one of vital importance to Lord Bracknell and myself. Is this Miss Prism a female of repellent aspect, remotely connected with education?

CHASUBLE. [*somewhat indignantly*] She is the most cultivated of ladies, and the very picture of respectability.

LADY BRACKNELL. It is obviously the same person. May I ask what position she holds in your household?

CHASUBLE. [*severely*] I am a celibate, madam.

JACK. [*interposing*] Miss Prism, Lady Bracknell, has been for the last three years Miss Cardew's esteemed governess and valued companion.

LADY BRACKNELL. In spite of what I hear of her, I must see her at once. Let her be sent for.

CHASUBLE. [*looking off*] She approaches; she is nigh.

[*Enter* MISS PRISM *hurriedly.*]

MISS PRISM. I was told you expected me in the vestry, dear Canon. I have been waiting for you there for an hour and three quarters. [*Catches sight of* LADY BRACKNELL *who has fixed her with a stony glare,* MISS PRISM *grows pale and quails. She looks anxiously round as if desirous to escape.*]

LADY BRACKNELL. [*in a severe, judicial voice*] Prism! [MISS PRISM *bows her head in shame.*] Come here, Prism! [MISS PRISM *approaches in a humble manner.*] Prism! Where is that baby? [*General consternation.* THE CANON *starts back in horror.* ALGERNON *and* JACK *pretend to be anxious to shield* CECILY *and* GWENDOLEN *from hearing the details of a terrible public scandal.*] Twenty-eight years ago, Prism, you left Lord Bracknell's house,

4. A radical Protestant sect of the 17th century, whose views about baptism were regarded as heretical by Anglicans.

5. A person employed at church services to usher worshipers to their pews and open the doors for them.

Number 104, Upper Grosvenor Street, in charge of a perambulator that contained a baby, of the male sex. You never returned. A
few weeks later, through the elaborate investigations of the Metropolitan police, the perambulator was discovered at midnight,
standing by itself in a remote corner of Bayswater. It contained
the manuscript of a three-volume novel of more than usually
revolting sentimentality. [MISS PRISM *starts in involuntary indignation.*] But the baby was not there! [*Everyone looks at* MISS
PRISM.] Prism! Where is that baby? [*A pause.*]

MISS PRISM. Lady Bracknell, I admit with shame that I do not
know. I only wish I did. The plain facts of the case are these. On
the morning of the day you mention, a day that is forever
branded on my memory, I prepared as usual to take the baby out
in its perambulator. I had also with me a somewhat old, but
capacious handbag, in which I had intended to place the manuscript of a work of fiction that I had written during my few unoccupied hours. In a moment of mental abstraction, for which I
never can forgive myself, I deposited the manuscript in the bassi-
nette, and placed the baby in the handbag.

JACK. [*who has been listening attentively*] But where did you
deposit the handbag?

MISS PRISM. Do not ask me, Mr. Worthing.

JACK. Miss Prism, this is a matter of no small importance to me. I
insist on knowing where you deposited the handbag that contained that infant.

MISS PRISM. I left it in the cloak room of one of the larger railway
stations in London.

JACK. What railway station?

MISS PRISM. [*quite crushed*] Victoria. The Brighton line. [*Sinks
into a chair.*]

JACK. I must retire to my room for a moment. Gwendolen, wait
here for me.

GWENDOLEN. If you are not too long, I will wait here for you all my
life.

[*Exit* JACK *in great excitement.*]

CHASUBLE. What do you think this means, Lady Bracknell?

LADY BRACKNELL. I dare not even suspect, Dr. Chasuble. I need
hardly tell you that in families of high position strange coinci-
dences are not supposed to occur. They are hardly considered the
thing.

[*Noises heard overhead as if someone was throwing trunks
about. Everyone looks up.*]

CECILY. Uncle Jack seems strangely agitated.

CHASUBLE. Your guardian has a very emotional nature.

LADY BRACKNELL. This noise is extremely unpleasant. It sounds as
if he was having an argument. I dislike arguments of any kind.
They are always vulgar, and often convincing.

CHASUBLE. [*looking up*] It has stopped now. [*The noise is redoubled.*]

LADY BRACKNELL. I wish he would arrive at some conclusion.

GWENDOLEN. This suspense is terrible. I hope it will last.

[*Enter* JACK *with a handbag of black leather in his hand.*]

JACK. [*rushing over to* MISS PRISM] Is this the handbag, Miss Prism? Examine it carefully before you speak. The happiness of more than one life depends on your answer.

MISS PRISM. [*calmly*] It seems to be mine. Yes, here is the injury it received through the upsetting of a Gower Street omnibus in younger and happier days. Here is the stain on the lining caused by the explosion of a temperance beverage, an incident that occurred at Leamington. And here, on the lock, are my initials. I had forgotten that in an extravagant mood I had had them placed there. The bag is undoubtedly mine. I am delighted to have it so unexpectedly restored to me. It has been a great inconvenience being without it all these years.

JACK. [*in a pathetic voice*] Miss Prism, more is restored to you than this handbag. I was the baby you placed in it.

MISS PRISM. [*amazed*] You!

JACK. [*embracing her*] Yes . . . mother!

MISS PRISM. [*recoiling in indignant astonishment*] Mr. Worthing! I am unmarried!

JACK. Unmarried! I do not deny that is a serious blow. But after all, who has the right to cast a stone against one who has suffered? Cannot repentance wipe out an act of folly? Why should there be one law for men, and another for women? Mother, I forgive you. [*Tries to embrace her again.*]

MISS PRISM. [*still more indignant*] Mr. Worthing, there is some error. [*Pointing to* LADY BRACKNELL.] There is the lady who can tell you who you really are.

JACK. [*after a pause*] Lady Bracknell, I hate to seem inquisitive, but would you kindly inform me who I am?

LADY BRACKNELL. I am afraid that the news I have to give you will not altogether please you. You are the son of my poor sister, Mrs. Moncrieff, and consequently Algernon's elder brother.

JACK. Algy's elder brother! Then I have a brother after all. I knew I had a brother! I always said I had a brother! Cecily—how could you have ever doubted that I had a brother? [*Seizes hold of* ALGERNON.] Dr. Chasuble, my unfortunate brother. Miss Prism, my unfortunate brother. Gwendolen, my unfortunate brother. Algy, you young scoundrel, you will have to treat me with more respect in the future. You have never behaved to me like a brother in all your life.

ALGERNON. Well, not till today, old boy, I admit. I did my best, however, though I was out of practice. [*Shakes hands.*]

GWENDOLEN. [*to* JACK] My own! But what own are you? What is your Christian name, now that you have become someone else?

JACK. Good heavens! . . . I had quite forgotten that point. Your decision on the subject of my name is irrevocable, I suppose?

GWENDOLEN. I never change, except in my affections.

CECILY. What a noble nature you have, Gwendolen!

JACK. Then the question had better be cleared up at once. Aunt Augusta, a moment. At the time when Miss Prism left me in the handbag, had I been christened already?

LADY BRACKNELL. Every luxury that money could buy, including christening, had been lavished on you by your fond and doting parents.

JACK. Then I was christened! That is settled. Now, what name was I given? Let me know the worst.

LADY BRACKNELL. Being the eldest son you were naturally christened after your father.

JACK. [*irritably*] Yes, but what was my father's christian name?

LADY BRACKNELL. [*meditatively*] I cannot at the present moment recall what the General's christian name was. But I have no doubt he had one. He was eccentric, I admit. But only in later years. And that was the result of the Indian climate, and marriage, and indigestion, and other things of that kind.

JACK. Algy! Can't you recollect what our father's christian name was?

ALGERNON. My dear boy, we were never even on speaking terms. He died before I was a year old.

JACK. His name would appear in the Army Lists of the period, I suppose, Aunt Augusta?

LADY BRACKNELL. The General was essentially a man of peace, except in his domestic life. But I have no doubt his name would appear in any military directory.

JACK. The Army Lists of the last forty years are here. These delightful records should have been my constant study. [*Rushes to bookcase and tears the books out.*] M. Generals . . . Mallam, Maxbohm,⁶ Magley, what ghastly names they have—Markby, Migsby, Mobbs, Moncrieff! Lieutenant 1840, Captain, Lieutenant Colonel, Colonel, General 1869, christian names, Ernest John. [*Puts book very quietly down and speaks quite calmly.*] I always told you, Gwendolen, my name was Ernest, didn't I? Well it is Ernest after all. I mean it naturally is Ernest.

LADY BRACKNELL. Yes, I remember now that the General was called Ernest. I knew I had some particular reason for disliking the name.

GWENDOLEN. Ernest! My own Ernest! I felt from the first that you could have no other name!

JACK. Gwendolen, it is a terrible thing for a man to find out suddenly that all his life he has been speaking nothing but the truth. Can you forgive me?

GWENDOLEN. I can. For I feel that you are sure to change.

JACK. My own one!

CHASUBLE. [*to* MISS PRISM] Laetitia! [*Embraces her.*]

MISS PRISM. [*enthusiastically*] Frederick! At last!

ALGERNON. Cecily! [*Embraces her.*] At last!

6. A play on the name of Max Beerbohm (1875–1956), who was to earn his name in the 20th century as a witty essayist.

JACK. Gwendolen! [*Embraces her.*] At last!

LADY BRACKNELL. My nephew, you seem to be displaying signs of triviality.

JACK. On the contrary, Aunt Augusta, I've now realized for the first time in my life the vital Importance of Being Earnest.

CURTAIN

performed, 1895   *published,* 1899

FRANCIS THOMPSON
(1859–1907)

Much of the poetry of the 1890's was written by members of groups such as the Rhymers' Club, of which Ernest Dowson and the young Yeats were members. Henley, too, had a band of writers associated with him who shared his views on life and poetry. Although Francis Thompson preferred to work more independently (he declined an invitation to join the Rhymers'), his poetry does have affinities with the writings of other poets of the time, in particular because of his Roman Catholicism, a religion which had attracted several converts during the 90's, including Dowson, Lionel Johnson (1867–1902), and the artist, Aubrey Beardsley (1872–98). Even Oscar Wilde, on his deathbed, declared himself a Roman Catholic.

Thompson's career seems like a tale from one of the novels of Graham Greene. The son of Roman Catholic converts, he was anxious to enter the priesthood but was not considered an eligible candidate. Later, after an unsuccessful attempt to complete medical school, he moved to London. Here he lived for several years as a tramp, suffering painfully not only from poverty but from an addiction to opium: when in his poems Thompson speaks of being an outcast, he speaks with the authority of experience. In 1888 he was rescued by a magazine editor, Wilfred Meynell, who recognized his literary talents and encouraged him to publish his poems. Owing to shattered health and also to a marked streak of indolence, Thompson's output in poetry was not extensive, but in his few best poems his achievement is impressive and distinctive. As his friend Coventry Patmore noted, *The Hound of Heaven* is one of the finest odes in English literature. In its fast-paced passages it reminds us of the odes of Shelley, about whom Thompson wrote an appreciative essay. An even more important influence than Shelley upon Thompson was that of the 17th-century metaphysical poets, and his poetry is therefore, like Browning's, a bridge to much of the poetry of the 20th century. Thompson was especially attracted by the 17th-century Roman Catholic poet Richard Crashaw. The Crashaw-like blending of religious fervor and striking conceits (such as "traitorous true-ness"), evident in the very title of *The Hound of Heaven*, seemed merely fantastic to some of Thompson's readers in the 1890's. To later readers, accustomed to the metaphysical devices of much 20th-century poetry, it has seemed less bizarre. Interesting comparisons may also be made between Thompson and Gerard Manley Hopkins, another Roman Catholic writer who likewise demonstrated, as the 19th century drew to its close, the remarkable variety in the poetry of the Victorian age.

The Hound of Heaven

I fled Him,[1] down the nights and down the days;
   I fled Him, down the arches of the years;
I fled Him, down the labyrinthine ways
   Of my own mind; and in the mist of tears
I hid from Him, and under running laughter.
         Up vistaed hopes I sped;
         And shot, precipitated,
Adown Titanic glooms of chasmed fears,
  From those strong Feet that followed, followed after.
       But with unhurrying chase,   10
       And unperturbéd pace,
   Deliberate speed, majestic instancy,[2]
     They beat—and a Voice beat
     More instant than the Feet—
  "All things betray thee, who betrayest Me."   15

     I pleaded, outlaw-wise,
By many a hearted casement, curtained red,
  Trellised with intertwining charities
(For, though I knew His love Who followed,
     Yet was I sore adread   20
Lest, having Him, I must have naught beside);[3]
But, if one little casement parted wide,
  The gust of His approach would clash it to.
  Fear wist not to evade, as Love wist to pursue.[4]
Across the margent[5] of the world I fled,   25
  And troubled the gold gateways of the stars,
  Smiting for shelter on their clangéd bars;
     Fretted to dulcet jars
And silvern chatter the pale ports o' the moon.[6]
I said to dawn, Be sudden; to eve, Be soon;   30
  With thy young skyey blossoms heap me over
     From this tremendous Lover!
Float thy vague veil about me, lest He see!
  I tempted all His servitors, but to find

1. Cf. St. Augustine, *Confessions* IV.iv. 7: "And lo, Thou wert close on the heels of those fleeing from Thee, God of vengeance and fountain of mercies, both at the same time, who turnest us to Thyself by most wonderful means."
2. Urgency.
3. The speaker, afraid that love of God will exclude other kinds of love, is seeking shelter in one of the warm dwellings associated with human love.

But his pursuer cuts off his escape, forcing him to remain outside, an outcast (lines 22–23).
4. This line apparently means that Fear did not know how to escape so effectively as Love knew how to pursue.
5. Boundary.
6. I.e., shook the gates of the moon until they gave forth soft and silvery sounds.

My own betrayal in their constancy,   35
In faith to Him their fickleness to me,
  Their traitorous trueness, and their loyal deceit.
To all swift things for swiftness did I sue;
  Clung to the whistling mane of every wind.
              But whether they swept, smoothly fleet,   40
              The long savannahs[7] of the blue;
                Or whether, Thunder-driven,
                They clanged his chariot 'thwart a heaven
Plashy with flying lightnings round the spurn o' their feet—
  Fear wist not to evade as Love wist to pursue.   45
              Still with unhurrying chase,
              And unperturbéd pace,
            Deliberate speed, majestic instancy,
              Came on the following Feet,
              And a Voice above their beat—   50
  "Naught shelters thee, who wilt not shelter Me."

I sought no more that after which I strayed
              In face of man or maid;
But still within the little children's eyes
              Seems something, something that replies;   55
They at least are for me, surely for me!
I turned me to them very wistfully;
But, just as their young eyes grew sudden fair
              With dawning answers there,
Their angel plucked them from me by the hair.   60
"Come then, ye other children, Nature's—share
With me," said I, "your delicate fellowship;
              Let me greet you lip to lip,
              Let me twine with you caresses,
                Wantoning   65
            With our Lady-Mother's[8] vagrant tresses,
                Banqueting
              With her in her wind-walled palace,
              Underneath her azured daïs,[9]
              Quaffing, as your taintless way is,   70
                From a chalice
Lucent-weeping out of the dayspring."[1]
                So it was done;
I in their delicate fellowship was one—
Drew the bolt of Nature's secrecies.   75
              I knew all the swift importings[2]
              On the willful face of skies;
              I knew how the clouds arise
              Spuméd of the wild sea-snortings;

7. Plains.
8. Mother Nature's.
9. Blue canopy of the sky.
1. Overflowing with shining light from

the sun (i.e., the children of Nature
drink the sunshine).
2. Meanings.

All that's born or dies 80
Rose and drooped with—made them shapers
Of mine own moods, or wailful or divine—
With them joyed and was bereaven.
I was heavy with the even,
When she lit her glimmering tapers 85
Round the day's dead sanctities.
I laughed in the morning's eyes.
I triumphed and I saddened with all weather,
Heaven and I wept together,
And its sweet tears were salt with mortal mine; 90
Against the red throb of its sunset-heart
I laid my own to beat,
And share commingling heat;
But not by that, by that, was eased my human smart.
In vain my tears were wet on Heaven's gray cheek. 95
For ah! we know not what each other says,
These things and I; in sound *I* speak—
Their sound is but their stir, they speak by silences.
Nature, poor stepdame, cannot slake my drouth;
Let her, if she would owe[3] me, 100
Drop yon blue bosom-veil of sky, and show me
The breasts o' her tenderness;
Never did any milk of hers once bless
My thirsting mouth.
Nigh and nigh draws the chase, 105
With unperturbéd pace,
Deliberate speed, majestic instancy;
And past those noiséd Feet
A voice comes yet more fleet—
"Lo naught contents thee, who content'st not Me." 110

Naked I wait Thy love's uplifted stroke!
My harness[4] piece by piece Thou hast hewn from me,
And smitten me to my knee;
I am defenseless utterly.
I slept, methinks, and woke, 115
And, slowly gazing, find me stripped in sleep.
In the rash lustihead of my young powers,
I shook the pillaring hours
And pulled my life upon me;[5] grimed with smears,
I stand amid the dust o' the mounded years— 120
My mangled youth lies dead beneath the heap.
My days have crackled and gone up in smoke,
Have puffed and burst as sun-starts[6] on a stream.
Yea, faileth now even dream

3. Own.
4. Armor.
5. Like Samson when he shook the pillars of the temple of Dagon and pulled down the roof on his head (Judges xvi).
6. Bubbles.

The dreamer, and the lute the lutanist;   125
Even the linked fantasies, in whose blossomy twist
I swung the earth a trinket at my wrist,
Are yielding;[7] cords of all too weak account
For earth with heavy griefs so overplussed.
           Ah! is Thy love indeed   130
A weed, albeit an amaranthine[8] weed,
Suffering no flowers except its own to mount?
           Ah! must—
           Designer infinite!—
Ah! must Thou char the wood ere Thou canst limn[9] with it?   135
My freshness spent its wavering shower i' the dust;
And now my heart is as a broken fount,
Wherein tear-drippings stagnate, spilt down ever
           From the dank thoughts that shiver
Upon the sightful branches of my mind.   140
           Such is; what is to be?
The pulp so bitter, how shall taste the rind?
I dimly guess what Time in mists confounds;
Yet ever and anon a trumpet sounds
From the hid battlements of Eternity;   145
Those shaken mists a space unsettle, then
Round the half-glimpséd turrets slowly wash again.
           But not ere him who summoneth
           I first have seen, enwound
With blooming robes, purpureal, cypress-crowned;   150
His name I know, and what his trumpet saith.
Whether man's heart or life it be which yields
           Thee harvest, must Thy harvest fields
           Be dunged with rotten death?

           Now of that long pursuit   155
           Comes on at hand the bruit;[1]
           That Voice is round me like a bursting sea:
              "And is thy earth so marred,
              Shattered in shard[2] on shard?
           Lo, all things fly thee, for thou fliest Me!   160
           Strange, piteous, futile thing,
Wherefore should any set thee love apart?
Seeing none but I makes much of naught," He said,
"And human love needs human meriting,
           How hast thou merited—   165
Of all man's clotted clay the dingiest clot?
           Alack, thou knowest not
How little worthy of any love thou art!
Whom wilt thou find to live ignoble thee

---

7. I.e., even his power of creating an imaginary world by poetry and song ("linked fantasies") is now inadequate.
8. Unfading and immortal.
9. Draw, as with charcoal.
1. Noise.
2. Fragment, as of broken pottery.

Save Me, save only Me?   170
All which I took from thee I did but take,
        Not for thy harms,
But just that thou might'st seek it in My arms.
        All which thy child's mistake
Fancies as lost, I have stored for thee at home;   175
        Rise, clasp My hand, and come!"

    Halts by me that footfall;
    Is my gloom, after all,
Shade of His hand, outstretched caressingly?
    "Ah, fondest,[3] blindest, weakest,   180
    I am He Whom thou seekest!
Thou dravest love from thee, who dravest Me."
1890–92   1893

The Kingdom of God[4]

"IN NO STRANGE LAND"

O world invisible, we view thee,
O world intangible, we touch thee,
O world unknowable, we know thee,
Inapprehensible, we clutch thee!

Does the fish soar to find the ocean,   5
The eagle plunge to find the air—
That we ask of the stars in motion
If they have rumor of thee there?

Not where the wheeling systems darken,
And our benumbed conceiving soars!—   10
The drift of pinions, would we hearken,
Beats at our own clay-shuttered doors.

The angels keep their ancient places—
Turn but a stone and start a wing!
'Tis ye, 'tis your estrangéd faces,   15
That miss the many-splendored thing.

But (when so sad thou canst not sadder)
Cry—and upon thy so sore loss
Shall shine the traffic of Jacob's ladder
Pitched betwixt Heaven and Charing Cross.[5]   20

Yea, in the night, my Soul, my daughter,
Cry—clinging Heaven by the hems;

---

3. Most foolish (archaic meaning).
4. Cf. Luke xvii.21: "The Kingdom of God is within you." See also Exodus
ii.22, and Psalms cxxxvii.4.
5. An intersection in London.

And lo, Christ walking on the water,
Not of Genesareth,[6] but Thames!

                                       1908

6. The Sea of Galilee (cf. Matthew xiv.25–33).

RUDYARD KIPLING
(1865–1936)

Kipling shares with an earlier Victorian, W. M. Thackeray, the distinction
of having been born in India and, at the age of 6, of having been sent
home to England to attend a private school. His views in later life were
deeply affected by the English schoolboy code of honor and duty, especially
when it involved loyalty to a group or team. At 17 he rejoined his parents
in India where his father was a teacher of sculpture at the Bombay School
of Art. For seven years he lived in India as a newspaper reporter and a
part-time writer before returning to England, where his poems and stories
(published while he was abroad) had brought him early fame. In 1892,
after his marriage to an American woman, he lived for a five-year interval in
Brattleboro, Vermont, until driven out in consequence of a quarrel with his
wife's relatives. So violent was the quarrel that in later trips to North
America, the Kiplings restricted their travels to Canada. Upon returning to
England from Vermont, Kipling settled on a country estate and purchased,
at the turn of the century, an expensive early-model automobile. He seems
to have been the first English author to own an automobile, which was
appropriate because of his keen interest in all kinds of machinery and feats
of engineering—one of many tastes in which he differed markedly from his
contemporaries in the 90's, the aesthetes. He was also the first English
author to receive the Nobel Prize for Literature (1907).

During his seven years in India in the 1880's, Kipling had discovered
new areas of human experience to exploit for his stories and poems. His stories in *Plain Tales from the Hills* (1888) explore some of the psychological
and moral problems of Englishmen and their wives living in the midst of a
subject people. In his two *Jungle Books* (1894, 1895) he ingeniously draws
upon the Indian scene to create a world of jungle animals. And although
Kipling never professed fully to understand the way of life of the Indians
themselves, or their religions, he was fascinated by them and tried to portray them with understanding. This effort is especially evident in his narrative, *Kim* (1901), in which the contemplative and religious way of life of
Indians is treated with no less sympathy than the active and this-worldly
way of life of the Victorian English governing classes. It is usually said that
Kipling, one of the great masters of the short story, and a superb craftsman,
was not as a rule successful with long narratives, but *Kim* disproves the
rule.

In his poems Kipling also draws upon the Indian scene, most commonly
as it is viewed through the eyes of private soldiers of the regular army, men
who had been sent out from England to garrison the country and fight off

invaders on the northwest frontiers. Kipling is usually thought of as the poet of British imperialism, as indeed he often was, but in these poems about ordinary British soldiers in India, there is little by way of flag-waving celebrations of the triumph of empire. The soldier who speaks in *The Widow of Windsor* is simply bewildered by the events in which he has taken part. As one of the soldiers of the queen (one of "Missis Victorier's sons") he has done his duty, but he does not see the course of empire as a divine design in which he has been a contributor. And the speaker in *The Ladies* looks back over his career in Far Eastern garrisons not from any political perspective but in terms of his love affairs with women of different races. Of this poem it may be noted that the speaker's attitudes towards colored races will strike many readers today as offensive, but his attitudes constitute an historically accurate account of how a late-19th-century British soldier viewed the strange lands in which he was stationed, as accurate as Mark Twain's presentation of Huck's mixed attitudes of affection and superiority towards the black slave, Jim, in *Huckleberry Finn*.

This fresh perspective of the common man upon events, expressed in the accent of the London cockney, was one of the qualities that gained Kipling an immediate audience for his *Barrack-Room Ballads* (1890, 1892). For many years Kipling was one of the most popular poets who has ever lived. What attracted his vast audience was not just the freshness of his subjects, but his mastery of swinging verse rhythms. Aside from his genius, Kipling's literary ancestry helps to explain his success. In part he learned his craft as a poet from traditional sources. He was not unsophisticated or unlearned; in his own family he had connections with the Pre-Raphaelites, and he was considerably influenced by such immediate literary predecessors as Swinburne and Browning. But the special influences on his style and rhythms were not traditional. One was the Protestant hymn. Both of his parents were children of Methodist clergymen, and hymn-singing, as well as preaching, affected him profoundly: "Three generations of Wesleyan ministers * * * lie behind me," he noted. The second influence came from what seems an antithetical secular quarter, the songs of the music hall. As a teenager in London, Kipling had enjoyed music-hall entertainments, which were to reach their peak of popularity in the 1890's. According to his biographer Angus Wilson, even though Kipling was, like Tennyson, the "most unmusical" of writers, he knew how to make poems that call to be set to music, such as *The Road to Mandalay*, or *Gentlemen Rankers*, with its memorable refrain (still popular in America): "We're poor little lambs who've lost our way, Baa! Baa! Baa!" Such a poem as *The Ladies* is ideal fare for a music-hall number and gains immeasurably by being sung.

Most of Kipling's best-known work was written before the death of Queen Victoria. In the 20th century, he continued to write prose and verse for 36 years, gaining some fresh notoriety as a result of his fierce outbursts against Germany during World War I. Some of his best post-Victorian poems are the songs in *Puck of Pook's Hill* (1906), celebrating in beautifully crafted verse the English past during the Roman and Anglo-Saxon periods.

Danny Deever

"What are the bugles blowin' for?" said Files-on-Parade.[1]
"To turn you out, to turn you out," the Color-Sergeant said.
"What makes you look so white, so white?" said Files-on-Parade.
"I'm dreadin' what I've got to watch," the Color-Sergeant said.
  For they're hangin' Danny Deever, you can hear the Dead March
    play,   5
  The regiment's in 'ollow square[2]—they're hanging' him today;
  They've taken of his buttons off an' cut his stripes[3] away,
  An they're hangin' Danny Deever in the mornin'.

"What makes the rear rank breathe so 'ard?" said Files-on-Parade.
"It's bitter cold, it's bitter cold," the Color-Sergeant said.   10
"What makes that front-rank man fall down?" said Files-on-Parade.
"A touch o' sun, a touch o' sun," the Color-Sergeant said.
  They are hangin' Danny Deever, they are marchin' of 'im round,
  They'ave 'alted Danny Deever by 'is coffin on the ground;
  An' 'e'll swing in 'arf a minute for a sneakin' shootin' hound— 15
  O they're hangin' Danny Deever in the mornin'!

" 'Is cot was right-'and cot to mine," said Files-on-Parade.
" 'E's sleepin' out an' far tonight," the Color-Sergeant said.
"I've drunk 'is beer a score o' times," said Files-on-Parade.
" 'E's drinkin bitter beer[4] alone," the Color-Sergeant said.   20
  They are hangin' Danny Deever, you must mark 'im to 'is place,
  For 'e shot a comrade sleepin'—you must look 'im in the face;
  Nine 'undred of 'is county[5] an' the Regiment's disgrace,
  While they're hangin' Danny Deever in the mornin'.

"What's that so black agin the sun?" said Files-on-Parade.   25
"It's Danny fightin' 'ard for life," the Color-Sergeant said.
"What's that that whimpers over'ead?" said Files-on-Parade.
"It's Danny's soul that's passin' now," the Color-Sergeant said.
  For they're done with Danny Deever, you can 'ear the quickstep
    play,
  The regiment's in column, an' they're marchin' us away;   30
  Ho! the young recruits are shakin', an' they'll want their beer
    today,
  After hangin' Danny Deever in the mornin'.

1890

---

1. Army private; "Color-Sergeant": high-ranking noncommissioned officer.
2. Ceremonial formation: the troops line four sides of a parade square, facing inward.
3. Chevrons denoting rank, worn by corporals and sergeants on the sleeves of their tunics.
4. "Bitter beer" or simply "bitter," a favorite variety of beer drunk in English pubs; the word "bitter" thus becomes a grim pun.
5. English regiments often bear the name of a particular county from which most of its men have been recruited (e.g., The Lancashire Fusiliers).

The Widow at Windsor

'Ave you 'eard o' the Widow at Windsor
  With a hairy gold crown on 'er 'ead?
She 'as ships on the foam—she 'as millions at 'ome,
  An' she pays us poor beggars in red.
    (Ow, poor beggars in red!)   5
There's 'er nick[1] on the cavalry 'orses,
  There's 'er mark on the medical stores—
An' 'er troopers[2] you'll find with a fair wind be'ind
  That takes us to various wars.
    (Poor beggars!—barbarious wars!)   10
      Then 'ere's to the Widow at Windsor,
        An' 'ere's to the stores an' the guns,
      The men an' the 'orses what makes up the forces
        O' Missis Victorier's sons.
      (Poor beggars! Victorier's sons!)   15

Walk wide o' the Widow at Windsor,
  For 'alf o' Creation she owns:
We 'ave bought 'er the same with the sword an' the flame,
  An' we've salted it down with our bones.
    (Poor beggars!—it's blue with our bones!)   20
Hands off o' the sons o' the widow,
  Hands off o' the goods in 'er shop,
For the kings must come down an' the emperors frown
  When the Widow at Windsor says "Stop!"
    (Poor beggars!—we're sent to say "Stop!")   25
      Then 'ere's to the Lodge o' the Widow,[3]
        From the Pole to the Tropics it runs—
      To the Lodge that we tile with the rank an' the file,
        An' open in form with the guns.
      (Poor beggars!—it's always they guns!)   30

We 'ave 'eard o' the Widow at Windsor,
  It's safest to leave 'er alone:
For 'er sentries we stand by the sea an' the land
  Wherever the bugles are blown.
    (Poor beggars!—an' don't we get blown!)   35
Take 'old o' the Wings o' the Mornin',
  An' flop round the earth till you're dead;
But you won't get away from the tune that they play
  To the bloomin' old rag over'ead.
    (Poor beggars!—it's 'ot over'ead!)   40

1. A nick on one of their hoofs identified army horses as property of the crown. The queen's "mark" was "V.R.I." (*"Victoria Regina et Imperatrix,"* Victoria Queen and Empress).

2. Troopships.
3 One of the lodges in the forest surrounding Windsor Castle where the queen and her family could relax in seclusion.

Then 'ere's to the sons o' the Widow,
    Wherever, 'owever they roam.
'Ere's all they desire, an' if they require
    A speedy return to their 'ome.
(Poor beggars!—they'll never see 'ome!)   45

1892

The Ladies

I've taken my fun where I've found it;
    I've rogued an' I've ranged in my time;
I've 'ad my pickin' o' sweethearts,
    An' four o' the lot was prime.
One was an 'arf-caste widow,   5
    One was a woman at Prome,[1]
One was the wife of a *jemadar-sais*,[2]
    An' one is a girl at 'ome.

Now I aren't no 'and with the ladies,
    For, takin' 'em all along,   10
You never can say till you've tried 'em,
    An' then you are like to be wrong.
There's times when you'll think that you mightn't,
    There's times when you'll know that you might;
But the things you will learn from the Yellow an' Brown,   15
    They'll 'elp you a lot with the White!

I was a young un at 'Oogli,[3]
    Shy as a girl to begin;
Aggie de Castrer she made me,
    An' Aggie was clever as sin;   20
Older than me, but my first un—
    More like a mother she were—
Showed me the way to promotion an' pay,
    An' I learned about women from 'er!

Then I was ordered to Burma,   25
    Actin' in charge o' Bazar,[4]
An' I got me a tiddy live 'eathen
    Through buyin' supplies off 'er pa.
Funny an' yellow an' faithful—
    Doll in a teacup she were—   30
But we lived on the square, like a true-married pair,
    An' I learned about women from 'er!

---

1. Town in Burma.
2. "Head-groom" [Kipling's note].
3. Hoogli, a town near Calcutta.

4. Shop selling provisions to troops. "Tiddy": tiny (slang).

Then we was shifted to Neemuch[5]
  (Or I might ha' been keepin' 'er now),
An' I took with a shiny she-devil,
  The wife of a nigger at Mhow;   35
'Taught me the gypsy-folks' *bolee;*[6]
  Kind o' volcano she were,
For she knifed me one night 'cause I wished she was white,
  And I learned about women from 'er!   40

Then I come 'ome in a trooper,
  'Long of a kid o' sixteen—
'Girl from a convent at Meerut,
  The straightest I ever 'ave seen.
Love at first sight was 'er trouble,   45
  She didn't know what it were;
An' I wouldn't do such, 'cause I liked 'er too much,
  But—I learned about women from 'er!

I've taken my fun where I've found it,
  An' now I must pay for my fun,   50
For the more you 'ave known o' the others
  The less will you settle to one;
An' the end of it's sittin' and thinkin',
  An' dreamin' Hell-fires to see;
So be warned by my lot (which I know you will not),   55
  An' learn about women from me!

What did the Colonel's Lady think?
  Nobody never knew.
Somebody asked the Sergeant's Wife,
  An' she told 'em true!   60
When you get to a man in the case,
  They're like as a row of pins—
For the Colonel's Lady an' Judy O'Grady
  Are sisters under their skins!

1896

Recessional[1]

1897

God of our fathers, known of old—
Lord of our far-flung battle-line—
Beneath whose awful Hand we hold

5. Nimach, Mhow (line 36), and Meerut (line 43) are all towns in India.
6. "Slang" [Kipling's note].
1. A hymn sung as the clergy and choir leave a church in procession at the end of a service. Kipling's hymn was written on the occasion of the Jubilee celebrations honoring the 60th anniversary of Queen Victoria's reign, celebrations which had prompted a good deal of boasting in the press about the greatness of her empire. *Recessional* was first published in the *Times,* and Kipling refused to accept any payments for its publication, then or later.

Dominion over palm and pine—
Lord God of Hosts, be with us yet   5
Lest we forget—lest we forget!

The tumult and the shouting dies—
    The Captains and the Kings depart—
Still stands Thine ancient Sacrifice,
    An humble and a contrite heart.[2]   10
Lord God of Hosts, be with us yet,
Lest we forget—lest we forget!

Far-called, our navies melt away—
    On dune and headland sinks the fire[3]—
Lo, all our pomp of yesterday   15
    Is one with Nineveh and Tyre![4]
Judge of the Nations, spare us yet,
Lest we forget—lest we forget!

If, drunk with sight of power, we loose
    Wild tongues that have not Thee in awe— 20
Such boasting as the Gentiles use
    Or lesser breeds without the Law[5]—
Lord God of Hosts, be with us yet,
Lest we forget—lest we forget!

For heathen heart that puts her trust   25
    In reeking tube and iron shard—
All valiant dust that builds on dust,
    And guarding calls not Thee to guard—
For frantic boast and foolish word,
Thy mercy on Thy People, Lord!   30

1897   1897, 1899

Harp Song of the Dane Women[1]

What is a woman that you forsake her,
And the hearth fire and the home acre,
To go with the old gray Widow-maker?

She[2] has no house to lay a guest in—
But one chill bed for all to rest in,   5
That the pale suns and the stray bergs nest in.

2. "The sacrifices of God are a broken spirit: a broken and a contrite heart, O God, thou wilt not despise" (Psalms li.17).
3. Bonfires were lit on high ground all over Britain on the night of the Jubilee.
4. Once capitals of great empires. The ruins of Nineveh, in Assyria, were discovered buried in desert sands by British archeologists in the 1850's. Tyre, in Phoenicia, had dwindled into a small Lebanese town.
5. "For when the Gentiles, which have not the law, do by nature the things contained in the law, these, having not the law, are a law unto themselves" (Romans ii.14).
1. From *Puck of Pook's Hill*, a book of stories about England in early times.
2. The sea.

She has no strong white arms to fold you,
But the ten-times-fingering weed to hold you—
Out on the rocks where the tide has rolled you.

Yet, when the signs of summer thicken,   10
And the ice breaks, and the birch buds quicken,
Yearly you turn from our side, and sicken—

Sicken again for the shouts and the slaughters.
You steal away to the lapping waters,
And look at your ship in her winter quarters.   15

You forget our mirth, and talk at the tables,
The kine[3] in the shed and the horse in the stables—
To pitch her sides and go over her cables.

Then you drive out where the storm clouds swallow,
And the sound of your oar blades, falling hollow,   20
Is all we have left through the months to follow.

Ah, what is Woman that you forsake her,
And the hearth fire and the home acre,
To go with the old gray Widow-maker?

1906

The Hyenas

After the burial-parties leave
    And the baffled kites[1] have fled;
The wise hyenas come out at eve
    To take account of our dead.

How he died and why he died   5
    Troubles them not a whit.
They snout the bushes and stones aside
    And dig till they come to it.

They are only resolute they shall eat
    That they and their mates may thrive,   10
And they know that the dead are safer meat
    Than the weakest thing alive.

(For a goat may butt, and a worm may sting,
    And a child will sometimes stand;
But a poor dead soldier of the king   15
    Can never lift a hand.)

---

3. Cows.
1. Birds of prey which feed on dead bodies.

They whoop and halloo and scatter the dirt
    Until their tushes[2] white
Take good hold in the army shirt,
    And tug the corpse to light,   20

And the pitiful face is shown again
    For an instant ere they close;
But it is not discovered to living men—
    Only to God and to those

Who, being soulless, are free from shame,   25
    Whatever meat they may find.
Nor do they defile the dead man's name—
    That is reserved for his kind.

                                        1918, 1919

2. Canine teeth.

ERNEST DOWSON
(1867–1900)

Ernest Christopher Dowson spent much of his childhood traveling with his father on the Continent, mostly in France. His education was thus irregular and informal, but he acquired a thorough knowledge of French and of his favorite French writers Gustave Flaubert, Honoré de Balzac, and Paul Verlaine, and a good knowledge of Latin poetry, especially Catullus, Propertius, and Horace. Dowson went to Oxford in 1886, but he did not take to regular academic instruction and left after a year. Though nominally assisting his father to manage a dock in the London district of Limehouse, Dowson spent most of his time writing poetry, stories, and essays, and talking with Lionel Johnson, W.B. Yeats, and other members of the Rhymers' Club, in which he played a prominent part. Between 1890 and 1894 Dowson, though leading the irregular life of so many of the 90's poets, produced his best work, and his volume of *Verses* came out in 1896. Late nights and excessive drinking impaired a constitution already threatened by tuberculosis. He moved to France in 1894, making a living by translating from the French for an English publisher, but growing steadily worse in health. After his return to England he was discovered in a dying condition by a friend, who took him to his home and nursed him until his death six weeks later.

Dowson was a member of what Yeats called "the tragic generation" of poets in the 90's who seemed to be driven by their own restless energies to dissipation and premature death. As a poet he was considerably influenced by Swinburne (whose feverish emotional tone he often captures very skillfully). He experimented with a variety of meters, and in *Cynara* used the alexandrine as the normal line of a six-line stanza in a manner more common in French than in English poetry. He was especially also interested in the work of the French Symbolist poets and in their theories of verbal suggestiveness and of poetry as incantation: he believed (as he once wrote in a letter) that a finer poetry could sometimes be achieved by "mere sound and music, with just a suggestion of sense."

[Cynara]

Non sum qualis eram bonae sub regno Cynarae[1]

Last night, ah, yesternight, betwixt her lips and mine
There fell thy shadow, Cynara! thy breath was shed
Upon my soul between the kisses and the wine;
And I was desolate and sick of an old passion,
    Yea, I was desolate and bowed my head: 5
I have been faithful to thee, Cynara! in my fashion.

All night upon mine heart I felt her warm heart beat,
Night-long within mine arms in love and sleep she lay;
Surely the kisses of her bought red mouth were sweet;
But I was desolate and sick of an old passion,   10
    When I awoke and found the dawn was gray:
I have been faithful to thee, Cynara! in my fashion.

I have forgot much, Cynara! gone with the wind,
Flung roses, roses riotously with the throng,
Dancing, to put thy pale, lost lilies out of mind;   15
But I was desolate and sick of an old passion,
    Yea, all the time, because the dance was long:
I have been faithful to thee, Cynara! in my fashion.

I cried for madder music and for stronger wine,
But when the feast is finished and the lamps expire,   20
Then falls thy shadow, Cynara! the night is thine;
And I am desolate and sick of an old passion,
    Yea, hungry for the lips of my desire:
I have been faithful to thee, Cynara! in my fashion.

        1891, 1896

Flos Lunae[2]

FOR YVANHOÉ RAMBOSSON[3]

I would not alter thy cold eyes,
Nor trouble the calm fount of speech

1. "I am not as I was under the reign of the good Cynara." This is the third and part of the fourth line of an ode of Horace (IV.1) in which the poet pleads with Venus to stop tormenting him with love since he is growing old and is no longer what he was when under the sway of Cynara (*Sin-ah-rah*), the girl he used to love. Of Dowson's "Cynara" Yeats later wrote: "Dowson, who seemed to drink so little and had so much dignity and reserve, was breaking his heart for the daughter of the keeper of an Italian eating house, in dissipation and drink * * * " Dowson's "Cynara" was, in fact, a Polish girl by the name of Adelaide Foltinowicz.
2. "Flower of the moon."
3. This name sounds too good to be true, and perhaps is. Desmond Flower's annotated edition of Dowson's poetical works identifies the other characters to whom Dowson dedicated poems but is silent on this one.

With aught of passion or surprise.
The heart of thee I cannot reach:
I would not alter thy cold eyes!   5

I would not alter thy cold eyes;
Nor have thee smile, nor make thee weep:
Though all my life droops down and dies,
Desiring thee, desiring sleep,
I would not alter thy cold eyes.   10

I would not alter thy cold eyes;
I would not change thee if I might,
To whom my prayers for incense rise,
Daughter of dreams! my moon of night!
I would not alter thy cold eyes.   15

I would not alter thy cold eyes,
With trouble of the human heart:
Within their glance my spirit lies.
A frozen thing, alone, apart:
I would not alter thy cold eyes.   20

                                            1891, 1896

[They Are Not Long]

Vitae summa brevis spem nos vetat incohare longam.[4]

They are not long, the weeping and the laughter,
    Love and desire and hate:
I think they have no portion in us after
    We pass the gate.

They are not long, the days of wine and roses: 5
    Out of a misty dream
Our path emerges for a while, then closes
    Within a dream.

                                            1896

Dregs

The fire is out, and spent the warmth thereof,
(This is the end of every song man sings!)
The golden wine is drunk, the dregs remain,
Bitter as wormwood and as salt as pain;
And health and hope have gone the way of love   5
Into the drear oblivion of lost things.
Ghosts go along with us until the end;
This was a mistress, this, perhaps, a friend.

---

4. "The shortness of life prevents us from entertaining far-off hopes"
(Horace, *Odes* I.4).

With pale, indifferent eyes, we sit and wait
For the dropped curtain and the closing gate;   10
This is the end of all the songs man sings.

                                                                1899

Exchanges

All that I had I brought.
  Little enough I know;
A poor rhyme roughly wrought,
  A rose to match thy snow:
All that I had I brought.   5

Little enough I sought;
  But a word compassionate,
A passing glance, or thought,
  For me outside the gate:
Little enough I sought.   10

Little enough I found:
  All that you had, perchance!
With the dead leaves on the ground,
  I dance the devil's dance.
All that you had I found   15

                                                                1899

Carthusians[1]

Through what long heaviness, assayed in what strange fire,
  Have these white monks been brought into the way of peace,
Despising the world's wisdom and the world's desire,
  Which from the body of this death bring no release?

Within their austere walls no voices penetrate;   5
  A sacred silence only, as of death, obtains;
Nothing finds entry here of loud or passionate;
  This quiet is the exceeding profit of their pains.

From many lands they came, in divers fiery ways;
  Each knew at last the vanity of earthly joys;   10
And one was crowned with thorns, and one was crowned with
  bays,[2]
  And each was tired at last of the world's foolish noise.

---

1. A monastic order founded in 1084 at Chartreuse in the French Alps. The Carthusian regimen is stringently ascetic; each white-robed monk is a silent solitary except when participating in services of worship. Cf. Arnold's *Stanzas from the Grande Chartreuse.*
2. A crown of bay leaves (or laurel) was awarded to poets whose work was admired.

It was not theirs with Dominic to preach God's holy wrath,
    They were too stern to bear sweet Francis' gentle sway;[3]
Theirs was a higher calling and a steeper path,   15
    To dwell alone with Christ, to meditate and pray.

A cloistered company, they are companionless,
    None knoweth here the secret of his brother's heart:
They are but come together for more loneliness,
    Whose bond is solitude and silence all their part.   20

O beatific life! Who is there shall gainsay,
    Your great refusal's victory, your little loss,
Deserting vanity for the more perfect way,
    The sweeter service of the most dolorous Cross.

Ye shall prevail at last! Surely ye shall prevail!   25
    Your silence and austerity shall win at last:
Desire and mirth, the world's ephemeral lights shall fail,
    The sweet star of your queen is never overcast.

We fling up flowers and laugh, we laugh across the wine;
    With wine we dull our souls and careful strains of art;   30
Our cups are polished skulls round which the roses twine:
    None dares to look at Death who leers and lurks apart.

Move on, white company, whom that has not sufficed!
    Our viols cease, our wine is death, our roses fail:
Pray for our heedlessness, O dwellers with the Christ!   35
    Though the world fall apart, surely ye shall prevail.

1891   1899

3. St. Dominic, founder of the Dominican order of friars (1215), whose preaching was especially directed to converting heathens to Christianity; St. Francis of Assisi, founder of the Franciscan order of friars in 1209, was a gentle and tender-spirited leader who worked and preached among the poor.

The Twentieth Century

1914–18: World War I.
1918: Gerard Manley Hopkins' poetry published.
1922: T. S. Eliot's *The Waste Land*.
1922: James Joyce's *Ulysses*.
1928: W. B. Yeats's *The Tower*.
1930: Period of depression and unemployment begins.
1939–45: World War II.

THE END OF VICTORIANISM—THE EDWARDIAN ERA—WORLD WAR I

Cultural movements do not proceed neatly by centuries, and this section, which for convenience we call "the twentieth century," begins really with the late 19th, when the sense of the passing of a major phase of English history was already in the air. Queen Victoria's Jubilee in 1887 and, even more, her Diamond Jubilee in 1897 were felt even by contemporaries to mark the end of an era. As the 19th century drew to a close there were many manifestations of a weakening of traditional stabilities. The aesthetic movement, with its insistence on "art for art's sake," assaulted the assumptions about the nature and function of art held by ordinary middle-class readers, deliberately, provocatively. It helped to widen the breach between artists and writers on the one hand and the "Philistine" public on the other —a breach whose earlier symptom was Matthew Arnold's war on the Philistines in *Culture and Anarchy* and which was later to result in the "alienation of the artist" that is now a commonplace of criticism. This was more than a purely English matter. From France came the tradition of the bohemian life that scorned the limits imposed by conventional ideas of respectability, together with other notions of the artist as rejecting and rejected by ordinary society, which in different ways fostered the view of the alienated artist. The life and work of the French Symbolist poets in France, the early novels of Thomas Mann in Germany (especially *Buddenbrooks*, 1901), and Joyce's *Portrait of the Artist as a Young Man* (1916) show some of the very different ways in which this attitude revealed itself in literature all over Europe. In England, the growth of popular education as a result of the Education Act of 1870, which finally made elementary education compulsory and universal, led to the rapid emergence of a large, unsophisticated literary public at whom new kinds of journalism, in particular the cheap "yellow press," were directed. A public that was literate but not in any real sense educated increased steadily throughout the 19th century, and one result of this was the splitting up of the audience for literature into "highbrows," "lowbrows," and "middlebrows." Although in earlier periods there had been different kinds of audience for different kinds of writing, the split now developed with unprecedented speed and to an unprecedented degree because of the mass production of "popular" literature for the semiliterate. The fragmentation of the reading public now merged with the artist's war on the Philistine (and indeed was one of the causes of that war in the first place) to widen the gap between popular art and art esteemed only by the sophisticated and the expert. This is part of the background of modern literature all over the Western world.

Another manifestation—or at least accompaniment—of the end of the Victorian age was the rise of various kinds of pessimism and stoicism. The novels and poetry of Thomas Hardy show one kind of pessimism (and it *was* pessimism, even if Hardy himself repudiated the term), and the poems of A. E. Housman show another variety, while a real or affected stoicism is to be found not only in these writers but also in many minor writers of the last decade of the 19th century and the first decade of the 20th. Examples of this stoicism—the determination to stand for human dignity by enduring bravely, with a "stiff upper lip," whatever fate may bring—range from Robert Louis Stevenson's essays and the rhetorically assertive poems of the editor and journalist W. E. Henley, to Rudyard Kipling's *Jungle Books* and many of his short stories, the last stanza of Housman's *The Chestnut Casts His Flambeaux* ("Bear them we can, and if we can we must") and Yeats's "They know that Hamlet and Lear are gay."

Although the high tide of anti-Victorianism was marked by the publication in 1918 of that classic of ironic debunking, *Eminent Victorians* by Lytton Strachey (1880–1932), the criticism of the normal attitudes and preconceptions of the Victorian middle classes first became really violent in the last two decades of the 19th century. No one could have been more savage in his attacks on the Victorian conceptions of the family, education, and religion than Samuel Butler, whose novel *The Way of All Flesh* (completed in 1884, posthumously published in 1903) is still the bitterest indictment in English literature of the Victorian way of life. The chorus of questioning of Victorian assumptions grew ever louder as the century drew to an end; sounding prominently in it was the voice of the young Bernard Shaw, one of Butler's greatest admirers. The position of women, too, was rapidly changing during this period. The Married Woman's Property Act of 1882, which allowed married women to own property in their own right; the admission of women to the universities at different times during the latter part of the century; the fight for women's suffrage, which was not won until 1918 (and not fully won until 1928)—these events marked a change in the attitude to women and in the part they played in the national life as well as in the relation between the sexes, which is reflected in a variety of ways in the literature of the period.

The Boer War (1899–1902), fought by the British to establish political and economic control over the Boer republics of South Africa, marked both the high point of and the reaction against British imperialism. It was a war against which many British intellectuals protested and one which the British in the end were slightly ashamed of having won. The development

of the British Empire into the British Commonwealth (i.e., into an association of self-governing countries) continued in fits and starts throughout
the first half of the 20th century, with imperialist and anti-imperialist
sentiment often meeting head on; writers as far apart as Kipling and E. M.
Forster occupied themselves with the problem. The Irish question also
caused a great deal of excitement from the beginning of the period until
well into the 1920's. A steadily rising Irish nationalism protested with increasing violence against the political subordination of Ireland to the
British Crown and government. In World War I some Irish nationalists
sought German help in rebelling against Britain, and this exacerbated feeling on both sides. No one can fully understand William Butler Yeats or
James Joyce without some awareness of the Irish struggle for independence,
the feelings of Anglo-Irish men of letters on this burning topic, and the
way in which the Irish Literary Revival of the late 19th and early 20th
centuries (with which Yeats was much concerned) reflected a determination
to achieve a vigorous national life culturally even if the road seemed
blocked politically.

Edwardian England (1901–10) was very conscious of being no longer
Victorian. Edward VII stamped his character on the decade in which
he reigned. It was a vulgar age of conspicuous enjoyment by those who
could afford it, and writers and artists kept well away from implication in
high society (though there were some conspicuous exceptions): in general,
there was no equivalent in this period of Queen Victoria's interest in Tennyson. The alienation of artists and intellectuals was proceeding apace. From
1910 (when George V came to the throne) until war broke out in August,
1914, Britain achieved a temporary equilibrium between Victorian earnestness and Edwardian flashiness; in retrospect that "Georgian" period seems
peculiarly golden, the last phase of assurance and stability before the old
order throughout Europe broke up in violence with results that are still
with us. Yet even then, under the surface, there was restlessness and experimentation. If this was the age of Rupert Brooke, it was also the age of
T. S. Eliot's first experiments in a disturbingly new kind of poetry.

"Edwardian" as a term applied to English cultural history suggests a
period in which the social and economic stabilities of the Victorian age—
country houses with numerous servants, a flourishing and confident middle
class, a strict hierarchy of social classes—remained unimpaired, though on
the level of ideas there was a sense of change and liberation. "Georgian"
refers largely to the lull before the storm of World War I. That war, as our
selection of the war poets makes clear, produced some major shifts in attitude.

THE POETIC REVOLUTION

A technical revolution in poetry was going on side by side with shifts
in attitude. The Imagist movement, influenced by T. E. Hulme's insistence on hard, clear, precise images and encouraged by Ezra Pound
when he lived in London just before World War I, fought against romantic fuzziness and facile emotionalism in poetry. The movement developed simultaneously on both sides of the Atlantic, and its early members
included Amy Lowell, Richard Aldington, Hilda Doolittle, John Gould

Fletcher, and F. S. Flint. As Flint explained in an article in March, 1913, Imagists insisted on "direct treatment of the 'thing,' whether subjective or objective," on the avoidance of all words "that did not contribute to the presentation," and on a freer metrical movement than a strict adherence to "the sequence of a metronome" could allow. All this encouraged precision in imagery and freedom of rhythmic movement, but more was required for the production of poetry of any real scope and interest. Imagism went in for the short, sharply etched, descriptive lyric, but it had no technique for the production of longer and more complex poems. Other new ideas about poetry helped to provide this technique. Sir Herbert Grierson's great edition of the poems of John Donne in 1912 both reflected and helped to encourage a new enthusiasm for 17th-century metaphysical poetry. The revival of interest in metaphysical wit brought with it a desire on the part of some pioneering poets to introduce into their poetry a much higher degree of intellectual complexity than had been found among the Victorians or the Georgians. The full subtlety of French Symbolist poetry also now came to be appreciated; it had been admired in the 90's, but for its dreamy suggestiveness rather than for its imagistic precision and complexity. At the same time a need was felt to bring poetic language and rhythms closer to those of conversation, or at least to spice the formalities of poetic utterance with echoes of the colloquial and even the slangy. Irony, which made possible several levels of discourse simultaneously, and wit, with the use of puns (banished from serious poetry for over 200 years), helped to achieve that union of thought and passion which T. S. Eliot, in his review of Grierson's anthology of metaphysical poetry (1921), saw as characteristic of the metaphysicals and wished to bring back into modern poetry. A new critical and a new creative movement in poetry went hand in hand, with Eliot the high priest of both. It was Eliot who extended the scope of Imagism by bringing the English metaphysicals and the French Symbolists (as well as the English Jacobean dramatists) to the rescue, thus adding new criteria of complexity and allusiveness to the criteria of concreteness and precision stressed by the Imagists. It was Eliot, too, who introduced into modern English and American poetry the kind of irony achieved by shifting suddenly from the formal to the colloquial or by oblique allusions to objects or ideas that contrasted sharply with those carried by the surface meaning of the poem. Thus between, say, 1911 (the first year of the Georgian poets) and 1922 (the year of the publication of *The Waste Land*) a major revolution occurred in English—and for that matter American—poetic theory and practice—a revolution which determined the way in which most serious poets and critics now think about their art. If one compares the poems in Palgrave's *Golden Treasury*, a Victorian anthology which was still used as a basic school text in Britain in the 1930's, with those in a number of academic anthologies of the mid-20th century, the change in poetic taste will become startlingly apparent. In the critical discussion, if not always in the allotment of space, Donne rather than Spenser becomes the great poet of the 16th- and 17th-century period; Gerard Manley Hopkins replaces Tennyson as the great 19th-century poet; and in general what one might call the metaphysical-Symbolist tradition predominates over both the cultivated self-pity of the Romantic-Victorian tradition and the Platonic-meditative strain of both the Elizabethans and (in his own way) Wordsworth.

The posthumous publication by Robert Bridges in 1918 of the poetry of Gerard Manley Hopkins encouraged further experimentation in language and rhythms. Hopkins combined absolute precision of the individual image with a complex ordering of images and a new kind of metrical patterning. The young poets of the early 1930's—W. H. Auden, Stephen Spender, C. Day Lewis—were much influenced by Hopkins as well as by Eliot (now the presiding genius of modern English and American poetry) and by a variety of other poets from the 16th-century John Skelton to Wilfred Owen. And even when the almost flamboyant new tones of Dylan Thomas were first sounded in the late 1930's, the influence of Hopkins could still be heard. It is only since World War II that a new generation of young English poets (including Donald Davie, Elizabeth Jennings, and Philip Larkin), searching for what has been called "purity of diction," have turned away from both the 17th century and the poetry of Hopkins and Eliot to seek a poetry which avoids all kinds of verbal excess in its desire for quiet luminosity and unpretentious truth.

Meanwhile the remarkable career of W. B. Yeats, stretching across the whole modern period, showed how a truly great poet can at the same time reflect the varying developments of his age and maintain an unmistakably individual accent. Beginning among the aesthetes of the 90's, turning later to a more tough and spare ironic language without losing his characteristic verbal magic, working out his own notions of symbolism and bringing them in different ways into his poetry, developing in his full maturity a rich symbolic and metaphysical poetry with its own curiously haunting cadences and its imagery both shockingly realistic and movingly suggestive, Yeats's work is itself a history of English poetry between 1890 and 1939. Yet he is always Yeats, unique and inimitable—without doubt the greatest English-speaking poet of his age.

Two important 20th-century poets stand somewhat apart from the main map of English poetry in the first half of the century. They are Robert Graves and Edwin Muir. Each has a highly individual voice and, the latter especially, a limited range. But they both show that there were strengths in the English poetic tradition untapped by Eliot and his followers. Graves, with a strong sense of tradition combined with a highly idiosyncratic poetic personality, has played a part in English poetry comparable to that played by Robert Frost in American. Muir's more quietist and mystical temperament was nourished by the unusual circumstances of his life, and his childhood in Orkney. In him, awareness of his native Scotland and a response to the heroic stories of ancient Greece were linked. Both poets were much concerned with time and the human response to time, and both had a deep sense of history.

BETWEEN THE WARS

The postwar disillusion of the 1920's was, it might be said, a spiritual matter, just as Eliot's Waste Land was a spiritual and not a literal wasteland. Depression and unemployment in the early 1930's, followed by the rise of Hitler and the cruel shadow of Fascism and Nazism over Europe, with its threat of another war, represented another sort of wasteland which produced another sort of effect on poets and novelists. The impotence of capitalist governments in the face of Hitlerism combined with economic dislocation to turn the majority of young intellectuals (and not only intellectuals) in the 1930's to the political Left. The 1930's were the Red decade, because only the Left seemed to offer any solution. The early poetry of W. H. Auden and his contemporaries cried out for "the death of the old gang" (in Auden's phrase) and a clean sweep politically and economically, while the Franco rebellion against the republican government in Spain, which started in the summer of 1936 and soon led to full-scale civil war, was regarded as a rehearsal for an inevitable second world war and thus further emphasized the inadequacy of politicians. Yet though all this is reflected passionately in the literature of the period, particularly in the poetry, it was not accompanied by any interesting developments in technique; many younger writers were more anxious to express their attitudes than to construct new kinds of works of art. The outbreak of World War II in September, 1939, following very shortly on Hitler's pact with Russia, which shocked and disillusioned so many of the young Left-wing writers, marked the sudden end of the Red decade; the concern of writers in Britain now was to maintain their integrity and indeed their existence in what was from the beginning expected to be a long and destructive war. This they did surprisingly well, but nevertheless this second war brought inevitable exhaustion: English literature has never quite recovered the vitality and interest in technical experimentation that marked the twenty years after about 1912.

These years—roughly 1912 to 1930—were the Heroic Age of the modern English novel. Joseph Conrad, James Joyce, and D. H. Lawrence are the giants, with Virginia Woolf and E. M. Forster brilliant minor figures—to name only the most outstanding writers. An important novelist of this period who stands rather apart from any of the movements discussed here is Ford Madox Ford (1873–1939), whose four novels about Christopher Tietjens published in the 1920's (and republished in a single volume as *Parade's End* in 1950) show meticulous craftsmanship and a deep sense of the changes wrought by the war on English life and character. The poet Robert Graves is similarly independent of movements and fashions in 20th-century literature: he developed and subtilized the Georgian tradition instead of adopting that of Eliot.

NEW METHODS IN FICTION

One can trace three major influences on the changes in attitude and technique in the modern novel. The first is the novelist's realization that the general background of belief which united him with his public in a common sense of what was significant in experience had disappeared. The public values of the Victorian novel, in which major crises of plot could be shown through changes in the social or financial or marital status of the chief characters, gave way to more personally conceived notions of value, dependent on the novelist's intuitions and sensibilities rather than on public agreement. "To believe that your impressions hold good for others," Virginia Woolf once wrote (discussing Jane Austen), "is to be released from the cramp and confinement of personality." The modern novelist could no longer believe this: he had to fall back on personality, drawing his criterion of significance in human affairs (and thus his principle of selection) from his own intuitions, so that he needed to find ways of convincing the reader that his own private sense of what was significant in experience was truly valid. A new technical burden was thus imposed on the novelist's prose, for it had now to build up a world of values instead of drawing on an existing world of values. Virginia Woolf tried to solve the problem by using some of the devices of poetry in order to suggest the novelist's own sense of value and vision of the world. Joyce, on the other hand, made no attempt to convey a single personal attitude, but reacted to the breakdown of public values by employing a kind of writing so multiple in its implications that it conveyed numerous points of view simultaneously, the author being totally objective and committed to none of them—a mode which required remarkable technical virtuosity.

The second influence on the changes in attitude and technique in the modern novel was a new view of time; time was not a series of chronological moments to be presented by the novelist in sequence with an occasional deliberate retrospect ("this reminded him of," "he recalled that"), but as a continuous flow in the consciousness of the individual, with the "already" continuously merging into the "not yet" and retrospect merging into anticipation. This influence is closely bound up with a third: the new notions of the nature of consciousness, which derived in a general way from Sigmund Freud and Carl Jung but were also part of the spirit of the age and discernible even in those novelists who had not read either psychologist. Consciousness is multiple; the past is always present in it at some level and is continually coloring one's present reaction. Marcel Proust in France, in his great novel sequence *Remembrance of Things Past* (1913–28), had explored the ways in which the past impinges on the present and consciousness is determined by memory. The view that a man *is* his memories, that his present is the sum of his past, that if we dig into a man's consciousness we can tell the whole truth about him without waiting for a chronological sequence of time to take him through a series of testing circumstances, inevitably led to a technical revolution in the novel. For now, by exploring in depth into consciousness and memory rather than proceeding lengthwise along the dimension of time, a novelist could write a novel concerned ostensibly with only one day of the hero's life (Joyce's *Ulysses* and Virginia Woolf's *Mrs. Dalloway*). This view of multiple levels of consciousness existing simultaneously, coupled with the view of time as a constant flow rather than a series of separate moments, meant that a novelist preferred to plunge into the consciousness of his characters in order to tell his story rather than to provide an external framework of chronological narrative. The "stream-of-consciousness" technique, where the author tries to render directly the very fabric of his character's consciousness without reporting it in formal, quoted remarks, was developed in the 1920's as an important new technique of the English novel. It made for more difficult reading, at least for those accustomed only to the methods of the older English novel. No "porch" was constructed at the front of the novel to put the reader in possession of necessary preliminary information: such information emerged, as the novel progressed, from the consciousness of each character as it responded to the present with echoes of its past. No conventional signposts were put up to tell the reader where he was, for that was felt to interfere with the immediacy of the impression. But once the reader learns how to find his way in this unsignposted territory, he is rewarded by new delicacies of perception and new subtleties of presentation.

Concentration on the "stream of consciousness" and on the association of ideas within the individual consciousness led inevitably to stress on the essential loneliness of the individual. For all consciousnesses are unique and isolated, and if this unique, private world is the real world in which men live, if the public values to which they must pay lip service in the social world in which they move are not the real values which give meaning to their personality, then each man is condemned to live in the prison of his own incommunicable consciousness. How is true communication possible in such a world? The public gestures imposed upon us by society never correspond to our real inward needs. They are conventional in the bad sense, mechanical, imposing a crude standardization on the infinite subtlety of experience. If we do try to give out a sign from our real selves, that sign is bound to be misunderstood when read by some other self in the light of that self's quite other personality. The theme of such modern fiction is thus the possibility of love, the establishment of emotional communication, in a community of private consciousnesses. This, is, in different ways, the theme of Joyce, of Lawrence, of Virginia Woolf, and of Forster, and (on a rather different scale and not always so directly) of Conrad. The search for communion and the inevitable isolation of Leopold Bloom in *Ulysses* is symbolic of the human condition as seen by the modern novelist. Similar investigations of this basic condition are Forster's explorations of the conventions which seem to be helps to living but which in fact prevent true human contacts, and Virginia Woolf's delicate projections of the relation between the self's need for privacy and the self's need for genuine communication. The theme of all Lawrence's novels is human relationships, the ideal of which he restlessly explored with shifting emphasis throughout his career; such relationships can be all too easily distorted by the mechanical conventions of society, by notions of respectability or propriety, by all the shams and frauds of middle-class life, by the demands of power or money or success. One might almost say that the greatest modern novels are about the difficulty, and at the same time the inevitability, of being human. The dilemma of the human condition is never really solved in these novelists; but knowledge that the dilemma is shared—a knowledge so brilliantly conveyed in *Ulysses* and so wryly proffered by Forster—can both illuminate and comfort.

Not all the novelists of the period, of course, were concerned with these themes or employed the new techniques appropriate to them. The "documentary" novelists, such as Arnold Bennett and John Galsworthy (and, in some at least of his novels, H. G. Wells), presented, often with great skill, the changing social scene, showing considerable insight and sympathy in recording aspects of it through the behavior of their imagined characters. Virginia Woolf called these writers "materialists," maintaining that they were content to deal with externals and did not go on to explore those aspects of consciousness, of the true inward life of men, in which human reality resides. She was perhaps judging unfairly, by standards that were not applicable to their sort of fiction; but modern criticism has on the whole agreed with her.

The short story in this period benefited from the new techniques of exploration in depth. A greater consciousness of the symbolic uses to which objects and incidents can be put and a greater subtlety in the ways in which patterns of suggestiveness are built up below the quietly realistic surface can be found in the short stories of writers so different from each other as Joyce, Katherine Mansfield, Lawrence, and Forster. Katherine Mansfield learned from the Russian short-story writer Anton Chekhov how to use the casual-seeming incidents of ordinary life in such a way as to set up haunting overtones of meaning. The apparently inconsequential surface masking the carefully organized substructure is found in much modern fiction (perhaps most of all in *Ulysses*): it is one of the results of the coming together, in the novel and the short story, of realism and symbolism, of contemporary probability and timeless significance. These things of course come together in great fiction of all ages; but the modern writer contrives their coexistence with greater self-consciousness than his predecessors.

THE DRAMA

Modern drama begins in a sense with the witty drawing-room comedies of Oscar Wilde; yet Wilde founded no dramatic school. His wit was personal and irresponsible, unlike the wit of Restoration comedy, which reflected an attitude to the relation between the sexes which was part of a view of society held by a whole (if a small) social class. Bernard Shaw brought still another kind of wit into drama—not Wilde's exhibitionist sparkle nor yet the assured sophistication of the Restoration dramatists, but the provocative paradox that was meant to tease and disturb, to challenge the complacency of the audience. Shaw's discussion plays were given dramatic life through the mastery of theatrical techniques which he learned during his years as a dramatic critic. In his general attitudes Shaw represents the anti-Victorianism of the late Victorians; his long life should not obscure the fact that his first—and some of his best—plays belong to the 90's. Other attempts by 20th-century dramatists to debate social questions on the stage—by Galsworthy, for example—deserve respect for their humanity and intelligence and sometimes for their theatrical craftsmanship, but they lack Shaw's verbal and intellectual brilliance and his superb capacity to entertain. We must turn to Ireland to find another really impressive variety of dramatic activity. The Irish Literary Theatre was founded in 1899, with Yeats's early play *The Countess Cathleen* as its first production. The founders—Yeats, Lady Gregory, George Moore, and Edward Martyn—wanted to make a contribution to an Irish literary revival, but they were influenced also by the Independent Theatre in London, founded in 1891 by J. T. Grein in order to encourage new developments in the drama. In 1902 the Irish Literary Theatre was able to maintain a permanent all-Irish company and changed its name to the Irish National Theatre, which moved in 1904 to the Abbey Theatre, by which name it has since been known. Many of the plays produced at the Abbey Theatre were only of local and ephemeral interest, but J. M. Synge's use of the speech and imagination of Irish country people, Yeats's powerful symbolic use of themes from old Irish legend, and Sean O'Casey's use of the Irish civil war as a background for plays combining tragic melodrama, humor of character, and irony of circumstance, brought new kinds of vitality to the theater. T. S. Eliot attempted with considerable success to revive a ritual poetic drama in England with his *Murder in the Cathedral* (1935). His later attempts to combine religious symbolism with the box-office appeal of amusing society comedy (as in *The Cocktail Party*, 1950), though impressive technical achievements, were not wholly successful: the combination of contemporary social chatter with profound religious symbolism produces an unevenness of tone and disturbing shifts in levels of realism. Elsewhere in modern drama the conflict between realism and symbolism (first clearly seen in Ibsen) is acted out in a variety of ways.

In spite of the achievements of Shaw, Yeats, and Eliot, it cannot be said of the drama as it can of poetry and fiction in this period that a technical revolution occurred which changed the whole course of literary history with respect to that particular literary form. The reformers of the 1890's invoked the name of the great Norwegian playwright Henrik Ibsen: like Shaw they saw him as essentially a critic of middle-class society rather than (as critics tend to see him today) as an essentially poetic dramatist experimenting with symbolic modes of expression. This may be the reason why the influence of Ibsen soon petered out in run-of-the-mill plays of humanitarian social concern. Harley Granville-Barker, actor, director, and Shakespeare scholar and critic as well as playwright, wrote four interesting and thoughtful plays in 1909 and 1910, but for all their intelligence they never really come alive theatrically. The staple of the London West End theater remained social comedy stiffened by occasional irony and sweetened by sentimentality (Noel Coward is one of the best purveyors of this sort of fare). The cleverly contrived sentimentalities of J. M. Barrie (1860–1937) were highly popular in their day; Barrie's plays showed a high theatrical skill and a determined cunning in the exploitation of the audience's reaction. That audience consisted for the most part of tired Philistines, and it was they who determined what was to be a box-office success. An original Scottish dramatist, who at one time appeared to be achieving singlehanded a new awakening in the Scottish theater but who in the end failed to do so, was James Bridie (pseudonym of Dr. O. H. Mavor, 1885–1951), whose witty and inventive plays show an intellectual liveliness sometimes reminiscent of Shaw.

The energy which the Irish movement gave to English drama has not lasted. Sean O'Casey's later plays, where he is influenced by expressionist techniques suggested by German dramatists as well as by Eugene O'Neill, have neither the vitality nor the vivid humor of those earlier plays in which he was able to give tragic meaning to the realities of contemporary Dublin life without denying its comic elements. Another Irish playwright, William Denis Johnston, has also experimented with expressionist techniques and has achieved in some of his plays a remarkable combination of the grotesque and the ironic. But vitality has not been coming into the English theater in the 1950's and early 1960's from this direction.

In the late 1940's and early 1950's it seemed that the verse plays of Christopher Fry were about to bring a new kind of poetic life into English drama. But Fry's exuberantly witty use of metaphor soon lost its appeal, and by the late 1950's a very different kind of drama brought vitality to the British theater. John Osborne's *Look Back in Anger* was produced at the Royal Court Theatre in 1956. Angrily, violently, and in an unadorned and sometimes brutally colloquial dialogue, it thrust upon the audience the revelation of psychological and social problems left unresolved, or even exacerbated, by the welfare state. *The Entertainer* (1957) was similar in its brash virtuosity; Osborne's third play, *Luther* (1960), shows him moving out of a preoccupation with a restricted part of the contemporary social scene to wider concerns and a freer use of imagination. Arnold Wesker was another Royal Court discovery. In a trilogy that began with *Chicken Soup with Barley* (1958), he explored, though less stridently than Osborne, related social and psychological problems. Joan Littlewood's Theatre Workshop introduced another kind of vigorous new theatricalism, with an impromptu-seeming kind of play made up of numerous small scenes; distinctive examples are Brendan Behan's *The Quare Fellow* (1956) and Shelagh Delaney's *A Taste of Honey* (1958). A third significant influence on recent English drama has been the director Peter Hall, who commissioned a number of important plays for his Aldwych productions, including Robert Bolt's *A Man for All Seasons* (1960) and John Arden's *Live Like Pigs* (1958). The man, however, who is emerging as the most important and individual dramatist is Harold Pinter, whose plays, including *The Birthday Party* (1958), *The Caretaker* (1960), and *The Homecoming* (1966), project disturbing symbolic meanings in a quietly colloquial language. These playwrights have the advantage of working with lively and innovative talent in the practical theater. In addition there is a constant and fruitful interaction between drama on the stage and drama in the film, the playwright himself usually working in both media.

LITERARY CRITICISM

Criticism occupies a much larger place on the map of modern literary culture than it has ever occupied before. New psychological and anthropological ideas have stimulated new kinds of critical activity; tools of critical analysis have been sharpened by the impact of linguistic philosophy; the increased difficulty of much modern writing, itself the result of the fragmentation of the audience for literature and the consequent withdrawal of serious writers into coteries using a more or less private symbolism, has increased the demand for critical interpretation. This is the great critical age, and criticism and creation have marched together (in Eliot's work, for example) to an unusual degree, although modern America has placed more emphasis on criticism than has modern Britain.

From one point of view, it could be maintained that Matthew Arnold is the father of modern literary criticism. Arnold thought literature was bound to replace religion as a source of inspiration and spiritual refreshment, and as a result insisted that we must have "the best" literature. If literature, rather than religion, is central to a civilization, and not a mere relaxation or optional pleasure, discrimination between good and bad literature is of the first importance, and critics become in a sense the equivalent of priests. F. R. Leavis, who edited the influential critical review *Scrutiny* from its foundation in 1932 until its demise in 1953, inherited from Arnold this view of the need to discover and proclaim "the best." His and his contributors' essays in *Scrutiny* were devoted to what they called "discrimination," to a determined winnowing of the little wheat from the abundant chaff by a careful technique of practical criticism which at first owed a great deal to I. A. Richards' methods in his Cambridge lectures. Leavis also inherited from Arnold his war against the Philistines and the view that the quality of literature which is produced and esteemed by a generation is bound up with the whole quality of its culture, of the way in which people live and work as well as think. *Culture and Environment*, by Leavis and Denys Thompson (1933), is similar in more than title to Arnold's *Culture and Anarchy*: it is an examination of the way in which the conditions of living imposed by some elements in modern civilization inhibit proper discrimination in literature as in other spheres. But Leavis repudiates any such simple ethical criterion as Arnold's "high seriousness," and sees the true moral vision of a writer embodied much more subtly and often indirectly in his work than Arnold did. In this view he has been influenced by Eliot's repudiation (in *Tradition and the Individual Talent*) of "any semi-ethical criterion of 'sublimity.'"

In general there has been in the last forty years or so—but again not to the same degree as in America—a repudiation of the older view of criticism as gentlemanly chat about books, the "hours in a library" sort of thing, in favor of a criticism much more rigorous and analytic. The revolution in taste proclaimed in the antiromantic essays of T. E. Hulme and developed in the influential essays of Eliot inevitably demanded a more strenuous kind of criticism. If poetic imagery was to be hard, dry, and precise and at the same time impregnated with metaphysical wit and irony, and if a new degree of intellectual complexity was to be demanded of poetry, then the critic had to provide himself with tools for the careful analysis of meaning and structure in order to demonstrate these qualities or the lack of them. Similarly, critics who agreed with Eliot that "the poet has, not a 'personality' to express, but a particular medium," became suspicious alike of autobiographical and exclamatory responses to literature and of the biographical approach which tended to assess literary quality in terms of the degree to which the writer genuinely expressed himself.

Thus the Arnoldian insistence on discrimination combined with the Hulme-Eliot tradition of precision and complexity to demand a more searchingly analytic kind of critical description and evaluation. At the same time I. A. Richards, interested in problems of communication and the different ways in which words work to communicate different sorts of meaning, developed his own technique of analysis of poetic imagery and structure, which had considerable influence on practical (i.e., applied) criticism. Richards turned to psychology for aid in his investigation of meaning and also for the construction of a theory of literary value. Psychology came into modern criticism in many other ways. Although the old-fashioned kind of biographical approach was now out of favor, the examination of the psychology of poetic creation became a respectable branch of criticism, sometimes used to reinforce an analytic account of how imagery works in a poem. On the whole, however, what might be called "genetic" criticism—explanation of the origins and development of a work, rather than of its present nature and value—went on apart from analytic and evaluative criticism. "Genetic" criticism could use psychology, with all the new resources brought in by Freud and Jung, or it could use sociology, studying the social factors that helped to condition particular writers and their works.

Psychology came into criticism in other ways also. Together with anthropology it helped to investigate the ways in which myth and symbol work in literature. Eliot had confessedly drawn on anthropological works in *The Waste Land,* thus virtually asking the critics to use such aids in examining the poem. They were not slow to take him up. Here Jung rather than Freud was the major influence, for Jung's view of racial memory (akin to Yeats's view of the "Great Memory," which preserved the meaning of symbols) was obviously relevant to any investigation of the way in which the mythical element in literature operates. Maud Bodkin's *Archetypal Patterns in Poetry* (1934) was a pioneer work in this field; it stimulated a host of further studies of myth and symbol on both sides of the Atlantic.

At the same time techniques of the analysis of meaning developed by Richards in his practical criticism were being developed to greater and sometimes provocative lengths by his onetime pupil, William Empson. Semantics was now an established tool of the analytic critic, used in many different ways. So the pattern is this: first, the necessity for discrimination (because we must have "the best") through rigorous critical analysis; further emphasis on critical rigor by the Hulme-Eliot tradition of precision, impersonality, and complexity; new tools for critical analysis through the study of semantics and linguistic philosophy; an interest in archetypal images through the psychological and anthropological incitements to the study of myth and symbol; side by side with all this, and sometimes interacting with it, psychological and sociological investigation of the way the creative process operates in given instances. All these elements are present in what has for many years now been called in America the "new criticism," for American critics, more than British critics, have taken up and developed, sometimes with great originality and persuasiveness, all of these critical strains.

In recent years the pattern of critical thought and practice has become less easily definable. New kinds of interests, social or linguistic and sometimes both, have emerged and interacted in varying ways with the procedures developed by Richards, Leavis, and others. The application of linguistics to the study of different styles—a branch of criticism now called stylistics—though not widely popular in Britain, is nevertheless being undertaken by some younger critics and points toward a new kind of sophistication in the analysis of literary language which may well give a new direction to the Empsonian tradition of analysis of ambiguity. Similarly, the anthropological study of myth, which has influenced the myth critics and the seekers of archetypes since the middle 1930's, has been given a new depth and complexity by the influences of the French social anthropologist Claude Lévi-Strauss. Strauss's theory of Structuralism is concerned with the way the human mind interprets and orders the phenomena perceived by the senses, and this helps to explain the symbols men use, the social structure they build, the myths they construct, and the language they employ. Thus new links between anthropology, sociology, psychology, linguistics, and literature are being forged which may well change radically the shape of literary criticism.

THOMAS HARDY
(1840–1928)

1872–96: Career as novelist, ending with *Jude the Obscure*.
1898:   *Wessex Poems*, first collection of poetry.

Thomas Hardy was born near Dorchester, in that area of southwest England that he was to make the "Wessex" of his novels. He attended local schools until the age of 15, when he was articled to a Dorchester architect with whom he worked for six years. In 1861 he went to London to continue his studies and to practice as an architect. Meanwhile he was completing his general education informally through his own erratic reading, and becoming more and more interested in both fiction and poetry. After some early attempts at writing both short stories and poems, he decided to concentrate on fiction. His first novel was rejected by the publishers in 1868 on the advice of George Meredith, who nevertheless advised Hardy to write another. The result was *Desperate Remedies*, published anonymously in 1871, followed the next year by his first real success (also published anonymously), *Under the Greenwood Tree*. Hardy's career as a novelist was now well launched; he gave up his architectural work and produced a series of novels that ended with *Jude the Obscure* in 1896. The hostile reception of this novel sent him back to poetry. His remarkable epic-drama of the Napoleonic Wars, *The Dynasts*, came out in three parts between 1903 and 1908; after this he wrote mostly lyric poetry.

Hardy's novels, set in a predominantly rural "Wessex," show the forces of nature outside and inside man combining to shape human destiny. Against a background of immemorial agricultural labor, with ancient monuments such as Stonehenge or an old Roman amphitheater reminding us of the human past, he presents characters at the mercy of their own passions or finding temporary salvation in the age-old rhythms of rural work or rural recreation. Men in Hardy's fiction are not masters of their fates; they are at the mercy of the indifferent forces which manipulate their behavior and their relations with others; but they can achieve dignity through endurance, and heroism through simple strength of character. The characteristic Victorian novelist—e.g., Dickens and Thackeray—was concerned with the behavior and problems of men in a given social milieu, which he described in detail; Hardy preferred to go directly for the elemental in human behavior with a minimum of contemporary social detail. Most of Hardy's novels are tragic, though *Under the Greenwood Tree* has an idyllic character possessed by no other of his novels. But even here the happy ending is achieved only by ending the story with the marriage of the hero and heroine and refusing to go further; the texture of the narrative, for all its moments of gaiety and charm, has already suggested the bitter ironies of which life is capable. His later work explores those ironies with sometimes an almost malevolent staging of coincidence in order to emphasize the disparity between human desire and ambition on the one hand and what fate has in store for the characters on the other. But fate is not a wholly external force. Men are driven by the demands of their own nature as much as by anything from outside them. *Tess of the D'Urbervilles* (1891) is the story of an intelligent and sensitive girl, daughter of a poor family, driven to murder and so to death by hanging, by a concatenation of events and circumstances so bitterly ironic that many readers find it the darkest of Hardy's novels, while others would award that distinction to *Jude the Obscure*, the disturbingly powerful account of an ambitious rustic trapped between his intellect and his sensuality and as a result delivered to destruction.

Hardy himself denied that he was a pessimist, calling himself a "meliorist," i.e., one who believes that the world may be made better by human effort. But there is little sign of "meliorism" in either his most important novels or his lyric poetry. In his poems—which alone are represented here because no extract could do justice to Hardy's power as a novelist—many of his characteristic attitudes and ideas and many of his favorite situations can be found. A number of his poems are verse anecdotes illustrating the perversity of fate, the disastrous or ironic coincidence. But his best poems go beyond this mood to present with quiet gravity and a carefully controlled elegiac feeling some aspect of human sorrow or loss or frustration or regret, always projected through a particular, fully realized situation. *Hap* shows Hardy in the characteristic mood of complaining about the irony of human destiny in a universe ruled by chance; but a poem such as *The Walk* (one of a group of poems written after the death of his first wife in 1912) gives, with remarkable power, concrete embodiment to a sense of loss. That power—we see it also in *A Broken Appointment* and *She Hears the Storm*—is achieved through a kind of verbal as well as an emotional integrity. Hardy's poetry, like his prose, often has a self-taught air about it; both can be odd or pretentious or awkward or clumsy. But at their best both his poetry and his prose have an air of persuasive authenticity. The association of a given emotion with particular visual memories in *Neutral Tones*, for example, is impressive because it carries such extraordinary conviction; and it carries that conviction because the rhythms and rhymes are handled so as to suggest the kind of utterance actually wrung from the poet (consider, e.g., the curious dead fall of "They had fallen from an ash, and were gray"). At the same time, Hardy will use an antique or a poetic word or phrase ("thereby," "a-wing") if it fits in with the movement of the poem and keeps him from having to stop and search for something more deft: the result is an effect not of artificiality but of spontaneity. Hardy's use of ballad rhythms often helps to give an elemental quality to his poetry, suggesting that this incident or situation, carefully particularized though it is, nevertheless stands for some profound and recurring themes in human experience.

Sometimes in Hardy's poetry the quiet lilt of the verse and the fall of the rhymes convey a deep but controlled emotion, as in *Drummer Hodge*, where the sense of a simple English soldier buried in a far distant land and mingling with an earth that will produce vegetation so different from anything known in England is poignantly expressed. *In Time of "The Breaking of Nations"* conveys with stark clarity the same awareness of the processes of nature continuing in spite of cataclysms caused by human folly in the novels. The sadness in Hardy—his inability to believe in the government of the world by a benevolent God, his sense of the waste and frustration involved in human life, his insistent irony when faced with moral or metaphysical questions—is part of the late Victorian mood. We can see something like it in A. E. Housman, and there is an earlier version of Victorian pessimism in Edward FitzGerald's *Rubáiyát of Omar Khay-yám*, published when Hardy was 19. Yet Hardy's characteristic themes and attitudes cannot be related simply to the reaction to new scientific and philosophical ideas (Darwin's theory of evolution, for example) that we see in so many forms in late 19th-century literature. The favorite poetic mood of both Tennyson and Arnold was also an elegiac one (e.g., in Tennyson's *Break, Break, Break* and Arnold's *Dover Beach*), but this is not Hardy's mood. The sad-sweet cadences of Victorian self-pity are not to be found in Hardy's poetry, which is sterner, as though braced by a long look at the worst. It is this sternness—sometimes amounting to rug-gedness—together with his verbal and emotional integrity, his refusal ever to surrender to mere poetic fashion, his quietly searching individual ac-cent, that has helped to bring about the steady rise in Hardy's poetic reputation in recent years, so that today he is regarded not only as a dis-tinguished novelist but also as a great English poet.

Hap[1]

If but some vengeful god would call to me
From up the sky, and laugh: "Thou suffering thing,
Know that thy sorrow is my ecstasy,
That thy love's loss is my hate's profiting!"

Then would I bear it, clench myself, and die,   5
Steeled by the sense of ire unmerited;
Half-eased in that a Powerfuller than I
Had willed and meted me the tears I shed.

But not so. How arrives it joy lies slain,
And why unblooms the best hope ever sown?   10
—Crass Casualty obstructs the sun and rain,
And dicing Time for gladness casts a moan. . . .
These purblind Doomsters[2] had as readily strown
Blisses about my pilgrimage as pain.

1866   1898

The Impercipient

(AT A CATHEDRAL SERVICE)

That with this bright believing band
      I have no claim to be,
That faiths by which my comrades stand
      Seem fantasies to me,

1. I.e., chance (as also "Casualty," line 11).
2. Half-blind judges.

And mirage-mists their Shining Land,   5
   Is a strange destiny.

Why thus my soul should be consigned
   To infelicity,
Why always I must feel as blind
   To sights my brethren see,   10
Why joys they've found I cannot find,
   Abides a mystery.

Since heart of mine knows not that ease
   Which they know; since it be
That He who breathes All's Well to these   15
   Breathes no All's-Well to me,
My lack might move their sympathies
   And Christian charity!

I am like a gazer who should mark
   An inland company   20
Standing upfingered, with, "Hark! hark!
   The glorious distant sea!"
And feel, "Alas, 'tis but yon dark
   And wind-swept pine to me!"

Yet I would bear my shortcomings   25
   With meet tranquillity,
But for the charge that blessed things
   I'd liefer not have be.
O, doth a bird deprived of wings
   Go earth-bound willfully!   30

.   .   .   .   .

Enough. As yet disquiet clings
   About us. Rest shall we.

                       1898

Neutral Tones

We stood by a pond that winter day,
And the sun was white, as though chidden of God,
And a few leaves lay on the starving sod;
     —They had fallen from an ash, and were gray.

Your eyes on me were as eyes that rove   5
Over tedious riddles of years ago;
And some words played between us to and fro
     On which lost the more by our love.

The smile on your mouth was the deadest thing
Alive enough to have strength to die;   10
And a grin of bitterness swept thereby
     Like an ominous bird a-wing. . . .

Since then, keen lessons that love deceives,
And wrings with wrong, have shaped to me
Your face, and the God-cursed sun, and a tree,   15
    And a pond edged with grayish leaves.

1867   1898

I Look into My Glass

I look into my glass,
And view my wasting skin,
And say, "Would God it came to pass
My heart had shrunk as thin!"

For then, I, undistressed   5
By hearts grown cold to me,
Could lonely wait my endless rest
With equanimity.

But Time, to make me grieve,
Part steals, lets part abide;   10
And shakes this fragile frame at eve
With throbbings of noontide.

1898

A Broken Appointment

    You did not come,
And marching Time drew on, and wore me numb.—
Yet less for loss of your dear presence there
Than that I thus found lacking in your make
That high compassion which can overbear   5
Reluctance for pure loving-kindness' sake
Grieved I, when, as the hope-hour stroked its sum,
    You did not come.

    You love not me,
And love alone can lend you loyalty;   10
—I know and knew it. But, unto the store
Of human deeds divine in all but name,
Was it not worth a little hour or more
To add yet this: Once you, a woman, came
To soothe a time-torn man; even though it be   15
    You love not me?

1902

Drummer Hodge

1

They throw in Drummer Hodge, to rest
    Uncoffined—just as found:

His landmark is a kopje-crest[1]
    That breaks the veldt around;
And foreign constellations west[2]   5
    Each night above his mound.

2

Young Hodge the Drummer never knew—
    Fresh from his Wessex home—
The meaning of the broad Karoo,[3]
    The Bush, the dusty loam,   10
And why uprose to nightly view
    Strange stars amid the gloam.

3

Yet portion of that unknown plain
    Will Hodge forever be;
His homely Northern breast and brain   15
    Grow to some Southern tree,
And strange-eyed constellations reign
    His stars eternally.

                                  1902

Lausanne[4]

IN GIBBON'S OLD GARDEN: 11–12 P.M.

JUNE 27, 1897

(The 110th anniversary of the completion of the Decline and Fall *at the same hour and place)*

A spirit seems to pass,
Formal in pose, but grave withal and grand:
He contemplates a volume in his hand,
And far lamps fleck him through the thin acacias.

  Anon the book is closed,   5
With "It is finished!" And at the alley's end
He turns, and when on me his glances bend
As from the Past comes speech—small, muted, yet composed.

  "How fares the Truth now?—Ill?
—Do pens but slily further her advance?   10

---

1. South African Dutch (Afrikaans) word for a small hill. "Veldt": Afrikaans for a plain or prairie. The poem is a lament for an English soldier killed in the Boer War (1899–1902). 2. Set. The "foreign constellations" are those visible only in the southern hemisphere. 3. A dry table-land region in South Africa (usually spelled "Karroo"). "The Bush": British Colonial word for an uncleared area of land. 4. Edward Gibbon finished his monumental *History of the Decline and Fall of the Roman Empire* (6 vols., 1776–88) in Lausanne, Switzerland, where he lived from 1783 until his death. Gibbon records in his *Memoirs of My Life and Writings* that "It was on the day, or rather night, of the 27th of June, 1787, that I wrote the last lines of the last page, in a summer-house in my garden," and goes on to describe his emotions on having completed his life's work. Gibbon, a skeptic, saw himself fighting for truth against prejudice and superstition.

May one not speed her but in phrase askance?[5]
Do scribes aver the Comic to be Reverend still?[6]

"Still rule those minds on earth
At whom sage Milton's wormwood words were hurled:
'Truth like a bastard comes into the world   15
Never without ill fame to him who gives her birth'?"[7]

1897   1902

The Darkling[1] Thrush

I leant upon a coppice gate[2]
    When Frost was specter-gray,
And Winter's dregs made desolate
    The weakening eye of day.
The tangled bine-stems[3] scored the sky   5
    Like strings of broken lyres,
And all mankind that haunted nigh
    Had sought their household fires.

The land's sharp features seemed to be
    The Century's corpse[4] outleant,   10
His crypt the cloudy canopy,
    The wind his death-lament.
The ancient pulse of germ and birth
    Was shrunken hard and dry,
And every spirit upon earth   15
    Seemed fervorless as I.

At once a voice arose among
    The bleak twigs overhead
In a fullhearted evensong
    Of joy illimited;   20
An aged thrush, frail, gaunt, and small,
    In blast-beruffled plume,
Had chosen thus to fling his soul
    Upon the growing gloom.

So little cause for carolings   25
    Of such ecstatic sound
Was written on terrestrial things
    Afar or nigh around,
That I could think there trembled through
    His happy good-night air   30
Some blessed Hope, whereof he knew
    And I was unaware.

1900   1902

5. Oblique.
6. I.e., do theological writers still claim respect for what is ridiculous on the grounds that it is ancient and venerable?
7. From Milton's *Areopagitica* (1644), defending liberty of the press.

1. In the dark.
2. Gate leading to a small wood or thicket.
3. Twining stems of shrubs.
4. This poem was written on December 31, 1900, the last day of the 19th century.

A Trampwoman's Tragedy
(182–)

1

From Wynyard's Gap [1] the livelong day,
    The livelong day,
We beat afoot the northward way
    We had traveled times before.
The sun-blaze burning on our backs,   5
Our shoulders sticking to our packs,
By fosseway,[2] fields, and turnpike tracks
    We skirted sad Sedge-Moor.

2

Full twenty miles we jaunted on,
    We jaunted on—   10
My fancy-man, and jeering John,
    And Mother Lee, and I.
And, as the sun drew down to west,
We climbed the toilsome Poldon [3] crest,
And saw, of landskip sights the best,   15
    The inn that beamed thereby.

3

For months we had padded side by side,
    Ay, side by side
Through the Great Forest, Blackmoor wide,
    And where the Parret ran.   20
We'd faced the gusts on Mendip ridge,
Had crossed the Yeo unhelped by bridge,
Been stung by every Marshwood midge,
    I and my fancy-man.

4

Lone inns we loved, my man and I,   25
    My man and I;
"King's Stag," "Windwhistle" [4] high and dry,
    "The Horse" on Hintock Green.
The cosy house at Wynyard's Gap,

1. The places here named are in Somerset, in southwest England on the northern edge of the area which Hardy called "Wessex" and of which his native Dorset, the county south and southwest of Somerset, reaching to the English Channel, was the major part.
2. Path running along a ditch. See note 4 below.
3. Sad (line 8) because of the Battle of Sedgemoor (1685) when the rebellion of the Duke of Monmouth against James II was crushed with excessive cruelty. "This plain [Sedgemoor], intersected by ditches known as *rhines*, * * * is broken by isolated hills and lower ridges, of which the most conspicuous are Brent Knoll near Burnham, the Isle of Avalon, rising with Glastonbury Tor as its highest point, and the long low ridge of Polden ending to the west in a steep bluff." *Encyclopaedia Britannica*, 11th edition, 1911.
4. "The highness and dryness of Windwhistle Inn was impressed upon the writer two or three years ago, when, after climbing on a hot afternoon to the beautiful spot near which it stands and entering the inn for tea, he was informed by the landlady that none could be had, unless he would fetch water from a valley half a mile off, the house containing not a drop, owing to its situation. However, a tantalizing row of full barrels behind her back testified to a wetness of a certain sort, which was not at that time desired" [Hardy's note].

"The Hut" renowned on Bredy Knap,   30
And many another wayside tap
  Where folk might sit unseen.

                    5
Now as we trudged—O deadly day,
    O deadly day!—
I teased my fancy-man in play   35
  And wanton idleness.
I walked alongside jeering John,
I laid his hand my waist upon;
I would not bend my glances on
  My lover's dark distress.   40

                    6
Thus Poldon top at last we won,
    At last we won,
And gained the inn at sink of sun
  Far-famed as "Marshal's Elm."⁵
Beneath us figured tor and lea,   45
From Mendip to the western sea—
I doubt if finer sight there be
  Within this royal realm.

                    7
Inside the settle all a-row—
    All four a-row   50
We sat, I next to John, to show
  That he had wooed and won.
And then he took me on his knee,
And swore it was his turn to be
My favored mate, and Mother Lee   55
  Passed to my former one.

                    8
Then in a voice I had never heard,
    I had never heard,
My only Love to me: "One word,
    My lady, if you please!   60
Whose is the child you are like to bear?—
His? After all my months o' care?"
God knows 'twas not! But, O despair!
  I nodded—still to tease.

                    9
Then up he sprung, and with his knife—   65
    And with his knife
He let out jeering Johnny's life,
    Yes; there, at set of sun.
The slant ray through the window nigh

---

5. "'Marshal's Elm,' so picturesquely situated, is no longer an inn, though the house, or part of it, still remains. It used to exhibit a fine old swinging sign" [Hardy's note].

Gilded John's blood and glazing eye,   70
Ere scarcely Mother Lee and I
   Knew that the deed was done.

10

The taverns tell the gloomy tale,
   The gloomy tale,
How that at Ivel-chester jail   75
   My Love, my sweetheart swung;
Though stained till now by no misdeed
Save one horse ta'en in time o' need;
(Blue Jimmy stole right many a steed
   Ere his last fling he flung).⁶   80

11

Thereaft I walked the world alone,
   Alone, alone!
On his death-day I gave my groan
   And dropt his dead-born child.
'Twas nigh the jail, beneath a tree,   85
None tending me; for Mother Lee
Had died at Glaston, leaving me
   Unfriended on the wild.

12

And in the night as I lay weak,
   As I lay weak,   90
The leaves a-falling on my cheek,
   The red moon low declined—
The ghost of him I'd die to kiss
Rose up and said: "Ah, tell me this!
Was the child mine, or was it his?   95
   Speak, that I rest may find!"

13

O doubt not but I told him then,
   I told him then,
That I had kept me from all men
   Since we joined lips and swore.   100
Whereat he smiled, and thinned away
As the wind stirred to call up day . . .
—'Tis past! And here alone I stray
   Haunting the Western Moor.

April, 1902   1909

6. " 'Blue Jimmy' was a notorious horse stealer of Wessex in those days, who appropriated more than a hundred horses before he was caught, among others one belonging to a neighbor of the writer's grandfather. He was hanged at the now demolished Ivel-chester or Ilchester jail above mentioned—that building formerly of so many sinister associations in the minds of the local peasantry, and the continual haunt of fever, which at last led to its condemnation. Its site is now an innocent-looking green meadow" [Hardy's note].

Let Me Enjoy

(MINOR KEY)

1

Let me enjoy the earth no less
Because the all-enacting Might
That fashioned forth its loveliness
Had other aims than my delight.

2

About my path there flits a Fair,   5
Who throws me not a word or sign;
I'll charm me with her ignoring air,
And laud the lips not meant for mine.

3

From manuscripts of moving song
Inspired by scenes and dreams unknown   10
I'll pour out raptures that belong
To others, as they were my own.

4

And some day hence, towards Paradise
And all its blest—if such should be—
I will lift glad, afar-off eyes,   15
Though it contain no place for me.

1909

The Rash Bride

AN EXPERIENCE OF THE MELLSTOCK QUIRE[1]

1

We Christmas-caroled down the Vale, and up the Vale, and
    round the Vale,
We played and sang that night as we were yearly wont to do—
A carol in a minor key, a carol in the major D,
Then at each house: "Good wishes: many Christmas joys to you!"

2

Next, to the widow's John and I and all the rest drew on.
    And I   5
Discerned that John could hardly hold the tongue of him for joy.
The widow was a sweet young thing whom John was bent on
    marrying,
And quiring at her casement seemed romantic to the boy.

3

"She'll make reply, I trust," said he, "to our salute? She must!"
    said he,
"And then I will accost her gently—much to her surprise!—   10

1. Choir.

For knowing not I am with you here, when I speak up and call
  her dear
A tenderness will fill her voice, a bashfulness her eyes."

4

So, by her window-square we stood; ay, with our lanterns there
  we stood,
And he along with us—not singing, waiting for a sign;
And when we'd quired her carols three a light was lit and out
  looked she,   15
A shawl about her bedgown, and her color red as wine.

5

And sweetly then she bowed her thanks, and smiled, and
  spoke aloud her thanks;
When lo, behind her back there, in the room, a man appeared.
I knew him—one from Woolcomb way—Giles Swetman—
  honest as the day,
But eager, hasty; and I felt that some strange trouble neared.   20

6

"How comes he there? . . . Suppose," said we, "she's wed of
  late! Who knows?" said we.
—"She married yestermorning—only mother yet has known
The secret o't!" shrilled one small boy. "But now I've told,
  let's wish 'em joy!"
A heavy fall aroused us: John had gone down like a stone.

7

We rushed to him and caught him round, and lifted him, and
  brought him round,   25
When, hearing something wrong had happened, oped the
  window she:
"Has one of you fallen ill?" she asked, "by these night
  labors overtasked?"
None answered. That she'd done poor John a cruel turn felt we.

8

Till up spoke Michael: "Fie, young dame! You've broke your
  promise, sly young dame,
By forming this new tie, young dame, and jilting John so true,   30
Who trudged tonight to sing to 'ee because he thought he'd
  bring to 'ee
Good wishes as your coming spouse. May ye such trifling rue!"

9

Her man had said no word at all; but being behind had heard
  it all,
And now cried: "Neighbors, on my soul I knew not 'twas
  like this!"
And then to her: "If I had known you'd had in tow not me
  alone,   35
No wife should you have been of mine. It is a dear bought bliss!"

10

She changed death-white, and heaved a cry: we'd never heard
  so grieved a cry

As came from her at this from him: heartbroken quite seemed
  she;
And suddenly, as we looked on, she turned, and rushed; and
  she was gone,
Whither, her husband, following after, knew not; nor knew we. 40

11

We searched till dawn about the house; within the house,
  without the house,
We searched among the laurel boughs that grew beneath the
  wall,
And then among the crocks and things, and stores for winter
  junketings,
In linhay,[2] loft, and dairy; but we found her not at all.

12

Then John rushed in: "O friends," he said, "hear this, this,
  this!" and bends his head: 45
"I've—searched round by the—*well*, and find the cover open
  wide!
I am fearful that—I can't say what . . . Bring lanterns, and
  some cords to knot."
We did so, and we went and stood the deep dark hole beside.

13

And then they, ropes in hand, and I—ay, John, and all the
  band, and I
Let down a lantern to the depths—some hundred feet and
  more;   50
It glimmered like a fog-dimmed star; and there, beside its light,
  afar,
White drapery floated, and we knew the meaning that it bore.

14

The rest is naught. . . . We buried her o' Sunday. Neighbors
  carried her;
And Swetman—he who'd married her—now miserablest
  of men,
Walked mourning first; and then walked John; just quivering,
  but composed anon;   55
And we the quire formed round the grave, as was the custom
  then.

15

Our old bass player, as I recall—his white hair blown—but why
  recall!—
His viol upstrapped, bent figure—doomed to follow her full
  soon—
Stood bowing, pale and tremulous; and next to him the rest
  of us. . . .
We sang the Ninetieth Psalm[3] to her—set to Saint Stephen's
  tune.   60

1909

2. Shed.
3. A favorite psalm at funerals, con- trasting God's eternity with the brevity
                                        of human life.

One We Knew

(M. H.[4] 1772–1857)

She told how they used to form for the country dances—
    "The Triumph," "The New-rigged Ship"—
To the light of the guttering wax in the paneled manses
    And in cots to the blink of a dip.[5]

She spoke of the wild "poussetting" and "allemanding" [6]   5
    On carpet, on oak, and on sod;
And the two long rows of ladies and gentlemen standing,
    And the figures the couples trod.

She showed us the spot where the maypole was yearly planted,
    And where the bandsmen stood   10
While breeched and kerchiefed partners whirled, and panted
    To choose each other for good.

She told of that far-back day when they learnt astounded
    Of the death of the King of France:
Of the Terror; and then of Bonaparte's unbounded   15
    Ambition and arrogance.

Of how his threats woke warlike preparations
    Along the southern strand,
And how each night brought tremors and trepidations
    Lest morning should see him land.   20

She said she had often heard the gibbet creaking
    As it swayed in the lightning flash,
Had caught from the neighboring town a small child's shrieking
    At the cart tail under the lash. . . .

With cap-framed face and long gaze into the embers—   25
    We seated around her knees—
She would dwell on such dead themes, not as one who remembers,
    But rather as one who sees.

She seemed one left behind of a band gone distant
    So far that no tongue could hail: 30
Past things retold were to her as things existent,
    Things present but as a tale.

May 20, 1902   1909

She Hears the Storm

There was a time in former years—
    While my rooftree was his—

---

4. Hardy's grandmother.
5. I.e., in cottages by the light of a candle.

6. To pousette is to dance round with hands joined; allemande is the name of a dance originating in Germany.

When I should have been distressed by fears
    At such a night as this!

I should have murmured anxiously,   5
    "The pricking rain strikes cold;
His road is bare of hedge or tree,
    And he is getting old."

But now the fitful chimney-roar,
    The drone of Thorncombe trees,   10
The Froom in flood upon the moor,
    The mud of Mellstock Leaze,[7]

The candle slanting sooty wicked,
    The thuds upon the thatch,
The eaves-drops on the window flicked,   15
    The clacking garden-hatch,[8]

And what they mean to wayfarers,
    I scarcely heed or mind;
He has won that storm-tight roof of hers
    Which Earth grants all her kind.   20

            1909

Channel Firing[1]

That night your great guns, unawares,
Shook all our coffins as we lay,
And broke the chancel window-squares,
We thought it was the Judgment Day
And sat upright. While drearisome   5
Arose the howl of wakened hounds:
The mouse let fall the altar-crumb,
The worms drew back into the mounds,

The glebe cow[2] drooled. Till God called, "No;
It's gunnery practice out at sea   10
Just as before you went below;
The world is as it used to be:

"All nations striving strong to make
Red war yet redder. Mad as hatters
They do no more for Christés[3] sake   15
Than you who are helpless in such matters.

---

7. The place names in Hardy's fictional "Wessex" were often invented ("Thorncombe," "Mellstock Leaze"), but he also used the names of real locations, as in "A Trampwoman's Tragedy." The standard edition of Hardy's novels has a map of "Wessex" showing the locale of both the real and the invented names. "The Froom" is presumably the river Frome, flowing through Dorsetshire and Somerset.
8. Gate.

1. Written in April, 1914, when Anglo-German naval rivalry was growing steadily more acute; the title refers to gunnery practice in the English Channel. Four months later (August 4) World War I broke out.
2. I.e., cow on a small plot of land belonging to a cottage (a "glebe" is a small field).
3. The archaic spelling and pronunciation suggest a ballad note of doom.

"That this is not the judgment hour
For some of them's a blessed thing,
For if it were they'd have to scour
Hell's floor for so much threatening. . . .   20

"Ha, ha. It will be warmer when
I blow the trumpet (if indeed
I ever do; for you are men,
And rest eternal sorely need)."

So down we lay again. "I wonder,   25
Will the world ever saner be,"
Said one, "than when He sent us under
In our indifferent century!"

And many a skeleton shook his head.
"Instead of preaching forty year,"   30
My neighbor Parson Thirdly said,
"I wish I had stuck to pipes and beer."

Again the guns disturbed the hour,
Roaring their readiness to avenge,
As far inland as Stourton Tower,   35
And Camelot, and starlit Stonehenge.[4]

1914   1914

The Convergence of the Twain

(LINES ON THE LOSS OF THE "TITANIC")[1]

1

In a solitude of the sea
Deep from human vanity,
And the Pride of Life that planned her, stilly couches she.

2

Steel chambers, late the pyres
Of her salamandrine fires,[2]
Cold currents thrid, and turn to rhythmic tidal lyres.   5

3

Over the mirrors meant
To glass the opulent
The sea worm crawls—grotesque, slimed, dumb, indifferent.

4. Again the "Wessex" place names from various sources: Stonehenge is the famous prehistoric stone circle on Salisbury Plain; Camelot was the legendary location of King Arthur's court and the Round Table. There is a real river Stour in Dorset, and a town called Stour Head, which Hardy calls "Stourton."
1. The *Titanic* was the largest and most luxurious ocean liner of her day. Considered unsinkable, she sank with great loss of life on April 15, 1912, on her maiden voyage from Southampton to America, after colliding with an iceberg.
2. Probably "fires in which nothing could survive" (although, since the salamander is a lizardlike animal supposed to be able to live in fire, "salamandrine" usually means "able to resist or to live in fire"). In the next line, "thrid" is the archaic past tense of the verb "thread."

4

Jewels in joy designed   10
  To ravish the sensuous mind
Lie lightless, all their sparkles bleared and black and blind.

5

Dim moon-eyed fishes near
  Gaze at the gilded gear
And query: "What does this vaingloriousness down here?" . . . 15

6

Well: while was fashioning
  This creature of cleaving wing,
The Immanent Will[3] that stirs and urges everything

7

Prepared a sinister mate
  For her—so gaily great—   20
A Shape of Ice, for the time far and dissociate.

8

And as the smart ship grew
  In stature, grace, and hue,
In shadowy silent distance grew the Iceberg too.

9

Alien they seemed to be: 25
  No mortal eye could see
The intimate welding of their later history,

10

Or sign that they were bent
  By paths coincident
On being anon twin halves of one august event,   30

11

Till the Spinner of the Years
  Said "Now!" And each one hears,
And consummation comes, and jars two hemispheres.
1912   1912, 1914

Ah, Are You Digging on My Grave?

"Ah, are you digging on my grave,
    My loved one?—planting rue?"[1]
—"No: yesterday he went to wed
One of the brightest wealth has bred.
'It cannot hurt her now,' he said,   5
    'That I should not be true.' "

"Then who is digging on my grave?
    My nearest dearest kin?"

3. The force (blind, but slowly gaining consciousness throughout history)
which drives the world, according to
Hardy's philosophy.

1. A yellow-flowered herb, traditionally an emblem of sorrow ("rue" is
also an archaic word for "sorrow").

—"Ah, no: they sit and think, 'What use!
What good will planting flowers produce?   10
No tendance of her mound can loose
    Her spirit from Death's gin.' "[2]

"But someone digs upon my grave?
    My enemy?—prodding sly?"
—"Nay: when she heard you had passed the Gate   15
That shuts on all flesh soon or late,
She thought you no more worth her hate,
    And cares not where you lie."

"Then, who is digging on my grave?
    Say—since I have not guessed!"   20
—"O it is I, my mistress dear,
Your little dog, who still lives near,
And much I hope my movements here
    Have not disturbed your rest?"

"Ah yes! *You* dig upon my grave . . .   25
    Why flashed it not on me
That one true heart was left behind!
What feeling do we ever find
To equal among human kind
    A dog's fidelity!"   30

"Mistress, I dug upon your grave
    To bury a bone, in case
I should be hungry near this spot
When passing on my daily trot.
I am sorry, but I quite forgot   35
    It was your resting place."

                       1914

Under the Waterfall

"Whenever I plunge my arm, like this,
In a basin of water, I never miss
The sweet sharp sense of a fugitive day
Fetched back from its thickening shroud of gray.
        Hence the only prime   5
        And real love-rhyme
        That I know by heart,
        And that leaves no smart,
Is the purl of a little valley fall
About three spans wide and two spans tall   10
Over a table of solid rock,
And into a scoop of the self-same block;
The purl of a runlet that never ceases

2. Trap.

In stir of kingdoms, in wars, in peaces;
With a hollow boiling voice it speaks   15
And has spoken since hills were turfless peaks."

"And why gives this the only prime
Idea to you of a real love rhyme?
And why does plunging your arm in a bowl
Full of spring water, bring throbs to your soul?"   20

"Well, under the fall, in a crease of the stone,
Though where precisely none ever has known,
Jammed darkly, nothing to show how prized,
And by now with its smoothness opalized,
   Is a drinking glass: 25
   For, down that pass
   My lover and I
   Walked under a sky
Of blue with a leaf-wove awning of green,
In the burn of August, to paint the scene,   30
And we placed our basket of fruit and wine
By the runlet's rim, where we sat to dine;
And when we had drunk from the glass together,
Arched by the oak-copse from the weather,
I held the vessel to rinse in the fall,   35
Where it slipped, and sank, and was past recall,
Though we stooped and plumbed the little abyss
With long bared arms. There the glass still is.
And, as said, if I thrust my arm below
Cold water in basin or bowl, a throe   40
From the past awakens a sense of that time,
And the glass we used, and the cascade's rhyme.
The basin seems the pool, and its edge
The hard smooth face of the brookside ledge,
And the leafy pattern of chinaware   45
The hanging plants that were bathing there.

"By night, by day, when it shines or lours,
There lies intact that chalice of ours,
And its presence adds to the rhyme of love
Persistently sung by the fall above.   50
No lip has touched it since his and mine
In turns therefrom sipped lovers' wine."

               1914

The Walk

  You did not walk with me
  Of late to the hilltop tree
    By the gated ways,
    As in earlier days;
    You were weak and lame,   5
    So you never came,

And I went alone, and I did not mind,
Not thinking of you as left behind.

I walked up there today
Just in the former way;   10
   Surveyed around
   The familiar ground
By myself again:
   What difference, then?
Only that underlying sense   15
Of the look of a room on returning thence.

               1914

During Wind and Rain

They sing their dearest songs—
He, she, all of them—yea,
Treble and tenor and bass,
   And one to play;
With the candles mooning each face. . . .   5
   Ah, no; the years O!
How the sick leaves reel down in throngs!

They clear the creeping moss—
Elders and juniors—aye,
Making the pathways neat   10
   And the garden gay;
And they build a shady seat. . . .
   Ah, no; the years, the years;
See, the white stormbirds wing across!

They are blithely breakfasting all—   15
Men and maidens—yea,
Under the summer tree,
   With a glimpse of the bay,
While pet fowl come to the knee. . . .
   Ah, no; the years O!   20
And the rotten rose is ripped from the wall.

They change to a high new house,
He, she, all of them—aye,
Clocks and carpets and chairs
   On the lawn all day,
And brightest things that are theirs. . . .   25
   Ah, no; the years, the years;
Down their carved names the raindrop plows.

               1917

In Time of "The Breaking of Nations"[1]

1
Only a man harrowing clods
In a slow silent walk

---

1. Cf. "Thou art my battle ax and weapons of war: for with thee will I break in pieces the nations" (Jeremiah li.20). The poem was written during World War I.

With an old horse that stumbles and nods
   Half asleep as they stalk.

2

Only thin smoke without flame   5
   From the heaps of couch-grass;
Yet this will go onward the same
   Though Dynasties pass.

3

Yonder a maid and her wight
   Come whispering by;   10
War's annals will cloud into night
   Ere their story die.

1915   1916

He Never Expected Much

[OR]

A CONSIDERATION

[*A reflection*] ON MY EIGHTY-SIXTH BIRTHDAY

Well, World, you have kept faith with me,
   Kept faith with me;
Upon the whole you have proved to be
   Much as you said you were.
Since as a child I used to lie   5
Upon the leaze[2] and watch the sky,
Never, I own, expected I
   That life would all be fair.

'Twas then you said, and since have said,
   Times since have said,   10
In that mysterious voice you shed
   From clouds and hills around:
"Many have loved me desperately,
Many with smooth serenity,
While some have shown contempt of me   15
   Till they dropped underground.

"I do not promise overmuch,
   Child; overmuch;
Just neutral-tinted haps and such,"
   You said to minds like mine.   20
Wise warning for your credit's sake!
Which I for one failed not to take,
And hence could stem such strain and ache
   As each year might assign.

1928

2. Pasture.

GERARD MANLEY HOPKINS
(1844–1889)

1866: Joins the Roman Catholic Church.
1877: Ordained.
1918: Posthumous publication of his poems by Bridges.

Gerard Manley Hopkins was educated at Highgate School, London, and at Balliol College, Oxford, where he studied classics and was influenced by the Oxford Movement, that revival of the ritualistic and dogmatic side of Christianity which began as a movement within the Church of England but which ended by taking many of its adherents, including the leading figure in the movement, John Henry Newman, to the Roman Catholic Church. After a period of spiritual turmoil Hopkins joined the Roman Catholic Church in 1866, sponsored by Newman, and two years later entered the Society of Jesus. He was ordained in 1877, and after serving as priest in a number of parishes, including one in a working-class area of Liverpool where the squalor disturbed him deeply, he was in 1884 appointed Professor of Classics at University College, Dublin.

A devoted Jesuit performing faithfully the duties assigned to him by his superiors, Hopkins was also a sensitive poet fascinated by language and rhythm and a passionately keen observer of the color and form and detail of the world of nature. The claims of religion and the duties of his religious profession were paramount, but his aesthetic interests (which included an interest in painting and music) asserted themselves with sometimes painful force, and it was not always easy for him to reconcile his religious vocation with his poetic genius. Before entering the Society of Jesus he burned his finished poems (though working copies survive) and did not write poetry again until late in 1875 or early in 1876. Hopkins went through periods of deep depression, of a listless sense of failure, and of that deep spiritual emptiness which mystics know as "the dark night of the soul" and see as one of the necessary stages on the road to spiritual fulfillment. This mood of spiritual desolation is expressed in the so-called "terrible sonnets," written between 1885 and 1889. But Hopkins also enjoyed moods of intense pleasure in the natural world, linked with a profound sense of natural beauty as a reflection of divine reality, and it is this combination of the most passionate and particularized apprehension of the sounds, shapes, and colors of the English countryside with the religious awareness of God as revealed through these sounds, shapes and colors, that is the theme of much of his poetry.

Hopkins' poems were never published in his lifetime. In spite of his eager interest in poetry and in technical problems of writing verse—an interest which is reflected in all its variety and intensity in the letters he wrote to his friends Robert Bridges (later poet laureate) and R. W. Dixon—Hopkins subordinated his poetry to his duties as a Jesuit and never sought any public fame as a poet. He resisted the suggestion made by

Bridges and others in 1879 that he publish some of his poems, as he felt that his religious superiors would not approve. It is doubtful in any case whether his poetry would have been appreciated or even understood in the 19th century, for it flouted most of the contemporary expectations of what poetry should be. One of his aims was to rejuvenate the language of poetry, and he did so in a variety of ways. Sometimes he placed a familiar and much-used word in a new and startling context to bring out a lost aspect of its original meaning (e.g., addressing God as "sir" in *Thou Art Indeed Just, Lord*); sometimes he revived older words or used dialect words or phrases (such as "all road ever" in *Felix Randal*); sometimes he coined new words on the analogy of existing ones (e.g., "leafmeal" in *Spring and Fall*). He also employed devices found in other poetic modes, such as Anglo-Saxon and Welsh, to find new ways of giving exact and arresting expression to an impression or an idea or a combination of both; and he used unusual combinations of words and unusual word order to achieve the exact curve of the meaning. His study of the medieval philosopher Duns Scotus had encouraged this interest in "individuation" or "this-ness" (*haecceitas*) as a clue to the nature of reality. The essential inward pattern of the expression, what he called "inscape," was his primary concern. "No doubt," he wrote to Bridges, "my poetry errs on the side of oddness * * * but as air, melody, is what strikes me most of all in music and design in painting, so design, pattern, or what I am in the habit of calling 'inscape' is what I above all aim at in poetry. Now it is the virtue of design, pattern, or inscape to be distinctive and it is the vice of distinctiveness to become queer. This vice I cannot have escaped." Bridges, though recognizing his friend's genius, was often more aware of the oddness than of the distinctiveness; a later generation, reacting against the mellifluous poeticizings of an attenuated Romantic tradition, saw in the power and originality of Hopkins' expression not only something tremendously impressive in itself but also an invitation to experiment in new uses of language and new poetic rhythms.

Hopkins' interest in rhythms was as great as his interest in words. In his letters he developed a theory of "sprung rhythm" which broke away from the standard conception of poetic rhythms as consisting of a number of metrical feet, each having a fixed number of syllables, some stressed and some unstressed, with a limited number of possible variations and substitutions. Intead, he saw rhythm in poetry as much more flexible, much more like time and tempo in music, where the rhythmic effects are controlled by the number of beats in the measure (rather than the number of notes) and the general pattern of rising or falling movement. He also experimented with various ways of running lines into each other and of manipulating groups of "slack" or unaccented syllables within the line. He often used accent marks, which draw the reader's attention to the way the stresses fall in the line. All these devices help to produce his characteristic "sprung rhythm," which gives his poetry a different sound from that of other Victorian verse, a sound in many respects more like that of English and American poetry since Eliot.

The remarkable swinging movement of the opening of *The Windhover* is a characteristic triumph of Hopkins' rhythmic effects. He called the rhythm here "falling," meaning that the stress comes first in each foot. (The first word, "I," is conceived of as an introductory light beat outside

the main movement of the line.) Hopkins himself scanned the first four
lines in this way:

I caught this morning mórning's mínion, king-
  dom of daylight's dáuphin, dapple-dáwn-drawn Falcon, in his riding
  Of the rólling level únderneáth him steady aír, and stríding
  High thére, how he rung upon the rein of a wimpling wing

The stressed syllables are marked ´, while the curved line underneath a
syllable marks what he called "hangers" or "outriders," which he defined
as "one, two, or three slack syllables added to a foot and not counted in
the nominal scanning." The curious plunging effect which this
rhythm achieves—reproducing so effectively the movement of the bird
which is being described—is heightened by the sense of urgent forward
movement achieved by splitting "kingdom" between two lines and rhyming the first syllable ("king-") with the unstressed syllable "ing" of "riding" in the next line as well as, more obviously, with "wing" in line 4.
The hyphenating of groups of words, as in "dapple-dawn-drawn," is another common device of Hopkins: it can achieve a variety of effects, with
each word in the hyphenated group modifying and coloring the other to
achieve a simultaneous blend of meaning both more immediate and more
subtle in its impact on the reader than the same words could produce if
linked more conventionally by conjunctions. Hopkins always tried to
squeeze all water out of his language, to avoid all unnecessary words that
are required only as grammatical signs and so are liable to dissipate the
meaning. To concentrate meaning (so that when the poem is finally made
out its meaning "explodes," as he once put it) rather than to dissipate it
was always Hopkins' aim.

Other devices used by Hopkins include patterns of alliteration (e.g.,
God's Grandeur, line 3: "It gathers to a greatness, like the *ooze* of *oil*");
internal rhymes (line 6: "And all is *seared* with trade; *bleared, smeared*
with toil"); varieties of assonance (lines 11–14: "West," "went,"
"breast"); and different kinds of sound patterns which he adapted from
the traditions of Welsh poetry.

In its kind of imagery, too, and in the way in which the imagery works,
Hopkins' poetry differs sharply from that of, say, Tennyson or Rossetti.
In such a poem as *The Starlight Night* we are struck not only by the
arresting imperatives with which it opens and the echoes of Anglo-Saxon
poetic devices in "fire-folk" and "circle-citadel" but also by the remarkable way in which excitement at an aspect of the natural world moves
into a religious affirmation. This is achieved partly by a punning use of
language unknown in serious English poetry since the 17th century. In
line 13, for example, the harvested sheaves ("shocks") are to be safely
housed in the barn. But "shocks" also suggests the other and more familiar
sense of the word—"the thousand natural shocks that flesh is heir to"
(*Hamlet*). By buying the beauty of nature with prayer (lines 8 ff.), we
learn to see God in nature and to possess both nature and God. Thus by
"owning" nature we have a home for it—and for ourselves, protecting
both the "shocks" of corn and ourselves from the shocks of life. At the
conclusion Christ and his saints are brought into this communion of the

sheltered and protected: it becomes now the communion of saints and that, we now learn, is what "the fire-folk sitting in the air" really suggested. And what other 19th-century poet would have used the language of the auction room in talking of, the beauty of nature and its relation to religious practices? ("Buy then! bid then!—What?—Prayer, patience, alms, vows.")

This combination of the startlingly colloquial and the strikingly unusual is an important feature of Hopkins' poetry. *The Lantern Out of Doors* begins with a simple, colloquial use of English ("And who goes there? / I think * * * "). The surface thought is also simple: we meet people in daily life who interest us momentarily, but our paths cross briefly and they disappear and we forget about them, because "out of sight is out of mind" (and notice the way Hopkins introduces a homely proverb here). Christ, on the other hand, never forgets people; He is always interested in them; He is their ransom, their rescue, and their eternal friend. There is, however, much more than this in the poem. The word "interests" in line 2 is not a normal poetic word; it arrests us by its very ordinariness. As the poem develops, it comes to suggest not only its obvious, primary meaning but its financial meaning (as in "to lend at interest"). The thought is: people whose character makes them valuable pass by but soon disappear when they are bought by death or distance. Although death or distance buys or consumes them, so that they are lost to sight, Christ continues to "mind" them—in the sense (still common in Scotland) of "remember" them as well as "look after" them, as a man minds his property. Christ's *interest* is their *ransom*: the implication is that Christ gives the interest on his property to ransom man—but of course the word "interest" is also used in its more obvious meaning. Or consider lines 5 and following. The sense is that men beautiful in "mould" (shape) disappear in the "mould" (the earth of the grave): their very beauty suggests their mortality. Or we could follow out the double meaning of "kind" in the phrase "foot follows kind." This combination of the colloquial and the formal, the building up of complex patterns of meaning through the multiple suggestiveness given to words in their poetic context, is what so excited 20th-century poets when they discovered Hopkins.

This discovery was made in 1918, long after Hopkins' death, when Bridges first brought out an edition of Hopkins' poems. By the time the second edition appeared, with an introduction by Charles Williams, in 1930, Hopkins' position was established; the younger poets, such as W. H. Auden and later Dylan Thomas, turned to him enthusiastically as one of their masters. Hopkins is thus in a sense a 20-century poet born out of his time who had to wait until the present century for posthumous appreciation and influence.

At the same time, Hopkins was very much a Victorian poet and we must not forget that there were Victorian poets, notably Browning, who broke away from the established conventions of 19th-century poetry—both the brooding simplicity of Wordsworth and the more sensuous and musical language of Keats and Tennyson—to arouse attention by a deliberate harshness or violence or eccentricity in both diction and rhythms. In this respect Hopkins shows many similarities to Browning. Hopkins was also very much of his period in his deep personal concern for the ethical meaning of Nature.

The text of the selections given here follows that of the fourth edition of Hopkins's poems (1970), edited by W. H. Gardner and N. H. MacKenzie, which is now the standard text.

God's Grandeur

The world is charged with the grandeur of God.
  It will flame out, like shining from shook foil;[1]
  It gathers to a greatness, like the ooze of oil
Crushed.[2] Why do men then now not reck his rod?
Generations have trod, have trod, have trod;   5
  And all is seared with trade; bleared, smeared with toil;
  And wears man's smudge and shares man's smell: the soil
Is bare now, nor can foot feel, being shod.

And for all this, nature is never spent;
  There lives the dearest freshness deep down things;   10
And though the last lights off the black West went
  Oh, morning, at the brown brink eastward, springs—
Because the Holy Ghost over the bent
  World broods with warm breast and with ah! bright wings.
1877   1918

The Starlight Night

Look at the stars! look, look up at the skies!
  O look at all the fire-folk sitting in the air!
  The bright boroughs, the circle-citadels there!
Down in dim woods the diamond delves! the elves'-eyes!
The grey lawns cold were gold,[3] where quickgold lies!   5
  Wind-beat whitebeam! airy abeles[4] set on a flare!
  Flake-doves sent floating forth at a farmyard scare!—
Ah well! it is all a purchase, all is a prize.

Buy then! bid then!—What?—Prayer, patience, alms, vows.
  Look, look: a May-mess,[5] like on orchard boughs!   10
    Look! March-bloom, like on mealed-with-yellow[6] sallows!

1. "I mean foil in the sense of leaf or tinsel * * * Shaken goldfoil gives off broad glares like sheet lightning and also, and this is true of nothing else, owing to its zigzag dints and creasings and network of small many cornered facets, a sort of fork lightning too" (Hopkins, *Letters*).
2. From olives.
3. Dewdrops, referred to also as "quickgold" (a word coined by analogy with "quicksilver" and thus suggesting the gleaming and volatile nature of dewdrops).
4. White poplars.
5. A profusion of May—i.e., suggesting a mass of May blossoms, such as pear blossoms ("like on orchard boughs"). "May" is also another name for the white hawthorn. There may be religious overtones, with "May" suggesting "Mary" (the Virgin) and "mess" suggesting "Mass" (the Catholic rite).
6. Yellow-spotted. "Sallows" are a variety of willow tree.

These are indeed the barn; withindoors house
The shocks.[7] This piece-bright paling[8] shuts the spouse
  Christ home, Christ and his mother and all his hallows.[9]
1877   1918

Spring

Nothing is so beautiful as Spring—
  When weeds, in wheels, shoot long and lovely and lush;
  Thrush's eggs look little low heavens, and thrush
Through the echoing timber does so rinse and wring
The ear, it strikes like lightnings to hear him sing;   5
  The glassy peartree leaves and blooms, they brush
  The descending blue; that blue is all in a rush
With richness; the racing lambs too have fair their fling.

What is all this juice and all this joy?
  A strain of the earth's sweet being in the beginning   10
In Eden garden.—Have, get, before it cloy,

  Before it cloud, Christ, lord, and sour with sinning,
Innocent mind and Mayday in girl and boy,
  Most, O maid's[1] child, thy choice and worthy the winning.
1877   1918

The Windhover[2]

TO CHRIST OUR LORD

I caught this morning morning's minion,[3] kingdom of daylight's dauphin,[4] dapple-dawn-drawn Falcon, in his
    riding

7. Sheaves of corn; see discussion of this poem in the Hopkins introduction.
8. Fencing. It is "piece-bright," i.e., bright as a gold or silver coin. "Piece" is this sense suggests the thirty pieces of silver for which Judas betrayed Christ, but line 9 implies that we can buy both Christ and the beauty of nature with a very different kind of coin.
9. Saints.
1. The Virgin Mary's. May is a popular form of the word "Mary," so "Mayday" in line 13 also suggests "Mary's day," day of innocence and purity. Cf. note 5 to *The Starlight Night.*
2. Kestrel, called "windhover" because it hovers in the air, head to wind. This poem has been variously explicated. The main thought seems to be that the ecstatic flying of the bird stirs the poet's heart ("in hiding," for the poet is a priest, with his heart hidden away from earthly things in the service of God). In the combination of beauty, strength, and glory which the poet sees in the bird, he sees an emblem of the beauty, strength, and glory of Christ, whom he addresses as "my chevalier" (line 11). It is "dangerous" to see these qualities in Christ, for we look to Christ for lessons in humility and the enduring of suffering. But it is "no wonder" (lines 12-14) that Christ's humility and suffering are bound up with His glory and pride; many things include their opposites: "sheer plod" can make the plowshare shine as it cuts its furrow, and a black coal in a fire can fall over and break and reveal its red-hot interior, its "gold-vermilion" gashes suggesting both beauty and pride and Christ's wounds and suffering.
3. Darling.
4. Heir (literally, the title of the eldest son of the king of France); the word carries overtones of chivalry and splendor.

Of the rolling level underneath him steady air, and striding
High there, how he rung upon the rein[5] of a wimpling wing
In his ecstasy! then off, off forth on swing,   5
    As a skate's heel sweeps smooth on a bow-bend: the hurl and
      gliding
    Rebuffed the big wind. My heart in hiding
Stirred for a bird,—the achieve of, the mastery of the thing!

Brute beauty and valour and act, oh, air, pride, plume, here
    Buckle![6] AND[7] the fire that breaks from thee then, a billion   10
Times told lovelier, more dangerous, O my chevalier!

No wonder of it: shéer plód makes plough down sillion[8]
Shine, and blue-bleak embers, ah my dear,
    Fall, gall themselves, and gash gold-vermilion.
1877   1918

Pied Beauty

Glory be to God for dappled things—
    For skies of couple-colour as a brinded[9] cow;
      For rose-moles all in stipple[1] upon trout that swim;
Fresh-firecoal chestnut-falls;[2] finches' wings;
    Landscape plotted and pieced[3]—fold, fallow, and plough;   5
    And áll trádes, their gear and tackle and trim.[4]

All things counter,[5] original, spare, strange;
    Whatever is fickle, freckled (who knows how?)
      With swift, slow; sweet, sour; adazzle, dim;
He fathers-forth whose beauty is past change: 10
              Praise him.
1877   1918

Hurrahing in Harvest

Summer ends now; now, barbarous in beauty, the stooks[6] rise
Around; up above, what wind-walks! what lovely behaviour

5. There is an implied comparison to a horse circling around its trainer at the end of a long rein. "Wimpling": rippling.

6. The obvious sense here is "join," though some critics have understood it as "bend" or "break" and some have taken it as an imperative in that sense. But see note 2. Hopkins is celebrating the point at which animal beauty, strength, bearing, and fine display all join.

7. Hopkins emphasizes the "AND" to draw attention from the admiration of the bird to the sense of Christ behind it which that admiration brings.

8. The ridge between two furrows of a plowed field. Hopkins uses this archaic word perhaps to suggest an overtone from "silica" (the mineral which in the form of gleaming particles of quartz often makes dull rocks shine).

9. Brindled, streaked.

1. Dots or small spots.

2. Chestnuts stripped of their husks after being roasted in "fresh-firecoal."

3. Divided into rectangles of different colors, as the English landscape appears. "Fold": enclosure for animals; "fallow": a field plowed but left unsown for a season.

4. Equipment.

5. Contrary, i.e., in contrasted patterns or colors. "Spare": rare.

6. Sheaves of corn placed upright, supporting each other at an angle, for drying.

Of silk-sack clouds! has wilder, wilful-wavier
Meal-drift moulded ever and melted across skies?

I walk, I lift up, I lift up heart, eyes,   5
Down all that glory in the heavens to glean our Saviour;
And, éyes, heárt, what looks, what lips yet gave you a
Rapturous love's greeting of realer, of rounder replies?

And the azurous hung hills are his world-wielding shoulder
Majestic—as a stallion stalwart, very-violet-sweet!—   10
These things, these things were here and but the beholder
Wanting; which two when they once meet,
The heart rears wings bold and bolder
And hurls for him, O half hurls earth for him off under his feet.
1877   1918

The Lantern out of Doors

Sometimes a lantern moves along the night.
    That interests our eyes. And who goes there?
    I think; where from and bound, I wonder, where,
With, all down darkness wide, his wading light?

Men go by me whom either beauty bright   5
    In mould or mind or what not else makes rare:
    They rain against our much-thick and marsh air
Rich beams, till death or distance buys them quite.

Death or distance soon consumes them: wind
    What most I may eye after,[7] be in at the end   10
I cannot, and out of sight is out of mind.

Christ minds: Christ's interest, what to avow or amend
    There, éyes them, heart wánts, care haúnts, foot fóllows
        kínd,
Their ránsom, théir rescue, ánd first, fást, last friénd.[8]
1877   1918

Binsey Poplars

FELLED 1879

My aspens dear, whose airy cages quelled,
    Quelled or quenched in leaves the leaping sun,
        All felled, felled, are all felled;

7. "I mean that the eye winds only in the sense that its focus or point of sight winds and that coincides with a point of the object and winds with that. For the object, a lantern passing further and further away and bearing now east now west of one right line, is truly and properly described as winding" (Hopkins, *Letters*).
8. For a discussion of the language in this poem, see the Hopkins introduction.

Of a fresh and following folded rank[9]
     Not spared, not one   5
       That dandled a sandalled
     Shadow that swam or sank
On meadow and river and wind-wandering weed-winding bank.

O if we but knew what we do
     When we delve[1] or hew—   10
Hack and rack[2] the growing green!
     Since country is so tender
To touch, her being só slender,
That, like this sleek and seeing ball[3]
But a prick will make no eye at all,   15
Where we, even where we mean
     To mend her we end her,
     When we hew or delve:
After-comers cannot guess the beauty been.
Ten or twelve, only ten or twelve   20
     Strokes of havoc únselve[4]
       The sweet especial scene,
     Rural scene, a rural scene,
     Sweet especial rural scene.

1879   1918

Duns Scotus's Oxford[5]

Towery city and branchy between towers;
Cuckoo-echoing, bell-swarmèd, lark-charmèd, rook-racked, river-
    rounded;
The dapple-eared lily below thee; that country and town did
Once encounter in, here coped[6] and poisèd powers;

Thou hast a base and brickish skirt[7] there, sours   5
That neighbour-nature thy grey beauty is grounded
Best in; graceless growth, thou hast confounded
Rural rural keeping[8]—folk, flocks, and flowers.

---

9. Row of trees with alternate trees set off at an angle, making the row "folded."
1. Dig.
2. Torture.
3. The eye.
4. Rob it of its "self" or individuality.
5. Duns Scotus, the 13th-century Scholastic philosopher, is supposed to have taught at Oxford ca. 1301. Hopkins admired him greatly; when he came upon two of Scotus's commentaries in 1872 he was "flush with a new stroke of enthusiasm. * * * When I took in any inscape of the sky or sea I thought of Scotus" (*Note-books*). In this poem he builds up an impression of medieval Oxford, then links this to Scotus through himself ("this air I gather and I release / He lived on") to end with a tribute to him.
6. Set off one against the other.
7. Refers to the appearance of 19th-century brick houses in north Oxford. Note the characteristic omission of the relative pronoun before "sours."
8. I.e., you have spoiled the effect of a rural city presiding over its rural environment.

Yet ah! this air I gather and I release
He lived on; these weeds and waters, these walls are what   10
He haunted who of all men most sways my spirits to peace;

Of realty[9] the rarest-veinèd unraveller; a not
Rivalled insight, be rival Italy or Greece;
Who fired France for Mary without spot.[1]
1879   1918

Felix Randal

Felix Randal the farrier,[2] O is he dead then? my duty all ended,
Who have watched his mould of man, big-boned and hardy-
    handsome
Pining, pining, till time when reason rambled in it and some
Fatal four disorders, fleshed there, all contended?

Sickness broke him. Impatient, he cursed at first, but mended   5
Being anointed and all; though a heavenlier heart began some
Months earlier, since I had our sweet reprieve and ransom
Tendered to him.[3] Ah well, God rest him all road ever[4] he
    offended!

This seeing the sick endears them to us, us too it endears.
My tongue had taught thee comfort, touch had quenched thy
    tears,   10
Thy tears that touched my heart, child, Felix, poor Felix Randal;

How far from then forethought of, all thy more boisterous years,
When thou at the random[5] grim forge, powerful amidst peers,
Didst fettle[6] for the great grey drayhorse his bright and battering
    sandal!
1880   1918

Spring and Fall

TO A YOUNG CHILD

Márgarét, áre you gríeving
Over Goldengrove unleaving?
Leáves, líke the things of man, you
With your fresh thoughts care for, can you?
Áh! ás the heart grows older   5
It will come to such sights colder
By and by, nor spare a sigh

9. Reality.
1. A reference to Scotus's work in
spreading the cult of the Virgin Mary
in France.
2. Blacksmith.
3. Had heard his confession and given

him absolution.
4. In whatever way.
5. Built with stones of irregular shapes
and sizes.
6. Prepare.

Though worlds of wanwood leafmeal[7] lie;
And yet you *will* weep and know why.
Now no matter, child, the name: 10
Sórrow's springs áre the same.
Nor mouth had, no nor mind, expressed
What heart heard of, ghost guessed:[8]
It ís the blight man was born for,
It is Margaret you mourn for.   15
1880   1918

Inversnaid[9]

This darksome burn,[1] horseback brown,
His rollrock highroad roaring down,
In coop and in comb[2] the fleece of his foam
Flutes and low to the lake falls home.

A windpuff-bonnet of fáwn-fróth   5
Turns and twindles[3] over the broth
Of a pool so pitchblack, féll-frówning,
It rounds and rounds Despair to drowning.

Degged[4] with dew, dappled with dew
Are the groins of the braes[5] that the brook treads through, 10
Wiry heathpacks, flitches[6] of fern,
And the beadbonny ash that sits over the burn.

What would the world be, once bereft
Of wet and of wildness? Let them be left,
O let them be left, wildness and wet;   15
Long live the weeds and the wilderness yet.
1881   1918

[Carrion Comfort][7]

Not, I'll not, carrion comfort, Despair, not feast on thee;
Not untwist—slack they may be—these last strands of man

---

7. "I take *wanwood* to be a noun (the meaning 'bloodless' being combined with the older meaning 'dark,' 'livid'—O.E. *wann*). *Leafmeal* I take for an adverb, made 'by substitution' from *piecemeal* on the analogy of Shakespeare's *inch-meal* and *limb-meal*: hence it suggests the leaves falling one by one, then rotting to form pale, mealy fragments" [W. H. Gardner's note].
8. "*Ghost*, spirit (of the living), with a proleptic suggestion of 'phantom'— the living spirit foreknowing, through sensory experience, its own state after death. Lines 8 and 14 connect the Fall of the Leaf with the Fall of Man: 'and unto dust shalt thou return' (Genesis iii.18)" [W. H. Gardner's note].
9. On Loch Lomondside, Scotland, famous for its rushing stream and waterfall.
1. Stream.
2. "Coop": hollow; "comb": crest.
3. Apparently Hopkins's coinage: twists and dwindles.
4. Sprinkled.
5. Hills.
6. Tufts, clumps.
7. Title supplied by Bridges in the 1918 edition. This is one of the "terrible sonnets," as are the two poems that follow.

In me ór, most weary, cry *I can no more*. I can;
Can something, hope, wish day come, not choose not to be.

But ah, but O thou terrible, why wouldst thou rude on me   5
Thy wring-world right foot rock?[8] lay a lionlimb against me?
    scan
With darksome devouring eyes my bruisèd bones? and fan,
O in turns of tempest, me heaped there; me frantic to avoid thee
    and flee?

Why? That my chaff might fly; my grain lie, sheer and clear.
Nay in all that toil, that coil,[9] since (seems) I kissed the rod,   10
Hand rather, my heart lo! lapped strength, stole joy, would
    laugh, chéer.
Cheer whom though? The hero whose heaven-handling flung
    me, fóot tród
Me? or me that fought him? O which one? is it each one? That
    night, that year
Of now done darkness I wretch lay wrestling with (my God!)
    my God.
1885   1918

[No Worst, There Is None][1]

No worst, there is none. Pitched past pitch of grief,
More pangs will, schooled at forepangs, wilder wring.
Comforter, where, where is your comforting?
Mary, mother of us, where is your relief?
My cries heave, herds-long;[2] huddle in a main, a chief-   5
woe, world-sorrow; on an age-old anvil wince and sing—
Then lull, then leave off. Fury had shrieked 'No ling-
ering! Let me be fell:[3] force I must be brief'.
O the mind, mind has mountains; cliffs of fall
Frightful, sheer, no-man-fathomed. Hold them cheap   10
May who ne'er hung there. Nor does long our small
Durance[4] deal with that steep or deep. Here! creep,
Wretch, under a comfort serves in a whirlwind: all
Life death does end and each day dies with sleep.
1885   1918

---

8. I.e., why wouldst thou turn roughly against me thy right foot that wrings the world?
9. Disturbance.
1. Untitled by Hopkins. Cf. the description of "desolation" in the *Spiritual Exercises* of St. Ignatius Loyola, founder of the Jesuit order: "a darkening of the soul, trouble of mind, movement to base and earthly things, restlessness of various agitations and temptations, moving to distrust, loss of hope, loss of love; when the soul feels herself thoroughly apathetic, sad, and as it were separated from her Creator and Lord."
2. Coming in large numbers and in a long series, like herds of cattle following each other. "Main" (like "chief") is an adjective, qualifying "woe."
3. Fierce. "Force" means here "perforce."
4. Endurance.

[Thou Art Indeed Just, Lord]

Justus quidem tu es, Domine, si disputem tecum; verumtamen
justa loquar ad te: Quare via impiorum prosperatur? &c.[5]

Thou art indeed just, Lord, if I contend
With thee; but, sir, so what I plead is just.
Why do sinners' ways prosper? and why must
Disappointment all I endeavour end?

Wert thou my enemy, O thou my friend,   5
How wouldst thou worse, I wonder, than thou dost
Defeat, thwart me? Oh, the sots and thralls of lust
Do in spare hours more thrive than I that spend,

Sir, life upon thy cause. See, banks and brakes[6]
Now, leavèd how thick! lacèd they are again   10
With fretty[7] chervil, look, and fresh wind shakes

Them; birds build—but not I build; no, but strain,
Time's eunuch, and not breed one work that wakes.
Mine,[8] O thou lord of life, send my roots rain.
1889   1918

5. The Latin is the Vulgate version of
Jeremiah xii.1, which reads in the King
James version: "Righteous are thou, O
Lord, when I plead with thee: yet let
me talk with thee of thy judgments:
Wherefore doth the way of the wicked
prosper? * * * " This Latin quotation
was Hopkins' title.
6. Clumps of fern.

7. Fretted, with interlacing pattern.
"Chervil" is a member of the parsley
family.
8. "Mine" may refer to "roots,"
emphasizing that the poet wants God to
send "*my* roots rain" since every other
creature is flourishing, or it may mean
"my God."

BERNARD SHAW
(1856–1950)

1876: Settles in London.
1892: *Widowers' Houses* produced.
1898: Publication of *Plays Pleasant and Unpleasant.*
1923: *Saint Joan.*

Bernard Shaw was born in Dublin of English stock, one of the galaxy of
Anglo-Irishmen (they include Swift, Sheridan, Edmund Burke, and Yeats)
who have contributed so brilliantly to English literature. He left school at
the age of 14 and worked for five years (1871–76) in a land agent's office.
He went to London in 1876, his mother having settled there in order to
improve her prospects as a music teacher, and began his literary career as
a writer of unsuccessful novels. He soon became interested in social reform:

in 1884 he was one of the founders of the Fabian Society, an organization dedicated to the promotion of socialism by gradual stages. Although he was friendly with the most important socialist thinkers in England in the late 19th century, including Sidney and Beatrice Webb and William Morris, Shaw was never a conventional socialist. His social and political attitude was affected by his belief in an active and individually *willed* kind of evolution, urged on by what he called the Life Force, and by his admiration of vitality and power. He inherited from his gifted mother a love of music and learned from her to know and admire Mozartian opera; he also became a great champion of Richard Wagner, and in his regular music criticism, first for the London *Star* and then for the *World*, not only displayed his enthusiasms with lively wit but also introduced a new standard in judging both performers and composers, often mocking conventional taste and fashionable preferences. In 1895 he became dramatic critic for the *Saturday Review* (a London periodical): his deliberately provocative reviews stirred up contemporary English ideas about plays and acting and enlarged the intellectual horizons of his readers. He championed Henrik Ibsen as well as Wagner, and published in 1891 a study of Ibsen entitled *The Quintessence of Ibsenism* which presented the Norwegian dramatist as a realistic and reforming playwright who addressed himself to the problems of modern life and introduced genuine *discussion* in his dialogue. The more profound and symbolic Ibsen whom we admire today was not Shaw's Ibsen, and it is significant that for him the great plays were those which attacked middle-class conventionality and hypocrisy rather than those which probed more subtly and poetically into deeper aspects of experience.

His training in music and dramatic criticism, his interest in social reform, his admiration for Wagner and Ibsen, the influence of Samuel Butler (author of *Erewhon* and *The Way of All Flesh* and the great satirist of Victorian life and thought) helped to make Shaw a playwright who on the one hand knew all the conventional tricks of the theater and on the other was determined to use the drama as he conceived Ibsen to have used it—as a means of shaking theater audiences out of their complacencies, hypocrisies, and thoughtless acquiescence in all kinds of social evil.

Reviewing new plays over a period of years had given Shaw an expert knowledge of the structural devices employed by the authors of the "well-made play" (adroitly plotted theatrical entertainment) of the late 19th century; and when he came to write his own plays he was able to use conventional dramatic structure and even conventional themes for highly unconventional purposes. From the beginning his aim as a dramatist was to shock his audiences into taking a new view of their society and the moral problems that arose out of it. "I must warn my readers," he wrote, "that my attacks are directed against themselves, not against my stage figures." Not only did he delight in standing the popular view on its head, but he went further: beginning by persuading his audience by means of dramatic action and dialogue that the conventional hero was the villain and the conventional villain was the hero, he would swing everything around again to show that the conventional hero was the hero after all, but in a very different sense from that which the audience had originally thought. He followed this pattern in *Man and Superman*, *Major Barbara*, and *Arms and the Man*. He used paradox, both in the action and even more in the dialogue, to dazzle and even bewilder his audiences—only to demonstate that their absurd conventional views and unconscious hypocrisies were responsible for their bewilderment. Having thus destroyed the audience's self-confidence he would organize the dialogue (or sometimes a monologue) in order to allow one of his splendidly vital (but never conventionally heroic) heroes to put across the Shavian vision of society or politics or religion or whatever was the main theme of the play. And all the time he entertained and fascinated by his wit as well as by his sheer sense of fun. Sometimes this sense of fun led him to conclude a serious critical comedy in sheer farce—as in *You Never Can Tell* (1900)—but on the whole Shaw combined entertainment and intellectual provocation to bring a new kind of critical wit into English drama. The wit of Oscar Wilde's comedies had no specific critical implications; it drew on the conventions of society not in order to expose them but in order to get the maximum number of epigrams out of their delightful inconsistencies and absurdities. Shaw's wit was put at the service of a genuine passion for reform, and even if he sometimes assumed the posture of a licensed clown—a posture which members of the public were all too ready to accept as his natural one, for it enabled them to laugh off the disturbing paradoxes he thrust at them—he remained to the end a crusader as well as an entertainer.

Shaw's first play, *Widowers' Houses* (produced in 1892), dealt in a characteristically provocative manner with the problem of slum landlordism: even here, with a subject easily compartmentalized into moral blacks and whites, Shaw's techniques of reversal and inversion keep revealing new aspects of the problem, so that, instead of merely condemning the landlord, the audience is forced to comprehend the entire complex of social and economic conditions that produced the problem. *Mrs. Warren's Profession*, written in 1893, was for a long time banned from the public theater because of its concern with the tabooed subject of prostitution; it is not, however, simply about prostitution, but about well-meaning brothel-keepers and the laws of supply and demand, which it explores with boldness and wit, again substituting the revelation of causes and consequences for simple moral indignation. In 1898 Shaw published *Plays Pleasant and Unpleasant*, with long provocative prefaces attacking a great variety of things, including theatrical censorship; the plays included *Arms and the Man, Candida, The Man of Destiny*, and (among the "unpleasant") *Widowers' Houses* and *Mrs. Warren's Profession*. Among his later plays, *John Bull's Other Island* (1904) is a characteristic contribution to the discussion of Ireland's grievances against the English; *Man and Superman* (1904) is an ambitious attempt to project through comedy his views of how the Life Force works in ordinary life and contains some brilliant scenes, though the play as a whole is rather too long and too talkative; *The Doctor's Dilemma* (1906) exposes both doctors and artists while exploring some of the moral problems in which they can become involved; *Major Barbara* (1907) shows Shaw's characteristic admiration of success and energy and his contempt for those evangelists who attempt to promote religion by giving soup to the poor instead of trying to convert the strong and successful; *Pygmalion* (1912) is a brilliant exploration of the relation between social class and accent in England, which has since been made into the extraordinarily popular musical comedy, *My Fair Lady*. *Heartbreak House* (1917), subtitled "a fantasia in the Russian manner on English themes," suggests the Russian dramatist Chekhov in its depiction of the imminent collapse of a civilization, but it is essentially Shavian, and the finest example of what Eric Bentley has called the "disquisitory" Shavian play, based on the inter-play of ideas in dialogue. *The Apple Cart* (1929) is a paradoxical treat-ment of the problems of monarchy and democracy done with a mischievous desire to shock equally both Left- and Right-wing thinkers and again shows that admiration of the strong man which is Shaw's personal heresy and goes oddly with his socialism.

Back to Methuselah (1921) was Shaw's most ambitious work, and the one which he considered his masterpiece. But it is in fact the dullest of his plays. Shaw's picture of the Life Force eventually enabling men to im-prove the human species to the point where they can live long enough to become little more than disembodied intellects reveals a curious coldness and abstraction at the heart of his thought. *Saint Joan* (1923), his one tragedy and often regarded as his finest play, is brilliant in its way, but it is really a comedy containing one tragic scene rather than a tragedy. Shaw had no historical imagination. He makes the past interesting by analogizing it to the present and gets his comic effects by interpreting his-torical characters as though they were the kind of characters who would be doing the same sort of thing today. The result is often very amusing, but it yields no real insight. Saint Joan as a girl with inspired common sense is a refreshing, funny, and, up to a point, a persuasive portrait—but this portrait is not compatible with the image of Joan as religious martyr, which Shaw does not know how to paint. Similarly, in that most entertain-ing play *Caesar and Cleopatra* (which is, incidentally, most brilliant the-atrically) Shaw's wit takes the form of interpreting the main characters as though they lived in the 19th century. Caesar becomes a 19th-century liberal and his secretary Britannicus is a Victorian Philistine: this gives a kind of reality to the past, but at the cost of losing a dimension.

Shaw wrote *Mrs. Warren's Profession* in 1893, but though it was pub-lished five years later, public performance on the stage was for long prohib-ited by the Lord Chamberlain, empowered by Act of Parliament to censor stage performances in Britain (the Lord Chamberlain no longer possesses this function). In 1902, the Stage Society, technically a private club and so not under the jurisdiction of the Lord Chamberlain, gave performances for its own members. The play was produced in New York in 1905, but it was at once closed down by the police, and the producer and his company were arrested; they were however eventually acquitted and the play was allowed to continue. Legal public performance in Britain had to wait until 1926.

Shaw's Preface to the play attacks the confusions and contradictions involved in the censorship of plays and contains an eloquent plea for the recognition of the seriousness and morality of *Mrs. Warren's Profession*. The play was written, he tells us, "to draw attention to the truth that pros-titution is caused, not by female depravity and male licentiousness, but simply by underpaying, undervaluing, and overworking women so shame-fully that the poorest of them are forced to resort to prostitution to keep body and soul together." He argues that Mrs. Warren's defense of herself in the play is "valid and unanswerable." "But it is no defence at all of the vice which she organizes. It is no defence of an immoral life to say that the alternative offered by society collectively to poor women is a miserable life, starved, overworked, fetid, ailing, ugly. Though it is quite natural and *right* for Mrs. Warren to choose what is, according to her lights, the least immoral alternative, it is none the less infamous of society to offer such alternatives. For the alternatives offered are not morality and immorality, but two sorts of immorality. The man who cannot see that starvation, overwork, dirt, and disease are as anti-social as prostitution—that they are the vices and crimes of a nation, and not merely its misfortunes—is (to put it as politely as possible) a hopelessly Private Person." (This is Shaw's way of saying that such a man is a hopeless idiot: the word "idiot" comes from the Greek *idiotes*, a private person, as distinct from one interested in public affairs.) Another theme of the play is the emergence of the "new woman," independent and sure of herself, represented by Vivie.

Shaw was an ardent believer in spelling reform, and, while awaiting a reformed alphabet and phonetic spelling, introduced some minor simplifications in his own spelling which he insisted on his publishers retaining. These simplifications (omission of the apostrophe in a number of contractions, and the use of widely spaced letters rather than italics to indicate emphasis, for example) are retained in the text here printed.

Mrs. Warren's Profession

Act I

Summer afternoon in a cottage garden on the eastern slope of a hill a little south of Haslemere in Surrey. Looking up the hill, the cottage is seen in the left hand corner of the garden, with its thatched roof and porch, and a large latticed window to the left of the porch. A paling completely shuts in the garden, except for a gate on the right. The common rises uphill beyond the paling to the sky line. Some folded canvas garden chairs are leaning against the side bench in the porch. A lady's bicycle is propped against the wall, under the window. A little to the right of the porch a hammock is slung from two posts. A big canvas umbrella, stuck in the ground, keeps the sun off the hammock, in which a young lady lies reading and making notes, her head towards the cottage and her feet towards the gate. In front of the hammock, and within reach of her hand, is a common kitchen chair, with a pile of serious-looking books and a supply of writing paper on it.

A gentleman walking on the common comes into sight from behind the cottage. He is hardly past middle age, with something of the artist about him, unconventionally but carefully dressed, and clean-shaven except for a moustache, with an eager susceptible face and very amiable and considerate manners. He has silky black hair, with waves of grey and white in it. His eyebrows are white, his moustache black. He seems not certain of his way. He looks over the paling; takes stock of the place; and sees the young lady.

THE GENTLEMAN. [*taking off his hat*] I beg your pardon. Can you
direct me to Hindhead View—Mrs Alison's?

THE YOUNG LADY. [*glancing up from her book*] This is Mrs Alison's. [*She resumes her work*]

THE GENTLEMAN. Indeed! Perhaps—may I ask are you Miss Vivie
Warren?

THE YOUNG LADY. [*sharply, as she turns on her elbow to get a
good look at him*] Yes.

THE GENTLEMAN. [*daunted and conciliatory*] I'm afraid I appear
intrusive. My name is Praed. [*Vivie at once throws her books
upon the chair, and gets out of the hammock*] Oh, pray dont let
me disturb you.

VIVIE. [*striding to the gate and opening it for him*] Come in, Mr
Praed. [*He comes in*] Glad to see you. [*She proffers her hand
and takes his with a resolute and hearty grip. She is an attractive
specimen of the sensible, able, highly-educated young middle-
class Englishwoman. Age 22. Prompt, strong, confident, self-possessed. Plain business-like dress, but not dowdy. She wears a
chatelaine*[1] *at her belt, with a fountain pen and a paper knife
among its pendants*]

PRAED. Very kind of you indeed, Miss Warren. [*She shuts the gate
with a vigorous slam. He passes in to the middle of the garden,
exercising his fingers, which are slightly numbed by her greeting*]
Has your mother arrived?

VIVIE. [*quickly, evidently scenting aggression*] Is she coming?

PRAED. [*surprised*] Didnt you expect us?

VIVIE. No.

PRAED. Now, goodness me, I hope Ive not mistaken the day. That
would be just like me, you know. Your mother arranged that she
was to come down from London and that I was to come over
from Horsham to be introduced to you.

VIVIE. [*not at all pleased*] Did she? Hm! My mother has rather
a trick of taking me by surprise—to see how I behave myself
when she's away, I suppose. I fancy I shall take my mother very
much by surprise one of these days, if she makes arrangements
that concern me without consulting me beforehand. She hasnt
come.

PRAED. [*embarrassed*] I'm really very sorry.

VIVIE. [*throwing off her displeasure*] It's not your fault, Mr Praed,
is it? And I'm very glad youve come. You are the only one of my
mother's friends I have ever asked her to bring to see me.

PRAED. [*relieved and delighted*] Oh, now this is really very good
of you, Miss Warren!

VIVIE. Will you come indoors; or would you rather sit out here and
talk?

PRAED. It will be nicer out here, dont you think?

VIVIE. Then I'll go and get you a chair. [*She goes to the porch for
a garden chair*]

PRAED. [*following her*] Oh, pray, pray! Allow me. [*He lays hands
on the chair*]

1. Clasp or hook.

VIVIE. [*letting him take it*] Take care of your fingers: theyre rather dodgy things, those chairs. [*She goes across to the chair with the books on it; pitches them into the hammock; and brings the chair forward with one swing*]

PRAED. `[*who has just unfolded his chair*] Oh, now d o let me take that hard chair. I like hard chairs.

VIVIE. So do I. Sit down, Mr Praed. [*This invitation she gives with genial peremptoriness, his anxiety to please her clearly striking her as a sign of weakness of character on his part. But he does not immediately obey*]

PRAED. By the way, though, hadnt we better go to the station to meet your mother?

VIVIE. [*coolly*] Why? She knows the way.

PRAED. [*disconcerted*] Er—I suppose she does. [*he sits down*]

VIVIE. Do you know, you are just like what I expected. I hope you are disposed to be friends with me.

PRAED. [*again beaming*] Thank you, my d e a r Miss Warren: thank you. Dear me! I'm glad your mother hasnt spoilt you!

VIVIE. How?

PRAED. Well, in making you too conventional. You know, my dear Miss Warren, I am a born anarchist. I hate authority. It spoils the relations between parent and child: even between mother and daughter. Now I was always afraid that your mother would strain her authority to make you very conventional. It's such a relief to find that she hasnt.

VIVIE. Oh! have I been behaving unconventionally?

PRAED. Oh no; oh dear no. At least not conventionally unconventionally, you understand. [*She nods and sits down. He goes on, with a cordial outburst*] But it was so charming of you to say that you were disposed to be friends with me! You modern young ladies are splendid: perfectly splendid!

VIVIE. [*dubiously*] Eh? [*watching him with dawning disappointment as to the quality of his brains and character*]

PRAED. When I was your age, young men and women were afraid of each other: there was no good fellowship. Nothing real. Only gallantry copied out of novels, and as vulgar and affected as it could be. Maidenly reserve! gentlemanly chivalry! always saying no when you meant yes! simple purgatory for shy and sincere souls.

VIVIE. Yes, I imagine there must have been a frightful waste of time. Especially women's time.

PRAED. Oh, waste of life, waste of everything. But things are improving. Do you know, I have been in a positive state of excitement about meeting you ever since your magnificent achievements at Cambridge: a thing unheard of in my day. It was perfectly splendid, you tieing with the third wrangler.[2] Just the right place, you know. The first wrangler is always a dreamy, morbid fellow, in whom the thing is pushed to the length of a disease.

2. A unique Cambridge term denoting distinction in a degree in mathematics. The person who achieved the top mark was the senior wrangler; then came the junior wrangler, and then the third wrangler.

VIVIE. It doesnt pay. I wouldnt do it again for the same money.

PRAED. [*aghast*] The same money!

VIVIE. I did it for £50.

PRAED. Fifty pounds!

VIVIE. Yes. Fifty pounds. Perhaps you dont know how it was. Mrs
Latham, my tutor at Newnham,[3] told my mother that I could
distinguish myself in the mathematical tripos if I went in for it
in earnest. The papers were full just then of Phillipa Summers
beating the senior wrangler. You remember about it, of course.

PRAED. [*shakes his head energetically*]!!!

VIVIE. Well anyhow she did; and nothing would please my mother
but that I should do the same thing. I said flatly it was not worth
my while to face the grind since I was not going in for teaching;
but I offered to try for fourth wrangler or thereabouts for £50.
She closed with me at that, after a little grumbling; and I was
better than my bargain. But I wouldnt do it again for that.
£200 would have been nearer the mark.

PRAED. [*much damped*] Lord bless me! Thats a very practical way
of looking at it.

VIVIE. Did you expect to find me an unpractical person?

PRAED. But surely it's practical to consider not only the work these
honors cost, but also the culture they bring.

VIVIE. Culture! My dear Mr Praed: do you know what the mathematical tripos means? It means grind, grind, grind for six to eight
hours a day at mathematics, and nothing but mathematics. I'm
supposed to know something about science; but I know nothing
except the mathematics it involves. I can make calculations for
engineers, electricians, insurance companies, and so on; but I
know next to nothing about engineering or electricity or insurance. I dont even know arithmetic well. Outside mathematics,
lawn-tennis, eating, sleeping, cycling, and walking, I'm a more
ignorant barbarian than any woman could possibly be who hadnt
gone in for the tripos.

PRAED. [*revolted*] What a monstrous, wicked, rascally system! I
knew it! I felt at once that it meant destroying all that makes
womanhood beautiful.

VIVIE. I dont object to it on that score in the least. I shall turn it
to very good account, I assure you.

PRAED. Pooh! In what way?

VIVIE. I shall set up in chambers in the City, and work at actuarial
calculations and conveyancing. Under cover of that I shall do
some law, with one eye on the Stock Exchange all the time. Ive
come down here by myself to read law: not for a holiday, as my
mother imagines. I hate holidays.

PRAED. You make my blood run cold. Are you to have no romance,
no beauty in your life?

VIVIE. I dont care for either, I assure you.

PRAED. You cant mean that.

---

3. Women's college at Cambridge University.

VIVIE. Oh yes I do. I like working and getting paid for it. When I'm tired of working, I like a comfortable chair, a cigar, a little whisky, and a novel with a good detective story in it.

PRAED. [*rising in a frenzy of repudiation*] I dont believe it. I am an artist; and I cant believe it: I refuse to believe it. It's only that you havnt discovered yet what a wonderful world art can open up to you.

VIVIE. Yes I have. Last May I spent six weeks in London with Honoria Fraser. Mamma thought we were doing a round of sightseeing together; but I was really at Honoria's chambers in Chancery Lane[4] every day, working away at actuarial calculations for her, and helping her as well as a greenhorn could. In the evenings we smoked and talked, and never dreamt of going out except for exercise. And I never enjoyed myself more in my life. I cleared all my expenses, and got intitiated into the business without a fee into the bargain.

PRAED. But bless my heart and soul, Miss Warren, do you call that discovering art?

VIVIE. Wait a bit. That wasnt the beginning. I went up to town on an invitation from some artistic people in Fitzjohn's Avenue: one of the girls was a Newnham chum. They took me to the National Gallery—

PRAED. [*approving*] Ah!! [*He sits down, much relieved*]

VIVIE. [*continuing*]—to the Opera—

PRAED. [*still more pleased*] Good!

VIVIE. —and to a concert where the band played all the evening: Beethoven and Wagner and so on. I wouldn't go through that experience again for anything you could offer me. I held out for civility's sake until the third day; and then I said, plump out, that I couldnt stand any more of it, and went off to Chancery Lane. N o w you know the sort of perfectly splendid modern young lady I am. How do you think I shall get on with my mother?

PRAED. [*startled*] Well, I hope—er—

VIVIE. It's not so much what you hope as what you believe, that I want to know.

PRAED. Well, frankly, I am afraid your mother will be a little disappointed. Not from any shortcoming on your part, you know: I dont mean that. But you are so different from her ideal.

VIVIE. Her what?!

PRAED. Her ideal.

VIVIE. Do you mean her ideal of ME?

PRAED. Yes.

VIVIE. What on earth is it like?

PRAED. Well, you must have observed, Miss Warren, that people who are dissatisfied with their own bringing-up generally think that the world would be all right if everybody were to be brought

---

4. I.e., office in the legal quarter of London.

up quite differently. Now your mother's life has been—er—I suppose you know—

VIVIE. Dont suppose anything, Mr Praed. I hardly know my mother. Since I was a child I have lived in England, at school or college, or with people paid to take charge of me. I have been boarded out all my life. My mother has lived in Brussels or Vienna and never let me go to her. I only see her when she visits England for a few days. I dont complain: it's been very pleasant; for people have been very good to me; and there has always been plenty of money to make things smooth. But dont imagine I know anything about my mother. I know far less than you do.

PRAED. [*very ill at ease*] In that case—[*He stops, quite at a loss. Then, with a forced attempt at gaiety*] But what nonsense we are talking! Of course you and your mother will get on capitally. [*He rises, and looks abroad at the view*] What a charming little place you have here!

VIVIE. [*unmoved*] Rather a violent change of subject, Mr Praed. Why wont my mother's life bear being talked about?

PRAED. Oh, you really mustnt say that. Isnt it natural that I should have a certain delicacy in talking to my old friend's daughter about her behind her back? You and she will have plenty of opportunity of talking about it when she comes.

VIVIE. No: s h e wont talk about it either. [*Rising*] However, I daresay you have good reasons for telling me nothing. Only, mind this, Mr Praed. I expect there will be a battle royal when my mother hears of my Chancery Lane project.

PRAED. [*ruefully*] I'm afraid there will.

VIVIE. Well, I shall win, because I want nothing but my fare to London to start there to-morrow earning my own living by devilling[5] for Honoria. Besides, I have no mysteries to keep up; and it seems she has. I shall use that advantage over her if necessary.

PRAED. [*greatly shocked*] Oh no! No, pray. Youd not do such a thing.

VIVIE. Then tell me why not.

PRAED. I really cannot. I appeal to your good feeling. [*She smiles at his sentimentality*] Besides you may be too bold. Your mother is not to be trifled with when she's angry.

VIVIE. You cant frighten me, Mr Praed. In that month at Chancery Lane I had opportunities of taking the measure of one or two women v e r y like my mother. You may back me to win. But if I hit harder in my ignorance than I need, remember that it is you who refuse to enlighten me. Now, let us drop the subject. [*She takes her chair and replaces it near the hammock with the same vigorous swing as before*]

PRAED. [*taking a desperate resolution*] One word, Miss Warren. I had better tell you. It's very difficult; but—

Mrs Warren and Sir George Crofts arrive at the gate. Mrs

---

5. Acting as assistant to a barrister (trial lawyer) as a way of gaining legal experience.

Warren is between 40 and 50, formerly pretty, showily dressed in a brilliant hat and a gay blouse fitting tightly over her bust and flanked by fashionable sleeves. Rather spoilt and domineering, and decidedly vulgar, but, on the whole, a genial and fairly presentable old blackguard of a woman.

Crofts is a tall powerfully-built man of about 50, fashionably dressed in the style of a young man. Nasal voice, reedier than might be expected from his strong frame. Clean-shaven bulldog jaws, large flat ears, and thick neck: gentlemanly combination of the most brutal types of city man, sporting man, and man about town.

VIVIE. Here they are [*Coming to them as they enter the garden*] How do, mater? Mr Praed's been here this half hour waiting for you.

MRS WARREN. Well, if youve been waiting, Praddy, it's your own fault: I thought youd have the gumption to know I was coming by the 3.10 train. Vivie: put your hat on, dear: youll get sunburnt. Oh, I forgot to introduce you. Sir George Crofts: my little Vivie.

Crofts advances to Vivie with his most courtly manner. She nods, but makes no motion to shake hands.

CROFTS. May I shake hands with a young lady whom I have known by reputation very long as the daughter of one of my oldest friends?

VIVIE. [*who has been looking him up and down sharply*] If you like. [*She takes his tenderly proffered hand and gives it a squeeze that makes him open his eyes; then turns away, and says to her mother*] Will you come in, or shall I get a couple more chairs [*She goes into the porch for the chairs*]

MRS WARREN. Well George, what do you think of her?

CROFTS. [*ruefully*] She has a powerful fist. Did you shake hands with her, Praed?

PRAED. Yes: it will pass off presently.

CROFTS. I hope so. [*Vivie reappears with two more chairs. He hurries to her assistance*] Allow me.

MRS WARREN. [*patronizingly*] Let Sir George help you with the chairs, dear.

VIVIE. [*pitching them into his arms*] Here you are. [*She dusts her hands and turns to Mrs Warren*] Youd like some tea, wouldnt you?

MRS WARREN. [*sitting in Praed's chair and fanning herself*] I'm dying for a drop to drink.

VIVIE. I'll see about it. [*She goes into the cottage*]

Sir George has by this time managed to unfold a chair and plant it beside Mrs Warren, on her left. He throws the other on the grass and sits down, looking dejected and rather foolish, with the handle of his stick in his mouth. Praed, still very uneasy, fidgets about the garden on their right.

MRS WARREN. [*to Praed, looking at Crofts*] Just look at him, Praddy: he looks cheerful, dont he? He's been worrying my life out these three years to have that little girl of mine shewn to him;

and now that Ive done it, he's quite out of countenance. [*Briskly*] Come! sit up, George; and take your stick out of your mouth. [*Crofts sulkily obeys*]

PRAED. I think, you know—if you dont mind my saying so—that we had better get out of the habit of thinking of her as a little girl. You see she has really distinguished herself; and I'm not sure, from what I have seen of her, that she is not older than any of us.

MRS WARREN. [*greatly amused*] Only listen to him, George! Older than any of us! Well, she has been stuffing you nicely with her importance.

PRAED. But young people are particularly sensitive about being treated in that way.

MRS WARREN. Yes; and young people have to get all that nonsense taken out of them, and a good deal more besides. Dont you interfere, Praddy: I know how to treat my own child as well as you do. [*Praed, with a grave shake of his head, walks up the garden with his hands behind his back. Mrs Warren pretends to laugh, but looks after him with perceptible concern. Then she whispers to Crofts*] Whats the matter with him? What does he take it like that for?

CROFTS. [*morosely*] Youre afraid of Praed.

MRS WARREN. What! Me! Afraid of dear old Praddy! Why, a fly wouldnt be afraid of him.

CROFTS. Y o u r e afraid of him.

MRS WARREN. [*angry*] I'll trouble you to mind your own business, and not try any of your sulks on me. I'm not afraid of y o u, anyhow. If you cant make yourself agreeable, youd better go home. [*She gets up, and, turning her back on him, finds herself face to face with Praed*] Come, Praddy, I know it was only your tender-heartedness. Youre afraid I'll bully her.

PRAED. My dear Kitty: you think I'm offended. Dont imagine that: pray dont. But you know I often notice things that escape you; and though you never take my advice, you sometimes admit afterwards that you ought to have taken it.

MRS WARREN. Well, what do you notice now?

PRAED. Only that Vivie is a grown woman. Pray, Kitty, treat her with every respect.

MRS WARREN. [*with genuine amazement*] Respect! Treat my own daughter with respect! What next, pray!

VIVIE. [*appearing at the cottage door and calling to Mrs Warren*] Mother: will you come to my room before tea?

MRS WARREN. Yes, dearie. [*She laughts indulgently at Praed's gravity, and pats him on the cheek as she passes him on her way to the porch*] Dont be cross, Praddy. [*She follows Vivie into the cottage*]

CROFTS. [*furtively*] I say, Praed.

PRAED. Yes.

CROFTS. I want to ask you a rather particular question.

PRAED. Certainly. [*He takes Mrs Warren's chair and sits close to Crofts*]

CROFTS. Thats right: they might hear us from the window. Look here: did Kitty ever tell you who that girl's father is?

PRAED. Never.

CROFTS. Have you any suspicion of who it might be?

PRAED. None.

CROFTS. [*not believing him*] I know, of course, that you perhaps might feel bound not to tell if she had said anything to you. But it's very awkward to be uncertain about it now that we shall be meeting the girl every day. We dont exactly know how we ought to feel towards her.

PRAED. What difference can that make? We take her on her own merits. What does it matter who her father was?

CROFTS. [*suspiciously*] Then you know who he was?

PRAED. [*with a touch of temper*] I said no just now. Did you not hear me?

CROFTS. Look here, Praed. I ask you as a particular favor. If you do know [*movement of protest from Praed*]—I only say, if you know you might at least set my mind at rest about her. The fact is, I feel attracted.

PRAED. [*sternly*] What do you mean?

CROFTS. Oh, dont be alarmed: it's quite an innocent feeling. Thats what puzzles me about it. Why, for all I know, I might be her father.

PRAED. You! Impossible!

CROFTS. [*catching him up cunningly*] You know for certain that I'm not?

PRAED. I know nothing about it, I tell you, any more than you. But really, Crofts—oh no, it's out of the question. Theres not the least resemblance.

CROFTS. As to that, theres no resemblance between her and her mother that I can see. I suppose she's not y o u r daughter, is she?

PRAED. [*rising indignantly*] Really, Crofts—!

CROFTS. No offence, Praed. Quite allowable as between two men of the world.

PRAED. [*recovering himself with an effort and speaking gently and gravely*] Now listen to me, my dear Crofts. [*He sits down again*] I have nothing to do with that side of Mrs Warren's life, and never had. She has never spoken to me about it; and of course I have never spoken to her about it. Your delicacy will tell you that a handsome woman needs s o m e friends who are not—well, not on that footing with her. The effect of her own beauty would become a torment to her if she could not escape from it occasionally. You are probably on much more confidential terms with Kitty than I am. Surely you can ask her the question yourself.

CROFTS. I have asked her, often enough. But she's so determined to keep the child all to herself that she would deny that it ever had a father if she could. [*Rising*] I'm thoroughly uncomfortable about it, Praed.

PRAED. [*rising also*] Well, as you are, at all events, old enough to be her father, I dont mind agreeing that we both regard Miss Vivie in a parental way, as a young girl whom we are bound to protect and help. What do you say?

CROFTS. [*aggressively*] I'm no older than you, if you come to that.

PRAED. Yes you are, my dear fellow: you were born old. I was born a boy: Ive never been able to feel the assurance of a grown-up man in my life. [*He folds his chair and carries it to the porch*]

MRS WARREN. [*calling from within the cottage*] Prad-dee! George! Tea-ea-ea-ea!

CROFTS. [*hastily*] She's calling us. [*He hurries in*]

Praed shakes his head bodingly, and is following Crofts when he is hailed by a young gentleman who has just appeared on the common, and is making for the gate. He is pleasant, pretty, smartly dressed, cleverly good-for-nothing, not long turned 20, with a charming voice and agreeably disrespectful manners. He carries a light sporting magazine rifle.

THE YOUNG GENTLEMAN. Hallo! Praed!

PRAED. Why, Frank Gardner! [*Frank comes in and shakes hands cordially*] What on earth are you doing here?

FRANK Staying with my father.

PRAED. The Roman father?[6]

FRANK. He's rector here. I'm living with my people this autumn for the sake of economy. Things came to a crisis in July: the Roman father had to pay my debts. He's stony broke in consequence; and so am I. What are you up to in these parts? Do you know the people here?

PRAED. Yes: I'm spending the day with a Miss Warren.

FRANK. [*enthusiastically*] What! Do you know Vivie? Isnt she a jolly girl? I'm teaching her to shoot with this [*putting down the rifle*] I'm so glad she knows you: youre just the sort of fellow she ought to know. [*He smiles, and raises the charming voice almost to a singing tone as he exclaims*] It's e v e r so jolly to find you here, Praed.

PRAED. I'm an old friend of her mother. Mrs Warren brought me over to make her daughter's acquaintance.

FRANK. The mother! Is s h e here?

PRAED. Yes: inside, at tea.

MRS WARREN. [*calling from within*] Prad-dee-ee-ee-eee! The tea-cake'll be cold.

PRAED. [*calling*] Yes, Mrs Warren. In a moment. Ive just met a friend here.

MRS WARREN. A what?

PRAED. [*louder*] A friend.

MRS WARREN. Bring him in.

PRAED. All right. [*To Frank*] Will you accept the invitation?

FRANK. [*incredulous, but immensely amused*] Is that Vivie's mother?

6. Not "Roman Catholic" (he is a Church of England priest) but a father with a Roman sense of duty. The word is used ironically.

PRAED. Yes.

FRANK. By jove! What a lark! Do you think she'll like me?

PRAED. Ive no doubt youll make yourself popular, as usual. Come in and try [*moving towards the house*]

FRANK. Stop a bit. [*Seriously*] I want to take you into my confidence.

PRAED. Pray dont. It's only some fresh folly, like the barmaid at Redhill.

FRANK. It's ever so much more serious than that. You say youve only just met Vivie for the first time?

PRAED. Yes.

FRANK. [*rhapsodically*] Then you can have no idea what a girl she is. Such character! Such sense! And her cleverness! Oh, my eye, Praed, but I can tell you she is clever! And—need I add?—she loves me.

CROFTS. [*putting his head out of the window*] I say, Praed: what are you about? D o come along [*He disappears*]

FRANK. Hallo! Sort of chap that would take a prize at a dog show, aint he? Who's he?

PRAED. Sir George Crofts, an old friend of Mrs Warren's. I think we had better come in.

On their way to the porch they are interrupted by a call from the gate. Turning, they see an elderly clergyman looking over it.

THE CLERGYMAN. [*calling*] Frank!

FRANK. Hallo! [*To Praed*] The Roman father. [*To the clergyman*] Yes, gov'nor: all right: presently. [*To Praed*] Look here, Praed: youd better go in to tea. I'll join you directly.

PRAED. Very good. [*He goes into the cottage*]

The clergyman remains outside the gate, with his hands on the top of it. The Rev. Samuel Gardner, a beneficed clergyman of the Established Church, is over 50. Externally he is pretentious, booming, noisy, important. Really he is that obsolescent social phenomenon the fool of the family dumped on the Church by his father, the patron, clamorously asserting himself as father and clergyman without being able to command respect in either capacity.

REV. S. Well, sir. Who are your friends here, if I may ask?

FRANK. Oh, it's all right, gov'nor! Come in.

REV. S. No sir; not until I know whose garden I am entering.

FRANK. It's all right. It's Miss Warren's.

REV. S. I have not seen her at church since she came.

FRANK. Of course not: she's a third wrangler. Ever so intellectual. Took a higher degree than you did; so why should she go to hear you preach?

REV. S. Dont be disrespectful, sir.

FRANK. Oh, it dont matter: nobody hears us. Come in. [*He opens the gate, unceremoniously pulling his father with it into the garden*] I want to introduce you to her. Do you remember the advice you gave me last July, gov'nor?

REV. S. [*severely*] Yes. I advised you to conquer your idleness and flippancy, and to work your way into an honorable profession and live on it and not upon me.

FRANK. No: thats what you thought of afterwards. What you actually said was that since I had neither brains nor money, I'd better turn my good looks to account by marrying somebody with both. Well, look here. Miss Warren has brains: you cant deny that.

REV. S. Brains are not everything.

FRANK. No, of course not: theres the money—

REV. S. [*interrupting him austerely*] I was not thinking of money, sir. I was speaking of higher things. Social position, for instance.

FRANK. I dont care a rap about that.

REV. S. But I do, sir.

FRANK. Well, nobody wants you to marry her. Anyhow, she has what amounts to a high Cambridge degree; and she seems to have as much money as she wants.

REV. S. [*sinking into a feeble vein of humor*] I greatly doubt whether she has as much money as y o u will want.

FRANK. Oh, come; I havnt been so very extravagant. I live ever so quietly; I dont drink; I dont bet much; and I never go regularly on the razzle-dazzle as you did when you were my age.

REV. S. [*booming hollowly*] Silence, sir.

FRANK. Well, you told me yourself, when I was making ever such an ass of myself about the barmaid at Redhill, that you once offered a woman £50 for the letters you wrote to her when—

REV. S. [*terrified*] Sh-sh-sh, Frank, for Heaven's sake! [*He looks round apprehensively. Seeing no one within earshot he plucks up courage to boom again, but more subduedly*] You are taking an ungentlemanly advantage of what I confided to you for your own good, to save you from an error you would have repented all your life long. Take warning by your father's follies, sir; and dont make them an excuse for your own.

FRANK. Did you ever hear the story of the Duke of Wellington and his letters?

REV. S. No, sir; and I dont want to hear it.

FRANK. The old Iron Duke didnt throw away £50: not he. He just wrote: "Dear Jenny: publish and be damned! Yours affectionately, Wellington." Thats what you should have done.

REV. S. [*piteously*] Frank, my boy: when I wrote those letters I put myself into that woman's power. When I told you about them I put myself, to some extent, I am sorry to say, in your power. She refused my money with these words, which I shall never forget. "Knowledge is power" she said; "and I never sell power." Thats more than twenty years ago; and she has never made use of her power or caused me a moment's uneasiness. You are behaving worse to me than she did, Frank.

FRANK. Oh yes I dare say! Did you ever preach at her the way you preach at me every day?

REV. S. [*wounded almost to tears*] I leave you sir. You are incorrigible. [*He turns towards the gate*]

FRANK. [*utterly unmoved*] Tell them I shant be home to tea, will you, gov'nor, like a good fellow? [*He moves towards the cottage door and is met by Praed and Vivie coming out*]

VIVIE. [*to Frank*] Is that your father, Frank? I do so want to meet him.

FRANK. Certainly. [*Calling after his father*] Gov'nor. Youre wanted. [*The parson turns at the gate, fumbling nervously at his hat. Praed crosses the garden to the opposite side, beaming in anticipation of civilities*] My father: Miss Warren.

VIVIE. [*going to the clergyman and shaking his hand*] Very glad to see you here, Mr Gardner. [*Calling to the cottage*] Mother: come along: youre wanted.

Mrs Warren appears on the threshold, and is immediately transfixed recognizing the clergyman.

VIVIE. [*continuing*] Let me introduce—

MRS WARREN. [*swooping on the Reverend Samuel*] Why, it's Sam Gardner, gone into the Church! Well, I never! Dont you know us, Sam? This is George Crofts, as large as life and twice as natural. Dont you remember me?

REV. S. [*very red*] I really—er—

MRS WARREN. Of course you do. Why, I have a whole album of your letters still: I came across them only the other day.

REV. S. [*miserably confused*] Miss Vavasour, I believe.

MRS WARREN. [*correcting him quickly in a loud whisper*] Tch! Nonsense! Mrs Warren: dont you see my daughter there?

Act II

Inside the cottage after nightfall. Looking eastward from within instead of westward from without, the latticed window, with its curtains drawn, is now seen in the middle of the front wall of the cottage, with the porch door to the left of it. In the left-hand side wall is the door leading to the kitchen. Farther back against the same wall is a dresser with a candle and matches on it, and Frank's rifle standing beside them, with the barrel resting in the plate-rack. In the centre a table stands with a lighted lamp on it. Vivie's books and writing materials are on a table to the right of the window, against the wall. The fireplace is on the right, with a settle: there is no fire. Two of the chairs are set right and left of the table.

The cottage door opens, shewing a fine starlit night without; and Mrs Warren, her shoulders wrapped in a shawl borrowed from Vivie, enters, followed by Frank, who throws his cap on the window seat. She has had enough of walking, and gives a gasp of relief as she unpins her hat; takes it off; sticks the pin through the crown; and puts it on the table.

MRS WARREN. O Lord! I dont know which is the worst of the country, the walking or the sitting at home with nothing to do. I could do with a whisky and soda now very well, if only they had such a thing in this place.

FRANK. Perhaps Vivie's got some.

MRS WARREN. Nonsense! What would a young girl like her be doing with such things! Never mind: it dont matter. I wonder how she passes her time here! I'd a good deal rather be in Vienna.

FRANK. Let me take you there. [*He helps her to take off her shawl, gallantly giving her shoulders a very perceptible squeeze as he does so*]

MRS WARREN. Ah! would you? I'm beginning to think youre a chip of the old block.

FRANK. Like the gov'nor, eh? [*He hangs the shawl on the nearest chair, and sits down*]

MRS WARREN. Never you mind. What do you know about such things? Youre only a boy. [*She goes to the hearth, to be farther from temptation*]

FRANK. Do come to Vienna with me? It'd be ever such larks.

MRS WARREN. No, thank you. Vienna is no place for you—at least not until youre a little older. [*She nods at him to emphasize this piece of advice. He makes a mock-piteous face, belied by his laughing eyes. She looks at him; then comes back to him*] Now, look here, little boy [*taking his face in her hands and turning it up to her*]; I know you through and through by your likeness to your father, better than you know yourself. Dont you go taking any silly ideas into your head about me. Do you hear?

FRANK. [*gallantly wooing her with his voice*] Cant help it, my dear Mrs Warren: it runs in the family.

She pretends to box his ears; then looks at the pretty laughing upturned face for a moment, tempted. At last she kisses him, and immediately turns away, out of patience with herself.

MRS WARREN. There! I shouldnt have done that. I am wicked. Never you mind, my dear: it's only a motherly kiss. Go and make love to Vivie.

FRANK. So I have.

MRS WARREN. [*turning on him with a sharp note of alarm in her voice*] What!

FRANK. Vivie and I are ever such chums.

MRS WARREN. What do you mean? Now see here: I wont have any young scamp tampering with my little girl. Do you hear? I wont have it.

FRANK. [*quite unabashed*] My dear Mrs Warren: dont you be alarmed. My intentions are honorable: ever so honorable; and your little girl is jolly well able to take care of herself. She dont need looking after half so much as her mother. She aint so handsome, you know.

MRS WARREN. [*taken aback by his assurance*] Well, you have got a nice healthy two inches thick of cheek all over you. I dont know where you got it. Not from your father, anyhow.

CROFTS. [*in the garden*] The gipsies, I suppose?

REV. S. [*replying*] The broomsquires[7] are far worse.

7. Small country landowners.

MRS WARREN. [*to Frank*] S-sh! Remember! youve had your warning.
Crofts and the Reverend Samuel come in from the garden, the
clergyman continuing his conversation as he enters.

REV. S. The perjury at the Winchester assizes[8] is deplorable.

MRS WARREN. Well? What became of you two? And wheres Praddy
and Vivie?

CROFTS. [*putting his hat on the settle and his stick in the chimney*
corner] They went up the hill. We went to the village. I wanted
a drink. [*He sits down on the settle, putting his legs up along*
the seat]

MRS WARREN. Well, she oughtnt to go off like that without telling
me. [*To Frank*] Get your father a chair, Frank: where are your
manners? [*Frank springs up and gracefully offers his father his*
chair; and then takes another from the wall and sits down at the
table, in the middle, with his father on his right and Mrs Warren
on his left] George: where are you going to stay to-night? You
cant stay here. And whats Praddy going to do?

CROFTS. Gardner'll put me up.

MRS WARREN. Oh no doubt youve taken care of yourself! But what
about Praddy?

CROFTS. Dont know. I suppose he can sleep at the inn.

MRS WARREN. Havnt you room for him, Sam?

REV. S. Well—er—you see, as rector here, I am not free to do as I
like. Er—what is Mr Praed's social position?

MRS WARREN. Oh, he's all right: he's an architect. What an old
stick-in-the-mud you are, Sam!

FRANK. Yes, it's all right, gov'nor. He built that place down in
Wales for the Duke. Caernarvon Castle they call it. You must
have heard of it. [*He winks with lightning smartness at Mrs*
Warren, and regards his father blandly]

REV. S. Oh, in that case, of course we shall only be too happy. I
suppose he knows the Duke personally.

FRANK. Oh, ever so intimately! We can stick him in Georgina's old
room.

MRS WARREN. Well, thats settled. Now if those two would only
come in and let us have supper. Theyve no right to stay out after
dark like this.

CROFTS. [*aggressively*] What harm are they doing you?

MRS WARREN. Well, harm or not, I dont like it.

FRANK. Better not wait for them, Mrs Warren. Praed will stay out
as long as possible. He has never known before what it is to stray
over the heath on a summer night with my Vivie.

CROFTS. [*sitting up in some consternation*] I say, you know!
Come!

REV. S. [*rising, startled out of his professional manner into real*
force and sincerity] Frank, once for all, it's out of the question.
Mrs Warren will tell you that it's not to be thought of.

CROFTS. Of course not.

FRANK. [*with enchanting placidity*] Is that so, Mrs Warren?

8. Law courts.

MRS WARREN. [*reflectively*] Well, Sam, I dont know. If the girl wants to get married, no good can come of keeping her unmarried.

REV. S. [*astounded*] But married to him!—your daughter to my son! Only think: it's impossible.

CROFTS. Of course it's impossible. Dont be a fool, Kitty.

MRS WARREN. [*nettled*] Why not? Isnt my daughter good enough for your son?

REV. S. But surely, my dear Mrs Warren, you know the reasons—

MRS WARREN. [*defiantly*] I know no reasons. If you know any, you can tell them to the lad, or to the girl, or to your congregation, if you like.

REV. S. [*collapsing helplessly into his chair*] You know very well that I couldnt tell anyone the reasons. But my boy will believe me when I tell him there a r e reasons.

FRANK. Quite right, Dad: he will. But has your boy's conduct ever been influenced by your reasons?

CROFTS. You cant marry her: and thats all about it. [*He gets up and stands on the hearth, with his back to the fireplace, frowning determinedly*]

MRS WARREN. [*turning on him sharply*] What have you go to do with it, pray?

FRANK. [*with his prettiest lyrical cadence*] Precisely what I was going to ask, myself, in my own graceful fashion.

CROFTS. [*to Mrs Warren*] I suppose you dont want to marry the girl to a man younger than herself and without either a profession or twopence to keep her on. Ask Sam, if you dont believe me. [*To the parson*] How much more money are you going to give him?

REV. S. Not another penny. He has had his patrimony; and he spent the last of it in July. [*Mrs Warren's face falls*]

CROFTS. [*watching her*] There! I told you. [*He resumes his place on the settle and puts up his legs on the seat again, as if the matter were finally disposed of*]

FRANK. [*plaintively*] This is ever so mercenary. Do you suppose Miss Warren's going to marry for money? If we love one another—

MRS WARREN. Thank you. Your love's a pretty cheap commodity, my lad. If you have no means of keeping a wife, that settles it: you cant have Vivie.

FRANK. [*much amused*] What do y o u say, gov'nor, eh?

REV. S. I agree with Mrs Warren.

FRANK. And good old Crofts has already expressed his opinion.

CROFTS. [*turning angrily on his elbow*] Look here: I want none of y o u r cheek.

FRANK. [*pointedly*] I'm ever so sorry to surprise you, Crofts, but you allowed yourself the liberty of speaking to me like a father a moment ago. One father is enough, thank you.

CROFTS. [*contemptuously*] Yah! [*He turns away again*]

FRANK. [*rising*] Mrs Warren: I cannot give my Vivie up, even for your sake.

MRS WARREN. [*muttering*] Young scamp!

FRANK. [*continuing*] And as you no doubt intend to hold out other prospects to her, I shall lose no time in placing my case before her. [*They stare at him; and he begins to declaim gracefully*]

> He either fears his fate too much,
> Or his deserts are small,
> That dares not put it to the touch
> To gain or lose it all.[9]

The cottage door opens whilst he is reciting; and Vivie and Praed come in. He breaks off. Praed puts his hat on the dresser. There is an immediate improvement in the company's behavior. Crofts takes down his legs from the settle and pulls himself together as Praed joins him at the fireplace. Mrs Warren loses her ease of manner and takes refuge in querulousness.

MRS WARREN. Wherever have you been, Vivie?

VIVIE. [*taking off her hat and throwing it carelessly on the table*] On the hill.

MRS WARREN. Well, you shouldnt go off like that without letting me know. How could I tell what had become of you? And night coming on too!

VIVIE. [*going to the door of the kitchen and opening it, ignoring her mother*] Now, about supper? [*All rise except Mrs Warren*] We shall be rather crowded in here, I'm afraid.

MRS WARREN. Did you hear what I said, Vivie?

VIVIE. [*quietly*] Yes, mother. [*Reverting to the supper difficulty*] How many are we? [*Counting*] One, two, three, four, five, six. Well, two will have to wait until the rest are done: Mrs. Alison has only plates and knives for four.

PRAED. Oh, it doesnt matter about me. I—

VIVIE. You have had a long walk and are hungry, Mr Praed: you shall have your supper at once. I can wait myself. I want one person to wait with me. Frank: are you hungry?

FRANK. Not the least in the world. Completely off my peck, in fact.

MRS WARREN. [*to Crofts*] Neither are you, George. You can wait.

CROFTS. Oh, hang it. Ive eaten nothing since tea-time. Cant Sam do it?

FRANK. Would you starve my poor father?

REV. S. [*testily*] Allow me to speak for myself, sir. I am perfectly willing to wait.

VIVIE. [*decisively*] Theres no need. Only two are wanted. [*She opens the door of the kitchen*] Will you take my mother in, Mr Gardner. [*The parson takes Mrs Warren; and they pass into the kitchen. Praed and Crofts follow. All except Praed clearly disapprove of the arrangement, but do not know how to resist it. Vivie stands at the door looking in at them*] Can you squeeze past to that corner, Mr Praed: it's rather a tight fit. Take care of your

9. From the poem *My Dear and Only Love*, by the Marquis of Montrose (1612–50).

coat against the white-wash: thats right. Now, are you all comfortable?

PRAED. [*within*] Quite, thank you.

MRS WARREN. [*within*] Leave the door open, dearie. [*Vivie frowns; but Frank checks her with a gesture, and steals to the cottage door, which he softly sets wide open*] Oh Lor, what a draught! Youd better shut it, dear.

Vivie shuts it with a slam, and then, noting with disgust that her mother's hat and shawl are lying about, takes them tidily to the window seat, whilst Frank noiselessly shuts the cottage door.

FRANK. [*exulting*] Aha! Got rid of em. Well, Vivvums: what do you think of my guvernor?

VIVIE. [*preoccupied and serious*] Ive hardly spoken to him. He doesnt strike me as being a particularly able person.

FRANK. Well, you know, the old man is not altogether such a fool as he looks. You see, he was shoved into the Church rather; and in trying to live up to it he makes a much bigger ass of himself than he really is. I dont dislike him as much as you might expect. He means well. How do you think youll get on with him?

VIVIE. [*rather grimly*] I dont think my future life will be much concerned with him, or with any of that old circle of my mother's, except perhaps Praed. [*She sits down on the settle*] What do you think of my mother?

FRANK. Really and truly?

VIVIE. Yes, really and truly.

FRANK. Well, she's ever so jolly. But she's rather a caution, isn't she? And Crofts! Oh my eye, Crofts! [*He sits beside her*]

VIVIE. What a lot, Frank!

FRANK. What a crew!

VIVIE. [*with intense contempt for them*] If I thought that *I* was like that—that I was going to be a waster, shifting along from one meal to another with no purpose, and no character, and no grit in me, I'd open an artery and bleed to death without one moment's hesitation.

FRANK. Oh no, you wouldnt. Why should they take any grind when they can afford not to? I wish I had their luck. No: what I object to is their form. It isnt the thing: it's slovenly, ever so slovenly.

VIVIE. Do you think your form will be any better when youre as old as Crofts, if you dont work?

FRANK. Of course I do. Ever so much better. Vivvums mustnt lecture: her little boy's incorrigible. [*He attempts to take her face caressingly in his hands*]

VIVIE. [*striking his hands down sharply*] Off with you: Vivvums is not in a humor for petting her little boy this evening. [*She rises and comes forward to the other side of the room*]

FRANK. [*following her*] How unkind!

VIVIE. [*stamping at him*] Be serious. I'm serious.

FRANK. Good. Let us talk learnedly. Miss Warren: do you know that all the most advanced thinkers are agreed that half the diseases of modern civilization are due to starvation of the affections in the young. Now, I—

VIVIE. [cutting him short] You are very tiresome. [She opens the inner door] Have you room for Frank there? He's complaining of starvation.

MRS WARREN. [within] Of course there is [clatter of knives and glasses as she moves the things on the table] Here! theres room now beside me. Come along, Mr Frank.

FRANK. Her little boy will be ever so even with his Vivvums for this. [He passes into the kitchen]

MRS WARREN. [within] Here, Vivie: come on you too, child. You must be famished. [She enters, followed by Crofts, who holds the door open for Vivie with marked deference. She goes out without looking at him; and he shuts the door after her] Why, George, you cant be done: youve eaten nothing. Is there anything wrong with you?

CROFTS. Oh, all I wanted was a drink. [He thrusts his hands in his pockets, and begins prowling about the room, restless and sulky]

MRS WARREN. Well, I like enough to eat. But a little of that cold beef and cheese and lettuce goes a long way. [With a sigh of only half repletion she sits down lazily on the settle]

CROFTS. What do you go encouraging that young pup for?

MRS WARREN. [on the alert at once] Now see here, George: what are you up to about that girl? Ive been watching your way of looking at her. Remember: I know you and what your looks mean.

CROFTS. Theres no harm in looking at her, is there?

MRS WARREN. I'd put you out and pack you back to London pretty soon if I saw any of your nonsense. My girl's little finger is more to me than your whole body and soul. [Crofts receives this with a sneering grin. Mrs Warren, flushing a little at her failure to impose on him in the character of a theatrically devoted mother, adds in a lower key] Make your mind easy: the young pup has no more chance than you have.

CROFTS. Maynt a man take an interest in a girl?

MRS WARREN. Not a man like you.

CROFTS. How old is she?

MRS WARREN. Never you mind how old she is.

CROFTS. Why do you make such a secret of it?

MRS WARREN. Because I choose.

CROFTS. Well, I'm not fifty yet; and my property is as good as ever it was—

MRS WARREN. [interrupting him] Yes; because youre as stingy as youre vicious.

CROFTS. [continuing] And a baronet isnt to be picked up every day. No other man in my position would put up with you for a mother-in-law. Why shouldnt she marry me?

MRS WARREN. You!

CROFTS. We three could live together quite comfortably. I'd die before her and leave her a bouncing widow with plenty of money. Why not? It's been growing in my mind all the time Ive been walking with that fool inside there.

MRS WARREN. [*revolted*] Yes; it's the sort of thing that would grow in your mind.

He halts in his prowling; and the two look at one another, she steadfastly, with a sort of awe behind her contemptuous disgust: he stealthily, with a carnal gleam in his eye and a loose grin.

CROFTS. [*suddenly becoming anxious and urgent as he sees no sign of sympathy in her*] Look here, Kitty: youre a sensible woman: you neednt put on any moral airs. I'll ask no more questions; and you need answer none. I'll settle the whole property on her; and if you want a cheque for yourself on the wedding day, you can name any figure you like—in reason.

MRS WARREN. So it's come to that with you, George, like all the other worn-out old creatures!

CROFTS. [*savagely*] Damn you!

Before she can retort the door of the kitchen is opened; and the voices of the others are heard returning. Crofts, unable to recover his presence of mind, hurries out of the cottage. The clergyman appears at the kitchen door.

REV. S. [*looking around*] Where is Sir George?

MRS WARREN. Gone out to have a pipe. [*The clergyman takes his hat from the table, and joins Mrs Warren at the fireside. Meanwhile Vivie comes in, followed by Frank, who collapses into the nearest chair with an air of extreme exhaustion. Mrs Warren looks round at Vivie and says, with her affectation of maternal patronage even more forced than usual*] Well, dearie: have you had a good supper?

VIVIE. You know what Mrs Alison's suppers are. [*She turns to Frank and pets him*] Poor Frank! was all the beef gone? did it get nothing but bread and cheese and ginger beer? [*Seriously, as if she had done quite enough trifling for one evening*] Her butter is really awful. I must get some down from the stores.

FRANK. Do, in Heaven's name!

Vivie goes to the writing-table and makes a memorandum to order the butter. Praed comes in from the kitchen, putting up his handkerchief, which he has been using as a napkin.

REV. S. Frank, my boy: it is time for us to be thinking of home. Your mother does not know yet that we have visitors.

PRAED. I'm afraid we're giving trouble.

FRANK. [*rising*] Not the least in the world; my mother will be delighted to see you. She's a genuinely intellectual artistic woman; and she sees nobody here from one year's end to another except the gov'nor; so you can imagine how jolly dull it pans out for her. [*To his father*] Y o u r e not intellectual or artistic are you, pater? So take Praed home at once; and I'll stay here and entertain Mrs Warren. Youll pick up Crofts in the garden. He'll be excellent company for the bull-pup.

PRAED. [*taking his hat from the dresser, and coming close to Frank*] Come with us, Frank. Mrs Warren has not seen Miss

Vivie for a long time; and we have prevented them from having a
moment together yet.

FRANK. [*quite softened, and looking at Praed with romantic admiration*] Of course. I forgot. Ever so thanks for reminding me.
Perfect gentleman, Praddy. Always were. My ideal through life.
[*He rises to go, but pauses a moment between the two older
men, and puts his hand on Praed's shoulder*] Ah, if you had only
been my father instead of this unworthy old man! [*He puts his
other hand on his father's shoulder*]

REV. S. [*blustering*] Silence, sir, silence: you are profane.

MRS WARREN. [*laughing heartily*] You should keep him in better
order, Sam. Goodnight. Here: take George his hat and stick with
my compliments.

REV. S. [*taking them*] Goodnight. [*They shake hands. As he
passes Vivie he shakes hands with her also and bids her goodnight. Then, in booming command, to Frank*] Come along, sir,
at once. [*He goes out*]

MRS WARREN. Byebye, Praddy.

PRAED. Byebye, Kitty.

They shake hands affectionately and go out together, she accompanying him to the garden gate.

FRANK. [*to Vivie*] Kissums?

VIVIE. [*fiercely*] No. I hate you. [*She takes a couple of books and
some paper from the writing-table, and sits down with them at
the middle table, at the end next the fireplace*]

FRANK. [*grimacing*] Sorry. [*He goes for his cap and rifle. Mrs.
Warren returns. He takes her hand*] Goodnight, d e a r Mrs
Warren. [*He kisses her hand. She snatches it away, her lips
tightening, and looks more than half disposed to box his ears. He
laughs mischievously and runs off, clapping-to the door behind
him*]

MRS WARREN. [*resigning herself to an evening of boredom now
that the men are gone*] Did you ever in your life hear anyone
rattle on so? Isnt he a tease? [*She sits at the table*] Now that I
think of it, dearie, dont you go on encouraging him. I'm sure he's
a regular good-for-nothing.

VIVIE. [*rising to fetch more books*] I'm afraid so. Poor Frank! I
shall have to get rid of him; but I shall feel sorry for him, though
he's not worth it. That man Crofts does not seem to me to be
good for much either: is he? [*She throws the books on the table
rather roughly*]

MRS WARREN. [*galled by Vivie's indifference*] What do you know
of men, child, to talk that way about them? Youll have to make
up your mind to see a good deal of Sir George Crofts, as he's a
friend of mine.

VIVIE. [*quite unmoved*] Why? [*She sits down and opens a
book*]. Do you expect that we shall be much together? You and
I, I mean?

MRS WARREN. [*staring at her*] Of course: until youre married.

Youre not going back to college again.

VIVIE. Do you think my way of life would suit you? I doubt it.

MRS WARREN. Y o u r way of life! What do you mean?

VIVIE. [*cutting a page of her book with the paper knife on her chatelaine*] Has it really never occurred to you, mother, that I have a way of life like other people?

MRS WARREN. What nonsense is this youre trying to talk? Do you want to shew your independence, now that youre a great little person at school? Dont be a fool, child.

VIVIE. [*indulgently*] Thats all you have to say on the subject, is it, mother?

MRS WARREN. [*puzzled, then angry*] Dont you keep on asking me questions like that. [*Violently*] Hold your tongue. [*Vivie works on, losing no time, and saying nothing*] You and your way of life, indeed! What next? [*She looks at Vivie again. No reply*] Your way of life will be what I please, so it will. [*Another pause*] Ive been noticing these airs in you ever since you got that tripos or whatever you call it. If you think I'm going to put up with them youre mistaken; and the sooner you find it out, the better. [*Muttering*] All I have to say on the subject, indeed! [*Again raising her voice angrily*] Do you know who youre speaking to, Miss?

VIVIE. [*looking across at her without raising her head from her book*] No. Who are you? What are you?

MRS WARREN. [*rising breathless*] You young imp!

VIVIE. Everybody knows my reputation, my social standing, and the profession I intend to pursue. I know nothing about you. What is that way of life which you invite me to share with you and Sir George Crofts, pray?

MRS WARREN. Take care. I shall do something I'll be sorry for after, and you too.

VIVIE. [*putting aside her books with cool decision*] Well, let us drop the subject until you are better able to face it. [*Looking critically at her mother*] You want some good walks and a little lawn tennis to set you up. You are shockingly out of condition: you were not able to manage twenty yards uphill today without stopping to pant; and your wrists are mere rolls of fat. Look at mine. [*She holds out her wrists*]

MRS WARREN. [*after looking at her helplessly, begins to whimper*] Vivie—

VIVIE. [*springing up sharply*] Now pray dont begin to cry. Anything but that. I really cannot stand whimpering. I will go out of the room if you do.

MRS WARREN. [*piteously*] Oh, my darling, how can you be so hard on me? Have I no rights over you as your mother?

VIVIE. Are you my mother?

MRS WARREN. [*appalled*] Am I your mother! Oh, Vivie!

VIVIE. Then where are our relatives? my father? our family friends? You claim the rights of a mother: the right to call me fool and child; to speak to me as no woman in authority over me at college dare speak to me; to dictate my way of life; and to force on me the acquaintance of a brute whom anyone can see to be the most vicious sort of London man about town. Before I give myself the trouble to resist such claims, I may as well find out whether they have any real existence.

MRS WARREN. [*distracted, throwing herself on her knees*] Oh no, no. Stop, stop. I am your mother: I swear it. Oh, you cant mean to turn on me—my own child! it's not natural. You believe me, dont you? Say you believe me.

VIVIE. Who was my father?

MRS WARREN. You dont know what youre asking. I cant tell you.

VIVIE. [*determinedly*] Oh yes you can, if you like. I have a right to know; and you know very well that I have that right. You can refuse to tell me, if you please; but if you do, you will see the last of me tomorrow morning.

MRS WARREN. Oh, it's too horrible to hear you talk like that. You wouldnt—you c o u l d n t leave me.

VIVIE. [*ruthlessly*] Yes, without a moment's hesitation, if you trifle with me about this. [*Shivering with disgust*] How can I feel sure that I may not have the contaminated blood of that brutal waster in my veins?

MRS WARREN. No, no. On my oath it's not he, nor any of the rest that you have ever met. I'm certain of that, at least.

Vivie's eyes fasten sternly on her mother as the significance of this flashes on her.

VIVIE. [*slowly*] You are certain of that, a t l e a s t. Ah! You mean that that is all you are certain of. [*Thoughtfully*] I see. [*Mrs Warren buries her face in her hands*] Dont do that, mother: you know you dont feel it a bit. [*Mrs Warren takes down her hands and looks up deplorably at Vivie, who takes out her watch and says*] Well, that is enough for tonight. At what hour would you like breakfast? Is half-past eight too early for you?

MRS WARREN. [*wildly*] My God, what sort of woman are you?

VIVIE. [*coolly*] The sort the world is mostly made of, I should hope. Otherwise I dont understand how it gets its business done. Come [*taking her mother by the wrist, and pulling her up pretty resolutely*]: pull yourself together. Thats right.

MRS WARREN. [*querulously*] Youre very rough with me, Vivie.

VIVIE. Nonsense. What about bed? It's past ten.

MRS WARREN. [*passionately*] Whats the use of my going to bed? Do you think I could sleep?

VIVIE. Why not? I shall.

MRS WARREN. You! youve no heart. [*She suddenly breaks out vehemently in her natural tongue—the dialect of a woman of the people—with all her affectations of maternal authority and conventional manners gone, and an overwhelming inspiration of true conviction and scorn in her*] Oh, I wont bear it: I wont put up with the injustice of it. What right have you to set yourself up above me like this? You boast of what you are to me—to m e, who gave you the chance of being what you are. What chance had I! Shame on you for a bad daughter and a stuck-up prude!

vivie. [*sitting down with a shrug, no longer confident; for her replies, which have sounded sensible and strong to her so far, now begin to ring rather woodenly and even priggishly against the new tone of her mother*] Dont think for a moment I set myself above you in any way. You attacked me with the conventional authority of a mother: I defended myself with the conventional superiority of a respectable woman. Frankly, I am not going to stand any of your nonsense; and when you drop it I shall not expect you to stand any of mine. I shall always respect your right to your own opinions and your own way of life.

mrs warren. My own opinions and my own way of life! Listen to her talking! Do you think I was brought up like you? able to pick and choose my own way of life? Do you think I did what I did because I liked it, or thought it right, or wouldnt rather have gone to college and been a lady if I'd had the chance?

vivie. Everybody has some choice, mother. The poorest girl alive may not be able to choose between being Queen of England or Principal of Newnham; but she can choose between ragpicking and flower-selling, according to her taste. People are always blaming their circumstances for what they are. I dont believe in circumstances. The people who get on in this world are the people who get up and look for the circumstances they want, and, if they cant find them, make them.

mrs warren. Oh, it's easy to talk, very easy, isnt it? Here! would you like to know what my circumstances were?

vivie. Yes: you had better tell me. Wont you sit down?

mrs warren. Oh, I'll sit down: dont you be afraid. [*She plants her chair farther forward with brazen energy, and sits down. Vivie is impressed in spite of herself*] D'you know what your gran'mother was?

vivie. No.

mrs warren. No you dont. I do. She called herself a widow and had a fried-fish shop down by the Mint, and kept herself and four daughters out of it. Two of us were sisters: that was me and Liz; and we were both good-looking and well made. I suppose our father was a well-fed man: mother pretended he was a gentleman; but I dont know. The other two were only half sisters: undersized, ugly, starved looking, hard working, honest poor creatures: Liz and I would have half-murdered them if mother hadnt half-murdered us to keep our hands off them. They were the respectable ones. Well, what did they get by their respectability? I'll tell you. One of them worked in a whitelead factory twelve hours a day for nine shillings a week until she died of lead poisoning. She only expected to get her hands a little paralyzed; but she died. The other was always held up to us as a model because she married a Government laborer in the Deptford victualling yard, and kept his room and the three children neat and tidy on eighteen shillings a week—until he took to drink. That was worth being respectable for, wasnt it?

VIVIE. [*now thoughtfully attentive*] Did you and your sister think so?

MRS WARREN. Liz didnt, I can tell you: she had more spirit. We both.went to a church school—that was part of the ladylike airs we gave ourselves to be superior to the children that knew nothing and went nowhere—and we stayed there until Liz went out one night and never came back. I know the school-mistress thought I'd soon follow her example; for the clergyman was always warning me that Lizzie'd end by jumping off Waterloo Bridge. Poor fool: that was all he knew about it! But I was more afraid of the whitelead factory than I was of the river; and so would you have been in my place. That clergyman got me a situation as a scullery maid in a temperance restaurant where they sent out for anything you liked. Then I was waitress; and then I went to the bar at Waterloo station: fourteen hours a day serving drinks and washing glasses for four shillings a week and my board. That was considered a great promotion for me. Well, one cold, wretched night, when I was so tired I could hardly keep myself awake, who should come up for a half of Scotch but Lizzie, in a long fur cloak, elegant and comfortable, with a lot of sovereigns in her purse.

VIVIE. [*grimly*] My aunt Lizzie!

MRS WARREN. Yes; and a very good aunt to have, too. She's living down at Winchester now, close to the cathedral, one of the most respectable ladies there. Chaperones girls at the county ball, if you please. No river for Liz, thank you! You remind me of Liz a little: she was a first-rate business woman—saved money from the beginning—never let herself look too·like what she was—never lost her head or threw away a chance. When she saw I'd grown up good-looking she said to me across the bar "What are you doing there, you little fool? wearing out your health and your appearance for other people's profit!" Liz was saving money then to take a house for herself in Brussels; and she thought we two could save faster than one. So she lent me some money and gave me a start; and I saved steadily and first paid her back, and then went into business with her as her partner. Why shouldnt I have done it? The house in Brussels was real high class: a much better place for a woman to be in than the factory where Anne Jane got poisoned. None of our girls were ever treated as I was treated in the scullery of that temperance place, or at the Waterloo bar, or at home. Would you have had me stay in them and become a worn out old drudge before I was forty?

VIVIE. [*intensely interested by this time*] No; but why did you choose that business? Saving money and good management will succeed in any business.

MRS WARREN. Yes, saving money. But where can a woman get the money to save in any other business? Could you save out of four shillings a week and keep yourself dressed as well? Not you. Of course, if youre a plain woman and cant earn anything more; or if you have a turn for music, or the stage, or newspaper-writing;

thats different. But neither Liz nor I had any turn for such things: all we had was our appearance and our turn for pleasing men. Do you think we were such fools as to let other people trade in our good looks by employing us as shopgirls, or barmaids, or waitresses, when we could trade in them ourselves and get all the profits instead of starvation wages? Not likely.

VIVIE. You were certainly quite justified—from the business point of view.

MRS WARREN. Yes; or any other point of view. What is any respectable girl brought up to do but to catch some rich man's fancy and get the benefit of his money by marrying him?—as if a marriage ceremony could make any difference in the right or wrong of the thing! Oh! the hypocrisy of the world makes me sick! Liz and I had to work and save and calculate just like other people; elseways we should be as poor as any good-for-nothing drunken waster of a woman that thinks her luck will last for ever. [*With great energy*] I despise such people: theyve no character; and if theres a thing I hate in a woman, it's want of character.

VIVIE. Come now, mother: frankly! Isnt it part of what you call character in a woman that she should greatly dislike such a way of making money?

MRS WARREN. Why, of course. Everybody dislikes having to work and make money; but they have to do it all the same. I'm sure Ive often pitied a poor girl; tired out and in low spirits, having to try to please some man that she doesnt care two straws for— some half-drunken fool that thinks he's making himself agreeable when he's teasing and worrying and disgusting a woman so that hardly any money could pay her for putting up with it. But she has to bear with disagreeables and take the rough with the smooth, just like a nurse in a hospital or anyone else. It's not work that any woman would do for pleasure, goodness knows; though to hear the pious people talk you would suppose it was a bed of roses.

VIVIE. Still, you consider it worth while. It pays.

MRS WARREN. Of course it's worth while to a poor girl, if she can resist temptation and is good-looking and well conducted and sensible. It's far better than any other employment open to her. I always thought that oughtnt to be. It c a n t be right, Vivie, that there shouldnt be better opportunities for women. I stick to that: it's wrong. But it's so, right or wrong; and a girl must make the best of it. But of course it's not worth while for a lady. If you took to it youd be a fool; but I should have been a fool if I'd taken to anything else.

VIVIE. [*more and more deeply moved*] Mother; suppose we were both as poor as you were in those wretched old days, are you quite sure that you wouldnt advise me to try the Waterloo bar, or marry a laborer, or even go into the factory?

MRS WARREN. [*indignantly*] Of course not. What sort of mother do you take me for! How could you keep your self-respect in such starvation and slavery? And whats a woman worth? whats life worth? without self-respect! Why am I independent and able to give my daughter a first-rate education, when other women that had just as good opportunities are in the gutter? Because I always knew how to respect myself and control myself. Why is Liz looked up to in a cathedral town? The same reason. Where would we be now if we'd minded the clergyman's foolishness? Scrubbing floors for one and sixpence a day and nothing to look forward to but the workhouse infirmary. Dont you be led astray by people who dont know the world, my girl. The only way for a woman to provide for herself decently is for her to be good to some man that can afford to be good to her. If she's in his own station of life, let her make him marry her; but if she's far beneath him she cant expect it: why should she? it wouldn't be for her own happiness. Ask any lady in London society that has daughters; and she'll tell you the same, except that I tell you straight and she'll tell you crooked. Thats all the difference.

VIVIE. [*fascinated, gazing at her*] My dear mother; you are a wonderful woman: you are stronger than all England. And are you really and truly not one wee bit doubtful—or—or—ashamed?

MRS WARREN. Well, of course, dearie, it's only good manners to be ashamed of it; it's expected from a woman. Women have to pretend to feel a great deal that they dont feel. Liz used to be angry with me for plumping out the truth about it. She used to say that when every woman could learn enough from what was going on in the world before her eyes, there was no need to talk about it to her. But then Liz was such a perfect lady! She had the true instinct of it; while I was always a bit of a vulgarian. I used to be so pleased when you sent me your photos to see that you were growing up like Liz: youve just her ladylike, determined way. But I cant stand saying one thing when everyone knows I mean another. Whats the use in such hypocrisy? If people arrange the world that way for women, theres no good pretending its arranged the other way. No: I never was a bit ashamed really. I consider I had a right to be proud of how we managed everything so respectably, and never had a word against us, and how the girls were so well taken care of. Some of them did very well: one of them married an ambassador. But of course now I darent talk about such things: whatever would they think of us! [*She yawns*] Oh dear! I do believe I'm getting sleepy after all. [*She stretches herself lazily, thoroughly relieved by her explosion, and placidly ready for her night's rest*]

VIVIE. I believe it is I who will not be able to sleep now. [*She goes to the dresser and lights the candle. Then she extinguishes the lamp, darkening the room a good deal*] Better let in some fresh air before locking up. [*She opens the cottage door, and finds that it is broad moonlight*] What a beautiful night! Look! [*She draws aside the curtains of the window. The landscape is seen bathed in the radiance of the harvest moon rising over Blackdown*]

MRS WARREN. [*with a perfunctory glance at the scene*] Yes, dear;

but take care you dont catch your death of cold from the night air.

VIVIE. [*contemptuously*] Nonsense.

MRS WARREN. [*querulously*] Oh yes: everything I say is nonsense, according to you.

VIVIE. [*turning to her quickly*] No: really that is not so, mother. You have got completely the better of me tonight, though I intended it to be the other way. Let us be good friends now.

MRS WARREN. [*shaking her head a little ruefully*] So it has been the other way. But I suppose I must give in to it. I always got the worst of it from Liz; and now I suppose it'll be the same with you.

VIVIE. Well, never mind. Come: goodnight, dear old mother [*She takes her mother in her arms*]

MRS WARREN. [*fondly*] I brought you up well, didnt I, dearie?

VIVIE. You did.

MRS WARREN. And youll be good to your poor old mother for it, wont you?

VIVIE. I will, dear. [*Kissing her*] Goodnight.

MRS WARREN. [*with unction*] Blessings on my own dearie darling! a mother's blessing!

She embraces her daughter protectingly, instinctively looking upward for divine sanction.

Act III

In the Rectory garden next morning, with the sun shining from a cloudless sky. The garden wall has a five-barred wooden gate, wide enough to admit a carriage, in the middle. Beside the gate hangs a bell on a coiled spring, communicating with a pull outside. The carriage drive comes down the middle of the garden and then swerves to its left, where it ends in a little gravelled circus opposite the Rectory porch. Beyond the gate is seen the dusty high road, parallel with the wall, bounded on the farther side by a strip of turf and an unfenced pine wood. On the lawn, between the house and the drive, is a clipped yew tree, with a garden bench in its shade. On the opposite side the garden is shut in by a box hedge; and there is a sundial on the turf, with an iron chair near it. A little path leads off through the box hedge, behind the sundial.

Frank, seated on the chair near the sundial, on which he has placed the morning papers, is reading The Standard. His father comes from the house, red-eyed and shivery, and meets Frank's eye with misgiving.

FRANK. [*looking at his watch*] Half-past eleven. Nice hour for a rector to come down to breakfast!

REV. S. Dont mock, Frank: dont mock. I am a little—er— [*Shivering*]—

FRANK. Off color?

REV. S. [*repudiating the expression*] No, sir: u n w e l l this morning. Wheres your mother?

FRANK. Dont be alarmed: she's not here. Gone to town by the
11.13 with Bessie. She left several messages for you. Do you feel
equal to receiving them now, or shall I wait til youve breakfasted?

REV. S. I h a v e breakfasted, sir. I am surprised at your mother
going to town when we have people staying with us. Theyll think
it very strange.

FRANK. Possibly she has considered that. At all events, if Crofts is
going to stay here, and you are going to sit up every night with
him until four, recalling the incidents of your fiery youth, it is
clearly my mother's duty, as a prudent housekeeper, to go up to
the stores and order a barrel of whisky and a few hundred
siphons.

REV. S. I did not observe that Sir George drank excessively.

FRANK. You were not in a condition to, gov'nor.

REV. S. Do you mean to say that *I*—?

FRANK. [*calmly*] I never saw a beneficed clergyman less sober. The
anecdotes you told about your past career were so awful that I
really dont think Praed would have passed the night under your
roof if it hadnt been for the way my mother and he took to one
another.

REV. S. Nonsense, sir. I am Sir George Croft's host. I must talk to
him about something; and he has only one subject. Where is Mr
Praed now?

FRANK. He is driving my mother and Bessie to the station.

REV. S. Is Crofts up yet?

FRANK. Oh, long ago. He hasnt turned a hair: he's in much better
practice than you. Has kept it up ever since, probably. He's
taken himself off somewhere to smoke.

*Frank resumes his paper. The parson turns disconsolately towards
the gate; then comes back irresolutely.*

REV. S. Er—Frank.

FRANK. Yes.

REV. S. Do you think the Warrens will expect to be asked here after
yesterday afternoon?

FRANK. Theyve been asked already.

REV. S. [*appalled*] What!!!

FRANK. Crofts informed us at breakfast that you told him to bring
Mrs Warren and Vivie over here today, and to invite them to
make this house their home. My mother then found she must go
to town by the 11.13 train.

REV. S. [*with despairing vehemence*] I never gave any such invitation. I never thought of such a thing.

FRANK. [*compassionately*] How do you know, gov'nor, what you
said and thought last night?

PRAED. [*coming in through the hedge*] Good morning.

REV. S. Good morning. I must apologize for not having met you at
breakfast. I have a touch of—of—

FRANK. Clergyman's sore throat, Praed. Fortunately not chronic.

PRAED. [*changing the subject*] Well, I must say your house is in a
charming spot here. Really most charming.

REV. S. Yes: it is indeed. Frank will take you for a walk, Mr Praed, if you like. I'll ask you to excuse me: I must take the opportunity to write my sermon while Mrs Gardner is away and you are all amusing yourselves. You wont mind, will you?

PRAED. Certainly not. Dont stand on the slightest ceremony with me.

REV. S. Thank you. I'll—er—er—[*He stammers his way to the porch and vanishes into the house*]

PRAED. Curious thing it must be writing a sermon every week.

FRANK. Ever so curious, if he did it. He buys em. He's gone for some soda water.

PRAED. My dear boy: I wish you would be more respectful to your father. You know you can be so nice when you like.

FRANK. My dear Praddy: you forget that I have to live with the governor. When two people live together—it doesnt matter whether theyre father and son or husband and wife or brother and sister—they cant keep up the polite humbug thats so easy for ten minutes on an afternoon call. Now the governor, who unites to many admirable domestic qualities the irresoluteness of a sheep and the pompousness and aggressiveness of a jackass—

PRAED. No, pray, pray, my dear Frank, remember! He is your father.

FRANK. I give him due credit for that. [*Rising and flinging down his paper*] But just imagine his telling Crofts to bring the Warrens over here! He must have been ever so drunk. You know, my dear Praddy, my mother wouldnt stand Mrs Warren for a moment. Vivie mustnt come here until she's gone back to town.

PRAED. But your mother doesnt know anything about Mrs Warren, does she? [*He picks up the paper and sits down to read it*]

FRANK. I don't know. Her journey to town looks as if she did. Not that my mother would mind in the ordinary way: she has stuck like a brick to lots of women who had got into trouble. But they were all nice women. Thats what makes the real difference. Mrs Warren, no doubt, has her merits; but she's ever so rowdy; and my mother simply wouldnt put up with her. So—hallo! [*This exclamation is provoked by the reappearance of the clergyman, who comes out of the house in haste and dismay*]

REV. S. Frank: Mrs Warren and her daughter are coming across the heath with Crofts: I saw them from the study windows. What am I to say about your mother?

FRANK. Stick on your hat and go out and say how delighted you are to see them; and that Frank's in the garden; and that mother and Bessie have been called to the bedside of a sick relative, and were ever so sorry they couldnt stop; and that you hope Mrs Warren slept well; and—and—say any blessed thing except the truth, and leave the rest to Providence.

REV. S. But how are we to get rid of them afterwards?

FRANK. Theres no time to think of that now. Here! [*He bounds into the house*]

REV. S. He's so impetuous. I dont know what to do with him, Mr Praed.

FRANK. [*returning with clerical felt hat, which he claps on his father's head*] Now: off with you. [*Rushing him through the gate*] Praed and I'll wait here, to give the thing an unpremeditated air. [*The clergyman, dazzed but obedient, hurries off*]

FRANK. We must get the old girl back to town somehow, Praed. Come! Honestly, dear Praddy, do you like seeing them together?

PRAED. Oh, why not?

FRANK. [*his teeth on edge*] Dont it make your flesh creep ever so little? that wicked old devil, up to every villainy under the sun, I'll swear, and Vivie—ugh!

PRAED. Hush, pray. Theyre coming.

The clergyman and Crofts are seen coming along the road, followed by Mrs Warren and Vivie walking affectionately together.

FRANK. Look: she actually has her arm round the old woman's waist. It's her right arm: she began it. She's gone sentimental, by God! Ugh! ugh! Now do you feel the creeps? [*The clergyman opens the gate; and Mrs Warren and Vivie pass him and stand in the middle of the garden looking at the house. Frank, in an ecstasy of dissimulation, turns gaily to Mrs Warren, exclaiming*] Ever so delighted to see you, Mrs Warren. This quiet old rectory garden becomes you perfectly.

MRS WARREN. Well, I never! Did you hear that, George? He says I look well in a quiet old rectory garden.

REV. S. [*still holding the gate for Crofts, who loafs through it, heavily bored*] You look well everywhere, Mrs Warren.

FRANK. Bravo, gov'nor! Now look here: lets have a treat before lunch. First lets see the church. Everyone has to do that. It's a regular old thirteenth century church, you know: the gov'nor's ever so fond of it, because he got up a restoration fund and had it completely rebuilt six years ago. Praed will be able to shew its points.

PRAED. [*rising*] Certainly, if the restoration has left any to shew.

REV. S. [*mooning hospitably at them*] I shall be pleased, I'm sure, if Sir George and Mrs Warren really care about it.

MRS WARREN. Oh, come along and get it over.

CROFTS. [*turning back towards the gate*] Ive no objection.

REV. S. Not that way. We go through the fields, if you dont mind. Round here [*He leads the way by the little path through the box hedge*]

CROFTS. Oh, all right. [*He goes with the parson*]

Praed follows with Mrs Warren. Vivie does not stir: she watches them until they have gone, with all the lines of purpose in her face marking it strongly.

FRANK. Aint you coming?

VIVIE. No. I want to give you a warning, Frank. You were making fun of my mother just now when you said that about the rectory garden. That is barred in future. Please treat my mother with as much respect as you treat your own.

FRANK. My dear Viv: she wouldnt appreciate it: the two cases require different treatment. But what on earth has happened to you? Last night we were perfectly agreed as to your mother and her set. This morning I find you attitudinizing sentimentally with your arm round your parent's waist.

VIVIE. [*flushing*] Attitudinizing!

FRANK. That was how it struck me. First time I ever saw you do a second-rate thing.

VIVIE. [*controlling herself*] Yes, Frank: there has been a change; but I dont think it a change for the worse. Yesterday I was a little prig.

FRANK. And today?

VIVIE. [*wincing; then looking at him steadily*] Today I know my mother better than you do.

FRANK. Heaven forbid!

VIVIE. What do you mean?

FRANK. Viv: theres a freemasonry among thoroughly immoral people that you know nothing of. Youve too much character. T h a t s the bond between your mother and me: thats why I know her better than youll ever know her.

VIVIE. You are wrong: you know nothing about her. If you knew the circumstances against which my mother had to struggle—

FRANK. [*adroitly finishing the sentence for her*] I should know why she is what she is, shouldnt I? What difference would that make? Circumstances or no circumstances, Viv, you wont be able to stand your mother.

VIVIE. [*very angrily*] Why not?

FRANK. Because she's an old wretch, Viv. If you ever put your arm round her waist in my presence again, I'll shoot myself there and then as a protest against an exhibition which revolts me.

VIVIE. Must I choose between dropping your acquaintance and dropping my mother's?

FRANK. [*gracefully*] That would put the old lady at ever such a disadvantage. No, Viv: your infatuated little boy will have to stick to you in any case. But he's all the more anxious that you shouldnt make mistakes. It's no use, Viv: your mother's impossible. She may be a good sort; but she's a bad lot, a very bad lot.

VIVIE. [*hotly*] Frank—! [*He stands his ground. She turns away and sits down on the bench under the yew tree, struggling to recover her self-command. Then she says*] Is she to be deserted by all the world because she's what you call a bad lot? Has she no right to live?

FRANK. No fear of that, Viv: s h e wont ever be deserted. [*He sits on the bench beside her*]

VIVIE. But I am to desert her, I suppose.

FRANK. [*babyishly, lulling her and making love to her with his voice*] Mustnt go live with her. Little family group of mother and daughter wouldnt be a success. Spoil our little group.

VIVIE. [*falling under the spell*] What little group?

FRANK. The babes in the wood: Vivie and little Frank. [*He nestles against her like a weary child*] Lets go and get covered up with leaves.

VIVIE. [*rhythmically, rocking him like a nurse*] Fast asleep, hand in hand, under the trees.

FRANK. The wise little girl with her silly little boy.

VIVIE. The dear little boy with his dowdy little girl.

FRANK. Ever so peaceful, and relieved from the imbecility of the little boy's father and the questionableness of the little girl's—

VIVIE. [*smothering the word against her breast*] Sh-sh-sh-sh! little girl wants to forget all about her mother. [*They are silent for some moments, rocking one another. Then Vivie wakes up with a shock, exclaiming*] What a pair of fools we are! Come: sit up. gracious! your hair. [*She smoothes it*] I wonder do all grown up people play in that childish way when nobody is looking. I never did it when I was a child.

FRANK. Neither did I. You are my first playmate. [*He catches her hand to kiss it, but checks himself to look round first. Very unexpectedly, he sees Crofts emerging from the box hedge*] Oh damn!

VIVIE. Why damn, dear?

FRANK. [*whispering*] Sh! Here's this brute Crofts. [*He sits farther away from her with an unconcerned air*]

CROFTS. Could I have a few words with you, Miss Vivie?

VIVIE. Certainly.

CROFTS. [*to Frank*] Youll excuse me, Gardner. Theyre waiting for you in the church, if you don't mind.

FRANK. [*rising*] Anything to oblige you, Crofts—except church. If you should happen to want me, Vivvums, ring the gate bell. [*He goes into the house with unruffled suavity*]

CROFTS. [*watching him with a crafty air as he disappears, and speaking to Vivie with an assumption of being on privileged terms with her*] Pleasant young fellow that, Miss Vivie. Pity he has no money, isnt it?

VIVIE. Do you think so?

CROFTS. Well, whats he to do? No profession. No property. Whats he good for?

VIVIE. I realize his disadvantages, Sir George.

CROFTS. [*a little taken aback at being so precisely interpreted*] Oh, it's not that. But while we're in this world we're in it; and money's money. [*Vivie does not answer*] Nice day, isnt it?

VIVIE. [*with scarcely veiled contempt for this effort at conversation*] Very.

CROFTS. [*with brutal good humor, as if he liked her pluck*] Well, thats not what I came to say. [*Sitting down beside her*] Now listen, Miss Vivie. I'm quite aware that I'm not a young lady's man.

VIVIE. Indeed, Sir George?

CROFTS. No; and to tell you the honest truth I dont want to be either. But when I say a thing I mean it; when I feel a sentiment I feel it in earnest; and what I value I pay hard money for. Thats the sort of man I am.

VIVIE. It does you great credit, I'm sure.

CROFTS. Oh, I dont mean to praise myself. I have my faults, Heaven knows: no man is more sensible of that than I am. I know I'm not perfect: thats one of the disadvantages of being a middle-aged man; for I'm not a young man, and I know it. But my code is a simple one, and, I think, a good one. Honor between man and man; fidelity between man and woman; and no cant about this religion or that religion, but an honest belief that things are making for good on the whole.

VIVIE. [with biting irony] "A power, not ourselves, that makes for righteousness," eh?

CROFTS. [taking her seriously] Oh certainly. Not ourselves, of course. You understand what I mean. Well, now as to practical matters. You may have an idea that Ive flung my money about; but I havnt: I'm richer today than when I first came into the property. Ive used my knowledge of the world to invest my money in ways that other men have overlooked; and whatever else I may be, I'm a safe man from the money point of view.

VIVIE. It's very kind of you to tell me all this.

CROFTS. Oh well, come, Miss Vivie: you neednt pretend you dont see what I'm driving at. I want to settle down with a Lady Crofts. I suppose you think me very blunt, eh?

VIVIE. Not at all: I am much obliged to you for being so definite and business-like. I quite appreciate the offer: the money, the position, L a d y C r o f t s, and so on. But I think I will say no, if you don't mind. I'd rather not. [She rises, and strolls across to the sundial to get out of his immediate neighborhood]

CROFTS. [not at all discouraged, and taking advantage of the additional room left him on the seat to spread himself comfortably, as if a few preliminary refusals were part of the inevitable routine of courtship] I'm in no hurry. It was only just to let you know in case young Gardner should try to trap you. Leave the question open.

VIVIE. [sharply] My no is final. I wont go back from it.

Crofts is not impressed. He grins; leans forward with his elbows on his knees to prod with his stick at some unfortunate insect in the grass; and looks cunningly at her. She turns away impatiently.

CROFTS. I'm a good deal older than you. Twenty-five years; quarter of a century. I shant live for ever; and I'll take care that you shall be well off when I'm gone.

VIVIE. I am proof against even that inducement, Sir George. Dont you think youd better take your answer? There is not the slightest chance of my altering it.

CROFTS. [rising after a final slash at a daisy, and coming nearer to her] Well, no matter. I could tell you some things that would change your mind fast enough; but I wont, because I'd rather win you by honest affection. I was a good friend to your mother: ask her whether I wasnt. She'd never have made the money that paid for your education if it hadnt been for my advice and help, not to mention the money I advanced her. There are not many men would have stood by her as I have. I put not less than

£40,000 into it, from first to last.

VIVIE. [*staring at him*] Do you mean to say you were my mother's business partner?

CROFTS. Yes. Now just think of all the trouble and the explanations it would save if we were to keep the whole thing in the family, so to speak. Ask your mother whether she'd like to have to explain all her affairs to a perfect stranger.

VIVIE. I see no difficulty, since I understand that the business is wound up, and the money invested.

CROFTS. [*stopping short, amazed*] Wound up! Wind up a business thats paying 35 per cent in the worst years! Not likely. Who told you that?

VIVIE. [*her color quite gone*] Do you mean that it is still—? [*She stops abruptly, and puts her hand on the sundial to support herself. Then she gets quickly to the iron chair and sits down*] What business are you talking about?

CROFTS. Well, the fact is it's not what would be considered exactly a high-class business in my set—the county set, you know—our set it will be if you think better of my offer. Not that theres any mystery about it: dont think that. Of course you know by your mother's being in it that it's perfectly straight and honest. Ive known her for many years; and I can say of her that she'd cut off her hands sooner than touch anything that was not what it ought to be. I'll tell you all about it if you like. I dont know whether youve found in travelling how hard it is to find a really comfortable private hotel.

VIVIE. [*sickened, averting her face*] Yes: go on.

CROFTS. Well, thats all it is. Your mother has a genius for managing such things. We've got two in Brussels, one in Ostend, one in Vienna, and two in Budapest. Of course there are others besides ourselves in it; but we hold most of the capital; and your mother's indispensable as managing director. Youve noticed, I daresay, that she travels a good deal. But you see you cant mention such things in society. Once let out the word hotel and everybody says you keep a public-house. You wouldnt like people to say that of your mother, would you? Thats why we're so reserved about it. By the way, youll keep it to yourself, wont you? Since it's been a secret so long, it had better remain so.

VIVIE. And this is the business you invite me to join you in?

CROFTS. Oh, no. My wife shant be troubled with business. Youll not be in it more than youve always been.

VIVIE. *I* always been! What do you mean?

CROFTS. Only that youve always lived on it. It paid for your education and the dress you have on your back. Dont turn up your nose at business, Miss Vivie: where would your Newnhams and Girtons be without it?

VIVIE. [*rising, almost beside herself*] Take care. I know what this business is.

CROFTS. [*staring, with a suppressed oath*] Who told you?

VIVIE. Your partner. My mother.

CROFTS. [*black with rage*] The old—
VIVIE. Just so.

He swallows the epithet and stands for a moment swearing and raging foully to himself. But he knows that his cue is to be sympathetic. He takes refuge in generous indignation.

CROFTS. She ought to have had more consideration for you. I'd never have told you.

VIVIE. I think you would probably have told me when we were married; it would have been a convenient weapon to break me in with.

CROFTS. [*quite sincerely*] I never intended that. On my word as a gentleman I didnt.

Vivie wonders at him. Her sense of the irony of his protest cools and braces her. She replies with contemptuous self-possession.

VIVIE. It does not matter. I suppose you understand that when we leave here today our acquaintance ceases.

CROFTS. Why? Is it for helping your mother?

VIVIE. My mother was a very poor woman who had no reasonable choice but to do as she did. You were a rich gentleman; and you did the same for the sake of 35 per cent. You are a pretty common sort of scoundrel, I think. That is my opinion of you.

CROFTS. [*after a stare: not at all displeased, and much more at ease on these frank terms than on their former ceremonious ones*] Ha! ha! ha! ha! Go it, little missie, go it: it doesnt hurt me and it amuses you. Why the devil shouldnt I invest my money that way? I take the interest on my capital like other people: I hope you dont think I dirty my own hands with the work. Come! you wouldnt refuse the acquaintance of my mother's cousin the Duke of Belgravia because some of the rents he gets are earned in queer ways. You wouldnt cut the Archbishop of Canterbury, I suppose, because the Ecclesiastical Commissioners have a few publicans and sinners among their tenants. Do you remember your Crofts scholarship at Newnham? Well, that was founded by my brother the M.P.[1] He gets his 22 per cent out of a factory with 600 girls in it, and not one of them getting wages enough to live on. How d'ye suppose they manage when they have no family to fall back on? Ask your mother. And do you expect me to turn my back on 35 per cent when all the rest are pocketing what they can, like sensible men? No such fool! If youre going to pick and choose your acquaintances on moral principles, youd better clear out of this country, unless you want to cut yourself out of all decent society.

VIVIE. [*conscience stricken*] You might go on to point out that I myself never asked where the money I spent came from. I believe I am just as bad as you.

CROFTS. [*greatly reassured*] Of course you are; and a very good thing too! What harm does it do after all? [*Rallying her jocularly*] So you dont think me such a scoundrel now you come to think it over. Eh?

---

1. Member of Parliament.

VIVIE. I have shared profits with you; and I admitted you just now to the familiarity of knowing what I think of you.

CROFTS. [*with serious friendliness*] To be sure you did. You wont find me a bad sort: I dont go in for being superfine intellectually; but Ive plenty of honest human feeling; and the old Crofts breed comes out in a sort of instinctive hatred of anything low, in which I'm sure youll sympathize with me. Believe me, Miss Vivie, the world isnt such a bad place as the croakers make out. As long as you dont fly openly in the face of society, society doesnt ask any inconvenient questions; and it makes precious short work of the cads who do. There are no secrets better kept than the secrets everybody guesses. In the class of people I can introduce you to, no lady or gentleman would so far forget themselves as to discuss my business affairs or your mother's. No man can offer you a safer position.

VIVIE. [*studying him curiously*] I suppose you really think youre getting on famously with me.

CROFTS. Well, I hope I may flatter myself that you think better of me than you did at first.

VIVIE. [*quietly*] I hardly find you worth thinking about at all now. When I think of the society that tolerates you, and the laws that protect you! when I think of how helpless nine out of ten young girls would be in the hands of you and my mother! the unmentionable woman and her capitalist bully—

CROFTS. [*livid*] Damn you!

VIVIE. You need not. I feel among the damned already.

She raises the latch of the gate to open it and go out. He follows her and puts his hand heavily on the top bar to prevent its opening.

CROFTS. [*panting with fury*] Do you think I'll put up with this from you, you young devil?

VIVIE. [*unmoved*] Be quiet. Some one will answer the bell. [*Without flinching a step she strikes the bell with the back of her hand. It clangs harshly; and he starts back involuntarily. Almost immediately Frank appears at the porch with his rifle*]

FRANK. [*with cheerful politeness*] Will you have the rifle, Viv; or shall I operate?

VIVIE. Frank: have you been listening?

FRANK. [*coming down into the garden*] Only for the bell, I assure you; so that you shouldn't have to wait. I think I shewed great insight into your character Crofts.

CROFTS. For two pins I'd take that gun from you and break it across your head.

FRANK. [*stalking him cautiously*] Pray dont. I'm ever so careless in handling firearms. Sure to be a fatal accident, with a reprimand from the coroner's jury for my negligence.

VIVIE. Put the rifle away, Frank: its quite unnecessary.

FRANK. Quite right, Viv. Much more sportsmanlike to catch him in a trap. [*Crofts, understanding the insult, makes a threatening movement*] Crofts: there are fifteen cartridges in the magazine here; and I am a dead shot at the present distance and at an object of your size.

CROFTS. Oh, you neednt be afraid. I'm not going to touch you.

FRANK. Ever so magnanimous of you under the circumstances! Thank you!

CROFTS. I'll tell you this before I go. It may interest you, since youre so fond of one another. Allow me, Mister Frank, to introduce you to your half-sister, the eldest daughter of the Reverend Samuel Gardner. Miss Vivie: your half-brother. Good morning. [*He goes out through the gate and along the road*]

FRANK. [*after a pause of stupefaction, raising the rifle*] Youll testify before the coroner that it's an accident, Viv. [*He takes aim at the retreating figure of Crofts. Vivie seizes the muzzle and pulls it round against her breast*]

VIVIE. Fire now. You may.

FRANK. [*dropping his end of the rifle hastily*] Stop! take care. [*She lets go. It falls on the turf*] Oh, youve given your little boy such a turn. Suppose it had gone off! ugh! [*He sinks on the garden seat, overcome*]

VIVIE. Suppose it had: do you think it would not have been a relief to have some sharp physical pain tearing through me?

FRANK. [*coaxingly*] Take it ever so easy, dear Viv. Remember; even if the rifle scared that fellow into telling the truth for the first time in his life, that only makes us the babes in the wood in earnest. [*He holds out his arms to her*] Come and be covered up with leaves again.

VIVIE. [*with a cry of disgust*] Ah, not that, not that. You make all my flesh creep.

FRANK. Why, whats the matter?

VIVIE. Goodbye. [*She makes for the gate*]

FRANK. [*jumping up*] Hallo! Stop! Viv! Viv! [*She turns in the gateway*] Where are you going to? Where shall we find you?

VIVIE. At Honoria Fraser's chambers, 67 Chancery Lane, for the rest of my life. [*She goes off quickly in the opposite direction to that taken by Crofts*]

FRANK. But I say—wait—dash it! [*He runs after her*]

Act IV

Honoria Fraser's chambers in Chancery Lane. An office at the top of New Stone Buildings, with a plate-glass window, distempered walls, electric light, and a patent stove. Saturday afternoon. The chimneys of Lincoln's Inn and the western sky beyond are seen through the window. There is a double writing table in the middle of the room, with a cigar box, ash pans, and a portable electric reading lamp almost snowed up in heaps of papers and books. This table has knee holes and chairs right and left and is very untidy. The clerk's desk, closed and tidy, with its high stool, is against the wall, near a door communicating with the inner rooms. In the opposite wall is the door leading to the public corridor. Its upper panel is of opaque glass, lettered in black on the outside, FRASER AND WARREN. A baize screen hides the corner between this door and the window.

Frank, in a fashionable light-colored coaching suit, with his stick, gloves, and white hat in his hands, is pacing up and down the office. Somebody tries the door with a key.

FRANK. [*calling*] Come in. It's not locked.

Vivie comes in, in her hat and jacket. She stops and stares at him.

VIVIE. [*sternly*] What are you doing here?

FRANK. Waiting to see you. Ive been here for hours. Is this the way you attend to your business? [*He puts his hat and stick on the table, and perches himself with a vault on the clerk's stool, looking at her with every appearance of being in a specially restless, teasing flippant mood*]

VIVIE. Ive been away exactly twenty minutes for a cup of tea. [*She takes off her hat and jacket and hangs them up behind the screen*] How did you get in?

FRANK. The staff had not left when I arrived. He's gone to play cricket on Primrose Hill. Why dont you employ a woman, and give your sex a chance?

VIVIE. What have you come for?

FRANK. [*springing off the stool and coming close to her*] Viv: lets go and enjoy the Saturday half-holiday somewhere, like the staff. What do you say to Richmond, and then a music hall, and a jolly supper?

VIVIE. Cant afford it. I shall put in another six hours work before I go to bed.

FRANK. Cant afford it, cant we? Aha! Look here. [*He takes out a handful of sovereigns and makes them chink*] Gold, Viv: gold!

VIVIE. Where did you get it?

FRANK. Gambling, Viv: gambling. Poker.

VIVIE. Pah! It's meaner than stealing it. No: I'm not coming. [*She sits down to work at the table, with her back to the glass door, and begins turning over the papers*]

FRANK. [*remonstrating piteously*] But, my dear Viv, I want to talk to you ever so seriously.

VIVIE. Very well: sit down in Honoria's chair and talk here. I like ten minutes chat after tea. [*He murmurs*] No use groaning: I'm inexorable. [*He takes the opposite seat disconsolately*] Pass that cigar box, will you?

FRANK. [*pushing the cigar box across*] Nasty womanly habit. Nice men dont do it any longer.

VIVIE. Yes: they object to the smell in the office; and weve had to take to cigarets. See! [*She opens the box and takes out a cigaret, which she lights. She offers him one; but he shakes his head with a wry face. She settles herself comfortably in her chair, smoking*] Go ahead.

FRANK. Well, I want to know what youve done—what arrangements youve made.

VIVIE. Everything was settled twenty minutes after I arrived here. Honoria has found the business too much for her this year; and she was on the point of sending for me and proposing a partner-

ship when I walked in and told her I hadnt a farthing in the
world. So I installed myself and packed her off for a fortnight's
holiday. What happened at Haslemere when I left?

FRANK. Nothing at all. I said youd gone to town on particular business.

VIVIE. Well?

FRANK. Well, either they were too flabbergasted to say anything, or
else Crofts had prepared your mother. Anyhow, she didnt say
anything; and Crofts didnt say anything; and Praddy only stared.
After tea they got up and went; and Ive not seen them since.

VIVIE. [*nodding placidly with one eye on a wreath of smoke*]
Thats all right.

FRANK. [*looking round disparagingly*] Do you intend to stick in
this confounded place?

VIVIE. [*blowing the wreath decisively away, and sitting straight
up*] Yes. These two days have given me back all my strength and
self-possession. I will never take a holiday again as long as I live.

FRANK. [*with a very wry face*] Mps! You look quite happy. And as
hard as nails.

VIVIE. [*grimly*] Well for me that I am!

FRANK. [*rising*] Look here, Viv: we must have an explanation.
We parted the other day under a complete misunderstanding.
[*He sits on the table, close to her*]

VIVIE. [*putting away the cigaret*] Well: clear it up.

FRANK. You remember what Crofts said?

VIVIE. Yes.

FRANK. That revelation was supposed to bring about a complete
change in the nature of our feeling for one another. It placed us
on the footing of brother and sister.

VIVIE. Yes.

FRANK. Have you ever had a brother?

VIVIE. No.

FRANK. Then you dont know what being brother and sister feels
like? Now I have lots of sisters; and the fraternal feeling is quite
familiar to me. I assure you my feeling for you is not the least in
the world like it. The girls will go their way; I will go mine; and
we shant care if we never see one another again. Thats brother
and sister. But as to you, I cant be easy if I have to pass a week
without seeing you. Thats not brother and sister. It's exactly
what I felt an hour before Crofts made his revelation. In short,
dear Viv, it's love's young dream.

VIVIE. [*bitingly*] The same feeling, Frank, that brought your
father to my mother's feet. Is that it?

FRANK. [*so revolted that he slips off the table for a moment*] I
very strongly object, Viv, to have my feelings compared to any
which the Reverend Samuel is capable of harboring; and I object
still more to a comparison of you to your mother. [*Resuming
his perch*] Besides, I dont believe the story. I have taxed my
father with it, and obtained from him what I consider tanta-
mount to a denial.

VIVIE. What did he say?

FRANK. He said he was sure there must be some mistake.

VIVIE. Do you believe him?

FRANK. I am prepared to take his word as against Crofts'.

VIVIE. Does it make any difference? I mean in your imagination or conscience; for of course it makes no real difference.

FRANK. [*shaking his head*] None whatever to m e.

VIVIE. Nor to me.

FRANK. [*staring*] But this is ever so surprising! [*He goes back to his chair*] I thought our whole relations were altered in your imagination and conscience, as you put it, the moment those words were out of the brute's muzzle.

VIVIE. No: it was not that. I didnt believe him. I only wish I could.

FRANK. Eh?

VIVIE. I think brother and sister would be a very suitable relation for us.

FRANK. You really mean that?

VIVIE. Yes. It's the only relation I care for, even if we could afford any other. I mean that.

FRANK. [*raising his eyebrows like one on whom a new light has dawned, and rising with quite an effusion of chivalrous senti-ment*] My dear Viv: why didnt you say so before? I am ever so sorry for persecuting you. I understand, of course.

VIVIE. [*puzzled*] Understand what?

FRANK. Oh, I'm not a fool in the ordinary sense: only in the Scriptural sense of doing all the things the wise man declared to be folly, after trying them himself on the most extensive scale. I see I am no longer Vivvum's little boy. Dont be alarmed: I shall never call you Vivvums again—at least unless you get tired of your new little boy, whoever he may be.

VIVIE. My new little boy!

FRANK. [*with conviction*] Must be a new little boy. Always happens that way. No other way, in fact.

VIVIE. None that you know of, fortunately for you.

Someone knocks at the door.

FRANK. My curse upon yon caller, whoe'er he be!

VIVIE. It's Praed. He's going to Italy and wants to say goodbye. I asked him to call this afternoon. Go and let him in.

FRANK. We can continue our conversation after his departure for Italy. I'll stay him out. [*He goes to the door and opens it*] How are you, Praddy? Delighted to see you. Come in.

Praed, dressed for travelling, comes in, in high spirits.

PRAED. How do you do, Miss Warren? [*She presses his hand cordially, though a certain sentimentality in his high spirits jars on her*] I start in an hour from Holborn Viaduct. I wish I could persuade you to try Italy.

VIVIE. What for?

PRAED. Why, to saturate yourself with beauty and romance, of course.

Vivie, with a shudder, turns her chair to the table, as if the work

waiting for her were a support to her. Praed sits opposite to her.
Frank places a chair near Vivie, and drops lazily and carelessly into
it, talking at her over his shoulder.

FRANK. No use, Praddy. Viv is a little Philistine. She is indifferent
to my romance, and insensible to my beauty.

VIVIE. Mr Praed: once for all, there is no beauty and no romance in
life for me. Life is what it is; and I am prepared to take it as it is.

PRAED. [*enthusiastically*] You will not say that if you come with
me to Verona and on to Venice. You will cry with delight at
living in such a beautiful world.

FRANK. This is most eloquent, Praddy. Keep it up.

PRAED. Oh, I assure you *I* have cried—I shall cry again, I hope—at
fifty! At your age, Miss Warren, you would not need to go so far
as Verona. Your spirits would absolutely fly up at the mere sight
of Ostend. You would be charmed with the gaiety, the vivacity,
the happy air of Brussels.

VIVIE. [*springing up with an exclamation of loathing*] Agh!

PRAED. [*rising*] Whats the matter?

FRANK. [*rising*] Hallo, Viv!

VIVIE. [*to Praed, with deep reproach*] Can you find no better
example of your beauty and romance than Brussels to talk to me
about?

PRAED. [*puzzled*] Of course it's very different from Verona. I
dont suggest for a moment that—

VIVIE. [*bitterly*] Probably the beauty and romance come to much
the same in both places.

PRAED. [*completely sobered and much concerned*] My dear Miss
Warren: I—[*looking inquiringly at Frank*] Is anything the
matter?

FRANK. She thinks your enthusiasm frivolous, Praddy. She's had
ever such a serious call.

VIVIE. [*sharply*] Hold your tongue, Frank. Dont be silly.

FRANK. [*sitting down*] Do you call this good manners, Praed?

PRAED. [*anxious and considerate*] Shall I take him away, Miss
Warren? I feel sure we have disturbed you at your work.

VIVIE. Sit down: I'm not ready to go back to work yet. [*Praed
sits*] You both think I have an attack of nerves. Not a bit of it.
But there are two subjects I want dropped, if you dont mind.
One of them [*to Frank*] is love's young dream in any shape or
form: the other [*to Praed*] is the romance and beauty of life,
especially Ostend and the gaiety of Brussels. You are welcome to
any illusions you may have left on these subjects: I have none. If
we three are to remain friends, I must be treated as a woman of
business, permanently single [*to Frank*] and permanently unromantic [*to Praed*].

FRANK. I also shall remain permanently single until you change
your mind. Praddy: change the subject. Be eloquent about something else.

PRAED. [*diffidently*] I'm afraid theres nothing else in the world
that I c a n talk about. The Gospel of Art is the only one I can

preach. I know Miss Warren is a great devotee of the Gospel of Getting On; but we cant discuss that without hurting your feelings, Frank, since you are determined not to get on.

FRANK. Oh, dont mind my feelings. Give me some improving advice by all means: it does me ever so much good. Have another try to make a successful man of me, Viv. Come; lets have it all: energy, thrift, foresight, self-respect, character. Dont you hate people who have no character, Viv?

VIVIE. [*wincing*] Oh, stop, stop: let us have no more of that horrible cant. Mr Praed: if there are really only those two gospels in the world, we had better all kill ourselves; for the same taint is in both, through and through.

FRANK. [*looking critically at her*] There is a touch of poetry about you today, Viv, which has hitherto been lacking.

PRAED. [*remonstrating*] My dear Frank: arnt you a little unsympathetic?

VIVIE. [*merciless to herself*] No: it's good for me. It keeps me from being sentimental.

FRANK. [*bantering her*] Checks your strong natural propensity that way, dont it?

VIVIE. [*almost hysterically*] Oh yes; go on: dont spare me. I was sentimental for one moment in my life—beautifully sentimental —by moonlight; and now—

FRANK. [*quickly*] I say, Viv: take care. Dont give yourself away.

VIVIE. Oh, do you think Mr Praed does not know all about my mother? [*Turning on Praed*] You had better have told me that morning, Mr Praed. You are very old fashioned in your delicacies, after all.

PRAED. Surely it is you who are a little old fashioned in your prejudices, Miss Warren, I feel bound to tell you, speaking as an artist, and believing that the most intimate human relationships are far beyond and above the scope of the law, that though I know that your mother is an unmarried woman, I do not respect her the less on that account. I respect her more.

FRANK. [*airily*] Hear! Hear!

VIVIE. [*staring at him*] Is that a l l you know?

PRAED. Certainly that is all.

VIVIE. Then you neither of you know anything. Your guesses are innocence itself compared to the truth.

PRAED. [*rising, startled and indignant, and preserving his politeness with an effort*] I hope not. [*More emphatically*] I hope not, Miss Warren.

FRANK. [*whistles*] Whew!

VIVIE. You are not making it easy for me to tell you, Mr Praed.

PRAED. [*his chivalry drooping before their conviction*] If there is anything worse—that is, anything else—are you sure you are right to tell us, Miss Warren?

VIVIE. I am sure that if I had the courage I should spend the rest of my life in telling everybody—stamping and branding it into them until they all felt their part in its abomination as I feel mine.

There is nothing I despise more than the wicked convention that protects these things by forbidding a woman to mention them. And yet I cant tell you. The two infamous words that describe what my mother is are ringing in my ears and struggling on my tongue; but I cant utter them: the shame of them is too horrible for me. [*She buries her face in her hands. The two men, astonished, stare at one another and then at her. She raises her head again desperately and snatches a sheet of paper and a pen*] Here: let me draft you a prospectus.

FRANK. Oh, she's mad. Do you hear, Viv? mad. Come! pull yourself together.

VIVIE. You shall see. [*She writes*] "Paid up capital: not less than £40,000 standing in the name of Sir George Crofts, Baronet, the chief shareholder. Premises at Brussels, Ostend, Vienna and Budapest. Managing director: Mrs Warren"; and now dont let us forget her qualifications: the two words. [*She writes the words and pushes the paper to them*] There! Oh no: dont read it: dont! [*She snatches it back and tears it to pieces; then seizes her head in her hands and hides her face on the table*]

Frank, who has watched the writing over his shoulder, and opened his eyes very widely at it, takes a card from his pocket; scribbles the two words on it; and silently hands it to Praed, who reads it with amazement, and hides it hastily in his pocket.

FRANK. [*whispering tenderly*] Viv, dear: thats all right. I read what you wrote: so did Praddy. We understand. And we remain, as this leaves us at present, yours ever so devotedly.

PRAED. We do indeed, Miss Warren. I declare you are the most splendidly courageous woman I ever met.

This sentimental compliment braces Vivie. She throws it away from her with an impatient shake, and forces herself to stand up, though not without some support from the table.

FRANK. Dont stir, Viv, if you dont want to. Take it easy.

VIVIE. Thank you. You can always depend on me for two things: not to cry and not to faint. [*She moves a few steps towards the door of the inner room, and stops close to Praed to say*] I shall need much more courage than that when I tell my mother that we have come to the parting of the ways. Now I must go into the next room for a moment to make myself neat again, if you dont mind.

PRAED. Shall we go away?

VIVIE. No; I shall be back presently. Only for a moment. [*She goes into the other room, Praed opening the door for her*]

PRAED. What an amazing revelation! I'm extremely disappointed in Crofts: I am indeed.

FRANK. I'm not in the least. I feel he's perfectly accounted for at last. But what a facer for me, Praddy! I cant marry her now.

PRAED. [*sternly*] Frank! [*The two look at one another, Frank unruffled, Praed deeply indignant*] Let me tell you, Gardner, that if you desert her now you will behave very despicably.

FRANK. Good old Praddy! Ever chivalrous! But you mistake: it's not the moral aspect of the case: it's the money aspect. I really cant bring myself to touch the old woman's money now.

PRAED. And was that what you were going to marry on?

FRANK. What else? *I* havnt any money, nor the smallest turn for making it. If I married Viv now she would have to support me; and I should cost her more than I am worth.

PRAED. But surely a clever bright fellow like you can make something by your own brains.

FRANK. Oh yes, a little [*He takes out his money again*] I made all that yesterday in an hour and a half. But I made it in a highly speculative business. No, dear Praddy: even if Bessie and Georgina marry millionaires and the governor dies after cutting them off with a shilling, I shall have only four hundred a year. And he wont die until he's three score and ten: he hasnt originality enough. I shall be on short allowance for the next twenty years. No short allowance for Viv, if I can help it. I withdraw gracefully and leave the field to the gilded youth of England. So thats settled. I shant worry her about it: I'll just send her a little note after we're gone. She'll understand.

PRAED. [*grasping his hand*] Good fellow, Frank! I heartily beg your pardon. But must you never see her again?

FRANK. Never see her again! Hang it all, be reasonable. I shall come along as often as possible, and be her brother. I can n o t understand the absurd consequences you romantic people expect from the most ordinary transactions. [*A knock at the door*] I wonder who this is. Would you mind opening the door? If it's a client it will look more respectable than if I appeared.

PRAED. Certainly. [*He goes to the door and opens it. Frank sits down in Vivie's chair to scribble a note*] My dear Kitty: come in: come in.

Mrs Warren comes in, looking apprehensively round for Vivie. She has done her best to make herself matronly and dignified. The brilliant hat is replaced by a sober bonnet, and the gay blouse covered by a costly black silk mantle. She is pitiably anxious and ill at ease: evidently panic-stricken.

MRS WARREN. [*to Frank*] What! Y o u r e here, are you?

FRANK. [*turning in his chair from his writing, but not rising*] Here, and charmed to see you. You come like a breath of spring.

MRS WARREN. Oh, get out with your nonsense. [*In a low voice*] Wheres Vivie?

Frank points expressively to the door of the inner room, but says nothing.

MR; WARREN. [*sitting down suddenly and almost beginning to cry*] Praddy: wont she see me, dont you think?

PRAED. My dear Kitty: dont distress yourself. Why should she not?

MRS WARREN. Oh, you never can see why not: youre too innocent. Mr Frank: did she say anything to you?

FRANK. [*folding his note*] She m u s t see you, if [*very expressively*] you wait til she comes in.

MRS WARREN. [*frightened*] Why shouldnt I wait?

Frank looks quizzically at her; puts his note carefully on the ink-bottle, so that Vivie cannot fail to find it when next she dips her pen; then rises and devotes his attention entirely to her.

FRANK. My dear Mrs Warren: suppose you were a sparrow—every so tiny and pretty a sparrow hopping in the roadway—and you saw a steam roller coming in your direction, would you wait for it?

MRS WARREN. Oh, dont bother me with your sparrows. What did she run away from Haslemere like that for?

FRANK. I'm afraid she'll tell you if you rashly await her return.

MRS WARREN. Do you want me to go away?

FRANK. No: I always want you to stay. But I a d v i s e you to go away.

MRS WARREN. What! And never see her again!

FRANK. Precisely.

MRS WARREN. [*crying again*] Praddy: dont let him be cruel to me. [*She hastily checks her tears and wipes her eyes*] She'll be so angry if she sees Ive been crying.

FRANK. [*with a touch of real compassion in his airy tenderness*] You know that Praddy is the soul of kindness, Mrs Warren. Praddy: what do y o u say? Go or stay?

PRAED. [*to Mrs Warren*] I really should be very sorry to cause you unnecessary pain; but I think perhaps you had better not wait. The fact is—[*Vivie is heard at the inner door*]

FRANK. Sh! Too late. She's coming.

MRS WARREN. Dont tell her I was crying. [*Vivie comes in. She stops gravely on seeing Mrs Warren, who greets her with hysterical cheerfulness*] Well, dearie. So here you are at last.

VIVIE. I am glad you have come: I want to speak to you. You said you were going, Frank, I think.

FRANK. Yes. Will you come with me, Mrs Warren? What do you say to a trip to Richmond, and the theatre in the evening? There is safety in Richmond. No steam roller there.

VIVIE. Nonsense, Frank. My mother will stay here.

MRS WARREN. [*scared*] I dont know: perhaps I'd better go. We're disturbing you at your work.

VIVIE. [*with quiet decision*] Mr Praed: please take Frank away. Sit down, mother. [*Mrs Warren obeys helplessly*]

PRAED. Come, Frank. Goodbye, Miss Vivie.

VIVIE. [*shaking hands*] Goodbye. A pleasant trip.

PRAED. Thank you: thank you. I hope so.

FRANK. [*to Mrs Warren*] Goodbye: youd ever so much better have taken my advice. [*He shakes hands with her. Then airily to Vivie*] Byebye, Viv.

VIVIE. Goodbye. [*He goes out gaily without shaking hands with her*]

PRAED. [*sadly*] Goodbye, Kitty.

MRS WARREN. [*sniveling*] —oobye!

Praed goes. Vivie, composed and extremely grave, sits down in Honoria's chair, and waits for her mother to speak. Mrs Warren, dreading a pause, loses no time in beginning.

MRS WARREN. Well, Vivie, what did you go away like that for with-out saying a word to me? How could you do such a thing! And what have you done to poor George? I wanted him to come with me; but he shuffled out of it. I could see that he was quite afraid of you. Only fancy: he wanted me not to come. As if [*trembling*] I should be afraid of you, dearie. [*Vivie's gravity deepens*] But of course I told him it was all settled and comfort-able between us, and that we were on the best of terms. [*She breaks down*] Vivie: whats the meaning of this? [*She produces a commercial envelope, and fumbles at the enclosure with trembling fingers*] I got it from the bank this morning.

VIVIE. It is my month's allowance. They sent it to me as usual the other day. I simply sent it back to be placed to your credit, and asked them to send you the lodgment receipt. In future I shall support myself.

MRS WARREN. [*not daring to understand*] Wasnt it enough? Why didnt you tell me? [*With a cunning gleam in her eye*] I'll double it: I was intending to double it. Only let me know how much you want.

VIVIE. You know very well that that has nothing to do with it. From this time I go my own way in my own business and among my own friends. And you will go yours. [*She rises*] Goodbye.

MRS WARREN. [*rising, appalled*] Goodbye?

VIVIE. Yes: Goodbye. Come: dont let us make a useless scene: you understand perfectly well. Sir George Crofts has told me the whole business.

MRS WARREN [*angrily*] Silly old— [*She swallows an epithet, and turns white at the narrowness of her escape from uttering it*]

VIVIE. Just so.

MRS WARREN. He ought to have his tongue cut out. But I thought it was ended: you said you didnt mind.

VIVIE. [*steadfastly*] Excuse me: I d o mind.

MRS WARREN. But I explained—

VIVIE. You explained how it came about. You did not tell me that it is still going on [*She sits*]

Mrs Warren, silenced for a moment, looks forlornly at Vivie, who waits, secretly hoping that the combat is over. But the cunning expression comes back into Mrs Warren's face; and she bends across the table, sly and urgent, half whispering.

MRS WARREN. Vivie: do you know how rich I am?

VIVIE. I have no doubt you are very rich.

MRS WARREN. But you dont know all that that means: youre too young. It means a new dress every day; it means theatres and balls every night; it means having the pick of all the gentlemen in Europe at your feet; it means a lovely house and plenty of servants; it means the choicest of eating and drinking; it means everything you like, everything you want, everything you can think of. And what are you here? A mere drudge, toiling and moiling early and late for your bare living and two cheap dresses a year. Think over it. [*Soothingly*] Youre shocked, I know. I can enter into your feelings; and I think they do you credit; but trust me, nobody will blame you: you may take my word for that. I know what young girls are; and I know youll think better of it when youve turned it over in your mind.

VIVIE. So thats how it's done, is it? You must have said all that to many a woman, mother, to have it so pat.

MRS WARREN. [*passionately*] What harm am I asking you to do? [*Vivie turns away contemptuously. Mrs Warren continues desperately*] Vivie: listen to me: you dont understand: youve been taught wrong on purpose: you dont know what the world is really like.

VIVIE. [*arrested*] Taught wrong on purpose! What do you mean?

MRS WARREN. I mean that youre throwing away all your chances for nothing. You think that people are what they pretend to be: that the way you were taught at school and college to think right and proper is the way things really are. But it's not: it's all only a pretence, to keep the cowardly slavish common run of people quiet. Do you want to find that out, like other women, at forty, when youve thrown yourself away and lost your chances; or wont you take it in good time now from your own mother, that loves you and swears to you that it's truth: gospel truth? [*Urgently*] Vivie: the big people, the clever people, the managing people, all know it. They do as I do, and think what I think. I know plenty of them. I know them to speak to, to introduce you to, to make friends of for you. I dont mean anything wrong; thats what you dont understand: your head is full of ignorant ideas about me. What do the people that taught you know about life or about people like me? When did they ever meet me, or speak to me, or let anyone tell them about me? the fools! Would they ever have done anything for you if I hadnt paid them? Havnt I told you that I want you to be respectable? Havnt I brought you up to be respectable? And how can you keep it up without my money and my influence and Lizzie's friends? Cant you see that youre cutting your own throat as well as breaking my heart in turning your back on me?

VIVIE. I recognize the Crofts philosophy of life, mother. I heard it all from him that day at the Gardners'.

MRS WARREN. You think I want to force that played-out old sot on you! I dont, Vivie: on my oath I dont.

VIVIE. It would not matter if you did: you would not succeed. [*Mrs Warren winces, deeply hurt by the implied indifference towards her affectionate intention. Vivie, neither understanding this nor concerning herself about it, goes on calmly*] Mother: you dont at all know the sort of person I am. I dont object to Crofts more than to any other coarsely built man of his class. To tell you the truth, I rather admire him for being strong-minded enough to enjoy himself in his own way and make plenty of money instead of living the usual shooting, hunting, dining-out, tailoring, loafing life of his set merely because all the rest do it.

And I'm perfectly aware that if I'd been in the same circumstances as my aunt Liz, I'd have done exactly what she did. I dont think I'm more prejudiced or straitlaced than you: I think I'm less. I'm certain I'm less sentimental. I know very well that fashionable morality is all a pretence, and that if I took your money and devoted the rest of my life to spending it fashionably, I might be as worthless and vicious as the silliest woman could possibly want to be without having a word said to me about it. But I dont want to be worthless. I shouldnt enjoy trotting about the park to advertize my dressmaker and carriage builder, or being bored at the opera to shew off a shopwindowful of diamonds.

MRS WARREN. [*bewildered*] But—

VIVIE. Wait a moment: Ive not done. Tell me why you continue your business now that you are independent of it. Your sister, you told me, has left all that behind her. Why dont you do the same?

MRS WARREN. Oh, it's all very easy for Liz: she likes good society, and has the air of being a lady. Imagine me in a cathedral town! Why, the very rooks in the trees would find me out even if I could stand the dulness of it. I must have work and excitement, or I should go melancholy mad. And what else is there for me to do? The life suits me: I'm fit for it and not for anything else. If I didnt do it somebody else would; so I dont do any real harm by it. And then it brings in money; and I like making money. No; it's no use: I cant give it up—not for anybody. But what need you know about it? I'll never mention it. I'll keep Crofts away. I'll not trouble you much: you see I have to be constantly running about from one place to another. Youll be quit of me altogether when I die.

VIVIE. No: I am my mother's daughter. I am like you: I must have work, and must make more money than I spend. But my work is not your work, and my way not your way. We must part. It will not make much difference to us: instead of meeting one another for perhaps a few months in twenty years we shall never meet: thats all.

MRS WARREN. [*her voice stifled in tears*] Vivie: I meant to have been more with you: I did indeed.

VIVIE. It's no use, mother: I am not to be changed by a few cheap tears and entreaties any more than you are, I daresay.

MRS WARREN. [*wildly*] Oh, you call a mother's tears cheap.

VIVIE. They cost you nothing; and you ask me to give you the peace and quietness of my whole life in exchange for them. What use would my company be to you if you could get it? What have we two in common that could make either of us happy together?

MRS WARREN. [*lapsing recklessly into her dialect*] We're mother and daughter. I want my daughter. Ive a right to you. Who is to care for me when I'm old? Plenty of girls have taken to me like daughters and cried at leaving me; but I let them all go because I had you to look forward to. I kept myself lonely for you. Youve no right to turn on me now and refuse to do your duty as a daughter.

VIVIE. [*jarred and antagonized by the echo of the slums in her mother's voice*] My duty as a daughter! I thought we should come to that presently. Now once for all, mother, you want a daughter and Frank wants a wife. I dont want a mother; and I dont want a husband. I have spared neither Frank nor myself in sending him about his business. Do you think I will spare y o u?

MRS WARREN. [*violently*] Oh, I know the sort you are: no mercy for yourself or anyone else. I know. My experience has done that for me anyhow: I can tell the pious, canting, hard, selfish woman when I meet her. Well, keep yourself to yourself: I dont want you. But listen to this. Do you know what I would do with you if you were a baby again? aye, as sure as there's a Heaven above us.

VIVIE. Strangle me, perhaps.

MRS WARREN. No: I'd bring you up to be a real daughter to me, and not what you are now, with your pride and your prejudices and the college education you stole from me: yes, stole: deny it if you can: what was it but stealing? I'd bring you up in my own house, I would.

VIVIE. [*quietly*] In one of your own houses.

MRS WARREN [*screaming*] Listen to her! listen to how she spits on her mother's grey hairs! Oh, may you live to have your own daughter tear and trample on you as you have trampled on me. And you will: you will. No woman ever had luck with a mother's curse on her.

VIVIE. I wish you wouldnt rant, mother. It only hardens me. Come: I suppose I am the only young woman you ever had in your power that you did good to. Dont spoil it all now.

MRS WARREN. Yes, Heaven forgive me, it's true; and you are the only one that ever turned on me. Oh, the injustice of it! the injustice! the injustice! I always wanted to be a good woman. I tried honest work; and I was slave-driven until I cursed the day I ever heard of honest work. I was a good mother; and because I made my daughter a good woman she turns me out as if I was a leper. Oh, if I only had my life to live over again! I'd talk to that lying clergyman in the school. From this time forth, so help me Heaven in my last hour, I'll do wrong and nothing but wrong. And I'll prosper on it.

VIVIE. Yes: it's better to choose your line and go through with it. If I had been you, mother, I might have done as you did; but I should not have lived one life and believed in another. You are a conventional woman at heart. That is why I am bidding you goodbye now. I am right, am I not?

MRS WARREN. [*taken aback*] Right to throw away all my money?

VIVIE. No: right to get rid of you? I should be a fool not to! Isnt that so?

MRS WARREN. [*sulkily*] Oh well, yes, if you come to that, I suppose you are. But Lord help the world if everybody took to doing

the right thing! And now I'd better go than stay where I'm not
wanted. [*She turns to the door*]

VIVIE. [*kindly*] Wont you shake hands?

MRS WARREN. [*after looking at her fiercely for a moment with a
savage impulse to strike her*] No, thank you. Goodbye.

VIVIE. [*matter-of-factly*] Goodbye. [*Mrs Warren goes out, slamming the door behind her. The strain on Vivie's face relaxes; her
grave expression breaks up into one of joyous content; her breath
goes out in a half sob, half laugh of intense relief. She goes
buoyantly to her place at the writing-table; pushes the electric
lamp out of the way; pulls over a great sheaf of papers; and is in
the act of dipping her pen in the ink when she finds Frank's
note. She opens it unconcernedly and reads it quickly, giving a
little laugh at some quaint turn of expression in it*] And goodbye,
Frank. [*She tears the note up and tosses the pieces into the wastepaper basket without a second thought. Then she goes at her
work with a plunge, and soon becomes absorbed in its figures*]

1893   1898

JOSEPH CONRAD
(1857–1924)

1875–94: Career as a seaman.
1895:   *Almayer's Folly.*
1904:   *Nostromo.*

Joseph Conrad was born Jozef Teodor Konrad Nalecz Korzeniowski in
Poland (then under Russian rule), son of a Polish patriot who suffered
exile in Russia for his Polish nationalist activities and died in 1869, leaving
Conrad to be brought up by a maternal uncle. At the age of 15 he amazed
everybody by announcing his passionate desire to go to sea; he was eventually allowed to go to Marseilles in 1874, and from there he made a number of voyages on French merchant ships to Martinique and the West
Indies. In 1878 he signed on an English ship which brought him to the
east coast English port of Lowestoft, where (still as an ordinary seaman)
he joined the crew of a small coasting vessel plying between Lowestoft
and Newcastle. In six voyages between these two ports he learned English.
Thus launched on a career in the British merchant service, Conrad sailed
on a variety of British ships to the Orient and elsewhere and eventually
gained his master's certificate in 1886, the year when he became a naturalized British subject. He received his first command in 1888, and in 1890
took a steamboat up the Congo River in nightmarish circumstances (described in *Heart of Darkness*) which produced severe illness and permanently haunted his imagination. In the early 1890's he was already thinking of turning some of his Malayan experiences into English fiction, and
in 1892–93, when serving as first mate on the *Torrens* sailing from London

to Adelaide, he revealed to a sympathetic passenger that he had begun a novel (*Almayer's Folly*), while on the return journey he impressed John Galsworthy, who was a passenger, with his conversation. Though possessed of a master's certificate, Conrad found it difficult to get the kind of job as master that he wished, and occasionally he had to serve in lesser capacities. His difficulty in obtaining a command, together with the interest aroused by *Almayer's Folly* when it was published in 1895, helped to turn him away from the sea to a career as a writer. He settled in London and in 1896 married an English girl; this son of a Polish patriot turned merchant seaman turned writer was henceforth an English novelist.

Conrad was for a long time regarded as a sea writer whose exotic descriptions of eastern landscapes and exploitation of the romantic atmosphere of Malaya and other unfamiliar regions gave his work a special kind of richness and splendor. But this is only one, and not in the last analysis the most important, aspect of his work. More and more Conrad used the sea and the circumstances of life on shipboard or in remote eastern settlements as means of exploring certain profound moral ambiguities in human experience. In *The Nigger of the "Narcissus"* (1897) he shows how a dying Negro seaman corrupts the morale of a ship's crew by the very fact that his plight produces sympathy, thus symbolically presenting one of his commonest themes—the necessity and at the same time the dangers of human contact. In *Lord Jim* (1900), using the device of an intermediate narrator, he probes the meaning of a gross failure of duty on the part of a romantic and idealistic young sailor, and by presenting the hero's history from a series of different points of view keeps the moral questioning continuing to the end. The use of intermediate narrators and multiple points of view is common in Conrad; it is his favorite way of suggesting the complexity of experience and the difficulty of judging human actions. In *Heart of Darkness* he draws on his Congo River experience to create an atmosphere of darkness and horror in the midst of which the hero recognizes a deep inner kinship with the corrupt villain, the Belgian trader who has lost all his earlier ideals to succumb to the worst elements in the native life he had hoped to improve.

This notion of the difficulty of true communion, coupled with the idea that communion can be unexpectedly forced on us—sometimes with someone who may be on the surface our moral opposite, so that we can at times be compelled into a mysterious recognition of our opposite as our true self—is found in many of Conrad's works; it provides one of the underlying themes of *The Secret Sharer* (1912). This story can be enjoyed for the clarity and power with which Conrad renders the atmosphere of the Gulf of Siam as felt by a young sea captain on taking on his first command, but it also uses situation and incident symbolically in order to suggest some of the paradoxes of identity and sympathy.

Other stories and novels explore the ways in which the codes we live by are tested in moments of crisis, revealing either their inadequacy or our own. Imagination can corrupt (as with Lord Jim), or save (as in *The Shadow Line*, 1917); and there are times when total lack of it can see a man through (Captain M'Whirr in *Typhoon*, 1902), though a similar lack in other circumstances can render a man comically ridiculous (Captain Mitchell in *Nostromo*, 1904).

Nostromo, a profound and subtle study of the corrupting effects of politics and "material interests" on personal relationships (set in an imaginary South American republic), is now generally regarded as Conrad's greatest work. His two other political novels—*The Secret Agent* (1906) and *Under Western Eyes* (1910)—have also recently come into their own. The latter is the story of a Russian student who becomes involuntarily associated with antigovernment violence in Czarist Russia and is irresistibly maneuvered by circumstances into a position where, although a government spy, he has to pretend to be a revolutionary among revolutionaries. This is the ultimate in human loneliness and incommunicability—when you must consistently pretend to be the opposite of what you are. It is a story of Dostoievskian power, and shows a very different Conrad from the picturesque sea-dreamer pictured by the earlier critics. Conrad was as much a pessimist as Hardy, but he projected his pessimism in subtler ways. He was also a great master of English prose, an astonishing fact when we realize that he was 21 before he learned any English, and that to the end of his life he spoke English with a thick foreign accent.

Preface to *The Nigger of the* "*Narcissus*"[1]

[The Task of the Artist]

A work that aspires, however humbly, to the condition of art should carry its justification in every line. And art itself may be defined as a single-minded attempt to render the highest kind of justice to the visible universe, by bringing to light the truth, manifold and one, underlying its every aspect. It is an attempt to find in its forms, in its colors, in its light, in its shadows, in the aspects of matter and in the facts of life, what of each is fundamental, what is enduring and essential—their one illuminating and convincing quality—the very truth of their existence. The artist, then, like the thinker or the scientist, seeks the truth and makes his appeal. Impressed by the aspect of the world the thinker plunges into ideas, the scientist into facts—whence, presently, emerging they make their appeal to those qualities of our being that fit us best for the hazardous enterprise of living. They speak authoritatively to our common-sense, to our intelligence, to our desire of peace or to our desire of unrest; not seldom to our prejudices, sometimes to our fears, often to our egoism—but always to our credulity. And their

1. *The Nigger of the "Narcissus"* was written in 1896–97, shortly after his marriage, and published first in *The New Review*, August–December 1897, and then in book form in 1898. The novel, in the words of Jocelyn Baines, Conrad's biographer, "is the culmination of Conrad's apprenticeship as a novelist." Conrad took particular pleasure in writing the book, and later called it "the story by which, as a creative artist, I stand or fall." It was with the feeling that he was now wholly dedicated to writing and had finally (in his own words) "done with the sea" that, a few months after finishing the novel, he wrote the preface in which he defined his aims as an artist. The preface first appeared in the 1898 edition.

words are heard with reverence, for their concern is with weighty matters: with the cultivation of our minds and the proper care of our bodies, with the attainment of our ambitions, with the perfection of the means and the glorification of our precious aims.

It is otherwise with the artist.

Confronted by the same enigmatical spectacle the artist descends within himself, and in that lonely region of stress and strife, if he be deserving and fortunate, he finds the terms of his appeal. His appeal is made to our less obvious capacities: to that part of our nature which, because of the warlike conditions of existence, is necessarily kept out of sight within the more resisting and hard qualities—like the vulnerable body within a steel armor. His appeal is less loud, more profound, less distinct, more stirring—and sooner forgotten. Yet its effect endures forever. The changing wisdom of successive generations discards ideas, questions facts, demolishes theories. But the artist appeals to that part of our being which is not dependent on wisdom: to that in us which is a gift and not an acquisition—and, therefore, more permanently enduring. He speaks to our capacity for delight and wonder, to the sense of mystery surrounding our lives; to our sense of pity, and beauty, and pain; to the latent feeling of fellowship with all creation—and to the subtle but invincible conviction of solidarity that knits together the loneliness of innumerable hearts, to the solidarity in dreams, in joy, in sorrow, in aspirations, in illusions, in hope, in fear, which binds men to each other, which binds together all humanity—the dead to the living and the living to the unborn.

It is only some such train of thought, or rather of feeling, that can in a measure explain the aim of the attempt, made in the tale which follows,[2] to present an unrestful episode in the obscure lives of a few individuals out of all the disregarded multitude of the bewildered, the simple and the voiceless. For, if any part of truth dwells in the belief confessed above, it becomes evident that there is not a place of splendor or a dark corner of the earth that does not deserve if only a passing glance of wonder and pity. The motive, then, may be held to justify the matter of the work; but this preface, which is simply an avowal of endeavor, cannot end here—for the avowal is not yet complete.

Fiction—if it at all aspires to be art—appeals to temperament. And in truth it must be, like painting, like music, like all art, the appeal of one temperament to all the other innumerable temperaments whose subtle and resistless power endows passing events with their true meaning, and creates the moral, the emotional atmosphere of the place and time. Such an appeal, to be effective, must be an impression conveyed through the senses; and, in fact, it cannot be made in any other way, because temperament, whether in-

2. I.e., *The Nigger of the "Narcissus."*

dividual or collective, is not amenable to persuasion. All art, therefore, appeals primarily to the senses, and the artistic aim when expressing itself in written words must also make its appeal through
the senses, if its high desire is to reach the secret spring of
responsive emotions. It must strenuously aspire to the plasticity
of sculpture, to the color of painting, and to the magic suggestiveness of music—which is the art of arts. And it is only through complete, unswerving devotion to the perfect blending of form and
substance; it is only through an unremitting, never-discouraged care
for the shape and ring of sentences that an approach can be made
to plasticity, to color, and that the light of magic suggestiveness may
be brought to play for an evanescent instant over the commonplace
surface of words: of the old, old words, worn thin, defaced by ages
of careless usage.

The sincere endeavor to accomplish that creative task, to go as
far on that road as his strength will carry him, to go undeterred by
faltering, weariness, or reproach, is the only valid justification for
the worker in prose. And if his conscience is clear, his answer to
those who in the fullness of a wisdom which looks for immediate
profit, demand specifically to be edified, consoled, amused; who
demand to be promptly improved, or encouraged, or frightened, or
shocked, or charmed, must run thus:—My task which I am trying
to achieve is, by the power of the written word, to make you hear,
to make you feel—it is, before all, to make you *see*. That—and no
more, and it is everything. If I succeed, you shall find there, according to your deserts, encouragement, consolation, fear, charm—
all you demand—and, perhaps, also that glimpse of truth for which
you have forgotten to ask.

To snatch, in a moment of courage, from the remorseless rush of
time a passing phase of life, is only the beginning of the task. The
task approached in tenderness and faith is to hold up unquestion-
ingly, without choice and without fear, the rescued fragment before
all eyes in the light of a sincere mood. It is to show its vibration,
its color, its form; and through its movement, its form, and its
color, reveal the substance of its truth—disclose its inspiring secret:
the stress and passion within the core of each convincing moment.
In a single-minded attempt of that kind, if one be deserving and
fortunate, one may perchance attain to such clearness of sincerity
that at last the presented vision of regret or pity, of terror or mirth,
shall awaken in the hearts of the beholders that feeling of unavoidable solidarity; of the solidarity in mysterious origin, in toil, in joy,
in hope, in uncertain fate, which binds men to each other and all
mankind to the visible world.

It is evident that he who, rightly or wrongly, holds by the convictions expressed above cannot be faithful to any one of the
temporary formulas of his craft. The enduring part of them—the
truth which each only imperfectly veils—should abide with him as

the most precious of his possessions, but they all—Realism, Romanticism, Naturalism, even the unofficial sentimentalism (which, like the poor,[3] is exceedingly difficult to get rid of)—all these gods must, after a short period of fellowship, abandon him—even on the very threshold of the temple—to the stammerings of his conscience and to the outspoken consciousness of the difficulties of his work. In that uneasy solitude the supreme cry of Art for Art, itself, loses the exciting ring of its apparent immorality. It sounds far off. It has ceased to be a cry, and is heard only as a whisper, often incomprehensible, but at times and faintly encouraging.

Sometimes, stretched at ease in the shade of a roadside tree, we watch the motions of a laborer in a distant field, and after a time, begin to wonder languidly as to what the fellow may be at. We watch the movements of his body, the waving of his arms; we see him bend down, stand up, hesitate, begin again. It may add to the charm of an idle hour to be told the purpose of his exertions. If we know he is trying to lift a stone, to dig a ditch, to uproot a stump, we look with a more real interest at his efforts; we are disposed to condone the jar of his agitation upon the restfulness of the landscape; and even, if in a brotherly frame of mind, we may bring ourselves to forgive his failure. We understand his object, and, after all, the fellow has tried, and perhaps he had not the strength—and perhaps he had not the knowledge. We forgive, go on our way—and forget.

And so it is with the workmen of art. Art is long and life is short,[4] and success is very far off. And thus, doubtful of strength to travel so far, we talk a little about the aim—the aim of art, which, like life itself, is inspiring, difficult—obscured by mists. It is not in the clear logic of a triumphant conclusion; it is not in the unveiling of one of those heartless secrets which are called the Laws of Nature. It is not less great, but only more difficult.

To arrest, for the space of a breath, the hands busy about the work of the earth, and compel men entranced by the sight of distant goals to glance for a moment at the surrounding vision of form and color, of sunshine and shadows; to make them pause for a look, for a sigh, for a smile—such is the aim, difficult and evanescent, and reserved only for a very few to achieve. But sometimes, by the deserving and the fortunate, even that task is accomplished. And when it is accomplished—behold!—all the truth of life is there: a moment of vision, a sigh, a smile—and the return to an eternal rest.

1897   1898

3. "For the poor always ye have with you." John xii.8.
4. Cf. the Latin proverb (deriving from a dictum of the Greek physician Hippocrates) *ars longa, vita brevis*, "art is long and life is short." Chaucer rendered it, "The lyf so short, the craft so long to lerne" (*The Parlement of Foules*) and Longfellow, "Art is long, and Time is fleeting" (*A Psalm of Life*).

The Brute

Dodging in from the rain-swept street, I exchanged a smile and a glance with Miss Blank in the bar of the Three Crows. This exchange was effected with extreme propriety. It is a shock to think that, if still alive, Miss Blank must be something over sixty now. How time passes!

Noticing my gaze directed inquiringly at the partition of glass and varnished wood, Miss Blank was good enough to say, encouragingly:

"Only Mr. Jermyn and Mr. Stonor in the parlor with another gentleman I've never seen before."

I moved towards the parlor door. A voice discoursing on the other side (it was but a matchboard partition), rose so loudly that the concluding words became quite plain in all their atrocity.

"That fellow Wilmot fairly dashed her brains out, and a good job, too!"

This inhuman sentiment, since there was nothing profane or improper in it, failed to do as much as to check the slight yawn Miss Blank was achieving behind her hand. And she remained gazing fixedly at the windowpanes, which streamed with rain.

As I opened the parlor door the same voice went on in the same cruel strain:

"I was glad when I heard she got the knock from somebody at last. Sorry enough for poor Wilmot, though. The man and I used to be chums at one time. Of course that was the end of him. A clear case if there ever was one. No way out of it. None at all."

The voice belonged to the gentleman Miss Blank had never seen before. He straddled his long legs on the hearthrug. Jermyn, leaning forward, held his pocket-handkerchief spread out before the grate. He looked back dismally over his shoulder, and as I slipped behind one of the little wooden tables, I nodded to him. On the other side of the fire, imposingly calm and large, sat Mr. Stonor, jammed tight into a capacious Windsor armchair. There was nothing small about him but his short, white side-whiskers. Yards and yards of extra superfine blue cloth (made up into an overcoat) reposed on a chair by his side. And he must just have brought some liner from sea, because another chair was smothered under his black waterproof, ample as a pall, and made of three-fold oiled silk, double-stitched throughout. A man's handbag of the usual size looked like a child's toy on the floor near his feet.

I did not nod to him. He was too big to be nodded to in that parlor. He was a senior Trinity pilot[1] and condescended to take his

---

1. I.e., official government pilot (Trinity House is the name of the government organization in charge of pilots, lighthouses, buoys, etc.).

turn in the cutter[2] only during the summer months. He had been many times in charge of royal yachts in and out of Port Victoria.[3] Besides, it's no use nodding to a monument. And he was like one. He didn't speak, he didn't budge. He just sat there, holding his handsome old head up, immovable, and almost bigger than life. It was extremely fine. Mr. Stonor's presence reduced poor old Jermyn to a mere shabby wisp of a man, and made the talkative stranger in tweeds on the hearthrug look absurdly boyish. The latter must have been a few years over thirty, and was certainly not the sort of individual that gets abashed at the sound of his own voice, because gathering me in, as it were, by a friendly glance, he kept it going without a check.

"I was glad of it," he repeated, emphatically. "You may be surprised at it, but then you haven't gone through the experience I've had of her. I can tell you, it was something to remember. Of course, I got off scot free myself—as you can see. She did her best to break up my pluck for me, though. She jolly near drove as fine a fellow as ever lived into a madhouse. What do you say to that—eh?"

Not an eyelid twitched in Mr. Stonor's enormous face. Monumental! The speaker looked straight into my eyes.

"It used to make me sick to think of her going about the world murdering people."

Jermyn approached the handkerchief a little nearer to the grate and groaned. It was simply a habit he had.

"I've seen her once," he declared, with mournful indifference. "She had a house——"

The stranger in tweeds turned to stare down at him, surprised.

"She had three houses," he corrected, authoritatively. But Jermyn was not to be contradicted.

"She had a house, I say," he repeated, with dismal obstinacy. "A great, big, ugly, white thing. You could see it from miles away—sticking up."

"So you could," assented the other readily. "It was old Colchester's notion, though he was always threatening to give her up. He couldn't stand her racket any more, he declared; it was too much of a good thing for him; he would wash his hands of her, if he never got hold of another—and so on. I daresay he would have chucked her, only—it may surprise you—his missus wouldn't hear of it. Funny, eh? But with women, you never know how they will take a thing, and Mrs. Colchester, with her moustaches and big eyebrows, set up for being as strong-minded as they make them. She used to walk about in a brown silk dress, with great gold cable flopping about her bosom. You should have heard her snapping out: 'Rubbish!' or 'Stuff and nonsense!' I daresay she knew when she was

---

2. I.e., his turn in the pilot boat, which ferried the pilot to the ship he was piloting.

3. Capital and chief port of the Seychelle Islands, Indian Ocean.

well off. They had no children, and had never set up a home anywhere. When in England she just made shift to hang out anyhow
in some cheap hotel or boardinghouse. I daresay she liked to get
back to the comforts she was used to. She knew very well she
couldn't gain by any change. And, moreover, Colchester, though a
first-rate man, was not what you may call in his first youth, and,
perhaps, she may have thought that he wouldn't be able to get hold
of another (as he used to say) so easily. Anyhow, for one reason or
another, it was 'Rubbish' and 'Stuff and nonsense' for the good
lady. I overheard once young Mr. Apse himself say to her confidentially: 'I assure you, Mrs. Colchester, I am beginning to feel quite
unhappy about the name she's getting for herself.' 'Oh,' says she,
with her deep little hoarse laugh, 'if one took notice of all the silly
talk,' and she showed Apse all her ugly false teeth at once. 'It would
take more than that to make me lose my confidence in her. I assure
you,' says she."

At this point, without any change of facial expression, Mr.
Stonor emitted a short, sardonic laugh. It was very impressive, but I
didn't see the fun. I looked from one to another. The stranger on
the hearthrug had an ugly smile.

"And Mr. Apse shook both Mrs. Colchester's hands, he was so
pleased to hear a good word said for their favorite. All these Apses,
young and old you know, were perfectly infatuated with that abominable, dangerous——"

"I beg your pardon," I interrupted, for he seemed to be addresing
himself exclusively to me; "but who on earth are you talking
about?"

"I am talking of the Apse family," he answered, courteously.

I nearly let out a damn at this. But just then the respected Miss
Blank put her head in, and said that the cab was at the door, if Mr.
Stonor wanted to catch the eleven three up.

At once the senior pilot arose in his mighty bulk and began to
struggle into his coat, with awe-inspiring upheavals. The stranger
and I hurried impulsively to his assistance, and directly we laid our
hands on him he became perfectly quiescent. We had to raise our
arms very high, and to make efforts. It was like caparisoning a
docile elephant. With a "Thanks, gentlemen," he dived under and
squeezed himself through the door in a great hurry.

We smiled at each other in a friendly way.

"I wonder how he manages to hoist himself up a ship's side-lad-
der," said the man in tweeds; and poor Jermyn, who was a mere
North Sea pilot,[4] without official status or recognition of any sort,
pilot only by courtesy, groaned.

"He makes eight hundred a year."

4. Pilot of coastal vessels plying
between North Sea ports on the east
coast of Britain, rather than of ocean-
going vessels.

"Are you a sailor?" I asked the stranger, who had gone back to his position on the rug.

"I used to be till a couple of years ago, when I got married," answered this communicative individual. "I even went to sea first in that very ship we were speaking of when you came in."

"What ship?" I asked, puzzled. "I never heard you mention a ship."

"I've just told you her name, my dear sir," he replied. "The *Apse Family*. Surely you've heard of the great firm of Apse & Sons, ship-owners. They had a pretty big fleet. There was the *Lucy Apse*, and the *Harold Apse*, and *Anne, John, Malcolm, Clara, Juliet*, and so on—no end of *Apses*. Every brother, sister, aunt, cousin, wife—and grandmother, too, for all I know—of the firm had a ship named after them. Good, solid, old-fashioned craft they were, too, built to carry and to last. None of your new-fangled, labor-saving appliances in them, but plenty of men and plenty of good salt beef and hard tack put aboard—and off you go to fight your way out and home again."

The miserable Jermyn made a sound of approval, which sounded like a groan of pain. Those were the ships for him. He pointed out in doleful tones that you couldn't say to labor-saving appliances: "Jump lively now, my hearties." No labor-saving appliance would go aloft on a dirty night with the sands under your lee.[5]

"No," assented the stranger, with a wink at me. "The Apses didn't believe in them either, apparently. They treated their people well—as people don't get treated nowadays, and they were awfully proud of their ships. Nothing ever happened to them. This last one, the *Apse Family*, was to be like the others, only she was to be still stronger, still safer, still more roomy and comfortable. I believe they meant her to last forever. They had her built composite—iron, teak-wood, and greenheart, and her scantling was something fabulous. If ever an order was given for a ship in a spirit of pride this one was. Everything of the best. The commodore captain of the employ was to command her, and they planned the accommodation for him like a house on shore under a big, tall poop[6] that went nearly to the mainmast. No wonder Mrs. Colchester wouldn't let the old man give her up. Why, it was the best home she ever had in all her married days. She had a nerve, that woman.

"The fuss that was made while the ship was building! Let's have this a little stronger, and that a little heavier; and hadn't that other thing better be changed for something a little thicker. The builders entered into the spirit of the game, and there she was, growing into the clumsiest, heaviest ship of her size right before all their eyes, without anybody becoming aware of it somehow. She was to be

---

5. I.e., would climb into the rigging on a stormy night with the treacherous Goodwin Sands on the sheltered side of the ship.

6. Raised deck on ships' stern.

2,000 tons register, or a little over; no less on any account. But see what happens. When they came to measure her she turned out 1,999 tons and a fraction. General consternation! And they say old Mr. Apse was so annoyed when they told him that he took to his bed and died. The old gentleman had retired from the firm twenty-five years before, and was ninety-six years old if a day, so his death wasn't, perhaps, so surprising. Still Mr. Lucian Apse was convinced that his father would have lived to a hundred. So we may put him at the head of the list. Next comes the poor devil of a shipwright[7] that brute caught and squashed as she went off the ways. They called it the launch of a ship, but I've heard people say that, from the wailing and yelling and scrambling out of the way, it was more like letting a devil loose upon the river. She snapped all her checks[8] like packthread, and went for the tugs in attendance like a fury. Before anybody could see what she was up to she sent one of them to the bottom, and laid up another for three months' repairs. One of her cables parted, and then, suddenly—you couldn't tell why— she let herself be brought up with the other as quiet as a lamb.

"That's how she was. You could never be sure what she would be up to next. There are ships difficult to handle, but generally you can depend on them behaving rationally. With *that* ship, whatever you did with her you never knew how it would end. She was a wicked beast. Or, perhaps, she was only just insane."

He uttered this supposition in so earnest a tone that I could not refrain from smiling. He left off biting his lower lip to apostrophize me.

"Eh! Why not? Why couldn't there be something in her build, in her lines corresponding to——What's madness? Only something just a tiny bit wrong in the make of your brain. Why shouldn't there be a mad ship—I mean mad in a shiplike way, so that under no circumstances could you be sure she would do what any other sensible ship would naturally do for you. There are ships that steer wildly, and ships that can't be quite trusted always to stay; others want careful watching when running in a gale; and, again, there may be a ship that will make heavy weather of it in every little blow. But then you expect her to be always so. You take it as part of her character, as a ship, just as you take account of a man's peculiarities of temper when you deal with him. But with her you couldn't. She was unaccountable. If she wasn't mad, then she was the most evil-minded, underhand, savage brute that ever went afloat. I've seen her run in a heavy gale beautifully for two days, and on the third broach to[9] twice in the same afternoon. The first time she flung the helmsman clean over the wheel, but as she didn't quite manage to kill him she had another try about three hours

7. Ship's carpenter.
8. Restraining ropes.

9. Come round with her broadside to the wind.

afterwards. She swamped herself fore and aft, burst all the canvas we had set, scared all hands into a panic, and even frightened Mrs. Colchester down there in these beautiful stern cabins that she was so proud of. When we mustered the crew there was one man missing. Swept overboard, of course, without being either seen or heard, poor devil! and I only wonder more of us didn't go.

"Always something like that. Always. I heard an old mate tell Captain Colchester once that it had come to this with him, that he was afraid to open his mouth to give any sort of order. She was as much of a terror in harbor as at sea. You could never be certain what would hold her. On the slightest provocation she would start snapping ropes, cables, wire hawsers, like carrots. She was heavy, clumsy, unhandy—but that does not quite explain that power for mischief she had. You know, somehow, when I think of her I can't help remembering what we hear of incurable lunatics breaking loose now and then."

He looked at me inquisitively. But, of course, I couldn't admit that a ship could be mad.

"In the ports where she was known," he went on, "they dreaded the sight of her. She thought nothing of knocking away twenty feet or so of solid stone facing off a quay or wiping off the end of a wooden wharf. She must have lost miles of chain and hundreds of tons of anchors in her time. When she fell aboard some poor unoffending ship it was the very devil of a job to haul her off again. And she never got hurt herself—just a few scratches or so, perhaps. They had wanted to have her strong. And so she was. Strong enough to ram Polar ice with. And as she began so she went on. From the day she was launched she never let a year pass without murdering somebody. I think the owners got very worried about it. But they were a stiff-necked generation all these Apses; they wouldn't admit there could be anything wrong with the *Apse Family*. They wouldn't even change her name. 'Stuff and nonsense,' as Mrs. Colchester used to say. They ought at least to have shut her up for life in some dry dock or other, away up the river, and never let her smell salt water again. I assure you, my dear sir, that she invariably did kill someone every voyage she made. It was perfectly well-known. She got a name for it, far and wide."

I expressed my surprise that a ship with such a deadly reputation could ever get a crew.

"Then, you don't know what sailors are, my dear sir. Let me just show you by an instance. One day in dock at home, while loafing on the forecastle head, I noticed two respectable salts come along, one a middle-aged, competent, steady man, evidently, the other a smart, youngish chap. They read the name on the bows and stopped to look at her. Says the elder man: '*Apse Family*. That's the sanguinary female dog' (I'm putting it in that way) 'of a ship,

Jack, that kills a man every voyage. I wouldn't sign in her—not for Joe, I wouldn't.' And the other says: 'If she were mine, I'd have her towed on the mud and set on fire, blamme if I wouldn't.' Then the first man chimes in: 'Much do they care! Men are cheap, God knows.' The younger one spat in the water alongside. 'They won't have me—not for double wages.'

"They hung about for some time and then walked up the dock. Half an hour later I saw them both on our deck looking about for the mate, and apparently very anxious to be taken on. And they were."

"How do you account for this?" I asked.

"What would you say?" he retorted. "Recklessness! The vanity of boasting in the evening to all their chums: 'We've just shipped in that there *Apse Family*. Blow her. She ain't going to scare us.' Sheer sailorlike perversity! A sort of curiosity. Well—a little of all that, no doubt. I put the question to them in the course of the voyage. The answer of the elderly chap was:

" 'A man can die but once.' The younger assured me in a mocking tone that he wanted to see 'how she would do it this time.' But I tell you what; there was a sort of fascination about the brute."

Jermyn, who seemed to have seen every ship in the world, broke in sulkily:

"I saw her once out of this very window towing up the river; a great black ugly thing, going along like a big hearse."

"Something sinister about her looks, wasn't there?" said the man in tweeds, looking down at old Jermyn with a friendly eye. "I always had a sort of horror of her. She gave me a beastly shock when I was no more than fourteen, the very first day—nay, hour—I joined her. Father came up to see me off, and was to go down to Gravesend with us. I was his second boy to go to sea. My big brother was already an officer then. We got on board about eleven in the morning, and found the ship ready to drop out of the basin, stern first. She had not moved three times her own length when, at a little pluck the tug gave her to enter the dock gates, she made one of her rampaging starts, and put such a weight on the check rope— a new six-inch hawser—that forward there they had no chance to ease it round in time, and it parted. I saw the broken end fly up high in the air, and the next moment that brute brought her quarter against the pier-head with a jar that staggered everybody about her decks. She didn't hurt herself. Not she! But one of the boys the mate had sent aloft on the mizzen to do something, came down on the poop deck—thump—right in front of me. He was not much older than myself. We had been grinning at each other only a few minutes before. He must have been handling himself carelessly, not expecting to get such a jerk. I heard his started cry—Oh! —in a high treble as he felt himself going, and looked up in time to see him go limp all over as he fell. Ough! Poor father was remarkably white about the gills when we shook hands in Gravesend. 'Are you all right?' he says, looking hard at me. 'Yes, father.' 'Quite sure?' 'Yes, father.' 'Well, then good-bye, my boy.' He told me afterwards that for half a word he would have carried me off home with him there and then. I am the baby of the family—you know," added the man in tweeds, stroking his moustache with an ingenuous smile.

I acknowledged this interesting communication by a sympathetic murmur. He waved his hand carelessly.

"This might have utterly spoiled a chap's nerve for going aloft, you know—utterly. He fell within two feet of me, cracking his head on a mooring-bitt. Never moved. Stone dead. Nice looking little fellow, he was. I had just been thinking we would be great chums. However that wasn't yet the worst that brute of a ship could do. I served in her three years of my time, and then I got transferred to the *Lucy Apse*, for a year. The sailmaker we had in the *Apse Family* turned up there, too, and I remember him saying to me one evening, after we had been a week at sea: 'Isn't she a meek little ship?' No wonder we thought the *Lucy Apse* a dear, meek, little ship after getting clear of that big, rampaging savage brute. It was like heaven. Her officers seemed to me the restfullest lot of men on earth. To me who had known no ship but the *Apse Family*, the *Lucy* was like a sort of magic craft that did what you wanted her to do of her own accord. One evening we got caught aback pretty sharply from right ahead. In about ten minutes we had her full again, sheets aft,[1] tacks down, decks cleared, and the officer of the watch leaning against the weather rail peacefully. It seemed simply marvelous to me. The other would have stuck for half an hour in irons, rolling her decks full of water, knocking the men about—spars cracking, braces snapping, yards[2] taking charge, and a confounded scare going on aft because of her beastly rudder, which she had a way of flapping about fit to raise your hair on end. I couldn't get over my wonder for days.

"Well, I finished my last year of apprenticeship in that jolly little ship—she wasn't so little either, but after that other heavy devil she seemed but a plaything to handle. I finished my time and passed; and then just as I was thinking of having three weeks of real good time on shore I got at breakfast a letter asking me the earliest day I could be ready to join the *Apse Family* as third mate. I gave my plate a shove that shot it into the middle of the table; dad looked up over his paper; mother raised her hands in astonishment, and I went out bareheaded into our bit of garden, where I walked round and round for an hour.

"When I came in again mother was out of the dining room, and

1. Sails towards the stern; "tacks":   2. Spars supporting sails.
lower fore-corners of the sails.

dad had shifted berth into his big armchair. The letter was lying on the mantelpiece.

" 'It's very creditable to you to get the offer, and very kind of them to make it,' he said. 'And I see also that Charles has been appointed chief mate of that ship for one voyage.'

"There was, over leaf, a P.S. to that effect in Mr. Apse's own handwriting, which I had overlooked. Charley was my big brother.

" 'I don't like very much to have two of my boys together in one ship,' father goes on, in his deliberate, solemn way. 'And I may tell you that I would not mind writing Mr. Apse a letter to that effect.'

"Dear old dad! He was a wonderful father. What would you have done? The mere notion of going back (and as an officer, too) to be worried and bothered, and kept on the jump night and day by that brute, made me feel sick. But she wasn't a ship you could afford to fight shy of. Besides, the most genuine excuse could not be given without mortally offending Apse & Sons. The firm, and I believe the whole family down to the old unmarried aunts in Lancashire, had grown desperately touchy about that accursed ship's character. This was the case for answering 'Ready now' from your very deathbed if you wished to die in their good graces. And that's precisely what I did answer—by wire, to have it over and done with at once.

"The prospect of being shipmates with my big brother cheered me up considerably, though it made me a bit anxious, too. Ever since I remember myself as a little chap he had been very good to me, and I looked upon him as the finest fellow in the world. And so he was. No better officer ever walked the deck of a merchant ship. And that's a fact. He was a fine, strong, upstanding, suntanned, young fellow, with his brown hair curling a little, and a eye like a hawk. He was just splendid. We hadn't seen each other for many years, and even this time, though he had been in England three weeks already, he hadn't showed up at home yet, but had spent his spare time in Surrey somewhere making up to Maggie Colchester, old Captain Colchester's niece. Her father, a great friend of dad's, was in the sugar-broking business, and Charley made a sort of second home of their house. I wondered what my big brother would think of me. There was a sort of sternness about Charley's face which never left it, not even when he was larking in his rather wild fashion.

"He received me with a great shout of laughter. He seemed to think my joining as an officer the greatest joke in the world. There was a difference of ten years between us, and I suppose he remembered me best in pinafores. I was a kid of four when he first went to sea. It surprised me to find how boisterous he could be.

" 'Now we shall see what you are made of,' he cried. And he held me off by the shoulders, and punched my ribs, and hustled me into his berth. 'Sit down, Ned. I am glad of the chance of having you with me. I'll put the finishing touch to you, my young officer, pro-viding you're worth the trouble. And, first of all, get it well into your head that we are not going to let this brute kill anybody this voyage. We'll stop her racket.'

"I perceived he was in dead earnest about it. He talked grimly of the ship, and how we must be careful and never allow this ugly beast to catch us napping with any of her damned tricks.

"He gave me a regular lecture on special seamanship for the use of the *Apse Family*; then changing his tone, he began to talk at large, rattling off the wildest, funniest nonsense, till my sides ached with laughing. I could see very well he was a bit above himself with high spirits. It couldn't be because of my coming. Not to that extent. But, of course, I wouldn't have dreamt of asking what was the matter. I had a proper respect for my big brother, I can tell you. But it was all made plain enough a day or two afterwards, when I heard that Miss Maggie Colchester was coming for the voyage. Uncle was giving her a sea trip for the benefit of her health.

"I don't know what would have been wrong with her health. She had a beautiful color, and a deuce of a lot of fair hair. She didn't care a rap for wind, or rain, or spray, or sun, or green seas, or any-thing. She was a blue-eyed, jolly girl of the very best sort, but the way she cheeked my big brother used to frighten me. I always expected it to end in an awful row. However, nothing decisive happened till after we had been in Sydney for a week. One day, in the men's dinner hour, Charley sticks his head into my cabin. I was stretched out on my back on the settee, smoking in peace.

" 'Come ashore with me, Ned,' he says, in his curt way.

"I jumped up, of course, and away after him down the gangway and up George Street. He strode along like a giant, and I at his elbow, panting. It was confoundedly hot. 'Where on earth are you rushing me to, Charley?' I made bold to ask.

" 'Here,' he says.

" 'Here' was a jeweler's shop. I couldn't imagine what he could want there. It seemed a sort of mad freak. He thrusts under my nose three rings, which looked very tiny on his big, brown palm, growling out—

" 'For Maggie! Which?'

"I got a kind of scare at this. I couldn't make a sound, but I pointed at the one that sparkled white and blue. He put it in his waistcoat pocket, paid for it with a lot of sovereigns, and bolted out. When we got on board I was quite out of breath. 'Shake hands, old chap,' I gasped out. He gave me a thump on the back. 'Give what orders you like to the boatswain when the hands turn-to,' says he; 'I am off duty this afternoon.'

"Then he vanished from the deck for a while, but presently he came out of the cabin with Maggie, and these two went over the gangway publicly, before all hands, going for a walk together on that awful, blazing hot day, with clouds of dust flying about. They came back after a few hours looking very staid, but didn't seem to have the slightest idea where they had been. Anyway, that's the answer they both made to Mrs. Colchester's question at teatime.

"And didn't she turn on Charley, with her voice like an old night cabman's! 'Rubbish. Don't know where you've been! Stuff and nonsense. You've walked the girl off her legs. Don't do it again.'

"It's surprising how meek Charley could be with that old woman. Only on one occasion he whispered to me, 'I'm jolly glad she isn't Maggie's aunt, except by marriage. That's no sort of relationship.' But I think he let Maggie have too much of her own way. She was hopping all over that ship in her yachting skirt and a red tam o' shanter like a bright bird on a dead black tree. The old salts used to grin to themselves when they saw her coming along, and offered to teach her knots or splices. I believe she liked the men, for Charley's sake, I suppose.

"As you may imagine, the fiendish propensities of that cursed ship were never spoken of on board. Not in the cabin, at any rate. Only once on the homeward passage Charley said, incautiously, something about bringing all her crew home this time. Captain Colchester began to look uncomfortable at once, and that silly, hard-bitten old woman flew out at Charley as though he had said something indecent. I was quite confounded myself; as to Maggie, she sat completely mystified, opening her blue eyes very wide. Of course, before she was a day older she wormed it all out of me. She was a very difficult person to lie to.

" 'How awful,' she said, quite solemn. 'So many poor fellows. I am glad the voyage is nearly over. I won't have a moment's peace about Charley now.'

"I assured her Charley was all right. It took more than that ship knew to get over a seaman like Charley. And she agreed with me.

"Next day we got the tug off Dungeness; and when the towrope was fast Charley rubbed his hands and said to me in an undertone—

" 'We've baffled her, Ned.'

" 'Looks like it,' I said, with a grin at him. It was beautiful weather, and the sea as smooth as a millpond. We went up the river without a shadow of trouble except once, when off Hole Haven, the brute took a sudden sheer and nearly had a barge anchored just clear of the fairway. But I was aft, looking after the steering, and she did not catch me napping that time. Charley came up on the poop, looking very concerned. 'Close shave,' says he.

" 'Never mind, Charley,' I answered, cherrily. 'You've tamed her.'

"We were to tow right up to the dock. The river pilot boarded us below Gravesend, and the first words I heard him say were: 'You may just as well take your port anchor inboard at once, Mr. Mate.'

"This had been done when I went forward. I saw Maggie on the forecastle head enjoying the bustle and I begged her to go aft, but she took no notice of me, of course. Then Charley, who was very busy with the head gear, caught sight of her and shouted in his biggest voice: 'Get off the forecastle head, Maggie. You're in the way here.' For all answer she made a funny face at him, and I saw poor Charley turn away, hiding a smile. She was flushed with the excitement of getting home again, and her blue eyes seemed to snap electric sparks as she looked at the river. A collier brig had gone round just ahead of us, and our tug had to stop her engines in a hurry to avoid running into her.

"In a moment, as is usually the case, all the shipping in the reach seemed to get into a hopeless tangle. A schooner and a ketch got up a small collision all to themselves right in the middle of the river. It was exciting to watch, and, meantime, our tug remained stopped. Any other ship than that brute could have been coaxed to keep straight for a couple of minutes—but not she! Her head fell off at once,[3] and she began to drift down, taking her tug along with her. I noticed a cluster of coasters at anchor within a quarter of a mile of us, and I thought I had better speak to the pilot. 'If you let her get amongst that lot,' I said, quietly, 'she will grind some of them to bits before we get her out again.'

" 'Don't I know her!' cries he, stamping his foot in a perfect fury. And he out with his whistle to make that bothered tug get the ship's head up again as quick as possible. He blew like mad, waving his arm to port, and presently we could see that the tug's engines had been set going ahead. Her paddles churned the water, but it was as if she had been trying to tow a rock—she couldn't get an inch out of that ship. Again the pilot blew his whistle, and waved his arm to port. We could see the tug's paddles turning faster and faster away, broad on our bow.

"For a moment tug and ship hung motionless in a crowd of moving shipping, and then the terrific strain that evil, stony-hearted brute would always put on everything, tore the towing-chock clean out. The towrope surged over, snapping the iron stanchions of the head-rail one after another as if they had been sticks of sealing wax. It was only then I noticed that in order to have a better view over our heads, Maggie had stepped upon the port anchor as it lay flat on the forecastle deck.

"It had been lowered properly into its hardwood beds, but there had been no time to take a turn with it. Anyway, it was quite secure as it was, for going into dock; but I could see directly that the towrope would sweep under the fluke[4] in another second. My

3. I.e., she stopped going forward.   4. Triangular piece of iron on each arm of the anchor.

heart flew up right into my throat, but not before I had time to yell out: 'Jump clear of that anchor!'

"But I hadn't time to shriek out her name. I don't suppose she heard me at all. The first touch of the hawser against the fluke threw her down; she was up on her feet again quick as lightning, but she was up on the wrong side. I heard a horrid, scraping sound, and then that anchor, tipping over, rose up like something alive; its great, rough iron arm caught Maggie round the waist, seemed to clasp her close with a dreadful hug, and flung itself with her over and down in a terrific clang of iron, followed by heavy ringing blows that shook the ship from stem to stern—because the ring stopper held!"

"How horrible!" I exclaimed.

"I used to dream for years afterwards of anchors catching hold of girls," said the man in tweeds, a little wildly. He shuddered. "With a most pitiful howl Charley was over after her almost on the instant. But, Lord! he didn't see as much as a gleam of her red tam o' shanter in the water. Nothing! nothing whatever! In a moment there were half a dozen boats around us, and he got pulled into one. I, with the boatswain and the carpenter, let go the other anchor in a hurry and brought the ship up somehow. The pilot had gone silly. He walked up and down the forecastle head wringing his hands and muttering to himself: 'Killing women, now! Killing women, now!' Not another word could you get out of him.

"Dusk fell, then a night black as pitch; and peering upon the river I heard a low, mournful hail, 'Ship, ahoy!' Two Gravesend watermen came alongside. They had a lantern in their wherry, and looked up the ship's side, holding on to the ladder without a word. I saw in the patch of light a lot of loose, fair hair down there."

He shuddered again.

"After the tide turned poor Maggie's body had floated clear of one of them big mooring buoys," he explained. "I crept aft, feeling half-dead, and managed to send a rocket up—to let the other searchers know, on the river. And then I slunk forward like a cur, and spent the night sitting on the heel of the bowsprit so as to be as far as possible out of Charley's way."

"Poor fellow!" I murmured.

"Yes. Poor fellow," he repeated, musingly. "That brute wouldn't let him—not even him—cheat her of her prey. But he made her fast in dock next morning. He did. We hadn't exchanged a word—not a single look for that matter. I didn't want to look at him. When the last rope was fast he put his hands to his head and stood gazing down at his feet as if trying to remember something. The men waited on the main deck for the words that end the voyage. Perhaps that is what he was trying to remember. I spoke for him. 'That'll do, men.'

"I never saw a crew leave a ship so quietly. They sneaked over the rail one after another, taking care not to bang their sea chests too heavily. They looked our way, but not one had the stomach to come up and offer to shake hands with the mate as is usual.

"I followed him all over the empty ship to and fro, here and there, with no living soul about but the two of us, because the old ship-keeper had locked himself up in the galley—both doors. Suddenly poor Charley mutters, in a crazy voice: 'I'm done here,' and strides down the gangway with me at his heels, up the dock, out at the gate, on towards Tower Hill. He used to take rooms with a decent old landlady in America Square, to be near his work.

"All at once he stops short, turns round, and comes back straight at me. 'Ned,' says he, 'I am going home.' I had the good luck to sight a four-wheeler and got him in just in time. His legs were beginning to give way. In our hall he fell down on a chair, and I'll never forget father's and mother's amazed, perfectly still faces as they stood over him. They couldn't understand what had happened to him till I blubbered out, 'Maggie got drowned, yesterday, in the river.'

"Mother let out a little cry. Father looks from him to me, and from me to him, as if comparing our faces—for, upon my soul, Charley did not resemble himself at all. Nobody moved; and the poor fellow raises his big brown hands slowly to his throat, and with one single tug rips everything open—collar, shirt, waistcoat—a perfect wreck and ruin of a man. Father and I got him upstairs somehow, and mother pretty nearly killed herself nursing him through a brain fever.'

The man in tweeds nodded at me significantly.

"Ah! there was nothing that could be done with that brute. She had a devil in her."

"Where's your brother?" I asked, expecting to hear he was dead. But he was commanding a smart steamer on the China coast, and never came home now.

Jermyn fetched a heavy sigh, and the handkerchief being now sufficiently dry, put it up tenderly to his red and lamentable nose.

"She was a ravening beast," the man in tweeds started again. "Old Colchester put his foot down and resigned. And would you believe it? Apse & Sons wrote to ask whether he wouldn't reconsider his decision! Anything to save the good name of the *Apse Family!* Old Colchester went to the office then and said that he would take charge again but only to sail her out into the North Sea and scuttle her there. He was nearly off his chump. He used to be darkish iron-gray, but his hair went snow-white in a fortnight. And Mr. Lucian Apse (they had known each other as young men) pretended not to notice it. Eh? Here's infatuation if you like! Here's pride for you!

"They jumped at the first man they could get to take her, for

fear of the scandal of the *Apse Family* not being able to find a skipper. He was a festive soul, I believe, but he stuck to her grim and
hard. Wilmot was his second mate. A harum-scarum fellow, and
pretending to a great scorn for all the girls. The fact is he was
really timid. But let only one of them do as much as lift her little
finger in encouragement, and there was nothing that could hold the
beggar. As apprentice, once, he deserted abroad after a petticoat,
and would have gone to the dogs then, if his skipper hadn't taken
the trouble to find him and lug him by the ears out of some house
of perdition or other.

"It was said that one of the firm had been heard once to express
a hope that this brute of a ship would get lost soon. I can hardly
credit the tale, unless it might have been Mr. Alfred Apse, whom
the family didn't think much of. They had him in the office, but he
was considered a bad egg altogether, always flying off to race meetings and coming home drunk. You would have thought that a ship
so full of deadly tricks would run herself ashore some day out of
sheer cussedness. But not she! She was going to last for ever. She
had a nose to keep off the bottom.'

Jermyn made a grunt of approval.

"A ship after a pilot's own heart, eh?" jeered the man in tweeds.
"Well, Wilmot managed it. He was the man for it, but even he,
perhaps, couldn't have done the trick without the green-eyed governess, or nurse, or whatever she was to the children of Mr. and
Mrs. Pamphilius.

"Those people were passengers in her from Port Adelaide to the
Cape. Well, the ship went out and anchored outside for the day.
The skipper—hospitable soul—had a lot of guests from town to a
farewell lunch—as usual with him. It was five in the evening before
the last shore boat left the side, and the weather looked ugly and
dark in the gulf. There was no reason for him to get under way.
However, as he had told everybody he was going that day, he imagined it was proper to do so anyhow. But as he had no mind after all
these festivities to tackle the straits in the dark, with a scant wind,
he gave orders to keep the ship under lower topsails and foresail as
close as she would lie, dodging along the land till the morning.
Then he sought his virtuous couch. The mate was on deck, having
his face washed very clean with hard rain squalls. Wilmot relieved
him at midnight.

"The *Apse Family* had, as you observed, a house on her poop . . ."

"A big, ugly white thing, sticking up," Jermyn murmured, sadly,
at the fire.

"That's it: a companion[5] for the cabin stairs and a sort of chart-
room combined. The rain drove in gusts on the sleepy Wilmot. The

5. Wooden hood covering stairway.

ship was then surging slowly to the southward, close hauled, with the coast within three miles or so to windward. There was nothing to look out for in that part of the gulf, and Wilmot went round to dodge the squalls under the lee of that chart-room, whose door on that side was open. The night was black, like a barrel of coal tar. And then he heard a woman's voice whispering to him.

"That confounded green-eyed girl of the Pamphilius people had put the kids to bed a long time ago, of course, but it seems couldn't get to sleep herself. She heard eight bells struck, and the chief mate come below to turn in. She waited a bit, then got into her dressing gown and stole across the empty saloon and up the stairs into the chart-room. She sat down on the settee near the open door to cool herself, I daresay.

"I suppose when she whispered to Wilmot it was as if somebody had struck a match in the fellow's brain. I don't know how it was they had got so very thick. I fancy he had met her ashore a few times before. I couldn't make it out, because, when telling the story, Wilmot would break off to swear something awful at every second word. We had met on the quay in Sydney, and he had an apron of sacking up to his chin, a big whip in his hand. A wagon driver. Glad to do anything not to starve. That's what he had come down to.

"However, there he was, with his head inside the door, on the girl's shoulder as likely as not—officer of the watch! The helmsman, on giving his evidence afterwards, said that he shouted several times that the binnacle lamp had gone out. It didn't matter to him, because his orders were to 'sail her close.' 'I thought it funny,' he said, 'that the ship should keep on falling off[6] in squalls, but I luffed her up every time as close as I was able. It was so dark I couldn't see my hand before my face, and the rain came in bucketfuls on my head.'

"The truth was that at every squall the wind hauled aft a little, till gradually the ship came to be heading straight for the coast, without a single soul in her being aware of it. Wilmot himself confessed that he had not been near the standard compass for an hour. He might well have confessed! The first thing he knew was the man on the lookout shouting blue murder forward there.

"He tore his neck free, he says, and yelled back at him: 'What do you say?'

" 'I think I hear breakers ahead, sir,' howled the man, and came rushing aft with the rest of the watch, in the 'awfulest blinding deluge that ever fell from the sky,' Wilmot says. For a second or so he was so scared and bewildered that he could not remember on which side of the gulf the ship was. He wasn't a good officer, but he

---

6. Deviating from her course; "luffed her up": brought the head of the ship nearer to the wind.

was a seaman all the same. He pulled himself together in a second, and the right orders sprang to his lips without thinking. They were to hard up with the helm[7] and shiver the main and mizzen-topsails.

"It seems that the sails actually fluttered. He couldn't see them, but he heard them rattling and banging above his head. 'No use! She was too slow in going off,' he went on, his dirty face twitching, and the damned carter's whip shaking in his hand. 'She seemed to stick fast.' And then the flutter of the canvas above his head ceased. At this critical moment the wind hauled aft again with a gust, filling the sails and sending the ship with a great way upon the rocks on her lee bow. She had overreached herself in her last little game. Her time had come—the hour, the man, the black night, the treacherous gust of wind—the right woman to put an end to her. The brute deserved nothing better. Strange are the instruments of Providence. There's a sort of poetical justice——"

The man in tweeds looked hard at me.

"The first ledge she went over stripped the false keel[8] off her. Rip! The skipper, rushing out of his berth, found a crazy woman, in a red flannel dressing gown, flying round and round the cuddy,[9] screeching like a cockatoo.

"The next bump knocked her clean under the cabin table. It also started the stern-post and carried away the rudder, and then that brute ran up a shelving, rocky shore, tearing her bottom out, till she stopped short, and the foremast dropped over the bows like a gangway."

"Anybody lost?" I asked.

"No one, unless that fellow, Wilmot," answered the gentleman, unknown to Miss Blank, looking round for his cap. "And his case was worse than drowning for a man. Everybody got ashore all right. Gale didn't come on till next day, dead from the West, and broke up that brute in a surprisingly short time. It was as though she had been rotten at heart." . . . He changed his tone, "Rain left off? I must get my bike and rush home to dinner. I live in Herne Bay— came out for a spin this morning."

He nodded at me in a friendly way, and went out with a swagger.

"Do you know who he is, Jermyn?" I asked.

The North Sea pilot shook his head, dismally. "Fancy losing a ship in that silly fashion! Oh, dear! oh dear!" he groaned in lugubrious tones, spreading his damp handkerchief again like a curtain before the glowing grate.

On going out I exchanged a glance and a smile (strictly proper) with the respectable Miss Blank, barmaid of the Three Crows.

1908

---

7. Put the tiller as far as possible to windward so as to turn the ship's head away from the wind; "shiver": cause to shake in the wind.

8. Additional keel attached to the bottom of the true keel for protection and to give stability.

9. Cabin.

The Secret Sharer

I

On my right hand there were lines of fishing stakes resembling a mysterious system of half-submerged bamboo fences, incomprehensible in its division of the domain of tropical fishes, and crazy of aspect as if abandoned forever by some nomad tribe of fishermen now gone to the other end of the ocean; for there was no sign of human habitation as far as the eye could reach. To the left a group of barren islets, suggesting ruins of stone walls, towers, and blockhouses, had its foundations set in a blue sea that itself looked solid, so still and stable did it lie below my feet; even the track of light from the westering sun shone smoothly, without that animated glitter which tells of an imperceptible ripple. And when I turned my head to take a parting glance at the tug which had just left us anchored outside the bar, I saw the straight line of the flat shore joined to the stable sea, edge to edge, with a perfect and unmarked closeness, in one leveled floor half brown, half blue under the enormous dome of the sky. Corresponding in their insignificance to the islets of the sea, two small clumps of trees, one on each side of the only fault in the impeccable joint, marked the mouth of the river Meinam we had just left on the first preparatory stage of our homeward journey; and, far back on the inland level, a larger and loftier mass, the grove surrounding the great Paknam pagoda, was the only thing on which the eye could rest from the vain task of exploring the monotonous sweep of the horizon. Here and there gleams as of a few scattered pieces of silver marked the windings of the great river; and on the nearest of them, just within the bar, the tug steaming right into the land become lost to my sight, hull and funnel and masts, as though the impassive earth had swallowed her up without an effort, without a tremor. My eye followed the light cloud of her smoke, now here, now there, above the plain, according to the devious curves of the stream, but always fainter and farther away, till I lost it at last behind the miter-shaped hill of the great pagoda. And then I was left alone with my ship, anchored at the head of the Gulf of Siam.

She floated at the starting point of a long journey, very still in an immense stillness, the shadows of her spars flung far to the eastward by the setting sun. At that moment I was alone on her decks. There was not a sound in her—and around us nothing moved, nothing lived, not a canoe on the water, not a bird in the air, not a cloud in the sky. In this breathless pause at the threshold of a long passage we seemed to be measuring our fitness for a long and arduous enterprise, the appointed task of both our existences to be carried out, far from all human eyes, with only sky and sea for spectators and for judges.

There must have been some glare in the air to interfere with one's sight, because it was only just before the sun left us that my roaming eyes made out beyond the highest ridge of the principal islet of the group something which did away with the solemnity of perfect solitude. The tide of darkness flowed on swiftly; and with tropical suddenness a swarm of stars came out above the shadowy earth, while I lingered yet, my hand resting lightly on my ship's rail as if on the shoulder of a trusted friend. But, with all that multitude of celestial bodies staring down at one, the comfort of quiet communion with her was gone for good. And there were also disturbing sounds by this time—voices, footsteps forward; the steward flitted along the main deck, a busily ministering spirit; a hand bell tinkled urgently under the poop deck. . . .

I found my two officers waiting for me near the supper table, in the lighted cuddy.[1] We sat down at once, and as I helped the chief mate, I said:

"Are you aware that there is a ship anchored inside the islands? I saw her mastheads above the ridge as the sun went down."

He raised sharply his simple face, overcharged by a terrible growth of whisker, and emitted his usual ejaculations: "Bless my soul, sir! You don't say so!"

My second mate was a sound-cheeked, silent young man, grave beyond his years, I thought; but as our eyes happened to meet I detected a slight quiver on his lips. I looked down at once. It was not my part to encourage sneering on board my ship. It must be said, too, that I knew very little of my officers. In consequence of certain events of no particular significance, except to myself, I had been appointed to the command only a fortnight before. Neither did I know much of the hands forward. All these people had been together for eighteen months or so, and my position was that of the only stranger on board. I mention this because it has some bearing on what is to follow. But what I felt most was my being a stranger to the ship; and if all the truth must be told, I was somewhat of a stranger to myself. The youngest man on board (barring the second mate), and untried as yet by a position of the fullest responsibility, I was willing to take the adequacy of the others for granted. They had simply to be equal to their tasks: but I wondered how far I should turn out faithful to that ideal conception of one's own personality every man sets up for himself secretly.

Meantime the chief mate, with an almost visible effect of collaboration on the part of his round eyes and frightful whiskers, was

1. Cabin.

trying to evolve a theory of the anchored ship. His dominant trait was to take all things into earnest consideration. He was of a pains-taking turn of mind. As he used to say, he "liked to account to himself" for practically everything that came in his way, down to a miserable scorpion he had found in his cabin a week before. The why and the wherefore of that scorpion—how it got on board and came to select his room rather than the pantry (which was a dark place and more what a scorpion would be partial to), and how on earth it managed to drown itself in the inkwell of his writing desk —had exercised him infinitely. The ship within the islands was much more easily accounted for; and just as we were about to rise from the table he made his pronouncement. She was, he doubted not, a ship from home lately arrived. Probably she drew too much water to cross the bar except at the top of spring tides. Therefore she went into that natural harbor to wait for a few days in prefer-ence to remaining in an open roadstead.

"That's so," confirmed the second mate, suddenly, in his slightly hoarse voice. "She draws over twenty feet. She's the Liverpool ship *Sephora* with a cargo of coal. Hundred and twenty-three days from Cardiff."

We looked at him in surprise.

"The tugboat skipper told me when he came on board for your letters, sir," explained the young man. "He expects to take her up the river the day after tomorrow."

After thus overwhelming us with the extent of his information he slipped out of the cabin. The mate observed regretfully that he "could not account for that young fellow's whims." What pre-vented him telling us all about it at once, he wanted to know.

I detained him as he was making a move. For the last two days the crew had had plenty of hard work, and the night before they had very little sleep. I felt painfully that I—a stranger—was doing something unusual when I directed him to let all hands turn in without setting an anchor watch.[2] I proposed to keep on deck my-self till one o'clock or thereabouts. I would get the second mate to relieve me at that hour.

"He will turn out the cook and the steward at four," I concluded, "and then give you a call. Of course at the slightest sign of any sort of wind we'll have the hands up and make a start at once."

He concealed his astonishment. "Very well, sir." Outside the cuddy he put his head in the second mate's door to inform him of my unheard-of caprice to take a five hours' anchor watch on myself. I heard the other raise his voice incredulously: "What? The cap-tain himself?" Then a few more murmurs, a door closed, then an-other. A few moments later I went on deck.

2. I.e., a part of the ship's crew kept on duty while the ship lies at anchor.

My strangeness, which had made me sleepless, had prompted that unconventional arrangement, as if I had expected in those solitary hours of the night to get on terms with the ship of which I knew nothing, manned by men of whom I knew very little more. Fast alongside a wharf, littered like any ship in port with a tangle of unrelated things, invaded by unrelated shore people, I had hardly seen her yet properly. Now, as she lay cleared for sea, the stretch of her main deck seemed to me very fine under the stars. Very fine, very roomy for her size, and very inviting. I descended the poop and paced the waist, my mind picturing to myself the coming passage through the Malay Archipelago, down the Indian Ocean, and up the Atlantic. All its phases were familiar enough to me, every characteristic, all the alternatives which were likely to face me on the high seas—everything! . . . except the novel responsibility of command. But I took heart from the reasonable thought that the ship was like other ships, the men like other men, and that the sea was not likely to keep any special surprises expressly for my discomfiture.

Arrived at that comforting conclusion, I bethought myself of a cigar and went below to get it. All was still down there. Everybody at the after end of the ship was sleeping profoundly. I came out again on the quarter-deck, agreeably at ease in my sleeping suit on that warm breathless night, barefooted, a glowing cigar in my teeth, and, going forward, I was met by the profound silence of the fore end of the ship. Only as I passed the door of the forecastle I heard a deep, quiet, trustful sigh of some sleeper inside. And suddenly I rejoiced in the great security of the sea as compared with the unrest of the land, in my choice of that untempted life presenting no disquieting problems, invested with an elementary moral beauty by the absolute straightforwardness of its appeal and by the singleness of its purpose.

The riding light in the fore-rigging burned with a clear, untroubled, as if symbolic, flame, confident and bright in the mysterious shades of the night. Passing on my way aft along the other side of the ship, I observed that the rope side ladder, put over, no doubt, for the master of the tug when he came to fetch away our letters, had not been hauled in as it should have been. I became annoyed at this, for exactitude in small matters is the very soul of discipline. Then I reflected that I had myself peremptorily dismissed my officers from duty, and by my own act had prevented the anchor watch being formally set and things properly attended to. I asked myself whether it was wise ever to interfere with the established routine of duties even from the kindest of motives. My action might have made me appear eccentric. Goodness only knew how that absurdly whiskered mate would "account" for my conduct, and what the whole ship thought of that informality of their new captain. I was vexed with myself.

Not from compunction certainly, but, as it were mechanically, I proceeded to get the ladder in myself. Now a side ladder of that sort is a light affair and comes in easily, yet my vigorous tug, which should have brought it flying on board, merely recoiled upon my body in a totally unexpected jerk. What the devil! . . . I was so astounded by the immovableness of that ladder that I remained stock-still, trying to account for it to myself like that imbecile mate of mine. In the end, of course, I put my head over the rail.

The side of the ship made an opaque belt of shadow on the darkling glassy shimmer of the sea. But I saw at once something elongated and pale floating very close to the ladder. Before I could form a guess a faint flash of phosphorescent light, which seemed to issue suddenly from the naked body of a man, flickered in the sleeping water with the elusive, silent play of summer lightning in a night sky. With a gasp I saw revealed to my stare a pair of feet, the long legs, a broad livid back immersed right up to the neck in a greenish cadaverous glow. One hand, awash, clutched the bottom rung of the ladder. He was complete but for the head. A headless corpse! The cigar dropped out of my gaping mouth with a tiny plop and a short hiss quite audible in the absolute stillness of all things under heaven. At that I suppose he raised up his face, a dimly pale oval in the shadow of the ship's side. But even then I could only barely make out down there the shape of his black-haired head. However, it was enough for the horrid, frost-bound sensation which had gripped me about the chest to pass off. The moment of vain exclamations was past, too. I only climbed on the spare spar and leaned over the rail as far as I could, to bring my eyes nearer to that mystery floating alongside.

As he hung by the ladder, like a resting swimmer, the sea lightning played about his limbs at every stir; and he appeared in it ghastly, silvery, fishlike. He remained as mute as a fish, too. He made no motion to get out of the water, either. It was inconceivable that he should not attempt to come on board, and strangely troubling to suspect that perhaps he did not want to. And my first words were prompted by just that troubled incertitude.

"What's the matter?" I asked in my ordinary tone, speaking down to the face upturned exactly under mine.

"Cramp," it answered, no louder. Then slightly anxious, "I say, no need to call anyone."

"I was not going to," I said.

"Are you alone on deck?"

"Yes."

I had somehow the impression that he was on the point of letting go the ladder to swim away beyond my ken—mysterious as he came. But, for the moment, this being appearing as if he had risen from the bottom of the sea (it was certainly the nearest land to the ship) wanted only to know the time. I told him. And he, down there, tentatively:

"I suppose your captain's turned in?"

"I am sure he isn't," I said.

He seemed to struggle with himself, for I heard something like the low, bitter murmur of doubt. "What's the good?" His next words came out with a hesitating effort.

"Look here, my man. Could you call him out quietly?"

I thought the time had come to declare myself.

"I am the captain."

I heard a "By Jove!" whispered at the level of the water. The phosphorescence flashed in the swirl of the water all about his limbs, his other hand seized the ladder.

"My name's Leggatt."

The voice was calm and resolute. A good voice. The self-possession of that man had somehow induced a corresponding state in myself. It was very quietly that I remarked:

"You must be a good swimmer."

"Yes. I've been in the water practically since nine o'clock. The question for me now is whether I am to let go this ladder and go on swimming till I sink from exhaustion, or—to come on board here."

I felt this was no mere formula of desperate speech, but a real alternative in the view of a strong soul. I should have gathered from this that he was young; indeed, it is only the young who are ever confronted by such clear issues. But at the time it was pure intuition on my part. A mysterious communication was established already between us two—in the face of that silent, darkened tropical sea. I was young, too; young enough to make no comment. The man in the water began suddenly to climb up the ladder, and I hastened away from the rail to fetch some clothes.

Before entering the cabin I stood still, listening in the lobby at the foot of the stairs. A faint snore came through the closed door of the chief mate's room. The second mate's door was on the hook, but the darkness in there was absolutely soundless. He, too, was young and could sleep like a stone. Remained the steward, but he was not likely to wake up before he was called. I got a sleeping suit out of my room and, coming back on deck, saw the naked man from the sea sitting on the main hatch, glimmering white in the darkness, his elbows on his knees and his head in his hands. In a moment he had concealed his damp body in a sleeping suit of the same gray-stripe pattern as the one I was wearing and followed me like my double on the poop. Together we moved right aft, bare-footed, silent.

"What is it?" I asked in a deadened voice, taking the lighted lamp out of the binnacle,[3] and raising it to his face.

"An ugly business."

He had rather regular features; a good mouth; light eyes under somewhat heavy, dark eyebrows; a smooth, square forehead; no growth on his cheeks; a small, brown mustache, and a well-shaped, round chin. His expression was concentrated, meditative, under the inspecting light of the lamp I held up to his face; such as a man thinking hard in solitude might wear. My sleeping suit was just right for his size. A well-knit young fellow of twenty-five at most. He caught his lower lip with the edge of white, even teeth.

"Yes," I said, replacing the lamp in the binnacle. The warm, heavy tropical night closed upon his head again.

"There's a ship over there," he murmured.

"Yes, I know. The *Sephora*. Did you know of us?"

"Hadn't the slightest idea. I am the mate of her—" He paused and corrected himself. "I should say I *was*."

"Aha! Something wrong?"

"Yes. Very wrong indeed. I've killed a man."

"What do you mean? Just now?"

"No, on the passage. Weeks ago. Thirty-nine south. When I say a man—"

"Fit of temper," I suggested, confidently.

The shadowy, dark head, like mine, seemed to nod imperceptibly above the ghostly gray of my sleeping suit. It was, in the night, as though I had been faced by my own reflection in the depths of a somber and immense mirror.

"A pretty thing to have to own up to for a Conway boy,"[4] murmured my double, distinctly.

"You're a Conway boy?"

"I am," he said, as if startled. Then, slowly . . . "Perhaps you too—"

It was so; but being a couple of years older I had left before he joined. After a quick interchange of dates a silence fell; and I thought suddenly of my absurd mate with his terrific whiskers and the "Bless my soul—you don't say so" type of intellect. My double gave me an inkling of his thoughts by saying:

"My father's a parson in Norfolk. Do you see me before a judge and jury on that charge? For myself I can't see the necessity. There are fellows that an angel from heaven—— And I am not that. He was one of those creatures that are just simmering all the time with

---

3. A stand on the deck, near the helm, on which the compass rests.

4. The *Conway* was a training ship on which student officers for the British merchant marine gained sea experience.

a silly sort of wickedness. Miserable devils that have no business to live at all. He wouldn't do his duty and wouldn't let anybody else do theirs. But what's the good of talking! You know well enough.the sort of ill-conditioned snarling cur—"

He appealed to me as if our experiences had been as identical as our clothes. And I knew well enough the pestiferous danger of such a character where there are no means of legal repression. And I knew well enough also that my double there was no homicidal ruffian. I did not think of asking him for details, and he told me the story roughly in brusque, disconnected sentences. I needed no more. I saw it all going on as though I were myself inside that other sleeping suit.

"It happened while we were setting a reefed foresail, at dusk. Reefed foresail! You understand the sort of weather. The only sail we had left to keep the ship running; so you may guess what it had been like for days. Anxious sort of job, that. He gave me some of his cursed insolence at the sheet. I tell you I was overdone with this terrific weather that seemed to have no end to it. Terrific, I tell you—and a deep ship. I believe the fellow himself was half crazed with funk. It was no time for gentlemanly reproof, so I turned round and felled him like an ox. He up and at me. We closed just as an awful sea made for the ship. All hands saw it coming and took to the rigging, but I had him by the throat, and went on shaking him like a rat, the men above us yelling, 'Look out! look out!' Then a crash as if the sky had fallen on my head. They say that for over ten minutes hardly anything was to be seen of the ship—just the three masts and a bit of the forecastle head and of the poop all awash driving along in a smother of foam. It was a miracle that they found us, jammed together behind the fore-bits. It's clear that I meant business, because I was holding him by the throat still when they picked us up. He was black in the face. It was too much for them. It seems they rushed us aft together, gripped as we were, screaming 'Murder!' like a lot of lunatics, and broke into the cuddy. And the ship running for her life, touch and go all the time, any minute her last in a sea fit to turn your hair gray only a-looking at it. I understand that the skipper, too, started raving like the rest of them. The man had been deprived of sleep for more than a week, and to have this sprung on him at the height of a furious gale nearly drove him out of his mind. I wonder they didn't fling me overboard after getting the carcass of their precious shipmate out of my fingers. They had rather a job to separate us, I've been told. A sufficiently fierce story to make an old judge and a respectable jury sit up a bit. The first thing I heard when I came to myself was the maddening howling of that endless gale, and on that the voice of the old man. He was hanging on to my bunk, staring into my face out of his sou'wester.

" 'Mr. Leggatt, you have killed a man. You can act no longer as chief mate of this ship.' "

His care to subdue his voice made it sound monotonous. He rested a hand on the end of the skylight to steady himself with, and all that time did not stir a limb, so far as I could see. "Nice little tale for a quiet tea party," he concluded in the same tone.

One of my hands, too, rested on the end of the skylight; neither did I stir a limb, so far as I knew. We stood less than a foot from each other. It occurred to me that if old "Bless my soul—you don't say so" were to put his head up the companion and catch sight of us, he would think he was seeing double, or imagine himself come upon a scene of weird witchcraft; the strange captain having a quiet confabulation by the wheel with his own gray ghost. I became very much concerned to prevent anything of the sort. I heard the other's soothing undertone.

"My father's a parson in Norfolk," it said. Evidently he had forgotten he had told me this important fact before. Truly a nice little tale.

"You had better slip down into my stateroom now," I said, moving off stealthily. My double followed my movements; our bare feet made no sound; I let him in, closed the door with care, and, after giving a call to the second mate, returned on deck for my relief.

"Not much sign of any wind yet," I remarked when he approached.

"No, sir. Not much," he assented, sleepily, in his hoarse voice, with just enough deference, no more, and barely suppressing a yawn.

"Well, that's all you have to look out for. You have got your orders."

"Yes, sir."

I paced a turn or two on the poop and saw him take up his position face forward with his elbow in the rat-lines of the mizzen-rigging before I went below. The mate's faint snoring was still going on peacefully. The cuddy lamp was burning over the table on which stood a vase with flowers, a polite attention from the ships' provision merchant—the last flowers we should see for the next three months at the very least. Two bunches of bananas hung from the beam symmetrically, one on each side of the rudder casing. Everything was as before in the ship—except that two of her captain's sleeping suits were simultaneously in use, one motionless in the cuddy, the other keeping very still in the captain's stateroom.

It must be explained here that my cabin had the form of the capital letter L, the door being within the angle and opening into the short part of the letter. A couch was to the left, the bed-place to the right; my writing desk and the chronometers' table faced the door. But anyone opening it, unless he stepped right inside, had no view of what I call the long (or vertical) part of the letter. It contained some lockers surmounted by a bookcase; and a few clothes, a thick jacket or two, caps, oilskin coat, and such like, hung on hooks. There was at the bottom of that part a door opening into my bathroom, which could be entered also directly from the saloon.[5] But that way was never used.

The mysterious arrival had discovered the advantage of this particular shape. Entering my room, lighted strongly by a big bulkhead lamp swung on gimbals[6] above my writing desk, I did not see him anywhere till he stepped out quietly from behind the coats hung in the recessed part.

"I heard somebody moving about, and went in there at once," he whispered.

I, too, spoke under my breath.

"Nobody is likely to come in here without knocking and getting permission."

He nodded. His face was thin and the sunburn faded, as though he had been ill. And no wonder. He had been, I heard presently, kept under arrest in his cabin for nearly seven weeks. But there was nothing sickly in his eyes or in his expression. He was not a bit like me, really; yet, as we stood leaning over my bed-place, whispering side by side, with our dark heads together and our backs to the door, anybody bold enough to open it stealthily would have been treated to the uncanny sight of a double captain busy talking in whispers with his other self.

"But all this doesn't tell me how you came to hang on to our side ladder," I inquired, in the hardly audible murmurs we used, after he had told me something more of the proceedings on board the *Sephora* once the bad weather was over.

"When we sighted Java Head I had had time to think all those matters out several times over. I had six weeks of doing nothing else, and with only an hour or so every evening for a tramp on the quarter-deck."

He whispered, his arms folded on the side of my bed-place, staring through the open port. And I could imagine perfectly the manner of this thinking out—a stubborn if not a steadfast operation; something of which I should have been perfectly incapable.

"I reckoned it would be dark before we closed with the land," he continued, so low that I had to strain my hearing, near as we were to each other, shoulder touching shoulder almost. "So I asked to speak to the old man. He always seemed very sick when he came to see me—as if he could not look me in the face. You know, that foresail saved the ship. She was too deep to have run long under bare poles. And it was I that managed to set it for him. Anyway,

5. I.e., the officers' dining room.
6. Device for suspending articles in order to keep them in a horizontal position whatever the ship's motion.

he came. When I had him in my cabin—he stood by the door looking at me as if I had the halter around my neck already—I asked him right away to leave my cabin door unlocked at night while the ship was going through Sunda Straits.[7] There would be the Java coast within two or three miles, off Angier Point. I wanted nothing more. I've had a prize for swimming my second year in the Conway."

"I can believe it," I breathed out.

"God only knows why they locked me in every night. To see some of their faces you'd have thought they were afraid I'd go about at night strangling people. Am I a murdering brute? Do I look it? By Jove! if I had been he wouldn't have trusted himself like that into my room. You'll say I might have chucked him aside and bolted out, there and then—it was dark already. Well, no. And for the same reason I wouldn't think of trying to smash the door. There would have been a rush to stop me at the noise, and I did not mean to get into a confounded scrimmage. Somebody else might have got killed—for I would not have broken out only to get chucked back, and I did not want any more of that work. He refused, looking more sick than ever. He was afraid of the men, and also of that old second mate of his who had been sailing with him for years—a gray-headed old humbug; and his steward, too, had been with him devil knows how long—seventeen years or more—a dogmatic sort of loafer who hated me like poison, just because I was the chief mate. No chief mate ever made more than one voyage in the *Sephora*, you know. Those two old chaps ran the ship. Devil only knows what the skipper wasn't afraid of (all his nerve went to pieces altogether in that hellish spell of bad weather we had)—of what the law would do to him—of his wife, perhaps. Oh, yes! she's on board. Though I don't think she would have meddled. She would have been only too glad to have me out of the ship in any way. The 'brand of Cain'[8] business, don't you see. That's all right. I was ready enough to go off wandering on the face of the earth—and that was price enough to pay for an Abel of that sort. Anyhow, he wouldn't listen to me. 'This thing must take its course. I represent the law here.' He was shaking life a leaf. 'So you won't?' 'No!' 'Then I hope you will be able to sleep on that,' I said, and turned my back on him. 'I wonder that *you* can,' cries he, and locks the door.

"Well, after that, I couldn't. Not very well. That was three weeks ago. We have had a slow passage through the Java Sea; drifted about Carimata[9] for ten days. When we anchored here they

---

7. Narrow passage between the islands of Sumatra and Java in the East Indies; the *Sephora* has been heading up from the Indian Ocean into the Java Sea.

8. After Cain killed his brother Abel, "the Lord set a mark upon Cain, lest any finding him should kill him" (Genesis iv.15).

9. Carimata (or Karimata) Strait, between the islands of Borneo and Billiton, connects the Java Sea with the South China Sea.

thought, I suppose, it was all right. The nearest land (and that's five miles) is the ship's destination; the consul would soon set about catching me; and there would have been no object in bolting to these islets there. I don't suppose there's a drop of water on them. I don't know how it was, but tonight that steward, after bringing me my supper, went out to let me eat it, and left the door unlocked. And I ate it—all there was, too. After I had finished I strolled out on the quarter-deck. I don't know that I meant to do anything. A breath of fresh air was all I wanted, I believe. Then a sudden temptation came over me. I kicked off my slippers and was in the water before I had made up my mind fairly. Somebody heard the splash and they raised an awful hullabaloo. 'He's gone! Lower the boats! He's committed suicide! No, he's swimming.' Certainly I was swimming. It's not so easy for a swimmer like me to commit suicide by drowning. I landed on the nearest islet before the boat left the ship's side. I heard them pulling about in the dark, hailing, and so on, but after a bit they gave up. Everything quieted down and the anchorage became as still as death. I sat down on a stone and began to think. I felt certain they would start searching for me at daylight. There was no place to hide on those stony things—and if there had been, what would have been the good? But now I was clear of that ship, I was not going back. So after a while I took off all my clothes, tied them up in a bundle with a stone inside, and dropped them in the deep water on the outer side of that islet. That was suicide enough for me. Let them think what they liked, but I didn't mean to drown myself. I meant to swim till I sank—but that's not the same thing. I struck out for another of these little islands, and it was from that one that I first saw your riding light. Something to swim for. I went on easily, and on the way I came upon a flat rock a foot or two above water. In the daytime, I dare say, you might make it out with a glass from your poop. I scrambled up on it and rested myself for a bit. Then I made another start. That last spell must have been over a mile."

His whisper was getting fainter and fainter, and all the time he stared straight out through the porthole, in which there was not even a star to be seen. I had not interrupted him. There was something that made comment impossible in his narrative, or perhaps in himself; a sort of feeling, a quality, which I can't find a name for. And when he ceased, all I found was a futile whisper: "So you swam for our light?"

"Yes—straight for it. It was something to swim for. I couldn't see any stars low down because the coast was in the way, and I couldn't see the land, either. The water was like glass. One might have been swimming in a confounded thousand-feet deep cistern with no place for scrambling out anywhere; but what I didn't like was the notion of swimming round and round like a crazed bullock before I gave out; and as I didn't mean to go back . . . No. Do you see me being hauled back, stark naked, off one of these little islands by the scruff of the neck and fighting like a wild beast? Somebody would have got killed for certain, and I did not want any of that. So I went on. Then your ladder—"

"Why didn't you hail the ship?" I asked, a little louder.

He touched my shoulder lightly. Lazy footsteps came right over our heads and stopped. The second mate had crossed from the other side of the poop and might have been hanging over the rail, for all we knew.

"He couldn't hear us talking—could he?" My double breathed into my very ear, anxiously.

His anxiety was an answer, a sufficient answer, to the question I had put to him. An answer containing all the difficulty of that situation. I closed the porthole quietly, to make sure. A louder word might have been overheard.

"Who's that?" he whispered then.

"My second mate. But I don't know much more of the fellow than you do."

And I told him a little about myself. I had been appointed to take charge while I least expected anything of the sort, not quite a fortnight ago. I didn't know either the ship or the people. Hadn't had the time in port to look about me or size anybody up. And as to the crew, all they knew was that I was appointed to take the ship home. For the rest, I was almost as much of a stranger on board as himself, I said. And at the moment I felt it most acutely. I felt that it would take very little to make me a suspect person in the eyes of the ship's company.

He had turned about meantime; and we, the two strangers in the ship, faced each other in identical attitudes.

"Your ladder—" he murmured, after a silence. "Who'd have thought of finding a ladder hanging over at night in a ship anchored out here! I felt just then a very unpleasant faintness. After the life I've been leading for nine weeks, anybody would have got out of condition. I wasn't capable of swimming round as far as your rudder chains. And, lo and behold! there was a ladder to get hold of. After I gripped it I said to myself, 'What's the good?' When I saw a man's head looking over I thought I would swim away presently and leave him shouting—in whatever language it was. I didn't mind being looked at. I—I liked it. And then you speaking to me so quietly—as if you had expected me—made me hold on a little longer. It had been a confounded lonely time—I don't mean while swimming. I was glad to talk a little to somebody that didn't belong to the *Sephora*. As to asking for the captain, that was a mere impulse. It could have been no use, with all the ship knowing about me and the other people pretty certain to be round here in the morning. I don't know—I wanted to be seen, to talk with some-body, before I went on. I don't know what I would have said. . . . 'Fine night, isn't it?' or something of the sort."

"Do you think they will be round here presently?" I asked with some incredulity.

"Quite likely," he said, faintly.

He looked extremely haggard all of a sudden. His head rolled on his shoulders.

"H'm. We shall see then. Meantime get into that bed," I whispered. "Want help? There."

It was a rather high bed-place with a set of drawers underneath. This amazing swimmer really needed the lift I gave him by seizing his leg. He tumbled in, rolled over on his back, and flung one arm across his eyes. And then, with his face nearly hidden, he must have looked exactly as I used to look in that bed. I gazed upon my other self for a while before drawing across carefully the two green serge curtains which ran on a brass rod. I thought for a moment of pinning them together for greater safety, but I sat down on the couch, and once there I felt unwilling to rise and hunt for a pin. I would do it in a moment. I was extremely tired, in a peculiarly intimate way, by the strain of stealthiness, by the effort of whisper-ing and the general secrecy of this excitement. It was three o'clock by now and I had been on my feet since nine, but I was not sleepy; I could not have gone to sleep. I sat there, fagged out, looking at the curtains, trying to clear my mind of the confused sensation of being in two places at once, and greatly bothered by an exasperating knocking in my head. It was a relief to discover suddenly that it was not in my head at all, but on the outside of the door. Before I could collect myself the words "Come in" were out of my mouth, and the steward entered with a tray, bringing in my morning coffee. I had slept, after all, and I was so frightened that I shouted, "This way! I am here, steward," as though he had been miles away. He put down the tray on the table next the couch and only then said, very quietly, "I can see you are here, sir." I felt him give me a keen look, but I dared not meet his eyes just then. He must have wondered why I had drawn the curtains of my bed before going to sleep on the couch. He went out, hooking the door open as usual.

I heard the crew washing decks above me. I knew I would have been told at once if there had been any wind. Calm, I thought, and I was doubly vexed. Indeed, I felt dual more than ever. The steward reappeared suddenly in the doorway. I jumped up from the couch so quickly that he gave a start.

"What do you want here?"

"Close your port, sir—they are washing decks."

"It is closed," I said, reddening.

"Very well, sir." But he did not move from the doorway and returned my stare in an extraordinary, equivocal manner for a time. Then his eyes wavered, all his expression changed, and in a voice unusually gentle, almost coaxingly:

"May I come in to take the empty cup away, sir?"

"Of course!" I turned my back on him while he popped in and out. Then I unhooked and closed the door and even pushed the bolt. This sort of thing could not go on very long. The cabin was as hot as an oven, too. I took a peep at my double, and discovered that he had not moved, his arm was still over his eyes; but his chest heaved; his hair was wet; his chin glistened with perspiration. I reached over him and opened the port.

"I must show myself on deck," I reflected.

Of course, theoretically, I could do what I liked, with no one to say nay to me within the whole circle of the horizon; but to lock my cabin door and take the key away I did not dare. Directly I put my head out of the companion I saw the group of my two officers, the second mate barefooted, the chief mate in long india-rubber boots, near the break of the poop, and the steward halfway down the poop ladder talking to them eagerly. He happened to catch sight of me and dived, the second ran down on the main deck shouting some order or other, and the chief mate came to meet me, touching his cap.

There was a sort of curiosity in his eye that I did not like. I don't know whether the steward had told them that I was "queer" only, or downright drunk, but I know the man meant to have a good look at me. I watched him coming with a smile which, as he got into point-blank range, took effect and froze his very whiskers. I did not give him time to open his lips.

"Square the yards by lifts and braces before the hands go to breakfast."

It was the first particular order I had given on board that ship; and I stayed on deck to see it executed, too. I had felt the need of asserting myself without loss of time. That sneering young cub got taken down a peg or two on that occasion, and I also seized the opportunity of having a good look at the face of every foremast man as they filed past me to go to the after braces. At breakfast time, eating nothing myself, I presided with such frigid dignity that the two mates were only too glad to escape from the cabin as soon as decency permitted; and all the time the dual working of my mind distracted me almost to the point of insanity. I was constantly watching myself, my secret self, as dependent on my actions as my own personality, sleeping in that bed, behind that door which faced me as I sat at the head of the table. It was very much like being mad, only it was worse because one was aware of it.

I had to shake him for a solid minute, but when at last he

opened his eyes it was in the full possession of his senses, with an inquiring look.

"All's well so far," I whispered. "Now you must vanish into the bathroom."

He did so, as noiseless as a ghost, and I then rang for the steward, and, facing him boldly, directed him to tidy up my stateroom while I was having my bath—" and be quick about it." As my tone admitted of no excuses, he said, "Yes, sir," and ran off to fetch his dustpan and brushes. I took a bath and did most of my dressing, splashing, and whistling softly for the steward's edification, while the secret sharer of my life stood drawn up bolt upright in that little space, his face looking very sunken in daylight, his eyelids lowered under the stern, dark line of his eyebrows drawn together by a slight frown.

When I left him there to go back to my room the steward was finishing dusting. I sent for the mate and engaged him in some insignificant conversation. It was, as it were, trifling with the terrific character of his whiskers; but my object was to give him an opportunity for a good look at my cabin. And then I could at last shut, with a clear conscience, the door of my stateroom and get my double back into the recessed part. There was nothing else for it. He had to sit still on a small folding stool, half smothered by the heavy coats hanging there. We listened to the steward going into the bathroom out of the saloon, filling the water bottles there, scrubbing the bath, setting things to rights, whisk, bang, clatter—out again into the saloon—turn the key—click. Such was my scheme for keeping my second self invisible. Nothing better could be contrived under the circumstances. And there we sat; I at my writing desk ready to appear busy with some papers, he behind me, out of sight of the door. It would not have been prudent to talk in daytime; and I could not have stood the excitement of that queer sense of whispering to myself. Now and then, glancing over my shoulder, I saw him far back there, sitting rigidly on the low stool, his bare feet close together, his arms folded, his head hanging on his breast—and perfectly still. Anybody would have taken him for me.

I was fascinated by it myself. Every moment I had to glance over my shoulder. I was looking at him when a voice outside the door said:

"Beg pardon, sir."

"Well!" . . . I kept my eyes on him, and so, when the voice outside the door announced, "There's a ship's boat coming our way, sir," I saw him give a start—the first movement he had made for hours. But he did not raise his bowed head.

"All right. Get the ladder over."

I hesitated. Should I whisper something to him? But what? His immobility seemed to have been never disturbed. What could I tell him he did not know already? . . . Finally I went on deck.

II

The skipper of the *Sephora* had a thin red whisker all round his face, and the sort of complexion that goes with hair of that color; also the particular, rather smeary shade of blue in the eyes. He was not exactly a showy figure; his shoulders were high, his stature but middling—one leg slightly more bandy than the other. He shook hands, looking vaguely around. A spiritless tenacity was his main characteristic, I judged. I behaved with a politeness which seemed to disconcert him. Perhaps he was shy. He mumbled to me as if he were ashamed of what he was saying; gave his name (it was something like Archbold—but at this distance of years I hardly am sure), his ship's name, and a few other particulars of that sort, in the manner of a criminal making a reluctant and doleful confession. He had had terrible weather on the passage out—terrible—terrible—wife aboard, too.

By this time we were seated in the cabin and the steward brought in a tray with a bottle and glasses. "Thanks! No." Never took liquor. Would have some water, though. He drank two tumblerfuls. Terrible thirsty work. Ever since daylight had been exploring the islands round his ship.

"What was that for—fun?" I asked, with an appearance of polite interest.

"No!" He sighed. "Painful duty."

As he persisted in his mumbling and I wanted my double to hear every word, I hit upon the notion of informing him that I regretted to say I was hard of hearing.

"Such a young man, too!" he nodded, keeping his smeary blue, unintelligent eyes fastened upon me. What was the cause of it—some disease? he inquired, without the least sympathy and as if he thought that, if so, I'd got no more than I deserved.

"Yes; disease," I admitted in a cheerful tone which seemed to shock him. But my point was gained, because he had to raise his voice to give me his tale. It is not worth while to record that version. It was just over two months since all this had happened, and he had thought so much about it that he seemed completely muddled as to its bearings, but still immensely impressed.

"What would you think of such a thing happening on board your own ship? I've had the *Sephora* for these fifteen years. I am a well-known shipmaster."

He was densely distressed—and perhaps I should have sympathized with him if I had been able to detach my mental vision from the unsuspected sharer of my cabin as though he were my second self. There he was on the other side of the bulkhead, four or five feet from us, no more, as we sat in the saloon. I looked politely at

Captain Archbold (if that was his name), but it was the other I saw, in a gray sleeping suit, seated on a low stool, his bare feet close together, his arms folded, and every word said between us falling into the ears of his dark head bowed on his chest.

"I have been at sea now, man and boy, for seven-and-thirty years, and I've never heard of such a thing happening in an English ship. And that it should be my ship. Wife on board, too."

I was hardly listening to him.

"Don't you think," I said, "that the heavy sea which, you told me, came aboard just then might have killed the man? I have seen the sheer weight of a sea kill a man very neatly, by simply breaking his neck."

"Good God!" he uttered, impressively, fixing his smeary blue eyes on me. "The sea! No man killed by the sea ever looked like that." He seemed positively scandalized at my suggestion. And as I gazed at him, certainly not prepared for anything original on his part, he advanced his head close to mine and thrust his tongue out at me so suddenly that I couldn't help starting back.

After scoring over my calmness in this graphic way he nodded wisely. If I had seen the sight, he assured me, I would never forget it as long as I lived. The weather was too bad to give the corpse a proper sea burial. So next day at dawn they took it up on the poop, covering its face with a bit of bunting; he read a short prayer, and then, just as it was, in its oilskins and long boots, they launched it amongst those mountainous seas that seemed ready every moment to swallow up the ship herself and the terrified lives on board of her.

"That reefed foresail saved you," I threw in.

"Under God—it did," he exclaimed fervently. "It was by a special mercy, I firmly believe, that it stood some of those hurricane squalls."

"It was the setting of that sail which—" I began.

"God's own hand in it," he interrupted me. "Nothing less could have done it. I don't mind telling you that I hardly dared give the order. It seemed impossible that we could touch anything without losing it, and then our last hope would have been gone."

The terror of that gale was on him yet. I let him go on for a bit, then said, casually—as if returning to a minor subject:

"You were very anxious to give up your mate to the shore people, I believe?"

He was. To the law. His obscure tenacity on that point had in it something incomprehensible and a little awful; something, as it were, mystical, quite apart from his anxiety that he should not be suspected of "countenancing any doings of that sort." Seven-and-thirty virtuous years at sea, of which over twenty of immaculate command, and the last fifteen in the *Sephora*, seemed to have laid him under some pitiless obligation.

"And you know," he went on, groping shamefacedly amongst his feelings, "I did not engage that young fellow. His people had some interest with my owners. I was in a way forced to take him on. He looked very smart, very gentlemanly, and all that. But do you know —I never liked him, somehow. I am a plain man. You see, he wasn't exactly the sort for the chief mate of a ship like the *Sephora*."

I had become so connected in thoughts and impressions with the secret sharer of my cabin that I felt as if I, personally, were being given to understand that I, too, was not the sort that would have done for the chief mate of a ship like the *Sephora*. I had no doubt of it in my mind.

"Not at all the style of man. You understand," he insisted, superfluously, looking hard at me.

I smiled urbanely. He seemed at a loss for a while.

"I suppose I must report a suicide."

"Beg pardon?"

"Sui-cide! That's what I'll have to write to my owners directly I get in."

"Unless you manage to recover him before tomorrow," I assented, dispassionately. . . . "I mean, alive."

He mumbled something which I really did not catch, and I turned my ear to him in a puzzled manner. He fairly bawled:

"The land—I say, the mainland is at least seven miles off my anchorage."

"About that."

My lack of excitement, of curiosity, of surprise, of any sort of pronounced interest, began to arouse his distrust. But except for the felicitous pretense of deafness I had not tried to pretend anything. I had felt utterly incapable of playing the part of ignorance properly, and therefore was afraid to try. It is also certain that he had brought some ready-made suspicions with him, and that he viewed my politeness as a strange and unnatural phenomenon. And yet how else could I have received him? Not heartily! That was impossible for psychological reasons, which I need not state here. My only object was to keep off his inquiries. Surlily? Yes, but surliness might have provoked a point-blank question. From its novelty to him and from its nature, punctilious courtesy was the manner best calculated to restrain the man. But there was the danger of his breaking through my defense bluntly. I could not, I think, have met him by a direct lie, also for psychological (not moral) reasons. If he had only known how afraid I was of his putting my feeling of identity with the other to the test! But, strangely enough—(I thought of it only afterward)—I believe that he was not a little disconcerted by the reverse side of that weird situation, by something in me that reminded him of the man he was seeking—suggested a mysterious similitude to the young fellow he had distrusted and disliked from the first.

However that might have been, the silence was not very prolonged. He took another oblique step.

"I reckon I had no more than a two-mile pull to your ship. Not a bit more."

"And quite enough, too, in this awful heat," I said.

Another pause full of mistrust followed. Necessity, they say, is mother of invention, but fear, too, is not barren of ingenious suggestions. And I was afraid he would ask me point-blank for news of my other self.

"Nice little saloon, isn't it?" I remarked, as if noticing for the first time the way his eyes roamed from one closed door to the other. "And very well fitted out, too. Here, for instance," I continued, reaching over the back of my seat negligently and flinging the door open, "is my bathroom."

He made an eager movement, but hardly gave it a glance. I got up, shut the door of the bathroom, and invited him to have a look round, as if I were very proud of my accommodation. He had to rise and be shown round, but he went through the business without any raptures whatever.

"And now we'll have a look at my stateroom," I declared, in a voice as loud as I dared to make it, crossing the cabin to the starboard side with purposely heavy steps.

He followed me in and gazed around. My intelligent double had vanished. I played my part.

"Very convenient—isn't it?"

"Very nice. Very comf . . ." He didn't finish, and went out brusquely as if to escape from some unrighteous wiles of mine. But it was not to be. I had been too frightened not to feel vengeful; I felt I had him on the run, and I meant to keep him on the run. My polite insistence must have had something menacing in it, because he gave in suddenly. And I did not let him off a single item; mate's room, pantry, storerooms, the very sail locker which was also under the poop—he had to look into them all. When at last I showed him out on the quarter-deck he drew a long, spiritless sigh, and mumbled dismally that he must really be going back to his ship now. I desired my mate, who had joined us, to see to the captain's boat.

The man of whiskers gave a blast on the whistle which he used to wear hanging round his neck, and yelled, "*Sephora's* away!" My double down there in my cabin must have heard, and certainly could not feel more relieved than I. Four fellows came running out from somewhere forward and went over the side, while my own men, appearing on deck too, lined the rail. I escorted my visitor to the gangway ceremoniously, and nearly overdid it. He was a tenacious beast. On the very ladder he lingered, and in that unique, guiltily conscientious manner of sticking to the point:

"I say . . . you . . . you don't think that—"

I covered his voice loudly:

"Certainly not. . . . I am delighted. Good-by."

I had an idea of what he meant to say, and just saved myself by the privilege of defective hearing. He was too shaken generally to insist, but my mate, close witness of that parting, looked mystified and his face took on a thoughtful cast. As I did not want to appear as if I wished to avoid all communication with my officers, he had the opportunity to address me.

"Seems a very nice man. His boat's crew told our chaps a very extraordinary story, if what I am told by the steward is true. I suppose you had it from the captain, sir?"

"Yes. I had a story from the captain."

"A very horrible affair—isn't it, sir?"

"It is."

"Beats all these tales we hear about murders in Yankee ships."

"I don't think it beats them. I don't think it resembles them in the least."

"Bless my soul—you don't say so! But of course I've no acquaintance whatever with American ships, not I, so I couldn't go against your knowledge. It's horrible enough for me. . . . But the queerest part is that these fellows seemed to have some idea the man was hidden aboard here. They had really. Did you ever hear of such a thing?"

"Preposterous—isn't it?"

We were walking to and fro athwart the quarter-deck. No one of the crew forward could be seen (the day was Sunday), and the mate pursued:

"There was some little dispute about it. Our chaps took offense. 'As if we would harbor a thing like that,' they said. 'Wouldn't you like to look for him in our coal hole?' Quite a tiff. But they made it up in the end. I suppose he did drown himself. Don't you, sir?"

"I don't suppose anything."

"You have no doubt in the matter, sir?"

"None whatever."

I left him suddenly. I felt I was producing a bad impression, but with my double down there it was most trying to be on deck. And it was almost as trying to be below. Altogether a nerve-trying situation. But on the whole I felt less torn in two when I was with him. There was no one in the whole ship whom I dared take into my confidence. Since the hands had got to know his story, it would have been impossible to pass him off for anyone else, and an accidental discovery was to be dreaded now more than ever. . . .

The steward being engaged in laying the table for dinner, we could talk only with our eyes when I first went down. Later in the afternoon we had a cautious try at whispering. The Sunday quietness of the ship was against us; the stillness of air and water around her was against us; the elements, the men were against us—everything was against us in our secret partnership; time itself—for this could not go on forever. The very trust in Providence was, I suppose, denied to his guilt. Shall I confess that this thought cast me down very much? And as to the chapter of accidents which counts for so much in the book of success, I could only hope that it was closed. For what favorable accident could be expected?

"Did you hear everything?" were my first words as soon as we took up our position side by side, leaning over my bed-place.

He had. And the proof of it was his earnest whisper, "The man told you he hardly dared to give the order."

I understood the reference to be to that saving foresail.

"Yes. He was afraid of it being lost in the setting."

"I assure you he never gave the order. He may think he did, but he never gave it. He stood there with me on the break of the poop after the maintopsail blew away, and whimpered about our last hope—positively whimpered about it and nothing else—and the night coming on! To hear one's skipper go on like that in such weather was enough to drive any fellow out of his mind. It worked me up into a sort of desperation. I just took it into my own hands and went away from him, boiling, and— But what's the use telling you? *You* know! . . . Do you think that if I had not been pretty fierce with them I should have got the men to do anything? Not it! The bosun perhaps? Perhaps! It wasn't a heavy sea—it was a sea gone mad! I suppose the end of the world will be something like that; and a man may have the heart to see it coming once and be done with it—but to have to face it day after day— I don't blame anybody. I was precious little better than the rest. Only—I was an officer of that old coal-wagon, anyhow—"

"I quite understand," I conveyed that sincere assurance into his ear. He was out of breath with whispering; I could hear him pant slightly. It was all very simple. The same strung-up force which had given twenty-four men a chance, at least, for their lives, had, in a sort of recoil, crushed an unworthy mutinous existence.

But I had no leisure to weigh the merits of the matter—footsteps in the saloon, a heavy knock. "There's enough wind to get under way with, sir." Here was the call of a new claim upon my thoughts and even upon my feelings.

"Turn the hands up," I cried through the door. "I'll be on deck directly."

I was going out to make the acquaintance of my ship. Before I left the cabin our eyes met—the eyes of the only two strangers on board. I pointed to the recessed part where the little campstool

awaited him and laid my finger on my lips. He made a gesture—
somewhat vague—a little mysterious, accompanied by a faint smile,
as if of regret.

This is not the place to enlarge upon the sensations of a man
who feels for the first time a ship move under his feet to his own
independent word. In my case they were not unalloyed. I was not
wholly alone with my command; for there was that stranger in
my cabin. Or rather, I was not completely and wholly with her.
Part of me was absent. That mental feeling of being in two places
at once affected me physically as if the mood of secrecy had penetrated my very soul. Before an hour had elapsed since the ship had
begun to move, having occasion to ask the mate (he stood by my
side) to take a compass bearing of the Pagoda, I caught myself
reaching up to his ear in whispers. I say I caught myself, but enough
had escaped to startle the man. I can't describe it otherwise than
by saying that he shied. A grave, preoccupied manner, as though he
were in possession of some perplexing intelligence, did not leave
him henceforth. A little later I moved away from the rail to look
at the compass with such a stealthy gait that the helmsman noticed it—and I could not help noticing the unusual roundness of
his eyes. These are trifling instances, though it's to no commander's
advantage to be suspected of ludicrous eccentricities. But I was
also more seriously affected. There are to a seaman certain words,
gestures, that should in given conditions come as naturally, as instinctively as the winking of a menaced eye. A certain order should
spring on to his lips without thinking; a certain sign should get itself made, so to speak, without reflection. But all unconscious alertness had abandoned me. I had to make an effort of will to recall
myself back (from the cabin) to the conditions of the moment. I
felt that I was appearing an irresolute commander to those people
who were watching me more or less critically.

And, besides, there were the scares. On the second day out, for
instance, coming off the deck in the afternoon (I had straw slippers on my bare feet) I stopped at the open pantry door and spoke
to the steward. He was doing something there with his back to
me. At the sound of my voice he nearly jumped out of his skin, as
the saying is, and incidentally broke a cup.

"What on earth's the matter with you?" I asked, astonished.

He was extremely confused. "Beg your pardon, sir. I made sure
you were in your cabin."

"You see I wasn't."

"No, sir. I could have sworn I had heard you moving in there
not a moment ago. It's most extraordinary . . . very sorry, sir."

I passed on with an inward shudder. I was so identified with my
secret double that I did not even mention the fact in those scanty,
fearful whispers we exchanged. I suppose he had made some slight

noise of some kind or other. It would have been miraculous if he hadn't at one time or another. And yet, haggard as he appeared, he looked always perfectly self-controlled, more than calm—almost invulnerable. On my suggestion he remained almost entirely in the bathroom, which, upon the whole, was the safest place. There could be really no shadow of an excuse for anyone ever wanting to go in there, once the steward had done with it. It was a very tiny place. Sometimes he reclined on the floor, his legs bent, his head sustained on one elbow. At others I would find him on the campstool, sitting in his gray sleeping suit and with his cropped dark hair like a patient, unmoved convict. At night I would smuggle him into my bed-place, and we would whisper together, with the regular footfalls of the officer of the watch passing and repassing over our heads. It was an infinitely miserable time. It was lucky that some tins of fine preserves were stowed in a locker in my stateroom; hard bread I could always get hold of; and so he lived on stewed chicken, paté de foie gras, asparagus, cooked oysters, sardines—on all sorts of abominable sham delicacies out of tins. My early morning coffee he always drank; and it was all I dared do for him in that respect.

Every day there was the horrible maneuvering to go through so that my room and then the bathroom should be done in the usual way. I came to hate the sight of the steward, to abhor the voice of that harmless man. I felt that it was he who would bring on the disaster of discovery. It hung like a sword over our heads.

The fourth day out, I think (we were then working down the east side of the Gulf of Siam, tack for tack, in light winds and smooth water)—the fourth day, I say, of this miserable juggling with the unavoidable, as we sat at our evening meal, that man, whose slightest movement I dreaded, after putting down the dishes ran up on deck busily. This could not be dangerous. Presently he came down again; and then it appeared that he had remembered a coat of mine which I had thrown over a rail to dry after having been wetted in a shower which had passed over the ship in the afternoon. Sitting stolidly at the head of the table I became terrified at the sight of the garment on his arm. Of course he made for my door. There was no time to lose.

"Steward," I thundered. My nerves were so shaken that I could not govern my voice and conceal my agitation. This was the sort of thing that made my terrifically whiskered mate tap his forehead with his forefinger. I had detected him using that gesture while talking on deck with a confidential air to the carpenter. It was too far to hear a word, but I had no doubt that this pantomime could only refer to the strange new captain.

"Yes, sir," the pale-faced steward turned resignedly to me. It was this maddening course of being shouted at, checked without rhyme or reason, arbitrarily chased out of my cabin, suddenly called into it, sent flying out of his pantry on incomprehensible errands, that accounted for the growing wretchedness of his expression.

"Where are you going with that coat?"

"To your room, sir."

"Is there another shower coming?"

"I'm sure I don't know, sir. Shall I go up again and see, sir?"

"No! never mind."

My object was attained, as of course my other self in there would have heard everything that passed. During this interlude my two officers never raised their eyes off their respective plates; but the lip of that confounded cub, the second mate, quivered visibly.

I expected the steward to hook my coat on and come out at once. He was very slow about it; but I dominated my nervousness sufficiently not to shout after him. Suddenly I became aware (it could be heard plainly enough) that the fellow for some reason or other was opening the door of the bathroom. It was the end. The place was literally not big enough to swing a cat in. My voice died in my throat and I went stony all over. I expected to hear a yell of surprise and terror, and made a movement, but had not the strength to get on my legs. Everything remained still. Had my second self taken the poor wretch by the throat? I don't know what I would have done next moment if I had not seen the steward come out of my room, close the door, and then stand quietly by the sideboard.

Saved, I thought. But, no! Lost! Gone! He was gone!

I laid my knife and fork down and leaned back in my chair. My head swam. After a while, when sufficiently recovered to speak in a steady voice, I instructed my mate to put the ship round at eight o'clock himself.

"I won't come on deck," I went on. "I think I'll turn in, and unless the wind shifts I don't want to be disturbed before midnight. I feel a bit seedy."

"You did look middling bad a little while ago," the chief mate remarked without showing any great concern.

They both went out, and I stared at the steward clearing the table. There was nothing to be read on that wretched man's face. But why did he avoid my eyes I asked myself. Then I thought I should like to hear the sound of his voice.

"Steward!"

"Sir!" Startled as usual.

"Where did you hang up that coat?"

"In the bathroom, sir." The usual anxious tone. "It's not quite dry yet, sir."

For some time longer I sat in the cuddy. Had my double vanished as he had come? But of his coming there was an explanation, whereas his disappearance would be inexplicable. . . . I went slowly into my dark room, shut the door, lighted the lamp, and for a time dared not turn round. When at last I did I saw him standing bolt upright in the narrow recessed part. It would not be true to say I had a shock, but an irresistible doubt of his bodily existence flitted through my mind. Can it be, I asked myself, that he is not visible to other eyes than mine? It was like being haunted. Motionless, with a grave face, he raised his hands slightly at me in a gesture which meant clearly, "Heavens! what a narrow escape!" Narrow indeed. I think I had come creeping quietly as near insanity as any man who has not actually gone over the border. That gesture restrained me, so to speak.

The mate with the terrific whiskers was now putting the ship on the other tack. In the moment of profound silence which follows upon the hands going to their stations I heard on the poop his raised voice: "Hard alee!" and the distant shout of the order repeated on the maindeck. The sails, in that light breeze, made but a faint fluttering noise. It ceased. The ship was coming round slowly; I held my breath in the renewed stillness of expectation; one wouldn't have thought that there was a single living soul on her decks. A sudden brisk shout, "Mainsail haul!" broke the spell, and in the noisy cries and rush overhead of the men running away with the main brace we two, down in my cabin, came together in our usual position by the bed-place.

He did not wait for my question. "I heard him fumbling here and just managed to squat myself down in the bath," he whispered to me. "The fellow only opened the door and put his arm in to hang the coat up. All the same—"

"I never thought of that," I whispered back, even more appalled than before at the closeness of the shave, and marveling at that something unyielding in his character which was carrying him through so finely. There was no agitation in his whisper. Whoever was being driven distracted, it was not he. He was sane. And the proof of his sanity was continued when he took up the whispering again.

"It would never do for me to come to life again."

It was something that a ghost might have said. But what he was alluding to was his old captain's reluctant admission of the theory of suicide. It would obviously serve his turn—if I had understood at all the view which seemed to govern the unalterable purpose of his action.

"You must maroon me as soon as ever you can get amongst these islands off the Cambodje[1] shore," he went on.

"Maroon you! We are not living in a boy's adventure tale," I protested. His scornful whispering took me up.

1. I.e., Cambodia.

"We aren't indeed! There's nothing of a boy's tale in this. But there's nothing else for it. I want no more. You don't suppose I am afraid of what can be done to me? Prison or gallows or whatever they may please. But you don't see me coming back to explain such things to an old fellow in a wig and twelve respectable tradesmen, do you? What can they know whether I am guilty or not—or of *what* I am guilty, either? That's my affair. What does the Bible say? 'Driven off the face of the earth.'[2] Very well. I am off the face of the earth now. As I came at night so I shall go."

"Impossible!" I murmured. "You can't."

"Can't? . . . Not naked like a soul on the Day of Judgment. I shall freeze on to this sleeping suit. The Last Day is not yet—and . . . you have understood thoroughly. Didn't you?"

I felt suddenly ashamed of myself. I may say truly that I understood—and my hesitation in letting that man swim away from my ship's side had been a mere sham sentiment, a sort of cowardice.

"It can't be done now till next night," I breathed out. "The ship is on the offshore tack and the wind may fail us."

"As long as I know that you understand," he whispered. "But of course you do. It's a great satisfaction to have got somebody to understand. You seem to have been there on purpose." And in the same whisper, as if we two whenever we talked had to say things to each other which were not fit for the world to hear, he added, "It's very wonderful."

We remained side by side talking in our secret way—but sometimes silent or just exchanging a whispered word or two at long intervals. And as usual he stared through the port. A breath of wind came now and again into our faces. The ship might have been moored in dock, so gently and on an even keel she slipped through the water, that did not murmur even at our passage, shadowy and silent like a phantom sea.

At midnight I went on deck, and to my mate's great surprise put the ship round on the other tack. His terrible whiskers flitted round me in silent criticism. I certainly should not have done it if it had been only a question of getting out of that sleepy gulf as quickly as possible. I believe he told the second mate, who relieved him, that it was a great want of judgment. The other only yawned. That intolerable cub shuffled about so sleepily and lolled against the rails in such a slack, improper fashion that I came down on him sharply.

"Aren't you properly awake yet?"

"Yes, sir! I am awake."

"Well, then, be good enough to hold yourself as if you were. And keep a lookout. If there's any current we'll be closing with

2. "And Cain said unto the Lord, ' * * * Behold, thou hast driven me   out this day from the face of the earth * * * ' " (Genesis iv.13–14).

some islands before daylight."

The east side of the gulf is fringed with islands, some solitary, others in groups. On the blue background of the high coast they seem to float on silvery patches of calm water, arid and gray, or dark green and rounded like clumps of evergreen bushes, with the larger ones, a mile or two long, showing the outlines of ridges, ribs of gray rock under the dark mantle of matted leafage. Unknown to trade, to travel, almost to geography, the manner of life they harbor is an unsolved secret. There must be villages—settlements of fishermen at least—on the largest of them, and some communication with the world is probably kept up by native craft. But all that forenoon, as we headed for them, fanned along by the faintest of breezes, I saw no sign of man or canoe in the field of the telescope I kept on pointing at the scattered group.

At noon I gave no orders for a change of course, and the mate's whiskers became much concerned and seemed to be offering themselves unduly to my notice. At last I said:

"I am going to stand right in. Quite in—as far as I can take her."

The stare of extreme surprise imparted an air of ferocity also to his eyes, and he looked truly terrific for a moment.

"We're not doing well in the middle of the gulf," I continued, casually. "I am going to look for the land breezes tonight."

"Bless my soul! Do you mean, sir, in the dark amongst the lot of all them islands and reefs and shoals?"

"Well—if there are any regular land breezes at all on this coast one must get close inshore to find them, mustn't one?"

"Bless my soul!" he exclaimed again under his breath. All that afternoon he wore a dreamy, contemplative appearance which in him was a mark of perplexity. After dinner I went into my stateroom as if I meant to take some rest. There we two bent our dark heads over a half-unrolled chart lying on my bed.

"There," I said. "It's got to be Koh-ring. I've been looking at it ever since sunrise. It has got two hills and a low point. It must be inhabited. And on the coast opposite there is what looks like the mouth of a biggish river—with some town, no doubt, not far up. It's the best chance for you that I can see."

"Anything. Koh-ring let it be."

He looked thoughtfully at the chart as if surveying chances and distances from a lofty height—and following with his eyes his own figure wandering on the blank land of Cochin China,[3] and then passing off that piece of paper clean out of sight into uncharted regions. And it was as if the ship had two captains to plan her course for her. I had been so worried and restless running up and down that I had not had the patience to dress that day. I had remained in my sleeping suit, with straw slippers and a soft floppy

---

3. South of Cambodia, with coast on the Gulf of Siam and the South China Sea.

hat. The closeness of the heat in the gulf had been most oppressive, and the crew were used to see me wandering in that airy attire.

"She will clear the south point as she heads now," I whispered into his ear. "Goodness only knows when, though, but certainly after dark. I'll edge her in to half a mile, as far as I may be able to judge in the dark—"

"Be careful," he murmured, warningly—and I realized suddenly that all my future, the only future for which I was fit, would perhaps go irretrievably to pieces in any mishap to my first command.

I could not stop a moment longer in the room. I motioned him to get out of sight and made my way on the poop. That unplayful cub had the watch. I walked up and down for a while thinking things out, then beckoned him over.

"Send a couple of hands to open the two quarter-deck ports," I said, mildly.

He actually had the impudence, or else so forgot himself in his wonder at such an incomprehensible order, as to repeat:

"Open the quarter-deck ports! What for, sir?"

"The only reason you need concern yourself about is because I tell you to do so. Have them open wide and fastened properly."

He reddened and went off, but I believe made some jeering remark to the carpenter as to the sensible practice of ventilating a ship's quarter-deck. I know he popped into the mate's cabin to impart the fact to him because the whiskers came on deck, as it were by chance, and stole glances at me from below—for signs of lunacy or drunkenness, I suppose.

A little before supper, feeling more restless than ever, I rejoined, for a moment, my second self. And to find him sitting so quietly was surprising, like something against nature, inhuman.

I developed my plan in a hurried whisper.

"I shall stand in as close as I dare and then put her round. I shall presently find means to smuggle you out of here into the sail locker, which communicates with the lobby. But there is an opening, a sort of square for hauling the sails out, which gives straight on the quarter-deck and which is never closed in fine weather, so as to give air to the sails. When the ship's way is deadened in stays and all the hands are aft at the main braces you shall have a clear road to slip out and get overboard through the open quarter-deck port. I've had them both fastened up. Use a rope's end to lower yourself into the water so as to avoid a splash—you know. It could be heard and cause some beastly complication."

He kept silent for a while, then whispered, "I understand."

"I won't be there to see you go," I began with an effort. "The rest . . . I only hope I have understood, too."

"You have. From first to last," and for the first time there seemed to be a faltering, something strained in his whisper. He caught hold of my arm, but the ringing of the supper bell made me start. He didn't, though; he only released his grip.

After supper I didn't come below again till well past eight o'clock. The faint, steady breeze was loaded with dew; and the wet, darkened sails held all there was of propelling power in it. The night, clear and starry, sparkled darkly, and the opaque, lightless patches shifting slowly against the low stars were the drifting islets. On the port bow there was a big one more distant and shadowily imposing by the great space of sky it eclipsed.

On opening the door I had a back view of my very own self looking at a chart. He had come out of the recess and was standing near the table.

"Quite dark enough," I whispered.

He stepped back and leaned against my bed with a level, quiet glance. I sat on the couch. We had nothing to say to each other. Over our heads the officer of the watch moved here and there. Then I heard him move quickly. I knew what that meant. He was making for the companion; and presently his voice was outside my door.

"We are drawing in pretty fast, sir. Land looks rather close."

"Very well," I answered. "I am coming on deck directly."

I waited till he was gone out of the cuddy, then rose. My double moved too. The time had come to exchange our last whispers, for neither of us was ever to hear each other's natural voice.

"Look here!" I opened a drawer and took out three sovereigns. "Take this, anyhow. I've got six and I'd give you the lot, only I must keep a little money to buy some fruit and vegetables for the crew from native boats as we go through Sunda Straits."

He shook his head.

"Take it," I urged him, whispering desperately. "No one can tell what—"

He smiled and slapped meaningly the only pocket of the sleeping jacket. It was not safe, certainly. But I produced a large old silk handkerchief of mine, and tying the three pieces of gold in a corner, pressed it on him. He was touched, I suppose, because he took it at last and tied it quickly round his waist under the jacket, on his bare skin.

Our eyes met; several seconds elapsed, till, our glances still mingled, I extended my hand and turned the lamp out. Then I passed through the cuddy, leaving the door of my room wide open. . . . "Steward!"

He was still lingering in the pantry in the greatness of his zeal, giving a rub-up to a plated cruet stand the last thing before going to bed. Being careful not to wake up the mate, whose room was opposite, I spoke in an undertone.

He looked round anxiously. "Sir!"

"Can you get me a little hot water from the galley?"

"I am afraid, sir, the galley fire's been out for some time now."

"Go and see."

He fled up the stairs.

"Now," I whispered, loudly, into the saloon—too loudly, perhaps, but I was afraid I couldn't make a sound. He was by my side in an instant—the double captain slipped past the stairs— through the tiny dark passage . . . a sliding door. We were in the sail locker, scrambling on our knees over the sails. A sudden thought struck me. I saw myself wandering barefooted, bareheaded, the sun beating on my dark poll. I snatched off my floppy hat and tried hurriedly in the dark to ram it on my other self. He dodged and fended off silently. I wonder what he thought had come to me before he understood and suddenly desisted. Our hands met gropingly, lingered united in a steady, motionless clasp for a second. . . . No word was breathed by either of us when they separated.

I was standing quietly by the pantry door when the steward returned.

"Sorry, sir. Kettle barely warm. Shall I light the spirit lamp?"

"Never mind."

I came out on deck slowly. It was now a matter of conscience to shave the land as close as possible—for now he must go overboard whenever the ship was put in stays. Must! There could be no going back for him. After a moment I walked over to leeward and my heart flew into my mouth at the nearness of the land on the bow. Under any other circumstances I would not have held on a minute longer. The second mate had followed me anxiously.

I looked on till I felt I could command my voice.

"She will weather," I said then in a quiet tone.

"Are you going to try that, sir?" he stammered out incredulously.

I took no notice of him and raised my tone just enough to be heard by the helmsman.

"Keep her good full."

"Good full, sir."

The wind fanned my cheek, the sails slept, the world was silent. The strain of watching the dark loom of the land grow bigger and denser was too much for me. I had shut my eyes—because the ship must go closer. She must! The stillness was intolerable. Were we standing still?

When I opened my eyes the second view started my heart with a thump. The black southern hill of Koh-ring seemed to hang right over the ship like a towering fragment of the everlasting night. On that enormous mass of blackness there was not a gleam to be seen, not a sound to be heard. It was gliding irresistibly toward us and yet seemed already within reach of the hand. I saw the vague figures of the watch grouped in the waist, gazing in awed silence.

"Are you going on, sir?" inquired an unsteady voice at my elbow. I ignored it. I had to go on.

"Keep her full. Don't check her way. That won't do now," I said warningly.

"I can't see the sails very well," the helmsman answered me, in strange, quavering tones.

Was she close enough? Already she was, I won't say in the shadow of the land, but in the very blackness of it, already swallowed up as it were, gone too close to be recalled, gone from me altogether.

"Give the mate a call," I said to the young man who stood at my elbow still as death. "And turn all hands up."

My tone had a borrowed loudness reverberated from the height of the land. Several voices cried out together: "We are all on deck, sir."

Then stillness again, with the great shadow gliding closer, towering higher, without a light, without a sound. Such a hush had fallen on the ship that she might have been a bark of the dead floating in slowly under the very gate of Erebus.[4]

"My God! Where are we?"

It was the mate moaning at my elbow. He was thunderstruck, and as it were deprived of the moral support of his whiskers. He clapped his hands and absolutely cried out, "Lost!"

"Be quiet," I said sternly.

He lowered his tone, but I saw the shadowy gesture of his despair. "What are we doing here?"

"Looking for the land wind."

He made as if to tear his hair, and addressed me recklessly.

"She will never get out. You have done it, sir. I knew it'd end in something like this. She will never weather, and you are too close now to stay. She'll drift ashore before she's round. O my God!"

I caught his arm as he was raising it to batter his poor devoted head, and shook it violently.

"She's ashore already," he wailed, trying to tear himself away.

"Is she? . . . Keep good full there!"

"Good full, sir," cried the helmsman in a frightened, thin, child-like voice.

I hadn't let go the mate's arm and went on shaking it. "Ready about, do you hear? You go forward"—shake—"and stop there" —shake—"and hold your noise"—shake—"and see these head sheets properly overhauled"—shake, shake—shake.

And all the time I dared not look toward the land lest my heart should fail me. I released my grip at last and he ran forward as if

4. Entry to Hades; place of pitch darkness.

fleeing for dear life.

I wondered what my double there in the sail locker thought of this commotion. He was able to hear everything—and perhaps he was able to understand why, on my conscience, it had to be thus close—no less. My first order "Hard alee!" re-echoed ominously under the towering shadow of Koh-ring as if I had shouted in a mountain gorge. And then I watched the land intently. In that smooth water and light wind it was impossible to feel the ship coming-to. No! I could not feel her. And my second self was making now ready to slip out and lower himself overboard. Perhaps he was gone already . . . ?

The great black mass brooding over our very mastheads began to pivot away from the ship's side silently. And now I forgot the secret stranger ready to depart, and remembered only that I was a total stranger to the ship. I did not know her. Would she do it? How was she to be handled?

I swung the mainyard and waited helplessly. She was perhaps stopped, and her very fate hung in the balance, with the black mass of Koh-ring like the gate of the everlasting night towering over her taffrail.[5] What would she do now? Had she way on her yet? I stepped to the side swiftly, and on the shadowy water I could see nothing except a faint phosphorescent flash revealing the glassy smoothness of the sleeping surface. It was impossible to tell—and I had not learned yet the feel of my ship. Was she moving? What I needed was something easily seen, a piece of paper, which I could throw overboard and watch. I had nothing on me. To run down for it I didn't dare. There was no time. All at once my strained, yearning stare distinguished a white object floating within a yard of the ship's side. White on the black water. A phosphorescent flash passed under it. What was that thing? . . . I recognized my own floppy hat. It must have fallen off his head . . . and he didn't bother. Now I had what I wanted—the saving mark for my eyes. But I hardly thought of my other self, now gone from the ship, to be hidden forever from all friendly faces, to be a fugitive and a vagabond on the earth, with no brand of the curse on his sane forehead to stay a slaying hand . . . too proud to explain.

And I watched the hat—the expression of my sudden pity for his mere flesh. It had been meant to save his homeless head from the dangers of the sun. And now—behold—it was saving the ship, by serving me for a mark to help out the ignorance of my strangeness. Ha! It was drifting forward, warning me just in time that the ship had gathered sternway.

"Shift the helm," I said in a low voice to the seaman standing still like a statue.

5. Rail across the stern.

The man's eyes glistened wildly in the binnacle light as he jumped round to the other side and spun round the wheel.

I walked to the break of the poop. On the overshadowed deck all hands stood by the forebraces waiting for my order. The stars ahead seemed to be gliding from right to left. And all was so still in the world that I heard the quiet remark "She's round," passed in a tone of intense relief between two seamen.

"Let go and haul."

The foreyards ran round with a great noise, amidst cheery cries. And now the frightful whiskers made themselves heard giving various orders. Already the ship was drawing ahead. And I was alone with her. Nothing! no one in the world should stand now between us, throwing a shadow on the way of silent knowledge and mute affection, the perfect communion of a seaman with his first command.

Walking to the taffrail, I was in time to make out, on the very edge of a darkness thrown by a towering black mass like the very gateway of Erebus—yes, I was in time to catch an evanescent glimpse of my white hat left behind to mark the spot where the secret sharer of my cabin and of my thoughts, as though he were my second self, had lowered himself into the water to take his punishment: a free man, a proud swimmer striking out for a new destiny.

1909   1912

A. E. HOUSMAN
(1859–1936)

Alfred Edward Housman was born in Fockbury, Worcestershire (close to the Shropshire border). After attending school at the nearby town of Bromsgrove he proceeded to Oxford where he studied classics and philosophy and in 1881 shocked his friends and teachers by failing his final examinations (he was at the time in a state of psychological turmoil resulting from his suppressed homosexual love for a fellow student). He obtained a civil service job and pursued his classical studies alone, gradually building up a reputation as a great textual critic of Latin literature by his contributions to learned periodicals. In 1892 he was appointed to the Chair of Latin at University College, London, and from 1911 until his death he was professor of Latin at Cambridge.

It was characteristic of Housman that his classical studies consisted of meticulous, impersonal textual investigations; there was something reserved and solitary about his life as there was about his scholarship, in which he allowed no trace of his feeling for literature to appear. That feeling nevertheless ran strong and deep, and in his lecture *The Name and Nature of Poetry* (1933) he expressed the view that poetry cannot be explained or analyzed, but is recognized by its almost physical effects on the reader as he reads. His own poetry was limited both in quantity and in range. Two "slim volumes"—*A Shropshire Lad* (1896) and *Last Poems* (1922) —were all that appeared during his lifetime, and after his death his brother Laurence Housman, playwright and poet, brought out another small book of *More Poems* (1936), on the whole inferior in quality to the first two.

Housman's writings on classical subjects consisted of articles and reviews marked by bitterly sarcastic exposure of the work of inferior editors punctuated by gloomy remarks about life. He was a very great textual critic of Latin poetry, but his remarks on the folly and incompetence of other textual critics go far beyond anything normally expected of superior scholarship talking of inferior. "If a man will comprehend the richness and variety of the universe, and inspire his mind with a due measure of wonder and of awe, he must contemplate the human intellect not only on its heights of genius but in its abysses of ineptitude. * * * Elias Stoeber['s] reprint * * * saw the light in 1767 at Strasburg, a city still famous for its geese. * * * Stoeber's mind, though that is no name to call it by, was one which turned as unswervingly to the false, the meaningless, the unmetrical, and the ungrammatical, as the needle to the pole" (Preface to *Manilius*, 1903).

Housman's aim as a poet was not to expand or develop the resources of English poetry but by limitation and concentration to achieve an utterance both compact and moving. He was influenced by Greek and Latin lyric poetry, by the traditional ballad, and by the lyrics of the early 19th-century German poet Heinrich Heine. His favorite theme is that of the doomed youth acting out the tragedy of his brief life in a context of agricultural activity and against a specific English background containing visual reminders of man's long history there. Nature is beautiful but indifferent and is to be enjoyed while we are still able to enjoy it. Love, friendship, and conviviality cannot last and may well result in betrayal or death, but are likewise to be relished while there is time. The wryly ironic tone sometimes degenerates into melodrama, and the stoicism seems at time histrionic, but at his best Housman's control of cadence enabled him to sound the note of resigned wisdom with quiet poignancy. Housman avoids self-pity by projecting the emotion through an imagined character, notably the "Shropshire lad," so that even the first-person poems seem to be distanced in some degree. At the same time the poems are distinguished sharply from the "gather ye rosebuds" tradition by the undertones of fatalism and even of doom.

Loveliest of Trees

Loveliest of trees, the cherry now
Is hung with bloom along the bough,
And stands about the woodland ride
Wearing white for Eastertide.

Now, of my threescore years and ten,   5
Twenty will not come again,
And take from seventy springs a score,
It only leaves me fifty more.

And since to look at things in bloom
Fifty springs are little room,   10
About the woodlands I will go
To see the cherry hung with snow.

                                                  1896

When I Was One-and-Twenty

When I was one-and-twenty
  I heard a wise man say,
"Give crowns and pounds and guineas
  But not your heart away;
Give pearls away and rubies   5
  But keep your fancy free."
But I was one-and-twenty,
  No use to talk to me.

When I was one-and-twenty
  I heard him say again,   10
"The heart out of the bosom
  Was never given in vain;
'Tis paid with sighs a plenty
  And sold for endless rue."
And I am two-and-twenty,   15
  And oh, 'tis true, 'tis true.

                                                  1896

To an Athlete Dying Young

The time you won your town the race
We chaired you through the market place;
Man and boy stood cheering by,
And home we brought you shoulder-high.

Today, the road all runners come,   5
Shoulder-high we bring you home,
And set you at your threshold down,
Townsman of a stiller town.

Smart lad, to slip betimes away
From fields where glory does not stay   10
And early though the laurel grows
It withers quicker than the rose.

Eyes the shady night has shut
Cannot see the record cut,
And silence sounds no worse than cheers   15
After earth has stopped the ears:

Now you will not swell the rout
Of lads that wore their honors out,

Runners whom renown outran
And the name died before the man.   20

So set, before its echoes fade,
The fleet foot on the sill of shade,
And hold to the low lintel up
The still defended challenge cup.

And round that early laureled head   25
Will flock to gaze the strengthless dead
And find unwithered on its curls
The garland briefer than a girl's.

1896

Bredon[1] Hill

In summertime on Bredon
    The bells they sound so clear;
Round both the shires they ring them
    In steeples far and near,
    A happy noise to hear.   5

Here of a Sunday morning
    My love and I would lie,
And see the colored counties,
    And hear the larks so high
    About us in the sky.   10

The bells would ring to call her
    In valleys miles away:
"Come all to church, good people;
    Good people, come and pray."
    But here my love would stay.   15

And I would turn and answer
    Among the springing thyme,
"O, peal upon our wedding,
    And we will hear the chime,
    And come to church in time."   20

But when the snows at Christmas
    On Bredon top were strown,
My love rose up so early
    And stole out unbeknown
    And went to church alone.   25

They tolled the one bell only,
    Groom there was none to see,
The mourners followed after,
    And so to church went she,
    And would not wait for me.   30

1. "Pronounced Breedon" [Housman's note]. The hill is in Worcestershire, adjacent to Shropshire.

The bells they sound on Bredon,
  And still the steeples hum,
"Come all to church, good people"—
  Oh, noisy bells, be dumb;   35
  I hear you, I will come.

1896

The Lent Lily

'Tis spring; come out to ramble
  The hilly brakes[1] around,
For under thorn and bramble
  About the hollow ground
  The primroses are found.   5

And there's the windflower[2] chilly
  With all the winds at play,
And there's the Lenten lily
  That has not long to stay
  And dies on Easter day.   10

And since till girls go maying
  You find the primrose still,
And find the windflower playing
  With every wind at will,
  But not the daffodil,   15

Bring baskets now, and sally
  Upon the spring's array,
And bear from hill and valley
  The daffodil away
  That dies on Easter day.   20

1896

On Wenlock Edge[3]

On Wenlock Edge the wood's in trouble;
  His forest fleece the Wrekin[4] heaves;
The gale, it plies the saplings double,
  And thick on Severn[5] snow the leaves.

'Twould blow like this through holt[6] and hanger   5
  When Uricon[7] the city stood:
'Tis the old wind in the old anger,
  But then it threshed another wood.

1. Clumps of bushes.
2. Anemone.
3. A sharp ridge, twenty miles long, in southeastern Shropshire.
4. A sugar-loaf hill at the northeast end of the Caradoc Hills in Shropshire.
5. The Severn River flows through Shropshire past the Wrekin into Wales.
6. Wooded hill; "hanger": wood on the side of a steep hill.
7. The Roman city of Uriconium (whose site is near Shrewsbury, the county seat of Shropshire).

Then, 'twas before my time, the Roman
   At yonder heaving hill would stare: 10
The blood that warms an English yeoman,
   The thoughts that hurt him, they were there.

There, like the wind through woods in riot,
   Through him the gale of life blew high;
The tree of man was never quiet: 15
   Then 'twas the Roman, now 'tis I.

The gale, it plies the saplings double,
   It blows so hard, 'twill soon be gone:
Today the Roman and his trouble
   Are ashes under Uricon.   20

                    1896

With Rue My Heart Is Laden

With rue my heart is laden
   For golden friends I had,
For many a rose-lipped maiden
   And many a lightfoot lad.

By brooks too broad for leaping   5
   The lightfoot boys are laid;
The rose-lipped girls are sleeping
   In fields where roses fade.

                    1896

Terence,[1] This Is Stupid Stuff

"Terence, this is stupid stuff:
You eat your victuals fast enough;
There can't be much amiss, 'tis clear,
To see the rate you drink your beer.
But oh, good Lord, the verse you make,   5
It gives a chap the bellyache.
The cow, the old cow, she is dead;
It sleeps well, the hornéd head:
We poor lads, 'tis our turn now
To hear such tunes as killed the cow.   10
Pretty friendship 'tis to rhyme
Your friends to death before their time
Moping melancholy mad:
Come, pipe a tune to dance to, lad."

1. *The Poems of Terence Hearsay* was Housman's intended title for *The Shropshire Lad.*

Why, if 'tis dancing you would be,   15
There's brisker pipes than poetry.
Say, for what were hopyards meant,
Or why was Burton built on Trent?[2]
Oh many a peer of England brews
Livelier liquor than the Muse,   20
And malt does more than Milton can
To justify God's ways to man.
Ale, man, ale's the stuff to drink
For fellows whom it hurts to think:
Look into the pewter pot   25
To see the world as the world's not.
And faith, 'tis pleasant till 'tis past:
The mischief is that 'twill not last.
Oh I have been to Ludlow[3] fair
And left my necktie God knows where,   30
And carried halfway home, or near,
Pints and quarts of Ludlow beer:
Then the world seemed none so bad,
And I myself a sterling lad;
And down in lovely muck I've lain,   35
Happy till I woke again.
Then I saw the morning sky.
Heigho, the tale was all a lie;
The world, it was the old world yet,
I was I, my things were wet,   40
And nothing now remained to do
But begin the game anew.

Therefore, since the world has still
Much good, but much less good than ill,
And while the sun and moon endure   45
Luck's a chance, but trouble's sure,
I'd face it as a wise man would,
And train for ill and not for good.
'Tis true the stuff I bring for sale
Is not so brisk a brew as ale: 50
Out of a stem that scored[4] the hand
I wrung it in a weary land.
But take it: if the smack is sour,
The better for the embittered hour;
It should do good to heart and head   55
When your soul is in my soul's stead;
And I will friend you, if I may,
In the dark and cloudy day.

---

2. Burton-on-Trent is the most famous of all English brewing towns; "many a peer" refers to the "beer barons," brewery magnates raised to the peerage.
3. A market town in Shropshire.
4. Cut.

There was a king reigned in the East:
There, when kings will sit to feast,   60
They get their fill before they think
With poisoned meat and poisoned drink.
He gathered all that springs to birth
From the many-venomed earth;
First a little, thence to more,   65
He sampled all her killing store;
And easy, smiling, seasoned sound,
Sate the king when healths went round.
They put arsenic in his meat
And stared aghast to watch him eat;   70
They poured strychnine in his cup
And shook to see him drink it up:
They shook, they stared as white's their shirt.
Them it was their poison hurt.
—I tell the tale that I heard told.   75
Mithridates, he died old.[5]

1896

The Chestnut Casts His Flambeaux[1]

The chestnut casts his flambeaux, and the flowers
    Stream from the hawthorn on the wind away,
The doors clap to, the pane is blind with showers.
    Pass me the can, lad; there's an end of May.

There's one spoilt spring to scant our mortal lot,   5
    One season ruined of our little store.
May will be fine next year as like as not:
    Oh ay, but then we shall be twenty-four.

We for a certainty are not the first
    Have sat in taverns while the tempest hurled   10
Their hopeful plans to emptiness, and cursed
    Whatever brute and blackguard made the world.

It is in truth iniquity on high
    To cheat our sentenced souls of aught they crave,
And mar the merriment as you and I   15
    Fare on our long fool's-errand to the grave.

Iniquity it is; but pass the can.
    My lad, no pair of kings our mothers bore;
Our only portion is the estate of man:
    We want the moon, but we shall get no more.   20

---

5. The story of Mithridates, king of
Pontus, who made himself immune to
poison by taking small doses daily, is
told in Pliny's *Natural History*.

1. Literally, torches. Housman is here
referring to the erect flower-clusters
(white, dashed with red and yellow)
of the horse-chestnut tree.

If here today the cloud of thunder lours
    Tomorrow it will hie on far behests;
The flesh will grieve on other bones than ours
    Soon, and the soul will mourn in other breasts.

The troubles of our proud and angry dust   25
    Are from eternity, and shall not fail.
Bear them we can, and if we can we must.
    Shoulder the sky, my lad, and drink your ale.

1922

Could Man Be Drunk Forever

Could man be drunk forever
    With liquor, love, or fights,
Lief should I rouse at morning
    And lief lie down of nights.

But men at whiles are sober   5
    And think by fits and starts,
And if they think, they fasten
    Their hands upon their hearts.

1896   1922

Epitaph on an Army of Mercenaries

These, in the day when heaven was falling,
    The hour when earth's foundations fled,
Followed their mercenary calling
    And took their wages and are dead.

Their shoulders held the sky suspended;   5
    They stood, and earth's foundations stay;
What God abandoned, these defended,
    And saved the sum of things for pay.

1922

Poetry of World War I

Britain declared war on Germany on August 4, 1914, after Germany had ignored Britain's appeal to refrain from violating Belgium's neutrality in her attack on France. The original spark that set off what proved to be the bloodiest and most widespread war that had yet been fought was the murder of the Archduke Ferdinand of Austria in the Balkan state of Serbia on June 28. Austria, supported by Germany, used the murder as a reason for declaring war on Serbia, which in turn was supported by her fellow-Slav country Russia. Since Russia was bound by a treaty obligation to both France and Britain, Russia and France were soon at war with Germany and Austria. The most effective way of attacking France was for Germany to go through Belgium, though all the powers had guaranteed Belgian neutrality. Although it was this attack on Belgium that brought Britain into the conflict, rival imperialisms, an international armaments race, French desire to regain Alsace-Lorraine which she had lost to Germany in 1870, and German and Austrian ambitions in the Balkans were some of the many other factors which helped to bring about the four-year struggle, a struggle which shook the world and seemed to mark the end of a whole phase of European civilization. Other countries joined in. Turkey joined Germany and Austria in October, 1914, and Bulgaria joined them the following year. Britain and France were joined by Japan late in August, 1914, by Italy (although Italy had in 1882 joined the "Triple Alliance" with Germany and Austria directed against France and Russia) in May, 1915, and by the United States in April, 1917.

Before the collapse of Germany followed by the armistice of November 11, 1918, some 8,700,000 lives had been lost (including 780,000 British) and the prolonged horrors of trench warfare had seared themselves into the minds of the survivors. For three years the battle line, "the Western Front," was stabilized between northwest France and Switzerland, with both sides dug in and making repeated, costly, and generally useless attempts to advance. The German use of poison gas at the second battle of Ypres in 1915, the massive German attack at Verdun in 1916, and the British introduction of tanks on the Somme in the same year failed to produce the breakthrough each side desired. Desolate, war-scarred landscapes with blasted trees and mud everywhere, trenches half-filled with water and infested with rats, miles of protective barbed wire strung out requiring to be cut by individual "volunteers" crawling through machine-gun fire to reach it before any advance could begin, long-continued massive bombardments by heavy artillery, and a sense of permanent stalemate which suggested to the soldiers involved that this living hell could go on for ever—all this was for long kept from the knowledge of the civilians at home, who continued to use the old patriotic slogans and write in old-fashioned romantic terms of the glories of war. But those poets who were involved on the front, however romantically they may have felt about the war when they first joined up, soon realized its full horror, and this realization affected both their

1916

imaginations and their poetic techniques. They had to find a way of expressing the terrible truths they had experienced, and even when they did not express them directly the underlying knowledge affected the way they wrote.

We must remember not only that the battle casualties of World War I were many times greater than those of World War II, wiping out virtually a whole generation of young men and shattering so many illusions and ideals, but also that people were wholly unprepared for the horrors of modern trench warfare. Before the outbreak of World War II the public had been educated by the war poetry and war novels of the previous war to understand its grim realities, and they had also read doom-laden books of prophecy showing destruction from the air and all the new technological means of producing mass death. When World War II began, many people in Britain expected even worse things to happen than did happen in terms of actual enemy attack. But World War I broke out on a largely innocent world, a world that still associated warfare with glorious cavalry charges and the noble pursuit of heroic ideals. That is why the poets of that war who spoke for the trauma of their generation were "war poets" of a special kind and why it is reasonable to break our chronological arrangement and discuss them as a group.

The "Georgian" poetry that was in vogue at the time the war broke out, and that some poets continued to write for some years afterwards, was marked by a quiet traditionalism that can be seen in much of the verse that appeared in the volumes of *Georgian Poetry* edited by Edward Marsh between 1911 and 1920. This represented an attempt to wall in the garden of English poetry against the disruptive forces of modern civilization. Cultured meditations of the English countryside ("I love the mossy quietness / That grows upon the great stone flags") alternated with self-conscious exercises in the exotic ("When I was but thirteen or so / I went into a golden land, / Chimporazo, Cotopaxi / Took me by the hand"). Sometimes the magical note was authentic, as in many of Walter de la Mare's poems, and sometimes the meditative strain was original and impressive, as in the poetry of Edward Thomas (although his style was toughened and tightened as a result of his war experiences). But as World War I went on, with more and more poets killed and the survivors increasingly disillusioned, the whole world on which the Georgian imagination rested came to appear unreal. A patriotic poem such as Rupert Brooke's *The Soldier* became a ridiculous anachronism in the face of the realities of trench warfare, and the even more blatantly patriotic note sounded by other Georgian poets (as in John Freeman's *Happy Is England Now*, which claimed that "there's not a nobleness of heart, hand, brain / But shines the purer; happiest is England now / In those that fight") came to seem positively obscene. The savage ironies of Siegfried Sassoon's war poems and the combination of pity and irony of those of Wilfred Owen portrayed a world undreamed of in the golden years from 1910 to 1914.

World War I left throughout Europe a sense that the bases of civilization had been destroyed, that all traditional values had been wiped out, and we see this reflected in the years immediately after the war in different ways in *The Waste Land* of T. S. Eliot and the early novels and stories of Aldous Huxley. But it was the poets who wrote during the war who most directly reflected the impact of the war experience.

RUPERT BROOKE
(1887–1915)

Rupert Brooke was educated at Rugby School and at King's College, Cambridge. Thereafter he traveled extensively in Europe, America, Canada, and the South Seas, writing poems and essays. In 1914, when World War I broke out, he saw service in Belgium; the next year he was dead of a fever on the Greek island of Skyros.

Brooke is often, and with considerable justice, taken as representative of the golden world of liberal culture immediately before World War I. His early death was symbolic of the death of a whole generation of dedicated English youth—brilliant and beautiful youth as they seemed in retrospect, for Brooke was noted for his physical beauty as well as for his talents. *The Soldier*, traditional both in its sonnet form and its idealistic patriotic mood, represents the last significant expression of an attitude that could not survive the horrors of trench warfare.

Brooke is the one poet represented here to whom the term "Georgian" can be applied without qualification. George V succeeded Edward VII in 1910 and "Georgian" refers to the early years of his reign, up to the 1914–18 World War. This term was first used of poets when Edward Marsh brought out in 1912 the first of a series of volumes, *Georgian Poetry*. For the most part, the poets represented in these anthologies were not interested in major changes in poetic technique and attitude; their subject matter was often the English countryside or else the exotic and the magical; their craftsmanship was on the whole traditional; their mood tended to be quietly meditative. Yet, though essentially conservative in his poetic tastes, Marsh was reasonably catholic in his choices: some of D. H. Lawrence's poems appeared first in *Georgian Poetry* (though Lawrence called Marsh a "bit of a policeman in poetry"). Brooke, however, was more at home in Marsh's poetic environment.

The Soldier[1]

If I should die, think only this of me,
    That there's some corner of a foreign field
That is forever England. There shall be
    In that rich earth a richer dust concealed;
A dust whom England bore, shaped, made aware,   5
    Gave, once, her flowers to love, her ways to roam,
A body of England's, breathing English air,
    Washed by the rivers, blest by suns of home.
And think, this heart, all evil shed away,
    A pulse in the Eternal mind, no less   10

1. The text given here follows Brooke's MS. in the British Museum.

Gives somewhere back the thoughts by England given,
Her sights and sounds; dreams happy as her day;
And laughter, learnt of friends; and gentleness,
In hearts at peace, under an English heaven.

1914   1915

EDWARD THOMAS
(1878–1917)

Edward Thomas was born in Lambeth, in south London. He began his literary career as a writer for the *Manchester Guardian* and at first wrote a great deal of prose which showed a Londoner's sentimentally idealizing attitude to the rural scene. But his move to a cottage in Sussex in the south of England, and his close friendship there with Robert Frost in the years immediately before World War I when Frost was living in England, turned him more and more to poetry, where Frost's influence was strengthening and disciplining. It was his experience as a soldier in the war that produced that further element of quiet toughness so characteristic of his best verse. In civilian life he was restless and often unhappy: his war experiences, in spite of the horror and the suffering that he witnessed, gave him a new confidence and a new technical assurance as a poet. This is evident in poems that do not directly refer to the war, but distill in a quietly intense way some aspect of English life—often but not always rural—that he had left behind. He was killed in action at Arras, in northeast France, in April, 1917.

Tears

It seems I have no tears left. They should have fallen—
Their ghosts, if tears have ghosts, did fall—that day
When twenty hounds streamed by me, not yet combed out
But still all equals in their rage of gladness
Upon the scent, made one, like a great dragon   5
In Blooming Meadow that bends towards the sun
And once bore hops: and on that other day
When I stepped out from the double-shadowed Tower
Into an April morning, stirring and sweet
And warm. Strange solitude was there and silence.   10
A mightier charm than any in the Tower
Possessed the courtyard. They were changing guard,
Soldiers in line, young English countrymen,
Fair-haired and ruddy, in white tunics. Drums
And fifes were playing "The British Grenadiers."   15
The men, the music piercing that solitude
And silence, told me truths I had not dreamed,
And have forgotten since their beauty passed.

1917

The Owl

Downhill I came, hungry, and yet not starved;
Cold, yet had heat within me that was proof
Against the north wind; tired, yet so that rest
Had seemed the sweetest thing under a roof.

Then at the inn I had food, fire, and rest,   5
Knowing how hungry, cold, and tired was I.
All of the night was quite barred out except
An owl's cry, a most melancholy cry

Shaken out long and clear upon the hill,
No merry note, nor cause of merriment,   10
But one telling me plain what I escaped
And others could not, that night, as in I went.

And salted was my food, and my repose,
Salted and sobered, too, by the bird's voice
Speaking for all who lay under the stars,   15
Soldiers and poor, unable to rejoice.

1917

The Path

Running along a bank, a parapet
That saves from the precipitous wood below
The level road, there is a path. It serves
Children for looking down the long smooth steep,
Between the legs of beech and yew, to where   5
A fallen tree checks the sight: while men and women
Content themselves with the road and what they see
Over the bank, and what the children tell.
The path, winding like silver, trickles on,
Bordered and even invaded by thinnest moss   10
That tries to cover roots and crumbling chalk
With gold, olive, and emerald, but in vain.
The children wear it. They have flattened the bank
On top, and silvered it between the moss
With the current of their feet, year after year.   15
But the road is houseless, and leads not to school.
To see a child is rare there, and the eye
Has but the road, the wood that overhangs
And underyawns it, and the path that looks
As if it led on to some legendary   20
Or fancied place where men have wished to go
And stay; till, sudden, it ends where the wood ends.

1917

Adlestrop[1]

Yes. I remember Adlestrop—
The name, because one afternoon
Of heat the express train drew up there
Unwontedly. It was late June.
The steam hissed. Someone cleared his throat.   5
No one left and no one came
On the bare platform. What I saw
Was Adlestrop—only the name.

And willows, willow herb, and grass,
And meadowsweet, and haycocks dry,   10
No whit less still and lonely fair
Than the high cloudlets in the sky.

And for that minute a blackbird sang
Close by, and round him, mistier,
Farther and farther, all the birds   15
Of Oxfordshire and Gloucestershire.

1917

The Gallows

There was a weasel lived in the sun
With all his family,
Till a keeper shot him with his gun
And hung him up on a tree,
Where he swings in the wind and rain,   5
In the sun and in the snow,
Without pleasure, without pain,
On the dead oak tree bough.

There was a crow who was no sleeper,
But a thief and a murderer   10
Till a very late hour; and this keeper
Made him one of the things that were,
To hang and flap in rain and wind,
In the sun and in the snow.
There are no more sins to be sinned   15
On the dead oak tree bough.

There was a magpie, too,
Had a long tongue and a long tail;
He could both talk and do—
But what did that avail?   20
He, too, flaps in the wind and rain

---

1. A small town in Gloucestershire.

Alongside weasel and crow,
Without pleasure, without pain,
On the dead oak tree bough.

And many other beasts   25
And birds, skin, bone, and feather,
Have been taken from their feasts
And hung up there together,
To swing and have endless leisure
In the sun and in the snow,   30
Without pain, without pleasure,
On the dead oak tree bough.

                                                   1917

Ambition

Unless it was that day I never knew
Ambition. After a night of frost, before
The March sun brightened and the Southwest blew,
Jackdaws began to shout and float and soar
Already, and one was racing straight and high   5
Alone, shouting like a black warrior
Challenges and menaces to the wide sky.
With loud long laughter then a woodpecker
Ridiculed the sadness of the owl's last cry.
And through the valley where all the folk astir   10
Made only plumes of pearly smoke to tower
Over dark trees and white meadows happier
Than was Elysium in that happy hour,
A train that roared along raised after it
And carried with it a motionless white bower   15
Of purest cloud, from end to end close-knit,
So fair it touched the roar with silence. Time
Was powerless while that lasted. I could sit
And think I had made the loveliness of prime,
Breathed its life into it and were its lord,   20
And no mind lived save this 'twixt clouds and rime.[1]
Omnipotent I was, nor even deplored
That I did nothing. But the end fell like a bell:
The bower was scattered; far off the train roared.
But if this was ambition I cannot tell.   25
What 'twas ambition for I know not well.

                                                   1918

A Private

This plowman dead in battle slept out of doors
Many a frozen night, and merrily

---

1. Hoarfrost.

Answered staid drinkers, good bedmen, and all bores:
"At Mrs. Greenland's Hawthorn Bush,"[2] said he,
"I slept." None knew which bush. Above the town, 5
Beyond "The Drover," a hundred spot the down
In Wiltshire. And where now at last he sleeps
More sound in France—that, too, he secret keeps.

1918

2. The name of a pub—as is "The Drover" (line 6).

SIEGFRIED SASSOON
(1886–1967)

Educated at Marlborough Grammar School and Clare College, Cambridge, Sassoon was fond of the life of the English country gentleman, to which he was brought up. His indirectly autobiographical *Memoirs of a Fox-Hunting Man* (1928) is a classic account of that kind of life and of his early war experiences, while his *Memoirs of an Infantry Officer* (1930) is an equally classic account of experiences in World War I.

Along with his passion for country sports (reflected in his autobiographical prose works), Sassoon had a lifelong passion for poetry. His early poetry reflects a somewhat faded romanticism, while the poetry of his later years, still employing traditional techniques, shows a meditative lyricism that reflects his growing religious feeling. But it is his war poetry that marks his most distinctive contribution to literature. He enlisted on the outbreak of war in 1914 and fought gallantly. But his growing horror at the grim realities of trench warfare produced a change in his verse and made him a pioneer of the new kind of war poetry—bitter, ironic, and dedicated to the exposure of the truth. Sassoon's war poetry is not subtle or complex: its power derives from its strength of feeling and sheer force of indignation.

Sassoon was wounded in 1917, and when he refused to go back to the front after his recovery he was sent to a sanitarium instead of being court-martialed. In the end (like Wilfred Owen, whom he befriended and influenced) he decided to return and be with his men, was wounded a second time, and promoted to the rank of captain.

Wirers

"Pass it along, the wiring party's[1] going out"—
And yawning sentries mumble, "Wirers going out."
Unraveling; twisting; hammering stakes with muffled thud,
They toil with stealthy haste and anger in their blood.

The Boche[2] sends up a flare. Black forms stand rigid there, 5
Stock-still like posts; then darkness, and the clumsy ghosts

1. Their job was to repair the barbed-wire fence protecting the trenches. 2. British army slang for German soldier.

Stride hither and thither, whispering, tripped by clutching snare
Of snags and tangles.
        Ghastly dawn with vaporous coasts
Gleams desolate along the sky, night's misery ended.

1918

Attack

At dawn the ridge emerges massed and dun
In the wild purple of the glow'ring sun,
Smoldering through spouts of drifting smoke that shroud
The menacing scarred slope; and, one by one,
Tanks creep and topple forward to the wire.   5
The barrage roars and lifts. Then, clumsily bowed
With bombs and guns and shovels and battle-gear,
Men jostle and climb to meet the bristling fire.
Lines of gray, muttering faces, masked with fear,
They leave their trenches, going over the top,   10
While time ticks blank and busy on their wrists,
And hope, with furtive eyes and grappling fists,
Flounders in mud. O Jesus, make it stop!

1918

The General

"Good-morning; good-morning!" the General said
When we met him last week on our way to the line.
Now the soldiers he smiled at are most of 'em dead,
And we're cursing his staff for incompetent swine.
"He's a cheery old card," grunted Harry to Jack   5
As they slogged up to Arras[3] with rifle and pack.

   ·   ·   ·   ·

But he did for them both by his plan of attack.

1918

Glory of Women

You love us when we're heroes, home on leave,
Or wounded in a mentionable place.
You worship decorations; you believe
That chivalry redeems the war's disgrace.
You make us shells.[4] You listen with delight,   5

3. A city in Northern France, in the front line throughout much of the war. The British assault on the Western Front that began on April 9, 1917, was known as the Battle of Arras. The British suffered casualties of 84,000 troops, inflicted casualties of 75,000 on the Germans, and took 13,000 prisoners. Canadian troops captured Vimy Ridge, which proved an invaluable defensive position against the German offensive of March, 1918.

4. Many women were recruited into munitions factories during the war.

By tales of dirt and danger fondly thrilled.
You crown our distant ardors while we fight,
And mourn our laureled memories when we're killed.
You can't believe that British troops "retire"
When hell's last horror breaks them, and they run,   10
Trampling the terrible corpses—blind with blood.
O German mother dreaming by the fire,
While you are knitting socks to send your son
His face is trodden deeper in the mud.

                                                                    1918

IVOR GURNEY
(1890–1937)

Ivor Bertie Gurney was born at Gloucester and early showed an aptitude
for music. After five years at the King's School, Gloucester, Gurney won a
scholarship to the Royal College of Music. His chief interest was now composing song-music, and it was as a composer rather than as a poet that he
first acquired a modest reputation. After war broke out in August, 1914, he
enlisted; his battalion was sent to France the following year, and Gurney
experienced all the horrors of the Western Front. He was wounded in
April, 1917, and when in hospital in Rouen sent some of his poems to
friends in London. The result was a volume published under the title
Severn and Somme in 1917. (The Severn is the English river at the head
of whose estuary Gloucester is situated; it appears often in his poetry. The
Somme is the river in northern France which was the scene of some of the
most murderous fighting in the war during the costly British and French
offensive of July to October, 1916.)

Gurney was returned to the front in time to take part in the grim Pas-
chendale offensive of the summer of 1917. He suffered the effects of a
poison-gas attack on August 22 and was sent to a mental hospital at War-
rington and then to another at St. Albans, but recovered sufficiently to be
released before the end of the war. He returned to the Royal College of
Music to study under the composer Vaughan Williams, and continued also
to write poetry. His second book of poems, *War's Emblems*, appeared in
1919.

By September, 1922, it was clear that Gurney's experiences of the war
had been so working on him that he suffered periodically from delusions.
He was confined at Barnwood House, a mental home in Gloucester, and
later, when the prospect of recovery seemed hopeless, to the City of
London Mental Hospital at Dartford, Kent, where he died on December
26, 1937. He continued to write poetry during his fifteen-year confinement
—like 19th-century poet John Clare, some of whose poems he set to music.

Gurney was one of the first English poets to feel the influence of Gerard
Manley Hopkins, and some of his poems of despair written in confinement
are reminiscent in tone and movement of Hopkins's "terrible" sonnets. A
greater influence on him was Edward Thomas, with whom he shares a

limpid directness of utterance. His poems descriptive of his experiences in
the war avoid all histrionics and attitudinizing, but with a painful quietness
recapture particular scenes and moments.

To His Love

> He's gone, and all our plans
>   Are useless indeed.
> We'll walk no more on Cotswold[1]
> Where the sheep feed
>   Quietly and take no heed.   5
>
> His body that was so quick
>   Is not as you
> Knew it, on Severn river
>   Under the blue
>   Driving our small boat through.   10
>
> You would not know him now . . .
>   But still he died
> Nobly, so cover him over
>   With violets of pride
>   Purple from Severn side.   15
>
> Cover him, cover him soon!
>   And with thickset
> Masses of memoried flowers—
>   Hide that red wet
>   Thing I must somehow forget.   20
>
>   1919

Towards Lillers[2]

> In October, marching taking the sweet air,
> Packs riding lightly, and home thoughts soft coming,
> "This is right marching, we are even glad to be here,
> Or very glad?" But looking upward to dark smoke foaming
> Chimneys on the clear crest, no more shades for roaming,   5
> Smoke covering sooty what men's heart holds dear,
> Lillers we approached, a quench for thirsty frames,
> And looked once more between houses and at queer names
> Of estaminets,[3] longed for cool wine or cold beer.
> This was war, we understood; moving and shifting about;   10
> To stand or be withstood in the mixed rout

---

1. Range of hills in Gloucestershire, in
western England.
2. In northwestern France, close to the
front line.
3. Cafés.

Of fight to come after this. But that was a good dream
Of justice or strength-test with steel tool a gleam
Made to the hand. But barbwire lay to the front,
Tiny aeroplanes circled as ever their work   15
High over the two ditches of heartsick men;
The times scientific, as evil as ever, again.
October lovely bathing with sweet air the plain.
Gone outward to the east and the new skies
Are aeroplanes, and flat there as tiny as bright   20
As insects wonderful colored after the night
Emerging lovely as ever into the new day's
First coolness and lucent gratefulness
Of the absorbing wide prayer of middle sight
Men clean their rifles insentient at that delight   25
Wonder increases as fast as the night dies.

Now up to the high above aeroplanes go
Swift bitter smoke puffs and spiteful flames,
None knows the pilots, none guesses at their names,
They fly unthought courses of common danger,   30
Honor rides on the frame with them through that anger,
As the heroes of Marathon[4] their renown we know.

                                                                      1933

Canadians[5]

We marched, and saw a company of Canadians,
Their coats weighed eighty pounds at least, we saw them
Faces infinitely grimed in, with almost dead hands
Bent, slouching downwards to billets[6] comfortless and dim.
Cave dwellers last of tribes they seemed, and a pity   5
Even from us just relieved, much as they were, left us
Lord, what a land of desolation, what iniquity
Of mere being, there of what youth that country bereft us;
Plagues of evil lay in Death's Valley we also
Had forded that up to the thighs in chill mud,   10
Gone for five days then any sign of life glow,
As the notched stumps or the gray clouds then we stood;
Dead past death from first hour and the needed mood
Of level pain shifting continually to and fro,
Saskatchewan, Ontario, Jack London[7] ran in   15
My own mind; what in others? these men who finely

4. The battle in which the Athenians
defeated the invading Persians in 490
B.C., thus ending the first Persian War.
5. Canada, like the other British
dominions, joined Britain in the war
immediately. Canadian forces were
involved in some of the most arduous
and costly operations.

6. Soldiers' lodgings (often ruined
buildings).
7. Novelist and short story writer
(1876–1916). Gurney was probably
thinking of his stories of the brutal
life of the Yukon (e.g., *The Son of the
Wolf*, 1900).

Perhaps had chosen danger for reckless and fine chance,
Fate had sent for suffering and dwelling obscenely
Vermin eaten, fed beastly, in vile ditches meanly.

1954

Crucifix Corner

There was a water dump[1] there, and regimental
Carts came every day to line up and fill full
Those rolling tanks with chlorinated clear mixture;
And curse the mud with vain veritable vexture.
Aveluy[2] across the valley, billets, shacks, ruins,   5
With time and time a crump there to mark doings.[3]
On New Year's Eve the marsh glowed tremulous
With rosy mist still holding late marvelous
Sun-glow, the air smelt home; the time breathed home.
Noel[4] not put away; new term not yet come,   10
All things said "Severn," the air was of those calm meadows;
Transport rattled somewhere in the southern shadows;
Stars that were not strange ruled the most quiet high-
Arch of soft sky, starred and most grave to see, most high.
What should break that but gun-noise or last Trump?   15
But neither came. At sudden, with light jump
Clarinet sang into "Hundred Pipers and A' "[5]
Aveluy's Scottish answered with pipers true call
"Happy we've been a' together." When nothing
Stayed of war-weariness or winter's loathing,   20
Crackers[6] with Christmas stockings hung in the heavens,
Gladness split discipline in sixes or sevens,
Hunger ebbed magically mixed with strange leavens;
Forgotten, forgotten the hard time's true clothing,
And stars were happy to see Man making Fate plaything.   25

1954

The Silent One

Who died on the wires,[7] and hung there, one of two—
Who for his hours of life had chattered through
Infinite lovely chatter of Bucks[8] accent:
Yet faced unbroken wires; stepped over, and went
A noble fool, faithful to his stripes—and ended.   5
But I weak, hungry, and willing only for the chance
Of line—to fight in the line, lay down under unbroken

1. Pool for water storage.
2. Village in N.E. France; "billets":
soldiers' lodgings.
3. Sound of a shell falling to mark
action.
4. Christmas.

5. A popular Scottish song and bagpipe
tune.
6. I.e., snap crackers.
7. The barbed wire protecting the front
from infantry attack.
8. Buckinghamshire.

Wires, and saw the flashes and kept unshaken,
Till the politest voice—a finicking accent, said:
"Do you think you might crawl through there: there's a hole"   10
Darkness, shot at: I smiled, as politely replied—
"I'm afraid not, Sir." There was no hole no way to be seen
Nothing but chance of death, after tearing of clothes
Kept flat, and watched the darkness, hearing bullets whizzing—
And thought of music—and swore deep heart's deep oaths   15
(Polite to God) and retreated and came on again,
Again retreated—and a second time faced the screen.

1954

December 30th

It is the year's end, the winds are blasting, and I
Write to keep madness and black torture away
A little—it is a hurt to my head not to complain.
In the world's places that honor earth, all men are thinking
Of centuries: all men of the ages of living and drinking;   5
Singing and company of all time till now—
(When the hate of Hell has this England's state plain).
By the places I know this night all the woods are battering
With the great blast, clouds fly low, and the moon
(If there is any) clamorous, dramatic, outspoken.   10
In such nights as this Lassington has been broken,
Severn flooded too high and banks overflown—
And the great words of *Lear* first tonight been spoken.
The boys of the villages growing up will say "I
Shall leave school, or have high wages,
    before another January—   15
Be grown up or free before again December's dark reign
Brights them to Christmas, dies for the year's memory."
May to them the gods make not all prayers vain.

Cotswold edge, Severn Valley that watches two
Magnificences; noble at right time or affectionate.   20
What power of these gods ever now call to you
For the folks in you of right noble; and of delight
In all Nature's things brought round in the year's circle,
Pray God in blasting, supplicate now in terrifical
Tempestuous movings about the high-sided night.   25

Men I have known fine, are dead in France, in exile,
One my friends is dumb, other friends dead also,
And I that loved you, past the soul am in torture's spite
Cursing the hour that bore me, pain that bred all
My greater longings; Love only to you, this last-year date.   30

1954

ISAAC ROSENBERG
(1890–1918)

Isaac Rosenberg was born in Bristol of a humble Anglo-Jewish family that moved to London in 1897. There, at Stepney, Rosenberg attended elementary schools until the age of fourteen, when he became apprenticed as an engraver in a firm of art publishers and attended evening classes at the Art School of Birkbeck College. His first ambition was to be a painter, and in 1911, when his apprenticeship was over, a group of three Jewish ladies provided the means for his studying at the Slade School of Art. His interest in writing poetry steadily developed, and with the encouragement of his married sister he circulated copies of his poems among members of London's literary set and gained a certain reputation, though neither his poetry nor his painting won him any material success. In 1912 he published the first of three pamphlets of poetry at his own expense, *Night and Day*. The other two were *Youth* (1915) and *Moses, A Play* (1916).

In 1914 Rosenberg went to South Africa for his health, and lived there with another of his sisters. He returned to England in 1915, enlisted in the army, and was killed in action on April 1, 1918. After his death his reputation steadily grew as an unusually interesting and original poet, who, though he never lived to reach maturity, nevertheless produced some poetry that broke new ground in imagery, rhythms, and the handling of dramatic effects. The fierce apprehension of the physical reality of war, the exclamatory directness of the language, and the vivid sense of involvement distinguish his poems from those of other war poets. Perhaps Rosenberg's lower-class background had something to do with this vividness: unlike the other poets we reprint, he served in the ranks.

Break of Day in the Trenches

The darkness crumbles away—
It is the same old druid[1] Time as ever.
Only a live thing leaps my hand—
A queer sardonic rat—
As I pull the parapet's[2] poppy   5
To stick behind my ear.
Droll rat, they would shoot you if they knew
Your cosmopolitan sympathies.
Now you have touched this English hand
You will do the same to a German—   10
Soon, no doubt, if it be your pleasure
To cross the sleeping green between.
It seems you inwardly grin as you pass
Strong eyes, fine limbs, haughty athletes

---

1. Member of a Celtic religious order found in ancient Gaul, Britain, and Ireland.
2. Wall protecting a trench.

Less chanced than you for life, 15
Bonds to the whims of murder,
Sprawled in the bowels of the earth,
The torn fields of France.
What do you see in our eyes
At the shrieking iron and flame 20
Hurled through still heavens?
What quaver—what heart aghast?
Poppies whose roots are in man's veins
Drop, and are ever dropping;
But mine in my ear is safe, 25
Just a little white with the dust.

1922

Louse Hunting

Nudes—stark and glistening,
Yelling in lurid glee.   Grinning faces
And raging limbs
Whirl over the floor one fire.
For a shirt verminously busy 5
Yon soldier tore from his throat, with oaths
Godhead might shrink at, but not the lice.
And soon the shirt was aflare
Over the candle he'd lit while we lay.

Then we all sprang up and stripped 10
To hunt the verminous brood.
Soon like a demons' pantomime
The place was raging.
See the silhouettes agape,
See the gibbering shadows 15
Mixed with the battled arms on the wall.
See gargantuan hooked fingers
Pluck in supreme flesh
To smutch supreme littleness.
See the merry limbs in hot Highland fling 20
Because some wizard vermin
Charmed from the quiet this revel
When our ears were half lulled
By the dark music
Blown from Sleep's trumpet. 25

1922

Returning, We Hear the Larks

Somber the night is.
And though we have our lives, we know
What sinister threat lurks there.

Dragging these anguished limbs, we only know
This poison-blasted track opens on our camp— 5
On a little safe sleep.

But hark! joy—joy—strange joy.
Lo! heights of night ringing with unseen larks.
Music showering on our upturned list'ning faces.

Death could drop from the dark 10
As easily as song—
But song only dropped,
Like a blind man's dreams on the sand
By dangerous tides,
Like a girl's dark hair for she dreams no ruin lies there, 15
Or her kisses where a serpent hides.

1922

Dead Man's Dump

The plunging limbers[1] over the shattered track
Racketed with their rusty freight,
Stuck out like many crowns of thorns,
And the rusty stakes like scepters old
To stay the flood of brutish men 5
Upon our brothers dear.

The wheels lurched over sprawled dead
But pained them not, though their bones crunched,
Their shut mouths made no moan.
They lie there huddled, friend and foeman, 10
Man born of man, and born of woman,
And shells go crying over them
From night till night and now.

Earth has waited for them,
All the time of their growth 15
Fretting for their decay:
Now she has them at last!
In the strength of their strength
Suspended—stopped and held.

What fierce imaginings their dark souls lit? 20
Earth! have they gone into you!
Somewhere they must have gone,
And flung on your hard back
Is their soul's sack
Emptied of God-ancestraled essences. 25
Who hurled them out?   Who hurled?

---

1. Two-wheeled vehicles for pulling guns or caissons.

None saw their spirits' shadow shake the grass,
Or stood aside for the half-used life to pass
Out of those doomed nostrils and the doomed mouth,
When the swift iron burning bee   30
Drained the wild honey of their youth.

What of us who, flung on the shrieking pyre,
Walk, our usual thoughts untouched,
Our lucky limbs as on ichor[2] fed,
Immortal seeming ever?   35
Perhaps when the flames beat loud on us,
A fear may choke in our veins
And the startled blood may stop.

The air is loud with death,
The dark air spurts with fire,   40
The explosions ceaseless are.
Timelessly now, some minutes past,
These dead strode time with vigorous life,
Till the shrapnel called "An end!"
But not to all.   In bleeding pangs   45
Some borne on stretchers dreamed of home,
Dear things, war-blotted from their hearts.

Maniac Earth! howling and flying, your bowel
Seared by the jagged fire, the iron love,
The impetuous storm of savage love.   50
Dark Earth! dark Heavens! swinging in chemic smoke,
What dead are born when you kiss each soundless soul
With lightning and thunder from your mined heart,
Which man's self dug, and his blind fingers loosed?

A man's brains splattered on   55
A stretcher-bearer's face;
His shook shoulders slipped their load,
But when they bent to look again
The drowning soul was sunk too deep
For human tenderness.   60

They left this dead with the older dead,
Stretched at the crossroads.

Burnt black by strange decay
Their sinister faces lie,
The lid over each eye,   65
The grass and colored clay
More motion have than they,
Joined to the great sunk silences.

2. In Greek mythology, the ethereal fluid that flowed in the veins of the
gods.

Here is one not long dead;
His dark hearing caught our far wheels,   70
And the choked soul stretched weak hands
To reach the living word the far wheels said,
The blood-dazed intelligence beating for light,
Crying through the suspense of far torturing wheels
Swift for the end to break   75
Or the wheels to break,
Cried as the tide of the world broke over his sight.

Will they come?   Will they ever come?
Even as the mixed hoofs of the mules,
The quivering-bellied mules,   80
And the rushing wheels all mixed
With his tortured upturned sight.
So we crashed round the bend,
We heard his weak scream,
We heard his very last sound,   85
And our wheels grazed his dead face.

                                                                      1922

WILFRED OWEN
(1893–1918)

Wilfred Owen was the most brilliantly promising of all the English poets
who were killed in World War I. In his early poems he had experimented
with new varieties of Keatsian sensuousness, but, under the influence of
his war experiences, he matured rapidly and remarkably. His powerful and
concentrated poems transcend bitterness to evoke what he called "the pity
of war" and to suggest the human waste and confusions involved in modern warfare.

Owen was also concerned to expand the resources of English poetic expression, but in a different way from Eliot and those influenced by Eliot.
His "pararhymes"—imperfect or half rhymes—and his flexible stanza forms
show him adapting rather than abandoning traditional techniques, while
his attitude, combining irony, compassion, and a sense of personal involvement in all human suffering, differs from characteristic Victorian poetic
attitudes without showing the studied objectivity of the early Eliot. Had
he lived, English poetry would almost certainly have been less dependent
upon the Eliot school; indeed, there might have developed an alternative
and equally valuable new tradition in postwar English poetry.

Owen's poems were collected and published posthumously (1920) by
his friend Siegfried Sassoon.

Greater Love

Red lips are not so red
  As the stained stones kissed by the English dead.
Kindness of wooed and wooer
Seems shame to their love pure.
O Love, your eyes lose lure   5
  When I behold eyes blinded in my stead!

Your slender attitude
  Trembles not exquisite like limbs knife skewed,
Rolling and rolling there
Where God seems not to care;   10
Till the fierce love they bear
  Cramps them in death's extreme decrepitude.

Your voice sings not so soft—
  Though even as wind murmuring through raftered loft—
Your dear voice is not dear,   15
Gentle, and evening clear,
As theirs whom none now hear,
  Now earth has stopped their piteous mouths that coughed.

Heart, you were never hot
  Nor large, nor full like hearts made great with shot;   20
And though your hand be pale,
Paler are all which trail
Your cross through flame and hail:
  Weep, you may weep, for you may touch them not.

1920

Futility

    Move him into the sun—
    Gently its touch awoke him once,
    At home, whispering of fields unsown.
    Always it woke him, even in France,
    Until this morning and this snow.   5
    If anything might rouse him now
    The kind old sun will know.

    Think how it wakes the seeds—
    Woke, once, the clays of a cold star.
    Are limbs, so dear-achieved, are sides,   10
    Full-nerved—still warm—too hard to stir?
    Was it for this the clay grew tall?
    —O what made fatuous sunbeams toil
    To break earth's sleep at all?

1920

Insensibility

I

Happy are men who yet before they are killed
Can let their veins run cold.
Whom no compassion fleers
Or makes their feet
Sore on the alleys cobbled with their brothers.   5
The front line withers,
But they are troops who fade, not flowers
For poets' tearful fooling:
Men, gaps for filling:
Losses, who might have fought   10
Longer; but no one bothers.

II

And some cease feeling
Even themselves or for themselves.
Dullness best solves
The tease and doubt of shelling,   15
And Chance's strange arithmetic
Comes simpler than the reckoning of their shilling.
They keep no check on armies' decimation.

III

Happy are those who lose imagination:
They have enough to carry with ammunition.   20
Their spirit drags no pack,
Their old wounds, save with cold, can not more ache.
Having seen all things red,
Their eyes are rid
Of the hurt of the colour of blood forever.   25
And terror's first constriction over,
Their hearts remain small-drawn.
Their senses in some scorching cautery[1] of battle
Now long since ironed,
Can laugh among the dying, unconcerned.   30

IV

Happy the soldier home, with not a notion
How somewhere, every dawn, some men attack,
And many sighs are drained.
Happy the lad whose mind was never trained:
His days are worth forgetting more than not.   35
He sings along the march
Which we march taciturn, because of dusk,
The long, forlorn, relentless trend
From larger day to huger night.

V

We wise, who with a thought besmirch   40
Blood over all our soul,
How should we see our task

---

1. Cauterization; searing with a hot iron.

But through his blunt and lashless eyes?
Alive, he is not vital overmuch;
Dying, not mortal overmuch;   45
Nor sad, nor proud,
Nor curious at all.
He cannot tell,
Old men's placidity from his.

VI

But cursed are dullards whom no cannon stuns,   50
That they should be as stones;
Wretched are they, and mean
With paucity that never was simplicity.
By choice they made themselves immune
To pity and whatever mourns in man   55
Before the last sea and the hapless stars;
Whatever mourns when many leave these shores;
Whatever shares
The eternal reciprocity of tears.

                                                               1920

Anthem for Doomed Youth

What passing-bells for these who die as cattle?
Only the monstrous anger of the guns.
Only the stuttering rifles' rapid rattle
Can patter out their hasty orisons.
No mockeries for them from prayers or bells,   5
Nor any voice of mourning save the choirs—
The shrill, demented choirs of wailing shells;
And bugles calling for them from sad shires.

What candles may be held to speed them all?
Not in the hands of boys, but in their eyes   10
Shall shine the holy glimmers of good-byes.
The pallor of girls' brows shall be their pall;
Their flowers the tenderness of patient minds,
And each slow dusk a drawing-down of blinds.

                                                               1920

Apologia Pro Poemate Meo[2]

I, too, saw God through mud—
    The mud that cracked on cheeks when wretches smiled.
War brought more glory to their eyes than blood,
    And gave their laughs more glee than shakes a child.

Merry it was to laugh there—   5
    Where death becomes absurd and life absurder.

2. "Apology for My Poem."

For power was on us as we slashed bones bare
Not to feel sickness or remorse of murder.

I, too, have dropped off fear—
Behind the barrage, dead as my platoon,
And sailed my spirit surging light and clear   10
Past the entanglement where hopes lay strewn;

And witnessed exultation—
Faces that used to curse me, scowl for scowl,
Shine and lift up with passion of oblation,   15
Seraphic for an hour; though they were foul.

I have made fellowships—
Untold of happy lovers in old song.
For love is not the binding of fair lips
With the soft silk of eyes that look and long,   20

By Joy, whose ribbon slips,
But wound with war's hard wire whose stakes are strong;
Bound with the bandage of the arm that drips;
Knit in the webbing of the rifle thong.

I have perceived much beauty   25
In the hoarse oaths that kept our courage straight;
Heard music in the silentness of duty;
Found peace where shell-storms spouted reddest spate.

Nevertheless, except you share
With them in hell the sorrowful dark of hell,   30
Whose world is but the trembling of a flare,
And heaven but as the highway for a shell,

You shall not hear their mirth:
You shall not come to think them well content
By any jest of mine. These men are worth   35
Your tears. You are not worth their merriment.

November, 1917   1920

Strange Meeting[1]

It seemed that out of battle I escaped
Down some profound dull tunnel, long since scooped

1. This poem, one of the last that Owen wrote, is unfinished. It shows his use of "pararhyme" (e.g., "groined," "groaned"; "hall," "Hell"), one of his technical experiments which have influenced later poets. The poem is "peculiarly a poem of the Western Front; it is a dream only a stage further on than the actuality of the tunneled dugouts with their muffled security, their smoky dimness, their rows of soldiers painfully sleeping, their officers and sergeants and corporals attempting to awaken those for duty, and the sense presently of 'going up' the ugly stairway to do someone in the uglier mud above a good turn. Out of these and similar materials Owen's transforming spirit has readily created his wonderful phantasma" (Edmund Blunden).

Through granites which titanic wars had groined.
Yet also there encumbered sleepers groaned,
Too fast in thought or death to be bestirred.   5
Then, as I probed them, one sprang up, and stared
With piteous recognition in fixed eyes,
Lifting distressful hands as if to bless.
And by his smile, I knew that sullen hall;
By his dead smile I knew we stood in Hell.   10
With a thousand pains that vision's face was grained;
Yet no blood reached there from the upper ground,
And no guns thumped, or down the flues made moan.
"Strange friend," I said, "here is no cause to mourn."
"None," said the other, "save the undone years,   15
The hopelessness. Whatever hope is yours,
Was my life also; I went hunting wild
After the wildest beauty in the world,
Which lies not calm in eyes, or braided hair,
But mocks the steady running of the hour,   20
And if it grieves, grieves richlier than here.
For by my glee might many men have laughed,
And of my weeping something had been left,
Which must die now. I mean the truth untold,
The pity of war, the pity war distilled.   25
Now men will go content with what we spoiled,
Or, discontent, boil bloody, and be spilled.
They will be swift with swiftness of the tigress,
None will break ranks, though nations trek from progress.
Courage was mine, and I had mystery,   30
Wisdom was mine, and I had mastery;
To miss the march of this retreating world
Into vain citadels that are not walled.
Then when much blood had clogged their chariot wheels
I would go up and wash them from sweet wells,   35
Even with truths that lie too deep for taint.
I would have poured my spirit without stint
But not through wounds; not on the cess² of war.
Foreheads of men have bled where no wounds were.
I am the enemy you killed, my friend.   40
I knew you in this dark; for so you frowned
Yesterday through me as you jabbed and killed.
I parried; but my hands were loath and cold.
Let us sleep now. . . ."

1918   1920

2. A somewhat archaic Anglo-Irish word meaning either "tax, levy" or (more probably, here) "luck"—as used in the phrase "bad cess to you" (may evil befall you).

DAVID JONES

(1895–1974)

David Jones was born in Brockley, Kent, son of a Welsh father and an English mother, and studied at the Camberwell School of Art before joining the army in January, 1915, to serve as a private soldier until the end of World War I. It is his experiences during the earlier part of this service that provided the material for his modern epic of war, *In Parenthesis*. He attended Westminster Art School after the war, and subsequently made a name for himself as an illustrator, engraver, and water colorist. In 1924 he worked with Eric Gill, the stone-carver and engraver whose strong Roman Catholic feeling and belief are reflected in his work, and under Gill's influence Jones also joined the Roman Catholic Church. Jones's joint Welsh and English origins, his visual sensitivity as an artist, and his interest in Catholic liturgy and ritual can be seen in his literary work, which includes the obscure but powerful long religious poem *The Anathémata* (1952) and *The Sleeping Lord and Other Fragments* (1973), as well as *In Parenthesis*, which combines prose and poetry with remarkable effect.

In Parenthesis, Jones's first literary work, was published in 1937 and won the Hawthornden Prize. It is an evocation in 40,000 words of the activities of members of a British infantry unit from its period of training in England to its participation in the murderous Somme offensive of July, 1916. The book is epic in scope and tone, echoing in carefully patterned moments themes from English and Welsh history and literature—especially the 6th-century heroic Welsh poem by Aneirin, *Y Gododdin*, which tells of an expedition of 300 Celtic warriors from Dineidyn (Edinburgh) against a vastly superior force of Saxons at Catraeth (Catterick) to perish except for three survivors, among them the bard himself. *In Parenthesis* avoids the traditional heroic poet's concentration on high-ranking heroes to build the narrative around very ordinary characters, both English and Welsh, who are presented in vivid silhouettes and sudden stabs of personal memory or reflections of them in the eyes of their fellow soldiers—Mr. Jenkins, Sergeant Snell, Corporal Quilter, Lance-Corporal Lewis, and (in a sense the central figure, suggesting the poet himself, the sole if wounded survivor of his unit at the end of the work) Private John Ball. Other characters flit in and out, some real, some legendary, some both. Here, for example, in a passage from Part 4, is a list of John Ball's companions (pp. 69–70):

> From where John Ball sat and did his brother-keeping, mirror-
> gazing, in the corner of the fire-bay, he could easily observe
> the dispositions of his companions, and the nature of the place
> the fully-come day had now exposed, and robbed of mystery.
> Bill Crower,
> Jack Float,
> Tom Thomas,
> Siôn Evans,
> Jones, rations,
> Jones Mitchell-Troy, with
> Lizzie Tallboy, with

Dai de la Cote male taille,
Watcyn, Wastebottom, and the rest,
his friends.

In a note to "Dai de la Cote male taille" Jones refers us to Malory, Book
9, Chapter 1, where we find the story of the knight called La Cote Male
Tayle, which Malory renders as "The Evyll-Shapyn Cote." "Dai" is the
familiar Welsh form of David; the addition of heroic echoes from Malory
gives this Welsh soldier of World War I another dimension, which the
author exploits some pages further on in putting into his mouth an epic
boast which is derived from both early Welsh and Anglo-Saxon poetry. He
is the same character as Dai Great-coat whom we see among the dead in
the concluding section, below.

In Parenthesis is in seven parts, beginning with a battalion parade in
England before embarkation for France and moving in later sections ever
nearer to the front lines, with a great number of incidental episodes and
widenings of reference, until (after a break in time from Christmas Day,
1915, to June, 1916) we reach the preparations for the offensive, with the
battalion moving up ready to attack, the terrible moments before zero hour,
and the final action in which John Ball's platoon is destroyed and he himself crawls wounded away from the action. Yet though the work has a
chronological sequence it is far from being a straightforward narrative; there
are multiple identifications of present characters with historical or mythological figures; echoes of Christian liturgy and ritual, suggesting that the soldiers are in some way acting out a ritual sacrifice, which contrast with or at
least are modified by echoes of Old English and Welsh epic poetry suggesting that the suffering is to some extent redeemed by willed heroic action.

This war poem (if poem it can be called) could not have been written
when Wilfred Owen and Siegfried Sassoon wrote their war poems. For
Jones is writing after James Joyce's *Ulysses* and T. S. Eliot's *Waste Land*
and is able to profit by the ways in which Joyce and Eliot brought mythology and ritual into narrative to give it a new kind of depth and scope. Eliot
himself, in an introduction to a new edition of the work (New York,
1961), pointed this out. Jones has brought together the committed pity
and irony of the serving soldier that we see in Owen with the distanced,
more elaborately illustrated, less immediately personal, more completely tex-
tured style of Eliot's long poem, and like Eliot he introduces notes to help
the reader in following the mythological and literary references. Another
significant difference between Jones and Owen is that Jones's is essentially a
religious work. There is a meaning in all this suffering and killing, and in
spite of ironies, comic or sardonic reference to popular soldier's songs, follies and vices and vanities and every kind of trivial behavior that goes to
make up the texture of experience for a group of men serving in an army
(and here again we can see parallels with similar aspects of *The Waste
Land*), the notes of ritual and mystery on the one hand and of history and
heroic myth on the other combine to suggest that, though the experience
of war was "in parenthesis," bracketed outside normal living, it had its own
secret meaning.

The extracts printed here are, first, from Jones's Preface, in which he
explains his intention and method, and, secondly, from Part 7, describing
events immediately before, during, and after the attack. At the beginning of

the last section quoted, Private John Ball, wounded, is crawling painfully toward the rear through the mingled bodies of British and German soldiers: in his fevered imagination he sees the Queen of the Woods distributing flowers to the dead. He then wonders whether he is able to continue carrying his rifle. (At the end of the *Chanson de Roland* the dying Roland tries in vain to shatter his sword Durendal to prevent it from being taken as a trophy by the Saracens; he finally puts it under his body. John Ball finally leaves his rifle under an oak tree.) In the end he lies still under the oak beside a dead German and a dead Englishman, hearing the reserves coming forward to continue the battle.

From In Parenthesis

From *Preface*

This writing has to do with some things I saw, felt, & was part of. The period covered begins early in December 1915 and ends early in July 1916. The first date corresponds to my going to France. The latter roughly marks a change in the character of our lives in the Infantry on the West Front. From then onward things hardened into a more relentless, mechanical affair, took on a more sinister aspect. The wholesale slaughter of the later years, the conscripted levies filling the gaps in every file of four, knocked the bottom out of the intimate, continuing, domestic life of small contingents of men, within whose structure Roland could find, and, for a reasonable while, enjoy, his Oliver. In the earlier months there was a certain attractive amateurishness, and elbow-room for idiosyncrasy that connected one with a less exacting past. The period of the individual rifle-man, of the "old sweat" of the Boer campaign, the "Bairnsfather"[1] war, seemed to terminate with the Somme battle. There were, of course, glimpses of it long after—all through in fact—but it seemed never quite the same. * * *

My companions in the war were mostly Londoners with an admixture of Welshmen, so that the mind and folk-life of those two differing racial groups are an essential ingredient to my theme. Nothing could be more representative. These came from London. Those from Wales. Together they bore in their bodies the genuine tradition of the Island of Britain, from Bendigeid Vran to Jingle and Marie Lloyd. These were the children of Doll Tearsheet. Those are before Caractacus[2] was. Both speak in parables, the wit of both

1. Bruce Bairnsfather, English cartoonist and journalist, best known for his sketches of life in the trenches during World War I.
2. Bendigeid Van, hero in Welsh heroic legend. Alfred Jingle, character in Dickens' *Pickwick Papers*. Marie Lloyd (real name Matilda Alice Victoria Wood), English music-hall comedian. Doll Tearsheet, prostitute in Shakespeare's *II Henry IV*. Caractacus or Caradoc, king of the Silures in the west of Britain during the reign of the Roman Emperor Claudius. He was taken to Rome as a prisoner in A.D. 51 but was pardoned by Claudius, who was impressed by his nobility of spirit.

is quick, both are natural poets; yet no two groups could well be
more dissimilar. It was curious to know them harnessed together,
and together caught in the toils of "good order and military discipline"; to see them shape together to the remains of an antique
regimental tradition, to see them react to the few things that united
us—the same jargon, the same prejudice against "other arms" and
against the Staff, the same discomforts, the same grievances, the
same maims, the same deep fears, the same pathetic jokes; to watch
them, oneself part of them, respond to the war landscape; for I
think the day by day in the Waste Land, the sudden violences and
the long stillnesses, the sharp contours and unformed voids of that
mysterious existence, profoundly affected the imaginations of those
who suffered it. It was a place of enchantment. It is perhaps best
described in Malory,[3] book iv, chapter 15—that landscape spoke
"with a grimly voice."

I suppose at no time did one so much live with a consciousness
of the past, the very remote, and the more immediate and trivial
past, both superficially and more subtly. No one, I suppose, however
much not given to association, could see infantry in tin-hats, with
ground-sheets over their shoulders, with sharpened pine-stakes in
their hands, and not recall

> . . . or may we cram,
> Within this wooden O . . .[4]

But there were deeper complexities of sight and sound to make ever
present

> the pibble pabble in Pompey's camp.[5]

Every man's speech and habit of mind were a perpetual showing:
now of Napier's expedition, now of the Legions at the Wall, now of
"train-band captain," now of Jack Cade, of John Ball, of the commons in arms. Now of *High Germany*, of *Dolly Gray*, of Bullcalf,
Wart and Poins; of Jingo largenesses, of things as small as the Kingdom of Elmet; of Wellington's raw shire recruits, of ancient border
antipathies, of our contemporary, less intimate, larger unities, of
John Barleycorn, of "sweet Sally Frampton." Now of Coel Hên—of
the Celtic cycle that lies, a subterranean influence as a deep water
troubling, under every tump[6] in this Island, like Merlin[7] complaining under his big rock.[8] * * *

---

3. Sir Thomas Malory, author of *Morte Darthur*.
4. Shakespeare's *Henry V*, prologue. The "wooden O" is the stage of the theater.
5. *Ibid.*, IV.i.
6. Mound or tumulus.

7. Merlin is the powerful enchanter of the Arthurian legends.
8. The mass of references here provide a wide area of historical and literary association, beginning with *Henry V* and going on to refer to Sir William Napier,

We who are of the same world of sense with hairy ass and furry wolf and who presume to other and more radiant affinities, are finding it difficult, as yet, to recognize these creatures of chemicals as true extensions of ourselves, that we may feel for them a native affection, which alone can make them magical for us. It would be interesting to know how we shall ennoble our new media as we have already ennobled and made significant our old—candle-light, fire-light, Cups, Wands and Swords, to choose at random.

Some of us ask ourselves if Mr. X adjusting his box-respirator can be equated with what the poet envisaged, in

I saw young Harry with his beaver on.[9]

We are in no doubt at all but what Bardolph's marching kiss for Pistol's "quondam Quickly" is[1] an experience substantially the same as you and I suffered on Victoria[2] platform. For the old authors there appears to have been no such dilemma—for them the embrace of battle seemed one with the embrace of lovers. For us it is different. There is no need to labour the point, nor enquire into the causes here. I only wish to record that for me such a dilemma exists, and that I have been particularly conscious of it during the making of this writing.

* * *

This writing is called *In Parenthesis* because I have written it in a kind of space between—I don't know between quite what—but as you turn aside to do something; and because for us amateur soldiers (and especially for the writer, who was not only amateur, but gro-tesquely incompetent, a knocker-over of piles, a parade's despair) the war itself was a parenthesis—how glad we thought we were to step outside its brackets at the end of '18—and also because our curious type of existence here is altogether in parenthesis.

D.J.

---

who fought in the Peninsular War and later wrote a famous history of that campaign; to the Roman legions who manned the Great Wall built by the Romans in Britain; to Jack Cade, who led an unsuccessful popular revolt against the misrule of Henry VI in 1450 and John Ball, a leader of the Peasants' Revolt of 1381; to a number of English ballads and popular songs and to characters in Shakespeare's *Henry IV*; to the ancient British kingdom of Elmet in southwest Yorkshire, overthrown by Anglo-Saxon invaders early in the 7th cen-tury; to Wellington's "raw shire recruits" who helped to win the Battle of Waterloo; and concluding with a reference to the old Celtic British myths that lie beneath everything.

9. Sir Richard Vernon's admiring description of the reformed Prince Hal ready for battle, *I Henry IV*, IV.i.104.

1. All are characters from *Henry IV*.

2. Victoria Station, London station for trains going to the south coast and hence the station for the Continent; troops for France left from Victoria.

From *Part 7: The Five Unmistakeable Marks*[1]
Gododdin I demand thy support.
It is our duty to sing: a meeting
place has been found.[2]

* * *

They shook out into a single line and each inclined his body to
the slope to wait.   21
And this is the manner of their waiting:
Those happy who had borne the yoke
who kept their peace
and these other in a like condemnation   25
to the place of a skull.

Immediately behind where Private 25201 Ball pressed his body to
the earth and the white chalk womb to mother him,
          Colonel Dell presumed to welcome
some other, come out of the brumous morning
at leisure and well-dressed and all at ease   30
as thriving on the nitrous air.
Well Dell!
          and into it they slide . . . of the admirable salads of Mrs. Cur-
tis-Smythe: they fall for her in Poona,[3] and its worth one's while
—but the comrade close next you screamed so after the last salvo
that it was impossible to catch any more the burthen of this white-
man talk.

And the place of their waiting a long burrow,
in the chalk a cutting, and steep clift—   35
but all but too shallow against his violence.
Like in long-ship, where you flattened face to kelson[4] for the shock-
breaking on brittle pavissed free-board, and the gunnel stove, and
no care to jettison the dead.

No one to care there for Aneirin Lewis spilled there
who worshipped his ancestors like a Chink
who sleeps in Arthur's lap   40
who saw Olwen-trefoils some moonlighted night
on precarious slats at Festubert,
on narrow foothold on le Plantin marsh—

1. "Carroll's *Hunting of the Snark*, Fit
the 2nd verse 15" [Jones's note]. Lewis
Carroll's mock-heroic nonsense poem
concerns the hunting of the elusive animal Snark, which may be known by
"five unmistakable marks."
2. "From *Y Gododdin*, early Welsh epi-
cal poem attributed to Aneirin (6th century); commemorates raid of 300 Welsh
of Gododdin (the territory of the Otad-
ini located near the Firth of Forth) into
English kingdom of Deira. Describes the
ruin of this 300 in battle at Catraeth

(perhaps Catterick in Yorkshire). Three
men alone escaped death, including the
poet, who laments his friends" [Jones's
note].
3. City in India, formerly headquarters
of the 6th division of the British southern army in India and a residence of the
governor of Bombay during the rainy
season; thus a symbol of the social life
of British India in the early part of this
century.
4. Inner keel fitted over the floor timbers
of a ship.

more shaved he is to the bare bone than
Yspaddadan Penkawr.   45
    Properly organized chemists can let make more riving power
than ever Twrch Trwyth;
more blistered he is than painted Troy Towers
and unwholer, limb from limb, than any of them fallen at Catraeth
or on the seaboard-down, by Salisbury,[5]
and no maker to contrive his funerary song.   50
    And the little Jew lies next him
cries out for Deborah his bride
and offers for stretcher-bearers
        gifts for their pains
and walnut suites in his delirium
        from Grays Inn Road.[6]   55

But they already look at their watches and it is zero minus seven
minutes.
Seven minutes to go . . . and seventy times seven times to the
minute,
this drumming of the diaphragm.
From deeply inward thumping all through you beating   60
no peace to be still in
and no one is there not anyone to stop
can't anyone—someone turn off the tap
or won't any one before it snaps.

Racked out to another turn of the screw   65
the acceleration heightens;
the sensibility of these instruments to register,
fails;
needle dithers disorientate.
The responsive mercury plays laggard to such fevers—you simply
can't take any more in.   70
And the surfeit of fear steadies to dumb incognition, so that when
they give the order to move upward to align with "A," hugged already just under the lip of the acclivity inches below where his tra-
versing machine-guns perforate to powder white—
white creature of chalk pounded
and the world crumbled away
and get ready to advance

5. "Arthur's lap. Cf. *Henry V*, Act II,
Sc. iii. [This is a comic mistake by the
hostess for "Abraham's bosom." To
sleep in Abraham's bosom is to be at
peace after death (cf. Luke xvi.22), and
the hostess is saying that Falstaff is at
peace after death. But when Jones takes
over the substitution of Arthur for Abraham, it is not a comic mistake but a deliberate introduction of the British Celtic
hero Arthur.] Olwen-trefoils. Cf.
Kulhwch ac Olwen [ancient Welsh
poem]: 'Four white trefoils sprang up

wherever she trod.' Yspaddaden Penkawr. The Giant task-setter in the
Kulhwch. "And Kaw of North Britain
came and shaved his beard, skin, and
flesh, clean to the very bone from ear to
ear. "Art shaved, man?" said Kulhwch.
"I am shaved," answered he.' Twrch
Trwyth. The mysterious destroying beast
which is the subject of much of the
Kulhwch story. Seaboard-down, by Salisbury. Refers to the Battle of Camlann.
Malory, book xxi, ch. 3" [Jones's note].
6. In London.

you have not capacity for added fear only the limbs are leaden to
negotiate the slope and rifles all out of balance, clumsied with long
auxiliary steel   75
seem five times the regulation weight—
it bitches the aim as well;
          and we ourselves as those small
cherubs, who trail awkwardly the weapons of the God in
                    Fine Art works.   80

The returning sun climbed over the hill, to lessen the shadows of
small and great things; and registered the minutes to zero hour.
Their saucer hats made dial for his passage: long thin line of them,
vivid domes of them,
cut elliptical with light
as cupola on Byzantine wall,
stout turrets to take the shock
and helmets of salvation.   85
Long side by side lie like friends lie
on daisy-down on warm days
cuddled close down kindly close with the mole
in down and silky rodent,
and if you look more intimately all manner of small creatures,   90
created-dear things creep about quite comfortably
yet who travail until now
beneath your tin-hat shade.
          He bawls at ear-hole:
Two minutes to go.   95
          Minutes to excuse me to make excuse.
Responde mihi?[7]
          for surely I must needs try them
so many, much undone
and lose on roundabouts as well and vari-colored polygram   100
to love and know
          and we have a little sister[8]
whose breasts will be as towers
and the gilly-flowers will blow next month
below the pound
with Fred Karno billed for *The Holloway*.[9]   105

He's getting it now more accurately and each salvo brackets more
narrowly and a couple right in, just as "D" and "C" are forming for
the second wave.

Wastebottom married a wife on his Draft-leave but the whinnying
splinter razored diagonal and mess-tin fragments drove inward and
toxined underwear.

---

7. ["Answer me."] "Cf. Dominican Lit-
tle Office of the Blessed Virgin Mary.
Office of the Dead, 2nd Nocturn, Lesson
IV (Job xiii. 22 to end of chapter)"
[Jones's note].
8. Cf. Song of Solomon viii. 8. "We

have a little sister, and she hath no
breasts."
9. The Holloway Empire Music Hall.
Fred Karno was a popular comedian
who performed there.

He maintained correct alignment with the others, face down,
and you never would have guessed.

* * *

The gentle slopes are green to remind you   281
of South English places, only far wider and flatter spread and
grooved and harrowed criss-cross whitely and the disturbed subsoil
heaped up albescent.[1]

Across upon this undulated board of verdure chequered bright
when you look to left and right
small, drab, bundled pawns severally make effort   285
moved in tenuous line
and if you looked behind—the next wave came slowly, as successive
surfs creep in to dissipate on flat shore;
and to your front, stretched long laterally,
and receded deeply,
the dark wood.   290

And now the gradient runs more flatly toward the separate scarred
saplings, where they make fringe for the interior thicket and you take
notice.
      There between the thinning uprights
at the margin
straggle tangled oak and flayed sheeny beech-bole, and fragile birch
      whose silver queenery is draggled and ungraced   295
and June shoots lopt
and fresh stalks bled
            runs the Jerry[2] trench.
And cork-screw stapled trip-wire
to snare among the briars   300
and iron warp with bramble weft
with meadow-sweet and lady-smock
for a fair camouflage.

Mr. Jenkins half inclined his head to them—he walked just barely
in advance of his platoon and immediately to the left of Private Ball.
      He makes the conventional sign   305
and there is the deeply inward effort of spent men who would make
response for him,
and take it at the double.
He sinks on one knee
and now on the other,
his upper body tilts in rigid inclination   310
this way and back;
weighted lanyard runs out to full tether,
           swings like a pendulum
             and the clock run down.

1. Becoming white.
2. British army slang for "German" in both World Wars.

Lurched over, jerked iron saucer over tilted brow,   315
clampt unkindly over lip and chin
nor no ventaille to this darkening
            and masked face lifts to grope the air
and so disconsolate;
enfeebled fingering at a paltry strap—   320
buckle holds,
holds him blind against the morning.
    Then stretch still where weeds pattern the chalk predella—
where it rises to his wire[3]—and Sergeant T. Quilter takes over.
                            * * *

It's difficult with the weight of the rifle.   636
Leave it—under the oak.
Leave it for a salvage-bloke
let it lie bruised for a monument
dispense the authenticated fragments to the faithful.   640
It's the thunder-besom for us
it's the bright bough borne
it's the tensioned yew for a Genoese jammed arbalest and a scarlet
square for a mounted *mareschal*,[4] it's that county-mob back to back.[5]
Majuba mountain and Mons Cherubim[6] and spreaded mats for
Sydney Street East,[7] and come to Bisley for a Silver Dish.[8] It's
R.S.M. O'Grady[9] says, it's the soldier's best friend if you care for
the working parts and let us be 'aving those springs released smartly
in Company billets on wet forenoons and clickerty-click and one up
the spout and you men must really cultivate the habit of treating
this weapon with the very greatest care and there should be a healthy
rivalry among you—it should be a matter of very proper pride and
    Marry it man! Marry it!   645
Cherish her, she's your very own.
    Coax it man coax it—it's delicately and ingeniously made—it's
an instrument of precision—it costs us tax-payers, money—I want
you men to remember that.

3. "The approach to the German trenches here rose slightly, in low chalk ridges" [Jones's note]; "predella": a platform or shelf (strictly, below or behind an altar).
4. "Mareschal": marshal (French); "arbalest": a powerful medieval crossbow.
5. "The Gloucestershire Regiment, during an action near Alexandria, in 1801, about-turned their rear rank and engaged the enemy back to back" [Jones's note].
6. The British were defeated by the Boers on Majuba Hill on Feb. 27, 1881. The "Angels of Mons" were angels (varying in number from two to a platoon) widely believed to have assisted the British to repel an attack at Mons by superior German forces on August 23, 1914.
7. In what became known as the Siege or Battle of Sydney Street, Winston Churchill, when he was Home Secretary in 1911, directed military operations in London against a group of anarchists. "It is said that in 'The Battle of Sydney Street' under Mr. Churchill's Home Secretaryship mats were spread on the pavement for troops firing from the prone position" [Jones's note].
8. At .Bisley, marksmen compete annually in rifle-shooting for such trophies as "a Silver Dish."
9. "R.S.M.": Regimental Sergeant-Major. "R.S.M. O'Grady," according to Jones's note, "refers to mythological personage figuring in Army exercises, the precise describing of which would be tedious. Anyway these exercises were supposed to foster alertness in dull minds—and were a curious blend of the parlor game and military drill."

Fondle it like a granny—talk to it—consider it as you would a friend—and when you ground these arms she's not a rooky's gas-pipe for greenhorns to tarnish.[1]

You've known her hot and cold.

You would choose her from among many.

You know her by her bias, and by her exact error at 300, and by the deep scar at the small, by the fair flaw in the grain, above the lower sling-swivel—

but leave it under the oak.   650

* * *

The secret princes between the leaning trees have diadems given them.   663

Life the leveller hugs her impudent equality—she may proceed at once to less discriminating zones.

The Queen of the Woods has cut bright boughs of various flowering.

These knew her influential eyes. Her awarding hands can pluck for each their fragile prize.

She speaks to them according to precedence. She knows what's due to this elect society. She can choose twelve gentle-men. She knows who is most lord between the high trees and on the open down.

Some she gives white berries
        some she gives brown

Emil has a curious crown it's   670
        made of golden saxifrage.

Fatty wears sweet-briar,
he will reign with her for a thousand years.

For Balder she reaches high to fetch his.

Ulrich smiles for his myrtle wand.   675

That swine Lillywhite has daisies to his chain—you'd hardly credit it.

She plaits torques of equal splendour for Mr. Jenkins and Billy Crower.

Hansel with Gronwy share dog-violets for a palm, where they lie in serious embrace beneath the twisted tripod.

Siôn gets St. John's Wort—that's fair enough.

Dai Great-coat,[2] she can't find him anywhere—she calls both high and low, she had a very special one for him.   680

Among this July noblesse she is mindful of December wood—when the trees of the forest beat against each other because of him.

She carries to Aneirin-in-the-nullah a rowan sprig,[3] for the

---

1. "I have employed here only such ideas as were common to the form of speech affected by Instructors in Musketry" [Jones's note].

2. See reference in introduction.

3. "Nullah": a river, stream, or riverbed. The rowan, or mountain ash, is a tree with magical properties in Celtic folklore.

glory of Guenedota.[4] You couldn't hear what she said to him, because she was careful for the Disciplines of the Wars.

At the gate of the wood you try a last adjustment, but slung so, it's an impediment, it's of detriment to your hopes, you had best be rid of it—the sagging webbing and all and what's left of your two fifty— but it were wise to hold on to your mask.

You're clumsy in your feebleness, you implicate your tin-hat rim with the slack sling of it.

 Let it lie for the dews to rust it, or ought you to decently cover the working parts.   685

 Its dark barrel, where you leave it under the oak, reflects the solemn star that rises urgently from Cliff Trench.

 It's a beautiful doll for us
it's the Last Reputable Arm.

 But leave it—under the oak.
leave it for a Cook's tourist to the Devastated Areas and crawl as far as you can and wait for the bearers.[5] 690

Mrs. Willy Hartington has learned to draw sheets and so has Miss Melpomené; and on the south lawns,
men walk in red white and blue
under the cedars
and by every green tree   695
and beside comfortable waters.
But why dont the bastards come—
Bearers!—stret-cher bear-errs!
or do they divide the spoils at the Aid-Post.[6]

 But how many men do you suppose could bear away a third of us:

drag just a little further—he yet may counter-attack. 700

Lie still under the oak
next to the Jerry
and Sergeant Jerry Coke.
 The feet of the reserves going up tread level with your fore-

---

4. The northwest parts of Wales. The last king of Wales, Llywelyn, was killed there in 1282. Jones refers to his death in another note on this part of Wales. He adds: "His [Llywelyn's] contemporary, Gruffydd ap yr Ynad Côch, sang of his death: 'The voice of lamentation is heard in every place . . . the course of nature is changed . . . the trees of the forest furiously rush against each other.' "
5. "This may appear to be an anachronism, but I remember in 1917 discussing with a friend the possibilities of tourist activity if peace ever came. I remember we went into details and wondered if the unexploded projectile lying near us would go up under a holiday-maker, and how people would stand up to be photographed on our parapets. I recall feeling very angry about this, as you do if you think of strangers ever occupying a house you live in, and which has, for you, particular associations" [Jones's note].
6. "The R.A.M.C." [Royal Army Medical Corps] was suspected by disgruntled men of the fighting units of purloining articles from the kit of the wounded and the dead. Their regimental initials were commonly interpreted: 'Rob All My Comrades' " [Jones's note].

head; and no word for you; they whisper one with another;
pass on, inward; 705
these latest succours:
green Kimmerii[7] to bear up the war.

Oeth and Annoeth's hosts they were
who in that night grew
younger men 710
younger striplings.[8]

The geste says this and the man who was on the field . . . and who
wrote the book . . . the man who does not know this has not understood anything.[9]

1937

7. Kimmerioi or Cimmerians, in Homer a fabulous people "on whom the sun never looks." They were, however, a real historical people who broke the power of Phrygia, overran Lydia, and invaded cities on the west coast of Greece.
8. "*Oeth and Annoeth's hosts . . . striplings.* Cf. Englyn 30 of the *Englynion y Beddeu*, 'The Stanzas of the Graves.' See Rhys, *Origin of the Englyn, Y Cymmrodor*, vol. xviii. Oeth and Annoeth's hosts occur in Welsh tradition as a mysterious body of troops that seem to have some affinity with the Legions. They were said to 'fight as well in the covert as in the open.' Cf. *The Iolo MSS*" [Jones's note].
9. "*The Geste says . . . anything.* Cf. *Chanson de Roland*, lines 2095–8:
'Co dit la geste e cil qui el camp fut,
[Li ber Gilie por qui Deus fait vertuz]
E fist la chartre [el muster de Loüm].
Ki tant ne set, ne l'ad prod entendut.'

I have used Mr. René Hague's translation" [Jones's note].

WILLIAM BUTLER YEATS
(1865–1939)

1891: Organization of the Rhymers' Club.
1899: Launching of the Irish National Theatre.
1914: *Responsibilities*.
1923: Nobel Prize.
1928: *The Tower*.

William Butler Yeats was born in Sandymount, Dublin. His father's family, of English stock, had been in Ireland for at least 200 years; his mother's, the Pollexfens, hailing originally from Devon, had been for some generations in Sligo, in the west of Ireland. J. B. Yeats, his father, had
abandoned the law to take up painting, at which he made a somewhat
precarious living. The Yeatses were in London from 1874 until 1883, when
they returned to Ireland—to Howth, a few miles from Dublin. On leaving high school in Dublin in 1883 Yeats decided to be an artist, with
poetry as his avocation, and attended art school; but he soon left, to concentrate on poetry. His first published poems appeared in the *Dublin University Review* in 1885.

Yeats's father was a religious skeptic, but he believed in the "religion of art." Yeats himself, religious by temperament but unable to believe in Christian orthodoxy, sought all his life for traditions of esoteric thought that would compensate for a lost religion. This search led him to various kinds of mysticism, to folklore, theosophy, spiritualism, and Neo-Platonism—not in any strict chronological order, for he kept returning to and reworking earlier aspects of his thought. In middle life he elaborated a symbolic system of his own, based on a variety of sources, which enabled him to strengthen the pattern and coherence of his poetic imagery. The student of Yeats is constantly coming up against this willful and sometimes baffling esotericism which he cultivated sometimes playfully, sometimes earnestly, sometimes treating it as though it were a body of truths and sometimes as though it were a convenient language of symbols. Modern scholarship has traced most of Yeats's mystical and quasi-mystical ideas to sources that were common to Blake and Shelley and which sometimes go far back into pre-Platonic beliefs and traditions. But his greatness as a poet lies in his ability to communicate the power and significance of his symbols, by the way he expresses and organizes them, even to readers who know nothing of his system.

Yeats's childhood and young manhood were spent between Dublin, London, and Sligo, and each of these places contributed something to his poetic development. In London in the 1890's he met the important poets of the day, and in 1891 was one of the founders of the Rhymers' Club, whose members included Lionel Johnson, Ernest Dowson, and many other characteristic figures of the 90's. Here he acquired ideas of poetry which were vaguely Pre-Raphaelite: he believed, in this early stage of his career, that a poet's language should be dreamy, evocative, and ethereal. From the countryside around Sligo he got something much more vigorous and earthy—a knowledge of the life of the peasantry and of their folklore. In Dublin he was influenced by the currents of Irish nationalism and, while often in disagreement with those who wished to use literature for crude political ends, he nevertheless learned to see his poetry as a contribution to a rejuvenated Irish culture. The three influences of Dublin, London, and Sligo did not develop in chronological order—he was going to and fro between these places throughout his early life—and we sometimes find a poem based on Sligo folklore in the midst of a group of dreamy poems written under the influence of the Rhymers' Club or an echo of Irish nationalist feeling in a lyric otherwise wholly Pre-Raphaelite in tone.

We can distinguish quite clearly, however, the main periods into which Yeats's poetic career falls. He began in the tradition of self-conscious romanticism which he learned from the London poets of the 90's. Spenser and Shelley, and a little later Blake, were also important influences. One of his early verse plays ends with a song:

> The woods of Arcady are dead
> And over is their antique joy;
> Of old the world on dreaming fed;
> Gray Truth is now her painted toy.

About the same time he was writing poems (e.g., *The Stolen Child*) deriving from his Sligo experience, with a quiet precision of natural imagery, country place names, and themes from folklore. A little later—i.e., in the latter part of his first period—Dublin literary circles sent him to Standish O'Grady's *History of Ireland: Heroic Period*, where he found the great stories of the heroic age of Irish history, and to George Sigerson's and Douglas Hyde's translations of Gaelic poetry into "that dialect which gets from Gaelic its syntax and keeps its still partly Tudor vocabulary." Even when he plays with Neo-Platonic ideas, as in *The Rose of the World* (also the product of the latter part of his early period), he can link them with Irish heroic themes and so give a dignity and a *style* to his imagery not normally associated with this sort of poetic dreaminess. Thus the heroic legends of old Ireland and the folk traditions of the modern Irish countryside provided Yeats with a stiffening for his early dreamlike imagery, which is why even his first, "90's" phase is productive of interesting poems. *The Lake Isle of Innisfree*, spoiled for some by overanthologizing, is nevertheless a fine poem of its kind: it is the clarity and control shown in the handling of the imagery which keeps all romantic fuzziness out of it and gives it its haunting quality. In *The Man Who Dreamed of Faeryland* he makes something peculiarly effective out of the contrast between human activities and the strangeness of nature. In *The Madness of King Goll* the disturbing sense of the *otherness* of the natural world drives the king mad. (Such contrasts are common in the early Yeats; in his later poetry he tries to resolve what he called these "antinomies" in inclusive symbols. See, for example, *Crazy Jane Talks to the Bishop*.)

It is important to realize that Yeats had a habit of revising his earlier poems in later printings, tightening up the language and getting rid of the more self-indulgent romantic imagery. The revised versions are found in his *Collected Poems*, which therefore present a somewhat muted picture of his poetic development. For the complete picture one should consult the Variorum Edition edited by Peter Allt and Russell K. Alspach, 1957.

It was Irish nationalism that first sent Yeats in search of a consistently simpler and more popular style. He tells in one of his autobiographical essays how he sought for a style in which to express the elemental facts about Irish life and aspirations. This led him to the concrete image, as did Hyde's translations from Gaelic folk songs, in which "nothing * * * was abstract, nothing worn-out." But other forces were also working on him. He began to feel more and more that his earlier poetic styles could not speak for the whole self. Looking back in 1906, he found that he had mistaken the poetic ideal. "Without knowing it, I had come to care for nothing but impersonal beauty. * * * We should ascend out of common interests, the thoughts of the newspapers, of the market place, but only so far as we can carry the normal, passionate, reasoning self, the personality as a whole." The result of the abandonment of "impersonal beauty," and of the desire to "carry the normal, passionate, reasoning self" into his poetry, is seen in the volumes of collected poems, *In the Seven Woods* (1903) and *The Green Helmet and Other Poems* (1910). *The Folly of Being Comforted, Adam's Curse*, and *The Old Men Admiring Themselves* are from the former of these, and one can see immediately how Yeats here combines the colloquial with the formal. This is characteristic of his "second period."

By this time Yeats had met the beautiful actress and violent Irish nationalist Maud Gonne, with whom he was desperately in love for many years, but who persistently refused to marry him. This affair is reflected in many of the poems of his second period, notably *No Second Troy*, published in *The Green Helmet*. He had also met Lady Gregory, Irish writer and promoter of Irish literature, in 1896 and she invited him to spend the following summer at her country house, Coole Park, in Galway. Yeats spent many holidays with Lady Gregory and discovered the attractiveness of the "country house ideal," seeing in an aristocratic life of elegance and leisure in a great house a method of imposing order on chaos and a symbol of the Neo-Platonic dance of life. He expresses this view many times in his poetry—e.g., at the end of *A Prayer for My Daughter*—and it became an important part of Yeats's complex of attitudes. The middle classes, with their Philistine money-grubbing, he detested, and for his ideal characters he looked either below them, to peasants and beggars, or above them, to the aristocracy, for each of these had their own traditions and lived according to them.

It was under Lady Gregory's influence that Yeats became involved in the founding of the Irish National Theatre in 1899. This led to his active participation in problems of play production, which included political problems of censorship, economic problems of paying carpenters and actors, and other aspects of "theater business, management of men." All this had an effect on his style. The reactions of Dublin audiences did not encourage Yeats's trust in popular judgment, and his bitterness with the "Paudeens," middle-class shopkeepers—who seemed to him to be without any dignity, or understanding, or nobility of spirit—produced some of the most effective poems (e.g., *September 1913* and *To a Shade*) of his third or middle period. This period is best represented by the volume *Responsibilities* (1914), whose title is significant of the change in Yeats's view of the poetic function. Yeats was now becoming more and more of a public figure. In 1922 he was appointed a senator of the recently established Irish Free State and served until 1928, playing an active part not only in promoting the arts but also in general political affairs, in which he supported the views of the Protestant landed class.

Meanwhile Yeats was responding in his own way to the change in poetic taste represented in the poetry and criticism of Ezra Pound and T. S. Eliot immediately before World War I. A gift for epigram had already begun to emerge in his poetry: in the volume entitled *The Wild Swans at Coole* (1919) he has a poem citing Walter Savage Landor (the 19th-century poet who wrote some fine lapidary verse) and John Donne as masters. To the precision, and the combination of colloquial and formal, which he had achieved early in the century, he now added a "metaphysical" as well as an epigrammatic element, and this is seen in the later poems of his third period. He also continued his experiments with different kinds of rhythm. At the same time he was continuing his search for a language of symbols and pursuing his esoteric studies. Yeats married in 1917, and his wife proved so sympathetic to his imaginative needs that the automatic writing which she produced (believed by Yeats to have been dictated by spirits, but apparently faked by Mrs. Yeats to help her husband) gave him the elements of a symbolic system which he later worked out in his book *A Vision* (1925, 1937) and which he used in all sorts of ways in much of his later poetry. The system was both a theory of the movements of history and a theory of the different types of personality, each movement and type being related in various complicated ways to a different phase of the moon. Some of Yeats's poetry is unintelligible without a knowledge of A Vision; but the better poems, such as the two on Byzantium, can be appreciated without such knowledge by the experienced reader who responds sensitively to the patterning of the imagery reinforced by the incantatory effect of the rhythms. Some recent criticism decries attempts by those who are not experts in the background of Yeats's esoteric thought to discuss his poetry and insists that only a detailed knowledge of Yeats's sources can yield his poetic meaning; but while it is true that some particular images do not yield all their significance to whose who are ignorant of the background, it is also true that too literal a paraphase of the symbolism in the light of the sources robs the poems of their power by reducing them to mere exercises in the use of a code.

The Tower (1928) and *The Winding Stair* (1933), from which the poems from *Sailing to Byzantium* through *After Long Silence* have been here selected, represent the mature Yeats at his very best—a realist-symbolist-metaphysical poet with an uncanny power over words. These volumes represent his fourth and greatest period. Here, in his poems of the 1920's and 1930's, winding stairs, spinning tops, "gyres," spirals of all kinds, are important symbols; not only are they connected with Yeats's philosophy of history and of personality, but they also serve as a means of resolving some of those contraries that had arrested him from the beginning. Life is a journey up a spiral staircase; as we grow older we cover the ground we have covered before, only higher up; as we look down the winding stair below us we measure our progress by the number of places where we were but no longer are. The journey is both repetitious and progressive; we go both round and upward Through symbolic images of this kind Yeats explores the paradoxes of time and change, of growth and identity, of love and age, of life and art, of madness and wisdom.

The Byzantium poems show Yeats trying to escape from the turbulence of life to the calm eternity of art. But in his fifth and final period he returned to the turbulence after (if only partly as a result of) undergoing the Steinach glandular operations in 1934, and his last poems have a controlled yet startling wildness. Yeats's return to life, to "the foul rag-and-bone shop of the heart," is one of the most impressive final phases of any poet's career. "I shall be a sinful man to the end, and think upon my deathbed of all the nights I wasted in my youth," he wrote in old age to a correspondent, and in his very last letter he wrote: "When I try to put all into a phrase I say, 'Man can embody truth but he cannot know it.' * * * The abstract is not life and everywhere draws out its contradictions. You can refute Hegel but not the Saint or the Song of Sixpence." When he died in January, 1939, he left a body of verse which, in variety and power, makes him beyond question the greatest 20th-century poet of the English language.

The Madness of King Goll[1]

I sat on cushioned otter skin:
My word was law from Ith to Emain,
And shook at Inver Amergin[2]
The hearts of the world-troubling seamen,
And drove tumult and war away   5
From girl and boy and man and beast;
The fields grew fatter day by day,
The wild fowl of the air increased;
And every ancient Ollave[3] said,
While he bent down his fading head,   10
"He drives away the Northern cold."
They will not hush, the leaves a-flutter round me, the
    beech leaves old.

I sat and mused and drank sweet wine;
A herdsman came from inland valleys,
Crying, the pirates drove his swine   15
To fill their dark-beaked hollow galleys.
I called my battle-breaking men
And my loud brazen battle cars
From rolling vale and rivery glen;
And under the blinking of the stars   20
Fell on the pirates by the deep,
And hurled them in the gulph of sleep:
These hands won many a torque of gold.
They will not hush, the leaves a-flutter round me, the
    beech leaves old.

But slowly, as I shouting slew   25
And trampled in the bubbling mire,
In my most secret spirit grew
A whirling and a wandering fire:
I stood: keen stars above me shone,
Around me shone keen eyes of men: 30
I laughed aloud and hurried on
By rocky shore and rushy fen;
I laughed because birds fluttered by,
And starlight gleamed, and clouds flew high,
And rushes waved and waters rolled.   35
They will not hush, the leaves a-flutter round me, the
    beech leaves old.

---

1. Yeats's first poem to be published in England (in *The Leisure Hour,* September, 1887). Its original title was *King Goll, An Irish Legend.* Like most of Yeats's early, poems, the text was later much revised, and it is the revised version that is printed here. (In all cases of revision, we print the version revised by Yeats for his *Collected Poems.*) The legend tells of an ancient Irish king, who went mad and hid himself in a valley near Cork, where all the madmen of Ireland were believed to wish to gather if they were free. Yeats's father painted his son (in the latter's words) "as King Goll, tearing the strings out of a harp, being insane with youth."
2. The ancient Irish place names evoke the old heroic legends of Ireland. Emain, said to have been founded by Queen Macha of the Golden Hair (3rd or 4th century B.C.), was in County Armagh (Armagh-Ard-macha, hill of Macha); it is now Navan Rath.
3. Learned man.

And now I wander in the woods
When summer gluts the golden bees,
Or in autumnal solitudes
Arise the leopard-colored trees;   40
Or when along the wintry strands
The cormorants shiver on their rocks;
I wander on, and wave my hands,
And sing, and shake my heavy locks.
The gray wolf knows me; by one ear   45
I lead along the woodland deer;
The hares run by me growing bold.
*They will not hush, the leaves a-flutter round me, the
    beech leaves old.*

I came upon a little town
That slumbered in the harvest moon,   50
And passed a-tiptoe up and down,
Murmuring, to a fitful tune,
How I have followed, night and day,
A tramping of tremendous feet,
And saw where this old tympan lay   55
Deserted on a doorway seat,
And bore it to the woods with me;
Of some inhuman misery
Our married voices wildly trolled.
*They will not hush, the leaves a-flutter round me, the
    beech leaves old.*   60

I sang how, when day's toil is done,
Orchil shakes out her long dark hair
That hides away the dying sun
And sheds faint odors through the air:
When my hand passed from wire to wire   65
It quenched, with sound like falling dew,
The whirling and the wandering fire;
But lift a mournful ulalu,
For the kind wires are torn and still,
And I must wander wood and hill   70
Through summer's heat and winter's cold.
*They will not hush, the leaves a-flutter round me, the
    beech leaves old.*

1887, 1888

The Stolen Child

Where dips the rocky highland
Of Sleuth Wood [4] in the lake,
There lies a leafy island

4. This and other places mentioned in the poem are in County Sligo, in north- western Ireland, where Yeats spent much of his childhood.

Where flapping herons wake
The drowsy water rats;
There we've hid our faery vats,
Full of berries
And of reddest stolen cherries.
Come away, O human child!
To the waters and the wild
With a faery, hand in hand,
For the world's more full of weeping than you can understand.

Where the wave of moonlight glosses
The dim gray sands with light,
Far off by furthest Rosses
We foot it all the night,
Weaving olden dances
Mingling hands and mingling glances
Till the moon has taken flight;
To and fro we leap
And chase the frothy bubbles,
While the world is full of troubles
And is anxious in its sleep.
Come away, O human child!
To the waters and the wild
With a faery, hand in hand,
For the world's more full of weeping than you can understand.

Where the wandering water gushes
From the hills above Glen-Car,
In pools among the rushes
That scarce could bathe a star,
We seek for slumbering trout
And whispering in their ears
Give them unquiet dreams;
Leaning softly out
From ferns that drop their tears
Over the young streams.
Come away, O human child!
To the waters and the wild
With a faery, hand in hand,
For the world's more full of weeping than you can understand.

Away with us he's going,
The solemn-eyed:
He'll hear no more the lowing
Of the calves on the warm hillside
Or the kettle on the hob
Sing peace into his breast,
Or see the brown mice bob
Round and round the oatmeal chest.
For he comes, the human child,
To the waters and the wild

5

10

15

20

25

30

35

40

45

50

With a faery, hand in hand,
From a world more full of weeping than he can understand.

1886, 1889

Down by the Salley Gardens[5]

Down by the salley gardens my love and I did meet;
She passed the salley gardens with little snow-white feet.
She bid me take love easy, as the leaves grow on the tree;
But I, being young and foolish, with her would not agree.

In a field by the river my love and I did stand,   5
And on my leaning shoulder she laid her snow-white hand.
She bid me take life easy, as the grass grows on the weirs;
But I was young and foolish, and now am full of tears.

1889

The Rose of the World[1]

Who dreamed that beauty passes like a dream?
For these red lips, with all their mournful pride,
Mournful that no new wonder may betide,
Troy passed away in one high funeral gleam,
And Usna's children died.[2]   5

We and the laboring world are passing by:
Amid men's souls, that waver and give place
Like the pale waters in their wintry race,
Under the passing stars, foam of the sky,
Lives on this lonely face.   10

Bow down, archangels, in your dim abode:
Before you were, or any hearts to beat,
Weary and kind one lingered by His seat;
He made the world to be a grassy road
Before her wandering feet.   15

1892

---

5. Originally entitled *An Old Song Resung*, with Yeats's footnote: "This is an attempt to reconstruct an old song from three lines imperfectly remembered by an old peasant woman in the village of Ballysodare, Sligo, who often sings them to herself." "Salley" is a variant of "sallow," a species of willow tree.
1. The Platonic Idea of eternal Beauty. "I notice upon reading these poems for the first time for several years that the quality symbolized as The Rose differs from the Intellectual Beauty of Shelley

and of Spenser in that I have imagined it as suffering with man and not as something pursued and seen from afar" (Yeats, in 1925).
2. In Old Irish legend, the Ulster warrior Naoise, son of Usna or Usnach (pronounced *Úshna*), carried off the beautiful Deirdre, whom King Conchubar of Ulster had intended to marry, and with his two brothers took her to Scotland. Eventually Conchubar lured the four of them back to Ireland and killed the three brothers.

The Lake Isle of Innisfree[3]

I will arise and go now, and go to Innisfree,
And a small cabin build there, of clay and wattles[4] made:
Nine bean-rows will I have there, a hive for the honeybee,
And live alone in the bee-loud glade.

And I shall have some peace there, for peace comes dropping slow,   5
Dropping from the veils of the morning to where the cricket sings;
There midnight's all a glimmer, and noon a purple glow,
And evening full of the linnet's wings.

I will arise and go now, for always night and day
I hear lake water lapping with low sounds by the shore;   10
While I stand on the roadway, or on the pavements gray,
I hear it in the deep heart's core.

1890, 1892

The Sorrow of Love

The brawling of a sparrow in the eaves,
The brilliant moon and all the milky sky,
And all that famous harmony of leaves,
Had blotted out man's image and his cry.

A girl arose that had red mournful lips   5
And seemed the greatness of the world in tears,
Doomed like Odysseus and the laboring ships
And proud as Priam murdered with his peers;[5]

Arose, and on the instant clamorous eaves,
A climbing moon upon an empty sky,   10
And all that lamentation of the leaves,
Could but compose man's image and his cry.

1892

When You Are Old[6]

When you are old and gray and full of sleep,
And nodding by the fire, take down this book,

3. Island in Lough Gill, County Sligo.
"My father had read to me some passage out of [Thoreau's] *Walden*, and I planned to live some day in a cottage on a little island called Innisfree * * * "
4. Stakes interwoven with twigs or branches.
5. Odysseus (whom the Romans called Ulysses), hero of Homer's *Odyssey* which describes how, after having fought in the siege of Troy, he wandered for ten years before reaching his home, the Greek island of Ithaca. Priam was king of Troy at the time of the siege and was killed when the Greeks captured the city.
6. A poem suggested by a sonnet of the 16th-century French poet Pierre de Ronsard; it begins *"Quand vous serez bien vieille, au soir, à la chandelle"* ("When you are old, sitting at evening by candle light"), but ends very differently from Yeats's poem.

And slowly read, and dream of the soft look
Your eyes had once, and of their shadows deep;

How many loved your moments of glad grace,   5
And loved your beauty with love false or true,
But one man loved the pilgrim soul in you,
And loved the sorrows of your changing face;

And bending down beside the glowing bars,
Murmur, a little sadly, how Love fled   10
And paced upon the mountains overhead
And hid his face amid a crowd of stars.

1892

Who Goes with Fergus?[7]

Who will go drive with Fergus now,
And pierce the deep wood's woven shade,
And dance upon the level shore?
Young man, lift up your russet brow,
And lift your tender eyelids, maid,   5
And brood on hopes and fear no more.

And no more turn aside and brood
Upon love's bitter mystery;
For Fergus rules the brazen cars,
And rules the shadows of the wood,   10
And the white breast of the dim sea
And all disheveled wandering stars.

1893

The Man Who Dreamed of Faeryland

He stood among a crowd at Dromahair;[8]
His heart hung all upon a silken dress,
And he had known at last some tenderness,
Before earth took him to her stony care;
But when a man poured fish into a pile,   5
It seemed they raised their little silver heads,
And sang what gold morning or evening sheds
Upon a woven world-forgotten isle
Where people love beside the raveled[9] seas;

---

7. In a late version of this Irish heroic legend, Fergus, "king of the proud Red Branch Kings," gave up his throne voluntarily to Conchubar to learn by dreaming and meditating the bitter wisdom of the poet and philosopher. This poem is quoted by Buck Mulligan in *Ulysses*, and a line of it also comes into Stephen Dedalus' mind.
8. This and other place names in the poem refer to places in County Sligo.
9. Tangled; hence here "turbulent."

That Time can never mar a lover's vows   10
Under that woven changeless roof of boughs:
The singing shook him out of his new ease.

He wandered by the sands of Lissadell;
His mind ran all on money cares and fears,
And he had known at last some prudent years   15
Before they heaped his grave under the hill;
But while he passed before a plashy place,
A lugworm with its gray and muddy mouth
Sang that somewhere to north or west or south
There dwelt a gay, exulting, gentle race   20
Under the golden or the silver skies;
That if a dancer stayed his hungry foot
It seemed the sun and moon were in the fruit:
And at that singing he was no more wise.

He mused beside the well of Scanavin,   25
He mused upon his mockers: without fail
His sudden vengeance were a country tale,
When earthy night had drunk his body in;
But one small knotgrass growing by the pool
Sang where—unnecessary cruel voice—   30
Old silence bids its chosen race rejoice,
Whatever raveled waters rise and fall
Or stormy silver fret the gold of day,
And midnight there enfold them like a fleece
And lover there by lover be at peace.   35
The tale drove his fine angry mood away.

He slept under the hill of Lugnagall;
And might have known at last unhaunted sleep
Under that cold and vapor-turbaned steep,
Now that the earth had taken man and all: 40
Did not the worms that spired about his bones
Proclaim with that unwearied, reedy cry
That God has laid his fingers on the sky,
That from those fingers glittering summer runs
Upon the dancer by the dreamless wave.   45
Why should those lovers that no lovers miss
Dream, until God burn Nature with a kiss?
The man has found no comfort in the grave.

                                    1891, 1892

The Secret Rose[1]

Far-off, most secret, and inviolate Rose,
Enfold me in my hour of hours; where those

1. The Rose is a symbol of beauty (see "The Rose of the World," below), and in this poem "this spiritual beauty was seen as part of Yeats's own belief that there would be a revelation due to the creation of Celtic mysteries (and a complete understanding between Yeats and Maud Gonne)" [A. N. Jeffares]. Yeats

Who sought thee in the Holy Sepulcher,
Or in the wine-vat, dwell beyond the stir
And tumult of defeated dreams; and deep   5
Among pale eyelids, heavy with the sleep
Men have named beauty. Thy great leaves enfold
The ancient beards, the helms of ruby and gold
Of the crowned Magi;[2] and the king whose eyes
Saw the Pierced Hands and Rood of elder rise   10
In Druid vapor and make the torches dim;
Till vain frenzy awoke and he died;[3] and him
Who met Fand walking among flaming dew
By a gray shore where the wind never blew,
And lost the world and Emer for a kiss;[4]   15
And him who drove the gods out of their liss,[5]
And till a hundred morns had flowered red
Feasted, and wept the barrows of his dead;
And the proud dreaming king who flung the crown
And sorrow away, and calling bard and clown   20
Dwelt among wine-stained wanderers in deep woods;[6]
And him who sold tillage, and house, and goods,
And sought through lands and islands numberless years,
Until he found, with laughter and with tears,
A woman of so shining loveliness   25
That men threshed corn at midnight by a tress,
A little stolen tress.[7] I, too, await

reveals how he used his sources in an interesting note: "I find that I have unintentionally changed the old story of Conchubar's death. He did not see the Crucifixion in a vision but was told of it * * * I have imagined Cuchulain meeting Fand 'walking among the flaming dew,' because, I think, of something in Mr. Standish O'Grady's books. [See above, p. 1563.] I have founded the man 'who drove the gods out of their liss,' or fort, upon something I have read about Caoilte after the battle of Gabhra, when almost all his companions were killed, driving the gods out of their liss, * * * I have founded 'the proud dreaming king' upon Fergus, the son of Rogh, but when I wrote my poem here, and in the song in my early book, 'Who will drive with Fergus now?' I only knew him in Mr. Standish O'Grady, * * * I have founded 'him who sold tillage, and house, and goods,' upon something in 'The Red Pony,' a folk-tale in Mr. Larminie's *West Irish Folk Tales*. A young man 'saw a light before him on the high-road. When he came as far, there was an open box on the road, and a light coming up out of it. He took up the box. There was a lock of hair in it. Presently he had to go to become the servant of a king for his living. There were eleven boys. When they were going out into the stable at ten o'clock, each of them took a light but he. He took no candle at all with

him. Each of them went into his own stable. When he went into his stable he opened the box. He left it in a hole in the wall. The light was great. It was twice as much as in the other stables.' The king hears of it, and makes him show him the box. The king says, 'You must go and bring me the woman to whom the hair belongs.' In the end the young man, and not the king, marries the woman."

2. The Magi are of course the "wise men" from the East who came to do homage to the infant Jesus. Mrs. Yeats told T. R. Henn that the image in lines 7–9 was "perhaps based on Botticelli's 'Adoration of the Magi,' with a Pre-Raphaelite overlay."

3. King Conchubar, in early Christian legend, is said to have died on the day of Christ's crucifixion in a fit of rage at hearing the news. Yeats, as his note explains, makes Conchubar see the crucifixion in a vision raised by the magic of the ancient Celtic priests, or Druids. The "Pierced Hands" are, of course, Christ's, and the "Rood" is the Cross.

4. The ancient Irish hero Cuchulain was seduced by Fand away from his wife Emer.

5. Fort. This is Caoilte, legendary Irish hero and companion of Oisin, son of Finn, poet and warrior.

6. The "proud dreaming king" is Fergus. See Yeats's note.

7. Yeats describes this tale in his note.

The hour of thy great wind of love and hate.
When shall the stars be blown about the sky,
Like the sparks blown out of a smithy, and die?   30
Surely thine hour has come, thy great wind blows,
Far-off, most secret, and inviolate Rose?

1896, 1897

The Folly of Being Comforted

One that is ever kind said yesterday:
"Your well-beloved's hair has threads of gray,
And little shadows come about her eyes;
Time can but make it easier to be wise
Though now it seem impossible, and so   5
All that you need is patience."

                             Heart cries, "No,
I have not a crumb of comfort, not a grain.
Time can but make her beauty over again:
Because of that great nobleness of hers
The fire that stirs about her, when she stirs,   10
Burns but more clearly. O she had not these ways
When all the wild summer was in her gaze."

O heart! O heart! if she'd but turn her head,
You'd know the folly of being comforted.

1902, 1903

Adam's Curse[1]

We sat together at one summer's end,
That beautiful mild woman, your close friend,
And you and I, and talked of poetry.
I said: "A line will take us hours maybe;
Yet if it does not seem a moment's thought,   5
Our stitching and unstitching has been naught.
Better go down upon your marrowbones
And scrub a kitchen pavement, or break stones
Like an old pauper, in all kinds of weather;
For to articulate sweet sounds together   10
Is to work harder than all these, and yet
Be thought an idler by the noisy set
Of bankers, schoolmasters, and clergymen
The martyrs call the world."

1. To work for a living was the curse imposed by God upon Adam after the Fall (see Genesis iii.17–19). The poem reflects an incident in Yeats's passionate but hopeless love for the beautiful actress Maud Gonne (see A. N. Jeffares, *W. B. Yeats: Man and Poet*, 1949, pp. 128–29).

And thereupon   15
That beautiful mild woman for whose sake
There's many a one shall find out all heartache
On finding that her voice is sweet and low
Replied: "To be born woman is to know—
Although they do not talk of it at school—   20
That we must labor to be beautiful."

I said: "It's certain there is no fine thing
Since Adam's fall but needs much laboring.
There have been lovers who thought love should be
So much compounded of high courtesy   25
That they would sigh and quote with learned looks
Precedents out of beautiful old books;
Yet now it seems an idle trade enough."

We sat grown quiet at the name of love;
We saw the last embers of daylight die,   30
And in the trembling blue-green of the sky
A moon, worn as if it had been a shell
Washed by time's waters as they rose and fell
About the stars and broke in days and years.

I had a thought for no one's but your ears: 35
That you were beautiful, and that I strove
To love you in the old high way of love;
That it had all seemed happy, and yet we'd grown
As weary-hearted as that hollow moon.

                                 1902, 1903

The Old Men Admiring Themselves in the Water

I heard the old, old men say,
"Everything alters,
And one by one we drop away."
They had hands like claws, and their knees
Were twisted like the old thorn trees   5
By the waters.
I heard the old, old men say,
"All that's beautiful drifts away
Like the waters."

                                 1903

No Second Troy[1]

Why should I blame her that she filled my days
With misery, or that she would of late
Have taught to ignorant men most violent ways,
Or hurled the little streets upon the great,
Had they but courage equal to desire?   5

1. Another poem about Maud Gonne, who was a passionate Irish nationalist, preaching violence to achieve Irish independence (see lines 3–5).

What could have made her peaceful with a mind
That nobleness made simple as a fire,
With beauty like a tightened bow, a kind
That is not natural in an age like this,
Being high and solitary and most stern?   10
Why, what could she have done, being what she is?
Was there another Troy for her to burn?[2]

1910

The Fascination of What's Difficult[3]

The fascination of what's difficult
Has dried the sap out of my veins, and rent
Spontaneous joy and natural content
Out of my heart. There's something ails our colt
That must, as if it had not holy blood   5
Nor on Olympus leaped from cloud to cloud,
Shiver under the lash, strain, sweat and jolt
As though it dragged road-metal. My curse on plays
That have to be set up in fifty ways,
On the day's war with every knave and dolt,   10
Theater business, management of men.
I swear before the dawn comes round again
I'll find the stable and pull out the bolt.

1910

September 1913[4]

What need you, being come to sense,
But fumble in a greasy till
And add the halfpence to the pence
And prayer to shivering prayer, until
You have dried the marrow from the bone?   5
For men were born to pray and save:
Romantic Ireland's dead and gone,
It's with O'Leary[5] in the grave.

Yet they were of a different kind,
The names that stilled your childish play,   10
They have gone about the world like wind,
But little time had they to pray

---

2. Helen of Troy was, of course, the cause of the destruction of the "first" Troy. The mixture of admiration and bitterness reflected here is characteristic of many of Yeats's poems about Maud Gonne.
3. Written when Yeats was director-manager of the Abbey Theatre. "Subject. To complain of the fascination of what's difficult. It spoils spontaneity and pleasure, and wastes time. Repeat the line ending difficult three times and rhyme on bolt, exalt, colt, jolt" (Yeats's diary for September, 1909).
4. The poem reflects Yeats's disillusion with the state of the Irish national movement (for independence from Great Britain). Contrast *Easter 1916*, where the heroism of the Easter Rebellion, 1916, has led him to withdraw his criticism.
5. John O'Leary, Irish nationalist of great spirit and integrity who died in 1907.

For whom the hangman's rope was spun,
And what, God help us, could they save?
Romantic Ireland's dead and gone,   15
It's with O'Leary in the grave.

Was it for this the wild geese spread
The gray wing upon every tide;
For this that all that blood was shed,
For this Edward Fitzgerald[6] died,   20
And Robert Emmet and Wolfe Tone,
All that delirium of the brave?
Romantic Ireland's dead and gone,
It's with O'Leary in the grave.

Yet could we turn the years again,   25
And call those exiles as they were
In all their loneliness and pain,
You'd cry, "Some woman's yellow hair
Has maddened every mother's son":
They weighed so lightly what they gave.   30
But let them be, they're dead and gone,
They're with O'Leary in the grave.

                                                     1913

To a Shade[1]

If you have revisited the town, thin Shade,
Whether to look upon your monument
(I wonder if the builder has been paid)
Or happier-thoughted when the day is spent
To drink of that salt breath out of the sea   5
When gray gulls flit about instead of men,
And the gaunt houses put on majesty:
Let these content you and be gone again;
For they are at their old tricks yet.

                          A man
Of your own passionate serving kind who had brought   10
In his full hands what, had they only known,
Had given their children's children loftier thought,
Sweeter emotion, working in their veins
Like gentle blood, has been driven from the place,
And insult heaped upon him for his pains,   15

---

6. Lord Edward Fitzgerald (1763–98), a British officer who, after being dismissed from the army for disloyal activities, joined the United Irishmen (an Irish nationalist organization), was arrested, and died in prison. Robert Emmet (1778–1803) was also an Irish patriot, executed for treason after a heroic career. Theobald Wolfe Tone (1763–98), one of the chief founders of the United Irishmen, committed suicide in prison in Dublin.

1. I.e., the spirit of the great Irish nationalist leader, Charles Stewart Parnell (1846–91). Yeats is here expressing his disgust at the grubby materialism and Philistinism of the Dublin middle classes.

And for his openhandedness, disgrace;[2]
Your enemy, an old foul mouth, had set
The pack upon him.
                    Go, unquiet wanderer,
And gather the Glasnevin[3] coverlet
About your head till the dust stops your ear,   20
The time for you to taste of that salt breath
And listen at the corners has not come;
You had enough of sorrow before death—
Away, away! You are safer in the tomb.

1913   1913

The Cold Heaven[4]

Suddenly I saw the cold and rook-delighting heaven
That seemed as though ice burned and was but the more ice,
And thereupon imagination and heart were driven
So wild that every casual thought of that and this
Vanished, and left but memories, that should be out of season   5
With the hot blood of youth, of love crossed long ago;
And I took all the blame out of all sense and reason,
Until I cried and trembled and rocked to and fro,
Riddled with light. Ah! when the ghost begins to quicken,[5]
Confusion of the deathbed over, is it sent   10
Out naked on the roads, as the books say, and stricken
By the injustice of the skies for punishment?

1912

The Wild Swans at Coole[1]

The trees are in their autumn beauty,
The woodland paths are dry,
Under the October twilight the water
Mirrors a still sky;
Upon the brimming water among the stones   5
Are nine-and-fifty swans.

2. Sir Hugh Lane, Lady Gregory's nephew, had collected a number of important modern French paintings which he wished to give to the city of Dublin, provided they were permanently housed in a suitable building. Fierce abuse of the paintings and of the proposed design of the gallery in the Dublin nationalist press caused Lane to send the pictures to the London National Gallery. (Lane was drowned on the *Lusitania* in 1915; after years of bitter court dispute over an unwitnessed çodicil to his will bequeathing the paintings to Dublin, an arrangement was reached in 1959 for the pictures to hang first in Dublin and then in London, for five years at a time.)
3. The cemetery where Parnell is buried.

4. Yeats told Maud Gonne, in answer to her inquiry, that this poem "was an attempt to describe the feelings aroused in him by the cold and detachedly beautiful winter sky. He felt alone and responsible in that loneliness for all the past mistakes that tortured his peace of mind. It was a momentary intensity of dreamlike perception, where physical surroundings remained fixed clear in the mind, to accentuate the years of thought and reality that passed in review in an instantaneous and yet eternal suspension of time" (A. N. Jeffares).
5. Come alive.
1. I.e., Coole Park, Lady Gregory's country estate, where Yeats was a frequent guest.

The nineteenth autumn has come upon me
Since I first made my count;[2]
I saw, before I had well finished,
All suddenly mount   10
And scatter wheeling in great broken rings
Upon their clamorous wings.

I have looked upon those brilliant creatures,
And now my heart is sore.
All's changed since I, hearing at twilight,   15
The first time on this shore,
The bell-beat of their wings above my head,
Trod with a lighter tread.

Unwearied still, lover by lover,
They paddle in the cold   20
Companionable streams or climb the air;
Their hearts have not grown old;
Passion or conquest, wander where they will,
Attend upon them still.

But now they drift on the still water,   25
Mysterious, beautiful;
Among what rushes will they build,
By what lake's edge or pool
Delight men's eyes when I awake some day
To find they have flown away?

1916   1917

Easter 1916[1]

I have met them at close of day
Coming with vivid faces
From counter or desk among gray
Eighteenth-century houses.
I have passed with a nod of the head   5
Or polite meaningless words,
Or have lingered awhile and said
Polite meaningless words,
And thought before I had done
Of a mocking tale or a gibe   10
To please a companion
Around the fire at the club,
Being certain that they and I
But lived where motley is worn:

2. His first visit had been in 1897
(nineteen years earlier).
1. On Easter Sunday of 1916, Irish nationalists launched a heroic but unsuccessful revolt against the British government; the week of street fighting
that followed is known as the Easter
Rebellion. As a result, a number of the
nationalists were executed: Britain, at
war with Germany, was in no mood to
tolerate Irish agitation for independence
—which was supported, for obvious
reasons, by Germany. Yeats knew the
chief rebels personally.

All changed, changed utterly: 15
A terrible beauty is born.

That woman's days were spent
In ignorant good will,
Her nights in argument
Until her voice grew shrill.   20
What voice more sweet than hers
When, young and beautiful,
She rode to harriers?[2]
This man had kept a school
And rode our wingéd horse;[3]   25
This other his helper and friend
Was coming into his force;
He might have won fame in the end,
So sensitive his nature seemed,
So daring and sweet his thought.   30
This other man I had dreamed
A drunken, vainglorious lout.[4]
He had done most bitter wrong
To some who are near my heart,
Yet I number him in the song;   35
He, too, has resigned his part
In the casual comedy;
He, too, has been changed in his turn,
Transformed utterly:
A terrible beauty is born.   40

Hearts with one purpose alone
Through summer and winter seem
Enchanted to a stone
To trouble the living stream.
The horse that comes from the road,   45
The rider, the birds that range
From cloud to tumbling cloud,
Minute by minute they change;
A shadow of cloud on the stream
Changes minute by minute;   50
A horse-hoof slides on the brim,
And a horse plashes within it;
The long-legged moorhens dive,
And hens to moorcocks call;
Minute by minute they live: 55
The stone's in the midst of all.

Too long a sacrifice
Can make a stone of the heart.
O when may it suffice?

2. Constance Gore-Booth (afterwards Countess Markiewicz), a member of the Sligo county aristocracy. A gay and beautiful girl, she had annoyed Yeats by becoming an embittered nationalist.
3. Patrick Pearse, who was a schoolmaster, a leader in the movement to restore the Gaelic language in Ireland, and a poet (hence the reference to "our wingéd horse"—Pegasus, the horse of the Muses). "His helper and friend" was Thomas MacDonagh.
4. Major John MacBride. Maud Gonne, to Yeats's great disgust, had married MacBride in 1903, only to be separated from him after two years.

That is Heaven's part, our part   60
To murmur name upon name,
As a mother names her child
When sleep at last has come
On limbs that had run wild.
What is it but nightfall?   65
No, no, not night but death;
Was it needless death after all?
For England may keep faith
For all that is done and said.
We know their dream; enough   70
To know they dreamed and are dead;
And what if excess of love
Bewildered them till they died?
I write it out in a verse—
MacDonagh and MacBride   75
And Connolly[5] and Pearse
Now and in time to be,
Wherever green is worn,
Are changed, changed utterly:
A terrible beauty is born.   80

                                        1916, 1920

On a Political Prisoner[1]

She that but little patience knew,
From childhood on, had now so much
A gray gull lost its fear and flew
Down to her cell and there alit,
And there endured her fingers' touch   5
And from her fingers ate its bit.

Did she in touching that lone wing
Recall the years before her mind
Became a bitter, an abstract thing,
Her thought some popular enmity: 10
Blind and leader of the blind
Drinking the foul ditch where they lie?

When long ago I saw her ride
Under Ben Bulben[2] to the meet,
The beauty of her countryside   15
With all youth's lonely wildness stirred,
She seemed to have grown clean and sweet
Like any rock-bred, sea-borne bird:

Sea-borne, or balanced on the air
When first it sprang out of the nest   20

5. James Connolly, Pearse's partner in leading the insurrection. Like the other rebels named here, he was executed by shooting.
1. Constance Gore-Booth Markiewicz, who was imprisoned after the Easter

Rebellion. She also figures in *Easter 1916.*
2. Mountain in County Sligo. The Gore-Booths lived at Lissadell, not far from Ben Bulben.

Upon some lofty rock to stare
Upon the cloudy canopy,
While under its storm-beaten breast
Cried out the hollows of the sea.

1920, 1921

The Second Coming[1]

Turning and turning in the widening gyre
The falcon cannot hear the falconer;
Things fall apart; the center cannot hold;
Mere anarchy is loosed upon the world,
The blood-dimmed tide is loosed, and everywhere   5
The ceremony of innocence is drowned;
The best lack all conviction, while the worst
Are full of passionate intensity.[2]

Surely some revelation is at hand;
Surely the Second Coming is at hand.   10
The Second Coming! Hardly are those words out
When a vast image out of *Spiritus Mundi*[3]
Troubles my sight: somewhere in sands of the desert
A shape with lion body and the head of a man,
A gaze blank and pitiless as the sun,   15
Is moving its slow thighs, while all about it
Reel shadows of the indignant desert birds.
The darkness drops again; but now I know
That twenty centuries of stony sleep
Were vexed to nightmare by a rocking cradle,[4]   20

1. This poem expresses Yeats's sense of the dissolution of the civilization of his time, the end of one cycle of history and the approach of another. He called each cycle of history a "gyre" (line 1) —literally a circular or spiral turn (Yeats pronounced it with a hard *g*). He imagines a falconer losing control of the falcon which sweeps in ever widening circles around him until it breaks away altogether, and sees this as a symbol of the end of the present gyre of civilization—what he once described as "all our scientific democratic fact-finding heterogeneous civilization." The birth of Christ brought to an end the cycle that had lasted from what Yeats called the "Babylonian mathematical starlight" (2000 B.C.) to the dissolution of Greco-Roman culture. "What if the irrational return?" Yeats asked in his prose work *A Vision*. "What if the circle begin again?" He speculates that "we may be about to accept the most implacable authority the world has known." The new Nativity ("the rough beast" of lines 21–22) is deliberately mysterious, both terrible and regenerative.

2. Lines 4–8 refer to the Russian Revolution of 1917, seen as a portent, but later Yeats accepted the poem as an unconscious prophecy of the rise of Fascism also. Speaking in 1924, Yeats declared: "It is impossible not to ask oneself to what great task of the nations we have been summoned in this transformed world where there is so much that is obscure and terrible." "The ceremony of innocence" suggests Yeats's view of ritual as the basis of civilized living. Cf. the last stanza of *A Prayer for My Daughter*.

3. The Spirit or Soul of the Universe, with which all individual souls are connected through the "Great Memory," which Yeats held to be a universal subconscious in which the human race preserves its past memories. It is thus a source of symbolic images for the poet.

4. I.e., the cradle of the infant Christ.

And what rough beast, its hour come round at last,
Slouches towards Bethlehem to be born?

1920, 1921

A Prayer for My Daughter[1]

Once more the storm is howling, and half hid
Under this cradle-hood and coverlid
My child sleeps on. There is no obstacle
But Gregory's wood[2] and one bare hill
Whereby the haystack- and roof-leveling wind,   5
Bred on the Atlantic, can be stayed;
And for an hour I have walked and prayed
Because of the great gloom that is in my mind.

I have walked and prayed for this young child an hour
And heard the sea-wind scream upon the tower,   10
And under the arches of the bridge, and scream
In the elms above the flooded stream;
Imagining in excited reverie
That the future years had come,
Dancing to a frenzied drum,   15
Out of the murderous innocence of the sea.[3]

May she be granted beauty and yet not
Beauty to make a stranger's eye distraught,
Or hers before a looking glass, for such,
Being made beautiful overmuch,   20
Consider beauty a sufficient end,
Lose natural kindness and maybe
The heart-revealing intimacy
That chooses right, and never find a friend.

Helen being chosen found life flat and dull   25
And later had much trouble from a fool,[4]
While that great Queen, that rose out of the spray,[5]
Being fatherless could have her way
Yet chose a bandy-leggéd smith for man.
It's certain that fine women eat   30
A crazy salad with their meat
Whereby the Horn of Plenty[6] is undone.

1. Yeats's daughter, christened Anne
Butler, was born on February 26, 1919,
in the refitted Norman tower of Thoor
Ballylee (Ballylee Castle) in Galway,
where Yeats lived: it is not far from
Coole Park. The wind from the Atlantic
roared in constantly (lines 1, 5–6).
2. Originally part of the Gregory estate, which had once also included
Thoor Ballylee.
3. A reference to Yeats's visions of the
future (cf. *The Second Coming*).

4. Presumably Paris, who carried Helen
off from her husband.
5. Venus, wife (in the *Odyssey* and
later accounts) of Vulcan, "bandy-
legged" god of fire and forge (line 29).
6. The traditional image of the "Horn
of Plenty" is generally associated by
Yeats not only with abundance of the
good things of the earth but also with
the good life, conceived to be based on
order and elegance (see concluding
lines).

In courtesy I'd have her chiefly learned;
Hearts are not had as a gift but hearts are earned
By those that are not entirely beautiful;   35
Yet many, that have played the fool
For beauty's very self, has charm made wise,
And many a poor man that has roved,
Loved and thought himself beloved,
From a glad kindness cannot take his eyes.   40

May she become a flourishing hidden tree
That all her thoughts may like the linnet[7] be,
And have no business but dispensing round
Their magnanimities of sound,
Nor but in merriment begin a chase,   45
Nor but in merriment a quarrel.
O may she live like some green laurel
Rooted in one dear perpetual place.

My mind, because the minds that I have loved,
The sort of beauty that I have approved,   50
Prosper but little, has dried up of late,
Yet knows that to be choked with hate
May well be of all evil chances chief.
If there's no hatred in a mind
Assault and battery of the wind   55
Can never tear the linnet from the leaf.

An intellectual hatred is the worst,
So let her think opinions are accursed.
Have I not seen the loveliest woman born[8]
Out of the mouth of Plenty's horn,   60
Because of her opinionated mind
Barter that horn and every good
By quiet natures understood
For an old bellows full of angry wind?

Considering that, all hatred driven hence,   65
The soul recovers radical innocence
And learns at last that it is self-delighting,
Self-appeasing, self-affrighting,
And that its own sweet will is Heaven's will;
She can, though every face should scowl   70
And every windy quarter howl
Or every bellows burst, be happy still.

And may her bridegroom bring her to a house
Where all's accustomed, ceremonious;
For arrogance and hatred are the wares   75
Peddled in the thoroughfares.
How but in custom and in ceremony
Are innocence and beauty born?

7. A small European songbird.   8. Maud Gonne.

Ceremony's a name for the rich horn,
And custom for the spreading laurel tree.   80
June, 1919   1919, 1921

Sailing to Byzantium[1]

1

That is no country for old men. The young
In one another's arms, birds in the trees
—Those dying generations—at their song,
The salmon-falls, the mackerel-crowded seas,
Fish, flesh, or fowl, commend all summer long   5
Whatever is begotten, born, and dies.
Caught in that sensual music all neglect
Monuments of unaging intellect.

2

An aged man is but a paltry thing,
A tattered coat upon a stick, unless   10
Soul clap its hands and sing, and louder sing
For every tatter in its mortal dress,
Nor is there singing school but studying
Monuments of its own magnificence;
And therefore I have sailed the seas and come   15
To the holy city of Byzantium.

3

O sages standing in God's holy fire
As in the gold mosaic of a wall,[2]
Come from the holy fire, perne in a gyre,[3]
And be the singing-masters of my soul.   20
Consume my heart away; sick with desire

1. This poem should be read together with *Byzantium*. Byzantium had become for Yeats the symbol of art or artifice as opposed to the natural world of biological activity, and as he grew older he turned away from the sensual world of growth and change to the timeless world of art (though he returned to the sensual world later on). He wrote in *A Vision:* "I think that if I could be given a month of antiquity and leave to spend it where I chose, I would spend it in Byzantium [modern Istanbul] a little before Justinian opened St. Sophia and closed the Academy of Plato [i.e., ca. A.D. 535]. * * * I think that in early Byzantium, maybe never before or since in recorded history, religious, aesthetic, and practical life were one, that architects and artificers * * * spoke to the multitude in gold and silver. The painter, the mosaic worker, the worker in gold and silver, the illuminator of sacred books were almost impersonal, almost perhaps without the consciousness of individual design, absorbed in their subject matter and that the vision of a whole people." In his old age, the poet repudiates the world of biological change (of birth, growth, and death), putting behind him images of breeding and sensuality to turn to "monuments of unaging intellect," in a world of art and artifice outside of time. The theme of this poem, though not the treatment, is similar to that of Keats's *Ode on a Grecian Urn.* Note that the stanza form is *ottava rima,* used with great originality in the placing of pauses.
2. Like the mosaic figures on the walls of the Church of Hagia Sophia ("Holy Wisdom") in Byzantium.
3. I.e., whirl round in a spiral motion. "Perne" (or "pirn") is literally a bobbin, reel, or spool, on which something is wound. It became a favorite word of Yeats's, used as a verb meaning "to spin round"; he associated the spinning with the spinning of fate. Here he asks the saints on the wall to descend in this symbolic spinning motion and help him to enter into their state.

And fastened to a dying animal
It knows not what it is; and gather me
Into the artifice of eternity.

4

Once out of nature I shall never take   25
My bodily form from any natural thing,
But such a form as Grecian goldsmiths make
Of hammered gold and gold enameling
To keep a drowsy Emperor awake;[4]
Or set upon a golden bough to sing   30
To lords and ladies of Byzantium
Of what is past, or passing, or to come.

1927   1927

Leda and the Swan[1]

A sudden blow: the great wings beating still
Above the staggering girl, her thighs caressed
By the dark webs, her nape caught in his bill,
He holds her helpless breast upon his breast.

How can those terrified vague fingers push   5
The feathered glory from her loosening thighs?
And how can body, laid in that white rush,
But feel the strange heart beating where it lies?

A shudder in the loins engenders there
The broken wall, the burning roof and tower[2]   10
And Agamemnon dead.

              Being so caught up,
So mastered by the brute blood of the air,
Did she put on his knowledge with his power
Before the indifferent beak could let her drop?

1923   1924, 1928

4. "I have read somewhere," Yeats wrote, "that in the Emperor's palace at Byzantium was a tree made of gold and silver, and artificial birds that sang." Cf. also Hans Christian Andersen's *Emperor's Nightingale*, which may have been in Yeats's mind at the time.
1. In Greek mythology Zeus visited Leda in the form of a swan. As a result of the union Leda gave birth to Helen and to Clytemnestra (wife of Agamemnon). Yeats saw Zeus's visit to Leda as an "annunciation," marking the beginning of Greek civilization: "I imagine the annunciation that founded Greece as made to Leda, remembering that they showed in a Spartan temple, strung up to the roof as a holy relic, an unhatched egg of hers, and that from one of her eggs came love and from the other war" (*A Vision*). In the original Cuala Press edition Yeats noted: "I wrote *Leda and the Swan* because the editor of a political review asked me for a poem. I thought, 'After the individualist, demagogic movement, founded by Hobbes and popularized by the Encyclopedists and the French Revolution, we have a soil so exhausted that it cannot grow that crop again for centuries.' Then I thought, 'Nothing is now possible but some movement from above preceded by some violent annunciation.' My fancy began to play with Leda and the Swan for metaphor, and I began this poem; but as I wrote, bird and lady took such possession of the scene that all politics went out of it, and my friend tells me that his 'conservative readers would misunderstand the poem.'" Note that this poem is in sonnet form; the placing of the pauses gives it a rhetorical pattern not normally associated with the sonnet.
2. I.e., the destruction of Troy, caused by Helen's elopement with the Trojan Paris. Agamemnon was murdered by his wife Clytemnestra, the other daughter of Leda and the Swan.

Among School Children

1

I walk through the long schoolroom questioning;
A kind old nun in a white hood replies;
The children learn to cipher and to sing,
To study reading-books and history,
To cut and sew, be neat in everything   5
In the best modern way—the children's eyes
In momentary wonder stare upon
A sixty-year-old smiling public man.

2

I dream of a Ledaean body,[1] bent
Above a sinking fire, a tale that she   10
Told of a harsh reproof, or trivial event
That changed some childish day to tragedy—
Told, and it seemed that our two natures blent
Into a sphere from youthful sympathy,
Or else, to alter Plato's parable,   15
Into the yolk and white of the one shell.[2]

3

And thinking of that fit of grief or rage
I look upon one child or t'other there
And wonder if she stood so at that age—
For even daughters of the swan can share   20
Something of every paddler's heritage—
And had that color upon cheek or hair,
And thereupon my heart is driven wild:
She stands before me as a living child.

4

Her present image floats into the mind—   25
Did Quattrocento[3] finger fashion it
Hollow of cheek as though it drank the wind
And took a mess of shadows for its meat?
And I though never of Ledaean kind
Had pretty plumage once—enough of that,   30
Better to smile on all that smile, and show
There is a comfortable kind of old scarecrow.

5

What youthful mother, a shape upon her lap
Honey of generation had betrayed,

---

1. "Ledaean": adjective from "Leda," meaning "like Helen of Troy" (Leda's daughter). The reference is to Maud Gonne (as also in lines 19–28).
2. In Plato's *Symposium* Aristophanes explains Love by supposing that "the primeval man was round and had four hands and four feet, back and sides forming a circle, one head with two faces," and was subsequently divided into two. "After the division, the two parts of man, each desiring his other half, came together, and threw their arms about one another eager to grow into one." The fact that Helen was born from an egg (as the daughter of Leda and the Swan) suggests Yeats's image for such a union.
3. 15th-century; a reference to Italian painters of the period, especially Botticelli (ca. 1444–1510).

And that must sleep, shriek, struggle to escape   35
As recollection or the drug decide,[4]
Would think her son, did she but see that shape
With sixty or more winters on its head,
A compensation for the pang of his birth,
Or the uncertainty of his setting forth?   40

6

Plato thought nature but a spume that plays
Upon a ghostly paradigm of things;
Solider Aristotle played the taws
Upon the bottom of a king of kings;[5]
World-famous golden-thighed Pythagoras[6]   45
Fingered upon a fiddle-stick or strings
What a star sang and careless Muses heard:
Old clothes upon old sticks to scare a bird.[7]

7

Both nuns and mothers worship images,[8]
But those the candles light are not as those   50
That animate a mother's reveries,
But keep a marble or a bronze repose.
And yet they too break hearts—O Presences
That passion, piety, or affection knows,
And that all heavenly glory symbolize—   55
O self-born mockers of man's enterprise;

8

Labor is blossoming or dancing where
The body is not bruised to pleasure soul,
Nor beauty born out of its own despair,
Nor blear-eyed wisdom out of midnight oil.   60
O chestnut tree, great-rooted blossomer,
Are you the leaf, the blossom, or the bole?
O body swayed to music, O brightening glance,
How can we know the dancer from the dance?[9]

1927

4. "I have taken the 'honey of generation' from Porphyry's essay on 'The Cave of the Nymphs,' but find no warrant in Porphyry for considering it the 'drug' that destroys the 'recollection' of prenatal freedom" [Yeats's note]. Porphyry was a Neo-Platonic philosopher of the 3rd century A.D. "Honey of generation," by blotting out the memory of prenatal happiness, "betrays" an infant to be born into this world. The infant will either "sleep" or "struggle to escape" (from this world) depending on whether the drug works or the recollection of blissful prenatal life overcomes the oblivion caused by the drug. 5. Plato thought nature was a mere appearance ("spume") veiling the ultimate spiritual and mathematical reality ("ghostly paradigm"); Aristotle was "solider" in that he believed that form really inhered in the matter of nature, and thus that nature itself had reality.

Aristotle was tutor to Alexander the Great, and disciplined him by applying the "taws" or strap. 6. Greek philosopher (early 6th century B.C.), interested in mathematics and the mathematical study of acoustics and music; his disciples, the Pythagoreans, developed a mystical philosophy of numerical relations and united the notions of astronomical and mathematical relations in the theory of the music of the spheres. Pythagoreans regarded their master with veneration as a god with a golden thigh. 7. A contemptuous description of the philosophies of Plato, Aristotle, and Pythagoras. 8. Nuns worship images of Christ or the Virgin; mothers worship their own inward images of their children. 9. Yeats's view of life as a cosmic dance, in which every human faculty joins harmoniously. The individual be-

A Dialogue of Self and Soul[1]

1

MY SOUL. I summon to the winding ancient stair;
    Set all your mind upon the steep ascent,
    Upon the broken, crumbling battlement,
    Upon the breathless starlit air,
    Upon the star that marks the hidden pole;   5
    Fix every wandering thought upon
    That quarter where all thought is done:
    Who can distinguish darkness from the soul?

MY SELF. The consecrated blade upon my knees
    Is Sato's ancient blade,[2] still as it was,   10
    Still razor-keen, still like a looking glass
    Unspotted by the centuries;
    That flowering, silken, old embroidery, torn
    From some court lady's dress and round
    The wooden scabbard bound and wound,   15
    Can, tattered, still protect, faded adorn.

MY SOUL. Why should the imagination of a man
    Long past his prime remember things that are
    Emblematical of love and war?
    Think of ancestral night that can,   20
    If but imagination scorn the earth
    And intellect its wandering
    To this and that and t'other thing,
    Deliver from the crime of death and birth.

MY SELF. Montashigi, third of his family, fashioned it   25
    Five hundred years ago, about it lie
    Flowers from I know not what embroidery—
    Heart's purple—and all these I set
    For emblems of the day against the tower
    Emblematical of the night,   30
    And claim as by a soldier's right
    A charter to commit the crime once more.

comes involved in the process, as the dancer becomes part of the dance. Yeats relates the idea of the cosmic dance to his views of ritual, elegance, and order (cf. "the ceremony of innocence" in *The Second Coming* and the end of *Prayer for my Daughter*), and sees it as a means of reconciling the conflicting opposites of ordinary life.

1. Yeats here debates two opposing claims: the soul's summons to wisdom, resignation from an active life, the spiritual ascent—symbolized by the winding stair, a symbol similar to that of Byzantium—against the summons to the life of action and passion, symbolized by the sword of the second stanza and championed by the "Self."

2. A Japanese called Sato had given Yeats a sword, telling him that it was a symbol of life and that its silk-embroidered sheath was a symbol of beauty. Thus the sword in its scabbard is "emblematical of love and war" (line 19) and represents the "day," as opposed to the "night" represented by the tower and the winding stair (lines 29–30).

My Soul. Such fullness in that quarter overflows
    And falls into the basin of the mind
    That man is stricken deaf and dumb and blind, 35
    For intellect no longer knows
    Is from the *Ought,* or *Knower* from the *Known*—
    That is to say, ascends to Heaven;
    Only the dead can be forgiven;
    But when I think of that my tongue's a stone. 40

2

My Self. A living man is blind and drinks his drop.
    What matter if the ditches are impure?
    What matter if I live it all once more?
    Endure that toil of growing up;
    The ignominy of boyhood; the distress 45
    Of boyhood changing into man;
    The unfinished man and his pain
    Brought face to face with his own clumsiness;

    The finished man among his enemies?—
    How in the name of Heaven can he escape 50
    That defiling and disfigured shape
    The mirror of malicious eyes
    Casts upon his eyes until at last
    He thinks that shape must be his shape?
    And what's the good of an escape 55
    If honor find him in the wintry blast?

    I am content to live it all again
    And yet again, if it be life to pitch
    Into the frog-spawn of a blind man's ditch,
    A blind man battering blind men; 60
    Or into that most fecund ditch of all,
    The folly that man does
    Or must suffer, if he woos
    A proud woman not kindred of his soul.

    I am content to follow to its source 65
    Every event in action or in thought;
    Measure the lot; forgive myself the lot!
    When such as I cast out remorse
    So great a sweetness flows into the breast
    We must laugh and we must sing, 70
    We are blest by everything,
    Everything we look upon is blest.

1929

For Anne Gregory

    "Never shall a young man,
    Thrown into despair
    By those great honey-colored

Ramparts at your ear,
Love you for yourself alone   5
And not your yellow hair."

"But I can get a hair-dye
And set such color there,
Brown, or black, or carrot,
That young men in despair   10
May love me for myself alone
And not my yellow hair."

"I heard an old religious man
But yesternight declare
That he had found a text to prove   15
That only God, my dear,
Could love you for yourself alone
And not your yellow hair."

1931, 1932

Byzantium[1]

The unpurged images of day recede;
The Emperor's drunken soldiery are abed;
Night resonance recedes, night-walkers' song
After great cathedral gong;
A starlit or a moonlit dome[2] disdains   5

1. The world of artifice and eternity to which Yeats journeyed in *Sailing to Byzantium* is now seen also as the world of death and spiritual purification from the "mire or blood" of life. As the poem opens, the "unpurged images of day" and then "night resonance" recede after the sounding of the gong at midnight (symbolic of the summons to death)—i.e., images of both the conscious (day) mind and the subconscious (night) mind depart, leaving the self in the hushed starlight or moonlight, purged of the "mere complexities" of flesh-and-blood life. This purified self "disdains" the confusion and murkiness of the unpurified self. In the second stanza the soul, released from what Yeats once called "the strain one upon another of opposites" of ordinary life, sees his spirit-guide leading him to the world of changelessness and purity. He hails this guide (a mediating figure between man, image, and shade) because he is now far enough beyond life to be able to do so. The third stanza shows the poet in the midst of the death-world of artifice and eternity, admiring the golden artifacts which, "in glory of changeless metal" (line 22), scorn the "complexities" and impurities of earthly creatures. In the next stanza the poet sees purgatorial fires burning away the "complexities" of bodily life; yet, unlike earthly flame which consumes as it burns, this flame "cannot singe a sleeve" (line 32). Finally, the poet finds himself no longer clearly in the world of pure spirit: he is pulled back by the tug of human emotion. He sees the smithies of the metalworkers buttressing the city against the dark tides of impurity and lust, while the dance of eternal life on the cold marble floor similarly helps to stem the flood (these are Platonic and Neo-Platonic images). But art and artifice cannot succeed in repelling the sensual life that beats against the city walls: in the end, human images break through and "beget" yet further images (cf. *Sailing to Byzantium*, in which he wanted to escape from "whatever is begotten, born, and dies"). The poem concludes on a note of human passion, "that dolphin-torn, that gong-tormented sea." In this instance, the gong is calling the poet back to life, not from life to death. He has discovered that art is nourished by life and in the end leads back to it. Yeats himself said that this poem was written "to warm myself back to life" after a serious illness.
2. "Starlit" and "moonlit" had a special symbolic significance for Yeats, as part of his theory of history and personality

All that man is,
All mere complexities,
The fury and the mire of human veins.

Before me floats an image, man or shade,
Shade more than man, more image than a shade;   10
For Hades' bobbin bound in mummy-cloth
May unwind the winding path;[3]
A mouth that has no moisture and no breath
Breathless mouths may summon;
I hail the superhuman;   15
I call it death-in-life and life-in-death.

Miracle, bird or golden handiwork,
More miracle than bird or handiwork,
Planted on the starlit golden bough,[4]
Can like the cocks of Hades crow,   20
Or, by the moon embittered, scorn aloud
In glory of changeless metal
Common bird or petal
And all complexities of mire or blood.

At midnight on the Emperor's pavement flit   25
Flames that no faggot feeds, nor steel has lit,
Nor storm disturbs, flames begotten of flame,
Where blood-begotten spirits come
And all complexities of fury leave,
Dying into a dance,   30
An agony of trance,
An agony of flame[5] that cannot singe a sleeve.

Astraddle on the dolphin's mire and blood,[6]
Spirit after spirit! The smithies break the flood,

in terms of the phases of the moon (in *A Vision*). The first phase—that of the dark of the moon, when only the stars shine—is the phase when "body is completely absorbed in its supernatural environment." The fifteenth phase—the full moon—is the phase of complete subjectivity, where the mind is "completely absorbed by being." Thus both phases are states of *being:* they reject the complexities of the world of *becoming* and change.

In the Cuala Press edition of 1932, "disdains" is printed as "distains" (i.e., discolors, pollutes); all subsequent printings, however, read "disdains." It has been argued that the first reading must be correct, but it makes less sense, and Yeats never corrected the "disdains" in later printings.
3. The spool of man's fate, which spins his destiny and which is symbolized by the wrappings around a mummy, may lead man, as it unwinds, to the realm of pure spirit (or up the winding stair, in another of Yeats's favorite images).
4. The "starlit golden bough" is part of the death-world of artifice and eter-

nity; it is opposed to a real, living bough, which would be lighted by the sun or the moon (cf. note 2). The bough is also associated with the mystical tree of the esoteric Hebrew doctrine of the cabala, in whose branches "the birds lodge and build their nests; that is, the souls or angels have their place." The "cocks of Hades" are the birds standing outside time whose crowing proclaims the cycles of rebirth to mortal beings: the golden birds of art, who live in the same tree, are similarly eternal.
5. The "agony of flame" was suggested to Yeats by a Japanese *Nō* play, *Motomezuka,* wherein a young girl suffers from perpetual burning, which is a sense of her own guilt. A priest tells her that the flames will cease if she no longer believes in their reality; she finds herself incapable of disbelief, however, and the play ends in "the dance of her agony."
6. The dolphin, in ancient art, was a symbol of the soul in transit from one state to another. Mounted on its back, the poet here is able to ride over the

The golden smithies of the Emperor!   35
Marbles of the dancing floor
Break bitter furies of complexity,
Those images that yet
Fresh images beget,
That dolphin-torn, that gong-tormented sea.   40

1930   1932

Crazy Jane Talks with the Bishop[1]

I met the Bishop on the road
And much said he and I.
"Those breasts are flat and fallen now,
Those veins must soon be dry;
Live in a heavenly mansion,   5
Not in some foul sty."

"Fair and foul are near of kin,
And fair needs foul," I cried.
"My friends are gone, but that's a truth
Nor grave nor bed denied,   10
Learned in bodily lowliness
And in the heart's pride.

"A woman can be proud and stiff
When on love intent;
But Love has pitched his mansion in   15
The place of excrement;
For nothing can be sole or whole
That has not been rent."

                                                       1932

After Long Silence

Speech after long silence; it is right,
All other lovers being estranged or dead,
Unfriendly lamplight hid under its shade,
The curtains drawn upon unfriendly night,
That we descant and yet again descant   5
Upon the supreme theme of Art and Song:
Bodily decrepitude is wisdom; young
We loved each other and were ignorant.

                                                       1932

---

sea of human passions—except that the
dolphin itself is made of "mire or
blood."
1. One of a series of poems dealing
with the paradox that wisdom may reside with fools and beggars (such as
Jane) rather than with the respectable
representatives of orthodoxy (such as
the Bishop). This poem also deals with
a favorite Yeatsian theme, the resolution of opposites, of what he called
elsewhere "all those antinomies / Of
day and night."

Lapis Lazuli[1]

(FOR HARRY CLIFTON)

I have heard that hysterical women say
They are sick of the palette and fiddle bow,
Of poets that are always gay,
For everybody knows or else should know
That if nothing drastic is done   5
Aeroplane and Zeppelin will come out,
Pitch like King Billy[2] bomb-balls in
Until the town lie beaten flat.

All perform their tragic play,
There struts Hamlet, there is Lear,   10
That's Ophelia, that Cordelia;
Yet they, should the last scene be there,
The great stage curtain about to drop,
If worthy their prominent part in the play,
Do not break up their lines to weep.   15
They know that Hamlet and Lear are gay;
Gaiety transfiguring all that dread.
All men have aimed at, found and lost;
Black out; Heaven blazing into the head:
Tragedy wrought to its uttermost.   20
Though Hamlet rambles and Lear rages,
And all the drop-scenes drop at once
Upon a hundred thousand stages,
It cannot grow by an inch or an ounce.

On their own feet they came, or on shipboard,   25
Camel-back, horse-back, ass-back, mule-back,
Old civilizations put to the sword.
Then they and their wisdom went to rack:
No handiwork of Callimachus,[3]
Who handled marble as if it were bronze,   30

1. A deep blue stone. "I notice that you have much lapis lazuli; someone has sent me a present of a great piece carved by some Chinese sculptor into the semblance of a mountain with temple, trees, paths, and an ascetic and pupil about to climb the mountain. Ascetic, pupil, hard stone, eternal theme of the sensual east. The heroic cry in the midst of despair. But no, I am wrong, the east has its solutions always and therefore knows nothing of tragedy. It is we, not the east, that must raise the heroic cry" (Yeats to Dorothy Wellesley, July 6, 1935).
2. King William III (William of Orange), who defeated the army of King James II at the Battle of the Boyne in 1690.
3. Greek sculptor (5th century B.C.), supposedly the originator of the Corinthian column and of the use of the running drill to imitate folds in drapery in statues. Yeats wrote of him: "With Callimachus pure Ionic revives again * * * and upon the only example of his work known to us, a marble chair, a Persian is represented, and may one not discover a Persian symbol in that bronze lamp, shaped like a palm * * * ? But he was an archaistic workman, and those who set him to work brought back public life to an older form" (*A Vision*).

Made draperies that seemed to rise
When sea wind swept the corner, stands;
His long lamp chimney shaped like the stem
Of a slender palm, stood but a day;
All things fall and are built again,   35
And those that build them again are gay.

Two Chinamen, behind them a third,
Are carved in lapis lazuli,
Over them flies a long-legged bird,
A symbol of longevity;   40
The third, doubtless a servingman,
Carries a musical instrument.

Every discoloration of the stone,
Every accidental crack or dent,
Seems a watercourse or an avalanche,   45
Or lofty slope where it still snows
Though doubtless plum or cherry branch
Sweetens the little halfway house
Those Chinamen climb towards, and I
Delight to imagine them seated there;   50
There, on the mountain and the sky,
On all the tragic scene they stare.
One asks for mournful melodies;
Accomplished fingers begin to play.
Their eyes mid many wrinkles, their eyes,   55
Their ancient, glittering eyes, are gay.

1938

Long-legged Fly[1]

That civilization may not sink,
Its great battle lost,
Quiet the dog, tether the pony
To a distant post;
Our master Caesar is in the tent   5
Where the maps are spread,
His eyes fixed upon nothing,
A hand under his head.
Like a long-legged fly upon the stream
His mind moves upon silence.   10

1. The first stanza shows Caesar planning one of his history-making campaigns: any disturbing noise now will
alter the course of civilization. In the
next stanza Helen of Troy as a child
practices a part: the future of Troy
and of the ancient world depends
on her being allowed to train herself to
be a woman. Finally, Michelangelo
works in the Sistine Chapel in Rome: he
must be undisturbed if his art is to be
unspoiled, so that it can give to future
generations of "girls at puberty" their
first disturbing thoughts of men.

That the topless towers[2] be burnt
And men recall that face,
Move most gently if move you must
In this lonely place.
She thinks, part woman, three parts a child,   15
That nobody looks; her feet
Practice a tinker shuffle
Picked up on a street.
Like a long-legged fly upon the stream
Her mind moves upon silence.   20

That girls at puberty may find
The first Adam in their thought,
Shut the door of the Pope's chapel,
Keep those children out.
There on that scaffolding reclines   25
Michael Angelo.
With no more sound than the mice make
His hand moves to and fro.
Like a long-legged fly upon the stream
His mind moves upon silence.   30

1939

The Circus Animals' Desertion[1]

1

I sought a theme and sought for it in vain,
I sought it daily for six weeks or so.
Maybe at last, being but a broken man,
I must be satisfied with my heart, although
Winter and summer till old age began   5
My circus animals were all on show,
Those stilted boys, that burnished chariot,
Lion and woman[2] and the Lord knows what.

2

What can I but enumerate old themes?
First that sea-rider Oisin[3] led by the nose   10
Through three enchanted islands, allegorical dreams,
Vain gaiety, vain battle, vain repose,
Themes of the embittered heart, or so it seems,
That might adorn old songs or courtly shows;

2. Of Troy. Cf. "Was this the face that
launched a thousand ships / And burnt
the topless towers of Ilium?" (Marlowe,
Dr. Faustus).

1. Yeats in old age looks back on some
of the main themes of his poems and
plays as circus animals that have now
deserted him, leaving him with only the
refuse of his human passions.

2. Cf. "On the gray rock of Cashel I

suddenly saw / A Sphinx with **woman**
breast and lion paw * * * " (Yeats,
*The Double Vision of Michael Ro-
bartes*).

3. Pronounced *Ushéen*. Hero of an Old
Irish legend, he was beguiled by a fairy
woman to the fairy world and returned
150 years later to find his friends dead
and Ireland Christian. Subject of an
early long poem by Yeats (1889).

But what cared I that set him on to ride,   15
I, starved for the bosom of his faery bride?

And then a counter-truth filled out its play,
The Countess Cathleen was the name I gave it;
She, pity-crazed, had given her soul away,
But masterful Heaven had intervened to save it.[4]   20
I thought my dear must her own soul destroy,
So did fanaticism and hate enslave it,
And this brought forth a dream and soon enough
This dream itself had all my thought and love.

And when the Fool and Blind Man stole the bread   25
Cuchulain fought the ungovernable sea;[5]
Heart-mysteries there, and yet when all is said
It was the dream itself enchanted me:
Character isolated by a deed
To engross the present and dominate memory.   30
Players and painted stage took all my love,
And not those things that they were emblems of.

3

Those masterful images because complete
Grew in pure mind, but out of what began?
A mound of refuse or the sweepings of a street,   35
Old kettles, old bottles, and a broken can,
Old iron, old bones, old rags, that raving slut
Who keeps the till. Now that my ladder's gone,
I must lie down where all the ladders start,
In the foul rag-and-bone shop of the heart.   40

1939

Under Ben Bulben[1]

1

Swear by what the sages spoke
Round the Mareotic Lake[2]

4. Title of an early Yeats play (1892) about an Irish countess who, although she sold her soul to the devil to get food for the starving people, goes to Heaven anyway, for God looks "on the motive, not the deed."
5. In Yeats's play *On Baile's Strand* (1904), where he probes for symbolic meanings in an old Irish legend.
1. One of Yeats's last poems, ending with the epitaph he wrote for himself. He wished to be buried in the churchyard of the village of Drumcliff, which lies "under Ben Bulben," mountain in County Sligo. Although he died on the French Riviera, his body was later brought back and buried at Drumcliff.

2. Lake Mareotis, bordering the city of Alexandria where a school of Neo-Pythagorean philosophers flourished in the 1st century A.D. By Lake Mareotis also flourished (3rd century A.D.) the Christian Neo-Platonists, in whom Yeats was much interested. The lake is mentioned in Shelley's poem *The Witch of Atlas*, a poem which Yeats admired and interpreted in his own way, seeing the Witch as a symbol of timeless, absolute beauty; hence what she "knew" and "spoke" and what "set the cocks a-crow" can be related to the "miracle" that "can like the cocks of Hades crow" in *Byzantium*.

That the Witch of Atlas knew,
Spoke and set the cocks a-crow.

Swear by those horsemen, by those women   5
Complexion and form prove superhuman,[3]
That pale, long-visaged company
That air in immortality
Completeness of their passions won;
Now they ride the wintry dawn   10
Where Ben Bulben sets the scene.

Here's the gist of what they mean.

2

Many times man lives and dies
Between his two eternities,
That of race and that of soul,   15
And ancient Ireland knew it all.
Whether man die in his bed
Or the rifle knocks him dead,
A brief parting from those dear
Is the worst man has to fear.   20
Though gravediggers' toil is long,
Sharp their spades, their muscles strong,
They but thrust their buried men
Back in the human mind again.

3

You that Mitchel's prayer have heard,   25
"Send war in our time, O Lord!"[4]
Know that when all words are said
And a man is fighting mad,
Something drops from eyes long blind,
He completes his partial mind,   30
For an instant stands at ease,
Laughs aloud, his heart at peace.
Even the wisest man grows tense
With some sort of violence
Before he can accomplish fate,   35
Know his work or choose his mate.

4

Poet and sculptor, do the work,
Nor let the modish painter shirk
What his great forefathers did,
Bring the soul of man to God,   40
Make him fill the cradles right.

Measurement began our might:
Forms a stark Egyptian thought,

3. The *sidhe* or fairy folk, who were believed to ride through the countryside near Ben Bulben. The gist of Yeats's thought here is: "Swear by those who speak superhuman, eternal truths." These truths are summed up in the second section of the poem: man has an afterlife both in the future of his individual soul and in the memory he leaves behind on earth.
4. John Mitchel, an Irish patriot imprisoned for his activities, wrote in his *Jail Journal:* "Give us war in our time, O Lord!"

Forms that gentler Phidias wrought.[5]
Michael Angelo left a proof   45
On the Sistine Chapel roof,
Where but half-awakened Adam
Can disturb globe-trotting Madam
Till her bowels are in heat,[6]
Proof that there's a purpose set   50
Before the secret working mind:
Profane perfection of mankind.

Quattrocento[7] put in paint
On backgrounds for a God or Saint
Gardens where a soul's at ease;   55
Where everything that meets the eye,
Flowers and grass and cloudless sky,
Resemble forms that are or seem
When sleepers wake and yet still dream,
And when it's vanished still declare,   60
With only bed and bedstead there,
That heavens had opened.
                       Gyres run on;
When that greater dream had gone
Calvert and Wilson, Blake and Claude,[8]
Prepared a rest for the people of God,   65
Palmer's phrase, but after that
Confusion fell upon our thought.

                       5
Irish poets, learn your trade,
Sing whatever is well made,
Scorn the sort now growing up   70
All out of shape from toe to top,
Their unremembering hearts and heads
Base-born products of base beds.
Sing the peasantry, and then
Hard-riding country gentlemen,   75
The holiness of monks, and after
Porter-drinkers' randy laughter;
Sing the lords and ladies gay
That were beaten into the clay
Through seven heroic centuries;   80

5. Greek sculptor (5th century B.C.), generally thought to have raised the classical ideal in art to its highest culmination. Yeats here itemizes steps in his history of knowledge and the arts, beginning with Babylonian mathematics ("measurement"), through "stark Egyptian thought," to the Renaissance of Michelangelo. Each of these steps is related to Yeats's cyclical theory of history.
6. Cf. *Long-Legged Fly*, stanza 3.
7. 15th-century Italian art.
8. Works by the five artists mentioned in lines 64–66 all provided images for Yeats's poetry: Edward Calvert, 19th-century wood-engraver; Richard Wilson, 18th-century landscape painter; William Blake, "one of the great mythmakers and mask-makers"; Claude Lorrain, 17th-century landscape painter; and (in line 66) Samuel Palmer, 19th-century landscape painter and etcher, one of whose works was "The Lonely Tower." Calvert, Blake, and Palmer knew each other and shared a view of the holiness of art. (See T. R. Henn, *The Lonely Tower*, 1950.)

Cast your mind on other days
That we in coming days may be
Still the indomitable Irishry.

6

Under bare Ben Bulben's head
In Drumcliff churchyard Yeats is laid.   85
An ancestor was rector there
Long years ago, a church stands near,
By the road an ancient cross.
No marble, no conventional phrase;
On limestone quarried near the spot   90
By his command these words are cut:
    Cast a cold eye
    On life, on death.
    Horseman, pass by!

September 4, 1938   1939

From Reveries over Childhood and Youth[1]
[*The Yeats Family*]

Some six miles off towards Ben Bulben and beyond the Channel,[2] as we call the tidal river between Sligo and the Rosses, and on top of a hill there was a little square two-storied house covered with creepers and looking out upon a garden where the box borders were larger than any I had ever seen, and where I saw for the first time the crimson steak of the gladiolus and awaited its blossom with excitement. Under one gable a dark thicket of small trees made a shut-in mysterious place, where one played and believed that something was going to happen. My great-aunt Micky lived there. Micky was not her right name for she was Mary Yeats and her father had been my great-grandfather, John Yeats, who had been Rector of Drumcliffe, a few miles further off, and died in 1847. She was a spare, high-colored, elderly woman and had the oldest-looking cat I had ever seen, for its hair had grown into matted locks of yellowy white. She farmed and had one old manservant, but could not have farmed at all, had not neighboring farmers helped to gather in the crops, in return for the loan of her farm implements and "out of respect for the family," for as Johnny Mac-Gurk, the Sligo barber said to me, "The Yeatses were always very respectable." She was full of family history; all her dinner knives were pointed like daggers through much cleaning, and there was a little

1. Yeats wrote a variety of autobiographical essays between 1914 and 1928: these were originally published separately and later collected as *The Autobiography of W. B. Yeats* (1936, 1953). The selections given here are from *Reveries over Childhood and Youth*, first published in 1915, and *The Trembling of the Veil*, first published in 1922.

2. Yeats's favorite County Sligo landscape. Cf. the places named in *The Stolen Child.*

James the First cream-jug with the Yeats motto and crest, and on her dining-room mantelpiece a beautiful silver cup that had belonged to my great-great-grandfather, who had married a certain Mary Butler. It had upon it the Butler crest and had been already old at the date 1534, when the initials of some bride and bridegroom were engraved under the lip. All its history for generations was rolled up inside it upon a piece of paper yellow with age, until some caller took the paper to light his pipe.

Another family of Yeats, a widow and her two children on whom I called sometimes with my grandmother, lived near in a long low cottage, and owned a very fierce turkey cock that did battle with their visitors; and some miles away lived the secretary to the Grand Jury and Land Agent, my great-uncle Mat Yeats and his big family of boys and girls; but I think it was only in later years that I came to know them well. I do not think any of these liked the Pollexfens, who were well off and seemed to them purse-proud, whereas they themselves had come down in the world. I remember them as very well-bred and very religious in the Evangelical way and thinking a good deal of Aunt Micky's old histories. There had been among our ancestors a King's County soldier, one of Marlborough's[3] generals, and when his nephew came to dine he gave him boiled pork, and when the nephew said he disliked boiled pork he had asked him to dine again and promised him something he would like better. However, he gave him boiled pork again and the nephew took the hint in silence. The other day as I was coming home from America, I met one of his descendants whose family has not another discoverable link with ours, and he too knew the boiled pork story and nothing else. We have the General's portrait, and he looks very fine in his armor and his long curly wig, and underneath it, after his name, are many honors that have left no tradition among us. Were we country people, we could have summarized his life in a legend. Other ancestors or great-uncles bore a part in Irish history; one saved the life of Sarsfield[4] at the battle of Sedgemoor; another, taken prisoner by King James's army, owed his to Sarsfield's gratitude; another, a century later, roused the gentlemen of Meath[5] against some local Jacquère,[6] and was shot dead upon a county road, and yet another "chased the United Irishmen[7] for a fortnight, fell into their hands and was hanged." The notorious

3. John Churchill, Duke of Marlborough (1650–1722), English general in the War of the Spanish Succession (1702–13).

4. Patrick Sarsfield (d. 1693), Irish Jacobite general who served in the battle of Sedgemoor (1685) when the Duke of Monmouth, illegitimate son of Charles II who was claiming the throne from his uncle James II, was defeated and captured.

5. Maritime county in province of Leinster, in the east of Ireland.

6. Peasant revolutionary. The "Jacquerie" was a peasants' revolt (1358) against the nobles in northern France (the term derived from *Jacques Bonhomme*, the nobility's contemptuous name for a peasant).

7. Irish society founded 1791 by Theobald Wolfe Tone which later was influential in causing the Irish rebellion of 1798.

Major Sirr, who arrested Lord Edward Fitzgerald[8] and gave him the bullet wound he died of in the jail, was godfather to several of my great-great-grandfather's children; while to make a balance, my great-grandfather had been Robert Emmett's[9] friend and was suspected and imprisoned though but for a few hours. One great-uncle fell at New Orleans in 1813, while another, who became Governor of Penang,[1] led the forlorn hope at the taking of Rangoon, and even in the last generation of all there had been lives of some power and pleasure. An old man who had entertained many famous people, in his eighteenth-century house, where battlement and tower showed the influence of Horace Walpole,[2] had but lately, after losing all his money, drowned himself, first taking off his rings and chain and watch as became a collector of many beautiful things; and once to remind us of more passionate life, a gunboat put into Rosses, commanded by the illegitimate son of some great-uncle or other. Now that I can look at their miniatures, turning them over to find the name of soldier, or lawyer, or Castle official,[3] and wondering if they cared for good books or good music, I am delighted with all that joins my life to those who had power in Ireland or with those anywhere that were good servants and poor bargainers, but I cared nothing as a child for Micky's tales. I could see my grandfather's ships come up the bay or the river, and his sailors treated me with deference, and a ship's carpenter made and mended my toy boats and I thought that nobody could be so important as my grandfather. Perhaps, too, it is only now that I can value those more gentle natures so unlike his passion and violence. An old Sligo priest has told me how my great-grandfather John Yeats always went into his kitchen rattling the keys, so much did he fear finding some one doing wrong, and of a speech of his when the agent of the great landowner of his parish brought him from cottage to cottage to bid the women send their children to the Protestant school. All promised till they came to one who cried, "Child of mine will never darken your door." "Thank you, my woman," he said, "you are the first honest woman I have met today." My uncle, Mat Yeats, the Land Agent, had once waited up every night for a week to catch some boys who stole his apples and when he caught them had given them sixpence and told them not to do it again. Perhaps it is only fancy or the softening touch of the miniaturist that makes me discover in their faces some courtesy and much gentleness. Two eighteenth-century faces interest me the

8. British officer (1763–98) who, after dismissal from the army for disloyal activities, joined the United Irishmen. Cf. *September 1913*, lines 19–22.
9. 1778–1803; Irish patriot, hanged at Dublin for treason.
1. Island in Malaya. Rangoon, capital of Burma, was taken by the British in 1824.

2. The 18th-century English author whose pseudo-Gothic house, Strawberry Hill, much influenced subsequent "Gothic" architecture in England and elsewhere.
3. I.e., official at Dublin Castle, where the Viceroy (representing the British Crown) lived with his staff before Irish independence was achieved in 1922.

most, one that of a great-great-grandfather, for both have under their powdered curling wigs a half-feminine charm, and as I look at them I discover a something clumsy and heavy in myself. Yet it was a Yeats who spoke the only eulogy that turns my head: "We have ideas and no passions, but by marriage with a Pollexfen we have given a tongue to the sea cliffs."

Among the miniatures there is a larger picture, an admirable drawing by I know not what master, that is too harsh and merry for its company. He was a connection and close friend of my great-grandmother Corbet, and though we spoke of him as "Uncle Beattie" in our childhood, no blood relation. My great-grandmother who died at ninety-three had many memories of him. He was the friend of Goldsmith and was accustomed to boast, clergyman though he was, that he belonged to a hunt club of which every member but himself had been hanged or transported for treason, and that it was not possible to ask him a question he could not reply to with a perfectly appropriate blasphemy or indecency.

[An Irish Literature]

From these debates, from O'Leary's[4] conversation, and from the Irish books he lent or gave me has come all I have set my hand to since. I had begun to know a great deal about the Irish poets who had written in English. I read with excitement books I should find unreadable today, and found romance in lives that had neither wit nor adventure. I did not deceive myself, I knew how often they wrote a cold and abstract language, and yet I who had never wanted to see the houses where Keats and Shelley lived would ask everybody what sort of place Inchedony was, because Callanan[5] had named after it a bad poem in the manner of *Childe Harold*. Walking home from a debate, I remember saying to some college student, "Ireland cannot put from her the habits learned from her old military civilization and from a church that prays in Latin. Those popular poets have not touched her heart, her poetry when it comes will be distinguished and lonely." O'Leary had once said to me, "Neither Ireland nor England knows the good from the bad in any art, but Ireland unlike England does not hate the good when it is pointed out to her." I began to plot and scheme how one might seal with the right image the soft wax before it began to harden. I had noticed that Irish Catholics among whom had been born so many political martyrs had not the good taste, the household courtesy and decency of the Protestant Ireland I had known, yet Protestant Ireland seemed to think of nothing but getting on in the world. I thought we might bring the halves together if we

---

4. John O'Leary (d. 1907), an Irish nationalist, for whom Yeats had great respect. Cf. *September 1913* ("Romantic Ireland's dead and gone, / It's with O'Leary in the grave").
5. Jeremiah John Callanan, Anglo-Irish poet, published *The Recluse of Inchedony and Other Poems* in 1830.

had a national literature that made Ireland beautiful in the memory, and yet had been freed from provincialism by an exacting criticism, an European pose.

1915

From The Trembling of the Veil
[London and Pre-Raphaelitism]

At the end of the 'eighties my father and mother, my brother and sisters and myself, all newly arrived from Dublin, were settled in Bedford Park in a red-brick house with several mantelpieces of wood, copied from marble mantelpieces designed by the brothers Adam,[1] a balcony and a little garden shadowed by a great horse-chestnut tree. Years before we had lived there, when the crooked ostentatiously picturesque streets with great trees casting great shadows had been a new enthusiasm: the Pre-Raphaelite movement at last affecting life. But now exaggerated criticism had taken the place of enthusiasm, the tiled roofs, the first in modern London, were said to leak, which they did not, and the drains to be bad, though that was no longer true; and I imagine that houses were cheap. I remember feeling disappointed because the co-operative stores, with their little seventeenth-century panes, had lost the romance I saw there when I passed them still unfinished on my way to school; and because the public-house, called The Tabard after Chaucer's Inn, was so plainly a common public-house; and because the great sign of a trumpeter designed by Rooke, the Pre-Raphaelite artist, had been freshened by some inferior hand. The big red-brick church had never pleased me, and I was accustomed, when I saw the wooden balustrade that ran along the slanting edge of the roof where nobody ever walked or could walk, to remember the opinion of some architect friend of my father's, that it had been put there to keep the birds from falling off. Still, however, it had some village characters and helped us to feel not wholly lost in the metropolis. I no longer went to church as a regular habit, but go I sometimes did, for one Sunday morning I saw these words painted on a board in the porch: "The congregation are requested to kneel during prayers; the kneelers are afterwards to be hung upon pegs provided for the purpose." In front of every seat hung a little cushion and these cushions were called "kneelers." Presently the joke ran through the community, where there were many artists who considered religion at best an unimportant accessory to good architecture and who disliked that particular church.

1. James and Robert, 18th-century Scottish architects and furniture designers who successfully adapted ancient Roman style in their work in England and Scotland.

I could not understand where the charm had gone that I had felt, when as a schoolboy of twelve or thirteen I had played among the unfinished houses, once leaving the marks of my two hands, blacked by a fall among some paint, upon a white balustrade.

Yet I was in all things Pre-Raphaelite. When I was fifteen or sixteen my father had told me about Rossetti and Blake and given me their poetry to read; and once at Liverpool on my way to Sligo I had seen Dante's *Dream* in the gallery there, a picture painted when Rossetti had lost his dramatic power and today not very pleasing to me, and its color, its people, its romantic architecture had blotted all other pictures away. It was a perpetual bewilderment that when my father, moved perhaps by some memory of his youth, chose some theme from poetic tradition, he would soon weary and leave it unfinished. I had seen the change coming bit by bit and its defense elaborated by young men fresh from the Paris art schools. "We must paint what is in front of us," or "A man must be of his own time," they would say, and if I spoke of Blake or Rossetti they would point out his bad drawing and tell me to admire Carolus Duran and Bastien-Lepage.[2] Then, too, they were very ignorant men; they read nothing, for nothing mattered but "knowing how to paint," being in reaction against a generation that seemed to have wasted its time upon so many things. I thought myself alone in hating these young men, their contempt for the past, their monopoly of the future, but in a few months I was to discover others of my own age, who thought as I did, for it is not true that youth looks before it with the mechanical gaze of a well-drilled soldier. Its quarrel is not with the past, but with the present, where its elders are so obviously powerful and no cause seems lost if it seem to threaten that power. Does cultivated youth ever really love the future, where the eye can discover no persecuted Royalty hidden among oak leaves,[3] though from it certainly does come so much proletarian rhetoric?

I was unlike others of my generation in one thing only. I am very religious, and deprived by Huxley and Tyndall,[4] whom I detested, of the simple-minded religion of my childhood, I had made a new religion, almost an infallible church of poetic tradition, of a fardel[5] of stories, and of personages, and of emotions, inseparable from their first expression, passed on from generation to generation by poets and painters with some help from philosophers and theologians. I wished for a world where I could discover this tradition

2. Carolus Duran (1837–1917) and Jules Bastien-Lepage (1848–84), French painters.
3. Charles II, after the decisive defeat of his father Charles I by the Parliamentarians at Naseby in 1645, hid in an oak tree before escaping abroad.
4. Thomas Henry Huxley (1825–95), biologist and popularizer of Darwin's ideas; John Tyndall (1820–93), physicist and active propagandist for science and materialism.
5. Bundle. This archaic word suggests Yeats's poetic attitude at the stage in his life which he is describing.

perpetually, and not in pictures and in poems only, but in tiles round the chimney piece and in the hangings that kept out the draft. I had even created a dogma: "Because those imaginary people are created out of the deepest instinct of man, to be his measure and his norm, whatever I can imagine those mouths speaking may be the nearest I can go to truth." When I listened they seemed always to speak of one thing only: they, their loves, every incident of their lives, were steeped in the supernatural. Could even Titian's "Ariosto"[6] that I loved beyond other portraits have its grave look, as if waiting for some perfect final event, if the painters before Titian had not learned portraiture, while painting into the corner of compositions full of saints and Madonnas, their kneeling patrons? At seventeen years old I was already an old-fashioned brass cannon full of shot, and nothing had kept me from going off but a doubt as to my capacity to shoot straight.

[Oscar Wilde]

My first meeting with Oscar Wilde was an astonishment. I never before heard a man talking with perfect sentences, as if he had written them all overnight with labor and yet all spontaneous. There was present that night at Henley's,[7] by right of propinquity or of accident, a man full of the secret spite of dullness, who interrupted from time to time, and always to check or disorder thought; and I noticed with what mastery he was foiled and thrown. I noticed, too, that the impression of artificiality that I think all Wilde's listeners have recorded came from the perfect rounding of the sentences and from the deliberation that made it possible. That very impression helped him, as the effect of meter, or of the antithetical prose of the seventeenth century, which is itself a true meter, helped its writers, for he could pass without incongruity from some unforeseen, swift stroke of wit to elaborate reverie. I heard him say a few nights later: "Give me *The Winter's Tale*, 'Daffodils that come before the swallow dare' but not *King Lear*. What is *King Lear* but poor life staggering in the fog?" and the slow, carefully modulated cadence sounded natural to my ears. That first night he praised Walter Pater's *Studies in the History of the Renaissance*: "It is my golden book; I never travel anywhere without it; but it is the very flower of decadence: the last trumpet should have sounded the moment it was written." "But," said the dull man, "would you not have given us time to read it?" "Oh no," was the retort, "there would have been plenty of time afterwards—in either world." I think he seemed to us, baffled as we were by youth, or by infirmity, a triumphant figure, and to some of us a figure from another age,

---

6. Titian (ca. 1477–1576), a Venetian painter, was thought to have painted a portrait of Lodovico Ariosto, the Italian poet and author of *Orlando Furioso*.

The painting is now described simply as "Portrait of a Man."
7. William Ernest Henley (1849–1903), poet, critic, and editor.

an audacious Italian fifteenth-century figure. A few weeks before I had heard one of my father's friends, an official in a publishing firm that had employed both Wilde and Henley as editors, blaming Henley who was "no use except under control" and praising Wilde, "so indolent but such a genius"; and now the firm became the topic of our talk. "How often do you go to the office?" said Henley. "I used to go three times a week," said Wilde, "for an hour a day but I have since struck off one of the days." "My God," said Henley, "I went five times a week for five hours a day and when I wanted to strike off a day they had a special committee meeting." "Furthermore," was Wilde's answer, "I never answered their letters. I have known men come to London full of bright prospects and seen them complete wrecks in a few months through a habit of answering letters." He too knew how to keep our elders in their place, and his method was plainly the more successful, for Henley had been dismissed. "No he is not an aesthete," Henley commented later, being somewhat embarrassed by Wilde's Pre-Raphaelite entanglement; "one soon finds that he is a scholar and a gentleman." And when I dined with Wilde a few days afterwards he began at once, "I had to strain every nerve to equal that man at all"; and I was too loyal to speak my thought: "You and not he said all the brilliant things." He like the rest of us had felt the strain of an intensity that seemed to hold life at the point of drama. He had said on that first meeting, "The basis of literary friendship is mixing the poisoned bowl"; and for a few weeks Henley and he became close friends till, the astonishment of their meeting over, diversity of character and ambition pushed them apart, and, with half the cavern helping, Henley began mixing the poisoned bowl for Wilde. Yet Henley never wholly lost that first admiration, for after Wilde's downfall he said to me: "Why did he do it? I told my lads to attack him and yet we might have fought under his banner."

[The Handiwork of Art]

Though I went to Sligo every summer, I was compelled to live out of Ireland the greater part of every year, and was but keeping my mind upon what I knew must be the subject matter of my poetry. I believed that if Morris[8] had set his stories amid the scenery of his own Wales, for I knew him to be of Welsh extraction and supposed wrongly that he had spent his childhood there, that if Shelley had nailed his *Prometheus*,[9] or some equal symbol, upon some Welsh or Scottish rock, their art would have entered more intimately, more microscopically, as it were, into our thought and

8. William Morris (1834–96), the poet, painter, and socialist.

9. A reference to Shelley's lyrical drama, *Prometheus Unbound*.

given perhaps to modern poetry a breadth and stability like that of ancient poetry. The statues of Mausolus and Artemisia[1] at the British Museum, private, half-animal, half-divine figures, all unlike the Grecian athletes and Egyptian kings in their near neighborhood, that stand in the middle of the crowd's applause, or sit above measuring it out unpersuadable justice, became to me, now or later, images of an unpremeditated joyous energy, that neither I nor any other man, racked by doubt and inquiry, can achieve; and that yet, if once achieved, might seem to men and women of Connemara or of Galway their very soul. In our study of that ruined tomb raised by a queen to her dead lover, and finished by the unpaid labor of great sculptors, after her death from grief, or so runs the tale, we cannot distinguish the handiwork of Scopas from that of Praxiteles,[2] and I wanted to create once more an art where the artist's handiwork would hide as under those half-anonymous chisels or as we find it in some old Scots ballads, or in some twelfth- or thirteenth-century Arthurian Romance. That handiwork assured, I had martyred no man for modeling his own image upon Pallas Athena's buckler; for I took great pleasure in certain allusions to the singer's life, one finds in old romances and ballads, and thought his presence there all the more poignant because we discover it half lost, like portly Chaucer, behind his own maunciple and pardoner upon the Canterbury roads. Wolfram von Eschenbach,[3] singing his German Parsifal, broke off some description of a famished city to remember that in his own house at home the very mice lacked food, and what old ballad singer was it who claimed to have fought by day in the very battle he sang by night? So masterful indeed was that instinct that when the minstrel knew not who his poet was, he must needs make up a man: "When any stranger asks who is the sweetest of singers, answer with one voice: 'A blind man; he dwells upon rocky Chios;[4] his songs shall be the most beautiful forever.'" Elaborate modern psychology sounds egotistical, I thought, when it speaks in the first person, but not those simple emotions which resemble the more, the more powerful they are, everybody's emotion, and I was soon to write many poems where an always personal emotion was woven into a general pattern of myth and symbol. When the Fenian poet[5] says that his heart has

1. Mausolus, king of Caria (in Asia Minor) in 4th century B.C. He married his sister Artemisia, who after his death built the famous monument named after him, the Mausoleum; a Greek statue of Mausolus and other sculptures from the Mausoleum is in the British Museum.

2. Greek sculptor of late 5th and early 4th century B.C. Scopas was a Greek sculptor of the 4th century B.C. who

went to Halicarnassus to superintend the sculpture of the Mausoleum (see previous note).

3. German poet of late 12th and early 13th century, who wrote the epic poem *Parzival*.

4. Greek island in the Aegean—one of the seven places which claimed Homer as its son.

5. I.e., a poet of Irish nationalism.

grown cold and callous—"For thy hapless fate, dear Ireland, and
sorrows of my own"—he but follows tradition and if he does not
move us deeply, it is because he has no sensuous musical vocabulary
that comes at need, without compelling him to sedentary toil and
so driving him out from his fellows. I thought to create that sensuous, musical vocabulary, and not for myself only, but that I
might leave it to later Irish poets, much as a medieval Japanese
painter left his style as an inheritance to his family, and I was
careful to use a traditional manner and matter, yet changed by
that toil, impelled by my share in Cain's curse,[6] by all that sterile
modern complication, by my "originality," as the newspapers call
it, did something altogether different. Morris set out to make a
revolution that the persons of his *Well at the World's End* or his
Waters of the Wondrous Isles, always, to my mind, in the likeness
of Artemisia and her man, might walk his native scenery; and I,
that my native scenery might find imaginary inhabitants, half-
planned a new method and a new culture. My mind began drifting
vaguely towards that doctrine of "the mask" which has convinced
me that every passionate man (I have nothing to do with mechanist,
or philanthropist, or man whose eyes have no preference) is, as it
were, linked with another age, historical or imaginary, where alone
he finds images that rouse his energy. Napoleon was never of his
own time, as the naturalistic writers and painters bid all men be,
but had some Roman emperor's image in his head and some con-
dottiere's[7] blood in his heart; and when he crowned that head at
Rome with his own hands he had covered, as may be seen from
David's[8] painting, his hesitation with that emperor's old suit.

[The Origin of The Lake Isle of Innisfree]

I had various women friends on whom I would call towards five
o'clock mainly to discuss my thoughts that I could not bring to a
man without meeting some competing thought, but partly because their tea and toast saved my pennies for the bus ride home;
but with women, apart from their intimate exchanges of thought, I
was timid and abashed. I was sitting on a seat in front of the British
Museum feeding pigeons when a couple of girls sat near and began
enticing my pigeons away, laughing and whispering to one another,
and I looked straight in front of me, very indignant, and presently
went into the Museum without turning my head towards them.

6. The curse imposed on Cain for killing his brother was to be "a fugitive
and a vagabond" (Genesis iv.12). Yeats
seems to be thinking of the curse imposed on *Adam*, that he should have to
work (Genesis iii.19).
7. Mercenary soldier (14th- and 15th-

century Italy)—usually hired as a
leader with a band of his followers.
8. Jacques Louis David (1748–1825),
French historical painter, court painter
to Napoleon: he painted a picture of
Napoleon's coronation.

Since then I have often wondered if they were pretty or merely very young. Sometimes I told myself very adventurous love stories with myself for hero, and at other times I planned out a life of lonely austerity, and at other times mixed the ideals and planned a life of lonely austerity mitigated by periodical lapses. I had still the ambition, formed in Sligo in my teens, of living in imitation of Thoreau on Innisfree, a little island in Lough Gill,[9] and when walking through Fleet Street very homesick I heard a little tinkle of water and saw a fountain in a shop window which balanced a little ball upon its jet, and began to remember lake water. From the sudden remembrance came my poem *Innisfree*, my first lyric with anything in its rhythm of my own music. I had begun to loosen rhythm as an escape from rhetoric and from that emotion of the crowd that rhetoric brings, but I only understood vaguely and occasionally that I must for my special purpose use nothing but the common syntax. A couple of years later I would not have written that first line with its conventional archaism—"Arise and go"— nor the inversion in the last stanza. * * *

[The Rhymers' Club]

I had already met most of the poets of my generation. I had said, soon after the publication of *The Wanderings of Usheen*,[1] to the editor of a series of shilling reprints, who had set me to compile tales of the Irish fairies, "I am growing jealous of other poets and we will all grow jealous of each other unless we know each other and so feel a share in each other's triumph." He was a Welshman, lately a mining engineer, Ernest Rhys,[2] a writer of Welsh translations and original poems, that have often moved me greatly though I can think of no one else who has read them. He was perhaps a dozen years older than myself and through his work as editor knew everybody who would compile a book for seven or eight pounds. Between us we founded The Rhymers' Club, which for some years was to meet every night in an upper room with a sanded floor in an ancient eating-house in the Strand called The Cheshire Cheese. Lionel Johnson, Ernest Dowson, Victor Plarr, Ernest Radford, John Davidson, Richard le Gallienne, T. W. Rolleston, Selwyn Image, Edwin Ellis, and John Todhunter came constantly for a time, Arthur Symons and Herbert Horne, less constantly, while William Watson joined but never came and Francis Thompson[3]

9. See *The Lake Isle of Innisfree*, above, and the note on it.
1. An early long poem by Yeats (1889). Yeats later spelled the name of the hero "Oisin."
2. 1859–1946; Welsh writer and editor; original editor of Everyman's Library.

3. The names here are of poets and writers of the 90's who were fellow members with Yeats of the Rhymers' Club. Francis Thompson (1859–1907), who "never joined," was the author of *The Hound of Heaven*.

came once but never joined; and sometimes if we met in a private house, which we did occasionally, Oscar Wilde came. It had been useless to invite him to The Cheshire Cheese for he hated Bohemia. "Olive Schreiner,"[4] he said once to me, "is staying in the East End because that is the only place where people do not wear masks upon their faces, but I have told her that I live in the West End because nothing in life interests me but the mask."

We read our poems to one another and talked criticism and drank a little wine. I sometimes say when I speak of the club, "We had such and such ideas, such and such a quarrel with the great Victorians, we set before us such and such aims," as though we had many philosophical ideas. I say this because I am ashamed to admit that I had these ideas and that whenever I began to talk of them a gloomy silence fell upon the room. A young Irish poet, who wrote excellently but had the worst manners, was to say a few years later, "You do not talk like a poet, you talk like a man of letters," and if all the Rhymers had not been polite, if most of them had not been to Oxford or Cambridge, the greater number would have said the same thing. I was full of thought, often very abstract thought, longing all the while to be full of images, because I had gone to the art school instead of a university. Yet even if I had gone to a university, and learned all the classical foundations of English literature and English culture, all that great erudition which once accepted frees the mind from restlessness, I should have had to give up my Irish subject matter, or attempt to found a new tradition. Lacking sufficient recognized precedent I must needs find out some reason for all I did. * * *

1922

4. South African novelist, author of *The Story of an African Farm* (1883).

E. M. FORSTER
(1879–1970)

Edward Morgan Forster was born in London; his father was an architect of Welsh extraction and his mother a member of a family distinguished during several generations for its evangelical religion and its philanthropic activities. He was educated at Tonbridge School (the "Sawston" of *The Longest Journey*), where he suffered the tribulations of a day boy at a boarding school, and King's College, Cambridge. The friends he made and the intellectual companionship he found at Cambridge have influenced his entire life. He visited Greece and spent some time in Italy in 1901, and this experience also had a permanent influence on him; throughout his life he has tended to set Greek and Italian peasant life in symbolic contrast to the stuffy and repressed life of middle-class England. Both Greek mythology and Italian Renaissance art opened up to him a world of what Matthew Arnold called "spontaneity of consciousness," and most of his work is concerned with ways of discovering such a quality in personal relationships amid the complexities and distortions of modern life. He began writing as a contributor to the newly founded liberal *Independent Review* in 1903, and in 1905 published his first novel, *Where Angels Fear to Tread*, a tragicomic projection of conflicts between refined English gentility and coarse Italian vitality.

English tutoring in Germany; an extended visit to India in 1912 and a shorter one in 1922; continuous intellectual companionship with members of the "Bloomsbury group" and others; and in 1946 an honorary fellowship at King's College, Cambridge, where he has mostly lived since, though with a good deal of traveling abroad—all this adds up to a civilized and humane existence, and (as Forster himself insists) an unusually happy one. His main interest has always been in personal relations, the "little society" we make for ourselves with our friends. But he has also cast a critical and reforming eye on the abuses of the world, his point of view being always that of the independent liberal, suspicious of all political slogans and catchwords.

Forster's second novel, *The Longest Journey* (1907), explores the differences between living and dead relationships with much incidental satire of English public-school education and English notions of respectability. *A Room with a View* (1908) explores the nature of love with a great deal of subtlety, using (as with his first novel) Italy as a liberating agent. *Howards End* (1910) probes the relation between inward feeling and outward action, between the kinds of reality in which people get involved in living. "Only connect!" exclaims one of the characters. "Only connect the prose and the passion, and both will be exalted, and human love will soon be at its height." But no one knew better than Forster that this is more easily said than done, and that false or premature connections, connections made by rule and not achieved through total realization of the personality, can destroy and corrupt. The halfway house to salvation is often grimmer than the starting point. In his last novel (for Forster has written no more fiction), *A Passage to India* (1924), he takes the relations between the English and the Indians in India in the early 1920's as a background against which to erect the most searching and complex of all his explorations of the possibilities and the limitations, the promises and the pitfalls, of human relationships. This remains his best-known novel, as well as his best.

Forster's short stories are as a rule much simpler in theme and treatment than his novels; many of them draw on Greek mythology to project the moment of escape or illumination for a character struggling against the meshes of convention. *The Road from Colonus* draws on themes from Greek tragedy to present a modern ironic picture of the moment of escape seen but not seized, with the inevitable consequence of loss and degeneration. There is a conscious use of symbolism here (for example, in the running water that so enchants Mr. Lucas in the magical spot in Greece, and his horror of the noise of running tap water at the end of the story) which is more successful than in most of his other short stories. Forster has also written critical, autobiographical and descriptive prose, notably *Aspects of the Novel* (1927), which, as a discussion of the techniques of fiction by a practicing novelist, has become a minor classic of criticism.

The Road from Colonus[1]

I

For no very intelligible reason, Mr. Lucas had hurried ahead of his party. He was perhaps reaching the age at which independence becomes valuable, because it is so soon to be lost. Tired of attention and consideration, he liked breaking away from the younger members, to ride by himself, and to dismount unassisted. Perhaps he also relished that more subtle pleasure of being kept waiting for lunch, and of telling the others on their arrival that it was of no consequence.

So, with childish impatience, he battered the animal's sides with his heels, and made the muleteer bang it with a thick stick and prick it with a sharp one, and jolted down the hillsides through clumps of flowering shrubs and stretches of anemones and asphodel, till he heard the sound of running water, and came in sight of the group of plane trees where they were to have their meal.

Even in England those trees would have been remarkable, so huge were they, so interlaced, so magnificently clothed in quivering green. And here in Greece they were unique, the one cool spot in that hard brilliant landscape, already scorched by the heat of an April sun. In their midst was hidden a tiny Khan or country inn, a frail and mud building with a broad wooden balcony in which sat an old woman spinning, while a small brown pig, eating orange peel, stood beside her. On the wet earth below squatted two children, playing some primeval game with their fingers; and their mother, none too clean either, was messing with some rice inside. As Mrs. Forman would have said, it was all very Greek, and the fastidious Mr. Lucas felt thankful that they were bringing their own food with them, and should eat it in the open air.

Still, he was glad to be there—the muleteer had helped him

1. Having been banished from Thebes on the discovery that he had unwittingly killed his father and married his mother, Oedipus wandered until he came to Colonus, and there with his daughter Antigone he rested on a rock within the sacred grove of the Furies. A passing native bade him depart, but, knowing that he had reached the last resting place appointed for him, he refused, and was eventually allowed to stay by Theseus, king of Athens. Shortly afterward he met his death mysteriously, having been taken by the gods in some unknown way to final rest. See Sophocles' play, *Oedipus at Colonus*.

off—and glad that Mrs. Forman was not there to forestall his opinions—glad even that he should not see Ethel for quite half an hour. Ethel was his youngest daughter, still unmarried. She was unselfish and affectionate, and it was generally understood that she was to devote her life to her father, and be the comfort of his old age. Mrs. Forman always referred to her as Antigone, and Mr. Lucas tried to settle down to the role of Oedipus, which seemed the only one that public opinion allowed him.

He had this in common with Oedipus, that he was growing old. Even to himself it had become obvious. He had lost interest in other people's affairs, and seldom attended when they spoke to him. He was fond of talking himself but often forgot what he was going to say, and even when he succeeded, it seldom seemed worth the effort. His phrases and gestures had become stiff and set, his anecdotes, once so successful, fell flat, his silence was as meaningless as his speech. Yet he had led a healthy, active life, had worked steadily, made money, educated his children. There was nothing and no one to blame: he was simply growing old.

At the present moment, here he was in Greece, and one of the dreams of his life was realized. Forty years ago he had caught the fever of Hellenism, and all his life he had felt that could he but visit that land, he would not have lived in vain. But Athens had been dusty, Delphi wet, Thermopylae flat, and he had listened with amazement and cynicism to the rapturous exclamations of his companions. Greece was like England: it was a man who was growing old, and it made no difference whether that man looked at the Thames or the Eurotas.[2] It was his last hope of contradicting that logic of experience, and it was failing.

Yet Greece had done something for him, though he did not know it. It had made him discontented, and there are stirrings of life in discontent. He knew that he was not the victim of continual ill-luck. Something great was wrong, and he was pitted against no mediocre or accidental enemy. For the last month a strange desire had possessed him to die fighting.

"Greece is the land for young people," he said to himself as he stood under the plane trees, "but I will enter into it, I will possess it. Leaves shall be green again, water shall be sweet, the sky shall be blue. They were so forty years ago; and I will win them back. I do mind being old, and I will pretend no longer."

He took two steps forward, and immediately cold waters were gurgling over his ankle.

"Where does the water come from?" he asked himself. "I do not even know that." He remembered that all the hillsides were dry; yet here the road was suddenly covered with flowing streams.

2. In ancient times, the river on which Sparta stood, in southern Greece (now the Iri or Iris).

He stopped still in amazement, saying: "Water out of a tree—out of a hollow tree? I never saw nor thought of that before."

For the enormous plane that leant towards the Khan was hollow—it had been burnt out for charcoal—and from its living trunk there gushed an impetuous spring, coating the bark with fern and moss, and flowing over the mule track to create fertile meadows beyond. The simple country folk had paid to beauty and mystery such tribute as they could, for in the rind of the tree a shrine was cut, holding a lamp and a little picture of the Virgin, inheritor of the Naiad's[3] and Dryad's joint abode.

"I never saw anything so marvelous before," said Mr. Lucas. "I could even step inside the trunk and see where the water comes from."

For a moment he hesitated to violate the shrine. Then he remembered with a smile his own thought—"the place shall be mine; I will enter it and possess it"—and leapt almost aggressively onto a stone within.

The water pressed up steadily and noiselessly from the hollow roots and hidden crevices of the plane, forming a wonderful amber pool ere it spilt over the lip of bark on to the earth outside. Mr. Lucas tasted it and it was sweet, and when he looked up the black funnel of the trunk he saw sky which was blue, and some leaves which were green; and he remembered, without smiling, another of his thoughts.

Others had been before him—indeed he had a curious sense of companionship. Little votive offerings to the presiding Power were fastened on to the bark—tiny arms and legs and eyes in tin, grotesque models of the brain or the heart—all tokens of some recovery of strength or wisdom or love. There was no such thing as the solitude of nature, for the sorrows and joys of humanity had pressed even into the bosom of a tree. He spread out his arms and steadied himself against the soft charred wood, and then slowly leant back, till his body was resting on the trunk behind. His eyes closed, and he had the strange feeling of one who is moving, yet at peace—the feeling of the swimmer, who, after long struggling with chopping seas, finds that after all the tide will sweep him to his goal.

So he lay motionless, conscious only of the stream below his feet, and that all things were a stream, in which he was moving.

He was aroused at last by a shock—the shock of an arrival perhaps, for when he opened his eyes, something unimagined, indefinable, had passed over all things, and made them intelligible and good.

There was meaning in the stoop of the old woman over her work, and in the quick motions of the little pig, and in her diminishing globe of wool. A young man came singing over the streams on a

3. Water nymph. "Dryad": wood nymph.

mule, and there was beauty in his pose and sincerity in his greeting. The sun made no accidental patterns upon the spreading roots of the trees, and there was intention in the nodding clumps of asphodel, and in the music of the water. To Mr. Lucas, who, in a brief space of time, had discovered not only Greece, but England and all the world and life, there seemed nothing ludicrous in the desire to hang within the tree another votive offering—a little model of an entire man.

"Why, here's papa, playing at being Merlin."

All unnoticed they had arrived—Ethel, Mrs. Forman, Mr. Graham, and the English-speaking dragoman.[4] Mr. Lucas peered out at them suspiciously. They had suddenly become unfamiliar, and all that they did seemed strained and coarse.

"Allow me to give you a hand," said Mr. Graham, a young man who was always polite to his elders.

Mr. Lucas felt annoyed. "Thank you, I can manage perfectly well by myself," he replied. His foot slipped as he stepped out of the tree, and went into the spring.

"Oh papa, my papa!" said Ethel, "what are you doing? Thank goodness I have got a change for you on the mule."

She tended him carefully, giving him clean socks and dry boots, and then sat him down on the rug beside the lunch basket, while she went with the others to explore the grove.

They came back in ecstasies, in which Mr. Lucas tried to join. But he found them intolerable. Their enthusiasm was superficial, commonplace, and spasmodic. They had no perception of the coherent beauty that was flowering around them. He tried at least to explain his feelings, and what he said was:

"I am altogether pleased with the appearance of this place. It impresses me very favorably. The trees are fine, remarkably fine for Greece, and there is something very poetic in the spring of clear running water. The people too seem kindly and civil. It is decidedly an attractive place."

Mrs. Forman upbraided him for his tepid praise.

"Oh, it is a place in a thousand!" she cried, "I could live and die here! I really would stop if I had not to be back at Athens! It reminds me of the Colonus of Sophocles."

"Well, *I* must stop," said Ethel. "I positively must."

"Yes, do! You and your father! Antigone and Oedipus. Of course you must stop at Colonus!"

Mr. Lucas was almost breathless with excitement. When he stood within the tree, he had believed that his happiness would be independent of locality. But these few minutes' conversation had undeceived him. He no longer trusted himself to journey through the world, for old thoughts, old wearinesses might be waiting to rejoin

4. Interpreter.

him as soon as he left the shade of the planes, and the music of the virgin water. To sleep in the Khan with the gracious, kind-eyed country people, to watch the bats flit about within the globe of shade, and see the moon turn the golden patterns into silver—one such night would place him beyond relapse, and confirm him forever in the kingdom he had regained. But all his lips could say was: "I should be willing to put in a night here."

"You mean a week, papa! It would be sacrilege to put in less."

"A week then, a week," said his lips, irritated at being corrected, while his heart was leaping with joy. All through lunch he spoke to them no more, but watched the place he should know so well, and the people who would so soon be his companions and friends. The inmates of the Khan only consisted of an old woman, a middle-aged woman, a young man and two children, and to none of them had he spoken, yet he loved them as he loved everything that moved or breathed or existed beneath the benedictory shade of the planes.

"En route!" said the shrill voice of Mrs. Forman. "Ethel! Mr. Graham! The best of things must end."

"Tonight," thought Mr. Lucas, "they will light the little lamp by the shrine. And when we all sit together on the balcony, perhaps they will tell me which offerings they put up."

"I beg your pardon, Mr. Lucas," said Graham, "but they want to fold up the rug you are sitting on."

Mr. Lucas got up, saying to himself: "Ethel shall go to bed first, and then I will try to tell them about my offering too—for it is a thing I must do. I think they will understand if I am left with them alone."

Ethel touched him on the cheek. "Papa! I've called you three times. All the mules are here."

"Mules? What mules?"

"Our mules. We're all waiting. Oh, Mr. Graham, do help my father on."

"I don't know what you're talking about, Ethel."

"My dearest papa, we must start. You know we have to get to Olympia tonight."

Mr. Lucas in pompous, confident tones replied: "I always did wish, Ethel, that you had a better head for plans. You know perfectly well that we are putting in a week here. It is your own suggestion."

Ethel was startled into impoliteness. "What a perfectly ridiculous idea. You must have known I was joking. Of course I meant I wished we could."

"Ah! if we could only do what we wished!" sighed Mrs. Forman, already seated on her mule.

"Surely," Ethel continued in calmer tones, "you didn't think I meant it."

"Most certainly I did. I have made all my plans on the supposition that we are stopping here, and it will be extremely inconvenient, indeed, impossible for me to start."

He delivered this remark with an air of great conviction, and Mrs. Forman and Mr. Graham had to turn away to hide their smiles.

"I am sorry I spoke so carelessly; it was wrong of me. But, you know, we can't break up our party, and even one night here would make us miss the boat at Patras."

Mrs. Forman, in an aside, called Mr. Graham's attention to the excellent way in which Ethel managed her father.

"I don't mind about the Patras boat. You said that we should stop here, and we are stopping."

It seemed as if the inhabitants of the Khan had divined in some mysterious way that the altercation touched them. The old woman stopped her spinning, while the young man and the two children stood behind Mr. Lucas, as if supporting him.

Neither arguments nor entreaties moved him. He said little, but he was absolutely determined, because for the first time he saw his daily life aright. What need had he to return to England? Who would miss him? His friends were dead or cold. Ethel loved him in a way, but, as was right, she had other interests. His other children he seldom saw. He had only one other relative, his sister Julia, whom he both feared and hated. It was no effort to struggle. He would be a fool as well as a coward if he stirred from the place which brought him happiness and peace.

At last Ethel, to humor him, and not disinclined to air her modern Greek, went into the Khan with the astonished dragoman to look at the rooms. The woman inside received them with loud welcomes, and the young man, when no one was looking, began to lead Mr. Lucas' mule to the stable.

"Drop it, you brigand!" shouted Graham, who always declared that foreigners could understand English if they chose. He was right, for the man obeyed, and they all stood waiting for Ethel's return.

She emerged at last, with close-gathered skirts, followed by the dragoman bearing the little pig, which he had bought at a bargain.

"My dear papa, I will do all I can for you, but stop in that Khan—no."

"Are there—fleas?" asked Mrs. Forman.

Ethel intimated that "fleas" was not the word.

"Well, I am afraid that settles it," said Mrs. Forman, "I know how particular Mr. Lucas is."

"It does not settle it," said Mr. Lucas. "Ethel, you go on. I do not want you. I don't know why I ever consulted you. I shall stop here alone."

"That is absolute nonsense," said Ethel, losing her temper. "How can you be left alone at your age? How would you get your meals or your bath? All your letters are waiting for you at Patras. You'll miss the boat. That means missing the London operas, and upsetting all your engagements for the month. And as if you could travel by yourself!"

"They might knife you," was Mr. Graham's contribution.

The Greeks said nothing; but whenever Mr. Lucas looked their way, they beckoned him towards the Khan. The children would even have drawn him by the coat, and the old woman on the balcony stopped her almost completed spinning, and fixed him with mysterious appealing eyes. As he fought, the issue assumed gigantic proportions, and he believed that he was not merely stopping because he had regained youth or seen beauty or found happiness, but because in that place and with those people a supreme event was awaiting him which would transfigure the face of the world. The moment was so tremendous that he abandoned words and arguments as useless, and rested on the strength of his mighty unrevealed allies: silent men, murmuring water, and whispering trees. For the whole place called with one voice, articulate to him, and his garrulous opponents became every minute more meaningless and absurd. Soon they would be tired and go chattering away into the sun, leaving him to the cool grove and the moonlight and the destiny he foresaw.

Mrs. Forman and the dragoman had indeed already started, amid the piercing screams of the little pig, and the struggle might have gone on indefinitely if Ethel had not called in Mr. Graham.

"Can you help me?" she whispered. "He is absolutely unmanageable."

"I'm no good at arguing—but if I could help you in any other way—" and he looked down complacently at his well-made figure.

Ethel hesitated. Then she said: "Help me in any way you can. After all, it is for his good that we do it."

"Then have his mule led up behind him."

So when Mr. Lucas thought he had gained the day, he suddenly felt himself lifted off the ground, and set sideways on the saddle, and at the same time the mule started off at a trot. He said nothing, for he had nothing to say, and even his face showed little emotion as he felt the shade pass and heard the sound of the water cease. Mr. Graham was running at his side, hat in hand, apologizing.

"I know I had no business to do it, and I do beg your pardon awfully. But I do hope that some day you too will feel that I was— damn!"

A stone had caught him in the middle of the back. It was thrown by the little boy, who was pursuing them along the mule track. He was followed by his sister, also throwing stones.

Ethel screamed to the dragoman, who was some way ahead with Mrs. Forman, but before he could rejoin them, another adversary appeared. It was the young Greek, who had cut them off in front, and now dashed down at Mr. Lucas' bridle. Fortunately Graham was an expert boxer, and it did not take him a moment to beat down the youth's feeble defense, and to send him sprawling with a bleeding mouth into the asphodel. By this time the dragoman had arrived, the children, alarmed at the fate of their brother, had desisted, and the rescue party, if such it is to be considered, retired in disorder to the trees.

"Little devils!" said Graham, laughing with triumph. "That's the modern Greek all over. Your father meant money if he stopped, and they consider we were taking it out of their pocket."

"Oh, they are terrible—simple savages! I don't know how I shall ever thank you. You've saved my father."

"I only hope you didn't think me brutal."

"No," replied Ethel with a little sigh. "I admire strength."

Meanwhile the cavalcade reformed, and Mr. Lucas, who, as Mrs. Forman said, bore his disappointment wonderfully well, was put comfortably on to his mule. They hurried up the opposite hillside, fearful of another attack, and it was not until they had left the eventful place far behind that Ethel found an opportunity to speak to her father and ask his pardon for the way she had treated him.

"You seemed so different, dear father, and you quite frightened me. Now I feel that you are your old self again."

He did not answer, and she concluded that he was not unnaturally offended at her behavior.

By one of those curious tricks of mountain scenery, the place they had left an hour before suddenly reappeared far below them. The Khan was hidden under the green dome, but in the open there still stood three figures, and through the pure air rose up a faint cry of defiance or farewell.

Mr. Lucas stopped irresolutely, and let the reins fall from his hand.

"Come, father dear," said Ethel gently.

He obeyed, and in another moment a spur of the hill hid the dangerous scene forever.

II

It was breakfast time, but the gas was alight, owing to the fog. Mr. Lucas was in the middle of an account of a bad night he had spent. Ethel, who was to be married in a few weeks, had her arms on the table, listening.

"First the door bell rang, then you came back from the theater. Then the dog started, and after the dog the cat. And at three in the morning a young hooligan passed by singing. Oh yes: then there was the water gurgling in the pipe above my head."

"I think that was only the bath water running away," said Ethel, looking rather worn.

"Well, there's nothing I dislike more than running water. It's perfectly impossible to sleep in the house. I shall give it up. I shall give notice next quarter. I shall tell the landlord plainly, 'The reason I am giving up the house is this: it is perfectly impossible to sleep in it.' If he says—says—well, what has he got to say?"

"Some more toast, father?"

"Thank you, my dear." He took it, and there was an interval of peace.

But he soon recommenced. "I'm not going to submit to the practicing next door as tamely as they think. I wrote and told them so—didn't I?"

"Yes," said Ethel, who had taken care that the letter should not reach. "I have seen the governess, and she has promised to arrange it differently. And Aunt Julia hates noise. It will be sure to be all right."

Her aunt, being the only unattached member of the family, was coming to keep house for her father when she left him. The reference was not a happy one, and Mr. Lucas commenced a series of half articulate sighs, which was only stopped by the arrival of the post.

"Oh, what a parcel!" cried Ethel. "For me! What can it be! Greek stamps. This is most exciting!"

It proved to be some asphodel bulbs, sent by Mrs. Forman from Athens for planting in the conservatory.

"Doesn't it bring it all back! You remember the asphodels, father. And all wrapped up in Greek newspapers. I wonder if I can read them still. I used to be able to, you know."

She rattled on, hoping to conceal the laughter of the children next door—a favorite source of querulousness at breakfast time.

"Listen to me! 'A rural disaster.' Oh, I've hit on something sad. But never mind. 'Last Tuesday at Plataniste, in the province of Messenia, a shocking tragedy occurred. A large tree'—aren't I getting on well?—'blew down in the night and'—wait a minute—oh, dear! 'crushed to death the five occupants of the little Khan there, who had apparently been sitting in the balcony. The bodies of Maria Rhomaides, the aged proprietress, and of her daughter, aged forty-six, were easily recognizable, whereas that of her grandson'—oh, the rest is really too horrid; I wish I had never tried it, and what's more I feel to have heard the name Plataniste before. We didn't stop there, did we, in the spring?"

"We had lunch," said Mr. Lucas, with a faint expression of trouble on his vacant face. "Perhaps it was where the dragoman bought the pig."

"Of course," said Ethel in a nervous voice. "Where the dragoman bought the little pig. How terrible!"

"Very terrible!" said her father, whose attention was wandering to the noisy children next door. Ethel suddenly started to her feet with genuine interest.

"Good gracious!" she exclaimed. "This is an old paper. It happened not lately but in April—the night of Tuesday the eighteenth —and we—we must have been there in the afternoon."

"So we were," said Mr. Lucas. She put her hand to her heart, scarcely able to speak.

"Father, dear father, I must say it: you wanted to stop there. All those people, those poor half savage people, tried to keep you, they're dead. The whole place, it says, is in ruins, and even the stream has changed its course. Father, dear, if it had not been for me, and if Arthur had not helped me, you must have been killed."

Mr. Lucas waved his hand irritably. "It is not a bit of good speaking to the governess, I shall write to the landlord and say, 'The reason I am giving up the house is this: the dog barks, the children next door are intolerable, and I cannot stand the noise of running water.'"

Ethel did not check his babbling. She was aghast at the narrowness of the escape, and for a long time kept silence. At last she said: "Such a marvelous deliverance does make one believe in Providence."

Mr. Lucas, who was still composing his letter to the landlord, did not reply.

1911

VIRGINIA WOOLF
(1882–1941)

1912: Marries Leonard Woolf.
1921: *Monday or Tuesday.*
1925: *Mrs. Dalloway.*

Virginia Woolf was born in London, daughter of Leslie Stephen, the late Victorian critic, philosopher, biographer, and scholar. She grew up as a member of a large and talented family, educating herself in her father's magnificent library, meeting in childhood many eminent Victorians, learning Greek from Walter Pater's sister. After her father's death in 1904 she settled with her sister and two brothers in Bloomsbury, that district of London which later was to become associated with her and the group among whom she moved. The "Bloomsbury group" included Lytton Strachey, the biographer; J. M. Keynes, the eminent economist; Roger Fry, an art critic; and E. M. Forster. When her sister Vanessa married Clive Bell, an art critic, in

1907, she and her brother took together another house in Bloomsbury, and there they entertained their literary and artistic friends at evening gatherings where the conversation sparkled. In 1912 she married Leonard Woolf, journalist, essayist, and political thinker; together they founded the Hogarth Press in 1917—a press which published some of the most interesting literature of our time, including an early volume of Eliot's poems (1919) and his *Homage to John Dryden* (1924) as well as her own novels. Her suicide in March, 1941, resulting from her fear that she was about to lose her mind and become a burden on her husband, first revealed to the public that she had been subject to periods of nervous depression, particularly after finishing a book, and that underneath the liveliness and wit so well known among the Bloomsbury group lay disturbing psychological tensions.

Woolf came naturally into the profession of writing. Moving among writers and artists, her world was from the beginning the cultured world of the middle-class and upper-middle-class London intelligentsia. She rebelled against what she called the "materialism" of such novelists as Arnold Bennett and John Galsworthy, and sought a more delicate rendering of those aspects of consciousness in which she felt that the truth of human experience really lay. After two novels cast rather cumbersomely in traditional form, she developed her own style, which handled the "stream of consciousness" with a carefully modulated poetic flow and brought into prose fiction something of the rhythms and the imagery of lyric poetry. The sketches in which she explored the possibilities of moving between action and contemplation, between specific external events in time and delicate tracings of the flow of consciousness where the mind moves between retrospect and anticipation, were collected in *Monday or Tuesday* (1921). These were technical experiments, and they made possible those later novels where her characteristic method is fully developed—*Jacob's Room* (1922); *Mrs. Dalloway* (1925), the first completely successful novel in her "new" style; *To the Lighthouse* (1927); *The Waves* (1931), the most stylized of her novels; and *Between the Acts* (1941), published after her death. Woolf was a skilled exponent of the "stream of consciousness" technique in her novels, exploring with great subtlety problems of personal identity and personal relationships as well as the significance of time, change, and memory for human personality. The delicate lyrical prose of her finest novels was a remarkable achievement.

She also wrote a great many reviews and critical essays, collected in *The Common Reader* (1925) and *The Second Common Reader* (1932); informal and personal in tone, her criticism is suggestive rather than authoritative and has an engaging air of spontaneity. She is equally concerned with her own craft as a writer and with what it was like to be a quite different person living in a different age.

Woolf was much concerned with the position of women, especially professional women, and the constrictions they suffered under. She wrote several cogent essays on the subject, notably in *A Room of One's Own* (1929) and *Three Guineas* (1938). Her novel *The Years* (1937) was originally to have included reflections on the position of women interspersed amid the action, but she later decided to publish them as a separate book, which became *Three Guineas*.

Monday or Tuesday

Lazy and indifferent, shaking space easily from his wings, knowing his way, the heron passes over the church beneath the sky. White and distant, absorbed in itself, endlessly the sky covers and uncovers, moves and remains. A lake? Blot the shores of it out! A mountain? Oh, perfect—the sun gold on its slopes. Down that falls. Ferns then, or white feathers, forever and ever—

Desiring truth, awaiting it, laboriously distilling a few words, forever desiring—(a cry starts to the left, another to the right. Wheels strike divergently. Omnibuses conglomerate in conflict)—forever desiring—(the clock asseverates with twelve distinct strokes that it is midday; light sheds gold scales; children swarm)—forever desiring truth. Red is the dome; coins hang on the trees; smoke trails from the chimneys; bark, shout, cry "Iron for sale"—and truth?

Radiating to a point men's feet and women's feet, black or gold-encrusted—(This foggy weather—Sugar? No, thank you—The commonwealth of the future)—the firelight darting and making the room red, save for the black figures and their bright eyes, while outside a van discharges, Miss Thingummy drinks tea at her desk, and plate glass preserves fur coats—

Flaunted, leaf-light, drifting at corners, blown across the wheels, silver-splashed, home or not home, gathered, scattered, squandered in separate scales, swept up, down, torn, sunk, assembled—and truth?

Now to recollect by the fireside on the white square of marble. From ivory depths words rising shed their blackness, blossom, and penetrate. Fallen the book; in the flame, in the smoke, in the momentary sparks—or now voyaging, the marble square pendant, minarets beneath and the Indian seas, while space rushes blue and stars glint—truth? or now, content with closeness?

Lacy and indifferent the heron returns; the sky veils her stars; then bares them.

1921

An Unwritten Novel

Such an expression of unhappiness was enough by itself to make one's eyes slide above the paper's edge to the poor woman's face—insignificant without that look, almost a symbol of human destiny with it. Life's what you see in people's eyes; life's what they learn, and, having learnt it, never, though they seek to hide it, cease to be aware of—what? That life's like that, it seems. Five faces opposite—five mature faces—and the knowledge in each face. Strange, though, how people want to conceal it! Marks of reticence are on all those faces: lips shut, eyes shaded, each one of the five doing something to hide or stultify his knowledge. One smokes; another reads; a third checks entries in a pocket book; a fourth stares at the map of the line framed opposite; and the fifth—the terrible thing about the fifth is that she does nothing at all. She looks at life. Ah, but my poor, unfortunate woman, do play the game—do, for all our sakes, conceal it!

As if she heard me, she looked up, shifted slightly in her seat, and sighed. She seemed to apologize and at the same time to say to me, "If only you knew!" Then she looked at life again. "But I do know" I answered silently, glancing at the *Times* for manners' sake. "I know the whole business. 'Peace between Germany and the Allied Powers was yesterday officially ushered in at Paris—Signor Nitti, the Italian Prime Minister—a passenger train at Doncaster was in collision with a goods train . . .' We all know—the *Times* knows—but we pretend we don't." My eyes had once more crept over the paper's rim. She shuddered, twitched her arm queerly to the middle of her back, and shook her head. Again I dipped into my great reservoir of life. "Take what you like," I continued, "births, deaths, marriages, Court Circular,[1] the habits of birds, Leonardo da Vinci, the Sandhills murder, high wages and the cost of living—oh, take what you like," I repeated, "it's all in the *Times*!" Again with infinite weariness she moved her head from side to side until, like a top exhausted with spinning, it settled on her neck.

The *Times* was no protection against such sorrow as hers. But other human beings forbade intercourse. The best thing to do against life was to fold the paper so that it made a perfect square, crisp, thick, impervious even to life. This done, I glanced up quickly, armed with a shield of my own. She pierced through my shield; she gazed into my eyes as if searching any sediment of courage at the depths of them and damping it to clay. Her twitch alone denied all hope, discounted all illusion.

So we rattled through Surrey and across the border into Sussex. But with my eyes upon life I did not see that the other travelers had left, one by one, till, save for the man who read, we were alone together. Here was Three Bridges station. We drew slowly down the platform and stopped. Was he going to leave us? I prayed both ways—I prayed last that he might stay. At that instant he roused himself, crumpled his paper contemptuously, like a thing done with, burst open the door, and left us alone.

---

1. The official account of the day's activities at court.

The unhappy woman, leaning a little forward, palely and color-lessly addressed me—talked of stations and holidays, of brothers at Eastbourne, and the time of year, which was, I forget now, early or late. But at last looking from the window and seeing, I knew, only life, she breathed, "Staying away—that's the drawback of it—" Ah, now we approached the catastrophe. "My sister-in-law"—the bitter-ness of her tone was like lemon on cold steel, and speaking, not to me, but to herself, she muttered, "nonsense, she would say—that's what they all say," and while she spoke she fidgeted as though the skin on her back were as a plucked fowl's in a poulterer's shop window.

"Oh, that cow!" she broke off nervously, as though the great wooden cow in the meadow had shocked her and saved her from some indiscretion. Then she shuddered, and then she made the awkward angular movement that I had seen before, as if, after the spasm, some spot between the shoulders burnt or itched. Then again she looked the most unhappy woman in the world, and I once more reproached her, though not with the same conviction, for if there were a reason, and if I knew the reason, the stigma was removed from life.

"Sisters-in-law," I said—

Her lips pursed as if to spit venom at the word; pursed they remained. All she did was to take her glove and rub hard at a spot on the windowpane. She rubbed as if she would rub something out forever—some stain, some indelible contamination. Indeed, the spot remained for all her rubbing, and back she sank with the shudder and the clutch of the arm I had come to expect. Something impelled me to take my glove and rub my window. There, too, was a little speck on the glass. For all my rubbing it remained. And then the spasm went through me; I crooked my arm and plucked at the middle of my back. My skin, too, felt like the damp chicken's skin in the poulterer's shop window; one spot between the shoulders itched and irritated, felt clammy, felt raw. Could I reach it? Surrep-titiously I tried. She saw me. A smile of infinite irony, infinite sorrow, flitted and faded from her face. But she had communicated, shared her secret, passed her poison; she would speak no more. Leaning back in my corner, shielding my eyes from her eyes, seeing only the slopes and hollows, grays and purples, of the winter's land-scape, I read her message, deciphered her secret, reading it beneath her gaze.

Hilda's the sister-in-law. Hilda? Hilda? Hilda Marsh—Hilda the blooming, the full bosomed, the matronly. Hilda stands at the door as the cab draws up, holding a coin. "Poor Minnie, more of a grass-hopper than ever—old cloak she had last year. Well, well, with two children these days one can't do more. No, Minnie, I've got it;

here you are, cabby—none of your ways with me. Come in, Minnie. Oh, I could carry *you*, let alone your basket!" So they go into the dining-room. "Aunt Minnie, children."

Slowly the knives and forks sink from the upright. Down they get (Bob and Barbara), hold out hands stiffly; back again to their chairs, staring between the resumed mouthfuls. [But this we'll skip; ornaments, curtains, trefoil china plate, yellow oblongs of cheese, white squares of biscuit—skip, oh, but wait! Halfway through luncheon one of those shivers; Bob stares at her, spoon in mouth. "Get on with your pudding, Bob"; but Hilda disapproves. "Why *should* she twitch?" Skip, skip, till we reach the landing on the upper floor; stairs brassbound; linoleum worn; oh, yes! little bedroom looking out over the roofs of Eastbourne—zigzagging roofs like the spines of caterpillars, this way, that way, striped red and yellow, with blue-black slating.] Now, Minnie, the door's shut; Hilda heavily descends to the basement; you unstrap the straps of your basket, lay on the bed a meager nightgown, stand side by side furred felt slippers. The looking glass—no, you avoid the looking glass. Some methodical disposition of hat pins. Perhaps the shell box has something in it? You shake it; it's the pearl stud there was last year—that's all. And then the sniff, the sigh, the sitting by the window. Three o'clock on a December afternoon; the rain drizzling! one light low in the skylight of a drapery emporium; another high in a servant's bedroom—this one goes out. That gives her nothing to look at. A moment's blankness—then, what are you thinking? (Let me peep across at her opposite; she's asleep or pretending it; so what would she think about sitting at the window at three o'clock in the afternoon? Health, money, hills, her God?) Yes, sitting on the very edge of the chair looking over the roofs of Eastbourne, Minnie Marsh prays to God. That's all very well; and she may rub the pane too, as though to see God better; but what God does she see? Who's the God of Minnie Marsh, the God of the back streets of Eastbourne, the God of three o'clock in the afternoon? I, too, see roofs, I see sky; but, oh, dear—this seeing of Gods! More like President Kruger than Prince Albert[2]—that's the best I can do for him; and I see him on a chair, in a black frock coat, not so very high up either; I can manage a cloud or two for him to sit on; and then his hand trailing in the cloud holds a rod, a truncheon is it?— black, thick, thorned—a brutal old bully—Minnie's God! Did he send the itch and the patch and the twitch? Is that why she prays? What she rubs on the window is the stain of sin. Oh, she committed some crime!

I have my choice of crimes. The woods flit and fly—in summer

---

2. Queen Victoria's consort (1819– 61); Stephanus Johannes Paulus   Kruger (1825–1906), president of the Boer Republic in South Africa.

there are bluebells; in the opening there, when spring comes, prim-roses. A parting, was it, twenty years ago? Vows broken? Not Min-nie's! . . . She was faithful. How she nursed her mother! All her sav-ings on the tombstone—wreaths under glass—daffodils in jars. But I'm off the track. A crime. . . . They would say she kept her sorrow, suppressed her secret—her sex, they'd say—the scientific people. But what flummery to saddle *her* with sex! No—more like this. Passing down the streets of Croydon twenty years ago, the violet loops of ribbon in the draper's window spangled in the electric light catch her eye. She lingers—past six. Still by running she can reach home. She pushes through the glass wing door. It's sale time. Shal-low trays brim with ribbons. She pauses, pulls this, fingers that with the raised roses on it—no need to choose, no need to buy, and each tray with its surprises. "We don't shut till seven," and then it *is* seven. She runs, she rushes, home she reaches, but too late. Neigh-bors—the doctor—baby brother—the kettle—scalded—hospital—dead—or only the shock of it, the blame? Ah, but the detail mat-ters nothing! It's what she carries with her; the spot, the crime, the thing to expiate, always there between her shoulders. "Yes," she seems to nod to me, "it's the thing I did."

Whether you did, or what you did, I don't mind; it's not the thing I want. The draper's window looped with violet—that'll do; a little cheap perhaps, a little commonplace—since one has a choice of crimes, but then so many (let me peep across again—still sleep-ing, or pretending sleep! white, worn, the mouth closed—a touch of obstinacy, more than one would think—no hint of sex)—so many crimes aren't *your* crime; your crime was cheap, only the retribution solemn; for now the church door opens, the hard wooden pew receives her; on the brown tiles she kneels; every day, winter, summer, dusk, dawn (here she's at it) prays. All her sins fall, fall, forever fall. The spot receives them. It's raised, it's red, it's burning. Next she twitches. Small boys point. "Bob at lunch today"—But elderly women are the worst.

Indeed now you can't sit praying any longer. Kruger's sunk beneath the clouds—washed over as with a painter's brush of liquid gray, to which he adds a tinge of black—even the tip of the trun-cheon gone now. That's what always happens! Just as you've seen him, felt him, someone interrupts. It's Hilda now.

How you hate her! She'll even lock the bathroom door overnight, too, though it's only cold water you want, and sometimes when the night's been bad it seems as if washing helped. And John at break-fast—the children—meals are worst, and sometimes there are friends—ferns don't altogether hide 'em—they guess, too; so out you go along the front,[3] where the waves are gray, and the papers

---

3. I.e., sea front, shore.

blow, and the glass shelters green and drafty, and the chairs cost tuppence—too much—for there must be preachers along the sands. Ah, that's a nigger—that's a funny man—that's a man with parakeets—poor little creatures! Is there no one here who thinks of God? —just up there, over the pier, with his rod—but no—there's nothing but gray in the sky or if it's blue the white clouds hide him, and the music—it's military music—and what they are fishing for? Do they catch them? How the children stare! Well, then home a back way—"Home a back way!" The words have meaning; might have been spoken by the old man with whiskers—no, no, he didn't really speak; but everything has meaning—placards leaning against doorways—names above shop windows—red fruit in baskets—women's heads in the hairdresser's—all say "Minnie Marsh!" But here's a jerk. "Eggs are cheaper!" That's what always happens! I was heading her over the waterfall, straight for madness, when, like a flock of dream sheep, she turns t'other way and runs between my fingers. Eggs are cheaper. Tethered to the shores of the world, none of the crimes, sorrows, rhapsodies, or insanities for poor Minnie Marsh; never late for luncheon; never caught in a storm without a mackintosh; never utterly unconscious of the cheapness of eggs. So she reaches home—scrapes her boots.

Have I read you right? But the human face—the human face at the top of the fullest sheet of print holds more, withholds more. Now, eyes open, she looks out; and in the human eye—how d'you define it?—there's a break—a division—so that when you've grasped the stem the butterfly's off—the moth that hangs in the evening over the yellow flower—move, raise your hand, off, high, away. I won't raise my hand. Hang still, then, quiver, life, soul, spirit, whatever you are of Minnie Marsh—I, too, on my flower— the hawk over the down—alone, or what were the worth of life? To rise; hang still in the evening, in the midday; hang still over the down. The flicker of a hand—off, up! then poised again. Alone, unseen; seeing all so still down there, all so lovely. None seeing, none caring. The eyes of others our prisons; their thoughts our cages. Air above, air below. And the moon and immortality. . . . Oh, but I drop to the turf! Are you down too, you in the corner, what's your name—woman—Minnie Marsh; some such name as that? There she is, tight to her blossom; opening her handbag, from which she takes a hollow shell—an egg—who was saying that eggs were cheaper? You or I? Oh, it was you who said it on the way home, you remember, when the old gentleman, suddenly opening his umbrella—or sneezing was it? Anyhow, Kruger went, and you came "home a back way," and scraped your boots. Yes. And now you lay across your knees a pocket handkerchief into which drop little angular fragments of eggshell—fragments of a map—a puzzle.

I wish I could piece them together! If you would only sit still. She's moved her knees—the map's in bits again. Down the slopes of the Andes the white blocks of marble go bounding and hurtling, crushing to death a whole troop of Spanish muleteers, with their convoy —Drake's[4] booty, gold and silver. But to return—

To what, to where? She opened the door, and, putting her umbrella in the stand—that goes without saying; so, too, the whiff of beef from the basement; dot, dot, dot. But what I cannot thus eliminate, what I must, head down, eyes shut, with the courage of a battalion and the blindness of a bull, charge and disperse are, indubitably, the figures behind the ferns, commercial travelers. There, I've hidden them all this time in the hope that somehow they'd disappear, or better still emerge, as indeed they must, if the story's to go on gathering richness and rotundity, destiny and tragedy, as stories should, rolling along with it two, if not three, commercial travelers and a whole grove of aspidistra. "The fronds of the aspidistra only partly concealed the commercial traveler—" Rhododendrons would conceal him utterly, and into the bargain give me my fling of red and white, for which I starve and strive; but rhododendrons in Eastbourne—in December—on the Marshes' table—no, no, I dare not; it's all a matter of crusts and cruets, frills and ferns. Perhaps there'll be a moment later by the sea. Moreover, I feel, pleasantly pricking through the green fretwork and over the glacis[5] of cut glass, a desire to peer and peep at the man opposite—one's as much as I can manage. James Moggridge is it, whom the Marshes call Jimmy? [Minnie, you must promise not to twitch till I've got this straight.] James Moggridge travels in[6]—shall we say buttons? —but the time's not come for bringing *them* in—the big and the little on the long cards, some peacock-eyed, others dull gold; cairngorms some, and others coral sprays—but I say the time's not come. He travels, and on Thursdays, his Eastbourne day, takes his meals with the Marshes. His red face, his little steady eyes—by no means altogether commonplace—his enormous appetite (that's safe; he won't look at Minnie till the bread's swamped the gravy dry), napkin tucked diamond-wise—but this is primitive, and, whatever it may do the reader, don't take me in. Let's dodge to the Moggridge household, set that in motion. Well, the family boots are mended on Sundays by James himself. He reads *Truth*.[7] But his passion? Roses—and his wife a retired hospital nurse—interesting—for God's sake let me have one woman with a name I like! But no; she's of the unborn children of the mind, illicit, none the less loved,

4. Sir Francis Drake (1540?–96), English sea captain, explorer, and adventurer.
5. Gentle slope.
6. I.e., is a traveling salesman for.
7. A British weekly popular earlier in this century, specializing in mild exposures.

like my rhododendrons. How many die in every novel that's written
—the best, the dearest, while Moggridge lives. It's life's fault.
Here's Minnie eating her egg at the moment opposite and at t'other
end of the line—are we past Lewes?—there must be Jimmy—
what's her twitch for?

There must be Moggridge—life's fault. Life imposes her laws; life
blocks the way; life's behind the fern; life's the tyrant; oh, but not
the bully! No, for I assure you I come willingly; I come wooed by
Heaven knows what compulsion across ferns and cruets, table
splashed and bottles smeared. I come irresistibly to lodge myself
somewhere on the firm flesh, in the robust spine, wherever I can
penetrate or find foothold on the person, in the soul, of Moggridge
the man. The enormous stability of the fabric; the spine tough as
whalebone, straight as oaktree; the ribs radiating branches; the flesh
taut tarpaulin; the red hollows; the suck and regurgitation of the
heart; while from above meat falls in brown cubes and beer gushes
to be churned to blood again—and so we reach the eyes. Behind
the aspidistra they see something: black, white, dismal; now the
plate again; behind the aspidistra they see elderly woman; "Marsh's
sister, Hilda's more my sort"; the tablecloth now. "Marsh would
know what's wrong with Morrises . . ." talk that over; cheese has
come; the plate again; turn it round—the enormous fingers; now
the woman opposite. "Marsh's sister—not a bit like Marsh;
wretched, elderly female. . . . You should feed your hens. . . . God's
truth, what's set her twitching? Not what *I* said? Dear, dear, dear!
these elderly women. Dear, dear!"

[Yes, Minnie; I know you've twitched, but one moment—James
Moggridge.]

"Dear, dear, dear!" How beautiful the sound is! like the knock of
a mallet on seasoned timber, like the throb of the heart of an
ancient whaler when the seas press thick and the green is clouded.
"Dear, dear!" what a passing bell for the souls of the fretful to
soothe them and solace them, lap them in linen, saying, "So long.
Good luck to you!" and then, "What's your pleasure?" for though
Moggridge would pluck his rose for her, that's done, that's over.
Now what's the next thing? "Madam, you'll miss your train," for
they don't linger.

That's the man's way; that's the sound that reverberates; that's
St. Paul's and the motor-omnibuses. But we're brushing the crumbs
off. Oh, Moggridge, you won't stay? You must be off? Are you driving through Eastbourne this afternoon in one of those little carriages? Are you the man who's walled up in green cardboard boxes,
and sometimes sits so solemn staring like a sphinx; and always there's
a look of the sepulchral, something of the undertaker, the coffin,
and the dusk about horse and driver? Do tell me—but the doors
slammed. We shall never meet again. Moggridge, farewell!

Yes, yes, I'm coming. Right up to the top of the house. One moment I'll linger. How the mud goes round in the mind—what a swirl these monsters leave, the waters rocking, the weeds waving and green here, black there, striking to the sand, till by degrees the atoms reassemble, the deposit sifts itself, and again through the eyes one sees clear and still, and there comes to the lips some prayer for the departed, some obsequy for the souls of those one nods to, the people one never meets again.

James Moggridge is dead now, gone forever. Well, Minnie—"I can face it no longer." If she said that—(Let me look at her. She is brushing the eggshell into deep declivities). She said it certainly, leaning against the wall of the bedroom, and plucking at the little balls which edge the claret-colored curtain. But when the self speaks to the self, who is speaking?—the emtombed soul, the spirit driven in, in, in to the central catacomb; the self that took the veil and left the world—a coward perhaps, yet somehow beautiful, as it flits with its lantern restlessly up and down the dark corridors. "I can bear it no longer," her spirit says. "That man at lunch—Hilda—the children." Oh, heavens, her sob! It's the spirit wailing its destiny, the spirit driven hither, thither, lodging on the diminishing carpets— meager footholds—shrunken shreds of all the vanishing universe— love, life, faith, husband, children, I know not what splendors and pageantries glimpsed in girlhood. "Not for me—not for me."

But then—the muffins, the bald elderly dog? Bead mats I should fancy and the consolation of underlinen. If Minnie Marsh were run over and taken to hospital, nurses and doctors themselves would exclaim. . . . There's the vista and the vision—there's the distance —the blue blot at the end of the avenue, while, after all, the tea is rich, the muffin hot, and the dog—"Benny, to your basket, sir, and see what mother's brought you!" So, taking the glove with the worn thumb, defying once more the encroaching demon of what's called going in holes, you renew the fortifications, threading the gray wool, running it in and out.

Running it in and out, across and over, spinning a web through which God himself—hush, don't think of God! How firm the stitches are! You must be proud of your darning. Let nothing disturb her. Let the light fall gently, and the clouds show an inner vest of the first green leaf. Let the sparrow perch on the twig and shake the raindrop hanging to the twig's elbow. . . . Why look up? Was it a sound, a thought? Oh, heavens! Back again to the thing you did, the plate glass with the violet loops? But Hilda will come. Ignomin-ies, humiliations, oh! Close the breach.

Having mended her glove, Minnie Marsh lays it in the drawer. She shuts the drawer with decision. I catch sight of her face in the glass. Lips are pursed. Chin held high. Next she laces her shoes. Then she touches her throat. What's your brooch? Mistletoe or merrythought? And what is happening? Unless I'm much mistaken, the pulse's quickened, the moment's coming, the threads are racing, Niagara's ahead. Here's the crisis! Heaven be with you! Down she goes. Courage, courage! Face it, be it! For God's sake don't wait on the mat now! There's the door! I'm on your side. Speak! Confront her, confound her soul!

"Oh, I beg your pardon! Yes, this is Eastbourne. I'll reach it down for you. Let me try the handle." [But Minnie, though we keep up pretenses, I've read you right—I'm with you now.]

"That's all your luggage?"

"Much obliged, I'm sure."

(But why do you look about you? Hilda won't come to the station, nor John; and Moggridge is driving at the far side of Eastbourne.)

"I'll wait by my bag, ma'am, that's safest. He said he'd meet me.... Oh, there he is! That's my son."

So they walk off together.

Well, but I'm confounded.... Surely, Minnie, you know better! A strange young man.... Stop! I'll tell him—Minnie!—Miss Marsh!—I don't know though. There's something queer in her cloak as it blows. Oh, but it's untrue, it's indecent.... Look how he bends as they reach the gateway. She finds her ticket. What's the joke? Off they go, down the road, side by side.... Well, my world's done for! What do I stand on? What do I know? That's not Minnie. There never was Moggridge. Who am I? Life's bare as bone.

And yet the last look of them—he stepping from the curb and she following him round the edge of the big building brims me with wonder—floods me anew. Mysterious figures! Mother and son. Who are you? Why do you walk down the street? Where tonight will you sleep, and then, tomorrow? Oh, how it whirls and surges— floats me afresh! I start after them. People drive this way and that. The white light splutters and pours. Plate glass windows. Carnations; chrysanthemums. Ivy in dark gardens. Milk carts at the door. Wherever I go, mysterious figures, I see you, turning the corner, mothers and sons; you, you, you. I hasten, I follow. This, I fancy, must be the sea. Gray is the landscape; dim as ashes; the water murmurs and moves. If I fall on my knees, if I go through the ritual, the ancient antics, it's you, unknown figures, you I adore; if I open my arms, it's you I embrace, you I draw to me—adorable world!

1921

The Mark on the Wall

Perhaps it was the middle of January in the present year that I first looked up and saw the mark on the wall. In order to fix a date it is necessary to remember what one saw. So now I think of the fire; the steady film of yellow light upon the page of my book; the three chrysanthemums in the round glass bowl on the mantelpiece. Yes, it must have been the wintertime, and we had just finished our tea, for I remember that I was smoking a cigarette when I looked up and saw the mark on the wall for the first time. I looked up through the smoke of my cigarette and my eye lodged for a moment upon the burning coals, and that old fancy of the crimson flag flapping from the castle tower came into my mind, and I thought of the cavalcade of red knights riding up the side of the black rock. Rather to my relief the sight of the mark interrupted the fancy, for it is an old fancy, an automatic fancy, made as a child perhaps. The mark was a small round mark, black upon the white wall, about six or seven inches above the mantelpiece.

How readily our thoughts swarm upon a new object, lifting it a little way, as ants carry a blade of straw so feverishly, and then leave it. . . . If that mark was made by a nail, it can't have been for a picture, it must have been for a miniature—the miniature of a lady with white powdered curls, powder-dusted cheeks, and lips like red carnations. A fraud of course, for the people who had this house before us would have chosen pictures in that way—an old picture for an old room. That is the sort of people they were— very interesting people, and I think of them so often, in such queer places, because one will never see them again, never know what happened next. They wanted to leave this house because they wanted to change their style of furniture, so he said, and he was in process of saying that in his opinion art should have ideas behind it when we were torn asunder, as one is torn from the old lady about to pour out tea and the young man about to hit the tennis ball in the back garden of the suburban villa as one rushes past in the train.

But for that mark, I'm not sure about it; I don't believe it was made by a nail after all; it's too big, too round, for that. I might get up, but if I got up and looked at it, ten to one I shouldn't be able to say for certain; because once a thing's done, no one ever knows how it happened. Oh! dear me, the mystery of life; the inaccuracy of thought! The ignorance of humanity! To show how very little control of our possessions we have—what an accidental affair this living is after all our civilization—let me just count over a few of the things lost in one lifetime, beginning, for that seems always the most mysterious of losses—what cat would gnaw, what rat would nibble—three pale blue canisters of bookbinding tools? Then there were the bird cages, the iron hoops, the steel skates, the Queen Anne coal scuttle, the bagatelle board, the hand organ—all gone, and jewels, too. Opals and emeralds, they lie about the roots of turnips. What a scraping paring affair it is to be sure! The wonder is that I've any clothes on my back, that I sit surrounded by solid furniture at this moment. Why, if one wants to compare life to anything, one must liken it to being blown through the Tube[1] at fifty miles an hour—landing at the other end without a single hairpin in one's hair! Shot out at the feet of God entirely naked! Tumbling head over heels in the asphodel meadows[2] like brown paper parcels pitched down a shoot in the post office! With one's hair flying back like the tail of a race horse. Yes, that seems to express the rapidity of life, the perpetual waste and repair; all so casual, all so haphazard. . . .

But after life. The slow pulling down of thick green stalks so that the cup of the flower, as it turns over, deluges one with purple and red light. Why, after all, should one not be born there as one is born here, helpless, speechless, unable to focus one's eyesight, groping at the roots of the grass, at the toes of the Giants? As for saying which are trees, and which are men and women, or whether there are such things, that one won't be in a condition to do for fifty years or so. There will be nothing but spaces of light and dark, intersected by thick stalks, and rather higher up perhaps, rose-shaped blots of an indistinct color—dim pinks and blues— which will, as time goes on, become more definite, become—I don't know what. . . .

And yet that mark on the wall is not a hole at all. It may even be caused by some round black substance, such as a small rose leaf, left over from the summer, and I, not being a very vigilant housekeeper—look at the dust on the mantelpiece, for example, the dust which, so they say, buried Troy three times over, only fragments of pots utterly refusing annihilation, as one can believe.

The tree outside the window taps very gently on the pane. . . . I want to think quietly, calmly, spaciously, never to be interrupted, never to have to rise from my chair, to slip easily from one thing to another, without any sense of hostility, or obstacle. I want to sink deeper and deeper, away from the surface, with its hard separate facts. To steady myself, let me catch hold of the first idea that passes . . . Shakespeare. . . . Well, he will do as well as another. A man who sat himself solidly in an armchair, and looked into the fire, so— A shower of ideas fell perpetually from some very high Heaven down through his mind. He leant his forehead on his hand,

---

1. London underground railway.
2. I.e., heaven, the next world (in

Greek mythology, asphodel flowers grow in the Elysian fields).

and people, looking in through the open door—for this scene is supposed to take place on a summer's evening— But how dull this is, this historical fiction! It doesn't interest me at all. I wish I could hit upon a pleasant track of thought, a track indirectly reflecting credit upon myself, for those are the pleasantest thoughts, and very frequent even in the minds of modest mouse-colored people, who believe genuinely that they dislike to hear their own praises. They are not thoughts directly praising oneself; that is the beauty of them; they are thoughts like this:

"And then I came into the room. They were discussing botany. I said how I'd seen a flower growing on a dust heap on the site of an old house in Kingsway.[3] The seed, I said, must have been sown in the reign of Charles the First. What flowers grew in the reign of Charles the First?" I asked— (But I don't remember the answer.) Tall flowers with purple tassels to them perhaps. And so it goes on. All the time I'm dressing up the figure of myself in my own mind, lovingly, stealthily, not openly adoring it, for if I did that, I should catch myself out, and stretch my hand at once for a book in self-protection. Indeed, it is curious how instinctively one protects the image of oneself from idolatry or any other handling that could make it ridiculous, or too unlike the original to be believed in any longer. Or is it not so very curious after all? It is a matter of great importance. Suppose the looking glass smashes, the image disappears, and the romantic figure with the green of forest depths all about it is there no longer, but only that shell of a person which is seen by other people—what an airless, shallow, bald, prominent world it becomes! A world not to be lived in. As we face each other in omnibuses and underground railways we are looking into the mirror; that accounts for the vagueness, the gleam of glassiness, in our eyes. And the novelists in future will realize more and more the importance of these reflections, for of course there is not one reflection but an almost infinite number; those are the depths they will explore, those the phantoms they will pursue, leaving the description of reality more and more out of their stories, taking a knowledge of it for granted, as the Greeks did and Shakespeare perhaps—but these generalizations are very worthless. The military sound of the word is enough. It recalls leading articles, cabinet ministers—a whole class of things indeed which, as a child, one thought the thing itself, the standard thing, the real thing, from which one could not depart save at the risk of nameless damnation. Generalizations bring back somehow Sunday in London, Sunday afternoon walks, Sunday luncheons, and also ways of speaking of the dead, clothes, and habits—like the habit of sitting all together in one room until a certain hour, although no-

3. Street in London.

body liked it. There was a rule for everything. The rule for table-cloths at that particular period was that they should be made of tapestry with little yellow compartments marked upon them, such as you may see in photographs of the carpets in the corridors of the royal palaces. Tablecloths of a different kind were not real tablecloths. How shocking, and yet how wonderful it was to discover that these real things, Sunday luncheons, Sunday walks, country houses, and tablecloths were not entirely real, were indeed half phantoms, and the damnation which visited the disbeliever in them was only a sense of illegitimate freedom. What now takes the place of those things I wonder, those real standard things? Men perhaps, should you be a woman; the masculine point of view which governs our lives, which sets the standard, which establishes Whitaker's Table of Precedency,[4] which has become, I suppose, since the war, half a phantom to many men and women, which soon, one may hope, will be laughed into the dustbin where the phantoms go, the mahogany sideboards and the Landseer[5] prints, Gods and Devils, Hell and so forth, leaving us all with an intoxicating sense of illegitimate freedom—if freedom exists. . . .

In certain lights that mark on the wall seems actually to project from the wall. Nor is it entirely circular. I cannot be sure, but it seems to cast a perceptible shadow, suggesting that if I ran my finger down that strip of the wall it would, at a certain point, mount and descend a small tumulus, a smooth tumulus like those barrows[6] on the South Downs which are, they say, either tombs or camps. Of the two I should prefer them to be tombs, desiring melancholy like most English people, and finding it natural at the end of a walk to think of the bones stretched beneath the turf. . . . There must be some book about it. Some antiquary must have dug up those bones and given them a name. . . . What sort of a man is an antiquary, I wonder? Retired Colonels for the most part, I daresay, leading parties of aged laborers to the top here, examining clods of earth and stone, and getting into correspondence with the neighboring clergy, which, being opened at breakfast time, gives them a feeling of importance, and the comparison of arrowheads necessitates cross-country journeys to the county towns, an agreeable necessity both to them and to their elderly wives, who wish to make plum jam or to clean out the study, and have every reason for keeping that great question of the camp or

---

4. Whitaker's Almanack, an annual compendium of information, prints a "Table of Precedency," which shows the order in which the various ranks in public life and society proceed on formal occasions.
5. Edwin Henry Landseer, 19th-century animal painter, reproductions of whose

"Stag at Bay," "Monarch of the Glen," and similar paintings were often found in Victorian homes.
6. Mounds of earth or stones erected by prehistoric peoples, usually as burial places; the South Downs are a range of low hills in southeastern England.

the tomb in perpetual suspension, while the Colonel himself feels agreeably philosophic in accumulating evidence on both sides of the question. It is true that he does finally incline to believe in the camp; and, being opposed, indites a pamphlet which he is about to read at the quarterly meeting of the local society when a stroke lays him low, and his last conscious thoughts are not of wife or child, but of the camp and that arrowhead there, which is now in the case at the local museum, together with the foot of a Chinese murderess, a handful of Elizabethan nails, a great many Tudor clay pipes, a piece of Roman pottery, and the wineglass that Nelson drank out of—proving I really don't know what.

No, no, nothing is proved, nothing is known. And if I were to get up at this very moment and ascertain that the mark on the wall is really—what shall we say?—the head of a gigantic old nail, driven in two hundred years ago, which has now, owing to the patient attrition of many generations of housemaids, revealed its head above the coat of paint, and is taking its first view of modern life in the sight of a white-walled firelit room, what should I gain? —Knowledge? Matter for further speculation? I can think sitting still as well as standing up. And what is knowledge? What are our learned men save the descendants of witches and hermits who crouched in caves and in woods brewing herbs, interrogating shrew-mice and writing down the language of the stars? And the less we honor them as our superstitions dwindle and our respect for beauty and health of mind increases. . . . Yes, one could imagine a very pleasant world. A quiet, spacious world, with the flowers so red and blue in the open fields. A world without professors or specialists or housekeepers with the profiles of policemen, a world which one could slice with one's thought as a fish slices the water with his fin, grazing the stems of the water lilies, hanging suspended over nests of white sea eggs. . . . How peaceful it is down here, rooted in the center of the world and gazing up through the gray waters, with their sudden gleams of light, and their reflections—if it were not for Whitaker's Almanack—if it were not for the Table of Precedency!

I must jump up and see for myself what that mark on the wall really is—a nail, a rose leaf, a crack in the wood?

Here is nature once more at her old game of self-preservation. This train of thought, she perceives, is threatening mere waste of energy, even some collision with reality, for who will ever be able to lift a finger against Whitaker's Table of Precedency? The Archbishop of Canterbury is followed by the Lord High Chancellor; the Lord High Chancellor is followed by the Archbishop of York. Everybody follows somebody, such is the philosophy of Whitaker; and the great thing is to know who follows whom. Whitaker knows, and let that, so Nature counsels, comfort you, instead of enraging you; and if you can't be comforted, if you must shatter this hour of peace, think of the mark on the wall.

I understand Nature's game—her prompting to take action as a way of ending any thought that threatens to excite or to pain. Hence, I suppose, comes our slight contempt for men of action— men, we assume, who don't think. Still, there's no harm in putting a full stop to one's disagreeable thoughts by looking at a mark on the wall.

Indeed, now that I have fixed my eyes upon it, I feel that I have grasped a plank in the sea; I feel a satisfying sense of reality which at once turns the two Archbishops and the Lord High Chancellor to the shadows of shades. Here is something definite, something real. Thus, waking from a midnight dream of horror, one hastily turns on the light and lies quiescent, worshiping the chest of drawers, worshiping solidity, worshiping reality, worshiping the impersonal world which is a proof of some existence other than ours. That is what one wants to be sure of. . . . Wood is a pleasant thing to think about. It comes from a tree; and trees grow, and we don't know how they grow. For years and years they grow, without paying any attention to us, in meadows, in forests, and by the side of rivers —all things one likes to think about. The cows swish their tails beneath them on hot afternoons; they paint rivers so green that when a moorhen dives one expects to see its feathers all green when it comes up again. I like to think of the fish balanced against the stream like flags blown out; and of water beetles slowly raising domes of mud upon the bed of the river. I like to think of the tree itself: first of the close dry sensation of being wood; then the grinding of the storm; then the slow, delicious ooze of sap; I like to think of it, too, on winter's nights standing in the empty field with all leaves close-furled, nothing tender exposed to the iron bullets of the moon, a naked mast upon an earth that goes tumbling, tumbling, all night long. The song of birds must sound very loud and strange in June; and how cold the feet of insects must feel upon it, as they make laborious progresses up the creases of the bark, or sun themselves upon the thin green awning of the leaves, and look straight in front of them with diamond-cut red eyes. . . . One by one the fibers snap beneath the immense cold pressure of the earth, than the last storm comes and, falling, the highest branches drive deep into the ground again. Even so, life isn't done with; there are a million patient, watchful lives still for a tree, all over the world, in bedrooms, in ships, on the pavement, living rooms, where men and women sit after tea, smoking cigaretts. It is full of peaceful thoughts, happy thoughts, this tree. I should like to take each one separately—but something is getting in the way. . . . Where was I? What has it all been about? A tree? A river? The Downs? Whitaker's Almanack? The fields of asphodel? I can't remember a thing.

Everything's moving, falling, slipping, vanishing. . . . There is a vast upheaval of matter. Someone is standing over me and saying:

"I'm going out to buy a newspaper."

"Yes?"

"Though it's no good buying newspapers. . . . Nothing ever happens. Curse this war; God damn this war! . . . All the same, I don't see why we should have a snail on our wall."

Ah, the mark on the wall! It was a snail.

1921

Modern Fiction

In making any survey, even the freest and loosest, of modern fiction, it is difficult not to take it for granted that the modern practice of the art is somehow an improvement upon the old. With their simple tools and primitive materials, it might be said, Fielding did well and Jane Austen even better, but compare their opportunities with ours! Their masterpieces certainly have a strange air of simplicity. And yet the analogy between literature and the process, to choose an example, of making motor cars scarcely holds good beyond the first glance. It is doubtful whether in the course of the centuries, though we have learnt much about making machines, we have learnt anything about making literature. We do not come to write better; all that we can be said to do is to keep moving, now a little in this direction, now in that, but with a circular tendency should the whole course of the track be viewed from a sufficiently lofty pinnacle. It need scarcely be said that we make no claim to stand, even momentarily, upon that vantage ground. On the flat, in the crowd, half blind with dust, we look back with envy to those happier warriors, whose battle is won and whose achievements wear so serene an air of accomplishment that we can scarcely refrain from whispering that the fight was not so fierce for them as for us. It is for the historian of literature to decide; for him to say if we are now beginning or ending or standing in the middle of a great period of prose fiction, for down in the plain little is visible. We only know that certain gratitudes and hostilities inspire us; that certain paths seem to lead to fertile land, others to the dust and the desert; and of this perhaps it may be worth while to attempt some account.

Our quarrel, then, is not with the classics, and if we speak of quarreling with Mr. Wells, Mr. Bennett, and Mr. Galsworthy,[1] it is partly that by the mere fact of their existence in the flesh their work has a living, breathing, everyday imperfection which bids us

---

1. The British novelists H. G. Wells (1866–1946), Arnold Bennett (1867– 1931), and John Galsworthy (1867– 1933).

take what liberties with it we choose. But it is also true that, while we thank them for a thousand gifts, we reserve our unconditional gratitude for Mr. Hardy, for Mr. Conrad, and in much lesser degree for the Mr. Hudson of *The Purple Land, Green Mansions,* and *Far Away and Long Ago.*[2] Mr. Wells, Mr. Bennett, and Mr. Galsworthy have excited so many hopes and disappointed them so persistently that our gratitude largely takes the form of thanking them for having shown us what they might have done but have not done; what we certainly could not do, but as certainly, perhaps, do not wish to do. No single phrase will sum up the charge or grievance which we have to bring against a mass of work so large in its volume and embodying so many qualities, both admirable and the reverse. If we tried to formulate our meaning in one word we should say that these three writers are materialists. It is because they are concerned not with the spirit but with the body that they have disappointed us, and left us with the feeling that the sooner English fiction turns its back upon them, as politely as may be, and marches, if only into the desert, the better for its soul. Naturally, no single word reaches the center of three separate targets. In the case of Mr. Wells it falls notably wide of the mark. And yet even with him it indicates to our thinking the fatal alloy in his genius, the great clod of clay that has got itself mixed up with the purity of his inspiration. But Mr. Bennett is perhaps the worst culprit of the three, inasmuch as he is by far the best workman. He can make a book so well constructed and solid in its craftsmanship that it is difficult for the most exacting of critics to see through what chink or crevice decay can creep in. There is not so much as a draft between the frames of the windows, or a crack in the boards. And yet—if life should refuse to live there? That is a risk which the creator of *The Old Wives' Tale,* George Cannon, Edwin Clayhanger,[3] and hosts of other figures, may well claim to have surmounted. His characters live abundantly, even unexpectedly, but it remains to ask how do they live, and what do they live for? More and more they seem to us, deserting even the well-built villa in the Five Towns,[4] to spend their time in some softly padded first-class railway carriage, pressing bells and buttons innumerable; and the destiny to which they travel so luxuriously becomes more and more unquestionably an eternity of bliss spent in the very best hotel in Brighton.[5] It can scarcely be said of Mr. Wells that he is a materialist in the sense

2. W. H. Hudson (1841–1922), naturalist and writer, was born in Argentina, though he later lived in London. *The Purple Land* (1885) is about South America; *Green Mansions* (1904), a novel set in South America, was his first real success.
3. Characters in Arnold Bennett's novels; *The Old Wives' Tale* (1908) is his best known novel.
4. The pottery towns of Staffordshire in which many of Bennett's novels and stories were set.
5. One-time fashionable seaside resort on southwest coast of England.

that he takes too much delight in the solidity of his fabric. His mind is too generous in its sympathies to allow him to spend much time in making things shipshape and substantial. He is a materialist from sheer goodness of heart, taking upon his shoulders the work that ought to have been discharged by Government officials, and in the plethora of his ideas and facts scarcely having leisure to realize, or forgetting to think important, the crudity and coarseness of his human beings. Yet what more damaging criticism can there be both of his earth and of his Heaven than that they are to be inhabited here and hereafter by his Joans and his Peters? Does not the inferiority of their natures tarnish whatever institutions and ideals may be provided for them by the generosity of their creator? Nor, profoundly though we respect the integrity and humanity of Mr. Galsworthy, shall we find what we seek in his pages.

If we fasten, then, one label on all these books, on which is one word, materialists, we mean by it that they write of unimportant things; that they spend immense skill and immense industry making the trivial and the transitory appear the true and the enduring.

We have to admit that we are exacting, and further, that we find it difficult to justify our discontent by explaining what it is that we exact. We frame our question differently at different times. But it reappears most persistently as we drop the finished novel on the crest of a sigh—Is it worth while? What is the point of it all? Can it be that, owing to one of those little deviations which the human spirit seems to make from time to time, Mr. Bennett has come down with his magnificent apparatus for catching life just an inch or two on the wrong side? Life escapes; and perhaps without life nothing else is worth while. It is a confession of vagueness to have to make use of such a figure as this, but we scarcely better the matter by speaking, as critics are prone to do, of reality. Admitting the vagueness which afflicts all criticism of novels, let us hazard the opinion that for us at this moment the form of fiction most in vogue more often misses than secures the thing we seek. Whether we call it life or spirit, truth or reality, this, the essential thing, has moved off, or on, and refuses to be contained any longer in such ill-fitting vestments as we provide. Nevertheless, we go on perseveringly, conscientiously, constructing our two and thirty chapters after a design which more and more ceases to resemble the vision in our minds. So much of the enormous labour of proving the solidity, the likeness to life, of the story is not merely the labor thrown away but labor misplaced to the extent of obscuring and blotting out the light of the conception. The writer seems constrained, not by his own free will but by some powerful and unscrupulous tyrant who has him in thrall, to provide a plot, to provide comedy, tragedy, love interest, and an air of probability embalming the whole so impeccable that if all his figures were to come to life they would find themselves dressed down to the last button of their coats in the fashion of the hour. The tyrant is obeyed; the novel is done to a turn. But sometimes, more and more often as time goes by, we suspect a momentary doubt, a spasm of rebellion, as the pages fill themselves in the customary way. Is life like this? Must novels be like this?

Look within and life, it seems, is very far from being "like this." Examine for a moment an ordinary mind on an ordinary day. The mind receives a myriad impressions—trivial, fantastic, evanescent, or engraved with the sharpness of steel. From all sides they come, an incessant shower of innumerable atoms; and as they fall, as they shape themselves into the life of Monday or Tuesday,[6] the accent falls differently from of old; the moment of importance came not here but there; so that, if a writer were a free man and not a slave, if he could write what he chose, not what he must, if he could base his work upon his own feeling and not upon convention, there would be no plot, no comedy, no tragedy, no love interest, or catastrophe in the accepted style, and perhaps not a single button sewn on as the Bond Street[7] tailors would have it. Life is not a series of gig-lamps[8] symmetrically arranged; life is a luminous halo, a semitransparent envelope surrounding us from the beginning of consciousness to the end. Is it not the task of the novelist to convey this varying, this unknown and uncircumscribed spirit, whatever aberration or complexity it may display, with as little mixture of the alien and external as possible? We are not pleading merely for courage and sincerity; we are suggesting that the proper stuff of fiction is a little other than custom would have us believe it.

It is, at any rate, in some such fashion as this that we seek to define the quality which distinguishes the work of several young writers, among whom Mr. James Joyce is the most notable, from that of their predecessors. They attempt to come closer to life, and to preserve more sincerely and exactly what interests and moves them, even if to do so they must discard most of the conventions which are commonly observed by the novelist. Let us record the atoms as they fall upon the mind in the order in which they fall, let us trace the pattern, however disconnected and incoherent in appearance, which each sight or incident scores upon the consciousness. Let us not take it for granted that life exists more fully in what is commonly thought big than in what is commonly thought small. Anyone who has read *A Portrait of the Artist as a Young Man* or, what promises to be a far more interesting work, *Ulysses*, now appearing[9] in the *Little Review*, will have hazarded some

---

6. *Monday or Tuesday* was the title of the collection of experimental stories and sketches that Woolf brought out in 1921.
7. Fashionable shopping street in London.
8. Carriage lamps.
9. "Written April, 1919" [Woolf's note].

theory of this nature as to Mr. Joyce's intention. On our part, with such a fragment before us, it is hazarded rather than affirmed; but whatever the intention of the whole, there can be no question but that it is of the utmost sincerity and that the result, difficult or unpleasant as we may judge it, is undeniably important. In contrast with those whom we have called materialists, Mr. Joyce is spiritual; he is concerned at all costs to reveal the flickerings of that innermost flame which flashes its messages through the brain, and in order to preserve it he disregards with complete courage whatever seems to him adventitious, whether it be probability, or coherence, or any other of these signposts which for generations have served to support the imagination of a reader when called upon to imagine what he can neither touch nor see. The scene in the cemetery,[1] for instance, with its brilliancy, its sordidity, its incoherence, its sudden lightning flashes of significance, does undoubtedly come so close to the quick of the mind that, on a first reading at any rate, it is difficult not to acclaim a masterpiece. If we want life itself, here surely we have it. Indeed, we find ourselves fumbling rather awkwardly if we try to say what else we wish, and for what reason a work of such originality yet fails to compare, for we must take high examples, with *Youth* or *The Mayor of Casterbridge*.[2] It fails because of the comparative poverty of the writer's mind, we might say simply and have done with it. But it is possible to press a little further and wonder whether we may not refer our sense of being in a bright yet narrow room, confined and shut in, rather than enlarged and set free, to some limitation imposed by the method as well as by the mind. Is it the method that inhibits the creative power? Is it due to the method that we feel neither jovial nor magnanimous, but centered in a self which, in spite of its tremor of susceptibility, never embraces or creates what is outside itself and beyond? Does the emphasis laid, perhaps didactically, upon indecency contribute to the effect of something angular and isolated? Or is it merely that in any effort of such originality it is much easier, for contemporaries especially, to feel what it lacks than to name what it gives? In any case it is a mistake to stand outside examining "methods." Any method is right, every method is right, that expresses what we wish to express, if we are writers; that brings us closer to the novelist's intention if we are readers. This method has the merit of bringing us closer to what we were prepared to call life itself; did not the reading of *Ulysses* suggest how much of life is excluded or ignored, and did it not come with a shock to open *Tristram Shandy* or even *Pendennis*[3] and be by them convinced that

1. The sixth episode ("Hades") of *Ulysses*, where Bloom goes to Paddy Dignam's funeral.
2. Stories by, respectively, Joseph Conrad and Thomas Hardy.
3. Novels by, respectively, Laurence Sterne (1713–68) and William Makepeace Thackeray (1811–63).

there are not only other aspects of life, but more important ones into the bargain.

However this may be, the problem before the novelist at present, as we suppose it to have been in the past, is to contrive means of being free to set down what he chooses. He has to have the courage to say that what interests him is no longer "this" but "that": out of "that" alone must he construct his work. For the moderns "that," the point of interest, lies very likely in the dark places of psychology. At once, therefore, the accent falls a little differently; the emphasis is upon something hitherto ignored; at once a different outline of form becomes necessary, difficult for us to grasp, incomprehensible to our predecessors. No one but a modern, no one perhaps but a Russian, would have felt the interest of the situation which Tchekov[4] has made into the short story which he calls "Gusev." Some Russian soldiers lie ill on board a ship which is taking them back to Russia. We are given a few scraps of their talk and some of their thoughts; then one of them dies and is carried away; the talk goes on among the others for a time, until Gusev himself dies, and looking "like a carrot or a radish" is thrown overboard. The emphasis is laid upon such unexpected places that at first it seems as if there were no emphasis at all; and then, as the eyes accustom themselves to twilight and discern the shapes of things in a room we see how complete the story is, how profound, and how truly in obedience to his vision Tchekov has chosen this, that, and the other, and placed them together to compose something new. But it is impossible to say "this is comic," or "that is tragic," nor are we certain, since short stories, we have been taught, should be brief and conclusive, whether this, which is vague and inconclusive, should be called a short story at all.

The most elementary remarks upon modern English fiction can hardly avoid some mention of the Russian influence, and if the Russians are mentioned one runs the risk of feeling that to write of any fiction save theirs is waste of time. If we want understanding of the soul and heart where else shall we find it of comparable profundity? If we are sick of our own materialism the least considerable of their novelists has by right of birth a natural reverence for the human spirit. "Learn to make yourself akin to people. . . . But let this sympathy be not with the mind—for it is easy with the mind —but with the heart, with love towards them." In every great Russian writer we seem to discern the features of a saint, if sympathy for the sufferings of others, love towards them, endeavor to reach some goal worthy of the most exacting demands of the spirit constitute saintliness. It is the saint in them which confounds us with a feeling of our own irreligious triviality, and turns so many of our

4. Anton Pavlovich Chekhov (1860–1904).

famous novels to tinsel and trickery. The conclusions of the Russian mind, thus comprehensive and compassionate, are inevitably, perhaps, of the utmost sadness. More accurately indeed we might speak of the inconclusiveness of the Russian mind. It is the sense that there is no answer, that if honestly examined life presents question after question which must be left to sound on and on after the story is over in hopeless interrogation that fills us with a deep, and finally it may be with a resentful, despair. They are right perhaps; unquestionably they see further than we do and without our gross impediments of vision. But perhaps we see something that escapes them, or why should this voice of protest mix itself with our gloom? The voice of protest is the voice of another and an ancient civilization which seems to have bred in us the instinct to enjoy and fight rather than to suffer and understand. English fiction from Sterne to Meredith[5] bears witness to our natural delight in humor and comedy, in the beauty of earth, in the activities of the intellect, and in the splendor of the body. But any deductions that we may draw from the comparison of two fictions so immeasurably far apart are futile save indeed as they flood us with a view of the infinite possibilities of the art and remind us that there is no limit to the horizon, and that nothing—no "method," no experiment, even of the wildest—is forbidden, but only falsity and pretense. "The proper stuff of fiction" does not exist; everything is the proper stuff of fiction, every feeling, every thought; every quality of brain and spirit is drawn upon; no perception comes amiss. And if we can imagine the art of fiction come alive and standing in our midst, she would undoubtedly bid us break her and bully her, as well as honor and love her, for so her youth is renewed and her sovereignty assured.

1925

From A Room of One's Own

[Shakespeare's Sister][1]

It was disappointing not to have brought back in the evening some important statement, some authentic fact. Women are poorer than men because—this or that. Perhaps now it would be better to give up seeking for the truth, and receiving on one's head an avalanche of opinion hot as lava, discolored as dishwater. It would be better to draw the curtains; to shut out distractions; to light the lamp; to narrow the inquiry and to ask the historian, who records

---

5. The novelist George Meredith (1828–1909).
1. The selection is drawn from Chapter Three and from the conclusion to the final chapter. In Chapter Two, she has been to the library of the British Museum, trying in vain to find answers to questions about the different fates of men and women.

not opinions but facts, to describe under what conditions women lived, not throughout the ages, but in England, say in the time of Elizabeth.

For it is a perennial puzzle why no woman wrote a word of that extraordinary literature when every other man, it seemed, was capable of song or sonnet. What were the conditions in which women lived, I asked myself; for fiction, imaginative work that is, is not dropped like a pebble upon the ground, as science may be; fiction is like a spider's web, attached ever so lightly perhaps, but still attached to life at all four corners. Often the attachment is scarcely perceptible; Shakespeare's plays, for instance, seem to hang there complete by themselves. But when the web is pulled askew, hooked up at the edge, torn in the middle, one remembers that these webs are not spun in midair by incorporeal creatures, but are the work of suffering human beings, and are attached to grossly material things, like health and money and the houses we live in.

I went, therefore, to the shelf where the histories stand and took down one of the latest, Professor Trevelyan's *History of England*.[2] Once more I looked up Women, found "position of," and turned to the pages indicated. "Wife-beating," I read, "was a recognized right of man, and was practiced without shame by high as well as low. . . . Similarly," the historian goes on, "the daughter who refused to marry the gentleman of her parents' choice was liable to be locked up, beaten, and flung about the room, without any shock being inflicted on public opinion. Marriage was not an affair of personal affection, but of family avarice, particularly in the 'chivalrous' upper classes. . . . Betrothal often took place while one or both of the parties was in the cradle, and marriage when they were scarcely out of the nurses' charge." That was about 1470, soon after Chaucer's time. The next reference to the position of women is some two hundred years later, in the time of the Stuarts. "It was still the exception for women of the upper and middle class to choose their own husbands, and when the husband had been assigned, he was lord and master, so far at least as law and custom could make him. Yet even so," Professor Trevelyan concludes, "neither Shakespeare's women nor those of authentic seventeenth-century memoirs, like the Verneys and the Hutchinsons,[3] seem wanting in personality and character." Certainly, if we consider it, Cleopatra must have had a way with her; Lady Macbeth, one would suppose, had a will of her own; Rosalind, one might conclude, was an attractive girl.[4]

2. G. M. Trevelyan's *History of England* (1926) long held its place as the standard one-volume history of the country.
3. "The ideal family life of the period [1640–50] that ended in such tragic political division has been recorded once for all in the *Memoirs of the Verney Family*" (Trevelyan, History of England). Lucy Hutchinson (b. 1628) wrote the biography of her husband, Col. John Hutchinson (1616–84); it was first published in 1806.
4. These three Shakespearean heroines are, respectively, in *Antony and Cleopatra*, *Macbeth*, and *As You Like It*.

Professor Trevelyan is speaking no more than the truth when he remarks that Shakespeare's women do not seem wanting in personality and character. Not being a historian, one might go even further and say that women have burnt like beacons in all the works of all the poets from the beginning of time—Clytemnestra, Antigone, Cleopatra, Lady Macbeth, Phèdre, Cressida, Rosalind, Desdemona, the Duchess of Malfi, among the dramatists; then among the prose writers: Millamant, Clarissa, Becky Sharp, Anna Karenina, Emma Bovary, Madame de Guermantes[5]—the names flock to mind, nor do they recall women "lacking in personality and character." Indeed, if woman had no existence save in the fiction written by men, one would imagine her a person of the utmost importance; very various; heroic and mean; splendid and sordid; infinitely beautiful and hideous in the extreme; as great as a man, some think even greater.[6] But this is woman in fiction. In fact, as Professor Trevelyan points out, she was locked up, beaten, and flung about the room.

A very queer, composite being thus emerges. Imaginatively she is of the highest importance; practically she is completely insignificant. She pervades poetry from cover to cover; she is all but absent from history. She dominates the lives of kings and conquerors in fiction; in fact she was the slave of any boy whose parents forced a ring upon her finger. Some of the most inspired words, some of the most profound thoughts in literature fall from her lips; in real life she could hardly read, could scarcely spell, and was the property of her husband.

It was certainly an odd monster that one made up by reading the historians first and the poets afterwards—a worm winged like an eagle; the spirit of life and beauty in a kitchen chopping up suet. But these monsters, however amusing to the imagination, have no existence in fact. What one must do to bring her to life was to

5. Characters in, respectively, Aeschylus's *Agamemnon*, Sophocles's *Antigone*, Shakespeare's *Antony and Cleopatra* and *Macbeth*, Racine's *Phèdre*, Shakespeare's *Troilus and Cressida, As You Like It* and *Othello*, Webster's *The Duchess of Malfi*, Congreve's *Way of the World*, Richardson's *Clarissa*, Thackeray's *Vanity Fair*, Tolstoy's *Anna Karenina*, Flaubert's *Madame Bovary*, and Proust's *A la Récherche du Temps Perdu*.

6. "'It remains a strange and almost inexplicable fact that in Athena's city, where women were kept in almost Oriental suppression as odalisques or drudges, the stage should yet have produced figures like Clytemnestra and Cassandra, Atossa and Antigone, Phèdre and Medea, and all the other heroines who dominate play after play of the "misogynist" Euripides. But the paradox of this world where in real life a respectable woman could hardly show her face alone in the street, and yet on the stage woman equals or surpasses man, has never been satisfactorily explained. In modern tragedy the same predominance exists. At all events, a very cursory survey of Shakespeare's work (similarly with Webster, though not with Marlowe or Jonson) suffices to reveal how this dominance, this initiative of women, persists from Rosalind to Lady Macbeth. So too in Racine; six of his tragedies bear their heroines' names; and what male characters of his shall we set against Hermione and Andromaque, Bérénice and Roxane, Phèdre and Athalie? So again with Ibsen; what men shall we match with Solveig and Nora, Hedda and Hilda Wangel and Rebecca West?'—F. L. Lucas, *Tragedy*, pp. 114–15" [Woolf's note].

think poetically and prosaically at one and the same moment, thus keeping in touch with fact—that she is Mrs. Martin, aged thirty-six, dressed in blue, wearing a black hat and brown shoes; but not losing sight of fiction either—that she is a vessel in which all sorts of spirits and forces are coursing and flashing perpetually. The moment, however, that one tries this method with the Elizabethan woman, one branch of illumination fails; one is held up by the scarcity of facts. One knows nothing detailed, nothing perfectly true and substantial about her. History scarcely mentions her. And I turned to Professor Trevelyan again to see what history meant to him. I found by looking at his chapter headings that it meant—

"The Manor Court and the Methods of Open-Field Agriculture . . . The Cistercians and Sheep-Farming . . . The Crusades . . . The University . . . The House of Commons . . . The Hundred Years' War . . . The Wars of the Roses . . . The Renaissance Scholars . . . The Dissolution of the Monasteries . . . Agrarian and Religious Strife . . . The Origin of English Sea-Power . . . The Armada . . ." and so on. Occasionally an individual woman is mentioned, an Elizabeth, or a Mary; a queen or a great lady. But by no possible means could middle-class women with nothing but brains and character at their command have taken part in any one of the great movements which, brought together, constitute the historian's view of the past. Nor shall we find her in any collection of anecdotes. Aubrey[7] hardly mentions her. She never writes her own life and scarcely keeps a diary; there are only a handful of her letters in existence. She left no plays or poems by which we can judge her. What one wants, I thought—and why does not some brilliant student at Newnham or Girton[8] supply it?—is a mass of information; at what age did she marry; how many children had she as a rule; what was her house like; had she a room to herself; did she do the cooking; would she be likely to have a servant? All these facts lie somewhere, presumably, in parish registers and account books; the life of the average Elizabethan woman must be scattered about somewhere, could one collect it and make a book of it. It would be ambitious beyond my daring, I thought, looking about the shelves for books that were not there, to suggest to the students of those famous colleges that they should rewrite history, though I own that it often seems a little queer as it is, unreal, lopsided; but why should they not add a supplement to history? calling it, of course, by some inconspicuous name so that women might figure there without impropriety? For one often catches a glimpse of them in the lives of the great, whisking away into the background, concealing, I sometimes think, a wink, a laugh, perhaps a tear. And, after all, we have lives enough

---

7. The diarist John Aubrey (1626–97).   8. The two women's colleges at Cambridge.

of Jane Austen; it scarcely seems necessary to consider again the influence of the tragedies of Joanna Baillie[9] upon the poetry of Edgar Allan Poe; as for myself, I should not mind if the homes and haunts of Mary Russell Mitford[1] were closed to the public for a century at least. But what I find deplorable, I continued, looking about the bookshelves again, is that nothing is known about women before the eighteenth century. I have no model in my mind to turn about this way and that. Here am I asking why women did not write poetry in the Elizabethan age, and I am not sure how they were educated; whether they were taught to write; whether they had sitting rooms to themselves; how many women had children before they were twenty-one; what, in short, they did from eight in the morning till eight at night. They had no money evidently; according to Professor Trevelyan they were married whether they liked it or not before they were out of the nursery, at fifteen or sixteen very likely. It would have been extremely odd, even upon this showing, had one of them suddenly written the plays of Shakespeare, I concluded, and I thought of that old gentleman, who is dead now, but was a bishop, I think, who declared that it was impossible for any woman, past, present, or to come, to have the genius of Shakespeare. He wrote to the papers about it. He also told a lady who applied to him for information that cats do not as a matter of fact go to heaven, though they have, he added, souls of a sort. How much thinking those old gentlemen used to save one! How the borders of ignorance shrank back at their approach! Cats do not go to heaven. Women cannot write the plays of Shakespeare.

Be that as it may, I could not help thinking, as I looked at the works of Shakespeare on the shelf, that the bishop was right at least in this; it would have been impossible, completely and entirely, for any woman to have written the plays of Shakespeare in the age of Shakespeare. Let me imagine, since facts are so hard to come by, what would have happened had Shakespeare had a wonderfully gifted sister, called Judith, let us say. Shakespeare himself went, very probably—his mother was an heiress—to grammar school, where he may have learnt Latin—Ovid, Virgil, and Horace—and the elements of grammar and logic. He was, it is well known, a wild boy who poached rabbits, perhaps shot a deer, and had, rather sooner than he should have done, to marry a woman in the neighborhood, who bore him a child rather quicker than was right. That escapade sent him to seek his fortune in London. He had, it seemed, a taste for the theater; he began by holding horses at the stage door. Very soon he got work in the theater, became a successful actor, and

9. Poet and dramatist (1762–1851) now forgotten, but admired by Walter Scott.   1. Poet and novelist (1787–1855) best known for her sketches of country life.

lived at the hub of the universe, meeting everybody, knowing everybody, practicing his art on the boards, exercising his wits in the streets, and even getting access to the palace of the queen. Meanwhile his extraordinarily gifted sister, let us suppose, remained at home. She was as adventurous, as imaginative, as agog to see the world as he was. But she was not sent to school. She had no chance of learning grammar and logic, let alone of reading Horace and Virgil. She picked up a book now and then, one of her brother's perhaps, and read a few pages. But then her parents came in and told her to mend the stockings or mind the stew and not moon about with books and papers. They would have spoken sharply but kindly, for they were substantial people who knew the conditions of life for a woman and loved their daughter—indeed, more likely than not she was the apple of her father's eye. Perhaps she scribbled some pages up in an apple loft on the sly, but was careful to hide them or set fire to them. Soon, however, before she was out of her teens, she was to be betrothed to the son of a neighboring wool-stapler.[2] She cried out that marriage was hateful to her, and for that she was severely beaten by her father. Then he ceased to scold her. He begged her instead not to hurt him, not to shame him in this matter of her marriage. He would give her a chain of beads or a fine petticoat, he said; and there were tears in his eyes. How could she disobey him? How could she break his heart? The force of her own gift alone drove her to it. She made up a small parcel of her belongings, let herself down by a rope one summer's night, and took the road to London. She was not seventeen. The birds that sang in the hedge were not more musical than she was. She had the quickest fancy, a gift like her brother's, for the tune of words. Like him, she had a taste for the theater. She stood at the stage door; she wanted to act, she said. Men laughed in her face. The manager —a fat, loose-lipped man—guffawed. He bellowed something about poodles dancing and women acting—no woman, he said, could possibly be an actress. He hinted—you can imagine what. She could get no training in her craft. Could she even seek her dinner in a tavern or roam the streets at midnight? Yet her genius was for fiction and lusted to feed abundantly upon the lives of men and women and the study of their ways. At last—for she was very young, oddly like Shakespeare the poet in her face, with the same gray eyes and rounded brows—at last Nick Greene the actor-manager took pity on her; she found herself with child by that gentleman and so—who shall measure the heat and violence of the poet's heart when caught and tangled in a woman's body?—killed herself one

2. A stapler is a dealer in staple goods (i.e., established goods in trade and marketing); hence a wool-stapler is a dealer in wool (one of the "staple" products of 16th-century England).

winter's night and lies buried at some crossroads where the omnibuses now stop outside the Elephant and Castle.[3]

That, more or less, is how the story would run, I think, if a
woman in Shakespeare's day had had Shakespeare's genius. But for
my part, I agree with the deceased bishop, if such he was—it is
unthinkable that any woman in Shakespeare's day should have had
Shakespeare's genius. For genius like Shakespeare's is not born
among laboring, uneducated, servile people. It was not born in England among the Saxons and the Britons. It is not born today among
the working classes. How, then, could it have been born among
women whose work began, according to Professor Trevelyan, almost
before they were out of the nursery, who were forced to it by their
parents and held to it by all the power of law and custom? Yet
genius of a sort must have existed among women as it must have
existed among the working classes. Now and again an Emily Brontë
or a Robert Burns blazes out and proves its presence. But certainly
it never got itself on to paper. When, however, one reads of a witch
being ducked, of a woman possessed by devils, of a wise woman selling herbs, or even of a very remarkable man who had a mother,
then I think we are on the track of a lost novelist, a suppressed
poet, of some mute and inglorious[4] Jane Austen, some Emily
Brontë who dashed her brains out on the moor or mopped and
mowed about the highways crazed with the torture that her gift had
put her to. Indeed, I would venture to guess that Anon, who wrote
so many poems without signing them, was often a woman. It was a
woman Edward Fitzgerald,[5] I think, suggested who made the ballads and the folk songs, crooning them to her children, beguiling
her spinning with them, or the length of the winter's night.

This may be true or it may be false—who can say?—but what is
true in it, so it seemed to me, reviewing the story of Shakespeare's
sister as I had made it, is that any woman born with a great gift in
the sixteenth century would certainly have gone crazed, shot herself, or ended her days in some lonely cottage outside the village,
half witch, half wizard, feared and mocked at. For it needs little
skill in psychology to be sure that a highly gifted girl who had tried
to use her gift for poetry would have been so thwarted and hindered
by other people, so tortured and pulled asunder by her own contrary
instincts, that she must have lost her health and sanity to a certainty. No girl could have walked to London and stood at a stage
door and forced her way into the presence of actor-managers without doing herself a violence and suffering an anguish which may

3. Suicides were buried at crossroads.
The Elephant and Castle was for long
a tavern south of the Thames where
roads went off to different parts of
southern England.

4. An echo of Thomas Gray's famous
line about "some mute inglorious
Milton" in *Elegy Written in a Country
Churchyard* (1751), line 59.
5. Poet and translator (1809–83).

have been irrational—for chastity may be a fetish invented by certain societies for unknown reasons—but were none the less inevitable. Chastity had then, it has even now, a religious importance in a woman's life, and has so wrapped itself round with nerves and instincts that to cut it free and bring it to the light of day demands courage of the rarest. To have lived a free life in London in the sixteenth century would have meant for a woman who was poet and playwright a nervous stress and dilemma which might well have killed her. Had she survived, whatever she had written would have been twisted and deformed, issuing from a strained and morbid imagination. And undoubtedly, I thought, looking at the shelf where there are no plays by women, her work would have gone unsigned. That refuge she would have sought certainly. It was the relic of the sense of chastity that dictated anonymity to women even so late as the nineteenth century. Currer Bell, George Eliot, George Sand,[6] all the victims of inner strife as their writings prove, sought ineffectively to veil themselves by using the name of a man. Thus they did homage to the convention, which if not implanted by the other sex was liberally encouraged by them (the chief glory of a woman is not to be talked of, said Pericles, himself a much-talked-of man), that publicity in women is detestable. Anonymity runs in their blood. The desire to be veiled still possesses them.

* * *

I told you in the course of this paper that Shakespeare had a sister; but do not look for her in Sir Sidney Lee's life of the poet.[7] She died young—alas, she never wrote a word. She lies buried where the omnibuses now stop, opposite the Elephant and Castle. Now my belief is that this poet who never wrote a word and was buried at the crossroads still lives. She lives in you and in me, and in many other women who are not here tonight, for they are washing up the dishes and putting the children to bed. But she lives; for great poets do not die; they are continuing presences; they need only the opportunity to walk among us in the flesh. This opportunity, as I think, it is now coming within your power to give her. For my belief is that if we live another century or so—I am talking of the common life which is the real life and not of the little separate lives which we live as individuals—and have five hundred a year each of us and rooms of our own; if we have the habit of freedom and the courage to write exactly what we think; if we escape a little from the common sitting room and see human beings not always in their relation to each other but in relation to reality; and the sky,

6. Male pseudonyms, respectively, of Charlotte Brontë, Marian Evans, and Amandine-Aurore-Lucie Dupin.
7. Sir Sidney Lee (1859–1926), biographer and Shakespeare scholar, published his *Life of William Shakespeare* in 1898.

too, and the trees or whatever it may be in themselves; if we look past Milton's bogey,[8] for no human being should shut out the view; if we face the fact, for it is a fact, that there is no arm to cling to, but that we go alone and that our relation is to the world of reality and not only to the world of men and women, then the opportunity will come and the dead poet who was Shakespeare's sister will put on the body which she has so often laid down. Drawing her life from the lives of the unknown who were he forerunners, as her brother did before her, she will be born. As for her coming without that preparation, without that effort on our part, without that determination that when she is born again she shall find it possible to live and write her poetry, that we cannot expect, for that would be impossible. But I maintain that she would come if we worked for her, and that so to work, even in poverty and obscurity, is worth while.

1929

Professions for Women[1]

When your secretary invited me to come here, she told me that your Society is concerned with the employment of women and she suggested that I might tell you something about my own professional experiences. It is true that I am a woman; it is true I am employed; but what professional experiences have I had? It is difficult to say. My profession is literature; and in that profession there are fewer experiences for women than in any other, with the exception of the stage—fewer, I mean, that are peculiar to women. For the road was cut many years ago—by Fanny Burney, by Aphra Behn, by Harriet Martineau,[2] by Jane Austen, by George Eliot— many famous women, and many more unknown and forgotten, have been before me, making the path smooth, and regulating my steps. Thus, when I came to write, there were very few material obstacles in my way. Writing was a reputable and harmless occupation. The family peace was not broken by the scratching of a pen. No demand was made upon the family purse. For ten and sixpence one can buy paper enough to write all the plays of Shakespeare—if one has a mind that way. Pianos and models, Paris, Vienna, and Berlin, masters and mistresses, are not needed by a writer. The cheapness of writing paper is, of course, the reason why women have succeeded

---

8. Milton, with his unhappy first marriage, his campaign for freedom of divorce, and his deliberate subordination of Eve to Adam in *Paradise Lost*, was and often still is held to be (not altogether accurately) an example of what the present age calls a "male chauvinist" attitude to women.

1. "A paper read to the Women's Service League" [Woolf's note].
2. Fanny Burney (1752–1840) was the author of *Evelina* and other novels; Mrs. Aphra Behn (1640–89) was a writer of romances and plays; Harriet Martineau (1802–76) was an economist, moralist, journalist, and novelist.

as writers before they have succeeded in the other professions.

But to tell you my story—it is a simple one. You have only got to figure to yourselves a girl in a bedroom with a pen in her hand. She had only to move that pen from left to right—from ten o'clock to one. Then it occurred to her to do what is simple and cheap enough after all—to slip a few of those pages into an envelope, fix a penny stamp in the corner, and drop the envelope into the red box at the corner. It was thus that I became a journalist; and my effort was rewarded on the first day of the following month—a very glorious day it was for me—by a letter from an editor containing a check for one pound ten shillings and sixpence. But to show you how little I deserve to be called a professional woman, how little I know of the struggles and difficulties of such lives, I have to admit that instead of spending that sum upon bread and butter, rent, shoes and stockings, or butcher's bills, I went out and bought a cat —a beautiful cat, a Persian cat, which very soon involved me in bitter disputes with my neighbors.

What could be easier than to write articles and to buy Persian cats with the profits? But wait a moment. Articles have to be about something. Mine, I seem to remember, was about a novel by a famous man. And while I was writing this review, I discovered that if I were going to review books I should need to do battle with a certain phantom. And the phantom was a woman, and when I came to know her better I called her after the heroine of a famous poem, The Angel in the House.[3] It was she who used to come between me and my paper when I was writing reviews. It was she who bothered me and wasted my time and so tormented me that at last I killed her. You who come of a younger and happier generation may not have heard of her—you may not know what I mean by The Angel in the House. I will describe her as shortly as I can. She was intensely sympathetic. She was immensely charming. She was utterly unselfish. She excelled in the difficult arts of family life. She sacrificed herself daily. If there was chicken, she took the leg; if there was a draft she sat in it—in short she was so constituted that she never had a mind or a wish of her own, but preferred to sympathize always with the minds and wishes of others. Above all—I need not say it—she was pure. Her purity was supposed to be her chief beauty—her blushes, her great grace. In those days—the last of Queen Victoria—every house had its Angel. And when I came to write I encountered her with the very first words. The shadow of her wings fell on my page; I heard the rustling of her skirts in the room. Directly, that is to say, I took my pen in my hand to review that novel by a famous man, she slipped behind me and whispered:

3. By Coventry Patmore (1823–96), published 1854–62.

"My dear, you are a young woman. You are writing about a book that has been written by a man. Be sympathetic; be tender; flatter; deceive; use all the arts and wiles of our sex. Never let anybody guess that you have a mind of your own. Above all, be pure." And she made as if to guide my pen. I now record the one act for which I take some credit to myself, though the credit rightly belongs to some excellent ancestors of mine who left me a certain sum of money—shall we say five hundred pounds a year?—so that it was not necessary for me to depend solely on charm for my living. I turned upon her and caught her by the throat. I did my best to kill her. My excuse, if I were to be had up in a court of law, would be that I acted in self-defense. Had I not killed her she would have killed me. She would have plucked the heart out of my writing. For, as I found, directly I put pen to paper, you cannot review even a novel without having a mind of your own, without expressing what you think to be the truth about human relations, morality, sex. And all these questions, according to the Angel of the House, cannot be dealt with freely and openly by women; they must charm, they must conciliate, they must—to put it bluntly—tell lies if they are to succeed. Thus, whenever I felt the shadow of her wing or the radiance of her halo upon my page, I took up the inkpot and flung it at her. She died hard. Her fictitious nature was of great assistance to her. It is far harder to kill a phantom than a reality. She was always creeping back when I thought I had despatched her. Though I flatter myself that I killed her in the end, the struggle was severe; it took much time that had better have been spent upon learning Greek grammar; or in roaming the world in search of adventures. But it was a real experience; it was an experience that was bound to befall all women writers at that time. Killing the Angel in the House was part of the occupation of a woman writer.

But to continue my story. The Angel was dead; what then remained? You may say that what remained was a simple and common object—a young woman in a bedroom with an inkpot. In other words, now that she had rid herself of falsehood, that young woman had only to be herself. Ah, but what is "herself"? I mean, what is a woman? I assure you, I do not know. I do not believe that you know. I do not believe that anybody can know until she has expressed herself in all the arts and professions open to human skill. That indeed is one of the reasons why I have come here—out of respect for you, who are in process of showing us by your experiments what a woman is, who are in process of providing us, by your failures and successes, with that extremely important piece of information.

But to continue the story of my professional experiences. I made one pound ten and six by my first review; and I bought a Persian cat with the proceeds. Then I grew ambitious. A Persian cat is all very well, I said; but a Persian cat is not enough. I must have a motorcar. And it was thus that I became a novelist—for it is a very strange thing that people will give you a motorcar if you will tell them a story. It is a still stranger thing that there is nothing so delightful in the world as telling stories. It is far pleasanter than writing reviews of famous novels. And yet, if I am to obey your secretary and tell you my professional experiences as a novelist, I must tell you about a very strange experience that befell me as a novelist. And to understand it you must try first to imagine a novelist's state of mind. I hope I am not giving away professional secrets if I say that a novelist's chief desire is to be as unconscious as possible. He has to induce in himself a state of perpetual lethargy. He wants life to proceed with the utmost quiet and regularity. He wants to see the same faces, to read the same books, to do the same things day after day, month after month, while he is writing, so that nothing may break the illusion in which he is living—so that nothing may disturb or disquiet the mysterious nosings about, feelings round, darts, dashes, and sudden discoveries of that very shy and illusive spirit, the imagination. I suspect that this state is the same both for men and women. Be that as it may, I want you to imagine me writing a novel in a state of trance. I want you to figure to yourselves a girl sitting with a pen in her hand, which for minutes, and indeed for hours, she never dips into the inkpot. The image that comes to my mind when I think of this girl is the image of a fisherman lying sunk in dreams on the verge of a deep lake with a rod held out over the water. She was letting her imagination sweep unchecked round every rock and cranny of the world that lies submerged in the depths of our unconscious being. Now came the experience that I believe to be far commoner with women writers than with men. The line raced through the girl's fingers. Her imagination had rushed away. It had sought the pools, the depths, the dark places where the largest fish slumber. And then there was a smash. There was an explosion. There was foam and confusion. The imagination had dashed itself against something hard. The girl was roused from her dream. She was indeed in a state of the most acute and difficult distress. To speak without figure, she had thought of something, something about the body, about the passions which it was unfitting for her as a woman to say. Men, her reason told her, would be shocked. The consciousness of what men will say of a woman who speaks the truth about her passions had roused her from her artist's state of unconsciousness. She could write no more. The trance was over. Her imagination could work no longer. This I believe to be a very common experience with women writers—they are impeded by the extreme conventionality of the other sex. For though men sensibly allow themselves great freedom in these respects, I doubt that they realize or can control the extreme severity with which they condemn such freedom in women.

These then were two very genuine experiences of my own. These were two of the adventures of my professional life. The first—killing the Angel in the House—I think I solved. She died. But the second, telling the truth about my own experiences as a body, I do not think I solved. I doubt that any woman has solved it yet. The obstacles against her are still immensely powerful—and yet they are very difficult to define. Outwardly, what is simpler than to write books? Outwardly, what obstacles are there for a woman rather than for a man? Inwardly, I think, the case is very different; she has still many ghosts to fight, many prejudices to overcome. Indeed it will be a long time still, I think, before a woman can sit down to write a book without finding a phantom to be slain, a rock to be dashed against. And if this is so in literature, the freest of all professions for women, how is it in the new professions which you are now for the first time entering?

Those are the questions that I should like, had I time, to ask you. And indeed, if I have laid stress upon these professional experiences of mine, it is because I believe that they are, though in different forms, yours also. Even when the path is nominally open—when there is nothing to prevent a woman from being a doctor, a lawyer, a civil servant—there are many phantoms and obstacles, as I believe, looming in her way. To discuss and define them is I think of great value and importance; for thus only can the labor be shared, the difficulties be solved. But besides this, it is necessary also to discuss the ends and the aims for which we are fighting, for which we are doing battle with these formidable obstacles. Those aims cannot be taken for granted; they must be perpetually questioned and examined. The whole position, as I see it—here in this hall surrounded by women practicing for the first time in history I know not how many different professions—is one of extraordinary interest and importance. You have won rooms of your own in the house hitherto exclusively owned by men. You are able, though not without great labor and effort, to pay the rent. You are earning your five hundred pounds a year. But this freedom is only a beginning; the room is your own, but it is still bare. It has to be furnished; it has to be decorated; it has to be shared. How are you going to furnish it, how are you going to decorate it? With whom are you going to share it, and upon what terms? These, I think are questions of the utmost importance and interest. For the first time in history you are able to ask them; for the first time you are able to decide for yourselves what the answers should be. Willingly would I stay and discuss those questions and answers—but not tonight. My time is up; and I must cease.

1942

JAMES JOYCE
(1882–1941)

1914: *Dubliners.*
1916: *A Portrait of the Artist as a Young Man.*
1922: *Ulysses.*
1939: *Finnegans Wake.*

James Joyce was born in Dublin, son of a talented but feckless father who is accurately described by Stephen Dedalus in *A Portrait of the Artist as a Young Man* as a man who had in his time been "a medical student, an oarsman, a tenor, an amateur actor, a shouting politician, a small landlord, a small investor, a drinker, a good fellow, a storyteller, somebody's secretary, something in a distillery, a tax-gatherer, a bankrupt, and at present a praiser of his own past." The elder Joyce drifted steadily down the financial and social scale, his family moving from house to house, each one less genteel and more shabby than the previous. James Joyce's whole education was Catholic, from the age of 6 to the age of 9 at Clongowes Wood College, and from 11 to 16 at Belvedere College, Dublin. Both were Jesuit institutions, and were normal roads to the priesthood. He then studied modern languages at University College, Dublin.

From a comparatively early age Joyce regarded himself as a rebel against the shabbiness and Philistinism of Dublin. In his early youth he was very religious, but in his last year at Belvedere he began to reject his Catholic faith in favor of a literary mission which he saw as involving rebellion and exile. He refused to play any part in the nationalist or other popular activities of his fellow students, and created some stir by his outspoken articles, one of which, on the Norwegian playwright Henrik Ibsen, appeared in the *Fortnightly Review* for April, 1900. He taught himself Norwegian to be able to read Ibsen and to write to him. When an article by Joyce, significantly entitled *The Day of the Rabblement*, was refused, on instructions of the faculty adviser, by the student magazine that had commissioned it, he had it printed privately. By 1902, when he received his B.A. degree, he was already committed to a career as exile and writer. For Joyce, as for his character Stephen Dedalus, the latter implied the former. To preserve his integrity, to avoid involvement in popular sentimentalities and dishonesties, and above all to be able to re-create with both total understanding and total objectivity the Dublin life he knew so well, he felt that he had to go abroad.

Joyce went to Paris after graduation, was recalled to Dublin by his mother's fatal illness, had a short spell there as a schoolteacher, then returned to the Continent in 1904 to teach English at Trieste and then at Zurich. He took with him Nora Barnacle, an uneducated Galway girl with no interest in literature; her native vivacity and peasant wit charmed Joyce, and the two lived in devoted companionship until Joyce's death, though they were not married until 1931. In 1920 Joyce settled in Paris, where he lived until December, 1940, when the war forced him to take refuge in Switzerland; he died in Zurich a few weeks later.

Proud, obstinate, absolutely convinced of his genius, given to fits of sudden gaiety and of sudden silence, Joyce was not always an easy person to get on with, yet he never lacked friends and throughout his 36 years on the Continent was always the center of a literary circle. Life was hard at first. At Trieste he had very little money, and he did not improve matters by drinking heavily, a habit checked somewhat by his brother Stanislaus who came out from Dublin to act (as Stanislaus put it much later) as his "brother's keeper." His financial position was much improved by the patronage of Mrs. Harold McCormick (Edith Rockefeller), who provided him with a monthly stipend from March, 1917, until September, 1919, when they quarreled, apparently because Joyce refused to submit to psychoanalysis by Carl Jung, who had been heavily endowed by Mrs. McCormick. The New York lawyer and art patron John Quinn, steered in Joyce's direction by Ezra Pound, also helped Joyce financially in 1917. A more permanent benefactor was the English feminist and editor Harriet Shaw Weaver, who not only subsidized Joyce generously from 1917 to the end of his life, but occupied herself indefatigably with arrangements for publishing his work.

Joyce's almost life-long exile from his native Ireland has something paradoxical about it. No writer has ever been more soaked in Dublin, its atmosphere, its history, its topography; in spite of doing most of his writing in Trieste, Zurich, and Paris, he wrote only and always about Dublin. He devised ways of expanding his accounts of Dublin, however, so that they became microcosms, small-scale models, of all human life, of all history and all geography. Indeed that was his life's work: to write about Dublin in such a way that he was writing about all of human experience.

Joyce began his career by writing a series of stories etching with extraordinary clarity aspects of Dublin life. But these stories—published as *Dubliners* in 1914—are more than sharp realistic sketches. In each, the detail is so chosen and organized that carefully interacting symbolic meanings are set up, and as a result *Dubliners* is a book about man's fate as well as a series of sketches of Dublin. (*Araby*, for example, is meticulously accurate in every physical detail, yet it is also a symbolic story about the relation between dreams and reality.) Further, the stories are presented in a particular order so that new meanings arise from the relation between them.

This was Joyce's first phase: he had to come directly to terms with the life he had rejected, to see it for what it was and for what it meant. Next, he had to come to terms with the meaning of his own development as a man dedicated to writing. He did this by weaving his autobiography into a novel so finely chiseled and carefully organized, so stripped of everything superfluous, that each word contributes to the presentation of the theme: the parallel movement toward art and toward exile. A part of Joyce's first draft has been posthumously published under the original title of *Stephen Hero* (1944): a comparison between it and the final version which Joyce gave to the world, *A Portrait of the Artist as a Young Man* (1916), will show how carefully Joyce reworked and compressed his material for maximum effect. The *Portrait* is not literally true as autobiography, though it has many autobiographical elements; but it is representatively true not only of Joyce but of the relation between the artist and society in the modern world.

In the *Portrait* Stephen worked out a theory of art which considers that art moves from the lyrical form—which is the simplest, the personal expression of an instant of emotion—through the narrative form—no longer purely personal—to the dramatic—the highest and most perfect form, where "the artist, like the God of creation, remains within or behind or beyond or above his handiwork, invisible, refined out of existence, indifferent, paring his fingernails." This view of art, which involves the objectivity, even the exile, of the artist (even though the artist uses only the materials provided for him by his own life) is related to that held by the poets of the 90's. More widely, it is related to the rejection by the artist of the ordinary world of middleclass values and activities which we see equally, though in different ways, in Matthew Arnold's war against the Philistines and in the concept (very un-Arnoldian) of the artist as bohemian. Joyce's career belongs to that long chapter in the history of the arts in Western civilization which begins with the artist's declaring his independence and ends with his feeling his inevitable "alienation." But if Joyce was alienated, as in certain ways he clearly was, he made his alienation serve his art: the kinds of writing represented by *Ulysses* and *Finnegans Wake* represent the most consummate craftsmanship put at the service of a humanely comic vision of all life. Some (though surprisingly few) of Joyce's innovations in organization and style have been imitated by other writers, but these books are, and will probably remain, unique in our literature. They are not freaks or historical oddities, but serious and exciting works.

From the beginning Joyce had trouble with the Philistines. Publication of *Dubliners* was held up for many years while he fought with both English and Irish publishers about certain words and phrases which they wished to eliminate. (It was the former who finally published the book.) His masterpiece *Ulysses* was banned in both Britain and America on its first appearance in 1922, its earlier serialization in the *Little Review* (March 1918–December 1920) having had to stop abruptly when the U.S. Post Office brought a charge of obscenity against it. Fortunately, Judge Woolsey's history-making decision in favor of *Ulysses* in the United States District Court on December 6, 1933, resulted in the lifting of the ban and the free circulation of the work first in America and soon afterwards in Britain.

ULYSSES

Ulysses is an account of one day in the lives of citizens of Dublin in the year 1904: it is thus the description of a limited number of events involving a limited number of people in a limited environment. Yet Joyce's ambition—which took him seven years to realize—is to make his action into a microcosm of all human experience. The events are not therefore told on a single level; the story is presented in such a manner that depth and implication are given to them and they become symbolic of the activity of Man in the World. The most obvious of the devices which Joyce employs in order to make clear the microcosmic aspect of his story is the parallel with Homer's *Odyssey*: every episode in *Ulysses* corresponds in some way to an episode in the *Odyssey*. Joyce regarded Homer's Ulysses as the most "complete" man in literature, a man who is shown in all his aspects—both coward and hero, cautious and reckless, weak and strong, husband and lover, father and son, sublime and ridiculous; so he makes his hero, Leopold Bloom, an Irish Jew, into a modern Ulysses, and by so doing helps to make him Everyman and to make Dublin the world.

The book opens at eight o'clock on the morning of June 16, 1904. Stephen Dedalus (the same character we saw in the *Portrait*, but this is two years after our last glimpse of him there) had been summoned back to Dublin by his mother's fatal illness and now lives in an old military tower on the shore with Buck Mulligan, a rollicking medical student, and an Englishman called Haines. In the first three episodes of *Ulysses*, which concentrate on Stephen, he is built up as an aloof, uncompromising artist, rejecting all advances by representatives of the normal world, the incomplete man, to be contrasted later with the complete Leopold Bloom, who is much more "normal" and conciliatory. After tracing Stephen through his early-morning activities and learning the main currents of his mind, we go, in the fourth episode, to the home of Bloom. We follow closely his every activity: attending a funeral, transacting his business, eating his lunch, walking through the Dublin streets, worrying about his wife's infidelity with Blazes Boylan—and at each point the contents of his mind, including retrospect and anticipation, are presented to the reader, until all his past history is revealed. Finally, Bloom and Stephen, who have just been missing each other all day, get together. By this time it is late, and Stephen, who has been drinking with some medical students, is the worse for liquor. Bloom, moved by a paternal feeling towards Stephen (his own son had died in infancy and in a symbolic way Stephen takes his place), follows him during subsequent adventures in the role of protector. The climax of the book comes when Stephen, far gone in drink, and Bloom, worn out with fatigue, succumb to a series of hallucinations where their subconscious and unconscious come to the surface in dramatic form and their whole personalities are revealed with a completeness and a frankness unique in literature. Then Bloom takes the unresponsive Stephen home and gives him a meal. After Stephen's departure Bloom retires to bed—it is now 2 A.M. on June 17—while his wife Molly, representing the principles of sex and reproduction on which all human life is based, closes the book with a long monologue in which her experiences as woman are remembered.

On the level of realistic description, *Ulysses* pulses with life and can be enjoyed for its evocation of early 20th-century Dublin. On the level of psychological exploration, it gives a profound and moving presentation of the personality and consciousness of Leopold Bloom and (to a lesser extent) Stephen Dedalus. On the level of style, it exhibits the most fascinating linguistic virtuosity. On a deeper symbolic level, the novel explores the paradoxes of human loneliness and sociability (for Bloom is both Jew and Dubliner, both exile and citizen, just as all men are in a sense both exiles and citizens), and it explores the problems posed by the relations between parent and child, between the generations, and between the sexes. At the same time, through its use of themes from Homer, Dante, and Shakespeare, from literature, philosophy, and history, the book weaves a subtle pattern of allusion and suggestion which illuminates many aspects of human experience. The more one reads *Ulysses* the more one finds in it, but at the same time one does not need to probe into the symbolic meaning in order to relish both its literary artistry and its human feeling. At the forefront stands Leopold Bloom, from one point of view a frustrated and confused outsider in the society in which he moves, from another a champion of kindness and justice whose humane curiosity about his fellows redeems him from mere vulgarity and gives the book its positive human foundation.

Readers who come to *Ulysses* with expectations about the way the story is to be presented derived from their reading of Victorian novels or even of such 20th-century novelists as Conrad and Lawrence will find much that is at first puzzling. Joyce presents the consciousness of his characters directly, without any explanatory comment which tells the reader whose consciousness is being rendered (this is the "stream-of-consciousness" method). He may move, in the same paragraph and without any sign that he is making such a transition, from a description of a character's action—e.g., Stephen walking along the shore or Bloom entering a restaurant —to an evocation of the character's mental response to this action. That response is always multiple: it derives partly from the character's immediate situation and partly from the whole complex of attitudes which his past history has created in him. To suggest this multiplicity, Joyce may vary his style, from the flippant to the serious or from a realistic description to a suggestive set of images which indicate what might be called the general tone of the character's consciousness. Past and present mingle in the texture of the prose because they mingle in the texture of consciousness; and this mingling can be indicated by puns, by sudden breaks into a new kind of style or a new kind of subject matter, or by some other device for keeping the reader constantly in sight of the shifting, kaleidoscopic nature of human awareness. With a little experience, the reader learns to follow the implications of Joyce's shifts in manner and content—even to follow that at first sight bewildering passage in the "Proteus" episode where Stephen does not go to visit his uncle and aunt but, passing the road that leads to their house, imagines the kind of conversation that would take place in his home *if* he had gone to visit his uncle and had then returned home and reported that he had done so. *Ulysses* must not be approached as though it were a novel written in a traditional manner; all preconceptions must be set aside and we must follow wherever the author leads us and let the language tell us what it has to say without our troubling whether language is being used "properly" or not.

FINNEGANS WAKE

Joyce's last work, *Finnegans Wake*, was published in 1939; it took more than fourteen years to write, and Joyce considered it his masterpiece. In *Ulysses* he had made the symbolic aspect of the novel at least as important as the realistic aspect, but in *Finnegans Wake* he gave up realism altogether. This vast story of a symbolic Irishman's cosmic dream develops by enormous reverberating puns a continuous expansion of meaning, the elements in the puns deriving from every conceivable source in history, literature, mythology, and Joyce's personal experience. The whole book being (on one level at least) a dream, Joyce invents his own dream language in which words are combined, distorted, created by fitting together bits of other words, used with several different meanings at once, often drawn from several different languages at once, and fused in all sorts of ways to achieve whole clusters of meaning simultaneously. In fact, so many echoing suggestions can be found in every word or phrase that a full annotation of even a few pages would require a large book. It has taken the co-operative work of a number of devoted readers to make clear the complex interactions of the multiple puns and pun-clusters through which the ideas are projected, and every rereading reveals new meanings. It is true that many readers find the efforts of explication demanded by *Finnegans Wake* too arduous; some, indeed, feel that the law of diminishing returns has now begun to operate, and that the effort of both author and reader is disproportionate. Nevertheless, the book has great beauty and fascination even for the casual reader. Students are advised to read aloud—or to listen to the record of Joyce reading aloud—the extract printed in this anthology, in order to appreciate the degree to which the rhythms of the prose assist in conveying the meaning.

To an even greater extent than *Ulysses*, *Finnegans Wake* aims at embracing all of human history. The title is from an Irish-American ballad about Tom Finnegan, a hod carrier who falls off a ladder when drunk and is apparently killed, but who revives when during the "wake" (the watch by the dead body) someone spills whiskey on him. The theme of death and resurrection, of cycles of change coming round in the course of history, is central to *Finnegans Wake*, which derives one of its main principles of organization from the cyclical theory of history put forward in 1725 by the Italian philosopher Giambattista Vico. Vico held that history passes through four phases: the divine or theocratic, when people are governed by their awe of the supernatural; the aristocratic (the "heroic age" reflected in Homer and in *Beowulf*); the democratic and individualistic; and the final stage of chaos, a fall into confusion which startles man back into supernatural reverence and starts the process once again. Joyce, like Yeats, saw his own generation as in the final stage awaiting the shock that will bring man back to the first.

A mere account of the narrative line of *Finnegans Wake* cannot, of course, give any idea of the content of the work. If one explains that it opens with Finnegan's fall, then introduces his successor Humphrey Chimpden Earwicker, who is Everyman, and whose dream constitutes the novel; that he is presented as having guilt feelings about an indecency he committed (or may have committed) in Phoenix Park, Dublin; that his wife Anna Livia Plurabelle or ALP (who is also Eve, Iseult, Ireland, the River Liffey) changes her role just as he does; that he has two sons Shem and Shaun (or Jerry and Kevin), who represent introvert and extrovert, artist and practical man, creator and popularizer, and symbolize this basic dichotomy in human nature by all kinds of metamorphoses; and if one adds that, in the four books into which *Finnegans Wake* is divided (after Vico's pattern), actions comic or grotesque or sad or tender or desperate or passionate or terribly ordinary (and very often several of these things at the same time) take place with all the shifting meanings of a dream, so that characters change into others or into inanimate objects and the setting keeps shifting—if we explain all this, we still have said very little about what makes *Finnegans Wake* what it is. The dreamer, whose initials HCE indicate his universality ("Here Comes Everybody"), is at the same time a particular person, who keeps a pub in Chapelizod, a Dublin suburb on the River Liffey near Phoenix Park. His mysterious misdemeanor in Phoenix Park is in a sense Original Sin: Earwicker is Adam as well as a primeval giant, the Hill of Howth, the Great Parent ("Haveth Childers

Everywhere" is another expansion of HCE), and Man in History. Other characters who flit and change through the book, such as the Twelve Customers (who are also twelve jurymen and public opinion) and the Four Old Men (who are also judges, the authors of the four Gospels, and the four elements), help to weave the texture of multiple significance so characteristic of the work. But always it is the punning language, extending significance downwards—rather than the plot, developing it lengthwise—that bears the main load of meaning.

Araby[1]

North Richmond Street, being blind, was a quiet street except at the hour when the Christian Brothers' School set the boys free.[2] An uninhabited house of two storeys stood at the blind end, detached from its neighbours in a square ground. The other houses of the street, conscious of decent lives within them, gazed at one another with brown imperturbable faces.

The former tenant of our house, a priest, had died in the back drawing-room. Air, musty from having been long enclosed, hung in all the rooms, and the waste room behind the kitchen was littered with old useless papers. Among these I found a few paper-covered books, the pages of which were curled and damp: *The Abbot*, by Walter Scott, *The Devout Communicant* and *The Memoirs of Vidocq*.[3] I liked the last best because its leaves were yellow. The wild garden behind the house contained a central apple-tree and a few straggling bushes under one of which I found the late tenant's rusty bicycle-pump. He had been a very charitable priest; in his will he had left all his money to institutions and the furniture of his house to his sister.

When the short days of winter came dusk fell before we had well eaten our dinners. When we met in the street the houses had

---

1. The third of the fifteen stories in *Dubliners*. This tale of the frustrated quest for beauty in the midst of drabness is both meticulously realistic in its handling of details of Dublin life and the Dublin scene and highly symbolic in that almost every image and incident suggests some particular aspect of the theme (e.g., the suggestion of the Holy Grail in the image of the chalice, mentioned in the fifth paragraph). Joyce was drawing on his own childhood recollections, and the uncle in the story is a reminiscence of Joyce's father. But in all the stories in *Dubliners* dealing with childhood, the child lives not with his parents but with an uncle and aunt—a symbol of that isolation and lack of proper relation between "consubstantial" ("in the flesh") parents and children which is a major theme in Joyce's

work. The text is that established by Robert Scholes in his edition of *Dubliners*.
2. The Joyce family moved to 17 North Richmond Street, Dublin, in 1894, and Joyce had earlier briefly attended the Christian Brothers' school a few doors away (the Christian Brothers are a Catholic religious community). The details of the house described here correspond exactly to those of No. 17.
3. François Eugène Vidocq (1775–1857) had an extraordinary career as soldier, thief, chief of the French detective force, and private detective. *The Abbot* is a historical novel dealing with Mary Queen of Scots, *The Devout Communicant* a Catholic religious manual.

grown sombre. The space of sky above us was the colour of ever-changing violet and towards it the lamps of the street lifted their feeble lanterns. The cold air stung us and we played till our bodies glowed. Our shouts echoed in the silent street. The career of our play brought us through the dark muddy lanes behind the houses where we ran the gantlet of the rough tribes from the cottages, to the back doors of the dark dripping gardens where odours arose from the ashpits, to the dark odorous stables where a coachman smoothed and combed the horse or shook music from the buckled harness. When we returned to the street light from the kitchen windows had filled the areas. If my uncle was seen turning the corner we hid in the shadow until we had seen him safely housed. Or if Mangan's sister came out on the doorstep to call her brother in to his tea we watched her from our shadow peer up and down the street. We waited to see whether she would remain or go in and, if she remained, we left our shadow and walked up to Mangan's steps resignedly. She was waiting for us, her figure defined by the light from the half-opened door. Her brother always teased her before he obeyed and I stood by the railings looking at her. Her dress swung as she moved her body and the soft rope of her hair tossed from side to side.

Every morning I lay on the floor in the front parlour watching her door. The blind was pulled down to within an inch of the sash so that I could not be seen. When she came out on the doorstep my heart leaped. I ran to the hall, seized my books and followed her. I kept her brown figure always in my eye and, when we came near the point at which our ways diverged, I quickened my pace and passed her. This happened morning after morning. I had never spoken to her, except for a few casual words, and yet her name was like a summons to all my foolish blood.

Her image accompanied me even in places the most hostile to romance. On Saturday evenings when my aunt went marketing I had to go to carry some of the parcels. We walked through the flaring streets, jostled by drunken men and bargaining women, amid the curses of labourers, the shrill litanies of shop-boys who stood on guard by the barrels of pigs' cheeks, the nasal chanting of street-singers, who sang a *come-all-you*[4] about O'Donovan Rossa, or a ballad about the troubles in our native land. These noises converged in a single sensation of life for me: I imagined that I bore my chalice safely through a throng of foes. Her name sprang to my lips at moments in strange prayers and praises which I myself did not understand. My eyes were often full of tears (I could not tell why) and at times a flood from my heart seemed to pour itself out into

4. Street ballad, so called from its opening words. This one was about the 19th-century Irish nationalist Jeremiah Donovan, popularly known as O'Donovan Rossa.

my bosom. I thought little of the future. I did not know whether I would ever speak to her or not or, if I spoke to her, how I could tell her of my confused adoration. But my body was like a harp and her words and features were like fingers running upon the wires.

One evening I went into the back drawing-room in which the priest had died. It was a dark rainy evening and there was no sound in the house. Through one of the broken panes I heard the rain impinge upon the earth, the fine incessant needles of water playing in the sodden beds. Some distant lamp or lighted window gleamed below me. I was thankful that I could see so little. All my senses seemed to desire to veil themselves and, feeling that I was about to slip from them, I pressed the palms of my hands together until they trembled, murmuring: *O love! O love!* many times.

At last she spoke to me. When she addressed the first words to me I was so confused that I did not know what to answer. She asked me was I going to *Araby*.[5] I forget whether I answered yes or no. It would be a splendid bazaar, she said; she would love to go.

—And why can't you? I asked.

While she spoke she turned a silver bracelet round and round her wrist. She could not go, she said, because there would be a retreat[6] that week in her convent. Her brother and two other boys were fighting for their caps and I was alone at the railings. She held one of the spikes, bowing her head towards me. The light from the lamp opposite our door caught the white curve of her neck, lit up her hair that rested there and, falling, lit up the hand upon the railing. It fell over one side of her dress and caught the white border of a petticoat, just visible as she stood at ease.

—It's well for you, she said.

—If I go, I said, I will bring you something.

What innumerable follies laid waste my waking and sleeping thoughts after that evening! I wished to annihilate the tedious intervening days. I chafed against the work of school. At night in my bedroom and by day in the classroom her image came between me and the page I strove to read. The syllables of the word *Araby* were called to me through the silence in which my soul luxuriated and cast an Eastern enchantment over me. I asked for leave to go to the bazaar Saturday night. My aunt was surprised and hoped it was not some Freemason affair.[7] I answered few questions in class. I watched my master's face pass from amiability to sternness; he

5. The bazaar, described by its "official catalogue" as a "Grand Oriental Fête," was actually held in Dublin on May 14–19, 1894.

6. Period of seclusion from ordinary activities devoted to religious exercises; "her convent" is, of course, her convent school.

7. His aunt shares her church's distrust of the Freemasons, an old European secret society, reputedly anti-Catholic.

hoped I was not beginning to idle. I could not call my wandering thoughts together. I had hardly any patience with the serious work of life which, now that it stood between me and my desire, seemed to me child's play, ugly monotonous child's play.

On Saturday morning I reminded my uncle that I wished to go to the bazaar in the evening. He was fussing at the hallstand, looking for the hat-brush, and answered me curtly:

—Yes, boy, I know.

As he was in the hall I could not go into the front parlour and lie at the window. I left the house in bad humour and walked slowly towards the school. The air was pitilessly raw and already my heart misgave me.

When I came home to dinner my uncle had not yet been home. Still it was early. I sat staring at the clock for some time and, when its ticking began to irritate me, I left the room. I mounted the staircase and gained the upper part of the house. The high cold empty gloomy rooms liberated me and I went from room to room singing. From the front window I saw my companions playing below in the street. Their cries reached me weakened and indistinct and, leaning my forehead against the cool glass, I looked over at the dark house where she lived. I may have stood there for an hour, seeing nothing but the brown-clad figure cast by my imagination, touched discreetly by the lamplight at the curved neck, at the hand upon the railings and at the border below the dress.

When I came downstairs again I found Mrs Mercer sitting at the fire. She was an old garrulous woman, a pawnbroker's widow, who collected used stamps for some pious purpose. I had to endure the gossip of the tea-table. The meal was prolonged beyond an hour and still my uncle did not come. Mrs Mercer stood up to go: she was sorry she couldn't wait any longer, but it was after eight o'clock and she did not like to be out late, as the night air was bad for her. When she had gone I began to walk up and down the room, clenching my fists. My aunt said:

—I'm afraid you may put off your bazaar for this night of Our Lord.

At nine o'clock I heard my uncle's latchkey in the hall-door. I heard him talking to himself and heard the hall-stand rocking when it had received the weight of his overcoat. I could interpret these signs. When he was midway through his dinner I asked him to give me the money to go to the bazaar. He had forgotten.

—The people are in bed and after their first sleep now, he said.

I did not smile. My aunt said to him energetically:

—Can't you give him the money and let him go? You've kept him late enough as it is.

My uncle said he was very sorry he had forgotten. He said he believed in the old saying: *All work and no play makes Jack a dull boy.* He asked me where I was going and, when I had told him a second time he asked me did I know *The Arab's Farewell to his Steed.*[8] When I left the kitchen he was about to recite the opening lines of the piece to my aunt.

I held a florin tightly in my hand as I strode down Buckingham Street towards the station. The sight of the streets thronged with buyers and glaring with gas recalled to me the purpose of my journey. I took my seat in a third-class carriage of a deserted train. After an intolerable delay the train moved out of the station slowly. It crept onward among ruinous houses and over the twinkling river. At Westland Row Station a crowd of people pressed to the carriage doors; but the porters moved them back, saying that it was a special train for the bazaar. I remained alone in the bare carriage. In a few minutes the train drew up beside an improvised wooden platform. I passed out on to the road and saw by the lighted dial of a clock that it was ten minutes to ten. In front of me was a large building which displayed the magical name.

I could not find any sixpenny entrance and, fearing that the bazaar would be closed, I passed in quickly through a turnstile, handing a shilling to a weary-looking man. I found myself in a big hall girdled at half its height by a gallery. Nearly all the stalls were closed and the greater part of the hall was in darkness. I recognised a silence like that which pervades a church after a service. I walked into the centre of the bazaar timidly. A few people were gathered about the stalls which were still open. Before a curtain, over which the words *Café Chantant*[9] were written in coloured lamps, two men were counting money on a salver. I listened to the fall of the coins.

Remembering with difficulty why I had come I went over to one of the stalls and examined porcelain vases and flowered tea-sets. At the door of the stall a young lady was talking and laughing with two young gentlemen. I remarked their English accents and listened vaguely to their conversation.

—Oh, I never said such a thing!

—O, but you did!

—O, but I didn't!

—Didn't she say that?

—Yes. I heard her.

—O, there's a . . . fib!

Observing me the young lady came over and asked me did I wish

8. Once-popular sentimental poem by Caroline Norton.
9. Literally "singing café" (café pro-viding musical entertainment, popular early in this century).

to buy anything. The tone of her voice was not encouraging; she seemed to have spoken to me out of a sense of duty. I looked humbly at the great jars that stood like eastern guards at either side of the dark entrance to the stall and murmured:

—No, thank you.

The young lady changed the position of one of the vases and went back to the two young men. They began to talk of the same subject. Once or twice the young lady glanced at me over her shoulder.

I lingered before her stall, though I knew my stay was useless, to make my interest in her wares seem the more real. Then I turned away slowly and walked down the middle of the bazaar. I allowed the two pennies to fall against the sixpence in my pocket. I heard a voice call from one end of the gallery that the light was out. The upper part of the hall was now completely dark.

Gazing up into the darkness I saw myself as a creature driven and derided by vanity; and my eyes burned with anguish and anger.

1914

Counterparts[1]

The bell rang furiously and, when Miss Parker went to the tube,[2] a furious voice called out in a piercing North of Ireland accent:

—Send Farrington here!

Miss Parker returned to her machine, saying to a man who was writing at a desk:

—Mr Alleyne wants you upstairs.

The man muttered *Blast him!* under his breath and pushed back his chair to stand up. When he stood up he was tall and of great bulk. He had a hanging face, dark wine-coloured, with fair eyebrows and moustache: his eyes bulged forward slightly and the whites of them were dirty. He lifted up the counter and, passing by the clients, went out of the office with a heavy step.

He went heavily upstairs until he came to the second landing, where a door bore a brass plate with the inscription *Mr Alleyne*. Here he halted, puffing with labour and vexation, and knocked. The shrill voice cried:

—Come in!

The man entered Mr Alleyne's room. Simultaneously Mr Alleyne, a little man wearing gold-rimmed glasses on a cleanshaven face,

---

1. The ninth story in *Dubliners*. The text is that established by Robert Scholes.

2. Primitive telephone used for communication between different rooms in the same building.

shot his head up over a pile of documents. The head itself was so pink and hairless that it seemed like a large egg reposing on the papers. Mr Alleyne did not lose a moment:

—Farrington? What is the meaning of this? Why have I always to complain of you? May I ask you why you haven't made a copy of that contract between Bodley and Kirwan? I told you it must be ready by four o'clock.

—But Mr Shelley said, sir—

—*Mr Shelley said, sir*. . . . Kindly attend to what I say and not to what *Mr Shelley says, sir*. You have always some excuse or another for shirking work. Let me tell you that if the contract is not copied before this evening I'll lay the matter before Mr Crosbie. . . . Do you hear me now?

—Yes, sir.

—Do you hear me now? . . . Ay and another little matter! I might as well be talking to the wall as talking to you. Understand once for all that you get a half an hour for your lunch and not an hour and a half. How many courses do you want, I'd like to know. . . . Do you mind me, now?

—Yes, sir.

Mr Alleyne bent his head again upon his pile of papers. The man stared fixedly at the polished skull which directed the affairs of Crosbie & Alleyne, gauging its fragility. A spasm of rage gripped his throat for a few moments and then passed, leaving after it a sharp sensation of thirst. The man recognised the sensation and felt that he must have a good night's drinking. The middle of the month was passed and, if he could get the copy done in time, Mr Alleyne might give him an order on the cashier. He stood still, gazing fixedly at the head upon the pile of papers. Suddenly Mr Alleyne began to upset all the papers, searching for something. Then, as if he had been unaware of the man's presence till that moment, he shot up his head again, saying:

—Eh? Are you going to stand there all day? Upon my word, Farrington, you take things easy!

—I was waiting to see . . .

—Very good, you needn't wait to see. Go downstairs and do your work.

The man walked heavily towards the door and, as he went out of the room, he heard Mr Alleyne cry after him that if the contract was not copied by evening Mr Crosbie would hear of the matter.

He returned to his desk in the lower office and counted the sheets which remained to be copied. He took up his pen and dipped it in the ink but he continued to stare stupidly at the last words he had written: *In no case shall the said Bernard Bodley be* . . . The evening was falling and in a few minutes they would be lighting the gas: then he could write. He felt that he must slake the thirst in his throat. He stood up from his desk and, lifting the counter as before, passed out of the office. As he was passing out the chief clerk looked at him inquiringly.

—It's all right, Mr. Shelley, said the man, pointing with his finger to the objective of his journey.

The chief clerk glanced at the hat-rack but, seeing the row complete, offered no remark. As soon as he was on the landing the man pulled a shepherd's plaid cap out of his pocket, put it on his head and ran quickly down the rickety stairs. From the street door he walked on furtively on the inner side of the path towards the corner and all at once dived into a doorway. He was now safe in the dark snug of O'Neill's shop, and, filling up the little window that looked into the bar with his inflamed face, the colour of dark wine or dark meat, he called out:

—Here, Pat, give us a g.p.,[3] like a good fellow.

The curate[4] brought him a glass of plain porter. The man drank it at a gulp and asked for a caraway seed. He put his penny on the counter and, leaving the curate to grope for it in the gloom, retreated out of the snug as furtively as he had entered it.

Darkness, accompanied by a thick fog, was gaining upon the dusk of February and the lamps in Eustace Street had been lit. The man went up by the houses until he reached the door of the office, wondering whether he could finish his copy in time. On the stairs a moist pungent odour of perfumes saluted his nose: evidently Miss Delacour had come while he was out in O'Neill's. He crammed his cap back again into his pocket and re-entered the office, assuming an air of absent-mindedness.

—Mr Alleyne has been calling for you, said the chief clerk severely. Where were you?

The man glanced at the two clients who were standing at the counter as if to intimate that their presence prevented him from answering. As the clients were both male the chief clerk allowed himself a laugh.

—I know that game, he said. Five times in one day is a little bit. . . . Well, you better look sharp and get a copy of our correspondence in the Delacour case for Mr Alleyne.

This address in the presence of the public, his run upstairs and the porter he had gulped down so hastily confused the man and, as he sat down at his desk to get what was required, he realised how hopeless was the task of finishing his copy of the contract before half past five. The dark damp night was coming and he longed to

---

3. Glass of porter (a dark brown beer).   4. Barman.

spend it in the bars, drinking with his friends amid the glare of gas and the clatter of glasses. He got out the Delacour correspondence and passed out of the office. He hoped Mr Alleyne would not discover that the last two letters were missing.

The moist pungent perfume lay all the way up to Mr Alleyne's room. Miss Delacour was a middle-aged woman of Jewish appearance. Mr Alleyne was said to be sweet on her or on her money. She came to the office often and stayed a long time when she came. She was sitting beside his desk now in an aroma of perfumes, smoothing the handle of her umbrella and nodding the great black feather in her hat. Mr Alleyne had swivelled his chair round to face her and thrown his right foot jauntily upon his left knee. The man put the correspondence on the desk and bowed respectfully but neither Mr Alleyne nor Miss Delacour took any notice of his bow. Mr Alleyne tapped a finger on the correspondence and then flicked it towards him as if to say: *That's all right: you can go.*

The man returned to the lower office and sat down again at his desk. He stared intently at the incomplete phrase: *In no case shall the said Bernard Bodley be* . . . and thought how strange it was that the last three words began with the same letter. The chief clerk began to hurry Miss Parker, saying she would never have the letters typed in time for post. The man listened to the clicking of the machine for a few minutes and then set to work to finish his copy. But his head was not clear and his mind wandered away to the glare and rattle of the public-house. It was a night for hot punches. He struggled on with his copy, but when the clock struck five he had still fourteen pages to write. Blast it! He couldn't finish it in time. He longed to execrate aloud, to bring his fist down on something violently. He was so enraged that he wrote *Bernard Bernard* instead of *Bernard Bodley* and had to begin again on a clean sheet.

He felt strong enough to clear out the whole office singlehanded. His body ached to do something, to rush out and revel in violence. All the indignities of his life enraged him. . . . Could he ask the cashier privately for an advance? No, the cashier was no good, no damn good: he wouldn't give an advance. . . . He knew where he would meet the boys: Leonard and O'Halloran and Nosey Flynn. The barometer of his emotional nature was set for a spell of riot.

His imagination had so abstracted him that his name was called twice before he answered. Mr Alleyne and Miss Delacour were standing outside the counter and all the clerks had turned round in anticipation of something. The man got up from his desk. Mr Alleyne began a tirade of abuse, saying that two letters were missing. The man answered that he knew nothing about them, that he had made a faithful copy. The tirade continued: it was so bitter and violent that the man could hardly restrain his fist from descending upon the head of the manikin before him.

—I know nothing about any other two letters, he said stupidly.

—*You—know—nothing*. Of course you know nothing, said Mr Alleyne. Tell me, he added, glancing first for approval to the lady beside him, do you take me for a fool? Do you think me an utter fool?

The man glanced from the lady's face to the little egg-shaped head and back again; and, almost before he was aware of it, his tongue had found a felicitous moment:

—I don't think, sir, he said, that that's a fair question to put to me.

There was a pause in the very breathing of the clerks. Everyone was astounded (the author of the witticism no less than his neighbours) and Miss Delacour, who was a stout amiable person, began to smile broadly. Mr Alleyne flushed to the hue of a wild rose and his mouth twitched with a dwarf's passion. He shook his fist in the man's face till it seemed to vibrate like the knob of some electric machine:

—You impertinent ruffian! You impertinent ruffian! I'll make short work of you! Wait till you see! You'll apologise to me for your impertinence or you'll quit the office instanter! You'll quit this, I'm telling you, or you'll apologise to me!

.   .   .   .

He stood in a doorway opposite the office watching to see if the cashier would come out alone. All the clerks passed out and finally the cashier came out with the chief clerk. It was no use trying to say a word to him when he was with the chief clerk. The man felt that his position was bad enough. He had been obliged to offer an abject apology to Mr Alleyne for his impertinence but he knew what a hornet's nest the office would be for him. He could remember the way in which Mr Alleyne had hounded little Peake out of the office in order to make room for his own nephew. He felt savage and thirsty and revengeful, annoyed with himself and with everyone else. Mr Alleyne would never give him an hour's rest; his life would be a hell to him. He had made a proper fool of himself this time. Could he not keep his tongue in his cheek? But they had never pulled together from the first, he and Mr Alleyne, ever since the day Mr Alleyne had overheard him mimicking his North of Ireland accent to amuse Higgins and Miss Parker: that had been the beginning of it. He might have tried Higgins for the money, but sure Higgins never had anything for himself. A man with two establishments to keep up, of course he couldn't. . . .

He felt his great body again aching for the comfort of the public-house. The fog had begun to chill him and he wondered could he touch Pat in O'Neill's. He could not touch him for more than a bob—and a bob was no use. Yet he must get money somewhere or other: he had spent his last penny for the g.p. and soon it would be too late for getting money anywhere. Suddenly, as he was fingering his watch-chain, he thought of Terry Kelly's pawn-office in Fleet Street. That was the dart! Why didn't he think of it sooner?

He went through the narrow alley of Temple Bar quickly, muttering to himself that they could all go to hell because he was going to have a good night of it. The clerk in Terry Kelly's said *A crown!* but the consignor held out for six shillings; and in the end the six shillings was allowed him literally. He came out of the pawn-office joyfully, making a little cylinder of the coins between his thumb and fingers. In Westmoreland Street the footpaths were crowded with young men and women returning from business and ragged urchins ran here and there yelling out the names of the evening editions. The man passed through the crowd, looking on the spectacle generally with proud satisfaction and staring masterfully at the office-girls. His head was full of the noises of tram-gongs and swishing trolleys and his nose already sniffed the curling fumes of punch. As he walked on he preconsidered the terms in which he would narrate the incident to the boys:

—So, I just looked at him—coolly, you know, and looked at her. Then I looked back at him again—taking my time, you know. *I don't think that that's a fair question to put to me,* says I.

Nosey Flynn was sitting up in his usual corner of Davy Byrne's and, when he heard the story, he stood Farrington a half-one, saying it was as smart a thing as ever he heard. Farrington stood a drink in his turn. After a while O'Halloran and Paddy Leonard came in and the story was repeated to them. O'Halloran stood tailors[5] of malt, hot, all round and told the story of the retort he had made to the chief clerk when he was in Callan's of Fownes's Street; but, as the retort was after the manner of the liberal shepherds in the eclogues,[6] he had to admit that it was not so clever as Farrington's retort. At this Farrington told the boys to polish off that and have another.

Just as they were naming their poisons who should come in but Higgins! Of course he had to join in with the others. The men asked him to give his version of it, and he did so with great vivacity for the sight of five small hot whiskies was very exhilarating. Everyone roared laughing when he showed the way in which Mr Alleyne

5. Tall glasses.
6. Eclogues are pastoral poems, but the reference is to *Hamlet* V.i.168. "Liberal" here means free-spoken.

shook his fist in Farrington's face. Then he imitated Farrington, saying, *And here was my nabs, as cool as you please,* while Farrington looked at the company out of his heavy dirty eyes, smiling and at times drawing forth stray drops of liquor from his moustache with the aid of his lower lip.

When that round was over there was a pause. O'Halloran had money but neither of the other two seemed to have any; so the whole party left the shop somewhat regretfully. At the corner of Duke Street Higgins and Nosey Flynn bevelled off to the left while the other three turned back towards the city. Rain was drizzling down on the cold streets and, when they reached the Ballast Office, Farrington suggested the Scotch House. The bar was full of men and loud with the noise of tongues and glasses. The three men pushed past the whining match-sellers at the door and formed a little party at the corner of the counter. They began to exchange stories. Leonard introduced them to a young fellow named Weathers who was performing at the Tivoli as an acrobat and knockabout *artiste.*[7] Farrington stood a drink all round. Weathers said he would take a small Irish and Apollinaris. Farrington, who had definite notions of what was what, asked the boys would they have an Apollinaris too; but the boys told Tim to make theirs hot. The talk became theatrical. O'Halloran stood a round and then Farrington stood another round, Weathers protesting that the hospitality was too Irish. He promised to get them in behind the scenes and introduce them to some nice girls. O'Halloran said that he and Leonard would go but that Farrington wouldn't go because he was a married man; and Farrington's heavy dirty eyes leered at the company in token that he understood he was being chaffed. Weathers made them all have just one little tincture at his expense and promised to meet them later on at Mulligan's in Poolbeg Street.

When the Scotch House closed they went round to Mulligan's. They went into the parlour at the back and O'Halloran ordered small hot specials all round. They were all beginning to feel mellow. Farrington was just standing another round when Weathers came back. Much to Farrington's relief he drank a glass of bitter this time. Funds were running low but they had enough to keep them going. Presently two young women with big hats and a young man in a check suit came in and sat at a table close by. Weathers saluted them and told the company that they were out of the Tivoli. Farrington's eyes wandered at every moment in the direction of one of the young women. There was something striking in her appearance. An immense scarf of peacock-blue muslin was wound round her hat and knotted in a great bow under her chin; and she wore bright

---

7. General music-hall performer.

yellow gloves, reaching to the elbow. Farrington gazed admiringly at the plump arm which she moved very often and with much grace; and when, after a little time, she answered his gaze he admired still more her large dark brown eyes. The oblique staring expression in them fascinated him. She glanced at him once or twice and, when the party was leaving the room, she brushed against his chair and said O' *pardon!* in a London accent. He watched her leave the room in the hope that she would look back at him, but he was disappointed. He cursed his want of money and cursed all the rounds he had stood, particularly all the whiskies and Apollinaris which he had stood to Weathers. If there was one thing that he hated it was a sponge. He was so angry that he lost count of the conversation of his friends.

When Paddy Leonard called him he found that they were talking about feats of strength. Weathers was showing his biceps muscle to the company and boasting so much that the other two had called on Farrington to uphold the national honour. Farrington pulled up his sleeve accordingly and showed his biceps muscle to the company. The two arms were examined and compared and finally it was agreed to have a trial of strength. The table was cleared and the two men rested their elbows on it, clasping hands. When Paddy Leonard said Go! each was to try to bring down the other's hand on to the table. Farrington looked very serious and determined.

The trial began. After about thirty seconds Weathers brought his opponent's hand slowly down on to the table. Farrington's dark wine-coloured face flushed darker still with anger and humiliation at having been defeated by such a stripling.

—You're not to put the weight of your body behind it. Play fair, he said.

—Who's not playing fair? said the other.

—Come on again. The two best out of three.

The trial began again. The veins stood out on Farrington's forehead, and the pallor of Weathers' complexion changed to peony. Their hands and arms trembled under the stress. After a long struggle Weathers again brought his opponent's hand slowly on to the table. There was a murmur of applause from the spectators. The curate, who was standing beside the table, nodded his red head towards the victor and said with loutish familiarity:

—Ah! that's the knack!

—What the hell do you know about it? said Farrington fiercely, turning on the man. What do you put in your gab for?

—Sh, sh! said O'Halloran, observing the violent expression of Farrington's face. Pony up, boys. We'll have just one little smahan more and then we'll be off.

A very sullen-faced man stood at the corner of O'Connell Bridge waiting for the little Sandymount tram to take him home. He was full of smouldering anger and revengefulness. He felt humiliated and discontented; he did not even feel drunk; and he had only twopence in his pocket. He cursed everything. He had done for himself in the office, pawned his watch, spent all his money; and he had not even got drunk. He began to feel thirsty again and he longed to be back again in the hot reeking public-house. He had lost his reputation as a strong man, having been defeated twice by a mere boy. His heart swelled with fury and, when he thought of the woman in the big hat who had brushed against him and said *Pardon!* his fury nearly choked him.

His tram let him down at Shelbourne Road and he steered his great body along in the shadow of the wall of the barracks. He loathed returning to his home. When he went in by the side-door he found the kitchen empty and the kitchen fire nearly out. He bawled upstairs:

—Ada! Ada!

His wife was a little sharp-faced woman who bullied her husband when he was sober and was bullied by him when he was drunk. They had five children. A little boy came running down the stairs.

—Who is that? said the man, peering through the darkness.

—Me, pa.

—Who are you? Charlie?

—No, pa. Tom.

—Where's your mother?

—She's out at the chapel.

—That's right. . . . Did she think of leaving any dinner for me?

—Yes, pa. I—

—Light the lamp. What do you mean by having the place in darkness? Are the other children in bed?

The man sat down heavily on one of the chairs while the little boy lit the lamp. He began to mimic his son's flat accent, saying half to himself: *At the chapel. At the chapel, if you please!* When the lamp was lit he banged his fist on the table and shouted:

—What's for my dinner?

—I'm going . . . to cook it, pa, said the little boy.

The man jumped up furiously and pointed to the fire.

—On that fire! You let the fire out! By God, I'll teach you to do that again!

He took a step to the door and seized the walking-stick which was standing behind it.

—I'll teach you to let the fire out! he said, rolling up his sleeve in order to give his arm free play.

The little boy cried O, *pa!* and ran whimpering round the table, but the man followed him and caught him by the coat. The little boy looked about him wildly but, seeing no way of escape fell upon his knees.

—Now, you'll let the fire out the next time! said the man, striking him viciously with the stick. Take that, you little whelp!

The boy uttered a squeal of pain as the stick cut his thigh. He clasped his hands together in the air and his voice shook with fright.

—O, pa! he cried. Don't beat me, pa! And I'll . . . I'll say a *Hail Mary* for you. . . . I'll say a *Hail Mary* for you, pa, if you don't beat me. . . . I'll say a *Hail Mary*. . . .

1914

From A Portrait of the Artist as a Young Man[1]

[*The Interview with the Director*]

The director stood in the embrasure of the window, his back to the light, leaning an elbow on the brown crossblind, and, as he spoke and smiled, slowly dangling and looping the cord of the other blind, Stephen stood before him, following for a moment with his eyes the waning of the long summer daylight above the roofs or

1. *A Portrait of the Artist as a Young Man* is the story of the development of Stephen Dedalus from earliest childhood until his full realization of his destiny as artist and of the implications of that destiny. There is a considerable amount of autobiography in the book, but it is far from straight autobiography. Everything is organized to show the parallel development of artist and exile: for Joyce, the writer can only achieve the objectivity proper to an artist by totally withdrawing from all implication in the life of the community from which he is to draw his material. In the novel Stephen rejects one by one his home, his religion, his country, growing ever more aloof and independent, exclaiming "*Non serviam*" ("I will not serve") to all the representatives of orthodoxy and convention, and even to the claims of friendship and personal affection. Stephen the artist comes into being at the moment when he has successfully resisted the temptation to enter the Jesuit order: he suddenly realizes that he is born to dwell apart, to look objectively on the world of men and record their doings with the artist's disinterested craftsmanship. He might well have become a priest, but the choice lay only between priest and artist, between "the

power of the keys, the power to bind and loose from sin," and the artist's godlike power to re-create the world with the word. That is why Stephen's rejection of the call to join the Jesuit order preludes the climax of the *Portrait* (which comes at the end of the second extract here printed). The first extract shows Stephen's response to that call, and the second shows him shortly afterwards experiencing his first true aesthetic vision as he looks at the girl standing with kilted skirts in the water and sees her without the desire either to possess or to convert but with the artist's joy in the presence of her reality.

As so often, Joyce in this book combines meticulous realism of detail with a persistent symbolism. The hero's name, for example, is itself symbolic. Stephen was the first Christian martyr, and in Greek mythology Daedalus was the first craftsman (or artist: the Greeks had one word for both), who made the labyrinth for King Minos at Crete; later, when Minos turned against him, he made himself wings and escaped by flying across the sea—symbol for Joyce of the artist's flight into necessary exile. The name "Daedalus" means "cunning craftsman": the artist for Joyce was both martyr and pioneer craftsman.

the slow deft movements of the priestly fingers. The priest's face was in total shadow, but the waning daylight from behind him touched the deeply grooved temples and the curves of the skull. Stephen followed also with his ears the accents and intervals of the priest's voice as he spoke gravely and cordially of indifferent themes, the vacation which had just ended, the colleges of the order abroad, the transference of masters. The grave and cordial voice went on easily with its tale, and in the pauses Stephen felt bound to set it on again with respectful questions. He knew that the tale was a prelude and his mind waited for the sequel. Ever since the message of summons had come for him from the director his mind had struggled to find the meaning of the message; and during the long restless time he had sat in the college parlour waiting for the director to come in his eyes had wandered from one sober picture to another around the walls and his mind wandered from one guess to another until the meaning of the summons had almost become clear. Then, just as he was wishing that some unforeseen cause might prevent the director from coming, he had heard the handle of the door turning and the swish of a soutane.[2]

The director had begun to speak of the Dominican and Franciscan orders and of the friendship between Saint Thomas and Saint Bonaventure.[3] The Capuchin dress, he thought, was rather too . . .

Stephen's face gave back the priest's indulgent smile and, not being anxious to give an opinion, he made a slight dubitative movement with his lips.

—I believe, continued the director, that there is some talk now among the Capuchins themselves of doing away with it and following the example of the other Franciscans.

—I suppose they would retain it in the cloisters? said Stephen.

—O, certainly, said the director. For the cloister it is all right, but for the street I really think it would be better to do away with, don't you?

—It must be troublesome, I imagine?

—Of course it is, of course. Just imagine when I was in Belgium I used to see them out cycling in all kinds of weather with this thing up about their knees! It was really ridiculous. *Les jupes*,[4] they call them in Belgium.

The vowel was so modified as to be indistinct.

—What do they call them?

—*Les jupes*.

2. Cassock.
3. St. Bonaventure, Italian Scholastic philosopher (known as "the seraphic doctor"), became general of the Franciscan order in 1256; his contemporary, St. Thomas Aquinas (*doctor angelicus*, or "the angelic doctor"), lead-

ing Scholastic philosopher, was a member of the Dominican order. The Capuchins were a special order of Franciscans, so called from the long pointed "capuche," or hood, which they wore.
4. Skirts.

—O!

Stephen smiled again in answer to the smile which he could not see on the priest's shadowed face, its image or spectre only passing rapidly across his mind as the low discreet accent fell upon his ear. He gazed calmly before him at the waning sky, glad of the cool of the evening and the faint yellow glow which hid the tiny flame kindling upon his cheek.

The names of articles of dress worn by women or of certain soft and delicate stuffs used in their making brought always to his mind a delicate and sinful perfume. As a boy he had imagined the reins by which horses are driven as slender silken bands and it shocked him to feel at Stradbrooke the greasy leather of harness. It had shocked him, too, when he had felt for the first time beneath his tremulous fingers the brittle texture of a woman's stocking for, retaining nothing of all he read save that which seemed to him an echo or a prophecy of his own state, it was only amid softworded phrases or within rosesoft stuffs that he dared to conceive of the soul or body of a woman moving with tender life.

But the phrase on the priest's lips was disingenuous for he knew that a priest should not speak lightly on that theme. The phrase had been spoken lightly with design and he felt that his face was being searched by the eyes in the shadow. Whatever he had heard or read of the craft of jesuits he had put aside frankly as not borne out by his own experience. His masters, even when they had not attracted him, had seemed to him always intelligent and serious priests, athletic and highspirited prefects. He thought of them as men who washed their bodies briskly with cold water and wore clean cold linen. During all the years he had lived among them in Clongowes[5] and in Belvedere he had received only two pandies[6] and, though these had been dealt him in the wrong, he knew that he had often escaped punishment. During all those years he had never heard from any of his masters a flippant word: it was they who had taught him christian doctrine and urged him to live a good life and, when he had fallen into grievous sin, it was they who had led him back to grace. Their presence had made him diffident of himself when he was a muff in Clongowes and it had made him diffident of himself also while he had held his equivocal position in Belvedere. A constant sense of this had remained with him up to the last year of his school life. He had never once disobeyed or allowed turbulent companions to seduce him from his habit of quiet obedience: and, even when he doubted some statement of a master, he had never presumed to doubt openly. Lately some of their judgments had sounded a little childish in his ears

5. The Jesuit school which Stephen (and the young Joyce) attended before going to Belvedere College.

6. Hard blows on the palm of the hand (for punishment).

and had made him feel a regret and pity as though he were slowly passing out of an accustomed world and were hearing its language for the last time. One day when some boys had gathered round a priest under the shed near the chapel, he heard the priest say:

—I believe that Lord Macaulay was a man who probably never committed a mortal sin in his life, that is to say, a deliberate mortal sin.[7]

Some of the boys had then asked the priest if Victor Hugo were not the greatest French writer. The priest had answered that Victor Hugo had never written half so well when he had turned against the church as he had written when he was a catholic.

—But there are many eminent French critics, said the priest, who consider that even Victor Hugo, great as he certainly was, had not so pure a French style as Louis Veuillot.[8]

The tiny flame which the priest's allusion had kindled upon Stephen's cheek had sunk down again and his eyes were still fixed calmly on the colourless sky. But an unresting doubt flew hither and thither before his mind. Masked memories passed quickly before him: he recognised scenes and persons yet he was conscious that he had failed to perceive some vital circumstance in them. He saw himself walking about the grounds watching the sports in Clongowes and eating slim jim out of his cricket-cap. Some jesuits were walking round the cycletrack in the company of ladies. The echoes of certain expressions used in Clongowes sounded in remote caves of his mind.

His ears were listening to these distant echoes amid the silence of the parlour when he became aware that the priest was addressing him in a different voice.

—I sent for you today, Stephen, because I wished to speak to you on a very important subject.

—Yes, sir.

—Have you ever felt that you had a vocation?

Stephen parted his lips to answer yes and then withheld the word suddenly. The priest waited for the answer and added:

—I mean have you ever felt within yourself, in your soul, a desire to join the order. Think.

—I have sometimes thought of it, said Stephen.

The priest let the blindcord fall to one side and, uniting his hands, leaned his chin gravely upon them, communing with himself.

—In a college like this, he said at length, there is one boy or perhaps two or three boys whom God calls to the religious life.

---

7. The life of the Whig historian Thomas Babington Macaulay (1800–59) was noted for its purity.
8. A 19th-century French journalist and leader of the French "Ultramontanes" (who supported the Pope's claim to be spiritual head of the church everywhere).

Such a boy is marked off from his companions by his piety, by the good example he shows to others. He is looked up to by them; he is chosen perhaps as prefect by his fellow sodalists. And you, Stephen, have been such a boy in this college, prefect of Our Blessed Lady's sodality.[9] Perhaps you are the boy in this college whom God designs to call to Himself.

A strong note of pride reinforcing the gravity of the priest's voice made Stephen's heart quicken in response. —To receive that call, Stephen, said the priest, is the greatest honour that the Almighty God can bestow upon a man. No king or emperor on this earth has the power of the priest of God. No angel or archangel in heaven, no saint, not even the Blessed Virgin herself has the power of a priest of God: the power of the keys, the power to bind and to loose from sin, the power of exorcism, the power to cast out from the creatures of God the evil spirits that have power over them, the power, the authority, to make the great God of Heaven come down upon the altar and take the form of bread and wine. What an awful power, Stephen!

A flame began to flutter again on Stephen's cheek as he heard in this proud address an echo of his own proud musings. How often had he seen himself as a priest wielding calmly and humbly the awful power of which angels and saints stood in reverence! His soul had loved to muse in secret on this desire. He had seen himself, a young and silentmannered priest, entering a confessional swiftly, ascending the altarsteps, incensing, genuflecting, accomplishing the vague acts of the priesthood which pleased him by reason of their semblance of reality and of their distance from it. In that dim life which he had lived through in his musings he had assumed the voices and gestures which he had noted with various priests. He had bent his knee sideways like such a one, he had shaken the thurible[1] only slightly like such a one, his chasuble[2] had swung open like that of such another as he turned to the altar again after having blessed the people. And above all it had pleased him to fill the second place in those dim scenes of his imagining. He shrank from the dignity of celebrant because it displeased him to imagine that all the vague pomp should end in his own person or that the ritual should assign to him so clear and final an office. He longed for the minor sacred offices, to be vested with the tunicle of subdeacon at high mass, to stand aloof from the altar, forgotten by the people, his shoulders covered with a humeral veil,[3] holding the paten within its folds or, when the sacrifice had been accomplished, to stand as

---

9. A religious fellowship.
1. Censer (container in which incense is burned).
2. Sleeveless outer garment worn by celebrant at Mass.

3. Veil covering the shoulders. "Paten": plate on which bread is placed in celebration of the Eucharist (Holy Communion).

deacon in a dalmatic of cloth of gold on the step below the celebrant, his hands joined and his face towards the people, and sing the chant, *Ite missa est*.[4] If ever he had seen himself celebrant it was as in the pictures of the mass in his child's massbook, in a church without worshippers, save for the angel of the sacrifice, at a bare altar and served by an acolyte scarcely more boyish than himself. In vague sacrificial or sacramental acts alone his will seemed drawn to go forth to encounter reality: and it was partly the absence of an appointed rite which had always constrained him to inaction whether he had allowed silence to cover his anger or pride or had suffered only an embrace he longed to give.

He listened in reverent silence now to the priest's appeal and through the words he heard even more distinctly a voice bidding him approach, offering him secret knowledge and secret power. He would know then what was the sin of Simon Magus[5] and what the sin against the Holy Ghost for which there was no forgiveness. He would know obscure things, hidden from others, from those who were conceived and born children of wrath. He would know the sins, the sinful longings and sinful thoughts and sinful acts, of others, hearing them murmured into his ears in the confessional under the shame of a darkened chapel by the lips of women and of girls: but rendered immune mysteriously at his ordination by the imposition of hands his soul would pass again uncontaminated to the white peace of the altar. No touch of sin would linger upon the hands with which he would elevate and break the host; no touch of sin would linger on his lips in prayer to make him eat and drink damnation to himself not discerning the body of the Lord. He would hold his secret knowledge and secret power, being as sinless as the innocent: and he would be a priest for ever according to the order of Melchisedec.[6]

—I will offer up my mass tomorrow morning, said the director, that Almighty God may reveal to you His holy will. And let you, Stephen, make a novena[7] to your holy patron saint, the first martyr who is very powerful with God, that God may enlighten your mind. But you must be quite sure, Stephen, that you have a vocation because it would be terrible if you found afterwards that you had none. Once a priest always a priest, remember. Your catechism tells you that the sacrament of Holy Orders is one of those which can be received only once because it imprints on the soul an indelible

---

4. "Go; it is sent forth." The traditional formula of dismissal at the end of the Mass.
5. The Simon who offered money in order to be given the power of laying on of hands possessed by the apostles (see Acts viii.18–19).
6. "Thou art a priest forever after the order of Melchisedec" (Hebrews v.6). Cf. Genesis xiv.18: "And Melchizedek king of Salem brought forth bread and wine: and he was the priest of the most high God."
7. Devotion consisting of prayers on nine consecutive days.

spiritual mark which can never be effaced. It is before you must weigh well, not after. It is a solemn question, Stephen, because on it may depend the salvation of your eternal soul. But we will pray to God together.

He held open the heavy hall door and gave his hand as if already to a companion in the spiritual life. Stephen passed out on to the wide platform above the steps and was conscious of the caress of mild evening air. Towards Findlater's church a quartette of young men were striding along with linked arms, swaying their heads and stepping to the agile melody of their leader's concertina. The music passed in an instant, as the first bars of sudden music always did, over the fantastic fabrics of his mind, dissolving them painlessly and noiselessly as a sudden wave dissolves the sandbuilt turrets of children. Smiling at the trivial air he raised his eyes to the priest's face and, seeing in it a mirthless reflection of the sunken day, detached his hand slowly which had acquiesced faintly in that companionship.

As he descended the steps the impression which effaced his troubled selfcommunion was that of a mirthless mask reflecting a sunken day from the threshold of the college. The shadow, then, of the life of the college passed gravely over his consciousness. It was a grave and ordered and passionless life that awaited him, a life without material cares. He wondered how he would pass the first night in the novitiate and with what dismay he would wake the first morning in the dormitory. The troubling odour of the long corridors of Clongowes came back to him and he heard the discreet murmur of the burning gasflames. At once from every part of his being unrest began to irradiate. A feverish quickening of his pulses followed and a din of meaningless words drove his reasoned thoughts hither and thither confusedly. His lungs dilated and sank as if he were inhaling a warm moist unsustaining air, and he smelt again the moist warm air which hung in the bath in Clongowes above the sluggish turfcoloured water.

Some instinct, waking at these memories, stronger than education or piety quickened within him at every near approach to that life, an instinct subtle and hostile, and armed him against acquiescence. The chill and order of the life repelled him. He saw himself rising in the cold of the morning and filing down with the others to early mass and trying vainly to struggle with his prayers against the fainting sickness of his stomach. He saw himself sitting at dinner with the community of a college. What, then, had become of that deeprooted shyness of his which had made him loth to eat or drink under a strange roof? What had come of the pride of his spirit which had always made him conceive himself as a being apart in every order?

The Reverend Stephen Dedalus, S. J.[8]

His name in that new life leaped into characters before his eyes and to it there followed a mental sensation of an undefined face or colour of a face. The colour faded and became strong like a changing glow of pallid brick red. Was it the raw reddish glow he had so often seen on wintry mornings on the shaven gills of the priests? The face was eyeless and sourfavoured and devout, shot with pink tinges of suffocated anger. Was it not a mental spectre of the face of one of the jesuits whom some of the boys called Lantern Jaws and others Foxy Campbell?

He was passing at that moment before the jesuit house in Gardiner Street, and wondered vaguely which window would be his if he ever joined the order. Then he wondered at the vagueness of his wonder, at the remoteness of his soul from what he had hitherto imagined her sanctuary, at the frail hold which so many years of order and obedience had of him when once a definite and irrevocable act of his threatened to end for ever, in time and in eternity, his freedom. The voice of the director urging upon him the proud claims of the church and the mystery and power of the priestly office repeated itself idly in his memory. His soul was not there to hear and greet it and he knew now that the exhortation he had listened to had already fallen into an idle formal tale. He would never swing the thurible before the tabernacle as priest. His destiny was to be elusive of social or religious orders. The wisdom of the priest's appeal did not touch him to the quick. He was destined to learn his own wisdom apart from others or to learn the wisdom of others himself wandering among the snares of the world.

The snares of the world were its ways of sin. He would fall. He had not yet fallen but he would fall silently, in an instant. Not to fall was too hard, too hard: and he felt the silent lapse of his soul, as it would be at some instant to come, falling, falling, but not yet fallen, still unfallen, but about to fall.

[The Walk on the Shore]

He could wait no longer.

From the door of Byron's publichouse to the gate of Clontarf Chapel, from the gate of Clontarf Chapel to the door of Byron's publichouse, and then back again to the chapel and then back again to the publichouse he had paced slowly at first, planting his steps scrupulously in the spaces of the patchwork of the footpath, then timing their fall to the fall of verses. A full hour had passed since his father had gone in with Dan Crosby, the tutor, to find out for him something about the university. For a full hour he had paced up and down, waiting: but he could wait no longer.

8. Society of Jesus (the Jesuit order).

He set off abruptly for the Bull,[9] walking rapidly lest his father's shrill whistle might call him back; and in a few moments he had rounded the curve at the police barrack and was safe.

Yes, his mother was hostile to the idea, as he had read from her listless silence. Yet her mistrust pricked him more keenly than his father's pride and he thought coldly how he had watched the faith which was fading down in his soul aging and strengthening in her eyes. A dim antagonism gathered force within him and darkened his mind as a cloud against her disloyalty: and when it passed, cloudlike, leaving his mind serene and dutiful towards her again, he was made aware dimly and without regret of a first noiseless sundering of their lives.

The university! So he had passed beyond the challenge of the sentries who had stood as guardians of his boyhood and had sought to keep him among them that he might be subject to them and serve their ends. Pride after satisfaction uplifted him like long slow waves. The end he had been born to serve yet did not see had led him to escape by an unseen path: and now it beckoned to him once more and a new adventure was about to be opened to him. It seemed to him that he heard notes of fitful music leaping upwards a tone and downwards a diminished fourth, upwards a tone and downwards a major third, like triple-branching flames leaping fitfully, flame after flame, out of a midnight wood. It was an elfin prelude, endless and formless; and, as it grew wilder and faster, the flames leaping out of time, he seemed to hear from under the boughs and grasses wild creatures racing, their feet pattering like rain upon the leaves. Their feet passed in pattering tumult over his mind, the feet of hares and rabbits, the feet of harts and hinds and antelopes, until he heard them no more and remembered only a proud cadence from Newman:[1]—

—Whose feet are as the feet of harts and underneath the everlasting arms.

The pride of that dim image brought back to his mind the dignity of the office he had refused. All through his boyhood he had mused upon that which he had so often thought to be his destiny and when the moment had come for him to obey the call he had turned aside, obeying a wayward instinct. Now time lay between: the oils of ordination would never anoint his body. He had refused. Why?

He turned seaward from the road at Dollymount and as he passed on to the thin wooden bridge he felt the planks shaking with the tramp of heavily shod feet. A squad of Christian Brothers was on its way back from the Bull and had begun to pass, two by two,

9. The places and buildings referred to in this extract are all in Dublin. The Bull is a long tongue of land by the sea, fortified to form a protecting sea wall.

1. John Henry Cardinal Newman.

across the bridge. Soon the whole bridge was trembling and resounding. The uncouth faces passed him two by two, stained yellow or red or livid by the sea, and as he strove to look at them with ease and indifference, a faint stain of personal shame and commiseration rose to his own face. Angry with himself he tried to hide his face from their eyes by gazing down sideways into the shallow swirling water under the bridge but he still saw a reflection therein of their topheavy silk hats, and humble tapelike collars and loosely hanging clerical clothes.

—Brother Hickey.

Brother Quaid.

Brother MacArdle.

Brother Keogh.

Their piety would be like their names, like their faces, like their clothes; and it was idle for him to tell himself that their humble and contrite hearts,[2] it might be, paid a far richer tribute of devotion than his had ever been, a gift tenfold more acceptable than his elaborate adoration. It was idle for him to move himself to be generous towards them, to tell himself that if he ever came to their gates, stripped of his pride, beaten and in beggar's weeds, that they would be generous towards him, loving him as themselves. Idle and embittering, finally, to argue, against his own dispassionate certitude, that the commandment of love bade us not to love our neighbour as ourselves with the same amount and intensity of love but to love him as ourselves with the same kind of love.

He drew forth a phrase from his treasure and spoke it softly to himself:

—A day of dappled seaborne clouds.—

The phrase and the day and the scene harmonised in a chord. Words. Was it their colours? He allowed them to glow and fade, hue after hue: sunrise gold, the russet and green of apple orchards, azure of waves, the greyfringed fleece of clouds. No, it was not their colours: it was the poise and balance of the period itself. Did he then love the rhythmic rise and fall of words better than their associations of legend and colour? Or was it that, being as weak of sight as he was shy of mind, he drew less pleasure from the reflection of the glowing sensible world through the prism of a language manycoloured and richly storied than from the contemplation of an inner world of individual emotions mirrored perfectly in a lucid supple periodic prose?

He passed from the trembling bridge on to firm land again. At that instant, as it seemed to him, the air was chilled; and looking

---

2. "The sacrifices of God are a broken spirit: a broken and a contrite heart, O God, thou wilt not despise" (Psalms li.17).

askance towards the water he saw a flying squall darkening and crisping suddenly the tide. A faint click at his heart, a faint throb in his throat told him once more of how his flesh dreaded the cold infra-human odour of the sea: yet he did not strike across the downs on his left but held straight on along the spine of rocks that pointed against the river's mouth.

A veiled sunlight lit up faintly the grey sheet of water where the river was embayed. In the distance along the course of the slow-flowing Liffey slender masts flecked the sky and, more distant still, the dim fabric of the city lay prone in haze. Like a scene on some vague arras, old as man's weariness, the image of the seventh city of Christendom was visible to him across the timeless air, no older nor more weary nor less patient of subjection than in the days of the thingmote.[3]

Disheartened, he raised his eyes towards the slowdrifting clouds, dappled and seaborne. They were voyaging across the deserts of the sky, a host of nomads on the march, voyaging high over Ireland, westward bound. The Europe they had come from lay out there beyond the Irish Sea, Europe of strange tongues and valleyed and woodbegirt and citadelled and of entrenched and marshalled races. He heard a confused music within him as of memories and names which he was almost conscious of but could not capture even for an instant; then the music seemed to recede, to recede, to recede: and from each receding trail of nebulous music there fell always one long-drawn calling note, piercing like a star the dusk of silence. Again! Again! Again! A voice from beyond the world was calling.

—Hello, Stephanos!

—Here comes The Dedalus!

—Ao! . . . Eh, give it over, Dwyer, I'm telling you or I'll give you a stuff in the kisser for yourself. . . . Ao!

—Good man, Towser! Duck him!

—Come along, Dedalus! Bous Stephanoumenos![4] Bous Stephaneforos!

—Duck him! Guzzle him now, Towser!

—Help! Help! . . . Ao!

He recognised their speech collectively before he distinguished their faces. The mere sight of that medley of wet nakedness chilled him to the bone. Their bodies, corpsewhite or suffused with a pallid golden light or rawly tanned by the suns, gleamed with the wet of the sea. Their divingstone, poised on its rude supports and rocking

---

3. Ancient Scandinavian public assembly; Dublin, "the seventh city of Christendom," was settled and ruled by the Danes in the 9th and 10th centuries.

4. Greek, "garlanded ox." "Stephanos" is the Greek for "crown," and sacrificial animals were crowned with garlands. "Bous Stephaneforos" means similarly "crown-bearing (or garland-bearing) ox."

under their plunges, and the rough-hewn stones of the sloping breakwater over which they scrambled in their horseplay, gleamed with cold wet lustre. The towels with which they smacked their bodies were heavy with cold seawater: and drenched with cold brine was their matted hair.

He stood still in deference to their calls and parried their banter with easy words. How characterless they looked: Shuley without his deep unbuttoned collar, Ennis without his scarlet belt with the snaky clasp, and Connolly without his Norfolk coat with the flapless sidepockets! It was a pain to see them and a sword-like pain to see the signs of adolescence that made repellent their pitiable nakedness. Perhaps they had taken refuge in number and noise from the secret dread in their souls. But he, apart from them and in silence, remembered in what dread he stood of the mystery of his own body.

—Stephanos Dedalos! Bous Stephanoumenos! Bous Stephaneforos!

Their banter was not new to him and now it flattered his mild proud sovereignty. Now, as never before, his strange name seemed to him a prophecy. So timeless seemed the grey warm air, so fluid and impersonal his own mood, that all ages were as one to him. A moment before the ghost of the ancient kingdom of the Danes had looked forth through the vesture of the hazewrapped city. Now, at the name of the fabulous artificer,[5] he seemed to hear the noise of dim waves and to see a winged form flying above the waves and slowly climbing the air. What did it mean? Was it a quaint device opening a page of some medieval book of prophecies and symbols, a hawklike man flying sunward above the sea, a prophecy of the end he had been born to serve and had been following through the mists of childhood and boyhood, a symbol of the artist forging anew in his workshop out of the sluggish matter of the earth a new soaring impalpable imperishable being?

His heart trembled; his breath came faster and a wild spirit passed over his limbs as though he were soaring sunward. His heart trembled in an ecstasy of fear and his soul was in flight. His soul was soaring in an air beyond the world and the body he knew was purified in a breath and delivered of incertitude and made radiant and commingled with the element of the spirit. An ecstasy of flight made radiant his eyes and wild his breath and tremulous and wild and radiant his windswept limbs.

—One! Two! . . . Look out!

—O, Cripes, I'm drownded!

—One! Two! Three and away!

—The next! The next!

5. The Greek craftsman Daedalus: see introductory note to *A Portrait*.

—One! . . . Uk!

—Stephaneforos!

His throat ached with a desire to cry aloud, the cry of a hawk or eagle on high, to cry piercingly of his deliverance to the winds. This was the call of life to his soul not the dull gross voice of the world of duties and despair, not the inhuman voice that had called him to the pale service of the altar. An instant of wild flight had delivered him and the cry of triumph which his lips withheld cleft his brain.

—Stephaneforos!

What were they now but the cerements shaken from the body of death—the fear he had walked in night and day, the incertitude that had ringed him round, the shame that had abased him within and without—cerements, the linens of the grave?

His soul had arisen from the grave of boyhood, spurning her graveclothes. Yes! Yes! Yes! He would create proudly out of the freedom and power of his soul, as the great artificer whose name he bore, a living thing, new and soaring and beautiful, impalpable, imperishable.

He started up nervously from the stoneblock for he could no longer quench the flame in his blood. He felt his cheeks aflame and his throat throbbing with song. There was a lust of wandering in his feet that burned to set out for the ends of the earth. On! On! his heart seemed to cry. Evening would deepen above the sea, night fall upon the plains, dawn glimmer before the wanderer and show him strange fields and hills and faces. Where?

He looked northward towards Howth. The sea had fallen below the line of seawrack on the shallow side of the breakwater and already the tide was running out fast along the foreshore. Already one long oval bank of sand lay warm and dry amid the wavelets. Here and there warm isles of sand gleamed above the shallow tides and about the isles and around the long bank and amid the shallow currents of the beach were lightclad figures, wading and delving.

In a few moments he was barefoot, his stockings folded in his pockets, and his canvas shoes dangling by their knotted laces over his shoulders and, picking a pointed salteaten stick out of the jetsam among the rocks, he clambered down the slope of the breakwater.

There was a long rivulet in the strand and, as he waded slowly up its course, he wondered at the endless drift of seaweed. Emerald and black and russet and olive, it moved beneath the current, swaying and turning. The water of the rivulet was dark with endless drift and mirrored the highdrifting clouds. The clouds were drifting above him silently and silently the seatangle was drifting below him; and the grey warm air was still: and a new wild life was singing in his veins.

Where was his boyhood now? Where was the soul that had hung back from her destiny, to brood alone upon the shame of her wounds and in her house of squalor and subterfuge to queen it in faded cerements and in wreaths that withered at the touch? Or where was he?

He was alone. He was unheeded, happy, and near to the wild heart of life. He was alone and young and wilful and wildhearted, alone amid a waste of wild air and brackish waters and the sea-harvest of shells and tangle and veiled grey sunlight and gayclad lightclad figures of children and girls and voices childish and girl-ish in the air.

A girl stood before him in midstream, alone and still, gazing out to sea. She seemed like one whom magic had changed into the like-ness of a strange and beautiful seabird. Her long slender bare legs were delicate as a crane's and pure save where an emerald trail of seaweed had fashioned itself as a sign upon the flesh. Her thighs, fuller and softhued as ivory, were bared almost to the hips where the white fringes of her drawers were like feathering of soft white down. Her slateblue skirts were kilted boldly about her waist and dovetailed behind her. Her bosom was as a bird's, soft and slight, slight and soft as the breast of some darkplumaged dove. But her long fair hair was girlish: and girlish, and touched with the wonder of mortal beauty, her face.

She was alone and still, gazing out to sea; and when she felt his presence and the worship of his eyes her eyes turned to him in quiet sufferance of his gaze, without shame or wantonness. Long, long she suffered his gaze and then quietly withdrew her eyes from his and bent them towards the stream, gently stirring the water with **her foot hither and thither. The first faint noise of gently moving water broke the silence, low and faint and whispering, faint as the bells of sleep; hither and thither, hither and thither: and a faint flame trembled on her cheek.**

—Heavenly God! cried Stephen's soul, in an outburst of profane joy.

He turned away from her suddenly and set off across the strand. His cheeks were aflame; his body was aglow; his limbs were trem-bling. On and on and on and on he strode, far out over the sands, singing wildly to the sea, crying to greet the advent of the life that had cried to him.

Her image had passed into his soul for ever and no word had broken the holy silence of his ecstasy. Her eyes had called him and his soul had leaped at the call. To live, to err, to fall, to triumph, to recreate life out of life! A wild angel had appeared to him, the angel of mortal youth and beauty, an envoy from the fair courts of life, to throw open before him in an instant of ecstasy the gates of all the ways of error and glory. On and on and on and on!

He halted suddenly and heard his heart in the silence. How far had he walked? What hour was it?

There was no human figure near him nor any sound borne to him over the air. But the tide was near the turn and already the day was on the wane. He turned landward and ran towards the shore and, running up the sloping beach, reckless of the sharp shingle, found a sandy nook amid a ring of tufted sandknolls and lay down there that the peace and silence of the evening might still the riot of his blood.

He felt above him the vast indifferent dome and the calm processes of the heavenly bodies; and the earth beneath him, the earth that had borne him, had taken him to her breast.

He closed his eyes in the languor of sleep. His eyelids trembled as if they felt the vast cyclic movement of the earth and her watchers, trembled as if they felt the strange light of some new world. His soul was swooning into some new world, fantastic, dim, uncertain as under sea, traversed by cloudy shapes and beings. A world, a glimmer, or a flower? Glimmering and trembling, trembling and unfolding, a breaking light, an opening flower, it spread in endless succession to itself, breaking in full crimson and unfolding and fading to palest rose, leaf by leaf and wave of light by wave of light, flooding all the heavens with its soft flushes, every flush deeper than other.

Evening had fallen when he woke and the sand and arid grasses of his bed glowed no longer. He rose slowly and, recalling the rapture of his sleep, sighed at its joy.

He climbed to the crest of the sandhill and gazed about him. Evening had fallen. A rim of the young moon cleft the pale waste of sky like the rim of a silver hoop embedded in grey sand; and the tide was flowing in fast to the land with a low whisper of her waves, islanding a few last figures in distant pools.

1904–14   1916

From Ulysses

[Proteus][1]

Ineluctable modality of the visible: at least that if no more, thought through my eyes.[2] Signatures of all things I am here to read, seaspawn and seawrack, the nearing tide, that rusty boot. Snotgreen, bluesilver, rust: coloured signs. Limits of the diaphane.[3] But he adds: in bodies. Then he was aware of them bodies before of them coloured. How? By knocking his sconce against them, sure. Go easy. Bald he was and a millionaire, *maestro di color che sanno*.[4] Limit of the diaphane in. Why in? Diaphane, adiaphane.[5] If you can put your five fingers through it, it is a gate, if not a door. Shut your eyes and see.

Stephen closed his eyes to hear his boots crush crackling wrack

1. "Proteus" is so titled because of the deliberate analogies that exist between it and the description of Proteus in *Odyssey* IV. (Joyce did not title any of the episodes in *Ulysses*, but the names are his; he used them in correspondence and in talk with friends.)

In Homer's *Odyssey*, Proteus is the changing sea god who continually alters his shape: when Telemachus, the son of Ulysses, asks Menelaus for help in finding his father, Menelaus tells him that he encountered Proteus by the seashore on the island of Pharos "in front of Egypt," and that, by holding on to him while he changed from one shape to another, he was able to force him to tell what had happened to Ulysses and the other Greek heroes of the Trojan war. In Joyce's narrative, Stephen Dedalus (who, like Homer's Telemachus, is looking for a father, but not in the literal "consubstantial" sense) is walking on the Dublin shore alone, "along Sandymount strand," speculating on the shifting shapes of things and the possibility of knowing truth by mere appearances.

First Stephen meditates on the "modality of the visible" and on the mystical notion that God writes his signature on all His works; then on the "modality of the audible," closing his eyes and trying to know reality simply through the sense of hearing. As he continues his walk, the people and objects he sees mingle in his thoughts with memories of his past relations with his family, of his schooldays, his residence in Paris whence he was recalled by his mother's fatal illness, his feeling of guilt about his mother's death (he had refused to kneel down and pray at her bedside, since he considered it would be a betrayal of his integrity as an unbeliever), and a variety of speculations about life and reality often derived from mystical works he had read "in the stagnant bay of Marsh's library" (in Dublin). This episode gives the reader a profound awareness of the nature of Stephen's sensibility and the contents of his conscious and subconscious mind and also sets going themes to be developed later in other episodes of *Ulysses*. The highly theoretical, inquiring, musing, speculating mind of Stephen is in sharp contrast to the practical, humane, sensual, concrete imagination of the book's real hero, Leopold Bloom, but there are also significant parallels between the streams of consciousness of the two. Some of the more important themes which emerge in Stephen's reverie are pointed out in footnotes.

The text given here has been collated with the Odyssey Press edition of *Ulysses* (1932), which is accepted as the "definitive standard edition."

2. I.e., the sense of sight provides an unavoidable way ("ineluctable modality") of knowing reality, the knowledge thus provided being a kind of "thought through [the] eyes." The phrase "signature of all things" comes from the German mystic Jakob Böhme, (1575–1624).

3. Transparency. Stephen is speculating on Aristotle's view of perception as developed in his *De Anima*.

4. There was a tradition that Aristotle was bald, with thin legs, small eyes, and a lisp. Aristotle is also traditionally supposed to have inherited considerable wealth and to have been presented with a fortune by his former pupil Alexander the Great. The Italian phrase is Dante's description of Aristotle in the *Inferno*, and means "the master of them that know."

5. What is not transparent (opposite of "diaphane").

and shells. You are walking through it howsomever. I am, a stride at a time. A very short space of time through very short times of space. Five, six: the *nacheinander*.[6] Exactly: and that is the ineluctable modality of the audible. Open your eyes. No. Jesus! If I fell over a cliff that beetles o'er his base,[7] fell through the *nebeneinander* ineluctably. I am getting on nicely in the dark. My ash sword hangs at my side. Tap with it: they do.[8] My two feet in his boots are at the end of my legs, *nebeneinander*. Sounds solid: made by the mallet of *Los Demiurgos*.[9] Am I walking into eternity along Sandymount strand? Crush, crack, crik, crick. Wild sea money. Dominie[1] Deasy kens them a'.

> *Won't you come to Sandymount,*
> *Madeline the mare?*

Rhythm begins, you see. I hear. A catalectic tetrameter[2] of iambs marching. No, agallop: *deline the mare*.

Open your eyes now. I will. One moment. Has all vanished since? If I open and am for ever in the black adiaphane. *Basta!*[3] I will see if I can see.

See now. There all the time without you: and ever shall be, world without end.

They came down the steps from Leahy's terrace prudently, *Frauenzimmer*:[4] and down the shelving shore flabbily their splayed feet sinking in the silted sand. Like me, like Algy,[5] coming down to our mighty mother. Number one swung lourdily[6] her midwife's

6. "After one another." Stephen, with eyes shut, is now sensing reality through the sense of sound only: unlike sight, sound falls on the sense of hearing in chronological sequence, one sound after another.

7. "What if it tempt you toward the flood, my lord, / Or to the dreadful summit of the cliff / That beetles o'er his base into the sea * * * " (*Hamlet* I.iv.69–71). "*Nebeneinander*": beside one another.

8. Stephen is still walking with his eyes shut, tapping with his "ash sword" (the walking stick of ash wood he always carried), as "they" (i.e., blind people) do. "His boots": Buck Mulligan's. Stephen, lacking boots of his own, had borrowed a castoff pair of Mulligan's.

9. The Demiurge, supernatural being who made the world in subordination to God. The mystical notion of the Demiurge who created the world haunts Stephen's mind; it is the Demiurge who writes his signature on created objects and whose mallet fashioned them. The world, sensed by the ear only, "sounds solid," as though made by the Demiurge's hammer.

1. Schoolmaster. Mr. Deasy was the headmaster of the school where Stephen taught (the previous episode has shown Stephen teaching). "Kens them a' ": knows them all; Stephen is putting Deasy into a mock-Scottish folk song.

2. The first of the two lines of popular verse which have come into Stephen's head consists metrically of four iambic feet ("tetrameter") with the unstressed syllable of the first iamb missing ("catalectic").

3. Italian, "Enough!"

4. "Midwives"; Stephen sees them coming from Leahy's Terrace, which runs by the beach.

5. Algernon Charles Swinburne, who wrote: "I will go back to the great sweet mother, / Mother and lover of men, the sea. I will go down to her, I and none other * * * " (*The Triumph of Time*).

6. Heavily (coined by Stephen from the French *lourd*). Stephen, like Joyce, had studied modern languages at University College, Dublin, and his preoccupation with words and languages is part of his character as potential literary artist. "Gamp": umbrella; and perhaps reference to Mrs. Gamp, the nurse in Dickens' *Martin Chuzzlewit*.

bag, the other's gamp poked in the beach. From the liberties, out for the day. Mrs. Florence MacCabe,[7] relict of the late Patk Mac-Cabe, deeply lamented, of Bride Street. One of her sisterhood lugged me squealing into life. Creation from nothing. What has she in the bag? A misbirth with a trailing navelcord, hushed in ruddy wool. The cords of all link back, strandentwining cable of all flesh. That is why mystic monks. Will you be as gods? Gaze in your omphalos. Hello. Kinch here. Put me on to Edenville. Aleph, alpha: nought, nought, one.[8]

Spouse and helpmate of Adam Kadmon:[9] Heva, naked Eve. She had no navel. Gaze. Belly without blemish, bulging big, a buckler of taut vellum, no, whiteheaped corn, orient and immortal, standing from everlasting to everlasting.[1] Womb of sin.

Wombed in sin darkness I was too, made not begotten. By them, the man with my voice and my eyes and a ghostwoman with ashes on her breath.[2] They clasped and sundered, did the coupler's will. From before the ages He willed me and now may not will me away or ever. A *lex eterna*[3] stays about Him. Is that then the divine substance wherein Father and Son are consubstantial? Where is poor dear Arius[4] to try conclusions? Warring his life long on the contransmagnificandjewbangtantiality.[5] Illstarred heresiarch.[6] In a Greek

7. Stephen imagines the first midwife is called Mrs. MacCabe. "Relict": widow.

8. Stephen is speculating on the mystical significance of the navel cord, seeing it as linking the generations, the combined navel cords stretching back to Adam and Eve. A mystic gazed in his *omphalos* (navel) to make contact with the first man. Stephen thinks of himself ("Kinch," his nickname) calling up Adam in "Edenville" through his navel, using the line of linked navel cords as a telephone line. Adam's telephone number, "Aleph, alpha: nought, nought, one," begins with the first letters of the Hebrew and of the Greek alphabet to suggest the great primeval number.

9. "Adam the Beginner," so called in Hebrew cabalistic literature of the Middle Ages; "Heva" is Hebrew for Eve. Because she was not born in the regular way, but created from Adam's rib, she had no navel.

1. Stephen is led, through reflection on Eve's navel-less "belly without blemish," to a recollection of the description of the original Eden (Paradise) by Thomas Traherne (ca. 1637–74), from whose prose *Centuries of Meditation* he quotes: "The corn was orient and immortal wheat, which should never be reaped, nor was ever sown. I thought it had stood from everlasting to everlasting. * * * " But immediately afterwards Stephen reflects that such language is inappropriate to Eve's body, as hers was the "womb of sin"—i.e., she first ate the fatal apple and brought

forth sin.

2. Stephen is haunted by thoughts of his mother in this guise.

3. Eternal law. God's eternal law, Stephen reflects, willed his birth from the beginning. He then goes on to speculate on the nature of the divine substance and whether God the Father and God the Son are of the same substance ("consubstantial").

4. 3rd-century theologian who "tried conclusions" on this matter, maintaining that Christ was less divine than God (Arius' views were condemned as heretical by the Council of Nicaea in 325).

5. Ironic "portmanteau word" made up of terms connected with the Arian controversy—"consubstantial," "transubstantial" (of a substance that changes into another)—and with the facts of Christ's nature (e.g., "Jew"; Jesus was a Jew, as Leopold Bloom in a later episode reminds an anti-Semitic Irishman).

6. Arch-heretic. Arius died suddenly in Constantinople in 336. He was never a bishop, and Stephen's image of him at the moment of death in full episcopal attire seems to combine recollections of other early "heresiarchs." In an earlier reverie Stephen had conjured up in his mind "a horde of heresies fleeing with mitres awry." These heretics are connected in Stephen's mind with argument about the relation between God the Father and God the Son and so with the problem of the true nature of paternity, which haunts him constantly.

watercloset he breathed his last: euthanasia. With beaded mitre and with crozier, stalled upon his throne, widower of a widowed see, with upstiffed omophorion, with clotted hinderparts.

Airs romped around him, nipping and eager airs. They are coming, waves. The whitemaned seahorses, champing, brightwind-bridled, the steeds of Mananaan.[7]

I mustn't forget his letter for the press. And after? The Ship, half twelve. By the way go easy with that money like a good young imbecile. Yes, I must.[8]

His pace slackened. Here. Am I going to Aunt Sara's or not? My consubstantial father's voice. Did you see anything of your artist brother Stephen lately? No? Sure he's not down in Strasburg terrace with his aunt Sally? Couldn't he fly a bit higher than that, eh? And and and and tell us Stephen, how is uncle Si? O weeping God, the things I married into. De boys up in de hayloft. The drunken little costdrawer and his brother, the cornet player. Highly respectable gondoliers. And skeweyed Walter sirring his father, no less. Sir. Yes, sir. No, sir. Jesus wept: and no wonder, by Christ.[9]

I pull the wheezy bell of their shuttered cottage: and wait. They take me for a dun, peer out from a coign of vantage.[1]

—It's Stephen, sir.

—Let him in. Let Stephen in.

A bolt drawn back and Walter welcomes me.

—We thought you were someone else.

In his broad bed nuncle Richie, pillowed and blanketed, extends over the hillock of his knees a sturdy forearm. Clean chested. He has washed the upper moiety.

—Morrow, nephew.

He lays aside the lapboard whereon he drafts his bills of costs for the eyes of Master Goff and Master Shapland Tandy, filing consents and common searches and a writ of *Duces Tecum*.[2] A bogoak frame over his bald head: Wilde's *Requiescat*.[3] The drone of his misleading whistle brings Walter back.

—Yes, sir?

—Malt[4] for Richie and Stephen, tell mother. Where is she?

7. Mananaan MacLir, Celtic sea god; his steeds are the "white horses" (still the name in Britain for the white foam on top of waves).
8. Mr. Deasy had given Stephen a letter to the press to be taken to the newspaper office. After that he has an appointment with Mulligan at The Ship, a tavern. "That money" is Mr. Deasy's last payment to him.
9. Stephen has been wondering whether to call on his uncle and aunt, Richie and Sara Goulding. He imagines his father interrogating him about the visit as if he had gone, and then pictures his cousins asking after his father, Simon Dedalus (his cousins' "uncle Si"). Simon Dedalus is contemptuous

of his wife's relations (Sara Goulding is his wife's sister). Stephen knows that any mention of them will bring on the familiar abuse of "the things I married into"—at best "highly respectable góndoliers" (from Gilbert and Sullivan's opera *The Gondoliers*). The scene that follows is also Stephen's purely imaginary picture of what the visit would be like.
1. Favorable corner.
2. "You shall take with you": opening words of search warrant. Goulding was a law clerk with Messrs. Goff and Tandy.
3. Poem by Oscar Wilde.
4. Whisky.

—Bathing Crissie, sir.

Papa's little bedpal. Lump of love.

—No, uncle Richie. . .

—Call me Richie. Damn your lithia water. It lowers. Whusky!

—Uncle Richie, really. . .

—Sit down or by the law Harry I'll knock you down.

Walter squints vainly for a chair.

—He has nothing to sit down on, sir.

—He has nowhere to put it, you mug. Bring in our Chippendale chair. Would you like a bite of something? None of your damned lawdeedaw air here; the rich of a rasher fried with a herring? Sure? So much the better. We have nothing in the house but backache pills.

All'erta![5]

He drones bars of Ferrando's *aria di sortita*. The grandest number, Stephen, in the whole opera. Listen.

His tuneful whistle sounds again, finely shaded, with rushes of the air, his fists bigdrumming on his padded knees.

This wind is sweeter.

Houses of decay, mine, his and all. You told the Clongowes gentry you had an uncle a judge and an uncle a general in the army.[6] Come out of them, Stephen. Beauty is not there. Nor in the stagnant bay of Marsh's library where you read the fading prophecies of Joachim Abbas.[7] For whom? The hundredheaded rabble of the cathedral close.[8] A hater of his kind ran from them to the wood of madness, his mane foaming in the moon, his eyeballs stars. Houyhnhnm, horsenostrilled.[9] The oval equine faces, Temple, Buck Mulligan, Foxy Campbell. Lantern jaws. Abbas father,[1] furious dean, what offence laid fire to their brains? Paff! *Descende, calve, ut ne nimium decalveris.*[2] A garland of grey hair

---

5. "Look out!" The first words of the *aria di sortita* (aria of a singer's entrance) sung by Ferrando, captain of the guard, in Verdi's opera *Il Trovatore*.
6. Stephen, reflecting on the steady social decline of his family, is remembering that, while at school at Clongowes Wood College, he had pretended to have important relations.
7. Abbot Joachim of Floris (the monastery of San Giovanni in Fiore, Italy), 12th-century mystic and theologian, whose prophetic work *Expositio in Apocalypsin* Stephen (i.e., Joyce) had read in Marsh's Library.
8. I.e., the precinct of a cathedral (Marsh's Library is in the close of St. Patrick's Cathedral).
9. St. Patrick's Close has recalled Jonathan Swift (who was Dean of St. Patrick's). Stephen remembers Swift's

misanthropy (he was "a hater of his kind") and his creation of the Houyhnhnms (noble horses) in Book IV of *Gulliver's Travels*. Then he thinks of people he knew who have horse-faces.
1. "Abbas" means literally "father."
2. "Go down, bald-head, lest you become even balder." This sentence, from Joachim's *Concordia* of the Old and New Testaments, is based on the mocking cry of the children to the prophet Elisha (II Kings ii.23: "Go up, thou bald head"); Joachim saw Elisha as a forerunner of St. Benedict—both had shaven or baldish heads. Stephen imagines the "comminated" (i.e., threatened) head of Joachim descending, clutching a "monstrance" (receptacle in which the consecrated host is exposed for adoration), in the midst of a nightmare church service.

on his comminated head see him me clambering down to the foot-pace (*descende*), clutching a monstrance, basiliskeyed. Get down, bald poll! A choir gives back menace and echo, assisting about the altar's horns, the snorted Latin of jackpriests moving burly in their albs, tonsured and oiled and gelded, fat with the fat of kidneys of wheat.

And at the same instant perhaps a priest round the corner is elevating it. Dringdring! And two streets off another locking it into a pyx.[3] Dringadring! And in a ladychapel another taking housel all to his own cheek. Dringdring! Down, up, forward, back. Dan Occam[4] thought of that, invincible doctor. A misty English morning the imp hypostasis tickled his brain. Bringing his host down and kneeling he heard twine with his second bell the first bell in the transept (he is lifting his) and, rising, heard (now I am lifting) their two bells (he is kneeling) twang in diphthong.

Cousin Stephen, you will never be a saint.[5] Isle of saints.[6] You were awfully holy, weren't you? You prayed to the Blessed Virgin that you might not have a red nose. You prayed to the devil in Serpentine avenue that the fubsy widow in front might lift her clothes still more from the wet street. *O si, certo!*[7] Sell your soul for that, do, dyed rags pinned round a squaw. More tell me, more still! On the top of the Howth tram alone crying to the rain: *naked women!* What about that, eh?

What about what? What else were they invented for?

Reading two pages apiece of seven books every night, eh? I was young. You bowed to yourself in the mirror, stepping forward to applause earnestly, striking face. Hurray for the Goddamned idiot! Hray! No-one saw: tell no-one. Books you were going to write with letters for titles. Have you read his F? O yes, but I prefer Q. Yes, but W is wonderful. O yes, W. Remember your epiphanies[8] on green oval leaves, deeply deep, copies to be sent if you died to all the great libraries of the world, including Alexandria? Someone was to read them there after a few thousand years, a mahamanvan-

---

3. Vessel in which the Host (consecrated bread or wafer) is kept. Stephen is imagining such a service, with himself officiating (he almost became a priest).
4. William of Occam or Ockham ("Dan" means "master"), 14th-century English theologian, who held that the individual thing is the reality and its name, the universal, an abstraction; he was concerned with "hypostasis"—the essential part of a thing as distinct from its attributes.
5. A parody of the words of Dryden to his distant relative Swift: "Cousin, you will never make a poet."
6. Ireland was called "*insula sanc-*

torum," ("isle of saints") in the Middle Ages.
7. "Oh yes, certainly!"
8. Joyce's own term for the prose poems he wrote as a young man. An epiphany, he said, was the sudden "revelation of the whatness of a thing" —of a gesture, a phrase, or a thought which he had experienced; he attempted to express, in the writing, the moment at which "the soul of the commonest object * * * seems to us radiant." Stephen's recollection of early and exotic literary ambitions is drawn directly from Joyce's own ambitions at the same age.

tara.[9] Pico della Mirandola like. Ay, very like a whale.[1] When one reads these strange pages of one long gone one feels that one is at one with one who once. . .

The grainy sand had gone from under his feet. His boots trod again a damp crackling mast, razorshells, squeaking pebbles, that on the unnumbered pebbles beats, wood sieved by the shipworm, lost Armáda. Unwholesome sandflats waited to suck his treading soles, breathing upward sewage breath. He coasted them, walking warily. A porterbottle stood up, stogged to its waist, in the cakey sand dough. A sentinel: isle of dreadful thirst.[2] Broken hoops on the shore; at the land a maze of dark cunning nets; farther away chalkscrawled backdoors and on the higher beach a dryingline with two crucified shirts. Ringsend: wigwams of brown steersmen and master mariners. Human shells.

He halted. I have passed the way to aunt Sara's. Am I not going there? Seems not. No-one about. He turned northeast and crossed the firmer sand towards the Pigeonhouse.[3]

—*Qui vous a mis dans cette fichue position?*

—*C'est le pigeon, Joseph.*

Patrice, home on furlough, lapped warm milk with me in the bar MacMahon. Son of the wild goose, Kevin Egan of Paris. My father's a bird, he lapped the sweet *lait chaud* with pink young tongue, plump bunny's face. Lap, *lapin*. He hopes to win in the *gros lots*. About the nature of women he read in Michelet. But he must send me *La Vie de Jésus* by M. Léo Taxil. Lent it to his friend.[4]

9. Cycle of change and recurrence, in Indian mystical thought. It is connected in Stephen's mind with the constant ebb and flow of the sea by which he is walking. Pico della Mirandola was a 15th-century mystical philosopher; his *Heptaplus* is a mystical account of the creation, much influenced by Jewish cabalistic thought.
1. Polonius to Hamlet (*Hamlet* III.ii.399) with reference to the changing shape of a cloud. The Protean theme of constant change, of ebb and flow, and of metempsychosis (i.e., transmigration of souls; a major theme in *Ulysses*), is working in Stephen's mind. The following sentence is a parody of an elegant, condescending modern essay on Pico or some other early mystic.
2. The atmosphere of the sandflats reminds Stephen of a desert island where men die of thirst. (The island of Pharos, where Menelaus found Proteus, was an "island of dreadful hunger.")
3. The Pigeon house in Ringsend, an old structure built on a breakwater in Dublin Bay and which in the course of time has served a great variety of purposes, suggests to Stephen the Dove

which is the symbol of the Holy Spirit, and this in turn suggests an irreverent dialogue (supposedly between Joseph and Mary when Mary is found to be pregnant: "Who has got you into this wretched condition?" "It was the pigeon [i.e., the Holy Dove], Joseph"). This he had picked up in Paris from the blasphemous M. Léo Taxil, whose book *La Vie de Jésus* ("The Life of Jesus") is mentioned in the next paragraph.
4. Stephen had first met Léo Taxil through Patrice, the son of "Kevin Egan of Paris," who in real life was the exiled nationalist Joseph Casey. The phrase "my father's a bird" comes from *The Song of the Cheerful Jesus*, a blasphemous poem by Buck Mulligan (actually Oliver Gogarty, who really wrote the poem); Stephen recalls Patrice reciting it as he drank warm milk ("*lait chaud*"), lapping it like a "*lapin*" ("rabbit"), and expressing the hope that he would win something substantial in the French national lottery (*gros lot:* "first prize"). Jules Michelet (1798–1874) was a French historian.

—*C'est tordant, vous savez. Moi je suis socialiste. Je ne crois pas en l'existence de Dieu. Faut pas le dire à mon père.*

—*Il croit?*

—*Mon père, oui.*

Schluss. He laps.[5]

My Latin quarter hat. God, we simply must dress the character. I want puce gloves. You were a student, weren't you? Of what in the other devil's name? Paysayenn. P. C. N., you know: *physiques, chimiques et naturelles.*[6] Aha. Eating your groatsworth of *mou en civet*, fleshpots of Egypt, elbowed by belching cabmen. Just say in the most natural tone: when I was in Paris, *boul' Mich',*[7] I used to. Yes, used to carry punched tickets to prove an alibi if they arrested you for murder somewhere. Justice. On the night of the seventeenth of February 1904 the prisoner was seen by two witnesses. Other fellow did it: other me. Hat, tie, overcoat, nose. *Lui, c'est moi.*[8] You seem to have enjoyed yourself.

Proudly walking. Whom were you trying to walk like? Forget: a dispossessed. With mother's money order, eight shillings, the banging door of the post office slammed in your face by the usher. Hunger toothache. *Encore deux minutes.* Look clock. Must get. *Fermé.* Hired dog! Shoot him to bloody bits with a bang shotgun, bits man spattered walls all brass buttons. Bits all khrrrrklak in place clack back. Not hurt? O, that's all right. Shake hands. See what I meant, see? O, that's all right. Shake a shake. O, that's all only all right.[9]

You were going to do wonders, what? Missionary to Europe after fiery Columbanus.[1] Fiacre and Scotus on their creepystools in heaven spilt from their pintpots, loudlatinlaughing: *Euge! Euge!*[2] Pretending to speak broken English as you dragged your valise, porter threepence, across the slimy pier at Newhaven. *Comment?* Rich booty you brought back; *Le tutu,* five tattered numbers of

5. Conversation between Stephen and Patrice: "It's screamingly funny, you know. I'm a socialist myself. I don't believe in the existence of God. Mustn't tell my father." "He is a believer?" "My father, yes." "*Schluss*": end.
6. I.e., the faculty of physics, chemistry, and biology at the École de Médecine in Paris, where Stephen, like Joyce, took a premedical course for a short time. The faculty was popularly known as "P. C. N." (pronounced "Paysayenn"). "*Mou en civet*": stew.
7. Popular Parisian abbreviation for the Boulevard Saint Michel.
8. "He is me"—a parody of Louis XIV's remark, "*L'état c'est moi*" ("I am the state").
9. A recollection of the occasion when, desperate for money, Stephen had received a money order for eight shillings from his mother. Afflicted with both hunger and toothache, he had gone to cash it at the post office—which was closed, even though, as he expostulated with the man at the door, there were still two minutes ("*encore deux minutes*") until the official closing time. In his retrospective rage he imagines himself shooting the "hired dog" to bits, and then in a revulsion of feeling has a mental reconciliation with him.
1. 6th-century Irish missionary on the Continent. Fiacre was a 6th-century Irish saint. Duns Scotus (ca. 1265–1308): Scholastic theologian and philosopher. "Creepystools": low stools.
2. "Well done!"

Pantalon Blanc et Culotte Rouge,[3] a blue French telegram, curiosity
to show:

—Mother dying come home father.[4]

The aunt thinks you killed your mother. That's why she won't.[5]

> *Then here's a health to Mulligan's aunt*
> *And I'll tell you the reason why.*
> *She always kept things decent in*
> *The Hannigan familèye.*

His feet marched in sudden proud rhythm over the sand furrows,
along by the boulders of the south wall. He stared at them proudly,
piled stone mammoth skulls. Gold light on sea, on sand, on boulders. The sun is there, the slender trees, the lemon houses.

Paris rawly waking, crude sunlight on her lemon streets. Moist
pith of farls[6] of bread, the froggreen wormwood, her matin incense,
court the air. Belluomo rises from the bed of his wife's lover's wife,
the kerchiefed housewife is astir, a saucer of acetic acid in her
hands. In Rodot's Yvonne and Madeleine newmake their tumbled
beauties, shattering with gold teeth *chaussons* of pastry, their
mouths yellowed with the *pus* of *flan breton*.[7] Faces of Paris men
go by, their wellpleased pleasers, curled conquistadores.[8]

Noon slumbers. Kevin Egan rolls gunpowder cigarettes through
fingers smeared with printer's ink,[9] sipping his green fairy as Patrice
his white. About us gobblers fork spiced beans down their gullets.
Un demi setier![1] A jet of coffee steam from the burnished caldron.
She serves me at his beck. *Il est irlandais. Hollandais? Non fromage.
Deux irlandais, nous, Irlande, vous savez? Ah oui!*[2] She thought
you wanted a cheese *hollandais*. Your postprandial, do you know
that word? Postprandial. There was a fellow I knew once in Bar-
celona, queer fellow, used to call it his postprandial. Well: *slainte!*[3]
Around the slabbed tables the tangle of wined breaths and grumbling gorges. His breath hangs over our saucestained plates, the
green fairy's fang thrusting between his lips. Of Ireland, the Dalcas-
sions, of hopes, conspiracies, of Arthur Griffith now.[4] To yoke me

---

3. Like the preceding name, name of French popular periodical.

4. This telegram was actually received by Joyce in Paris.

5. Stephen recalls Buck Mulligan's telling him that his (Mulligan's) aunt disapproved of Stephen because, by refusing to pray at his dying mother's bedside, he had hastened her death. Stephen then tries to laugh away his feeling of guilt by quoting mentally a (slightly parodied) verse of a popular song.

6. Thin circular cakes.

7. Memories of a restaurant in Paris: "*chaussons*" are pastry turnovers; "*flan breton*" is a pastry filled with custard.

8. Conquerors (Spanish).

9. Egan (i.e., Joseph Casey) became a typesetter for the Parisian edition of the *New York Herald*.

1. Abusive Parisian slang for a liquid measure (about one fourth of a liter) —here, presumably, of wine or beer.

2. "He is Irish. Dutch? Not cheese. We are two Irishmen, Ireland, you understand? Oh, yes!"

3. Gaelic, "Your health!"

4. Two extremes of Irish history: from the Dalcassian line came the early kings of Munster (from A.D. 300 on); Arthur Griffith (1872–1922) was an Irish revolutionary leader, founder of the Sinn Fein ("We Ourselves") movement.

as his yokefellow, our crimes our common cause. You're your father's son. I know the voice. His fustian shirt, sanguineflowered,
trembles its Spanish tassels at his secrets. M. Drumont,[5] famous
journalist, Drumont, know what he called queen Victoria? Old
hag with the yellow teeth. *Vieille ogresse* with the *dents jaunes*.
Maud Gonne, beautiful woman, *La Patrie*, M. Millevoye, Félix
Faure,[6] know how he died? Licentious men. The froeken, *bonne
à tout faire*,[7] who rubs male nakedness in the bath at Upsala. *Moi
faire*, she said. *Tous les messieurs*.[8] Not this *Monsieur*, I said. Most
licentious custom. Bath a most private thing. I wouldn't let my
brother, not even my own brother, most lascivious thing. Green
eyes, I see you. Fang, I feel. Lascivious people.

The blue fuse burns deadly between hands and burns clear.
Loose tobacco shreds catch fire: a flame and acrid smoke light our
corner. Raw facebones under his peep of day boy's hat. How the
head centre got away, authentic version. Got up as a young bride,
man, veil, orangeblossoms, drove out the road to Malahide. Did,
faith. Of lost leaders, the betrayed, wild escapes. Disguises, clutched
at, gone, not here.[9]

Spurned lover. I was a strapping young gossoon[1] at that time,
I tell you, I'll show you my likeness one day. I was, faith. Lover,
for her love he prowled with colonel Richard Burke, tanist[2] of his
sept, under the walls of Clerkenwell[3] and, crouching, saw a flame
of vengeance hurl them upward in the fog. Shattered glass and
toppling masonry. In gay Paree he hides, Egan of Paris, unsought
by any save by me. Making his day's stations, the dingy printing-
case, his three taverns, the Montmartre lair he sleeps short night
in, rue de la Goutte-d'Or, damascened with flyblown faces of the
gone. Loveless, landless, wifeless. She is quite nicey comfy without
her outcast man,[4] madame, in rue Gît-le-Coeur, canary and two
buck lodgers. Peachy cheeks, a zebra skirt, frisky as a young thing's.
Spurned and undespairing. Tell Pat[5] you saw me, won't you? I
wanted to get poor Pat a job one time. *Mon fils*, soldier of France.
I taught him to sing. *The boys of Kilkenny are stout roaring blades*.

5. Edouard Drumont (1844–1917),
French politician and bitter anti-Sem-
ite.
6. Maud Gonne, the beautiful actress
and violent Irish nationalist whom
Yeats loved; *"La Patrie"*: journal edited
by Lucien Millevoye, French Nationalist
Deputy and Maud Gonne's lover; Félix
Faure, 19th century French statesman.
7. Maid-of-all-work (French, translating the preceding Swedish word).
8. "I do all the gentlemen" (in broken
French).
9. Another Protean theme of change.
Egan had told Stephen of his cousin
James Stephens' escape from prison dis-

guised as a bride (Stephens was really
the cousin of Casey, the original of
Egan in this episode).
1. Boy.
2. Successor-apparent to a Celtic chief.
"Sept": clan.
3. District in east central London.
Stephen is recalling Egan's conversation about the Fenian violence in London which necessitated his fleeing to
France.
4. I.e., Egan's wife, who is "quite nicey
comfy" in the metaphorical "rue Gît-le-
Cœur" (i.e., the street where the heart
lies dead) back home in Ireland.
5. Patrice, Egan's son.

Know that old lay? I taught Patrice that. Old Kilkenny:[6] saint Canice, Strongbow's castle on the Nore. Goes like this. O, O. He takes me, Napper Tandy,[7] by the hand.

> O, O the boys of
> Kilkenny. . .

Weak wasting hand on mine. They have forgotten Kevin Egan, not he them. Remembering thee, O Sion.[8]

He had come nearer the edge of the sea and wet sand slapped his boots. The new air greeted him, harping in wild nerves, wind of wild air of seeds of brightness. Here, I am not walking out to the Kish lightship, am I? He stood suddenly, his feet beginning to sink slowly in the quaking soil. Turn back.

Turning, he scanned the shore south, his feet sinking again slowly in new sockets. The cold domed room of the tower[9] waits. Through the barbicans[1] the shafts of light are moving ever, slowly ever as my feet are sinking, creeping duskward over the dial floor. Blue dusk, nightfall, deep blue night. In the darkness of the dome they wait, their pushedback chairs, my obelisk valise, around a board of abandoned platters. Who to clear it? He has the key.[2] I will not sleep there when this night comes. A shut door of a silent tower entombing their blind bodies, the panthersahib and his pointer.[3] Call: no answer. He lifted his feet up from the suck and turned back by the mole of boulders. Take all, keep all. My soul walks with me, form of forms. So in the moon's midwatches I pace the path above the rocks, in sable silvered, hearing Elsinore's tempting flood.[4]

The flood is following me. I can watch it flow past from here. Get back then by the Poolbeg road to the strand there. He climbed over the sedge and eely oarweeds and sat on a stool of rock, resting his ashplant in a grike.

A bloated carcass of a dog lay lolled on bladderwrack. Before him the gunwale of a boat, sunk in sand. *Un coche ensablé.*[5] Louis Veuil-

6. Kilkenny is called after the Irish St. Canice (its Irish name is Cill Chainnigh), on the river Nore, where Strongbow (the second Earl of Pembroke, who invaded Ireland in the 12th century), had his stronghold.

7. James Napper Tandy (1740–1803), Irish revolutionary, hero of the song *The Wearing of the Green.*

8. Cf. Psalm cxxxvii.1 (in the King James Bible): "we wept, when we remembered Zion." But "Zion" in the Douay (Roman Catholic) Bible, is spelled "Sion," and the Book of Common Prayer has "When we remembered thee, O Sion."

9. Where Stephen lived with Buck Mulligan.

1. Outworks of a castle.

2. In the preceding episode, Mulligan asked for and got the key of the tower

from Stephen.

3. I.e., Mulligan and the Englishman Haines, who live with Stephen in the tower. Stephen thinks of them as calling for him in vain, since he has decided not to return.

4. Cf. *Hamlet* I.ii.242, where the ghost of Hamlet's murdered father is described as having a beard of "sable silver'd." Allusions to *Hamlet* occur often in *Ulysses;* in a later episode Stephen expounds the theory that Shakespeare is to be identified, not with Hamlet himself, but with his betrayed father.

5. "A coach embedded in the sand." Louis Veuillot was a 19th-century French journalist; Théophile Gautier, a 19th-century French poet, novelist, and critic.

lot called Gautier's prose. These heavy sands are language tide and
wind have silted here. And there, the stoneheaps of dead builders,
a warren of weasel rats. Hide gold there. Try it. You have some.
Sands and stones. Heavy of the past. Sir Lout's toys. Mind you
don't get one bang on the ear. I'm the bloody well gigant rolls all
them bloody well boulders, bones for my steppingstones. Feefaw-
fum. I zmells de bloodz oldz an Iridzman.[6]

A point, live dog, grew into sight running across the sweep of
sand. Lord, is he going to attack me? Respect his liberty. You will
not be master of others or their slave. I have my stick. Sit tight.
From farther away, walking shoreward across from the crested tide,
figures, two. The two maries. They have tucked it safe among the
bulrushes. Peekaboo. I see you. No, the dog. He is running back
to them. Who?

Galleys of the Lochlanns[7] ran here to beach, in quest of prey,
their bloodbeaked prows riding low on a molten pewter surf. Dane
vikings, torcs of tomahawks aglitter on their breasts when Malachi
wore the collar of gold. A school of turlehide whales stranded in
hot noon, spouting, hobbling in the shallows. Then from the starving cagework city a horde of jerkined dwarfs, my people, with flay-
ers' knives, running, scaling, hacking in green blubbery whalemeat.
Famine, plague and slaughters. Their blood is in me, their lusts my
waves. I moved among them on the frozen Liffey, that I, a changeling, among the spluttering resin fires. I spoke to no-one: none to
me.

The dog's bark ran towards him, stopped, ran back.[8] Dog of
my enemy. I just simply stood pale, silent, bayed about. *Terribilia
meditans.*[9] A primrose doublet, fortune's knave, smiled on my fear.
For that are you pining, the bark of their applause? Pretenders:
live their lives. The Bruce's brother, Thomas Fitzgerald, silken
knight, Perkin Warbeck, York's false scion, in breeches of silk of
whiterose ivory, wonder of a day, and Lambert Simnel, with a tail
of nans and sutlers, a scullion crowned.[1] All kings' sons. Paradise
of pretenders then and now. He saved men from drowning[2] and
you shake at a cur's yelping. But the courtiers who mocked Guido
in Or san Michele were in their own house. House of . . . We

6. Stephen is thinking of the boulders
on the shore as the work of a large
but clumsy giant ("Sir Lout"). "They
[Sir Lout and his family] were giants
right enough * * * My Sir Lout has
rocks in his mouth instead of teeth. He
articulates badly" (Joyce to Frank
Budgen, reported in Budgen's *James
Joyce and the Making of Ulysses*,
1934).
7. Scandinavians (Gaelic). Stephen is
meditating on the Vikings who settled
Dublin; it was here that they came
ashore, he thinks.

8. The dog in this and subsequent paragraphs keeps changing in appearance;
he "is the mummer among beasts—the
Protean animal" (Joyce to Budgen).
Joyce himself was afraid of dogs.
9. "Meditating terrible things."
1. Stephen is meditating on pretenders (i.e., false claimants): the names
here are those of pretenders who have
figured in English history. This is the
Proteus theme again—disguises and
changes.
2. Mulligan had saved a man from
drowning.

don't want any of your medieval abstrusiosities. Would you do what he did? A boat would be near, a lifebuoy. *Natürlich*,[3] put there for you. Would you or would you not? The man that was drowned nine days ago off Maiden's rock. They are waiting for him now. The truth, spit it out. I would want to. I would try. I am not a strong swimmer. Water cold soft. When I put my face into it in the basin at Clongowes. Can't see! Who's behind me? Out quickly, quickly! Do you see the tide flowing quickly in on all sides, sheeting the lows of sands quickly, shellcocoacoloured? If I had land under my feet. I want his life still to be his, mine to be mine. A drowning man. His human eyes scream to me out of horror of his death. I. . . With him together down . . . I could not save her.[4] Waters: bitter death: lost.

A woman and a man. I see her skirties. Pinned up, I bet.

Their dog ambled about a bank of dwindling sand, trotting, sniffing on all sides. Looking for something lost in a past life. Suddenly he made off like a bounding hare, ears flung back, chasing the shadow of a lowskimming gull. The man's shrieked whistle struck his limp ears. He turned, bounded back, came nearer, trotted on twinkling shanks. On a field tenney a buck, trippant, proper, unattired.[5] At the lacefringe of the tide he halted with stiff forehoofs, seawardpointed ears. His snout lifted barked at the wavenoise, herds of seamorse. They serpented towards his feet, curling, unfurling many crests, every ninth, breaking, plashing, from far, from farther out, waves and waves.

Cocklepickers.[6] They waded a little way in the water and, stooping, soused their bags, and, lifting them again, waded out. The dog yelped running to them, reared up and pawed them, dropping on all fours, again reared up at them with mute bearish fawning. Unheeded he kept by them as they came towards the drier sand, a rag of wolf's tongue redpanting from his jaws. His speckled body ambled ahead of them and then loped off at a calf's gallop. The carcass lay on his path. He stopped, sniffed, stalked round it, brother, nosing closer, went round it, sniffling rapidly like a dog all over the dead dog's bedraggled fell. Dogskull, dogsniff, eyes on the ground, moves to one great goal. Ah, poor dogsbody. Here lies poor dogsbody's body.

—Tatters! Out of that, you mongrel.

The cry brought him skulking back to his master and a blunt

3. Of course.
4. A man had been drowned off the coast, and his body had not yet been recovered. As Stephen thinks of the horror of drowning he recalls once again his mother's death.
5. At this point in its constantly changing appearance the dog looks like a heraldic animal and is described in the language of heraldry; the sentence "On a field * * * unattired" means: "On an orange-brown (tawny) background, a buck, tripping, in natural colors, without horns."
6. Stephen recognizes the man and woman on the beach as gypsy cocklepickers (cockles are edible shellfish, like mussels).

bootless kick sent him unscathed across a spit of sand, crouched in flight. He slunk back in a curve. Doesn't see me. Along by the edge of the mole he lolloped, dawdled, smelt a rock and from under a cocked hindleg pissed against it. He trotted forward and, lifting his hindleg, pissed quick short at an unsmelt rock. The simple pleasures of the poor. His hindpaws then scattered sand: then his forepaws dabbled and delved. Something he buried there, his grandmother.[7] He rooted in the sand, dabbling, delving and stopped to listen to the air, scraped up the sand again with a fury of his claws, soon ceasing, a pard,[8] a panther, got in spousebreach,[9] vulturing the dead.

After he woke me up last night same dream or was it? Wait. Open hallway. Street of harlots. Remember. Haroun al Raschid.[1] I am almosting it. That man led me, spoke. I was not afraid. The melon he had he held against my face. Smiled: creamfruit smell. That was the rule, said. In. Come. Red carpet spread. You will see who.

Shouldering their bags they trudged, the red Egyptians.[2] His blued feet out of turnedup trousers slapped the clammy sand, a dull brick muffler strangling his unshaven neck. With woman steps she followed: the ruffian and his strolling mort.[3] Spoils slung at her back. Loose sand and shellgrit crusted her bare feet. About her windraw face her hair trailed. Behind her lord his helpmate, bing awast, to Romeville.[4] When night hides her body's flaws calling under her brown shawl from an archway where dogs have mired. Her fancyman is treating two Royal Dublins in O'Loughlin's of Blackpitts. Buss her, wap in rogue's rum lingo, for, O, my dimber wapping dell.[5] A shefiend's whiteness under her rancid rags. Fumbally's lane that night: the tanyard smells.

> *White thy fambles, red thy gan*
> *And thy quarrons dainty is.*

7. Reference to a joke Stephen had made to his pupils in school that morning about "the fox burying his grandmother under a hollybush." This has many symbolic reverberations throughout *Ulysses*. The buried grandmother suggests Stephen's mother, the Church, and Ireland (the "Poor Old Woman"), while the hollybush, evergreen tree of life, represents resurrection in which, in spite of his religious disbelief, Stephen is much interested and about which (as about metempsychosis) he is continually brooding.
8. Leopard or panther.
9. I.e., begotten in adultery.
1. Stephen's dream of the famous Caliph of Baghdad, of the "street of harlots," and of his meeting a man with

a melon, foreshadows his meeting later in the day with Leopold Bloom and his visit to the brothel area of Dublin.
2. I.e., gypsies. As Stephen watches the gypsy cockle-pickers with their dog he imagines their vagabond life and recalls fragments of gypsy speech and of thieves' slang.
3. Gypsies' "freewoman" (i.e., a harlot). "Spoils": the association gypsy-Egyptian reminds Stephen of the Israelites "spoiling the Egyptians" in Exodus xii.36.
4. Go away to London.
5. 17th-century thieves' slang—"buss": kiss; "wap": copulate with; "rum": good; "dimber": pretty; "wapping dell": whore.

Couch a hogshead with me then.
In the darkmans clip and kiss.[6]

Morose delectation Aquinas tunbelly calls this, *frate porcospino*.[7]
Unfallen Adam rode and not rutted. Call away let him:[8] *thy quar-*
rons dainty is. Language no whit worse than his. Monkwords, mary-
beads jabber on their girdles: roguewords, tough nuggets patter in
their pockets.

Passing now.

A side-eye at my Hamlet hat. If I were suddenly naked here as
I sit? I am not. Across the sands of all the world, followed by the
sun's flaming sword, to the west, trekking to evening lands. She
trudges, schlepps, trains, drags, trascines her load.[9] A tide westering, moondrawn, in her wake. Tides, myriadislanded, within her,
blood not mine, *oinopa ponton*,[1] a winedark sea. Behold the handmaid of the moon. In sleep the wet sign calls her hour, bids her
rise. Bridebed, childbed, bed of death, ghostcandled.[2] *Omnis caro*
ad te veniet. He comes, pale vampire, through storm his eyes, his
bat sails bloodying the sea, mouth to her mouth's kiss.[3]

Here. Put a pin in that chap, will you? My tablets.[4] Mouth to
her kiss. No. Must be two of em. Glue 'em well. Mouth to her
mouth's kiss.

His lips lipped and mouthed fleshless lips of air: mouth to her
womb. Oomb, allwombing tomb.[5] His mouth moulded issuing
breath, unspeeched: ooeeehah: roar of cataractic planets, globed,
blazing, roaring wayawayawayawayawayaway. Paper. The bank-
notes, blast them. Old Deasy's letter. Here. Thanking you for hospitality tear the blank end off. Turning his back to the sun he bent
over far to a table of rock and scribbled words.[6] That's twice I forgot to take slips from the library counter.

His shadow lay over the rocks as he bent, ending. Why not endless till the farthest star? Darkly they are there behind this light,

6. More thieves' slang: "fambles":
hands; "gan": mouth; "quarrons":
body; "couch a hogshead": come to bed;
"darkmans": night; "clip": kiss. These
four lines and some of the phrases in
the preceding paragraph are quoted
from a song of the period, *The Rogue's*
Delight in Praise of His Strolling Mort
(cf. note 3).
7. "Brother porcupine" (Italian), a reference to the fat ("tunbelly") but
prickly philosopher, St. Thomas Aquinas.
8. The gypsy is calling his dog.
9. All words suggesting moving or dragging. " 'I like that crescendo of verbs,'
he [Joyce] said. 'The irresistible tug
of the tides' " (Budgen).
1. "Winedark sea" (Homer).
2. He is thinking of his mother again.
The Latin (from the burial service)

means: "All flesh will come to thee."
3. Death comes like the Flying Dutchman in a phantom ship to give the fatal
kiss.
4. Cf. Hamlet I.v.107: "My tablets!"
5. Stephen's consciousness here can be
illuminated with reference to Blake's
poem *The Gates of Paradise*, which
concludes: "The door of death I open
found / And the worm weaving in the
ground: / Thou'rt my mother from the
womb, / Wife, sister, daughter, to the
tomb * * * " Cf. also "the earth that's
nature's mother is her tomb. / What
is her burying ground that is her womb
* * * " (*Romeo and Juliet*, II.iii.9–10).
6. Stephen tears off the blank end of
Mr. Deasy's letter to the press and
writes a poem that will be quoted later
in the novel.

darkness shining in the brightness, delta of Cassiopeia, worlds. Me sits there with his augur's rod of ash, in borrowed sandals, by day beside a livid sea, unbeheld, in violet night walking beneath a reign of uncouth stars.[7] I throw this ended shadow from me, manshape ineluctable, call it back. Endless, would it be mine, form of my form? Who watches me here? Who ever anywhere will read these written words? Signs on a white field. Somewhere to someone in your flutiest voice. The good bishop of Cloyne[8] took the veil of the temple out of his shovel hat: veil of space with coloured emblems hatched on its field. Hold hard. Coloured on a flat: yes, that's right. Flat I see, then think distance, near, far, flat I see, east, back. Ah, see now. Falls back suddenly, frozen in stereoscope. Click does the trick. You find my words dark. Darkness is in our souls, do you not think? Flutier. Our souls, shamewounded by our sins, cling to us yet more, a woman to her lover clinging, the more the more.

She trusts me, her hand gentle, the longlashed eyes. Now where the blue hell am I bringing her beyond the veil?[9] Into the ineluctable modality of the ineluctable visuality. She, she, she. What she? The virgin at Hodges Figgis' window on Monday looking in for one of the alphabet books you were going to write. Keen glance you gave her. Wrist through the braided jess of her sunshade. She lives in Leeson park, with a grief and kickshaws, a lady of letters. Talk that to some else, Stevie: a pickmeup. Bet she wears those curse of God stays suspenders and yellow stockings, darned with lumpy wool. Talk about apple dumplings, *piuttosto*.[1] Where are your wits?

Touch me. Soft eyes. Soft soft soft hand. I am lonely here. O, touch me soon, now. What is that word known to all men? I am quiet here alone. Sad too. Touch, touch me.

He lay back at full stretch over the sharp rocks, cramming the scribbled note and pencil into a pocket, his hat tilted down on his eyes. That is Kevin Egan's movement I made nodding for his nap, sabbath sleep. *Et vidit Deus. Et erant valde bona.*[2] Alo! *Bonjour*, welcome as the flowers in May. Under its leaf he watched through peacocktwittering lashes the southing sun. I am caught in this burn-

7. He imagines himself as the constellation Cassiopeia, supposed to represent the wife of Cepheus (an Ethiopian king) seated in a chair and holding up her arms. His ash walking stick he thinks of as an "augur's [Roman soothsayer's] rod of ash."
8. George Berkeley, Bishop of Cloyne (in Ireland), 1685-1753, who argued that the external world has no objective reality but exists only in the mind of the perceiver. Stephen (as at the opening of this episode) is experiment-

ing again with ways of sensing reality.
9. "She" is Psyche, the soul, whom he is bringing from "beyond the veil." But from metaphysical speculations on reality and the soul Stephen is led (by the Psyche association) to think of "the virgin at Hodges Figgis' window."
1. Rather, sooner.
2. Connecting two phrases from the Vulgate: "And God saw" (Genesis i.4) and "And they were very good" (Genesis i.31).

ing scene. Pan's hour, the faunal noon. Among gumheavy serpent-plants, milkoozing fruits, where on the tawny waters leaves lie wide. Pain is far.

And no more turn aside and brood.[3]

His gaze brooded on his broadtoed boots, a buck's castoffs *nebeneinander.* He counted the creases of rucked leather wherein another's foot had nested warm. The foot that beat the ground in tripudium, foot I dislove. But you were delighted when Esther Osvalt's shoe went on you: girl I knew in Paris. *Tiens, quel petit pied!*[4] Staunch friend, a brother soul: Wilde's love that dare not speak its name. He now will leave me. And the blame? As I am. As I am. All or not at all.

In long lassoes from the Cock lake the water flowed full, covering greengoldenly lagoons of sand, rising, flowing. My ashplant will float away. I shall wait. No, they will pass on, passing chafing against the low rocks, swirling, passing. Better get this job over quick. Listen: a fourworded wavespeech: seesoo, hrss, rsseeiss ooos. Vehement breath of waters amid seasnakes, rearing horses, rocks. In cups of rocks it slops: flop, slop, slap: bounded in barrels. And, spent, its speech ceases. It flows purling, widely flowing, floating foampool, flower unfurling.

Under the upswelling tide he saw the writhing weeds lift languidly and sway reluctant arms, hising up their petticoats,[5] in whispering water swaying and upturning coy silver fronds. Day by day: night by night: lifted, flooded and let fall. Lord, they are weary: and, whispered to, they sigh. Saint Ambrose heard it, sigh of leaves and waves, waiting, awaiting the fullness of their times, *diebus ac noctibus iniurias patiens ingemiscit.*[6] To no end gathered: vainly then released, forth flowing, wending back: loom of the moon. Weary too in sight of lovers, lascivious men, a naked woman shining in her courts, she draws a toil of waters.

Five fathoms out there. Full fathom five thy father lies.[7] At one he said. Found drowned. High water at Dublin bar. Driving before it a loose drift of rubble, fanshoals of fishes, silly shells. A corpse rising saltwhite from the undertow, bobbing landward, a pace a pace a porpoise. There he is. Hook it quick. Sunk though he be beneath the watery floor. We have him. Easy now.

3. The first line of the second (and last) stanza of Yeats's poem *Who Goes with Fergus,* which is often in Stephen's mind. The line expresses for him the mood of noontide stillness and of lotos-eating in a lush oriental scene which overcomes him momentarily when he realizes that it is 12 o'clock, the hour of the Greek nature god Pan, "faunal noon." This oriental lotos-eating theme, which is associated also with Bloom, is important in the *Ulysses.*
4. "Look, what a little foot!"
5. A phrase from a vulgar song sung by Mulligan earlier that morning.
6. "Night and day he patiently groaned forth his wrongs" (St. Ambrose).
7. The theme of the drowned man is important in this episode (cf. the drowned sailor in Eliot's *Waste Land*). This line is from Ariel's song in *The Tempest* (I.ii.396).

Bag of corpsegas sopping in foul brine. A quiver of minnows, fat of a spongy titbit, flash though the slits of his buttoned trouser-fly. God becomes man becomes fish becomes barnacle goose becomes featherbed mountain. Dead breaths I living breathe, tread dead dust, devour a urinous offal from all dead. Hauled stark over the gunwale he breathes upward the stench of his green grave, his leprous nosehole snoring to the sun.

A seachange this, brown eyes saltblue. Seadeath, mildest of all deaths known to man. Old Father Ocean. *Prix de Paris:*[8] beware of imitations. Just you give it a fair trial. We enjoyed ourselves immensely.

Come. I thirst. Clouding over. No black clouds anywhere, are there?[9] Thunderstorm. Allbright he falls, proud lightning of the intellect, *Lucifer, dico, qui nescit occasum.*[1] No. My cockle hat and staff and his my sandal shoon.[2] Where? To evening lands. Evening will find itself.

He took the hilt of his ashplant, lunging with it softly, dallying still. Yes, evening will find itself in me, without me. All days make their end. By the way next when is it? Tuesday will be the longest day. Of all the glad new year, mother,[3] the rum tum tiddledy tum. Lawn Tennyson, gentleman poet. *Già.*[4] For the old hag with the yellow teeth. And Monsieur Drumont, gentleman journalist. *Già.* My teeth are very bad. Why, I wonder? Feel. That one is going too. Shells. Ought I go to a dentist, I wonder, with what money? That one. Toothless Kinch, the superman. Why is that, I wonder, or does it mean something perhaps?

My handkerchief. He threw it. I remember. Did I not take it up?

His hand groped vainly in his pockets. No, I didn't. Better buy one.

He laid the dry snot picked from his nostril on a ledge of rock, carefully. For the rest let look who will.

Behind. Perhaps there is someone.

He turned his face over a shoulder, rere regardant.[5] Moving

---

8. "Prize of Paris"; the reference is probably to the Paris Exposition of 1889, where prizes were awarded in various categories of food, etc.: the prize-winning commodities bear the seal of the prize on the label (hence, "beware of imitations"). Stephen mentally awards the prize to death by drowning. "Seachange" is from Ariel's song, once more.

9. Stephen is looking up to make sure the sky does not threaten a thunderstorm; like Joyce, he hates thunder.

1. Thunder and lightning recall the Fall of Lucifer, "Lucifer, I say, who knows not his fall."

2. From Ophelia's mad song (*Hamlet*, IV.v.23–26): "How should I your

true-love know / From another one? / By his cockle hat and staff, / And his sandal shoon." Ophelia, too, was drowned.

3. "You must wake and call me early, call me early, mother dear; / Tomorrow 'ill be the happiest time of all the glad New Year * * * " From *The May Queen* by Alfred, Lord Tennyson ("Lawn Tennyson").

4. Of course!

5. Looking behind him (heraldic terminology). Stephen, as we leave him sitting by the shore, is described in a highly stylized, heraldic language, as though he had himself become a work of art.

through the air high spars of a threemaster, her sails brailed up on the crosstrees,[6] homing, upstream, silently moving, a silent ship.

[Lestrygonians][1]

Pineapple rock, lemon platt, butter scotch. A sugarsticky girl shovelling scoopfuls of creams for a christian brother. Some school treat. Bad for their tummies. Lozenge and comfit manufacturer to His Majesty the King. God. Save. Our. Sitting on his throne, sucking red jujubes white.

A sombre Y. M. C. A. young man, watchful among the warm sweet fumes of Graham Lemon's, placed a throwaway in a hand of Mr Bloom.

Heart to heart talks.

Bloo . . . Me? No.

Blood of the Lamb.[2]

His slow feet walked him riverward, reading. Are you saved? All are washed in the blood of the lamb. God wants blood victim. Birth, hymen, martyr, war, foundation of a building, sacrifice, kidney burntoffering, druid's altars. Elijah is coming. Dr John Alex-

6. When Budgen pointed out to Joyce that "crosstrees" was not the proper nautical term for the spars to which the sails are bent, Joyce thanked him but added: "But the word 'crosstrees' is essential. It comes in later on and I can't change it. After all, a yard is also a crosstree for the onlooking landlubber." Joyce later uses "crosstree" in a reference to the crucifixion of Christ, so that the suggestion here is of Stephen as both artist and martyr (as his name implies). But the ship is also a real ship, which actually arrived in Dublin on June 16, 1904.

1. It is lunch time in Dublin and Leopold Bloom, as he walks through the city in no great hurry (for he likes to linger and watch what goes on around him), thinks of food. The Lestrygonians in Book X of the *Odyssey* are cannibals, and throughout this episode there are suggestions of the slaughter of living creatures for food, or of food as something disgusting, which make somewhat tenuous contact with Homer's description of the cannibals spearing Ulysses' men for food; the parallel is not, however, profound or very important. What is most important about this episode is that it shows us Bloom's consciousness responding to the sights and sounds of Dublin. His humane curiosity, his desire to learn and to improve the human lot, his sympathetic concern for Mrs. Breen and Mrs. Purefoy, his feeding the gulls, his recollections of a happier time when his daugh-

ter was a baby and his relations with his wife Molly were thoroughly satisfactory, his interest in opera, his continuous shying away from thoughts of his wife's rendezvous with the dashing Blazes Boylan—all this helps to build up his character in depth and to differentiate him sharply from Stephen. Unlike Stephen, Bloom's interest in language is confined to simple puns and translations, his interest in poetry is obvious and sentimental; his interest in the nature of reality takes the form of half-forgotten fragments of science remaining in his mind from schooldays. Everything about him is concrete, practical, sensual, and middlebrow or lowbrow, as distinct from the abstract, theoretical, esoteric speculations of Stephen in the "Proteus" episode. For example, when Stephen saw seagulls, he speculated on Daedalus and on flying as a symbol of the artist going into exile; when Bloom sees them, he thinks they must be hungry and buys a bun to feed them. There are parallels between their two streams of consciousness. Bloom's thoughts, in a sense, include Stephen's, but in a popularized and even vulgarized form.

The text of this selection has also been collated with the Odyssey Press edition of 1932.

2. Bloom has been handed a religious leaflet ("throwaway") containing the phrase "Blood of the Lamb." He at first mistakes "Blood" for "Bloom."

ander Dowie, restorer of the church in Zion, is coming.[3]

Is coming! Is coming!! Is coming!!!
All heartily welcome.

Paying game. Torry and Alexander last year. Polygamy. His wife will put the stopper on that. Where was that ad some Birmingham firm the luminous crucifix? Our Saviour. Wake up in the dead of night and see him on the wall, hanging. Pepper's ghost idea. Iron nails ran in.

Phosphorous it must be done with. If you leave a bit of codfish for instance. I could see the bluey silver over it. Night I went down to the pantry in the kitchen. Don't like all the smells in it waiting to rush out. What was it she wanted?[4] The Malaga raisins. Thinking of Spain. Before Rudy[5] was born. The phosphorescence, that bluey greeny. Very good for the brain.

From Butler's monument house corner he glanced along Bachelor's walk. Dedalus' daughter there still outside Dillon's auctionrooms. Must be selling off some old furniture. Knew her eyes at once from the father. Lobbing about waiting for him. Home always breaks up when the mother goes. Fifteen children he had. Birth every year almost. That's in their theology or the priest won't give the poor woman the confession, the absolution. Increase and multiply. Did you ever hear such an idea? Eat you out of house and home. No families themselves to feed. Living on the fat of the land. Their butteries and larders. I'd like to see them do the black fast Yom Kippur.[6] Crossbuns. One meal and a collation for fear he'd collapse on the altar. A housekeeper of one of those fellows if you could pick it out of her. Never pick it out of her. Like getting L s. d.[7] out of him. Does himself well. No guests. All for number one. Watching his water. Bring your own bread and butter. His reverence. Mum's the word.

Good Lord, that poor child's dress is in flitters. Underfed she looks too. Potatoes and marge, marge and potatoes. It's after they feel it. Proof of the pudding. Undermines the constitution.

As he set foot on O'Connell bridge a puffball of smoke plumed up from the parapet. Brewery barge with export stout. England. Sea air sours it, I heard. Be interesting some day get a pass through Hancock to see the brewery. Regular world in itself. Vats of potter, wonderful. Rats get in too. Drink themselves bloated as big as a collie floating. Dead drunk on the porter. Drink till they puke again

---

3. Dowie was a Scottish-American evangelist who established the "Christian Catholic Apostolic Church in Zion" (i.e., Zion City, Illinois) in 1901.
4. "She" is Bloom's wife Molly, born in Gibraltar.

5. Their son, who had died in infancy eleven years before.
6. Jewish Day of Atonement.
7. I.e., cash: £, s., d. are the abbreviations, respectively, for pounds, shillings, and pence.

like christians. Imagine drinking that! Rats: vats. Well of course if we knew all the things.

Looking down he saw flapping strongly, wheeling between the gaunt quay walls, gulls. Rough weather outside. If I threw myself down? Reuben J's son must have swallowed a good bellyful of that sewage.[8] One and eightpence too much. Hhhhm. It's the droll way he comes out with the things. Knows how to tell a story too.

They wheeled lower. Looking for grub. Wait.

He threw down among them a crumpled paper ball. Elijah thirtytwo feet per sec is com.[9] Not a bit. The ball bobbed unheeded on the wake of swells, floated under by the bridge piers. Not such damn fools. Also the day I threw that stale cake out of the Erin's King picked it up in the wake fifty yards astern. Live by their wits. They wheeled, flapping.

> *The hungry famished gull*
> *Flaps o'er the waters dull.*

That is how poets write, the similar sounds. But then Shakespeare has no rhymes: blank verse. The flow of the language it is. The thoughts. Solemn.

> *Hamlet, I am thy father's spirit*
> *Doomed for a certain time to walk the earth.*[1]

—Two apples a penny! Two for a penny!

His gaze passed over the glazed apples serried on her stand. Australians they must be this time of year. Shiny peels: polishes them up with a rag or a handkerchief.

Wait. Those poor birds.

He halted again and bought from the old applewoman two Banbury cakes for a penny and broke the brittle paste and threw its fragments down into the Liffey. See that? The gulls swooped silently two, then all, from their heights, pouncing on prey. Gone. Every morsel.

Aware of their greed and cunning he shook the powdery crumb from his hands. They never expected that. Manna.[2] Live on fishy flesh they have to, all sea birds, gulls, seagoose. Swans from Anna

---

8. Reuben J. Dodd, Dublin solicitor (lawyer), whose son had been rescued from the Liffey River by a man to whom Reuben J. had given two shillings as a reward—"one and eightpence too much," as Simon Dedalus had remarked to Bloom earlier that morning when they were discussing the incident. It is Dedalus' comment that Bloom is thinking of in the following sentences.

9. I.e., Elijah is coming, accelerating at the rate of 32 feet per second per second, the acceleration rate of falling bodies. ("Elijah is coming" is the legend on the handbill Bloom is tossing away). 1. *Hamlet* I.v.9–10 (slightly misquoted).
2. The divine food (small, round, and white) which the children of Israel ate in the wilderness (Exodus xvi.14–15).

Liffey[3] swim down here sometimes to preen themselves. No accounting for tastes. Wonder what kind is swanmeat. Robinson Crusoe had to live on them.

They wheeled, flapping weakly. I'm not going to throw any more. Penny quite enough. Lot of thanks I get. Not even a caw. They spread foot and mouth disease too. If you cram a turkey, say, on chestnut meal it tastes like that. Eat pig like pig. But then why is it that saltwater fish are not salty? How is that?

His eyes sought answer from the river and saw a rowboat rock at anchor on the treacly swells lazily its plastered board.

Kino's
11/-
Trousers.[4]

Good idea that. Wonder if he pays rent to the corporation. How can you own water really? It's always flowing in a stream, never the same, which in the stream of life we trace. Because life is a stream. All kinds of places are good for ads. That quack doctor for the clap used to be stuck up in all the greenhouses. Never see it now. Strictly confidential. Dr Hy Franks. Didn't cost him a red like Maginni the dancing master self advertisement. Got fellows to stick them up or stick them up himself for that matter on the q. t. running in to loosen a button. Fly by night. Just the place too. POST NO BILLS. POST NO PILLS. Some chap with a dose burning him. If he. . .

O!

Eh?

No . . . No.

No, no. I don't believe it. He wouldn't surely?

No, no.[5]

Mr Bloom moved forward raising his troubled eyes. Think no more about that. After one. Timeball on the ballast office is down. Dunsink time. Fascinating little book that is of Sir Robert Ball's.[6] Parallax. I never exactly understood. There's a priest. Could ask

---

3. The Liffey flows from the Wicklow Mountains northeast and east to Dublin Bay.
4. I.e., eleven shillings ("11/-") for Kino's Trousers. Bloom is a canvasser for advertisements: he receives commissions from newspapers for getting tradesmen to place advertisements with them.
5. Blazes Boylan, flashy philanderer, is due to call on Molly Bloom that afternoon, to discuss the program of a concert which he is managing for her (Molly is a singer). Bloom knows that Boylan and his wife will commit adultery together. Here it suddenly occurs to him that Boylan might give Molly

a "dose" of venereal disease, but he puts the thought from him as incredible.
6. The "timeball on the ballastoffice" registers the official time of the observatory at Dunsink. Noticing that the timeball is down, which means that it is after 1 o'clock, Bloom is reminded of the observatory, then of the Irish astronomer Sir Robert Ball's popular book on astronomy, *The Story of the Heavens* (1886), and of the astronomical term "parallax" he found in the book but which he "never exactly understood."

him. Par it's Greek: parallel, parallax. Met him pikehoses[7] she called it till I told her about the transmigration. O rocks!

Mr Bloom smiled O rocks at two windows of the ballast office. She's right after all. Only big words for ordinary things on account of the sound. She's not exactly witty. Can be rude too. Blurt out what I was thinking. Still I don't know. She used to say Ben Dollard had a base barreltone voice. He has legs like barrels and you'd think he was singing into a barrel. Now, isn't that wit? They used to call him big Ben. Not half as witty as calling him base barreltone. Appetite like an albatross. Get outside of a baron of beef. Powerful man he was at storing away number one Bass.[8] Barrel of Bass. See? It all works out.

A procession of whitesmocked men marched slowly towards him along the gutter, scarlet sashes across their boards. Bargains. Like that priest they are this morning: we have sinned: we have suffered. He read the scarlet letters on their five tall white hats: H. E. L. Y. S. Wisdom Hely's. Y lagging behind drew a chunk of bread from under his foreboard, crammed it into his mouth and munched as he walked. Our staple food. Three bob a day, walking along the gutters, street after street. Just keep skin and bone together, bread and skilly. They are not Boyl: no: M'Glade's men. Doesn't bring in any business either. I suggested to him about a transparent show cart with two smart girls sitting inside writing letters, copybooks, envelopes, blotting paper. I bet that would have caught on. Smart girls writing something catch the eye at once. Everyone dying to know what she's writing. Get twenty of them round you if you stare at nothing. Have a finger in the pie. Women too. Curiosity. Pillar of salt. Wouldn't have it of course because he didn't think of it himself first. Or the inkbottle I suggested with a false stain of black celluloid. His ideas for ads like Plumtree's potted under the obituaries, cold meat department. You can't lick 'em. What? Our envelopes. Hello! Jones, where are you going? Can't stop, Robinson, I am hastening to purchase the only reliable inkeraser *Kansell*, sold by Hely's Ltd, 85 Dame Street. Well out of that ruck I am. Devil of a job it was collecting accounts of those convents. Tranquilla convent. That was a nice nun there, really sweet face. Wimple suited her small head. Sister? Sister? I am sure she was crossed in love by her eyes. Very hard to bargain with that sort of woman. I disturbed her at her devotions that morning. But glad to communicate with the outside world. Our great day, she said.

7. Molly's way of pronouncing "metempsychosis." When Bloom had explained metempsychosis to her that morning, she had exclaimed "O rocks" at the pretentious term. He now mentally repeats "O rocks!" at the thought of the word "parallax."
8. A popular British beer.

Feast of Our Lady of Mount Carmel. Sweet name too: caramel. She knew, I think she knew by the way she. If she had married she would have changed. I suppose they really were short of money. Fried everything in the best butter all the same. No lard for them. My heart's broke eating dripping. They like buttering themselves in an out. Molly tasting it, her veil up. Sister? Pat Claffey, the pawnbroker's daughter. It was a nun they say invented barbed wire.

He crossed Westmoreland street when apostrophe S had plodded by. Rover cycleshop. Those races are on today. How long ago is that? Year Phil Gilligan died. We were in Lombard street west. Wait, was in Thom's. Got the job in Wisdom Hely's year we married. Six years. Ten years ago: ninetyfour he died, yes that's right, the big fire at Arnott's. Val Dillon was lord mayor. The Glencree dinner. Alderman Robert O'Reilly emptying the port into his soup before the flag fell, Bobbob lapping it for the inner alderman. Couldn't hear what the band played. For what we have already received may the Lord make us. Milly[9] was a kiddy then. Molly had that elephantgrey dress with the braided frogs. Mantailored with selfcovered buttons. She didn't like it because I sprained my ankle first day she wore choir picnic at the Sugarloaf. As if that. Old Goodwin's tall hat done up with some sticky stuff. Flies' picnic too. Never put a dress on her back like it. Fitted her like a glove, shoulder and hips. Just beginning to plump it out well. Rabbit pie we had that day. People looking after her.

Happy. Happier then. Snug little room that was with the red wallpaper, Dockrell's, one and ninepence a dozen. Milly's tubbing night. American soap I bought: elderflower. Cosy smell of her bathwater. Funny she looked soaped all over. Shapely too. Now photography.[1] Poor papa's daguerreotype atelier he told me of. Hereditary taste.

He walked along the curbstone.

Stream of life. What was the name of that priestlylooking chap was always squinting in when he passed? Weak eyes, woman. Stopped in Citron's saint Kevin's parade. Pen something. Pendennis? My memory is getting. Pen . . . ? of course it's years ago. Noise of the trams probably. Well, if he couldn't remember the dayfather's name that he sees every day.

Bartell d'Arcy was the tenor, just coming out then. Seeing her home after practice. Conceited fellow with his waxedup moustache. Gave her that song *Winds that blow from the south.*

Windy night that was I went to fetch her there was that lodge meeting on about those lottery tickets after Goodwin's concert in the supper room or oakroom of the mansion house. He and I be-

---

9. Bloom's 15-year-old daughter.   1. Milly is working at a photographer's.

hind. Sheet of her music blew out of my hand against the high school railings. Lucky it didn't. Thing like that spoils the effect of a night for her. Professor Goodwin linking her in front. Shaky on his pins, poor old sot. His farewell concerts. Positively last appearance on any stage. May be for months and may be for never. Remember her laughing at the wind, her blizzard collar up. Corner of Harcourt road remember that gust? Brrfoo! Blew up all her skirts and her boa nearly smothered old Goodwin. She did get flushed in the wind. Remember when we got home raking up the fire and frying up those pieces of lap of mutton for her supper with the Chutney sauce she liked. And the mulled rum. Could see her in the bedroom from the hearth unclamping the busk of her stays. White.

Swish and soft flop her stays made on the bed. Always warm from her. Always liked to let herself out. Sitting there after till near two, taking out her hairpins. Milly tucked up in beddyhouse. Happy. Happy. That was the night. . .

—O, Mr Bloom, how do you do?

—O, how do you do, Mrs Breen?[2]

—No use complaining. How is Molly those times? Haven't seen her for ages.

—In the pink, Mr Bloom said gaily, Milly has a position down in Mullingar, you know.

—Go away! Isn't that grand for her?

—Yes, in a photographer's there. Getting on like a house on fire. How are all your charges?

—All on the baker's list, Mrs Breen said.

How many has she? No other in sight.

—You're in black I see. You have no. . .

—No, Mr Bloom said. I have just come from a funeral.

Going to crop up all day, I foresee. Who's dead, when and what did he die of? Turn up like a bad penny.

—O dear me, Mrs Breen said, I hope it wasn't any near relation.

May as well get her sympathy.

—Dignam, Mr Bloom said. An old friend of mine. He died quite suddenly, poor fellow. Heart trouble, I believe. Funeral was this morning.

> *Your funeral's tomorrow*
> *While you're coming through the rye.*
> *Diddlediddle dumdum*
> *Diddlediddle. . .*

—Sad to lose the old friends, Mrs Breen's woman eyes said melancholily.

Now that's quite enough about that. Just quietly: husband.

2. Mrs. Breen had been an old sweetheart of Bloom's.

—And your lord and master?

Mrs Breen turned up her two large eyes. Hasn't lost them anyhow.

—O, don't be talking, she said. He's a caution to rattlesnakes. He's in there now with his lawbooks finding out the law of libel. He has me heartscalded. Wait till I show you.

Hot mockturtle vapour and steam of newbaked jampuffs rolypoly poured out from Harrison's. The heavy noonreek tickled the top of Mr Bloom's gullet. Want to make good pastry, butter, best flour, Demerara sugar, or they'd taste it with the hot tea. Or is it from her? A barefoot arab stood over the grating, breathing in the fumes. Deaden the gnaw of hunger that way. Pleasure or pain is it? Penny dinner. Knife and fork chained to the table.

Opening her handbag, chipped leather, hatpin: ought to have a guard on those things. Stick it in a chap's eye in the tram. Rummaging. Open. Money. Please take one. Devils if they lose sixpence. Raise Cain. Husband barging. Where's the ten shillings I gave you on Monday? Are you feeding your little brother's family? Soiled handkerchief: medicinebottle. Pastille that was fell. What is she? . . .

—There must be a new moon out, she said. He's always bad then.[3] Do you know what he did last night?

Her hand ceased to rummage. Her eyes fixed themselves on him, wide in alarm, yet smiling.

—What? Mr Bloom asked.

Let her speak. Look straight in her eyes. I believe you. Trust me.

—Woke me up in the night, she said. Dream he had, a nightmare.

Indiges.

—Said the ace of spades[4] was walking up the stairs.

—The ace of spades! Mr Bloom said.

She took a folded postcard from her handbag.

—Read that, she said. He got it this morning.

—What is it? Mr Bloom asked, taking the card. U. P.?

—U. P.: up, she said. Someone taking a rise out of him. It's a great shame for them whoever he is.

—Indeed it is, Mr Bloom said.

She took back the card, sighing.

—And now he's going round to Mr Menton's office. He's going to take an action for ten thousand pounds, he says.

She folded the card into her untidy bag and snapped the catch.

Same blue serge dress she had two years ago, the nap bleaching. Seen its best days. Wispish hair over her ears. And that dowdy

---

3. Mr. Breen is mentally disturbed.   4. Symbol of death.

toque, three old grapes to take the harm out of it. Shabby genteel. She used to be a tasty dresser. Lines round her mouth. Only a year or so older than Molly.

See the eye that woman gave her, passing. Cruel. The unfair sex.

He looked still at her, holding back behind his look his discontent. Pungent mockturtle oxtail mulligatawny. I'm hungry too. Flakes of pastry on the gusset of her dress: daub of sugary flour stuck to her cheek. Rhubarb tart with liberal fillings, rich fruit interior. Josie Powell that was. In Luke Doyle's long ago, Dolphin's Barn, the charades. U. P.: up.

Change the subject.

—Do you ever see anything of Mrs Beaufoy, Mr Bloom asked.

—Mina Purefoy? she said.

Philip Beaufoy I was thinking. Playgoer's club.[5] Matcham often thinks of the masterstroke. Did I pull the chain? Yes. The last act.

—Yes.

—I just called to ask on the way in is she over it. She's in the lying-in hospital in Holles street. Dr Horne got her in. She's three days bad now.

—O, Mr Bloom said. I'm sorry to hear that.

—Yes, Mrs Breen said. And a houseful of kids at home. It's a very stiff birth, the nurse told me.

—O, Mr Bloom said.

His heavy pitying gaze absorbed her news. His tongue clacked in compassion. Dth! Dth!

—I'm sorry to hear that, he said. Poor thing! Three days! That's terrible for her.

Mrs Breen nodded.

—She was taken bad on the Tuesday. . .

Mr Bloom touched her funnybone gently, warning her.

—Mind! Let this man pass.

A bony form strode along the curbstone from the river, staring with a rapt gaze into the sunlight through a heavy stringed glass. Tight as a skullpiece a tiny hat gripped his head. From his arm a folded dustcoat, a stick and an umbrella dangled to his stride.

—Watch him, Mr Bloom said. He always walks outside the lampposts. Watch!

—Who is he if it's a fair question, Mrs. Breen asked. Is he dotty?

—His name is Cashel Boyle O'Connor Fitzmaurice Tisdall Farrell, Mr Bloom said, smiling. Watch!

5. Bloom is thinking of the story *Matcham's Masterstroke*, by "Mr. Philip Beaufoy, Playgoers' club, London," which he had read in the toilet that morning. He then mentally quotes the opening sentence.

—He has enough of them, she said. Denis will be like that one of these days.

She broke off suddenly.

—There he is, she said. I must go after him. Goodbye. Remember me to Molly, won't you?

—I will, Mr Bloom said.

He watched her dodge through passers towards the shopfronts. Denis Breen in skimpy frockcoat and blue canvas shoes shuffled out of Harrison's hugging two heavy tomes to his ribs. Blown in from the bay. Like old times. He suffered her to overtake him without surprise and thrust his dull grey beard towards her, his loose jaw wagging as he spoke earnestly.

Meshuggah.[6] Off his chump.

Mr Bloom walked on again easily, seeing ahead of him in sunlight the tight skullpiece, the dangling stick, umbrella, dustcoat. Going the two days. Watch him! Out he goes again. One way of getting on in the world. And that other old mosey lunatic in those duds. Hard time she must have with him.

U. P.: up. I'll take my oath that's Alf Bergan or Richie Goulding. Wrote it for a lark in the Scotch house, I bet anything. Round to Menton's office. His oyster eyes staring at the postcard. Be a feast for the gods.

He passed the *Irish Times*. There might be other answers lying there. Like to answer them all. Good system for criminals. Code. At their lunch now. Clerk with the glasses there doesn't know me. O, leave them there to simmer. Enough bother wading through fortyfour of them. Wanted smart lady typist to aid gentleman in literary work. I called you naughty darling because I do not like that other world. Please tell me what is the meaning. Please tell me what perfume does your wife.[7] Tell me who made the world. The way they spring those questions on you. And the other one Lizzie Twigg. My literary efforts have had the good fortune to meet with the approval of the eminent poet A. E. (Mr Geo Russell).[7a] No time to do her hair drinking sloppy tea with a book of poetry.

Best paper by long chalks for a small ad. Got the provinces now. Cook and general, exc cuisine, housemaid kept. Wanted live man for spirit counter. Resp girl (R. C.) wishes to hear of post in fruit or pork shop. James Carlisle made that. Six and a half per cent

---

6. Yiddish, "mad."

7. Bloom is mentally quoting a letter written to him by the typist Martha Clifford, with whom he is carrying on a purely epistolary love affair (she had misspelled "word" as "world": "I do not like that other *world*"). Lizzie Twigg was one of the other typists who had answered his advertisement for a

secretary "to aid gentleman in literary work" (Bloom's pretext for beginning such an affair).

7a. A. E. (George Russell, 1867–1935), the Irish poet mentioned as a reference by Lizzie Twigg when she answered Bloom's advertisement, is later encountered by Bloom with a woman who Bloom speculates might be Lizzie.

dividend. Made a big deal on Coates's shares. Ca'canny. Cunning old Scotch hunks. All the toady news. Our gracious and popular vicereine.[8] Bought the *Irish Field* now. Lady Mountcashel has quite recovered after her confinement and rode out with the Ward Union staghounds at the enlargement yesterday at Rathoath. Uneatable fox. Pothunters too. Fear injects juices make it tender enough for them. Riding astride. Sit her horse like a man. Weightcarrying huntress. No sidesaddle or pillion for her, not for Joe. First to the meet and in at the death. Strong as a brood mare some of those horsey women. Swagger around livery stables. Toss off a glass of brandy neat while you'd say knife. That one at the Grosvenor this morning. Up with her on the car: wishwish. Stonewall or fivebarred gate put her mount to it. Think that pugnosed driver did it out of spite. Who is this she was like? O yes! Mrs Miriam Dandrade that sold me her old wraps and black underclothes in the Shelbourne hotel. Divorced Spanish American. Didn't take a feather out of her my handling them. As if I was her clotheshorse. Saw her in the viceregal party when Stubbs the park ranger got me in with Whelan of the *Express*. Scavenging what the quality left. High tea. Mayonnaise I poured on the plums thinking it was custard. Her ears ought to have tingled for a few weeks after. Want to be a bull for her. Born courtesan. No nursery work for her, thanks.

Poor Mrs Purefoy! Methodist husband. Method in his madness. Saffron bun and milk and soda lunch in the educational dairy. Eating with a stopwatch, thirtytwo chews to the minute. Still his muttonchop whiskers grew. Supposed to be well connected. Theodore's cousin in Dublin Castle. One tony relative in every family. Hardy annuals he presents her with. Saw him out at the Three Jolly Topers marching along bareheaded and his eldest boy carrying one in a marketnet. The squallers. Poor thing! Then having to give the breast year after year all hours of the night. Selfish those t.t's are. Dog in the manger. Only one lump of sugar in my tea, if you please.

He stood at Fleet street crossing. Luncheon interval a six penny at Rowe's? Must look up that ad in the national library.[9] An eightpenny in the Burton. Better. On my way.

He walked on past Bolton's Westmoreland house. Tea. Tea. Tea. I forgot to tap Tom Kernan.[1]

Sss. Dth, dth, dth! Three days imagine groaning on a bed with a vinegared handkerchief round her forehead, her belly swollen out!

---

8. Wife of the Viceroy, who represented the British Crown in Ireland; Bloom is thinking of the society column in the *Irish Times*.
9. Bloom's goal, on his walk through Dublin, is the National Library, where he wants to look up an advertisement in a back number of the *Kilkenny People*.
1. A Dublin tea merchant and friend of Bloom's, whom Bloom had earlier intended to ask ("tap") for some tea.

Phew! Dreadful simply! Child's head too big: forceps. Doubled up inside her trying to butt its way out blindly, groping for the way out. Kill me that would. Lucky Molly got over hers lightly. They ought to invent something to stop that. Life with hard labour. Twilight-sleep idea: queen Victoria was given that. Nine she had. A good layer. Old woman that lived in a shoe she had so many children. Suppose he was consumptive. Time someone thought about it instead of gassing about the what was it the pensive bosom of the silver effulgence. Flapdoodle to feed fools on. They could easily have big establishments. Whole thing quite painless out of all the taxes give every child born five quid at compound interest up to twentyone, five per cent is a hundred shillings and five tiresome pounds, multiply by twenty decimal system, encourage people to put by money save hundred and ten and a bit twentyone years want to work it out on paper come to a tidy sum, more than you think.

Not stillborn of course. They are not even registered. Trouble for nothing.

Funny sight two of them together, their bellies out. Molly and Mrs Moisel. Mothers' meeting. Phthisis retires for the time being, then returns. How flat they look after all of a sudden! Peaceful eyes. Weight off their minds. Old Mrs Thornton was a jolly old soul. All my babies, she said. The spoon of pap in her mouth before she fed them. O, that's nyumyum. Got her hand crushed by old Tom Wall's son. His first bow to the public. Head like a prize pumpkin. Snuffy Dr Murren. People knocking them up at all hours. For God's sake doctor. Wife in her throes. Then keep them waiting months for their fee. To attendance on your wife. No gratitude in people. Humane doctors, most of them.

Before the huge high door of the Irish house of parliament a flock of pigeons flew. Their little frolic after meals. Who will we do it on? I pick the fellow in black. Here goes. Here's good luck. Must be thrilling from the air. Apjohn, myself and Owen Goldberg up in the trees near Goose green playing the monkeys. Mackerel they called me.

A squad of constables debouched from College street, marching in Indian file. Goose step. Foodheated faces, sweating helmets, patting their truncheons. After their feed with a good load of fat soup under their belts. Policeman's lot is oft a happy one. They split up into groups and scattered, saluting towards their beats. Let out to graze. Best moment to attack one in pudding time. A punch in his dinner. A squad of others, marching irregularly, rounded Trinity railings, making for the station. Bound for their troughs. Prepare to receive cavalry. Prepare to receive soup.

He crossed under Tommy Moore's roguish finger. They did right to put him up over a urinal: meeting of the waters.[2] Ought to be places for women. Running into cakeshops. Settle my hat straight. *There is not in this wide world a vallee.* Great song of Julia Morkan's. Kept her voice up to the very last. Pupil of Michael Balfe's wasn't she?

He gazed after the last broad tunic. Nasty customers to tackle. Jack Power could a tale unfold: father a G man. If a fellow gave them trouble being lagged they let him have it hot and heavy in the bridewell.[3] Can't blame them after all with the job they have especially the young hornies. That horse policeman the day Joe Chamberlain was given his degree in Trinity he got a run for his money.[4] My word he did! His horse's hoofs clattering after us down Abbey street. Luck I had the presence of mind to dive into Manning's or I was souped. He did come a wallop, by George. Must have cracked his skull on the cobblestones. I oughtn't to have got myself swept along with those medicals. And the Trinity jibs[5] in their mortarboards. Looking for trouble. Still I got to know that young Dixon who dressed that sting for me in the Mater and now he's in Holles street where Mrs Purefoy. Wheels within wheels. Police whistle in my ears still. All skedaddled. Why he fixed on me. Give me in charge. Right here it began.

—Up the Boers!

—Three cheers for De Wet![6]

—We'll hang Joe Chamberlain on a sourapple tree.

Silly billies: mob of young cubs yelling their guts out. Vinegar hill. The Butter exchange band. Few years time half of them magistrates and civil servants. War comes on: into the army helterskelter: same fellows used to whether on the scaffold high.

Never know who you're talking to. Corney Kelleher he has Harvey Duff in his eye. Like that Peter or Denis or James Carey that blew the gaff on the invincibles. Member of the corporation too. Egging raw youths on to get in the know. All the time drawing secret service pay from the castle.[7] Drop him like a hot potato. Why those plain clothes men are always courting slaveys. Easily twig a man used to uniform. Squarepushing up against a backdoor. Maul her a bit. Then the next thing on the menu. And who is the gentleman does be visiting there? Was the young master saying anything? Peeping Tom through the keyhole. Decoy duck. Hotblooded young student fooling round her fat arms ironing.

---

2. *The Meeting of the Waters* was a famous poem by the much-loved Irish poet Thomas Moore (1779–1852) whose statue Bloom now passes.
3. Prison.
4. When Joseph Chamberlain, the British Colonial Secretary, came to Dublin to receive an honorary degree from Trinity College, a group of medical students rioted against him and against the Boer War.
5. Trinity College students.
6. Boer general.
7. I.e., from the British government, whose representative lived at Dublin Castle.

—Are those yours, Mary?

—I don't wear such things. . . Stop or I'll tell the missus on you. Out half the night.

—There are great times coming, Mary. Wait till you see.

—Ah, get along with your great times coming.

Barmaids too. Tobacco shopgirls.

James Stephens'[8] idea was the best. He knew them. Circles of ten so that a fellow couldn't round on more than his own ring. Sinn Fein.[9] Back out you get the knife. Hidden hand. Stay in. The firing squad. Turnkey's daughter got him out of Richmond, off from Lusk. Putting up in the Buckingham Palace hotel under their very noses. Garibaldi.[1]

You must have a certain fascination: Parnell.[2] Arthur Griffith is a squareheaded fellow but he has no go in him for the mob. Want to gas about our lovely land. Gammon and spinach. Dublin Bakery Company's tearoom. Debating societies. That republicanism is the best form of government. That the language question should take precedence of the economic question. Have your daughters inveigling them to your house. Stuff them up with meat and drink. Michaelmas goose. Here's a good lump of thyme seasoning under the apron for you. Have another quart of goosegrease before it gets too cold. Halffed enthusiastists. Penny roll and a walk with the band. No grace for the carver. The thought that the other chap pays best sauce in the world. Make themselves thoroughly at home. Shove us over those apricots, meaning peaches. The not far distant day. Home Rule sun rising up in the northwest.[3]

His smile faded as he walked, a heavy cloud hiding the sun slowly, shadowing Trinity's surly front. Trams passed one another, ingoing, outgoing, clanging. Useless words. Things go on same; day after day: squads of police marching out, back: trams in, out. Those two loonies mooching about. Dignam carted off. Mina Purefoy swollen belly on a bed groaning to have a child tugged out of her. One born every second somewhere. Other dying every second. Since I fed the birds five minutes. Three hundred kicked the bucket. Other three hundred born, washing the blood off, all are washed in the blood of the lamb, bawling maaaaaa.

Cityful passing away, other cityful coming, passing away too: other coming on, passing on. Houses, lines of houses, streets, miles

8. Irish nationalist revolutionary.
9. Irish revolutionary movement; the Gaelic words mean "We Ourselves."
1. Bloom is thinking of a variety of nationalist conspirators who escaped from danger, among them the 19th-century Italian patriot and general Giuseppe Garibaldi.

2. Charles Stewart Parnell (1846–91), Irish nationalist political leader. Arthur Griffith was founder of the Sinn Fein.
3. Reference to Arthur Griffith's comment on the *Freeman* masthead, which showed the sun rising in the northwest from behind the bank of Ireland. Bloom has a *Freeman* in his pocket.

of pavements, piledup bricks, stones. Changing hands. This owner, that. Landlord never dies they say. Other steps into his shoes when he gets his notice to quit. They buy the place up with gold and still they have all the gold. Swindle in it somewhere. Piled up in cities, worn away age after age. Pyramids in sand. Built on bread and onions. Slaves Chinese wall. Babylon. Big stones left. Round towers. Rest rubble, sprawling suburbs, jerrybuilt, Kerwan's mushroom houses, built of breeze. Shelter for the night.

No one is anything.

This is the very worst hour of the day. Vitality. Dull, gloomy: hate this hour. Feel as if I had been eaten and spewed.

Provost's house. The reverend Dr Salmon: tinned salmon. Well tinned in there. Wouldn't live in it if they paid me. Hope they have liver and bacon today. Nature abhors a vacuum.

The sun freed itself slowly and lit glints of light among the silver ware in Walter Sexton's window opposite by which John Howard Parnell[4] passed, unseeing.

There he is: the brother. Image of him. Haunting face. Now that's a coincidence. Course hundreds of times you think of a person and don't meet him. Like a man walking in his sleep. No-one knows him. Must be a corporation meeting today. They say he never put on the city marshal's uniform since he got the job. Charley Boulger used to come out on his high horse, cocked hat, puffed, powdered and shaved. Look at the woebegone walk of him. Eaten a bad egg. Poached eyes on ghost. I have a pain. Great man's brother: his brother's brother. He'd look nice on the city charger. Drop into the D. B. C. probably for his coffee, play chess there. His brother used men as pawns. Let them all go to pot. Afraid to pass a remark on him. Freeze them up with that eye of his. That's the fascination: the name. All a bit touched. Mad Fanny and his other sister Mrs Dickinson driving about with scarlet harness. Bolt upright like surgeon M'Ardle. Still David Sheehy beat him for south Meath. Apply for the Chiltern Hundreds and retire into public life. The patriot's banquet. Eating orangepeels in the park. Simon Dedalus said when they put him in parliament that Parnell would come back from the grave and lead him out of the House of Commons by the arm.

—Of the twoheaded octopus, one of whose heads is the head upon which the ends of the world have forgotten to come while the other speaks with a Scotch accent. The tentacles. . .

They passed from behind Mr Bloom along the curbstone. Beard and bicycle. Young woman.

And there he is too. Now that's really a coincidence: secondtime. Coming events cast their shadows before. With the approval of the

4. C. S. Parnell's brother.

eminent poet Mr Geo Russell.[5] That might be Lizzie Twigg with him. A. E.: what does that mean? Initials perhaps. Albert Edward, Arthur Edmund, Alphonsus Eb Ed El Esquire. What was he saying? The ends of the world with a Scotch accent. Tentacles: octopus. Something occult: symbolism. Holding forth. She's taking it all in. Not saying a word. To aid gentleman in literary work.

His eyes followed the high figure in homespun, beard and bicycle, a listening woman at his side. Coming from the vegetarian. Only weggebobbles and fruit. Don't eat a beefsteak. If you do the eyes of that cow will pursue you through all eternity. They say it's healthier. Wind and watery though. Tried it. Keep you on the run all day. Bad as a bloater. Dreams all night. Why do they call that thing they gave me nutsteak? Nutarians. Fruitarians. To give you the idea you are eating rumpsteak. Absurd. Salty too. They cook in soda. Keep you sitting by the tap all night.

Her stockings are loose over her ankles. I detest that: so tasteless. Those literary ethereal people they are all. Dreamy, cloudy, symbolistic. Esthetes they are. I wouldn't be surprised if it was that kind of food you see produces the like waves of the brain the poetical. For example one of those policemen sweating Irish stew into their shirts; you couldn't squeeze a line of poetry out of him. Don't know what poetry is even. Must be in a certain mood.

> *The dreamy cloudy gull*
> *Waves o'er the waters dull.*

He crossed at Nassau street corner and stood before the window of Yeates and Son, pricing the field glasses. Or will I drop into old Harris's and have a chat with young Sinclair? Wellmannered fellow. Probably at his lunch. Must get those old glasses of mine set right. Gœrz lenses, six guineas. Germans making their way everywhere. Sell on easy terms to capture trade. Undercutting. Might chance on a pair in the railway lost property office. Astonishing the things people leave behind them in trains and cloak rooms. What do they be thinking about? Women too. Incredible. Last year travelling to Ennis had to pick up that farmer's daughter's bag and hand it to her at Limerick junction. Unclaimed money too. There's a little watch up there on the roof of the bank to test those glasses by.

His lids came down on the lower rims of his irides. Can't see it. If you imagine it's there you can almost see it. Can't see it.

He faced about and, standing between the awnings, held out his right hand at arm's length towards the sun. Wanted to try that often. Yes: completely. The tip of his little finger blotted out the

5. Bloom wonders whether the woman with A.E. might be Lizzie Twigg and then goes on to speculate on the meaning of "A.E." and on Russell's mystical ideas.

sun's disk. Must be the focus where the rays cross. If I had black glasses. Interesting. There was a lot of talk about those sunspots when we were in Lombard street west. Terrific explosions they are. There will be a total eclipse this year: autumn some time.

Now that I come to think of it, that ball falls at Greenwich time. It's the clock is worked by an electric wire from Dunsink. Must go out there some first Saturday of the month. If I could get an introduction to professor Joly or learn up something about his family. That would do to: man always feels complimented. Flattery where least expected. Nobleman proud to be descended from some king's mistress. His foremother. Lay it on with a trowel. Cap in hand goes through the land. Not go in and blurt out what you know you're not to: what's parallax? Show this gentleman the door.

Ah.

His hand fell again to his side.

Never know anything about it. Waste of time. Gasballs spinning about, crossing each other, passing. Same old dingdong always. Gas, then solid, then world, then cold, then dead shell drifting around, frozen rock like that pineapple rock. The moon. Must be a new moon out, she said. I believe there is.

He went on by la Maison Claire.

Wait. The full moon was the night we were Sunday fortnight exactly there is a new moon. Walking down by the Tolka. Not bad for a Fairview moon. She was humming: The young May moon she's beaming, love. He other side of her. Elbow, arm. He. Glowworm's la-amp is gleaming, love. Touch. Fingers. Asking. Answer. Yes.

Stop. Stop. If it was it was.[6] Must.

Mr Bloom, quick breathing, slowlier walking, passed Adam court.

With a deep quiet relief, his eyes took note: this is street here middle of the day Bob Doran's bottle shoulders. On his annual bend, M'Coy said. They drink in order to say or do something or *cherchez la femme*.[7] Up in the Coombe with chummies and streetwalkers and then the rest of the year as sober as a judge.

Yes. Thought so. Sloping into the Empire. Gone. Plain soda would do him good. Where Pat Kinsella had his Harp theater before Whitbread ran the Queen's.[8] Broth of a boy. Dion Boucicault business with his harvestmoon face in a poky bonnet. Three Purty Maids from School. How time flies eh? Showing long red pantaloons under his skirts. Drinkers, drinking, laughed spluttering, their drink against their breath. More power, Pat. Coarse red: fun for drunkards: guffaw and smoke. Take off that white hat. His parboiled eyes. Where is he now? Beggar somewhere. The harp that

6. Bloom is thinking again of his wife's infidelities.

7. "Look for the woman" (in the case).

8. The Queen's Theatre. Dion Boucicault was an Irish-born American dramatist, manager, and actor.

2120 · *James Joyce*

once did starve us all.[9]

I was happier then. Or was that I? Or am I now I? Twentyeight I was. She twentythree when we left Lombard street west something changed. Could never like it again after Rudy. Can't bring back time. Like holding water in your hand. Would you go back to then? Just beginning then. Would you? Are you not happy in your home, you poor little naughty boy? Wants to sew on buttons for me. I must answer. Write it in the library.

Grafton street gay with housed awnings lured his senses. Muslin prints silk, dames and dowagers, jingle of harnesses, hoofthuds lowringing in the baking causeway. Thick feet that woman has in the white stockings. Hope the rain mucks them up on her. Country bred chawbacon. All the beef to the heels were in. Always gives a woman clumsy feet. Molly looks out of plumb.

He passed, dallying, the windows of Brown Thomas, silk mercers. Cascades of ribbons. Flimsy China silks. A tilted urn poured from its mouth a flood of bloodhued poplin: lustrous blood. The huguenots brought that here. *La causa è santa!*[1] Tara tara. Great chorus that. Tara. Must be washed in rainwater. Meyerbeer. Tara: bom bom bom.

Pincushions. I'm a long time threatening to buy one. Stick them all over the place. Needles in window curtains.

He bared slightly his left forearm. Scrape: nearly gone. Not today anyhow. Must go back for that lotion. For her birthday perhaps. Junejuly augseptember eighth. Nearly three months off. Then she mightn't like it. Women won't pick up pins. Say it cuts lo.

Gleaming silks, petticoats on slim brass rails, rays of flat silk stockings.

Useless to go back. Had to be. Tell me all.

High voices. Sunwarm silk. Jingling harnesses. All for a woman, home and houses, silk webs, silver, rich fruits, spicy from Jaffa. Agendath Netaim.[2] Wealth of the world.

A warm human plumpness settled down on his brain. His brain yielded. Perfume of embraces all him assailed. With hungered flesh obscurely, he mutely craved to adore.

Duke street. Here we are. Must eat. The Burton. Feel better then.

He turned Combridge's corner, still pursued. Jingling hoofthuds. Perfumed bodies, warm, full. All kissed, yielded: in deep summer fields, tangled pressed grass, in trickling hallways of tenements, along sofas, creaking beds.

9. A reference to the lack of financial success of the Harp Theatre through a punning reworking (almost worthy of Stephen Dedalus) of Tom Moore's famous *Harp That Once Through Tara's Halls*.
1. "The cause is sacred," chorus from Meyerbeer's opera *Les Huguenots*, which Bloom is recalling. The Huguenots were

16th- and 17th-century French Protestants, many of whom fled to Britain to escape persecution.
2. "Planters' Company" (Hebrew). Bloom recalls a leaflet advertising an early Zionist settlement which he had seen that morning and is still carrying in his pocket.

—Jack, love!
—Darling!
—Kiss me, Reggy!
—My boy!
—Love!³

His heart astir he pushed in the door of the Burton restaurant. Stink gripped his trembling breath: pungent meatjuice, slop of greens. See the animals feed.

Men, men, men.

Perched on high stools by the bar, hats shoved back, at the tables calling for more bread no charge, swilling, wolfing gobfuls of sloppy food, their eyes bulging, wiping wetted moustaches. A pallid suetfaced young man polished his tumbler knife fork and spoon with his napkin. New set of microbes. A man with an infant's saucestained napkin tucked round him shovelled gurgling soup down his gullet. A man spitting back on his plate: halfmasticated gristle: no teeth to chewchewchew it. Chump chop from the grill. Bolting to get it over. Sad booser's eyes. Bitten off more than he can chew. Am I like that? See ourselves as others see us. Hungry man is an angry man. Working tooth and jaw. Don't! O! A bone! That last pagan king of Ireland Cormac in the schoolpoem choked himself at Sletty southward of the Boyne.⁴ Wonder what he was eating. Something galoptious. Saint Patrick converted him to Christianity. Couldn't swallow it all however.

—Roast beef and cabbage.
—One stew.

Smells of men. His gorge rose. Spaton sawdust, sweetish warmish cigarette smoke, reek of plug, spilt beer, men's beery piss, the stale of ferment.

Couldn't eat a morsel here. Fellow sharpening knife and fork, to eat all before him, old chap picking his tootles. Slight spasm, full, chewing the cud. Before and after. Grace after meals. Look on this picture then on that. Scoffing up stewgravy with sopping sippets of bread. Lick it off the plate, man! Get out of this.

He gazed round the stooled and tabled eaters, tightening the wings of his nose.

—Two stouts here.
—One corned and cabbage.

That fellow ramming a knifeful of cabbage down as if his life depended on it. Good stroke. Give me the fidgets to look. Safer to eat from his three hands. Tear it limb from limb. Second nature to

3. Sensual images are leading Bloom to imagine love scenes from a sentimental novel. The cannibal Lestrygonians had used "the handsome daughter of Lestrygonian Antiphates" as a decoy to lure Ulysses' men to her father, and Bloom is drawn by his sensual and sexual imagination to enter Burton's restaurant —only to be disgusted by the grossness of the atmosphere.
4. Bloom is recalling a "schoolpoem" about a legendary incident in Irish history.

him. Born with a silver knife in his mouth. That's witty, I think. Or no. Silver means born rich. Born with a knife. But then the allusion is lost.

An illgirt server gathered sticky clattering plates. Rock, the bailiff, standing at the bar blew the foamy crown from his tankard. Well up: it splashed yellow near his boot. A diner, knife and fork upright, elbows on table, ready for a second helping stared towards the foodlift across his stained square of newspaper. Other chap telling him something with his mouth full. Sympathetic listener. Table talk. I munched hum un thu Unchster Bunk un Munchday. Ha? Did you, faith?

Mr Bloom raised two fingers doubtfully to his lips. His eyes said.

—Not here. Don't see him.[5]

Out. I hate dirty eaters.

He backed towards the door. Get a light snack in Davy Byrne's. Stopgap. Keep me going. Had a good breakfast.

—Roast and mashed here.

—Pint of stout.

Every fellow for his own, tooth and nail. Gulp. Grub. Gulp. Gobstuff.

He came out into clearer air and turned back towards Grafton street. Eat or be eaten. Kill! Kill!

Suppose that communal kitchen years to come perhaps. All trotting down with porringers and tommycans to be filled. Devour contents in the street. John Howard Parnell example the provost of Trinity every mother's son don't talk of your provosts and provost of Trinity women and children, cabmen, priests, parsons, fieldmarshals, archbishops. From Ailesbury road, Clyde road, artisan's dwellings north Dublin union, lord mayor in his gingerbread coach, old queen in a bathchair. My plate's empty. After you with our incorporated drinkingcup. Like sir Philip Crampton's fountain. Rub off the microbes with your handkerchief. Next chap rubs on a new batch with his. Father O'Flynn would make hares of them all. Have rows all the same. All for number one. Children fighting for the scrapings of the pot. Want a soup pot as big as the Phoenix Park. Harpooning flitches and hindquarters out of it. Hate people all around you. City Arms hotel *table d'hôte* she called it. Soup, joint and sweet. Never know whose thoughts you're chewing. Then who'd wash up all the plates and forks? Might be all feeding on tabloids that time. Teeth getting worse and worse.

After all there's a lot in that vegetarian fine flavour of things from the earth garlic, of course, it stinks Italian organgrinders crisp of onions, mushrooms truffles. Pain to animal too. Pluck and draw fowl. Wretched brutes there at the cattlemarket waiting for the

5. He pretends he is looking for someone he cannot see, so that he has an excuse to leave without eating.

poleaxe to split their skulls open. Moo. Poor trembling calves. Meh. Staggering bob. Bubble and squeak. Butchers' buckets wobble lights. Give us that brisket off the hook. Plup. Rawhead and bloody bones. Flayed glasseyed sheep hung from their haunches, sheepsnouts bloodypapered sniveling nosejam on sawdust. Top and lashers going out. Don't maul them pieces, young one.

Hot fresh blood they prescribe for decline. Blood always needed. Insidious. Lick it up, smoking hot, thick sugary. Famished ghosts.

Ah, I'm hungry.

He entered Davy Byrne's. Moral pub. He doesn't chat. Stands a drink now and then. But in leapyear once in four. Cashed a cheque for me once.

What will I take now? He drew his watch. Let me see now. Shandygaff?

—Hello, Bloom! Nosey Flynn said from his nook.

—Hello, Flynn.

—How's things?

—Tiptop . . . Let me see. I'll take a glass of burgundy and . . . let me see.

Sardines on the shelves. Almost taste them by looking. Sandwich? Ham and his descendants mustered and bred there. Potted meats. What is home without Plumtree's potted meat? Incomplete. What a stupid ad! Under the obituary notices they stuck it. All up a plumtree. Dignam's potted meat. Cannibals would with lemon and rice. White missionary too salty. Like pickled pork. Except the chief consumes the parts of honour. Ought to be tough from exercise. His wives in a row to watch the effect. *There was a right royal old nigger. Who ate or something the somethings of the reverend Mr MacTrigger.* With it an abode of bliss. Lord knows what concoction. Cauls mouldy tripes windpipes faked and minced up. Puzzle find the meat. Kosher. No meat and milk together. Hygiene that was what they call now. Yom kippur fast spring cleaning of inside. Peace and war depend on some fellow's digestion. Religions. Christmas turkeys and geese. Slaughter of innocents. Eat, drink and be merry. Then casual wards full after. Heads bandaged. Cheese digests all but itself. Mighty cheese.

—Have you a cheese sandwich?

—Yes, sir.

Like a few olives too if they had them. Italian I prefer. Good glass of burgundy; take away that. Lubricate. A nice salad, cool as a cucumber. Tom Kernan can dress. Puts gusto into it. Pure olive oil. Milly served me that cutlet with a sprig of parsley. Take one Spanish onion. God made food, the devil the cooks. Devilled crab.

—Wife well?

—Quite well, thanks . . . A cheese sandwich, then. Gorgonzola, have you?

—Yes, sir.

Nosey Flynn sipped his grog.

—Doing any singing those times?

Look at his mouth. Could whistle in his own ear. Flap ears to match. Music. Knows as much about it as my coachman. Still better tell him. Does no harm. Free ad.

—She's engaged for a big tour end of this month. You may have heard perhaps.

—No. O, that's the style. Who's getting it up?

The curate[6] served.

—How much is that?

—Seven d., sir . . . Thank you, sir.

Mr Bloom cut his sandwich into slender strips. *Mr MacTrigger. Easier than the dreamy creamy stuff. His five hundred wives. Had the time of their lives.*

—Mustard, sir?

—Thank you.

He studded under each lifted strip yellow blobs. *Their lives.* I have it. *It grew bigger and bigger and bigger.*

—Getting it up? he said. Well, it's like a company idea, you see. Part shares and part profits.

—Ay, now I remember, Nosey Flynn said, putting his hand in his pocket to scratch his groin. Who is this was telling me? Isn't Blazes Boylan mixed up in it?

A warm shock of air heat of mustard haunched on Mr Bloom's heart. He raised his eyes and met the stare of a bilious clock. Two. Pub clock five minutes fast. Time going on. Hands moving. Two. Not yet.[7]

His midriff yearned then upward, sank within him, yearned more longly, longingly.

Wine.

He smellsipped the cordial juice and, bidding his throat strongly to speed it, set his wineglass delicately down.

—Yes, he said. He's the organiser in point of fact.

No fear. No brains.

Nosey Flynn snuffed and scratched. Flea having a good square meal.

—He had a good slice of luck, Jack Mooney was telling me, over that boxing match Myler Keogh won again that soldier in the Portobello barracks. By God, he had the little kipper down in the county Carlow he was telling me. . . .

Hope that dewdrop doesn't come down into his glass. No, snuffled it up.

—For near a month, man, before it came off. Sucking duck eggs

---

6. Bartender.

7. I.e., not yet time for Boylan to visit Molly.

by God till furthers orders. Keep him off the boose, see? O, by God, Blazes is a hairy chap.

Davy Byrne came forward from the hindbar in tuckstitched shirt sleeves, cleaning his lips with two wipes of his napkin. Herring's blush. Whose smile upon each feature plays with such and such replete. Too much fat on the parsnips.

—And here's himself and pepper on him, Nosey Flynn said. Can you give us a good one for the Gold cup?

—I'm off that, Mr Flynn, Davy Byrne answered. I never put anything on a horse.

—You're right there, Nosey Flynn said.

Mr. Bloom ate his strips of sandwich, fresh clean bread, with relish of disgust, pungent mustard, the feety savour of green cheese. Sips of his wine soothed his palate. Not logwood that. Tastes fuller this weather with the chill off.

Nice quiet bar. Nice piece of wood in that counter. Nicely planed. Like the way it curves there.

—I wouldn't do anything at all in that line, Davy Byrne said. It ruined many a man the same horses.

Vintners' sweepstake. Licensed for the sale of beer, wine and spirits for consumption on the premises. Heads I win tails you lose.

—True for you, Nosey Flynn said. Unless you're in the know. There's no straight sport going now. Lenehan gets some good ones. He's giving Sceptre today. Zinfandel's the favourite, lord Howard de Walden's, won at Epsom. Morny Cannon is riding him. I could have got seven to one against Saint Amant a fortnight before.

—That so? Davy Byrne said. . . .

He went towards the window and, taking up the petty cash book, scanned its pages.

—I could, faith, Nosey Flynn said snuffling. That was a rare bit of horseflesh. Saint Frusquin was her sire. She won in a thunderstorm, Rothschild's filly, with wadding in her ears. Blue jacket and yellow cap. Bad luck to big Ben Dollard and his John O'Gaunt. He put me off it. Ay.

He drank resignedly from his tumbler, running his fingers down the flutes.

—Ay, he said, sighing.

Mr Bloom, champing standing, looked upon his sigh. Nosey numskull. Will I tell him that horse Lenehan?[8] He knows already. Better let him forget. Go and lose more. Fool and his money. Dewdrop coming down again. Cold nose he'd have kissing a woman. Still they might like. Prickly beards they like. Dog's cold noses. Old Mrs. Riordan with the rumbling stomach's Skye terrier in the City Arms hotel. Molly fondling him in her lap. O the big doggybow-

---

8. Bloom is wondering whether to pass on a tip from Lenehan, who wrote for the racing paper *Sport*.

wowsywowsy!

Wine soaked and softened rolled pith of bread mustard a moment mawkish cheese. Nice wine it is. Taste it better because I'm not thirsty. Bath of course does that. Just a bite or two. Then about six o'clock I can. Six, six. Time will be gone then. She. . .

Mild fire of wine kindled his veins. I wanted that badly. Felt so off colour. His eyes unhungrily saw shelves of tins, sardines, gaudy lobster's claws. All the odd things people pick up for food. Out of shells, periwinkles with a pin, off trees, snails out of the ground the French eat, out of the sea with bait on a hook. Silly fish learn nothing in a thousand years. If you didn't know risky putting anything into your mouth. Poisonous berries. Johnny Magories. Roundness you think good. Gaudy colour warns you off. One fellow told another and so on. Try it on the dog first. Led on by the smell or the look. Tempting fruit. Ice cones. Cream. Instinct. Orangegroves for instance. Need artificial irrigation. Bleibtreustrasse.[9] Yes but what about oysters. Unsightly like a clot of phlegm. Filthy shells. Devil to open them too. Who found them out? Garbage, sewage they feed on. Fizz and Red bank oysters. Effect on the sexual. Aphrodis. He was in the Red bank this morning. Was he oyster old fish at table. Perhaps he young flesh in bed. No. June has no ar no oysters. But there are people like tainted game. Jugged hare. First catch your hare. Chinese eating eggs fifty years old, blue and green again. Dinner of thirty courses. Each dish harmless might mix inside. Idea for a poison mystery. That archduke Leopold was it. No. Yes, or was it Otto one of those Habsburgs? Or who was it used to eat the scruff off his own head? Cheapest lunch in town. Of course, aristocrats. Then the others copy to be in the fashion. Milly too rock oil and flour. Raw pastry I like myself. Half the catch of oysters they throw back in the sea to keep up the price. Cheap. No one would buy. Caviare. Do the grand. Hock in green glasses. Swell blowout. Lady this. Powdered bosom pearls. The *élite*. *Crème de la crème*.[1] They want special dishes to pretend they're. Hermit with a platter of pulse keep down the stings of the flesh. Know me come eat with me. Royal sturgeon. High sheriff, Coffey, the butcher, right to venisons of the forest from his ex.[2] Send him back the half of a cow. Spread I saw down in the Master of the Rolls' kitchen area. Whitehatted *chef* like a rabbi. Combustible duck. Curly cabbage *à la duchesse de Parme*. Just as well to write it on the bill of fare so you can know what you've eaten too many drugs spoil the broth. I know it myself. Dosing it with Edward's desiccated soup. Geese stuffed silly for them. Lobsters boiled alive. Do ptake some

9. The Berlin street which contained the offices of the "Planters' Company."
1. "Cream of the cream" (i.e., the very best, socially).
2. All sturgeon caught in or off Britain were the property of the king, according to the ancient traditional rights to certain kinds of fish or game. Bloom goes on to imagine a Dublin butcher having a "right to venisons of the forest from his ex[cellency]"—i.e., the Viceroy.

ptarmigan. Wouldn't mind being a waiter in a swell hotel. Tips, evening dress, halfnaked ladies. May I tempt you to a little more filleted lemon sole, miss Dubedat? Yes, do bedad. And she did bedad. Huguenot name I expect that. A miss Dubedat lived in Killiney I remember. *Du, de la*, French. Still it's the same fish, perhaps old Micky Hanlon of Moore street ripped the guts out of making money, hand over fist, finger in fishes' gills, can't write his name on a cheque, think he was painting the landscape with his mouth twisted. Moooikill A Aitcha Ha. Ignorant as a kish of brogues,[3] worth fifty thousand pounds.

Stuck on the pane two flies buzzed, stuck.

Glowing wine on his palate lingered swallowed. Crushing in the winepress grapes of Burgundy. Sun's heat it is. Seems to a secret touch telling me memory. Touched his sense moistened remembered. Hidden under wild ferns on Howth. Below us bay sleeping sky. No sound. The sky. The bay purple by the Lion's head. Green by Drumleck. Yellowgreen towards Sutton. Fields of undersea, the lines faint brown in grass, buried cities. Pillowed on my coat she had her hair, earwigs in the heather scrub my hand under her nape, you'll toss me all. O wonder! Coolsoft with ointments her hand touched me, caressed: her eyes upon me did not turn away. Ravished over her I lay, full lips full open, kissed her mouth. Yum. Softly she gave me in my mouth the seedcake warm and chewed. Mawkish pulp her mouth had mumbled sweet and sour with spittle. Joy: I ate it: joy. Young life, her lips that gave me pouting. Soft, warm, sticky gumjelly lips. Flowers her eyes were, take me, willing eyes. Pebbles fell. She lay still. A goat. No-one. High on Ben Howth rhododendrons a nannygoat walking surefooted, dropping currants. Screened under ferns she laughed warmfolded. Wildly I lay on her, kissed her; eyes, her lips, her stretched neck, beating, woman's breasts full in her blouse of nun's veiling, fat nipples upright. Hot I tongued her. She kissed me. I was kissed. All yielding she tossed my hair. Kissed, she kissed me.[4]

Me. And me now.

Stuck, the flies buzzed.

His downcast eyes followed the silent veining of the oaken slab. Beauty: it curves: curves are beauty. Shapely goddesses, Venus, Juno: curves the world admires. Can see them library museum standing in the round hall, naked goddesses. Aids to digestion. They don't care what man looks. All to see. Never speaking, I mean to

---

3. A basket of shoes.
4. Bloom is remembering when he first proposed to Molly, on the Hill of Howth, near Dublin. Molly also recalls this in the final "Penelope" episode, which is her soliloquy: " * * * we were lying on the rhododendrons on Howth head in the grey tweed suit and his straw hat the day I got him to propose to me yes * * * my God after that long kiss I near lost my breath * * * I saw he understood or felt what a woman is and I knew I could always get round him and I gave him all the pleasure I could leading him on * * * "

say to fellows like Flynn. Suppose she did Pygmalion and Galatea[5] what would she say first? Mortal! Put you in your proper place. Quaffing nectar at mess with gods, golden dishes, all ambrosial. Not like a tanner lunch we have, boiled mutton, carrots and turnips, bottle of Allsop. Nectar, imagine it drinking electricity: god's food. Lovely forms of woman sculped Junonian. Immortal lovely. And we stuffing food in one hole and out behind: food, chyle, blood, dung, earth, food: have to feed it like stoking an engine. They have no. Never looked. I'll look today. Keeper won't see. Bend down let something fall see if she.

Dribbling a quiet message from his bladder came to go to do not to do there to do. A man and ready he drained his glass to the lees and walked, to men too they gave themselves, manly conscious, lay with men lovers, a youth enjoyed her, to the yard.

When the sound of his boots had ceased Davy Byrne said from his book:

—What is this he is? Isn't he in the insurance line?

—He's out of that long ago, Nosey Flynn said. He does canvassing for the *Freeman*.

—I know him well to see, Davy Byrne said. Is he in trouble?

—Trouble? Nosey Flynn said. Not that I heard of. Why?

—I noticed he was in mourning.

—Was he? Nosey Flynn said. So he was, faith. I asked him how was all at home. You're right, by God. So he was.

—I never broach the subject, Davy Byrne said humanely, if I see a gentleman is in trouble that way. It only brings it up fresh in their minds.

—It's not the wife anyhow, Nosey Flynn said. I met him the day before yesterday and he coming out of that Irish farm dairy John Wyse Nolan's wife has in Henry street with a jar of cream in his hand taking it home to his better half. She's well nourished, I tell you. Plovers on toast.

—And is he doing for the *Freeman*? Davy Byrne said.

Nosey Flynn pursed his lips.

—He doesn't buy cream on the ads he picks up. You can make bacon of that.

—How so? Davy Byrne asked, coming from his book.

Nosey Flynn made swift passes in the air with juggling fingers. He winked.

—He's in the craft,[6] he said.

—Do you tell me so? Davy Byrne said.

—Very much so, Nosey Flynn said. Ancient free and accepted

5. Pygmalion was the sculptor whose statue of Galatea came alive.
6. I.e., in the "free and accepted order" of Freemasons, one of the oldest European secret societies; it was not in good repute in predominantly Roman Catholic countries like Ireland.

order. Light, life and love, by God. They give him a leg up. I was
told that by a, well, I won't say who.

—Is that a fact?

—O, it's a fine order, Nosey Flynn said. They stick to you when
you're down. I know a fellow was trying to get into it, but they're
as close as damn it. By God they did right to keep the women out of
it.

Davy Byrne smiledyawnednodded all in one:

—Iiiiiichaaaaaaach!

—There was one woman, Nosey Flynn said, hid herself in a clock
to find out what they do be doing. But be damned but they smelt
her out and swore her in on the spot a master mason. That was
one of the Saint Legers of Doneraile.

Davy Byrne, sated after his yawn, said with tearwashed eyes:

—And is that a fact? Decent quiet man he is. I often saw him
in here and I never once saw him, you know, over the line.

—God Almighty couldn't make him drunk, Nosey Flynn said
firmly. Slips off when the fun gets too hot. Didn't you see him look
at his watch? Ah, you weren't there. If you ask him to have a drink
first thing he does he outs with the watch to see what he ought to
imbibe. Declare to God he does.

—There are some like that, Davy Byrne said. He's a safe man,
I'd say.

—He's not too bad, Nosey Flynn said, snuffling it up. He has
been known to put his hand down too to help a fellow. Give the
devil his due. O, Bloom has his good points. But there's one thing
he'll never do.

His hand scrawled a dry pen signature beside his grog.

—I know, Davy Byrne said.

—Nothing in black and white, Nosey Flynn said.

Paddy Leonard and Bantam Lyons came in. Tom Rochford followed, a plaining hand on his claret waistcoat.

—Day, Mr. Byrne.

—Day, gentlemen.

They paused at the counter.

—Who's standing? Paddy Leonard asked.

—I'm sitting anyhow, Nosey Flynn answered.

—Well, what'll it be? Paddy Leonard asked.

—I'll take a stone ginger, Bantam Lyons said.

—How much? Paddy Leonard cried. Since when, for God's sake?
What's yours, Tom?

—How is the main drainage? Nosey Flynn asked, sipping.

For answer Tom Rochford pressed his hand to his breastbone
and hiccupped.

—Would I trouble you for a glass of fresh water, Mr Byrne? he
said.

—Certainly, sir.

Paddy Leonard eyed his alemates.

—Lord love a duck, he said, look at what I'm standing drinks to! Cold water and gingerpop! Two fellows that would suck whisky off a sore leg. He has some bloody horse up his sleeve for the Gold cup. A dead snip.

—Zinfandel is it? Nosey Flynn asked.

Tom Rochford spilt powder from a twisted paper into the water set before him.

—That cursed dyspepsia, he said before drinking.

—Breadsoda is very good, Davy Byrne said.

Tom Rochford nodded and drank.

—Is it Zinfandel?

—Say nothing, Bantam Lyons winked. I'm going to plunge five bob on my own.

—Tell us if you're worth your salt and be damned to you, Paddy Leonard said. Who gave it to you?

Mr Bloom on his way out raised three fingers in greeting.

—So long, Nosey Flynn said.

The others turned.

—That's the man now that gave it to me, Bantam Lyons whispered.

—Prrwht! Paddy Leonard said with scorn. Mr Byrne, sir, we'll take two of your small Jamesons after that and a. . .

—Stone ginger, Davy Byrne added civilly.

—Ay, Paddy Leonard said. A suckingbottle for the baby.

Mr Bloom walked towards Dawson street, his tongue brushing his teeth smooth. Something green it would have to be: spinach say Then with those Röntgen rays searchlight you could.

At Duke lane a ravenous terrier choked up a sick knuckly cud on the cobble stones and lapped it with new zest. Surfeit. Returned with thanks having fully digested the contents. First sweet then savoury. Mr Bloom coasted warily. Ruminants. His second course. Their upper jaw they move. Wonder if Tom Rochford will do anything with that invention of his. Wasting time explaining it to Flynn's mouth. Lean people long mouths. Ought to be a hall or a place where inventors could go in and invent free. Course then you'd have all the cranks pestering.

He hummed, prolonging in solemn echo, the closes of the bars:

> *Don Giovanni, a cenar teco*
> *M'invitasti.*[8]

8. Since Molly is a singer, Bloom is familiar with opera. Here he recalls the song sung by the Commendatore's statue in Mozart's *Don Giovanni*, and translates accurately the Italian words he quotes, except for "*teco*" ("with you"). This opera supplies some of the key themes in *Ulysses*, and the famous duet between Don Giovanni and Zerlina. "*Là ci darèm la mano*" ("There we will join hands"), haunts Bloom's mind continually throughout the day. It is on the program of Molly's concert which she is discussing with Boylan that after-

Feel better. Burgundy. Good pick me up. Who distilled first? Some chap in the blues. Dutch courage. That *Kilkenny People* in the national library now I must.

Bare clean closestools, waiting, in the window of William Miller, plumber, turned back his thoughts. They could: and watch it all the way down, swallow a pin sometimes come out of the ribs years after, tour round the body, changing biliary duct, spleen squirting liver, gastric juice coils of intestines like pipes. But the poor buffer would have to stand all the time with his insides entrails on show. Science.

—*A cenar teco.*

What does that *teco* mean? Tonight perhaps.

> *Don Giovanni, thou hast me invited*
> *To come to supper tonight,*
> *The rum the rumdum.*

Doesn't go properly.

Keyes: two months if I get Nannetti[9] to. That'll be two pounds ten, about two pounds eight. Three Hynes owes me. Two eleven. Presscott's ad. Two fifteen. Five guineas about. On the pig's back.

Could buy one of those silk petticoats for Molly, colour of her new garters.

Today. Today. Not think.[1]

Tour the south then. What about English watering places? Brighton, Margate. Piers by moonlight. Her voice floating out. Those lovely sideside girls. Against John Long's a drowsing loafer lounged in heavy thought, gnawing a crusted knuckle. Handy man wants job. Small wages. Will eat anything.

Mr Bloom turned at Gray's confectioner's window of unbought tarts and passed the reverend Thomas Connellan's bookstore. *Why I left the church of Rome?* Bird's Nest. Women run him. They say they used to give pauper children soup to change to protestants in the time of the potato blight. Society over the way papa went to for the conversion of poor jews. Same bait. Why we left the church of Rome?

A blind stripling stood tapping the curbstone with his slender cane. No tram in sight. Wants to cross.

—Do you want to cross? Mr Bloom asked.

The blind stripling did not answer. His wall face frowned weakly. He moved his head uncertainly.

—You're in Dawson street, Mr Bloom said. Molesworth street is opposite. Do you want to cross? There's nothing in the way.

noon, and Bloom associates it with her adultery with Boylan.

9. Proofreader and business manager of the *Freeman's Journal*, and in charge of the advertising Bloom is trying to get for the paper. If he will add a complimentary reference to Keyes, a grocer, in a gossip column, Keyes promises to renew his advertisement, which means a commission for Bloom.

1. I.e., of Molly and Boylan.

The cane moved out trembling to the left. Mr Bloom's eye followed its line and saw again the dyeworks' van drawn up before Drago's. Where I saw his brilliantined hair just when I was. Horse drooping. Driver in John Long's. Slaking his drouth.

—There's a van there, Mr Bloom said, but it's not moving. I'll see you across. Do you want to go to Molesworth street?

—Yes, the stripling answered. South Frederick street.

—Come, Mr Bloom said.

He touched the thin elbow gently: then took the limp seeing hand to guide it forward.

Say something to him. Better not do the condescending. They mistrust what you tell them. Pass a common remark.

—The rain kept off.

No answer.

Stains on his coat. Slobbers his food, I suppose. Tastes all different for him. Have to be spoonfed first. Like a child's hand his hand. Like Milly's was. Sensitive. Sizing me up I daresay from my hand. Wonder if he has a name. Van. Keep his cane clear of the horse's legs tired drudge get his doze. That's right. Clear. Behind a bull: in front of a horse.

—Thanks, sir.

Knows I'm a man. Voice.

—Right now? First turn to the left.

The blind stripling tapped the curbstone and went on his way, drawing his cane back, feeling again.

Mr Bloom walked behind the eyeless feet, a flatcut suit of herringbone tweed. Poor young fellow! How on earth did he know that van was there? Must have felt it. See things in their foreheads perhaps. Kind of sense of volume. Weight would he feel it if something was removed. Feel a gap. Queer idea of Dublin he must have, tapping his way round by the stones. Could he walk in a beeline if he hadn't that cane? Bloodless pious face like a fellow going in to be a priest.

Penrose! That was that chap's name.

Look at all the things they can learn to do. Read with their fingers. Tune pianos. Or we are surprised they have any brains. Why we think a deformed person or a hunchback clever if he says something we might say. Of course the other senses are more. Embroider. Plait baskets. People ought to help. Work basket I could buy Molly's birthday. Hates sewing. Might take an objection. Dark men they call them.

Sense of smell must be stronger too. Smells on all sides bunched together. Each person too. Then the spring, the summer: smells. Tastes. They say you can't taste wines with your eyes shut or a cold in the head. Also smoke in the dark they say get no pleasure.

And with a woman, for instance. More shameless not seeing.

That girl passing the Stewart institution, head in the air. Look at me. I have them all on. Must be strange not to see her. Kind of a form in his mind's eye. The voice temperature when he touches her with fingers must almost see the lines, the curves. His hands on her hair, for instance. Say it was black for instance. Good. We call it black. Then passing over her white skin. Different feel perhaps. Feeling of white.

Postoffice. Must answer.[2] Fag today. Send her a postal order two shillings half a crown. Accept my little present. Stationer's just here too. Wait. Think over it.

With a gentle finger he felt ever so slowly the hair combed back above his ears. Again. Fibres of fine fine straw. Then gently his finger felt the skin of his right cheek. Downy hair there too. Not smooth enough. The belly is the smoothest. No-one about. There he goes into Frederick street. Perhaps to Levenston's dancing academy piano. Might be settling my braces.

Walking by Doran's public house he slid his hand between waistcoat and trousers and, pulling aside his shirt gently, felt a slack fold of his belly. But I know it's whiteyellow. Want to try in the dark to see.

He withdrew his hand and pulled his dress to.

Poor fellow! Quite a boy. Terrible. Really terrible. What dreams would he have, not seeing. Life a dream for him. Where is the justice being born that way. All those women and children excursion beanfeast burned and drowned in New York.[3] Holocaust. Karma they call that transmigration for sins you did in a past life the reincarnation met him pikehoses.[4] Dear, dear, dear. Pity of course: but somehow you can't cotton on to them someway.

Sir Frederick Falkiner going into the freemasons' hall. Solemn as Troy. After his good lunch in Earlsfort terrace. Old legal cronies cracking a magnum. Tales of the bench and assizes and annals of the bluecoat school.[5] I sentenced him to ten years. I suppose he'd turn up his nose at that stuff I drank. Vintage wine for them, the year marked on a dusty bottle. Has his own ideas of justice in the recorder's court. Wellmeaning old man. Police chargesheets crammed with cases get their percentage manufacturing crime. Sends them to the rightabout. The devil on moneylenders. Gave Reuben J. a great strawcalling. Now he's really what they call a dirty jew. Power those judges have. Crusty old topers in wigs. Bear with a sore paw. And may the Lord have mercy on your soul.

Hello, placard. Mirus bazaar. His excellency the lord lieuten-

2. Martha Clifford's letter.
3. This terrible disaster on an excursion steamer on the Hudson took place on June 15, 1904, and was reported in the Dublin papers on June 16.
4. I.e., metempsychosis: Bloom is remembering again their morning conversation on this subject, when Molly exclaimed "O rocks!"
5. Sir Frederick Falkiner wrote the history of the "bluecoat school" in Oxmantown, Dublin. The Dublin "bluecoat school" was founded by Charles II for poor children.

ant. Sixteenth today it is. In aid of funds for Mercer's hospital. *The Messiah* was first given for that. Yes. Handel. What about going out there. Ballsbridge. Drop in on Keyes. No use sticking to him like a leech. Wear out my welcome. Sure to know someone on the gate.

Mr Bloom came to Kildare street. First I must. Library.

Straw hat in sunlight. Tan shoes. Turnedup trousers. It is. It is.[6]

His heart quopped softly. To the right. Museum. Goddesses. He swerved to the right.

Is it? Almost certain. Won't look. Wine in my face. Why did I? Too heady. Yes, it is. The walk. Not see. Not see. Get on.

Making for the museum gate with long windy strides he lifted his eyes. Handsome building. Sir Thomas Deane designed. Not following me?

Didn't see me perhaps. Light in his eyes.

The flutter of his breath came forth in short sighs. Quick. Cold statues: quiet there. Safe in a minute.

No, didn't see me. After two. Just at the gate.

My heart!

His eyes beating looked steadfastly at cream curves of stone. Sir Thomas Deane was the Greek architecture.

Look for something I.

His hasty hand went quick into a pocket, took out, read unfolded Agendath Netaim. Where did I?

Busy looking for.

He thrust back quickly Agendath.

Afternoon she said.

I am looking for that. Yes, that. Try all pockets. Handker. *Freeman*. Where did I? Ah, yes. Trousers. Purse. Potato. Where did I?

Hurry. Walk quietly. Moment more. My heart.

His hand looking for the where did I put found in his hip pocket soap lotion have to call tepid paper stuck. Ah, soap there! Yes. Gate.[7]

Safe!

1914–21   1922

---

6. Bloom catches a glimpse of Boylan and tries to avoid an encounter.

7. Anxious to avoid Boylan, Bloom pretends to admire the architecture of the Museum and National Library building, and then pretends to be looking for something in his pockets, where he finds the "Agendath Netaim" leaflet. He continues to search desperately in his pock-

ets to avoid looking up and seeing Boylan, discovers the potato he carries as a remedy against rheumatism and a cake of soap he had bought that morning (the soap reminds him that he must call at the chemist's to collect a face lotion he had ordered for Molly). At last he goes through the National Library gate and feels safe.

From Finnegans Wake[1]

From *Anna Livia Plurabelle*

* * * Well, you know or don't you kennet[2] or haven't I told you every telling has a taling and that's the he and the she of it. Look, look, the dusk is growing! My branches lofty are taking root. And my cold cher's[3] gone ashley. Fieluhr?[4] Filou! What age is at? It saon[5] is late. 'Tis endless now senne[6] eye or erewone[7] last saw Waterhouse's clogh.[8] They took it asunder, I hurd thum sigh. When will they reassemble it? O, my back, my back, my bach![9] I'd want to go to Aches-les-Pains.[10] Pingpong! There's the Belle for Sexaloitez![11] And Concepta de Send-us-pray! Pang! Wring out the clothes! Wring in the dew![12] Godavari,[13] vert the showers! And

1. Because the meanings in *Finnegans Wake* are developed not by action but by language—a great network of multiple puns that echo themes back and forth throughout the book—the careful reading of a single passage, even out of context, will convey more than any summary of the "plot" (some discussion of the general plan of the work is given in the Joyce introduction). The particular passage selected here was one of Joyce's favorites, and there exists a phonograph recording of it made by himself. It consists of the closing pages of the eighth chapter of Book I; the chapter was published separately as *Anna Livia Plurabelle* in 1928 and 1930, although the finished book omits this title.

The entire chapter is a dialogue, and the scene is the river Liffey: two washerwomen are washing in public the dirty linen of HCE and ALP (the "hero" and "heroine"; see the Joyce introduction), and gossiping as they work. As this excerpt opens, it is growing dark; things become gradually less and less distinct, so that the washerwomen cannot be sure what the objects seen in the dusk really are. As it grows darker, the river becomes wider (we get nearer its mouth) and the wind rises, so that the women have more and more difficulty hearing each other. At last, as night falls, they become part of the landscape, an elm tree and a stone on the river bank. Toward the end of the dialogue they ask to hear a tale of Shem and Shaun (HCE's two sons), and this question points the way to Book II, which opens with the two boys (metamorphosed for the moment into Glugg and Chuff) playing in front of the tavern in the evening.

A complete annotation of even this brief passage is, of course, a physical impossibility in this anthology. The notes that are provided are intended to indicate the nature of what Joyce does with language and to enable the reader

to see what is going on. But there are all sorts of suggestions built up in the language that are not referred to in the notes: each reader will find some for himself.

2. Ken it ("know it") + Kennet (river in England). Rivers in *Finnegans Wake* symbolize the flow of life, and thousands of river names are suggested throughout the book in allusive pun-combinations, as here.

3. Cold cheer (i.e., cold comfort) + cold chair + (perhaps) culture. "Gone ashley": gone to ashes. Going to ashes suggests the fiery death and rebirth of the mythical phoenix: from the ashes of the dead phoenix rises a new one. Modern culture, which can provide only cold cheer, is in the state of decay, the "going to ashes," which precedes the stage of rebirth into a new cultural cycle (according to Giambattista Vico's cyclical theory of history, which is important to *Finnegans Wake*). "Gone ashley" also means "turned into an ash tree" (i.e., it is so cold that the speaker feels herself turning into a tree).

4. *Viel Uhr?* (German, "What's the time?") "Filou": pickpocket, thief (French). The question echoes so as to suggest that time is a thief.

5. Soon + Saône (river in France).

6. Since + Senne (river in Belgium).

7. E'er a one + *Erewhon* (novel by Samuel Butler—"Nowhere" spelled backwards).

8. Clock or bell (Irish) + the name of an Irish river.

9. Brook (German) + dear (Welsh).

10. Cf. Aix-les-Bains, France.

11. *Sex* (Latin, "six") + *laüten* (German, "to ring [the bells]"). The Angelus bell is rung every six hours.

12. Cf. "Ring out the old, ring in the new" (Tennyson, *In Memoriam*).

13. God of Eire; also the name of a river in India. "Vert": avert + *vert* (French, "green"), for "the showers" make grass green.

grant thaya grace! Aman. Will we spread them here now? Ay, we will. Flip! Spread on your bank and I'll spread mine on mine. Flep! It's what I'm doing. Spread! It's churning chill. Der went[14] is rising. I'll lay a few stones on the hostel sheets. A man and his bride embraced between them. Else I'd have sprinkled and folded them only. And I'll tie my butcher's apron here. It's suety yet. The strollers will pass it by. Six shifts, ten kerchiefs, nine to hold to the fire and this for the code,[15] the convent napkins, twelve, one baby's shawl. Good mother Jossiph[16] knows, she said. Whose head? Mutter snores? Deataceas![17] Wharnow are alle her childer, say? In kingdome gone or power to come or gloria be to them farther? Allalivial, allalluvial![18] Some here, more no more, more again lost alla stranger.[19] I've heard tell that same brooch of the Shannons[20] was married into a family in Spain. And all the Dunders de Dunnes[21] in Markland's[22] Vineland beyond Brendan's herring pool[23] takes number nine in yangsee's[24] hats. And one of Biddy's[25] beads went bobbing till she rounded up lost histereve[26] with a marigold and a cobbler's candle in a side strain of a main drain of a manzinahurries[27] off Bachelor's Walk. But all that's left to the last of the Meaghers[28] in the loup of the years prefixed and between is one kneebuckle and two hooks in the front. Do you tell me that now? I do in troth. Orara por Orbe and poor Las Animas![29]

---

14. *Der Wind* (German, "the wind") + Derwent (river in England).
15. Cold + code (i.e., the code in which the book is written). The numbers in this sentence have special meanings indicated in other episodes.
16. Joseph + *joss* (pidgin English, "God") + gossip (which derives from *god-sib*, Middle English, "godparent").
17. Latin, "Goddess, may you be silent!" Dea Tacita, in Roman mythology, is the name sometimes given to Acca Laurentia, mistress of Hercules and foster-mother of Romulus and Remus.
18. Multiple punning—Anna Livia + all alive + *la lluvia* (Spanish, "rain") + alluvial—suggesting the mother-river-fertility associations of ALP. At least two other meanings are also present: All alive O! (street cry of shellfish vendors) + Alleluia (Vulgate Latin form of "Hallelujah").
19. Cf. *à l'étranger* (French, "abroad").
20. Ornament and branch of the Shannons (family and river).
21. The form of the name suggests an aristocratic Anglo-Norman family. "Dunder" suggests thunder; *dun* is an Irish word meaning "hill," "fort on a hill."
22. Borderland + land of the mark (i.e., land of money, or America; "Vineland" or Vinland was the Norse name for America). Both King Mark of Cornwall (a character in the Tristan and

Iseult story) and Mark of the Gospels are primary symbolic characters in *Finnegans Wake*.
23. The Atlantic Ocean; St. Brendan was an Irish monk who sailed out into the Atlantic to find the terrestrial paradise.
24. Yankees' + Yangtze (river in China). The de Dunnes have swollen heads now that they have emigrated to America.
25. Diminutive form of the name Bridget; St. Brigid (or Bridget) is a patron saint of Ireland. "Biddy" is also a term for an Irish maidservant.
26. Yester eve (last night) + eve of history. The sentence may be paraphrased: "Irish history got lost when she went off in a side branch of the main Roman Catholic Church, and Biddy (i.e., Ireland) landed herself in the dirt." There are also Freudian implications here.
27. Man's in a hurry + Manzanares (river in Spain).
28. Thomas Francis Meagher, Irish patriot and revolutionary, who was transported to Van Diemen's Land in 1849 and escaped to America in 1852. "Loup": loop + *loup* (French, "wolf" and also "solitary man"). Cf. Wolfe Tone, the ill-fated Irish revolutionist.
29. *Ora pro nobis* (Latin, "pray for us") + Orara (river in New South Wales) + *pro orbe* (Latin, "for the world") + Orbe (river in France). "Las Animas": souls (Spanish); also

Ussa, Ulla, we're umbas[30] all! Mezha, didn't you hear it a deluge
of times, ufer[31] and ufer, respund to spond?[32] You deed, you deed!
I need, I need! It's that irrawaddyng[33] I've stoke in my aars. It all
but husheth the lethest zswound. Oronoko![34] What's your trouble?
Is that the great Finnleader[35] himself in his joakimono on his statue
riding the high horse there forehengist?[36] Father of Otters,[37] it is
himself! Yonne there! Isset that? On Fallareen Common? You're
thinking of Astley's Amphitheayter where the bobby restrained you
making sugarstuck pouts to the ghostwhite horse of the Peppers.[38]
Throw the cobwebs from your eyes, woman, and spread your washing proper! It's well I know your sort of slop. Flap! Ireland sober
is Ireland stiff. Lord help you, Maria, full of grease, the load is
with me! Your prayers. I sonht zo![39] Madammangut! Were you
lifting your elbow, tell us, glazy cheeks, in Conway's Carrigacurra
canteen? Was I what, hobbledyhips?[40] Flop! Your rere gait's creak-
orheuman bitts your butts disagrees.[41] Amn't I up since the damp
dawn, marthared mary allacook, with Corrigan's pulse and varicoarse
veins, my pramaxle smashed, Alice Jane in decline and my oneeyed
mongrel twice run over, soaking and bleaching boiler rags, and
sweating cold, a widow like me, for to deck my tennis champion
son, the laundryman with the lavandier flannels? You won your
limpopo[42] limp fron the husky[43] hussars when Collars and Cuffs
was heir to the town and your slur gave the stink to Carlow.[44] Holy
Scamander,[45] I sar it again! Near the golden falls. Icis on us! Seints
of light! Zezere![46] Subdue your noise, you hamble creature! What

the name of a river in Colorado. The
entire sentence may be read: "Pray for
us and for all souls."
30. *Umbra* (Latin, "shade") + Umba
(river in Africa). "Ussa," "Ulla," and
"Mezha" are also river names; each
contains a number of other meanings.
31. Bank (of river).
32. *Spund* (German, "bung").
33. A multiple pun: Irrawady (river in
Burma) + irritating + wadding. This
and the following sentence may be
paraphrased: "It's that wadding I've
stuck in my ears. It hushes the least
sound."
34. *Oroonoko* (novel by Mrs. Aphra
Behn about a "noble savage," published
ca. 1678).
35. Fionn mac Cumhail (Finn Mac-
Cool), legendary hero of ancient Ireland. "Joakimono": i.e., comic kimono;
joki is the Finnish word for river; the
name Joachim is perhaps also implied.
36. Hengist was the Jute invader of
England (with Horsa), ca. 449; he
founded the kingdom of Kent.
37. Father of Waters (i.e., the Mis-
sissippi) + Father of Orders (i.e., Saint
Patrick).
38. Philip Astley's Royal Amphithea-
tre was a famous late 18th-century English circus, specializing in trained

horses; "Pepper's Ghost" was a popular circus act. One of the washerwomen
has been reproving the other, who
thought she saw the great Finn himself riding his high horse, by telling her
that once before she had to be restrained by a policeman for making
"sugarstuck pouts" at a circus horse.
39. I thought so + Izontzo (river in
Italy).
40. Hobbledehoy + wobbly hips.
41. The sentence is a punning discussion of her hard work and ailments.
The first four words may also be read:
"Your rear get (i.e., your last child) is
Greek or Roman."
42. Name of a river in south Africa.
43. Cf. *uisge* (Gaelic, "whisky," but
literally, "water [of life]").
44. I.e., "You got a slur on your reputation carrying on with soldiers in the
Age of Elegance, and the scandal was
all over Ireland" (ALP is being addressed, and some of her many lovers
are mentioned). "Carlow" is a county
in Ireland.
45. River near Troy, famous in classical legend. "I sar": I saw + Isar (river
in Germany).
46. See there + Zezere (river in Portugal).

is it but a blackburry growth or the dwyergray ass them four old codgers[47] owns. Are you meanam[48] Tarpey and Lyons and Gregory? I meyne now, thank all, the four of them, and the roar of them, that draves[49] that stray in the mist and old Johnny MacDougal along with them. Is that the Poolbeg flasher beyant,[50] pharphar, or a fireboat coasting nyar[51] the Kishtna or a glow I behold within a hedge or my Garry come back from the Indes? Wait till the honeying of the lune,[52] love! Die eve, little eve, die![53] We see that wonder in your eye. We'll meet again, we'll part once more. The spot I'll seek if the hour you'll find. My chart shines high where the blue milk's upset. Forgivemequick, I'm going! Bubye! And you, pluck your watch, forgetmenot. Your evenlode.[54] So save to jurna's[55] end! My sights are swimming thicker on me by the shadows to this place. I sow[56] home slowly now by own way, moyvalley way. Towy[57] I too, rathmine.

Ah, but she was the queer old skeowsha anyhow, Anna Livia, trinkettoes! And sure he was the quare old buntz too, Dear Dirty Dumpling,[58] foostherfather of fingalls[59] and dotthergills. Gammer and gaffer we're all their gangsters. Hadn't he seven dams to wive him? And every dam had her seven crutches. And every crutch had its seven hues.[60] And each hue had a differing cry. Sudds[61] for me and supper for you and the doctor's bill for Joe John. Befor! Bifur![62] He married his markets, cheap by foul, I know, like any Etrurian

---

47. The Four Old Men, who represent, among other things, the authors of the Gospels and the four elements.
48. Meaning + Menam (river in Thailand). The precise connotations of the three proper names that follow escape the present annotator.
49. Drives + Drave (river in Hungary).
50. I.e., the Poolbeg Lighthouse beyond (this lighthouse is in Dublin Bay); "pharphar": far far + Pharphar (river in Damascus) + *pharos* (Greek, "lighthouse").
51. Near + Nyar (river in India). "Kishtna": Kish (city in ancient Mesopotamia, traditionally the ruling city after the Flood) + Krishna (Hindu god of joy) + Kistna (river in India) + the Kish lightship (in Dublin Bay).
52. Loon (Scottish, "boy") + *luna* (Latin, "moon"). "Honeying of the lune": honeymoon, etc.
53. This sentence suggests traditional lovers' prayers for the day to die and night to come, and it also recalls the death of "little Eva" in *Uncle Tom's Cabin*. The sentences that follow are echoes of popular songs.
54. Evening load + Evenlode (river in England).
55. Journey + Jurna (river in Brazil).
56. Sow (river in England).
57. Name of a river in Wales. Moy is

the name of an Irish river, and Moyvalley and Rathmine are names of Dublin suburbs.
58. "Dumpling" suggests Humpty Dumpty, whose fall is one of the many involved in the vastly symbolic fall of Finnegan. The phrase "Dear Dirty Dublin" occurs in *Ulysses*.
59. A pun-cluster: Fine Gael (the United Ireland Party) + fine Gaels + Fingal (river in Tasmania) + *Fingal* (the poem by James Macpherson, supposedly a translation from the Gaelic original of Ossian, an ancient Gaelic poet and son of Fingal—who is the same as Fionn mac Cumhail or Finn MacCool).
60. Colors of the rainbow (suggested a few lines later by "pinky limony creamy" and "turkiss indienne mauves"). In these sentences Joyce is punningly parodying the nursery rhyme, "As I was going to St. Ives / I met a man with seven wives * * * "
61. Suds (slang term for beer) + soapsuds + sudd (the floating vegetable matter which often obstructs navigation on the White Nile).
62. Bifurcated creature! This image of man as a forked being suggests HCE (cf. "Etrurian Catholic Heathen"). HCE's marital history, in his role as the Great Parent or generator, is one of the themes in this passage.

Catholic Heathen, in their pinky limony creamy birnies[63] and their turkiss indienne mauves. But at milkidmass[64] who was the spouse? Then all that was was fair. Tys Elvenland![65] Teems of times and happy returns. The seim anew.[66] Ordovico[67] or viricordo. Anna was, Livia is, Plurabelle's to be. Northmen's thing made southfolk's place but howmulty plurators made eachone in person?[68] Latin me that, my trinity scholard, out of eure sanscreed into oure eryan![69] *Hircus Civis Eblanensis!*[70] He had buckgoat paps on him, soft ones for orphans. Ho,[71] Lord! Twins of his bosom. Lord save us! And ho! Hey? What all men. Hot? His tittering daughters of. Whawk?

Can't hear with the waters of. The chittering waters of. Flittering bats, fieldmice bawk talk. Ho! Are you not gone ahome? What Thom Malone? Can't hear with bawk of bats, all thim liffeying waters of. Ho, talk save us! My foos won't moos.[72] I feel as old as yonder elm. A tale told of Shaun or Shem? All Livia's daughter-sons. Dark hawks hear us. Night! Night! My ho head halls. I feel as heavy as yonder stone. Tell me of John or Shaun? Who were Shem and Shaun the living sons or daughters of? Night now! Tell me, tell me, tell me, elm! Night night! Telmetale of stem or stone.[73] Beside the rivering waters of, hitherandthithering waters of. Night!

1923–38   1939

63. Coats of mail.

64. Milking time + Michaelmas (September 29).

65. 'Tis the land of Elves + Tys Elv (Norway).

66. The same again + Seim (river in Ireland).

67. The Ordovices were an ancient British tribe in northern Wales, and Ordovician is a term for a geological period. "Ordovico" is also a pun on Vico and his order of historical phases. Joyce is here suggesting the cyclical nature of things: the marital history of HCE is the history of ever-renewing life ("the seim anew"), and HCE's bride is Everywoman, past, present, and future ("Anna was, Livia is, Plurabelle's to be"). "Viricordo" is another verbal twist to Vico and his cycles, suggesting his *ricorso* ("recurrence," i.e., the 4th stage of the cycle which brings back the 1st), as well as overtones from the Latin *vir* (man) and *cor* (heart): the heart of man beats on, through all phases of civilization.

68. This sentence may be paraphrased: "The assembly of the Norsemen made the South-folk's place (i.e., as the Vikings settled Dublin), but how many marital pluralists (the word 'plurators'

suggests men who had many wives or mistresses) went into the making of each of us?" The question is another link with the theme of HCE as the Great Parent.

69. I.e., out of your Sanskrit into your Aryan. "Sanscreed" has further punning meanings: *sans* screed (without script) + *sans* creed (without faith). Thus the phrase can read: "out of your illiteracy or faithlessness into Irish" (Eire-an). The greatest skeptic must pause in reverence before the endless flow of life, represented by Irish history.

70. Latin, "The Goat-Citizen of Dublin!" The goat is the symbol of lust and so of fecundity; *"Eblanensis"* is the adjective form of Eblana, the name given by the 3rd-century Alexandrian geographer Ptolemy to what may have been the site of the modern Dublin.

71. Chinese, "river."

72. Move + *Moos* (German, "moss"). Her foot ("foos") won't move; it is also turning to moss.

73. Stone and elm tree are important symbols in *Finnegans Wake*. Signifying permanence and change, time and space, mercy and justice, they undergo many changes of symbolic meaning throughout the book.

· D. H. LAWRENCE
(1885–1930)

> 1912: Gives up school teaching for literature.
> 1915: *The Rainbow*, first of the "new" novels.

David Herbert Lawrence was born in the Midland mining village of East-wood, Nottinghamshire. His father was a miner; his mother, better educated than her husband and self-consciously genteel, fought all her married life to lift her children out of the working class. Lawrence was aware from an early age of the struggle between his parents; he was very much on his mother's side during his childhood, resenting his father's coarse and sometimes drunken behavior and allying himself with his mother's delicacy and refinement. After the death of an elder brother he became the center of his mother's emotional life and played in his own relation to her a loving and protective role. His mother's claims on him kept frustrating his relationships with girls, and the personal problems and conflicts that resulted are presented in his first really distinguished novel, *Sons and Lovers* (1913), where, against a background of paternal coarseness and vitality conflicting with maternal refinement and gentility, he sets the theme of the demanding mother who has given up the prospect of achieving a true emotional life with her husband and turns to her sons with a stultifying and possessive love. Many years later Lawrence came to feel that he had misjudged his father, whose coarseness represented after all a genuine vitality and some wholeness of personality, even if these qualities were impoverished and distorted by the civilization in which he lived.

Spurred on by his mother, Lawrence escaped through education from the mining world of his father. He won a scholarship to Nottingham high school and later, after working first as a clerk and then as an elementary school teacher (1902–6), studied for two years at Nottingham University College, where he obtained his teacher's certificate in 1908. Meanwhile he was reading on his own a great deal of literature and some philosophy and was working on his first novel, encouraged (as he was in all his early writing) by Jessie Chambers, the "Miriam" of *Sons and Lovers*. His first published work was a group of poems which appeared in the *English Review* for November, 1909. The following February the same periodical published his first short story. He was now regarded in London literary circles as a promising young writer; his first novel, *The White Peacock* (1910), was received with respect. From 1908 to 1912 he taught school in Croydon, a southern suburb of London, but he gave this up after falling in love with Frieda von Richthofen, the German wife of a Professor of French at Nottingham. They went to Germany together and married in 1914, after Frieda had been divorced by her first husband.

Abroad with Frieda, Lawrence finished *Sons and Lovers*, the autobiographical novel at which he had been working off and on for years. The war brought them back to England, where Frieda's German origins and Lawrence's fierce objection to the war gave him trouble with the authorities. More and more—especially after the banning of his next novel, *The Rainbow*, in 1915—Lawrence came to feel that the forces of modern civilization were arrayed against him. As soon as he could leave England after the war he sought refuge in Italy, Australia, Mexico, then again in Italy, and finally in the south of France, often desperately ill, restlessly searching for an ideal, or at least a tolerable, community in which to live. He died of tuberculosis in the south of France on the 2nd of March, 1930, at the early age of 44.

Shortly before his death he had written:

> Give me the moon at my feet
> Put my feet upon the crescent, like a Lord!
> O let my ankles be bathed in moonlight, that I may go
> sure and moon-shod, cool and bright-footed
> towards my goal.
>
> For the sun is hostile, now
> his face is like the red lion . . .

In these elemental images he invoked his end, a gesture at once heroic and desperate. It was typical of him to symbolize his passing with reference to the sun and moon, for Lawrence was at home with such cosmic images as no other English writer except Blake has ever been; he was at home, one might say, with the universe, with all that is deep-rooted and elemental in man and nature, and at constant war with the mechanical and artificial, with the constraints and hypocrisies that civilization imposes on man's fundamental self. His most characteristic writings are essentially a record in symbolic terms of his explorations of human individuality and of all that hindered it and all that might fulfill it, whether in the natural world or in the world of other individuals.

This is not what the English novel is generally supposed to do, and Lawrence, with new things to say and a new way of using the novel form, was not easily or quickly appreciated. His early novels, *The White Peacock*, *The Trespasser*, and even the original and impressive *Sons and Lovers*, were more conventional in style and treatment; they aroused contemporary interest and even acclaim, and it appeared that he might be on his way to becoming one of the acknowledged and popular Georgian novelists. But with the publication of *The Rainbow* in 1915 the true, original Lawrence first emerged clearly, and the critics turned away in bewilderment and condemnation. *The Rainbow* was suppressed as indecent a month after its publication, and the war between Lawrence and the world of timid convention was on. The rest of his life, during which he produced about a dozen more novels and many poems, short stories, sketches, and miscellaneous articles, was, in his own words, "a savage enough pilgrimage," marked by incessant struggle and by moments of frustration and despair. Lawrence was one of those artists who had to create the taste by which he could be appreciated. He had no gift for explaining his attitude and literary technique in simple expository prose. He could explain himself only by performing, by operating in his own way as an artist, letting the work of art speak with its own voice and pulse with its own life. When he tried to talk *about* his ideas, instead of projecting them symbolically in art, he was often irritatingly and vaguely rhetorical. "Sense of truth," "supreme impulse" are phrases characteristic of Lawrence's belief in intuition, in the dark forces of the inner self, that must not be allowed to be swamped by the rational faculties but must be brought into a harmonious relation with them. It was a point of view—or rather, a perception, a passionate insight—which could not be convincingly expressed in argument, but demanded direct projection in art.

The genteel culture of Lawrence's mother came more and more to represent death for Lawrence. In much of his later work, and especially in some of his short stories, he sets the deadening restrictiveness of middle-class conventional living against the forces of liberation that are often represented by an outsider—a peasant, a gypsy, a working man, a primitive of some kind, someone free by circumstance or personal effort. The recurring theme of his short stories—which contain some of his best work—is the distortion of love by possessiveness or gentility or a false romanticism or a false conception of the life of the artists, and the achievement of a living relation between a man and a woman against the pressure of class-feeling or tradition or habit or prejudice.

His two masterpieces, *The Rainbow* and *Women in Love* (both of which developed out of what was originally conceived as a single novel to be called *The Sisters*), are to be read as symbolic and dramatic poems in prose. In these novels Lawrence probes with both subtlety and power into various aspects of relationship—the relationship between man and his environment, the relationship between the generations, the relationship between man and woman, the relationship between instinct and intellect, and above all the proper basis for the marriage relationship as he conceived it. He is concerned too with the impact of modern industrial civilization on human sensibility, and finds many ways, at once realistic and symbolic, of projecting this. At the very opening of *The Rainbow*, where Lawrence is dealing with the family history of the Brangwens, whose annals he is about to tell, he makes clear even by the rhythms of his prose, as well as by his tone and imagery, that this is not to be a chronicle family novel like Galsworthy's *Forsyte Saga*.

The Rainbow is built on sets of human relationships, both horizontal and vertical. Thus we first see the marriage of Tom Brangwen with the Polish widow Lydia Lensky; then Tom's relationship with his step-daughter Anna; then Anna's relationship with her husband Will; then Will's relationship with his daughters Ursula and Gudrun; and so on. The truth of emotional detail in the presentation of these developing relationships is rendered with extraordinary force and subtlety. A fine example is in the extract below, which shows Tom Brangwen comforting his little step-daughter Anna.

In the relationship of Anna and Will in marriage we begin to find the true Laurentian doctrine that marriage is a fight and at the same time, if properly realized, a means of mystic knowledge through the awareness by one partner (in ultimate intimacy) of the essential *otherness* of the other. After the amorous luxury and mutual discovery of the first few days of marriage, Anna suddenly turns into the brisk housewife and sends the bewildered Will out of doors while she sets about her housework. Lawrence's view of marriage as a struggle derived from his own relationship with his strong-minded German-born wife Frieda. There are more and bitterer lovers' quarrels in Lawrence's novels than anywhere else in English literature. Lawrence's "crockery-throwing" view of love could become tedious, except that, as he presents it, it is bound up with the deepest rhythms and most profound instincts of the man-woman relationship. It is even more strong in *Women in Love*, which deals with Ursula and Gudrun Brangwen and their search for an adequate love relationship. The novel is, however, very much more than the traditional love quest, the developing relationships of Ursula and Rupert Birkin on the one hand and Gudrun and Gerald Crich on the other.

In Rupert there is more than a little of Lawrence himself, yet Lawrence is still able occasionally to laugh at him. Gerald, coldly handsome son of a powerful Midland mineowner, accumulates for himself, as the novel progresses, all the deadening and distorting effects of modern industrial civilization. Lawrence does not simply make Gerald's behavior inadequate or offensive; he is able to invent for his characters actions which while wholly realistic on the surface, or social level, are at the same time profoundly symbolic. This symbolism does not always come off, but when it does the effect is remarkable, as in a scene where Gerald forces his terrified mare to stand by the railway line while a shunting train hisses and clanks back and forth. The novel reveals a deep sense of English provincial life, in which—in spite of all Lawrence's wanderings abroad and of the foreign setting of many of his novels—his sensibility was really deeply rooted, much as George Eliot's was. His intimacy with the English scene, especially with provincial middle-class and working-class patterns of thought and feeling and the relation between them, is revealed again and again in the short stories, notably in "Fanny and Annie," "Daughters of the Vicar," "The Fox," "The Christening," and "Tickets Please."

In *The Rainbow* and *Women in Love*, then, Lawrence is developing a radically new kind of novel in which he explores kinds of human relationships with a combination of uncanny psychological precision and intense poetic feeling. They have an acute surface realism, a sharp sense of time and place, and brilliant topographical detail, and at the same time their high poetic symbolism, both of the total pattern of action and of incidents and objects within it, establishes a rhythm of meaning that is missed by those who read the novels with the conventional categories of "plot" and "characters" in mind. His next novel, *Aaron's Rod* (1922), is more uneven; in it Lawrence, employing many of his own experiences, explores problems of human relations under the question of moral and political leadership, which for a time obsessed him. He was concerned with the struggle for leadership in marriage as well as in politics. Two other novels on the theme of leadership, *Kangaroo* (1923), set in Australia, and *The Plumed Serpent* (1926), set in Mexico, similarly uneven, show him trying to give symbolic fictional form to his own problems and preoccupations. But *Kangaroo* in particular has its moments of uncanny perceptiveness, and it is extraordinary how Lawrence, drawing on his experiences during a short stay in Australia, was able to get beneath the skin of the country and evoke so much of the essential reality of both place and people.

It is hard to think of another English novelist whose best and most characteristic work makes such a disquieting assault on our normal patterns of thought and feeling. It is not simply that Lawrence is a rebel against convention—many writers have been that—or that his views are startling, though they sometimes are. It is rather that the whole response to life, and in particular to the problems posed by human relationships, that emerges from his novels and stories seems to come so profoundly from the deepest recesses of his being and therefore assault the deepest recesses of *our* being, that the challenge seems to go beyond that which is normally asserted by a work of art. It is difficult to escape the challenge; to make any attempt to respond fully to what he is saying is to be drawn into his world, forced to share his vision.

Although there are complex critical reasons for the posthumous triumph of this writer who was so much reviled in his lifetime, there is also a simple and striking reason that must not be forgotten. Lawrence had vision; he had a poetic sense of life; he had a keen ear and a piercing eye for every kind of vitality and color and sound in the world, for landscape—be it of England or Italy or New Mexico—for the individuality and concreteness of things in nature, and for the individuality and concreteness of people. His travel sketches are as impressive in their way as his novels; he seizes both on the symbolic incident and on the concrete reality, and each is interpreted in terms of the other. He looked at the world freshly, with his own eyes, avoiding formulas and clichés; and he forged for himself a kind of utterance which, at his best, was able to convey powerfully and vividly what his fresh, original vision showed him. This kind of originality has its drawbacks; he was sometimes shrill, sometimes repetitive, sometimes almost hysterical; some scenes in his novels are murky with unachieved symbolism or splutter with unresolved passion. But the great Lawrence remains.

This restless pilgrim with his uncanny perceptions into the depths of physical things, with his uncompromising honesty and originality in his view of men and the world, cannot be dismissed as merely a great eccentric. Nor is he a great prophet. He is essentially an artist; it is his *rendering* of life in his art, not his preaching about life's meaning, that matters.

Odor of Chrysanthemums

I

The small locomotive engine, Number 4, came clanking, stumbling down from Selston with seven full wagons. It appeared round the corner with loud threats of speed, but the colt that it startled from among the gorse,[1] which still flickered indistinctly in the raw afternoon, out-distanced it at a canter. A woman, walking up the railway line to Underwood, drew back into the hedge, held her basket aside, and watched the footplate of the engine advancing. The trucks[2] thumped heavily past, one by one, with slow inevitable movement, as she stood insignificantly trapped between the jolting black wagons and the hedge; then they curved away towards the coppice[3] where the withered oak leaves dropped noiselessly, while the birds, pulling at the scarlet hips beside the track, made off into the dusk that had already crept into the spinney.[4] In the open, the smoke from the engine sank and cleaved to the rough grass. The fields were dreary and forsaken, and in the marshy strip that led to the whimsey,[5] a reedy pit pond, the fowls had already abandoned their run among the alders, to roost in the tarred fowl house. The pit bank loomed up beyond the pond, flames like red sores licking its ashy sides, in the afternoon's stagnant light. Just beyond rose the tapering chimneys and the clumsy black headstocks of Brinsley Colliery.[6] The two wheels were spinning fast up against the sky, and the winding engine rapped out its little spasms. The miners were being turned up.

The engine whistled as it came into the wide bay of railway lines beside the colliery, where rows of trucks stood in harbor.

Miners, single, trailing, and in groups, passed like shadows diverging home. At the edge of the ribbed level of sidings squat a low cottage, three steps down from the cinder track. A large bony vine clutched at the house, as if to claw down the tiled roof. Round the bricked yard grew a few wintry primroses. Beyond, the long garden sloped down to a bush-covered brook course. There were some twiggy apple trees, winter-crack trees, and ragged cabbages. Beside the path hung disheveled pink chrysanthemums, like pink cloths hung on bushes. A woman came stooping out of the felt-covered fowl house, halfway down the garden. She closed and

1. Also known as furze or whin, a prickly bush with yellow flowers common on heaths, moors, and hillsides all over Britain.
2. Open freight cars.
3. A wood of small trees or shrubs.
4. Copse, thicket.
5. Machine for raising ore or water from a mine.
6. Coal mine; "headstocks" support revolving parts of a machine.

padlocked the door, then drew herself erect, having brushed some bits from her white apron.

She was a tall woman of imperious mien, handsome, with definite black eyebrows. Her smooth black hair was parted exactly. For a few moments she stood steadily watching the miners as they passed along the railway: then she turned towards the brook course. Her face was calm and set, her mouth was closed with disillusionment. After a moment she called:

"John!" There was no answer. She waited, and then said distinctly:

"Where are you?"

"Here!" replied a child's sulky voice from among the bushes. The woman looked piercingly through the dusk.

"Are you at that brook?" she asked sternly.

For answer the child showed himself before the raspberry canes that rose like whips. He was a small, sturdy boy of five. He stood quite still, defiantly.

"Oh!" said the mother, conciliated. "I thought you were down at that wet brook—and you remember what I told you——"

The boy did not move or answer.

"Come, come on in," she said more gently, "it's getting dark. There's your grandfather's engine coming down the line!"

The lad advanced slowly, with resentful, taciturn movement. He was dressed in trousers and waistcoat of cloth that was too thick and hard for the size of the garments. They were evidently cut down from a man's clothes.

As they went slowly towards the house he tore at the ragged wisps of chrysanthemums and dropped the petals in handfuls among the path.

"Don't do that—it does look nasty," said his mother. He refrained, and she, suddenly pitiful, broke off a twig with three or four wan flowers and held them against her face. When mother and son reached the yard her hand hesitated, and instead of laying the flower aside, she pushed it in her apron-band. The mother and son stood at the foot of the three steps looking across the bay of lines at the passing home of the miners. The trundle of the small train was imminent. Suddenly the engine loomed past the house and came to a stop opposite the gate.

The engine-driver, a short man with round gray beard, leaned out of the cab high above the woman.

"Have you got a cup of tea?" he said in a cheery, hearty fashion.

It was her father. She went in, saying she would mash.[7] Directly,

---

7. Infuse the tea, i.e., let it stand after pouring boiling water over the tea leaves in order to gain strength.

she returned.

"I didn't come to see you on Sunday," began the little gray-bearded man.

"I didn't expect you," said his daughter.

The engine driver winced; then, reassuming his cheery, airy manner, he said:

"Oh, have you heard then? Well, and what do you think——?"

"I think it is soon enough," she replied.

At her brief censure the little man made an impatient gesture, and said coaxingly, yet with dangerous coldness:

"Well, what's a man to do? It's no sort of life for a man of my years, to sit at my own hearth like a stranger. And if I'm going to marry again it may as well be soon as late—what does it matter to anybody?"

The woman did not reply, but turned and went into the house. The man in the engine-cab stood assertive, till she returned with a cup of tea and a piece of bread and butter on a plate. She went up the steps and stood near the footplate of the hissing engine.

"You needn't 'a' brought me bread an' butter," said her father. "But a cup of tea"—he sipped appreciatively—"it's very nice." He sipped for a moment or two, then: "I hear as Walter's got another bout on," he said.

"When hasn't he?" said the woman bitterly.

"I heerd tell of him in the Lord Nelson braggin' as he was going to spend that b—— afore he went: half a sovereign that was."

"When?" asked the woman.

"A' Sat'day night—I know that's true."

"Very likely," she laughed bitterly. "He gives me twenty-three shillings."

"Aye, it's a nice thing, when a man can do nothing with his money but make a beast of himself!" said the gray-whiskered man. The woman turned her head away. Her father swallowed the last of his tea and handed her the cup.

"Aye," he sighed, wiping his mouth. "It's a settler,[8] it is——"

He put his hand on the lever. The little engine strained and groaned, and the train rumbled towards the crossing. The woman again looked across the metals. Darkness was settling over the spaces of the railway and trucks: the miners, in gray somber groups, were still passing home. The winding engine pulsed hurriedly, with brief pauses. Elizabeth Bates looked at the dreary flow of men, then she went indoors. Her husband did not come.

The kitchen was small and full of firelight; red coals piled glowing up the chimney mouth. All the life of the room seemed in the

---

8. Crushing (or final) blow.

white, warm hearth and the steel fender reflecting the red fire. The cloth was laid for tea; cups glinted in the shadows. At the back, where the lowest stairs protruded into the room, the boy sat struggling with a knife and a piece of white wood. He was almost hidden in the shadow. It was half-past four. They had but to await the father's coming to begin tea. As the mother watched her son's sullen little struggle with the wood, she saw herself in his silence and pertinacity; she saw the father in her child's indifference to all but himself. She seemed to be occupied by her husband. He had probably gone past his home, slunk past his own door, to drink before he came in, while his dinner spoiled and wasted in waiting. She glanced at the clock, then took the potatoes to strain them in the yard. The garden and fields beyond the brook were closed in uncertain darkness. When she rose with the saucepan, leaving the drain steaming into the night behind her, she saw the yellow lamps were lit along the high road that went up the hill away beyond the space of the railway lines and the field.

Then again she watched the men trooping home, fewer now and fewer.

Indoors the fire was sinking and the room was dark red. The woman put her saucepan on the hob, and set a batter pudding near the mouth of the oven. Then she stood unmoving. Directly, gratefully, came quick young steps to the door. Someone hung on the latch a moment, then a little girl entered and began pulling off her outdoor things, dragging a mass of curls, just ripening from gold to brown, over her eyes with her hat.

Her mother chid her for coming late from school, and said she would have to keep her at home the dark winter days.

"Why, mother, it's hardly a bit dark yet. The lamp's not lighted, and my father's not home."

"No, he isn't. But it's a quarter to five! Did you see anything of him?"

The child became serious. She looked at her mother with large, wistful blue eyes.

"No, mother, I've never seen him. Why? Has he come up an' gone past, to Old Brinsley? He hasn't, mother, 'cos I never saw him."

"He'd watch that," said the mother bitterly, "he'd take care as you didn't see him. But you may depend upon it, he's seated in the Prince o' Wales. He wouldn't be this late."

The girl looked at her mother piteously.

"Let's have our teas, mother, should we?" said she.

The mother called John to table. She opened the door once more and looked out across the darkness of the lines. All was deserted:

she could not hear the winding-engines.

"Perhaps," she said to herself, "he's stopped to get some ripping [9] done."

They sat down to tea. John, at the end of the table near the door, was almost lost in the darkness. Their faces were hidden from each other. The girl crouched against the fender slowly moving a thick piece of bread before the fire. The lad, his face a dusky mark on the shadow, sat watching her who was transfigured in the red glow.

"I do think it's beautiful to look in the fire," said the child.

"Do you?" said her mother. "Why?"

"It's so red, and full of little caves—and it feels so nice, and you can fair smell it."

"It'll want mending directly," replied her mother, "and then if your father comes he'll carry on and say there never is a fire when a man comes home sweating from the pit. A public house is always warm enough."

There was silence till the boy said complainingly: "Make haste, our Annie."

"Well, I am doing! I can't make the fire do it no faster, can I?"

"She keeps wafflin' it about so's to make 'er slow," grumbled the boy.

"Don't have such an evil imagination, child," replied the mother.

Soon the room was busy in the darkness with the crisp sound of crunching. The mother ate very little. She drank her tea determinedly, and sat thinking. When she rose her anger was evident in the stern unbending of her head. She looked at the pudding in the fender, and broke out:

"It is a scandalous thing as a man can't even come home to his dinner! If it's crozzled up to a cinder I don't see why I should care. Past his very door he goes to get to a public house, and here I sit with his dinner waiting for him——"

She went out. As she dropped piece after piece of coal on the red fire, the shadows fell on the walls, till the room was almost in total darkness.

"I canna see," grumbled the invisible John. In spite of herself, the mother laughed.

"You know the way to your mouth," she said. She set the dustpan outside the door. When she came again like a shadow on the hearth, the lad repeated, complaining sulkily:

"I canna see."

"Good gracious!" cried the mother irritably, "you're as bad as your father if it's a bit dusk!"

9. Taking out or cutting away coal or stone (a mining and quarrying term).

Nevertheless, she took a paper spill from a sheaf on the mantel-piece and proceeded to light the lamp that hung from the ceiling in the middle of the room. As she reached up, her figure displayed itself just rounding with maternity.

"Oh, mother——!" exclaimed the girl.

"What?" said the woman, suspended in the act of putting the lamp glass over the flame. The copper reflector shone handsomely on her, as she stood with uplifted arm, turning to face her daughter.

"You've got a flower in your apron!" said the child, in a little rapture at this unusual event.

"Goodness me!" exclaimed the woman, relieved. "One would think the house was afire." She replaced the glass and waited a moment before turning up the wick. A pale shadow was seen floating vaguely on the floor.

"Let me smell!" said the child, still rapturously, coming forward and putting her face to her mother's waist.

"Go along, silly!" said the mother, turning up the lamp. The light revealed their suspense so that the woman felt it almost unbearable. Annie was still bending at her waist. Irritably, the mother took the flowers out from her apron band.

"Oh, mother—don't take them out!" Annie cried, catching her hand and trying to replace the sprig.

"Such nonsense!" said the mother, turning away. The child put the pale chrysanthemums to her lips, murmuring:

"Don't they smell beautiful!"

Her mother gave a short laugh.

"No," she said, "not to me. It was chrysanthemums when I married him, and chrysanthemums when you were born, and the first time they ever brought him home drunk, he'd got brown chrysanthemums in his buttonhole."

She looked at the children. Their eyes and their parted lips were wondering. The mother sat rocking in silence for some time. Then she looked at the clock.

"Twenty minutes to six!" In a tone of fine bitter carelessness she continued: "Eh, he'll not come now till they bring him. There he'll stick! But he needn't come rolling in here in his pit dirt, for *I* won't wash him. He can lie on the floor——Eh, what a fool I've been, what a fool! And this is what I came here for, to this dirty hole, rats and all, for him to slink past his very door. Twice last week—he's begun now——"

She silenced herself, and rose to clear the table.

While for an hour or more the children played, subduedly intent, fertile of imagination, united in fear of the mother's wrath, and in dread of their father's home-coming, Mrs. Bates sat in her

rocking chair making a "singlet" of thick cream-colored flannel,
which gave a dull wounded sound as she tore off the gray edge. She
worked at her sewing with energy, listening to the children, and her
anger wearied itself, lay down to rest, opening its eyes from time to
time and steadily watching, its ears raised to listen. Sometimes
even her anger quailed and shrank, and the mother suspended her
sewing, tracing the footsteps that thudded along the sleepers outside; she would lift her head sharply to bid the children "hush," but
she recovered herself in time, and the footsteps went past the gate,
and the children were not flung out of their play-world.

But at last Annie sighed, and gave in. She glanced at her wagon
of slippers, and loathed the game. She turned plaintively to her
mother.

"Mother!"—but she was inarticulate.

John crept out like a frog from under the sofa. His mother
glanced up.

"Yes," she said, "just look at those shirt-sleeves!"

The boy held them out to survey them, saying nothing. Then
somebody called in a hoarse voice away down the line, and suspense
bristled in the room, till two people had gone by outside, talking.

"It is time for bed," said the mother.

"My father hasn't come," wailed Annie plaintively. But her
mother was primed with courage.

"Never mind. They'll bring him when he does come—like a
log." She meant there would be no scene. "And he may sleep on
the floor till he wakes himself. I know he'll not go to work tomorrow after this!"

The children had their hands and faces wiped with a flannel.
They were very quiet. When they had put on their nightdresses,
they said their prayers, the boy mumbling. The mother looked
down at them, at the brown silken bush of intertwining curls in the
nape of the girl's neck, at the little black head of the lad, and her
heart burst with anger at their father, who caused all three such
distress. The children hid their faces in her skirts for comfort.

When Mrs. Bates came down, the room was strangely empty,
with a tension of expectancy. She took up her sewing and stitched
for some time without raising her head. Meantime her anger was
tinged with fear.

II

The clock struck eight and she rose suddenly, dropping her sewing on her chair. She went to the stair-foot door, opened it, listening. Then she went out, locking the door behind her.

Something scuffled in the yard, and she started, though she
knew it was only the rats with which the place was over-run. The

night was very dark. In the great bay of railway lines, bulked with trucks, there was no trace of light, only away back she could see a few yellow lamps at the pit top, and the red smear of the burning pit bank on the night. She hurried along the edge of the track, then, crossing the converging lines, came to the stile by the white gates, whence she emerged on the road. Then the fear which had led her shrank. People were walking up to New Brinsley; she saw the lights in the houses; twenty yards farther on were the broad windows of the Prince of Wales, very warm and bright, and the loud voices of men could be heard distinctly. What a fool she had been to imagine that anything had happened to him! He was merely drinking over there at the Prince of Wales. She faltered. She had never yet been to fetch him, and she never would go. So she continued her walk towards the long straggling line of houses, standing back on the highway. She entered a passage between the dwellings.

"Mr. Rigley?—Yes! Did you want him? No, he's not in at this minute."

The raw-boned woman leaned forward from her dark scullery and peered at the other, upon whom fell a dim light through the blind of the kitchen window.

"Is it Mrs. Bates?" she asked in a tone tinged with respect.

"Yes. I wondered if your Master was at home. Mine hasn't come yet."

"'Asn't 'e! Oh, Jack's been 'ome an' 'ad 'is dinner an' gone out. 'E's just gone for 'alf an hour afore bedtime. Did you call at the Prince of Wales?"

"No——"

"No, you didn't like——! It's not very nice." The other woman was indulgent. There was an awkward pause. "Jack never said nothink about—about your Master," she said.

"No!—I expect he's stuck in there!"

Elizabeth Bates said this bitterly, and with recklessness. She knew that the woman across the yard was standing at her door listening, but she did not care. As she turned:

"Stop a minute! I'll just go an' ask Jack if 'e knows anythink," said Mrs. Rigley.

"Oh no—I wouldn't like to put——!"

"Yes, I will, if you'll just step inside an' see as th' childer doesn't come downstairs and set theirselves afire."

Elizabeth Bates, murmuring a remonstrance, stepped inside. The other woman apologized for the state of the room.

The kitchen needed apology. There were little frocks and trousers and childish undergarments on the squab and on the floor, and a litter of playthings everywhere. On the black American cloth [1] of the table were pieces of bread and cake, crusts, slops, and a teapot with cold tea.

"Eh, ours is just as bad," said Elizabeth Bates, looking at the woman, not at the house. Mrs. Rigley put a shawl over her head and hurried out, saying:

"I shanna be a minute."

The other sat, noting with faint disapproval the general untidiness of the room. Then she fell to counting the shoes of various sizes scattered over the floor. There were twelve. She sighed and said to herself: "No wonder!"—glancing at the litter. There came the scratching of two pairs of feet on the yard, and the Rigleys entered. Elizabeth Bates rose. Rigley was a big man, with very large bones. His head looked particularly bony. Across his temple was a blue scar, caused by a wound got in the pit, a wound in which the coal dust remained blue like tattooing.

"'Asna 'e come whoam yit?" asked the man, without any form of greeting, but with deference and sympathy. "I couldna say wheer he is—'e's non ower theer!"—he jerked his head to signify the Prince of Wales.

"'E's 'appen gone up to th' Yew," said Mrs. Rigley.

There was another pause. Rigley had evidently something to get off his mind:

"Ah left 'im finishin' a stint," he began. "Loose-all [2] 'ad bin gone about ten minutes when we com'n away, an' I shouted: 'Are ter comin', Walt?' an' 'e said: 'Go on, Ah shanna be but a'ef a minnit,' so we com'n ter th' bottom, me an' Bowers, thinkin' as 'e wor just behint, an' 'ud come up i' th' next bantle [3]——"

He stood perplexed, as if answering a charge of deserting his mate. Elizabeth Bates, now again certain of disaster, hastened to reassure him:

"I expect 'e's gone up to th' Yew Tree, as you say. It's not the first time. I've fretted myself into a fever before now. He'll come home when they carry him."

"Ay, isn't it too bad!" deplored the other woman.

"I'll just step up to Dick's an' see if 'e *is* theer," offered the man, afraid of appearing alarmed, afraid of taking liberties.

"Oh, I wouldn't think of bothering you that far," said Elizabeth Bates, with emphasis, but he knew she was glad of his offer.

As they stumbled up the entry, Elizabeth Bates heard Rigley's wife run across the yard and open her neighbor's door. At this, suddenly all the blood in her body seemed to switch away from her

1. Oilcloth.
2. Signal for end of work.
3. Group.

heart.

"Mind!" warned Rigley. "Ah've said many a time as Ah'd fill up them ruts in this entry, sumb'dy 'll be breakin' their legs yit."

She recovered herself and walked quickly along with the miner.

"I don't like leaving the children in bed, and nobody in the house," she said.

"No, you dunna!" he replied courteously. They were soon at the gate of the cottage.

"Well, I shanna be many minnits. Dunna you be frettin' now, 'e'll be all right," said the butty.[4]

"Thank you very much, Mr. Rigley," she replied.

"You're welcome!" he stammered, moving away. "I shanna be many minnits."

The house was quiet. Elizabeth Bates took off her hat and shawl, and rolled back the rug. When she had finished, she sat down. It was a few minutes past nine. She was startled by the rapid chuff of the winding engine at the pit, and the sharp whirr of the brakes on the rope as it descended. Again she felt the painful sweep of her blood, and she put her hand to her side, saying aloud: "Good gracious!—it's only the nine o'clock deputy [5] going down," rebuking herself.

She sat still, listening. Half an hour of this, and she was wearied out.

"What am I working myself up like this for?" she said pitiably to herself, "I s'll only be doing myself some damage."

She took out her sewing again.

At a quarter to ten there were footsteps. One person! She watched for the door to open. It was an elderly woman, in a black bonnet and a black woolen shawl—his mother. She was about sixty years old, pale, with blue eyes, and her face all wrinkled and lamentable. She shut the door and turned to her daughter-in-law peevishly.

"Eh, Lizzie, whatever shall we do, whatever shall we do!" she cried.

Elizabeth drew back a little, sharply.

"What is it, mother?" she said.

The elder woman seated herself on the sofa.

"I don't know, child, I can't tell you!"—she shook her head slowly. Elizabeth sat watching her, anxious and vexed.

"I don't know," replied the grandmother, sighing very deeply. "There's no end to my troubles, there isn't. The things I've gone through, I'm sure it's enough——!" She wept without wiping her

---

4. Workmate (cf. "buddy"). Among English coal-miners it has the special meaning of "a supervisor intermediary between the employers and the men."
5. Minor coal-mine official.

eyes, the tears running.

"But, mother," interrupted Elizabeth, "what do you mean? What is it?"

The grandmother slowly wiped her eyes. The fountains of her tears were stopped by Elizabeth's directness. She wiped her eyes slowly.

"Poor child! Eh, you poor thing!" she moaned. "I don't know what we're going to do, I don't—and you as you are—it's a thing, it is indeed!"

Elizabeth waited.

"Is he dead?" she asked, and at the words her heart swung violently, though she felt a slight flush of shame at the ultimate extravagance of the question. Her words sufficiently frightened the old lady, almost brought her to herself.

"Don't say so, Elizabeth! We'll hope it's not as bad as that; no, may the Lord spare us that, Elizabeth. Jack Rigley came just as I was sittin' down to a glass afore going to bed, an' 'e said: ' 'Appen you'll go down th' line, Mrs. Bates. Walt's had an accident. 'Appen you'll go an' sit wi' 'er till we can get him home.' I hadn't time to ask him a word afore he was gone. An' I put my bonnet on an' come straight down, Lizzie. I thought to myself: 'Eh, that poor blessed child, if anybody should come an' tell her of a sudden, there's no knowin' what'll 'appen to 'er.' You mustn't let it upset you, Lizzie —or you know what to expect. How long is it, six months—or is it five, Lizzie? Ay!"—the old woman shook her head—"time slips on, it slips on! Ay!"

Elizabeth's thoughts were busy elsewhere. If he was killed— would she be able to manage on the little pension and what she could earn?—she counted up rapidly. If he was hurt—they wouldn't take him to the hospital—how tiresome he would be to nurse!—but perhaps she'd be able to get him away from the drink and his hateful ways. She would—while he was ill. The tears offered to come to her eyes at the picture. But what sentimental luxury was this she was beginning? She turned to consider the children. At any rate she was absolutely necessary for them. They were her business.

"Ay!" repeated the old woman, "it seems but a week or two since he brought me his first wages. Ay—he was a good lad, Elizabeth, he was, in his way. I don't know why he got to be such a trouble, I don't. He was a happy lad at home, only full of spirits. But there's no mistake he's been a handful of trouble, he has! I hope the Lord'll spare him to mend his ways. I hope so, I hope so. You've had a sight o' trouble with him, Elizabeth, you have indeed. But he was a jolly enough lad wi' me, he was, I can assure you. I don't know how it is. . . ."

The old woman continued to muse aloud, a monotonous irritating sound, while Elizabeth thought concentratedly, startled once, when she heard the winding engine chuff quickly, and the brakes skirr with a shriek. Then she heard the engine more slowly, and the brakes made no sound. The old woman did not notice. Elizabeth waited in suspense. The mother-in-law talked, with lapses into silence.

"But he wasn't your son, Lizzie, an' it makes a difference. Whatever he was, I remember him when he was little, an' I learned to understand him and to make allowances. You've got to make allowances for them——"

It was half-past ten, and the old woman was saying: "But it's trouble from beginning to end; you're never too old for trouble, never too old for that——" when the gate banged back, and there were heavy feet on the steps.

"I'll go, Lizzie, let me go," cried the old woman, rising. But Elizabeth was at the door. It was a man in pit clothes.

"They're bringin' 'im, Missis," he said. Elizabeth's heart halted a moment. Then it surged on again, almost suffocating her. "Is he—is it bad?" she asked.

The man turned away, looking at the darkness:

"The doctor says 'e'd been dead hours. 'E saw 'im i' th' lamp-cabin."

The old woman, who stood just behind Elizabeth, dropped into a chair, and folded her hands, crying: "Oh, my boy, my boy!"

"Hush!" said Elizabeth, with a sharp twitch of a frown. "Be still, mother, don't waken th' children: I wouldn't have them down for anything!"

The old woman moaned softly, rocking herself. The man was drawing away. Elizabeth took a step forward.

"How was it?" she asked.

"Well, I couldn't say for sure," the man replied, very ill at ease. "'E wor finishin' a stint an' th' butties 'ad gone, an' a lot o' stuff come down atop 'n 'im."

"And crushed him?" cried the widow, with a shudder.

"No," said the man, "it fell at th' back of 'im. 'E wor under th' face an' it niver touched 'im. It shut 'im in. It seems 'e wor smothered."

Elizabeth shrank back. She heard the old woman behind her cry:

"What?—what did 'e say it was?"

The man replied, more loudly: "'E wor smothered!"

Then the old woman wailed aloud, and this relieved Elizabeth.

"Oh, mother," she said, putting her hand on the old woman, "don't waken th' children, don't waken th' children."

She wept a little, unknowing, while the old mother rocked herself and moaned. Elizabeth remembered that they were bringing him home, and she must be ready. "They'll lay him in the parlor," she said to herself, standing a moment pale and perplexed.

Then she lighted a candle and went into the tiny room. The air was cold and damp, but she could not make a fire, there was no fireplace. She set down the candle and looked round. The candlelight glittered on the luster-glasses, on the two vases that held some of the pink chrysanthemums, and on the dark mahogany. There was a cold, deathly smell of chrysanthemums in the room. Elizabeth stood looking at the flowers. She turned away, and calculated whether there would be room to lay him on the floor, between the couch and the chiffonier. She pushed the chairs aside. There would be room to lay him down and to step round him. Then she fetched the old red tablecloth, and another old cloth, spreading them down to save her bit of carpet. She shivered on leaving the parlor; so, from the dresser drawer she took a clean shirt and put it at the fire to air. All the time her mother-in-law was rocking herself in the chair and moaning.

"You'll have to move from there, mother," said Elizabeth. "They'll be bringing him in. Come in the rocker."

The old mother rose mechanically, and seated herself by the fire, continuing to lament. Elizabeth went into the pantry for another candle, and there, in the little penthouse under the naked tiles, she heard them coming. She stood still in the pantry doorway, listening. She heard them pass the end of the house, and come awkwardly down the three steps, a jumble of shuffling footsteps and muttering voices. The old woman was silent. The men were in the yard.

Then Elizabeth heard Matthews, the manager of the pit, say: "You go in first, Jim. Mind!"

The door came open, and the two women saw a collier backing into the room, holding one end of a stretcher, on which they could see the nailed pit boots of the dead man. The two carriers halted, the man at the head stooping to the lintel of the door.

"Wheer will you have him?" asked the manager, a short, white-bearded man.

Elizabeth roused herself and came from the pantry carrying the unlighted candle.

"In the parlor," she said.

"In there, Jim!" pointed the manager, and the carriers backed round into the tiny room. The coat with which they had covered the body fell off as they awkwardly turned through the two doorways, and the women saw their man, naked to the waist, lying stripped for work. The old woman began to moan in a low voice of horror.

"Lay th' stretcher at th' side," snapped the manager, "an' put 'im on th' cloths. Mind now, mind! Look you now——!"

One of the men had knocked off a vase of chrysanthemums. He stared awkwardly, then they set down the stretcher. Elizabeth did not look at her husband. As soon as she could get in the room, she went and picked up the broken vase and the flowers.

"Wait a minute!" she said.

The three men waited in silence while she mopped up the water with a duster.

"Eh, what a job, what a job, to be sure!" the manager was saying, rubbing his brow with trouble and perplexity. "Never knew such a thing in my life, never! He'd no business to ha' been left. I never knew such a thing in my life! Fell over him clean as a whistle, an' shut him in. Not four foot of space, there wasn't— yet it scarce bruised him."

He looked down at the dead man, lying prone, half naked, all grimed with coal dust.

"'Sphyxiated', the doctor said. It *is* the most terrible job I've ever known Seems as if it was done o' purpose. Clean over him, an' shut 'im in, like a mouse-trap"—he made a sharp, descending gesture with his hand.

The colliers standing by jerked aside their heads in hopeless comment.

The horror of the thing bristled upon them all.

Then they heard the girl's voice upstairs calling shrilly: "Mother, mother—who is it? Mother, who is it?"

Elizabeth hurried to the foot of the stairs and opened the door:

"Go to sleep!" she commanded sharply. "What are you shouting about? Go to sleep at once—there's nothing——"

Then she began to mount the stairs. They could hear her on the boards, and on the plaster floor of the little bedroom. They could hear her distinctly:

"What's the matter now?—what's the matter with you, silly thing?"—her voice was much agitated, with an unreal gentleness.

"I thought it was some men come," said the plaintive voice of the child. "Has he come?"

"Yes, they've brought him. There's nothing to make a fuss about. Go to sleep now, like a good child."

They could hear her voice in the bedroom, they waited whilst she covered the children under the bedclothes.

"Is he drunk?" asked the girl, timidly, faintly.

"No! No—he's not! He—he's asleep."

"Is he asleep downstairs?"

"Yes—and don't make a noise."

There was silence for a moment, then the men heard the frightened child again:

"What's that noise?"

"It's nothing, I tell you, what are you bothering for?"

The noise was the grandmother moaning. She was oblivious of everything, sitting on her chair rocking and moaning. The manager put his hand on her arm and bade her "Sh—sh!!"

The old woman opened her eyes and looked at him. She was shocked by this interruption, and seemed to wonder.

"What time is it?" the plaintive thin voice of the child, sinking back unhappily into sleep, asked this last question.

"Ten o'clock," answered the mother more softly. Then she must have bent down and kissed the children.

Matthews beckoned to the men to come away. They put on their caps and took up the stretcher. Stepping over the body, they tiptoed out of the house. None of them spoke till they were far from the wakeful children.

When Elizabeth came down she found her mother alone on the parlor floor, leaning over the dead man, the tears dropping on him.

"We must lay him out," the wife said. She put on the kettle, then returning knelt at the feet, and began to unfasten the knotted leather laces. The room was clammy and dim with only one candle, so that she had to bend her face almost to the floor. At last she got off the heavy boots and put them away.

"You must help me now," she whispered to the old woman. Together they stripped the man.

When they arose, saw him lying in the naïve dignity of death, the woman stood arrested in fear and respect. For a few moments they remained still, looking down, the old mother whimpering. Elizabeth felt countermanded. She saw him, how utterly inviolable he lay in himself. She had nothing to do with him. She could not accept it. Stooping, she laid her hand on him, in claim. He was still warm, for the mine was hot where he had died. His mother had his face between her hands, and was murmuring incoherently. The old tears fell in succession as drops from wet leaves; the mother was not weeping, merely her tears flowed. Elizabeth embraced the body of her husband, with cheek and lips. She seemed to be listening, inquiring, trying to get some connection. But she could not. She was driven away. He was impregnable.

She rose, went into the kitchen, where she poured warm water into a bowl, brought soap and flannel and a soft towel. "I must wash him," she said.

Then the old mother rose stiffly, and watched Elizabeth as she carefully washed his face, carefully brushing his big blond moustache from his mouth with the flannel. She was afraid with a bottomless fear, so she ministered to him. The old woman, jealous, said:

"Let me wipe him!"—and she kneeled on the other side drying slowly as Elizabeth washed, her big black bonnet sometimes brushing the dark head of her daughter-in-law. They worked thus in silence for a long time. They never forgot it was death, and the touch of the man's dead body gave them strange emotions, different in each of the women; a great dread possessed them both, the mother felt the lie was given to her womb, she was denied; the wife felt the utter isolation of the human soul, the child within her was a weight apart from her.

At last it was finished. He was a man of handsome body, and his face showed no traces of drink. He was blond, full fleshed, with fine limbs. But he was dead.

"Bless him," whispered his mother, looking always at his face, and speaking out of sheer terror. "Dear lad—bless him!" She spoke in a faint, sibilant ecstasy of fear and mother love.

Elizabeth sank down again to the floor, and put her face against his neck, and trembled and shuddered. But she had to draw away again. He was dead, and her living flesh had no place against his. A great dread and weariness held her: she was so unavailing. Her life was gone like this.

"White as milk he is, clear as a twelve-month baby, bless him, the darling!" the old mother murmured to herself. "Not a mark on him, clear and clean and white, beautiful as ever a child was made," she murmured with pride. Elizabeth kept her face hidden.

"He went peaceful, Lizzie—peaceful as sleep. Isn't he beautiful, the lamb? Ay—he must ha' made his peace, Lizzie. 'Appen he made it all right, Lizzie, shut in there. He'd have time. He wouldn't look like this if he hadn't made his peace. The lamb, the dear lamb. Eh, but he had a hearty laugh. I loved to hear it. He had the heartiest laugh, Lizzie, as a lad——"

Elizabeth looked up. The man's mouth was fallen back, slightly open under the cover of the moustache. The eyes, half shut, 'did not show glazed in the obscurity. Life with its smoky burning gone from him, had left him apart and utterly alien to her. And she knew what a stranger he was to her. In her womb was ice of fear, because of this separate stranger with whom she had been living as one flesh. Was this what it all meant—utter, intact separateness, obscured by heat of living? In dread she turned her face away. The fact was too deadly. There had been nothing between them, and yet they had come together, exchanging their nakedness repeatedly. Each time he had taken her, they had been two isolated beings, far apart as now. He was no more responsible than she. The child was like ice in her womb. For as she looked at the dead man, her mind, cold and detached, said clearly: "Who am I? What have I been doing? I have been fighting a husband who did not exist. *He* existed all the time. What wrong have I done? What was that I have been living with? There lies the reality, this man." And her soul died in her for fear: she knew she had never seen him, he had never seen her, they had met in the dark and had fought in the dark, not knowing whom they met or whom they fought. And now she saw, and turned silent in seeing. For she had been wrong. She had said he was something he was not; she had felt familiar with him. Whereas he was apart all the while, living as she never lived, feeling as she never felt.

In fear and shame she looked at his naked body, that she had known falsely. And he was the father of her children. Her soul was torn from her body and stood apart. She looked at his naked body and was ashamed, as if she had denied it. After all, it was itself. It seemed awful to her. She looked at his face, and she turned her own face to the wall. For his look was other than hers, his way was not her way. She had denied him what he was—she saw it now. She had refused him as himself. And this had been her life, and his life. She was grateful to death, which restored the truth. And she knew she was not dead.

And all the while her heart was bursting with grief and pity for him. What had he suffered? What stretch of horror for this helpless man! She was rigid with agony. She had not been able to help him. He had been cruelly injured, this naked man, this other being, and she could make no reparation. There were the children—but the children belonged to life. This dead man had nothing to do with them. He and she were only channels through which life had flowed to issue in the children. She was a mother—but how awful she knew it now to have been a wife. And he, dead now, how awful he must have felt it to be a husband. She felt that in the next world he would be a stranger to her. If they met there, in the beyond, they would only be ashamed of what had been before. The children had come, for some mysterious reason, out of both of them. But the children did not unite them. Now he was dead, she knew how eternally he was apart from her, how eternally he had nothing more to do with her. She saw this episode of her life closed. They had denied each other in life. Now he had withdrawn. An anguish came over her. It was finished then: it had become hopeless between them long before he died. Yet he had been her husband. But how little!

"Have you got his shirt, 'Lizabeth?"

Elizabeth turned without answering, though she strove to weep and behave as her mother-in-law expected. But she could not, she was silenced. She went into the kitchen and returned with the garment.

"It is aired," she said, grasping the cotton shirt here and there to try. She was almost ashamed to handle him; what right had she or anyone to lay hands on him; but her touch was humble on his body. It was hard work to clothe him. He was so heavy and inert. A terrible dread gripped her all the while: that he could be so heavy and utterly inert, unresponsive, apart. The horror of the distance between them was almost too much for her—it was so infinite a gap she must look across.

At last it was finished. They covered him with a sheet and left him lying, with his face bound. And she fastened the door of the little parlor, lest the children should see what was lying there. Then, with peace sunk heavy on her heart, she went about making tidy the kitchen. She knew she submitted to life, which was her immediate master. But from death, her ultimate master, she winced with fear and shame.

1911, 1914

From The Rainbow

From *Chapter II. They Live at the Marsh* [1]

One afternoon, the pains began, Mrs. Brangwen was put to bed, the midwife came. Night fell, the shutters were closed, Brangwen came in to tea, to the loaf and the pewter teapot, the child, silent and quivering, playing with glass beads, the house, empty, it seemed, or exposed to the winter night, as if it had no walls.

Sometimes there sounded, long and remote in the house, vibrating through everything, the moaning cry of a woman in labor. Brangwen, sitting downstairs, was divided. His lower, deeper self

1. Tom Brangwen, a Nottinghamshire farmer, married Lydia Lensky, widow of a Polish émigré doctor. Anna is Lydia's child by her first marriage. The scene is Marsh Farm, a few miles south of East- wood, where Lawrence was born, and just across the Nottinghamshire-Derbyshire border from the town of Ilkeston where Lawrence trained as a teacher. Lydia is about to have her first child by Tom.

was with her, bound to her, suffering. But the big shell of his body remembered the sound of owls that used to fly round the farmstead when he was a boy. He was back in his youth, a boy, haunted by the sound of the owls, waking up his brother to speak to him. And his mind drifted away to the birds, their solemn, dignified faces, their flight so soft and broad-winged. And then to the birds his brother had shot, fluffy, dust-colored, dead heaps of softness with faces absurdly asleep. It was a queer thing, a dead owl.

He lifted his cup to his lips, he watched the child with the beads. But his mind was occupied with owls, and the atmosphere of his boyhood, with his brothers and sisters. Elsewhere, fundamental, he was with his wife in labor, the child was being brought forth out of their one flesh. He and she, one flesh, out of which life must be put forth. The rent was not in his body, but it was of his body. On her the blows fell, but the quiver ran through to him, to his last fiber. She must be torn asunder for life to come forth, yet still they were one flesh, and still, from further back, the life came out of him to her, and still he was the unbroken that has the broken rock in its arms, their flesh was one rock from which the life gushed, out of her who was smitten and rent, from him who quivered and yielded.

He went upstairs to her. As he came to the bedside she spoke to him in Polish.

"Is it very bad?" he asked.

She looked at him, and oh, the weariness to her, of the effort to understand another language, the weariness of hearing him, attending to him, making out who he was, as he stood there fair-bearded and alien, looking at her. She knew something of him, of his eyes. But she could not grasp him. She closed her eyes.

He turned away, white to the gills.

"It's not so very bad," said the midwife.

He knew he was a strain on his wife. He went downstairs.

The child glanced up at him, frightened.

"I want my mother," she quavered.

"Ay, but she's badly," he said mildly, unheeding.

She looked at him with lost, frightened eyes.

"Has she got a headache?"

"No—she's going to have a baby."

The child looked round. He was unaware of her. She was alone again in terror.

"I want my mother," came the cry of panic.

"Let Tilly undress you," he said. "You're tired."

There was another silence. Again came the cry of labor.

"I want my mother," rang automatically from the wincing, panic-stricken child, that felt cut off and lost in a horror of desolation.

Tilly came forward, her heart wrung.

"Come an' let me undress her then, pet lamb," she crooned. "You s'll have your mother in th' mornin', don't you fret, my duckie; never mind, angel."

But Anna stood upon the sofa, her back to the wall.

"I want my mother," she cried, her little face quivering, and the great tears of childish, utter anguish falling.

"She's poorly, my lamb, she's poorly tonight, but she'll be better by mornin'. Oh, don't cry, don't cry, love, she doesn't want you to cry, precious little heart, no, she doesn't."

Tilly took gently hold of the child's skirts. Anna snatched back her dress, and cried, in a little hysteria:

"No, you're not to undress me—I want my mother,"—and her child's face was running with grief and tears, her body shaken.

"Oh, but let Tilly undress you. Let Tilly undress you, who loves you, don't be wilful tonight. Mother's poorly, she doesn't want you to cry."

The child sobbed distractedly, she could not hear.

"I want my mother," she wept.

"When you're undressed, you s'll go up to see your mother— when you're undressed, pet, when you've let Tilly undress you, when you're a little jewel in your nightie, love. Oh, don't you cry, don't you——"

Brangwen sat stiff in his chair. He felt his brain going tighter. He crossed over the room, aware only of the maddening sobbing.

"Don't make a noise," he said.

And a new fear shook the child from the sound of his voice. She cried mechanically, her eyes looking watchful through her tears, in terror, alert to what might happen.

"I want—my—mother," quavered the sobbing, blind voice.

A shiver of irritation went over the man's limbs. It was the utter, persistent unreason, the maddening blindness of the voice and the crying.

"You must come and be undressed," he said, in a quiet voice that was thin with anger.

And he reached his hand and grasped her. He felt her body catch in a convulsive sob. But he too was blind, and intent, irritated into mechanical action. He began to unfasten her little apron. She would have shrunk from him, but could not. So her small body remained in his grasp, while he fumbled at the little buttons and tapes, unthinking, intent, unaware of anything but the irritation of her. Her body was held taut and resistant, he pushed off the little dress and the petticoats, revealing the white arms. She kept stiff, overpowered, violated, he went on with his task. And all the while she sobbed, choking:

"I want my mother."

He was unheedingly silent, his face stiff. The child was now incapable of understanding, she had become a little, mechanical thing of fixed will. She wept, her body convulsed, her voice repeating the same cry.

"Eh, dear o' me!" cried Tilly, becoming distracted herself. Brangwen, slow, clumsy, blind, intent, got off all the little garments, and stood the child naked in its shift upon the sofa.

"Where's her nightie?" he asked.

Tilly brought it, and he put it on her. Anna did not move her limbs to his desire. He had to push them into place. She stood, with fixed, blind will, resistant, a small, convulsed, unchangeable thing weeping ever and repeating the same phrase. He lifted one foot after the other, pulled off slippers and socks. She was ready.

"Do you want a drink?" he asked.

She did not change. Unheeding, uncaring, she stood on the sofa, standing back, alone, her hands shut and half lifted, her face, all tears, raised and blind. And through the sobbing and choking came the broken:

"I—want—my—mother."

"Do you want a drink?" he said again.

There was no answer. He lifted the stiff, denying body between his hands. Its stiff blindness made a flash of rage go through him. He would like to break it.

He set the child on his knee, and sat again in his chair beside the fire, the wet, sobbing, inarticulate noise going on near his ear, the child sitting stiff, not yielding to him or anything, not aware.

A new degree of anger came over him. What did it all matter? What did it matter if the mother talked Polish and cried in labor, if this child were stiff with resistance, and crying? Why take it to heart? Let the mother cry in labor, let the child cry in resistance, since they would do so. Why should he fight against it, why resist? Let it be, if it were so. Let them be as they were, if they insisted.

And in a daze he sat, offering no fight. The child cried on, the minutes ticked away, a sort of torpor was on him.

It was some little time before he came to, and turned to attend to the child. He was shocked by her little wet, blinded face. A bit dazed, he pushed back the wet hair. Like a living statue of grief, her blind face cried on.

"Nay," he said, "not as bad as that. It's not as bad as that, Anna, my child. Come, what are you crying for so much? Come, stop now, it'll make you sick. I wipe you dry, don't wet your face any more. Don't cry any more wet tears, don't, it's better not to. Don't cry—it's not so bad as all that. Hush now, hush—let it be enough."

His voice was queer and distant and calm. He looked at the child.

She was beside herself now. He wanted her to stop, he wanted it all to stop, to become natural.

"Come," he said, rising to turn away, "we'll go an' supper-up the beast."

He took a big shawl, folded her round, and went out into the kitchen for a lantern.

"You're never taking the child out, of a night like this," said Tilly.

"Ay, it'll quieten her," he answered.

It was raining. The child was suddenly still, shocked, finding the rain on its face, the darkness.

"We'll just give the cows their something-to-eat, afore they go to bed," Brangwen was saying to her, holding her close and sure.

There was a trickling of water into the butt, a burst of raindrops sputtering on to her shawl, and the light of the lantern swinging, flashing on a wet pavement and the base of a wet wall. Otherwise it was black darkness: one breathed darkness.

He opened the doors, upper and lower, and they entered into the high, dry barn, that smelled warm even if it were not warm. He hung the lantern on the nail and shut the door. They were in another world now. The light shed softly on the timbered barn, on the whitewashed walls, and the great heap of hay; instruments cast their shadows largely, a ladder rose to the dark arch of a loft. Outside there was the driving rain, inside, the softly illuminated stillness and calmness of the barn.

Holding the child on one arm, he set about preparing the food for the cows, filling a pan with chopped hay and brewer's grains and a little meal. The child, all wonder, watched what he did. A new being was created in her for the new conditions. Sometimes, a little spasm, eddying from the bygone storm of sobbing, shook her small body. Her eyes were wide and wondering, pathetic. She was silent, quite still.

In a sort of dream, his heart sunk to the bottom, leaving the surface of him still, quite still, he rose with the panful of food, carefully balancing the child on one arm, the pan in the other hand. The silky fringe of the shawl swayed softly, grains and hay trickled to the floor; he went along a dimly lit passage behind the mangers, where the horns of the cows pricked out of the obscurity. The child shrank, he balanced stiffly, rested the pan on the manger wall, and tipped out the food, half to this cow, half to the next. There was a noise of chains running, as the cows lifted or dropped their heads sharply; then a contented, soothing sound, a long snuffing as the beasts ate in silence.

The journey had to be performed several times. There was the rhythmic sound of the shovel in the barn, then the man returned walking stiffly between the two weights, the face of the child peering out from the shawl. Then the next time, as he stooped, she freed her arm and put it round his neck, clinging soft and warm, making all easier.

The beasts fed, he dropped the pan and sat down on a box, to arrange the child.

"Will the cows go to sleep now?" she said, catching her breath as she spoke.

"Yes."

"Will they eat all their stuff up first?"

"Yes. Hark at them."

And the two sat still listening to the snuffing and breathing of cows feeding in the sheds communicating with this small barn. The lantern shed a soft, steady light from one wall. All outside was still in the rain. He looked down at the silky folds of the paisley shawl. It reminded him of his mother. She used to go to church in it. He was back again in the old irresponsibility and security, a boy at home.

The two sat very quiet. His mind, in a sort of trance, seemed to become more and more vague. He held the child close to him. A quivering little shudder, re-echoing from her sobbing, went down her limbs. He held her closer. Gradually she relaxed, the eyelids began to sink over her dark, watchful eyes. As she sank to sleep, his mind became blank.

When he came to, as if from sleep, he seemed to be sitting in a timeless stillness. What was he listening for? He seemed to be listening for some sound a long way off, from beyond life. He remembered his wife. He must go back to her. The child was asleep, the eyelids not quite shut, showing a slight film of black pupil between. Why did she not shut her eyes? Her mouth was also a little open.

He rose quickly and went back to the house.

"Is she asleep?" whispered Tilly.

He nodded. The servant woman came to look at the child who slept in the shawl, with cheeks flushed hot and red, and a whiteness, a wanness round the eyes.

"God-a-mercy!" whispered Tilly, shaking her head.

He pushed off his boots and went upstairs with the child. He became aware of the anxiety grasped tight at his heart, because of his wife. But he remained still. The house was silent save for the wind outside, and the noisy trickling and splattering of water in the water butts. There was a slit of light under his wife's door.

He put the child into bed wrapped as she was in the shawl, for the sheets would be cold. Then he was afraid that she might not be able to move her arms, so he loosened her. The black eyes opened, rested on him vacantly, sank shut again. He covered her up. The last little quiver from the sobbing shook her breathing.

This was his room, the room he had had before he married. It was familiar. He remembered what it was to be a young man, untouched.

He remained suspended. The child slept, pushing her small fists from the shawl. He could tell the woman her child was asleep. But he must go to the other landing. He started. There was the sound of the owls—the moaning of the woman. What an uncanny sound! It was not human—at least to a man.

He went down to her room, entering softly. She was lying still, with eyes shut, pale, tired. His heart leapt, fearing she was dead. Yet he knew perfectly well she was not. He saw the way her hair went loose over her temples, her mouth was shut with suffering in a sort of grin. She was beautiful to him—but it was not human. He had a dread of her as she lay there. What had she to do with him? She was other than himself.

Something made him go and touch her fingers that were still grasped on the sheet. Her brown-gray eyes opened and looked at him. She did not know him as himself. But she knew him as the man. She looked at him as a woman in childbirth looks at the man who begot the child in her: an impersonal look, in the extreme hour, female to male. Her eyes closed again. A great, scalding peace went over him, burning his heart and his entrails, passing off into the infinite.

When her pains began afresh, tearing her, he turned aside, and could not look. But his heart in torture was at peace, his bowels were glad. He went downstairs, and to the door, outside, lifted his face to the rain, and felt the darkness striking unseen and steadily upon him.

The swift, unseen threshing of the night upon him silenced him and he was overcome. He turned away indoors, humbly. There was the infinite world, eternal, unchanging, as well as the world of life.

1912–14   1915

The Horse Dealer's Daughter

"Well, Mabel, and what are you going to do with yourself?" asked Joe, with foolish flippancy. He felt quite safe himself. Without listening for an answer, he turned aside, worked a grain of tobacco to the tip of his tongue, and spat it out. He did not care about anything, since he felt safe himself.

The three brothers and the sister sat round the desolate break-fast-table, attempting some sort of desultory consultation. The morning's post had given the final tap to the family fortunes, and all was over. The dreary dining-room itself, with its heavy mahogany furniture, looked as if it were waiting to be done away with.

But the consultation amounted to nothing. There was a strange air of ineffectuality about the three men, as they sprawled at table, smoking and reflecting vaguely on their own condition. The girl was alone, a rather short, sullen-looking young woman of twenty-seven. She did not share the same life as her brothers. She would have been good-looking, save for the impressive fixity of her face, "bull-dog," as her brothers called it.

There was a confused tramping of horses' feet outside. The three men all sprawled round in their chairs to watch. Beyond the dark holly bushes that separated the strip of lawn from the high-road, they could see a cavalcade of shire horses swinging out of their own yard, being taken for exercise. This was the last time. These were the last horses that would go through their hands. The young men watched with critical, callous look. They were all frightened at the collapse of their lives, and the sense of disaster in which they were involved left them no inner freedom.

Yet they were three fine, well-set fellows enough. Joe, the eldest, was a man of thirty-three, broad and handsome in a hot, flushed way. His face was red, he twisted his black moustache over a thick finger, his eyes were shallow and restless. He had a sensual way of uncovering his teeth when he laughed, and his bearing was stupid. Now he watched the horses with a glazed look of helplessness in his eyes, a certain stupor of downfall.

The great draught horses swung past. They were tied head to tail, four of them, and they heaved along to where a lane branched off from the highroad, planting their great hoofs floutingly in the fine black mud, swinging their great rounded haunches sumptuously, and trotting a few sudden steps as they were led into the lane, round the corner. Every movement showed a massive, slumbrous strength, and a stupidity which held them in subjection. The groom at the head looked back, jerking the leading rope. And the cavalcade moved out of sight up the lane, the tail of the last horse, bobbed up tight and stiff, held out taut from the swinging great haunches as they rocked behind the hedges in a motion-like sleep.

Joe watched with glazed hopeless eyes. The horses were almost like his own body to him. He felt he was done for now. Luckily he was engaged to a woman as old as himself, and therefore her father, who was steward of a neighboring estate, would provide him with a job. He would marry and go into harness. His life was over, he would be a subject animal now.

He turned uneasily aside, the retreating steps of the horses echoing in his ears. Then, with foolish restlessness, he reached for the scraps of bacon rind from the plates, and making a faint whistling sound, flung them to the terrier that lay against the fender. He watched the dog swallow them, and waited till the creature looked into his eyes. Then a faint grin came on his face, and in a high, foolish voice he said:

"You won't get much more bacon, shall you, you little b——?"

The dog faintly and dismally wagged its tail, then lowered its haunches, circled round, and lay down again.

There was another helpless silence at the table. Joe sprawled uneasily in his seat, not willing to go till the family conclave was dissolved. Fred Henry, the second brother, was erect, clean-limbed, alert. He had watched the passing of the horses with more *sang froid.* If he was an animal, like Joe, he was an animal which controls, not one which is controlled. He was master of any horse, and he carried himself with a well-tempered air of mastery. But he was not master of the situations of life. He pushed his coarse brown moustache upwards, off his lip, and glanced irritably at his sister, who sat impassive and inscrutable.

"You'll go and stop with Lucy for a bit, shan't you?" he asked. The girl did not answer.

"I don't see what else you can do," persisted Fred Henry.

"Go as a skivvy," [1] Joe interpolated laconically.

The girl did not move a muscle.

"If I was her, I should go in for training for a nurse," said Malcolm, the youngest of them all. He was the baby of the family, a young man of twenty-two, with a fresh, jaunty *museau.* [2]

But Mabel did not take any notice of him. They had talked at her and round her for so many years, that she hardly heard them at all.

The marble clock on the mantelpiece softly chimed the half-hour, the dog rose uneasily from the hearth-rug and looked at the party at the breakfast-table. But still they sat on an ineffectual conclave.

"Oh, all right," said Joe suddenly, apropos of nothing. "I'll get a move on."

He pushed back his chair, straddled his knees with a downward jerk, to get them free, in horsey fashion, and went to the fire. Still he did not go out of the room; he was curious to know what the

---

1. Servant girl.   2. Face (French slang).

others would do or say. He began to charge his pipe, looking down at the dog and saying in a high, affected voice:

"Going wi' me? Going wi' me are ter? Tha'rt goin' further than tha counts on just now, dost hear?"

The dog faintly wagged his tail, the man stuck out his jaw and covered his pipe with his hands, and puffed intently, losing himself in the tobacco, looking down all the while at the dog with an absent brown eye. The dog looked up at him in mournful distrust. Joe stood with his knees stuck out, in real horsey fashion.

"Have you had a letter from Lucy?" Fred Henry asked of his sister.

"Last week," came the neutral reply.

"And what does she say?"

There was no answer.

"Does she *ask* you to go and stop there?" persisted Fred Henry.

"She says I can if I like."

"Well, then, you'd better. Tell her you'll come on Monday."

This was received in silence.

"That's what you'll do then, is it?" said Fred Henry, in some exasperation.

But she made no answer. There was a silence of futility and irritation in the room. Malcolm grinned fatuously.

"You'll have to make up your mind between now and next Wednesday," said Joe loudly, "or else find yourself lodgings on the curbstone."

The face of the young woman darkened, but she sat on immutable.

"Here's Jack Ferguson!" exclaimed Malcolm, who was looking aimlessly out of the window.

"Where?" exclaimed Joe loudly.

"Just gone past."

"Coming in?"

Malcolm craned his neck to see the gate.

"Yes," he said.

There was a silence. Mabel sat on like one condemned, at the head of the table. Then a whistle was heard from the kitchen. The dog got up and barked sharply. Joe opened the door and shouted:

"Come on."

After a moment a young man entered. He was muffled up in overcoat and a purple woolen scarf, and his tweed cap, which he did not remove, was pulled down on his head. He was of medium height, his face was rather long and pale, his eyes looked tired.

"Hello, Jack! Well, Jack!" exclaimed Malcolm and Joe. Fred

Henry merely said: "Jack."

"What's doing?" asked the newcomer, evidently addressing Fred Henry.

"Same. We've got to be out by Wednesday. Got a cold?"

"I have—got it bad, too."

"Why don't you stop in?"

"*Me* stop in? When I can't stand on my legs, perhaps I shall have a chance." The young man spoke huskily. He had a slight Scotch accent.

"It's a knockout, isn't it," said Joe, boisterously, "if a doctor goes round croaking with a cold. Looks bad for the patients, doesn't it?"

The young doctor looked at him slowly.

"Anything the matter with *you*, then?" he asked sarcastically.

"Not as I know of. Damn your eyes, I hope not. Why?"

"I thought you were very concerned about the patients, wondered if you might be one yourself."

"Damn it, no, I've never been patient to no flaming doctor, and hope I never shall be," returned Joe.

At this point Mabel rose from the table, and they all seemed to become aware of her existence. She began putting the dishes together. The young doctor looked at her, but did not address her. He had not greeted her. She went out of the room with the tray, her face impassive and unchanged.

"When are you off then, all of you?" asked the doctor.

"I'm catching the eleven-forty," replied Malcolm. "Are you goin' down wi' th' trap, Joe?"

"Yes, I've told you I'm going down wi' th' trap, haven't I?"

"We'd better be getting her in then. So long, Jack, if I don't see you before I go," said Malcolm, shaking hands.

He went out, followed by Joe, who seemed to have his tail between his legs.

"Well, this is the devil's own," exclaimed the doctor, when he was left alone with Fred Henry. "Going before Wednesday, are you?"

"That's the orders," replied the other.

"Where, to Northampton?"

"That's it."

"The devil!" exclaimed Ferguson, with quiet chagrin.

And there was silence between the two.

"All settled up, are you?" asked Ferguson.

"About."

There was another pause.

"Well, I shall miss yer, Freddy, boy," said the young doctor.

"And I shall miss thee, Jack," returned the other.

"Miss you like hell," mused the doctor.

Fred Henry turned aside. There was nothing to say. Mabel came in again, to finish clearing the table.

"What are *you* going to do, then, Miss Pervin?" asked Ferguson. "Going to your sister's, are you?"

Mabel looked at him with her steady, dangerous eyes, that always made him uncomfortable, unsettling his superficial ease.

"No," she said.

"Well, what in the name of fortune *are* you going to do? Say what you mean to do," cried Fred Henry, with futile intensity.

But she only averted her head, and continued her work. She folded the white table cloth, and put on the chenille cloth.

"The sulkiest bitch that ever trod!" muttered her brother.

But she finished her task with perfectly impassive face, the young doctor watching her interestedly all the while. Then she went out.

Fred Henry stared after her, clenching his lips, his blue eyes fixing in sharp antagonism, as he made a grimace of sour exasperation.

"You could bray her into bits, and that's all you'd get out of her," he said, in a small, narrowed tone.

The doctor smiled faintly.

"What's she *going* to do, then?" he asked.

"Strike me if *I* know!" returned the other.

There was a pause. Then the doctor stirred.

"I'll be seeing you tonight, shall I?" he said to his friend.

"Ay—where's it to be? Are we going over to Jessdale?"

"I don't know. I've got such a cold on me. I'll come round to the Moon and Stars, anyway."

"Let Lizzie and May miss their night for once, eh?"

"That's it—if I feel as I do now."

"All's one——"

The two young men went through the passage and down to the back door together. The house was large, but it was servantless now, and desolate. At the back was a small bricked house yard and beyond that a big square, graveled fine and red, and having stables on two sides. Sloping, dank, winter-dark fields stretched away on the open sides.

But the stables were empty. Joseph Pervin, the father of the family, had been a man of no education, who had become a fairly large horse dealer. The stables had been full of horses, there was a great turmoil and come-and-go of horses and of dealers and grooms. Then the kitchen was full of servants. But of late things had declined. The old man had married a second time, to retrieve his fortunes. Now he was dead and everything was gone to the dogs, there was nothing but debt and threatening.

For months, Mabel had been servantless in the big house,

keeping the home together in penury for her ineffectual brothers. She had kept house for ten years. But previously it was with unstinted means. Then, however brutal and coarse everything was, the sense of money had kept her proud, confident. The men might be foul-mouthed, the women in the kitchen might have had reputations, her brothers might have illegitimate children. But so long as there was money, the girl felt herself established, and brutally proud, reserved.

No company came to the house, save dealers and coarse men. Mabel had no associates of her own sex, after her sister went away. But she did not mind. She went regularly to church, she attended to her father. And she lived in the memory of her mother, who had died when she was fourteen, and whom she had loved. She had loved her father, too, in a different way, depending upon him, and feeling secure in him, until at the age of fifty-four, he married again. And then she had set hard against him. Now he had died and left them all hopelessly in debt.

She had suffered badly during the period of poverty. Nothing, however, could shake the curious, sullen, animal pride that dominated each member of the family. Now, for Mabel, the end had come. Still she would not cast about her. She would follow her own way just the same. She would always hold the keys of her own situation. Mindless and persistent, she endured from day to day. Why should she think? Why should she answer anybody? It was enough that this was the end, and there was no way out. She need not pass any more darkly along the main street of the small town, avoiding every eye. She need not demean herself any more, going into the shops and buying the cheapest food. This was at an end. She thought of nobody, not even of herself. Mindless and persistent, she seemed in a sort of ecstasy to be coming nearer to her fulfilment, her own glorification, approaching her dead mother, who was glorified.

In the afternoon, she took a little bag, with shears and sponge and a small scrubbing-brush, and went out. It was a gray, wintry day, with saddened, dark green fields and an atmosphere blackened by the smoke of foundries not far off. She went quickly, darkly along the causeway, heeding nobody, through the town to the churchyard.

There she always felt secure, as if no one could see her, although as a matter of fact she was exposed to the stare of everyone who passed along under the churchyard wall. Nevertheless, once under the shadow of the great looming church, among the graves, she felt immune from the world, reserved within the thick churchyard wall as in another country.

Carefully she clipped the grass from the grave, and arranged the pinky-white, small chrysanthemums in the tin cross. When this was done, she took an empty jar from a neighboring grave, brought water, and carefully, most scrupulously sponged the marble head-stone and the coping-stone.

It gave her sincere satisfaction to do this. She felt in immediate contact with the world of her mother. She took minute pains, went through the park in a state bordering on pure happiness, as if in performing this task she came into a subtle, intimate con-nection with her mother. For the life she followed here in the world was far less real than the world of death she inherited from her mother.

The doctor's house was just by the church. Ferguson, being a mere hired assistant, was slave to the countryside. As he hurried now to attend to the out-patients in the surgery, glancing across the graveyard with his quick eye, he saw the girl at her task at the grave. She seemed so intent and remote, it was like looking into another world. Some mystical element was touched in him. He slowed down as he walked, watching her as if spellbound.

She lifted her eyes, feeling him looking. Their eyes met. And each looked again at once, each feeling, in some way, found out by the other. He lifted his cap and passed on down the road. There remained distinct in his consciousness, like a vision, the memory of her face, lifted from the tombstone in the churchyard, and looking at him with slow, large, portentous eyes. It *was* por-tentous, her face. It seemed to mesmerize him. There was a heavy power in her eyes which laid hold of his whole being, as if he had drunk some powerful drug. He had been feeling weak and done before. Now the life came back into him, he felt delivered from his own fretted, daily self.

He finished his duties at the surgery as quickly as might be, hastily filling up the bottles of the waiting people with cheap drugs. Then, in perpetual haste, he set off again to visit several cases in another part of his round, before tea-time. At all times he preferred to walk if he could, but particularly when he was not well. He fancied the motion restored him.

The afternoon was falling. It was gray, deadened, and wintry, with a slow, moist, heavy coldness sinking in and deadening all the faculties. But why should he think or notice? He hastily climbed the hill and turned across the dark green fields, following the black cinder-track. In the distance, across a shallow dip in the country, the small town was clustered like smouldering ash, a tower, a spire, a heap of low, raw, extinct houses. And on the nearest fringe of the town, sloping into the dip, was Oldmeadow, the Pervins' house. He could see the stables and the outbuildings distinctly, as they lay towards him on the slope. Well, he would not go there many more times! Another resource would be lost to him, another place gone: the only company he cared for in the alien, ugly little town he was losing. Nothing but work, drudgery, constant hastening from dwelling to dwelling among the colliers and the iron-workers. It wore him out, but at the same time he had a craving for it. It was a stimulant to him to be in the homes of the working people, moving, as it were, through the innermost body of their life. His nerves were excited and gratified. He could come so near, into the very lives of the rough, inarticulate, powerfully emotional men and women. He grumbled, he said he hated the hellish hole. But as a matter of fact it excited him, the contact with the rough, strongly-feeling people was a stimulant applied direct to his nerves.

Below Oldmeadow, in the green, shallow, soddened hollow of fields, lay a square, deep pond. Roving across the landscape, the doctor's quick eye detected a figure in black passing through the gate of the field, down towards the pond. He looked again. It would be Mabel Pervin. His mind suddenly became alive and attentive.

Why was she going down there? He pulled up on the path on the slope above, and stood staring. He could just make sure of the small black figure moving in the hollow of the failing day. He seemed to see her in the midst of such obscurity, that he was like a clairvoyant, seeing rather with the mind's eye than with ordinary sight. Yet he could see her positively enough, whilst he kept his eye attentive. He felt, if he looked away from her, in the thick, ugly falling dusk, he would lose her altogether.

He followed her minutely as she moved, direct and intent, like something transmitted rather than stirring in voluntary activity, straight down the field towards the pond. There she stood on the bank for a moment. She never raised her head. Then she waded slowly into the water.

He stood motionless as the small black figure walked slowly and deliberately towards the center of the pond, very slowly, gradually moving deeper into the motionless water, and still moving forward as the water got up to her breast. Then he could see her no more in the dusk of the dead afternoon.

"There!" he exclaimed. "Would you believe it?"

And he hastened straight down, running over the wet, soddened fields, pushing through the hedges, down into the depression of callous wintry obscurity. It took him several minutes to come to the pond. He stood on the bank, breathing heavily. He could see nothing. His eyes seemed to penetrate the dead water. Yes, perhaps that was the dark shadow of her black clothing beneath the surface of the water.

He slowly ventured into the pond. The bottom was deep, soft clay, he sank in, and the water clasped dead cold round his legs.

As he stirred he could smell the cold, rotten clay that fouled up into the water. It was objectionable in his lungs. Still, repelled and yet not heeding, he moved deeper into the pond. The cold water rose over his thighs, over his loins, upon his abdomen. The lower part of his body was all sunk in the hideous cold element. And the bottom was so deeply soft and uncertain, he was afraid of pitching with his mouth underneath. He could not swim, and was afraid.

He crouched a little, spreading his hands under the water and moving them round, trying to feel for her. The dead cold pond swayed upon his chest. He moved again, a little deeper, and again, with his hands underneath, he felt all around under the water. And he touched her clothing. But it evaded his fingers. He made a desperate effort to grasp it.

And so doing he lost his balance and went under, horribly, suffocating in the foul earthy water, struggling madly for a few moments. At last, after what seemed an eternity, he got his footing, rose again into the air and looked around. He gasped, and knew he was in the world. Then he looked at the water. She had risen near him. He grasped her clothing, and drawing her nearer, turned to take his way to land again.

He went very slowly, carefully, absorbed in the slow progress. He rose higher, climbing out of the pond. The water was now only about his legs; he was thankful, full of relief to be out of the clutches of the pond. He lifted her and staggered on to the bank, out of the horror of wet, gray clay.

He laid her down on the bank. She was quite unconscious and running with water. He made the water come from her mouth, he worked to restore her. He did not have to work very long before he could feel the breathing begin again in her; she was breathing naturally. He worked a little longer. He could feel her live beneath his hands; she was coming back. He wiped her face, wrapped her in his overcoat, looked round into the dim, dark gray world, then lifted her and staggered down the bank and across the fields.

It seemed an unthinkably long way, and his burden so heavy he felt he would never get to the house. But at last he was in the stable yard, and then in the house yard. He opened the door and went into the house. In the kitchen he laid her down on the hearthrug and called. The house was empty. But the fire was burning in the grate.

Then again he kneeled to attend to her. She was breathing regularly, her eyes were wide open and as if conscious, but there seemed something missing in her look. She was conscious in herself, but unconscious of her surroundings.

He ran upstairs, took blankets from a bed, and put them before the fire to warm. Then he removed her saturated, earthy-smelling clothing, rubbed her dry with a towel, and wrapped her naked in the blankets. Then he went into the dining room, to look for spirits. There was a little whisky. He drank a gulp himself, and put some into her mouth.

The effect was instantaneous. She looked full into his face, as if she had been seeing him for some time, and yet had only just become conscious of him.

"Dr. Ferguson?" she said.

"What?" he answered.

He was divesting himself of his coat, intending to find some dry clothing upstairs. He could not bear the smell of the dead, clayey water, and he was mortally afraid for his own health.

"What did I do?" she asked.

"Walked into the pond," he replied. He had begun to shudder like one sick, and could hardly attend to her. Her eyes remained full on him, he seemed to be going dark in his mind, looking back at her helplessly. The shuddering became quieter in him, his life came back to him, dark and unknowing, but strong again.

"Was I out of my mind?" she asked, while her eyes were fixed on him all the time.

"Maybe, for the moment," he replied. He felt quiet, because his strength had come back. The strange fretful strain had left him.

"Am I out of my mind now?" she asked.

"Are you?" he reflected a moment. "No," he answered truthfully. "I don't see that you are." He turned his face aside. He was afraid now, because he felt dazed, and felt dimly that her power was stronger than his, in this issue. And she continued to look at him fixedly all the time. "Can you tell me where I shall find some dry things to put on?" he asked.

"Did you dive into the pond for me?" she asked.

"No," he answered. "I walked in. But I went in overhead as well."

There was silence for a moment. He hesitated. He very much wanted to go upstairs to get into dry clothing. But there was another desire in him. And she seemed to hold him. His will seemed to have gone to sleep, and left him, standing there slack before her. But he felt warm inside himself. He did not shudder at all, though his clothes were sodden on him.

"Why did you?" she asked.

"Because I didn't want you to do such a foolish thing," he said.

"It wasn't foolish," she said, still gazing at him as she lay on the floor, with a sofa cushion under her head. "It was the right thing to do. *I* knew best, then."

"I'll go and shift these wet things," he said. But still he had not the power to move out of her presence, until she sent him. It was as if she had the life of his body in her hands, and he could not extricate himself. Or perhaps he did not want to.

Suddenly she sat up. Then she became aware of her own immediate condition. She felt the blankets about her, she knew her own limbs. For a moment it seemed as if her reason were going. She looked round, with wild eye, as if seeking something. He stood still with fear. She saw her clothing lying scattered.

"Who undressed me?" she asked, her eyes resting full and inevitable on his face.

"I did," he replied, "to bring you round."

For some moments she sat and gazed at him awfully, her lips parted.

"Do you love me, then?" she asked.

He only stood and stared at her, fascinated. His soul seemed to melt.

She shuffled forward on her knees, and put her arms round him, round his legs, as he stood there, pressing her breasts against his knees and thighs, clutching him with strange, convulsive certainty, pressing his thighs against her, drawing him to her face, her throat, as she looked up at him with flaring, humble eyes of transfiguration, triumphant in first possession.

"You love me," she murmured, in strange transport, yearning and triumphant and confident. "You love me. I know you love me, I know."

And she was passionately kissing his knees, through the wet clothing, passionately and indiscriminately kissing his knees, his legs, as if unaware of everything.

He looked down at the tangled wet hair, the wild, bare, animal shoulders. He was amazed, bewildered, and afraid. He had never thought of loving her. He had never wanted to love her. When he rescued her and restored her, he was a doctor, and she was a patient. He had had no single personal thought of her. Nay, this introduction of the personal element was very distasteful to him, a violation of his professional honor. It was horrible to have her there embracing his knees. It was horrible. He revolted from it, violently. And yet—and yet—he had not the power to break away.

She looked at him again, with the same supplication of powerful love, and that same transcendent, frightening light of triumph. In view of the delicate flame which seemed to come from her face like a light, he was powerless. And yet he had never intended to love her. He had never intended. And something stubborn in him could not give way.

"You love me," she repeated, in a murmur of deep, rhapsodic assurance. "You love me."

Her hands were drawing him, drawing him down to her. He was afraid, even a little horrified. For he had, really, no intention of loving her. Yet her hands were drawing her towards her. He put out his hand quickly to steady himself, and grasped her bare shoulder. A flame seemed to burn the hand that grasped her soft shoulder. He had no intention of loving her: his whole will was against his yielding. It was horrible. And yet wonderful was the touch of her shoulders, beautiful the shining of her face. Was she perhaps mad? He had a horror of yielding to her. Yet something in him ached also.

He had been staring away at the door, away from her. But his hand remained on her shoulder. She had gone suddenly very still. He looked down at her. Her eyes were now wide with fear, with doubt, the light was dying from her face, a shadow of terrible grayness was returning. He could not bear the touch of her eyes' question upon him, and the look of death behind the question.

With an inward groan he gave way, and let his heart yield towards her. A sudden gentle smile came on his face. And her eyes, which never left his face, slowly, slowly filled with tears. He watched the strange water rise in her eyes, like some slow fountain coming up. And his heart seemed to burn and melt away in his breast.

He could not bear to look at her any more. He dropped on his knees and caught her head with his arms and pressed her face against his throat. She was very still. His heart, which seemed to have broken, was burning with a kind of agony in his breast. And he felt her slow, hot tears wetting his throat. But he could not move.

He felt the hot tears wet his neck and the hollows of his neck, and he remained motionless, suspended through one of man's eternities. Only now it had become indispensable to him to have her face pressed close to him; he could never let her go again. He could never let her head go away from the close clutch of his arm. He wanted to remain like that for ever, with his heart hurting him in a pain that was also life to him. Without knowing, he was looking down on her damp, soft brown hair.

Then, as it were suddenly, he smelt the horrid stagnant smell of that water. And at the same moment she drew away from him and looked at him. Her eyes were wistful and unfathomable. He was afraid of them, and he fell to kissing her, not knowing what he was doing. He wanted her eyes not to have that terrible, wistful, unfathomable look.

When she turned her face to him again, a faint delicate flush was glowing, and there was again dawning that terrible shining of joy in her eyes, which really terrified him, and yet which he now wanted to see, because he feared the look of doubt still more.

"You love me?" she said, rather faltering.

"Yes." The word cost him a painful effort. Not because it wasn't true. But because it was too newly true, the *saying* seemed to tear open again his newly torn heart. And he hardly wanted it to be true, even now.

She lifted her face to him, and he bent forward and kissed her on the mouth, gently, with the one kiss that is an eternal pledge. And as he kissed her his heart strained again in his breast. He never intended to love her. But now it was over. He had crossed over the gulf to her, and all that he had left behind had shriveled and become void.

After the kiss, her eyes again slowly filled with tears. She sat still, away from him, with her face drooped aside, and her hands folded in her lap. The tears fell very slowly. There was complete silence. He too sat there motionless and silent on the hearth rug. The strange pain of his heart that was broken seemed to consume him. That he should love her? That this was love! That he should be ripped open in this way! Him, a doctor! How they would all jeer if they knew! It was agony to him to think they might know.

In the curious naked pain of the thought he looked again **to** her. She was sitting there drooped into a muse. He saw a tear fall, and his heart flared hot. He saw for the first time that one of her shoulders was quite uncovered, one arm bare, he could see one of her small breasts; dimly, because it had become almost dark in the room.

"Why are you crying?" he asked, in an altered voice.

She looked up at him, and behind her tears the consciousness of her situation for the first time brought a dark look of shame to her eyes.

"I'm not crying, really," she said, watching him, half frightened.

He reached his hand, and softly closed it on her bare arm.

"I love you! I love you!" he said in a soft, low vibrating voice, unlike himself.

She shrank, and dropped her head. The soft, penetrating grip of his hand on her arm distressed her. She looked up at him.

"I want to go," she said. "I want to go and get you some dry things."

"Why?" he said. "I'm all right."

"But I want to go," she said. "And I want you to change your things."

He released her arm, and she wrapped herself in the blanket, looking at him, rather frightened. And still she did not rise.

"Kiss me," she said wistfully.

He kissed her, but briefly, half in anger.

Then, after a second, she rose nervously, all mixed up in the blanket. He watched her in her confusion as she tried to extricate herself and wrap herself up so that she could walk. He watched her relentlessly, as she knew. And as she went, the blanket trailing, and as he saw a glimpse of her feet and her white leg, he tried to remember her as she was when he had wrapped her in the blanket. But then he didn't want to remember, because she had been nothing to him then, and his nature revolted from remembering her as she was when she was nothing to him.

A tumbling muffled noise from within the dark house startled him. Then he heard her voice: "There are clothes." He rose and went to the foot of the stairs, and gathered up the garments she had thrown down. Then he came back to the fire, to rub himself down and dress. He grinned at his own appearance when he had finished.

The fire was sinking, so he put on coal. The house was now quite dark, save for the light of a street-lamp that shone in faintly from beyond the holly trees. He lit the gas with matches he found on the mantelpiece. Then he emptied the pockets of his own clothes, and threw all his wet things in a heap into the scullery. After which he gathered up her sodden clothes, gently, and put them in a separate heap on the copper-top in the scullery.

It was six o'clock on the clock. His own watch had stopped. He ought to go back to the surgery. He waited, and still she did not come down. So he went to the foot of the stairs and called:

"I shall have to go."

Almost immediately he heard her coming down. She had on her best dress of black voile, and her hair was tidy, but still damp. She looked at him—and in spite of herself, smiled.

"I don't like you in those clothes," she said.

"Do I look a sight?" he answered.

They were shy of one another.

"I'll make you some tea," she said.

"No, I must go."

"Must you?" And she looked at him again with the wide, strained, doubtful eyes. And again, from the pain of his breast, he knew how he loved her. He went and bent to kiss her, gently, passionately, with his heart's painful kiss.

"And my hair smells so horrible," she murmured in distraction. "And I'm so awful, I'm so awful! Oh no, I'm too awful." And she broke into bitter, heart-broken sobbing. "You can't want to love me, I'm horrible."

"Don't be silly, don't be silly," he said, trying to comfort her, kissing her, holding her in his arms. "I want you, I want to marry you, we're going to be married, quickly, quickly—tomorrow if I can."

But she only sobbed terribly, and cried:

"I feel awful. I feel awful. I feel I'm horrible to you."

"No, I want you, I want you," was all he answered, blindly, with that terrible intonation which frightened her almost more than her horror lest he should *not* want her.

1922

The Princess

To her father, she was The Princess. To her Boston aunts and uncles she was just *Dollie Urquhart, poor little thing*.

Colin Urquhart was just a bit mad. He was of an old Scottish family, and he claimed royal blood. The blood of Scottish kings flowed in his veins. On this point, his American relatives said, he was just a bit "off." They could not bear any more to be told *which* royal blood of Scotland blued his veins. The whole thing was rather ridiculous, and a sore point. The only fact they remembered was that it was not Stuart.[1]

He was a handsome man, with a wide-open blue eye that seemed sometimes to be looking at nothing, soft black hair brushed rather low on his low, broad brow, and a very attractive body. Add to this a most beautiful speaking voice, usually rather hushed and diffident, but sometimes resonant and powerful like bronze, and you have the sum of his charms. He looked like some old Celtic hero. He looked as if he should have worn a grayish kilt and a sporran, and shown his knees. His voice came direct out of the hushed Ossianic past.[2]

For the rest, he was one of those gentlemen of sufficient but not excessive means who fifty years ago wandered vaguely about, never arriving anywhere, never doing anything, and never definitely being anything, yet well received in the good society of more than one country.

He did not marry till he was nearly forty, and then it was a wealthy Miss Prescott, from New England. Hannah Prescott at twenty-two was fascinated by the man with the soft black hair not yet touched by gray, and the wide, rather vague blue eyes. Many women had been fascinated before her. But Colin Urquhart, by his very vagueness, had avoided any decisive connection.

Mrs. Urquhart lived three years in the mist and glamour of her husband's presence. And then it broke her. It was like living with a fascinating specter. About most things he was completely, even ghostly oblivious. He was always charming, courteous, perfectly gra-

---

1. The name of the famous royal house of Scotland.
2. Ossian was a near-legendary Gaelic bard of the 3rd century whose heroic poetry was "discovered" and "translated" (but actually largely invented) by James Macpherson in the 18th century.

cious in that hushed, musical voice of his. But absent. When all came to all, he just wasn't there. "Not all there," as the vulgar say.

He was the father of the little girl she bore at the end of the first year. But this did not substantiate him the more. His very beauty and his haunting musical quality became dreadful to her after the first few months. The strange echo: he was like a living echo! His very flesh, when you touched it, did not seem quite the flesh of a real man.

Perhaps it was that he was a little bit mad. She thought it definitely the night her baby was born.

"Ah, so my little princess has come at last!" he said, in his throaty, singing Celtic voice, like a glad chant, swaying absorbed.

It was a tiny, frail baby, with wide, amazed blue eyes. They christened it Mary Henrietta. She called the little thing *My Dollie*. He called it always *My Princess*.

It was useless to fly at him. He just opened his wide blue eyes wider, and took a childlike, silent dignity there was no getting past.

Hannah Prescott had never been robust. She had no great desire to live. So when the baby was two years old she suddenly died.

The Prescotts felt a deep but unadmitted resentment against Colin Urquhart. They said he was selfish. Therefore they discontinued Hannah's income, a month after her burial in Florence, after they had urged the father to give the child over to them, and he had courteously, musically, but quite finally refused. He treated the Prescotts as if they were not of his world, not realities to him: just casual phenomena, or gramophones, talking-machines that had to be answered. He answered them. But of their actual existence he was never once aware.

They debated having him certified unsuitable to be guardian of his own child. But that would have created a scandal. So they did the simplest thing, after all—washed their hands of him. But they wrote scrupulously to the child, and sent her modest presents of money at Christmas, and on the anniversary of the death of her mother.

To The Princess her Boston relatives were for many years just a nominal reality. She lived with her father, and he traveled continually, though in a modest way, living on his moderate income. And never going to America. The child changed nurses all the time. In Italy it was a contadina; in India she had an ayah,[3] in Germany she had a yellow-haired peasant girl.

Father and child were inseparable. He was not a recluse. Wherever he went he was to be seen paying formal calls going out to luncheon or to tea, rarely to dinner. And always with the child.

---

3. Native nursemaid; "contadina": peasant.

People called her Princess Urquhart, as if that were her christened name.

She was a quick, dainty little thing with dark gold hair that went a soft brown, and wide, slightly prominent blue eyes that were at once so candid and so knowing. She was always grown up; she never really grew up. Always strangely wise, and always childish.

It was her father's fault.

"My little Princess must never take too much notice of people and the things they say and do," he repeated to her. "People don't know what they are doing and saying. They chatter-chatter, and they hurt one another, and they hurt themselves very often, till they cry. But don't take any notice, my little Princess. Because it is all nothing. Inside everybody there is another creature, a demon which doesn't care at all. You peel away all the things they say and do and feel, as cook peels away the outside of the onions. And in the middle of everybody there is a green demon which you can't peel away. And this green demon never changes, and it doesn't care at all about all the things that happen to the outside leaves of the person, all the chatter-chatter, and all the husbands and wives and children, and troubles and fusses. You peel everything away from people, and there is a green, upright demon in every man and woman; and this demon is a man's real self, and a woman's real self. It doesn't really care about anybody, it belongs to the demons and the primitive fairies, who never care. But, even so, there are big demons and mean demons, and splendid demonish fairies, and vulgar ones. But there are no royal fairy women left. Only you, my little Princess. You are the last of the royal race of the old people; the last, my Princess. There are no others. You and I are the last. When I am dead there will be only you. And that is why, darling, you will never care for any of the people in the world very much. Because their demons are all dwindled and vulgar. They are not royal. Only you are royal, after me. Always remember that. And always remember, it is a *great secret*. If you tell people, they will try to kill you, because they will envy you for being a Princess. It is our great secret, darling. I am a prince, and you a princess, of the old, old blood. And we keep our secret between us, all alone. And so, darling, you must treat all people very politely, because *noblesse oblige*.[4] But you must never forget that you alone are the last of Princesses; and that all other are less than you are, less noble, more vulgar. Treat them politely and gently and kindly, darling. But you are the Princess, and they are commoners. Never try to think of them as if they were like you. They are not. You will find, always, that they are lacking, lacking in the royal touch, which only you have———"

4. "High rank has its obligations."

The Princess learned her lesson early—the first lesson, of absolute reticence, the impossibility of intimacy with any other than her father; the second lesson, of naïve, slightly benevolent politeness. As a small child, something crystallized in her character, making her clear and finished, and as impervious as crystal.

"Dear child!" her hostesses said of her. "She is so quaint and old-fashioned; such a lady, poor little mite!"

She was erect, and very dainty. Always small, nearly tiny in physique, she seemed like a changeling beside her big, handsome, slightly mad father. She dressed very simply, usually in blue or delicate grays, with little collars of old Milan point, or very finely-worked linen. She had exquisite little hands, that made the piano sound like a spinet[5] when she played. She was rather given to wearing cloaks and capes, instead of coats, out of doors, and little eighteenth-century sort of hats. Her complexion was pure apple-blossom.

She looked as if she had stepped out of a picture. But no one, to her dying day, ever knew exactly the strange picture her father had framed her in and from which she never stepped.

Her grandfather and grandmother and her Aunt Maud demanded twice to see her, once in Rome and once in Paris. Each time they were charmed, piqued, and annoyed. She was so exquisite and such a little virgin. At the same time so knowing and so oddly assured. That odd, assured touch of condescension, and the inward coldness, infuriated her American relations.

Only she really fascinated her grandfather. He was spellbound; in a way, in love with the little faultless thing. His wife would catch him brooding, musing over his grandchild, long months after the meeting, and craving to see her again. He cherished to the end the fond hope that she might come to live with him and her grandmother.

"Thank you so much, grandfather. You are so very kind. But Papa and I are such an old couple, you see, such a crochety old couple, living in a world of our own."

Her father let her see the world—from the outside. And he let her read. When she was in her teens she read Zola and Maupassant, and with the eyes of Zola and Maupassant[6] she looked on Paris. A little later she read Tolstoy and Dostoevsky. The latter confused her. The others, she seemed to understand with a very shrewd, canny understanding, just as she understood the Decameron stories as she read them in their old Italian, or the Nibelung poems.[7] Strange and *uncanny*, she seemed to understand things in

5. Small kind of harpsichord, a fore-runner of the piano.
6. Emile Zola (1840–1902), French naturalistic novelist, wrote the novel series *Les Rougon-Macquart*, the chief monument of the French Naturalist movement. Guy de Maupassant (1850–93), French short-story writer and novelist, was known for the frankness of his realism.
7. The *Decameron* is a collection of tales written by the Italian writer and humanist Giovanni Boccaccio (1313–75); the *Nibelungenlied* is a mythic German poem of the 13th century.

a cold light perfectly, with all the flush of fire absent. She was something like a changeling, not quite human.

This earned her, also, strange antipathies. Cabmen and railway porters, especially in Paris and Rome, would suddenly treat her with brutal rudeness, when she was alone. They seemed to look on her with sudden violent antipathy. They sensed in her curious impertinence, an easy, sterile impertinence towards the things *they* felt most. She was so assured, and her flower of maidenhood was so scentless. She could look at a lusty, sensual Roman cabman as if he were a sort of grotesque, to make her smile. She knew all about him, in Zola. And the peculiar condescension with which she would give him her order, as if she, frail, beautiful thing, were the only reality, and he, coarse monster, was a sort of Caliban[8] floundering in the mud on the margin of the pool of the perfect lotus, would suddenly enrage the fellow, the real Mediterranean who prided himself on his *beauté male*, and to whom the phallic mystery was still the only mystery. And he would turn a terrible face on her, bully her in a brutal, coarse fashion—hideous. For to him she had only the blasphemous impertinence of her own sterility.

Encounters like these made her tremble, and made her know she must have support from the outside. The power of her spirit did not extend to these low people, and they had all the physical power. She realized an implacability of hatred in their turning on her. But she did not lose her head. She quietly paid out money and turned away.

Those were dangerous moments, though, and she learned to be prepared for them. The Princess she was, and the fairy from the North, and could never understand the volcanic phallic rage with which coarse people could turn on her in a paroxysm of hatred. They never turned on her father like that. And quite early she decided it was the New England mother in her whom they hated. Never for one minute could she see with the old Roman eyes, see herself as sterility, the barren flower taking on airs and an intolerable impertinence. This was what the Roman cabman saw in her. And he longed to crush the barren blossom. Its sexless beauty and its authority put him in a passion of brutal revolt.

When she was nineteen her grandfather died, leaving her a considerable fortune in the safe hands of responsible trustees. They would deliver her her income, but only on condition that she resided for six months in the year in the United States.

"Why should they make me conditions?" she said to her father. "I refuse to be imprisoned six months in the year in the United States. We will tell them to keep their money."

"Let us be wise, my little Princess, let us be wise. No, we are almost poor, and we are never safe from rudeness. I cannot allow

8. The savage and deformed slave in Shakespeare's *Tempest*.

anybody to be rude to me. I hate it, I hate it!" His eyes flamed as he said it. "I could kill any man or woman who is rude to me. But we are in exile in the world. We are powerless. If we were really poor, we should be quite powerless, and then I should die. No, my Princess. Let us take their money, then they will not dare to be rude to us. Let us take it, as we put on clothes, to cover ourselves from their aggressions."

There began a new phase, when the father and daughter spent their summers on the Great Lakes or in California, or in the Southwest. The father was something of a poet, the daughter something of a painter. He wrote poems about the lakes or the redwood trees, and she made dainty drawings. He was physically a strong man, and he loved the out-of-doors. He would go off with her for days, paddling in a canoe and sleeping by a camp fire. Frail little Princess, she was always undaunted, always undaunted. She would ride with him on horseback over the mountain trails till she was so tired she was nothing but a bodiless consciousness sitting astride her pony. But she never gave in. And at night he folded her in her blanket on a bed of balsam pine twigs, and she lay and looked at the stars unmurmuring. She was fulfilling her role.

People said to her as the years passed, and she was a woman of twenty-five, then a woman of thirty, and always the same virgin dainty Princess, "knowing" in a dispassionate way, like an old woman, and utterly intact:

"Don't you ever think what you will do when your father is no longer with you?"

She looked at her interlocutor with that cold, elfin detachment of hers:

"No, I never think of it," she said.

She had a tiny, but exquisite little house in London, and another small, perfect house in Connecticut, each with a faithful housekeeper. Two homes, if she chose. And she knew many interesting literary and artistic people. What more?

So the years passed imperceptibly. And she had that quality of the sexless fairies, she did not change. At thirty-three she looked twenty-three.

Her father, however, was ageing, and becoming more and more queer. It was now her task to be his guardian in his private madness. He spent the last three years of life in the house in Connecticut. He was very much estranged, sometimes had fits of violence which almost killed the little Princess. Physical violence was horrible to her; it seemed to shatter her heart. But she found a woman a few years younger than herself, well-educated and sensitive, to be a sort of nurse-companion to the mad old man. So the fact of madness was never openly admitted. Miss Cummins, the companion, had a passionate loyalty to the Princess, and a curious affection, tinged with love, for the handsome, white-haired, courteous old man, who was never at all aware of his fits of violence once they passed.

The Princess was thirty-eight years old when her father died. And quite unchanged. She was still tiny, and like a dignified, scentless flower. Her soft brownish hair, almost the color of beaver fur, was bobbed, and fluffed softly round her apple-blossom face, that was modeled with an arched nose like a proud old Florentine portrait. In her voice, manner, and bearing she was exceedingly still, like a flower that has blossomed in a shadowy place. And from her blue eyes looked out the Princess's eternal laconic challenge, that grew almost sardonic as the years passed. She was the Princess, and sardonically she looked out on a princeless world.

She was relieved when her father died, and at the same time, it was as if everything had evaporated around her. She had lived in a sort of hothouse, in the aura of her father's madness. Suddenly the hothouse had been removed from around her, and she was in the raw, vast, vulgar open air.

Quoi faire? What was she to do? She seemed faced with absolute nothingness. Only she had Miss Cummins, who shared with her the secret, and almost the passion for her father. In fact, the Princess felt that her passion for her mad father had in some curious way transferred itself largely to Charlotte Cummins during the last years. And now Miss Cummins was the vessel that held the passion for the dead man. She herself, the Princess, was an empty vessel.

An empty vessel in the enormous warehouse of the world.

Quoi faire? What was she to do? She felt that, since she could not evaporate into nothingness, like alcohol from an unstoppered bottle, she must *do* something. Never before in her life had she felt the incumbency. Never, never had she felt she must *do* anything. That was left to the vulgar.

Now her father was dead, she found herself on the *fringe* of the vulgar crowd, sharing their necessity to *do* something. It was a little humiliating. She felt herself becoming vulgarized. At the same time she found herself looking at men with a shrewder eye: an eye to marriage. Not that she felt any sudden interest in men, or attraction towards them. No. She was still neither interested nor attracted towards men vitally. But *marriage*, that peculiar abstraction, had imposed a sort of spell on her. She thought that *marriage*, in the blank abstract, was the thing she ought to *do*. That *marriage* implied a man she also knew. She knew all the facts. But the man seemed a property of her own mind rather than a thing in himself, another thing.

Her father died in the summer, the month after her thirty-eighth birthday. When all was over, the obvious thing to do, of course, was to travel. With Miss Cummins. The two women knew each other intimately, but they were always Miss Urquhart and Miss Cummins to one another, and a certain distance was instinctively maintained. Miss Cummins, from Philadelphia, of scholastic stock, and intelligent but untraveled, four years younger than the Princess, felt herself immensely the junior of her "lady." She had a sort of passionate veneration for the Princess, who seemed to her ageless, timeless. She could not see the rows of tiny, dainty, exquisite shoes in the Princess's cupboard without feeling a stab at the heart, a stab of tenderness and reverence, almost of awe.

Miss Cummins also was virginal, but with a look of puzzled surprise in her brown eyes. Her skin was as pale and clear, her features well modeled, but there was a certain blankness in her expression, where the Princess had an odd touch of Renaissance grandeur. Miss Cummins's voice was also hushed almost to a whisper; it was the inevitable effect of Colin Urquhart's room. But the hushedness had a hoarse quality.

The Princess did not want to go to Europe. Her face seemed turned west. Now her father was gone, she felt she would go west, westwards, as if forever. Following, no doubt, the March of Empire,[9] which is brought up rather short on the Pacific coast, among swarms of wallowing bathers.

No, not the Pacific coast. She would stop short of that. The Southwest was less vulgar. She would go to New Mexico.

She and Miss Cummins arrived at the Rancho del Cerro Gordo towards the end of August, when the crowd was beginning to drift back east. The ranch lay by a stream on the desert some four miles from the foot of the mountains, a mile away from the Indian pueblo of San Cristobal. It was a ranch for the rich; the Princess paid thirty dollars a day for herself and Miss Cummins. But then she had a little cottage to herself, among the apple trees of the orchard, with an excellent cook. She and Miss Cummins, however, took dinner at evening in the large guest-house. For the Princess still entertained the idea of *marriage*.

The guests at the Rancho del Cerro Gordo were of all sorts, except the poor sort. They were practically all rich, and many were romantic. Some were charming, others were vulgar, some were movie people, quite quaint and not unattractive in their vulgarity, and many were Jews. The Princess did not care for Jews, though they were usually the most interesting to *talk* to. So she talked a good deal with the Jews, and painted with the artists, and rode with the young men from college, and had altogether quite a good time.

9. The line "Westward the course of empire takes its way" (from *Verses on the Prospects of Planting Arts and* *Learning in America*, by Bishop Berkeley, 1685–1753) was often misquoted as "march of empire."

And yet she felt something of a fish out of water, or a bird in the wrong forest. And *marriage* remained still completely in the abstract. No connecting it with any of these young men, even the nice ones.

The Princess looked just twenty-five. The freshness of her mouth, the hushed, delicate-complexioned virginity of her face gave her not a day more. Only a certain laconic look in her eyes was disconcerting. When she was *forced* to write her age, she put twenty-eight, making the figure *two* rather badly, so that it just avoided being a three.

Men hinted marriage at her. Especially boys from college suggested it from a distance. But they all failed before the look of sardonic ridicule in the Princess's eyes. It always seemed to her rather preposterous, quite ridiculous, and a tiny bit impertinent on their part.

The only man that intrigued her at all was one of the guides, a man called Romero—Domingo Romero. It was he who had sold the ranch itself to the Wilkiesons, ten years before, for two thousand dollars. He had gone away, then reappeared at the old place. For he was the son of the old Romero, the last of the Spanish family that had owned miles of land around San Cristobal. But the coming of the white man and the failure of the vast flocks of sheep, and the fatal inertia which overcomes all men, at last, on the desert near the mountains, had finished the Romero family. The last descendants were just Mexican peasants.

Domingo, the heir, had spent his two thousand dollars, and was working for white people. He was now about thirty years old, a tall, silent fellow, with a heavy closed mouth and black eyes that looked across at one almost sullenly. From behind he was handsome, with a strong, natural body, and the back of his neck very dark and well-shapen, strong with life. But his dark face was long and heavy, almost sinister, with that peculiar heavy meaningless in it, characteristic of the Mexicans of his own locality. They are strong, they seem healthy. They laugh and joke with one another. But their physique and their natures seem static, as if there were nowhere, nowhere at all for their energies to go, and their faces, degenerating to mis-shapen heaviness, seem to have no *raison d'être*,[1] no radical meaning. Waiting either to die or to be aroused into passion and hope. In some of the black eyes a queer, haunting mystic quality, sombre and a bit gruesome, the skull-and-cross-bones look of the Penitentes.[2] They had found their *raison d'être* in self-torture and death-worship. Unable to wrest a *positive* significance for themselves from the vast, beautiful, but vindictive landscape they were

1. "Reason for being."
2. Religious flagellant societies who flourished in Mexico and New Mexico.

born into, they turned on their own selves, and worshiped death through self-torture. The mystic gloom of this showed in their eyes.

But as a rule the dark eyes of the Mexicans were heavy and half alive, sometimes hostile, sometimes kindly, often with the fatal Indian glaze on them, or the fatal Indian glint.

Domingo Romero was *almost* a typical Mexican to look at, with the typical heavy, dark, long face, clean-shaven, with an almost brutally heavy mouth. His eyes were black and Indian looking. Only, at the center of their hopelessness was a spark of pride, or self-confidence, or dauntlessness. Just a spark in the midst of the blackness of static despair.

But this spark was the difference between him and the mass of men. It gave a certain alert sensitiveness to his bearing and a certain beauty to his appearance. He wore a low-crowned black hat, instead of the ponderous headgear of the usual Mexican, and his clothes were thinnish and graceful. Silent, aloof, almost imperceptible in the landscape, he was an admirable guide, with a startling quick intelligence that anticipated difficulties about to rise. He could cook, too, crouching over the camp fire and moving his lean deft brown hands. The only fault he had was that he was not forthcoming, he wasn't chatty and cozy.

"Oh, don't send Romero with us," the Jews would say. "One can't get any response from him."

Tourists come and go, but they rarely *see* anything, inwardly. None of them ever saw the spark at the middle of Romero's eye; they were not alive enough to see it.

The Princess caught it one day, when she had him for a guide. She was fishing for trout in the canyon, Miss Cummins was reading a book, the horses were tied under the trees, Romero was fixing a proper fly on her line. He fixed the fly and handed her the line, looking up at her. And at that moment she caught the spark in his eye. And instantly she knew that he was a gentleman, that his "demon," as her father would have said, was a fine demon. And instantly her manner towards him changed.

He had perched her on a rock over a quiet pool, beyond the cottonwood trees. It was early September, and the canyon already cool, but the leaves of the cottonwoods were still green. The Princess stood on her rock, a small but perfectly-formed figure, wearing a soft, close gray sweater and neatly-cut gray riding-breeches, with tall black boots, her fluffy brown hair straggling from under a little gray felt hat. A woman? Not quite. A changeling of some sort, perched in outline there on the rock, in the bristling wild canyon. She knew perfectly well how to handle a line. Her father had made a fisherman of her.

Romero, in a black shirt and with loose black trousers pushed into wide black riding-boots, was fishing a little farther down. He had put his hat on a rock behind him; his dark head was bent a little forward, watching the water. He had caught three trout. From time to time he glanced upstream at the Princess, perched there so daintily. He saw she had caught nothing.

Soon he quietly drew in his line and came up to her. His keen eye watched her line, watched her position. Then, quietly, he suggested certain changes to her, putting his sensitive brown hand before her. And he withdrew a little, and stood in silence, leaning against a tree, watching her. He was helping her across the distance. She knew it, and thrilled. And in a moment she had a bite. In two minutes she landed a good trout. She looked round at him quickly, her eyes sparkling, the color heightened in her cheeks. And as she met his eyes a smile of greeting went over his dark face, very sudden, with an odd sweetness.

She knew he was helping her. And she felt in his presence a subtle, insidious male *kindliness* she had never known before waiting upon her. Her cheek flushed, and her blue eyes darkened.

After this, she always looked for him, and for that curious dark beam of a man's kindliness which he could give her, as it were, from his chest, from his heart. It was something she had never known before.

A vague, unspoken intimacy grew up between them. She liked his voice, his appearance, his presence. His natural language was Spanish; he spoke English like a foreign language, rather slow, with a slight hesitation, but with a sad, plangent sonority lingering over from his Spanish. There was a certain subtle correctness in his appearance; he was always perfectly shaved; his hair was thick and rather long on top, but always carefully groomed behind. And his fine black cashmere shirt, his wide leather belt, his well-cut, wide black trousers going into the embroidered cowboy boots had a certain inextinguishable elegance. He wore no silver rings or buckles. Only his boots were embroidered and decorated at the top with an inlay of white suede. He seemed elegant, slender, yet he was very strong.

And at the same time, curiously, he gave her the feeling that death was not far from him. Perhaps he too was half in love with death.[3] However that may be, the sense she had that death was not far from him made him "possible" to her.

Small as she was, she was quite a good horsewoman. They gave her at the ranch a sorrel mare, very lovely in color, and well-made, with a powerful broad neck and the hollow back that betokens a swift runner. Tansy, she was called. Her only fault was the usual

---

3. Cf. "I have been half in love with easeful Death" (Keats, *Ode to a Nightingale*, line 52).

mare's failing, she was inclined to be hysterical.

So that every day the Princess set off with Miss Cummins and Romero, on horseback, riding into the mountains. Once they went camping for several days, with two more friends in the party.

"I think I like it better," the Princess said to Romero, "when we three go alone."

And he gave her one of his quick, transfiguring smiles.

It was curious no white man had ever showed her this capacity for subtle gentleness, this power to *help* her in silence across a distance, if she were fishing without success, or tired of her horse, or if Tansy suddenly got scared. It was as if Romero could send her *from his heart* a dark beam of succor and sustaining. She had never known this before, and it was very thrilling.

Then the smile that suddenly creased his dark face, showing the strong white teeth. It creased his face almost into a savage grotesque. And at the same time there was in it something so warm, such a dark flame of kindliness for her, she was elated into her true Princess self.

Then that vivid, latent spark in his eye, which she had seen, and which she knew he was aware she had seen. It made an inter-recognition between them, silent and delicate. Here he was delicate as a woman in this subtle inter-recognition.

And yet his presence only put to flight in her the *idée fixe*[4] of "marriage." For some reason, in her strange little brain, the idea of *marrying him* could not enter. Not for any definite reason. He was in himself a gentleman, and she had plenty of money for two. There was no actual obstacle. Nor was she conventional.

No, now she came down to it, it was as if their two "daemons"[5] could marry, were perhaps married. Only their two *selves*, Miss Urquhart and Señor Domingo Romero, were for some reason incompatible. There was a peculiar subtle intimacy of inter-recognition between them. But she did not see in the least how it would lead to marriage. Almost she could more easily marry one of the nice boys from Harvard or Yale.

The time passed, and she let it pass. The end of September came, with aspens going yellow on the mountain heights, and oak-scrub going red. But as yet the cottonwoods in the valley and canyons had not changed.

"When will you go away?" Romero asked her, looking at her fixedly, with a blank black eye.

"By the end of October," she said. "I have promised to be in Santa Barbara at the beginning of November."

He was hiding the spark in his eye from her. But she saw the

4. "Fixed idea."
5. The Greek spelling differentiates the word from the normal English "demon" and indicates the original Greek meaning of the word: protective or inner spirit.

peculiar sullen thickening of his heavy mouth.

She had complained to him many times that one never saw any wild animals, except chipmunks and squirrels, and perhaps a skunk and a porcupine. Never a deer, or a bear, or a mountain lion.

"Are there no bigger animals in these mountains?" she asked, dissatisfied.

"Yes," he said. "There are deer—I see their tracks. And I saw the tracks of a bear."

"But why can one never see the animals themselves?" She looked dissatisfied and wistful like a child.

"Why, it's pretty hard for you to see them. They won't let you come close. You have to keep still, in a place where they come. Or else you have to follow their tracks a long way."

"I can't bear to go away till I've seen them: a bear, or a deer——" The smile came suddenly on his face, indulgent.

"Well, what do you want? Do you want to go up into the mountains to some place, to wait till they come?"

"Yes," she said, looking up at him with a sudden naïve impulse of recklessness.

And immediately his face became somber again, responsible.

"Well," he said, with slight irony, a touch of mockery of her. "You will have to find a house. It's very cold at night now. You would have to stay all night in a house."

"And there are no houses up there?" she said.

"Yes," he replied. "There is a little shack that belongs to me, that a miner built a long time ago, looking for gold. You can go there and stay one night, and maybe you see something. Maybe! I don't know. Maybe nothing come."

"How much chance is there?"

"Well, I don't know. Last time when I was there I see three deer come down to drink at the water, and I shot two raccoons. But maybe this time we don't see anything."

"Is there water there?" she asked.

"Yes, there is a little round pond, you know, below the spruce trees. And the water from the snow runs into it."

"Is it far away?" she asked.

"Yes, pretty far. You see that ridge there"—and turning to the mountains he lifted his arm in the gesture which is somehow so moving, out in the West, pointing to the distance—"that ridge where there are no trees, only rock"—his black eyes were focused on the distance, his face impassive, but as if in pain—"you go round that ridge, and along, then you come down through the spruce trees to where that cabin is. My father bought that placer claim from a miner who was broke, but nobody ever found any gold or anything, and nobody ever goes there. Too lonesome!"

The Princess watched the massive, heavy-sitting, beautiful bulk of the Rocky Mountains. It was early in October, and the aspens were already losing their gold leaves; high up, the spruce and pine seemed to be growing darker; the great flat patches of oak scrub on the heights were red like gore.

"Can I go over there?" she asked, turning to him and meeting the spark in his eye.

His face was heavy with responsibility.

"Yes," he said, "you can go. But there'll be snow over the ridge, and it's awful cold, and awful lonesome."

"I should like to go," she said, persistent.

"All right," he said. "You can go if you want to."

She doubted, though, if the Wilkiesons would let her go; at least alone with Romero and Miss Cummins.

Yet an obstinacy characteristic of her nature, an obstinacy tinged perhaps with madness, had taken hold of her. She wanted to look over the mountains into their secret heart. She wanted to descend to the cabin below the spruce trees, near the tarn of bright green water. She wanted to see the wild animals move about in their wild unconsciousness.

"Let us say to the Wilkiesons that we want to make the trip round the Frijoles canyon," she said.

The trip round the Frijoles canyon was a usual thing. It would not be strenuous, nor cold, nor lonely: they could sleep in the log house that was called an hotel.

Romero looked at her quickly.

"If you want to say that," he replied, "you can tell Mrs. Wilkieson. Only I know she'll be mad with me if I take you up in the mountains to that place. And I've got to go there first with a pack horse, to take lots of blankets and some bread. Maybe Miss Cummins can't stand it. Maybe not. It's a hard trip."

He was speaking, and thinking, in the heavy, disconnected Mexican fashion.

"Never mind!" The Princess was suddenly very decisive and stiff with authority. "I want to do it. I will arrange with Mrs. Wilkieson. And we'll go on Saturday."

He shook his head slowly.

"I've got to go up on Sunday with a pack horse and blankets," he said. "Can't do it before."

"Very well!" she said, rather piqued. "Then we'll start on Monday."

She hated being thwarted even the tiniest bit.

He knew that if he started with the pack on Sunday at dawn he would not be back until late at night. But he consented that they should start on Monday morning at seven. The obedient Miss

Cummins was told to prepare for the Frijoles trip. On Sunday Romero had his day off. He had not put in an appearance when the Princess retired on Sunday night, but on Monday morning, as she was dressing, she saw him bringing in the three horses from the corral. She was in high spirits.

The night had been cold. There was ice at the edges of the irrigation ditch, and the chipmunks crawled into the sun and lay with wide, dumb, anxious eyes, almost too numb to run.

"We may be away two or three days," said the Princess.

"Very well. We won't begin to be anxious about you before Thursday, then," said Mrs. Wilkieson, who was young and capable: from Chicago. "Anyway," she added, "Romero will see you through. He's so trustworthy."

The sun was already on the desert as they set off towards the mountains, making the greasewood and the sage pale as pale-gray sands, luminous the great level around them. To the right glinted the shadows of the adobe pueblo, flat and almost invisible on the plain, earth of its earth. Behind lay the ranch and the tufts of tall, plumy cottonwoods, whose summits were yellowing under the perfect blue sky.

Autumn breaking into color in the great spaces of the Southwest.

But the three trotted gently along the trail, towards the sun that sparkled yellow just above the dark bulk of the ponderous mountains. Side-slopes were already gleaming yellow, flaming with a second light, under coldish blue of the pale sky. The front slopes were in shadow, with submerged luster of red oak scrub and dull-gold aspens, blue-black pines and grayblue rock. While the canyon was full of a deep blueness.

They rode single file, Romero first, on a black horse. Himself in black, made a flickering black spot in the delicate pallor of the great landscape, where even pine trees at a distance take a film of blue paler than their green. Romero rode on in silence past the tufts of furry greasewood. The Princess came next, on her sorrel mare. And Miss Cummins, who was not quite happy on horseback, came last, in the pale dust that the others kicked up. Sometimes her horse sneezed, and she started.

But on they went at a gentle trot. Romero never looked round. He could hear the sound of the hoofs following, and that was all he wanted.

For the rest, he held ahead. And the Princess, with that black, unheeding figure always traveling away from her, felt strangely helpless, withal elated.

They neared the pale, round foothills, dotted with the round dark piñon and cedar shrubs. The horses clinked and trotted among the stones. Occasionally a big round greasewood held out fleecy tufts of flowers, pure gold. They wound into blue shadow, then up a steep stony slope, with the world lying pallid away behind and below. Then they dropped into the shadow of the San Cristobal canyon.

The stream was running full and swift. Occasionally the horses snatched at a tuft of grass. The trail narrowed and became rocky; the rocks closed in; it was dark and cool as the horses climbed and climbed upwards, and the tree trunks crowded in the shadowy, silent tightness of the canyon. They were among cottonwood trees that ran straight up and smooth and round to an extraordinary height. Above, the tips were gold, and it was sun. But away below, where the horses struggled up the rocks and wound among the trunks, there was still blue shadow by the sound of waters and an occasional gray festoon of old man's beard, and here and there a pale, dripping crane's-bill flower among the tangle and the debris of the virgin place. And again the chill entered the Princess's heart as she realized what a tangle of decay and despair lay in the virgin forests.

They scrambled downwards, splashed across stream, up rocks and along the trail of the other side. Romero's black horse stopped, looked down quizzically at the fallen trees, then stepped over lightly. The Princess's sorrel followed, carefully. But Miss Cummins's buckskin made a fuss, and had to be got round.

In the same silence, save for the clinking of the horses and the splashing as the trail crossed stream, they worked their way upwards in the tight, tangled shadow of the canyon. Sometimes, crossing stream, the Princess would glance upwards, and then always her heart caught in her breast. For high up, away in heaven, the mountain heights shone yellow, dappled with dark spruce firs, clear almost as speckled daffodils against the pale turquoise blue lying high and serene above the dark-blue shadow where the Princess was. And she would snatch at the blood-red leaves of the oak as her horse crossed a more open slope, not knowing what she felt.

They were getting fairly high, occasionally lifted above the canyon itself, in the low groove below the speckled, gold-sparkling heights which towered beyond. Then again they dipped and crossed stream, the horses stepping gingerly across a tangle of fallen, frail aspen stems, then suddenly floundering in a mass of rocks. The black emerged ahead, his black tail waving. The Princess let her mare find her own footing; then she too emerged from the clatter. She rode on after the black. Then came a great frantic rattle of the buckskin behind. The Princess was aware of Romero's dark face looking round, with a strange, demonlike watchfulness, before she herself looked round, to see the buckskin scrambling rather lamely beyond the rocks, with one of his pale buff knees already red with blood.

"He almost went down!" called Miss Cummins.

But Romero was already out of the saddle and hastening down the path. He made quiet little noises to the buckskin, and began examining the cut knee.

"Is he hurt?" asked Miss Cummins anxiously, and she climbed hastily down.

"Oh, my goodness!" she cried, as she saw the blood running down the slender buff leg of the horse in a thin trickle. "Isn't that *awful*?" She spoke in a stricken voice, and her face was white.

Romero was still carefully feeling the knee of the bucksin. Then he made him walk a few paces. And at last he stood up straight and shook his head.

"Not very bad!" he said. "Nothing broken."

Again he bent and worked at the knees. Then he looked up at the Princess.

"He can go on," he said. "It's not bad."

The Princess looked down at the dark face in silence.

"What, go on right up there?" cried Miss Cummins. "How many hours?"

"About five!" said Romero simply.

"Five hours!" cried Miss Cummins. "A horse with a lame knee! And a steep mountain! Why-y!"

"Yes, it's pretty steep up there," said Romero, pushing back his hat and staring fixedly at the bleeding knee. The buckskin stood in a stricken sort of dejection. "But I think he'll make it all right," the man added.

"Oh!" cried Miss Cummins, her eyes bright with sudden passion of unshed tears. "I wouldn't think of it. I wouldn't ride him up there, not for any money."

"Why wouldn't you?" asked Romero.

"It *hurts* him."

Romero bent down again to the horse's knee.

"Maybe it hurts him a little," he said. "But he can make it all right, and his leg won't get stiff."

"What! Ride him five hours up the steep mountains?" cried Miss Cummins. "I couldn't. I just couldn't do it. I'll lead him a little way and see if he can go. But I *couldn't* ride him again. I couldn't. Let me walk."

"But Miss Cummins, dear, if Romero says he'll be all right?" said the Princess.

"I know it hurts him. Oh, I just couldn't bear it."

There was no doing anything with Miss Cummins. The thought of a hurt animal always put her into a sort of hysterics.

They walked forward a little, leading the buckskin. He limped rather badly. Miss Cummins sat on a rock.

"Why, it's agony to see him!" she cried. "It's *cruel*!"

"He won't limp after a bit, if you take no notice of him," said Romero. "Now he plays up, and limps very much, because he wants to make you see."

"I don't think there can be much playing up," said Miss Cummins bitterly. "We can *see* how it must hurt him."

"It don't hurt much," said Romero.

But now Miss Cummins was silent with antipathy.

It was a deadlock. The party remained motionless on the trail, the Princess in the saddle, Miss Cummins seated on a rock, Romero standing black and remote near the drooping buckskin.

"Well!" said the man suddenly at last. "I guess we go back, then."

And he looked up swiftly at his horse, which was cropping at the mountain herbage and treading on the trailing reins.

"No!" cried the Princess. "Oh no!" Her voice rang with a great wail of disappointment and anger. Then she checked herself.

Miss Cummins rose with energy.

"Let me lead the buckskin home," she said, with cold dignity, "and you two go on."

This was received in silence. The Princess was looking down at her with a sardonic, almost cruel gaze.

"We've only come about two hours," said Miss Cummins. "I don't mind a bit leading him home. But I *couldn't* ride him. I *couldn't* have him ridden with that knee."

This again was received in dead silence. Romero remained impassive, almost inert.

"Very well, then," said the Princess. "You lead him home. You'll be quite all right. Nothing can happen to you, possibly. And say to them that we have gone on and shall be home tomorrow—or the day after."

She spoke coldly and distinctly. For she could not bear to be thwarted.

"Better all go back, and come again another day," said Romero —noncommittal.

"There will never *be* another day," cried the Princess. "I want to go on."

She looked at him square in the eyes, and met the spark in his eye.

He raised his shoulders slightly.

"If you want it," he said. "I'll go on with you. But Miss Cummins can ride my horse to the end of the canyon, and I lead the buckskin. Then I come back to you."

It was arranged so. Miss Cummins had her saddle put on Romero's black horse, Romero took the buckskin's bridle, and they started back. The Princess rode very slowly on, upwards, alone. She was at first so angry with Miss Cummins that she was blind to everything else. She just let her mare follow her own inclinations.

The peculiar spell of anger carried the Princess on, almost unconscious, for an hour or so. And by this time she was beginning to climb pretty high. Her horse walked steadily all the time. They emerged on a bare slope, and the trail wound through frail aspen stems. Here a wind swept, and some of the aspens were already bare. Others were fluttering their disks of pure, solid yellow leaves, so *nearly* like petals, while the slope ahead was one soft, glowing fleece of daffodil yellow; fleecy like a golden foxskin, and yellow as daffodils alive in the wind and the high mountain sun.

She paused and looked back. The near great slopes were mottled with gold and the dark hue of spruce, like some unsinged eagle, and the light lay gleaming upon them. Away through the gap of the canyon she could see the pale blue of the egglike desert, with the crumpled dark crack of the Rio Grande Canyon. And far, far off, the blue mountains like a fence of angels on the horizon.

And she thought of her adventure. She was going on alone with Romero. But then she was very sure of herself, and Romero was not the kind of man to do anything to her against her will. This was her first thought. And she just had a fixed desire to go over the brim of the mountains, to look into the inner chaos of the Rockies. And she wanted to go with Romero, because he had some peculiar kinship with her; there was some peculiar link between the two of them. Miss Cummins anyhow would have been only a discordant note.

She rode on, and emerged at length in the lap of the summit. Beyond her was a great concave of stone and stark, dead-gray trees, where the mountain ended against the sky. But nearer was the dense black, bristling spruce, and at her feet was the lap of the summit, a flat little valley of sere grass and quiet-standing yellow aspens, the stream trickling like a thread across.

It was a little valley or shell from which the stream was gently poured into the lower rocks and trees of the canyon. Around her was a fairylike gentleness, the delicate sere grass, the groves of delicate-stemmed aspens dropping their flakes of bright yellow. And the delicate, quick little stream threading though the wild, sere grass.

Here one might expect deer and fawns and wild things, as in a little paradise. Here she was to wait for Romero, and they were to have lunch.

She unfastened her saddle and pulled it to the ground with a crash, letting her horse wander with a long rope. How beautiful Tansy looked, sorrel, among the yellow leaves that lay like a patina on the sere ground. The Princess herself wore a fleecy sweater of a pale, sere buff, like the grass, and riding-breeches of a pure orange-tawny colour. She felt quite in the picture.

From her saddle-pouches she took the packages of lunch, spread a little cloth, and sat to wait for Romero. Then she made a little fire. Then she ate a deviled egg. Then she ran after Tansy, who was straying across-stream. Then she sat in the sun, in the stillness near the aspens, and waited.

The sky was blue. Her little alp was soft and delicate as fairyland. But beyond and up jutted the great slopes, dark with the pointed feathers of spruce, bristling with gray dead trees among gray rock, or dappled with dark and gold. The beautiful, but fierce, heavy cruel mountains, with their moments of tenderness.

She saw Tansy start, and begin to run. Two ghostlike figures on horseback emerged from the black of the spruce across the stream. It was two Indians on horseback, swathed like seated mummies in their pale-gray cotton blankets. Their guns jutted beyond the saddles. They rode straight towards her, to her thread of smoke.

As they came near, they unswathed themselves and greeted her, looking at her curiously from their dark eyes. Their black hair was somewhat untidy, the long rolled plaits on their shoulders were soiled. They looked tired.

They got down from their horses near her little fire—a camp was a camp—swathed their blankets round their hips, pulled the saddles from their ponies and turned them loose, then sat down. One was a young Indian whom she had met before, the other was an older man.

"You all alone?" said the younger man.

"Romero will be here in a minute," she said, glancing back along the trail.

"Ah, Romero! You with him? Where are you going?"

"Round the ridge," she said. "Where are you going?"

"We are going down to Pueblo."

"Been out hunting? How long have you been out?"

"Yes. Been out five days." The young Indian gave a little meaningless laugh.

"Got anything?"

"No. We see tracks of two deer—but not got nothing."

The Princess noticed a suspicious-looking bulk under one of the saddles—surely a folded-up deer. But she said nothing.

"You must have been cold," she said.

"Yes, very cold in the night. And hungry. Got nothing to eat since yesterday. Eat it all up." And again he laughed his little meaningless laugh. Under their dark skins, the two men looked peaked and hungry. The Princess rummaged for food among the saddlebags. There was a lump of bacon—the regular stand-back—and some bread. She gave them this, and they began toasting slices of it on long sticks at the fire. Such was the little camp Romero saw as he rode down the slope: the Princess in her orange breeches, her head tied in a blue-and-brown silk kerchief, sitting opposite the two dark-headed Indians across the camp-fire, while one of the Indians was leaning forward toasting bacon, his two plaits of braid-hair dangling as if wearily.

Romero rode up, his face expressionless. The Indians greeted him in Spanish. He unsaddled his horse, took food from the bags, and sat down at the camp to eat. The Princess went to the stream for water, and to wash her hands.

"Got coffee?" asked the Indians.

"No coffee this outfit," said Romero.

They lingered an hour or more in the warm midday sun. Then Romero saddled the horses. The Indians still squatted by the fire. Romero and the Princess rode away, calling *Adios!* to the Indians over the stream and into the dense spruce whence two strange figures had emerged.

When they were alone, Romero turned and looked at her curiously, in a way she could not understand, with such a hard glint in his eyes. And for the first time she wondered if she was rash.

"I hope you don't mind going alone with me," she said.

"If you want it," he replied.

They emerged at the foot of the great bare slope of rocky summit, where dead spruce trees stood sparse and bristling like bristles on a gray dead hog. Romero said the Mexicans, twenty years back, had fired the mountains, to drive out the whites. This gray concave slope of summit was corpselike.

The trail was almost invisible. Romero watched for the trees which the Forest Service had blazed. And they climbed the stark corpse slope, among dead spruce, fallen and ash-gray, into the wind. The wind came rushing from the west, up the funnel of the canyon, from the desert. And there was the desert, like a vast mirage tilting slowly upwards towards the west, immense and pallid, away beyond the funnel of the canyon. The Princess could hardly look.

For an hour their horses rushed the slope, hastening with a great working of the haunches upwards, and halting to breathe, scrambling again, and rowing their way up length by length, on the livid, slanting wall. While the wind blew like some vast machine.

After an hour they were working their way on the incline, no longer forcing straight up. All was gray and dead around them; the horses picked their way over the silver-gray corpses of the spruce. But they were near the top, near the ridge.

Even the horses made a rush for the last bit. They had worked round to a scrap of spruce forest near the very top. They hurried in, out of the huge, monstrous, mechanical wind, that whistled inhu-

manly and was palely cold. So, stepping through the dark screen of
trees, they emerged over the crest.

In front now was nothing but mountains, ponderous, massive,
down-sitting mountains, in a huge and intricate knot, empty of life
or soul. Under the bristling black feathers of spruce near-by lay
patches of white snow. The lifeless valleys were concaves of rock
and spruce, the rounded summits and the hog-backed summits of
gray rock crowded one behind the other like some monstrous herd
in arrest.

It frightened the Princess, it was *so* inhuman. She had not
thought it could be so inhuman, so, as it were, anti-life. And yet
now one of her desires was fulfilled. She had seen it, the massive,
gruesome, repellent core of the Rockies. She saw it there beneath
her eyes, in its gigantic heavy gruesomeness.

And she wanted to go back. At this moment she wanted to turn
back. She had looked down into the intestinal knot of these mountains. She was frightened. She wanted to go back.

But Romero was riding on, on the lee side of the spruce forest,
above the concaves of the inner mountains. He turned round to her
and pointed at the slope with a dark hand.

"Here a miner has been trying for gold," he said. It was a gray
scratched-out heap near a hole—like a great badger hole. And it
looked quite fresh.

"Quite lately?" said the Princess.

"No, long ago—twenty, thirty years." He had reined in his horse
and was looking at the mountains. "Look!" he said. "There goes
the Forest Service trail—along those ridges, on the top, way over
there till it comes to Lucytown, where is the Government road. We
go down there—no trail—see behind that mountain—you see the
top, no trees, and some grass?"

His arm was lifted, his brown hand pointing, his dark eyes piercing
into the distance, as he sat on his black horse twisting round to her.
Strange and ominous, only the demon of himself, he seemed to her.
She was dazed and a little sick, at that height, and she could not
see any more. Only she saw an eagle turning in the air beyond, and
the light from the west showed the pattern on him underneath.

"Shall I ever be able to go so far?" asked the Princess faintly, pet-
ulantly.

"Oh yes! All easy now. No more hard places."

They worked along the ridge, up and down, keeping on the lee
side, the inner side, in the dark shadow. It was cold. Then the trail
laddered up again, and they emerged on a narrow ridge-track, with
the mountain slipping away enormously on either side. The Princess
was afraid. For one moment she looked out, and saw the desert, the
desert ridges, more desert, more blue ridges, shining pale and very

vast, far below, vastly palely tilting to the western horizon. It was ethereal and terrifying in its gleaming, pale, half-burnished immensity, tilted at the west. She could not bear it. To the left was the ponderous, involved mass of mountains all kneeling heavily.

She closed her eyes and let her consciousness evaporate away. The mare followed the trail. So on and on, in the wind again.

They turned their backs to the wind, facing inwards to the mountains. She thought they had left the trail; it was quite invisible.

"No," he said, lifting his hand and pointing. "Don't you see the blazed trees?"

And making an effort of consciousness, she was able to perceive on a pale-gray dead spruce stem the old marks where an ax had chipped a piece away. But with the height, the cold, the wind, her brain was numb.

They turned again and began to descend; he told her they had left the trail. The horses slithered in the loose stones, picking their way downward. It was afternoon, the sun stood obtrusive and gleaming in the lower heavens—about four o'clock. The horses went steadily, slowly, but obstinately onwards. The air was getting colder. They were in among the lumpish peaks and steep concave valleys. She was barely conscious at all of Romero.

He dismounted and came to help her from her saddle. She tottered, but would not betray her feebleness.

"We must slide down here," he said. "I can lead the horses."

They were on a ridge, and facing a steep bare slope of pallid, tawny mountain grass on which the western sun shone full. It was steep and concave. The Princess felt she might start slipping, and go down like a toboggan into the great hollow.

But she pulled herself together. Her eye blazed up again with excitement and determination. A wind rushed past her; she could hear the shriek of spruce trees far below. Bright spots came on her cheeks as her hair blew across. She looked a wild, fairylike little thing.

"No," she said. "I will take my horse."

"Then mind she doesn't slip down on top of you," said Romero. And away he went, nimbly dropping down the pale, steep incline, making from rock to rock, down the grass, and following any little slanting groove. His horse hopped and slithered after him, and sometimes stopped dead, with forefeet pressed back, refusing to go farther. He, below his horse, looked up and pulled the reins gently, and encouraged the creature. Then the horse once more dropped his forefeet with a jerk, and the descent continued.

The Princess set off in blind, reckless pursuit, tottering and yet nimble. And Romero, looking constantly back to see how she was faring, saw her fluttering down like some queer little bird, her orange breeches twinkling like the legs of some duck, and her head, tied in the blue and buff kerchief, bound round and round like the head of some blue-topped bird. The sorrel mare rocked and slipped behind her. But down came the Princess in a reckless intensity, a tiny, vivid spot on the great hollow flank of the tawny mountain. So tiny! Tiny as a frail bird's egg. It made Romero's mind go blank with wonder.

But they had to get down, out of that cold and dragging wind. The spruce trees stood below, where a tiny stream emerged in stones. Away plunged Romero, zigzagging down. And away behind, up the slope, fluttered the tiny, bright-colored Princess, holding the end of the long reins, and leading the lumbering, four-footed, sliding mare.

At last they were down. Romero sat in the sun, below the wind, beside some squaw-berry bushes. The Princess came near, the color flaming in her cheeks, her eyes dark blue, much darker than the kerchief on her head, and glowing unnaturally.

"We make it," said Romero.

"Yes," said the Princess, dropping the reins and subsiding on to the grass, unable to speak, unable to think.

But, thank heaven, they were out of the wind and in the sun.

In a few minutes her consciousness and her control began to come back. She drank a little water. Romero was attending to the saddles. Then they set off again, leading the horses still a little farther down the tiny stream-bed. Then they could mount.

They rode down a bank and into a valley grove dense with aspens. Winding through the thin, crowding, pale-smooth stems, the sun shone flickering beyond them, and the disklike aspen leaves, waving queer mechanical signals, seemed to be splashing the gold light before her eyes. She rode on in a splashing dazzle of gold.

Then they entered shadow and the dark, resinous spruce trees. The fierce boughs always wanted to sweep her off her horse. She had to twist and squirm past.

But there was a semblance of an old trail. And all at once they emerged in the sun on the edge of the spruce grove, and there was a little cabin, and the bottom of a small, naked valley with gray rock and heaps of stones, and a round pool of intense green water, dark green. The sun was just about to leave it.

Indeed, as she stood, the shadow came over the cabin and over herself; they were in the lower gloom, a twilight. Above, the heights still blazed.

It was a little hole of a cabin, near the spruce trees, with an earthen floor and an unhinged door. There was a wooden bed-bunk, three old sawn-off log-lengths to sit on as stools, and a sort of fireplace; no room for anything else. The little hole would hardly contain two people. The roof had gone—but Romero had laid on thick spruce boughs.

The strange squalor of the primitive forest pervaded the place, the squalor of animals and their droppings, the squalor of the wild. The Princess knew the peculiar repulsiveness of it. She was tired and faint.

Romero hastily got a handful of twigs, set a little fire going in the stove grate, and went out to attend to the horses. The Princess vaguely, mechanically, put sticks on the fire, in a sort of stupor, watching the blaze, stupefied and fascinated. She could not make much fire—it would set the whole cabin alight. And smoke oozed out of the dilapidated mud-and-stone chimney.

When Romero came in with the saddle-pouches and saddles, hanging the saddles on the wall, there sat the little Princess on her stump of wood in front of the dilapidated fire-grate, warming her tiny hands at the blaze, while her orange breeches glowed almost like another fire. She was in a sort of stupor.

"You have some whiskey now, or some tea? Or wait for some soup?" he asked.

She rose and looked at him with bright, dazed eyes, half comprehending; the color glowing hectic in her cheeks.

"Some tea," she said, "with a little whiskey in it. Where's the kettle?"

"Wait," he said. "I'll bring the things."

She took her cloak from the back of her saddle, and followed him into the open. It was a deep cup of shadow. But above the sky was still shining, and the heights of the mountains were blazing with aspen like fire blazing.

Their horses were cropping the grass among the stones. Romero clambered up a heap of gray stones and began lifting away logs and rocks, till he had opened the mouth of one of the miner's little old workings. This was his cache. He brought out bundles of blankets, pans for cooking, a little petrol camp-stove, an ax, the regular camp outfit. He seemed so quick and energetic and full of force. This quick force dismayed the Princess a little.

She took a saucepan and went down the stones to the water. It was very still and mysterious, and of a deep green color, yet pure, transparent as glass. How cold the place was! How mysterious and fearful.

She crouched in her dark cloak by the water, rinsing the saucepan, feeling the cold heavy above her, the shadow like a vast weight upon her, bowing her down. The sun was leaving the mountaintops, departing, leaving her under profound shadow. Soon it would crush her down completely.

Sparks? Or eyes looking at her across the water? She gazed, hypnotized. And with her sharp eyes she made out in the dusk the pale form of a bobcat crouching by the water's edge, pale as the stones amongst which it crouched, opposite. And it was watching her with cold, electric eyes of strange intentness, a sort of cold, icy wonder and fearlessness. She saw its *museau*[6] pushed forward, its tufted ears pricking intensely up. It was watching her with cold, animal curiosity, something demonish and conscienceless.

She made a swift movement, spilling her water. And in a flash the creature was gone, leaping like a cat that is escaping; but strange and soft in its motion, with its little bobtail. Rather fascinating. Yet that cold, intent, demonish watching! She shivered with cold and fear. She knew well enough the dread and repulsiveness of the wild.

Romero carried in the bundles of bedding and the camp outfit. The windowless cabin was already dark inside. He lit a lantern, and then went out again with the ax. She heard him chopping wood as she fed sticks to the fire under her water. When he came in with an armful of oak-scrub faggots, she had just thrown the tea into the water.

"Sit down," she said, "and drink tea."

He poured a little bootleg whiskey into the enamel cups, and in the silence the two sat on the log-ends, sipping the hot liquid and coughing occasionally from the smoke.

"We burn these oak sticks," he said. "They don't make hardly any smoke."

Curious and remote he was, saying nothing except what had to be said. And she, for her part, was as remote from him. They seemed far, far apart, worlds apart, now they were so near.

He unwrapped one bundle of bedding, and spread the blankets and the sheepskin in the wooden bunk.

"You lie down and rest," he said, "and I make the supper."

She decided to do so. Wrapping her cloak round her, she lay down in the bunk, turning her face to the wall. She could hear him preparing supper over the little petrol stove. Soon she could smell the soup he was heating; and soon she heard the hissing of fried chicken in a pan.

"You eat your supper now?" he said.

With a jerky, despairing movement, she sat up in the bunk, tossing back her hair. She felt cornered.

"Give it me here," she said.

He handed her first the cupful of soup. She sat among the blankets, eating it slowly. She was hungry. Then he gave her an enamel plate with pieces of fried chicken and currant jelly, butter and

6. French, "muzzle, snout."

bread. It was very good. As they ate the chicken he made the coffee. She said never a word. A certain resentment filled her. She was cornered.

When supper was over he washed the dishes, dried them, and put everything away carefully, else there would have been no room to move in the hole of a cabin. The oak-wood gave out a good bright heat.

He stood for a few moments at a loss. Then he asked her:

"You want to go to bed soon?"

"Soon," she said. "Where are you going to sleep?"

"I make my bed here——" he pointed to the floor along the wall. "Too cold out of doors."

"Yes," she said. "I suppose it is."

She sat immobile, her cheeks hot, full of conflicting thoughts. And she watched him while he folded the blankets on the floor, a sheepskin underneath. Then she went out into night.

The stars were big. Mars sat on the edge of a mountain, for all the world like the blazing eye of a crouching mountain lion. But she herself was deep, deep below in a pit of shadow. In the intense silence she seemed to hear the spruce forest crackling with electricity and cold. Strange, foreign stars floated on that unmoving water. The night was going to freeze. Over the hills came the far sobbing-singing howling of the coyotes. She wondered how the horses would be.

Shuddering a little, she turned to the cabin. Warm light showed through its chinks. She pushed at the rickety, half-opened door.

"What about the horses?" she said.

"My black, he won't go away. And your mare will stay with him. You want to go to bed now?"

"I think I do."

"All right. I feed the horses some oats."

And he went out into the night.

He did not come back for some time. She was lying wrapped up tight in the bunk.

He blew out the lantern, and sat down on his bedding to take off his clothes. She lay with her back turned. And soon, in the silence, she was asleep.

She dreamed it was snowing, and the snow was falling on her through the roof, softly, softly, helplessly, and she was going to be buried alive. She was growing colder and colder, the snow was weighing down on her. The snow was going to absorb her.

She awoke with a sudden convulsion, like pain. She was really very cold; perhaps the heavy blankets had numbed her. Her heart seemed unable to beat, she felt she could not move.

With another convulsion she sat up. It was intensely dark. There was not even a spark of fire, the light wood had burned right away. She sat in thick oblivious darkness. Only through a chink she could see a star.

What did she want? Oh, what did she want? She sat in bed and rocked herself woefully. She could hear the steady breathing of the sleeping man. She was shivering with cold; her heart seemed as if it could not beat. She wanted warmth, protection, she wanted to be taken away from herself. And at the same time, perhaps more deeply than anything, she wanted to keep herself intact, intact, untouched, that no one should have any power over her, or rights to her. It was a wild necessity in her that no one, particularly no man, should have any rights or power over her, that no one and nothing should possess her.

Yet that other thing! And she was so cold, so shivering, and her heart could not beat. Oh, would not someone help her heart to beat?

She tried to speak, and could not. Then she cleared her throat.

"Romero," she said strangely; "it is so cold."

Where did her voice come from, and whose voice was it, in the dark?

She heard him at once sit up, and his voice, startled, with a resonance that seemed to vibrate against her, saying:

"You want me to make you warm?"

"Yes."

As soon as he had lifted her in his arms, she wanted to scream to him not to touch her. She stiffened herself. Yet she was dumb.

And he was warm, but with a terrible animal warmth that seemed to annihilate her. He panted like an animal with desire. And she was given over to this thing.

She had never, never wanted to be given over to this. But she had *willed* that it should happen to her. And according to her will, she lay and let it happen. But she never wanted it. She never wanted to be thus assailed and handled, and mauled. She wanted to keep herself to herself.

However, she had willed it to happen, and it had happened. She panted with relief when it was over.

Yet even now she had to lie within the hard, powerful clasp of this other creature, this man. She dreaded to struggle to go away. She dreaded almost too much the icy cold of that other bunk.

"Do you want to go away from me?" asked his strange voice. Oh, if it could only have been a thousand miles away from her! Yet she had willed to have it thus close.

"No," she said.

And she could feel a curious joy and pride surging up again in him: at her expense. Because he had got her. She felt like a victim there. And he was exulting in his power over her, his possession, his pleasure.

When dawn came, he was fast asleep. She sat up suddenly.

"I want a fire," she said.

He opened his brown eyes wide, and smiled with a curious tender luxuriousness.

"I want you to make a fire," she said.

He glanced at the chinks of light. His brown face hardened to the day.

"All right," he said. "I'll make it."

She did her face while he dressed. She could not bear to look at him. He was so suffused with pride and luxury. She hid her face almost in despair. But feeling the cold blast of air as he opened the door, she wriggled down into the warm place where he had been. How soon the warmth ebbed, when he had gone!

He made a fire and went out, returning after a while with water.

"You stay in bed till the sun comes," he said. "It very cold."

"Hand me my cloak."

She wrapped the cloak fast round her, and sat up among the blankets. The warmth was already spreading from the fire.

"I suppose we will start back as soon as we've had breakfast?"

He was crouching at his camp-stove making scrambled eggs. He looked up suddenly, transfixed, and his brown eyes, so soft and luxuriously widened, looked straight at her.

"You want to?" he said.

"We'd better get back as soon as possible," she said, turning aside from his eyes.

"You want to get away from me?" he asked, repeating the question of the night in a sort of dread.

"I want to get away from here," she said decisively. And it was true. She wanted supremely to get away, back to the world of people.

He rose slowly to his feet, holding the aluminum frying pan.

"Don't you like last night?" he asked.

"Not really," she said. "Why? Do you?"

He put down the frying pan and stood staring at the wall. She could see she had given him a cruel blow. But she did not relent. She was getting her own back. She wanted to regain possession of all herself, and in some mysterious way she felt that he possessed some part of her still.

He looked round at her slowly, his face grayish and heavy.

"You Americans," he said, "you always want to do a man down."

"I am not American," she said. "I am British. And I don't want to do any man down. I only want to go back now."

"And what will you say about me, down there?"

"That you were very kind to me, and very good."

He crouched down again, and went on turning the eggs. He gave her her plate, and her coffee, and sat down to his own food.

But again he seemed not to be able to swallow. He looked up at her.

"You don't like last night?" he asked.

"Not really," she said, though with some difficulty. "I don't care for that kind of thing."

A blank sort of wonder spread over his face at these words, followed immediately by a black look of anger, and then a stony, sinister despair.

"You don't?" he said, looking her in the eyes.

"Not really," she replied, looking back with steady hostility into his eyes.

Then a dark flame seemed to come from his face.

"I make you," he said, as if to himself.

He rose and reached her clothes, that hung on a peg: the fine linen underwear, the orange breeches, the fleecy jumper, the blue-and-bluff kerchief; then he took up her riding-boots and her bead moccasins. Crushing everything in his arms, he opened the door. Sitting up, she saw him stride down to the dark-green pool in the frozen shadow of that deep cup of a valley. He tossed the clothing and the boots out on the pool. Ice had formed. And on the pure, dark green mirror, in the slaty shadow, the Princess saw her things lying, the white linen, the orange breeches, the black boots, the blue moccasins, a tangled heap of color. Romero picked up rocks and heaved them out at the ice, till the surface broke and the fluttering clothing disappeared in the rattling water, while the valley echoed and shouted again with the sound.

She sat in despair among the blankets, hugging tight her pale-blue cloak. Romero strode straight back to the cabin.

"Now you stay here with me," he said.

She was furious. Her blue eyes met his. They were like two demons watching one another. In his face, beyond a sort of unrelieved gloom, was a demonish desire for death.

He saw her looking round the cabin, scheming. He saw her eyes on his rifle. He took the gun and went out with it. Returning, he pulled out her saddle, carried it to the tarn, and threw it in. Then he fetched his own saddle, and did the same.

"Now will you go away?" he said, looking at her with a smile.

She debated within herself whether to coax him and wheedle him. But she knew he was already beyond it. She sat among her blankets in a frozen sort of despair, hard as hard ice with anger.

He did the chores, and disappeared with the gun. She got up in her blue pajamas, huddled in her cloak, and stood in the doorway.

The dark-green pool was motionless again, the stony slopes were pallid and frozen. Shadow still lay, like an after-death, deep in this valley. Always in the distance she saw the horses feeding. If she could catch one! The brilliant yellow sun was halfway down the mountain. It was nine o'clock.

All day she was alone, and she was frightened. What she was frightened of she didn't know. Perhaps the crackling in the dark spruce wood. Perhaps just the savage, heartless wildness of the mountains. But all day she sat in the sun in the doorway of the cabin, watching, watching for hope. And all the time her bowels were cramped with fear.

She saw a dark spot that probably was a bear, roving across the pale grassy slope in the far distance, in the sun.

When, in the afternoon, she saw Romero approaching, with silent suddenness, carrying his gun and a dead deer, the cramp in her bowels relaxed, then became colder. She dreaded him with a cold dread.

"There is deer-meat," he said, throwing the dead doe at her feet.

"You don't want to go away from here," he said. "This is a nice place."

She shrank into the cabin.

"Come into the sun," he said, following her. She looked up at him with hostile, frightened eyes.

"Come into the sun," he repeated, taking her gently by the arm, in a powerful grasp.

She knew it was useless to rebel. Quietly he led her out, and seated himself in the doorway, holding her still by the arm.

"In the sun it is warm," he said. "Look, this is a nice place. You are such a pretty white woman, why do you want to act mean to me? Isn't this a nice place? Come! Come here! It is sure warm here."

He drew her to him, and in spite of her stony resistance, he took her cloak from her, holding her in her thin blue pajamas.

"You sure are a pretty little white woman, small and pretty," he said. "You sure won't act mean to me—you don't want to, I know you don't."

She, stony and powerless, had to submit to him. The sun shone on her white, delicate skin.

"I sure don't mind hell fire," he said. "After this."

A queer, luxurious good humor seemed to possess him again. But though outwardly she was powerless, inwardly she resisted him, absolutely and stonily.

When later he was leaving her again, she said to him suddenly:

"You think you can conquer me this way. But you can't. You can never conquer me."

He stood arrested, looking back at her, with many emotions conflicting in his face—wonder, surprise, a touch of horror, and an unconscious pain that crumpled his face till it was like a mask. Then he went out without saying a word, hung the dead deer on a bough, and started to flay it. While he was at this butcher's work, the sun sank and cold night came on again.

"You see," he said to her as he crouched, cooking the supper, "I ain't going to let you go. I reckon you called to me in the night, and I've some right. If you want to fix it up right now with me, and say you want to be with me, we'll fix it up now and go down to the ranch tomorrow and get married or whatever you want. But you've got to say you want to be with me. Else I shall stay right here, till something happens."

She waited a while before she answered:

"I don't want to be with anybody against my will. I don't dislike you; at least, I didn't, till you tried to put your will over mine. I won't have anybody's will put over me. You can't succeed. Nobody could. You can never get me under your will. And you won't have long to try, because soon they will send someone to look for me."

He pondered this last, and she regretted having said it. Then somber, he bent to the cooking again.

He could not conquer her, however much he violated her. Because her spirit was hard and flawless as a diamond. But he could shatter her. This she knew. Much more, and she would be shattered.

In a somber, violent excess he tried to expend his desire for her. And she was racked with agony, and felt each time she would die. Because, in some peculiar way, he had got hold of her, some unrealized part of her which she never wished to realize. Racked with a burning, tearing anguish, she felt that the thread of her being would break, and she would die. The burning heat that racked her inwardly.

If only, only she could be alone again, cool and intact! If only she could recover herself again, cool and intact! Would she ever, ever, ever be able to bear herself again?

Even now she did not hate him. It was beyond that. Like some racking, hot doom. Personally he hardly existed.

The next day he would not let her have any fire, because of attracting attention with the smoke. It was a gray day, and she was cold. He stayed round, and heated soup on the petrol stove. She lay motionless in the blankets.

And in the afternoon she pulled the clothes over her head and broke into tears. She had never really cried in her life. He dragged the blankets away and looked to see what was shaking her. She sobbed in helpless hysterics. He covered her over again and went outside, looking at the mountains, where clouds were dragging and leaving a little snow. It was a violent, windy, horrible day, the evil of winter rushing down.

She cried for hours. And after this a great silence came between them. They were two people who had died. He did not touch her any more. In the night she lay and shivered like a dying dog. She felt that her very shivering would rupture something in her body, and she would die.

At last she had to speak.

"Could you make a fire? I am so cold," she said, with chattering teeth.

"Want to come over here?" came his voice.

"I would rather you made me a fire," she said, her teeth knocking together and chopping the words in two.

He got up and kindled a fire. At last the warmth spread, and she could sleep.

The next day was still chilly, with some wind. But the sun shone. He went about in silence, with a dead-looking face. It was now so dreary and so like death she wished he would do anything rather than continue in this negation. If now he asked her to go down with him to the world and marry him, she would do it. What did it matter? Nothing mattered any more.

But he would not ask her. His desire was dead and heavy like ice within him. He kept watch around the house.

On the fourth day as she sat huddled in the doorway in the sun, hugged in a blanket, she saw two horsemen come over the crest of the grassy slope—small figures. She gave a cry. He looked up quickly and saw the figures. The men had dismounted. They were looking for the trail.

"They are looking for me," she said.

"*Muy bien*,"[7] he answered in Spanish.

He went and fetched his gun, and sat with it across his knees.

"Oh!" she said. "Don't shoot!"

He looked across at her.

"Why?" he said. "You like staying with me?"

"No," she said. "But don't shoot."

"I ain't going to Pen," he said.

"You won't have to go to Pen," she said. "Don't shoot!"

"I'm going to shoot," he muttered.

And straightway he kneeled and took very careful aim. The Princess sat on in an agony of helplessness and hopelessness.

The shot rang out. In an instant she saw one of the horses on the pale grassy slope rear and go rolling down. The man had dropped in the grass, and was invisible. The second man clambered on his

7. "Very well" or "O.K."

horse, and on that precipitous place went at a gallop in a long swerve towards the nearest spruce tree cover. Bang! Bang! went Romero's shots. But each time he missed, and the running horse leaped like a kangaroo towards cover.

It was hidden. Romero now got behind a rock; tense silence, in the brilliant sunshine. The Princess sat on the bunk inside the cabin, crouching, paralyzed. For hours, it seemed, Romero knelt behind this rock, in his black shirt, bareheaded, watching. He had a beautiful, alert figure. The Princess wondered why she did not feel sorry for him. But her spirit was hard and cold, her heart could not melt. Though now she would have called him to her, with love.

But no, she did not love him. She would never love any man. Never! It was fixed and sealed in her, almost vindictively.

Suddenly she was so startled she almost fell from the bunk. A shot rang out quite close from behind the cabin. Romero leaped straight into the air, his arms fell outstretched, turning as he leaped. And even while he was in the air, a second shot rang out, and he fell with a crash, squirming, his hands clutching the earth towards the cabin door.

The Princess sat absolutely motionless, transfixed, staring at the prostrate figure. In a few moments the figure of a man in the Forest Service appeared close to the house; a young man in a broad-brimmed Stetson hat, dark flannel shirt, and riding-boots, carrying a gun. He strode over to the prostrate figure.

"Got you, Romero!" he said aloud. And he turned the dead man over. There was already a little pool of blood where Romero's breast had been.

"H'm!" said the Forest Service man. "Guess I got you nearer than I thought."

And he squatted there, starring at the dead man.

The distant calling of his comrade aroused him. He stood up.

"Hullo, Bill!" he shouted. "Yep! Got him! Yep! Done him in, apparently."

The second man rode out of the forest on a gray horse. He had a ruddy, kind face, and round brown eyes, dilated with dismay.

"He's not passed out?" he asked anxiously.

"Looks like it," said the first young man coolly.

The second dismounted and bent over the body. Then he stood up again, and nodded.

"Yea-a!" he said. "He's done in all right. It's him all right, boy! It's Domingo Romero."

"Yep! I know it" replied the other.

Then in perplexity he turned and looked into the cabin, where the Princess squatted, staring with big owl eyes from her red blanket.

"Hello!" he said, coming towards the hut. And he took his hat off. Oh, the sense of ridicule she felt! Though he did not mean any.

But she could not speak, no matter what she felt.

"What'd this man start firing for?" he asked.

She fumbled for words, with numb lips.

"He had gone out of his mind!" she said, with solemn, stammering conviction.

"Good Lord! You mean to say he'd gone out of his mind? Whew! That's pretty awful! That explains it then. H'm!"

He accepted the explanation without more ado.

With some difficulty they succeeded in getting the Princess down to the ranch. But she, too, was not a little mad.

"I'm not quite sure where I am," she said to Mrs. Wilkieson, as she lay in bed. "Do you mind explaining?"

Mrs. Wilkieson explained tactfully.

"Oh yes!" said the Princess. "I remember. And I had an accident in the mountains, didn't I? Didn't we meet a man who'd gone mad, and who shot my horse from under me?"

"Yes, you met a man who had gone out of his mind."

The real affair was hushed up. The Princess departed east in a fortnight's time, in Miss Cummins's care. Apparently she had recovered herself entirely. She was the Princess, and a virgin intact.

But her bobbed hair was gray at the temples, and her eyes were a little mad. She was slightly crazy.

"Since my accident in the mountains, when a man went mad and shot my horse from under me, and my guide had to shoot him dead, I have never felt quite myself."

So she put it.

Later, she married an elderly man, and seemed pleased.

1925

From Mornings in Mexico

The Dance of the Sprouting Corn

Pale, dry, baked earth, that blows into dust of fine sand. Low hills of baked pale earth, sinking heavily, and speckled sparsely with dark dots of cedar bushes. A river on the plain of drought, just a cleft of dark, reddish-brown water, almost a flood. And over all, the blue, uneasy, alkaline sky.

A pale, uneven, parched world, where a motorcar rocks and lurches and churns in sand. A world pallid with dryness, inhuman with a faint taste of alkali. Like driving in the bed of a great sea that dried up unthinkable ages ago, and now is drier than any other dryness, yet still reminiscent of the bottom of the sea, sandhills sinking, and straight, cracked mesas, like cracks in the dry-mud bottom of the sea.

So, the mud church standing discreetly outside, just outside the pueblo, not to see too much. And on its façade of mud, under the timbered mud-eaves, two speckled horses rampant, painted by the Indians, a red piebald and a black one.

Swish! Over the logs of the ditch-bridge, where brown water is flowing full. There below is the pueblo, dried mud like mud-pie houses, all squatting in a jumble, prepared to crumble into dust and be invisible, dust to dust returning, earth to earth.

That they don't crumble is the mystery. That these little squarish mud-heaps endure for centuries after centuries, while Greek marble tumbles asunder, and cathedrals totter, is the wonder. But then, the naked human hand with a bit of new soft mud is quicker than time, and defies the centuries.

Roughly the low, square, mud-pie houses make a wide street where all is naked earth save a doorway or a window with a pale-blue sash. At the end of the street, turn again into a parallel wide, dry street. And there, in the dry, oblong aridity, there tosses a small forest that is alive; and thud—thud—thud goes the drum, and the deep sound of men singing is like the deep soughing of the wind, in the depths of a wood.

You realize that you had heard the drum from the distance, also the deep, distant roar and boom of the singing, but that you had not heeded, as you don't heed the wind.

It all tosses like young, agile trees in a wind. This is the dance of the sprouting corn, and everybody hold a little, beating branch of green pine. Thud—thud—thud—thud—thud! goes the drum, heavily the men hop and hop and hop, sway, sway, sway, sway go the little branches of green pine. It tosses like a little forest, and the deep sound of men's singing is like the booming and tearing of a wind deep inside a forest. They are dancing the Spring Corn Dance.

This is the Wednesday after Easter, after Christ Risen and the corn germinated. They dance on Monday and on Tuesday. Wednesday is the third and last dance of this green resurrection.

You realize the long lines of dancers, and a solid cluster of men singing near the drum. You realize the intermittent black-and-white fantasy of the hopping Koshare, the jesters, the Delight-Makers. You become aware of the ripple of bells on the knee-garters of the dancers, a continual pulsing ripple of little bells; and of the sudden wild, whooping yells from near the drum. Then you become aware of the seedlike shudder of the gourd-rattles, as the dance changes, and the swaying of the tufts of green pine-twigs stuck behind the arms of all the dancing men, in the broad green arm-bands.

Gradually comes through to you the black, stable solidity of the dancing women, who poise like solid shadow, one woman behind each rippling, leaping male. The long, silky black hair of the women, streaming down their backs, and the equally long, streaming, gleaming hair of the males, loose over broad, naked, orange-brown shoulders.

Then the faces, the impassive, rather fat, golden-brown faces of the women, with eyes cast down, crowned above with the green tableta, like a flat tiara. Something strange and noble about the impassive, barefoot women in the short black cassocks, as they subtly tread the dance, scarcely moving, and yet edging rhythmically along, swaying from each hand the green spray of pine-twig out—out—out—out, to the thud of the drum, immediately behind the leaping fox-skin of the men dancers. And all the emerald-green, painted tabletas, the flat wooden tiaras shaped like a castle gateway, rise steady and noble from the soft, slightly bowed heads of the women, held by a band under the chin. All the tabletas down the line, emerald green, almost steady, while the bright black heads of the men leap softly up and down, between.

Bit by bit you take it in. You cannot get a whole impression, save of some sort of wood tossing, a little forest of trees in motion, with gleaming black hair and gold-ruddy breasts that somehow do not destroy the illusion of forest.

When you look at the women, you forget the men. The bare-armed, bare-legged, barefoot women with streaming hair and lofty green tiaras, impassive, downward-looking faces, twigs swaying outwards from subtle, rhythmic wrists; women clad in the black, prehistoric short gown fastened over one shoulder, leaving the other shoulder bare, and showing at the arm-place a bit of pink or white undershirt; belted also round the waist with a woven woolen sash, scarlet and green on the handwoven black cassock. The noble, slightly submissive bending of the tiara-ed head. The subtle measure of the bare, breathing, birdlike feet, that are flat, and seem to cleave to earth softly, and softly lift away. The continuous outward swaying of the pine-sprays.

But when you look at the men, you forget the women. The men are naked to the waist, and ruddy-golden, and in the rhythmic, hopping leap of the dance their breasts shake downwards, as the strong, heavy body comes down, down, down, down, in the downward plunge of the dance. The black hair streams loose and living down their backs, the black brows are level, the black eyes look out unchanging from under the silky lashes. They are handsome, and absorbed with a deep rhythmic absorption, which still leaves them awake and aware. Down, down, down they drop, on the heavy, ceaseless leap of the dance, and the great necklaces of shell-cores spring on the naked breasts, the neck-shell flaps up and down, the short white kilt of woven stuff, with the heavy woolen embroidery, green and red and black, opens and shuts slightly to the strong lifting of the knees: the heavy whitish cords that hang from the kilt-band at the side sway and coil forever down the side of the right leg, down to the ankle, the bells on the red-woven garters under the knees ripple without end, and the feet, in buckskin boots furred round the ankle with a beautiful band of skunk fur, black with a white tip, come down with a lovely, heavy, soft precision, first one, then the other, dropping always plumb to earth. Slightly bending forward, a black gourd rattle in the right hand, a small green bough in the left, the dancer dances the eternal drooping leap, that brings his life down, down, down, down from the mind, down from the broad, beautiful, shaking breast, down to the powerful pivot of the knees, then to the ankles, and plunges deep from the ball of the foot into the earth, towards the earth's red center, where these men belong, as is signified by the red earth with which they are smeared.

And meanwhile, the shell-cores from the Pacific sway up and down, ceaselessly, on their breasts.

Mindless, without effort, under the hot sun, unceasing, yet never perspiring nor even breathing heavily, they dance on and on. Mindless, yet still listening, observing. They hear the deep, surging singing of the bunch of old men, like a great wind soughing. They hear the cries and yells of the man waving his bough by the drum. They catch the word of the song, and at a moment, shudder the black rattles, wheel, and the line breaks, women from men, they thread across to a new formation. And as the men wheel round, their black hair gleams and shakes, and the long fox-skin sways, like a tail.

And always, when they form into line again, it is a beautiful long straight line, flexible as life, but straight as rain.

The men round the drum are old, or elderly. They are all in a bunch, and they wear day dress, loose cotton drawers, pink or white cotton shirt, hair tied up behind with the red cords, and banded round the head with a strip of pink rag, or white rag, or blue. There they are, solid like a cluster of bees, their black heads with the pink rag circles all close together, swaying their pine-twigs with rhythmic, windswept hands, dancing slightly, mostly on the right foot, ceaselessly, and singing, their black bright eyes absorbed, their dark lips pushed out, while the deep strong sound rushes like wind, and the unknown words form themselves in the dark.

Suddenly the solitary man pounding the drum swings his drum round, and begins to pound on the other end, on a higher note, pang—pang—pang! instead of the previous brumm! brumm! brumm! of the bass note. The watchful man next the drummer yells and waves lightly, dancing on bird-feet. The Koshare make strange, eloquent gestures to the sky.

And again the gleaming bronze-and-dark men dancing in the rows shudder their rattles, break the rhythm, change into a queer, beautiful two-step, the long lines suddenly curl into rings, four rings of dancers, the leaping, gleaming-seeming men between the solid, subtle, submissive blackness of the women who are crowned with emerald-green tiaras, all going subtly round in rings. Then slowly they change again, and form a star. Then again, unmingling, they come back into rows.

And all the while, all the while the naked Koshare are threading about. Of bronze-and-dark men-dancers there are some forty-two, each with a dark, crowned woman attending him like a shadow. The old men, the bunch of singers in shirts and tied-up black hair, are about sixty in number, or sixty-four. The Koshare are about twenty-four.

They are slim and naked, daubed with black-and-white earth, their hair daubed white and gathered upwards to a great knot on top of the head, whence springs a tuft of corn-husks, dry corn-leaves. Though they wear nothing but a little black square cloth, front and back, at their middle, they do not seem naked, for some are white with black spots, like a leopard, and some have broad black lines or zigzags on their smeared bodies, and all their faces are blackened with triangles or lines till they look like weird masks. Meanwhile their hair, gathered straight up and daubed white and sticking up from the top of the head with corn-husks, completes the fantasy. They are anything but natural. Like blackened ghosts of a dead corncob, tufted at the top.

And all the time, running like queer spotted dogs, they weave nakedly through the unheeding dance, comical, weird, dancing the dance-step naked and fine, prancing through the lines, up and down the lines, and making fine gestures with their flexible hands, calling something down from the sky, calling something up from the earth, and dancing forward all the time. Suddenly as they catch a word from the singers, name of a star, of a wind, a name for the sun, for a cloud, their hands soar up and gather in the air, soar down with a slow motion. And again, as they catch a word that means earth, earth deeps, water within the earth, or red-earth-quickening, the hands flutter softly down, and draw up the water, draw up the earth-quickening, earth to sky, sky to earth, influences above to influences below, to meet in the germ-quick of corn, where life is.

And as they dance, the Koshare watch the dancing men. And if a fox-skin is coming loose at the belt, they fasten it as the man dances, or they stoop and tie another man's shoe. For the dancer must not hesitate to the end.

And then, after some forty minutes, the drum stops. Slowly the dancers file into one line, woman behind man, and move away, threading towards their kiva, with no sound but the tinkle of knee-bells in the silence.

But at the same moment the thud of an unseen drum, from beyond, the soughing of deep song approaching from the unseen. It is the other half, the other half of the tribe coming to continue the dance. They appear round the kiva—one Koshare and one dancer leading the rows, the old men all abreast, singing already in a great strong burst.

So, from ten o'clock in the morning till about four in the afternoon, first one-half then the other. Till at last, as the day wanes, the two halves meet, and the two singings like two great winds surge one past the other, and the thicket of the dance becomes a real forest. It is the close of the third day.

Afterwards, the men and women crowd on the roofs of the two low round towers, the kivas, while the Koshare run round jesting and miming, and taking big offerings from the women, loaves of bread and cakes of blue-maize meal. Women come carrying big baskets of bread and guayava, on two hands, an offering.

And the mystery of germination, not procreation, but *putting forth*, resurrection, life springing within the seed, is accomplished. The sky has its fire, its waters, its stars, its wandering electricity, its winds, its fingers of cold. The earth has its reddened body, its invisible hot heart, its inner waters and many juices and unaccountable stuffs. Between them all, the little seed: and also man, like a seed that is busy and aware. And from the heights and from the depths man, the caller, calls: man, the knower, brings down the influences and brings up the influences, with his knowledge: man, so vulnerable, so subject, and yet even in his vulnerability and subjection, a master, commands the invisible influences and is obeyed. Commands in that song, in that rhythmic energy of dance, in that still-submissive mockery of the Koshare. And he accomplishes his end, as master. He partakes in the springing of the corn, in the rising and budding and earing of the corn. And when he eats his bread, at last, he recovers all he once sent forth, and partakes again of the energies he called to the corn, from out of the wide universe.

1927

Why the Novel Matters

We have curious ideas of ourselves. We think of ourselves as a body with a spirit in it, or a body with a soul in it, or a body with a mind in it. *Mens sana in corpore sano.* The years drink up the wine, and at last throw the bottle away, the body, of course, being the bottle.

It is a funny sort of superstition. Why should I look at my hand, as it so cleverly writes these words, and decide that it is a mere nothing compared to the mind that directs it? Is there really any huge difference between my hand and my brain? Or my mind? My hand is alive, it flickers with a life of its own. It meets all the strange universe in touch, and learns a vast number of things, and knows a vast number of things. My hand, as it writes these words, slips gaily along, jumps like a grasshopper to dot an *i*, feels the table rather cold, gets a little bored if I write too long, has its own rudiments of thought, and is just as much *me* as is my brain, my mind, or my soul. Why should I imagine that there is a *me* which is more *me* than my hand is? Since my hand is absolutely alive, me alive.

Whereas, of course, as far as I am concerned, my pen isn't alive at all. My pen *isn't me* alive. Me alive ends at my finger tips.

Whatever is me alive is me. Every tiny bit of my hands is alive, every little freckle and hair and fold of skin. And whatever is me alive is me. Only my fingernails, those ten little weapons between me and an inanimate universe, they cross the mysterious Rubicon [1] between me alive and things like my pen, which are not alive, in my own sense.

So, seeing my hand is all alive, and me alive, wherein is it just a bottle, or a jug, or a tin can, or a vessel of clay, or any of the rest of that nonsense? True, if I cut it it will bleed, like a can of cherries. But then the skin that is cut, and the veins that bleed, and the bones that should never be seen, they are all just as alive as the blood that flows. So the tin can business, or vessel of clay, is just bunk.

And that's what you learn, when you're a novelist. And that's what you are very liable *not* to know, if you're a parson, or a philosopher, or a scientist, or a stupid person. If you're a parson, you talk about souls in heaven. If you're a novelist, you know that paradise is in the palm of your hand, and on the end of your nose, because both are alive; and alive, and man alive, which is more than you can say,

---

1. When Julius Caesar crossed the River Rubicon (near Rimini, Italy) in 49 B.C., in defiance of the Senate's orders, this indicated his intention of advancing against Pompey and thus involving the country in civil war. Hence to "cross the Rubicon" means to take an important and irrevocable decision.

for certain, of paradise. Paradise is after life, and I for one am not keen on anything that is *after* life. If you are a philosopher, you talk about infinity, and the pure spirit which knows all things. But if you pick up a novel, you realize immediately that infinity is just a handle to this self-same jug of a body of mine; while as for knowing, if I find my finger in the fire, I know that fire burns, with a knowledge so emphatic and vital, it leaves Nirvana merely a conjecture. Oh, yes, my body, me alive, *knows*, and knows intensely. And as for the sum of all knowledge, it can't be anything more than an accumulation of all the things I know in the body, and you, dear reader, know in the body.

These damned philosophers, they talk as if they suddenly went off in steam, and were then much more important than they are when they're in their shirts. It is nonsense. Every man, philosopher included, ends in his own finger tips. That's the end of his man alive. As for the words and thoughts and sighs and aspirations that fly from him, they are so many tremulations in the ether, and not alive at all. But if the tremulations reach another man alive, he may receive them into his life, and his life may take on a new color, like a chameleon creeping from a brown rock on to a green leaf. All very well and good. It still doesn't alter the fact that the so-called spirit, the message or teaching of the philosopher or the saint, isn't alive at all, but just a tremulation upon the ether, like a radio message. All this spirit stuff is just tremulations upon the ether. If you, as man alive, quiver from the tremulation of the ether into new life, that is because you are man alive, and you take sustenance and stimulation into your alive man in a myriad ways. But to say that the message, or the spirit which is communicated to you, is more important than your living body, is nonsense. You might as well say that the potato at dinner was more important.

Nothing is important but life. And for myself, I can absolutely see life nowhere but in the living. Life with a capital L is only man alive. Even a cabbage in the rain is cabbage alive. All things that are alive are amazing. And all things that are dead are subsidiary to the living. Better a live dog than a dead lion. But better a live lion than a live dog. *C'est la vie!*

It seems impossible to get a saint, or a philosopher, or a scientist, to stick to this simple truth. They are all, in a sense, renegades. The saint wishes to offer himself up as spiritual food for the multitude. Even Francis of Assisi turns himself into a sort of angel-cake, of which anyone may take a slice. But an angel-cake is rather less than man alive. And poor St. Francis might well apologize to his body, when he is dying: "Oh, pardon me, my body, the wrong I did you through the years!" It was no wafer, for others to eat.

The philosopher, on the other hand, because he can think, decides that nothing but thoughts matter. It is as if a rabbit, because he can make little pills, should decide that nothing but little pills matter. As for the scientist, he has absolutely no use for me so long as I am man alive. To the scientist, I am dead. He puts under the microscope a bit of dead me, and calls it me. He takes me to pieces, and says first one piece, and then another piece, is me. My heart, my liver, my stomach have all been scientifically me, according to the scientist; and nowadays I am either a brain, or nerves, or glands, or something more up-to-date in the tissue line.

Now I absolutely flatly deny that I am a soul, or a body, or a mind, or an intelligence, or a brain, or a nervous system, or a bunch of glands, or any of the rest of these bits of me. The whole is greater than the part. And therefore, I, who am man alive, am greater than my soul, or spirit, or body, or mind, or consciousness, or anything else that is merely a part of me. I am a man, and alive. I am man alive, and as long as I can, I intend to go on being man alive.

For this reason I am a novelist. And being a novelist, I consider myself superior to the saint, the scientist, the philosopher, and the poet, who are all great masters of different bits of man alive, but never get the whole hog.

The novel is the one bright book of life. Books are not life. They are only tremulations on the ether. But the novel as a tremulation can make the whole man alive tremble. Which is more than poetry, philosophy, science, or any other book-tremulation can do.

The novel is the book of life. In this sense, the Bible is a great confused novel. You may say, it is about God. But it is really about man alive. Adam, Eve, Sarai, Abraham, Isaac, Jacob, Samuel, David, Bath-Sheba, Ruth, Esther, Solomon, Job, Isaiah, Jesus, Mark, Judas, Paul, Peter: what is it but man alive, from start to finish? Man alive, not mere bits. Even the Lord is another man alive, in a burning bush, throwing the tablets of stone at Moses's head.

I do hope you begin to get my idea, why the novel is supremely important, as a tremulation on the ether. Plato makes the perfect ideal being tremble in me. But that's only a bit of me. Perfection is only a bit, in the strange make-up of man alive. The Sermon on the Mount makes the selfless spirit of me quiver. But that, too, is only a bit of me. The Ten Commandments set the old Adam shivering in me, warning me that I am a thief and a murderer, unless I watch it. But even the old Adam is only a bit of me.

I very much like all these bits of me to be set trembling with life and the wisdom of life. But I do ask that the whole of me shall tremble in its wholeness, some time or other.

And this, of course, must happen in me, living.

But as far as it can happen from a communication, it can only happen when a whole novel communicates itself to me. The Bible —but *all* the Bible—and Homer, and Shakespeare: these are the supreme old novels. These are all things to all men. Which means that in their wholeness they affect the whole man alive, which is the man himself, beyond any part of him. They set the whole tree trembling with a new access of life, they do not just stimulate growth in one direction.

I don't want to grow in any one direction any more. And, if I can help it, I don't want to stimulate anybody else into some particular direction. A particular direction ends in a *cul-de-sac*. We're in a *cul-de-sac* at present.

I don't believe in any dazzling revelation, or in any supreme Word. "The grass withereth, the flower fadeth, but the Word of the Lord shall stand for ever." That's the kind of stuff we've drugged ourselves with. As a matter of fact, the grass withereth, but comes up all the greener for that reason, after the rains. The flower fadeth, and therefore the bud opens. But the Word of the Lord, being man-uttered and a mere vibration on the ether, becomes staler and staler, more and more boring, till at last we turn a deaf ear and it ceases to exist, far more finally than any withered grass. It is grass that renews its youth like the eagle, not any Word.

We should ask for no absolutes, or absolute. Once and for all and for ever, let us have done with the ugly imperialism of any absolute. There is no absolute good, there is nothing absolutely right. All things flow and change, and even change is not absolute. The whole is a strange assembly of apparently incongruous parts, slipping past one another.

Me, man alive, I am a very curious assembly of incongruous parts. My yea! of today is oddly different from my yea! of yesterday. My tears of tomorrow will have nothing to do with my tears of a year ago. If the one I love remains unchanged and unchanging, I shall cease to love her. It is only because she changes and startles me into change and defies my inertia, and is herself staggered in her inertia by my changing, that I can continue to love her. If she stayed put, I might as well love the pepper pot.

In all this change, I maintain a certain integrity. But woe betide me if I try to put my finger on it. If I say of myself, I am this, I am that!—then, if I stick to it, I turn into a stupid fixed thing like a lamp-post. I shall never know wherein lies my integrity, my individuality, my me. I *can* never know it. It is useless to talk about my ego. That only means that I have made up an *idea* of myself, and that I am trying to cut myself out to pattern. Which is no good. You can cut your cloth to fit your coat, but you can't clip bits off your living body, to trim it down to your idea. True, you can put yourself into ideal corsets. But even in ideal corsets, fashions change.

Let us learn from the novel. In the novel, the characters can do nothing but *live*. If they keep on being good, according to pattern, or bad, according to pattern, or even volatile, according to pattern, they cease to live, and the novel falls dead. A character in a novel has got to live, or it is nothing.

We, likewise, in life have got to live, or we are nothing.

What we mean by living is, of course, just as indescribable as what we mean by *being*. Men get ideas into their heads, of what they mean by Life, and they proceed to cut life out to pattern. Sometimes they go into the desert to seek God, sometimes they go into the desert to seek cash, sometimes it is wine, woman, and song, and again it is water, political reform, and votes. You never know what it will be next: from killing your neighbor with hideous bombs and gas that tears the lungs, to supporting a Foundlings Home and preaching infinite Love, and being co-respondent in a divorce.

In all this wild welter, we need some sort of guide. It's no good inventing Thou Shalt Nots!

What then? Turn truly, honorably to the novel, and see wherein you are man alive, and wherein you are dead man in life. You may love a woman as man alive, and you may be making love to a woman as sheer dead man in life. You may eat your dinner as man alive, or as a mere masticating corpse. As man alive you may have shot at your enemy. But as a ghastly simulacrum of life you may be firing bombs into men who are neither your enemies nor your friends, but just things you are dead to. Which is criminal, when the things happen to be alive.

To be alive, to be man alive, to be whole man alive: that is the point. And at its best, the novel, and the novel supremely, can help you. It can help you not to be dead man in life. So much of a man walks about dead and a carcass in the street and house, today: so much of women is merely dead. Like a pianoforte with half the notes mute.

But the novel you can see, plainly, when the man goes dead, the woman goes inert. You can develop an instinct for life, if you will, instead of a theory of right and wrong, good and bad.

In life, there is right and wrong, good and bad, all the time. But what is right in one case is wrong in another. And in the novel you see one man becoming a corpse, because of his so-called goodness, another going dead because of his so-called wickedness. Right and wrong is an instinct: but an instinct of the whole consciousness in a man, bodily, mental, spiritual at once. And only in the novel are *all* things given full play, or at least, they may be given full play, when we realize that life itself, and not inert safety, is the reason for living. For out of the full play of all things emerges the only thing that is anything, the wholeness of a man, the wholeness of a woman, man alive, and live woman.

1936

Love on the Farm[1]

What large, dark hands are those at the window
Grasping in the golden light
Which weaves its way through the evening wind
    At my heart's delight?

Ah, only the leaves! But in the west   5
I see a redness suddenly come
Into the evening's anxious breast—
    'Tis the wound of love goes home!

The woodbine creeps abroad
Calling low to her lover: 10
    The sunlit flirt who all the day
    Has poised above her lips in play
    And stolen kisses, shallow and gay
    Of pollen, now has gone away—
    She woos the moth with her sweet, low word;   15
And when above her his moth-wings hover
Then her bright breast she will uncover
And yield her honey-drop to her lover.

Into the yellow, evening glow
Saunters a man from the farm below;   20
Leans, and looks in at the low-built shed
Where the swallow has hung her marriage bed.
    The bird lies warm against the wall.
    She glances quick her startled eyes
    Towards him, then she turns away   25
    Her small head, making warm display
    Of red upon the throat. Her terrors sway
    Her out of the nest's warm, busy ball,
    Whose plaintive cry is heard as she flies
    In one blue stoop from out the sties   30
    Into the twilight's empty hall.
Oh, water-hen, beside the rushes
Hide your quaintly scarlet blushes,
Still your quick tail, lie still as dead,
Till the distance folds over his ominous tread!   35

The rabbit presses back her ears,
Turns back her liquid, anguished eyes
And crouches low; then with wild spring
Spurts from the terror of *his* oncoming;
To be choked back, the wire ring   40
Her frantic effort throttling:

---

1. Called *Cruelty and Love* when first published in 1913, and *Love on the Farm* when it appeared in *Collected Poems* (1928).

Piteous brown ball of quivering fears!
Ah, soon in his large, hard hands she dies,
And swings all loose from the swing of his walk!
Yet calm and kindly are his eyes   45
And ready to open in brown surprise
Should I not answer to his talk
Or should he my tears surmise.

I hear his hand on the latch, and rise from my chair
Watching the door open; he flashes bare   50
His strong teeth in a smile, and flashes his eyes
In a smile like triumph upon me; then careless-wise
He flings the rabbit soft on the table board
And comes towards me: ah! the uplifted sword
Of his hand against my bosom! and oh, the broad   55
Blade of his glance that asks me to applaud
His coming! With his hand he turns my face to him
And caresses me with his fingers that still smell grim
Of the rabbit's fur! God, I am caught in a snare!
I know not what fine wire is round my throat;   60
I only know I let him finger there
My pulse of life, and let him nose like a stoat
Who sniffs with joy before he drinks the blood.

And down his mouth comes to my mouth! and down
His bright dark eyes come over me, like a hood   65
Upon my mind! his lips meet mine, and a flood
Of sweet fire sweeps across me, so I drown
Against him, die, and find death good.

                                                 1913, 1928

Piano

Softly, in the dusk, a woman is singing to me;
Taking me back down the vista of years, till I see
A child sitting under the piano, in the boom of the tingling
    strings
And pressing the small, poised feet of a mother who smiles
    as she sings.

In spite of myself, the insidious mastery of song   5
Betrays me back, till the heart of me weeps to belong
To the old Sunday evenings at home, with winter outside
And hymns in the cozy parlor, the tinkling piano our guide.

So now it is vain for the singer to burst into clamor
With the great black piano appassionato. The glamor   10
Of childish days is upon me, my manhood is cast
Down in the flood of remembrance, I weep like a child for the
    past.

                                                       1918

Tortoise Shell[1]

The Cross, the Cross
Goes deeper in than we know,
Deeper into life;
Right into the marrow
And through the bone.   5
Along the back of the baby tortoise
The scales are locked in an arch like a bridge,
Scale-lapping, like a lobster's sections
Or a bee's.

Then crossways down his sides   10
Tiger-stripes and wasp-bands.

Five, and five again, and five again,
And round the edges twenty-five little ones,
The sections of the baby tortoise shell.

Four, and a keystone;   15
Four, and a keystone;
Four, and a keystone;
Then twenty-four, and a tiny little keystone.

It needed Pythagoras[2] to see life playing with counters on the
    living back
Of the baby tortoise;   20
Life establishing the first eternal mathematical tablet,
Not in stone, like the Judean Lord,[3] or bronze, but in life-
    clouded, life-rosy tortoise shell.

The first little mathematical gentleman
Stepping, wee mite, in his loose trousers
Under all the eternal dome of mathematical law.   25

Fives, and tens,
Threes and fours and twelves,
All the *volte face*[4] of decimals,
The whirligig of dozens and the pinnacle of seven.

Turn him on his back,   30
The kicking little beetle,
And there again, on his shell-tender, earth-touching belly,
The long cleavage of division, upright of the eternal cross

---

1. The first of six poems known as the
"Tortoise sequence," first published in
a volume called *Tortoises* in 1921.
2. Greek mathematician and philosopher (6th century B.C.).

3. The God of the Jews who delivered
the stone tablets of the Law to Moses.
4. French, "art of turning to face the
opposite direction."

And on either side count five,
On each side, two above, on each side, two below   35
The dark bar horizontal.

The Cross!
It goes right through him, the sprottling[5] insect,
Through his crosswise cloven psyche,
Through his five-fold complex-nature.   40

So turn him over on his toes again;
Four pinpoint toes, and a problematical thumb-piece,
Four rowing limbs, and one wedge-balancing head,
Four and one makes five, which is the clue to all mathematics.

The Lord wrote it all down on the little slate   45
Of the baby tortoise.
Outward and visible indication of the plan within,
The complex, manifold involvedness of an individual creature
Plotted out
On this small bird, this rudiment,   50
This little dome, this pediment
Of all creation,
This slow one.

1921

Tortoise Shout

I thought he was dumb,
I said he was dumb,
Yet I've heard him cry.

First faint scream,
Out of life's unfathomable dawn,   5
Far off, so far, like a madness, under the horizon's dawning rim,
Far, far off, far scream.

Tortoise *in extremis.*

Why were we crucified into sex?
Why were we not left rounded off, and finished in ourselves,   10
As we began,
As he certainly began, so perfectly alone?

A far, was-it-audible scream,
Or did it sound on the plasm direct?

Worse than the cry of the newborn,   15
A scream,

5. Sprawling.

A yell,
A shout,
A paean,
A death-agony,
A bird-cry,   20
A submission,
All tiny, tiny, far away, reptile under the first dawn.

War-cry, triumph, acute-delight, death-scream reptilian,
Why was the veil torn?[1]   25
The silken shriek of the soul's torn membrane?
The male soul's membrane
Torn with a shriek half music, half horror.

Crucifixion.
Male tortoise, cleaving behind the hovel-wall of that dense female,
Mounted and tense, spread-eagle, outreaching out of the shell
In tortoise-nakedness,
Long neck, and long vulnerable limbs extruded, spread-eagle over
    her house-roof,
And the deep, secret, all-penetrating tail curved beneath her
    walls,
Reaching and gripping tense, more reaching anguish in utter-
    most tension   35
Till suddenly, in the spasm of coition, tupping like a jerking
    leap, and oh!
Opening its clenched face from his outstretched neck
And giving that fragile yell, that scream.
Super-audible,
From his pink, cleft, old-man's mouth,   40
Giving up the ghost,
Or screaming in Pentecost,[2] receiving the ghost.

His scream, and his moment's subsidence,
The moment of eternal silence,
Yet unreleased, and after the moment, the sudden, startling jerk
    of coition, and at once   45
The inexpressible faint yell—
And so on, till the last plasm of my body was melted back
To the primeval rudiments of life, and the secret.

So he tups, and screams
Time after time that frail, torn scream   50
After each jerk, the longish interval,
The tortoise eternity,

1. Cf. Matthew xxvii, describing
Christ's death: "And Jesus cried again
with a loud voicer and gave up the
ghost. And behold, the veil [curtain] of
the temple was torn in two, from top
to bottom; and the earth shook, and
the rocks were split."
2. The religious holiday celebrating the
descent of the Holy Ghost upon
Christ's apostles.

Age-long, reptilian persistence,
Heartthrob, slow heartthrob, persistent for the next spasm.

I remember, when I was a boy,   55
I heard the scream of a frog, which was caught with his foot in
      the mouth of an up-starting snake;
I remember when I first heard bull-frogs break into sound in the
      spring;
I remember hearing a wild goose out of the throat of night
Cry loudly, beyond the lake of waters;
I remember the first time, out of a bush in the darkness, a night-
      ingale's piercing cries and gurgles startled the depths of my
      soul;   60
I remember the scream of a rabbit as I went through a wood at
      midnight;
I remember the heifer in her heat, blorting and blorting through
      the hours, persistent and irrepressible;
I remember my first terror hearing the howl of weird, amorous
      cats;
I remember the scream of a terrified, injured horse, the sheet
      lightning,
And running away from the sound of a woman in labor, some-
      thing like an owl whooing,   65
And listening inwardly to the first bleat of a lamb,
The first wail of an infant,
And my mother singing to herself,
And the first tenor singing of the passionate throat of a young
      collier,[3] who has long since drunk himself to death,
The first elements of foreign speech   70
On wild dark lips.

And more than all these,
And less than all these,
This last,
Strange, faint coition yell   75
Of the male tortoise at extremity,
Tiny from under the very edge of the farthest far-off horizon of
      life.

The cross,
The wheel on which our silence first is broken,
Sex, which breaks up our integrity, our single inviolability, our
      deep silence,   80
Tearing a cry from us.

Sex, which breaks us into voice, sets us calling across the deeps,
      calling, calling for the complement,

3. Coal miner.

Singing, and calling, and singing again, being answered, having
    found.
Torn, to become whole again, after long seeking for what is lost,
The same cry from the tortoise as from Christ, the Osiris-cry[4] of
    abandonment,   85
That which is whole, torn asunder,
That which is in part, finding its whole again throughout the
    universe.

1921

Bavarian Gentians

Not every man has gentians in his house
in Soft September, at slow, Sad Michaelmas.

Bavarian gentians, big and dark, only dark
darkening the daytime torchlike with the smoking blueness of
    Pluto's gloom,[1]
ribbed and torchlike, with their blaze of darkness spread blue   5
down flattening into points, flattened under the sweep of white day
torch-flower of the blue-smoking darkness, Pluto's dark-blue daze,
black lamps from the halls of Dis, burning dark blue,
giving off darkness, blue darkness, as Demeter's pale lamps give off
    light,
lead me then, lead me the way.   10

Reach me a gentian, give me a torch
let me guide myself with the blue, forked torch of this flower
down the darker and darker stairs, where blue is darkened on blue-
    ness.
even where Persephone[2] goes, just now, from the frosted September
to the sightless realm where darkness was awake upon the dark   15
and Persephone herself is but a voice
or a darkness invisible enfolded in the deeper dark
of the arms Plutonic, and pierced with the passion of dense gloom,
among the splendor of torches of darkness, shedding darkness on
    the lost bride and her groom.

1923

---

4. Osiris, the Egyptian vegetation god,
was murdered by his brother Set, who
cut the corpse into 14 pieces and scattered them throughout Egypt; Osiris,
like Christ, was resurrected, and
became an important ruler in the other
world.
1. Pluto was god of the underworld
in classical mythology; he was also
called "Dis" (line 8).
2. Bride of Pluto, who abducted her

from the earth, and daughter of Demeter, goddess of the fruits of the
earth (line 14). She was allowed to
return to earth every spring but had
to descend again to Hades in the autumn, "the frosted September." Demeter and Persephone were central figures in ancient fertility myths, where
Persephone's annual descent and return were linked with the death and
rebirth of vegetation.

Snake

A snake came to my water trough
On a hot, hot day, and I in pajamas for the heat,
To drink there.

In the deep, strange-scented shade of the great dark carob tree
I came down the steps with my pitcher 5
And must wait, must stand and wait, for there he was at the trough
     before me.

He reached down from a fissure in the earth-wall in the gloom
And trailed his yellow-brown slackness soft-bellied down, over the
     edge of the stone trough
And rested his throat upon the stone bottom,
And where the water had dripped from the tap, in a small clear-
     ness, 10
He sipped with his straight mouth,
Softly drank through his straight gums, into his slack long body,
Silently.

Someone was before me at my water trough,
And I, like a second-comer, waiting. 15

He lifted his head from his drinking, as cattle do,
And looked at me vaguely, as drinking cattle do,
And flickered his two-forked tongue from his lips, and mused a
     moment,
And stooped and drank a little more,
Being earth-brown, earth-golden from the burning bowels of the
     earth 20
On the day of Sicilian July, with Etna smoking.

The voice of my education said to me
He must be killed,
For in Sicily the black black snakes are innocent, the gold are veno-
     mous.

And voices in me said, If you were a man 25
You would take a stick and break him now, and finish him off.

But must I confess how I liked him,
How glad I was he had come like a guest in quiet, to drink at my
     water trough
And depart peaceful, pacified, and thankless
Into the burning bowels of this earth? 30

Was it cowardice, that I dared not kill him?
Was it perversity, that I longed to talk to him?
Was it humility, to feel so honored?
I felt so honored.

And yet those voices: 35
If you were not afraid, you would kill him!

And truly I was afraid, I was most afraid,
But even so, honored still more
That he should seek my hospitality
From out the dark door of the secret earth.   40

He drank enough
And lifted his head, dreamily, as one who has drunken,
And flickered his tongue like a forked night on the air, so black,
Seeming to lick his lips,
And looked around like a god, unseeing, into the air,   45
And slowly turned his head,
And slowly, very slowly, as if thrice adream
Proceeded to draw his slow length curving round
And climb the broken bank of my wall-face.

And as he put his head into that dreadful hole,   50
And as he slowly drew up, snake-easing his shoulders, and entered
    further,
A sort of horror, a sort of protest against his withdrawing into that
    horrid black hole,
Deliberately going into the blackness, and slowly drawing himself
    after,
Overcame me now his back was turned.

I looked round, I put down my pitcher,   55
I picked up a clumsy log
And threw it at the water trough with a clatter.

I think it did not hit him;
But suddenly that part of him that was left behind convulsed in un-
    dignified haste,
Writhed like lightning, and was gone   60
Into the black hole, the earth-lipped fissure in the wall-front
At which, in the intense still noon, I stared with fascination.

And immediately I regretted it.
I thought how paltry, how vulgar, what a mean act!
I despised myself and the voices of my accursed human education. 65

And I thought of the albatross,[1]
And I wished he would come back, my snake.

For he seemed to me again like a king,
Like a king in exile, uncrowned in the underworld,
Now due to be crowned again.   70

And so, I missed my chance with one of the lords
Of life.
And I have something to expiate:
A pettiness.

                                                               1923

1. Coleridge's *Ancient Mariner*.

Cypresses[2]

Tuscan cypresses,
What is it?

Folded in like a dark thought
For which the language is lost,
Tuscan cypresses,   5
Is there a great secret?
Are our words no good?

The undeliverable secret,
Dead with a dead race and a dead speech, and yet
Darkly monumental in you,   10
Etruscan cypresses.

Ah, how I admire your fidelity,
Dark cypresses!

Is it the secret of the long-nosed Etruscans?[3]
The long-nosed, sensitive-footed, subtly-smiling Etruscans,   15
Who made so little noise outside the cypress groves?

Among the sinuous, flame-tall cypresses
That swayed their length of darkness all around
Etruscan-dusky, wavering men of old Etruria:
Naked except for fanciful long shoes,   20
Going with insidious, half-smiling quietness
And some of Africa's imperturbable sangfroid
About a forgotten business.

What business, then?
Nay, tongues are dead, and words are hollow as hollow
    seedpods,   25
Having shed their sound and finished all their echoing
Etruscan syllables,
That had the telling.

Yet more I see you darkly concentrate,
Tuscan cypresses,   30
On one old thought:
On one old slim imperishable thought, while you remain

---

2. The cypress is a tall dark evergreen coniferous tree, associated with mourning.

3. The Etruscans were the most important of the pre-Roman inhabitants of Italy; they spread out from their original territory (modern Tuscany, a region in central Italy) to dominate about a third of Italy, but were in their turn conquered by the Romans. Scholars are still uncertain about the precise identity of the Etruscans, and inscriptions in their language have never been deciphered. Lawrence had long been interested in them and in their art.

Etruscan cypresses;
Dusky, slim marrow-thought of slender, flickering men of Etruria,
Whom Rome called vicious.   35

Vicious, dark cypresses:
Vicious, you supple, brooding, softly-swaying pillars of dark flame.
Monumental to a dead, dead race
Embowered in you!

Were they then vicious, the slender, tender-footed   40
Long-nosed men of Etruria?
Or was their way only evasive and different, dark, like cypress
    trees in a wind?

They are dead, with all their vices,
And all that is left
Is the shadowy monomania of some cypresses   45
And tombs.

The smile, the subtle Etruscan smile still lurking
Within the tombs,
Etruscan cypresses.
He laughs longest who laughs last;   50
Nay, Leonardo[4] only bungled the pure Etruscan smile.

What would I not give
To bring back the rare and orchidlike
Evil-yclept Etruscan?
For as to the evil   55
We have only Roman word for it,
Which I, being a little weary of Roman virtue,
Don't hang much weight on.

For oh, I know, in the dust where we have buried
The silenced races and all their abominations,   60
We have buried so much of the delicate magic of life.

There in the deeps
That churn the frankincense and ooze the myrrh,
Cypress shadowy,
Such an aroma of lost human life!   65

They say the fit survive,
But I invoke the spirits of the lost.
Those that have not survived, the darkly lost,
To bring their meaning back into life again,
Which they have taken away   70

4. Leonardo da Vinci (1452–1519) the   as the *Mona Lisa* or *La Gioconda* has
Italian painter, whose portrait known   a famous mysterious smile.

And wrap inviolable in soft cypress trees,
Etruscan cypresses.

Evil, what is evil?
There is only one evil, to deny life
As Rome denied Etruria   75
And mechanical America Montezuma[5] still.

                                                                 1923

How Beastly the Bourgeois Is

How beastly the bourgeois is
especially the male of the species—

Presentable, eminently presentable—
shall I make you a present of him?

Isn't he handsome? Isn't he healthy? Isn't he a fine specimen?   5
Doesn't he look the fresh clean Englishman, outside?
Isn't it God's own image? tramping his thirty miles a day
after partridges, or a little rubber ball?
wouldn't you like to be like that, well off, and quite the thing?

Oh, but wait!   10
Let him meet a new emotion, let him be faced with another
        man's need,
let him come home to a bit of moral difficulty, let life face him
        with a new demand on his understanding
and then watch him go soggy, like a wet meringue.
Watch him turn into a mess, either a fool or a bully.
Just watch the display of him, confronted with a new demand on
        his intelligence,   15
a new life-demand.

How beastly the bourgeois is
especially the male of the species—

Nicely groomed, like a mushroom
standing there so sleek and erect and eyeable—   20
and like a fungus, living on the remains of bygone life
sucking his life out of the dead leaves of greater life than his
        own.

And even so, he's stale, he's been there too long.
Touch him, and you'll find he's all gone inside
just like an old mushroom, all wormy inside, and hollow   25
under a smooth skin and an upright appearance.

---

5. Aztec war chief or "emperor" of   Spanish conquest in the early 16th cen-
ancient Mexico at the time of the   tury.

Full of seething, wormy, hollow feelings
rather nasty—
How beastly the bourgeois is!

Standing in their thousands, these appearances, in damp
    England   30
what a pity they can't all be kicked over
like sickening toadstools, and left to melt back, swiftly
into the soil of England.

                                                 1929

The Ship of Death

1

Now it is autumn and the falling fruit
and the long journey towards oblivion.

The apples falling like great drops of dew
to bruise themselves an exit from themselves.

And it is time to go, to bid farewell   5
to one's own self, and find an exit
from the fallen self.

2

Have you built your ship of death, O have you?
O build your ship of death, for you will need it.

The grim frost is at hand, when the apples will fall   10
thick, almost thundrous, on the hardened earth.

And death is on the air like a smell of ashes!
Ah! can't you smell it?

And in the bruised body, the frightened soul
finds itself shrinking, wincing from the cold   15
that blows upon it through the orifices.

3

And can a man his own quietus make
with a bare bodkin?

With daggers, bodkins, bullets, man can make
a bruise or break of exit for his life;   20
but is that a quietus, O tell me, is it quietus?

Surely not so! for how could murder, even self-murder
ever a quietus make?

4

O let us talk of quiet that we know,
that we can know, the deep and lovely quiet   25
of a strong heart at peace!

How can we this, our own quietus, make?

5

Build then the ship of death, for you must take
the longest journey, to oblivion.

And die the death, the long and painful death   30
that lies between the old self and the new.

Already our bodies are fallen, bruised, badly bruised,
already our souls are oozing through the exit
of the cruel bruise.

Already the dark and endless ocean of the end   35
is washing in through the breaches of our wounds,
already the flood is upon us.

Oh build your ship of death, your little ark
and furnish it with food, with little cakes, and wine
for the dark flight down oblivion.   40

6

Piecemeal the body dies, and the timid soul
has her footing washed away, as the dark flood rises.

We are dying, we are dying, we are all of us dying
and nothing will stay the death-flood rising within us
and soon it will rise on the world, on the outside world.   45

We are dying, we are dying, piecemeal our bodies are
        dying
and our strength leaves us,
and our soul cowers naked in the dark rain over the flood,
cowering in the last branches of the tree of our life.

7

We are dying, we are dying, so all we can do   50
is now to be willing to die, and to build the ship
of death to carry the soul on the longest journey.

A little ship, with oars and food
and little dishes, and all accoutrements
fitting and ready for the departing soul.   55

Now launch the small ship, now as the body dies
and life departs, launch out, the fragile soul
in the fragile ship of courage, the ark of faith
with its store of food and little cooking pans
and change of clothes,   60
upon the flood's back waste
upon the waters of the end
upon the sea of death, where still we sail
darkly, for we cannot steer, and have no port.

There is no port, there is nowhere to go   65
only the deepening blackness darkening still
blacker upon the soundless, ungurgling flood
darkness at one with darkness, up and down

and sideways utterly dark, so there is no direction any
    more
and the little ship is there; yet she is gone.   70
She is not seen, for there is nothing to see her by.
She is gone! gone! and yet
somewhere she is there.
Nowhere!

8

And everything is gone, the body is gone   75
completely under, gone, entirely gone.
The upper darkness is heavy as the lower,
between them the little ship
is gone
It is the end, it is oblivion.

9

And yet out of eternity a thread   80
separates itself on the blackness,
a horizontal thread
that fumes a little with pallor upon the dark.

Is it illusion? or does the pallor fume
A little higher?
Ah wait, wait, for there's the dawn,   85
the cruel dawn of coming back to life
out of oblivion

Wait, wait, the little ship
drifting, beneath the deathly ashy gray
of a flood-dawn.   90

Wait, wait! even so, a flush of yellow
and strangely, O chilled wan soul, a flush of rose.

A flush of rose, and the whole thing starts again.

10

The flood subsides, and the body, like a worn sea-shell
emerges strange and lovely.   95
And the little ship wings home, faltering and lapsing
on the pink flood,
and the frail soul steps out, into her house again
filling the heart with peace.

Swings the heart renewed with peace   100
even of oblivion.

Oh build your ship of death, oh build it!
for you will need it.
For the voyage of oblivion awaits you.

1929–30   1933

EDWIN MUIR
(1887–1959)

Edwin Muir was born on a farm in the Orkney Islands, Scotland, but moved with his family to Glasgow at the age of 14. This move from a simple farming community with deep roots in the past to a large, dirty, industrial city represented a change that haunted his imagination for the rest of his life and which he described vividly in his autobiography, *The Story and the Fable*, 1940. His life in Glasgow was for some years wretched and poverty-stricken. Father, mother, and two brothers died in rapid succession. Muir worked at a variety of jobs in the city—officeboy in a law office, then with an engineering firm, then with a publishing firm, clerk in the office of a beer-bottling factory—before getting a job in a bone factory in Fairport where "except for making a return of the weight of the bones and enduring their stench during the various stages they passed through, I had nothing to do with the stuff out of which the firm ground its profits." Meanwhile he was reading widely and educating himself in both literature and politics. In 1919 he married the novelist and critic Willa Anderson and moved to London. He was by now making his living as a literary journalist on the staff of the periodical *The New Age*. The Muirs lived on the continent for a while, then settled in St. Andrews, still making a precarious living by writing. After World War II Muir was head of the British Council in Prague until the Communists took over Czechoslovakia; he then became Warden of Newbattle Abbey, near Edinburgh. The last few years of his life he spent in a small village near Cambridge.

Muir published his first volume of poems in 1925, and thereafter his poems were to be found regularly (though never in any great number) in periodicals and in nine further slim volumes. He also published several books of criticism, notably *The Structure of the Novel* (1928) and *Scott and Scotland* (1936). He also, with his wife, translated Kafka's novels from the German. It was only on the publication of his last book of poems, *One Foot in Eden* (1956), that more than a small minority of perceptive critics came to recognize his poetic stature. With the posthumous publication of his *Collected Poems* in 1960 his reputation as one of the most original poets of the 20th century was assured.

Muir's range is limited: he was always fascinated by time, by links between generations, by the modern meaning of ancient myths, by the question of identity and change. These interests provide the themes of almost all his poetry. Yet if he had but few themes, the grave precision of his language, the translucent quality of his imagery, the supple, unforced rhythms, and the delicacy of observation and of sensibility that underlies all this, combine to make poetry of remarkable individuality and power. Writing in his autobiography of his first few years in Glasgow, Muir described them as "so stupidly wretched, such a meaningless waste of inherited virtue, that I cannot write of them even now without confused grief and anger." "Inherited virtue" meant much to him, and its waste was to him always a tragedy. For all the sophistication and the knowledge of modern psychology and political theory that Muir acquired, he never ceased to be aware that his roots had been torn from the primitive traditions of Orkney, and he sought to replant these with new ways. He was far from being a rustic escapist or an idealizer of the country life. His poetry is often grim and sometimes nightmarish. But the integrity of feeling, the delicacy and precision of awareness, and the quiet, seemingly effortless, mastery of a supple language that we find in his poetry produce in the end a reassurance. Muir belonged to no modern school and followed no contemporary fashion. Like Graves, but in a very different manner, he found his own way of relating traditional myth to the tensions of modern life.

Troy[1]

He all that time among the sewers of Troy
Scouring for scraps. A man so venerable
He might have been Priam's self, but Priam was dead,
Troy taken. His arms grew meager as a boy's,
And all that flourished in that hollow famine   5
Was his long, white, round beard. Oh, sturdily
He swung his staff and sent the bold rats skipping
Across the scurfy hills and worm-wet valleys,
Crying: "Achilles, Ajax, turn and fight!
Stop cowards!" Till his cries, dazed and confounded,   10
Flew back at him with: "Coward, turn and fight!"
And the wild Greeks yelled round him.
Yet he withstood them, a brave, mad old man,
And fought the rats for Troy. The light was rat-gray,
The hills and dells, the common drain, his Simois,   15
Rat-gray. Mysterious shadows fell
Affrighting him whenever a cloud offended
The sun up in the other world. The rat-hordes,
Moving, were gray dust shifting in gray dust.
Proud history has such sackends. He was taken   20
At last by some chance robber seeking treasure
Under Troy's riven roots. Dragged to the surface.
And there he saw Troy like a burial ground
With tumbled walls for tombs, the smooth sward wrinkled
As Time's last wave had long since passed that way,   25
The sky, the sea, Mount Ida and the islands,
No sail from edge to edge, the Greeks clean gone.
They stretched him on a rock and wrenched his limbs,
Asking: "Where is the treasure?" till he died.

1937

1. Priam was king of Troy at the time it was besieged and finally captured and destroyed by the Greeks. He himself was killed by the victorious Greek army. Achilles (hero of Homer's *Iliad*) and Ajax were Greek heroes in the Trojan War. Simois (line 15) was the river that flowed across the Trojan plain.

The Return

I see myself sometimes, an old old man
Who has walked so long with time as time's true servant,
That he's grown strange to me—who was once myself—
Almost as strange as time, and yet familiar
With old man's staff and legendary cloak,   5
For see, it is I, it is I. And I return
So altered, so adopted, to the house
Of my own life. There all the doors stand open
Perpetually, and the rooms ring with sweet voices,
And there my long life's seasons sound their changes,   10
Childhood and youth and manhood all together,
And welcome waits, and not a room but is
My own, beloved and longed for. And the voices,
Sweeter than any sound dreamt of or known,
Call me, recall me. I draw near at last,   15
An old old man, and scan the ancient walls
Rounded and softened by the compassionate years,
The old and heavy and long-leaved trees that watch
This my inheritance in friendly darkness.
And yet I cannot enter, for all within   20
Rises before me there, rises against me,
A sweet and terrible labyrinth of longing,
So that I turn aside and take the road
That always, early or late, runs on before.

1947, 1949

The Animals

They do not live in the world,
Are not in time and space.
From birth to death hurled
No word do they have, not one
To plant a foot upon,   5
Were never in any place.

For with names the world was called
Out of the empty air,
With names was built and walled,
Line and circle and square,   10
Dust and emerald;
Snatched from deceiving death
By the articulate breath.

But these have never trod
Twice the familiar track,   15
Never never turned back
Into the memoried day.
All is new and near

In the unchanging Here
Of the fifth great day of God,[2]   20
That shall remain the same,
Never shall pass away.

On the sixth day we came.

1949, 1952

Adam's Dream

They say the first dream Adam our father had
After his agelong daydream in the Garden [3]
When heaven and sun woke in his wakening mind,
The earth with all its hills and woods and waters,
The friendly tribes of trees and animals,   5
And earth's last wonder Eve (the first great dream
Which is the ground of every dream since then)—
They say he dreamt lying on the naked ground,
The gates shut fast behind him as he lay
Fallen in Eve's fallen arms, his terror drowned   10
In her engulfing terror, in the abyss
Whence there's no further fall, and comfort is—
That he was standing on a rocky ledge
High on the mountainside, bare crag behind,
In front a plain as far as eye could reach,   15
And on the plain a few small figures running
That were like men and women, yet were so far away
He could not see their faces. On they ran,
And fell, and rose again, and ran, and fell,
And rising were the same yet not the same,   20
Identical or interchangeable,
Different in indifference. As he looked
Still there were more of them, the plain was filling
As by an alien arithmetical magic
Unknown in Eden, a mechanical   25
Addition without meaning, joining only
Number to number in no mode or order,
Weaving no pattern. For these creatures moved
Towards no fixed mark even when in growing bands
They clashed against each other and clashing fell   30
In mounds of bodies. For they rose again,
Identical or interchangeable,
And went their way that was not like a way;

2. God created fish and fowl on the fifth day; then he created the land animals on the sixth day, and after that (still on the sixth day) created man (Genesis i). Muir seems to have put the animals together with the birds and fishes in the fifth day.

3. I.e., after the Fall. After they had eaten of the forbidden Tree of the Knowledge of Good and Evil, Adam and Eve were expelled from the Garden of Eden: Muir here imagines Adam's first dream after the expulsion.

Some back and forward, back and forward, some
In a closed circle, wide or narrow, others   35
In zigzags on the sand. Yet all were busy,
And tense with purpose as they cut the air
Which seemed to press them back. Sometimes they paused
While one stopped one—fortuitous assignations
In the disorder, whereafter two by two   40
They ran awhile,
Then parted and again were single. Some
Ran straight against the frontier of the plain
Till the horizon drove them back. A few
Stood still and never moved. Then Adam cried   45
Out of his dream, "What are you doing there?"
And the crag answered "Are you doing there?"
"What are you doing there?"—"you doing there?"
The animals had withdrawn and from the caves
And woods stared out in fear or condemnation,   50
Like outlaws or like judges. All at once
Dreaming or half-remembering, "This is time,"
Thought Adam in his dream, and time was strange
To one lately in Eden. "I must see,"
He cried, "the faces. Where are the faces? Who   55
Are you all out there?" Then in his changing dream
He was a little nearer, and he saw
They were about some business strange to him
That had a form and sequence past their knowledge;
And that was why they ran so frenziedly.   60
Yet all, it seemed, made up a story, illustrated
By these the living, the unknowing, cast
Each singly for his part. But Adam longed
For more, not this mere moving pattern, not
This illustrated storybook of mankind   65
Always a-making, improvised on nothing.
At that he was among them, and saw each face
Was like his face, so that he would have hailed them
As sons of God but that something restrained him.
And he remembered all, Eden, the Fall,   70
The Promise, and his place, and took their hands
That were his hands, his and his children's hands,
Cried out and was at peace, and turned again
In love and grief in Eve's encircling arms.

1950, 1952

The Horses

Barely a twelvemonth after
The seven days war that put the world to sleep,
Late in the evening the strange horses came.
By then we had made our covenant with silence,

But in the first few days it was so still   5
We listened to our breathing and were afraid.
On the second day
The radios failed; we turned the knobs; no answer.
On the third day a warship passed us, heading north,
Dead bodies piled on the deck. On the sixth day   10
A plane plunged over us into the sea. Thereafter
Nothing. The radios dumb;
And still they stand in corners of our kitchens,
And stand, perhaps, turned on, in a million rooms
All over the world. But now if they should speak,   15
If on a sudden they should speak again,
If on the stroke of noon a voice should speak,
We would not listen, we would not let it bring
That old bad world that swallowed its children quick[4]
At one great gulp. We would not have it again.   20
Sometimes we think of the nations lying asleep,
Curled blindly in impenetrable sorrow,
And then the thought confounds us with its strangeness.
The tractors lie about our fields; at evening
They look like dank sea-monsters couched and waiting.   25
We leave them where they are and let them rust:
"They'll molder away and be like other loam."
We make our oxen drag our rusty plows,
Long laid aside. We have gone back
Far past our fathers' land.
                                And then, that evening   30
Late in the summer the strange horses came.
We heard a distant tapping on the road,
A deepening drumming; it stopped, went on again
And at the corner changed to hollow thunder.
We saw the heads   35
Like a wild wave charging and were afraid.
We had sold our horses in our fathers' time
To buy new tractors. Now they were strange to us
As fabulous steeds set on an ancient shield
Or illustrations in a book of knights.   40
We did not dare go near them. Yet they waited,
Stubborn and shy, as if they had been sent
By an old command to find our whereabouts
And that long-lost archaic companionship.
In the first moment we had never a thought   45
That they were creatures to be owned and used.
Among them were some half a dozen colts
Dropped in some wilderness of the broken world,
Yet new as if they had come from their own Eden.
Since then they have pulled our plows and borne our loads, 50
But that free servitude still can pierce our hearts.
Our life is changed; their coming our beginning.

                                                    1956

4. Alive.

EDITH SITWELL
(1887–1964)

Edith Sitwell and her younger brothers, the poet, essayist, and novelist Osbert and the poet, essayist, and art historian Sacheverel, constituted one of the most extraordinary literary families in the England of their time. Their father was an eccentric English baronet (whose character is brilliantly captured in Osbert's autobiography). Sitwell herself was an eccentrically gifted poet who objected to the subdued rural descriptions and reflections of the Georgian poets and reacted in favor of a highly abstract verbal clowning that exploited the sounds and rhythms and suggestions of words and phrases, often with remarkable pyrotechnic display. She edited and was a substantial contributor to the six "cycles" of *Wheels* (1916–21) in which she displayed her verbal and rhythmic virtuosity and encouraged others to follow her example. Her poem-sequence *Façade* (1922), with its cunning exploration of rhymes and rhythms, was set to music by the composer Sir William Walton, whose intensely sympathetic setting of the words enhanced their impact in a remarkable way. The first performance in January 1922 was a sensation: Sitwell read the poems from behind a screen, and Walton conducted the orchestra.

But Edith Sitwell was more than a juggler of colored balls. There is always a human meaning hinted at, sometimes with mocking laughter, sometimes with anguish, in her poetry, and in her later work she uses her shock tactics to attack the pettiness and philistinism of the life of high society of her time. Her last poems are much concerned with the horrors of war, the varieties of human suffering produced by modern civilization, and the healing powers of a faith in God combined with a sense of the richness and variety of nature. She never found a style in which this later attitude could be fully and distinctively rendered, so that while her last poems remain the most moving and sympathetic in terms of their subject matter, they are often less successful and certainly less exciting than the earlier poems by which she will be best remembered. Edith Sitwell "discovered" the young Dylan Thomas and remained his friend and champion throughout his life.

From Façade

Clowns' Houses

Beneath the flat and paper sky
The sun, a demon's eye,
Glowed through the air, that mask of glass;
All wand'ring sounds that pass

Seemed out of tune, as if the light   5
Were fiddle-strings pulled tight.
The market-square with spire and bell
Clanged out the hour in Hell.

The busy chatter of the heat
Shrilled like a parakeet;   10
And shuddering at the noonday light
The dust lay dead and white

As powder on a mummy's face,
Or fawned with simian grace
Round booths with many a hard bright toy   15
And wooden brittle joy:

The cap and bells of Time the Clown
That, jangling, whistled down,
Young cherubs hidden in the guise
Of every bird that flies;   20

And star-bright masks for youth to wear,
Lest any dream that fare
—Bright pilgrim—past our ken, should see
Hints of Reality.

Upon the sharp-set grass, shrill-green,   25
Tall trees like rattles lean,
And jangle sharp and dizzily;
But when night falls they sigh

Till Pierrot[1] moon steals slyly in,
His face more white than sin,   30
Black-masked, and with cool touch lays bare
Each cherry, plum, and pear.

Then underneath the veiléd eyes
Of houses, darkness lies—
Tall houses; like a hopeless prayer   35
They cleave the sly dumb air.

Blind are those houses, paper-thin;
Old shadows hid therein,
With sly and crazy movements creep
Like marionettes, and weep.   40

Tall windows show Infinity;
And, hard reality,
The candles weep and pry and dance
Like lives mocked at by Chance.

The rooms are vast as Sleep within: 45
When once I ventured in,
Chill Silence, like a surging sea
Slowly enveloped me.

1. Traditional clown character in   and wide pantaloons.
French pantomime, with whitened face

Trio for Two Cats and a Trombone

Long steel grass—
The white soldiers pass—
The light is braying like an ass.
See
The tall Spanish jade   5
With hair black as nightshade
Worn as a cockade!
Flee
Her eyes' gasconade[2]
And her gown's parade,   10
(As stiff as a brigade).
Tee-hee!
The hard and braying light
Is zebra'd black and white
It will take away the slight   15
And free,
Tinge of the mouth-organ sound,
(Oyster-stall notes) oozing round
Her flounces as they sweep the ground.
The   20
Trumpet and the drum
And the martial cornet come
To make the people dumb—
But we
Won't wait for sly-foot night   25
(Moonlight, watered milk-white, bright)
To make clear the declaration
Of our Paphian[3] vocation,
Beside the castanetted sea,
Where stalks Il Capitaneo   30
Swaggart braggadocio
Sword and mustachio—
He
Is green as a cassada[4]
And his hair is an armada.   35
To the jade "Come kiss me harder"
He called across the battlements as she
Heard our voices thin and shrill
As the steely grasses' thrill,
Or the sound of the onycha[5]   40
When the phoca has the pica[6]
In the palace of the Queen Chinee!

2. Extravagant boasting; the natives of Gascony in France had the reputation of being great boasters and braggarts.
3. Amorous; Paphos, the ancient Greek city on Cyprus, was famous for the temple of Aphrodite, the goddess of love.
4. Or cassava, a plant with fleshy tuberous roots; "armada": fleet of ships.
5. The plate which closes the aperture of the shell of a certain species of marine mollusc. Sitwell is apparently thinking of the sound made by blowing into a conch or spiral univalve marine shell.
6. One suspects that Sitwell has chosen these words more for sound than sense: "phoca" is Latin for "seal" (the animal), "Pica" is medieval Latin for magpie.

When Sir Beelzebub

When
Sir
Beelzebub called for his syllabub in the hotel in Hell
       Where Proserpine[7] first fell,
  Blue as the gendarmerie were the waves of the sea,   5

      (Rocking and shocking the barmaid).

Nobody comes to give him his rum but the
Rim of the sky hippopotamus-glum
Enhances the chances to bless with a benison
Alfred Lord Tennyson crossing the bar[8] laid   10
With cold vegetation from pale deputations
Of temperance workers (all signed In Memoriam)
Hoping with glory to trip up the Laureate's feet,

      (Moving in classical meters) . . .

Like Balaclava,[9] the lava came down from the   15
Roof, and the sea's blue wooden gendarmerie
Took them in charge while Beelzebub roared for his rum.

    . . . None of them come!

            1922

The Day Grew Water-Pale and Cool as Eves

    The day grew water-pale and cool as eves. . . .
    A lady sang through water-rippling leaves:

    "The mauve summer rain
    Is falling again—
    It soaks through the eaves   5
    And the ladies' sleeves—
    It soaks through the eaves

    That like silver fish fall
    In the fountains, recall
    Afternoons when I   10
    Was a child small and shy
    In the palace. . . . Fish lie

7. Roman name for the Greek Persephone, carried off by Hades, god of the
underworld, to be his queen there.
8. A reference to Tennyson's poem
Crossing the Bar; there is a reference
two lines further on to the same poet's
In Memoriam (1850—the year he

became poet laureate).
9. Site of a famous battle in the Crimean War (1854); also the name
given to a knitted woolen helmet covering both head and shoulders, worn by
British soldiers on active service from
1892.

On the grass with lives darkling.
Our laughter falls sparkling
As the mauve raindrops bright   15
When they fall through the light
With the briefest delight.

The pavilions float
On the lake like a boat. . . .
Mauve rains from trees fall   20
Like wisteria flowers . . . all
My life is like this
And drifts into nothingness!

The strange ladies sigh
'The autumn is nigh' . . .   25
The King bows and mutters. . . .
His eyelids seem shutters
Of a palace pavilion
Deserted a million

Echoing years ago.   30

Oh, but the rain falls slow."

1924

The Poet Laments the Coming of Old Age

I see the children running out of school;
They are taught that Goodness means a blinding hood
Or is heaped by Time like the hump on an agéd back,
And that Evil can be cast like an old rag
And Wisdom caught like a hare and held in the golden sack   5
Of the heart. . . . But I am one who must bring back sight to the
    blind.

Yet there was a planet dancing in my mind
With a gold seed of Folly . . . long ago. . . .
And where is that grain of Folly? . . . with the hare-wild wind
Of my spring it has gone from one who must bring back sight to
    the blind.   10

For I, the fool, was once like the philosopher
Sun who laughs at evil and at good:
I saw great things mirrored in littleness,
Who now see only that great Venus wears Time's filthy dress—
A toothless crone who once had the Lion's mouth.   15

The Gold Appearances from Nothing rise
In sleep, by day[1] . . . two thousand years ago
There was a man who had the Lion's leap,
Like the Sun's, to take the worlds and loves he would,
But (laughed the philosopher Sun, and I, the fool)   20

Great golden Alexander[2] and his thunder-store
Are now no more
Than the armored knight who buzzed on the windowpane
And the first drops of rain.

He lies in sleep. . . . But still beneath a thatch   25
Of hair like sunburnt grass, the thieving sweet thoughts move
Toward the honey-hive. . . . And another sweet-tooth Alexander
     runs
Out of the giant shade that is his school,
To take the dark knight's world, the honeycomb.

The Sun's simulacrum, the gold-sinewed man   30
Lies under a hump of grass, as once I thought to wear
With patience, Goodness like a hump on my agéd back.
. . . But Goodness grew not with age, although my heart must
     bear
The weight of all Time's filth, and Wisdom is not a hare in the
     golden sack

Of the heart. . . . It can never be caught. Though I bring back
     sight to the blind   35
My seed of Folly has gone, that could teach me to bear
That the gold-sinewed body that had the blood of all the earth
     in its veins
Has changed to an old rag of the outworn world
And the great heart that the first Morning made
Should wear all Time's destruction for a dress.   40

                                                                    1945

---

1. "This is a reference to a passage in Plato's *The Sophist*" [Sitwell's note]. Plato's dialogue *The Sophist* discusses the question of "being" and "not-being": "If the name is distinguished from the thing, that supposes two things * * * And yet he who identifies the name with the thing will be com-pelled to say that the name is of nothing, or if he says that the name is of something, then the name will be the name of a name, and of nothing else." 2. Alexander the Great (356–23 B.C.), king of Macedonia and conqueror of the Persian empire.

T. S. ELIOT
(1888–1965)

1915: Settles in London.
1917: *Prufrock and Other Observations.*
1922: *The Waste Land.*
1927: Becomes British subject; confirmed in Anglican Church.
1944: *Four Quartets.*

Thomas Stearns Eliot was born in St. Louis, Missouri, of New England stock. He entered Harvard in 1906, and was influenced there by the anti-romanticism of Irving Babbitt and the philosophical and critical interests of George Santayana, as well as by the enthusiasm that prevailed in certain Harvard circles for Elizabethan and Jacobean literature, the Italian Renaissance, and Indian mystical philosophy. His philosophical studies included intensive work on the English idealist philosopher F. H. Bradley, on whom he eventually wrote his Harvard dissertation. (Bradley's emphasis on the private nature of individual experience, "a circle enclosed on the outside," had considerable influence on the private imagery of Eliot's poetry and on the view of the relation between the individual and other individuals reflected in much of his poetry.) Later Eliot studied literature and philosophy in France and Germany, before going to England shortly after the outbreak of World War I in 1914. He studied Greek philosophy at Oxford, taught school in London, and then obtained a position with Lloyd's Bank which he held until 1925, when he joined the London publishing firm of Faber and Gwyer, becoming a director when the firm became Faber and Faber in 1929.

Eliot started writing literary and philosophical reviews soon after settling in London. He wrote for the *Athenaeum* and the *Times Literary Supplement*, among other periodicals, and was assistant editor of the *Egoist* from 1917 to 1919. In 1922 he founded the influential quarterly, the *Criterion*, which he edited until it ceased publication in 1939. His poetry first appeared in 1915, when *The Love Song of J. Alfred Prufrock* was printed in *Poetry* magazine (Chicago) and a few other short poems were published in the short-lived periodical, *Blast*. His first published collection of poems was *Prufrock and Other Observations*, 1917; two other small collections followed in 1919 and 1920; in 1922 *The Waste Land* appeared, first in the *Criterion* in October, then in the *Dial* (in America) in November, and finally in book form. *Poems 1909–25* (1925) collected these earlier poems. Meanwhile he was also publishing collections of his critical essays, notably *The Sacred Wood* in 1920 and *Homage to John Dryden* in 1924. *For Lancelot Andrewes* followed in 1928 and in 1932 he included most of these earlier essays with some new ones in *Selected Essays*. Eliot became a British subject and joined the Church of England in 1927.

"Our civilization comprehends great variety and complexity, and this variety and complexity, playing upon a refined sensibility, must produce various and complex results. The poet must become more and more com-

2256 · *T. S. Eliot*

prehensive, more allusive, more indirect, in order to force, to dislocate if necessary, language into his meaning." This remark, from Eliot's essay on *The Metaphysical Poets* (1921), gives one clue to his poetic method from *Prufrock* through *The Waste Land*. In the attenuated romantic tradition of the Georgian poets who were active when he settled in London, in their quietly meditative pastoralism, faded exoticism, or self-consciously realistic descriptions of urban life, he saw an exhausted poetic mode being employed, with no verbal excitement or original craftsmanship. He sought to make poetry more subtle, more suggestive, and at the same time more precise. He had learned from the Imagists the necessity of clear and precise images, and he learned, too, from T. E. Hulme and from his early supporter and adviser Ezra Pound to fear romantic softness and to regard the poetic medium rather than the poet's personality as the important factor. At the same time, the "hard dry" images advocated by Hulme were not enough for him; he wanted wit, allusiveness, irony. He saw in the metaphysical poets how wit and passion could be combined, and he saw in the French Symbolists how an image could be both absolutely precise in what it referred to physically and at the same time endlessly suggestive in the meanings it set up because of its relationship to other images. The combination of precision, symbolic suggestion, and ironic mockery in the poetry of the late 19th-century French poet Jules Laforgue attracted and influenced him, and he was influenced too by other 19th-century French poets: by Théophile Gautier's artful carving of impersonal shapes of meaning; by Charles Baudelaire's strangely evocative explorations of the symbolic suggestions of objects and images; by the Symbolist poets Paul Verlaine, Arthur Rimbaud, and Stéphane Mallarmé. He also found in the Jacobean dramatists a flexible blank verse with overtones of colloquial movement: Middleton, Tourneur, Webster, and others, taught him as much—in the way of verse movement, imagery, the counterpointing of the accent of conversation and the note of terror—as either the metaphysicals or the French Symbolists.

Hulme's protests against the romantic concept of poetry fitted in well enough with what Eliot had learned from Irving Babbitt at Harvard; yet for all his severity with such poets as Shelley, for all his conscious cultivation of a classical viewpoint and his insistence on order and discipline rather than on mere self-expression in art, one side of Eliot's poetic genius is, in one sense of the word, romantic. The Symbolist influence on his imagery, his interest in the evocative and the suggestive, such lines as "And fiddled whisper music on those strings / And bats with baby faces in the violet light / Whistled, and beat their wings," and such recurring images as the hyacinth girl and the rose garden, all show what could be called a romantic element in his poetry. But it is combined with a dry ironic allusiveness, a play of wit, and a colloquial element, which are not normally found in poets of the romantic tradition.

Eliot's real novelty—and the cause of much bewilderment when his poems first appeared—was his deliberate elimination of all merely connective and transitional passages, his building up of the total pattern of meaning through the immediate juxtaposition of images without overt explanation of what they are doing, together with his use of oblique references to other works of literature (some of them quite obscure to most contemporary readers). *Prufrock* presents a symbolic landscape where the meaning emerges from the mutual interaction of the images, and that meaning is enlarged by echoes, often ironic, of Hesiod and Dante and Shakespeare. *The Waste Land* is a series of scenes and images with no author's voice intervening to tell us where we are, but with the implications developed through multiple contrasts and through analogies with older literary works often referred to in a distorted quotation or half-concealed allusion. Further, the works referred to are not necessarily works which are central in the Western literary tradition: besides Dante and Shakespeare there are pre-Socratic philosophers, minor (as well as major) 17th-century poets and dramatists, works of anthropology, history, and philosophy, and other echoes of the poet's private reading. In a culture where there is no longer any assurance on the part of the poet that his public has a common cultural heritage, a common knowledge of works of the past, Eliot felt it necessary to build up his own body of references. It is this which marks the difference between Eliot's use of earlier literature and, say, Milton's. Both poets are difficult to the modern reader, who needs editorial assistance in recognizing and understanding many of the allusions—but Milton was drawing on a body of knowledge common to educated men in his day. Nevertheless, this aspect of Eliot can be exaggerated: the fact remains that the nature of his imagery together with the movement of his verse generally succeed in setting the tone he requires, in establishing the area of meaning to be developed, so that even a reader ignorant of most of the literary allusions can often get the "feel" of the poem and achieve some understanding of what it says.

Eliot's early poetry, until at least the middle 1920's, is mostly concerned in one way or another with the Waste Land, with aspects of the decay of culture in the modern Western world. After his formal acceptance of Anglican Christianity we find a penitential note in much of his verse, a note of quiet searching for spiritual peace, with considerable allusion to Biblical, liturgical, and mystical religious literature and to Dante. *Ash Wednesday* (1930), a poem in six parts, much less fiercely concentrated in style than the earlier poetry, explores with gentle insistence a mood both penitential and questioning. The so-called "Ariel" poems (the title is accidental, and has nothing to do with their form or content) present or explore aspects of religious doubt or discovery or revelation, sometimes, as in *Marina*, using a purely secular imagery and sometimes, as in *Journey of the Magi*, drawing on Biblical incident. In *Four Quartets* (of which the first, *Burnt Norton*, appeared in the *Collected Poems* of 1935, though all four were not completed until 1943, when they were published together) Eliot further explored essentially religious moods, dealing with the relation between time and eternity and the cultivation of that selfless passivity which can yield the moment of timeless revelation in the midst of time. The mocking irony, the savage humor, the deliberately startling juxtaposition of the sordid and the romantic, give way in these later poems to a quieter poetic idiom, often still complexly allusive but never deliberately shocking.

Eliot's criticism was the criticism of a practicing poet who worked out in relation to his reading of older literature what he needed to hold and to admire. He lent the growing weight of his authority to that shift in literary taste that replaced Milton by Donne as the great 17th-century English poet, and replaced Tennyson in the 19th century by Hopkins. His often-quoted description of the late 17th-century "dissociation of sensibility"—keeping wit and passion in separate compartments—which he saw as determining the course of English poetry throughout the 18th and 19th centuries, is both a contribution to the rewriting of English literary history and an explanation of what he was aiming at in his own poetry: the re-establishment of that *unified* sensibility he found in Donne and other early 17th-century poets and dramatists. His view of tradition, his dislike of the poetic exploitation of the author's own personality, his advocacy of what he called "orthodoxy," made him suspicious of what he considered eccentric geniuses such as Blake and D. H. Lawrence. On the other side, his dislike of the grandiloquent and his insistence on complexity and on the mingling of the formal with the conversational made him distrustful of the influence of Milton on English poetry. He considered himself "classicist in literature, royalist in politics, and Anglo-Catholic in religion" (*For Lancelot Andrewes*, 1928), in favor of order against chaos, tradition against eccentricity, authority against rampant individualism; yet his own poetry is in many respects untraditional and certainly highly individual in tone. His conservative and even authoritarian habit of mind has alienated some who admire—and some whose own poetry has been much influenced by—his poetry.

Eliot's plays have all been, directly or indirectly, on religious themes. *Murder in the Cathedral* (1935) deals with the murder of Archbishop Thomas à Becket in an appropriately ritual manner, with much use of a chorus and with the central speech in the form of a sermon by the archbishop in his cathedral shortly before his murder. *The Family Reunion* (1939) deals with the problem of guilt and redemption in a modern upper-class English family; it makes a deliberate attempt to combine choric devices from Greek tragedy with a poetic idiom subdued to the accents of drawing-room conversation. In his three later plays, all written in the 1950's, *The Cocktail Party*, *The Confidential Clerk*, and *The Elder Statesman*, he achieved popular success by casting a serious religious theme in the form of a sophisticated modern social comedy, using a verse that is so conversational in movement that when spoken in the theater it does not sound like verse at all.

Critics differ on the degree to which Eliot succeeded in his last plays in combining box-office success with dramatic effectiveness. But there is no disagreement on his importance as one of the great renovators of the English poetic dialect, whose influence on a whole generation of poets, critics, and intellectuals generally was enormous. His range as a poet is limited, and his interest in the great middle ground of human experience (as distinct from the extremes of saint and sinner) deficient: but when in 1948 he was awarded the rare honor of the Order of Merit by King George VI and also gained the Nobel Prize in literature, his positive qualities were widely and fully recognized—his poetic cunning, his fine craftsmanship, his original accent, his historical and representative importance as *the* poet of the modern Symbolist-metaphysical tradition.

The Love Song of J. Alfred Prufrock[1]

*S'io credesse che mia risposta fosse
A persona che mai tornasse al mondo,
Questa fiamma staria senza piu scosse.
Ma perciocche giammai di questo fondo
Non torno vivo alcun, s'i'odo il vero,
Senza tema d'infamia ti rispondo.*[2]

Let us go then, you and I,
When the evening is spread out against the sky
Like a patient etherized[3] upon a table;
Let us go, through certain half-deserted streets,
The muttering retreats   5
Of restless nights in one-night cheap hotels
And sawdust restaurants with oyster shells:
Streets that follow like a tedious argument
Of insidious intent
To lead you to an overwhelming question . . .   10
Oh, do not ask, "What is it?"
Let us go and make our visit.

In the room the women come and go
Talking of Michelangelo.

The yellow fog that rubs its back upon the windowpanes,   15
The yellow smoke that rubs its muzzle on the windowpanes
Licked its tongue into the corners of the evening,
Lingered upon the pools that stand in drains,
Let fall upon its back the soot that falls from chimneys,
Slipped by the terrace, made a sudden leap,   20

1. A dramatic monologue in which the speaker builds up a mood of social futility and inadequacy through the thoughts and images which haunt his consciousness and by means of the symbolic landscape in which he moves. The title implies an ironic contrast between the romantic suggestions of "love song" and the dully prosaic name, "J. Alfred Prufrock." The quotation from Dante's *Inferno* which stands at the head of the poem adds to this contrast a note of profound hopelessness. Prufrock himself, middle-aged and unhappy, is not really at home in the society in which he is condemned to live; he is aware of the futility of such visits as he is paying, of his own awkwardness and maladjustment, and his self-conscious response to the demands made on him. He is haunted not only by a knowledge of the pettiness and triviality of this world, but also by a sense of his own sexual inadequacy and a feeling that once, somewhere, he had had a vision of a life more real and

more beautiful, but that he has long since strayed from that reality to the artificial and barren existence in which he now suffocates. The lost dreamworld was paradoxically the only real world, man's true element, and out of it he drowns.
2. "If I thought that my reply would be to one who would ever return to the world, this flame would stay without further movement; but since none has ever returned alive from this depth, if what I hear is true, I answer you without fear of infamy." Dante, *Inferno* XXVII.61–66. Guido da Montefeltro, shut up in his flame (the punishment given to false counselors), tells the shame of his evil life to Dante because he believes Dante will never return to earth to report it.
3. A contrast is perhaps here implied between "ether" as the free sky or the heavens and the word's medical connotations—helplessness, disease, the elimination of consciousness and personality.

And seeing that it was a soft October night,
Curled once about the house, and fell asleep.

And indeed there will be time[4]
For the yellow smoke that slides along the street,
Rubbing its back upon the windowpanes;
There will be time, there will be time
To prepare a face to meet the faces that you meet;
There will be time to murder and create,
And time for all the works and days of hands[5]
That lift and drop a question on your plate;
Time for you and time for me,
And time yet for a hundred indecisions,
And for a hundred visions and revisions,
Before the taking of a toast and tea.

In the room the women come and go
Talking of Michelangelo.

And indeed there will be time
To wonder, "Do I dare?" and, "Do I dare?"
Time to turn back and descend the stair,
With a bald spot in the middle of my hair—
(They will say: "How his hair is growing thin!")
My morning coat, my collar mounting firmly to the chin,
My necktie rich and modest, but asserted by a simple pin—
(They will say: "But how his arms and legs are thin!")
Do I dare
Disturb the universe?
In a minute there is time
For decisions and revisions which a minute will reverse.

For I have known them all already, known them all—
Have known the evenings, mornings, afternoons,
I have measured out my life with coffee spoons;
I know the voices dying with a dying fall[6]
Beneath the music from a farther room.
    So how should I presume?

And I have known the eyes already, known them all—
The eyes that fix you in a formulated phrase,
And when I am formulated, sprawling on a pin,
When I am pinned and wriggling on the wall,
Then how should I begin
To spit out all the butt-ends of my days and ways?
    And how should I presume?

And I have known the arms already, known them all—
Arms that are braceleted and white and bare

---

4. Cf. Andrew Marvell's *To His Coy Mistress*: "Had we but world enough and time * * *"
5. *Works and Days* is a poem about the farming year by Hesiod, Greek poet of 8th century B.C. Eliot's contrast is between useful agricultural labor and the futile "works and days of hands" engaged in meaningless social gesturing.
6. Ironic recollection of Orsino's speech in *Twelfth Night* (I.i.4): "That strain again! It had a dying fall."

(But in the lamplight, downed with light brown hair!)
Is it perfume from a dress   65
That makes me so digress?
Arms that lie along a table, or wrap about a shawl.
　　And should I then presume?
　　And how should I begin?

· · · ·

Shall I say, I have gone at dusk through narrow streets   70
And watched the smoke that rises from the pipes
Of lonely men in shirt-sleeves, leaning out of windows? . . .

I should have been a pair of ragged claws
Scuttling across the floors of silent seas.[7]

· · · ·

And the afternoon, the evening, sleeps so peacefully!   75
Smoothed by long fingers,
Asleep . . . tired . . . or it malingers,
Stretched on the floor, here beside you and me.
Should I, after tea and cakes and ices,
Have the strength to force the moment to its crisis?   80
But though I have wept and fasted, wept and prayed,
Though I have seen my head (grown slightly bald) brought in upon
　　a platter,[8]
I am no prophet—and here's no great matter;
I have seen the moment of my greatness flicker,
And I have seen the eternal Footman hold my coat, and snicker,   85
And in short, I was afraid.

And would it have been worth it, after all,
After the cups, the marmalade, the tea,
Among the porcelain, among some talk of you and me,
Would it have been worth while,   90
To have bitten off the matter with a smile,
To have squeezed the universe into a ball
To roll it toward some overwhelming question,
To say: "I am Lazarus,[9] come from the dead,
Come back to tell you all, I shall tell you all"—   95
If one, settling a pillow by her head,
　　Should say: "That is not what I meant at all.
　　That is not it, at all."

And would it have been worth it, after all,
Would it have been worth while,   100
After the sunsets and the dooryards and the sprinkled streets,

7. I.e., he would have been better as a
crab on the ocean bed. Perhaps, too, the
motion of a crab suggests futility and
growing old; cf. *Hamlet* II.ii.205–6:
"for you yourself, sir, should be old as
I am, if, like a crab, you could go backward."

8. Like that of John the Baptist. See
Mark vi.17–28 and Matthew xiv.3–11.
9. Cf. Luke xvi.19–31 and John xi.1–
44.

After the novels, after the teacups, after the skirts that trail along
    the floor—
And this, and so much more?—
It is impossible to say just what I mean!
But as if a magic lantern threw the nerves in patterns on a
    screen: 105
Would it have been worth while
If one, settling a pillow or throwing off a shawl,
And turning toward the window, should say:
    "That is not it at all,
    That is not what I meant, at all."   110

                              . . . .

No! I am not Prince Hamlet, nor was meant to be;
Am an attendant lord, one that will do
To swell a progress,[1] start a scene or two,
Advise the prince; no doubt, an easy tool,
Deferential, glad to be of use,   115
Politic, cautious, and meticulous;
Full of high sentence,[2] but a bit obtuse;
At times, indeed, almost ridiculous—
Almost, at times, the Fool.

I grow old . . . I grow old . . .   120
I shall wear the bottoms of my trousers rolled.

Shall I part my hair behind? Do I dare to eat a peach?
I shall wear white flannel trousers, and walk upon the beach.
I have heard the mermaids singing, each to each.

I do not think that they will sing to me.   125

I have seen them riding seaward on the waves
Combing the white hair of the waves blown back
When the wind blows the water white and black.

We have lingered in the chambers of the sea
By sea-girls wreathed with seaweed red and brown   130
Till human voices wake us, and we drown.
1910–11   1915, 1917

From Landscapes[3]
Rannoch, by Glencoe[4]

Here the crow starves, here the patient stag
Breeds for the rifle. Between the soft moor

1. In the Elizabethan sense of a state
journey made by a royal or noble person. Elizabethan plays sometimes
showed such "progresses" crossing the
stage.
2. In its older meanings, "opinions,"

"sententiousness."
3. Under this title Eliot grouped five
short poems, each dealing with a specific
place. The last two are reprinted here.
4. In Scotland.

And the soft sky, scarcely room
To leap or soar. Substance crumbles, in the thin air
Moon cold or moon hot. The road winds in   5
Listlessness of ancient war
Languor of broken steel,
Clamor of confused wrong, apt
In silence. Memory is strong
Beyond the bone. Pride snapped,   10
Shadow of pride is long, in the long pass
No concurrence of bone.

Cape Ann⁵

O quick quick quick, quick hear the song sparrow,
Swamp sparrow, fox sparrow, vesper sparrow
At dawn and dusk. Follow the dance
Of the goldfinch at noon. Leave to chance
The Blackburnian warbler, the shy one. Hail   5
With shrill whistle the note of the quail, the bobwhite
Dodging by baybush. Follow the feet
Of the walker, the water thrush. Follow the flight
Of the dancing arrow, the purple martin. Greet
In silence the bullbat. All are delectable. Sweet sweet sweet   10
But resign this land at the end, resign it
To its true owner, the tough one, the sea gull.
The palaver is finished.

1933–34   1936

Sweeney among the Nightingales¹

ὤμοι, πέπληγμαι καιρίαν πληγὴν ἔσω.²

Apeneck Sweeney spreads his knees
Letting his arms hang down to laugh,
The zebra stripes along his jaw
Swelling to maculate³ giraffe

5. On the northern coast of Massachusetts, not far from the New Hampshire border; a wilderness area in the middle of the cape is inhabited by the birds Eliot here describes.
1. This poem shows Eliot's characteristic method of presenting his meaning through multiple parallels and contrasts. Lust, cruelty, and violence have always existed in the world; but in heroic periods of history they have sprung from grand passions of love or hate and have later been embodied in meaningful myths. The nightingale, in Greek myth, was the symbol of the transformation of human lust into art: Philomela, having been ravished and had her tongue cut out by her sister's husband Tereus, was turned into a nightingale and sings eternally. The horrors of Agamemnon's murder are similarly subsumed in the search for and achievement of divine justice (cf. Aeschylus' dramatic trilogy, the *Oresteia*). But the shabby animality of Sweeney and his drunken lady friend (significantly anonymous), frolicking lewdly in a restaurant, is unrelieved by any such transmutation. In Sweeney's world violence is limited to overturning a coffee cup and tearing at grapes, and lust has become only a "gambit," easily "declined."
2. "Alas, I am struck with a mortal blow within" (Aeschylus, *Agamemnon*, line 1343). The voice of Agamemnon heard crying out from the palace as he is murdered by his wife Clytemnestra.
3. Spotted, stained.

The circles of the stormy moon   5
Slide westward toward the River Plate,[4]
Death and the Raven drift above
And Sweeney guards the hornéd gate.[5]

Gloomy Orion and the Dog
Are veiled;[6] and hushed the shrunken seas;   10
The person in the Spanish cape
Tries to sit on Sweeney's knees

Slips and pulls the tablecloth
Overturns a coffee cup,
Reorganized upon the floor   15
She yawns and draws a stocking up;

The silent man in mocha brown
Sprawls at the window sill and gapes;
The waiter brings in oranges
Bananas figs and hothouse grapes;   20

The silent vertebrate in brown
Contracts and concentrates, withdraws;
Rachel *née* Rabinovitch
Tears at the grapes with murderous paws;

She and the lady in the cape   25
Are suspect, thought to be in league;
Therefore the man with heavy eyes
Declines the gambit, shows fatigue,

Leaves the room and reappears
Outside the window, leaning in,   30
Branches of wistaria
Circumscribe a golden grin;

The host with someone indistinct
Converses at the door apart,
The nightingales are singing near   35
The Convent of the Sacred Heart,

And sang within the bloody wood
When Agamemnon cried aloud,[7]
And let their liquid siftings fall
To stain the stiff dishonored shroud.   40

1918, 1919

4. Estuary on South American coast between Argentina and Uruguay, formed by the Uruguay and Paraná rivers.
5. The gates of horn, in Hades, through which true dreams come to the upper world.
6. "Orion" and the "Dog" are the constellations. For Sweeney and his friend, the gate of vision is blocked and the great mythmaking constellations are "veiled."
7. Agamemnon was not murdered in a "bloody wood," but in his bath. Eliot is here telescoping Agamemnon's murder with the wood where Philomela was ravished and also with the "bloody wood" of Nemi, where, in ancient times, the old priest was slain by his successor (as described in the first chapter of Sir James Frazer's *Golden Bough*). The great myths of regeneration represented by this ritual slaying are meaningless for Sweeney and his friends, as are the song of the nightingales and the spiritual reality represented by the Convent of the Sacred Heart.

Whispers of Immortality[1]

Webster[2] was much possessed by death
And saw the skull beneath the skin;
And breastless creatures under ground
Leaned backward with a lipless grin.

Daffodil bulbs instead of balls   5
Stared from the sockets of the eyes!
He knew that thought clings round dead limbs
Tightening its lusts and luxuries.

Donne,[3] I suppose, was such another
Who found no substitute for sense,   10
To seize and clutch and penetrate;
Expert beyond experience,

He knew the anguish of the marrow
The ague of the skeleton;
No contact possible to flesh   15
Allayed the fever of the bone.

    ·   ·   ·   ·

Grishkin is nice: her Russian eye
Is underlined for emphasis;
Uncorseted, her friendly bust
Gives promise of pneumatic bliss.   20

The couched Brazilian jaguar
Compels the scampering marmoset
With subtle effluence of cat;
Grishkin has a maisonette;

The sleek Brazilian jaguar   25
Does not in its arboreal gloom
Distil so rank a feline smell
As Grishkin in a drawing room.

And even the Abstract Entities
Circumambulate her charm;   30
But our lot crawls between dry ribs
To keep our metaphysics warm.

1918, 1919

---

1. The effects are here again achieved
by contrasts and parallels. The Elizabethan and Jacobean poets and dramatists were obsessed by death and suffered the anguish of those for whom all
knowledge comes through the senses but
who know that the senses, doomed to
decay, cannot satisfy the ultimate longings. By contrast Grishkin, high-class
prostitute, is wholly committed to the
flesh, like an animal; even abstract philosophy is seduced by her charms.
2. John Webster, Jacobean dramatist,
author of *The Duchess of Malfi* and
The White Devil.
3. The poet John Donne (1572–1631).

The Waste Land

is a poem about spiritual dryness, about the kind of existence in which no regenerating belief gives significance and value to men's daily activities, sex brings no fruitfulness, and death heralds no resurrection. Eliot himself gives one of the main clues to the theme and structure of the poem in a general note, in which he stated that "not only the title, but the plan and a good deal of the symbolism of the poem were suggested by Miss Jessie L. Weston's book on the Grail legend: *From Ritual to Romance*" (1920). He further acknowledged a general indebtedness to Sir James Frazer's *Golden Bough* (12 volumes, 1890–1915), "especially the two volumes *Adonis, Attis, Osiris*," in which Frazer deals with ancient vegetation myths and fertility ceremonies. Miss Weston's study, drawing on material from Frazer and other anthropologists, traced the relationship of these myths and rituals to Christianity and most especially to the legend of the Holy Grail. She found an archetypal fertility myth in the story of the Fisher King whose death, infirmity, or impotence (there are many forms of the myth) brought drought and desolation to the land and failure of the power to reproduce themselves among both men and beasts. This symbolic Waste Land can be revived only if a "questing knight" goes to the Chapel Perilous, situated in the heart of it, and there asks certain ritual questions about the Grail (or Cup) and the Lance—originally fertility symbols, female and male respectively. The proper asking of these questions revives the king and restores fertility to the land. The relation of this original Grail myth to fertility cults and rituals found in many different civilizations, and represented by stories of a dying god who is later resurrected (e.g., Tammuz, Adonis, Attis), shows their common origin in a response to the cyclical movement of the seasons, with vegetation dying in winter to be resurrected again in the spring. Christianity, according to Miss Weston, gave its own spiritual meaning to the myth; it "did not hesitate to utilize the already existing medium of instruction, but boldly identified the Deity of Vegetation, regarded as Life Principle, with the God of the Christian Faith." The Fisher King is related to the use of the fish symbol in early Christianity. Miss Weston states "with certainty that the Fish is a Life symbol of immemorial antiquity, and that the title of Fisher has, from the earliest ages, been associated with the Deities who were held to be specially connected with the origin and preservation of Life." Eliot, following Miss Weston, thus uses a great variety of mythological and religious material, both occidental and oriental, in order to paint a symbolic picture of the modern Waste Land and the need for regeneration. The terror of that life—its loneliness, emptiness, and irrational apprehensions—as well as its misuse of sexuality are vividly presented, but, paradoxically, the poem ends with a benediction. Another significant general source for the poem is the composer Richard Wagner, some of whose operas (*Götterdämmerung* ["Twilight of the Gods"], *Parsifal, Rheingold*, and *Tristan and Isolde*) are drawn on.

The poem as published owed a great deal to the severe pruning of Ezra Pound; recently the original manuscript, with Pound's excisions and comments, has turned up, providing fascinating information about the genesis and development of the poem. It was reproduced in facsimile in 1971, edited by Eliot's widow Valerie Eliot, who also supplied notes supplementing those that Eliot himself added when the poem was first published in book form in 1922 and which are included with the present editor's footnotes to the poem.

The Waste Land

"Nam Sibyllam quidem Cumis ego ipse oculis meis vidi in ampulla pendere, et cum illi pueri dicerent: Σίβυλλα τί θέλεις; respondebat illa: ἀποθανεῖν θέλω."[1]

FOR EZRA POUND[2]

il miglior fabbro

I. The Burial of the Dead[3]

April is the cruelest month, breeding
Lilacs out of the dead land, mixing
Memory and desire, stirring
Dull roots with spring rain.
Winter kept us warm, covering   5
Earth in forgetful snow, feeding
A little life with dried tubers.
Summer surprised us, coming over the Starnbergersee[4]
With a shower of rain; we stopped in the colonnade,
And went on in sunlight, into the Hofgarten,[5]   10
And drank coffee, and talked for an hour.
Bin gar keine Russin, stamm' aus Litauen, echt deutsch.[6]
And when we were children, staying at the archduke's,

1. From the *Satyricon* of Petronius (1st century A.D.): "For once I myself saw with my own eyes the Sibyl at Cumae hanging in a cage, and when the boys said to her 'Sibyl, what do you want?' she replied, 'I want to die.'" The Cumaean Sibyl was the most famous of the Sibyls, the prophetic old women of Greek mythology: she guided Aeneas through Hades in the *Aeneid*. She had been granted immortality by Apollo, but since she forgot to ask for perpetual youth, she shrank into withered old age and her authority declined. Cf. other prophets in the poem: Madame Sosostris and Tiresias.
2. Ezra Pound (1885–), the American expatriate poet who was a key figure in the modern movement in poetry, helped Eliot with the final revisions. *"Il miglior fabbro"* (i.e., the better craftsman) was a tribute originally paid to the Provencal poet Arnaut Daniel in Dante's *Purgatorio* XXVI.117.
3. The title comes from the Anglican burial service. April is the cruelest month because it brings no true renewal but instead tortures us with vain recollections. The seasons as they are here described do not form part of a living cycle; the people whose chatter we hear in international holiday resorts do not wish a really new life, and April is thus cruel in another sense because it suggests resurrection to those who do not wish it. With a sudden shift in tone the voice becomes suggestive of the prophet Ezekiel announcing the dryness and hopeless fragmentation of civilization; then this voice gives way to songs of romantic passion and memories of lost opportunities for love. We next see the mysteries of ancient religion transformed into fashionable fortune-telling by a fake Egyptian clairvoyante; the elemental symbols of the ancient Tarot pack of cards have degenerated into a trickster's patter (but still immensely evocative, and with each character in the pack related to themes to be developed later in the poem). Then the vision changes to a more direct picture of modern civilization: Baudelaire's Paris, modern London, Dante's Limbo, all three seen as really the same; the feverish speaker turns the great resurrection ritual into a mad and sinister question about gardening; and the author rounds on the reader to insist that he see himself in the same situation.
4. Lake near Munich. The scene in this and the following eight lines, which evokes European decadence before World War I, seems to have been suggested by an autobiographical work by Countess Marie Larisch, *My Past* (London, 1913), but Valerie Eliot says that Eliot had never read the book and got his information from the Countess directly, in conversations with her.
5. A small public park in Munich.
6. "I am not Russian at all; I come from Lithuania, a true German."

My cousin's, he took me out on a sled,
And I was frightened. He said, Marie,   15
Marie, hold on tight. And down we went.
In the mountains, there you feel free.
I read, much of the night, and go south in the winter.

What are the roots that clutch, what branches grow
Out of this stony rubbish? Son of man,[7]   20
You cannot say, or guess, for you know only
A heap of broken images, where the sun beats,
And the dead tree gives no shelter, the cricket no relief,[8]
And the dry stone no sound of water. Only
There is shadow under this red rock,[9]   25
(Come in under the shadow of this red rock),
And I will show you something different from either
Your shadow at morning striding behind you
Or your shadow at evening rising to meet you;
I will show you fear in a handful of dust.   30

> Frisch weht der Wind
> Der Heimat zu
> Mein Irisch Kind,
> Wo weilest du?[1]

"You gave me hyacinths first a year ago;   35
They called me the hyacinth girl."
—Yet when we came back, late, from the Hyacinth garden,
Yours arms full, and your hair wet, I could not
Speak, and my eyes failed, I was neither
Living nor dead, and I knew nothing,   40
Looking into the heart of light, the silence.
Oed' und leer das Meer.[2]

Madame Sosostris,[3] famous clairvoyante,
Had a bad cold, nevertheless
Is known to be the wisest woman in Europe,   45

7. "Cf. Ezekiel II, i" [Eliot's note].
Here God is addressing Ezekiel, "Son
of man." God continues, "stand upon
thy feet, and I will speak unto thee."
8. "Cf. Ecclesiastes XII, v" [Eliot's
note]. The verse cited by Eliot is part
of the Preacher's picture of the desolation of old age, "when they shall
be afraid of that which is high, and
fears shall be in the way, and the almond tree shall flourish, and the grasshopper shall be a burden, and desire
shall fail * * * "
9. Cf. Isaiah xxxii.2: the "righteous
king" "shall be * * * as rivers of
water in a dry place, as the shadow of
a great rock in a weary land."
1. "V. Tristan und Isolde, I, verses
5–8" [Eliot's note]. In Wagner's opera,
a sailor recalls the girl he has left be-

hind: "Fresh blows the wind to the
homeland; my Irish child, where are
you waiting?"
2. "Id. III, verse 24" [Eliot's note].
In Act III of Tristan und Isolde, Tristan lies dying. He is waiting for Isolde
to come to him from Cornwall, but a
shepherd, appointed to watch for her
sail, can only report, "Waste and empty
is the sea."
3. A mock Egyptian name (suggested
to Eliot by "Sesostris, the Sorceress of
Ecbatana," the name assumed by a
character in Aldous Huxley's novel
Crome Yellow who dresses up as a
gypsy to tell fortunes at a fair). The
anticlimactic effect of "had a bad
cold" is deliberate; it is intended to be
ironic and debunking.

With a wicked pack of cards.[4] Here, said she,
Is your card, the drowned Phoenician Sailor,[5]
(Those are pearls that were his eyes. Look!)
Here is Belladonna, the Lady of the Rocks,[6]
The lady of situations.   50
Here is the man with three staves,[7] and here the Wheel,
And here is the one-eyed merchant,[8] and this card,
Which is blank, is something he carries on his back,
Which I am forbidden to see. I do not find
The Hanged Man.[9] Fear death by water.   55
I see crowds of people, walking round in a ring.
Thank you. If you see dear Mrs. Equitone,
Tell her I bring the horoscope myself:
One must be so careful these days.

4. I.e., the Tarot deck of cards. The four suits of the Tarot pack, discussed by Jessie Weston in *From Ritual to Romance*, are the cup, lance, sword, and dish—the life symbols found in the Grail story. Miss Weston noted that "today the Tarot has fallen somewhat into disrepute, being principally used for purposes of divination." Some of the cards mentioned in lines 46–56 are discussed by Eliot in his note to this passage: "I am not familiar with the exact constitution of the Tarot pack of cards, from which I have obviously departed to suit my own convenience. The Hanged Man, a member of the traditional pack, fits my purpose in two ways: because he is associated in my mind with the Hanged God of Frazer, and because I associate him with the hooded figure in the passage of the disciples to Emmaus in Part V. The Phoenician Sailor and the Merchant appear later; also the 'crowds of people,' and Death by Water is executed in Part IV. The Man with Three Staves (an authentic member of the Tarot pack) I associate, quite arbitrarily, with the Fisher King himself."

5. See Part IV. Phlebas the Phoenician and Mr. Eugenides, the Smyrna merchant—both of whom appear later in the poem—are different phases of the same symbolic character, here identified as the "Phoenician Sailor." Mr. Eugenides exports "currants" (line 210); the drowned Phlebas floats in the "current" (line 315). The line that follows is from Shakespeare's *Tempest* (I.ii.398). Ariel's song to the shipwrecked Ferdinand, who was "sitting on a bank / Weeping again the King my father's wrack," when "this music crept by me on the waters." The song is about the supposed drowning of Ferdinand's father, Alonso. *The Waste Land* contains many references to *The Tempest*: the supposed drowning of Alonso and Ferdinand is regarded as their purification by water, and the

"sea change" suffered by Alonso typifies, from one point of view, suffering transmuted into art (Eliot was impressed by the ritual element in Shakespeare's last plays). Ferdinand is also associated with Phlebas and Mr. Eugenides and therefore with the "drowned Phoenician Sailor." Drowning and sea change are both, of course, the work of water. Symbol of purification, baptism, refreshment, and growth, water plays diverse roles in the poem.

6. "Belladonna": beautiful lady. The word also suggests Madonna (the Virgin Mary) and therefore the Madonna of the Rocks (as in Leonardo da Vinci's painting); the rocks symbolize the Church. But there are other rocks—the rocks of dryness, of the Waste Land (e.g., lines 331 ff.). Belladonna is also an eye-cosmetic and a poison—the "deadly" nightshade. In the next line, the woman-figure of the Virgin becomes "the lady of situations," foreshadowing the neurasthenic lady of intrigue in Part II.

7. Life-force symbol, associated by Eliot with the Fisher King. The "Wheel" is the wheel of fortune, whose turning represents the reversals of human life.

8. Mr. Eugenides, "one-eyed" because the figure is in profile on the card and also as a suggestion of evil or crookedness. The mysterious burden on his back may be the mysteries of the fertility cults which, Miss Weston emphasizes, Phoenician merchants carried throughout the Mediterranean, or simply "the burthen of the mystery," "the heavy and the weary weight / Of all this unintelligible world" in Wordsworth's *Tintern Abbey*.

9. On his card in the Tarot pack he is shown hanging from one foot from a T-shaped cross. He symbolizes the self-sacrifice of the fertility god who is killed in order that his resurrection may bring fertility once again to land and people.

Unreal City,[1]   60
Under the brown fog of a winter dawn,
A crowd flowed over London Bridge, so many,[2]
I had not thought death had undone so many.
Sighs, short and infrequent, were exhaled,[3]
And each man fixed his eyes before his feet.   65
Flowed up the hill and down King William Street,
To where Saint Mary Woolnoth kept the hours
With a dead sound on the final stroke of nine.[4]
There I saw one I knew, and stopped him, crying: "Stetson![5]
You who were with me in the ships at Mylae![6]   70
That corpse you planted last year in your garden,
Has it begun to sprout?[7] Will it bloom this year?
Or has the sudden frost disturbed its bed?
Oh keep the Dog far hence, that's friend to men,
Or with his nails he'll dig it up again![8]   75
You! hypocrite lecteur!—mon semblable—mon frère!"[9]

1. "Cf. Baudelaire: 'Fourmillante cité, cité pleine de rêves, / Où le spectre en plein jour raccroche le passant' [Eliot's note]. The lines are quoted from Les Sept Vieillards ("The Seven Old Men") by Charles Baudelaire (1821–67); it is poem XCIII of Les Fleurs du Mal ("The Flowers of Evil"). The lines may be translated: "Swarming city, city full of dreams, / Where the specter in broad daylight accosts the passerby."
2. "Cf. Inferno III, 55–57 * * *" [Eliot's note]. The note goes on to quote Dante's lines, which may be translated: "So long a train of people, / that I should never have believed / That death had undone so many." Dante, just outside the gate of Hell, has seen "the wretched souls of those who lived without disgrace and without praise." In his essay on Baudelaire Eliot argued that in a sense it was better to be positively evil than to be neither good nor evil.
3. "Cf. Inferno IV, 25–27 * * *" [Eliot's note]. In Limbo, the first circle of Hell, Dante has found the virtuous heathen, who lived before Christianity and are therefore eternally unable to achieve their desire of seeing God. Dante's lines, cited by Eliot, mean: "Here, so far as I could tell by listening, / there was no lamentation except sighs, / which caused the eternal air to tremble."
4. "A phenomenon which I have often noticed" [Eliot's note]. St. Mary Woolnoth is a church in the "City" of London (the financial district); the crowd is flowing across London Bridge to work in the City.
5. Presumably representing the "aver-

age businessman."
6. The battle of Mylae (260 B.C.) in the First Punic War, which, like World War I, was fought for economic reasons.
7. A distortion of the ritual death of the fertility god.
8. "Cf. the Dirge in Webster's White Devil" [Eliot's note]. In the play by John Webster (d. 1625), the dirge, sung by Cornelia, has the lines: "But keep the wolf far thence, that's foe to men, / For with his nails he'll dig them up again." Eliot makes the "wolf" into a "Dog," which is not a "foe" but a "friend" to man. The image may be intended to suggest the ultimate degeneration of the fertility ritual, where the dying god is something buried in a suburban back garden to be dug up again by a friendly dog. There may be a reference to Sirius, the Dog Star, which is important in Egyptian mythology as heralding the fertilizing floods of the Nile (this is discussed by Miss Weston). But most important in this passage is the feverish nightmare atmosphere which it develops.
9. "V. Baudelaire, Preface to Fleurs du Mal" [Eliot's note]. The passage is the last line of the introductory poem Au Lecteur ("To the Reader") in Baudelaire's Fleurs du Mal; it may be translated: "Hypocrite reader!—my likeness—my brother!" Au Lecteur describes man as sunk in stupidity, sin, and evil; but the worst in "each man's foul menagerie of sin" is Boredom, the "monstre délicat"—"You know him, reader * * *" Like Baudelaire, Eliot is here shocking the reader into full participation in the poem.

II. A Game of Chess[1]

The Chair she sat in, like a burnished throne,[2]
Glowed on the marble, where the glass
Held up by standards wrought with fruited vines
From which a golden Cupidon peeped out   80
(Another hid his eyes behind his wing)
Doubled the flames of sevenbranched candelabra
Reflecting light upon the table as
The glitter of her jewels rose to meet it,
From satin cases poured in rich profusion;   85
In vials of ivory and colored glass
Unstoppered, lurked her strange synthetic perfumes,
Unguent, powdered, or liquid—troubled, confused
And drowned the sense in odors; stirred by the air
That freshened from the window, these ascended   90
In fattening the prolonged candle flames,
Flung their smoke into the laquearia,[3]
Stirring the pattern on the coffered ceiling.
Huge sea-wood fed with copper
Burned green and orange, framed by the colored stone,   95
In which sad light a carvèd dolphin swam.
Above the antique mantel was displayed
As though a window gave upon the sylvan scene[4]
The change of Philomel,[5] by the barbarous king

1. The title suggests two plays by Thomas Middleton (1580–1627): *A Game at Chess* and, more significantly, *Women Beware Women*, which has a scene in which a mother-in-law is distracted by a game of chess while her daughter-in-law is seduced: every move in the chess game represents a move in the seduction. Section II opens with a bored woman of leisure sitting before her dressing table in an atmosphere where the ornaments, the perfumes, the sheer excess of objects stifle the senses, while works of art emphasize the distinction between grandeur and futility. The neurasthenia and mounting hysteria revealed by the dialogue (or an interior monologue, or the remarks in quotation marks) may be spoken by the lady and those not in quotation marks may represent her husband's unspoken answers) and the degeneration of culture through parody and jazzing up of lines from Shakespeare culminate in the meaningless yet terrifying "knock." This at once becomes the barman's knock on the counter as he calls closing time, and thus the scene changes to the lower end of the social scale, with women talking in a pub about methods of abortion—another aspect of that sterility and misuse of sex which help to make up the modern Waste Land.
2. "Cf. *Antony and Cleopatra*, II, ii, 1. 190" [Eliot's note]. In Shakespeare's play, Enobarbus' famous description of the first meeting of Antony and Cleopatra begins, "The barge she sat in, like a burnish'd throne, / Burn'd on the water. * * * " Eliot's language in the opening lines of Part II is full of ironic distortions of Enobarbus' speech.
3. "Laquearia. V. *Aeneid*, I, 726 * * * " [Eliot's note]. *Laquearia* means "a paneled ceiling," and Eliot's note quotes the passage in the *Aeneid* which was his source for the word. The passage may be translated: "Blazing torches hang from the gold-paneled ceiling [*laquearibus aureis*], and torches conquer the night with flames." Virgil is here describing the banquet given by Dido, queen of Carthage, for Aeneas, with whom she fell in love. (Carthage is the scene of more "unholy loves" later in the poem; cf. line 307 and Eliot's note on it.)
4. "Sylvan scene. V. Milton, *Paradise Lost*, IV, 140" [Eliot's note]. The phrase is part of the first description of Eden, which we see through Satan's eyes.
5. "V. Ovid, *Metamorphoses*, VI, Philomela" [Eliot's note]. The note is a reference to Ovid's version of the Greek myth of the rape of Philomela by "the barbarous king" Tereus, husband of her sister Procne. Philomela was transformed into a nightingale. Eliot's note for line 100 refers ahead to his elaboration of the nightingale's song.

So rudely forced; yet there the nightingale   100
Filled all the desert with inviolable voice
And still she cried, and still the world pursues,
"Jug Jug"[6] to dirty ears.
And other withered stumps of time
Were told upon the walls; staring forms   105
Leaned out, leaning, hushing the room enclosed.
Footsteps shuffled on the stair.
Under the firelight, under the brush, her hair
Spread out in fiery points
Glowed into words, then would be savagely still.   110

"My nerves are bad tonight. Yes, bad. Stay with me.
Speak to me. Why do you never speak. Speak.
    What are you thinking of? What thinking? What?
I never know what you are thinking. Think."

I think we are in rats' alley[7]   115
Where the dead men lost their bones.

"What is that noise?"
                         The wind under the door.[8]
"What is that noise now? What is the wind doing?"
                         Nothing again nothing.   120
                                    "Do
You know nothing? Do you see nothing? Do you remember
Nothing?"

        I remember
Those are pearls that were his eyes.   125
"Are you alive, or not? Is there nothing in your head?"
                                          But
O O O O that Shakespeherian Rag—
It's so elegant
So intelligent
"What shall I do now? What shall I do?"   130
"I shall rush out as I am, and walk the street
With my hair down, so. What shall we do tomorrow?
What shall we ever do?"
                         The hot water at ten.   135
And if it rains, a closed car at four.
And we shall play a game of chess,[1]
Pressing lidless eyes and waiting for a knock upon the door.

When Lil's husband got demobbed,[2] I said—
I didn't mince my words, I said to her myself,   140

6. Conventional representation of nightingale's song in Elizabethan poetry. The
tragic myth has become degraded into
a dirty story.
7. "Cf. Part III, l. 195" [Eliot's note].
8. "Cf. Webster: 'Is the wind in that
door still?'" [Eliot's note]. The line
cited in the note is from John Webster's *The Devil's Law Case* (III.ii.162).
1. "Cf. the game of chess in Middleton's *Women Beware Women*" [Eliot's
note]. The significance of this chess
game is discussed in note 1 for this section.
2. British slang for "demobilized" (discharged from the army).

HURRY UP PLEASE ITS TIME[3]
Now Albert's coming back, make yourself a bit smart.
He'll want to know what you done with that money he gave you
To get yourself some teeth. He did, I was there.
You have them all out, Lil, and get a nice set,   145
He said, I swear, I can't bear to look at you.
And no more can't I, I said, and think of poor Albert,
He's been in the army four years, he wants a good time,
And if you don't give it him, there's others will, I said.
Oh is there, she said. Something o' that, I said.   150
Then I'll know who to thank, she said, and give me a straight look.
HURRY UP PLEASE ITS TIME
If you don't like it you can get on with it, I said.
Others can pick and choose if you can't.
But if Albert makes off, it won't be for lack of telling.   155
You ought to be ashamed, I said, to look so antique.
(And her only thirty-one.)
I can't help it, she said, pulling a long face,
It's them pills I took, to bring it off, she said.
(She's had five already, and nearly died of young George.)   160
The chemist[4] said it would be all right, but I've never been the
    same.
You *are* a proper fool, I said.
Well, if Albert won't leave you alone, there it is, I said,
What you get married for if you don't want children?
HURRY UP PLEASE ITS TIME   165
Well, that Sunday Albert was home, they had a hot gammon,[5]
And they asked me in to dinner, to get the beauty of it hot—
HURRY UP PLEASE ITS TIME
HURRY UP PLEASE ITS TIME
Goonight Bill. Goonight Lou. Goonight May. Goonight.   170
Ta ta. Goonight. Goonight.
Good night, ladies, good night, sweet ladies, good night, good night.[6]

III. The Fire Sermon[7]

The river's tent is broken: the last fingers of leaf
Clutch and sink into the wet bank. The wind

3. The traditional call of the British bartender at closing time.
4. Druggist.
5. Ham or bacon.
6. Cf. the mad Ophelia's departing words (*Hamlet* IV.v.72). Ophelia, too, met "death by water."
7. Just as water both purifies and drowns, so fire both purges and destroys: in this part, the roles of fire are emphasized. The Fire Sermon itself was preached by the Buddha against the fires of lust and other passions which destroy men and prevent their regeneration. The section opens with an autumn scene on the Thames, which is made increasingly sinister by such devices as ironic references to or distortions of famous passages in literature and the mocking equation of noble rituals of the past with modern trivialities and obscenities. We turn briefly to Mr. Eugenides, degenerate descendant of the Syrian merchants who had once spread the fertility cults throughout the Mediterranean, and then to the deliberately horrible scene of modern lust, sex without meaning. Seductions on the Thames, old and new, with parodic echoes of Wagner, Shakespeare, and Dante, lead to a further expression of the sense of nothingness and meaninglessness that characterizes the modern Waste Land, and the section ends with the Occidental St. Augustine echoing the Oriental Buddha in a call for the renunciation of lust.

Crosses the brown land, unheard. The nymphs are departed.   175
Sweet Thames, run softly, till I end my song.[8]
The river bears no empty bottles, sandwich papers,
Silk handkerchiefs, cardboard boxes, cigarette ends
Or other testimony of summer nights. The nymphs are departed.
And their friends, the loitering heirs of city directors;   180
Departed, have left no addresses.
By the waters of Leman I sat down and wept . . .[9]
Sweet Thames, run softly till I end my song,
Sweet Thames, run softly, for I speak not loud or long.
But at my back in a cold blast I hear[1]   185
The rattle of the bones, and chuckle spread from ear to ear.
A rat crept softly through the vegetation
Dragging its slimy belly on the bank
While I was fishing[2] in the dull canal
On a winter evening round behind the gashouse   190
Musing upon the king my brother's wreck[3]
And on the king my father's death before him.
White bodies naked on the low damp ground
And bones cast in a little low dry garret,
Rattled by the rat's foot only, year to year.   195
But at my back from time to time I hear[4]
The sound of horns and motors, which shall bring
Sweeney to Mrs. Porter in the spring.[5]
O the moon shone bright on Mrs. Porter
And on her daughter   200
They wash their feet in soda water[6]
Et O ces voix d'enfants, chantant dans la coupole![7]

8. "V. Spenser, *Prothalamion*" [Eliot's note]. Eliot's line is the refrain from Spenser's marriage song, which is also set by the Thames in London—but a very different Thames from the modern littered river.
9. Cf. Psalms cxxxvii.1, in which the exiled Hebrews mourn for their homeland: "By the rivers of Babylon, there we sat down, yea, we wept, when we remembered Zion." Lake Leman is another name for Lake Geneva; Eliot wrote *The Waste Land* in Lausanne, by that lake. The common noun "leman" is an archaic word meaning, in the bad sense, an illicit sweetheart or mistress; hence "the waters of Leman" become associated with the fires of lust.
1. An ironic distortion of Andrew Marvell's famous lines from *To His Coy Mistress*: "But at my back I always hear / Time's wingèd chariot hurrying near * * *." Cf. line 196.
2. To fish is to seek eternity and salvation (cf. the Fisher King), but this activity is now degraded and dirtied.
3. "Cf. *The Tempest*, I, ii" [Eliot's note]. See line 48.
4. "Cf. Marvell, *To His Coy Mistress*" [Eliot's note].
5. "Cf. Day, *Parliament of Bees*: 'When

of the sudden, listening, you shall hear, / A noise of horns and hunting, which shall bring / Actaeon to Diana in the spring, / Where all shall see her naked skin . . .'" [Eliot's note]. Actaeon was changed to a stag and hunted to death after he saw Diana, the goddess of chastity, bathing with her nymphs. In parodying the poem by John Day (1574–ca. 1640), Eliot is implying that Actaeon's fate indicates a very different set of values from those represented by the association of Sweeney and Mrs. Porter.
6. "I do not know the origin of the ballad from which these lines are taken: it was reported to me from Sydney, Australia" [Eliot's note]. One of the less vulgar versions of the song, which was popular among Australian troops in World War I, went as follows: "O the moon shines bright on Mrs. Porter / And on the daughter / Of Mrs. Porter. / They wash their feet in soda water / And so they oughter / To keep them clean."
7. "V. Verlaine, *Parsifal*" [Eliot's note]. The line is translated, "And O those children's voices singing in the dome!" Verlaine's sonnet describes Parsifal, the questing knight, resisting all

Twit twit twit
Jug jug jug jug jug jug
So rudely forc'd.   205
Tereu[8]

Unreal City
Under the brown fog of a winter noon
Mr. Eugenides, the Smyrna[9] merchant
Unshaven, with a pocket full of currants
C.i.f.[1] London: documents at sight,   210
Asked me in demotic French[2]
To luncheon at the Cannon Street Hotel[3]
Followed by a weekend at the Metropole.

At the violet hour, when the eyes and back   215
Turn upward from the desk, when the human engine waits
Like a taxi throbbing waiting,
I Tiresias,[4] though blind, throbbing between two lives,
Old man with wrinkled female breasts, can see
At the violet hour, the evening hour that strives   220
Homeward, and brings the sailor home from sea,[5]
The typist home at teatime, clears her breakfast, lights

sensual temptations to keep himself pure for the Grail; Wagner's *Parsifal* had his feet washed before entering the castle of the Grail.

8. "Tereu" is a reference to Tereus, who "rudely forc'd" Philomela; it was also one of the conventional words for a nightingale's song in Elizabethan poetry. Cf. the song from John Lyly's *Alexander and Campaspe* (1564): "Oh, 'tis the ravished nightingale. / *Jug, jug, jug, jug, tereu!* she cries," and lines 100 ff.

9. Seaport in western Turkey; here associated with Carthage and the ancient Phoenician and Syrian merchants (unlike those of modern Smyrna), who spread the old mystery cults. The sort of cult spread by Mr. Eugenides is indicated by his suggestion of "a weekend at the Metropole" (a luxury hotel at Brighton).

1. "The currants were quoted at a price 'carriage and insurance free to London'; and the Bill of Lading etc. were to be handed to the buyer upon payment of the sight draft" [Eliot's note].

2. Popular, vulgar French.

3. By the station which was then chief terminus for travelers to the continent; hence, a favorite meeting place for businessmen going or coming from abroad.

4. "Tiresias, although a mere spectator and not indeed a 'character,' is yet the most important personage in the poem, uniting all the rest. Just as the one-eyed merchant, seller of currants, melts into the Phoenician Sailor, and the latter is not wholly distinct from Ferdinand Prince of Naples, so all the women are one woman, and the two

sexes meet in Tiresias. What Tiresias *sees*, in fact, is the substance of the poem. The whole passage from Ovid is of great anthropological interest * * * " [Eliot's note]. The note then quotes the Latin text of Ovid's *Metamorphoses* which tells the story of Tiresias' change of sex. The Latin may be translated: "[The story goes that once Jove, having drunk a great deal,] jested with Juno. He said, 'Your pleasure in love is really greater than that enjoyed by men.' She denied it; so they decided to seek the opinion of the wise Tiresias, for he knew both aspects of love. For once, with a blow of his staff, he had committed violence on two huge snakes as they copulated in the green forest; and—wonderful to tell—was turned from a man into a woman and thus spent seven years. In the eighth year he saw the same snakes again and said: 'If a blow struck at you is so powerful that it changes the sex of the giver, I will now strike at you again.' With these words he struck the snakes, and his former shape was restored to him and he became as he had been born. So he was appointed arbitrator in the playful quarrel, and supported Jove's statement. It is said that Saturnia [i.e., Juno] was quite disproportionately upset, and condemned the arbitrator to perpetual blindness. But the almighty father (for no god may undo what has been done by another god), in return for the sight that was taken away, gave him the power to know the future and so lightened the penalty paid by the honor."

5. "This may not appear as exact as Sappho's lines, but I had in mind the

Her stove, and lays out food in tins.
Out of the window perilously spread
Her drying combinations touched by the sun's last rays.[5a]   225
On the divan are piled (at night her bed)
Stockings, slippers, camisoles, and stays.
I Tiresias, old man with wrinkled dugs
Perceived the scene, and foretold the rest—
I too awaited the expected guest.   230
He, the young man carbuncular,[6] arrives,
A small house agent's clerk, with one bold stare,
One of the low on whom assurance sits
As a silk hat on a Bradford[7] millionaire.
The time is now propitious, as he guesses,   235
The meal is ended, she is bored and tired,
Endeavors to engage her in caresses
Which still are unreproved, if undesired.
Flushed and decided, he assaults at once;
Exploring hands encounter no defense;   240
His vanity requires no response,
And makes a welcome of indifference.
(And I Tiresias have foresuffered all
Enacted on this same divan or bed;
I who have sat by Thebes[8] below the wall   245
And walked among the lowest of the dead.)
Bestows one final patronizing kiss,
And gropes his way, finding the stairs unlit . . .

She turns and looks a moment in the glass,
Hardly aware of her departed lover;   250
Her brain allows one half-formed thought to pass;
"Well now that's done: and I'm glad it's over."
When lovely woman stoops to folly and
Paces about her room again, alone,
She smoothes her hair with automatic hand,   255
And puts a record on the gramophone.[9]

"This music crept by me upon the waters"[1]
And along the Strand, up Queen Victoria Street.

'longshore' or 'dory' fisherman, who returns at nightfall" [Eliot's note]. Sappho's poem addressed Hesperus, the evening star, as the star that brings everyone home from work to evening rest; her poem is here distorted by Eliot. There is also an echo of Robert Louis Stevenson's *Requiem* in line 221 ("Home is the sailor, home from sea").
5a. The present editor has been informed that this and the preceding line constitute a "great allusion" to Keats's lines "Charmed magic casements, opening on the foam/ Of perilous seas, in faery lands forlorn" (*Ode to a Nightingale*, lines 69–70) but he remains skeptical. It is, however, certainly a powerful anti-romantic image.
6. Pimply.

7. A Yorkshire woolen-manufacturing town, where many rapid fortunes were made in World War I.
8. Tiresias lived in Thebes for many generations, where he witnessed the tragic fates of Oedipus and Creon; he prophesied in the market place by the wall of Thebes.
9. "V. Goldsmith, the song in *The Vicar of Wakefield*" [Eliot's note]. Olivia, a character in Oliver Goldsmith's novel, sings the following song when she returns to the place where she was seduced: "When lovely woman stoops to folly / And finds too late that men betray / What charm can soothe her melancholy, / What art can wash her guilt away? / The only art her guilt to cover, / To hide her shame from every

O City city, I can sometimes hear
Beside a public bar in Lower Thames Street,   260
The pleasant whining of a mandolin
And a clatter and a chatter from within
Where fishmen lounge at noon: where the walls
Of Magnus Martyr hold
Inexplicable splendor of Ionian white and gold [2]   265

        The river sweats[3]
        Oil and tar
        The barges drift
        With the turning tide
        Red sails   270
        Wide
        To leeward, swing on the heavy spar.
        The barges wash
        Drifting logs
        Down Greenwich reach   275
        Past the Isle of Dogs.[4]
            Weialala leia
            Wallala leialala

        Elizabeth and Leicester[5]
        Beating oars   280
        The stern was formed
        A gilded shell
        Red and gold
        The brisk swell
        Rippled both shores   285
        Southwest wind
        Carried down stream
        The peal of bells

---

eye, / To give repentance to her lover / And wring his bosom—is to die."
1. "V. *The Tempest*, as above" [Eliot's note]. Cf. line 48. (The line is from Ferdinand's speech, continuing after "weeping again the King my father's wrack.")
2. "The interior of St. Magnus Martyr is to my mind one of the finest among [Sir Christopher] Wren's interiors. * * * " [Eliot's note]. In these lines, the "pleasant" music, the "fishmen" resting after labor, and the splendor of the church interior all suggest a world of true values, where work and relaxation are both real and take place in a context of religious meaning. It is but a momentary glimpse of an almost lost world.
3. "The Song of the (three) Thames-daughters begins here. From line 292 to 306 inclusive they speak in turn. V. *Götterdämmerung*, III, i: the Rhine-daughters" [Eliot's note]. The Thames-daughters, both old and new, reflect a barren world of shabbiness and lust. Eliot parallels them with the Rhine-maidens in Wagner's opera *Die Götter-*

dämmerung ("The Twilight of the Gods") who lament that, with the gold of the Nibelungs stolen, the beauty of the river is gone. The refrain in lines 277–78 is borrowed from Wagner.
4. Greenwich is a borough in London on the south side of the Thames; opposite is the Isle of Dogs (a peninsula): Eliot presumably intends a reference to the earlier theme of the Dog.
5. The fruitless love of Queen Elizabeth and the Earl of Leicester (Sir Robert Dudley) is recalled in Eliot's note: "V. [J. A.] Froude, *Elizabeth*, Vol. I, ch. iv, letter of De Quadra to Philip of Spain: 'In the afternoon we were in a barge, watching the games on the river. (The queen) was alone with Lord Robert and myself on the poop, when they began to talk nonsense, and went so far that Lord Robert at last said, as I was on the spot there was no reason why they should not be married if the queen pleased.'" Even these two great figures from the 16th century represent no past glory and no contrast to present sordidness. (Queen Elizabeth was born in the old Green-

White towers
>Weialala leia   290
>Wallala leialala

"Trams and dusty trees.
Highbury bore me. Richmond and Kew
Undid me.[6] By Richmond I raised my knees
Supine on the floor of a narrow canoe."   295

"My feet are at Moorgate,[7] and my heart
Under my feet. After the event
He wept. He promised 'a new start.'
I made no comment. What should I resent?"

"On Margate[8] Sands.   300
I can connect
Nothing with nothing.
The broken fingernails of dirty hands.
My people humble people who expect
Nothing."   305

>la la

To Carthage then I came[9]

Burning burning burning burning[1]
O Lord Thou pluckest me out[2]
O Lord Thou pluckest   310

burning

IV. Death by Water[3]

Phlebas the Phoenician, a fortnight dead,
Forgot the cry of gulls, and the deep sea swell

wich House, by the river, where Greenwich Hospital now stands.)
6. "Cf. *Purgatorio*, V, 133 * * * *" [Eliot's note]. The *Purgatorio* lines, which Eliot here parodies, may be translated: "Remember me, who am La Pia. / Siena made me, Maremma undid me." Highbury is a residential London suburb; Richmond is a pleasant part of London westward up the Thames, with boating and riverside hotels; Kew, adjoining Richmond, has the famous Kew Gardens.
7. Slum area in east London.
8. Popular seaside resort on Thames estuary.
9. "V. St. Augustine's *Confessions:* 'to Carthage then I came, where a caldron of unholy loves sang all about mine ears'" [Eliot's note]. The passage from the *Confessions* quoted here occurs in St. Augustine's account of his youthful life of lust. Cf. line 92 and its note.
1. "The complete text of the Buddha's Fire Sermon (which corresponds in importance to the Sermon on the Mount) from which these words are taken, will be found translated in the late Henry

Clarke Warren's *Buddhism in Translation* (Harvard Oriental Series). * * * *" [Eliot's note]. In the sermon, the Buddha instructs his priests that all things "are on fire. * * * The eye * * * is on fire; forms are on fire; eye-consciousness is on fire; impressions received by the eye are on fire; and whatever sensation, pleasant, unpleasant, or indifferent, originates in dependence on impressions received by the eye, that also is on fire. And with what are these on fire? With the fire of passion, say I, with the fire of hatred, with the fire of infatuation * * * *" For Christ's Sermon on the Mount see Matthew v-vii.
2. "From St. Augustine's *Confessions* again. The collocation of these two representatives of eastern and western asceticism, as the culmination of this part of the poem, is not an accident" [Eliot's note]. Cf. also Zechariah iii.2, where God, rebuking Satan, speaks of Joshua the high priest as "a brand plucked out of the fire."
3. This section has been interpreted in two ways: either it signifies death by water without resurrection (water *mis-*

And the profit and loss.
                           A current under sea   315
Picked his bones in whispers. As he rose and fell
He passed the stages of his age and youth
Entering the whirlpool.
                        Gentile or Jew
O you who turn the wheel and look to windward,   320
Consider Phlebas, who was once handsome and tall as you.

V. *What the Thunder Said*[4]

After the torchlight red on sweaty faces
After the frosty silence in the gardens
After the agony in stony places
The shouting and the crying   325
Prison and palace and reverberation
Of thunder of spring over distant mountains
He who was living is now dead[5]
We who were living are now dying
With a little patience   330

Here is no water but only rock
Rock and no water and the sandy road
The road winding above among the mountains
Which are mountains of rock without water
If there were water we should stop and drink   335
Amongst the rock one cannot stop or think
Sweat is dry and feet are in the sand
If there were only water amongst the rock
Dead mountain mouth of carious teeth that cannot spit
Here one can neither stand nor lie nor sit   340

used), or it symbolizes the sacrificial death which precedes rebirth. It is true that Phlebas is purged of his commercial interests and vanities when he suffers a sea change, and Miss Weston tells of the annual casting into the sea at Alexandria of an effigy of the head of Adonis—to be taken out after seven days by jubilant celebrators of the cult. The majority of interpreters, however, see Phlebas' drowning as a death by water which brings no resurrection, although there is a strange sense of peace in the death. Cf. line 47 and its note. 4. "In the first part of Part V three themes are employed: the journey to Emmaus, the approach to the Chapel Perilous (see Miss Weston's book), and the present decay of eastern Europe" [Eliot's note]. The journey to Emmaus (see line 360 and its note) is a significant feature in the story of Christ, and in this section the Waste Land is more clearly related to that story. Christ is associated with the slain fertility god, but there is still no resurrection. The rocky landscape is described with a new and agonizing intensity until everything breaks down in hallucination in which visions of the decay of the great cities of Western civilization give way to nightmare images of horror. Then the scene changes to the Chapel Perilous in the midst of the Waste Land: it seems empty and derelict and apparently the quest has been in vain. But suddenly the cock crows, the lightning flashes, and the fertilizing rain falls. The thunder peals and gives its message of salvation in terms of Oriental wisdom, the Sanskrit words for "Give, Sympathize, Control." But we are too timidly prudent to give properly, too shut in within our own individualities to be able to sympathize properly, and we can more easily respond to control than exercise it. Salvation remains problematical. 5. These lines, containing allusions to Christ's imprisonment and trial, and to Gethsemane and Golgotha, suggest the hopeless days between Good Friday and Easter, between the Crucifixion and the Resurrection—associated with the death of the Fisher King and the moment of despair in the Waste Land when regeneration seems impossible.

There is not even silence in the mountains
But dry sterile thunder without rain
There is not even solitude in the mountains
But red sullen faces sneer and snarl
From doors of mudcracked houses 345
                       If there were water

   And no rock
   If there were rock
   And also water
   And water 350
   A spring
   A pool among the rock
   If there were the sound of water only
   Not the cicada[6]
   And dry grass singing 355
   But sound of water over a rock
   Where the hermit thrush[7] sings in the pine trees
   Drip drop drip drop drop drop drop
   But there is no water

Who is the third who walks always beside you?[8] 360
When I count, there are only you and I together
But when I look ahead up the white road
There is always another one walking beside you
Gliding wrapped in a brown mantle, hooded
I do not know whether a man or a woman 365
—But who is that on the other side of you?

What is that sound high in the air[9]
Murmur of maternal lamentation
Who are those hooded hordes swarming
Over endless plains, stumbling in cracked earth 370
Ringed by the flat horizon only
What is the city over the mountains
Cracks and reforms[1] and bursts in the violet air
Falling towers

6. Grasshopper. Cf. the prophecy of Ecclesiastes, "the grasshopper shall be a burden, and desire shall fail * * * " (and cf. also line 23 and its note).
7. "This is * * * the hermit thrush which I have heard in Quebec County. * * * Its 'water-dripping song' is justly celebrated" [Eliot's note].
8. "The following lines were stimulated by the account of one of the Antarctic expeditions (I forget which, but I think one of Shackleton's): it was related that the party of explorers, at the extremity of their strength, had the constant delusion that there was *one more member* than could actually be counted" [Eliot's note]. This reminiscence is associated with the journey of Christ's disciples to Emmaus given in Luke xxiv.13–16: "And it came to pass, that,

while they communed together and reasoned, Jesus himself drew near, and went with them. But their eyes were holden that they should not know him."
9. Eliot's note for lines 367–77 is: "Cf. Herman Hesse, *Blick ins Chaos* ["A Glimpse into Chaos"] * * * " The note then quotes a passage from the German text, which is translated: "Already half of Europe, already at least half of Eastern Europe, on the way to Chaos, drives drunk in sacred infatuation along the edge of the precipice, sings drunkenly, as though hymn singing, as Dmitri Karamazov [in Dostoyevski's *Brothers Karamazov*] sang. The offended bourgeois laughs at the songs; the saint and the seer hear them with tears."
1. Used ironically.

Jerusalem Athens Alexandria 375
Vienna London
Unreal

A woman drew her long black hair out tight
And fiddled whisper music on those strings
And bats with baby faces in the violet light 380
Whistled, and beat their wings
And crawled head downward down a blackened wall
And upside down in air were towers
Tolling reminiscent bells, that kept the hours
And voices singing out of empty cisterns and exhausted wells. 385

In this decayed hole among the mountains
In the faint moonlight, the grass is singing
Over the tumbled graves, about the chapel
There is the empty chapel, only the wind's home.[2]
It has no windows, and the door swings, 390
Dry bones can harm no one.
Only a cock stood on the rooftree
Co co rico co co rico[3]
In a flash of lightning. Then a damp gust
Bringing rain 395

Ganga[4] was sunken, and the limp leaves
Waited for rain, while the black clouds
Gathered far distant, over Himavant.[5]
The jungle crouched, humped in silence.
Then spoke the thunder 400
Da[6]
Datta: what have we given?
My friend, blood shaking my heart
The awful daring of a moment's surrender
Which an age of prudence can never retract 405
By this, and this only, we have existed
Which is not to be found in our obituaries
Or in memories draped by the beneficent spider[7]
Or under seals broken by the lean solicitor

2. Suggesting the moment of near despair before the Chapel Perilous, when the questing knight sees nothing there but decay. This illusion of nothingness is the knight's final test.
3. The crowing of the cock signals the departure of ghosts and evil spirits. Cf. *Hamlet* I.i.157 ff.
4. The river Ganges.
5. I.e., snowy mountain; the name of a peak in the Himalayas.
6. "'Datta, dayadhvam, damyata' (Give, sympathize, control). The fable of the meaning of the Thunder is found in the *Brihadaranyaka—Upanishad*, 5, 1. * * * " [Eliot's note]. The Hindu fable referred to is that of gods, men, and demons each in turn asking of

their father Prajapati, "Speak to us, O Lord." To each he replied with the one syllable "*DA*," and each group interpreted it in a different way: "*Datta*," to give alms; "*Dayadhvam*," to have compassion; "*Damyata*," to practice self-control. The fable concludes, "This is what the divine voice, the Thunder, repeats when he says: *DA, DA, DA:* 'Control yourselves; give alms; be compassionate.' Therefore one should practice these three things: self-control, alms-giving, and compassion."
7. "Cf. Webster, *The White Devil*, V, vi: '. . . they'll remarry / Ere the worm pierce your winding-sheet, ere the spider / Make a thin curtain for your epitaphs' " [Eliot's note].

In our empty rooms   410
DA
Dayadhvam: I have heard the key[8]
Turn in the door once and turn once only
We think of the key, each in his prison
Thinking of the key, each confirms a prison   415
Only at nightfall, ethereal rumours
Revive for a moment a broken Coriolanus[9]
DA
Damyata: The boat responded
Gaily, to the hand expert with sail and oar
The sea was calm, your heart would have responded   420
Gaily, when invited, beating obedient
To controlling hands

                              I sat upon the shore
Fishing,[1] with the arid plain behind me   425
Shall I at least set my lands in order?[2]
London Bridge is falling down falling down falling down[3]
Poi s'ascose nel foco che gli affina[4]
Quando fiam uti chelidon[5]—O swallow swallow

8. "Cf. *Inferno*, XXXIII, 46 * * * "
[Eliot's note]. In this passage from
the *Inferno* Ugolino recalls his imprisonment in the tower with his children,
where they starved to death: "And I
heard below the door of the horrible
tower being locked up." Eliot implies
that we cannot obey the command to
sympathize because we are imprisoned
within the circle of our own egotism.
Eliot's note for this line goes on to
quote F. H. Bradley, *Appearance and
Reality*, p. 346, as follows: " 'My external sensations are no less private
to myself than are my thoughts or my
feelings. In either case my experience
falls within my own circle, a circle
closed on the outside; and, with all its
elements alike, every sphere is opaque
to the others which surround it. . . .
In brief, regarded as an existence which
appears in a soul, the whole world for
each is peculiar and private to that
soul.' "
9. Coriolanus, who acted out of pride
rather than duty, is an obvious example of a man locked in the prison of
his own self. He led the enemy against
his native city out of injured pride
(cf. Shakespeare's *Coriolanus*).
1. "V. Weston: *From Ritual to Romance;* chapter on the Fisher King"
[Eliot's note].
2. The inclusive "I," who sits in the
symbolic act of fishing (seeking salvation, regeneration, eternity) with the
Waste Land behind him, wonders how
far he can order his affairs. There is
a note of subdued hope or at least of
determination in these lines. The "at
least" suggests a reasonable minimum
of achievement.

3. One of the later lines of this nursery
rhyme is: "Take the key and lock her
up, my fair lady."
4. "V. *Purgatorio*, XXVI, 148 * * * "
[Eliot's note]. The note goes on to
quote lines 145–48 of the *Purgatorio*,
in which Arnaut Daniel, the Provençal
poet, addresses Dante: " 'Now I pray
you, by that virtue which guides you
to the summit of the stairway, be mindful in due time of my pain.' " Then
(in the line Eliot quotes here) "he
hid himself in the fire which refines
them." The purgatorial vision of refining fire—as distinct from the fires
of lust—represents one of the hopeful
fragments shored up by the seeker for
regeneration and order.
5. "V. *Pervigilium Veneris*. Cf. Philomela in Parts II and III" [Eliot's
note]. The Latin phrase in the text
means, "When shall I be as the swallow?" It comes from the *Pervigilium
Veneris* ("Vigil of Venus"), an anonymous late Latin poem combining a
hymn to Venus with a description of
spring. In the last two stanzas of the
Pervigilium occurs a recollection of the
Tereus-Procne-Philomela myth (except
that in this version the swallow is identified with Philomela); the anonymous
poet's mood changes to one of sadness,
combined with hope for renewal: "The
maid of Tereus sings under the poplar
shade, so that you would think musical
trills of love came from her mouth and
not a sister's complaint of a barbarous
husband. * * * She sings, we are silent. When will my spring come? When
shall I be as the swallow that I may
cease to be silent? I have lost the Muse
in silence, and Apollo regards me not

Le Prince d'Aquitaine à la tour abolie[6]
These fragments I have shored against my ruins[7]   430
Why then Ile fit you. Hieronymo's mad againe.[8]
Datta. Dayadhvam. Damyata.
          Shantih   shantih   shantih[9]

1921   1922

Journey of the Magi[1]

"A cold coming we had of it,
Just the worst time of the year
For a journey, and such a long journey:
The ways deep and the weather sharp,
The very dead of winter."[2]
And the camels galled, sore-footed, refractory,   5
Lying down in the melting snow.
There were times we regretted
The summer palaces on slopes, the terraces,
And the silken girls bringing sherbet.
Then the camel men cursing and grumbling   10
And running away, and wanting their liquor and women,
And the night-fires going out, and the lack of shelters,
And the cities hostile and the towns unfriendly
And the villages dirty and charging high prices: 15
A hard time we had of it.

* * * " For "O swallow swallow" cf. Swinburne's *Itylus*, which begins, "Swallow, my sister, O sister swallow, / How can thine heart be full of spring?" and Tennyson's lyric in *The Princess*: "O Swallow, Swallow, flying, flying south * * * "

6. "V. Gerard de Nerval, Sonnet *El Desdichado*" [Eliot's note]. The French line may be translated, "The Prince of Aquitaine in the ruined tower." One of the cards in the Tarot pack is "the tower struck by lightning." The ruined tower is symbolic of a decayed tradition.

7. This may refer to the whole poem —fragments assembled by the poet in the attempt to come to terms with his situation.

8. "V. Kyd's *Spanish Tragedy*" [Eliot's note]. Subtitled "Hieronymo's Mad Againe," Kyd's play (1594) is an early example of the Elizabethan tragedy of revenge. Hieronymo, driven mad by the murder of his son, has his revenge when he is asked to write a court entertainment. He replies, "Why then Ile fit you!" (i.e., accommodate you), and assigns the parts in the entertainment so that, in the course of the action, his son's murderers are killed.

9. "Shantih. Repeated as here, a formal ending to an Upanishad. 'The Peace which passeth understanding' is our equivalent to this word" [Eliot's note]. The Upanishads are poetic dialogues on Hindu metaphysics, written after the Vedas, the ancient Hindu scriptures, and in part commenting on them. The fact that the benediction is in a language so foreign to Western tradition may indicate that the solution is willed, not achieved. The fragments with which the poem ends seem like a desperate attempt at ordering chaos, but it breaks down in madness ("Hieronymo's mad againe"). We end with the threefold message repeated and the benediction uttered; but the issue remains in doubt.

1. One of the three wise men who came from the east to Jerusalem to do homage to the infant Jesus (Matthew ii.1–12) is recalling in old age the meaning of the experience.

2. Adapted from a passage in a Nativity sermon by the 17th-century divine Lancelot Andrewes: "A cold coming they had of it at this time of the year, just the worst time of the year to take a journey, and specially a long journey in. The ways deep, the weather sharp, the days short, the sun farthest off, *in solstitio brumali*, 'the very dead of winter.' "

At the end we preferred to travel all night,
Sleeping in snatches,
With the voices singing in our ears, saying
That this was all folly.   20

Then at dawn we came down to a temperate valley,
Wet, below the snow line, smelling of vegetation;
With a running stream and a water mill beating the darkness,
And three trees on the low sky,
And an old white horse galloped away in the meadow.[3]   25
Then we came to a tavern with vine-leaves over the lintel,
Six hands at an open door dicing for pieces of silver,[4]
And feet kicking the empty wineskins.
But there was no information, and so we continued
And arrived at evening, not a moment too soon   30
Finding the place; it was (you may say) satisfactory.

All this was a long time ago, I remember,
And I would do it again, but set down
This set down
This: were we led all that way for   35
Birth or Death? There was a Birth, certainly,
We had evidence and no doubt. I had seen birth and death,
But had thought they were different; this Birth was
Hard and bitter agony for us, like Death, our death.
We returned to our places, these Kingdoms,   40
But no longer at ease here, in the old dispensation,
With an alien people clutching their gods.
I should be glad of another death.

                                                               1927

Marina[1]

Quis hic locus, quae regio, quae mundi plaga?[2]

What seas what shores what gray rocks and what islands
What water lapping the bow

3. A series of images of freshness and renewal, combined with anticipations of disaster. The "three trees on the low sky" suggest the three crosses, with Christ crucified on the center one; the men dicing for pieces of silver suggest the soldiers dicing for Christ's garments and Judas' betrayal of him for thirty pieces of silver.
4. "Why, for all of us, out of all that we have heard, seen, felt, in a lifetime, do certain images recur, charged with emotion, rather than others? * * * six ruffians seen through an open window playing cards at night at a small French railway junction where there was a water mill" (Eliot, *The Use of*

Poetry and the Use of Criticism).
1. Marina is Pericles' daughter in Shakespeare's play *Pericles Prince of Tyre:* she was born at sea, lost to her father, then as a young woman found by him again. This poem evokes the mood of hushed wonder with which Pericles rediscovered his daughter, who had almost miraculously preserved her innocence and virtue through harrowing experiences. The situation is of course symbolic: a mood is established of regeneration, of escape from lust into love and from violence and confusion into peace. The symbolic boat on which the reunion takes place was originally made by the speaker, but for

And scent of pine and the woodthrush singing through the fog
What images return
O my daughter.   5

Those who sharpen the tooth of the dog, meaning
Death
Those who glitter with the glory of the hummingbird, **meaning**
Death
Those who sit in the sty of contentment, meaning   10
Death
Those who suffer the ecstasy of the animals, meaning
Death

Are become unsubstantial, reduced by a wind,
A breath of pine, and the woodsong fog   15
By this grace dissolved in place

What is this face, less clear and clearer
The pulse in the arm, less strong and stronger—
Given or lent? more distant than stars and nearer than the eye

Whispers and small laughter between leaves and hurrying feet   20
Under sleep, where all the waters meet.

Bowsprit cracked with ice and paint cracked with heat.
I made this, I have forgotten
And remember.
The rigging weak and the canvas rotten   25
Between one June and another September.
Made this unknowing, half conscious, unknown, my own.
The garboard strake[3] leaks, the seams need calking.
This form, this face, this life
Living to live in a world of time beyond me; let me   30
Resign my life for this life, my speech for that unspoken,
The awakened, lips parted, the hope, the new ships.

What seas what shores what granite islands towards my timbers
And woodthrush calling through the fog
My daughter.   35

1930

---

a purpose he cannot remember; it is
battered and frail; but it serves its
purpose, having led him to this moment
of grace, dedication, and new hope.
One must not be too literal in pressing a meaning on each of the images:
this is the most delicately evocative of
all Eliot's poems.
2. "What place is this, what country,
what region of the world?" Spoken by
Hercules on regaining sanity after having killed his children in his madness,
in Seneca's play *Hercules Furens* ("The

Mad Hercules"). This is a situation
contrary to the one evoked in the poem.
Eliot once wrote to a correspondent
that he wished to achieve a "crisscross"
between the scenes in the Senecan and
the Shakespearean plays. He appears to
be making that association between
birth and death which he uses so often
(as in *The Waste Land* and *Journey
of the Magi*).
3. The planking nearest to the boat's
keel—hence its most vital spot.

From Four Quartets
Little Gidding[1]

I

Midwinter spring is its own season
Sempiternal[2] though sodden towards sundown,
Suspended in time, between pole and tropic.
When the short day is brightest, with frost and fire,
The brief sun flames the ice, on pond and ditches,   5
In windless cold that is the heart's heat,
Reflecting in a watery mirror
A glare that is blindness in the early afternoon.
And glow more intense than blaze of branch, or brazier,
Stirs the dumb spirit: no wind, but pentecostal fire[3]   10
In the dark time of the year. Between melting and freezing

1. This is the fourth of Eliot's *Four Quartets*, four related poems each divided into five "movements" in a manner reminiscent of the structure of a quartet or a sonata and each dealing with some aspect of the relation of time and eternity, the meaning of history, the achievement of the moment of timeless insight. Though the *Four Quartets* constitute a unified sequence, they were each written separately and can be read as individual poems. "*Little Gidding* can be understood by itself, without reference to the preceding poems, which it yet so beautifully completes" (Helen Gardner). Each of the four is named after a place. Little Gidding is a village in Huntingdonshire where in 1625 Nicholas Ferrar established an Anglican religious community; it was broken up in 1647, toward the end of the Civil War, by the victorious Puritans; the chapel, however, was rebuilt in the 19th century and still exists. The poet recalls a midwinter visit to the chapel; he evokes the scene and uses it for a starting point for a meditation on England's past and present, on the possibility of redemption through purgation. Eliot wrote the poem in 1942, when he was a fire-watcher during World War II, and he looks back at the history and meaning of Little Gidding from his own war experience in order to project its present significance.

The first section or movement is itself in three parts of which the first sets the scene and the season, the second asserts the significance of this place at any season, and the third reminds us of the original purpose of the community and suggests what these dead can communicate to us now, to achieve "the intersection of the timeless moment." The second movement is much more lyrical in tone, and broods over change and decay. It then changes to a Dan-

tesque verse form (suggesting Dante's *terza rima*, but unrhymed) in which the poet describes himself walking at dawn after an air raid and encountering a "dead master" returned temporarily from Purgatory. (The scene also recalls Dante's meeting his own dead master Brunetto Latini in Hell.) The spirit talks of the relation between past and present, their common concern with language, and the slow and difficult progress toward purgation; he disappears when the All Clear sounds. The third movement broods over the uses of memory and attitudes toward history; recalls that the combatants in that earlier war are now "folded in a single party"; concedes that one cannot revive lost causes; and suggests that in detachment and in the view of past suffering as purgation a sense of peace and of renewal might be achieved. The short lyrical fourth movement elaborates the notion of purgation (the dove of peace has become the bombing plane), sees fire as purgative as well as destructive, and emphasizes the dual nature of love and the alternative of the two kinds of fire. The final movement accepts the movements of history and sees history as "a pattern of timeless moments," so that here at this moment in Little Gidding "while the light fails / On a winter afternoon, in a secluded chapel / History is now and England." The poet now sees the rose of life and the yew tree of death interpenetrating at each moment and ends with a vision of suffering and love, the fire and the rose, as one.
2. Eternal, everlasting.
3. On the Pentecost day after the death and resurrection of Christ, there appeared to His apostles "cloven tongues like as of fire * * * And they were all filled with the Holy Ghost" (Acts ii).

The soul's sap quivers. There is no earth smell
Or smell of living thing. This is the springtime
But not in time's covenant. Now the hedgerow
Is blanched for an hour with transitory blossom   15
Of snow, a bloom more sudden
Than that of summer, neither budding nor fading,
Not in the scheme of generation.
Where is the summer, the unimaginable
Zero summer?

         If you came this way,   20
Taking the route you would be likely to take
From the place you would be likely to come from,
If you came this way in may time, you would find the hedges
White again, in May, with voluptuary sweetness.
It would be the same at the end of the journey,   25
If you came at night like a broken king,[4]
If you came by day not knowing what you came for,
It would be the same, when you leave the rough road
And turn behind the pigsty to the dull façade
And the tombstone. And what you thought you came for   30
Is only a shell, a husk of meaning
From which the purpose breaks only when it is fulfilled
If at all. Either you had no purpose
Or the purpose is beyond the end you figured
And is altered in fulfillment. There are other places   35
Which also are the world's end, some at the sea jaws,
Or over a dark lake, in a desert or a city—
But this is the nearest, in place and time,
Now and in England.

         If you came this way,
Taking any route, starting from anywhere,   40
At any time or at any season,
It would always be the same: you would have to put off
Sense and notion. You are not here to verify,
Instruct yourself, or inform curiosity
Or carry report. You are here to kneel   45
Where prayer has been valid. And prayer is more
Than an order of words, the conscious occupation
Of the praying mind, or the sound of the voice praying.
And what the dead had no speech for, when living,
They can tell you, being dead: the communication   50
Of the dead is tongued with fire beyond the language of the living.
Here, the intersection of the timeless moment
Is England and nowhere. Never and always.

II

Ash on an old man's sleeve
Is all the ash the burnt roses leave.   55

4. I.e., Charles I. King Charles visited Ferrar's community more than once, and is said to have paid his last visit in secret after his final defeat in the Civil War.

Dust in the air suspended
Marks the place where a story ended.
Dust inbreathed was a house—
The wall, the wainscot, and the mouse.
The death of hope and despair,   60
    This is the death of air.[5]

There are flood and drouth
Over the eyes and in the mouth,
Dead water and dead sand
Contending for the upper hand.   65
The parched eviscerate soil
Gapes at the vanity of toil,
Laughs without mirth.
    This is the death of earth.

Water and fire succeed   70
The town, the pasture, and the weed.
Water and fire deride
The sacrifice that we denied.
Water and fire shall rot
The marred foundations we forgot,   75
Of sanctuary and choir.
    This is the death of water and fire.

In the uncertain hour before the morning
  Near the ending of interminable night
    At the recurrent end of the unending   80
After the dark dove with the flickering tongue
  Had passed below the horizon of his homing
    While the dead leaves still rattled on like tin
Over the asphalt where no other sound was
  Between three districts whence the smoke arose   85
  I met one walking, loitering and hurried
As if blown towards me like the metal leaves
  Before the urban dawn wind unresisting.
    And as I fixed upon the down-turned face
That pointed scrutiny with which we challenge   90
  The first-met stranger in the waning dusk
    I caught the sudden look of some dead master
Whom I had known, forgotten, half recalled
  Both one and many; in the brown baked features
    The eyes of a familiar compound ghost[6]·   95
Both intimate and unidentifiable.

<hr>

5. "The death of air," like that of "earth" and of "water and fire" in the succeeding stanzas, recalls the theory of the creative strife of the four elements propounded by Heraclitus (Greek philosopher of 4th and 5th centuries B.C.): "Fire lives in the death of air; air lives in the death of fire; water lives in the death of earth; and earth lives in the death of water." But at this point in the poem, unlike Heraclitus' theory, death is not intermingled with life.

6. Cf. Shakespeare, Sonnet 86, line 9: 'that affable familiar ghost." W. B. Yeats is the "dead master" who is an important part of this "compound ghost."

So I assumed a double part,[7] and cried
    And heard another's voice cry: "What! are *you* here?"
Although we were not. I was still the same,
    Knowing myself yet being someone other—   100
    And he a face still forming; yet the words sufficed
To compel the recognition they preceded.
    And so, compliant to the common wind,
    Too strange to each other for misunderstanding,
In concord at this intersection time   105
    Of meeting nowhere, no before and after,
    We trod the pavement in a dead patrol.
I said: "The wonder that I feel is easy,
    Yet ease is cause of wonder. Therefore speak:
    I may not comprehend, may not remember."   110
And he: "I am not eager to rehearse
    My thought and theory which you have forgotten.
    These things have served their purpose: let them be.
So with your own, and pray they be forgiven
    By others, as I pray you to forgive   115
    Both bad and good. Last season's fruit is eaten
And the fullfed beast shall kick the empty pail.
    For last year's words belong to last year's language
    And next year's words await another voice.
But, as the passage now presents no hindrance   120
    To the spirit unappeased and peregrine[8]
    Between two worlds become much like each other,
So I find words I never thought to speak
    In streets I never thought I should revisit
    When I left my body on a distant shore.   125
Since our concern was speech, and speech impelled us
    To purify the dialect of the tribe[9]
    And urge the mind to aftersight and foresight,
Let me disclose the gifts reserved for age
    To set a crown upon your lifetime's effort.   130
    First, the cold friction of expiring sense
Without enchantment, offering no promise
    But bitter tastelessness of shadow fruit
    As body and soul begin to fall asunder.
Second, the conscious impotence of rage   135
    At human folly, and the laceration
    Of laughter at what ceases to amuse.
And last, the rending pain of re-enactment
    Of all that you have done, and been; the shame
    Of motives late revealed, and the awareness   140
Of things ill done and done to others' harm

---

7. Two interpretations have been suggested: either the poet assumes the part of Dante as he accosted people in Hell or Purgatory, or else he assumes the part of his own other self.
8. Foreign, coming from abroad.
9. A rendering of the line *"Donner un sens plus pur aux mots de la tribu"* in Stéphane Mallarmé's sonnet *Le Tombeau d'Edgar Poe* ("The Tomb of Edgar Poe"). There are many less direct literary echoes in this passage, some recalling Milton, some various Jacobean dramatists, some Dante.

Which once you took for exercise of virtue.
Then fools' approval stings, and honor stains.
From wrong to wrong the exasperated spirit
  Proceeds, unless restored by that refining fire[1]   145
  Where you must move in measure, like a dancer."
The day was breaking. In the disfigured street
  He left me, with a kind of valediction,
  And faded on the blowing of the horn.[2]

III

There are three conditions which often look alike   150
Yet differ completely, flourish in the same hedgerow:
Attachment to self and to things and to persons, detachment
From self and from things and from persons; and, growing between
    them, indifference
Which resembles the others as death resembles life,
Being between two lives—unflowering, between   155
The live and the dead nettle. This is the use of memory:
For liberation—not less of love but expanding
Of love beyond desire, and so liberation
From the future as well as the past. Thus, love of a country
Begins as attachment to our own field of action   160
And comes to find that action of little importance
Though never indifferent. History may be servitude,
History may be freedom. See, now they vanish,
The faces and places, with the self which, as it could, loved them,
To become renewed, transfigured, in another pattern.   165

Sin is Behovely, but
All shall be well, and
All manner of thing shall be well.[3]
If I think, again, of this place,
And of people, not wholly commendable,   170
Of no immediate kin or kindness,
But some of peculiar genius,
All touched by a common genius,
United in the strife which divided them;
If I think of a king at nightfall,[4]   175

1. Cf. *The Waste Land*, line 428 and its note.
2. Cf. *Hamlet*, I.ii.157. "It faded on the crowing of the cock." The horn is the All Clear signal after an air raid (the dialogue has taken place between the dropping of the last bomb and the sounding of the All Clear). Eliot called the section which ends with this line "the nearest equivalent to a canto of the *Inferno* or *Purgatorio*" that he could achieve, and spoke of his intention to present "a parallel, by means of contrast, between the *Inferno* and the *Purgatorio* * * * and a hallucinated scene after an air raid."
3. A quotation from the 14th-century English mystic, Dame Juliana of Norwich: "Sin is behovabil [inevitable], but all shall be well and all shall be

well and all manner of thing shall be well." It is the accent of genuine mystical experience and authority that Eliot wishes to convey in using Dame Juliana's words. The thought expressed— that in spite of sin or even through sin all shall be well—is a variation of the "fortunate fall" (*felix culpa*) idea found in Milton and elsewhere.
4. Charles I. He died "on the scaffold" in 1649, while his principal advisers, Archbishop Laud and Thomas Wentworth, Earl of Strafford, were both executed earlier by the victorious Parliamentary forces. Eliot is here meditating on the English Civil War and refusing to take sides, for history subsumes both sides. The war becomes a symbol of purgation through suffering. Cf. conclusion of this section.

Of three men, and more, on the scaffold
And a few who died forgotten
In other places, here and abroad,
And of one who died blind and quiet[5]
Why should we celebrate   180
These dead men more than the dying?
It is not to ring the bell backward
Nor is it an incantation
To summon the specter of a Rose.
We cannot revive old factions   185
We cannot restore old policies
Or follow an antique drum.
These men, and those who opposed them
And those whom they opposed
Accept the constitution of silence   190
And are folded in a single party.
Whatever we inherit from the fortunate
We have taken from the defeated
What they had to leave us—a symbol:
A symbol perfected in death.   195
And all shall be well and
All manner of thing shall be well
By the purification of the motive
In the ground of our beseeching.

                        IV   200

The dove descending breaks the air
With flame of incandescent terror
Of which the tongues declare
The one discharge from sin and error.
The only hope, or else despair
   Lies in the choice of pyre or pyre—   205
   To be redeemed from fire by fire.

Who then devised the torment? Love.
Love is the unfamiliar Name
Behind the hands that wove
The intolerable shirt of flame[6]
Which human power cannot remove.   210
  We only live, only suspire
  Consumed by either fire or fire.

                        V

What we call the beginning is often the end
And to make an end is to make a beginning.   215
The end is where we start from. And every phrase
And sentence that is right (where every word is at home,
Taking its place to support the others,
The word neither diffident nor ostentatious,

---

5. Milton.
6. Out of love for her husband Hercules, Deianira gave him the poisoned
shirt of Nessus. She had been told

that it would increase his love for
her, but instead it so corroded his flesh
that in his agony he mounted a funeral
pyre and burned himself to death.

An easy commerce of the old and the new,   220
The common word exact without vulgarity,
The formal word precise but not pedantic,
The complete consort[7] dancing together)
Every phrase and every sentence is an end and a beginning,
Every poem an epitaph. And any action   225
Is a step to the block, to the fire, down the sea's throat
Or to an illegible stone: and that is where we start.
We die with the dying:
See, they depart, and we go with them.
We are born with the dead: 230
See, they return, and bring us with them.
The moment of the rose and the moment of the yew tree
Are of equal duration. A people without history
Is not redeemed from time, for history is a pattern
Of timeless moments. So, while the light fails   235
On a winter's afternoon, in a secluded chapel
History is now and England.

With the drawing of this Love and the voice of this Calling[8]
We shall not cease from exploration
And the end of all our exploring   240
Will be to arrive where we started
And know the place for the first time.
Through the unknown, remembered gate
When the last of earth left to discover
Is that which was the beginning;   245
At the source of the longest river
The voice of the hidden waterfall
And the children in the apple tree
Not known, because not looked for
But heard, half-heard, in the stillness   250
Between two waves of the sea.[9]
Quick now, here, now, always—
A condition of complete simplicity
(Costing not less than everything)
And all shall be well and   255
All manner of thing shall be well
When the tongues of flame are in-folded
Into the crowned knot of fire
And the fire and the rose are one.

1942   1942, 1943

7. The word means both "company" and "harmony of sounds."
8. This line is from an anonymous 14th-century mystical work, the *Cloud of Unknowing.*
9. The voice of the children in the apple tree symbolizes the sudden moment of insight. Cf. the conclusion to

Burnt Norton (the first of the *Four Quartets*), where the laughter of the children in the garden has a like meaning: "Sudden in a shaft of sunlight / Even while the dust moves / There rises the hidden laughter / Of children in the foliage / Quick now, here, now, always * * * "

Tradition and the Individual Talent[1]

I

In English writing we seldom speak of tradition, though we occasionally apply its name in deploring its absence. We cannot refer to "the tradition" or to "a tradition"; at most, we employ the adjective in saying that the poetry of So-and-so is "traditional" or even "too traditional." Seldom, perhaps, does the word appear except in a phrase of censure. If otherwise, it is vaguely approbative, with the implication, as to the work approved, of some pleasing archaeological reconstruction. You can hardly make the word agreeable to English ears without this comfortable reference to the reassuring science of archaeology.

Certainly the word is not likely to appear in our appreciations of living or dead writers. Every nation, every race, has not only its own creative, but its own critical turn of mind; and is even more oblivious of the shortcomings and limitations of its critical habits than of those of its creative genius. We know, or think we know, from the enormous mass of critical writing that has appeared in the French language the critical method or habit of the French; we only conclude (we are such unconscious people) that the French are "more critical" than we, and sometimes even plume ourselves a little with the fact, as if the French were the less spontaneous. Perhaps they are; but we might remind ourselves that criticism is as inevitable as breathing, and that we should be none the worse for articulating what passes in our minds when we read a book and feel an emotion about it, for criticizing our own minds in their work of criticism. One of the facts that might come to light in this process is our tendency to insist, when we praise a poet, upon those aspects of his work in which he least resembles anyone else. In these aspects or parts of his work we pretend to find what is individual, what is the peculiar essence of the man. We dwell with satisfaction upon the poet's difference from his predecessors, especially his immediate predecessors; we endeavor to find something that can be isolated in order to be enjoyed. Whereas if we approach a poet without this prejudice we shall often find that not only the best, but the most individual parts of his work may be those in which the dead poets, his ancestors, assert their immortality most vigorously. And I do not mean the impressionable period of adolescence, but the period of full maturity.

Yet if the only form of tradition, of handing down, consisted in

1. First published in the *Egoist* (1919) and later collected in *The Sacred Wood* (1920), this essay is one of Eliot's most influential pieces of criticism.

following the ways of the immediate generation before us in a blind or timid adherence to its successes, "tradition" should positively be discouraged. We have seen many such simple currents soon lost in the sand; and novelty is better than repetition. Tradition is a matter of much wider significance. It cannot be inherited, and if you want it you must obtain it by great labor. It involves, in the first place, the historical sense, which we may call nearly indispensable to any one who would continue to be a poet beyond his twenty-fifth year; and the historical sense involves a perception, not only of the pastness of the past, but of its presence; the historical sense compels a man to write not merely with his own generation in his bones, but with a feeling that the whole of the literature of Europe from Homer and within it the whole of the literature of his own country has a simultaneous existence and composes a simultaneous order. This historical sense, which is a sense of the timeless as well as of the temporal and of the timeless and of the temporal together, is what makes a writer traditional. And it is at the same time what makes a writer most acutely conscious of his place in time, of his own contemporaneity.

No poet, no artist of any art, has his complete meaning alone. His significance, his appreciation is the appreciation of his relation to the dead poets and artists. You cannot value him alone; you must set him, for contrast and comparison, among the dead. I mean this as a principle of aesthetic, not merely historical, criticism. The necessity that he shall conform, that he shall cohere, is not onesided; what happens when a new work of art is created is something that happens simultaneously to all the works of art which preceded it. The existing monuments form an ideal order among themselves, which is modified by the introduction of the new (the really new) work of art among them. The existing order is complete before the new work arrives; for order to persist after the supervention of novelty, the *whole* existing order must be, if ever so slightly, altered; and so the relations, proportions, values of each work of art toward the whole are readjusted; and this is conformity between the old and the new. Whoever has approved this idea of order, of the form of European, of English literature will not find it preposterous that the past should be altered by the present as much as the present is directed by the past. And the poet who is aware of this will be aware of great difficulties and responsibilities.

In a peculiar sense he will be aware also that he must inevitably be judged by the standards of the past. I say judged, not amputated, by them; not judged to be as good as, or worse or better than, the dead; and certainly not judged by the canons of dead critics. It is a judgment, a comparison, in which two things are measured by each other. To conform merely would be for the new work not really to conform at all; it would not be new, and would therefore not be a work of art. And we do not quite say that the new is more valuable because it fits in; but its fitting in is a test of its value—a test, it is true, which can only be slowly and cautiously applied, for we are none of us infallible judges of conformity. We say: it appears to conform, and is perhaps individual, or it appears individual, and may conform; but we are hardly likely to find that it is one and not the other.

To proceed to a more intelligible exposition of the relation of the poet to the past: he can neither take the past as a lump, an indiscriminate bolus,[2] nor can he form himself wholly on one or two private admirations, nor can he form himself wholly upon one preferred period. The first course is inadmissible, the second is an important experience of youth, and the third is a pleasant and highly desirable supplement. The poet must be very conscious of the main current, which does not at all flow invariably through the most distinguished reputations. He must be quite aware of the obvious fact that art never improves, but that the material of art is never quite the same. He must be aware that the mind of Europe— the mind of his own country—a mind which he learns in time to be much more important than his own private mind—is a mind which changes, and that this change is a development which abandons nothing en route, which does not superannuate either Shakespeare, or Homer, or the rock drawing of the Magdalenian[3] draftsmen. That this development, refinement perhaps, complication certainly, is not, from the point of view of the artist, any improvement. Perhaps not even an improvement from the point of view of the psychologist or not to the extent which we imagine; perhaps only in the end based upon a complication in economics and machinery. But the difference between the present and the past is that the conscious present is an awareness of the past in a way and to an extent which the past's awareness of itself cannot show.

Someone said: "The dead writers are remote from us because we *know* so much more than they did." Precisely, and they are that which we know.

I am alive to a usual objection to what is clearly part of my program for the métier of poetry. The objection is that the doctrine requires a ridiculous amount of erudition (pedantry), a claim which can be rejected by appeal to the lives of poets in any pantheon. It will even be affirmed that much learning deadens or perverts poetic sensibility. While, however, we persist in believing that a poet ought to know as much as will not encroach upon his necessary receptivity and necessary laziness, it is not desirable to confine knowledge to whatever can be put into a useful shape for examinations, drawing rooms, or the still more pretentious modes of pub-

2. A round mass of anything: a large pill.
3. The most advanced culture of the European Paleolithic period (from discoveries at La Madeleine, France).

licity. Some can absorb knowledge, the more tardy must sweat for it. Shakespeare acquired more essential history from Plutarch[4] than most men could from the whole British Museum. What is to be insisted upon is that the poet must develop or procure the consciousness of the past and that he should continue to develop this consciousness throughout his career.

What happens is a continual surrender of himself as he is at the moment to something which is more valuable. The progress of an artist is a continual self-sacrifice, a continual extinction of personality.

There remains to define this process of depersonalization and its relation to the sense of tradition. It is in this depersonalization that art may be said to approach the condition of science. I, therefore, invite you to consider, as a suggestive analogy, the action which takes place when a bit of finely filiated[5] platinum is introduced into a chamber containing oxygen and sulphur dioxide.

II

Honest criticism and sensitive appreciation are directed not upon the poet but upon the poetry. If we attend to the confused cries of the newspaper critics and the *susurrus*[6] of popular repetition that follows, we shall hear the names of poets in great numbers; if we seek not Blue-book[7] knowledge but the enjoyment of poetry, and ask for a poem, we shall seldom find it. I have tried to point out the importance of the relation of the poem to other poems by other authors, and suggested the conception of poetry as a living whole of all the poetry that has ever been written. The other aspect of this Impersonal theory of poetry is the relation of the poem to its author. And I hinted, by an analogy, that the mind of the mature poet differs from that of the immature one not precisely in any valuation of "personality," not being necessarily more interesting, or having "more to say," but rather by being a more finely perfected medium in which special, or very varied, feelings are at liberty to enter into new combinations.

The analogy was that of the catalyst.[8] When the two gases previously mentioned are mixed in the presence of a filament of platinum, they form sulphurous acid. This combination takes place only if the platinum is present; nevertheless the newly formed acid contains no trace of platinum, and the platinum itself is apparently unaffected; has remained inert, neutral, and unchanged. The mind of the poet is the shred of platinum. It may partly or exclusively operate upon the experience of the man himself; but, the more perfect the artist, the more completely separate in him will be the

4. Greek biographer (1st century A.D.) of Greek and Roman celebrities, from whose work Shakespeare drew the plots of his Roman plays.
5. Drawn out like a thread.
6. Murmuring, buzzing.

7. British official government publication.
8. Substance that triggers a chemical change without itself being affected by the reaction.

man who suffers and the mind which creates; the more perfectly will the mind digest and transmute the passions which are its material.

The experience, you will notice, the elements which enter the presence of the transforming catalyst, are of two kinds: emotions and feelings. The effect of a work of art upon the person who enjoys it is an experience different in kind from any experience not of art. It may be formed out of one emotion, or may be a combination of several; and various feelings, inhering for the writer in particular words or phrases or images, may be added to compose the final result. Or great poetry may be made without the direct use of any emotion whatever: composed out of feelings solely. Canto XV of the *Inferno* (Brunetto Latini)[9] is a working up of the emotion evident in the situation; but the effect, though single as that of any work of art, is obtained by considerable complexity of detail. The last quatrain gives an image, a feeling attaching to an image, which "came," which did not develop simply out of what precedes, but which was probably in suspension in the poet's mind until the proper combination arrived for it to add itself to.[1] The poet's mind is in fact a receptacle for seizing and storing up numberless feelings, phrases, images, which remain there until all the particles which can unite to form a new compound are present together.

If you compare several representative passages of the greatest poetry you see how great is the variety of types of combination, and also how completely any semi-ethical criterion of "sublimity" misses the mark. For it is not the "greatness," the intensity, of the emotions, the components, but the intensity of the artistic process, the pressure, so to speak, under which the fusion takes place, that counts. The episode of Paolo and Francesca[2] employs a definite emotion, but the intensity of the poetry is something quite different from whatever intensity in the supposed experience it may give the impression of. It is no more intense, furthermore, than Canto XXVI,[3] the voyage of Ulysses, which has not the direct dependence upon an emotion. Great variety is possible in the process of transmutation of emotion: the murder of Agamemnon,[4] or the agony of Othello, gives an artistic effect apparently closer to a possible

9. Dante meets in Hell his old master Brunetto Latini, suffering eternal punishment for unnatural lust, yet still loved and admired by Dante, who addresses him with affectionate courtesy. It is one of the most moving passages in the *Inferno*.
1. Dante's strange interview with Brunetto is over, and Brunetto moves off to continue his punishment: "Then he turned round, and seemed like one of those / Who run for the green cloth [in the footrace] at Verona / In the

field; and he seemed among them / Not the loser but the winner."
2. Illicit lovers whom Dante meets in the second circle of Hell (*Inferno* V) and at whose punishment and sorrows he swoons with pity.
3. Of the *Inferno*. Ulysses, suffering in Hell for "false counseling," tells Dante of his final voyage.
4. By his wife Clytemnestra; the central action of Aeschylus' play *Agamemnon*.

original than the scenes from Dante. In the *Agamemnon*, the artistic emotion approximates to the emotion of an actual spectator; in *Othello* to the emotion of the protagonist himself. But the difference between art and the event is always absolute; the combination which is the murder of Agamemnon is probably as complex as that which is the voyage of Ulysses. In either case there has been a fusion of elements. The ode of Keats contains a number of feelings which have nothing particular to do with the nightingale, but which the nightingale, partly, perhaps, because of its attractive name, and partly because of its reputation, served to bring together.

The point of view which I am struggling to attack is perhaps related to the metaphysical theory of the substantial unity of the soul: for my meaning is, that the poet has, not a "personality" to express, but a particular medium, which is only a medium and not a personality, in which impressions and experiences combine in peculiar and unexpected ways. Impressions and experiences which are important for the man may take no place in the poetry, and those which become important in the poetry may play quite a negligible part in the man, the personality.

I will quote a passage which is unfamiliar enough to be regarded with fresh attention in the light—or darkness—of these observations:

> And now methinks I could e'en chide myself
> For doting on her beauty, though her death
> Shall be revenged after no common action.
> Does the silkworm expend her yellow labors
> For thee? For thee does she undo herself?
> Are lordships sold to maintain ladyships
> For the poor benefit of a bewildering minute?
> Why does yon fellow falsify highways,
> And put his life between the judge's lips,
> To refine such a thing—keeps horse and men
> To beat their valors for her? . . .[5]

In this passage (as is evident if it is taken in its context) there is a combination of positive and negative emotions: an intensely strong attraction toward beauty and an equally intense fascination by the ugliness which is contrasted with it and which destroys it. This balance of contrasted emotion is in the dramatic situation to which the speech is pertinent, but that situation alone is inadequate to it. This is, so to speak, the structural emotion, provided by the drama. But the whole effect, the dominant tone, is due to the fact that a number of floating feelings, having an affinity to this emotion by no means superficially evident, have combined with it to give us a new art emotion.

It is not in his personal emotions, the emotions provoked by par-

5. From Cyril Tourneur's *The Revenger's Tragedy* (1607), III.iv.

ticular events in his life, that the poet is in any way remarkable or interesting. His particular emotions may be simple, or crude, or flat. The emotion in his poetry will be a very complex thing, but not with the complexity of the emotions of people who have very complex or unusual emotions in life. One error, in fact, of eccentricity in poetry is to seek for new human emotions to express; and in this search for novelty in the wrong place it discovers the perverse. The business of the poet is not to find new emotions, but to use the ordinary ones and, in working them up into poetry, to express feelings which are not in actual emotions at all. And emotions which he has never experienced will serve his turn as well as those familiar to him. Consequently, we must believe that "emotion recollected in tranquility"[6] is an inexact formula. For it is neither emotion, nor recollection, nor, without distortion of meaning, tranquility. It is a concentration, and a new thing resulting from the concentration, of a very great number of experiences which to the practical and active person would not seem to be experiences at all; it is a concentration which does not happen consciously or of deliberation. These experiences are not "recollected," and they finally unite in an atmosphere which is "tranquil" only in that it is a passive attending upon the event. Of course this is not quite the whole story. There is a great deal, in the writing of poetry, which must be conscious and deliberate. In fact, the bad poet is usually unconscious where he ought to be conscious, and conscious where he ought to be unconscious. Both errors tend to make him "personal." Poetry is not a turning loose of emotion, but an escape from emotion; it is not the expression of personality, but an escape from personality. But, of course, only those who have personality and emotions know what it means to want to escape from these things.

III

ὁ δὲ νοῦς ἴσως Θειότερόν τι χαὶ ἀπαθές ἐστιν.[7]

This essay proposes to halt at the frontier of metaphysics or mysticism, and confine itself to such practical conclusions as can be applied by the responsible person interested in poetry. To divert interest from the poet to the poetry is a laudable aim: for it would conduce to a juster estimation of actual poetry, good and bad. There are many people who appreciate the expression of sincere emotion in verse, and there is a smaller number of people who can appreciate technical excellence. But very few know when there is an expression of *significant* emotion, emotion which has its life in the poem and not in the history of the poet. The emotion of art is impersonal. And the poet cannot reach this impersonality with-

6. Wordsworth, Preface to *Lyrical Ballads*, 2nd edition (1800). Wordsworth said that poetry "takes its origin from emotion recollected in tranquility."

7. "The mind is doubtless something more divine and unimpressionable." Aristotle, *De Anima* ("On the Soul"), I.4.

out surrendering himself wholly to the work to be done. And he is not likely to know what is to be done unless he lives in what is not merely the present, but the present moment of the past, unless he is conscious, not of what is dead, but of what is already living.

1919, 1920

The Metaphysical Poets

By collecting these poems[1] from the work of a generation more often named than read, and more often read than profitably studied, Professor Grierson has rendered a service of some importance. Certainly the reader will meet with many poems already preserved in other anthologies, at the same time that he discovers poems such as those of Aurelian Townshend or Lord Herbert of Cherbury here included. But the function of such an anthology as this is neither that of Professor Saintsbury's admirable edition of Caroline poets nor that of the *Oxford Book of English Verse*. Mr. Grierson's book is in itself a piece of criticism and a provocation of criticism; and we think that he was right in including so many poems of Donne, elsewhere (though not in many editions) accessible, as documents in the case of "metaphysical poetry." The phrase has long done duty as a term of abuse or as the label of a quaint and pleasant taste. The question is to what extent the so-called metaphysicals formed a school (in our own time we should say a "movement"), and how far this so-called school or movement is a digression from the main current.

Not only is it extremely difficult to define metaphysical poetry, but difficult to decide what poets practice it and in which of their verses. The poetry of Donne (to whom Marvell and Bishop King are sometimes nearer than any of the other authors) is late Elizabethan, its feeling often very close to that of Chapman. The "courtly" poetry is derivative from Jonson, who borrowed liberally from the Latin; it expires in the next century with the sentiment and witticism of Prior. There is finally the devotional verse of Herbert, Vaughan, and Crashaw (echoed long after by Christina Rossetti and Francis Thompson); Crashaw, sometimes more profound and less sectarian than the others, has a quality which returns through the Elizabethan period to the early Italians. It is difficult to find any precise use of metaphor, simile, or other conceit, which is common to all the poets and at the same time important enough as an element of style to isolate these poets as a group. Donne, and

1. *Metaphysical Lyrics and Poems of the Seventeenth Century:* Donne to Butler. Selected and edited, with an Essay, by Herbert J. C. Grierson (1921). Eliot's essay was originally a review of this book in the London *Times Literary Supplement*.

often Cowley, employ a device which is sometimes considered characteristically "metaphysical"; the elaboration (contrasted with the condensation) of a figure of speech to the farthest stage to which ingenuity can carry it. Thus Cowley develops the commonplace comparison of the world to a chessboard through long stanzas (*To Destiny*), and Donne, with more grace, in A *Valediction*,[2] the comparison of two lovers to a pair of compasses. But elsewhere we find, instead of the mere explication of the content of a comparison, a development by rapid association of thought which requires considerable agility on the part of the reader.

> On a round ball
> A workman that hath copies by, can lay
> An Europe, Afrique, and an Asia,
> And quickly make that which was nothing, all;
> So doth each tear,
> Which thee doth wear,
> A globe, yea world, by that impression grow,
> Till thy tears mixed with mine do overflow
> This world; by waters sent from thee, my heaven dissolvéd so.[3]

Here we find at least two connections which are not implicit in the first figure, but are forced upon it by the poet: from the geographer's globe to the tear, and the tear to the deluge. On the other hand, some of Donne's most successful and characteristic effects are secured by brief words and sudden contrasts:

> A bracelet of bright hair about the bone,[4]

where the most powerful effect is produced by the sudden contrast of associations of "bright hair" and of "bone." This telescoping of images and multiplied associations is characteristic of the phrase of some of the dramatists of the period which Donne knew: not to mention Shakespeare, it is frequent in Middleton, Webster, and Tourneur, and is one of the sources of the vitality of their language.

Johnson, who employed the term "metaphysical poets," apparently having Donne, Cleveland, and Cowley chiefly in mind, remarks of them that "the most heterogeneous ideas are yoked by violence together."[5] The force of this impeachment lies in the failure of the conjunction, the fact that often the ideas are yoked but not united; and if we are to judge of styles of poetry by their abuse, enough examples may be found in Cleveland to justify Johnson's condemnation. But a degree of heterogeneity of material compelled into unity by the operation of the poet's mind is omnipresent in poetry. We need not select for illustration such a line as:

---

2. I.e., *A Valediction: Forbidding Mourning.*
3. Donne's *A Valediction: Of Weeping*, lines 10–18.

4. *The Relique*, line 6.
5. See Samuel Johnson's *Life of Cowley.*

Notre âme est un trois-mâts cherchant son Icarie;[6]

we may find it in some of the best lines of Johnson himself (*The Vanity of Human Wishes*):

> His fate was destined to a barren strand,
> A petty fortress, and a dubious hand;
> He left a name at which the world grew pale,
> To point a moral, or adorn a tale.

where the effect is due to a contrast of ideas, different in degree but the same in principle, as that which Johnson mildly reprehended. And in one of the finest poems of the age (a poem which could not have been written in any other age), the *Exequy* of Bishop King, the extended comparison is used with perfect success: the idea and the simile become one, in the passage in which the Bishop illustrates his impatience to see his dead wife, under the figure of a journey:

> Stay for me there; I will not fail
> To meet thee in that hollow Vale.
> And think not much of my delay;
> I am already on the way,
> And follow thee with all the speed
> Desire can make, or sorrows breed.
> Each minute is a short degree,
> And ev'ry hour a step towards thee.
> At night when I betake to rest,
> Next morn I rise nearer my West
> Of life, almost by eight hours sail,
> Than when sleep breathed his drowsy gale. . . .
> But hark! My pulse, like a soft drum
> Beats my approach, tells Thee I come;
> And slow howe'er my marches be,
> I shall at last sit down by Thee.

(In the last few lines there is that effect of terror which is several times attained by one of Bishop King's admirers, Edgar Poe.) Again, we may justly take these quatrains from Lord Herbert's Ode,[7] stanzas which would, we think, be immediately pronounced to be of the metaphysical school:

> So when from hence we shall be gone,
> And be no more, nor you, nor I,
> As one another's mystery,
> Each shall be both, yet both but one.

6. "Our soul is a three-masted ship searching for her Icarie"; a line from Charles Baudelaire's poem, *Le Voyage* (Icarie is an imaginary utopia in *Voyage en Icarie*, 1840, a novel by the French socialist Etienne Cabet).

7. Lord Herbert of Cherbury (1583–1648), brother of George Herbert. The "Ode" is his *Ode upon a Question moved, whether Love should continue forever?*

> This said, in her uplifted face,
>   Her eyes, which did that beauty crown,
>   Were like two stars, that having faln down,
> Look up again to find their place:
>
> While such a moveless silent peace
>   Did seize on their becalméd sense,
>   One would have thought some influence
> Their ravished spirits did possess.

There is nothing in these lines (with the possible exception of the stars, a simile not at once grasped, but lovely and justified) which fits Johnson's general observations on the metaphysical poets in his essay on Cowley. A good deal resides in the richness of association which is at the same time borrowed from and given to the word "becalmed"; but the meaning is clear, the language simple and elegant. It is to be observed that the language of these poets is as a rule simple and pure; in the verse of George Herbert this simplicity is carried as far as it can go—a simplicity emulated without success by numerous modern poets. The *structure* of the sentences, on the other hand, is sometimes far from simple, but this is not a vice; it is a fidelity to thought and feeling. The effect, at its best, is far less artificial than that of an ode by Gray. And as this fidelity induces variety of thought and feeling, so it induces variety of music. We doubt whether, in the eighteenth century, could be found two poems in nominally the same meter, so dissimilar as Marvell's *Coy Mistress* and Crashaw's *Saint Teresa*; the one producing an effect of great speed by the use of short syllables, and the other an ecclesiastical solemnity by the use of long ones:

> Love, thou art absolute sole lord
> Of life and death.

If so shrewd and sensitive (though so limited) a critic as Johnson failed to define metaphysical poetry by its faults, it is worth while to inquire whether we may not have more success by adopting the opposite method: by assuming that the poets of the seventeenth century (up to the Revolution[8]) were the direct and normal development of the precedent age; and, without prejudicing their case by the adjective "metaphysical," consider whether their virtue was not something permanently valuable, which subsequently disappeared, but ought not to have disappeared. Johnson has hit, perhaps by accident, on one of their peculiarities, when he observes that "their attempts were always analytic"; he would not agree that, after the dissociation, they put the material together again in a new unity.

It is certain that the dramatic verse of the later Elizabethan and early Jacobean poets expresses a degree of development of sensibil-

8. Of 1688; when James II was replaced by William and Mary.

ity which is not found in any of the prose, good as it often is. If
we except Marlowe, a man of prodigious intelligence, these dramatists were directly or indirectly (it is at least a tenable theory)
affected by Montaigne. Even if we except also Jonson and Chapman, these two were probably erudite, and were notably men who
incorporated their erudition into their sensibility: their mode of
feeling was directly and freshly altered by their reading and thought.
In Chapman especially there is a direct sensuous apprehension of
thought, or a recreation of thought into feeling, which is exactly
what we find in Donne:

> in this one thing, all the discipline
> Of manners and of manhood is contained;
> A man to join himself with th' Universe
> In his main sway, and make in all things fit
> One with that All, and go on, round as it;
> Not plucking from the whole his wretched part,
> And into straits, or into nought revert,
> Wishing the complete Universe might be
> Subject to such a rag of it as he;
> But to consider great Necessity.[9]

We compare this with some modern passage:

> No, when the fight begins within himself,
> A man's worth something. God stoops o'er his head,
> Satan looks up between his feet—both tug—
> He's left, himself, i' the middle; the soul wakes
> And grows. Prolong that battle through his life![1]

It is perhaps somewhat less fair, though very tempting (as both
poets are concerned with the perpetuation of love by offspring),
to compare with the stanzas already quoted from Lord Herbert's
Ode the following from Tennyson:

> One walked between his wife and child,
> With measured footfall firm and mild,
> And now and then he gravely smiled.
> The prudent partner of his blood
> Leaned on him, faithful, gentle, good,
> Wearing the rose of womanhood.
> And in their double love secure,
> The little maiden walked demure,
> Pacing with downward eyelids pure.
> These three made unity so sweet,
> My frozen heart began to beat,
> Remembering its ancient heat.[2]

---

9. From *The Revenge of Bussy d'Am-*
bois (IV.i.137–46).
1. Robert Browning's *Bishop Blou-*
gram's Apology, lines 693–97.
2. Tennyson's *The Two Voices,* lines
412–23.

The difference is not a simple difference of degree between poets. It is something which had happened to the mind of England between the time of Donne or Lord Herbert of Cherbury and the time of Tennyson and Browning; it is the difference between the intellectual poet and the reflective poet. Tennyson and Browning are poets, and they think; but they do not feel their thought as immediately as the odor of a rose. A thought to Donne was an experience; it modified his sensibility. When a poet's mind is perfectly equipped for its work, it is constantly amalgamating disparate experience; the ordinary man's experience is chaotic, irregular, fragmentary. The latter falls in love, or reads Spinoza, and these two experiences have nothing to do with each other, or with the noise of the typewriter or the smell of cooking; in the mind of the poet these experiences are always forming new wholes.

We may express the difference by the following theory: The poets of the seventeenth century, the successors of the dramatists of the sixteenth, possessed a mechanism of sensibility which could devour any kind of experience. They are simple, artificial, difficult, or fantastic, as their predecessors were; no less nor more than Dante, Guido Cavalcanti, Guinicelli, or Cino.[3] In the seventeenth century a dissociation of sensibility set in, from which we have never recovered; and this dissociation, as is natural, was aggravated by the influence of the two most powerful poets of the century, Milton and Dryden. Each of these men performed certain poetic functions so magnificently well that the magnitude of the effect concealed the absence of others. The language went on and in some respects improved; the best verse of Collins, Gray, Johnson, and even Goldsmith satisfies some of our fastidious demands better than that of Donne or Marvell or King. But while the language became more refined, the feeling became more crude. The feeling, the sensibility, expressed in the *Country Churchyard* (to say nothing of Tennyson and Browning) is cruder than that in the *Coy Mistress*.

The second effect of the influence of Milton and Dryden followed from the first, and was therefore slow in manifestation. The sentimental age began early in the eighteenth century, and continued. The poets revolted against the ratiocinative, the descriptive; they thought and felt by fits, unbalanced; they reflected. In one or two passages of Shelley's *Triumph of Life*, in the second *Hyperion*, there are traces of a struggle toward unification of sensibility. But Keats and Shelley died, and Tennyson and Browning ruminated.

After this brief exposition of a theory—too brief, perhaps, to

3. These last three poets, all of whom lived in the 13th century, were members of the Tuscan school of lyric love poets (Guido Guinicelli was hailed by Dante in the *Purgatorio* as "father of Italian poets"; Cino da Pistoia was a friend of Dante and Petrarch).

carry conviction—we may ask, what would have been the fate of
the "metaphysical" had the current of poetry descended in a direct
line from them, as it descended in a direct line to them? They
would not, certainly, be classified as metaphysical. The possible interests of a poet are unlimited; the more intelligent he is the better;
the more intelligent he is the more likely that he will have interests:
our only condition is that he turn them into poetry, and not merely
meditate on them poetically. A philosophical theory which has
entered into poetry is established, for its truth or falsity in one
sense ceases to matter, and its truth in another sense is proved.
The poets in question have, like other poets, various faults. But
they were, at best, engaged in the task of trying to find the verbal
equivalent for states of mind and feeling. And this means both that
they are more mature, and that they wear better, than later poets
of certainly not less literary ability.

It is not a permanent necessity that poets should be interested
in philosophy, or in any other subject. We can only say that it
appears likely that poets in our civilization, as it exists at present,
must be *difficult*. Our civilization comprehends great variety and
complexity, and this variety and complexity, playing upon a refined
sensibility, must produce various and complex results. The poet
must become more and more comprehensive, more allusive, more
indirect, in order to force, to dislocate if necessary, language into
his meaning. (A brilliant and extreme statement of this view, with
which it is not requisite to associate oneself, is that of M. Jean
Epstein, *La Poésie d'aujourd'hui.*[4]) Hence we get something which
looks very much like the conceit—we get, in fact, a method curiously similar to that of the "metaphysical poets," similar also in its
use of obscure words and of simple phrasing.

> *O géraniums diaphanes, guerroyeurs sortilèges,*
> *Sacrilèges monomanes!*
> *Emballages, dévergondages, douches! O pressoirs*
> *Des vendanges des grands soirs!*
> *Layettes aux abois,*
> *Thyrses au fond des bois!*
> *Transfusions, représailles,*
> *Relevailles, compresses et l'éternal potion,*
> *Angélus! n'en pouvoir plus*
> *De débâcles nuptiales! de débâcles nuptiales!*[5]

4. "Poetry of Today."
5. "O transparent geraniums, warrior
incantations, / Monomaniac sacrileges!
/ Packing materials, shamelessnesses,
shower baths! O wine presses / Of
great evening vintages! / Hard-pressed
baby linen, / Thyrsis in the depths of
the woods! / Transfusions, reprisals,
/ Churchings, compresses, and the eternal potion, / Angelus! no longer to be

borne [are] / Catastrophic marriages!
catastrophic marriages!" This passage
is from *Derniers vers X* ("Last Poems,"
1890), by Jules Laforgue (1860–87).
Eliot oddly sees a similarity between
this kind of hysterical free association
and the strictly ordered imagery of the
metaphysicals. But it is the combination of "obscure words and simple
phrasing" that strikes him in both.

The same poet could write also simply:

> *Elle est bien loin, elle pleure,*
> *Le grand vent se lamente aussi . . .*[6]

Jules Laforgue, and Tristan Corbière[7] in many of his poems, are nearer to the "school of Donne" than any modern English poet. But poets more classical than they have the same essential quality of transmuting ideas into sensations, of transforming an observation into a state of mind.

> *Pour l'enfant, amoureux de cartes et d'estampes,*
> *L'univers est égal à son vaste appétit.*
> *Ah, que le monde est grand à la clarté des lampes!*
> *Aux yeux du souvenir que le monde est petit!*[8]

In French literature the great master of the seventeenth century —Racine—and the great master of the nineteenth—Baudelaire— are in some ways more like each other than they are like any one else. The greatest two masters of diction are also the greatest two psychologists, the most curious explorers of the soul. It is interesting to speculate whether it is not a misfortune that two of the greatest masters of diction in our language, Milton and Dryden, triumph with a dazzling disregard of the soul. If we continued to produce Miltons and Drydens it might not so much matter, but as things are it is a pity that English poetry has remained so incomplete. Those who object to the "artificiality" of Milton or Dryden sometimes tell us to "look into our hearts and write." But that is not looking deep enough; Racine or Donne looked into a good deal more than the heart. One must look into the cerebral cortex, the nervous system, and the digestive tracts.

May we not conclude, then, that Donne, Crashaw, Vaughan, Herbert and Lord Herbert, Marvell, King, Cowley at his best, are in the direct current of English poetry, and that their faults should be reprimanded by this standard rather than coddled by antiquarian affection? They have been enough praised in terms which are implicit limitations because they are "metaphysical" or "witty," "quaint" or "obscure," though at their best they have not these attributes more than other serious poets. On the other hand, we must not reject the criticism of Johnson (a dangerous person to disagree with) without having mastered it, without having assimilated the Johnsonian canons of taste. In reading the celebrated passage in his essay on Cowley we must remember that by wit he clearly means something more serious than we usually mean today;

---

6. "She is far away, she weeps, / The great wind mourns also." From *Derniers vers XI, Sur une défunte* ("On a Dead Woman").

7. 1845–75; also a French Symbolist poet.

8. From Baudelaire's *Le Voyage:* "For the child, in love with maps and prints, / The universe matches his vast appetite. / Ah, how big the world is by lamplight! How small the world is to the eyes of memory!"

in his criticism of their versification we must remember in what a narrow discipline he was trained, but also how well trained; we must remember that Johnson tortures chiefly the chief offenders, Cowley and Cleveland. It would be a fruitful work, and one requiring a substantial book, to break up the classification of Johnson (for there has been none since) and exhibit these poets in all their difference of kind and of degree, from the massive music of Donne to the faint, pleasing tinkle of Aurelian Townshend—whose *Dialogue Between a Pilgrim and Time* is one of the few regrettable omissions from the excellent anthology of Professor Grierson.

1921

KATHERINE MANSFIELD
(1888–1923)

Katherine Mansfield was born in Wellington, New Zealand, third daughter of Harold (later Sir Harold) Beauchamp, an energetic businessman. After early schooling in New Zealand she spent four years "finishing" at Queen's College in London, before returning to New Zealand in 1906. Ambitious, and dissatisfied with the life of a successful merchant's daughter, she went to London again in 1908 in order to embark on a literary career. Her first year there was disastrous. She made an unfortunate marriage, left her husband, and became pregnant by another man. She retreated to Germany to have her baby, but lost it by miscarriage. Disillusioned and unhappy, she wrote a series of bitter sketches of life as she observed it in Germany (published in 1911 as *In a German Pension*). In 1910 she was back in London, writing stories for the *New Age* (where some of her German stories first appeared). In 1912 she met the editor and critic John Middleton Murry, and though she was not able to marry him until 1918, when her first husband divorced her, their life together began at this time.

In the two following years she wrote stories for the two periodicals successively edited by Murry, *Rhythm* and the *Blue Review*. In 1916, after the death of her much loved brother in World War I, she embarked on a series of stories with New Zealand settings, drawing on recollections of her childhood with him; *Prelude*, the first and longest of these, was published in 1918. It was included in *Bliss and Other Stories* (1920) which, with *The Garden Party and Other Stories* (1922) and *The Dove's Nest and Other Stories* (1923), contains her best work. All this time she was vainly seeking health in the south of France, in Switzerland, and elsewhere, for, as early as 1917, she knew she had tuberculosis. She stopped writing altogether in 1922, and died suddenly in January, 1923.

Katherine Mansfield is essentially a short-story writer. The quiet clarity of detail, the symbolic use of objects and incidents presented with extraordinary physical accuracy, the ability to distill an atmosphere, to suggest by a few details a whole way of life, both individual and social, are the most striking features of her best stories. She works through suggestion rather than explicit development; *The Daughters of the Late Colonel*, for example, with its subdued elegiac sense of wasted lives, is potential tragedy, but the surface is restrained comedy. The meaning is achieved most of all through the atmosphere, and the atmosphere is built up through the accumulation of small strokes, none of which seems in itself more than a piece of shrewdly observed realistic detail. The ability to manipulate time is another quality Katherine Mansfield shows in her best work: she makes particularly effective use of the unobtrusive flash back, where we find ourselves in an earlier phase of the action without quite knowing how we got there although fully aware of its relevance to the total action and atmosphere. Her most characteristic stories are never shrill or violent or obvious; she rarely approaches her subject head-on. Her work was an influential contribution to the subtilization of technique in the short story which has been the main contribution of the 20th century to this genre.

The Daughters of the Late Colonel

1

The week after was one of the busiest weeks of their lives. Even when they went to bed it was only their bodies that lay down and rested; their minds went on, thinking things out, talking things over, wondering, deciding, trying to remember where . . .

Constantia lay like a statue, her hands by her sides, her feet just overlapping each other, the sheet up to her chin. She stared at the ceiling.

"Do you think father would mind if we gave his top hat to the porter?"

"The porter?" snapped Josephine. "Why ever the porter? What a very extraordinary idea!"

"Because," said Constantia slowly, "he must often have to go to funerals. And I noticed at—at the cemetery that he only had a bowler." She paused. "I thought then how very much he'd appreciate a top hat. We ought to give him a present, too. He was always very nice to father."

"But," cried Josephine, flouncing on her pillow and staring across the dark at Constantia, "father's head!" And suddenly, for one awful moment, she nearly giggled. Not, of course, that she felt in the least like giggling. It must have been habit. Years ago, when they had stayed awake at night talking, their beds had simply heaved. And now the porter's head, disappearing, popped out, like a candle, under father's hat. . . . The giggle mounted, mounted; she clenched her hands; she fought it down; she frowned fiercely at the dark and said "Remember" terribly sternly.

"We can decide tomorrow," she sighed.

Constantia had noticed nothing; she sighed.

"Do you think we ought to have our dressing gowns dyed as well?"

"Black?" almost shrieked Josephine.

"Well, what else?" said Constantia. "I was thinking—it doesn't seem quite sincere, in a way, to wear black out of doors and when we're fully dressed, and then when we're at home——"

"But nobody sees us," said Josephine. She gave the bedclothes such a twitch that both her feet became uncovered, and she had to creep up the pillows to get them well under again.

"Kate does," said Constantia. "And the postman very well might."

Josephine thought of her dark-red slippers, which matched her dressing gown, and of Constantia's favorite indefinite green ones which went with hers. Black! Two black dressing gowns and two pairs of black woolly slippers, creeping off to the bathroom like black cats.

"I don't think it's absolutely necessary," said she.

Silence. Then Constantia said, "We shall have to post the papers with the notice in them tomorrow to catch the Ceylon mail. . . . How many letters have we had up till now?"

"Twenty-three."

Josephine had replied to them all, and twenty-three times when she came to "We miss our dear father so much" she had broken down and had to use her handkerchief, and on some of them even to soak up a very light-blue tear with an edge of blotting paper. Strange! She couldn't have put it on—but twenty-three times. Even now, though, when she said over to herself sadly, "We miss our dear father *so* much" she could have cried if she'd wanted to.

"Have you got enough stamps?" came from Constantia.

"Oh, how can I tell?" said Josephine crossly. "What's the good of asking me that now?"

"I was just wondering," said Constantia mildly.

Silence again. There came a little rustle, a scurry, a hop.

"A mouse," said Constantia.

"It can't be a mouse because there aren't any crumbs," said Josephine.

"But it doesn't know there aren't," said Constantia.

A spasm of pity squeezed her heart. Poor little thing! She wished she'd left a tiny piece of biscuit on the dressing table. It was awful to think of it not finding anything. What would it do?

"I can't think how they manage to live at all," she said slowly.

"Who?" demanded Josephine.

And Constantia said more loudly than she meant to, "Mice."

Josephine was furious. "Oh, what nonsense, Con!" she said. "What have mice got to do with it? You're asleep."

"I don't think I am," said Constantia. She shut her eyes to make sure. She was.

Josephine arched her spine, pulled up her knees, folded her arms so that her fists came under her ears, and pressed her cheek hard against the pillow.

2

Another thing which complicated matters was they had Nurse Andrews staying on with them that week. It was their own fault; they had asked her. It was Josephine's idea. On the morning—well, on the last morning, when the doctor had gone, Josephine had said to Constantia, "Don't you think it would be rather nice if we asked Nurse Andrews to stay on for a week as our guest?"

"Very nice," said Constantia.

"I thought," went on Josephine quickly, "I should just say this afternoon, after I've paid her, 'My sister and I would be very pleased, after all you've done for us, Nurse Andrews, if you would stay on for a week as our guest.' I'd have to put that in about being our guest in case——"

"Oh, but she could hardly expect to be paid!" cried Constantia.

"One never knows," said Josephine sagely.

Nurse Andrews had, of course, jumped at the idea. But it was a bother. It meant they had to have regular sit-down meals at the proper times, whereas if they'd been alone they could just have asked Kate if she wouldn't have minded bringing them a tray wherever they were. And meal times now that the strain was over were rather a trial.

Nurse Andrews was simply fearful about butter. Really they couldn't help feeling that about butter, at least, she took advantage of their kindness. And she had that maddening habit of asking for just an inch more bread to finish what she had on her plate, and then, at the last mouthful, absent-mindedly—of course it wasn't absent-mindedly—taking another helping. Josephine got very red when this happened, and she fastened her small, beadlike eyes on the tablecloth as if she saw a minute strange insect creeping through the web of it. But Constantia's long, pale face lengthened and set, and she gazed away—away—far over the desert, to where that line of camels unwound like a thread of wool. . . .

"When I was with Lady Tukes," said Nurse Andrews, "she had such a dainty little contrayvance for the buttah. It was a silvah Cupid balanced on the—on the bordah of a glass dish, holding a tayny fork. And when you wanted some buttah you simply pressed his foot and he bent down and speared you a piece. It was quite a gayme."

Josephine could hardly bear that. But "I think those things are very extravagant" was all she said.

"But whey?" asked Nurse Andrews, beaming through her eyeglasses. "No one, surely, would take more buttah than one wanted—would one?"

"Ring, Con," cried Josephine. She couldn't trust herself to reply.

And proud young Kate, the enchanted princess, came in to see what the old tabbies wanted now. She snatched away their plates of mock something or other and slapped down a white, terrified blanc-mange.

"Jam, please, Kate," said Josephine kindly.

Kate knelt and burst open the sideboard, lifted the lid of the jam pot, saw it was empty, put it on the table, and stalked off.

"I'm afraid," said Nurse Andrews a moment later, "there isn't any."

"Oh, what a bother!" said Josephine. She bit her lip. "What had we better do?"

Constantia looked dubious. "We can't disturb Kate again," she said softly.

Nurse Andrews waited, smiling at them both. Her eyes wandered, spying at everything behind her eyeglasses. Constantia in despair went back to her camels. Josephine frowned heavily—concentrated. If it hadn't been for this idiotic woman she and Con would, of course, have eaten their blanc-mange without. Suddenly the idea came.

"I know," she said. "Marmalade. There's some marmalade in the sideboard. Get it, Con."

"I hope," laughed Nurse Andrews, and her laugh was like a spoon tinkling against a medicine glass—"I hope it's not very bittah marmalayde."

3

But, after all, it was not long now, and then she'd be gone for good. And there was no getting over the fact that she had been very kind to father. She had nursed him day and night at the end. Indeed, both Constantia and Josephine felt privately she had rather overdone the not leaving him at the very last. For when they had gone in to say good-by Nurse Andrews had sat beside his bed the whole time, holding his wrist and pretending to look at her watch. It couldn't have been necessary. It was so tactless, too. Supposing father had wanted to say something—something private to them. Not that he had. Oh, far from it! He lay there, purple, a dark, angry purple in the face, and never even looked at them when they came in. Then, as they were standing there, wondering what to do, he had suddenly opened one eye. Oh, what a difference it would have made, what a difference to their memory of him, how much easier to tell people about it, if he had only opened both! But no—one eye only. It glared at them a moment and then . . . went out.

4

It had made it very awkward for them when Mr. Farolles, of St. John's, called the same afternoon.

"The end was quite peaceful, I trust?" were the first words he said as he glided towards them through the dark drawing room.

"Quite," said Josephine faintly. They both hung their heads.

Both of them felt certain that eye wasn't at all a peaceful eye.

"Won't you sit down?" said Josephine.

"Thank you, Miss Pinner," said Mr. Farolles gratefully. He folded his coat-tails and began to lower himself into father's arm-chair, but just as he touched it he almost sprang up and slid into the next chair instead.

He coughed. Josephine clasped her hands; Constantia looked vague.

"I want you to feel, Miss Pinner," said Mr. Farolles, "and you, Miss Constantia, that I'm trying to be helpful. I want to be helpful to you both, if you will let me. These are the times," said Mr. Farolles, very simply and earnestly, "when God means us to be helpful to one another."

"Thank you very much, Mr. Farolles," said Josephine and Constantia.

"Not at all," said Mr. Farolles gently. He drew his kid gloves through his fingers and leaned forward. "And if either of you would like a little Communion, either or both of you, here *and* now, you have only to tell me. A little Communion is often very help—a great comfort," he added tenderly.

But the idea of a little Communion terrified them. What! In the drawing room by themselves—with no—no altar or anything! The piano would be much too high, thought Constantia, and Mr. Farolles could not possibly lean over it with the chalice. And Kate would be sure to come bursting in and interrupt them, thought Josephine. And supposing the bell rang in the middle? It might be somebody important—about their mourning. Would they get up reverently and go out, or would they have to wait . . . in torture?

"Perhaps you will send round a note by your good Kate if you would care for it later," said Mr. Farolles.

"Oh yes, thank you very much!" they both said.

Mr. Farolles got up and took his black straw hat from the round table.

"And about the funeral," he said softly. "I may arrange that—as your dear father's old friend and yours, Miss Pinner—and Miss Constantia?"

Josephine and Constantia got up too.

"I should like it to be quite simple," said Josephine firmly, "and not too expensive. At the same time, I should like——"

"A good one that will last," thought dreamy Constantia, as if Josephine were buying a nightgown. But of course Josephine didn't say that. "One suitable to our father's position." She was very nervous.

"I'll run round to our good friend Mr. Knight," said Mr. Farolles soothingly. "I will ask him to come and see you. I am sure you will find him very helpful indeed."

5

Well, at any rate, all that part of it was over, though neither of them could possibly believe that father was never coming back. Josephine had had a moment of absolute terror at the cemetery, while the coffin was lowered, to think that she and Constantia had done this thing without asking his permission. What would father say when he found out? For he was bound to find out sooner or later. He always did. "Buried. You two girls had me *buried!*" She heard his stick thumping. Oh, what would they say? What possible excuse could they make? It sounded such an appallingly heartless thing to do. Such a wicked advantage to take of a person because he happened to be helpless at the moment. The other people seemed to treat it all as a matter of course. They were strangers; they couldn't be expected to understand that father was the very last person for such a thing to happen to. No, the entire blame for it all would fall on her and Constantia. And the expense, she thought, stepping into the tight-buttoned cab. When she had to show him the bills. What would he say then?

She heard him absolutely roaring, "And do you expect me to pay for this gimcrack excursion of yours?"

"Oh," groaned poor Josephine aloud, "we shouldn't have done it, Con!"

And Constantia, pale as a lemon in all that blackness, said in a frightened whisper, "Done what, Jug?"

"Let them bu-bury father like that," said Josephine, breaking down and crying into her new, queer-smelling mourning handkerchief.

"But what else could we have done?" asked Constantia wonderingly. "We couldn't have kept him, Jug—we couldn't have kept him unburied. At any rate, not in a flat that size."

Josephine blew her nose; the cab was dreadfully stuffy.

"I don't know," she said forlornly. "It is all so dreadful. I feel we ought to have tried to, just for a time at least. To make perfectly sure. One thing's certain"—and her tears sprang out again—"father will never forgive us for this—never!"

6

Father would never forgive them. That was what they felt more than ever when, two mornings later, they went into his room to go through his things. They had discussed it quite calmly. It was even down on Josephine's list of things to be done. *Go through father's things and settle about them.* But that was a very different matter from saying after breakfast:

"Well, are you ready, Con?"

"Yes, Jug—when you are."

"Then I think we'd better get it over."

It was dark in the hall. It had been a rule for years never to disturb father in the morning, whatever happened. And now they were going to open the door without knocking even. . . . Constantia's eyes were enormous at the idea; Josephine felt weak in the knees.

"You—you go first," she gasped, pushing Constantia.

But Constantia said, as she always had said on those occasions, "No, Jug, that's not fair. You're eldest."

Josephine was just going to say—what at other times she wouldn't have owned to for the world—what she kept for her very last weapon, "But you're tallest," when they noticed that the kitchen door was open, and there stood Kate. . . .

"Very stiff," said Josephine, grasping the door-handle and doing her best to turn it. As if anything ever deceived Kate!

It couldn't be helped. That girl was . . . Then the door was shut behind them, but—but they weren't in father's room at all. They might have suddenly walked through the wall by mistake into a different flat altogether. Was the door just behind them? They were too frightened to look. Josephine knew that if it was it was holding itself tight shut; Constantia felt that, like the doors in dreams, it hadn't any handle at all. It was the coldness which made it so awful. Or the whiteness—which? Everything was covered. The blinds were down, a cloth hung over the mirror, a sheet hid the bed; a huge fan of white paper filled the fireplace. Constantia timidly put out her hand; she almost expected a snowflake to fall. Josephine felt a queer tingling in her nose, as if her nose was freezing. Then a cab klop-klopped over the cobbles below, and the quiet seemed to shake into little pieces.

"I had better pull up a blind," said Josephine bravely.

"Yes, it might be a good idea," whispered Constantia.

They only gave the blind a touch, but it flew up and the cord flew after, rolling round the blind-stick, and the little tassel tapped as if trying to get free. That was too much for Constantia.

"Don't you think—don't you think we might put it off for another day?" she whispered.

"Why?" snapped Josephine, feeling, as usual, much better now that she knew for certain that Constantia was terrified. "It's got to be done. But I do wish you wouldn't whisper, Con."

"I didn't know I was whispering," whispered Constantia.

"And why do you keep on staring at the bed?" said Josephine, raising her voice almost defiantly. "There's nothing *on* the bed."

"Oh, Jug, don't say so!" said poor Connie. "At any rate, not so loudly."

Josephine felt herself that she had gone too far. She took a wide swerve over to the chest of drawers, put out her hand, but quickly drew it back again.

"Connie!" she gasped, and she wheeled round and leaned with her back against the chest of drawers.

"Oh, Jug—what?"

Josephine could only glare. She had the most extraordinary feeling that she had just escaped something simply awful. But how could she explain to Constantia that father was in the chest of drawers? He was in the top drawer with his handkerchiefs and neckties, or in the next with his shirts and pajamas, or in the lowest of all with his suits. He was watching there, hidden away—just behind the door handle—ready to spring.

She pulled a funny old-fashioned face at Constantia, just as she used to in the old days when she was going to cry.

"I can't open," she nearly wailed.

"No, don't, Jug," whispered Constantia earnestly. "It's much better not to. Don't let's open anything. At any rate, not for a long time."

"But—but it seems so weak," said Josephine, breaking down.

"But why not be weak for once, Jug?" argued Constantia, whispering quite fiercely. "If it is weak." And her pale stare flew from the locked writing table—so safe—to the huge glittering wardrobe, and she began to breathe in a queer, panting way. "Why shouldn't we be weak for once in our lives, Jug? It's quite excusable. Let's be weak—be weak, Jug. It's much nicer to be weak than to be strong."

And then she did one of those amazingly bold things that she'd done about twice before in their lives; she marched over to the wardrobe, turned the key, and took it out of the lock. Took it out of the lock and held it up to Josephine, showing Josephine by her extraordinary smile that she knew what she'd done, she'd risked deliberately father being in there among his overcoats.

If the huge wardrobe had lurched forward, had crashed down on Constantia, Josephine wouldn't have been surprised. On the contrary, she would have thought it the only suitable thing to happen. But nothing happened. Only the room seemed quieter than ever, and bigger flakes of cold air fell on Josephine's shoulders and knees. She began to shiver.

"Come, Jug," said Constantia, still with that awful callous smile, and Josephine followed just as she had that last time, when Constantia had pushed Benny into the round pond.

7

But the strain told on them when they were back in the dining room. They sat down, very shaky, and looked at each other.

"I don't feel I can settle to anything," said Josephine, "until I've had something. Do you think we could ask Kate for two cups of hot water?"

"I really don't see why we shouldn't," said Constantia carefully. She was quite normal again. "I won't ring. I'll go to the kitchen door and ask her."

"Yes, do," said Josephine, sinking down into a chair. "Tell her, just two cups, Con, nothing else—on a tray."

"She needn't even put the jug on, need she?" said Constantia, as though Kate might very well complain if the jug had been there.

"Oh no, certainly not! The jug's not at all necessary. She can pour it direct out of the kettle," cried Josephine, feeling that would be a labor-saving indeed.

Their cold lips quivered at the greenish brims. Josephine curved her small red hands round the cup; Constantia sat up and blew on the wavy stream, making it flutter from one side to the other.

"Speaking of Benny," said Josephine.

And though Benny hadn't been mentioned Constantia immediately looked as though he had.

"He'll expect us to send him something of father's, of course. But it's so difficult to know what to send to Ceylon."

"You mean things get unstuck so on the voyage," murmured Constantia.

"No, lost," said Josephine sharply. "You know there's no post. Only runners."

Both paused to watch a black man in white linen drawers running through the pale fields for dear life, with a large brown-paper parcel in his hands. Josephine's black man was tiny; he scurried along glistening like an ant. But there was something blind and tireless about Constantia's tall, thin fellow, which made him, she decided, a very unpleasant person indeed. . . . On the veranda, dressed all in white and wearing a cork helmet, stood Benny. His right hand shook up and down, as father's did when he was impatient. And behind him, not in the least interested, sat Hilda, the unknown sister-in-law. She swung in a cane rocker and flicked over the leaves of the *Tatler*.

"I think his watch would be the most suitable present," said Josephine.

Constantia looked up; she seemed surprised.

"Oh, would you trust a gold watch to a native?"

"But of course I'd disguise it," said Josephine. "No one would know it was a watch." She liked the idea of having to make a parcel such a curious shape that no one could possibly guess what it was. She even thought for a moment of hiding the watch in a narrow cardboard corset-box that she'd kept by her for a long time, waiting for it to come in for something. It was such beautiful firm cardboard. But, no, it wouldn't be appropriate for this occasion. It had lettering on it: *Medium Women's 28. Extra Firm Busks*. It would be almost too much of a surprise for Benny to open that and find father's watch inside.

"And of course it isn't as though it would be going—ticking, I mean," said Constantia, who was still thinking of the native love of jewelry. "At least," she added, "it would be very strange if after all that time it was."

8

Josephine made no reply. She had flown off on one of her tangents. She had suddenly thought of Cyril. Wasn't it more usual for the only grandson to have the watch? And then dear Cyril was so appreciative, and a gold watch meant so much to a young man. Benny, in all probability, had quite got out of the habit of watches; men so seldom wore waistcoats in those hot climates. Whereas Cyril in London wore them from year's end to year's end. And it would be so nice for her and Constantia, when he came to tea, to know it was there. "I see you've got on grandfather's watch, Cyril." It would be somehow so satisfactory.

Dear boy! What a blow his sweet, sympathetic little note had been! Of course they quite understood; but it was most unfortunate.

"It would have been such a point, having him," said Josephine.

"And he would have enjoyed it so," said Constantia, not thinking what she was saying.

However, as soon as he got back he was coming to tea with his aunties. Cyril to tea was one of their rare treats.

"Now, Cyril, you mustn't be frightened of our cakes. Your Auntie Con and I bought them at Buszard's this morning. We know what a man's appetite is. So don't be ashamed of making a good tea."

Josephine cut recklessly into the rich dark cake that stood for her winter gloves or the soling and heeling of Constantia's only respectable shoes. But Cyril was most unmanlike in appetite.

"I say, Aunt Josephine, I simply can't. I've only just had lunch, you know."

"Oh, Cyril, that can't be true! It's after four," cried Josephine. Constantia sat with her knife poised over the chocolate-roll.

"It is, all the same," said Cyril. "I had to meet a man at Victoria,[1] and he kept me hanging about till . . . there was only time to get lunch and to come on here. And he gave me—phew"—Cyril put his hand to his forehead—"a terrific blowout," he said.

It was disappointing—today of all days. But still he couldn't be expected to know.

"But you'll have a meringue, won't you, Cyril?" said Aunt Josephine. "These meringues were bought specially for you. Your dear father was so fond of them. We were sure you are, too."

"I *am*, Aunt Josephine," cried Cyril ardently. "Do you mind if I take half to begin with?"

"Not at all, dear boy; but we mustn't let you off with that."

"Is your dear father still so fond of meringues?" asked Auntie Con gently. She winced faintly as she broke through the shell of hers.

---

1. London railroad station, connecting with the Channel ports.

"Well, I don't quite know, Auntie Con," said Cyril breezily.

At that they both looked up.

"Don't know?" almost snapped Josephine. "Don't know a thing like that about your own father, Cyril?"

"Surely," said Auntie Con softly.

Cyril tried to laugh it off. "Oh, well," he said, "it's such a long time since——" He faltered. He stopped. Their faces were too much for him.

"Even so," said Josephine.

And Auntie Con looked.

Cyril put down his teacup. "Wait a bit," he cried. "Wait a bit, Aunt Josephine. What am I thinking of?"

He looked up. They were beginning to brighten. Cyril slapped his knee.

"Of course," he said, "it was meringues. How could I have forgotten? Yes, Aunt Josephine, you're perfectly right. Father's most frightfully keen on meringues."

They didn't only beam. Aunt Josephine went scarlet with pleasure; Auntie Con gave a deep, deep sigh.

"And now, Cyril, you must come and see father," said Josephine. "He knows you were coming today."

"Right," said Cyril, very firmly and heartily. He got up from his chair; suddenly he glanced at the clock.

"I say, Auntie Con, isn't your clock a bit slow? I've got to meet a man at—at Paddington[2] just after five. I'm afraid I shan't be able to stay very long with grandfather."

"Oh, he won't expect you to stay *very* long!" said Aunt Josephine.

Constantia was still gazing at the clock. She couldn't make up her mind if it was fast or slow. It was one or the other, she felt almost certain of that. At any rate, it had been.

Cyril still lingered. "Aren't you coming along, Auntie Con?"

"Of course," said Josephine, "we shall all go. Come on, Con."

9

They knocked at the door, and Cyril followed his aunts into grandfather's hot, sweetish room.

"Come on," said Grandfather Pinner. "Don't hang about. What is it? What've you been up to?"

He was sitting in front of a roaring fire, clasping his stick. He had a thick rug over his knees. On his lap there lay a beautiful pale yellow silk handkerchief.

"It's Cyril, father," said Josephine shyly. And she took Cyril's hand and led him forward.

"Good afternoon, grandfather," said Cyril, trying to take his hand out of Aunt Josephine's. Grandfather Pinner shot his eyes

2. London railroad station, serving the west of England and Wales.

at Cyril in the way he was famous for. Where was Auntie Con? She stood on the other side of Aunt Josephine; her long arms hung down in front of her; her hands were clasped. She never took her eyes off grandfather.

"Well," said Grandfather Pinner, beginning to thump, "what have you got to tell me?"

What had he, what had he got to tell him? Cyril felt himself smiling like a perfect imbecile. The room was stifling, too.

But Aunt Josephine came to his rescue. She cried brightly, "Cyril says his father is still very fond of meringues, father dear."

"Eh?" said Grandfather Pinner, curving his hand like a purple meringue-shell over one ear.

Josephine repeated, "Cyril says his father is still very fond of meringues."

"Can't hear," said old Colonel Pinner. And he waved Josephine away with his stick, then pointed with his stick to Cyril. "Tell me what she's trying to say," he said.

(My God!) "Must I?" said Cyril, blushing and staring at Aunt Josephine.

"Do, dear," she smiled. "It will please him so much."

"Come on, out with it!" cried Colonel Pinner testily, beginning to thump again.

And Cyril leaned forward and yelled, "Father's still very fond of meringues."

At that Grandfather Pinner jumped as though he had been shot. "Don't shout!" he cried. "What's the matter with the boy? *Meringues!* What about 'em?"

"Oh, Aunt Josephine, must we go on?" groaned Cyril desperately.

"It's quite all right, dear boy," said Aunt Josephine, as though he and she were at the dentist's together. "He'll understand in a minute." And she whispered to Cyril, "He's getting a bit deaf, you know." Then she leaned forward and really bawled at Grandfather Pinner, "Cyril only wanted to tell you, father dear, that *his* father is still very fond of meringues."

Colonel Pinner heard that time, heard and brooded, looking Cyril up and down.

"What an esstrordinary thing!" said old Grandfather Pinner. "What an esstrordinary thing to come all this way here to tell me!"

And Cyril felt it *was*.

"Yes, I shall send Cyril the watch," said Josephine.

"That would be very nice," said Constantia. "I seem to remember last time he came there was some little trouble about the time."

10

They were interrupted by Kate bursting through the door in her usual fashion, as though she had discovered some secret panel in the wall.

"Fried or boiled?" asked the bold voice.

Fried or boiled? Josephine and Constantia were quite bewildered for the moment. They could hardly take it in.

"Fried or boiled what, Kate?" asked Josephine, trying to begin to concentrate.

Kate gave a loud sniff. "Fish."

"Well, why didn't you say so immediately?" Josephine reproached her gently. "How could you expect us to understand, Kate? There are a great many things in this world, you know, which are fried or boiled." And after such a display of courage she said quite brightly to Constantia, "Which do you prefer, Con?"

"I think it might be nice to have it fried," said Constantia. "On the other hand, of course boiled fish is very nice. I think I prefer both equally well . . . Unless you . . . In that case———"

"I shall fry it," said Kate, and she bounced back, leaving their door open and slamming the door of her kitchen.

Josephine gazed at Constantia; she raised her pale eyebrows until they rippled away into her pale hair. She got up. She said in a very lofty, imposing way, "Do you mind following me into the drawing room, Constantia? I've something of great importance to discuss with you."

For it was always to the drawing room they retired when they wanted to talk over Kate.

Josephine closed the door meaningly. "Sit down, Constantia," she said, still very grand. She might have been receiving Constantia for the first time. And Con looked round vaguely for a chair, as though she felt indeed quite a stranger.

"Now the question is," said Josephine, bending forward, "whether we shall keep her or not."

"That is the question," agreed Constantia.

"And this time," said Josephine firmly, "we must come to a definite decision."

Constantia looked for a moment as though she might begin going over all the other times, but she pulled herself together and said, "Yes, Jug."

"You see, Con," explained Josephine, "everything is so changed now." Constantia looked up quickly. "I mean," went on Josephine, "we're not dependent on Kate as we were." And she blushed faintly. "There's not father to cook for."

"That is perfectly true," agreed Constantia. "Father certainly doesn't want any cooking now, whatever else———"

Josephine broke in sharply. "You're not sleepy, are you, Con?"

"Sleepy, Jug?" Constantia was wide-eyed.

"Well, concentrate more," said Josephine sharply, and she returned to the subject. "What it comes to is, if we did"—and this she barely breathed, glancing at the door—"give Kate notice"—she raised her voice again—"we could manage our own food."

"Why not?" cried Constantia. She couldn't help smiling. The idea was so exciting. She clasped her hands. "What should we live on, Jug?"

"Oh, eggs in various forms!" said Jug, lofty again. "And, besides, there are all the cooked foods."

"But I've always heard," said Constantia, "they are considered so very expensive."

"Not if one buys them in moderation," said Josephine. But she tore herself away from this fascinating bypath and dragged Constantia after her.

"What we've got to decide now, however, is whether we really do trust Kate or not."

Constantia leaned back. Her flat little laugh flew from her lips.

"Isn't it curious, Jug," said she, "that just on this one subject I've never been able to quite make up my mind?"

11

She never had. The whole difficulty was to prove anything. How did one prove things, how could one? Suppose Kate had stood in front of her and deliberately made a face. Mightn't she very well have been in pain? Wasn't it impossible, at any rate, to ask Kate if she was making a face at her? If Kate answered "No"—and of course she would say "No"—what a position! How undignified! Then again Constantia suspected, she was almost certain that Kate went to her chest of drawers when she and Josephine were out, not to take things but to spy. Many times she had come back to find her amethyst cross in the most unlikely places, under her lace ties or on top of her evening bertha.[3] More than once she had laid a trap for Kate. She had arranged things in a special order and then called Josephine to witness.

"You see, Jug?"

"Quite, Con."

"Now we shall be able to tell."

But, oh dear, when she did go to look, she was as far off from a proof as ever! If anything was displaced, it might so very well have happened as she closed the drawer; a jolt might have done it so easily.

"You come, Jug, and decide. I really can't. It's too difficult."

But after a pause and a long glare Josephine would sigh. "Now you've put the doubt into my mind, Con, I'm sure I can't tell myself."

"Well, we can't postpone it again," said Josephine. "If we postpone it this time——"

But at that moment in the street below a barrel organ struck up.

---

3. Detachable lace collar for low-necked dresses.

Josephine and Constantia sprang to their feet together.

"Run, Con," said Josephine. "Run quickly. There's sixpence on the——"

Then they remembered. It didn't matter. They would never have to stop the organ-grinder again. Never again would she and Constantia be told to make that monkey take his noise somewhere else. Never would sound that loud, strange bellow when father thought they were not hurrying enough. The organ-grinder might play there all day and the stick would not thump.

> It never will thump again,
> It never will thump again,

played the barrel-organ.

What was Constantia thinking? She had such a strange smile; she looked different. She couldn't be going to cry.

"Jug, Jug," said Constantia softly, pressing her hands together. "Do you know what day it is? It's Saturday. It's a week today, a whole week."

> A week since father died,
> A week since father died,

cried the barrel organ. And Josephine, too, forgot to be practical and sensible; she smiled faintly, strangely. On the Indian carpet there fell a square of sunlight, pale red; it came and went and came—and stayed, deepened—until it shone almost golden.

"The sun's out," said Josephine, as though it really mattered.

A perfect fountain of bubbling notes shook from the barrel organ, round, bright notes, carelessly scattered.

Constantia lifted her big, cold hands as if to catch them, and then her hands fell again. She walked over to the mantelpiece to her favorite Buddha. And the stone and gilt image, whose smile always gave her such a queer feeling, almost a pain and yet a pleasant pain, seemed today to be more than smiling. He knew something; he had a secret. "I know something that you don't know," said her Buddha. Oh, what was it, what could it be? And yet she had always felt there was . . . something.

The sunlight pressed through the windows, thieved its way in, flashed its light over the furniture and the photographs. Josephine watched it. When it came to mother's photograph, the enlargement over the piano, it lingered as though puzzled to find so little remained of mother, except the earrings shaped like tiny pagodas and a black feather boa. Why did the photographs of dead people always fade so? wondered Josephine. As soon as a person was dead their photograph died too. But, of course, this one of mother was very old. It was thirty-five years old. Josephine remembered standing on a chair and pointing out that feather boa to Constantia and telling her that it was a snake that had killed their mother in Ceylon. . . . Would everything have been different if mother hadn't died? She didn't see why. Aunt Florence had lived with them until they had left school, and they had moved three times and had their yearly holiday and . . . and there'd been changes of servants, of course.

Some little sparrows, young sparrows they sounded, chirped on the window ledge. Y*eep—eyeep—yeep*. But Josephine felt they were not sparrows, not on the window ledge. It was inside her, that queer little crying noise. Y*eep—eyeep—yeep*. Ah, what was it crying, so weak and forlorn?

If mother had lived, might they have married? But there had been nobody for them to marry. There had been father's Anglo-Indian friends before he quarreled with them. But after that she and Constantia never met a single man except clergymen. How did one meet men? Or even if they'd met them, how could they have got to know men well enough to be more than strangers? One read of people having adventures, being followed, and so on. But nobody had ever followed Constantia and her. Oh yes, there had been one year at Eastbourne[4] a mysterious man at their boarding-house who had put a note on the jug of hot water outside their bedroom door! But by the time Connie had found it the steam had made the writing too faint to read; they couldn't even make out to which of them it was addressed. And he had left next day. And that was all. The rest had been looking after father, and at the same time keeping out of father's way. But now? But now? The thieving sun touched Josephine gently. She lifted her face. She was drawn over to the window by gentle beams. . . .

Until the barrel organ stopped playing Constantia stayed before the Buddha, wondering, but not as usual, not vaguely. This time her wonder was like longing. She remembered the times she had come in here, crept out of bed in her nightgown when the moon was full, and lain on the floor with her arms outstretched, as though she was crucified. Why? The big, pale moon had made her do it. The horrible dancing figures on the carved screen had leered at her and she hadn't minded. She remembered too how, whenever they were at the seaside, she had gone off by herself and got as close to the sea as she could, and sung something, something she had made up, while she gazed all over that restless water. There had been this other life, running out, bringing things home in bags, getting things on approval, discussing them with Jug, and taking them back to get more things on approval, and arranging father's trays and trying not to annoy father. But it all seemed to have happened in a kind of tunnel. It wasn't real. It was only when she

---

4. Seaside resort on Sussex coast.

came out of the tunnel into the moonlight or by the sea or into a thunderstorm that she really felt herself. What did it mean? What was it she was always wanting? What did it all lead to? Now? Now?

She turned away from the Buddha with one of her vague gestures. She went over to where Josephine was standing. She wanted to say something to Josephine, something frightfully important, about—about the future and what . . .

"Don't you think perhaps—" she began.

But Josephine interrupted her. "I was wondering if now——" she murmured. They stopped; they waited for each other.

"Go on, Con," said Josephine.

"No, no, Jug; after you," said Constantia.

"No, say what you were going to say You began," said Josephine.

"I . . . I'd rather hear what you were going to say first," said Constantia.

"Don't be absurd, Con."

"Really, Jug."

"Connie!"

"Oh, *Jug!*"

A pause. Then Constantia said faintly, "I can't say what I was going to say, Jug, because I've forgotten what it was . . . that I was going to say."

Josephine was silent for a moment. She stared at a big cloud where the sun had been. Then she replied shortly, "I've forgotten too."

1920   1922

HUGH MacDIARMID

(1892–1978)

1925:   *Sangschaw*.
1926:   *A Drunk Man Looks at the Thistle*.
1933-42: Lives in Whalsay, Shetland Islands.
1955:   *In Memoriam James Joyce*.

Hugh MacDiarmid is the pen name of Christopher Murray Grieve, who was born in the Scottish Border town of Langholm, son of a rural postman. The family lived below the town library of over 12,000 books, almost all of which MacDiarmid later claimed to have read. This passion for reading independently of any academic program stayed with him all his life, and helps to explain the air of massive self-education that pervades much of his later writing. At school he was lucky enough to have for his English teacher the Scottish composer Francis George Scott, who remained a lifelong friend and composed brilliant settings to many of his lyrics. MacDiarmid relied heavily on Scott's encouragement and criticism of his early poetry. He went from Langholm to Broughton Junior Student Centre in Edinburgh to train as a teacher, but on his father's death in 1911 he gave up this training and embarked on a career as a journalist. During World War I he served with the Royal Army Medical Corps in Salonika, Italy, and France. In 1920 he settled in Montrose, an attractive town on the east coast of Scotland, and worked for the *Montrose Review*. Shortly after, he brought out three volumes of new Scottish poetry by different hands, which he edited under the title *Northern Numbers, Being Representative Selections from Certain Living Scottish Poets*. The aim of these volumes was to do for Scottish poetry what *Georgian Poetry* had done for English, though Grieve's own poetry had even at this stage little in common with anything that can be considered characteristically Georgian. It was uneven and sometimes wordy, though marked by a highly individual sense of language and a fondness for cosmological imagery. Though at this stage he was writing in standard English rather than Scots, he had already developed a deep concern for Scottish literary culture, which he saw as decayed and requiring rejuvenation by association with all that was best in new literary ideas and movements throughout Europe.

MacDiarmid lived in Montrose until 1929, becoming active as a Labour member of the Town Council and as a founding member of the Scottish Center of the international literary organization P. E. N. and of the National Party of Scotland, but his highly individual political views led to conflict with all these organizations. His most important activity was to champion a Scottish Renaissance Movement, to redeem Scottish culture from the sentimentality and pallid imitativeness which he saw as its chief faults. An unhappy period in England from 1930 to 1932, when he engaged in a variety of occupations, strengthened his passion for Scotland and forced on him a reappraisal of his own social and political views. In 1932 he called himself a Communist (though still a Scottish Nationalist) and he joined the Communist Party in 1934. He was expelled because of his Scottish Nationalism in 1938 and rejoined in 1957, but he was always a very special kind of Communist. As he once explained,

> * * * I must be a Bolshevik
> Before the Revolution, but I'll cease to be one quick
> When Communism rules the roost.

He also wrote: "As a Socialist * * * I am * * * interested only in a very subordinate way in the politics of socialism as a political theory; my real concern with Socialism is as an artist's organized approach to the interdependencies of life."

The true emergence of "Hugh MacDiarmid" came with the publication of *Sangschaw* in 1925. The adoption of this pen name served notice that he associated himself with the Celtic element in Scottish history and culture, and later he was to associate Scotland with Ireland, Wales, and Cornwall as part of a Celtic ring of peoples who could produce an alternative culture to that of Anglo-Saxondom. But more significant than this new name was the kind of poetry he was now producing. This consisted largely of short lyrics in Scots, which is not a Celtic language at all (as Scottish Gaelic is), but the language originally identical with that spoken in northern England and developed into a powerful literary medium by the great medieval poets of Scotland, notably Robert Henryson and William Dunbar. The growth of standard English as the written language of Scotland, encouraged as early as the late 16th century by the adoption of an English translation of the Bible by Scottish Protestants, accelerated by the departure of the Scottish Court, with its Court poets, for England in 1603 when James VI of Scotland inherited the throne of England, and given still greater impetus by the disappearance of Scotland as a separate political entity by the "incorporating union" between Scotland and England in 1707, drove the Scots language into the position of a spoken vernacular that was no longer a fully developed literary language, and it was largely by concentration on the folk tradition that 18th-century Scottish poets, notably Robert Burns, were able to use Scots vigorously in their poetry. But in the 19th century the Burns tradition became debased and sentimentalized. MacDiarmid's great achievement was to recognize that the Scottish poetic tradition needed to be radically reshaped and that the decadent post-Burns tradition was beyond disciplining into a poetry of any maturity or originality.

MacDiarmid therefore looked back to Scottish poetry of the 15th century and saw that it was written in a rich and assured Scottish language that grew out of a living speech yet reached far beyond it. He saw too that the poetry of the Scottish "makars" (as the medieval Scottish poets were called) was European in scope, that it combined its genuinely distinctive Scottishness with a relaxed air of being at home in the culture of Europe as a whole. In this respect he saw Scotland as less provincial, less insular in attitude than England: Scotland's long alliance with France and the long tradition of Scotsmen going to Europe to study or soldier or offer services of one kind or another gave some historical evidence for such a view, which in some degree lay behind MacDiarmid's often expressed Anglophobia.

At this stage MacDiarmid believed that a truly creative Scottish poetry had to be in some form of Scots, yet not the emasculated dialect Scots of the post-Burns tradition, and not standard English, which he did not see as able to tap the real roots of Scottish experience. He therefore ransacked the rich vocabulary of Dunbar and Henryson and used it together with modern dialect Scots and standard English. This revived Scots, or "Lallans" (i.e., Lowland Scots) as it was often called, was unashamedly synthetic, put together out of a combination of older Scots words and modern words. Some of the words were culled from dictionaries. Like Joyce, MacDiarmid had an enormous linguistic curiosity and wanted to increase the expressiveness of his poetic speech by every resource of vocabulary he could lay his hands on. In his later poetry, when he wrote in English, he ransacked the technical vocabularies of the sciences in the same spirit. His Scots lyrics have much more energy and vitality than the English poems he had hitherto written, homing in on their subject without any verbal padding or traditional "poetic" language (which can be seen in some of his earlier verse) and using Scots words, in conjunction with English, in ways that startle and shake the reader.

The lyrics of *Sangschaw* and his next volume *Penny Wheep* (1926) vindicated MacDiarmid's choice of Scots. They display a wonderful verbal delicacy which combines precise observation of natural objects with a tense mystical clarity of vision. He had a vision of the contradictions that lie deep in the heart of man and nature and of the possibility of reconciling them by tense concentration on the individual reality of separate things. This is bound up with his view that the proper *naming* of objects can in some way release their energies and place them all in their rich selfhood in the total pattern of the universe. Hence MacDiarmid could be simultaneously a passionate Scot and an internationalist who embraced with excited affection every odd little language, everything different and challenging and offbeat and *itself*. (His view of the self-ness, the individual reality of natural objects, is very like the concept of *haecceitas*, "this-ness," which Gerard Manley Hopkins got from Duns Scotus.)

MacDiarmid's early Scots lyrics are brilliant poems, but they are miniatures, small and finely etched pieces, which avoid large pronouncements. In *A Drunk Man Looks at the Thistle* (1936), however, he builds up an epic statement about Scotland out of a series of related lyrics and passages of descriptive and reflective poetry. It is in a way a modern version of the medieval dream poem, in which drunkenness plays the part that sleep plays in the medieval tradition, being used as a means of removing the speaker's inhibitions and getting him into that visionary predicament. Like William Dunbar, MacDiarmid is a poet of sharply contrasting moods, and in *A Drunk Man* he alternates between lyricism, savage satire, comic irony, philosophic reflection, and personal confession. It is MacDiarmid's masterpiece.

In 1933 Hugh MacDiarmid and his second wife, the Cornish Valda Trevlyn who shared his pan-Celticism and always supported him with enormous loyalty, settled in a small cottage on the island of Whalsay, in the remote Shetland Islands, and lived there with their small son, often in acute poverty. For though MacDiarmid had now thoroughly established himself as an explosive force in Scottish literature and as the creator of a Scottish Renaissance, his books did not provide him with a reasonable income and his continuous fight against the Establishment led to his condemnation by large numbers of respectable and influential people. "The poetry I want turns its back contemptuously on all the cowardly and brainless staples of Anglo-Scottish literature," he wrote in his autobiographical *Lucky Poet* (1943), "—the whole base business of people who do not act but are acted upon * * * though they include every irresponsible who occupies a 'responsible position' in Scotland today, * * *" He wanted to get rid of "the whole gang of high mucky-mucks, famous fatheads, old wives of both sexes, stuffed shirts, hollow men with headpieces stuffed with straw, bird-wits, lookers-under-beds, trained seals, creeping Jesuses, Scots Wha Ha'evers, village idiots, policemen, leaders of white-mouse factions and noted connoisseurs of bread and butter, glorified gangsters, and what 'Billy' Phelps calls Medlar Novelists (the medlar being a fruit that becomes rotten before it is ripe), Commercial Calvinists, makers of 'noises like a turnip,' and all the touts, toadies and lickspittles of the English Ascendancy, and their infernal women-folk, and all their skunkoil skulduggery." This kind of invective, which MacDiarmid indulged in with enormous relish, is part of the old Scottish tradition of "flyting," or mutual rhetorical abuse by two opponents; for him, however, it was not a game, but passionately meant.

MacDiarmid remained on Whalsay until 1942, cut off from the "civilization" of the mainland and, worst of all, from new books and periodicals. But his isolation gave him a period of retrenchment and new development.

His encounter with the stark geographical and geological realities of his remote island increased his awareness of the strange reality of natural objects. He became interested in rocks and stones and in the technical vocabulary used to describe and classify them. The volume *Stony Limits and Other Poems* reflects this interest. He was now writing more and more in English rather than Scots, but an English with its own kind of vocabulary. His use of geological terms in the opening of *On a Raised Beach*, the longest and finest poem in the collection, and other aspects of that poem's individual use of language, show his interest in exploring new ways of engaging the strange reality he was trying to come to terms with. These attempts to reach out through language to a way of expressing the uncanny "quiddity" of natural objects and their relation to human feelings went on side by side with his political and social polemics, yet in a sense they were related, for MacDiarmid's political vision was hardly political at all, but a vision of a society redeemed from all second-handness in living, united in an intense relishing of the reality of experience. This involved a discipline that transcended all known norms and a view of life which went beyond humanism to something that can only be called trans-humanist.

In 1942 MacDiarmid was directed to a war job in a steel factory in Glasgow, and from this he moved to the Merchant Service to work on ships engaged in duties in the Clyde estuary until the end of the war. In 1951 he settled in a little cottage in Biggar, Lanarkshire. To the disappointment of many who considered his Scots lyrics his finest achievement, he turned more and more to what he called "the poetry of fact," trying to embrace, sometimes with an almost desperate use of enormous catalogues, all the new scientific and technological knowledge that the modern world had brought into being and to relate it to human awareness. He included a great deal of this kind of poetry in *Lucky Poet*, especially in a remarkable chapter entitled "The Kind of Poetry I Want," which includes the lines:

> I dream of poems like the bread-knife
> Which cuts three slices at once;
> Of poems concerned with technical matters * * *
> Or in cut-gem clearness surpass even Huxley's
> Prose account of the endophragmal system of the crayfish
> And his Anatomy of the Vertebrata; * * *

But perhaps the most remarkable example of MacDiarmid's later style was *In Memoriam James Joyce: from A Vision of a World Language* (1955). This is a poem—and presented as part of a longer one—of over 6,000 lines, written (more or less) in English, with an enormous number of quotations from and references to other languages and literatures. It is built of verse paragraphs of varying length, unrhymed for the most part, with the lines expanding or contracting according to the flow of the thought and the meter free and flexible. The movement of the verse is essentially colloquial; the rhythms are those of conversation; but the rise and fall of the sound and the carefully controlled shifts in tempo provide enough underlying formal pattern to prevent the poem from disintegrating into mere discursiveness. Its theme might be described as the essential kinship of everything in the world that is fully realized and properly possessed of its identity.

This was a favorite subject of Walt Whitman. Whitman accepted and celebrated everything in the world so long as it was true to itself and not faked or (to use one of his characteristic terms) "dandified." Whitman, like MacDiarmid, used in his poems the long catalogue; he taught himself how to give a meaning to lists of things by placing them in a context in terms of which each list became a confession of faith in all that was of value in the world. MacDiarmid's poem is a confession of faith. The world language he talks about is the ever-sought, never wholly attainable, ideal means of expression which will be able, merely by describing things, to reveal the glory of their essential quiddity. But the paradox is that in order to make a complete statement about anything you must refer, however obliquely, both by way of contrast and of comparison, to everything else. The ideal world language must thus consist of cosmic puns, in which everything is said when anything is said and which nevertheless at the same time identifies individual things with the utmost precision. Joyce went further towards the realization of such a language than any other writer has done: it is therefore appropriate that a poem in memory of Joyce should have this theme.

MacDiarmid is now generally recognized as the greatest Scottish poet since Burns (and some see him as greater than Burns), and one of a trilogy with Burns and Dunbar. He early achieved fame in France, but in later years he has achieved recognition all over Europe, and he made many a triumphant progress in Communist countries, including China. His wide-ranging curiosity about and sympathy with other literatures is one reason for his international fame. His output has been very large, and it is not consistent in quality. Some of his later work, with its enormous catalogues, lists of names, quotations from scientific and philosophical authorities, its apparent garrulity, has defeated some critics who have the highest admiration for his lyrics. MacDiarmid was awarded a Civil List pension in 1950, and he felt ever since very much as Dr. Johnson did when he accepted a pension from George III; he might well have used Johnson's words: "My pension is more out of the usual course of things than any instance that I have known. Here, Sir, was a man avowedly no friend to Government at the time, who got a pension without asking for it. I never courted the great; they sent for me; but I think they now give me up." Neither his pension nor the honorary doctorate of laws he received from Edinburgh University in 1957 in any way diminished his attack on governmental and university establishments. A long discursive poem in his later style published in 1957 was entitled *The Battle Continues*.

The list of books edited, written, or translated by MacDiarmid amounts to over 70. In addition to poems in his different styles, he wrote critical, historical, and political essays, edited other poets (including Dunbar and Burns) and founded or edited five periodicals. He belongs with Yeats and Eliot, both of whom were friends and admirers of his, as one of the strikingly original poets of the modern world, and he belongs especially with Joyce, whom he greatly admired, as one who strove to push back the limits of literary speech. He was also the greatest example in modern history of the Poet as Rebel. He himself has said that he would like to have engraved on his tombstone simply his name and the dates of his birth and death and the words:

"A Disgrace to the community."—Mr. Justice Mugge.

The Watergaw[1]

Ae weet forenicht i' the yow-trummle[2]
I saw yon antrin thing,
A watergaw wi' its chitterin' licht
Ayont the on-ding;
5 An' I thocht° o' the last wild look ye gied°   *thought / gave*
Afore ye deed!°   *died*

There was nae reek i' the laverock's hoose
That nicht—an' nane i' mine;
But I hae thocht o' that foolish licht
10 Ever sin' syne;
An' I think that mebbe at last I ken
What your look meant then.

1922   1925

The Bonnie Broukit Bairn[1]

Mars is braw° in crammasy,°   *brave / red*
Venus in a green silk goun,°   *gown*
The auld mune[2] shak's her gowden° feathers,   *golden*
Their starry talk's a wheen o' blethers,[3]
5 Nane for thee a thochtie[4] sparin',
Earth, thou bonnie broukit bairn!
—But greet,° an' in your tears ye'll droun   *cry*
The haill clanjamfrie![5]

1925

---

1. "Watergaw" is a Fifeshire word meaning "the fragment of a rainbow appearing on the horizon." MacDiarmid himself, as C. M. Grieve, editor of *The Scottish Chapbook*, where this poem (his first written in Scots) originally appeared, commented on it as follows: "Doric economy of expressiveness is impressively illustrated in the first four lines of Mr. MacDiarmid's poem. Translate them into English. That is the test. You will find that the shortest possible translation runs something like this: 'One wet afternoon (or early evening) in the cold weather in July after the sheepshearing I saw that rare thing—an indistinct rainbow, with its shivering light, above the heavily-falling rain.'" The second stanza may be rendered: "There was no smoke in the lark's house that night [meaning, MacDiarmid explains, "it was a dark and stormy night"], and none in mine ["and my heart was dark and stormy too"]. But I have thought of that foolish light ever since then; and I think that maybe at last I know what your look meant then."

2. The "yow-trummle," literally "ewe-tremble," refers to a cold snap after the summer sheep-shearing, which makes the sheared sheep tremble with cold; it is the kind of expressive Scots word that appealed to MacDiarmid.

1. The pretty, neglected child.
2. Old moon.
3. A lot of meaningless chatter.
4. Diminutive of thought.
5. The whole collection. (Jamieson's *Dictionary of the Scottish Language*, which was much used by MacDiarmid, explains "clanjamfrie" as "a term used to denote low, worthless people, or those who are viewed in this light" and cites Scott's use of the word in this sense in *Guy Mannering*.)

Moonstruck[1]

When the warl's couped soon' as a peerie
That licht-lookin' craw o' a body, the moon,
Sits on the fower cross-win's
Peerin' a' roon'.

5   She's seen me—she's seen me—an' straucht°   *straight*
Loupit° clean on the quick o' my hert.°   *leaped / heart*
The quhither o' cauld gowd's fairly
Gi'en me a stert.[2]

An' the roarin' o' oceans noo'
10   Is peerieweerie[3] to me:
Thunner's° a tinklin' bell: an' Time   *thunder's*
Whuds° like a flee.°   *flits / fly*

1925

The Eemis Stane[4]

I' the how-dumb-deid o' the cauld hairst nicht
The warl' like an eemis stane
Wags i' the lift;
An' my eerie memories fa'
5   Like a yowdendrift.

Like a yowdendrift so's I couldna read
The words cut oot i' the stane
Had the fug o' fame
An' history's hazelraw
10   No' yirdit thaim.

1925

From A Drunk Man Looks at the Thistle

1. Farewell to Dostoevski

The wan leafs shak, atour° us like the snaw.   *around*
Here is the cavaburd[1] in which Earth's tint.°   *lost*

1. This is one of a series of four lyrics
entitled *Au Clair de la Lune* ("By the
light of the moon"). MacDiarmid has
written of it: "The first two lines of
Moonstruck mean: 'When the world is
dozed like a top at the height of its
spin, that light-looking crow of a body,
the moon * * *' I can think of no English equivalent which can bring out the
complicated sense of that description of
the moon, at once insubstantial and disreputable looking, radiant and yet dark
with sinister influences."
2. The quiver of the cold gold's fairly
given me a start.

3. Diminished to a mere thread of
sound.
4. The whole poem may be rendered:
"In the still center of the cold harvest
night the world like a teetering stone
sways in the sky, and my eerie memories
fall like snow driven by the wind. Like
snow driven by the wind, so that I
couldn't read the words cut out in the
stone even if the moss of fame and the
lichen of history had not buried them."
It is only in the 7th line that the stone
is revealed as a tombstone.
1. Dense snowstorm.

There's naebody but Oblivion and us,
Puir gangrel° buddies, waunderin' hameless in't.   *wanderer*

5   The stars are larochs° o' auld cottages,   *foundations*
And a' Time's glen is fu' o' blinnin' stew.[2]
Nae freen'ly lozen° skimmers:° and the   *window / gleams /*
    wund°   *wind*
Rises and separates even me and you.

I ken nae Russian and you ken nae Scots.
10   We canna tell oor voices frae the wund.
The snaw is seekin' everywhere: oor herts
At last like roofless ingles° it has f'und.   *hearths*

And gethers there in drift on endless drift,
Oor broken herts that it can never fill;
15   And still—its leafs like snaw, its growth like wund—
The thistle[3] rises and forever will!

                                        1926

2. *Yet Ha'e I Silence Left*

Yet ha'e I Silence left, the croon° o' a'.   *crown*

No' her, wha on the hills langsyne° I saw   *long ago*
Liftin' a foreheid o' perpetual snaw.

No' her, wha in the how-dumb-deid o' nicht[1]
5   Kyths,[2] like Eternity in Time's despite.

No' her, withooten° shape, wha's name is   *without /*
    Daith,°   *Death*
No' Him, unkennable° abies° to faith   *unknowable / except*

—God whom, gin° e'er He saw a Man, 'ud be   *if*
E'en mair dumfooner'd[3] at the sicht° than he.   *sight*

10   —But Him, whom nocht° in man or Deity,   *nothing*
Or Daith or Dreid or Laneliness can touch,
Wha's deed owre often and has seen owre much.[4]

    O I ha'e Silence left.

                                        1926

---

2. A storm through which it is impossible to see.
3. The thistle is the emblem of Scotland.
1. The still center of night.

2. Makes herself known, appears.
3. More dumbfounded.
4. Who has died too often and seen too
much.

From To Circumjack Cencrastus

Lourd on My Hert

<table>
<tr><td></td><td>Lourd° on my hert as winter lies</td><td>*heavy*</td></tr>
<tr><td></td><td>The state that Scotland's in the day.</td><td></td></tr>
<tr><td></td><td>Spring to the North has aye come slow</td><td></td></tr>
<tr><td></td><td>But noo° dour[1] winter's like to stay</td><td>*now*</td></tr>
<tr><td>5</td><td>For guid,°</td><td>*good*</td></tr>
<tr><td></td><td>And no' for guid!</td><td></td></tr>
</table>

O wae's me on the weary days
When it is scarce grey licht° at noon; *light*
It maun° be a' the stupid folk *must*
10 Diffusin' their dullness roon and roon
Like soot
That keeps the sunlicht oot.

Nae wonder if I think I see
A lichter° shadow than the neist° *lighter / next*
15 I'm fain to cry: "The dawn, the dawn!
I see it brakin' in the East."
But ah
—It's juist mair snaw![2]

1930

From On a Raised Beach

All is lithogenesis[1]—or lochia,
Carpolite[2] fruit of the forbidden tree,
Stones blacker than any in the Caaba,[3]
Cream-colored caen-stone, chatoyant pieces,[4]

1. Hard, stern.
2. Just more snow.

1. From Greek *lithos*, stone, and *genesis*, origin. This word is apparently a coinage of MacDiarmid's, on the analogy of "lithology," the study of stones and rocks. Stones and rocks, and their relation to human experience, is the theme of this long poem, which deliberately uses a strange technical vocabulary to communicate the poet's sense of the mysterious otherness of the natural world of geology. The massing of geological and other technical words that follow illustrates MacDiarmid's joy in harnessing to his poetry specialist terms from the sciences.
2. An adjective from the Greek *karpos*, fruit (cf. "carpology," that branch of plant anatomy relating to the structure of fruit and seeds); following the em-

phatic word "lithogenesis," the origin or birth of the rock structure of the earth, and the reference to "lochia," a discharge from the uterus after childbirth, the word helps to build up the suggestion of some primeval birth of the earth's crust.
3. More usually Ka'ba or Kaaba, the sacred shrine of Mohammedanism, containing the famous "black stone" in the middle of the great mosque at Mecca.
4. The Caen stone of Normandy is a well-known stone of the Bathonian series; "chatoyant": glistening, shot through with gleaming colors; "celadon" (also from the French) is a pale, soft, sea-green color; "corbeau" (literally "raven" in French) is the same as corbel, an architectural term meaning a projection from the face of a wall, supporting a weight.

5 Celadon and corbeau, bistre and beige,[5]
Glaucous, hoar, enfouldered, cyathiform,[6]
Making mere faculae[7] of the sun and moon,
I study you glout° and gloss, but have   frown
No cadrans[8] to adjust you with, and turn again
10 From optik to haptik[9] and like a blind man run
My fingers over you, arris by arris, burr by burr,[1]
Slickensides,[2] truité,° rugas,[3] foveoles,[4]   speckled
Bringing my aesthesis° in vain to bear,   perception
An angle-titch[5] to all your corrugations and coigns,°   corners
15 Hatched foraminous[6] cavo-rilieva[7] of the world,
Diectic,[8] fiducial[9] stones. Chiliad by chiliad
What bricole[1] piled you here, stupendous cairn?[2]
What artist poses the Earth écorché[3] thus,
Pillar of creation engouled[4] in me?
20 What eburnation[5] augments you with men's bones,
Every energumen[6] an Endymion[7] yet?
All the other stones are in this hæcceity[8] it seems,
But where is the Christophanic[9] rock that moved?
What Cabirian[1] song from this catasta[2] comes?

25 Deep conviction or preference can seldom
Find direct terms in which to express itself.

---

5. Color words, meaning respectively dark brown, the color of natural wood, grayish-blue (or grayish-green), white (or gray).
6. The word "enfouldered" occurs once in Spenser's *Faerie Queene* ("with foul enfouldred smoake") and is thought to mean "like a thundercloud." MacDiarmid apparently uses it to denote a shape, for he is here moving on from color to shape; he seems to have invented "cyathiform" to mean "shaped like a cup" (Greek *kyathos* + *form*).
7. Bright spots or streaks on the surface of the sun.
8. A machine for cutting gems and adjusting the angles of the facets.
9. From sight to touch.
1. Rough edge or ridge. "Arris": the edge formed by the meeting of two straight or curved surfaces.
2. Surfaces of rocks that have been ground against each other.
3. Wrinkled, presumably from Latin *ruga*, a wrinkle; the normal English word derived from *ruga* and meaning wrinkled is "rugate."
4. Small depressions or pits.
5. Apparently an invented word, perhaps meaning the poet's particular tilt or angle of observation.
6. Having foramina, which are small perforations or openings.
7. A style of relief in which the highest portions of the figures are on a level with the general surface.

8. Perhaps equivalent to diecious, a term in zoology and botany indicating the separation of the sexes.
9. Probably used in the technical sense employed by astronomers, surveyors, and others, to mean a line, point, etc., used as a fixed basis of comparison. "Chiliad": a thousand years.
1. A medieval engine for throwing stones or bolts; a catapult.
2. A heap of stones.
3. Anatomical figure with the skin removed for the study of muscles.
4. In heraldry, referring to bends, crosses, etc., which enter the mouths of animals.
5. A term in pathology, meaning the act or process of becoming hard and dense like ivory.
6. Someone possessed by a devil.
7. In Greek mythology, a young man loved by Selene, the moon goddess.
8. The *haecceitas* or "this-ness," specific individuality, that so interested the medieval philosopher Duns Scotus.
9. Indicating the appearance of Christ (Christophany is the theological term for the appearance of Christ).
1. Adjective from Cabiri, a group of non-Hellenic deities (perhaps Phyrigian) about whose nature and function there is considerable mystery.
2. A block on which slaves stood for sale. The Latin word means simply a scaffold.

Today on this shingle[3] shelf
I understand this pensive reluctance so well,
This not discommendable obstinacy,
These contrivances of an inexpressive critical feeling,
These stones with their resolve that Creation shall not
    be
Injured by iconoclasts and quacks. Nothing has stirred
Since I lay down this morning an eternity ago
But one bird. The widest open door is the least liable to
    intrusion,
Ubiquitous as the sunlight, unfrequented as the sun.
The inward gates of a bird are always open.
It does not know how to shut them.
That is the secret of its song,
But whether any man's are ajar is doubtful.
I look at these stones and know little about them,
But I know their gates are open too,
Always open, far longer open, than any bird's can be,
That every one of them has had its gates wide open far
    longer
Than all birds put together, let alone humanity,
Though through them no man can see,
No man nor anything more recently born than them-
    selves
And that is everything else on the Earth.
I too lying here have dismissed all else.
Bread from stones is my sole and desperate dearth,
From stones, which are to the Earth as to the sunlight
Is the naked sun which is for no man's sight.
I would scorn to cry to any easier audience
Or, having cried, to lack patience to await the response.
I am no more indifferent or ill-disposed to life than
    death is;
I would fain accept it all completely as the soil does;
Already I feel all that can perish perishing in me
As so much has perished and all will yet perish in these
    stones.
I must begin with these stones as the world began.

Shall I come to a bird quicker than the world's course
    ran?
    To a bird, and to myself, a man?
    And what if I do, and further?
I shall only have gone a little way to go back again
And be like a fleeting deceit of development,
Iconoclasts, quacks. So these stones have dismissed
All but all of evolution, unmoved by it,

Line numbers in margin: 30, 35, 40, 45, 50, 55, 60, 65

3. Beds of small stones on the seashore.

(Is there anything to come they will not likewise
        dismiss?)
As the essential life of mankind in the mass
Is the same as their earliest ancestors' yet.

Actual physical conflict or psychological warfare
70   Incidental to love or food
Brings out animal life's bolder and more brilliant
        patterns
        Concealed as a rule in habitude.
        There is a sudden revelation of color,
        The protrusion of a crest,
75   The expansion of an ornament,
—But no general principle can be guessed
From these flashing fragments we are seeing,
These foam-bells on the hidden currents of being.
The bodies of animals are visible substances
And must therefore have color and shape, in the first
80   place
Depending on chemical composition, physical structure,
        mode of growth,
Psychological rhythms and other factors in the case,
But their purposive function is another question.
Brilliant-hued animals hide away in the ocean deeps;
85 The mole has a rich sexual coloring in due season
Under the ground; nearly every beast keeps
Brighter colors inside it than outside.
What the seen shows is never anything to what it's
        designed to hide,
The red blood which makes the beauty of a maiden's
        cheek
90 Is as red under a gorilla's pigmented and hairy face.
Varied forms and functions though life may seem to
        have shown
They all come back soon to the likeness of stone,
So to the intervening stages we can best find a clue
In what we all came from and return to.
95 There are no twirly bits in this ground bass.

We must be humble. We are so easily baffled by appear-
        ances
And do not realize that these stones are one with the
        stars.
It makes no difference to them whether they are high
        or low,
Mountain peak or ocean floor, palace, or pigsty.
There are plenty of ruined buildings in the world but
100   no ruined stones.
No visitor comes from the stars

But is the same as they are.
—Nay, it is easy to find a spontaneity here,
An adjustment to life, an ability
105 To ride it easily, akin to "the buoyant
Prelapsarian[4] naturalness of a country girl
Laughing in the sun, not passion-rent,
But sensing in the bound of her breasts vigors to come
Powered to make her one with the stream of earth-life
    round her,"
110 But not yet as my Muse is, with this ampler scope,
This more divine rhythm, wholly at one
With the earth, riding the Heavens with it, as the stones do
And all soon must.
But it is wrong to indulge in these illustrations
115 Instead of just accepting the stones.
It is a paltry business to try to drag down
The arduus furor of the stones to the futile imaginings of men,
To all that fears to grow roots into the common earth,
As it soon must, lest it be chilled to the core,
120 As it will be—and none the worse for that.
Impatience is a poor qualification for immortality.
Hot blood is of no use in dealing with eternity.
It is seldom that promises or even realizations
Can sustain a clear and searching gaze.
125 But an emotion chilled is an emotion controlled;
This is the road leading to certainty,
Reasoned planning for the time when reason can no longer avail.
It is essential to know the chill of all the objections
That come creeping into the mind, the battle between
    opposing ideas
130 Which gives the victory to the strongest and most universal
Over all others, and to wage it to the end
With increasing freedom, precision, and detachment
A detachment that shocks our instincts and ridicules our desires.
All else in the world cancels out, equal, capable
135 Of being replaced by other things (even as all the ideas
That madden men now must lose their potency in a few years
And be replaced by others—even as all the religions,
All the material sacrifices and moral restraints,
That in twenty thousand years have brought us no nearer to God
140 Are irrelevant to the ordered adjustments
Out of the reach of perceptive understanding
Forever taking place on the Earth and in the unthinkable
    regions around it;
This cats' cradle of life; this reality volatile yet determined;
This intense vibration in the stones
145 That makes them seem immobile to us)

4. From before the Fall of Man.

But the world cannot dispense with the stones.
They alone are not redundant. Nothing can replace them
Except a new creation of God.

* * *

All is lithogenesis—or lochia;
And I can desire nothing better,
An immense familiarity with other men's imaginings
Convinces me they cannot either
305 (If they could, it would instantly be granted
—The present order must continue till then)
Though, of course, I still keep an open mind,
A mind as open as the grave.
You may say that the truth cannot be crushed out,
310 That the weight of the whole world may be tumbled on it,
And yet, in puny, distorted, phantasmal shapes albeit,
It will braird° again; it will force its way up   sprout
Through unexpectable fissures? look over this beach.
What ruderal° and rupestrine° growth is here?   stony / rocky
315 What crop confirming any credulities?
Conjure a fescue[5] to teach me with from this
And I will listen to you, but until then
Listen to me—Truth is not crushed;
It crushes, gorgonizes[6] all else into itself.
320 The trouble is to know it when you see it?
You will have no trouble with it when you do.
Do not argue with me. Argue with these stones.
Truth has no trouble in knowing itself.
This is it. The hard fact. The inoppugnable[7] reality,
325 Here is something for you to digest.
Eat this and we'll see what appetite you have left
For a world hereafter.
I pledge you in the first and last crusta,[8]
The rocks rattling in the bead-proof seas.

* * *

1934

From In Memoriam James Joyce

We Must Look at the Harebell[1]

We must look at the harebell as if
We had never seen it before.
Remembrance gives an accumulation of satisfaction

---

5. A genus of grass.
6. Turns into stone, as in Greek mythology the Gorgon did to beholders.
7. Not to be fought against.
8. Crustacean, class of aquatic creatures

(crabs, lobsters, etc.) covered with a horny shell.
1. The Scottish bluebell, a blue flower with a bell-shaped blossom.

Yet the desire for change is very strong in us
And change is in itself a recreation.   5
To those who take any pleasure
In flowers, plants, birds, and the rest
An ecological change is recreative.
(Come. Climb with me. Even the sheep are different
And of new importance.   10
The coarse-fleeced, hardy Herdwick,
The Hampshire Down, artificially fed almost from birth,
And butcher-fat from the day it is weaned,
The Lincoln-Longwool, the biggest breed in England,
With the longest fleece, and the Southdown   15
Almost the smallest—and between them thirty other breeds,
Some whitefaced, some black,
Some with horns and some without,
Some long-wooled, some short-wooled,
In England where the men, and women too,   20
Are almost as interesting as the sheep.)
Everything is different, everything changes,
Except for the white bedstraw which climbs all the way
Up from the valleys to the tops of the high passes
The flowers are all different and more precious   25
Demanding more search and particularity of vision.
Look! Here and there a pinguicula[2] eloquent of the Alps
Still keeps a purple-blue flower
On the top of its straight and slender stem.
Bog-asphodel, deep-gold, and comely in form,   30
The queer, almost diabolical, sundew,
And when you leave the bog for the stag moors and the rocks
The parsley fern—a lovelier plant
Than even the proud Osmunda Regalis[3]—
Flourishes in abundance   35
Showing off oddly contrasted fronds
From the cracks of the lichened stones.
It is pleasant to find the books
Describing it as "very local."
Here is a change indeed!   40
The universal *is* the particular.

                                                                        1955

In the Children's Hospital

"Does it matter? Losing your legs?"
Siegfried Sassoon

Now let the legless boy show the great lady
How well he can manage his crutches.

---

2. The butterwort, a genus of small
herbs whose leaves secrete a sticky substance in which small insects are caught.

3. The "flowering fern" or "royal fern,"
a plant with large fronds.

It doesn't matter though the Sister[1] objects,
"He's not used to them yet," when such is
The will of the Princess. Come, Tommy,[2]   5
Try a few desperate steps through the ward.
Then the hand of Royalty will pat your head
And life suddenly cease to be hard.
For a couple of legs are surely no miss
When the loss leads to such an honour as this!   10
One knows, when one sees how jealous the rest
Of the children are, it's been all for the best!—
But would the sound of your sticks on the floor
Thundered in her skull for evermore!

1935

Another Epitaph on an Army of Mercenaries[3]

It is a God-damned lie to say that these
Saved, or knew, anything worth any man's pride.
They were professional murderers and they took
Their blood money and impious risks and died.
In spite of all their kind some elements of worth   5
With difficulty persist here and there on earth.

1935

1. Head nurse in charge of a hospital ward.
2. Common name for British soldier, but here just the actual name of the child.

3. "In reply to A. E. Housman's" [MacDiarmid's note]. See A. E. Housman's poem *Epitaph on an Army of Mercenaries*.

ROBERT GRAVES
(1895–)

Robert Ranke Graves was born in London of partly Anglo-Irish and partly German descent—his great-uncle was the distinguished German historian Leopold von Ranke—but his voice is peculiarly English. He left Charter-house School to go immediately into the army, serving in World War I until he was invalided out in 1917. After the war he went to Oxford, took a B.Litt. degree and in 1926 began a brief period as Professor of English at the Egyptian University in Cairo. In 1929 he published *Goodbye to All That*, an account of his experiences in the war, which, as he himself put it, "paid my debts and enabled me to set up in Majorca as a writer." He returned to Majorca after World War II and has made his home there ever since.

Graves began as a Georgian poet, but from an early stage it was clear that he was a Georgian with a difference. The mingling of the colloquial and the visionary in his vocabulary, the accent of conversation underlying the regular rhythms of his stanzas, the tension between a romantic indulgence in emotion and a cool appraisal of its significance—these are qualities found even in his early poetry, though it is only in his later work that we find them more consistently employed and effectively disciplined. His best work combines the ironic and the visionary in a highly individual manner, and he is also capable of a down-to-earth poetry, often ironical and mocking in tone and dealing with simple domestic facts or the more annoying of personal relationships, which nevertheless is seen on further reading to reach out to ever wider and deeper implications. He himself has said: "I write poems for poets, and satires or grotesques for wits. For people in general I write prose, and am content that they should be unaware that I do anything else. To write poems for other than poets is wasteful" (Foreword to *Poems 1938–45*). But this is mischievous exaggeration. "What Mr. Graves means," Lionel Trilling has observed, "is that, in our day, only poets can be counted on not to be misled by the lightness and clarity of his verse, by the irony and the humor; that only poets will be sufficiently aware of the tradition in which he writes, and of hearing the truth that lies not only in the doctrinal statements that the poem makes but also in the justice of its diction, in the pitch and tone of its voice * * * " (*A Gathering of Fugitives*, p. 23).

Graves has long made his living by his prose, which is extensive and varied and includes, in addition to *Goodbye to All That*, a number of historical novels in which characters and events from the classical or Biblical past are reconstructed in a lively modern idiom: the most notable of his historical novels are *I, Claudius* (1934), *Claudius the God* (1934), and *King Jesus* (1946). Graves is a good classical and Biblical scholar, though an eccentric one. His interest in classical and Biblical myth is closely related to his theory of poetry and of poetic inspiration, which he expressed in *The White Goddess* (1948), a study of mythology drawn from a great variety of sources but essentially original in its main emphases and interpretations. The book begins as a history of myth, develops into an attack on fashionable kinds of poetry, and ends with his own view of poetry. It preserves the secret wisdom of a people and derives from the great female inspirational principle which he called the White Goddess. Only a return to goddess-worship and an abandonment of patriarchy in favor of matriarchal society can help modern poetry to recover its lost force, clarity, and mythic wisdom. There is often a note of willful exaggeration or mocking mischief in Graves' criticism: he loves to flutter the academic dovecotes, and in the lectures he gave as Clark Lecturer at Cambridge in 1954–55 (*The Crowning Privilege*, 1955) and as Professor of Poetry at Oxford (the professorship of poetry at Oxford is not a regular academic appointment but a visiting lectureship chosen by the vote of all Oxford M.A.'s) in 1964–65 (*Poetic Craft and Principle*, 1967) he deliberately provoked the local academics by contemptuously dismissing most of the accepted great figures of English poetry.

Among the early influences on Graves' poetry were the late 15th- and early 16th-century poet John Skelton, the ballads, Welsh and Irish heroic and popular poetry, and Thomas Hardy (one of the few poets surviving into his own lifetime whom he admired). From 1925 to 1939 the American poet Laura Riding was in Europe and Graves worked closely with and was much influenced by her: they collaborated in the influential critical work, *A Survey of Modernist Poetry* (1927). But for Graves modernism was not represented by the later Yeats or by Pound or Eliot; it had more in common with the work of the American poets John Crowe Ransom, E. E. Cummings, and William Carlos Williams. In his own later poetry Graves becomes more and more the poet of personal relationships, especially of love between the sexes.

In successive editions of his poems Graves has ruthlessly pruned away what he has come to dislike or believes to represent a phase of his poetic career that he has outgrown. He has published over 15 volumes of poetry, of which *Collected Poems* 1959 represents most of what he wants to preserve. He has continued to publish slim volumes of new poetry (*New Poems* 1961; *New Poems* 1962), but the 1959 volume well represents the range and quality of his genius. Its publication was the sign for clear critical affirmation, on both sides of the Atlantic, that Graves is a major English poet of our time. He won the Russell Loines Award for Poetry in 1958 and the Gold Medal of the National Poetry Society of America in 1960.

Down, Wanton, Down!

Down, wanton, down! Have you no shame
That at the whisper of Love's name,
Or Beauty's, presto! up you raise
Your angry head and stand at gaze?

Poor bombard-captain, sworn to reach   5
The ravelin and effect a breach—
Indifferent what you storm or why,
So be that in the breach you die!

Love may be blind, but Love at least
Knows what is man and what mere beast;   10
Or Beauty wayward, but requires
More delicacy from her squires.

Tell me, my witless, whose one boast
Could be your staunchness at the post,
When were you made a man of parts   15
To think fine and profess the arts?

Will many-gifted Beauty come
Bowing to your bald rule of thumb,
Or Love swear loyalty to your crown?
Be gone, have done! Down, wanton, down!   20

1933

The Reader Over My Shoulder

You, reading over my shoulder, peering beneath
My writing arm—I suddenly feel your breath
  Hot on my hand or on my nape,

So interrupt my theme, scratching these few
Words on the margin for you, namely you, 5
 Too-human shape fixed in that shape:—

All the saying of things against myself
And for myself I have well done myself.
 What now, old enemy, shall you do
But quote and underline, thrusting yourself 10
Against me, as ambassador of myself,
 In damned confusion of myself and you?

For you in strutting, you in sycophancy,
Have played too long this other self of me,
 Doubling the part of judge and patron 15
With that of creaking grind-stone to my wit.
Know me, have done: I am a proud spirit
 And you forever clay. Have done.

          1938

The Devil's Advice to Story-tellers

Lest men suspect your tale to be untrue,
Keep probability—some say—in view.
But my advice to story-tellers is:
Weigh out no gross of probabilities,
Nor yet make diligent transcriptions of 5
Known instances of virtue, crime or love.
To forge a picture that will pass for true,
Do conscientiously what liars do—
Born liars, not the lesser sort that raid
The mouths of others for their stock-in-trade: 10
Assemble, first, all casual bits and scraps
That may shake down into a world perhaps;
People this world, by chance created so,
With random persons whom you do not know—
The teashop sort, or travelers in a train 15
Seen once, guessed idly at, not seen again;
Let the erratic course they steer surprise
Their own and your own and your readers' eyes;
Sigh then, or frown, but leave (as in despair)
Motive and end and moral in the air; 20
Nice contradiction between fact and fact
Will make the whole read human and exact.

          1938

A Love Story

The full moon easterly rising, furious,
Against a winter sky ragged with red;

The hedges high in snow, and owls raving—
Solemnities not easy to withstand:
A shiver wakes the spine.   5

In boyhood, having encountered the scene,
I suffered horror: I fetched the moon home,
With owls and snow, to nurse in my head
Throughout the trials of a new Spring,
Famine unassuaged.   10

But fell in love, and made a lodgement
Of love on those chill ramparts.
Her image was my ensign:[1] snows melted,
Hedges sprouted, the moon tenderly shone,
The owls trilled with tongues of nightingale.   15

These were all lies, though they matched the time,
And brought me less than luck; her image
Warped in the weather, turned beldamish.
Then back came winter on me at a bound,
The pallid sky heaved with a moon-quake.   20

Dangerous it had been with love-notes
To serenade Queen Famine.
In tears I recomposed the former scene,
Let the snow lie, watched the moon rise, suffered the owls,
Paid homage to them of unevent.   25

1945

Gulls and Men

The naturalists of the Bass Rock [2]
    On this vexatious point agree:
That sea-birds of all sorts that flock
    About the Bass, repeatedly
        Collide in mid-flight,   5

And neither by design, in play,
    Nor by design, in shrewd assault,
But (as these patient watchers say,
    Eyes that are seldom proved at fault)
        By lack of foresight.   10

Stupidity, which poor and rich
    Hold the recognizance of man,
Precious stupidity, of which
    Let him denude himself who can
        And stand at God's height—   15

1. Flag.
2. A small, roughly circular, rocky island in the Firth of Forth, Scotland,
on which there are a lighthouse and
huge numbers of sea birds.

2346 · *Robert Graves*

Stupidity that brings to birth
   More, always more, than to the grave,
The burden of all songs on earth,
   And by which men are brave
     And women contrite—   20

This jewel bandied from a cliff
   By gulls and razor-bills and such!
Where is man's vindication if
   Perfectibility's as much
     Bird-right as man-right?   25

1947, 1948

The White Goddess[3]

All saints revile her, and all sober men
Ruled by the God Apollo's golden mean—
In scorn of which we sailed to find her
In distant regions likeliest to hold her
Whom we desired above all things to know,   5
Sister of the mirage and echo.

It was a virtue not to stay,
To go our headstrong and heroic way
Seeking her out at the volcano's head,
Among pack ice, or where the track had faded   10
Beyond the cavern of the seven sleepers: [4]
Whose broad high brow was white as any leper's,
Whose eyes were blue, with rowan-berry lips,
With hair curled honey-colored to white hips.

Green sap of Spring in the young wood astir   15
Will celebrate the Mountain Mother,
And every song-bird shout awhile for her;
But we are gifted, even in November
Rawest of seasons, with so huge a sense
Of her nakedly worn magnificence   20
We forget cruelty and past betrayal,
Heedless of where the next bright bolt may fall.

1953

The Straw

Peace, the wild valley streaked with torrents,
A hoopoe [5] perched on his warm rock. Then why
This tremor of the straw between my fingers?

---

3. The significance of the White Goddess for Graves is explained in the introductory headnote.
4. Cf. Donne, *The Good-Morrow*—"Or snorted we in the seven sleepers' den."
5. Bird with pinkish-cinnamon mantle and breast, prominent black-tipped crest, and barred black-and-white wings and tail.

What should I fear? Have I not testimony
In her own hand, signed with her own name   5
That my love fell as lightning on her heart?

These questions, bird, are not rhetorical.
Watch how the straw twitches and leaps
As though the earth quaked at a distance.

Requited love; but better unrequited   10
If this chance instrument gives warning
Of cataclysmic anguish far away.

Were she at ease, warmed by the thought of me,
Would not my hand stay steady as this rock?
Have I undone her by my vehemence?   15

1951, 1953

Dialogue on the Headland

SHE: You'll not forget these rocks and what I told you?
HE: How could I? Never: whatever happens.
SHE: What do you think might happen?
     Might you fall out of love?—did you mean that?
HE: Never, never! "Whatever" was a sop   5
     For jealous listeners in the shadows.
SHE: You haven't answered me. I asked:
     "What do you think might happen?"
HE: Whatever happens: though the skies should fall
     Raining their larks and vultures in our laps—   10
SHE: "Though the seas turn to slime"—say that—
     "Though water-snakes be hatched with six heads."
HE: Though the seas turn to slime, or tower
     In an arching wave above us, three miles high—
SHE: "Though she should break with you," —dare you say that?—   15
     "Though she deny her words on oath."
HE: I had that in my mind to say, or nearly;
     It hurt so much I choked it back.
SHE: How many other days can't you forget?
     How many other loves and landscapes?   20
HE: You are jealous?
SHE: Damnably.
HE: The past is past.
SHE: And this?
HE: Whatever happens, this goes on.   25
SHE: Without a future? Sweetheart, tell me now:
     What do you want of me? I must know that.
HE: Nothing that isn't freely mine already.
SHE: Say what is freely yours and you shall have it.
HE: Nothing that, loving you, I could dare take.   30
SHE: O, for an answer with no "nothing" in it!

HE: Then give me everything that's left.
SHE: Left after what?
HE: After whatever happens:
Skies have already fallen, seas are slime,   35
Water-snakes poke and peer six-headedly—
SHE: And I lie snugly in the Devil's arms.
HE: I said: "Whatever happens." Are you crying?
SHE: You'll not forget me—ever, ever, ever?

                                   1952, 1953

The Blue-fly

Five summer days, five summer nights,
The ignorant, loutish, giddy blue-fly
Hung without motion on the cling peach,
Humming occasionally: "O my love, my fair one!"
    As in the Canticles.[6]   5

Magnified one thousand times, the insect
Looks farcically human; laugh if you will!
Bald head, stage-fairy wings, blear eyes,
A caved-in chest, hairy black mandibles,
    Long spindly thighs.   10

The crime was detected on the sixth day.
What then could be said or done? By anyone?
It would have been vindictive, mean and what-not
To swat that fly for being a blue-fly,
    For debauch of a peach.   15

Is it fair, either, to bring a microscope
To bear on the case, even in search of truth?
Nature, doubtless, has some compelling cause
To glut the carriers of her epidemics—
    Nor did the peach complain.   20

                                     1952, 1953

A Plea to Boys and Girls

You learned Lear's *Nonsense Rhymes* by heart, not rote;
    You learned Pope's *Iliad* by rote, not heart;
These terms should be distinguished if you quote
    My verses, children—keep them poles apart—
And call the man a liar who says I wrote   5
    All that I wrote in love, for love of art.

                                     1956, 1958

6. The Biblical Song of Songs, or Song of Solomon.

Friday Night

Love, the sole Goddess fit for swearing by,
Concedes us graciously the little lie:
The white lie, the half-lie, the lie corrective
Without which love's exchange might prove defective,
Confirming hazardous relationships
By kindly *maquillage* [7] of Truth's pale lips.
This little lie was first told, so they say,
On the sixth day (Love's planetary day)
When, meeting her full-bosomed and half dressed,
Jove roared out suddenly: "Hell take the rest!
Six hard days of Creation are enough"—
And clasped her to him, meeting no rebuff.

Next day he rested, and she rested too.
The busy little lie between them flew:
"If this be not perfection," Love would sigh,
"Perfection is a great, black, thumping lie . . ."
Endearments, kisses, grunts, and whispered oaths;
But were her thoughts on breakfast, or on clothes?

1957, 1958

A Slice of Wedding Cake

Why have such scores of lovely, gifted girls
  Married impossible men?
Simple self-sacrifice may be ruled out,
  And missionary endeavor, nine times out of ten.

Repeat "impossible men": not merely rustic,
  Foul-tempered or depraved
(Dramatic foils chosen to show the world
  How well women behave, and always have behaved).

Impossible men: idle, illiterate,
  Self-pitying, dirty, sly,
For whose appearance even in City parks
  Excuses must be made to casual passers-by.

Has God's supply of tolerable husbands
  Fallen, in fact, so low?
Or do I always over-value woman
  At the expense of man?
            Do I?
                It might be so.

1959

7. Make-up (French).

F. R. LEAVIS

(1895–1978)

Frank Raymond Leavis was born at Cambridge and educated there at the Perse School and Emmanuel College. In 1936 he became Fellow of Downing College, Cambridge, where he directed English studies and rapidly made the college a distinctive English school within the university. His insistence on rigorous evaluative criticism, his championship of T. S. Eliot and D. H. Lawrence before either was academically respectable, his scorn for the genteel academic tradition with its catholicity of taste and gentlemanly tone, and his contemptuous dismissal of all literature except the small amount of genuinely realized work which represented the "great tradition" made him an isolated and embattled figure, but an immensely influential one. He was one of the founders of the periodical *Scrutiny* (1932–53) through which his influence was exercised. On his retirement from Cambridge teaching in 1962 he was for some years professor at the new English University of York.

Literature and Society[1]

Two or three years back, or at any time in the Marxizing decade,[2] having been invited to discourse on "Literature and Society," I should have known what was expected of me—and what to expect. I should have been expected to discuss, or to give opportunities for discussing, the duty of the writer to identify himself with the working class, the duty of the critic to evaluate works of literature in terms of the degree in which they seemed calculated to further (or otherwise) the proper and predestined outcome of the class struggle, and the duty of the literary historian to explain literary history as the reflection of changing economic and material realities (the third adjective, "social," which I almost added here would be otiose). I should have been braced for such challenges as the proposition that D. H. Lawrence, though he

> was unquestionably aware of and tried to describe the outside forces that were undermining the bourgeois society into which he made his way . . . saw those forces from a *bourgeois* viewpoint, as destroyers to be combated. Consequently he misrepresented reality.[3]

1. "This is the substance, reconstructed in a condensed form from the notes used on the occasion, of an address given to the Students' Union of the London School of Economics and Politics" [Leavis's note].

2. The 1930's, when many intellectuals were influenced by Marxism.
3. "*The Mind in Chains* (edited by C. Day Lewis, reviewed in *Scrutiny* for September, 1937)" [Leavis's note].

What was wrong with his work was that he "shared the life of a social class which has passed its prime."

I assume that the expectation I should have had to address myself to in those not so very remote days isn't entertained at all generally on the present occasion, and I assume it gladly. But that does leave me with a large undirected formula on my hands: "Literature and Society" might, in fact, seem to be daunting and embarrassing in the wealth of possibilities it covers. However, certain major interests of my own respond to it quite comfortably and I had no difficulty in concluding that I should be expected to do what, in accordance with those interests, it would suit me to do: that is, to try and define on what grounds and in what ways the study of literature—literature as it concerns me, who am avowedly in the first place a literary critic—should, I think, be seen as intimately relevant to what may be presumed to be the major interests of students at the London School of Economics.[4]

For if the Marxist approach to literature seems to me unprofitable, that is not because I think of literature as a matter of isolated works of art, belonging to a realm of pure literary values (whatever *they* might be); works regarding the production of which it is enough to say that individuals of specific creative gifts were born and created them. No one interested in literature who began to read and think immediately after the last war—at a time, that is coincident with the early critical work of T. S. Eliot—can fail to have taken stock, for conscious rejection, of the Romantic critical tradition (if it can be called that): the set of ideas and attitudes about literary creation coming down through the nineteenth century. That tradition laid all the stress on inspiration and the individual genius. How do masterpieces arrive? Gifted individuals occur, inspiration sets in, creation results. Mr. Eliot, all of whose early prose may be said to have been directed against the Romantic tradition, which till then had not been effectively challenged, lays the stress on the other things (or some of them) besides individual talent and originative impulse from within that have to be taken account of when we try to understand any significant achievement in art. Of course, it was no discovery that there are these things to be taken account of: criticism and literary history had for generations dealt in influences, environments, and the extra-literary conditions of literary production. But we are apt to be peculiarly under the influence of ideas and attitudes of which we are not fully conscious, they prevail until rejected, and the Romantic set—an atmosphere of the unformulated and vague—may be said to have pre-

---

4. A college of the University of London specializing in economics, philosophy, and sociology, at this time containing some distinguished left-wing professors.

vailed until Mr. Eliot's criticism, cooperating with his poetry, made unconsciousness impossible and rejection inevitable.

Something like the idea of Tradition so incisively and provocatively formulated by him plays, I think, an essential part in the thinking of everyone today who is seriously interested in literature. If I say that idea represents a new emphasis on the social nature of artistic achievement, I ought to add at once that the word "social" probably doesn't occur in the classical essay, *Tradition and the Individual Talent* (the word that takes Mr. Eliot's stress is "impersonal"). The "society" implied in this "social"—and (which is, of course, my point) in the idea of Tradition—is not the Marxist concept; and the difference is what I have my eye on. But let me first remind you of the idea as Mr. Eliot formulates it. The individual writer is to be aware that his work is *of* the Literature to which it belongs and not merely added externally to it. A literature, that is, must be thought of as essentially something more than an accumulation of separate works: it has an organic form, or constitutes an organic order, in relation to which the individual writer has his significance and his being. "Mind" is the analogy (if this is the right word) used:

> He must be aware that the mind of Europe—the mind of his own country—a mind which he learns in time to be much more important than his own private mind—is a mind which changes . . .

and so on.

Something, I said, in the nature of this way of thinking seems to me inevitable for anyone who thinks about literature at all. The ways in which it is at odds with Marxist theories of culture are obvious. It stresses, not economic and material determinants, but intellectual and spiritual, so implying a different conception from the Marxist of the relation between the present of society and the past, and a different conception of society. It assumes that, enormously—no one will deny it—as material conditions count, there is a certain measure of spiritual autonomy in human affairs, and that human intelligence, choice, and will do really and effectively operate, expressing an inherent human nature. There *is* a human nature —that is how, from the present point of view, we may take the stress as falling; a human nature an understanding of which is of primary importance to students of society and politics. And here is the first way that presents itself of indicating the kind of importance literature—the literary critic's literature—should be recognized to have for such students: the study of it is, or should be, an intimate study of the complexities, potentialities, and essential conditions of human nature.

But that, by itself, is too large a proposition to take us anywhere.

Let me, by way of moving towards more discussible particularity, make another obvious note on the difference between the Marxist kind of attitude toward literature and that represented by the idea of Tradition I've invoked. It's true that this latter stresses the social aspect of creative achievement as the Romantic attitude didn't; but it allows for the individual aspect more than the Marxist does. This is inevitably a crude way of putting it—as you'll see, that "inevitably" is my point. But to postpone that for a moment: you can't be interested in literature and forget that the creative individual is indispensable. Without the individual talent there is no creation. While you are in intimate touch with literature no amount of dialectic, or of materialistic interpretation, will obscure for long the truth that human life lives only in individuals: I might have said, the truth that it is only in individuals that society lives.

The point I wanted to make is this: you can't contemplate the nature of literature without acquiring some inhibition in respect to that antithesis, "the individual and society," and losing any innocent freedom you may have enjoyed in handling it; without, that is, acquiring some inhibiting apprehensions of the subtleties that lie behind the antithesis.

An illustration presents itself readily. I have spoken of the "Romantic" attitude, and the phrase might be called misleading, since the actual poets of the Romantic period—Wordsworth, Coleridge, Byron, Shelley, Keats—differ widely among themselves. No general description worth offering will cover them. Though as influences they merge later in a Romantic tradition, they themselves do not exemplify any common Romanticism. What they have in common is that they belong to the same age; and in belonging to the same age they have in common something negative: the absence of anything to replace the very positive tradition (literary, and more than literary—hence its strength) that had prevailed till towards the end of the eighteenth century. It is this tradition, the Augustan, that I want to consider briefly first.

It originated in the great changes in civilization that make the second part of the seventeenth century look so unlike the first, and its early phase may be studied in the works of John Dryden. The conventions, standards, and idiom of its confident maturity offer themselves for contemplation in *The Tatler* and *The Spectator*. The relevant point to be made about it for the present purpose is that it laid a heavy stress on the social. Its insistence that man is a social being was such as to mean in effect that all his activities, inner as well as outer, that literature took cognizance of were to belong to an overtly social context. Even the finest expressions of the spirit were to be in resonance with a code of Good Form—for with such a code the essential modes and idioms of Augustan culture were intimately associated. The characteristic movements and dictions of the eighteenth century, in verse as well as prose, convey a suggestion of social deportment and company manners.

An age in which such a tradition gets itself established is clearly an age in which the writer feels himself very much at one with society. And the Augustan heyday, the Queen Anne period,[5] was a period very confident of its flourishing cultural health. But we should expect such an insistence on the social to have in time a discouraging effect on the deeper sources of originality, the creative springs in the individually experiencing mind. We should expect to find evidence of this in the field of poetry, and we find it. This is no place to pretend to give a fair account of the Augustan decline, which was a complex affair: I'm merely stressing an aspect that is relevant to my present purpose. Where, then, a tradition like that I have adumbrated prevails there is bound before long to be a movement of protest in minds of the kind that ought to be creative. They will feel that conventional expression—that which, nevertheless, seems natural and inevitable to the age—imposes a conventional experience, and that this, suppressing, obtruding, muffling, and misrepresenting, is at odds with their own. There will be a malaise, a sense of blunted vitality, that would express itself to this effect if it were fully conscious. Full consciousness is genius, and manifests itself in technical achievement, the new use of words. In the seventeen-eighties it is William Blake.

Blake in his successful work says implicitly: "It is I who see and feel. I see only what *I* see and feel only what *I* feel. My experience is mine, and in its specific quality lies its significance." He may be said to have reversed for himself the shift of stress that occurred at the Restoration. But to such a reversal there is clearly a limit. Blake uses the English language, and not one of his own invention; and to say that he uses it is not to say that it is for him a mere instrument. His individuality has developed in terms of the language, with the ways of experiencing, as well as of handling experience, that it involves. The mind and sensibility that he has to express are *of* the language.

I may seem here to be handling a truism of the kind that there's no point in recalling. But I believe that the familiar truths that we contemplate when we contemplate the nature of language—in the way, that is, in which we have to when we take a critical interest in literature—have the familiarity of the familiar things that we tend to lose sight of when we begin to think. And what I have just been touching on is perhaps the most radical of the ways in which the literary critic's interest in literature leads to a new recognition of the essentially social nature of the individual—and (I may add) of the "reality" he takes for granted.

5. The age of Pope and Swift (1702–14), which liked to consider itself an "Augustan" age (i.e., comparable to the age of the Emperor Augustus in Rome) and was both socially and culturally full of confidence.

In any case, I want to pass at once to an order of consideration that will probably seem to have more discussible bearings on the normal preoccupations of the student of society. The measure of social collaboration and support represented by the English language didn't make Blake prosperously self-sufficient; he needed something more—something that he didn't get. This is apparent in a peculiar kind of difficulty that his work offers to the critic. I am thinking of the difficulty one so often has in deciding what kind of thing it is one has before one.

> A petty sneaking knave I knew—
> O! Mr. Cromek, how do ye do?[6]

—that is clearly a private blow-off. *The Tyger* is clearly a poem (in spite of the abandoned job of the third stanza).[7] But again and again one comes on the thing that seems to be neither wholly private nor wholly a poem. It seems not to know what it is or where it belongs, and one suspects that Blake didn't know. What he did know—and know deep down in himself—was that he had no public: he very early gave up publishing in any serious sense. One obvious consequence, or aspect, of this knowledge is the carelessness that is so apparent in the later prophetic books. Blake had ceased to be capable of taking enough trouble. The uncertainty I have just referred to is a more radical and significant form of the same kind of disability. In the absence, we may put it, of adequate social collaboration (the sense, or confident prospect, of a responsive community of minds was the minimum he needed) his powers of attaining in achieved creation to that peculiar impersonal realm to which the work of art belongs and in which minds can meet—it is as little a world of purely private experience as it is the public world of the laboratory—failed to develop as, his native endowment being what it was, they ought to have done.[8]

The inevitable way in which serious literary interest develops towards the sociological is suggested well enough here. What better conditions, one asks, can one imagine for a Blake? Can one imagine him in a tradition that should have nurtured his genius rather than have been something it had to escape from, and in a society that should have provided him with the best conceivable public? But what is the best conceivable public? And so one is led on to inquire

---

6. An epigram by Blake, whose poem *The Tyger* is then contrasted with it.
7. "The second interrogative sentence of the stanza Blake made a number of attempts at completing before he threw up the job" [Leavis's note].
8. "The following, both in its curiously striking qualities—it clearly comes from a remarkable poet, and in what I take to be its lack of self-sufficiency as a poem, seems to be a representatively suggestive document of the case I have

been trying to describe: "Truly, my Satan, thou art but a dunce, / And dost not know the garment from the man; / Every harlot was a virgin once, / Nor canst thou ever change Kate to Nan. / Though thou art worshippd by the names divine / Of Jesus and Jehovah, thou art still / The Son of Morn in weary night's decline, / The lost traveler's dream under the hill" [Leavis's note].

into the nature and conditions of cultural health and prosperity.

I will illustrate with a line of reflection that has occupied myself a good deal. Harking back from Blake one notes that the establishment of the Augustan tradition was associated with—indeed, it involved—a separation, new and abrupt, between sophisticated culture and popular. Anticipating the problem of bringing home as convincingly and vividly as possible to (say) students of modern social and political questions what is meant by saying that there was, in the seventeenth century, a real culture of the people, one thinks first of Dryden's contemporary, Bunyan.[9] If *The Pilgrim's Progress* is a humane masterpiece, that is in spite of the bigoted sectarian creed that Bunyan's allegory, in detail as in sum, directs itself to enforcing. In spite of his aim, a humane masterpiece resulted because he belonged to the civilization of his time, and that meant, for a small-town "mechanick," participating in a rich traditional culture.

It is on the reader approaching as a literary critic that this truth compels itself (others seem to miss it). Take, for instance, this passage, which such a reader would fix on as representative of Bunyan's art:

> Christian: Pray, who are your kindred there, if a man may be so bold?
>
> By-ends: Almost the whole town; and in particular, my lord Turn-about, my lord Timeserver, my lord Fair-speech, (from whose ancestors that town first took its name), also Mr. Smoothman, Mr. Facing-both-ways, Mr. Anything; and the parson of our parish, Mr. Two-tongues, was my mother's own brother by father's side; and to tell you the truth, I am become a gentleman of good quality; yet my great grandfather was but a waterman, looking one way and rowing another; and I got most of my estate by the same occupation.
>
> Christian: Are you a married man?
>
> By-ends: Yes, and my wife is a very virtuous woman, the daughter of a virtuous woman; she was my lady Faining's daughter, therefore she came of a very honorable family, and is arrived to such a pitch of breeding, that she knows how to carry it to all, even to prince and peasant. 'Tis true we somewhat differ in religion from those of the stricter sort, yet but in two small points: first, we never strive against wind and tide; secondly, we are always most zealous when religion goes in his silver slippers; we love much to walk with him in the street, if the sun shines, and the people applaud him.

9. John Bunyan (1628–88) wrote his famous religious allegory *The Pilgrim's Progress* in 1675.

The critic notes that the names and racy turns of speech here are organically *of* the style; a style that clearly (and not the less so for there being literary associations) concentrates and intensifies the life of popular idiom. This life, running so richly into the placing nickname and the proverbial epitome, is unmistakably the expression of a vigorous humane culture. For what is involved is not merely an idiomatic raciness of speech, expressing a strong vitality, but a traditional art of social living, with its mature habits of judgment and valuation. We must beware of idealizing uncritically, but the fact is plain. There would have been no Bunyan (as there would before him have been no Shakespeare) if in his time, with all its disadvantages from a modern point of view, there had not been, living in the daily life of the people, a rich traditional culture—a culture that has disappeared so completely that modern revolutionaries, social reformers, and Utopists do not commonly seem to have any notion of the kind of thing that has been lost.

This then is what the literary critic has to deduce from his reading. If he finds that others, interested primarily in social reform and social history, do not seem properly impressed by such evidence, he can, by way of bringing home to them in how full a sense there is, behind the literature, a social culture and an art of living, call attention to Cecil Sharp's introduction to *English Folk Songs from the Southern Appalachians*. Hearing that the English folk song still persisted in the remoter valleys of those mountains Sharp, during the last war, went over to investigate, and brought back a fabulous haul. More than that, he discovered that the tradition of song and dance (and a reminder is in place at this point of the singing and dancing with which the pilgrims punctuate their progress in the second part of Bunyan's Calvinistic allegory) had persisted so vigorously because the whole context to which folk song and folk dance belong was there too: he discovered, in fact, a civilization or "way of life" (in our Democratic parlance) that was truly an art of social living.

The mountaineers were descended from settlers who had left this country in the eighteenth century.

The region is from its inaccessibility a very secluded one . . . the inhabitants have for a hundred years or more been completely isolated and shut off from all traffic with the rest of the world. Their speech is English, not American, and, from the number of expressions they use that have long been obsolete elswhere, and the old-fashioned way in which they pronounce many of their words, it is clear that they are talking the language of a past day. They are a leisurely, cheery people in their quiet way, in whom the social instinct is very highly developed . . . They know their Bible intimately and subscribe to an austere creed, charged with Calvinism and the unrelenting doctrines of determinism or fatal-

ism . . . They have an easy unaffected bearing and the unselfcon-
scious manners of the well-bred . . . A few of those we met were
able to read and write, but the majority were illiterate. They are
however good talkers, using an abundant vocabulary racily and
often picturesquely.

That the illiterate may nevertheless reach a high level of culture will surprise only those who imagine that education and cultivation are convertible terms. The reason, I take it, why these
mountain people, albeit unlettered, have acquired so many of the
essentials of culture, is partly to be attributed to the large amount
of leisure they enjoy, without which, of course, no cultural development is possible, but chiefly to the fact that they have one and
all entered at birth into the full enjoyment of their racial inheritance. Their language, wisdom, manners, and the many graces of
life that are theirs, are merely racial attributes which have been
gradually acquired and accumulated in past centuries and handed
down generation by generation, each generation adding its quota
to what it received . . .

. . . Of the supreme value of an inherited tradition, even when
unenforced by any formal school education, our mountain community in the Southern Highlands is an outstanding example.

Correlation of Cecil Sharp's introduction with Bunyan should
sufficiently confirm and enforce the significance attributed to
Bunyan above. And Bunyan himself shows how the popular culture
to which he bears witness could merge with literary culture at the
level of great literature. The converse, regarding the advantages
enjoyed by the literary writer, the "intellectual," need not be
stated: they are apparent in English literature from Shakespeare to
Marvell. We see Marvell—it is, of course, for this reason I name
him—as pre-eminently refined, European in sophistication, and intimately related to a tradition of courtly urbanity; but his refinement
involves no insulation from the popular—the force of which judgment is brought out by contrast with Pope. In prose, compare Halifax with Dryden. Halifax (the Trimmer)[1] is "easy," "natural," and
urbane, a master of the spoken tone and movement: in short he is
unmistakably of the Restoration; but his raciness and idiomatic life
relate him as unmistakably to Bunyan. I don't think I am being
fanciful when I say that when Dryden gets lively, as in the preface
to *All for Love*, he tends towards the Cockney; he assimilates, in
fact, with L'Estrange.[2] At least, his polite idiomatic ease is wholly
of the coffeehouse, that new organ of metropolitan culture the
vibration of which seems essentially to exclude any intimate relations with Bunyan's world. The exclusive, or insulating, efficacy of

1. George Savile, Marquess of Halifax
(1633–95), politician and pioneer
essayist; one of his essays, *The Character of a Trimmer*, sums up his own
political and religious views, which
"trimmed" between extremes.
2. Sir Roger L'Estrange (1616–1704),
journalist and pamphleteer.

the politeness of Augustan verse, even in Pope, whose greatness manifests itself in his power of transcending the Augustan, is at any rate obvious; and Pope's politeness belongs to the same world as the politeness of Addison's prose. Where, in short, Augustan convention and idiom, with their social suggestion, prevail, sophisticated culture cuts itself off from the traditional culture of the people.

The eighteenth century, significantly, had a habit of attempting the naïve, and, characteristically, evoked its touching simplicities of low life in modes that, Augustan tone and movement being inescapable, evoked at the same time the elegant and polite. It is one of the manifestations of Blake's genius that he, unique in this, can— the evidence is apparent here and there in *Poetical Sketches* (1783) —be genuinely, in verse that has nothing Augustan about it, of the people (popular London in his time was clearly still something of a "folk"). The mention of this aspect of Blake serves to bring out by contrast the significance of Wordsworth's kind of interest in humble and rustic life. It is essentially—in so far as it is more than nominal—an interest in something felt as external to the world to which he himself belongs, and very remote from it: the reaction that Wordsworth represents against the Augustan century doesn't mean any movement towards re-establishing the old organic relations betwen literary culture and the sources of vitality in the general life. By Wordsworth's death, the Industrial Revolution had done its work, and the traditional culture of the people was no longer there, except vestigially.

No one, then, seriously interested in modern literature can feel that it represents a satisfactory cultural order. But if anyone should conclude that it ought therefore—the literature that the literary critic finds significant—to be contemned, and that a really significant contemporary literature would have the Marxizing or Wellsian[3] kind of relation to social, political, and economic problems, he may be reminded that but for the persisting literary tradition, the history I have so inadequately sketched would have been lost, and our notions of what a popular culture might be, and what relations might exist between it and a "highbrow" culture, would have been very different. And it needs stressing that where there isn't, in the literary critic's sense, a significant contemporary literature the literary tradition—the "mind" (and mind includes memory)—is not fully live. To have a vital literary culture we must have a literature that is a going concern; and that will be what, under present conditions of civilization, it has to be. *Where* it is can be determined only by the literary critic's kind of judgment.

What one has to suggest in general by way of urging on students

3. A reference to the novelist H. G. Wells (1866–1946) and his belief in the perfectibility of man through scientific progress.

of politics and society the claims of literary studies (I don't mean the ordinary academic kind) to be regarded as relevant and important is that thinking about political and social matters ought to be done by minds of some real literary education, and done in an intellectual climate informed by a vital literary culture. More particularly, of course, there are, capable of endless development and illustration, the hints for the social historian and the sociologist I have thrown out in the course of my argument. These all involve the principle that literature will yield to the sociologist, or anyone else, what it has to give only if it is approached as literature. For what I have in mind is no mere industrious searching for "evidence," and collecting of examples, in whatever happens to have been printed and preserved. The "literature" in question is something in the definition of which terms of value judgment figure essentially, and something accessible only to the reader capable of intelligent and sensitive criticism.

I am thinking, in this instance, not of the actual business of explicit valuation, but of the ability to respond appropriately and appreciatively to the subtleties of the artist's use of language and to the complexities of his organizations. And I am not thinking merely of poetry. It is to poetry, mainly, that I have made my illustrative references, but if one were enumerating the more obvious kinds of interest that literature has to offer the sociologist, prose fiction, it is plain, would figure very largely. There seems to be a general view that anyone can read a novel; and the uses commonly made of novels as evidence, sociological or other, would seem to illustrate that view. Actually, to use as evidence or illustration the kinds of novel that are most significant and have most to offer requires an uncommon skill, the product of a kind of training that few readers submit themselves to. For instance, the sociologist can't learn what Jane Austen has to teach about the part played by the family in the life, individual and social, of her times, so different in this respect from ours, without being, in reading her, a much more intelligent critic than any professional authority he is likely to have gone to for guidance. Nor, without being an original critic, adverted and sensitized by experience and the habit of critical analysis, can the social psychologist learn what Conrad has to teach about the social nature of the individual's "reality."

These instances must suffice—I choose them for their suggestive diversity. Instead of offering any further, I will end by making a general contention in other terms. Without the sensitizing familiarity with the subtleties of language, and the insight into the relations between abstract or generalizing thought and the concrete or human experience, that the trained frequentation of literature alone can bring, the thinking that attends social and political studies will not have the edge and force it should.

1943

STEVIE SMITH
(1902–1971)

Stevie Smith's real name was Florence Margaret Smith, but she was nicknamed "Stevie," and used the name in all her writing, because of her small stature—the reference being to the famous jockey Steve Donoghue. She was born in Hull, Yorkshire, but at the age of three went with her mother and sister to live with an aunt in Palmer's Green, an unfashionable and out-of-the-way suburb of London. She had a good high school education, concentrating on French and the classics, but did not go on to a university. She obtained a position as secretary to the magazine-publishing firm of Newnes, Pearson, eventually becoming private secretary to the two principals in the firm, while continuing to live with her aunt, to whom she was devoted. When her aunt grew old and feeble Smith gave up her job to look after her, although she herself was often in ill health. At the same time she managed somehow to lead a lively social life in London and was known for the vividness and variety of her conversation at parties.

Stevie Smith first appeared as a novelist, with *Novel on Yellow Paper* (1936). This was followed by two further novels and nine volumes of poetry. It was *Novel on Yellow Paper* and her first volume of poetry, *A Good Time Was Had By All* (1937) that established her reputation, and her poems began to appear frequently in newspapers and periodicals.

Stevie Smith is one of the absolute originals of English literature, whose work fits into no category and shows none of the characteristic influences of the age. Sometimes she is reminiscent of Blake, sometimes of Ogden Nash, sometimes of Edward Lear, but her voice is always her own. Her language is sometimes simple and matter-of-fact, sometimes deliberately archaic (where it is often suggestive of old ballads), while her verse movement ranges from free conversational rhythms to traditional verse patterns, on occasion becoming—deliberately, with ironic effect—almost doggerel. The simple matter-of-fact speech can exist in the same poem as a more deliberately "poetic" language; in *Is it Wise?*, for example, we encounter "a song of Melancholy," "a garland of sighs," "a martyr's dowry," and then the simple refrain "No, it is not wise." She illustrated many of her poems with quaint drawings ("doodles" as she called them) which have the same kind of oddity as the poetry. She was a religious skeptic who was at the same time fascinated by theological speculation, the language of the Bible, and religious experience. Her concern with death and suicide may seem morbid, but it was genuine: and in *Not Waving but Drowning* (published in the volume of that name in 1957) a deep pessimism is clothed in wit and even humor. Her unique quality is perhaps her ability to be simultaneously tragic, visionary, and amusing.

Is It Wise?

Is it wise
To hug misery
To make a song of Melancholy
To weave a garland of sighs

To abandon hope wholly?　　　　　　　　　5
No, it is not wise.

Is it wise
To love Mortality
To make a song of Corruptibility
A chain of linked lies　　　　　　　　　10
To bind Mutability?
No, it is not wise.

Is it wise
To endure
To call up Old Fury　　　　　　　　　15
And Pain for a martyr's dowry
When Death's a prize
Easy to carry?
No, it is not wise.

　　　　　　　　　　　　　　　1937

Our Bog Is Dood

Our Bog is dood, our Bog is dood,
They lisped in accents mild,
But when I asked them to explain
They grew a little wild.
How do you know your Bog is dood　　　5
My darling little child?

We know because we wish it so
That is enough, they cried,
And straight within each infant eye
Stood up the flame of pride,　　　　　10
And if you do not think it so
You shall be crucified.

Then tell me, darling little ones,
What's dood, suppose Bog is?
Just what we think, the answer came,　　15
Just what we think it is.
They bowed their heads. Our Bog is ours
And we are wholly his.

But when they raised them up again
They had forgotten me　　　　　　　20
Each one upon each other glared
In pride and misery
For what was dood, and what their Bog
They never could agree.

Oh sweet it was to leave them then,　　25
And sweeter not to see,

And sweetest of all to walk alone
Beside the encroaching sea,
The sea that soon should drown them all,
That never yet drowned me.   30

                                              1950

Not Waving but Drowning

Nobody heard him, the dead man,
But still he lay moaning:
I was much further out than you thought
And not waving but drowning.

Poor chap, he always loved larking   5
And now he's dead
It must have been too cold for him his heart gave way,
They said.

Oh, no no no, it was too cold always
(Still the dead one lay moaning)   10
I was much too far out all my life
And not waving but drowning.

                                              1957

The New Age

Shall I tell you the signs of a New Age coming?
It is a sound of drubbing and sobbing
Of people crying, We are old, we are old
And the sun is going down and becoming cold
Oh sinful and sad and the last of our kind   5
If we turn to God now do you think He will mind?
Then they fall on their knees and begin to whine
That the state of Art itself presages decline
As if Art has anything or ever had
To do with civilization whether good or bad.   10
Art is wild as a cat and quite separate from civilization
But that is another matter that is not now under consideration.
Oh these people are fools with their sighing and sinning
Why should Man be at an end? he is hardly beginning.
This New Age will slip in under cover of their cries   15
And be upon them before they have opened their eyes.
Well, say geological time is a one-foot rule
Then Man's only been here about half an inch to play the fool
Or be wise if he likes, as he often has been
Oh heavens how these crying people spoil the beautiful
    geological scene.   20

                                              1957

Can It Be?

Can it be, can it be
That beasts are of various bravery,
Some brave by nature, some not at all,
Some trying to be against a fall?

I saw a cat. Beside a lily tank,   5
Paved level with the grass, she stood, this cat,
Considering her leap.
Three times she backed for jumping, gathered tight
(So tight, thought landed her already over)
And did not jump. And then,   10
After a pause, as scolding humanly
"Not nervy, eh? We'll see."
She jumped. And what a jump that was!
Quite twice as long
And high   15
As it need be,
Now why
Did this cat jump at all, so force herself?
There was a path around the tank,
She could have walked.   20

Can it be, can it be
That beasts are of various bravery,
Some simply brave, some not, some taking thought
(Most curiously) to cast themselves aloft?

1957

In the Park

Walking one day in the park in winter
I heard two silvered gentlemen talking,
Two old friends, elderly, walking, talking
There by the silver lake mid-pooled black in winter.

"Pray for the Mute who have no word to say,"   5
Cried the one old gentleman, "Not because they are dumb,
But they are weak. And the weak thoughts beating in the brain
Generate a sort of heat, yet cannot speak.
Thoughts that are bound without sound
In the tomb of the brain's room, wound. Pray for the Mute."   10

"But" (said his friend) "see how they swim
Free in the element best loved, so wet; yet breathe

As a visitor to the air come; plunge then, rejoicing more,
Having left it briefly for the visited shore, to come
Home to the wet   15
Windings that are yet
Best loved though familiar; and oh so right the wet
Stream and the wave; he is their pet."

Finished, the mild friend
Smiled, put aside his well-tuned hearing instrument   20
And it seemed
The happiness he spoke of
Irradiated all his members, and his heart
Barked with delight to stress
So much another's happiness.   25

But which other's? The somber first
Speaker reversed
The happy moment; cried again
(Mousing for pain) "Pray for the Mute" (a tear drops)
"They are like the brute."   30

Struck by the shout
That he may not know what it's about
The deaf friend again
Up-ends his hearing instrument to relieve the strain.
What? Oh shock, " 'Pray for the Mute'?   35
I thought you said the newt."

Now which is Christianer pray, of these old friends, the one who
    will say
For pain's sake pray, pray; or the deaf other that rejoices
So much that the cool amphibian
Shall have his happiness, all things rejoicing with him?   40

But wait; the first speaker now, the old somber one,
Is penetrated quite by his friend's sun
And, "Oh blesséd you," he cries, "to show
So in simplicity what is true."
All his face is suffused with happy tears and as he weeps he sings
    a happy song,   45
Happier even than his friend's song was, righting the wrong.
So two, better than one, finally strike truth in his happy songs:

"Praise," cries the weeping softened one,
    Not pray, praise, all men,
Praise is the best prayer, the least self's there, that least's
    release."   50

1957

Thoughts About the Person from Porlock[1]

Coleridge received the Person from Porlock
And ever after called him a curse,
Then why did he hurry to let him in?
He could have hid in the house.

It was not right of Coleridge in fact it was wrong   5
(But often we all do wrong)
As the truth is I think he was already stuck
With Kubla Khan.

He was weeping and wailing: I am finished, finished,
I shall never write another word of it,   10
When along comes the Person from Porlock
And takes the blame for it.

It was not right, it was wrong,
But often we all do wrong.

May we inquire the name of the Person from Porlock?
Why, Porson, didn't you know?   15
He lived at the bottom of Porlock Hill
So had a long way to go.

He wasn't much in the social sense
Though his grandmother was a Warlock,   20
One of the Rutlandshire ones I fancy
And nothing to do with Porlock.

And he lived at the bottom of the hill as I said
And had a cat named Flo,
And had a cat named Flo.   25

I long for the Person from Porlock
To bring my thoughts to an end,
I am becoming impatient to see him
I think of him as a friend,

Often I look out of the window   30
Often I run to the gate
I think, He will come this evening,
I think it is rather late.

1. S. T. Coleridge tells us in a prefatory note to *Kubla Khan* that he wrote the poem in "a lonely farmhouse between Porlock and Linton, on the Exmoor confines of Somerset and Devonshire." He had taken "an anodyne" (opium) to relieve "a slight indisposition" and then fell asleep and had a strange dream. He began to evoke the dream in *Kubla Khan* after he woke up, but was interrupted "by a person on business from Porlock" and could never recover the original inspiration so as to complete the poem.

I am hungry to be interrupted
Forever and ever amen   35
O Person from Porlock come quickly
And bring my thoughts to an end.

•

I felicitate the people who have a Person from Porlock
To break up everything and throw it away
Because then there will be nothing to keep them   40
And they need not stay.

Why do they grumble so much?
He comes like a benison
They should be glad he has not forgotten them
They might have had to go on.   45

•

These thoughts are depressing I know. They are depressing,
I wish I was more cheerful, it is more pleasant,
Also it is a duty, we should smile as well as submitting
To the purpose of One Above who is experimenting
With various mixtures of human character which goes best,   50
All is interesting for him it is exciting, but not for us.
There I go again. Smile, smile, and get some work to do
Then you will be practically unconscious without positively
        having to go.

                                                                          1962

Pretty

Why is the word pretty so underrated?
In November the leaf is pretty when it falls
The stream grows deep in the woods after rain
And in the pretty pool the pike stalks

He stalks his prey, and this is pretty too,   5
The prey escapes with an underwater flash
But not for long, the great fish has him now
The pike is a fish who always has his prey

And this is pretty. The water rat is pretty
His paws are not webbed, he cannot shut his nostrils   10
As the otter can and the beaver, he is torn between
The land and water. Not "torn," he does not mind.

The owl hunts in the evening and it is pretty
The lake water below him rustles with ice
There is frost coming from the ground, in the air mist   15
All this is pretty, it could not be prettier.

Yes, it could always be prettier, the eye abashes
It is becoming an eye that cannot see enough,
Out of the wood the eye climbs. This is prettier
A field in the evening, tilting up.   20

The field tilts to the sky. Though it is late
The sky is lighter than the hill field
All this looks easy but really it is extraordinary
Well, it is extraordinary to be so pretty.

And it is careless, and that is always pretty   25
This field, this owl, this pike, this pool are careless,
As Nature is always careless and indifferent
Who sees, who steps, means nothing, and this is pretty.

So a person can come along like a thief—pretty!—
Stealing a look, pinching the sound and feel,
Lick the icicle broken from the bank   30
And still say nothing at all, only cry pretty.

Cry pretty, pretty, pretty and you'll be able
Very soon not even to cry pretty
And so be delivered entirely from humanity   35
This is prettiest of all, it is very pretty.

                                                                        1962

The Galloping Cat

Oh I am a cat that likes to
Gallop about doing good
So
One day when I was
Galloping about doing good, I saw   5
A Figure in the path; I said:
Get off! (Be-
cause
I am a cat that likes to
Gallop about doing good)
But he did not move, instead   10
He raised his hand as if
To land me a cuff
So I made to dodge so as to
Prevent him bringing it orf,
Un-for-tune-ately I slid   15
On a banana skin
Some Ass had left instead
Of putting in the bin. So
His hand caught me on the cheek   20

I tried
To lay his arm open from wrist to elbow
With my sharp teeth
Because I am
A cat that likes to gallop about doing good.   25
Would you believe it?
He wasn't there
My teeth met nothing but air,
But a Voice said: Poor cat,
(Meaning me) and a soft stroke   30
Came on me head
Since when
I have been bald.
I regard myself as
A martyr to doing good.   35
Also I heard a swoosh
As of wings, and saw
A halo shining at the height of
Mrs Gubbins's backyard fence,
So I thought: What's the good   40
Of galloping about doing good
When angels stand in the path
And do not do as they should
Such as having an arm to be bitten off
All the same I   45
Intend to go on being
A cat that likes to
Gallop about doing good
So
Now with my bald head I go,   50
Chopping the untidy flowers down, to and fro,
An' scooping up the grass to show
Underneath
The cinder path of wrath
Ha ha ha ha, ho,   55
Angels aren't the only ones who do not know
What's what and that
Galloping about doing good
Is a full-time job
That needs   60
An experienced eye of earthly
Sharpness, worth I dare say
(If you'll forgive a personal note)
A good deal more
Than all that skyey stuff   65
Of angels that make so bold as
To pity a cat like me that
Gallops about doing good.

1971

GEORGE ORWELL
(1903–1950)

George Orwell was the pseudonym of Eric Blair, who was born in India where his father was a British civil servant. He was sent to private school in England, and won a scholarship to Eton, the foremost "public school" (i.e., private boarding school) in the country. It was at Eton that he first became conscious of the difference between his own background and the wealthy background of many of his schoolmates. On leaving school he joined the Imperial Police in Burma (both Burma and India were then still part of the British Commonwealth and Empire). His service in Burma from 1922 to 1927 produced a sense of guilt about British colonialism and a feeling that he must make some kind of personal expiation for it. He was now determined to be a writer, and adopted a pseudonym as one way of escaping from the class position in which his birth and education had placed him. He went to Paris to try to make a living by teaching while he made his first attempts at writing. He found he could keep alive in Paris only by taking the most menial jobs, and even then he barely survived. His experience there was followed by a spell as a tramp in England, and both experiences are vividly recorded in his first book, *Down and Out in Paris and London* (1933). Orwell did not have to suffer the dire poverty which he seems to have actually courted (he had influential friends who would have been glad to help him); he wanted, however, to learn about the life of the poor at first hand, partly out of humane curiosity, partly because, as he wrote, if he did so "part of my guilt would drop from me."

The Road to Wigan Pier (1937) discusses the experiences Orwell shared with the unemployed in the north of England. The book pleased neither the Left nor the Right, for by now Orwell was showing what was to become his characteristic independence of mind on political and social questions: he wrote of what he knew at first hand to be true and was contemptuous of ideologies. He never joined a political party, but regarded himself as a man of the uncommitted and independent Left. He took part on the Republican side in the Spanish Civil War, which broke out in 1936 when Franco raised his rebellion against the Republican government, and returned to write *Homage to Catalonia* (1938). This book strongly criticized the Communist part in the civil war and showed from his own experience how the Communist Party in Spain was out to destroy Anarchists, Trotskyists and any others on the Republican side who were suspected of not toeing the Stalinist line; it aroused great indignation on the Left in Britain and elsewhere, for Leftists believed that they should solidly support the Soviet Union and the Communist Party as the natural leaders in the struggle against international fascism. Orwell never wavered in his belief that while profound social change was necessary and desirable in capitalist countries of the west, the so-called socialism established in Soviet Russia was a perversion of socialism and a wicked tyranny. In *Animal Farm* (1945) he wrote an animal fable showing how such a perversion of socialism could develop, while in *Nineteen Eighty-Four* (1949), when he was an embittered man dying of tuberculosis, he wrote a savagely powerful novel depicting a totalitarian future in an England where the government used the language of socialism to cover a tyranny that systematically destroys the human spirit.

It was Orwell's independent innocence of eye that made him both a permanent misfit politically and a brilliantly original writer. He was an outstanding journalist, and the essays he wrote regularly for the left-wing British journal *Tribune* and other periodicals include some of his best work.

Some Thoughts on the Common Toad

Before the swallow, before the daffodil, and not much later than the snowdrop, the common toad salutes the coming of spring after his own fashion, which is to emerge from a hole in the ground, where he has lain buried since the previous autumn, and crawl as rapidly as possible towards the nearest suitable patch of water. Something—some kind of shudder in the earth, or perhaps merely a rise of a few degrees in the temperature—has told him that it is time to wake up: though a few toads appear to sleep the clock round and miss out a year from time to time—at any rate, I have more than once dug them up, alive and apparently well, in the middle of the summer.

At this period, after his long fast, the toad has a very spiritual look, like a strict Anglo-Catholic towards the end of Lent. His movements are languid but purposeful, his body is shrunken, and by contrast his eyes look abnormally large. This allows one to notice, what one might not at another time, that a toad has about the most beautiful eye of any living creature. It is like gold, or more exactly it is like the golden-colored semiprecious stone which one some times sees in signet rings, and which I think is called a chrysoberyl.

For a few days after getting into the water the toad concentrates on building up his strength by eating small insects. Presently he has swollen to his normal size again, and then he goes through a phase of intense sexiness. All he knows, at least if he is a male toad, is that he wants to get his arms round something, and if you offer him a stick, or even your finger, he will cling to it with surprising strength and take a long time to discover that it is not a female toad. Frequently one comes upon shapeless masses of ten or twenty toads rolling over and over in the water, one clinging to another without distinction of sex. By degrees, however, they sort themselves out into couples, with the male duly sitting on the female's back. You can now distinguish males from females, because the male is smaller, darker, and sits on top, with his arms tightly clasped round the female's neck. After a day or two the spawn is laid in long strings which wind themselves in and out of the reeds and soon become invisible. A few more weeks, and the water is alive with masses of tiny tadpoles which rapidly grow larger, sprout hind-legs, then forelegs, then shed their tails: and finally, about the middle of the summer, the new generation of toads, smaller than one's thumbnail but perfect in every particular, crawl out of the water to begin the game anew.

I mention the spawning of the toads because it is one of the phenomena of spring which most deeply appeal to me, and because the toad, unlike the skylark and the primrose, has never had much of a boost from the poets. But I am aware that many people do not like reptiles or amphibians, and I am not suggesting that in order to enjoy the spring you have to take an interest in toads. There are also the crocus, the missel-thrush, the cuckoo, the blackthorn, etc. The point is that the pleasures of spring are available to everybody, and cost nothing. Even in the most sordid street the coming of spring will register itself by some sign or other, if it is only a brighter blue between the chimney pots or the vivid green of an elder sprouting on a blitzed site. Indeed it is remarkable how Nature goes on existing unofficially, as it were, in the very heart of London. I have seen a kestrel flying over the Deptford gasworks, and I have heard a first-rate performance by a blackbird in the Euston Road. There must be some hundreds of thousands, if not millions, of birds living inside the four-mile radius, and it is rather a pleasing thought that none of them pays a halfpenny of rent.

As for spring, not even the narrow and gloomy streets round the Bank of England are quite able to exclude it. It comes seeping in everywhere, like one of those new poison gases which pass through all filters. The spring is commonly referred to as "a miracle," and during the past five or six years this worn-out figure of speech has taken on a new lease of life. After the sort of winters we have had to endure recently, the spring does seem miraculous, because it has become gradually harder and harder to believe that it is actually going to happen. Every February since 1940 I have found myself thinking that this time winter is going to be permanent. But Persephone, like the toads, always rises from the dead at about the same moment.[1] Suddenly, towards the end of March, the miracle happens and the decaying slum in which I live is transfigured. Down in the square the sooty privets[2] have turned bright green, the leaves are thickening on the chestnut trees, the daffodils are out, the wallflowers are budding, the policeman's tunic looks positively a pleasant shade of blue, the fishmonger greets his customers with a smile, and even the sparrows are quite a different color, having felt the balminess of the air and nerved themselves to take a bath, their first since last September.

1. In the Greek myth Persephone was carried off to Hades, the lower world, by Pluto, but was allowed to spend some months of the year back on earth. The myth is symbolic of the burying of the seed in the ground and its later growth.

2. Hedges of privet, an evergreen shrub.

Is it wicked to take a pleasure in spring and other seasonal changes? To put it more precisely, is it politically reprehensible, while we are all groaning, or at any rate ought to be groaning, under the shackles of the capitalist system, to point out that life is frequently more worth living because of a blackbird's song, a yellow elm tree in October, or some other natural phenomenon which does not cost money and does not have what the editors of left-wing newspapers call a class angle? There is no doubt that many people think so. I know by experience that a favourable reference to "Nature" in one of my articles is liable to bring me abusive letters, and though the key word in these letters is usually "sentimental," two ideas seem to be mixed up in them. One is that any pleasure in the actual process of life encourages a sort of political quietism. People, so the thought runs, ought to be discontented, and it is our job to multiply our wants and not simply to increase our enjoyment of the things we have already. The other idea is that this is the age of machines and that to dislike the machine, or even to want to limit its domination, is backward-looking, reactionary and slightly ridiculous. This is often backed up by the statement that a love of Nature is a foible of urbanized people who have no notion what Nature is really like. Those who really have to deal with the soil, so it is argued, do not love the soil, and do not take the faintest interest in birds or flowers, except from a strictly utilitarian point of view. To love the country one must live in the town, merely taking an occasional weekend ramble at the warmer times of year.

This last idea is demonstrably false. Medieval literature, for instance, including the popular ballads, is full of an almost Georgian[3] enthusiasm for Nature, and the art of agricultural peoples such as the Chinese and Japanese centers always round trees, birds, flowers, rivers, mountains. The other idea seems to me to be wrong in a subtler way. Certainly we ought to be discontented, we ought not simply to find out ways of making the best of a bad job, and yet if we kill pleasure in the actual process of life, what sort of future are we preparing for ourselves? If a man cannot enjoy the return of spring, why should he be happy in a labor-saving Utopia? What will he do with the leisure that the machine will give him? I have always suspected that if our economic and political problems are ever really solved, life will become simpler instead of more complex, and that the sort of pleasure one gets from finding the first primrose will loom larger than the sort of pleasure one gets from eating an ice to the tune of a Wurlitzer. I think that by retaining one's childhood love of such things as trees, fishes, butterflies and

3. A reference to the Georgian poets (ca. 1910–1920) and their love of nature.

—to return to my first instance—toads, one makes a peaceful and
decent future a little more probable, and that by preaching the
doctrine that nothing is to be admired except steel and concrete,
one merely makes it a little surer that human beings will have no
outlet for their surplus energy except in hatred and leader worship.

At any rate, spring is here, even in London N.1, and they can't
stop you enjoying it. This is a satisfying reflection. How many a
time have I stood watching the toads mating, or a pair of hares
having a boxing match in the young corn, and thought of all the
important persons who would stop me enjoying this if they could.
But luckily they can't. So long as you are not actually ill, hungry,
frightened, or immured in a prison or a holiday camp, spring is still
spring. The atom bombs are piling up in the factories, the police
are prowling through the cities, the lies are streaming from the
loudspeakers, but the earth is still going round the sun, and neither
the dictators nor the bureaucrats, deeply as they disapprove of the
process, are able to prevent it.

1946, 1968

SAMUEL BECKETT
(1906–)

1937: Moved to Paris.
1952: *Waiting for Godot.*
1969: Nobel Prize.

Samuel Beckett, born near Dublin, took a degree at Trinity College (Dublin's Protestant university), but then went abroad and settled for good in
Paris in 1937. He has lived in Paris ever since, teaching in French *lycées*,
and serving occasionally as Joyce's secretary, translator and critical defender
—but mostly writing. Since the mid-1940's, he generally writes in French
as a first tongue and then sometimes translates his French into an eloquent,
Irish-tinged English. Shortly after the war, he published three interrelated
novels, *Molloy*, *Malone Dies*, and *The Unnamable*. They may well be
thought his masterpiece some day, but Beckett's first major public recognition came as a result of a somber, static, and hilarious stage-vaudeville titled
Waiting for Godot. The play is simplicity itself. Vladimir and Estragon, a
pair of derelicts, are waiting in a bleak place for Godot, who tantalizes
them by promising to come but never doing so. They talk, they complain,
they try to kill time; the play ends with them still waiting. It is a play without plot or intrigue, which uses brilliantly the idea of nothing happening
on stage, the vacancy experienced when something is expected but never
found. It is a despairing and funny play. In 1958, *Endgame*, even more
despairing and just as funny, repeated the success of *Godot*; and despite

wiseacre predictions that each grotesque, hilarious work would be his last, Beckett has remained vigorously active in fiction, in drama for stage and radio, in mime, and in film. In 1969 he received the Nobel Prize for Literature.

His work is always stripped, severe, grotesquely comic, and haunted by the theme of nonexistence. He seeks to represent the mind purified down to its last bitter, almost unbearably pure negation—and kept alive simply by the force of that negation. From René Descartes, the 17th-century French thinker, and his follower Arnold Geulincx, Beckett took over premises regarding the separation of body and mind which led him to represent, almost uniformly throughout his work, mind under the compulsion of questioning itself. Fastened to a dying animal, as Yeats said, the mind of a Beckett character seeks constantly to reassure itself of its own existence by developing a brilliant, sterile dialectic of its own. The old scarecrows and crones who animate what a clever undergraduate once called Beckett's "crucifictions" live in a disgusting world and are themselves disintegrating. They all have stories to tell, and as long as they can keep talking, can keep some sort of empty verbal game going, they need not despair of their being. But any sort of comfort or security beyond the absolute minimum eludes them. They take no action, they preach no doctrine, they know nothing save their own ignorance, they are kicked and cuffed by society, they stink, they sulk, they snarl at their own disgusting condition. And yet in some dark way, they represent mankind, "without the courage to end or the strength to go on"—as the narrator of *The End* describes himself. In clinging to hopelessness as their one hope, they bear witness, as more comfortable folk could not, to the essential holiness of existence.

The End[1]

They clothed me and gave me money. I knew what the money was for, it was to get me started. When it was gone I would have to get more, if I wanted to go on. The same for the shoes, when they were worn out I would have to get them mended, or get myself another pair, or go on barefoot, if I wanted to go on. The same for the coat and trousers, needless to say, with this difference, that I could go on in my shirtsleeves, if I wanted. The clothes—shoes, socks, trousers, shirt, coat, hat—were not new, but the deceased must have been about my size. That is to say, he must have been a little shorter, a little thinner, for the clothes did not fit me so well in the beginning as they did at the end, the shirt especially, and it was many a long day before I could button it at the neck, or profit by the collar that went with it, or pin the skirts together between my legs in the way my mother had taught me. He must have put

1. *The End* was written in French and partially published in *Les Temps Modernes* for July, 1946; still in French, it appeared complete in *Nouvelles et textes pour rien* (1955). It was translated into English by Richard Seaver in collaboration with the author, as part of the collection, *Stories and Texts for Nothing* (1967).

on his Sunday best to go to the consultation, perhaps for the first time, unable to bear it any longer. Be that as it may the hat was a bowler, in good shape. I said, Keep your hat and give me back mine. I added, Give me back my greatcoat. They replied that they had burnt them, together with my other clothes. I understood then that the end was near, at least fairly near. Later on I tried to exchange this hat for a cap, or a slouch which could be pulled down over my face, but without much success. And yet I could not go about bareheaded, with my skull in the state it was. At first this hat was too small, then it got used to me. They gave me a tie, after long discussion. It seemed a pretty tie to me, but I didn't like it. When it came at last I was too tired to send it back. But in the end it came in useful. It was blue, with kinds of little stars. I didn't feel well, but they told me I was well enough. They didn't say in so many words that I was as well as I would ever be, but that was the implication. I lay inert on the bed and it took three women to put on my trousers. They didn't seem to take much interest in my private parts which to tell the truth were nothing to write home about, I didn't take much interest in them myself. But they might have passed some remark. When they had finished I got up and finished dressing unaided. They told me to sit on the bed and wait. All the bedding had disappeared. It made me angry that they had not let me wait in the familiar bed, instead of leaving me standing in the cold, in these clothes that smelt of sulphur. I said, You might have left me in bed till the last moment. Men all in white came in with mallets in their hands. They dismantled the bed and took away the pieces. One of the women followed them out and came back with a chair which she set before me. I had done well to pretend I was angry. But to make it quite clear to them how angry I was that they had not left me in my bed, I gave the chair a kick that sent it flying. A man came in and made a sign to me to follow him. In the hall he gave me a paper to sign. What's this, I said, a safe-conduct? It's a receipt, he said, for the clothes and money you have received. What money? I said. It was then I received the money. To think I had almost departed without a penny in my pocket. The sum was not large, compared to other sums, but to me it seemed large. I saw the familiar objects, companions of so many bearable hours. The stool, for example, dearest of all. The long afternoons together, waiting for it to be time for bed. At times I felt its wooden life invade me, till I myself became a piece of old wood. There was even a hole for my cyst. Then the window pane with the patch of frosting gone, where I used to press my eye in the hour of need, and rarely in vain. I am greatly obliged to you, I said, is there a law which prevents you from throwing me out naked and penniless? That would damage our reputation in the long run, he replied.

Could they not possibly keep me a little longer, I said, I could make myself useful. Useful, he said, joking apart you would be willing to make yourself useful? A moment later he went on, If they believed you were really willing to make yourself useful they would keep you, I am sure. The number of times I had said I was going to make myself useful, I wasn't going to start that again. How weak I felt! Perhaps, I said, they would consent to take back the money and keep me a little longer. This is a charitable institution, he said, and the money is a gift you receive when you leave. When it is gone you will have to get more, if you wish to go on. Never come back here whatever you do, you would not be let in. Don't go to any of our branches either, they would turn you away. Exelmans![2] I cried. Come come, he said, and anyway no one understands a tenth of what you say. I'm so old, I said. You are not so old as all that, he said. May I stay here just a little longer, I said, till the rain is over. You may wait in the cloister, he said, the rain will go on all day. You may wait in the cloister till six o'clock, you will hear the bell. If anyone challenges you, you need only say you have permission to shelter in the cloister. Whose name will I give? I said. Weir, he said.

I had not been long in the cloister when the rain stopped and the sun came out. It was low and I reckoned it must be getting on for six, considering the season. I stayed there looking through the archway at the sun as it went down behind the cloister. A man appeared and asked me what I was doing. What do you want? were the words he used. Very friendly. I replied that I had Mr Weir's permission to stay in the cloister till six o'clock. He went away, but came back immediately. He must have spoken to Mr Weir in the interim, for he said, You must not loiter in the cloister now the rain is over.

Now I was making my way through the garden. There was that strange light which follows a day of persistent rain, when the sun comes out and the sky clears too late to be of any use. The earth makes a sound as of sighs and the last drops fall from the emptied, cloudless sky. A small boy, stretching out his hands and looking up at the blue sky, asked his mother how such a thing was possible. Fuck off, she said. I suddenly remembered I had not thought of asking Mr Weir for a piece of bread. He would surely have given it to me. I had as a matter of fact thought of it during our conversation in the hall. I had said to myself, Let us first finish our conversation, then I'll ask. I knew well they would not keep me. I would gladly have turned back, but I was afraid one of the guards would

2. René Joseph Isidore Exelmans was one of Napoleon's bravest and most capable field marshals. The narrator's cry here may relate to some incident of unusual ruthlessness on the part of Exelmans.

stop me and tell me I would never see Mr Weir again. That might have added to my sorrow. And anyway I never turned back on such occasions.

In the street I was lost. I had not set foot in this part of the city for a long time and it seemed greatly changed. Whole buildings had disappeared, the palings had changed position, and on all sides I saw, in great letters, the names of tradesmen I had never seen before and would have been at a loss to pronounce. There were streets where I remembered none, some I did remember had vanished and others had completely changed their names. The general impression was the same as before. It is true I did not know the city very well. Perhaps it was quite a different one. I did not know where I was supposed to be going. I had the great good fortune, more than once, not to be run over. My appearance still made people laugh, with that hearty jovial laugh so good for the health. By keeping the red part of the sky as much as possible on my right hand I came at last to the river. Here all seemed at first sight more or less as I had left it. But if I had looked more closely I would doubtless have discovered many changes. And indeed I subsequently did so. But the general appearance of the river, flowing between its quays and under its bridges, had not changed. Yes, the river still gave the impression it was flowing in the wrong direction. That's all a pack of lies I feel. My bench was still there. It was shaped to fit the curves of the seated body. It stood beside a watering trough, gift of a Mrs Maxwell to the city horses, according to the inscription. During the short time I rested there several horses took advantage of this monument. The iron shoes approached and the jingle of the harness. Then silence. That was the horse looking at me. Then the noise of pebbles and mud that horses make when drinking. Then the silence again. That was the horse looking at me again. Then the pebbles again. Then the silence again. Till the horse had finished drinking or the driver deemed it had drunk its fill. The horses were uneasy. Once, when the noise stopped, I turned and saw the horse looking at me. The driver too was looking at me. Mrs Maxwell would have been pleased if she could have seen her trough rendering such services to the city horses. When it was night, after a tedious twilight, I took off my hat which was paining me. I longed to be under cover again, in an empty place, close and warm, with artificial light, an oil lamp for choice, with a pink shade for preference. From time to time someone would come to make sure I was all right and needed nothing. It was long since I had longed for anything and the effect on me was horrible.

In the days that followed I visited several lodgings, without much success. They usually slammed the door in my face, even when I showed my money and offered to pay a week in advance, or even two. It was in vain I put on my best manners, smiled and spoke distinctly, they slammed the door in my face before I could even finish my little speech. It was at this time I perfected a method of doffing my hat at once courteous and discreet, neither servile nor insolent. I slipped it smartly forward, held it a second poised in such a way that the person addressed could not see my skull, then slipped it back. To do that naturally, without creating an unfavorable impression, is no easy matter. When I deemed that to tip my hat would suffice, I naturally did no more than tip it. But to tip one's hat is no easy matter either. I subsequently solved this problem, always fundamental in time of adversity, by wearing a kepi[3] and saluting in military fashion, no, that must be wrong, I don't know, I had my hat at the end. I never made the mistake of wearing medals. Some landladies were in such need of money that they let me in immediately and showed me the room. But I couldn't come to an agreement with any of them. Finally I found a basement. With this woman I came to an agreement at once. My oddities, that's the expression she used, did not alarm her. She nevertheless insisted on making the bed and cleaning the room once a week, instead of once a month as I requested. She told me that while she was cleaning, which would not take long, I could wait in the area. She added, with a great deal of feeling, that she would never put me out in bad weather. This woman was Greek, I think, or Turkish. She never spoke about herself. I somehow got the idea she was a widow or at least that her husband had left her. She had a strange accent. But so had I with my way of assimilating the vowels and omitting the consonants.

Now I didn't know where I was. I had a vague vision, not a real vision, I didn't see anything, of a big house five or six stories high, one of a block perhaps. It was dusk when I got there and I did not pay the same heed to my surroundings as I might have done if I had suspected they were to close about me. And by then I must have lost all hope. It is true that when I left this house it was a glorious day, but I never look back when leaving. I must have read somewhere, when I was small and still read, that it is better not to look back when leaving. And yet I sometimes did. But even without looking back it seems to me I should have seen something when leaving. But there it is. All I remember is my feet emerging from my shadow, one after the other. My shoes had stiffened and the sun brought out the cracks in the leather.

I was comfortable enough in this house, I must say. Apart from a few rats I was alone in the basement. The woman did her best to respect our agreement. About noon she brought me a big tray of

3. A military cap, as worn notably by the French Foreign Legion.

food and took away the tray of the previous day. At the same time she brought me a clean chamber pot. The chamber pot had a large handle which she slipped over her arm, so that both her hands were free to carry the tray. The rest of the day I saw no more of her except sometimes when she peeped in to make sure nothing had happened to me. Fortunately I did not need affection. From my bed I saw the feet coming and going on the sidewalk. Certain evenings, when the weather was fine and I felt equal to it, I fetched my chair into the area and sat looking up into the skirts of the women passing by. Once I sent for a crocus bulb and planted it in the dark area, in an old pot. It must have been coming up to spring, it was probably not the right time for it. I left the pot outside, attached to a string I passed through the window. In the evening, when the weather was fine, a little light crept up the wall. Then I sat down beside the window and pulled on the string to keep the pot in the light and warmth. That can't have been easy, I don't see how I managed it. It was probably not the right thing for it. I manured it as best I could and pissed on it when the weather was dry. It may not have been the right thing for it. It sprouted, but never any flowers, just a wilting stem and a few chlorotic[4] leaves. I would have liked to have a yellow crocus, or a hyacinth, but there, it was not to be. She wanted to take it away, but I told her to leave it. She wanted to buy me another, but I told her I didn't want another. What lacerated me most was the din of the newspaper boys. They went pounding by every day at the same hours, their heels thudding on the sidewalk, crying the names of their papers and even the headlines. The house noises disturbed me less. A little girl, unless it was a little boy, sang every evening at the same hour, somewhere above me. For a long time I could not catch the words. But hearing them day after day I finally managed to catch a few. Strange words for a little girl, or a little boy. Was it a song in my head or did it merely come from without? It was a sort of lullaby, I believe. It often sent me to sleep, even me. Sometimes it was a little girl who came. She had long red hair hanging down in two braids. I didn't know who she was. She lingered awhile in the room, then went away without a word. One day I had a visit from a policeman. He said I had to be watched, without explaining why. Suspicious, that was it, he told me I was suspicious. I let him talk. He didn't dare arrest me. Or perhaps he had a kind heart. A priest too, one day I had a visit from a priest. I informed him I belonged to a branch of the reformed church. He asked me what kind of clergyman I would like to see. Yes, there's that about the reformed church, you're lost, it's unavoidable. Perhaps he had a kind heart. He told me to let him know if I ever needed a helping hand. A helping hand! He

4. Anemic.

gave me his name and explained where I could reach him. I should have made a note of it.

One day the woman made me an offer. She said she was in urgent need of cash and that if I could pay her six months in advance she would reduce my rent by one fourth during that period, something of that kind. This had the advantage of saving six weeks' (?) rent and the disadvantage of almost exhausting my small capital. But could you call that a disadvantage? Wouldn't I stay on in any case till my last penny was gone, and even longer, till she put me out? I gave her the money and she gave me a receipt.

One morning, not long after this transaction, I was awakened by a man shaking my shoulder. It could not have been much past eleven. He requested me to get up and leave his house immediately. He was most correct, I must say. His surprise, he said, was no less than mine. It was his house. His property. The Turkish woman had left the day before. But I saw her last night, I said. You must be mistaken, he said, for she brought the keys to my office no later than yesterday afternoon. But I just paid her six months' rent in advance, I said. Get a refund, he said. But I don't even know her name, I said, let alone her address. You don't know her name? he said. He must have thought I was lying. I'm sick, I said, I can't leave like this, without any notice. You're not so sick as all that, he said. He offered to send for a taxi, even an ambulance if I preferred. He said he needed the room immediately for his pig which even as he spoke was catching cold in a cart before the door and no one to look after him but a stray urchin whom he had never set eyes on before and who was probably busy tormenting him. I asked if he couldn't let me have another place, any old corner where I could lie down long enough to recover from the shock and decide what to do. He said he could not. Don't think I'm being unkind, he added. I could live here with the pig, I said, I'd look after him. The long months of peace, wiped out in an instant! Come now, come now, he said, get a grip on yourself, be a man, get up, that's enough. After all it was no concern of his. He had really been most patient. He must have visited the basement while I was sleeping.

I felt weak. Perhaps I was. I stumbled in the blinding light. A bus took me into the country. I sat down in a field in the sun. But it seems to me that was much later. I stuck leaves under my hat, all the way round, to make a shade. The night was cold. I wandered for hours in the fields. At last I found a heap of dung. The next day I started back to the city. They made me get off three buses. I sat down by the roadside and dried my clothes in the sun. I enjoyed doing that. I said to myself, There's nothing more to be done now, not a thing, till they are dry. When they were dry I brushed them with a brush, I think a kind of currycomb, that I found in a stable.

Stables have always been my salvation. Then I went to the house and begged a glass of milk and a slice of bread and butter. They gave me everything except the butter. May I rest in the stable? I said. No, they said. I still stank, but with a stink that pleased me. I much preferred it to my own which moreover it prevented me from smelling, except a waft now and then. In the days that followed I took the necessary steps to recover my money. I don't know exactly what happened, whether I couldn't find the address, or whether there was no such address, or whether the Greek woman was unknown there. I ransacked my pockets for the receipt, to try and decipher the name. It wasn't there. Perhaps she had taken it back while I was sleeping. I don't know how long I wandered thus, resting now in one place, now in another, in the city and in the country. The city had suffered many changes. Nor was the country as I remembered it. The general effect was the same. One day I caught sight of my son. He was striding along with a briefcase under his arm. He took off his hat and bowed and I saw he was as bald as a coot. I was almost certain it was he. I turned round to gaze after him. He went bustling along on his duck feet, bowing and scraping and flourishing his hat left and right. The insufferable son of a bitch.

One day I met a man I had known in former times. He lived in a cave by the sea. He had an ass that grazed winter and summer, over the cliffs, or along the little tracks leading down to the sea. When the weather was very bad this ass came down to the cave of his own accord and sheltered there till the storm was past. So they had spent many a night huddled together, while the wind howled and the sea pounded on the shore. With the help of this ass he could deliver sand, sea wrack[5] and shells to the townsfolk, for their gardens. He couldn't carry much at a time, for the ass was old and small and the town was far. But in his way he earned a little money, enough to keep him in tobacco and matches and to buy a piece of bread from time to time. It was during one of these excursions that he met me, in the suburbs. He was delighted to see me, poor man. He begged me to go home with him and spend the night. Stay as long as you like, he said. What's wrong with your ass? I said. Don't mind him, he said, he doesn't know you. I reminded him that I wasn't in the habit of staying more than two or three minutes with anyone and that the sea did not agree with me. He seemed deeply grieved to hear it. So you won't come, he said. But to my amazement I got up on the ass and off we went, in the shade of the red chestnuts springing from the sidewalk. I held the ass by the mane, one hand in front of the other. The little boys jeered and threw stones, but their aim was poor, for they only hit me once, on the hat. A policeman stopped us and accused us of disturbing the

5. Eelgrass, seaweed, etc.

peace. My friend replied that we were as nature had made us, the boys too were as nature had made them. It was inevitable, under these conditions, that the peace should be disturbed from time to time. Let us continue on our way, he said, and order will soon be restored throughout your beat. We followed the quiet, dustwhite inland roads with their hedges of hawthorn and fuchsia and their footpaths fringed with wild grass and daisies. Night fell. The ass carried me right to the mouth of the cave, for in the dark I could not have found my way down the path winding steeply to the sea. Then he climbed back to his pasture.

I don't know how long I stayed there. The cave was nicely arranged, I must say. I treated my crablice with salt water and seaweed, but a lot of nits must have survived. I put compresses of seaweed on my skull, which gave me great relief, but not for long. I lay in the cave and sometimes looked out at the horizon. I saw above me a vast trembling expanse without islands or promontories. At night a light shone into the cave at regular intervals. It was here I found the phial in my pocket. It was not broken, for the glass was not real glass. I thought Mr Weir had confiscated all my belongings. My host was out most of the time. He fed me on fish. It is easy for a man, a proper man, to live in a cave, far from everybody. He invited me to stay as long as I liked. If I preferred to be alone he would gladly prepare another cave for me farther on. He would bring me food every day and drop in from time to time to make sure I was all right and needed nothing. He was kind. Unfortunately I did not need kindness. You wouldn't know of a lake dwelling? I said. I couldn't bear the sea, its splashing and heaving, its tides and general convulsiveness. The wind at least sometimes stops. My hands and feet felt as though they were full of ants. This kept me awake for hours on end. If I stayed here something awful would happen to me, I said, and a lot of good that would do me. You'd get drowned, he said. Yes, I said, or I'd jump off the cliff. And to think I couldn't live anywhere else, he said, in my cabin in the mountains I was very unhappy. Your cabin in the mountains? I said. He repeated the story of his cabin in the mountains, I had forgotten it, it was as though I were hearing it for the first time. I asked him if he still had it. He replied he had not seen it since the day he fled from it, but that he believed it was still there, a little decayed no doubt. But when he urged me to take the key I refused, saying I had other plans. You will always find me here, he said, if you ever need me. Ah people. He gave me his knife.

What he called his cabin was a sort of wooden shed. The door had been removed, for firewood, or for some other purpose. The glass had disappeared from the window. The roof had fallen in at several places. The interior was divided, by the remains of a partition, into two unequal parts. If there had been any furniture it was gone. The vilest acts had been committed on the ground and against the walls. The floor was strewn with excrements, both human and animal, with condoms and vomit. In a cowpad a heart had been traced, pierced by an arrow. And yet there was nothing to attract tourists. I noticed the remains of abandoned nosegays. They had been greedily gathered, carried for miles, then thrown away, because they were cumbersome or already withered. This was the dwelling to which I had been offered the key.

The scene was the familiar one of grandeur and desolation.

Nevertheless it was a roof over my head. I rested on a bed of ferns, gathered at great labor with my own hands. One day I couldn't get up. The cow saved me. Goaded by the icy mist she came in search of shelter. It was probably not the first time. She can't have seen me. I tried to suck her, without much success. Her udder was covered with dung. I took off my hat and summoning all my energy, began to milk her into it. The milk fell to the ground and was lost, but I said to myself, No matter, it's free. She dragged me across the floor, stopping from time to time only to kick me. I didn't know our cows too could be so inhuman. She must have recently been milked. Clutching the dug with one hand I kept my hat under it with the other. But in the end she prevailed. For she dragged me across the threshold and out into the giant streaming ferns, where I was forced to let go.

As I drank the milk I reproached myself with what I had done. I could no longer count on this cow and she would warn the others. More master of myself I might have made a friend of her. She would have come every day, perhaps accompanied by other cows. I might have learnt to make butter, even cheese. But I said to myself, No, all is for the best.

Once on the road it was all downhill. Soon there were carts, but they all refused to take me up. In other clothes, with another face, they might have taken me up. I must have changed since my expulsion from the basement. The face notably seemed to have attained its climacteric.[6] The humble, ingenuous smile would no longer come, nor the expression of candid misery, showing the stars and the distaff.[7] I summoned them, but they would not come. A mask of dirty old hairy leather, with two holes and a slit, it was too far gone for the old trick of please your honor and God reward you and pity upon me. It was disastrous. What would I crawl with in future? I lay down on the side of the road and began to writhe each time I heard a cart approaching. That was so they would not think I was sleeping or resting. I tried to groan, Help! Help! But the tone

---

6. Crucial point. For numerological reasons, the grand climacteric of human life is supposed to come when seven crosses nine—at the age of 63.
7. The beggar's expression may dis-creetly intimate that he is a victim of fate—the stars being agents that con-trol one's fate and the classical Fates (Moirae or Parcae) traditionally carry-ing a distaff.

that came out was that of polite conversation. My hour was not yet come and I could no longer groan. The last time I had cause to groan I had groaned as well as ever, and no heart within miles of me to melt. What was to become of me? I said to myself, I'll learn again. I lay down across the road at a narrow place, so that the carts could not pass without passing over my body, with one wheel at least, or two if there were four. But the day came when, looking round me, I was in the suburbs, and from there to the old haunts it was not far, beyond the stupid hope of rest or less pain.

So I covered the lower part of my face with a black rag and went and begged at a sunny corner. For it seemed to me my eyes were not completely spent, thanks perhaps to the dark glasses my tutor had given me. He had given me the *Ethics* of Geulincx.[8] They were a man's glasses, I was a child. They found him dead, crumpled up in the water closet, his clothes in awful disorder, struck down by an infarctus.[9] Ah what peace. The *Ethics* had his name (Ward) on the flyleaf, the glasses had belonged to him. The bridge, at the time I am speaking of, was of brass wire, of the kind used to hang pictures and big mirrors, and two long black ribbons served as wings. I wound them round my ears and then down under my chin where I tied them together. The lenses had suffered, from rubbing in my pocket against each other and against the other objects there. I thought Mr Weir had confiscated all my belongings. But I had no further need of these glasses and used them merely to soften the glare of the sun. I should never have mentioned them. The rag gave me a lot of trouble. I got it in the end from the lining of my greatcoat, no, I had no greatcoat now, of my coat then. The result was a gray rag rather than a black, perhaps even checkered, but I had to make do with it. Till afternoon I held my face raised towards the southern sky, then towards the western till night. The bowl gave me a lot of trouble. I couldn't use my hat because of my skull. As for holding out my hand, that was quite out of the question. So I got a tin and hung it from a button of my greatcoat, what's the matter with me, of my coat, at pubis level. It did not hang plumb, it leaned respectfully towards the passerby, he had only to drop his mite. But that obliged him to come up close to me, he was in danger of touching me. In the end I got a bigger tin, a kind of big tin box, and I placed it on the sidewalk at my feet. But people who give alms don't much care to toss them, there's something contemptuous about this gesture which is repugnant to sensitive natures. To say nothing of their having to aim. They are prepared to give, but not for their gift to go rolling under the passing feet or under the passing wheels, to be picked up perhaps by some undeserving

8. The *Ethics* of Arnold Geulincx (1624–69), like most of his important works, were published posthumously. They teach that we cannot alter the exterior world, and that, accordingly, the chief moral virtue is humility, expressing itself in submission.
9. Heart attack.

person. So they don't give. There are those, to be sure, who stoop, but generally speaking people who give alms don't much care to stoop. What they like above all is to sight the wretch from afar, get ready their penny, drop it in their stride and hear the God bless you dying away in the distance. Personally I never said that, nor anything like it, I wasn't much of a believer, but I did make a noise with my mouth. In the end I got a kind of board or tray and tied it to my neck and waist. It jutted out just at the right height, pocket height, and its edge was far enough from my person for the coin to be bestowed without danger. Some days I strewed it with flowers, petals, buds, and that herb which men call fleabane, I believe, in a word whatever I could find. I didn't go out of my way to look for them, but all the pretty things of this description that came my way were for the board. They must have thought I loved nature. Most of the time I looked up at the sky, but without focusing it, for why focus it? Most of the time it was a mixture of white, blue, and gray, and then at evening all the evening colors. I felt it weighing softly on my face, I rubbed my face against it, one cheek after the other, turning my head from side to side. Now and then to rest my neck I dropped my head on my chest. Then I could see the board in the distance, a haze of many colors. I leaned against the wall, but without nonchalance, I shifted my weight from one foot to the other and my hands clutched the lapels of my coat. To beg with your hands in your pockets makes a bad impression, it irritates the workers, especially in winter. You should never wear gloves either. There were guttersnipes who swept away all I had earned, under cover of giving me a coin. It was to buy sweets. I unbuttoned my trousers discreetly to scratch myself. I scratched myself in an upward direction, with four nails. I pulled on the hairs, to get relief. It passed the time, time flew when I scratched myself. Real scratching is superior to masturbation, in my opinion. One can masturbate up to the age of seventy, and even beyond, but in the end it becomes a mere habit. Whereas to scratch myself properly I would have needed a dozen hands. I itched all over, on the privates, in the bush up to the navel, under the arms, in the arse, and then patches of eczema and psoriasis that I could set raging merely by thinking of them. It was in the arse I had the most pleasure. I stuck my forefinger up to the knuckle. Later, if I had to shit, the pain was atrocious. But I hardly shat any more. Now and then a flying machine flew by, sluggishly it seemed to me. Often at the end of the day I discovered the leg of my trousers all wet. That must have been the dogs. I personally pissed very little. If by chance the need came on me a little squirt in my fly was enough to relieve it. Once at my post I did not leave it till nightfall. I had no appetite, God tempered the wind to me. After work I bought a bottle of milk and drank it in the evening in the shed. Better still, I got a little boy to buy it for me, always the same, they wouldn't serve me, I don't know why. I gave him a penny for his pains. One day I witnessed a strange scene. Normally I didn't see a great deal. I didn't hear a great deal either. I didn't pay attention. Strictly speaking I wasn't there. Strictly speaking I believe I've never been anywhere. But that day I must have come back. For some time past a sound had been scarifying me. I did not investigate the cause, for I said to myself, It's going to stop. But as it did not stop I had no choice but to find out the cause. It was a man perched on the roof of a car and haranguing the passersby. That at least was my interpretation. He was bellowing so loud that snatches of his doctrine reached my ears. Union . . . brothers . . . Marx . . . capital . . . bread and butter . . . love. It was all Greek to me. The car was drawn up against the curb, just in front of me, I saw the orator from behind. All of a sudden he turned and pointed at me, as at an exhibit. Look at this down and out, he vociferated, this leftover. If he doesn't go down on all fours, it's for fear of being impounded. Old, lousy, rotten, ripe for the muckheap. And there are a thousand like him, worse than him, ten thousand, twenty thousand—. A voice, Thirty thousand. Every day you pass them by, resumed the orator, and when you have backed a winner you fling them a farthing. Do you ever think? The voice, God forbid. A penny, resumed the orator, tuppence—. The voice, Thruppence. It never enters your head, resumed the orator, that your charity is a crime, an incentive to slavery, stultification, and organized murder. Take a good look at this living corpse. You may say it's his own fault. Ask him if it's his own fault. The voice, Ask him yourself. Then he bent forward and took me to task. I had perfected my board. It now consisted of two boards hinged together, which enabled me, when my work was done, to fold it and carry it under my arm. I liked doing little odd jobs. So I took off the rag, pocketed the few coins I had earned, untied the board, folded it, and put it under my arm. Do you hear me, you crucified bastard! cried the orator. Then I went away, although it was still light. But generally speaking it was a quiet corner, busy but not overcrowded, thriving and well-frequented. He must have been a religious fanatic, I could find no other explanation. Perhaps he was an escaped lunatic. He had a nice face, a little on the red side.

I did not work every day. I had practically no expenses. I even managed to put a little aside, for my very last days. The days I did not work I spent lying in the shed. The shed was on a private estate, or what had once been a private estate, on the riverside. This estate, the main entrance to which opened on a narrow, dark, and silent street, was enclosed with a wall, except of course on the river front, which marked its northern boundary for a distance of about thirty yards. From the last quays beyond the water the eyes rose to a confusion of low houses, wasteland, hoardings, chimneys, steeples,

and towers. A kind of parade ground was also to be seen, where soldiers played football all the year round. Only the ground-floor windows—no, I can't. The estate seemed abandoned. The gates were
locked and the paths were overgrown with grass. Only the ground-
floor windows had shutters. The others were sometimes lit at night,
faintly, now one, now another. At least that was my impression.
Perhaps it was reflected light. In this shed, the day I adopted it, I
found a boat, upside down. I righted it, chocked it up with stones
and pieces of wood, took out the thwarts, and made my bed inside.
The rats had difficulty in getting at me, because of the bulge of the
hull. And yet they longed to. Just think of it, living flesh, for in
spite of everything I was still living flesh. I had lived too long
among rats, in my chance dwellings, to share the dread they inspire
in the vulgar. I even had a soft spot in my heart for them. They
came with such confidence towards me, it seemed without the least
repugnance. They made their toilet with catlike gestures. Toads at
evening, motionless for hours, lap flies from the air. They like to
squat where cover ends and open air begins, they favour thresholds.
But I had to contend now with water rats, exceptionally lean and
ferocious. So I made a kind of lid with stray boards. It's incredible
the number of boards I've come across in my lifetime, I never
needed a board but there it was, I had only to stoop and pick it up.
I liked doing little odd jobs, no, not particularly, I didn't mind. It
completely covered the boat, I'm referring again to the lid. I pushed
it a little towards the stern, climbed into the boat by the bow,
crawled to the stern, raised my feet, and pushed the lid back to the
bow till it covered me completely. But what did my feet push
against? They pushed against a cross bar I nailed to the lid for that
purpose, I liked these little odd jobs. But it was better to climb into
the boat by the stern and pull back the lid with my hands till it
completely covered me, then push it forward in the same way when
I wanted to get out. As holds for my hands I planted two spikes
just where I needed them. These little odds and ends of carpentry,
if I may so describe it, carried out with whatever tools and material
I chanced to find, gave me a certain pleasure. I knew it would soon
be the end, so I played the part, you know, the part of—how shall I
say, I don't know. I was comfortable enough in this boat, I must
say. The lid fitted so well I had to pierce a hole. It's no good closing your eyes, you must leave them open in the dark, that is my
opinion. I am not speaking of sleep, I am speaking of what I believe
is called waking. In any case, I slept very little at this period, I
wasn't sleepy, or I was too sleepy, I don't know, or I was afraid, I
don't know. Flat then on my back I saw nothing except, dimly, just
above my head, through the tiny chinks, the gray light of the shed.
To see nothing at all, no, that's too much. I heard faintly the cries
of the gulls ravening about the mouth of the sewer near by. In a

spew of yellow foam, if my memory serves me right, the filth gushed into the river and the slush of birds above screaming with hunger and fury. I heard the lapping of water against the slip and against the bank and the other sound, so different, of open wave, I heard it too. I too, when I moved, felt less boat than wave, or so it seemed to me, and my stillness was the stillness of eddies. That may seem impossible. The rain too, I often heard it, for it often rained. Sometimes a drop, falling through the roof of the shed, exploded on me. All that composed a rather liquid world. And then of course there was the voice of the wind or rather those, so various, of its playthings. But what does it amount to? Howling, soughing, moaning, sighing. What I would have liked was hammer strokes, bang bang bang, clanging in the desert. I let farts to be sure, but hardly ever a real crack, they oozed out with a sucking noise, melted in the mighty never. I don't know how long I stayed there. I was very snug in my box, I must say. It seemed to me I had grown more independent of recent years. That no one came any more, that no one could come any more, to ask me if I was all right and needed nothing, distressed me then but little. I was all right, yes, quite so, and the fear of getting worse was less with me. As for my needs, they had dwindled as it were to my dimensions and become, if I may say so, of so exquisite a quality as to exclude all thought of succor. To know I had a being, however faint and false, outside of me, had once had the power to stir my heart. You become unsociable, it's inevitable. It's enough to make you wonder sometimes if you are on the right planet. Even the words desert you, it's as bad as that. Perhaps it's the moment when the vessels stop communicating, you know, the vessels. There you are still between the two murmurs, it must be the same old song as ever, but Christ you wouldn't think so. There were times when I wanted to push away the lid and get out of the boat and couldn't, I was so indolent and weak, so content deep down where I was. I felt them hard upon me, the icy, tumultuous streets, the terrifying faces, the noises that slash, pierce, claw, bruise. So I waited till the desire to shit, or even to piss, lent me wings. I did not want to dirty my nest! And yet it sometimes happened, and even more and more often. Arched and rigid I edged down my trousers and turned a little on my side, just enough to free the hole. To contrive a little kingdom, in the midst of the universal muck, then shit on it, ah that was me all over. The excrements were me too, I know, I know, but all the same. Enough, enough, the next thing I was having visions, I who never did, except sometimes in my sleep, who never had, real visions, I'd remember, except perhaps as a child, my myth will have it so. I knew they were visions because it was night and I was alone in my boat. What else could they have been? So I was in my boat and gliding on the waters. I didn't have to row, the ebb was carrying me out. Anyway I saw no oars, they must have taken them away. I had a board, the remains of a thwart perhaps, which I used when I came too close to the bank, or when a pier came bearing down on me or a barge at its moorings. There were stars in the sky, quite a few. I didn't know what the weather was doing, I was neither cold nor warm and all seemed calm. The banks receded more and more, it was inevitable, soon I saw them no more. The lights grew fainter and fewer as the river widened. There on the land men were sleeping, bodies were gathering strength for the toil and joys of the morrow. The boat was not gliding now, it was tossing, buffeted by the choppy waters of the bay. All seemed calm and yet foam was washing aboard. Now the sea air was all about me, I had no other shelter than the land, and what does it amount to, the shelter of the land, at such a time. I saw the beacons, four in all, including a lightship. I knew them well, even as a child I had known them well. It was evening, I was with my father on a height, he held my hand. I would have liked him to draw me close with a gesture of protective love, but his mind was on other things. He also taught me the names of the mountains. But to have done with these visions I also saw the lights of the buoys, the sea seemed full of them, red and green, and to my surprise even yellow. And on the slopes of the mountain, now rearing its unbroken bulk behind the town, the fires turned from gold to red, from red to gold. I knew what it was, it was the gorse burning. How often I had set a match to it myself, as a child. And hours later, back in my home, before I climbed into bed, I watched from my high window the fires I had lit. That night then, all aglow with distant fires, on sea, on land, and in the sky, I drifted with the currents and the tides. I noticed that my hat was tied, with a string I suppose, to my buttonhole. I got up from my seat in the stern and a great clanking was heard. That was the chain. One end was fastened to the bow and the other round my waist. I must have pierced a hole beforehand in the floorboards, for there I was down on my knees prying out the plug with my knife. The hole was small and the water rose slowly. It would take a good half hour, everything included, barring accidents. Back now in the stern-sheets, my legs stretched out, my back well propped against the sack stuffed with grass I used as a cushion, I swallowed my calmative. The sea, the sky, the mountains, and the islands closed in and crushed me in a mighty systole,[1] then scattered to the uttermost confines of space. The memory came faint and cold of the story I might have told, a story in the likeness of my life, I mean without the courage to end or the strength to go on.

1946, 1955, French; 1967, English

---

1. The two motions of the heart are systole and diastole, contraction and expansion. The word is used here meta- phorically for a mighty compression of the universe.

W. H. AUDEN
(1907–1973)

Wystan Hugh Auden was born in York and educated at Gresham's School, Holt, Cheshire, and Christ Church, Oxford. After leaving Oxford he taught school from 1930 to 1935 and later worked for a government film unit. His sympathies in the 1930's were with the Left, like those of most intellectuals of his age, and he spent a short time as an ambulance driver on the republican side in the Spanish Civil War. He traveled in Iceland and China before coming to America in 1939; in 1946 he became an American citizen. He has taught at a number of American colleges, and was elected Professor of Poetry at Oxford for the 1956–60 tenure (the position requires the giving of only a few lectures a year).

Auden was the most active of the group of young English poets who, in the late 1920's and early 1930's, saw themselves bringing new techniques and attitudes to English poetry. Stephen Spender and Cecil Day Lewis were at the time the most prominent of the other members of the new school, which soon afterward fell apart, each poet going his own separate way. Like all his generation, Auden learned poetic wit and irony from Eliot, and he also learned metrical and verbal techniques from Hopkins and from Wilfred Owen. His English studies at Oxford familiarized him with the rhythms and long alliterative line of Anglo-Saxon poetry as well as with the rapid and rollicking short lines (a sort of inspired doggerel) of the early 16th-century poet John Skelton: both influenced his own versification. He learned, too, from the songs of the English music hall and, later, from American blues singers.

The depression which upset America in 1929 hit England soon afterwards, and Auden and his contemporaries looked out at an England of industrial stagnation and mass unemployment, seeing not the metaphorical Waste Land of Eliot but a more literal Waste Land of poverty and "depressed areas." His early poetry is much concerned with a diagnosis of the ills of his country. This diagnosis, conducted in a verse which combined deliberate irreverence and sometimes even clowning with a cunning verbal craftsmanship, drew on both Freud and Marx to show England now as a nation of neurotic invalids who must learn to "throw away their rugs," and now as the victim of an antiquated economic system. The liveliness and nervous force of this early poetry of Auden's made a great impression, even though an uncertainty about his audience led him to introduce purely private symbols, intelligible only to a few friends, in some of his poems.

Gradually, Auden learned to clarify his imagery and control his desire to shock, and he produced, in the years around 1940, some poems (such as, in this anthology, *Lullaby*) of finely disciplined movement, pellucid clarity, and deep yet unsentimental feeling. At the same time he was developing a more complex view of the world, moving from his earlier diagnosis of modern ills in terms of Freud and Marx to a more religious view of personal responsibility and traditional value without, however, abandoning the ideas and terms he had learned from modern psychology. But he never lost his ear for popular speech or his ability to combine elements from popular art with an extreme technical formality. He was always the experimenter, particularly in ways of bringing together high artifice and a colloquial tone.

Some of Auden's most exciting work is found in his early volumes, *Poems* (1930) and *On This Island* (1937). *Another Time* (1940) shows greater control and less violence. Of his later volumes, *Nones* (1951) shows most clearly his characteristic ways of combining or alternating the grave and the flippant. For the first part of his career—the English and the early American phase—Auden was very much the poet of his times, first of the Depression and then of the Age of the Refugee. In the poems of this period he preferred to confront modern problems directly rather than to filter them, as Eliot did, through symbolic situations. The poems of the last phase of his career, notably those in *About the House* (1967) and *City without Walls* (1970), are increasingly personal in tone and combine an apparent air of offhand informality with remarkable technical skill in versification. Auden grew increasingly hostile to the modern world and skeptical of all remedies offered for modern ills: he took refuge in friendship, grounded in an ever deepening but rarely obtrusive religious feeling. In the last year of his life he returned to England to live in Oxford, feeling the need to be part of a university community as a protection against loneliness. An uneven poet, a poet who in the opinion of some critics never quite fulfilled the enormous promise of his early work, Auden is nevertheless now generally recognized as one of the masters of 20th-century English poetry, a thoughtful, seriously playful (if one may put it in this paradoxical way) poet whom more than one critic has compared to Dryden in his combination of lively intelligence and immense craftsmanship.

This Lunar Beauty[1]

This lunar beauty
Has no history
Is complete and early;
If beauty later
Bear any feature   5
It had a lover
And is another.

This like a dream
Keeps other time
And daytime is   10
The loss of this;
For time is inches
And the heart's changes
Where ghost has haunted
Lost and wanted.   15

1. The poem contrasts "lunar beauty," which is complete, changeless, and impersonal, to the beauty of daylight, which is involved in time and changing human passion.

But this was never
A ghost's endeavor
Nor finished this,
Was ghost at ease;
And till it pass   20
Love shall not near
The sweetness here
Nor sorrow take
His endless look.

1930

Petition

Sir, no man's enemy, forgiving all
But will its negative inversion, be prodigal:
Send to us power and light, a sovereign touch[1]
Curing the intolerable neural itch,
The exhaustion of weaning, the liar's quinsy,[2]   5
And the distortions of ingrown virginity.
Prohibit sharply the rehearsed response
And gradually correct the coward's stance;
Cover in time with beams those in retreat
That, spotted, they turn though the reverse were great;   10
Publish each healer that in city lives
Or country houses at the end of drives;
Harrow the house of the dead; look shining at
New styles of architecture, a change of heart.

1930

On This Island

Look, stranger, on this island now
The leaping light for your delight discovers,
Stand stable here
And silent be,
That through the channels of the ear   5
May wander like a river
The swaying sound of the sea.

Here at the small field's ending pause
When the chalk wall falls to the foam, and its tall ledges
Oppose the pluck   10
And knock of the tide,
And the shingle scrambles after the suck-
-ing surf, and the gull lodges
A moment on its sheer side.

1. The "king's touch" was often regarded as a miraculous cure for disease (cf. "sovereign" as an adjective,
meaning "the best").
2. Tonsillitis.

Far off like floating seeds the ships   15
Diverge on urgent voluntary errands;
And the full view
Indeed may enter
And move in memory as now these clouds do,
That pass the harbor mirror   20
And all the summer through the water saunter.

1936

Spain 1937[1]

Yesterday all the past. The language of size
Spreading to China along the trade routes; the diffusion
            Of the counting-frame and the cromlech;[2]
Yesterday the shadow-reckoning in the sunny climates.

Yesterday the assessment of insurance by cards,   5
The divination of water; yesterday the invention
            Of cart wheels and clocks, the taming of
Horses; yesterday the bustling world of the navigators.

Yesterday the abolition of fairies and giants;
The fortress like a motionless eagle eyeing the valley,   10
            The chapel built in the forest;
Yesterday the carving of angels and of frightening gargoyles.

The trial of heretics among the columns of stone;
Yesterday the theological feuds in the taverns
            And the miraculous cure at the fountain;   15
Yesterday the Sabbath of Witches. But today the struggle.

Yesterday the installation of dynamos and turbines;
The construction of railways in the colonial desert;
            Yesterday the classic lecture
On the origin of Mankind. But today the struggle.   20

Yesterday the belief in the absolute value of Greek;
The fall of the curtain upon the death of a hero;
            Yesterday the prayer to the sunset,
And the adoration of madmen. But today the struggle.

As the poet whispers, startled among the pines   25
Or, where the loose waterfall sings, compact, or upright
            On the crag by the leaning tower:
"O my vision. O send me the luck of the sailor."

---

1. Written when the Spanish Civil War was raging. The rebellion by General Franco's Right-wing army against the Left-wing Spanish government, which broke out in 1936 and provoked full-scale civil war, was viewed by British liberal intellectuals at the time as a testing struggle between fascism and democracy. The poem first appeared separately in 1937, the proceeds of its sale going to "Medical Aid for Spain." This is Auden's revised version of 1940. 2. Ancient stone circle (archaeological term).

And the investigator peers through his instruments
At the inhuman provinces, the virile bacillus   30
　　　　Or enormous Jupiter finished:
"But the lives of my friends. I inquire, I inquire."

And the poor in their fireless lodgings dropping the sheets
Of the evening paper: "Our day is our loss. O show us
　　　　History the operator, the   35
Organizer, Time the refreshing river."

And the nations combine each cry, invoking the life
That shapes the individual belly and orders
　　　　The private nocturnal terror:
"Did you not found once the city-state of the sponge,   40

"Raise the vast military empires of the shark
And the tiger, establish the robin's plucky canton?[3]
　　　　Intervene. O descend as a dove or
A furious papa or a mild engineer: but descend."

And the life, if it answers at all, replies from the heart   45
And the eyes and the lungs, from the shops and squares of the city:
　　　　"O no, I am not the Mover,
Not today, not to you. To you I'm the
"Yes-man, the bar-companion, the easily-duped:
I am whatever you do; I am your vow to be   50
　　　　Good, your humorous story;
I am your business voice; I am your marriage.

"What's your proposal? To build the Just City? I will.
I agree. Or is it the suicide pact, the romantic
　　　　Death? Very well, I accept, for   55
I am your choice, your decision: yes, I am Spain."

Many have heard it on remote peninsulas,
On sleepy plains, in the aberrant fishermen's islands,
　　　　In the corrupt heart of the city;
Have heard and migrated like gulls or the seeds of a flower.   60

They clung like burrs to the long expresses that lurch
Through the unjust lands, through the night, through the alpine
　　　tunnel;
　　　　They floated over the oceans;
They walked the passes: they came to present their lives.

On that arid square, that fragment nipped off from hot   65
Africa, soldered so crudely to inventive Europe,
　　　　On that tableland scored by rivers,
Our fever's menacing shapes are precise and alive.

Tomorrow, perhaps, the future: the research on fatigue
And the movements of packers; the gradual exploring of all the   70
　　　　Octaves of radiation;
Tomorrow the enlarging of consciousness by diet and breathing.

3. District.

Tomorrow the rediscovery of romantic love;
The photographing of ravens; all the fun under
        Liberty's masterful shadow;   75
Tomorrow the hour of the pageant-master and the musician.

Tomorrow, for the young, the poets exploding like bombs,
The walks by the lake, the winter of perfect communion;
        Tomorrow the bicycle races
Through the suburbs on summer evenings: but today the struggle. 80

Today the inevitable increase in the chances of death;
The conscious acceptance of guilt in the fact of murder;
        Today the expending of powers
On the flat ephemeral pamphlet and the boring meeting.

Today the makeshift consolations; the shared cigarette;   85
The cards in the candle-lit barn and the scraping concert,
        The masculine jokes; today the
Fumbled and unsatisfactory embrace before hurting.

The stars are dead; the animals will not look:
We are left alone with our day, and the time is short and   90
        History to the defeated
May say Alas but cannot help or pardon.
1937   1937, 1940

Musée des Beaux Arts[1]

About suffering they were never wrong,
The Old Masters: how well they understood
Its human position; how it takes place
While someone else is eating or opening a window or just walking
    dully along;
How, when the aged are reverently, passionately waiting   5
For the miraculous birth, there always must be
Children who did not specially want it to happen, skating
On a pond at the edge of the wood:
They never forgot
That even the dreadful martyrdom must run its course   10
Anyhow in a corner, some untidy spot
Where the dogs go on with their doggy life and the torturer's horse
Scratches its innocent behind on a tree.

In Brueghel's *Icarus*,[2] for instance: how everything turns away
Quite leisurely from the disaster; the plowman may   15

1. "Museum of Fine Arts." The reference is to the Museum of Fine Arts in Brussels, which contains Brueghel's *Icarus*.
2. Icarus was the son of Daedalus, the cunning craftsman of ancient legend. Together they flew on artificial wings fastened to their shoulders with wax, but Icarus ventured too near the sun, which melted the wax, and so he fell and perished. The painting of the fall of Icarus is by the Flemish painter Pieter Brueghel (ca. 1520–69): Icarus' legs are disappearing into the sea in one corner of the picture, the rest of which has nothing to do with him.

Have heard the splash, the forsaken cry,
But for him it was not an important failure; the sun shone
As it had to on the white legs disappearing into the green
Water; and the expensive delicate ship that must have seen
Something amazing, a boy falling out of the sky,   20
Had somewhere to get to and sailed calmly on.

1940

Lullaby

Lay your sleeping head, my love,
Human on my faithless arm;
Time and fevers burn away
Individual beauty from
Thoughtful children, and the grave   5
Proves the child ephemeral:
But in my arms till break of day
Let the living creature lie,
Mortal, guilty, but to me
The entirely beautiful.   10

Soul and body have no bounds:
To lovers as they lie upon
Her tolerant enchanted slope
In their ordinary swoon,
Grave the vision Venus sends   15
Of supernatural sympathy,
Universal love and hope;
While an abstract insight wakes
Among the glaciers and the rocks
The hermit's sensual ecstasy.   20

Certainty, fidelity
On the stroke of midnight pass
Like vibrations of a bell,
And fashionable madmen raise
Their pedantic boring cry: 25
Every farthing of the cost,
All the dreaded cards foretell,
Shall be paid, but from this night
Not a whisper, not a thought,
Not a kiss nor look be lost.   30

Beauty, midnight, vision dies:
Let the winds of dawn that blow
Softly round your dreaming head
Such a day of sweetness show
Eye and knocking heart may bless,   35
Find the mortal world enough;
Noons of dryness see you fed
By the involuntary powers,
Nights of insult let you pass
Watched by every human love.   40

1940

In Memory of W. B. Yeats

(D. JAN. 1939)

1

He disappeared in the dead of winter:
The brooks were frozen, the airports almost deserted,
And snow disfigured the public statues;
The mercury sank in the mouth of the dying day.
O all the instruments agree   5
The day of his death was a dark cold day.

Far from his illness
The wolves ran on through the evergreen forests,
The peasant river was untempted by the fashionable quays;
By mourning tongues   10
The death of the poet was kept from his poems.

But for him it was his last afternoon as himself,
An afternoon of nurses and rumors;
The provinces of his body revolted,
The squares of his mind were empty,   15
Silence invaded the suburbs,
The current of his feeling failed: he became his admirers.

Now he is scattered among a hundred cities
And wholly given over to unfamiliar affections;
To find his happiness in another kind of wood   20
And be punished under a foreign code of conscience.
The words of a dead man
Are modified in the guts of the living.

But in the importance and noise of tomorrow
When the brokers are roaring like beasts on the floor of the
    Bourse,[1]   25
And the poor have the sufferings to which they are fairly
    accustomed,
And each in the cell of himself is almost convinced of his freedom;
A few thousand will think of this day
As one thinks of a day when one did something slightly unusual.
O all the instruments agree   30
The day of his death was a dark cold day.

2

You were silly like us: your gift survived it all;
The parish of rich women, physical decay,
Yourself; mad Ireland hurt you into poetry.
Now Ireland has her madness and her weather still,   35
For poetry makes nothing happen: it survives
In the valley of its saying where executives
Would never want to tamper; it flows south

1. Stock exchange.

From ranches of isolation and the busy griefs,
Raw towns that we believe and die in; it survives,
A way of happening, a mouth.   40

3

Earth, receive an honored guest;
William Yeats is laid to rest:
Let the Irish vessel lie
Emptied of its poetry.   45

Time that is intolerant
Of the brave and innocent,
And indifferent in a week
To a beautiful physique,

Worships language and forgives   50
Everyone by whom it lives;
Pardons cowardice, conceit,
Lays its honours at their feet.

Time that with this strange excuse
Pardoned Kipling and his views,   55
And will pardon Paul Claudel,
Pardons him for writing well.[4]

In the nightmare of the dark
All the dogs of Europe bark,
And the living nations wait,   60
Each sequestered in its hate;

Intellectual disgrace
Stares from every human face,
And the seas of pity lie
Locked and frozen in each eye.   65

Follow, poet, follow right
To the bottom of the night,
With your unconstraining voice
Still persuade us to rejoice;

With the farming of a verse   70
Make a vineyard of the curse,
Sing of human unsuccess
In a rapture of distress;

In the deserts of the heart
Let the healing fountain start,   75
In the prison of his days
Teach the free man how to praise.

1940

4. Kipling's "views" were imperialistic
and jingoistic; Paul Claudel (1868–
1955), French poet, dramatist, and dip-
lomat, was an extreme Right-winger in
his political ideas. Yeats's own politics
were at times antidemocratic and appeared to favor dictatorship.

Their Lonely Betters

As I listened from a beach-chair in the shade
To all the noises that my garden made,
It seemed to me only proper that words
Should be withheld from vegetables and birds.

A robin with no Christian name ran through   5
The Robin-Anthem which was all it knew,
And rustling flowers for some third party waited
To say which pairs, if any, should get mated.

No one of them was capable of lying,
There was not one which knew that it was dying   10
Or could have with a rhythm or a rhyme
Assumed responsibility for time.

Let them leave language to their lonely betters
Who count some days and long for certain letters;
We, too, make noises when we laugh or weep,   15
Words are for those with promises to keep.

1951

In Praise of Limestone

If it form the one landscape that we the inconstant ones
    Are consistently homesick for, this is chiefly
Because it dissolves in water. Mark these rounded slopes
    With their surface fragrance of thyme and beneath
A secret system of caves and conduits; hear these springs   5
    That spurt out everywhere with a chuckle
Each filling a private pool for its fish and carving
    Its own little ravine whose cliffs entertain
The butterfly and the lizard; examine this region
    Of short distances and definite places: 10
What could be more like Mother or a fitter background
    For her son, for the nude young male who lounges
Against a rock displaying his dildo, never doubting
    That for all his faults he is loved, whose works are but
Extensions of his power to charm? From weathered outcrop   15
    To hill-top temple, from appearing waters to
Conspicuous fountains, from a wild to a formal vineyard,
    Are ingenious but short steps that a child's wish
To receive more attention than his brothers, whether
    By pleasing or teasing, can easily take.   20

Watch, then, the band of rivals as they climb up and down
    Their steep stone gennels [1] in twos and threes, sometimes

---

1. A "gennel," in the dialect of Auden's native Yorkshire and other northern counties, is a long narrow passage between houses. Here it is a passage between rocks.

Arm in arm, but never, thank God, in step; or engaged
   On the shady side of a square at midday in
Voluble discourse, knowing each other too well to think   25
   There are any important secrets, unable
To conceive a god whose temper-tantrums are moral
   And not to be pacified by a clever line
Or a good lay: for, accustomed to a stone that responds,
   They have never had to veil their faces in awe   30
Of a crater whose blazing fury could not be fixed;
   Adjusted to the local needs of valleys
Where everything can be touched or reached by walking,
   Their eyes have never looked into infinite space
Through the lattice-work of a nomad's comb; [2] born lucky,   35
   Their legs have never encountered the fungi
And insects of the jungle, the monstrous forms and lives
   With which we have nothing, we like to hope, in common.
So, when one of them goes to the bad, the way his mind works
   Remains comprehensible: to become a pimp   40
Or deal in fake jewelry or ruin a fine tenor voice
   For effects that bring down the house could happen to all
But the best and the worst of us . . .
                         That is why, I suppose,
   The best and worst never stayed here long but sought   45
Immoderate soils where the beauty was not so external,
   The light less public and the meaning of life
Something more than a mad camp. "Come!" cried the granite wastes,
   "How evasive is your humor, how accidental
Your kindest kiss, how permanent is death." (Saints-to-be
   Slipped away sighing.) "Come!" purred the clays and gravels.   50
"On our plains there is room for armies to drill; rivers
   Wait to be tamed and slaves to construct you a tomb
In the grand manner: soft as the earth is mankind and both
   Need to be altered." (Intendant Caesars rose and
Left, slamming the door.) But the really reckless were fetched   55
   By an older colder voice, the oceanic whisper:
"I am the solitude that asks and promises nothing;
   That is how I shall set you free. There is no love;
There are only the various envies, all of them sad."

They were right, my dear, all those voices were right   60
And still are; this land is not the sweet home that it looks,
   Nor its peace the historical calm of a site
Where something was settled once and for all: A backward
   And delapidated province, connected
To the big busy world by a tunnel, with a certain   65
   Seedy appeal, is that all it is now? Not quite:
It has a worldly duty which in spite of itself

2. The context suggests that this might be a popular name for a plant or tree (cf. "traveler's joy" and "traveler's palm"), but Auden is probably using the phrase quite literally to suggest that these people have never led a nomad's (wanderer's) life. The "nomad's comb" might be the fringe of unkempt hair through which the nomad peers at wild landscapes.

It does not neglect, but calls into question
All the Great Powers assumed; it disturbs our rights. The poet,
   Admired for his earnest habit of calling   70
The sun the sun, his mind Puzzle, is made uneasy
   By these solid statues which so obviously doubt
His antimythological myth; and these gamins,
   Pursuing the scientist down the tiled colonnade
With such lively offers,[3] rebuke his concern for Nature's   75
   Remotest aspects: I, too, am reproached, for what
And how much you know. Not to lose time, not to get caught,
   Not to be left behind, not, please! to resemble
The beasts who repeat themselves, or a thing like water
   Or stone whose conduct can be predicted, these   80
Are our Common Prayer, whose greatest comfort is music
   Which can be made anywhere, is invisible,
And does not smell. In so far as we have to look forward
   To death as a fact, no doubt we are right: But if
Sins can be forgiven, if bodies rise from the dead,   85
   These modifications of matter into
Innocent athletes and gesticulating fountains,
   Made solely for pleasure, make a further point:
The blessed will not care what angle they are regarded from,
   Having nothing to hide. Dear, I know nothing of   90
Either, but when I try to imagine a faultless love
   Or the life to come, what I hear is the murmur
Of underground streams, what I see is a limestone landscape.

                                 1948, 1951

3. These are not to be taken as literal statues of gamins (urchins) or man-made colonnades; they suggest rather that limestone is easily worked (by nature as well as by art) into shapes that remind us of familiar objects in the customary human world, unlike the "granite wastes" (line 47) and other sterner landscapes with which the limestone landscape is contrasted. The scientist, concerned with "Nature's remotest aspects," is "rebuked" by the familiar limestone shapes which suggest that man and his ordinary needs are more important. A basic theme of the poem is that easily weathered and easily worked limestone joins the natural to the human world, so that there is an easy transition "From weathered outcrop / To hilltop temple, from appearing waters to / Con-spicuous fountains, from a wild to a formal vineyard" (lines 15–18). Saints, would-be world conquerors, and solitary mystics prefer less comfortable landscapes; and even the limestone landscape is not as reassuring as it may seem ("this land is not the sweet home that it looks," line 61). But it asserts the primacy of the ordinary human, and as an ordinary man, not a saint, the poet finds in it the only satisfactory symbol of the good life. The landscape of this poem derives from Auden's native Yorkshire. Cf. "New Year Letter": "I see the nature of my kind / As a locality I love / Those limestone moors that stretch from Brough / To Hexham on the Roman Wall / That is my symbol of us all."

LOUIS MacNEICE
(1907–1963)

Louis MacNeice was born in Belfast, Northern Ireland, and educated at Marlborough and at Merton College, Oxford, where he studied classics.

For the next ten years he lectured in classics—at the University of Birmingham from 1930 to 1936, and at Bedford College for Women, London, from 1936 to 1940. He was feature-writer and producer for the British Broadcasting Corporation from 1941 to 1949, and after that became director of the British Institute in Athens.

MacNeice uses the modern tradition of irony in his own way. His dry, precise style has none of Auden's verbal brilliance, but it can be highly effective through its very restraint. He has never joined any of the movements in modern English poetry. A carefully controlled melancholy underlies much of his poetry; he has a somber sense of modern life, of its tragicomedies and futilities, and above all of the sadness that underlies all modern attempts to recapture, in memories of youth or by sudden emotion when listening to a street singer or watching a landscape, a sense of significance in daily living. His best poetry has always been fairly lowpressured, sardonic in a subdued manner, but with an occasional burst of wild Celtic irony. There is an integrity of feeling and a consistently high level of craftsmanship in his work that give his poems their special air of full realization: one never finds on a second reading that one had been taken in by an initial showiness. MacNeice is coming to be regarded more and more in England as second only to Auden among poets of his generation.

Sunday Morning

Down the road someone is practicing scales,
The notes like little fishes vanish with a wink of tails,
Man's heart expands to tinker with his car
For this is Sunday morning, Fate's great bazaar,
Regard these means as ends, concentrate on this Now,   5
And you may grow to music or drive beyond Hindhead[1] anyhow,
Take corners on two wheels until you go so fast
That you can clutch a fringe or two of the windy past,
That you can abstract this day and make it to the week of time
A small eternity, a sonnet self-contained in rhyme.   10

But listen, up the road, something gulps, the church spire
Opens its eight bells out, skulls' mouths which will not tire
To tell how there is no music or movement which secures
Escape from the weekday time. Which deadens and endures.

         1935

The Sunlight on the Garden

The sunlight on the garden
Hardens and grows cold,

---

1. This upland district in Surrey is a usual place to stop on the typical Sunday outing.

We cannot cage the minute
Within its nets of gold;
When all is told   5
We cannot beg for pardon.

Our freedom as free lances
Advances towards its end;
The earth compels, upon it
Sonnets and birds descend;   10
And soon, my friend,
We shall have no time for dances.

The sky was good for flying
Defying the church bells
And every evil iron   15
Siren and what it tells:
The earth compels,
We are dying, Egypt, dying[2]

And not expecting pardon,
Hardened in heart anew,   20
But glad to have sat under
Thunder and rain with you,
And grateful too
For sunlight on the garden.

1937   1938

Bagpipe Music

It's no go the merrygoround, it's no go the rickshaw,
All we want is a limousine and a ticket for the peepshow.
Their knickers are made of crepe-de-chine, their shoes are made of
    python,
Their halls are lined with tiger rugs and their walls with heads of
    bison.

John MacDonald found a corpse, put it under the sofa,   5
Waited till it came to life and hit it with a poker,
Sold its eyes for souvenirs, sold its blood for whisky,
Kept its bones for dumbbells to use when he was fifty.

It's no go the Yogi-Man, it's no go Blavatsky,[3]
All we want is a bank balance and a bit of skirt in a taxi.   10

Annie MacDougall went to milk, caught her foot in the heather,
Woke to hear a dance record playing of Old Vienna.
It's no go your maidenheads, it's no go your culture,
All we want is a Dunlop tire and the devil mend the puncture.

2. Cf. Antony's speech in *Antony and Cleopatra:* "I am dying, Egypt, dying" (IV.xv.41).
3. Madame Blavatsky (1831–91), the famous theosophist whose ideas were popular in some quarters in Britain in the 1930's.

The Laird o' Phelps spent Hogmanay⁴ declaring he was sober,⠀⠀⠀15
Counted his feet to prove the fact and found he had one foot over.
Mrs. Carmichael had her fifth, looked at the job with repulsion,
Said to the midwife, "Take it away; I'm through with overproduc-
⠀⠀⠀tion."

It's no go the gossip column, it's no go the Ceilidh,⁵
All we want is a mother's help and a sugar-stick for the baby.⠀⠀⠀20

Willie Murray cut his thumb, couldn't count the damage,
Took the hide of an Ayrshire cow and used it for a bandage.
His brother caught three hundred cran⁶ when the seas were lavish,
Threw the bleeders back in the sea and went upon the parish.⁷

It's no go the Herring Board, it's no go the Bible,
All we want is a packet of fags⁸ when our hands are idle.

It's no go the picture palace, it's no go the stadium,
It's no go the country cot with a pot of pink geraniums.
It's no go the Government grants, it's no go the elections,
Sit on your arse for fifty years and hang your hat on a pension.⠀⠀⠀30

It's no go my honey love, it's no go my poppet;
Work your hands from day to day, the winds will blow the profit.
The glass is falling hour by hour, the glass will fall forever,
But if you break the bloody glass you won't hold up the weather.

⠀⠀⠀⠀⠀⠀⠀⠀⠀⠀⠀⠀⠀⠀⠀⠀⠀⠀⠀⠀⠀1938

Mahabalipuram⁹

All alone from his dark sanctum the lingam¹ fronts, affronts the
⠀⠀⠀sea,
The world's dead weight of breakers against sapling, bull and candle
⠀⠀⠀Where worship comes no more,
Yet how should these cowherds and gods continue to dance in the
⠀⠀⠀rock
All the long night along ocean in this lost border between⠀⠀⠀5
That thronging gonging mirage of paddy and toddy² and dung
⠀⠀⠀And this uninhabited shore?
Silent except for the squadrons of water, the dark grim chargers
⠀⠀⠀launched from Australia,
Dark except for their manes of phosphorus, silent in spite of the
⠀⠀⠀rockhewn windmill

---

4. New Year's Eve.
5. Pronounced *kaley*: a Scottish Gaelic word meaning a social evening spent in singing and story-telling.
6. A measure of fresh herrings, about 750 fish. The Scottish herring industry failed in the 1930's; the Herring Board (line 25) was a government attempt to provide helpful direction.
7. I.e., "went on the county" (on re-lief).

8. Cigarettes.
9. Mahabalipuram, a fishing village south of Madras on the eastern coast of India, is near an enclave of ruined ancient Hindu temples.
1. Phallus; here an emblem of Shiva, the Hindu god of generative energy but also primarily of destruction.
2. In India, palm wine.

That brandishes axe and knife[3]—   10
The many-handed virgin facing, abasing the Oaf, the Demon;
Dark in spite of the rockhewn radiance of Vishnu[4] and Shiva and
    silent
In spite of the mooing of Krishna's herds;[5] yet in spite of this dark-
    ness and silence
        Behold what a joy of life—

Which goes with an awe and a horror; the innocence which sur-
    mounted the guilt   15
Thirteen centuries back when an artist eyeing this litter of granite
    Saw it for waste and took
A header[6] below the rockface, found there already like a ballet of
    fishes
Passing, repassing each other, these shapes of gopi and goblin,
Of elephant, serpent and antelope, saw them and grasped his mallet
    And cried with a clear stroke: Look!   21
And now we look, we to whom mantra and mudra[7] mean little,
And who find in this Hindu world a zone that is ultra-violet
    Balanced by an infra-red,
Austerity and orgy alike being phrased, it seems, in a strange dead
    language   25
But now that we look without trying to learn and only look in the
    act of leaping
After the sculptor into the rockface, now we can see, if not hear,
    those phrases
        To be neither strange nor dead.

Not strange for all their ingrown iconography, not so strange as our
    own dreams
Because better ordered, these are the dreams we have needed   30
    Since we forgot how to dance;
This god asleep on the snake[8] is the archetype of the sleep that we
    lost
When we were born, and these wingless figures that fly
Merely by bending the knee are the earnest of what we aspire to
    Apart from science and chance.   35

And the largest of all these reliefs, forty foot high by a hundred,
Is large in more senses than one, including both heaven and the
    animal kingdom
    And a grain of salt as well
For the saint stands always above on one leg fasting

---

3. Kali, the four-armed goddess of death
and destruction, who was the wife of
Shiva.
4. The god of preservation.
5. Krishna was said to have been an incarnation of Vishnu. Raised as a cow-
herd, he was notorious for his dalliance
with milkmaids (or Gopis).
6. That is, a head-first dive.

7. A mantra is a mystical incantation;
mudras, in Hindu temple dancing, are
stylized positions of the hands by which
the dancer conveys states of mind.
8. Between the cycles of creation, each
of which was attended by an incarnation
of Vishnu, the god slept on a coiled
snake resting on the waters of the cosmos.

Acquiring power while the smug hypocritical cat beneath him   40
Stands on his hindlegs too admired by the mice
    Whom the sculptor did not tell.

Nor did he tell the simple and beautiful rustics
Who saved from their doom by Krishna are once more busy and
    happy
    Absorbed in themselves and Him,   45
That trapped in this way in the rock their idyl would live to excite
And at once annul the lust and the envy of tourists
Taking them out of themselves and to find themselves in a world
    That has neither rift nor rim:

A monochrome world that has all the indulgence of color,   50
A still world whose every harmonic is audible,
    Largesse of spirit and stone;
Created things for once and for all featured in full while for once
    and never
The creator who is destroyer stands at the last point of land
Featureless; in a dark cell, a phallus of granite, as abstract   55
    As the North Pole; as alone.

But the visitor must move on and the waves assault the temple,
Living granite against dead water, and time with its weathering
    action
    Make phrase and feature blurred;
Still from today we know what an avatar[9] is, we have seen   60
God take shape and dwell among shapes, we have felt
Our aging limbs respond to those ageless limbs in the rock
    Reliefs. Relief is the word.

                                   1948

Good Dream

    He woke in his usual room, decided
    Feeling completely awake to switch
    The reading lamp on and read—but where
    Is the switch? No switch no light. No light
    No chapter nor verse. Competely awake   5
    He gropes for the switch and finds the book
    He left in the dark but what is a book
    Left in the dark? He feels the book
    Suddenly gently taken away
    By someone's hand and warm voice   10
    Begins, beginneth, aloud in the dark:

9. The incarnation of a Hindu deity, such as Krishna.

Here beginneth the first chapter—
But it wasn't the first, he was half way through.
No, says the voice, *the first chapter*
At the first verse in the first voice,   15
Which is mine, none other's: Here beginneth—
But I tell you, he says, I was half way through,
I am completely awake, I can prove it;
Where is the switch? I will show you the place
Half way through.
             There is no switch,   20
The voice replies; *in the beginning*
Is darkness upon the face of the earth
In which you must wait for me till I
Show you the place not half way through
But just begun, the place you never   25
Knew was here.
           But I know this place,
It is my usual room, except
The switch has gone.
           The switch was never
There to start with; which is why
You refuse to wake.
           But I am completely   30
Awake, I told you.
           You will tell me
Once you are. Here beginneth—
I tell you this is my usual room;
I can put my hand from the bed and feel the . . .
Yes?
        The wall—but I can't. Where   35
Has the wall gone? My bed was against it.
What was against it?
           Why is your voice
Moving away? Why do I hear
Water over it?
           There is water
Between us, I am here on the bank,   40
You will have to row.
           Row?
               What
Is a boat for? I am here on the bank
But I need light to row.
           No.
No light until you reach this bank.
Feel for your oars.
           Here are my oars.   45
Then loose that rope. Are you ready? Row.
Here beginneth. . . .
           He dips his oars
And knows the walls receding, hears

The ripples round the chair legs, hears
Larksong high in the chimney, hears   50

Rustling leaves in the wardrobe, smells
All the smells of a river, and yet
Feeling, smelling, hearing, knowing,
Still cannot see. This boat has no
Switch. No switch no light.
                              No light?   55
          Pull on your oars. I am here.
                              He pulls.
Splutter of water, crackle and grinding
Of reeds and twigs; then bump. The hand
That stole the book that was left in the dark
Comes out of the dark, the hand that is hers,   60
Hers, none other's, and seizes his
To help him on to the bank.
                              "And God

Said Let there be light"[1]

                              His usual room

Has lost its usual walls and found
Four walls of sky, incredible blue
Enclosing incredible green enclosing   65
Her, none other.

                              Completely awake.

1. Genesis i.3. "And God said, let there be light: and there was light."

                                                          1961

DYLAN THOMAS
(1914–1953)

Dylan Thomas was born in Swansea, Wales, and educated at Swansea Grammar School. After working for a time as a newspaper reporter, he was "discovered" as a poet in 1933 through a poetry contest in a popular newspaper. The following year his *Eighteen Poems* caused considerable excitement because of the strange violence of their imagery and their powerfully suggestive obscurity. It looked as though a new kind of strength and romantic picturesqueness had been restored to English poetry after the deliberately muted tones of Eliot and his followers. Thomas did not, however, turn out to be the founder of a neo-romantic movement, though some early critics took him to be so. As his poetry became better known, and after he had clarified the somewhat clotted imagery of his early style in his later volumes—*The Map of Love* (1939), *Deaths and Entrances* (1946), *Collected Poems* (1953)—it became clear that Thomas was an extremely craftsmanlike poet, and not the shouting rhapsodist that some

had taken him to be. His images were most carefully ordered in a patterned sequence, and his major theme was the unity of all life, the continuing *process* of life and death and new life which linked the generations
to each other. Thomas saw the workings of biology as a magical transformation producing unity out of diversity, and again and again in his poetry he
sought a poetic ritual to celebrate this unity ("The force that through
the green fuse drives the flower / Drives my green age"). He saw man
locked in a round of identities—with the beginning of growth also the
first movement toward death, the beginning of love leading to procreation,
new growth, and so in turn to death again and to life again, and because
of this view he comforted himself with the unity of man and nature, of
past and present, of life and death, and so "refused to mourn the death
of a child." In his best poems the closely woven imagery (deriving from
the Bible, Welsh folklore and preaching, and Freud) is organized to present aspects of this theme. His more open-worked poems of reminiscence
and autobiographical emotion, such as *Poem in October,* communicate
more immediately to the reader through their fine lyrical feeling and compelling use of simple natural images. His autobiographical work *Portrait
of the Artist as a Young Dog* and his radio play *Under Milk Wood* reveal
a vividness of observation and a combination of violence and tenderness
in expression that shows he could handle prose as excitingly as verse.

Thomas was a brilliant talker (when he felt like it), a considerable
drinker, a reckless and impulsive man whose short life was packed with
emotional ups and downs. His poetry readings in America between 1950
and 1953 were enormous successes, in spite of his sometimes reckless
antics and his deliberately offensive behavior to academic stuffed shirts
or those he imagined to be such. He died suddenly in New York, on his
third American trip, in November 1953. He acted the bohemian poet
as that role had not been played since the 90's; some thought this behavior wonderful, though others deplored it. He was a brilliant reader
of his own and others' poems, and many people who do not normally
read poetry were drawn to Thomas's by the magic of his own reading.
After his premature death a reaction set in: some critics declared that he
had been overrated as a poet because of the sensational role he had played
in life. But a balanced view is now possible; it is clear that at his best he
was an original poet of great power and beauty.

The Force That Through the Green Fuse
Drives the Flower

The force that through the green fuse drives the flower
Drives my green age; that blasts the roots of trees
Is my destroyer.
And I am dumb to tell the crooked rose
My youth is bent by the same wintry fever.   5

The force that drives the water through the rocks
Drives my red blood; that dries the mouthing streams
Turns mine to wax.
And I am dumb to mouth unto my veins
How at the mountain spring the same mouth sucks.   10

The hand that whirls the water in the pool
Stirs the quicksand; that ropes the blowing wind
Hauls my shroud sail.
And I am dumb to tell the hanging man
How of my clay is made the hangman's lime.   15

The lips of time leech to the fountain head;
Love drips and gathers, but the fallen blood
Shall calm her sores.
And I am dumb to tell a weather's wind
How time has ticked a heaven round the stars.   20

And I am dumb to tell the lover's tomb
How at my sheet goes the same crooked worm.

1933

This Bread I Break

This bread I break was once the oat,
This wine upon a foreign tree
Plunged in its fruit;
Man in the day or wind at night
Laid the crops low, broke the grape's joy.   5

Once in this wine the summer blood
Knocked in the flesh that decked the vine,
Once in this bread
The oat was merry in the wind;
Man broke the sun, pulled the wind down.   10

This flesh you break, this blood you let
Make desolation in the vein,
Were oat and grape
Born of the sensual root and sap;
My wine you drink, my bread you snap.   15

1936

After the Funeral[1]

(IN MEMORY OF ANN JONES)

After the funeral, mule praises, brays,
Windshake of sailshaped ears, muffle-toed tap
Tap happily of one peg in the thick
Grave's foot, blinds down the lids, the teeth in black,
The spittled eyes, the salt ponds in the sleeves,   5
Morning smack of the spade that wakes up sleep,
Shakes a desolate boy who slits his throat
In the dark of the coffin and sheds dry leaves,
That breaks one bone to light with a judgment clout,
After the feast of tear-stuffed time and thistles   10
In a room with a stuffed fox and a stale fern,
I stand, for this memorial's sake, alone
In the sniveling hours with dead, humped Ann
Whose hooded, fountain heart once fell in puddles
Round the parched worlds of Wales and drowned each sun   15
(Though this for her is a monstrous image blindly
Magnified out of praise; her death was a still drop;
She would not have me sinking in the holy
Flood of her heart's fame; she would lie dumb and deep
And need no druid[2] of her broken body).   20
But I, Ann's bard on a raised hearth, call all
The seas to service that her wood-tongued virtue
Babble like a bellbuoy over the hymning heads,
Bow down the walls of the ferned and foxy woods
That her love sing and swing through a brown chapel,   25
Bless her bent spirit with four, crossing birds.
Her flesh was meek as milk, but this skyward statue
With the wild breast and blessed and giant skull
Is carved from her in a room with a wet window
In a fiercely mourning house in a crooked year.   30
I know her scrubbed and sour humble hands
Lie with religion in their cramp, her threadbare
Whisper in a damp word, her wits drilled hollow,
Her fist of a face died clenched on a round pain;
And sculptured Ann is seventy years of stone.   35
These cloud-sopped, marble hands, this monumental
Argument of the hewn voice, gesture and psalm,
Storm me forever over her grave until
The stuffed lung of the fox twitch and cry Love
And the strutting fern lay seeds on the black sill.   40

1938, 1939

1. Ann Jones was Thomas's aunt; she lived in a farmhouse in the Welsh landscape described in *Poem in October*. The opening lines of the poem describe, in deliberately mixed metaphors and "transferred epithets," the insincerity of the behavior at the funeral in contrast to the genuine grief of the "desolate boy" who in imagination is already dead (lines 7 ff.).
2. Priest of the ancient Celtic pagans (forefathers of the modern Welsh).

There Was a Saviour

There was a saviour
Rarer than radium,
Commoner than water, crueller than truth;
Children kept from the sun
Assembled at his tongue   5
To hear the golden note turn in a groove,
Prisoners of wishes locked in their eyes
In the jails and studies of his keyless smiles.

The voice of children says
From a lost wilderness
There was calm to be done in his safe unrest,   10
When hindering man hurt
Man, animal, or bird
We hid our fears in that murdering breath,
Silence, silence to do, when earth grew loud,   15
In lairs and asylums of the tremendous shout.

There was glory to hear
In the churches of his tears,
Under his downy arm you sighed as he struck,
O you who could not cry   20
On to the ground when a man died
Put a tear for joy in the unearthly flood
And laid your cheek against a cloud-formed shell:
Now in the dark there is only yourself and myself.

Two proud, blacked brothers cry,   25
Winter-locked side by side,
To this inhospitable hollow year,
O we who could not stir
One lean sigh when we heard
Greed on man beating near and fire neighbor   30
But wailed and nested in the sky-blue wall
Now break a giant tear for the little known fall,

For the drooping of homes
That did not nurse our bones,
Brave deaths of only ones but never found,   35
Now see, alone in us,
Our own true strangers' dust
Ride through the doors of our unentered house.
Exiled in us we arouse the soft,
Unclenched, armless, silk and rough love that breaks all rocks. 40

1940

The Hunchback in the Park

The hunchback in the park
A solitary mister
Propped between trees and water
From the opening of the garden lock
That lets the trees and water enter   5
Until the Sunday somber bell at dark

Eating bread from a newspaper
Drinking water from the chained cup
That the children filled with gravel
In the fountain basin where I sailed my ship   10
Slept at night in a dog kennel
But nobody chained him up.

Like the park birds he came early
Like the water he sat down
And Mister they called Hey mister   15
The truant boys from the town
Running when he had heard them clearly
On out of sound

Past lake and rockery
Laughing when he shook his paper   20
Hunchbacked in mockery
Through the loud zoo of the willow groves
Dodging the park keeper
With his stick that picked up leaves.

And the old dog sleeper   25
Alone between nurses and swans
While the boys among willows
Made the tigers jump out of their eyes
To roar on the rockery stones
And the groves were blue with sailors   30

Made all day until bell time
A woman figure without fault
Straight as a young elm
Straight and tall from his crooked bones
That she might stand in the night   35
After the locks and chains

All night in the unmade park
After the railings and shrubberies
The birds the grass the trees the lake
And the wild boys innocent as strawberries   40
Had followed the hunchback
To his kennel in the dark.

1941

Poem in October

It was my thirtieth year to heaven
Woke to my hearing from harbor and neighbor wood
    And the mussel pooled and the heron
                Priested shore
                The morning beckon   5
With water praying and call of seagull and rook
And the knock of sailing boats on the net webbed wall
                Myself to set foot
                That second
In the still sleeping town and set forth.   10

    My birthday began with the water-
Birds and the birds of the winged trees flying my name
    Above the farms and the white horses
                And I rose
                In rainy autumn   15
And walked abroad in a shower of all my days.
High tide and the heron dived when I took the road
                Over the border
                And the gates
Of the town closed as the town awoke.   20

    A springful of larks in a rolling
Cloud and the roadside bushes brimming with whistling
    Black birds and the sun of October
                Summery
                On the hill's shoulder,   25
Here were fond climates and sweet singers suddenly
Come in the morning where I wandered and listened
                To the rain wringing
                Wind blow cold
In the wood faraway under me.   30

    Pale rain over the dwindling harbor
And over the sea wet church the size of a snail
    With its horns through mist and the castle
                Brown as owls
                But all the gardens   35
Of spring and summer were blooming in the tall tales
Beyond the border and under the lark full cloud.
                There could I marvel
                My birthday
Away but the weather turned around.   40

    It turned away from the blithe country
And down the other air and the blue altered sky
    Streamed again a wonder of summer
                With apples
                Pears and red currants   45
And I saw in the turning so clearly a child's
Forgotten mornings when he walked with his mother

Through the parables
Of sun light
And the legends of the green chapels   50

And the twice told fields of infancy
That his tears burned my cheeks and his heart moved in mine.
These were the woods the river and sea
Where a boy
In the listening   55
Summertime of the dead whispered the truth of his joy
To the trees and the stones and the fish in the tide.
And the mystery
Sang alive
Still in the water and singingbirds.   60

And there could I marvel my birthday
Away but the weather turned around. And the true
Joy of the long dead child sang burning
In the sun.
It was my thirtieth   65
Year to heaven stood there then in the summer noon
Though the town below lay leaved with October blood.
O may my heart's truth
Still be sung
On this high hill in a year's turning.   70

1945, 1946

Do Not Go Gentle into That Good Night

Do not go gentle into that good night,
Old age should burn and rave at close of day;
Rage, rage against the dying of the light.

Though wise men at their end know dark is right,
Because their words had forked no lightning they   5
Do not go gentle into that good night.

Good men, the last wave by, crying how bright
Their frail deeds might have danced in a green bay,
Rage, rage against the dying of the light.

Wild men who caught and sang the sun in flight,   10
And learn, too late, they grieved it on its way,
Do not go gentle into that good night.

Grave men, near death, who see with blinding sight
Blind eyes could blaze like meteors and be gay,
Rage, rage against the dying of the light.   15

And you, my father, there on the sad height,
Curse, bless, me now with your fierce tears, I pray.
Do not go gentle into that good night.
Rage, rage against the dying of the light.

1951, 1952

DORIS LESSING

(1919–   )

Born in Persia of British parents, Doris Lessing (née Tayler) lived on a Southern Rhodesian farm from 1924 to 1949 before settling in England. Her novel tetralogy with the general title *Children of Violence* (beginning with *Martha Quest*, 1952) combines elements of psychological autobiography with powerful exploration of the relationship between black and white in Africa. Her combination of psychological introspection, political analysis, social documentary, and feminism gives a characteristic tone to her novels and short stories. These elements are powerfully combined in her novel *The Golden Notebook* (1962), which explores the sexual problems of an independent woman in a man's world with unexhibitionist frankness while at the same time probing the political conscience of an ex-communist and the needs and dilemmas of a creative writer. Some of her short stories, which deal with racial and social dilemmas as well as with loneliness, the claims of politics, the problems of aging (especially for women), the conflict between the generations, and a whole spectrum of problems of alienation and isolation, have a pungency and force lacking in her more discursive novels. Mrs. Lessing (she uses the name of her second husband, though both her marriages have been dissolved) is very much a writer of her time, deeply involved with the changing patterns of thought, feeling, and culture during the last quarter century. One feels that there is an absolute continuity between her life and her work. The story below is taken from her volume of short stories, *A Man and Two Women*.

To Room Nineteen

This is a story, I suppose, about a failure in intelligence: the Rawlings' marriage was grounded in intelligence.

They were older when they married than most of their married friends: in their well-seasoned late twenties. Both had had a number of affairs, sweet rather than bitter; and when they fell in love—for they did fall in love—had known each other for some time. They joked that they had saved each other "for the real thing." That they had waited so long (but not too long) for this real thing was to them a proof of their sensible discrimination. A good many of their friends had married young, and now (they felt) probably regretted lost opportunities; while others, still unmarried, seemed to them arid, self-doubting, and likely to make desperate or romantic marriages.

Not only they, but others, felt they were well matched: their friends' delight was an additional proof of their happiness. They had played the same roles, male and female, in this group or set, if such a wide, loosely connected, constantly changing constellation of people could be called a set. They had both become, by virtue of their moderation, their humor, and their abstinence from painful experience people to whom others came for advice. They could be, and were, relied on. It was one of those cases of a man and a woman linking themselves whom no one else had ever thought of linking, probably because of their similarities. But then everyone exclaimed: Of course! How right! How was it we never thought of it before!

And so they married amid general rejoicing, and because of their foresight and their sense for what was probable, nothing was a surprise to them.

Both had well-paid jobs. Matthew was a subeditor on a large London newspaper, and Susan worked in an advertising firm. He was not the stuff of which editors or publicized journalists are made, but he was much more than "a subeditor," being one of the essential background people who in fact steady, inspire and make possible the people in the limelight. He was content with this position. Susan had a talent for commercial drawing. She was humorous about the advertisements she was responsible for, but she did not feel strongly about them one way or the other.

Both, before they married, had had pleasant flats, but they felt it unwise to base a marriage on either flat, because it might seem like a submission of personality on the part of the one whose flat it was not. They moved into a new flat in South Kensington on the clear understanding that when their marriage had settled down (a process they knew would not take long, and was in fact more a humorous concession to popular wisdom than what was due to themselves) they would buy a house and start a family.

And this is what happened. They lived in their charming flat for two years, giving parties and going to them, being a popular young married couple, and then Susan became pregnant, she gave up her job, and they bought a house in Richmond. It was typical of this couple that they had a son first, then a daughter, then twins, son and daughter. Everything right, appropriate, and what everyone would wish for, if they could choose. But people did feel these two had chosen; this balanced and sensible family was no more than what was due to them because of their infallible sense for *choosing* right.

And so they lived with their four children in their gardened house in Richmond and were happy. They had everything they had wanted and had planned for.

And yet . . .

Well, even this was expected, that there must be a certain flatness. . . .

Yes, yes, of course, it was natural they sometimes felt like this. Like what?

Their life seemed to be like a snake biting its tail. Matthew's job for the sake of Susan, children, house, and garden—which caravanserai needed a well-paid job to maintain it. And Susan's practical intelligence for the sake of Matthew, the children, the house and the garden—which unit would have collapsed in a week without her.

But there was no point about which either could say: "For the sake of *this* is all the rest." Children? But children can't be a center of life and a reason for being. They can be a thousand things that are delightful, interesting, satisfying, but they can't be a wellspring to live from. Or they shouldn't be. Susan and Matthew knew that well enough.

Matthew's job? Ridiculous. It was an interesting job, but scarcely a reason for living. Matthew took pride in doing it well; but he could hardly be expected to be proud of the newspaper: the newspaper he read, *his* newspaper, was not the one he worked for.

Their love for each other? Well, that was nearest it. If this wasn't a center, what was? Yes, it was around this point, their love, that the whole extraordinary structure revolved. For extraordinary it certainly was. Both Susan and Matthew had moments of thinking so, of looking in secret disbelief at this thing they had created: marriage, four children, big house, garden, charwomen, friends, cars . . . and this *thing*, this entity, all of it had come into existence, been blown into being out of nowhere, because Susan loved Matthew and Matthew loved Susan. Extraordinary. So that was the central point, the wellspring.

And if one felt that it simply was not strong enough, important enough, to support it all, well whose fault was that? Certainly neither Susan's nor Matthew's. It was in the nature of things. And they sensibly blamed neither themselves nor each other.

On the contrary, they used their intelligence to preserve what they had created from a painful and explosive world: they looked around them, and took lessons. All around them, marriages collapsing, or breaking, or rubbing along (even worse, they felt). They must not make the same mistakes, they must not.

They had avoided the pitfall so many of their friends had fallen into—of buying a house in the country *for the sake of the children*; so that the husband became a weekend husband, a weekend father, and the wife always careful not to ask what went on in the town flat which they called (in joke) a bachelor flat. No, Matthew was a full-time husband, a full-time father, and at nights, in the big married bed in the big married bedroom (which had an attractive view of the river) they lay beside each other talking and he told her about his day, and what he had done, and whom he had met; and she told him about her day (not as interesting, but that was not her fault) for both knew of the hidden resentments and deprivations of the woman who has lived her own life—and above all, has earned her own living—and is now dependent on a husband for outside interests and money.

Nor did Susan make the mistake of taking a job for the sake of her independence, which she might very well have done, since her old firm, missing her qualities of humor, balance, and sense, invited her often to go back. Children needed their mother to a certain age, that both parents knew and agreed on; and when these four healthy wisely brought-up children were of the right age, Susan would work again, because she knew, and so did he, what happened to women of fifty at the height of their energy and ability, with grown-up children who no longer needed their full devotion.

So here was this couple, testing their marriage, looking after it, treating it like a small boat full of helpless people in a very stormy sea. Well, of course, so it was. . . . The storms of the world were bad, but not too close—which is not to say they were selfishly felt: Susan and Matthew were both well-informed and responsible people. And the inner storms and quicksands were understood and charted. So everything was all right. Everything was in order. Yes, things were under control.

So what did it matter if they felt dry, flat? People like themselves, fed on a hundred books (psychological, anthropological, sociological) could scarcely be unprepared for the dry, controlled wistfulness which is the distinguishing mark of the intelligent marriage. Two people, endowed with education, with discrimination, with judgment, linked together voluntarily from their will to be happy together and to be of use to others—one sees them everywhere, one knows them, one even is that thing oneself: sadness because so much is after all so little. These two, unsurprised, turned toward each other with even more courtesy and gentle love: this was life, that two people, no matter how carefully chosen, could not be everything to each other. In fact, even to say so, to think in such a way, was banal, they were ashamed to do it.

It was banal, too, when one night Matthew came home late and confessed he had been to a party, taken a girl home and slept with her. Susan forgave him, of course. Except that forgiveness is hardly the word. Understanding, yes. But if you understand something, you don't forgive it, you are the thing itself: forgiveness is for what you *don't* understand. Nor had he *confessed*—what sort of word is that?

The whole thing was not important. After all, years ago they had joked: Of course I'm not going to be faithful to you, no one can be faithful to one other person for a whole lifetime. (And there was the word *faithful*—stupid, all these words, stupid, belonging to a savage old world.) But the incident left both of them irritable. Strange, but they were both bad-tempered, annoyed. There was something unassimilable about it.

Making love splendidly after he had come home that night, both had felt that the idea that Myra Jenkins, a pretty girl met at a party, could be even relevant was ridiculous. They had loved each other for over a decade, would love each other for years more. Who, then, was Myra Jenkins?

Except, thought Susan, unaccountably bad-tempered, she was (is?) the first. In ten years. So either the ten years' fidelity was not important, or she isn't. (No, no, there is something wrong with this way of thinking, there must be.) But if she isn't important, presumably it wasn't important either when Matthew and I first went to bed with each other that afternoon whose delight even now (like a very long shadow at sundown) lays a long, wand-like finger over us. (Why did I say sundown?) Well, if what we felt that afternoon was not important, nothing is important, because if it hadn't been for what we felt, we wouldn't be Mr. and Mrs. Rawlings with four children, etc., etc. The whole thing is *absurd*—for him to have come home and told me was absurd. For him not to have told me was absurd. For me to care, or for that matter not to care, is absurd . . . and who is Myra Jenkins? Why, no one at all.

There was only one thing to do, and of course these sensible people did it: they put the thing behind them, and consciously, knowing what they were doing, moved forward into a different phase of their marriage, giving thanks for past good fortune as they did so.

For it was inevitable that the handsome, blond, attractive, manly man, Matthew Rawlings, should be at times tempted (oh, what a word!) by the attractive girls at parties she could not attend because of the four children; and that sometimes he would succumb (a word even more repulsive, if possible) and that she, a good-looking woman in the big well-tended garden at Richmond, would sometimes be pierced as by an arrow from the sky with bitterness. Except that bitterness was not in order, it was out of court. Did the casual girls touch the marriage? They did not. Rather it was they who knew defeat because of the handsome Matthew Rawlings' marriage body and soul to Susan Rawlings.

In that case why did Susan feel (though luckily not for longer than a few seconds at a time) as if life had become a desert, and that nothing mattered, and that her children were not her own?

Meanwhile her intelligence continued to assert that all was well. What if her Matthew did have an occasional sweet afternoon, the odd affair? For she knew quite well, except in her moments of aridity, that they were very happy, that the affairs were not important.

Perhaps that was the trouble? It was in the nature of things that the adventures and delights could no longer be hers, because of the four children and the big house that needed so much attention. But perhaps she was secretly wishing, and even knowing that she did, that the wildness and the beauty could be his. But he was married to her. She was married to him. They were married inextricably. And therefore the gods could not strike him with the real magic, not really. Well, was it Susan's fault that after he came home from an adventure he looked harassed rather than fulfilled? (In fact, that was how she knew he had been *unfaithful*, because of his sullen air, and his glances at her, similar to hers at him: What is it that I share with this person that shields all delight from me?) But none of it by anybody's fault. (But what did they feel ought to be somebody's fault?) Nobody's fault, nothing to be at fault, no one to blame, no one to offer or to take it ... and nothing wrong, either, except that Matthew never was really struck, as he wanted to be, by joy; and that Susan was more and more often threatened by emptiness. (It was usually in the garden that she was invaded by this feeling: she was coming to avoid the garden, unless the children or Matthew were with her.) There was no need to use the dramatic words, unfaithful, forgive, and the rest: intelligence forbade them. Intelligence barred, too, quarreling, sulking, anger, silences of withdrawal, accusations and tears. Above all, intelligence forbids tears.

A high price has to be paid for the happy marriage with the four healthy children in the large white gardened house.

And they were paying it, willingly, knowing what they were doing. When they lay side by side or breast to breast in the big civilized bedroom overlooking the wild sullied river, they laughed, often, for no particular reason; but they knew it was really because of these two small people, Susan and Matthew, supporting such an edifice on their intelligent love. The laugh comforted them; it saved them both, though from what, they did not know.

They were now both fortyish. The older children, boy and girl, were ten and eight, at school. The twins, six, were still at home. Susan did not have nurses or girls to help her: childhood is short; and she did not regret the hard work. Often enough she was bored, since small children can be boring; she was often very tired; but she regretted nothing. In another decade, she would turn herself back into being a woman with a life of her own.

Soon the twins would go to school, and they would be away from home from nine until four. These hours, so Susan saw it, would be the preparation for her own slow emancipation away from the role of hub-of-the-family into woman-with-her-own life. She was already planning for the hours of freedom when all the children would be "off her hands." That was the phrase used by Matthew and by Susan and by their friends, for the moment when the youngest child went off to school. "They'll be off your hands, darling Susan, and you'll have time to yourself." So said Matthew, the intelligent husband, who had often enough commended and consoled Susan, standing by her in spirit during the years when her soul was not her own, as she said, but her children's.

What it amounted to was that Susan saw herself as she had been at twenty-eight, unmarried; and then again somewhere about fifty, blossoming from the root of what she had been twenty years before. As if the essential Susan were in abeyance, as if she were in cold storage. Matthew said something like this to Susan one night: and she agreed that it was true—she did feel something like that. What, then, was this essential Susan? She did not know. Put like that it sounded ridiculous, and she did not really feel it. Anyway, they had a long discussion about the whole thing before going off to sleep in each other's arms.

So the twins went off to their school, two bright affectionate children who had no problems about it, since their older brother and sister had trodden this path so successfully before them. And now Susan was going to be alone in the big house, every day of the school term, except for the daily woman who came in to clean.

It was now, for the first time in this marriage, that something happened which neither of them had foreseen.

This is what happened. She returned, at nine-thirty, from taking the twins to the school by car, looking forward to seven blissful hours of freedom. On the first morning she was simply restless, worrying about the twins "naturally enough" since this was their first day away at school. She was hardly able to contain herself until they came back. Which they did happily, excited by the world of school, looking forward to the next day. And the next day Susan took them, dropped them, came back, and found herself reluctant to enter her big and beautiful home because it was as if something was waiting for her there that she did not wish to confront. Sensibly, however, she parked the car in the garage, entered the house, spoke to Mrs. Parkes the daily woman about her duties, and went up to her bedroom. She was possessed by a fever which drove her out again, downstairs, into the kitchen, where Mrs. Parkes was making cake and did not need her, and into the garden. There she sat on a bench and tried to calm herself, looking at trees, at a brown glimpse of the river. But she was filled with tension, like a panic: as if an enemy was in the garden with her. She spoke to herself severely, thus: All this is quite natural. First, I spent twelve years of my adult life working, *living my own life*. Then I married, and from the moment I became pregnant for the first time I signed myself over, so to speak, to other people. To the children. Not for one moment in twelve years have I been alone, had time to myself. So now I have to learn to be myself again. That's all.

And she went indoors to help Mrs. Parkes cook and clean, and found some sewing to do for the children. She kept herself occupied every day. At the end of the first term she understood she felt two contrary emotions. First: secret astonishment and dismay that during those weeks when the house was empty of children she had in fact been more occupied (had been careful to keep herself occupied) than ever she had been when the children were around her needing her continual attention. Second: that now she knew the house would be full of them, and for five weeks, she resented the fact she would never be alone. She was already looking back at those hours of sewing, cooking (but by herself), as at a lost freedom which would not be hers for five long weeks. And the two months of term which would succeed the five weeks stretched alluringly open to her—freedom. But what freedom—when in fact she had been so careful *not* to be free of small duties during the last weeks? She looked at herself, Susan Rawlings, sitting in a big chair by the window in the bedroom, sewing shirts or dresses, which she might just as well have bought. She saw herself making cakes for hours at a time in the big family kitchen: yet usually she bought cakes. What she saw was a woman alone, that was true, but she had not felt alone. For instance, Mrs. Parkes was always somewhere in the house. And she did not like being in the garden at all, because of the closeness there of the enemy—irritation, restlessness, emptiness, whatever it was, which keeping her hands occupied made less dangerous for some reason.

Susan did not tell Matthew of these thoughts. They were not sensible. She did not recognize herself in them. What should she say to her dear friend and husband Matthew? "When I go into the garden, that is, if the children are not there, I feel as if there is an enemy there waiting to invade me." "What enemy, Susan darling?" "Well I don't know, really. . . ." "Perhaps you should see a doctor?"

No, clearly this conversation should not take place. The holidays began and Susan welcomed them. Four children, lively, energetic, intelligent, demanding: she was never, not for a moment of her day, alone. If she was in a room, they would be in the next room, or waiting for her to do something for them; or it would soon be time for lunch or tea, or to take one of them to the dentist. Something to do: five weeks of it, thank goodness.

On the fourth day of these so welcome holidays, she found she was storming with anger at the twins, two shrinking beautiful children who (and this is what checked her) stood hand in hand looking at her with sheer dismayed disbelief. This was their calm mother, shouting at them. And for what? They had come to her with some game, some bit of nonsense. They looked at each other, moved closer for support, and went off hand in hand, leaving Susan holding on to the windowsill of the living room, breathing deep, feeling sick. She went to lie down, telling the older children she had a headache. She heard the boy Harry telling the little ones: "It's all right, Mother's got a headache." She heard that *It's all right* with pain.

That night she said to her husband: "Today I shouted at the twins, quite unfairly." She sounded miserable, and he said gently: "Well, what of it?"

"It's more of an adjustment than I thought, their going to school."

"But Susie, Susie darling. . . ." For she was crouched weeping on the bed. He comforted her: "Susan, what is all this about? You shouted at them? What of it? If you shouted at them fifty times a day it wouldn't be more than the little devils deserve." But she wouldn't laugh. She wept. Soon he comforted her with his body. She became calm. Calm, she wondered what was wrong with her, and why she should mind so much that she might, just once, have behaved unjustly with the children. What did it matter? They had forgotten it all long ago: Mother had a headache and everything was all right.

It was a long time later that Susan understood that that night, when she had wept and Matthew had driven the misery out of her with his big solid body, was the last time, ever in their married life, that they had been—to use their mutual language—with each other. And even that was a lie, because she had not told him of her real fears at all.

The five weeks passed, and Susan was in control of herself, and good and kind, and she looked forward to the holidays with a mixture of fear and longing. She did not know what to expect. She took the twins off to school (the elder children took themselves to school) and she returned to the house determined to face the enemy wherever he was, in the house, or the garden or—where?

She was again restless, she was possessed by restlessness. She cooked and sewed and worked as before, day after day, while Mrs. Parkes remonstrated: "Mrs. Rawlings, what's the need for it? I can do that, it's what you pay me for."

And it was so irrational that she checked herself. She would put the car into the garage, go up to her bedroom, and sit, hands in her lap, forcing herself to be quiet. She listened to Mrs. Parkes moving around the house. She looked out into the garden and saw the branches shake the trees. She sat defeating the enemy, restlessness. Emptiness. She ought to be thinking about her life, about herself. But she did not. Or perhaps she could not. As soon as she forced her mind to think about Susan (for what else did she want to be alone for?) it skipped off to thoughts of butter or school clothes. Or it thought of Mrs. Parkes. She realized that she sat listening for the movements of the cleaning woman, following her every turn, bend, thought. She followed her in her mind from kitchen to bathroom, from table to oven, and it was as if the duster, the cleaning cloth, the saucepan, were in her own hand. She would hear herself saying: No, not like that, don't put that there. . . . Yet she did not give a damn what Mrs. Parkes did, or if she did it at all. Yet she could not prevent herself from being conscious of her, every minute. Yes, this was what was wrong with her: she needed, when she was alone, to be really alone, with no one near. She could not endure the knowledge that in ten minutes or in half an hour Mrs. Parkes would call up the stairs: "Mrs. Rawlings, there's no silver polish. Madam, we're out of flour."

So she left the house and went to sit in the garden where she was screened from the house by trees. She waited for the demon to appear and claim her, but he did not.

She was keeping him off, because she had not, after all, come to an end of arranging herself.

She was planning how to be somewhere where Mrs. Parkes would not come after her with a cup of tea, or a demand to be allowed to telephone (always irritating since Susan did not care who she telephoned or how often), or just a nice talk about something. Yes, she needed a place, or a state of affairs, where it would not be necessary to keep reminding herself: In ten minutes I must telephone Matthew about . . . and at half past three I must leave early for the children because the car needs cleaning. And at ten o'clock tomorrow I must remember. . . . She was possessed with resentment that the seven hours of freedom in every day (during weekdays in the school term) were not free, that never, not for one second, ever, was she free from the pressure of time, from having to remember this or that. She could never forget herself; never really let herself go into forgetfulness.

Resentment. It was poisoning her. (She looked at this emotion and thought it was absurd. Yet she felt it.) She was a prisoner. (She looked at this thought too, and it was no good telling herself it was a ridiculous one.) She must tell Matthew—but what? She was filled with emotions that were utterly ridiculous, that she despised, yet that nevertheless she was feeling so strongly she could not shake them off.

The school holidays came round, and this time they were for nearly two months, and she behaved with a conscious controlled decency that nearly drove her crazy. She would lock herself in the bathroom, and sit on the edge of the bath, breathing deep, trying to let go into some kind of calm. Or she went up into the spare room, usually empty, where no one would expect her to be. She heard the children calling "Mother, Mother," and kept silent, feeling guilty. Or she went to the very end of the garden, by herself, and looked at the slow-moving brown river; she looked at the river and closed her eyes and breathed slow and deep, taking it into her being, into her veins.

Then she returned to the family, wife and mother, smiling and responsible, feeling as if the pressure of these people—four lively children and her husband—were a painful pressure on the surface of her skin, a hand pressing on her brain. She did not once break down into irritation during these holidays, but it was like living out a prison sentence, and when the children went back to school, she sat on a white stone seat near the flowing river, and she thought: It is not even a year since the twins went to school, since *they were off my hands* (What on earth did I think I meant when I used that stupid phrase?) and yet I'm a different person. I'm simply not myself. I don't understand it.

Yet she had to understand it. For she knew that this structure—big white house, on which the mortgage still cost four hundred a year, a husband, so good and kind and insightful, four children, all doing so nicely, and the garden where she sat, and Mrs. Parkes the cleaning woman—all this depended on her, and yet she could not understand why, or even what it was she contributed to it.

She said to Matthew in their bedroom: "I think there must be something wrong with me."

And he said: "Surely not, Susan? You look marvelous—you're as lovely as ever."

She looked at the handsome blond man, with his clear, intelligent, blue-eyed face, and thought: Why is it I can't tell him? Why not? And she said: "I need to be alone more than I am."

At which he swung his slow blue gaze at her, and she saw what she had been dreading: Incredulity. Disbelief. And fear. An incredulous blue stare from a stranger who was her husband, as close to her as her own breath.

He said: "But the children are at school and off your hands."

She said to herself: I've got to force myself to say: Yes, but do you realize that I never feel free? There's never a moment I can say to myself: There's nothing I have to remind myself about, nothing I have to do in half an hour, or an hour, or two hours. . . .

But she said: "I don't feel well."

He said: "Perhaps you need a holiday."

She said, appalled: "But not without you, surely?" For she could not imagine herself going off without him. Yet that was what he meant. Seeing her face, he laughed, and opened his arms, and she went into them, thinking: Yes, yes, but why can't I say it? And what is it I have to say?

She tried to tell him, about never being free. And he listened and said: "But Susan, what sort of freedom can you possibly want— short of being dead! Am I ever free? I go to the office, and I have to be there at ten—all right, half past ten, sometimes. And I have to do this or that, don't I? Then I've got to come home at a certain time—I don't mean it, you know I don't—but if I'm not going to be back home at six I telephone you. When can I ever say to myself: I have nothing to be responsible for in the next six hours?"

Susan, hearing this, was remorseful. Because it was true. The good marriage, the house, the children, depended just as much on his voluntary bondage as it did on hers. But why did he not feel bound? Why didn't he chafe and become restless? No, there was something really wrong with her and this proved it.

And that word *bondage*—why had she used it? She had never felt marriage, or the children, as bondage. Neither had he, or surely they wouldn't be together lying in each other's arms content after twelve years of marriage.

No, her state (whatever it was) was irrelevant, nothing to do with her real good life with her family. She had to accept the fact that after all, she was an irrational person and to live with it. Some people had to live with crippled arms, or stammers, or being deaf. She would have to live knowing she was subject to a state of mind she could not own.

Nevertheless, as a result of this conversation with her husband, there was a new regime next holidays.

The spare room at the top of the house now had a cardboard sign saying: PRIVATE! DO NOT DISTURB! on it. (This sign had been drawn in coloured chalks by the children, after a discussion between the parents in which it was decided this was psychologically the right thing.) The family and Mrs. Parkes knew this was "Mother's Room" and that she was entitled to her privacy. Many serious conversations took place between Matthew and the children about not taking Mother for granted. Susan overheard the first, between father and Harry, the older boy, and was surprised at her irritation over it. Surely she could have a room somewhere in that big house and retire into it without such a fuss being made? Without it being so solemnly discussed? Why couldn't she simply have announced: "I'm going to fit out the little top room for myself, and when I'm in it I'm not to be disturbed for anything short of fire"? Just that, and finished; instead of long earnest discussions. When she heard Harry and Matthew explaining it to the twins with Mrs. Parkes coming in—"Yes, well, a family sometimes gets on top of a woman"—she had to go right away to the bottom of the garden until the devils of exasperation had finished their dance in her blood.

But now there was a room, and she could go there when she liked, she used it seldom: she felt even more caged there than in her bedroom. One day she had gone up there after a lunch for ten children she had cooked and served because Mrs. Parkes was not there, and had sat alone for a while looking into the garden. She saw the children stream out from the kitchen and stand looking up at the window where she sat behind the curtains. They were all— her children and her friends—discussing Mother's Room. A few minutes later, the chase of children in some game came pounding up the stairs, but ended as abruptly as if they had fallen over a ravine, so sudden was the silence. They had remembered she was there, and had gone silent in a great gale of "Hush! Shhhhhh! Quiet, you'll disturb her. . . ." And they went tiptoeing downstairs like criminal conspirators. When she came down to make tea for them, they all apologized. The twins put their arms around her, from front and back, making a human cage of loving limbs, and promised it would never occur again. "We forgot, Mummy, we forgot all about it!"

What it amounted to was that Mother's Room, and her need for privacy, had become a valuable lesson in respect for other people's rights. Quite soon Susan was going up to the room only because it was a lesson it was a pity to drop. Then she took sewing up there, and the children and Mrs. Parkes came in and out: it had become another family room.

She sighed, and smiled, and resigned herself—she made jokes at her own expense with Matthew over the room. That is, she did from the self she liked, she respected. But at the same time, something inside her howled with impatience, with rage. . . . And she was frightened. One day she found herself kneeling by her bed and praying: "Dear God, keep it away from me, keep him away from me." She meant the devil, for she now thought of it, not caring if she were irrational, as some sort of demon. She imagined him, or it, as a youngish man, or perhaps a middle-aged man pretending to be young. Or a man young-looking from immaturity? At any rate, she saw the young-looking face which, when she drew closer, had dry lines about mouth and eyes. He was thinnish, meager in build. And he had a reddish complexion, and ginger hair. That was he—a gingery, energetic man, and he wore a reddish hairy jacket, unpleasant to the touch.

Well, one day she saw him. She was standing at the bottom of the garden, watching the river ebb past, when she raised her eyes and saw this person, or being, sitting on the white stone bench. He was looking at her, and grinning. In his hand was a long crooked stick, which he had picked off the ground, or broken off the tree above him. He was absent-mindedly, out of an absent-minded or freakish impulse of spite, using the stick to stir around in the coils of a blindworm or a grass snake (or some kind of snakelike creature: it was whitish and unhealthy to look at, unpleasant). The snake was twisting about, flinging its coils from side to side in a kind of dance of protest against the teasing prodding stick.

Susan looked at him thinking: Who is the stranger? What is he doing in our garden? Then she recognized the man around whom her terrors had crystalized. As she did so, he vanished. She made herself walk over to the bench. A shadow from a branch lay across thin emerald grass, moving jerkily over its roughness, and she could see why she had taken it for a snake, lashing and twisting. She went back to the house thinking: Right, then, so I've seen him with my own eyes, so I'm not crazy after all—there *is* a danger because I've seen him. He is lurking in the garden and sometimes even in the house, and he wants *to get into me and to take me over*.

She dreamed of having a room or a place, anywhere, where she could go and sit, by herself, no one knowing where she was.

Once, near Victoria, she found herself outside a news agent that had Rooms to Let advertised. She decided to rent a room, telling no one. Sometimes she could take the train in to Richmond and sit alone in it for an hour or two. Yet how could she? A room would cost three or four pounds a week, and she earned no money, and how could she explain to Matthew that she needed such a sum? What for? It did not occur to her that she was taking it for granted she wasn't going to tell him about the room.

Well, it was out of the question, having a room; yet she knew she must.

One day, when a school term was well established, and none of the children had measles or other ailments, and everything seemed in order, she did the shopping early, explained to Mrs. Parkes she was meeting an old school friend, took the train to Victoria, searched until she found a small quiet hotel, and asked for a room for the day. They did not let rooms by the day, the manageress said, looking doubtful, since Susan so obviously was not the kind of woman who needed a room for unrespectable reasons. Susan made a long explanation about not being well, being unable to shop without frequent rests for lying down. At last she was allowed to rent the room provided she paid a full night's price for it. She was taken up by the manageress and a maid, both concerned over the state of her health . . . which must be pretty bad if, living at Richmond (she had signed her name and address in the register), she needed a shelter at Victoria.

The room was ordinary and anonymous, and was just what Susan needed. She put a shilling in the gas fire, and sat, eyes shut, in a dingy armchair with her back to a dingy window. She was alone. She was alone. She could feel pressures lifting off her. First the sounds of traffic came very loud; then they seemed to vanish; she might even have slept a little. A knock on the door: it was Miss Townsend the manageress, bringing her a cup of tea with her own hands, so concerned was she over Susan's long silence and possible illness.

Miss Townsend was a lonely woman of fifty, running this hotel with all the rectitude expected of her, and she sensed in Susan the possibility of understanding companionship. She stayed to talk. Susan found herself in the middle of a fantastic story about her illness, which got more and more improbable as she tried to make it tally with the large house at Richmond, well-off husband, and four children. Suppose she said instead: Miss Townsend, I'm here in your hotel because I need to be alone for a few hours, above all *alone and with no one knowing where I am.* She said it mentally, and saw, mentally, the look that would inevitably come on Miss Townsend's elderly maiden's face. "Miss Townsend, my four children and my husband are driving me insane, do you understand that? Yes, I can see from the gleam of hysteria in your eyes that comes from loneliness controlled but only just contained that I've got everything in the world you've ever longed for. Well, Miss Townsend, I don't want any of it. You can have it, Miss Townsend. I wish I was absolutely alone in the world, like you. Miss Townsend, I'm besieged by seven devils, Miss Townsend, Miss Townsend, let me stay here in your hotel where the devils can't get me. . . ." Instead of saying all this, she described her anemia, agreed to try Miss Townsend's remedy for it, which was raw liver, minced, between whole-meal bread, and said yes, perhaps it would be better if she stayed at home and let a friend do shopping for her. She paid her bill and left the hotel, defeated.

At home Mrs. Parkes said she didn't really like it, no, not really, when Mrs. Rawlings was away from nine in the morning until five. The teacher had telephoned from school to say Joan's teeth were paining her, and she hadn't known what to say; and what was she to make for the children's tea, Mrs. Rawlings hadn't said.

All this was nonsense, of course. Mrs. Parkes's complaint was that

Susan had withdrawn herself spiritually, leaving the burden of the big house on her.

Susan looked back at her day of "freedom" which had resulted in her becoming a friend to the lonely Miss Townsend, and in Mrs. Parkes's remonstrances. Yet she remembered the short blissful hour of being alone, really alone. She was determined to arrange her life, no matter what it cost, so that she could have that solitude more often. An absolute solitude, where no one knew her or cared about her.

But how? She thought of saying to her old employer: I want to back you up in a story with Matthew that I am doing part-time work for you. The truth is that . . . but she would have to tell him a lie too, and which lie? She could not say: I want to sit by myself three or four times a week in a rented room. And besides, he knew Matthew, and she could not really ask him to tell lies on her behalf, apart from his being bound to think it meant a lover.

Suppose she really took a part-time job, which she could get through fast and efficiently, leaving time for herself. What job? Addressing envelopes? Canvassing?

And there was Mrs. Parkes, working widow, who knew exactly what she was prepared to give to the house, who knew by instinct when her mistress withdrew in spirit from her responsibilities. Mrs. Parkes was one of the servants of this world, but she needed someone to serve. She had to have Mrs. Rawlings, her madam, at the top of the house or in the garden, so that she could come and get support from her: "Yes, the bread's not what it was when I was a girl. . . . Yes, Harry's got a wonderful appetite, I wonder where he puts it all. . . . Yes, it's lucky the twins are so much of a size, they can wear each other's shoes, that's a saving in these hard times. . . . Yes, the cherry jam from Switzerland is not a patch on the jam from Poland, and three times the price. . . ." And so on. That sort of talk Mrs. Parkes must have, every day, or she would leave, not knowing herself why she left.

Susan Rawlings, thinking these thoughts, found that she was prowling through the great thicketed garden like a wild cat: she was walking up the stairs, down the stairs, through the rooms, into the garden, along the brown running river, back, up through the house, down again. . . . It was a wonder Mrs. Parkes did not think it strange. But on the contrary, Mrs. Rawlings could do what she liked, she could stand on her head if she wanted, provided she was *there*. Susan Rawlings prowled and muttered through her house, hating Mrs. Parkes, hating poor Miss Townsend, dreaming of her hour of solitude in the dingy respectability of Miss Townsend's hotel bedroom, and she knew quite well she was mad. Yes, she was mad.

She said to Matthew that she must have a holiday. Matthew

agreed with her. This was not as things had been once—how they had talked in each other's arms in the marriage bed. He had, she knew, diagnosed her finally as *unreasonable*. She had become someone outside himself that he had to manage. They were living side by side in this house like two tolerably friendly strangers.

Having told Mrs. Parkes, or rather, asked for her permission, she went off on a walking holiday in Wales. She chose the remotest place she knew of. Every morning the children telephoned her before they went off to school, to encourage and support her, just as they had over Mother's Room. Every evening she telephoned them, spoke to each child in turn, and then to Matthew. Mrs. Parkes, given permission to telephone for instructions or advice, did so every day at lunchtime. When, as happened three times, Mrs. Rawlings was out on the mountainside, Mrs. Parkes asked that she should ring back at such and such a time, for she would not be happy in what she was doing without Mrs. Rawlings' blessing.

Susan prowled over wild country with the telephone wire holding her to her duty like a leash. The next time she must telephone, or wait to be telephoned, nailed her to her cross. The mountains themselves seemed trammeled by her unfreedom. Everywhere on the mountains, where she met no one at all, from breakfast time to dusk, excepting sheep, or a shepherd, she came face to face with her own craziness which might attack her in the broadest valleys, so that they seemed too small; or on a mountaintop from which she could see a hundred other mountains and valleys, so that they seemed too low, too small, with the sky pressing down too close. She would stand gazing at a hillside brilliant with ferns and bracken, jeweled with running water, and see nothing but her devil, who lifted inhuman eyes at her from where he leaned negligently on a rock, switching at his ugly yellow boots with a leafy twig.

She returned to her home and family, with the Welsh emptiness at the back of her mind like a promise of freedom.

She told her husband she wanted to have an *au pair* girl.

They were in their bedroom, it was late at night, the children slept. He sat, shirted and slippered, in a chair by the window, looking out. She sat brushing her hair and watching him in the mirror. A time-hallowed scene in the connubial bedroom. He said nothing, while she heard the arguments coming in to his mind, only to be rejected because every one was *reasonable*.

"It seems strange to get one now, after all, the children are in school most of the day. Surely the time for you to have help was when you were stuck with them day and night. Why don't you ask Mrs. Parkes to cook for you? She's even offered to—I can understand if you are tired of cooking for six people. But you know that an *au pair* girl means all kinds of problems, it's not like having an ordinary char in during the day. . . ."

Finally he said carefully: "Are you thinking of going back to work?"

"No," she said, "no, not really." She made herself sound vague, rather stupid. She went on brushing her black hair and peering at herself so as to be oblivious of the short uneasy glances her Matthew kept giving her. "Do you think we can't afford it?" she went on vaguely, not at all the old efficient Susan who knew exactly what they could afford.

"It's not that," he said, looking out of the window at dark trees, so as not to look at her. Meanwhile she examined a round, candid, pleasant face with clear dark brows and clear grey eyes. A sensible face. She brushed thick healthy black hair and thought: Yet that's the reflection of a madwoman. How very strange! Much more to the point if what looked back at me was the gingery green-eyed demon with his dry meager smile. . . . Why wasn't Matthew agreeing? After all, what else could he do? She was breaking her part of the bargain and there was no way of forcing her to keep it: that her spirit, her soul, should live in this house, so that the people in it could grow like plants in water, and Mrs. Parkes remain content in their service. In return for this, he would be a good loving husband, and responsible towards the children. Well, nothing like this had been true of either of them for a long time. He did his duty, perfunctorily; she did not even pretend to do hers. And he had become like other husbands, with his real life in his work and the people he met there, and very likely a serious affair. All this was her fault.

At last he drew heavy curtains, blotting out the trees, and turned to force her attention: "Susan, are you really sure we need a girl?" But she would not meet his appeal at all: She was running the brush over her hair again and again, lifting fine black clouds in a small hiss of electricity. She was peering in and smiling as if she were amused at the clinging hissing hair that followed the brush.

"Yes, I think it would be a good idea on the whole," she said, with the cunning of a madwoman evading the real point.

In the mirror she could see her Matthew lying on his back, his hands behind his head, staring upwards, his face sad and hard. She felt her heart (the old heart of Susan Rawlings) soften and call out to him. But she set it to be indifferent.

He said: "Susan, the children?" It was an appeal that *almost* reached her. He opened his arms, lifting them from where they had lain by his sides, palms up, empty. She had only to run across and fling herself into them, onto his hard, warm chest, and melt into herself, into Susan. But she could not. She would not see his lifted arms. She said vaguely: "Well, surely it'll be even better for them? We'll get a French or a German girl and they'll learn the language."

In the dark she lay beside him, feeling frozen, a stranger. She felt as if Susan had been spirited away. She disliked very much this woman who lay here, cold and indifferent beside a suffering man, but she could not change her.

Next morning she set about getting a girl, and very soon came Sophie Traub from Hamburg, a girl of twenty, laughing, healthy, blue-eyed, intending to learn English. Indeed, she already spoke a good deal. In return for a room—"Mother's Room"—and her food, she undertook to do some light cooking, and to be with the children when Mrs. Rawlings asked. She was an intelligent girl and understood perfectly what was needed. Susan said: "I go off sometimes, for the morning or for the day—well, sometimes the children run home from school, or they ring up, or a teacher rings up. I should be here, really. And there's the daily woman. . . ." And Sophie laughed her deep fruity *Fräulein's* laugh, showed her fine white teeth and her dimples, and said: "You want some person to play mistress of the house sometimes, not so?"

"Yes, that is just so," said Susan, a bit dry, despite herself, thinking in secret fear how easy it was, how much nearer to the end she was than she thought. Healthy Fräulein Traub's instant understanding of their position proved this to be true.

The *au pair* girl, because of her own common sense, or (as Susan said to herself with her new inward shudder) because she had been *chosen* so well by Susan, was a success with everyone, the children liking her, Mrs. Parkes forgetting almost at once that she was German, and Matthew finding her "nice to have around the house." For he was now taking things as they came, from the surface of life, withdrawn both as a husband and a father from the household.

One day Susan saw how Sophie and Mrs. Parkes were talking and laughing in the kitchen, and she announced that she would be away until teatime. She knew exactly where to go and what she must look for. She took the District Line to South Kensington, changed to the Circle, got off at Paddington, and walked around looking at the smaller hotels until she was satisfied with one which had FRED'S HOTEL painted on windowpanes that needed cleaning. The façade was a faded shiny yellow, like unhealthy skin. A door at the end of a passage said she must knock; she did, and Fred appeared. He was not at all attractive, not in any way, being fattish, and run-down, and wearing a tasteless striped suit. He had small sharp eyes in a white creased face, and was quite prepared to let Mrs. Jones (she chose the farcical name deliberately, staring him out) have a room three days a week from ten until six. Provided of course that she paid in advance each time she came? Susan produced fifteen shillings (no price had been set by him) and held it out, still fixing him with a bold unblinking challenge she had not known until then she could use at will. Looking at her still, he took up a ten-shilling note from her palm between thumb and forefinger, fingered it; then shuffled up two half crowns, held out his own palm with these bits of money displayed thereon, and let his gaze lower broodingly at them. They were standing in the passage, a red-shaded light above, bare boards beneath, and a strong smell of floor polish rising about them. He shot his gaze up at her over the still-extended palm, and smiled as if to say: What do you take me for? "I shan't," said Susan, "be using this room for the purposes of making money." He still waited. She added another five shillings, at which he nodded and said: "You pay, and I ask no questions." "Good," said Susan. He now went past her to the stairs, and there waited a moment: the light from the street door being in her eyes, she lost sight of him momentarily. Then she saw a sober-suited, white-faced, white-balding little man trotting up the stairs like a waiter, and she went after him. They proceeded in utter silence up the stairs of this house where no questions were asked—Fred's Hotel, which could afford the freedom for its visitors that poor Miss Townsend's hotel could not. The room was hideous. It had a single window, with thin green brocade curtains, a three-quarter bed that had a cheap green satin bedspread on it, a fireplace with a gas fire and a shillling meter by it, a chest of drawers, and a green wicker armchair.

"Thank you," said Susan, knowing that Fred (if this was Fred, and not George, or Herbert or Charlie) was looking at her, not so much with curiosity, an emotion he would not own to, for professional reasons, but with a philosophical sense of what was appropriate. Having taken her money and shown her up and agreed to everything, he was clearly disapproving of her for coming here. She did not belong here at all, so his look said. (But she knew, already, how very much she did belong: the room had been waiting for her to join it.) "Would you have me called at five o'clock, please?" and he nodded and went downstairs.

It was twelve in the morning. She was free. She sat in the armchair, she simply sat, she closed her eyes and sat and let herself be alone. She was alone and no one knew where she was. When a knock came on the door she was annoyed, and prepared to show it: but it was Fred himself, it was five o'clock and he was calling her as ordered. He flicked his sharp little eyes over the room—bed, first. It was undisturbed. She might never have been in the room at all. She thanked him, said she would be returning the day after tomorrow, and left. She was back home in time to cook supper, to put the children to bed, to cook a second supper for her husband and herself later. And to welcome Sophie back from the pictures where she had gone with a friend. All these things she did cheerfully, willingly. But she was thinking all the time of the hotel room, she was longing for it with her whole being.

Three times a week. She arrived promptly at ten, looked Fred in the eyes, gave him twenty shillings, followed him up the stairs, went into the room, and shut the door on him with gentle firmness. For Fred, disapproving of her being here at all, was quite ready to let friendship, or at least acquaintanceship, follow his disapproval, if only she would let him. But he was content to go off on her dismissing nod, with the twenty shillings in his hand.

She sat in the armchair and shut her eyes.

What did she *do* in the room? Why, nothing at all. From the chair, when it had rested her, she went to the window, stretching her arms, smiling, treasuring her anonymity, to look out. She was no longer Susan Rawlings, mother of four, wife of Matthew, employer of Mrs. Parkes and of Sophie Traub, with these and those relations with friends, schoolteachers, tradesmen. She no longer was mistress of the big white house and garden, owning clothes suitable for this and that activity or occasion. She was Mrs. Jones, and she was alone, and she had no past and no future. Here I am, she thought, after all these years of being married and having children and playing those roles of responsibility—and I'm just the same. Yet there have been times I thought that nothing existed of me except the roles that went with being Mrs. Matthew Rawlings. Yes, here I am, and if I never saw any of my family again, here I would still be . . . how very strange that is! And she leaned on the sill, and looked into the street, loving the men and women who passed, because she did not know them. She looked at the downtrodden buildings over the street, and at the sky, wet and dingy, or sometimes blue, and she felt she had never seen buildings or sky before. And then she went back to the chair, empty, her mind a blank. Sometimes she talked aloud, saying nothing—an exclamation, meaningless, followed by a comment about the floral pattern on the thin rug, or a stain on the green satin coverlet. For the most part, she wool-gathered—what word is there for it?—brooded, wandered, simply went dark, feeling emptiness run deliciously through her veins like the movement of her blood.

This room had become more her own than the house she lived in. One morning she found Fred taking her a flight higher than usual. She stopped, refusing to go up, and demanded her usual room, Number 19. "Well, you'll have to wait half an hour then." he said. Willingly she descended to the dark disinfectant-smelling hall, and sat waiting until the two, man and woman, came down the stairs, giving her swift indifferent glances before they hurried out into the street, separating at the door. She went up to the room, *her* room, which they had just vacated. It was no less hers, though the windows were set wide open, and a maid was straightening the bed as she came in.

After these days of solitude, it was both easy to play her part as mother and wife, and difficult—because it was so easy: she felt an imposter. She felt as if her shell moved here, with her family, answering to Mummy, Mother, Susan, Mrs. Rawlings. She was surprised no one saw through her, that she wasn't turned out of doors, as a fake. On the contrary, it seemed the children loved her more; Matthew and she "got on" pleasantly, and Mrs. Parkes was happy in her work under (for the most part, it must be confessed) Sophie Traub. At night she lay beside her husband, and they made love again, apparently just as they used to, when they were really married. But she, Susan, or the being who answered so readily and improbably to the name of Susan, was not there: she was in Fred's Hotel, in Paddington, waiting for the easing hours of solitude to begin.

Soon she made a new arrangement with Fred and with Sophie. It was for five days a week. As for the money, five pounds, she simply asked Matthew for it. She saw that she was not even frightened he might ask what for: he would give it to her, she knew that, and yet it was terrifying it could be so, for this close couple, these partners, had once known the destination of every shilling they must spend. He agreed to give her five pounds a week. She asked for just so much, not a penny more. He sounded indifferent about it. It was as if he were paying her, she thought: *paying her off*—yes, that was it. Terror came back for a moment, when she understood this, but she stilled it: things had gone too far for that. Now, every week, on Sunday nights, he gave her five pounds, turning away from her before their eyes could meet on the transaction. As for Sophie Traub, she was to be somewhere in or near the house until six at night, after which she was free. She was not to cook, or to clean, she was simply to be there. So she gardened or sewed, and asked friends in, being a person who was bound to have a lot of friends. If the children were sick, she nursed them. If teachers telephoned, she answered them sensibly. For the five daytimes in the school week, she was altogether the mistress of the house.

One night in the bedroom, Matthew asked: "Susan, I don't want to interfere—don't think that, please—but are you sure you are well?"

She was brushing her hair at the mirror. She made two more strokes on either side of her head, before she replied: "Yes, dear, I am sure I am well."

He was again lying on his back, his big blond head on his hands, his elbows angled up and part-concealing his face. He said: "Then Susan, I have to ask you this question, though you must understand, I'm not putting any sort of pressure on you." (Susan heard the word pressure with dismay, because this was inevitable, of course she could not go on like this.) "Are things going to go on like this?"

"Well," she said, going vague and bright and idiotic again, so as to escape: "Well, I don't see why not."

He was jerking his elbows up and down, in annoyance or in pain, and, looking at him, she saw he had got thin, even gaunt; and restless angry movements were not what she remembered of him. He said: "Do you want a divorce, is that it?"

At this, Susan only with the greatest difficulty stopped herself from laughing: she could hear the bright bubbling laughter she *would* have emitted, had she let herself. He could only mean one thing: she had a lover, and that was why she spent her days in London, as lost to him as if she had vanished to another continent.

Then the small panic set in again: she understood that he hoped she did have a lover, he was begging her to say so, because otherwise it would be too terrifying.

She thought this out, as she brushed her hair, watching the fine black stuff fly up to make its little clouds of electricity, hiss, hiss, hiss. Behind her head, across the room, was a blue wall. She realized she was absorbed in watching the black hair making shapes against the blue. She would be answering him. "Do *you* want a divorce, Matthew?"

He said: "That surely isn't the point, is it?"

"You brought it up, I didn't," she said, brightly, suppressing meaningless tinkling laughter.

Next day she asked Fred: "Have inquiries been made for me?"

He hesitated, and she said: "I've been coming here a year now. I've made no trouble, and you've been paid every day. I have a right to be told."

"As a matter of fact, Mrs. Jones, a man did come asking."

"A man from a detective agency?"

"Well, he could have been, couldn't he?"

"I was asking you . . . well, what did you tell him?"

"I told him a Mrs. Jones came every weekday from ten until five or six and stayed in Number Nineteen by herself."

"Describing me?"

"Well Mrs. Jones, I had no alternative. Put yourself in my place."

"By rights I should deduct what that man gave you for the information."

He raised shocked eyes: she was not the sort of person to make jokes like this! Then he chose to laugh: a pinkish wet slit appeared across his white crinkled face: his eyes positively begged her to laugh, otherwise he might lose some money. She remained grave, looking at him.

He stopped laughing and said: "You want to go up now?"—returning to the familiarity, the comradeship, of the country where no questions are asked, on which (and he knew it) she depended completely.

She went up to sit in her wicker chair. But it was not the same.

Her husband had searched her out. (The world had searched her out.) The pressures were on her. She was here with his connivance. He might walk in at any moment, here, into Room 19. She imagined the report from the detective agency: "A woman calling herself Mrs. Jones, fitting the description of your wife (etc., etc., etc.), stays alone all day in Room No. 19. She insists on this room, waits for it if it is engaged. As far as the proprietor knows, she receives no visitors there, male or female." A report something on these lines, Matthew must have received.

Well of course he was right: things couldn't go on like this. He had to put an end to it all simply by sending the detective after her.

She tried to shrink herself back into the shelter of the room, a snail perked out of its shell and trying to squirm back. But the peace of the room had gone. She was trying consciously to revive it, trying to let go into the dark creative trance (or whatever it was) that she had found there. It was no use, yet she craved for it, she was as ill as a suddenly deprived addict.

Several times she returned to the room, to look for herself there, but instead she found the unnamed spirit of restlessness, a prickling fevered hunger for movement, an irritable self-consciousness that made her brain feel as if it had colored lights going on and off inside it. Instead of the soft dark that had been the room's air, were now waiting for her demons that made her dash blindly about, muttering words of hate; she was impelling herself from point to point like a moth dashing itself against a windowpane, sliding to the bottom, fluttering off on broken wings, then crashing into the invisible barrier again. And again and again. Soon she was exhausted, and she told Fred that for a while she would not be needing the room, she was going on holiday. Home she went, to the big white house by the river. The middle of a weekday, and she felt guilty at returning to her own home when not expected. She stood unseen, looking in at the kitchen window. Mrs. Parkes, wearing a discarded floral overall of Susan's, was stooping to slide something into the oven. Sophie, arms folded, was leaning her back against a cupboard and laughing at some joke made by a girl not seen before by Susan—a dark foreign girl, Sophie's visitor. In an armchair Molly, one of the twins, lay curled, sucking her thumb and watching the grownups. She must have some sickness, to be kept from school. The child's listless face, the dark circles under her eyes, hurt Susan: Molly was looking at the three grownups working and talking in exactly the same way Susan looked at the four through the kitchen window: she was remote, shut off from them.

But then, just as Susan imagined herself going in, picking up the little girl, and sitting in an armchair with her, stroking her probably heated forehead, Sophie did just that: she had been standing on one leg, the other knee flexed, its foot set against the wall. Now she let her foot in its ribbon-tied red shoe slide down the wall, stood solid on two feet, clapping her hands before and behind her, and sang a couple of lines in German, so that the child lifted her heavy eyes at her and began to smile. Then she walked, or rather skipped, over to the child, swung her up, and let her fall into her lap at the same moment she sat herself. She said "Hopla! Hopla! Molly . . ." and began stroking the dark untidy young head that Molly laid on her shoulder for comfort.

Well. . . . Susan blinked the tears of farewell out of her eyes, and went quietly up the house to her bedroom. There she sat looking at the river through the trees. She felt at peace, but in a way that was new to her. She had no desire to move, to talk, to do anything at all. The devils that had haunted the house, the garden, were not there; but she knew it was because her soul was in Room 19 in Fred's Hotel; she was not really here at all. It was a sensation that should have been frightening: to sit at her own bedroom window, listening to Sophie's rich young voice sing German nursery songs to her child, listening to Mrs. Parkes clatter and move below, and to know that all this had nothing to do with her: she was already out of it.

Later, she made herself go down and say she was home: it was unfair to be here unannounced. She took lunch with Mrs. Parkes, Sophie, Sophie's Italian friend Maria, and her daughter Molly, and felt like a visitor.

A few days later, at bedtime, Matthew said: "Here's your five pounds," and pushed them over at her. Yet he must have known she had not been leaving the house at all.

She shook her head, gave it back to him, and said, in explanation, not in accusation: "As soon as you knew where I was, there was no point."

He nodded, not looking at her. He was turned away from her: thinking, she knew, how best to handle this wife who terrified him.

He said: "I wasn't trying to . . . it's just that I was worried."

"Yes, I know."

"I must confess that I was beginning to wonder . . ."

"You thought I had a lover?"

"Yes, I am afraid I did."

She knew that he wished she had. She sat wondering how to say: "For a year now I've been spending all my days in a very sordid hotel room. It's the place where I'm happy. In fact, without it I don't exist." She heard herself saying this, and understood how terrified he was that she might. So instead she said: "Well, perhaps you're not far wrong."

Probably Matthew would think the hotel proprietor lied: he would want to think so.

"Well," he said, and she could hear his voice spring up, so to speak, with relief: "in that case I must confess I've got a bit of an affair on myself."

She said, detached and interested: "Really? Who is she?" and saw Matthew's startled look because of this reaction.

"It's Phil. Phil Hunt."

She had known Phil Hunt well in the old unmarried days. She was thinking: No, she won't do, she's too neurotic and difficult. She's never been happy yet. Sophie's much better: Well Matthew will see that himself, as sensible as he is.

This line of thought went on in silence, while she said aloud: "It's no point telling you about mine, because you don't know him."

Quick, quick, invent, she thought. Remember how you invented all that nonsense for Miss Townsend.

She began slowly, careful not to contradict herself: "His name is Michael"—(*Michael What?*)—"Michael Plant." (What a silly name!) "He's rather like you—in looks, I mean." And indeed, she could imagine herself being touched by no one but Matthew himself. "He's a publisher." (Really? Why?) "He's got a wife already and two children."

She brought out this fantasy, proud of herself.

Matthew said: "Are you two thinking of marrying?"

She said, before she could stop herself: "Good God, *no!*"

She realized, if Matthew wanted to marry Phil Hunt, that this was too emphatic, but apparently it was all right, for his voice sounded relieved as he said: "It is a bit impossible to imagine one-self married to anyone else, isn't it?" With which he pulled her to him, so that her head lay on his shoulder. She turned her face into the dark of his flesh, and listened to the blood pounding through her ears saying: I am alone, I am alone, I am alone.

In the morning Susan lay in bed while he dressed.

He had been thinking things out in the night, because now he said: "Susan, why don't we make a foursome?"

Of course, she said to herself, of course he would be bound to say that. If one is sensible, if one is reasonable, if one never allows one-self a base thought or an envious emotion, naturally one says: Let's make a foursome!

"Why not?" she said.

"We could all meet for lunch. I mean, it's ridiculous, you sneak-ing off to filthy hotels, and me staying late at the office, and all the lies everyone has to tell."

What on earth did I say his name was?—she panicked, then said: "I think it's a good idea, but Michael is away at the moment. When he comes back though—and I'm sure you two would like each other."

"He's away, is he? So that's why you've been . . . ." Her husband put his hand to the knot of his tie in a gesture of male coquetry she would not before have associated with him; and he bent to kiss her cheek with the expression that goes with the words: Oh you naughty little puss! And she felt its answering look, naughty and coy, come onto her face.

Inside she was dissolving in horror at them both, at how far they had both sunk from honesty of emotion.

So now she was saddled with a lover, and he had a mistress! How ordinary, how reassuring, how jolly! And now they would make a foursome of it, and go about to theaters and restaurants. After all, the Rawlings could well afford that sort of thing, and presumably the publisher Michael Plant could afford to do himself and his mistress quite well. No, there was nothing to stop the four of them developing the most intricate relationship of civilized tolerance, all enveloped in a charming afterglow of autumnal passion. Perhaps they would all go off on holidays together? She had known people who did. Or perhaps Matthew would draw the line there? Why should he, though, if he was capable of talking about "foursomes" at all?

She lay in the empty bedroom, listening to the car drive off with Matthew in it, off to work. Then she heard the children clattering off to school to the accompaniment of Sophie's cheerfully ringing voice. She slid down into the hollow of the bed, for shelter against her own irrelevance. And she stretched out her hand to the hollow where her husband's body had lain, but found no comfort there: he was not her husband. She curled herself up in a small tight ball under the clothes: she could stay here all day, all week, indeed, all her life.

But in a few days she must produce Michael Plant, and—but how? She must presumably find some agreeable man prepared to impersonate a publisher called Michael Plant. And in return for which she would—what? Well, for one thing they would make love. The idea made her want to cry with sheer exhaustion. Oh no, she had finished with all that—the proof of it was that the words "make love," or even imagining it, trying hard to revive no more than the pleasures of sensuality, let alone affection, or love, made her want to run away and hide from the sheer effort of the thing. . . . Good Lord, why make love at all? Why make love with anyone? Or if you are going to make love, what does it matter who with? Why shouldn't she simply walk into the street, pick up a man and have a roaring sexual affair with him? Why not? Or even with Fred? What difference did it make?

But she had let herself in for it—an interminable stretch of time with a lover, called Michael, as part of a gallant civilized foursome. Well, she could not, and she would not.

She got up, dressed, went down to find Mrs. Parkes, and asked her for the loan of a pound, since Matthew, she said, had forgotten to leave her money. She exchanged with Mrs. Parkes variations on the theme that husbands are all the same, they don't think, and without saying a word to Sophie, whose voice could be heard upstairs from the telephone, walked to the underground, traveled to South Kensington, changed to the Inner Circle, got out at Paddington, and walked to Fred's Hotel. There she told Fred that she wasn't going on holiday after all, she needed the room. She would have to wait an hour, Fred said. She went to a busy tearroom-cum-restaurant around the corner, and sat watching the people flow in and out the door that kept swinging open and shut, watched them mingle and merge and separate, felt her being flow into them, into their movement. When the hour was up she left a half crown for her pot of tea, and left the place without looking back at it, just as she had left her house, the big, beautiful white house, without another look, but silently dedicating it to Sophie. She returned to Fred, received the key of No. 19, now free, and ascended the grimy stairs slowly, letting floor after floor fall away below her, keeping her eyes lifted, so that floor after floor descended jerkily to her level of vision, and fell away out of sight.

No. 19 was the same. She saw everything with an acute, narrow, checking glance: the cheap shine of the satin spread, which had been replaced carelessly after the two bodies had finished their convulsions under it; a trace of powder on the glass that topped the chest of drawers; an intense green shade in a fold of the curtain. She stood at the window, looking down, watching people pass and pass and pass until her mind went dark from the constant movement. Then she sat in the wicker chair, letting herself go slack. But she had to be careful, because she did not want, today, to be surprised by Fred's knock at five o'clock.

The demons were not here. They had gone forever, because she was buying her freedom from them. She was slipping already into the dark fructifying dream that seemed to caress her inwardly, like the movement of her blood . . . but she had to think about Matthew first. Should she write a letter for the coroner? But what should she say? She would like to leave him with the look on his face she had seen this morning—banal, admittedly, but at least confidently healthy. Well, that was impossible, one did not look like that with a wife dead from suicide. But how to leave him believing she was dying because of a man—because of the fascinating publisher Michael Plant? Oh, how ridiculous! How absurd! How humiliating! But she decided not to trouble about it, simply not to think about the living. If he wanted to believe she had a lover, he would believe it. And he *did* want to believe it. Even when he had found out that there was no publisher in London called Michael Plant, he would think: Oh poor Susan, she was afraid to give me his real name.

And what did it matter whether he married Phil Hunt or Sophie? Though it ought to be Sophie, who was already the mother of those children ... and what hypocrisy to sit here worrying about the children, when she was going to leave them because she had not got the energy to stay.

She had about four hours. She spent them delightfully, darkly, sweetly, letting herself slide gently, gently, to the edge of the river. Then, with hardly a break in her consciousness, she got up, pushed the thin rug against the door, made sure the windows were tight shut, put two shillings in the meter, and turned on the gas. For the first time since she had been in the room she lay on the hard bed that smelled stale, that smelled of sweat and sex.

She lay on her back on the green satin cover, but her legs were chilly. She got up, found a blanket folded in the bottom of the chest of drawers, and carefully covered her legs with it. She was quite content lying there, listening to the faint soft hiss of the gas that poured into the room, into her lungs, into her brain, as she drifted off into the dark river.

1963

HAROLD PINTER
(1930–)

Harold Pinter is in many ways the most challenging and original of the lively new playwrights who have emerged in Britain in the last 20 years. No one else has his special combination of realistic dialogue and subtly elusive meaning. He is a very private character, avoiding public appearances, declarations of intention and policy, and any hints of autobiography. His plays are aloof and self-contained works, often mysterious in the sense that it is impossible to extract a meaning or a message: the play is the play, not a dramatized argument.

Pinter was born in Hackney, East London, in 1930. He studied briefly at the Academy of Dramatic Art and from the age of 19 to the age of 27 acted in a repertory company. His first play (in one act), *The Room*, was written and produced in 1957 and was followed immediately by *The Dumb Waiter* and (his first real success) *The Birthday Party*. He has written for both the theater and television. *The Caretaker* won the *Evening Standard* Drama Award for 1960 and the Page 1 Award of the Newspaper Guild of New York. His later plays include *The Homecoming* (1965), *Landscape* (1968), and *Old Times* (1971). He has also written a number of screenplays based on novels by other writers: these include *The Servant, The Pumpkin Eater*, and *The Go-Between*, and a screenplay of Proust's *A la Recherche du Temps Perdu*, published in 1977. Pinter has also directed plays.

Pinter's kind of play has been called "comedy of menace," for while the wit, the lively inconsequence of the dialogue, and the sense of the irrationality of much human behavior make for comedy, there is always some sense of menace, of threat to the security of home (often a symbolic room—a refuge, a prison, a sign of selfhood, a trap, the world itself) and identity. The source of the threat appears to be external, but the suggestion seems to be that it may well come from within the characters themselves.

Pinter's earlier plays show the influence of the "theater of the absurd," especially of Samuel Beckett and the French playwright Eugène Ionesco, but his originality puts a highly individual stamp on all his work. He has a remarkable ear for the language and rhythms of ordinary spoken English and a haunting sense of the difficulties of human communication and the ways in which language can be used to evade as much as to reveal.

The Dumb Waiter

Scene: A basement room. Two beds, flat against the back wall. A serving hatch, closed, between the beds. A door to the kitchen and lavatory, left. A door to a passage, right.

BEN *is lying on a bed, left, reading a paper.* GUS *is sitting on a bed, right, tying his shoelaces, with difficulty. Both are dressed in shirts, trousers and braces.*
Silence.
GUS *ties his laces, rises, yawns and begins to walk slowly to the door, left. He stops, looks down, and shakes his foot.*
BEN *lowers his paper and watches him.* GUS *kneels and unties his shoelace and slowly takes off the shoe. He looks inside it and brings out a flattened matchbox. He shakes it and examines it. Their eyes meet.* BEN *rattles his paper and reads.* GUS *puts the matchbox in his pocket and bends down to put on his shoe. He ties his lace, with difficulty.* BEN *lowers his paper and watches him.* GUS *walks to the door, left, stops, and shakes the other foot. He kneels, unties his shoelace, and slowly takes off the shoe. He looks inside it and brings out a flattened cigarette packet. He shakes it and examines it. Their eyes meet.* BEN *rattles his paper and reads.* GUS *puts the packet in his pocket, bends down, puts on his shoe and ties the lace.*
He wanders off, left.
BEN *slams the paper down on the bed and glares after him. He picks up the paper and lies on his back, reading.*
Silence.
A lavatory chain is pulled twice off, left, but the lavatory does not flush.
Silence.
GUS *re-enters, left, and halts at the door, scratching his head.*
BEN *slams down the paper.*
BEN. Kaw!
　　[*He picks up the paper.*].
What about this? Listen to this!

[*He refers to the paper.*]
A man of eighty-seven wanted to cross the road. But there was a lot of traffic, see? He couldn't see how he was going to squeeze through. So he crawled under a lorry.[1]

GUS. He what?

BEN. He crawled under a lorry. A stationary lorry.

GUS. No?

BEN. The lorry started and ran over him.

GUS. Go on!

BEN. That's what it says here.

GUS. Get away.

BEN. It's enough to make you want to puke, isn't it?

GUS. Who advised him to do a thing like that?

BEN. A man of eighty-seven crawling under a lorry!

GUS. It's unbelievable.

BEN. It's down here in black and white.

GUS. Incredible.

> [*Silence.*]
> [GUS *shakes his head and exits.* BEN *lies back and reads.*]
> [*The lavatory chain is pulled once off left, but the lavatory does not flush.*]
> [BEN *whistles at an item in the paper.*]
> [GUS *re-enters.*]

I want to ask you something.

BEN. What are you doing out there?

GUS. Well, I was just—

BEN. What about the tea?

GUS. I'm just going to make it.

BEN. Well, go on, make it.

GUS. Yes, I will. [*He sits in a chair. Ruminatively.*] He's laid on some very nice crockery this time, I'll say that. It's sort of striped. There's a white stripe.

> [BEN *reads.*]

It's very nice. I'll say that.

> [BEN *turns the page.*]

You know, sort of round the cup. Round the rim. All the rest of it's black, you see. Then the saucer's black, except for right in the middle, where the cup goes, where it's white.

> [BEN *reads.*]

Then the plates are the same, you see. Only they've got a black stripe—the plates—right across the middle. Yes, I'm quite taken with the crockery.

BEN [*still reading.*] What do you want plates for? You're not going to eat.

GUS. I've brought a few biscuits.

BEN. Well, you'd better eat them quick.

GUS. I always bring a few biscuits. Or a pie. You know I can't drink tea without anything to eat.

BEN. Well, make the tea then, will you? Time's getting on.

---

1. Truck.

[GUS *brings out the flattened cigarette packet and examines it.*]

GUS. You got any cigarettes? I think I've run out.

[*He throws the packet high up and leans forward to catch it.*]

I hope it won't be a long job, this one.

[*Aiming carefully, he flips the packet under his bed.*]

Oh, I wanted to ask you something.

BEN [*slamming his paper down*]. Kaw!

GUS. What's that?

BEN. A child of eight killed a cat!

GUS. Get away.

BEN. It's a fact. What about that, eh? A child of eight killing a cat!

GUS. How did he do it?

BEN. It was a girl.

GUS. How did she do it?

BEN. She—

[*He picks up the paper and studies it.*]

It doesn't say.

GUS. Why not?

BEN. Wait a minute. It just says—Her brother, aged eleven, viewed the incident from the toolshed.

GUS. Go on!

BEN. That's bloody ridiculous.

[*Pause.*]

GUS. I bet he did it.

BEN. Who?

GUS. The brother.

BEN. I think you're right.

[*Pause.*]

[*Slamming down the paper.*] What about that, eh? A kid of eleven killing a cat and blaming it on his little sister of eight! It's enough to—

[*He breaks off in disgust and seizes the paper.* GUS *rises.*]

GUS. What time is he getting in touch?

[BEN *reads.*]

What time is he getting in touch?

BEN. What's the matter with you? It could be any time. Any time.

GUS [*moves to the foot of* BEN's *bed*]. Well, I was going to ask you something.

BEN. What?

GUS. Have you noticed the time that tank takes to fill?

BEN. What tank?

GUS. In the lavatory.

BEN. No. Does it?

GUS. Terrible.

BEN. Well, what about it?

GUS. What do you think's the matter with it?

BEN. Nothing.

GUS. Nothing?
BEN. It's got a deficient ballcock, that's all.
GUS. A deficient what?
BEN. Ballcock.
GUS. No? Really?
BEN. That's what I should say.
GUS. Go on! That didn't occur to me.

[GUS *wanders to his bed and presses the mattress.*]

I didn't have a very restful sleep today, did you? It's not much of a bed. I could have done with another blanket too. [*He catches sight of a picture on the wall.*] Hello, what's this? [*Peering at it.*] "The First Eleven."[2] Cricketers. You seen this, Ben?

BEN [*reading*]. What?
GUS. The first eleven.
BEN. What?
GUS. There's a photo here of the first eleven.
BEN. What first eleven?
GUS [*studying the photo*]. It doesn't say.
BEN. What about that tea?
GUS. They all look a bit old to me.

[GUS *wanders downstage, looks out front, then all about the room.*]

I wouldn't like to live in this dump. I wouldn't mind if you had a window, you could see what it looked like outside.

BEN. What do you want a window for?
GUS. Well, I like to have a bit of a view, Ben. It whiles away the time.

[*He walks about the room.*]

I mean, you come into a place when it's still dark, you come into a room you've never seen before, you sleep all day, you do your job, and then you go away in the night again.

[*Pause.*]

I like to get a look at the scenery. You never get the chance in this job.

BEN. You get your holidays, don't you?
GUS. Only a fortnight.
BEN [*lowering the paper*]. You kill me. Anyone would think you're working every day. How often do we do a job? Once a week? What are you complaining about?
GUS. Yes, but we've got to be on tap though, haven't we? You can't move out of the house in case a call comes.
BEN. You know what your trouble is?
GUS. What?
BEN. You haven't got any interests.
GUS. I've got interests.
BEN. What? Tell me one of your interests.

[*Pause.*]

GUS. I've got interests.

2. A school's top team of cricketers.

BEN. Look at me. What have I got?

GUS. I don't know. What?

BEN. I've got my woodwork. I've got my model boats. Have you ever seen me idle? I'm never idle. I know how to occupy my time, to its best advantage. Then when a call comes, I'm ready.

GUS. Don't you ever get a bit fed up?

BEN. Fed up? What with?

[*Silence.*]

[BEN *reads.* GUS *feels in the pocket of his jacket, which hangs on the bed.*]

GUS. You got any cigarettes? I've run out.

[*The lavatory flushes off left.*]

There she goes.

[GUS *sits on his bed.*]

No, I mean, I say the crockery's good. It is. It's very nice. But that's about all I can say for this place. It's worse than the last one. Remember that last place we were in? Last time, where was it? At least there was a wireless there. No, honest. He doesn't seem to bother much about our comfort these days.

BEN. When are you going to stop jabbering?

GUS. You'd get rheumatism in a place like this, if you stay long.

BEN. We're not staying long. Make the tea, will you? We'll be on the job in a minute.

[GUS *picks up a small bag by his bed and brings out a packet of tea. He examines it and looks up.*]

GUS. Eh, I've been meaning to ask you.

BEN. What the hell is it now?

GUS. Why did you stop the car this morning, in the middle of that road?

BEN [*lowering the paper*]. I thought you were asleep.

GUS. I was, but I woke up when you stopped. You did stop, didn't you?

[*Pause.*]

In the middle of that road. It was still dark, don't you remember? I looked out. It was all misty. I thought perhaps you wanted to kip,[3] but you were sitting up dead straight, like you were waiting for something.

BEN. I wasn't waiting for anything.

GUS. I must have fallen asleep again. What was all that about then? Why did you stop?

BEN [*picking up the paper*]. We were too early.

GUS. Early? [*He rises.*] What do you mean? We got the call, didn't we, saying we were to start right away. We did. We shoved out on the dot. So how could we be too early?

BEN [*quietly*]. Who took the call, me or you?

GUS. You.

BEN. We were too early.

GUS. Too early for what?

3. Nap.

[*Pause.*]

You mean someone had to get out before we got in?

[*He examines the bedclothes.*]

I thought these sheets didn't look too bright. I thought they ponged[4] a bit. I was too tired to notice when I got in this morning. Eh, that's taking a bit of a liberty, isn't it? I don't want to share my bed-sheets. I told you things were going down the drain. I mean, we've always had clean sheets laid on up till now. I've noticed it.

BEN. How do you know those sheets weren't clean?

GUS. What do you mean?

BEN. How do you know they weren't clean? You've spent the whole day in them, haven't you?

GUS. What, you mean it might be my pong? [*He sniffs sheets.*] Yes. [*He sits slowly on bed.*] It could be my pong, I suppose. It's difficult to tell. I don't really know what I pong like, that's the trouble.

BEN [*referring to the paper*]. Kaw!

GUS. Eh, Ben.

BEN. Kaw!

GUS. Ben.

BEN. What?

GUS. What town are we in? I've forgotten.

BEN. I've told you. Birmingham.

GUS. Go on!

[*He looks with interest about the room.*]

That's in the Midlands. The second biggest city in Great Britain. I'd never have guessed.

[*He snaps his fingers.*]

Eh, it's Friday today, isn't it? It'll be Saturday tomorrow.

BEN. What about it?

GUS [*excited*]. We could go and watch the Villa.[5]

BEN. They're playing away.

GUS. No, are they? Caarr! What a pity.

BEN. Anyway, there's no time. We've got to get straight back.

GUS. Well, we have done in the past, haven't we? Stayed over and watched a game, haven't we? For a bit of relaxation.

BEN. Things have tightened up, mate. They're tightened up.

[*GUS chuckles to himself.*]

GUS. I saw the Villa get beat in a cup tie once. Who was it against now? White shirts. It was one-all at half time. I'll never forget it. Their opponents won by a penalty. Talk about drama. Yes, it was a disputed penalty. Disputed. They got beat two–one, anyway, because of it. You were there yourself.

BEN. Not me.

GUS. Yes, you were there. Don't you remember that disputed penalty?

4. Smelled.
5. Aston Villa, popularly known simply as "the Villa," Birmingham's football team.

BEN. No.

GUS. He went down just inside the area. Then they said he was just acting. I didn't think the other bloke touched him myself. But the referee had the ball on the spot.

BEN. Didn't touch him! What are you talking about? He laid him out flat!

GUS. Not the Villa. The Villa don't play that sort of game.

BEN. Get out of it.

[*Pause.*]

GUS. Eh, that must have been here, in Birmingham.

BEN. What must?

GUS. The Villa. That must have been here.

BEN. They were playing away.

GUS. Because you know who the other team was? It was the Spurs. It was Tottenham Hotspur.[6]

BEN. Well, what about it?

GUS. We've never done a job in Tottenham.

BEN. How do you know?

GUS. I'd remember Tottenham.

[BEN *turns on his bed to look at him.*]

BEN. Don't make me laugh, will you?

[BEN *turns back and reads.* GUS *yawns and speaks through his yawn.*]

GUS. When's he going to get in touch?

[*Pause.*]

Yes, I'd like to see another football match. I've always been an ardent football fan. Here, what about coming to see the Spurs tomorrow?

BEN [*tonelessly*]. They're playing away.

GUS. Who are?

BEN. The Spurs.

GUS. Then they might be playing here.

BEN. Don't be silly.

GUS. If they're playing away they might be playing here. They might be playing the Villa.

BEN [*tonelessly*]. But the Villa are playing away.

[*Pause. An envelope slides under the door, right.* GUS *sees it. He stands, looking at it.*]

GUS. Ben.

BEN. Away. They're all playing away.

GUS. Ben, look here.

BEN. What?

GUS. Look.

[BEN *turns his head and sees the envelope. He stands.*]

BEN. What's that?

GUS. I don't know.

BEN. Where did it come from?

GUS. Under the door.

---

6. A football team; Tottenham is in north London.

BEN. Well, what is it?

GUS. I don't know.

[*They stare at it.*]

BEN. Pick it up.

GUS. What do you mean?

BEN. Pick it up!

[GUS *slowly moves towards it, bends and picks it up.*]

What is it?

GUS. An envelope.

BEN. Is there anything on it?

GUS. No.

BEN. Is it sealed?

GUS. Yes.

BEN. Open it.

GUS. What?

BEN. Open it!

[GUS *opens it and looks inside.*]

What's in it?

[GUS *empties twelve matches into his hand.*]

GUS. Matches.

BEN. Matches?

GUS. Yes.

BEN. Show it to me.

[GUS *passes the envelope.* BEN *examines it.*]

Nothing on it. Not a word.

GUS. That's funny, isn't it?

BEN. It came under the door?

GUS. Must have done.

BEN. Well, go on.

GUS. Go on where?

BEN. Open the door and see if you can catch anyone outside.

GUS. Who, me?

BEN. Go on!

[GUS *stares at him, puts the matches in his pocket, goes to his bed and brings a revolver from under the pillow. He goes to the door, opens it, looks out and shuts it.*]

GUS. No one.

[*He replaces the revolver.*]

BEN. What did you see?

GUS. Nothing.

BEN. They must have been pretty quick.

[GUS *takes the matches from pocket and looks at them.*]

GUS. Well, they'll come in handy.

BEN. Yes.

GUS. Won't they?

BEN. Yes, you're always running out, aren't you?

GUS. All the time.

BEN. Well, they'll come in handy then.

GUS. Yes.

BEN. Won't they?

GUS. Yes, I could do with them. I could do with them too.

BEN. You could, eh?

GUS. Yes.

BEN. Why?

GUS. We haven't any.

BEN. Well, you've got some now, haven't you?

GUS. I can light the kettle now.

BEN. Yes, you're always cadging matches. How many have you got there?

GUS. About a dozen.

BEN. Well, don't lose them. Red too. You don't even need a box.
   [GUS *probes his ear with a match.*]
   [*Slapping his hand*]. Don't waste them! Go on, go and light it.

GUS. Eh?

BEN. Go and light it.

GUS. Light what?

BEN. The kettle.

GUS. You mean the gas.

BEN. Who does?

GUS. You do.

BEN [*his eyes narrowing*]. What do you mean, I mean the gas?

GUS. Well, that's what you mean, don't you? The gas.

BEN [*powerfully*]. If I say go and light the kettle I mean go and light the kettle.

GUS. How can you light a kettle?

BEN. It's a figure of speech! Light the kettle. It's a figure of speech!

GUS. I've never heard it.

BEN. Light the kettle! It's common usage!

GUS. I think you've got it wrong.

BEN [*menacing*]. What do you mean?

GUS. They say put on the kettle.

BEN [*taut*]. Who says?
   [*They stare at each other, breathing hard.*]
   [*Deliberately.*] I have never in all my life heard anyone say put on the kettle.

GUS. I bet my mother used to say it.

BEN. Your mother? When did you last see your mother?

GUS. I don't know, about—

BEN. Well, what are you talking about your mother for?
   [*They stare.*]
   Gus, I'm not trying to be unreasonable. I'm just trying to point out something to you.

GUS. Yes, but—

BEN. Who's the senior partner here, me or you?

GUS. You.

BEN. I'm only looking after your interests, Gus. You've got to learn, mate.

GUS. Yes, but I've never heard—

BEN [*vehemently*]. Nobody says light the gas! What does the gas light?

GUS. What does the gas—?

BEN [*grabbing him with two hands by the throat, at arm's length*]. THE KETTLE, YOU FOOL!

     [GUS *takes the hands from his throat.*]

GUS. All right, all right.

     [*Pause.*]

BEN. Well, what are you waiting for?

GUS. I want to see if they light.

BEN. What?

GUS. The matches.

     [*He takes out the flattened box and tries to strike.*]

  No.

     [*He throws the box under the bed.*]

     [BEN *stares at him.*]

     [GUS *raises his foot.*]

  Shall I try it on here?

     [BEN *stares.* GUS *strikes a match on his shoe. It lights.*]

  Here we are.

BEN [*wearily*]. Put on the bloody kettle, for Christ's sake.

     [BEN *goes to his bed, but, realizing what he has said, stops and half turns. They look at each other.* GUS *slowly exits, left.* BEN *slams his paper down on the bed and sits on it, head in hands.*]

GUS [*entering*]. It's going.

BEN. What?

GUS. The stove.

     [GUS *goes to his bed and sits.*]

  I wonder who it'll be tonight.

     [*Silence.*]

  Eh, I've been wanting to ask you something.

BEN [*putting his legs on the bed*]. Oh, for Christ's sake.

GUS. No. I was going to ask you something.

     [*He rises and sits on* BEN's *bed.*]

BEN. What are you sitting on my bed for?

     [GUS *sits.*]

  What's the matter with you? You're always asking me questions. What's the matter with you?

GUS. Nothing.

BEN. You never used to ask me so many damn questions. What's come over you?

GUS. No, I was just wondering.

BEN. Stop wondering. You've got a job to do. Why don't you just do it and shut up?

GUS. That's what I was wondering about.

BEN. What?

GUS. The job.

BEN. What job?

GUS [*tentatively*]. I thought perhaps you might know something.

     [BEN *looks at him.*]

I thought perhaps you—I mean—have you got any idea—who it's going to be tonight?

BEN. Who what's going to be?

[*They look at each other.*]

GUS [*at length*]. Who it's going to be.

[*Silence.*]

BEN. Are you feeling all right?

GUS. Sure.

BEN. Go and make the tea.

GUS. Yes, sure.

[*GUS exits, left, BEN looks after him. He then takes his revolver from under the pillow and checks it for ammunition. GUS re-enters.*]

The gas has gone out.

BEN. Well, what about it?

GUS. There's a meter.

BEN. I haven't got any money.

GUS. Nor have I.

BEN. You'll have to wait.

GUS. What for?

BEN. For Wilson.

GUS. He might not come. He might just send a message. He doesn't always come.

BEN. Well, you'll have to do without it, won't you?

GUS. Blimey.

BEN. You'll have a cup of tea afterwards. What's the matter with you?

GUS. I like to have one before.

[*BEN holds the revolver up to the light and polishes it.*]

BEN. You'd better get ready anyway.

GUS. Well, I don't know, that's a bit much, you know, for my money.

[*He picks up a packet of tea from the bed and throws it into the bag.*]

I hope he's got a shilling, anyway, if he comes. He's entitled to have. After all, it's his place, he could have seen there was enough gas for a cup of tea.

BEN. What do you mean, it's his place?

GUS. Well, isn't it?

BEN. He's probably only rented it. It doesn't have to be his place.

GUS. I know it's his place. I bet the whole house is. He's not even laying on any gas now either.

[*GUS sits on his bed.*]

It's his place all right. Look at all the other places. You go to this address, there's a key there, there's a teapot, there's never a soul in sight—[*He pauses.*] Eh, nobody ever hears a thing, have you ever thought of that? We never get any complaints, do we, too much noise or anything like that? You never see a soul, do you? —except the bloke who comes. You ever noticed that? I wonder if the walls are soundproof. [*He touches the wall above his bed.*] Can't tell. All you do is wait, eh? Half the time he doesn't even bother to put in an appearance, Wilson.

BEN. Why should he? He's a busy man.

GUS [*thoughtfully*]. I find him hard to talk to, Wilson. Do you know that, Ben?

BEN. Scrub round it, will you?

> [*Pause.*]

GUS. There are a number of things I want to ask him. But I can never get round to it, when I see him.

> [*Pause.*]

I've been thinking about the last one.

BEN. What last one?

GUS. That girl.

> [BEN *grabs the paper, which he reads.*]
>
> [*Rising, looking down at* BEN.] How many times have you read that paper?
>
> [BEN *slams the paper down and rises.*]

BEN [*angrily*]. What do you mean?

GUS. I was just wondering how many times you'd—

BEN. What are you doing, criticizing me?

GUS. No, I was just—

BEN. You'll get a swipe round your earhole if you don't watch your step.

GUS. Now look here, Ben—

BEN. I'm not looking anywhere [*He addresses the room.*] How many times have I—! A bloody liberty!

GUS. I didn't mean that.

BEN. You just get on with it, mate. Get on with it, that's all.

> [BEN *gets back on the bed.*]

GUS. I was just thinking about that girl, that's all.

> [GUS *sits on his bed.*]

She wasn't much to look at, I know, but still. It was a mess though, wasn't it? What a mess. Honest, I can't remember a mess like that one. They don't seem to hold together like men, women. A looser texture, like. Didn't she spread, eh? She didn't half spread. Kaw! But I've been meaning to ask you.

> [BEN *sits up and clenches his eyes.*]

Who clears up after we've gone? I'm curious about that. Who does the clearing up? Maybe they don't clear up. Maybe they just leave them there, eh? What do you think? How many jobs have we done? Blimey, I can't count them. What if they never clear anything up after we've gone.

BEN [*pityingly*]. You mutt. Do you think we're the only branch of this organization? Have a bit of common. They got departments for everything.

GUS. What cleaners and all?

BEN. You birk!

GUS. No, it was that girl made me start to think—

> [*There is a loud clatter and racket in the bulge of wall between the beds, of something descending. They grab their*

revolvers, jump up and face the wall. The noise comes to a
stop. Silence. They look at each other. BEN *gestures sharply*
towards the wall. GUS *approaches the wall slowly. He bangs*
it with his revolver. It is hollow. BEN *moves to the head of*
his bed, his revolver cocked. GUS *puts his revolver on his bed*
and pats along the bottom of the center panel. He finds a
rim. He lifts the panel. Disclosed is a serving-hatch, a
"dumb waiter." A wide box is held by pulleys. GUS *peers*
into the box. He brings out a piece of paper.]

BEN. What is it?

GUS. You have a look at it.

BEN. Read it.

GUS [*reading*]. Two braised steak and chips. Two sago puddings.
Two teas without sugar.

BEN. Let me see that. [*He takes the paper.*]

GUS [*to himself*]. Two teas without sugar.

BEN. Mmnn.

GUS. What do you think of that?

BEN. Well—
[*The box goes up,* BEN *levels his revolver.*]

GUS. Give us a chance! They're in a hurry, aren't they?
[BEN *rereads the note.* GUS *looks over his shoulder.*]
That's a bit—that's a bit funny, isn't it?

BEN [*quickly*]. No. it's not funny. It probably used to be a café
here, that's all. Upstairs. These places change hands very quickly.

GUS. A café?

BEN. Yes.

GUS. What, do you mean this was the kitchen, down here?

BEN. Yes, they change hands overnight, these places. Go into liqui-
dation. The people who run it, you know, they don't find it a
going concern, they move out.

GUS. You mean the people who ran this place didn't find it a going
concern and moved out?

BEN. Sure.

GUS. WELL, WHO'S GOT IT NOW?
[*Silence.*]

BEN. What do you mean, who's got it now?

GUS. Who's got it now? If they moved out, who moved in?

BEN. Well, that all depends—
[*The box descends with a clatter and bang.* BEN *levels his*
revolver. GUS *goes to the box and brings out a piece of*
paper.]

GUS [*reading*]. Soup of the day. Liver and onions. Jam tart.
[*A pause.* GUS *looks at* BEN. BEN *takes the note and reads it.*
He walks slowly to the hatch. GUS *follows.* BEN *looks into*
the hatch but not up it. GUS *puts his hand on* BEN'S *shoul-*
der. BEN *throws if off.* GUS *puts his finger to his mouth. He*
leans on the hatch and swiftly looks up it. BEN *flings him*
away in alarm. BEN *looks at the note. He throws his revolver*
on the bed and speaks with decision.]

BEN. We'd better send something up.

GUS. Eh?

BEN. We'd better send something up.

GUS. Oh! Yes. Yes. Maybe you're right.

> [*They are both relieved at the decision.*]

BEN [*purposefully*]. Quick! What have you got in that bag?

GUS. Not much.

> [GUS *goes to the hatch and shouts up it.*]

Wait a minute!

BEN. Don't do that!

> [GUS *examines the contents of the bag and brings them out, one by one.*]

GUS. Biscuits. A bar of chocolate. Half a pint of milk.

BEN. That all?

GUS. Packet of tea.

BEN. Good.

GUS. We can't send the tea. That's all the tea we've got.

BEN. Well, there's no gas. You can't do anything with it, can you?

GUS. Maybe they can send us down a bob.[7]

BEN. What else is there?

GUS [*reaching into bag*]. One Eccles cake.

BEN. One Eccles cake?[8]

GUS. Yes.

BEN. You never told me you had an Eccles cake.

GUS. Didn't I?

BEN. Why only one? Didn't you bring one for me?

GUS. I didn't think you'd be keen.

BEN. Well, you can't send up one Eccles cake, anyway.

GUS. Why not?

BEN. Fetch one of those plates.

GUS. All right.

> [GUS *goes towards the door, left, and stops.*]

Do you mean I can keep the Eccles cake then?

BEN. Keep it?

GUS. Well, they don't know we've got it, do they?

BEN. That's not the point.

GUS. Can't I keep it?

BEN. No, you can't. Get the plate.

> [GUS *exits, left.* BEN *looks in the bag. He brings out a packet of crisps.[9] Enter* GUS *with a plate.*]

[*Accusingly, holding up the crisps.*] Where did these come from?

GUS. What?

BEN. Where did these crisps come from?

GUS. Where did you find them?

BEN [*hitting him on the shoulder*]. You're playing a dirty game, my lad!

GUS. I only eat those with beer!

---

7. I.e., a shilling (to insert in the gas meter).

8. A small cake originally made in the Lancashire town of Eccles.

9. Potato chips.

BEN. Well, where were you going to get the beer?

GUS. I was saving them till I did.

BEN. I'll remember this. Put everything on the plate.

[*They pile everything on to the plate. The box goes up without the plate.*]

Wait a minute!

[*They stand.*]

GUS. It's gone up.

BEN. It's all your stupid fault, playing about!

GUS. What do we do now?

BEN. We'll have to wait till it comes down.

[BEN *puts the plate on the bed, puts on his shoulder holster, and starts to put on his tie.*]

You'd better get ready.

[GUS *goes to his bed, puts on his tie, and starts to fix his holster.*]

GUS. Hey, Ben.

BEN. What?

GUS. What's going on here?

[*Pause.*]

BEN. What do you mean?

GUS. How can this be a café?

BEN. It used to be a café.

GUS. Have you seen the gas stove?

BEN. What about it?

GUS. It's only got three rings.

BEN. So what?

GUS. Well, you couldn't cook much on three rings, not for a busy place like this.

BEN [*irritably*]. That's why the service is slow!

[BEN *puts on his waistcoat.*]

GUS. Yes, but what happens when we're not here? What do they do then? All these menus coming down and nothing going up. It might have been going on like this for years.

[BEN *brushes his jacket.*]

What happens when we go?

[BEN *puts on his jacket.*]

They can't do much business.

[*The box descends. They turn about.* GUS *goes to the hatch and brings out a note.*]

GUS [*reading*]. Macaroni Pastitsio. Ormitha Macarounada.

BEN. What was that?

GUS. Macaroni Pastitsio. Ormitha Macarounada.

BEN. Greek dishes.

GUS. No.

BEN. That's right.

GUS. That's pretty high class.

BEN. Quick before it goes up.

[GUS *puts the plate in the box.*]

GUS [*calling up the hatch*]. Three McVitie and Price! One Lyons

Red Label! One Smith's Crisps![1] One Eccles cake! One Fruit and Nut!

BEN. Cadbury's.[2]

GUS [*up the hatch*]. Cadbury's!

BEN [*handing the milk*]. One bottle of milk.

GUS [*up the hatch*]. One bottle of milk! Half a pint! [*He looks at the label.*] Express Dairy! [*He puts the bottle in the box.*]

[*The box goes up.*]

Just did it.

BEN. You shouldn't shout like that.

GUS. Why not?

BEN. It isn't done.

[BEN *goes to his bed.*]

Well, that should be all right, anyway, for the time being.

GUS. You think so, eh?

BEN. Get dressed, will you? It'll be any minute now.

[GUS *puts on his waistcoat.* BEN *lies down and looks up at the ceiling.*]

GUS. This is some place. No tea and no biscuits.

BEN. Eating makes you lazy, mate. You're getting lazy, you know that? You don't want to get slack on your job.

GUS. Who me?

BEN. Slack, mate, slack.

GUS. Who me? Slack?

BEN. Have you checked your gun? You haven't even checked your gun. It looks disgraceful, anyway. Why don't you ever polish it?

[GUS *rubs his revolver on the sheet.* BEN *takes out a pocket mirror and straightens his tie.*]

GUS. I wonder where the cook is. They must have had a few, to cope with that. Maybe they had a few more gas stoves. Eh! Maybe there's another kitchen along the passage.

BEN. Of course there is! Do you know what it takes to make an Ormitha Macarounada?

GUS. No, what?

BEN. An Ormitha—! Buck your ideas up, will you?

GUS. Takes a few cooks, eh?

[GUS *puts his revolver in its holster.*]

The sooner we're out of this place the better.

[*He puts on his jacket.*]

Why doesn't he get in touch? I feel like I've been here years. [*He takes his revolver out of its holster to check the ammunition.*] We've never let him down though, have we? We've never let him down. I was thinking only the other day, Ben. We're reliable, aren't we?

[*He puts his revolver back in its holster.*]

Still, I'll be glad when it's over tonight.

[*He brushes his jacket.*]

I hope the bloke's not going to get excited tonight, or anything.

---

1. Brands, respectively, of cookies, tea, and potato chips.　　2. A brand of chocolate bar.

I'm feeling a bit off. I've got a splitting headache.

[*Silence.*]

[*The box descends.* BEN *jumps up.*]

[GUS *collects the note.*]

[*Reading.*] One Bamboo Shoots, Water Chestnuts, and Chicken. One Char Siu and Beansprouts.

BEN. Beansprouts?

GUS. Yes.

BEN. Blimey.

GUS. I wouldn't know where to begin.

[*He looks back at the box. The packet of tea is inside it. He picks it up.*]

They've sent back the tea.

BEN [*anxious*]. What'd they do that for?

GUS. Maybe it isn't teatime.

[*The box goes up. Silence.*]

BEN [*throwing the tea on the bed, and speaking urgently*]. Look here. We'd better tell them.

GUS. Tell them what?

BEN. That we can't do it, we haven't got it.

GUS. All right then.

BEN. Lend us your pencil. We'll write a note.

[GUS, *turning for a pencil, suddenly discovers the speaking tube, which hangs on the right wall of the hatch facing his bed.*]

GUS. What's this?

BEN. What?

GUS. This.

BEN [*examining it*]. This? It's a speaking tube.

GUS. How long has that been there?

BEN. Just the job. We should have used it before, instead of shouting up there.

GUS. Funny I never noticed it before.

BEN. Well, come on.

GUS. What do you do?

BEN. See that? That's a whistle.

GUS. What, this?

BEN. Yes, take it out. Pull it out.

[GUS *does so.*]

That's it.

GUS. What do we do now?

BEN. Blow into it.

GUS. Blow?

BEN. It whistles up there if you blow. Then they know you want to speak. Blow.

[GUS *blows. Silence.*]

GUS [*tube at mouth*]. I can't hear a thing.

BEN. Now you speak! Speak into it!

[GUS *looks at* BEN, *then speaks into the tube.*]

GUS. The larder's bare!

BEN. Give me that!

[*He grabs the tube and puts it to his mouth.*]

[*Speaking with great deference.*] Good evening. I'm sorry to
—bother you, but we just thought we'd better let you know that
we haven't got anything left. We sent up all we had. There's no
more food down here.

[*He brings the tube slowly to his ear.*]

What?

[*To mouth.*]

What?

[*To ear. He listens. To mouth.*]

No, all we had we sent up.

[*To ear. He listens. To mouth.*]

Oh, I'm very sorry to hear that.

[*To ear. He listens. To* GUS.]

The Eccles cake was stale.

[*He listens. To* GUS.]

The chocolate was melted.

[*He listens. To* GUS.]

The milk was sour.

GUS. What about the crisps?

BEN [*listening*]. The biscuits were moldy.

[*He glares at* GUS. *Tube to mouth.*]

Well, we're sorry about that.

[*Tube to ear.*]

What?

[*To mouth.*]

What?

[*To ear.*]

Yes. Yes.

[*To mouth.*]

Yes certainly. Right away.

[*To ear. The voice has ceased. He hangs up the tube.*]

[*Excitedly*]. Did you hear that?

GUS. What?

BEN. You know what he said? Light the kettle! Not put on the
kettle! Not light the gas! But light the kettle!

GUS. How can we light the kettle?

BEN. What do you mean?

GUS. There's no gas.

BEN [*clapping hand to head*]. Now what do we do?

GUS. What did he want us to light the kettle for?

BEN. For tea. He wanted a cup of tea.

GUS. *He* wanted a cup of tea! What about me? I've been wanting a
cup of tea all night!

BEN [*despairingly*]. What do we do now?

GUS. What are we supposed to drink?

[BEN *sits on his bed, staring.*]

What about us?

[BEN *sits.*]

I'm thirsty too. I'm starving. And he wants a cup of tea. That beats the band, that does.

[BEN *lets his head sink on to his chest.*]

I could do with a bit of sustenance myself. What about you? You look as if you could do with something too.

[GUS *sits on his bed.*]

We send him up all we've got and he's not satisfied. No, honest, it's enough to make the cat laugh. Why did you send him up all that stuff? [*Thoughtfully.*] Why did I sent it up?

[*Pause.*]

Who knows what he's got upstairs? He's probably got a salad bowl. They must have something up there. They won't get much from down here. You notice they didn't ask for any salads? They've probably got a salad bowl up there. Cold meat, radishes, cucumbers. Watercress. Roll mops.

[*Pause.*]

Hardboiled eggs.

[*Pause.*]

The lot. They've probably got a crate of beer too. Probably eating my crisps with a pint of beer now. Didn't have anything to say about those crisps, did he? They do all right, don't worry about that. You don't think they're just going to sit there and wait for stuff to come up from down here, do you? That'll get them nowhere.

[*Pause.*]

They do all right.

[*Pause.*]

And he wants a cup of tea.

[*Pause.*]

That's past a joke, in my opinion.

[*He looks over at* BEN, *rises, and goes to him.*]

What's the matter with you? You don't look too bright. I feel like an Alka-Seltzer myself.

[BEN *sits up.*]

BEN [*in a low voice*]. Time's getting on.

GUS. I know. I don't like doing a job on an empty stomach.

BEN [*wearily*]. Be quiet a minute. Let me give you your instructions.

GUS. What for? We always do it the same way, don't we?

BEN. Let me give you your instructions.

[GUS *sighs and sits next to* BEN *on the bed. The instructions are stated and repeated automatically.*]

When we get the call, you go over and stand behind the door.

GUS. Stand behind the door.

BEN. If there's a knock on the door you don't answer it.

GUS. If there's a knock on the door I don't answer it.

BEN. But there won't be a knock on the door.

GUS. So I won't answer it.

BEN. When the bloke comes in—

GUS. When the bloke comes in—

BEN. Shut the door behind him.

GUS. Shut the door behind him.

BEN. Without divulging your presence.

GUS. Without divulging my presence.

BEN. He'll see me and come towards me.

GUS. He'll see you and come towards you.

BEN. He won't see you.

GUS [*absently*]. Eh?

BEN. He won't see you.

GUS. He won't see me.

BEN. But he'll see me.

GUS. He'll see you.

BEN. He won't know you're there.

GUS. He won't know you're there.

BEN. He won't know *you're* there.

GUS. He won't know I'm there.

BEN. I take out my gun.

GUS. You take out your gun.

BEN. He stops in his tracks.

GUS. He stops in his tracks.

BEN. If he turns round—

GUS. If he turns round—

BEN. You're there.

GUS. I'm here.

[BEN *frowns and presses his forehead.*]

You've missed something out.

BEN. I know. What?

GUS. I haven't taken my gun out, according to you.

BEN. You take your gun out—

GUS. After I've closed the door.

BEN. After you've closed the door.

GUS. You've never missed that out before, you know that?

BEN. When he sees you behind him—

GUS. Me behind him—

BEN. And me in front of him—

GUS. And you in front of him—

BEN. He'll feel uncertain—

GUS. Uneasy.

BEN. He won't know what to do.

GUS. So what will he do?

BEN. He'll look at me and he'll look at you.

GUS. We won't say a word.

BEN. We'll look at him.

GUS. He won't say a word.

BEN. He'll look at us.

GUS. And we'll look at him.

BEN. Exactly.

[*Pause.*]

GUS. What do we do if it's a girl?

BEN. We do the same.

GUS. Exactly the same?
BEN. Exactly.
  [*Pause.*]
GUS. We don't do anything different?
BEN. We do exactly the same.
GUS. Oh.
  [GUS *rises, and shivers.*]
  Excuse me.
  [*He exits through the door on the left.* BEN *remains sitting on the bed, still.*]
  [*The lavatory chain is pulled once off left, but the lavatory does not flush.*]
  [*Silence.*]
  [GUS *re-enters and stops inside the door, deep in thought. He looks at* BEN, *then walks slowly across to his own bed. He is troubled. He stands, thinking. He turns and looks at* BEN. *He moves a few paces towards him.*]
[*Slowly in a low, tense voice.*] Why did he send us matches if he knew there was no gas?
  [*Silence.*]
  [BEN *stares in front of him.* GUS *crosses to the left side of* BEN, *to the foot of his bed, to get to his other ear.*]
  Ben. Why did he send us matches if he knew there was no gas?
  [BEN *looks up.*]
  Why did he do that?
BEN. Who?
GUS. Who sent us those matches?
BEN. What are you talking about?
  [GUS *stares down at him.*]
GUS [*thickly*]. Who is it upstairs?
BEN [*nervously*]. What's one thing to do with another?
GUS. Who is it, though?
BEN. What's one thing to do with another?
  [BEN *fumbles for his paper on the bed.*]
GUS. I asked you a question.
BEN. Enough!
GUS [*with growing agitation*]. I asked you before. Who moved in? I asked you. You said the people who had it before moved out. Well, who moved in?
BEN [*hunched*]. Shut up.
GUS. I told you, didn't I?
BEN [*standing*]. Shut up!
GUS [*feverishly*]. I told you before who owned this place, didn't I? I told you.
  [BEN *hits him viciously on the shoulder.*]
  I told you who ran this place, didn't I?
  [BEN *hits him viciously on the shoulder.*]
[*Violently.*] Well, what's he playing all these games for? That's what I want to know. What's he doing it for?
BEN. What games?

GUS [*passionately, advancing*]. What's he doing it for? We've been through our tests, haven't we? We got right through our tests, years ago, didn't we? We took them together, don't you remember, didn't we? We've proved ourselves before now, haven't we? We've always done our job. What's he doing all this for? What's the idea? What's he playing these games for?

> [*The box in the shaft comes down behind them. The noise is this time accompanied by a shrill whistle, as it falls.* GUS *rushes to the hatch and seizes the note.*]

[*Reading.*] Scampi!

> [*He crumples the note, picks up the tube, takes out the whistle, blows and speaks.*]

WE'VE GOT NOTHING LEFT! NOTHING! DO YOU UNDERSTAND?

> [BEN *seizes the tube and flings* GUS *away. He follows* GUS *and slaps him hard, back-handed, across the chest.*]

BEN. Stop it! You maniac!

GUS. But you heard!

BEN [*savagely*]. That's enough! I'm warning you!

> [*Silence.*]
> [BEN *hangs the tube. He goes to his bed and lies down. He picks up his paper and reads.*]
> [*Silence.*]
> [*The box goes up.*]
> [*They turn quickly, their eyes meet.* BEN *turns to his paper.*]
> [*Slowly* GUS *goes back to his bed, and sits.*]
> [*Silence.*]
> [*The hatch falls back into place.*]
> [*They turn quickly, their eyes meet.* BEN *turns back to his paper.*]
> [*Silence.*]
> [BEN *throws his paper down.*]

BEN. Kaw!

> [*He picks up the paper and looks at it.*]

Listen to this!

> [*Pause.*]

What about that, eh?

> [*Pause.*]

Kaw!

> [*Pause.*]

Have you ever heard such a thing?

GUS [*dully*]. Go on!

BEN. It's true.

GUS. Get away.

BEN. It's down here in black and white.

GUS [*very low*]. Is that a fact?

BEN. Can you imagine it.

GUS. It's unbelievable.

BEN. It's enough to make you want to puke, isn't it?

GUS [*almost inaudible*]. Incredible.

[BEN *shakes his head. He puts the paper down and rises. He fixes the revolver in his holster.*]

[GUS *stands up. He goes towards the door on the left.*]

BEN. Where are you going?

GUS. I'm going to have a glass of water.

[*He exits.* BEN *brushes dust off his clothes and shoes. The whistle in the speaking tube blows. He goes to it, takes the whistle out and puts the tube to his ear. He listens. He puts it to his mouth.*]

BEN. Yes.

[*To ear. He listens. To mouth.*]

Straight away. Right.

[*To ear. He listens. To mouth.*]

Sure we're ready.

[*To ear. He listens. To mouth.*]

Understood. Repeat. He has arrived and will be coming in straight away. The normal method to be employed. Understood.

[*To ear. He listens. To mouth.*]

Sure we're ready.

[*To ear. He listens. To mouth.*]

Right.

[*He hangs the tube up.*]

Gus!

[*He takes out a comb and combs his hair, adjusts his jacket to diminish the bulge of the revolver. The lavatory flushes off left.* BEN *goes quickly to the door, left.*]

Gus!

[*The door right opens sharply.* BEN *turns, his revolver leveled at the door.*]

[GUS *stumbles in.*]

[*He is stripped of his jacket, waistcoat, tie, holster, and revolver.*]

[*He stops, body stooping, his arms at his sides.*]

[*He raises his head and looks at* BEN.]

[*A long silence.*]

[*They stare at each other.*]

CURTAIN

1960

Poetry after Mid-Century

In sharp contrast to the literature of anti-culture and alienation represented by some of the most interesting English drama of the 1950's, there emerged about the same time less divided figures, of more modest dimensions, more clearly devoted to revivifying inherited artistic forms and the humanist tradition of Western cultural values. This group of young poets and critics has been known generically since the middle 1950's as "the Movement." These are not by any means the hardshelled traditionalists of the traditional Anglican-royalist-and-classical persuasion; they reject the rigidity of the T. S. Eliot formulations as earnestly as the near-nihilism of the extreme existentialists, and have tried to carve out a middle course of their own. Perhaps the most significant critical champion of the Movement is the poet, critic, and scholar Donald Davie, whose revealingly entitled book, *Purity of Diction in English Verse* (1952), sets out to demonstrate the eighteenth-century virtues of plainness, clarity, economy of metaphor, and urbanity of statement in which the Augustan poets excelled and the romantic poets were often deficient. His second critical work, *Articulate Energy: An Inquiry into the Syntax of English Poetry* (1955) urges the advantages of retaining prose syntax in poetry and concludes with a frontal attack on Northrop Frye's view as expressed in the following quotation: "Language in a human mind is not a list of words with their customary meanings attached, but a single interlocking structure, one's total power of expressing oneself. Literature is the objective counterpart of this, a total form of verbal expression which is re-created in miniature whenever a new poem is written." Not so, argues Davie:

> The appeal of theories such as Mr. Frye's is manifest in the loaded words that their promoters use, in recommending them. A poetry in which the syntax articulates only "the world of the poem" is said to be "pure," "absolute," "sheer," "self-sufficient." Wordsworth's poems are "impure" because they have about them the smell of soil and soiled flesh, the reek of humanity. Their syntax is not "pure" syntax because it refers to, it mimes, something outside itself and outside the world of its poem, something that smells of the human, of generation and hence of corruption. It is my case against the symbolist theorists that, in trying to remove the human smell from poetry, they are only doing harm. For poetry to be great, it must reek of the human as Wordsworth's poetry does. This is not a novel contention; but perhaps it is one of those things that cannot be said too often.

The miniature anthology of English poetry of the fifties, sixties, and seventies presented below begins with some examples of Movement poets and then presents work by poets who, in one direction or another, break out of the chastened humanism of the Movement. For new forces kept coming in during the sixties and seventies. British poetry today is more diverse than any critical schematization would suggest, ranging from various kinds of pop poetry associated with jazz and intended for performance at large gatherings —this is often a poetry containing much facile rhetoric and devices which strike the ear impressively but which fail to yield anything further to reading and reflection—to delicate, sophisticated verse in which the meaning is set off and enhanced by reticence. Between these two extremes are a great variety of poets with a great variety of talents. Since the end of the 1950's a new element of both rhetoric and myth (or at least legend) has been coming into English poetry. At the same time, there remains an important difference betwen some of the most interesting and significant recent English poetry and recent American poetry. The English poets do not risk everything in what M. L. Rosenthal has called a "bitter grappling with the gross, the anti-human, the inarticulable," but prefer to face modern experience in the light of coherent knowledge of how the world has grown to be what it is, and how the language they use can be accommodated to express modern experience without sacrificing lucidity to power or control to anguish.

The charge sometimes brought against modern English poetry is that it is too reticent, too genteel, and at the same time too fond of a "humane articulateness" (in Rosenthal's phrase). We can recognize in this charge some of the characteristics of the Movement poets. It is perhaps true that English poets of today have a greater sense of responsibility toward the language they use, a greater desire not to force on it meanings or emotions greater than it can semantically bear, than modern American poets. But they have their own strengths. The young English poet Alan Brownjohn, writing on English poetry in the 1970's, has stressed these strengths and pleaded for a proper awareness of them: "We move daily deeper into a complex and alarming kind of technical, late capitalist civilization where the surfaces get smoother and the realities ever more violent, irrational, and ruthless. One's first, instinctive response is to resort to the counter-irrationality of a counter-culture. But the only effective response, in the long term, will come from a rational, skeptical temperament which will calmly and wisely dismantle the machinery of horror and organize the commonwealth of decency."

Not all recent English poets would agree with this, but in general it can be said that they feel the importance of not losing control, of using their art to combat rather than to embody disorder. In the largest sense this is a classical position.

DONALD DAVIE
(1922–)

Donald Davie was born at Barnsley and attended St. Catherine's College, Cambridge. He has pursued an academic career and has held teaching posts at Trinity College, Dublin, Cambridge University, and the University of Essex before taking up his present position as professor of English at Stanford University. He is the most influential critic among the English poets of his generation, and although now living in America he participates frequently in critical debates going on in England.

For Doreen: A Voice from the Garden

We have a lawn of moss.
The next house is called The Beeches.

A towering squirrel-haunted
Trellis of trees, across
Our matt and trefoil, reaches   5
Shade where our guests have sauntered.

Cars snap by in the road.
In a famous photographed village
The High Street is our address.
Our guests write from abroad   10
Delighted to envisage
Rose-arbor and wilderness.

They get them, and the lilacs.
Some frenzy in us discards
Lilacs and all, and will harden,   15
However England stacks
Her dear discolored cards
Against us, us to her garden.

Anglophobia rises
In Brooklyn to hysteria   20
At some British verses.
British, one sympathizes.
Diesel-fumes cling to wistaria.
One conceives of worse reverses.

The sough of the power-brake   25
Makes every man an island;
But we are the island race.
We must be mad to take
Offense at our poisoned land
And the gardens that pock her face.   30
                                                    1963

Across the Bay

A queer thing about those waters: there are no
Birds there, or hardly any.
I did not miss them, I do not remember
Missing them, or thinking it uncanny.

The beach so-called was a blinding splinter of limestone,   5
A quarry outraged by hulls.
We took pleasure in that: the emptiness, the hardness
Of the light, the silence, and the water's stillness.

But this was the setting for one of our murderous scenes.
This hurt, and goes on hurting: 10
The venomous soft jelly, the undersides.
We could stand the world if it were hard all over.

                                                    1964

To Certain English Poets

My dears, don't I know? I esteem you more than you think,
    you modest and quietly spoken, you stubborn and unper-
      suaded.
    Your civil dislikes hum over a base that others
    shudder at, as at some infernal cold.
But pits full of smoky flame are sunk in the English
    Gehenna,[1]   5
    where suffering souls like ours are bound and planted
    now in the one hot spot, now in another.
The operator is an imagination of Dante[2]
    that plucks us out of the one and plugs us at once in
      another
    with an obedient pip-pip-pip at the switchboard.   10
Like you I look with astonished fear and revulsion
    at the gross and bearded, articulate and good-humored
    Franco-American torso, pinned across
    the plane of human action, twitching and roaring.[3]
Yet a restlessness less than divine comes over us, doesn't it,
    sometimes,   15
    to string our whole frames, ours also, in scintillant items,
    with an unabashed crackle of intercom and static?
Or will you, contained, still burn with that surly pluck?

                                              1968, 1972

To Helen Keller

Yours was the original freak-out: Samuel Beckett's
mutilated prodigies,[1] for whose
sake these last years we bought so many tickets
and read so many books, were hotter news
when your and Anne Sullivan Macy's[2] iron will,   5
back in the 'twenties, stooped to vaudeville.

One will, two persons . . . yes, let campus rebels
account for education at that level,

1. Originally, a valley near Jerusalem, where children were sacrificed to Moloch; hence, Hell.
2. A reference to Dante's vision of Hell in his *Inferno*.
3. Davie is thinking of writers of action and violence, such as Ernest Hemingway in Paris in the 1920's, more recent American poets of unconventional action (e.g. Allen Ginsberg), and French student activists like Danny Le Rouge. The poem was written during the period of recent student "revolt" and partly expresses Davie's embarrassment at and distaste for the violent scenes that occurred (with the approval of some writers in both France and America) in his own University of Essex.
1. A not inaccurate description of the protagonists in the stories and plays of the Irish-born Samuel Beckett (1906); see *The End*, above. His work was especially popular among the intelligentsia in the 1950's and 60's.
2. The dedicated teacher of the deaf and blind Helen Keller.

that give, that take. I wonder if it troubles
our modish masters of sardonic revel   10
that you, who seemed typecast for it, were not
conscious of Black Comedy[3] in the plot.

You were by force of circumstance, by force
of your afflictions, I suppose, the most
literary person ever was.   15
No sight nor sound for you was more than a ghost;
and yet because you called each phantom's name,
tame to your paddock chords and colors came.

This too, at this, the mind of our time is appalled.
The Gutenberg era, the era of rhyme, is over.   20
It's an end to the word-smith now, an end to the Skald,[4]
an end to the erudite, elated rover
threading a fiord of words. Four-letter expletives
are all of that ocean's plankton that still lives.

You, who had not foreseen it, you endured it: 25
a life that is stripped, stripped down to the naked,
asking what ground it has, what has ensured it.
Your answer was: the language, for whose sake it
seemed worthwhile in Tuscumbia, Alabama,[5]
month after month to grope and croak and stammer.   30

1968, 1972

3. Term used (loosely) to describe the cynically perverse comedies of various writers in the 60's, such as (in Britain) Joe Orton, Tom Stoppard, and Harold Pinter (see above), or (in America) Terry Southern (*M*A*S*H*). 4. Poetic historian or reciter of poetic histories (Scandinavian): hence, poet. The "Gutenberg era" is the age of the printed book (the 15th-century German Johannes Gutenberg is considered to have invented printing in Europe). 5. Birthplace of Helen Keller, where she spent her early years.

PHILIP LARKIN

(1922–)

Philip Larkin was born in Coventry and studied at Oxford, after which he worked as a university librarian in a number of universities; he is now librarian of the University of Hull. He is perhaps the most quietly English of all the Movement poets. He has edited the controversial *Oxford Book of Twentieth-Century English Verse* (1973).

Lines on a Young Lady's Photograph Album

At last you yielded up the album, which,
Once open, sent me distracted. All your ages
Matt and glossy on the thick black pages!

Too much confectionery, too rich:
I choke on such nutritious images.   5

My swivel eye hungers from pose to pose—
In pigtails, clutching a reluctant cat;
Or furred yourself, a sweet girl-graduate;
Or lifting a heavy-headed rose
Beneath a trellis, or in a trilby hat   10

(Faintly disturbing, that, in several ways)—
From every side you strike at my control,
Not least through these disquieting chaps who loll
At ease about your earlier days:
Not quite your class, I'd say, dear, on the whole.   15

But O, photography! as no art is,
Faithful and disappointing! that records
Dull days as dull, and hold-it smiles as frauds,
And will not censor blemishes
Like washing-lines, and Hall's-Distemper boards,   20

But shows the cat as disinclined, and shades
A chin as doubled when it is, what grace
Your candor thus confers upon her face!
How overwhelmingly persuades
That this is a real girl in a real place,   25

In every sense empirically true!
Or is it just *the past?* Those flowers, that gate,
These misty parks and motors, lacerate
Simply by being over; you
Contract my heart by looking out of date.   30

Yes, true; but in the end, surely, we cry
Not only at exclusion, but because
It leaves us free to cry. We know *what was*
Won't call on us to justify
Our grief, however hard we yowl across   35

The gap from eye to page. So I am left
To mourn (without a chance of consequence)
You, balanced on a bike against a fence;
To wonder if you'd spot the theft
Of this one of you bathing; to condense,   40

In short, a past that no one now can share,
No matter whose your future; calm and dry,
It holds you like a heaven, and you lie

Unvariably lovely there,
Smaller and clearer as the years go by.   45

1956

Faith Healing

Slowly the women file to where he stands
Upright in rimless glasses, silver hair,
Dark suit, white collar. Stewards tirelessly
Persuade them onwards to his voice and hands,
Within whose warm spring rain of loving care   5
Each dwells some twenty seconds. *Now, dear child,*
What's wrong, the deep American voice demands,
And, scarcely pausing, goes into a prayer
Directing God about this eye, that knee.
Their heads are clasped abruptly; then, exiled   10

Like losing thoughts, they go in silence; some
Sheepishly stray, not back into their lives
Just yet; but some stay stiff, twitching and loud
With deep hoarse tears, as if a kind of dumb
And idiot child within them still survives   15
To reawake at kindness, thinking a voice
At last calls them alone, that hands have come
To lift and lighten; and such joy arrives
Their thick tongues blort, their eyes squeeze grief, a crowd
Of huge unheard answers jam and rejoice—   20

What's wrong! Moustached in flowered frocks they shake:
By now, all's wrong. In everyone there sleeps
A sense of life lived according to love.
To some it means the difference they could make
By loving others, but across most it sweeps   25
As all they might have done had they been loved.
That nothing cures. An immense slackening ache,
As when, thawing, the rigid landscape weeps,
Spreads slowly through them—that, and the voice above
Saying *Dear child,* and all time has disproved.   30

1964

Ambulances

Closed like confessionals, they thread
Loud noons of cities, giving back
None of the glances they absorb.
Light glossy gray, arms on a plaque,
They come to rest at any curb: 5
All streets in time are visited.

Then children strewn on steps or road,
Or women coming from the shops
Past smells of different dinners, see
A wild white face that overtops   10
Red stretcher-blankets momently
As it is carried in and stowed,

And sense the solving emptiness
That lies just under all we do,
And for a second get it whole,   15
So permanent and blank and true.
The fastened doors recede. *Poor soul,*
They whisper at their own distress;

For borne away in deadened air
May go the sudden shut of loss   20
Round something nearly at an end,
And what cohered in it across
The years, the unique random blend
Of families and fashions, there

At last begin to loosen. Far   25
From the exchange of love to lie
Unreachable inside a room
The traffic parts to let go by
Brings closer what is left to come,
And dulls to distance all we are.   30

                                              1964

High Windows

When I see a couple of kids
And guess he's fucking her and she's
Taking pills or wearing a diaphragm,
I know this is paradise

Everyone old has dreamed of all their lives—   5
Bonds and gestures pushed to one side
Like an outdated combine harvester,
And everyone young going down the long slide

To happiness, endlessly. I wonder if
Anyone looked at me, forty years back,   10
And thought, *That'll be the life;*
No God any more, or sweating in the dark

About hell and that, or having to hide
What you think of the priest. He

And his lot will all go down the long slide   15
Like free bloody birds. And immediately

Rather than words comes the thought of high windows:
The sun-comprehending glass,
And beyond it, the deep blue air, that shows
Nothing, and is nowhere, and is endless.   20

                                                  1974

Sad Steps

Groping back to bed after a piss
I part thick curtains, and am startled by
The rapid clouds, the moon's cleanliness.

Four o'clock: wedge-shadowed gardens lie
Under a cavernous, a wind-picked sky.   5
There's something laughable about this,

The way the moon dashes through clouds that blow
Loosely as cannon-smoke to stand apart
(Stone-colored light sharpening the roofs below)

High and preposterous and separate—   10
Lozenge[1] of love! Medallion of art!
O wolves of memory! Immensements! No,

One shivers slightly, looking up there.
The hardness and the brightness and the plain
Far-reaching singleness of that wide stare   15

Is a reminder of the strength and pain
Of being young; that it can't come again,
But is for others undiminished somewhere.

                                                  1974

1. Diamond-shaped pattern.

MOLLY HOLDEN
(1927–)

Molly Holden was born in London and educated at Commonweal Grammar School, Swindon. She married Alan Holden in 1949. She was crippled
in 1946 by multiple sclerosis, and has been paralyzed ever since. She lives in
Bromsgrove, Worcestershire, in the west of England. She writes about trees,
flowers, country scenes remembered or glimpsed from a car, country people,
love, childbirth, illness. But her work is not in the Georgian tradition of
rural poetry that these subjects may suggest. The perceptiveness and lucid-

ity with which she records her observations of country life derive from an essential toughness and are reminiscent sometimes of Thomas Hardy (whose poetry certainly influenced her), sometimes of the later Edward Thomas, and sometimes of Robert Frost. The tone is both familiar and formal, the language at times something like that of casually spoken observations yet always controlled and shaped. Holden has also written four novels.

Photograph of Haymaker, 1890

It is not so much the image of the man
that's moving—he pausing from his work
to whet his scythe, trousers tied
below the knee, white shirt lit by
another summer's sun, another century's—   5
as the sight of the grasses beyond
his last laid swathe, so living yet
upon the moment previous to death;
for as the man stooping straightened up
and bent again they died before his blade.   10

Sweet hay and gone some seventy years ago
and yet they stand before me in the sun,
stems damp still where their neighbors' fall
uncovered them, succulent and straight,
immediate with moon-daisies.   15

1960

Some Men Create

Some men create an unintended
    beauty by default,
never cut back the creeping ivy
    so its stragglers vault

from crumbling wall to neighboring bridge   5
    beside the arched lane.
to swing like hair from the parapet,
    shining with spring rain;

never gravel out the timber pile
    nor lop the dead oak   10
so that the seeding traveler's joy
    smothers them like smoke.

So among orderly husbandry
    leave some plots alone
that the eye may reap with pleasure what   15
    the hand has not sown.

1960

Seaman, 1941

This was not to be expected.

Waves, wind, and tide brought him again
to Barra.[1] Clinging to driftwood many hours
the night before, he had not recognized
the current far offshore his own nor   5
known he drifted home. He gave up, anyway,
some time before the smell of land reached out
or dawn outlined the morning gulls.

                        They found him
on the white sand southward of the ness,[2]   10
not long enough in the sea to be
disfigured, cheek sideways as in sleep;
old men who had fished with his father
and grandfather knew him at once,
before they even turned him on his back, by the set   15
of the dead shoulders, and were shocked.

This was not to be expected.

His mother, with hot eyes, preparing the parlor
for his corpse, would have preferred, she thought,
to have been told by telegram rather   20
than so to know that convoy, ship, and son
had only been a hundred miles northwest
of home when the torpedoes struck.
She could have gone on thinking that
he'd had no chance; but to die offshore,   25
in Hebridean tides, as if he'd stayed
a fisherman for life and never gone to war
was not to be expected.

                            1971

My Debt to Farmers

I prate of trees and meadows but am
no countrywoman. I have nothing
in common with farmers save perhaps
a liking for plenty of room and a knowledge
of seasons as they turn the farming year.   5
I am hardly even envious as I see them
stand and talk in atmospheric yards.
Some I hate, those who deny
sun to their hens, space to their hedges,

1. A small island in the Hebrides (cf.   2. Promontory.
line 26) off Scotland's west coast.

full life to life; and even those whose men   10
and boys on bikes and burr-eared dogs
still drive their cattle comfortably on
golden evenings on warm roads, for whom
we stop and wait delightedly, would not
care for my appreciation of their beasts'   15
taking their time to milking, their
uninhibited bowels, their melancholy.

But I am more than grateful to farmers.
The raw material of their livelihood
is also mine, valuable for different   20
and various reasons—fine grass, for hay,
the soil-conserving trees, the field of wheat
ripe-full as any harbor with the tide—profit
for them and properties for me. Even more
I like, though, what they curse, the places where   25
men's organization has not quite succeeded
or even been defied, where the nettled wild
creeps back at the corner of a barn
or lichens viridify the gatepost's ridge.

So what's marginal land to them, rank corners,   30
unwelcome poppies, is for me the haunt
of a sharp-scented spirit which persists
in such tall edges of fields, in standing pools
among alders, and which provides me with
the solid food of a curious poetry.   35

1971

Upstairs Light

That particular light begins about halfway
upstairs—a brighter daylight than in kitchen,
hall, or living room, less overshadowed and reduced
by neighbors' walls or lilacs given their heads.
It sparkles. It floods the upper stairwell,   5
the austere landing, bleaches the bedspreads,
slides along walls, glares from the bathroom tiles.
I, at ground level now, remember it longingly.[3]

Philosophically speaking, of course, it still exists
although, because I do not see it now, it seems   10
a thing of the past; I used to see, from upstairs windows,
the crystal bases of clouds, the sunset, the lupins
next-door-but-two, the winter stars. It lit

3. Confined to a wheelchair since her paralysis, Molly Holden has long been
unable to go upstairs.

the morning ritual of making beds, or making up.
It spiced afternoon lovemaking. It illumined   15
the heads of children asleep.

        It was a brighter world, upstairs.

                                    1971

The Double Nature of White

White orchards are the earliest, stunning
the spirit resigned to winter's black; white thorn
sprays first the bare wet branches of the hedge.
We should purely delight. Yet, when one
who gazes on this brilliance turns to look   5
into a companion's eyes, who gazes on the same,
he sees an evil look, as if of cataract.
This is but reflection of the whitely-gorgeous blossom
but is uncomfortable, seems a malignity.

What's in white that's so ambiguous? for   10
the symbol of virginity is, too, unnatural
—like the albino animal, the parasitic plant,
the ghost. And bridal finery is gladly cast aside
for the colors of consummation.

Ah, after these white orchards, bright   15
and cold as youth and as swiftly shed,
will come through these same crooked lanes
(though differently positioned in the hedge
and on the verge) the green of tiny leaf, apples'
tender pink—carnation of bud and coral   20
of fuller flower—and then the creaminess
of pear, may,[4] hemlock, crown, of meadowsweet;
and we'll forget this leprous dawn.

Not until next year's spring will
the ambiguity of white so trouble us again   25
and then—again—only momentarily.

                                    1975

T. H.[5]

He hardly ever looked directly at
the camera or the painters of his portraits,
though twice he nearly gave himself away.
Once, when old, in a Dorset lane, caught

---

4. Hawthorn.   5. Thomas Hardy.

off his guard perhaps, or proud   5
of the bicycle he held and forgetting
his reticence, he seems to be looking along
the hedge straight at the distant friend
with the camera; and once, again perhaps
betrayed by friendship, he looks up   10
—young, handsome, hair soft, waved back,
moustache most neatly trimmed—easily, as if
a friend had called: "Come on, Tom! give us a snap!"
(Though it may have been a studio set,
arm along the back of the chair, white gloves,   15
book neatly open on his knee.) In either case,
he remains elusive, giving nothing away,
body turned sideways, looking over his shoulder,
upwards certainly but sidelong, his glance
sliding past the lens and even going beyond   20
the shoulder of the photographer.

He looked down as he walked, too, friends said,
noting the patterns of frost on the road;
but we know from his work that he never missed
the beauty of a passing girl or the glint   25
of sunlight on distant farm machinery.

His look is always the look of the proud
and reticent peasant, of the men who kept
themselves to themselves, whose masters
must not know too much about their men   30
—even though it be no more than a small superstition,
a family phrase, probably not even, at worst,
a bastardy. I doubt he had much to hide;
it was just in his nature to be secretive,
to remain lifelong the close boy from Bockhampton.   35
Certainly, before he died, he destroyed much
in bonfires on the lawns but probably
nothing as vital as we would like to think.
Men have always enjoyed bonfires.

Since I perceived this indirectness in him, though,   40
the younger portrait reminds me of a young
dog fox I met one morning slipping along
a hedgerow (he out late, I early). I remember
he glanced at me in just that way, independent
and unabashed, the handsome sidelong look   45
that went round and about but never directly
met my eyes, for that would betray his soul.
He was not being sly, only careful. That quick look
told him all he wanted—my kind, the direction
in which I traveled, even my intention. It was enough.   50
He was discreet; he had his own business

to be about, and a rich life several fields away.
He knew more of the land we walked than I ever would
—the slightest shadowing of slope in a field that
could camouflage a traveler, the brooks to be crossed   55
and used to break a scent. I presented no danger.

I see now how much alike these Wessex creatures,
fox and man, in their wariness were; for the latter also,
despite his downcast eyes, saw everything he needed
about his fellow-men and the world, marking it all   60
upon the full-mapped country of his mind and memory.

                                                              1975

THOM GUNN

(1929–)

Son of a London journalist, Thom Gunn was educated at University College School, London and at Trinity College, Cambridge. His poems show that insistence on exactness of image and movement can produce something more than agreeable verse craftsmanship. Reminiscent sometimes of Graves, sometimes of Muir, sometimes of the American poet Yvor Winters (with whom Gunn studied in California), Gunn's poems have a special kind of modest and honest individuality which makes them, if not continually exciting, at least always engaging. His long stay in America has turned him into what one critic has called "a mid-Atlantic or Anglo-American poet," and he is one of the few English poets who has on occasion adopted the method of composition by syllable count (rather than stress patterns) which has been so significant in modern American poetry.

Considering the Snail

The snail pushes through a green
night, for the grass is heavy
with water and meets over
the bright path he makes, where rain
has darkened the earth's dark. He   5
moves in a wood of desire,

pale antlers barely stirring
as he hunts. I cannot tell
what power is at work, drenched there
with purpose, knowing nothing.   10
What is a snail's fury? All
I think is that if later

I parted the blades above
the tunnel and saw the thin
trail of broken white across   15
litter, I would never have
imagined the slow passion
to that deliberate progress.

                                                1956

Human Condition

Now it is fog, I walk
Contained within my coat;
No castle more cut off
By reason of its moat:
Only the sentry's cough,   5
The mercenaries' talk.

The street lamps, visible,
Drop no light on the ground,
But press beams painfully
In a yard of fog around.   10
I am condemned to be
An individual.

In the established border
There balances a mere
Pinpoint of consciousness.   15
I stay, or start from, here:
No fog makes more or less
The neighboring disorder.

Particular, I must
Find out the limitation
Of mind and universe,   20
To pick thought and sensation
And turn to my own use
Disordered hate or lust.

I seek, to break, my span.   25
I am my one touchstone.
This is a test more hard
Than any ever known.
And thus I keep my guard
On that which makes me man.   30

Much is unknowable.
No problem shall be faced
Until the problem is;
I, born to fog, to waste,
Walk through hypothesis,   35
An individual.

                                                1957

Moly[1]

Nightmare of beasthood, snorting, how to wake.
I woke. What beasthood skin she made me take?

Leathery toad that ruts for days on end,
Or cringing dribbling dog, man's servile friend,

Or cat that prettily pounces on its meat,   5
Tortures it hours, then does not care to eat:

Parrot, moth, shark, wolf, crocodile, ass, flea.
What germs, what jostling mobs there were in me.

These seem like bristles, and the hide is tough.
No claw or web here: each foot ends in hoof.   10

Into what bulk has method disappeared?
Like ham, streaked. I am gross—gray, gross, flap-eared.

The pale-lashed eyes my only human feature.
My teeth tear, tear. I am the snouted creature

That bites through anything, root, wire, or can.   15
If I was not afraid I'd eat a man.

Oh a man's flesh already is in mine.
Hand and foot poised for risk. Buried in swine.

I root and root, you think that it is greed,
It is, but I seek out a plant I need.   20

Direct me gods, whose changes are all holy,
To where it flickers deep in grass, the moly:

Cool flesh of magic in each leaf and shoot,
From milk flower to the black forked root.

From this fat dungeon I could rise to skin   25
And human title, putting pig within.

I push my big gray wet snout through the green,
Dreaming the flower I have never seen.

1971

1. A magic herb of Greek mythology. The enchantress Circe transformed Odysseus' shipmates into swine; Odysseus, protected by the herb moly which he had been given by the gods' messenger Hermes, compelled her to restore them to human shape.

Hampstead: The Horse Chestnut Trees

At the top of a low hill
two stand together, green
bobbings contained within
the general sway. They
must be about my age.   5
My brother and I
rode between them and
down the hill and the impetus
took us on without pedaling
to be finally braked by   10
a bit of sullen marsh
(no longer there) where the mud
was colored by the red-brown
oozings of iron. It
was autumn
           or was it?   15

Nothing to keep it there, the
smell of leaf in May
sweet and powerful as rutting
confuses me now, it's all
getting lost, I started   20
forgetting it even as I wrote.

Forms remain, not the life
of detail or hue
then the forms are lost and
only a few dates stay with you.   25

But the trees have no sentiments
their hearts are wood
and preserve nothing
           their
boles get great, they are
embraced by the wind they   30
rushingly embrace,
they spread outward
and upward
           without regret
hardening tender green   35
to insensate lumber.

1976

TED HUGHES

(1930–)

Ted Hughes was born in Yorkshire, brought up in the West Country, and educated at Cambridge. His first wife was the intense and anguished American poet Sylvia Plath, who committed suicide at 31. His poetry from the beginning showed a greater urgency of both imagery and feeling than is found in the Movement poets. He was early influenced by Hopkins and by the later Yeats, but his anthropological sense of history and of nature is very much his own. He shares, however, with some other contemporary poets an ambivalent attitude to nature—seen as both startlingly apart from human sensitivities and simultaneously parallel to and symbolic of the human situation. His poems show an inventiveness, a joy in the exercise of his art, that exists side by side with a curiosity which is sometimes compassionate, sometimes simply fierce. The English critic A. Alvarez wrote that "Hughes * * * now joins the select band of survivor-poets whose work is adequate to the destructive reality we inhabit," adding that he believes that "he is the only British poet to have done so."

Wind

This house has been far out at sea all night,
The woods crashing through darkness, the booming hills,
Winds stampeding the fields under the window
Floundering black astride and blinding wet

Till day rose; then under an orange sky   5
The hills had new places, and wind wielded
Blade-light, luminous and emerald,
Flexing like the lens of a mad eye.

At noon I scaled along the house-side as far as
The coal-house door. I dared once to look up—   10
Through the brunt wind that dented the balls of my eyes
The tent of the hills drummed and strained its guyrope,

The fields quivering, the skyline a grimace,
At any second to bang and vanish with a flap:
The wind flung a magpie away and a black-   15
Back gull bent like an iron bar slowly. The house

Rang like some fine green goblet in the note
That any second would shatter it. Now deep
In chairs, in front of the great fire, we grip
Our hearts and cannot entertain book, thought,   20

Or each other. We watch the fire blazing,
And feel the roots of the house move, but sit on,
Seeing the window tremble to come in,
Hearing the stones cry out under the horizons.

1957

A Dream of Horses

We were born grooms, in stable-straw we sleep still,
All our wealth horse-dung and the combings of horses,
And all we can talk about it what horses ail.

Out of the night that gulfed beyond the palace-gate
There shook hooves and hooves and hooves of horses: 5
Our horses battered their stalls; their eyes jerked white.

And we ran out, mice in our pockets and straw in our hair,
Into darkness that was avalanching to horses
And a quake of hooves. Our lantern's little orange flare

Made a round mask of our each sleep-dazed face,   10
Bodiless, or else bodied by horses
That whinnied and bit and cannoned the world from its place.

The tall palace was so white, the moon was so round,
Everything else this plunging of horses
To the rim of our eyes that strove for the shapes of the sound.   15

We crouched at our lantern, our bodies drank the din,
And we longed for a death trampled by such horses
As every grain of the earth had hooves and mane.

We must have fallen like drunkards into a dream
Of listening, lulled by the thunder of the horses.   20
We awoke stiff; broad day had come.

Out through the gate the unprinted desert stretched
To stone and scorpion; our stable-horses
Lay in their straw, in a hag-sweat, listless and wretched.

Now let us, tied, be quartered by these poor horses,   25
If but doomsday's flames be great horses,
    he forever itself a circling of the hooves of horses.

1960

Relic

I found this jawbone at the sea's edge:
There crabs, dogfish, broken by the breakers or tossed
To flap for half an hour and turn to a crust
Continue the beginning. The deeps are cold:

In that darkness camaraderie does not hold: 5
Nothing touches but, clutching, devours. And the jaws,
Before they are satisfied or their stretched purpose
Slacken, go down jaws; go gnawn bare. Jaws
Eat and are finished and the jawbone comes to the beach:
This is the sea's achievement; with shells,   10
Vertebrae, claws, carapaces, skulls.

Time in the sea eats its tail, thrives, casts these
Indigestibles, the spars of purposes
That failed far from the surface. None grow rich
In the sea. This curved jawbone did not laugh   15
But gripped, gripped and is now a cenotaph.

                                                                            1960

Examination at the Womb-Door

Who owns these scrawny little feet? *Death.*
Who owns this bristly scorched-looking face? *Death.*
Who owns these still-working lungs? *Death.*
Who owns this utility coat of muscles? *Death.*
Who owns these unspeakable guts? *Death.*   5
Who owns these questionable brains? *Death.*
All this messy blood? *Death.*
These minimum-efficiency eyes? *Death.*
This wicked little tongue? *Death.*
This occasional wakefulness? *Death.*   10

Given, stolen, or held pending trial?
Held.

Who owns the whole rainy, stony earth? *Death.*
Who owns all of space? *Death.*

Who is stronger than hope? *Death.*   15
Who is stronger than the will? *Death.*
Stronger than love? *Death.*
Stronger than life? *Death.*

But who is stronger than death?
                              Me, evidently.

Pass, Crow.   20
                                                                            1970

A Disaster

There came news of a word.
Crow saw it killing men. He ate well.
He saw it bulldozing

Whole cities to rubble. Again he ate well.
He saw its excreta poisoning seas. 5
He became watchful.
He saw its breath burning whole lands
To dusty char.
He flew clear and peered.

The word oozed its way, all mouth, 10
Earless, eyeless.
He saw it sucking the cities
Like the nipples of a sow
Drinking out all the people
Till there were none left, 15
All digested inside the word.

Ravenous, the word tried its great lips
On the earth's bulge, like a giant lamprey—
There it started to suck.

But its effort weakened. 20
It could digest nothing but people.
So there it shrank, wrinkling weaker,
Puddling
Like a collapsing mushroom.
Finally, a drying salty lake. 25
Its era was over.
All that remained of it a brittle desert
Dazzling with the bones of earth's people

Where Crow walked and mused.

1970

The Seven Sorrows

The first sorrow of autumn
Is the slow goodbye
Of the garden who stands so long in the evening
A brown poppy head.
The stalk of a lily, 5
And still cannot go.

The second sorrow
Is the empty feet
Of the pheasant who hangs from a hook with his brothers.
The woodland of gold 10
Is folded in feathers
With its head in a bag.

And the third sorrow
Is the slow goodbye
Of the sun who has gathered the birds and who gathers　　15
The minutes of evening
The golden and holy
Ground of the picture.

The fourth sorrow
Is the pond gone black　　　　　　　　　　　　　　20
Ruined and sunken the city of water—
The beetle's palace,
The catacombs
Of the dragonfly.

And the fifth sorrow　　　　　　　　　　　　　　　25
Is the slow goodbye
Of the woodland that quietly breaks up its camp.
One day it's gone.
It has left only litter—
Firewood, tentpoles.　　　　　　　　　　　　　　30

And the sixth sorrow
Is the fox's sorrow
The joy of the huntsman, the joy of the hounds,
The hooves that pound
Till earth closes her ear　　　　　　　　　　　　　35
To the fox's prayer.

And the seventh sorrow
Is the slow goodbye
Of the face with its wrinkles that looks through the window
As the year packs up　　　　　　　　　　　　　　40
Like a tatty fairground
That came for the children.

　　　　　　　　　　　　　　　　　　　　1976

JON SILKIN

(1930–　)

Jon Silkin was born in London, and before winning a Gregory Poetry Fellowship at Leeds University spent some years working as a manual laborer. He took a degree in English at Leeds and then did research on the poets of World War I, which bore fruit in his book *Out of Battle: The Poetry of the Great War* (1972). He has been editor of the important "little magazine" *Stand* since 1952. Silkin's early poetry is characterized by a direct and violent imagery that conveys a sense of moral yearning, an awareness of the built-in obstacles to peace and fulfillment that exist in both man and nature. His later poetry manages to give a new dimension to an imagery still often elemental, exploring the complex relations between man and nature and linking this exploration to an awareness of social and psychological problems. Silkin has visited America several times, and some of his poems have American themes.

Nature with Man

The lank summer grass
As it is, bent and wailing;
A scorching wind
Scours a whole plain of it.
Dust still oppresses. Then   5
As if the earth received
A bruise a pool of brown
Slime erupts slowly
From among the stems. Summer mud . . .
Hot and stagnant. The grass stalks   10
Stand pricked without root
In the rimless mud . . . in what eye.
On some field of gray stone
A white sud of saliva,
So fine it seems a mildew,   15
Agonizes over the crop.

But are the humans here? Nature
Had a human head. The mouth
Turned on its long neck, biting through
Scale, sinew; and the blood   20
Carried through the flesh
Beyond the ends of veins
As the severed head
Rolled into the bulrushes.
This limp and useless   25
Going off among tall weeds
Has soured the earth, whose body
Decays and perishes.
As for the pain
That suds onto the stone;   30
That, simply, is pain.

How much else is there?
There is only one head.
But it has several minds
Which still give out   35
Great reticulations
Of ideas, nets willful and sharp

Over it; binding it
In pride and thought that cut
The smiling face of pleasure.   40

"O pity, pity, pity"?
But the weedy soul is shrinking.
Nor can it see how
To join itself unto
The membered flesh. The whole   45
Of nature is turning slowly
Into an eye that searches
For its most developed
And treacherous creature, man.
Monstrous and huge eye: 50
The entire process
Of nature perverted
Into the search for him.

                                                       1965

A Bluebell[1]

Most of them in the first tryings
Of nature, hang at angles,
Like lamps. These though
Look round, like young birds,
Poised on their stems. Closer,   5
In all their sweetness, malevolent. For there is
In the closed, blue flower, gas-colored,
A seed-like dark green eye.
Carroway, grained, supple,
And watching; it is always there,   10
Fibrous, alerted,
Coarse grained enough to print
Out all your false delight
In "sweet nature." This is struggle.
The beetle exudes rot: the bee   15
Grapples the reluctant nectar
Coy, suppurating, and unresigned.
Buds print the human passion
Pure now not still immersed
In fighting wire worms.   20

                                                       1965

---

1. *A Bluebell* is one of a series of "Flower Poems" of which Silkin has written: "The method is to take one particular species of flower, and to look at the flower quite closely. I also try to characterize the life and process of the flower and, in making all three substantial, to suggest certain correspondences with human types and situations. Yet although the poems are not only, and not simply, about flowers, they are not only or simply about human beings and their predicaments. They hover tentatively between the two, although whatever object or situation they temporarily absent themselves to they never lose sight of the flower. . . ."

Creatures

Shells are now found
Of creatures not still subsisting,
Chipped from the hardened mud under
Which oil lurks.

Men came with their chipped diamonds   5
And a pole with these smelted onto it
To bore rock. Oil broke out
Into the clear American air.

Barely noticed at the time
Among the soil screwed from   10
Above the crude useful oil,
Shells, about half an inch.
They were whorled, and chipped from
What they had been hardening in,
Falling through the glistening mud   15
They filled with the spiral
Wriggling creature gone from them.
It is a spiral horn, silent;
And shaped like an inert
Clammy-skinned spring.   20

They grew property:
An amnion,[1] a house;
Their grave no more special,
No more particular than
A pattern, a repetition of curving   25
Continuous shape, for survival.

1971

Untitled Poem

The perfume on your body, and the musk of it.
The second is on me, I smell the first
on you as a sign.

I wear the undelicate odor.

Shuffling through the city, my mildness deceit. Hungry   5
and light-headed with venom. The adder silks
to refuse bins.

1. Membrane enclosing the fetus before birth.

Fastened to the street: the working men's hostel past
two bins. A man beat me to those. I was afraid,
and the pulps he left stayed unfingered.   10

I had not thought of you: timidly
I spent my pence. In a dormitory
my body covered my trousers.

Along your flesh drifts your hair, a tree bearing
concupiscence, and your smile shows.   15
This is enough almost.

Your arms are slim, your fingers' amazing strength.
The tree's whole self blurts through long hair.
It's not grief, not joy; saffron spills
milk on the road.

A friend working through television gave   20
me a brass thruppence;
I bought tea with it, bearing nausea.

In Jerusalem the hills, bare; soft-haired goats
made of teeth; all the shoots are champed.
Hunger drifts through plains, over the declivities   25
of London; delicate smoky flakes of it.

On the rock splinters cold air; a coward
felt another's bruises in his groin.
He fears the cold air, its true match. Love, I love you.
Can I mean more?   30

You smile among four friends; three of us speak
and you say nothing. It hurts; your speech
is a silent woman.

Each night the kicked man screams.
If I help you. If I can lift you. His stain   35
over stone is blue, feather light.

The feet of police emboss the sidewalk.
                                        Linked
by my penis, our child could grow.
                                Fear
synchronizes with us.

I enter you. Local as a root. I wait   40
for you to get your breath. We measure each other.

We are prepared, lassitude melts. The hair
is naked, the piled spaces of hunger, and I touch
our candor;

the flesh in abandon robes gently 45
the tenderness. The candle's flame curves
round its inner light.

Your hair is seaweed. You smile monstrously.
Memory flushes me through.
Your salt skin rustles on me. Of love, this entirely 50
is not what we were taught.

Thin black coffee in a pan flicks
beads of heat. The flaking city mounds
stillness, and amiable sleep
spreads our flesh. 55

We will not last, love, as we are. Love,
I would have us stay, ever, like this.

My conscience, my fear, and our sex, stir.

1976

At Nightfall

Night-fall unfastens the door, and the font
baptizes the raw body; womb
and its flesh pule to each other.

The mother's milk: clear and sweet
dropping from the soft pointed opening. 5

It's the stars count, and they flee us
inundating their absences
with our terse lives. When we die
we are dead forever.

It comes clear finally. The Milky Way 10
vents its glowing hugenesses over
what's not there. The galaxies
pour their milk away.

Nothing's going to last

the clear baptismal water, twice welcome, 15
like two good hands

like the olive with
its stone of oil.

1976

The Church Is Getting Short of Breath

Sabbaths of the pensive spread buttocks.

Conscience, the size of a dried pea,
chafes over the pews flesh sweating

its Sabbath juice.

Douser of burning wax: old man   5
hugs remorse like a first wife. What labor
will such bridal pains be fruitful with?

First night of marriage wakes the bride
to shimmering kindness; our hemisphere
dishes the Sabbath, dead prayers,   10

the dulled rose of texts, desert mica.
Air breeds to the shy nibbling tourist.
Work-day fingers the rosary of work-days.

Work's necessary bead; the mechanic
wrenches the thread by which our lives   15
fasten to us.

Coming first to church, sharp
as the warrior wren. Morning dews
the prompt mind, tourist of the holy
places pious with no use.   20

This is the true debating ground,
and here the praying hands consume
the life they build. I shall do what I can.

The question loses its memory,
and the dense shade, in the spaces, runs   25
to hydrogen

laconic as its dull copulars.

Sneck[1] the latch-door; Adam from sculpted
wood raises Eve with himself
to the bridal shapes. Love congregating   30

the bench will have its forked play
of their clasped forms: I have come to an end

1. Close by bringing down the latch.

of the ancient days. Labored tweed
surplices the rich man.

My lovely parents, when you shaded   35
each in the other's thought, and flesh
pleaded one anatomy, of life,

endless life, death's frail nucleus
sweated to come alive, its soul
in our flesh. I loved my origins.   40

But you midwifed death. So I became
man, and as others judged me you
I judged. O gentle God, with both hands

you lathed prayer, a chariot's flange, God
of hope. The stars' system contracts,   45
that, or they flee us. Of such fountains

we lie in the solar ground, and the question
loses its mark.

1976

ELAINE FEINSTEIN
(1930–)

Elaine Cooklin was born in Bootle, Lancashire; she received her education
at Wyggeston Grammar School, Leicester, and at Newnham College, Cambridge. In 1966 she married Dr. Arnold Feinstein. She now lives with her
family in London. Hers is a restrained and meditative poetry which captures
the ordinariness of daily existence together with its strangeness. Her impressive translations of Russian women poets have widened her consciousness
and enabled her to provide a special kind of resonance to her rendering of a
response to what is often an essentially English scene. She has learned
something from the verbal adventurousness of modern American poetry, but
makes only occasional gestures in this direction. Like Molly Holden, she
shows a determination to use language expressively without shattering the
limits of consensus about language shared by reader and writer. This is a
very British concern, and differentiates most British poetry written today
from much that is written on the Continent and in America. Elaine Feinstein is also the author of four novels.

Anniversary

Suppose I took out a slender ketch from
under the pokes of Palace pier tonight to
catch a sea going fish for you

or dressed in antique goggles and wings and
flew down through sycamore leaves into the park   5

or luminescent through some planetary strike
put one delicate flamingo leg over the sill of your lab

Could I surprise you? or would you insist on
keeping a pattern to link every transfiguration?

Listen, I shall have to whisper it   10
into your heart directly: we are all
supernatural / every day
we rise new creatures / cannot be predicted

                                                                  1971

Out

The diesel stops. It is morning. Gray sky
is falling into the mud. At the waterside
two builders' cranes are sitting like birds

and the yellow gorse pushes up
like camel-thorn between oil-drums and old cars.   5
Who shall I take for my holy poet

to lead me out of this plain? I want an
innocent spirit of invention: a Buster Keaton[1]
to sail unnaturally overhead by simple leverage and

fire the machinery. Then we should all spring out of our   10
heads, dazzled with hope, even the white-faced ticket
collector dozing over his fag,[2] at such an intervention

suddenly in this stopped engine, we should
see the white gulls rising out of the rain over
the fen: and know our own freedom.   15
                                                                  1971

Waiting

The house is sick. When I come down
at night to the broken kitchen, the open wall, and find
a gray-haired and courteous old
cat asleep in a design of gypsum on the ground:
I sense between iron girders and old   5
gas-pipes how many more ill-lit creatures of a damp

1. A comic film actor who specialized   pers and similar situations.
in astonishing feats of surviving while   2. Cigarette.
clinging onto window ledges of skyscra-

garden are waiting. Under the provisional blossom
of a plum tree they threaten a long siege
whispering: they shall eat sorrow
which is the flesh of the rat, the   10
dead limb in the locked room.
And I can hardly remember the dream of sunlight and
hot sweet wallflowers that led us to break through
to the almost forgotten lord of the dark outside
whose specters are part of his word, and whose promise of 15
home always demands the willingness to move on: who
forces me to acknowledge his ancient sign.

1971

Night Thoughts

Uncurtained, my long room floats on
    darkness, moored in rain,
my shelves of orange skillets
    lie out in the black grass.
Tonight I can already taste   5
    the wet soil of their ghosts.
And my spirit looks through the glass:
    I cannot hold on forever.

No tenure, in garden trees, I
    hang like a leaf, and stare   10
at cartilaginous shapes
    my shadow their visitor.
And words cannot brazen it out.
    Nothing can hold forever.

1973

November Songs

1

The air is rising tonight and the leaf dust is
    burning in cadmium bars, the skinny beeches
are alight in the town fire of their own humus.
    There is oxblood in the sky. No month to be surly. .

The attic cracks and clicks as we ride the night   5
    our bodies spiced with salt and olive sweetness:
but a savory smoke is hanging in our hair,
    for the earth turns, and the air of the earth rises.

And it blows November spores over the sash.
    The sky is a red lichen in the mirror,   10
As the air rises we already breathe in the
    oracular resins of the season.

II

And now what aureole possesses the fine
    extremities of my leafless trees? They are
Florentine[3] today, their fen wood is ocher   15

an afternoon's bewildering last
    sunlight honors their sunken
life with an alien radiance:

and we, who are restless by the
    same accident that gives their   20
vegetable patience   grace

may worship the tranquility of
    waiting, but will not
find such blessing in the human face.

                                    1973

3. Florence, the Italian city, is famous alike for the beauty of its location (on the river Arno, at the foot of spurs of the Apennines) and the splendor of its art collections. Hence "Florentine" here implies a natural beauty combined with suggestions of art.

GEOFFREY HILL
(1932–)

Geoffrey Hill, born at Bromsgrove, Worcestershire and educated at Bromsgrove County High School and Keble College, Oxford, is a university teacher of English with a highly sophisticated critical mind which can be seen at work in his poetry. His precise and subtle use of imagery is combined with a disciplined irony and a fine sense of form. His *Mercian Hymns* (1971) shows a powerful sense of early English history and of the strengths of the Anglo-Saxon poetic language working through a very modern English consciousness.

September Song[1]

born 19.6.32—deported 24.9.42

Undesirable you may have been, untouchable
you were not. Not forgotten
or passed over at the proper time.

As estimated, you died. Things marched,
sufficient, to that end.   5

1. The poem is about the gassing of Jews in German extermination camps; Zyklon-B (line 6) was the gas used. Hill's fellow poet Jon Silkin has drawn attention to the kind of wit involved in the subtitle, "where the natural event is placed, simply, beside the human and murderous 'deported' as if the latter were of the same order and inevitability for the victim"; he discusses, too, "the irony of conjuncted meanings between 'undesirable' (touching on both sexual desire and racism) and 'untouchable,' which exploits a similar ambiguity but reverses the emphases," and is "unusually dense *and* simple."

Just so much Zyklon and leather, patented
terror, so many routine cries.

(I have made
an elegy for myself it
is true)   10

September fattens on vines. Roses
flake from the wall. The smoke
of harmless fires drifts to my eyes.

This is plenty. This is more than enough.

                                                                  1968

From Funeral Music[2]

3

They bespoke doomsday and they meant it by
God, their curved metal rimming the low ridge.
But few appearances are like this. Once
Every five hundred years a comet's
Over-riding stillness might reveal men   5
In such array, livid and featureless,
With England crouched beastwise beneath it all.
"Oh, that old northern business . . ." A field
After battle utters its own sound
Which is like nothing on earth, but is earth.   10
Blindly the questing snail, vulnerable
Mole emerge, blindly we lie down, blindly
Among carnage the most delicate souls
Tup in their marriage-blood, gasping "Jesus."

7

"Prowess, vanity, mutual regard,
It seemed I stared at them, they at me.
That was the gorgon's[3] true and mortal gaze:
Averted conscience turned against itself."
A hawk and a hawk-shadow. "At noon,   5
As the armies met, each mirrored the other;
Neither was outshone. So they flashed and vanished .
And all that survived them was the stark ground
Of this pain. I made no sound, but once
I stiffened as though a remote cry   10
Had heralded my name. It was nothing . . ."

2. These two poems are from a
sequence of eight poems suggested by
certain episodes in the 15th-century
English civil wars known as the War
of the Roses. "In this sequence I was
attempting a florid grim music broken
by grunts and shrieks," the poet has
written. He explains that there is "no
overt narrative or dramatic structure"
in the sequence: "the whole inference,
though, has value if it gives a key to
the ornate and heartless music puncu-
tated by mutterings, blasphemies, and
cries for help."
3. Greek mythological snake-haired
woman whose terrible aspect turned the
viewer to stone.

Reddish ice tinged the reeds; dislodged, a few
Feathers drifted across; carrion birds
Strutted upon the armor of the dead.

1968

From Mercian Hymns[1]

VI

The princes of Mercia were badger and raven. Thrall
    to their freedom, I dug and hoarded. Orchards
    fruited above clefts. I drank from honeycombs of
    chill sandstone.

"A boy at odds in the house, lonely among brothers."   5
    But I, who had none, fostered a strangeness; gave
    myself to unattainable toys.

Candles of gnarled resin, apple-branches, the tacky
    mistletoe. "Look" they said and again "look." But
    I ran slowly; the landscape flowed away, back to   10
    its source.

In the schoolyard, in the cloakrooms, the children
    boasted their scars of dried snot; wrists and
    knees garnished with impetigo.

VII

Gasholders,[2] russet among fields. Milldams, marlpools
    that lay unstirring. Eel-swarms. Coagulations of
    frogs: once, with branches and half-bricks, he
    battered a ditchful; then sidled away from the
    stillness and silence.   5

Ceolred[3] was his friend and remained so, even after
    the day of the lost fighter: a biplane, already
    obsolete and irreplaceable, two inches of heavy
    snub silver. Ceolred let it spin through a hole in
    the classroom floorboards, softly, into the   10
    rat droppings and coins.

After school he lured Ceolred, who was sniggering
    with fright, down to the old quarries, and flayed

1. "The historical Offa reigned over Mercia (and the greater part of England south of the Humber) in the years A.D. 757–796. During early medieval times he was already becoming a creature of legend. The Offa who figures in this sequence might perhaps most usefully be regarded as the presiding genius of the West Midlands, his dominion enduring from the middle of the eighth century until the middle of the twentieth (and possibly beyond). The indication of such a timespan will, I trust, explain and to some extent justify a number of anachronisms" [Hill's note].

2. Or gasometers, large metal receptacles for gas. "Marlpools": pools in deposits of crumbling clay and chalk.

3. Ceolred was a 9th-century bishop of Leicester, but the name is here used as a characteristic Anglo-Saxon Mercian name.

him. Then, leaving Ceolred, he journeyed for hours,
calm and alone, in his private derelict sandlorry[4]   15
named *Albion*.

VIII

The mad are predators. Too often lately they harbor
against us. A novel heresy exculpates all maimed
souls. Abjure it! I am the King of Mercia, and
I know.

Threatened by phone calls at midnight, venomous let-   5
ters, forewarned I have thwarted their imminent
devices.

Today I name them; tomorrow I shall express the new
law. I dedicate my awakening to this matter.

X

He adored the desk, its brown-oak inlaid with ebony,
assorted prize pens, the seals of gold and base
metal into which he had sunk his name.

It was there that he drew upon grievances from the
people; attended to signatures and retributions;   5
forgave the death-howls of his rival. And there
he exchanged gifts with the Muse of History.

What should a man make of remorse, that it might
profit his soul? Tell me. Tell everything to
Mother, darling, and God bless.   10

He swayed in sunlight, in mild dreams. He tested the
little pears. He smeared catmint on his palm for
his cat Smut to lick. He wept, attempting to master *ancilla* and *servus*.[5]

XVI

Clash of salutation. As keels thrust into shingle.
Ambassadors, pilgrims. What is carried over? The
Frankish[6] gift, two-edged, regaled with slaughter.

The sword is in the king's hands; the crux a craftsman's triumph. Metal effusing its own fragrance,   5
a variety of balm. And other miracles, other
exchanges.

Shafts from the winter sun homing upon earth's rim.
Christ's mass: in the thick of a snowy forest the
flickering evergreen fissured with light.   10

4. Sand truck. Albion was an old
Celtic name for England; it is also the
name of a famous make of British
truck.
5. "Maidservant" and "manservant"
(or slave).
6. The Franks were members of a confederation of German tribes who
formed the Frankish Empire in the
Dark Ages. In the 9th century they
gave way to the medieval kingdoms
that became known as France, Germany, and Italy.

Attributes assumed, retribution entertained. What is
  borne amongst them? Too much or too little. Indulgences of bartered acclaim; an expenditure, a
  hissing. Wine, urine, and ashes.

XXVIII

Processes of generation; deeds of settlement. The
  urge to marry well; wit to invest in the properties of healing-springs. Our children and our
  children's children, o my masters.

Tracks of ancient occupation. Frail ironworks rust-   5
  ing in the thorn-thicket. Hearthstones; charred
  lullabies. A solitary ax-blow that is the echo
  of a lost sound.

Tumult recedes as though into the long rain. Groves
  of legendary holly; silverdark the ridged gleam.   10

XXX

And it seemed, while we waited, he began to walk towards us   he vanished

he left behind coins, for his lodging, and traces of
  red mud.

1971

SEAMUS HEANEY

(1939–)

Seamus Heaney was born in Northern Ireland and brought up on a farm in
County Derry. He attended Queen's University, Belfast, and at Belfast
became friendly with Henry Chambers, editor of *Phoenix*, originally a liter-
ary-cum-political magazine founded in 1959 and professing "a faith in
words and all that reflects ordinary human activity." Heaney, who had
already published two "slim volumes" of poetry, appeared in *Phoenix* in
1967, and his work has some of the qualities associated with that magazine.
There is no cultural posturing or calculated incoherence in Heaney's quietly
human poems, which project their subject with an objectivity of mood and
imagery that sets off rather than conceals the underlying sympathy with
daily rhythms of ordinary experience. Some of Heaney's early poems seem
at first sight to possess the sort of realism we associate with Flemish painting; they are subtler than they at first appear and show considerable formal
skill and delicacy.

In 1969 Heaney, who had become to some extent involved in Irish radical politics, read a book that gave a new theme to his poetry. This was
The Bog People, by P. V. Glob, a Danish archeologist, who described the
discoveries, in bogs in northwestern Europe, of the bodies of men and
women who had lived in the early centuries of the Christian era. The
bodies were astonishingly well preserved (because of the special properties

of the soil acids in the bog water), and looked as if they had died only recently. The condition of the bodies suggests that they had been, in one way or another, ritually sacrificed in winter or early spring to assure a good growth of crops. As Heaney said in a lecture in 1974, he "began to get an idea of bog as the memory of the landscape, or as a landscape that remembered everything that happened in and to it. In fact, if you go round the National Museum in Dublin, you will realize that a great proportion of the most cherished material heritage of Ireland was 'found in a bog' " (one of Heaney's critics reminds us that "bog" is one of the few words of Irish origin to enter the English language). He was deeply impressed by the photographs in Glob's book, which he called "unforgettable," and said that they blended in his mind "with photographs of atrocities, past and present, in the long rites of Irish political and religious struggles."

Churning Day

A thick crust, coarse-grained as limestone rough-cast,
hardened gradually on top of the four crocks
that stood, large pottery bombs, in the small pantry.
After the hot brewery of gland, cud and udder
cool porous earthenware fermented the buttermilk   5
for churning day, when the hooped churn was scoured
with plumping kettles and the busy scrubber
echoed daintily on the seasoned wood.
It stood then, purified, on the flagged kitchen floor.

Out came the four crocks, spilled their heavy lip   10
of cream, their white insides, into the sterile churn.
The staff, like a great whisky muddler fashioned
in deal wood, was plunged in, the lid fitted.
My mother took first turn, set up rhythms
that slugged and thumped for hours. Arms ached.   15
Hands blistered. Cheeks and clothes were spattered
with flabby milk.

              Where finally gold flecks
began to dance. They poured hot water then,
sterilized a birchwood-bowl   20
and little corrugated butter-spades.
Their short stroke quickened, suddenly
a yellow curd was weighting the churned up white,
heavy and rich, coagulated sunlight
that they fished, dripping, in a wide tin strainer,   25
heaped up like gilded gravel in the bowl.

The house would stink long after churning day,
acrid as a sulfur mine. The empty crocks
were ranged along the wall again, the butter
in soft printed slabs was piled on pantry shelves.   30
And in the house we moved with gravid ease,

our brains turned crystals full of clean deal churns,
the plash and gurgle of the sour-breathed milk,
the pat and slap of small spades on wet lumps.

1966

Poor Women in a City Church

The small wax candles melt to light,
Flicker in marble, reflect bright
Asterisks on brass candlesticks:
At the Virgin's altar on the right
Blue flames are jerking on wicks.   5

Old dough-faced women with black shawls
Drawn down tight kneel in the stalls.
Cold yellow candle-tongues, blue flame
Mince and caper as whispered calls
Take wing up to the Holy Name.   10

Thus each day in the sacred place
They kneel. Golden shrines, altar lace,
Marble columns and cool shadows
Still them. In the gloom you cannot trace
A wrinkle on their beeswax brows.   15

1966

Viking Dublin: Trial Pieces[1]

I

It could be a jawbone
or a rib or a portion cut
from something sturdier:
anyhow, a small outline

was incised, a cage   5
or trellis to conjure in.[2]
Like a child's tongue
following the toils

of his calligraphy,
like an eel swallowed   10
in a basket of eels,
the line amazes itself

eluding the hand
that fed it,

1. The Vikings (Norsemen) attacked and took Dublin in the 9th century; they ruled in Dublin and the province of Munster intermittently from the early 9th century on, until they were driven out by the Anglo-Normans in 1171.
2. The poet is talking about an object (a piece of bone with a pattern carved on it) excavated among other Viking remains in a bog near Dublin.

a bill in flight,
a swimming nostril.

II

These are trial pieces,
the craft's mystery
improvised on bone:
foliage, bestiaries,

interlacings elaborate
as the netted routes
of ancestry and trade.
That have to be

magnified on display
so that the nostril
is a migrant prow
sniffing the Liffey,[3]

swanning it up to the ford,
dissembling itself
in antler combs, bone pins,
coins, weights, scalepans.[4]

III

Like a long sword
sheathed in its moisting
burial clays,
the keel stuck fast

in the slip of the bank,
its clinker-built hull
spined and plosive
as *Dublin*.[5]

And now we reach in
for shards of the vertebrae,
the ribs of hurdle,
the mother-wet caches—

and for this trial piece
incised by a child,
a longship, a buoyant
migrant line.

IV

That enters my longhand,
turns cursive, unscarfing
a zoomorphic wake,
a worm of thought

15

20

25

30

35

40

45

50

---

3. The river which flows through
Dublin; the "migrant prow" is a
Viking ship.
4. The tip of the bone is shaped like
the prow of a Viking ship, but the pattern on the bone suggests combs made
of antlers, pins made of bone, etc.
"Swanning": gliding effortlessly.
5. I.e., as the sound of the word
"Dublin."

I follow in the mud.
I am Hamlet the Dane,[6]
skull-handler, parablist,   55
smeller of rot

in the state, infused
with its poisons,
pinioned by ghosts
and affections,   60

murders and pieties,
coming to consciousness
by jumping in graves,
dithering, blathering.

V

Come fly with me,   65
come sniff the wind
with the expertise
of the Vikings—

neighborly, scoretaking
killers, haggers[7]   70
and hagglers, gombeen-men,[8]
hoarders of grudges and gain.

With a butcher's aplomb
they spread out your lungs
and made you warm wings   75
for your shoulders.

Old fathers, be with us.
Old cunning assessors
of feuds and of sites
for ambush or town.   80

VI

"Did you ever hear tell,"
said Jimmy Farrell,
"of the skulls they have
in the city of Dublin?

White skulls and black skulls   85
and yellow skulls, and some
with full teeth, and some
haven't only but one,"

and compounded history
in the pan[9] of "an old Dane,   90

6. Cf. Hamlet's cry when he leaps into Ophelia's grave: "This is I, / Hamlet the Dane" (V.i.224–25) (some of the Vikings, or Norsemen, were Danes). In the next lines (55–64) Heaney effectively sums up a number of the main themes and situations of Shakespeare's play.
7. Hackers.
8. Usurers.
9. I.e., brainpan.

maybe, was drowned
in the Flood."

My words lick around
cobbled quays, go hunting
lightly as pampooties[1]   95
over the skullcapped ground.

1975

The Grauballe Man[2]

As if he had been poured
in tar, he lies
on a pillow of turf
and seems to weep

the black river of himself.   5
The grain of his wrists
is like bog oak,
the ball of his heel

like a basalt egg.
His instep has shrunk   10
cold as a swan's foot
or a wet swamp root.

His hips are the ridge
and purse of a mussel,
his spine an eel arrested   15
under a glisten of mud.

The head lifts,
the chin is a visor
raised above the vent
of his slashed throat   20

that has tanned and toughened.
The cured wound
opens inwards to a dark
elderberry place.

Who will say "corpse"   25
to his vivid cast?

1. (Irish) sandals of undressed cow-
skin.
2. The body of the "Grauballe man"
was discovered in a bog in the village
of Grauballe (Denmark) in 1952. In
The Bog People, P. V. Glob describes
the discovery and the condition of the
body in detail, and reproduces a
number of photographs (cf. lines 32–
36), including pictures of the hands
and feet. The Grauballe man was
clearly a ritual sacrifice: his throat had
been cut, in order that the sacrificial
blood might pour out in a stream in
honor of the fertility goddess. He lived
between 210 and 410 A.D.

Who will say "body"
to his opaque repose?

And his rusted hair,
a mat unlikely
as a fetus's.
I first saw his twisted face

in a photograph,
a head and shoulder
out of the peat,
bruised like a forceps baby,

but now he lies
perfected in my memory,
down to the red horn
of his nails,

hung in the scales
with beauty and atrocity:
with the Dying Gaul[3]
too strictly compassed

on his shield,
with the actual weight
of each hooded victim,
slashed and dumped.

1975

Punishment[4]

I can feel the tug
of the halter at the nape
of her neck, the wind
on her naked front.

3. A reference to the ancient statue (in the Capitoline Museum, Rome), which depicts graphically the sufferings of the dying man.
4. In 1951 the body of a young girl, who lived in the late 1st century A.D., was recovered from a bog in Windeby (Germany). As P. V. Glob describes her in *The Bog People,* she "lay naked in the hole in the peat, a bandage over the eyes and a collar round the neck. The band across the eyes was drawn tight and had cut into the neck and the base of the nose. We may feel sure that it had been used to close her eyes to this world. There was no mark of strangulation on the neck, so that it had not been used for that purpose." Her hair "had been shaved off with a razor on the left side of the head * * * When the brain was removed the convolutions and folds of the surface could be clearly seen [Glob reproduces a photograph of her brain] * * * this girl of only fourteen had had an inadequate winter diet * * * To keep the young body under, some birch branches and a big stone were laid upon her." According to the Roman historian Tacitus, the Germanic peoples punished adulterous women by shaving off their hair and then scourging them out of the village or killing them.

It blows her nipples   5
to amber beads,
it shakes the frail rigging
of her ribs.

I can see her drowned
body in the bog,   10
the weighing stone,
the floating rods and boughs.

Under which at first
she was a barked sapling
that is dug up   15
oak-bone, brain-firkin:

her shaved head
like a stubble of black corn,
her blindfold a soiled bandage,
her noose a ring   20

to store
the memories of love.
Little adulteress,
before they punished you

you were flaxen-haired,   25
undernourished, and your
tar-black face was beautiful.
My poor scapegoat,

I almost love you
but would have cast, I know,   30
the stones of silence.
I am the artful voyeur

of your brain's exposed
and darkened combs,
your muscles' webbing   35
and all your numbered bones:

I who have stood dumb
when your betraying sisters,
cauled in tar,
wept by the railings,   40

who would connive
in civilized outrage
yet understand the exact
and tribal, intimate revenge.

1975

Poems in Process

Poets in all ages have claimed that their poems were not willed but were inspired, whether by a muse, by divine visitation, or by sudden emergence from the poet's subconscious mind. But as the poet Richard Aldington has remarked, "genius is not enough; one must also work." The working manuscripts of the greatest poets show that, however involuntary the origin of a poem, vision was usually followed by laborious revision before the work achieved the seeming inevitability of its final form.

Although some earlier poetic manuscripts have survived, it was not until the 19th century that the working drafts of poets began to be widely preserved, and so remain abundantly available. The examples from major poets which are transcribed here represent various stages in the evolution of a poem, and a variety of procedures in the mode of composition by individual poets. The selections from Blake, Byron, Shelley, and Keats are drafts of some of their best poems, written, emended, crossed-out, and rewritten in the heat of first invention; while poems by Wordsworth, Hopkins, and Yeats are shown in successive stages of revision over an extended period of time. Shelley's *O World, O Life, O Time* originated in a few key nouns, together with an abstract rhythmic pattern which was only later fleshed out with words, while Yeats's *After Long Silence* began as a prose sketch which gradually and laboriously was reshaped into a metric and stanzaic form. Still other poems—Tennyson's *The Lady of Shalott*, Yeats's *The Sorrow of Love*—were subjected to radical revision long after the initial versions had been committed to print. In all these examples we look on as each poet, no matter how rapidly he achieves a result he is willing to let stand, carries on his inevitably tentative efforts to meet the multiple requirements of meaning, syntax, meter, sound pattern, and the constraints imposed by his chosen stanza. And because these are all very good poets, the seeming conflict between the necessities of significance and form results not in the distortion but in the perfection of the poetic statement.

Our transcriptions from the poets' drafts attempt to reproduce, as accurately as the change from script to print will allow, the appearance of the original manuscript page. A poet's first attempt at a line or phrase is reproduced in larger type, his emendations in smaller type. The line numbers in the headings which identify an excerpt are those of the final form of the complete poem, as reprinted in the text of this anthology, above. Within the transcriptions themselves, whether of a manuscript or an early printed version of a poem, the only line numbers are those which occur in the original.

SELECTED BIBLIOGRAPHY

Autograph Poetry in the English Language, 2 vols., 1973, compiled by P. J. Croft, reproduces and transcribes one or more pages of manuscript in the poet's own hand, from the 14th century to the present time; Volume I includes Blake and Burns; Volume II includes many of the other poets represented in this volume of *The Norton Anthology of English Literature*, from Wordsworth to Dylan Thomas. Books which discuss the process of composition and revision, with examples from the manuscripts and printed versions of poems, are: Charles D. Abbott, ed., *Poets at Work*, 1948; Phyllis Bartlett, *Poems in Process*, 1951; A. F. Scott, *The Poet's Craft*, 1957. In *Word for Word: A Study of Authors' Alterations*, 1965, Wallace Hildick analyzes the composition of prose fiction as well as poems; a shorter version, *Word for Word: The Rewriting of Fiction*, 1965, discusses the revision of novels by George Eliot, Samuel Butler, Hardy, Lawrence, James, and Woolf. Byron's "*Don Juan*," edited by T. G. Steffan and W. W. Pratt, 4 vols., 1957, transcribes the manuscript drafts; the Cornell Wordsworth, in process, reproduces, transcribes, and discusses all versions of Wordsworth's poems from the first manuscript drafts to the final publication in his lifetime; the three volumes published as of 1978 are *The Salisbury Plain Poems*, 1975; *The Prelude, 1798–1799*, 1977; and *Home at Grasmere*, 1977. M. R. Ridley has written a study of the poet's manuscripts in *Keats's Craftsmanship*, 1933; and Jon Stallworthy, *Between the Lines: Yeats's Poetry in the Making*, 1963, reproduces and analyzes the sequential drafts of a number of Yeats's major poems. Valerie Eliot has edited T. S. Eliot's *The Waste Land: A Facsimile and Transcript of the Original Drafts Including the Annotations of Ezra Pound*, 1971, while Dame Helen Gardner has transcribed and analyzed the manuscript drafts of Eliot's *Four Quartets* in *The Composition of Four Quartets*, 1978.

WILLIAM BLAKE
The Tyger[1]

[First Draft]

The Tyger

1
Tyger Tyger burning bright
In the forests of the night
What immortal hand or eye
~~Dare~~ ~~Could~~ frame thy fearful symmetry

2
Burnt in
~~In what~~ distant deeps or skies
~~The cruel~~ ~~Burnt the~~ fire of thine eyes
On what wings dare he aspire
What the hand dare sieze the fire

3
And what shoulder & what art
Could twist the sinews of thy heart
And when thy heart began to beat
What dread hand & what dread feet

~~Could fetch it from the furnace deep~~
~~And in thy horrid ribs dare steep~~

1. These drafts have been taken from a notebook used by William Blake, called The Rossetti MS because it was once owned by Dante Gabriel Rossetti, the Victorian poet and painter; David V. Erdman's edition of *The Notebook of William Blake* (1973) contains a photographic facsimile. The stanza and line numbers were written by Blake in the manuscript.

~~In the well of sanguine woe~~
~~In what clay & what mould~~
~~Were thy eyes of fury rolld~~

4   ~~Where~~
    ~~What~~ the hammer ~~what~~ the chain
    In what furnace was thy brain

                                    dread grasp
    What the anvil what ~~the arm~~ ~~arm~~ ~~grasp~~ ~~clasp~~
Dare ~~Could~~ its deadly terrors ~~clasp~~ ~~grasp~~ clasp

6   Tyger Tyger burning bright
    In the forests of the night
    What immortal hand & eye
                    frame
    Dare ~~form~~ thy fearful symmetry

                [*Trial Stanzas*]

    Burnt in distant deeps or skies
    The cruel fire of thine eye,
    Could heart descend or wings aspire
    What the hand dare sieze the fire

                    dare he ~~smile~~ ~~laugh~~
5   And ~~did he laugh~~ his work to see
                    ankle
    ~~What the shoulder what the knee~~
            Dare
4   ~~Did~~ he who made the lamb make thee
1   When the stars threw down their spears
2   And waterd heaven with their tears

            [*Second Full Draft*]

    Tyger Tyger burning bright
    In the forests of the night
    What Immortal hand & eye
    Dare frame thy fearful symmetry

    And what shoulder & what art
    Could twist the sinews of thy heart
    And when thy heart began to beat
    What dread hand & what dread feet

    When the stars threw down their spears
    And waterd heaven with their tears
    Did he smile his work to see
    Did he who made the lamb make thee

    Tyger Tyger burning bright
    In the forests of the night
    What immortal hand & eye
    Dare frame thy fearful symmetry

[*Final Version, 1794*][2]

The Tyger

Tyger Tyger, burning bright,
In the forests of the night;
What immortal hand or eye,
Could frame thy fearful symmetry?

In what distant deeps or skies
Burnt the fire of thine eyes!
On what wings dare he aspire?
What the hand, dare sieze the fire?

And what shoulder, & what art,
Could twist the sinews of thy heart?
And when thy heart began to beat,
What dread hand? & what dread feet?

What the hammer? what the chain,
In what furnace was thy brain?
What the anvil? what dread grasp,
Dare its deadly terrors clasp?

When the stars threw down their spears
And water'd heaven with their tears:
Did he smile his work to see?
Did he who made the Lamb make thee?

Tyger, Tyger burning bright,
In the forests of the night:
What immortal hand or eye,
Dare frame thy fearful symmetry?

WILLIAM WORDSWORTH
She Dwelt Among the Untrodden Ways

[*Version in a Letter to Coleridge, December, 1798, or January, 1799*][1]

My hope was one, from cities far
    Nursed on a lonesome heath:
Her lips were red as roses are,
    Her hair a woodbine wreath.

She lived among the untrodden ways
    Beside the springs of Dove,

---

2. As published in *Songs of Experience.*
1. Printed in Ernest de Selincourt's *Early Letters of William and Dorothy Wordsworth* (1935). Simply by deleting two weak stanzas from this draft, and making a few verbal changes, Wordsworth converted a rather conventional poem into one of the great dirges in the language.

A maid whom there were none to praise,
    And very few to love;

A violet by a mossy stone
    Half-hidden from the eye!
Fair as a star when only one
    Is shining in the sky!

And she was graceful as the broom[2]
    That flowers by Carron's side;
But slow distemper checked her bloom,
    And on the Heath she died.

Long time before her head lay low
    Dead to the world was she:
But now she's in her grave, and Oh!
    The difference to me!

[*Final Version, 1800*][3]

Song

She dwelt among th' untrodden ways
    Beside the springs of Dove,
A Maid whom there were none to praise
    And very few to love.

A Violet by a mossy stose
    Half-hidden from the Eye!
—Fair, as a star when only one
    Is shining in the sky!

She *liv'd* unknown, and few could know
    When Lucy ceas'd to be;   10
But she is in her Grave, and Oh!
    The difference to me.

LORD BYRON
From Don Juan[1]

[*First Draft: Canto III, Stanza* 9]

~~Life is a play and men~~
All tragedies are finished by a death,
All Comedies are ended by a marriage,

---

2. A shrub with long slender branches and yellow flowers; the Carron is a river in northwestern Scotland.
3. As published in the second edition of *Lyrical Ballads*.

1. Reproduced from transcripts made of Byron's manuscripts in T. G. Steffan and W. W. Pratt, *Byron's "Don Juan"* (1957). The stanzas were published by Byron in their emended form.

~~For Life can go no further~~
These two form the last gasp of Passion's breath
~~All further is a blank   I won't disparage~~
~~That holy state   but certainly beneath~~
~~The Sun   of human things~~
~~These two are levellers, and human breath~~
~~So   These point the epigram of human breath~~
~~Or any~~ The future states of both are left to faith,
~~Though Life and love I like not to disparage~~
~~The~~ For authors ~~think~~ description might disparage
                          fear
~~Tis strange that poets never try to wreathe~~ [sic?]
~~With eith   'Tis strange that poets of the Catholic faith~~
~~Neer go beyond—and   but seem to dread miscarriage~~
~~So dramas close with death or settlement for life~~
~~Veiling   Leaving the future states of Love and Life~~
~~The paradise beyond like that of life~~
~~And neer describing either~~
~~To mere conjecture of a devil   and   or wife~~
~~And don't say much of paradise or wife~~
The worlds to come of both—~~&~~ or fall beneath,
And ~~all   both the worlds would blame them for miscarriage~~
And then both worlds would punish their miscarriage—
~~So leaving both with priest & prayerbook ready~~
So leaving ~~Clerg both a~~ each their Priest and prayerbook ready,
They say no more of death or of the Lady.

[First Draft: Canto XIV, Stanza 95]

Alas! ~~I speak by~~ Experience ~~never~~ yet
        quote   seldom
~~I had a paramour and I've had many~~
~~To whom I did not cause a deep~~ regret—
                                   some small
~~Whom I had not some reason to~~ regret
~~For Whom   I did not feel myself~~ a Zany—
Alas! by all experience, seldom yet
(I merely quote what I have heard from many)
Had lovers not some reason to regret
The passion which made Solomon a Zany.
~~I also had a wife~~—not to forget—
I've also seen some wives—not to forget—
The marriage state—the best or worst of any—
Who ~~was~~ the very ~~paragon~~ of wives,
    were   paragons
Yet made the misery of ~~both our~~ lives.
                        many
                        several
                        of at least two

PERCY BYSSHE SHELLEY

The three stages of this poem labeled "First Draft" are scattered through one of Shelley's notebooks, now in the Huntington Library, California; these drafts have been transcribed and analyzed by Bennett Weaver, "Shelley Works Out the Rhythm of *A Lament*," *PMLA* (1932), pp. 570–76. They show Shelley working with fragmentary words and phrases, and simultaneously with a wordless pattern of pulses which marked out the meter of the single lines and the shape of the lyric stanzas. Shelley left this draft unfinished.

Apparently at some later time, Shelley returned to the poem and wrote what is here called the "Second Draft"; from this he then made, on a second page, a revised fair copy which provided the text that Mary Shelley published in 1824, after the poet's death. These two manuscript pages are now in the Bodleian Library, Oxford; the first page is photographically reproduced and discussed by John Carter and John Sparrow, "Shelley, Swinburne, and Housman," *Times Literary Supplement* (1968), pp. 1318–19.

O World, O Life, O Time

[*First Draft, Stage 1*]

Ah time, oh night, oh day
~~Ni nal ni na, na ni~~
~~Ni na ni na, ni na~~
Oh life O death, O time
Time a di
~~Never Time~~
Ah time, a time O-time
~~Time!~~

[*First Draft, Stage 2*]

Oh time, oh night oh day
~~O day oh night, alas~~
  O Death time night ~~oh~~
Oh, Time
Oh time o night oh day

[*First Draft, Stage 3*]

Na na, na na ná na
Nă nă na na na—nă nă
  Nă nă nă nă nă nă
Na na nã nã nâ ă na

Na na na—nă nă—na na
  Na na na na—na na na na na
Na na na na na.
    Na na
Na na na na na
    Na na
Na na na na na ˘ na!

Oh time, oh night, o day
     alas
  O day ~~serenest~~, o day
  O day alas the day
That thou shouldst sleep when we awake to say

O time time—o death—o day
      for
O day, o death life is far from thee
O thou wert never free
For death is now with thee
~~And life is far from~~
O death, o day for life is far from thee

[Second Draft][1]

Out of the day & night   I am
A joy has taken flight   despair
Fresh spring & summer   & winter hoar
  Fill my faint heart with grief, but with
                       delight
      No more — o never more!

~~We~~ O World, o life, o time
  ~~Will ye~~ On whose last steps I climb
Trembling at those which I have trod[2] before
When will return the glory of yr prime
   No more   Oh never more

       Out of the day & night
       A joy has taken flight—
             autumn
~~From~~ Green spring, & ~~summer~~ gra[3] & winter hoar

[FAIR COPY]

O World   o Life   o Time
On whose last steps I climb
Trembling at that where I had stood before
When will return the glory of yr prime?
   No more, o never more

2

Out of the day & night
A joy has taken flight

---

1. Shelley apparently wrote the first stanza of this draft low down on the page, and ran out of space after crowding in the third line of the second stanza; he then, in a lighter ink, wrote a revised form of the whole of the second stanza at the top of the page. In this revision, he left a space after "summer" in line 3, indicating that he planned an insertion that would fill out the four-foot meter of this line, and so make it match the five feet in the corresponding line of the first stanza.

In the upper right-hand corner of this manuscript page Shelley wrote "I am despair"—seemingly to express his bleak mood at the time he wrote the poem.

For this, and for the transcript of the Fair Copy that follows, the editor is indebted to Donald H. Reiman of The Pforzheimer Library.

2. Shelley at first wrote "trod," then overwrote that with "stood." In the following line, Shelley at first wrote "yr," then overwrote "thy."

3. Not clearly legible; it is either "gra" or "gre." A difference in the ink from the rest of the line indicates that Shelley, having left a blank space, later started to fill it in, but thought better of it and crossed out the fragmentary insertion.

Fresh spring & summer   [4] & winter hoar
Move my faint heart with grief but with delight
No more, o, never more

JOHN KEATS
From The Eve of St. Agnes[1]

[*Stanza 26*]

But soon his heart revives—her prayers said

She ~~lays aside her veil~~   pearled

strips her hair of all its wreath~~ed pearl~~

~~Unclasps her bosom jewels~~

~~And twists it in one knot upon her head~~

soon.

But soon his heart revives—her prayers (ing) done,

Sh(Of)   all her (its) wreathed pearl she strips her hair

Unclasps her warmed jewels one by one

her bursting

Loosens ~~her boddice from her~~

~~her Boddice lace string~~

~~her Boddice and her bosom bar~~

her

[HERE KEATS BEGINS A NEW SHEET]

Loosens her fragrant ~~boddice~~ and doth bare

Her

Anon

~~But soon~~ his heart revives—her praying done

frees

Of all its wreathéd pearl her hair she ~~strips~~

Unclasps her warmed jewels one by one

by degrees

~~to her knees~~

Loosens her fragrant boddice: ~~and down slips~~

Her sweet attire ~~falls light creeps down by~~

creeps rusteling to her knees

Mermaid   in sea weed

Half hidden like a ~~Syren of the Sea~~

~~And more melodious~~   dreaming

She stands awhile in thought, and sees

---

4. This Fair Copy of the Second Draft retains, and even enlarges, the blank space, indicating that Shelley still hasn't made up his mind what to insert after the word "summer"; we may speculate, by reference to the fragmentary version of this stanza in the Second Draft, that he had in mind as possibilities either an adjective, "gray" or "green," or else the noun "autumn." Mary Shelley closed up this space when she published the poem in 1824, with the result that later editors, following Mary Shelley's version, have until very recently printed this line as though Shelley had intended it to be one metric foot shorter than the corresponding line of stanza 1.

1. Transcribed from what is probably the best known of all manuscripts, that which contains Keats's first draft of all but the first seven stanzas of *The Eve of St. Agnes*; it is now in the Houghton Library, Harvard University. Keats's published version of the poem, above, contains some further changes in wording.

In fancy fair Saint Agnes in her bed
But dares not look behind or all the charm is ~~fled~~ dead

[*Stanza 30*]

~~But~~
~~And still she slept:~~
And still she slept an azure-lidded sleep
In blanched linen smooth and lavender'd;
While he from frorth the closet brought a heap

     ~~fruits~~
Of candied ~~sweets sweets with~~ and plumb and gourd
    apple Quince
         creamed
With jellies soother than the ~~dairy~~ curd
      tinct
And lucent syrups ~~smooth~~ with crannamon
~~And sugar'd dates from that o'er Euphrates fard~~
    ~~in Brigantine transferrd~~
        ~~transferrd~~
  Manna and daites in Bragine ~~wild transferrd~~
      ~~and Manna~~
~~And Manna wild and~~
        ~~Bragantine~~
       ~~sugar'd~~ dates transferrd
argosy ~~In Brigantine from Fez~~
From fez—and spiced danties every one
  ~~glutted~~
From ~~wealthy~~ Sa⟨l⟩marchand to cedard lebanon
  silken

To Autumn[2]

Season of Mists and mellow fruitfulness
 Close bosom friend of the naturing sun;
Conspiring with him how to load and bless
  The Vines with fruit that round the thatch eves run
  To bend with apples the mosſ'd Cottage trees
   And fill all furuits with sweeness to the core
    To swell the gourd, and plump the hazle shells
  With a white kernel; to set budding more
   And still more later flowers for the bees
   Until they think wam days with never cease
    For Summer has o'erbrimm'd their clammy cells—

      oft amid thy stores?
Who hath not seen thee⟨ ⟩~~for thy haunts are many~~
      abroad
Sometimes whoever seeks ~~for thee~~ may find
Thee sitting careless on a granary floorn
Thy hair soft lifted by the winnowing wind

---

2. From the only extant manuscript of the poem—evidently Keats's first draft, at least of stazas 2 and 3—in the Houghton Library, Harvard University. The many pen-slips and errors in spelling indicate that Keats wrote rapidly, in a state of creative excitement. Keats made a few further changes before publishing the poem in the form included in the selections from Keats, above.

husky
~~While bright the Sun slants through the barn;~~
on on a half reap'd furrow sound asleep
~~Or sound asleep in a half reaped field~~
Dos'd with read poppies; while thy reeping hook
~~Spares form   Some slumbrous~~
—minutes while wam slumpers creep

Or on a half reap'd furrow sound asleep
Dos'd with the fume of poppies, while thy hook
spares the next swath and all its twined nowers
~~Spares for some slumbrous minutes the next swath;~~
And sometimes like a gleans thost dost keep
Steady thy laden head across the brook;
Or by a Cyder-press with patent look
Thou watchest the last oozing hours by hours

[Stanza 3]

Where are the songs of Sping? Aye where are they?
Think not of them thou hast thy music too—
barred   bloom
While ~~a gold~~ cloud ˢ ~~gilds~~ the soft-dying day
And
~~And~~ Touching ~~the~~ the stubble plains rosy hue—
with
Then in a waiful quire the small gnats mourn
Among the river sallows, ~~on the~~ borne afots
Or sinking as the light wind lives and dies;
And full grown Lambs loud bleat from hilly bourn,
Hedge crickets sing, and now again full soft
The Redbreast whistles from a garden croft:
~~And new flock still~~
And Gathering Swallows twiter in the Skies—

ALFRED, LORD TENNYSON

From The Lady of Shalott[1]

[Version of 1832]

PART THE FIRST.

On either side the river lie
Long fields of barley and of rye,
That clothe the wold, and meet the sky.
And thro' the field the road runs by
To manytowered Camelot.

1. First published in Tennyson's *Poems* of 1832 (dated 1833 on the title page). The volume was severely criticized by some reviewers; partly in response to this criticism, Tennyson radically revised a number of the poems, including *The Lady of Shalott*, before reprinting them in his *Poems* (1842).

Parts I and IV are reproduced here in the version of 1832. The final form of the poem reprinted in the selections from Tennyson, above, differs from the revised version that Tennyson published in 1842 only in line 157, which in 1842 read: "A corse between the houses high"; Tennyson changed the line to "Dead-pale between the houses high" in 1855.

The yellowleavèd waterlily,
The greensheathèd daffodilly,
Tremble in the water chilly,
   Round about Shallot.

Willows whiten, aspens shiver,
The sunbeam-showers break and quiver
In the stream that runneth ever
By the island in the river,
   Flowing down to Camelot.
Four gray walls and four gray towers
Overlook a space of flowers,
And the silent isle imbowers
   The Lady of Shallot.

Underneath the bearded barley,
The reaper, reaping late and early,
Hears her ever chanting cheerly,
Like an angel, singing clearly,
   O'er the stream of Camelot.
Piling the sheaves in furrows airy,
Beneath the moon, the reaper weary
Listening whispers, " 'tis the fairy
   Lady of Shalott."

The little isle is all inrailed
With a rose-fence, and overtrailed
With roses: by the marge unhailed
The shallop flitteth silkensailed,
   Skimming down to Camelot.
A pearlgarland winds her head:
She leaneth on a velvet bed,
Full royally apparellèd,
   The Lady of Shalott.

*   *   *

PART THE FOURTH.
———

In the stormy eastwind straining
The pale-yellow woods were waning,
The broad stream in his banks complaining,
Heavily the low sky raining
   Over towered Camelot:
Outside the isle a shallow boat
Beneath a willow lay afloat,
Below the carven stern she wrote,
   THE LADY OF SHALOTT.

A cloudwhite crown of pearl she dight.
All raimented in snowy white

That loosely flew, (her zone in sight,
Clasped with one blinding diamond bright,)
      Her wide eyes fixed on Camelot,
Though the squally eastwind keenly
Blew, with folded arms serenely
By the water stood the queenly
      Lady of Shalott.

With a steady, stony glance—
Like some bold seer in a trance,
Beholding all his own mischance,
Mute, with a glassy countenance—
      She looked down to Camelot.
It was the closing of the day,
She loosed the chain, and down she lay,
The broad stream bore her far away,
      The Lady of Shalott.

As when to sailors while they roam,
By creeks and outfalls far from home,
Rising and dropping with the foam,
From dying swans wild warblings come,
      Blown shoreward; so to Camelot
Still as the boathead wound along
The willowy hills and fields among,
They heard her chanting her deathsong,
      The Lady of Shalott.

A longdrawn carol, mournful, holy,
She chanted loudly, chanted lowly,
Till her eyes were darkened wholly,
And her smooth face sharpened slowly
      Turned to towered Camelot:
For ere she reached upon the tide
The first house by the waterside,
Singing in her song she died,
      The Lady of Shalott.

Under tower and balcony,
By gardenwall and gallery,
A pale, pale corpse she floated by,
Deadcold, between the houses high.
      Dead into towered Camelot.
Knight and burgher, lord and dame,
To the plankèd wharfage came:
Below the stern they read her name,
      "The Lady of Shalott."

They crossed themselves, their stars they blest,

Knight, minstrel, abbot, squire and guest.
There lay a parchment on her breast,
That puzzled more than all the rest,
        The wellfed wits at Camelot.
"The web was woven curiously
The charm is broken utterly,
Draw near and fear not—this is I,
        The Lady of Shalott."

From Tithonus[2]

[Lines 1–10]

[TRINITY COLLEGE MANUSCRIPT]

Ay me! Ay me! the woods decay & fall
~~The stars blaze out & never rise again.~~
                                    the
The vapours weep their substance to ground
Man‸ comes & tills the earth & lies beneath
And after many summers dies the ~~rose~~ swan
Me only fatal immortality
Consumes: I wither slowly in thine arms:
Here at the quiet limit of the world
                            e yet
A white-haired shado~~w~~ roaming like a dream
The ever-silent spaces of the East
Far-folded mists & gleaming halls of morn.

[HEATH MANUSCRIPT]

Tithon

Ay me! ay me! the woods decay and fall,
The vapours weep their substance to the ground,
Man comes and tills the earth and lies beneath,
And after many summers dies the rose.
Me only fatal immortality
Consumes: I wither slowly in thine arms,
Here at the quiet limit of the world,
A white-haired shadow roaming like a dream
The ever-silent spaces of the East,
Far-folded mists, and gleaming halls of morn.

2. Three manuscript drafts of *Tithonus* are extant. Two are in Tennyson's Notebooks Nos. 20 and 21, at Trinity College, Cambridge; a third one, written 1833, is in the Commonplace Book compiled by Tennyson's friend, J. M. Heath, which is in the Fitzwilliam Museum at Cambridge University. According to Tennyson's editor, Christopher Ricks, the Heath version is later than those in the Trinity Manuscripts. The transcriptions here of Tennyson's opening lines are from the first draft (Trinity College manuscript, Notebook 20), and from the Heath manuscript, where the poem is titled "Tithon." These are followed by the final version of *Tithonus* that Tennyson published in 1864. As late as in the edition of 1860, the opening words had remained "Ay me! ay me!" and "field" (line 3) had remained "earth."

[AS PRINTED IN 1864]
Tithonus

The woods decay, the woods decay and fall,
The vapours weep their burthen to the ground,
Man comes and tills the field and lies beneath,
And after many a summer dies the swan.
Me only cruel immortality
Consumes: I wither slowly in thine arms,
Here at the quiet limit of the world,
A white-haired shadow roaming like a dream
The ever-silent spaces of the East,
Far-folded mists, and gleaming halls of morn.

GERARD MANLEY HOPKINS
[Thou Art Indeed Just, Lord][1]

Justus quidem tu es, Domine, si disputem te-
cum; verumtamen justa loquar ad te: quare
via impiorum prosperatur? etc.—Jer. xii 1.

March 17 1889

Thou art indeed just, ~~were I to~~ contend
  ^{Lord, if I}
With thee; but, ~~Lord,~~ so what I ~~speak~~ is just.
     ^{sir,}   ^{plead}

Why do sinners' ways prosper? and why must

Disappointment all I endeavour end?

Wert thou my enemy, O thou my friend,

How wouldst thou worse, I wonder, than thou dost

Defeat, thwart me? ~~Ah! sots, revellers,~~ thralls ~~to~~ lust
            ^{O the sots and}   ^{of}

~~In~~ spare hours ~~do~~ more thrive than I ~~who~~ spend,
^{Do in}   ^{that}

1. From a manuscript in the Bodleian Library, Oxford University; it is a clean copy, made after earlier drafts, which Hopkins went on to revise further. Differences in the ink show that the emendation "lacèd they are" (line 10) was made during the first writing, but that the other verbal changes were made later. The interlinear markings are Hopkins's metrical indicators; he explains their significance in the "Author's Pre-face," included in *Poems of Gerard Manley Hopkins* (1970), edited by W. H. Gardner and N. H. MacKenzie.

The epigraph is from the Vulgate translation of Jeremiah xii.1; a literal translation of the Latin is: "Thou art indeed just, Lord, [even] if I plead with Thee; nevertheless I will speak what is just to Thee: Why does the way of the wicked prosper? etc."

                        great   see,
/ / Sir, ~~my~~ life on thy cause. ~~Look,~~ banks and brakes
/ Now, leavèd   lacèd they are
\   ~~Leavèd~~ how thick! ~~broiderèd all~~ again
 \   look
  \ With fretty chervil, ~~now,~~ and fresh wind shakes
 / Them; birds build—but not I build; no, but strain,
 / Time's eunuch, and not breed one work that wakes.
 \ Mine, O   send my
  \ ~~Then send,~~ thou lord of life, ~~these~~ roots ~~their~~ rain.

WILLIAM BUTLER YEATS

Yeats usually composed very slowly and with painful effort. He tells us
in his *Autobiography* that "five or six lines in two or three laborious
hours were a day's work, and I longed for somebody to interrupt me."
His manuscripts show the slow evolution of his best poems, which sometimes began with a prose sketch, were then versified, and underwent
numerous revisions. Even after many of his poems had been published,
Yeats continued to revise them repeatedly, sometimes drastically, in later
printings.

The Sorrow of Love[1]

[*Manuscript, 1891*][2]

The quarrel of the sparrows in the eaves,
The full round moon and the star-laden sky,
The song of the ever-singing leaves,
Had hushed away earth's old and weary cry.

And then you came with those red mournful lips,
And with you came the whole of the world's tears,
And all the sorrows of her labouring ships,
And all the burden of her million years.

And now the angry sparrows in the eaves,
The withered moon, the white stars in the sky,
The wearisome loud chanting of the leaves,
Are shaken with earth's old and weary cry.

[*First Printed Version, 1892*][3]

The quarrel of the sparrows in the eaves,
The full round moon and the star-laden sky,

---

1. Originally composed in Yeats's Pre-
Raphaelite mode of the early 1890's, *The
Sorrow of Love* was one of his most
popular poems. Nonetheless, some 30
years after publication, Yeats rewrote
the lyric to give it the greater precision
and colloquial vigor of his poetic style in

the 1920's.
2. Manuscript version composed in October, 1891, as transcribed by Jon Stallworthy, *Between the Lines: Yeats's Poetry in the Making* (Oxford University
Press, 1963), pages 47–48.
3. From Yeats's *The Countess Kathleen*

And the loud song of the ever-singing leaves
   Had hid away earth's old and weary cry.

And then you came with those red mournful lips,
   And with you came the whole of the world's tears,
And all the sorrows of her labouring ships,
   And all burden of her myriad years.

And now the sparrows warring in the eaves,
   The crumbling moon, the white stars in the sky,
And the loud chanting of the unquiet leaves,
   Are shaken with earth's old and weary cry.

[Final Printed Version, 1925][4]

The brawling of a sparrow in the eaves,
The brilliant moon and all the milky sky,
And all that famous harmony of leaves,
Had blotted out man's image and his cry.

A girl arose that had red mournful lips
And seemed the greatness of the world in tears,
Doomed like Odysseus and the labouring ships
And proud as Priam murdered with his peers;

Arose, and on the instant clamorous eaves,
A climbing moon upon an empty sky,
And all that lamentation of the leaves,
Could but compose man's image and his cry.

Leda and the Swan[5]

[First Version]

Annunciation

Now can the swooping Godhead have his will
Yet hovers, though her helpless thighs are pressed
By the webbed toes; and that all powerful bill

---

and Various Legends and Lyrics (1892). In a corrected page proof for this printing, now in the Garvan Collection of the Yale University Library, lines 7–8 originally read: "And all the sorrows of his labouring ships, / And all the burden of his married years." Also, in lines 4 and 12, the adjective was "bitter" instead of "weary." In his *Poems* (1895), Yeats inserted the missing "the" in line 8, and changed "sorrows" (line 7) to "trouble"; "burden" (line 8) to "trouble"; and "crumbling moon'" (line 10) to "curd-pale moon."

4. In *Early Poems and Stories* (1925). Yeats wrote in his *Autobiography* (New York, 1938), page 371, that "in later

years" he had "learnt that occasional prosaic words gave the impression of an active man speaking," so that "certain words must be dull and numb. Here and there in correcting my early poems I have introduced such numbness and dullness, turned, for instance, 'the curd-pale moon' into the 'brilliant moon,' that all might seem, as it were, remembered with indifference, except some one vivid image." Yeats, however, did not recall his emendations accurately. He had in 1925 altered "the full round moon" (line 2) to "the brilliant moon," and "the curd-pale moon" (line 10, version of 1895) to "a climbing moon."

5. From Yeats's manuscript *Journal*,

Has suddenly bowed her face upon his breast.
How can those terrified vague fingers push
The feathered glory from her loosening thighs?
All the stretched body's laid on that white rush
       strange
And feels the ~~strong~~ heart beating where it lies
A shudder in the loins engenders there
The broken wall, the burning roof and tower
And Agamemnon dead . . . .
                    Being so caught up
Did nothing pass before her in the air?
Did she put on his knowledge with his power
Before the indifferent beak could let her drop.
                  Sept 18 1923

      swooping
The ~~trembl~~ godhead is half hovering still,
     climbs
Yet ~~climbs~~ upon her trembling body pressed
    webbed
By the toes; & ~~through~~ that all powerful bill
       ~~thrown~~ bowed
Has suddenly ~~bowed~~ her face upon his breast.
How can those terrified vague fingers push
The feathered glory from her loosening thighs
           laid
All the stretched body ~~leans~~ on that white rush
          or
~~Her falling body thrown on the white~~ white rush
Can feel etc
or Her body can but lean on the white rush

    But mounts until her trembling thighs are pressed[6]
  ~~B~~
By the webbed toes; & that all powerful bill
Has suddenly bowed her head on his breast

Sections 248 and 250. This *Journal,* including facsimiles and transcriptions of the drafts of *Leda and the Swan,* has been published in W. B. Yeats, *Memoirs,* edited by Denis Donoghue (Macmillan, London, 1972).

The first version, entitled "Annunciation," seems to be a clean copy of earlier drafts; Yeats went on to revise it further, especially the opening octave. Neither of the other two complete drafts, each of which Yeats labeled "Final Version," was in fact final. Yeats himself crossed out the first draft. The second, although Yeats published it in 1924, was subjected to further revision before he published the poem in *The Tower* (1928), in the final form reprinted in the selections from Yeats, above.

Yeats's handwriting is hasty and very difficult to decipher. The readings of some words, both in the manuscripts of this poem and of *After Long Silence,* below, are uncertain.

6. This passage is written across the blank page opposite the first version; Yeats drew a line indicating that it was to replace the revised lines 2–4, which he had written below the first version.

Can hold

Final Version
Annunciation

The swooping godhead is half hovering still
But mounts, until her trembling thighs are pressed
By the webbed toes, & that all powerful bill
Has hung her helpless body
~~Has suddenly bowed her head up~~on his breast.
How can those terrified vague fingers push
The feathered glory from her loosening thighs?
How now its body leans on
With her body ~~laid on the white rush~~
all the stretched body laid on the white rush
and ~~Can~~ feel the strange heart beating where it lies?
A shudder in the loins engenders there
The broken wall, the burning roof & tower
And Agamemnon dead . . .

Being mastered so
~~Being so caught up~~

So
~~And~~ mastered by the brute blood of the air
~~Being mastered so~~
~~Did nothing pass before her in the air?~~
Did she put on his knowledge with his power
Before the indifferent beak could let her drop.

WBY. Sept 18 1923

swoop
A ~~rush~~ upon great wings & hovering still
~~He sinks until~~
~~He has sunk on her down, & her hair~~
~~The great bird sinks, till~~
The bird descends, & her frail ~~thigh~~ thighs are pressed
By the webbed toes, & that all

that
Now ~~all~~ her body's laid on that white rush[7]
~~All the stretched body, laid on that white rush~~
~~Now that whole~~
Now that her body, on the white rush
Can feel

Final Version
Leda & the Swan

A rush, a sudden wheel and
~~A swoop upon great wings &~~ hovering still
sinks down·   bare frail
stet The bird ~~descends~~ & her ~~frail~~ thighs are pressed
By the ~~toes~~ webbed toes, & that all powerful bill

7. Written on the blank page across from the complete version, with an arrow indicating that it was a revision of the seventh line.

      laid
Has ~~driven~~ her helpless face upon his breast.
How can those terrified vague fingers push
The feathered glory from her loosening thighs?
     s laid
All the stretched body ~~laid~~ on that white rush
And ~~feel~~ feels the strange heart beating where it lies.
A shudder in the loins engenders there
The broken wall, the burning roof & tower
And Agamemnon dead.
                Being so caught up
So mastered by the ~~br~~ brute blood of the air
Did she put on his knowledge with his power
Before the indifferent beak could let her drop.

After Long Silence[8]

[Draft 1]

Subject

Your hair is white
My hair is white
Come let us talk of love
What other theme do we know
When we were young
We were in love with one another
~~A O~~ And therefore ignorant

[Draft 2]

Those
~~Your~~ other lover[s] being dead & gone

                              friendly light
                              hair is white

              ~~on love descant~~   descant
Upon the ~~sole theme~~ supreme theme of art &   song
Wherein there's theme so fitting for the aged.   ;young
We loved each other & were ignorant

8. The drafts of *After Long Silence* are interspersed with other materials on seven pages of a manuscript book, begun in 1928, which includes a number of additional poems that were published in *The Winding Stair and Other Poems* (1933). It begins, like many of Yeats's poems, with a prose sketch, and is labeled simply "Subject." It then passes through a tentative versified stage (Draft 2) in which Yeats sets down four complete lines and a set of possible rhyme words; is subjected to various drafts and revisions; and concludes with the final text that Yeats published in 1933. Yeats did not add the title *After Long Silence* until he wrote out a fair copy for his typist at some time after August 14, 1931.

David R. Clark, "After 'Silence,' The 'Supreme Theme': Eight Lines of Yeats," includes photocopies and transcripts of the drafts of this poem, together with a discussion of its biographical occasion and its interpretation (in *Myth and Reality in Irish Literature*, edited by Joseph Ronsley, Waterloo, Canada, 1977, pages 149–73).

[*Draft 3*]

~~I h~~

Once more I have kissed your hand & it is right—
All other lovers being estranged or dead
~~The heavy curtain drawn—the candle-light~~
~~Waging a doubtful battle with the shade~~

descant,
~~We call our wisdom up upon our wisdom & descant~~
~~Upon the supreme theme of art & song~~
Decrepitude increases wisdom—young
We loved each other & were ~~ignorant ignor~~ ignorant

[*Draft 4*]

Un
~~The~~ friendly lamplight hidden by its shade
~~And shutters clapped upon the deepening night~~
~~The candle hidden by its friendly shade~~
Those curtains drawn upon the deepening night—

s
~~The curtain drawn on the unfriendly night~~
That we descant & yet again descant
supreme theme
Upon the ~~supreme theme~~ of ~~art & song~~   art & song—
Bodily decrepitude is wisdom—young

[*Final MS Version*]

Speech after long silence; ~~&~~ it is right—
or
All other lovers being estranged ~~&~~ dead,
hid
Unfriendly lamp-light ~~hid~~ under its shade,
upon
The curtain's drawn ~~upon~~ unfriendly night—
That we descant & yet again descant
Upon the supreme theme of art & song;
Bodily decrepitude is wisdom; young
We loved each other & were ignorant

Nov
~~Oct~~ 1929

Selected Bibliographies

The Selected Bibliographies incorporate a list of Suggested General Readings on English literature, followed by bibliographies for each of the periods in this volume. For ease of reference, the authors within each period are arranged in alphabetical order. In those instances where there are also general readings for a group of authors (such as "The Nineties" or "Poetry of World War I"), the title of the group, with its entries, appears in its alphabetical place. Those entries are followed by the names of all the authors in that group; the bibliographical listing for each of those authors will also be found in its proper alphabetical place.

SUGGESTED GENERAL READINGS

Histories of England and of English Literature

George Macaulay Trevelyan's *History of England*, rev., 1945, is an excellent survey in one volume; for detailed studies of single periods, see *The Oxford History of England*, 15 vols., 1934 ff., by a variety of historians. For single books in the comprehensive 12-volume *Oxford History of English Literature*, edited by F. P. Wilson and Bonamy Dobrée, 1945 ff., see the listings below. *A Guide to English Literature*, ed. Boris Ford, 1954–61, is available in 6 paperback volumes. Useful one-volume histories are Albert C. Baugh and others, *A Literary History of England*, rev., 1967; Hardin Craig and others, *A History of English Literature*, 1950; and (less densely factual, and more a running literary appreciation) David Daiches, *A Critical History of English Literature*, 2 vols., 1961. *Annals of English Literature, 1475–1950*, ed. J. C. Ghosh and others, rev. 1961, lists important publications year by year, together with the significant literary events in each year. Ellen Moers, *Literary Women*, 1976, is a history of the circumstances, inter-influences, and distinctive features of literature written by women.

Drama

Allardyce Nicoll, *British Drama*, rev., 1962, and *A History of English Drama, 1660–1900*, 6 vols., rev., 1952–59.

The Novel

The most detailed, although somewhat pedestrian, history is Ernest A. Baker's *History of the English Novel*, 10 vols., 1924–39. Among the short histories are Walter A. Raleigh, *The English Novel*, rev., 1911, which stops at Walter Scott; and, more up-to-date, Arnold Kettle, *An Introduction to the English Novel*, 2 vols., 1951–53; Walter Allen, *The English Novel*, 1954; Ian Watt, *The Rise of the Novel*, 1957; and Lionel Stevenson, *The English Novel*, 1960.

Poetry

W. J. Courthope, *A History of English Poetry*, 6 vols., 1895–1910, and H. J. C. Grierson and J. C. Smith, *A Critical History of English Poetry*, rev., 1947. In addition, Douglas Bush's two books, *Mythology and the Renaissance Tradition in English Poetry*, 1932, 1957, and *Mythology and the Romantic Tradition in English Poetry*, 1937, 1957, constitute an excellent running account, from their special perspective, of English poetry from the 16th century through T. S. Eliot. Another book which ranges widely in English poetry from the Middle Ages through the 18th century is E. M. W. Tillyard, *The English Epic and Its Background*, 1954.

Literary Criticism

George Saintsbury, *A History of English Criticism*, 1911, is still referred to. More recent histories of English criticism are M. H. Abrams, *The Mirror and the Lamp: Romantic Theory and the Critical Tradition*, 1953; W. K. Wimsatt, Jr. and Cleanth Brooks, *Literary Criticism: A Short History*, 1957; George Watson, *The Literary Critics*, 1962; and René Wellek, *A History of Modern Criticism: 1750–1950*, 1955, of which four of the projected five volumes have been published. René Wellek and Austin Warren, *Theory of Literature*, rev. 1970, is a useful introduction to the variety of scholarly and critical approaches to the study of literature.

Reference Works

The New Cambridge Bibliography of English Literature, ed. George Watson and I. R. Willison, 1969–77, lists all the books of the major and many minor British authors, together with a large selection from biographical, scholarly, and critical works written about these authors. Literary biographies and critical books published since that time can be found in the "Annual Bibliography" *PMLA*; for separate periods, see listings below. F. W. Bateson, ed., *A Guide to English Literature*, rev., 1968, is a selected list of editions, and of scholarly and critical treatments, of all important English writers; for poetry only see A. E. Dyson, ed., *English Poetry: Select Bibliographical Guides*, 1971. *Poetry Explication*, rev. by Joseph M. Kuntz, 1962, lists close analyses of English poems, old and recent, and I. F. Bell and Donald Baird, *The English Novel, 1578–1956*, 1958, provides a useful list of 20th-century criticisms of fiction. Further bibliographical aids are described in Richard D. Altick and Andrew Wright, *Selective Bibliography for the Study of English and American Literature*, 1971, and Arthur G. Kennedy, *A Concise Bibliography for Students of English*, rev., 1972.

For compact biographies of English authors, see the multi-volumed *Dictionary of National Biography*, edited by Leslie Stephen and Sidney Lee in 1885–1900, with supplements that carry the work to persons who died up to 1960; condensed biographies will be found in the *Concise Dictionary of National Biography*, Part I (1953) and Part II (1961). Handy reference books on authors, works, and various literary terms and allusions are *The Oxford Companion to English Literature*, edited by Paul Harvey, rev., 1970; *The Reader's Companion to World Literature*, edited by Calvin S. Brown, 1956; *The Oxford Companion to the Theater*, edited by Phyllis Hartnoll, rev., 1967; *Dictionary of World Literature*, edited by Joseph T. Shipley, rev., 1953; and *Encyclopedia of Poetry and Poetics*, edited by Alex Preminger and others, 1965. Low-priced handbooks which define and illustrate literary concepts and terms are: M. H. Abrams, *A Glossary of Literary Terms*, rev., 1971; W. F. Thrall and Addison Hibbard, *A Handbook to Literature*, revised by G. Hugh Holman, 1960; and Lee T. Lemon, *A Glossary for the Study of English*, 1971. A useful and concise reference book is G. M. Kirkwood, *A Short Guide to Classical Mythology*, 1959.

Albert C. Baugh, *A History of the English Language*, rev., 1957, will be found helpful, as will various treatments of English meters and stanza forms, such as: R. M. Alden, *English Verse*, 1903; Karl Shapiro and Robert Beum, *A Prosody Handbook*, 1965; Paul Fussell, Jr., *Poetic Meter and Poetic Form*, 1966; and *The Structure of Verse: Modern Essays in Prosody*, ed. Harvey Gross, 1966.

Intellectual History and Criticism

Students interested in intellectual history as a background for reading English literature will profit from Arthur T. Lovejoy, *The Great Chain of Bering*, 1936, and *Essays in the History of Ideas*, 1948; Marjorie Nicolson, *The Breaking of the Circle*, 1950, *Science and Imagination*, 1956, and *Mountain Gloom and Mountain Glory*, 1959; John Herman Randall, Jr., *The Making of the Modern Mind*, rev., 1940; Basil Willey, *The Seventeenth Century Background*, 1934, *The Eighteenth Century Background*, 1940, and *Nineteenth Century Studies*, 1949; and M. H. Abrams, *Natural Supernaturalism: Tradition and Revolution in Romantic Literature*, 1971. In addition, the following is a selection from those books in literary history and criticism which have been notably influential in shaping modern approaches to English literature and literary forms; Erich Auerbach, *Mimesis: The Representation of Reality in Western Literature*, 1953; Maud Bodkin, *Archetypal Patterns in Poetry*, 1934; Cleanth Brooks, *The Well Wrought Urn*, 1947; Ronald Crane, *The Languages of Criticism and the Structure of Poetry*, 1953, *The Idea of the Humanities*, 2 vols., 1967, and, as editor, *Critics and Criticism, Ancient and Modern*, 1952; T. S. Eliot, *Selected Essays*, 3rd edition, 1951, and *On Po-*

etry and Poets, 1957; William Empson, *Seven Types of Ambiguity*, 3rd edition, 1953; William K. Wimsatt, *The Verbal Icon*, 1954; Francis Fergusson, *The Idea of a Theater*, 1949; Northrop Frye, *Anatomy of Criticism*, 1957; Henry James, *The Art of the Novel: Critical Prefaces*, 1934; F. R. Leavis, *Revaluation*, 1936, and *The Great Tradition* (i.e., in the novel), 1948; C. S. Lewis, *The Allegory of Love*, rev., 1938; John Livingston Lowes, *The Road to Xanadu*, rev., 1930; Percy Lubbock, *The Craft of Fiction*, 1926; I. A. Richards, *Principles of Literary Criticism*, 5th edition, 1934, and *Practical Criti-*

cism, 1930; Caroline Spurgeon, *Shakespeare's Imagery*, 1935; Lionel Trilling, *The Liberal Imagination*, 1950, and *The Opposing Self*, 1955; Edmund Wilson, *Axel's Castle: A Study in the Imaginative Literature of 1870–1930*, 1936, and *The Wound and the Bow*, 1941; Wayne C. Booth, *The Rhetoric of Fiction*, 1961, and *A Rhetoric of Irony*, 1974; W. J. Bate, *The Burden of the Past and the English Past*, 1970; and Harold Bloom, *The Anxiety of Influence*, 1973. A convenient introduction to recent structuralist approaches to literary study is Jonathan Culler's *Structuralist Poetics*, 1975.

THE ROMANTIC PERIOD

Bibliographies

The most convenient starting point is to consult the surveys by Frank Jordan and other editors, *The English Romantic Poets, a Review of Research and Criticism*, rev., 1972, on Wordsworth, Coleridge, Byron, Shelley, and Keats; and Carolyn W. Houtchens and Lawrence H. Houtchens, *The English Romantic Poets and Essayists*, rev., 1966, on Blake, the lesser poets, and the major essayists. A short bibliography, designed for students, is *Romantic Poets and Prose Writers*, compiled by R. H. Fogle, 1967. Annual bibliographies of publications about these writers are to be found in *ELH*, 1937–49; *Philological Quarterly*, 1950–64· and *English Language Notes*, 1965–

Political and Social Background

Succinct and reliable treatments of the political and social events in this period are the relevant chapters of G. M. Trevelyan's *British History of the Nineteenth Century*, 2nd edition, 1937, and *English Social History*, 1942. More detailed histories are Elie Halévy, *England in 1815*, rev., 1949, and *The Liberal Awakening, 1815–1830*, rev., 1949; J. Steven Watson, *The Reign of George III, 1760–1815*, 1960; and Asa Briggs, *The Making of Modern England: 1783–1867*, 1959. Gilbert Slater, *The Growth of Modern England*, 1932, deals especially with the industrial revolution. For English literary relations to the French Revolution, see Edward Dowden, *The French Revolution and English Literature*, 1897; A. E. Hancock, *The French Revolution and the English Poets*, 1899; and Howard Mumford Jones, *Revolution and Romanticism*, 1974.

Intellectual Background

Illuminating analyses of important intellectual movements will be found in A. O. Lovejoy's *The Great Chain of Being*, 1936, Chapters IX and X, and *Essays in the History of Ideas*, 1948. Other particularly useful works on intellectual history are Basil Willey, *The Eighteenth Century Background*, 1940, and *Nineteenth Century Studies: Coleridge to Matthew Arnold*, 1949; Joseph Warren Beach, *The Concept of Nature in Nineteenth-Century English Poetry*, 1936; Hoxie Neale Fairchild, *Religious Trends in English Poetry*, of which Vol. III (1949) deals with 1780–1830); H. W. Piper, *The Active Universe: Pantheism and the Concept of Imagination in the English Romantic Poets*, 1962; and Carl Woodring's excellent survey of *Politics in English Romantic Poetry*, 1970. On Romantic literature in its social matrix, see the relevant chapters in Raymond Williams, *Culture and Society, 1780–1950*, 1960. In *Romanticism: Points of View*, rev., 1970, Robert F. Gleckner and Gerald E. Enscoe reprint major essays on the defining features of "Romanticism"; see also the essays in *Romanticism Reconsidered*, ed. Northrop Frye, 1963, and David Thorburn and Geoffrey Hartman, eds., *Romanticism: Vistas, Instances, Continuities*, 1973.

Literary History and Criticism

Among the histories of Romantic literature are: Oliver Elton, *A Survey of English Literature, 1780–1830*, 2 vols., 1928; W. L. Renwick's rather inadequate *English Literature 1789–1815*, 1963; and Ian Jack's *English Literature, 1815–1832*, 1963. Mario Praz's *The Romantic Agony*, 2nd ed., 1951, treats Satanism, sadism, vampirism, and others of the more exotic literary interests of the time; G. R. Thompson has edited *The Gothic Imagination: Essays in Dark Romanticism*, 1974; and Peter Thorsley's

The Byronic Hero, 1962, discusses the solitary or alienated hero in other writers, as well as Byron; see also Frank Kermode's *Romantic Image,* 1957, on the concept of the poet at odds with society, from the Romantic period to Yeats. Douglas Bush's *Mythology and the Romantic Tradition in English Poetry,* 1937, is so broad in its range that it constitutes an excellent survey of Romantic poetry in general. The older negative appraisals of the Romantic achievement by the neohumanist, Irving Babbitt, in *Rousseau and Romanticism,* 1919, and *On Being Creative and Other Essays,* 1932, has been taken up and expanded by Edward E. Bostetter in *The Romantic Ventriloquists,* 1963. G. Wilson Knight, *The Starlit Dome,* 1941, reprinted 1960, is an influential early example of the approach to Romantic poets by the analysis of characteristic patterns of imagery. Harold Bloom, *The Visionary Company,* rev., 1971, which relates these poets to the prophetic tradition of Spenser and Milton, includes brief and stimulating commentaries on each of the important poems; Bloom's *The Ringers of the Tower,* 1971, consists of influential essays on both 19th- and 20th-century "Romantic" writers. David Perkins treated *The Quest for Permanence* in Wordsworth, Shelley, and Keats, 1951; and Northrop Frye presents an archetypal overview in *A Study of English Romanticism,* 1968. In *Natural Supernaturalism: Tradition and Revolution in Romantic Literature,* 1971, M. H. Abrams deals with persistent themes, concepts, and designs in English and German Romantic literature, and stresses their relation both to the biblical tradition and the intellectual ambiance of a revolutionary age. Other recent books to be noted are Michael G. Cooke, *The Romantic Will,* 1976; Thomas Weiskel, *The Romantic Sublime: Studies in the Structure and Psychology of Transcendence,* 1976; and Morse Beckham, *Romanticism and Behavior,* 1976. *English Romantic Poets: Modern Essays and Criticism,* edited by M. H. Abrams, 1960, is a collection of broadly representative essays by major contemporary critics; *Romanticism and Consciousness: Essays in Criticism,* edited by Harold Bloom, 1970, focuses on some leading topics in Romantic literature. See also the essays in Frederick W. Hilles and Harold Bloom, eds., *From Sensibility to Romanticism,* 1965. For critical opinions of the poets during their own lifetime, see Donald A. Reiman's *The Romantics Reviewed: Contemporary Reviews of British Romantic Writers,* 9 vols., 1972.

Following are studies of various forms of Romantic literature. On literary criticism: M. H. Abrams, *The Mirror and the Lamp: Romantic Theory and the Critical Tradition,* 1953; René Wellek, *A History of Modern Criticism: 1750–1950,* Vol. II, *The Romantic Age,* 1955. On narrative poetry: Kark Kroeber, *Romantic Narrative Art,* 1960, and Brian Wilkie, *Romantic Poets and Epic Tradition,* 1965. On the novel: Ernest A. Baker, *The History of the English Novel,* Vol. V, 1961; Montague Summers, *The Gothic Quest: A History of the Gothic Novel,* 1938; and Robert Kiely, *The Romantic Novel in England,* 1972. On drama: Allardyce Nicoll, *History of Early Nineteenth-Century Drama, 1800–50,* 2 vols., rev. ed. 1955. On the essay: William F. Bryan and Ronald S. Crane, Introduction, *The English Familiar Essay,* 1916; Marie H. Law, *The English Familiar Essay in the Early Nineteenth Century,* 1934.

Thomas Lovell Beddoes

The standard edition of Beddoes's writings, including his manuscript remains, is the *Works,* edited by H. W. Donner, 1935. The same scholar has edited a good selection of the *Plays and Poems,* 1950, and has written the best biography, *Thomas Lovell Beddoes: The Making of a Poet,* 1935. See also R. H. Snow, *Thomas Lovell Beddoes,* 1928.

William Blake

The beautifully printed *The Complete Writings of William Blake,* edited by Geoffrey Keynes, 1957, has now been replaced as the scholar's edition by *The Poetry and Prose of William Blake,* edited by David Erdman and Harold Bloom, 1965, which includes painstaking textual notes and brief commentaries on many of the poems. Erdman has also prepared a modernized text of all Blake's verse, with copious explanatory notes by W. H. Stevenson, *The Poems of William Blake* (Longman-Norton Annotated English Poets), 1971. There is a *Life of William Blake* by Mona Wilson, 1927, rev., 1948, and Raymond Lister's *William Blake: An Introduction to the Man and His Work,* 1968; but the first full account, Alexander Gilchrist's *The Life of William Blake,* which appeared in 1863, is a charming work which has been a source book for all later biographers and is available (expertly edited and supplemented by Ruthven Todd) in Everyman's Library, 1945.

The modern era of the scholarly explication of Blake symbolism was begun by S. Foster Damon's *William*

Blake: His Philosophy and Symbols, 1924; the same scholar has also published a very helpful Blake Dictionary: The Ideas and Symbols of William Blake, 1965. Of more recent books perhaps the most useful are: Northrop Frye's classic analysis of Blake's moral allegory, Fearful Symmetry, 1947; Mark Schorer's study emphasizing Blake's characteristic union of political, moral, and religious radicialism, William Blake: The Politics of Vision, 1946; David V. Erdman's detailed investigation of the relation of Blake's poetry to the historical events of his time, Blake: Prophet Against Empire, rev., 1969; Peter Fisher's incisive exposition of Blake's thought, The Valley of Vision, 1961; Harold Bloom's commentaries on the individual poems, Blake's Apocalypse: A Study in Poetic Argument, 1963; Thomas R. Frosch's The Awakening of Albion: The Renovation of the Body in the Poetry of William Blake, 1973; and J. A. Wittreich's Angel of Apocalypse: Blake's Idea of Milton, 1975.

Modern critical essays are collected in Blake, edited by Northrop Frye, 1966, and in Blake's Visionary Forms Dramatic, edited by D. V. Erdman and J. E. Grant, 1970. H. M. Margoliouth's William Blake, 1951, and Martin K. Nurmi's William Blake, 1976, are useful general introductions to the man and his work. Studies emphasizing the shorter poems are: Hazard Adams, William Blake: A Reading of the Shorter Poems, 1963; Robert F. Gleckner, The Piper and the Bard, 1959; and E. D. Hirsch, Jr., Innocence and Experience: An Introduction to Blake, 1964. Blake's Sublime Allegory, edited by Stuart Curran and Joseph Anthony Wittreich, Jr., 1973, includes essays by diverse scholars on the major prophecies, The Four Zoas, Milton, and Jerusalem; while Susan Fox's Poetic Form in Blake's "Milton" is an admirably lucid analysis of that poem, and of Blakes' other mythographic poems. A Concordance to the Writings of William Blake, edited by David Erdman, 1967, is an important aid in elucidating his symbolism. On Blake's graphic work, see David Bindman, Blake as an Artist, 1977; there is a large and growing list of books which reproduce (some of them in color) Blake's etched poems, drawings, and engravings; especially useful is The Illuminated Blake, edited by David V. Erdman, 1974, of which the subtitle describes the contents: "All of William Blake's Illuminated Works with a Plate-by-Plate Commentary"; and Erdman's reproduction, with transcripts and commentary, of The

Notebooks of William Blake, revised 1977. The Blake Bibliography, edited by G. E. Bentley, Jr., and Martin K. Nurmi, 1964, is supplemented by Bentleys' Blake Records, 1969, and his Blake Books, 1977.

William Lisle Bowles

The Poetical Works, ed. G. Gilfillan, 1855. G. Greeve, A Wiltshire Parson and His Friends: The Correspondence of W. L. Bowles, 1926.

Robert Burns

The standard references for Burns's poems are the Centenary Edition, edited in 4 vols. by W. E. Henley and T. F. Henderson, 1896–97, and The Poems and Songs of Robert Burns, ed. James Kinsley, 3 vols., 1968. A good one-volume edition is that by James Kinsley, Oxford Standard Authors, 1969; and a useful selection has been edited by John Delancey Ferguson, Selected Poems of Robert Burns, 1926. Ferguson has also given us a reliable edition of The Letters of Robert Burns, 2 vols., 1931, and a brilliant portrait of Burns, Pride and Passion, 1939. A detailed and thoroughly documented biography is by Franklyn Bliss Snyder, The Life of Robert Burns, 1932; and David Daiches has provided a useful survey of Robert Burns and His World, 1971. James C. Dick has written an excellent study of the texts and music of The Songs of Robert Burns, 1903. David Daiches's Robert Burns, 1950, provides a critical analysis of all the major poems, while Thomas Crawford's Burns: A Study of the Poems and Songs, 1960, is a detailed and comprehensive commentary. See also James Kinsley, ed., Scottish Poetry, A Critical Survey, 1955, and Donald A. Low, ed., Critical Essays on Robert Burns, 1975.

George Gordon, Lord Byron

The Works of Lord Byron, 1898–1904, contains seven volumes of Poetry, edited by Ernest Hartley Coleridge, and six volumes of Letters and Journals, edited by Rowland E. Prothero; the latter are being superseded by Leslie A. Marchand's superb edition of the Letters and Journals, of which 6 volumes (up to 1819) have been published. There are numerous editions of the collected poems: a well-chosen and annotated selection has been published in two volumes in the Odyssey Press Series: Don Juan and Other Satiric Poems, edited by Louis I. Bredvold, 1935, and Childe Harold's Pilgrimage and Other Romantic Poems, edited by Samuel C. Chew, 1936. A full new selection, ed. Frank D. McConnell, is *Byron's Poetry*, a Norton Critical Edition, 1978. Selections from the letters have been prepared by V. H. Collins, *Lord Byron in His Letters*, 1927, and by R. G. Howarth, *Letters of Lord Byron*, 1933. *His Very Self and Voice*, by Ernest J. Lovell, Jr., 1954, is a compilation of Byron's conversations, and *Byron: A Self-Portrait*, edited by Peter Quennell, 2 vols., 1950, reprints selected letters and the text of his diaries.

The standard biography, a circumstantial and objective narrative, is Leslie A. Marchand's *Byron: A Biography*, 3 vols., 1957; a one-volume condensation is *Byron, a Portrait*, 1970. A very readable short life is Peter Quennell, *Byron*, 1934. Among the many recent books on Byron as poet are: G. Wilson Knight's symbolic interpretations and praises of Byron, *The Burning Oracle*, 1939, and *Lord Byron: Christian Virtues*, 1954; E. J. Lovell, Jr., *Byron: The Record of a Quest*, 1950; Paul West, *Byron and the Spoiler's Art*, 1960; Andrew Rutherford, *Byron*, 1961; L. A. Marchand, *Byron's Poetry: A Critical Introduction*, 1965; and Jerome L. McGann, *Fiery Dust: Byron's Poetic Development*, 1968. Bernard Blackstone's *Byron: A Survey*, 1975, is a readable, though somewhat idiosyncratic, introduction to the writer; and Charles Robinson, *Byron and Shelley: The Snake and the Eagle Wreathed in Fight*, 1975, discusses the relations and inter-influences of these two poets. *Byron*, 1963, edited by Paul West, is a collection of 20th-century essays in criticism.

An edition of *Don Juan* which incorporates the changes Byron made in his manuscripts is *Byron's Don Juan*, edited by T. G. Steffan and W. W. Pratt, 4 vols., 1957; the first volume, by Steffan, is a full commentary on his poem. Other discussions of Byron's masterpiece are: P. G. Trueblood, *The Flowering of Byron's Genius: Studies in Byron's Don Juan*, 1945; E. F. Boyd, *Byron's Don Juan: A Critical Study*, 1945; George M. Ridenour, *The Style of "Don Juan,"* 1960; Jerome L. McGann, *"Don Juan" in Context*, 1976; and E. E. Bostetter's collection of *Twentieth-Century Interpretations of "Don Juan,"* 1969.

John Clare

The fullest selection from Clare's published poems and from the great mass of his unpublished remains is *The Poems of John Clare*, edited by J. W. Tibble, 2 vols., 1935. The same scholar, with Anne Tibble, has written *Clare: His Life and Poetry*, rev.,

1972, and has edited *The Prose*, 1951, and *The Letters*, 1951. Shorter selections, edited independently from the manuscripts, are Geoffrey Grigson's editions of *Poems of John Clare's Madness*, 1949, and *Selected Poems*, 1950; and *Selected Poems and Prose*, edited by Eric Robinson and Geoffrey Summerfield, 1967. The essays on Clare by J. M. Murry, collected in his *John Clare and Other Studies*, 1959, will indicate the sudden leap forward of Clare's reputation when he was "rediscovered" in the 1920's. See also John Barrell, *The Idea of Landscape and the Sense of Place, 1730–1840: An Approach to the Poetry of John Clare*, 1972; Mark Storey, *The Poetry of John Clare: A Critical Introduction*, 1974; and Greg Crosson, *A Relish for Eternity: The Process of Divinization in the Poetry of John Clare*, 1976.

Samuel Taylor Coleridge

The *Complete Works*, ed. W. G. T. Shedd, 7 vols., 1853, 1844, though far from complete, is the most inclusive collection of Coleridge's works; it will be superseded by the edition of Coleridge's writings now in process under the general editorship of Kathleen Coburn, 1969– ; the works so far edited in this series by various scholars are: *Lectures 1795 on Politics and Religion; The Watchman; Essays on His Times; The Friend; Lay Sermons;* and *On the Constitution of the Church and State*. The edition of the *Complete Poetical Works* is by E. H. Coleridge, 2 vols., 1912; a one-volume edition of the *Poetical Works* by the same editor is available in Oxford Standard Authors. The most fully annotated edition of *Biographia Literaria* is by John Shawcross, 2 vols., 1907; a good reprint of the critical classic was edited by George Watson, rev., 1965. Thomas Middleton Raysor has edited the fragmentary remains of *Coleridge's Shakespearean Criticism*, 2 vols., 1930, and *Coleridge's Miscellaneous Criticism*, 1936. The definitive edition of Coleridge's *Collected Letters* is edited by E. L. Griggs, 6 vols., 1956–62. The first three volumes of Coleridge's extraordinary *Notebooks* are available, meticulously edited by Kathleen Coburn, 1957–71.

E. K. Chambers, *Samuel Taylor Coleridge*, 1938, gives a condensed and unsympathetic factual account of Coleridge's life. Lawrence Hanson, *The Life of S. T. Coleridge: The Early Years*, 1938, is an extensive study of the poet's life and writings to 1800; there is a good short study of the life and works by Walter J. Bate, *Coleridge*, 1968, and, with emphasis on the philosophical and religious writings, by Basil Willey, *Samuel Taylor Coleridge*, 1972. H. M. Margoliouth has described the most fruitful literary association on record in his *Wordsworth and Coleridge, 1795–1834*, 1953. The best inclusive critique of Coleridge as poet is by Humphry House, *Coleridge*, 1953; for a more modern analysis, see *The Poetic Voices of Coleridge*, by Max F. Schulz, 1963. John Beer has explored *Coleridge the Visionary*, 1959; and Reeve Parker has written a revealing study of the "conversation poems" in *Coleridge's Meditative Art*, 1975. *The Road to Xanadu*, 1927, rev., 1930, by J. L. Lowes, which investigates the sources and composition of *The Ancient Mariner* and *Kubla Khan*, has achieved the status of a critical classic. Recent discussion of Coleridge as critic will be found in M. H. Abrams, *The Mirror and the Lamp*, 1953, René Wellek, *A History of Modern Criticism 1750–1950*, Vol. II, 1955, Richard Harter Fogle, *The Idea of Coleridge's Criticism*, 1962, and J. A. Appleyard, *Coleridge's Philosophy of Literature*, 1965. Norman Fruman, *Coleridge, The Damaged Archangel*, 1971, collects all the charges and evidence concerning Coleridge's "plagiarism." Among the excellent recent studies of Coleridge's philosophical, theological, and moral interests and achievements are: Richard Haven, *Patterns of Consciousness*, 1969; Thomas McFarland's important and wide-ranging study of *Coleridge and the Pantheist Tradition*, 1969; Owen Barfield, *What Coleridge Thought*, 1971, and Lawrence S. Lockridge, *Coleridge the Moralist*, 1977. On opium and Coleridge's poetry, see M. H. Abrams, *The Milk of Paradise*, new edition, 1970; Elisabeth Schneider, *Coleridge, Opium and Kubla Khan*, 1953; and Alethea Hayter, *Opium and the Romantic Imagination*, 1968. Modern essays in criticism have been collected by Kathleen Coburn, *Coleridge*, 1967, and by John Beer, *Coleridge's Variety*, 1974.

George Darley

Complete Poetical Works, edited by Ramsay Colles, 1908; C. C. Abbott, *The Life and Letters of George Darley*, 1928. See the section on Darley in J. Heath-Stubbs, *The Darkling Plain*, 1950.

Thomas De Quincey

The Collected Writings, edited by David Masson, 14 vols., 1889–90, although incomplete, is still the standard edition of De Quincey's writings; other essays will be found in *Uncollected Writings*, ed. James Hogg, 2 vols., 1890, and *Posthumous Writings*, ed. A. H. Japp, 2 vols., 1891–93. There are numerous books of selections from De Quincey, and *The Confessions of an English Opium-Eater*, has been frequently reprinted. Horace Ainsworth Eaton's *Thomas De Quincey: A Biography*, 1936, is a detailed and reliable biography; Edward Sackville-West's *A Flame in Sunlight*, 1936, offers a speculative depth-analysis of De Quincey's temperament. Good short biographies and critiques are Malcolm Elwin's *De Quincey*, 1935, and J. C. Metcalf's *De Quincey: A Portrait*, 1940; see also John E. Jordan, *De Quincey to Wordsworth: A Biography of a Relationship*, 1962. For the effect of opium-addiction on his writings, see M. H. Abrams, *The Milk of Paradise*, rev., 1970, and Alethea Hayter, *Opium and the Romantic Imagination*, 1968. John E. Jordan has edited the critical essays in *De Quincey as Critic*, 1973. On his critical theories, see Jordan, *Thomas De Quincey, Literary Critic*, 1952, and on his thought, the section in J. Hillis Miller, *The Disappearance of God: Five Nineteenth-Century Writers*, 1963.

William Hazlitt

The Complete Works of William Hazlitt, 21 vols., 1930–34, has been well edited by P. P. Howe; the final volume includes a full general index, as well as an index of Hazlitt's quotations. Useful selections of Hazlitt's writings are *Selected Essays*, edited by Geoffrey Keynes, 1930, and *Hazlitt on English Literature*, edited by Jacob Zeitlin, 1926. P. P. Howe's largely factual *Life of William Hazlitt*, 1947, has been superseded by Catherine M. Maclean's *Born Under Saturn*, 1944, and by Herschel Baker's comprehensive study of his thought and writings, *William Hazlitt*, 1962; the most recent and detailed critical biography is *Hazlitt*, by Ralph M. Wardle, 1971. Stewart C. Wilcox described *Hazlitt in the Workshop*, 1943. The chapter on Hazlitt in Oliver Elton's *A Survey of English Literature 1780–1830* 2 vols., 1912, remains a useful comment on Hazlitt as essayist and prose stylist. Virginia Woolf includes an appreciation of Hazlitt in *The Second Common Reader*, 1932. On Hazlitt as a critic of literature and the arts, see the Introduction in Jacob Zeitlin's anthology, *Hazlitt on English Literature*, 1913; Elizabeth Schneider, *The Aesthetics of William Hazlitt*, 1933; W. J. Bate's comments in *Criticism: The Major Texts*, 1952; and René Wellek, *A History of Modern Criticism 1750–1950*, Vol. II, 1955.

Leigh Hunt

Hunt's complete journalistic output (it is estimated that it would take up between 50 and 60 volumes) has never been collected. Following are the best editions and useful selections of various types of his writings: *Poetical Works*, edited by H. S. Milford, Oxford Standard Authors, 1923; *Leigh Hunt's Literary Criticism*, edited by Carolyn W. and Lawrence H. Houtchens, 1956 (it includes a general appreciation of Hunt as a man of letters by C. D. Thorpe), and by the same editors, *Leigh Hunt's Dramatic Criticism, 1808–1831*, 1949; *Selected Essays*, edited by J. B. Priestley, 1929. Hunt's *Autobiography* is available in The World's Classics. The best English biography is Edmund Blunden's *Leigh Hunt: A Biography*, 1930, but the fullest and most scholarly is in French, the first volume of Louis Landré's monumental *Leigh Hunt* (1935–36); the second volume of this treatise constitutes the best critical survey of all of Hunt's writings.

John Keats

The standard edition of the poetry is now Jack Stillinger's *The Poems of John Keats*, 1978, replacing H. W. Garrod's *Poetical Works*, rev., 1958. Miriam Allott's *The Poems of John Keats*, 1970, is copiously annotated. Hyder E. Rollins's *The Letters of John Keats*, 2 vols., 1958, is an exact reprint from the manuscripts.

The best biography is W. J. Bate's notable study of the poet's life, writings, and place in the English poetic tradition, *John Keats*, 1963. Shorter critical biographies are Aileen Ward, *John Keats: The Making of a Poet*, 1963, Douglas Bush, *John Keats*, 1966, and Robert Gittings, *John Keats*, 1968. Among the many critical writings on the poet, the following are especially useful: C. D. Thorpe, *The Mind of John Keats*, 1926 (on Keats's thought); M. R. Ridley, *Keats's Craftsmanship*, 1933 (based on the revisions in Keats's manuscripts); R. H. Fogle, *The Imagery of Keats and Shelley*, 1949 (a study of Keats's characteristic diction and figurative language); Earl Wasserman, *The Finer Tone*, 1953 (a close and sometimes oversubtle analysis of the major poems); E. C. Pettet, *On the Poetry of Keats*, 1957; Morris Dickstein, *Keats and His Poetry*, 1971; Stuart Sperry's illuminating book on *Keats the Poet*, 1973; Christopher Ricks's lively and wide-ranging study of *Keats and Embarrassment*, 1974; Stuart Ende, *Keats and the Sublime*, 1976; and Robert K. Ryan's analysis of Keats's personal creed, against the background of the religious views of his age, *Keats: The Religious Sense*, 1976. *Keats*, edited by W. J. Bate, 1964, reprints a number of recent critical essays.

Charles Lamb

We are indebted to E. V. Lucas for the standard *Works of Charles and Mary Lamb*, 7 vols., 1903–5; for the standard edition of their *Letters*, 3 vols., 1935; and for the standard *Life of Charles Lamb*, 2 vols., rev., 1921. A new edition of *The Letters of Charles and Mary Anne Lamb*, by Edwin W. Marrs, Jr., is in process; the two volumes so far published include the letters up to 1809. *Charles Lamb*, written by Alfred Ainger for the English Men of Letters series in 1882, is still a useful critical biography. The influential essay on Lamb by Walter Pater in his *Appreciations* set the tone for much of the standard commentary on the essayist; Edmund Blunden's *Charles Lamb and His Contemporaries*, 1933, is an appreciation by a more recent devotee; Denys Thompson's "Our Debt to Lamb," in *Determinations*, edited by F. R. Leavis, 1934, offers a contrary view. A recent book on Lamb, with a Freudian point of view, is Fred V. Randall's *The World of Elia: Charles Lamb's Essayistic Romanticism*, 1975. A selection from his critical writings, *Lamb's Criticism*, 1923, was edited by E. M. W. Tillyard, and includes an introductory essay on "Lamb as a Literary Critic." On the criticism see also René Wellek, *History of Modern Criticism*, Vol. II, 1955.

Walter Savage Landor

The Complete Works have been edited by T. E. Welby and Stephen Wheeler, 16 vols., 1927–36, and the poems alone by Stephen Wheeler in 3 vols., 1937. A more reliable edition of the prose writings is by C. G. Crump, 2 vols., 1891–93. There is a volume of selected *Poetry and Prose*, edited by E. K. Chambers, 1946. The official biography is *Walter Savage Landor*, by his friend, John Forster, 2 vols., 1869, but it is long and dull; a recent, full, and readable biography is R. H. Super's *Landor: A Biography*, 1954. For criticism, see also Malcolm Elwin, *Landor: A Replevin*, 1958; Chapter VII in Douglas Bush, *Mythology and the Romantic Tradition*, 1937 and Robert Pinsky, *Landor's Poetry*, 1968.

Thomas Moore

Poetical Works, edited by A. D. Godley, 1910; a selection of *Lyrics and Satires*, edited by Sean O'Faolain, 1929; *Memoirs, Journals, and Correspondence*, edited by Lord John Russell, 8 vols., 1853–56. A selection from the memoirs was published as *Tom Moore's Diary*, edited by J. B. Priestley, 1925. The best biography is Howard M. Jones's lively *The Harp That Once—A Chronicle of the Life of Thomas Moore*, 1937.

Thomas Love Peacock

The Works have been edited by H. F. B. Brett-Smith and C. E. Jones in 10 vols., 1924–34, and the poems alone by R. B. Johnson, 1906. The novels have been often reprinted, singly and collectively. There are good lives of Peacock by Carl Van Doren, 1911, by J. B. Priestley, 1927, and by Felix Felton, 1973. For a critical analysis of his writings, see Carl Dawson, *His Fine Wit: A Study of T. L. Peacock*, 1970.

Sir Walter Scott

Scott's novels have been often reprinted, both collectively and individually, and most of the best ones are available in cheap editions. A useful collection of the *Poetical Works* is that in the Oxford Standard Authors, edited in 1904 by J. L. Robertson. The letters have been edited by H. J. C. Grierson in 12 vols., 1932–37, and the *Journal* has been edited by J. G. Tait in 3 vols., 1939–46. The official *Memoirs of the Life of Sir Walter Scott* by Scott's son-in-law, J. G. Lockhart, 7 vols., 1837–38, is an English classic; its facts and evaluations are supplemented by H. J. C. Grierson's *Sir Walter Scott, Bart.*, 1938, and by the full-scale biography, Edgar Johnson's *Sir Walter Scott: The Great Unknown*, 2 vols., 1970. There is also a lively and engaging life, *Sir Walter Scott*, by the novelist John Buchan, 1932, and a useful study by David Daiches of *Sir Walter Scott and His World*, 1971. See also James T. Hillhouse, *The Waverly Novels and their Critics*, 1936, and the many treatments of Scott as poet and novelist listed in Chapter IV of *The English Romantic Poets and Essayists*, edited by Carolyn W. and Lawrence H. Houtchens, rev., 1966.

Mary Wollstonecraft Shelley

There is no collected edition of Mary Shelley's works, and only a limited (though increasing) number of titles have been recently reprinted; see W. H. Lyles, *Mary Shelley: An Annotated Bibliography*, 1975. *Frankenstein* (1818) is available in a number of modern reprints; especially noteworthy are the scholarly editions by James Rieger, 1974, and the Norton Critical Edition by J. Paul Hunter (in preparation), which have reliable texts, changes from the first to the third editions of 1818 and 1831, and much useful supplementary material. Another fine novel, *The Last Man* (1826) has been reprinted in an edition by Hugh J. Luke, Jr., 1965. *Mathilda*, a novella of 1819 which the author left in manuscript, was printed for the first time by Elizabeth Nitchie, 1959. The short fictional writings have been excellently edited by Charles E. Robinson, *Mary Shelley, Collected Tales and Stories*, 1976. Her prefaces and notes to her husband's poems are conveniently accessible in Oxford Standard Authors, *The Complete Poetical Works of Percy Bysshe Shelley*, edited by Thomas Hutchinson and revised by G. M. Matthews, 1970.

Frederick L. Jones has edited *The Letters of Mary W. Shelley*, 1946, and *Mary Shelley's Journal*, 1947. The first modern life, and still one of the best, is R. Glynn Grylls, *Mary Shelley, A Biography*, 1938. The novelist Muriel Spark wrote a lively and sympathetic biography, *Child of Light: A Reassessment of Mary Shelley*, in 1951. Elizabeth Nitchie's *Mary Shelley, Author of "Frankenstein"*, 1953, is especially useful for its study of the extent to which Mary wrote herself, her family history, and her husband and friends into her fictional works. William A. Walling's *Mary Shelley*, 1972, in Twayne's English Authors Series, offers a compact treatment of Mary's life and critiques of her major writings.

Percy Bysshe Shelley

The nearest to a complete collection of Shelley's writings is *The Complete Works*, edited in 10 vols. by Roger Ingpen and Walter E. Peck, 1926–30. The most widely used single volume of the poems has been that in the Oxford Standard Authors, edited by Thomas Hutchinson and revised by G. M. Matthews, 1970. *Shelley's Prose* was collected by David Lee Clark in 1954; and *The Letters* were edited by Frederick L. Jones in 2 vols., 1964. Because of the erratic way in which Shelley's poems and essays were published, all the collected editions are faulty; Shelley's writings are now in the process of being revised and reprinted by a number of editors. Neville Rogers's new edition of *The Complete Poetical Works*, of which two volumes are in print, has been severely criticized by scholars. The best texts are those in *The Lyrics of Shelley*, edited and sensitively interpreted by Judith Chernaik, 1972; and in the large selection of *Shelley's Poetry and Prose*, A Norton Critical Edition, edited by Donald H. Reiman and Sharon B. Powers, 1977, which also includes a collection of recent critical essays on Shelley.

The classic life is Newman Ivey White's *Shelley*, 2 vols., 1940, which is also available in a condensed single volume, *Portrait of Shelley*, 1945. Richard Holmes's *Shelley: The Pursuit*, 1974, is not as detailed as White's biography, but provides a vivid sense of Shelley as a human being. Kenneth Neill Cameron, in *The Young Shelley*, 1950, and in the sequel, *Shelley: The Golden Years*, 1974, emphasizes the development of Shelley's radical social and political thinking. C. E. Pulos, *The Deep Truth: A Study of Shelley's Scepticism*, 1954, a valuable corrective of standard views of Shelley, emphasizes the philosophic scepticism at the center of his idealism.

Shelley's Major Poetry, by Carlos Baker, 1948, provides useful analyses of the longer poems which stress their ideational content; Carl H. Grabo, in *A Newton Among Poets*, 1930, and Desmond King-Hele, in *Shelley: His Thought and Work*, 1960, deal with Shelley's conversion of scientific knowledge into poetic imagery. *The Imagery of Keats and Shelley*, 1949, by Richard H. Fogle, is an analysis of the stylistic qualities of Shelley's poetry.

As early as 1900, W. B. Yeats, in "The Philosophy of Shelley's Poetry" (reprinted in *Essays*, 1924) dealt with Shelley as one of the great symbolist poets.

Recent treatments of Shelley's symbolic imagery are Peter Butter, *Shelley's Idols of the Cave*, 1954, and Harold Bloom's innovative study, *Shelley's Mythmaking*, 1959, which puts Shelley in the line of the visionary poets whose imaginative processes were instinctively mythopoeic. Earl Wasserman's *Shelley: A Critical Reading*, 1971, replaces his earlier treatments of Shelley; it is a massive and illuminating series of close readings of Shelley's most important poems and essays. Other recent critiques are Milton Wilson, *Shelley's Later Poetry*, 1959; R. G. Woodman, *The Apocalyptic Tradition in the Poetry of Shelley*, 1964; Donald Reiman, *Percy Bysshe Shelley*, 1969; and Stuart Curran's fine study of *Shelley's Annus Mirabilis: The Maturing of an Epic Vision*, 1975. Charles Robinson discusses the personal and poetic relations of *Byron and Shelley: The Snake and the Eagle Wreathed in Fight*, 1975. *Shelley*, edited by George M. Ridenour, 1965, is an anthology of modern critical essays.

Robert Southey

The *Poetical Works*, edited by Southey himself, are in 10 vols., 1837–38, reprinted, 1860; the best one-volume selection is *Poems*, edited by M. H. Fitzgerald, 1909. The prose works have not been collected. There is a *Life and Correspondence*, edited in 6 vols. by C. C. Southey in 1849–50, and a selection of the *Letters*, edited by M. H. Fitzgerald for World's Classics, 1912. For biography see Edward Dowden's *Southey*, 1874; William Haller's *The Early Life*, 1917; Jack Simmons' *Southey*, 1945; and Robert Carnall's *Robert Southey and His Age*, 1960.

Mary Wollstonecraft

We still lack an edition of all of Mary Wollstonecraft's writings or a collective edition of her letters. Her single works, however, are available in modern reprints. Of these the most important are: *A Vindication of the Rights of Men* (1790), facsimile edition by Eleanor Louise Nicholes, 1960; *A Vindication of the Rights of Woman* (1792), A Norton Critical Edition, edited by Carol H. Poston, 1975; *Letters Written during a Short Residence in Sweden, Norway, and Denmark* (1796), edited by Carol H. Poston, 1976; and a reprint in a single volume (edited by Gary Kelly, 1976) of her two novels, the early *Mary, A Fiction* (1788), and *The Wrongs of Woman; or Maria*, which she left unfinished at her death.

Biographers rely for many facts on William Godwin's candid *Memoirs of the Author of "A Vindication of the Rights of Woman"*, 1798. The first modern critical biography is Ralph Wardle's *Mary Wollstonecraft*, 1951; see also Eleanor Flexner, *Mary Wollstonecraft: A Biography*, 1972, and Claire Tomlin's lively book, stressing the foibles and complex motivations of her subject, *The Life and Death of Mary Wollstonecraft*, 1974. A recent detailed life is Emily Sunstein's *A Different Face: The Life of Mary Wollstonecraft*, 1975. Excellent short introductions to the author are the admiring essays by Virginia Woolf, "Mary Wollstonecraft." *The Second Common Reader*, 1932 (reprinted in Carol Poston's edition of *A Vindication of the Rights of Woman*), and by Ruth Benedict, "Mary Wollstonecraft," in *An Anthropologist at Work*, edited by Margaret Mead, 1959. See also the treatment of Mary Wollstonecraft as a major figure in literature, in Ellen Moers, *Literary Women*, 1976.

Dorothy Wordsworth

The biography is by Ernest de Selincourt, *Dorothy Wordsworth*, 1933. Her letters are collected with those of her brother in *The Letters of William and Dorothy Wordsworth*, 6 vols., 1935–39, now in the process of revision by C. L. Shaver and others, 1967–. *The Journals of Dorothy Wordsworth* were edited by Ernest de Selincourt in 2 vols., 1941; a more accurate version of the early Alfoxden and Grasmere Journals (1798–1803) is now available, *Journals of Dorothy Wordsworth*, edited by Mary Moorman, 1971. See also Catherine Macdonald Maclean, *Dorothy Wordsworth, the Early Years*, 1932.

William Wordsworth

Ernest de Selincourt has edited *The Poetical Works* (with Helen Darbishire), 5 vols., 1940–49; the variorum edition of *The Prelude*, with the texts of 1805 and 1850 on facing pages (revised by Helen Darbishire, 1959); and *The Letters of William and Dorothy Wordsworth*, 6 vols., 1935–39 (now being revised by C. L. Shaver and others, 1967–). Newly edited texts of the 1805 and 1850 *Preludes* on facing pages, together with the "Two-Part *Prelude*" of 1799, various manuscript fragments of *The Prelude*, and a selection of recent critical essays on the poem, are available in *The Prelude: 1799, 1805, 1850*, A Norton Critical Edition, edited by Jonathan Wordsworth, M. H. Abrams, and Stephen Gill, 1979. Wordsworth's poems in one volume were edited for Oxford Standard Authors by Thomas Hutchinson and revised by Ernest de Selincourt, 1950. A new series, the Cornell Wordsworth, 1975– , will print texts of Wordsworth's long poems, together with all variant readings from the manuscripts (which are reproduced and transcribed) through the final printing in Wordsworth's lifetime; the volumes already published, by diverse editors, are *The Salisbury Plain Poems; The Prelude, 1798–1799;* and *Home at Grasmere*. W. J. B. Owen and Jane Worthington Smyser have edited *The Prose Works*, 3 vols., 1973; Owen has also printed from this edition a convenient collection of *Wordsworth's Literary Criticism*, 1974.

Until recently, the standard biography was George McLean Harper, *William Wordsworth: His Life,* *Works, and Influence*, 2 vols., 1916, rev., 1929; Mary Moormans' *William Wordsworth*, Vol. I, rev. 1968, and Vol. II, 1965, takes advantage of the greatly expanded scholarship of the last three decades. Edith Batho, *The Later Wordsworth*, 1933, and W. L. Sperry, *Wordsworth's Anti-Climax*, 1935, are studies of the poet after 1805. H. M. Margoliouth deals briefly with the relations between two great poets in *Wordsworth and Coleridge, 1795–1835*, 1953. Mark L. Reed's scrupulous work, dating precisely Wordsworth's poems, manuscripts, and the events of his daily life, has reached two volumes, *Wordsworth: The Chronology of the Early Years*, 1967, and *The Chronology of the Middle Years*, 1975.

Walter Raleigh's *Wordsworth*, 1903, Helen Darbishire's *The Poet Wordsworth*, 1950, and Carl Woodring's *Wordsworth*, 1965, are useful introductions to Wordsworth's poetry. Paul D. Sheats has written a fine study of the early poems, *The Making of Wordsworth's Poetry, 1785–1798*, 1973. The current interest in *Lyrical Ballads* is shown in three good books: Stephen M. Parrish, *The Art of the "Lyrical Ballads"*, 1973; Mary Jacobus, *Tradition and Experiment in Wordsworth's "Lyrical Ballads" (1798)*, 1976; and John E. Jordan, *Why the "Lyrical Ballads"?*, 1976. *The Mind of a Poet*, by Raymond D. Havens, 2 vols., 1941, is a detailed study of *The Prelude;* Herbert Lindenberger, *On Wordsworth's Prelude*, 1963, is a more recent and lively exploration; Richard J. Onorato, *The Character of the Poet: Wordsworth in "The Prelude,"* 1971, applies psychoanalytic concepts to the poem; and Frank D. McConnell has written *The Confessional Imagination: A Reading of Wordsworth's "Prelude,"* 1974. Various aspects of Wordsworth's thought are discussed in Basil Willey, *The Eighteenth Century Background*, 1940; N. P. Stallknecht, *Strange Seas of Thought*, 2nd ed., 1958, and Geoffrey Durrant, *Wordsworth and the Great System*, 1970. Prominent among recent books on Wordsworth's poetry are: John Jones, *The Egotistical Sublime*, 1954; David Ferry, *The Limits of Mortality*, 1959; David Perkins, *Wordsworth and the Poetry of Sincerity*, 1964; and Geoffrey Hartman's impressive study of *Wordsworth's Poetry, 1787–1814*, 1964. The range and diversity of critical studies is represented in *Wordsworth: A Collection of Critical Essays*, edited by M. H. Abrams, 1972.

THE VICTORIAN AGE

Studies of the Victorian age and its point of view include Richard D. Altick, *Victorian People and Ideas: A Companion for the Modern Reader of Victorian Literature*, 1973; Asa Briggs, *The Age of Improvement*, 1962; W. L. Burn, *The Age of Equipoise: A study of the Mid-Victorian Generation*, 1964; Marcus Cunliffe, *The Age of Expansion: 1848–1917*, 1974; Jerome Buckley, *The Victorian Temper*, 1951; Walter E. Houghton, *The Victorian Frame of Mind, 1830–1870*, 1957; J. B. Schneewind, *Backgrounds of English Victorian Literature*, 1970 and G. M. Young, *Victorian England: Portrait of an Age*, 1936 (republished in 1977 with 215 pages of explanatory notes by George Kitson Clark). Young's essay is a brilliant synthesis, but it can be incomprehensible to readers who are not yet adequately familiar with the history of the age. Such readers should consult David Thomson's *England in the Nineteenth Century*, 1950, or Derek Beales, *From Castlereagh to Gladstone: 1815–1885*, 1970. Also useful historically is the readable biography of Queen Victoria by Elizabeth Longford, *Victoria R. I.*, 1964. Studies of special aspects of the age include Richard Altick, *The English Common Reader*, 1957; Jerome Buckley, *The Triumph of Time*, 1966; E. P. Thompson, *The Making of the English Working Class*, 1963; Steven Marcus, *The Other Victorians: A Study of Sexuality and Pornography in Mid-Nineteenth-Century England*, 1964; Herbert Sussman, *Victorians and the Machine*, 1968; Martha Vicinus, ed., *Suffer and Be Still: Women in the Victorian Age*, 1972, and *The Victorian City*, edited by H. J. Dyos and Michael Wolff, 2 vols., 1973. For pictures and paintings of the Victorian scene, see Jeremy Maas, *Victorian Painters*, 1969, and J. B. Priestley, *Victorian Heyday* (with 200 pictures), 1971. Also revealing are the illustrations for Henry Mayhew's *London Labour and London Poor*, originally published 1851, reprinted 1967, and Gustav Doré's *London: A Pilgrimage*, originally published 1872 and reprinted 1970. *Nature and the Victorian Imagination*, edited by U. C. Knoepflmacher and G. B. Tennyson, 1977, features valuable essays on literature and the visual arts. Studies of Victorian literature include Patricia Ball, *The Heart's Events: The Victorian Poetry of Relationships*, 1976; Harold Bloom, *The Ringers in the Tower*, 1971; Douglas Bush, *Mythology and the Romantic Tradition*, 1937; Carol T. Christ, *The Finer Optic: The Aesthetic of Particularity in Victorian Poetry*, 1975; Oliver Elton, *A Survey of English Literature*, 1920, vols. 3 and 4; George Ford, *Keats and the Victorians*, 1944; E. D. H. Johnson, *The Alien Vision of Victorian Poetry*, 1952; F. L. Lucas, *Ten Victorian Poets*, 1940; Robert Langbaum, *The Poetry of Experience*, 1957, and *The Modern Spirit: Essays on the Continuity of * * * Literature*, 1970; J. Hillis Miller, *The Disappearance of God: Five Nineteenth-Century Writers*, 1963; Morse Peckham, *Beyond the Tragic Vision*, 1962; John R. Reed, *Victorian Conventions*, 1975; René Wellek, *A History of Modern Criticism*, Vol. 4, 1965. Helpful collections of critical essays have been compiled by Robert Preyer in his *Victorian Literature: Selected Essays*, 1965; Richard Levine in his *Backgrounds to Victorian Literature*, 1967; Isabel Armstrong, *The Major Victorian Poets: Reconsiderations*, 1969; and by Michael Timko in *Victorian Poetry*, Spring, 1978. Especially noteworthy is *The Art of Victorian Prose*, edited by George Levine and William Madden, 1968.

For classified or annotated lists of other books and articles, see *The Victorian Poets: A Guide to Research*, edited by F. E. Faverty, rev., 1968; *Victorian Fiction: A Guide to Research*, edited by Lionel Stevenson, 1964; *Victorian Fiction: A Second Guide to Research*, edited by George H. Ford, 1978; and *Victorian Prose: A Guide to Research*, edited by David J. DeLaura, 1973.

For developments in prose fiction during the period see Walter Allen, *The English Novel*, 1954; Lionel Stevenson, *The English Novel: A Panorama*, 1960; and Kathleen Tillotson, *The Novel of the Eighteen-Forties*, 1956. For special critical issues, see J. Hillis Miller, *The Form of Victorian Fiction*, 1968.

Matthew Arnold

The Works, 1903, is an incomplete collection of Arnold's writings; it must be supplemented by later editions such as *The Poetical Works*, edited by C. B. Tinker and H. F. Lowry, 1950, and the elaborately annotated *Poems of Arnold*, edited by Kenneth Allott, 1965; the *Note-Books*, edited by H. F. Lowry, Karl Young, and W. H. Dunn, 1952; and *The Letters of Arnold to * * * Clough*, edited by H. F. Lowry, 1932. A complete collection of Arnold's letters is in preparation. R. H. Super has produced an authoritative edition of *The*

Complete Prose Works in 11 volumes, 1960–77 (Super is also the author of *The Time Spirit of Matthew Arnold,* 1970). For a study of those prose works see William Robbins' *The Ethical Idealism of Matthew Arnold,* 1959.

Lionel Trilling's excellent *Matthew Arnold,* 1949, remains a standard critical and biographical study, but see also W. Stacy Johnson's *The Voices of Matthew Arnold,* 1961; Dwight Culler's *Imaginative Reason,* 1966; G. Robert Stange's *The Poet as Humanist,* 1967, and Douglas Bush's *Matthew Arnold,* 1972. Two useful investigations of Arnold's literary and intellectual background are Leon Gottfried's *Matthew Arnold and the Romantics,* 1963, and Edward Alexander's *Arnold and John Stuart Mill,* 1965. See also Alexander's *Matthew Arnold, John Ruskin, and the Modern Temper,* 1973, and Kenneth Allott's *Matthew Arnold,* 1975.

Emily Brontë

The Complete Poems were edited by C. W. Hatfield in 1941. Information about the Gondal narrative is supplied by Fannie R. Ratchford's *The Brontës' Web of Childhood,* 1941, and *Gondal's Queen, A Novel in Verse,* 1955. The most satisfactory biography is Winifred Gerin's *Emily Brontë,* 1971. Several of the essays in *The Art of Emily Brontë,* edited by Anne Smith, 1977, are devoted to the poetry. A useful edition of her most important novel is *Wuthering Heights; A Norton Critical Edition,* edited by William M. Sale, Jr., rev., 1972.

Elizabeth Barrett Browning

The standard *Complete Works* were edited by Charlotte Porter and Helen Clarke, 6 vols., 1900. Cora Kaplan's edition of *Aurora Leigh and Other Poems,* 1978, is a useful selection. A reasonable biography is Gardner B. Taplin's *The Life of Elizabeth Barrett Browning,* 1957. See also Alethea Hayter, *Elizabeth Barrett Browning,* 1965.

Robert Browning

In 1969 was published the first of 13 projected volumes of a variorum edition of Browning's *Complete Works* (edited by Roma A. King, Jr., and others). A standard edition has been that edited by F. G. Kenyon, 10 vols., 1912; a one-volume collection was edited by Ian Jack, 1971. W. Hall Griffin and H. C. Minchin's *The Life of Robert Browning,* 1910, rev., 1938, has been the standard biogra-

phy but is now superseded by *The Book, The Ring, and the Poet* by William Irvine and Park Honan, 1974. More eccentric but lively is the psychoanalytic study by Betty Miller, *Robert Browning: A Portrait,* 1952. For a special study of the poet's early years, see John Maynard, *Browning's Youth,* 1977. W. C. DeVane's *A Browning Handbook,* rev., 1955, is a model compilation of factual data concerning each of Browning's poems: sources, composition, and reputation. Further information is supplied by Norman B. Crowell, *A Reader's Guide to Robert Browning,* 1972, which also offers simplified summaries of critical discussions for 23 monologues.

The critical assessments in G. K. Chesterton's *Robert Browning,* 1903, are colorfully expressed and often shrewd. Roma A. King, Jr.'s *The Bow and the Lyre,* 1957, and *The Focusing Artifice,* 1969, contain detailed discussions of some of the principal monologues. Robert Langbaum's *The Poetry of Experience* is an admirable attempt to relate Browning's monologues to some of the main developments in modern literature. See also Donald Hair, *Browning's Experiments with Genre,* 1972, and Ian Jack, *Browning's Major Poetry,* 1973. For an understanding of Browning's ideas, W. O. Raymond's *The Infinite Moment,* 1965, is suggestive. Many of the best discussions of Browning's achievement, especially discussions of individual poems, have been conveniently assembled in two collections that rarely overlap each other: *Robert Browning: A Collection of Critical Essays,* edited by Philip Drew, 1966, and *The Browning Critics,* edited by Boyd Litzinger and K. L. Knickerbocker, 1965. The latter collection also includes an extensive bibliography. Litzinger has also edited (with Donald Smalley) *Browning: The Critical Heritage,* 1970. See also the collection of essays edited by Isabel Armstrong, *Robert Browning,* 1974.

Thomas Carlyle

The *Works* have been edited by H. D. Traill, 30 vols., 1898–1901. Seven volumes of the *Collected Letters,* projected to extend to 30 volumes, have been published since 1971 (edited by C. R. Sanders and others). C. F. Harrold's edition of *Sartor Resartus,* 1937, is helpful concerning Carlyle's debt to German literature, as is Louis Cazamian's *Carlyle,* translated in 1932, concerning his religious background. J. A. Froude's *Thomas Carlyle,* 1882–84, remains, despite its inaccuracies, the standard biography.

Recommended as studies of Carlyle's thought are Emery Neff, *Carlyle and Mill*, 1926; Eric Bentley, *A Century of Hero-Worship*, 1944; and Philip Rosenberg, *The Seventh Hero: Thomas Carlyle and the Theory of Radical Activism*, 1974. That he has affinities with 20-century "myth-makers" such as D. H. Lawrence is argued by Albert J. LaValley in *Carlyle and the Idea of the Modern*, 1968. John Holloway's *The Victorian Sage*, 1953, includes a chapter analyzing Carlyle's rhetoric. George B. Tennyson's *Sartor Called Resartus*, 1965, is an important critical study. See also George Levine's *The Boundaries of Fiction*, 1968, on Carlyle, Macaulay, and Newman, and the collection of essays edited by K. J. Fielding and Rodger L. Tarr, *Carlyle Past and Present*, 1976.

Lewis Carroll

The Complete Writings of Lewis Carroll, 1939. A highly recommended selection is *Alice in Wonderland*, A Norton Critical Edition, edited by Donald J. Gray, 1971. See also Derek Hudson, *Lewis Carroll*, 1954; William Empson, *Some Versions of Pastoral*, 1935; Martin Gardner, *The Annotated Snark*, 1962; and Virginia Woolf, *The Moment and Other Essays*, 1948.

See also entries under **Light Verse**.

Arthur Hugh Clough

The Poems were edited by H. F. Lowry, A. L. F. Norrington, and F. L. Mulhauser, 1951. In 1974 Mulhauser edited a revised edition, with some poems previously omitted. Mulhauser was also editor of *The Correspondence*, 1957. *A. H. Clough: The Uncommitted Mind*, by Katherine Chorley, 1962, is a lively but frequently misleading study. *The Poetry of Clough* by Walter Houghton, 1963, contends that Clough is a major satirical poet. On Clough's religious and intellectual background see Paul Veyriras, *A. H. Clough*, 1965 (in French). See also the judicious study by Robindra Biswas, *Arthur Hugh Clough: Towards a Reconsideration*, 1972.

Ernest Dowson

The standard modern edition of Dowson's poems is *The Poetical Works of Ernest Christopher Dowson*, edited with an introduction by Desmond Flower, 3rd ed., 1967. *Dilemmas*, 1895, reprinted 1971, is a collection of his stories, as is *The Stories of Ernest Dowson*, edited by J. M. Longaker, 1947. Much lively and illuminating comment on Dowson will be found in W. B. Yeats's *Autobiography*, 1955. *Ernest Dowson*, by J. M. Longaker, 1944, and *Ernest Dowson*, by T. B. Swann, 1965, are critical biographies; a short chapter on Dowson in *Essays in Criticism and Research*, by Geoffrey Tillotson, 1967, assesses his relationship with other poets. See also *Letters of Ernest Dowson*, edited by Desmond Flower and Henry Maas, 1967.

See also entries under **The Nineties**.

Edward FitzGerald

George Bentham edited *The Variorum Edition of the * * * Writings of Edward FitzGerald*, 7 vols., 1902. A. McKinley Terhune, *The Life of Edward FitzGerald*, 1947; A. J. Arberry, *The Romance of the Rubáiyát*, 1959.

W. S. Gilbert

Gilbert's librettos for Sullivan in their finally revised form comprise *The Complete Plays of Gilbert and Sullivan*, 1976. The earliest published versions, often substantially different from those performed today, are reprinted in Reginald Allen's *The First Night Gilbert and Sullivan*, 1958. Vocal scores of the most popular songs and ensembles, reproduced from 19th-century editions, are given in *The Authentic Gilbert and Sullivan Songbook*, 1977. Earlier works by Gilbert include *The Bab Ballads*, edited by James Ellis, 1970, and *Gilbert Before Sullivan: Six Comic Plays*, 1967, edited by Jane W. Stedman, 1967. Hesketh Pearson's *Gilbert: His Life and Strife*, 1957, is the best modern biography, and one of many good accounts of the Gilbert/Sullivan partnership is Christopher Hibbert's *Gilbert & Sullivan and Their Victorian World*, 1976. A sampling of Gilbert criticism is offered by John B. Hones in *W. S. Gilbert: A Century of Scholarship and Commentary*, 1970.

See also entries under **Light Verse**.

William Ernest Henley

The Works, 5 volumes, were published in 1921. See B. Ifor Evans, *English Poetry in the Later Nineteenth Century*, 1933, chapter XII, and Jerome H. Buckley, *William Ernest Henley: A Study of the "Counter-Decadence" of the Nineties*, 1945. Also useful on Henley as a figure of the Nineties is a study (in French) by André Guillaume, *William Ernest Henley et son groupe*, 1973.

See also entries under **The Nineties**.

Thomas Henry Huxley

The Life and Letters of Thomas Henry Huxley, by Leonard Huxley,

2 vols., 1900, is the standard biography. William Irvine, *Apes, Angels, and Victorians,* 1955, is lively and informative. See also *1859: Entering an Age of Crisis,* edited by P. Appleman, W. A. Madden, and M. Wolff, 1959, and, especially, Harold Cyril Bibby, *Scientist Extraordinary: The Life and Scientific Work of Thomas Henry Huxley,* 1972.

Rudyard Kipling

The Sussex Edition of the complete works, 35 vols., 1937–39, is the standard complete edition. *Rudyard Kipling's Verse: Definitive Edition,* 1940, contains all the poetry. T. S. Eliot has edited, with an appreciative and discerning introduction, *A Choice of Kipling's Verse,* 1941. His letters appear in various books, among them *Kipling to Rider Haggard,* edited by M. N. Cohen, 1965. Charles E. Carrington's *Rudyard Kipling,* 1955, is the official biography, but three others are worthy of note: J. I. M. Stewart's *Rudyard Kipling,* 1966; Philip Mason's *Kipling: The Glass, the Shadow and the Fire,* 1975, an informative account of Kipling's complex relationship with India; and Angus Wilson's *The Strange Ride of Rudyard Kipling,* 1978, a judicious and readable interpretation of Kipling's life and attitudes. Three important midcentury critics have written interesting essays on Kipling: Edmund Wilson in *The Wound and the Bow,* 1941; George Orwell in *Critical Essays,* 1946, and Lionel Trilling in *The Liberal Imagination,* 1950. *Rudyard Kipling, Realist and Fabulist,* by Bonamy Dobrée, 1967, and *Aspects of Kipling's Art,* by C. A. Bodelson, 1964, are perceptive critical studies, and there are three useful collections of critical essays: *Kipling's Mind and Art,* edited by Andrew Rutherford, 1964; *Kipling and the Critics,* edited by E. L. Gilbert, 1965; and *Rudyard Kipling,* edited by John Gross, 1972. R. L. Green has edited *Rudyard Kipling* in the Critical Heritage Series, 1971.

See also entries under **The Nineties.**

Edward Lear

The Complete Nonsense, edited by Holbrook Jackson, 1947. Angus Davidson, *Edward Lear: Landscape Painter and Nonsense Poet,* 1938; Elizabeth Sewell, *The Field of Nonsense,* 1952. Edward Gorey's *Gorey x3,* 1976, provides delightful illustrations for Lear's *The Jumblies* and *The Dong with the Luminous Nose.* See also Thomas Byrom, *Nonsense and Wonder: The Poems and Cartoons of Edward Lear,* 1978.

See also entries under **Light Verse.**

Light Verse

Interesting collections of assorted kinds of light verse include *A Century of Parody and Imitation,* edited by Walter Jerrold and R. M. Leonard, 1913, 1968; *Parodies: An Anthology from Chaucer to Beerbohm,* edited by Dwight Macdonald, 1960; *The Oxford Book of Light Verse,* edited by W. H. Auden, 1938, and *The New Oxford Book of Light Verse,* edited by Kingsley Amis, 1978.

See also entries under **Lewis Carroll, W. S. Gilbert,** and **Edward Lear.**

George Meredith

Phyllis Bartlett's edition of the *Poems,* 1978, supersedes G. M. Trevelyan's edition of 1928. *The Letters,* edited by C. L. Cline, were published in 3 volumes in 1970. See Lionel Stevenson, *The Ordeal of George Meredith,* 1953; C. Day Lewis, *Introduction to Modern Love,* 1948; and Norman Kelvin, *A Troubled Eden,* 1961. A Norton Critical Edition of his novel, *The Egoist* was edited by Robert M. Adams in 1979.

John Stuart Mill

Since 1963 more than half of the projected 25 volumes of the *Collected Works* have been published (general editors are F. E. L. Priestley and John Robson). This collection includes 6 volumes of Mill's letters, edited by Francis Mineka and Dwight Lindley. *On Liberty* has been edited by David Spitz in the Norton Critical Editions series, 1975. *The Life of J. S. Mill* by M. St. J. Packe, 1954, is the standard biography. Studies include A. W. Benn, *The History of English Rationalism in the Nineteenth Century,* 2 vols., 1906; Karl Britton, *John Stuart Mill,* 1953; Emery Neff, *Carlyle and Mill,* 1926; John Robson, *The Improvement of Mankind,* 1968; and Alan Ryan, *John Stuart Mill,* 1970.

William Morris

Collected Works, 24 vols., 1910–15; J. W. Mackail, *The Life of William Morris,* 2 vols., 1899; George Bernard Shaw, *William Morris, As I Knew Him,* 1936; Graham Hough, *The Last Romantics,* 1949; Peter Faulkner, *William Morris and William Butler Yeats,* 1962, and Peter Faulkner, ed., *William Morris: The Critical Heritage,* 1973. E. P. Thompson's Marxist approach in *William Morris: Romantic to Revolutionary,* 1977 (a revised version of an earlier book) offers the best study of Morris's politics.

John Henry Cardinal Newman

The 41 volumes of Newman's works were published over a period of years, but no standard edition has as yet appeared. Twenty-one of the projected 30 volumes of the *Letters and Diaries*, edited by C. S. Dessain, have been published since 1961. For a useful text, with criticism, of *Apologia pro Vita Sua*, see David J. De-Laura's Norton Critical Edition, 1968. Meriol Trevor's *New Man*, 2 vols., 1962, is a comprehensive biography. For Newman's religious background and development, two of the most helpful studies are R. W. Church's *The Oxford Movement*, 1891, and Charles F. Harold's *John Henry Newman*, 1945. His literary skill is analyzed in John Holloway's *The Victorian Sage*, 1953, Chapter VI; Walter E. Houghton's *The Art of Newman's "Apologia,"* 1945; and Martin J. Svaglic's "The Structure of Newman's *Apologia*," *PMLA*, LXVI (1951), 138–48. Especially recommended is Dwight Culler's *The Imperial Intellect*, 1955. William Robbins's *The Newman Brothers*, 1966, develops an interesting contrast between Newman and his free-thinking brother, Francis Newman.

The Nineties

On the special qualities of the literature of the 1890's see Richard Ellman, ed., *Edwardians and Late Victorians*, 1960. See also Holbrook Jackson, *The Eighteen Nineties*, 1913, rev., 1976; Osbert Burdett, *The Beardsley Period*, 1925; Graham Hough, *The Last Romantics*, 1947; and Ian Fletcher, *The 1890's: A Lost Decade*, 1961. Three useful anthologies of the period are *An Anthology of "Nineties" Verse*, edited by A. J. A. Symons, 1928; *British Poetry of the Eighteen-Nineties*, edited by Donald Davidson, 1937; and *Aesthetes and Decadents in the 1890's: An Anthology of British Poetry and Prose*, edited by K. Beckson, 1966.

See also entries under **Ernest Dowson, William Ernest Henley, Rudyard Kipling, Francis Thompson,** and **Oscar Wilde.**

Walter Pater

Works, 10 vols., 1910. Thomas Wright, *The Life of Walter Pater*, 2 vols., 1907; German d'Hangest, *Walter Pater: l'homme et l'oeuvre*, 2 vols., 1962. Critical essays include T. S. Eliot's "Arnold and Pater" in *Selected Essays 1917–32*, 1932; Graham Hough, *The Last Romantics*, 1949, Chapter IV; Ruth Z. Temple, "The Ivory Tower as Lighthouse" in *Edwardians and Late Victorians*, edited by Richard Ellman, 1960; U. C. Knoepflmacher, *Religious Humanism and the Victorian Novel*, 1965, and David J. DeLaura, *Hebrew and Hellene in Victorian England: Newman, Arnold, and Pater*, 1969. Highly recommended is Laurence Evans's excellent chapter on Pater in *Victorian Prose: A Guide to Research,* ed. David J. DeLaura, 1973.

Christina Rossetti

The standard edition of the *Poetical Works of Christina Rossetti* was edited by W. M. Rossetti in 1904. Virginia Woolf's *The Second Common Reader*, 1932, contains an essay on the poet. Also useful are Marya Zaturenska, *Christina Rossetti: A Portrait*, 1949; H. N. Fairchild, *Religious Trends in English Poetry*, 1957, Vol. IV, Chapter 10; and Lona M. Packer, *Christina Rossetti*, 1963.

Dante Gabriel Rossetti

Rossetti's *Works* were edited by W. M. Rossetti, 1911; *The House of Life* was edited by P. F. Baum, 1928, and *The Letters* by Oswald Doughty and J. R. Wahl, 4 vols., 1965–67 (an incomplete collection). See Oswald Doughty's *D. G. Rossetti: A Victorian Romantic*, 1960, and Lionel Stevenson, *The Pre-Raphaelite Poets*, 1973. Jerome McGann's "Rossetti's Significant Details," *Victorian Poetry*, Spring, 1969, is also recommended.

John Ruskin

The *Works* were edited by E. T. Cook and Alexander Wedderburn, 39 vols., 1903–12. Ruskin's biography is being at present rewritten, but meanwhile E. T. Cook's *The Life of Ruskin*, 2 vols., 1911, is informative. His *Diaries*, edited by Joan Evans and J. H. Whitehouse, were published in 1956. An interesting digest of his aesthetic theories was compiled by Joan Evans in *The Lamp of Beauty: Writings on Art by John Ruskin*, 1958. Also recommended are R. H. Wilenski, *John Ruskin*, 1933; John D. Rosenberg, *The Darkening Glass*, 1961; and George P. Landow, *The Aesthetic and Critical Theories of John Ruskin*, 1971.

Algernon Charles Swinburne

Complete Works, edited by E. W. Gosse and T. J. Wise, 20 vols., 1925–27; *The Swinburne Letters*, edited by Cecil Y. Lang, 6 vols., 1959–62; G. Lafourcade, *Swinburne: A Literary Biography*, 1932. For an attack on Swinburne's shortcomings as a poet, see A. E. Housman's essay of 1910, first published in *American Scholar*, Winter 1969–70. For more sympathetic readings see the special Swinburne issue of *Victorian Poetry*, Spring-Summer 1971, and also see the exceptionally fine study by Jerome J. McGann: *Swinburne: An Experiment in Criticism*, 1972.

Alfred, Lord Tennyson

Tennyson's *Works* were edited by his son Hallam, Lord Tennyson, in 9 vols., 1907–8. The *Poems*, in one volume, were edited by Christopher Ricks, 1969. Norton Critical Editions of Tennyson's work are *Tennyson's Poetry*, edited by Robert W. Hill, Jr., 1972, and *In Memoriam*, edited by Robert H. Ross, 1974. Hallam Tennyson's *Alfred, Lord Tennyson: A Memoir*, 2 vols., 1897, is a mine of scattered anecdotes and valuable information. A full-scale biography is being prepared by Robert Martin; meanwhile the best available is Sir Charles Tennyson's *Alfred Tennyson*, 1949. Sir Harold Nicolson's *Tennyson*, 1923, a critical study more than a biography, gives a lively but distorted assessment of Tennyson's achievement. A number of critical studies have successively corrected Nicolson's oversights and have variously demonstrated that Tennyson is one of the finest of poets. These include Jerome H. Buckley's *Tennyson: The Growth of a Poet*, 1961; Valerie Pitt's *Tennyson Laureate*, 1962; Christopher Ricks's *Tennyson*, 1972; F. E. L. Priestley's *Language and Structure in Tennyson's Poetry*, 1973; James R. Kincaid's *Tennyson's Major Poems: The Comic and Ironic Patterns*, 1975; W. David Shaw's *Tennyson's Style*, 1976; and, most especially to be recommended, *The Poetry of Tennyson* by A. Dwight Culler, 1977.

Some of the most interesting discussions are in introductory essays to Tennyson's poems by T. S. Eliot, 1936; W. H. Auden, 1944; H. Marshall McLuhan, 1956; Jerome Buckley, 1958; and George MacBeth, 1971. Also useful are *A Commentary on Tennyson's "In Memoriam,"* by A. C. Bradley, 1901; *The Alien Vision of Victorian Poetry*, by E. D. H. Johnson, 1952; and *Critical Essays on the Poetry of Tennyson*, edited by John Kilham, 1960. Book-length studies of the *Idylls* have been published by Clyde de L. Ryals, 1967, John R. Reed, 1969, and John D. Rosenberg, 1973. A collection of critical essays on *In Memoriam* was edited by John Dixon Hunt, 1970.

Francis Thompson

Complete Poetical Works were edited by Wilfred Meynell, 3 vols., 1913. Biographies are Paul van K. Thompson, *Francis Thompson*, 1961, and John Walsh, *Strange Harp * * * the Life of Francis Thompson*, 1967.

See also entries under **The Nineties.**

Oscar Wilde

For a full-scale guide to editions of Wilde and studies of his life and work see the long essay by Ian Fletcher and John Stokes in *Anglo-Irish Literature: A Review of Research*, edited by Richard J. Finneran, 1976, pp. 48–137. There are many modern selections of Wilde's work; a convenient one-volume edition of *The Complete Works of Oscar Wilde* has been edited by J. B. Foreman, with an introduction by Wilde's son, Vyvyan Holland, new edition, 1966. The *Letters* were edited by Rupert Hart-Davis, 1962, and a selection of Wilde's critical essays, *The Artist as Critic* was edited by Richard Ellmann in 1968. Ellmann is also preparing a full-scale biography of Wilde which promises to become standard (see his *Golden Codgers: Biographical Speculations*, 1974). Meanwhile there are earlier books: *Oscar Wilde: His Life and Confessions*, by Frank Harris, 1916, 1960, is full of anecdotes which, though not always factually accurate, often indicate psychological truths about Wilde; *Oscar Wilde and the Yellow Nineties*, by Francis Winwar, 1940, gives a picture of Wilde in his setting; *The Life of Oscar Wilde, His Life and Wit*, by Hesketh Pearson, 1946, concentrates on his life rather than his work; and *Oscar Wilde: A Biography*, by H. Montgomery Hyde, 1975, offers a lively narrative and contains a useful bibliography. *Oscar Wilde, A Pictorial Biography*, by Vyvyan Holland, 1960, has splendid photographs of Wilde and his contemporaries and also provides a concise factual account of his life.

Oscar Wilde: A Collection of Critical Essays, edited by Richard Ellmann, 1969, is valuable for its coverage of responses to Wilde by other writers such as Yeats and Shaw. *Oscar Wilde: The Critical Heritage*, edited by Kenneth Beckson, 1970, is especially helpful with regard to the plays; it covers the period 1881–1927. On *The Importance of Being Earnest* see also a perceptive essay by Ian Gregor, "Comedy and Oscar Wilde" in *Sewanee Review*, Spring, 1966, pp. 501–21.

See also entries under **The Nineties.**

THE TWENTIETH CENTURY

The following critical works deal with some general aspects of modern English Literature: *New Bearings in English Poetry*, by F. R. Leavis, 2nd ed., 1950; *Forces in Modern British Literature*, by William Y. Tindall, 1947, 1956; *The Modern Writer and His World*, by G. S. Fraser, 1953; *The Present Age in British Literature*, by David Daiches, 1958; *The Novel and the Modern World*, by David Daiches, 2nd ed., 1960; *The Modern Poets, A Critical Introduction*, 1960, and *The New Modern Poetry*, 1967, both by M. L. Rosenthal; *The New Poetic*, by C. K. Stead, 1964; *The Modern Tradition: Backgrounds of Modern Literature*, edited by Richard Ellmann and Charles Feidelson, 1965; *The Struggle of the Modern*, by Stephen Spender, 1963; *The Idea of the Modern*, by Irving Howe, 1968; and *Twentieth-Century British Literature: A Reference Guide and Bibliography*, by Ruth Z. Temple, 1968. *Eight Modern Writers*, by J. I. M. Stewart (*Oxford History of English Literature*, Vol. XII), 1963, includes valuable chapters on Hardy, Shaw, Conrad, Kipling, Yeats, Joyce, and Lawrence, and a comprehensive bibliography. *The Modern Age*, Vol. 7 of *The Pelican Guide to English Literature*, 1961, edited by B. Ford, contains some helpful critical essays and a bibliography. *Contemporary British Literature*, by Fred B. Millett, 1935, and *Anglo-Irish Literature: A Review of Research*, edited by Richard J. Finneran, 1976, contain bibliographies of modern British and Anglo-Irish writers, respectively, up to their dates of publication. Bibliographies also appear in the periodical *20th-Century Literature*. The first three chapters of *Image and Experience: Studies in a Literary Revolution*, by Graham Hough, 1960, attempt to put the whole modern movement in perspective.

The social and political background is well covered in *The Great War and Modern Memory*, by Paul Fussell, 1975; *The Long Week-End: A Social History of Great Britain 1918–1939*, by Robert Graves and Alan Hodge, 1940; *The Baldwin Age*, edited by John Raymond, 1960; *The Thirties*, by Julian Symons, rev., 1975; *The Auden Generation: Literature and Politics in England in the 1930s*, by Samuel Hynes, 1976; and *The Social Context of Modern English Literature*, by Malcolm Bradbury, 1971.

Vol. 4 of *The New Cambridge Bibliography of English Literature*, edited by I. R. Willison, 1972, deals with the period 1900–1950 and gives a full list of critical and scholarly works about the authors of the period produced up to 1970.

W. H. Auden

W. H. Auden: Collected Poems, edited by Edward Mendelson, 1976, contains all the poems that the author wished to preserve, in the texts that received his final approval. *The English Auden. Poems, Essays and Dramatic Writings 1927–1939*, edited by Edward Mendelson, 1977, reprints in their original versions all the poems Auden published in book form during the 1930's, together with some previously unpublished and uncollected poems and a selection of Auden's early prose writings. *The Dyer's Hand and Other Essays*, 1968, brings together a selection of his stimulating literary-critical articles, lectures, and reviews. *Forewords and Afterwords*, 1973, is a comparable collection. Auden edited a number of anthologies, including (with Norman Pearson) *Poets of the English Language*, 5 vols., 1950; (with Noah Greenberg and Charles Kallman) *An Elizabethan Songbook*, 1955; and *The Elder Edda: A Selection*, 1969. *Auden: An Introductory Essay*, by Richard Hoggart, 1951; *The Making of the Auden Canon*, by J. W. Beach, 1957; *The Poetry of W. H. Auden*, by M. K. Spears, 1963; *Auden*, by Barbara Everett, 1964; *The Poetic Art of W. H. Auden*, by J. G. Blair, 1965; *Auden's Poetry*, by Justin Replogle, 1969; and *The Case of the Helmeted Airman: A Study of W. H. Auden's Poetry*, by François Duchene, 1972, are critical studies. *A Reader's Guide to W. H. Auden*, by John Fuller, 1970, provides a commentary on Auden's poetry and drama in chronological order; while *The Auden Generation: Literature and Politics in England in the 1930s*, by Samuel Hynes, 1976, is an illuminating study of Auden and his contemporaries in their historical context.

Samuel Beckett

The standard bibliography, *Samuel Beckett: His Works and His Critics*, edited by Raymond Federman and John Fletcher, 1970, deals with the criticism only through 1966. Deirdre Blair's *Samuel Beckett: A Biography*, 1978, may change the direction of Beckett studies; meanwhile, the best introduction to the works themselves is Hugh Kenner's *Reader's Guide to Samuel Beckett*, 1973. Beckett's philosophical and religious ideas are well presented in *The Ship of Chaos*, by David T. Hesla, 1971; and

Beckett/Beckett, by Vivian Mercier, 1977, shows that the Paris flowering grew from Dublin soil. Colin Duckworth's English introduction to his edition of *En attendant Godot,* 1966, is the classic essay on the classic play, *Waiting for Godot.* Textual study of Beckett is in its infancy; there is a Beckett Archive at the University of Reading; a twice-yearly *Journal of Beckett Studies* began publication in 1976.

Rupert Brooke

The Poetical Works, 2nd edition, 1970, and *The Letters,* 1968, are both edited by G. L. Keynes. *The Prose* is edited by Christopher Hassall, 1956, who wrote the standard biography, *Rupert Brooke,* 1964. There are critical discussions in "Rupert Brooke and the Intellectual Imagination," an essay by Walter de la Mare, collected in his *Pleasures and Speculations,* 1940; *English Poetry of the First World War,* by John H. Johnston, 1964; *Heroes' Twilight,* by Bernard Bergonzi, 1965; and *Rupert Brooke: A Reappraisal and Selection from his Writings, Some Hitherto Unpublished,* edited by Timothy Rogers, 1971.

See also entries under **Poetry of World War I.**

Joseph Conrad

Standard is *The Uniform Edition of the Works of Joseph Conrad,* 22 vols., 1923–28, reprinted in 1946 ff. as *The Collected Edition of the Works of Joseph Conrad.* Other collections are the Concord Edition, 22 vols., 1923–28, and the Memorial Edition, 21 vols., 1925. When completed, the Cambridge University Press's variorum edition will be the standard edition. Many of the novels are available in individual paperbound editions; among the most notable are the Norton Critical Editions of *Heart of Darkness,* edited by Robert Kimbrough, rev., 1972; *Lord Jim,* edited by Thomas C. Moser, 1968; and *The Nigger of the "Narcissus,"* edited by Robert Kimbrough, 1979.

Two perceptive critical studies are *Conrad the Novelist,* by Albert J. Guerard, 1958, and *Joseph Conrad, Achievement and Decline,* by Thomas C. Moser, 1957. *The Portable Conrad,* edited by Morton D. Zabel, 1947, contains a good selection with a helpful introduction. The discussion of Conrad in *The Great Tradition,* by F. R. Leavis, 1949, is valuable, as is the chapter on Conrad in *The Novel and the Modern World,* by David Daiches, 2nd ed., 1960. There is a brilliant essay on *Lord Jim* in *The English Novel: Form and Function,* by Dorothy Van Ghent, 1953, and

the Introduction to the Modern Library edition of *Nostromo,* edited by Robert Penn Warren, 1951, is an essential piece. The important studies of the political novels are *The Political Novels of Joseph Conrad,* by Eloise Knapp Hay, 1953; *Paradise of Snakes,* by Claire Rosenfield, 1967; and *Conrad's Politics: Community and Anarchy in the Fiction of Joseph Conrad,* by Avrom Fleishman, 1967. *Joseph Conrad,* by Jocelyn Baines, 1960, is the standard biography, and until the publication of Frederick Karl's long-awaited edition of Conrad's letters, *Joseph Conrad: Life and Letters,* edited by G. Jean-Aubry, 2 vols., 1927, will remain the standard if very incomplete edition. This should be supplemented by *Letters from Joseph Conrad,* edited by Edward Garnett, 1928, and *Joseph Conrad's Letters to R. B. Cunninghame Graham,* edited by C. T. Watts, 1969.

Donald Davie

Collected Poems, 1972, has been followed by *The Shires,* 1975, and *In the Stopping Train,* 1978. As with other distinguished poet-critics, Davie's critical writings on other poets—notably *Purity of Diction in English Verse,* 1952, *Articulate Energy,* 1955, and *Thomas Hardy and British Poetry,* 1972—also illuminate his own work. Critical discussion of Davie's poetry is to be found in *Eight Contemporary Poets,* by Calvin Bedient, 1974; *British Poetry since 1960: A Critical Survey,* edited by Michael Schmidt and Grevel Lindop, 1972; *Donald Davie, Charles Tomlinson, Geoffrey Hill,* edited for the Open University by G. Martin, M. Dodsworth, M. Edwards, and J. Purkis, 1976; and *Agenda*: Donald Davie Special Issue, Vol. 14, No. 2, Summer, 1976.

See also entries under **Poetry after Mid-Century.**

T. S. Eliot

The fullest one-volume collections of Eliot's poetry are *Collected Poems, 1909–1963,* 1963, and *The Complete Poems and Plays* (including *Poems Written in Early Youth*), 1969. Some critical essays are in *Selected Essays,* 3rd ed., 1972; *On Poetry and Poets,* 1957; and *Selected Prose of T.S. Eliot,* edited by Frank Kermode, 1975. T. S. Eliot, *The Waste Land: A Facsimile and Transcript of the Original Drafts including the Annotations of Ezra Pound,* edited by Valerie Eliot, 1971, is an indispensable tool for study of *The Waste Land. T. S. Eliot, The Waste Land,* by Helen Williams, 2nd rev. ed., 1973, is a critical study of the poem taking full account of the new material made available in Valerie Eliot's edition, *T. S. Eliot, Poems in the Making,* by Gertrude Patterson, 1971, also makes use of the rediscovered Eliot manuscripts of *The Waste Land* but ranges widely throughout Eliot's work. *The Composition of Four Quartets,* by Helen Gardner, 1978, describes the growth of the poem from the drafts and includes new information on its sources.

Among the many books on Eliot, *The Achievement of T. S. Eliot,* by F. O. Matthiessen, rev., 1947, has the enthusiasm of a pioneer work; *T. S. Eliot: A Study of His Writings by Various Hands,* edited by B. Rajan, 1947, and *T. S. Eliot, a Selected Critique,* edited by Leonard Unger, 1948, bring together a variety of critical essays including some helpful explications of *The Waste Land,* and *Four Quartets*; *The Art of T. S. Eliot,* by Helen Gardner, is a perceptive critical study of his poetry; *T. S. Eliot, the Design of his Poetry,* by Elizabeth Drew, 1950, is a systematic chronological survey and explanation; *A Reader's Guide to T. S. Eliot,* by George Williamson, 1953, is thorough and informative in its explanation of obscurities and references; and *T. S. Eliot's Poetry and Plays,* by Grover Smith, Jr., 1956, goes through the poems and plays in an exhaustive and even exhausting manner. The best short critical books on Eliot are *T. S. Eliot,* by Northrop Frye, 1963, and *T. S. Eliot,* by Bernard Bergonzi, 1972. In the absence of a full-scale biography, one is the more grateful for *T. S. Eliot: The Man and His Work,* a collection of memoirs, edited by Allen Tate, 1967; *Notes on Some Figures behind T. S. Eliot,* by Herbert Howarth, 1965; and *Eliot's Early Years,* by Lyndall Gordon, 1977. *T. S. Eliot: A Bibliography,* edited by Donald Gallup, rev., 1969, lists the extensive criticism on Eliot through 1967.

Elaine Feinstein

Some Unease and Angels: Selected Poems, 1977, includes poems from *In a Green Eye,* 1966; *The Magic Apple Tree,* 1971; and *The Celebrants and Other Poems,* 1973. She has translated *Marina Tsvetayeva: Selected Poems,* 1971, and written six novels: *The Circle,* 1970; *The Aberstone Exit,* 1972; *The Glass Alembic,* 1974; *The Children of the Rose,* 1974; *The Ecstasy of Doctor Miriam Garner,* 1976; and *The Shadow Master,* 1978. For some critical comment, see *British Poetry since 1960: A Critical Survey,* edited by Michael Schmidt and Grevel Lindop, 1972, pp. 79–80.

See also entries under **Poetry after Mid-Century.**

E. M. Forster

Forster's five major novels—*Where Angels Fear to Tread,* 1905; *The Longest Journey,* 1907; *A Room With a View,* 1910; *Howards End,* 1910; and *A Passage to India,* 1924—are available in various editions. The best and most recent is The Abinger Edition of Forster's works, edited by Oliver Stallybrass, which will eventually include all Forster's writings. A sixth novel, *Maurice,* was finished in 1914 but published posthumously in 1971. A homosexual romance, it adds nothing to Forster's reputation as a novelist. *The Collected Tales of E. M. Forster* appeared in 1947, *The Life to Come and Other Stories* posthumously in 1972. *Abinger Harvest,* a collection of some eighty essays, was published in 1927, *Two Cheers for Democracy,* a second collection, in 1951. Forster's casual but provocative study of fictional technique, *Aspects of the Novel,* appeared in 1927. His biography of his aunt, *Marianne Thornton,* 1956, is an illuminating contribution to Victorian social history.

Among the many critical studies of Forster's work, of particular interest are *E. M. Forster* by Lionel Trilling, 2nd rev. ed., 1965; *The Cave and the Mountain: a Study of E. M. Forster,* by Wilfred Stone, 1966; and *E. M. Forster: The Perils of Humanism,* by Frederick Crews, 1962. A candid biography has just been published: *E. M. Forster, a Life,* Vols. 1 and 2, 1977 and 1978, by P. N. Furbank.

Robert Graves

Collected Poems 1975, 1975, the most recent and fullest of several *Collected* volumes, has a biographical introduction by James McKinley. Of Graves's many prose works, the most relevant to a study of his poetry are *Good-bye to All That,* 1929, rev., 1957, an autobiography written when he was 33; *On Poetry: Collected Talks and Essays,* 1969; and *The White Goddess,* 1948, enlarged edition, 1966. *Robert Graves,* by J. M. Cohen, 1960; *Swifter than Reason, The Poetry and Criticism of Robert Graves,* by Douglas Day, 1963; *The Poetry of Robert Graves,* by Michael Kirkham, 1969; and *Robert Graves: Peace-Weaver,* by James S. Mehoke, 1975, are critical studies, the last containing a useful bibliography.

Thom Gunn

Gunn's publications include *Fighting Terms,* 1954, rev., 1962; *The Sense of Movement,* 1957; *The Mis-*

2554 · *Selected Bibliographies*

anthrope, 1958; *My Sad Captains*, 1961; *Touch*, 1967; *Positives*, 1967; *Poems 1950–1966*, 1969; *Moly*, 1971; and *Jack Straw's Castle*, 1975. There is some critical discussion of his poetry in *Rule and Energy: Trends in British Poetry since the Second World War*, by John Press, 1963, and *British Poetry since 1960: A Critical Survey*, edited by Michael Schmidt and Grevel Lindop, 1972.

See also entries under **Poetry after Mid-Century.**

Ivor Gurney

Two collections of poems were published in Gurney's lifetime: *Severn and Somme*, 1917, and *War's Embers*, 1919. A selection of hitherto unpublished *Poems by Ivor Gurney*, edited by Edmund Blunden, appeared in 1954. A fuller but still far from satisfactory selection, of 139 poems both published and unpublished, appeared as *Poems of Ivor Gurney 1890–1937* in 1973, with Blunden's introduction reprinted and a biographical note by Leonard Clark. There still exist in various notebooks some 700 unpublished poems. A critical discussion of Gurney's poetry is to be found in *Out of Battle*, by Jon Silkin, 1972, Chapter 6.

See also entries under **Poetry of World War I.**

Thomas Hardy

Hardy published over a dozen volumes of poetry in his lifetime; *The Collected Poems* were issued in one volume in 1932; and *The Complete Poems*, edited by James Gibson, in 1976. There are several collected editions of Hardy's complete work, notably the Wessex Edition, 21 vols., 1912–14, and the Mellstock Edition, 37 vols., 1919–20. Many of the novels are in paperbound editions; among the most notable are the Norton Critical Editions of *Jude the Obscure*, edited by Norman Page, 1978; *The Mayor of Casterbridge*, edited by James K. Robinson, 1977; *The Return of the Native*, edited by James Gindin, 1969; and *Tess of the D'Urbervilles*, edited by Scott Elledge, rev., 1979.

The best biographical treatment is to be found in *Young Thomas Hardy*, 1975, and *Thomas Hardy's Later Years*, 1978, both by Robert Gittings. Hardy himself dictated much of his second wife's biography, *The Early Life of Thomas Hardy*, 1928, and *The Later Years of Thomas Hardy*, 1930. The Hardy Centennial Number of *The Southern Review*, 1940, was influential in shaping Hardy's critical reputation: the special Hardy Issue of *Agenda*, 1970,

contains much of the most interesting recent criticism. *Hardy: A Collection of Critical Essays*, edited by Albert Guerard, 1963, treats both the prose and the poetry, as does *Thomas Hardy: Distance and Desire*, by J. Hillis Miller, 1970, and *An Essay on Hardy*, by John Bayley, 1978. *The Pattern of Hardy's Poetry*, by Samuel Hynes, 1956, remains sound and useful; *Thomas Hardy and British Poetry*, by Donald Davie, 1973, is worth consulting; and *A Commentary on the Poems of Thomas Hardy*, by F. B. Pinion, 1976, is helpful on individual poems.

Seamus Heaney

Heaney has published four volumes of poetry: *Death of a Naturalist*, 1966; *Door into the Dark*, 1969; *Wintering Out*, 1972; and *North*, 1975.

See also entries under **Poetry after Mid-Century.**

Geoffrey Hill

Hill's first three collections of poems—*For the Unfallen*, 1959; *King Log*, 1968; and *Mercian Hymns*, 1971—were published together in the U.S. under the title *Somewhere is Such a Kingdom*, with an introduction by Harold Bloom, 1975. This has been followed by *Tenebrae*, 1978. Jon Silkin contributed a chapter-length account of Hill's poetry to *British Poetry since 1960: A Critical Survey*, edited by Michael Schmidt and Grevel Lindop, 1972, and there is some useful information in *Donald Davie, Charles Tomlinson, Geoffrey Hill*, edited for the Open University by G. Martin, M. Dodsworth, M. Edwards, and J. Purkis, 1976.

See also entries under **Poetry after Mid-Century.**

Molly Holden

She has published three collections of poems: *To Make Me Grieve*, 1968, *Air and Chill Earth*, 1971, and *The Country Over*, 1975; *The Unfinished Feud*, 1971, a children's novel; and three other novels: *A Tenancy of Flint*, 1971, *White Rose and Wanderer*, 1972, and *Reiver's Weather*, 1973. There is some critical account of Molly Holden's poetry in *British Poetry since 1960: A Critical Survey*, edited by Michael Schmidt and Grevel Lindop, 1972.

See also entries under **Poetry after Mid-Century.**

Gerard Manley Hopkins

Robert Bridges edited the first (posthumous) edition of Hopkins's poems in 1918; a second edition, in 1930, and a third, in 1948; each added further unpublished poems. A fourth, in 1967, edited by W. H. Gardner and N. H. MacKenzie, brought together all the known poems and verse fragments in both English and Latin.

In addition to the poems, Hopkins's letters and parts of his notebooks have been published, and these are of great interest to students of Hopkins's mind and of his poetic techniques: *The Letters of Gerard Manley Hopkins to Robert Bridges* and *The Correspondence of G. M. Hopkins and Richard Watson Dixon*, edited by C. C. Abbot, 2 vols., 1935; *Further Letters of Gerard Manley Hopkins*, edited by C. C. Abbot, 1937, rev., 1956; and *Notebooks and Papers of Gerard Manley Hopkins*, edited by Humphry House, 1937. House has also edited *Journals and Papers*, 1959; the edition was completed by Graham Storey. This, together with *Sermons and Devotional Writings*, edited by Christopher Devlin, 1959, constitutes a revised edition of the *Notebooks and Papers*. A useful selection of Hopkins's poetry and prose is *A Hopkins Reader*, edited by John Pick, 1953.

The most elaborate study of Hopkins is *G. M. Hopkins: A Study of Poetic Idiosyncrasy in Relation to Poetic Tradition*, by W. H. Gardner, 2 vols., 1944, 1949. Other stimulating studies include *Gerard Manley Hopkins: A Critical Eassy towards the Understanding of his Poetry*, by W. A. M. Peters, 1948; *Hopkins*, by N. H. MacKenzie, 1968; *The Dragon in the Gate: Studies in the Poetry of G. M. Hopkins*, 1968; and *A Commentary on the Complete Poems of Gerard Manley Hopkins*, by Paul L. Mariani, 1970. There are three good collections of critical essays: *Gerard Manley Hopkins*, by the Kenyon Critics, 1945; *Immortal Diamond: Studies in Gerard Manley Hopkins*, edited by Norman Weyand and Raymond Schoder, 1949; and *Hopkins: A Collection of Critical Essays*, edited by Geoffrey H. Hartman, 1966.

The only biography covering the poet's whole career is *Gerard Manley Hopkins: A Life*, by Eleanor Ruggles, 1944, but *Gerard Manley Hopkins: Priest and Poet*, by John Pick, 2nd ed., 1966, is also recommended.

A. E. Housman

Housman's three volumes of poetry —*A Shropshire Lad*, 1896; *Last Poems*, 1922; and the posthumous *More Poems*, 1936—were brought together in *Collected Poems*, rev., 1971. A *Complete Poems*, edited by Basil Davenport, with a history of the text by Tom Burns Haber, was published in 1959. *Selected Prose*, ed. John Carter, 1961, includes some of the notorious prefaces. *The Letters of A. E. Housman* were edited by Henry Maas in 1971. The best criticism is to be found in *A Collection of Critical Essays*, edited by Christopher Ricks, 1968; *A. E. Housman: A Divided Life*, by George L. Watson, 1957, is a biography.

Ted Hughes

Hughes's publications include *The Hawk in the Rain*, 1957; *Lupercal*, 1960; *Wodwo*, 1967; *Crow*, 1970; *Gaudete*, 1977; and *Cave Birds*, 1978. There is critical discussion of his work in *Rule and Energy: Trends in British Poetry since the Second World War*, by John Press, 1963, and *Eight Contemporary Poets*, by Calvin Bedient, 1974.

See also entries under **Poetry after Mid-Century.**

David Jones

Jones's long poems, *In Parenthesis*, 1937 and 1963, and *The Anathémata*, 1952, are both available in paperback, and some of his more important prose is to be found in *Epoch and Artist, Selected Writings*, edited by Harman Grisewood, 1959. Publication details of his shorter poems, prose writings, and the secondary literature on his work are listed in the bibliography to *David Jones: Artist and Writer*, by David Blamires, 1972, the most comprehensive critical study to date. There are chapter-length discussions of *In Parenthesis* in *English Poetry of the First World War*, by John H. Johnston, 1964; *Heroes' Twilight*, by Bernard Bergonzi, 1965; and *Out of Battle*, by Jon Silkin, 1972.

See also entries under **Poetry of World War I.**

James Joyce

The Viking Critical Editions of *Dubliners*, edited by Robert Scholes and A. Walton Litz, 1969, and *A Portrait of the Artist as a Young Man*, edited by Chester Anderson, 1968, include criticism, detailed commentary, and bibliography. *Ulysses* was first published in the United States in 1934; a text with some improvements was published in 1961, and *Ulysses: A Facsimile of the Manuscript*, with a critical introduction by Harry Levin, in 1975. *Finnegans Wake* was published in 1939, and a revised text, incorporating the author's corrections, in 1958. There are three volumes of Joyce's *Letters*, the first edited by Stuart Gilbert, 1957, and the second and third by Richard Ellmann, 1966.

Good general accounts of Joyce's work will be found in *James Joyce,* by Harry Levin, 1941, and *James Joyce*, by A. Goldman, 1968. Two useful critical works on *Dubliners* are *Twentieth-Century Interpretations of Dubliners: A Collection of Critical Essays*, edited by P. K. Garrett, 1968, and *James Joyce's Dubliners: Critical Essays*, edited by Clive Hart, 1969. The most helpful of many critical studies of *Ulysses* are *The Book as World: James Joyce's Ulysses*, by Marilyn French, 1976; *James Joyce: The Citizen and the Artist*, by C. H. Peake, 1976; *James Joyce's Ulysses: Critical Essays*, edited by Clive Hart and David Hayman, 1974; *Allusions in Ulysses*, by Weldon Thornton, 1973; *Notes for Joyce: An Annotation of James Joyce's Ulysses*, by Don Gifford and Robert Seidman, 1974; *The Classical Temper: A Study of James Joyce's Ulysses*, by S. L. Goldberg, 1961; and *Joyce and Shakespeare*, by William Schutte, 1957. *Surface and Symbol*, by Robert M. Adams, 1963, studies the raw material of actual Dublin life in *Ulysses*. Illuminating books on *Finnegans Wake* include *The Books at the Wake*, by J. S. Atherton, 1974; *A Third Census of Finnegans Wake*, by Adaline Glasheen, 1976; and *Structure and Motif in Finnegans Wake*, by Clive Hart, 1962.

James Joyce, by Richard Ellmann, is the standard biography; his *Ulysses on the Liffey*, 1973, and *The Consciousness of Joyce*, 1977, are also highly recommended.

Philip Larkin

In addition to two early novels—*Jill*, 1946, and *A Girl in Winter*, 1947—and a collection of essays on jazz (*All that Jazz: A Record Diary 1961–68*, 1970), Philip Larkin has published four books of poems: *The North Ship*, 1945; rev., 1966; *The Less Deceived*, 1955; *The Whitsun Weddings*, 1964; and *High Windows*, 1974. He edited *The Oxford Book of Twentieth-Century English Verse*, 1973. *Philip Larkin*, by David Timms, 1973, is a full-length study of his poetry, and there are good critical essays in *Phoenix*: Philip Larkin Issue 11/12 Autumn and Winter 1973/4, and *Eight Contemporary Poets*, by Calvin Bedient, 1974.

See also entries under **Poetry after Mid-Century.**

D. H. Lawrence

The standard edition of the collected works is the Phoenix Edition, 1955. *Collected Poems* appeared in 1928 and 1932; *Selected Poems* (selected by Richard Aldington) in 1934; and *Complete Poems*, 3 vols.,

in 1964. *Studies in Classical American Literature*, was published in 1923. Most of Lawrence is available in Penguin/Viking editions, including the invaluable papers collected in *Phoenix* and *Phoenix* II. The announced Cambridge Edition should become standard when completed.

Lawrence: Novelist, by F. R. Leavis, 1955, is an impassioned argument for Lawrence's supreme greatness and, more than any other book, is responsible for the Lawrence revival. The best critical study is *The Forked Flame*, by H. M. Daleski, 1965, which explains Lawrence's art in terms of his ideas. *The Deed of Life: The Novels and Tales of D. H. Lawrence*, by J. Moynahan, 1966, is a splendid critical study of the novels and stories. *Double Measure*, by George Ford, 1965, is an excellent study of *Women in Love* and *The Rainbow*, and various short stories that illustrate the same themes. Other important studies include *The Dark Sun*, by Graham Hough, 1956, which contains a perceptive chapter on Lawrence's poetry, and *D. H. Lawrence and the New World*, by David Cavitch, 1969. *D. H. Lawrence*, by Frank Kermode, 1971, is a very helpful introduction. The Viking Critical Edition of *Sons and Lovers*, edited by J. Moynahan, 1968, contains vital scholarly and critical material. Another useful work on this novel is *D. H. Lawrence and "Sons and Lovers": Sources and Criticism*, by E. W. Tedlock, 1965. The best biography is *The Intelligent Heart*, by Harry T. Moore, 1954; but Lawrence's own *Letters*, edited by Aldous Huxley, 1932, and much more fully but still incompletely by Harry T. Moore in 1962, provide the best introduction to his life. His wife's memoir, *Not I, but the Wind . . .*, by Frieda Lawrence, 1934, is an important and moving book. *D. H. Lawrence*, by E. T. [Jessie Chambers], 1935 and 1965 (2nd ed.), offers a revealing account of his youth and is crucial to an understanding of *Sons and Lovers*.

F. R. Leavis

Among Leavis's important books are *Revaluation*, 1936, 1950; *New Bearings in English Poetry*, 1932; *For Continuity*, 1933; *The Great Tradition*, 1948; *The Common Pursuit*, 1952; *Anna Karenina and Other Essays*, 1967; *Lectures in America*, 1969 (with Q. D. Leavis); *Letters in Criticism*, edited and with an introduction by John Tasker, 1974; and *The Living Principle: "English" as a Discipline of Thought*, 1975. Leavis edited the critical periodical *Scrutiny* from 1932 to 1953. *Leavis*, by Ronald Hayman, 1976, is a biography with a good bibliography.

Doris Lessing

Most of Lessing's collections of short stories, plays, and novels, including the five-volume *Children of Violence*, 1952–69, and *The Golden Notebook*, 1962, are available in paperback. *A Small Personal Voice*, edited by Paul Schleuter, 1974, is a selection of Lessing's essays on her life and writings, on other writers, and on Africa, where she lived before settling in England. Critical studies of her work include *Doris Lessing*, by Dorothy Brewster, 1965; *The Novels of Doris Lessing*, by Paul Schleuter, 1973; *The City and the Veld*, by Mary Ann Singleton, 1977; and *Doris Lessing: Critical Essays*, edited by Annis Pratt and L. S. Dembo, 1974, which includes a useful bibliography.

Hugh MacDiarmid

Collected Poems of Hugh MacDiarmid, revised edition with enlarged glossary prepared by John C. Weston, 1967, is the most convenient volume for American readers of MacDiarmid's poetry, but, though it contains a great deal, it is far from complete and, in spite of Weston's corrections of errors in the first edition, it still contains too many mistakes. And it prints *A Drunk Man Looks at the Thistle* as a series of separate poems with individual titles, thus obscuring the structure and unity of the work. However, Weston's admirable edition of *A Drunk Man* with critical and explanatory notes, published by the University of Massachusetts Press in 1971, provides a first-rate text for American readers. MacDiarmid was first introduced to American readers in a volume of selected lyrics, *Speaking for Scotland*, 1946. His principal volumes, in addition to those mentioned in the headnote, are *First Hymn to Lenin, and Other Poems*, 1931; *Second Hymn to Lenin*, 1932; *Scots Unbound, and Other Poems*, 1932; *At the Sign of the Thistle: a Collection of Essays*, 1934; *The Golden Treasury of Scottish Poetry* (ed.), 1940; *Cornish Heroic Song for Valda Trevlyn*, 1943; *A Kist of Whistles: New Poems*, 1947; *Lucky Poet*, 1943, reprinted 1972; and *The Company I've Kept* (autobiographical), 1966.

Two useful selections of MacDiarmid's prose are: *The Uncanny Scot: A Selection of Prose by Hugh MacDiarmid*, edited with an introduction by Kenneth Buthlay, 1968, and *Selected Essays of Hugh MacDiarmid*, edited with an introduction by Duncan Glen, 1969.

The best general account of MacDiarmid and his poetry is *Hugh MacDiarmid*, by Kenneth Buthlay, 1964. A good account of the Scottish cultural background and of MacDiarmid's part in Scottish literary movements is *Hugh MacDiarmid and the Scottish Renaissance*, by Ducann Glen, 1964. *Hugh MacDiarmid, A Festschrift*, edited by K. D. Duval and Sydney Goodsir Smith, published in 1962 on the occasion of the poet's 70th birthday, contains 15 essays by different hands on aspects of his life and work and is the most important single critical book on MacDiarmid. *Hugh MacDiarmid: A Critical Survey*, edited by Duncan Glen, 1972, also contains 15 essays by different critics, together with a comprehensive bibliography. *MacDiarmid: an Illustrated Biography*, by Gordon Wright, 1977, is a vivid presentation of 85 years of the poet's life in photographs, caricatures, poems, press-cuttings, and other documents.

Louis MacNeice

All of MacNeice's poetry has now been collected in one volume, *Collected Poems*, 1967. *The Strings Are False*, 1966, is a posthumously published unfinished autobiography. *Varieties of Parable*, 1965, are lectures on poetry given at Cambridge. MacNeice made verse translations of Aeschylus' *Agamemnon*, 1937, and, with E. L. Stahl, of Goethe's *Faust* (an abridged version of parts I and II), 1951. Critical studies include *Apollo's Blended Dream: A Study of the Poetry of Louis MacNeice*, by William T. McKinnon, 1971, and *Louis MacNeice: The Skeptical Vision*, by Terence Brown, 1975; while critical essays supplement personal recollections of friends and relatives in *Time Was Away*, edited by Terence Brown, 1974.

Katherine Mansfield

There is a convenient complete one-volume edition of Katherine Mansfield's stories, *The Short Stories of Katherine Mansfield*, 1937. Her *Journal* was edited by Middleton Murry, definitive ed., 1954, and *Letters and Journals of Katherine Mansfield: A Selection*, by C. K. Stead, 1977. *Katherine Mansfield, a Critical Study*, by S. Berkman, 1951; *Katherine Mansfield*, by Leslie Moore [Ida Constance Baker], 1971; *Katherine Mansfield, a Biography*, by A. Alpers, 1953; and *Lives and Letters*, by John Carswell, 1978, a reminiscence, are the most helpful of the several books about her and her work.

Edwin Muir

Collected Poems 1921–1958, 1960, is the standard complete edition. His *Selected Poems* were edited with a preface by T. S. Eliot in 1965 and his *Selected Letters* edited by P. H. Butter in 1974. In addition to the works mentioned in the headnote, Muir wrote *John Knox: Portrait of a Calvinist*, 1929; *The Estate of Poetry*, 1962; and three collections of critical essays: *Latitudes*, 1924; *Transition*, 1926; and *Essays on Literature and Society*, 2nd ed., 1965. *Edwin Muir*, by P. H. Butter, 1962; *The Poetry of Edwin Muir*, by E. L. Huberman, 1971; and *Barbarous Knowledge: Myth in the Poetry of Yeats, Graves, and Muir*, by D. Hoffman, 1967, are critical studies; and *Edwin Muir, Man and Poet*, by P. H. Butter, 1966, is the standard biography. Muir's *An Autobiography*, 1954, is complemented by *Belonging: A Memoir*, by Willa Muir, 1968.

George Orwell

After *Down and Out in Paris and London*, 1933, Orwell wrote two works of fiction: *Burmese Days*, 1934, and *Keep the Aspidistra Flying*, 1936. There followed *The Road to Wigan Pier*, 1937; *Homage to Catalonia*, 1938; *Coming up for Air*, 1939, a novel; *Inside the Whale*, 1940, a collection of essays; *The Lion and the Unicorn*, 1941, an analysis of the English character; and four further volumes of essays: *Critical Essays*, 1946; *Shooting an Elephant*, 1950; *England Your England*, 1953; and *Such, Such Were the Joys*, 1953. *The Collected Essays, Journalism and Letters*, edited by S. Orwell and I. Angus, appeared in 4 volumes in 1968.

Among the many critical studies of Orwell are *"Nineteen Eighty-Four"*, edited by I. Howe, 1963; *Orwell*, by E. M. Thomas, 1965; *The Last Man in Europe*, by Alan Sandison, 1974; *The Paradox of George Orwell*, by R. J. Voorhees, 1961; *George Orwell; A Collection of Critical Essays*, edited by R. Williams, 1974; *The Crystal Spirit*, by G. Woodcock, 1967; and *George Orwell*, edited by J. Meyers, 1975, a volume in the Critical Heritage Series. *Chronicles of Conscience*, by J. Calder, 1968, is a comparative study of Orwell and Arthur Koestler. *The Unknown Orwell*, by P. Stansky and W. Abrahams, 1972, is biographical.

Wilfred Owen

The Collected Poems, edited by C. Day Lewis, 1963, is more complete but less accurate than *Wilfred Owen: War Poems and Others*, edited by Dominic Hibberd, 1973. Both will be replaced in due course by *The Complete Poems*, edited by Jon Stallworthy.

The best critical studies are *Wilfred Owen*, by D. S. R. Welland, 2nd ed., 1978, and *Wilfred Owen*, by Gertrude M. White, 1969. *Wilfred Owen* by Dominic Hibberd, 1975, is a useful introduction to the poet's life and work, and *Wilfred Owen*, by Jon Stallworthy, 1974, is the standard biography. Major sources of biographical information are *The Collected Letters*, edited by Harold Owen and John Bell, 1967, and *Journey from Obscurity: Memoirs of the Owen Family*, by Harold Owen, Vol. 1, 1963; Vol. 2, 1964; Vol. 3, 1965.

See also entries under **Poetry of World War I**.

Harold Pinter

Four volumes of Pinter's writings were published in 1977: *Complete Works: One*, *Complete Works: Two*, *Poems and Prose 1949–1977*, and *The Proust Screenplay*, written with the collaboration of Joseph Losey and Barbara Bray. Critical studies of his work include *Harold Pinter*, by Arnold H. Hinchliffe, 1967; *Harold Pinter*, by Walter Kerr, 1967; *Harold Pinter: The Poetics of Silence*, by James R. Hollis, 1970; *Pinter: A Study of His Plays*, by Martin Esslin, 1976; *Strategems to Uncover Nakedness: The Dramas of Harold Pinter*, by Lois G. Gordon, 1969; *Harold Pinter*, by Arlene Sykes, 1970; *The Plays of Harold Pinter: An Assessment*, by Simon Trussler, 1973; and *Pinter: A Collection of Critical Essays*, edited by Arthur Ganz, 1972.

Poetry after Mid-Century

Critical materials may be found in *Rule and Energy: Trends in British Poetry since the Second World War*, by John Press, 1963; *The New Poets*, by M. L. Rosenthal, 1967; *A Vision of Reality*, by F. Grubb, 1965; *Eight Contemporary Poets*, by Calvin Bedient, 1974; *British Poetry since 1960: A Critical Survey*, edited by Michael Schmidt and Grevel Lindop, 1972 (which contains, in an appendix, a list of nearly 250 living British poets and their works and a list of 42 anthologies of modern British poetry); and *Thomas Hardy and British Poetry*, by Donald Davie, 1972.

The most important anthologies of the period are *New Lines*, 1957, and *New Lines 2*, 1963, both edited by Robert Conquest; *The Oxford Book of Twentieth-Century English Verse*, edited by Philip Larkin, 1973; *British Poetry since 1945*, edited by E. Lucie-Smith, 1970; *The New Poetry*, edited by A. Alvarez, 1962; and *The Young British Poets*, edited by Jeremy Robson, 1971. British poets are well represented, with biographical and critical notes and bibliographies, in *The Norton Anthology of Modern Poetry*, edited by Richard Ellmann and Robert O'Clair, 1973.

See also entries under **Donald Davie, Elaine Feinstein, Thom Gunn, Seamus Heaney, Geoffrey Hill, Molly Holden, Ted Hughes, Philip Larkin**, and **Jon Silkin.**

Poetry of World War I

The best anthologies are *Up the Line to Death: The War Poets, 1914–1918*, edited by Brian Gardner, 1964, and *Men who March Away: Poems of the First World War*, edited by I. M. Parsons, 1965. These poems are set in a much needed new perspective by *Drummer Hodge: The Poetry of the Anglo-Boer War 1899–1902* by M. van Wyk Smith, 1978. *Heroes' Twilight: A Study of the Literature of the Great War*, by Bernard Bergonzi, 1965, is a balanced introduction to both the poetry and literary prose of the period, while one of the many strengths of *The Great War and Modern Memory*, by Paul Fussell, 1975, is a range of reference that includes nonliterary as well as literary writing. *English Poetry of the First World War: A Study in the Evolution of Lyric and Narrative Form*, by John H. Johnston, 1964, and *Out of Battle: The Poetry of the Great War*, by Jon Silkin, 1972, are more conventional critical studies.

See also entries under **Rupert Brooke, Ivor Gurney, David Jones, Wilfred Owen, Isaac Rosenberg, Siegfried Sassoon**, and **Edward Thomas.**

Isaac Rosenberg

The Collected Poems, edited by Gordon Bottomley and Denys Harding, 2nd edition, 1949, will shortly be superseded as the standard edition by *The Complete Poems*, edited by Ian Parsons. There are three critical biographies: *Isaac Rosenberg: The Half Used Life*, by Jean Liddiard, 1975; *Isaac Rosenberg: Poet and Painter*, by Jean Moorcraft Wilson, 1975; and *Journey to the Trenches: The Life of Isaac Rosenberg, 1890–1918*, by Joseph Cohen, 1975.

See also entries under **Poetry of World War I.**

Siegfried Sassoon

The "war poems" included in *Collected Poems 1908–1956*, 1961, should be read in conjunction with Sassoon's prose works: *Memoirs of an Infantry Officer*, 1930; *Sherston's*

Progress, 1936; and *Siegfried's Journey*, 1945. All are discussed in *Siegfried Sassoon: A Critical Study*, by Michael Thorpe, 1966, and *The Great War and Modern Memory*, by Paul Fussell, 1975. The poetry is considered in "The Literature of the First World War," by D. J. Enright, in *The Modern Age* (Penguin Companion to English Literature, Vol. 7), 1961; *Heroes' Twilight: A Study of the Literature of the Great War*, by Bernard Bergonzi, 1965; *English Poetry of the First World War: A Study in the Evolution of Lyric and Narrative Form*, by John H. Johnston, 1964; and *Out of Battle: The Poetry of the Great War*, by Jon Silkin, 1972.

See also entries under **Poetry of World War I.**

Bernard Shaw

The Collected Works of Bernard Shaw, in the Ayot St. Lawrence Edition, 30 vols., appeared in 1930 ff. *Collected Plays with their Prefaces*, 7 vols., 1975, contains the finally revised text of all the published plays, together with historical data and miscellaneous Shavian pronouncements on each play. Many of the plays are also available in inexpensive reprints; note especially *Bernard Shaw's Plays*, A Norton Critical Edition, edited by Warren Sylvester Smith, 1970. Selections of his prose include *Bernard Shaw, Selected Prose*, edited by Diarmuid Russell, 1952; *Plays and Players* (drama criticism), edited by A. C. Ward, 1952; *The Nondramatic Literary Criticism of Bernard Shaw*, edited by Stanley Weintraub, 1972; *Shaw on Music*, edited by Eric Bentley, 1955; and *Bernard Shaw on Language*, edited by Abraham Tauber, 1963.

A still useful critical study is Eric Bentley's *Bernard Shaw: A Reconsideration*, 1947. *Shaw the Dramatist*, by Louis Crompton, 1969, examines twelve major plays from the standpoint of their social, historical, and philosophical backgrounds. Edmund Wilson's essay, "Shaw at Eighty," in *The Triple Thinkers*, 1952, is a stimulating discussion of Shaw as thinker and playwright. *G. B. S. 90: Aspects of Shaw's Life and Works*, edited by S. Winsten, 1946, contains recollections of Shaw's contemporaries together with essays by a variety of writers. Also useful is *G. B. Shaw, A Collection of Critical Essays*, edited by R. J. Kaufmann, 1965.

The most reliable biography is *Man of the Century*, by Archibald Henderson, 1956. Also of interest is *George Bernard Shaw: His Life and Personality*, by Hesketh Pearson, 1963. The *Collected Letters of Ber-*

nard Shaw, edited by Dan H. Laurence, 4 vols., 1965, contains 3,000 of a postulated 100,000 that he wrote.

Jon Silkin

Silkin's volumes of poetry include *The Portrait and Other Poems,* 1951; *The Peaceable Kingdom,* 1954; *The Re-ordering of the Stones,* 1961; *Nature with Man,* 1965; *Poems New and Selected,* 1966; *Amana Grass,* 1971; and *The Principle of Water,* 1974. He has also published a critical book, *Out of Battle: The Poetry of the Great War,* 1972. There is some critical discussion of his poetry in *British Poetry since 1960: A Critical Survey,* edited by Michael Schmidt and Grevel Lindop, 1972.

See also entries under **Poetry after Mid-Century.**

Edith Sitwell

In addition to more than thirty volumes of poetry, culminating in *Collected Poems,* 1957, and *Selected Poems,* with an introduction by John Lehmann, 1965, Edith Sitwell produced a variety of critical and other prose works. These include *Alexander Pope,* 1930; *The English Eccentrics,* rev., 1957; *Aspects of Modern Poetry,* 1934; *A Poet's Notebook,* 1950; and *Taken Care Of: An Autobiography,* 1965. John Lehmann and Derek Parker edited *Edith Sitwell: Selected Letters 1919–1964* and Lehmann has written an informative account of her family and background in *A Nest of Tigers: Edith, Osbert and Sacheverell Sitwell in their Times,* 1968. There is critical discussion of her work in *Edith Sitwell: The Symbolist Order,* by J. D. Brophy, 1968; *A Map of Modern English Verse,* by John Press, 1969; "Poets Old and New: Edith Sitwell" in *Assays,* by K. Rexroth, 1961; and *The Last Years of a Rebel: A Memoir of Edith Sitwell,* by E. Salter, 1967.

Stevie Smith

Stevie Smith's best books of poetry include her first, *A Good Time Was Had By All,* 1937; *Harold's Leap,* 1950; *Not Waving But Drowning,* 1957; and *Scorpion and Other Poems,* published posthumously with an introduction by Patric Dickinson in 1972; she was also the author of three novels. Both the *Selected Poems,* 1962, and the *Collected Poems,* 1976, reproduce many of her drawings, which she often printed with the poems.

There is at present no substantial critical work on Smith; two interviews, in *The Poet Speaks,* edited by Peter Orr, 1966, and *Ivy and Stevie,* by Kay Dick, 1971, are worth consulting. Also useful are: a chapter in *Eight Contemporary Poets,* by Calvin Bedient, 1974; Philip Larkin's essay, "Frivolous and Vulnerable" (*New Statesman,* September 28, 1962); and an anonymous review entitled "The Voice of Genteel Decay" (*Times Literary Supplement,* July 14, 1972).

Dylan Thomas

The Poems of Dylan Thomas, rev., 1974, is the fullest collection of Thomas's poetry. He also wrote the autobiographical prose *Portrait of the Artist as a Young Dog,* 1940; *Adventures in the Skin Trade,* 1955; a radio play, *Under Milk Wood,* 1954, which has proved a great popular success; and *Quite Early One Morning,* 1954, a collection of stories, essays, and minor pieces. In 1957 Vernon Watkins edited *Thomas's Letters to Vernon Watkins,* and *The Notebooks of Dylan Thomas* were edited by Ralph N. Maud in 1967. Maud's *Entrances to Dylan Thomas's Poetry,* 1963, is a good introduction to the workings of the poet's mind; *The Poetry of Dylan Thomas,* by Elder Olsen, 1954, is a helpful if somewhat oversystematized discussion of his poetry; and *Dylan Thomas: The Poet and his Critics,* by R. B. Kershner, 1976, is an evaluation of Thomas criticism with a useful bibliography. *The Life of Dylan Thomas,* by Constantine Fitzgibbon, 1965, and *Dylan Thomas: A Biography,* by Paul Ferris, 1977, are good biographies, while *The Days of Dylan Thomas,* by Bill Read, 1964, supplements a straightforward narrative with many photographs.

Edward Thomas

The Collected Poems of Edward Thomas, edited by R. George Thomas, 1978, is the standard scholarly edition, but also available are the plain-text *Collected Poems,* edited by Walter de la Mare, 1974, and *Selected Poems,* 1964. The best studies of Thomas's life and work are *Edward Thomas: A Critical Biography,* by William Cooke, 1970, and *Edward Thomas,* by R. George Thomas, 1972. Also of biographical and critical importance are *Letters from Edward Thomas to Gordon Bottomley,* edited by R. George Thomas, 1968; *The Diary of Edward Thomas: 1 January–8 April 1917,* with an introduction by Roland Gant, 1977; the moving memoirs of the poet's wife, *As it Was* and *World Without End,* by Helen Thomas, 1956; and *Edward Thomas: The Last Four Years,* by Eleanor Farjeon, 1958.

See also entries under **Poetry of World War I.**

Virginia Woolf

All ten novels are available in paperback. The *Collected Essays*, 4 vols., 1966–67, are supplemented by *Books and Portraits*, edited by Mary Lyon, 1977, which includes many of her literary sketches of famous writers. The first volume of *The Diary of Virginia Woolf*, edited by Anne Olivier Bell, 5 vols., appeared in 1977, as have three volumes of the projected six-volume *Letters of Virginia Woolf*, edited by Nigel Nicholson, 1975 ff.

The most detailed critical study of the novels and essays is *Virginia Woolf and Her Works*, by Jean Guiget (trans. Jean Stewart), 1965. *Virginia Woolf, the Inward Voyage*, by Havena Richter, 1970, analyzes her use of the subjective mode in the development of her characters, and *Virginia Woolf: A Collection of Critical Essays*, edited by Thomas Lewis, 1975, contains useful studies of individual novels. Other critical works include *Virginia Woolf*, by David Daiches, rev., 1963; *Virginia Woolf: Her Art as a Novelist*, by Joan Bennett, 2nd ed., 1964; and *Feminism and Art: A Study of Virginia Woolf*, by Herbert Marder, 1968, which emphasizes the social relevance of her novels, a topic illuminated by Woolf's own *A Room of One's Own*, 1929, and *Three Guineas*, 1938.

A balanced biography is *Virginia Woolf*, by Quentin Bell, 2 vols., 1972; *Moments of Being*, edited by Jeanne Schulkind, 1976, contains satirical and hilarious autobiographical fragments, as well as a helpful introduction. Of interest also are Leonard Woolf's five volumes of autobiography, *Sowing*, 1960; *Growing*, 1961; *Beginning Again*, 1964; *Downhill All the Way*, 1967; and *The Journey Not the Arrival Matters*, 1975. See also *The Bloomsbury Group*, by J. K. Johnstone, 1954, and *Bloomsbury*, by Quentin Bell, 1968.

William Butler Yeats

In addition to poems and verse plays, Yeats published essays, stories, and autobiographical writings, and produced editions of William Blake (with Edwin Ellis) and of some poems of Spenser. He also edited *The Oxford Book of Modern Verse*, 1936. *Collected Poems*, Definitive Edition, 1956, and *Collected Plays*, 2nd edition, 1952, collect Yeats's main work into two convenient volumes, although the standard editions are *The Variorum Edition of the Poems*, edited by Peter Allt and Russell K. Alspach, 1957, corrected 3rd printing, 1966, and *The Variorum Edition of the Plays*, edited by Russell K. Alspach, 1966, corrected 2nd printing, 1966. The fullest and most representative selection of the voluminous correspondence, a multi-volume edition of which is now in preparation, is *The Letters of W. B. Yeats*, edited by Allan Wade, 1954. Yeats's mystical work *A Vision* was first published in 1925; a much revised edition appeared in 1937. His autobiographical writings are combined in *The Autobiography of W. B. Yeats*, 1938 ff. Neither the first draft of Yeats's *Autobiography* nor his *Journals* were published until 1972, when Denis Donoghue edited them under the title *Memoirs*. *Mythologies*, 1959, contains the bulk of Yeats's prose fiction; *Essays and Introductions*, 1961, the most important of his critical prose; and *Explorations*, 1962, miscellaneous prose pieces not readily available elsewhere.

The critical literature on Yeats is more extensive than that on any other 20th-century poet, and the best guide to this is "W. B. Yeats" in *Anglo-Irish Literature: A Review of Research*, edited by Richard J. Finneran, 1976. *W. B. Yeats: A Critical Introduction*, by Balachandra Rajan, 2nd ed., 1969, is the most satisfactory of many short introductory studies, though less substantial than *The Identity of Yeats*, by Richard Ellmann, 2nd ed., 1964, and *The Lonely Tower: Studies in the Poetry of W. B. Yeats*, by T. R. Henn, 2nd ed., 1965, the best general accounts of Yeats's work. *The Permanence of Yeats*, edited by James Hall and Martin Steinmann, 1950; *Yeats: A Collection of Critical Essays*, edited by John Unterecker, 1963; and *In Excited Reverie*, edited by A. N. Jaffares and K. G. W. Cross, 1965, are three of several useful collections of critical essays. The most helpful commentaries are *A Commentary on the Collected Poems of W. B. Yeats*, 1968, and *A Commentary on The Collected Plays of W. B. Yeats*, 1975, both by A. N. Jeffares. Three specialist critical studies of important areas of Yeats's work are *W. B. Yeats Self Critic: A Study of His Early Verse*, by Thomas Parkinson, 1951, reprinted 1971 with *The Later Poetry* and a new foreword; *Between the Lines: W. B. Yeats's Poetry in the Making*, by Jon Stallworthy, 1963, corrected 2nd imp., 1965; and *Swan and Shadow: Yeats's Dialogue with History*, by Thomas R. Whitaker, 1964.

The first authorized biography was *W. B. Yeats 1865–1939*, by Joseph Hone, 2nd ed., 1962, and another, by F. S. L. Lyons, is now in preparation. The best critical biography is *Yeats: The Man and the Masks*, by Richard Ellmann, 1948; and *Yeats*, by Frank Tuohy, 1976, supplements a straightforward narrative with many excellent illustrations.

Poetic Forms and
Literary Terminology

RHYTHM AND METER

Verse is generally distinguished from prose as a more compressed and more regularly rhythmic form of statement. This approximate truth underlines the importance of **meter** in poetry, as the means by which rhythm is measured and described.

In the classical languages, meter was established on a **quantitative** basis, by the regular alternation of long and short syllables (that is, syllables classified according to the time taken to pronounce them). Outside of a few experiments (and the songs of Thomas Campion), this system has never proved congenial to English, which distinguishes, instead, between **stressed** and **unstressed,** or accented and unaccented syllables. Two varieties of accented stress may be distinguished. On the one hand, there is the natural stress pattern of words themselves; *sýllable* is accented on the first syllable, *deplórable* on the second, and so on. Then there is the sort of stress which indicates rhetorical emphasis. If the sentence "You went to Greece?" is given a pronounced accent on the last word, it implies "Greece (of all places)?" If the accent falls on the first word, it implies "you (of all people)?" The meter of poetry—that is, its rhythm—is ordinarily built up out of a regular recurrence of accents, whether established as **word accents** or **rhetorical accents;** once started in the reader's mind, it has (like all rhythm) a persistent effect of its own.

The unit which is repeated to give steady rhythm to a poem is called a **poetic foot;** in English it usually consists of accented and unaccented syllables in one of five fairly simple patterns:

The **iambic foot** (or **iamb**) consists of an unstressed followed by a stressed syllable, as in *uníte, repeát,* or *insíst.* Most English verse falls naturally into the iambic pattern.

The **trochaic foot** (**trochee**) inverts this order; it is a stressed followed by an unstressed syllable—for example, *únit, réaper,* or *ínstant.*

The **anapestic foot** (**anapest**) consists of two unstressed syllables followed by a stressed syllable, as in *intercéde, disarránge,* or *Cameróon.*

The **dactylic foot** (**dactyl**) consists of a stressed syllable followed by two unstressed syllables, as in *Wáshington, Écuador,* or *ápplejack.*

The **spondaic foot** (**spondee**) consists of two successive stressed syllables, as in *heartbreak, headline,* or *Kashmir.*

2562

In all the examples above, word accent and the quality of the metrical foot coincide exactly. But the metrical foot may well consist of several words, or, on the other hand, one word may well consist of several metrical feet. *Phótolithógraphy* consists of two excellent dactyls in a single word; *dárk and with spóts on it,* though it consists of six words rather than one, is also two dactyls—not quite such good ones. When we read a piece of poetry with the intention of discovering its underlying metrical pattern, we are said to **scan** it—that is, we go through it line by line, indicating by conventional signs which are the accented and which the unaccented syllables within the feet (the ictus ' generally designates accented, the mora ˘ unaccented syllables). We also count the number of feet in each line, or, more properly, **verse**—since a single poetic line is generally called a "verse." Verse lengths are conventionally described in terms derived from the Greek:

Monometer: one foot (of rare occurrence)
Dimeter: two feet (also rare)
Trimeter: three feet
Tetrameter: four feet
Pentameter: five feet
Hexameter: six feet (six iambic feet make an **Alexandrine**)
Heptameter: seven feet (also rare)

Doctor Johnson's little parody of simpleminded poets would thus be scanned this way:

> Ĭ pút mў hát ŭpón mў héad
> Ănd wálked ĭntó thĕ Stránd,
> Ănd thére Ĭ mét ănóthĕr mán
> Whŏse hát wăs ín hĭs hánd.

The poem is iambic in rhythm, alternating tetrameter and trimeter in verse length. The fact that it scans so nicely is, however, no proof that it is good poetry. Quite the contrary. Many of poetry's most subtle effects are achieved by establishing an underlying rhythm and then varying it by means of a whole series of devices, some dramatic and expressive, others designed simply to lend variety and interest to the verse. A well-known sonnet of Shakespeare's (116) begins,

> Let me not to the marriage of true minds
> Admit impediments. Love is not love
> Which alters when it alteration finds,
> Or bends with the remover to remove.

It is perfectly possible, if one crushes all one's sensitivities, to read the first line of this poem as mechanical iambic pentameter:

> Lĕt mé nŏt tó thĕ márrĭage óf trúe mínds.

But of course nobody ever reads it that way, except to make a point; read with normal English accent and some sense of what it is saying, the line would probably form a pattern something like this:

> Lĕt mĕ nŏt tŏ thĕ márrĭage ŏf trúe mínds,

which is neither pentameter nor in any way iambic. The second line is a little more iambic, but, read for expression, falls just as far short of pentameter:

Ădmĭt ĭmpédĭmĕnts. Lóve ĭs nŏt lóve.

Only in the third and fourth lines of the sonnet do we get verses which read as well as scan like five iambic feet.

The fact is that perfectly regular metrical verse is easy to write and dull to read. Among the devices in common use for varying too regular a pattern are, for instance, the insertion of a trochaic foot among iambics, especially at the opening of a line, where the soft first syllable of the iambic foot often needs stiffening (see line 1 above); the more or less free addition of extra unaccented syllables; and the use of **caesura,** or strong grammatical pause within a line (conventionally indicated, in scanning, by the sign ||). The second line of the sonnet above is a good example of caesura:

Admit impediments. || Love is not love.

The strength of the caesura, and its placing in the line, may be varied to produce striking variations of effect. More broadly, the whole relation between the poem's sound- and rhythm-patterns and its pattern as a sequence of assertions (phrases, clauses, sentences) may be manipulated by the poet. Sometimes his statements fit neatly within the lines, so that each line ends with a strong mark of punctuation; they are then known as **end-stopped lines.** Sometimes the sense flows over the ends of the lines, creating **run-on lines;** this process is also known, from the French, as **enjambment** (literally, "straddling").

End-stopped lines (Marlowe, *Hero and Leander*, lines 45–48):

> So lovely fair was Hero, Venus' nun,
> As Nature wept, thinking she was undone,
> Because she took more from her than she left
> And of such wondrous beauty her bereft.

Run-on lines (Keats, *Endymion* I.89–93):

> Full in the middle of this pleasantness
> There stood a marble altar, with a tress
> Of flowers budded newly; and the dew
> Had taken fairy fantasies to strew
> Daisies upon the sacred sward, * * *

Following the example of such poets as Blake, Rimbaud, and Whitman, many poets of the 20th century have undertaken to write what is called **free verse**—that is, verse which has neither a fixed metrical foot, nor (consequently) a fixed number of feet in its lines, but which depends for its rhythm on a pattern of cadences, or the rise and fall of the voice in utterance. All freedom in art is of course relative; free verse, with its special aptitude for metrical variety and nervous, colloquial phrasing—its total responsiveness, in other words, to its subject matter—has so successfully established itself that it is now widely recognized as a new and rather demanding form of artistic discipline.

SENSE AND SOUND

The very words of which poetic lines—whether free or traditional—are composed cause them to have different sounds and produce different effects. Polysyllables, being pronounced fast, often cause a line to move swiftly; monosyllables, especially when heavy and requiring distinct accents, may cause it to move heavily, as in Milton's famous line (*Paradise Lost* II.621):

> Rocks, caves, lakes, fens, bogs, dens, and shades of death.

Poetic assertions are often dramatized and reinforced by means of **alliteration**—that is, the use of several nearby words or stressed syllables beginning with the same consonant. When Shakespeare writes (*Sonnet* 64),

> Ruin hath taught me thus to ruminate
> That Time will come and take my love away,

the rich, round, vague echoes of the first line contrast most effectively with the sharp anxiety and directness of the alliterative *t*'s in the second. When Dryden starts *Absalom and Achitophel* with that wicked couplet,

> In pious times, ere priestcraft did begin,
> Before polygamy was made a sin,

the satiric undercutting is strongly reinforced by the triple alliteration which links "*p*ious" with "*p*riestcraft" and "*p*olygamy."

Assonance, or repetition of the same or similar vowel sounds within a passage (usually in accented syllables), also serves to enrich it, as in two lines from Keats's *Ode on Melancholy:*

> For shade to shade will come too drowsily,
> And drown the wakeful anguish of the soul.

It is clear that the round, hollow tones of "drowsily," repeated in "drown" and darkening to the full *o*-sound of "soul," have much to do with the effect of the passage. A related device is **consonance,** or the repetition of a pattern of consonants with changes in the intervening vowels—for example: *linger, longer, languor; rider, reader, raider, ruder.*

Direct verbal imitation of natural sounds (known as **onomatopoeia**) has has been much attempted, from Virgil's galloping horse—

> *Quadrupedante putrem sonitu quatit ungula campum*—

to Tennyson's account, in *The Princess,* of

> The moan of doves in immemorial elms,
> And murmuring of innumerable bees.

Often ingeniously exploited as a side effect, onomatopoeia is essentially a trick, with about the same value in poetry as it has in music.

RHYME AND STANZA

Rhyme consists of a repetition of accented sounds in words, usually those falling at the end of verse lines. If the rhyme sound is the very last syllable of the line (*rebound, sound*), the rhyme is called **masculine;** if the accented syllable is followed by an unaccented syllable (*hounding, bounding*), the rhyme is called **feminine.** Rhymes amounting to three or more syllables, like forced rhymes, generally have a comic effect in English, and have been freely used for this purpose, e.g., by Ogden Nash (*opportunity, impunity; failure, azalea*). Rhymes occurring within a single line are called **internal**; for instance, the Mother-Goose rhyme, "Mary, Mary, quite contrary," or Coleridge's *Ancient Mariner* ("We were the first that ever burst / Into that silent sea"). **Eye rhymes** are words used as rhymes which look alike but actually sound different (for example, *alone, done; remove, love*); **off rhymes** (sometimes called **partial, imperfect,** or **slant rhymes**) are occasionally the result of pressing exigencies or lack of skill, but are also, at times, used deliberately by modern poets for special effects. For instance, a sonnet by Dylan Thomas contains such "rhymes" as *knees, toes; Eve, grave; van, bone;* and *winter, ladder* (*Holy Sonnet* 3). Pairings like the last two are sometimes loosely described as consonance, rather than rhyme.

Blank verse is unrhymed iambic pentameter; until the recent advent of free verse, it was the only unrhymed measure to achieve general popularity in English. First used by the Earl of Surrey, blank verse was during the 16th century largely dramatic in character. *Paradise Lost* was one of the first nondramatic poems in English to use blank verse. But Milton's authority and his success were so great that during the 18th and 19th centuries blank verse came to be used for a great variety of discursive, descriptive, and philosophical poems—besides remaining the standard metrical form for epics. Thomson's *Seasons*, Cowper's *Task*, Wordsworth's *Prelude*, and Tennyson's *Idylls of the King* were all written in blank verse.

A **stanza** is a recurring unit of a poem, consisting of a number of verses. Certain poetic forms (as a notable example, Pindaric odes) have stanzas comprising a variable number of verses, of varying lengths. Others are more regular, hence easier to describe.

The simplest form of stanza is the **couplet**; it is simply two lines rhyming together. When a single couplet is considered in isolation, it is sometimes called a **distich**; when it includes a complete unified thought, ending with a terminal mark of punctuation, it is called a **closed couplet.** The iambic pentameter couplet seems to work best when it is strict and regular, but to regularize it was a work of considerable time and practice. Even as skillful a versifier as Ben Jonson, though he writes iambic pentameter couplets in a poem like *To Penshurst*, has not yet mastered what we call the **heroic couplet.** This is a strictly iambic pentameter couplet, strongly end-stopped, and with the couplets prevailingly closed. Heroic couplets generally are varied by means of a decided caesura, and limited to precisely ten syllables per line. The heroic couplet is the principal form of English neoclassical style. A model of its swift, keen, yet weighty wit is the opening of Dryden's *Absalom and Achitophel*. Occasionally, as in this poem, heroic couplets are varied by the introduction of a third rhyme, to make a **tercet** (usually enclosed by a marginal brace); and a striking terminal effect is sometimes achieved by the introduction of an Alexandrine (a line of iambic hexameter) as the third line of the tercet.

Another customary and challenging form of couplet is the **tetrameter,** or **four-beat couplet.** The more closely rhymes recur, the harder couplets are to manage; in addition, a four-beat line is hard to divide by caesura without splitting it into two tick-tock dimeters. For this reason, tetrameter couplets have posed a perpetual challenge to poets, and still provide an admirable finger-exercise for aspiring versifiers. A model of tetrameter couplets managed with marvelous variety, complexity, and expressiveness is Marvell's *To His Coy Mistress*:

> Thou by the Indian Ganges' side
> Shouldst rubies find; I by the tide
> Of Humber would complain. I would
> Love you ten years before the flood,
> And you should, if you please, refuse
> Till the conversion of the Jews.

English has not done much with rhymes grouped in threes, but has borrowed from Italian the form known as *terza rima,* in which Dante composed his *Divine Comedy*. This form consists of linked groups of three rhymes according to the following pattern: *aba bcb cdc ded,* etc. Shelley's *Ode to the West Wind* is composed in stanzas of *terza rima,* the poem as a whole ending with a couplet.

Quatrains are stanzas of four lines; the lines usually rhyme alternately, *abab,* or in the second and fourth lines, *abcb.* When they alternate tetrameter and trimeter lines, as in Johnson's little poem about men in hats (above), or as in *Sir Patrick Spens,* they are called **ballad stanza.** Dryden's *Annus Mirabilis* and Gray's *Elegy Written in a Country Churchyard* are in heroic quatrains; these rhyme alternately, and employ five-stress iambic verse throughout. Tennyson used for *In Memoriam* a tetrameter quatrain rhymed *abba,* and FitzGerald translated *The Rubáiyát of Omar Khayyám* into a pentameter rhymed *aaba;* but these forms have not been very generally adopted.

Chaucer's *Troilus and Criseyde* is an early example in English of **rime royal,** a seven-line iambic pentameter stanza consisting essentially of a quatrain dovetailed onto two couplets, according to the rhyme scheme *ababbcc* (the fourth line serves both as the final line of the quatrain and the first line of the first couplet). Closely akin to rime royal, but differentiated by an extra *a*-rhyme between the two *b*-rhymes, is **ottava rima,** that is, an eight-line stanza rhyming *abababcc.* As its name suggests, ottava rima is of Italian origin; it was first used in English by Wyatt. Its final couplet, being less prepared for than in rime royal, and usually set off as a separate verbal unit, has a special witty snap to it, for which Byron found good use in *Don Juan.*

The longest and most intricate stanza generally used for narrative purposes in English is that devised by Edmund Spenser for *The Faerie Queene.* The **Spenserian stanza** has nine lines rhyming *ababbcbcc;* the first eight lines are pentameter, the last line an Alexandrine. Slow-moving, intricate of pattern, and demanding in its rhyme scheme (the *b*-sound recurs four times, the *c*-sound three), the Spenserian stanza has nonetheless appealed widely to poets seeking a rich and complicated metrical form. Keats's *Eve of St. Agnes* and Shelley's *Adonais* are brilliantly successful 19th-century examples of its use.

The **sonnet,** originally a stanza of Italian origin which has developed into an independent lyric form, is usually defined as fourteen lines of iambic pentameter. None of the elements in this definition is absolute. The first sonnet of Sidney's *Astrophel and Stella* is in hexameters, and Milton has one sonnet of twenty lines (*On the New Forcers of Conscience*), while Meredith wrote a whole series of sixteen-line sonnets (*Modern Love*). Most sonnets, however, conform to the definition. Sonnets generally follow one of two conventional rhyme schemes. The **Petrarchan** or **Italian sonnet** is divided into sections of eight lines (**octave**) and six lines (**sestet**), rhyming *abba abba* and *cdecde*. (There are many variations of the rhyme scheme in the sestet; that described is the most frequent.) Under this arrangement, the poet tends to use his octave to state the problem and his sestet to resolve it. The **English** or **Shakespearean** sonnet takes the form of three quatrains and a final couplet, rhyming *abab cdcd efef gg*. The couplet is ideally suited for producing a summary statement or witty twist after the problem has been turned about in the three quatrains. Both these forms represent ideal models, not absolute prescriptions. Many sonnets approximate these patterns without following them precisely; indeed, the term ' sonnet" was slow in acquiring any meaning more specific than that of "short lyric poem." Among Donne's *Songs and Sonnets* there is just one sonnet in the more modern sense, *The Token*, and it has eighteen lines.

In the Elizabethan period, the sonnet underwent its most intensive cultivation in connection with themes of courtly love. Perhaps in revulsion, Donne used the sonnet mostly to express religious devotion (*Holy Sonnets, La Corona*), while Milton employed it on satiric, social, or political themes. In Wordsworth, it expanded in the direction of moral reflection and commentary, while G. M. Hopkins loaded it with a rich philosophical and rhetorical complexity which sometimes threatened to swamp the form altogether. But the applications of the sonnet are truly limitless, for it is a form just long and complex enough to provide compressed yet dignified statement of almost any major theme.

In blank verse or irregularly rhymed verse, where stanzaic divisions do not exist or are indistinct, the poetry sometimes falls into **verse paragraphs,** which are in effect divisions of sense like prose paragraphs. This division can be clearly seen in Milton's *Lycidas* or Spenser's *Epithalamion*. In the latter poem, it is reinforced by a **refrain,** which is simply a line repeated at the end of each stanza. Ballads also customarily have refrains; for example, the refrain of *Lord Randall* is

> mother, make my bed soon,
> For I'm weary wi' hunting, and fain wald lie down.

FIGURATIVE LANGUAGE

The act of bringing words together into rich and vigorous poetic lines is complex and demanding, chiefly because so many variables require control. There is the "thought" of the lines, their verbal texture, their emotional resonance, the developing perspective of the reader—all these to be managed at once. One of the poet's chief resources toward this end is figurative language. Here, as in matters of meter, one may distinguish a great variety of devices, some of which we use in everyday speech without special awareness of their names and natures. When we say someone eats "like a horse" or "like a bird," we are using a **simile,** that is, a comparison marked out by a specific word of likening—"like" or "as." When we omit the word of comparison but imply a likeness—as in the sentence, "That hog has guzzled all the champagne"—we are making use of **metaphor.** The **epic simile,** frequent in epic poetry, is an extended simile in which the thing compared is described as an object in its own right, beyond its point of likeness with the main subject. Milton starts to compare Satan to Leviathan, but concludes his simile with the story of a sailor who moored his ship by mistake, one night, to a whale (*Paradise Lost* I.200–208). Metaphors and similes have been complexly but usefully distinguished according to their special effects; they may be, for instance, violent, comic, degrading, decorative.

When we speak of "forty head of cattle" or ask someone to "lend a hand" with a job, we are using **synecdoche,** a figure which substitutes the part for the whole. When we speak of a statement "coming from the White House," or a man much interested in "the turf," we are using **metonymy,** or the substitution of one term for another with which it is closely associated. **Antithesis** is a device for placing opposing ideas in grammatical parallel, as, for example, in the following passage from Pope's *Rape of the Lock* (V.25–30), where there are more examples of antithesis than there are lines:

> But since, alas! frail beauty must decay,
> Curled or uncurled, since locks will turn to gray;
> Since painted, or not painted, all shall fade,
> And she who scorns a man must die a maid,
> What then remains but well our power to use,
> And keep good humor still whate'er we lose?

Irony is a verbal device which implies an attitude quite different from (and often opposite to) that which is literally expressed. When Job answers his comforters, saying "No doubt but ye are the people, and wisdom shall die with you" (Job xii.2), he is using irony thick to the point of sarcasm. When Eliot writes, in *Whispers of Immortality,* that "Grishkin is nice," the adjective is carefully chosen to let an ironic grimace of distaste appear. And when Donne "proves," in *The Canonization,* that he and his mistress are going to found a new religion of love, he seems to be inviting us to take a subtly ironic attitude toward religion as well as love.

Because it is easy to see through, **hyperbole,** or willful exaggeration, is a favorite device of irony—which is not to say that it may not be "serious" as well. When she hears that a young man is "dying for love" of her, a sensible girl does not accept this statement literally, but it may convey a serious meaning to her nonetheless. The **pun,** or play on words (known to the learned, sometimes, as **paronomasia**), may also be serious or comic in intent; witness, for example, the famous series of puns in Donne's *Hymn to God the Father.* **Oxymoron** is a figure of flat contradiction—for instance, Milton's famous description of hell as containing "darkness visible" (*Paradise Lost* I.63). A **paradox** is a statement which seems absurd but turns out to have rational meaning after all, usually in some unexpected sense; Donne speaks of fear being great courage and high valor (*Satire III,* line 16), and turns out to mean that fear of God is greater courage than any earthly bravery. The **Petrarchan conceit** was an ingenious, complimentary comparison or turn of thought; Wyatt compares the state of a lover to a ship tossed in a storm, and a hundred different sonneteers explored the possibility of describing their ladies' anatomy in conventional Petrarchan conceits—her teeth like pearls, lips like rubies, hair like finespun gold, etc. On the other hand, the **metaphysical conceit** was a more ingenious many-leveled comparison, worked out in some detail and giving a strong sense of the poet's ingenuity in overcoming obstacles—for instance, Donne's comparison of separated lovers to the legs of a compass (*A Valediction: Forbidding Mourning*) or Herbert's comparison of devotion to a pulley (*The Pulley*).

Images are often described as "mental pictures"; it is more accurate to say that they are verbal representations of something capable of being visualized: some readers have such mental pictures, some do not. Images not only convey what things look like, but direct us, by their pattern of associated and involved feelings, in our reactions to what is being represented. Indeed, there may be such a weight of meaning or feeling behind the image that the verbal picture itself becomes transparent and its "meaning" becomes primary. Abstract ideas can get attached to specific images—water, snake, bird, sun, worm, lion, whatever—in a multitude of ways, of which the reader need sometimes only be reminded. Of course the poet can also be arbitrary about it, letting his reader know simply that Red Cross "stands for" Holiness and Archimago "stands for" Hypocrisy. If that's as far as it goes, we have a primitive variety of **allegory.** But the relation between the tenor of the image (its abstract meaning) and the vehicle (the concrete picture) can be much more indefinite and insubstantial. If the poet mentions a peacock, he may or may not intend his reader to think of immortality, because the unfolding of the peacock's tail and the opening of its "eyes" has traditionally suggested the rebirth of the soul after death. If that is the way the image works, then it is a **symbol.** Or again, if the poet mentions a fish, he may well intend the reader to think of Christ. This isn't because of any similarity between the fish and Christ; the identification depends on a mildly esoteric bit of information, that the Greek word for fish, *ichthys*, forms an anagram of the Greek words for "Jesus Christ, Son of God, Savior." When the connection between tenor and vehicle is arbitrary, or involves the elements of a puzzle, the image may be referred to as an **emblem.** In the 16th and 17th centuries, emblems often took the form of puzzling little drawings, the meaning of which was explained in appended verses: for an example see the emblem prefixed to Crashaw's poem *To the Countess of Denbigh* (in Volume 1).

Personification is the attribution of human qualities to an inanimate object (for example, the Sea) or an abstract concept (Freedom); a special variety of it is called (in a **term** of John Ruskin's invention) the **pathetic fallacy.** When we speak of leaves "dancing" or a lake "smiling," we attribute human traits to nonhuman objects. Ruskin thought this was false and therefore "morbid"; modern criticism tends to view the practice as artistically and morally neutral. A more formal and abstract variety of personification is **allegory,** in which a narrative (such as *Pilgrim's Progress*) is constructed by representing general concepts (Faithfulness, Sin, Despair) as persons. A **fable** (like the Nun's Priest's Tale) represents beasts behaving like humans; a **parable** is a brief story, or simply an observation, with strong moral application; and an **exemplum** is a story told to illustrate a point in a sermon. A special series of devices, nearly obsolete today, used to be available to poets who could count on readers trained in the classics. These were the devices of **classical epithet** and **allusion.** In their simplest form, the classic myths used to provide a repertoire of agreeable stage properties, and a convenient shorthand for expressing emotional attitudes. Picturesque creatures like centaurs, satyrs, and sphinxes, heroes and heroines like Hector and Helen, and the whole pantheon of Olympic deities could be used to make ready reference to a great many aspects of human nature. One does not have to explain the problems of a man who is "cleaning the Augean stables"; if he is afflicted with an "Achilles' heel," or is assailing "Hydra-headed difficulties," his state is clear. These epithets, or descriptive phrases, making reference to mythological stories, suggest in a phrase situations which would normally require cumbersome explanations. Conceivably other mythologies might have served the same end in analogous ways. But because they could be taken for granted as the common possession of all educated readers, the classic myths entered into English literature as early as Chaucer, and are only now passing away as a viable system of allusions. In poets like Spenser and Milton, classical allusion becomes a kind of enormously learned game, in which the poet seeks to make his points as indirectly as possible. For instance, Spenser writes in the *Epithalamion*, lines 328–29:

> Lyke as when Jove with fayre Alcmena lay,
> When he begot the great Tirynthian **groome.**

The mere mention of Alcmena in the first line suggests, to the knowing reader, Hercules; Spenser's problem in the second line is to find a way of referring to him which is neither redundant nor heavy-handed. "Tirynthian" reminds us of his long connection with the city of Tiryns, stretching our minds (as it were) across his whole career; and **"groome"** compresses references to a man-child, a servant, and a bridegroom, all of which apply to different aspects of Hercules' history. Thus, far from simply avoiding redundancy, Spenser has enriched the whole texture of his verse, thought, and feeling by his gift for precise classical epithet.

Index

2572